GOVERNORS STATE UNIVERSITY LIBRARY
3 1611 00173 4208
W9-BRY-383

Grade 11

Annotated Teacher's Edition

Prentice Hall

LITERATURE

Timeless Voices, Timeless Themes

THE AMERICAN EXPERIENCE

PRENTICE HALL
Upper Saddle River, New Jersey
Needham, Massachusetts
Glenview, Illinois

Copyright © 2000 by Prentice-Hall, Inc., Upper Saddle River, New Jersey 07458. All rights reserved. No part of this book may be reproduced or transmitted in any form or by any means, electronic or mechanical, including photocopying, recording, or by any information storage and retrieval system, without permission in writing from the publisher. Printed in the United States of America.

ISBN 0-13-050429-7

4 5 6 7 8 9 10   03 02 01 00

An outstanding array of

Only Prentice Hall gives you an outstanding array of print and technology support, developed to let you customize easily to your teaching style and local or state curriculum.

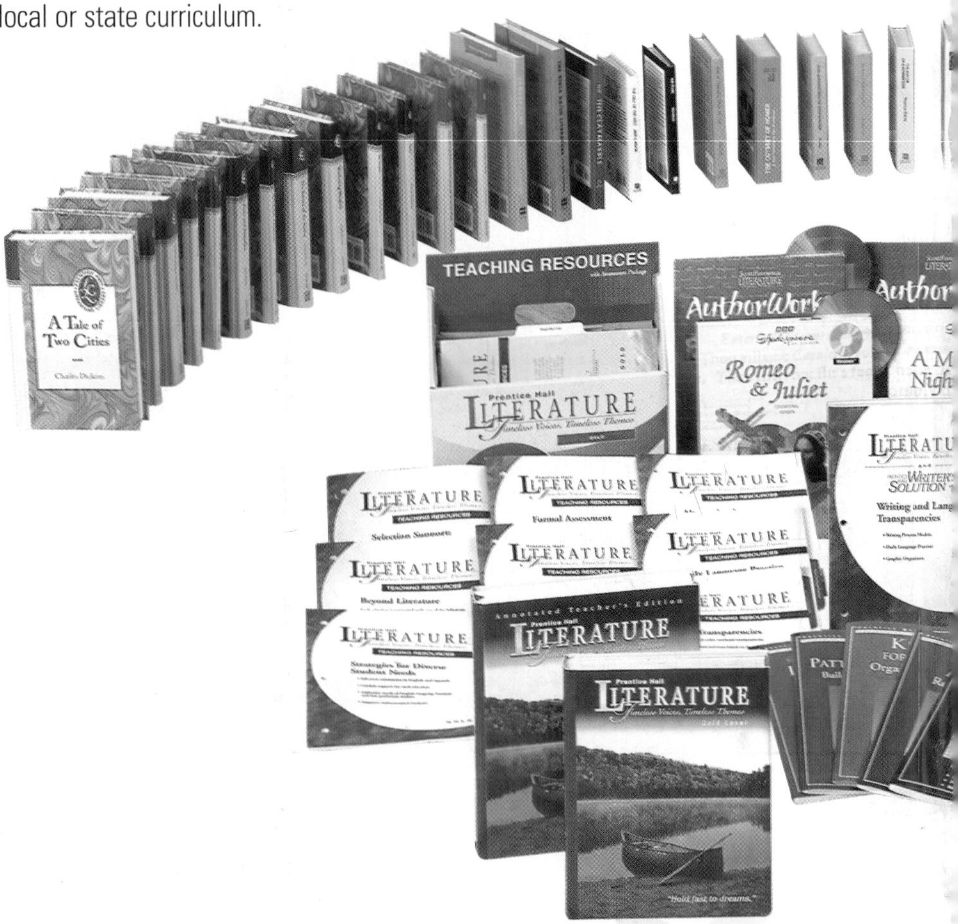

Print components and Transparency Resources

- Student Edition
- Annotated Teacher's Edition
- Teaching Resources
  - Selection Support
  - Formal Assessment with Assessment Resources Software CD-ROM
  - Alternative Assessment
  - Beyond Literature
  - Strategies for Diverse Student Needs
  - Art Transparencies
  - Professional Development Library
    - Assess Student Work
    - Kick Off for Success
    - Putting Patterns to Work
    - Manage Instruction in the Block
  - Daily Language Practice
- *Resource Pro*® CD-ROM with Local Objectives Editor
  - Exclusive *Planning Express*® software with Local Objectives Editor
  - Instant access to all teaching resources
  - 100 additional selections per grade level
- Writer's Companion
- Grammar Practice Book
- Writing and Language Transparencies
- Fine Arts Posters
- Spanish Language Support

Plus...Technology Resources

- Assessment Resources Software CD-ROM
- *Got It!* Videotapes
- Interactive Student Tutorial CD-ROM
- Literature Companion Web Site
- *Looking at Literature* Videotapes
- *Looking at Literature* Videodiscs
- *Humanities* Videotapes
- Student Book on Audiocassettes
- *AuthorWorks* CD-ROM series
- *BBC Shakespeare* CD-ROM series
- *Writer's Solution Writing Lab* CD-ROM
- *Writer's Solution Language Lab* CD-ROM
- *Writers at Work* Videotapes
- *Writers at Work* Videodiscs

print and technology resources

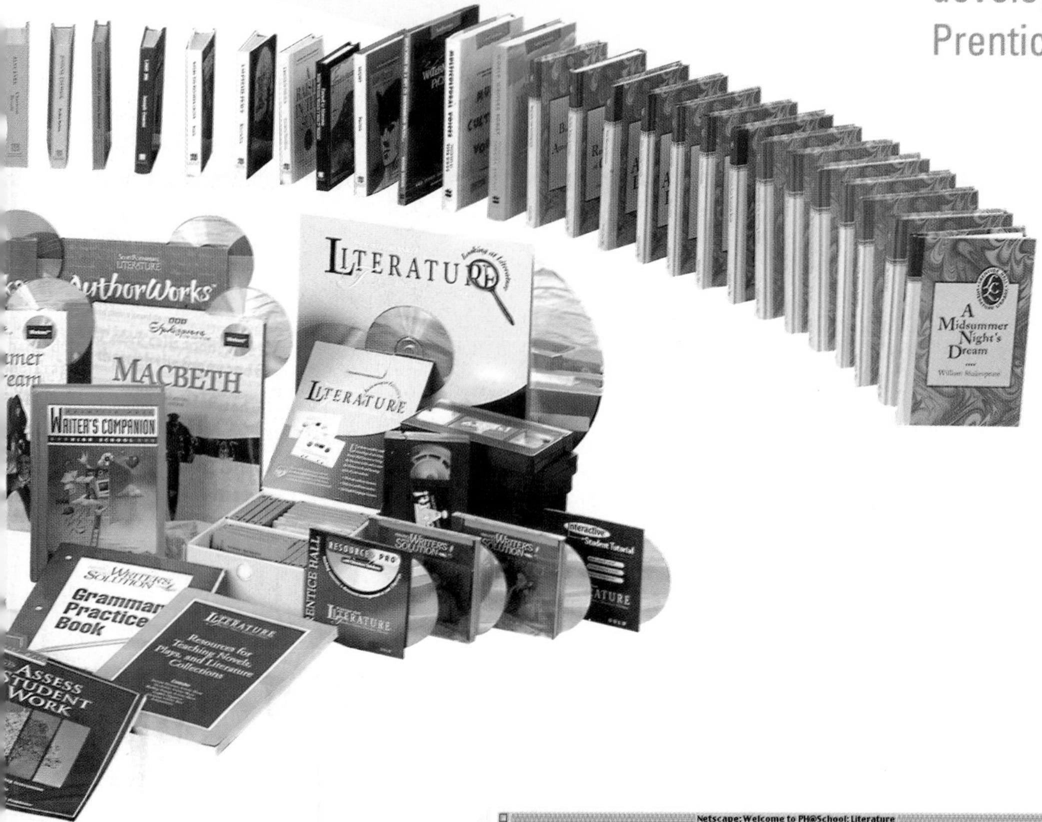

Grade 9 components shown.

Introducing a Web site developed specifically for Prentice Hall Literature.

On-line Student Resources

- Current Events Writing Workshop keeps students up to date with two fully developed writing assignments, updated twice each year.
- Activities incorporate Internet resources for nearly every selection.
- Multiple-choice tests—scored-online—for every selection.
- Hot links provide instant access to sites supporting every selection.

On-line Teacher Resources

- Teachers can consult with colleagues through the Faculty Forum.
- Teaching links provide instant access to sites providing teaching support for every selection.

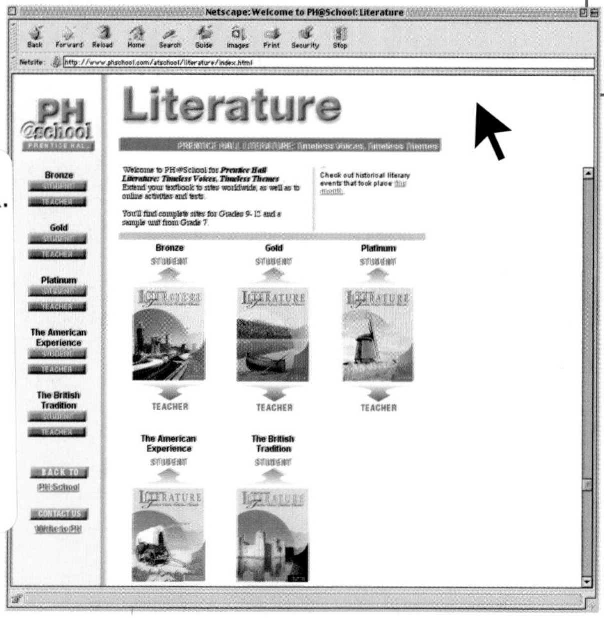

Access a wide range of interactive tools at **www.phlit.phschool.com**

Prentice Hall literature
[redacted]
MAT-CTR.
LT
PN
59
.P7451
2001
v.6

Outstanding blend of classic, contemporary, and

Prentice Hall *Literature:*

Timeless Voices, Timeless Themes

combines an outstanding blend of time-tested classics, the finest contemporary literature, and inspirational literature to create a new enthusiasm for literature.

Classic literature opens your classroom to lives and cultures across time and place. From Homer to Mark Twain, we give you the classic literature that you love to teach.

inspirational literature

Contemporary literature is relevant to students' lives. Prentice Hall gives you the finest selections of today to engage your students and foster an appreciation of literature. Prentice Hall also offers an extensive sampling of real-world texts that help students build skills for success in both school and work.

Inspirational literature evokes in students the passion a writer feels for life and literature. In turn, students gain a sense of a living literature—writing that explores the immediate wonders and beauty of the world around them.

Unmatched skills instruction

ONLY **PRENTICE HALL**

- Teaches literary elements before, during, and after every selection.
- Integrates strategic reading instruction before, during, and after every selection, making the finest literature accessible to all students.
- Motivates students to read through real-world connections before, during, and after every selection.
- Teaches vocabulary-building strategies with every selection.
- Provides more writing and grammar instruction than any other literature program.
- Offers an Authors in Depth study for at least one key author for every unit.

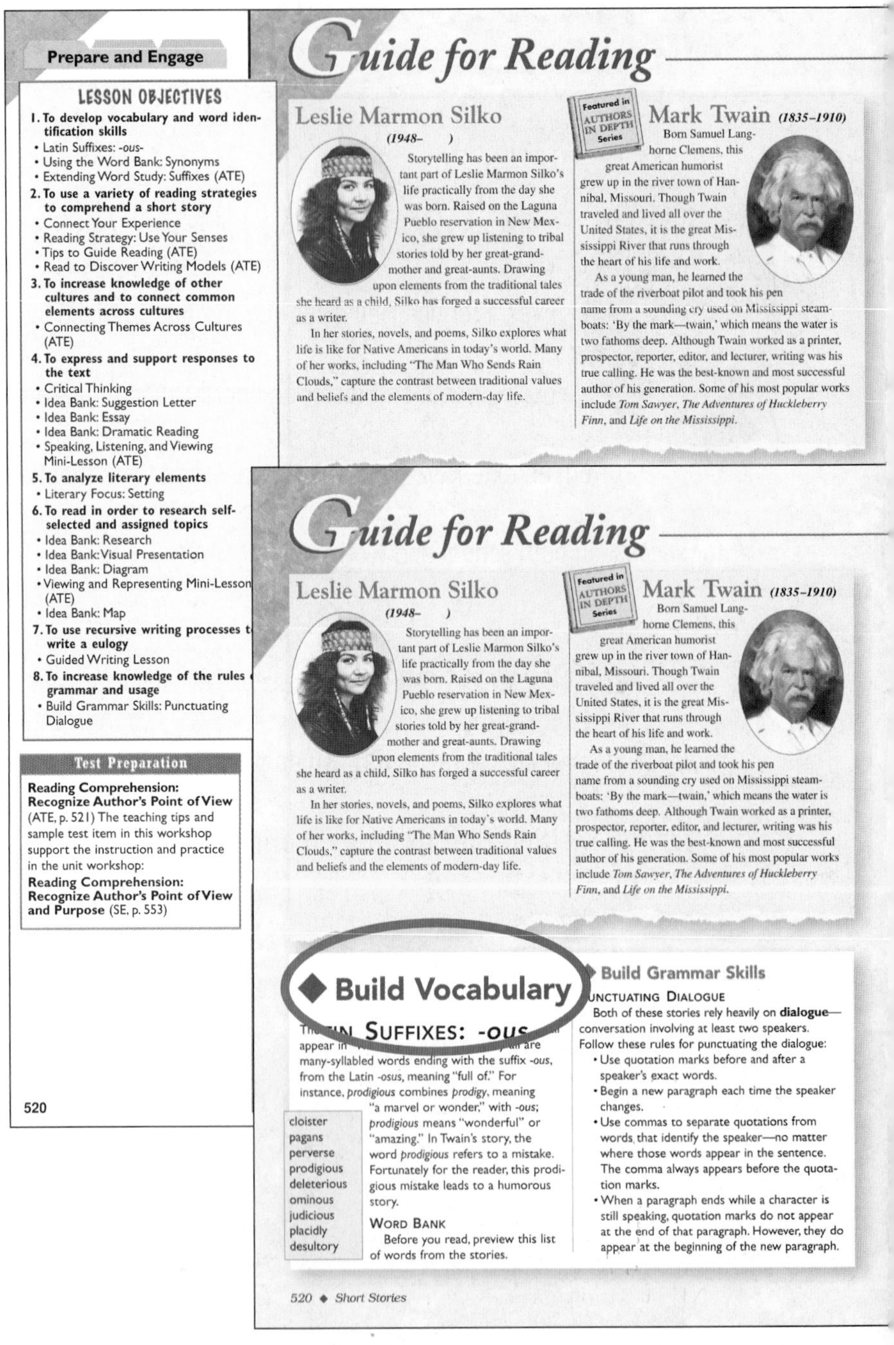

Prepare and Engage

LESSON OBJECTIVES

1. **To develop vocabulary and word identification skills**
   - Latin Suffixes: -*ous*-
   - Using the Word Bank: Synonyms
   - Extending Word Study: Suffixes (ATE)
2. **To use a variety of reading strategies to comprehend a short story**
   - Connect Your Experience
   - Reading Strategy: Use Your Senses
   - Tips to Guide Reading (ATE)
   - Read to Discover Writing Models (ATE)
3. **To increase knowledge of other cultures and to connect common elements across cultures**
   - Connecting Themes Across Cultures (ATE)
4. **To express and support responses to the text**
   - Critical Thinking
   - Idea Bank: Suggestion Letter
   - Idea Bank: Essay
   - Idea Bank: Dramatic Reading
   - Speaking, Listening, and Viewing Mini-Lesson (ATE)
5. **To analyze literary elements**
   - Literary Focus: Setting
6. **To read in order to research self-selected and assigned topics**
   - Idea Bank: Research
   - Idea Bank: Visual Presentation
   - Idea Bank: Diagram
   - Viewing and Representing Mini-Lesson (ATE)
   - Idea Bank: Map
7. **To use recursive writing processes t[o] write a eulogy**
   - Guided Writing Lesson
8. **To increase knowledge of the rules [of] grammar and usage**
   - Build Grammar Skills: Punctuating Dialogue

Test Preparation

Reading Comprehension: Recognize Author's Point of View (ATE, p. 521) The teaching tips and sample test item in this workshop support the instruction and practice in the unit workshop: **Reading Comprehension: Recognize Author's Point of View and Purpose** (SE, p. 553)

520

Guide for Reading

Leslie Marmon Silko (*1948–*)

Storytelling has been an important part of Leslie Marmon Silko's life practically from the day she was born. Raised on the Laguna Pueblo reservation in New Mexico, she grew up listening to tribal stories told by her great-grandmother and great-aunts. Drawing upon elements from the traditional tales she heard as a child, Silko has forged a successful career as a writer.

In her stories, novels, and poems, Silko explores what life is like for Native Americans in today's world. Many of her works, including "The Man Who Sends Rain Clouds," capture the contrast between traditional values and beliefs and the elements of modern-day life.

Featured in AUTHORS IN DEPTH Series

Mark Twain (*1835–1910*)

Born Samuel Langhorne Clemens, this great American humorist grew up in the river town of Hannibal, Missouri. Though Twain traveled and lived all over the United States, it is the great Mississippi River that runs through the heart of his life and work.

As a young man, he learned the trade of the riverboat pilot and took his pen name from a sounding cry used on Mississippi steamboats: 'By the mark—twain,' which means the water is two fathoms deep. Although Twain worked as a printer, prospector, reporter, editor, and lecturer, writing was his true calling. He was the best-known and most successful author of his generation. Some of his most popular works include *Tom Sawyer, The Adventures of Huckleberry Finn*, and *Life on the Mississippi*.

◆ Build Vocabulary

[LAT]IN SUFFIXES: -ous

Th[e] ... appear in ... are many-syllabled words ending with the suffix -*ous*, from the Latin -*osus*, meaning "full of." For instance, *prodigious* combines *prodigy*, meaning "a marvel or wonder," with -*ous*; *prodigious* means "wonderful" or "amazing." In Twain's story, the word *prodigious* refers to a mistake. Fortunately for the reader, this prodigious mistake leads to a humorous story.

WORD BANK

Before you read, preview this list of words from the stories.

cloister
pagans
perverse
prodigious
deleterious
ominous
judicious
placidly
desultory

◆ Build Grammar Skills

[P]UNCTUATING DIALOGUE

Both of these stories rely heavily on **dialogue**—conversation involving at least two speakers. Follow these rules for punctuating the dialogue:

- Use quotation marks before and after a speaker's exact words.
- Begin a new paragraph each time the speaker changes.
- Use commas to separate quotations from words that identify the speaker—no matter where those words appear in the sentence. The comma always appears before the quotation marks.
- When a paragraph ends while a character is still speaking, quotation marks do not appear at the end of that paragraph. However, they do appear at the beginning of the new paragraph.

520 ◆ Short Stories

▲

Build Vocabulary introduces a vocabulary-building strategy with every selection.

Reading Strategy provided before, during, and after every selection.

The Man to Send Rain Clouds
◆ The Invalid's Story ◆

◆ Literature and Your Life

CONNECT YOUR EXPERIENCE
At some time, everyone has to deal with the loss of a loved o… People cope with this in different ways. They may try to preserve the loved one's memory, or they may look to fulfill the person's last wishes. These stories present two very different sets of circumstances surrounding a person's death and others' responses to it.

THEMATIC FOCUS: FACING CONFLICTS
As these stories reveal, dealing with death can involve working out difficult and sometimes unexpected issues and situations.

◆ Background for Understanding

CULTURE
"The Man to Send Rain Clouds" explores the traditions of the Pueblo Indians. The Pueblos have lived in the southwestern United States for nearly 3,000 years. They first came into contact with Europeans when the Spanish arrived in the 1500's. During the twentieth century, the Pueblos have incorporated many aspects of the …

◆ Reading Strategy

…E YOUR SENSES
… your senses a real workout. As you read each one, **use your senses** to picture the setting and the characters in your mind.
Draw from your own experiences to see, hear, smell, taste, or feel what each author describes. For example, when Twain describes a piece of cheese with an overpowering odor, search your memory to recall when you've smelled especially pungent cheese, and try to re-create the sensation in your mind.

Interest Grabber Have students name movies that they've seen—one involving humorous treatment of the events surrounding death and one involving reflections …n the honor and respect arising from death. Discuss the ways that death can provoke such different responses. Tell students that the contrasting views of death in the movies parallel the views of death in these stories.

Connecting Themes Across Cultures
Each of these stories deals with death and survivors' reactions to it. In both cases, the survivors follow a set of rules dictated by their culture. Ask students to share their knowledge of mourning customs from their own culture or other cultures they know. For example, in Judaism, a body is usually buried within 24 hours of death, while in other religions, a …

The Man to Send Rain Clouds
◆ The Invalid's Story ◆

◆ Literature and Your Life

CONNECT YOUR EXPERIENCE
At some time, everyone has to deal with the loss of a loved one. People cope with this in different ways. They may try to preserve the loved one's memory, or they may look to fulfill the person's last wishes. These stories present two very different sets of circumstances surrounding a person's death and others' responses to it.

THEMATIC FOCUS: FACING CONFLICTS
As these stories reveal, dealing with death can involve working out difficult and sometimes unexpected issues and situations.

◆ Background for Understanding

CULTURE
"The Man to Send Rain Clouds" explores the traditions of the Pueblo Indians. The Pueblos have lived in the southwestern United States for nearly 3,000 years. They first came into contact with Europeans when the Spanish arrived in the 1500's. During the twentieth century, the Pueblos have incorporated many aspects of the industrial world into their lives. Nevertheless, they have tried to maintain their ancient traditions and beliefs—including the view that if they keep themselves in harmony with the natural world, nature will give them what they need, such as sufficient rainfall for their crops. The Pueblos' balancing of modern ways with their own customs and views provides the central conflict in Silko's story.

Journal Writing Jot down what you know about the Pueblo… …cultures.

◆ Reading Strategy

USE YOUR SENSES
A dry wintry desert waiting for rain. A stifling boxcar with a smelly package. The setting of each story gives your senses a real workout. As you read each one, **use your senses** to picture the setting and the characters in your mind.

Draw from your own experiences to see, hear, smell, taste, or feel what each author describes. For example, when Twain describes a piece of cheese with an overpowering odor, search your memory to recall when you've smelled especially pungent cheese, and try to re-create the sensation in your mind.

Use a graphic organizer like this one to help you record key details appealing to each sense.

Sights	Sounds	Smells	Tastes	Physical Sensation

◆ Literary Focus

…TING
In… …etting—the place and ti… …, the setting simply provides a backdrop for the actions and characters. In other stories—including these—the setting shapes the characters' actions.

In addition to time and place, a story's setting includes the **cultural background** against which the action takes place: the customs, ideas, values, and beliefs of the society in which it occurs. The cultural background for "The Man to Send Rain Clouds" consists of the customs and beliefs of the Pueblo people.

Guide for Reading ◆ 521

Customize for
Less Proficient Readers
Twain's long sentences may pos… …lem for these studen… result, … with them to break down some of the long sentences toward the beginning of the story. For example, show that the second sentence in the second paragraph includes a long series of details relating to the circumstances surrounding the narrator's discovery of his friend's death. Have students list each of the details separately; then show how they fit together.

Customize for
Pre-AP Students
Challenge students to retell Silko's story from Father Paul's or Louise's point of view and Twain's story from the expressman's point of view. Afterward, hold a group discussion to evaluate the presentations.

Customize for
English Language Learners
Help these students by clarifying confusing passages in the Twain story, such as "He gasped once or twice, then moved toward the cof—gun-box . . ." or ". . . here he scrambled to his feet and broke a pane. . . ." You might also help with words written in dialect, such as "How long has he *ben* dead?"

521

Customize for… notes in the Teacher's Edition offer strategies and tips for helping readers of all levels.

Literary Focus teaches literary elements before, during, and after every selection.

Motivation for today's students

ONLY PRENTICE HALL

- Makes the finest collection of classic and contemporary literature relevant to students.
- Engages students with *Literature and Your Life* sections before, during, and after every selection.
- Features *Connections to Today's World* that link high-interest contemporary selections to thematically related classic literature.
- Explores cross-curricular, career, community, and media connections in the *Beyond Literature* feature.
- Offers an outstanding array of videos, software, and technology to make literature accessible to today's multimedia generation.

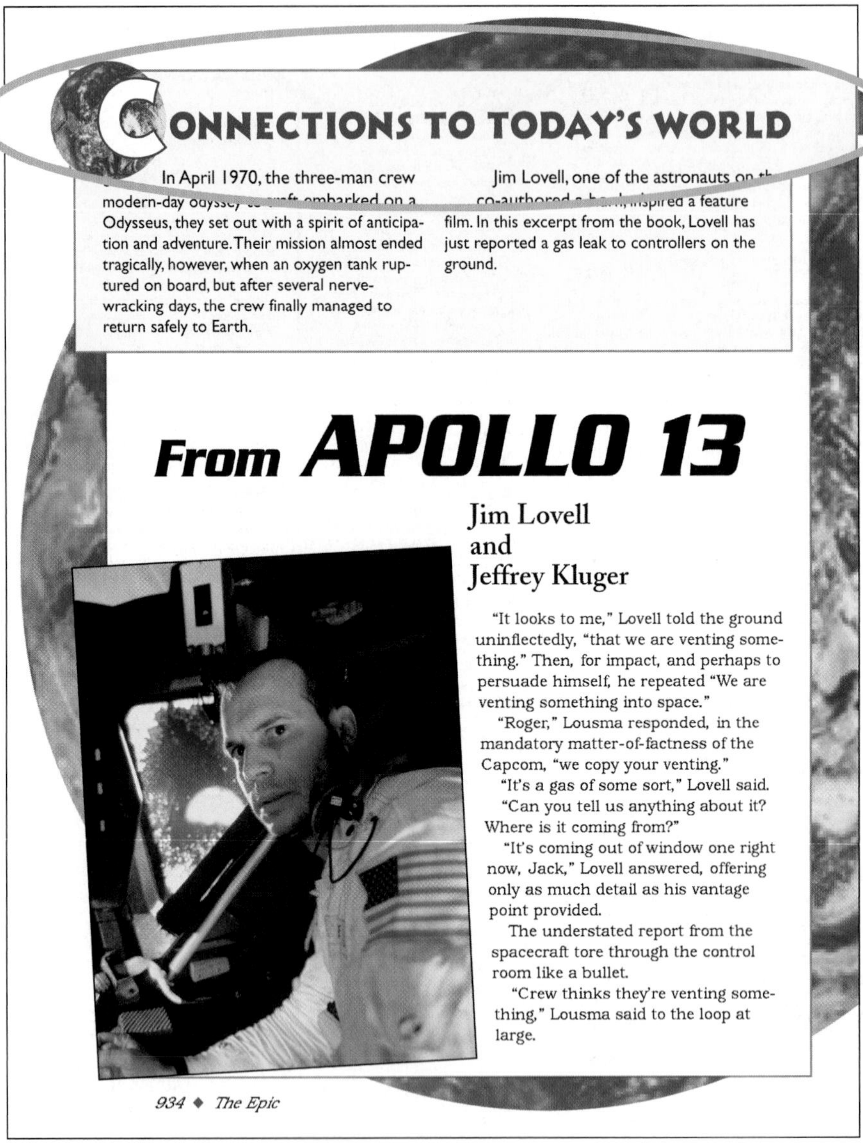

CONNECTIONS TO TODAY'S WORLD

In April 1970, the three-man crew modern-day odyssey ... craft embarked on a Odysseus, they set out with a spirit of anticipation and adventure. Their mission almost ended tragically, however, when an oxygen tank ruptured on board, but after several nerve-wracking days, the crew finally managed to return safely to Earth.

Jim Lovell, one of the astronauts on th... co-authored a book, inspired a feature film. In this excerpt from the book, Lovell has just reported a gas leak to controllers on the ground.

From APOLLO 13

Jim Lovell and Jeffrey Kluger

"It looks to me," Lovell told the ground uninflectedly, "that we are venting something." Then, for impact, and perhaps to persuade himself, he repeated "We are venting something into space."

"Roger," Lousma responded, in the mandatory matter-of-factness of the Capcom, "we copy your venting."

"It's a gas of some sort," Lovell said.

"Can you tell us anything about it? Where is it coming from?"

"It's coming out of window one right now, Jack," Lovell answered, offering only as much detail as his vantage point provided.

The understated report from the spacecraft tore through the control room like a bullet.

"Crew thinks they're venting something," Lousma said to the loop at large.

934 ♦ *The Epic*

▲

Connections to Today's World links classic literature to high-interest contemporary writings.

MODEL SELECTION

The Gift of the Magi

◆ Literature and Your Life

...ECT YOUR EXPERIENCE

Qu... your birthday gift. You open the box—and your spirits sink. Your gift is a lopsided sweater, made by an inexperienced knitter in your least favorite color. Hiding your disappointment, you thank the giver enthusiastically. After all, it's the thought that counts.

Gifts are sometimes less appropriate or more meaningful than they first appear. In this story, a husband and wife discover the unexpected problems and joys of giving gifts.

THEMATIC FOCUS: WORKING TOWARD A GOAL

As this story shows, a person may strive toward a goal with the best of intentions, only to find that his or her effort was misdirected. How can people redirect their efforts in such a situation?

Journal Writing In your journal, describe an incident—real or imagined—in which someone tried to do something nice but had his or her plans go awry. Explain what, if anything, the person did to fix problems resulting from his or her actions.

◆ Background for Understanding

ECONOMICS

When you read a story that was written more than ten years ago, you will find that prices or amounts of money seem ridiculously low. This is because the United States has experienced inflation over the years. Inflation is a continual increase in most or all major prices throughout an economy. Although the causes of inflation are hotly debated, the effects are clear: The purchasing power of a unit of currency goes down. In the story, which was written at the beginning of the twentieth century, $32 is a month's rent for Della and Jim. Today, $32 would not even pay for a night in an inexpensive motel.

...iterary Focus

...OT

The events in a story make up its **plot,** which is traditionally divided into five parts: *exposition, rising action, climax, falling action,* and *resolution.* The exposition provides background information and sets the scene for the conflict—a struggle between opposing people or forces that drives the action of the story. The introduction of the conflict marks the beginning of the rising action, in which the conflict intensifies until it reaches the high point, or climax, of the story. After the climax, the action falls to a resolution. The resolution shows how the situation turns out and ties up loose ends.

As you read the story, jot down events associated with the different parts of the plot on a diagram like this one.

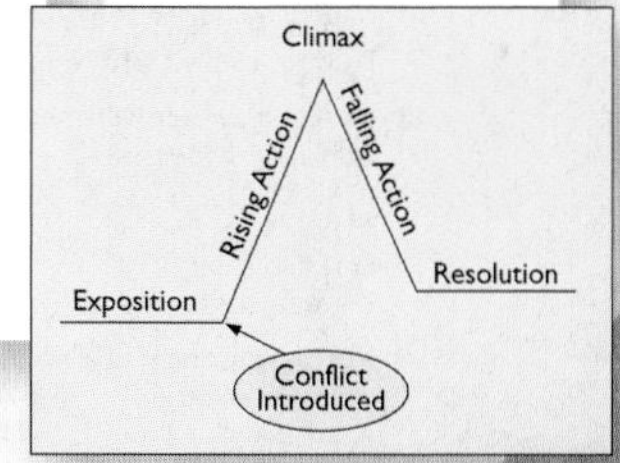

Guide for Reading ◆ 457

◀ **Literature and Your Life** sections before, during, and after every selection connect literature to students' lives.

A wide array of videos, software, and technology makes literature come alive for today's students. ▶

Assessment success

ONLY PRENTICE HALL

- Integrates standardized test preparation activities and strategies with every selection.
- Provides point-of-use test-taking strategies in the Teacher's Edition.
- Provides the most support and practice for national tests, such as the SAT and ACT, as well as state and local tests.
- Provides the most comprehensive array of print and technology to prepare students for standardized tests.

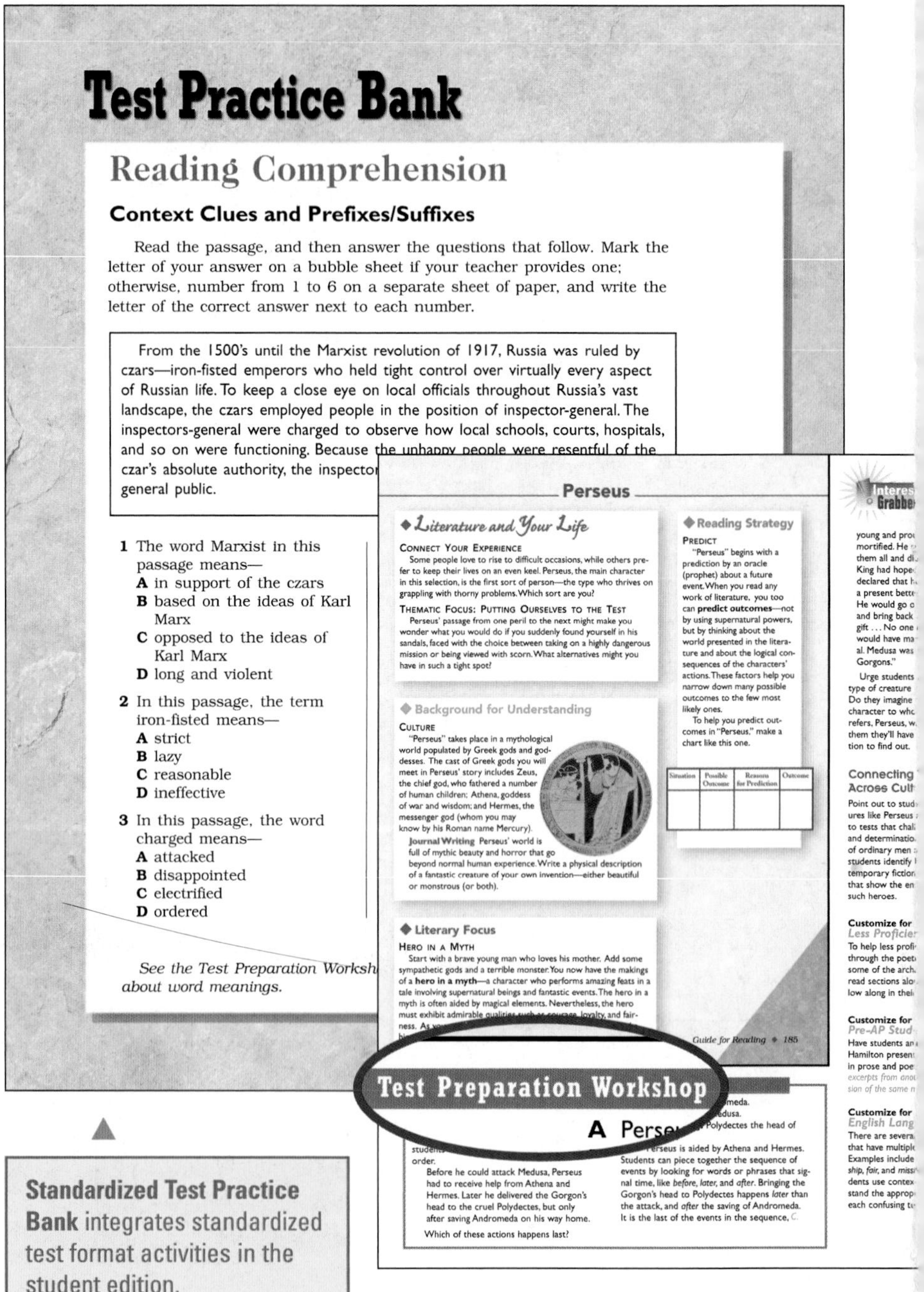
Test Practice Bank

Reading Comprehension

Context Clues and Prefixes/Suffixes

Read the passage, and then answer the questions that follow. Mark the letter of your answer on a bubble sheet if your teacher provides one; otherwise, number from 1 to 6 on a separate sheet of paper, and write the letter of the correct answer next to each number.

From the 1500's until the Marxist revolution of 1917, Russia was ruled by czars—iron-fisted emperors who held tight control over virtually every aspect of Russian life. To keep a close eye on local officials throughout Russia's vast landscape, the czars employed people in the position of inspector-general. The inspectors-general were charged to observe how local schools, courts, hospitals, and so on were functioning. Because the unhappy people were resentful of the czar's absolute authority, the inspector... general public.

1 The word Marxist in this passage means—
A in support of the czars
B based on the ideas of Karl Marx
C opposed to the ideas of Karl Marx
D long and violent

2 In this passage, the term iron-fisted means—
A strict
B lazy
C reasonable
D ineffective

3 In this passage, the word charged means—
A attacked
B disappointed
C electrified
D ordered

See the Test Preparation Worksh... about word meanings.

Perseus

Literature and Your Life

Reading Strategy

Background for Understanding

Literary Focus

Test Preparation Workshop

Standardized Test Practice Bank integrates standardized test format activities in the student edition.

Standardized Test Preparation Workshops at point-of-use in the Teacher's Edition help you plan for student assessment success.

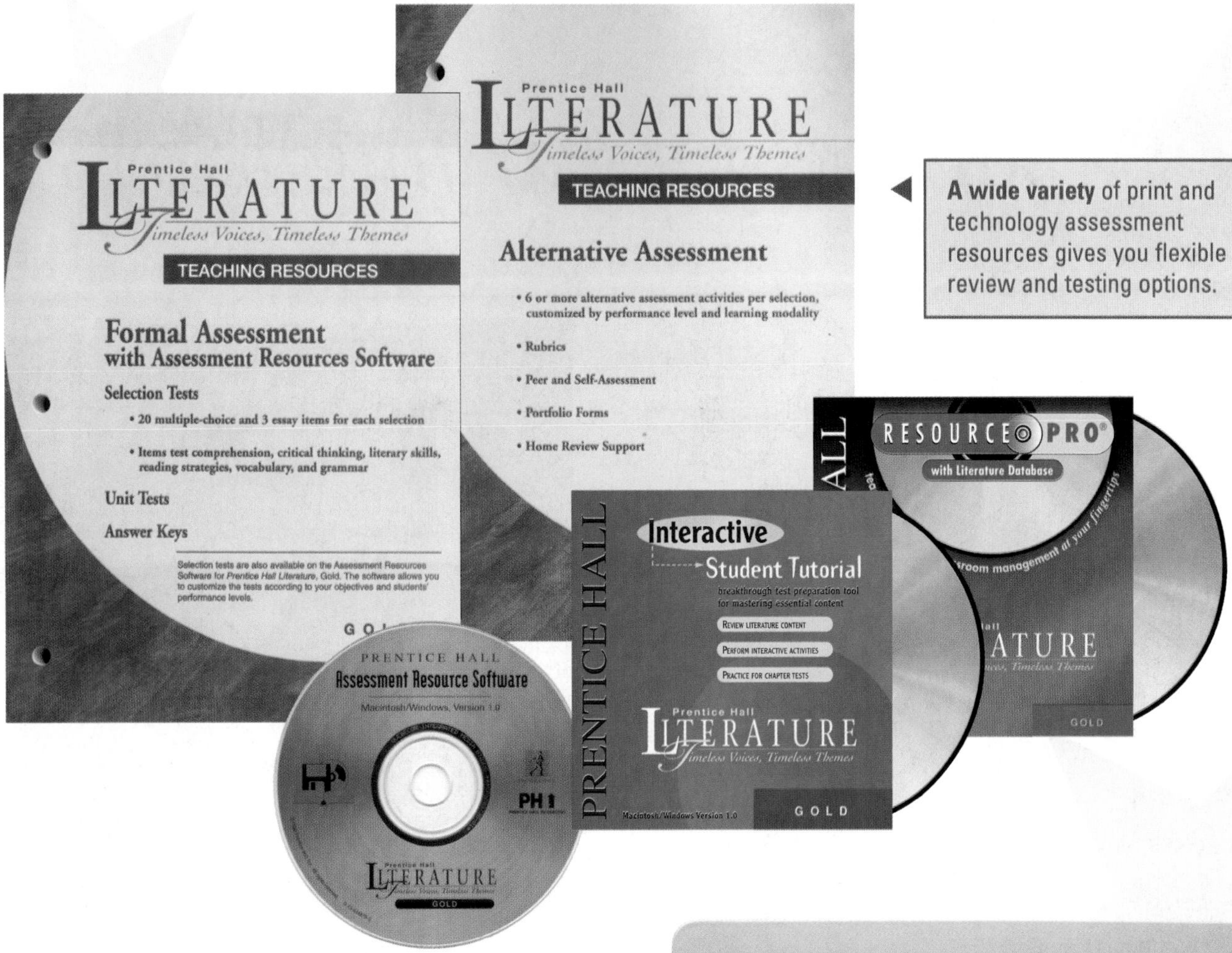

Prentice Hall
LITERATURE
Timeless Voices, Timeless Themes
TEACHING RESOURCES
Formal Assessment
with Assessment Resources Software
Selection Tests
• 20 multiple-choice and 3 essay items for each selection
• Items test comprehension, critical thinking, literary skills, reading strategies, vocabulary, and grammar
Unit Tests
Answer Keys
Prentice Hall
LITERATURE
Timeless Voices, Timeless Themes
TEACHING RESOURCES
Alternative Assessment
• 6 or more alternative assessment activities per selection, customized by performance level and learning modality
• Rubrics
• Peer and Self-Assessment
• Portfolio Forms
• Home Review Support
PRENTICE HALL
Assessment Resource Software
Macintosh/Windows, Version 1.0
RESOURCE PRO
with Literature Database
PRENTICE HALL
Interactive
Student Tutorial
breakthrough test preparation tool for mastering essential content
REVIEW LITERATURE CONTENT
PERFORM INTERACTIVE ACTIVITIES
PRACTICE FOR CHAPTER TESTS
GOLD

A wide variety of print and technology assessment resources gives you flexible review and testing options.

Resource Pro® CD-ROM with Local Objectives Editor lets you customize your lessons by importing local or state objectives.

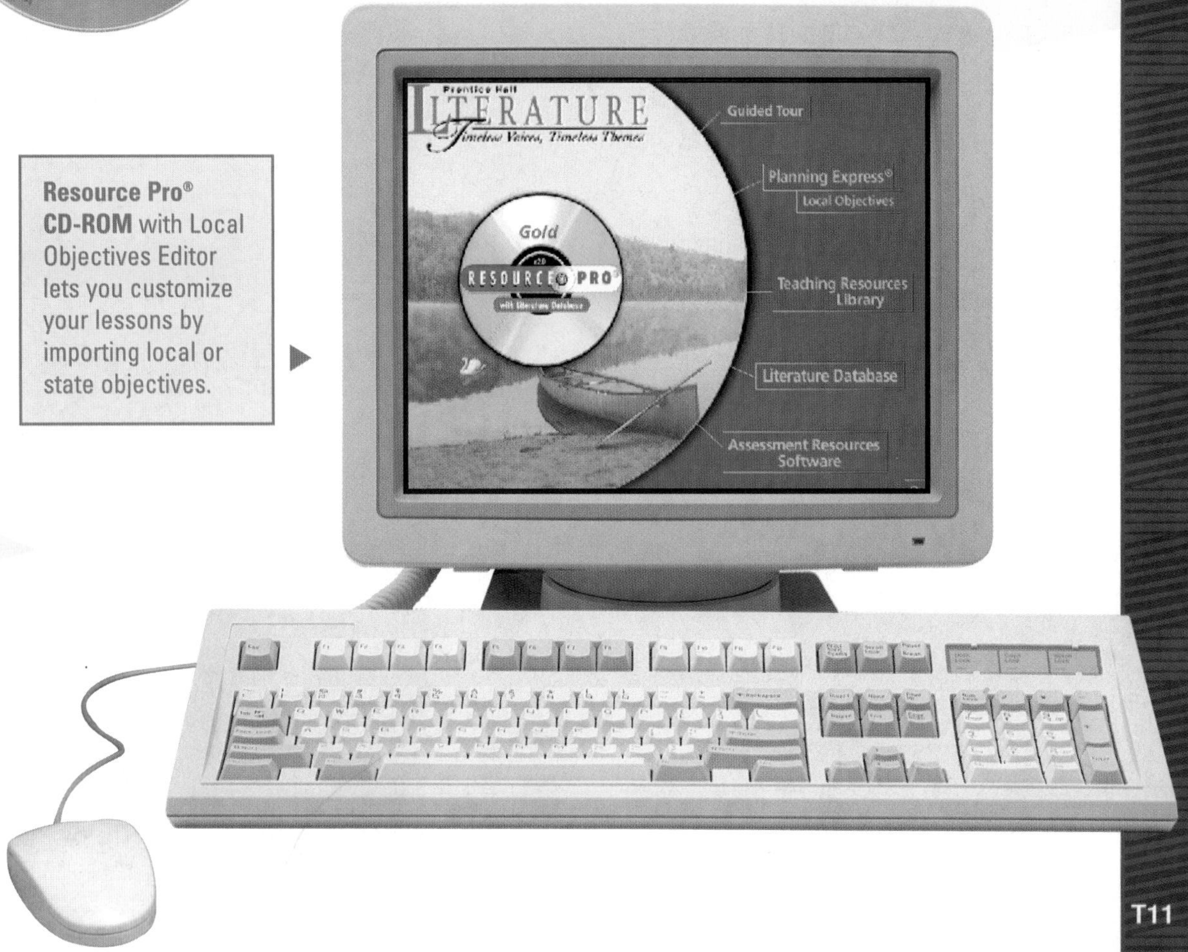

Resources for varying learning

ONLY **PRENTICE HALL**

- Recognizes diverse learning styles and provides appropriate teaching support.
- Features integrated reading support before, during, and after every selection.
- Provides *Customize for…* teacher notes that offer strategies for various student populations.
- Offers *Idea Bank* activities geared to all types of learners.
- Features *Interest Grabber* notes at the beginning of every selection.
- Provides selection support pages for students of all learning modalities.

Develop Understanding

One-Minute Insight "Jade Flower Palace" is a lyric poem that expresses the speaker's feeling about the impermanence of power and glory. The setting includes images of scurrying rats, ruins, and ghost fires that convey the message that power and glory are fleeting. In contrast, the setting of "The Moon at the Fortified Pass" is an active kingdom—its people alive and its armies on the move. Yet it is in a lonely moment in time in the mountain setting that the speaker portrays the soldiers' homesickness and fear of death in order to emphasize the senselessness of war.

◆ **Reading Strategy**

❶ **Read in Sentences** Ask a student to read from "The stream …" to "tiles" in order to notice the stops and to emphasize the short, simple sentences.

◆ **Build Grammar Skills**

❷ **Adjectival Modifiers** Ask students to find a participial phrase used as an adjectival modifier in lines 4–5. What noun does it modify? *"Standing in ruins" is a participial phrase modifying the noun "palace."*

◆ **Critical Thinking**

❸ **Infer** Ask students which images in this passage convey the idea that things are not permanent. *The images of ghost fires and shattered pavements that are all washed away convey the idea of impermanence.*

◆ **Reading Strategy**

❹ **Read in Sentences** Point out that the word "Only" (line 14) begins a sentence that crosses a stanza break. Ask a volunteer to read the sentence aloud.

◆ **Literary Focus**

❺ **Lyric Poetry** Encourage students to suggest what feelings the speaker in this lyric poem expresses. *Suggeste… expresses… fulness, lo… of resign…*

858

Jade Flower Palace

Tu Fu
Translated by
Kenneth Rexroth

❶ The stream swirls. The wind moans in
The pines. Gray rats scurry over
Broken tiles. What prince, long ago,
❷ Built this palace, standing in
Ruins beside the cliffs? There are
Green ghost fires in the black rooms.
❸ The shattered pavements are all
Washed away. Ten thousand organ
Pipes whistle and roar. The storm
Scatters the red autumn leaves.
His dancing girls are yellow dust.
Their painted cheeks have crumbled
Away. His gold chariots
And courtiers are gone. Only
❹
A stone horse is left of his
Glory. I sit on the grass and
Start a poem, but the pathos of
❺ It overcomes me. The future
Slips imperceptibly away.
Who can say what the years will bring?

◆ **Build Vocabulary**

pathos (pā' thäs) *n.*: Quality in something experienced or observed that arouses feelings of pity, sorrow, sympathy, or compassion

wistful (wist' fəl) *adj.*: Expressing longing

858 ◆ Poetry

Block Scheduling Strategies

Consider these suggestions to take advantage of extended class time:

- Have students complete the journal activity in Literature and Your Life (p. 855). After they … ıem to search for ways in … ıinate the themes they … ts to look for other … :he themes addressed in these two poems. Have students share poems they've found with the rest of the class.
- Invite students to prepare and present the Visual Presentation activity, in the Idea Bank on p. 863. Use the Viewing and Representing Mini-Lesson on p. 859, to get students started.
- Have students complete the Guided Writing Lesson, p. 863. Use the instruction on p. 863 of the ATE to help them draft their poems.

Prentice Hall
LITERATURE
Timeless Voices, Timeless Themes
TEACHING RESOURCES
Strategies for Diverse Student Needs
• Selection summaries in English and Spanish
• Guided support for each selection
• Addresses needs of English language learners and less proficient readers
• Supports mainstreamed students
GOLD

◀ **Strategies for Diverse Student Needs** offers guided support for every selection.

styles and ability levels

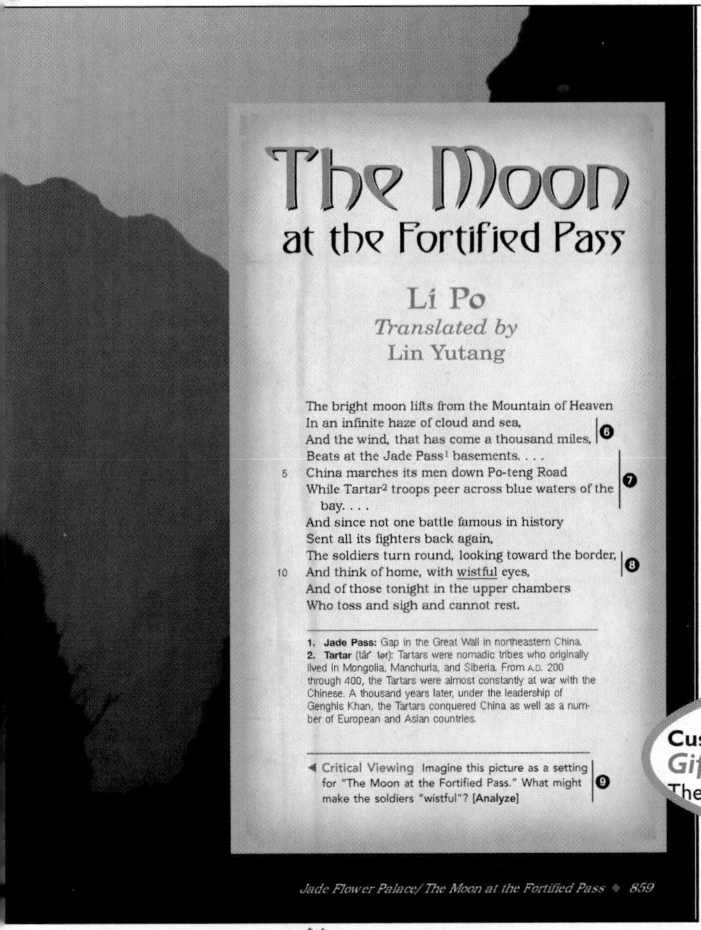

The Moon at the Fortified Pass

Lí Po
Translated by
Lin Yutang

The bright moon lifts from the Mountain of Heaven
In an infinite haze of cloud and sea, ❻
And the wind, that has come a thousand miles,
Beats at the Jade Pass[1] basements. . . .
China marches its men down Po-teng Road ❼
While Tartar[2] troops peer across blue waters of the bay. . . .
And since not one battle famous in history
Sent all its fighters back again,
The soldiers turn round, looking toward the border, ❽
And think of home, with wistful eyes,
And of those tonight in the upper chambers
Who toss and sigh and cannot rest.

1. **Jade Pass:** Gap in the Great Wall in northeastern China.
2. **Tartar** (tär′ tər): Tartars were nomadic tribes who originally lived in Mongolia, Manchuria, and Siberia. From A.D. 200 through 400, the Tartars were almost constantly at war with the Chinese. A thousand years later, under the leadership of Genghis Khan, the Tartars conquered China as well as a number of European and Asian countries.

◀ Critical Viewing Imagine this picture as a setting for "The Moon at the Fortified Pass." What might make the soldiers "wistful"? [Analyze] ❾

Jade Flower Palace/The Moon at the Fortified Pass ◆ 859

◆ Build Grammar Skills

❻ **Adjectival Modifiers** Challenge students to identify the adjectival modifiers for "haze" (line 2) and "wind" (line 3) and to state what type each is. *The prepositional phrase "of cloud and sea" modifies the noun "haze." The adjective clause "that has come a thousand miles" modifies the noun "wind."*

◆ Literary Focus

❼ **Lyric Poetry** Point out that since this is a lyric poem, its historical situation is described in only two lines. In a narrative poem, much more about the history of this conflict would have been explained. Ask students to describe the setting for this event. *Sample answer: The place is the Jade Pass, a fortified gap in the Great Wall in northeastern China. The setting is moonlit, hazy, windy, and far from home.*

◆ Critical Thinking

❽ **Infer** What descriptive words in this passage indicate the soldiers' feeling, and what is that feeling? *The phrases "looking toward the border," "And think of home," reflect the soldiers' feeling, which is one of homesickness.*

▶Critical Viewing◀

❾ **Analyze** *Suggested response: These aspects of the setting would make the soldiers ... of night;*

Customize for *Gifted/Talented Students*

These students might be interest... ...ssing the theme ... form; for example, a journal entry, a brief musical interpretation, a painting, or a dance. Suggest that they begin by jotting down the theme, then decide which art form would best express the feelings they associate with that theme.

Cultural Connection

Community Gathering Places The speaker in Rosellen Brown's poem suggests that friends make life more enjoyable. Many communities and different cultures host events where people gather to share friendship and good times. Holiday activities, parades, block parties, town picnics, and concerts in the park are just a few types of gatherings that are sponsored by communities.

Challenge students to generate a list of places around the world where friends gather—they can research, as needed. In France, outdoor cafes are popular summertime gathering places; in Greece, the town square; in other locations it might be church or the community hall. What events or gathering places does your own community offer?

Discuss with them how community gathering places may have changed over time. What might have caused changes? Encourage them to consider the impact of technological advances such as cars, TV, air conditioning, and so forth. Ask them to speculate about future gathering places.

859

▲ **A wide range** of technology support appeals to varying learning styles.

◀ **Customize for**... notes in the Teacher's Edition make it easy to tailor instruction to varying student populations.

The largest literature library

ONLY **PRENTICE HALL**

- Combines over 80 titles to give you the classic and contemporary fiction, nonfiction, and drama that you love to teach.
- Offers exclusive thematic anthologies.
- Provides you with all of the teaching resources you need to explore each title.

PLUS...

bn.com BARNES & NOBLE

We give you a choice of over 8 million books, videos, audiotapes, and software through our partnership with barnesandnoble.com.

Choose the books that you want to teach!

available

WORLD WRITERS TODAY
THE BIBLE AS/IN LITERATURE
MULTICULTURAL VOICES
A SEPARATE PLACE
JOHNNY TREMAIN
Esther Forbes
LORD JIM
Joseph Conrad
A RAISIN IN THE SUN
Lorraine Hansberry
THE PEARL
Steinbeck
THE CLAY MARBLE
Workplace Writing
PRENTICE HALL LITERATURE LIBRARY
The Red Badge of Courage
Stephen Crane
A Midsummer Night's Dream
William Shakespeare
THE CALL OF THE WILD
BY JACK LONDON

The only literature program

ONLY **PRENTICE HALL**

- Choose from over 8 million books, videos, audiotapes, and software—the world's largest selection.
- Find exactly the resources you want for you and your students.
- Take advantage of a bookstore that never closes.
- Visit www.phlit.phschool.com to find details on this exciting partnership.

bn.com
BARNES & NOBLE

The nation's leading literature program now comes with the world's largest bookstore.

that comes with a bookstore!

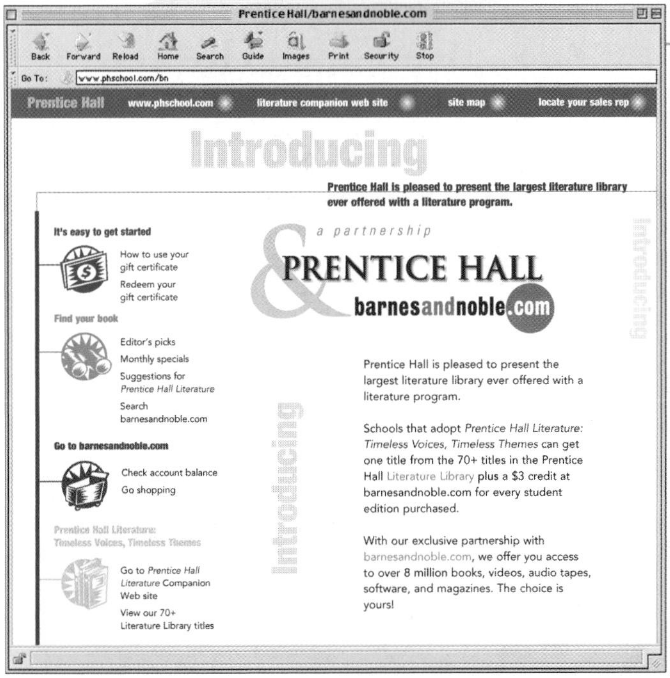

Exclusive partnership!

Prentice Hall is pleased to present the largest literature library ever offered with a literature program. With our exclusive partnership with barnesandnoble.com, we offer you access to over *8 million titles. We make it easy to get what you want.* Log on to www.phlit.phschool.com/bn and see how.

Key features help you find your book

- Editor's picks guide you to titles our editors enjoy and recommend.
- Bargain books help you shop and get the best deals.
- Suggestions for *Prentice Hall Literature* always correlate to the title you teach.
- Search barnesandnoble.com and choose from over 8 million books, videos, audio-tapes, and software.

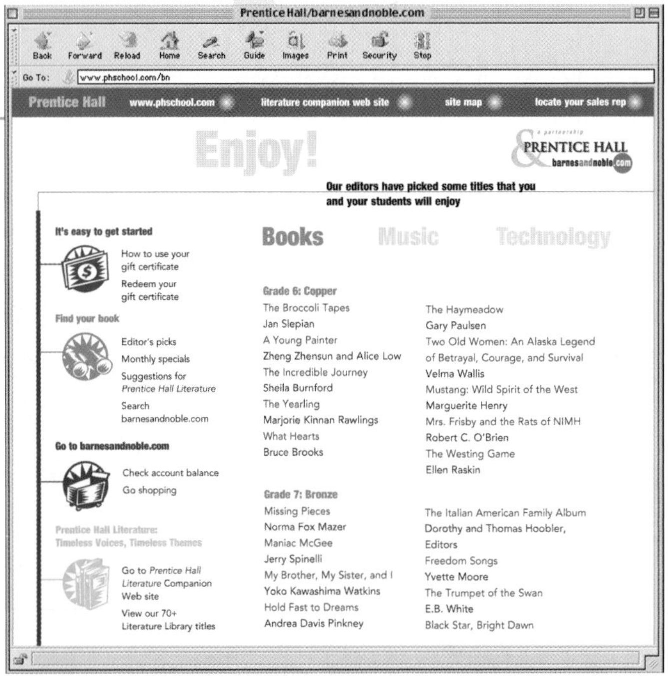

Outstanding array of technology resources

ONLY **PRENTICE HALL**

- Motivates students with a wide range of fully integrated technology.
- Makes teachers' planning easier with the groundbreaking *Resource Pro® CD-ROM with Local Objectives Editor.*
- Grabs students' attention with videos for each selection.
- Helps varying learning styles with selections on tape and video segments that hook students.
- Features the award-winning interactive writing instruction of *Writer's Solution.*
- Gives you a dedicated companion Web site at www.phlit.phschool.com to access a full-range of interactive, Internet-based activities.

Listening to Literature Audiocassettes bring literature to life and meet the diverse needs and learning styles of your students.

A wide array of **Video Series** are fully integrated into the textbook and feature point-of-use notes in the Teacher's Edition.

Resource Pro® with Local Objectives Editor CD-ROM gives you the tools to customize your lessons.

Writer's Solution, Prentice Hall's award-winning interactive writing instruction program, has been fully integrated into *Prentice Hall Literature: Timeless Voices, Timeless Themes.*

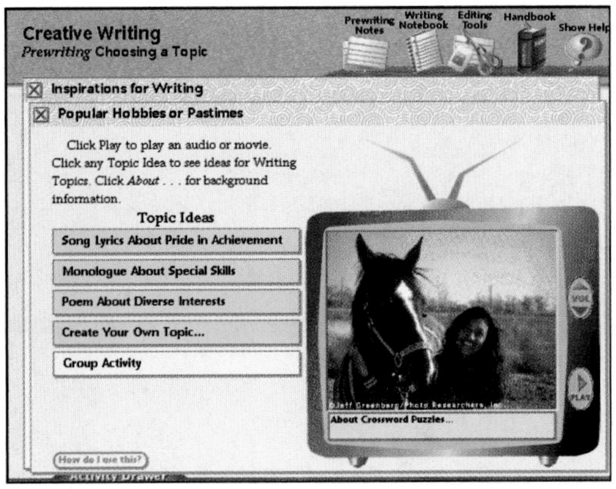

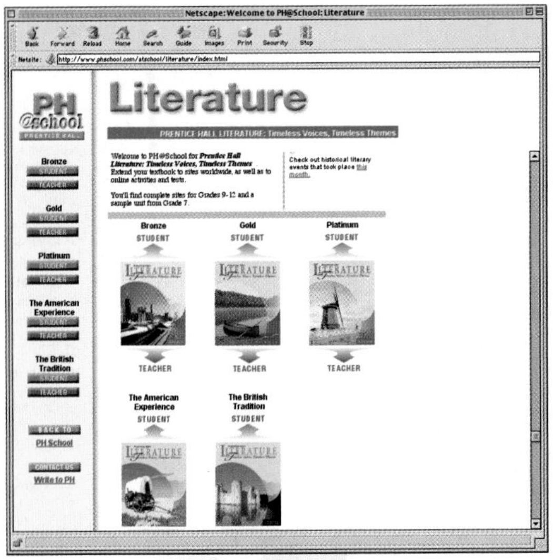

Internet Home Page, at www.phlit.phschool.com provides features that support *Prentice Hall Literature: Timeless Voices, Timeless Themes.*

Literature CD-ROM Library features multimedia presentations; hyperlinks to glossaries, indexes, and encyclopedias; and complete on-line testing; as just some of the outstanding features on these interactive CD-ROMs.

Formal Assessment CD-ROM allows you to gauge your students' ability levels and establish your own skills objectives.

Support for block scheduling

ONLY **PRENTICE HALL**

- Provides block scheduling lesson suggestions with every selection.
- Offers a full range of activities and workshops to create opportunities for in-depth exploration of a topic.
- Supports the use of a variety of instructional models.
- Encourages students to demonstrate their knowledge and understanding of concepts and content through alternative assessment.
- Features the award-winning *Resource Pro® with Planning Express® CD-ROM* to help you manage block scheduling lesson planning and manage resources.

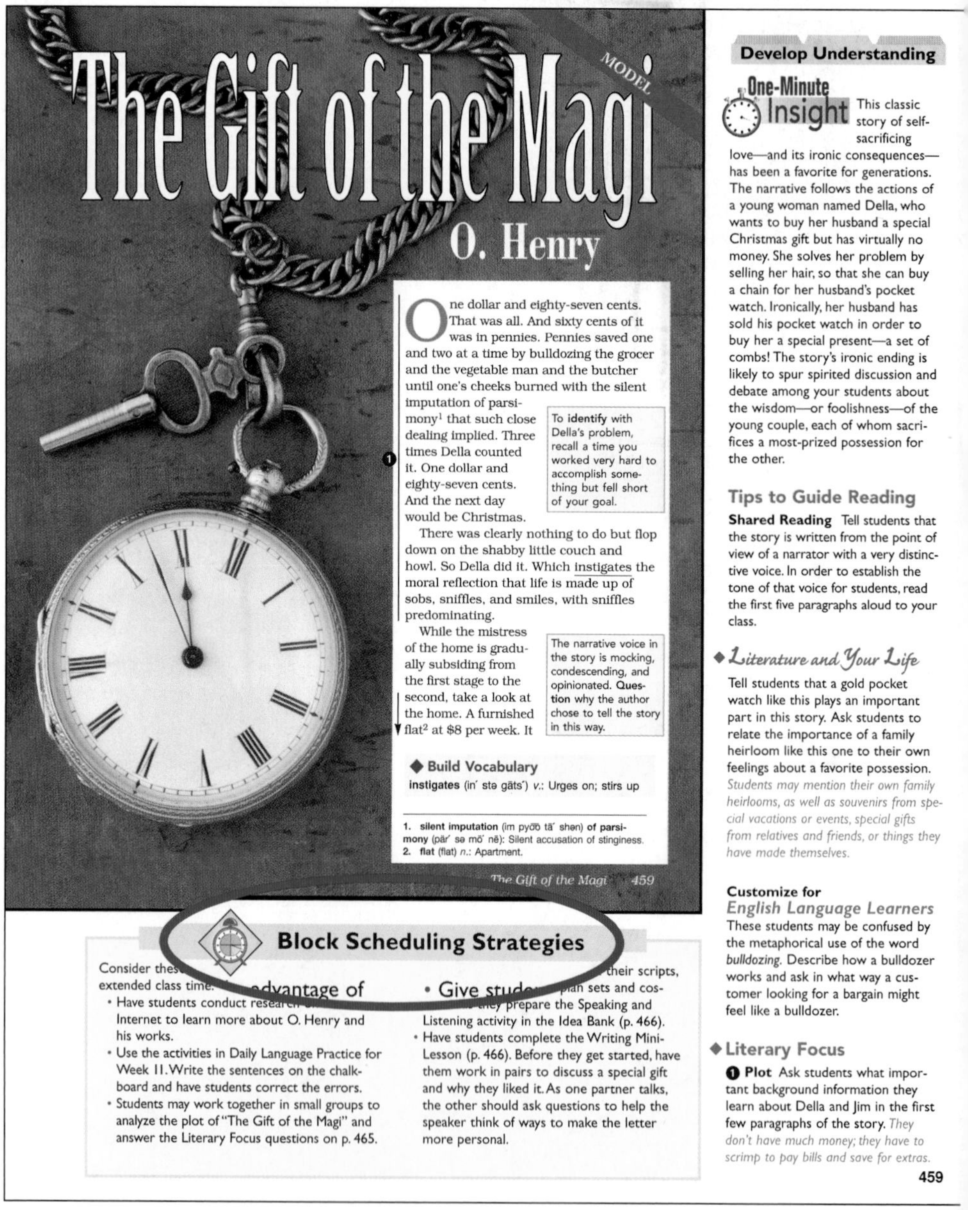

The Gift of the Magi

MODEL

O. Henry

One dollar and eighty-seven cents. That was all. And sixty cents of it was in pennies. Pennies saved one and two at a time by bulldozing the grocer and the vegetable man and the butcher until one's cheeks burned with the silent imputation of parsimony[1] that such close dealing implied. Three times Della counted it. One dollar and eighty-seven cents. And the next day would be Christmas.

To **identify** with Della's problem, recall a time you worked very hard to accomplish something but fell short of your goal.

There was clearly nothing to do but flop down on the shabby little couch and howl. So Della did it. Which instigates the moral reflection that life is made up of sobs, sniffles, and smiles, with sniffles predominating.

While the mistress of the home is gradually subsiding from the first stage to the second, take a look at the home. A furnished flat[2] at $8 per week. It

The narrative voice in the story is mocking, condescending, and opinionated. **Question** why the author chose to tell the story in this way.

◆ **Build Vocabulary**

instigates (in′ stə gāts′) *v.*: Urges on; stirs up

1. **silent imputation** (im pyo͞o tā′ shən) **of parsimony** (pär′ sə mō′ nē): Silent accusation of stinginess.
2. **flat** (flat) *n.*: Apartment.

The Gift of the Magi 459

Develop Understanding

One-Minute Insight This classic story of self-sacrificing love—and its ironic consequences—has been a favorite for generations. The narrative follows the actions of a young woman named Della, who wants to buy her husband a special Christmas gift but has virtually no money. She solves her problem by selling her hair, so that she can buy a chain for her husband's pocket watch. Ironically, her husband has sold his pocket watch in order to buy her a special present—a set of combs! The story's ironic ending is likely to spur spirited discussion and debate among your students about the wisdom—or foolishness—of the young couple, each of whom sacrifices a most-prized possession for the other.

Tips to Guide Reading

Shared Reading Tell students that the story is written from the point of view of a narrator with a very distinctive voice. In order to establish the tone of that voice for students, read the first five paragraphs aloud to your class.

◆ ***Literature and Your Life***

Tell students that a gold pocket watch like this plays an important part in this story. Ask students to relate the importance of a family heirloom like this one to their own feelings about a favorite possession. *Students may mention their own family heirlooms, as well as souvenirs from special vacations or events, special gifts from relatives and friends, or things they have made themselves.*

Customize for
English Language Learners
These students may be confused by the metaphorical use of the word *bulldozing*. Describe how a bulldozer works and ask in what way a customer looking for a bargain might feel like a bulldozer.

◆ **Literary Focus**

❶ **Plot** Ask students what important background information they learn about Della and Jim in the first few paragraphs of the story. *They don't have much money; they have to scrimp to pay bills and save for extras.*

Block Scheduling Strategies

Consider thes extended class time. dvantage of

- Have students conduct researc Internet to learn more about O. Henry and his works.
- Use the activities in Daily Language Practice for Week 11. Write the sentences on the chalkboard and have students correct the errors.
- Students may work together in small groups to analyze the plot of "The Gift of the Magi" and answer the Literary Focus questions on p. 465.
- Give stud their scripts, plan sets and cos- prepare the Speaking and Listening activity in the Idea Bank (p. 466).
- Have students complete the Writing Mini-Lesson (p. 466). Before they get started, have them work in pairs to discuss a special gift and why they liked it. As one partner talks, the other should ask questions to help the speaker think of ways to make the letter more personal.

459

Block Scheduling Strategies give you point-of-use suggestions with every selection.

Resource Pro® with Planning Express® CD-ROM helps you manage lesson planning and resources.

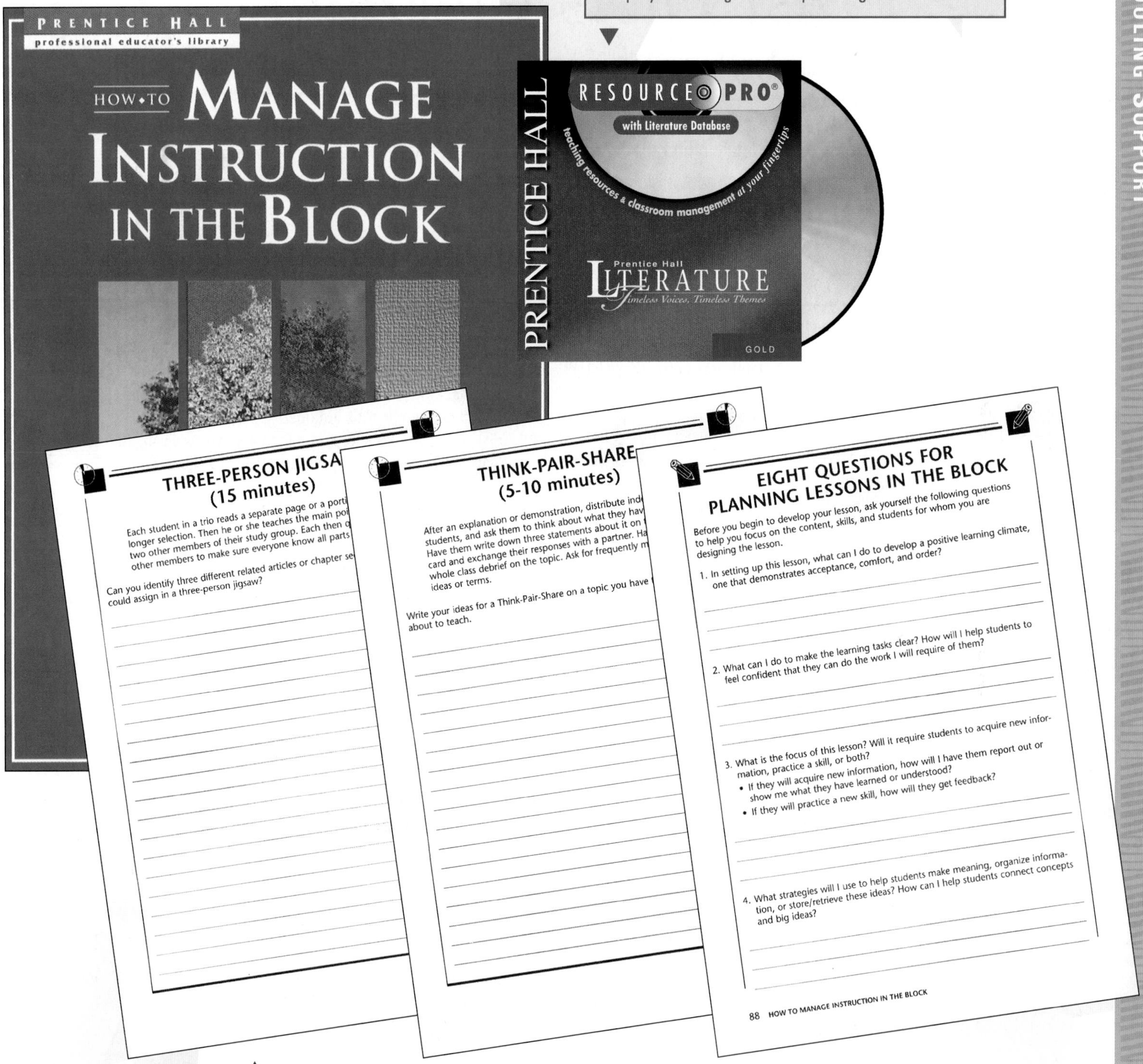
PRENTICE HALL
professional educator's library
HOW•TO MANAGE INSTRUCTION IN THE BLOCK
PRENTICE HALL
RESOURCE PRO®
with Literature Database
teaching resources & classroom management at your fingertips
Prentice Hall
LITERATURE
Timeless Voices, Timeless Themes
GOLD
THREE-PERSON JIGSA
(15 minutes)
THINK-PAIR-SHARE
(5-10 minutes)
EIGHT QUESTIONS FOR PLANNING LESSONS IN THE BLOCK
Before you begin to develop your lesson, ask yourself the following questions to help you focus on the content, skills, and students for whom you are designing the lesson.
1. In setting up this lesson, what can I do to develop a positive learning climate, one that demonstrates acceptance, comfort, and order?
2. What can I do to make the learning tasks clear? How will I help students to feel confident that they can do the work I will require of them?
3. What is the focus of this lesson? Will it require students to acquire new information, practice a skill, or both?
• If they will acquire new information, how will I have them report out or show me what they have learned or understood?
• If they will practice a new skill, how will they get feedback?
4. What strategies will I use to help students make meaning, organize information, or store/retrieve these ideas? How can I help students connect concepts and big ideas?
88 HOW TO MANAGE INSTRUCTION IN THE BLOCK

Teaching Resources give you guidance and support for managing time, adapting curriculum materials, and designing lessons.

Fast Facts Calendar

What happened on this day in . . .

The following list calls out important dates in literary history as well as other historical dates, which appear in italics. You may use this information as a quick enrichment activity to start classes or as the basis for students' writing assignments, research projects, collaborative work, or cross-curricular study.

January

1 1660 Samuel Pepys records the first entry in his Diary: "This morning (we lying lately in the garret) I rose, put on my suit with great skirts, having not lately worn any other clothes but them."

2 1920 Isaac Asimov is born in Petrovichi, Russia.

3 1882 Docking in New York City, Oscar Wilde is asked by customs officials if he has anything to declare. "Nothing but my genius," he replies.

4 1960 Albert Camus is killed in an automobile accident.

6 1840 Fanny Burney, Mme d'Arbley, dies in Bath, England, at age 87.

1878 Carl Sandburg, winner of Pulitzer Prizes in history (1940) and poetry (1951), is born in Galesburg, Illinois.

7 1841 Victor Hugo is elected to the Académie Française.

1903 Zora Neale Hurston is born in Eatonville, Florida.

8 1913 In London, Robert Frost and Ezra Pound meet for the first time at the opening of the Poetry Bookshop.

9 1946 Harlem Renaissance poet Countee Cullen dies in New York.

10 1845 Elizabeth Barrett and Robert Browning begin corresponding after she receives a note from him saying "I love you."

11 1928 Thomas Hardy dies at his home near Dorchester, England.

12 1876 Jack London is born in San Francisco, California.

13 1695 Jonathan Swift is ordained an Anglican priest.

14 1894 Inaugural issue of *Vogue* features two stories by Kate Chopin.

15 1846 Fyodor Dostoyevsky publishes his first novel at age 25.

17 1706 Benjamin Franklin is born in Boston, Massachusetts.

1860 Anton Chekhov is born in Taganrog, Russia.

23 1936 George Orwell writes: "I worshipped Kipling at 13, loathed him at 17, enjoyed him at 20, despised him at 25, and now again rather admire him."

27 1302 Dante Alighieri is expelled from Florence when a political group he opposes seizes control.

29 1963 Robert Frost dies in Boston, Massachusetts.

30 1935 Ezra Pound meets Benito Mussolini and reads aloud several lines from a draft of the *Cantos.* The dictator finds the reading entertaining.

February

1 1902 Langston Hughes is born in Joplin, Missouri.

2 1870 Mark Twain marries Olivia Langdon in Elmira, New York.

1922 On James Joyce's 40th birthday, *Ulysses* is published.

3 1874 Gertrude Stein is born in Allegheny, Pennsylvania. She will later boast: "I have been the creative mind of the century."

4 1818 At an evening at Leigh Hunt's, John Keats, Hunt, and Percy Bysshe Shelley vie with each other in composing sonnets on the subject of the Nile. Hunt's is deemed the best.

1938 Thorton Wilder's Pulitzer Prize-winning play *Our Town* opens.

7 1812 Lord Byron, in his first speech in the House of Lords, denounces a measure that would provide the death penalty for rebellious laborers.

1885 Sinclair Lewis, the first American to win the Nobel Prize for Literature (1930), is born in Sauk Centre, Minnesota.

9 1944 Alice Walker, winner of the 1983 Pulitzer Prize for Fiction for *The Color Purple,* is born.

10 1846 Edward Lear's *A Book of Nonsense* is published.

12 1959 On the 150th anniversary of Lincoln's birth, Carl Sandburg addresses a joint session of the United States Congress.

13 1974 Alexander Solzhenitsyn is expelled from the Soviet Union. He settles in the United States two years later.

16 1751 Thomas Gray anonymously publishes "Elegy Written in a Country Churchyard."

18 1931 Toni Morrison is born in Lorain, Ohio.

19 *1878 Thomas Alva Edison receives the first patent for a phonograph.*

1927 Carson McCullers is born in Columbus, Georgia.

20 1950 Dylan Thomas arrives in New York for his first series of American poetry readings.

23 1821 John Keats dies in Rome, Italy, of tuberculosis.

27 1807 Henry Wadsworth Longfellow is born in Portland, Maine.

1902 John Steinbeck is born in Salinas, California.

1934 N. Scott Momaday is born in Lawton, Oklahoma.

28 1916 Henry James dies in London. His last words are: "So here it is at last, the distinguished thing."

29 1960 James Thurber writes in the *New York Post* that "Humor is emotional chaos remembered in tranquillity."

9780131324770

March

1 1914 Ralph Ellison is born in Oklahoma City, Oklahoma.
2 1942 D. H. Lawrence dies of tuberculosis at age 45.
4 1916 Playwright Horton Foote is born. Foote goes on to write the Pulitzer Prize-winning play *The Young Man From Atlanta*.
1921 E. M. Forster (*A Passage to India*) sets out for India.
5 *1770 Five American colonists are killed in the Boston Massacre.*
6 1928 Gabriel García Márquez is born in Antarctica, Colombia. He wins the Nobel Prize for Literature in 1982.
7 1870 Thomas Hardy meets Emma Gifford, who will become his first wife. When she dies in 1912, Hardy leaves his desk calendar on her death date until his own death in 1928.
8 1941 Sherwood Anderson dies after eating a toothpick along with an hors d'oeuvre.
10 1948 Zelda Fitzgerald, wife of F. Scott Fitzgerald, dies in a fire at Highland Hospital.
11 1818 Mary Shelley's *Frankenstein* is published. It begins as a simple ghost story to entertain house guests, who encourage her to develop the story.
13 1818 John Keats writes to a friend: "I am sometimes so very skeptical as to think poetry is a mere Jack-o'-Lantern to whoever may chance to be struck with its brilliance."
1943 Stephen Vincent Benét dies of a heart attack at age 44.
14 *1841 David Livingstone arrives in Cape Town, South Africa, beginning a lifelong exploration of Africa's southern interior.*
16 1850 Nathaniel Hawthorne's *The Scarlet Letter* is published.
1904 James Joyce is awarded a bronze medal in a singing contest in Dublin. He immediately throws the medal in the river.
18 1932 John Updike, winner of the 1982 Pulitzer Prize for Fiction, is born in Shillington, Pennsylvania.
19 1842 As a publicity stunt for his play *Les Ressources de Quinola*, Honoré de Balzac starts a rumor that tickets are scarce. The plan backfires when his potential audience stays home upon hearing the news.
20 1828 Henrik Ibsen is born in Skien, Norway.
1852 Harriet Beecher Stowe's *Uncle Tom's Cabin* is published.
21 1843 Robert Southey, poet laurete, dies in Keswick, England.
23 1913 Jack London writes to Winston Churchill, Bernard Shaw, and H. G. Wells to ask what they are paid for their "stuff."
25 1811 Percy Bysshe Shelley is expelled from Oxford for refusing to admit writing *The Necessity of Atheism*.
26 1874 Robert Frost, winner of four Pulitzer Prizes for Poetry (1924, 1931, 1937, 1943), is born in San Francisco, California.
1892 Walt Whitman dies in Camden, New Jersey.
1911 Tennessee Williams is born in Columbus, Mississippi.
28 1775 Samuel Johnson says of poet Thomas Gray: "He was dull in company, dull in his closet, dull everywhere. He was dull in a new way, and that made people think him great."
29 1952 E. B. White writes to his daughter about *Charlotte's Web*: "Whether children will find anything amusing in it only time will tell."
31 1631 John Donne dies in London.
1914 Octavio Paz is born in Mexico City, Mexico.

April

1 1816 When the secretary of the Prince Regent asks her to write a "historical romance," Jane Austen responds: "I could not seriously sit down to write a serious romance under any other motive than to save my life."
2 1836 Charles Dickens and Catherine Hogarth are married in London.
1846 Nathaniel Hawthorne is appointed Surveyor of the Salem Custom House.
3 1783 Washington Irving is born in New York, New York.
4 1928 Maya Angelou is born in St. Louis, Missouri.
6 1327 Petrarch sees a beautiful woman in church. Smitten, he will write 366 poems to "Laura."
7 1770 William Wordsworth is born in Cumberland, England.
1889 Gabriela Mistral is born. She will be the first South American to win the Nobel Prize for Literature.
9 1821 Charles Baudelaire is born in Paris, France.
10 1925 F. Scott Fitzgerald's *The Great Gatsby* is published.
11 1914 Bernard Shaw's *Pygmalion* opens in London.
1931 Dorothy Parker steps down as drama critic for *The New Yorker*.
12 1709 Richard Steele publishes the first issue of *The Tatler*.
1861 Confederate guns fire on Fort Sumter, in Charleston Harbor, South Carolina, starting the American Civil War.
13 1845 Victor Hugo is made a peer of France, Vicomte Hugo.
1909 Eudora Welty is born in Jackson, Mississippi.
14 1828 Noah Webster's dictionary, 22 years in the making, is published.
15 1755 Samuel Johnson's *A Dictionary of the English Language* is published.
1947 Jackie Robinson, the first African American baseball player in the major leagues, plays his first game with the Brooklyn Dodgers.
16 1994 Ralph Ellison dies in New York.
17 1884 Isak Dinesen is born in Rungsted, Denmark.
1897 Thornton Wilder is born in Madison, Wisconsin.
18 *1774 On his Midnight Ride, Paul Revere warns colonists of a British attack.*
1958 A Federal Court decides that because Ezra Pound is insane, he cannot be held for treason and can be released from custody.
19 1824 George Gordon, Lord Byron, dies at age 36.
20 1859 The first volume of Charles Dickens's *A Tale of Two Cities* is published.
21 1910 Mark Twain dies in Redding, Connecticut.
23 1564 William Shakespeare is born in Stratford-upon-Avon, England.
1850 William Wordsworth dies in the Lake District.
24 1905 Robert Penn Warren is born in Guthrie, Kentucky.
25 1719 After several rejections, Daniel Defoe's *Robinson Crusoe* is published.
26 1914 Bernard Malamud is born in Brooklyn, New York.
27 1667 John Milton sells the copyright for *Paradise Lost* for 10 pounds to Samuel Simmons.
1945 Dramatist August Wilson is born in Pittsburgh, Pennsylvania.
1994 Nelson Mandela is elected president in the first election open to all races in South Africa.
28 1926 Harper Lee, author of *To Kill a Mockingbird* (1960), is born in Monroeville, Alabama.
30 1922 A. E. Housman dies at age 77.

May

1 1700 John Dryden dies in London.
1931 The Empire State Building opens in New York City.
2 1936 The manuscript of Edna St. Vincent Millay's *Conversation at Midnight* is destroyed in a hotel fire.
1945 Colette becomes the first female member of the Académie Goncourt, a literary honor.
3 *Under Milkwood,* by Dylan Thomas, is given its first American reading.
4 1940 Nora Joyce, wife of James Joyce, tells her husband: "Well, Jim, I haven't read any of your books, but I'll have to someday because they must be good considering how well they sell."
5 1902 Bret Harte dies in London at age 65.
1926 Sinclair Lewis declines the Pulitzer Prize, saying that such prizes tend to make writers "safe, polite, obedient, and sterile."
1927 Virginia Woolf publishes *To the Lighthouse*.
6 1862 Henry David Thoreau dies in Concord, Massachusetts.
1940 John Steinbeck's *The Grapes of Wrath* wins the Pulitzer Prize.
7 1812 Robert Browning is born in London.
1945 World War II ends in Europe.
10 *1869 The Transcontinental Railroad is completed.*
12 1812 Edward Lear is born in Highgate, England.
1828 Dante Gabriel Rossetti is born in London.
13 1906 Willa Cather becomes editor of *McClure's Magazine*.
14 1900 Hal Borland is born in Sterling, Colorado.
1931 Her coffee plantation a failure, Isak Dinesen leaves Africa. Five years later, *Out of Africa* makes her internationally famous.
15 1886 Emily Dickinson dies in Amherst, Massachusetts.
1890 Pulitzer Prize-winning author Katherine Anne Porter is born in Texas. She goes on to write *Ship of Fools*.
16 1763 James Boswell first meets Samuel Johnson. His biography of Johnson will be published 28 years later.
1836 Edgar Allan Poe marries his cousin, Virginia Clemm.
18 1593 After dramatist Christopher Marlow is falsely accused of heresy by his roommate, a warrant is issued for Marlowe's arrest.
19 1795 James Boswell, Dr. Johnson's biographer, dies in London.
1930 Lorraine Hansberry is born in Chicago, Illinois.
20 1845 Robert Browning pays his first visit to Elizabeth Barrett.
1932 Amelia Earhart begins her first solo flight across the Atlantic Ocean.
21 1688 Alexander Pope is born in London, England.
22 1859 Sir Arthur Conan Doyle is born in Edinburgh, Scotland.
1969 Langston Hughes dies in New York.
23 1839 Henry Wadsworth Longfellow says of Jane Austen: "Her writings are a capital picture of real life, with all the little wheels and machinery laid bare like a patent clock. But she explains and fills out too much."
25 1808 Ralph Waldo Emerson is born in Boston, Massachusetts.
1908 Theodore Roethke is born in Saginaw, Michigan.
26 735 The Venerable Bede dies at Jarrow.
27 1907 Rachel L. Carson is born in Springdale, Pennsylvania.
29 1906 T. H. White is born in Bombay, India.
1953 Sir Edmund Hillary and Nepalese mountaineer Tenzing Norgay make the first ascent of Mount Everest (29,028 feet).
30 1903 Countee Cullen is born in Louisville, Kentucky.
1909 The National Conference on the Negro convenes, which will lead to the founding of the NAACP.
31 1819 Walt Whitman is born in West Hills, Long Island.

June

1 1898 Bernard Shaw marries Charlotte Payne-Townsend.
2 1825 Emily Brontë leaves Cowan Bridge School, where officials have noted in her record: "Subsequent career—governess."
3 1936 Author Larry McMurtry is born in Texas. He goes go on to write the Pulitzer Prize-winning *Lonesome Dove*.
4 1962 William Faulkner's last novel, *The Reivers*, is published posthumously and wins the Pulitzer Prize for Fiction the following year.
5 1900 Stephen Crane dies of tuberculosis in Germany.
6 *1944 The D-Day invasion of France by Allied troops in World War II takes place.*
7 1899 Elizabeth Bowen is born in Dublin, Ireland.
8 1374 Chaucer is appointed Comptroller for the Customs and Subsidy of Wools at £10 a year.
9 1870 Charles Dickens dies at age 58.
11 1899 Kawabata Yasunari is born. In 1968, he is the first Japanese to win the Nobel Prize for Literature.
12 1929 Anne Frank is born in Frankfurt-am-Main, Germany.
13 1865 William Butler Yeats is born in Dublin, Ireland.
1894 Poet Mark Van Doren is born in Hope Park, Illinois.
15 *1215 King John of England signs the Magna Carta.*
16 1938 Joyce Carol Oates is born in Lockport, New York.
17 1719 Joseph Addison dies at age 47. He is buried in Westminster Abbey.
1914 John Hersey is born in Tientsin, China.
1917 Gwendolyn Brooks is born in Topeka, Kansas.
18 *1983 Sally Ride becomes the first American woman in space.*
21 1956 Playwright Arthur Miller refuses to betray his left-wing associates before the House Committee on Un-American Activities.
24 1842 Ambrose Bierce is born in Meigs County, Ohio.
1916 John Ciardi is born in Boston, Massachusetts.
25 1903 George Orwell is born in Motihari, India.
26 *1945 Fifty nations sign the charter of the United Nations in San Francisco.*
27 1872 Paul Laurence Dunbar is born in Dayton, Ohio.
1936 Lucille Clifton is born in Depew, New York.
28 1888 Robert Louis Stevenson leaves San Francisco on his first voyage to the South Seas.
1914 Archduke Francis Ferdinand is assassinated, touching off World War I.
29 1613 The Globe Theater catches fire and burns to the ground during a performance of Shakespeare's *Henry VIII*.
30 1911 Czeslaw Milosz, winner of the Nobel Prize for Literature, is born near Vilna, Lithuania.

July

1 *1997* *Great Britain gives up control of Hong Kong to China.*
2 1961 Ernest Hemingway dies in Ketcham, Idaho.
3 1883 Franz Kafka is born in Prague, Czechoslovakia.
4 *1776* *American Declaration of Independence is signed.*
1804 Nathaniel Hawthorne is born in Salem, Massachusetts.
1855 Walt Whitman prints the first edition of his *Leaves of Grass.*
5 1880 Bernard Shaw leaves his job with the Edison Telephone Company. He later said, "You must not suppose, because I am a man of letters, that I never tried to earn an honest living."
6 1895 O. Henry, trying to flee a charge of embezzlement, boards a train headed for New Orleans.
7 1535 Sir Thomas More is beheaded for refusing to acknowledge Henry VIII as supreme authority of the Church.
8 1822 Percy Bysshe Shelley is drowned while sailing off the coast of Italy.
9 1942 Anne Frank and her family go into hiding.
10 *1962* *Telstar, the first communications satellite, transmits the first television pictures from the United States to Europe.*
11 1937 Dylan Thomas marries Caitlin Macnamara.
12 1904 Pablo Neruda is born in Parral, Chile.
14 *1789* *The French Revolution begins in Paris.*
1904 Isaac Bashevis Singer is born in Radzymin, Poland.
1986 Jorge Luis Borges dies in Geneva, Switzerland.
16 1660 Even as he is being ordered into custody, Milton works on *Paradise Lost*, which he publishes 7 years later.
17 1886 Poet Gerard Manley Hopkins converts to Roman Catholicism.
18 1817 Jane Austen dies in Winchester, England.
19 *1848* *The first U.S. women's rights convention in Seneca Falls, N.Y., begins, led by Lucretia Mott and Elizabeth Cady Stanton.*
20 1869 Mark Twain's *Innocents Abroad* is published.
1969 Neil Armstrong becomes the first person to set foot on the moon.
22 1898 Stephen Vincent Benét is born in Bethlehem, Pennsylvania.
23 1846 Thoreau is jailed for refusing to pay a $1 poll tax; this moves him to write *Civil Disobedience*.
25 1897 Jack London heads for the Klondike aboard the steamer *Umatilla*.
26 1892 Pearl S. Buck, winner of the 1932 Pulitzer Prize in fiction and the 1938 Nobel Prize in Literature, is born in Hillsboro, West Virginia.
29 1805 Statesman and writer Alexis de Tocqueville is born in Paris, France.
31 1703 After having written *The Shortest Way with Dissenters*, Daniel Defoe is forced to stand in the pillory in front of Temple Bar. He draws sympathetic crowds who pelt him with flowers instead of mud.

August

1 1819 Herman Melville is born in New York, New York.
2 1924 James Baldwin is born in New York, New York.
3 1887 Wartime poet Rupert Brooke is born in Warwickshire, England.
5 1850 Guy de Maupassant is born near Dieppe, France.
6 1637 Ben Jonson dies in London at the age of 65.
1809 Alfred, Lord Tennyson, poet laureate of England, is born in Lincolnshire, England.
7 1804 William Blake writes to William Hayley: "Money flies from me. Profit never ventures upon my threshold."
8 1884 Sara Teasdale is born in St. Louis, Missouri.
9 1842 Herman Melville escapes from a one-month captivity by South Sea Island cannibals.
10 1824 Charlotte Brontë is sent to Cowan Bridge School by her widowed father.
11 1921 Pulitzer Prize-winning author Alex Haley is born in Ithaca, New York.
12 1827 William Blake dies at age 70 in London.
14 1925 Journalist Russell Baker is born.
15 1771 Sir Walter Scott is born in Edinburgh, Scotland.
17 1917 Wilfred Owen and Siegfried Sassoon, both recuperating from battle fatigue at the Craiglockhart War Hospital, meet and form an intense friendship.
1930 Ted Hughes is born in West Yorkshire, England.
18 *1920* *The Nineteenth Amendment, giving women the right to vote, is ratified.*
19 *1691* *Six people are hanged in Salem Village, Massachusetts, for witchcraft.*
21 1762 Lady Wortley Montague dies. Her last words are: "It has all been very interesting."
22 1904 Kate Chopin dies in her hometown of St. Louis, Missouri.
1920 Ray Bradbury is born in Waukegan, Illinois.
23 1869 Edgar Lee Masters is born in Garnett, Kansas.
24 1847 Charlotte Brontë's *Jane Eyre* is sent to the publisher under the name Currer Bell.
25 1836 Bret Harte is born in Albany, New York.
26 1893 Jack London returns to San Francisco after spending eight months on a seal-hunting expedition aboard the *Sophia Sutherland*.
1914 Julio Cortázar is born in Brussels, Belgium.
27 1660 John Milton's books are burned in London after Milton, in his pamphlets, repeatedly attacks King Charles II.
28 *1963* *Martin Luther King, Jr., delivers his "I have a dream" speech to more than 200,000 people in Washington, D.C.*
29 1809 Oliver Wendell Holmes is born in Cambridge, Massachusetts.
1962 Robert Frost leaves for a goodwill tour of the U.S.S.R., sponsored by the U.S. State Department.
30 1797 Mary Wollstonecraft Shelley, author of *Frankenstein*, is born in London.

September

2 *1945 Japan signs a peace treaty to end World War II.*
3 1849 Sarah Orne Jewett is born in South Berwick, Maine.
1962 E. E. Cummings dies in North Conway, New Hampshire.
4 1908 Richard Wright is born near Natchez, Mississippi.
6 1890 Joseph Conrad becomes master of the *Roi des Belges*, an experience he will draw upon later in his writing.
7 1892 John Greenleaf Whittier dies of a stroke in Hampton Falls, New Hampshire.
8 *1522 Ferdinand Magellan's crew arrives in Seville, Spain, becoming the first people to circumnavigate the globe.*
1947 Ann Beattie is born in Washington, D.C.
9 1828 Leo Tolstoy is born in Tula, a province of Russia.
10 1886 Poet H. D. (Hilda Doolittle) is born in Bethlehem, Pennsylvania.
11 1862 William Sidney Porter, later known as O. Henry, is born. He would spend a good portion of his life in Texas, and go on to write "The Gift of the Magi" and other short stories.
12 1846 Elizabeth Barrett and Robert Browning secretly marry.
13 1876 Sherwood Anderson is born in Camden, Ohio. F. Scott Fitzgerald would later describe him as "the possessor of a brilliant and almost inimitable prose style, and of scarcely any ideas at all."
14 *1814 British end bombardment of Fort McHenry, inspiring Francis Scott Key to write the words to "The Star-Spangled Banner."*
1851 James Fennimore Cooper dies in Cooperstown, New York.
16 1672 Anne Bradstreet dies in Andover, Massachusetts.
17 1883 William Carlos Williams, winner of the 1963 Pulitzer Prize for Poetry, is born in Rutherford, New Jersey.
18 1709 Samuel Johnson is born in Staffordshire, England.
19 1985 Italo Calvino dies in Siena, Italy.
20 1923 T. S. Eliot's *The Waste Land* receives scathing reviews in the *Times Literary Supplement.*
22 1598 Ben Jonson is indicted for manslaughter after killing another actor in a duel.
24 1896 F. Scott Fitzgerald is born in St. Paul, Minnesota.
25 1897 William Faulkner, winner of the 1949 Nobel Prize for Literature and of the 1955 and 1963 Pulitzer Prizes for Fiction, is born in New Albany, Mississippi.
26 1888 T. S. Eliot is born in St. Louis, Missouri.
28 1891 Herman Melville dies in New York, having never achieved literary recognition.
1909 Poet Stephen Spender is born in London.
29 1973 W. H. Auden dies in Vienna, Austria, at age 66.
30 1598 Edmund Spenser is appointed Sheriff of Cork, Ireland.
1937 Albert Camus writes: "It is in order to shine sooner that authors refuse to rewrite. Despicable. Begin again."

October

1 *1847 American astronomer Maria Mitchell records the first comet (Comet Mitchell) viewed by a telescope.*
2 1836 Charles Darwin returns from his voyage on H.M.S. *Beagle*.
1904 Graham Greene is born in Hertfordshire, England.
3 1895 Stephen Crane's *The Red Badge of Courage* is published.
1916 James Herriot is born in Sunderland, Scotland.
4 1910 Jack London buys nine plot outlines from Sinclair Lewis for $52.50.
6 1599 William Shakespeare's *Romeo and Juliet* is published.
7 1849 Edgar Allan Poe dies in Baltimore, Maryland. He is 40 years old.
8 1779 William Blake begins his studies at the Royal Academy.
9 1950 Edna St. Vincent Millay dies in Austerlitz, New York.
10 1935 George Gershwin's *Porgy and Bess*, the first American-theme opera, opens in New York City.
12 *1492 Columbus and crew arrive at the islands now known as the West Indies.*
1908 Ann Petry is born in Old Saybrook, Connecticut.
14 1888 Katherine Mansfield is born in Wellington, New Zealand.
15 1897 Stephen Crane and Joseph Conrad have lunch together, marking the start of a famous friendship.
17 1586 Sir Philip Sidney, fighting a war in Holland, dies of battle wounds at age 32.
1915 Arthur Miller is born in New York City.
19 1745 Jonathan Swift dies in Dublin, Ireland.
20 1854 Arthur Rimbaud is born in Charlesville, France.
21 1929 Ursula Le Guin is born in Berkeley, California.
22 1919 Doris Lessing is born in Kermanshah, Iran.
24 1923 Denise Levertov is born in Essex, England.
25 1400 Geoffrey Chaucer dies in London, possibly of the plague.
1498 Amerigo Vespucci returns to Cadiz, Spain, from the lands that will later be named after him, the Americas.
26 1880 In Hartford, Connecticut, Mark Twain remarks, "I don't mind what the opposition says of me, so long as they don't tell the truth."
27 1914 Dylan Thomas is born in Swansea, Wales.
28 *1886 The Statue of Liberty is dedicated to the United States by France.*
29 1618 Sir Walter Raleigh is executed in the Tower of London.
1929 The New York Stock Exchange crashes, signaling the start of a worldwide economic depression.
31 1795 John Keats is born in Finsbury Pavement, England.

November

1 1871 Stephen Crane is born in Newark, New Jersey.
1930 Ernest Hemingway breaks his arm in a car crash following a hunting trip with John Dos Passos.
2 1927 T. S. Eliot becomes a British subject.
4 1918 Wilfred Owen dies in France at age 25.
1948 T. S. Eliot receives the Nobel Prize for Literature.
5 1644 Samuel Pepys records in his *Diary* that *Macbeth* is "a pretty good play."
6 1315 Dante Alighieri is sentenced to death when he refuses to return to Florence following his exile. He dies of malaria in Ravenna six years later.
7 1913 Albert Camus is born in Mondoni, Algeria.
8 1674 John Milton dies in London at age 65.
9 1953 Dylan Thomas dies in New York City.
11 *1620 The Mayflower Compact is signed off Cape Cod, Massachusetts.*
12 1935 Theodore Roethke is hospitalized with delusions brought on by hypothermia after spending a night in the Michigan woods.
13 1797 Samuel Taylor Coleridge and William Wordsworth begin work on *The Rime of the Ancient Mariner*.
14 1851 Herman Melville's *Moby-Dick* is published.
15 1887 Marianne Moore, winner of the 1952 Pulitzer Prize for Poetry, is born in St. Louis, Missouri.
16 1849 Fyodor Doestoevsky is sentenced to death for his socialist activities. The sentence is later lessened to four-years' hard labor in Siberia.
18 *1805 The Lewis and Clark expedition reaches the Pacific Ocean and claims the Oregon region for the United States.*
1865 Mark Twain's "The Celebrated Jumping Frog of Calaveras County" appears in the *Saturday Press*.
19 *1863 Lincoln delivers the Gettysburg Address.*
21 1694 Voltaire is born in Paris, France.
1910 Leo Tolstoy dies en route to the Caucasus.
22 1621 John Donne is elected dean of St. Paul's Cathedral.
1916 Jack London dies in Santa Rosa, California.
24 1868 Scott Joplin, the "King of Ragtime" music, is born near Linden, Texas.
26 1862 On meeting Harriet Beecher Stowe, Abraham Lincoln comments: "So this is the little lady who made the big war."
27 1970 Fearing that he will not be allowed to return home, Alexander Solzhenitsyn writes that he cannot go to Stockholm, Sweden, to receive the Nobel Prize.
28 1757 William Blake is born in London, England.
29 *1929 Richard E. Byrd makes the first flight over the South Pole.*
30 1667 Jonathan Swift is born in Dublin, Ireland.
1835 Mark Twain (Samuel Longhorn Clemens) is born in Florida, Missouri.

December

1 1860 The first installment of Charles Dickens's *Great Expectations* is published.
1955 Rosa Parks is arrested for refusing to give up her seat on a bus in Montgomery, Alabama.
2 1793 Samuel Taylor Coleridge enlists in the Light Dragoons.
1867 Charles Dickens gives his first readings in New York City. The lines at the box office stretch for miles.
3 1857 Joseph Conrad is born in the Polish Ukraine, then under Russian rule.
5 1830 Christina Rossetti is born in London, England.
1934 Joan Didion is born in Sacramento, California.
6 1712 Joseph Addison and Richard Steele publish the last issue of *The Spectator*.
7 *1941 A surprise attack is launched on the American naval base at Pearl Harbor.*
9 1854 Alfred, Lord Tennyson, publishes "The Charge of the Light Brigade" six weeks after the Battle of Balaclava.
10 1830 Emily Dickinson is born in Amherst, Massachusetts.
11 1875 Robert Louis Stevenson says of Robert Browning's writing: "He floods acres of paper with brackets and inverted commas."
12 1889 Robert Browning dies in Venice, Italy.
13 1927 Poet James Wright is born in Martin's Ferry, Ohio.
14 1953 Marjorie Kinnan Rawlings dies in Saint Augustine, Florida.
15 *1790 The U.S. Bill of Rights takes effect.*
1936 George Orwell leaves England to help in the war effort in Spain.
16 *1773 The Boston Tea Party takes place.*
1775 Jane Austen is born in Hampshire, England.
1917 Arthur C. Clarke is born in Somerset, England.
17 1843 *A Christmas Carol*, by Charles Dickens, is published.
18 1870 Saki (H. H. Munro) is born in Burma.
19 1732 Ben Franklin publishes *Poor Richard's Almanack*, a best seller in colonial America.
20 1871 In the *Chicago Tribune,* Mark Twain compares himself with George Washington: "I have a higher and greater standard of principle. Washington could not lie. I *can* lie but I won't."
21 1767 The Newport, Rhode Island, *Mercury* publishes a poem by 13-year-old African American poet Phillis Wheatley.
22 1869 Edwin Arlington Robinson is born in Head Tide, Maine.
24 1881 Poet Juan Ramón Jiménez, winner of the 1956 Nobel Prize for Literature, is born in Andalusia, Spain.
25 1642 Isaac Newton is born in Lincolnshire, England.
26 1606 William Shakespeare's *King Lear* is performed at court.
1913 Ambrose Bierce, while serving in Pancho Villa's army, writes his last letter and is never heard from again.
29 *1845 U.S. President James K. Polk signs legislation making Texas the twenty-eighth state of the United States.*
30 1816 Percy Bysshe Shelley marries Mary Godwin.
1865 Rudyard Kipling is born in Bombay, India.
31 1900 Edward Everett Hale welcomes in the new century, presiding at a Boston civic ceremony.

Selection	Reading	Literary Elements/Forms	Vocabulary	Grammar
from ***Journal of the First Voyage to America,* C. Columbus,** SE p. 15	Reading Level: Average • Reading for Success: Literal Comprehension Strategies, SE pp. 14, 18; TR Selection Support, pp. 3–4 • Break Down Sentences, TR Str. for Diverse St. Needs, p. 1	• Journals, SE pp. 13, 18; TR Selection Support, p. 5	• Latin Word Roots: *-flict-*, SE pp. 13, 18; TR Selection Support, p. 1 Word Bank: exquisite, p. 15; affliction, indications, abundance, p. 17	• Action Verbs and Linking Verbs, SE pp. 13, 18; TR Selection Support, p. 2 • WS Language Lab CD-ROM, Action Verbs, Linking Verbs
"The Earth . . . ," Onondaga; "When Grizzlies . . . ," Modoc; from ***The Navajo Origin . . . ,* Navajo;** from ***The Iroquois Constitution,* Iroquois,** SE pp. 22, 24, 26, 28	Reading Levels: Easy, Easy, Easy, Average • Recognize Cultural Details, SE pp. 21, 30; TR Selection Support, p. 8 • Summarize Main Idea, TR Str. for Diverse St. Needs, p. 2	• Origin Myths, SE pp. 21, 30; TR Selection Support, p. 9	• Latin Suffixes: *-tion*, SE pp. 21, 30; TR Selection Support, p. 6 Word Bank: ablutions, protruded, p. 27; confederate, disposition, deliberation, p. 29	• Compound Sentences, SE pp. 21, 30; TR Selection Support, p. 7 • WS Language Lab CD-ROM, Kinds of Sentences, Subjects and Predicates, Compound Sentence Parts
"A Journey Through Texas," A. N. Cabeza de Vaca; "Boulders Taller Than . . . ," G. López de Cárdenas, SE pp. 34, 38	Reading Levels: Average, Average • Signal Words, SE pp. 33, 40; TR Selection Support, p. 12 • Sequence Events, TR Str. for Diverse St. Needs, p. 3	• Exploration Narrative, SE pp. 33, 40; TR Selection Support, p. 13	• Latin Word Roots: *-mort-*, SE pp. 33, 40; TR Selection Support, p. 10 Word Bank: entreated, feigned, mortality, p. 35; subsisted, traversed, p. 37; dispatched, p. 38	• Past and Past Perfect Verb Tenses, SE pp. 33, 40; TR Selection Support, p. 11 • WS Language Lab CD-ROM, Tense
from ***The Interesting Narrative of the Life of Olaudah Equiano,* O. Equiano,** SE p. 44	Reading Level: Average • Summarize, SE pp. 43, 48; TR Selection Support, p. 16 • Classify Descriptive Details, TR Str. for Diverse St. Needs, p. 4	• Slave Narratives, SE pp. 43, 48; TR Selection Support, p. 17 • Analyze a Movie Review, ATE, p. 45	• Latin Word Roots: *-vid-*, SE pp. 43, 48; TR Selection Support, p. 14 Word Bank: loathsome, pestilential, copious, improvident, avarice, p. 44; pacify, p. 47	• Active and Passive Voice, SE pp. 43, 48; TR Selection Support, p. 15 • WS Language Lab CD-ROM, Strengthening Sentences, Active and Passive Voice
"Diamond Island: Alcatraz," D. B. Wilson; "Big Yellow Taxi" J. Mitchell, SE pp. 51, 56	Reading Levels: Average, Easy	• Analyze an Author's Comment, ATE, p. 52	Word Bank: expended, redolence, p. 53; autonomous, p. 55	• WS Gram. Pr. Book, pp. 60–61
from ***The General History of Virginia,* J. Smith;** from ***Of Plymouth Plantation,* W. Bradford,** SE pp. 66, 71	Reading Levels: Challenging, Challenging • Break Down Sentences, SE pp. 65, 76; TR Selection Support, p. 22 • Paraphrase, TR Str. for Diverse St. Needs, p. 5	• Narrative Accounts, SE pp. 65, 76; TR Selection Support, p. 23 • Analyze a Movie Review, ATE, p. 69	• Related Words: Forms of *Peril;* SE pp. 65, 76; TR Selection Support, p. 20 Word Bank: pilfer, palisades, conceits, p. 67; mollified, p. 69; peril, loath, sundry, p. 72; recompense, p. 74	• Plural and Possessive Nouns, SE pp. 65, 76; TR Selection Support, p. 21 • WS Language Lab CD-ROM, Types of Nouns
from ***The Right Stuff,* T. Wolfe,** SE p. 79	Reading Level: Average		• TR Selection Support, p. 24 Word Bank: malevolent, obliterated, trajectory, jettisoned, p. 80	
"To My Dear and Loving Husband," A. Bradstreet; "Huswifery," E. Taylor, SE pp. 90, 92	Reading Levels: Average, Challenging • Paraphrase, SE pp. 89, 94; TR Selection Support, p. 28 • Restate Poetic Language, TR Str. for Diverse St. Needs, p. 6	• The Puritan Plain Style, SE pp. 89, 94; TR Selection Support, p. 29	• Anglo-Saxon Suffixes: *-fold*, SE pp. 89, 94; TR Selection Support, p. 26 Word Bank: recompense, manifold, persevere, p. 91	• Direct Address, SE pp. 89, 94; TR Selection Support, p. 27 • WS Language Lab CD-ROM, Commas
from ***Sinners in the Hands of an Angry God,* J. Edwards,** SE p. 98	Reading Level: Challenging • Context Clues, SE pp. 97, 102; TR Selection Support, p. 32 • Question Author's Purpose, TR Str. for Diverse St. Needs, p. 7	• Sermon, SE pp. 97, 102; TR Selection Support, p. 33	• Latin Prefixes: *omni-*, SE pp. 97, 102; TR Selection Support, p. 30 Word Bank: omnipotent, p. 99; ineffable, dolorous, p. 101	• Forms of Adjectives and Adverbs, SE pp. 97, 102; TR Selection Support, p. 31 • WS Language Lab CD-ROM, Forms of Comparison • WS Gram. Pr. Book, pp. 73–74
"Iron Bird: Cal Ripken's Work Ethic," S. Wulf, SE p. 105	Reading Level: Easy		• TR Selection Support, p. 34 Word Bank: purported, p. 105; artifice, untoward, malaise, malingered, immersed, p. 106	

Writing	Speaking, Listening, and Viewing	Researching and Representing	Assessment	Technology
• Journal, Continuation, Comparing Journals, SE p. 19 • Oral Report, SE p. 19 • Report, TR Alt. Assess., p. 1 • New Ending, Origin Myth, Essay, SE p. 31	• Informative Speech, Native American Art, SE p. 19 • Debate, TR Alt. Assess., p. 1	• Map, Columbus Collection, SE p. 19 • Research Skills Mini-Lesson: Internet, ATE p. 16 • Science Display, TR Alt. Assess., p. 1	• Selection Test, TR Formal Assessment, pp. 1–3; Assess. Res. Software • Description Rubric [for Wr. Lesson], TR Alt. Assess., p. 112	• from *Journal of the First Voyage to America*, LL Audiocassettes • WS Writing Lab CD-ROM, Description Tutorial; Wr. at Work Videodisc, Ch. 1
• Guided Writing Lesson: Retelling of a Myth [Effective Repetition], SE p. 31 • Constitution Updating, TR Alt. Assess., p. 2 • Journal Entry, Creative Description, Comparison-and-Contrast Essay, SE p. 41	• Native American Chant, Dramatic Enactment, SE p. 31 • Musical Reading, TR Alt. Assess., p. 2	• Totem Pole, Logo, SE p. 31 • Origin Myth, TR Alt. Assess., p. 2	• Selection Test, TR Formal Assessment, pp. 4–6; Assess. Res. Software • Fictional Narrative Rubric [for Wr. Lesson], TR Alt. Assess., p. 110 • TR Alt. Assess., p. 2	• "The Earth. . .," "When Grizzlies. . .," from *The Navajo Origin. . .*, from *The Iroquois Constitution*, LL Audiocassettes • Looking at Lit., Ch. 1 • WS Writing Lab CD-ROM, Response to Literature Tutorial
• Guided Writing Lesson: Journal [Precise Details], SE p. 41 • Explorer Profiles, TR Alt. Assess., p. 3 • Activist List, Editorial, Character Sketch, SE p. 49	• Persuasive Speech, Southwest Guide, SE p. 41 • Skit, TR Alt. Assess., p. 3	• "America the Beautiful" Presentation, Television Series, SE p. 41 • V/R Mini-Lessons: Presentation, ATE p. 36; Southwest Guide, ATE p. 38 • Mural, TR Alt. Assess., p. 3	• Selection Test, TR Formal Assessment, pp. 7–9; Assess. Res. Software • Description Rubric [for Wr. Lesson], TR Alt. Assess., p. 112 • TR Alt. Assess., p. 3	• "A Journey Through Texas," "Boulders Taller Than. . . , LL Audiocassettes • WS Writing Lab CD-ROM, Description Tutorial; Wr. at Work Videodisc, Ch. 1 • Lit. CD-ROM: *History of Am. Lit.*
• Guided Writing Lesson: Museum Placard [Sequence of Events], SE p. 49 • Pamphlet, TR Alt. Assess., p. 4 • Cultural Story, Museum Brochure, Persuasive Essay, SE p. 58	• Debate, Antislavery Speech, SE p. 49 • Speaking, Listening, and Viewing Mini-Lesson: Antislavery Speech, ATE p. 46 • Folk Song, TR Alt. Assess., p. 4	• Internet Research, Movie Poster, SE p. 49 • Artifacts of Slavery, TR Alt. Assess., p. 4	• Selection Test, TR Formal Assessment, pp. 10–12; Assess. Res. Software • Summary Rubric [for Wr. Lesson], TR Alt. Assess., p. 113 • TR Alt. Assess., p. 4	• from *The Interesting Narrative of the Life of Olaudah Equiano,* LL Audiocassettes • WS Writing Lab CD-ROM, Exposition Tutorial; Wr. at Work Videodisc, Ch. 3 • Lit. CD-ROM: *History of Am. Lit.*
• Memorial Speech, Dramatic Scene, News Article, SE p. 77	• Television Interview, SE p. 58	• Time Capsule, SE p. 58	• Selection Test, TR Formal Assessment, pp. 13–14; Assess. Res. Software	• "Diamond Island: Alcatraz," LL Audiocassettes
• Guided Writing Lesson: Comparison of Narratives [Clear Organization], SE p. 77 • Report, TR Alt. Assess., p. 5	• Persuasive Speech, Early American Art, SE p. 77	• Advertisement, Menu, SE p. 77 • Diagram, TR Alt. Assess., p. 5 • V/R: Early Am. Art, ATE p. 68 • Research: Drawing Conclusions from Research, ATE p. 70 • V/R: Advertisement, ATE p. 732	• Selection Test, TR Formal Assessment, pp. 19–21; Assess. Res. Software • Comparison/Contrast Rubric [for Wr. Lesson], TR Alt. Assess., p. 118 • TR Alt. Assess., p. 5	• from *The General History of Virginia*, from *Of Plymouth Plantation*, LL Audiocassettes • WS Writing Lab CD-ROM, Response to Literature Tutorial • Lit. CD-ROM: *History of Am. Lit.*
• Dialogue, News Article, Sci-Fi Story, SE p. 82	• Debriefing Speech, SE p. 82	• Diagram, SE p. 82	• Selection Test, TR Formal Assessment, pp. 22–23; Assess. Res. Software	• from *The Right Stuff,* LL Audiocassettes
• Letter, Magazine Article, Poem, SE p. 95 • Guided Writing Lesson: Editorial [Anticipation of Opposing Arguments], SE p. 95 • Puritan Plain Style, TR Alt. Assess., p. 6	• Informal Debate, Love Song, SE p. 95 • Speaking, Listening, and Viewing Mini-Lesson: Informal Debate, ATE p. 92 • Book Chat, TR Alt. Assess., p. 6	• Bradstreet Sampler, Graphic Display, SE p. 95 • Puritan Arts, TR Alt. Assess., p. 6	• Selection Test, TR Formal Assessment, pp. 27–29; Assess. Res. Software • Persuasion Rubric [for Wr. Lesson], TR Alt. Assess., p. 120 • TR Alt. Assess., p. 6	• "To My Dear and Loving Husband," "Huswifery," LL Audiocassettes • WS Writing Lab CD-ROM, Persuasion Tutorial; Wr. at Work Videodisc, Ch. 4 • Lit. CD-ROM: *History of Am. Lit.*
• Diary Entry, Newscast, Public Letter, SE p. 103 • Guided Writing Lesson: Evaluation of Persuasion [Unity], SE p. 103 • The Puritan Legacy, TR Alt. Assess., p. 7	• Oral Interpretation, Oral Report, SE p. 103 • Speaking, Listening, and Viewing Mini-Lesson: Oral Interpretation, ATE p. 100 • Persuasive Speech, TR Alt. Assess., p. 7	• Television Commercial, Puritan Handbook, SE p. 103 • Puritan Preachers, TR Alt. Assess., p. 7	• Selection Test, TR Formal Assessment, pp. 30–32; Assess. Res. Software • Evaluation/Review Rubric [for Wr. Lesson], TR Alt. Assess., p. 119 • TR Alt. Assess., p. 7	• from *Sinners in the Hands of an Angry God*, LL Audiocassettes • WS Writing Lab CD-ROM, Response to Literature; Wr. at Work Videodisc, Ch. 7 • Lit. CD-ROM: *History of Am. Lit.*
• Newspaper Editorial, Character Defense, Baseball Poem, SE p. 109	• Group Debate, SE p. 109 • Speaking, Listening, and Viewing Mini-Lesson: Group Debate, ATE p. 106	• Reference Guide, SE p. 109 • Research Skills Mini-Lesson: Finding Quotations, ATE p. 105	• Selection Test, TR Formal Assessment, pp. 33–34; Assess. Res. Software	• "Iron Bird: Cal Ripken's Work Ethic," LL Audiocassettes

Selection	Reading	Literary Elements/Forms	Vocabulary	Grammar
from ***The Autobiography*, B. Franklin,** SE p. 131	Reading Level: Challenging • Reading for Success: Strategies for Constructing Meaning, SE pp. 130, 136; TR Selection Support, pp. 38–39 • Identify Paragraph Topics, TR Str. for Diverse St. Needs, p. 8	• Autobiography, SE pp. 129, 136; TR Selection Support, p. 40	• Latin Word Roots: *-vigil-*, SE pp. 129, 136; TR Selection Support, p. 36 Word Bank: arduous, avarice, p. 131; foppery, felicity, p. 134	• Pronoun Case, SE pp. 129, 136; TR Selection Support, p. 37 • WS Language Lab CD-ROM, Pronoun Case • WS Gram. Pr. Book, pp. 62–64
"The Declaration of Independence," T. Jefferson; from ***The Crisis, Number 1*, T. Paine,** SE pp. 140, 144	Reading Levels: Challenging, Average • Recognizing Charged Words, SE pp. 139, 146; TR Selection Support, p. 43 • Simplify Long Sentences, TR Str. for Diverse St. Needs, p. 9	• Persuasion, SE pp. 139, 146; TR Selection Support, p. 44	• Latin Word Roots: *-fid-*, SE pp. 139, 146; TR Selection Support, p. 41 Word Bank: unalienable, usurpations, p. 140; perfidy, redress, magnanimity, consanguinity, acquiesce, p. 142; impious, infidel, p. 145	• Parallelism, SE pp. 139, 146; TR Selection Support, p. 42 • WS Language Lab CD-ROM, Strengthening Sentences • WS Gram. Pr. Book, pp. 49–50
"To His Excellency, . . . ," "An Hymn to the Evening," P. Wheatley, SE pp. 150, 152	Reading Levels: Challenging, Average • Clarify Meaning, SE pp. 149, 154; TR Selection Support, p. 47 • Restate Poetic Language, TR Str. for Diverse St. Needs, p. 10	• Personification, SE pp. 149, 154; TR Selection Support, p. 48	• Latin Prefixes: *re-*, SE pp. 149, 154; TR Selection Support, p. 45 Word Bank: celestial, refulgent, propitious, refluent, pensive, p. 151; placid, scepter, p. 152	• Subject and Verb Agreement, SE pp. 149, 154; TR Selection Support, p. 46 • WS Language Lab CD-ROM, Subject-Verb Agreement • WS Gram. Pr. Book, pp. 66–68
from ***Letter From Birmingham City Jail*, Dr. M. L. King, Jr,** SE p. 157	Reading Level: Average		• TR Selection Support, p. 49 Word Bank: motives, p. 157; vitality, impelled, flagrant, profundity, monotony, scintillating, p. 158	
"Speech in the Virginia Convention," P. Henry; "Speech in the Convention," B. Franklin, SE pp. 169, 172	Reading Levels: Challenging, Challenging • Evaluating Persuasive Appeals, SE pp. 167, 174; TR Selection Support, p. 53 • List Key Ideas, TR Str. for Diverse St. Needs, p. 11	• Speeches, SE pp. 167, 174; TR Selection Support, p. 54	• Latin Suffixes: *-ity*, SE pp. 167, 174; TR Selection Support, p. 51 Word Bank: arduous, p. 169; insidious, subjugation, vigilant, p. 170; infallibility, despotism, salutary, unanimity, posterity, manifest, p. 173	• Double Negatives, SE pp. 167, 174; TR Selection Support, p. 52 • WS Language Lab CD-ROM, Avoiding Double Negatives • WS Gram. Pr. Book, Negative Sentences, pp. 78–79
"Inaugural Address," J. F. Kennedy, SE p.177	Reading Level: Average		• TR Selection Support, p. 55 Word Bank: heirs, p. 177; tyranny, alliance, invective, adversary, invoke, eradicate, p. 178	
from ***Poor Richard's Almanack*, B. Franklin,** SE p. 188	Reading Level: Easy	• Aphorisms, SE pp. 187, 190; TR Selection Support, p. 60	• Words With Multiple Meanings, SE pp. 187, 190; TR Selection Support, p. 57 Word Bank: fasting, squander, p. 189	• Irregular Comparison of Adj. and Adv., SE pp. 187, 190; TR Selection Support, p. 58 • WS Language Lab CD-ROM, Irregular Comparisons • WS Gram. Pr. Book, p. 74
"Letter to Her Daughter . . . ," A. S. Adams; from ***Letters From an American Farmer*, M. J. de Crèvecoeur,** SE pp. 195, 197	Reading Levels: Average, Challenging • Relate to Your Experiences, SE pp. 187, 190; TR Selection Support, p. 59 • Give Examples, TR Str. for Diverse St. Needs, p. 12	• Private and Public Letter (Epistles), SE pp. 193, 200; TR Selection Support, p. 64	• Word Origins, SE pp. 193, 200; TR Selection Support, p. 61 Word Bank: extricate, agues, p. 195; asylum, penury, despotic, subsistence, p. 199	• Semicolons, SE pp. 193, 200; TR Selection Support, p. 62 • WS Language Lab CD-ROM, Semicolons • WS Gram. Pr. Book, p. 89
from ***Roots*, A. Haley,** SE p. 203	Reading Level: Average • Distinguish Between Fact and Opinion, SE pp. 193, 200; TR Selection Support, p. 63 • Summarize Main Idea, TR Str. for Diverse St. Needs, p. 13		• TR Selection Support, p. 65 Word Bank: congealed, p. 204, crux, p. 204; cacophony, p. 206	

A Nation Is Born (1750–1800)

Writing	Speaking, Listening, and Viewing	Researching and Representing	Assessment	Technology
• Guided Lesson: Autobiographical Account [Show Cause and Effect], SE p. 137 • Advertisement, Improvement Plan, Report, SE p. 137 • Newspaper Column, TR Alt. Assess., p. 8	• Oral Interpretation, Interview, SE p. 137 • Mini-Lesson: Interview, ATE p. 133 • Philosophical Presentation, TR Alt. Assess., p. 8	• Poster, Travel Brochure, SE p. 137 • Virtue Video, TR Alt. Assess., p. 8	• Selection Test, TR Formal Assessment, pp. 38–40; Assess. Res. Software • Narrative Based on Personal Experience Rubric [for Mini-Lesson], TR Alt. Assess., p. 111 • TR Alt. Assess., p. 8	• from *The Autobiography*, LL Audiocassettes • Looking at Lit., Ch. 3 • WS Writing Lab CD-ROM, Narration Tutorial; Wr. at Work Videodisc, Ch. 2 • Lit. CD-ROM: *History of Am. Lit.*
• Guided Lesson: A Proposal to the Principal [Use Forceful Language], SE p. 147 • Letter, Precis, Newspaper Stories, SE p. 147 • Character Sketch, TR Alt. Assess., p. 9	• Oral Presentation, Dramatic Reading, SE p. 147 • Dramatized Debate, TR Alt. Assess., p. 9	• Poster, Class Discussion on Paine, SE p. 147 • Stamp Design, TR Alt. Assess., p. 9 • Research Mini-Lesson: Using Multiple Sources, ATE p. 143	• Selection Test, TR Formal Assessment, pp. 41–43; Assess. Res. Software • Persuasion Rubric [for Wr. Lesson], TR Alt. Assess., p. 120 • TR Alt. Assess., p. 9	• "The Declaration of Independence," from *The Crisis, Number 1*, LL Audiocassettes • WS Writing Lab CD-ROM, Persuasion Tutorial; Wr. at Work Videodisc, Ch. 4
• Guided Lesson: Inscription for a Monument [Persuasive Tone], SE p. 155 • Letter, Diary Entry, Poem or Essay, SE p. 155 • Book Review, TR Alt. Assess., p. 10	• Dramatic Reading, Political Cartoons, SE p. 155 • Background Music, TR Alt. Assess., p. 10	• Graphic Display on Washington, Portrait, SE p. 155 • Pictures of Evening, TR Alt. Assess., p. 10 • Viewing and Representing Mini-Lesson: Graphic Display on Washington, ATE p. 158	• Selection Test, TR Formal Assessment, pp. 44–46; Assess. Res. Software • Description Rubric [for Wr. Lesson], TR Alt. Assess., p. 112 • TR Alt. Assess., p. 10	• "To His Excellency, General Washington," "An Hymn to the Evening," LL Audiocassettes • Looking at Lit., Ch. 4 • WS Writing Lab CD-ROM, Description Tutorial; Wr. at Work Videodisc, Ch. 1 • Lit. CD-ROM: *History of Am. Lit.*
• Poem for a Prisoner, Essay, Editorial, SE p. 160	• Oration, Freedom Survey, SE p. 160 • Speaking, Listening, and Viewing Mini-Lesson: Dramatic Delivery, ATE p. 170	• Voices of Freedom Booklet, Report on Dr. King, SE p. 160	• Selection Test, TR Formal Assessment, pp. 47–48; Assess. Res. Software	• from *Letter from Birmingham City Jail*, LL Audiocassettes
• Guided Lesson: Commentary on a Speech [Anticipating Questions], SE p. 175 • Diary Entry, Speech, Critique, SE p. 175 • Political Editorial, TR Alt. Assess., p. 11	• Dramatic Delivery, Debate, SE p. 175 • Point/Counterpoint, TR Alt. Assess., p. 11	• Display of Famous Speeches, Multimedia Present., SE p. 175 • Constitutional Convention, TR Alt. Assess., p. 11 • Viewing and Representing Mini-Lesson: Multimedia Presentation, ATE p. 172	• Selection Test, TR Formal Assessment, pp. 53–55; Assess. Res. Software • Evaluation/Review Rubric [for Wr. Lesson], TR Alt. Assess., p. 119 • TR Alt. Assess., p. 11	• "Speech in the Virginia Convention," "Speech in the Convention," LL Audiocassettes • WS Writing Lab CD-ROM, Response to Literature Tutorial; Wr. at Work Videodisc, Ch. 7
• Summation, Research Writing, Comparative Essay, SE p. 180	• Volunteerism Survey, SE p. 180	• Video Record, SE p. 180	• Selection Test, TR Formal Assessment, pp. 56–57; Assess. Res. Software	• "Inaugural Address," LL Audiocassettes
• Guided Lesson: Internet Page for Aphorisms [Style Appropriate to Medium], SE p. 191 • Personal Narrative, Magazine Article, Folk Tale, SE p. 191	• Rap, Oral Presentation, SE p. 191 • Survey, TR Alt. Assess., p. 12	• Instruction Manual, Board Game, SE p. 191 • Picture This, TR Alt. Assess., p. 12	• Selection Test, TR Formal Assessment, pp. 61–63; Assess. Res. Software • Definition/Classification Rubric [for Wr. Lesson], TR Alt. Assess., p. 114 • TR Alt. Assess., p. 12	• from *Poor Richard's Almanack*, LL Audiocassettes • WS Writing Lab CD-ROM, Exposition Tutorial; Wr. at Work Videodisc, Ch. 3
• Guided Lesson: Personal Letter [Necessary Context/Background], SE p. 201 • Descriptive Letter, Reflective Essay, "Melting Pot" Epistle, SE p. 201 • Two Letters, TR Alt. Assess., p. 13	• Letter Reading, Immigrant Interview, SE p. 201 • "Melting Pot" Debate, TR Alt. Assess., p. 13	• American Interpretation, Advertising Campaign, SE p. 201 • Political Cartoon, TR Alt. Assess., p. 13	• Selection Test, TR Formal Assessment, pp. 64–66; Assess. Res. Software • Comparison/Contrast Rubric [for Wr. Lesson], TR Alt. Assess., p. 118 • TR Alt. Assess., p. 13	• "Letter to Her Daughter . . . ," from *Letters From an American Farmer*, LL Audiocassettes • WS Writing Lab CD-ROM, Exposition Tutorial; Wr. at Work Videodisc, Ch. 3
• Journal Entry, Director's Notes, Book Jacket, SE p. 207	• Informal Debate, SE p. 207 • Speaking, Listening, and Viewing Mini-Lesson: Informal Debate, ATE p. 204	• Multimedia Roots Presentation, Cultural Heritage Display, SE p. 207 • Viewing and Representing Mini-Lesson: Multimedia Presentation, ATE p. 203	• Selection Test, TR Formal Assessment, pp. 67–68; Assess. Res. Software	• from *Roots*, LL Audiocassettes

Selection	Reading	Literary Elements/Forms	Vocabulary	Grammar
from ***The Announcement of* The Dial, M. Fuller and R. W. Emerson,** SE p. 229	Reading Level: Challenging • Reading for Success: Strat. for Reading Critically, SE pp. 228, 232; TR Sel. Support, pp. 67–71 • Rephrase Complicated Sent., TR Str. for Diverse St. Needs, p. 14	• Announcement, SE pp. 227, 232; TR Selection Support, p. 71	• Latin Roots: *-spect-*, SE pp. 227, 232; TR Sel. Sup., p. 67 Word Bank: compunctions, privations, rudiments, pittance, contingent, superseding, circumspection, reiterate, inappeasable, polemics, p. 231	• Commonly Confused Words: *Principal* and *Principle*, SE pp. 227, 232; TR Selection Support, p. 68
"The Devil and Tom Walker," W. Irving, SE p. 236	Reading Level: Average • Infer Cultural Attitudes, SE pp. 235, 246; TR Selection Support, p. 74 • Summarize Paragraphs, TR Str. for Diverse St. Needs, p. 15	• Omniscient Narrator, SE pp. 235, 246; TR Selection Support, p. 75	• Latin Prefixes: *ex-*, SE pp. 235, 246; TR Selection Support, p. 72 Word Bank: avarice, p. 240; usurers, extort, ostentation, parsimony, p. 243	• Adjective Clauses, SE pp. 235, 246; TR Selection Support, p. 73 • WS Gram. Pr. Book, p. 35
"A Psalm of Life," "The Tide Rises, The Tide Falls," H. W. Longfellow, SE pp. 250, 252	Reading Levels: Average, Easy • Associate Images With Life, SE pp. 249, 254; TR Selection Support, p. 78 • Recognize Metaphors, TR Str. for Diverse St. Needs, p. 16	• Stanza Forms, SE pp. 249, 254; TR Selection Support, p. 79 Analyze Literary Criticism, ATE, p. 269	• Latin Word Roots: *-face-*, SE pp. 249, 254; TR Selection Support, p. 76 Word Bank: bivouac, sublime, p. 251; efface, p. 253	• Inverted Word Order, SE pp. 249, 254; TR Selection Support, p. 77 • WS Gram. Pr. Book, p. 26
"Thanatopsis," W. C. Bryant; "Old Ironsides," O. W. Holmes; "The First Snowfall," J. R. Lowell; from ***Snowbound,* J. G. Whittier,** SE pp. 259, 262, 264, 267	Reading Levels: Challenging, Average, Easy, Average • Summarize, SE pp. 258, 272; TR Selection Support, p. 82 • Explain Poetic Phrases, TR Str. for Diverse St. Needs, p. 17	• Meter, SE pp. 258, 272; TR Selection Support, p. 83	• Latin Word Roots: *-patr-*, SE pp. 258, 272; TR Selection Support, p. 80 Word Bank: sepulcher, pensive, venerable, p. 261; gloaming, p. 265; ominous, p. 267; querulous, patriarch, p. 268	• Participles as Adjectives, SE pp. 258, 272; TR Selection Support, p. 81 • WS Language Lab CD-ROM, Misplaced Modifiers • WS Gram. Pr. Book, p. 32
"Crossing the Great Divide," M. Lewis; "The Most Sublime . . . ," J. W. Powell, SE pp. 276, 278	Reading Levels: Average, Average • Noting Spatial Relationships, SE pp. 275, 282; TR Selection Support, p. 86 • Outline Main Idea/Sup. Det., TR Str. for Diverse St. Needs, p. 18	• Description, SE pp. 275, 282; TR Selection Support, p. 87	• Latin Prefixes: *multi-*, SE pp. 275, 282; TR Selection Support, p. 84 Word Bank: conspicuous, p. 277; sublime, labyrinth, excavated, demarcation, p. 279; multifarious, multitudinous, p. 281	• Participial Phrases, SE pp. 275, 282; TR Selection Support, p. 85 • WS Language Lab CD-ROM, Misplaced Modifiers • WS Gram. Pr. Book, p. 32
from ***Pilgrim at Tinker Creek: Seeing,* A. Dillard,** SE p. 285	Reading Level: Average		• TR Selection Support, p. 88	
"The Fall of the House of Usher," "The Raven;" E. A. Poe, SE p. 297, 309	Reading Levels: Challenging, Average • Break Down Long Sent., SE pp. 295, 314; TR Sel. Support, p. 92 • Sequence Events, TR Str. for Diverse St. Needs, p. 19	• Single Effect, SE pp. 295, 314; TR Selection Support, p. 93 • Analyze Literary Criticism, ATE p. 300	• Latin Word Roots: *-voc-*, SE pp. 295, 314; TR Sel. Support, p. 90 Word Bank: importunate, munificent, equivocal, appellation, specious, p. 298; anomalous, p. 300; sentience, p. 303; obeisance, craven, p. 310	• Coordinate Adjectives, SE pp. 295, 314; TR Selection Support, p. 91 • WS Language Lab CD-ROM, Commas • WS Gram. Pr. Book, p. 86
"The Minister's Black Veil," N. Hawthorne, SE p. 318	Reading Level: Challenging • Evaluate the Author's Messages, SE pp. 317, 328; TR Selection Support, p. 96 • Analyze Characters, TR Str. for Diverse St. Needs, p. 20	• Allegory, SE pp. 317, 328; TR Selection Support, p. 97	• Latin Word Roots: *-equi-*, SE pp. 317, 328; TR Sel. Sup., p. 94 Words: venerable, iniquity, indecorous, ostentatious, sagacious, vagary, p. 321; tremulous, waggery, impertinent, obstinacy, p. 323	• Varying Sentence Openers, SE pp. 317, 328; TR Selection Support, p. 95 • WS Language Lab CD-ROM, Varying Sentence Structure • WS Gram. Pr. Book, pp. 110–112
from ***Moby Dick,* H. Melville,** SE p. 332	Reading Level: Challenging • Recognize Symbols, SE pp. 331, 346; TR Selection Support, p. 100 • Identify Chain of Events, TR Str. for Diverse St. Needs, p. 21	• Symbol, SE pp. 331, 346; TR Selection Support, p. 101 • Analyze a Movie Review, ATE p. 336 • Analyze an Author's Comment, ATE, p. 353	• Latin Prefixes: *mal-*, SE pp. 331, 346; TR Selection Support, p. 98 Word Bank: inscrutable, p. 335; maledictions, p. 337; prescient, p. 340; pertinaciously, p. 342	• Agreement With Collective Nouns, SE pp. 331, 346; TR Selection Support, p. 99 • WS Language Lab CD-ROM, Subject-Verb Agreement • WS Gram. Pr. Book, p. 68
"Where *Is* Here?," J. C. Oates, SE p. 349	Reading Level: Average		• TR Selection Support, p. 102 Word Bank: genial, gregarious, covertly, p. 349; avuncular, galvanic, p. 354	

A Growing Nation (1800–1870)

Writing	Speaking, Listening, and Viewing	Researching and Representing	Assessment	Technology
• Guided Writing Lesson: Proposal [A Clear and Consistent Purpose], SE p. 233 • Letter, Persuasive Credo, Persuasive Essay, SE p. 233 • Custom Announcements, TR Alt. Assess., p. 14	• Literary Reading, Panel Discussion, SE p. 233 • On the Air, TR Alt. Assess., p. 14	• Journal Review, Graphic Display, SE p. 233 • Announcement Planner, TR Alt. Assess., p. 14	• Selection Test, TR Formal Assessment, pp. 72–74; Assess. Res. Software • Persuasion Rubric [for Wr. Lesson], TR Alt. Assess., p. 120	• from *The Announcement of The Dial,* LL Audiocassettes • WS Writing Lab CD-ROM, Practical and Technical Writing Tutorial • Lit. CD-ROM: *History of Am. Lit.*
• Correspondence, Revised Ending, Analysis, SE p. 247 • Writing Lesson: Updating a Story [Audience], SE p. 247 • A Happy Ending?, TR Alt. Assess., p. 15	• Enactment, Impromptu Speech, SE p. 247 • Folk Song, TR Alt. Assess., p. 15	• Board Game, Exhibition, SE p. 247 • Viewing and Representing: Board Game, ATE p. 239 • Research, ATE p. 241 • Dramatization, TR Alt. Assess., p. 15	• Selection Test, TR Formal Assessment, pp. 75–77; Assess. Res. Software • Fictional Narrative Rubric [for Wr. Lesson], TR Alt. Assess., p. 110	• "The Devil and Tom Walker," LL Audiocassettes • WS Writing Lab CD-ROM, Response to Literature Tutorial
• Guided Writing Lesson: Credo [Persuasive Tone], SE p. 255 • Epitaph, Personal Response, Essay, SE p. 255 • Poetry Critic, TR Alt. Assess., p. 16	• Audio Presentation/Discussion, SE p. 255 • Mini-Lesson: Commencement Address, ATE p. 251 • Poetic Recording, TR Alt. Assess., p. 16	• Performance, Graphic Display, SE p. 255 • Poetic Images, TR Alt. Assess., p. 16	• Selection Test, TR Formal Assessment, pp. 78–80; Assess. Res. Software • Expression and Persuasion Rubrics [for Wr. Lesson], TR Alt. Assess., pp. 109, 120	• "A Psalm of Life," "The Tide Rises, The Tide Falls," LL Audiocassettes • Looking at Lit., Ch. 5 • WS Writing Lab CD-ROM, Pers. Tut.; Wr. at Work Videodisc, Ch. 4
• Guided Writing Lesson: Précis [Clear Beginning, Middle and End], SE p. 273 • Letter, Poem, Analytical Essay, SE p. 273 • Documentary Introduction, TR Alt. Assess., p. 17	• Dramatic Reading, Poetry Critique, SE p. 273 • Speaking, Listening, and Viewing Mini-Lesson: Dramatic Reading, ATE p. 270	• Oral Presentation, Graphic Display, SE p. 273 • Research Skills Mini-Lesson: Outlining, ATE p. 267 • Video Director, TR Alt. Assess., p. 17	• Selection Test, TR Formal Assessment, pp. 81–83; Assess. Res. Software • Summary Rubric [for Wr. Lesson], TR Alt. Assess., p. 113	• "Thanatopsis," "Old Ironsides," "The First Snowfall," LL Audiocassettes • WS Writing Lab CD-ROM, Exp. Tut. • Lit. CD-ROM: *History of Am. Lit.*
• Guided Writing Lesson: Description [Use Transitions to Show Place], SE p. 283 • Abstract, Advertisement, News Article, SE p. 283 • Report, TR Alt. Assess., p. 18	• Speech, TV Doc., SE p. 283 • Speaking, Listening, and Viewing Mini-Lesson: Speech, ATEp. 278 • Hear What I Hear, TR Alt. Assess., p. 18	• Expedition Map, Research Report, SE p. 283 • Going Further, TR Alt. Assess., p. 18	• Selection Test, TR Formal Assessment, pp. 84–86; Assess. Res. Software • Description Rubric [for Wr. Lesson], TR Alt. Assess., p. 112	• "Crossing the Great Divide," Meriwether Lewis; "The Most Sublime . . .," LL Audiocassettes • WS Writing Lab CD-ROM, Description Tutorial; Wr. at Work Videodisc, Ch. 1
• Folk Ballad, Desc., Comparison/ Contrast Essay, SE p. 288	• Music Critique, SE p. 288	• Nature Journal, SE p. 288	• Selection Test, TR Formal Assessment, pp. 87–88; Assess. Res. Software	• from *Pilgrim at Tinker Creek: Seeing,* LL Audiocassettes
• Guided Writing Lesson: Intro. to a Radio Show [Appropriateness for Medium], SE p. 315 • Letter, Obit., Essay, SE p. 315 • Essay on an Early Detective Story, TR Alt. Assess., p. 19	• Dramatic Reading, Movie Analysis, SE p. 315 • S/L/V Mini-Lesson: Movie Analysis, ATE p. 310 • Folksong Setting, TR Alt. Assess., p. 19	• Report, Set Design, SE p. 315 • V/R Mini-Lesson: Set Design, ATE p. 298 • Research: Resources for Lit. Research, ATE p. 302 • Raven Mythology, TR Alt. Assess., p. 19	• Selection Test, TR Formal Assessment, pp. 93–95; Assess. Res. Software • Response to Literature Rubric [for Wr. Lesson], TR Alt. Assess., p. 125	• "The Fall of the House of Usher," "The Raven," LL Audiocassettes • WS Writing Lab CD-ROM, Response to Literature Tutorial • Lit. CD-ROM: *History of Am. Lit.*
• Writing Lesson: Resp. to a Short Story [Prec. Det.], SE p. 329 • Letter, Memo to New Ministers, Essay, SE p. 329 • Analysis of Parables, TR Alt. Assess., p. 20	• Debate, Soundtrack, SE p. 329 • Speaking, Listening, and Viewing Mini-Lesson: Debate, ATE p. 324	• Reading Report, Illus., SE p. 329 • V/R Lesson: Illus., ATE p. 323 • Research Skills Mini-Lesson: Taking Notes, ATE p. 320 • Diff. Med., TR Alt. Assess., p. 20	• Selection Test, TR Formal Assessment, pp. 96–98; Assess. Res. Software • Response to Literature Rubric [for Wr. Lesson], TR Alt. Assess., p. 125	• "The Minister's Black Veil," LL Audiocassettes • WS Writing Lab CD-ROM, Response to Literature Tutorial; Wr. at Work Videodisc, Ch. 7 • Lit. CD-ROM: *History of Am. Lit.*
• Writing Lesson: A Dramatic Scene [Realistic Dial.], SE p. 347 • Eulogy, Character Sketch, Essay, SE p. 347 • Description and Analysis, TR Alt. Assess., p. 21	• Monologue, Reader's Theater, SE p. 347 • Speaking, Listening, and Viewing Mini-Lesson: Readers Theatre, ATE p. 344 • Movie Rev., TR Alt. Assess., p. 21	• Model, Report, SE p. 347 • Viewing and Representing Mini-Lesson: Model, ATE p. 329 • Obsession, TR Alt. Assess., p. 21	• Selection Test, TR Formal Assessment, pp. 99–101; Assess. Res. Software • Drama Rubric [for Wr. Lesson], TR Alt. Assess., p. 124	• from *Moby Dick,* LL Audiocassettes • WS Writing Lab CD-ROM, Creative Writing Tutorial • Lit. CD-ROM: *History of Am. Lit.*
• Diary Entry, Comparison and Contrast, Essay, SE p. 356	• Radio Presentation, SE p. 356	• Floor Plans, SE p. 356 • Research Skills Mini-Lesson: Using Text Organizers, ATE p. 351	• Selection Test, TR Formal Assessment, pp. 102–103; Assess. Res. Software	• "Where *Is* Here?," LL Audiocassettes

Program Planner Unit 3

Selection	Reading	Literary Elements/Forms	Vocabulary	Grammar
from ***Nature***, from ***Self Reliance***, **"The Snowstorm," "Concord Hymn," R. W. Emerson,** SE pp. 364, 366, 368, 369	Reading Levels: Average, Average, Average, Average • Challenge the Text, SE pp. 363, 370; TR Selection Support, p. 106 • Reword Author's Ideas, TR Str. for Diverse St. Needs, p. 22	• Transcendentalism, SE pp. 363, 370; TR Selection Support, p. 107	• Latin Word Roots: *-radi-*, SE pp. 363, 370; TR Selection Support, p. 104 Word Bank: blithe, connate, p. 364; chaos, aversion, suffrage, divines, p. 367; radiant, tumultuous, bastions, p. 368	• Vary Sent. Length, SE pp. 363, 370; TR Selection Support, p. 105 • WS Language Lab CD-ROM • WS Gram. Pr. Book, p. 110
from ***Walden***, from ***Civil Disobedience***, **H. D. Thoreau,** SE pp. 374, 380	Reading Levels: Challenging, Avg. • Evaluate Writer's Statement of Philosophy, SE pp. 373, 382; TR Selection Support, p. 110 • Identify Key Ideas, TR Str. for Diverse St. Needs, p. 23	• Style, SE pp. 373, 382; TR Selection Support, p. 111	• Latin Roots: *-flu-*, SE pp. 373, 382; TR Selection Support, p. 108 Words: dilapidated, p. 375; sublime, superfluous, evitable, p. 377; magnanimity, p. 379; expedient, posterity, alacrity, p. 381	• Infinitives and Infinitive Phrases, SE pp. 373, 382; TR Selection Support, p. 109 • WS Language Lab CD-ROM, Verb Phrases • WS Gram. Pr. Book, p. 34
"Gardening," B. White; "Hammer and a Nail," E. Saliers, SE pp. 385, 387	Reading Levels: Easy, Average		• TR Selection Support, p. 112 Word Bank: filigree, p. 386; hovel, abyss, p. 387	
E. Dickinson's Poetry, SE pp. 396, 397, 398, 399, 400, 401	Reading Levels: Chall., Avg., Chall., Chall., Chall., Avg., Avg. • Analyze Images, SE pp. 395, 402; TR Selection Support, p. 116 • Form a Mental Picture, TR Str. for Diverse St. Needs, p. 24	• Slant Rhyme, SE pp. 395, 402; TR Selection Support, p. 117	• Latin Roots: *-finis-*, SE pp. 395, 402; TR Selection Support, p. 114 Word Bank: cornice, surmised, p. 397; oppresses, p. 399; finite, infinity, p. 400	• Gerunds, SE pp. 395, 402; TR Selection Support, p. 115 • WS Gram. Pr. Book, p. 33
W. Whitman's Poetry, SE pp. 406, 408, 413, 414, 414, 415	Reading Levels: Challenging, Avg., Easy, Avg., Avg., Easy • Infer the Poet's Attitude, SE pp. 405, 416; TR Sel. Sup., p. 120 • Identify Theme, TR Str. for Diverse St. Needs, p. 25	• Free Verse, SE pp. 405, 416; TR Selection Support, p. 121	• Latin Roots: *-fus-*, SE pp. 405, 416; TR Selection Support, p. 118 Word Bank: abeyance, p. 409, effuse, p. 411	• Pronoun and Antecedent Agreement, SE pp. 405, 416; TR Selection Support, p. 119 • WS Language Lab CD-ROM, Pronouns and Antecedents • WS Gram. Pr. Book, pp. 69–70
"I, Too," L. Hughes; "To Walt Whitman," A. de Hoyos, SE pp. 419, 420	Reading Levels: Easy, Easy			

Program Planner Unit 4

Selection	Reading	Literary Elements/Forms	Vocabulary	Grammar
"An Episode of War," S. Crane; "Willie Has Gone to the War," S. Foster, SE pp. 443, 447	Reading Levels: Average, Easy • Reading for Success: Interactive Strategies, SE pp. 442, 448; TR Sel. Sup., pp. 125–126 • Form a Mental Picture, TR Str. for Diverse St. Needs, p. 26	• Realism and Naturalism, SE pp. 441, 448; TR Selection Support, p. 127	• Latin Word Roots: *-greg-*, SE pp. 441, 448; TR Selection Support, p. 123 Word Bank: precipitate, aggregation, inscrutable, p. 444; disdainfully, p. 446; glade, p. 447	• Correct Use of *Like* and *As*, SE pp. 441, 448; TR Selection Support, p. 124
"Swing Low, Sweet Chariot," "Go Down, Moses," SE pp. 452, 453	Reading Levels: Easy, Average • Listen, SE pp. 451, 454; TR Selection Support, p. 130 • Explain Poetic Phrases, TR Str. for Diverse St. Needs, p. 27	• Refrain, SE pp. 451, 454; TR Selection Support, p. 131	• Latin Word Roots: *-press-*, SE pp. 451, 454; TR Selection Support, p. 128 Word Bank: oppressed, smite, p. 453	• Direct Address, SE pp. 451, 454; TR Selection Support, p. 129
from ***My Bondage and My Freedom***, **F. Douglass,** SE p. 458	Reading Level: Challenging • Establish a Purpose, SE pp. 457, 464; TR Sel. Support, p. 134 • Reword Author's Ideas, TR Str. for Diverse St. Needs, p. 28	• Autobiography, SE pp. 457, 464; TR Selection Support, p. 135	• Latin Roots: *-bene-*, SE pp. 457, 464; TR Sel. Support, p. 132 Word Bank: congenial, benevolent, stringency, depravity, p. 459; consternation, p. 461; redolent, p. 462	• Correlative Conjunctions, SE pp. 457, 464; TR Selection Support, p. 133 • WS Gram. Pr. Book, p. 13
"An Occurrence at Owl Creek Bridge," A. Bierce, SE p. 468	Reading Level: Average • Chronological Order, SE pp. 467, 476; TR Selection Support, p. 138 • Plot a Story Map, TR Str. for Diverse St. Needs, p. 29	• Point of View, SE pp. 467, 476; TR Selection Support, p. 139 • Analyze Literary Criticism, ATE p. 472	• Latin Word Roots: *-sum-*, SE pp. 467, 476; TR Selection Support, p. 136 Word Bank: etiquette, deference, p. 469; imperious, dictum, summarily, p. 470; effaced, oscillation, p. 471; apprised, p. 472; malign, ineffable, p. 475	• Semicolons in Compound Sentences, SE pp. 467, 476; TR Selection Support, p. 137 • WS Language Lab CD-ROM, Semicolons • WS Gram. Pr. Book, p. 89

A Growing Nation (1800–1870)

Writing	Speaking, Listening, and Viewing	Researching and Representing	Assessment	Technology
• Guided Writing Lesson: Letter to the Editor [Elaboration], SE p. 371 • Poem, Advertisement, Critical Evaluation, SE p. 371 • A Man of His Time?, TR Alt. Assess., p. 22	• Public Service Announcement, Analysis, SE p. 371 • The Transcendentalists, TR Alt. Assess., p. 22	• Art, Research, SE p. 371 • Snow Art, TR Alt. Assess., p. 22	• Selection Test, TR Formal Assessment, pp. 107–109; Assess. Res. Software • Analysis/Interpretation Rubric [for Wr. Lesson], TR Alt. Assess., p. 127	• from *Nature*, from *Self Reliance*, "The Snowstorm," "Concord Hymn," LL Audio • WS Writing Lab CD-ROM, Persuasion Tutorial; Wr. at Work Videodisc, Ch. 4 • Lit. CD-ROM: *History of Am. Lit.*
• Writing Lesson: Persuasive Essay [Cause/Effect Org.], SE p. 383 • Letter/Ed., Report, Comparison/Contrast Essay, SE p. 383 • Words to Live By, TR Alt. Assess., p. 23	• TV Script, Debate, SE p. 383 • Speaking, Listening, and Viewing Mini-Lesson: Television Script, ATE p. 378 • Courtroom Drama, TR Alt. Assess., p. 23	• Walden Pond Research, Nature Journal, SE p. 383 • Thoreau's Cabin, TR Alt. Assess., p. 23	• Selection Test, TR Formal Assessment, pp. 110–112; Assess. Res. Software • Persuasion Rubric [for Wr. Lesson], TR Alt. Assess., p. 120	• from *Walden*, from *Civil Disobedience*, LL Audiocassettes • Looking at Lit., Ch. 6 • WS Writing Lab CD-ROM, Persuasion Tutorial • Lit. CD-ROM: *History of Am. Lit.*
• Personal Anecdote, Grant Proposal, Critique, SE p. 388	• Music Analysis, SE p. 388	• Drawing, SE p. 388	• Selection Test, TR Formal Assessment, pp. 113–114; Assess. Res. Software	• "Gardening," "Hammer and a Nail," LL Audiocassettes
• Writing Lesson: Letter to an Author [Clear/Logical Org.], SE p. 403 • Poem, Editor's Letter, Critical Response, SE p. 403 • Fashion Symbolism, TR Alt. Assess., p. 24	• Oral Interpretation, Musical Interpretation, SE p. 403 • S/L/V Mini-Lesson: Musical Interpretation, ATE p. 398 • Cathedral Tunes, TR Alt. Assess., p. 24	• Painting, Report, SE p. 403 • Art and Nature, TR Alt. Assess., p. 24	• Selection Test, TR Formal Assessment, pp. 118–120; Assess. Res. Software • Resp. to Lit. Rubric [for Wr. Lesson], TR Alt. Assess., p. 125 • TR Alt. Assess., p. 24	• Emily Dickinson's Poetry, LL Audiocassettes • WS Writing Lab CD-ROM, Response to Literature Tutorial • Lit. CD-ROM: *History of Am. Lit.*
• Writing Lesson: Imitation of Style [Cons. Style], SE p. 417 • Inscription, Poem, Speculative Essay, SE p. 417 • Song of Yourself, TR Alt. Assess., p. 25	• Collage, Oral Interpretation, SE p. 417 • Speaking, Listening, and Viewing Mini-Lesson: Oral Interpretation, ATE p. 411 • Debate, TR Alt. Assess., p. 25	• Graphic Display, Report, SE p. 417 • Producing Whitman's Poetry on Stage, TR Alt. Assess., p. 25	• Sel., TR Form. Assess., pp. 121–123; Assess. Res. Software • Poetry Rubric [for Wr. Lesson], TR Alt. Assess., p. 123 • TR Alt. Assess., p. 25	• Walt Whitman's Poetry, LL Audiocassettes • WS Writing Lab CD-ROM, Creative Writing Tutorial; Wr. at Work Ch. 6 • Lit. CD-ROM: *History of Am. Lit.*
• Letter, Comparison-and-Contrast Essay, Poetic Response, SE p. 421	• Group Discussion, SE p. 421	• Diptych, SE p. 421	• Selection Test, TR Formal Assessment, pp. 124–125; Assess. Res. Software	• "I, Too," "To Walt Whitman," LL Audiocassettes

Division, Reconciliation, and Expansion (1850–1914)

• Letter, Editorial, Definition Essay, SE p. 449 • Writing Lesson: Field Report [Precise Details], SE p. 449 • Diary Entry, TR Alt. Assess., p. 26	• Enactment, Music Performance, SE p. 449 • S/L/V Mini-Lesson: Music Performance, ATE p. 445 • Speech! Speech!, TR Alt. Assess., p. 26	• Soldier's Scrapbook, Oral Presentation, SE p. 449 • A Soldier's Diet, TR Alt. Assess., p. 26	• Selection Test, TR Formal Assessment, pp. 129–131; Assess. Res. Software • Description Rubric [for Wr. Lesson], TR Alt. Assess., p. 112 • TR Alt. Assess., p. 26	• "An Episode of War," "Willie Has Gone to the War," LL Audiocassettes • Looking at Lit., Ch. 7 • WS Writing Lab CD-ROM, Exp. Tutorial; Wr. at Work Ch. 3
• Letter, Spiritual, Reflective Essay, SE p. 455 • Guided Writing Lesson: Song [Effective Repetition], SE p. 455 • Concert Program, TR Alt. Assess., p. 27	• Choral Reading, Music Appreciation SE p. 455 • Story-telling, TR Alt. Assess., p. 27	• Map, Logo, SE p. 455 • Glossary of Freedom, TR Alt. Assess., p. 27	• Selection Test, TR Formal Assessment, pp. 132–134; Assess. Res. Software • Poetry Rubric [for Wr. Lesson], TR Alt. Assess., p.123 • TR Alt. Assess., p. 27	• "Swing Low, Sweet Chariot," "Go Down, Moses," LL Audiocassettes • WS Writing Lab CD-ROM, Creative Writing Tutorial; Wr. at Work Videodisc Ch. 6
• Diary Entry, New Version, Essay, SE p. 465 • Writing Lesson: Adm. Essay [Clear/Logical Org.], SE p. 465 • Attorney's Brief, TR Alt. Assess., p. 28	• Dramatic Dialogue, Oral Interpretation, SE p. 465 • S/L/V Mini-Lesson: Dramatic Dialogue, ATE p. 462 • Songs of Freedom, TR Alt. Assess., p. 28	• Interpretive Dance, Graphic Display, SE p. 465 • Dramatized Debate, TR Alt. Assess., p. 28	• Sel. Test, TR Formal Assess., pp. 135–137; Assess. Software • Cause-Effect Rubric [for Wr. Lesson], TR Alt. Assess., p. 117 • TR Alt. Assess., p. 28	• from *My Bondage and My Freedom*, LL Audiocassettes • Looking at Lit., Ch. 8 • WS Writing Lab CD-ROM, Practical/Tech. Writing Tutorial
• Farewell Letter, Prequel, Critical Essay, SE p. 477 • Writing Lesson: Fictional News Article [Objective Tone], SE p. 477 • Essay, TR Alt. Assess., p. 29	• Viewing, Oral Presentation, SE p. 477 • S/L/V Mini-Lesson: Spoken Review, ATE p. 474 • Film Rev., TR Alt. Assess., p. 29	• Chart, Graphic Display, SE p. 477 • V/R Lesson: Video, ATE p. 469 • Poster, TR Alt. Assess., p. 29 • Research Skills Mini-Lesson: Note Cards, ATE p. 470	• Selection Test, TR Formal Assessment, pp. 138–140; Assess. Res. Software • Fict. Narrative Rubric [for Wr. Lesson], TR Alt. Assess., p. 110 • TR Alt. Assess., p. 29	• "An Occurrence at Owl Creek Bridge," LL Audiocassettes • WS Writing Lab CD-ROM, Narration Tutorial

Selection	Reading	Literary Elements/Forms	Vocabulary	Grammar
"The Gettysburg Address," "Second Inaugural Address," A. Lincoln; "Letter to His Son," R. E. Lee, SE pp. 480, 481, 482	• Use Background Knowledge, SE pp. 479, 484; TR Selection Support, p. 142 • Summarize Main Idea, TR Str. for Diverse St. Needs, p. 30	• Diction, SE pp. 479, 484; TR Selection Support, p. 143	pp. 479, 484; TR Selection Support, p. 140 Word Bank: consecrate, hallow, p. 480; deprecated, insurgents, p. 481; discern, scourge, malice, p. 482; anarchy, redress, p. 483	• Parallel Structure, SE pp. 479, 484; TR Selection Support, p. 141
"For What It's Worth," S. Stills, SE p. 487	Reading Level: Average		Word Bank: paranoia, p. 487	
Civil War Diaries, Journals, and Letters, SE pp. 496, 499, 500, 501, 502, 503	Reading Levels: Avg., Average, Average, Easy, Easy, Easy • Dist. Fact/Opinion, SE pp. 495, 504; TR Sel. Support, p. 147 • Identify Chain of Events, TR Str. for Diverse St. Needs, p. 31	• Diaries, Journals, and Letters, SE pp. 495, 504; TR Selection Support, p. 148	• Latin Prefixes: *ob-*, SE pp. 495, 504; TR Sel. Support, p. 145; Word Bank: capitulate, audaciously, foreboding, obstinate, imprecations, p. 497; serenity, p. 498	• Capitalization of Proper Nouns, SE pp. 495, 504; TR Selection Support, p. 146 • WS Language Lab CD-ROM, Capitalization • WS Gram. Pr. Book pp. 81–82
from ***A Woman at War,* M. Moore,** SE p. 507	Reading Level: Average		• TR Selection Support, p. 149	
"The Boys' Ambition" from ***Life on the Mississippi,* "The Notorious Jumping Frog," M. Twain,** SE pp. 521, 525	Reading Levels: Average, Challenging • Regional Dialect, SE pp. 519, 530; TR Sel. Support, p. 153 • Recognize Humor, TR Str. for Diverse St. Needs, p. 32	• Humor, SE pp. 519, 530; TR Selection Support, p. 154 • Analyze Literary Criticism, ATE, p. 527	• Greek Prefixes: *mono-*, SE pp. 519, 530; TR Sel. Support, p. 151 Words: transient, p. 521; prodigious, eminence, p. 523; garrulous, conjectured, monotonous, interminable, p. 525; ornery, p. 526	• Double Negatives, SE pp. 519, 530; TR Selection Support, p. 152 • WS Language Lab CD-ROM, Avoiding Double Negatives • WS Gram. Pr. Book, pp. 78–79
"The Outcasts of Poker Flat," B. Harte, SE p. 534	Reading Level: Average • Question the Text, SE pp. 533, 542; TR Selection Support, p. 153 • Make a Character Chart, TR Str. for Diverse St. Needs, p. 33	• Regionalism, SE pp. 533, 542; TR Selection Support, p. 158 • Analyze a Film Review, ATE, p. 536	• Latin Word Roots: *-bel-*, SE pp. 533, 542; TR Sel. Support, p. 155 Words: expatriated, anathema, bellicose, recumbent, equanimity, p. 536; vociferation, vituperative, p. 539; querulous, p. 540	• Coordinating Conjunctions in Compound Sentences, SE pp. 533, 542; TR Selection Support, p. 156
"Heading West," M. D. Colt; "I Will Fight No More Forever," Chief Joseph, SE pp. 546, 551	Reading Levels: Easy, Easy • Respond, SE pp. 545, 552; TR Selection Support, p. 161 • Chain of Events Organizer, TR Str. for Diverse St. Needs, p. 34	• Tone, SE pp. 545, 552; TR Selection Support, p. 162	• Words From Latin: *Terra Firma*, SE pp. 545, 552; TR Selection Support, p. 159 Word Bank: genial, p. 546; pervading, terra firma, emigrants, p. 547; profusion, depredations, p. 548; nonplused, p. 549	• Sent. Fragments, SE pp. 545, 552; TR Selection Support, p. 160 • WS Lang. Lab CD-ROM, Fragments and Run-on Sentences • WS Gram. Pr. Book, pp. 45–46
"To Build a Fire," J. London, SE p. 556	Reading Level: Average • Predict, SE pp. 555, 566; TR Selection Support, p. 165 • Identify Sensory Images, TR Str. for Diverse St. Needs, p. 35	• Conflict, SE pp. 555, 566; TR Selection Support, p. 166 • Analyze Literary Criticism, ATE, p. 563	• Latin Roots: *-ject-*, SE pp. 555, 566; TR Selection Support, p. 163 Word Bank: conjectural, unwonted, p. 557; conflagration, p. 561; peremptorily, p. 563	• Adverb Clauses, SE pp. 555, 566; TR Selection Support, p. 164 • WS Language Lab CD-ROM, Varying Sentence Structure • WS Gram. Pr. Book, p. 36
"Pecos Bill Becomes a Coyote," "The Legend of Gregorio Cortez," "The Streets of Laredo," SE pp. 570, 574, 575	Reading: Average, Easy, Easy • Recognize Cultural Details, SE pp. 569, 576; TR Sel. Sup., p. 169 • Summarize Narrative, TR Str. for Diverse St. Needs, p. 36	• Folk Literature, SE pp. 569, 576; TR Selection Support, p. 170 • Analyze an Author's Comment, ATE, p. 581	• Suffixes: *-ance* and *-ence*, SE pp. 569, 576; TR Selection Support, p. 167 Word Bank: defiance, p. 573; pall, p. 575	• Compound Predicates, SE pp. 569, 576; TR Selection Support, p. 168 • WS Language Lab CD-ROM, Compoud Sentence Parts
from ***Lonesome Dove,* L. McMurtry,** SE p. 579	Reading Level: Average		• TR Selection Support, p. 171 Word Bank: aggrieved, p. 579	
"The Story of an Hour," K. Chopin, SE p. 592	Reading Level: Average • Recognize Ironic Details, SE pp. 591, 596; TR Selection Support, p. 175 • Analyze Characters' Behavior, TR Str. for Div. St. Needs, p. 37	• Irony, SE pp. 591, 596; TR Selection Support, p. 176	• Anglo-Saxon Prefixes: *fore-*, SE pp. 591, 596; TR Selection Support, p. 173 Word Bank: forestall, repression, elusive, tumultuously, importunities, p. 594	• Appositives and Appositive Phrases, SE pp. 591, 596; TR Selection Support, p. 174 • WS Language Lab CD-ROM, Identifying Appositives • WS Gram. Pr. Book, pp. 30–31

Division, Reconciliation, and Expansion (1850–1914)

Writing	Speaking, Listening, and Viewing	Researching and Representing	Assessment	Technology
• Guided Writing Lesson: Research Query [Appropriate Language for Purpose], SE p. 485 • Letter of Response, Diary Entry, Newspaper Column, SE p. 485 • Journ. Ent., TR Alt. Assess., p. 30	• Reenactment, Mock Court, SE p. 485 • Model and Demonstration, TR Alt. Assess., p. 30	• Graphic Display, Web Site, SE p. 485 • Civil War Exhibit, TR Alt. Assess., p. 30	• Selection Test, TR Formal Assessment, pp. 141–143; Assess. Res. Software • Business Letter Rub. [for Wr. Lesson], TR Alt. Assess.,p. 128 • TR Alt. Assess., p. 30	• "The Gettysburg Address," "Second Inaugural Address," "Letter to His Son," LL Audio • WS Writing Lab CD-ROM, Pract./Tech. Writing Tutorial; Wr. at Work Videodisc Ch. 5
• Updated Lyrics, Interpretation, Evaluation, SE p. 488	• Interview/Group Discussion, SE p. 488	• Graphic Display, SE p. 488	• Selection Test, TR Formal Assessment, pp. 144–145; Assess. Res. Software	
• Summary, Book Jacket, Reflective Essay, SE p. 505 • Writing Lesson: Firsthand Bio. [Vivid Verbs], SE p. 505 • Civil War Report, TR Alt. Assess., p. 31	• Viewing, Dramatic Reading, SE p. 505 • Music and the Civil War, TR Alt. Assess., p. 31	• Timeline, Model/Map, SE p. 505 • Viewing and Representing Mini-Lesson: Timeline, ATE p. 500 • Eyewitness Accounts, TR Alt. Assess., p. 31	• Selection Test, TR Formal Assessment, pp. 150–152; Assess. Res. Software • Nar./Pers. Exp, Rub. [for Wr. Lesson], TR Alt. Assess., p. 111 • TR Alt. Assess., p. 31	• Civil War Diaries, Journals, and Letters, LL Audiocassettes • WS Writing Lab CD-ROM, Narration Tutorial; Wr. at Work Videodisc Ch. 2
• Telegram, News Story, Critical Essay, SE p. 512	• Debate, SE p. 512	• Poster, SE p. 512	• Selection Test, TR Formal Assessment, pp. 153–154; Assess. Res. Software	• from *A Woman at War*, LL Audiocassettes
• Cartoon, Obituary, Analytic Essay, SE p. 531 • Guided Writing Lesson: Humorous Anecdote [Elaboration for Vividness], SE p. 531 • Explan., TR Alt. Assess.,p. 32	• Interview, Oral Interp., SE p. 531 • S/L/V Mini-Lesson: Oral Interpretation, ATE p. 528 • Oral Reading, TR Alt. Assess., p. 32	• Multimedia Presentation, Illustration, SE p. 531 • Research Skills Mini-Lesson: Citing Sources, ATE p. 522 • Song, TR Alt. Assess., p. 32	• Sel. Test, TR Form. Assess., pp. 158–160; Assess. Res. Software • Fict. Narrative Rubric [for Wr. Lesson], TR Alt. Assess., p. 110 • TR Alt. Assess., p. 32	• "The Boys' Ambition," "The Notorious Jumping Frog," LL Audiocassettes • WS Writing Lab CD-ROM Nar. Tut.; Wr. at Work Videodisc Ch. 2 • Lit. CD-ROM: *History of Am. Lit.*
• Visitor's Guide, Review, Newspaper Editorial, SE p. 543 • Guided Writing Lesson: Description of a Place [Precise Details], SE p. 543 • Account, TR Alt. Assess., p. 33	• Literary Discussion, Eulogy, SE p. 543 • Speaking, Listening, and Viewing Mini-Lesson: Eulogy, ATE p. 540 • Perf., TR Alt. Assess., p. 33	• Boom Towns, In Search of Gold, SE p. 543 • Illustration, TR Alt. Assess., p. 33	• Selection Test, TR Formal Assessment, pp. 161–163; Assess. Res. Software • Description Rubric [for Wr. Lesson], TR Alt. Assess., p. 112 • TR Alt. Assess., p. 33	• "The Outcasts of Poker Flat," LL Audiocassettes • WS Writing Lab CD-ROM, Desc. Tut.; Wr. at Work Videodisc Ch. 1 • Lit. CD-ROM: *History of Am. Lit.*
• Poem, Character Sketch, Speech, SE p. 553 • Guided Writing Lesson: Position Paper [Coherence], SE p. 553 • Movie Rev., TR Alt. Assess., p. 34	• Oral Interpretation, Viewing, SE p. 553 • S/L/V Mini-Lesson: Oral Interpretation, ATE p. 550 • Oral Rep., TR Alt. Assess., p. 34	• Brochure, Quilt, SE p. 553 • Viewing and Representing Mini-Lesson: Brochure, ATE p. 549 • Map of the Journey, TR Alt. Assess., p. 34	• Selection Test, TR Formal Assessment, pp. 164–166; Assess. Res. Software • Persuasion Rubric [for Wr. Lesson], TR Alt. Assess., p. 120 • TR Alt. Assess., p. 34	• "Heading West," "I Will Fight No More Forever," LL Audiocassettes • WS Writing Lab CD-ROM, Pers. Tut.; Wr. at Work Videodisc Ch. 4
• Diary Entry, Sequel, Character. Analysis, SE p. 567 • Writing Lesson: Lit. Analysis [Support an Argument], SE p. 567 • Scene, TR Alt. Assess., p. 35	• Enactment, Oral Storytelling, SE p. 567 • Television News Broadcast, TR Alt. Assess., p. 35	• Graph. Disp., Pamph., SE p. 567 • Research: Using Museums for Research, ATE p. 557 • Viewing and Representing Mini-Lesson: Pamphlet, ATE p. 560 • Exhibit, TR Alt. Assess., p. 35	• Selection Test, TR Formal Assessment, pp. 167–169; Assess. Res. Software • Interpretation Rubric [for Wr. Lesson], TR Alt. Assess., p. 127 • TR Alt. Assess., p. 35	• "To Build a Fire," LL Audiocassettes • WS Writing Lab CD-ROM, Response to Literature Tutorial; Wr. at Work Videodisc Ch. 7 • Lit. CD-ROM: *History of Am. Lit.*
• Fantasy Creature, Dialogue, Analytic Essay, SE p. 577 • Guided Writing Lesson: Legend [Elaboration], SE p. 577 • Autobiographical Folk Tale, TR Alt. Assess., p. 36	• Oral Report, Prosecution Argument, SE p. 577 • S/L/V Mini-Lesson: Oral Report, ATE p. 573 • Native American Folk Tale, TR Alt. Assess., p. 36	• Western Ballads, Graphic Display, SE p. 577 • Folk Literature Web site, TR Alt. Assess., p. 36	• Sel. Test, TR Form. Assess., pp. 170–172; Assess. Res. Software • Fict. Narrative Rubric [for Wr. Lesson], TR Alt. Assess., p. 110 • TR Alt. Assess., p. 36	• "Pecos Bill Becomes a Coyote," "The Legend of Gregorio Cortez," LL Audiocassettes • WS Writing Lab CD-ROM Narration Tutorial; Wr. at Work Videodisc Ch. 2
• Western Scenario, Literary Critique, SE p. 584	• Audition, SE p. 584	• Report, Annotated Movie List, SE p. 584	• Sel. Test, TR Form. Assess., pp. 173–174; Assess. Res. Software • Sel. Test, TR Form. Assess., pp. 179–181; Assess. Res. Software	• from *Lonesome Dove*, LL Audiocassettes
• Diary Entry, New Version, Commentary, SE p. 597 • Writing Lesson: Reflective Essay [Personal Tone], SE p. 597 • Screenplay, TR Alt. Assess., p. 37	• Soliloquy, Cultural Comparison, SE p. 597 • Informal Debate, TR Alt. Assess., p. 37	• Visual Interpretation, Pantomime, SE p. 597 • Interview, TR Alt. Assess., p. 37	• Description Rubric [for Wr. Lesson], TR Alt. Assess., p. 112 • TR Alt. Assess., p. 37	• "The Story of an Hour," LL Audiocassettes • WS Writing Lab CD-ROM, Description Tutorial

Program Planner Unit 4

Selection	Reading	Literary Elements/Forms	Vocabulary	Grammar
"Douglass," "We Wear the Mask," P. L. Dunbar, SE pp. 600, 601	Reading Levels: Average, Average • Interpret, SE pp. 599, 602; TR Selection Support, p. 179 • Rephrase Poetry as Prose, TR Str. for Diverse St. Needs, p. 38	• Rhyme, SE pp. 599, 602; TR Selection Support, p. 180	• Related Words: Forms of *Guile;* SE pp. 599, 602; TR Selection Support, p. 177 Word Bank: salient, tempest, stark, p. 600; guile, myriad, p. 601	• Punctuation of Interjections, SE pp. 599, 602; TR Selection Support, p. 178 • WS Language Lab CD-ROM, Exclamation Marks • WS Gram. Pr. Book, p. 85
"Luke Havergal," "Richard Cory," E. A. Robinson; "Lucinda Matlock," "Richard Bone," E. L. Masters, SE pp. 606, 607, 608, 609	Reading Levels: Average, Average, Average, Average • Recognize Attitudes, SE pp. 605, 610; TR Sel. Sup., p. 183 • Gather Character Evidence , TR Str. for Diverse St. Needs, p. 39	• Speaker, SE pp. 605, 610; TR Selection Support, p. 184	• Latin Word Roots: *-pose-*, SE pp. 605, 610; TR Selection Support, p. 181 Word Bank: imperially, p. 607; repose, degenerate, p. 608; epitaph, p. 609	• Noun Clauses, SE pp. 605, 610; TR Selection Support, p. 182 • WS Gram. Pr. Book, p. 37
"A Wagner Matinee," W. Cather, SE p. 614	Reading Level: Challenging • Clarifying, SE pp. 613, 620; TR Selection Support, p. 187 • Outline Main Idea and Supporting Details, TR Str. for Diverse St. Needs, p. 40	• Characterization, SE pp. 613, 620; TR Selection Support, p. 188	• Words From Music: *Prelude;* SE pp. 613, 620; TR Sel. Sup., p. 185 Word Bank: reverential, p. 615; tremulously, semi-somnambu-lant, p. 616; inert, p. 617; pre-lude, p. 618; jocularity, p. 619	• Reflexive and Intensive Pronouns, SE pp. 613, 620; TR Selection Support, p. 186
"Cats," A. Quindlen, SE p. 623	Reading Level: Average		• TR Selection Support, p. 189	

Program Planner Unit 5

"The Love Song of J. Alfred Prufrock," T. S. Eliot, SE p. 647	Reading Level: Challenging • Reading for Success: Strategies for Reading Poetry, SE pp. 646, 652; TR Selection Support, pp. 193–194 • Paraphrase, TR Str. for Diverse St. Needs, p. 41	• Dramatic Monologue, SE pp. 645, 652; TR Selection Support, p. 195	• Greek Prefixes: *di-*, SE pp. 645, 652; TR Selection Support, p. 191 Word Bank: insidious, p. 647; digress, p. 649; malingers, meticulous, obtuse, p. 650	• Adjectival Modifiers, SE pp. 645, 652; TR Sel. Support, p. 192 • WS Language Lab CD-ROM, Misplaced Modifiers • WS Gram. Pr. Book, pp. 47–48
The Imagist Poets: E. Pound, W. C. Williams, H. D. (Hilda Doolittle), SE pp. 657, 660, 661, 662, 662, 663, 664, 665	Reading Levels: Challenging, Avg., Easy, Avg., Avg., Avg., Avg., Avg. • Engage Your Senses, SE pp. 656, 666; TR Sel. Sup., pp. 198 • Identify Sensory Imagery, TR Str. for Diverse St. Needs, p. 42	• Imagist Poetry, SE pp. 656, 666; TR Selection Support, p. 199 • Analyze Literary Criticism, ATE, p. 663	• Forms of *Appear;* SE pp. 656, 666; TR Selection Support, p. 196 Word Bank: voluminous, dogma, p. 657; apparition, p. 661	• Concrete/Abstract Nouns, SE pp. 656, 666; TR Sel. Sup., p. 197 • WS Language Lab CD-ROM, Types of Nouns • WS Gram. Pr. Book, p. 5
"Winter Dreams," F. S. Fitzgerald, SE p. 670	Reading Level: Average • Draw Conclusions About Characters, SE pp. 669, 684; TR Selection Support, p. 202 • Respond to Characters' Actions, TR Str. for Div. St. Needs, p. 43	• Characterization, SE pp. 669, 684; TR Selection Support, p. 203	• Latin Roots: *-somn-*, SE pp. 669, 684; TR Sel. Sup., p. 200 Words: fallowness, p. 670; prepos-terous, fortuitous, p. 672; sinuous, p. 675; mundane, p. 676; poignant, 679; pugilistic, somnolent, p. 681	• Dashes, SE pp. 669, 684; TR Selection Support, p. 201 • WS Language Lab CD-ROM, Dashes • WS Gram. Pr. Book, p. 93
"The Turtle," J. Steinbeck, SE p. 688	Reading Level: Average • Find Clues To Theme, SE pp. 687, 690; TR Sel. Support, p. 206 • Outline Main Idea/Sup. Details, TR Str. for Div. St. Needs, p. 44	• Theme, SE pp. 687, 690; TR Selection Support, p. 207	• Latin Prefixes: *pro-*, SE pp. 687, 690; TR Selection Support, p. 204 Word Bank: embankment, pro-truded, p. 689	• Parallel Structure, SE pp. 687, 690; TR Selection Support, p. 205 • WS Language Lab CD-ROM, Strengthening Sentences • WS Gram. Pr. Book, pp. 49–50
"anyone lived . . . ," "old age sticks," E. E. Cummings; "The Unknown Citizen," W. H. Auden, SE pp. 694, 695, 696	Reading Levels: Chall., Chall., Avg. • Relate Struct. to Meaning, SE pp. 693, 698; TR Sel. Sup., p. 210 • Interpret Poetic Images, TR Str. for Diverse St. Needs, p. 45	• Satire, SE pp. 693, 698; TR Selection Support, p. 211	• Greek Roots: *-psych-*, SE pp. 693, 698; TR Selection Support, p. 208 Word Bank: statistics, psychology, p. 697	• Parentheses, SE pp. 693, 698; TR Selection Support, p. 209 • WS Gram. Pr. Book, p. 94
"The Far and the Near," T. Wolfe, SE p. 702	Reading Level: Challenging • Predict, SE pp. 701, 706; TR Selection Support, p. 214 • Identify Key Ideas, TR Str. for Diverse St. Needs, p. 46	• Climax and Anticlimax, SE pp. 701, 706; TR Selection Support, p. 215	• Latin Roots: *-temp-*, SE pp. 701, 706; TR Selection Support, p. 212 Word Bank: tempo, p. 703; sallow, sullen, timorous, visage, p. 705	• Restrictive and Nonrestrictive Participial Phrases, SE pp. 701, 706; TR Selection Support, p. 213 • WS Gram. Pr. Book, p. 32

Division, Reconciliation, and Expansion (1850–1914)

Writing	Speaking, Listening, and Viewing	Researching and Representing	Assessment	Technology
• Diary Entry, Report, Literary Analysis, SE p. 603 • Guided Writing Lesson: Poem [Main Impression], SE p. 603 • Newspaper Editorial, TR Alt. Assess., p. 38	• Panel Discussion, Oral Interpretation, SE p. 603 • Oral Reading, TR Alt. Assess., p. 38	• Other Cultures, Timeline, SE p. 603 • Performance Work, TR Alt. Assess., p. 38	• Selection Test, TR Formal Assessment, pp. 182–184; Assess. Res. Software • Poetry Rubric [for Wr. Lesson], TR Alt. Assess., p. 123 • TR Alt. Assess., p. 38	• "Douglass," "We Wear the Mask," LL Audiocassettes • WS Writing Lab CD-ROM, Creative Writing Tutorial; Wr. at Work Videodisc Ch. 6
• Biographical Sketch, Comparison/Contrast, Letter, SE p. 611 • Guided Writing Lesson: Firsthand Biography [Transitions to Show Order of Importance], SE p. 611 • Short Story, TR Alt. Assess., p. 39	• Music Appreciation, Dramatic Reading, SE p. 611 • Improvisational Skit, TR Alt. Assess., p. 39	• Illustration, Map, SE p. 611 • Poetry to Music, TR Alt. Assess., p. 39	• Selection Test, TR Formal Assessment, pp. 185–187; Assess. Res. Software • Narrative Based on Personal Experience Rubric [for Wr. Lesson], TR Alt. Assess., p. 111 • TR Alt. Assess., p. 39	• "Luke Havergal," "Richard Cory," "Lucinda Matlock," "Richard Bone," LL Audiocassettes • WS Writing Lab CD-ROM, Narration Tutorial; Wr. at Work Videodisc Ch. 2
• Diary Entry, School Brochure, Editorial, SE p. 621 • Guided Writing Lesson: Travel Brochure [Sensory Details], SE p. 621 • Desc., TR Alt. Assess., p. 40	• Debate, Oral Storytelling, SE p. 621 • S/L/V Mini-Lesson: Debate, ATE p. 618 • Oral Presentation, TR Alt. Assess., p. 40	• A Wagner Matinee, Research Project, SE p. 621 • Illustration, TR Alt. Assess., p. 40	• Selection Test, TR Formal Assessment, pp. 188–190; Assess. Res. Software • Description Rubric [for Wr. Lesson], TR Alt. Assess., p. 112 • TR Alt. Assess., p. 40	• "A Wagner Matinee," LL Audiocassettes • WS Writing Lab CD-ROM, Description Tutorial • Lit. CD-ROM: *History of Am. Lit.*
• Epitaph, Letter to the Editor, Song, Character Sketch, SE p. 625	• Dramatic Monologue, SE p. 625	• Report, SE p. 625	• Selection Test, TR Formal Assessment, pp. 191–192; Assess. Res. Software	• "Cats," LL Audiocassettes

Disillusion, Defiance, and Discontent (1914–1946)

• Letter, Character Analysis, Allusions Essay, SE p. 653 • Guided Writing Lesson: Monologue [Consistent Point of View], SE p. 653 • Poem of Free Associations, TR Alt. Assess., p. 41	• Oral Interpretation, Role Play, SE p. 653 • Speaking, Listening, and Viewing Mini-Lesson: Role Play, ATE p. 649 • Perf., TR Alt. Assess., p. 41	• Report, Art Exhibit, SE p. 653 • Illustration, TR Alt. Assess., p. 41	• Sel. Test, TR Form. Assess. pp. 197–199; Assess. Res. Software • Fict. Narrative Rubric [for Wr. Lesson], TR Alt. Assess., p. 110 • TR. Alt. Assess., p. 41	• "The Love Song of J. Alfred Prufrock," LL Audiocassettes • WS Writing Lab CD-ROM, Creative Writing Tutorial • Lit. CD-ROM: *History of Am. Lit.*
• Description, Poem, Critical Essay, SE p. 667 • Writing Lesson: An Editor's Rev. of Ms. [Brevity/Clarity], SE p. 667 • Explanation of Metaphor, TR Alt. Assess., p. 42	• Informal Debate, Oral Interpretation, SE p. 667 • Oral Reports, TR Alt. Assess., p. 42	• Art, Poetry Collection, SE p. 667 • Research Skills Mini-Lesson: Formulating Questions, ATE p. 657 • Musical Performance, TR Alt. Assess., p. 42	• Sel. Test, TR Form. Assess. pp. 200–202; Assess. Res. Software • Resp. to Lit. Rubric [for Wr. Lesson], TR Alt. Assess., p. 125 • TR Alt. Assess., p. 42	• The Imagist Poets, LL Audiocassettes • WS Writing Lab CD-ROM, Response to Literature Tutorial; Wr. at Work Videodisc Ch. 7 • Lit. CD-ROM: *History of Am. Lit.*
• Diary Entry, Résumé, Essay, SE p. 685 • Writing Lesson: Character Analysis, [Elaboration, SE p. 685 • Two Viewpoints, TR Alt. Assess., p. 43	• Enactment, Musical Interpretation, SE p. 685 • Speaking, Listening, and Viewing Mini-Lesson: Enactment, ATE p. 672	• Montage, Report, SE p. 685 • Movie Scene, TR Alt. Assess., p. 43	• Sel. Test, TR Form. Assess. pp. 203–205; Assess. Res. Software • Lit. Analysis/ Interp. Rub. [for Wr. Lesson], TR Alt. Assess., p. 127 • TR Alt. Assess., p. 43	• "Winter Dreams," LL Audiocassettes • WS Wr. Lab CD-ROM, Resp. to Lit. Tut.; Wr. at Wrk Videodisc Ch. 7 • Lit. CD-ROM: *History of Am. Lit.*
• Description, Lite. Analysis, Hist. Content Essay, SE p. 691 • Writing Lesson: Sci. Observ. [Clear Seq. of Events], SE p. 691 • Character Sketches, TR Alt. Assess., p. 44	• Interview, Monologue, SE p. 691 • Radio Advertisement, TR Alt. Assess., p. 44	• Environmental Report, Cartoon, SE p. 691 • Set Design, TR Alt. Assess., p. 44	• Sel. Test, TR Form. Assess. pp. 206–208; Assess. Res. Software • Tech. Desc./ Expl. Rub. [for Wr. Lesson], TR Alt. Assess., p. 130 • TR Alt. Assess., p. 44	• "The Turtle," LL Audiocassettes • WS Writing Lab CD-ROM, Desc. Tut. Wr. at Work Videodisc Ch. 1 • Lit. CD-ROM: *History of Am. Lit.*
• Summary, Double Diary Entry, Critical Essay, SE p. 699 • Guided Writing: Poetry Reading [Types of Support], SE p. 699 • Sat. Poem, TR Alt. Assess., p. 45	• Poetry Reading, Group Discussion, SE p. 699 • Speaking, Listening, and Viewing Mini-Lesson: Poetry Reading, ATE p. 696	• Internet Research, Art, SE p. 699 • Stage Setting, TR Alt. Assess., p. 45	• Sel. Test, TR Form. Assess., pp. 209–211; Assess. Res. Software • Comp/Cont Rub. [for Wr. Lesson], TR Alt. Assess., p. 118 • TR Alt. Assess., p. 45	• "anyone lived . . .," "old age sticks," "The Unknown Citizen," LL Audiocassettes • WS Writing Lab CD-ROM, Response to Literature Tutorial
• Guided Writing Lesson: Brochure [Accuracy], SE p. 707 • Desc., First Person Account, Comp/Cont Essay, SE p. 707 • Job Desc., TR Alt. Assess., p. 46	• Interview, Music Critique, SE p. 707 • S/L/V Mini-Lesson: Music Critique, ATE p. 704 • Song Lyr., TR Alt. Assess., p. 46	• Railroad Report, Map, SE p. 707 • Portrait of the Seasons, TR Alt. Assess., p. 46	• Sel. Test, TR Form. Assess., pp. 212–214; Assess. Res. Software • Description Rubric [for Wr. Lesson], TR Alt. Assess., p. 112 • TR Alt. Assess, p. 46	• "The Far and the Near," LL Audiocassettes • WS Writing Lab CD-ROM, Description Tutorial • Lit. CD-ROM: *History of Am. Lit.*

Selection	Reading	Literary Elements/Forms	Vocabulary	Grammar
"Of Modern Poetry," "Anecdote of the Jar," W. Stevens; "Ars Poetica," A. Macleish; "Poetry," M. Moore, SE pp. 710, 711, 712, 714	Reading Levels: Chall., Chall., Chall., Chall. • Paraphrase, SE pp. 709, 716; TR Selection Support, p. 218 • Explain and Resp. to Poetry, TR Str. for Diverse St. Needs, p. 47	• Simile, SE pp. 709, 716; TR Selection Support, p. 219	• Latin Roots: *-satis-*, SE pp. 709, 716; TR Selection Support, p. 216 Word Bank: suffice, insatiable, p. 710; slovenly, dominion, p. 711; palpable, p. 713; derivative, literalists, p. 715	• Subject Complements, SE pp. 709, 716; TR Selection Support, p. 217 • WS Gram. Pr. Book, p. 21
"Allentown," B. Joel, SE p. 719	Reading Level: Easy			
"In Another Country," E. Hemingway; "The Corn Planting," S. Anderson; "A Worn Path," E. Welty, SE pp. 731, 735, 740	Reading Levels: Average, Easy, Challenging • Identify with Characters, SE pp. 730, 746; TR Selection Support, p. 223 • Make a Character Chart, TR Str. for Diverse St. Needs, p. 48	• Point of View, SE pp. 730, 746; TR Selection Support, p. 224 • Analyze an Author's Comment, ATE, p. 741	• Latin Roots: *-val-*, SE pp. 730, 746; TR Selection Support, p. 221 Word Bank: invalided, p. 734; grave, limber, p. 741; obstinate, p. 745	• Punctuating Dialogue, SE pp. 730, 746; TR Selection Support, p. 222 • WS Language Lab CD-ROM, Quotation Marks, Colons, and Semicolons • WS Gram. Pr. Book, pp. 90–91
"Anxiety," G. Paley, SE p. 749	Reading Level: Average		• TR Selection Support, p. 225	
"April Showers," E. Wharton, SE p. 760	Reading Level:Average • Anticipate Events, SE pp. 759, 766; TR Selection Support, p. 229 • Identify Chain of Events, TR Str. for Diverse St. Needs, p. 49	• Elements of Plot, SE pp. 759, 766; TR Selection Support, p. 230	• Latin Roots: *man-*, *manu-,* SE pp. 759, 766; TR Sel. Sup., p. 227 Word Bank: admonitory, retrospective, antagonism, p. 761; contrition, manuscript, p. 763; commiseration, p. 765	• Gerund Phrases, SE pp. 759, 766; TR Selection Support, p. 228 • WS Language Lab CD-ROM, Recognizing and Using Phrases • WS Gram. Pr. Book, p. 33
"Chicago," "Grass," C. Sandburg, SE pp. 770, 771	Reading Levels: Easy, Average • Respond, SE pp. 769, 772; TR Selection Support, p. 233 • Reword Poet's Ideas, TR Str. for Diverse St. Needs, p. 50	• Apostrophe, SE pp. 769, 772; TR Selection Support, p. 234	• Related Words: *Brutal*, SE pp. 769, 772; TR Selection Support, p. 231 Word Bank: brutal, wanton, cunning, p. 771	• Four Types of Sentences, SE pp. 769, 772; TR Sel. Sup., p. 232 • WS Language Lab CD-ROM, Kinds of Sentences • WS Gram. Pr. Book, p. 19
"The Jilting of Granny Weatherall," K. A. Porter, SE p. 776	Reading Level: Average • Clarify Seq. of Events, SE pp. 775, 782; TR Sel. Support, p. 237 • Make a Timeline, TR Str. for Diverse St. Needs, p. 51	• Stream of Consciousness, SE pp. 775, 782; TR Selection Support, p. 238	• Greek Prefixes: *dys-*, SE pp. 775, 782; TR Selection Support, p. 235; Word Bank: piety, frippery, dyspepsia, p. 781	• Imperative Sentences, SE pp. 775, 782; TR Selection Support, p. 236
"Race at Morning," "Nobel Prize Accept. Speech," W. Faulkner, SE pp. 786, 798	Reading Levels: Average, Easy • Break Down Long Sent., SE pp. 785, 800; TR Sel. Support, p. 241 • Dialect, Sum. Main Idea, TR Str. for Diverse St. Needs, p. 52	• Dialect, SE pp. 785, 800; TR Selection Support, p. 242 • Analyze Literary Criticism, ATE p. 789	• Latin Suffixes: *-ery*, SE pp. 785, 800; TR Sel. Support, p. 239 Word Bank: bayou, distillery, buck, p. 787; moiling, switch, p. 789; scrabbling, p. 791; swag, glade, p. 793	• Correct Use of Irregular Verb Forms, SE pp. 785, 800; TR Selection Support, p. 240 • WS Lang. Lab CD-ROM, Correct and Effective Use of Verbs • WS Gram. Pr. Book, p. 55
R. Frost Poetry, SE pp. 804, 806, 808, 810, 811, 812	Reading Levels: Avg., Avg., Avg., Easy, Avg., Challenging • Reading Blank Verse, SE pp. 803, 814; TR Sel. Sup., p. 245 • Restate Poetry as Prose, TR Str. for Diverse St. Needs, p. 53	• Blank Verse, SE pp. 803, 814; TR Selection Support, p. 246	• Latin Roots: *-lum-*, SE pp. 803, 814; TR Selection Support, p. 243 Word Bank: poise, p. 805; rueful, p. 808; luminary, p. 811	• Uses of Infinitives, SE pp. 803, 814; TR Selection Support, p. 244 • WS Language Lab CD-ROM, Recognizing and Using Phrases
"The Night the Ghost Got In," J. Thurber; from ***Here Is New York,* E. B. White,** SE pp. 818, 822	Reading Levels: Average, Easy • Recognize Hyperbole, SE pp. 817, 826; TR Selection Support, p. 249 • Identify Paragraph Topics, TR Str. for Diverse St. Needs, p. 54	• Informal Essay, SE pp. 817, 826; TR Selection Support, p. 250 • Analyze and Author's Comment, ATE p. 822	• Latin Word Roots: *-terr-*, SE pp. 817, 826; TR Sel. Support, p. 247 Word Bank: intuitively, p. 819; blaspheming, p. 820; aspiration, subterranean, p. 823; claustrophobia, cosmopolitan, p. 824	• Commas in Series, SE pp. 817, 826; TR Selection Support, p. 248 • WS Language Lab CD-ROM, Commas • WS Gram. Pr. Book, p. 86
from ***Dust Tracks on a Road,* Z. N. Hurston,** SE p. 830	Reading Level: Average • Analyze How a Writer Achieves Purpose, SE pp. 829, 836; TR Selection Support, p. 253 • Analyze Characters, TR Str. for Diverse St. Needs, p. 55	• Purpose in Autobiography, SE pp. 829, 836; TR Selection Support, p. 254	• Greek Roots: *-graph-*, SE pp. 829, 836; TR Selection Support, p. 251 Word Bank: foreknowledge, brazenness, caper, p. 831; exalted, geography, p. 833; avarice, p. 834	• Parallelism in Coordinate Elements, SE pp. 829, 836; TR Selection Support, p. 252 • WS Language Lab CD-ROM, Strengthening Sentences • WS Gram. Pr. Book, pp. 49–50

Disillusion, Defiance, and Discontent (1914–1946)

Writing	Speaking, Listening, and Viewing	Researching and Representing	Assessment	Technology
• Guided Writing Lesson: Definition [Background], SE p. 717 • Ars Poetica, Comp/Contrast, Response to Criticism, SE p. 717 • Poetry Review, TR Alt. Assess., p. 47	• Round Table Discussion, Introduction, SE p. 717 • S/L/V Mini-Lesson: Round Table Discussion, ATE p. 713 • Multimedia Poetry Reading, TR Alt. Assess., p. 47	• Illustration, Poetry Collection, SE p. 717 • Poetry Exhibit, TR Alt. Assess., p. 47 • V/R Mini-Lesson: Illustration, ATE p. 711	• Selection Test, TR Formal Assessment, pp. 215–217; Assess. Res. Software • Definition Rubric [for Wr. Lesson], TR Alt. Assess., p. 114 • TR Alt. Assess., p. 47	• "Of Modern Poetry," "Anecdote of the Jar," "Ars Poetica," "Poetry," LL Audiocassettes • WS Writing Lab CD-ROM, Exp. Tut.; Wr. at Work Videodisc Ch. 3 • Lit. CD-ROM: *History of Am. Lit.*
• Application Essay, Letter to Congress, Newspaper Interview, SE p. 722	• Enactment, Interview, SE p. 722 • Mini-Lesson: Interview, ATE p. 719	• Diagram, City Profile, SE p. 722	• Selection Test, TR Formal Assessment, pp. 218–219; Assess. Res. Software	
• Memorial Speech, Magazine Article, Grant Proposal, SE p. 747 • Guided Writing Lesson: Personal Narrative [Elaboration to Add Emotional Depth], SE p. 747 • Prequel, TR Alt. Assess., p. 48	• Oral Story, Enactment, SE p. 747 • S/L/V Mini-Lesson: Enactment, ATE p. 739 • Interview, TR Alt. Assess., p. 48	• Report, Mil. Report, SE p. 747 • Map, TR Alt. Assess., p. 48 • Res.: Report Visuals, ATE p. 730 • V/R Mini-Lesson: Military Report, ATE p. 735 • Research: Reports, ATE p. 737	• Selection Test, TR Formal Assessment, pp. 224–226; Assess. Res. Software • Nar. Based on Pers. Exp. Rub. [for Wr. Lesson], TR Alt. Assess., p. 111 • TR Alt. Assess., p. 48	• "In Another Country," "The Corn Planting," "A Worn Path,"LL Audio • Looking at Lit., Ch. 9 • WS Wr. Lab CD-ROM, Nar. Tut.; Wr. at Work Videodisc Ch. 2
• Dialogue, Expository Essay, Critical Analysis, SE p. 752	• Interview, SE p. 752	• Historical Newspaper, Future Projection, SE p. 752	• Selection Test, TR Formal Assessment, pp. 227–228; Assess. Res. Software	• "Anxiety," LL Audiocassettes
• Flier Copy, Movie Scene, Critical Response, SE p. 767 • Guided Writing Lesson: Short Story [Mood], SE p. 767 • Essay, TR Alt. Assess., p. 49	• Casting Discussion, Dramatic Monologue, SE p. 767 • S/L/V Mini-Lesson: Casting Discussion, ATE p. 762 • Radio Play, TR Alt. Assess., p. 49	• Interior Design Project, Contest Announcement, SE p. 767 • Demonstration, TR Alt. Assess., p. 49	• Selection Test, TR Formal Assessment, pp. 232–234; Assess. Res. Software • Fict. Narrative Rubric [for Wr. Lesson], TR Alt. Assess., p. 110 • TR Alt. Assess., p. 49	• "April Showers," LL Audiocassettes • WS Writing Lab CD-ROM, Narration Tutorial; Wr. at Work Videodisc Ch. 2
• Writing Lesson: Description [Precise Details], SE p. 773 • Letter/Ed., TR Alt. Assess., p. 50 • Postcard, Apostrophe, Analysis of Repetition, SE p. 773	• Disagreement, Stand-up Routine, SE p. 773 • S/L/V Mini-Lesson: Disagreement, ATE p. 770 • Oral Report, TR Alt. Assess., p. 50	• Research Project, Population Breakdown, SE p. 773 • Collage, TR Alt. Assess., p. 50	• Selection Test, TR Formal Assessment, pp. 235–237; Assess. Res. Software • Description Rubric [for Wr. Lesson], TR Alt. Assess., p. 112	• "Chicago," "Grass," LL Audiocassettes • WS Writing Lab CD-ROM, Description Tutorial • Lit. CD-ROM: *History of Am. Lit.*
• Writing Lesson: Monologue [Characterization], SE p. 783 • Report, Letter, Course Description, SE p. 783 • Letter, TR Alt. Assess., p. 51	• Convers., Lecture, SE p. 783 • S/L/V Mini-Lesson: Conversation, ATE p. 780 • Monologue, TR Alt. Assess., p. 51	• Free Painting, Report on Hospice Care, SE p. 783 • Magazine, TR Alt. Assess., p. 51 • V/R Mini-Lesson: Free Painting, ATE p. 770	• Sel. Test, TR Form. Assess., pp. 238–240; Assess. Res. Software • Drama Rubric [for Wr. Lesson], TR Alt. Assess., p. 124 • TR Alt. Assess., p. 51	• "The Jilting of Granny Weatherall," LL Audiocassettes • WS Writing Lab CD-ROM, Creative Writing Tutorial
• Writing Lesson: Crit. Rev. [Elab. to Support an Arg.], SE p. 801 • Letter, Acceptance Speech, Analysis, SE p. 801 • Analysis, TR Alt. Assess., p. 52	• Debate, Broadcast, SE p. 801 • Speaking, Listening, and Viewing Mini-Lesson: Broadcast, ATE p. 796 • Interview, TR Alt. Assess., p. 52	• Pantomime, Musical Research, SE p. 801 • Map of the Hunt, TR Alt. Assess., p. 52 • Research: Finding Up-to-Date Information, ATE, p. 780	• Selection Test, TR Formal Assessment, pp. 241–243; Assess. Res. Software • Crit. Review Rubric [for Wr. Lesson], TR Alt. Assess., p. 126 • TR Alt. Assess., p. 52	• "Race at Morning," "Nobel Prize Acceptance Speech," LL Audio • WS Writing Lab CD-ROM, Response to Literature • Lit. CD-ROM: *History of Am. Lit.*
• Writing Lesson: Introduction to an Anthology [Transitions to Show Examples], SE p. 815 • Character Sketch, News Story, Essay, SE p. 815 • Speech, TR Alt. Assess., p. 53	• Eulogy, Poetry Reading, SE p. 815 • Speaking/Listening/Viewing Mini-Lesson: Eulogy, ATE p. 812 • Percussive Poetry, TR Alt. Assess., p. 53	• Graphic Display, Travel Brochure, SE p. 815 • Group Poem, TR Alt. Assess., p. 53	• Sel. Test, TR Form. Assess. pp. 244–246; Assess. Res. Software • Lit. Analysis/ Interp. Rub. [for Wr. Lesson], TR Alt. Assess., p. 127 • TR Alt. Assess., p. 53	• Robert Frost Poetry, LL Audio • Looking at Lit., Ch. 10 • WS Writing Lab CD-ROM, Exp. Tut.; Wr. at Work Videodisc Ch. 3 • Lit. CD-ROM: *History of Am. Lit.*
• Guided Writing: Toast at a Party [Grab Listeners' Atten.], SE p. 827 • Tourist Guide, Police Report, Critical Response, SE p. 827 • Humorous Narrative, TR Alt. Assess., p. 54	• Audition, Essay Critique, SE p. 827 • S/L Mini-Lesson: Audition, ATE p. 824 • Screenplay, TR Alt. Assess., p. 54	• Historical Re-creation, Set Design, SE p. 827 • Board Game, TR Alt. Assess., p. 54	• Sel. Test, TR Formal Assess., pp. 247–249; Assess. Res. Software • Expression Rubric [for Wr. Lesson], TR Alt. Assess., p. 109 • TR Alt. Assess., p. 54	• "The Night the Ghost Got In," from *Here Is New York,* LL Audiocassettes • WS Writing Lab CD-ROM, Description Tutorial
• Guided Writing: Inspiration [Show, Don't Tell], SE p. 837 • Autobiographical Episode, Eulogy, Opinion Essay, SE p. 837 • Autobiographical. Review, TR Alt. Assess., p. 55	• Campaign Speech, Interview, SE p. 837 • Speaking, Listening, and Viewing Mini-Lesson: Campaign Speech, ATE p. 834	• Reading List, Folk-Tale Collection, SE p. 837 • Dramatization, TR Alt. Assess., p. 55	• Selection Test, TR Formal Assessment, pp. 250–252; Assess. Res. Software • Nar./Pers. Exp. Rub. [for Wr. Lesson], TR Alt. Assess., p. 111 • TR Alt. Assess., p. 55	• from *Dust Tracks on a Road,* LL Audiocassettes • WS Writing Lab CD-ROM, Narration Tutorial; Wr. at Work Videodisc Ch. 2

Program Planner — Unit 5

Selection	Reading	Literary Elements/Forms	Vocabulary	Grammar
"Refugee in . . . ," "Ardella," "The Negro Speaks . . . ," "Dream Variations," L. Hughes; "The Tropics . . . ," C. McKay, SE pp. 840, 841, 842, 843	Reading Levels: Avg., Avg., Chall., Chall., Chall., Chall. • Draw Inferences About the Speaker, SE pp. 839, 844; TR Selection Support, p. 257 • React to Poetry, TR Str. for Diverse St. Needs, p. 56	• Speaker, SE pp. 839, 844; TR Selection Support, p. 258	• Latin Word Roots: *-lib-*, SE pp. 839, 844; TR Selection Support, p. 255 Word Bank: liberty, lulled, dusky, p. 841	• Verb Tenses: Past and Present Perfect, SE pp. 839, 844; TR Selection Support, p. 256 • WS Language Lab CD-ROM, Correct and Effective Use of Verbs • WS Gram. Pr. Book, pp. 54–58
"From/Dark Tower," C. Cullen; "A Black Man Talks . . . ," A. Bontemps; "Storm Ending," J. Toomer, SE pp. 848, 850, 851	Reading Levels: Average, Challenging, Average • Connect to Hist. Context, SE pp. 847, 852; TR Sel. Sup., p. 261 • Explain Poetic Images, TR Str. for Diverse St. Needs, p. 57	• Metaphor, SE pp. 847, 852; TR Selection Support, p. 262	• Latin Word Roots: *-cre-*, SE pp. 847, 852; TR Sel. Support, p. 259 Word Bank: increment, countenance, beguile, p. 849; stark, reaping, glean, p. 850	• Placement of Adjectives, SE pp. 847, 852; TR Selection Support, p. 260
"i yearn," R. Sánchez, SE p. 855	Reading Level: Average		• TR Selection Support, p. 263	

Program Planner — Unit 6

"The Life You Save May Be Your Own," F. O'Connor, SE p. 879	Reading Level: Average • Reading for Success: Strat. for Reading Fiction, SE pp. 878, 888; TR Sel. Support, pp. 267–268 • Analyze Characters' Behavior, TR Str. for Div. St. Needs, p. 58	• Grotesque Characters, SE pp. 877, 888; TR Selection Support, p. 269	• Latin Word Roots: *-sol-*, SE pp. 877, 888; TR Sel. Support, p. 265 Word Bank: desolate, listed, p. 879; ominous, ravenous, p. 883; morose, p. 885; guffawing, p. 886	• Subjunctive Mood, SE pp. 877, 888; TR Selection Support, p. 266 • WS Lang. Lab CD-ROM, Correct and Effective Use of Verbs • WS Gram. Pr. Book, p. 59
"The First Seven Years," B. Malamud, SE p. 893	Reading Level: Average • Identify with Characters, SE pp. 891, 900; TR Sel. Sup., p. 272 • Make a Timeline, TR Str. for Diverse St. Needs, p. 59	• Epiphany, SE pp. 891, 900; TR Selection Support, p. 273 • Analyze and Author's Comment, ATE p. 896	• Latin Roots: *-liter-*, SE pp. 891, 900; TR Selection Support, p. 270 Word Bank: diligence, connivance, illiterate, unscrupulous, p. 894; repugnant, discern, p. 897	• Correct Use of *Who/Whom*, SE pp. 891, 900; TR Sel. Sup., p. 271 • WS Language Lab CD-ROM, Pronoun Case • WS Gram. Pr. Book, p. 65
"The Brown Chest," J. Updike, SE p. 904	Reading Level: Average • Break Down Long Sent., SE pp. 903, 910; TR Sel. Sup., p. 276 • Form a Mental Picture, TR Str. for Diverse St. Needs, p. 60	• Atmosphere, SE pp. 903, 910; TR Selection Support, p. 277	• Latin Word Roots: *-sim-*, SE pp. 903, 910; TR Sel. Support, p. 274 Words: mottled, p. 905; assimilate, unfathomable, egregious, p. 907; proprietorial, evanescent, p. 909	• Begin. Sent. w/ Adv. Clauses, SE pp. 903, 910; TR Sel. Sup., p. 275 • WS Language Lab CD-ROM, Varying Sentence Structure • WS Gram. Pr. Book, pp. 110–111
"Hawthorne," R. Lowell; "Gold Glade," R. P. Warren; "The Light . . . ," "The Adamant," T. Roethke; "Traveling Through . . . ," W. Stafford, SE pp. 914, 916, 918, 919, 920	Reading Levels: Chall., Chall., Avg., Chall., Easy • Paraphrase, SE pp. 913, 922; TR Selection Support, p. 280 • Restate Poetry as Prose, TR Str. for Diverse St. Needs, p. 61	• Diction and Style, SE pp. 913, 922; TR Selection Support, p. 281	• Related Words: *Exhaust*, SE pp. 913, 922; TR Sel. Sup., p. 278 Word Bank: brooding, furtive, meditation, p. 915; declivity, p. 916; vestiges, p. 918; exhaust, p. 921	• Subject /Verb Agreement, SE pp. 913, 922; TR Sel. Sup., p. 279 • WS Lang. Lab CD-ROM, Agree. in Numb. or Spec. Probs in Agree. • WS Gram. Pr. Book, pp. 66–68
"Average Waves in Unprotected Waters," A. Tyler, SE p. 926	Reading Level: Average • Order Events, SE pp. 925, 932; TR Selection Support, p. 284 • Identify Chain of Events, TR Str. for Diverse St. Needs, p. 62	• Foreshadowing, SE pp. 925, 932; TR Selection Support, p. 285	• Latin Prefixes: *trans-*, SE pp. 925, 932; TR Sel. Sup., p. 282; Word Bank: orthopedic, transparent, p. 927; stocky, staunch, viper, p. 929	• Correct Use of Adjectives and Adverbs, SE pp. 925, 932; TR Selection Support, p. 283
from ***The Names,* N. S. Momaday; "Mint Snowball," N. S. Nye; "Suspended," J. Harjo,** SE pp. 936, 940, 942	Reading Levels: Easy, Easy, Easy • Relate to Experiences, SE pp. 935, 944; TR Sel. Support, p. 288 • Summarize Paragraphs, TR Str. for Diverse St. Needs, p. 63	• Anecdotes, SE pp. 935, 944; TR Selection Support, p. 289 • Analyze a Book Review, ATE p. 938	• Latin Prefixes: *con-*, SE pp. 935, 944; TR Sel. Support, p. 286 Word Bank: supple, p. 937; concocted, flamboyant, elixir, permeated, replicate, p. 941; revelatory, confluence, p. 943	• Elliptical Clauses, SE pp. 935, 944; TR Selection Support, p. 287

Disillusion, Defiance, and Discontent (1914–1946)

Writing	Speaking, Listening, and Viewing	Researching and Representing	Assessment	Technology
• Guided Writing: Profile of an Immigrant Grp. [Obj. Tone], SE p. 845 • Journal Entry, Description, Poem, SE p. 845 • Poem, TR Alt. Assess., p. 56	• Speech, Viewing, SE p. 845 • Oral Presentation, TR Alt. Assess., p. 56	• Posters, Travel Brochure, SE p. 845	• Selection Test, TR Formal Assessment, pp. 253–255; Assess. Res. Software • Res. Report/Paper Rub. [for Wr. Lesson], TR Alt. Assess., p. 121 • TR Alt. Assess., p. 56	• "Refugee in . . . ," "Ardella," "The Negro Speaks . . . ," "Dream Variations," "The Tropics . . . ," LL Audiocassettes • WS Wr. Lab CD-ROM, Res. Wr. Tut.; Wr. at Work Videodisc Ch. 5 • Lit. CD-ROM: *History of Am. Lit.*
• Guided Writing: Desc. of Weather Cond. [Vivid Verbs], SE p. 853 • List, Poem, Essay, SE p. 853 • Synopsis, TR Alt. Assess., p. 57	• Weather Report, Visual Display, SE p. 853 • Oral Reading, TR Alt. Assess., p. 57	• Research Report, Painting, SE p. 853 • Compilation, TR Alt. Assess., p. 57 • V/R Mini-Lesson: Painting, ATE p. 850	• Sel. Test, TR Form. Assess., pp. 256–258; Assess. Res. Software • Description Rubric [for Wr. Lesson], TR Alt. Assess., p. 112 • TR Alt. Assess., p. 57	• "From the Dark Tower," "A Black Man Talks . . . ," "Storm Ending," LL Audiocassettes • WS Writing Lab CD-ROM, Description Tutorial; Wr. at Work Videodisc Ch. 1
• Dear Ricardo, You Yearn, Literary Analysis, SE p. 857	• Interview, SE p. 857	• Graph, SE p. 857	• Selection Test, TR Formal Assessment, pp. 259–260; Assess. Res. Software	• "i yearn," LL Audiocassettes

Prosperity and Protest (1946–Present)

Writing	Speaking, Listening, and Viewing	Researching and Representing	Assessment	Technology
• Report, Moral Analysis, Short Story, SE p. 889 • Writing: Deposition [Transitions to Show Cause/ Effect], SE p. 889 • Newspaper Article, TR Alt. Assess., p. 58	• Staged Reading, Body Language Presentation, SE p. 889 • S/L/V Mini-Lesson: Staged Reading, ATE p. 886 • Oral Presentation, TR Alt. Assess., p. 58	• Magazine Illustration, Special Education Research, SE p. 889 • Career Profile, TR Alt. Assess., p. 58	• Selection Test, TR Formal Assessment, pp. 265–267; Assess. Res. Software • Cause/Effect Rubric [for Wr. Lesson], TR Alt. Assess., p. 117	• "The Life You Save May Be Your Own," LL Audiocassettes • WS Writing Lab CD-ROM, Exposition Tutorial • Lit. CD-ROM: *History of Am. Lit.*
• Diary Entry, Letter, Literary Analysis, SE p. 901 • Guided Writing: Personality Profile [Elaboration], SE p. 901 • Story Rev., TR Alt. Assess., p. 59	• Group Disc, Role Play, SE p. 901 • S/L/V Mini-Lesson: Role Play, ATE p. 895 • Process Explanation, TR Alt. Assess., p. 59	• Cultural Research, Accounting Curriculum, SE p. 901 • Graph, TR Alt. Assess., p. 59	• Sel. Test, TR Form. Assess., pp. 268–270; Assess. Res. Software • Description Rubric [for Wr. Lesson], TR Alt. Assess., p. 112	• "The First Seven Years," LL Audiocassettes • WS Writing Lab CD-ROM, Description Tutorial
• Inventory, Poem, Analysis of a Symbol, SE p. 911 • Guided Writing Lesson: Guide [Clear/Logical Org.], SE p. 911 • Vivid Description, TR Alt. Assess., p. 60	• Bequest, Conv., SE p. 911 • S/L/V Mini-Lesson: Bequest, ATE p. 907 • Calligraphy Demonstration, TR Alt. Assess., p. 60	• Fashion Report, Music, SE p. 911 • Class "Brown Chest," TR Alt. Assess., p. 60	• Sel. Test, TR Form. Assess., pp. 271–273; Assess. Res. Software • How-to/Process Exp. Rub. [for Wr. Lesson], TR Alt. Assess., p. 115	• "The Brown Chest," LL Audiocassettes • WS Writing Lab CD-ROM, Practical and Tech. Wr. Tutorial • Lit. CD-ROM: *History of Am. Lit.*
• Explanation, Poem, Critical Response, SE p. 923 • Guided Writing: Writer Reviews Another [Suit. Criteria], SE p. 923 • Metaphor Poem, TR Alt. Assess., p. 61	• Oral Presentation, Movie Summary, SE p. 923 • S/L/V Mini-Lesson: Oral Presentation, ATE p. 919 • Multimedia Presentation, TR Alt. Assess., p. 61	• Mural, Dictionary, SE p. 923 • Viewing/Representing: Mural, ATE p. 916 • Portrait, TR Alt. Assess., p. 61	• Selection Test, TR Formal Assessment, pp. 274–276; Assess. Res. Software • Eval./Review Rubric [for Wr. Lesson], TR Alt. Assess., p. 119	• "Hawthorne," "Gold Glade," "The Light . . . ," "The Adamant," "Traveling Through . . . ," LL Audio • WS Wr. Lab CD-ROM, Resp. to Lit. Tut.; Wr. at Wrk. Videodisc, Ch. 7 • Lit. CD-ROM: *History of Am. Lit.*
• New Version, Letter, Critical Response, SE p. 933 • Guided Writing: Social Worker's Report [Transitions], SE p. 933 • Adv. Col., TR Alt. Assess., p. 62	• Conversation, Political Speech, SE p. 933 • S/L/V Mini-Lesson: Political Speech, ATE p. 930	• Fact-Finding Report, Medical Brochure, SE p. 933 • Research: Fact-Finding Report, ATE p. 928 • Biblio., TR Alt. Assess., p. 62	• Sel. Test, TR Form. Assess., pp. 277–279; Assess. Res. Software • Cause/Effect Rubric [for Wr. Lesson], TR Alt. Assess., p. 117	• "Average Waves in Unprotected Waters," LL Audiocassettes • WS Writing Lab CD-ROM, Exposition Tutorial
• Recipe, Description, Analytical Essay, SE p. 945 • Guided Writing: Oral Hist. [Necessary Context], SE p. 945 • Critical Response, TR Alt. Assess., p. 63	• Evocative Music, Movie Review SE p. 945 • Response to Jazz, TR Alt. Assess., p. 63	• Photographs and Memories, Illustration, SE p. 945 • Mural, TR Alt. Assess., p. 63	• Sel. Test, TR Form. Assess., pp. 280–282; Assess. Res. Software • Tech. Desc./Explan. Rub. [for Wr. Lesson], TR Alt. Assess., p. 130	• from *The Names*, "Mint Snowball," "Suspended," LL Audiocassettes • WS Wr. Lab CD-ROM, Exp. Tut.; Wr. at Work Videodisc, Ch. 3

Selection	Reading	Literary Elements/Forms	Vocabulary	Grammar
"Everyday Use," A. Walker, SE p. 948	Reading Level: Average • Contrasting Characters, SE pp. 947, 954; TR Sel. Sup., p. 292 • Analyze Characters, TR Str. for Diverse St. Needs, p. 64	• Character's Motivation, SE pp. 947, 954; TR Selection Support, p. 293	• Latin Roots: *-doc-/-doct-*, SE pp. 947, 954; TR Sel. Sup., p. 290 Word Bank: furtive, lye, oppress, doctrines, p. 951	• Sentence Fragments, SE pp. 947, 954; TR Sel. Sup., p. 291 • WS Lang. Lab CD-ROM, Frag. and Run-On Sentences • WS Gram. Pr. Book, p. 45
from ***The Woman Warrior,* M. H. Kingston,** SE p. 958	Reading Level: Average • Apply Background Info., SE pp. 957, 962; TR Sel. Sup., p. 296 • Identify Paragraph Topics, TR Str. for Diverse St. Needs, p. 65	• Memoirs, SE pp. 957, 962; TR Selection Support, p. 297 • Analyze Literary Criticism, ATE p. 958	• Latin Roots: *-aud-*, SE pp. 957, 962; TR Selection Support, p. 294 Word Bank: hysterically, encampment, p. 959; inaudibly, gravity, oblivious, p. 960	• Punct. a Quote w/in a Quote, SE pp. 957, 962; TR Sel. Sup., p. 295 • WS Lang. Lab CD-ROM, Quotations, Colons, and Semicolons • WS Gram. Pr. Book, p. 91
"Antojos," J. Alvarez, SE p. 966	Reading Level: Easy • Identify w/Character, SE pp. 965, 974; TR Sel. Support, p. 300 • Sequence Events, TR Str. for Diverse St. Needs, p. 66	• Flashback, SE pp. 965, 974; TR Selection Support, p. 301	• Words From Spanish: SE pp. 965, 974; TR Sel. Sup., p. 298 Words: dissuade, loath, p. 969; appease, machetes, collusion, docile, p. 971; enunciated, p. 973	• Absolute Phrases, SE pp. 965, 974; TR Selection Support, p. 299
"Freeway 280," L. D. Cervantes; "Who Burns . . . ," M. Espada; "Hunger in . . . ," S. Ortiz; "Most Satisfied . . . ," D. Chang; "What For," G. Hongo, SE pp. 978, 979, 980. 981, 982	Reading Levels: Chall., Easy, Avg., Avg., Chall. • Summarize, SE pp. 977, 985; TR Selection Support, p. 304 • Reword Poets' Ideas, TR Str. for Diverse St. Needs, p. 67	• Voice, SE pp. 977, 985; TR Selection Support, p. 305	• Greek Prefixes: *auto-*, SE pp. 977, 985; TR Sel. Support, p. 302 Word Bank: crevices, p. 979; automation, p. 980; pervade, p. 981; liturgy, conjure, calligraphy, trough, p. 982	• Participial Phrases, SE pp. 977, 985; TR Selection Support, p. 303 • WS Language Lab CD-ROM, Misplaced Modifiers • WS Gram. Pr. Book, p. 32
from ***The Mortgaged Heart,* C. McCullers; "Onomatopoeia," W. Safire; "Coyote v. Acme," I. Frazier,** SE pp. 994, 996, 998	Reading Levels: Challenging, Easy, Average • ID Line of Reasoning, SE pp. 993, 1002; TR Sel. Sup., p. 308 • Paraphrase, TR Str. for Diverse St. Needs, p. 68	• Essays, SE pp. 993, 1002; TR Selection Support, p. 309	• Latin Roots: *-ten-*, SE pp. 993, 1002; TR Sel. Sup. p. 306 Word Bank: pristine, corollary, aesthetic, maverick, p. 994; contiguous, precipitate, caveat, p. 999; tensile, p. 1001	• Pron. with Appositives, SE pp. 993, 1002; TR Sel. Sup., p. 307
"Straw Into Gold," S. Cisneros; "For the Love of Books," R. Dove; "Mother Tongue," A. Tan, SE pp. 1006, 1010, 1012	Reading Levels: Avg., Easy, Avg. • Eval. a Writer's Mess., SE pp. 1005, 1017; TR Sel. Sup., p. 312 • Summarize Main Idea, TR Str. for Diverse St. Needs, p. 69	• Reflective Essay, SE pp. 1005, 1017; TR Selection Support, p. 313	• Latin Roots: *-scrib-* and *-script-*, SE pp. 1005, 1017; TR Selection Support, p. 310 Word Bank: nomadic, p. 1008; transcribed, empirical, p. 1013; benign, semantic, p. 1015; quandary, nascent, p. 1016	• Varying Sent. Structure, SE pp. 1005, 1017; TR Sel. Sup., p. 311 • WS Language Lab CD-ROM, Varying Sentence Structure • WS Gram. Pr. Book, pp. 110–111
"The Rockpile," J. Baldwin, SE p. 1026	Reading Level: Average • Analyze Cause/Effect, SE pp. 1025, 1032; TR Sel. Sup., p. 316 • Rephrase Characters' Speech, TR Str. for Div. St. Needs, p. 70	• Setting, SE pp. 1025, 1032; TR Selection Support, p. 317	• Latin Prefixes: *mal-*, SE pp. 1025, 1032; TR Sel. Sup., p. 314 Word Bank: intriguing, benevolent, decorously, latent, p. 1027; engrossed, jubilant, arrested, p. 1028; malevolence, perdition, p. 1031	• Restrictive and Nonrestrictive Adj. Clauses, SE pp. 1025, 1032; TR Sel. Sup., p. 315 • WS Gram. Pr. Book, p. 87
from ***Hiroshima,* J. Hersey; "Losses," "The Death of the Ball Turret Gunner," R. Jarrell,** SE pp. 1036, 1044, 1045	Reading Levels: Challenging, Easy, Easy • Draw Inf. About Theme, SE pp. 1035, 1046; TR Sel. Sup., p. 320 • Question Author's Purpose, TR Str. for Diverse St. Needs, p. 71	• Implied Theme, SE pp. 1035, 1046; TR Sel. Support, p. 321 • Analyze a Literary Criticism, ATE p. 1038	• Latin Roots: *-vol-*, SE pp. 1035, 1046; TR Sel. Sup. p. 318 Word Bank: evacuated, volition, rendezvous, p. 1037; philanthropies, p. 1039; incessant, convivial, p. 1042	• Trans., Trans. Phrases, SE pp. 1035, 1046; TR Sel. Sup., p. 319 • WS Language Lab CD-ROM, Transition and Words, Unity and Coherence in Paragraphs • WS Gram. Pr. Book, p. 114
"Mirror," S. Plath; "In a Classroom," A. Rich; "The Explorer," G. Brooks; "Frederick Douglass," "Runagate Runagate," R. Hayden, SE pp. 1050, 1051, 1052, 1053, 1054	Reading Levels: Avg., Challenging, Challenging, Easy, Easy • Interpret, SE pp. 1049, 1056; TR Selection Support, p. 324 • Interpret and Explain Poetry, TR Str. for Diverse St. Needs, p. 72	• Theme and Context, SE pp. 1049, 1056; TR Sel. Sup., p. 325	• Latin Word Roots: *-cep-* and *-cept-*, SE pp. 1049, 1056; TR Selection Support, p. 322 Word Bank: preconceptions, meditate, p. 1050, din, wily, p. 1052	• Par. Struct., SE pp. 1049, 1056; TR Selection Support, p. 323 • WS Language Lab CD-ROM, Strengthening Sentences • WS Gram. Pr. Book, pp. 49–50

Prosperity and Protest (1946–Present)

Writing	Speaking, Listening, and Viewing	Researching and Representing	Assessment	Technology
• Journal Entry, Speech, Character Analysis, SE p. 955 • Guided Writing: Review of a Short Story [Accuracy], SE p. 955 • Essay, TR Alt. Assess., p. 64	• TV Talk Show, Debate, SE p. 955 • S/L/V Mini-Lesson: Debate, ATE p. 952 • Dialogue, TR Alt. Assess., p. 64	• Heritage Exhibit, African Languages Project, SE p. 955 • Research: Non-Print Resources, ATE p. 951 • Quilt Rep., TR Alt. Assess., p. 64	• Sel. Test, TR Form. Assess., pp. 283–285; Assess. Res. Software • Crit. Review Rub. [for Wr. Lesson], TR Alt. Assess.,p. 126	• "Everyday Use," LL Audio • WS Wr. Lab CD-ROM, Res. to Lit. Tut.; Wr. at Wrk Videodisc, Ch. 7 • Lit. CD-ROM: *History of Am. Lit.*
• Diary Entry, Prequel, Character Analysis, SE p. 963 • Writing: Guide/Planning a Family Reunion [Exp. a Proc.], SE p. 963 • Autobiographical Sketch, TR Alt. Assess., p. 65	• Talk Story, Panel Disc., SE p. 963 • S/L/V Mini-Lesson: Talk Story, ATE p. 960 • Role-Play, TR Alt. Assess., p. 65	• Written Report, Historical Travelogue, SE p. 963 • Ellis Island Report, TR Alt. Assess., p. 65	• Sel. Test, TR Form. Assess., pp. 286–288; Assess. Res. Software • How-to/Proc. Explan. Rub. [for Wr. Lesson], TR Alt. Assess., p. 115	• from *The Woman Warrior,* LL Audiocassettes • WS Writing Lab CD-ROM, Practical and Tech. Writing Tutorial • Lit. CD-ROM: *History of Am. Lit.*
• Postcard, New Version, Personal Essay, SE p. 975 • Guided Writing Lesson: Travel Safety [Transitions,] SE p. 975 • Adventure Story, TR Alt. Assess., p. 66	• Multimedia Report, Dialogue, SE p. 975 • S/L/V Mini-Lesson: Newscast, ATE p. 972 • Scene, TR Alt. Assess., p. 66	• Flowchart, Set Design, SE p. 975 • V/R Mini-Lesson: Set Design, ATE p. 972 • Ad Study, TR Alt. Assess., p. 66	• Sel. Test, TR Form. Assess., pp. 289–291; Assess. Res. Software • How-to/Proc. Explan. Rub. [for Wr. Lesson], TR Alt. Assess., p. 115	• "Antojos," LL Audiocassettes • WS Writing Lab CD-ROM, Exposition Tutorial
• Letter, Editorial, Compare-and-Contrast Essay, SE p. 986 • Guided Writing: Observ. of a Storm [Fig. Lang.], SE p. 986 • Point-of-View Poem, TR Alt. Assess., p. 67	• Interview, Oral Interpretation, SE p. 986 • S/L/V Mini-Lesson: Interview, ATE p. 983 • Present., TR Alt. Assess., p. 67	• Cultural Report, Anthology, SE p. 986 • Res.: Eval. Resources, ATE p. 982 • Grp Poem, TR Alt. Assess., p. 67	• Sel. Test, TR Form. Assess., pp. 292–294; Assess. Res. Software • Tech. Desc./Explan. Rub. [for Wr. Lesson], TR Alt. Assess., p. 130	• "Freeway 280," "Who Burns . . .," "Hunger in . . . ," "Most Satisfied . . . ," "What For," LL Audio • Looking at Lit., Ch. 11 • WS Wr. Lab CD-ROM, Desc. Tut.; Wr. at Work Videodisc, Ch. 1
• Letter, News Article, Analytical Essay, SE p. 1003 • Writing: Résumé for Wile E. Coyote [Format], SE p. 1003 • Product Description, TR Alt. Assess., p. 68	• Opening Statement for the Defense, Inv. Words, SE p. 1003 • S/L/V Mini-Lesson: Opening State. for the Def., ATE p. 998 • Song, TR Alt. Assess., p. 68	• Essay Collection, Cartoon Strip, SE p. 1003 • Catalog Illustration, TR Alt. Assess., p. 68	• Sel. Test, TR Form. Assess., pp. 299–301; Assess. Res. Software • Résumé/Cover Letter Rub. [for Wr. Lesson], TR Alt. Assess., p. 129	• from *The Mortgaged Heart,* "Onomatopoeia," "Coyote v. Acme," LL Audiocassettes • WS Writing Lab CD-ROM, Practical and Tech. Wr. Tutorial
• Letter, Science-Fiction Story, Television Pilot, SE p. 1018 • Guided Writing Lesson: Memory [Main Impression], SE p. 1018 • How-To Instructions, TR Alt. Assess., p. 69	• Speech, Monologue, SE p. 1018 • S/L/V Mini-Lesson: Speech, ATE p. 1013	• Icons, Readers' Club, SE p. 1018 • Classify Books, TR Alt. Assess., p. 69	• Sel. Test, TR Form. Assess., pp. 302–304; Assess. Res. Software • Description Rubric [for Wr. Lesson], TR Alt. Assess., p. 112	• "Straw Into Gold," "For the Love of Books," "Mother Tongue," LL Audiocassettes • WS Wr. Lab CD-ROM, Desc. Tut.; Wr. at Work Videodisc, Ch. 1
• Flyer, Movie Proposal, Psychological Profile, SE p. 1033 • Guided Writing: Roy's Journal [Personal Tone], SE p. 1033 • Community Profile, TR Alt. Assess., p. 70	• Radio Play, Public-Service Announcement, SE p. 1033 • S/L/V Mini-Lesson: Public Serv. Announcement, ATE p. 1028 • Role-Play, TR Alt. Assess., p. 70	• Book Jacket, Illustrated Report, SE p. 1033 • Model, TR Alt. Assess., p. 70	• Sel. Test, TR Form. Assess., pp. 308–310; Assess. Res. Software • Resp. to Literature Rubric [for Wr. Lesson], TR Alt. Assess., p. 125	• "The Rockpile," LL Audiocassettes • WS Writing Lab CD-ROM, Response to Literature Tutorial
• Journ., Poem, Essay, SE p. 1047 • Guided Writing: Intro. to a Documentary [Knowledge Level of Readers], SE p. 1047 • Wr. Treaty, TR Alt. Assess., p. 71	• Debate, Dramatic Reading, SE p. 1047 • S/L/V Mini-Lesson: Dramatic Reading, ATE p. 1044 • Oral Reading, TR Alt. Assess., p. 71	• Map, Res. Rep., SE p. 1047 • V/R Lesson: Map, ATE p. 1039 • Illus., TR Alt. Assess., p. 71	• Sel. Test, TR Form. Assess., pp. 311–313; Assess. Res. Software • Summary Rubric [for Wr. Lesson], TR Alt. Assess., p. 113	• from *Hiroshima,* "Losses," "The Death of the Ball Turret Gunner," LL Audiocassettes • Looking at Lit., Ch. 2 • WS Wr. Lab CD-ROM, Res. Wr. Tut.; Wr. at Work Videodisc, Ch. 5
• Letter, Poem or Paragraph, Comparison and Contrast Essay, SE p. 1057 • Guided Writing: Lit. Analysis [Specific Examples], SE p. 1057 • Editorial, TR Alt. Assess., p. 72	• Oral Interpretation, Debate, SE p. 1057 • Panel Discussion, TR Alt. Assess., p. 72	• Multimedia Presentation, Collage, SE p. 1057 • Protest Poster, TR Alt. Assess., p. 72	• Sel. Test, TR Form. Assess., pp. 314–316; Assess. Res. Software • Lit. Analysis/Interp. Rub. [for Wr. Lesson], TR Alt. Assess., p. 127	• "Mirror," "In a Classroom," "The Explorer," "Frederick Douglass," "Runagate Runagate," LL Audio • WS Wr. Lab CD-ROM, Resp. to Lit. Tut.; Wr. at Wrk Videodisc, Ch. 7 • Lit. CD-ROM: *History of Am. Lit.*

Selection	Reading	Literary Elements/Forms	Vocabulary	Grammar
"For My Children," C. McElroy; "Bidwell Ghost," L. Erdrich, SE pp. 1060, 1062	Reading Levels: Average, Average • Read in Sent., SE pp. 1059, 1064; TR Sel. Support, p. 328 • Identify Sensory Words, TR Str. for Diverse St. Needs, p. 73	• Lyric Poetry, SE pp. 1059, 1064; TR Selection Support, p. 329	• Related Words: *Heritage*, SE pp. 1059, 1064; TR Sel. Sup., p. 326 Word Bank: shackles, heritage, effigies, p. 1061	• Sequence of Tenses, SE pp. 1059, 1064; TR Sel. Sup., p. 327 • WS Lang. Lab CD-ROM, Correct and Effective Use of Verbs • WS Gram. Pr. Book, p. 58
"The Writer in the Family," E. L. Doctorow, SE p. 1068	Reading Level: Average • Judge Char. Actions, SE pp. 1067, 1076; TR Sel. Sup., p. 332 • Resp. to Char. Actions, TR Str. for Diverse St. Needs, p. 74	• Static and Dynamic Characters, SE pp. 1067, 1076; TR Selection Support, p. 333	• Greek Suffixes: *-itis*, SE pp. 1067, 1076; TR Sel. Sup., p. 330 Word Bank: bronchitis, cronies, barometer, p. 1069; anthology, p. 1071	• Commonly Confused Words: *Affect* and *Effect*, SE pp. 1067, 1076; TR Sel. Sup., p. 331 • WS Gram. Pr. Book, p. 80
"Camouflaging the . . . ," Y. Komunyakaa; "Ambush" from ***The Things They Carried,*** **T. O'Brien,** SE pp. 1080, 1082	Reading Levels: Chall., Avg. • Envision the Action, SE pp. 1079, 1084; TR Sel. Sup., p. 336 • Form a Mental Picture, TR Str. for Diverse St. Needs, p. 75	• First-Person Nar., SE pp. 1079, 1084; TR Sel. Sup., p. 337	• Words From War: SE pp. 1079, 1084; TR Select. Support, p. 334 Word Bank: refuge, p. 1081; ambush, ammunition, muzzle, gape, p. 1083	• Noun Clauses, SE pp. 1079, 1084; TR Sel. Support, p. 335 • WS Gram. Pr. Book, p. 37
Crucible, **Act I, A. Miller,** SE p. 1089	Reading Level: Challenging • Question the Characters' Motives, SE pp. 1088, 1112; TR Selection Support, p. 340 • Make a Character Chart, TR Str. for Diverse St. Needs, p. 76	• Drama: Dialogue and Stage Directions, SE pp.1088, 1112; TR Selection Support, p. 341	• Latin Word Roots: *-grat-*, SE pp. 1088, 1112; TR Select. Support, p. 338 Word Bank: predilection, ingratiating, p.1091; dissembling, p. 1093; calumny, p. 1098; inculcation, propitiation, p. 1105; licentious, p. 1107	• Pronoun Case in Incomplete Constructions, SE pp. 1088, 1112; TR Select. Support, p. 339 • WS Language Lab CD-ROM, Pronoun Case • WS Gram. Pr. Book, p. 65
Crucible, **Act II, A. Miller,** SE p. 1114	Reading Level: Challenging • Read Drama, SE pp. 1113, 1130; TR Selection Support, p. 344 • Paraphrase Dialogue, TR Str. for Diverse St. Needs, p. 77	• Allusion, SE pp. 1113, 1130; TR Selection Support, p. 345	• Greek Suffixes: *-logy*, SE pp. 1113, 1130; TR Select. Support, p. 342 Word Bank: pallor, ameliorate, p. 1117; avidly, p. 1119; base, deference, theology, p. 1121; quail, p. 1125; gingerly, p. 1126; abomination, blasphemy. p. 1128	• Commas After Introductory Words, SE pp. 1113, 1130; TR Selection Support, p. 343 • WS Language Lab CD-ROM, Commas • WS Gram. Pr. Book, p. 87
Crucible, **Act III, A. Miller,** SE p. 1132	Reading Level: Challenging • Categorize Characters by Role, SE pp. 1131, 1152; TR Selection Support, p. 348 • Use a Story Map Organizer, TR Str. for Diverse St. Needs, p. 78	• Dramatic and Verbal Irony, SE pp. 1131, 1152; TR Selection Support, p. 349	• Legal Terms: SE pp. 1131, 1152; TR Selection Support, p. 346 Word Bank; contentious, p. 1133; deposition, p. 1135; imperceptible, deferentially, p. 1137; anonymity, prodigious, effrontery, p. 1139; confounded, p. 1141; incredulously, p. 1143; blanched, p. 1146	• Subject and Verb Agreement, SE pp. 1131, 1152; TR Selection Support, p. 347 • WS Language Lab CD-ROM, Special Problems in Agreement • WS Gram. Pr. Book, p. 26
Crucible, **Act IV, A. Miller,** SE p. 1154	Reading Level: Challenging • Apply Themes to Contemporary Events, SE p. 1153, 1168; TR Selection Support. pp. 352 • Prepare a Reader's Theater, TR Str. for Diverse St. Needs, p. 79	• Theme, SE pp. 1153, 1168; TR Selection Support, p. 353	• Words From Myths: Tantalize, SE pp. 1153, 1168; TR Selection Support, p. 350 Word Bank; agape, p. 1156; conciliatory, beguile, floundering, retaliation, adamant, cleave, p. 1159; sibilance, p. 1161; tantalized, p. 1163; purged, p. 1165	• Commonly Confused Words: Raise and Rise, SE pp. 1153, 1168; TR Selection Support, p.351 • WS Gram. Pr. Book, p.80

Prosperity and Protest (1946–Present)

Writing	Speaking, Listening, and Viewing	Researching and Representing	Assessment	Technology
• Letter, Song Lyrics, Comp/ Contrast Essay, SE p. 1065 • Guided Writing: Ghost Story [Sensory Details], SE p. 1065 • Childhood Story, TR Alt. Assess., p. 73	• Legend, Oral Report, SE p. 1065	• Drawing/Painting, Illustrated Report, SE p. 1065 • Fam. Map, TR Alt. Assess., p. 73	• Sel. Test, TR Form. Assess., pp. 317–319; Assess. Res. Software • Fict. Narrative Rubric [for Wr. Lesson], TR Alt. Assess., p. 110	• "For My Children," "Bidwell Ghost," LL Audiocassettes • WS Wr. Lab CD-ROM, Nar. Tut.; Wr. at Work Videodisc, Ch. 2
• Final Letter, Eulogy, Critical Essay, SE p. 1077 • Guided Writing Lesson: Advice Column [Elaboration], SE p. 1077 • Comparison-Contrast Essay, TR Alt. Assess., p. 74	• Family Conference, Debate, SE p. 1077 • S/L/V Mini-Lesson: Family Conference, ATE p. 1070 • Interview, TR Alt. Assess., p. 74	• Costume Proposal, Grief Hotline, SE p. 1077 • Report, TR Alt. Assess., p. 74	• Sel. Test, TR Form. Assess., pp. 320–322; Assess. Res. Software • Problem–Solution Rub. [for Wr. Lesson], TR Alt. Assess., p. 116	• "The Writer in the Family," LL Audiocassettes • WS Wr. Lab CD-ROM, Pers. Tut.; Wr. at Work Videodisc, Ch. 4
• Letter, Newspaper Article, Lit. Analysis, SE p. 1085 • Guided Writing: Personal Account [Suspense], SE p. 1085 • Autobiographical Essay, TR Alt. Assess., p. 75	• Interview, Choral Reading, SE p. 1085 • S/L/V Mini-Lesson: Interview, ATE p. 1082 • Debate, TR Alt. Assess., p. 75	• Dance, Multimedia Presentation, SE p. 1085 • Map, TR Alt. Assess., p. 75	• Sel. Test, TR Form. Assess., pp. 323–325; Assess. Res. Software • Nar./Pers. Exp. Rubric [for Wr. Lesson], TR Alt. Assess., p. 111	• "Camouflaging the . . . ," "Ambush," from *The Things They Carried,* LL Audiocassettes • WS Writing Lab CD-ROM, Nar. Tut.; Wr. at Work Videodisc, Ch. 2 • Lit. CD-ROM: *How to Read and Understand Drama*
• Medical Chart, News Account, SE p. 1112 • Book Jacket, TR Alt. Assess., p.76	• Oral Presentation, Dramatization, SE p. 1112 • Mini-Lesson: Dramatization, ATE p. 1098 • Persuasive Speech, TR Alt. Assess., p. 76	• Sketch, TR Alt. Assess., p. 76	• Selection Test, TR Formal Assessment, pp. 326–328; Assess. Res. Software	• Lit. CD-ROM: *How to Read and Understand Drama*
• Wanted Poster, Additional Scene, SE p. 1130 • Musicology Report, TR Alt. Assess., p. 77	• Scene, TR Alt. Assess., p. 77	• Pantomime, SE p. 1130 • Travel Brochure, TR Alt. Assess., p. 76	• Selection Test, TR Formal Assessment, pp. 329–331; Assess. Res. Software	
• Character Sketch, Letter to the Editor, SE p. 1152 • Deposition, TR Alt. Assess., p. 78	• Soliloquy, SE p. 1152 • Mini-Lesson: Soliloquy ATE p. 1134 • Courtroom Speech, TR Alt. Assess., p. 78	• Casting Call, TR Alt. Assess., p. 76	• Selection Test, TR Formal Assessment, pp. 332–334;	
• Casting Profiles, Analysis, Critical Response, SE p. 1169 • Mini-Lesson: Defend [Pro-and-Con Argument], SE p. 1169 • Indictment, TR Alt. Assess., p. 79	• Mock Trail, Group Discussion, SE p. 1169 • Mini-Lesson: Mock Trail, ATE p. 1163 • Sound TRack, TR Alt. Assess., p. 79	• Comparison and Contrast Chart, Memorial, SE p. 1169 • Memoir, TR Alt. Assess., p. 79	• Selection Test, TR Formal Assessment, pp. 335–337; Assess. Res. Software • Persuasion Rubric [for Mini-Lesson], TR Alt. Assess., p.120	• WS Writing Lab CD-ROM, Persuasion Tutorial; Wr. at Work Videodisc, Ch. 4

Skills Workshops

Unit	Writing Process Workshops	Applying Language Skills	Student Success Workshops	Speaking, Listening, and Viewing Workshops	Test Preparation Workshops
Beginnings–1750	Cause-and-Effect Essay, p. 59 Annotated Bibliography, p. 83 Persuasive Essay, p. 110	Correct Run-on Sentences; Avoid Stringy Sentences, pp. 60, 61 Citing Sources; Avoiding Vague Statements, pp. 84, 85 Comparative and Superlative Forms; Complex Sentences, pp. 111, 112	Reading a Map, p. 62 Establish a Purpose for Reading, p. 86 Using Vocabulary References, p. 113	Interpreting Literature Orally, p. 114	Summarizing Written Texts, p. 115
A Nation Is Born (1750–1800)	Editorial, p. 161 Informative Speech, p. 181 Multimedia Presentation, p. 208	Prepositional Phrases; Varying Sentence Beginnings, pp. 162, 163 Misplaced or Dangling Modifiers; Using Transitions, pp. 182, 183 Vague or Ambiguous Pronoun Reference; Adverb or Adjective?, pp. 209, 210	Evaluating Sources of Information, p. 164 Understanding Connotation and Denotation, p. 184 Evaluate a Writer's Motivation, p. 211	Delivering a Persuasive Speech, p. 212	Recognize Cause and Effect; Predict Outcomes, p. 213
A Growing Nation (1800–1870)	Travel Brochure, p. 289 Video Script, p. 357 Reflective Essay, p. 389 Critical Evaluation, p. 422	Appositives; Figurative Language, pp. 290, 291 Eliminating Unnecessary Words; Spoken vs. Written Language, pp. 358, 359 Precise Nouns; Pronoun Case, pp. 390, 391 Quotations and Quotation Marks; Indirect and Direct Quotations, pp. 423, 424	Recognizing Modes of Persuasion, p. 292 Monitoring Reading Strategies, p. 360 Understanding Analogies, p. 392 Analyzing Reviews, p. 425	Handling a College or Job Interview, p. 426	Analyze Information to Make Inferences and Generalizations, p. 427
Division, Reconciliation, and Expansion (1850–1914)	Problem-and-Solution Essay, p. 489 Historical Narrative, p. 513 Comparison-and-Contrast Essay, p. 585 Character Profile, p. 626	Active and Passive Voice; Avoiding Logical Fallacies, pp. 490, 491 Avoiding Shifts in Tense; Punctuating Dialogue, pp. 514, 515 Avoiding Faulty Logic; Inverted Sentences, pp. 586, 587 Using Quotations; Combining Sentences, pp. 627, 628	Graphic Devices for Reading Comprehension, p. 492 Locating Information on the Internet, p. 516 Using Print Resources, p. 588 Reading an Application Form, p. 629	Verbal and Nonverbal Performance Techniques, p. 630	Using Context, p. 631
Disillusion, Defiance, and Discontent (1914–1946)	Essay for Test, p. 723 Literary Analysis, p. 753 Statistical Report, p. 858	Sentence Fragments; Language Variety, pp. 724, 725 Parallel Structure; Infinitives and Infinitive Phrases, pp. 754, 755 Semicolons; Accuracy of Charts and Graphs, pp. 859, 860	Using Study Strategies, p. 726 Read Silently for Extended Periods, p. 756 Analyzing Text Structures, p. 861	Viewing Media Critically, p. 862	Sentence Completion Questions, p. 863
Prosperity and Protest (1946–Present)	Research Paper, p. 987 Job Portfolio, p. 1019 Position Paper, p. 1138	Topic and Supporting Sentences; Proper Bibliographic Form, pp. 988, 989 Capitalization; Action Verbs, pp. 1020, 1021 Connotation and Denotation; Varying Sentence Length, pp. , 1139, 1140	Tailoring Research Papers to Specific Audiences, p. 990 Using Text Organizers as a Research Tool, p. 1022 Drawing Conclusions From Researched Information, p. 1141	Interpreting Literature for Varied Audiences, p. 1142	Punctuation, Usage, and Sentence Structure, p. 1143

Prentice Hall

LITERATURE

Timeless Voices, Timeless Themes

THE AMERICAN EXPERIENCE

PRENTICE HALL
Upper Saddle River, New Jersey
Needham, Massachusetts
Glenview, Illinois

Copyright © 2000 by Prentice-Hall, Inc., Upper Saddle River, New Jersey 07458. All rights reserved. No part of this book may be reproduced or transmitted in any form or by any means, electronic or mechanical, including photocopying, recording, or by any information storage and retrieval system, without permission in writing from the publisher. Printed in the United States of America.

ISBN 0-13-050289-8
4 5 6 7 8 9 10   03 02 01 00

PRENTICE HALL

ACKNOWLEDGMENTS

Grateful acknowledgment is made to the following for permission to reprint copyrighted material:

Addison-Wesley Longman Inc. "Gardening" from *Mama Makes Up Her Mind* by Bailey White. Copyright © 1993 by Bailey White. Reprinted by permission of Addison-Wesley Longman Inc.
American Demographics Inc. "Most Immigrants Find the Dream" by Brad Edmondson from *Forecast,* May 1997. © 1997 Cowles Business Media. Reprinted with permission of American Demographics Inc.
Amistad Research Center, administered by Thompson and Thompson "From the Dark Tower" by Countee Cullen, published in *Copper Sun,* Harper & Bros., © 1927, renewed 1954 by Ida Cullen. Copyrights held by the Amistad Research Center, administered by Thompson and Thompson, New York, NY. Reprinted by permission.
Arte Público Press "To Walt Whitman" by Angela de Hoyos from *In Other Words: Literature by Latinas of the United States* (Houston: Arte Público Press, University of Houston, 1994). "The Salamanders" / "Las Salamandras" by Tomás Rivera from *Tomás Rivera: The Complete Works,* edited by Julián Olivares (Houston: Arte Público Press, University of Houston, 1992). Reprinted with permission from the publisher, Arte Público Press.
James Baldwin Estate "The Rockpile" is collected in *Going to Meet the Man* by James Baldwin, ©1965 by James Baldwin, copyright renewed. Published by Vintage Books. Reprinted by arrangement with the James Baldwin Estate.
Peter Basch, Literary Agent "When Grizzlies Walked Upright" (Modoc) from *American Indian Myths and Legends,* selected and edited by Richard Erdoes and Alfonso Ortiz, published by Pantheon Books. Copyright © 1984 by Richard Erdoes and Alfonso Ortiz.
Susan Bergholz Literary Services "Antojos" by Julia Alvarez, copyright © 1991 by Julia Alvarez. Later published in a slightly different form in *How the Garcia Girls Lost Their Accents,* copyright © 1991 by Julia Alvarez. Published by Plume, an imprint of Dutton Signet, a division of Penguin USA, Inc., and originally in hardcover by Algonquin Books of Chapel Hill. "Straw Into Gold," copyright © 1987 by Sandra Cisneros. First published in *The Texas Observer,* September 1987. Reprinted by permission of Susan Bergholz Literary Services, New York. All rights reserved.

(Acknowledgments continue on page 1292.)

Prentice Hall

LITERATURE

Timeless Voices, Timeless Themes

Copper

Bronze

Silver

Gold

Platinum

The American Experience

The British Tradition

World Masterpieces

Program Authors

The program authors guided the direction and philosophy of *Prentice Hall Literature, Timeless Voices, Timeless Themes.* Working with the development team, they contributed to the pedagogical integrity of the program and to its relevance for today's teachers and students.

Reading Specialist
Linda Ellis teaches reading and language arts methods courses at Stephen F. Austin State University and for five years has sponsored the school's Student Reading Council.

Reading Specialist
Jacqueline Parten Gerla teaches reading education classes at The University of Texas at Tyler and has received numerous teaching awards.

Writing Specialist
Joyce Armstrong Carroll has taught every grade level in her forty years in the profession. She is co-director of the New Jersey Writing Project, serving as a consultant in all aspects of the language arts.

Writing Specialist
Edward E. Wilson, a former editor of English, is co-director of the New Jersey Writing Project, working as a writing/reading/literature consultant for school districts nationwide.

Language Specialist
Richard Lederer, who taught for twenty-seven years, is the author of such best-selling titles as *Anguished English* and *Pun & Games.* He writes a syndicated column, "Looking at Language," and hosts a weekly radio show, *A Way With Words.*

Assessment Specialist
Argelia Arizpe Guadarrama, secondary curriculum coordinator in the Pharr-San Juan-Alamo Independent School District, is also the program developer for English as a Second Language and at-risk students.

Assessment Specialist
Peggy Leeman, in addition to teaching full time and handling administrative duties, is an adjunct English professor at Dallas County Community College and a consultant to the College Board for Advanced Placement English.

Speaking, Listening, Viewing, & Representing Specialist
Jocelyn Chadwick-Joshua, Director of American Studies at the Dallas Institute of Humanities and Culture, is a teacher, lecturer, author, and consultant to school districts.

Program Advisors

The program advisors provided ongoing input throughout the development of *Prentice Hall Literature: Timeless Voices, Timeless Themes*. Their valuable insights ensure that the perspectives of the teachers throughout the country are represented within this literature series.

Diane Cappillo
Language Arts Department Chair
Barbara Goleman Senior High School
Miami, Florida

Anita Clay
English Instructor
Gateway Institute of Technology
St. Louis, Missouri

Nancy M. Fahner
Language Arts Instructor
Charlotte High School
Charlotte, Michigan

Terri Fields
Language Arts and Communication Arts Teacher, Author
Sunnyslope High School
Phoenix, Arizona

V. Pauline Hodges
Teacher and Educational Consultant
Forgan High School
Forgan, Oklahoma

Jennifer Huntress
Secondary Language Arts Coordinator
Putnam City Schools
Oklahoma City, Oklahoma

Angelique McMath Jordan
English Teacher
Dunwoody High School
Dunwoody, Georgia

Nancy L. Monroe
English and Speed Reading Teacher
Bolton High School
Alexandria, Louisiana

Rosemary A. Naab
English Chairperson
Ryan High School
Archdiocese of Philadelphia
Philadelphia, Pennsylvania

Ann Okamura
English Teacher
Laguna Creek High School
Elk Grove, California

Jonathan L. Schatz
English Teacher/Team Leader
Tappan Zee High School
Orangeburg, New York

John Scott
English Teacher
Hampton High School
Hampton, Virginia

Ken Spurlock
Assistant Principal
Boone County High School
Florence, Kentucky

Multicultural Review Board

Clara M. Chu
Assistant Professor, Department of Library and Information Science
UCLA
Los Angeles, California

Nora A. Little Light Bird
Bilingual Project Director
Lodge Grass Public Schools
Lodge Grass, Montana

K. Tsianina Lomawaima
Associate Professor, American Indian Studies
University of Arizona
Tucson, Arizona

Larry L. Martin
Chair of History, Geography, and International Studies
Coppin State College
Baltimore, Maryland

Sunita Sunder Mukhi
Program Associate, Cultural Programs Division, Asia Society
New York, New York

Julio Noboa Polanco
Professor, Department of Teaching
The University of Northern Iowa, San Antonio Center
San Antonio, Texas

Alfredo Samone
Educational Consultant
Region 4, Education Service Center
Houston, Texas

A. J. Williams-Meyers
Professor, Black Studies Department
SUNY-College at New Paltz
New Paltz, New York

Contributing Writers

Amy Duer
Former English Teacher, Expert on Special Needs
Palm Beach Lakes High School
Palm Beach, Florida

Emily Hutchinson
Former English Teacher
Los Angeles Unified School District
Los Angeles, California

Eileen Oshinsky
Former ESL Teacher
New York City Public Schools
Brooklyn, New York

Stacey Sparks
Former Librarian
Cuyahoga County Public Library System
Cuyahoga County, Ohio

David Pence, Jr.
Former English Teacher
Morse High School
Bath, Maine

Diane Tasca
Former Literature and Writing Instructor
University of Illinois
Urbana, Illinois

Unit 1

Beginnings–1750

Unit 1

Part 2 Focus on Literary Forms: Narrative Accounts

Part 3 The Emerging American Identity: The Puritan Influence

Unit 2

A Nation Is Born (1750–1800)

Unit 2

Part 3 The Emerging American Identity: Defining an American

Unit 3

A Growing Nation (1800–1870)

Part 2 Shadows of the Imagination

Part 3 The Emerging American Identity: The Human Spirit and the Natural World

PART 4 FOCUS ON LITERARY FORMS: POETRY

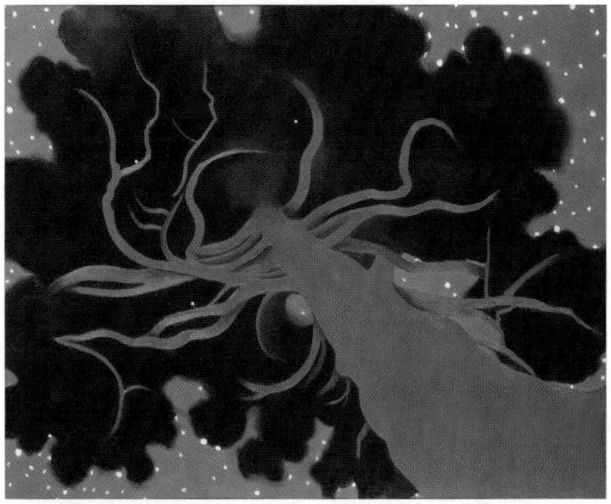

Unit

4 *Division, Reconciliation, and Expansion (1850–1914)*

PART 2 FOCUS ON LITERARY FORMS: DIARIES, JOURNALS, AND LETTERS

PART 3 FORGING NEW FRONTIERS

Unit 4

Part 4 Living in a Changing World

Unit 5

Disillusion, Defiance, and Discontent (1914–1946)

Unit 5

Part 2 Focus on Literary Forms: The Short Story

Part 3 From Every Corner of the Land

The Harlem Renaissance

Unit 6 Prosperity and Protest (1946–Present)

PART I LITERATURE CONFRONTS THE EVERYDAY

Part 2 Focus on Literary Forms: Essay

Part 3 The Emerging American Identity: Social Protest

Unit 7

Connections to World Literature

Additional Readings and Resources

Analyzing Real-World Texts

Literature in Translation: Paired Readings in English and Spanish

Planning Instruction and Assessment

Unit Objectives

1. To read selections from the beginnings of the American literary tradition through 1750
2. To apply literal comprehension strategies, appropriate for reading these selections
3. To analyze literary elements
4. To use a variety of strategies to read unfamiliar words and to build vocabulary
5. To learn elements of grammar, usage, and style
6. To use recursive writing processes to write in a variety of forms
7. To express and support responses to various types of texts
8. To prepare, organize, and present literary interpretations

Meeting the Objectives

With each selection, you will find instructional material and portfolio opportunities through which students can meet these objectives. You will find additional practice pages for reading strategies, literary elements, vocabulary, and grammar in the ***Selection Support*** booklet in the ***Teaching Resources*** box.

Test Preparation

The end of unit workshop, **Reading Comprehension: Summarizing Written Texts** (SE, p. 115), is supported by teaching tips and a sample test item in the ATE workshop with each selection grouping.

- **Summarizing Written Texts** (ATE, pp. 13, 21, 43, 89)
- **Stated Main Idea** (ATE, p. 33)
- **Supporting Details** (ATE, p. 65)
- **Paraphrasing** (ATE, p. 97)

The following additional workshops in the ATE give teaching tips and a sample test item for applying the skill taught in the Student Success Workshops:

- **Reading a Map** (ATE, p. 62)
- **Establish a Purpose for Reading** (ATE, p. 86)
- **Using Vocabulary References** (ATE, p. 113)

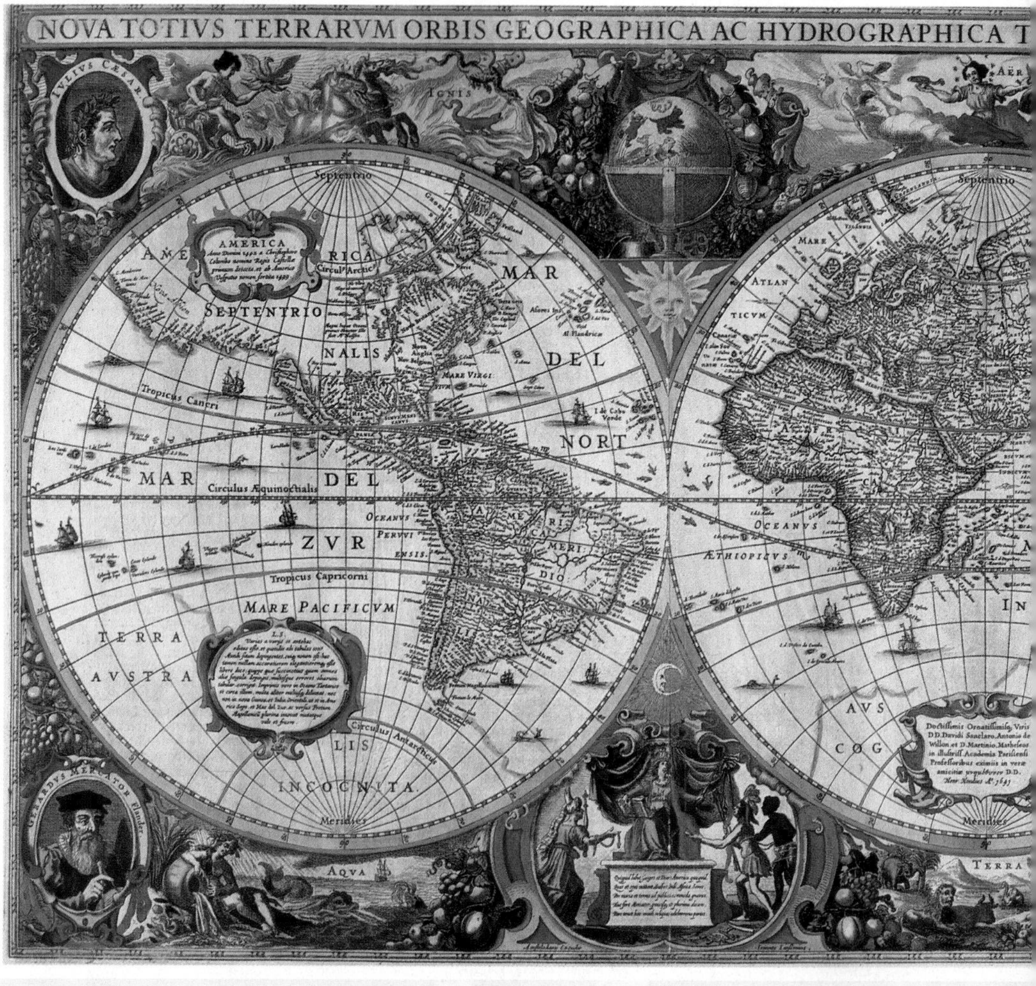

World Map, 1630, The Huntington Library, Art Collections and Botanical Gardens, San Marino, CA

Humanities: Art

World Map, 1630.

This map of the world from 1630 contains much detail. The Latin legend on the top reads New Geographic and Hydrographic Map of All the Lands of the Globe. Details on the map show scenes depicting the four basic elements. Fire is at the upper left, water at the lower left, air at the upper right, and earth at the lower right. The map also features portraits at the four corners, including those of Julius Caesar at the upper left and the mapmaker Mercatur at the lower left.

Have students link the map to Unit 1 by answering these questions:

1. How much of the New World had been explored by 1630? *The outlines of South and Central America are roughly accurate, as are the eastern coasts of Canada and the United States, suggesting that these coastlines had been explored.*
2. Which of the 13 colonies had been founded? *Virginia, Massachusetts, and New York had been founded.*

UNIT 1

Beginnings – 1750

"We shall be as a City upon a Hill, the eyes of all people are upon us; so that if we shall deal falsely with our God in this work we have undertaken and so cause him to withdraw his present help from us, we shall be made a story and a by-word through the world."

—John Winthrop,
Governor of the Massachusetts
Bay Colony

Assessing Student Progress

The following tools are available to measure the degree to which students meet the unit objectives:

Informal Assessment

The questions on the Guide for Responding sections are a first level of response to the concepts and skills presented with the selection. Students' responses are a brief informal measure of their grasp of the material. Their responses on this level can indicate where further instruction and practice are needed. You may then follow up with the practice pages in the ***Selection Support*** booklet.

You will find literature and reading guides in the ***Alternative Assessment*** booklet, which you may give students on an individual basis for informal assessment of their performance.

Formal Assessment

In the ***Formal Assessment*** booklet, you will find selection tests and a unit test.

Selection Tests The selection tests measure comprehension and skills acquisition for each selection or group of selections.

Unit Test The unit test, which calls on students to read a passage of literature they have not previously seen, applies the unit skills on a broader level. The Critical Reading section measures Unit Objectives 1, 2, and 3. The Vocabulary and Grammar section measures Objectives 4 and 5. The Essay section measures Objectives 1 and 6. Both the Critical Reading and Vocabulary and Grammar sections use formats similar to those found on many standardized tests, including the SAT.

Alternative Assessment

Portfolios As you review individual pieces or the collected work in students' portfolios, you will find assessment sheets available in the portfolio section of the ***Alternative Assessment*** booklet.

Scoring Rubrics You will find scoring rubrics for writing modes in the ***Alternative Assessment*** booklet. You can apply these to Guided Writing Lessons and to Writing Process Workshop lessons.

Speaking, Listening, and Viewing The ***Alternative Assessment*** booklet contains assessment sheets for speaking, listening, and viewing activities.

Learning Modalities The ***Alternative Assessment*** booklet contains activities that appeal to different learning styles. You may use these too as an alternative measurement of students' growth.

Using the Timeline

The Timeline can serve a number of instructional purposes, as follows:

Getting an Overview Use the Timeline to help students get a quick overview of themes and events of the period. This approach will benefit all students but may be especially helpful for visually oriented students, English language learners, and those less proficient in reading. (For strategies in using the Timeline as an overview, see the bottom of this page.)

Thinking Critically Have students answer paired comprehension and critical thinking questions about the Timeline to help them establish the *so what* behind the *what happened.* (For Check Your Comprehension, Critical Thinking, and Critical Viewing questions, see the bottom and side column of the facing page.)

Connecting to Selections Have students refer back to the Timeline when beginning to read individual selections. By consulting the Timeline regularly, they will gain a better sense of the period's chronology. In addition, they will appreciate what was occurring in the world that gave rise to these works of literature.

Projects Students can use the Timeline as a launching pad for projects like these:

- **Customized Timeline** Have students create a period timeline in their notebooks, adding key dates as they read new selections. They can use dates from this Timeline as a starting framework.
- **Special Reports** Have students scan the Timeline for items that interest them, research these further, and report on them to the class.

Timeline

1490–1750

1490 | 1542 | 1594

American Events

- **1492** Native American groups first encounter European explorers.
- **1492** Christopher Columbus lands in the Bahamas. ◀

- **1515** Juan Ponce de Léon lands on the Florida peninsula.
- **1515** Vasco Núñez de Balboa reaches the Pacific Ocean.
- **1540** Francisco Vázquez de Coronado explores the Southwest.

- **1565** St. Augustine, Florida, first permanent settlement in U.S., founded by Pedro Menendez.
- **1586** English colony at Roanoke Island disappears; known as the Lost Colony.
- **1590** Iroquois Confederacy established to stop warfare among the Five Nations.

- **1607** First permanent English settlement at Jamestown, Virginia.
- **1608** Captain John Smith writes *A True Relation . . . of Virginia.* ◀
- **1619** House of Burgesses established in Virginia; first legislature in the Western Hemisphere.
- **1620** Pilgrims land at Plymouth, Massachusetts. ▶

- **1620** William Bradford begins writing *Of Plymouth Plantation*; completed in 1651.
- **1636** Harvard College founded in Massachusetts.
- **1640** First printing press in English-speaking North America arrives in Massachusetts. ◀
- **1640** *Bay Psalm Book* published; first book printed in the colonies.

World Events

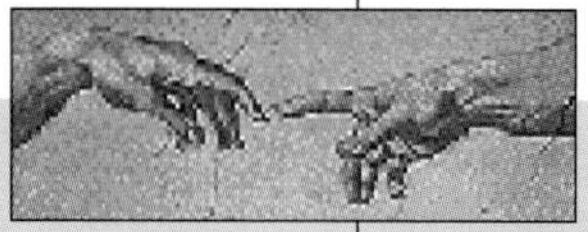

- **1499** England: 20,000 die in London plague.
- **1503** Italy: Leonardo da Vinci paints the *Mona Lisa.*
- **1508** Italy: Michelangelo paints ceiling of Sistine Chapel. ▲
- **1518** Africa: Barbarossa drives the Spanish from Algiers and most of Algeria.
- **1519** Spain: Chocolate introduced to Europe.
- **1520** Magellan sails around the world. ◀

- **1520** Mexico: Cortez conquers Aztecs.
- **1531** Peru: Pizarro conquers Incas.

- **1558** England: Elizabeth I inherits throne. ▶
- **1560** Brazil: Smallpox epidemic kills millions.
- **1566** Belgium: Bruegel paints *The Wedding Dance.*
- **1580** France: Montaigne's *Essays* published.

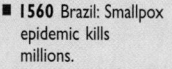

- **1595** England: Shakespeare completes *A Midsummer Night's Dream.*
- **1605** Spain: Cervantes publishes Part I of *Don Quixote.*
- **1609** Italy: Galileo builds first telescope. ▲
- **1630** Japan: All Europeans expelled.
- **1633** England: John Donne publishes *Poems.*
- **1640** India: English establish settlement at Madras.
- **1642** Holland: Rembrandt paints *Night Watch.*
- **1643** England: Civil War begins.
- **1644** China: Ming Dynasty ends. ◀

Getting an Overview of the Period

Introduction To give students an overview of the period, indicate the span of dates along the top of the Timeline. How much time is covered in this unit? *The span is from 1490 to 1750, 260 years.* Point out the division of the Timeline into American and World Events, and have them practice scanning the Timeline to look at both these categories. Finally, tell them that the events in the Timeline often represent beginnings, turning points, and endings. For example, in 1492, Native Americans first encounter European explorers.

Key Events One "story" this Timeline tells is that of the discovery and colonization of the North American continent by Europeans. Have students select items in the American Events section that help tell this story. *Examples include 1492, Christopher Columbus lands in the Bahamas; 1607, First permanent English settlement at Jamestown, Virginia; 1647, Massachusetts establishes free public schools.* Have them look at American Events from 1698–1750 and identify trends. *The colonies were in the midst of a religious revival.*

1646 — 1698 — 1750

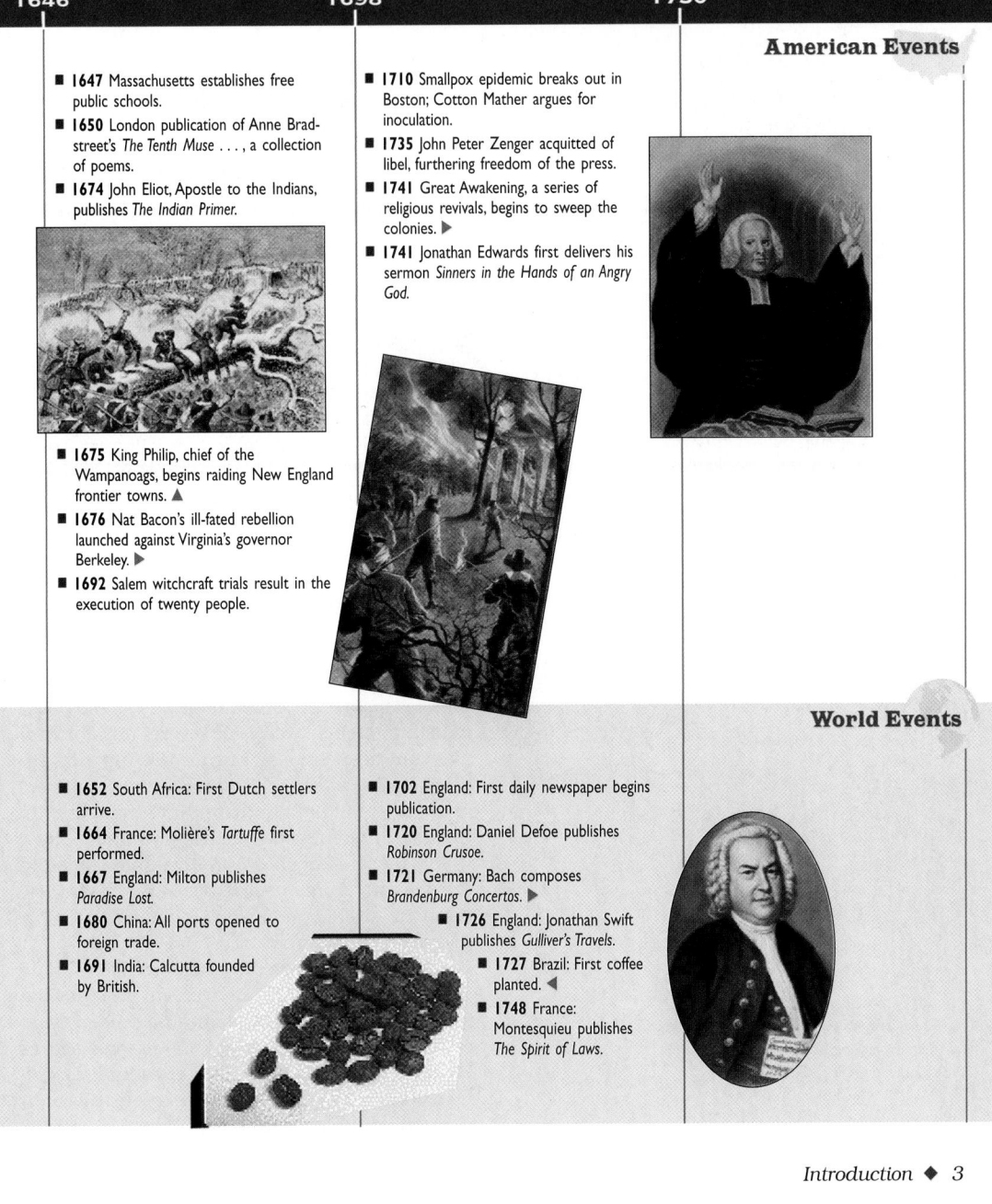

American Events

- **1647** Massachusetts establishes free public schools.
- **1650** London publication of Anne Bradstreet's *The Tenth Muse . . .*, a collection of poems.
- **1674** John Eliot, Apostle to the Indians, publishes *The Indian Primer.*

- **1675** King Philip, chief of the Wampanoags, begins raiding New England frontier towns. ▲
- **1676** Nat Bacon's ill-fated rebellion launched against Virginia's governor Berkeley. ▶
- **1692** Salem witchcraft trials result in the execution of twenty people.

- **1710** Smallpox epidemic breaks out in Boston; Cotton Mather argues for inoculation.
- **1735** John Peter Zenger acquitted of libel, furthering freedom of the press.
- **1741** Great Awakening, a series of religious revivals, begins to sweep the colonies. ▶
- **1741** Jonathan Edwards first delivers his sermon *Sinners in the Hands of an Angry God.*

World Events

- **1652** South Africa: First Dutch settlers arrive.
- **1664** France: Molière's *Tartuffe* first performed.
- **1667** England: Milton publishes *Paradise Lost.*
- **1680** China: All ports opened to foreign trade.
- **1691** India: Calcutta founded by British.

- **1702** England: First daily newspaper begins publication.
- **1720** England: Daniel Defoe publishes *Robinson Crusoe.*
- **1721** Germany: Bach composes *Brandenburg Concertos.* ▶
- **1726** England: Jonathan Swift publishes *Gulliver's Travels.*
- **1727** Brazil: First coffee planted. ◀
- **1748** France: Montesquieu publishes *The Spirit of Laws.*

◆ Critical Thinking

1. (a) Name four explorers who helped open the North American continent to Europeans. (b) Judging by their names, which country was especially active in sending out explorers? **[Infer]** *(a) Columbus, Ponce de Leon, Balboa, and Coronado. (b) Their names suggest that Spain was especially active.*
2. (a) How many years elapsed between the first European encounter with Native Americans and the first permanent settlement? (b) What might account for the time span? **[Hypothesize]** *(a) A period of 73 years elapsed from the first encounter in 1492 to the settlement of St. Augustine in 1565. (b) Reasonable answers include: Fear of the unknown and the difficulty of the journey may have prevented people from settling the Americas.*
3. (a) Name three key developments in colonial life. (b) Show how each indicates that life in the colonies was steadily improving. **[Interpret]** *(a) Reasonable answers include: 1636, Harvard University founded; 1640, First printing press, Bay Psalm Book published; 1647, Massachusetts establishes free public schools. (b) These developments point to the spread of learning and information.*
4. (a) In the period 1646–1698, what event resulted in executions? (b) What does this event suggest about life in the colonies? **[Analyze]** *(a) The Salem witchcraft trials were held in 1692 and led to executions. (b) These trials indicate religious fervor and a climate of fear.*
5. (a) What occurred in the field of health and medicine in the period 1698–1750? (b) What does it reveal? **[Draw Conclusions]** *(a) A smallpox epidemic broke out in 1710. (b) That Cotton Mather had to argue for inoculations suggests that health measures were still primitive.*

▶Critical Viewing◀

1. In the picture of Columbus landing (1492), what does his pose indicate? **[Analyze]** *His pose might indicate that something dramatic is happening and that he is taking possession of a new land.*
2. What does the picture of the pilgrims' ship (1620) suggest about the experience of voyaging from Europe to North America? **[Infer]** *The ship seems to list precariously to the side, suggesting that the voyage was probably difficult and dangerous.*
3. How would a press like the one established in 1640 affect life in the colonies? **[Speculate]** *It would make possible the publishing of local newspapers and the dissemination of information.*
4. What do the pictures of King Philip's raid (1675) and Nat Bacon's rebellion (1676) suggest about life in the colonies? **[Draw Conclusions]** *Colonial life had its dangerous side, with external and internal conflicts.*
5. What does the picture accompanying the Great Awakening (1741) disclose about the style of Puritan preachers? **[Analyze]** *The gesture indicates a dramatic style of preaching.*

Develop Understanding

Customize for
Less Proficient Readers
Have students preview the art and illustrations in A Graphic Look at the Period and answer the questions about them before reading The Story of the Times.

Customize for
English Language Learners
Have these students use A Graphic Look at the Period, without the questions, to speculate about the era. Also have them glance at the bold heads in The Story of the Times and formulate questions that the sections introduced by these heads might answer.

Customize for
Visual/Spatial Learners
Students with a visual or spatial orientation will benefit by using the maps on pages 4 and 9 to identify Native American cultures and the countries from which European colonists came.

Customize for
AP Students
Challenge more advanced students to use evidence from A Graphic Look at the Period and The Story of the Times to draw conclusions about differences in values between Native Americans and Europeans.

Answers to

A GRAPHIC LOOK

Read a Map (a) The tribes in the Southwest culture areas are Navajo, Hopi, Pueblo, and Apache. (b) The Cherokees are in the Southeast culture area. (c) Geographic features like bodies of water, terrain, and climate might affect ways of life.

Connect Rooms for winter cooking and roofs for work suggest the varied climate of the Southwest.

A GRAPHIC LOOK AT THE PERIOD

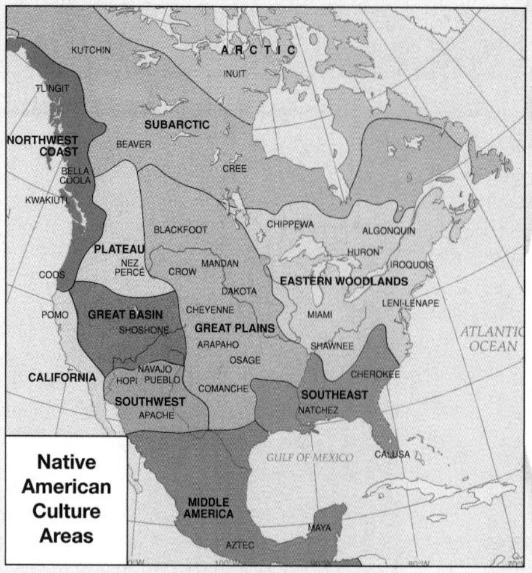

▲ **Read a Map** As Native Americans spread out to populate North America, they developed varied cultures. (a) Name two tribes in the Southwest culture area. (b) With which area are the Cherokees associated? (c) What geographic features might have led to the development of different ways of life?

▲ **Connect** How does this pueblo dwelling reflect the southwestern environment in which it was built?

The Story of the Times
Beginnings to 1750

More than a century after European explorers first landed in North America, there were still no permanent settlements in the Western Hemisphere north of St. Augustine, Florida. By 1607, however, a small group of English settlers was struggling to survive on a marshy island in the James River in the present state of Virginia. In 1611, Thomas Dale, governor of the colony, wrote a report to the king expressing the colonists' determination to succeed. Despite disease and starvation, Jamestown did survive.

The first settlers were entranced by the native inhabitants they met. They did not at first realize that these earlier Americans, like Europeans, had cultural values and literary traditions of their own. Their literature was entirely oral, for the tribes of North America had not yet developed writing systems. This extensive oral literature, along with the first written works of the colonists, forms the beginning of the American literary heritage.

Historical Background

When Christopher Columbus reached North America in 1492, the continent was already populated, though sparsely, by several hundred Native American tribes. Europeans did not encounter these tribes all at one time. Explorers from different nations came into contact with them at different times. As we now know, these widely dispersed tribes of Native Americans differed greatly from one another in language, government, social organization, customs, housing, and methods of survival.

The Native Americans No one knows for certain when or how the first Americans arrived in what is now the United States. It may have been as recently as 12,000 years ago or as long ago as 70,000 years. Even if the shorter estimate is correct, Native Americans have been on the continent thirty times longer than the Europeans.

Cross-Curricular Connection: Social Studies

The Origins of Native Americans
Remind students that Native Americans had probably been living in the Americas for thousands of years before Europeans arrived. Scholars now believe that Native Americans came to this continent from Asia by way of a land bridge across the Bering Strait. In several waves of migrations, they traveled southward and eastward from Alaska. That Native peoples came from Asia explains what is similar in their appearance. However, the existence of different phases in the migration accounts for the different linguistic and cultural groups indicated on the map in A Graphic Look at the Period, p. 4.

Ask students to speculate about the types of adaptations Native groups had to make in order to live in different regions. *Students may mention use of wood to build shelter in forested areas and the need of plains groups to follow buffalo herds.*

Colonists from Europe did not begin arriving on the east coast of North America until the late 1500's.

What were the earliest Americans doing for those many centuries? To a great extent, the answer is shrouded in mystery. No written story of the Native Americans exists. Archaeologists have deduced a great deal from artifacts, however, and folklorists have recorded a rich variety of songs, legends, and myths.

What we do know is that the Native Americans usually, but by no means always, greeted the earliest European settlers as friends. They instructed the newcomers in their agriculture and woodcraft, introduced them to maize, beans, squash, maple sugar, snowshoes, toboggans, and birch bark canoes. Indeed, many more of the European settlers would have succumbed to the bitter northeastern winters had it not been for the help of these first Americans.

Pilgrims and Puritans A small group of Europeans sailed from England on the *Mayflower* in 1620. The passengers were religious reformers—Puritans who were critical of the Church of England. Having given up hope of "purifying" the Church from within, they chose instead to withdraw from the Church. This action earned them the name Separatists. We know them as the Pilgrims. They landed in North America and established a settlement at what is now Plymouth, Massachusetts. With help from friendly tribes of Native Americans, the Plymouth settlement managed to survive the rigors of North America. The colony never grew very large, however. Eventually, it was engulfed by the Massachusetts Bay Colony, the much larger settlement to the north.

Like the Plymouth Colony, the Massachusetts Bay Colony was also founded by religious reformers. These reformers, however, did not withdraw from the Church of England. Unlike the Separatists, they were Puritans who intended instead to reform the Church from within. In America, the Puritans hoped to establish what John Winthrop, governor of the Colony, called a "city upon a hill," a model community guided in all aspects by the Bible. Their form of government would be a theocracy, a state under the immediate guidance of God.

▲ **Make an Inference** What Puritan values does this painting illustrate?

▲ **Analyze Art** These Puritan children posed for a portrait about 1670. Like other Puritans, they could expect to live twice as long as children in other colonies, where life was harder. What evidence of prosperity do you see in this painting?

More About the Puritans

Religion affected every aspect of Puritan life, although the Puritans were not always as stern and otherworldly as they are sometimes pictured. Their writings occasionally revealed a sense of humor, and the hardships of daily life forced them to be practical. In one sense, the Puritans were radical, since they demanded fundamental changes in the Church of England. In another sense, however, they were conservative. They preached a plain, unadorned Christianity that contrasted sharply with the cathedrals, vestments, ceremony, and hierarchy of the Church of England.

Connection to the Literature

- Students will encounter Native American works from several of the culture areas shown on the map on p. 4. These works include an Onondaga origin myth, "The Earth on Turtle's Back," p. 22 (Eastern Woodlands), and an excerpt from *The Navajo Origin Legend,* p. 26 (Southwest).
- Students will gain greater insight into Puritan style and values as they read Anne Bradstreet's "To My Dear and Loving Husband," p. 90, and the excerpt from Jonathan Edwards's sermon "Sinners in the Hands of an Angry God," p. 98.

Answers to

A GRAPHIC LOOK

Make an Inference This painting illustrates the Puritan values of hard work, cooperation, and a sense of community.

Analyze Art Evidence of prosperity includes the fine clothing that the children are wearing and the fan that the girl in the center is carrying.

Cross-Curricular Connection: Social Studies

Puritan Values

Use A Graphic Look at the Period to help students imagine Puritan life in the colonies (see the portrait of Puritan children, p. 5, bottom, and the comparison of living quarters, p. 7, bottom).

Point out to them that, although Puritans seem like distant figures from an ancient time, they bequeathed us a legacy that is still vital: Puritan values. Write some of these values on the chalkboard: self-examination and self-discipline; a concern for education; an unwillingness to spend freely; and a commitment to self-reliance and hard work.

Have students identify the ways in which these values still influence us today. *Students may answer that politicians, parents, and teachers stress the importance of education and educational standards; the importance of hard work is recognized not only in business but also in professional sports; many politicians argue against overspending.*

Historical Background

Comprehension Check ☑

1. Who was populating the North American continent when Christopher Columbus arrived in 1492? *Several hundred Native American tribes were living on the continent.*
2. What kind of greeting did Native Americans usually give the newly arrived Europeans? *They usually gave them a friendly greeting.*
3. What was a key difference between Pilgrims and Puritans? *Pilgrims chose to withdraw from the Church of England. Puritans still hoped to reform the Church of England.*
4. What were the central beliefs of the Puritans? *They believed that humans exist for the glory of God, that the Bible is the sole expression of God's will, and that God has already chosen who will be saved.*
5. From what social class did southern plantation owners come? *They were aristocrats.*

◆ Critical Thinking

1. What motives might have prompted the earliest European explorers to come to North America? **[Speculate]** *These motives might have included a search for wealth in the form of gold or new trading routes and a love of adventure.*
2. What aspect of Native American literature might have led Europeans to overlook it? **[Deduce]** *Native American literature was entirely oral; it did not exist in books.*
3. Were Puritan ideals especially suited to the task of colonizing a new and wild place? Explain. **[Connect]** *The commitment to hard work, frugality, and self-reliance does seem compatible with the difficult labor of establishing a new colony.*
4. In what way were the roots of the American Civil War planted during colonial times? **[Analyze]** *Southern plantations relied more heavily on enslaved Africans than northern farms did. The institution of slavery was already part of the southern way of life.*

Answers to A Graphic Look

Draw a Conclusion These drawings might show potential settlers animals and plants that could be sources of food or trouble.

▲ **Draw a Conclusion** John White, a colonist at Roanoke, made these vivid drawings and others that gave many Europeans the first glimpse of the plants and animals of the Americas. Why would White's drawings be of value to Europeans who planned to settle in North America?

Among the Puritans' central beliefs were the ideas that human beings exist for the glory of God and that the Bible is the sole expression of God's will. They also believed in predestination—John Calvin's doctrine that God has already decided who will achieve salvation and who will not. The elect, or saints, who are to be saved cannot take election for granted, however. Because of that, all devout Puritans searched their souls with great rigor and frequency for signs of grace. The Puritans felt that they could accomplish good only through continual hard work and self-discipline. When people today speak of the "Puritan ethic," that is what they mean.

Puritanism was in decline throughout New England by the early 1700's, as more liberal Protestant congregations attracted followers. A reaction against this new freedom, however, set in around 1720. The Great Awakening, a series of religious revivals led by such eloquent ministers as the famous Jonathan Edwards and George Whitefield, swept through the colonies. The Great Awakening attracted thousands of converts to many Protestant groups, but it did little to revive old-fashioned Puritanism. Nevertheless, Puritan ideals of hard work, frugality, self-improvement, and self-reliance are still regarded as basic American virtues.

The Southern Planters The Southern Colonies differed from New England in climate, crops, social organization, and religion. Prosperous coastal cities grew up in the South, just as in the North, but beyond the southern cities lay large plantations, not small farms. Despite its romantic image, the plantation was in fact a large-scale agricultural enterprise and a center of commerce. Up to a thousand people, many of them enslaved, might live and work on a single plantation.

The first black slaves were brought to Virginia in 1619, a year before the Pilgrims landed at Plymouth. The plantation system and the institution of slavery were closely connected from the very beginning, although slavery existed in every colony, including Massachusetts.

Most of the plantation owners were Church of England members who regarded themselves as aristocrats. The first generation of owners, the men who established the great plantations,

Cross-Curricular Connection: Science

Plants and Animals of the New World
Explain to students that Europeans coming to North America for the first time encountered many plant and animal species that were previously unknown to them.

Among the new types of trees were the *locust*, the *live oak*, and the *hickory*. New types of food crops included *eggplant, persimmon, pecan, sweet potato,* and *squash*.

For some of the new animals, the colonists adopted Indian names—for example, *skunk, opposum, chipmunk, moose,* and *raccoon*. For other new animals, colonists made up descriptive terms of their own: *bullfrog, garter snake, mud hen, potato bug, groundhog,* and *reed bird*.

Have students pretend to be colonists arriving in their region for the first time. Ask them to think up their own descriptive terms for a few of the region's plants or animals. *There are no wrong answers, but you might have students model their responses on the descriptive terms used by colonists. You might even analyze some of these with students.*

were ambitious, energetic, self-disciplined, and resourceful, just as the Puritans were. The way of life on most plantations, however, was more sociable and elegant than that of any Puritan. By 1750, Puritanism was in decline everywhere, and the plantation system in the South was just reaching its peak.

Literature of the Period

It was an oddly assorted group that established the foundations of American literature: the Native Americans with their oral traditions, the Puritans with their preoccupation with sin and salvation, and the southern planters with their busy social lives. Indeed, much of the literature that the colonists read was not produced in the colonies—it came from England. Yet, by 1750, there were the clear beginnings of a native literature that would one day be honored throughout the English-speaking world.

Native American Tradition For a long time, Native American literature was viewed mainly as folklore. The consequence was that song lyrics, hero tales, migration legends, and accounts of the creation were studied more for their content than for their literary qualities. In an oral tradition, the telling of the tale may change with each speaker, and the words are almost sure to change over time. Thus, no fixed versions of such literary works exist. Still, in cases where the words of Native American lyrics or narratives have been captured in writing, the language is often poetic and moving. As might be expected in an oral setting, oratory was much prized among Native Americans. The names of certain orators, such as Logan and Red Jacket, were widely known.

The samples of Native American literature in this unit reveal the depth and power of those original American voices.

"In Adam's Fall/We Sinned All" Just as religion dominated the lives of the Puritans, it also dominated their writings—most of which would not be considered literary works by modern standards. Typically, the Puritans wrote theological studies, hymns, histories, biographies, and autobiographies. The purpose of such writing was to provide spiritual insight and instruction. When Puritans wrote for themselves in journals

▲ **Make an Inference** Like native artists throughout Central America, Mexican artists crafted elaborate works of gold. Their designs were rich in symbolism and natural references. How do you think the fine quality of gold ornaments like this one reinforced the European desire to conquer the Western Hemisphere?

▲ **Compare and Contrast** These rooms from Colonial Williamsburg illustrate the living quarters of white landowners and African slaves. (a) What do these rooms have in common? (b) What are the major differences?

More About Native American Literature Native American literature and language is closer to us than students usually realize. Tell them that they can find one-word examples of various tribal languages simply by looking at a map or road signs. A remarkable number of American place names come from Native American words.

Connection to the Literature

- In reading Native American pieces like "When Grizzlies Walked Upright," p. 24, students should try to "hear" them as if they are being told. This technique will help students remember that Native American literature was part of an oral tradition.
- In Jonathan Edwards's "Sinners in the Hands of an Angry God," p. 98, students will encounter a type of literature that is characteristically Puritan: the sermon.

Answers to

A GRAPHIC LOOK

Make an Inference Fine golden ornaments like this one may have excited the greed of Europeans and encouraged their belief in legendary cities of gold. This greed, in turn, may have spurred them to further conquest.

Compare and Contrast (a) These rooms have in common chair and table, utensils and dishes. (b) The landowners' living quarters, below, are far more luxurious. The walls are not made of logs, as in the slaves' quarters. Also, in the landowners' quarters, dishes and silverware are more elegant, there is a cabinet for fine dishes, and there are pictures on the wall.

Humanities: Music

Native American and Puritan Music
Play for students the following pieces from the **Listening to Music** Audio CD: *The American Experience* "Navajo Night Chant" and "Psalm 100" from the *Bay Psalm Book.*

Have students find the Navajos on the map on p.4. *They are in the Southwest.* Tell students that the "Navajo Night Chant" is performed on the final night of a three-to-seven-day healing ceremony. This ceremony is meant to cure sickness by restoring the harmony among the individual, the group, and the universe.

Because Puritans believed that the melody of a religious song should not interfere with its message, the psalms were set to simple tunes.

Both pieces of music were used for religious purposes. What are the main differences between them? *Students may contrast the melody of the psalm with the apparently nonmelodic chant.*

More About *The New England Primer* Compiled by Benjamin Harris, this book might have sold up to two million copies in the 1700's and was the standard text from which most colonial children learned to read. Moral instruction was interwoven throughout the book, and letters of the alphabet were taught through such inspirational couplets as "The idle Fool / Is whipt at School."

More About the *Bay Psalm Book* The book was published at Cambridge in 1640. Its full title was *The Whole Book of Psalms Faithfully Translated into English Metre.* The intention of the authors was to make a faithful rather than an elegant translation.

More About Cotton Mather As a result of conflicts with Native Americans, Cotton Mather was not sympathetic toward them. When he heard that the wife and son of a Native American leader had been captured by settlers and sold into slavery, Mather declared (perhaps with a sense of victory):

> It must be bitter as death to him to lose his wife and only son, for the Indians are marvelously fond and affectionate toward their children.

Answers to

A GRAPHIC LOOK

Interpret Place Names This fact reveals that the group was still attached to the land they fled. They kept alive the old place names by re-bestowing them on the new places they founded.

Link Past to Present Modern magazine and book covers place a much greater emphasis on graphics and color to attract a reader's eye. The cover of this 1640 hymnal cover stresses the descriptive text. It is for the most part unadorned.

▲ **Interpret Place Names** The Puritans founded Harvard College at Newtowne in 1636. Three years later, they renamed the city Cambridge to honor the British city where many of the colonists had studied. What does this fact reveal about the group who fled England?

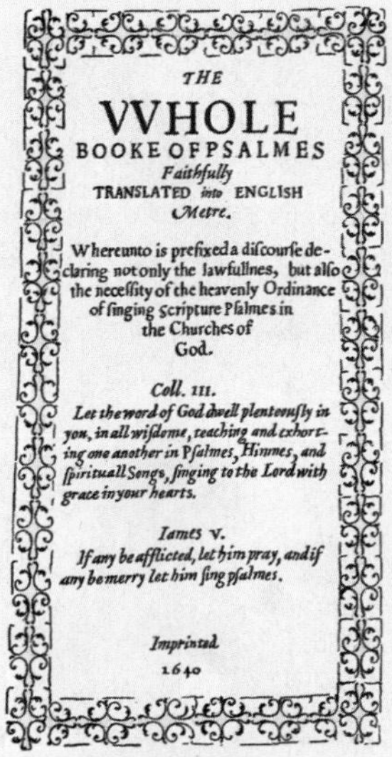

THE
VVHOLE
BOOKE OF PSALMES
Faithfully
TRANSLATED into ENGLISH
Metre.
Whereunto is prefixed a diſcourſe declaring not only the lawfullnes, but alſo the neceſſity of the heavenly Ordinance of ſinging Scripture Pſalmes in the Churches of God.

Coll. III.
Let the word of God dwell plenteouſly in you, in all wiſdome, teaching and exhorting one another in Pſalmes, Himnes, and ſpirituall Songs, ſinging to the Lord with grace in your hearts.

James v.
If any be afflicted, let him pray, and if any be merry let him ſing pſalmes.

Imprinted
1640

▲ **Link Past to Present** Many of the books printed in the colonies were religious publications. Compare this 1640 hymnal cover with covers of modern magazines and printed material.

or diaries, their aim was the serious kind of self-examination they practiced in other aspects of their lives. The Puritans produced neither fiction nor drama because they regarded both as sinful. The Puritans did write poetry, however, as a vehicle of spiritual enlightenment. Although they were less concerned with a poem's literary form than with its message, some writers were naturally more gifted than others. A few excellent Puritan poets emerged in the 1600's, among them Anne Bradstreet and Edward Taylor. Anne Bradstreet's moving, personal voice and Edward Taylor's devotional intensity shine through the conventional Puritanism of their themes.

The Puritans had a strong belief in education for both men and women. In 1636, they founded Harvard College to ensure a well-educated ministry. Two years later, they set up the first printing press in the colonies. In 1647, free public schools were established in Massachusetts. *The New England Primer*, first published around 1690, combined instruction in spelling and reading with moralistic teachings, such as "In Adam's fall/We sinned all."

One of the first books printed in the colonies was the *Bay Psalm Book*, the standard hymnal of the time. Increase Mather, one of the book's three authors, served for many years as pastor of the North Church in Boston. He was also the author of some 130 books. *Cases of Conscience Concerning Evil Spirits*, published in 1693, was a discourse on the Salem witchcraft trials of the previous year. The trials, conducted in an atmosphere of hysteria, resulted in the hanging of twenty people as witches.

Increase's eldest son, Cotton Mather, far exceeded his father's literary output, publishing at least 400 works in his lifetime. Cotton Mather, like his father, is remembered in part because of his connection with the Salem witchcraft trials. Although he did not actually take part in the trials, his works on witchcraft had helped to stir up some of the hysteria. Still, Cotton Mather was one of the most learned men of his time, a power in the state and a notable author. His theory of writing was simple (although his writing was not): The more information a work contains, the better its style.

Cross-Curricular Connection: Social Studies

African American Culture
African Americans in South Carolina and Georgia made up the majority of the population, and they generally had regular contact with only a handful of colonists. As a result, they were able to exercise greater control over their day-to-day existence than those enslaved in other colonies and to preserve many of their cultural traditions. Many had come to South Carolina and Georgia directly from Africa. They still practiced the crafts of their homeland, such as basket weaving and pottery, and they continued making the music they loved and telling the stories their parents and grandparents had passed down to them. In some cases, they kept their culture alive in their speech. The most well-known example is the Gullah language, a combination of English and African. As late as the 1940's, speakers of Gullah were using four thousand words from the languages of more than twenty-one separate groups in West Africa. African Americans even preserved the African manner of burial.

Ask students how the dissemination of African American stories differed from that of European literature. *African American tales were part of an oral tradition.*

In fact, the Puritans in general had a theory of literary style. They believed in a plain style of writing—one in which clear statement is the highest goal. An ornate or clever style would be a sign of vanity and, as such, would not be in accordance with God's will. Despite the restrictions built into their life and literature, the Puritans succeeded in producing a small body of excellent writing.

Southern Voices Considering the number of brilliantly literate statesmen who would later emerge in the South, especially in Virginia, it seems surprising that only a few notable southern writers appeared prior to 1750. As in Puritan New England, those who were educated produced a substantial amount of writing, but it was mostly of a practical nature. For example, John Smith, the leader of the settlement at Jamestown, Virginia, wrote *The General History of Virginia* to describe his experiences for Europeans. In addition to accounts like Smith's, letters written by southern planters also provide insight into this time period. Unlike the Puritans, southerners did not oppose fiction or drama, and the first theater in America opened in Williamsburg, Virginia, in 1716.

The Planter From Westover The important literature of the pre-Revolutionary South can be summed up in one name—William Byrd. Byrd lived at Westover, a magnificent plantation on the James River bequeathed to him by his wealthy father. Commissioned in 1728 to survey the boundary line between Virginia and North Carolina, Byrd kept a journal of his experiences. That journal served as the basis for his book, *The History of the Dividing Line,* which was circulated in manuscript form among Byrd's friends in England. Published nearly a century after Byrd's death, the book was immediately recognized as a minor humorous masterpiece. More of Byrd's papers were published later, establishing his reputation as the finest writer in the pre-Revolutionary South.

The writers whose work appears in this unit are not the great names in American literature. They are the founders, the men and women who laid the groundwork for the towering achievements that followed. The modest awakening of American literature seen in this unit had repercussions that echoed down the years.

▲ **Make an Inference** John Smith was the leader of the Jamestown settlement at Virginia. What does the clothing in this portrait reveal about his social stature or rank?

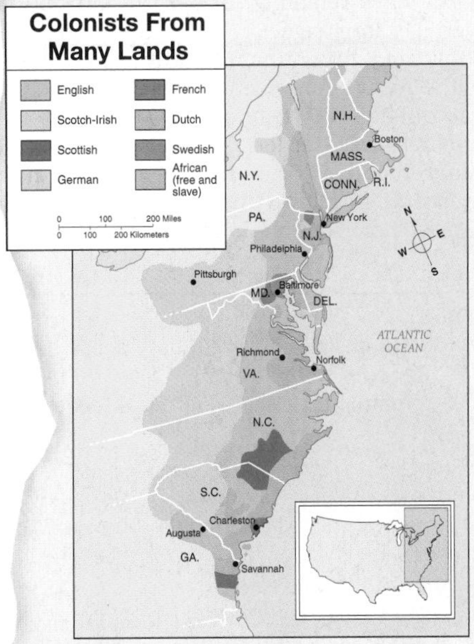

▲ **Draw a Conclusion** New immigrants from Europe, as well as enslaved Africans, carried their own cultures to the American colonies. (a) Which group settled in all the colonies? (b) What would explain this?

Literature of the Period

Comprehension Check ☑

1. Name three groups that contributed to early American literature. *Native Americans, Puritans, and southern planters were three contributing groups.*
2. What subject dominated the writings of Puritans? *Religion tended to dominate their writings.*
3. Cite two facts supporting the idea that Puritans had a strong belief in education. *In 1636, they founded Harvard College, and, in 1638, they set up the first printing press in the colonies. Also, free public schools were established in Massachusetts in 1647.*
4. Why was the first theater in America established in the South? *Unlike Puritans, southerners did not object to fiction or drama.*
5. Who was the author of the most important literary work in the pre-Revolutionary South? *That writer was William Byrd.*

◆ Critical Thinking

1. What attitude toward Native Americans may have led settlers to classify Native American literature as folklore? **[Speculate]** *An attitude of superiority may have led settlers to classify it in this way.*
2. Why do you think Puritans viewed fiction and drama as sinful? **[Infer]** *They may have viewed these forms as sources of entertainment rather than spiritual enlightenment.*
3. Why do you think early Americans mostly read work that had been produced in England? **[Draw Conclusions]** *They probably relied on what was familiar, and they may have been too busy establishing themselves to produce a great body of literary work. Also, Puritans tended to distrust fiction and drama.*
4. In what way are today's self-help books a reflection of Puritan values? **[Relate]** *Puritans stressed self-reliance, education, and hard work, as do these books.*

Activities

1. **Graphic Organization of Ideas** Give students the Outline Organizer in ***Writing and Language Transparencies,*** p. 95. Have them use the form to outline the major points in The Story of the Times.
2. **Panels of Experts** Have each student choose a section of The Story of the Times on which to become an expert. Within small groups, have student-experts present what they have learned and then lead a discussion on the subject.
3. **Annotated Map** Have students create an annotated map to illustrate some of the key events that are described in The Story of the Times.
4. **Connect to the Literature** Challenge students to find passages from the literature in this section that illustrate key ideas in the The Story of the Times. Then ask them to read these passages aloud to the class and explain how they illustrate an idea or insight from The Story of the Times.

Answers to A GRAPHIC LOOK

Make an Inference The clothing reveals that he was high ranking. It seems to be of good quality, and he is apparently carrying a fine sword.

Draw a Conclusion (a) English settled in all the colonies. (b) For most of the seventeenth century, England controlled these colonies, and most settlers came from England.

Develop Understanding

◆ Critical Thinking

1. If the animal and plant species that settlers encountered had been the same as those in Europe, how might our language have been different? **[Speculate]** *In those circumstances, the settlers probably wouldn't have adopted Native American terms for plants and animals.*
2. What does the Anglicizing of Native American terms suggest about the influence of a language on the terms it borrows from other languages? **[Generalize]** *This example suggests that when a language borrows terms from another language, it generally changes them so that speakers can recognize and pronounce them more easily.*

▶Critical Viewing◀

1. What does the chart reveal about the foods eaten by the Algonquin group of Native Americans? **[Infer]** *It discloses that they ate hominy, pecan, and pone.*

Answers to Activities

1. Among states with Native American names are the following: Alabama (name of a tribe in the Creek Confederacy), Alaska (Aleutian for "mainland"), Arizona (Papago for "place of the little springs"), Arkansas (Sioux for "downstream people"), Connecticut (Algonquian for "place of the long river"), Idaho (Shoshone for "behold the sun coming down the mountains"), Illinois (Illini for "superior people"), Iowa (Ioway for "beautiful land"), Kansas (Sioux for "south wind people"), Kentucky (Cherokee for "meadowland"), Massachusetts (Massachuset for "great hill place"), and Michigan (Chippewa for "great water").
2. Answers will vary depending on the region where students live. You might suggest that students use a road map to pick out names of local places. In searching out the origins of names, try consulting with local historical societies or with Native American organizations.

*T*he Development of American English

OUR NATIVE AMERICAN HERITAGE

by Richard Lederer

If you had been one of the early explorers or settlers of North America, you would have found many things in your new environment unknown to you. The handiest way of filling voids in your vocabulary would have been to ask local Native Americans what words they used. The early colonists began borrowing words from friendly Native Americans almost from the moment of their first contact, and many of those shared words have remained in our everyday language.

Anglicizing Pronouncing many of the Native American words was difficult for the early explorers and settlers. In many instances, they shortened and simplified the names. For example, *otchock* became "woodchuck," *rahaugcum* turned to "raccoon," and the smelly *segankw* transformed into a "skunk." The North American menagerie brought more new words into the English language including caribou (Micmac), chipmunk (Ojibwa), moose (Algonquian), muskrat (Abenaki), and porgy (Algonquian).

The Poetry of Place Names William Penn said he did not know "a language spoken in Europe that hath words of more sweetness and greatness." To Walt Whitman, *Monongahela* "rolls with venison richness upon the palate." Some of our loveliest place names—*Susquehanna, Shenandoah, Rappahannock*—began life as Native American words. Such names are the stuff of poetry.

If you look at a map of the United States, you will realize how freely settlers used words of Indian origin to name our states, cities, towns, mountains, lakes, rivers, and ponds. Five of our six Great Lakes and exactly half of our states have names that were borrowed from Native American words. Many other bodies of water and land have taken on names we have come to know as part of the American language.

Food	
squash (Natick)	pecan (Algonquian)
hominy (Algonquian)	pone (Algonquian)
pemmican (Cree)	succotash (Narraganset)
People	
sachem (Narraganset)	papoose (Narraganset)
squaw (Massachuset)	mugwump (Natick)
Native American life	
moccasin (Chippewa)	toboggan (Algonquian)
tomahawk (Algonquian)	wigwam (Abenaki)
tepee (Dakota)	caucus (Algonquian)
pow-wow (Narraganset)	wampum (Massachuset)
bayou (Choctaw)	potlatch (Chinook)
hogan (Navajo)	hickory (Algonquian)
kayak (Inuit)	totem (Ojibwa)

Activities

1. Brainstorm for a list of the states that have Native American names. Research the origin of each name.
2. With help from an encyclopedia or other source, find out what Native American tribes live or once lived in your part of the country. Do their languages survive in many place names? Pick out ten names of places in your state—cities, towns, mountains, or bodies of water—that have Native American names. Try to find their exact origins. What can you find out about the history of your state that will help explain why these names were chosen?

Cross-Curricular Connection: Social Studies

Linguistic Contributions of Immigrants
In addition to borrowing words from Native Americans, colonists borrowed terms from the languages of various immigrant groups.

The Dutch, who colonized New York and the surrounding area before the English, contributed words for types of food, like *cruller, cookie,* and *cole slaw.* They also contributed a word it is hard to imagine doing without: *boss.* Two other words with Dutch origins are *stoop* and *scow.*

The French colonists contributed words that reflect their activities in and around Canada, northern New York, the Ohio River, and New Orleans: *levee, cache, caribou, bayou, chowder,* and *portage,* among others.

German immigrants contributed the names of foods like *sauerkraut, noodle,* and *pretzel.*

Many Spanish contributions reflect the colonial activities of Spain in the New World: *alligator, armadillo, canoe,* and *maize,* to name a few.

Have students create a chart showing the linguistic contributions of various immigrant groups. They can use these examples and add to them by consulting histories of English.

Part 1

Meeting of Cultures

Oneida Chieftain Shikellamy
Unknown American Artist
Philadelphia Museum of Art

Humanities: Art

Oneida Chieftain Shikellamy, 1820, by unknown American artist.

Like other Iroquoian-speaking tribes, the Oneida, who lived in New York, raised corn and formed permanent settlements, living together in longhouses that sheltered extended families. By the nineteenth century, most Oneida were living either in Oneida, in Ontario, Canada, or in Green Bay, Wisconsin. Today, around 3,000 descendants of the Oneida are concentrated in these areas.

Have your students link the artwork to the focus of Part 1, Meeting of Cultures, by answering the following questions:

1. What attitude toward the chief would you say the artist—an American—communicates? *The artist communicates respect through his portrayal of Shikellamy as a handsome, impressive figure in his full regalia. The chief's posture also suggests that the painter admires him.*
2. How does this painting portray the state of relations between the European and Oneida cultures? *The fact that the chief possesses a gun but just stands with it implies that the Oneida and the American people trusted one another.*

One-Minute Planning Guide

This section introduces students to the cultural groups that staked their place in the early American wilderness. Columbus's *Journal of the First Voyage to America* describes the explorer's first encounters with local natives. The origin myths and constitution that follow offer a closer look at the culture of several Native American nations. The focus shifts to the Southwest with two accounts of Spanish quests to explore the New World. Olaudah Equiano's "Interesting Narrative" offers a graphic, firsthand look at how enslaved Africans reached American soil. Part 1 closes with a contemporary short story and song lyrics that help students relate the "meeting of cultures" theme to modern life.

Customize for *Varying Student Needs*

When assigning the selections in this part, keep these factors in mind:

from *Journal of the First Voyage to America*
- Brief journal excerpt
- Less proficient readers may need help with formal diction

"The Earth on Turtle's Back," "When Grizzlies Walked Upright," from *The Navajo Origin Legend,* and from *The Iroquois Constitution*
- Myths are brief, accessible, and easy to read
- Constitution excerpt contains strong visual imagery

"A Journey Through Texas" and "Boulders Taller Than the Great Tower of Seville"
- Exploration journals
- Less proficient readers may need to break down lengthy sentences in "A Journey"

from *The Interesting Narrative of the Life of Olaudah Equiano*
- High-interest nonfiction account of passage on a slave ship

"Diamond Island: Alcatraz" and "Big Yellow Taxi"
- Contemporary short story and song lyrics
- High-interest, accessible connections to Part 1 theme

Prepare and Engage

LESSON OBJECTIVES

1. **To develop vocabulary and word identification skills**
   - Latin Word Roots: *-flict-*
   - Using the Word Bank: Synonyms
   - Extending Word Study
2. **To use a variety of reading strategies to comprehend nonfiction**
   - Connect Your Experience
   - Reading for Success: Literal Comprehension Strategies
3. **To increase knowledge of other cultures and to connect common elements across cultures**
   - Connecting Themes Across Cultures (ATE)
   - Idea Bank: Informative Speech
   - Idea Bank: Native American Art
4. **To express and support responses to the text**
   - Critical Thinking
   - Idea Bank: Continuation
   - Idea Bank: Map
5. **To analyze literary elements**
   - Literary Focus: Journals
6. **To read in order to research self-selected and assigned topics**
   - Idea Bank: Comparing Journals
   - Idea Bank: Columbus Collection
   - Research Skills Mini-Lesson
   - Questions for Research
7. **To plan, prepare, organize, and present literary interpretations**
   - Idea Bank: Crew Member's Journal
8. **To use recursive writing processes to write an oral report**
   - Guided Writing Lesson
9. **To increase knowledge of the rules of grammar and usage**
   - Grammar and Style: Action Verbs and Linking Verbs

Test Preparation

Reading Comprehension: Summarizing Written Texts
(ATE, p. 13)
The teaching tips and sample test item in this workshop support the instruction and practice in the unit workshop:
Reading Comprehension: Summarizing Written Texts
(SE, p. 115)

Guide for Interpreting

Christopher Columbus

(1451–1506)

Not much is known about the early life of Christopher Columbus, one of history's most famous explorers. Evidently, he left his home in Genoa, Italy, and went to sea at a young age. At age 25, he was shipwrecked off the coast of Portugal. Once back on land, Columbus studied mapmaking and navigation. He also learned Latin and read Marco Polo's account of the riches of Asia.

Between 1480 and 1482, Columbus sailed to the Azores and to the Canary Islands off Africa. He then began to dream of more challenging voyages.

> ***One goal became the focus of Columbus's life: reaching the fabled cities of Asia by sailing westward around the world.***

First, Columbus tried to convince King John II of Portugal to fund a westward voyage. When his requests were rejected there, Columbus sought funding from other European rulers. After a series of unsuccessful attempts, Columbus won the support of Queen Isabella of Spain.

A Hard Bargain Queen Isabella and her husband, King Ferdinand, agreed to finance Columbus's first voyage in 1492. In forging the agreements, the explorer had negotiated favorable terms. In addition to funding, he asked for and received the right to rule any lands he conquered. He would also be entitled to 10 percent of all wealth from those lands.

The Famous Voyage Columbus set sail on August 3. On October 12, he reached one of the Bahama islands, which he mistook for an island off India. Columbus named the island San Salvador. Then he continued to explore the Caribbean. Over the next twelve years, he made three more transatlantic voyages, ever convinced that he had reached Asia and always hopeful of finding Marco Polo's fabled cities.

◆ Background for Understanding

HISTORY: THE ERA OF EXPLORATION

In the 1450's, the only known way to India from Europe involved traveling through Turkey. When the Turks announced a new tax on Europe's profitable overland trade with India in 1453, Portugal and Spain began to look for an alternate sea route to India. Their search brought Europe into contact with North and South America. Within a century, much of these two vast continents would come under European control. It was not until 1498 that Vasco da Gama found the all-sea route to India—around the horn of Africa.

As this map shows, Columbus's voyages took him from Lisbon, Portugal, to Palos, Spain, and the Canary Islands before crossing the Atlantic. He landed first on the island of San Salvador, where this account begins.

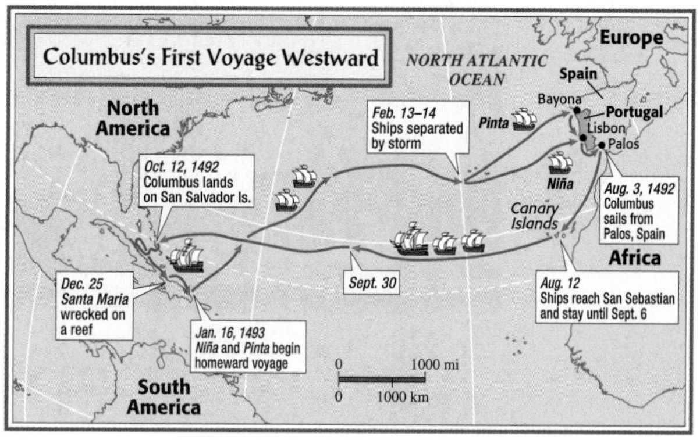

Prentice Hall Literature Program Resources

REINFORCE / RETEACH / EXTEND

Selection Support Pages
Build Vocabulary: Word Roots: *-flict-*, p. 1
Grammar and Style: Action and Linking Verbs, p. 2
Reading for Success: Literal Comprehension, pp. 3–4
Literary Focus: Journals, p. 5

Strategies for Diverse Student Needs, p. 1

Beyond Literature
Cross-Curricular Connection: Social Studies, p. 1

Formal Assessment Selection Test, pp. 1–3; Assessment Resources Software

Alternative Assessment, p. 1

Writing and Language Transparencies
Descriptive and Observational Writing, pp. 9–12

Resource Pro CD-ROM

Literature CD-ROM

Listening to Literature Audiocassettes

from Journal of the First Voyage to America

◆ Literature and Your Life

Connect Your Experience

"If you can dream it, you can do it," one motivational motto asserts. However, to fulfill the desire to circle the globe in a boat or discover the cure for a deadly disease takes much more than sheer will. A dreamer needs financial resources. Even Christopher Columbus had to secure and retain backers for his voyages. Many of his journal entries stressed the rich potential of the new lands, so that, upon reading them, Queen Isabella would decide to continue her sponsorship.

Journal Writing How would you have sold the idea of traveling around the globe to people who believed it would not be worth the expense? Write a convincing argument in your journal.

Thematic Focus: Meeting of Cultures

The earliest days of European exploration of North America brought native peoples into contact with curious newcomers. What kind of things can happen when cultures first meet?

◆ Build Vocabulary

Latin Word Roots: *-flict-*

Columbus calls his ignorance of botany an *affliction*. Words like *afflict, conflict,* and *inflict* contain the Latin root *-flict-*, meaning "to strike." An *affliction* is anything causing pain or misery.

Word Bank

Before you read, preview this list of words from the journal.

indications
abundance
exquisite
affliction

◆ Grammar and Style

Action Verbs and Linking Verbs

Action verbs—like *anchored, found,* and *saw*—express physical or mental action. **Linking verbs**—such as *be, become,* and *look*—express a state of being. Linking verbs are followed by a noun or pronoun that renames the subject or by an adjective that describes it.

Action Verb: We arrived at a cape off the island.

Linking Verb: Groves of trees are abundant.

Action verbs make writing more lively. Notice that Columbus often relies on action verbs to describe his experience.

◆ Literary Focus

Journals

The European encounters with and conquest of the Americas are recorded in the journals of the explorers. A **journal** is an individual's day-by-day account of events. It provides valuable details that can be supplied only by a participant or an eyewitness. As a record of personal reactions, a journal reveals much about the writer.

While offering insight into the life of the writer, a journal is not necessarily a reliable record of facts. The writer's impressions may color the telling of events, particularly when he or she is a participant. Journals written for publication rather than private use are even less likely to be objective. As you read Columbus's journal, look for evidence that the explorer was writing for an audience.

Interest Grabber Prepare students to read the selection by giving them the following assignment in advance. Begin by asking: If someone agreed to finance your venture, where would your dreams take you? Where would you go or what would you do if you could make a lifelong dream into a reality? Ask volunteers to share their responses with the class. Then explain that they are about to read an account written by a man who believed that he had made his lifelong dreams into reality by going where no European had gone before.

Connecting Themes Across Cultures

Students will be familiar with the fact that Columbus' discovery led to the massive migrations that have shaped and defined this nation. Point out to students that this is just as true for Central and South America as it is for the United States. Latin America has a highly diverse population, including those descended from enslaved Africans and immigrants from every land, including large Asian and Jewish populations.

Customize for
Less Proficient Readers
This journal, which comes from a sixteenth-century manuscript, may prove to be a challenge for less proficient readers. To help them work through it, organize these students into small groups. Emphasize key ideas and de-emphasize extraneous details to aid comprehension.

Customize for
AP Students
Encourage these students to be on the lookout for ways in which Columbus's purpose for writing affected the tone of his entries.

Customize for
English Language Learners
Have these students follow along in their text as you read aloud to them or they listen to the recording of the selection. For additional support, provide any or all of the following, as needed: historical background, young adult literature, or illustrated books on Columbus's journey.

Listening to Literature Audiocassettes

Test Preparation Workshop

Reading Comprehension: Summarizing Written Texts Many standardized tests ask students to identify the best summary of a passage. Use the following sample test item to demonstrate the skill to students.

In forging the agreement, Columbus had negotiated favorable terms. In addition to funding, he asked for and received the right to rule any lands he conquered. He would also be entitled to 10 percent of all wealth from those lands.

Which of the following is the best summary of this passage?

A Columbus would earn wealth through the agreement.
B Columbus expected to be a ruler.
C Columbus made an agreement which would bring him both wealth and the right to rule.
D Columbus was not only an explorer, but a shrewd politician.

Responses *A* and *B* contain accurate information contained in the passage, but only *C* presents all the key points.

Reading for Success

The Reading for Success page in each unit presents a set of problem-solving procedures to help readers understand authors' words and ideas on multiple levels. Good readers develop a bank of strategies from which they can draw as needed.

Unit 1 introduces strategies for literal comprehension. It is important for students to understand a work on its literal level before they apply higher-level critical thinking strategies. These strategies for literal comprehension give readers an approach for attacking text on a surface level—understanding, vocabulary, sentence structure, and sometimes complex language.

These strategies for literal comprehension are modeled with *Journal of the First Voyage to America.* Each green box shows an example of the thinking process involved in applying one of these strategies.

How to Use the Reading for Success Page

- Introduce the literal comprehension strategies, presenting each as a problem-solving procedure. Be sure students understand what each strategy involves and under what circumstances to apply it.
- Before students read the story, have them preview it, looking at the annotations in the green boxes that model the strategies.
- To reinforce these strategies after students have read the selection, have students do the Reading for Success pages in ***Selection Support,*** pp. 3–4. These pages give students an opportunity to read a selection and practice literal comprehension strategies by writing their own annotations.

Reading for Success

Literal Comprehension Strategies

Before you can begin to analyze or critique a piece of literature, you must be certain that you understand what the writer is saying. Some writing you'll encounter is easy to understand—it is written plainly and uses language familiar to you. However, if a writer uses long, complex sentences, a word order you don't recognize, or language that is archaic, you may run into difficulty. These strategies will offer you pathways to understanding complex writing.

Recognize the historical context of the literature.

Knowing about the historical period in which a work was written will help you comprehend the writer's words and ideas. The introduction to this unit provides background on the period. Read the selections in the context of this information.

Reread or read ahead.

- Reread a sentence or a paragraph to find the connections among the words, or connect the ideas in several sentences to get the sense of a passage.
- Read ahead. A detail you don't understand may become clear further on.

Break down long or confusing sentences.

- Read sentences in meaningful sections, not word by word.
- Figure out the subject (what the sentence is about). Then determine what the sentence is saying about the subject. Sometimes you may need to rearrange the parts of a sentence or to take other groups of words out of the way to do this.

Use context clues.

Context refers to the words, phrases, and sentences that surround a word. You can often use clues in the context to figure out the meaning of a word. Look, for example, at this passage from Columbus's journal:

After having *dispatched* a meal, I went ashore . . .

The word *dispatched* may be unfamiliar to you, but the word *meal* provides a clue that *dispatch* probably deals in this case with eating or finishing.

Restate for understanding.

- Paraphrase or restate a sentence or paragraph in your own words.
- Summarize at appropriate points—reviewing the main ideas of what has happened. Notice story details that seem to be important.

Look for signal words.

Signal words indicate chronological order and importance or other relationships between ideas.

As you read the following passage from the journal of Columbus, notice the notes along the side. The notes demonstrate how to apply these strategies to your reading.

Reading Strategies: Support and Reinforcement

Appropriate Reading Strategies Students are given a reading strategy to apply in reading each selection. In those selections where surface language may be challenging, students are given one of these literal comprehension strategies. In other selections a strategy is suggested that is appropriate to the selection.

Reading Prompts To encourage application of the given reading strategy, there are occasional prompts, within green boxes, at appropriate and significant points.

In addition, there are red boxes prompting application of the Literary Focus concept and maroon boxes prompting students to connect with their lives.

Using the Boxed Annotations and Prompts

The material in the green, red, and maroon boxes along the sides of selections is intended to help students apply the literary element and the reading strategy and to make a connection with their lives.

You may use the boxed material in these ways:

- Have students pause when they come to a box and respond to its prompt before they continue reading.
- Urge students to read through the selection ignoring the boxes. After they have read the selection completely, they may go back and review the selection, responding to the prompts.

MODEL

from Journal of the First Voyage to America

Christopher Columbus

This account begins nine days after Columbus landed on San Salvador.

Sunday, Oct. 21st [1492]. At 10 o'clock, we arrived at a cape of the island,[1] and anchored, the other vessels in company. After having dispatched a meal, I went ashore, and found no habitation save a single house, and that without an occupant; we had no doubt that the people had fled in terror at our approach, as the house was completely furnished. I suffered nothing to be touched, and went with my captains and some of the crew to view the country. This island even exceeds the others in beauty and fertility. Groves of lofty and flourishing trees are abundant, as also large lakes, surrounded and overhung by the foliage, in a most enchanting manner. Everything looked as green as in April in Andalusia.[2] The melody of the birds was so exquisite that

Read ahead to see whether Columbus retains this level of respect for the island natives.

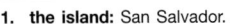

❶ ❷

1. **the island:** San Salvador.
2. **Andalusia** (an′ də lo͞o′ zhə): A region of Spain.

◆ Build Vocabulary

exquisite (eks′ kwi zit) *adj.*: Very beautiful; delicate; carefully wrought

▲ **Critical Viewing** The astrolabe was an invention that made the age of exploration possible. What features of this one suggest that it is an instrument of navigation? **[Support]** ❸

Develop Understanding

One-Minute Insight

This excerpt from Christopher Columbus's journal portrays the explorer's observations and impressions of San Salvador and states his plans for further exploration. He appears to have been taken with the natural beauty of the island and with the friendliness of its inhabitants. However, his choice of language and details make it clear that his purpose in writing was to impress the king and queen, who were financing his expedition and expecting a return on their investment.

Cultural Connection

Before students read this selection, you may wish to mention that it, like some of the others that follow, presents the point of view of a particular European explorer. Remind students that these explorers did not actually "discover" the Americas, since at the time of their arrival Native Americans had been in the hemisphere for thousands of years. Also point out that many of the Native Americans who tried to defend their land and their ways were badly treated by the invaders; those who faced Columbus were no exception.

◆ Reading for Success

❶ Recognize Historical Context Guide students to appreciate Columbus's motivation—to impress his royal backers with the success of his expedition. Here, and throughout the piece, he believes he is close to Asia and the riches it promises. He makes a point of presenting his observations in the best light.

◆ Grammar and Style

❷ Action Verbs and Linking Verbs Although Columbus uses several linking verbs here, he enlivens the passage with descriptive writing and figurative language.

▶Critical Viewing◀

❸ Support Students should note that the astrolabe has a needle and markings around its perimeter similar to those of a navigational compass.

Block Scheduling Strategies

Consider these suggestions to take advantage of extended class time:

- Divide the class into groups to brainstorm for what they already know about Christopher Columbus and his voyages to the New World. They can refer to the Background for Understanding feature on p. 12 for details.
- Have students listen to all or part of the selection on audiocassette. As they listen, they can focus on the lithograph on p. 16 for a visual image to accompany the text. Do they think that the artist has captured what they hear in Columbus's own words?
- Allow time for students to research Columbus on the Internet before or after they read.
- Set up peer groups in which students can discuss how the active reading strategies (p. 14) apply to this selection.
- Encourage individuals or groups to select, plan, and begin their choice of Idea Bank projects or assignments (p. 19). Necessary research can take place in the class or in the school library.

▶Critical Viewing◀

❶ **Evaluate; Support** Students can say that the artist is emphasizing the success, significance, and pageantry of the landing.

◆Reading for Success

❷ **Use Context Clues** Students can use the surrounding text in this passage to determine that a "league" is a measure of distance. A league is a length that has varied in different times and countries. In English-speaking countries it is about 3 miles long.

Humanities: Art

Columbus Landing in the New World

This lithograph was made by an unknown artist. The lithography process was invented in the late 1700's and was used as an alternative to engraving for reproducing paintings and drawings for books. It differs from engraving in that the printing surface is neither etched nor cut. Rather, an image is drawn with a greasy crayon on a slab of limestone. Then the stone is sponged with water, and the greasy areas repel the water. Next, an inking roller is passed over the stone, and the greased areas attract the ink, while the wet areas repel it. Paper is then pressed onto the prepared surface and pulled away to reveal the print. A stone lithograph produced a black-and-white image. Color was introduced by hand after the print was made.

Use these questions for discussion:

1. Does this lithograph present a romanticized view of Columbus's landing? If so, how? *Students may say that the scene is romanticized because everyone is dressed in formal attire for the ceremony, and the land seems beautiful and hospitable.*
2. What can you learn about Columbus's crew from this lithograph? *Students may cite the crew's religious inclinations, their formal dress, their pageantry, and their seriousness.*

Extending Word Study

Encyclopedia Columbus uses archaic measurement terms such as *span, league,* and *quintal. Span* derived from the linear distance across an outspread hand. Have students use encyclopedias to learn more about the origins of these and more current terms of measurement, such as *inch, mile,* and *meter.*

❶ ▲ **Critical Viewing** Evaluate the artist's interpretation of Columbus's landing in the Western Hemisphere. What aspects of the moment does he emphasize? **[Evaluate; Support]**

one was never willing to part from the spot, and the flocks of parrots obscured the heavens. The diversity in the appearance of the feathered tribe from those of our country is extremely curious. A thousand different sorts of trees, with their fruit were to be met with, and of a wonderfully delicious odor. It was a great affliction to me to be ignorant of their natures, for I am very certain they are all valuable; specimens of them and of the plants I have preserved. Going round one of these lakes, I saw a snake, which we killed, and I have kept the skin for your Highnesses; upon being discovered he took to the water, whither[3] we followed him, as it was not deep, and dispatched him with our lances; he was seven spans[4] in length; I think there are many more such about here. I discovered also the aloe tree, and am determined to take on board the ship tomorrow, ten quintals[5] of it, as I am told it is valuable. While we were in search of some good water we came upon a village of the natives about half a league from the place where the ships lay; the

Connect to the historical context. Columbus may want to flatter his financial backers in order to get future funding.

Use **context clues** to discover that *dispatched* used this way means "to finish off" or "kill."

Columbus uses the **signal words** "While we were in search of some good water" to show that the group is not just touring, but is looking with a purpose. ❷

3. **whither:** To which place.
4. **spans** *n.*: Units of measure, each equal to about nine inches.
5. **quintals** (kwint′əlz) *n.*: Units of weight, each equal to 100 kilograms, or 220.46 pounds.

Research Skills Mini-Lesson

Internet

Introduce the Concept Tell students that when they conduct research for an assignment such as the Columbus Collection activity on page 19, a good way to approach the work is through the Internet.

Develop Background Point out that several search engines on the Web can connect students with resource-rich sources such as news media, museums, colleges, and universities. Encourage students to visit Yahoo!, Kids Web, Altavista, or webcrawler.

Apply the Information Have students work in pairs to test out search engines. Ask each pair to conduct a simple search for "Christopher Columbus," noting the number of usable links they find. Direct students to keep a running list of key-words they've used and the results they've achieved. Have students keep a record of what they find in their search on note cards.

Assess Evaluate these records on the quality of what students find, including the applicability of their findings to the Columbus Connections activity.

Reread this sentence to conclude that Columbus is maintaining his level of respect for the property of others.

inhabitants on discovering us abandoned their houses, and took to flight, carrying off their goods to the mountain. I ordered that nothing which they had left should be taken, not even the value of a pin. Presently we saw several of the natives advancing towards our party, and one of them came up to us, to whom we gave some hawk's bells and glass beads, with which he was delighted. We asked him in return, for water, and after I had gone on board the ship, the natives came down to the shore with their calabashes[6] full, and showed great pleasure in presenting us with it. I ordered more glass beads to be given them, and they promised to return the next day. It is my wish to fill all the water casks of the ships at this place, which being executed, I shall depart immediately, if the weather serve, and sail round the island, till I succeed in meeting with the king, in order to see if I can acquire any of the gold, which I hear he possesses. Afterwards I shall set sail for another very large island which I believe to be *Cipango*,[7] according to the indications I receive from the Indians on board. They call the Island *Colba*,[8] and say there are many large ships, and sailors there. This other island they name *Bosio*[9] and inform me that it is very large; the others which lie in our course, I shall examine on the passage, and according as I find gold or spices in abundance, I shall determine what to do; at all events I am determined to proceed on to the continent, and visit the city of Guisay[10] where I shall deliver the letters of your Highnesses to the *Great Can*,[11] and demand an answer, with which I shall return.

Break down this long sentence by separating clauses and deleting descriptive details. You will be left with this: I want to fill the water tanks and leave. I'll sail around the island to meet the king. I want the gold he has.

Paraphrase this sentence this way: On my travels, I will look for riches. My main goal is to get to the continent. At Guisay, I will meet with the Great Can and act as a diplomat for the king and queen.

6. **calabashes** (kal´ ə bash´ əz) *n.*: Dried, hollow shells of gourds used as cups or bowls.
7. **Cipango** (si paŋ´ gō): Old name for a group of islands east of Asia, probably what is now Japan.
8. **Colba** (kôl´ bə): Cuba.
9. **Bosio** (bō´ sē ō): Probably the island on which the Dominican Republic and Haiti are now located.

10. **Guisay** (gē sā´): The City of Heaven, the name given by Marco Polo to the residence of Kublai Khan (ko͞o´ blī kän), the ruler of China from A.D. 1260–1294.
11. ***Great Can*** (kän): Kublai Khan.

◆ Build Vocabulary

affliction (ə flik´ shən) *n.*: Something causing pain or suffering

indications (in´ di kā´ shənz) *n.*: Signs; things that point out or signify

abundance (ə bun´ dəns) *n.*: A great supply; more than enough

Guide for Responding

◆ Literature and Your Life

Reader's Response If you had sponsored Columbus's voyage, how would you feel upon reading this account of his experience?

Thematic Focus Columbus's journals record one of the earliest meetings of Europeans and native North Americans. What kind of interaction did the two groups have? What evidence does the journal offer to help you decide?

Questions for Research Explore the motives of the early explorers. Which of their motives was strongest: the desire for gold, the desire for fame, the desire to Christianize? Read the journals of an early explorer and generate researchable questions about his motives.

☑ Check Your Comprehension

1. What is Columbus's reaction to the landscape?
2. According to Columbus, why are the houses empty when he and his crew arrive?
3. How long does Columbus plan to spend on this island?

◆ Reading for Success

❸ Restate for Understanding Some students will be better able to comprehend this complicated sentence by paraphrasing it. For example: Many natives came toward us and one came right up to us. He was delighted with the gifts we gave him.

◆ Reading for Success

❹ Look for Signal Words The signal word "Afterwards" indicates a time order; first Columbus will sail around San Salvador to acquire gold from its kings, then he'll head for Cipango.

Reinforce and Extend

Reteach

It is worthwhile to remind students about the basic nature of journals. They are a day-by-day record kept by individuals, and reflect only what these individuals perceive and wish to record. They can be of great help or interest to students, but, though we may classify them as nonfiction, journals are limited in perspective and often factually inaccurate. Columbus's journal, for instance, shows that believed he was off the coast of Asia.

Literature CD-ROM Have students use the CD-ROM *The History of American Literature,* Part 1, Disk 1, Feature 2, to learn more about European exploration of the Americas.

Answers

◆ Literature and Your Life

Reader's Response Students may express pride or surprise in Columbus's successes.

Thematic Focus While the interactions were not violent, there is some suggestion that the natives were frightened of Columbus. The journal describes at least two occasions when the natives "fled in terror at [Columbus's] approach."

☑ Check Your Comprehension

1. Columbus thought the landscape was beautiful and lush.
2. He believes that the island's inhabitants had fled in fear.
3. Columbus wanted to stay on the island only until they had collected enough water to continue the voyage.

Beyond the Selection

FURTHER READING

Works About Columbus

Columbus Then and Now: A Life Reexamined, Miles H. Davidson

Christopher Columbus, Mariner, Samuel Eliot Morison

The Crown of Columbus, Michael Dorris and Louise Erdrich

We recommend that you preview these texts before recommending them to students.

INTERNET

You and your students may find additional information about Columbus and his voyages on the Internet. We suggest the following site. Please be aware, however, that the site may have changed from the time we published this information.

For more information about Columbus, go to **http://sunsite.unc.edu/expo/1492.exhibit/c-Columbus/columbus.html**

We *strongly recommend* that you preview the site before you send students to it.

Answers

◆ Critical Thinking

1. Columbus describes the island in great detail, stressing the richness of the landscape.
2. He seemed to look for things that appeared valuable or exotic, such as the snake skin and the plant specimens.
3. Columbus says the meeting went very well, although he acknowledges that the natives may have been fearful. He stresses the peacefulness of the interaction.
4. Students may respond that Columbus did a good job of justifying his explorations by stressing the beauty of the new land, the value of its botanical specimens, and the potential for finding valuable spices and gold on nearby islands.
5. Suggested response: Although a crew member may also have been impressed by the landscape, a sailor's account may have included more details about the way Columbus treated his crew.
6. Suggested response: A Native American's account would include more details about the native's perspective. It might have revealed concern, worry, shock, or fear about the foreign visitors.

◆ Reading for Success

1. *Habitation* means housing. Clues include "a single house."
2. Once Columbus leaves the island, he will meet with a king, sail for Cipango, continue to look for riches, and go to Guisay.
3. Columbus wants to find riches to convince his financial backers that their investment was justified.

◆ Literary Focus

1. Columbus includes monetary references to keep his financial supporters interested. Details about the wealth of the island may persuade the king and queen to invest even more money in Columbus's exploration.
2. Columbus describes a paradise. Here, fruit falls off the trees, the landscape is beautiful and the people are friendly and helpful.

◆ Build Vocabulary

Using the Latin Word Root *-flict-*

1. Things that can be described as conflicting clash or strike against each other. Sample response: Columbus and the Native Americans had conflicting ideas about the importance of gold.
2. Inflict means to strike with something that causes pain. Sample response: Don't inflict that terrible casserole on me—eat your own leftovers!
3. Someone with an affliction has been struck with an illness or injury that causes suffering. Sample response: His affliction kept him bedridden for three months.

Using the Word Bank

1. b 2. a 3. b 4. c

◆ Grammar and Style

1. linking; linking
2. action
3. linking
4. action; action
5. linking

Writing Application Students should discover that action verbs make writing more lively and linking verbs make it more detached.

Guide for Responding (continued)

◆ Critical Thinking

INTERPRET

1. How can you tell that Columbus was struck by the beauty of the island? **[Support]**

2. What appears to have been Columbus's primary consideration in choosing "specimens" to send back to Spain? **[Analyze]**

3. According to Columbus, how did the first meeting with the natives go? **[Generalize]**

EVALUATE

4. If Columbus was writing to generate further support, how well did he justify the value of his explorations? **[Make a Judgment]**

APPLY

5. How would this account be different if it had been written by a crew member? **[Hypothesize]**

6. How would this account be different if it had been written by a Native American observing the acts of the crew members? **[Hypothesize]**

◆ Reading for Success

LITERAL COMPREHENSION STRATEGIES

Review the reading strategies and the notes showing how to comprehend a writer's words and intention. Then apply them to answer the following:

1. Using context clues, identify the meaning of *habitation* on p. 15.

2. Based on the the signal word *Afterwards* on p. 17, list the four things Columbus plans to do when he leaves the island.

3. Apply historical context to explain why Columbus hoped to find "gold or spices in abundance."

◆ Literary Focus

JOURNALS

A **journal** is an individual's day-by-day account of events and personal reactions. Although most journals are kept solely as personal records, Columbus chronicled his voyage to the Americas for his investors, the king and queen of Spain.

1. Why do you think Columbus often refers to the monetary value of things he has seen?

2. What impression of the Americas does Columbus seem to be trying to convey?

◆ Build Vocabulary

USING THE LATIN ROOT *-flict-*

The following words contain the Latin root *-flict-*, which means "to strike." Look at the definitions provided. Explain how the root contributes to the meaning of each word. Then write a sentence for each.

1. conflicting: fighting; battling

2. inflict: to give or cause pain

3. affliction: the condition of pain and suffering

USING THE WORD BANK: Synonyms

In your notebook, write the letter of the word that is closest in meaning to the first word.

1. indication: (a) delight, (b) sign, (c) value

2. abundance: (a) overflow, (b) dearth, (c) preservation

3. exquisite: (a) shocking, (b) beautiful, (c) sorrowful

4. affliction: (a) extension, (b) gift, (c) trouble

◆ Grammar and Style

ACTION AND LINKING VERBS

Action verbs show physical or mental action and tell what the subject is doing. **Linking verbs** express a state of being and connect the subject to a word that renames or describes the subject.

Practice On your paper, indicate whether each italicized word is an action verb or a linking verb.

1. I *am* very certain that they *are* all valuable.

2. Presently, we *saw* several of the natives advancing toward our party.

3. The diversity in the appearance of the feathered tribe from those of our country *is* extremely curious.

4. I *ordered* more glass beads to be given them and they *promised* to return the next day.

5. Everything *looked* as green as in April in Andalusia.

Writing Application Write two descriptive paragraphs—one using only linking verbs and the other using only action verbs. Contrast the two paragraphs to draw a conclusion about how these verb types produce different effects. Share your conclusion with your classmates.

Grammar Reinforcement

For additional instruction and practice, see the lesson on Writing With Nouns and Verbs in the **Language Lab CD-ROM** and the practice page on Action and Linking Verbs (p. 7) in the *Writer's Solution Grammar Practice Book.*

Build Your Portfolio

Idea Bank

Writing

1. **Crew Member's Journal** Imagine that you are one of Columbus's crew members, and rewrite this account from your point of view.
2. **Continuation** Pick up where Columbus left off. Write a journal entry in which you describe your thoughts as you explore the Caribbean. Use the map on page 12, along with your imagination, to come up with details.
3. **Comparing Journals** Columbus went on to make many more voyages, but never achieved his goal of reaching Asia. Use library sources to locate journals from one of Columbus's later voyages. Write an essay comparing the mood of the later journal entry with this one. Offer an explanation of the differences. **[Social Studies Link]**

Speaking, Listening, and Viewing

4. **Informative Speech** Native Americans inhabited the Americas centuries before the arrival of the European explorers. Some historians have begun to rethink Columbus's legacy. Research this issue and present a brief speech on your findings. **[Social Studies Link]**
5. **Native American Art** Many Native American cultures have artistic traditions. Find pictures of the various Native American art forms and compare these forms to European art from the same time period. Make a chart summarizing major similarities and differences. **[Art Link]**

Researching and Representing

6. **Map** Draw a map of the island, showing where Columbus landed and the areas he explored.
7. **Columbus Collection** Demonstrate Columbus's presence in today's world. Find prominent public places named for him (parks and cities, for example) and learn how Columbus Day is celebrated in different parts of the country. Present your findings in a scrapbook.

Online Activity www.phlit.phschool.com

Guided Writing Lesson

Oral Report on the Voyage

Columbus's funding depended on his ability to sell his experiences to an audience who hadn't seen the lands he explored. As Columbus, write and present an oral report you would give to the king and queen of Spain upon your return to Europe.

Writing Skills Focus: Elaboration for Vividness

To help you listeners share your experiences, **elaborate** by providing in-depth, detailed descriptions. Include sensory details, which tell what can be seen, heard, felt, touched, or smelled. In this model, Columbus helps readers imagine what they have never experienced.

Model From the Journal

Groves of lofty and flourishing trees are abundant, as also large lakes, surrounded and overhung by the foliage in a most enchanting manner. Everything looked as green as in April in Andalusia. The melody of the birds was so exquisite that one was never willing to part from the spot, and the flocks of parrots obscured the heavens.

By using sensory details to describe the island, Columbus elaborates on his idea that the fertile landscape was beautiful.

Prewriting Imagine the landscape of the island Columbus visited. List the tropical sights, sounds, textures, smells, and tastes that he may have encountered.

Drafting As your describe the island, include as many sensory details as you can. Instead of telling your audience how lovely the island was, include details to show the lushness of the region.

Revising Add details to strengthen each image you've described. Add smells to descriptions that appeal only to sight and sound; consider adding details about texture or taste where appropriate.

Idea Bank

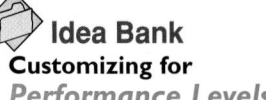

Customizing for
Performance Levels
Following are suggestions for matching Idea Bank topics with your students' performance levels
Less Advanced Students: 1, 5, 6
Average Students: 2, 5, 7
More Advanced Students: 3, 4

Customizing for
Learning Modalities
Following are suggestions for matching Idea Bank topics with your students' learning modalities:
Visual/Spatial: 6, 7
Verbal/Linguistic: 4, 5
Logical/Mathematical: 6
Bodily/Kinesthetic: 7

Guided Writing Lesson

Writing and Language Transparencies Use the Descriptive and Observational ***Writing Transparencies,*** pp. 9–12, to model descriptive writing.

Writers at Work Videodisc
Have students view the videodisc segment (Ch. 1) featuring writer Rita Dove in which she discusses her ideas about descriptive writing. Have students discuss why even a professional writer like Dove has to work to find just the right details and language for her audience.

Play frames 335 to 10985

Writing Lab CD-ROM
Have students complete the tutorial on Description. Follow these steps:
1. Direct students to the Interactive Writing Models of descriptive details in the Narrowing Your Topic section. Students will see examples of how sensory details, vivid verbs, and precise nouns can add impact to their descriptions.
2. Use the Sensory Word Bins to help students create vivid descriptions.
3. Have students draft on computer.
4. Use the Vague Adjectives Checker to aid revision.

ASSESSMENT OPTIONS

Formal Assessment, Selection Test, pp. 1–3, and Assessment Resources Software. The selection test is designed so that it can be easily customized to the performance levels of your students.

Alternative Assessment, p. 1, includes options for less advanced students, more advanced students, verbal/linguistic learners, and interpersonal learners.

PORTFOLIO ASSESSMENT
Use the following rubrics in the ***Alternative Assessment*** booklet to assess student writing:
Crew Member's Journal: Narrative Based on Personal Experience Rubric, p. 111
Continuation: Expression Rubric, p. 109
Comparing Journals: Comparison/Contrast Rubric, p. 118
Guided Writing Lesson: Description Rubric, p. 112

Prepare and Engage

LESSON OBJECTIVES

1. To develop vocabulary and word identification skills
- Latin Suffixes: *-tion*
- Using the Word Bank: Synonyms

2. To use a variety of reading strategies to comprehend nonfiction
- Connect Your Experience
- Reading Strategy: Recognize Cultural Details

3. To increase knowledge of other cultures and to connect common elements across cultures
- Background for Understanding
- Idea Bank: Dramatic Enactment

4. To express and support responses to the text
- Critical Thinking
- Idea Bank: New Ending
- Idea Bank: Logo

5. To analyze literary elements
- Literary Focus: Origin Myths

6. To read in order to research self-selected and assigned topics
- Idea Bank: Native American Chant
- Idea Bank: Totem Pole
- Beyond Literature

7. To plan, prepare, organize, and present literary interpretations
- Idea Bank: Origin Myth
- Idea Bank: Essay

8. To use recursive writing processes to write an observation
- Guided Writing Lesson

9. To increase knowledge of the rules of grammar and usage
- Grammar and Style : Compound Sentences

Test Preparation

Reading Comprehension: Summarizing Written Texts
(ATE, p. 21)
The teaching tips and sample test item in this workshop support the instruction and practice in the unit workshop:
Reading Comprehension: Summarizing Written Texts
(SE, p. 115)

Guide for Interpreting

Onondaga

As one of the original five member nations, the Onondaga were an influential force in the Iroquois Confederation, a league of Iroquoian-speaking Native Americans. The Onondaga live in what is now central New York State, in villages of wood and bark longhouses occupied by related families. Following the breakup of the Iroquois Confederation after the American Revolution, factions of Onondaga scattered to various parts of the country, but the majority returned to their ancestral valley in New York, where the Onondaga reservation now exists.

Modoc

The Modoc once lived in villages in the area of Oregon and northern California, where they farmed, fished, and hunted. Though each village was independent and had its own leaders, in times of war they would band together. In the mid-nineteenth century, the Modoc were forced onto a reservation in Oregon. A band of Modoc, under the leadership of a subchief known as Captain Jack, later fled the reservation. The result was several years of hostilities with United States troops and the eventual relocation of Captain Jack's followers to Oklahoma. They were later allowed to return to the Oregon reservation, which was dissolved in the mid-1950's.

Navajo

Today, the Navajo nation is the largest Native American nation in the United States, with more than 100,000 members. Many live on the Navajo reservation, which covers 24,000 square miles of Arizona, Utah, and New Mexico. Fierce warriors and hunters, the ancient Navajo settled in the Southwest about 1,000 years ago and eventually intermarried with the peaceful Pueblo people, who taught them to weave and raise crops. In 1864, after decades of fighting off encroaching American settlers, the Navajo were driven from their territory by the United States Army. They were eventually allowed to return to a reservation on Navajo land. Many Navajo still carry on traditional customs, living in earth-and-log structures and practicing the tribal religion.

Iroquois

The powerful Iroquois nation lived in what is now the northeastern United States. During the fourteenth century, an Iroquoian mystic and prophet named Dekanawidah traveled from village to village urging the Iroquois-speaking people to stop fighting and band together in peace and brotherhood. Dekanawidah's efforts led to the formation of the Iroquois Confederation of the Five Nations, a league of five Iroquois tribes: Mohawk, Oneida, Seneca, Cayuga, and Onondaga.

◆ Background for Understanding

CULTURE: HUMANS AND THE NATURAL WORLD

Native Americans have great respect for the natural world. They believe that each creature has its own power by which it maintains itself and affects others. Each Native American culture has its own name for this power, but early white settlers learned the Algonquian term *manito*. Manitos come in all shapes and sizes, but many Native American cultures recognize a chief manito, or Great Spirit—an invisible power that is the source of life and good for humans.

Many of the animals that helped feed and clothe the early Native Americans are revered as powerful manitos. Native American folklore and art, much of which portrays animals, reflect this great respect.

Journal Writing Look closely at the images of the moose and bear on this piece of Native American pottery. Given what you now know about Native American beliefs, explain what the arrows might symbolize.

Prentice Hall Literature Program Resources

REINFORCE / RETEACH / EXTEND

Selection Support Pages
Build Vocabulary: Latin Suffixes: *-tion*, p. 6
Grammar and Style: Compound Sentences, p. 7
Reading Strategy: Recognize Cultural Details, p. 8
Literary Focus: Origin Myths, p. 9

Strategies for Diverse Student Needs, p. 2

Beyond Literature
Cultural Connection: Native American Myths, p. 2

Formal Assessment Selection Test, p. 4–6; Assessment Resources Software

Alternative Assessment, p. 2

Resource Pro CD-ROM

Literature CD-ROM

Listening to Literature Audiocassettes

The Earth on Turtle's Back ◆ When Grizzlies Walked Upright
from The Navajo Origin Legend ◆ *from* The Iroquois Constitution

◆ Literature and Your Life

Connect Your Experience

"What was I like when I was born?" "What do you remember about my great-grandparents?" You ask questions like these for the same reason we all ask them. We share a fundamental desire to understand our origins—where we come from, our place in the world. Just as you collect stories of your family history, cultures create stories to explain the world as they know it.

Thematic Focus: Meeting of Cultures

Think of these origin stories as Native American responses to the universal questions of how and why we came to be. Notice as you read them that all four works are filled with images from nature.

What role does nature play in explaining—and maintaining—Native American life?

◆ Build Vocabulary

Latin Suffixes: *-tion*

The word *deliberation* contains the frequently used Latin suffix *-tion*, which forms a noun from the verb to which it is added. The literal meaning of *deliberation*, then, is "the act of deliberating." In *The Iroquois Constitution,* Dekanawidah tells the lords not to take actions without carefully considering them.

Word Bank

As you read these four works, you will encounter the words on this list. Each word is defined on the page where it first appears. Preview the list before you read.

- ablutions
- protruded
- confederate
- disposition
- deliberation

◆ Grammar and Style

Compound Sentences

In oral, as well as in written, language, compound sentences provide a natural way to link ideas. A **compound sentence** has two or more main clauses linked by a coordinating conjunction—*and, or,* or *but*—or by a semicolon. A main clause is a complete thought that contains a subject (which tells who or what the sentence is about) and a predicate (which tells what the subject is or does).

subj. pred. subj. pred.
The snow melted in his footsteps, and the water ran down in rivers.

◆ Literary Focus

Origin Myths

The need to explain how life began gave birth to **myths**, traditional stories, often about immortal beings, that are passed down from generation to generation. When these stories recount the origins of earthly life, we call them **origin myths.** Myths often explain many other phenomena, including customs, institutions, or religious rites; natural landmarks, such as a great mountain; or events beyond people's control. As you read each myth, note who or what is responsible for the start of life on Earth, and look for explanations of natural phenomena.

◆ Reading Strategy

Recognize Cultural Details

The Navajo Origin Legend excerpt opens with an image of the spirit men and women drying themselves with cornmeal. The gods they call appear carrying ears of corn. The myth's repeated references to corn reflect its importance to the Navajo way of life.

Literature mirrors the culture that produced it. As you read, **recognize cultural details** by noticing references to objects, animals, or practices that signal how the people of a culture live, think, or worship.

Test Preparation Workshop

Reading Comprehension: Summarizing Written Texts Students will need to recognize accurate summaries on standardized tests. Use this sample test item to help students practice:

> The need to explain how life began gave birth to myths, traditional stories, often about immortal beings, that are passed down from generation to generation. Myths often explain other phenomena, including customs, institutions, or religious rites and natural landmarks, such as a great mountain; or events beyond people's control.

Which of the following is the best summary of this passage?

A Myths are created to help explain those things that can't be otherwise understood.
B Myths are created to explain religious rites.
C Myths explain how life began.
D Myths are passed through the generations.

Choices *B, C,* and *D* offer accurate but incomplete information. *A* is the best summary.

Interest Grabber

Hook students' interest in origin myths by asking them to put aside, for a moment, all modern scientific knowledge. Have them imagine a simpler time when people asked the same "big picture" questions they ask today, such as "Why am I here?" or "How did the earth get this way?" Form small groups in which students can share nonscientific explanations they have heard for these questions or for other natural phenomena, such as why the moon changes shape or why tides ebb and flow. Have them speculate how and why people created and shared myths or legends, and why they still have universal appeal. Tell them they are about to read a series of myths that Native Americans created in response to the "big picture" questions they just discussed.

Customize for *Less Proficient Readers*

Because these selections are brief and are written in simple language and short sentences, they will most likely pose little difficulty for these students. However, to avoid confusion, you may want to point out that most of the characters are gods, animals, or elements. Students should recognize that capitalization is used to signify character names.

Customize for *AP Students*

Challenge students to find links to modern scientific thought in the works in this grouping. For example, the Onondaga myth acknowledges an understanding that humans must live on land, not water. The Modoc tale recognizes that humans and bears share some physical traits.

Customize for *English Language Learners*

Students new to American culture may not realize the diversity among Native American nations—their varied ways of life, languages, habits, and cultures. Familiarize students with the general locations of the Native American nations represented in this selection and identify specific geographic features that can help them better appreciate the cultural details.

Develop Understanding

One-Minute Insight This myth from the Onondaga relates a story of the creation of the world. In this version, the Earth forms as an offshoot of a celestial place called Skyland.

Literature CD-ROM To build background on Native Americans and the oral tradition, use the CD-ROM *The History of American Literature,* Part 1, Disk 1, Feature 2.

Looking at Literature Videodisc Play Chapter One of the videodisc. This segment provides background on Native American peoples. Discuss which Native American cultural values contribute to the ideas conveyed in this selection.

Chapter 1

◆ Reading Strategy

❶ Recognize Cultural Details Students may say that the Onondaga believe that dreams are powerful messages, which must be obeyed.

◆ Critical Thinking

❷ Predict Ask students to predict what will happen as a result of this accident. Students may say that the wife and her child will become the first people on Earth or that the seeds will grow into Earth's new plants.

◆ Reading Strategy

❸ Recognize Cultural Details Draw attention to the animals: They demonstrate human traits of speech, cooperation, concern, and tenacity. Discuss the Onondaga respect for all living creatures.

The Earth on Turtle's Back

Onondaga

Retold by Michael J. Caduto and Joseph Bruchac

Connections to World Literature, *page 1146*

Before this Earth existed, there was only water. It stretched as far as one could see, and in that water there were birds and animals swimming around. Far above, in the clouds, there was a Skyland. In that Skyland there was a great and beautiful tree. It had four white roots which stretched to each of the sacred directions,[1] and from its branches all kinds of fruits and flowers grew.

There was an ancient chief in the Skyland. His young wife was expecting a child, and one night she dreamed that she saw the Great Tree uprooted. The next day she told her husband the story.

> ◆ **Reading Strategy** What do the Chief's words to his wife tell you about the beliefs of the Onondaga?

❶ He nodded as she finished telling her dream. "My wife," he said, "I am sad that you had this dream. It is clearly a dream of great power and, as is our way, when one has such a powerful dream we must do all we can to make it true. The Great Tree must be uprooted."

Then the Ancient Chief called the young men together and told them that they must pull up the tree. But the roots of the tree were so deep, so strong, that they could not budge it. At last the Ancient Chief himself came to the tree. He wrapped his arms around it, bent his knees and strained. At last, with one great effort, he uprooted the tree and placed it on its side. ❷ Where the tree's roots had gone deep into the Skyland there was now a big hole. The wife of the chief came close and leaned over to look down, grasping the tip of one of the Great Tree's branches to steady her. It seemed as if she saw something down there, far below, glittering like water. She leaned out further to look and, as she leaned, she lost her balance and fell into the hole. Her grasp slipped off the tip of the branch, leaving her with only a handful of seeds as she fell, down, down, down, down.

Far below, in the waters, some of the birds and animals looked up.

"Someone is falling toward us from the sky," said one of the birds.

❸ "We must do something to help her," said another. Then two Swans flew up. They caught the Woman From The Sky between their wide wings. Slowly, they began to bring her down toward the water, where the birds and animals were watching.

"She is not like us," said one of the animals. "Look, she doesn't have webbed feet. I don't think she can live in the water."

"What shall we do then?" said another of the water animals.

"I know," said one of the water birds. "I have heard that there is Earth far below the waters. If we dive down and bring up Earth, then she will have a place to stand."

So the birds and animal decided that someone would have to bring up Earth. One by one they tried.

The Duck dove first, some say. He swam down and down, far beneath the surface, but could not reach the bottom and floated back up. Then the Beaver tried. He went even deeper, so deep that all was dark, but he could not reach the bottom either. The Loon tried, swimming with his strong wings. He was gone a long, long time, but he, too, failed to bring up Earth. Soon it seemed that all had tried and all had failed. Then a small voice spoke.

1. **the sacred directions:** North, South, East, and West.

Block Scheduling Strategies

Consider these suggestions to take advantage of extended class time:

- In order to better appreciate the richness and variety of the oral tradition, have students listen to all or part of the selections in this grouping on audiocassette. Discuss how hearing the myths, which originated in oral tradition, compares with reading them.
- Students may benefit from researching origin myths, oral tradition, or Native Americans either in resource books or on the Internet.
- Have students work in discussion groups to answer the Critical Thinking questions that follow each selection.
- Before students complete the Guided Writing Lesson (p. 31), stage a class discussion on the effective use of repetition. Have students look for specific examples of repetition in the myths in this selection, and discuss how it adds to the stories.
- Invite students to share their myth retellings by reading them aloud for classmates.

"I will bring up Earth or die trying."

They looked to see who it was. It was the Tiny Muskrat. She dove down and swam and swam. She was not as strong or as swift as the others, but she was determined. She went so deep that it was all dark, and still she swam deeper. She swam so deep that her lungs felt ready to burst, but she swam deeper still. At last, just as she was becoming unconscious, she reached out one small paw and grasped at the bottom, barely touching it before she floated up, almost dead. ❹

When the other animals saw her break the surface they thought she had failed. Then they saw her right paw was held tightly shut.

"She has the Earth," they said. "Now where can we put it?"

"Place it on my back," said a deep voice. It was the Great Turtle, who had come up from the depths.

They brought the Muskrat over to the Great Turtle and placed her paw against his back. To this day there are marks at the back of the Turtle's shell which were made by the Muskrat's paw. The tiny bit of Earth fell on the back of the Turtle. Almost immediately, it began to grow larger and larger and larger until it became the whole world. ❺

Then the two Swans brought the Sky Woman down. She stepped onto the new Earth and opened her hand, letting the seeds fall onto the bare soil. From those seeds the trees and the grass sprang up. Life on Earth had begun.

▲ Critical Viewing What characteristics of this turtle are explained in this origin myth? **[Connect]** ❻

Guide for Responding

◆ Literature and Your Life

Reader's Response If you had been the Ancient Chief, would you have pulled up the Great Tree? Explain your answer.

Thematic Focus How do the animals portrayed in this myth embody the best aspects of human nature?

Informal Debate Work with a group of classmates to stage an informal debate on whether Muskrat or Turtle deserves more credit for the creation of the Earth.

☑ Check Your Comprehension

1. According to the myth, what existed before this Earth?
2. What starts the chain of events that eventually leads to Earth's creation?
3. What does the Sky Woman bring with her from Skyland, and how does it affect the Earth?

◆ Critical Thinking

INTERPRET

1. Name at least two things that are lost or sacrificed in the Skyland so there would be life on Earth. **[Analyze]**
2. How do the animals in this myth exhibit human virtues? **[Interpret]**
3. Whom do you think the Onondaga ultimately credit with bringing Earth into existence? **[Infer]**
4. What can you conclude from this myth about the relationship between the Onondaga and their natural environment? Explain your answer. **[Draw Conclusions]**

EXTEND

5. Muskrat was willing to give up her life to save the Sky Woman. Describe someone you know from literature or real life who has also acted selflessly. **[Synthesize]**

◆ Grammar and Style

❹ Compound Sentences This passage has some examples of compound sentences, as well as short simple sentences. Have students rework all the sentences in this excerpt so that it consists only of simple sentences. Ask them to read the revision aloud to appreciate the impact of sentence variety on the effectiveness of the passage.

◆ Literary Focus

❺ Origin Myths Point out that this passage explains the existence of something that can be seen to this day: marks on the back of the turtle's shell. Discuss why the Onondaga myth would include such a connection. *Students may say that this gives the tale credibility, or shows why the people should show respect for the animals.* Encourage students to look for other such examples throughout this and other myths in this grouping.

▶Critical Viewing◀

❻ Connect Students should respond that the marks on the turtle's shell are explained as the pawprints left by Muskrat's muddied claws.

Reinforce and Extend

Answers

◆ Literature and Your Life

Reader's Response Some students may respond that they would not have pulled up such a sacred tree on the basis of a dream; others may say that, like the Ancient Chief, they would have taken the dream seriously and uprooted the tree.

Thematic Focus The animals are concerned, sympathetic, cooperative, and willing to risk even their lives to help another.

☑ Check Your Comprehension

1. Water, filled with animals and birds, and Skyland and its inhabitants existed before this Earth.
2. The ancient Skyland chief's young wife has a dream in which she sees the Great Tree uprooted.
3. The Sky Woman brings the seeds she pulled from the Great Tree's branch as she fell into the hole. The trees and grass on Earth spring from those seeds.

◆ Critical Thinking

1. The Great Tree is pulled up, the Ancient Chief loses his young wife, and Muskrat loses (or almost loses) her life.
2. They exhibit concern, kindness, generosity, heroism, and quick thinking. They unite their efforts to help the falling Sky Woman: The Swans catch her in their wings; the Duck, Beaver, Loon, and Muskrat risk their lives to bring up Earth; and Turtle offers to bear the weight of the world on his shell.
3. Suggested response: The Onondaga credit the animals of the waters.
4. The Onondaga have great respect and even affection for all of nature, particularly the water animals. They recognize that they inhabit a world that belonged first to animals.
5. Students should cite people or characters who clearly exhibit selfless behavior.

Develop Understanding

One-Minute Insight This Modoc legend tells the story of how American Indians were created and how bears came to walk on four legs. It tells of how the daughter of the Chief of the Sky Spirits falls off a mountain and is rescued by bears. The grizzlies raise her, and she eventually marries one of them and has children. Years later, when the Chief of the Sky Spirits is reunited with his daughter and learns of her children, he punishes the grizzlies by making them walk on four legs. The children of his daughter become the first Indians and refuse to ever kill grizzlies.

▶Critical Viewing◀

❶ **Assess** The bear, feathers, pawprint, and hides are part of the natural world; the shield and spear are the work of humans. The artwork reflects the Native Americans' sense of harmony with the natural world.

◆ *Literature and Your Life*

❷ Ask students to relate features of this story to elements of creation stories they tell in their own cultures. What is the appeal of such straightforward explanations? *Students may say that they provide answers to almost unfathomable questions and they are easy to recall and pass on in the oral tradition.*

◆ Literary Focus

❸ **Origin Myths** Encourage students to contrast creation, as presented in this Modoc myth, with creation in the Onondaga myth. *In the Onondaga myth, existing animals are instrumental in creating Earth itself; in the Modoc myth, the Sky Spirit creates both Earth and its creatures.*

When Grizzlies Walked Upright

Modoc

Retold by Richard Erdoes and Alfonso Ortiz

❶ ▲ **Critical Viewing** Which elements of the natural world are included in this image? Which elements represent the human world? What is the effect of the presentation of both together? **[Assess]**

Before there were people on earth, the Chief of the Sky Spirits grew tired of his home in the Above World, because the air was always brittle with an icy cold. So he carved a hole in the sky with a stone and pushed all the snow and ice down below until he made a great mound that reached from the earth almost to the sky. Today it is known as Mount Shasta.

Then the Sky Spirit took his walking stick, stepped from a cloud to the peak, and walked down to the mountain. When he was about halfway to the valley below, he began to put his finger to the ground here and there, here and there. Wherever his finger touched, a tree grew. The snow melted in his footsteps, and the water ran down in rivers.

The Sky Spirit broke off the small end of his giant stick and threw the pieces into the rivers. The longer pieces turned into beaver and otter; ❷ the smaller pieces became fish. When the ❸ leaves dropped from the trees, he picked them up, blew upon them, and so made the birds. Then he took the big end of his giant stick and made all the animals that walked on the earth, the biggest of which were the grizzly bears.

Now when they were first made, the bears were covered with hair and had sharp claws, just as they do today, but they walked on two feet and could talk like people. They looked so fierce that the Sky Spirit sent them away from him to live in the forest at the base of the mountain.

Pleased with what he'd done, the Chief of the Sky Spirits decided to bring his family down and live on earth himself. The mountains of snow and ice became their lodge. He made a big fire in the center of the mountain and a hole in the top so ❹

Humanities: Art

Dreamwalker by Nancy Wood Taber.

Nancy Wood Taber lives in the Manzano Mountains outside Albuquerque, New Mexico. Her art consists of detailed, lifelike colored-pencil drawings or alkyd paintings of the birds and animals of the wilderness near her home. She infuses her art with Native American mythology and spiritualism. She hopes to encourage viewers to experience a deeper appreciation for the importance of animals in their lives.

This colored-pencil drawing is part of Taber's "Spirit Shield" series. It shows a bear who has chosen "to take the earth walk among the two-leggeds." The bear's hibernation represents introspection and the quest for inner knowledge and strength.

Use these questions for discussion:

1. In what way does the artist blend the natural and human worlds? *Students may say that the shield and spear are objects made by people, using animal products such as feathers and leather. By placing them behind the bear, the artist suggests that people should learn from the bear's innate wisdom.*
2. What might the artist suggest about the bear by portraying it in the upright position? *Students might say that since the bear is one of the only creatures besides humans that walks upright, the artist believes in a connection between this formidable animal and humans.*

that the smoke and sparks could fly out. When
4 he put a big log on the fire, sparks would fly up and the earth would tremble.

Late one spring while the Sky Spirit and his family were sitting round the fire, the Wind Spirit sent a great storm that shook the top of the mountain. It blew and blew and roared and roared. Smoke blown back into the lodge hurt their eyes, and finally the Sky Spirit said to his youngest daughter, "Climb up to the smoke hole and ask the Wind Spirit to blow more gently. Tell him I'm afraid he will blow the mountain over."

As his daughter started up, her father said, "But be careful not to stick your head out at the top. If you do, the wind may catch you by the hair and blow you away."

The girl hurried to the top of the mountain and stayed well inside the smoke hole as she spoke to the Wind Spirit. As she was about to climb back down, she remembered that her father had once said you could see the ocean from the top of their lodge. His daughter wondered what the ocean looked like, and her curiosity got the better of her. She poked her head out of the hole and turned toward the west, but before she could see anything, the Wind Spirit caught her long hair, pulled her out of the mountain, and blew her down over the snow and ice. She landed among the scrubby fir trees at the edge of the timber and snow line, her long red hair trailing over the snow.

5 **◆ Reading Strategy**
What detail about the way Native American women wear their hair is revealed here?

There a grizzly bear found the little girl when he was out hunting food for his family. He carried her home with
6 him, and his wife brought her up with their family of cubs. The little red-haired girl and the cubs ate together, played together, and grew up together.

When she became a young woman, she and the eldest son of the grizzly bears were married. In the years that followed they had many children, who were not as hairy as the grizzlies, yet did not look exactly like their spirit mother, either.

All the grizzly bears throughout the forests were so proud of these new creatures that they made a lodge for the red-haired mother and her children. They placed the lodge near Mount Shasta—it is called Little Mount Shasta today.

After many years had passed, the mother grizzly bear knew that she would soon die. Fearing that she should ask of the Chief of the Sky Spirits to forgive her for keeping his daughter, she gathered all the grizzlies at the lodge they had built. Then she sent her eldest grandson in a cloud to the top of Mount Shasta, to tell the Spirit Chief where he could find his long-lost daughter.

When the father got this news he was so glad that he came down the mountainside in giant strides, melting the snow and tearing up the land under his feet. Even today his tracks can be seen in the rocky path on the south side of Mount Shasta.

As he neared the lodge, he called out, "Is this where my little daughter lives?"

He expected his child to look exactly as she had when he saw her last. When he found a grown woman instead, and learned that the strange creatures she was taking care of were his grandchildren, he became very angry. A new race had been created that was not of his
making! He frowned on the old grandmother so 7
sternly that she promptly fell dead. Then he
cursed all the grizzlies: 8

"Get down on your hands and knees. You have wronged me, and from this moment all of you will walk on four feet and never talk again."

He drove his grandchildren out of the lodge, put his daughter over his shoulder, and climbed back up the mountain. Never again did he come to the forest. Some say that he put out the fire in the center of his lodge and took his daughter back up to the sky to live.

Those strange creatures, his grandchildren, scattered and wandered over the earth. They were the first Indians, the ancestors of all the Indian tribes.

That's why the Indians living around Mount Shasta would never kill a grizzly bear. Whenever a grizzly killed an Indian, his body was burned on the spot. And for many years all who passed that way cast a stone there until a great pile of stones marked the place of his death.

◆ Literary Focus

4 Origin Myths Ask students: The origin of what natural phenomenon is explained here? *This passage explains the origin of the volcano. Mount Shasta, in present-day California, about fifty miles south of the Oregon border, is a volcanic peak.*

◆ Reading Strategy

5 Recognize Cultural Details This passage reveals that Native American woman wore their hair long.

◆ Critical Thinking

6 Synthesize Ask students to relate the girl being taken in by the bear to similar myths or legends in which a human is rescued or raised by caring animals. Students might recall the stories of Tarzan or Mowgli, or characters from other folktales they have read. They can use these to predict what may happen as a result of the relationship between the girl and the bears.

◆ Reading Strategy

7 Recognize Cultural Details Discuss what kind of god the Modoc believe the Sky Spirit is. *Students may say that the Modoc Sky Spirit is proud, easily angered, vengeful, and quick to exert his authority.*

◆ *Literature and Your Life*

8 In this myth, the grizzlies take pity on the lost girl and raise her as their own. Yet they are punished forever by the Sky Spirit. Ask students to think of times in their own lives when they did something that they believed at the time was an act of kindness or generosity, but which led to an unexpected negative result.

Customize for
Gifted/Talented Students
This myth explains a natural landmark—a trail visible on Mt. Shasta. This kind of explanation of natural features is common in many traditional cultures. For example, Greek mythology explains the formation of the constellation Cancer, or the Crab. The goddess Hera lifted a crab up into the heavens as a reward. The crab had bitten and been killed by Hercules, one of Hera's many enemies. Have students invent such an explanation for some natural feature in your region.

Cultural Connection

Every culture has its own origin myths or *pourquoi* (the French word for "why?") tales, which attempt to explain natural phenomena. Encourage interested students to find other examples of origin myths from around the world. Groups can select a trio of myths from three different cultures. Challenge them to find in that trio recurring themes or elements, unique explanations, and cultural details that both distinguish the myths and form common bonds among them. Students can present their findings in a multimedia presentation or as an oral or written report.

Develop Understanding

One-Minute Insight This creation story tells of how the first man and first woman were created from the wind and ears of corn. The wind comes to represent life, reflected in the fact that people must breathe in order to survive. In addition to capturing the Navajo belief in the sacredness of the wind, the legend reflects other Navajo values, such as the importance of corn as a source of sustenance.

Customize for *Logical/Mathematical Learners*
Have these students look for number patterns in this myth and offer logical explanations for them. For instance, students may notice that the ceremony in this myth begins on the *twelfth* day. Twelve is a number often used in literature to indicate a year, a full life cycle, or other indeterminate period of long wait.

▶Critical Viewing◀

❶ **Compare** Students may notice around the central circle a set of four ovals: black, white, blue, and yellow, which are the colors of the four Navajo gods. They will see two humanlike figures, one whose head points east, the other west.

Read to Understand

Myths often reflect important elements of a society's most fundamental beliefs. Have students consider what this legend suggests about the Navajos. For instance, students might ask whether the gods seem benign or capricious, and what the answer might

from The Navajo Origin Legend

Navajo

Retold by Washington Matthews

On the morning of the twelfth day the people washed themselves well. The women dried themselves with yellow cornmeal; the men with white cornmeal. Soon after the ablutions were completed they heard the distant call of the approaching gods.[1] It was shouted, as before, four times—nearer and louder at each repetition—and, after the fourth call, the gods appeared. Blue Body and Black Body each carried a sacred buckskin. White Body carried two ears of corn, one yellow, one white, each covered at the end completely with grains.

1. **the approaching gods:** The four Navajo gods: White Body, Blue Body, Yellow Body, and Black Body.

▼ **Critical Viewing** This painting depicts the Blessingway chant, which is based on another Navajo legend. Compare the ceremony depicted in the painting with the one described in this excerpt of *The Navajo Origin Legend.* Which elements are common to both? **[Compare]** ❶

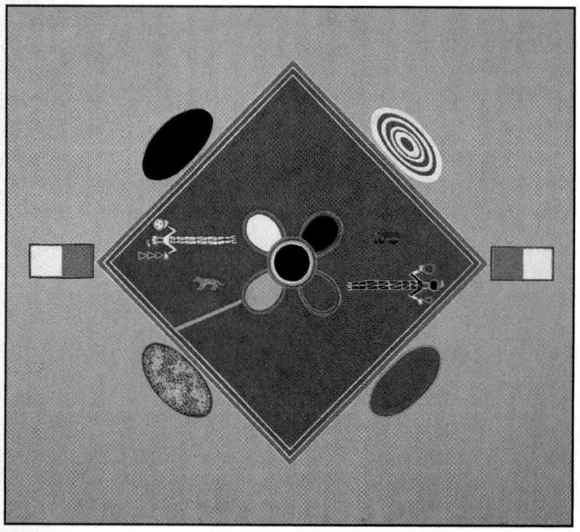

The Place of Emergence and the Four Worlds, 1938, Navajo, Wheelwright Museum of the American Indian

Humanities: Art

The Place of Emergence and the Four Worlds, 1938, by Pierre Woodman.

This painting captures the creation of the Earth Surface People by the Holy People, as described in the Blessingway chant. The square blue figure represents water. The human figures represent Changing Woman and House of White Shell Woman. The central black circle is the place of emergence. The Big Reed, with seven steps on it, leads to the border of the blue rectangle. Just north of this is the figure of a coyote. On the northeast side is a brown badger, whose feet are black because it stepped in mud as it emerged into the fourth world. The outside ovals represent mountains: San Francisco Peak to the southwest; Big Sheep Mountain to the northwest; Blanca Peak to the northeast; and to the southeast, Mount Taylor.

Use these questions for discussion:

1. How does the Navajo sacred number four appear in this work? *Responses include four mountains, four ovals around the place of emergence, four corners, two four-legged animals, four squares (two white, two blue).*
2. How does the artist use symmetry and asymmetry to convey the Navajo world view? *Students may say that symmetry implies a universe of order and purpose, but the asymmetrical staircase suggests the unknown parts of life that everyone must face.*

2 The gods laid one buckskin on the ground with the head to the west: on this they placed the two ears of corn, with their tips to the east, and over the corn they spread the other buckskin with its head to the east; under the white ear they put the feather of a white eagle, under the yellow ear the feather of a yellow eagle. Then they told the people to stand at a distance and allow the wind to enter. The white wind blew from the east, and the yellow wind blew from the west, between the skins. While the wind was blowing, eight of the Mirage People[2] came and walked around the objects on the ground four times, and as they walked the eagle feathers, whose tips protruded from between the buckskins, were seen to move. When the Mirage People had finished their walk the upper buckskin was lifted; the ears of corn had disappeared, a man and a woman lay there in their stead.

The white ear of corn had been changed into a man, the yellow ear into a woman. It was the wind that gave them life. It is the wind that comes out of our mouths now that gives us life. When this ceases to blow we die. In the skin at the tips of our fingers we see the trail of the wind; it shows us where the wind blew when our ancestors were created.

◆ Literary Focus Why might the Navajo have viewed the wind as the source of life? 3

The pair thus created were First Man and First Woman (Atsé Hastin and Atsé Estsán). The gods directed the people to build an enclosure of brushwood for the pair. When the enclosure was finished, First Man and First Woman entered it, and the gods said to them: "Live together now as husband and wife."

2. **Mirage People:** Mirages personified.

◆ Build Vocabulary

ablutions (ab lo͞o´ shənz) *n.*: Washing or cleansing the body as part of a religious rite

protruded (prō tro͞od´ id) *v.*: Jutted out

Guide for Responding

◆ Literature and Your Life

Reader's Response What words would you use to describe the images in these tales and the impression they made on you?

Thematic Focus What happens when the spirit and natural worlds meet?

Group Activity *The Navajo Origin Legend* describes a ritual performed by the gods and the Mirage People. What formal and informal rituals are part of our lives today? Consider social, religious, educational, and even sports-related rituals, such as tossing a coin to start a game. List suggestions on the chalkboard.

☑ Check Your Comprehension

1. According to the Modoc myth, how are the landscape and creatures of the Earth formed?
2. Summarize the Navajo creation ceremony.

◆ Critical Thinking

INTERPRET

1. (a) In the eyes of the Modoc Sky Spirit, what was the true crime of the grizzly bears? (b) What does his reaction reveal about him? **[Analyze]**
2. What is the meaning of the Modoc custom of marking the site where an Indian was killed by a grizzly? **[Interpret]**
3. Why do the Navajo associate the tips of the fingers with the trail of the wind? **[Interpret]**
4. Find evidence in the passage that suggests that four is a sacred number for the Navajo. **[Analyze]**

COMPARE LITERARY WORKS

5. In what ways do these tales differ from each other? **[Contrast]**

◆ Critical Thinking

1. (a) They created a new race without him. (b) Suggested response: It reveals that he was proud of his role as creator of the earth, and did not want anyone else to share his powers of creation.
2. Suggested response: It's a sign of respect or a tribute to both the Indian who lost his life and the spirit of their ancestor or "brother" grizzly bear.
3. The tips of the fingers have lines (fingerprints). The Navajos believe that these markings were made by the wind when it brought their ancestors to life.
4. Two of the most sacred acts in the passage—the call of the gods and the walk of the Mirage People—occur four times.
5. Students may note that, unlike the first two origin myths, the Navajo legend does not explain the formation of the Earth. While animals play a key role in bringing human life to Earth in the first two myths, vegetation (corn) is the key to life in the Navajo tale.

Customize for
Bodily/Kinesthetic and Visual/Spatial Learners

2 Help students clarify the action by suggesting that they act it out, make a storyboard, or construct a simple model that fits the description.

◆ Literary Focus

3 **Origin Myths** Students may respond that the wind is a major climatic force in the part of the country where the Navajo live, so they came to ascribe many powers to it. Also, since they know that to breathe means to be alive, they may compare wind to breath.

◆ Critical Thinking

Hypothesize The footnote refers to Yellow Body as the fourth Navajo god, yet he is not directly mentioned in this myth. Ask students how they might explain this apparent omission. *Students may say that it is Yellow Body who provides the life-giving wind.*

Reinforce and Extend

Answers

◆ Literature and Your Life

Reader's Response The impressions created by the works will vary from tale to tale and student to student.

Thematic Focus In these tales, new life or new creation results from the meeting of the two worlds.

☑ Check Your Comprehension

1. The Chief of the Sky Spirits pushes all of the snow and ice in the Above World down to Earth to form Mount Shasta, then descends the mountain, forming trees and rivers as he walks. Pieces of his walking stick become beaver, otter, and fish in the rivers, and larger pieces of his stick form the rest of the creature of the earth.
2. The spirit people cleanse and dry themselves, then call forth the four gods. Two appear carrying buckskin; two carry ears of corn. They place the corn on one buckskin, cover it with the other, then tuck eagle feathers under each ear of corn. As eight Mirage People circled the buckskins four times, the winds blew in from the east and west, transforming the ears into people.

One-Minute Insight The Iroquois Constitution tells how and why representatives of the Iroquois nations should hold formal councils to discuss and decide issues of concern to all. When Dekanawidah presented his *Kaianerekowa,* or Great Law of Peace, much of the world was beset by persecution, plague, and power struggles. His plan led to the most far-reaching and notable political unit north of the Aztec civilization. The sense of mutual respect, cooperation, and ritual it expressed served as a model for later European settlers who came to North America.

❶ **Clarification** Students may know the term *Confederate* as a proper noun for a rebellious secessionist of the American Civil War. Here, *confederate* is an adjective that broadly describes those united in alliance for a common goal.

▶Critical Viewing◀

❷ **Analyze** Students should note how the artist's portrayal of Red Jacket's serious, penetrating stare, defiant stance, face paint, and ceremonial objects—a tomahawk, a peace pipe, and a beaded belt—reflect the dignity and nobility of his subject.

◆ Literature and Your Life

❸ Have students respond to the ritual for opening the council by linking its elements to rituals they have experienced, whether religious, cultural, or social. Discuss the purpose of ritual and the impact it can have on the attitudes of a group.

◆ Reading Strategy

❹ **Recognize Cultural Details** Students may respond that the Iroquois show deep respect for their pantheistic religion, which worships the Earth and all its bounties by acknowledging the many spirits who provide all life.

from The Iroquois Constitution

Iroquois

Translated by Arthur C. Parker

Red Jacket, George Catlin, The Thomas Gilcrease Institute of American History and Art, Tulsa, Oklahoma

▲ **Critical Viewing** How does this portrait reflect a belief in the dignity and nobility of the Native Americans? **[Analyze]** ❷

❶ I am Dekanawidah and with the Five Nations[1] confederate lords I plant the Tree of the Great Peace. I name the tree the Tree of the Great Long Leaves. Under the shade of this Tree of the Great Peace we spread the soft white feathery down of the globe thistle as seats for you, Adodarhoh, and your cousin lords.

We place you upon those seats, spread soft with the feathery down of the globe thistle, there beneath the shade of the spreading branches of the Tree of Peace. There shall you sit and watch the council fire of the confederacy of the Five Nations, and all the affairs of the Five Nations shall be transacted at this place before you.

Roots have spread out from the Tree of the Great Peace, one to the north, one to the east, one to the south and one to the west. The name of these roots is the Great White Roots and their nature is peace and strength.

If any man or any nation outside the Five Nations shall obey the laws of the Great Peace and make known their disposition to the lords of the confederacy, they may trace the roots to the tree and if their minds are clean and they are obedient and promise to obey the wishes of the confederate council, they shall be welcomed to take shelter beneath the Tree of the Long Leaves.

We place at the top of the Tree of the Long Leaves an eagle who is able to see afar. If he sees in the distance any evil approaching or any danger threatening he will at once warn the people of the confederacy.

The smoke of the confederate council fire shall ever ascend and pierce the sky so that other nations who may be allies may see the council fire of the Great Peace . . .

Whenever the confederate lords shall assemble for the purpose of holding a council, the Onondaga lords shall open it by expressing their gratitude to their cousin lords and greeting them, and they shall make an address and offer thanks to the earth where men dwell, to the streams of water, the pools, the springs and the lakes, to the maize and the fruits, to the medicinal herbs and trees, to the forest trees for their usefulness, to the animals that serve as food and give their pelts for clothing, to the ❸ great winds and the lesser winds, to the thunderers, to the sun, the mighty warrior, to the moon, to the messengers of the Creator who reveal his wishes and to the Great Creator who dwells in the heavens above, who gives all the things useful to men, and who is the source and the ruler of health and life.

> **◆ Reading Strategy** What can you learn about the Iroquois culture from the items on this list? ❹

Then shall the Onondaga lords declare the council open . . .

1. **Five Nations:** The Mohawk, Oneida, Onondaga, Cayuga, and Seneca tribes. Together, these tribes formed the Iroquois Confederation.

Humanities: Art

Red Jacket by George Catlin.

George Catlin was born in Wilkes-Barre, Pennsylvania. To please his father, he practiced law until 1832, at which time he became intrigued by "the dignity and nobility of the Native Americans." It was then that Catlin decided to devote himself to art and to becoming a historian of Native Americans.

This Native American portrait depicts fiery Seneca orator Sagoyewatha, who reluctantly followed his people into an alliance with the British. He received a red coat from the British as a ritual gift. In this portrait he is not wearing the red coat that led to his English nickname, but he does wear a large medal given to him by George Washington after the American Revolution.

Use these questions for discussion:

1. What personality traits has the artist tried to capture in this portrait? *Suggested response: Strength, determination, and pride.*
2. How are these traits related to the values and ideas set forth in the Iroquois Constitution? *The Constitution said a leader needed wisdom, patience, and a sense of duty—all of which require the inner strength and determination captured in the portrait.*

All lords of the Five Nations' Confederacy must be honest in all things . . . It shall be a serious wrong for anyone to lead a lord into trivial affairs, for the people must ever hold their lords high in estimation out of respect to their honorable positions.

5 When a candidate lord is to be installed he shall furnish four strings of shells (or wampum)[2] one span in length bound together at one end. Such will constitute the evidence of his pledge to the confederate lords that he will live according to the constitution of the Great Peace and exercise justice in all affairs.

When the pledge is furnished the speaker of the council must hold the shell strings in his hand and address the opposite side of the council fire and he shall commence his address saying: "Now behold him. He has now become a confederate lord. See how splendid he looks." An address may then follow. At the end of it he shall send the bunch of shell strings to the opposite side and they shall be received as evidence of the pledge. Then shall the opposite side say:

6 "We now do crown you with the sacred emblem of the deer's antlers, the emblem of your lordship. You shall now become a mentor of the people of the Five Nations. The thickness of your skin shall be seven spans—which is to say that you shall be proof against anger, offensive actions and criticism. Your heart shall be filled with peace and good will and your mind filled with a yearning for the welfare of the people of the confederacy. With endless patience you shall carry out your duty and your firmness shall be tempered with tenderness for your people. Neither anger nor fury shall find lodgement in your mind and all your words and actions shall be marked with calm deliberation. In all of your deliberations in the confederate council, in your efforts at 6
law making, in all your official acts, self-interest shall be cast into oblivion. Cast not over your shoulder behind you the warnings of the nephews and nieces should they chide you for any error or wrong you may do, but return to the way of the Great Law which is just and right. Look and listen for the welfare of the whole people and have always in view not only the present but also the coming generations, even those whose faces are yet beneath the surface of the ground—the unborn of the future nation."

2. **wampum** (wäm´ pəm) *n.*: Small beads made of shells.

◆ Build Vocabulary

confederate (kən fed´ ər it) *adj.*: United with others for a common purpose

disposition (dis´ pə zish´ ən) *n.*: An inclination or tendency

deliberation (di lib´ ə rā´ shən) *n.*: Careful consideration

Guide for Responding

◆ Literature and Your Life

Reader's Response If you were the chief of a Native American nation, would this speech persuade you to join the confederation? Explain.

Thematic Focus How does Dekanawidah use images from nature in the Iroquois Constitution? What do these references tell you about the Iroquois?

☑ Check Your Comprehension

1. What three natural images does Dekanawidah use in association with the Great Peace?
2. Summarize the qualities and conduct required of council lords by the Iroquois Constitution.

◆ Critical Thinking

INTERPRET

1. The constitution tells the lords to "offer thanks to the earth where men dwell." What does this decree suggest about the Iroquois? **[Infer]**
2. What do you learn about Dekanawidah from the constitution he created? **[Infer]**

EVALUATE

3. Explain whether you believe a tree can effectively represent peace. **[Evaluate]**

APPLY

4. The constitution outlines Iroquois leadership qualities. What qualities do you think modern leaders should possess? Explain. **[Synthesize]**

Beyond the Selection

FURTHER READING

Other Origin Myths

"The Coming of Gluscabi" (Abenaki), retold by Michael J. Caduto and Joseph Bruchac

Pictographs from the Walam Olum (Delaware)

Beginnings: Earth, Sky, Life, Death by Sophia Lyon Fahs and Dorothy T. Spoerl

Other Works with the Theme of Origins

"The Origin of Fire," Ella E. Clark

"The Creation," James Weldon Johnson

We recommend that you preview these texts before recommending them to students.

INTERNET

The Internet provides excellent opportunities for students to learn more about Native Americans. We suggest the following site. Please be aware, however, that the site may have changed since this information was published.

To view a site with many links to cyber-resources on Native Americans, go to **http://encarta.msn.com/schoolhouse/nativeam/nativeam.asp**

We *strongly recommend* that you preview this and related sites before sending students to them.

5 Clarification The *span* is a unit of measure equal to the length from the tip of the thumb to the tip of the pinkie on an outstretched hand.

◆ Reading Strategy

6 Recognize Cultural Details Have students use this passage to determine the Iroquois view of the attributes a lord should possess. Ask them which of those attributes, if any, they observe in today's leaders. *Students may say that the Iroquois believe a lord should have the qualities of self-confidence and an ability to look toward the future.*

Reinforce and Extend

Answers

◆ Literature and Your Life

Reader's Response Students should support their response with clear reasoning.

Thematic Focus Dekanawidah uses the image of a tree, its leaves, and its roots to symbolize the peace he wishes to establish between the five nations. Clearly, the Iroquois deeply respect nature.

☑ Check Your Comprehension

1. He uses the image of the Tree of the Long Leaves which is strongly rooted and shelters those who seek peace, the eagle who can see afar and warn of danger, and the council fire whose smoke will be a visible reminder of the Great Peace.
2. They must be honest in all things, slow to anger, and full of peace, good will, and a desire for the welfare of their people. Their actions should always exhibit farsightedness, deliberation, and compassion.

◆ Critical Thinking

1. They respected their environment and were conscious of their dependence on the earth.
2. He had a great vision for his people. He saw the weaknesses of their society and hoped to overcome them by uniting the Native American people.
3. Suggested response: The tree is an effective image because it is familiar, memorable, and easily understandable for all the Iroquois.
4. Students may respond that leaders should be responsible, just, honest, unbiased, and farsighted.

Answers

◆ Reading Strategy

Suggested responses:

Onondaga ("The Earth on Turtle's Back"): The Onondaga are ruled by chiefs. They believe strongly in the power of dreams. Water and water animals like swans, ducks, beavers, loons, muskrats, and turtles are important to them.

Modoc ("When Grizzlies Walked Upright"): The Modoc are ruled by chiefs. They live in an environment of mountains, valleys, volcanoes, and rivers, and Mount Shasta is an important place to them. Animals such as birds, beaver, otter, fish, and especially grizzly bears are a big part of their lives. They live in lodges with holes in the roof to let out the smoke of their fires.

Navajo *(The Navajo Origin Legend)*: Corn, in the form of cornmeal and whole ears, is central to Navajo life. The wind is also very important. Eagles (for their feathers) and deer (for buckskin) are also special to the Navajo.

Iroquois *(The Iroquois Constitution)*: Natural symbols like trees and fire have great significance for the Iroquois culture. The Iroquois believe in peace, obedience, honesty, patience, and goodwill. The earth, water, all types of trees, plants, and medicinal herbs, animals that provide food and clothing, the winds, the sun, the moon, and the Great Creator "who is the source and the ruler of health and life" are the central elements in Iroquois life. Wampum are considered valuable.

◆ Literary Focus

1. "When Grizzlies Walked Upright" explains the creation of trees, rivers, beaver, otter, fish, birds, Mount Shasta and the paths down its side, volcanoes, and Little Mount Shasta. The tale also explains why grizzly bears walk on all fours and can't speak, why Modoc don't kill grizzlies, why they burn the body of anyone killed by a grizzly, and why Modoc mark the site of a grizzly victim's death with stones.
2. (a) The Sky Spirit's daughter and the grizzly bear; (b) The Sky Woman and the animals, particularly Muskrat and Turtle; (c) The four Navajo gods, the Mirage People, and the winds.

Guide for Responding *(continued)*

◆ Reading Strategy

Recognize Cultural Details

Cultural details—those that reflect aspects of daily life or prevalent attitudes—can provide insight into the culture behind the literature. Drawing on the details you noted while reading, write two or three sentences describing what each selection reveals about the culture that created it.

◆ Literary Focus

Origin Myths

Ears of corn transform into people. Immortal beings and mystical events like this are typical of **origin myths**—stories passed from generation to generation to explain the creation of the world and all it holds.

1. Describe the natural phenomena, customs, and creatures (other than humans) explained in "When Grizzlies Walked Upright."
2. List those who share in the process of bringing about human life on Earth in (a) "When Grizzlies Walked Upright," (b) "The Earth on Turtle's Back," and (c) *The Navajo Origin Legend.*

Beyond Literature

History Connection

The United States Constitution From the fourteenth-century Iroquois Constitution to the Pilgrim's 1620 Mayflower Compact to the 1787 United States Consti-tution, legal documents governing societies have flourished on North American soil.

In more than two centuries, the original United States Constitution has been amended only twenty-seven times. The first ten amendments, known as the Bill of Rights, outline the relationship of government and citizen rights.

Read a copy of the United States Constitution. In what ways is it similar to the Iroquois document? In what ways is it different?

◆ Build Vocabulary

Using the Latin Suffix *-tion*

Change each of the following verbs to a noun by adding the suffix *-tion*. Make any other necessary spelling changes (check a dictionary if you're not sure). Then use each new word in a sentence.

1. constitute: to set up in a legal form; establish
2. estimate: to form an opinion or judgment
3. dispose: to tend or incline

Using the Word Bank: Synonyms

For each grouping, write the letter of the word whose meaning does not match the other two:

1. (a) cleansings, (b) imaginings, (c) ablutions
2. (a) deliberation, (b) consideration, (c) commotion
3. (a) protruded, (b) dangled, (c) jutted
4. (a) disposition, (b) inclination, (c) assumption
5. (a) varied, (b) confederate, (c) united

◆ Grammar and Style

Compound Sentences

Closely related main clauses are often joined to form **compound sentences.** Each clause of a compound sentence contains its own subject and predicate and can stand alone as a complete thought.

A **compound sentence** has two or more main clauses linked by a coordinating conjunction—*and, or,* and *but*—or by a semicolon.

Writing Application On your paper, rewrite the following paragraph so that it contains at least three compound sentences. You may need to add or change some words. Then underline the subject and predicate in each clause.

Then the Beaver tried. He went deeper into the darkness. He could not reach the bottom. Next, the loon dove into the water. Even he could not reach the bottom. He floated back up. Then a voice spoke, "I will bring up Earth or die trying."

◆ Build Vocabulary

Using the Latin Suffix *-tion*

1. constitution: Sample response: The people's rights are spelled out in the constitution.
2. estimation: Sample response: The lords held Dekanawidah high in their estimation.
3. disposition: Sample response: Only those with a peaceful disposition could remain in the group.

Using the Word Bank

1. b 2. c 3. b 4. c 5. a

◆ Grammar and Style

Suggested response: Then the Beaver tried. He went even deeper into the darkness, but he could not reach the bottom, either. The Loon dove next, swimming deep into the water. Even his strong wings could not reach the bottom, and he floated back up. Then a small voice spoke. "I will bring up Earth, or I will die trying."

Grammar Reinforcement

For additional instruction and practice, use the practice page (p. 43) in the *Writer's Solution Grammar Practice Book.*

Reteach

To reteach this section, use ***Strategies for Diverse Student Needs*** booklet, p. 2.

Build Your Portfolio

Idea Bank

Writing

1. New Ending According to "The Earth on Turtle's Back," Muskrat was responsible for creating the "new Earth." Draft a new ending for the myth that includes an explanation of how the Sky Spirits reward her.

2. Origin Myth Write a myth that explains the origin of a local natural landmark, such as a nearby lake, valley, or cliff.

3. Essay The Iroquois Constitution had to hold the listener's attention. In an essay, analyze how this document uses imagery and phrasing to create a memorable impression.

Speaking, Listening, and Viewing

4. Native American Chant Locate information about and recordings of Native American chants. Then present a brief oral report on Native American music and play a chant for your class. **[Music Link]**

5. Dramatic Enactment Enact a council meeting at which a new Iroquois lord is to be installed. Create the roles of the Onondaga lords, the candidate lord, the speaker of the council, and the gathering of council lords. Perform the scene for your class. **[Performing Arts Link]**

Researching and Representing

6. Totem Pole Research the Native American practice of carving vertical logs decorated with images. On a totem you research or create, identify each image on the totem with a label and caption explaining its significance.

7. Logo Using the images contained in the Iroquois Constitution for inspiration, design a logo representing the Iroquois Confederation. **[Art Link]**

Online Activity www.phlit.phschool.com

Guided Writing Lesson

Retelling of a Myth

Myths are oral forms of communication, repeated over the years by storytellers, all of whom added something of their own to the retelling. Select a myth with which you're familiar and retell it to a friend. Keep the structure and sequence of events, but rewrite the tale to appeal to your audience. For example, you might update the setting.

Writing Skills Focus: Effective Repetition

Effective repetition—the practice of repeating actions, phrases, or words to produce a desired effect—can make an oral tale more memorable and create drama and heighten suspense.

Repetition of the boldfaced and italicized words in this passage from "The Earth on Turtle's Back" creates both rhythm and drama.

Model From the Story

[Muskrat] dove down and **swam and swam**. *She was not as strong* or as swift as the others, but *she was determined*. She went so **deep** that it was all dark, and **still she swam deeper**.

As you formulate your retelling, look for ways to use repetition to captivate your audience.

Prewriting Create a rough plot outline based on what you remember about the myth. Then make a list of elements of the myth that you will retain and elements that you will adapt.

Drafting Following your plot outline, create a rough draft. Look for places where you can use repetition to create drama and establish rhythm.

Revising Read your tale aloud and decide whether it is dramatic and memorable. Does your use of repetition succeed in creating the sound you hoped for? Polish your writing to get the effect you want.

Idea Bank

Customizing for *Performance Levels*

Following are suggestions for matching Idea Bank topics with your students' performance levels:
Less Advanced Students: 1, 7
Average Students: 2, 5, 6
More Advanced Students: 3, 4

Customizing for *Learning Modalities*

Following are suggestions for matching Idea Bank topics with your students' learning modalities:
Musical/Rhythmic: 4
Bodily/Kinesthetic: 5
Visual/Spatial: 6, 7

Guided Writing Lesson

Refer students to the Writing Handbook, p. 1192, for instruction on the writing process, and page 1196 for further information on Response to Literature.

Writing and Language Transparencies Use the Story Map Transparency, p. 99, to help students organize their retelling of a myth.

Writing Lab CD-ROM

Have students complete the tutorial on Response to Literature. Follow these steps:

1. Direct students to the Audio-annotated Literary Model of a retelling of a literary work in the About Response to Literature section.
2. Have students draft on computer.
3. Use the Revision Checker for language variety to highlight repeated words and phrases so that students can check for effective use of repetition.

✓ ASSESSMENT OPTIONS

Formal Assessment, Selection Test, pp. 4–6, and Assessment Resources Software. The selection test is designed so that it can be easily customized to the performance levels of your students.

Alternative Assessment, p. 2, includes options for less advanced students, more advanced students, musical/rhythmic learners, interpersonal learners, and verbal/linguistic learners.

PORTFOLIO ASSESSMENT

Use the following rubrics in the ***Alternative Assessment*** booklet to assess student writing:
New Ending: Fictional Narrative Rubric, p. 110
Origin Myth: Fictional Narrative Rubric, p. 110
Essay: Literary Analysis/Interpretation Rubric, p. 127
Guided Writing Lesson: Fictional Narrative Rubric, p. 110

Prepare and Engage

LESSON OBJECTIVES

1. **To develop vocabulary and word identification skills**
   - Latin Word Roots: *-mort-*
   - Using the Word Bank: Sentence Completions
2. **To use a variety of reading strategies to comprehend an exploration narrative**
   - Connect Your Experience
   - Reading Strategy: Signal Words
   - Tips to Guide Reading
3. **To increase knowledge of other cultures and to connect common elements across cultures**
   - Connecting Themes Across Cultures (ATE)
4. **To express and support responses to the text**
   - Critical Thinking
   - Idea Bank: Journal Entry
   - Idea Bank: Creative Description
5. **To analyze literary elements**
   - Literary Focus
   - Idea Bank: Comparison-and Contrast Essay
6. **To read in order to research self-selected and assigned topics**
   - Idea Bank: "America the Beautiful" Presentation
   - Idea Bank: Television Series
7. **To plan, prepare, organize, and present literary interpretations**
   - Idea Bank: Persuasive Speech
   - Idea Bank: Southwest Guide
8. **To use recursive writing processes to write an explorer's journal**
   - Guided Writing Lesson: Explorer's Journal
9. **To increase knowledge of the rules of grammar and usage**
   - Grammar and Style: Past Tenses of Verbs

Test Preparation

Reading Comprehension: Stated Main Idea (ATE, p. 33)
The teaching tips and sample test item in this workshop support the instruction and practice in the unit workshop:
Reading Comprehension: Summarizing Written Texts (SE p. 115)

Guide for Interpreting

Alvar Núñez Cabeza de Vaca

(1490?–1557?)

In 1528, Pánfilo de Narváez and 400 Spanish soldiers landed near Tampa Bay and set out to explore Florida's west coast. Alvar Núñez Cabeza de Vaca (äl´ bär nōōn´ yes kä bä´ sä dā bä´ kä) was second in command. Beset by illness and the prospect of starvation, Narváez and his men set sail for Mexico in five flimsy boats. He and most of the men drowned. Cabeza de Vaca and a party of about sixty reached the Texas shore.

Only fifteen of the group lived through the winter. In the end, Cabeza de Vaca and three others survived. They were captured by Indians and spent the next several years as captives. Cabeza de Vaca gained a reputation as a medicine man and trader. The four Spaniards finally escaped and wandered for eighteen months across the Texas plains. In 1536, the survivors finally reached Mexico City.

Cabeza de Vaca's adventures and his reports on the richness of Texas sparked exploration of the region. In this passage, he speaks of Estevanico, the first African to set foot in Texas.

García López de Cárdenas

(c. 1540)

García López de Cárdenas (gär sē´ ä lō´ pes dä kär´ dā näs) is best remembered as the first European to visit the Grand Canyon. As a leader of Francisco Vásquez de Coronado's expedition to New Mexico (1540–1542), Cárdenas was dispatched from Cibola (Zuni) in western New Mexico to see a river that the Moqui Native Americans of northeastern Arizona had described to one of Coronado's captains. The river was the Colorado. López de Cárdenas departed on August 25, 1540, and reached the Grand Canyon after a westward jaunt of about twenty days. He became the first explorer to view the canyon and its river, which from the vantage of the canyon's rim they believed to be a stream merely six feet across! Unable to descend to the river, they brought back descriptions that attempted to record the magnitude of the great sight.

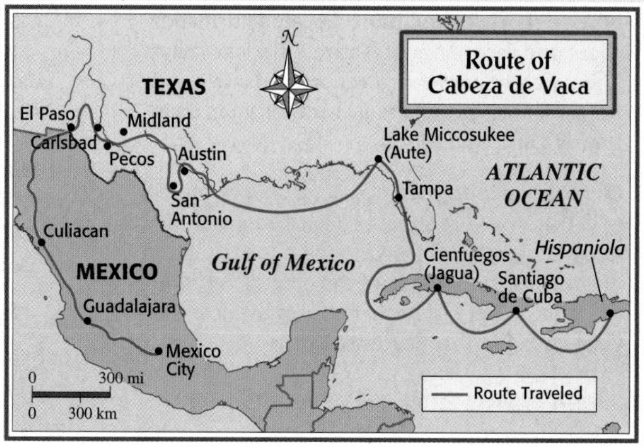

◆ Background for Understanding

HISTORY: EXPEDITIONS IN THE SOUTHWEST

In March of 1536, Cabeza de Vaca and the three remaining members of his party stumbled out of the desert and into history as the first Europeans to have crossed North America from Florida to Mexico. The party of Spaniards who came across a raving, half-naked white man (Cabeza de Vaca) on Mexico's northern frontier did not at first understand who he was. Once Cabeza de Vaca told his tale, however, the Spanish viceroy ordered that it be recorded.

Cabeza de Vaca's account gave rise to rumors of cities of great wealth north of the Rio Grande. In response, conquistador Francisco Vásquez de Coronado, in 1540, led a two-year expedition to what is now New Mexico.

Prentice Hall Literature Program Resources

REINFORCE / RETEACH / EXTEND

Selection Support Pages
Build Vocabulary: Word Roots: *-mort-*, p. 10
Grammar and Style: Verb Tenses, p. 11
Reading Strategy: Signal Words, p. 12
Literary Focus: Exploration Narrative, p. 13

Strategies for Diverse Student Needs, p. 3

Beyond Literature
Career Connection: Travel Guide, p. 3

Formal Assessment Selection Test, pp. 7–9; Assessment Resources Software

Alternative Assessment, p. 3

Writing and Language Transparencies
Descriptive and Observational Writing, pp. 9–12

Resources Pro CD-ROM

Listening to Literature Audiocassettes

◆ A Journey Through Texas ◆
Boulders Taller Than the Great Tower of Seville

◆ Literature and Your Life

CONNECT YOUR EXPERIENCE

If you ever traveled to a new place, the first thing you probably did upon your return was tell your friends what you saw. Just imagine the tales you would have told if, like the authors of these two selections, you were among the first Europeans to travel the southwestern region of North America and meet the native inhabitants.

THEMATIC FOCUS: MEETING OF CULTURES

Often people have difficulty appreciating a culture radically different from their own. How do the Spaniards respond to the native inhabitants of the Southwest?

Journal Writing Write about the knowledge you gained from meeting someone from a different culture.

◆ Literary Focus

EXPLORATION NARRATIVE

The European men who trail-blazed the Americas recounted their experiences in **exploration narratives**—firsthand accounts that tell the story of their experiences. The purpose of these accounts was to provide information to the people back home in Europe, so the explorers were careful to record in detail what they observed during their travels. Exploration narratives generally are factual, although the viewpoints expressed in them are sometimes distinctly personal. The writers often described the difficulties and discoveries of their explorations to impress others and perhaps to inspire readers to follow in their footsteps.

◆ Grammar and Style

PAST AND PAST PERFECT VERB TENSES

The **past tense** shows an action or condition that began and ended at a given time in the past. The **past perfect tense** shows a past action or condition that ended before another past action began. Verbs in the past perfect consist of *had*, followed by the past participle. Look at these examples:

After five days they had not returned [past perfect] and the Indians explained [past] that it might be because they had not found [past perfect] anybody.

◆ Reading Strategy

SIGNAL WORDS

When you read a detailed narrative account, it's easy to lose track of the order of events. One way to avoid having this happen, however, is to pay close attention to **signal words**—words that point out relationships among ideas and events. Often signal words show time relationships. They can also indicate level of importance, cause-and-effect relationships, or contrasts. Look at these examples:

Words signaling

time: *After five days*, they had not *yet* returned.

contrast: . . . *although* this was the warm season, no one could live in this canyon because of the cold.

◆ Build Vocabulary

LATIN WORD ROOTS: *-mort-*

The word *mortality* has as its root the Latin *-mort-*, meaning "death." You may already know the word *mortal*, a term commonly used to distinguish humans, who are subject to death, from the *immortal* gods of mythology.

WORD BANK

Before you read, preview this list of words from the narratives.

entreated
feigned
mortality
subsisted
traversed
dispatched

Test Preparation Workshop

Reading Comprehension: Stated Main Idea Some standardized tests require students to identify stated main ideas in reading passages. Use the following sample test question to help students practice identifying a stated main idea.

Cabeza de Vaca's exploration was beset by danger. Five flimsy boats sank, causing many of the crew to drown. Some survivors of that ordeal didn't make it through a harsh winter. In the end, only four men survived.

What is the main idea of this passage?

A Five boats sank.
B A severe winter killed many of the crew.
C Cabeza deVaca was brave.
D Cabeza deVaca's exploration met with danger.

Choices *A* and *B* contain details found in the passage, but they do not convey the central idea. Choice *C* is not supported by the paragraph. *D* is the correct answer, because it expresses the general idea of the passage.

Interest Grabber Tell students: Imagine what it would be like to find yourself among people whose language and customs were unknown to you. How would it feel to be a "stranger in a strange land" for years with no hope of returning to familiar customs? On whom could you depend for help? Point out that Cabeza de Vaca and his followers spent eight years in just such a situation. Direct students to keep thinking about how they might have acted in similar circumstances.

Connecting Themes Across Cultures

Ask students to recall a time when they visited an unusual place or met a group of people whose ideas, behavior, customs, and/or traditions were quite different from their own. Invite students to describe their reactions to the circumstance and to evaluate how the experience broadened their understanding. Remind students of the different ethnic neighborhoods within the United States.

Customize for
Less Proficient Readers

Guide students to break lengthy sentences into shorter ones, paraphrasing as needed. Have them practice on this sentence:

> "In truth, we were very much concerned about it, for, seeing the great mortality, we dreaded that all of them might die or forsake us in their terror, while those further on, upon learning of it, would get out of our way hereafter."

Customize for
AP Students

Guide these students to keep in mind the chronicler's purpose as they read. Have them consider that the narrator knows that he's making history. Have students evaluate how this knowledge might affect the narrator's way of recording events and his bias in interpreting events and results.

Customize for
English Language Learners

These narratives contain archaic syntax and unfamiliar language. Guide students to work with native speakers to help them paraphrase these sentences to ease comprehension.

Develop Understanding

One-Minute Insight Cabeza de Vaca was a Spanish adventurer whose views and beliefs were dramatically altered as a result of his extraordinary experiences living with Native Americans. This narrative describes his journey into what is now Texas as he and his followers attempted to reach the Spanish settlements in Mexico City. Cabeza de Vaca reluctantly came to understand something about the people whose land he traveled through. His perspective differs considerably from that of Narváez and the other conquistadors, whose goal was to plunder the local resources and forcibly convert the Native Americans to Catholicism.

Literature CD-ROM To build background, use the CD-ROM *The History of American Literature:* Part 1, Disk 1, Feature 2, which discusses the European explorers' written accounts of their discoveries.

◆ Background for Understanding

History Between 1492 and 1540, exploration and expansion fever spread through western Europe. By the time Cabeza de Vaca landed in Texas, the Spanish had gained a solid foothold in the Caribbean basin and in Mexico. Ponce de León had explored the coasts of what is now Florida, Verrazano had been up the Atlantic coast all the way to Newfoundland, and Magellan's ships had made it around South America and across the Pacific Ocean. Failure was no deterrent to the European kings and queens as voyage followed voyage. No European explorer before Cabeza de Vaca had as yet ventured inland in North America.

▶Critical Viewing◀

1 Speculate Students should note that the landscape appears to be hot, sunny, and very dry. Such terrain would probably supply little food or water, and travelers might easily starve, dehydrate, or suffer heatstroke.

A Journey Through Texas

Alvar Núñez Cabeza de Vaca

1 ▲ **Critical Viewing** How would a landscape like this one pose difficulty for the expeditions that explored it? **[Speculate]**

Alvar Núñez Cabeza de Vaca and his three countrymen wandered for months through Texas as they journeyed toward the Spanish settlement in Mexico City. In the course of his travels, Cabeza de Vaca healed a Native American by performing the first recorded surgery in Texas. His resulting fame attracted so many followers that Cabeza de Vaca noted in his journal, "the number of our companions became so large that we could no longer control them." As they continued traveling westward, the group was well received by the Native Americans they encountered.

The same Indians led us to a plain beyond the chain of mountains, where people came to meet us from a long distance. By those we were treated in the same manner as before, and they made so many presents to the Indians who came with us that, unable to carry all, they left half of it. . . . We told these people our route was towards sunset, and they replied that in that direction people lived very far away. So we ordered them to send there and inform the inhabitants that we were coming and how. From this they begged to be excused, because the others were their enemies, and they did not want us to go to them. Yet they did not venture to disobey in the end,

Block Scheduling Strategies

Consider these suggestions to take advantage of extended class time:

- Have students complete the journal activity in Literature and Your Life (p. 33) and discuss their entries in small groups.
- Use the Viewing and Representing Mini-Lesson in the teacher edition (p. 38) to help students complete the Southwest Guide activity in the Speaking, Listening, and Viewing section of the Idea Bank (p. 41). Allow time for students to work in small groups to develop appropriate questions and answers. You may wish to have students videotape their interviews, then have the class view and critique each interview.
- Encourage students to research these explorers or their historical narratives on the Internet either before or after they read.
- Have students complete the Guided Writing Lesson (p. 41). Before they get started have a class discussion on the importance of including precise details when writing an explorer's journal.

and sent two women, one of their own and the other a captive. They selected women because these can trade everywhere, even if there be war.

We followed the women to a place where it ❷ had been agreed we should wait for them. After five days they had not yet returned, and the Indians explained that it might be because they had not found anybody. So we told them to take us north, and they repeated that there were no people, except very far away, and neither food nor water. Nevertheless we insisted, saying that we wanted to go there, and they still excused themselves as best they could, until at last we became angry.

❸ One night I went away to sleep out in the ❹ field apart from them; but they soon came to where I was, and remained awake all night in great alarm, talking to me, saying how frightened they were. They entreated us not to be angry any longer, because, even if it was their death, they would take us where we chose. We feigned to be angry still, so as to keep them in suspense, and then a singular[1] thing happened.

On that same day many fell sick, and on the next day eight of them died! All over the country, where it was known, they became so afraid that it seemed as if the mere sight of us would kill them. They besought[2] us not to be angry nor to procure the death of any more of their number, for they were convinced that we killed ❺ them by merely thinking of it. In truth, we were very much concerned about it, for, seeing the great mortality, we dreaded that all of them might die or forsake us in their terror, while those further on, upon learning of it, would get out of our way hereafter. We prayed to God our Lord to assist us, and the sick began to get well. Then we saw something that astonished us very much, and it was that, while the parents, brothers and wives of the dead had shown deep grief at their illness, from the moment they died the survivors made no demonstration whatsoever, and showed not the slightest feeling; nor did they dare to go near the bodies until we ordered their burial. . . .

The sick being on the way of recovery, when we had been there already three days, the women whom we had sent out returned, saying that they had met very few people, nearly all having gone after the cows, as it was the season. So we ordered those who had been sick to remain, and those who were well to accompany us, and that, two days' travel from there, the same women should go with us and get people to come to meet us on the trail for our reception.

The next morning all those who were strong enough came along, and at the end of three journeys we halted. Alonso del Castillo and Estevanico,[3] the negro, left with the women as guides, and the woman who was a captive took them to a river that flows between mountains, where there was a village, in which her father lived, and these were the first abodes we saw that were like unto real houses. Castillo and Estevanico went to these and, after holding parley[4] with the Indians, at the end of three days Castillo returned to where he had left us, bringing with him five or six of the Indians. He told how he had found permanent houses, inhabited, the people of which ate beans and squashes, and that he had also seen maize.

Of all things upon earth this caused us the greatest pleasure, and we gave endless thanks to our Lord for this news. Castillo also said that the negro was coming to meet us on the way, near by, with all the people of the houses. For that reason we started, and after going a league and a half met the negro and the people that came to receive us, who gave us beans and many squashes to eat, gourds to carry water in, robes of cowhide, and other things. As those people and the Indians of our company were enemies, and did not understand each other, we took leave of the latter, leaving them all that had been given to us, while we went on with the former and, six leagues beyond, when night was already approaching, reached their houses, where they received us with great ceremonies. Here we remained one day, and left on the next, taking them with us to other permanent

1. **singular:** Strange.
2. **besought:** (bē sôt´) Pleaded with.

3. **Estevanico** (es´ tä vä nē´ kō): Of Moorish extraction, Estevanico was the first African man to set foot in Texas.
4. **holding parley** (pär´ lē): Conferring.

◆ Build Vocabulary

entreated (en trēt´ id) *v.*: Begged; pleaded

feigned (fānd) *v.*: Pretended; faked

mortality (môr tal´ ə tē) *n.*: Death on a large scale, as from disease or war

◆ Grammar and Style

❷ Past and Past Perfect Verb Tenses Guide students to understand the use of the past perfect tense in this sentence. Help them see that the agreement as to where they were to wait occurred *before* Cabeza de Vaca and the women traveled to the place.

◆ Critical Thinking

❸ Make Inferences Ask students to describe the character of the Spanish explorers as shown by the way they interacted with their accommodating hosts. *Students may call the Spaniards single-minded, uncompromising, and manipulative.*

◆ Reading Strategy

❹ Signal Words Alert students to the many signal words in these sentences, such as *nevertheless, but, because,* and *then.* Discuss the relationship each signals and how each contributes to the unity and coherence of the passage.

❺ Clarification Discuss with students how the Europeans brought more than new customs and religious beliefs to the Native Americans they encountered; they brought diseases as well, including some for which the Native Americans had no natural immunity.

Tips to Guide Reading

Silent Reading Suggest that students read "A Journey Through Texas" silently, monitoring their understanding of the order of events in the narrative. Have students look for signal words that show time relationships and cause-and-effect relationships.

Beyond the Classroom

Career Connection

Cultural Anthropologist In "A Journey Through Texas," Cabeza de Vaca describes the experience of living within a culture utterly different from his own. Cultural anthropologists observe peoples of the world in their own habitats. They record all aspects of their daily routines and how they live: what they eat and drink, how they dress, how they treat the young and elderly, how they get along with neighbors and outsiders, what they value and believe, what ceremonies and rituals they practice, and so on. Students interested in the field of cultural anthropology can visit a natural history museum or university and talk with anthropologists there. They can also read about the groundbreaking work of Margaret Mead, Sylvia Ashton-Warner, and others.

Community Connection

Local Life Have students imagine that a cultural anthropologist from another culture is visiting your community. Challenge them to prepare a description of features of public and private life that would help that visitor better understand life in your community. Students in pairs or groups can brainstorm for a list of key categories they can use to prepare their descriptions.

◆ Literary Focus

❶ **Exploration Narrative** How does this passage exemplify a portion of an exploration narrative? *Students should respond that Cabeza de Vaca provides a clear picture for readers of how these Native Americans acted and how they dressed. They can note that he also expresses his personal reactions to their abilities and qualities, as well as to the treatment he received from them.*

◆ Critical Thinking

❷ **Hypothesize** Ask students to explain how Cabeza de Vaca and his hosts were able to share all this information, given the language barrier. *Some students may point out that, by now, Cabeza de Vaca had been among different Indian groups for several years, and that he would probably have picked up bits and pieces of several languages.*

▶Critical Viewing◀

❸ **Infer** Students may respond that the Native Americans seem respectful or even slightly in awe of the Spaniards. They bring their sick to the Spaniards, then give them room to work their healing.

▶Critical Viewing◀

❹ **Analyze** Students may say that the picture shows Cabeza de Vaca as a serious and thoughtful man, who carried himself with dignity.

Humanities: Art

Painting of Cabeza de Vaca, Esteban, and their companions by Tom Mirrat.

This work portrays the encounter between the Spanish explorer and his men and the sick Indians, as described in Cabeza de Vaca's journal. Use these questions for discussion:

1. How can you tell the Spaniards from the Indians? *Students may say that the Spaniards are the ones with beards. Three Spaniards kneel beside sick Indians, and Esteban is the African man standing to the left.*
2. What are the people doing? *Students may say that the Spaniards are praying over the victims or offering sympathy or comfort, while the frightened and worried Indians, whose own healing practices have failed them, stand aside, curiously looking on.*

houses, where they subsisted on the same food also, and thence on we found a new custom.

❶ The people who heard of our approach did not, as before, come out to meet us on the way, but we found them at their homes, and they had other houses ready for us. . . . There was nothing they would not give us. They are the best formed people we have seen, the liveliest and most capable; who best understood us and answered our questions. We called them "of the cows," because most of the cows die near there, and because for more than fifty leagues up that stream they go to kill many of them. Those people go completely naked, after the manner of the first we met. The women are covered with deerskins, also some men, especially the old ones, who are of no use any more in war.

❷ The country is well settled. We asked them why they did not raise maize, and they replied that they were afraid of losing the crops, since for two successive years it had not rained, and the seasons were so dry that the moles had eaten the corn, so that they did not dare to plant any more until it should have rained very hard. And they also begged us to ask Heaven for rain, which we promised to do. We also wanted to know from where they brought their maize, and they said it came from where the sun sets, and that it was found all over that country, and the shortest way to it was in that direction. We asked them to tell us how to go, as they did not want to go themselves, to tell us about the way.

They said we should travel up the river towards the north, on which trail for seventeen days we would not find a thing to eat, except a fruit called *chacan*, which they grind between stones; but even then it cannot be eaten, being so coarse and dry; and so it was, for they showed it to us and we could not eat it. But they also said that, going upstream, we could always travel among people who were their enemies, although speaking the

▲ **Critical Viewing** This stamp was issued in Spain to commemorate the four-hundredth anniversary of the discovery of Florida. What does the portrait suggest about Cabeza de Vaca's character? **[Analyze]** ❹

❸ ▼ **Critical Viewing** What does this painting suggest about the relationship between Cabeza de Vaca and the Native Americans? Why? **[Infer]**

Painting of Cabeza de Vaca, Esteban, and their companions among various Texas Indian tribes, Tom Mirrat, The Institute of Texan Cultures, San Antonio, Texas

Viewing and Representing Mini-Lesson

This mini-lesson supports the "America the Beautiful" Presentation on p. 41.

Introduce the Concept Tell students that they will create a multimedia presentation on the beauty of some aspect of our country's landscape. Remind students to use a variety of resources, including almanacs, encyclopedias, photographic texts, periodicals, the Internet, and audio and video recordings.

Develop Background Have students generate a list of national parks, memorable sites, and spectacular regions of the country to research. In small groups, have students collect information on the region of their choice.

Apply the Information Tell students to review their research material to determine if it's complete. Help groups divide the tasks involved in the presentation: assembling photographs or a video, choosing music, or writing the narrative.

Assess the Outcome Assess students' work on their ability to choose appropriate and relevant materials, to combine a variety of media, and to make a logical, coherent presentation.

same language, and who could give us no food, but would receive us very willingly, and give us many cotton blankets, hides and other things; but that it seemed to them that we ought not to take that road.

In doubt as to what should be done, and which was the best and most advantageous road to take, we remained with them for two days. They gave us beans, squashes, and calabashes.[5] Their way of cooking them is so new and strange that I felt like describing it here, in order to show how different and queer are the devices and industries of human beings. They have no pots. In order to cook their food they fill a middle-sized gourd with water, and place into a fire such stones as easily become heated, and when they are hot to scorch they take them out with wooden tongs, thrusting them into the water of the gourd, until it boils. As soon as it boils they put into it what they want to cook, always taking out the stones as they cool off and throwing in hot ones to keep the water steadily boiling. This is their way of cooking.

> ◆ Literary Focus
> 5 Why does the author include these cooking customs in his exploration narrative?

6 After two days were past we determined to go in search of maize, and not to follow the road to the cows, since the latter carried us to the north, which meant a very great circuit, as we held it always certain that by going towards sunset we should reach the goal of our wishes.

So we went on our way and traversed the whole country to the South Sea,[6] and our resolution was not shaken by the fear of great starvation, which the Indians said we should suffer (and indeed suffered) during the first seventeen days of travel. All along the river, and in the course of these seventeen days we received plenty of cowhides, and did not eat of their famous fruit (*chacan*), but our food consisted (for each day) of a handful of deer-tallow, which for 6 that purpose we always sought to keep, and so 7 endured these seventeen days, at the end of which we crossed the river and marched for seventeen days more. At sunset, on a plain between very high mountains, we met people who, for one-third of the year, eat but powdered straw, and as we went by just at that time, had to eat it also, until, at the end of that journey we found some permanent houses, with plenty of harvested maize, of which and of its meal they gave us great quantities, also squashes and beans, and blankets of cotton. . . .

5. **calabashes** (kal′ ə bash′ əz) *n.*: Dried, hollow shells of gourds used to hold food or beverages.

6. **the South Sea:** The Gulf of Mexico.

◆ Build Vocabulary

subsisted (səb sist′ id) *v.*: Remained alive; were sustained

traversed (trə vurst′) *v.*: Moved over, across, or through

Guide for Responding

◆ Literature and Your Life

Reader's Response Would you find the many stops in the journey through Texas to be frustrating or fascinating? Explain your answer.

Thematic Focus How might Cabeza de Vaca's experiences with Native American cultures have changed him as a person?

☑ Check Your Comprehension

1. Why do the Spaniards order the Native Americans to travel with them?
2. Why do the Spaniards become fearful when Native Americans in their company die?

◆ Critical Thinking

INTERPRET

1. Why do the Native Americans obey the orders of the Spaniards? **[Infer]**
2. (a) What do the Native Americans believe was the cause of the sickness that struck them on the journey? (b) What are some of the more likely explanations for the illness? **[Draw Conclusions]**

EXTEND

3. Do you think the Native Americans would have extended a warm welcome to Cabeza de Vaca if he had been the hundredth Spaniard to journey through their lands? Explain. **[Social Studies Link]**

◆ Literary Focus

5 Exploration Narrative
Responses should include that any detailed information about how the Native Americans performed everyday tasks helped to create a thorough and new description of their culture and civilization, potentially illuminating readers back in Europe.

Customize for
Visual/Spatial Learners
6 Some students may benefit from and enjoy referring back to the map on p. 32 in the Guide for Interpreting, as well as to a modern-day map of the region. They can use the map(s) to orient themselves and may even attempt to follow Cabeza's route from Cuba all the way to Mexico City.

Customize for
Logical/Mathematical Learners
7 Logical/mathematical learners may wish to estimate the explorers' walking speed to figure out about how far they actually traveled during the portion of their journey described in this passage.

Reinforce and Extend

Answers

◆ Literature and Your Life

Reader's Response Some students may say that they would be frustrated by any delays in reaching the Spanish settlement. Other students might respond that they would be fascinated by the encounters with new cultures.

Thematic Focus Sample response: He may have learned to understand and appreciate cultures other than his own.

☑ Check Your Comprehension

1. They wanted them to serve as guides.
2. They were afraid that the Native Americans would flee in terror and leave them stranded, and that other Native Americans would then avoid them.

◆ Critical Thinking

1. Suggested response: The Native Americans may have been afraid of the Spaniards.
2. (a) The Native Americans thought the Spaniards had the power to wish fatal illnesses on them. (b) The illnesses may have stemmed from a disease or virus, or from weakness due to lack of food or rest.
3. Suggested response: They probably would not have welcomed him as warmly because the novelty of greeting a visitor from another land would have begun to wear off, and the Native Americans might also have come to resent the Spaniards as trespassers on their lands.

One-Minute Insight By the time of Coronado's expedition in 1540, the Spanish knew there was gold and silver in the Americas. Although Coronado's search for the Seven Cities of Cibola led only to impoverished villages in today's New Mexico, the group he dispatched northward led to European discovery of the Grand Canyon. García López de Cárdenas, with the help of Hopi guides from nearby mesas, became the first European to see this natural wonder. Unable to find water or cross the canyon, Cárdenas eventually left in frustration.

◆ Background for Understanding

❶ History Students may be interested to know that Don Pedro de Tovar's name remains alive today in the form of El Tovar, the rustic but majestic 1905 guest lodge that is perched on the south rim of the Grand Canyon.

Within the park boundaries, there are about 2,000 sites once inhabited by the Anasazi—the name given to the Native American peoples who lived in settlements throughout the plateau country of the Southwest. Tusayán pueblo, constructed in 1185 and once occupied by about thirty people, is the most impressive of these. By the time Cárdenas arrived, the Anasazi were gone and the canyon rim was inhabited by the Navajo, who came from the northwest in about 1400.

◆ Critical Thinking

❷ Hypothesize Ask students to estimate how far the expedition traveled in the twenty days from Tusayán to the settlements. Have them explain their reasoning. *Students can guess that since the twenty days of traveling was over rough terrain and the men were laden with supplies, their hiking speed is not likely to have been much more than 10 miles per day, and that the trip was perhaps about 150–200 miles.*

❸ Clarification Although the Spaniards found no trail from the canyon rim to the river, there are four trails that hikers can take today: Bright Angel, South Kaibab, Hermit, and Grandview.

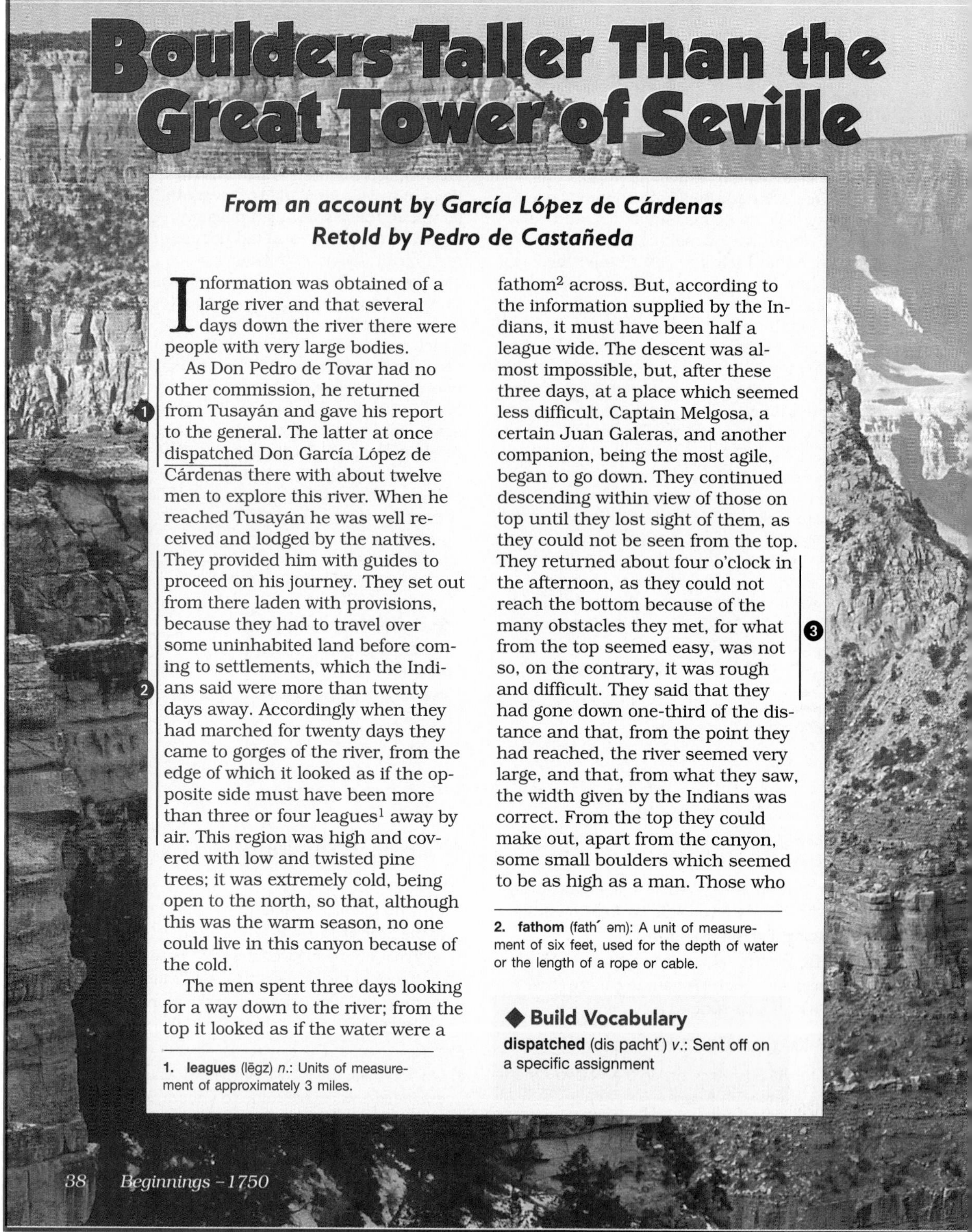

Boulders Taller Than the Great Tower of Seville

From an account by García López de Cárdenas
Retold by Pedro de Castañeda

Information was obtained of a large river and that several days down the river there were people with very large bodies.

As Don Pedro de Tovar had no other commission, he returned [1] from Tusayán and gave his report to the general. The latter at once dispatched Don García López de Cárdenas there with about twelve men to explore this river. When he reached Tusayán he was well received and lodged by the natives. They provided him with guides to proceed on his journey. They set out from there laden with provisions, because they had to travel over some uninhabited land before coming to settlements, which the Indians [2] said were more than twenty days away. Accordingly when they had marched for twenty days they came to gorges of the river, from the edge of which it looked as if the opposite side must have been more than three or four leagues[1] away by air. This region was high and covered with low and twisted pine trees; it was extremely cold, being open to the north, so that, although this was the warm season, no one could live in this canyon because of the cold.

The men spent three days looking for a way down to the river; from the top it looked as if the water were a fathom[2] across. But, according to the information supplied by the Indians, it must have been half a league wide. The descent was almost impossible, but, after these three days, at a place which seemed less difficult, Captain Melgosa, a certain Juan Galeras, and another companion, being the most agile, began to go down. They continued descending within view of those on top until they lost sight of them, as they could not be seen from the top. They returned about four o'clock in the afternoon, as they could not reach the bottom because of the many obstacles they met, for what from the top seemed easy, was not [3] so, on the contrary, it was rough and difficult. They said that they had gone down one-third of the distance and that, from the point they had reached, the river seemed very large, and that, from what they saw, the width given by the Indians was correct. From the top they could make out, apart from the canyon, some small boulders which seemed to be as high as a man. Those who

1. **leagues** (lēgz) *n.*: Units of measurement of approximately 3 miles.

2. **fathom** (fath´ əm): A unit of measurement of six feet, used for the depth of water or the length of a rope or cable.

◆ Build Vocabulary

dispatched (dis pacht´) *v.*: Sent off on a specific assignment

Viewing and Representing Mini-Lesson

This mini-lesson supports the Southwest Guide activity in the Idea Bank on p. 41.

Introduce the Concept Review the purpose of "survival" guides. Remind students that these manuals give information to travelers about the dangers of traveling through a region. You may choose to brainstorm for a list of survival tips for something more contemporary—surviving life at a mall or surviving American literature.

Develop Background To understand what the southwestern landscape was like before the growth of large cities, encourage students to search for old photographs and fine art of the region from earlier periods in American history.

Apply the Information Have students draw conclusions about southwestern climate and vegetation. Suggest that they consult an atlas to help them. Remind students to include information on changes in seasons, different elevations, food, clothing, tools, and medicines.

Assess the Outcome Assess students' ability to make sound inferences about the climate and vegetation, on the completeness of their guide, and its relevance to the 1500's.

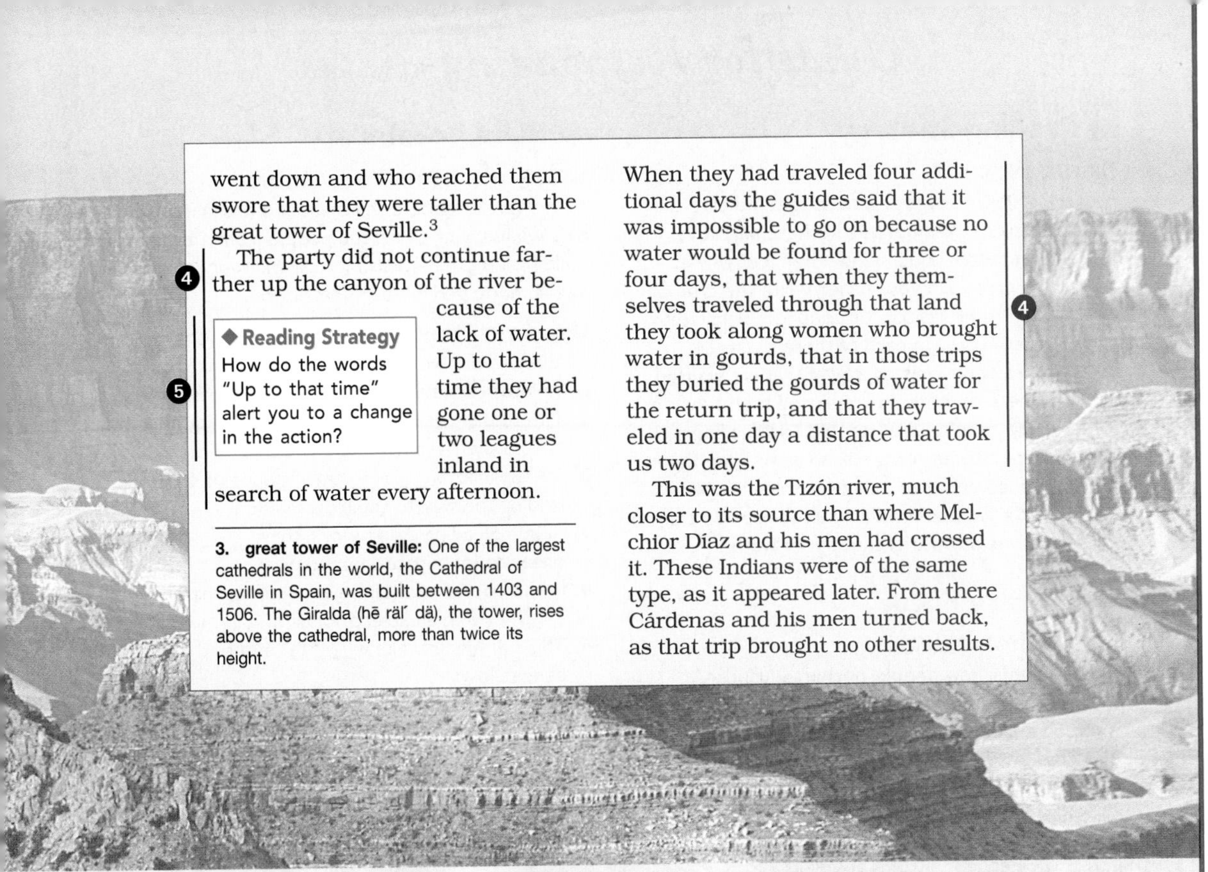

went down and who reached them swore that they were taller than the great tower of Seville.[3]

4 The party did not continue farther up the canyon of the river because of the lack of water. Up to that time they had gone one or two leagues inland in search of water every afternoon.

5 **◆ Reading Strategy**
How do the words "Up to that time" alert you to a change in the action?

When they had traveled four additional days the guides said that it was impossible to go on because no water would be found for three or four days, that when they themselves traveled through that land they took along women who brought water in gourds, that in those trips they buried the gourds of water for the return trip, and that they traveled in one day a distance that took us two days. 4

This was the Tizón river, much closer to its source than where Melchior Díaz and his men had crossed it. These Indians were of the same type, as it appeared later. From there Cárdenas and his men turned back, as that trip brought no other results.

3. **great tower of Seville:** One of the largest cathedrals in the world, the Cathedral of Seville in Spain, was built between 1403 and 1506. The Giralda (hē räl′ dä), the tower, rises above the cathedral, more than twice its height.

Guide for Responding

◆ *Literature and Your Life*

Reader's Response How does this description compare with your knowledge of the Grand Canyon?

Thematic Focus How does the help provided by Native Americans make it possible for the explorers to experience the wonders of the Grand Canyon?

☑ Check Your Comprehension

1. What factual details do you learn about the canyon from this account?
2. What two factors prevent the group from finding their way down to the river?

◆ Critical Thinking

INTERPRET

1. How do the author's experiences with the rough terrain affect which details he chooses to include in this account? **[Analyze]**

APPLY

2. The explorers are searching for a river. How does their mission affect the way they perceive the Grand Canyon? Explain your answer. **[Apply]**

EXTEND

3. How might this account have been different if it had been written to secure future funding? **[Social Studies Link]**

◆ Critical Thinking

4 Speculate Ask students to think about and discuss why a lack of water can influence the decisions that explorers and settlers make.

◆ Reading Strategy

5 Signal Words Students should respond that "up to that time" signals a change in the course of the journey.

Reinforce and Extend

Answers

◆ *Literature and Your Life*

Reader's Response Students who have never visited the canyon may be surprised that the Spaniards were unable to descend.

Thematic Focus The natives provide guides and provisions for the journey to the canyon.

☑ Check Your Comprehension

1. A wide canyon is in the middle of a desert; it is so deep that men climbing down the precipices cannot always be seen from the top; the river at the base of the canyon is approximately half a league wide.
2. First, the land was rough and difficult to cross. Second, the lack of water prevented them from going any further up the canyon.

◆ Critical Thinking

1. Because the author has experienced the challenges presented by travel in such rough terrain, he includes details about distances, terrain, water supply, and other factors that affect survival.
2. Since the explorers' goal is to investigate the river at the bottom of the canyon, they are frustrated by the steep canyon walls and water shortage that curtail their explorations. They are too preoccupied with the physical difficulties of their quest to record their reaction to the beauty.
3. The account might contain detailed descriptions of the canyon's impressive size and beauty in order to convince financial backers that exploration of the canyon could potentially bring them fame, glory, and riches.

Beyond the Selection

FURTHER READING

Other Works by the Authors

"Relación," Alvar Núñez Cabeza de Vaca [other portions of the explorer's narrative]

The Narrative of the Expedition of Coronado, Pedro de Castañeda [the account from which the selection is taken]

Related Works

The Odyssey of Cabeza de Vaca, Morris Bishop

Wilderness at Dawn, Ted Morgan

INTERNET

The Internet provides excellent opportunities for students to learn more about the conquistadors. We suggest the following site. Please be aware, however, that the site may have changed since we published this information:

http://www.utmb.edu/galveston/history/devaca.html

We *strongly recommend* that you preview this site before sending students to it.

Answers

◆ Reading Strategy

1. contrast; time
2. reason; time
3. reason

◆ Literary Focus

1. The awe-inspiring height of the great tower would have been well known among López de Cárdenas's contemporaries.
2. Suggested response: Cabeza de Vaca probably wanted to share the harrowing experiences and many new discoveries he made while living among people and landscapes unlike any known to his fellow Spaniards. López de Cárdenas may have felt a certain amount of pride at having discovered a place so awe-inspiring that his country's greatest landmark was dwarfed by comparison.
3. The land of Cabeza de Vaca's narrative is filled with friendly natives, but is basically barren and hostile. López de Cárdenas describes a land of gargantuan proportions and natural wonders unlike any he's seen before.
4. While both writers seem to find the Natives Americans friendly and cooperative, neither appears to consider them as equals. Cabeza de Vaca, however, interacts freely with the Native Americans and describes their diets, customs, and practices in greater detail than López de Cárdenas, who does not record his reactions to his Native American guides.
5. Suggested responses include: Ponce de León explored the land he named Florida. Cortés came upon the lower peninsula of California. Lewis and Clark explored westward from the Louisiana territory to the Oregon territory.

◆ Build Vocabulary

Using the Latin Root *-mort-*
Sample response: The body of the firefighter, who had been *mortally* injured in the blaze, was carried to the *mortuary* so that the *mortician* could prepare it for burial. The mayor, who delivered the eulogy at the funeral, said that the brave man would be *immortalized* in the hearts and minds of his fellow citizens.

Using the Word Bank
1. dispatched; 2. entreated; 3. feigned; 4. traversed; 5. subsisted; 6. mortality

Guide for Responding *(continued)*

◆ Reading Strategy

SIGNAL WORDS

Staying alert to **signal words** that indicate the relationships between events in these narratives helped you better understand when and why actions took place. On your paper, write the type of relationship (time, reason, or contrast) signaled by the italicized words in each of these passages:

1. *Nevertheless* we insisted, saying that we wanted to go there, and they still excused themselves as best they could, *until* at last we became angry.
2. We feigned to be angry still, *so as* to keep them in suspense, and *then* a singular thing happened.
3. The party did not continue farther up the canyon of the river *because* of the lack of water.

◆ Literary Focus

EXPLORATION NARRATIVE

New sights, new people, uncharted lands—these are the basic ingredients of **exploration narratives** like those of Cabeza de Vaca and López de Cárdenas. These narratives recount the experiences of the first Europeans to set foot in unexplored regions of North America.

Though it may have been years or even centuries before their work was published (the account of the Coronado expedition wasn't printed until 1896), these narratives offer readers insight into these explorers' achievements.

1. Why do the men who descend into the Grand Canyon use the image of the great tower of Seville to convey the size of the boulders they see?
2. What do you think motivated each explorer to record the things he saw?
3. What impression of the Americas does each writer convey?
4. Compare and contrast the two writers' reactions to the Native Americans they encounter in their explorations.
5. Both writers documented territories previously unknown to the Spaniards. What other searches have led to settlement of specific areas of what is now the United States?

◆ Build Vocabulary

USING THE LATIN ROOT *-mort-*

In your notebook, write about a firefighter who dies while trying to rescue people from a burning building. Use the words *mortally, mortuary, mortician,* and *immortalized* in your description.

USING THE WORD BANK: Sentence Completions

Choose the word from the Word Bank that best completes each of the following sentences.

1. The soldier was __?__ by the expedition leader to find the river they had heard so much about.
2. The Spaniards __?__ their guides to continue leading the way to their destination.
3. When pleading didn't work, they __?__ anger in order to intimidate their guides.
4. In the course of their seventeen-day march, they __?__ a barren stretch of land.
5. The starving travelers __?__ on mouthfuls of deer tallow.
6. The conquistadors were alarmed by the __?__ that befell the natives.

◆ Grammar and Style

PAST TENSES OF VERBS

The **past tense** of a verb shows an action that began and ended at a given time in the past. The **past perfect tense** indicates an action that ended before another past action began. It is formed with the helping verb *had* and the past participle of the verb.

Practice In your notebook, write the tense of the italicized verb.

1. We *followed* the women to a place where it *had been agreed* we should wait for them.
2. Many *fell* sick.
3. On the next day eight of them *died*!
4. They *had gone* down one third of the distance.
5. Until then, they *had gone* one or two leagues inland in search of water.

Writing Application Write a description of an activity you recently completed that you'd worked on for some time. Use both the past and past perfect tenses.

◆ Grammar and Style

Practice
1. past; past perfect
2. past
3. past
4. past perfect
5. past perfect

Writing Application
Students' descriptions should make proper use of both past and past perfect tenses in order to show the time relationship between the various steps or processes involved in the activity.

Grammar Reinforcement

For additional instruction and practice, use the lesson on Using Verbs and the practice pages on verb tense (pp. 54–57) in the *Writer's Solution Grammar Practice Book.*

Reteach

To reteach the selection, use ***Strategies for Diverse Student Needs,*** p. 3.

Build Your Portfolio

Idea Bank

Writing

1. **Journal Entry** After years of wanderings in the wilderness, what would you feel upon finally gaining sight of a town? In a journal entry, describe the experience of rejoining "civilization."
2. **Creative Description** Select an awe-inspiring natural wonder such as Niagara Falls or a towering mountain. Write a description conveying its majesty to someone who has never seen it.
3. **Comparison-and-Contrast Essay** Each writer had a unique purpose for relating his experiences. In an essay, compare and contrast the circumstances and attitudes revealed in each account.

Speaking, Listening, and Viewing

4. **Persuasive Speech** As a member of the small party that explored the Grand Canyon with López de Cárdenas, give a speech to convince the general that the view of the canyon is well worth a trip by the entire Coronado expedition.
5. **Southwest Guide** Look at pictures of the Southwest. From the pictures, make inferences about the climate and vegetation of the area. Then compile a survival guide for sixteenth-century travelers to this region. **[Media Link]**

Researching and Representing

6. **"America the Beautiful" Presentation** Create a multimedia presentation using photographs or videos that capture the beauty of our country's varied terrain. Set the presentation to music, and provide narration. **[Media Link]**
7. **Television Series** Create a concept for a television series rooted in exploration. Describe the premise of the series, along with its setting and characters. **[Media Link]**

Online Activity www.phlit.phschool.com

Guided Writing Lesson

Explorer's Journal

Imagine that like Cabeza de Vaca and López de Cárdenas, you have begun to explore a territory where no one has gone before. Write a journal that details what you discover. Be as descriptive as possible so that others may follow in your footsteps.

Writing Skills Focus: Precise Details

To make your explorer's journal useful to others who may want to study your experiences, use **precise details** in your account. For example, instead of vaguely reporting that the trees flowered in a *variety of bright hues*, identify the colors by name.

To introduce readers to a completely unfamiliar fruit, notice how Cabeza de Vaca uses specific details:

Model From the Journal

. . . except a fruit called chacan, which they grind between stones; but even then it cannot be eaten, being so coarse and dry . . .

This factual—almost scientific—description would be more informative than an empty notation that called the fruit "strangely exotic."

Prewriting First, choose the location that you will explore. It can be a place you've visited or one you've only read about or seen on television. Gather details to include in your journal. If you've never been to the place, you'll need to do some research.

Drafting Limit your journal entry to a specific day or moment. Focus on a few objects to describe in full. Keep in mind that you're writing for an audience unfamiliar with these objects.

Revising Ask a partner to read your first draft and comment on the level of detail you provide. If your reader can't "see" an item you've described, add more information to flesh out the image.

ASSESSMENT OPTIONS

Formal Assessment, Selection Test, pp. 7–9, and Assessment Resources Software. The selection test is designed so that it can be easily customized to the performance levels of your students.

Alternative Assessment, p. 3, includes options for less advanced students, more advanced students, verbal/linguistic learners, bodily/kinesthetic learners, and visual/spatial learners.

PORTFOLIO ASSESSMENT
Use the following rubrics in the ***Alternative Assessment*** booklet to assess student writing:
Journal Entry: Expression Rubric, p. 109
Creative Description: Description Rubric, p. 112
Comparison-and-Contrast Essay: Comparison/Contrast Rubric, p. 118
Guided Writing Lesson: Description Rubric, p. 112

Idea Bank

Customizing for *Performance Levels*
Following are suggestions for matching Idea Bank topics with your students' performance levels:
Less Advanced Students: 1, 4
Average Students: 2, 5, 7
More Advanced Students: 3, 6

Customizing for *Learning Modalities*
Following are suggestions for matching Idea Bank topics with your students' learning modalities:
Verbal/Linguistic: 4, 7
Interpersonal: 5
Visual/Spatial: 6
Logical/Mathematical: 4

Guided Writing Lesson

Writing and Language Transparencies Use the transparencies on Descriptive and Observational Writing, pp. 9–12, to model descriptive writing.

Writers at Work Videodisc
Have students view the videodisc segment (Ch. 1) featuring author Rita Dove to learn how she gathers details for descriptive writing. Have students discuss what Dove means when she refers to details that "will recreate a world."

Play frames 335 to 10985

Writing Lab CD-ROM
Have students complete the tutorial on Description. Follow these steps:
1. Use the Sensory Details Word Bins and Interactive Writing Model to help students gather details for their explorer's journals.
2. Have students draft on computer.
3. Revise using the Revision Checker for vague or overused adjectives to help students sharpen their descriptive details.

Prepare and Engage

LESSON OBJECTIVES

1. To develop vocabulary and word identification skills
- Latin Word Roots: *-vid-*
- Using the Word Bank: Synonym or Antonym?
- Extending Word Study (ATE)

2. To use a variety of reading strategies to comprehend an autobiography
- Connect Your Experience
- Reading Strategy: Summarize

3. To express and support responses to the text
- Critical Thinking
- Idea Bank: Activist List
- Idea Bank: Editorial
- Idea Bank: Character Sketch
- Idea Bank: Movie Poster
- Analyze a Movie Review

4. To analyze literary elements
- Literary Focus: Slave Narrative

5. To read in order to research self-selected and assigned topics
- Idea Bank: Internet Research

6. To plan, prepare, organize, and present literary interpretations
- Idea Bank: Debate
- Idea Bank: Antislavery Speech
- Speaking, Listening and Viewing Mini-lesson

7. To use recursive writing processes to write a museum placard
- Guided Writing Lesson

8. To increase knowledge of the rules of grammar and usage
- Grammar and Style: Active and Passive Voice

Test Preparation

Reading Comprehension: Summarizing Written Texts (ATE, p. 43)
The teaching tips and sample test item in this workshop support the instruction and practice in the unit workshop:

Reading Comprehension: Summarizing Written Texts (SE, p. 115)

Guide for Interpreting

Olaudah Equiano *(1745–1797)*

When published in 1789, the autobiography of Olaudah Equiano (ō lä o͞o´ dä ek´ wē än´ ō) created a sensation.

The Interesting Narrative ***made society face the cruelties of slavery and contributed to the banning of the slave trade in both the United States and England.***

The son of a tribal elder in the powerful kingdom of Benin, Equiano might have followed in his father's footsteps had he not been sold into slavery. When Equiano was eleven years old, he and his sister were kidnapped from their home in West Africa and sold to British slave traders. Separated from his sister, Equiano was taken first to the West Indies, then to Virginia, where he was purchased by a British captain and employed at sea.

Saving to Buy Liberty Renamed Gustavus Vassa, Equiano was enslaved for nearly ten years. After managing his Philadelphia master's finances and making his own money in the process, Equiano amassed enough to buy his freedom. In later years, he settled in England and devoted himself to the abolition of slavery. To publicize the plight of slaves, he wrote his two-volume autobiography, *The Interesting Narrative.* Although Equiano's writing raised concern about the less than humane conditions inherent in slavery, the slave trade in the United States was not abolished by law until 1808, nearly twenty years after its publication.

◆ Background for Understanding

History: The Slave Trade

The slave trade Equiano describes was in full operation during the colonization of the Western Hemisphere. While many people came to the new world in search of wealth or riches, many others were brought against their will.

Between 1500 and 1800, about 15 million Africans were captured and shipped to the Western Hemisphere. As Equiano attests, the conditions of the Atlantic crossing, known as "the middle passage," were atrocious. For six to ten weeks, Africans were crammed below deck in spaces sometimes less than five feet high. Families were torn apart; men and women placed in separate holds. During the voyage, men were often shackled together in pairs. Overcrowding, disease, and despair claimed many lives. Some Africans mutinied, and others tried to starve themselves or jump overboard. Historians estimate that nearly 2 million slaves died before reaching their destination. This map shows the most common routes of the middle passage.

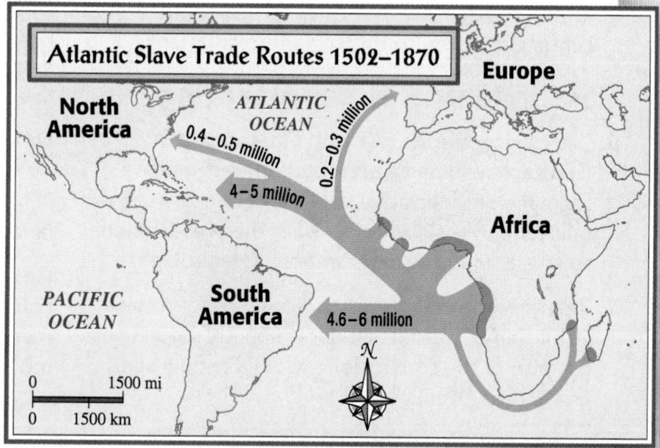

Prentice Hall Literature Program Resources

REINFORCE / RETEACH / EXTEND

Selection Support Pages
Build Vocabulary: Word Roots: *-vid-*, p. 14
Grammar and Style: Active and Passive Voice, p. 15
Reading Strategy: Summarize, p. 16
Literary Focus: Slave Narratives, p. 17

Strategies for Diverse Student Needs, p. 4

Beyond Literature Media Connection: Film Portrayals of the Slave Trade, p. 4

Formal Assessment Selection Test, pp. 10–12; Assessment Resources Software

Alternative Assessment, p. 4

Resource Pro CD-ROM

Literature CD-ROM

Listening to Literature Audiocassettes

from The Interesting Narrative of the Life of Olaudah Equiano

◆ *Literature and Your Life*

Connect Your Experience

Imagine knowing that members of your community were valuable merchandise and that your family could be shipped away to a distant land to perform forced labor! Living in a world where slavery existed, you might develop a new attitude about the sweetness of freedom and the value of life.

Journal Writing How would you feel if you were sent to another country against your will? Jot down your thoughts.

Thematic Focus: Meeting of Cultures

European traditions and ideas often came into conflict with Native American customs. However, these were not the only cultures clashing on this continent. Equiano, an African brought against his will, represents another culture to be absorbed into the American scene.

◆ Literary Focus

Slave Narratives

Equiano's account of the middle passage is an early example of a slave narrative. A uniquely American literary genre, a **slave narrative** is an autobiographical account of life as a slave. Often written to expose the horrors of human bondage, it documents a slave's experiences from his or her own point of view.

Encouraged by abolitionists, many freed or escaped slaves published narratives in the years before the Civil War.

◆ Grammar and Style

Active and Passive Voice

A verb is in the **active voice** when the subject of the sentence performs the action. A verb is in the **passive voice** when the action is performed on the subject. When the performer of an action is not known or is not important, the writer uses the passive voice.

Active Voice: . . . they tossed the remaining fish into the sea . . .
(The subject, *they*, performs the action of the verb *tossed*.)

Passive Voice: This situation was aggravated by the galling of the chains . . .
(The subject *situation* receives the action of the verb.)
What is the effect of Equiano's use of the passive voice?

◆ Reading Strategy

Summarize

As you read material published in another time period or written in an unfamiliar style, it is often helpful to summarize the main points. When you **summarize,** you state briefly in your own words the main ideas and supporting details of the text. You might pause to summarize each page, each event, or even each paragraph. For example, you might summarize Equiano's first paragraph in this way:

> The slaves were kept below deck in tight confinement. The conditions were unbearable. People were chained in pairs and disease ran rampant. Many died. Equiano himself, although allowed to stay on deck, often wished to die.

◆ Build Vocabulary

Latin Word Roots: *-vid-*

Equiano calls his captors *improvident*. The root *-vid-*, which comes from the Latin *videre*, means "to see." The word *provident* means "to have foresight." *Improvident* describes someone who lacks foresight.

Word Bank

Before you read, preview this list of words from the selection.

- loathsome
- pestilential
- copious
- improvident
- avarice
- pacify

Interest Grabber Students are probably familiar with common expressions using the term *slave,* which inadvertently trivialize the true horrors of slavery. It's likely that many have used some like these: "slave over homework," "slave to fashion," or "cyber-slave." But have students ever really thought about what it meant to be a slave, forcibly captured and transported like cargo in the hold of ship? To help students begin to appreciate such an experience, and to give them a sense of the graphic descriptions in the account they're about to read, have a student volunteer read aloud the first five or six sentences describing the conditions in which Africans were kept as they were transported into slavery. Then, before having students read the rest of the account, allow a few minutes for students to share their reactions to what they just heard. Had they been aware that conditions were so harsh on slave ships?

Customize for
Less Proficient Readers
To help these students through the archaic vocabulary and syntax in this slave narrative, encourage them to focus on one sentence at a time, make sure they understand it, then read on.

Customize for
AP Students
Guide these students to notice the evenhanded approach Equiano takes to his subject. They can appreciate that the narrative is realistic, descriptive, and poignant, that it makes its points vividly without exaggeration or embellishment. Ask them to consider how the narrative might have been received by European readers in 1789.

Customize for
English Language Learners
Students learning English may have difficulty understanding the many lengthy sentences Equiano wrote in the passive voice. Model how to break them into shorter sentences and to rephrase them in the active voice to facilitate comprehension. Suggest that these students work together in pairs to apply this strategy as they read.

Test Preparation Workshop

Reading Comprehension: Summarizing Written Texts: Implied Main Idea When the main idea is not directly stated, students must infer the main focus of the passage. Some standardized tests require students to identify the implied main idea of a reading passage. Have students reread pp. 44–45. Then have them choose the **implied main idea** of the first paragraph from the following responses.

A Most slaves were kept in the hold below the deck.
B Death seemed better than life to slaves on the African slave ships.
C Slave ships from Africa were filthy, overcrowded and cruelly managed, which caused many slaves to sicken and die.
D Equiano wrote a journal about life on an African slave ship.

Choice *A* is a supporting detail and choices *B* and *D* present background information. *C* contains the implied main idea.

Develop Understanding

One-Minute Insight Like Harriet Beecher Stowe's *Uncle Tom's Cabin,* which appeared in 1853, Equiano's work had a significant effect on the institution of slavery. Stowe's explosive bestseller, by exposing the cruelty of slavery, helped to ignite the Civil War and end slavery in America. Similarly, Equiano's narrative revealed the horrors of the slave trade and contributed to its demise. Unlike *Uncle Tom's Cabin,* which was a novel, *The Interesting Narrative* was a first-hand account of an actual event. Its strength is in its readability. Equiano clearly communicates the horrors of slavery without hyperbole or histrionics. In this excerpt, the matter-of-fact descriptions of life aboard a slave ship speak for themselves.

Customize for ***Visual/Spatial and Bodily/Kinesthetic Learners***
To get a hint of the desperately crowded and deadly conditions on a slave ship, students can recall the experience of being packed like sardines on a rush-hour subway or bus or of being stuck in a huge immobile crowd trying to leave or enter a concert or sporting event.

❶ **Clarification** Point out that Equiano and others were months in transit prior to boarding the ship, and that they then spent several weeks on board before setting sail. Tell students that adult captives were chained together at the ankles and wrists and that the shackles were removed only when one of the pair became very sick or died. You may wish to explain that "necessary tubs" were crude buckets or troughs used communally as toilets.

from

The Interesting Narrative of the Life of Olaudah Equiano

Olaudah Equiano

In the first several chapters, Equiano describes how he and his sister were kidnapped from their home in West Africa by slave traders and transported to the African coast. During this six- or seven-month journey, Equiano was separated from his sister and held at a series of way stations. After reaching the coast, Equiano was shipped with other slaves to this continent. The following account describes this horrifying journey.

At last when the ship we were in, had got in all her cargo, they made ready with many fearful noises, and we were all put under deck, so that we could not see how they managed the vessel. But this disappointment was the least of my sorrow. The stench of the hold while we were on the coast was so intolerably loathsome, that it was dangerous to remain there for any time, and some of us had been permitted to stay on the deck for the fresh air; but now that the whole ship's cargo were confined together, it became absolutely pestilential. ❶ The closeness of the place, and the heat of the climate, added to the number in the ship, which was so crowded that each had scarcely room to turn himself, almost suffocated us. This produced copious perspirations, so that the air soon became unfit for respiration, from a variety of loathsome smells, and brought on a sickness among the slaves, of which many died—thus falling victims to the improvident avarice, as I may call it, of their purchasers. This wretched situation was again aggravated by the galling of the chains, now become insupportable, and the

◆ Build Vocabulary

loathsome (lōth´ səm) *adj.*: Hateful; detestable

pestilential (pes´ tə len´ shəl) *adj.*: Likely to cause disease

copious (kō´ pē əs) *adj.*: Plentiful; abundant

improvident (im präv´ ə dənt) *adj.*: Shortsighted; failing to provide for the future

avarice (av´ ər is) *n.*: Greed for riches

Block Scheduling Strategies

Consider these suggestions to take advantage of extended class time:

- Have students complete the journal activity in Literature and Your Life (p. 43) and discuss their entries in small groups.
- Introduce the Reading Strategy by demonstrating how summarizing as they read can help students clarify the main points of a passage. For practice, assign the Reading Strategy page on summarizing, p. 16, in ***Selection Support,*** either before or after students have read the selection.
- Have students listen to all or part of the selection on audiocassette. Hold a class discussion about the effect of hearing the selection. Did the account seem more vivid when it was spoken aloud as though Equiano was describing the scene for them?
- Encourage students to spend some time researching on the Internet either before or after reading the selection. Students can research the slave trade and the middle passage, or they can use the Internet to complete the Internet Research project in the Idea Bank on p. 49.
- Have students complete the Guided Writing Lesson (p. 49). Before students begin, have a class discussion on using transitional words to clarify the sequence of events. You may also wish to use the **Writers at Work Videodisc** or **Writing Lab CD-ROM** to help students complete their writing assignments.

Slaves Below Deck (detail), Lt. Francis Meynell, National Maritime Museum, Greenwich

2 ▲ **Critical Viewing** The artist portrays conditions on a slave ship. Compare and contrast this image with the one that Equiano describes. **[Compare and Contrast]**

1 filth of the necessary tubs, into which the children often fell, and were almost suffocated. The shrieks of the women, and the groans of the dying, rendered the whole a scene of horror almost inconceivable. Happily perhaps, for myself, I was soon reduced so low here that it was thought necessary to keep me almost always on deck; and from my extreme youth I was not put in fetters.[1] In this situation I expected every hour to share the fate of my companions, some of whom were almost daily brought upon deck at the point of death, which I began to hope would soon put an end to my miseries. Often did I think many of the inhabitants of the deep much more happy than myself. I envied them the freedom they enjoyed, and as often wished I could change my condition for theirs. Every circumstance I met with, served only to render my state more painful, and heightened my apprehensions, and my opinion of the cruelty of the whites.

3 ◆ **Reading Strategy**
Summarize the conditions on the ship.

4

One day they had taken a number of fishes; and when they had killed and satisfied themselves with as many as they thought fit, to our astonishment who were on deck, rather than give any of them to us to eat, as we expected, they tossed the remaining fish into the sea again, although we begged and prayed for some as well as we could, but in vain; and some of my countrymen, being pressed by hunger, took an opportunity, when they thought no one saw them, of trying to get a little privately; but they were discovered, and the attempt procured them some very severe floggings. One day, when we had a smooth sea and moderate wind, two of my wearied countrymen who were chained together

1. **fetters** (fet′ ərz) *n.*: Chains.

▶Critical Viewing◀

2 Compare and Contrast Students may respond that life on the slave ship depicted in the painting does not accurately reflect the one Equiano described. In contrast to the thoroughly horrifying experience he recounts, the image presented in the picture is one of a seemingly content group of captives, unchained and chatting among themselves in a relatively uncrowded space.

◆ Reading Strategy

3 Summarize Students should respond that the stench and heat were suffocating, the rubbing of the chains was unbearable, and people shrieked and moaned in misery and pain.

◆ Literary Focus

4 Slave Narratives In this sentence, Equiano could be referring either to the fish or to those who had died or had jumped overboard. Ask students to respond to this ambiguity.

Humanities: Art

Slaves Below Deck (detail) by Lt. Francis Meynell.

This picture depicts a scene aboard a Spanish slaveship on its way to the West Indies. Here we see the slaves crammed into the dark, airless hull.

Ask students to consider whether the artist or Equiano best captures the horror of the voyage. Students should explain their answers. *Students may respond that Equiano's description seems more horrible than the scene portrayed in the painting. They may defend or explain their answer by pointing out that the written account details the stench, the pain of the shackles, and the mistreatment the slaves endured—none of which are clearly communicated by the painting.*

Analyze a Movie Review

In making the movie *Amistad,* Steven Spielberg took up the challenge of recreating the conditions on board a slave ship much like the one Equiano describes. Spielberg made every effort to capture the ugliness of the passage across the Atlantic.

One reviewer said that the "harrowing Middle Passage scenes will not be forgotten by anyone who sees Spielberg's movie: the horrors of the slave trade have rarely been captured in such indelible, painful images."

While Spielberg's true story was set in the middle of the 19th century and Equiano's memoir recounts a crossing made nearly a century earlier, students can use Equiano's narrative to test the movie's general faithfulness to the history of the slave trade. Have them answer the following questions:

1. Does the movie present a generally accurate portrayal of conditions on board a slaver?
2. Were any elements of Equiano's account left out of the movie?

▶Critical Viewing◀

❶ **Draw Conclusions** Students' estimates will vary, and may be obtained by estimating the number of slaves per row and then multiplying by the number of rows. Although it is impossible for students to know what the artist thought of slavery, they can surmise from the overcrowding that the ship's captain, owner, designer, or builder had little regard for its cargo.

◆ Critical Thinking

❷ **Synthesize** Stopping a ship that was under sail to retrieve slaves clearly demonstrates the value placed on them. Since slaves were so valuable, how could the traders have justified their treatment of them? *Students may respond that though the slave traders considered slaves to be valuable cargo, they thought of them as nothing more than cargo—the traders did not think of the slaves as human beings and mistreated them accordingly.*

◆ Literary Focus

❸ **Slave Narratives** Students can say that the captors wanted docile slaves and they wanted them alive. They can respond to the terrible cruelty of the slave traders toward their "cargo."

Extending Word Study

Context Clues Draw students' attention to the words *was suffered* on p. 46. Here, the word *suffered* has a different meaning from "endured pain." Ask students to find clues to the meaning of the word in the rest of the sentence. (The clue "on account of his illness . . . out of irons" suggests that the meaning here is "to be allowed" or "to be permitted.") Explain the importance of using context clues to figuring out meanings of words.

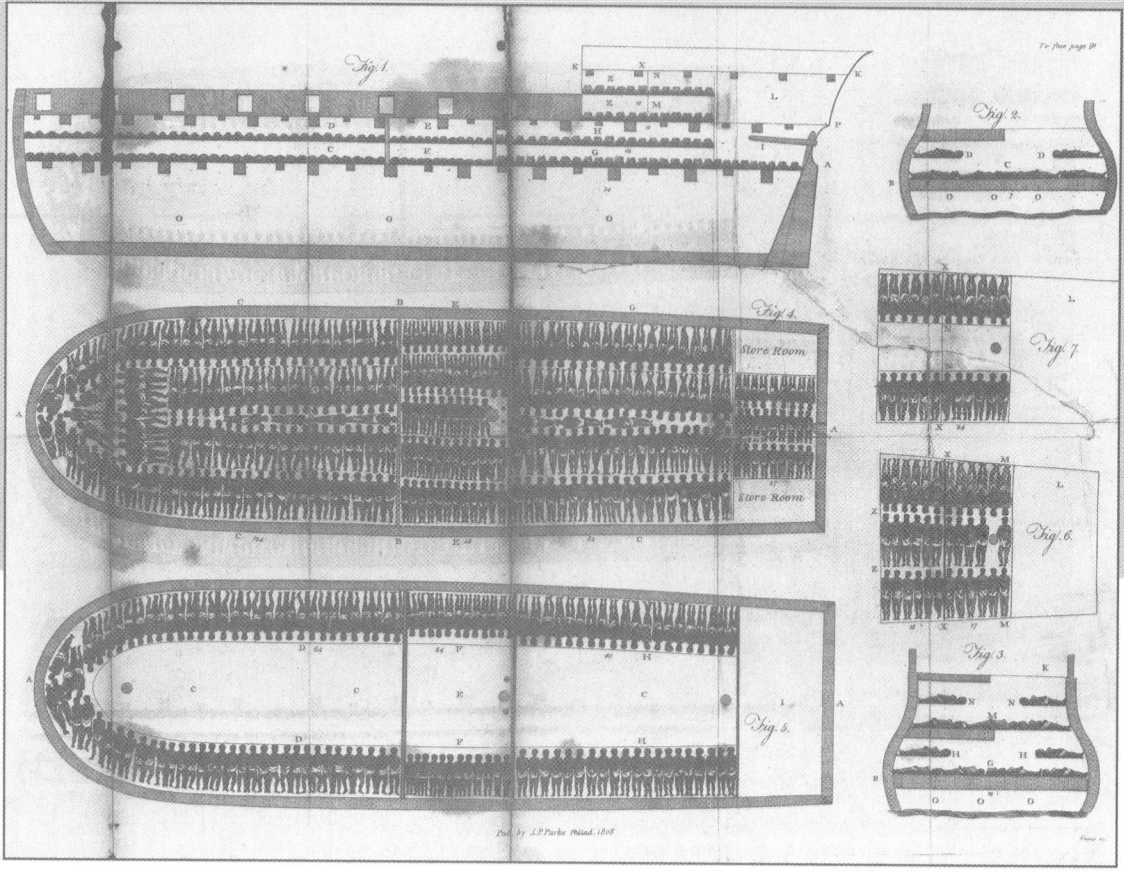

❶ ▲ **Critical Viewing** Estimate the number of slaves that this ship can carry. What do the drawings suggest about the ship designer's attitude toward slavery? **[Draw Conclusions]**

(I was near them at the time), preferring death to such a life of misery, somehow made through the nettings and jumped into the sea; immediately, another quite dejected fellow, who, on account of his illness, was suffered to be out of irons, also followed their example; and I believe many more would very soon have done the same, if they had not been prevented by the ship's crew, who were instantly alarmed. Those of us that were the most active, were in a moment put down under the deck; and there was such a noise and confusion amongst the people of the ship as I never heard before, to stop her, and get the boat out to go after the slaves. However, two of the wretches were drowned, but they got the other, and afterwards flogged him unmercifully, for thus attempting to prefer death to slavery. ❷ ❸

> ◆ **Literary Focus** What does this detail reveal about the captors' attitude?

In this manner we continued to undergo more hardships than I can now relate, hardships which are inseparable from this accursed trade. Many a time we were near suffocation from the want of fresh air, which we were often without for whole days together. This, and the stench of the necessary tubs, carried off many.

During our passage, I first saw flying fishes, which surprised me very much; they used

Speaking, Listening, and Viewing Mini-Lesson

Antislavery Speech

This mini-lesson supports the Speaking, Listening, and Viewing activity in the Idea Bank on p. 49.

Introduce the Concept Discuss how speeches can be used to influence public opinion on important issues or to persuade an audience to think or act a certain way. Explain that a good persuasive speech is clear, well-organized, accurate, and convincing. You may wish to have students read or listen to speeches by some of our nation's great orators, such as Martin Luther King, Jr., or Abraham Lincoln.

Develop Background In addition to using what they have learned about the slave trade, students can research to find out more about the American political climate in 1789 and the attitudes that legislators were likely to have toward slavery. You might have a few volunteers prepare background information for the class. More advanced students might look into the tone and style of speechmaking in 1789 and use their findings as they prepare their own speeches.

Apply the Information Have students draft their antislavery speeches, using their impressions of Equiano's narrative to strengthen their arguments. Each student should then present his or her speech to fellow group members.

Assess the Outcome Invite class members to critique the speeches. They can evaluate their effectiveness based on clarity, organization, accuracy of information, and persuasiveness. Use the Peer Assessment: Speaker/Speech Rubric, p. 133 in ***Alternative Assessment.***

frequently to fly across the ship, and many of them fell on the deck. I also now first saw the use of the quadrant;[2] I had often with astonishment seen the mariners make observations with it, and I could not think what it meant. They at last took notice of my surprise; and one of them, willing to increase it, as well as to
❹ gratify my curiosity, made me one day look through it. The clouds appeared to me to be land, which disappeared as they passed along. This heightened my wonder; and I was now more persuaded than ever, that I was in another world, and that every thing about me was magic. At last, we came in sight of the island of Barbados, at which the whites on board gave a great shout, and made many signs of joy to us. We did not know what to think of this; but as the vessel drew nearer, we plainly saw the harbor, and other ships of different kinds and sizes, and we soon anchored amongst them, off Bridgetown.[3] Many merchants and planters now came on board, though it was in the evening. They put us in separate parcels,[4] and examined us attentively. They also made us jump, and pointed to the land, signifying we were to go there. We thought by this, we should be eaten by these ugly men, as they appeared to us; and, when soon after we were all put down under the deck again, there was much dread and trembling among us, and nothing ❺
but bitter cries to be heard all the night from these apprehensions, insomuch, that at last the white people got some old slaves from the land to pacify us. They told us we were not to be eaten, but to work, and were soon to go on land, where we should see many of our country people. This report eased us much. And sure
enough, soon after we were landed, there came ❻
to us Africans of all languages.

We were conducted immediately to the merchant's yard, where we were all pent up together, like so many sheep in a fold, without regard to sex or age. . . . We were not many
days in the merchant's custody, before we were ❼
sold after their usual manner, which is this: On a signal given (as the beat of a drum), the buyers rush at once into the yard where the slaves are confined, and make choice of that parcel they like best. . . .

---

2. **quadrant** (kwä´ drənt) *n.*: An instrument used by navigators to determine the position of a ship.
3. **Bridgetown** *n.*: The capital of Barbados.
4. **parcels** (pär´ səlz) *n.*: Groups.

◆ Build Vocabulary

pacify (pas´ ə fī´) *v.*: Calm; soothe

Guide for Responding

◆ Literature and Your Life

Reader's Response Based on his narrative, what is your impression of Equiano?

Thematic Focus When one culture dominates another, what troubles might a society face?

Journel Writing Jot down your reactions to Equiano's account. What emotions did it stir up?

☑ Check Your Comprehension

1. How did Equiano's age affect his experiences during the voyage?
2. (a) For what crimes were slaves punished? (b) What was the punishment?
3. Summarize the conditions for the slaves on board the ship.

◆ Critical Thinking

❹ **Infer** What does this passage reveal about the author? *Students may say that Equiano was curious and thoughtful, that the awful circumstances did not squash his interest in learning.*

❺ **Clarification** From the beginning of the voyage, there had been rumors among the captives that sailors and other whites were cannibals. Point out that this assumption was not entirely unreasonable, given the fact that the captives had probably interacted with few, if any, white people, other than the sailors and traders who treated them so harshly.

◆ Critical Thinking

❻ **Draw Conclusions** Ask students to explain what a variety of languages indicates about the slave trade. *Students should say that the slave trade was widespread throughout Africa.*

◆ Grammar and Style

❼ **Active and Passive Voice** Point out that the extensive use here of the passive voice reinforces the idea that the slaves were recipients—not initiators—of actions.

Reinforce and Extend

Answers

◆ Literature and Your Life

Reader's Response Students may be impressed by Equiano's curiosity and eagerness to learn. They may also react to his high level of education as demonstrated by his diction.

Thematic Focus Students may point out that domination of cultures can lead to misunderstanding, disrespect, loss of freedoms and rights, and ultimately dehumanization.

☑ Check Your Comprehension

1. Equiano was granted certain privileges because of his age. For example, he was often kept on deck rather in the cramped quarters below.
2. (a) Slaves tried to eat leftover fish and tried to jump overboard. (b) They were flogged.
3. Slaves were kept in poorly ventilated, cramped quarters. Sanitary conditions were unhealthy; slaves were chained and poorly fed.

Beyond the Selection

FURTHER READING

Other Works About the Middle Passage

The Middle Passage: White Ships Black Cargo, Tom Feelings and John Henrick
Roots, Alex Haley
Middle Passage, Charles Johnson

We recommend that you preview these texts before assigning them to students.

INTERNET

You and your students may find additional information about Equiano's experiences on the Internet. We suggest the following site. Please be aware, however, that the site may have changed from the time we published this information.

For information about Olaudah Equiano and slavery in America, go to **http://www.atomicage.com/equiano/life.html**

We *strongly recommend* that you preview this and related sites before you send students to them.

Answers

◆ Critical Thinking

1. Equiano believes that the traders' greed led them to load the ships with more slaves than was actually healthy. This greed led to unsanitary conditions and illness.
2. He wanted to learn, which suggests that he hadn't given up completely. For example, Equiano was curious about the workings of the ship and the quadrant.
3. He shows that human beings chose to jump overboard to certain death rather than stay. He describes a system in which people were treated as animals, fed poorly, and whipped for minor infractions.
4. Suggested response: Colonists and explorers did not know what they would find; however, they made the choice to take such a risk. Equiano's voyage is made against his will under horrible conditions.

◆ Reading Strategy

Summaries should include the following main points: Olaudah Equiano traveled across the Atlantic Ocean in a slave ship. The conditions on board were detestable; most slaves were confined to an overheated, cramped space. The crew treated the slaves as less than human, often flogging them for trespasses. When the ship arrived on shore the slaves were frightened by their situation. Finally, they were brought to auction and sold.

◆ Literary Focus

1. Equiano stresses the unsanitary conditions.
2. The slaves felt complete despair. Many expressed a desire to die rather than endure the ordeal.
3. Possible response: The traders gave the slaves very little living space on board ship. They routinely flogged slaves to punish them.
4. The traders indulged Equiano's curiosity by allowing him to use the quadrant. The traders allowed younger slaves to be kept out of chains and above deck.
5. The traders' main motivation was to make as much money as possible.

Reteach

To help students understand the Reading Strategy in the selection, refer to the booklet ***Strategies for Diverse Student Needs,*** p. 2.

Guide for Responding *(continued)*

◆ Critical Thinking

INTERPRET

1. Why does Equiano blame the illness aboard the ship on the "improvident avarice" of the traders? **[Support]**

2. How can you tell that Equiano has a great zest for life despite his assertion that he wanted to die? Provide examples from the story. **[Support]**

APPLY

3. Equiano's narrative was instrumental in the fight to ban the slave trade in America. What persuasive evidence does his description of the middle passage offer? **[Defend]**

EXTEND

4. How does Equiano's voyage compare with those of explorers and colonists? **[Social Studies Link]**

◆ Reading Strategy

SUMMARIZE

When you **summarize** a piece of writing, you state the main ideas and supporting details of a selection.

Write a summary of Equiano's narrative, identifying at least three main ideas the author conveys about the voyage.

◆ Literary Focus

SLAVE NARRATIVE

A **slave narrative** is an autobiographical account of life as a slave. In describing significant events in his or her life, the writer often documents the horrors of slavery. This selection from Equiano's narrative provides a grim description of the middle passage and the operation of the slave trade.

1. What aspect of the conditions aboard ship does Equiano stress in this account?

2. What was the general feeling of the slaves toward their situation?

3. Cite two examples of the slave traders' cruelty to the slaves.

4. Cite two examples that show the traders' concern for the slaves' well-being.

5. What might have motivated the traders' behavior toward their human cargo? Explain.

◆ Build Vocabulary

USING THE LATIN ROOT *-vid-*

Considering the meaning of the Latin root *-vid-*, "to see," answer these questions:

1. Why is *evidence* useful in establishing guilt?

2. How would *video* technology change telephone habits?

USING THE WORD BANK: Synonym or Antonym?

Decide whether the words in each of the following pairs are synonyms or antonyms. On your paper, write *A* for *Antonym* or *S* for *Synonym.*

1. loathsome/hateful

2. pestilential/sanitary

3. copious/sparse

4. improvident/cautious

5. avarice/greed

6. pacify/torment

◆ Grammar and Style

ACTIVE AND PASSIVE VOICE

When Equiano explains, ". . . they were discovered," he uses the **passive voice** to emphasize the slaves rather than their captors. The use of the passive voice was common when Equiano wrote, but today, most writers choose the **active voice** whenever possible to make their writing more forceful and effective.

A verb is in the **active voice** when the subject of the sentence performs the action. A verb is in the **passive voice** when the action is performed on the subject.

Practice Rewrite the following sentences using the active voice. You may need to add words to indicate who performed the action.

1. Some of us had been permitted to stay on the deck for the fresh air.

2. We thought we should be eaten by these ugly men.

3. I was soon reduced low here.

4. It was thought necessary to keep me almost always on deck.

◆ Build Vocabulary

Using the Latin Root *-vid-*

Suggested responses:

1. Evidence can establish guilt because others can see proof of what took place.
2. People using video phones might become more concerned with their own appearance before picking up a telephone.

Using the Word Bank

1. S 2. A 3. A 4. A
5. S 6. A

◆ Grammar and Style

Suggested responses:

1. The crew permitted some of us to stay on the deck for fresh air.
2. We thought these ugly men would eat us.
3. The conditions soon reduced me low.
4. The crew thought it necessary to keep me almost always on deck.

Grammar Reinforcement

For additional instruction, use the Strengthening Sentences lesson on the **Language Lab CD-ROM** and the pages on Voice, pp. 60–61, in the *Writer's Solution Grammar Practice Book.*

Build Your Portfolio

Idea Bank

Writing

1. Activist List Equiano's autobiography contributed to the end of the slave trade. Create a list of problems facing today's society, and offer suggestions for how people could be educated about each problem. **[Social Studies Link]**

2. Editorial Imagine that you are an American newspaper publisher in 1789 when Equiano's *The Interesting Narrative* was released. As an abolitionist who would like to ban slavery, write the editorial you might have printed in response to the book. **[Career Link]**

3. Character Sketch As a director staging a production of *The Interesting Narrative*, write a description of the character of Equiano. Include Equiano's strengths and weaknesses in order to enable an actor to portray him.

Speaking, Listening, and Viewing

4. Debate Is it possible for slavery to exist in today's society? With a group of classmates, debate this question. **[Social Studies Link]**

5. Antislavery Speech Prepare and deliver a speech arguing against slavery in the newly formed Union to present to the 1789 Congress. Use Equiano's narrative to bolster your argument. **[Social Studies Link]**

Researching and Representing

6. Internet Research Organizations such as Amnesty International work to increase awareness of injustices around the world. Use the Internet or the library to learn about Amnesty International and the causes it publicizes. Report your findings to the class. **[Technology Link]**

7. Movie Poster Design a poster to advertise a Hollywood version of Equiano's narrative. You may want to retitle the work for film audiences.

Online Activity www.phlit.phschool.com

Guided Writing Lesson

Museum Placard

To educate today's audiences, institutions like Detroit's Museum of African American History have been developing exhibits that document the slave trade of the 1800's. Imagine that you've been asked to write the introductory material that will appear on a large placard at the beginning of such an exhibit. Explain the sequence of events of the slave trade, beginning with the capture of Africans on their native continent, and conclude with the auctioning of enslaved Africans in the Americas. Use this tip to help you develop your placard.

Writing Skills Focus: Sequence of Events

A chronological **sequence** leads readers clearly from the first step to the next in the order in which events took place. Outline the sequence you'll be describing. Follow these suggestions:

- Begin with what happens first and continue in time order.
- Use words like *next, then,* and *finally* to make the sequence as clear to readers as possible.
- Avoid shifts in time sequence.

Prewriting Use library sources to gather facts about the slave trade. Organize your information graphically, perhaps by drawing a map on which you can indicate the routes of the slave trade, dates, and other key details.

Drafting Refer to your notes as you begin writing. Keep events in chronological order and use transition words—such as *at first, next, while, then, finally,* and *after*—to ensure that the order is clear.

Revising Reread your work to confirm that the placard will highlight the important stages of the slave trade. Eliminate any nonessential details, and add transitions to sharpen the sequence of events.

Idea Bank

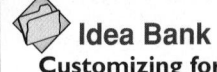

Customizing for
Performance Levels

Following are suggestions for matching Idea Bank topics with your students' performance levels:
Less Advanced Students: 1, 7
Average Students: 2, 5, 6
More Advanced Students: 3, 4

Customizing for
Learning Modalities

Following are suggestions for matching Idea Bank topics with your students' learning modalities:
Logical/Mathematical: 4, 5
Bodily/Kinesthetic: 6
Visual/Spatial: 7

Guided Writing Lesson

Writers at Work Videodisc

Have students view the videodisc segment (Ch. 3) featuring museum writer Thom Harrington to learn his tips on how to be concise and accurate when writing to inform. Ask students to discuss what Harrington identifies as common pitfalls to avoid in expository writing. Students may also find it helpful to adopt Harrington's strategy of using an outline to help organize ideas.

Play frames 23159 to 33243

Writing Lab CD-ROM

Have students complete the tutorial on Exposition. Follow these steps:

1. Direct students to review the interactive Writing Model of a summary.
2. Students can use the Timeline Activity to help them organize the sequence of the events they will summarize in their placards.
3. Have students complete their drafts on the computer.
4. Use the Revision Checker for Transition Words to help students revise.

✓ ASSESSMENT OPTIONS

Formal Assessment, Selection Test, pp. 10–12, and Assessment Resources Software. The selection test is designed so that it can be easily customized to the performance levels of your students.

Alternative Assessment, p. 4, includes options for less advanced students, more advanced students, musical/rhythmic learners, verbal/linguistic learners, visual/spatial learners, and bodily/kinesthetic learners.

PORTFOLIO ASSESSMENT

Use the following rubrics in the **Alternative Assessment** booklet to assess student writing:
Activist List: Problem-Solution Rubric, p. 116
Editorial: Persuasion Rubric, p. 120
Character Sketch: Literary Analysis/Interpretation Rubric, p. 127
Guided Writing Lesson: Summary Rubric, p. 113

LESSON OBJECTIVES

1. To use a variety of reading strategies to comprehend a short story and a song
- Tips to Guide Reading (ATE)
- Read to Take Action (ATE)

2. To increase knowledge of other cultures and to connect common elements across cultures
- Thematic Connection

3. To express and support responses to the text
- Critical Thinking
- Idea Bank: Cultural Story
- Idea Bank: Museum Brochure
- Idea Bank: Persuasive Essay
- Idea Bank: Time Capsule
- Analyze an Author's Comment

4. To read in order to research self-selected and assigned topics
- Questions for Research

5. To plan, prepare, organize, and present literary interpretations
- Idea Bank: Television Interview

Interest Grabber Give students the following advance assignment: If you could ask an ancestor—a great-grandparent, for example—a question about the past, what would you want to know? What knowledge has been lost that you feel should be preserved for future generations? Ask volunteers to share their responses.

Explain that when cultures meet—including the cultures of older and newer generations—benefits emerge, yet other things may be lost forever.

Darryl Babe Wilson was aware of this problem. He writes of his grandfather, "The volumes of knowledge that were buried with him are lost to my generation." Tell students that to rescue a part of his knowledge and experiences, Wilson's grandfather chose to share one very important tale from his past with his grandson. The story they are about to read describes how the elderly Native American ensured that at least one piece of his knowledge was preserved.

CONNECTIONS TO TODAY'S WORLD

Diamond Island: Alcatraz
Darryl Babe Wilson

Big Yellow Taxi
Joni Mitchell

Thematic Connection

MEETING OF CULTURES

Though quite different, the works in Part I share one thing in common: they record impressions of the world, of new experiences, of new people seen through the filter of the writer's experiences and culture. The Native Americans saw nature as the source of earthly life. The conquistadors viewed new lands and people within the framework of European values. Olaudah Equiano vividly portrayed the consequences of one culture's belief in its right to dominate another. Each of their stories contributes uniquely to our understanding of the country that would become the United States of America.

Today, the distinct lines that separated these cultures have blurred into a shared "American experience." America is still celebrated as a melting pot of cultures from around the world, but there are those who feel that some of the values that once shaped the nation are in danger of being left behind.

O BEAUTIFUL FOR SPACIOUS SKIES . . .

The Native Americans who saw the Earth as the handiwork of gods, enchanted animals, and magical winds could not have foreseen a world paved over with parking lots, such as folk singer Joni Mitchell describes in "Big Yellow Taxi." The early Native Americans, who lived in harmony with their environment, would have been shocked to discover how much of the American wilderness has given way to development. Today, the wide open spaces and awe-inspiring sights that greeted the explorers still exist, but they are fewer and farther between.

KEEPING THE FLAME ALIVE

The last two centuries have also seen the gradual disappearance of many of the cultures and customs of Native American peoples. Darryl Babe Wilson preserves in writing the memories of Native American elders. Wilson confronts the elders' fear that the younger generation of Native Americans are unenlightened about their ancestral heritage. Wilson strives to bring about a "meeting of cultures" *within* his Native American nation, as well as from without.

DARRYL BABE WILSON (1939–)

Darryl Babe Wilson is a Native American poet and short-story writer. He lives in California's San Francisco Bay area and teaches writing at two local colleges. Before moving to California in 1997, Wilson taught Native American studies at the University of Arizona, where he earned his Ph.D. in Comparative Culture and Literary Studies. Wilson often writes about the struggles of his people. For his book *Voices from the Earth*, he interviewed Native Americans from Barrow, Alaska, to the Mayan Peninsula of Mexico and Guatemala.

JONI MITCHELL (1943–)

Joni Mitchell is a well-loved and influential folk singer-songwriter. Born in Ft. MacLeod, Alberta, Canada, she began performing while in her twenties at local coffeehouses. After cutting her first album in 1968, she produced a title almost every year through 1982. Her album *Clouds* won a Grammy award for best folk performance.

Customize for
Less Proficient Readers
To help these students, present a simple chronology of the events described in "Diamond Island: Alcatraz": the piece, written in 1989, records a conversation held in 1971 about an event that happened sometime between 1850 and 1870.

Prentice Hall Literature Program Resources

REINFORCE / RETEACH / EXTEND

Selection Support Pages
Build Vocabulary, p. 18
Thematic Connection: Meeting of Cultures, p. 19

Formal Assessment Selection Test, pp. 13–14; Assessment Resources Software

Resource Pro CD-ROM

Diamond Island: Alcatraz

Allisti Ti-Tanin-Miji
(Rock Rainbow)

Darryl Babe Wilson

CONNECTIONS TO TODAY'S WORLD

San Francisco, 1849, Attributed to Joshua Pierce

▲ Critical Viewing This painting shows Alcatraz as seen from a San Francisco hilltop at twilight. What is the mood created by this depiction of the island? [Describe] ❶

There was a single letter in the mailbox. Somehow it seemed urgent. The address, although it was labored over, could hardly be deciphered—square childlike print that did not complete the almost individual letters. Inside, five pages written on both sides. Blunt figures. Each word pressed heavily into the paper. I could not read it but I could feel the message. "Al traz" was in the first paragraph, broken and

Develop Understanding

One-Minute Insight Places or events can hold different meanings and mysteries for different generations or cultures. The essayist offers his beliefs and attitudes as he shares a story his grandfather told him years earlier. A bold escape from Alcatraz a century before was a key event in the history of his people, yet is little known today. The writer wonders how and if later generations will come to understand and appreciate their heritage.

Enrichment *Isla de los Alcatraces,* or Island of the Pelicans, was once home to thousands of birds. Early settlers drove the birds away; eventually Anglo settlers remade the island as a fortress, a military prison, then a maximum-security penitentiary. Strong, cold currents churn past "The Rock," supposedly making escape impossible. After 1962, when the prison closed, Alcatraz lay vacant, but for a caretaker. In 1969 a group of "Indians of All Nations" took over the old prison, claiming that unused federal property could be returned to reservation status. They hoped to establish a Native American cultural center there, but left the island in 1971. Today Alcatraz is one of San Francisco's most popular tourist attractions.

▶Critical Viewing◀

❶ **Describe** Students may say that Alcatraz Island seems isolated and mysterious, as it sits alone in the middle of the bay in the eerie purple twilight. They may also note that the island seems to form a boundary between the populated city in the foreground and the distant empty hills.

Humanities: Art

San Francisco, 1849, by Joshua Pierce.

Little is known of American painter Joshua H. Pierce other than that he lived and worked in the San Francisco area from 1841 to 1859. His body of work consists of full-size paintings and miniatures (about the size of a playing card) of the San Francisco landscape. His works are valuable for their beauty and for the historical record they provide of the area.

This oil painting shows San Francisco in 1849. In the harbor are sailing ships and Alcatraz Island. The scene would have looked much like this when Grandfather's family was imprisoned there. Use these questions for discussion:

1. How well does this depiction of Alcatraz reflect Grandfather's description? *Responses should relate their responses to Grandfather's description of Alcatraz as a big rock in the middle of great salt water.*
2. If Grandfather's ancestors were to view a current photograph of this same scene, do you think they would still recognize the site as Alcatraz Island? Why or why not? *Students should note that the addition of the Golden Gate Bridge, skyscrapers, electric lights, cars, supertankers, and so on, has dramatically changed the San Francisco Bay area.*

◆ Critical Thinking

❶ **Draw Conclusions** Ask students why Thanksgiving may remind the narrator of Grandfather's ordeal. What inference can students draw from the use of the word *ordeal?* *While Thanksgiving is often a time for reflection, it also celebrates the cooperative spirit between Native Americans and colonists. Ordeal suggests Grandfather has been through something terrible.*

Thematic Connection

❷ **Meeting of Cultures** Cultures often disagree about how to describe a place or tell when and how it was first discovered or occupied. Ask students to summarize the point the author makes about cultural conflict in this passage. *Responses should reflect the author's belief that Native Americans knew about Alcatraz and held it sacred generations before Ayala "discovered" it in 1775.*

Comprehension Check ☑

❸ Ask students to identify the natural event that the Native Americans describe to explain the creation of San Francisco Bay and Alcatraz Island. *It was an earthquake.*

◆ Reading Strategy

❹ **Form a Mental Picture** Ask students to imagine the setting. Encourage them to conjure up not only the visual scene, but how the place smells and sounds, and how it might feel actually to be there.

Customize for *Verbal/Linguistic Learners*

The old man's story in "Diamond Island: Alcatraz" is from oral tradition; "Big Yellow Taxi" was written to be sung. Ask volunteers to read Grandfather's words aloud, or play a recording of "Big Yellow Taxi" to appreciate the pieces as oral works.

Tips to Guide Reading

Buddy Reading Have students work in pairs to read the selection silently. Suggest that they stop at the end of each page to order the chronology of the story and to resolve any questions they might have. Tell them that since the story moves back and forth in time, it might be helpful for them to track the chronology of events closely.

scattered, but there. At the very bottom of the final page—running out of space—he scrawled his name. It curved down just past the right-hand corner. The last letter of his name, *n*, did not fit: *Gibso*. It was winter, 1971. I hurried to his home.

Grandfather lived at Atwam, 100 miles east of Redding, California, in a little shack out on the flat land. His house was old and crooked just like in a fairy tale. His belongings were few and they, too, were old and worn. I always wanted to know his age and often asked some of the older of our people if they could recall when Grandfather was born. After silences that sometimes seemed more than a year, they always shook their silver-gray heads and answered: "I dunno. He was old and wrinkled with white hair for as long as I can remember. Since I was just a child." He must have been born between 1850 and 1870.

❶ Thanksgiving weekend, 1989. It is this time of the year when I think about Grandfather and his ordeal. I keep promising myself that I will write his story down because it is time to give the island of Alcatraz a proper identity and a "real" history. It is easy for modern people to

❷ think that the history of Alcatraz began when a foreign ship sailed into the bay and a stranger named Don Juan Manuel de Ayala[1] observed the "rock" and recorded "Alcatraz" in a log book in 1775. That episode, that sailing and that recording was only moments ago.

❸ Grandfather said that long ago the Sacramento Valley was a huge freshwater lake, that it was "as long as the land" (from the northern part of California to the southern), and that a great shaking of an angry spirit within the earth caused part of the coastal range to crumble into the outer-ocean. When the huge lake finally drained and the waves from the earthquake finally settled, there was the San Francisco Bay, and there, in isolation and containing a "truth," was Diamond Island (Alcatraz).

He told me the story one winter in his little one-room house in Atwam. It is bitter cold there during winters. I arrived late in the evening, tires of my truck spinning up his driveway. The driveway was a series of frozen, broken mudholes in a general direction across a field to his home. The headlights bounced out of control.

My old 1948 Chevy pickup was as cold inside as it was outside. The old truck kept going, but it was a fight to make it go in the winter. It was such a struggle that we called it "Mr. Miserable." Mr. Miserable and I came to a jolting halt against a snowbank that was the result of someone shoveling a walk in the front yard. We expended our momentum. The engine died with a sputtering cough. Lights flopped out.

It was black outside but the crusted snow lay like a ghost upon the earth and faded away in every direction. The night sky trembled with the fluttering of a million stars—all diamond blue. Wind whipped broken tumbleweeds across his neglected yard. The snow could not conceal the yard's chaos. ❹

The light in the window promised warmth. Steam puffing from every breath, I hurried to his door. The snow crunched underfoot, sounding like a horse eating a crisp apple. The old door lurched open with a complaint. Grandfather's fatigued, centenarian[2] body a black silhouette against the brightness—bright although he had but a single shadeless lamp to light the entire house. I saw a skinned bear once. It looked just like Grandfather. Short, stout arms and bowed legs. Compact physique. Muscular—not fat. Thick chest. Powerful. Natural.

Old powder-blue eyes strained to see who was out there in the dark. "Hallo. You're just the man I'm lookin' for." Coffee aroma exploded from the open door. Coffee. Warmth!

Grandfather stood back and I entered the comfort of his jumbled little bungalow. It was cozy in there. He was burning juniper wood. Juniper, cured for a summer, has a clean, delicate aroma—a perfume. After a healthy handshake we huddled over steaming cups of coffee. Grandfather looked long at me. I think that he was not totally convinced that I was there. The hot coffee was good. It was not a fancy Colombian, aromatic blend, but it was so good!

---

1. **Don Juan Manuel de Ayala** (dän hwän män wel´ dā ä yä´ lä): An eighteenth-century Spanish explorer who was the first European to enter San Francisco Bay.

2. **centenarian** (sen´ tə ner´ ē ən) *adj.*: At least one hundred years old.

Analyze an Author's Comment

As these pages suggest, Darryl B. Wilson's attachment to land and family is deep. He is the son of A'juma'wi and Atsuge'wi Indians, whose homeland was the northeastern corner of California. Some of his happiest memories from childhood included hunting, fishing, and hiking with his father in the Northern California mountains. The family closeness he treasured came to a shattering end, though, when his mother and baby brother were killed in an automobile accident.

Though Wilson disliked school, and found his family a refuge from formal education, his writing career blossomed. Wilson cited his father's influence and once said, "He always wanted an artist in the family. He said he wanted 'a good drawer.' I cannot draw pictures with a brush or pencil and pen, so I attempt to create pictures with words."

Read these words to students and have them answer the following questions:

A Does Wilson succeed in "creating pictures with words" when he writes? Explain.

B In what way is his devotion to family consistent in the words quoted here and in "Diamond Island: Alcatraz"?

We were surrounded by years of Grandfather's collections. It was like a museum. Everything was very old and worn. It seemed that every part of the clutter had a history—sometimes a history that remembered the origin of the earth, like the bent pail filled with obsidian[3] that he had collected from Glass Mountain many summers before, "just in case."

5 He also had a radio that he was talked into purchasing when he was a young working man in the 1920's. The radio cost $124. I think he got conned by that merchant and the episode magnified in mystery when he recalled that it was not until 1948 before he got the electric company to put a line to his home. By that time he forgot about the radio and he did not remember to turn it on until 1958. It worked. There was an odor of oldness—like a mouse that died then dried to a stiffness through the years—a redolence of old neglected newspapers.

6 The old person in the old house under the old moon began to tell the story of his escape from "the rock" long ago. He gathered himself together and reached back into a painful past. The silence was long and I thought that he might be crying silently. Then, with a quiver in his voice, he started telling the story that he wanted me to know:

"Alcatraz Island. Where the Pit River runs into the sea is where I was born, long ago. *Alcatraz*, that's the white man's name for it. To our people, in our legends, we always knew it as *Allisti Ti-tanin-miji* [Rock Rainbow], Diamond Island. In our legends, that's where the Mouse Brothers, the twins, were told to go when they searched for a healing treasure for our troubled people long, long ago. They were to go search at the end of *It A-juma* [Pit River]. They found it. They brought it back. But it is lost now. It is said, the 'diamond' was to bring goodness to all our people, everywhere.

"We always heard that there was a 'diamond' on an island near the great salt water. We were always told that the 'diamond' was a thought, or a truth. Something worth very much. It was not a jewelry. It sparkled and it shined, but it was not a jewelry. It was more. Colored lights came from inside it with every movement. That is why we always called it [Alcatraz] *Allisti Ti-Tanin-miji."* With a wave of an ancient hand and words filled with enduring knowledge, Grandfather spoke of a time long past.

In one of the many raids upon our people of the Pit River country, his pregnant mother was taken captive and forced, with other Indians, to make the long and painful march to Alcatraz in the winter. At that same time, the military was "sweeping" California. Some of our people were "removed" to the Round Valley Reservation at Covelo; others were taken east by train in open cattle cars during the winter to Quapa, Oklahoma. Still others were taken out into the ocean at Eureka and thrown overboard into icy waters. 7

Descendants of those that were taken in chains to Quapa are still there. Some of those cast into the winter ocean at Eureka made it back to land and returned to Pit River country. A few of those defying confinement, the threat of being shot by "thunder sticks," and dark winter nights of a cold Alcatraz-made-deadly by churning, freezing currents, made it back to Pit River country, too.

Grandfather said, "I was very small, too small to remember, but my grandmother remembered it all. The guards allowed us to swim around the rock. Every day, my mother swam. Every day, the people swam. We were not just swimming. We were gaining strength. We were learning the currents. We had to get home.

"When it was time, we were ready. We left at darkness. Grandmother said that I was a baby and rode my mother's back, clinging as she swam from Alcatraz to solid ground in night. My Grandmother remembered that I pulled so hard holding on that I broke my mother's necklace. It is still there in the water . . . somewhere." With a pointing of a stout finger southward, Grandfather indicated where "there" was. 8

Quivering with emotion, he hesitated. He trembled. "I do not remember if I was scared,"

---

3. **obsidian** (əb sid′ ē ən) *n.*: Hard, dark-colored or black volcanic glass.

◆ Build Vocabulary

expended (ek spend′ id) *v.*: To have spent or used by consuming

redolence (red′ əl əns) *n.*: Scent; smell

CONNECTIONS TO TODAY'S WORLD

◆ Critical Thinking

5 Infer Ask students what kind of person Grandfather is, based on this anecdote and the other information the author has revealed so far. *Students may say that Grandfather is disinterested in material things, and focuses more on daily survival; some may suggest that he leads a more spiritual life.*

◆ Critical Thinking

6 Speculate Ask students to give a possible reason for Grandfather's apparent urgency to tell his story. *Students may say that Grandfather senses that his life is nearly over and that he wants to share a powerful family story with his grandson before it's too late.*

7 Clarification The Round Valley Reservation is in northern California, about twenty miles inland from the Pacific and about 175 miles north of San Francisco. Oklahoma, which has the greatest Native American population in the United States (California is second), was a destination for many Native Americans who were "removed" from their traditional lands.

Customize for
AP Students

8 Challenge these students by asking: How can the necklace be interpreted as a symbol of the clash between Grandfather's culture and another that disrespected it? *Students may say that the necklace stands for the traditions of the past, which encircled the mother, and were broken as a result of the persecution and imprisonment. Because its fragments lie in San Francisco Bay near Alcatraz, the necklace may also be said to represent parts of the Native American tradition that remain for the interested ones to seek out and hopefully restore.*

Customize for
Gifted/Talented

Grandfather speaks of the "diamond" or healing treasure of his troubled people. Have students create a story about the "diamond," imagining its loss or discovery and interpreting its importance and symbolism for Grandfather's people.

Cultural Connection

Respect for elders is a feature common to many cultures. Native Americans, and other cultures that have a long oral tradition, value elders as members of the group who can bridge the past and the future as they pass traditional wisdom from generation to generation. Not only do they keep alive a people's history, legends, myths, dances, songs, and customs, they also advise the young on how to live good and productive lives. Have students find out more about traditional Native American values. Challenge them to give examples of how the traditional wisdom is still applicable today.

▶Critical Viewing◀

1 Connect Students may say that the man's weatherworn face reflects the experiences of many years. Although very old, he still looks strong as he faces the camera directly. The unkempt hair suggests a wild, free person who is not concerned with trivial things.

Thematic Connection

2 Meeting of Cultures Ask students to explain how Grandfather's efforts to recollect his tale for a grandson who "wrote things down on paper" represents a meeting of cultures. *Grandfather realizes that his grandson's work is part of a written tradition, which can be used to preserve for others what he offers in his traditional oral manner.*

Thematic Connection

3 Meeting of Cultures Ask students to respond to the feelings the narrator expresses when he realizes how different he and his grandfather are. What does the narrator respect most? Invite students to share any similar reactions they may have had with family members or friends who come from other cultures.

Read to Take Action

Explain that sometimes students read text that influences them to take a position on an issue and to act on it. When they read text to take action, they should look for opinions, reasons, and facts that support a position.

Direct students to the first full paragraph on page 55. Have students discuss what Darryl Babe Wilson is advocating. *He is encouraging Native Americans to take action, in order "to survive as a distinct and autonomous people."* Ask students to discuss what specific action persuaded readers might take.

Photo of a Native American male (Wailaki tribe), Edward S. Curtis, Southwest Museum, Los Angeles

▲ **Critical Viewing** How does this portrait convey the wisdom of the grandfather in the story? **[Connect]**

Grandfather said, crooked, thick fingers rubbing a creased and wrinkled chin covered with white stubble. "I must have been."

When those old, cloudy eyes dripped tears down a leathery, crevassed[4] face, and long silences were between his sentences, often I trembled too. He softly spoke of his memory.

Our cups were long empty; *maliss* (fire) needed attention. The moon was suspended in the frozen winter night—round, bright, scratched and scarred—when Grandfather finally paused in his thinking. The old castiron heater grumbled and screamed (1) when I slid open the top to drop in a fresh log. Sparks flew up into the darkness then disappeared. I slammed the top closed. Silence, again.

Grandfather continued, "There was not real diamonds on the island. At least I don't think so. I always thought the diamonds were not diamonds but some kind of understanding, some kind of good thought—or something." He shook a white, shaggy head and looked off into the distance into a time that was so long ago that the mountains barely remembered. For long moments he reflected, he gathered his thoughts. (2) He knew that I "wrote things down on paper."

The night was thick. To the north a coyote howled. Far to the west an old coyote rasped a call to the black wilderness, a supreme presence beneath starry skies with icy freedom all around.

"When first I heard about the 'diamond,' I thought it might be a story of how we escaped. But after I heard that story so many times, I don't think so. I think there was a truth there that the Mouse Brothers were instructed to get and bring back long ago to help our people. I don't think that I know where that truth is now. Where can it be? It must be deep *inside Axo-Yet* [Mount Shasta][5] or *Sa Titt* [Medicine Lake]. It hides from our people. The truth hides from us. It must not like us. It denies us."

The One-as-Old-as-the-Mountains made me wonder about this story. It seems incredible that there was such an escape from Alcatraz. Through American propaganda I have been trained to believe that it was impossible to escape from that isolated rock because of the currents and because of the freezing temperature as the powerful ocean and the surging rivers merged in chaos. I was convinced—until I heard Grandfather's story and until I realized that he dwelled within a different "time," a different "element." He dwelled within a spirituality of a natural source. In his world, I was only (3) a foreign infant. It is true today that when I talk with the old people I feel like *nilladuwi*—(a white man). I feel like some domesticated creature addressing original royalty—knowing that the old ones were pure savage, born into the wild, free.

In his calm manner, Grandfather proceeded. "We wandered for many nights. We hid during the day. It is said that we had to go south for three nights before we could turn north. [My people landed at San Francisco and had to sneak to what is now San Jose, traveling at night with no food until they could turn northward.] They [the U.S. Army] were after us. They were after us all. We had to be careful. We had to be careful and not make mistakes. We headed north for two nights.

"We came to a huge river. We could not cross it. It was swift. My mother walked far upstream then jumped in. Everybody followed. The river washed us to the other shore [possibly the Benicia Straits]. We rested for two days eating dead fish that we found along the river. We could not build a fire because they would see the smoke and catch us so we must eat it [fish] raw. At night we traveled again. Again we traveled, this time for two nights also.

"There is a small island of mountains in the

4. **crevassed** (krə vast′) *adj.*: Deeply cracked.
5. **Mount Shasta** (shas′ tə): A volcanic mountain in northern California.

Humanities: Photography

Photo of a Native American Male (Wailaki tribe) by Edward S. Curtis (1868–1952).

The work of Edward Sherrif Curtis is remarkable for its sensitivity to the displaced Native American tribes of the Northwest. Sponsored by millionaire J. P. Morgan and endorsed by President Theodore Roosevelt, Curtis created a photographic and written record of these tribes that is a classic in recorded anthropology. This photo is one of 20,000 that accompanied Curtis's twenty-volume masterwork, *The North American Indian.*

His goal was to portray Native Americans as a proud people of noble heritage. Use these questions for discussion:

1. What do you think the man in this portrait is feeling? *Some students might say that he is feeling sadness; others, that he is feeling pride.*
2. What effect is created by the use of black-and-white, rather than color, photography? *Students may say that it makes the man seem older or from a more distant time.*

great valley [Sutter Buttes]. When we reached that place one of the young men climbed the highest peak. He was brave. We were all brave. It was during the sunlight. We waited for him to holler as was the plan. We waited a long, long time. Then we heard: *'Axo-Yet! Axo-Yet! To-ho-ja-toki! To-ho-ja-toki Tanjan'* [Mount Shasta! Mount Shasta! North direction!]. Our hearts were happy. We were close to home. My mother squeezed me to her. We cried. I know we cried. I was there. So was my mother and grandmother."

❹ Grandfather has been within the earth for many snows now. The volumes of knowledge that were buried with him are lost to my generation, a generation that needs original knowledge now more than ever, if we are to survive as a distinct and autonomous people. Perhaps a generation approaching will be more aware, more excited with tradition and custom and less satisfied to being off balance somewhere between the world of the "white man" and the world of the "Indian," and will seek this knowledge.

It is nearing winter, 1989. Snows upon *Axo-Yet* (Mount Shasta) are deep. The glaring white makes Grandfather's hair nearly yellow—now that I better recall the coarse strands that I often identified as "silver." That beautiful mountain. The landmark that caused the hunted warrior 140 years ago to forget the tragic episode that could have been the termination of our nation, and, standing with the sun shining full upon him, hollered to a frightened people waiting below: *"Axo-Yet! Axo-Yet! To-ho-ja-toki Tanjan!"*

CONNECTIONS TO TODAY'S WORLD

❺ Perhaps the approaching generation will seek and locate *Allisti Ti-tanin-miji* within the mountains. Possibly that generation will reveal many truths to this world society that is immense and confused in its immensity. An old chief of the Pit River country, "Charlie Buck," said often: "Truth. It is truth that will set us free." Along with Grandfather, I think that it was a "truth" that the Mouse Brothers brought to our land from Diamond Island long ago. A truth that needs to be understood, appreciated, and acknowledged. A truth that needs desperately to be found and known for its value.

Grandfather's letter is still in my files. I still can't read it, but if I could, I am sure that the message would be the same as this story that he gave to me as the moon listened and the winds whispered across a frozen Atwam, during a sparkling winter night long ago.

◆ Build Vocabulary

autonomous (ô tän′ ə məs) *adj.*: Independent

Guide for Responding

◆ Literature and Your Life

Reader's Response If you could ask Grandfather a question about his story, what would you ask? Why?

Thematic Focus Wilson implies that the existence of Native American culture is endangered today just as it was more than one hundred years ago when his ancestors were persecuted by those who didn't understand or value their culture. What is the source of the modern threat to the survival of his people's heritage?

☑ Check Your Comprehension

1. How did Grandfather learn the story of his family's escape from Alcatraz—an event that took place when he was a small boy?
2. According to the story, what does the "diamond" of Diamond Island represent?
3. What does Grandfather believe has become of the "diamond"?

("Critical Thinking" questions appear on p. 57.)

Beyond the Selection

FURTHER READING

Other Works by Darryl Babe Wilson

Dear Christopher: Letters to Christopher Columbus by Contemporary Native Americans

Surviving in Two Worlds: Contemporary Native American Voices

We recommend that you preview the texts before assigning them to students.

INTERNET

You and your students may find additional information about Alcatraz Island, including the Native American occupation of 1969–1971, on the Internet. We suggest the following site. Please be aware, however, that sites may have changed since this information was published.

For information about Alcatraz and its history, go to the official Web Site sponsored by the National Parks Service at **http://www.nps.gov/alcatraz/**

We *strongly recommend* that you preview sites before you send students to them.

Customize for
English Language Learners

❹ Help these students understand this passage by clarifying idiomatic phrases. Guide them to grasp the meaning of "been within the earth for many snows now" *It can be restated as "has died and been buried for many winters, or years."* Explain that "original knowledge" refers to an understanding of one's past, based on the stories of his or her heritage; being "off balance somewhere" means that people caught between cultures cannot feel as secure as they would if they knew their roots.

◆ Literature and Your Life

❺ Discuss with students what kinds of truths they believe that their generation seeks, or should seek, and how truths can set them free.

Reinforce and Extend

Customize for
Less Proficient Readers

These students will benefit greatly from rereading all or part of the essay. In reviewing it, suggest that students focus on separate elements, such as the story of the Alcatraz escape, the circumstances of the meeting between grandfather and grandson, and the reflections the narrator makes about "truth."

Answers

◆ Literature and Your Life

Reader's Response Students' responses should reflect a careful reading of Grandfather's story.

Thematic Focus Wilson suggests that the threat comes both from within and from without the Native American culture: from a modern society that is "confused in its immensity"; and from his own younger generation of Native Americans, who are torn between the "white man" and the "Indian" and have little interest in keeping tradition alive.

☑ Check Your Comprehension

1. The story was told to him by his grandmother.
2. The diamond is not a jewel but a truth to be discovered and passed on.
3. He doesn't know where the truth that was supposed to help their people has gone. He believes it may be hiding deep inside Mount Shasta.

One-Minute Insight Mitchell regrets that we rarely appreciate the things that enrich our lives—natural beauty, a clean, safe environment, a good relationship—until it's too late to salvage them.

◆ Critical Thinking

❶ **Speculate** Point out that Mitchell intentionally uses incorrect grammar in the first line of the repeating chorus. Ask students why they think she chose to include this "error." *Students may say that she used "poetic license" to select words that fit the spirit and rhythm of her melody.*

❷ **Clarification** DDT is the popular nickname for the chemical compound DichloroDiphenyl Trichloroethane, a powerful insecticide that is known to cause environmental damage.

❸ **Clarification** Point out that in the slang of the 1960's, "old man" means boyfriend, not father.

◆ Critical Thinking

❹ **Interpret** Have students consider the double meaning of the last stanza: it bemoans environmental loss and personal loss, neither of which the speaker valued enough until it was too late.

◆ Critical Thinking

Evaluate Ask students to explain whether they feel that the Manhattan street scene pictured on these pages is an accurate representation of the world of "Big Yellow Taxi." *Students may regard the street scene as an example of a former paradise now paved over. Others may say that the song is less about taxis than it is about fear of ruining our world unless we care for it while it still exists.*

Reinforce and Extend

Customize for ***Musical/Rhythmic Learners***
This song's rhythmic, upbeat feel contrasts with the serious concerns it conveys. If possible, play the song, which appears on Mitchell's *Ladies of the Canyon* album. Alternatively, play other artists' interpretations of the song. Consider the version by Amy Grant or Janet Jackson.

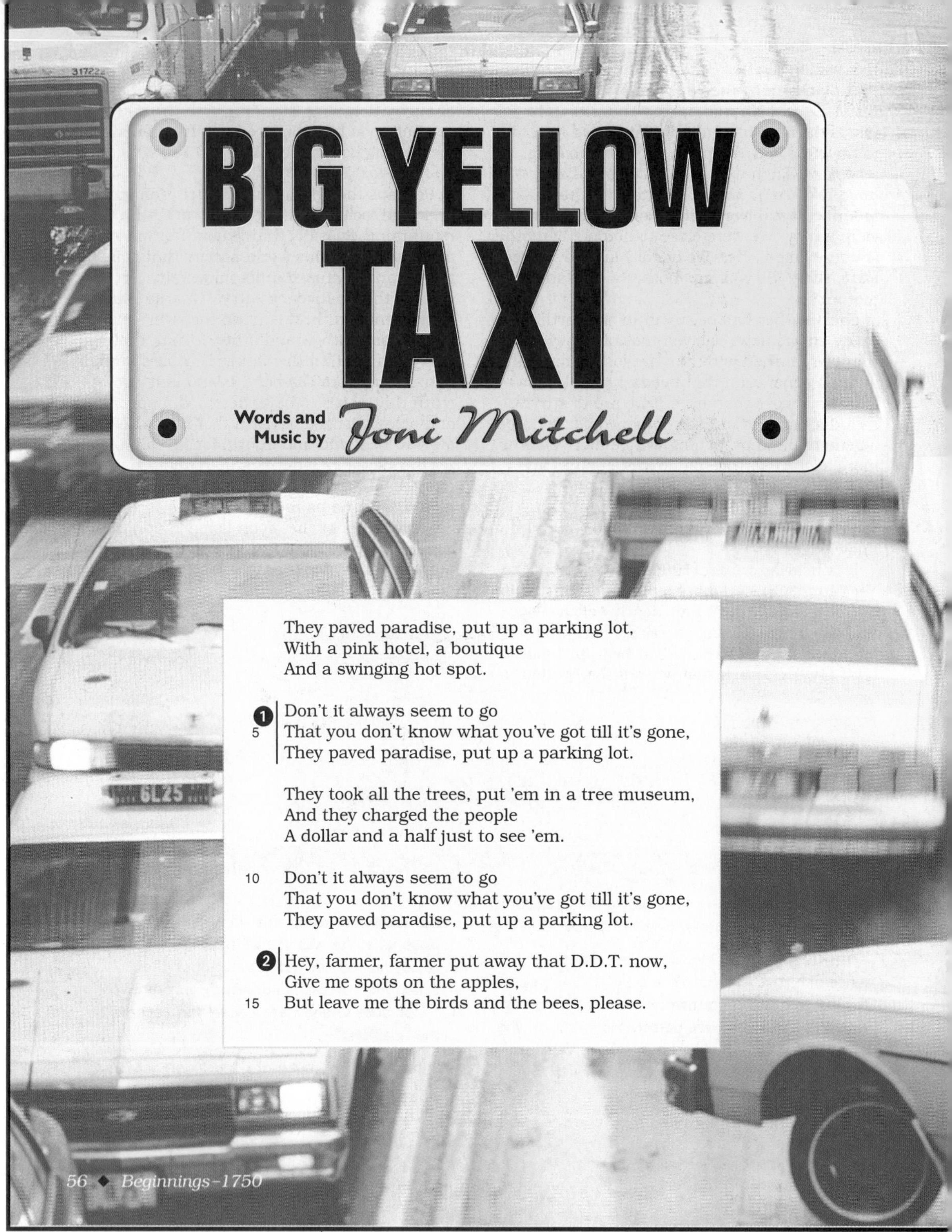

BIG YELLOW TAXI

Words and Music by *Joni Mitchell*

They paved paradise, put up a parking lot,
With a pink hotel, a boutique
And a swinging hot spot.

❶ Don't it always seem to go
That you don't know what you've got till it's gone,
They paved paradise, put up a parking lot.

They took all the trees, put 'em in a tree museum,
And they charged the people
A dollar and a half just to see 'em.

Don't it always seem to go
That you don't know what you've got till it's gone,
They paved paradise, put up a parking lot.

❷ Hey, farmer, farmer put away that D.D.T. now,
Give me spots on the apples,
But leave me the birds and the bees, please.

Beyond the Classroom

Career Connection

Singer-Songwriter Like Joni Mitchell, Paul Simon, Shawn Colvin, and others, some talented people combine a love of music and words to become singer-songwriters. They write lyrics, compose and arrange the music, and record or perform their work. Some singer-songwriters specialize in certain types of music, such as the blues, political ballads, or children's songs. Others explore a range of musical styles. Inform students that not all singer-songwriters are performing artists. Many work in the commercial side of the industry, writing song lyrics and music for soundtracks to television shows, television and radio commercials, and movies of all kinds.

Invite interested students to identify current singer-songwriters they enjoy, and learn about their backgrounds. They might interview people who have written songs to get a clearer understanding of the breadth of the task, necessary equipment, training, and so on. You might invite emerging singer-songwriters in your school to perform for the class and talk about their craft.

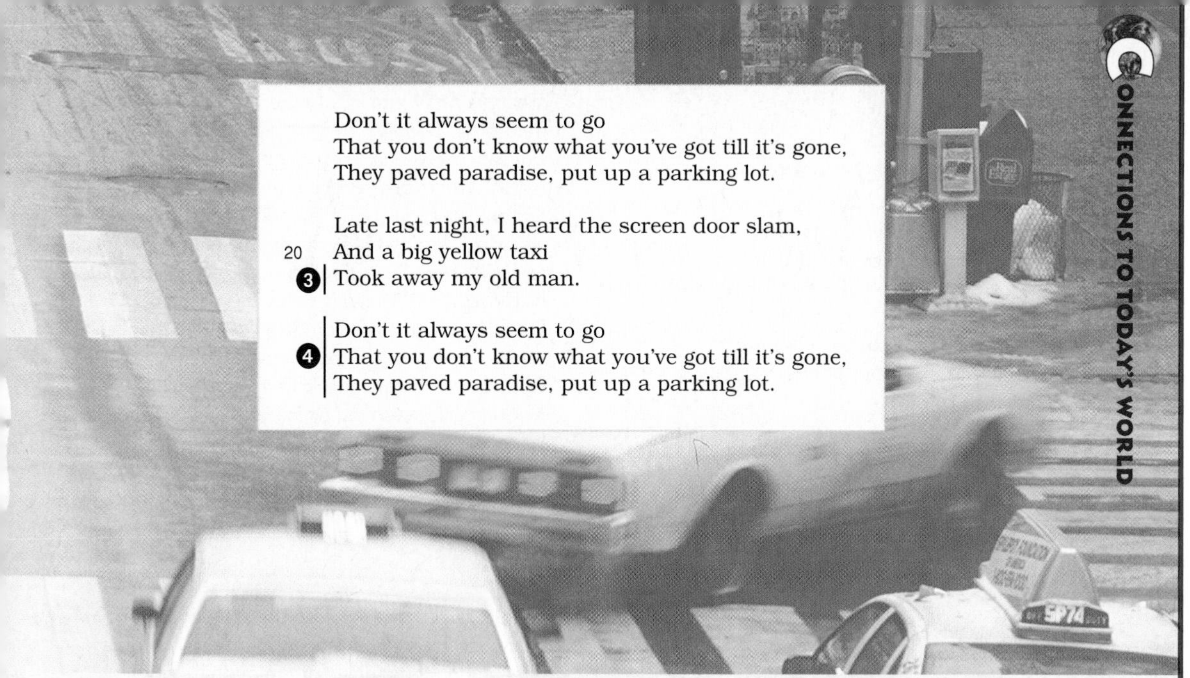

Don't it always seem to go
That you don't know what you've got till it's gone,
They paved paradise, put up a parking lot.

Late last night, I heard the screen door slam,
And a big yellow taxi
❸ Took away my old man.

Don't it always seem to go
❹ That you don't know what you've got till it's gone,
They paved paradise, put up a parking lot.

Guide for Responding

◆ Literature and Your Life

Reader's Response Give an example of someone or something you didn't fully appreciate until it was too late.

Thematic Focus What are the two "cultures" represented in "Big Yellow Taxi"? How would Mitchell describe the interaction of these cultures?

Questions for Research Find out about some measures taken to preserve natural spaces. Think of relevant questions about wilderness areas, such as these: What legislation maintains these areas? Which laws reduce it? How does a national forest differ from a national park?

☑ Check Your Comprehension

1. What human creations replace nature in "Big Yellow Taxi"?
2. What happens to the trees?
3. What examples does Mitchell provide to prove "you don't know what you've got till it's gone"?

◆ Critical Thinking

INTERPRET

1. Why does Grandfather ask the narrator to visit in "Diamond Island: Alcatraz"?
2. Explain why Darryl Babe Wilson's generation needs "original knowledge" in order to survive. **[Infer]**
3. What do the apples with spots symbolize in this song? **[Interpret]**

EVALUATE

4. How do you think the Native American creators of the origin myths would feel about the world Mitchell describes in "Big Yellow Taxi"? Explain. **[Speculate]**

EXTEND

5. Wilson writes about preserving a heritage. What do people in your culture do to preserve their identity as a culture? **[Community Link].**
6. How can the phrase "you don't know what you've got till it's gone" be applied to Darryl Babe Wilson's efforts as a writer? **[Literature Link]**

Beyond the Selection

Other Songs by Joni Mitchell
"The Circle Game"
"Woodstock"
"Both Sides Now"
"Chelsea Morning"

We recommend that you preview these songs before sharing them with students.

INTERNET

You and your students may find additional information about Joni Mitchell on the Internet. We suggest the following sites. Please be aware, however, that sites may have changed since this information was published.

For information about Mitchell's live and music, visit her home page at **http://www. jonimitchell.com/**

We *strongly recommend* that you preview sites before you send students to them.

Answers

◆ Literature and Your Life

Reader's Response Students may cite friends, family members, pets, or things that they have lost or left behind.

Thematic Focus Mitchell implies that there is no interaction between the two cultures: modern society obliterates the natural world.

☑ Check Your Comprehension

1. A parking lot, a hotel, a boutique, and a nightclub replace nature.
2. They are preserved in a museum.
3. She provides the following examples: losing a natural paradise to a parking lot; losing the trees to a museum; losing the birds and bees to insecticides; and losing her boyfriend.

◆ Critical Thinking

1. Before he dies, Grandfather wants to tell the narrator the story of his people's escape from Diamond Island and their trek to Mount Shasta. Grandfather probably feels confident that the truths in the story—as well as the facts—will be recorded.
2. The author's generation needs "original knowledge" to survive as a people because their heritage is in the minds of their elders, not in academic history texts.
3. The apples are in their natural state; they symbolize an environment that people have not yet tampered with.
4. Suggested response: The early Native Americans would be horrified by a world in which nature has nearly been wiped out by "civilization." They would probably agree with Mitchell that we will not fully appreciate what we have lost until it is too late to get it back.
5. Students may describe specific traditions or religious and holiday celebrations where food, music, and stories characteristic of their particular culture are shared.
6. Wilson is striving to preserve the heritage that he fears is slipping away as the "ancient ones" who retain the history and heritage of the Native American people in their hearts and heads begin to dwindle in number.

Answers
Thematic Connection

1. Because they have been born into modern American society and lack the cultural knowledge of their elders, Wilson feels that his generation of Native Americans is part of a different culture from that of the elders who were "born into the wild."
2. (a) The word "paradise" symbolizes nature, which is being lost to the forces of progress or urbanization. (b) Once built up and paved over, the land is absorbed into cities and towns and it becomes almost impossible to restore the landscape to its natural state.
3. Students' responses should reflect their understanding of the many subtle forms of "culture" that exist and the resulting potential for the exchange—or clash—of ideas.

Idea Bank

Customizing for
Performance Levels

Following are suggestions for matching Idea Bank topics with your students' performance levels:
Less Advanced Students: 1, 5
Average Students: 2, 4
More Advanced Students: 3

Customizing for
Learning Modalities

Following are suggestions for matching Idea Bank topics with your students' learning modalities:
Intrapersonal: 1
Interpersonal: 4
Verbal/Linguistic: 4
Body/Kinesthetic: 5

Thematic Connection

Meeting of Cultures

Though Cabeza de Vaca's experiences with Native Americans he encountered while traveling through Texas are a classic example of the meeting of two very different cultures, this theme can take many different forms. Sometimes, as illustrated in "Big Yellow Taxi" and "Diamond Island: Alcatraz," there can be a conflict between different aspects of the same culture or a clash between opposing values of different cultures.

1. Wilson says that he feels like a domesticated creature or "white man" when he talks to the elders of his people. In what ways does the relationship between younger and more elderly Native Americans reflect a "meeting of cultures"?

2. Explain how the saying "Paradise once lost can never be regained" relates to "Big Yellow Taxi." (a) What does "paradise" symbolize, and to what is it lost? (b) Why can it never be regained?

3. Describe a situation from your own life or observations that you feel represents a "meeting of cultures." What are the "cultures" involved? Is the meeting characterized by friendly exchange, or is it more a clash of cultures?

Idea Bank

Writing

1. Cultural Story Think of a story that you believe represents your culture or deserves to be handed down to future generations. Then preserve it in writing. The story may be about an incident from your own life or that of a relative or family friend.

2. Museum Brochure "Big Yellow Taxi" paints a picture of a world so far removed from its natural state that trees are a rarity seen only in a "tree museum." In such a world, what else might be found only in museums? Create a brochure for a museum of the future that exhibits endangered objects. Include an overview of the museum's collection and background information on where or how several important display items were obtained. **[Career Link]**

3. Persuasive Essay Though often dominated by colonists who did not understand or respect their cultures, both Native Americans and enslaved Africans clung tightly to the unifying strength of their respective heritage. Thanks to that determination, many Native and African Americans still practice the customs and religions of their ancestors. Write an essay in which you persuade your readers to explore and preserve their own cultural heritage for themselves and for future generations. Use the selections you have read to argue the need for greater awareness and understanding of the richness of the many cultures that form the American mosaic. **[Social Studies Link]**

Speaking, Listening, and Viewing

4. Television Interview Work with a classmate to stage an interview with Grandfather for a television program called "Native American Focus." Begin by developing a set of interview questions about Grandfather's memories of his childhood escape from Alcatraz. Then outline Grandfather's answers using information from the selection. Use your prepared notes to stage the interview for your class. **[Media Link]**

Researching and Representing

5. Time Capsule How would you represent modern American culture to future generations or a different culture? Work in a small group to create a time capsule of items that you believe capture the time in which you live. Choose a range of items that reflect current events, popular culture, trends, and attitudes. Once you have gathered at least a half dozen items, create identifying labels for each. Present your finished time capsule to your class, and explain the rationale for selecting each item. **[Social Studies Link]**

Online Activity www.phlit.phschool.com

ASSESSMENT OPTIONS

Formal Assessment, Selection Test, pp. 13–14, and Assessment Resources Software. The selection test is designed so that it can be easily customized to the performance levels of your students.

PORTFOLIO ASSESSMENT
Use the following rubrics in the ***Alternative Assessment*** booklet to assess student writing:
Cultural Story: Narrative Based on Personal Experience Rubric, p. 111
Museum Brochure: Description Rubric, p. 112
Persuasive Essay: Persuasion Rubric, p. 120

Writing Process Workshop

Cause-and-Effect Essay

When Europeans stepped onto North American soil, they opened the door for more settlements and the eventual creation of a new nation. They set off a chain of events that changed the world. The European settlement of North America is an ideal topic for a **cause-and-effect essay**—an essay that examines the reasons behind an event or phenomenon and explains the effects of that event. Write a cause-and-effect essay explaining an event or phenomenon that interests you. The following skills, introduced in this section's Guided Writing Lessons, will help you write your essay.

Writing Skills Focus

- ▶ **Use precise details** to support your explanations. (See p. 41.)
- ▶ **Use effective repetition** to emphasize your main points. (See p. 31.)
- ▶ **Outline the sequence of events** to make it easy for readers to follow the causes and effects. (See p. 49.)

Note that in this example, Olaudah Equiano gives several causes for a single effect—his awe and amazement at the unfamiliar things he observes while on a slave ship.

MODEL FROM LITERATURE

from *The Interesting Narrative of the Life of Olaudah Equiano*
by Olaudah Equiano

During our passage, I first saw flying fishes, which surprised me very much; they used frequently to fly across the ship, and many of them fell on the deck. ① I also now first saw the use of the quadrant; I had often with astonishment seen mariners make observations with it, and I could not think what it meant. They at last took notice of my surprise; and one of them, willing to increase it, as well as to gratify my curiosity, made me one day look through it. The clouds appeared to me to be land, which disappeared as they passed along. This heightened my wonder; ② and I was now more persuaded than ever that I was in another world, and that every thing about me was magic . . . ③

① This precise detail about flying fish helps the reader see why this sight inspired awe in Equiano.

② Equiano emphasizes his amazement through repeated references to his feelings.

③ Equiano provides a list of causes—from flying fish to unusual clouds—that contribute to his amazement.

Prepare and Engage

LESSON OBJECTIVES

- To use recursive writing processes to write a cause-and-effect essay
- To recognize and correct run-on sentences
- To recognize and correct stringy sentences

Distribute the Cause-Effect scoring rubric (p. 117 in the ***Alternative Assessment*** booklet) to make students aware of the criteria on which their work will be evaluated. See the suggestions on page 61 for customizing the rubric to this workshop.

You may also want to present to the class the Cause-and-Effect Organizer from the ***Writing and Language Transparencies*** Graphic Organizers.

Writers at Work Videodisc
To introduce students to key characteristics of expository writing, and to show them how curator Thom Harrington uses elements of cause-and-effect essays when writing about history, play the videodisc segment on Exposition (Ch. 3).

Play frames 23159 to 33243

Writing Lab CD-ROM
If your students have access to computers, you may want to have them work in the tutorial on Exposition to complete all or part of their cause-and-effect essays. Have students follow these steps:

1. Review the audio-annotated model of a cause-and-effect essay.
2. Complete an interactive questionnaire and a chain of events activity designed to help gather details.
3. Draft their essays on computer.
4. Respond to an interactive Self-Evaluation Checklist to judge the effectiveness of their essay.

Cross-Curricular Connection: Social Studies

Use the example provided of the European settlement of North America as a springboard for a class discussion about causal analyses of historical forces. Students may be familiar with reasons—or causes—for establishing such settlements: Many Europeans migrated to North America to escape persecution in their homelands; others were tempted by the "spirit of exploration"; still others had economic motivations. Though these causes are different, the impact (or effect) was ultimately the same on Native Americans: an encroachment on their land and way of life. Point out that historians and other social scientists employ cause-and-effect analyses not only to gain insight into events but also into the lives of groups or individuals. Ask, what are some of the writing purposes social scientists might use? *Student responses might include that social scientists explore events in history in order to determine what, if anything, might have been done differently to avoid particular outcomes. They also notice parallels between widely differing events in order to formulate general theories.*

Develop Student Writing

Prewriting Strategy

As students choose a topic for the essays, remind them that they may need to narrow their initial topics to avoid tackling subjects that are too complex to be dealt with in a single essay. Discuss how the three topic ideas provided in the student edition might be narrowed in scope.

Use a trifold to have students explore more specific levels of each topic.

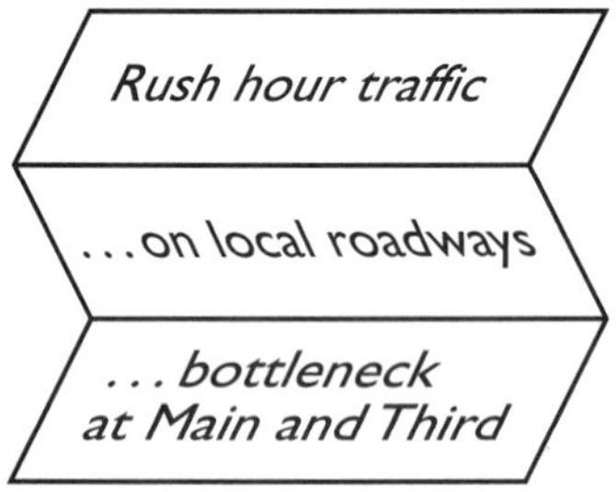

Customize for ***Visual/Spatial Learners***

Ask these students how they might improve the type of flowchart shown to help them with their own essays. At the publishing stage, encourage visual/spatial learners to design a more detailed, graphically-enhanced chart that can be provided to readers as a visual aid.

Writing Lab CD-ROM

Have students review the audio-annotated examples of different types of details in the Gathering Details section of the tutorial. They can see examples of how statistics, quotations, and comparisons lend their writing credibility.

Elaboration Strategy

Though students are instructed to bear in mind the introduction-body-conclusion method of organization, make clear that causes and effects should not map discretely to these sections. That is, writers should not limit their discussion of effects to the conclusion alone.

Applying Language Skills: Correct Run-on Sentences

A run-on sentence has two or more main clauses incorrectly punctuated as a single sentence.

Run-on Sentence:

The strike hurt baseball, fans lost interest.

To correct a run-on sentence, divide the main clauses into separate sentences, add a semicolon, or use a comma and a conjunction between main clauses.

Revised Sentences:

The strike hurt baseball. Fans lost interest in the game.

or

The strike hurt baseball; fans lost interest in the game.

or

The strike hurt baseball, and fans lost interest in the game.

Practice Revise this sentence three ways.

Ticket prices went up, fans stayed away.

Writing Application Revise your essay to eliminate any run-on sentences.

Writer's Solution Connection
Language Lab

For more practice correcting run-on sentences, complete the Language Lab lesson on Fragments and Run-on Sentences.

Prewriting

Choose a Topic Your essay can explain the cause of a current effect (for example, why the stock market is surging or sagging) or predict the future effects of current causes (where the stock market will be next year). You can also choose one of the topic ideas listed here.

Topic Ideas

- The causes of rush-hour traffic jams on local roadways
- The effects of expansion on a professional sport
- The effects of a certain school rule on student behavior

Gather Details Conduct research to learn more about causes and effects related to your topic. Generate questions like these to guide your research. To direct your exploration toward the most relevant points, address these key questions about your subject:

- ▶ Who are the people involved?
- ▶ How are they affected?
- ▶ What are the causes?
- ▶ What can be done to change the situation?

Outline the Sequence of Events Once you've finished gathering information, use a graphic organizer like this flowchart to outline the sequence of causes and effects. Keep in mind that the cause of a subsequent event may itself be the effect of a preceding cause.

Baseball strike results in the cancellation of 1994 World Series.
↕
Attendance remains low.
↕
Owners introduce limited regular season interleague play.
↕
Temporary surge in attendance.

Drafting

Organize Your Material Into an Introduction, Body, and Conclusion To arrange your material in the most readable and understandable way, introduce your topic clearly, develop it fully in the body of your essay, and restate it persuasively in your conclusion.

Applying Language Skills

Correct Run-on Sentences In the example run-on sentence provided ("The strike hurt baseball, fans lost interest"), the writer may be trying to express a cause and its effect in a single sentence. However, explain to students that the poor grammar makes the relationship unclear because it is difficult for readers to see where one idea ends and another begins. When reviewing the three possible ways of correcting the run-on sentence provided, ask students which method they prefer and why. Remind them that they need to make the same sort of thoughtful choices while drafting and revising their essays.

Answers

1. Ticket prices went up. Fans stayed away.
2. Ticket prices went up; fans stayed away.
3. Ticket prices went up, and fans stayed away.

Grammar Reinforcement

In addition to the **Language Lab CD-ROM** lesson cited in the student edition, you might have students complete the practice pages on run-on sentences (p. 45), end marks (p. 85), and semicolons (p. 89) in the *Writer's Solution Grammar Practice Book.*

Note Places for Further Development If your first draft has passages that could use more specific details, don't stop to fill them in. Complete your draft, but mark those sections for further development.

Revising

Use a Checklist Refer to the Writing Skills Focus on p. 59, and use the items as a checklist to evaluate and revise your essay.

- Have I used precise details?
  Replace vague or abstract details with more precise language and images. Fill in any spots that you marked for later development.
- Have I used repetition effectively?
  Look for places where you can reinforce key points through repetition.
- Have I clearly outlined the sequence of events?
  Ask a peer reviewer to restate the chain of causes and effects. If the relationships are unclear, refer to your outline and add transitions to strengthen connections between ideas.

Revision Model

The dramatic impact of interleague play was especially visible in New York in 1997, when the New York Yankees met the New York Mets [at Yankee Stadium] ① before a [capacity] ② crowd ~~that was much larger than usual.~~ [of 56,000. The roaring enthusiasm of the huge crowd left no doubt that the temporary experiment had a long future.] ③

① The writer fills in missing details.
② The writer replaces a long phrase with a single precise word.
③ The writer adds a prediction about the future.

Publishing

- **Informative Speech** Present your essay in a speech to classmates. Use charts, graphs, or diagrams to clarify the cause-and-effect relationships you describe.

APPLYING LANGUAGE SKILLS: Avoid Stringy Sentences

Stringy sentences contain many ideas connected by words like *and, so, or,* and *then.*

Stringy Sentence:

The players went on strike, and the fans became angry, because they were aware of the players' huge salaries, and knew the owners were very wealthy.

To revise stringy sentences, decide which ideas are closely related and which are not. Break separate ideas into distinct sentences.

Revised Sentences:

When the players went on strike, the fans became angry. Fans were aware that players made huge salaries, and knew that the owners were very wealthy.

Writing Application As you revise your cause-and-effect essay, be on the lookout for stringy sentences. Revise any you find by breaking them up into shorter sentences.

Writer's Solution Connection Writing Lab

For help gathering details, use the self-interview questionnaire in the Exposition tutorial in the Writing Lab.

Revision Strategy

Both the Writing Skills Focus and the checklist here identify the repetition of main points as a key skill. However, point out to students that they should revise to avoid nearly identical *expressions* of those ideas. Encourage them to vary sentence structure and word choice.

Publishing

If students wish to prepare an oral presentation of their essays as suggested in the student edition, guide them to the effective use of flip pads and markers, or overhead transparencies.

Applying Language Skills

Avoid Stringy Sentences Point out that in the stringy sentence provided, the writer attempts to make several causal links in the space of a single sentence. In the revised sentences the different causes and effects are separated, but are linked closely enough to express the relationship between the different ideas.

Grammar Reinforcement

For additional instruction and practice, have students complete practice page 110 in the *Writer's Solution Grammar Practice Book.*

Reinforce and Extend

Reflect on Writing Ask students what new things they learned about their topics by approaching them from a cause-and-effect angle.

Prentice Hall Writing and Grammar For more prewriting, elaboration, and revision strategies, see *Prentice Hall Writing and Grammar.*

ASSESSMENT		4	3	2	1
PORTFOLIO ASSESSMENT Use the Cause-Effect rubric in ***Alternative Assessment*** (p. 117) to assess students' writing. Add these criteria to customize the rubric to this assignment.	**Avoids Stringy Sentences**	The writer consistently avoids using stringy sentences by breaking ideas into distinct sentences.	The writer occasionally uses stringy sentences, but usually makes ideas distinct by using different sentences.	The writer often has trouble breaking down stringy sentences into shorter ones.	The writer consistently uses stringy sentences, making the essay difficult to read.
	Effective Repetition	The writer repeats main ideas at appropriate points in the essay in a way that clearly supports the thesis.	The writer repeats main points, but not always in a way that supports the thesis.	The writer avoids repeating main points, or does so in largely ineffective manner.	The writer does not repeat the essay's main points at all, weakening the overall unity of the essay.

Prepare and Engage

LESSON OBJECTIVES

- To read in varied sources, such as maps
- To use text organizers such as overviews, headings, and graphic features to locate and categorize information

Apply the Strategies

One way to guide students to "connect the dots" is to have them note the region in which the Bosnian troops are located; the three icons in the western section of the map are on the Bosnian controlled border. In contrast, the Serb troops are surrounding the city of Sarajevo.

Answers

1. Fighting was most intense in the areas immediately around Sarajevo, with many battles taking place only five or ten miles outside the city.
2. Fighting was intense in this area because both sides realized the importance of capturing Sarajevo.
3. The Bosnian government seems to have made protecting key urban areas such as Breza, Visoko, and Kiseljak a priority.
4. The city of Sarajevo is surrounded by mountains and waterways, making an invasion difficult.
5. If Bosnian leaders could have clearly seen the direction of the Serb troop movements, they might have redirected more Bosnian forces to defend Sarajevo instead of the outlying areas.

Student Success Workshop

Real-World Reading Skills — Reading a Map

Strategies for Success

When you think of a map, the first thing that comes to mind may be an atlas or a history textbook. Maps are also common in newspapers, news magazines, and many other written texts. By offering a visual representation of a place, a map can help give you a clearer picture of a scene that an author describes using words.

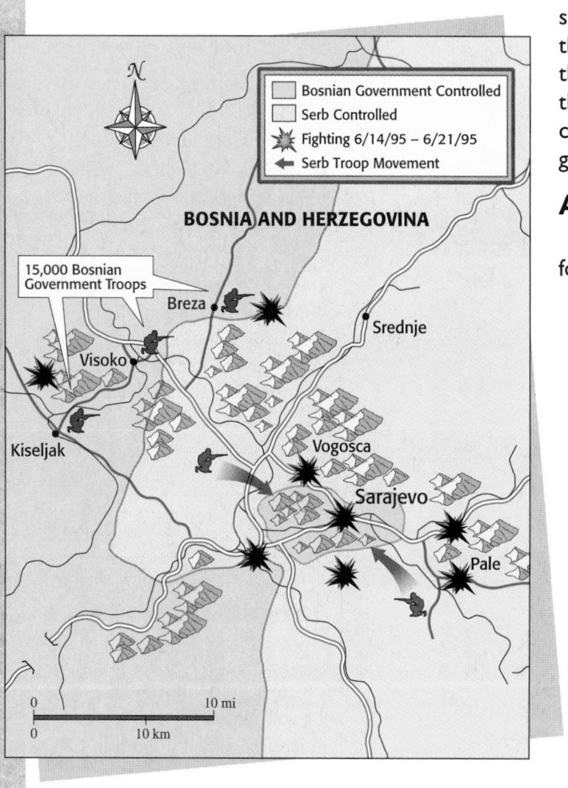

Read Between the Lines Like a book, a map must be read carefully to be properly understood. Most maps have a legend that provides distance scales and explains any symbols included on the map.

Connect the Dots The map on this page shows fighting that took place in and around the city of Sarajevo in a one-week period during the civil war in Bosnia. If you look closely, you'll see symbols representing Serb troop movement in the direction of the city of Sarajevo. Judging by the direction of the arrows, you can conclude that the Serbs' goal was to capture the city. By connecting the symbols in this way, you can gather important information from the map.

Apply the Strategies

Using the map on the left, answer the following questions.

1. Where was the fighting most intense during the week of June 14–21, 1995?
2. Why do you think the fighting was most intense in this area?
3. What can you infer about the priorities of the Bosnian government, judging by where it placed its troops?
4. What features would hinder an invasion of the city of Sarajevo?
5. How might this map have been of use to Bosnian government leaders?

Here are other situations in which you can apply map-reading skills:

- Reading news magazines
- Reading historical novels
- Traveling

Test Preparation Workshop

Reading Comprehension:
Reading a Map Reading and interpreting the information on a map is a skill that will help students perform on standardized tests.

Point out to students that many maps include a scale that can be used to calculate distances; this map provides a scale marker in both miles and kilometers.

Write this sample test item on the board to help students read a map:

Approximately how far in miles would troops have to travel to go from Visoko to Pale?

A 10 miles
B 15 miles
C 20 miles
D 25 miles

By measuring the distance with a ruler, then converting that figure to "real world" distances by using the scale, students should determine that the distance between Visoko and Pale is approximately 20 miles. Therefore, *C* is the correct answer. Discuss with students the ways in which understanding the distances between points on a map can make a map especially useful.

PART 2 *Focus on Literary Forms:*

Narrative Accounts

Building the Fort, Julien Binford, The Jamestown/Yorktown Educational Trust

The settlers who journeyed across a hostile ocean and forged homes in a new land were generally far too busy just surviving to create poems and other types of literature that matched those of other areas of the world. The early settlers did succeed, however, in writing vivid narrative accounts—a literary form that has remained popular to this day.

One-Minute Planning Guide

This section explores narrative accounts, both as a literary form and as a firsthand look at the lives of some of America's first European settlers. John Smith's *The General History of Virginia* is a colorful and subjective account of the establishment of Jamestown Colony. Smith's account is paired with William Bradford's modest, straightforward retelling of the Pilgrims' plight in *Of Plymouth Plantation.* Though quite different in tone, both accounts describe the Native Americans' important role in helping the settlers survive in the New World. The exploration of new worlds jumps to the space age in *The Right Stuff,* a contemporary account of the Mercury space program.

Customize for
Varying Student Needs

When assigning the selections in this part, keep in mind the following factors:

from *The General History of Virginia*

from *Of Plymouth Plantation*

- Firsthand accounts of New World settlements
- Less proficient readers may need help with complex language and lengthy sentences

from *The Right Stuff*

- High-interest, contemporary nonfiction account of space exploration
- Brief and accessible; some specialized vocabulary

Humanities: Art

Building the Fort, c. 1960, by Julien Binford.

This oil painting depicts the building of the fort at the colony at Jamestown, Virginia, in May 1607. According to historical accounts, Captain Smith ordered that the fort be built almost as soon as the colonists landed on shore. However, since many of the colonists had been gentlemen in England, they were reluctant to perform manual labor. During this early phase of construction, the colonists were taken by surprise by natives' bow-and-arrow attacks, and a number of them died. This violence persuaded the men to finish the fort quickly and they became more willing to do whatever laborious tasks were required.

Have your students link the painting to Part 2, "Narrative Accounts," by answering the following questions:

1. Looking at the image, would you say that the painter's attitude toward the Jamestown settlement was positive or negative? Why? *Most students will say that the painter's attitude was positive, based on such details as the warm colors in the painting; the settlers' orderly, cooperative labor; the sense of calm authority projected by the men who seem to be directing the work.*
2. What does the fact that the men are building a fort rather than engaged in some other activity suggest about the life of a settler in the New World? *It suggests that a settler's life was perceived as being endangered and in need of the collective bulwark of a fort.*

Prepare and Engage

LESSON OBJECTIVES

1. To develop vocabulary and word identification skills
- Related Words: Forms of *peril*
- Using the Word Bank: Antonym or Synonym?
- Extending Word Study: Prefixes (ATE)

2. To use a variety of reading strategies to comprehend historical fiction
- Connect Your Experience
- Reading Strategy: Break Down Sentences
- Read to Understand

3. To increase knowledge of other cultures and to connect common elements across cultures
- Background for Understanding: History

4. To express and support responses to the text
- Critical Thinking
- Analyze a Book Review (ATE)

5. To analyze literary elements
- Literary Focus: Narrative Accounts

6 To read in order to research self-selected and assigned topics
- Idea Bank: News Article
- Research Skills Mini-Lesson (ATE)
- Viewing and Representing Mini-Lesson (ATE)
- Idea Bank: Art
- Idea Bank: Advertisement
- Idea Bank: Menu

7. To plan, prepare, organize, and present literary interpretations
- Idea Bank: Memorial Speech
- Idea Bank: Dramatic Scene
- Idea Bank: Persuasive Speech

8. To use recursive writing processes to write a comparison of narratives
- Guided Writing Lesson

9. To increase knowledge of the rules of grammar and usage
- Grammar and Style: Plural and Possessive Nouns

Test Preparation

Supporting Details (ATE, p. 65) The teaching tips and sample test item in this workshop support the instruction and practice in the unit workshop:

Reading Comprehension: Summarizing Written Texts (SE, p. 115)

Guide for Interpreting

John Smith *(1580–1631)*

If John Smith were alive today, he'd be starring opposite Arnold Schwarzenegger in blockbuster adventure films—at least, that's probably where he'd see himself. Adventurer, poet, mapmaker, and egotist are just a few of the labels that apply to Smith, who earned a reputation as one of England's most famous explorers by helping to lead the first successful English colony in America. Stories of his adventures, often embellished by his own pen, fascinated readers of his day and continue to provide details about early exploration of the Americas.

Following a ten-year career as a soldier, Smith led a group of colonists to this continent, where they landed in Virginia in 1607 and founded Jamestown. As president of the colony from 1608 to 1609, Smith helped to obtain food, enforce discipline, and deal with the local Native Americans.

Though Smith returned to England in 1609, he made two more voyages to America to explore the New England coast. He published several works in the course of his life, including *The General History of Virginia, New England, and the Summer Isles* (1624).

William Bradford *(1590–1657)*

Survival in North America was a matter of endurance, intelligence, and courage. William Bradford had all three. Thirteen years after the founding of Jamestown, Bradford helped lead the Pilgrims to what is now Massachusetts.

Bradford, who was born in Yorkshire, England, joined a group of Puritan extremists who believed the Church of England was corrupt and wished to separate from it. In the face of stiff persecution, they eventually fled to Holland and from there sailed to North America.

After the death of the colony's first leader, the Pilgrims elected William Bradford governor. He was reelected thirty times. During his tenure, he organized the repayment of debts to financial backers, encouraged new immigration, and established good relations with the Native Americans, without whose help the colony never would have survived.

In 1630, Bradford began writing *Of Plymouth Plantation,* a firsthand account of the Pilgrims' struggle to endure, sustained only by courage and unbending faith. The work, written in the simple language known as Puritan Plain Style, was not published until 1856.

◆ Background for Understanding

History: The Colonial Experience

The trading company that financed the Jamestown expedition mistakenly believed that there was much money to be made in North America. John Smith was nearly sent to prison for not meeting his backers' financial expectations. It is not surprising, then, that Smith sometimes exaggerated the exploits of the settlers as they struggled to survive in the new land.

The Jamestown settlers weren't the only ones struggling. In 1620, after a difficult voyage aboard the tiny *Mayflower,* the Pilgrims landed not in Virginia, as intended, but much farther north near Cape Cod, Massachusetts. It was mid-December before they could build shelters and move ashore. During those dreary weeks of waiting on the ship, William Bradford's wife, Dorothy, fell overboard and was drowned.

Once ashore, the Pilgrims found the hardships of settling in a strange land worsened by a harsh winter and disputes over the validity of their charter, which had been for Virginia. The conflict led the settlers to create the "Mayflower Compact," the first agreement for self-government made by the colonists and a model for later settlements.

Prentice Hall Literature Program Resources

REINFORCE / RETEACH / EXTEND

Selection Support Pages
Build Vocabulary: Forms of *Peril,* p. 20
Grammar and Style: Possessive Nouns, p. 21
Reading Strategy: Break Down Sentences, p. 22
Literary Focus: Historical Narrative, p. 23

Strategies for Diverse Student Needs, p. 5

Beyond Literature
Humanities: Art, p. 5

Formal Assessment Selection Test, p. 19–21; Assessment Resources Software

Alternative Assessment, p. 5

Resource Pro CD-ROM

from The General History of Virginia ◆ *from* Of Plymouth Plantation ◆

◆ *Literature and Your Life*

CONNECT YOUR EXPERIENCE

You can probably remember a point in your life when everything seemed to be going against you. Consider what the early American colonists faced: starvation, exhaustion, illness, and the terror of the unknown. As the narratives show, determination pushed them on.

Journal Writing Write down your thoughts about what you imagine it was like to be an early settler.

THEMATIC FOCUS: MEETING OF CULTURES

The settlers faced many terrible risks for a chance at a new life. Would they have survived without the help of the Native Americans?

◆ Reading Strategy

BREAK DOWN SENTENCES

Break down the meaning of complex sentences by considering one section at a time. Separate the essential parts of the sentence (the *who* and *what)* from difficult language. Mentally bracket any descriptions that aren't essential. Below, John Smith explains why establishing a colony at Jamestown was so difficult.

> Such actions have [ever since the world's beginning] been subject to such accidents, [and everything of worth is found full of difficulties,] but nothing so difficult as to establish a commonwealth so far remote from men and means.

When you ignore the passages in brackets, you can easily get at the central point: *Actions like these have resulted in accidents before, but nothing as hard as establishing a commonwealth so far away from people and resources.*

◆ Grammar and Style

PLURAL AND POSSESSIVE NOUNS

In their narratives, Smith and Bradford use **possessive** nouns to show kinship and ownership. Notice that they follow these rules:

- Add an apostrophe and -*s* to show the possessive case of most singular nouns: the King's dearest daughter
- Add an apostrophe to show the possessive of plural nouns ending in -*s* or -*es*: in two or three months' time
- Add an apostrophe and -*s* to show the possessive of plural nouns that do not end in -*s* or -*es:* where men's minds are so untoward

◆ Literary Focus

NARRATIVE ACCOUNTS

Narrative accounts tell the story of real-life events. The selections that follow are **historical narratives,** narrative accounts that record significant historical events. Some historical narratives, including these, are firsthand accounts by people who lived through the events. Others are secondhand, or secondary, accounts by people who researched, but did not live through, the events. As you read, keep in mind that firsthand accounts are sometimes subjective because of the writer's personal involvement in the events.

◆ Build Vocabulary

RELATED WORDS: FORMS OF *PERIL*

In *Of Plymouth Plantation*, the Pilgrims found themselves in *peril,* or danger. You could describe their journey as *perilous,* an adjective meaning "full of danger." You could also say that undertaking such a risky voyage could *imperil* their lives. Now you've learned a verb that means "to place in danger."

WORD BANK

Preview this list of words from the selections.

pilfer
palisades
conceits
mollified
peril
loath
sundry
recompense

Test Preparation Workshop

Summarizing Written Texts: Supporting Details Many standardized tests require students to recognize summaries by identifying main ideas and supporting details. Students should recognize which details are important to the main idea and which are not. Present the following sample test item:

> With this lodging and diet, our extreme toil in bearing and planting palisades so strained and bruised us and our continual labor in the extremity of the heat had so weakened us, as were cause sufficient to have made us so miserable in our native country or any other place in the world.

Which of the following does NOT support the main idea that early Virginians were miserable in their new country?

A They were weak from planting their crops.
B They had little food.
C The heat was extreme.
D They were attacked by Native Americans.

All of these support the main idea EXCEPT choice D.

Interest Grabber

Write the following "Help Wanted" advertisement on the chalkboard:

> Wanted: Experienced leader capable of inspiring and governing people in life-threatening crisis situations. Ability to mediate disputes and maintain order in the face of chaos. Good interpersonal and communication skills. Community outreach efforts require overcoming language and cultural barriers. Basic bookkeeping, homebuilding, farming, trading, and political skills. Salary cannot be guaranteed; job security is nonexistent.

Ask students whether they would apply for this job. Then tell students that the narratives they are about to read were written by two men whose lives were the inspiration for this ad. They held one of the most challenging jobs imaginable: They were leaders of expeditions to the New World.

Customize for *Less Proficient Readers*

Have students work in pairs or small groups. Guide them to go *slowly* and to pause after each paragraph to paraphrase for one another. Encourage them to reread passages several times, breaking down sentences to get at their essence.

Customize for *AP Students*

Guide students to look for words used as different parts of speech or that have meanings other than those they are familiar with. Point out, for example, the word *fortuned* as a verb in the first sentence of Smith's narrative.

Customize for *English Language Learners*

Help students who are learning English by pointing out that the meanings of several words used in these narratives have changed since the accounts were written. You may wish to pair these students with more advanced readers who can help them to use context clues, to break down sentences, or to use dictionaries to figure out the meanings of these words, such as *wanted* and *demeaned.*

One-Minute Insight In this excerpt from *The General History of Virginia,* John Smith describes the rough beginning of the founding of Jamestown Colony. He emphasizes the struggle to cross the ocean, to find nourishment, and to live side by side with the Native Americans who preceded them. The narrative, which contains the romantic tale of Smith's rescue by Pocahontas, is not always completely historically accurate, as it strives to present the writer's deeds in a favorable light. It is, however, a firsthand account of a significant event and provides a rare look at the life of a historical figure written in his own words.

◆ Literature and Your Life

Point out to students that they are about to read firsthand accounts of historical events that have often been altered and romanticized by later popularized versions. Guide them to compare the events and people as seen by Smith and then Bradford with their more familiar popularized portrayal.

◆ Background for Understanding

History The events of Smith's narrative took place in 1607, nineteen years after England's defeat of the Spanish Armada left the seas almost entirely open to the British. The London Trading Company was the financial backer of the Jamestown expedition and operated the settlement as a private venture from 1607 to 1624. Bearing a close resemblance to some savings-and-loan companies of the 1980's, the London Trading Company sold "junk bonds" to finance this speculative real-estate venture. The company and its investors knew very little about the wilderness of North America and were unrealistic in their expectations of material gain from the colony.

▶Critical Viewing◀

❶ **Infer** Students may respond that the artist's portrayal indicates that he views the Native Americans as hostile or savage; they are shown in body paint and carry brutal-looking weapons.

from The General History of Virginia

John Smith

What Happened Till the First Supply

Connections to World Literature, *page 1150*

Founding of the First Permanent English Settlement in America, A. C. Warren, New York Public Library

❶ ▲ **Critical Viewing** What can you infer about the artist's attitude toward Native Americans from the way he depicts them? **[Infer]**

Block Scheduling Strategies

Consider these suggestions to take advantage of extended class time:

- Introduce the selection with the Interest Grabber on p. 65 of the teacher edition, then prepare students to read the text by reviewing the Literature and Your Life section (p. 65) or by playing the Literature CD-ROM feature on Smith and Bradford in *The History of American Literature:* Disk 1, Part 1, Feature 3.
- Present the Reading Strategy lesson (p. 65) and model this technique. Assign the Break Down Sentences page in ***Selection Support,*** p. 22, either before or after students have read the text.
- After reading the selections, use the Viewing and Representing Mini-Lesson in the teacher edition (p. 69) to support the Early American Art activity described in the Idea Bank (p. 77).
- Introduce the Guided Writing Lesson (p. 77) and review the basics of point-by-point and subject-by-subject organizations. Use the Comparison-and-Contrast Transparency, p. 87 in ***Writing and Language Transparencies,*** to help students organize their pre-writing notes.

2 Being thus left to our fortunes, it fortuned[1] that within ten days, scarce ten amongst us could either go[2] or well stand, such extreme weakness and sickness oppressed us. And thereat none need marvel if they consider the cause and reason, which was this: 3 While the ships stayed, our allowance was somewhat bettered by a daily proportion of biscuit which the sailors would pilfer to sell, give, or exchange with us for money, sassafras,[3] or furs. But when they departed, there remained neither tavern, beer house, nor place of relief but the common kettle.[4] Had we been as free from all sins as gluttony and drunkenness we might have been canonized for saints, but our President[5] would never have been admitted for engrossing to his private,[6] oatmeal, sack,[7] oil, aqua vitae,[8] beef, eggs, or what not but the kettle; that indeed he allowed equally to be distributed, and that was half a pint of wheat and as much barley boiled with water for a man a day, and this, having fried some twenty-six weeks in the ship's hold, contained as many worms as grains so that we might truly call it rather so much bran than corn; our drink was water, our lodgings castles in the air.

With this lodging and diet, our extreme toil in bearing and planting palisades so strained and bruised us and our continual labor in the extremity of the heat had so weakened us, as were cause sufficient to have made us as miserable in our native country or any other place in the world.

From May to September, those that escaped lived upon sturgeon and sea crabs. Fifty in this time we buried; the rest seeing the President's projects to escape these miseries in our pinnace[9] by flight (who all this time had neither felt want nor sickness) so moved our dead spirits as we deposed him and established Ratcliffe in his place . . .

4 But now was all our provision spent, the sturgeon gone, all helps abandoned, each hour expecting the fury of the savages; when God, the patron of all good endeavors, in that desperate extremity so changed the hearts of the savages that they brought such plenty of their fruits and provision as no man wanted.

> **◆ Reading Strategy**
> "Buried" in this long sentence is an important turn of events for the colonists. Break the sentence down to understand its meaning.

5 And now where some affirmed it was ill done of the Council[10] to send forth men so badly provided, this incontradictable reason will show them plainly they are too ill advised to nourish such ill conceits: First, the fault of our going was our own; what could be thought fitting or necessary we had, but what we should find, or want, or where we should be, we were all ignorant and supposing to make our passage in two months, with victual to live and the advantage of the spring to work; we were at sea five months where we both spent our victual and lost the opportunity of the time and season to plant, by the unskillful presumption of our ignorant transporters that understood not at all what they undertook.

Such actions have ever since the world's beginning been subject to such accidents, and everything of worth is found full of difficulties, but nothing so difficult as to

1. **fortuned** *v.*: Happened.
2. **go** *v.*: Be active.
3. **sassafras** (sas´ ə fras´) *n.*: A tree, the root of which was valued for its supposed medicinal qualities.
4. **common kettle:** Communal cooking pot.
5. **President:** Wingfield, the leader of the colony.
6. **engrossing to his private:** Taking for his own use.
7. **sack** *n.*: Type of white wine.
8. **aqua vitae** (ak´ wə vit´ ē): Brandy.
9. **pinnace** (pin´ is) *n.*: Small sailing ship.
10. **Council:** The seven persons in charge of the expedition.

◆ Build Vocabulary

pilfer (pil´ fər) *v.*: Steal

palisades (pal´ə sādz´) *n.*: Large, pointed stakes set in the ground to form a fence used for defense

conceits (kən sētz´) *n.*: Strange or fanciful ideas

◆ Reading Strategy

2 Break Down Sentences You may wish to break down the first sentence and restate it so that it is easier to follow. Encourage students to use this strategy throughout this piece and the next to help them figure out the meanings of difficult passages.

Comprehension Check ☑

3 Ask students how the settlers were able to supplement their meager diets while the ship that brought them to Virginia was still docked nearby. *Students should respond that they bought or traded for rations of biscuits from the ship's crew.* Make sure students understand that the ship soon left to return to England and only the colonists remained.

◆ Reading Strategy

4 Break Down Sentences Students should respond that Smith explains that when all seemed lost, God saw to it that the Native Americans came to the rescue of the desperate settlers with plentiful gifts of food.

◆ Literary Focus

5 Narrative Accounts Ask students: What is Smith's motive for writing this passage? *Students should respond that he is trying to shift blame away from himself and other expedition leaders by recounting the chain of events, decisions, and assumptions that resulted in the desperate situation in Virginia.*

Humanities: Art

Founding of the First Permanent English Settlement in America, c. 19th century, by Asa Coolidge Warren (1819–1904).

This engraving illustrates the moment when Pocahontas, Powhatan's daughter, came to the rescue of the English captive, John Smith.

Warren, the son of a Boston portrait painter, showed an early interest in engraving and then apprenticed to an engraver. After years of engraving and also drawing on wood for other engravers, he had to stop altogether when he lost the sight in one eye. Thereafter, Warren turned to painting instead.

Use these questions for discussion:

1. Imagine that you were present in the scene depicted here. How would you describe it? *Students' answers can include the looks of surprise and confusion many express, the eagerness the young men seem to show to do Smith harm, and the body language of those in the scene. Responses can also describe weapons, clothing, hairstyles, ornaments, and jewelry.*
2. The engraving describes Smith's account of the incident. Do you believe it happened this way? Did it happen at all? *Students will have differing opinions about the accuracy of Smith's account; they should be prepared to explain the reasoning behind their answers.*

◆ Critical Thinking

❶ **Analyze** Most historians consider Smith's account inaccurate on several occasions. Have students look for examples of Smith's subjectivity in this passage and elsewhere. *In the bracketed passage, students should cite Smith's discussion of his own good qualities.*

◆ Literary Focus

❷ **Narrative Accounts** Students should respond that Smith gives himself altogether too much credit for escaping and saving the settlement. They can say that it is unlikely that he was held in such high esteem by the Native Americans.

❸ **Clarification** Point out Smith's use of the terms *barbarians* and *savages* in this passage and elsewhere in his account. Discuss how this language shows his Eurocentrism and reveals how little he understood Native American cultures.

◆ Critical Thinking

❹ **Speculate** Ask students to explain why the Native Americans let Smith live, while killing the others in his party. *Students can respond that they respected him for being a leader or that they were impressed by the way he defended himself from them.*

◆ Literature and Your Life

❺ Ask students whether they have ever tried to impress or dazzle someone with their knowledge, as Smith does here. Invite volunteers who say they have had this experience to describe the circumstances and explain how it turned out.

Extending Word Study

Prefixes Remind students that knowing the meaning of a prefix will help them unlock the meanings of new words. Write the word *antipode* on the board and ask a student to give the meaning of the prefix and the word. Suggest that students form two groups to play a word game using the prefix *anti-*. The first group makes a list of ten words with the prefix *anti-*. The second group is challenged to write the definitions of the list of words. Then the second group creates a list of words for the first group to define. To verify definitions, the words must be checked in a dictionary.

establish a commonwealth so far remote from men and means and where men's minds are so untoward[11] as neither do well themselves nor suffer others. But to proceed.

❶ The new President and Martin, being little beloved, of weak judgment in dangers, and less industry in peace, committed the managing of all things abroad[12] to Captain Smith, who, by his own example, good words, and fair promises, set some to mow, others to bind thatch, some to build houses, others to thatch them, himself always bearing the greatest task for his own share, so that in short time he provided most of them lodgings, neglecting any for himself. . . .

Leading an expedition on the Chickahominy River, Captain Smith and his men are attacked by Indians, and Smith is taken prisoner.

When this news came to Jamestown, much was their sorrow for his loss, few expecting what ensued.

> **◆ Literary Focus**
> How does this paragraph alert you to the fact that Smith's account is not completely objective?

❷ ❸ Six or seven weeks those barbarians kept him prisoner, many strange triumphs and conjurations they made of him, yet he so demeaned himself amongst them, as he not only diverted them from surprising the fort, but procured his own liberty, and got himself and his company such estimation amongst them, that those savages admired him.

The manner how they used and delivered him is as followeth:

The savages having drawn from George Cassen whither Captain Smith was gone, prosecuting that opportunity they followed him with three hundred bowmen, conducted by the King of Pamunkee,[13] who in divisions searching the turnings of the river found Robinson and Emry by the fireside; those they shot full of arrows and slew. Then finding the Captain, as is said, that used the savage that was his guide as his shield (three of them being slain and divers[14] others so galled),[15] all the rest would not come near him. Thinking thus to have returned to his boat, regarding them, as he marched, more than his way, slipped up to the middle in an oozy creek and his savage with him; yet dared they not come to him till being near dead with cold he threw away his arms. Then according to their compositions[16] they drew him forth and led him to the fire where his men were slain. Diligently they chafed his benumbed limbs. ❹

He demanding for their captain, they showed him Opechancanough, King of Pamunkee, to whom he gave a round ivory double compass dial. Much they marveled at the playing of the fly and needle,[17] which they could see so plainly and yet not touch it because of the glass that covered them. But when he demonstrated by that globe-like jewel the roundness of the earth and skies, the sphere of the sun, moon, and stars, and how the sun did chase the night round about the world continually, the greatness of the land and sea, the diversity of nations, variety of complexions, and how we were to them antipodes[18] and many other such like matters, they all stood as amazed with admiration. ❺

Nothwithstanding, within an hour after, they tied him to a tree, and as many as could stand about him prepared to shoot him, but the King holding up the compass in his hand, they all laid down their bows

11. **untoward** *adj.*: Stubborn.
12. **abroad** *adv.*: Outside the palisades.
13. **Pamunkee:** Pamunkee River.
14. **divers** (dī′ vərz) *adj.*: Several.
15. **galled** *v.*: Wounded.
16. **composition** *n.*: Ways.
17. **fly and needle** *n.*: Parts of a compass.
18. **antipodes** (an tip′ ə dēz′) *n.*: Two places on opposite sides of the Earth.

Viewing and Representing Mini-Lesson

Early American Art
This mini-lesson supports activity 5, p. 77.

Introduce the Concept Have students look at p. 66 for an example of early American art. Explain that artists' interpretations were based on their own views. Ask students to consider ways that artists can convey messages through their paintings.

Develop the Background Students may meet in groups to identify artists of early American art and to research their work. Suggest that they use the library and Internet to gather material about various artists.

Apply the Information Students should begin with a list of research questions, for example: What artist is most noted for portraits, landscapes, or political scenes? How did historical events influence the artists' representations? What views on life and people are represented in the artists' work?

Assess the Outcome Evaluate students on their ability to present a variety of artists and on their interpretations of the artists' work.

and arrows and in a triumphant manner led him to Orapaks where he was after their manner kindly feasted and well used. . . .

At last they brought him to Werowocomoco, where was Powhatan, their Emperor. Here more than two hundred of those grim courtiers stood wondering at him, as he had been a monster, till Powhatan and his train had put themselves in their greatest braveries. Before a fire upon a seat like a bedstead, he sat covered with a great robe made of raccoon skins and all the tails hanging by. On either hand did sit a young wench of sixteen or eighteen years and along on each side the house, two rows of men and behind them as many women, with all their heads and shoulders painted red, many of their heads bedecked with the white down of birds, but every one with something, and a great chain of white beads about their necks.

6 At his entrance before the King, all the people gave a great shout. The queen of Appomattoc was appointed to bring him water to wash his hands, and another brought him a bunch of feathers, instead of a towel, to dry them; having feasted him after their best barbarous manner they could, a long consultation was held, but the conclusion was, two great stones were brought before Powhatan: then as many as could, laid hands on him, dragged him to them, and thereon laid his head and being ready with their clubs to beat out his brains, Pocahontas, the King's dearest daughter, when no entreaty could prevail, got his head in her arms and laid her own upon his to save him from death; whereat the Emperor was contented he should live to make him hatchets, and her bells, beads, and copper, for they thought him as well of all occupations as themselves.[19] For the King himself will make his own robes, shoes, bows, arrows, pots; plant, hunt, or do anything so well as the rest.

◆ Reading Strategy
7 Break down this long sentence to clarify the sequence of events.

Two days after, Powhatan, having disguised himself in the most fearfulest manner he could, caused Captain Smith to be brought forth to a great house in the woods and there upon a mat by the fire to be left alone. Not long after, from behind a mat that divided the house, was made the most dolefulest noise he ever heard; then Powhatan more like a devil than a man, with some two hundred more as black as himself, came unto him and told him now they were friends, and presently he should go to Jamestown to send him two great guns and a grindstone for which he would give him the country of Capahowasic and forever esteem him as his son Nantaquond.

So to Jamestown with twelve guides Powhatan sent him. That night they quartered in the woods, he still expecting (as he had done all this long time of his imprisonment) every hour to be put to one death or other, for all their feasting. But almighty God (by His divine providence) had mollified the hearts of those stern barbarians with compassion. The next morning betimes they came to the fort, where Smith having used the savages with what kindness he could, he showed Rawhunt, Powhatan's trusty servant, two demiculverins[20] and a millstone to carry Powhatan; they found them somewhat too heavy, but when they did see him discharge them, being loaded with stones, among the boughs of a great tree loaded with icicles, the ice and branches came so tumbling down that the poor savages ran away half dead with fear. But at last we regained some conference with them and gave them such toys and sent to Powhatan, his women, and children such presents as gave them in general full content. 8

19. **as well . . . themselves:** Capable of making them just as well as they could themselves.

20. **demiculverins** (dem′ ē kul′ vər inz): Large cannons.

◆ Build Vocabulary

mollified (mäl′ ə fīd′) *v.*: Soothed; calmed

◆ Background for Understanding

6 History The accuracy of Smith's account of his rescue by Pocahontas has been questioned by historians for several reasons. For one thing, in his early accounts of his capture, he never mentioned that she was twelve or thirteen at the time and he was twenty-eight. For another, no other contemporary accounts substantiate it. In addition, in other writings, Smith describes similar adventures with other admiring women.

◆ Reading Strategy

7 Break Down Sentences Students should begin by breaking the sentence down at each colon or semicolon. They can then further divide each portion into a series of individual events. Suggest that students may find it helpful to replace the many pronouns with nouns for clarification, as needed.

◆ Literary Focus

8 Narrative Accounts Ask students how Smith's depiction of the Native Americans changes toward the end of his captivity. Ask them to explain how he might have hoped this change would affect the reader's opinion of him. *Students can respond that Smith wants the reader to think well of him, because he outwitted the suddenly docile natives, dazzled them with European power, and won them over with kindness and generosity.*

Analyze a Movie Review

Steven Spielberg is known to be exceptionally careful about historical accuracy when making films. In making the movie *Amistad,* Spielberg took up the challenge of recreating the conditions on board a slave ship much like the one in which Olaudah Equiano sailed across the Atlantic. Working closely with Debbie Allen, producer of the film, Spielberg made every effort to capture on film the ugliness of the Middle Passage. As one actor said later, "It was hard not to cry. . . . Because you knew this was what my people went through."

Did Spielberg and Allen succeed? One reviewer said that the "harrowing Middle Passage scenes will not be forgotten by anyone who sees Spielberg's movie: the horrors of the slave trade have rarely been captured in such indelible, painful images." While Spielberg's true story was set in the middle of the 19th century and Equiano's memoir recounts a crossing made nearly a century earlier, students can use Equiano's narrative to test the movie's general faithfulness to the history of the slave trade. Have students view the movie and answer the following questions:

1. Does the movie present a generally accurate portrayal of conditions on board a slaver?
2. Were any elements of Equiano's account left out of the movie? What were they?

◆ Critical Thinking

❶ Compare and Contrast Discuss with students how Smith's attitude concerning the settlers' situation has changed since the early part of his account. *Students may say that Smith felt optimistic when he realized that the area provided food for those who knew how to obtain it. They may also point out that he probably felt more hopeful after he'd established a better relationship with the Native Americans.*

◆ Literary Focus

❷ Narrative Accounts Students may say that Smith wants his financial backers to know that despite many challenges, the colony is still afloat. He wants them to think that the success is largely due to his endeavors—and God's help.

Reinforce and Extend

Answers

◆ Literature and Your Life

Reader's Response Some students may point out that the voyage back to England might well have been just as dangerous as staying in Jamestown.

Thematic Focus Suggested responses: They were hoping to get rich or they had a sense of adventure.

☑ Check Your Comprehension

1. They are low on food and are weak and sick.
2. While the ships stay, the sailors trade provisions for money, sassafras, or furs. Later, the Native Americans bring them food.
3. He describes them as unpopular, poor in judgment, and lazy.
4. He praises his own good leadership, self-sacrifice, and hard work.

◆ Critical Thinking

1. Suggested response: He seems to be a vain man, impressed by his own cleverness, and a resourceful, capable and influential man.
2. He finds them to be backward, ignorant, and dangerous.
3. Suggested response: He does this to distance himself from the work, and make it seem less subjective.
4. Suggested response: Smith seems to have embellished and exaggerated some of his adventures.
5. Responses should reflect Smith's energy, ambition, and leadership qualities.

Now in Jamestown they were all in combustion,[21] the strongest preparing once more to run away with the pinnace; which, with the hazard of his life, with saker falcon[22] and musket shot, Smith forced now the third time to stay or sink.

Some, no better than they should be, had plotted with the President the next day to have him put to death by the Levitical law,[23] for the lives of Robinson and Emry; pretending the fault was his that had led them to their ends: but he quickly took such order with such lawyers that he laid them by their heels till he sent some of them prisoners for England.

Now every once in four or five days, Pocahontas with her attendants brought him so much provision that saved many of their lives, that else for all this had starved with hunger.

His relation of the plenty he had seen, especially at Werowocomoco, and of the state and bounty of Powhatan (which till that time was unknown), so revived their dead spirits (especially the love of Pocahontas) as all men's fear was abandoned. ❶

Thus you may see what difficulties still crossed any good endeavor; and the good success of the business being thus oft brought to the very period of destruction; yet you see by what strange means God hath still delivered it. ❷

◆ Literary Focus What does this last paragraph reveal about Smith's purpose in creating his narrative account?

21. **combustion** (kəm bəs´ chən) *n.*: Tumult.
22. **saker falcon**: Small cannon.
23. **Levitical law**: "He that killeth man shall surely be put to death" (Leviticus 24:17).

Guide for Responding

◆ Literature and Your Life

Reader's Response Would you have returned to England at the earliest opportunity or stayed on at Jamestown? Why?

Thematic Focus What might have prompted colonists to leave England and start new lives in America?

☑ Check Your Comprehension

1. What hardships do the colonists face during their first several months in this country?
2. What assistance do the colonists receive?
3. What criticisms does Smith make of the new president and colonist Martin?
4. Who or what does Smith praise in this account?

◆ Critical Thinking

INTERPRET

1. What impression of Smith do you get from this account? **[Infer]**
2. Describe Smith's attitude toward the Native Americans. **[Analyze]**
3. Why do you think Smith writes in the third person, referring to himself as "he" instead of "I"? **[Draw Conclusions]**

EVALUATE

4. Do you think that Smith's account is accurate down to the last detail? Why or why not? **[Evaluate]**

EXTEND

5. If Smith were alive today, what career might he have? Explain. **[Career Link]**

Research Skills Mini-Lesson

Drawing Conclusions from Research
This mini-lesson supports the Menu activity in the Idea Bank on p. 77.

Introduce the Concept Explain to students that after gathering facts, details, and other information, they can draw conclusions about the topic they have researched.

Develop the Background In doing the research for the Menu activity, students should generate their questions related to the foods colonists ate, the crops they planted, and the kinds of foods that were *not* in their diet. Explain that the more details they gather in their research about the topic, the more accurate their conclusions will be.

Apply the Information Before creating a menu, it may be helpful for students to organize the information in a chart. They might state their conclusions with references to the chart.

Assess the Outcome Evaluate students on their ability to draw conclusions based on the information they have researched. Use the Scoring Rubric: Research Report/Paper on p. 121 in the ***Alternative Assessment*** booklet.

from

Of Plymouth Plantation

William Bradford

The Coming of the Mayflower, N. C. Wyeth, from the Collection of the Metropolitan Life Insurance Company, New York City

3 ▲ **Critical Viewing** Is this an idealized or a realistic depiction of the *Mayflower's* Atlantic crossing? Explain your decision. **[Judge; Support]**

Of Their Voyage and How They Passed the Sea; and of Their Safe Arrival at Cape Cod

After they had enjoyed fair winds and weather for a season, they were encountered many times with cross winds and met with many fierce storms with which the ship was shroudly[1] shaken, and her upper works made very leaky; and one of the main beams in the midships was bowed and cracked, which put them in some fear that the ship

1. **shroudly** (shrood´ lē) *adv.*: Wickedly.

Humanities: Art

The Coming of the Mayflower by Newell Convers Wyeth (1882–1945).

N. C. Wyeth was a prolific American illustrator. He illustrated many popular and well-known works and became involved in the difficult art of mural painting. Wyeth's last mural commission was a series of eight huge pieces that express the spirit and heritage of New England. *The Coming of the Mayflower* was included in this series. Wyeth died before completing the project, but his son, the artist Andrew Wyeth, and his son-in-law, John McCoy, finished the work for him.

Use these questions for discussion:

1. What viewpoint does Wyeth use to lend drama to the scene? *The view is from land—perhaps the famous Plymouth Rock—toward which the ship appears to be headed. There is a sense of excitement and expectation.*
2. Wind plays a key role in the first part of Bradford's account. How does Wyeth demonstrate the power of wind in this mural? *Responses can point to the billowing sails, the listing ship, and the whitecaps in the choppy seas.*

Develop Understanding

One-Minute Insight In Puritan Plain Style, William Bradford presents a firsthand description of the initial experiences of the Massachusetts settlers known to us as the Pilgrims. Historians consider this to be a factually accurate account. Bradford relates how this community of families, united in their goals and religious beliefs, began the task of building a new settlement in the harsh wilderness. His account reflects his faith in God, whom he credits for the settlers' peaceful, beneficial relationship with their Native American neighbors.

Clarification Inform students that at the time Bradford wrote, *plantation* was a term for a new colony or settlement, and did not connote the presence of slavery.

Customize for
Interpersonal Learners
As students begin this narrative, have them think about what kinds of issues potentially hostile neighbors must work out to survive in such close proximity. They can consider the difficulties all parties will face trying to do so.

▶Critical Viewing◀

3 Judge; Support Students may respond that the colorful painting serves to glorify or romanticize the crossing because it does not portray the hardships endured by the ship's passengers. Others might say that the painting realistically depicts the rough seas the *Mayflower* was certain to have faced.

Customize for
Gifted/Talented Students
Students may be challenged by creating a dramatization of the meeting between Captain Smith and the Native Americans. Have them compose a drama for presentation to the class. Remind students to use what they have learned about writing dialogue, including appropriate verbal and nonverbal gestures, and representing history accurately.

Customize for
Visual/Spatial Learners
To help students picture the repairs made to the ship, display a photo or painting of the *Mayflower II* or of another vessel similar to the original *Mayflower.*

Comprehension Check ☑

❶ Ask students to describe the "difference of opinion" that divides the sailors. *Students should reply that the mariners were debating whether to continue on with the second half of a dangerous trip and collect their wages, or to turn back to attempt to save their lives.*

◆ Reading Strategy

❷ **Break Down Sentences** By breaking this sentence into shorter, simpler parts, students can more easily comprehend its meaning. They can understand that the sailors examined the ship and found it seaworthy, and that the carpenter and master figured out how to stabilize the main beam by using a large iron screw and a post bound firmly in the lower deck.

◆ Literary Focus

❸ **Narrative Accounts** Ask students: How does Bradford blur the line between firsthand and secondhand historical narrative? *Students can respond that Bradford blurs the line by using the pronouns* they *and* them, *which suggest a secondhand telling. Students may also point out that Bradford includes observations about how the sailors felt, and inserts his own first-person comments in parentheses.*

◆ Literary Focus

❹ **Narrative Accounts** Guide students to notice how Bradford uses the stolid Puritan writing style here. He describes the intense excitement the weary seafarers must have felt when they spotted land with the understated words . . . *not a little joyful.*

Connecting to Real World Texts

To connect this selection to a Web site, see p. 1208

could not be able to perform the voyage. So some of the chief of the company, perceiving the mariners to fear the sufficiency of the ship as appeared by their mutterings, they entered into serious consultation with the master and other officers of the ship, to consider in time of the danger, and rather to return than to cast themselves into a desperate and inevitable peril. And truly there was great distraction and difference of opinion amongst the mariners themselves: fain would they do what
❶ could be done for their wages' sake (being now near half the seas over) and on the other hand they were loath to hazard their lives too desperately. But in examining of all opinions, the master and others affirmed they knew the ship to be strong and firm under water; and for the buckling of the main beam, there was a great iron screw the passengers brought out of Holland, which would raise the beam into his place; the which being done, the carpenter and master affirmed that with a post put under it, set firm in the lower deck and otherways bound, he would make it sufficient. And as for the decks and upper works, they would caulk them as well as they could, and though with the working of the ship they would not long keep staunch, yet there would otherwise be no great danger, if they did not overpress her with sails. So they committed themselves to the will of God and resolved to proceed.

> **◆ Reading Strategy**
> ❷ Many ideas and actions are expressed in this lengthy sentence. To better comprehend its meaning, break the passage down into shorter sentences.

In sundry of these storms the winds were so fierce and the seas so high, as they could not bear a knot of sail, but were forced to hull[2] for divers days together. And in one of them, as they thus lay at hull in a mighty storm, a lusty[3] young man called John Howland, coming upon some occasion above the gratings was, with a seel[4] of the ship, thrown into sea; but it pleased God that he caught hold of the topsail halyards[5] which hung overboard and ran out at length. Yet he held his hold (though he was sundry fathoms under water) till he was hauled up by the same rope to the brim of the water, and then with a boat hook and other means got into the ship again and his life saved. And though he was something ill with it, yet he lived many years after and became a profitable member both in church and commonwealth. In all this voyage there died but one of the passengers, which was William Butten, a youth, servant to Samuel Fuller, when they drew near the coast.

But to omit other things (that I may be brief) after long beating at sea they fell with that land which is called Cape Cod; the which being made and certainly known to be it, they were not a little joyful. After some deliberation had amongst themselves and with the master of the ship, they tacked about and resolved to stand for the southward (the wind and weather being fair) to find some place about
Hudson's River for their habitation. But after ❸
they had sailed that course about half the ❹
day, they fell amongst dangerous shoals and roaring breakers, and they were so far entangled therewith as they conceived themselves in great danger; and the wind shrinking upon them withal,[6] they resolved to bear up again for the Cape and thought themselves happy to get out of those dangers before night overtook them, as by God's good providence they did. And the next day they got into the Cape Harbor[7] where they rid in safety.

Being thus arrived in a good harbor, and brought safe to land, they fell upon their knees and blessed the God of Heaven who had brought them over the vast and furious ocean, and delivered them from all the perils and miseries thereof, again to set their feet on the firm and stable earth, their proper element.

2. **hull** *v.*: Drift with the wind.
3. **lusty** *adj.*: Strong; hearty.
4. **seel** *n.*: Rolling.
5. **halyards** (hal´ yərdz) *n.*: Ropes for raising or lowering sails.

6. **withal** (with´ ôl) *adv.*: Also.
7. **Cape Harbor:** Now Provincetown Harbor.

◆ Build Vocabulary

peril (per´ əl) *n.*: Danger

loath (lōth) *adj.*: Reluctant; unwilling

sundry (sun´ drē) *adj.*: Various; different

Cultural Connection

The Pilgrims and the Jamestown colonists needed great fortitude to succeed in the New World. Discuss with students that today's immigrants face their own different kinds of hardships. Have groups discuss the opportunities and hardships that greet today's newcomers to America. These include overcoming language barriers, securing housing and jobs, dealing with different cultural traditions, facing discrimination, and adjusting to life in a new place. Have students compare and contrast the seventeenth-century obstacles with the obstacles of today. Ask them to suggest and list the skills and strengths people must have to overcome these obstacles. Some students may have firsthand knowledge of this challenge; invite them to share personal or family experiences.

5 ▲ **Critical Viewing** What can you learn about the lifestyle at Plymouth Plantation from this photograph of an authentic re-creation of the settlement? **[Infer]**

6 The Starving Time

But that which was most sad and lamentable was, that in two or three months' time half of their company died, especially in January and February, being the depth of winter, and wanting houses and other comforts: being infected with the scurvy[8] and other diseases which this long voyage and their inaccommodate[9] condition had brought upon them. So as there died sometimes two or three of a day in the foresaid time, that of one hundred and odd persons, scarce fifty remained. And of these, in the time of most distress, there was but six or seven sound persons who to their great commendations, be it spoken, spared no pains night or day, but with abundance of toil and hazard of their own health, fetched them wood, made them fires, dressed them meat, made their beds, washed their loathsome clothes, clothed and unclothed them. In a word, did all the homely[10] and necessary offices for them which dainty and queasy stomachs cannot endure to hear named; and all this willingly and cheerfully, without any grudging in the least, showing herein their true love unto their friends and brethren; a rare example and worthy to be remembered. Two of these seven were Mr. William Brewster, their reverend Elder, and Myles Standish, their 7

8. **scurvy** (skur´ vē) *n.*: Disease caused by vitamin C deficiency.
9. **inaccommodate** (in´ ə käm´ ə dət) *adj.*: Unfit.
10. **homely** (hōm´ lē) *adj.*: Domestic.

▶Critical Viewing◀

5 Infer Students may respond that the photo indicates that life at the stark seaside plantation was hard. There is nothing lush or prosperous about the plain, unadorned buildings. Student responses should reflect the idea that the Pilgrims have struggled to create a settlement that is at the mercy of the rugged environment.

◆Literary Focus

6 Narrative Accounts Draw attention to the subheads Bradford uses. Guide students to see that these serve to partition the narrative, to make it easier to follow the chronicler's account and point of view.

◆Critical Thinking

7 Synthesize Ask students how Bradford's description of the few who were not afflicted by disease reflects his moral values. What does he want his readers to think about these people? What does he hope his readers will gain from learning of this experience? *Students should respond that the care and concern the Pilgrims exhibit is a function of their strong common religious beliefs and the powerful sense of community they share. Bradford wants his readers to understand how the settlers' faith influenced their behavior toward one another.*

Read to Understand

Explain that one purpose for reading historical fiction is to understand the topic or time period of the selection. In "Of Plymouth Plantation," students will experience the settlers' lives through the text, learning how they survived through hardships and dangers to start a new life in a new land. One way to understand the text is for students to put themselves in the place of a settler at Plymouth plantation. Students might set this purpose for reading and then follow up by writing a diary page from the point of view of a settler living in Plymouth Plantation.

Viewing and Representing Mini-Lesson

Advertisement

This mini-lesson supports activity 6 on p. 77.

Introduce the Concept Remind students that an advertisement is a form of persuasion, and that in order to be convincing, the advertisement must be accurate, pleasing, and specific to the intended audience. It should also have information that the viewer needs, wants, or enjoys.

Develop the Background Have students create a list of information they want to include in the poster about life at Plymouth Plantation. What views of life would attract people to join the Pilgrims? How can the poster represent life as it was then? Should the poster include drawings? What persuasive language should be used to convince people to journey to America?

Apply the Information Have students display their posters and entertain questions from prospective Plantation settlers. "Advertisers" should explain why Plymouth Plantation is the place to live.

Assess the Outcome You may want to use the Scoring Rubric: Persuasion on p. 120 in ***Alternative Assessment.***

◆ Literary Focus

❶ **Narrative Accounts** Considering the many cases of extreme sickness in the colony, it is unlikely that a secondhand account would have included the minor incident Bradford described.

❷ **Clarification** Students may be surprised at the behavior described here. Tell students that less than half of the hundred and two passengers on the *Mayflower* were Pilgrims. Forty people were recruited in England without regard to religious beliefs; there were also eighteen servants and three hired workers. In all, there were fifty men, twenty women, and thirty-two children.

◆ Literary Focus

❸ **Narrative Accounts** Point out the contrast between Bradford's portrayal of passengers' treatment of their ailing companions and the Pilgrims' treatment of one another. Guide students to see that Bradford presents this anecdote to teach a lesson about community and compassion.

❹ **Enrichment** Massasoit (c. 1580–1661), one of the most powerful Native American leaders in New England, was chief of the Wampanoag Indians. He faithfully observed the 1621 treaty with the Pilgrims.

English-speaking Squanto had been kidnapped by an English slave trader in 1615. When he finally returned to his people, the Patuxets, in 1618, he found that the entire tribe had been wiped out by disease.

◆ *Literature and Your Life*

❺ Ask students whether they would be willing to live by this agreement. Have them explain their responses. *Many will respond favorably to the sense of reciprocity and camaraderie written into the agreement.*

Captain and military commander, unto whom myself and many others were much beholden in our low and sick condition. And yet the Lord so upheld these persons as in this general calamity they were not at all infected either with sickness or lameness. And what I have said of these I may say of many others who died in this general visitation,[11] and others yet living: that whilst they had health, yea, or any strength continuing, they were not wanting to any that had need of them. And I doubt not but their recompense is with the Lord.

But I may not here pass by another remarkable passage not to be forgotten. As this calamity fell among the passengers that were to be left here to plant, and were hasted ashore and made to drink water that the seamen might have the more beer, and one[12] in his sickness desiring but a small can of beer, it was answered that if he were their own father he should have none. The disease began to fall amongst them also, so as almost half of their company died before they went away, and many of their officers and lustiest men, as the boatswain, gunner, three quartermasters, the cook and others. At which the Master was something strucken and sent to the sick ashore and told the Governor he should send for beer for them that had need of it, though he drunk water homeward bound.

> **◆ Literary Focus** ❶
> Do you think Bradford's illness would have been included in a secondhand narrative account?

❷ But now amongst his company there was far another kind of carriage[13] in this misery than amongst the passengers. For they that before had been boon[14] companions in drinking and jollity in the time of their health and welfare, began now to desert one another in this calamity, saying they would not hazard their lives for them, they should be infected by coming to help them in their cabins; and so, after they came to lie by it, would do little or nothing for them but, "if they died, let them die." But such of the passengers as were yet aboard showed them what mercy they could which made some of their hearts relent, as the boatswain (and some others) who was a proud young man and would often curse and scoff at the passengers. But when he grew weak, they had compassion on him and helped him; then he confessed he did not deserve it at their hands, he had abused them in word and deed. "Oh!" (saith he) "you, I now see, show your love like Christians indeed one ❷ to another, but we let one another lie and die ❸ like dogs." Another lay cursing his wife, saying if it had not been for her he had never come this unlucky voyage, and anon cursing his fellows, saying he had done this and that for some of them; he had spent so much and so much amongst them, and they were now weary of him and did not help him, having need. Another gave his companion all he had, if he died, to help him in his weakness; he went and got a little spice and made him a mess[15] of meat once or twice. And because he died not so soon as he expected, he went amongst his fellows and swore the rogue would cozen[16] him, he would see him choked before he made him any more meat; and yet the poor fellow died before morning.

Indian Relations

All this while the Indians came skulking about them, and would sometimes show themselves aloof off, but when any approached near them, they would run away; and once they stole away their tools where they had been at work and were gone to dinner. But about the sixteenth of March, a certain Indian came boldly amongst them and spoke to them in broken English, which they could well understand but marveled at it. At length they understood by discourse with him, that he was not of these parts, but

11. **visitation** *n.*: Affliction.
12. **one:** William Bradford.
13. **carriage** *n.*: Behavior.
14. **boon** *adj.*: Close.

15. **mess** *n.*: Meal.
16. **cozen** (kuz´ ən) *v.*: Cheat.

◆ Build Vocabulary

recompense (rek´ əm pens´) *n.*: Reward; repayment

Beyond the Classroom

Career Connection

Interpreter For much of the time Squanto was involved with the Pilgrims, he proved to be untrustworthy. However, he was so useful in his role as interpreter that the settlers chose to overlook his misdeeds. The Pilgrims felt very fortunate to know someone who could translate for them.

Have students brainstorm for a list of jobs for those interested in languages and careers as interpreters or translators. *Sample responses include: tour guide, translator at international company, position at a foreign embassy to the United States.* Guide students to recognize the distinctions between interpreter and translator: A translator generally works with written documents, while an interpreter orally translates spoken words—speeches, conversations, negotiations, and so on—and facilitates communication between people who speak different languages.

If possible, invite a student to interview someone currently working as an interpreter or translator to find out what the job entails, what conflicts or issues arise (as in diplomacy), and what special skills and understanding are required (absolute fluency, good communications, writing, and interpersonal skills).

belonged to the eastern parts where some English ships came to fish, with whom he was acquainted and could name sundry of them by their names, amongst whom he had got his language. He became profitable to them in acquainting them with many things concerning the state of the country in the east parts where he lived, which was afterwards profitable unto them; as also of the people here, of their names, number and strength, of their situation and distance from this place, and who was chief amongst them. His name was Samoset. He told them also of another Indian whose name was Squanto, a native of this place, who had been in England and could speak better English than himself.

Being, after some time of entertainment and gifts dismissed, a while after he came again, and five more with him, and they brought again all the tools that were stolen away before, and made way for the coming of
4 their great Sachem,[17] called Massasoit. Who, about four or five days after, came with the chief of his friends and other attendance, with the aforesaid Squanto. With whom, after friendly entertainment and some gifts given him, they made a peace with him (which hath now continued this twenty-four years) in these terms:

1. That neither he nor any of his should injure or do hurt to any of their people.
2. That if any of his did hurt to any of theirs, he should send the offender, that they might punish him.
3. That if anything were taken away from any of theirs, he should cause it to be restored; and they should do the like to his.
4. If any did unjustly war against him, they would aid him; if any did war against them, he should aid them. 5
5. He should send to his neighbors confederates to certify them of this, that they might not wrong them, but might be likewise comprised in the conditions of peace.
6. That when their men came to them, they should leave their bows and arrows behind them.

After these things he returned to his place called Sowams, some 40 miles from this place, but Squanto continued with them and was their interpreter and was a special instrument sent of God for their good beyond 6
their expectation. He directed them how to set their corn, where to take fish, and to procure other commodities, and was also their pilot to bring them to unknown places for their profit, and never left them till he died.

17. Sachem (sā´ chəm): Chief.

Guide for Responding

◆ *Literature and Your Life*

Reader's Response If you had been making the journey on the *Mayflower*, what would you have done differently to better prepare for life in America?

Thematic Focus How has this account changed your impression of the Pilgrims?

Check Your Comprehension

1. What hardships do the Pilgrims endure during their trip across the Atlantic?
2. What hardships do they encounter during their first winter at Plymouth?
3. (a) In what ways does Samoset help the Pilgrims? (b) What does Squanto do for them?

◆ Critical Thinking

INTERPRET

1. How would you characterize the Pilgrims' reactions to the hardships they encountered during their first winter in Plymouth? **[Classify]**
2. Find two statements that convey the Pilgrims' belief that they were being guided and protected by God. **[Analyze]**

COMPARE LITERARY WORKS

3. Do you feel that the changing attitudes of the settlers and the Native Americans reflect typical experiences with newcomers? Why or why not? **[Synthesize]**

◆ Critical Thinking

6 Compare and Contrast Have students compare Bradford's and Smith's attitudes toward the Native Americans. *Smith condescended to the Native Americans, whom he viewed as savages, and was willing to take advantage of them as he saw fit. Bradford treated the Native Americans with respect and came to believe that they appeared as God's instrument on the Pilgrims' behalf.*

Reinforce and Extend

Answers

◆ *Literature and Your Life*

Reader's Response Students' responses should show an understanding of the settlers' hardships.

Thematic Focus Students may not have realized how hard the Pilgrims had to struggle to establish themselves in the New World.

Check Your Comprehension

1. They encounter fierce storms, and their ship falls into disrepair.
2. They lack shelter, warmth, and food. Many suffer from scurvy or die of other illnesses.
3. (a) Samoset helps acquaint the Pilgrims with the local terrain, convinces the Native Americans to return the tools they took, helps negotiate peace with Massasoit, and introduces the settlers to Squanto. (b) Squanto acted as their interpreter and guide, and taught them how to plant, fish, and find provisions.

◆ Critical Thinking

1. The Pilgrims react to hardships with strength, determination, and a loving, cooperative spirit.
2. Suggested responses include: "Being thus arrived in a good harbor, and brought safe to land, they fell upon their knees and blessed the God of Heaven who had brought them over the vast and furious ocean. . . ." and ". . . but Squanto continued with them and was their interpreter and was a special instrument sent of God for their good. . . ."
3. Suggested response: Yes, at first strangers are usually apprehensive with one another. Once they become familiar with one another, the fear and nervousness diminish.

Beyond the Selection

FURTHER READING

Other Works by the Authors

The True Travels, Adventures and Observations of Captain J. Smith, John Smith
Mourt's Relation, William Bradford

Other Works About Early Colonial Settlement

Jamestown, Carl Bridenbaugh
William Bradford, Perry D. Westbrook
Founding Fathers: The Puritans in England and America, John Adair

INTERNET

You and your students may find additional information about Smith, Bradford, and European colonial settlement in America on the Internet. We suggest the following site. Please be aware, however, that sites may have changed from the time we published this information.

For information about the Mayflower and Plymouth Plantation, go to:

http://www. plmoth. org

We *strongly recommend* that you preview sites before you send students to them.

Answers

◆ Reading Strategy

Students should select appropriately complex or lengthy sentences and break them down into components that are more manageable or easily understood. Look for slashes or brackets at logical points in the sentence. Paraphrases should include the main points in each sentence.

◆ Literary Focus

1. Suggested responses include: In the seventh paragraph, Smith is subjective when he contrast the president and colonist Martin with himself. In the tenth paragraph, Smith calls the Native Americans "barbarians" and glorifies his own cleverness. The entire episode in which Pocahontas saves Smith from death is also believed to be an exaggeration of both the actual danger Smith faced and Pocahontas's feelings for him.
2. (a) Smith's purpose is to give his version of the settlement of Jamestown and to encourage others to join it. He also strives to entertain his readers, while boasting about his own strength and cleverness. (b) Bradford seems more interested in recording for posterity a factual and modest account of the Pilgrims' experience. He wishes to credits God, rather than people, with any of the good things that happened to them.

Beyond Literature

Students may respond that artifacts can reveal details about the objects and activities that were part of daily life in the settlements. They can also demonstrate the type of craftsmanship or materials the colonists used. Smith or Bradford may have neglected to mention these details because their contemporaries were already familiar with many of them.

◆ Build Vocabulary

Using Related Words
1. c 2. a 3. b

Using the Word Bank
1. A 2. S 3. S 4. A 5. A 6. A
7. A 8. S

Guide for Responding (continued)

◆ Reading Strategy

Break Down Sentences

When you **break down sentences** into simpler parts, you can get at the meaning of even lengthy or difficult sentences. Scan the narratives for a sentence that you found particularly challenging. Write the sentence on your paper, then do the following:

1. Use brackets or slashes to show how you broke the sentence down.
2. Write the meaning of the sentence as you understand it.

◆ Literary Focus

Narrative Accounts

These selections are both **narrative accounts**, stories about real-life experiences. Both are also firsthand **historical narratives**, written about key events by people who experienced them. Firsthand accounts capture the flavor of the time, the setting, and what it was like to participate in the event. The information presented is not always accurate, however, since the writer often tries to persuade or entertain readers.

1. Find two examples in which Smith exaggerates or displays subjectivity in recounting events.
2. (a) What do you think Smith's purpose was in writing this narrative? (b) How was Bradford's purpose different?

Beyond Literature

History Connection

Archaeologists Unearth the Jamestown Fort In 1996, a team of archaeologists located the remains of a fort built by John Smith and Jamestown's original inhabitants. It was long believed that the fort had been washed away by the James River. When archaeologist William Kelso found a shard of pottery that he believed dated back to 1545, however, he kept digging and found more than 100,000 artifacts—armor, coins, musket balls—from the seventeenth-century colony.

What can artifacts reveal about a colony that might be missing from a written account?

◆ Build Vocabulary

Using Related Words

Use the definitions you have learned to understand the meaning of other forms of the words in the Word Bank. On your paper, write the letter of the word that best answers each question.

a. mollification **b.** pilferer **c.** conceited

1. Which word describes people who are full of fanciful dreams of themselves?
2. Which word refers to the act of soothing or calming someone?
3. Which word describes someone who steals?

Using the Word Bank: Antonym or Synonym?

Decide whether the words in each of the following pairs are antonyms or synonyms. On your paper, write *A* for *Antonymn* or *S* for *Synonym.*

1. pilfer, donate
2. palisades, fences
3. conceits, fantasies
4. mollified, angered
5. peril, safety
6. loath, willing
7. sundry, single
8. recompense, reward

◆ Grammar and Style

Plural and Possessive Nouns

The **possessive** form of nouns indicates kinship and ownership. Add an apostrophe and *-s* to form the possessive singular of most nouns. Add an apostrophe to form the possessive of plural nouns that end in *-s* or *-es*.

Incorrect: All the passenger's spirits were flagging.

Correct: All the passengers' spirits were flagging.

Use the apostrophe *only* for the possessive form; do *not* use it to form simple plurals.

Writing Application Rewrite this paragraph, correcting any mistakes in plurals or possessives.

Much to *Bradfords* amazement, Samoset spoke to the *Pilgrims* in broken English. Samoset convinced his fellow *Indians'* to return the *settler's* tools. He persuaded Massasoit to pay his *respects* to the *Pilgrims*, and introduced them to one of his *friend's*, Squanto.

Reteach

Break Down Sentences To help students use the strategy of breaking down sentences, use the visual device shown here. Have students choose a long sentence from the text and respond to the questions. Not all the parts will be filled in for each passage. Explain that this separates the essential information from the descriptions and nonessential text. Then have students read what they have written to extract the main idea from the passage.

Who? ______________
What? ______________
When ? ______________
Where? ______________
Why ? ______________

◆ Grammar and Style

Bradford's (singular possessive); Pilgrims (plural); Indians (plural); settlers' (plural possessive); respects (plural); Pilgrims (plural); friends (plural)

Grammar Reinforcement

For additional practice, use the Types of Nouns lesson in the Nouns and Pronouns unit of the **Language Lab CD-ROM.**

Build Your Portfolio

Idea Bank

Writing

1. Memorial Speech As a Jamestown settler, you have been asked to speak at a memorial service for John Smith. Write a speech in which you describe Smith's adventures and accomplishments.

2. Dramatic Scene Write a scene that captures Samoset's first meeting with the Plymouth settlers. Include dialogue and stage directions. **[Performing Arts Link]**

3. News Article Pocahontas married a Jamestown settler and traveled to England. As a reporter for *The London Times,* research Pocahontas's life. Write an article about her visit to England.

Speaking, Listening, and Viewing

4. Persuasive Speech Imagine that you are Samoset. Deliver a persuasive speech in which you make the case for fostering peace between the settlers and your tribe. **[Social Studies Link]**

5. Early American Art Artists represented the many encounters settlers had with the Native Americans. Give a presentation to your class showing works by several artists. In your presentation, discuss how the representations might be accurate or biased. **[Social Studies Link]**

Researching and Representing

6. Advertisement Create a poster advertising life at Plymouth Plantation. Encourage others to journey to America to join the Pilgrim settlers.

7. Menu Many Pilgrims suffered from scurvy, a disease caused by a diet lacking in vitamin C. Learn more about the foods the colonists ate and the crops they planted. Then create a historically accurate menu for a typical day in the life of an early colonist. **[Health Link]**

Online Activity www.phlit.phschool.com

Guided Writing Lesson

Comparison of Narratives

These narratives leave the reader with the impression that Smith and Bradford were very different people with distinctly different outlooks on life. Write a comparison of these firsthand accounts.

Writing Skills Focus: Clear Organization

When you are comparing and contrasting, use a **clear organization**—one that will help to define the similarities and differences between your subjects. Two basic types of comparison-and-contrast organization are point by point and subject by subject:

- In a point-by-point organization, discuss each aspect of your subject in turn. For example, discuss one aspect of Smith's tone and immediately contrast it with an aspect of Bradford's tone.
- In a subject-by-subject organization, discuss all the qualities of one subject—say, the tone *and* content of Smith's narrative—and then the qualities of the other.

Prewriting Review the two narratives, noting each author's style, purpose, and objectivity. To help you gather and organize details, use a Venn diagram like this one.

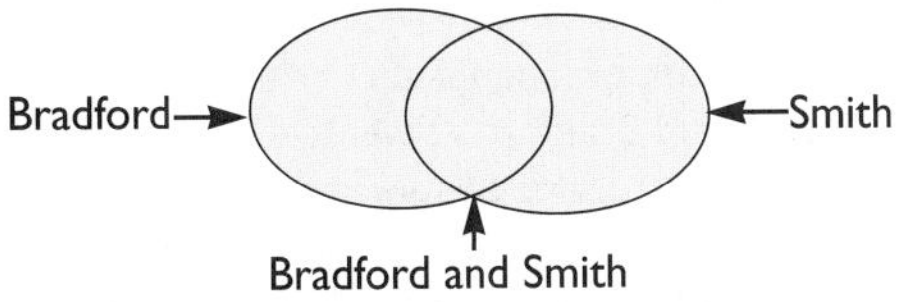

Drafting Focus each paragraph on a single author or point of comparison. To connect paragraphs and keep the relationships of ideas clear, use transitions such as *similarly, also, likewise, equally, in contrast, but, although, however, instead, on the other hand.*

Revising Revise your paper, reordering information to make the organization clearer and adding details when appropriate to strengthen your points.

Idea Bank

Customizing for
Performance Levels
Following are suggestions for matching Idea Bank topics with your students' performance levels:
Less Advanced Students: 1, 6
Average Students: 2, 4
More Advanced Students: 3, 5, 7

Customizing for
Learning Modalities
Following are suggestions for matching Idea Bank topics with your students' learning modalities:
Verbal/Linguistic: 4, 5
Logical/Mathematical: 7
Visual/Spatial: 6

Guided Writing Lesson

Writing and Language Transparencies Use the Comparison-and-Contrast Organizer (pp. 87–89) to help students record the differences and similarities between the two narratives. For prewriting, elaboration, and revising strategies, see *Prentice Hall Writing and Grammar.*

Writing Lab CD-ROM
Have students complete the tutorial on Response to Literature. Follow these steps:

1. Have students review the Audio-annotated Literary Model of a comparative analysis of two literary works.
2. Use the Venn Diagram activity in the Gathering Details section. Have students draft on the computer.
4. Students can use the Self-Evaluation Checklist in the Revising and Editing section to aid revisions

✓ ASSESSMENT OPTIONS

Formal Assessment, Selection Test, pp. 19–21, and Assessment Resources Software. The selection test is designed so that it can be easily customized to the performance levels of your students.

Alternative Assessment, p. 5, includes options for less advanced students, more advanced students, visual/spatial learners, and verbal/linguistic learners.

PORTFOLIO ASSESSMENT
Use the following rubrics in the ***Alternative Assessment*** booklet to assess student writing:
Memorial Speech: Expression Rubric, p. 109
Dramatic Scene: Drama Rubric, p. 124
News Article: Research Report/Paper Rubric, p. 121
Guided Writing Lesson: Comparison/Contrast Rubric, p. 118

Prepare and Engage

LESSON OBJECTIVES

1. **To develop vocabulary and word identification skills**
   - Extending Word Study: Prefixes
2. **To use a variety of reading strategies to comprehend a narrative account**
   - Read to Be Entertained
3. **To express and support responses to the text**
   - Critical Thinking
4. **To read in order to research self-selected and assigned topics**
   - Idea Bank: Diagram
5. **To plan, prepare, organize, and present literary interpretations**
   - Idea Bank: Debriefing Speech
   - Idea Bank: Dialogue

Interest Grabber Play *The Right Stuff* film adaptation of the scene described in this selection. Ask students: What must Glenn have been thinking and feeling as he became the first person to orbit Earth? *Students will probably say that Glenn was elated or incredibly excited and proud.* After students have shared their responses, tell them that the selection they are about to read paints a picture that might surprise them.

Customize for
Less Proficient Readers
To help students with this work, guide them to break apart long sentences into smaller segments to better follow the narrative.

Customize for
English Language Learners
This piece is rich with technical terms and space jargon that may be unfamiliar to students. To prepare them to read, use a model or photograph of a rocket to help students understand such terms as *liftoff, rocket, capsule, supersonic,* and *orbit,* in addition to the Build Vocabulary and footnoted words.

CONNECTIONS TO TODAY'S WORLD

The Right Stuff
Tom Wolfe

Thematic Connection

THE PIONEER SPIRIT

The early American settlers struggled through rough seas, sickness, and starvation to carve out a home in a new land. They would have offered many different reasons to explain why—religious freedom, economic opportunity, political autonomy. At heart, it was a hunger for uncharted territory that drove the settlers to sail across the wide ocean and set foot on a forbidding continent. That spirit kept Americans going for three more centuries, setting their feet ever westward, blazing trails across the continent.

On the brink of a new millennium, the frontier has given way to a network of highways, airports, and shopping malls. When the frontier disappeared, the pioneer spirit had nowhere to go but up. In the twentieth century, this spirit pushed Americans into tiny, cramped capsules. The new pioneers have defied gravity itself and leaped upward into space. Tom Wolfe's book *The Right Stuff* documents this new American exploration.

Literary Connection

NARRATIVE ACCOUNTS

John Smith, William Bradford, and Tom Wolfe all wrote historical **narrative accounts**—factual reports of notable events. You will notice big differences between Wolfe's twentieth-century account of John Glenn's brief zooms around the planet and Smith's and Bradford's seventeenth-century chronicles of the colonists' struggles to survive. One obvious difference is in the style, the shift from the formal vocabulary of seventeenth-century men of authority to the more casual, slang-filled language of a twentieth-century journalist.

Wolfe's account represents a great departure from the nonfiction writing of his own day. Just as the astronauts pushed the limits of human experience, stretching it beyond the Earth, Wolfe's writing broke out of the tradition of narrative nonfiction to incorporate the more imaginative techniques of fiction writing. Wolfe and other practitioners of the "New Journalism" of the 1960's highlight vivid details of character and setting and call attention to the way the observer feels about what is being observed.

TOM WOLFE
(1930–)

Born in a Virginia far different from the one that John Smith knew, Tom Wolfe began his career working as a reporter and Latin America correspondent for the *Washington Post.* He then turned to magazine writing and eventually published essays, articles, and, later, full-length books that focused on various aspects of the contemporary American scene. He described elements of popular culture in *The Kandy-Kolored Tangerine Flake Streamline Baby* and dissected the art world in *The Painted Word.* Many critics regard *The Right Stuff,* an account of the Mercury space program, as Wolfe's best work.

Prentice Hall Literature Program Resources

REINFORCE / RETEACH / EXTEND

Selection Support Pages
Build Vocabulary, p. 24
Thematic and Literary Connections, p. 25

Formal Assessment Selection Test, pp. 22–23; Assessment Resources Software

Resource Pro CD-ROM

CONNECTIONS TO TODAY'S WORLD

from *The Right Stuff*

Tom Wolfe

1 ▲ Critical Viewing How do you imagine the astronauts' impressions of a liftoff differ from the views of spectators? **[Hypothesize]**

Here he is!—within twenty seconds of liftoff, and the only strange thing is how little adrenaline[1] is pumping when the moment comes . . . He can hear the rumble of the Atlas engines building up down there below his back. All the same, it isn't terribly loud. The huge squat rocket shakes a bit and struggles to overcome its own weight. It all happens very slowly in the first few seconds, like an extremely heavy elevator rising. They've lit the candle and there's no turning

1. **adrenaline** (ə dren´ ə lin´) *n.*: Stress-related hormone secreted by the adrenal gland. When released, it increases heartbeat and raises blood pressure.

Develop Understanding

One-Minute Insight

This excerpt mixes journalistic fact with vivid narrative writing to capture the drama and excitement of John Glenn's pioneering space flight in 1962. Readers follow the countdown as if they are privy to Glenn's thoughts. The account describes the effects of gravity, g-forces, weightlessness, and the extraordinary moment when Glenn realizes that he is in orbit.

◆ Background for Understanding

History On February 20, 1962, Lt. Col. John H. Glenn, Jr., became the first American to experience orbital space flight. A Mercury-Atlas-6 rocket shot the small capsule known as *Friendship 7,* with Glenn aboard, into space. He orbited the Earth three times, spending four hours and fifty-five minutes in space. In a then-remarkable feat of technology, millions of Americans watched his historic flight on their TV sets.

▶Critical Viewing◀

1 Hypothesize Students' responses should contrast the astronauts' unique perspective and sensations within the space capsule with the very dramatic, fiery site experienced by those watching on the ground.

Read to Be Entertained

Have students preview the selection to see that the writing is lively and entertaining. The writer takes the reader on the journey into space with John Glenn to experience the "you are there" feeling. Have students note the use of ellipses to create a suspension in thought and anticipation for the reader. After reading the selection, have students share other characteristics of the text that fulfilled their purpose for reading to be entertained.

❶ Clarification Shepard and Grissom were among the original group of men selected for NASA's manned space program because they had "the right stuff." Alan B. Shepard, Jr., and Virgil I. "Gus" Grissom were the first and second Americans in space (April 5 and July 21, 1961), but neither went into earth orbit. Their flights were very brief —only fifteen minutes, but they provided the only firsthand experiences Glenn could draw upon during his own training.

◆ Critical Thinking

❷ Compare and Contrast Have students consider the preparatory training and knowledge Glenn had to acquire in advance of his pioneering flight. Ask them to compare his thorough preparation with the limited knowledge earlier travelers to the unknown, such as Christopher Columbus, John Smith, or William Bradford, might have had before their pioneering journeys. Debate whether advanced preparation minimizes, eliminates, or increases fears and concerns. How else can good preparation help a pioneer? What can it never do?

Thematic Connection

❸ The Pioneer Spirit Remind students that Columbus, the Puritans, and other early pioneers chronicled the events of their journeys because they were aware that they were making history. Have students draw parallels between their purposes for writing and the expectations for communication facing John Glenn during his flight.

Extending Word Study

Prefixes On the board, write *transonic* and *supersonic*. Have students figure out the meanings of these words using the prefixes *trans-* and *super-*. Then have students find other words in the dictionary using these prefixes and create a crossword puzzle using the words and their meanings.

back, and yet there's no surge inside him. His pulse rises only to 110, no more than the minimum rate you should have if you have to deal with a sudden emergency. How strange that it should be this way! He has been more wound up for a takeoff in an F-102.[2]

"The clock is operating," he said, "We're underway."

It was all very smooth, much smoother than ❶ the centrifuge[3] . . . just as Shepard and Grissom said it would be. He had gone through the same g-forces[4] so many times . . . he hardly noticed them as they built up. It would have bothered him much more if they had been less. Nothing novel! No excitement, please! It took thirteen seconds for the huge rocket to reach transonic speed. The vibrations started. It was ❷ just as Shepard and Grissom said: it was much gentler than the centrifuge. He was still lying flat on his back, and the g-forces drove him deeper and deeper into the seat, but it all felt so familiar. He barely noticed it. He kept his eyes on the instrument panel the whole time . . . All quite normal, every little needle and switch in the right place . . . No malevolent instructor feeding *Abort* problems into the loop . . . As the rocket entered the transonic zone, the vibration became intense. The vibrations all but obliterated the roar of the engines. He was entering the area of "max q," maximum aerodynamic pressure, in which the pressure of the shaft of the Atlas forcing its way through the atmosphere at supersonic speed would reach almost a thousand pounds per square foot. Through the cockpit window he could see the sky turning black. Almost 5 g's were driving him back into his seat. And yet . . . *easier than the centrifuge* . . . All at once he was through *max q*, as if through a turbulent strait, and the trajectory was smooth and he was supersonic and the rumble of the rocket engines was more muffled than ever and he could hear all the little fans and recorders and the busy little kitchen, the humming little shop . . . . The pressure on his chest reached 6 g's. The rocket pitched down. For the first time he could see clouds and the horizon. In a moment—*there it was*—the Atlas rocket's two booster engines shut down and were jettisoned from the side of the shaft and his body was slammed forward, as if he were screeching to a halt, and the g-forces suddenly dropped to 1.25, almost as if he were on earth and not accelerating at all, but the central sustainer engine and two smaller engines were still driving him up through the atmosphere . . . A flash of white smoke went up past the window . . . . *No! The escape tower was firing early—but the* JETTISON TOWER *light wasn't on!* . . . He didn't see the tower go . . . Wait a minute . . . There went the tower, on schedule . . . The JETTISON TOWER light came on green . . . The smoke must have been from the booster rockets as they left the shaft . . . The rocket pitched back up . . . going straight up . . . The sky was very black now . . . The g-forces began pushing him back into his seat again . . . 3 g's . . . 4 g's . . . 5 g's . . . Soon he would be forty miles up . . . the last critical moment of powered flight, as the capsule separated from the rocket and went into its orbital trajectory . . . or didn't . . . *Hey!* . . . All at once the whole capsule was whipping up and down, as if it were tied to the end of a diving board, a springboard. The g-forces built up and the capsule whipped up and down. Yet no sooner had it begun than Glenn knew what it was. The weight of the rocket on the launch pad had been 260,000 pounds, practically all of it rocket fuel, the liquid oxygen. This was being consumed at such a furious rate, about one ton per second, that the rocket was becoming merely a skeleton with a thin skin of metal stretched over it, a tube so long and light that it was flexing. The g-forces reached six and

2. **F-102:** U.S. Air Force fighter plane.
3. **centrifuge** (sen´ trə fyo͞oj´) *n.*: A machine using force to pull a rotating object outward from a center. This type of machine was used to train the astronauts for the effects of spaceflight.
4. **g-forces** *n.*: Units measuring inertial pressure on a body during rapid acceleration. Units represent multiples of the acceleration of gravity.

◆ Build Vocabulary

malevolent (mə lev´ ə lənt) *adj.*: Mean-spirited; showing ill will

obliterated (ə blit´ ər āt´ id) *v.*: Blotted out; destroyed

trajectory (trə jek´ tə rē) *n.*: The curved path of an object hurtling through space

jettisoned (jet´ ə sənd) *v.*: Thrown overboard to lighten the weight of a ship

Beyond the Classroom

Career Connection

Today's Pioneers Who are today's pioneers? Students may identify them as computer wizards, medical researchers, astronomers, oceanographers, or avant-garde artists, among others. Have interested groups discuss what kind of "right stuff" modern-day pioneers need to succeed in breaking new ground in their particular field. Encourage each group to explore a different groundbreaking career, gathering information on education and skills requirements, qualifications, and job descriptions. Students can use library reference materials or the Internet to find this information, or they can interview family friends who work in related fields. Have students list key qualifications or characteristics that these "pioneers" share with pioneers of old. Each group can present its findings to the class in an oral report.

then he was weightless, just like that. The sudden release made him feel as if he were tumbling head over heels, as if he had been catapulted off the end of that same springboard and was falling through the air doing forward rolls. But he had felt this same thing on the centrifuge when they ran the g-forces up to seven and then suddenly cut the speed. At the same moment, right on schedule . . . a loud report . . . the posigrade rockets fired, throwing the capsule free of the rocket shaft . . . the capsule began its automatic turnabout, and all the proper green lights went on in front of him, and he knew he was "through the gate," as they said.

"Zero-g and I feel fine," he said. "Capsule is turning around . . ."

Glenn knew he was weightless. From the instrument readings and through sheer logic he knew it, but he couldn't feel it, just as Shepard and Grissom had never felt it. The turnaround brought him up to a sitting position, vertical to the earth, and that was the way he felt. He was sitting in a chair, upright, in a very tiny cramped quiet little cubicle 125 miles above the earth, a little metal closet, silent except for the humming of its electrical system, the inverters, the gyros, the cameras, the radio . . . *the radio* . . . He had been specifically instructed to violate the Fighter Jock code of No Chatter. He was supposed to radio back every sight, every sensation, and otherwise give the taxpayers the juicy stuff they wanted to hear. Glenn, more than any of the others, was fully capable of doing the job. Yet it was an awkward thing. It seemed unnatural. ❸

"Oh!" he said. "That view is tremendous!"

Well, it was a start. In fact, the view was not particularly extraordinary. It was extraordinary that he was up here in orbit about the earth. He could see the exhausted Atlas rocket following him. It was tumbling end over end from the force of the small rockets throwing the capsule free of it.

He could hear Alan Shepard, who was serving as capcom[5] in the Mercury Control Center at the Cape. His voice came in very clearly. He was saying, "You have a go, at least seven orbits."

"Roger," said Glenn. "Understand Go for at least seven orbits . . . This is *Friendship 7*. Can see clear back, a big cloud pattern way back across toward the Cape. Beautiful sight."

5. **capcom** (kap´ käm) *n. jargon*: Capsule communicator; person speaking directly to astronaut.

Guide for Responding

◆ Literature and Your Life

Reader's Response How would you have felt if you had been in that space capsule instead of John Glenn? What struck you as the most exciting part of his first few minutes in space?

Thematic Focus What takes more courage: riding in a capsule into space like the astronauts or making a new life in an uncharted land like the early settlers? Why?

☑ Check Your Comprehension

1. What does Glenn find so strange about his physical reactions on liftoff?
2. What had Shepard and Grissom told Glenn about their own experiences in space?
3. Why does Glenn radio the comment, "That view is tremendous"? How does he actually feel about the view?

◆ Critical Thinking

INTERPRET

1. What would you say are John Glenn's principal attributes, as shown in this excerpt? **[Analyze]**
2. Why do you think Glenn keeps comparing his training experiences in the centrifuge with his experiences during the actual spaceflight? **[Infer]**
3. Why is Glenn supposed to "radio back every sight . . . and otherwise give taxpayers the juicy stuff they wanted to hear"? **[Interpret]**

APPLY

4. Imagine that Glenn was heading to Mars to start the first human settlement. How might his thoughts have been different? What kind of "right stuff" would be necessary for such a venture? **[Synthesize]**

Reinforce and Extend

Customize for
Less Proficient Readers
These students will benefit from rereading all or part of the narrative account, and from watching the excerpt from the film adaptation of *The Right Stuff*. Help students focus on Glenn's responses to the events unfolding around him.

Answers

◆ Literature and Your Life

Reader's Response Students' responses should reflect the excitement or apprehension they might have felt. Some may say the liftoff was the most exciting moment; others might refer to the moment Glenn became weightless.

Thematic Focus Students should support their responses based on their interpretations of Smith's, Bradford's, and Wolfe's accounts.

☑ Check Your Comprehension

1. Glenn is surprised that his vital signs remain calm and consistent.
2. They told him that the experience would be much gentler than the training and that he wouldn't feel his weightlessness.
3. Glenn knows many people are listening for his reactions. He doesn't think the view is as tremendous as he had hoped.

◆ Critical Thinking

1. Suggested response: Students may call Glenn calm, confident, and serious.
2. Glenn has trained for so long that he expects the experience to go a certain way. When it doesn't, he compares the reality to what he trained for.
3. Glenn's flight was important to the space program. His commentary would be broadcast to the many Americans who were following the flight.
4. Suggested response: If Glenn had been leaving Earth to stake out a life on Mars, he might have wondered about his safety, his future, and his chances of returning to Earth. Such a traveler would need to be brave, physically fit, and able to deal with stress calmly.

Beyond the Selection

FURTHER READING

Other Works About Astronauts and Space Travel

The Other Side of the Moon, Neil Armstrong
A Man on the Moon, Andrew Chaikin
Men From Earth, Buzz Aldrin and Malcolm McConnell
Deke!, Donald "Deke" Slayton, with Michael Cassutt

We suggest you preview these texts before assigning them to students.

INTERNET

You and your students may find additional information about John Glenn, the Mercury space mission, and NASA on the Internet. We recommend the following Web site. Please be aware that sites may have changed since this information was published.

For information on America's space program, go to the NASA site at **http://www.nasa. gov**

You may also find information on space travel on the Internet. We *strongly recommend* that you preview sites before you send students to them.

Answers
Thematic Connection

1. Both Glenn and the colonists were undertaking something that had never been done before. Both took a risk in order to explore.
2. Glenn was able to use technology to help him prepare for his flight. For the most part, he knew exactly what would happen. Some students will say his preparation enhanced his experience because it allowed him to be successful.
3. Suggested response: Glenn's right stuff was his bravery and control in a potentially frightening situation. John Smith or William Bradford would have defined "the right stuff" as the ability to lead in a time of crisis, to withstand hard work on a meager diet, and to trust in God.

Literary Connection

1. Sample responses: ***Wolfe:*** sarcastic, casual, friendly. Wolfe writes in an easy style, including Glenn's thoughts so that a reader feels involved in the action. ***Bradford and Smith:*** severe, distant, formal. The colonists report in a dry, narrative style that reads more like a memo than an anecdote.
2. Wolfe's narrative shows that American society has come to appreciate personal insights and emotional information about a given event. The colonists, on the other hand, were more interested in leaving a record of the events themselves—an account that reflected their stoic approach to life.

Idea Bank

Customizing for
Performance Levels
Following are suggestions for matching Idea Bank topics with your students' performance levels:
Less Advanced Students: 1
Average Students: 2, 5
More Advanced Students: 3, 4

Customizing for
Learning Modalities
Following are suggestions for matching Idea Bank topics with your students' learning modalities:
Visual/Spatial: 5
Logical/Mathematical: 4, 5

Thematic Connection

The Pioneer Spirit

In the early 1960's, when the space age was just dawning, President Kennedy referred to space as our "new ocean," likening the advances in the space program to the discovery, exploration, and settlement of America by Europeans centuries before.

1. In what ways is John Glenn's experience similar to that of the Europeans who crossed the Atlantic Ocean and settled in America?
2. How do twentieth-century advances make Glenn's experience different from that of the colonists? Do you think these advances enhance his experience or diminish it? Why?
3. Tom Wolfe's title, *The Right Stuff,* refers to the qualities test pilots needed to fly higher, faster, and farther than anyone had ever done before. What personal qualities give John Glenn "the right stuff"? How do you think John Smith or William Bradford would have defined "the right stuff" needed to make a home in the American wilderness?

Literary Connection

Narrative Accounts

Narrative accounts, like other types of writing, reflect their times. As you consider Tom Wolfe's account of the spaceflight, think of the specific differences between it and either John Smith's or William Bradford's chronicle of life in an early American colony.

1. List three words to describe each narrative account you read. Defend your choices.
2. Explain what each narrative tells you about the frame of mind of the people who lived during that time.

Idea Bank

Writing

1. **Dialogue** Write a dialogue between John Glenn and William Bradford, in which Glenn argues why it is important for humans to explore space and Bradford argues why such exploration is wrong.
2. **News Article** Write the lead for a contemporary news article about the New England colonists' early struggles. Be sure to cover the *who, what, when, where, why,* and *how* of their experiences. **[Career Link]**
3. **Sci-Fi Story** Recent discoveries suggest that life may have existed on Mars at some time. Write a science-fiction story set in the twenty-first century, in which John Smith is heading toward Mars with a group of colonists to set up the first station on that planet.

Speaking, Listening, and Viewing

4. **Debriefing Speech** This excerpt continually refers to the pre-flight practice Glenn and the other astronauts endured. Write the debriefing comments Glenn may have given after his flight. Include the details future astronauts would find useful in preparation for flight. **[Science Link]**

Researching and Representing

5. **Diagram** Do some research about Glenn's vehicle, then draw a diagram showing the rocket with the space capsule. Label the various parts of the diagram. Then read about the *Mayflower* (or similar ships), and draw a diagram of the kind of boat that took the Pilgrims across the ocean. Use a similar scale for your two diagrams to show how small *Friendship 7* is compared with the *Mayflower.* **[Science Link; Art Link]**

Online Activity www.phlit.phschool.com

✓ ASSESSMENT OPTIONS

Formal Assessment, Selection Test, pp. 22–23, and Assessment Resources Software. The selection test is designed so that it can be easily customized to the performance levels of your students.

PORTFOLIO ASSESSMENT
Use the following rubrics in the ***Alternative Assessment*** booklet to assess student writing:
Dialogue: Persuasion Rubric, p. 120
News Article: Description Rubric, p. 112
Sci-Fi Story: Fictional Narrative Rubric, p. 110

Writing Process Workshop

Annotated Bibliography

Since no one has yet invented a time machine, the selections in this unit are as close as you are likely to come to knowing the texture and feel of the life of our forebears in early America. Historians often use such accounts—along with other kinds of sources—to reconstruct the past. For students and scholars, one invaluable resource is an **annotated bibliography**—a list of materials on a certain topic. Beyond source information such as titles, authors, and publication dates, an annotated bibliography includes summaries or reviews of the material.

The following skills will help you to create an annotated bibliography.

Writing Skills Focus

- **Use clear organization** in summarizing the major elements of the book. (See p. 77.)
- **Communicate the main ideas** briefly and clearly.
- **Present publishing information** accurately so that readers can find the sources you include.

The following is a sample item from an annotated bibliography covering historical novels about pre-1750 America. Note how the writer clearly organizes the material into distinct areas.

MODEL

Rinaldi, Ann. *A Break With Charity: A Story About the Salem Witch Trials.* New York: Harcourt Brace Jovanovich/Gulliver Books, 1992. Fiction.

The 1692 witchcraft trials caused mass hysteria in the once tranquil Massachusetts town of Salem. Susanna English, the fictional heroine of this novel, her family, and her friends find their lives sucked into the controversy. ① Susanna's determined character springs to life as she grapples with this tragedy and sets out to stop the madness in her community. ② The issues of individual conscience and the pressures of social conformity emerge with compelling clarity. ③ The author's meticulous research is evident in the historically authentic details of character and setting that embellish this excellent novel. ④

① The author immediately states the basic plot and setting.

② The entry provides a strong sense of the protagonist's character.

③ The entry includes a brief statement of theme.

④ The writer offers an overall evaluation of the work.

Prepare and Engage

LESSON OBJECTIVES

- To use recursive writing processes to write an annotated bibliography
- To rely on the conventions and mechanics of written English to write clearly and effectively

You may want to distribute the scoring rubric for Research Report (p. 121) and Summary (p. 113) in ***Alternative Assessment*** to make students aware of some of the criteria on which their work will be evaluated. See the suggestions on p. 85 for customizing these rubrics to this workshop.

You may also want to present to the class the Writing Process Model for Research Report (pp. 41–50) or Written Evaluation (pp. 25–31) in the ***Writing and Language Transparencies.***

Writing Lab CD-ROM

If your students have access to computers, you may want to have them work in the tutorial on Research to complete all or part of their annotated bibliographies. Have students follow these steps:

1. Review the model of an annotated bibliography.
2. Learn from audio-annotated instruction on how to take notes to organize their information.
3. Draft their annotated bibliographies on the computer.
4. Respond to an interactive Self-Evaluation Checklist to help them judge the effectiveness of their annotated bibliographies.

Career Connection

Library Science Although library card catalogs or their computer-based equivalent are a convenient way of storing source information, the original data must be entered by a professional who inspects each item. Point out the numerous career opportunities that exist outside of the familiar settings of school and community libraries. Large university library systems, for example, often maintain several specialized libraries on campus, such as ones devoted to art history, math, or psychology. Research institutions as well as corporations require libraries whose collections must be kept up-to-date. Librarians employed by such companies fill a vital role in the information society, often hold several advanced degrees, and command good salaries. Ask students how the skills used in writing annotated bibliographies might serve a librarian well, or, by contrast, how these skills might differ from other librarian expertises. *Students might respond that though librarians may not provide personal evaluations and critiques in their summaries of materials, their knowledge of an item's content—not just where it can be found—is often highly valued by library patrons. For example, if a person is confronted with an entire shelf of books on a given topic, it may be the librarian's job to offer concise, opinionated summaries of the options that match the person's needs.*

Develop Student Writing

Prewriting Strategy

To provide students with a sense of the type of pertinent information that should be in their annotated bibliographies, use the topic ideas provided to brainstorm for a list of items they might include for readers interested in those topics. For example, since science is constantly coming up with new findings in this area, readers looking for sources of nutritional advice may want to know how current the information is. Similarly, an evaluation of college guides should probably tell readers the sources of the guides' findings—is it the college admission offices, surveys taken of students, or the personal opinion of the author?

Customize for
Less Advanced Students

Some students may be intimidated by the prospect of compiling an annotated bibliography, assuming that they should first have a thorough firsthand knowledge of all the books in a given field. You might consider reviewing certain reading skills with these students—for example, scanning for key information. Also, let students know that it is acceptable to read reviews and summaries found elsewhere in order to feel more comfortable during the information gathering stage.

Writing Lab CD-ROM

Have students use the Annotated Bibliography Topic Bin in the Choosing a Topic section of the tutorial. They can explore an interactive topic list to help them find a subject for their own writing.

Elaboration Strategy

Before and while students draft their annotated bibliographies, review the key characteristics of the form that they should bear in mind. While they will have to sum up information, what they are producing is not just a summary. Nor are they strictly "writing about literature." Instead, they should be drawing upon skills related to these other types of writing while keeping the focus on research.

Applying Language Skills: Citing Sources

Any bibliography should list source information thoroughly and accurately and in alphabetical order. Note the title, author, publication date, and publisher of each source you cite.

Book With One Author:
Myerhoff, Barbara. *Number Our Days.* New York: Touchstone, 1978.

Book With More Than One Author:
Jaffe, Nina, and Steve Zeitlin. *While Standing on One Foot.* New York: Henry Holt, 1993.

Magazine Article:
Squires, Sally. "The Heart Is a Hungry Hunter." *Cooking Light,* May 1996: 50–56.

If you cannot use italicized type, underline titles of full works.

Writing Application As you finalize your annotated bibliography, be sure the order and punctuation of each entry are correct.

Writer's Solution Connection
Writing Lab

For more information about citing and crediting sources, use the Drafting section of the Writing Lab Research tutorial.

Prewriting

Choose a Topic American history provides an almost endless store of fascinating ideas for research. Think about an aspect of the American past that especially interests you, or choose one of the topic ideas listed here.

Topic Ideas

- Political biographies
- Nutrition advice for adolescents
- Detective stories
- College guides

Gather Information When preparing an annotated bibliography, it is helpful to consider the widest possible array of resources to locate appropriate print and nonprint information.

- Consult the library's card catalog or computer databases using key words related to your subject.
- Look in fiction, poetry, drama, social science, and general nonfiction sections of the library.
- Use the *Readers' Guide* to locate articles in magazines, newspapers, and journals. To find sources on the Internet, use search networks, such as AltaVista.

Record the Information When You Find It As you find and review material, note the publishing information accurately. Doing so will save you time in the drafting, revising, and proofreading stages.

Plan a Clear Organization Make a list of the key areas you wish to cover in your comments about each source—for nonfiction: topic, time period, scope; and for fiction: plot, character, and theme—and then take notes on each item.

Drafting

Organize Your Entries Whether you organize your bibliography in a "best" to "worst" order or list the entries alphabetically by title, implement that plan as you draft. Within each entry, follow a logical order that provides both factual summaries and your critical evaluation.

Use Correct Format Your teacher might ask you to use the MLA (Modern Language Association) style for proper bibliographic form. Follow that format or use the information in the Apply Language Skills lesson on this page to make sure your entries consistently follow an appropriate format.

Applying Language Skills

Citing Sources Emphasize that citing sources in a consistent and accurate manner is an area where students should aspire to perfection. For example, a small error in the spelling of an author's name (or not listing multiple authors in the correct order) may mean that a researcher using the annotated bibliography will not be able to locate a book even if it is readily available. Alternatively, if writers forget to cite the specific pages in a long work or magazine, they may in effect be asking a future researcher to conduct a time-consuming search once they have located the source.

Grammar Reinforcement

In addition to the **Writing Lab CD-ROM** section cited in the student edition, the *Sourcebook* contains a Developing Your Style lesson on Citing and Crediting Sources (p. 161). For further instruction, see the practice pages on Library and Reference Skills (pp. 169–171) in the *Writer's Solution Grammar Practice Book.*

Revising

Cut Out Unnecessary Information To keep your annotations brief, delete any information that wouldn't be essential to someone researching your topic.

Proofread Your Work Any errors a writer makes in grammar or mechanics can distract or confuse a reader. Proofread your work carefully to eliminate errors. Use this checklist:

- ▶ Are all your sentences complete?
- ▶ Does every verb agree with its subject?
- ▶ Is your punctuation correct?
- ▶ Does your bibliographic entry follow the standard form specified in a reliable style guide?

Revision Model

The son of a Scottish earl, James Gour is only fifteen ~~yaers~~ ① years old when he is kidnapped and sent to prerevolutionary North Carolina under a new name, John Scot. ~~He has exciting adventures. . . .~~ ② He eventually joins the revolutionary struggle for independence from the British.

① The writer corrects a typographical error.

② This sentence offers more information than the vague one it replaces.

Publishing

▶ **Create a Class Collection of Annotated Bibliographies** Publish your own anthology of annotated bibliographies. Make this resource available to other students in the library.

▶ **Go On-line** Find the appropriate Web site for your topic, and share your annotated bibliography with a wider audience. You might even update your work with input from Web browsers.

Applying Language Skills: Avoiding Vague Statements

Make your sentences as clear and informative as possible by eliminating any vague statements.

Vague Sentence:

This biography of a Houston mayor is interesting.

Revision:

Because it reveals the obstacles he overcame while in office, this biography of a Houston mayor is an inspiration to readers.

Notice how the added details provide specific reasons why the biography is being praised.

Practice Revise the following sentences to make them less vague.

1. The library's collection of biographies is large.
2. The author creates a good setting.

Writing Application As you revise your annotated bibliography, add details as necessary to eliminate any vague sentences.

Writer's Solution Connection
Language Lab

For more information about revising vague sentences, complete the Language Lab lesson on Writing With Nouns and Verbs.

Revision Strategy

If students are working with peer reviewers to proofread bibliographic entries for style, make sure each reviewer has a copy of the style guide the writer followed. Point out that as long as the writer consistently follows a form set forth in an authoritative guide, entries should be considered correct.

Publishing

Consider making students' bibliographies available by distributing them to teachers of other subject areas that might require research-based writing or term papers.

Applying Language Skills

Avoid Vague Statements Explain to students that while annotated bibliography entries should be concise, they also need to provide meaningful information to the reader.

Answers

Suggested responses:

1. The library's collection of biographies is the largest in Iowa, with 50,000 volumes.
2. The author effectively contrasts the stark, bleak setting of the moors with the colorful drama that takes place there.

Grammar Reinforcement

For additional instruction and practice, complete the **Language Lab CD-ROM** lesson on Strengthening Sentences and pages on Sentence Style (pp. 110–113) in the *Writer's Solution Grammar Practice Book.*

Reinforce and Extend

Prentice Hall Writing and Grammar For more prewriting, elaboration, and revision strategies, see *Prentice Hall Writing and Grammar.*

✓ ASSESSMENT

		4	3	2	1
PORTFOLIO ASSESSMENT Use the rubrics on Summary (p. 113) and Research Report/Paper (p. 121) in the ***Alternative Assessment*** to assess students' writing. Add the following criteria to further customize the rubrics to this assignment.	**Clear Organization**	The writer uses a clear organization throughout the annotated bibliography, making it a useful research tool.	The writer's organization is mostly clear, but some entries vary the presentation of the book's elements.	Each summary is somewhat organized, but no attempt is made to use a single method throughout the bibliography.	The writer does not use a clear organization, so readers spend excessive time and effort searching for information.
	Avoiding Vague Statements	The writer consistently uses sufficient details to avoid making vague statements.	The writer includes some statements that could be clearer, but mostly uses details effectively.	The writer includes too many statements that are vague and lack distinctive details.	The writer consistently uses vague statements, making it difficult for readers to gather meaningful information.

Prepare and Engage

LESSON OBJECTIVES

- To establish and adjust a purpose for reading such as to find out, to understand, to interpret, to enjoy, and to solve problems
- To read to be entertained, to appreciate a writer's craft, to be informed, to take action, and to discover models to use in his/her own writing

Apply the Strategies

Customize for
Intrapersonal Learners

Encouraging students to keep track of what they read and why they read it will reinforce self-directed reading. Have students create a reading log. Students should note the date, time, text, purpose for reading, and amount of time they spent reading. Any text that they spend at least five minutes reading should be entered in the log.

Answers

1. Possible answer: The writer looks to the future and recognizes potential problems.
2. Possible answer: Morristown has the lowest recycling rate in the state. I am hesitant to accept all the writer has to say, however, because he discusses trash disposal and recycling in the same breath, and they are not the same thing.
3. Possible answer: After reading the letter, I might look into ways to improve the local recycling effort without too much cost.

Student Success Workshop

Real-World Reading Skills — Establish a Purpose for Reading

Strategies for Success

To be an effective reader, know your purpose for reading. Your experience will be more enjoyable, and you'll absorb more of what you read. Purposes for reading vary from text to text and from person to person, but establishing your purpose when you begin to read will help you focus on the task at hand.

Why determine a purpose? Your purpose for reading will affect the way you approach a text. For example, when you read a scientific article, your purpose may be to understand all the details. You would read slowly and carefully. However, you might also read the same article to be entertained or simply to be informed about the issue. In this case, you would read more quickly and less intensely.

Purposes for Reading Use the following purposes to direct your reading:

- ▶ *To be entertained.* You may read simply for the fun of it.
- ▶ *To be informed.* If you pick up a newsmagazine, you may read to be informed or to learn about an issue of interest.
- ▶ *To take action.* In order to act upon your beliefs, it is important to know the issues. Perhaps you have environmental concerns. Reading with the purpose of taking action will help you take the first step in getting involved.
- ▶ *To find writing models.* You can also read with the purpose of appreciating a writer's craft or discovering models to use in your own writing.

To the Editor:

I can't understand why the city council rejected the new increased recycling plan for our town. In Morristown, we recycle only 6% of our waste, which is the lowest rate in the state. They said it was not economically positive, but that only applies for the moment. In fifteen months, the North End landfill closes, and the Springfield Acres landfill will close in less than two years. At that time, the cost for Waste Management to transport trash to distant landfills will so far surpass the cost of initiating a recycling program that our leaders will be kicking themselves. Also, as long as we're talking economics, since when did doing good become a decision based on profit?

Sincerely,

Apply the Strategies

Imagine that you lived in the town described in this letter. Answer the following questions.

1. What aspects of this passage might you use as a model for your own writing of a letter to the editor?
2. What information could you get about local recycling from this letter? What aspects of the letter might make you hesitant to accept all the writer has to say?
3. What action might this letter prompt you to take?

✔ *Here are situations in which to apply varied purposes for reading:*
- ▶ Using a computer software manual
- ▶ Reading movie reviews
- ▶ Rereading your favorite novel

Test Preparation Workshop

Establish a Purpose for Reading
Establishing a purpose before they begin reading passages on standardized tests will help students recognize the ideas and concepts they must understand in order to answer test items.

Explain that some test items will ask students to recognize an author's main idea. Have students return to the letter on this page, then answer this sample test item:

With which statement might the author agree?

A Recycling efforts, while good for the environment, are too hard on the pocketbook.

B The city council has not spent enough time discussing the increased recycling plan.

C Decisions based on economic reasons can have more expensive consequences down the line.

D Town officials often ignore the voices of the citizens they are supposed to represent.

Guide students to recognize that *C* is the best answer, as it is the only one that clearly echoes statements the author makes.

PART 3 The Puritan Influence

Pilgrims Going to Church (detail)
George Henry Boughton
© Collection of The New York Historical Society

The Puritans—who came to America in the 1600's for religious freedom—were characterized by a strict moral code and a strong work ethic. Although Puritanism eventually died out, many Puritan values, including a belief in the importance of hard work and an unbending faith in the face of adversity, have remained an important part of the American identity.

One-Minute Planning Guide

This section explores the Puritan influence on America's emerging literary identity. The poetry of Anne Bradstreet and Edward Taylor exemplifies the Puritan Plain Style, though Bradstreet's "To My Dear and Loving Husband" is unusual for its treatment of marital—rather than religious—love. Like the Puritans who first heard it, students are sure to find Jonathan Edwards's fiery sermon "Sinners in the Hands of an Angry God" to be an eye-opening look at Puritanism. Part 3 ends with "Iron Bird: Cal Ripken's Work Ethic," a contemporary portrait of a baseball hero who embodies many of the Puritan principles that shaped our national identity.

Customize for
Varying Student Needs

When assigning the selections in this part, keep in mind these factors:

"To My Dear and Loving Husband" and "Huswifery"

- Two brief lyric poems
- Simple language and religious imagery convey marital and religious devotion
- Intrapersonal learners may relate to the devotion and dedication the poems emphasize.

"Sinners in the Hands of an Angry God"

- Excerpt from a sermon
- Antiquated language and imagery may challenge less proficient readers
- Verbal/linguistic learners may be amazed that despite Edwards' flat delivery, the language of his fire-and-brimstone sermon caused intense reactions in the congregation

"Iron Bird: Cal Ripken's Work Ethic"

- High-interest contemporary character profile of a living baseball legend

Humanities: Art

Pilgrims Going to Church, 1967, by George Henry Boughton.

George Henry Boughton (1833–1905) was born in Norwich, England. From 1852 to 1858, he lived in Albany, New York, concentrating on landscape painting. After a year in New York City, he went to Europe and settled back in England in the 1860's. Throughout his career, Boughton's work was exhibited in both England and the United States. He became known primarily as a painter of "subject pictures" like *Pilgrims Going to Church.*

Have your students link the art to the theme of Part 3, The Emerging American Identity: The Puritan Influence, by answering the following questions:

1. What does the way people are looking around and holding their guns tell you about their state of mind as they go to church? Why might they feel this way? *They seem to be wary of some kind of danger. Perhaps there have been incidents in which colonists have been ambushed by natives or attacked by animals, or perhaps they are afraid because they are in an unknown land, where anything might happen.*
2. What do the details of the painting—the weather, the setting, the colors, the posture of the people—reveal about life in the early days of the Puritan settlement? *The frozen landscape, the darkness at the edges of the painting, the stark colors, the watchful posture of the people suggest that life among the Puritans was harsh, joyless, and possibly filled with danger.*

LESSON OBJECTIVES

1. **To develop vocabulary and word identification skills**
   - Anglo-Saxon Suffixes: *-fold*
   - Using the Word Bank: Connotations
2. **To use a variety of reading strategies to comprehend poetry**
   - Reading Strategy: Paraphrase
3. **To express and support responses to the text**
   - Critical Thinking
   - Idea Bank: Love Song
   - Idea Bank: Informal Debate
   - Idea Bank: Letter
   - Idea Bank: Magazine Article
4. **To analyze literary elements**
   - Literary Focus: Puritan Plain Style
   - Idea Bank: Poem
5. **To read in order to research self-selected and assigned topics**
   - Idea Bank: Graphic Display
6. **To plan, prepare, organize, and present literary interpretations**
   - Idea Bank: Bradstreet Sampler
7. **To use recursive writing processes to write an editorial**
   - Guided Writing Lesson
8. **To increase knowledge of the rules of grammar and usage**
   - Grammar and Style: Direct Address

Test Preparation

Reading Comprehension: Summarizing Written Texts (ATE, p. 89)

The teaching tips and sample test item in this workshop support the instruction and practice in the unit workshop:

Reading Comprehension: Summarizing Written Texts (ATE, p. 115)

Guide for Interpreting

Featured in AUTHORS IN DEPTH Series

Anne Bradstreet

(1612–1672)

Anne Bradstreet and her husband, Simon, arrived in the Massachusetts Bay Colony in 1630, when she was only eighteen. Armed with the strength of her Puritan upbringing, she left behind her hometown of Northampton, England, to start afresh in America. It was not an easy life for Bradstreet, who raised eight children and faced many hardships.

Despite the hardships she faced, Bradstreet was able to devote her spare moments to the very "unladylike" occupation of writing. In 1650, a collection of her scholarly poems, *The Tenth Muse Lately Sprung Up in America, By a Gentlewoman of Those Parts*, was published in England. Bradstreet's later poems, such as "To My Dear and Loving Husband," are more personal, expressing her feelings about the joys and difficulties of everyday Puritan life.

Bradstreet's poetry reflects the Puritans' knowledge of the stories and language of the Bible, as well as their awareness of the relationship between earthly and heavenly life. Her work also exhibits some of the characteristics of the French and English poetry of her day.

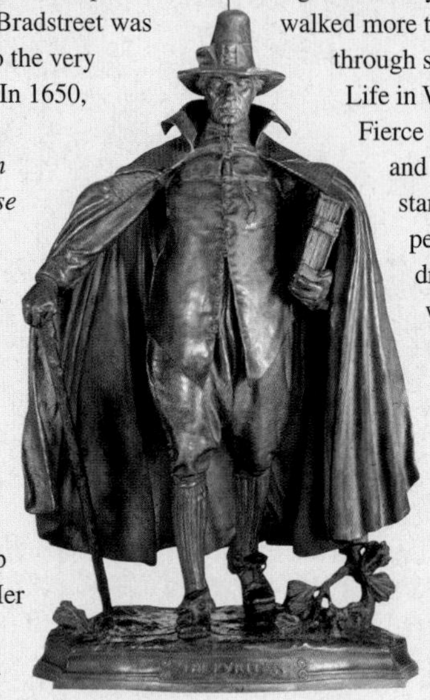

The Puritan, Augustus Saint-Gaudens, The Metropolitan Museum of Art

Featured in AUTHORS IN DEPTH Series

Edward Taylor

(1642–1729)

Before the English government's lack of tolerance for his Puritan beliefs prompted him to emigrate to America, Edward Taylor worked as a teacher in England. Upon arriving in Boston in 1668, Taylor entered Harvard College, graduating in 1671. He accepted the position of minister and physician in the small farming community of Westfield, Massachusetts, then walked more than one hundred miles, much of it through snow, to his new home.

Life in Westfield was filled with hardships. Fierce battles between the Native Americans and the colonists left the community in constant fear. Taylor also experienced many personal tragedies. Five of his eight children died in infancy; then his wife died while still a young woman. He remarried and had five or six more children. (Biographers differ on the exact number.)

Edward Taylor is now generally regarded as the best of the colonial poets. Yet, because Taylor thought of his poetry as a form of personal worship, he allowed only two stanzas to be published while he was alive. Few people knew about his work until his poems were published more than two centuries after his death.

◆ Background for Understanding

LITERATURE: PURITAN WRITING

For the Puritans, the sole purpose of literature was moral instruction. They were aware of the emotional power of poetry but approved of it only if, like the Psalms, it "moved hearts to righteousness." There were many writers of verse in Puritan times, but few were women. Bradstreet was aware that writing was considered unacceptable behavior for women, but she persevered nonetheless.

Taylor's work was generally unknown during his lifetime. Some believe that he chose not to publish his poems because their joyousness and delight in sensory experience ran counter to New England attitudes. The discovery of a stash of Taylor's poetry in the 1930's is considered one of the major literary finds of the twentieth century.

Prentice Hall Literature Program Resources

REINFORCE / RETEACH / EXTEND

Selection Support Pages
Build Vocabulary: Suffixes: *-fold,* p. 26
Grammar and Style: Direct Address, p. 27
Reading Strategy: Paraphrase, p. 28
Literary Focus: Puritan Plain Style, p. 29

Strategies for Diverse Student Needs, p. 6

Beyond Literature
Cross-Curricular Connection: Performing Arts, p. 6

Formal Assessment, Selection Test, p. 27–29; Assessment Resources Software

Alternative Assessment, p. 6

Writing and Language Transparencies
Writing Process Model: Persuasive Essay, pp. 33–36

Resource Pro CD-ROM

Listening to Literature Audiocassettes

◆ Literature and Your Life

Connect Your Experience

If preserved, your belongings would convey a sense of your individuality to people born centuries from now. Puritans had few possessions, dressed somberly and uniformly, and didn't believe in expressing themselves creatively. Because they have left so little behind, they remain a mystery in many ways.

Journal Writing List the five personal possessions that best express your individuality. What would they tell future generations about your lifestyle and personality?

Thematic Focus: The Puritan Influence

These poems are like a glimpse behind the thick curtain of Puritanism at the thoughts and feelings of real people. How do the beliefs they express make these poems distinctly Puritan?

◆ Literary Focus

The Puritan Plain Style

The writing style of the Puritans reflected the plain style of their lives—spare, simple, and straightforward. The **Puritan Plain Style** is characterized by short words, direct statements, and references to ordinary, everyday objects. Puritans believed that poetry should serve God by clearly expressing only useful or religious ideas. Poetry appealing to the senses or emotions was viewed as dangerous.

◆ Build Vocabulary

Anglo-Saxon Suffixes: *-fold*

Although you may not know the word *manifold,* you've heard references to returning good wishes *tenfold* or increasing an investment *fourfold.* These words describe actions performed *ten* ways and *four* times. Applying this pattern, you can determine that *manifold* describes an action performed "many ways or times." The Anglo-Saxon suffix *-fold,* meaning "a specific number of times or ways," is used to form both adjectives and adverbs.

Word Bank

Preview this list of words from the poems.

recompense
manifold
persevere

◆ Reading Strategy

Paraphrase

While these poems truly capture the essence of Puritan life, they can also present a challenge to the reader. To help you better absorb the meaning of each poem, take time to **paraphrase,** or restate ideas expressed by the poets in your own words.

Bradstreet's Version

My love is such that rivers
cannot quench,
Nor ought but love from
thee, give recompense.

Paraphrased

My love is so strong that
rivers cannot relieve its thirst;
only your love will satisfy it.

Use the information in the footnotes to help you paraphrase unfamiliar references.

◆ Grammar and Style

Direct Address

In the opening line, the speaker in "Huswifery" calls upon God with the words, "Make me, O Lord, Thy spinning wheel complete." The phrase "O Lord," which is set off by commas, signals that the speaker is addressing God directly. As used here, "O Lord" is a term of **direct address**—a name or phrase used when speaking directly to someone or something. As you read, think about the reasons why the poets use terms of direct address in their poems.

Test Preparation Workshop

Summarizing Written Texts
Several standardized tests measure students' ability to identify the best summary of a passage. Explain that summarizing is especially useful when reading poetry. After students have reread the poem on p. 91, have them pick the best summary from the choices below.

A The author wants to live forever with her husband.
B The author's love for her husband, which she values more than gold and riches, will never die.
C The author owes her husband money.
D The author wants heaven to reward her husband.

Choices *A* and *D* make only partially complete claims; *C* presents incorrect information. *B* is the best summary.

Interest Grabber

Give students the following homework assignment in advance. Ask them to think of one or two love songs they know and enjoy. Have them jot down the lyrics and/or bring to class a recording of the song(s). Introduce Bradstreet's and Taylor's poems to the class by inviting volunteers to read the lyrics or play excerpts from their favorite love songs. Encourage students to explain why they find the songs moving.

Then write the following quotation on the chalkboard: "If ever two were one, then surely we." Tell students that it is a line from a love poem not yet set to music, and ask them to respond to it. Finally, reveal to them that the poet/speaker was a Puritan woman who lived more than three hundred years ago and that the line comes from a poem they are about to read in which she expresses her deep love for her husband.

Customize for
Less Proficient Readers
Have less proficient readers read the poems in segments. Model how to break each poem into small chunks: couplets for the Bradstreet, stanzas for the Taylor. Help students rephrase or summarize the meaning of each chunk to grasp the poem's meaning.

Customize for
AP Students
In addition to examining the poems for their meaning and evidence of Puritan views, students can also analyze each poem in terms of its form, structure, and rhyme scheme.

Customize for
English Language Learners
Help these students understand the archaic singular form of the pronouns *thee, thou,* or *thy.* Such pronouns rarely appear in modern English. Model how to replace these words with the more familiar pronouns *you* or *your.*

Customize for
Intrapersonal Learners
As students read, have them look for ways the speakers show how they feel toward their subjects. Challenge them to list other ways people can demonstrate their devotion to or feelings for others.

Develop Understanding

One-Minute Insight Simon Bradstreet was often away from home on business for months at a time. Anne wrote this poem during one of his absences. In it, she expresses her deep love and admiration for her husband as well as her own spiritual conviction in the simple and direct "plain style." In closing, she prays that their love may continue eternally even after they have left this life. This work is rare in its declaration of marital love, rather than love for God, which may be more expected in a Puritan poem.

◆ Background for Understanding

Literature Lyric poems, or lyrics, are brief poems expressing the poet's personal feelings and thoughts. Unlike a narrative poem, a lyric focuses on producing a single, unified effect. These poems, which the ancient Greeks sang to the accompaniment of a small harplike instrument called a lyre, tend to be melodic. You might discuss the meanings of the words *lyrical, lyricism,* and *lyre* with students to help them grasp the concept of lyric poetry. Point out that song lyrics may also be considered a form of lyric poetry.

Literature CD-ROM Introduce students to Bradstreet's and Taylor's works using the CD-ROM *The History of American Literature:* Part 1, Disk 1, Feature 4.

▶Critical Viewing◀

❶ **Analyze** Students may say that the figures are modestly clothed and do not touch or show physical affection. They are part of their world without standing out from it.

To My Dear and Loving Husband

Anne Bradstreet

Eighteenth-century pastoral scene in needlework, Mary Whitehead, c. 1750, Lyman Allyn Art Museum, New London, Connecticut, USA

▲ Critical Viewing Anne Bradstreet embroidered silk and linen samplers like this one. Which Puritan values are reflected in this scene? **[Analyze]** ❶

Block Scheduling Strategies

Consider these suggestions to take advantage of extended class time:

- Divide the class into groups to share their views on marriage and on the rights and responsibilities of each partner in a good marriage. You might direct students to the Group Discussion on p. 91.
- Introduce the lesson skills you will cover (p. 89) and assign the corresponding ***Selection Support*** pages as homework.
- Set up peer groups in which students can analyze how the Puritan Plain Style is evident in the two poems. Ask each group to answer the Literary Focus questions in the Guide for Responding (p. 94).
- Present the Humanities: Art activity that appears in the Teacher's Edition on page 91. Interested students can research Puritan crafts or try some of them themselves, if materials can be obtained.
- Introduce the Guided Writing Lesson (p. 95). You might share sample editorials from local newspapers to acquaint students with the usual style and format of a position piece. Use the Writing and Language Transparencies for Persuasive Essay, pp. 33–36, and the Argument Organizer, pp. 75–77, to help students through the Prewriting and Drafting stages.
- If time permits, ask volunteers to share their completed Mini-Lesson editorials. Ask the class to comment on the strength of the arguments presented.

If ever two were one, then surely we.
If ever man were lov'd by wife, then thee; ❷
If ever wife was happy in a man,
Compare with me ye women if you can. ❸

I prize thy love more than whole mines of gold,
Or all the riches that the East doth hold. ❹
My love is such that rivers cannot quench,
Nor ought[1] but love from thee, give recompense.
Thy love is such I can no way repay,
The heavens reward thee manifold, I pray.
Then while we live, in love let's so persevere,[2]
That when we live no more, we may live ever. ❺

1. **ought** (ôt) *n.*: Anything whatever.
2. **persevere**: Pronounced *per se´ ver* in the seventeenth century, and thus rhymed with the word *ever*.

◆ Build Vocabulary

recompense (rek´ əm pens´) *n.*: Repayment; something given or done in return for something else

manifold (man´ ə fōld´) *adv.*: In many ways

persevere (pur sə vir´) *v.*: Persist; be steadfast in purpose

Guide for Responding

◆ Literature and Your Life

Reader's Response What is your image of Anne Bradstreet after reading this poem? Does she fit your concept of a Puritan? Why or why not?

Thematic Focus How does this poem express emotions that are distinctly Puritan yet universally human?

Group Discussion With a group of classmates, discuss the advice on how to make a marriage work that the Bradstreets might give modern couples.

☑ Check Your Comprehension

1. In the first four lines of the poem, what is Bradstreet saying about her relationship with her husband?
2. According to Bradstreet, what is the only thing that can match or reward her unquenchable love for her husband?

◆ Critical Thinking

INTERPRET

1. What does Bradstreet mean by the apparent paradox, or contradiction, in the last two lines: ". . . let's so persevere, / That when we live no more, we may live ever"? **[Interpret]**
2. How do Bradstreet's repetition and images help to convey the strength of the emotion being expressed? **[Analyze]**
3. Why might some of Bradstreet's Puritan contemporaries have considered this poem inappropriate? **[Infer]**

APPLY

4. Do you think personal devotion is as much esteemed today as it was in Anne Bradstreet's day? Support your answer. **[Apply]**

Humanities: Art

Puritan homes generally had few works of art. This may be due to the Puritan attitude against finery or because there was little extra money or time to spend on anything but necessities. Puritan women, however, often did arts and crafts, such as embroidery and quilting, and men sometimes did fine leather work, bookbinding, or metal smithing. Students may be interested to learn that the crewel work depicted on p. 92 is attributed to Anne Bradstreet.

Invite students to research typical arts and crafts of the seventeenth-century Puritan communities. They can find information on the Internet or in the library. Artistic or hands-on learners may wish to try some of these colonial crafts to create modern-day replicas of them.

◆ Reading Strategy

❷ **Paraphrase** Have students paraphrase the opening couplet to get a sense for the poem's main idea. *Sample response: We must be the ideal couple; you are the most beloved husband.*

◆ Literary Focus

❸ **Puritan Plain Style** Bradstreet uses straightforward words to express a deep feeling in a modest way.

❹ **Clarification** Tell students that "the East" refers to Asia: China, India, or other far-off lands that few Europeans had ever seen, but about which tales of wealth were common.

◆ Literary Focus

❺ **Puritan Plain Style** Guide students to read the final couplet as an example of Puritan Plain Style. The poet's simple words express her dream that the couple's love will be so strong that it will endure even when their earthly bodies die.

Answers

Reinforce and Extend

◆ Literature and Your Life

Reader's Response Students may express surprise that Bradstreet was a passionate woman.

Thematic Focus The poem deals with the universal sentiment of romantic love expressed within the Puritan religious framework.

☑ Check Your Comprehension

1. Her relationship with her husband is the model of happiness.
2. Her husband's love is her only reward for her devotion.

◆ Critical Thinking

1. If they are true in this life, they will be together eternally in heaven.
2. Repetition emphasizes her thoughts. The images make her feelings easier to comprehend by relating them to concrete objects.
3. The poem deals with the personal emotion of love for a spouse, rather than a more clearly religious theme.
4. Students should support responses with reasoning and/or observations or experiences.

Develop Understanding

One-Minute Insight This poem is an extended metaphor expressing Edward Taylor's deep belief in God and in God's presence in all parts of daily life. "Huswifery" compares the housekeeping task of making cloth with the gift of God's salvation. The poem is like a prayer imploring God to guide the speaker, as a worker masters his tools, to do His bidding. Taylor wants to live a modest life, to act according to God's laws, and to submit to God's will; by so doing he hopes to achieve eternal glory.

Customize for ***AP Students***
This version of Taylor's poem has modern spelling and capitalization. More advanced students might try to read it in its original version.

◆ Background for Understanding

Literature A *conceit* is a kind of figurative language that draws an elaborate and unusual comparison between two startlingly different subjects. Taylor makes an intricate, extended comparison between the making of cloth and the granting of God's grace. Help students see how this conceit mirrors Taylor's belief in the close relationship between God and the natural world. Even in Puritan Plain Style, Taylor speaks fervently and personally to God.

▶Critical Viewing◀

❶ **Make a Judgment** The needlework was created around the same time as the poem and that it reflects the bright colors and "varnished flowers" of the needlework that Taylor describes in "Huswifery."

Huswifery

Edward Taylor

Crewel work chair seat cover, Gift of Samuel Bradstreet, Museum of Fine Arts, Boston

❶ ▲ Critical Viewing What makes this sampler an effective illustration to accompany Taylor's poem? **[Make a Judgment]**

Speaking, Listening, and Viewing Mini-Lesson

Informal Debate
This mini-lesson supports the Speaking, Listening, and Viewing activity in the Idea Bank on p. 95.

Introduce the Concept Discuss the mechanics of debating. Individuals or teams state their opposing views on a given issue. Participants are given the opportunity to respond to the opposition's comments. Be sure students understand that a debate is more than an argument; it has a set form, and participants rely on logic and research to build and present their points.

Develop Background Have students brainstorm for values they attribute to the Puritans, such as devotion, hard work, modesty, and obedience. Then have students list values they ascribe to modern Americans, such as love of freedom, mobility, generosity (or selfishness), and so on.

Apply the Information Form two teams. Assign one team to argue that American identity is still shaped by Puritan values; the other team argues against this idea. Allow teams time to gather supporting evidence, prepare their arguments, plan rebuttals, and practice delivering their points. Hold the debate.

Assess the Outcome Encourage students in the audience to listen carefully to the logic behind each point and to evaluate each team's performance based on the effectiveness of its arguments. How thoroughly and persuasively did each side state its case?

Make me, O Lord, Thy spinning wheel complete.
Thy holy word my distaff[1] make for me.
Make mine affections[2] Thy swift flyers[3] neat
And make my soul Thy holy spoole to be.
My conversation make to be Thy reel
And reel the yarn thereon spun of Thy wheel.

Make me Thy loom then, knit therein this twine:
And make Thy holy spirit, Lord, wind quills:[4]
Then weave the web Thyself. The yarn is fine.
Thine ordinances[5] make my fulling mills.[6] ❷
Then dye the same in heavenly colors choice. ❸
All pinked[7] with varnished flowers of paradise.

Then clothe therewith mine understanding, will,
Affections, judgment, conscience, memory
My words, and actions, that their shine may fill
My ways with glory and Thee glorify.
Then mine apparel shall display before Ye
That I am clothed in holy robes for glory.

1. **distaff** (dis´ taf) *n.*: Staff on which flax or wool is wound for use in spinning.
2. **affections** (ə fek´ shenz) *n.*: Emotions.
3. **flyers** *n.*: Part of a spinning wheel that twists fibers into yarn.
4. **quills** *n.*: Weaver's spindles or bobbins.
5. **ordinances** (ôrd´ ən əns əz) *n.*: Sacraments or religious rites.
6. **fulling mills** *n.*: Machines that shrink and thicken cloth to the texture of felt.
7. **pinked** *v.*: Decorated.

Guide for Responding

◆ *Literature and Your Life*

Reader's Response *Huswifery* means "housekeeping." Given the title, were you surprised by the content of this poem? Explain.

Thematic Focus How did Puritans find opportunities for worship even in everyday tasks and objects?

Class Poll Conduct a quick poll to determine whether your classmates feel "Huswifery" should be considered a prayer or a poem.

☑ Check Your Comprehension

1. To what household task does the speaker liken the granting of salvation?
2. What does the speaker want to do with God's handiwork?

◆ Critical Thinking

INTERPRET

1. What does the poem suggest about the speaker's attitude toward God? **[Infer]**
2. How do the final two lines convey Taylor's belief that religious grace comes as a gift from God, rather than as a result of a person's efforts? **[Analyze]**
3. What does Taylor's comparison of a household task with the granting of grace suggest about his perception of God's relationship to the earthly world? **[Infer]**

APPLY

4. What process might Taylor describe if he were writing this poem today? **[Synthesize]**

Beyond the Selection

FURTHER READING

Other Works by the Authors

The Works of Anne Bradstreet, 1612–1672, Anne Bradstreet

Poetical Works, Edward Taylor

Other Works About Puritanism

Day of Doom, Michael Wigglesworth

The Crucible, Arthur Miller

The Puritans: A Sourcebook of Their Writings, edited by Perry Miller and Thomas H. Johnson

INTERNET

You and your students may find additional information about Anne Bradstreet on the Internet. We suggest the following site. Please be aware, however, that sites may have changed from the time we published this information.

For information about the life and poetical works of Anne Bradstreet, go to **http:// www.vcu.edu/ engweb/ eng391/bradbio. html**

You may also find related information on Puritanism on the Internet. We *strongly recommend* that you preview the sites before you send students to them.

◆ Literary Focus

❷ **Puritan Plain Style** Guide students to recognize that although this poem uses simple words to describe common, everyday items, the Puritan poet has created a rich multilayered metaphor. Increasingly complex connections—spinning wheel to yarn to loom to cloth to holy robes—represent steps he hopes he can follow in life to glorify God and to achieve a state of grace.

◆ Critical Thinking

❸ **Analyze** Taylor's poetry provides insight into the Puritan view of the meaning of life. Invite students to share what they already know about Puritanism and identify Puritan values and attitudes in the poem.

Reinforce and Extend

Answers

◆ *Literature and Your Life*

Reader's Response Students may respond that they did not predict the poem's subject.

Thematic Focus Puritans saw God's will at work in every aspect of their lives. Everything they did—even the daily tasks of housekeeping—had a deeper meaning in light of their constant search for signs that God had chosen them for personal salvation.

☑ Check Your Comprehension

1. It is likened to the task of spinning and weaving yarn to make cloth.
2. He wants to clothe his heart and mind with the cloth of salvation so that their shine glorifies both his actions and God.

◆ Critical Thinking

1. It suggests that he is devoted to God and that he desires to be completely at God's mercy, as a machine is completely in the hands of its operator.
2. They say that the speaker—his thoughts and actions—is clothed by God in salvation. He does not earn this through any acts or merits of his own; rather, it is bestowed on him as "holy robes."
3. It suggests that he believes God is actively involved in the everyday affairs of the world.
4. Students may suggest modern tasks such as using a computer or driving a car.

Answers

◆ Reading Strategy

Suggested responses:

1. Your love is so strong I can't repay it, so I pray heaven will reward you for it in many ways.
2. Weave the web yourself. The yarn is delicate. Your sacraments clean and thicken it. Then dye it in the best heavenly colors, decorated with bright flowers of paradise.

◆ Build Vocabulary

Using the Suffix *-fold*

1. The savvy investor watched the value of his stock increase *threefold.*
2. Since having quadruplets last spring, Sandy claims her laundry has grown *fourfold.*

Using the Word Bank: Connotations

1. b 2. c 3. b

◆ Literary Focus

Puritan Plain Style

1. (a) Simple language (most words are only one syllable), religious conviction ("The heavens reward thee manifold, I pray"), and a direct style that goes immediately to the heart of the subject ("If ever two were one, then surely we") are characteristic of the Puritan Plain Style. (b) The personal, emotional subject of love for her husband, and vivid, exotic images, such as "whole mines of gold, /Or all the riches that the East doth hold" are not associated with the style.
2. (a) References to everyday objects (spinning wheel, loom), religious theme and references (the entire poem is addressed to God as a prayer for salvation; " . . . My ways with glory and Thee glorify"), and a direct style that uses language typical of seventeenth-century everyday conversation ("Then weave the web Thyself. The yarn is fine") are typical of the Puritan Plain Style. (b) The extended use of metaphors ("Make me Thy loom then . . . / And make Thy holy spirit, Lord, wind quills:") and vivid images ("All pinked with varnished flowers of paradise") is not normally associated with the Puritan Plain Style.

Guide for Responding *(continued)*

◆ Reading Strategy

PARAPHRASE

When you **paraphrase** by restating important ideas in your own words as you read, you better absorb the meaning of difficult or old-fashioned language, such as you encountered in these poems.

In your notebook, paraphrase these passages from the poems as though you were explaining their meaning to a friend. Wherever applicable, use the information in the poems' footnotes to help you.

1. Thy love is such I can no way repay,
The heavens reward thee manifold, I pray.

2. Then weave the web Thyself. The yarn is fine.
Thine ordinances make my fulling mills.
Then dye the same in heavenly colors choice,
All pinked with varnished flowers of paradise.

◆ Build Vocabulary

USING THE ANGLO-SAXON SUFFIX *-fold*

Replace the italicized phrase with a word with the same meaning that contains the suffix *-fold.*

1. The savvy investor watched the value of his stock increase *to three times its size.*

2. Since having quadruplets last spring, Sandy claims her laundry has grown *in four ways.*

USING THE WORD BANK: Connotations

Identify the letter of the situation that best demonstrates the meaning of the first phrase.

1. well-deserved recompense: (a) getting a flat tire while taking your grandmother to the doctor, (b) getting a day off after working long hours, (c) cleaning a messy room after a tiring day

2. to increase manifold: (a) to receive a 15 percent salary increase, (b) to add a drop of water to an overflowing bucket, (c) to get a 300 percent return on an investment

3. persevere: (a) quit when you get tired of playing, (b) practice until you improve your average, (c) argue with a referee

◆ Literary Focus

PURITAN PLAIN STYLE

In "To My Dear and Loving Husband," Bradstreet expresses her deep love for her husband as well as her own spiritual convictions in the simple and direct **Puritan Plain Style.** This style of poetry is characterized by the use of short, easily understood words, common to seventeenth-century conversation. Although "Huswifery" is written in a more ornate style, with unusual metaphors and decorative language, it also reflects a strict Puritan view of the world.

1. (a) Identify three aspects of the Puritan Plain Style reflected in "To My Dear and Loving Husband." Support your answer with examples from the poem. (b) Which aspects of the poem are not typical of the Puritan Plain Style?

2. (a) Identify three aspects of the Puritan Plain Style reflected in "Huswifery." Support your answer with examples from the poem.
(b) In what ways is the poem not typical of the Puritan Plain Style?

◆ Grammar and Style

DIRECT ADDRESS

Use commas to separate a word or phrase of **direct address** from the rest of the sentence.

Middle: Make me, O Lord, Thy spinning wheel complete.

End: May you be rewarded for your love, dear husband.

Practice On your paper, rewrite the following passages, adding punctuation where needed. Underline the word or phrase of direct address in each.

1. Baa, baa, Black Sheep have you any wool?

2. Swing low sweet chariot / Coming for to carry me home. . . .

3. I could not love thee dear so much, / Loved I not honor more.

4. Are you sleeping Brother John?

Looking at Style Explain why you think the two writers used direct address in their poems.

◆ Grammar and Style

1. Baa, baa, Black Sheep, have you any wool?
2. Swing low, sweet chariot, /Coming for to carry me home . . .
3. I could not love thee, dear, so much, / Loved I not honor more.
4. Are you sleeping, Brother John?

Looking at Style By addressing her husband directly in her poem, Bradstreet makes the expression of her love for him even more personal. Taylor uses direct address in order to emphasize that he is asking or praying God for a special favor.

Grammar Reinforcement

For additional instruction and practice, use the lesson on commas in the Capitalization and Punctuation unit of the **Language Lab CD-ROM.** The lesson includes a model of how to punctuate nouns of direct address.

Build Your Portfolio

Idea Bank

Writing

1. Letter Choose a character from literature or life who loved with an intensity equal to Bradstreet's. Writing as that character, compose a letter to your loved one, using comparisons to express the depth of your feelings.

2. Magazine Article People today could learn a lot about personal devotion from these poems. Write a magazine article stressing the need for people to show such devotion to their loved ones and to the values in which they believe.

3. Poem Create a modern version of "Huswifery," replacing the spinning wheel with a contemporary image that is equally appropriate to the theme of personal religious devotion.

Speaking, Listening, and Viewing

4. Informal Debate Foremost among the Puritan values were a strong work ethic and devotion to God and family. Stage a debate to argue whether these Puritan values exist in today's society.

5. Love Song Create a love song based on Bradstreet's poem. Set your lyrics to music and perform the song for your class. **[Music Link]**

Researching and Representing

6. Bradstreet Sampler On paper, design a sampler like the one on p. 90 for the Bradstreet home. Include a motto that expresses Bradstreet's beliefs and concerns as reflected in her poetry. **[Art Link]**

7. Graphic Display Research the process of spinning yarn and weaving cloth as it was practiced in the colonial era. Create a graphic display that identifies the steps and tools referenced in "Huswifery," and write the corresponding line(s) of verse next to each. **[Social Studies Link]**

Online Activity www.phlit.phschool.com

Guided Writing Lesson

Editorial: Men and Housework

We do not generally associate men with tasks such as spinning and weaving—chores normally delegated to colonial women. Today, however, men are taking on more of what was once classified as "women's work." In a newspaper editorial, address the need for men to do their share of housework.

Writing Skills Focus: Anticipation of Opposing Arguments

You can expect that some readers might disagree with your proposals. **Anticipate opposing arguments** by considering objections your readers might raise and addressing them up front in your editorial. For example, to answer an argument that a man who works all day should not have to scrub floors when he comes home, you might observe that many women who work away from home face those tasks when they return from work. Build your case by addressing each of the opposing arguments you anticipate.

Prewriting In order to anticipate opposing arguments, use a problem-and-solution chart. List tasks to be completed in the average household. For each task, list objections or obstacles in the "problem" column; in the "solution" column, identify ways to get them done by both the men and women of the household.

Drafting Clearly state your position in the opening paragraph, then support your reasoning in the body of the editorial. Use the ideas you developed in your problem-and-solution chart to deflate opposing arguments by confronting them head on.

Revising Ask a classmate to critique your editorial and strengthen any weak spots he or she identifies. Was the editorial persuasive? Were there any points you omitted that could leave you open to objections?

✓ ASSESSMENT OPTIONS

Formal Assessment, Selection Test, pp. 27–29, and Assessment Resources Software. The selection test is designed so that it can be easily customized to the performance levels of your students.

Alternative Assessment, p. 6, includes options for less advanced students, more advanced students, verbal/linguistic learners, intrapersonal learners and interpersonal learners.

PORTFOLIO ASSESSMENT

Use the following rubrics in the ***Alternative Assessment*** booklet to assess student writing:
Letter: Expression Rubric, p. 109
Magazine Article: Expression Rubric, p. 109
Poem: Poetry Rubric, p. 123
Guided Writing Lesson: Persuasion Rubric, p. 120

Idea Bank

Customizing for ***Performance Levels***

Following are suggestions for matching Idea Bank topics with your students' performance levels:
Less Advanced Students: 1, 6
Average Students: 2, 5, 7
More Advanced Students: 3, 4

Customizing for ***Learning Modalities***

Following are suggestions for matching Idea Bank topics with your students' learning modalities:
Logical/Mathematical: 4, 7
Musical/Rhythmic: 5
Visual/Spatial: 6

Guided Writing Lesson

For more prewriting, elaboration, and revision strategies, see *Prentice Hall Writing and Grammar.*

Writers at Work Videodisc

Have students view the videodisc segment (Ch. 4) featuring Gasby Greely, to see how she approaches persuasion. Discuss how Greely organizes her ideas before she begins to write. How might her approach help students organize their editorials?

Play frames 33643 to 43235

Writing Lab CD-ROM

Have students complete the tutorial on Persuasion. Follow these steps:

1. Review the audio-annotated models of an editorial and a persuasive essay.
2. Use the Pros and Cons Chart to help students anticipate opposing arguments.
3. After students have drafted on the computer, have them use the Persuasive Word Bins to strengthen their editorials.

Reteach

If some students need more help understanding how to paraphrase, refer to the Restate Poetic Language strategy, p. 10 in ***Strategies for Diverse Student Needs.***

Prepare and Engage

LESSON OBJECTIVES

1. **To develop vocabulary and word identification skills**
   - Latin Prefixes: *omni-*
   - Using the Word Bank: Context
   - Reading Strategy: Context Clues
2. **To use a variety of reading strategies to comprehend a sermon**
   - Tips to Guide Reading (ATE)
3. **To increase knowledge of other cultures and to connect common elements across cultures**
   - Connecting Themes Across Cultures (ATE)
4. **To express and support responses to the text**
   - Critical Thinking
   - Idea Bank: Diary Entry
   - Idea Bank: Television Commercial
   - Idea Bank: Public Letter
   - Idea Bank: Newscast
5. **To analyze literary elements**
   - Literary Focus: Sermon
6. **To read in order to research self-selected and assigned topics**
   - Idea Bank: Oral Report
   - Idea Bank: Puritan Handbook
7. **To plan, prepare, organize, and present literary interpretations**
   - Idea Bank: Oral Interpretation
8. **To use recursive writing processes to write an evaluation**
   - Guided Writing Lesson
9. **To increase knowledge of the rules of grammar and usage**
   - Grammar and Style: Forms of Adjectives and Adverbs

Test Preparation

Summarizing Written Texts: Paraphrasing (ATE, p. 97)
The teaching tips and sample test item in this workshop support the instruction and practice in the unit workshop:
Reading Comprehension: Summarizing Written Texts (SE, p.115)

Guide for Interpreting

Jonathan Edwards *(1703–1758)*

Jonathan Edwards is so synonymous with "fire and brimstone"—a phrase symbolizing the torments of hell endured by sinners—that his name alone was enough to make many eighteenth-century Puritans shake in their shoes.

This great American theologian and powerful Puritan preacher was born in East Windsor, Connecticut, where he grew up in an atmosphere of devout discipline.

As a young boy, Edwards is said to have preached sermons to his playmates from a makeshift pulpit he built behind his home.

A brilliant academic, he learned Latin, Greek, and Hebrew by the age of twelve, entered Yale at thirteen, and graduated four years later as class valedictorian. He went on to earn his master's degree in theology.

A Preacher Born and Raised Edwards began his preaching career in 1727 as assistant to his grandfather, Solomon Stoddard, pastor of the church at Northampton, Massachusetts, one of the largest and wealthiest congregations in the Puritan world. Edwards also preached as a visiting minister throughout New England. Strongly desiring a return to the orthodoxy and fervent faith of the Puritan past, he became a leader of the Great Awakening, a religious revival that swept the colonies in the 1730's and 1740's.

Changing Attitudes The Great Awakening did not last, however, and in 1750 Edwards was dismissed from his position after his extreme conservatism alienated much of the congregation. He continued to preach and write until his death in 1758, shortly after becoming president of the College of New Jersey (now Princeton University).

Edwards's highly emotional sermon "Sinners in the Hands of an Angry God" is by far his most famous work. It was delivered to a congregation in Enfield, Connecticut, in 1741, and it is said to have caused listeners to rise from their seats in a state of hysteria.

◆ Background for Understanding

HISTORY: EDWARDS IN THE PULPIT

You would never guess from looking at the intimidating cover of this contemporary reprint that Edwards preached this "fire and brimstone" sermon in a speaking style that was quiet and restrained. According to one account, he read the six-hour sermon in a level voice, staring over the heads of his congregation at the bell rope that hung against the back wall "as if he would stare it in two." In spite of his calm demeanor, his listeners are said to have groaned and screamed in terror. Edwards reportedly had to stop several times and ask for silence. Without once resorting to dramatic techniques, he was able to build religious emotion to a fever pitch through effective use of vivid imagery and repetition of his main points.

SINNERS
IN THE HANDS OF AN
ANGRY GOD.
A
SERMON
Preached at ENFIELD, July 8th, 1741.
At a Time of great Awakenings; and attended with remarkable Impressions on many of the Hearers.
By JONATHAN EDWARDS, A.M.
Pastor of the Church of CHRIST, in NORTHAMPTON.

Journal Activity Think about why Edwards might have chosen to use a quiet, level tone rather than a more dramatic or emotional delivery. Explain why you think listeners might find a quiet style even more terrifying than an overly dramatic one.

Prentice Hall Literature Program Resources

REINFORCE / RETEACH / EXTEND

Selection Support Pages
Build Vocabulary: Prefixes: *omni-*, p. 30
Grammar and Style: Forms of Adjectives and Adverbs, p. 31
Reading Strategy: Context Clues, p. 32
Literary Focus: Sermon, p. 33

Strategies for Diverse Student Needs, p. 7

Beyond Literature
Workplace Skills, p. 7

Formal Assessment Selection Test, pp. 30–32; Assessment Resources Software

Alternative Assessment, p. 7

Writing and Language Transparencies
Written Evaluation, pp. 25–31

Daily Language Practice,
Weeks 2 and 3, pp.109,110

Resource Pro CD-ROM

Listening to Literature Audiocassettes

from Sinners in the Hands of an Angry God

◆ Literature and Your Life

Connect Your Experience

Suppose your younger brother is involved with the "wrong crowd." Perhaps all you can do to get him back on track is paint a bleak picture of the awful future that may await him if he doesn't turn himself around. Jonathan Edwards had the same concerns about his fellow worshipers. He believed many were walking a path of certain destruction, and he desperately wanted to turn them toward repentance and heaven. Edwards achieved his goal by filling his sermons with terrifying descriptions of the horrors that awaited those who did not mend their ways.

Thematic Focus: The Puritan Influence

Is "scaring them straight" an effective way to change people's behavior for the better?

◆ Build Vocabulary

Latin Prefixes: *omni-*

Edwards describes how the wrath of God could rush down with *omnipotent* power upon sinners. The adjective *potent* means "strong or powerful." The addition of the Latin prefix *omni-*, meaning "all or everywhere," creates a new word, *omnipotent*, which literally means "all powerful."

Word Bank

Preview this list of words from the sermon.

omnipotent
ineffable
dolorous

◆ Grammar and Style

Forms of Adjectives and Adverbs

The power of Edwards's sermon is largely a result of his use of vivid modifiers. Most adjectives and adverbs have three forms. The **basic,** or **positive, form** is used when a comparison is *not* being made. The **comparative form** shows two things being compared. The **superlative form** identifies one or more of the members of a group as having the most or least of a certain characteristic.

Positive: holy, mercifully, good/well
Comparative: holier, more/less mercifully, better
Superlative: holiest, most/least mercifully, best

Most one-syllable and some two-syllable adjectives and adverbs use *-er* to form the comparative and *-est* to form the superlative. For all other adjectives and adverbs, use *more* or *less* to form the comparative and *most* or *least* to form the superlative.

◆ Literary Focus

Sermon

Though often associated with stern lectures or "fire and brimstone" speeches like this one, sermons can also be instructional or inspiring. A **sermon** is broadly defined as a speech given from a pulpit in a house of worship, usually as part of a religious service. Like its written counterpart, the essay, a sermon expresses the message or point of view its author wishes to convey to his or her audience, called a congregation. The atmosphere of colonial America helped the sermon flourish as a popular literary form.

◆ Reading Strategy

Context Clues

Searching the **context**—the surrounding words, phrases, and sentences—for clues can help you come up with the meaning of unfamiliar words as you read. Look at the word *abominable* in this passage:

> . . . you are ten thousand times more *abominable* in his [God's] eyes, than the most hateful venomous serpent is in ours. . . .

The context clue comes in the form of a comparison: Edwards likens the way the sinner appears in God's eye with our view of "the most hateful venomous serpent." From this clue, you can determine that *abominable* must be close in meaning to *disgusting* or *horrible*—words evoked by the image of a deadly snake.

Test Preparation Workshop

Summarizing Written Texts: Paraphrasing Many standardized tests require students to identify the best summary of a written passage. Being able to paraphrase information will help students recognize accurate summaries. Present the following sample, and ask students to choose the best paraphrase.

> However you may have reformed your life in many things, and may have had religious affections, and may keep up a form of religion in your families and closets, and in the house of God, it is nothing but his mere pleasure that keeps you from being this moment swallowed up in everlasting destruction.

A God can still condemn you even if you live virtuously, pray privately, and go to church.
B People should pray and lead virtuous lives.
C God will pardon you if you go to church.
D People should be religious in order to win God's approval.

B is an accurate, but incomplete, statement. Choices *C* and *D* are misleading: praying and being religious don't necessarily secure God's grace. *A* is the best paraphrase.

Interest Grabber

Most students know the persuasive power of media ads, of peer pressure, and of other methods used to influence actions or attitudes. Have groups brainstorm for approaches or techniques that they find to be persuasive. Then hook students' interest in Jonathan Edwards's persuasive sermon by reading the following quotation to them:

> O sinner! Consider the fearful danger you are in: it is a great furnace of wrath, a wide and bottomless pit, full of the fire of wrath, that you are held over in the hand of that God. . . .

Ask students to characterize the approach (emotional or intellectual) Edwards, a conservative Puritan preacher, uses. Have them respond to it and predict how Edwards will attempt to persuade the congregation to accept his message.

Connecting Themes Across Cultures

Invite students to identify belief systems, in their own and other cultures, that agree or disagree with Puritan notions of how to convince individuals to live a virtuous lifestyle. For example, they might compare and contrast Puritan beliefs with what they know about the beliefs of Islamic Fundamentalism, Hinduism, or varieties of Buddhism.

Customize for
Less Proficient Readers

Jonathan Edwards uses repetition to emphasize his points in recurring phrases such as "it is nothing but air" or "the mere pleasure of God." Have students look for words and phrases that repeat in the sermon, and derive from these repetitions the essence of Edwards's message.

Customize for
AP Students

In contrast to the spirited tone his fervent sermon seems to demand, Edwards gave his speech in a calm, even-tempered voice. Challenge more advanced students to deliver the sermon as Edwards did to emphasize the contrast between the medium and the message. Discuss the impact of this contradiction.

Develop Understanding

One-Minute Insight Edwards's sermon is based on the Puritan belief in a life of hard work, self-discipline, and religious devotion. His sermon was delivered to strike fear in his listeners and to convince them that they must observe lives of humility and righteousness if they have any hope of achieving God's grace. What listeners might find most fearful in the speech may be the idea that an angry and powerful God could be indifferent to human misery, and that redemption lay in God's whim of mercy, which mortals can hope to receive only by observing His laws completely.

Clarification *Brimstone* is the archaic name for sulfur, a chemical whose noxious odor is typically associated with the fires of Hell. It is used in biblical passages, such as Genesis 19:24, where an angry God "... rained down fire and brimstone from the skies ..."

◆ Literary Focus

❶ Sermon Ask students to find details that characterize this piece as a sermon. They may cite the use of religious references to Christ and God or the repetition of words to heighten a sense of warning to the congregants. Also have them look for examples of figurative language, such as the personification of Hell's "wide gaping mouth open," which add poetic and dramatic impact to the piece.

◆ Critical Thinking

❷ Analyze Ask students to explain Edwards's view of man's place in the universe. *Students may say that man is a puppet of God, and so must do what God wants or risk abandonment.*

from Sinners in the Hands of an Angry God

Jonathan Edwards

Connections to World Literature, *page 1154*

This is the case of every one of you that are out of Christ:[1] That world of misery, that lake of burning brimstone, is extended abroad under you. There is the dreadful pit of the glowing flames of the wrath of God; there is Hell's wide gaping mouth open; and you have nothing to stand upon, nor anything to take hold of; there is nothing between you and Hell but the air; it is
❶ only the power and mere pleasure of God that
❷ holds you up.

You probably are not sensible of this; you find you are kept out of Hell, but do not see the hand of God in it; but look at other things, as the good state of your bodily constitution, your care of your own life, and the means you use for your own preservation. But indeed these things are nothing; if God should withdraw his hand, they would avail no more to keep you from falling than the thin air to hold up a person that is suspended in it.

Your wickedness makes you as it were heavy as lead, and to tend downwards with great weight and pressure towards Hell; and if God should let you go, you would immediately sink and swiftly descend and plunge into the bottomless gulf, and your healthy constitution, and your own care and prudence, and best contrivance, and all your righteousness, would have no more influence to uphold you and keep you out of Hell, than a spider's web would have to stop a fallen rock. Were it not for the sovereign pleasure of God, the earth would not bear you one moment . . . The world would spew you out, were it not for the sovereign hand of Him who hath subjected it in hope. There are black clouds of God's wrath now hanging directly over your heads, full of the dreadful storm, and big with thunder; and were it not for the restraining hand of God, it would immediately burst forth upon you. The sovereign pleasure of God, for the present, stays[2] his rough wind; otherwise it would come with fury, and your destruction would come like a whirlwind, and you would be like the chaff of the summer threshing floor.

The wrath of God is like great waters that are dammed for the present; they increase more and more, and rise higher and higher, till
an outlet is given; and the longer the stream is ❸
stopped, the more rapid and mighty is its course, when once it is let loose. It is true, that

1. **out of Christ:** Not in God's grace.

2. **stays:** Restrains.

Block Scheduling Strategies

Consider these suggestions to take advantage of extended class time:

- Discuss with students the Thematic Focus question on p. 97. Stress the relevance of the sermon during the historical period in which it was delivered.
- To build background on the Puritans and to add more grammar, usage, and mechanics instruction, use the Daily Language Practice pages for Weeks 2 and 3.
- Have students listen to all or part of the sermon on audiocassette. Discuss the impact of the delivery and whether listening to the sermon influences students' appreciation of it.
- To give students a strategy for unlocking the unfamiliar words in the sermon, discuss the Reading Strategy: Context Clues, for the selection. Do the Reading Strategy activity (p. 102).
- Before students begin the Guided Writing Lesson (p. 103), discuss the importance of a unified approach in a persuasive piece. Ask students to find examples of unity in Edwards's sermon, and to explain how these elements add to the sermon's impact.

judgment against your evil works has not been executed hitherto; the Hoods of God's vengeance have been withheld; but your guilt in the meantime is constantly increasing, and you are every day treasuring up more wrath; the waters are constantly rising, and waxing more and more mighty; and there is nothing but the mere pleasure of God, that holds the waters back, that are unwilling to be stopped, and press hard to go
❸ forward. If God should only withdraw his hand from the floodgate, it would immediately fly open, and the fiery floods of the fierceness and wrath of God, would rush forth with inconceivable fury, and would come upon you with omnipotent power; and if your strength were ten thousand times greater than it is, yea, ten thousand times greater than the strength of the stoutest, sturdiest devil in Hell, it would be nothing to withstand or endure it.

The bow of God's wrath is bent, and the arrow made ready on the string, and justice bends the arrow at your heart, and strains the bow, and it is nothing but the mere pleasure of God, and that of an angry God, without any promise or obligation at all, that keeps the arrow one moment from being made drunk with your blood. Thus all you that never passed under a great change of heart, by the mighty power of the spirit of God upon your souls; all you that were never born again, and made new creatures, and raised from being dead in sin, to a state of

The Puritan, 1898, Frank E. Schoonover, Collection of the Brandywine River Museum

▲ Critical Viewing What words from the text would you apply to describe the mood of this painting? **[Analyze]** ❹

◆ Build Vocabulary

omnipotent (äm nip′ ə tənt) *adj.*: All-powerful

◆ Literary Focus

❸ Invite students to evaluate the effectiveness of water imagery as a tool for persuasion. *Students may say that because water is an ever-present, familiar, powerful, and dramatic force of life or death, it gives Edwards many potent images he can use to convey his ideas.*

▶Critical Viewing◀

❹ **Analyze** Citations may include "your own care and prudence," "unexperienced light," "infinite gloom," "fierceness," "moral and strict, sober and religious," "miserable condition that you are in."

Customize for *Musical/Rhythmic Learners*

Edwards uses the poetic sound devices of onomatopoeia and alliteration to heighten the drama of his message. Invite students to read passages aloud to experience the *wind* of repeated *f's* or *s's*, or the *smash* of repeated *t's* or *d's*.

Customize for *Verbal/Linguistic Learners*

Invite volunteers to select a portion of this sermon to practice and deliver to classmates, who can critique the delivery and the overall persuasive effect.

Tips to Guide Reading

Shared Reading To help students monitor their comprehension as they read, guide them into the tone and language of the selection by reading the first few paragraphs aloud. Then have students continue reading silently.

Humanities: Art

The Puritan, 1898, by Frank E. Schoonover (1877–1922).

Frank Schoonover was an American illustrator. A student of the famous illustrator Howard Pyle, Schoonover illustrated magazines and books, such as *LaFitte,* the *Pirate of the Gulf,* and the *Hopalong Cassidy* series of westerns. His paintings show great precision of detail. This piece not only accurately illustrates Puritan garb, but conveys the austere attitude of the Puritans. Use these questions for discussion:

1. This is a "formal" portrait, one in which the subject was posed by the artist. How does this concept echo the sermon? *The artist influences how we perceive the Puritan by presenting him in a certain stance, with certain objects, and in a muted light. In the sermon, Jonathan Edwards paints a portrait of the Puritan in words by describing the state of the moral life of the Puritan as well as how that life can be improved.*
2. From this painting alone, what can you infer about the way of life of the Puritans? *Students may say that the Puritans lived an austere and serious life.*

Cultural Connection

Edwards's apparent belief in an afterlife is typical of the followers of most major religions. According to the ancient Greeks, people who led a good life were sent to Elysium, a paradise filled with fields of flowers and sunlight. In Norse mythology heroes slain in battle went to Valhalla, a golden palace in the homeland of the gods. There they would do battle each morning and feast each noon. In Buddhism and Hinduism, the soul is reincarnated, or reborn in another body or form, until it achieves a state of spiritual perfection.

Encourage students to choose a culture and investigate its beliefs about life after death. They may report their findings in a presentation to the class.

◆ Literary Focus

❶ Sermon Ask students to describe God as envisioned by Edwards. *Students may describe the Puritan God as cruel, imperious, condescending, vengeful, and easily provoked.*

◆ Reading Strategy

❷ Context Clues Students may say that the words *provoked* and *incensed* mean "stirred up" and "enraged," respectively.

◆ Reading Strategy

❸ Context Clues Have students use clues in this sentence to determine the meaning of the words *duration* and *mitigation*. *The word* duration *means "the time that something lasts." The word* mitigation *means "respite, rest, or rescue."*

new, and before altogether unexperienced light and life, are in the hands of an angry God. However you may have reformed your life in many things, and may have had religious affections, and may keep up a form of religion in your families and closets,[3] and in the house of God, it is nothing but His mere pleasure that keeps you from being this moment swallowed up in everlasting destruction. However unconvinced you may now be of the truth of what you hear, by and by you will be fully convinced of it.

Those that are gone from being in the like circumstances with you, see that it was so with them; for destruction came suddenly upon most of them; when they expected nothing of it, and while they were saying, peace and safety: now they see, that those things on which they depended for peace and safety, were nothing but thin air and empty shadows.

❶ The God that holds you over the pit of Hell, much as one holds a spider, or some loathsome insect over the fire, abhors you, and is dreadfully provoked: his wrath towards you burns like fire; he looks upon you as worthy of nothing else, but to be cast into the fire; he is of purer eyes than to bear to have you in his sight; you are ten thousand times more abominable in his eyes, than the most hateful venomous serpent is in ours. . . .

O sinner! Consider the fearful danger you are in: it is a great furnace of wrath, a wide and bottomless pit, full of the fire of wrath, that you are held over in the hand of that God, whose wrath is provoked and incensed as much against you, as against many of the damned in Hell. You hang by a slender thread, with the flames of divine wrath flashing about it, and ready every moment to singe it, and burn it asunder; and you have no interest in any mediator, and nothing to lay hold of to save yourself, nothing to keep off the flames of wrath, nothing of your own, nothing that you ever have done, nothing that you can do, to induce God to spare you one moment. . . .

❷ **◆ Reading Strategy** Use the reference to "furnace of wrath" as a clue to the meaning of *provoked* and *incensed.*

When God beholds the ineffable extremity of your case, and sees your torment to be so vastly disproportioned to your strength, and sees how your poor soul is crushed, and sinks down, as it were, into an infinite gloom; he will have no compassion upon you, he will not forbear the executions of his wrath, or in the least lighten his hand; there shall be no moderation or mercy, nor will God then at all stay his rough wind; he will have no regard to your welfare, nor be at all careful lest you should suffer too much in any other sense, than only that you shall *not suffer beyond what strict justice requires*. . . .

God stands ready to pity you; this is a day of mercy; you may cry now with some encouragement of obtaining mercy. But once the day of mercy is past, your most lamentable and dolorous cries and shrieks will be in vain; you will be wholly lost and thrown away of God, as to any regard to your welfare. God will have no other use to put you to, but to suffer misery; you shall be continued in being to no other end; for you will be a vessel of wrath fitted to destruction; and there will be no other use of this vessel, but to be filled full of wrath. . . .

Thus it will be with you that are in an unconverted state, if you continue in it; the infinite might, and majesty, and terribleness of the omnipotent God shall be magnified upon you, in the ineffable strength of your torments. You shall be tormented in the presence of the holy angels, and in the presence of the Lamb,[4] and when you shall be in this state of suffering, the glorious inhabitants of Heaven shall go forth and look on the awful spectacle, that they may see what the wrath and fierceness of the Almighty is; and when they have seen it, they will fall down and adore that great power and majesty. . . .

It would be dreadful to suffer this fierceness and wrath of Almighty God one moment; but you must suffer it to all eternity. There will be no end to this exquisite horrible misery. When you look forward, you shall see a long forever, a boundless duration before you, which will swallow up your thoughts and amaze your soul; and you will absolutely despair of ever having any deliverance, any end, any mitigation, any rest at all. . . . ❸

How dreadful is the state of those that are daily and hourly in the danger of this great

3. **closets** *n.*: Small, private rooms for meditation.

4. **the Lamb:** Jesus.

Speaking, Listening, and Viewing Mini-Lesson

Oral Interpretation

This mini-lesson supports the Speaking, Listening, and Viewing activity in the Idea Bank on p. 103.

Introduce the Concept Explain that an oral interpretation is a dramatic reading similar to an actor's performance. However, in a reading, the performer need not memorize the lines or prepare costume, props, or scenery to enhance the production.

Develop Background Select a brief descriptive passage from a narrative for students to interpret. Discuss elements a dramatic reader employs to make a passage more accessible to an audience, such as gestures, correct pronunciation, appropriate reading rate, volume, pitch, and tone. Point out that all of the elements must be properly utilized to achieve just the right mood for the piece.

Apply the Information Readers should familiarize themselves with the selected passage and practice its delivery. After rehearsing, students should present the passage to the class.

Assess the Outcome Students should evaluate the interpretations using the following criteria: use of appropriate gestures and correct pronunciation; effective use of volume, pitch, tone; and rate of reading.

wrath and infinite misery! But this is the dismal case of every soul in this congregation that has not been born again, however moral and strict, sober and religious, they may otherwise be. Oh that you would consider it, whether you be young or old! . . . Those of you that finally continue in a natural condition, that shall keep you out of Hell longest will be there in a little time! Your damnation does not slumber; it will come swiftly, and, in all probability, very suddenly upon many of you. You have reason to wonder that you are not already in Hell. It is doubtless the case of some whom you have seen and known, that never deserved Hell more than you, and that heretofore appeared as likely to have been now alive as you. Their case is past all hope; they are crying in extreme misery and perfect despair; but here you are in the land of the living and in the house of God, and have an opportunity to obtain salvation. What would not those poor damned hopeless souls give for one day's opportunity such as you now enjoy!

4

And now you have an extraordinary opportunity, a day wherein Christ has thrown the door of mercy wide open, and stands in calling and crying with a loud voice to poor sinners; a day wherein many are flocking to him, and pressing into the kingdom of God. Many are daily coming from the east, west, north and south; many that were very lately in the same miserable condition that you are in, are now in a happy state, with their hearts filled with love to him who has loved them, and washed them from their sins in his own blood, and rejoicing in hope of the glory of God. How awful is it to be left behind at such a day! To see so many others feasting, while you are pining and perishing! To see so many rejoicing and singing for joy of heart, while you have cause to mourn for sorrow of heart, and howl for vexation of spirit! . . .

5 ◆ *Literature and Your Life*

What does the image of a door that's "wide open" mean to you?

Therefore, let everyone that is out of Christ now awake and fly from the wrath to come. The wrath of Almighty God is now undoubtedly hanging over a great part of this congregation: let everyone fly out of Sodom.[5] "Haste and escape for your lives, look not behind you, escape to the mountain, lest you be consumed."[6]

---

5. **Sodom** (säd′ əm): In the Bible, a city destroyed by fire because of the sinfulness of its people.

6. **"Haste . . . consumed":** From Genesis 19:17, the angels' warning to Lot, the only virtuous man in Sodom, to flee the city before they destroy it.

◆ Build Vocabulary

ineffable (in ef′ ə bəl) *adj.*: Inexpressible; unable to be spoken

dolorous (dō′ lər əs) *adj.*: Sad; mournful

Guide for Responding

◆ Literature and Your Life

Reader's Response How do you think you would have reacted if you had heard Edwards deliver this sermon?

Thematic Focus In the fifteen years of the Great Awakening, Edwards succeeded in converting thousands to Puritanism before his congregation rebelled against his conservative beliefs and dismissed him from his position. Do you think Edwards's message and tactics would be well received today?

Journal Activity Do you think scare tactics like those of Edwards are an effective way of changing people's behavior? Think about the impact Edwards made on his congregation as you answer this question in your journal.

✓ Check Your Comprehension

1. According to the opening paragraph, what keeps sinners from falling into Hell?
2. Describe at least two images Edwards uses to depict the wrath of God.
3. (a) Toward the end of the sermon, what does Edwards say that sinners can obtain? (b) What must they do to obtain it?

Beyond the Selection

FURTHER READING

Other Works by Jonathan Edwards

A Faithful Narrative (1737)

Some Thoughts Concerning the Present Revival (1743)

Other Works About Puritanism

The Wonders of the Invisible World, Cotton Mather

Jonathan Edwards, Pastor, Patricia Tracy

The Crucible, Arthur Miller

We recommend that you preview these texts before assigning them to students.

INTERNET

You and your students may find additional information about Jonathan Edwards and Puritanism on the Internet. We suggest the following site. Please be aware, however, that the site may have changed from the time we published this information. Go to **http://ourworld.compuserve.com/homepages/WCarson/homepage.htm**

We *strongly recommend* that you preview the site before sending students to it.

4 **Clarification** *Natural condition*, in this context, refers to what Edwards believes to be the original, unsaved state of all humans because of Adam's fall from grace in the Garden of Eden.

◆ Literature and Your Life

5 Students may respond that the image suggests the unexpected opportunity to be welcomed in.

Reinforce and Extend

Answers

◆ Literature and Your Life

Reader's Response Some students may say that the sermon would have frightened or upset them.

Thematic Focus Some students may say that Edwards's message and tactics would not be well-received today because most contemporary religious views do not characterize God as vengeful or angry.

✓ Check Your Comprehension

1. The hand of God keeps sinners from falling into Hell.
2. Sample response: Edwards describes the wrath of God as black clouds hanging over the heads of sinners and as dammed waters waiting to burst through the floodgate.
3. (a) Sinners can obtain mercy and salvation. (b) To obtain it sinners must repent.

Reteach

Students may benefit from a demonstration of how to use context clues. Invite them to identify a paragraph which includes one or more unfamiliar words or phrases. Write the passage on the board, underlining the difficult words. Then circle the surrounding context which can help students determine the meaning of the words. For example, in the top paragraph of the right column on p. 100, students might not understand the archaic use of the word *stay*. You might circle the preceding phrase *there shall be no moderation or mercy*, and circle the metaphor, *his rough wind*, which follows. Putting the sense of the preceding phrase together with the metaphor (which students should readily infer to mean "his anger"), guide students to interpret the connotation of *stay* in this context ("stop or cause to cease").

Answers

◆ Critical Thinking

1. Edwards's description of Hell is designed to instill fear in the congregation.
2. (a) The repetition of the word *wrath* drives home Edwards's message: that God's anger toward sinners is building and that they will suffer unless they repent. (b) The images are familiar, concrete images, like dammed waters and a bent bow, that show the potential for great danger and pain.
3. Students may say that Edwards's approach would not be effective today. Many of today's worshippers do not hold the same severe beliefs as Edwards did.
4. Students may say that scare tactics are justified in situations where someone's habits or actions endanger his or her health or well-being, or where attempts to reason with or educate the person are unsuccessful in getting him or her to change.

◆ Reading Strategy

1. *Waxing* means "growing or building." References to water that is "constantly increasing" and "constantly rising" and the words "more and more" indicate something that is getting larger in size.
2. *Abhors* means "detests or is disgusted by." If God feels towards the listener as he might toward a spider or "some loathsome insect," then *abhor* must be associated with feelings of hatred or disgust.

◆ Literary Focus

1. Edwards is trying to convince people of the need to repent and convert to Puritanism to save themselves.
2. (a) Edwards appeals to the people's sense of fear and uncertainty. (b) This is appropriate because the listeners may have been feeling insecure about the strength of their faith or less than confident in the virtuousness of their behavior. Their fear of damnation would make them convert.

◆ Build Vocabulary

Using the Prefix *omni-*

1. b 2. a 3. c

Guide for Responding *(continued)*

◆ Critical Thinking

INTERPRET

1. Why do you think Edwards opens this portion of his sermon with a description of Hell? **[Infer]**
2. (a) What impact is created by the repeated use of the word *wrath*? (b) How do the many symbols and images of God's wrath add to the impact? **[Analyze]**

EVALUATE

3. Would Edwards's sermon and style of delivery be as effective on a modern congregation? Why or why not? **[Evaluate; Support]**

APPLY

4. In which situations, if any, is it justifiable to use fear to get a person to improve his or her behavior? Explain your answer. **[Synthesize]**

◆ Reading Strategy

CONTEXT CLUES

Using the **context**—the surrounding words or sentences—can be an effective way to unlock the meaning of an unfamiliar word. Use the context in the passages below to define the italicized words.

1. . . . you are every day treasuring up more wrath; the waters are constantly rising, and *waxing* more and more mighty . . .
2. The God that holds you over the pit of Hell, much as one holds a spider, or some loathsome insect over the fire, *abhors* you, and is dreadfully provoked . . .

◆ Literary Focus

SERMON

Jonathan Edwards fought his crusade for salvation with words that often took the form of a **sermon**—a speech that has a definite point of view and is delivered from the pulpit during a worship service.

1. What point of view or message is Edwards conveying in this sermon?
2. (a) To what emotion does he appeal in his effort to motivate the congregation? (b) Considering Edwards's purpose, why is this an appropriate choice? Explain your answer.

◆ Build Vocabulary

USING THE LATIN PREFIX ***omni-***

Each of these adjectives contains the Latin prefix *omni-*, meaning "all" or "every." Use the information in parentheses to match each adjective with the situation to which it best applies.

1. omnipotent (*potent* = powerful)
2. omniscient (*sciens* = knowing)
3. omnivorous (*vor* = to eat)

a. how a student might describe a smart teacher
b. how a prisoner might describe his powerful jailer
c. how a zoologist might describe an animal that eats both meat and plants

USING THE WORD BANK: Context

Write this sentence in your notebook, filling each blank with the appropriate word from the Word Bank:

The citizens of Oz sighed with a __?__ air, indicating their __?__ sadness at learning that the Wizard they considered __?__ was just an ordinary man, hiding behind a curtain.

◆ Grammar and Style

FORMS OF ADJECTIVES AND ADVERBS

The **comparative** form of adjectives and adverbs is used to compare two things or ideas; the **superlative** form is used when comparing more than two things or ideas.

Writing Application Rewrite the following paragraph in your notebook, correcting all errors in comparisons:

> When we think of great preachers, Edwards is the name that quickliest comes to mind. Of the many Puritan sermonizers who rose to fame during the Great Awakening, Edwards is still considered the more influential. Most of his writing appealed to reason and logic; "Sinners in the Hands of an Angry God" is his most emotional and more famous work.

Looking at Style Review the sermon and find an adjective and an adverb in each form that you feel is especially vivid. Explain how Edwards uses each one you've chosen to create a powerful image.

Using the Word Bank: Context

The citizens of Oz sighed with a dolorous air, indicating their ineffable sadness at learning that the Wizard they considered omnipotent was just an ordinary man, hiding behind a curtain.

◆ Grammar and Style

When we think of great preachers, Edwards is the name that most quickly comes to mind. Of the many Puritan sermonizers who rose to fame during the Great Awakening, Edwards is still considered the most influential. Most of his writing appealed to reason and logic; "Sinners in the Hands of an Angry God" is his most emotional and most famous work.

Grammar Reinforcement

For additional instruction and practice, use the lesson in the **Language Lab CD-ROM** on Forms of Comparison and the practice pages (pp. 73–74) in the *Writer's Solution Grammar Practice Book*.

Build Your Portfolio

Idea Bank

Writing

1. Diary Entry You are a devout member of the Enfield, Connecticut, congregation. In a diary entry, describe your feelings after listening to all six hours of Edwards's sermon.

2. Newscast Edwards was dismissed as pastor of the Northampton congregation after he publicly named members who he believed had lapsed in their devotion. Write a newscast announcing the dismissal and the reasons for it. **[Media Link]**

3. Public Letter As Edwards, write an open letter defending the actions that led to your dismissal. Explain why you publicly denounced members of the congregation.

Speaking, Listening, and Viewing

4. Oral Interpretation Read an excerpt from the sermon in your choice of dramatic style. Invite your classmates to critique the impact of your delivery. **[Performing Arts Link]**

5. Oral Report Sermons like those of Dr. Martin Luther King, Jr., still have the power to inspire us. Research Dr. King's sermons and their role in the civil rights movement. Give a brief oral report on your findings. **[Social Studies Link]**

Researching and Representing

6. Television Commercial Create a commercial to persuade people to adopt a healthier lifestyle. Include music or sound effects as you share your commercial with your class. **[Media Link]**

7. Puritan Handbook Gather information about Puritan beliefs and the famous "work ethic." Create a handbook that includes guidelines and rules for living and worshiping as a proper Puritan.

Online Activity www.phlit.phschool.com

Guided Writing Lesson

Evaluation of Persuasion

A speaker's choice of persuasive techniques should depend on the audience and the occasion. At Enfield, Edwards decided to appeal to the congregation's emotions. Was it the best choice? Write an evaluation of the persuasive techniques Edwards used. Discuss the response he evoked in his listeners and the ways in which he achieved it. Are his techniques an appropriate and effective means of persuading the audience? Why or why not? Your evaluation will have greater clarity and strength if its elements work together to create a unified effect.

Writing Skills Focus: Unity

Unity refers to a singleness of effect. A piece of writing is unified when its elements or paragraphs express one main idea; a paragraph has unity when each sentence relates to a single topic.

Note how this paragraph conveys a single idea that supports the overall theme of the sermon.

Model From the Sermon

Therefore, let everyone that is out of Christ, now awake and fly from the wrath to come. The wrath of Almighty God is now undoubtedly hanging over a great part of this congregation: let everyone fly out of Sodom. "Haste and escape for your lives, look not behind you, escape to the mountains, lest you be consumed."

Prewriting To help focus your writing, summarize Edwards's techniques and your evaluation of their effectiveness in a clearly defined statement.

Drafting Use the statement you created as the basis for a strong, focused opening paragraph. Support your main point in the paragraphs that follow.

Revising Read your evaluation as though you were seeing it for the first time. Eliminate any information that's unrelated to the main idea.

Idea Bank

Customizing for
Performance Levels
Following are suggestions for matching Idea Bank topics with your students' performance levels:
Less Advanced Students: 1, 6
Average Students: 2, 4
More Advanced Students: 3, 5, 7

Customizing for
Learning Modalities
Musical/Rhythmic: 4
Verbal/Linguistic: 5
Interpersonal: 6
Logical/Mathematical: 5, 7

Guided Writing Lesson

For more prewriting, elaboration, and revision strategies, see *Prentice Hall Writing and Grammar.*

Writing and Language Transparencies To help students write their evaluations, use the Writing Process Model 5: Written Evaluation, pp. 25–31.

Have students view the videodisc segment (Ch. 7) featuring literary agent Theresa Park discussing how she evaluates manuscripts. Ask students whether they can use Park's method of evaluation.

Play frames 26321 to 29738

Writing Lab CD-ROM
Have students complete the tutorial on Response to Literature. Follow these steps:

1. Use the Evaluation Word Bins to select precise adverbs and adjectives to capture their reactions exactly.
2. Have students draft on the computer.
3. Use the Proofreading Checklist to aid revision.

✓ ASSESSMENT OPTIONS

Formal Assessment, Selection Test, pp. 30–32. The selection test is designed so that it can be easily customized to the performance levels of your students.

Alternative Assessment, p. 7, includes options for less advanced students, more advanced students, verbal/linguistic learners, and bodily/kinesthetic learners.

PORTFOLIO ASSESSMENT
Use the following rubrics in the ***Alternative Assessment*** booklet to assess student writing:
Diary Entry: Expression Rubric, p. 109
Newscast: Summary Rubric, p. 113
Public Letter: Cause-Effect Rubric, p. 117
Guided Writing Lesson: Evaluation/Review Rubric, p. 119

Prepare and Engage

LESSON OBJECTIVES

1. **To increase knowledge of other cultures and to connect common elements across cultures**
   - Thematic Connection
2. **To express and support responses to the text**
   - Critical Thinking
   - Idea Bank: Newspaper Editorial
   - Idea Bank: Character Defense
3. **To read in order to research self-selected and assigned topics**
   - Idea Bank: Reference Guide
   - Research Skills Mini-Lesson (ATE)
4. **To plan, prepare, organize, and present literary interpretations**
   - Idea Bank: Debate
   - Speaking, Listening, and Viewing Mini-Lesson (ATE)

Interest Grabber Ask students: What might a modern sports superstar have in common with Anne Bradstreet, Edward Taylor, and Jonathan Edwards? After students have had a chance to respond, write these maxims on the board: "Whatever it takes"; "If you're going to do it, you might as well do it correctly"; and "Nothing's worth doing halfway." Tell them that athlete Cal Ripken, Jr., of the Baltimore Orioles, said these words. Explain that the feature article they are about to read will help them see a connection between Ripken and America's most famous Puritan poets and preachers.

Customize for
English Language Learners
This piece contains baseball jargon, names of baseball greats, and figures of speech, such as "look a gift horse in the mouth." English language learners who are unfamiliar with the history of American baseball may not understand the significance of many of the references in the article. Ask students who are baseball fans to volunteer to partner with English language learners to help them comprehend and appreciate the piece.

CONNECTIONS TO TODAY'S WORLD

Iron Bird: Cal Ripken's Work Ethic

Steve Wulf

Thematic Connection

THE PURITAN INFLUENCE

Stand tall, speak plainly, work hard, and put all you've got into the game—every game, year in and year out. While it may not exactly qualify as a Puritan credo, Cal Ripken Jr.'s approach to playing baseball is firmly rooted in the Puritan ethic. Though it's doubtful the Puritans would have endorsed professional sports, they almost certainly would have approved of Ripken, the Baltimore Orioles shortstop known for his unwavering work ethic, modesty, and dedication to his fans.

ONE FOR THE RECORD BOOKS

On September 6, 1995, Ripken shattered Lou Gehrig's famous streak by playing his 2,131st consecutive game. Ripken's streak was a long time in the making; in the process, he won the admiration of fans, colleagues, and the sports media. He's been hailed as a true sports hero, an increasingly rare accolade in an age where salaries and endorsements, rather than love of the game, seem to come first in the hearts of many professional athletes.

Ripken, however, does not consider himself a hero, just a hard worker, a trait he claims to have learned from his father. When Cal Ripken Sr. became manager of the Orioles' Double A team in 1972, Cal Jr. was old enough to help out—and to notice how his dad dedicated himself to his team. "I think that's when I first picked up my work ethic," says Cal Jr. "My dad did everything. He was not only the manager but also the pitching coach, the batting coach, the batting-practice pitcher, the groundkeeper."

PURITAN AND PROUD OF IT

Hard work and heroism are closely linked in the American mind, due largely to the influence of the Puritans. The self-discipline and steadfastness that characterize Ripken have their roots in the Puritans' simple code of faithful endurance. Life for the Puritans was not easy, but they believed in meeting the challenge with perseverance and fidelity. Today, we still respect people like Ripken who approach their personal and professional lives in the same way. Whether the game is life or simply baseball, we continue to admire those who embody the principles prized by the Puritans centuries ago.

STEVE WULF
(1950–)

Steve Wulf loves baseball. Not that baseball is the only subject he covers: as a senior writer, Wulf has written for every section of *Time* since joining the newsweekly in 1995. His *Time* cover story on the assassination of Israeli President Yitzhak Rabin even won one of the Overseas Press Club's highest honors in 1996. Wulf had plenty of opportunities to write about baseball during his seventeen years as a reporter, writer, and editor with *Sports Illustrated.* He's also authored several popular books, including *Baseball Anecdotes.* Most recently, he co-authored *I Was Right on Time,* the autobiography of the Negro Leagues' legend Buck O'Neil. Wulf, who was also a consultant for Ken Burns's acclaimed documentary *Baseball*, has appeared on numerous national television programs and networks.

104 ◆ *Beginnings –1750*

Prentice Hall Literature Program Resources

REINFORCE / RETEACH / EXTEND

Selection Support Pages
Build Vocabulary, p. 34
Thematic Connection: The Puritan Influence, p. 35

Formal Assessment
Selection Test, pp. 33–34;
Assessment Resources Software

Resource Pro CD-ROM

Listening to Literature Audiocassettes

❶ # Iron Bird: Cal Ripken's Work Ethic

Steve Wulf

In early September 1995, baseball fans everywhere waited in anticipation for Cal Ripken to break the record set by baseball great Lou Gehrig for most consecutive games played. As the big day drew closer, the self-effacing Ripken found himself at the center of a whirlwind of national media attention. This article appeared in Time *magazine shortly before Ripken earned his place in the record books.*

The streak is such an inadequate description for something that began 2,127 games, 29 different double-play partners and 13¼ years ago. ❷ If you pitch 59 consecutive shutout innings or hit in 56 straight games, you are on a streak. But if you play so long that 3,695 other major leaguers have gone on the disabled list since the last time you spent an entire game on the bench, so continuously that more than 50 million fans have seen nobody but you start the game at your position, you are not on a streak. You are on a river, a long, meandering river like, say, the Susquehanna, which begins its 444-mile journey in Cooperstown, New York,[1] the purported cradle of baseball. From there the Susquehanna finds its way to Oneonta, the home of 1950 National League MVP Jim Konstanty; dips down into Pennsylvania before recrossing the border near Binghamton, where Wee Willie Keeler and Whitey Ford cut their professional teeth; winds back down south toward Wilkes-Barre,

1. **Cooperstown, New York:** Site of the National Baseball Hall of Fame and considered by some to be the place where baseball was invented in 1839.

◆ Build Vocabulary

purported (pər pôrt′ id) *adj.*: Supposed

CONNECTIONS TO TODAY'S WORLD

❸ ▶ Critical Viewing Decide whether Cal Ripken appears comfortable in the spotlight as he accepts the crowd's applause for setting the record for most consecutive games played. Explain your answer. **[Assess]**

Develop Understanding

One-Minute Insight This *Time* magazine feature article explores the dedication to and love for baseball that enabled Cal Ripken to shatter Lou Gehrig's long-standing record of 2,130 consecutive games played. The writer examines the influences that shaped the sports hero's personal and professional character, including his legendary temper and his solid work ethic, to conclude that Ripken is simply doing "whatever it takes."

❶ **Enrichment** Tell students that the nickname Steve Wulf uses to describe Cal Ripken in the title is a play on words. Lou Gehrig, whose streak Ripken broke, was called the "Iron Horse." Because Ripken plays for the Baltimore Orioles, Wulf calls him the "Iron *Bird*."

❷ **Clarification** Be sure students realize that these are actual Major League Baseball records. Orel Hershiser pitched 59 consecutive shutout innings for the Los Angeles Dodgers in 1988. In 1941, Joe DiMaggio of the New York Yankees hit in 56 straight games.

▶Critical Viewing◀

❸ **Assess** Responses will vary, but students should support their answers. Some students may respond that Ripken does not seem to be comfortable in the spotlight since he appears to be reserved or even shy during the greatest moment of his career.

Research Skills Mini-Lesson

Finding Quotations

Introduce Tell students that when they have a research assignment or project such as the Reference Guide on p. 109, a useful skill is knowing how to find quotations. Apt quotations can add interest or humor to a presentation, report, or magazine article. Interesting quotations can make the difference between dull and fascinating biographical writing. A good quotation can even spice up a personal Web site.

Develop Point out that quotations can be found in various sources, including anthologies, such as *Bartlett's*; collections of quotations on particular themes; journals, letters, biographies, memoirs, and autobiographies; magazine and newspaper interviews; and Internet Web sites devoted to quotations.

Apply Direct partners to locate quotations at the library, using the subject, title, and author catalogues. Encourage them also to make use of the Internet, typing in key words such as "Puritanism," "quotations," or the names of individuals, after accessing an Internet search engine such as Yahoo or Lycos. Emphasize that students should take care to record their quotations accurately, paying special attention to original punctuation, spelling, and capitalization. They may find it useful to record each quotation on a separate notecard.

Assess Evaluate students on their ability to locate a variety of apt and interesting quotations from a variety of sources.

◆ **Critical Thinking**

❶ **Generalize** Ask students what this passage can reveal about record breakers in general. *Students may say that to persevere, one must possess drive, passion, tenacity, and the will to win.*

◆ **Critical Thinking**

❷ **Compare and Contrast** Guide students to analyze the writer's comparison of two athletes: Gehrig and Ripken. According to the writer, in what ways did Gehrig excel? *Gehrig was a stronger offensive player.* In what ways does Wulf say Ripken is stronger? *Ripken is more "durable," Ripken plays harder; Ripken may enjoy the game more.*

Thematic Connection

❸ **The Puritan Influence** Discuss with students the author's view that Cal Ripken's attitude and demeanor seem like throwbacks to earlier times. Like the Puritans, Ripken dedicates himself fully to what he loves. He maintains a positive attitude, and although well-paid, stays loyal to his team when the lure of more money could have caused him to change teams. You might have students contrast the attitude of many superstar players today with the Puritan ethic.

Pennsylvania, where Joe McCarthy managed his first team; meets up with the West Branch, which flows past Williamsport, the birthplace of Little League Baseball, and Lewisburg, home of Christy Mathewson's alma mater, Bucknell University; bisects Harrisburg, where Hall of Fame pitcher Vic Willis got his start; rushes past York, which once knew Brooks Robinson as a second baseman; crosses the border into Maryland and—at long last—enters the Chesapeake Bay at Havre de Grace, which happens to be the birthplace of Calvin Edwin Ripken Jr.

Unless something unforeseen or unthinkable happens, Cal Ripken, the 35-year-old shortstop for the Baltimore Orioles, will play in his 2,131st straight game on Sept. 6, against the California Angels in Oriole Park at Camden Yards. That will break the record set by Lou Gehrig, the first baseman for the New York Yankees from 1925 until 1939. The "Streak," as it has come to be called, officially began on May 30, 1982, when Orioles manager Earl Weaver started Ripken at third base, which was then his position, against the Toronto Blue Jays. The previous day, Weaver had rested the 21-year-old rookie in the second game of a doubleheader.

Unofficially, the Streak probably began in the late '60s in the basement of the Ripken household, by then in Aberdeen, Maryland. Says Vi Ripken, the matriarch of the Ripken clan (daughter Ellen, sons Cal Jr., Fred and Billy): "I wish I had a nickel for every time I heard 'Just one more game, Mom.' The kids would be playing Ping Pong in the basement, and it was always a struggle to get them to come upstairs for dinner, and even more of a struggle to get them to go to bed. Nobody liked to end the night on a loss, especially Junior. 'Just one more game, Mom.' " ❶

Just one more game. Therein lies the true beauty of the Streak. Ripken never set out to eclipse the "Iron Horse," who he modestly and somewhat mistakenly believes was a much better ballplayer than himself. "I'm not even in Gehrig's league," says Ripken. Offensively speaking, Ripken may be right, although he has had two MVP, Gehrigian seasons (1983 and 1991). But defensively Ripken plays a much tougher position than Gehrig did, and he does a much better job of it at that. As durable as Lou was, he played every inning of every game for only one season; Ripken played every inning of 904 straight games from 1982 to '87—only his father, then the manager of the Orioles, could sit him down. While Gehrig occasionally resorted to artifice to extend his streak, Ripken has never done anything untoward to keep *his* alive, or played anything less than hard. Gehrig was literally afraid of leaving the lineup; Ripken is in it for the fun. "There's a joy to Cal's game that never ceases to amaze me," says Mike Flanagan, the Orioles' pitching coach who has played for Cal Sr. and played with Cal Jr. "People who think he's out for glory just don't get it." Indeed, fans who think that Ripken will sit down shortly after No. 2,131 are mistaken. Barring injury or sudden ineptitude, Ripken will play in Nos. 2,132, 2,133, 2,134 . . . The Iron Bird. ❷

Occasionally given to slumps, Ripken is approaching the Streak in something of a hitting malaise that has dropped his average into the .260s. But he still plays his position with amazing grace; at 6 ft. 4 in. he is not only the tallest shortstop in history but also one of the smoothest. And rather than go into a shell to protect his privacy this season, he has been making a concerted effort to meet the needs of the media and the wants of the fans. At the All-Star Game in Arlington, Texas, he worked his way from dugout to dugout in 100°F heat, signing everything put in his way. In Baltimore this summer, he has been conducting after-the-game autograph sessions to make up for lost time and repair the wounds of the baseball strike.[2]

There are times in which Ripken seems not just a throwback but the last true sports hero. He carries the requisite superstar salary—$6 million annually for two more years—but almost none of the other baggage that has come to be associated with the modern-day profes- ❸

2. **the baseball strike:** A Major League Baseball Players Association strike put an early end to the 1994 baseball season and resulted in a delayed start to the 1995 season.

◆ **Build Vocabulary**

artifice (ärt´ ə fis) *n.*: Artful trickery

untoward (un tō´ ərd) *adj.*: Inappropriate or improper

malaise (ma lāz´) *n.*: Decline or slump

malingered (mə liŋ´ gərd) *v.*: Escaped work or duty by pretending to be ill

immersed (im murst´) *v.*: Plunged or completely submerged

Speaking, Listening, and Viewing Mini-Lesson

Group Debate

This mini-lesson supports the Speaking, Listening, and Viewing activity in the Idea Bank on p. 109.

Introduce Explain that in a formal debate, two teams argue for and against a given proposition or question. Each team takes a single point of view on the issue.

Develop Tell team members to discuss the most important points, in order to present their position persuasively. They should also decide what types of evidence to gather to effectively support their main points. As they put together their "case" or position, each team should also predict what arguments the other team may make against them, and plan counterarguments.

Apply Each team should elect a captain who will clearly, calmly, and persuasively summarize the team's main position and conclusions. In speeches timed by two student judges, each captain should present the team's argument and evidence. After listening carefully to both sides of the debate, team members may huddle to discuss strategies for refuting the other team's reasoning, looking for flaws in its "evidence" or logic. In timed rebuttal speeches, the team captains may then take one turn each to refute the other side's position. They should conclude by reminding the audience and judges why their team's case is strongest.

Assess Have student judges determine which team has won the debate by most persuasively presenting its argument.

sional athlete. He has never sulked, malingered, strutted, whined, wheedled or referred to himself in the third person. He has turned down several
3 opportunities to become a free agent, preferring to remain an Oriole and a Baltimorean. He has endorsements, to be sure, but his most famous one
4 is for milk.

▲ **Critical Viewing** From this photograph, what can you learn about Ripken's relationship with his fans? **[Infer]**

America never stops moaning about the absence of heroes—"Where have you gone, Joe DiMaggio?"—yet when it has someone who daily displays grit, generosity, spirit and skill, not to mention incredibly blue eyes, what does it do? It looks this generation's gift horse in the mouth. Robert Lipsyte, the respected New York *Times* columnist, recently suggested that Ripken take a seat rather than sully Gehrig's memory. And the hate mail that Ripken has received this summer has been of such volume and venom that Major League Baseball has had to beef up the security around him.

Opponents and teammates alike hold Ripken in the same awe in which he holds Gehrig. Says the Toronto Blue Jays' veteran designated hitter Paul Molitor: "As someone who has spent a few years of my life on the disabled list, I can tell you that what Cal has done and is still doing is be-
5 yond my comprehension. He plays the second toughest position on the field every day, often on artificial turf, sometimes in day games after night games, sometimes after flying all night. He's still a dangerous hitter, still the most reliable shortstop out there, and he is the essence of class on and off the field. He's enough to make you sick."

The Streak has had two close calls. The first came during game No. 444 in April 1985, when Ripken sprained his ankle on a pick-off play in the third inning. Although he continued playing, his ankle was badly swollen and discolored after the game. Fortunately, the Orioles had scheduled an exhibition game against the Naval Academy the next day. The second near-miss came as a result of a bench-clearing mêlée[3] with the Seattle Mariners during game No. 1,790 in June of '93. Ripken twisted his knee, and when he woke up the next morning, he couldn't put his weight on it. He told his wife Kelly he might not be able to play that night. According to Kelly, "Just before he left 6 for the ball park, I said, 'Maybe you could just play one inning and then come out.' He snapped, 'No! Either I play the whole game or I don't play at all.' I told him, 'Just checking, dear.' "

Ripken did play the full nine innings that night. In fact, he has played in 99.2% of every Orioles game since the Streak began. The percentage would be even higher had Ripken not been ejected from two games in the first inning. . . .

If Ripken does have a flaw, it is his temper.
He doesn't tolerate incompetence on the part of 7
umpires or teammates. "I'm also stubborn," he says. "I think that's one trait I share with Gehrig." But by and large he conducts himself with consideration and intelligence and good humor. His parents have something to do with that, but so does the Orioles' organization, which has a unique tradition of encouraging players to become active in the community. Ripken is particularly involved in an adult-literacy program in Baltimore.

It's not easy being Ripken, especially these days. Before a recent 7:30 P.M. game with the Cleveland Indians, he arrived at the ball park at 12:30 for a two-hour discussion with Oriole officials on the plans for "Streak Week." At 2:45 he had a photo shoot with the Rawlings Sporting Goods company. At 3 he did a CNN interview; at 3:30 two local TV interviews; at 4:05 an ESPN interview. After that he immersed himself in his pregame routine, stretching and laughing with Brady Anderson, taking his cuts in batting practice, prancing around his shortstop territory in infield practice—how can any man find so much enjoyment in a ground ball, much less his 100,000,000th ground ball? Then he went off to work on his swing on the indoor batting tee for 15 minutes, and then he went over scouting reports on the Indians. Once the game started,

CONNECTIONS TO TODAY'S WORLD

3. **mêlée** (mā′ lā′) *n.*: Noisy, confused fight.

▶Critical Viewing◀

4 **Infer** Students may say that Ripken seems unhurried and interested in talking with his fans.

◆ *Literature and Your Life*

5 Ask students who participate in an organized sport to comment on the difficulty of playing every game, being at every practice, and never missing an event. Elicit similar comments from students who take part in organized arts activities, such as band or chorus, where consistency and teamwork are also necessary. Encourage students to identify the sacrifices this consistency requires them to make.

Thematic Connection

6 **The Puritan Influence** Discuss Cal Ripken's "all or nothing" attitude toward playing baseball as an extension of the Puritan ethic. Like the Puritans, Ripken is willing to make the necessary sacrifices—including playing with a painful injury—in order to be true to his belief in the importance of persevering and meeting commitments.

◆ Critical Thinking

7 **Evaluate** Point out that the writer identifies a negative aspect of Ripken's character. Ask students to determine the effect of the clause *"If Ripkin does have a flaw." It implies that Ripkin has no flaws.* Ask students to identify the writer's attitude toward his subject. *Wulf is effervescent in his praise for Ripkin.* Remind students that this article appeared in *Time* the week before Ripken broke Gehrig's record. Then ask whether they think Wulf's bias is acceptable. *Some students will say that excitement and praise would be expected at that time; others might call for more objective reporting.*

Beyond the Classroom

Career Connection

Attendance In this article and among sports fans, Cal Ripken is glorified for his dependability and consistency. As he approached the milestone of his 2,131st game, he was celebrated in the media as a hero. Full-time workers in particular understand the demands and difficulties of maintaining an excellent attendance record in the workplace.

Since they work on a ten-month calendar, your students may be unaware of these demands. Share the realities of the entry-level job market with students. Employees in many jobs are given a two-week vacation, an average of ten company holidays, and a small bank of sick days and personal days each year.

Lead a discussion to explore the necessity of a good attendance record in the business world. Point out that frequently, tasks or projects are assigned to each worker and an absence might put a deadline in jeopardy, cause inconvenience to others, or even lose business. In addition, a poor attendance record might become part of an employee's file, and if an attendance problem becomes severe enough, it could even be cause for termination.

Ask students to interview adults about the attendance requirements at various jobs and share their findings with the class.

Thematic Connection

❶ The Puritan Influence Discuss Cal Ripken's acceptance of "the Streak" in his life and ask students to relate it to Puritan values. *Students may say that, like the Puritans, Ripken accepts what life sets before him and works his hardest to deal with it.*

Enrichment On September 20, 1998, Cal Ripken ended his streak at 2632 games. While some expected the streak to be broken by injury or illness, Ripken surprised fans by electing to sit a game out. Ripken said, "It just reached a time when I thought it was time to change the subject, restore the focus to the team, and move on." Ripken returned to the line-up on September 22.

Reinforce and Extend

Customize for
Intrapersonal Learners
These students may wish to extend their understanding of Cal Ripken by reading his autobiography, *The Only Way I Know.*

Answers

◆ *Literature and Your Life*

Reader's Response Some students may respond that they would take any risk to maintain their streak; more cautious students may say that they would not want to take the chance of permanently injuring themselves.

☑ **Check Your Comprehension**

Ripken's 2,131st game breaks the record set by baseball legend Lou Gehrig for most consecutive games played.

◆ Critical Thinking

1. The writer shows Ripken's ability to work hard, enjoy the game, and still spend time with his fans, despite his celebrity status.
2. Students should explain the reasoning behind their answers. Some students may say that Ripken's hard work and dedication qualify him for the title of hero; others may argue that Ripken is only doing what he is paid millions of dollars to do and therefore does not qualify as a hero.

he went hitless and drew a walk, but played his position flawlessly. (A shortstop has some special responsibility on every play that's not a strikeout.) And when the 3-hr. 16-min. 8-5 defeat was over, Ripken didn't just dress and go home. He went back out onto the field for one of his post game autograph sessions, signing for and kibitzing[4] with 2,000 fans. "Cal Ripken personifies everything that is right with baseball," said Bob Seal, 33, an engineer for the Norfolk Southern Railroad who came up to the game from Chattanooga, Tennessee.

A Ripken autograph session is illuminating because he doesn't just sign, sign, sign in the joyless way that many other ballplayers do. He engages people in conversation, talking to them as one baseball fan would to another. ("Man, did you see the stuff Mussina had tonight?" says Ripken, the fan.) If he sees a child with a rival's hat on, he'll kid him or her and maybe even exchange the cap for one of his own.

Actually, Ripken's easy way with the fans had something to do with the way he met his wife. Kelly Geer's mother chatted him up at a restaurant signing one night in 1983, telling him about her eligible daughter, and Cal signed the ball to Kelly, "If you look like your mother, I'm sorry I missed you. Cal Ripken." As Kelly recalls, "My reaction was, 'Who's Cal Ripken?' But a couple of months later, I was in a restaurant where he was signing, and when I thanked him for being so nice to my mom, he said, 'You must be Kelly. You're 6 ft. tall, blond, you have green eyes, you went to the University of Maryland, and you work for the airlines.' The next day he called."

4. **kibitzing** (kib′ its iŋ) *v.*: Giving advice or making observations.

Kelly and Cal were married four years later. They now have two children: Rachel, who was born in November 1989, and Ryan, who was born in July 1993 on—somebody up there likes Cal—an off day.

Both the Orioles and Ripken feared that this season might be overwhelming for him, but it has become quite the opposite. "This is the most relaxed I've seen Cal in years," says Kelly. "He's at peace with himself. He realizes that even though the Streak will always be a part of his identity, it's a positive thing." ❶

When Ripken is asked how he's changed during the Streak, he responds, "Less and grayer hair." But then he gives a more thoughtful answer: "I'm much better with people, kids particularly. When I was young and fans would give me their babies to hold for a picture, the babies always ended up crying. But now that I have kids of my own, I find it easier not only to hold them, but to talk to them. And they ask—no offense—the best questions. Like 'How come you're not crying? How come you're not mad you lost the game?' And I tell them, 'I am mad, but I've learned not to show it.' Or they'll ask, 'What's it like to hit a home run to win the game? Is it the best feeling in the world?' And I tell them, 'It is the best feeling.' The kids reduce the game to its most basic level, and they remind me why it is I love baseball so much."

Travel upriver from Havre de Grace all the way to Cooperstown, and right there on Main Street is a statue of a boy called *The Sandlot Kid.* He's barefoot, and he's wearing a straw hat. But he holds his bat over his shoulder a little like Cal Ripken. Just one more game.

Guide for Responding

◆ *Literature and Your Life*

Reader's Response If you were Ripken, would you have risked playing with injuries rather than miss a game and end your streak? Explain.

☑ **Check Your Comprehension**

Why is Cal Ripken's 2,131st game such an important one?

◆ Critical Thinking

INTERPRET

1. What impression does the writer convey with the complete account of Ripken's schedule on the day of the Cleveland Indians game? **[Analyze]**

EVALUATE

2. Do you believe that Ripken has earned the right to be called a hero? Explain. **[Evaluate]**

Beyond the Selection

FURTHER READING

Other Works by Steve Wulf
Baseball Anecdotes
I Was Right on Time

By Cal Ripken, Jr.
The Only Way I Know

We recommend that you preview these texts before assigning them to students.

INTERNET

You and your students can find additional information about Cal Ripken, Jr., on the Internet. We suggest the following site. Please be aware, however, that the site may have changed since this information was published.

To learn more about Ripken, visit:
http://www.2131.com/

You may also find related information on baseball legends on the Internet. We *strongly recommend* that you preview sites before you send students to them.

Thematic Connection

The Puritan Influence: Alive and Well and Living in the United States?

At first glance, modern American lifestyles and values might seem to have little in common with those of the Puritans. Scratch the surface, however, and you'd be surprised at what you find. At the heart of our culture, for instance, is an enduring belief in the "American dream," the promise that anyone who works hard enough will succeed in life. Though the media are filled with stories and statistics that suggest that the American dream is in danger of becoming just that—a dream—the United States still has a special place in its collective heart for those who "pull themselves up by their bootstraps." Self-made individuals who succeed through merit and honest hard work will always be among our most respected heroes.

Puritan ethics have also left their mark on much of what is considered uniquely American culture. The Puritans' belief in simplicity is evident in everything from the simple lines of traditional American furniture and architecture to the value we place on traits like forthright speech: "Mean what you say and say what you mean" are still words to live by for many. Though life in the United States seems to grow increasingly complicated, the renewed emphasis on "family values" shows that our nation still cherishes simple Puritan virtues—honesty, hard work, and devotion to religion, family, and neighbor.

1. How does Ripken's involvement in an adult-literacy program reflect Puritan virtues?
2. What might Jonathan Edwards and his Puritan followers have admired about Cal Ripken's character?

Idea Bank

Writing

1. **Newspaper Editorial** As the editor of *The Puritan Plain Speaker,* you have decided to write an editorial celebrating Cal Ripken's new record for most consecutive games played. Explain in your editorial why you believe the achievement is worthy of the attention of the Puritan community.

2. **Character Defense** Imagine that Jonathan Edwards has just condemned Cal Ripken for "wasting his life in the idle pursuit of a child's game." Write an open letter to the Puritan community in which you defend Ripken's character. Explain how Ripken's career embodies so many of the traits that Puritans value most.

3. **Baseball Poem** Compose a poem in the Puritan Plain Style that praises Ripken's baseball skill, dedication, and hard work. List words or phrases that describe Ripken's virtues as both a person and a player. Use each word or phrase as the basis for one or two lines of your poem.

Speaking, Listening, and Viewing

4. **Group Debate** Work with a group of classmates to stage a debate. The topic of your debate is the Puritan influence: Making a comeback or gone for good? Group members should work in two teams to develop and outline the main points of their arguments before staging the debate for the class.

Researching and Representing

5. **Reference Guide** "A place for everything and everything in its place." "Silence is golden." "A penny saved is a penny earned." These and many more of the sayings we still repeat have their roots in Puritan values and virtues. Work with a partner to gather famous quotations that reflect a Puritan influence. Ask a librarian to help you locate potential sources, such as Benjamin Franklin's *Poor Richard's Almanack* (an excerpt of the *Almanack* begins on p. 188 of this book). Compile your collection into a reference guide. Annotate each saying with a brief explanation of how it relates to Puritanism.

Online Activity www.phlit.phschool.com

ASSESSMENT OPTIONS

Formal Assessment, Selection Test, pp. 26–27, and Assessment Resources Software. The selection test is designed so that it can be easily customized to the performance levels of your students.

PORTFOLIO ASSESSMENT

Use the following rubrics in the ***Alternative Assessment*** booklet to assess student writing:
Newspaper Editorial: Persuasion Rubric, p. 120
Character Defense: Persuasion Rubric, p. 120
Baseball Poem: Poetry Rubric, p. 123

Answers

Thematic Connection

1. Ripken's willingness to volunteer his time and efforts to help others reflects the Puritan belief in self-sacrifice and dedication to neighbor.
2. Edwards and the Puritans probably would have admired Ripken's modesty, hard work, perseverance, and dedication to his fans and to helping others.

Idea Bank

Customizing for *Performance Levels*

Following are suggestions for matching Idea Bank topics with your students' performance levels:
Less Advanced Students: 3
Average Students: 2, 4
More Advanced Students: 1, 5

Customizing for *Learning Modalities*

Following are suggestions for matching Idea Bank topics with your students' learning modalities:
Interpersonal: 4
Logical/Mathematical: 4
Verbal/Linguistic: 4, 5

Prepare and Engage

LESSON OBJECTIVES

- To use recursive writing processes to write a persuasive essay
- To compose increasingly more involved sentences and correctly use comparative and superlative forms

You may want to distribute the scoring rubric for Persuasion (p. 120) in ***Alternative Assessment*** to make students aware of the criteria on which their work will be evaluated. For suggestions on how you can customize the rubric to this workshop see page 112.

You may also want to present to the class the Writing Process Model of a Persuasive Essay from the ***Writing and Language Transparencies.***

Connect to Literature Unit 3, A Growing Nation, includes an excerpt of a persuasive essay: Henry David Thoreau's "Civil Disobedience" (p. 380). You might wish to have students look at this selection to see how Thoreau uses persuasive language.

Writers at Work Videodisc To introduce students to key elements and to show them how Gasby Greely uses persuasive writing, play the videodisc segment on Persuasion (Ch. 4).

Play frames 33643 to 43235

Writing Lab
If your students have access to computers, you may want to have them work in the tutorial on Persuasion. Have them follow these steps:

1. Use the interactive instruction on detecting bias in sources while gathering evidence.
2. Draft their persuasive essays on the computer.
3. Revise for emphasis by using word bins of persuasive and transitional words or phrases.

Persuasive Essay — Writing Process Workshop

There are various levels of persuasion: for example, a teenager trying to coax the car keys from Dad, grass-roots volunteers encouraging voter registration, or Puritan minister Jonathan Edwards warning his awestruck congregants to save their souls from eternal damnation.

You can polish your powers to sway and convince by writing a **persuasive essay**—a short piece of writing that tries to influence readers to take an action or accept a position on a particular issue. The following skills, introduced in this section's Guided Writing Lessons, will help you write a persuasive essay.

Writing Skills Focus

- ▶ **Anticipate opposing arguments** so that you can address likely objections to your position in the course of your essay. (See p. 95.)
- ▶ **Evaluate persuasive techniques** to decide how best to appeal to your audience: through logic, shared experience, humor, emotion, or some combination of these. (See p. 103.)

Jonathan Edwards, for example, churns up a powerful emotional whirlwind in his famous sermon.

MODEL FROM LITERATURE

from "Sinners in the Hands of an Angry God"
by Jonathan Edwards

How dreadful ① is the state of those that are daily and hourly in the danger of this great wrath and infinite misery! But this is the dismal case of every soul in this congregation that has not been born again, however moral and strict, sober and religious, ② they may otherwise be. Oh that you would consider it, whether you be young or old! . . .

① Edwards paints a frightening picture, playing on his audience's fear.

② Edwards anticipates his listeners' possible descriptions of themselves and turns their ideas against them.

Beyond the Classroom

Career Connection

Sales The persuasive techniques mentioned in the student edition—logic, shared experience, humor, and so on—are the same tools that an experienced salesperson uses to "close a deal." Retail salespeople, telemarketers, and fund-raisers rely on their persuasive skills every day. Explain that salespersons often tailor their presentations to the personality type and experience of potential clients as well as to the product or service offered. Salespeople "consider audience and purpose" in much the same way that a persuasive writer does. Ask students what persuasive advantages an in-person sales presentation might have when compared with the persuasive techniques available to the essay writer. *Possible advantages of an in-person presentation over persuasive writing: establishing a personal bond through eye contact and body language; being able to judge midstream whether a persuasive technique is effective, and if not, to adjust accordingly; being able to repeat information as needed.*

Prewriting

Choose a Topic Have a friend or classmate conduct an interview with you about local or national issues. Review your responses, and choose the issue that's most important to you. As an alternative, you may want to choose to take a stand on one of the following issues.

Topic Ideas

- HDTV: bright future or sales gimmick?
- Business downsizing: problem or solution?
- Television rating system: helpful guide or form of censorship?

Clarify Your Position Although many issues entail more than two perspectives, it will help you organize your thoughts if you start out with the two major poles of the controversy and decide where you stand.

Gather and Evaluate Evidence To make your viewpoint convincing, you have to back it up with **facts**—statements that can be verified or proved—and not just pile up more **opinions**—personal beliefs that cannot be proved true or false. Unless you are already an expert on your topic, you will need to do research at the library, on the Internet, or through your own interviews, surveys, and experiments.

Use Pro-and-Con Organization You won't convince anybody by ignoring opposing ideas; the best strategy is to anticipate them, meet them head-on, and knock them down through use of the pro-and-con structure. Here's an example:

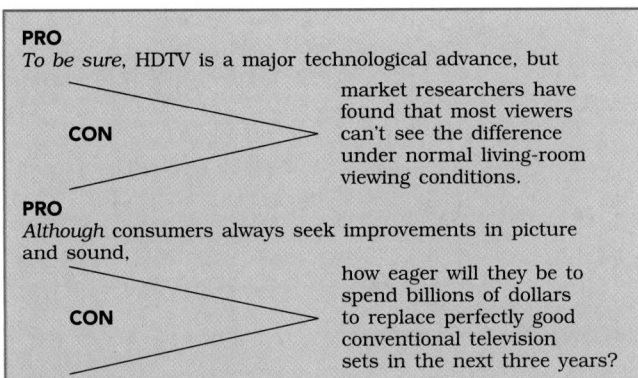

PRO
To be sure, HDTV is a major technological advance, but

CON
market researchers have found that most viewers can't see the difference under normal living-room viewing conditions.

PRO
Although consumers always seek improvements in picture and sound,

CON
how eager will they be to spend billions of dollars to replace perfectly good conventional television sets in the next three years?

Applying Language Skills: Comparative and Superlative Forms

Most adjectives have a **positive form**, a **comparative form** for comparing two items, and a **superlative form** for comparing more than two items.

Positive	Comparative	Superlative
slow	slower	slowest
arid	more arid	most arid

When in doubt about how to form the comparative or superlative, check a dictionary. If no acceptable *-er* or *-est* forms are listed, use *more* and *most.*

Practice Choose the appropriate form for each example.

1. Of all the new technology, HDTV offers the (clearer, clearest) reception.
2. I'd prefer the (less, least) costly of the two models.

Writing Application Look for places in your essay in which you compare items. Revise any incorrect comparative and superlative forms.

Writer's Solution Connection
Writing Lab

For more topic ideas for your essay, use the Inspirations in the Writing Lab tutorial on Persuasion.

Develop Student Writing

Prewriting Strategy

Use the topic ideas provided as the basis for a class brainstorming session on where one might gather evidence to support a given position. For example, a student writing a persuasive essay supporting the introduction of HDTV might find evidence by writing or calling for the standard marketing and promotional material that a manufacturer makes available to the public. A writer taking the counter-position on the same topic might find evidence by examining consumer reports and contacting consumer advocacy groups that might provide information on hidden or unforeseen costs of adopting the new system.

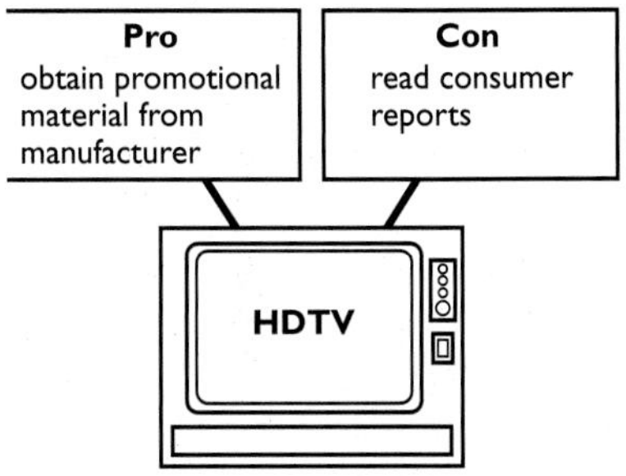

Writing Lab CD-ROM

Have students complete the Audience Profile, and review the audio-annotated models of writing for different purposes. These can be found in the Prewriting section of the tutorial. In the first activity, students answer questions to help them focus on their intended audiences; in the second, they can examine how writing on the same subject differs when the purpose does.

Applying Language Skills

Comparative and Superlative Forms

Introduce the skill by explaining to students that persuasion often requires comparison. While their point may very well be valid, their position will be undermined if they use incorrect forms such as "preciousest" or "more bad," or double comparisons such as "most best."

Answers

1. Of all the new technology, HDTV offers the clearest reception.
2. I'd prefer the less costly of the two models.

Grammar Reinforcement

For additional instruction and practice, complete the lesson on Forms of Comparisons in the **Language Lab CD-ROM** and practice p. 73 in the *Writer's Solution Grammar Practice Book.*

Elaboration Strategy

As they draft their persuasive essays students may decide not to use certain points they planned to make. Unless such a point is central to their argument, students should have no problem omitting it—although when revising and editing they should make sure that the essay is still coherent and smooth.

Revision Strategy

Coach reviewers to offer suggestions that help serve the writer's goals—not simply debate the writer's position if they happen to disagree with it.

Publishing

Students who wish to deliver their essays as speeches might benefit from the strategies in the Speaking and Listening Workshop on page 114.

Applying Language Skills

Answers

1. Because we watch hours of television, we would benefit from the sharpest images.
2. Although the first models proved to be the most expensive, later ones were more affordable.

Grammar Reinforcement

For additional instruction and practice, complete the Varying Sentence Structure lesson in the **Language Lab CD-ROM.**

Reinforce and Extend

Prentice Hall Writing and Grammar For more prewriting, elaboration, and revision, see *Prentice Hall Writing and Grammar.*

Applying Language Skills: Complex Sentences

A **complex sentence** has one main clause and one or more subordinate clauses. A **subordinate clause,** underlined here, has a subject and a predicate but cannot stand alone as a sentence.

Although truer colors would improve the picture, we can still appreciate the movie this way.

Use conjunctions such as *after, as, before, although,* and *unless* to create subordinate clauses.

Practice Combine clauses to make complex sentences. Use the conjunctions provided.

1. We watch hours of television. We would benefit from the sharpest images. (because)
2. The first models proved to be the most expensive. Later ones were more affordable. (although)

Writing Application To add variety to your essay, replace short, choppy sentences with complex sentences.

Writer's Solution Connection Language Lab

For more practice, complete the Language Lab lesson on Varying Sentence Structure.

Drafting

Evaluate Persuasive Techniques As you begin writing, consider whether you should appeal to your audience's emotions, sense of reason, or both.

Organize Into Introduction, Body, and Conclusion Begin with an introduction that grabs your readers and states your viewpoint clearly. In the body, develop your supporting evidence as you address opposing ideas. Conclude by reinforcing your argument with a decisive restatement of your main point.

Revising

Use a Peer Reviewer Have a friend or classmate read your draft to see whether he or she is convinced by your argument. Note any holes or weak spots the reviewer brings to your attention.

Self-Evaluation Use the following criteria for a good persuasive essay to guide your revisions.

- Is your viewpoint clearly stated in the introduction?
- Have you presented enough supporting facts and evidence?
- Have you anticipated and addressed opposing arguments?
- Is there a suitable balance of logic and emotion that will sway your intended audience?

Revision Model

① Maybe the sound quality of the new technology is slightly improved, but ^ How many times are we going to ^ spend hundreds to ② revamp our entire entertainment library?

① The writer anticipates an objection by noting the benefits of the technology.

② This reference to money provides a financial reason to persuade readers.

Publishing

Here are some ways to reach a larger audience:

- **Speak Out** Deliver your essay as a speech to your class or to a local civic group.
- **Local News** Send your piece to the op-ed editor of your daily newspaper.

✓ ASSESSMENT		4	3	2	1
PORTFOLIO ASSESSMENT Use the rubric on Persuasion in ***Alternative Assessment*** (p. 120) to assess students' writing. Add these criteria to customize the rubric to this assignment.	**Persuasive Techniques**	The writer uses persuasive techniques that are appropriate to the essay's audience and purpose.	The writer is fairly effective at persuading but at times relies on the same technique regardless of the context.	The writer's attempts to persuade do not always work, nor are particular techniques used when they would be most effective.	The writer consistently fails to persuade or does so in an unclear or ineffective manner.
	Complex Sentences	The writer consistently uses complex sentences effectively	At times, the writer creates complex sentences.	The writer rarely uses complex sentences.	The writer avoids using complex sentences or uses them incorrectly.

Student Success Workshop

Vocabulary Development — Using Vocabulary References

Strategies for Success

Using reference tools is a fundamental way to build your vocabulary. Consult the following to define and understand unfamiliar words.

Use a Dictionary or Glossary The easiest way to determine what a word means is to look it up in a dictionary. Along with listing the definitions in order of common usage, a dictionary will also provide the word's pronunciation and origin.

Many texts, such as textbooks and manuals, contain a glossary of terms. These glossaries explain the meaning of terms as they are used in that specific text. If, for example, you were following a recipe that required you to *blanch* an ingredient, you could go to the glossary of the cookbook for the definition of that term.

Consult a Thesaurus A thesaurus provides lists of words with similar meanings. Knowing the shades of meaning for synonymous words such as *meeting, assembly,* and *convention* can give you a more precise understanding of what you read.

Make Use of Available Technology Many software programs and on-line services have reference tools that can assist you with vocabulary. Glossaries, dictionaries, and thesauruses are often built in or linked for easy access. Also, since print dictionaries do not always include the latest "new" words, you can examine available technologies, such as on-line dictionary updates, to help you find and define recently coined words and terms.

Here are some other situations in which you might use vocabulary references:

- Completing tax forms
- Reading legal documents, such as contracts

Apply the Strategies

Read this article from the "Science Club Newsletter" about the Mars space program. Then answer the questions that follow.

NASA Says Faster Isn't Necessarily Better

You might be surprised to learn that the computer used in the 1997 Pathfinder mission to Mars was a dinosaur in its own time. Its 20 megahertz microprocessor could never compete with the average 100 megahertz home computer. Still, the RAD6000 guided Pathfinder more than 300 million miles to the red planet. Why didn't NASA use a more advanced computer?

Reliability Is Priority #1

Supported by complex computers at NASA's Earth stations, Pathfinder doesn't need lightning-speed processing. What it demands, however, is reliability. After all, it's a long way to a repair shop. On-board computers must also be lighter, more energy efficient, and tolerant of radiation and vacuum. RAD6000 does have some bells and whistles—128 megabytes of memory and an operating system that understands the importance of precision timing when opening the air bags. As NASA's Brian Schneider said, "Your computer may be faster and more powerful than ours, but it wouldn't get the job done in space."

1. What is the *Pathfinder*? What reference sources could confirm your answer?
2. Besides a dictionary, where might you find the meaning of *radiation*?
3. Why do you think the writer used the word *tolerant* in the article? Locate synonyms to see if they could be successfully substituted.
4. The words *microprocessor, megahertz,* and *megabytes* are fairly recent terms. Conduct a search in reference sources other than a dictionary to define them.
5. What is the meaning of *dinosaur* as used in the article? Of *bells* and *whistles*? What sources might confirm your answer?

Prepare and Engage

LESSON OBJECTIVES

- To use reference materials such as glossary, dictionary, thesaurus, and available technology to determine precise meaning and usage

Customize for
Visual/Spatial Learners
In order to "see" the various reference tools, have students create a visual organizer of the different vocabulary references and the information they provide. The organizer should also include information about when to turn to each reference source. Encourage students to explore the various reference sources to gain firsthand information about their uses.

Apply the Strategies

Answers

1. A glossary from a recent text on space, various on-line resources, and software programs could all provide information on the *Pathfinder.*
2. The glossary of a science textbook would probably provide the meaning of radiation, as would on-line sources and software programs.
3. The writer may have used *tolerant* to help illustrate that on-board computers in space will face adverse conditions. Synonyms such as withstand or endure might also be used.
4. Students may consult glossaries, software programs, and on-line reference sources to define the terms.
5. *Dinosaur* is used to mean something old and out of date. *Bells and whistles* refers to "extras" that are meant to be enticing. Checking a standard dictionary, or a dictionary of slang or phrases, could confirm the meanings.

Test Preparation Workshop

Using Vocabulary References
Vocabulary development will help students perform well on standardized tests. Using reference sources will help students gain a broader knowledge of word meanings that will help them answer test questions relating to vocabulary.

Point out that by using reference sources, students will learn that *tolerant* has more than one meaning. Students can use this knowledge to correctly answer the following sample test item:

Which of the following is the best definition of <u>tolerant</u> as it is used in the passage?

A resigned to
B liberal
C able to ignore
D able to withstand

Guide students to recognize that D is the best answer, because this meaning of *tolerant* indicates that the word was used to denote the adverse conditions in space that a computer must withstand. While *B* is another meaning for *tolerant,* the context of the passage does not support this meaning.

Prepare and Engage

LESSON OBJECTIVES

- To make valid interpretations of a variety of literary texts

Discuss with students that some literary texts, such as poems, plays, and some essays and stories, were meant to be read aloud or performed. Have students share experiences about performances they may have seen that really illuminated the work for them. Invite students to compare the experience of reading a play or a poem with viewing a performance of the same work. Students may have seen a performance or interpretation that did not, for any number of reasons, seem "true" to them. Encourage students to describe why they felt the performance was not a valid interpretation of the work.

Apply the Strategies

1. Remind students that stage directions not only indicate suggestions for movement or tone; they may also provide background information on the characters.
2. Remind listeners that the interpretations are not competing with each other, but serve to illustrate how preparation and research can improve oral interpretations.
3. Point out that students might want to do some research on the story for their guides, or provide a list of areas for others to explore.

Speaking, Listening, and Viewing Workshop

Interpreting Literature Orally

Through the oral interpretation of a literary text—such as a poem, story, essay, or play—an audience sees a work come to life. A valid interpretation retains the message or tone of the original piece; thus, some preparation is required for a successful literary interpretation. Use these strategies for interpreting literature orally:

Prepare and Organize Your Interpretation After choosing a literary work for interpretation, decide how you will organize your presentation. Think about the kind of background information your audience will need. Finding information about the author, the cultural-historic context of the piece, and the work's relation to other works by the same author will guide your understanding and assure authenticity in your interpretation. If you plan to use props, begin to organize and prepare them early.

Rehearse Your Presentation Rehearsal is the key to the success of your presentation. Since familiarity with the text is most important, read the work many times, both silently and aloud. Without altering the meaning of the work in any significant way, explore different tones of voice, facial expressions, and gestures until you feel comfortable with your interpretation of the work. Record yourself, and listen for any unnatural places in your interpretation. Finally, rehearse in front of a friend or family member, and ask for feedback—you'll grow more confident about your performance, too.

Apply the Strategies

Experiment with oral interpretations of different literary genres.

1. With a small group of classmates, present a scene from a play. Use stage directions to arrive at a valid interpretation of the written words.
2. Orally interpret a poem for your class. Then, ask a classmate who is not as familiar with the poem to read it aloud. With classmates, discuss the different impacts of the two interpretations.
3. Find a short story with a message you like. Write a guide that would help others interpret the story orally.

Tips for Presenting an Interpretation

When interpreting literature orally, follow these strategies:

- *Make sure your interpretation is valid; it should reflect the meaning of the original work.*
- *Experiment with different ways of interpreting the work, using your voice, body, and facial expressions.*
- *Practice your performance until it looks and sounds natural.*

Beyond the Classroom

Community Connection

Spread the Word Community events that include oral interpretations are often well received in various community settings. Museums, local libraries, elder services, elementary classes, and preschools often sponsor performances of all kinds. The audiences may be diverse or homogeneous, depending on the setting and occasion.

Encourage students to arrange and prepare a presentation of several oral interpretations for a specific community audience. Invite class members to take some part in producing the presentation, even if they do not perform. Have students discuss and plan the presentation for the specific audience, setting, and occasion.

Test Preparation Workshop

Reading Comprehension — Summarizing Written Texts

Strategies for Success

The reading sections of standardized tests often require you to identify the implied main idea in a passage. They also require you to choose the best summary of a passage. Use these strategies to help you answer test questions on these skills:

Implied Main Idea An implied main idea is not stated directly. To identify the implied main idea, ask yourself, "What general idea is the writer expressing?" Focus on the writer's theme or conclusions. Look at the following example:

Haiku are three-line poems in which the first and third lines contain five syllables and the second line contains seven syllables. This form of poetry, which originated in Japan, reflects Japanese views of simplicity and nature. Bashō, a seventeenth-century Japanese poet, is credited with making haiku an important art form.

Born into a wealthy family, Bashō left home to become a poor wanderer and study Zen Buddhism, history, and classical Chinese poetry. His nomadic life increased the popularity of haiku, as he wrote and shared his verse in the communities through which he passed. Bashō's lightness, humor, and sensitivity to nature greatly influenced the eighteenth-century masters of haiku.

1 Which of the following choices best expresses the main idea implied in the first paragraph?

- **A** Haiku originated in Japan.
- **B** Bashō was the first great haiku poet.
- **C** Haiku is a unique and important art form in Japan.
- **D** People have been writing haiku for 300 years.

Answers **A, B,** and **D** give background information. **C** contains the implied main idea.

Effective Summaries A summary is a concise restating of the key points of a text. Ask yourself, "Which sentence best expresses the main ideas without unnecessary details?" Look at the following example:

2 Which of the following best summarizes the first paragraph?

- **A** Uniquely Japanese, haiku is a concise poetic form popularized by the seventeenth-century poet Bashō.
- **B** Haiku is a type of poetry.
- **C** Haiku is a Japanese form of poetry.
- **D** Bashō, a seventeenth-century poet, was the first to make haiku a separate art form.

Answers **B** and **D** say nothing about Japan. Although **C** is true, it does not include all of the key points. **A** is the correct answer.

Apply the Strategies

1 Which of the following is the implied main idea in the second paragraph on haiku?

- **A** Bashō set the standard for haiku poetry.
- **B** Bashō's learning and life helped define haiku.
- **C** Haiku grew because of Bashō's travels.
- **D** Other poets followed Bashō's example.

2 Which of the following is the best summary of the second paragraph?

- **A** Bashō's poetic life and ideas raised haiku to an art form in seventeenth-century Japan.
- **B** Bashō's wide-ranging travels contributed to the popularity of haiku in Japan.
- **C** Bashō studied history, Zen Buddhism, and classical Chinese poetry.
- **D** Haiku was an important art form in seventeenth-century Japan.

Correlations to Standardized Tests

The reading comprehension skills reviewed in this workshop correspond to the following standardized test sections:

SAT Reading

ACT Reading

Test Preparation

Each ATE workshop in Unit 1 supports the instruction here by providing teaching suggestions and a sample test item:

- Summarizing Written Texts (ATE, pp. 13, 21, 43, 89)
- Stated Main Idea (ATE, pp. 33)
- Supporting Details (ATE, pp. 65)
- Paraphrasing (ATE, pp. 97)

Prepare and Engage

LESSON OBJECTIVES

- To produce summaries of texts by identifying main ideas and their supporting details

Answers

1. (B) Bashō's learning and life helped define haiku.
2. (B) Bashō's wide-ranging travels contributed to the popularity of haiku in Japan.

Test-Taking Tip

Identifying the Best Answer
Point out to students that many items on standardized tests ask them to identify the best answer to a test item. Students should read the answer choices carefully and may need to decide between two choices that seem correct.

For example, discuss question 2 in Apply the Strategies. Answers *C* and *D* can be eliminated, as *C* is not a strong summary statement and *D* does not give enough information about the second paragraph. On first glance, both *A* and *B* seem to be reasonable choices. However, by rereading the question and noting that the summary statement should focus solely upon the second paragraph, students should recognize that *A* would be a better summary statement for the entire passage. B, which sums up the information in the second paragraph, is the correct answer.

Planning Instruction and Assessment

Unit Objectives

1. To read selections from the American literary tradition written between 1750 and 1800
2. To apply a variety of reading strategies, particularly strategies for constructing meaning, to reading these selections
3. To analyze literary elements
4. To use a variety of strategies to build vocabulary
5. To learn elements of grammar, usage, and style
6. To use recursive writing processes to write in a variety of forms
7. To express and support responses to various types of texts
8. To prepare, organize, and present literary interpretations

Meeting the Objectives

With each selection, you will find instructional material and portfolio opportunities through which students can meet these objectives. You will also find practice pages for reading strategies, literary elements, vocabulary, and grammar in the ***Selection Support*** booklet in the ***Teaching Resources*** box.

Test Preparation

The unit workshop, **Reading Comprehension: Recognize Cause and Effect; Predict Outcomes** (SE, p. 213), is supported by teaching tips and a sample test item in the ATE workshop with each selection grouping.

- **Recognize Cause and Effect** (ATE, pp. 129, 139, 187, 193)
- **Predict Outcomes** (ATE, pp. 149, 167)

The following additional workshops in the ATE give teaching tips and a sample test item for applying the skill taught in the Student Success Workshops:

- **Evaluate Sources of Information** (ATE, p. 164)
- **Understand Connotation and Denotation** (ATE, p. 184)
- **Evaluating a Writer's Motivation** (ATE, p. 211)

Washington Crossing the Delaware, Emanuel Gottlieb Leutze, Metropolitan Museum of Art

Humanities: Art

Washington Crossing the Delaware, 1851, by Emanuel Gottlieb Leutze.

Gottlieb Leutze (1816–1864) was an American painter who lived in Germany for two decades, painting subjects from American history.

Washington Crossing the Delaware is one of the best-known paintings in the world. On Christmas night, 1776, General George Washington led 2,400 American soldiers from Pennsylvania across the Delaware River to Trenton, New Jersey, where they surprised German-born Hessian mercenaries who were unprepared for battle. In the Battle of Trenton, the Americans lost only 10 soldiers and took 900 Hessian prisoners.

Use this question for discussion:

What elements in the painting add to the heroic stature of George Washington and link him to the destiny of the newly emerging nation? *His posture is commanding and unflinching; his head is the highest of all those in the painting; his position parallels that of the windswept flag.*

UNIT 2

A Nation Is Born (1750–1800)

"The time is now near at hand which must probably determine whether Americans are to be freemen or slaves; whether they are to have any property they can call their own; whether their houses and farms are to be pillaged and destroyed and themselves consigned to a state of wretchedness from which no human efforts will deliver them. The fate of unborn millions will now depend, under God, on the courage and conduct of this army. Our cruel and unrelenting enemy leaves us only the choice of brave resistance, or the most abject submission. We have, therefore, to resolve to conquer or die."

—George Washington,
addressing the Continental Army
before the battle of Long Island, August 27, 1776.

Assessing Student Progress

The following tools are available to measure the degree to which students meet the unit objectives:

Informal Assessment

The questions on the Guide for Responding sections are a first level of response to the concepts and skills presented within the selection. Students' responses are a brief, informal measure of their grasp of the material. Their responses on this level can indicate where further instruction and practice are needed. You may then follow up with the practice pages in the ***Selection Support*** booklet.

You will find literature and reading guides in the ***Alternative Assessment*** booklet, which you may give students on an individual basis for informal assessment of their performance.

Formal Assessment

In the ***Formal Assessment*** booklet, you will find selection tests and part tests.

Selection Tests The selection tests measure comprehension and skills acquisition for each selection or group of selections.

Part Tests Each part test, which calls on students to read a passage of literature they have not previously seen, applies the unit skills on a broader level. The Critical Reading section measures Unit Objectives 1, 2, and 3. The Vocabulary and Grammar section measures Objectives 4 and 5. The Essay section measures Objectives 1 and 6. Both the Critical Reading and Vocabulary and Grammar sections use formats similar to those found on many standardized tests, including the SAT.

Alternative Assessment

Portfolios As you review individual pieces or the collected work in students' portfolios, you will find assessment sheets available in the portfolio section of the ***Alternative Assessment*** booklet.

Scoring Rubrics You will find scoring rubrics for writing modes in the ***Alternative Assessment*** booklet. You can apply these to Guided Writing Lessons and to Writing Process Workshop lessons.

Speaking, Listening, and Viewing The ***Alternative Assessment*** booklet contains assessment sheets for speaking, listening, and viewing activities.

Learning Modalities The ***Alternative Assessment*** booklet contains activities that appeal to different learning styles. You may use these tools as an alternative measurement of students' growth.

Using the Timeline

The Timeline can serve a number of instructional purposes, as follows:

Getting an Overview Use the timeline to help students get a quick overview of themes and events of the period. This approach will benefit all students but may be especially helpful for visually oriented students, English language learners, and those less proficient in reading. (For strategies in using the Timeline as an overview, see the bottom of this page.)

Thinking Critically Questions are provided on the facing page. Use these questions to have students review the events, discuss their significance, and examine the *so what* behind the *what happened.*

Connecting to Selections Have students refer back to the Timeline when beginning to read individual selections. By consulting the Timeline regularly, they will gain a better sense of the period's chronology. In addition, they will appreciate what was occurring in the world that gave rise to these works of literature.

Projects Students can use the Timeline as a launching pad for projects like these:

- **Customized Timeline** Have students create a period timeline in their notebooks, adding key dates as they read new selections. They can use dates from this Timeline as a starting framework, but they may want to customize their timeline by giving it a thematic focus, for example, events relating to the American Revolution.
- **Special Reports** Have students scan the Timeline for items that interest them, research these further, and report on them to the class. Students might want to report on one of the important inventions of this period, for example: the first striking clock with all parts made in America (1753), an improved steam engine (1769), or the cotton gin (1793).

Timeline

1750–1800

1750 | 1760 | 1770

American Events

- **1748** *Poor Richard's Almanack* sold to new owner after 25 years under Benjamin Franklin. ▶

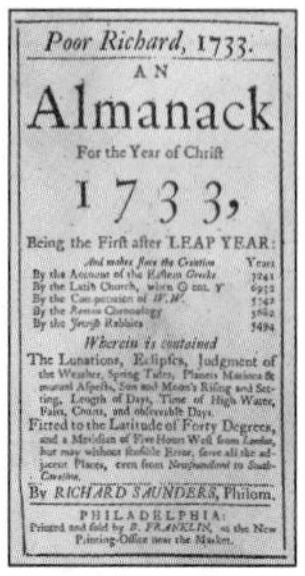

- **1752** Benjamin Franklin conducts his kite and key experiment with lightning. ▼
- **1753** Benjamin Banneker constructs the first striking clock with all parts made in America. The clock keeps perfect time for the next 40 years.
- **1754** French and Indian War begins.

- **1759–63** France gives up claims to North American territory.
- **1765** Stamp Act passed by British Parliament; colonists protest bitterly.
- **1767** Townshend Acts impose new taxes, angering colonists further.

- **1771** Benjamin Franklin begins his *Autobiography*.
- **1773** Parliament's Tea Act prompts Boston Tea Party. ▲
- **1773** Phillis Wheatley's *Poems on Various Subjects* published in England. ◀
- **1774** First Continental Congress meets in Philadelphia.
- **1775** Patrick Henry gives his "liberty or death" speech.
- **1775** The American Revolution begins.
- **1776** Second Continental Congress adopts Declaration of Independence. ▼
- **1776** Congress approves the enlistment of African American men.
- **1778** France recognizes U.S. independence and signs treaty of alliance.

World Events

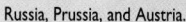

- **1755** France: School for deaf opens in Paris. ▼
- **1755** England: Samuel Johnson publishes *Dictionary of the English Language.*
- **1757** England: Robert Clive defeats native army at Plassey, India.
- **1759** France: Voltaire publishes *Candide*, satirizing optimism of Rousseau.

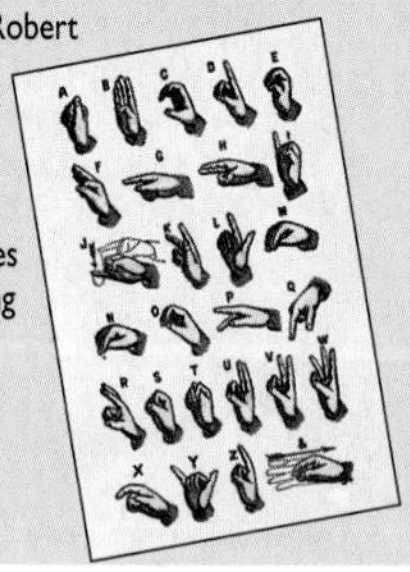

- **1762** France: Jean Jacques Rousseau states his political philosophy in *The Social Contract.*
- **1763** Seven Years War ends.
- **1769** Scotland: James Watt invents an improved steam engine.
- **1769** England: Richard Arkwright invents a frame for spinning; helps bring about factory system.

- **1770** Germany: Ludwig von Beethoven is born. ▶

- **1772** Poland: First of three partitions of Poland gives land to Russia, Prussia, and Austria.
- **1774** England: Joseph Priestley discovers oxygen, named later by Lavoisier.
- **1779** England: Captain James Cook becomes first European to see Hawaii.
- **1779** South Africa: First of Kaffir wars between blacks and whites breaks out.

Getting an Overview of the Period

Introduction To give students an overview of the period, indicate the span of dates along the top of the Timeline. How much time is covered in this unit? *A period of 50 years.* Next, point out that the Timeline is divided into specifically American Events (on top) and World Events (on bottom). Have them practice scanning the Timeline across, looking both at the American Events and the World Events. Finally, point out that the events in the Timeline often represent beginnings, turning points, or endings. *The British surrender to Washington (1781) is an example.*

Key Events Tell students that this Timeline tells the "story" of how America won its independence from Britain. Have them find key events leading up to the American Revolution. *Examples include the British imposition of the Stamp Act and the Townshend Acts (1765, 1767) and the meeting of the First Continental Congress (1774).* Then have them locate the beginning and ending dates of the American Revolution. *These are 1775 and 1783, respectively.* What events after the Revolution show how the nation's identity was developing? *One example is the first census in 1790.*

1780 1790 1800

American Events

- **1780** James Derham becomes the first black man licensed to practice medicine in the U.S.
- **1781** General Cornwallis surrenders British army to George Washington at Yorktown. ▲
- **1782** Michel-Guillaume Jean de Crèvecoeur's *Letters From an American Farmer* published in London.
- **1783** Noah Webster's *Spelling Book* first appears; 60 million copies would be sold.
- **1783** Revolutionary War ends.
- **1787** Constitutional Convention meets in Philadelphia to draft Constitution.
- **1789** George Washington elected first President of United States. ▼
- **1790** First federal U.S. census shows approximately 757,208 blacks in the U.S., nearly 20% of the total population. 59,557 are free.
- **1793** Eli Whitney invents cotton gin. ▶
- **1795** University of North Carolina opens as America's first state university.
- **1801** Thomas Jefferson, principal author of Declaration of Independence, elected President.

World Events

- **1781** England: William Herschel discovers planet Uranus. ▼
- **1782** Germany: Goethe begins 50 years of work on the poem *Faust.*
- **1785** France: Jean-Pierre Blanchard makes first balloon crossing of English Channel.
- **1786** Scotland: Robert Burns is widely acclaimed for his first book of poems.
- **1786** Austria: Wolfgang Amadeus Mozart creates the comic opera *The Marriage of Figaro.*
- **1789** France: Storming of Bastille in Paris sets off French Revolution.
- **1791** England: James Boswell publishes *The Life of Samuel Johnson.* ▲
- **1793** France: King Louis XVI and Marie Antoinette executed.
- **1796** England: Edward Jenner develops smallpox vaccine.
- **1796** France: Napoleon Bonaparte comes to power in France. ▶
- **1797** Spain: Goya creates *Los Caprichos* etchings.
- **1798** England: William Wordsworth and Samuel Taylor Coleridge publish *Lyrical Ballads.*
- **1800** Germany: Ludwig von Beethoven composes *First Symphony.*

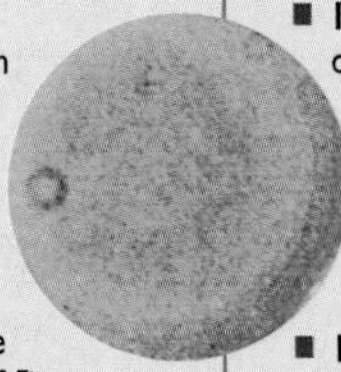

◆ Critical Thinking

1. (a) What two entries about Benjamin Franklin appear in the period 1750–1760? (b) What do these entries reveal about Franklin's interests? **[Draw Conclusions]** *(a) In 1748, Franklin sold his publication* Poor Richard's Almanack *to a new owner. In 1752, he conducted an experiment with lightning. (b) These activities suggest that Franklin had wide-ranging interests; some of them were literary, and others scientific.*
2. (a) What did France give up in the period 1759 to 1763? (b) What events might logically have led up to this one? **[Infer]** *(a) France gave up its claim to North American territory. (b) This renunciation of territory suggests that France may have engaged in a contest for it, probably with the British. France's giving up of this territory suggests that it lost this conflict.*
3. (a) What actions did Congress take in the period 1770-1780 (b) What ongoing story do these actions tell? **[Speculate]** *(a) The first Continental Congress met in Philadelphia (1774), the Second Continental Congress adopted the Declaration of Independence (1776), and Congress approved the enlistment of African American men (1776). (b) These actions tell the story of America organizing for resistance to Britain, declaring that resistance, and taking measures to support it.*
4. (a) Name two technological events that occurred in England in 1769. (b) In what ways might these events have affected people's lives? **[Speculate]** *(a) An improved steam engine and a frame for spinning were invented. The latter helped bring about the factory system. (b) Factories might have attracted people from the country to work in the city. They probably produced quantities of less expensive goods.*
5. (a) When was the first federal census taken? (b) What does it indicate about the status of blacks in the new country. **[Interpret]** *(a) The first federal census was taken in 1790. (b) It indicates that blacks were a substantial minority in the country but that most of them were enslaved.*

▶Critical Viewing◀

1. What did the deaf learn in their new school (1755)? **[Infer]** *The picture suggests that they learned sign language.*
2. What does the picture reveal about Franklin's experiments with lightning (1752)? **[Infer]** *Franklin used a kite to get a bolt of lightning to strike. Perhaps it was meant to strike the key dangling from the kite string. Students may also indicate that the bottle by Franklin's foot played a part in the experiment.*
3. In what kind of ships did the British bring tea into the colonies (1773)? **[Analyze]** *The picture suggests that the British transported tea in large sailing ships with several masts.*
4. How do the writing implements related to the entry on the Declaration of Independence (1776) help you imagine the writing of that document? **[Connect]** *The implements suggest that Jefferson wrote the Declaration with a quill pen like this one. The quill appears to be dipped in an inkwell.*
5. What does the picture indicate about the British surrender (1781)? **[Infer]** *Judging from the picture, the surrender seems to have been conducted with a great deal of ceremony.*

Develop Understanding

Customize for
Less Proficient Readers
Have students preview the maps and charts on pages 121, 122, and 125 of A Graphic Look at the Period. Have them discuss what these graphics reveal about the birth of a new nation.

Customize for
English Language Learners
Have these students choose a picture from A Graphic Look at the Period, study it carefully, and give a brief oral presentation on it for other students.

Customize for
Intrapersonal Learners
Have students with an intrapersonal orientation write a journal entry expressing what the events described in the Story of the Times mean to them.

Customize for
AP Students
Challenge more advanced students to use evidence from A Graphic Look at the Period and The Story of the Times to answer this question: Did the military and political revolution America accomplished have its counterpart in literature? Explain.

Answers to

A GRAPHIC LOOK

Assess Technology Newspapers, letters, and pamphlets can fan the flames of revolution in a community by spreading news and ideas quickly.

Make an Inference Ports became major cities because they were the gateways of commerce. Their busy harbors received new immigrants and shipments of goods from abroad. All the activity surrounding commerce created many jobs and a need for many people to do them.

A GRAPHIC LOOK AT THE PERIOD

▲ **Assess Technology** Colonial printers played an important role in uniting colonists against the British. Why are newspapers, letters, and pamphlets critical to inspiring revolution?

▼ **Make an Inference** Almost from its founding in 1682, Philadelphia was a thriving port. This painting shows the busy Philadelphia waterfront in 1720. Why did ports become the major cities of the colonies?

The Story of the Times
1750–1800

Historical Background

It is easy to forget how long the thirteen original states had been colonies. By 1750, there were fourth- and fifth-generation Americans of European descent living in Virginia and New England. These people were English subjects, and, on the whole, they were well satisfied with that status. In fact, as late as the early 1760's, few Americans had given much thought to the prospect of independence.

Between the mid-1760's and the mid-1770's, however, attitudes changed dramatically. King George III and Parliament imposed a number of regulations that threatened the liberties of the colonists. With each succeeding measure, the outrage in America grew, finally erupting into war.

The Age of Reason Great upheavals in history occur when circumstances are ripe. The American Revolution was such an upheaval, and the groundwork for it had been laid by European writers and thinkers as well as by the English king and Parliament. The eighteenth century is often characterized as the Enlightenment, or the Age of Reason. Spurred by the work of many seventeenth-century thinkers—such as scientists Galileo and Sir Isaac Newton, philosophers Voltaire and Jean Jacques Rousseau, and political theorist John Locke, the writers and thinkers of the Enlightenment valued reason over faith. Unlike the Puritans, they had little interest in the

Cross-Curricular Connection: Social Studies

Effects of the French and Indian War Point out to students how the French and Indian War (1754–1763) prepared the way for the American Revolution. For example, it strained the previously good relations between the colonies and the home country. The arrogance of British officers offended American military leaders like Washington. Also, many New Englanders were shocked by what they regarded as the immorality of British troops.

Acquiring a new sense of identity, colonists began to see themselves as different from the British. They saw themselves as less formal than the British, but with a superior sense of right and wrong. They came to think of the British as a corrupt people who had departed from the path of righteousness.

Ask students how this new sense of identity may have paved the way for revolution. *Believing they were morally superior, Americans could justify self-rule.*

hereafter, believing instead in the power of reason and science to further human progress. They spoke of a social contract that forms the basis of government. Above all, they believed that people are by nature good, not evil. A perfect society seemed to them to be more than just an idle dream.

The American statesmen of the Revolutionary period were themselves figures of the Enlightenment. No history of the period would be complete without mention of the ideas and writings of Benjamin Franklin, Thomas Paine, and Thomas Jefferson. These Americans not only expressed the ideas of the Age of Reason, but they also helped to put them spectacularly into practice.

Toward a Clash of Arms The American Revolution was preceded by the French and Indian War, a struggle between England and France for control of North America. The conflict broke out in 1754 and continued for nearly a decade. When the war officially ended in 1763, defeated France gave up its claims to North American territory. There was general jubilation in the thirteen English colonies.

The good feelings were short-lived, however. The British government, wanting to raise revenue in the colonies to pay its war debt, passed the Stamp Act in 1765. Colonial reaction to the Stamp Act, which required the buying and affixing of stamps to each of 54 ordinary items, was swift and bitter. Stamps were burned. Stamp distributors were beaten and their shops destroyed. Eventually, the Stamp Act was repealed.

Other acts and reactions followed. The Townshend Acts of 1767 taxed paper, paint, glass, lead, and tea. When the colonists organized a boycott, the British dissolved the Massachusetts legislature and sent two regiments of British troops to Boston. In 1770, these Redcoats fired into a taunting mob, causing five fatalities. This so-called Boston Massacre further inflamed colonial passions. Parliament repealed the Townshend duties except for the tax on tea, but a separate Tea Act giving an English company a virtual monopoly soon greeted the colonists. Furious, a group of Bostonians dressed as Mohawks dumped a shipment of tea

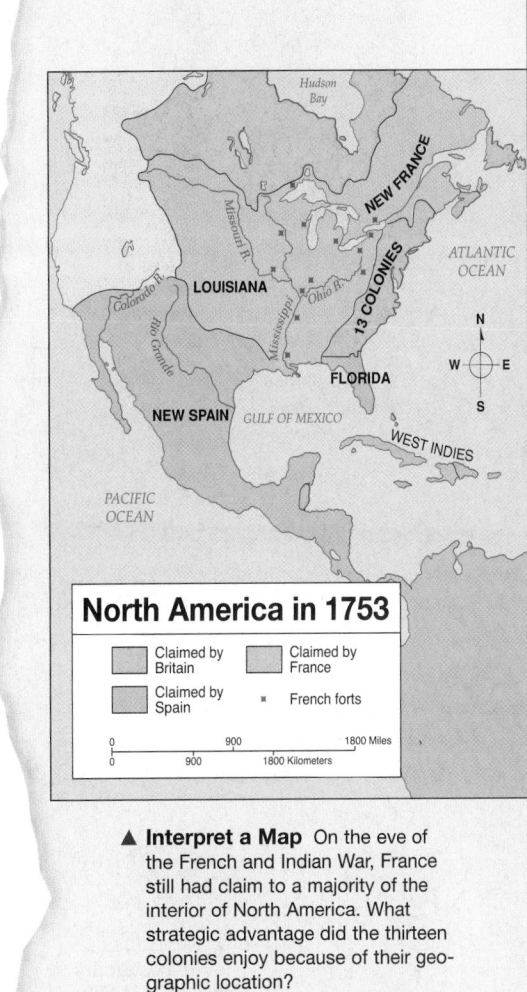

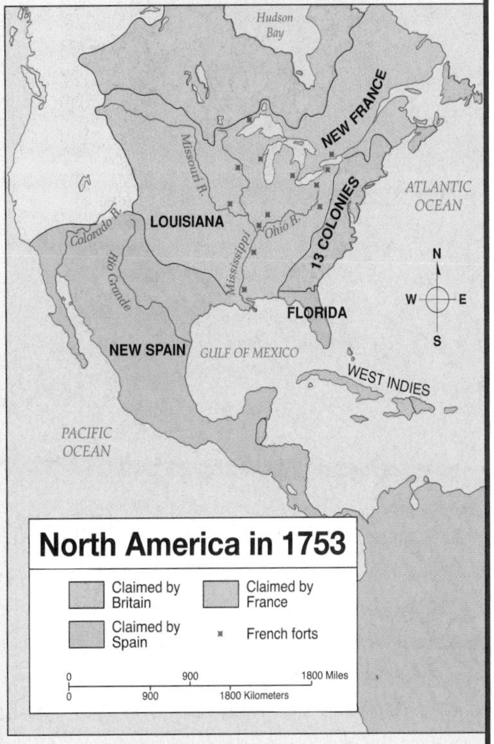

▲ **Interpret a Map** On the eve of the French and Indian War, France still had claim to a majority of the interior of North America. What strategic advantage did the thirteen colonies enjoy because of their geographic location?

More About the Boston Massacre Paul Revere, a silversmith and patriot, did an engraving of the Boston Massacre (p. 124). It shows British troops firing on unarmed citizens and is intended to prompt anger at the British. Revere's engraving does not show the events leading up to this end result. The incident began when boys threw ice at a sentry guarding the Customs House. This minor confrontation brought a mob from a nearby square. A British captain responded to a call for help, bringing seven soldiers with him. When they were attacked by the mob, these soldiers opened fire, killing five citizens.

Connection to the Literature

- In "Speech in the Virginia Convention," p. 169, Patrick Henry demonstrates the fiery oratorical style that helped inspire Americans to revolutionary fervor.
- In selections like "The Declaration of Independence," p. 140, and the excerpt from *The Crisis, Number 1*, p. 144, students will find eloquent expression of the American wish for independence.

Answers to

A GRAPHIC LOOK

Interpret a Map The thirteen colonies enjoyed the strategic advantage of a long coastline. With several major ports, like New York and Philadelphia, they could easily receive shipments of goods and troop transports.

Humanities: Music

"Chester," William Billings.

Use the ***Listening to Music*** Audio CD: *The American Experience* to show students how American music of the late 1700's reflected the struggle for independence. Play the song "Chester" written by William Billings (1746–1800).

"Chester" represents a new form of American popular music, the political song. It proudly expresses the determination and optimism of Americans as they strive for independence. During the American Revolution, this song became a source of inspiration for American troops, many of whom knew it by heart. Provide students with its lyrics:

Let tyrants shake their iron rod,
And Slav'ry clank her galling chains,
We fear them not, we trust in God
New England's God for ever reigns.

When God inspir'd us for the fight,
Their ranks were broke, their lines forc'd.
Their Ships were Shatter'd in our sight,
Or swiftly driven from our Coast.

What grateful Off'ring shall we bring?
What shall we render to the Lord?
Loud Hallelujahs let us Sing,
And praise his name on ev'ry Chord.

Ask students to describe the song's mood. *They may call it defiant and strong.*

More About the Revolution

At the Concord skirmish on April 19, 1775, two Americans fell but so did three Redcoats. The British commander ordered a retreat to Boston. American snipers fired on the British troops all the way back, causing a total of 273 casualties.

In June, the Americans killed or wounded more than a thousand British soldiers at the Battle of Bunker Hill. Although all the fighting up to this point had taken place in Massachusetts, the revolt involved all the colonies. Two days before Bunker Hill, the Second Continental Congress, meeting in Philadelphia, had named a commander in chief of the official American army. He was George Washington of Virginia.

The Battle of Saratoga, in the fall of 1777, marked a turning point in the war. At Saratoga, in upstate New York, the British were surrounded and forced to surrender more than 5,000 men. When news of this American victory reached Paris, the government of France formally recognized the independence of the United States. Soon afterward, France began to commit troops to aid the American cause.

Answers to

A Graphic Look

(from page 122)

Assess The picture indicates that cold weather probably posed a challenge for soldiers. The coats these soldiers are wearing don't appear to be very warm. Snow and ice also create hazards for troops as they travel.

Identify Cause and Effect Many Patriots probably left Philadelphia in 1777 because troops of General Howe entered that city and Washington's army retreated to Valley Forge.

(from page 123)

Hypothesize A new country might glorify its wartime heroes out of gratitude for their leadership in the fighting.

Draw a Conclusion The clothing of these men suggests that prominent and well-to-do citizens were generally elected to the Virginia House of Burgesses.

▲ **Assess** Many critical battles of the American Revolution were fought in New York, New Jersey, and Pennsylvania during the fall and winter of 1776 to 1777. What challenges would the weather pose for the soldiers?

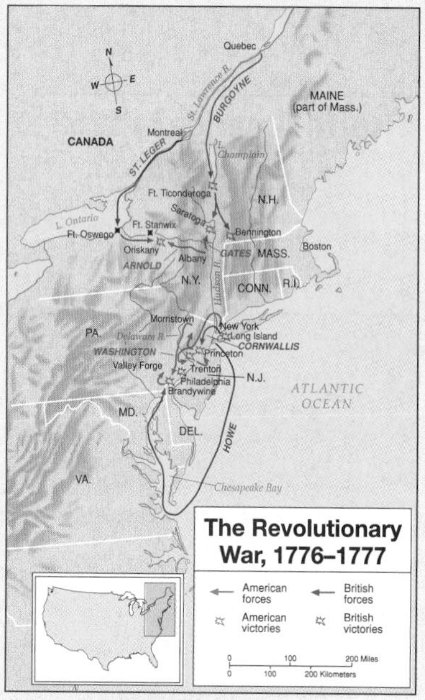

▲ **Identify Cause and Effect** Based on this map, why do you think many Patriots left Philadelphia in 1777?

into Boston harbor. As punishment for this Boston Tea Party, the English Parliament passed the Coercive Acts. Because they shut down the port of Boston, forbade meetings other than annual town meetings, and insisted that British troops could be housed in colonists' homes, colonists immediately dubbed these laws the Intolerable Acts.

In September 1774, colonial leaders, although not speaking openly of independence, met in Philadelphia for the First Continental Congress. The British, their authority slipping away, appointed General Thomas Gage governor of Massachusetts. The stage was set for war.

"The Shot Heard Round the World" On April 19, 1775, 700 British troops met some 70 colonial minutemen on the Lexington green. A musket shot was fired (from which side, no one knows), and before the shooting that followed was over, eight Americans lay dead. The British marched west to Concord, where another skirmish took place. The encounters at Lexington and Concord, a landmark in American history, have been referred to as "the shot heard round the world." The American Revolution had begun, and there would be no turning back.

More than a year would pass before the colonies declared their independence. After six years of fighting, the war finally came to an end at Yorktown, Virginia, on October 19, 1781. Aided by the French army and the French navy, and enlisting the service of black soldiers, General Washington's army bottled up the 8,000-man British force under General Cornwallis. Seeing that escape was impossible, General Cornwallis surrendered.

The New Nation The path to self-government was not always smooth, however. After the Revolution, the Articles of Confederation established a "league of friendship" among the new states. This arrangement did not work well. The federal Constitution that replaced the Articles required many compromises and was ratified only after a long fight. Even then, a Bill of Rights had to be added to placate those who feared the centralized power that the Constitution conferred.

Cross-Curricular Connection: Social Studies

A People's War Tell students that about 200,000 fighters served at one time or another in the American cause. Most of them were young, relatively poor men. They and their officers were paid badly, if at all, and poorly fed and clothed.

Some 5,000 African American men also took part in the war, on both sides. African American and white women served on both sides as well. Many women followed husbands, lovers, or fathers into battle, cared for them, and nursed them. A few women actually fought in battles. Deborah Sampson, for example, disguised herself as a man, calling herself Robert Shurtleff, and served from May 1782 to October 1783. Her husband became the only man to receive a pension as the "widow" of a veteran!

Ask students to speculate why most of the fighters were poor men. *Reasonable answers include: There were more poor men than rich men; poor men had less to lose and were more influenced by radical ideas.*

The old revolutionaries, by and large, remained true to their principles and continued their public duties. George Washington became the nation's first president. John Adams, a signer of the Declaration of Independence, succeeded him in that office. Then, in 1800, Americans elected as their president the brilliant statesman who had drafted the Declaration, one of the heroes of the Enlightenment, Thomas Jefferson.

Literature of the Period

A Time of Crisis In contrast to the private soul-searching of the Puritans of New England, much of what was produced during the Revolutionary period was public writing. By the time of the War for Independence, nearly fifty newspapers had been established in the coastal cities. At the time of Washington's inauguration, there were nearly forty magazines. Almanacs were popular from Massachusetts to Georgia.

The mind of the nation was on politics. Journalists and printers provided a forum for the expression of ideas. After 1763, those ideas were increasingly focused on relations with Great Britain and, more broadly, on the nature of government. As the literature presented in this unit testifies, the writing of permanent importance from the Revolutionary era is mostly political writing.

Politics as Literature The public writing and speaking of American statesmen in two tumultuous decades, the 1770's and 1780's, helped to reshape not only the nation but also the world.

Patrick Henry was a spellbinding orator whose speech against the Stamp Act in the Virginia House of Burgesses brought cries of "Treason!" Ten years later, his electrifying speech to the Virginia Convention expressed the rising sentiment for independence.

Thomas Paine was perhaps more influential than any other in swaying public opinion in favor of independence. His 1776 pamphlet *Common Sense* swept the colonies, selling 100,000 copies in three months.

The Declaration of Independence was first drafted by Thomas Jefferson in June 1776. The finished document is largely his work, although

▲ **Hypothesize** This cotton handkerchief, probably made in 1777, honors General George Washington. Why might a new country glorify its wartime heroes?

▲ **Draw a Conclusion** When Patrick Henry railed against the Stamp Act, Virginia became the first colony officially to protest the new tax law. Based on this painting, what type of citizen do you think was generally elected to serve in the Virginia House of Burgesses?

Historical Background

Comprehension Check ☑

1. What name is often given to the age that influenced American statesmen of the Revolution? *It is often called the Age of Reason.*
2. After the French and Indian War, what British measures enraged the colonists? *The colonists were enraged by taxes to pay off the British war debt.*
3. Where did the first battles of the Revolution take place? *They took place at Lexington and Concord, Massachusetts.*
4. Describe how Washington ended the war on October 19, 1781. *In Yorktown, Washington's army bottled up a force led by General Cornwallis while the French navy blockaded the port. Cornwallis surrendered.*
5. After the Revolution, what document replaced the Articles of Confederation? *The Constitution replaced the Articles.*

◆ Critical Thinking

1. Why did the Enlightenment idea that people are basically good prove a spur to revolution? **[Analyze]** *If people are basically good, then it must be the wrong form of government that creates unhappiness. People are therefore justified in changing their government.*
2. In what way did the American Revolution begin with the French and Indian War? **[Analyze]** *The war brought about the debt that prompted England to tax the colonies. These taxes provoked rebellion.*
3. Why do you think the colonists were able to defeat England, a great world power? **[Analyze]** *The colonists were fighting on their home ground and used effective guerrilla tactics. Also, the British may have spread themselves too thin in trying to cover all of the colonies.*

Cross-Curricular Connection: Social Studies

Thomas Paine When Thomas Paine wrote *Common Sense,* he was a recent immigrant from England. Nevertheless, he was able to capture the revolutionary mood of the country. His pamphlet sold a total of about 150,000 copies, compared to the few hundred copies that accounted for the distribution of most political pamphlets.

One secret of Paine's success is his plain, direct style. An artisan with little formal education, Paine did not refer to Greek and Latin literature that only the educated could appreciate. Instead, he supported his points with references to the Bible, a book that people of all classes had read.

During the American Revolution, Paine wrote 16 pamphlets that were collectively called *The Crisis* (see p. 144 for an excerpt from *The Crisis, Number 1*). These pamphlets had a wide readership among Patriots.

Shortly after the Revolution, Paine returned to England. There he wrote a tract titled *The Rights of Man,* which was a defense of the French Revolution. In this work, Paine argued that people enjoy natural rights and that governments have an obligation to guarantee these rights.

Ask students if they can think of anyone today whose life resembles Paine's. *Students may name people like Martin Luther King, Jr. Have them support their answers.*

More About the Constitution
Not everyone in 1787 was pleased with the Constitution. Alexander Hamilton called it a "weak and worthless fabric," and Benjamin Franklin supported it only because "I expect no better." (See Franklin's speech to the Constitutional Convention, p. 172)

The doubts of the framers were reflected in the controversy over ratification. Delaware ratified the Constitution within three months, thus becoming the first state in the Union. However, the ratification of nine states was necessary before the document could go into effect. The last few states proved difficult. The contest between supporters and opponents was especially hard-fought in New York. Alexander Hamilton, whose opinion of the Constitution was none too high, nevertheless wanted to see it pass in his home state. With James Madison and John Jay, he wrote a series of essays that were first published as letters to three New York newspapers. These essays, collected as *The Federalist,* served their immediate purpose. New York ratified the constitution by a vote of 30 to 27. Over time, they have also come to be recognized as authoritative statements on the principles of American government.

Answers to A GRAPHIC LOOK

(from page 124)

Make an Inference The many papers on the floor suggest that the document went through many revisions and that the writing of it was hard work.

Analyze Bias The civilian crowd, which seems to include women, seems neither armed nor hostile. The calm dog in the foreground creates viewer sympathy for the colonists. Some of them have already fallen. It is not immediately apparent from the picture, but the incident did not occur at Butcher's Hall as shown; also, Revere exaggerated the number killed.

(from page 125)

Identify Problems One state might not honor the currency of another state. Also, the currencies of different states might not be comparable in value.

Read a Chart The government's income during this period was $4,418,000. The government owed $81,497,000.

▲ **Make an Inference** This painting captures the writing of the Declaration of Independence. What do the many papers on the floor of the room suggest about the writing of the Declaration?

▲ **Analyze Bias** Paul Revere's engraving of the Boston Massacre played a major role in whipping up colonial fury against the British. Revere purposefully distorted the events. For example, notice that Revere shows the British general giving orders to shoot. Eyewitnesses have said this never happened. What other details suggest the artist was pro-colonist?

a committee of five statesmen, including Benjamin Franklin, was involved in its creation. The Declaration, despite some exaggerated charges against King George III, is one of the most influential political statements ever made.

Another Revolutionary period document written by committee that has stood the test of time is the Constitution of the United States, drafted in 1787. The framers, whose new nation boasted about four million people, hoped that the Constitution would last at least a generation. It still survives, amended only 27 times, as the political foundation of a superpower of 50 states and more than 250 million people.

The Cultural Scene While politics dominated the literature of the Revolutionary period, not every writer of note was a statesman. Verse appeared in most of the newspapers, and numerous broadside ballads were published. (A broadside ballad is a single sheet of paper, printed on one or both sides, dealing with a current topic.) One of the most popular broadside ballads was called "The Dying Redcoat," supposedly written by a British sergeant mortally wounded in the Revolution.

Two other poets of the day whose works were more sophisticated than the broadside ballads were Joel Barlow and Phillis Wheatley. Barlow, a 1778 Yale graduate, is best remembered for "The Hasty Pudding," a mock-heroic tribute to cornmeal mush. Phillis Wheatley, born in Africa and brought to Boston in childhood as a slave, showed early signs of literary genius. A collection of her poems was published in England while she was still a young woman.

Another writer of the Revolutionary period recorded his impressions of everyday American life. Born into an aristocratic French family, Michel-Guillaume Crèvecoeur became a soldier of fortune, a world traveler, and a farmer. For fifteen years, he owned a plantation in Orange County, New York, and his impressions of life there were published in London in 1782 as *Letters From an American Farmer.*

Perhaps the best-known writing of the period outside the field of politics was done by Benjamin Franklin. His *Poor Richard's Almanack* became familiar to most households in the colonies. A statesman, printer, author, inventor,

Humanities: Architecture

Planning a Capital City.
To establish its identity, the new country needed an impressive capital. On Jefferson's recommendation, George Washington appointed an African American mathematician and inventor, Benjamin Banneker, to the commission in charge of surveying the District of Columbia. Pierre Charles L'Enfant, a French artist and architect who had fought for the United States during the Revolution, developed the city plan. L'Enfant designed a capital with broad streets, public walks, a mansion for the President, a pedestrian mall, and the Capitol. Although the federal government moved to the District in 1800, it took decades longer to realize the L'Enfant plan in its entirety.

Washington, D.C., with its great boulevards, marble buildings in the Roman style, and public monuments, is the most obvious legacy of the Federalists' grand plans for the United States.

Ask students what ideas and feelings such architecture is meant to call up in visitors and residents alike. *It is meant to inspire respect, even awe, and to emphasize the notion that human institutions can be organized in a rational way.*

and scientist, Franklin was a true son of the Enlightenment. His *Autobiography*, covering only his early years, is regarded as one of the finest autobiographies in any language.

Culture and Art During the Revolutionary period, America began to establish a cultural identity of its own. Theaters were built from New York to Charleston. A number of new colleges were established after the war, especially in the South. Several outstanding painters were at work in the colonies and the young republic. Among them were John Singleton Copley, Gilbert Stuart, John Trumbull, and Charles Willson Peale. Patience Wright, famous in the colonies as a sculptor of wax portraits, moved to London before the war. While there, she acted as a Revolutionary spy. In music, William Billings produced *The New England Psalm-Singer* and a number of patriotic hymns. This was a turbulent time—a time of action—and its legacy was cultural as well as political.

American Literature at Daybreak By the early 1800's, America could boast a small body of national literature. The Native Americans had contributed haunting poetry and legends through their oral traditions. The Puritans had written a number of powerful, inward-looking works. The statesmen of the Revolutionary period had produced political documents for the ages. A few poets and essayists had made a permanent mark on the literature of the young republic. There were, however, no American novels or plays of importance, and the modern short story had yet to be invented.

As the eighteenth century came to a close, however, the raw materials for a great national literature were at hand, waiting to be used. The nation stood on the threshold of a territorial and population explosion unique in the history of the world. It would take almost exactly a century to close the frontier on the vast and varied continent beyond the Appalachians. During that century, American literature would burst forth with a vitality that might have surprised even the farsighted founders of the nation. The colonial age ended with a narrow volume of memorable literature. The nineteenth century would close with a library of works that form a major part of America's literary heritage.

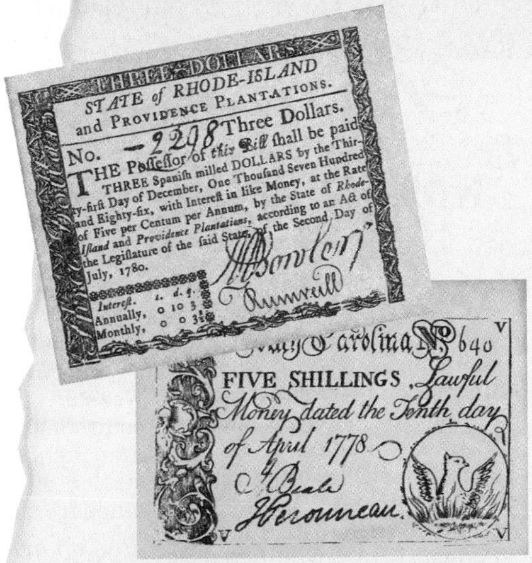

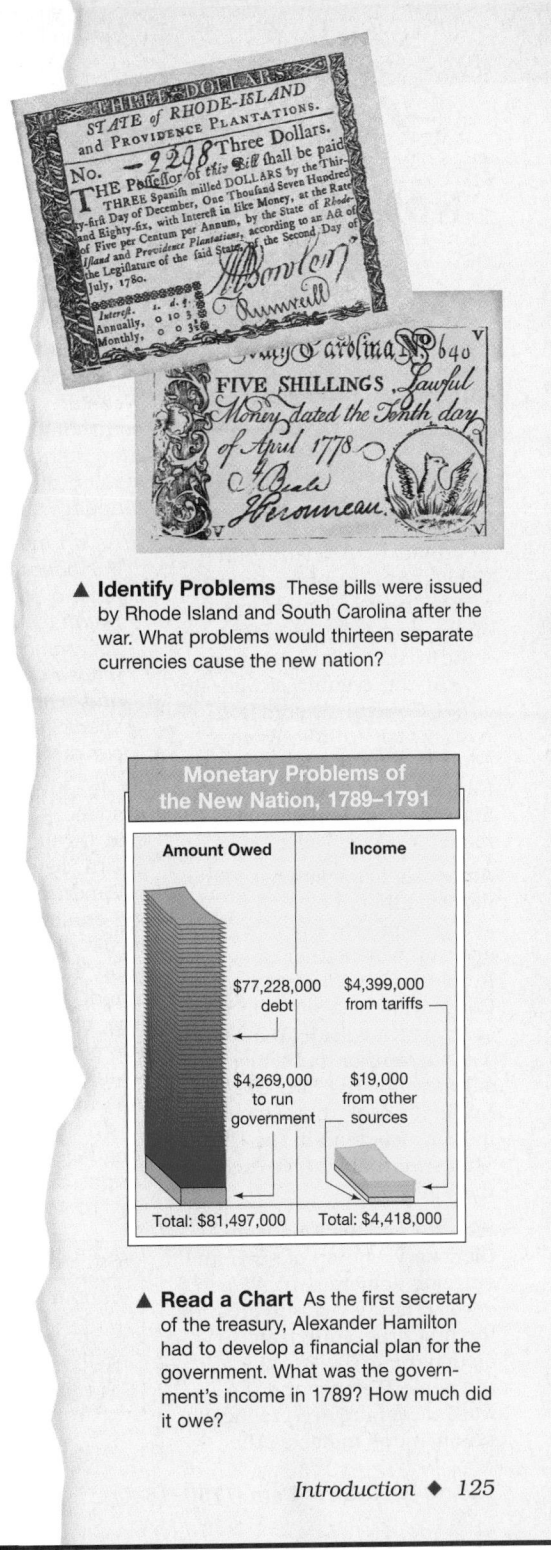

▲ **Identify Problems** These bills were issued by Rhode Island and South Carolina after the war. What problems would thirteen separate currencies cause the new nation?

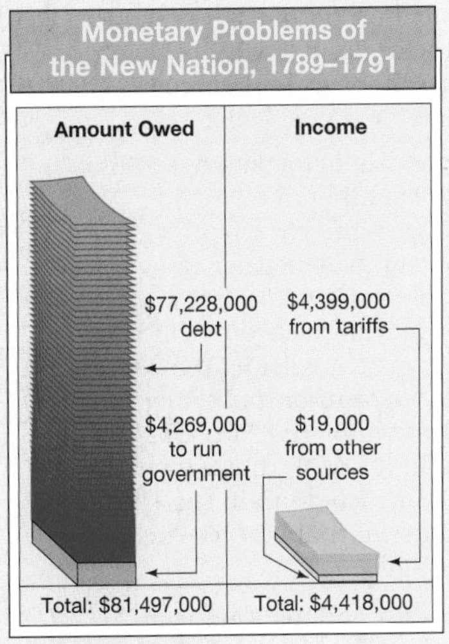

▲ **Read a Chart** As the first secretary of the treasury, Alexander Hamilton had to develop a financial plan for the government. What was the government's income in 1789? How much did it owe?

Literature of the Period

Comprehension Check ☑

1. In what way was the writing produced during this period different from that produced by the Puritans? *The Puritans were concerned with private soul searching, while this writing was public.*
2. Name three important public writers or speakers of this era. *Among the important public writers or speakers of the era were Patrick Henry, Thomas Paine, and Thomas Jefferson.*
3. What are two key political documents that were written by committee and that have stood the test of time? *The Declaration of Independence and the Constitution are two such documents.*
4. Outside the field of politics, what writer produced the best-known works? *Benjamin Franklin produced the best works outside the field of politics.*
5. As the eighteenth century came to a close, what types of literature were still largely untried by American authors? *American authors had not yet written important novels or plays.*

◆ Critical Thinking

1. Why do you think most of the important writing of this era was political? **[Infer]** *People were concerned with the relationship between the colonies and Great Britain. Their minds were on political matters.*
2. Why did many people cooperate in the writing of the Declaration of Independence and the Constitution? **[Draw Conclusions]** *Many opinions were required because these documents would have to represent the collective thought of the American people.*
3. Why do you think plays and novels lagged behind poetry and essays in the literature of the new country? **[Speculate]** *Reasonable answers include: American writers were timid about competing with great European writers in these genre; these types of literature require a more settled society and an established audience.*

Activities

1. **Graphic Organization of Ideas** Give students the Problem/Solution Organizer, p. 79, in the ***Writing and Language Transparencies.*** Have them use it to analyze the problem the colonists faced in deciding whether to rebel.
2. **Debate** Have students divide into teams, the Patriots and the Loyalists. These groups will debate this resolution: The colonies will be better off if they rebel against British control. Debaters should review The Story of the Times for arguments.
3. **Annotated Literary Map** Use the information in The Story of the Times as a source in creating an annotated literary map of America for the period 1750–1800. Link authors and works to their locations.
4. **Proposal** As an adviser to President Washington, write a proposal to encourage the arts in America. Use The Story of the Times to summarize what has already been accomplished. Then indicate what needs to be done and how the government can help.

◆ Critical Thinking

1. Why do you think Washington called on Noah Webster? **[Speculate]** *Washington may have been interested in Webster's attempt to "declare independence" for American English. This movement in linguistics paralleled the successful Revolution that he had just led.*
2. Why do you think it was necessary for Webster to travel across America? **[Infer]** *He had to travel in order to discover the new words that people in all regions were using.*
3. In what ways do Webster's efforts reflect a drive to standardize and a respect for innovation? **[Draw Conclusions]** *Webster wanted to standardize American spellings, but he also wanted to differentiate them from British spellings and to recognize the new words that were part of American English.*

▶Critical Viewing◀

1. Judging by the chart of British and American spellings, what can you deduce about the changes in spelling that Webster introduced? **[Deduce]** *Webster's changes seem to be simplifications and deletions. For example, he removes the k from ck endings and the u from ou combinations. Also he replaces ugh with w in plow.*

Answers to Activities

1. Help students understand the format of an *Oxford English Dictionary* entry so that they can trace the history of the word they choose. Point out to them, for instance, that under each numbered definition, there are dated examples of usage in chronological order.
2. (a) suspenders; (b) elevator; (c) truck; (d) gas; (e) television.
   Following are additional words that distinguish Americans from British citizens:

British	American
biscuit	cookie
bonnet	hood (of a car)
circus	traffic circle
dustbin	garbage can
pram	baby carriage
tin	can
windscreen	windshield

The Development of American English

NOAH WEBSTER AND THE AMERICAN LANGUAGE

by Richard Lederer

Travel back in time to May 1787 to the city of Philadelphia. It is thronged with important visitors, including Benjamin Franklin, Alexander Hamilton, James Madison, and the brightest of these luminaries—George Washington. They have come to attend the Constitutional Convention "in order to form a more perfect Union" of states that have recently won a surprising military victory.

On the evening of May 26, 1787, General Washington pays a visit to talk about education with a 28-year-old New Englander who is teaching school in Philadelphia. His name is Noah Webster.

America's Schoolmaster Why did Washington call on a young man scarcely half his age who was neither a Revolutionary War hero nor a Convention delegate? One reason was that Noah Webster was the author, publisher, and salesman of *The Blue-Backed Speller*, a book that was then more widely read in the United States than any other except the Bible.

Webster and the American Dictionary On top of such an amazing achievement, Webster devoted thirty years to creating the first great American dictionaries. The fact that the name *Webster* and the word *dictionary* are practically synonymous indicates the enduring brightness of Webster's reputation.

Throughout his life, Noah Webster was afire with the conviction that the United States should have its own version of the English language. In 1789, he wrote:

> *As an independent nation, our honor requires us to have a system of our own, in language as well as government. Great Britain, whose children we are and whose language we speak, should no longer be our standard.*

In putting this theory into practice, Noah Webster traveled throughout the East and South, listening to the speech of American people, and taking endless notes. He included in his dictionaries an array of shiny new American words, among them *applesauce, bullfrog, chowder, handy, hickory, succotash, tomahawk*—and *skunk*: "a quadruped remarkable for its smell."

In shaping the American language, Noah Webster also taught a new nation a new way to spell.

British spelling	Webster's spelling
honour, humour	honor, humor
musick, publick	music, public
centre, theatre	center, theater
plough	plow

Activities

1. Dictionary-makers are the biographers of words. Pick a word from the *Oxford English Dictionary* and write its "biography"—when the word was born and how it acquired new meanings over the course of its life.
2. Give the American equivalent of each of the following British words: (a) braces, (b) lift, (c) lorry, (d) petrol, (e) telly. Identify additional words that distinguish Americans from British citizens.

Cross-Curricular Connection: Social Studies

Noah Webster Today it is difficult for us to fully appreciate the influence that Noah Webster had on American English and American spelling. These statistics may help: In 1850, when the population of the country was about 23 million, Webster's famous "Blue-backed Speller" sold about one million copies annually.

In fact, Webster's schoolbooks sold so well that he was able to devote the latter part of his life to compiling dictionaries. *The American Dictionary of the English Language*, which appeared in 1828, achieved annual sales of about 300,000. In addition to providing excellent definitions of some 70,000 words, it helped teach Americans how to pronounce these words in a uniform way.

Ask students to explain what accounted for the popularity of Webster's books. *Early Americans may have felt a pride in embracing and learning about their version of English.*

PART 1

Voices for Freedom

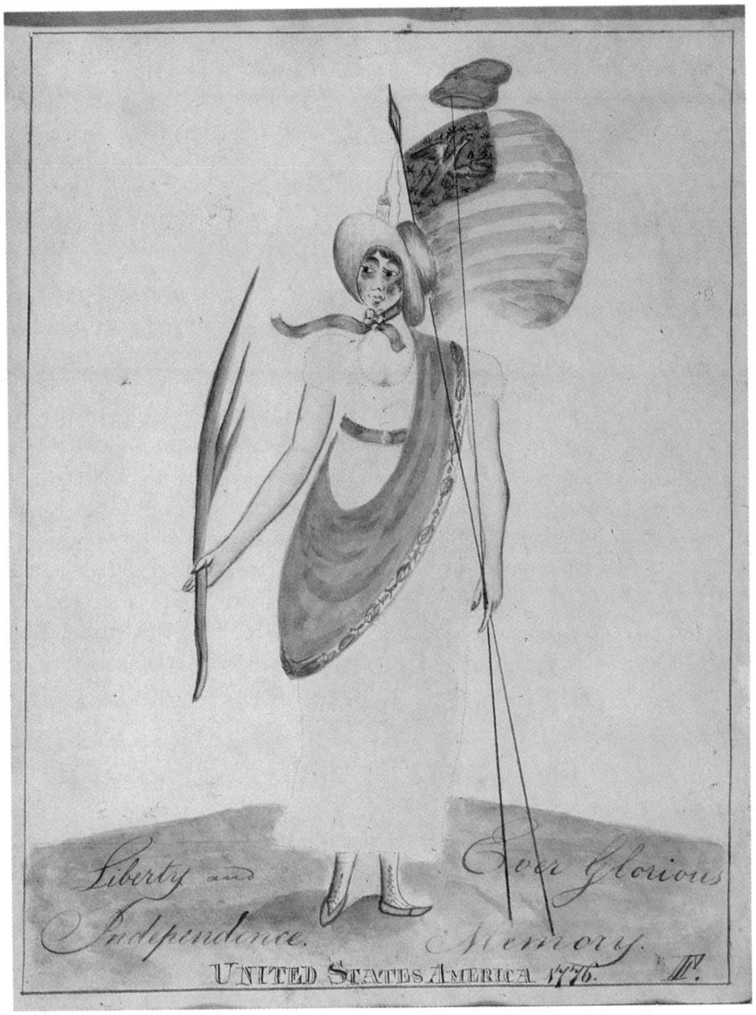

Miss Liberty, Abby Aldrich Rockefeller Folk Art Center, Williamsburg, Virginia

One-Minute Planning Guide

The selections in this section present some of colonial America's greatest revolutionary voices. The excerpt from *The Autobiography* presents the self-disciplined, practical wisdom of Benjamin Franklin. In *The Crisis, Number 1*, the voice of Thomas Paine rings with a call to fight for freedom. *The Declaration of Independence*, authored by Thomas Jefferson, contains some of the finest prose on the rights of man ever written. Two poems by Phillis Wheatley, an African American who spoke eloquently of the promise of America, follow. The first, "To His Excellency, General Washington," is a exhilarating tribute to Washington and the cause of freedom. The second, "An Hymn to the Evening," presents a calmer voice reflecting on the restorative powers of night and sleep. Part 1 ends with an excerpt from *Letter from Birmingham City Jail*, which contains the words of a more contemporary great voice of freedom, Martin Luther King, Jr.

Customize for *Varying Student Needs*

When assigning the selections in this part, keep in mind these factors:

from *The Autobiography*
- Less proficient readers may need help with unfamiliar vocabulary and and unusual sentence structure
- Logical/mathematic students may be intrigued by Franklin's approach to self-improvement

from *The Crisis, Number 1*
- This emotional call to arms will appeal to most students

"The Declaration of Independence"
- This inspirational document will appeal to most students
- Difficult vocabulary may cause problems for less proficient readers

"To His Excellency, General Washington"
- This moving tribute contains difficult vocabulary and sentence structure

"An Hymn to the Evening"
- The captivating rhymes of this poem will draw all readers in

from *Letter from Birmingham City Jail*
- Background on the civil-rights movement may be necessary for understanding

Humanities: Art

Miss Liberty.

Compared to fine art, folk art is produced by artists without formal training. It usually expresses the values of a group. Much folk art has a rough, awkward quality that more sophisticated artists admire and imitate.

As a composition, *Miss Liberty* expresses the ideals of the independent-minded colonists. The brown cap on the top one of the staffs carried by Miss Liberty is a farmer's cap, signifying that the movement for American independence was strongly supported by citizen farmers.

Have your students link the art to the focus of Part 1, Voices for Freedom, by answering the following questions:

1. What ideas about liberty does the artist express by personifying the quality as a young woman? *Sample response: The artist emphasizes the naturalness and innocence of liberty.*
2. What items does Miss Liberty carry? What significance might they have? *Sample response: She carries an American flag, identifying liberty with the new nation; she carries a farmer's cap and a plant, linking liberty with citizen farmers.*

Prepare and Engage

LESSON OBJECTIVES

1. **To develop vocabulary and word identification skills**
   - Latin Word Roots: *-vigil-*
   - Using the Word Bank: Analogies
   - Extending Word Study: Connotations
2. **To use a variety of reading strategies to comprehend nonfiction**
   - Connect Your Experience
   - Reading for Success: Strategies for Constructing Meaning
3. **To increase knowledge of other cultures and to connect common elements across cultures**
   - Idea Bank: Poster
4. **To express and support responses to the text**
   - Critical Thinking
   - Idea Bank: Advertisement
   - Idea Bank: Travel Brochure
5. **To analyze literary elements**
   - Literary Focus: Autobiography
6. **To read in order to research self-selected and assigned topics**
   - Idea Bank: Report
   - Idea Bank: Interview
   - Questions for Research
7. **To plan, prepare, organize, and present literary interpretations**
   - Idea Bank: Oral Interpretation
8. **To use recursive writing processes to write an observation**
   - Guided Writing Lesson
9. **To increase knowledge of the rules of grammar and usage**
   - Grammar and Style: Pronoun Case

Test Preparation

Reading Comprehension: Recognize Cause and Effect (ATE, p. 129)
The teaching tips and sample test item in this workshop support the instruction and practice in the unit workshop:
Reading Comprehension: Recognize Cause and Effect; Predict Outcomes (SE, p. 213)

Guide for Interpreting

Featured in AUTHORS IN DEPTH Series

Benjamin Franklin

(1706–1790)

No other colonial American more closely embodied the promise of America than Benjamin Franklin. Through hard work, dedication, and ingenuity, Franklin was able to rise out of poverty to become a wealthy, famous, and influential person. Although he never received a formal education, Franklin made important contributions in a variety of fields, including literature, journalism, science, diplomacy, education, and philosophy.

Early Years Franklin, one of seventeen children, was born in Boston. After leaving school at the age of ten, he spent two years working for his father before becoming an apprentice to his older brother, who was a printer. When he was seventeen, Franklin left Boston and traveled to Philadelphia, hoping to open his own print shop. Once he established himself as a printer, Franklin began producing a newspaper and an annual publication called *Poor Richard's Almanack,* which contained information, observations, and advice. The *Almanack*, published from 1732 through 1757, was very popular and earned Franklin a reputation as a talented writer.

Man of Science When Franklin was forty-two, he retired from the printing business to devote himself to science. He proved to be as successful a scientist as he had been a printer. Over the course of his lifetime, Franklin was responsible for inventing the lightning rod, bifocals, and a new type of stove; confirming the laws of electricity; and contributing to the scientific understanding of earthquakes and ocean currents. In spite of all these achievements, Franklin is best remembered for his career in politics.

Statesman and Diplomat Franklin played an important role in drafting the Declaration of Independence, enlisting French support during the Revolutionary War, negotiating a peace treaty with Britain, and drafting the United States Constitution. In his later years, he was ambassador first to England and then to France.

Even before Washington, Franklin was considered "the father of his country."

The Story Behind the Story

Franklin wrote the first section of *The Autobiography* in 1771 at the age of sixty-five. At the urging of friends, he wrote three more sections—the last shortly before his death—but succeeded only in bringing the account of his life to the years 1757 to 1759. Though never completed, his *Autobiography,* filled with his opinions and suggestions, provides not only a record of his achievements but also an understanding of his character. (For more on Franklin, see pp.166 and 186.)

◆ Background for Understanding

HISTORY: FRANKLIN IN PHILADELPHIA

Benjamin Franklin greatly influenced daily life in colonial Philadelphia. He helped establish the city's public library and fire department, as well as its first college. In addition, through his efforts Philadelphia became the first city in the colonies to have street lights.

Philadelphia was an important center of activity during the period leading up to the American Revolution. It was here that the Declaration of Independence, establishing the United States as an independent nation, was written and signed.

In Philadelphia today, you can still walk down cobblestone streets and visit historic sites. Independence Hall, where the Declaration of Independence was signed, the Liberty Bell, and the home of Betsy Ross are within walking distance for tourists and history enthusiasts.

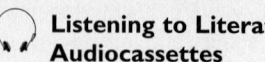

Prentice Hall Literature Program Resources

REINFORCE / RETEACH / EXTEND

Selection Support Pages
Build Vocabulary: Latin Word Roots: *-vigil-*, p. 36
Grammar and Style: Pronoun Case, p. 37
Reading Strategy: Constructing Meaning, pp. 38–39
Literary Focus: Autobiography, p. 40

Strategies for Diverse Student Needs, p. 18

Beyond Literature, p. 14

Formal Assessment Selection Test, pp. 38–40

Alternative Assessment, p. 8

Writing and Language Transparencies
Cause-and-Effect Organizer, p. 91

Resource Pro CD-ROM

Listening to Literature Audiocassettes

Literature CD-ROM

MODEL SELECTION

from The Autobiography

◆ Literature and Your Life

Connect Your Experience

Real-life stories can provide as much excitement as any fictional drama. It's not surprising, then, that bestseller lists frequently include the autobiographies of celebrities; we want to know how people have achieved fame and dealt with adversity. Autobiographies of historical figures, such as Franklin, can be equally gripping, allowing us a firsthand look at events that have helped shape our world.

Journal Writing List the experiences you would choose to write about if you were preparing an autobiography.

Thematic Focus: Voices for Freedom

Beyond throwing out the British government, people living at the time of the American Revolution wanted to create a uniquely American way of life. In many ways, Franklin represents that new American. *The Autobiography* describes his desire to improve himself. He writes of this ambition to help others follow in his path.

◆ Build Vocabulary

Latin Word Roots: *-vigil-*

The word *vigilance,* used in *The Autobiography,* contains the Latin root *-vigil-,* which means, "the act or period of remaining awake so as to guard or observe something." The meaning of *-vigil-* can help you define *vigilance* as "watchfulness."

Word Bank

Preview this list of words from *The Autobiography*.

arduous
avarice
vigilance
disposition
foppery
felicity

◆ Grammar and Style

Pronoun Case

Pronouns are words that replace nouns. **Pronoun case** refers to the form that a pronoun takes to indicate its function in a sentence. **Subjective case** pronouns—such as *I, we, you, he, she, it,* and *they*—are used when the pronoun is the subject of the sentence. **Objective case** pronouns—such as *me, us, him, her, it* and *them*—are used when the pronoun receives the action of the verb (direct object) or serves as the object of a preposition. Look at this example:

subj. obj. of prep.
I always carried my little book with *me*.

◆ Literary Focus

Autobiography

Benjamin Franklin's *Autobiography* set the standard for what was then a new genre. An **autobiography** is a person's account of his or her life. Generally written in the first person, with the author speaking as "I," autobiographies present life events as the writer views them. In addition to providing inside details about the writer's life, autobiographies offer insights into the beliefs and perceptions of the author. Autobiographies also offer a glimpse of what it was like to live in the author's setting and time frame. Autobiographies often provide a view of historical events that you won't find in history books.

As you read, use an organizer like this one to note what the selection reveals about Franklin's life, his attitudes, and the period in which he lived.

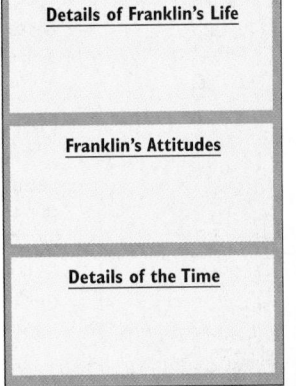

Details of Franklin's Life
Franklin's Attitudes
Details of the Time

Interest Grabber Write the following quotation of Franklin's on the chalkboard: "I wished to live without committing any fault at any time." Ask students to think about whether they could apply this quotation to everything they have said and done in the past twenty-four hours. Discuss reasons it would be difficult to never commit a fault at any time. Ask students to look for the difficulties Franklin may have faced in achieving this goal.

Customize for
Less Proficient Readers
Have students work in pairs to paraphrase the text. For a large group of students, make each pair responsible for only a portion of the text. Then put the paraphrases together.

Customize for
AP Students
Ask students to compare William Bennett's ten virtues (*Book of Virtues*) with Franklin's thirteen. Ask how their comparisons prove or disprove Franklin's observation that "different writers included more or fewer ideas under the same name."

Customize for
English Language Learners
Have students copy the first sentence from each of Franklin's paragraphs. With your help or the help of a native-speaking partner, have them write the "translation" of each sentence into simple language.

Customize for
Gifted/Talented Students
Reading Franklin's autobiography offers a special challenge to the reader. Franklin seems well-known, but the autobiography gives an account of his life that may be foreign to students. Though challenging, students should interpret Franklin on his own terms. One strategy to accomplish this is to allow one or more students to speak in Franklin's voice, defending his way of living.

Test Preparation Workshop

Reading Comprehension:
Cause and Effect In many standardized tests students will have to identify causes and effects. Use the following sample test item to demonstrate.

> I proposed to myself, for the sake of clearness, to use rather more names [for virtues] with fewer ideas annexed to each, than a few names with more ideas: and I included under thirteen names of virtues all that at that time occurred to me as necessary or desirable.

Why did Franklin name more virtues instead of fewer?

A He wanted to be clear.
B He wanted to measure the virtue of his friends.
C He thought thirteen was a lucky number.
D He decided there were only thirteen virtues.

Choices *B* and *C* do not contain any information from the passage. Students may be tempted by choice *D,* but should recognize that *A* is the best answer.

Reading for Success

The Reading for Success page in each unit presents a set of problem-solving procedures to help readers understand authors' words and ideas on multiple levels. Good readers develop a bank of strategies from which they can draw as needed.

When students are able to bring their own knowledge to a literary work, they build meaning by examining the author's ideas in light of their own experience. Unit 2 introduces strategies for constructing meaning. These strategies give readers a method for reading that will facilitate understanding of what they read.

Six strategies for constructing meaning are modeled with an excerpt from *The Autobiography* by Benjamin Franklin. Each green box shows an example of the thinking process involved in applying one of these strategies.

How to Use the Reading for Success Page

- Introduce the constructing meaning strategies, presenting each as a problem solving procedure. Be sure students understand what each strategy involves and under what circumstances to apply it.
- Before students read the selection, have them preview it, looking at the annotations in the green boxes that model the strategies.
- To reinforce these strategies after students have read the selection, have students do the Reading for Success pages in ***Selection Support***, pp. 38–39. These pages give students an opportunity to read another selection and practice constructing meaning strategies by writing their own annotations.

Reading for Success

Strategies for Constructing Meaning

When you read a work of literature, you look for what it means. Why did the author write it? What does he or she want to convey? What does the work mean to you? In looking for answers to questions like these, you construct the meaning that the work has for you.

Constructing meaning from a work of literature is a process in which you examine the author's ideas in the light of what you already know. There are many ways that you can construct meaning from a text. Here are a few strategies to direct you through the process:

Make inferences.

Writers don't always tell you everything. You need to "read between the lines" to arrive at ideas writers suggest but don't say. Often writers provide details and actions of a character from which you infer information about the author's message.

Draw conclusions.

A conclusion is a general statement that you can make based on details in the text. A series of inferences can lead you to a conclusion.

Recognize the writer's motivation or bias.

Be aware of the writer's views on an issue. A writer who is strongly inclined toward one position or another may not present an issue impartially. Consider the writer's motivation. Does the writer want you to believe as he or she does? This factor can affect the meaning that you take from a work.

Distinguish fact from opinion.

A fact is a statement that can be proved. An opinion is someone's belief, not necessarily supported by proof. An opinion carries more weight if it is supported by facts. Take care not to think that an opinion is a fact, and look to see whether a writer has supported his or her opinions.

Interpret the information.

- ▶ Explain to yourself the meaning or the significance of what the author is saying.
- ▶ Restate the author's message.

Use your knowledge of the historical time period.

The political climate and the intellectual trends of a specific time period are reflected in the writing that comes out of it. Apply the information from the introduction to this unit as you read the selections.

As you read the following excerpt from Benjamin Franklin's *Autobiography,* look at the notes along the sides. These notes demonstrate how to apply these strategies to a work of literature.

Reading Strategies: Support and Reinforcement

Appropriate Reading Strategies Students are given a reading strategy to apply in reading each selection. In those selections where constructing meaning may be challenging, students are given one of these constructing meaning strategies. In other selections, a strategy is suggested that is appropriate to the selection.

Reading Prompts To encourage application of the given reading strategy, there are occasional prompts, within green boxes, at appropriate and significant points.

In addition, there are red boxes prompting application of the Literary Focus concept and maroon boxes prompting students to connect with their lives.

Using the Boxed Annotations and Prompts The material in the green, red, and maroon boxes along the sides of selections is intended to help students apply the literary element and the reading strategy and to make a connection with their lives.

You may use the boxed material in several ways:

- Have students pause when they come to a box and respond to its prompt before they continue reading.
- Urge students to read through the selection ignoring the boxes. After they have read the selection completely, they may go back and review the selection, responding to the prompts.

MODEL

from The Autobiography

Benjamin Franklin

It was about this time I conceived the bold and arduous project of arriving at moral perfection. I wished to live without committing any fault at any time; I would conquer all that either natural inclination, custom, or company might lead me into. As I knew, or thought I knew, what was right and wrong, I did not see why I might not always do the one
❶ and avoid the other. But I soon found I had undertaken a task of more difficulty than I had imagined. While my care was employed in guarding against one fault, I was often surprised by another; habit took the advantage of inattention; inclination was sometimes too strong for reason. I concluded, at length, that the mere speculative conviction that it was our interest to be completely virtuous was not sufficient to prevent our slipping; and that the contrary habits must be broken, and good ones acquired and established, before we can have any dependence on a steady, uniform rectitude of conduct. For this purpose I therefore contrived the following method.

> Franklin's **motivation** seems to be to impress readers with his good intentions and his diligent efforts.

> ❷ Franklin begins this paragraph by stating **factually** how he planned to achieve moral perfection. He concludes the paragraph with his **opinion** that virtue is not inborn but must be steadily worked at.

In the various enumerations of the moral virtues I had met with in my reading, I found the catalog more or less numerous, as different writers included more or fewer ideas under the same name. Temperance, for example, was by some confined to eating and drinking, while by others it was extended to mean the moderating every other pleasure, appetite, inclination, or passion, bodily or mental, even to our avarice and ambition. I proposed to myself, for the sake of clearness, to use rather more names, with fewer ideas annexed to each, than a few names with more ideas; and I included under thirteen names of virtues all that at that time occurred to me as necessary or desirable, and annexed to each a short precept, which fully expressed the extent I gave to its meaning. ❹

Benjamin Franklin as a Young Printer in Philadelphia, The Granger Collection, New York

◀ **Critical Viewing** What does the expression on Franklin's face suggest about his personality? **[Infer]** ❸

◆ Build Vocabulary

arduous (är′ jo͞o wəs) *adj.*: Difficult

avarice (av′ ər is) *n.*: Greed

Humanities: Art

Benjamin Franklin as a Young Printer in Philadelphia.

While most people are familiar with a grandfatherly, spectacled image of Franklin, this engraving provides a rare glimpse of Benjamin Franklin in his youth. Here we see the young Franklin carrying the tools of his trade, that of a printer.

Young Franklin was a hard worker with purpose and self-discipline. After serving as a printer's apprentice in Boston under his brother James, Benjamin went off on his own to Philadelphia. By age twenty-four Franklin was publishing his own newspaper, *The Pennsylvania Gazette.*

Discuss with students the calm confidence that radiates from Franklin's posture and expression.

Use these questions for discussion:

1. What can we learn about Franklin from this picture? *We can learn of Franklin's occupation, personality traits, and the era in which he lived.*
2. How is this picture related to the selection it illustrates? *The picture shows a hard-working, self-disciplined Franklin, just the sort of person who might reach for moral perfection.*

Develop Understanding

One-Minute Insight

This excerpt shows Franklin's struggle to reach moral perfection, a subject he writes about with the fervent hope that others will imitate the effort. Naming thirteen virtues, Franklin focuses on one at a time, the perfection of one leading to ease of perfecting the next. As years pass, he devotes more time to attaining each virtue before advancing to the next. In telling his story, Franklin displays his fastidious nature, detailed mind, logic in addressing the virtues, daily organization, and harsh self-evaluations. Finally, he claims the result of his life-long struggle has been happiness.

Looking at Literature Videodisc Play Chapter 3 of the videodisc. This segment focuses on Franklin's ideas of moral perfection. Discuss with students the elements of autobiography. What can we learn from this kind of writing?

Chapter 3

◆ Critical Thinking

❶ **Interpret** Ask students: What problem does Franklin encounter in his search for moral perfection? *He immediately finds that his task is more difficult than he expected.*

Customize for
Less Proficient Readers
❷ Show students how to break long sentences, such as the one cited, into shorter units of thought by using punctuation—especially commas and semicolons—as a guide.

▶Critical Viewing◀

❸ **Infer** The expression suggests that Franklin is a calm, confident and serious individual.

◆ Critical Thinking

❹ **Classify** Help students see Franklin's difficulty in assigning the elements of a given virtue by asking students to do the same for another virtue, frugality. *Elements may include recycling; buying generic or sale items; walking or bicycling (not driving); having no television or other electronic luxuries.*

Literature CD-ROM To build background, use the CD-ROM *The History of American Literature:* Part 1, Disc 1, Feature 9. This feature focuses in part on Benjamin Franklin.

◆ Critical Thinking

❶ **Connect** Ask students: What additional virtues do you think would be appropriate for this list both in Franklin's lifetime and in contemporary times? *Additional virtues may include kindness, courage, patience, and generosity, among others.*

◆ Reading for Success

❷ **Interpret the Information** Ask students: Why does Franklin decide he needs a method for checking his progress? *Students may say he needs to track his daily struggle in order to see progress.*

Customize for *Visual/Spatial Learners*

❸ Ask these students to construct a likeness of a page from Franklin's little book. Be sure students use a red pencil or pen to make the page as authentic in appearance as possible.

Extending Word Study

Connotations Remind students that a word's connotation is the set of ideas associated with it, in addition to its explicit meaning. Use *frugality* as an example. It is a noun denoting a quality of thriftiness or economy. Frugality is generally thought to be a positive quality, but another word that denotes nearly the same thing—*stinginess*—is thought to have negative connotations. Have students discuss the positive, negative, or neutral connotations of other words in the selection.

These names of virtues, with their precepts, were:

1. TEMPERANCE Eat not to dullness; drink not to elevation.
2. SILENCE Speak not but what may benefit others or yourself; avoid trifling conversation.
3. ORDER Let all your things have their places; let each part of your business have its time.
4. RESOLUTION Resolve to perform what you ought; perform without fail what you resolve.
5. FRUGALITY Make no expense but to do good to others or yourself; i.e., waste nothing.
6. INDUSTRY Lose no time; be always employed in something useful; cut off all unnecessary actions.
7. SINCERITY Use no hurtful deceit; think innocently and justly, and, if you speak, speak accordingly.
8. JUSTICE Wrong none by doing injuries, or omitting the benefits that are your duty.
9. MODERATION Avoid extremes; forebear resenting injuries so much as you think they deserve.
10. CLEANLINESS Tolerate no uncleanliness in body, clothes, or habitation.
11. TRANQUILLITY Be not disturbed at trifles, or at accidents common or unavoidable.
12. CHASTITY
13. HUMILITY Imitate Jesus and Socrates.[1]

From this list, you can **infer** that Franklin is organized and diligent.

My intention being to acquire the *habitude* of all these virtues, I judged it would be well not to distract my attention by attempting the whole at once but to fix it on one of them at a time; and, when I should be master of that, then to proceed to another, and so on, till I should have gone through the thirteen; and, as the previous acquisition of some might facilitate the acquisition of certain others, I arranged them with that view, as they stand above. *Temperance* first, as it tends to procure that coolness and clearness of head, which is so necessary where constant vigilance was to be kept up, and guard maintained against the unremitting attraction of ancient habits and the force of perpetual temptations. This being acquired and established, *Silence* would be more easy; and my desire being to gain knowledge at the same time that I improved in virtue, and considering that in conversation it was obtained rather by the use of the ears than of the tongue, and therefore wishing to break a habit I was getting into of prattling, punning, and joking, which only made me acceptable to trifling company, I gave *Silence* the second place. This and the next, *Order,* I expected would allow me more time for attending to my project and my studies. *Resolution,* once become habitual, would keep me firm in my endeavors to obtain all the subsequent virtues; *Frugality* and *Industry* freeing me from my remaining debt and producing affluence and independence, would make more easy the practice of *Sincerity* and *Justice,* etc., etc. Conceiving then, that, agreeably to the advice of Pythagoras[2] in his *Golden Verses,* daily examination would be necessary, I contrived the following method for conducting that examination.

I made a little book, in which I allotted a page for each of the virtues. I ruled each page with red ink, so as to have seven columns, one for each day of the week, marking each column with a letter for the day. I crossed these columns with thirteen red lines, marking the beginning of each line with the first letter of one of the virtues, on which line and in its proper column I might mark, by a little black spot, every fault I found upon examination to have been committed respecting that virtue upon that day.

The details of Franklin's methodical approach lead you to **infer** that Franklin is seriously dedicated to his goal.

I determined to give a week's strict attention to each of the virtues successively. Thus, in the

1. **Socrates** (säk´ rə tēz´): Greek philosopher and teacher (470?–399 B.C.).

2. **Pythagoras** (pi thag´ ə rəs): Greek philosopher and mathematician who lived in the sixth century B.C.

◆ Build Vocabulary

vigilance (vij´ ə ləns) *n.*: Watchfulness
disposition (dis´ pə zish´ ən) *n.*: Management

Block Scheduling Strategies

Consider these suggestions to take advantage of extended class time:

- To build background, have students view Part 1, Disc 1, Feature 9 of *The History of American Literature* on the **Literature CD-ROM.** This segment focuses in part on Benjamin Franklin. Discuss with students Franklin's many achievements.
- Discuss the Literary Focus with the class. Ask what kinds of information autobiographies can provide for the reader.
- Have students apply each of the six Strategies for Constructing Meaning. You might use a jigsaw approach and divide the class into six small groups, assigning one strategy to a group. Ask each group to annotate a new selection. As a class, apply all six Strategies to this selection from *The Autobiography.*
- Create a team competition for answering the Critical Thinking questions (p. 136). Give groups time to prepare answers, but explain that any individual must be able to answer the team's question.
- Have students who complete the Report in the Writing section of the Idea Bank (p. 137) share their reports with the class.
- To help students choose an appropriate experience to write about for the Guided Writing Lesson on page 137, review with them the characteristics of an autobiography (see Literary Focus, p. 129).

first week, my great guard was to avoid every[3] the least offense against *Temperance*, leaving the other virtues to their ordinary chance, only marking every evening the faults of the day. Thus, if in the first week I could keep my first line, marked *T.* clear of spots, I supposed the habit of that virtue so much strengthened, and its opposite weakened, that I might venture extending my attention to include the next, and for the following week keep both lines clear of spots. Proceeding thus to the last, I could go through a course complete in thirteen weeks, and four courses in a year. And like him who, having a garden to weed, does not attempt to eradicate all the bad herbs at once, which would exceed his reach and his strength, but works on one of the beds at a time, and, having accomplished the first, proceeds to a second, (4) so I should have, I hoped, the encouraging pleasure of seeing on my pages the progress I made in virtue, by clearing successively my lines of their spots, till in the end, by a number of courses, I should be happy in viewing a clean book, after a thirteen weeks' daily examination. . . .

(5) The precept of *Order* requiring that *every part of my business should have its allotted time,* one page in my little book contained the following scheme of employment for the twenty-four hours of a natural day.

(6)

THE MORNING. *Question.* What good shall I do this day?	5 6 7	Rise, wash, and address *Powerful Goodness!* Contrive day's business, and take the resolution of the day; prosecute the present study, and breakfast.
	8 9 10 11	Work.
NOON.	12 1	Read, or overlook my accounts, and dine.
	2 3 4	Work.
EVENING. *Question.* What good have I done today?	6 7 8 9	Put things in their places. Supper. Music or diversion, or conversation. Examination of the day.
	10 11 12	
NIGHT.	1 2 3 4	Sleep.

3. **every:** Even.

I entered upon the execution of this plan for self-examination, and continued it with occasional intermissions for some time. I was surprised to find myself so much fuller of faults than I had imagined; but I had the satisfaction of seeing them diminish. To avoid the trouble of renewing now and then my little book, which, by scraping out the marks on the paper of old faults to make room for new ones in a new course, became full of holes, I transferred my tables and precepts to the ivory leaves of a memorandum book, on which the lines were drawn with red ink that made a durable stain, and on those lines I marked my faults with a black-lead pencil, which marks I could easily wipe out with a wet sponge. After a while I went through one course only in a year, and afterward only one in several years, till at length I omitted them entirely, being employed in voyages and business abroad, with a multiplicity of affairs that interfered; but I always carried my little book with me. (7)

Interpret this passage to mean that Franklin expects that he will eventually achieve the perfection he seeks.

My scheme of *Order* gave me the most trouble; and I found that, though it might be practicable where a man's business was such as to leave him the disposition of his time, that of a journeyman printer, for instance, it was not possible to be exactly observed by a master, who must mix with the world and often receive people of business at their own hours. (8) *Order*, too, with regard to places for things,

◆ Reading for Success

4 Interpret the Information Ask students what simile Franklin uses in this passage to illustrate his system of attending to each virtue. How does the simile help the reader to understand the system? *Franklin compares working on one virtue at a time to weeding one planting bed at a time. The simile helps the reader understand Franklin's system by comparing it to a well-known gardening procedure.*

◆ Reading for Success

5 Recognize the Writer's Purpose or Bias Ask students: What is Franklin's purpose in keeping the daily record? *Suggested response: He does so to make sure that he doesn't waste time or stray from his disciplined and purposeful way of living.*

◆ Literature and Your Life

6 Point out the importance of detailed journals in showing autobiographical details otherwise forgotten in the broad picture that remains after the passage of much time. World leaders often keep detailed journals or diaries that become invaluable resources in writing an autobiography or a biography.

◆ Critical Thinking

7 Interpret Ask students: Is Franklin's excuse for changing habits valid? Explain. *Students who say it is invalid may cite his earlier demands on himself; those who say it is valid may say years of practice make the effort easier.*

◆ Reading for Success

8 Use Your Knowledge of the Historical Time Period Point out that for little or no pay a journeyman printer worked with a master to learn the business.

Speaking, Listening, and Viewing Mini-Lesson

Interview

This mini-lesson supports the Speaking, Listening, and Viewing activity in the Idea Bank on page 137.

Introduce the Concept Point out that Franklin wrote for the benefit of his offspring. Have students discuss the idea of learning from older relatives. Ask them to share such a learning experience they or someone they know has had.

Develop Background Before students begin their interview plans, brainstorm with the class about topics interviewers should ask about, such as school, social events, world affairs, technology, work, and so on. As a class, develop a list of good interview questions. Remind students to set up interviews courteously, calling ahead, arranging a time, planning good use of the time, bringing pad and pen or recording equipment. Remind students to follow their planned list of questions but to be versatile enough to follow up on an interesting response to gain further detail.

Apply the Information When the interviews are complete, have students focus on one or two main ideas or lessons from each interview to share with the class, perhaps reinforcing the presentation with clips from recordings.

Assess the Outcome Have students evaluate their own and other's interviews using these criteria: Clarity of Organization, Adequacy of Summary, Communication of Main Idea or Lesson.

❶ **Clarification** Explain that a blacksmith, often called a "smith" or "smithy," used hand tools and a hot fire to shape iron items like horseshoes, gate latches, and ax heads. The wheel is a large sharpening stone used for smoothing or forming a cutting edge.

◆ Critical Thinking

❷ **Interpret** Ask students: How does the story of the speckled ax reflect a search for perfection? *Some students may say that people may tire of the on-going struggle toward perfection and so settle for less. Other students might say that although people may constantly strive for perfection, they will never reach it.*

▶Critical Viewing◀

❸ **Draw Conclusions** In the painting, students may note discipline in worshippers' attention, their head coverings, the separation of sexes, their row seats. Similarly, in *The Autobiography*, students may note Franklin shows discipline in his use of the little book and daily schedules.

◆ Grammar and Style

❹ **Pronoun Case** Point out that Franklin switches from first person to third. The subjective *I* becomes *he*; the objective *me* becomes *him*.

Reteach

Use an optical illusion to reteach historical context. Show students a simple illusion like the one below, point out that what they "see" is influenced by the surrounding circumstances. In the same way, what they "see" in a literary selection is influenced by the circumstances of the time during which it was written.

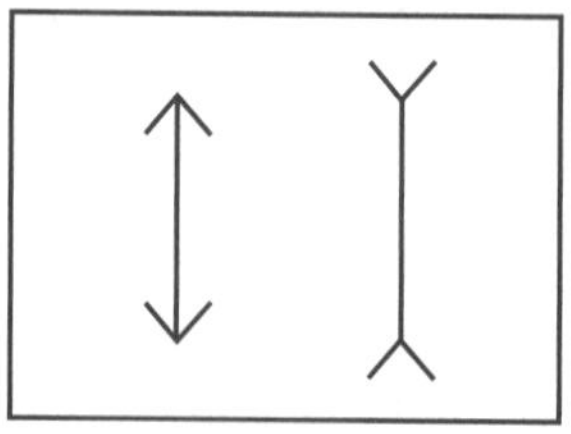

Quaker Meeting, British, fourth quarter 18th century or first quarter 19th century, Museum of Fine Arts, Boston

▲ **Critical Viewing** Relate this picture to *The Autobiography*. What does each suggest about discipline and order? **[Draw Conclusions]** ❸

papers, etc., I found extremely difficult to acquire. I had not been early accustomed to it, and, having an exceeding good memory, I was not so sensible of the inconvenience attending want of method. This article, therefore, cost me so much painful attention, and my faults in it vexed me so much, and I made so little progress in amendment, and had such frequent relapses, that I was almost ready to give up the attempt, and content myself with a faulty character in that respect, like the man
❶ who, in buying an ax of a smith, my neighbor,
desired to have the whole of its surface as
❷ bright as the edge. The smith consented to grind it bright for him if he would turn the wheel; he turned, while the smith pressed the broad face of the ax hard and heavily on the stone, which made the turning of it very fatiguing. The man came every now and then from the wheel to see how the work went on, and at length would take his ax as it was, without farther grinding. "No," said the smith, "turn on, turn on; we shall have it bright by and by; as yet, it is only speckled." "Yes," says the man, *"but I think I like a speckled ax best."* And I believe this may have been the case with many, who, having, for want of some such means as I employed, found the difficulty of obtaining good

From this information and your previous inferences, **draw the conclusion** that despite his efforts, Franklin failed to achieve perfection.

The **historical context** makes this anecdote about the ax appropriate. Axes were in common use at that time. ❶ ❷

◆ Build Vocabulary

foppery (fäp´ ər ē) *n.*: Foolishness

felicity (fə lis´ ə tē) *n.*: Happiness; bliss

Humanities: Art

Quaker Meeting, British, fourth quarter 18th century or first quarter 19th century, artist unknown.

This painting is based on a print of a Quaker meeting by Egbert von Heemkirk of London (c. 1670), now in the Quaker collection at Haverford College in Haverford, Pennsylvania. It depicts a sense of Quaker order and virtue.

Use these questions for discussion:

1. Choose a few of the figures in the painting. What do you suppose each is saying or thinking? *Some might be praying; others closing their eyes to listen more carefully to the speaker. Some may be thinking about the hard benches; some may be drifting off to sleep.*
2. What contributes to the severe mood of the painting? *The artist's use of browns, black, and white and the obvious lack of any bright colors; the dark background; the somber expressions; the parallel rows; and the shaded eyes of some characters all contribute to the mood.*

1 and breaking bad habits in other points of vice and virtue, have given up the struggle, and
2 concluded that *"a speckled ax was best"*; for something, that pretended to be reason, was every now and then suggesting to me that such extreme nicety as I exacted of myself might be a kind of foppery in morals, which, if it were known, would make me ridiculous; that a perfect character might be attended with the inconvenience of being envied and hated; and that a benevolent man should allow a few faults in himself, to keep his friends in countenance.

> Recognize Franklin's **opinion** that people detest success in others. He uses this belief as an excuse for not becoming "perfect."

In truth, I found myself incorrigible with respect to *Order;* and now I am grown old, and my memory bad, I feel very sensibly the want of it. But, on the whole, though I never arrived at the perfection I had been so ambitious of obtaining, but fell far short of it, yet I was, by the endeavor, a better and a happier man than I otherwise should have been if I had not attempted it; as those who aim at perfect writing by imitating the engraved copies, though they never reached the wished-for excellence of those copies, their hand is mended by the endeavor, and is tolerable while it continues fair and legible.

> **Interpret** this passage to mean that Franklin doesn't regret that he never achieved perfection, but he is a better person for trying.

It may be well my posterity should be informed that to this little artifice, with the blessing of God, their ancestor owed the constant felicity of his life, down to his seventy-ninth year in which this is written. 4 What reverses may attend the remainder is in the hand of Providence; but, if they arrive, the reflection on past happiness enjoyed ought to help his bearing them with more resignation. To *Temperance* he ascribes his long-continued health, and what is still left to him of a good constitution; to *Industry* and *Frugality,* the early easiness of his circumstances and acquisition of his fortune, with all that knowledge that enabled him to be a useful citizen, and obtained for him some degree of reputation among the learned; to *Sincerity* and *Justice,* the confidence of his country, and the honorable employs it conferred upon him; and to the joint influence of the whole mass of the virtues, even in the imperfect state he was able to acquire them, all that evenness of temper, and that cheerfulness in conversation, which makes his company still sought for, and agreeable even to his younger acquaintance. 5 I hope, therefore, that some of my descendants may follow the example and reap the benefit. 6

> Franklin admits to the **motivation** of wanting to look good in the eyes of his descendants. He also wants to show he produced some positive results in his life.

Guide for Responding

◆ Literature and Your Life

Reader's Response What do you think of Franklin's plan? Why?

Thematic Focus Autobiographies reflect the time period in which they are written. What elements of Franklin's *Autobiography* suggest that it was written at the dawn of American independence?

Questions for Research From *The Autobiography,* make a list of relevant questions about values in the northern colonies, such as these: Was it important to be on time? Was work or relaxation more important?

☑ Check Your Comprehension

1. In your own words, outline Franklin's plan to achieve moral perfection.
2. Explain why Franklin included *Silence* among his list of virtues.
3. Under the virtue of *Order,* Franklin lays out a basic daily schedule. What are the activities for which he provides time each day?
4. What aspects of Franklin's plan did not go as he expected?

Beyond the Selection

FURTHER READING

Other Works by Benjamin Franklin

The Autobiography of Benjamin Franklin and Other Writings, L. Jesse Lemisch, ed.

Benjamin Franklin's The Art of Virtue: His Formula for Successful Living, George L. Rogers, ed.

Letters to the Press, 1758–1775, Verner W. Crane, ed.

We suggest that you preview these works before recommending them to students.

INTERNET

You and your students can find more information on the Internet at the following sites. Please be aware, however, that the sites may have changed from the time we published this information.

See Franklin and His Printing Press at **http://sln.fi.edu/franklin/printer/printer.html**

For a time line of Franklin's life, go to **http://falcon.jmu.edu/~ramseyil/amlitcol.htm**

We *strongly recommend* that you preview the sites before you send the students to them.

◆ Reading for Success

5 Distinguish Fact From Opinion Ask students: What part of this passage is fact; what part is opinion? *Students may note that it is fact that he feels good about his struggle; it is opinion that it brings good health, wealth, and reputation.*

◆ Critical Thinking

6 Analyze Ask students: What is Franklin's final message to his readers? *He wants others to follow in his footsteps.*

Reinforce and Extend

Answers

◆ Literature and Your Life

Reader's Response Students should be able to support their answers with examples from the selection.

Thematic Focus Responses should touch upon the different style of writing. Franklin writes in a formal style, using long sentences and unfamiliar words. Students may feel that his concern with virtue is reflective of that time. They may feel that a modern autobiography would tend to focus more on one's flaws than on one's attempts to achieve "perfection."

☑ Check Your Comprehension

1. Franklin's plan is to devote one week to each of the thirteen virtues and to master the virtue in that time, thus completing his plan for moral perfection in thirteen weeks.
2. He feels you can learn more when you are listening than when you are talking.
3. Franklin allots himself only four hours of sleep. Other activities include meals, work, washing, reading, entertainment, reviewing accounts, cleaning up, and reviewing the day.
4. He finds he has many more flaws than he thought and that each time he eradicates one, he discovers another. He does not make as much progress with the virtue of *order* as he would like, and he finds that the whole process takes far longer than he expected.

Answers

◆ Critical Thinking

1. He includes the story mainly to explain that he comes to accept his inability to achieve perfection in the virtue of *order*. Readers may feel the story shows the broader point of coming to accept one's own limitations.
2. He comes to wonder if "it might be better to allow oneself to keep a few faults so that one doesn't end up . . . envied and hated . . . ."
3. While he never achieves moral perfection, he feels he does improve himself, and that the effort was well worth it. He believes he is a better and much happier person than he would otherwise have been, and attributes much of his success in life to this effort.
4. Analyzing behavior can lead to insights about how to best change behavior to achieve personal growth.
5. Organizers or daily planners help users stick to a schedule or complete tasks. Some people feel that a "to do" list allows them to focus on jobs to complete. Without an organizer, some feel they would forget certain items.

◆ Reading for Success

1. Possible response: One opinion that Franklin presents as a fact is that his virtues are responsible for his health and success.
2. Possible response: Franklin is a self-disciplined individual who adheres as best he can to ideals of behavior.
3. Suggested response: Franklin may have felt that his plan and the beginning of the new nation were in some way connected. For America to succeed, each individual American must succeed. Therefore, Americans should have a strong work ethic and adhere to good values.

Guide for Responding *(continued)*

◆ Critical Thinking

Interpret

1. Why does Franklin include the story about the man with the speckled ax? **[Analyze]**
2. How does Franklin's perspective about the importance of achieving moral perfection change over time? **[Compare and Contrast]**
3. What does Franklin see as the long-term benefits of his efforts to achieve moral perfection? **[Analyze Cause and Effect]**

Apply

4. How can analyzing behavior contribute to personal growth? **[Synthesize]**

Extend

5. Many people use daily planners organized like Franklin's daily activity sheet. What are the benefits of such a system? **[Career Link]**

◆ Reading for Success

Strategies for Constructing Meaning

Review the reading strategies and the notes showing how to construct meaning. Then apply them to answer the following:

1. Identify an opinion of Franklin's that he presents as a fact.
2. Draw a conclusion about Franklin from this segment of *The Autobiography.*
3. Explain in terms of the historical context why Franklin was interested in sharing his plan with future generations.

◆ Literary Focus

Autobiography

An **autobiography** is the story of a person's life written by that person. Because the author's attitudes, thoughts, and feelings color the self-portrayal, the autobiography is subjective. For example, Franklin's sense of morality is revealed in this excerpt from *The Autobiography.*

1. What does Franklin convey about his character?
2. How would this selection be different if it were written *about* Frankin rather than by him?

◆ Build Vocabulary

Using the Latin Root *-vigil-*

The Latin root *-vigil-* means "the act or period of remaining awake so as to guard or observe something." Use the definition of *-vigil-*, as well as the context, to write a definition of the italicized word in each sentence.

1. His mother said that she would be *vigilant* in her efforts to make sure he did his homework.
2. To restore safety, members of a *vigilante* group began patroling the neighborhood at night.

Using the Word Bank: Analogies

In your notebook, complete each of these analogies with a word from the Word Bank.

1. *Permission* is to *authorization* as ___?___ is to *greed.*
2. *Danger* is to *peril* as ___?___ is to *silliness.*
3. *Tragedy* is to *comedy* as ___?___ is to *negligence.*
4. *Order* is to *chaos* as ___?___ is to *sadness.*
5. *Exceptional* is to *common* as ___?___ is to *easy.*
6. *Error* is to *mistake* as ___?___ is to *arrangement.*

◆ Grammar and Style

Pronoun Case

The **subjective case** is used when the pronoun is the subject of the sentence or renames the subject after a linking verb. The **objective case** is used when the pronoun is a direct or indirect object of the verb or the object of a preposition.

Practice Choose the correct pronoun to complete each sentence.

1. At length a fresh difference arose between my brother and (I, me).
2. It was time for (we, us) to leave that place.
3. Though I did not give them any dissatisfaction, (they, them) dismissed me from my position.
4. (We, Us) two undertook to move to Boston.
5. Wilson and (he, him) took care to prevent my getting employment anywhere else.

◆ Literary Focus

1. He is disciplined and organized (although he finds *order* the most troublesome virtue); he is a serious, self-confident, optimistic person who believes in the possibility of self-improvement.
2. Suggested response: Another writer would not have been able to write as much about what Franklin was thinking at the time. Another writer might have pointed out contradictions between Franklin's aims and instances where he did not live up to these ideals. Another writer may have presented Franklin in a less positive light.

◆ Build Vocabulary

1. Watchful.
2. A group of people watching out for the public good; A volunteer that without authority assumes police powers, such as pursuing and punishing criminal suspects.

Using the Word Bank

1. avarice; 2. foppery
3. vigilance; 4. felicity
5. arduous; 6. disposition

◆ Grammar and Style

1. me 2. us 3. they
4. we 5. he

Grammar Reinforcement

For additional instruction and practice, use the lesson in the **Language Lab CD-ROM** on Pronoun Case and the practice pages on case (pp. 62–64) in the *Grammar Practice Book.*

Build Your Portfolio

Idea Bank

Writing

1. **Advertisement** Write an advertisement for Franklin's book, designed to appear in a Philadelphia newspaper of Franklin's time.

2. **Personal Improvement Plan** Think of a few areas in which you'd like to improve. Then consider what you can do to improve in these areas. Present your ideas in a written plan. **[Health Link]**

3. **Report** *The Autobiography* shows the world a certain side of Franklin's life. Find out about his political achievements. Compare what you learn from *The Autobiography* with Franklin's career as a statesman. Share your findings in a short paper. **[Social Studies Link]**

Speaking, Listening, and Viewing

4. **Oral Interpretation** Choose a short portion of the selection to read out loud. Practice it until you feel comfortable with the old-fashioned way it is written, then perform it for the class. **[Performing Arts Link]**

5. **Interview** Ask an older relative to tell you about his or her own life. Summarize the interview for your class, identifying the lessons someone else's life has taught you.

Researching and Representing

6. **Poster** Find out more about Franklin's accomplishments in the field of science. Create a poster that highlights some of his inventions. **[Science Link]**

7. **Travel Brochure** Create a brochure for tourists visiting Philadelphia. Highlight Franklin's accomplishments and include pictures of some of the relevant historic sites.

Online Activity www.phlit.phschool.com

Guided Writing Lesson

Autobiographical Account

Anyone can write an autobiography. With your activities, friendships, family and school events, successes, and failures, you have a vast amount of material from which to choose. Choose an important experience in your life and write an autobiographical account of the experience. Tell what made this moment memorable and what you've learned from it.

Writing Skills Focus: Show Cause and Effect

In your account, clearly show the effects of an experience on your life. Notice how Franklin deliberately anticipates the effect of each virtue:

Model From the Autobiography

Resolution, once become habitual, would keep me firm in my endeavors to obtain all the subsequent virtues; *Frugality* and *Industry,* freeing me from my remaining debt and producing affluence and independence, would make more easy the practice of *Sincerity* and *Justice,* etc. . . .

Prewriting Brainstorm for a list of details from the experience you want to describe. Note what happened, what you felt, and what you may have learned. Include as many specific details as you can.

Drafting Write your autobiographical account, incorporating those details that will make the event and its significance clear to readers. Remember to show the cause-and-effect relationship between the event or experience and your life. Use transition words such as *since, if/then,* and *consequently* to highlight the relationship for readers.

Revising When you revise, pay attention to cause-and-effect relationships. Whenever a transition would make cause and effect more obvious, add one.

✓ ASSESSMENT OPTIONS

Formal Assessment, Selection Test, pp. 38–40, and Assessment Resources Software. The selection test is designed so that it can be easily customized to the performance levels of your students.

Alternative Assessment, p. 8, includes options for less advanced students, more advanced students, visual/spatial learners, bodily/kinesthetic learners, and interpersonal learners.

PORTFOLIO ASSESSMENT
Use the following rubrics in the ***Alternative Assessment*** booklet to assess student writing:
Advertisement: Persuasion Rubric, p. 120
Personal Improvement Plan: How-to/Process Explanation Rubric, p. 115
Report: Comparison/Contrast Rubric, p. 118
Guided Writing Lesson: Narrative Based on Personal Experience Rubric, p. 111

Idea Bank

Customizing for *Performance Levels*
Following are suggestions for matching Idea Bank topics with your students' performance levels:
Less Advanced Students: 1
Average Students: 2, 4, 6
More Advanced Students: 3, 5, 7

Customizing for *Learning Modalities*
Following are suggestions for matching Idea Bank topics with your students' learning modalities:
Musical/Rhythmic: 4
Interpersonal: 5
Visual/Spatial: 6, 7

Guided Writing Lesson

For more instruction on prewriting, elaboration, and revision, see *Prentice Hall Writing and Grammar.*

Writing and Language Transparencies Have students use the Cause-and-Effect Organizer, p. 91, to help them show the effects that an experience had on their life.

Writers at Work Videodisc
Have students view the videodisc segment (Ch. 2) featuring novelist, poet, and essayist N. Scott Momaday who speaks about choosing a topic for a narrative. Ask students how discussing something with a person or listening to music can trigger a writing idea.

Play frames 11644 to 20980

Writing Lab CD-ROM
Have students complete the tutorial on Narration. Have students follow these steps:
1. Use the Purpose Profile to help focus on their intended purpose.
2. Use the Video tip on drafting.
3. Use the Self-Evaluation Checklist to aid revision.

Prepare and Engage

LESSON OBJECTIVES

1. To develop vocabulary and word identification skills
- Latin Word Roots: *-fid-*
- Using the Word Bank: True or False?
- Extending Word Study: Word Origins

2. To use a variety of reading strategies to comprehend nonfiction
- Connect Your Experience

3. To increase knowledge of other cultures and to connect common elements across cultures
- Connecting Themes Across Cultures (ATE)

4. To express and support responses to the text
- Critical Thinking
- Idea Bank: Letter
- Idea Bank: Précis
- Idea Bank: Newspaper Stories
- Idea Bank: Poster

5. To critically evaluate texts and the authority of sources
- Reading Strategy: Recognizing Charged Words
- Literary Focus: Persuasion

6. To read in order to research self-selected and assigned topics
- Idea Bank: Oral Presentation
- Idea Bank: Class Discussion on Paine

7. To plan, prepare, organize, and present literary interpretations
- Idea Bank: Dramatic Reading

8. To use recursive writing processes to write an observation
- Guided Writing Lesson

9. To increase knowledge of the rules of grammar and usage
- Grammar and Style: Parallelism

Test Preparation

Reading Comprehension: Recognize Cause and Effect (ATE, p. 139)
The teaching tips and sample test item in this workshop support the instruction and practice in the unit workshop:
Reading Comprehension: Recognizing Cause and Effect; Predict Outcomes (SE, p. 213)

Guide for Interpreting

Thomas Jefferson
(1743–1826)

When you look at all the things Thomas Jefferson accomplished in his lifetime, it seems there was virtually nothing that Jefferson couldn't do. Not only did he help our nation win its independence and serve as its third president, but he also founded the University of Virginia, helped establish the public school system, designed his own home, invented a type of elevator for sending food from floor to floor, and created the decimal system for American money. He was also a skilled violinist, an art enthusiast, and a brilliant writer.

Born into a wealthy Virginia family, Jefferson attended the College of William and Mary and went on to earn a law degree. While serving in the Virginia House of Burgesses, he became an outspoken defender of American rights. When conflict between the colonists and the British erupted into a revolution, Jefferson emerged as a leader in the effort to win independence.

When the war ended, Jefferson served as the American minister to France for several years. He then served as the nation's first secretary of state and second vice president before becoming president in 1801. While in office, Jefferson nearly doubled the size of the nation by authorizing the purchase of the Louisiana Territory from France.

Thomas Paine
(1737–1809)

Thomas Paine met Benjamin Franklin in London, and the introduction changed his life—and American history. Paine emigrated to the colonies from England in 1774. With a letter of introduction from Franklin, Paine began a career as a journalist. In January 1776, he published *Common Sense*, in which he argued that Americans must fight for independence. The pamphlet created a national mood for revolution.

Paine enlisted in the American army toward the end of 1776. At that time, the army had just suffered a crushing defeat by the British in New Jersey and had retreated into Pennsylvania. They were suffering from freezing weather, a shortage of provisions, and low morale. Paine was writing the first of a series of essays entitled *The American Crisis*. Washington ordered Paine's essay read to his troops before they crossed the Delaware to defeat the Hessians at the Battle of Trenton.

Paine's later works supported the French Revolution (*The Rights of Man*, 1792). His attack on organized religion (*The Age of Reason*, 1794) turned American public opinion against him, and when he died in 1809, he was a broken man. Years later, however, he was once again recognized as a hero of the Revolution.

◆ Background for Understanding

History: Jefferson and the Declaration

In 1776, Jefferson was chosen (with Franklin, Adams, and others) to write a declaration of the colonies' independence. The draft presented to the Second Continental Congress was largely Jefferson's work. To his disappointment, however, Congress made changes before approving the document. They dropped Jefferson's condemnation of the British for tolerating a corrupt Parliament, and they struck out a strong statement against slavery.

Despite these changes, what remained was plainly treasonous, and the penalty for treason was death. Considering that the odds were heavily stacked against the colonists at the time, it took tremendous bravery for members of Congress to sign the document and send it off to King George III. Had the colonists failed to win the war, all who had signed the Declaration would most likely have been executed.

Prentice Hall Literature Program Resources

REINFORCE / RETEACH / EXTEND

Selection Support Pages
Build Vocabulary: Latin Word Roots: *-fid-*, p. 41
Grammar and Style: Parallelism, p. 42
Reading Strategy: Charged Words, p. 43
Literary Focus: Persuasion, p. 44

Strategies for Diverse Student Needs, Simplify Long Sentences, p. 9

Beyond Literature Beyond the Classroom: Community Connection, p. 9

Formal Assessment, Selection Test, pp. 41–43; Assessment Resources Software

Alternative Assessment, p. 9

Writing and Language Transparencies Problem and Solution Organizer, p. 79

Resource Pro CD-ROM

Listening to Literature Audiocassettes

Literature CD-ROM

The Declaration of Independence
◆ *from* The Crisis, Number 1 ◆

◆ Literature and Your Life

Connect Your Experience

When shouts for freedom are transformed into military force, we recognize the signs of revolution. Today, we experience revolutions through images and reports in the news media. The best way to experience what our own Revolution was like, however, is to read documents that capture the spirit that enabled the colonists to win their independence.

Journal Writing Write about the concept of freedom. Are there different types of freedom?

Thematic Focus: Voices for Freedom

Jefferson and Paine were eloquent speakers for American freedom. How are their voices similar, and how are they distinct?

◆ Build Vocabulary

Latin Word Roots: *-fid-*

Paine and Jefferson use two related words—*infidel* and *perfidy*—in the selections that follow. These words contain the Latin root *-fid-*, which means "faith" or "trust." An *infidel* is a person without faith, and *perfidy* is a betrayal of trust.

Word Bank

Preview this list of words from the selections.

- unalienable
- usurpations
- perfidy
- redress
- magnanimity
- consanguinity
- acquiesce
- impious
- infidel

◆ Grammar and Style

Parallelism

Parallelism refers to the repeated use of phrases, clauses, or sentences that are similar in structure or meaning. Writers use this technique to emphasize important ideas and create rhythm. Jefferson uses parallelism to list the reasons that Americans declared their independence. Note Jefferson's rhythmic use of parallel verbs and direct objects in the following sentence:

He has *plundered our seas, ravaged our coasts, burned our towns,* and *destroyed the lives* of our people.

◆ Literary Focus

Persuasion

Persuasion is writing meant to convince readers to think or act in a certain way. A persuasive writer appeals to emotions or reason, offers opinions, and urges action.

Jefferson wrote to persuade the king that the colonists were justified in declaring their independence. Paine wrote to convince American citizens of the justness of revolution and to lift the spirits of American soldiers on the battlefield. Notice the techniques each writer uses to persuade readers to share his views.

◆ Reading Strategy

Recognizing Charged Words

As you read these documents, be sensitive to each writer's use of **charged words**—words with strong connotations likely to produce an emotional response. For example, Paine uses *tyranny*, a word meaning "oppressive power." The word may evoke feelings of fear or outrage, as well as images of cruel political leaders.

It's important to avoid being swayed by charged words. Look for thorough support—facts, statistics, quotations from authorities—to back up the words.

Interest Grabber Jefferson and Paine wrote inspirational words that roused colonial Americans to action. How could words help sustain the morale of a tattered army? Set the scene for students by having them imagine themselves as soldiers fighting in the Revolutionary War. Ask students to imagine the following situation. They are dressed in ragged clothes. It's winter; snow and ice surround them. A few have light jackets; only some have shoes. All are hungry, huddled in tents without floors. Badly defeated in the last battle, they think of home.

What spoken words could keep these desperate soldiers fighting for independence? Have students answer in their journals, writing in the first person as a Revolutionary War soldier. Discuss their responses. Then explain that they are about to read two pieces that inspired those soldiers.

Connecting Themes Across Cultures

When representatives from the thirteen colonies signed the Declaration of Independence, they were forging a path that other nations would soon follow. In Latin America, a campaign for independence from Spain took shape early in the nineteenth century, led by Simon Bolivar. His dream was to create a nation of united ex-colonies, a kind of United States of Central and South America.

Customize for
Less Proficient Readers

Glorious oratory inspires listeners. Help less proficient readers "hear" Paine's inspiring rhetoric by playing the audiocassette as they read silently. Then play the cassette a second time, asking students to read aloud quietly with the recording.

Listening to Literature Audiocassettes

Customize for
AP Students

Have these students examine Paine's comparisons, particularly those connecting a thief with the British. What effect do Paine's comparisons have?

Test Preparation Workshop

Reading Comprehension:
Recognize Cause and Effect Standardized tests require students to perceive the effects that are caused by certain actions, events, or ideas. To help students understand cause-and-effect relationships, have them reread pp. 140–141. Then ask:

Which of the following actions of the British king was NOT a cause of the American colonists' Declaration of Independence?

A His refusal to pass laws created by the colonists
B His dissolution of colonial houses of representatives
C His interference with the American justice system
D His personal visit to the thirteen colonies

Choices *A*, *B*, and *C* all contributed to the Americans' decision to declare independence from Britain. *D* is the correct choice, because it is NOT a stated cause of the revolution.

Develop Understanding

One-Minute Insight Perhaps the most influential document in American history, *The Declaration of Independence* provides the philosophy of the colonial revolutionaries and outlines their experiences with what they call a tyrannical king.

In this famous battlecry of freedom, Jefferson identifies what he calls "self-evident" truths, pointing out the equality of men and the tenuous contract of government. Then, in a list of the objectionable acts of King George III, arranged from least offensive to most, Jefferson outlines the reasons that the colonials are dissatisfied with their government. Jefferson reaches the reasoned conclusion that the colonists have tried every logical means of solving the problems with the British without results and therefore must become independent of Britain.

◆ Reading Strategy

1 Recognizing Charged Words Ask students: Why did Jefferson include phrases like "laws of nature" and "nature's God"? *Students may say that Jefferson implies that the separation from Britain was a natural, logical, and ethical matter.*

◆ Critical Thinking

2 Infer Ask students: What does Jefferson want readers to infer from this line? *He wants them to infer that there can be no argument about the obvious truth of the statements that follow.*

◆ Critical Thinking

3 Analyze Guide students to see that a generalization like this one would not be convincing on its own. In the paragraphs that follow, have students take note of how Jefferson supports this charge against the king by providing a list of grievances.

The Declaration of Independence

Thomas Jefferson

When in the course of human events, it becomes necessary for one people to dissolve the political bands which have connected them with another, and to assume among the powers of the earth, the separate and equal station to which the laws of nature and of nature's God entitle them, a decent respect to the opinions of mankind requires that they should declare the causes which impel them to the separation. 1

2 We hold these truths to be self-evident: that all men are created equal; that they are endowed by their Creator with certain unalienable rights; that among these are life, liberty and the pursuit of happiness; that to secure these rights, governments are instituted among men, deriving their just powers from the consent of the governed; that whenever any form of government becomes destructive of these ends, it is the right of the people to alter or to abolish it, and to institute new government, laying its foundation on such principles and organizing its powers in such form, as to them shall seem most likely to effect their safety and happiness. Prudence, indeed, will dictate that governments long established should not be changed for light and transient causes; and accordingly all experience hath shown, that mankind are more disposed to suffer while evils are sufferable than to right themselves by abolishing the forms to which they are accustomed. But when a long train of abuses and usurpations, pursuing invariably the same object, evinces a design to reduce them under absolute despotism,[1] it is their right, it is their duty, to throw off such government, and to provide new guards for their future security. Such has been the patient sufferance of these colonies; and such is now the necessity which constrains[2] them to alter their former systems of government. The history of the present king of Great Britain is a history of repeated injuries and usurpations, all having in direct object the establishment of an 3

1. **despotism** (des´ pə tiz əm) *n.*: Tyranny.
2. **constrains** *v.*: Forces.

◆ Build Vocabulary

unalienable (un āl´ yən ə bəl) *adj.*: Not to be taken away

usurpations (yo͞o´ sər pā´ shənz) *n.*: Unlawful seizures of rights or privileges

Block Scheduling Strategies

Consider these suggestions to take advantage of extended class time:

- To help students understand the historical significance of the selections, have them complete the journal activity on page 139. Discuss what personal sacrifice freedom is worth.
- Introduce the Grammar and Style lesson on parallelism, page 139, and the activity on page 146. Students can complete the Grammar and Style page in ***Selection Support,*** (p. 42).
- To prepare students for the tone of these selections, have them do the Reading Strategy activities on Recognizing Charged Words, (p. 146). Follow up with the Reading Strategy page in ***Selection Support,*** (p. 43).
- Encourage students to work in groups to complete the Dramatic Reading activity on page 147.
- To provide students with a tool for completing the Guided Writing Lesson (p. 147), discuss the power of connotation in persuasive writing.

The Declaration of Independence, John Trumbull, Yale University Art Gallery

4 ▲ **Critical Viewing** What is the mood of this painting? How does the mood suit the occasion? **[Relate]**

absolute tyranny over these states. To prove this, let facts be submitted to a candid world.

He has refused his assent to laws the most wholesome and necessary for the public good.

He has forbidden his governors to pass laws of immediate and pressing importance, unless suspended in their operation till his assent should be obtained; and when so suspended, he has utterly neglected to attend to them.

5 He has refused to pass other laws for the accommodation of large districts of people, unless those people would relinquish the right of representation in the legislature, a right inestimable to them and formidable to tyrants only.

He has called together legislative bodies at places unusual, uncomfortable, and distant from the depository of their public records, for the sole purpose of fatiguing them into compliance with his measures.

He has dissolved representative houses repeatedly, for opposing with manly firmness his invasions on the rights of the people.

He has refused for a long time after such dissolutions to cause others to be elected, whereby the legislative powers, incapable of annihilation, have returned to the people at large for their exercise, the state remaining in the mean time exposed to all the dangers of invasion from without, and convulsions within.

He has endeavored to prevent the population of these states; for that purpose obstructing the laws for naturalization of foreigners, refusing to pass others to encourage their migration hither, and raising the conditions of new appropriations of lands. 6

He has obstructed the administration of justice, by refusing his assent to laws for establishing judiciary powers.

He has made judges dependent on his will alone, for the tenure of their offices, and the

▶Critical Viewing◀

4 Relate The mood of this painting is dignified, stately, and triumphant. The mood certainly suits one of the most important occasions in world history, the signing of *The Declaration of Independence.* Note that the light comes from above, lighting faces and documents. The artist may be suggesting that, to the signers, *The Declaration of Independence* is a document that is the result of divine will.

◆Reading Strategy

5 Recognizing Charged Words Discuss with students the charged word in this passage, the definition of that word, and what that word implies about the king. *The charged word is tyrant, which means "a cruel or oppressive ruler." Jefferson uses tyrant to suggest that the king's behavior is not just politically unacceptable; it is inhuman.*

Literature CD-ROM To build background, use the CD-ROM *The History of American Literature:* Part 1, Disc 1, Feature 7. This video focuses in part on Thomas Jefferson and Thomas Paine.

◆Critical Thinking

6 Analyze Ask students to examine the paragraph structure Jefferson employs in this section of the document. What do they notice? *Students should notice that each paragraph begins with the parallel statement, "He has . . . ." Each paragraph states a different complaint that the colonist bring against the king.*

Humanities: Art

The Declaration of Independence, 1786, by John Trumbull.

The son of the governor of Connecticut, John Trumbull (1756–1843) was one of the first American aristocrats to paint seriously. Since Trumbull had lost the sight in one eye in an accident, the artist Benjamin West urged him to paint small pictures that his one eye could encompass.

This painting is only thirty inches wide, yet it contains forty-eight figures, grouped naturally and convincingly. Seated at the table is John Hancock; standing in front of him are Benjamin Franklin, Thomas Jefferson, Robert R. Livingston, Roger Sherman, and John Adams. Trumbull's placement of the heads of his subjects and the sweep of banners in the background add action and excitement to what might have been a very placid composition.

Use these questions for discussion:

1. How might a photograph of this event have differed from the artistic interpretation? *The lighting might be more generalized and made individual faces less identifiable.*
2. How does the composition of the painting add to the feeling that this is a historic moment? *Suggested response: The fact that so many figures are present in dignified dress and poses, focusing their attention on the dignitaries and documents at the front of the room, adds a historic feeling.*

▶Critical Viewing◀

❶ **Contrast** Stars on the 1781 flag and current flags represent the number of states. Today's flag has thirteen stripes to represent the thirteen original colonies.

❷ **Clarification** The colonists, under order of the king, had to provide lodging for the British armed forces.

◆ **Literary Focus**

❸ **Persuasion** One way to strengthen the impact of persuasion is to express consecutive key ideas that are increasingly more important. Ask students to review the text up to this point for a pattern of increasingly important ideas.

◆ **Literary Focus**

❹ **Persuasion** Students may say that by showing the king as an unfit ruler, Jefferson answers every argument readers may have for remaining loyal to Britain, thus using superior persuasive techniques.

◆ **Critical Thinking**

❺ **Infer** Ask students to characterize Jefferson's attitude toward Native Americans. *Jefferson holds Native Americans in low esteem, calling them "merciless Indian savages."*

Extending Word Study

Word Origins When Jefferson described King George III as behaving like a *tyrant*, he was using a word charged with 2,500 years of bloody history. Have students look up the meaning of *tyrant* in a dictionary and explain whether Jefferson's description of the King's behavior merited the charge of tyranny. You might extend the discussion by asking if any students can name the dinosaur that carries a "tyrannous" name. *Tyrannosaurus rex.*

Washington's headquarters standard flag, Courtesy of The Valley Forge Historical Society

▲ **Critical Viewing** Contrast this 1781 flag with today's American flag. What do the stars on this one and the current one represent? How does today's flag reflect the importance of the thirteen stars shown here? **[Contrast]** ❶

amount and payment of their salaries.

He has erected a multitude of new offices, and sent hither swarms of officers to harass our people and eat out their substance.

He has kept among us in times of peace standing armies without the consent of our legislatures.

He has affected to render the military independent of, and superior to, the civil power.

He has combined with others to subject us to a jurisdiction foreign to our constitution and unacknowledged by our laws, giving his assent to their acts of pretended legislation: ❷ for quartering large bodies of armed troops among us; for protecting them by a mock trial from punishment for any murders which they should commit on the inhabitants of these states; for cutting off our trade with all parts of the world; for imposing taxes on us without our consent; for depriving us, in many cases, of the benefits of trial by jury; for transporting us beyond seas to be tried for pretended offenses; for abolishing the free system of English laws in a neighboring province,[3] establishing therein an arbitrary government, and enlarging its boundaries, so as to render it at once an example and fit instrument for introducing the same absolute rule into these colonies; for taking away our charters, abolishing our most valuable laws, and altering fundamentally the forms of our governments; for suspending our own legislatures, and declaring themselves invested with power to legislate for us in all cases whatsoever.

He has abdicated government here, by declaring us out of his protection and waging war against us. ❸

He has plundered our seas, ravaged our coasts, burned our towns, and destroyed the lives of our people.

He is at this time transporting large armies of foreign mercenaries to complete the works of death, desolation, and tyranny, already begun with circumstances of cruelty and perfidy scarcely paralleled in the most barbarous ages, and totally unworthy the head of a civilized nation.

He has constrained our fellow citizens taken captive on the high seas to bear arms against their country, to become the executioners of their friends and brethren, or to fall themselves by their hands.

He has excited domestic insurrections amongst us, and has endeavored to bring on the inhabitants of our frontiers, the merciless Indian savages, whose known rule of warfare is an undistinguished destruction of all ages, sexes, and conditions. ❹ ❺

◆ **Literary Focus** How does this catalog of offenses support Jefferson's argument?

In every stage of these oppressions we have petitioned for redress in the most humble terms. Our repeated petitions have been answered only by repeated injury.

◆ **Build Vocabulary**

perfidy (pʉr´ fə dē) *n.*: Betrayal of trust

redress (ri dres´) *n.*: Compensation for a wrong done

magnanimity (mag´ nə nim´ ə tē) *n.*: Ability to rise above pettiness or meanness

consanguinity (kän´ saŋ gwin´ ə tē) *n.*: Kinship

acquiesce (ak´ wē es´) *v.*: Agree without protest

3. **neighboring province:** Quebec.

Beyond the Classroom

Career Connection

Speech Writing Jefferson was chosen to write *The Declaration of Independence* because of his broad understanding of political thought and his ability to write. Today, most high-ranking politicians and business people turn to others whose knowledge and writing skills can help them communicate more effectively. Beyond drafting and revising, speech writers do research, conduct interviews, and study policy. They prepare speeches for a variety of audiences and purposes. For example, since the first lady may deliver a speech on education to a group of students and address the same topic at a fundraising dinner, her speech writer will use language to suit each occasion.

Have students spend a week analyzing the "sound bites" they see in the news. Ask them to look for evidence of strong composition, such as a logical order of ideas, clear explanation of problems, and the use of evidence to support an argument. Ask students if they suspect the work of any behind-the-scenes writers.

A prince whose character is thus marked by every act which may define a tyrant is unfit to be the ruler of a free people.

6 Nor have we been wanting in attentions to our British brethren. We have warned them from time to time of attempts by their legislature to extend an unwarrantable jurisdiction over us. We have reminded them of the circumstances of our emigration and settlement here. We have appealed to their native justice and magnanimity and we have conjured[4] them by the ties of our common kindred to disavow these usurpations which would inevitably interrupt our connections and correspondence. They too have been deaf to the voice of justice and of consanguinity. We must therefore acquiesce in the necessity which denounces[5] our separation and hold them, as we hold the rest of mankind, enemies in war, in peace friends.

We, therefore, the representatives of the United States of America in general congress assembled, appealing to the Supreme Judge of the world for the rectitude of our intentions, do in the name and by authority of the good people of these colonies, solemnly publish and declare that these united colonies are and of right ought to be free and independent states; that they are absolved from all allegiance to the British Crown, and that all political connection between them and the state of Great Britain is and ought to be totally dissolved; and that as free and independent states, they have full power to levy war, conclude peace, contract alliances, establish commerce, and to do all other acts and things which independent states may of right do.

And for the support of this declaration, with a firm reliance on the protection of divine providence, we mutually pledge to each other our lives, our fortunes and our sacred honor.

4. **conjured** *v.*: Solemnly appealed to.
5. **denounces** *v.*: Here, announces.

Guide for Responding

◆ Literature and Your Life

Reader's Response What feelings does this document evoke? Why?

Thematic Focus What do you think is the difference between a "voice for freedom" and a "voice of treason"? Explain.

☑ Check Your Comprehension

1. What are the three "unalienable rights" listed in the second paragraph?
2. According to Jefferson, when should a government be abolished?
3. List three statements presented to support his claim that the king's objective is "the establishment of an absolute tyranny over these states."
4. (a) What does Jefferson claim the colonists have done at "every stage of these oppressions"? (b) How has the king responded to the colonists' actions?

◆ Critical Thinking

INTERPRET

1. What effect does Jefferson's list of grievances have on his argument? **[Analyze]**
2. Why does Jefferson focus his attack on King George III rather than on the British Parliament or people? **[Deduce]**
3. How is the eighteenth-century faith in reason reflected in the Declaration? **[Connect]**

APPLY

4. Considering Jefferson's views concerning the purpose of a government, which governments in today's world might he find objectionable? Why? **[Hypothesize]**

EXTEND

5. Could the Declaration of Independence be delivered effectively as a speech? Why or why not? **[Performing Arts Link]**

◆ Critical Thinking

6 Compare and Contrast
Discuss with students why Jefferson uses the word *brethren* rather than *brothers*. *The word brothers often refers to family members while the word brethren usually refers to people linked by a common cause or faith. The choice of words implies that the colonists no longer feel a strong bond with the English subjects living in Britain.*

Reinforce and Extend

Answers

◆ Literature and Your Life

Reader's Response Students may say they have feelings of patriotism or excitement.

Thematic Focus A "voice for freedom" addresses an unjust government; a "voice of treason" speaks against a just government.

☑ Check Your Comprehension

1. They are life, liberty and the pursuit of happiness.
2. When a government denies the "unalienable rights," it should be altered or abolished.
3. Among the facts that Jefferson presents are the king's refusal to assent to new laws, his dissolution of representative houses, and his refusal to hold elections.
4. (a) At every stage they have petitioned the king for redress. (b) Repeated petitions have been met "by repeated injury."

◆ Critical Thinking

1. The list of grievances adds both credibility and momentum.
2. Suggested response: The focus of Jefferson's argument is on tyranny and, therefore, on the tyrant.
3. The Declaration presents a well-reasoned argument consisting of a list of grievances that leads to the logical conclusion of independence.
4. Suggested response: He would abhor governments that do not uphold "unalienable" rights.
5. Suggested response: Because it is filled with forceful, precise language and rhetorical devices such as repetition and parallelism, the "Declaration of Independence" would make a stunning speech.

Research Skills Mini-Lesson

Using Multiple Sources

Introduce Tell students that when they conduct research for an activity like Class Discussion on Paine, in the Idea Bank, p. 147, they should use multiple sources to ensure that the information they get is balanced and full.

Develop Tom Paine was a leading opinion-maker in the years of the Revolutionary War. Being controversial, he had detractors, as well as many admirers. Therefore, if students plan to lead a discussion on Paine, they should be aware of the varied opinions that color the history of his career.

Apply Suggest that students consult some or all of the following sources:

- magazines that specialize in American history
- encyclopedias
- biographies of both Paine and his detractors
- Internet sources

Have students keep an annotated list of the sources they find.

Assess Evaluate students on the variety of sources they find for clarifying and deepening the class discussion suggested in the Idea Bank activity.

Develop Understanding

One-Minute Insight Paine's rhetoric, designed to build morale among the soldiers, promises that the severity of their situation makes triumph more glorious. He also vows that God would never desert those who fight for just causes. He denigrates the Tories, praises those who still stand, and calls upon all to put their shoulders to the wheel, focusing on the positive of what can still be done. He labels those who step aside as evil, cold-hearted, cowardly, and unprincipled and concludes with a story comparing the British position to that of a thief—and the punishment they both deserve.

❶ **Clarification** Paine wrote sixteen essays titled "Crisis," the last announcing that the Revolution was "gloriously and happily accomplished."

▶Critical Viewing◀

❷ **Connect** By placing the recruit centrally in strong light and the recruiter, elevated, also in the light, arms raised toward the heavens like a preacher, and all others in the dark, the artist conveys a mood of salvation. Fighting for independence took on a religious fervor.

❸ **Clarification** The quotation is from the Declaratory Act of Parliament (February, 1766) that asserted Britain's complete authority over the American colonies.

◆ Literary Focus

❹ **Persuasion** Ask students what persuasive appeal Paine uses in this passage. *He appeals to the reader's sense of morality.*

◆ Reading Strategy

❺ **Recognizing Charged Words** Paine's use of the charged word *thousands* creates a specific image of the large number of young men needed, especially when the population numbered only thousands.

Connecting to World Literature

To connect this selection to world literature, see p. 1182, "Nelson Mandela."

❶ *from* The Crisis, Number 1

Thomas Paine

Connections to World Literature, *page 1158*

Recruiting for the Continental Army, c. 1857–59, William T. Ranney, Munson-Williams-Proctor Institute, Museum of Art, Utica, New York

❷ ▲ **Critical Viewing** How does this image capture the patriotic fervor of Paine's essay? **[Connect]**

These are the times that try men's souls. The summer soldier and the sunshine patriot will in this crisis, shrink from the service of his country; but he that stands it NOW, deserves the love and thanks of man and woman. Tyranny, like hell, is not easily conquered; yet we have this consolation with us, that the harder the conflict, the more glorious the triumph. What we obtain too cheap, we esteem too lightly; 'tis dearness only that gives everything its value. Heaven knows how to put a proper price upon its goods; and it would be strange indeed, if so celestial an article as FREEDOM should not be highly rated. Britain, with an army to enforce her tyranny, has declared that ❸ she has a right (*not only to* TAX) but "to BIND *us in* ALL CASES WHATSOEVER," and if being *bound in that manner,* is not slavery, then is there not such a thing as slavery upon earth. Even the expression is impious, for so unlimited a power can belong only to God . . .

I have as little superstition in me as any man living, but my secret opinion has ever been, and still is, that God Almighty will not give up a people to military destruction, or leave them unsupportedly to perish, who have so earnestly and so repeatedly sought to avoid the calamities of war, by every decent method which wisdom could invent. Neither have I so much of the infidel in me, as to suppose that he has relinquished the government of the world, and given us up to the care of devils; and as I do not, I cannot see on what grounds the king of Britain can look up to heaven for help against us: a common murderer, a highwayman, or a housebreaker, has as good a pretense as he . . . ❹

I once felt all that kind of anger, which a man ought to feel, against the mean[1] principles that are held by the Tories:[2] a noted one, who kept a tavern at Amboy, was standing at his door, with as pretty a child in his hand, about eight or nine years old, as I ever saw, and after speaking his mind as freely as he thought was prudent, finished with this unfatherly expression, *"Well! give me peace in my day."* Not a man lives on the continent but fully believes that a separation must some time or other finally take place, and a generous parent should have said, *"If there must be trouble let it be in my day, that my child may have peace";* and this single reflection, well applied, is sufficient to awaken every man to duty. Not a place upon earth might be so happy as America. Her situation is remote from all the wrangling world, and she has nothing to do but to trade with them. A man can distinguish himself between temper and principle, and I am as confident, as I am that God governs the world, that America will never be happy till she gets clear of foreign dominion. Wars, without ceasing, will

1. **mean** *adj.*: Here, small-minded.
2. **Tories:** Colonists who remained loyal to Great Britain.

Humanities: Art

Recruiting for the Continental Army, c. 1857–1859, by William T. Ranney.

This painting was not done to illustrate Thomas Paine's words but rather has been chosen to accompany them here. Ranney has captured what must have been the energy of the moment through artistic dramatization and excitement. The image as a whole rings of patriotism. Since a recruit was paid less than seven dollars a month, from which the cost of his clothing was deducted, an appeal to patriotism was a chief recruiting strategy.

Use these questions for discussion:

1. Although this is not an action-packed picture, how does the artist convey the feeling of excitement that must have existed at such a moment? *The speaker's upraised arms, the focus of the painting on the act of signing, and the women and children looking on, all convey a great moment.*
2. Why is this painting an appropriate choice to illustrate Paine's essay? *The artist assumes the same near-religious fervor as Paine in depicting the noble act of signing to fight for independence.*

break out till that period arrives, and the continent must in the end be conqueror; for though the flame of liberty may sometimes cease to shine, the coal can never expire . . .

I turn with the warm ardor of a friend to those who have nobly stood, and are yet determined to stand the matter out: I call not upon a few, but upon all; not on *this* state or *that* state, but on *every* state; up and help us; lay your shoulders to the wheel; better have too much force than too little, when so great an object is at stake. Let it be told to the future world, that in the depth of winter, when nothing but hope and virtue could survive, that the city and the country, alarmed at one common danger, came forth to meet and to repulse it. Say not that
5 thousands are gone, turn out your tens of thousands; throw not the burden of the day upon Providence, but "*show your faith by your works*," that God may bless you. It matters not where you live, or what rank of life you hold, the evil or the blessing will reach you all. The far and the near, the home counties and the back, the rich and the poor, will suffer or rejoice alike. The heart that feels not now, is dead: the blood of his children will curse his cowardice, 6
who shrinks back at a time when a little might have saved the whole, and made *them* happy. (I love the man that can smile at trouble; that can gather strength from distress, and grow brave by reflection.) 'Tis the business of little minds to shrink; but he whose heart is firm, and whose conscience approves his conduct, will pursue his principles unto death. My own line of reasoning is to myself as straight and clear as a ray of light. Not all the treasures of the world, so far as I believe, could have induced me to support an offensive war, for I 7
think it murder; but if a thief breaks into my house, burns and destroys my property, and kills or threatens to kill me, or those that are in it, and to "*bind me in all cases whatsoever*," to his absolute will, am I to suffer it? What signifies it to me, whether he who does it is a king or a common man: my countryman, or not my countryman; whether it be done by an individual villain or an army of them? If we reason to the root of things we shall find no difference; neither can any just cause be assigned why we should punish in the one case and pardon in the other.

◆ Build Vocabulary

impious (im´ pē əs) *adj.*: Lacking reverence for God

infidel (in´ fə dəl) *n.*: A person who holds no religious belief

Guide for Responding

◆ *Literature and Your Life*

Reader's Response Which of Thomas Paine's images of the American Revolution do you find most stirring or memorable? Why?

Thematic Focus Do you find Paine's voice compelling? Do you think Paine is trustworthy as a reporter? Explain.

☑ Check Your Comprehension

1. Of what is Paine confident in the third paragraph?
2. What opinion of offensive wars does Paine express in the final paragraph?

◆ Critical Thinking

INTERPRET

1. Name two emotions to which the author appeals in this essay. **[Classify]**
2. (a) What is the main idea of the essay? (b) How does Paine develop his main idea? **[Support]**

APPLY

3. In your opinion, how persuasive is Paine's essay? Support your answer. **[Evaluate]**
4. How might a colonist who had remained loyal to the British react to Paine's argument? **[Hypothesize]**

Beyond the Selection

FURTHER READING

Other Works by Jefferson and Paine

The Complete Jefferson, Saul K. Padover, ed.

Common Sense, The Rights of Man, and Other Essential Writing of Thomas Paine

Other Works About Voices for Freedom

April Morning, Howard Fast

Paul Revere and the World He Lived In, Esther Forbes

We recommend that you preview these texts before assigning them to students.

INTERNET

You and your students can find more information on the Internet. We suggest the following site. Please be aware, however, that the site may have changed since we published this information.

For more on both Jefferson's life and works and Paine's works, go to the James Madison University Web site at **http://falcon.jmu.edu/~ramseyil/amlitfirst.htm.**

We *strongly recommend* that you preview the site before you send students to it.

◆ Literary Focus

❻ **Persuasion** Have students point out the charged words in this sentence and explain their persuasive impact. *The charged words are* dead, blood of his children, curse, cowardice, *and* shrinks. *Their persuasive impact is strong because no reader wants them attached to himself.*

◆ Critical Thinking

❼ **Infer** Ask students: What inference can you draw from this statement? *Paine wants to appear supportive of war only in extreme situations.*

Reinforce and Extend

Answers

◆ *Literature and Your Life*

Reader's Response Students' responses should reflect a detailed knowledge of the selection.

Thematic Connection Students will probably find Paine's voice compelling. Paine does, however, exaggerate at times, such as when he equates British rule with slavery.

☑ Check Your Comprehension

1. Paine is confident that America will never be happy until she is free of foreign dominion.
2. Paine likens offensive wars to murder.

◆ Critical Thinking

1. Possible response: He appeals to the emotions of fear and anger.
2. (a) The main idea of the essay is that the colonists are fighting for a just cause; thus they should endure the difficult times and not lose sight of their purpose. (b) Possible response: He uses aphorisms and the story of the tavern-keeper at Amboy.
3. Possible response: Paine's vivid descriptions of the American predicament and his comparisons between British behavior and the actions of common criminals make his argument very persuasive.
4. Possible response: He or she might have been angered by Paine's remarks.

Answers

◆ Reading Strategy

1. (a) *Liberty* suggests an ideal life, characterized by freedom.
   (b) *Justice* can be associated with fairness, freedom, and equality.
   (c) *Honor* evokes a sense of morality and dignity.
   (d) *Barbarous* suggests cruel and animalistic behavior.
2. Students should be able to explain the connotations of the words they choose. For example, the words *mankind, humanity,* and *human events* from the Declaration of Independence suggest universality not limited to the colonists. The words *destruction* and *perish,* from "The Crisis, Number 1," are stronger words than *end* or *death.*

◆ Build Vocabulary

1. *confident:* certain; self-assured
2. *fidelity:* faithful devotion to duty or vows
3. *confidential:* maintaining a trust

Using the Word Bank

1. True; 2. True; 3. True; 4. False
5. False; 6. False 7. False 8. False
9. False

◆ Literary Focus

1. The grievances become more serious. This serves to give the Declaration a momentum leading the reader to a single conclusion.
2. Possible response: Two of many examples of Paine's use of opinion include: "What we obtain too cheap, we esteem too lightly; 'tis dearness only that gives everything its value" and "Even the expression is impious, for so unlimited a power can belong only to God . . ."
3. Suggested response: Paine appeals more to readers' emotions. For example, he uses numerous charged words, such as *crisis, tyranny, hell, heaven, freedom,* and *slavery.* Also, his anecdote about the tavernkeeper at Amboy is designed to excite the emotions of readers interested in making a safe, free world for their children.
4. Students who prefer Jefferson may say that the logical list of grievances is very persuasive. Students who prefer Paine may say that it is more emotionally effective.

Guide for Responding (continued)

◆ Reading Strategy

RECOGNIZING CHARGED WORDS

These two political works are filled with **charged words**—words chosen to evoke emotional responses. In "The Crisis," for example, Paine uses the charged word *thief* to characterize the colonists' British caretakers. Had Paine used a kinder word, such as *custodian* or *supporters,* he would have tapped a different response in his audience.

1. What responses are evoked by these words from the Declaration of Independence?

a. liberty **b.** justice **c.** honor **d.** barbarous

2. Cite two other charged words in these selections and identify the connotations of each.

◆ Build Vocabulary

USING THE LATIN ROOT *-fid-*

Use the Latin root *-fid-,* meaning "faith" or "trust," to help you define each of the following words:

1. confident **2.** fidelity **3.** confidential

USING THE WORD BANK: True or False?

Indicate which of the following statements are true and which are false. Explain the reasoning behind each answer.

1. If a child *acquiesces* about being put to bed, she accepts her bedtime.
2. *Magnanimity* is a desirable trait in elected officials.
3. There is no need for *redress* if no wrong has been committed.
4. American citizens would not be within their rights to protest *usurpations* of their property.
5. Enemies at war feel *consanguinity* toward one another.
6. The woman felt grateful for the *perfidy* I had demonstrated toward her.
7. *Unalienable* rights must be agreed upon annually.
8. *Infidels* observe certain religious holidays.
9. A pastor's *impious* behavior would be celebrated by his parishioners.

◆ Literary Focus

PERSUASION

Both the Declaration of Independence and "The Crisis, Number 1" are examples of **persuasion**—writing that attempts to convince an audience to think or act in a certain way. In the Declaration of Independence, Jefferson presents a long list of grievances to support his argument. Paine, on the other hand, presents a variety of types of information—anecdotes, opinions, facts, and examples—to persuade his audience that fighting the British is just.

1. Do the charges in the Declaration of Independence get more serious as the list of grievances continues? What is the effect of this kind of organization?
2. Give two examples of Paine's use of opinions in "The Crisis."
3. In your opinion, does Paine appeal more to readers' emotions or reason in this essay? Explain.
4. Which selection do you find more persuasive? Why?

◆ Grammar and Style

PARALLELISM

Parallelism—like Lincoln's "Gettysburg Address" lines "*of the people, by the people, for the people*"—emphasizes ideas, creates rhythm, and makes writing forceful.

Parallelism is the use of the same grammatical structure to present several ideas of equal importance.

Practice Rewrite each sentence to correct errors in parallel structure.

1. Thomas Jefferson was patriotic, intelligent, imaginative, and he had courage.
2. Jefferson wrote the Declaration, designed his home at Monticello, and was one of the people who founded the University of Virginia.
3. Patrick Henry was a brilliant speaker; Thomas Jefferson was a gifted writer; and the talented military leader was George Washington.

Writing Application Write one or two paragraphs presenting your opinion on an issue about which you have strong feelings. Use parallelism to emphasize your key points.

◆ Grammar and Style

1. Thomas Jefferson was patriotic, intelligent, imaginative, and courageous.
2. Jefferson wrote the Declaration of Independence, designed his home at Monticello, and co-founded the University of Virginia.
3. Patrick Henry was a brilliant speaker; Thomas Jefferson was a gifted writer; George Washington was a talented military leader.

Grammar Reinforcement

For additional instruction and practice, use the lesson in the **Language Lab CD-ROM** on Strengthening Sentences and the practice pages on Faulty Parallelism (pp. 49–50) in the *Writer's Solution Grammar Practice Book.*

Reteach

To reteach persuasion, students create lists of persuasive techniques employed by Jefferson and Paine in these selections. For example, Jefferson cataloged specific ways in which King George violated American rights, and Paine used highly charged words in making his case. Both served well to persuade people to support the American cause.

Build Your Portfolio

Idea Bank

Writing

1. Letter In a December 1776 letter, George Washington wrote, "I am wearied to death. I think the game is pretty near up." As Washington, write a letter conveying your thoughts after hearing Paine's essay.

2. Précis A précis is a concise summary of essential points or statements. Write a précis of Jefferson's Declaration. **[Social Studies Link]**

3. Newspaper Stories As a colonial journalist, write an article recounting the signing of the Declaration. Then write the version of the story that might have appeared in a London paper following the receipt of the document.

Speaking, Listening, and Viewing

4. Oral Presentation The song "Yankee Doodle Dandy" helped spur American troops on to victory. Investigate the surprising origin of the song. Share your findings in an oral presentation.

5. Dramatic Reading With a small group of classmates, rehearse and prepare a dramatic reading of the Declaration of Independence. **[Performing Arts Link]**

Researching and Representing

6. Poster Design a Revolutionary War recruitment poster based on Paine's ideas. Like Paine, you might also deride "the summer soldier and the sunshine patriot." **[Art Link]**

7. Class Discussion on Paine Research Paine's early years. Prepare notes to help you lead a class discussion on Paine's contributions to the Revolutionary cause. **[Social Studies Link]**

Online Activity www.phlit.phschool.com

Guided Writing Lesson

A Proposal to the Principal

With a group of classmates, choose a problem or situation in your school that you think should be changed. Then draft a proposal to the principal explaining why the situation needs attention and how you think it should be corrected.

Writing Skills Focus: Use Forceful Language

Forceful words can make your argument more effective. Use language with positive connotations to present ideas you want your audience to accept; use language with negative connotations to present ideas you wish your audience to reject. Notice how Paine uses the negative power of words:

Model From the Essay

> . . . I cannot see on what grounds the king of Britain can look up to heaven for help against us: a common murderer, a highwayman, or a housebreaker, has as good a pretense as he . . .

Paine compares royalty to an average criminal—a comparison that would elicit a strong response. In your proposal, use words that can have such a powerful impact.

Prewriting List the reasons that the situation in your school should be changed. Write details—including facts, examples, explanations—supporting each reason.

Drafting Use terms such as *superior* and *wise* to reinforce the soundness of your proposal. Where appropriate, use words with negative connotations to present opposing points. Keep in mind, however, that you are writing for your principal.

Revising Carefully review your proposal and revise any statements that seem unreasonable. Check that you have offered evidence to support your argument.

Idea Bank

Customizing for *Performance Levels*
Following are suggestions for matching Idea Bank topics with your students' performance levels:
Less Advanced Students: 1, 5
Average Students: 3, 4, 6
More Advanced Students: 2, 7

Customizing for *Learning Modalities*
Following are suggestions for matching Idea Bank topics with your students' learning modalities:
Musical/Rhythmic: 4
Interpersonal: 5, 7
Visual/Spatial: 6

Guided Writing Lesson

For more instruction on prewriting, elaboration, and revision, see *Prentice Hall Writing and Grammar.*

Writing and Language Transparencies Have students use the Problem/ Solution Organizer, p. 79, to organize their prewriting details.

Have students view the videodisc segment (Ch. 4) featuring Gasby Greely, the Vice President of Communications for the National Urban League, speaking about persuasive writing. Ask students to summarize what Greely says about the significance of words in persuasive writing.

Play frames 33643 to 43235

Writing Lab CD-ROM
Have students complete the tutorial on Persuasion. Have students follow these steps:

1. Use the Interactive Instruction on choosing an organization.
2. Review the sections on audience and purpose. Draft on the computer.
3. Use the Word Bins to select persuasive words for revision.

ASSESSMENT OPTIONS

Formal Assessment, Selection Test, pp. 41–43. The selection test is designed so that it can be easily customized to the performance levels of your students.

Alternative Assessment, p. 9, includes options for less advanced students, more advanced students, visual/spatial learners, bodily/kinesthetic learners, and verbal/linguistic learners.

PORTFOLIO ASSESSMENT
Use the following rubrics in the ***Alternative Assessment*** booklet to assess student writing:
Letter: Expression Rubric, p. 109
Précis: Summary Rubric, p. 113
Newspaper Stories: Summary Rubric, p. 113
Guided Writing Lesson: Persuasion Rubric, p. 120

Prepare and Engage

LESSON OBJECTIVES

1. **To develop vocabulary and word identification skills**
   - Latin Prefixes: *re-*
   - Using the Word Bank: Antonyms
2. **To use a variety of reading strategies to comprehend a poem**
   - Connect Your Experience
   - Reading Strategy: Clarify Meaning
3. **To increase knowledge of other cultures and to connect common elements across cultures**
   - Background for Understanding
4. **To express and support responses to the text**
   - Critical Thinking
   - Idea Bank: Letter
   - Idea Bank: Diary Entry
   - Idea Bank: Poem or Essay
   - Idea Bank: Portrait
5. **To analyze literary elements**
   - Literary Focus: Personification
   - Idea Bank: Political Cartoons
6. **To read in order to research self-selected and assigned topics**
   - Idea Bank: Graphic Display on Washington
7. **To plan, prepare, organize, and present literary interpretations**
   - Idea Bank: Dramatic Reading
8. **To use recursive writing processes to write an inscription**
   - Guided Writing Lesson
9. **To increase knowledge of the rules of grammar and usage**
   - Grammar and Style: Subject and Verb Agreement

Test Preparation

Reading Comprehension: Predict Outcomes (ATE, p. 149) The teaching tips and sample test item in this workshop support the instruction and practice in the unit workshop:

Reading Comprehension: Recognize Cause and Effect; Predict Outcomes (SE, p. 213)

Guide for Interpreting

Featured in AUTHORS IN DEPTH Series

Phillis Wheatley
(1753?–1784)

Phillis Wheatley, an African slave known in Boston for her poetic gift, attracted great attention at an early age.

Wheatley was one of the finest American poets of her day—an amazing feat, considering that few women in the colonies and even fewer slaves could read or write.

Brought to America from West Africa on a slave ship when she was about eight years old, Phillis Wheatley was purchased by a Boston merchant named John Wheatley in 1761. The Wheatleys recognized the girl's high intelligence and taught her to read and write. She avidly read the Bible, Latin and Greek classics, and works by contemporary English poets. At age thirteen, she saw her first poem published.

Fame Abroad at an Early Age In 1772, Wheatley met several British aristocrats who admired her poetry and helped her to publish *Poems on Various Subjects: Religious and Moral* in London in 1773. This text was probably the first book published by an African.

The Story Behind the Poem During the Revolutionary War, Wheatley wrote a poem addressed to the commander of the American forces, George Washington. In October 1775, Wheatley sent the poem to Washington. He responded:

> I thank you most sincerely for your polite notice of me in the elegant lines you enclosed; and however undeserving I may be of such encomium [high praise] and panegyric [tribute], the style and manner exhibit a striking proof of your poetical talents; in honor of which, and as a tribute justly due you, I would have published the poem, had I not been apprehensive that, while I only meant to give the world this new instance of your genius, I might have incurred the imputation of vanity. . . .

Slide From Glory Despite being freed by John Wheatley in 1773, Phillis Wheatley lived with hardship and sorrow as the years went on. Two of her children died in infancy, her husband was jailed for debt, and she fell into obscurity as a poet. After she died in poverty around the age of thirty, her *Poems on Various Subjects: Religious and Moral* finally found an American publisher.

◆ Background for Understanding

HISTORY: PHILLIS WHEATLEY'S EXAM

Getting a volume of verse published in 1773 was difficult for Phillis Wheatley: Publishers were skeptical that an African girl of eighteen was capable of writing such sophisticated poems. Consequently, Boston's leading political and intellectual lights—led by Governor Thomas Hutchinson—administered an oral examination to her. Apparently, Wheatley made impressive responses to each question, for her inquisitors eventually drafted a two-paragraph letter to the public stating, in part:

> We . . . assure the World, that the POEMS specified in the following Page, were (as we verily believe) written by PHILLIS, a young Negro Girl, who was but a few Years since, brought . . . from *Africa.*

This judgment was crucial in getting *Poems on Various Subjects: Religious and Moral* published in England. However, Boston publishers refused to print the work for thirteen years.

Prentice Hall Literature Program Resources

REINFORCE / RETEACH / EXTEND

Selection Support Pages
Build Vocabulary: Latin Prefixes: *re-*, p. 45
Grammar and Style: Subject and Verb Agreement, p. 46
Reading Strategy: Clarify Meaning, p. 47
Literary Focus: Personification, p. 48

Strategies for Diverse Student Needs, p. 10

Beyond Literature
Humanities: Art, p. 10

Formal Assessment, Selection Test, pp. 44–46

Alternative Assessment, p. 10

Writing and Language Transparencies
Branching Organizer, p. 67

Resource Pro CD-ROM

Listening to Literature Audiocassettes

Literature CD-ROM

To His Excellency, General Washington
◆ An Hymn to the Evening ◆

◆ Literature and Your Life

Connect Your Experience

A movie, a haircut, a suggestion—you may informally praise several things or people every day. You probably find colorful ways to explain why you admire a subject. At times you may express praise in a more formal way—in a song, essay, or poem—as Phillis Wheatley does in these poems.

Journal Writing Write a paragraph praising an unusual subject. Vividly convey why you find the subject praiseworthy.

Thematic Focus: Voices for Freedom

As the spirit of revolution spread, General Washington became a symbol of freedom. His image graced flags, teacups, and other items. Wheatley helped to forge Washington's fame.

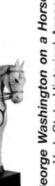

George Washington on a Horse, New York State Historical Association, Cooperstown

◆ Build Vocabulary

Latin Prefixes: *re-*

In Phillis Wheatley's poetry, you will find the words *refulgent* and *refluent.* The Latin prefix *re-*, which means "again" or "back," can help you define these words. Coming from the Latin word *refulgere,* meaning "to flash back," *refulgent* has come to mean "brilliant." The Latin word *fluere* means "to flow," and *refluent* can be defined as "flowing back."

Word Bank

Before you read, preview this list of words from the poems.

celestial
refulgent
propitious
refluent
pensive
placid
scepter

◆ Grammar and Style

Subject and Verb Agreement

Even in poetry, the rules of **subject-verb agreement** apply. Verbs become either singular or plural to agree with their subject in number. Singular subjects take singular verb forms; plural subjects take plural verb forms. Look at these lines from Wheatley's poems:

Singular: <u>She</u> (s) <u>flashes</u> (v) dreadful in refulgent arms.

Plural: And <u>nations</u> (s) <u>gaze</u> (v) at scenes before unknown!

◆ Literary Focus

Personification

When writers attribute human powers and characteristics to something that is not human, such as an object, an aspect of nature, or an idea, they're using **personification.**

For instance, in the line "Astonish'd ocean feels the wild uproar," the sea is personified with a human emotion (astonishment) and sensibility (feeling the wild uproar).

Eighteenth-century English poets often personified concepts as gods or goddesses. Similarly, Wheatley personifies America, England, and the west wind as gods or goddesses in these poems.

◆ Reading Strategy

Clarify Meaning

You may need to **clarify** the meaning of passages of complex prose or poetry, such as these poems, by figuring out grammatical structures and checking the definition of every word.

For example, this line from "To His Excellency, General Washington" may pose some difficulty:

> See mother earth her off-
> spring's fate bemoan . . .

By reordering the words and defining *offspring* and *bemoan,* you may unlock the meaning:

> See mother earth weep over
> the fate of her children.

Interest Grabber Understanding Wheatley's poems depends on recognizing personification. Write a list of common items on the board, such as rubber band, wind, table, cloud, car, newspaper, snow, rock, sparrow, leaf, and book. In small groups, ask students to provide sentences that give each item a human characteristic, such as "The *wind* gripped the tree and shook it violently." Put each group's sentences on the chalkboard. Compare the effect of various personifications. For instance, a leaf that dances in the wind takes on a different characteristic than one that hangs on tenaciously, shouldering the brutal buffeting of the wind.

Customize for
Less Proficient Readers
Have these students work in pairs to paraphrase the poem. Make sure they attack ideas sentence by sentence, using the reading strategy to clarify meaning. Have them share the paraphrases with the class.

Customize for
AP Students
Have these students generate a list of all of the examples of personification found in the poems. Use the list and the Interest Grabber activity as a basis for class discussion.

Customize for
English Language Learners
With a dictionary and a thesaurus, have students generate a glossary for the poems, listing any words they do not understand, along with simpler synonyms. Share the glossary with the class prior to discussion of the poems.

Customize for
Visual/Spatial Learners
Have these students find a picture or a statue of the goddess Columbia. You might remind them that a statue of Columbia sits atop the dome of the Capitol in Washington, D. C. Ask students to compare a sculptor's interpretation with Wheatley's.

Test Preparation Workshop

Reading Comprehension:
Predict Outcomes Many standardized tests measure students' ability to make accurate predictions based on information in a reading passage. Have students answer this sample test item:

> Brought to America from West Africa on a slave ship when she was about eight years old, Phillis Wheatley quickly learned to speak, read, and write English. She avidly read classic works as well as those by contemporary English poets. When publishers didn't believe she wrote the poems she claimed to have written, they gave her a test.
>
> Phillis most likely—
> **A** failed the test
> **B** passed the test
> **C** refused to take the test
> **D** was too nervous to take the test

Choices *A, C,* and *D* are possible outcomes, but they are not supported by textual evidence. Choice *B* is the most likely outcome based on what students learn in the text.

Develop Understanding

One-Minute Insight This poem glorifies the bravery and goodness of the revolutionary cause by personifying America as the goddess Columbia. Mother Earth sympathizes with her daughter's fight as she faces her enemies. The poem then praises George Washington as "first in peace and honors," famous for both his bravery and goodness, the perfect leader for a nation defended by heaven, a leader who has the moral support of other nations which hope America will win the war against Britain. The poem asks Washington to proceed, guided by the goddess; and Wheatley suggests that he will be rewarded with a crown, a mansion, and a golden throne.

Customize for *Gifted/Talented Students*
In her poem, Phillis Wheatley personifies things in nature, such as the ocean, autumn, and mother earth. Have students choose an object or idea of their own to personify. It might be something in nature or an idea like freedom. Encourage students to communicate their personification in performance or in art.

❶ **Clarification** Point out to students that the olive branch is a symbol of peace and the laurel, a symbol of victory.

◆ Literary Focus

❷ **Personification** Ask students: How are heaven, the ocean, and autumn personified? *Heaven has a "fair face"; the ocean is "astonished" by the wind's "wild uproar"; autumn has a "golden reign."*

▶Critical Viewing◀

❸ **Interpret** Students may note that Columbia holds the British crown beneath her foot while she places the laurel wreath, a symbol of victory, on Washington's head. This suggests Washington's leadership in the colonists' victory over England.

To His Excellency, General Washington

Phillis Wheatley

Liberty and Washington, New York State Historical Association, Cooperstown

▲ **Critical Viewing** Noting the symbols of the Revolutionary conflict, explain the action of the painting. **[Interpret]** ❸

Celestial choir! enthron'd in realms of light,
  Columbia's[1] scenes of glorious toils I write.
While freedom's cause her anxious breast alarms,
She flashes dreadful in refulgent arms.
See mother earth her offspring's fate bemoan,
And nations gaze at scenes before unknown!
See the bright beams of heaven's revolving light
Involved in sorrows and the veil of night!
  The goddess comes, she moves divinely fair, ❶
Olive and laurel binds her golden hair:
Wherever shines this native of the skies,
Unnumber'd charms and recent graces rise.
  Muse![2] bow propitious while my pen relates
How pour her armies through a thousand gates,
As when Eolus[3] heaven's fair face deforms,
Enwrapp'd in tempest and a night of storms;
Astonish'd ocean feels the wild uproar, ❷
The refluent surges beat the sounding shore;
Or thick as leaves in Autumn's golden reign,
Such, and so many, moves the warrior's train.
In bright array they seek the work of war,

1. **Columbia:** America personified as a goddess.
2. **Muse:** A Greek goddess, in this case Erato, who is thought to inspire poets. She is one of nine muses presiding over literature, the arts, and the sciences.
3. **Eolus** (ē´ ə ləs): The Greek god of the winds.

Block Scheduling Strategies

Consider these suggestions to take advantage of extended class time:

- Build background by having students view Chapter 4 of the **Looking at Literature Videodisc,** which focuses on "To His Excellency, George Washington."
- Reinforce the Literary Focus of Personification by having students complete the Literary Focus page of ***Selection Support,*** p. 47.
- In cooperative groups, have students apply the Reading Strategy (p. 149) to the poems, clarifying sentences for understanding.
- Create a team competition for answering the Critical Thinking questions (pp. 151, 153). Give groups time to prepare answers, but explain that any individual must be able to answer the team's question.
- Before students begin the Guided Writing Lesson on page 155, let the class brainstorm for a list of historical figures.

Where high unfurl'd the ensign[4] waves in air.
Shall I to Washington their praise recite?
Enough thou know'st them in the fields of fight.
Thee, first in peace and honors,—we demand
The grace and glory of thy martial band.
Fam'd for thy valor, for thy virtues more,
Hear every tongue thy guardian aid implore!
One century scarce perform'd its destined round,
When Gallic[5] powers Columbia's fury found;
And so may you, whoever dares disgrace
The land of freedom's heaven-defended race! ❹
Fix'd are the eyes of nations on the scales,
For in their hopes Columbia's arm prevails.
Anon Britannia[6] droops the pensive head,
While round increase the rising hills of dead.
Ah! cruel blindness to Columbia's state!
Lament thy thirst of boundless power too late.
Proceed, great Chief, with virtue on thy side,
Thy ev'ry action let the goddess guide.
A crown, a mansion, and a throne that shine,
With gold unfading, WASHINGTON! be thine. ❺

4. **ensign** (en´ sin): Flag.
5. **Gallic** (gal´ ik): French. The colonists, led by Washington, defeated the French in the French and Indian War (1754–1763).
6. **Britannia:** England.

◆ Build Vocabulary

celestial (sə les´ chəl) *adj.*: Of the heavens

refulgent (ri ful´ jənt) *adj.*: Radiant; shining

propitious (prō pish´ əs) *adj.*: Favorably inclined or disposed

refluent (ref´ lo͞o ənt) *adj.*: Flowing back

pensive (pen´ siv) *adj.*: Thinking deeply or seriously

Guide for Responding

◆ Literature and Your Life

Reader's Response Do you think that Columbia and General Washington are worthy subjects of the poet's praise? Why or why not?

Thematic Focus In your opinion, is there a contradiction between freedom and war? Explain your answer.

☑ Check Your Comprehension

1. To whom is the poem addressed?
2. Whom does the speaker praise?
3. Which two nations does the speaker describe as being in military opposition to America?

◆ Critical Thinking

INTERPRET

1. According to the poet, what is the nature of the relationship between God and the American cause? **[Analyze]**
2. What do the comparisons in lines 13–20 suggest? **[Interpret]**

EVALUATE

3. How successful is Wheatley in conveying the power and righteousness of American military forces? **[Assess]**

EXTEND

4. How might a historian's treatment of the British-American conflict differ from Wheatley's treatment of the same subject? **[Social Studies Link]**

Humanities: Art

Liberty and Washington

This folk art image glorifies Washington in many of the same ways as Wheatley's poem does.

Many folk artists may have thought of themselves as craftspeople and not as artists and therefore never signed their works. Consequently, although the folk art of earlier centuries remains, the names of the artists are lost forever. Only a few folk artists from earlier times are well known: those who developed a distinct style or were very prolific. Despite the anonymity of the creators, American folk art is widely collected and displayed in museums around the United States.

Use this question for discussion:
How do the words on the pedestal add to an interpretation of the art? *Citizens had already used the motto to praise Washington. Liberty's laurel wreath reinforces this praise.*

▶Critical Thinking◀

❹ **Interpret** Ask students to speculate about why Wheatley calls America's fight for freedom a "heaven-defended race." *Students may note the recurring attitude among many patriots that God is on the side of right.*

❺ **Clarification** "A crown, a mansion, and a throne" are biblical allusions to the rewards that await those who perform the will of God.

Reinforce and Extend

Answers

◆ Literature and Your Life

Reader's Response Suggested response: Columbia and Washington are worthy of the poet's praise because the army commander and the whole nation are fighting for something invaluable—political freedom.

Thematic Focus Suggested response: There is no real freedom in fighting and death; yet war can promote or allow future freedom. In this way, the two terms are not contradictory.

☑ Check Your Comprehension

1. It is addressed to General George Washington.
2. The speaker praises the goddess Columbia and General Washington.
3. The nations are France and Britain.

◆ Critical Thinking

1. Because the American colonists are fighting for a virtuous cause, they are supported by God's power.
2. America's armies are as mighty, valiant, and powerful as the forces of nature.
3. Wheatley's idealistic praise conveys quite successfully the power and righteousness of American military forces.
4. Students may note that a scholarly historian would probably rely almost entirely on facts and would attempt to avoid bias and the appearance of nationalism.

One-Minute Insight Wheatley directs her attention to the close of day by describing a sunset and the night's restorative powers. Beginning after sunrise, storms have shaken the earth. After the rain, however, the aroma of blossoms, the sound of water in streams and the songs of birds make music. By evening, the western sky is the most beautiful—a deep red. Grateful to God for the light, the narrator asks for a peaceful night of sleep and to awaken the next morning ready to strive for the pure life.

Literature CD-ROM To build background, use the CD-ROM *The History of American Literature,* Part 1, Disc 1, Feature 4. This segment focuses in part on Phillis Wheatley.

◆ Literary Focus

❶ Personification Ask students: How is the wind personified in these lines? *The wind breathes and exhales incense.*

Customize for
Less Proficient Readers
These students might more easily understand the meaning of this poem by making a chart in which they list the different parts of the day the poem mentions—the daylight hours,sunset, and night—as well as the corresponding line numbers of the poem.

Reteach

To help students clarify the meaning of difficult lines, use this strategy: Suggest that students write out any difficult lines and then use different colored markers to circle the subject, underline the verb, and double underscore the object of the verb. Afterward, suggest that they write the sentence again, reordering the words.

An Hymn to

Phillis Wheatley

Soon as the sun forsook the eastern main
The pealing thunder shook the heav'nly plain;
❶ Majestic grandeur! From the zephyr's[1] wing,
Exhales the incense of the blooming spring.
Soft purl[2] the streams, the birds renew their notes,
And through the air their mingled music floats.

Through all the heav'ns what beauteous dyes are spread!
But the west glories in the deepest red:
So may our breasts with ev'ry virtue glow,
The living temples of our God below!

1. **zephyr's** (zef´ ərz) *n.*: Belonging to the west wind.
2. **purl** (pʉrl) *v.*: To move in ripples or with a murmuring sound.

◆ Build Vocabulary

placid (plas´ id) *adj.*: Tranquil; calm; quiet

scepter (sep´ tər) *n.*: A rod or staff held by rulers as a symbol of sovereignty

Cultural Connection

Black Female Poets The publication of Phillis Wheatley's work merits special note for several reasons. First, she was female; few female authors anywhere had gained recognition by the eighteenth century. Second, she was African American; that group, too, had been denied literary recognition. Third, she was a slave; slaves generally could neither read nor write. Thus, Wheatley earned many "firsts." Nevertheless, for years she stood alone as a black female author before other black women joined the literary ranks.

Have students compile a list of other well-known black female poets. On the Internet, Wheatley's name will lead to Web sites with links to black female poets. See the Internet note in Beyond the Selection at right. You might have students research each of the poets and report their findings to the class.

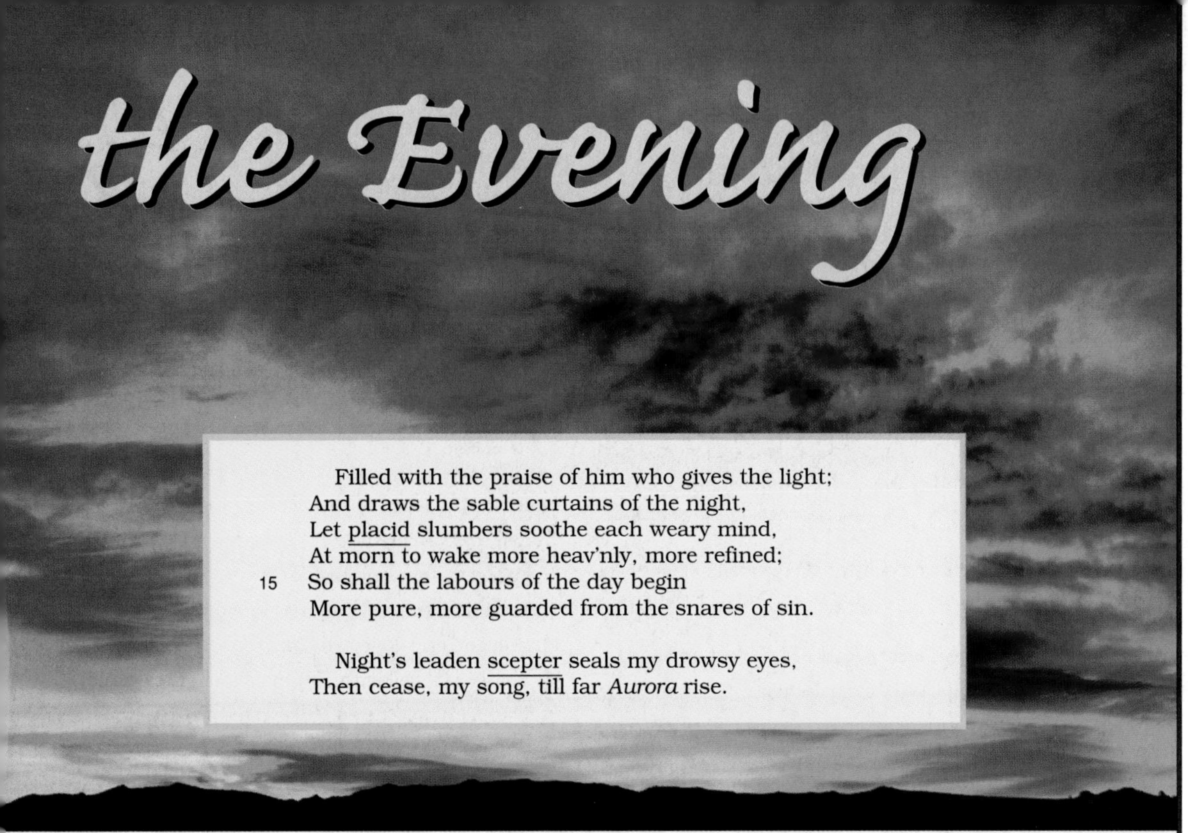

the Evening

Filled with the praise of him who gives the light;
And draws the sable curtains of the night,
Let placid slumbers soothe each weary mind,
At morn to wake more heav'nly, more refined;
So shall the labours of the day begin
More pure, more guarded from the snares of sin.

Night's leaden scepter seals my drowsy eyes,
Then cease, my song, till far *Aurora* rise.

Guide for Responding

◆ Literature and Your Life

Reader's Response Did you find this poem inspiring? Why or why not?

Thematic Focus How does this poem relate to the concept of freedom?

Group Discussion Phillis Wheatley's poem in praise of evening contains many descriptive details about the natural world. Would it be possible to praise evening in a poem containing descriptions of an urban setting? Why or why not?

☑ Check Your Comprehension

1. What happens in the first stanza?
2. According to the poet, what are "living temples of our God below"?
3. When are human beings "more pure"?

◆ Critical Thinking

INTERPRET

1. What does the poet find praiseworthy about the evening? **[Analyze]**
2. Given her comments in lines 14 and 16, why do you think Wheatley focuses her praise on evening rather than on morning? **[Infer]**

EVALUATE

3. In your view, how accurate is Wheatley's contrast of a person's state of mind at night and in the morning? **[Evaluate]**

COMPARE LITERARY WORKS

4. Wheatley writes in elevated and powerful language. Compare the two poems in this section. Are there similarities in her dramatic use of language? Without seeing her name, could you tell they are by the same poet? **[Compare and Contrast]**

Beyond the Selection

FURTHER READING

Other Works by Phillis Wheatley

Life and Works of Phillis Wheatley
Memoir and Poems of Phillis Wheatley

Other Works About Washington

Washington: The Indispensable Man, James Thomas Flexner
George Washington: A Biography, John R. Alden

We recommend that you review these texts before assigning them to students.

INTERNET

You and your students may find more information about Phillis Wheatley on the Internet. We suggest the following site. Please be aware, however, that sites may have changed from the time we published this information.

For more about Wheatley, go to **http://falcon.jmu.edu/~ramseyil/amlit.htm#J**

We *strongly recommend* that you preview the site before you send students to it.

▶Critical Thinking◀

❷ **Interpret** Ask students: What effect does Wheatley suggest sleep has on the mind? *She implies that sleep soothes the mind and makes it more pure.*

❸ **Clarification** Aurora is the Roman goddess of the dawn.

Reinforce and Extend

Answers

◆ **Literature and Your Life**

Reader's Response Students should support their opinions with citations from the poem.

Thematic Focus Possible response: Although the poet does not speak of freedom explicitly, this kind of meditation would probably not occur in a society in which people felt themselves to be not free.

☑ **Check Your Comprehension**

1. On a spring afternoon, a brief thunder shower occurs; the aroma of flowers is blown through the air by the wind; the sounds of streams and birds blend together.
2. People are the living temples.
3. According to the poet, human beings are most pure in the morning, after sleep.

◆ **Critical Thinking**

1. She finds the evening praiseworthy for its beautiful colors and for its ability to soothe and refresh the minds and spirits of human beings.
2. Suggested response: While people are "more pure" in the morning, it is evening and night that have the power to transform people's mental and spiritual well-being.
3. Students who agree with Wheatley may cite their own experiences with the refreshing powers of sleep. Those who disagree may explain they feel anxiety in the mornng about the day that lies ahead and calmer at night.
4. Students may say that the use of exclamation points and the formal, often inverted, sentence structure, as well as the elevated language make the poems similar enough to be the work of a single poet.

Answers

◆ Reading Strategy

1. The word *unnumber'd* means "numerous" and *graces* means "beauties." *Wherever this native of the skies shines, unnumber'd charms and recent graces rise. Muse! bow propitious while my pen relates how her armies pour through a thousand gates.*
2. Sample responses: "An Hymn" line 9: *Our breasts may glow with every virtue.* "To His Excellency. . ." line 2: *I write of Columbia's glorious work.*
3. The writing seems more flowery, more poetic, and less straightforward.

◆ Literary Focus

1. Columbia is characterized as a powerful, flashing, resplendent goddess.
2. (a) The goddess moves divinely, and her hair is gold and bound by olive and laurel. (b) They imply that America is beautiful and powerful.
3. Eolus personifies the unbeatable American forces.
4. Britain is personified as Britannia, a defeated warrior with a drooping head.
5. Wheatley personifies the sun, the wind, and dawn.

◆ Build Vocabulary

Using the Latin Prefix *re-*

1. c 2. d 3. a 4. b

Using the Word Bank: Analogies

1. b 2. a 3. c 4. a 5. c
6. b 7. a

◆ Grammar and Style

1. thunder shakes
2. powers find
3. breasts glow
4. slumbers soothe
5. hills increase

Grammar Reinforcement

For additional instruction and practice, use the lesson in the **Language Lab CD-ROM** on Agreement in Number and the practice pages on Subject and Verb Agreement (pp. 66–68) in the *Writer's Solution Grammar Practice Book.*

Guide for Responding *(continued)*

◆ Reading Strategy

Clarifying Meaning

Poetry often requires close reading. It's necessary to look at each passage very carefully and **clarify the meaning** of any sections that seem confusing or unclear. To do so, check the definition of any unfamiliar words, and rephrase passages that are written in unusual word orders. In these poems, Wheatley frequently inverts common sentence order by placing a verb before its subject. Rephrase the wording to interpret the meaning.

1. Clarify lines 11–14 of "To His Excellency, General Washington" by explaining the meaning of *unnumber'd* and *graces* and reordering the sentence parts.
2. Find two more examples of inverted subject and verb order in these poems and restate the poet's meaning.
3. What is the effect of inverted subject and verb order on the style of the poetry?

◆ Literary Focus

Personification

Personification is the attribution of human powers or qualities to something that is not human, such as an inanimate object, an aspect of nature, or an abstract idea. For centuries, writers have used personification to satisfy a desire to understand the world in human terms. For example, the ocean was personified as the god Poseidon by ancient Greeks and as the god Neptune by ancient Romans. Today, phrases like "a raging fire" are so common that we rarely think of them as personifications. In "To His Excellency, General Washington," Phillis Wheatley personifies America as the goddess Columbia.

1. In "To His Excellency, General Washington," how does the poet characterize Columbia?
2. (a) What details does she use in describing Columbia's physical appearance? (b) How do these details contribute to an overall impression of Columbia?
3. What does the god Eolus (line 15) personify?
4. How does Wheatley personify Britain?
5. In "An Hymn to the Evening," what nonhuman subjects does Wheatley personify?

◆ Build Vocabulary

Using the Latin Prefix *re-*

The common Latin prefix *re-* means "back" or "again." In your notebook, match each word in the left column with its definition in the right column.

1. revolve	**a.** repeat from memory
2. relate	**b.** make new again
3. recite	**c.** turn or roll again and again
4. renew	**d.** link back to; connect

Using the Word Bank: Antonyms

On your paper, write the word whose meaning is most nearly opposite that of the first word:

1. celestial: (a) heavenly, (b) earthbound, (c) windy
2. refulgent: (a) tarnished, (b) sparkling, (c) colorful
3. propitious: (a) evil, (b) lucky, (c) inopportune
4. refluent: (a) surging, (b) stagnant, (c) ebbing
5. pensive: (a) reflective, (b) mournful, (c) carefree
6. placid: (a) unfettered, (b) agitated, (c) generous
7. scepter: (a) trinket, (b) emblem, (c) wand

◆ Grammar and Style

Subject and Verb Agreement

A verb must agree in number with its subject. Singular subjects take **singular verbs**; plural subjects take **plural verbs.** In this example, the subject and verb are separated by other parts of the sentence:

Shall I (s) to Washington their praise recite (v)?

Practice In your notebook, copy the following lines. Underline the subject, and then choose the correct form of the verb in parentheses.

1. The thunder (shake, shakes) the heavenly plain.
2. When Gallic powers Columbia's fury (find, finds).
3. So may our breasts with every virtue (glow, glows).
4. Slumbers (soothe, soothes) each weary mind.
5. While round (increase, increases) the rising hills of dead.

Viewing and Representing Mini-Lesson

Graphic Display

This mini-lesson supports the Graphic Display on Washington in the Idea Bank on page 155.

Introduce the Concept Tell students to first research different aspects of Washington's life—his family, education, military career, and the presidency. Remind students to use a variety of resources in their research, including texts, photographs, illustrations, fine art, and the Internet.

Develop Background Divide students into small groups and have each choose one aspect of Washington's life to focus on. Suggest that they consider graphics such as: pictures of Washington on coins or bills, paintings or illustrations of him; maps of his military tactics or the location of battles; cartoons; posters; or documents from the Revolutionary War era.

Apply the Information Have groups evaluate their materials to determine what is relevant, interesting, important, and artistically pleasing.

Assess the Outcome Assess students' work on the quality of their research, the variety and relevance of the graphics they chose, and creativity of the display.

Build Your Portfolio

Idea Bank

Writing

1. **Letter** Imagine that Phillis Wheatley is still alive. Write a letter to her, asking questions about her work, giving your reactions to it, and praising her accomplishments.

2. **Diary Entry** Write the diary entry that Wheatley might have composed the night before her oral examination in the Boston courthouse.

3. **Poem or Essay** Develop a list of traits that express the ideals of today's society. In a poem or essay, describe the appearance and behavior of someone who personifies these traits.

Speaking, Listening, and Viewing

4. **Dramatic Reading** When read aloud, poems gain richness because sound devices—rhyme, meter, alliteration, assonance—become fully animated. Rehearse one of Wheatley's poems and present a dramatic reading for your classmates. **[Performing Arts Link]**

5. **Political Cartoons** During the Revolutionary period, people often expressed their views about leaders and issues through humor. Find some political cartoons from this time. Show them to your class, and compare them with political cartoons today. **[Social Studies Link]**

Researching and Representing

6. **Graphic Display on Washington** Research George Washington's military career, political life, or youth. Create a graphic display that highlights some important events in his life. **[Social Studies Link]**

7. **Portrait** Draw an image depicting today's America as a person. Compare and contrast your work with the illustration of Columbia. **[Art Link]**

Online Activity www.phlit.phschool.com

Guided Writing Lesson

Inscription for a Monument

Washington is one of the most revered men in American history. Choose a figure from history whom you admire. Imagine that you have been hired to write an inscription for a monument or statue honoring this individual. Speak volumes in very few words and convey the heroic qualities of this historical figure.

Writing Skills Focus: Persuasive Tone

To write an inscription that is honest and accurate, you'll need to choose language that emphasizes the subject's greatness. Use a **persuasive tone** and words with positive connotations. Look at this celebration of George Washington:

Model of Persuasive Tone

A man of supreme courage and skill, George Washington was an inspiring general, a true patriot, and a fearless leader—a conqueror who not only risked his life, but left a legacy of liberty for generations to savor.

By using positive adjectives such as *supreme* and *fearless*, as well as charged words like *conqueror* and *liberty*, the writer emphasizes qualities that communicate Washington's heroism.

Prewriting You may wish to research your chosen historical subject. Make a list of specific accomplishments and notable qualities—both personal and professional.

Drafting Use forceful nouns and adjectives that have positive connotations. For example, use *trailblazer* instead of *worker,* or *tireless* in place of *good.*

Revising Reread your inscription, looking for opportunities to be more economical and precise with your word choices. Check that you've included the figure's most important accomplishments.

Idea Bank

Customizing for *Performance Levels*
Following are suggestions for matching Idea Bank topics with your students' performance levels:
Less Advanced Students: 1
Average Students: 2, 4, 6, 7
More Advanced Students: 3, 5

Customizing for *Learning Modalities*
Following are suggestions for matching Idea Bank topics with your students' learning modalities:
Musical/Rhythmic: 4
Logical/Mathematical: 5, 6
Visual/Spatial: 7

Guided Writing Lesson

For more instruction on prewriting, elaboration, see *Prentice Hall Writing and Grammar*.

Writing and Language Transparencies Have students use the Branching Organizer, p. 67, to organize their subject's accomplishments and notable qualities.

Writing Lab CD-ROM
Have students complete the tutorial on Description. Have students follow these steps:
1. Use the Word Bins to choose words that enhance descriptive writing.
2. In the Drafting section, refer to the tips on focusing a main idea. Draft on the computer.
3. Use the Proofreading Checklist to aid revision.

ASSESSMENT OPTIONS

Formal Assessment, Selection Test, pp. 44–46, and Assessment Resources Software. The selection test is designed so that it can be easily customized to the performance levels of your students.

Alternative Assessment, p. 10, includes options for less advanced students, more advanced students, visual/spatial learners, musical/rhythmic learners, and intrapersonal learners.

PORTFOLIO ASSESSMENT
Use the following rubrics in the ***Alternative Assessment*** booklet to assess student writing:
Letter: Literary Analysis/Interpretation Rubric, p. 127
Diary Entry: Summary Rubric, p. 113
Poem or Essay: Description Rubric, p. 112
Guided Writing Lesson: Description Rubric, p. 112

LESSON OBJECTIVES

1. **To use a variety of reading strategies to comprehend a letter**
   - Read to Interpret (ATE)
2. **To increase knowledge of other cultures and to connect common elements across cultures**
   - Thematic Connection: Voices of Freedom
3. **To express and support responses to the text**
   - Critical Thinking
   - Idea Bank: Editorial
   - Idea Bank: Freedom Survey
4. **To analyze literary elements**
   - Idea Bank: Poem for a Prisoner
   - Idea Bank: Essay
5. **To read in order to research self-selected and assigned topics**
   - Idea Bank: Voices of Freedom Booklet
   - Idea Bank: Report on Dr. King
   - Research Skills Mini-Lesson (ATE)
6. **To plan, prepare, organize, and present literary interpretations**
   - Idea Bank: Oration
   - Speaking Listening, and Viewing Mini-Lesson (ATE)

Interest Grabber

Write this quotation on the chalkboard:

"We will win our freedom because the sacred heritage of our nation and the eternal will of God are embodied in our echoing demands."

Ask students to estimate when these words were written. Some students may say that the quotation is from a time in the distant past, perhaps during the Revolutionary War. Explain that the words were written by Martin Luther King, Jr., a civil-rights leader who sought the freedoms that were fought for by the American colonists so long ago. Ask students to find parallels, as they read the letter, between King's words and those of Americans during the Revolutionary War period.

CONNECTIONS TO TODAY'S WORLD

from Letter From Birmingham City Jail

Martin Luther King, Jr.

Thematic Connection

VOICES FOR FREEDOM

The voices who cried out for freedom during the Revolutionary period began a tradition that has carried on to this day. In recent years, a wide spectrum of Americans have raised insistent voices in the name of personal, social, and political freedoms. We have lobbied for women's rights, protested against wars, petitioned for election reform, and championed causes as varied as reduced taxes and illiteracy. Among the most eloquent of these voices for freedom was Martin Luther King, Jr.

TWENTIETH-CENTURY CALLS FOR FREEDOM

Martin Luther King, Jr., and other American civil rights leaders of the 1950's and 1960's shared similar ideas of freedom expressed by early Americans such as Paine, Jefferson, and Wheatley. In his sermons and speeches, King addressed some of the same themes as his Revolutionary forebears did—freedom, the fundamental importance of justice, and strategies for fighting oppression. Like Paine's, King's language was vivid; like Wheatley's, his words alluded to deities and heroes; and like Jefferson's, his voice called for boldness, wisdom, and morality.

Arrested in 1963 for protesting racial segregation in Birmingham, Alabama, King sat in jail and read a newspaper article in which eight white clergymen chastised him for "unwise and untimely" demonstrations. Without proper writing paper, King drafted a response—the "Letter From Birmingham City Jail"—in the cramped margins of that newspaper. King's impassioned words focus both protest and hope on his small audience of white peers. A few months later, King would lead the March on Washington. On this occasion, more than 200,000 Americans of all races would gather around the Lincoln Memorial and hear his voice ring out again for the causes of racial justice and freedom.

MARTIN LUTHER KING, JR. (1929–1968)

A charismatic Baptist minister and civil rights leader, Martin Luther King, Jr., struggled to bring African Americans into the political and economic mainstream of American life in the 1950's and 1960's. King drew inspiration from the Christian ideals of his father and grandfather, both of whom were also Baptist ministers.

Armed with the philosophy of Mohandas K. Gandhi, the Indian leader, Dr. King insisted that political and social freedoms were attainable through nonviolent actions. Starting in his native Atlanta and moving to Montgomery and Birmingham, Alabama, King led boycotts, marches, and sit-ins to protest segregation. He became a national figure, organizing the March on Washington and speaking out against discrimination. King stressed nonviolence; however, he became an American martyr for freedom when he was assassinated at the age of 39. His widow, Coretta Scott King, works to keep King's message and achievements alive.

Prentice Hall Literature Program Resources

REINFORCE / RETEACH / EXTEND

Selection Support Pages
Build Vocabulary, p. 49
Thematic Connection, p. 50

Formal Assessment, Selection Test, pp. 47–48; Assessment Resources Software

Resource Pro CD-ROM

Listening to Literature Audiocassettes

from

Letter From Birmingham City Jail

CONNECTIONS TO TODAY'S WORLD

Dr. Martin Luther King, Jr.

I hope the church as a whole will meet the challenge of this decisive hour. But even if the church does not come to the aid of justice, I have no despair about the future. I have no fear about the outcome of our struggle in Birmingham, even if our motives **1** are presently misunderstood. We will reach the goal of freedom in

◆ **Build Vocabulary**

motives (mōt′ ivz) *n.*: Reasons for action; inner drives

◀ Critical Viewing To prevent others from joining this African American sitting at a "whites only" lunch counter, the other seats were piled with linen supplies. Basing your response on their posture and activity, what might the customer and the waitress be feeling? **[Hypothesize]**

Speaking, Listening, and Viewing Mini-Lesson

Oration

This mini-lesson supports the Oration activity in the Idea Bank on page 160.

Introduce the Concept Explain that an oration is a formal speech that is logical and persuasive and appeals to the emotions. Remind students that an effective oration should have a clear introduction and conclusion and a logical sequence of ideas.

Develop Background Have students reread King's speech and brainstorm for ideas about freedom, leadership, and causes. Tell them to choose a topic and formulate a position. Before they begin writing, have students analyze the persuasive techniques that King used in his speech.

Apply the Information Before finalizing their speeches, have students evaluate the techniques that they have used and make revisions where necessary. Suggest that they ask themselves if they've used strong persuasive images, memorable statements, relevant and accurate information, arguments backed up by facts, and repetition.

Assess the Outcome Assess students' on their use of persuasive techniques, as well as their use of eye contact and information.

One-Minute Insight Like Thomas Paine, Martin Luther King, Jr., expresses certainty in the cause of freedom and its outcome. Just as early voices for freedom criticized the British crown and called on a sense of morality, King criticizes the ministers' praise of the Birmingham police, whose ugly treatment of women and children, old men and young boys left King sickened. Ministers especially, King points out, should know that it is wrong to use moral means to achieve immoral ends. Like Phillis Wheatley, King showers elegant praise on the courage of the nonviolent demonstrators. He praises the young and old, the men and women, who nonviolently sit at lunch counters and in the fronts of busses, going willingly to jail "for conscience's sake," standing for what Thomas Jefferson and his peers set out in the Declaration of Independence.

Customize for
Less Proficient Readers
Have less proficient readers work in teams to paraphrase parts of the letter. Put the team paraphrases together for a complete summary.

Customize for
AP Students
Suggest that these students read the entire *Letter From Birmingham City Jail.* (See the Internet note in Beyond the Selection on page 159 of the teacher edition for a possible source.) Ask students to share their additional insights with the class.

Customize for
English Language Learners
Hearing the letter read aloud may help English language learners follow the meaning. Play the audiocassette, and ask these students to follow in their texts.

Customize for
Interpersonal Learners
Suggest that these students try to identify with King as he sits in his jail cell writing this letter. Ask them to share the feelings they think King may have experienced.

▶Critical Viewing◀

1 **Hypothesize** Students might say that the customer feels nervous and afraid while the waitress feels annoyed and angry.

◆ Critical Thinking

❶ Compare and Contrast Ask students: How does King's comment here compare to those made by Jefferson, Paine, and Wheatley? *Students may say that King, like the other writers, frames his statement in Biblical reference.*

◆ Critical Thinking

❷ Compare and Contrast Ask students: Which of the other voices for freedom does King's statement echo here? *Students should note the similarity between this statement and Thomas Paine's.*

◆ Critical Thinking

❸ Analyze Point out King's use of specific examples to support his argument and identify the "real heroes" of the South. Ask students who these heroes are. *They are the people who bravely sat at counters and faced hostility for the cause of integration and freedom.*

◆ Critical Thinking

❹ Compare and Contrast Ask students: How do King's words echo those of Jefferson, Paine, and Wheatley? *Students should note similarities to Jefferson's opening paragraph of "The Declaration of Independence," Paine's closing paragraph in "The Crisis, Number 1," and Wheatley's praise of a hero.*

Read to Interpret

King's letter from jail is a call for freedom, justice, and equality. Explain to students that when they read primary material such as letters, or public addresses such as speeches or editorials, they must understand the events and ideas that the work comes from. To help students interpret "Letter from a Birmingham City Jail," read with them the Thematic Connection on p. 156.

Birmingham and all over the nation, because the goal of America is freedom. Abused and scorned though we may be, our destiny is tied up with the destiny of America. Before the Pilgrims landed at Plymouth we were here. Before the pen of Jefferson etched across the pages of history the majestic words of the Declaration of Independence, we were here. For more than two centuries our foreparents labored in this country without wages; they made cotton king; and they built the homes of their masters in the midst of brutal injustice and shameful humiliation—and yet out of a bottomless vitality they continued to thrive and develop. If the inexpressible cruelties of slavery could not stop us, the opposition we now face will surely fail. ❶ We will win our freedom because the sacred heritage of our nation and the eternal will of God are embodied in our echoing demands.

Before the pen of Jefferson etched across the pages of history the majestic words of the Declaration of Independence, we were here.

I must close now. But before closing I am impelled to mention one other point in your statement that troubled me profoundly. You warmly commended the Birmingham police force for keeping "order" and "preventing violence." I don't believe you would have so warmly commended the police force if you had seen its angry violent dogs literally biting six unarmed, nonviolent Negroes. I don't believe you would so quickly commend the policemen if you would observe their ugly and inhuman treatment of Negroes here in the city jail; if you would watch them push and curse old Negro women and young Negro girls; if you would see them slap and kick old Negro men and young Negro boys; if you will observe them, as they did on two occasions, refuse to give us food because we wanted to sing our grace together. I'm sorry that I can't join you in your praise for the police department.

It is true that they have been rather disciplined in their public handling of the demonstrators. In this sense they have been rather publicly "nonviolent." But for what purpose? To preserve the evil system of segregation. Over the last few years I have consistently preached that nonviolence demands that the means we use must be as pure as the ends we seek. So I have tried to make it clear that it is wrong to use immoral means to attain moral ends. ❷ But now I must affirm that it is just as wrong, or even more so, to use moral means to preserve immoral ends. Maybe Mr. Connor and his policemen have been rather publicly nonviolent, as Chief Pritchett was in Albany, Georgia, but they have used the moral means of nonviolence to maintain the immoral end of flagrant racial injustice. T. S. Eliot has said that there is no greater treason than to do the right deed for the wrong reason.

❸ I wish you had commended the Negro sit-inners and demonstrators of Birmingham for their sublime courage, their willingness to suffer and their amazing discipline in the midst of the most inhuman provocation. One day the South will recognize its real heroes. They will be the James Merediths, courageously and with a majestic sense of purpose facing jeering and hostile mobs and the agonizing loneliness that characterizes the life of the pioneer. They will be old, oppressed, battered Negro women, symbolized in a seventy-two-year-old woman of Montgomery, Alabama, who rose up with a sense of dignity and with her people decided not to

◆ Build Vocabulary

vitality (vī tal′ ə tē) *n.*: Power to endure or survive; life force

impelled (im peld′) *v.*: Moved; forced

flagrant (flā′ grənt) *adj.*: Glaring, outrageous

profundity (prō fun′ də tē) *n.*: Intellectual depth

monotony (mə nät′ ən ē) *n.*: Tiresome, unchanging sameness; lack of variety

scintillating (sint′ əl āt′ iŋ) *adj.*: Sparkling

Research Skills Mini-Lesson

Locating and Using Primary Sources This mini-lesson supports the Report on Dr. King activity on p. 160.

Introduce the Concept Tell students that to write a report on Dr. King using primary sources, they will need to use a variety of print and nonprint information, including texts, databases, and the Internet. Explain that a primary source is the original or first source of information—for example, an exact copy of what King wrote or said.

Develop Background In researching important events in King's life, suggest that they use newspaper accounts, such as those found in *The New York Times* or the *Los Angeles Times*, that quoted his speeches or reprinted his letters. Direct students to the writings of King's wife, Coretta Scott King. Have students search library databases.

Apply the Information After researching primary sources and gathering information, have students narrow their focus to one event in King's life. Have them evaluate their information to determine if it is complete and relevant.

Assess the Outcome Assess students on their ability to locate and use primary source materials and to present information logically and completely. You might have students use the Scoring Rubric for Research Report/Paper, p. 121 in ***Alternative Assessment.***

ride the segregated buses, and responded to one who inquired about her tiredness with ungrammatical profundity: "My feet is tired, but my soul is rested." They will
3 be the young high school and college students, young ministers of the gospel and a host of their elders courageously and nonviolently sitting-in at lunch counters and willingly going to jail for conscience's sake. One day the South will know that when these disinherited children of God sat down at lunch counters they were in reality standing up for the best in the American dream and the most sacred values in
4 our Judeo-Christian heritage, and thusly, carrying our whole nation back to those great wells of democracy which were dug deep by the Founding Fathers in the formulation of the Constitution and the Declaration of Independence.

Never before have I written a letter this long (or should I say a book?). I'm afraid that it is much too long to take your precious time. I can assure you that it would have been much shorter if I had been writing from a comfortable desk, but what else is there to do when you are alone for days in the dull monotony of a narrow jail cell other than write long letters, think strange thoughts, and pray long prayers?

If I have said anything in this letter that is an overstatement of the truth and is indicative of an unreasonable impatience, I beg you to forgive me. If I have said anything in this letter that is an understatement of the truth and is indicative of my having a patience that makes me patient with anything less than brotherhood, I beg God to forgive me.

I hope this letter finds you strong in the faith. I also hope that circumstances will soon make it possible for me to meet each of you, not as an integrationist or a civil rights leader, but as a fellow clergyman and a Christian brother. Let us all hope that the dark clouds of racial prejudice will soon pass away and the deep fog of misunderstanding will be lifted from our fear-drenched communities and in some not too distant tomorrow the radiant stars of love and brotherhood will shine over our great nation with all of their scintillating beauty.

Yours for the cause of Peace
and Brotherhood,
Martin Luther King, Jr.

Guide for Responding

◆ Literature and Your Life

Reader's Response What are your thoughts about King's ideas of justice, freedom, and heroism?

Thematic Focus How does King's reference to Jefferson add to his argument?

Journal Writing King notes the importance of making means and ends equally "pure." In your mind, how does a specific goal direct the way you achieve it? Discuss your ideas in a journal entry.

☑ Check Your Comprehension

1. What is the author's opinion of the Birmingham police officers' behavior?
2. Which people does the author identify as unsung heroes of the South?

◆ Critical Thinking

INTERPRET

1. What does the author mean by the statement, "the goal of America is freedom"? **[Interpret]**
2. Why do you think King finds the comment "My feet is tired, but my soul is rested" heroic and profound? **[Infer]**

APPLY

3. How might the effect of this letter have been different if it had been written from "a comfortable desk" rather than "a narrow jail cell"? **[Hypothesize]**

COMPARE LITERARY WORKS

4. Compare Martin Luther King's letter with the Declaration of Independence. Explain how themes in the letter echo those in the Declaration. **[Connect]**

Reinforce and Extend

Answers

◆ Literature and Your Life

Readers Response Students may say that King's ideas of justice, freedom, and heroism are correct, noble, and applicable to everyone.

Thematic Focus King's reference to Jefferson illustrates that the freedoms that King is seeking are the same ones fought for by colonial Americans. Therefore, King's argument is rooted in American history.

☑ Check Your Comprehension

1. King believes that Birmingham police officers have acted with brutality, ugliness, and inhumanity.
2. The unsung heroes of the South are the courageous, dignified, disciplined, and visionary black citizens who nonviolently insisted on their own freedom.

◆ Critical Thinking

1. Suggested response: King's statement suggests that America was founded to preserve individual freedom for its citizenry. His words also imply that maintenance of freedom is an ongoing process.
2. Suggested response: The comment reflects both the worldly and philosophical aspects of the fight for freedom: winning the struggle yields both exhaustion and peace of mind. The grammatical error may also elicit sympathy and awe.
3. Suggested response: Because King is in jail, his letter may be more persuasive. He shows that he is a man who is willing to be arrested for what he believes is right.
4. Students should identify themes such as individual rights, equality, and shared responsibility.

Beyond the Selection

FURTHER READING

Other Works by Martin Luther King, Jr.

A Testament of Hope: The Essential Writings of Martin Luther King, Jr.

Other Works About the Civil Rights Movement

Think About Our Rights: Civil Liberties and the United States, Reginald Wilson

An Oral History of the Civil Rights Movement from the 1950's through the 1980's, Henry Hampton

We recommend that you preview these texts before assigning them to students.

INTERNET

You and your students may find more information on the Internet. We suggest the following site. Please be aware, however, the site may have changed since we published this information.

For more about King, including a biography, and his papers, go to the Martin Luther King, Jr., Directory From the MLK Center in Atlanta at **http://www-leland.stanford. edu/group/King**

We *strongly recommend* that you preview the site before you send students to it.

Answers

Thematic Connection

1. Suggested response: The "great wells of democracy" contain freedom. King's incarceration underscores both the lack of freedom for African Americans in Alabama in 1963 and his own insistence on seizing that freedom for the future.
2. Possible response: The Revolution was a full-scale war with Britain; King's "war" is being waged with non-violent tactics.

Idea Bank

Customizing for *Performance Levels*

Following are suggestions for matching Idea Bank topics with your students' performance levels:
Less Advanced Students: 1
Average Students: 2, 4, 5,
More Advanced Students: 3, 6, 7

Customizing for *Learning Modalities*

Following are suggestions for matching Idea Bank topics with your students' learning modalities:
Musical/Rhythmic: 4
Interpersonal: 5
Visual/Spatial: 6
Logical/Mathematical: 7

Thematic Connection

Voices for Freedom

Paine, Jefferson, and Wheatley did not merely record a momentous period of history; their voices resounded on battlefields and in palaces and helped bring freedom to the citizens of the new United States of America. Similarly, Martin Luther King's calls for freedom and justice were heard not only by his immediate audience, but also eventually by millions of people across America.

1. How is King's imprisonment related to "those great wells of democracy which were dug deep by the Founding Fathers in the formulation of the Constitution and the Declaration of Independence"?
2. Both "Letter From Birmingham City Jail" and "To His Excellency, General Washington" glorify freedom. What similarities and differences can you identify between the war for independence and the struggle for civil rights?

Idea Bank

Writing

1. **Poem for a Prisoner** If Phillis Wheatley had known Martin Luther King, Jr., she might have written poetry to celebrate his courage and beliefs. Use your knowledge of Wheatley and King to write a poem she might have written in tribute to him. **[Literature Link]**
2. **Essay** In "Letter From Birmingham City Jail," Martin Luther King makes a brief comparison between "the inexpressible cruelties of slavery" and "the opposition we now face." Write an essay in which you compare and contrast more extensively the situation of slaves and the situation of segregated blacks in the early 1960's.
3. **Editorial** Write an editorial to bring King's imprisonment to light. Use Paine's emotional persuasive style or Jefferson's logical persuasive style to argue against the actions of the Birmingham police force.

Speaking, Listening, and Viewing

4. **Oration** Use a portion of "Letter From Birmingham City Jail" as a springboard for a speech about leadership, freedom, or devotion to a cause. Carefully analyze the text to discover stylistic or rhetorical techniques—such as repetition, parallelism, alliteration, and so on—that could contribute to a stirring oral performance. **[Performing Arts Link]**
5. **Freedom Survey** Spending time in jail might teach a prisoner about a loss of freedom. However, the presence of freedom may be more difficult to observe. Ask a variety of people to share their definitions of freedom. Then compile their responses into a report. **[Career Link]**

Researching and Representing

6. **Voices of Freedom Booklet** Create a booklet that celebrates the American tradition of fighting for freedom. Include the colonists and also more contemporary citizens who have worked to earn rights and fight injustice. Briefly identify and highlight the causes and achievements of the voices you have chosen. Include copies of photographs, drawings, news headlines and articles, and other images. **[Art Link]**
7. **Report on Dr. King** Using primary sources such as newspaper accounts, letters or speeches, prepare an oral or written report on an important moment in Dr. King's eventful life. Consider the 1955 Montgomery bus boycott, the 1965 march from Selma to Montgomery, the 1960 sit-ins at lunch counters, or the 1963 March on Washington.

Online Activity www.phlit.phschool.com

ASSESSMENT OPTIONS

Formal Assessment, Selection Test, pp. 47–48, and Assessment Resources Software. The selection test is designed so that it can be easily customized to the performance levels of your students.

PORTFOLIO ASSESSMENT

Use the following rubrics in the ***Alternative Assessment*** booklet to assess student writing:
Poem for a Prisoner: Poetry Rubric, p. 123
Essay: Comparison/Contrast Rubric, p. 118
Editorial: Persuasion Rubric, p. 120

Writing Process Workshop

Editorial

An **editorial**—essentially a brief persuasive essay—is the form in which the management of a newspaper, magazine, or radio or television station airs its views on major political and social issues. *The Crisis, Number 1,* Thomas Paine's stirring summons to revolution, departs from this definition in two respects: It is longer than a typical editorial, and it wasn't just part of a publication—it *was* the publication, a pamphlet published by Paine himself. Its urgency and powerful impact, however, have made *The Crisis* a model for editorial writers for more than two hundred years.

The following skills, introduced in this section's Guided Writing Lessons, will help you write an effective editorial of your own:

Recruiting for the Continental Army, (detail), William T. Ranney, Munson-Williams-Proctor Institute, Museum of Art, Utica, New York

Writing Skills Focus

- **Show causes and effects** to help readers see the implications of decisions or courses of action. (See p. 137.)
- **Use forceful language** to command your readers' attention and bolster the impact of your arguments. (See p. 147.)
- **Adopt a persuasive tone** by using positive, emotionally charged words. (See p. 155.)

Notice how this excerpt from an editorial illustrates these skills.

Writing Model

Introduction to an editorial arguing against congressional term limits

Because Franklin Delano Roosevelt had been elected to unprecedented third and fourth terms during World War II, Congress subsequently enacted a two-term limit for the presidency in order to discourage dictatorial ambitions in the chief of state. ① The recent movement to dose the sluggish House and Senate with the same two-term medicine is a misguided attack on the very core of the democracy it claims to bolster. ②

① Terms such as "because" and "in order to" establish a clear cause-and-effect relationship between issues and events.

② Forceful language such as "dose," "sluggish" and "misguided attack" creates a compelling argument.

Prepare and Engage

LESSON OBJECTIVES

- To use recursive writing processes to write an editorial
- To recognize and use prepositional phrases
- To vary sentence beginnings

You may want to distribute the scoring rubric for Persuasion (p. 120) in ***Alternative Assessment*** to make students aware of the criteria on which their work will be evaluated. See the suggestions on page 163 for customizing the rubric to this workshop.

You may also want to present the Argument Organizer in **Writing and Language Transparencies**, p. 75.

Connect to Literature Have students review this unit's excerpt from *The Crisis, Number 1,* by Thomas Paine (p. 144), which contains many key elements of an editorial.

Writing Lab CD-ROM
If your students have access to computers, you may want to have them use the tutorial on Persuasion to write their editorials. Have students follow these steps:

- Review the interactive model of an editorial.
- Use the interactive instruction on detecting bias in sources while gathering evidence, and then organize that evidence with the graphic organizers provided.
- Draft their editorials on the computer.
- Use the Self-Evaluation Checklist to help them revise their editorials.

Beyond the Classroom

Career Connection

Journalism Both print and broadcast journalism offer career opportunities for students interested in writing editorials on a regular basis. Explain that usually such opportunities for subjective writing present themselves only after a writer has served as a field reporter or features writer for some time. Point out that editors' responsibilities may include not only writing the editorials themselves, but helping determine the *editorial position* of the periodical or broadcast station. This duty can encompass diverse tasks: deciding the topics for editorials; hiring writers that represent a particular perspective or political belief; or commissioning pieces that express a specific viewpoint. Ask students for their opinions about the potential pros and cons associated with directing editorial policy in this way. *Students may respond that consistently coming up with well-informed editorials on a daily or weekly basis may pose too great a challenge. Others may claim that hiring others to conduct the necessary research for editorials could help them accomplish this.*

Writers at Work Videodisc To show how Gasby Greely uses persuasive techniques in writing public service announcements, play the videodisc segment on Persuasion (Ch. 4).

Play frames 33643 to 43235

Develop Student Writing

Prewriting Strategy

To enhance the brainstorming activity on forceful language, make a thesaurus available and review how to use it. Explain that many writers will use a thesaurus in conjunction with a dictionary because it may not clarify the different shades of meaning between possible word choices.

Customize for
Interpersonal Learners

These students may benefit from informally "trying out" the basic pro and con arguments of their editorial with a partner in order to gain confidence about their positions.

Grammar Reinforcement

Writing Lab CD-ROM

Have students review the interactive instruction on using library resources, an activity that appears in the Gathering Details section of the tutorial. Students can learn about using the following resources: library catalogs, encyclopedias, magazine articles (through the *Readers' Guide to Periodical Literature*), CD-ROM's and on-line services.

Elaboration Strategy

Guide students to elaborate on their main points using a *SEE* technique of Statement, Extension, and Elaboration. Using a basic statement from a student's work, create a graphic and sample like the one shown here.

S	Voting should not not be taken for granted.
E	It is a responsibility as well as a right.
E	As a self-governing people, we have a duty to choose leaders who will make fair decisions for the good of the nation.

Applying Language Skills: Prepositional Phrases

A **prepositional phrase** is a group of words that includes a preposition—such as *for, in, because, throughout*—and a noun or pronoun. The noun or pronoun that generally follows the preposition is the object of the preposition.

Prepositional Phrases

Prepositions	Objects of Prepositions
for	*her*
through	*the years*
because of	*his inspiring patriotism*

Practice Write each prepositional phrase from the passage below on your paper. Then underline each preposition and circle each object.

In difficult times, people are often capable of great things. Without sufficient provisions or fuel, the ragged army of volunteers under General Washington managed to beat back well-trained British troops.

Writer's Solution Connection
Writing Lab

To help you develop a balanced argument, use the Pros and Cons organizer in the Tutorial on Persuasion.

Prewriting

Choose a Topic Because editorials focus on issues of current concern, you might brainstorm with classmates to learn the issues that concern or involve them. You can get additional ideas by scanning a newspaper or watching television news programs. You might also choose one of these topic suggestions.

Topic Ideas

- Term limits
- Local environmental concerns
- Television content ratings
- Rap lyrics
- School uniforms
- Volunteerism

Gather Evidence Consider your topic and point of view. Do you know everything you need to know in order to make a persuasive argument? To help build your case, conduct research in the library's computer databases or on the Internet to find relevant magazine articles or reference works.

Brainstorm for "Forceful Language" If you don't feel strongly about your topic, neither will your readers. That's why it's important to use forceful language to convey your views. Notice the difference between the impact of the weak "opinion" words and their more forceful alternatives in the chart below. Jot down a list of forceful words that you can use to make your argument persuasive and effective.

Weak	Forceful
disapprove	deplore
support	applaud
should	must
ask	implore

Drafting

Use a Condensed Essay Structure Use the basic structure of introduction-body-conclusion to organize and present your thoughts. Begin with an introduction that grabs your readers' attention and states your argument clearly. Develop and support your main points in the body, showing logical cause-and-effect relationships between ideas. In the conclusion, restate your point of view and any call to action on the readers' part.

Maintain a Positive Tone Readers can be turned off by an overly negative approach. If you have a criticism to make, state it concisely and fairly. Then devote at least as much space to explaining and defending a constructive alternative, using positive, persuasive language.

Applying Language Skills

Prepositional Phrases To introduce this language skill, explain that prepositional phrases represent an important way of adding or clarifying information in sentences. An understanding of the ways that prepositions and their objects work together can help make writing more efficient. To illustrate the function of prepositional phrases in context, you may want to have students use the phrases provided (*for her; through the years; because of his inspiring patriotism*) in a series of sentences.

Answers

In (difficult times,) people are often capable of (great things.) Without (sufficient provisions or fuel,) the ragged army of (volunteers) under (General Washington) managed to beat back well-trained British troops.

Grammar Reinforcement

For additional instruction and practice, use the **Language Lab CD-ROM** lesson Recognizing and Using Phrases and practice pages 12 and 30 in the *Writer's Solution Grammar Practice Book.*

Revising

Work With a Peer Reviewer Ask a classmate to read and evaluate your editorial, using the following checklist.

- ▶ Does the editorial successfully communicate the writer's views on the issue?
- ▶ Is it coherent and organized, with a clear introduction, body, and conclusion?
- ▶ Are ideas developed and supported with clear cause-and-effect statements?
- ▶ Is the language forceful and compelling? Does it succeed in persuading you to adopt the writer's point of view?

Use your reviewer's responses to these questions to help you improve your editorial.

Revision Model

Americans know that ~~there has been no real~~ ① congressional gridlock has stalled action on key issues, such as national health care, campaign financing, education reform, poverty, and so on. The answer to our problems, however, is more democracy, not less. ② Term limits for Congress would infringe on our freedom of choice by automatically eliminating two-term incumbents from the election race. Let the voters, not the legislators, decide if and when they want to "throw the bums out"; and even more to the point, let's ~~not give up~~ ③ preserve our right not to throw out the ~~people we want.~~ ④ dedicated public servants who have earned our trust.

① The writer uses more forceful language.

② This addition of a clear cause-and-effect relationship strengthens the writer's case.

③–④ These revisions adopt a more persuasive tone by substituting positive, emotionally charged language.

Publishing

Consider sharing your editorial with others:

- ▶ **Newspapers** Submit your editorial to the school newspaper or to the op-ed page of your town's newspaper.
- ▶ **Send to Appropriate Recipients** Send your editorial, with a brief cover letter, to an appropriate civic leader or elected official.

Applying Language Skills: Varying Sentence Beginnings

To avoid monotony and enhance your writing, use a variety of sentence openers. Below are just a few of the structures you can use to begin a sentence.

Examples:

Subject first: British troops were sent to destroy colonial munitions at Concord.

Adjective first: Enraged, colonial minutemen challenged them on the Lexington green.

Prepositional phrase first: From out of nowhere, a shot rang out.

Adverb first: Immediately, the firing became widespread, leaving eight Americans dead.

Practice Write a five-sentence paragraph about a work from this section. Begin each sentence with a different structure.

Writing Application Use a variety of sentence openers to enliven your editorial.

Writer's Solution Connection
Writing Lab

To ensure variety in your sentences, use the revision checker for sentence openers in the Revising and Editing section of the tutorial on Persuasion.

Revision Strategy

Encourage students to reenter their writing, identifying and articulating the reasons for paragraph arrangement. After discussion, students may choose to reformulate some paragraphs for emphasis or coherence.

Grammar Reinforcement

Writing Lab CD-ROM
The Word Bin activity for persuasive words in the Revising and Editing section of the tutorial can help students emphasize their main points.

Publishing

As an alternative to sending their editorials to elected officials as posted letters, students might consider e-mail.

Applying Language Skills

Varying Sentence Beginnings
Explain that varying sentence beginnings is a natural complement to other stylistic devices that engage readers such as using forceful language.

Answers
Make sure that at least three different types of beginnings are used in students' paragraphs.

Grammar Reinforcement

For additional instruction, use the **Language Lab CD-ROM** lesson Varying Sentence Structure and practice page 112 in the *Writer's Solution Grammar Practice Book.*

Reinforce and Extend

Reflect on Writing Have the class read editorials drawn from the day's newspapers, and analyze why they are—or are not—effective. For more instruction on prewriting, elaboration, and revision, see *Prentice Hall Writing and Grammar.*

✓ ASSESSMENT

PORTFOLIO ASSESSMENT
Use the rubric on Persuasion in ***Alternative Assessment*** (p. 120) to assess students' writing. Add these criteria to customize the rubric to this assignment.

	4	3	2	1
Varying Sentence Beginnings	The writer consistently varies sentence beginnings in a way that greatly enhances the writing.	The writer occasionally varies sentence beginnings to avoid monotony.	The writer rarely varies sentence beginnings.	The writer consistently uses the same type of sentence be-ginning, which makes the writing sound flat.
Forceful Language	The writer consistently uses emotionally-charged, forceful language that heightens the persuasiveness of the editorial.	The writer frequently uses forceful rather than weak language.	The writer rarely uses forceful language, or does so in an unclear manner with word choices that are not always appropriate.	The writer uses weak language throughout the editorial, seriously hampering its ability to persuade.

Introduce the Strategy

LESSON OBJECTIVES

- To evaluate the credibility of information sources, including how the writer's motivation might affect that credibility
- To recognize logical, deceptive, and/or faulty modes of persuasion in texts

Customize for
Logical/Mathematical Learners

Encourage students to evaluate the flyer as a puzzle which selectively provides the reader with certain pieces of information. Challenge logical/mathematical learners to hypothetically omit or include specific phrases or words and then explore how the overall meaning might change. For example, if the phrase "of African Studies" were absent from the second line, readers might logically surmise that though Matho is a professor who holds a doctorate degree, her qualifications might be in a field unrelated to Africa.

Apply the Strategies

Answers

1. She is a Professor of African Studies.
2. Dr. Matho's information is first-hand, and she is an expert in this subject area. However, readers cannot tell from the poster alone how long she spent in Africa nor the range of her experiences there.
3. The book's subtitle indicates a subjective view of Africa because it states that it is based on "personal observations."
4. Because the purpose of the poster is to increase attendance at the talk, the writing must heavily promote the speaker's background and expertise.

Student Success Workshop

Real-World Reading Skills — Evaluating Sources of Information

Strategies for Success

Just because a piece of writing has been published doesn't mean it's accurate and reliable. Often, the writer has a particular motive or point of view that may slant the piece in one direction. A writer may even include incorrect information. That's why it's critical to evaluate carefully the source you use when you gather information on a topic.

Examine the Source Ask questions like these to determine the credibility of each source:

- ▶ What are the author's qualifications? Are they appropriate to the topic?
- ▶ If the source is a periodical, what is its reputation for accuracy and thoroughness? Who is its intended audience?
- ▶ What, if any, evidence of bias appears in the information? Might the source have an interest in slanting the information to support a specific point of view?
- ▶ Is the information supported with verifiable facts?

MEET THE AUTHOR!

Well-known travel writer and Professor of African Studies Alice Matho shares the experiences that inspired her latest book about Africa

Traveling My Homeland:
My personal observations of changing life in today's Africa

Slide show * Lecture * Discussion
8:00 P.M. Monday—Rolly Hall Auditorium

Copies of Dr. Matho's earlier books on Africa will also be available at the lecture.

Apply the Strategies

You want to gather information about contemporary African life before applying to a cultural exchange program. The poster on this page advertises a lecture and book about Africa. As you consider attending the lecture, evaluate the credibility of the poster, lecture, and book as information sources.

1. What credentials does Dr. Matho have for writing about Africa?
2. How reliable do you think Dr. Matho's information about Africa will be? Explain.
3. Do you think *Traveling My Homeland* will present an objective or a subjective view of Africa?
4. What is the purpose of the poster? How might that purpose result in a biased presentation of information?

Here are other situations in which it's important to evaluate information sources:

- ▶ *Research reports*
- ▶ *Political campaigns*
- ▶ *Product packaging claims*

Test Preparation Workshop

Evaluating Sources of Information Many standardized tests measure students' ability to evaluate sources of information. Have students answer this sample test item:

Based on information on the poster, Alice Matho's lecture and book would be a good source for—

A a report on African history
B a report on life in modern Africa
C a report on travel writing
D a report on African animals

Lead students to see that B is the best answer because the subtitle of the lecture mentions "changing life in today's Africa." According to the poster, Matho has no credentials regarding African history, which disqualifies answer *A*. *C* is not a good answer because although Mathos is a travel writer, travel writing is not the focus of her lecture. *D* should be discounted because although the poster shows a photograph of a giraffe, there is no information that Matho will talk about animals.

PART 2 # *Focus on Literary Forms:* *Speeches*

George Washington Standing on the Platform,
Pennsylvania State Capitol, Harrisburg

The colonial period of American history witnessed speeches and oratory powerful enough to start the Revolution. In speeches that rang through the halls of government, speakers such as Patrick Henry and Benjamin Franklin turned away from colonial loyalty toward a spirit of independence.

One-Minute Planning Guide

The selections in this section feature three of the finest orators in American history. In "Speech in the Convention," Benjamin Franklin shows how the wisdom that comes with age can help resolve a clashing of the minds. Patrick Henry then rouses his countrymen to battle for freedom with his famous "Speech in the Virginia Convention." This part concludes with an example of a modern inspirational speech, President John F. Kennedy's Inaugural Address.

Customize for
Varying Student Needs

When assigning the selections in this part, keep these factors in mind:

"Speech in the Convention"
- Circuitous reasoning within this speech may cause problems for less proficient readers

"Speech in the Virginia Convention"
- Fiery spirit will appeal to most students
- Unfamiliar vocabulary may cause problems

"Inaugural Address"
- This modern appeal for freedom at home and abroad will appeal to students
- Background of the cold war essential for understanding

Humanities: Art

George Washington.

This painting depicts George Washington as President of the Constitutional Convention that met in the Pennsylvania State House in May, 1787. The words arching over the painting are taken from Washington's address to the Convention, in which he told the delegates to forge a worthy document that they could strongly support. Four months later, in September, 1787, the Constitution was signed by a majority of the men who had met to draft it.

Have your students link the art to the focus of Part 2, Speeches, by answering the following questions:

1. Compare the image of George Washington in this painting to that in Leutze's *Washington Crossing the Delaware* (page 116). What elements in this painting suggest that Washington will be a successful leader for the new nation? *Sample answer: His posture suggests confidence and vision. As in the Leutze painting, no head is higher than Washington's, and several of the delegates to the Convention have turned their heads to listen to him.*
2. What is the effect of showing Washington's words as they are arranged here, arching over the speaker and his audience? *Sample answer: The painter suggests that these words in particular go to the heart of Washington's address and that they have become immortal.*

LESSON OBJECTIVES

1. **To develop vocabulary and word identification skills**
   - Latin Suffixes: *-ity*
   - Using the Word Bank: Definitions
   - Extending Word Study: Word Origins
2. **To use a variety of reading strategies to comprehend historical speeches**
   - Connect Your Experience
   - Tips to Guide Reading (ATE)
   - Read to Understand (ATE)
3. **To increase knowledge of other cultures and to connect common elements across cultures**
   - Connecting Themes Across Cultures (ATE)
4. **To express and support responses to the text**
   - Critical Thinking
   - Analyze a Commentary (ATE)
   - Idea Bank: Speech
   - Idea Bank: Critique
   - Idea Bank: Diary Entry
5. **To evaluate texts and the authority of sources**
   - Reading Strategy: Evaluating Persuasive Appeals
   - Literary Focus: Speeches
6. **To read in order to research self-selected and assigned topics**
   - Questions for Research
   - Idea Bank: Display of Speeches
   - Idea Bank: Multimedia Presentation
   - Idea Bank: Video Record
7. **To plan, prepare, organize, and present literary interpretations**
   - Speaking, Listening, and Viewing Mini-Lesson (ATE)
   - Idea Bank: Volunteerism Survey
   - Idea Bank: Dramatic Delivery
   - Idea Bank: Debate
8. **To use recursive writing processes to write a commentary on a speech**
   - Guided Writing Lesson
9. **To increase knowledge of the rules of grammar and usage**
   - Grammar and Style: Double Negatives

Test Preparation

Reading Comprehension: Predict Outcomes (ATE, p. 167) The teaching tips and sample test item in this workshop support the instruction and practice in the unit workshop:

Reading Comprehension: Recognize Cause and Effect; Predict Outcomes (SE, p. 213)

Guide for Interpreting

Patrick Henry *(1736–1799)*

It was said that Patrick Henry could move his listeners to anger, fear, or laughter more easily than the most talented actor. Remembered most for his fiery battle cry "Give me liberty or give me death," Henry is considered the most powerful orator of the American Revolution. He helped to inspire colonists to unite in an effort to win their independence. Shortly after his 1765 election to the Virginia House of Burgesses, Henry delivered one of his most powerful speeches, declaring his opposition to the Stamp Act. Over the protests of some of the most influential members, the Virginia House adopted Henry's resolutions.

Voice of Protest In 1775, Henry delivered his most famous speech at the Virginia Provincial Convention. While most of the speakers that day argued that the colony should seek a compromise with the British, Henry boldly urged armed resistance to England. His speech had a powerful impact on the audience, feeding the Revolutionary spirit that led to the signing of the Declaration of Independence.

In the years that followed, Henry continued to be an important political leader, serving as governor of Virginia and member of the Virginia General Assembly.

Featured in AUTHORS IN DEPTH Series

Benjamin Franklin *(1706–1790)*

Although his achievements spanned a wide range of areas—including science, literature, journalism, and education—Benjamin Franklin is most remembered as a statesman. He is the only American to sign the four documents that established the nation: the Declaration of Independence, the treaty of alliance with France, the peace treaty with England, and the Constitution.

A Persuasive Diplomat Franklin was a leader in the movement for independence. In 1776, Congress sent him to France to enlist desperately needed aid for the American Revolution. Franklin's persuasive powers proved effective, as he was able to achieve his goal—a pivotal breakthrough that may have been the deciding factor in the war.

Helping Forge a Nation In 1783, Franklin signed the peace treaty that ended the war and established the new nation. He returned home to serve as a delegate to the Constitutional Convention in Philadelphia. There, as politicians clashed over plans for the new government, Franklin worked to resolve conflicts and ensure ratification of the Constitution. (For more on Franklin, see pp. 128 and 186.)

◆ Background for Understanding

HISTORY: PATRICK HENRY'S BRAVERY

Today, it's hard for us to imagine the bravery it took for speakers like Patrick Henry to publicly denounce the British king. England was the most powerful country in the world, and the odds were overwhelmingly against the colonies' winning their freedom. By criticizing the king, Patrick Henry and other colonial leaders were putting their lives on the line. If the colonies' efforts to win their independence had failed, Henry could have been executed for treason.

Henry was quite aware of this. In fact, he had openly been accused of treason when he delivered his speech in opposition to the Stamp Act in 1765. On that occasion, Henry had referred to two leaders who had been killed for political reasons and declared that King George III of Britain might "profit by their example." This shocked the members of the audience so much that they screamed out, accusing him of treason. Henry is reported to have replied, "If this be treason, make the most of it!"

Prentice Hall Literature Program Resources

REINFORCE / RETEACH / EXTEND

Selection Support Pages
Build Vocabulary: Latin Suffixes: *-ity*, p. 51
Grammar and Style: Double Negatives, p. 52
Reading Strategy: Evaluating Persuasive Appeals, p. 53
Literary Focus: Speeches, p. 54

Strategies for Diverse Student Needs, p. 11

Beyond Literature
Beyond the Classroom: Workplace Skills, p. 11

Formal Assessment Selection Test, pp. 53–55, Assessment Resources Software

Alternative Assessment, p. 11

Writing and Language Transparencies
Writing Process Model 5: Written Evaluation, pp. 25–31

Resource Pro CD-ROM

Listening to Literature Audiocassettes

Speech in the Virginia Convention
◆ Speech in the Convention ◆

◆ Literature and Your Life

Connect Your Experience

You're probably already familiar with lines from many famous speeches— even though you may not be aware of it. Lines like Martin Luther King's "I have a dream" and John F. Kennedy's "Ask not what your country can do for you" have become a part of most Americans' vocabularies. The reason why those lines have become so famous is that they come from speeches—like the two you're about to read—that have shaped our nation's history.

Journal Writing What slogans or mottoes capture the attention of your generation? Choose one—from politics, music, or advertisements—and explain why it works.

Thematic Focus: A Nation Is Born

What ideas about "life, liberty, and the pursuit of happiness" that the Constitution promises are planted in the speeches of Henry and Franklin?

◆ Build Vocabulary

Latin Suffixes: *-ity*

Benjamin Franklin warns colleagues not to be overconfident of their infallibility. The Latin suffix *-ity* turns adjectives into nouns. Added to the adjective *infallible,* meaning "incapable of error," it creates the noun *infallibility,* meaning "the state of being infallible."

Word Bank

Preview this list of words from the speeches.

arduous
insidious
subjugation
vigilant
infallibility
despotism
salutary
unanimity
posterity
manifest

◆ Grammar and Style

Double Negatives

Today, it is not acceptable to use **double negatives**—two negative words where only one is needed. In previous centuries, however, double negatives were sometimes used to emphasize an idea. For example, Benjamin Franklin uses this sentence in his speech:

I am *not* sure I shall *never* approve it.

Franklin was stressing a possibility. The context of his statement suggests that Franklin might approve at a later date.

As you read these speeches, look for double negatives. Evaluate whether they effectively emphasize an idea.

◆ Literary Focus

Speeches

Speeches have played an important role in American politics—from the Revolutionary period to the present. An effective speaker uses a variety of techniques to emphasize important points:

- *Restatement:* repeating an idea in a variety of ways
- *Repetition:* restating an idea using the same words
- *Parallelism:* repeating grammatical structures
- *Rhetorical question:* asking a question whose answer is self-evident; intended to stir emotions.

◆ Reading Strategy

Evaluating Persuasive Appeals

To stir an audience, speakers often appeal to people's emotions—their hopes, fears, likes, and dislikes. Speakers can also appeal to their audience's sense of reason. When you read a persuasive speech, it's important to recognize and evaluate the types of appeals that the speaker makes. Ask yourself: What is the speaker's motivation in evoking these emotions? What arguments and evidence does the speaker offer to back up his or her emotional appeals? How well do the appeals suit the audience and occasion?

Interest Grabber Patrick Henry concluded his speech with the famous words, "Give me liberty or give me death." Write the words on the board. Have students spend six or seven minutes freewriting in their journals in response to this question: What is worth dying for? Encourage students to share their thoughts, and then point out the circumstances under which Henry made his exclamatory statement. Ask students to imagine that they were members of the Virginia Convention. Ask them what Henry would have to say to convince them that they, too, should be willing to die for liberty.

Connecting Themes Across Cultures

Have students think of individuals who have led entire nations to freedom. What do these leaders possess that enables them to inspire others? Why are the goals of life, liberty, and happiness not limited to one people or one culture?

Customize for *Less Proficient Readers*

Use a jigsaw strategy in which each pair or small group of less proficient readers becomes the expert team for a portion of the speech and shares their expertise with (i.e., teaches) their peers.

Customize for *AP Students*

Ask students to read portions of James Alexander Thom's *From Sea to Shining Sea,* an account of the George Rogers Clark family who knew and worked with Thomas Jefferson, Patrick Henry, and Benjamin Franklin. Ask them to share the account with the class and point out differences in perspectives.

Customize for *English Language Learners*

To understand the impact of the oratory, have students listen two or more times to the audiocassette, following the text in their books.

Listening to Literature Audiocassettes

Test Preparation Workshop

Reading Comprehension: Predict Outcomes Many standardized tests require students to make predictions. Use this sample test item:

Have we [colonists] shown ourselves so unwilling to be reconciled that [English] force must be called in to win back our love? Let us not deceive ourselves, sir. These are the implements of war and subjugation—the last arguments to which kings resort.

Based on this passage, what will happen if the British assemble their armies and navies?

A The British will remain peaceful.
B The colonists will monitor the British military in order to avoid armed conflict.
C The British will decrease their show of military strength after they threaten the colonists.
D The British will attempt to use force against the colonists, and the two sides will go to war against each other.

Although the first three choices are possible outcomes, choice D is most likely based on the information in the text.

Develop Understanding

One-Minute Insight Patrick Henry's speech in the convention was critically timed. Henry's persuasive argument helped turn colonial government sentiment against negotiation and toward war. Henry begins his speech with a respectful rebuttal of the previous speeches. Then he defends his own position.

Judging by the conduct of the British, he says, they are preparing for war. Colonists have tried every argument; discussion can no longer avert the coming storm. Colonists are being ignored; the only retreat is into slavery. The time for peaceful compliance is over; the war has already begun. Henry concludes his masterfully persuasive speech by declaring that he would rather die than live without liberty.

Tips to Guide Reading

Buddy Reading Suggest that students pair off in a "buddy" reading configuration to use this strategy. Partners read silently and stop at the end of a paragraph or other designated point to summarize the text. They may individually write their summary statements, then compare notes. By discussing their summaries, they will identify and work out the main ideas.

Customize for *Less Proficient Readers*

This speech contains many long sentences of unusual grammatical construction, as well as eloquent words and allusions that may be unfamiliar to these students. Instruct these students to paraphrase each sentence while they read. By doing so, they will be better able to understand the message of Patrick Henry's speech.

▶Critical Viewing◀

❶ **Evaluate** Some students may say that the painting shows dramatic impact, with the speech causing incredulous characters to talk among themselves or to rise in reaction. Other students may classify those same depictions as examples of a lack of attention.

Patrick Henry Before the Virginia House of Burgesses, Peter F. Rothermel, Red Hill, The Patrick Henry National Memorial

❶ ▲ **Critical Viewing** Patrick Henry's dramatic speeches swayed sentiment away from loyalty to the British crown and toward armed resistance. How effectively does the artist convey the power of Henry's oratory? **[Evaluate]**

Humanities: Art

Patrick Henry Before the Virginia House of Burgesses, 1852, by Peter F. Rothermel.

In the mid-1800's, Philadelphia was the capital of book and magazine publishing and had its own group of painters of historical subjects. The leader of these artists was Rothermel. In his paintings he mixed historical reconstruction with contemporary sentiment. In this painting, Rothermel presents his interpretation of Patrick Henry delivering his famous address to the Virginia House of Burgesses on May 29, 1765.

Use these questions for discussion:

1. Which figure is Patrick Henry? *He is the man standing with his arm raised.*
2. How has the artist created a dramatic atmosphere in this painting? *Henry is on a raised platform; his lighted face is set against a dark background; other actions, frozen in time, depict animated responses from the listeners; the character in the foreground grips the chair and table; a glove lies forgotten on the floor.*

SPEECH IN THE VIRGINIA CONVENTION

Connections to World Literature, *page 1160*

Patrick Henry

Mr. President: No man thinks more highly than I do of the patriotism, as well as abilities, of the very worthy gentlemen who have just addressed
❷ the house. But different men often see the same subject in different lights; and, therefore, I hope it will not be thought disrespectful to those gentlemen, if, entertaining, as I do, opinions of a character very opposite to theirs, I shall speak forth my sentiments freely and without reserve. This is no time for ceremony. The question before the house is one of awful moment[1] to this country. For my own part, I consider it as nothing less than a question of freedom or slavery. And in proportion to the magnitude of the subject ought to be the freedom of the debate. It is only in this way that we can hope to arrive at truth, and fulfill the great responsibility which we hold to God and our country. Should I keep back my opinions at such a time, through fear of giving offense, I should consider myself as guilty of treason toward my country, and of an act of disloyalty toward the Majesty of Heaven, which I revere above all earthly kings.

Mr. President, it is natural to man to indulge in the illusions of hope. We are apt to ❸
shut our eyes against a painful truth, and listen to the song of that siren till she transforms us into beasts.[2] Is this the part of wise men, engaged in a great and <u>arduous</u> struggle ❹
for liberty? Are we disposed to be of the

1. **moment:** Importance.

2. **listen . . . beasts:** In Homer's *Odyssey,* the enchantress Circe transforms men into swine after charming them with her singing.

◆ Build Vocabulary

arduous (är′ jo͞o wəs) *adj.*: Difficult

◆ Literary Focus

❷ **Speeches** Notice how Henry starts his oration by declaring his respect for those who have stated their disapproval for the Revolution, while pointing out that he disagrees with these men. This important rhetorical device is known as a "concession" to the opposition.

◆ Critical Thinking

❸ **Interpret** Ask students: Why does Henry make this statement when his intent is to shatter hope? *Students may say that it is part of the persuasive process to begin where the audience is comfortable, and many of the listeners still hoped for peace.*

◆ Reading Strategy

❹ **Evaluating Persuasive Appeals** Ask students: How does Henry appeal to the vanity of the Virginia Convention? *Students should point out that he flatters them, calling them wise.*

Read to Understand

Guide students in setting this purpose for reading by having them preview the text. Ask students to give their ideas about the text and to suggest how they might read to understand Henry's speech. Students may read to find out why Henry made the speech and the reasons for his argument. Suggest that students make notes of the main ideas in his argument. They may also make notes of questions they may want to research later.

Block Scheduling Strategies

Consider these suggestions to take advantage of extended class time:

- Discuss with students the Literature and Your Life section on page 167. Ask students to elaborate on political speeches they have heard on radio or television. Ask what makes those speeches memorable.
- Have students listen to the speeches on the Listening to Literature Audiocassettes. Discuss with students how the dramatic use of the voice accentuates the message of the speaker.
- Introduce the Grammar and Style lesson by explaining that double negatives are now considered incorrect, though they were acceptable in the past. Reinforce learning by having students use the Grammar and Style page in ***Selection Support,*** p. 52.
- Have students work in small groups to answer the Critical Thinking questions on pages 171 and 173.
- Answer the Reading Strategy questions on page 174 as a class. Be sure students understand the difference between appeals to emotion and appeals to reason.
- Before having students complete the Guided Writing Lesson on page 175, provide guidance by using Writing Process Model 5: Written Evaluation, pp. 25–31, in ***Writing and Language Transparencies.***

◆ **Literary Focus**

❶ **Speeches** Ask students to identify the speech technique Patrick Henry is using in these lines. What is its effect? *Henry is using rhetorical questions. The effect is to enhance Henry's argument because the answers to the questions depict a government of Britain that is about to use military action to force the colonists into submitting to British demands.*

◆ **Literary Focus**

❷ **Speeches** Elicit the following response: These questions have the effect of countering every argument the anti-war segment has.

◆ **Critical Thinking**

❸ **Analyze** Ask students to name the speech techniques that Henry uses in this passage. *Henry uses both repetition and parallelism.*

◆ **Reading Strategy**

❹ **Evaluating Persuasive Appeals** In this passage, Henry rebuts an opposing argument. Ask students why this is so effective. *By anticipating and answering an opposing argument, Henry weakens the argument by declaring it illogical.*

◆ **Reading Strategy**

❺ **Evaluating Persuasive Appeals** Elicit the following response: By suggesting that God is on the colonists' side, Henry appeals to his audience's religious faith.

◆ **Reading Strategy**

❻ **Evaluating Persuasive Appeals** Ask students how this famous final sentence strengthens Henry's argument. *This sentence strengthens Henry's argument both by appealing to the emotions of his audience and by stating that he is willing to make the ultimate sacrifice to secure liberty.*

Customize for
Gifted/Talented Students
Students may be challenged to write a speech to be delivered in the United States Congress on issues that are important today. Suggest that students write an emotional, persuasive speech and deliver it to the class in much the same way Patrick Henry may have delivered his speech.

number of those who having eyes see not, and having ears hear not,[3] the things which so nearly concern their temporal salvation? For my part, whatever anguish of spirit it may cost, I am willing to know the whole truth; to know the worst and to provide for it.

I have but one lamp by which my feet are guided, and that is the lamp of experience. I know of no way of judging of the future but by the past. And judging by the past, I wish to know what there has been in the conduct of the British ministry for the last ten years to justify those hopes with which gentlemen have been pleased to solace themselves and the house? Is it that insidious smile with which our petition has been lately received? Trust it not, sir; it will prove a snare to your feet. Suffer not yourselves to be betrayed with a kiss.[4] Ask yourselves how this gracious reception of our petition comports with those warlike preparations which cover our waters and darken our land. Are fleets and armies necessary to a work of love and reconciliation? Have we shown ourselves so unwilling to be reconciled that force must be called in to win back our love? Let us not deceive ourselves, sir. These are the implements of war and subjugation—the last arguments to which kings resort.

❶ I ask gentlemen, sir, what means this martial array, if its purpose be not to force us to submission? Can gentlemen assign any other possible motive for it? Has Great Britain any enemy in this quarter of the world, to call for all this accumulation of navies and armies? No, sir, she has none. They are meant for us: they can be meant for no other. They are sent over to bind and rivet upon us those chains which the British ministry have been so long forging.

And what have we to oppose to them? Shall we try argument? Sir, we have been trying that for the last ten years. Have we anything new to offer upon the subject? Nothing. We have held the subject up in every light of which it is capable; but it has been all in vain. Shall we resort to entreaty and humble supplication? What terms shall we find which have not been already exhausted? Let us not, I beseech you, sir, deceive ourselves longer. Sir, we have done everything that could be done to avert the storm which is now coming on. We have petitioned; we have remonstrated; we have supplicated; we have prostrated ourselves before the throne, and have implored its interposition[5] to arrest the tyrannical hands of the ministry and Parliament. Our petitions have been slighted; our remonstrances have produced additional violence and insult; our supplications have been disregarded; and we have been spurned with contempt from the foot of the throne! In vain, after these things, may we indulge the fond[6] hope of peace and reconciliation. There is no longer any room for hope. If we wish to be free, if we mean to preserve inviolate those inestimable privileges for which we have been so long contending, if we mean not basely to abandon the noble struggle in which we have been so long engaged, and which we have pledged ourselves never to abandon until the glorious object of our contest shall be obtained—we must fight! I repeat it, sir, we must fight! An appeal to arms and to the God of Hosts is all that is left us! ❸

They tell us, sir, that we are weak—unable to cope with so formidable an adversary. But when shall we be stronger? Will it be the next week, or the next year? Will it be when we are totally disarmed, and when a British guard shall be stationed in every house? Shall we gather strength by irresolution and inaction? Shall we acquire the means of effectual ❹

◆ **Literary Focus**
What is the effect of these rhetorical questions? ❷

3. **having eyes . . . hear not:** In Ezekiel 12:2, those "who have eyes to see, but see not, who have ears to hear, but hear not" are addressed.
4. **betrayed with a kiss:** In Luke 22:47–48, Jesus is betrayed with a kiss.

5. **interposition:** Intervention.
6. **fond:** Foolish.

◆ **Build Vocabulary**

insidious (in sid′ ē əs) *adj.*: Deceitful; treacherous

subjugation (sub′ jə gā′ shən) *n.*: The act of conquering

vigilant (vij′ ə lənt) *adj.*: Alert to danger

Speaking, Listening, and Viewing Mini-Lesson

Dramatic Delivery
This mini-lesson supports the activity on p. 175.

Introduce the Concept Explain that in order to give an effective presentation, students should emphasize the points in the speech with gestures, eye contact, and body language.

Develop the Background Have students list characteristics of Henry's speeches, including emotions, language, and style. Ask them to think about how to adapt these characteristics in their own speeches. Have them mark a copy of the speech and use it as a prompt during rehearsal.

Apply the Information Have students present their Patrick Henry speech.

Assess the Outcome Evaluate students on evidence of preparation, on effective use of gestures and voice, and on appropriate eye contact and body language. Students can assess one another using Peer Assessment: Speaker/Speech form, p. 133 in ***Alternative Assessments.***

resistance by lying supinely on our backs and hugging the delusive phantom of hope until our enemies shall have bound us hand and foot? Sir, we are not weak, if we make a proper use of those means which the God of nature hath placed in our power. Three millions of people, armed in the holy cause of liberty, and in such a country as that which we possess, are invincible by any force which our enemy can send against us. Besides, sir, we shall not fight our battles alone. There is a just God who presides over the destinies of nations and who will raise up friends to fight our battles for us. The battle, sir, is not to the strong alone;[7] it is to the vigilant, the active, the brave. Besides, sir, we have no election;[8] if we were base enough to desire it, it is now too late to retire from the contest. There is no retreat but in submission and slavery! Our chains are forged! Their clanging may be heard on the plains of Boston! The war is inevitable—and let it come! I repeat it, sir, let it come!

> ◆ **Reading Strategy** (5)
> How does Henry appeal to emotions in this passage?

It is in vain, sir, to extenuate the matter. Gentlemen may cry, "Peace, peace"—but there is no peace. The war is actually begun! The next gale that sweeps from the north[9] will bring to our ears the clash of resounding arms! Our brethren are already in the field! Why stand we here idle? What is it that gentlemen wish? What would they have? Is life so dear, or peace so sweet, as to be purchased at the price of chains and slavery? Forbid it, Almighty God! I know not what course others may take; but as for me, give me liberty or give me death! (6)

7. The battle . . . alone: "The race is not to the swift, nor the battle to the strong." (Ecclesiastes 9:11)
8. election: Choice.
9. The next gale . . . north: In Massachusetts, some colonists had already shown open resistance to the British.

Guide for Responding

◆ Literature and Your Life

Reader's Response What is your impression of Patrick Henry? Based on this speech, do you think his reputation as a powerful orator was deserved? Explain.

Thematic Focus How important of a role can a political speech like Henry's play in a time of crisis? Explain.

Questions for Research Do Patrick Henry's dramatic speeches reflect his vibrant personality, or was he just a good orator? List questions that could guide research about him.

☑ Check Your Comprehension

1. How does Henry say that he judges the future?
2. (a) What does Henry say is the reason for the British military buildup in America? (b) What course of action must the colonists take?
3. What does Henry say "the next gale that sweeps from the north" will bring?

◆ Critical Thinking

INTERPRET

1. Why do you think Henry begins by stating his opinions of the previous speakers? **[Infer]**
2. Why does Henry believe that compromise with the British is not a workable solution? **[Support]**
3. How does Henry answer the objection that the colonists are not ready to fight? **[Analyze]**
4. To what does Henry compare the colonists' situation? **[Analyze]**

APPLY

5. What occasion or situation might prompt a statesman to deliver such a formal, dramatic speech today? **[Relate]**

EXTEND

6. Compare Henry's speech with political speeches today. What speakers, if any, measure up to his power? **[Social Studies Link]**

Beyond the Classroom

Workplace Skills Connection

Leadership Today, persuasion is not restricted to the halls of government. All businesses—including education, retail, advertising, and non-profit organizations—call for individuals to "sell" ideas to their co-workers and the public.

In many businesses, a new idea of the concept for a new product must be "sold" internally before money is budgeted for its creation. Fact sheets, marketability reports, and cost analyses require detailed planning. Presentations call for polished speeches that sing the praises of an idea.

With students, brainstorm for a list of workplace situations that call for persuasive techniques. *They include: asking for a raise; motivating employees to work harder; and generating new advertising, product, or design ideas.*

Reinforce and Extend

Answers

◆ Literature and Your Life

Reader's Response Invite students to share their impressions. Ask students to identify the language or techniques that they find effective.

Thematic Focus Such a speech can unite people in a time of crisis and provide direction for future action.

☑ Check Your Comprehension

1. He judges the future by the past.
2. (a) He believes the purpose of the British military buildup is to force the colonists into submission.
   (b) The colonists must fight the British.
3. "The next gale that sweeps from the north" will bring the cries of war.

◆ Critical Thinking

1. Suggested response: By stating his respect for the previous speakers, he creates the impression that he has given consideration to their opinions and makes them more willing to listen to his opinion.
2. Compromise is not a workable solution because the British have responded to the previous petitions of the colonists with increased repression.
3. Henry answers the objection by saying that if they wait, they will give the British time to build up their forces. He disputes the charge that the colonists are weak.
4. Henry compares the colonists' situation to slavery.
5. Suggested response: The threat of war might prompt a speaker to deliver a similar speech.
6. Students should explain why their chosen speakers measure up to Henry.

Extending Word Study

Research Word Origins Have students look up the origin of *vigilant* and discuss the meaning of the word *vigil*. Discuss how knowing a word's origin can sometimes help students determine its meaning and spelling. For example, if they know the origin of *vigil*, they know that it is spelled with *i*. Have students think of other words with this origin, spell them, define them, and then verify their answers in a dictionary.

Develop Understanding

One-Minute Insight In an interesting coda to his career as an American statesman, Benjamin Franklin uses his years of experience to urge his colleagues to accept the United States Constitution. Franklin admits that he does not entirely approve of the newly framed Constitution, but he recognizes the limitations of any such document. He says, to create any legal document by means of a committee means it will have some inherent weaknesses. In fact, though, the form of government will more likely fail because of the people who administer it than because of the document that establishes it. He proposes, therefore, that it is better to endorse unanimously a document that does mostly what is intended than to find fault and thereby subject it to the possibility of failure. This speech paves the way for the acceptance of one of America's most important and lasting documents.

◆ Reading Strategy

❶ Evaluating Persuasive Appeals Ask students: What appeal does Franklin use here? *Students should see Franklin's admission of age and his growing wisdom to doubt his own judgment as an example of appealing through humility or modesty.*

◆ Critical Thinking

❷ Interpret Ask students: For what purpose does Franklin insert this observation? *Students may say that he adds humor to a tense situation but also makes a point about infallibility.*

◆ Reading Strategy

❸ Evaluating Persuasive Appeal Ask students what kind of appeal Franklin is using in this passage and why it may prove effective in getting delegates to vote in favor of the Constitution. *Suggested response: Franklin appeals to the pride and vanity of the delegates by saying the document is closer to perfection than he imagined possible. Such a favorable assessment of their work may lead the delegates to put aside minor objections and vote favorably.*

Speech in the Convention

Benjamin Franklin

Mr. President,

I confess, that I do not entirely approve of this Constitution at present; but, Sir, I am not sure I shall never approve it; for, having lived long, I have experienced many instances of being obliged, ❶ by better information or fuller consideration, to change my opinions even on important subjects, which I once thought right, but found to be otherwise. It is therefore that, the older I grow, the more apt I am to doubt my own judgment of others. Most men, indeed, as well as most sects in religion, think themselves in possession of all truth, and that wherever others differ from them, it is so far error. . . . Though many private Persons think almost as highly of their own infallibility as of that of their Sect, few express it so naturally ❷ as a certain French Lady, who, in a little dispute with her sister, said, "But I meet with nobody but myself that is *always* in the right." *"Je ne trouve que moi qui aie toujours raison."*

In these sentiments, Sir, I agree to this Constitution, with all its faults,—if they are such; because I think a general Government necessary for us, and there is no form of government but what may be a blessing to the people, if well administered; and I believe, farther, that this is likely to be well administered for a course of years, and can only end in despotism, as other forms have done before it, when the people shall become so corrupted as to need despotic government, being incapable of any other. I doubt, too, whether any other Convention we can obtain, may be able to make a better constitution; for, when you assemble a number of men, to have the advantage of their joint wisdom, you inevitably assemble with those men all their ❸ prejudices, their passions, their errors of opinion, their local interests, and their selfish views. From such an assembly can a *perfect* production be expected? It therefore astonishes me, Sir, to find this system approaching so near to perfection as it does; and I think it

Viewing and Representing Mini-Lesson

Multimedia Presentation

This mini-lesson supports the Researching and Representing activity 7 on p. 175.

Introduce Tell students that aspects of the American Revolution have been depicted in a many forms that can be used in an effective presentation. Have students think of some sources they might use to do their research. Delegate students to work in small groups to plan and organize the research.

Develop Suggest that students include print and nonprint materials in their presentations. Tell them to consider maps, illustrations, and charts. Suggest that students also look for videos, films, and music to convey life during this period in American history.

Apply Have students present background about the American Revolution to introduce their presentation. Invite the class to ask questions.

Assess Evaluate students on their ability to present a variety of media that accurately represents the American Revolution. You can use the Scoring Rubric for Multimedia Presentation, p. 122 in ***Alternative Assesment.***

will astonish our enemies, who are waiting with confidence to hear, that our councils are confounded like those of the builders of Babel, and that our States are on the point of separation, only to meet hereafter for the purpose of cutting one another's throats. Thus I consent, Sir, to this Constitution, because I expect no better, and because I am not sure that it is not the best. The opinions I have had of its *errors* I sacrifice to the public good. I have never whispered a syllable of them abroad. Within these walls they were born, and here they shall die. If every one of us, in returning to our Constituents, were to report the objections he has had to it, and endeavour to gain Partisans in support of them, we might prevent its being generally received, and thereby lose all the salutary effects and great advantages resulting naturally in our favour among foreign nations, as well as among ourselves, from our real or apparent unanimity. 4 Much of the strength and efficiency of any government, in procuring and securing happiness to the people, depends on *opinion*, on the general opinion of the goodness of that government, as well as of the wisdom and integrity of its governors. I hope, therefore, for our own sakes, as a part of the people, and for the sake of our posterity, that we shall act heartily and unanimously in recommending this Constitution, wherever our Influence may extend, and turn our future thoughts and endeavors to the means of having it *well administered.*

On the whole, Sir, I cannot help expressing a wish, that every member of the Convention who may still have objections to it, would with me on this occasion doubt a little of his own infallibility, and, to make *manifest* our *unanimity*, put his name to this Instrument.

◆ Build Vocabulary

infallibility (in fal′ ə bil′ ə tē) *n.*: Inability to be wrong; reliability

despotism (des′ pət iz′ əm) *n.*: Government by absolute rule; tyranny

salutary (sal′ yo͞o ter′ ē) *adj.*: Beneficial; promoting a good purpose

unanimity (yo͞o′ nə nim′ ə tē) *n.*: Complete agreement

posterity (päs ter′ ə tē) *n.*: All succeeding generations

manifest (man′ ə fest′) *adj.*: Evident; obvious; clear

Guide for Responding

◆ Literature and Your Life

Reader's Response Based on Franklin's argument, would you have ratified the Constitution? Why or why not?

Thematic Focus How does Franklin use his experience as a diplomat to persuade his audience?

☑ Check Your Comprehension

1. What three reasons does Franklin give for agreeing to the Constitution?
2. Of what has Franklin "never whispered a syllable . . . abroad"?
3. What advantage does Franklin see in the unanimity of the delegates?

◆ Critical Thinking

INTERPRET

1. What effect does Franklin achieve by his "confession" in the first paragraph? **[Interpret]**
2. Why does Franklin acknowledge the "faults" of the Constitution? **[Infer]**
3. What is Franklin's purpose in suppressing his "opinions" for "the public good"? **[Analyze]**

EVALUATE

4. How effective is the overall organization of Franklin's speech? Explain. **[Evaluate]**

EXTEND

5. In the excerpt from his *Autobiography* on p. 131, Franklin details his attempt to achieve moral perfection. Compare and contrast the younger Franklin described there with the one who delivered this speech. **[Literature Link]**

Beyond the Selection

FURTHER READING

Other Works by and About Henry

Correspondence and Speeches, W. W. Henry, editor
Patrick Henry, Richard R. Beeman

Other Works by and About Franklin

Letters to the Press, 1758–1775, Verner W. Crane, editor
Franklin of Philadelphia, Esmond Wright

We suggest that you preview these works before recommending them to students.

INTERNET

You and your students can find information on the Internet. Please note that the following sites may have changed from the time we published this information. For more about Henry, go to **http://www.inmind.com/schools/lessons/PatrickHenry/index.html**

For more about Franklin, go to **http://sln.fi.edu/tfi/preview/ benlearn.html**

We *strongly recommend* that you preview these sites before sending students to them.

◆ Literature and Your Life

4 Ask students: Do you think Franklin's statement is true of today's government? *Students may agree but may point out that some of today's governors may lack integrity.*

Reinforce and Extend

Answers

◆ Literature and Your Life

Reader's Response Most students may agree with Franklin's argument that unanimity is critical.

Thematic Focus Franklin says that in his years of experience, he has never found a document that completely satisfied everyone.

☑ Check Your Comprehension

1. Reasons include general government is necessary; probably no other convention could make a better constitution; and enemies of the colonies are hoping for disagreement among the separate states.
2. He has never mentioned his qualms about the Constitution.
3. Unanimity will mean a united group of states whose people will be resolute in the cause of revolution.

◆ Critical Thinking

1. His confession makes him seem honest and modest, and thus more persuasive.
2. Franklin shows that he has objections like the other delegates, but is able to set those objections aside for the common good.
3. Franklin wants the people to become united as one in the cause of liberty.
4. Franklin's moves from individual doubt to positive, unanimous accord. This movement is effective in carrying away skepticism and opening the gate for consensus and agreement.
5. While the younger Franklin believed that perfection might be achievable, the older Franklin realizes that perfection in life is an impossibility.

Answers

◆ Reading Strategy

1. Henry must appeal to reason because he must persuade intelligent individuals that his argument is correct. He must appeal to emotion to get the audience fired up about the idea of fighting the British.
2. He probably ended his speech with an emotional appeal so that the audience would be inspired to take action.

◆ Literary Focus

1. (a and b) The following series of rhetorical questions leads the listener to understand that the British intend to subdue the colonists through force: "... what means this martial array, it its purpose be not to force us to submission? Can gentlemen assign any other possible motive for it? Has Great Britain any enemy in this quarter of the world, to call for all this accumulation of navies and armies?"
2. Here is an instance of repetition: "... we must fight! I repeat it, sir, we must fight!"
3. (a) 1. "... I do not entirely approve of this Constitution at present," "... I agree to this Constitution, with all its faults." 2. "It therefore astonishes me, Sir, to find this system approaching so near to perfection as it does." "... I consent, Sir, to this Constitution, because I expect no better." 3. "Most men, indeed, as well as most sects in religion, think themselves in possession of all truth ..." "... many private Persons think almost as highly of their own infallibility as of that of their Sect ..." (b) The restatement amplifies each key point.
4. Franklin uses parallel structure when he says, "... doubt my own judgment of others." "... doubt a little of his own infallibility ..." Parallelism reinforces the main idea.

Beyond Literature

The benefits of a televised convention include: universal access to a party's platform and ideals, and generated interest in an election. However, the drawbacks of a heightened awareness of a television audience can reduce the true exchange of ideas and create what some have called a "media circus."

Guide for Responding (continued)

◆ Reading Strategy

Evaluating Persuasive Appeals

An effective speaker uses a variety of **persuasive appeals.** Patrick Henry uses a blend of appeals to reason and to emotion in his speech.

1. Considering the purpose of Henry's speech, why are these two techniques appropriate?
2. Why do you think Henry chose to end his speech with an emotional appeal?

◆ Literary Focus

Speeches

In these **speeches**, Henry and Franklin use a variety of devices, including rhetorical questions, restatement, repetition, and parallelism (see definitions on p. 167) to emphasize their points.

1. (a) Find an instance where Henry uses a series of rhetorical questions. (b) What purpose does this series of questions serve?
2. Find an instance where Henry uses repetition.
3. (a) List three examples of restatement from Franklin's speech. (b) What is the effect of this restatement?
4. Find an example of parallelism in Franklin's speech. What effect does this have?

Beyond Literature

Cultural Connection

Elections Around the World In the United States, voters elect a president every four years through the electoral college system. The president serves a four-year term and may be reelected one time. This system is unique to the United States, however, as each country chooses its leaders in a different way. Some countries use only indirect methods of election, and some do not place limits on a president's term. Read about other systems of election. If you were to design a new framework for leadership, would you model it after the one in the United States or does another system seem better?

◆ Build Vocabulary

Using the Latin Suffix *-ity*

The Latin suffix *-ity* creates nouns that mean "the state of [the original adjective]." Write a definition for each of the following words:

1. complexity **2.** flexibility **3.** unanimity

Using the Word Bank: Definitions

On your paper, match the word from the Word Bank with its definition.

1. arduous	**a.** beneficial
2. insidious	**b.** evident; clear
3. subjugation	**c.** deceitful; treacherous
4. vigilant	**d.** complete agreement
5. infallibility	**e.** succeeding generations
6. despotism	**f.** the act of conquering
7. salutary	**g.** alert to danger
8. unanimity	**h.** difficult
9. posterity	**i.** reliability
10. manifest	**j.** tyranny

◆ Grammar and Style

Double Negatives

Although orators in the Revolutionary period sometimes used **double negatives** to stress their opinions, it is no longer considered acceptable to use double negatives in speaking or in writing.

Incorrect: I do*n't hardly* know where to begin. Here, the negatives are *n't* (*not*) and *hardly*. Use only one to make a negative sentence.

Correct: I don't know where to begin.

Practice On your paper, revise each sentence below that contains a double negative. If a sentence is correct, write "correct."

1. Don't sign nothing until you hear from me.
2. You don't have enough information.
3. I don't think you'll want hardly anything from me.
4. I didn't have any idea that he wouldn't show up.
5. It wouldn't make no difference to me if they cancelled the meeting.

◆ Build Vocabulary

1. *Complexity* means "the state of being complicated."
2. *Flexibility* means "the state of being easily bent."
3. *Unanimity* means "the state of being united in opinion."

Using the Word Bank

1. h 2. c 3. f 4. g 5. i
6. j 7. a 8. d 9. e 10. b

◆ Grammar and Style

Possible answers:

1. Don't sign anything until you hear from me.
2. Correct
3. I don't think you'll want anything from me.
4. I didn't have any idea that he would show up.
5. It wouldn't make any difference to me if they cancelled the meeting.

Grammar Reinforcement

For additional instruction and practice, use the lesson in the **Language Lab CD-ROM** on Problems With Modifiers and the practice pages on Negative Sentences (pp. 78–79) in the *Writer's Solution Grammar Practice Book.*

Build Your Portfolio

Idea Bank

Writing

1. **Diary Entry** As a member of the Virginia House of Burgesses, you have just heard Henry's powerful speech. Write a diary entry in which you record your feelings.

2. **Speech** Imagine that you are a speaker in the Virginia Provincial Convention and that you do not agree with Patrick Henry. Write a speech in which you rebut each of Henry's points.

3. **Critique** According to critic Richard Beeman, Henry had a remarkable "ability to comprehend the essential meaning and import of the political issues [of the day. He was] one of the most powerful, effective, and generally constructive local politicians that America had ever produced." Using evidence from the speech, write a brief essay in which you respond to Beeman's assessment.

Speaking, Listening, and Viewing

4. **Dramatic Delivery** How would Patrick Henry deliver a speech today? Present one of his speeches using a variety of visual aids for support.

5. **Debate** Use either speech as the subject of a debate. With a group, present arguments for and against independence or the ratification of the Constitution. **[Social Studies Link]**

Researching and Representing

6. **Display of Famous Speeches** Collect speeches from different periods of history, along with photographs or illustrations. Create a display highlighting key passages from the speeches.

7. **Multimedia Presentation** Use illustrations, maps, and music to create a multimedia presentation that brings the American Revolution to life for your class. **[Technology Link]**

Online Activity www.phlit.phschool.com

Guided Writing Lesson

Commentary on a Speech

Patrick Henry had the ability to deliver a moving speech at a moment's notice. Choose a speech by a skilled modern orator—such as Mario Cuomo, Ronald Reagan, or Jesse Jackson—and write a commentary that evaluates the way in which the speaker leads an audience to agree with his or her ideas.

Writing Skills Focus: Anticipating Questions

If you think about the questions or objections your audience may have, you can address those issues and eliminate the questions from readers' minds. Notice how Henry uses these rhetorical questions to **anticipate objections** from his audience:

Model From the Speech

And what have we to oppose to them? Shall we try argument? Sir, we have been trying that for the last ten years. Have we anything new to offer upon the subject? Nothing.

By summing up and responding to possible objections before they are voiced, Henry controls the direction his argument takes.

Prewriting Review the speech you've chosen several times to outline the speaker's key points or note the persuasive techniques the writer uses. Then critically analyze how well the speaker has supported his or her key points and how effectively he or she has used persuasive techniques.

Drafting Focus each of your paragraphs on a single point. For example, one paragraph might focus on the speaker's appeals to emotions.

Revising Anticipate your critics' questions. Review your essay as you would if someone disagreed with it. Note the points you might refute or the questions you might ask. Then go back and respond to those potential objections.

✓ ASSESSMENT OPTIONS

Formal Assessment, Selection Test, pp. 53–55, and Assessment Resources Software. The selection test is designed so that it can be easily customized to the performance levels of your students.

Alternative Assessment, p. 11, includes options for less advanced students, more advanced students, verbal/linguistic learners, musical/rhythmic learners, and interpersonal learners.

PORTFOLIO ASSESSMENT

Use the following rubrics in the ***Alternative Assessment*** booklet to assess student writing:
Diary Entry: Summary Rubric, p. 113
Speech: Persuasion Rubric, p. 120
Critique: Evaluation/Review Rubric, p. 119
Guided Writing Lesson: Evaluation/Review Rubric, p. 119

Idea Bank

Customizing for *Performance Levels*

Following are suggestions for matching Idea Bank topics with your students' performance levels:
Less Advanced Students: 1
Average Students: 2, 4, 6
More Advanced Students: 3, 5, 7

Customizing for *Learning Modalities*

Following are suggestions for matching Idea Bank topics with your students' learning modalities:
Bodily/Kinesthetic: 4
Interpersonal: 5
Visual/Spatial: 6, 7

Guided Writing Lesson

For more instruction on prewriting, elaboration, and revision, see *Prentice Hall Writing and Grammar.*

Writing and Language Transparencies Guide students in writing their commentaries by using the Writing Process Model 5: Written Evaluation, pp. 25–31.

Writers at Work Videodisc Have students view the videodisc segment (Ch. 7) featuring literary agent Theresa Park speaking about response to literature. Ask students in what ways Park responds to a piece of literature.

Play frames 22209 to 31154

Writing Lab CD-ROM
Have students complete the tutorial on Response to Literature. Have students follow these steps:
1. Use the Evaluation Word Bins for words that capture precise reactions to speeches.
2. Draft on the computer.
3. Use the Interactive Self-Evaluation Checklist to aid revision.

LESSON OBJECTIVES

1. **To critically evaluate texts and the authority of sources**
   - Literary Connection: Speeches
2. **To increase knowledge of other cultures and to connect common elements across cultures**
   - Thematic Connection
3. **To express and support responses to the text**
   - Critical Thinking
   - Idea Bank: Summation
   - Idea Bank: Comparative Essay
   - Analyze a Commentary (ATE)

Interest Grabber Ask students to share what they know about John F. Kennedy. In a discussion, explain Kennedy's ideals. Tell students that Kennedy's inaugural address—and his brief administration—challenged the "new generation of Americans" to do their part to ensure freedom and human rights at home and abroad. Discuss with students what their generation can and should do to preserve the freedoms that President Kennedy and the founders of the United States fought to preserve.

CONNECTIONS TO TODAY'S WORLD

Inaugural Address

John F. Kennedy

Thematic Connection

AMERICAN SPEECHMAKING

"Give me liberty or give me death!" "Four score and seven years ago . . ." "We have nothing to fear but fear itself." "Ask not what your country can do for you, ask what you can do for your country." "I have a dream . . ." All these lines from famous speeches cry out from the pages of American history, forming an important part of our nation's identity. Public speaking has been an important American tradition from the Revolutionary period to the present. Speeches provide a valuable record of the events and issues that have been pivotal in shaping our nation.

Many of our nation's most memorable speeches were delivered in difficult or troubled times. Patrick Henry's speech was delivered at a time when the colonies were on the brink of war with England. Benjamin Franklin's speech was presented during the heated struggle to forge our Constitution.

When John F. Kennedy took office in 1961, the United States was locked in a potentially explosive stalemate with the Soviet Union and its allies. Fierce adversaries, the United States and the Soviet Union were stockpiling nuclear weapons, creating the possibility of a disastrous war that could destroy the Earth. In his now-famous inaugural address, Kennedy addressed our nation's fears and reached out to our adversaries, while reaffirming our nation's strength.

Literary Connection

SPEECHES

The issues that Kennedy addresses in his speech are very different from those presented in Henry's and Franklin's speeches. However, Kennedy uses many of the same techniques as his predecessors. That's because while the world has changed tremendously since America won its independence, effective speakers still use many of the same persuasive techniques. These include rhetorical questions, or questions asked only for effect; repetition, the presentation of the same idea using the same language; the restatement of the same idea in different ways; and parallelism, the use of a repeated grammatical structure.

JOHN F. KENNEDY

(1917–1963)

Elected thirty-fifth president of the United States, John Fitzgerald Kennedy was the youngest person ever to serve in that office. The era over which Kennedy presided during his brief presidency witnessed events as diverse as the launch of the first communication satellite, Telstar, and the signing of the first nuclear nonproliferation treaty with the Soviet Union. The United States teetered on the brink of nuclear war during the Cuban missile crisis and put its first astronaut into orbit around the Earth. Tragically, Kennedy was assassinated on November 22, 1963, after serving only two years and ten months in office.

Prentice Hall Literature Program Resources

REINFORCE / RETEACH / EXTEND

Selection Support Pages
Build Vocabulary, p. 55
Thematic Connection: American Speechmaking p. 56

Formal Assessment Selection Test, pp. 56–57, Assessment Resources Software

Resource Pro CD-ROM

Inaugural Address

CONNECTIONS TO TODAY'S WORLD

John F. Kennedy

Vice President Johnson, Mr. Speaker, Mr. Chief Justice, President Eisenhower, Vice President Nixon, President Truman,[1] *reverend clergy, fellow citizens,* we observe today not a victory of party, but a celebration of freedom—symbolizing an end, as well as a beginning—signifying renewal, as well as change. For I have sworn before you and Almighty God the same solemn oath our forebears prescribed nearly a century and three quarters ago.

The world is very different now. For man holds in his mortal hands the power to abolish all forms of human poverty and all forms of human life. And yet the same revolutionary beliefs for which our forebears fought are still at issue around the globe—the belief that the rights of man come not from the generosity of the state, but from the hand of God.

2 We dare not forget today that we are the heirs of that first revolution. Let the word go forth from this time and place, to friend and foe alike, that the torch has been passed to a new generation of Americans—born in this century, tempered by war, disciplined by a hard and bitter peace, proud of our ancient heritage—and unwilling to witness or permit the slow undoing of those human rights to which this Nation has always been committed, and to which we are committed today at home and around the world.

3 Let every nation know, whether it wishes us well or ill, that we shall pay any price, bear any burden, meet any hardship, support any friend, oppose any foe, in order to assure the survival and the success of liberty.

This much we pledge—and more.

To those old allies whose cultural and spiritual origins we share, we pledge the loyalty of faithful friends. United, there is little we cannot do in a host of cooperative ventures. Divided, there is little we can do—for we dare not meet a powerful challenge at odds and split asunder.[2]

Retroactive I, Robert Rauschenberg, 1964, Wadsworth Atheneum, Hartford, Connecticut
© Robert Rauschenberg/Licensed by VAGA, New York, N.Y.

1 ▲ **Critical Viewing** What do the images in this montage—and the unfinished quality of the upper right corner—suggest about Kennedy? **[Infer]**

1. Vice President . . . Truman: Present at Kennedy's inauguration were Lyndon B. Johnson, Kennedy's vice president; 34th president Dwight D. Eisenhower and his vice president, Richard M. Nixon; and 33rd president Harry S. Truman.

2. United . . . Divided . . . split asunder: Kennedy echoes the famous lines from Abraham Lincoln's second inaugural address: "United we stand . . . divided we fall."

◆ Build Vocabulary

heirs (erz) *n.*: People who carry on the tradition of predecessors

Develop Understanding

One-Minute Insight

In his inaugural address, John F. Kennedy, cites the revolutionary ideals of the founders of the United States, and pledges to do his part to preserve freedom and to work toward peace everywhere. Like Patrick Henry and Benjamin Franklin, Kennedy was a charismatic speaker. All could stir a crowd. All strove to "explore what problems unite us instead of belaboring those problems which divide us." Ironically, it was Kennedy who said, "In the long history of the world, only a few generations have been granted the role of defending freedom in its hour of maximum danger." He joins Henry and Franklin as being among those few.

Customize for *English Language Learners*

Students may have difficulty with metaphors like "beachhead of cooperation" and "jungle of suspicion." Ask them to make a list of similar word groups they find puzzling. Discuss the meanings of the word groups with the class.

▶Critical Viewing◀

1 Infer The images seem to reflect the unsettling, cold-war period during which Kennedy served as President. The unfinished quality of the upper right corner may signify the unfinished presidential term of Kennedy.

◆ Critical Thinking

2 Speculate Ask students: Why do you think Kennedy refers to himself and his audience as "heirs of that first revolution"? *He is establishing a feeling of patriotism by connecting the present time with the patriotic fervor of the Revolutionary War period.*

◆ Critical Thinking

3 Compare Ask students: How does this paragraph echo Patrick Henry's and Benjamin Franklin's speeches? *The phrases show parallelism and repetition and show concern over the "success of liberty."*

Humanities: Art

Retroactive I, 1964, by Robert Rauschenberg.

This work of art, created from oils and silk-screen on canvas, uses Kennedy's image to create a reflection of the young president's era.

Born in Port Arthur, Texas, Robert Rauschenberg (1925–   ) is an American artist who experiments with different combinations of various materials and techniques. Beginning in the early 1960's, Rauschenberg began to combine media images with printmaking techniques to create striking works like the one shown here.

Use these questions for discussion:

1. What impression about the Kennedy era do you get from this work? *Students might say the period was chaotic, complex, or uncertain.*
2. Does the work capture the mood and content of the inaugural address? Why or why not? *Student opinions should be supported by citations from the speech.*

Customize for
Less Proficient Readers
Help these students see that paragraph beginnings within the speech show parallel thoughts. Point out that six paragraphs begin "To . . ." (with the sixth beginning, "Finally, to . . ."). Explain that each of these specifies what Kennedy is pledging and is introduced by the single-line paragraph, "This much we pledge—and more."

Customize for
AP Students
Have these students work in teams to analyze the grammatical parallels in portions of Kennedy's speech. They may choose to develop a graphic organizer to show the similar grammatical structures.

Customize for
Musical/Rhythmic Learners
What makes a speech memorable is its use of language, usually a rhythmic pattern involving parallelism and/or repetition. Have these students reread the speech and identify the musical/rhythmic phrases and sentences.

❶ **Clarification** Explain to students that in the years immediately following World War II, the United States and other non-communist nations were in a state of "cold war," or rivalry and mutual distrust, with the former Soviet Union and other communist nations. During the Cold War, many Americans feared the possibility of catastrophic nuclear war with the Soviet Union. In addition, many United States government officials believed that communist nations would try to install communist governments in many developing countries throughout the world.

◆ ***Literature and Your Life***

❷ Ask students to discuss if and how Kennedy's sentence, referring to international peace, also applies to their own interpersonal peace. Discussion should include reference to the importance of negotiation, rather than violence, in solving differences.

◆ ***Literature and Your Life***

❸ Ask students: What can you do for your country? *Encourage students to brainstorm for a list of responses.*

To those new States whom we welcome to the ranks of the free, we pledge our word that one form of colonial control shall not have passed away merely to be replaced by a far more iron tyranny. We shall not always expect to find them supporting our view. But we shall always hope to find them strongly supporting their own freedom—and to remember that, in the past, those who foolishly sought power by riding the back of the tiger ended up inside.

❶ To those peoples in the huts and villages across the globe struggling to break the bonds of mass misery, we pledge our best efforts to help them help themselves, for whatever period is required—not because the Communists may be doing it, not because we seek their votes, but because it is right. If a free society cannot help the many who are poor, it cannot save the few who are rich.

My fellow citizens of the world: Ask not what America will do for you, but what together we can do for the freedom of man.

To our sister republics south of our border, we offer a special pledge—to convert our good words into good deeds—in a new alliance for progress—to assist free men and free governments in casting off the chains of poverty. But this peaceful revolution of hope cannot become the prey of hostile powers. Let all our neighbors know that we shall join with them to oppose aggression or subversion anywhere in the Americas. And let every other power know that this Hemisphere intends to remain the master of its own house.

To that world assembly of sovereign states, the United Nations, our last best hope in an age where the instruments of war have far outpaced the instruments of peace, we renew our pledge of support—to prevent it from becoming merely a forum for invective—to strengthen its shield of the new and the weak—and to enlarge the area in which its writ may run.

Finally, to those nations who would make themselves our adversary, we offer not a pledge but a request: that both sides begin anew the quest for peace, before the dark powers of destruction[3] unleashed by science engulf all humanity in planned or accidental self-destruction.

We dare not tempt them with weakness. For only when our arms are sufficient beyond doubt can be we certain beyond doubt that they will never be employed.

But neither can two great and powerful groups of nations take comfort from our present course—both sides overburdened by the cost of modern weapons, both rightly alarmed by the steady spread of the deadly atom, yet both racing to alter that uncertain balance of terror that stays the hand of mankind's final war.

So let us begin anew—remembering on both sides that civility is not a sign of weakness, and sincerity is always subject to proof. Let us never negotiate out of fear. But let us never fear to negotiate. ❷

Let both sides explore what problems unite us instead of belaboring those problems which divide us.

Let both sides, for the first time, formulate serious and precise proposals for the inspection and control of arms—and bring the absolute power to destroy other nations under the absolute control of all nations.

Let both sides seek to invoke the wonders of science instead of its terrors. Together let us explore the stars, conquer the deserts, eradicate disease, tap the ocean depths, and encourage the arts and commerce.

Let both sides unite to heed in all corners of the earth the command of Isaiah—to "undo the heavy burdens . . . and to let the oppressed go free."[4]

◆ Build Vocabulary

tyranny (tir′ ə nē) *n.*: Oppressive and unjust government

alliance (ə lī′əns) *n.*: Union of nations for a specific purpose

invective (in vek′ tiv) *n.*: Verbal attack; strong criticism

adversary (ad′ vər ser′ ē) *n.*: Opponent; enemy

invoke (in vōk′) *v.*: Call on for help, inspiration, or support

eradicate (e rad′ i kāt′) *v.*: Get rid of; wipe out; destroy

3. **dark powers of destruction:** Nuclear war.
4. **Isaiah:** The quotation refers to the passage in Isaiah 58:6.

Analyze a Commentary

Tell students that the images from John F. Kennedy's inauguration are remembered as among the most powerful of his presidency. No part of the inauguration made a greater impression than the speech. Years later one observer remarked, "his inaugural address really inspired people; it was a feeling of renewal." George McGovern, was less positive: "that business of bearing any burden and taking on any foe was great at the time, but looking back on it, I think it was really quite arrogant."

Have students answer the following questions in their journal:

1. What aspects of Kennedy's speech might you have found inspiring? *The possibility of abolishing poverty, the image of Americans as heirs to a revolution, as torchbearers may inspire some students.*
2. Why do you think George McGovern considered Kennedy's statement arrogant? *Some students may identify Kennedy's assumption of such power as arrogant.*

And if a beachhead of cooperation may push back the jungle of suspicion, let both sides join in creating a new endeavor, not a new balance of power, but a new world of law, where the strong are just and the weak secure and the peace preserved.

All this will not be finished in the first 100 days. Nor will it be finished in the first 1,000 days, nor in the life of this Administration, nor even perhaps in our lifetime on this planet. But let us begin.

In your hands, my fellow citizens, more than in mine, will rest the final success or failure of our course. Since this country was founded, each generation of Americans has been summoned to give testimony to its national loyalty. The graves of young Americans who answered the call to service surround the globe.

Now the trumpet summons us again—not as a call to bear arms, though arms we need; not as a call to battle, though embattled we are—but a call to bear the burden of a long twilight struggle, year in and year out, "rejoicing in hope, patient in tribulation"[5]—a struggle against the common enemies of man: tyranny, poverty, disease, and war itself.

Can we forge against these enemies a grand and global alliance, North and South, East and West, that can assure a more fruitful life for all mankind? Will you join in that historic effort?

In the long history of the world, only a few generations have been granted the role of defending freedom in its hour of maximum danger. I do not shrink from this responsibility—I welcome it. I do not believe that any of us would exchange places with any other people or any other generation. The energy, the faith, the devotion which we bring to this endeavor will light our country and all who serve it—and the glow from that fire can truly light the world.

And so, my fellow Americans: Ask not what your country can do for you—ask what you can do for your country. 3

My fellow citizens of the world: Ask not what America will do for you, but what together we can do for the freedom of man.

Finally, whether you are citizens of America or citizens of the world, ask of us the same high standards of strength and sacrifice which we ask of you. With a good conscience our only sure reward, with history the final judge of our deeds, let us go forth to lead the land we love, asking His blessing and His help, but knowing that here on earth God's work must truly be our own.

5. **"rejoicing . . . tribulation":** From Romans 12:12. In Paul's letter to the Romans, he enjoins people to work together in love and mutual respect.

CONNECTIONS TO TODAY'S WORLD

Guide for Responding

◆ Literature and Your Life

Reader's Response Which lines or phrases from Kennedy's speech do you find most memorable? Why? Which have you heard quoted elsewhere?

Thematic Focus What does Kennedy's speech reveal about the time in which it was delivered?

☑ Check Your Comprehension

1. What is the "end, as well as a beginning" to which Kennedy refers?
2. List two specific pledges Kennedy makes.

◆ Critical Thinking

INTERPRET

1. Why does Kennedy make reference to the founders of the country? **[Infer]**
2. What do the "new generation of Americans" have in common with the Revolutionary colonists? **[Compare]**
3. What strategy does Kennedy defend with "We dare not tempt . . . with weakness"? **[Interpret]**
4. What do you think Kennedy saw as the country's greatest challenge? **[Draw Conclusions]**

EXTEND

5. Locate evidence in this speech to prove that Kennedy believed in volunteerism. **[Social Studies Link]**

Prepare and Engage

Answers

◆ Literature and Your Life

Reader's Response Students could cite lines such as the following:

"Let us never negotiate out of fear . . . ," or "Ask not what your country . . ."

Thematic Focus The speech reveals that Kennedy spoke in a time of international tension.

☑ Check Your Comprehension

1. Kennedy refers to the end of one political administration and the beginning of another.
2. Kennedy pledges to support the success of liberty and to help poor emerging nations through building an alliance for progress.

◆ Critical Thinking

1. He mentions the founders of the country to illustrate that the same revolutionary belief in human rights must still be upheld in modern society.
2. They both have a commitment to human rights.
3. Kennedy defends the strategy of negotiating from strength—the strength of an ample supply of nuclear weapons as a deterrent to keep other nations from starting a nuclear war.
4. Response may include the challenge of defending human rights and freedoms at home and abroad or reducing the number of nuclear weapons worldwide.
5. Perhaps the greatest evidence is the famous statement, "Ask not what your country can do for you—ask what you can do for your country."

Beyond the Selection

FURTHER READING

Other Works by John F. Kennedy
Profiles in Courage

Other Speeches
Great American Speeches 1898–1963, John Graham

Works About John F. Kennedy
John F. Kennedy, Judie Mills
One Brief Shining Moment, William Manchester

We suggest that you preview these works before recommending them to students.

INTERNET

You and your students may find additional information about John F. Kennedy on the Internet. We suggest the following sites. Please be aware, however, that the sites may have changed from the time we published this information.

For more about Kennedy, visit the John Fitzgerald Kennedy National Historic Site at **http://www.nps.gov/jofi/** or visit the J. F. K. Library and Museum at **http://www.cs.umb.edu/jfklibrary/index.htm**

We *strongly recommend* that you preview the sites before you send students to them.

Answers
Thematic Connection

1. (a) You expect to be persuaded or directed to take a particular course of action. (b) Kennedy urges his audience to think positively about the future they will build.
2. (a) A setting such as the steps of the Capitol can add to the perceived formality or importance of a speech. (b) On radio, the speech might have been perceived as more intimate or personal.
3. Students should support their comparisons with examples from the speeches.

Literary Connection

1. (a) This excerpt uses the techniques of a carefully turned phrase and of parallelism.
(b) This excerpt uses the techniques of repetition and parallelism.
2. Sentences should mimic the style of the chosen passage.

Idea Bank
Customizing for ***Performance Levels***
Following are suggestions for matching Idea Bank topics with your students' performance levels:
Less Advanced Students: 1
Average Students: 2, 4
More Advanced Students: 3, 5

Customizing for ***Learning Modalities***
Following are suggestions for matching Idea Bank topics with your students' learning modalities:
Interpersonal: 4
Visual/Spatial: 5

Thematic Connection

AMERICAN SPEECHMAKING

You may not consider yourself an audience for speechmakers, but modern media, especially television, has put speakers and audiences in closer contact today than ever before in history. Even the most casual channel surfer will encounter news clips from speeches at fund-raisers or political gatherings or the floor of the legislature. In fact, in this age of instant news, some speakers anticipate a reporter's need for brief quotations and include succinct phrases for the "sound bites" that will appear in newscasts.

1. (a) What expectations do you have when listening to a political speaker? (b) How does Kennedy's speech fulfill those expectations?
2. (a) How does setting—the Oval Office, the steps of the Capitol, or the halls of Congress—affect the way a speech is received? (b) How would Kennedy's speech be different if it were presented as a radio address?
3. How does Kennedy's speech compare with other political speeches you've heard or seen?

Literary Connection

SPEECHES

American leaders have delivered speeches to announce new beginnings, calm a worried public, or set a firm stance against our enemies. For some speakers, the style of the message is just as important as the message itself. A carefully turned phrase, a memorable line, or the slightest hint of poetry can make a speech more moving. Other persuasive techniques include parallelism, the repeated use of a grammatical structure; repetition, the presentation of the same idea using the same language; and the restatement of an idea in different ways.

1. For each of the following lines from Kennedy's speech, identify the technique used.
a. If a free society cannot help the many who are poor, it cannot save the few who are rich.
b. Let us never negotiate out of fear. But let us never fear to negotiate.
2. Choose one of the two preceding passages. Then write two sentences of your own that follow the pattern Kennedy used in that passage.

Idea Bank

Writing

1. Summation Recall an effective speech that you have heard. Write an essay that sums up the main ideas the speaker expressed.

2. Research Writing Use the Internet to find the transcript, audio, or video of another president's inaugural speech. Read or listen carefully and compare the one you choose with the speeches of Kennedy, Franklin, and Henry. Sum up your findings in a brief essay. **[Technology Link]**

3. Comparative Essay Compare Kennedy's oratorical skills with those of either Franklin or Henry. Decide what elements are unique to each speaker's style and clarify points of contrast. End by offering your opinion on which man was the better speech writer. Back up your opinion with details from the two speeches.

Speaking, Listening, and Viewing

4. Volunteerism Survey Kennedy's belief in humanity's ability to help one another was the driving force behind the founding of the Peace Corps. Find out about volunteer opportunities in your community. To learn what attracts people to their work, interview people who volunteer. Collate their responses and share your findings with your class. **[Community Link]**

Researching and Representing

5. Video Record Put together a videotape of a program of student speakers or a local community meeting. Edit the recording to illustrate effective speechmaking techniques the speakers have used. Present your edited video to the class and invite their critiques. **[Technology Link]**

Online Activity www.phlit.phschool.com

ASSESSMENT OPTIONS

Formal Assessment, Selection Test, pp. 56–57, and Assessment Resources Software. The selection test is designed so that it can be easily customized to the performance levels of your students.

PORTFOLIO ASSESSMENT
Use the following rubrics in the ***Alternative Assessment*** booklet to assess student writing:
Summation: Summary Rubric, p. 113
Research Writing: Research Report/Paper Rubric, p. 121
Comparative Essay: Comparison/Contrast Rubric, p. 118

Writing Process Workshop

Informative Speech

What comes to mind when you hear the word **speech**? The science talk on black holes that fired your imagination? Martin Luther King at the Washington Monument, searing the conscience of a nation? Or, Patrick Henry changing the course of history? These are examples of oratory at its best: combining the power of the word and the drama of the human voice to inform, entertain, persuade, inspire.

Most of the speeches you are likely to encounter—television sales pitches, campaign talks, or Patrick Henry's address to the Virginia legislature—seek to persuade. Speeches can be just as effective in educating and informing, however. The following skills will help you to deliver an effective informative speech.

Writing Skills Focus

- **Anticipate questions** by considering your likely audience and listing the questions that your listeners are likely to have. Try to answer as many of these questions as possible. (See p. 175.)
- **Use transitional words and phrases** to make clear connections among your ideas.
- **Check the accuracy** of the facts you are reporting.

Patrick Henry Before the Virginia House of Burgesses, (detail), Peter F. Rothermel, Red Hill, the Patrick Henry National Memorial

Writing Model

Imagine learning that your only hope for survival is a heart transplant! ① In the United States, your chances of finding a heart for transplant are the best in the world. Yet ② you have no guarantees: Last year 52,000 people waited for organ transplants, but only 19,410 were actually performed. Consider your quandary, then, if you lived in Japan, where a stricter definition of the moment of death has led to a shortage of donated organs. The result: ③ Each year, hundreds of Japanese lives are lost.

④ What exactly is the difference in the way Japan and the Western countries define the end of life?

① The writer immediately grabs the listeners, using their imaginations to place them in a suspenseful situation.

② The speaker leads into a statistic with a transitional word.

③ The speaker maintains a conversational tone by varying the length of sentences.

④ The speaker anticipates listeners' questions and thereby fastens on the main topic.

Prepare and Engage

LESSON OBJECTIVES

- To use recursive writing processes to write an informative speech
- To recognize and correct misplaced or dangling modifiers
- To use transitions for coherence

Establish Writing Guidelines

Distribute the scoring rubrics for Summary (p. 113), Definition/ Classification (p. 114), and How-to/ Process Explanation (p. 115) in ***Alternative Assessment.*** See the suggestions on page 183 for customizing the rubrics to this workshop.

Distribute the Outline Graphic Organizer (pp. 95–97) in the ***Writing and Language Transparencies*** to help students organize their ideas.

Connect to Literature Students may benefit from reviewing the ways the speeches by Henry and Franklin (p. 168 and p. 172) demonstrate different speech-writing techniques.

Writers at Work Videodisc

To show students how Transit Museum curator Thom Harrington gives informative tours, play the videodisc segment on Exposition (Ch. 3). Ask students to compare and contrast his live presentations with the delivery of a formal speech.

Play frames 23159 to 33243

Writing Lab CD-ROM

If your students have access to computers, you may want to have them work in the tutorial on Exposition. Have students follow these steps:

1. Review the audio-annotated model of an informative speech.
2. Complete a Topic Wheels activity specifically designed to help find topics for informative speeches.
3. Draft on the computer.
4. Use the Self-Evaluation Checklist to help judge the effectiveness of their speeches.

Beyond the Classroom

Workplace Skills Connection

Lecturing Students will be familiar with informative speeches given in academic settings by teachers. Point out, however, that classroom teaching is not the only profession in which a person might be required to speak to the public with an informative purpose. Park rangers, tour guides, spokespersons in the fields of fire prevention and public safety, human resource trainers who instruct the work force—frequently give talks that are similar to informative speeches. In addition, highly regarded experts in a given field such as politics or the sciences may also be asked to speak at colleges or universities, or to address large groups at conventions or fund-raising events.

Ask students to decide which strategies for writing informative speeches would be most helpful to (a) tour guide; (b) a presidential spokesperson; and (c) a trainer. *Students should note that audience and purpose will affect the speeches each presents.*

Prewriting Strategy
Suggest that students use a topic web to brainstorm for different aspects of their topics.

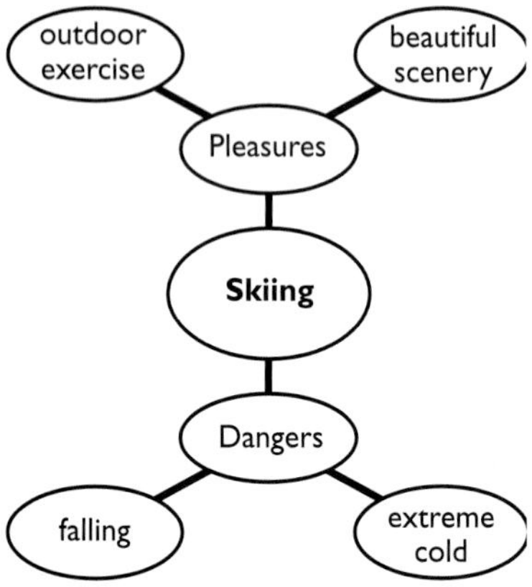

Customize for
Interpersonal Learners
Encourage these students to interview their peers as necessary to gain an understanding of what their audience might expect from an informative speech on a given topic.

Writing Lab CD-ROM
Have students use the many audio-annotated models in the Drafting section of the tutorial. They can explore writing models of introductions, bodies, and conclusions as well as a student model.

Elaboration Strategy
If students decide to use the note card method of delivering their informative speeches, provide them with this tip: Write the topic of a particular card at the top using large, bold letters resembling a headline, and then write the actual detailed text in a smaller hand beneath it. This way the speaker can decide whether the note card should be used simply as a memory prompt for improvising or expanding, or as the full text to be read verbatim.

Applying Language Skills: Misplaced or Dangling Modifiers
A modifying word or phrase should be placed as close as possible to the modified words in order to avoid confusing or even unintentionally comical results.

Misplaced Modifier:
Entering the main exhibition hall, the dinosaur display was breathtaking. (dangling participle)

Corrected:
Entering the main exhibition hall, we found the dinosaur display breathtaking.

Notice that the participle "entering," which absurdly seems to modify "dinosaur display" in the first sentence, correctly modifies "we" in the corrected version.

Practice On your paper, correct the following misplaced modifiers.

1. Careening down the ski slope, a tree suddenly appeared directly in my path.
2. The mechanic said that he only works on weekdays.
3. Yesterday we heard a fascinating lecture about quasars in the auditorium.

Writing Application Review your informative speech for any misplaced or dangling modifiers, and correct them by placing them as close as possible to the word or words they modify.

Prewriting
Choose a Topic You can't fake interest or enthusiasm: If you're not genuinely interested in your topic, you will likely have an audience of squirmy clock-watchers. Make a list of topics that really interest you, that you'd like to know more about, and that you would enjoy sharing with others. Keep in mind that your informative speech is really an expository essay adapted to the spoken word, so a wide array of topical categories are suitable: comparison and contrast, problem and solution, cause and effect, consumer report, or summary.

Topic Ideas
- Dog-training techniques
- The history of women's professional basketball
- Skiing: pleasures and dangers
- The effect of pollution on global warming
- Summary of a favorite novel or movie
- Personal guide to local hiking trails

Research Your Topic Unless your topic is something in which you already possess considerable expertise (say, skiing or hiking), you will have to gather enough material to make your presentation truly informative to your listeners. Ask interesting and relevant questions about your topic to help guide your research. Use key words from these questions to search the Internet and computer databases and card catalogs in the library. Don't stint on research: Be sure your listeners will really learn something from your talk.

Drafting
Organize Your Ideas Decide whether it's best to develop your ideas chronologically or in order of importance.

Decide Between Note Cards and Writing Out the Text Speeches that are read verbatim from a text often have a stiff, inexpressive quality. Consider the possibility of jotting down your key ideas on note cards and expanding on your notes informally as you give your talk.

Think of a Snappy Opening Most often you will either win or lose your audience in the first few minutes of your speech. A snappy, lively opening is crucial in "hooking" your audience. If appropriate to the topic, a time-tested way to engage your listeners is to open with a joke or humorous anecdote.

Applying Language Skills
Misplaced or Dangling Modifiers Because misplaced modifiers often create unintentional humor, you may want to engage students by inviting them to come up with their own comic sentences to share with the class. You may also want to help students distinguish between dangling and misplaced modifiers by pointing out that in the former the item that should be modified is usually missing completely from the sentence.

Answers
1. Careening down the ski slope, *I gasped as* a tree suddenly appeared directly in my path.
2. The mechanic said that he works on weekdays *only.*
3. Yesterday *in the auditorium* we heard a fascinating lecture about quasars.

Grammar Reinforcement
For additional instruction and practice, use Misplaced Modifiers lesson in the **Language Lab CD-ROM,** and practice pages 47 and 48 in the *Writer's Solution Grammar Practice Book.*

Use a Varied Rhythm and Structure Avoid a monotonous, sing-song delivery that will lull your listeners into dreamland. It's equally important to vary sentence length, although shorter sentences, even the occasional fragment, work best in oral presentations.

Practice Tape yourself, stand in front of a mirror, or ask someone to listen to your speech.

Revising

As you revise your speech following your rehearsal, ask yourself these questions:

- Are my ideas presented clearly and logically?
- Did I "hook" my listeners with a lively opening?
- Did I use transitional words and phrases?
- Did I vary the length of my sentences?
- Have I anticipated my listeners' questions?

Revision Model

Many Japanese believe that death occurs when the heart stops beating ~~, whereas~~ ① . In contrast, Western medicine defines death as the moment when the brain stops functioning, even if the heart is still beating with the help of a respirator ~~, an~~ ② . This outlook ~~that~~ makes it easier to obtain healthy, functioning organs for transplant to ~~others.~~ other patients whose lives hang in the balance. ③

① ② The speaker breaks up two longer sentences into shorter ones with transitional phrases to make the speech easier to follow.

③ This insertion of punchier, more emotive language enlivens the presentation.

Publishing

Deliver Your Speech As you deliver your speech, vary the volume and tone of your voice to emphasize key ideas. In addition, use hand gestures as a means of reinforcing your ideas. Try to avoid focusing your eyes on a single person. Instead, scan your audience, trying to meet as many eyes as possible.

Applying Language Skills: Using Transitions

Transitional words or phrases can help you make your writing more coherent by clarifying various kinds of relationships among ideas: in time, space, order of importance, cause and effect, comparison and contrast, or example.

No Transition: Flying is the fastest way of getting there. Taking the train allows you to see the country close up.

Transition: Flying is the fastest way of getting there, but taking the train allows you to see the country close up.

The addition of "but" drives home the contrast between the two forms of travel.

Practice On your paper, join the following ideas with the appropriate transitional word or phrase.

1. Vicky is a talented singer. Yolanda is a more versatile performer.
2. The frost was severe. The orange crop is in danger.
3. A serious hobby can be very satisfying. Marco enjoys building furniture in his workshop.

Writing Application As you draft your informative speech, look for relationships between ideas that could be clarified through the use of transitional words or phrases.

Revision Strategy

Invite students to use peer reviewers to act as a "rehearsal audience" for their speeches.

Publishing

You might want to videotape students' delivery of their informative speeches to present them to a wider audience.

Applying Language Skills

Using Transitions Explain to students that the effective use of transitions will help an audience follow their speeches better.

Answers

Suggested Responses:

1. Vicky is a talented singer, but Yolanda is a more versatile performer.
2. The frost was severe, so the orange crop is in danger.
3. A serious hobby can be very satisfying; for example, Marco enjoys building furniture in his workshop.

Grammar Reinforcement

For additional instruction and practice, use the **Language Lab CD-ROM** lesson on Unity and Coherence in Paragraphs and practice page 114 in the *Writer's Solution Grammar Practice Book.*

Reinforce and Extend

For more prewriting, elaboration, and revision strategies, see *Prentice Hall Writing and Grammar.*

Reflect on Writing Because this workshop contained elements of both writing and speaking, ask students to compare and contrast their skill and enjoyment level for each.

✓ ASSESSMENT		4	3	2	1
PORTFOLIO ASSESSMENT Use the expository writing rubrics in ***Alternative Assessment.*** For example, you might use Summary (p. 113); Definition/Classification (p. 114); or How-to/Process Explanation (p. 115) to assess students' writing. Add the following criteria to customize rubrics to this assignment.	**Using Transitions**	The writer consistently provides transitional words and phrases that signal the relationships between ideas.	The writer includes transitional words and phrases, using them correctly.	The writer provides transitional words and phrases infrequently or unclearly.	The writer consistently avoids using transitional words and phrases, thus making the speech hard to follow.
	Anticipates Questions	The writer consistently anticipates listeners' questions and answers them effectively.	The writer occasionally anticipates listeners' questions and answers them.	The writer rarely anticipates listeners' questions, and/or fails to answer them effectively.	The writer avoids anticipating or answering questions one might expect from listeners.

Prepare and Engage

LESSON OBJECTIVES

- To discriminate between connotative and denotative meanings and interpret the connotative power of words

Customize for
English Language Learners
As they encounter examples of connotation, have students create and add to a vocabulary log to reinforce the ways words can be used for particular effects. Students may want to create word webs to show how certain words are related but different in their denotative and connotative meanings. Encourage students to explore how similar words and meanings are expressed in their first language.

Apply the Strategies

Answers
Possible responses:

1. *Bask* means "to expose pleasantly to warmth," which is a meaning used in the passage, but as it refers to both the warmth of the sun and the coolness of tropical breezes, it connotes more than simple warmth; *bask* becomes closer in meaning to *luxuriate*.
2. Some synonyms for *crave* include *want, wish for, long for,* and *hanker*. These synonyms are not as precise as *crave*, as it is used in the passage. *Crave* connotes hunger and desire simultaneously, so it is an effective choice here.
3. *Monday* cannot be replaced with another day of the week because it signals the beginning of a long work week.

Student Success Workshop

Vocabulary Development — Understanding Connotation and Denotation

Strategies for Success

Good writers choose their words carefully. They use the direct and implied meanings of words to say exactly what they mean. **Denotation** is the literal, exact meaning of a word as it is found in a dictionary. For example, a *home* is defined as "one's place of residence." **Connotation,** however, describes the various associations a word brings with it and involves the reader's emotional response to a word. The connotations of *home* may include *security* and *a sense of one's own place* or *belonging.*

Distinguish Between Connotation and Denotation Recognizing the differences between connotation and denotation will help you in your reading and writing. Confusion can arise when a word's connotations are so strong or familiar that they replace the word's denotative meaning in daily use. When you are not sure of the meaning of a word, or the effect of its connotations, use a dictionary and thesaurus to help in your understanding.

Interpret Connotative Meanings Words that are similar in meaning can have different connotative meanings. For example, *politician* and *statesman* both describe a person involved in public affairs. Connotatively, however, *politician* implies someone more involved in the day-to-day processes of public affairs, whereas statesman refers to someone who works more on its philosophical aspects. When you read, check the context of a word. What connotative clues does the context offer? Also, be alert for how certain words make you feel. Your response will further help you interpret a word's connotative meaning.

Apply the Strategies

The front page of this travel brochure contains only words. Evaluate the use of connotation and denotation in this excerpt, and answer the questions that follow.

> Imagine yourself on a sun-drenched beach. You're gazing at an endless emerald sea. The warm rays of the sun feel good against your skin and find contrast in the late-afternoon tropical breeze. You bask in both, not sure which you crave more. And then you think of everyone back in the office. It's a Monday, and they still have the whole week to go. . . .
>
> Why don't you make your reservation with us today and begin reveling in your next vacation?

1. Look up the underlined words in a dictionary. Do their denotative meanings create a feeling different from their connotative meanings? Explain.
2. Do synonyms of the underlined words have the same connotative power? Explain why the writer might have chosen these words instead of their synonyms.
3. Can you replace the word *Monday* and get the same effect? What other words or phrases were chosen specifically for their connotative impact?

✔ *Here are other situations in which you might need to evaluate the connotative meanings of words:*
- ▶ *Sales materials*
- ▶ *Job-performance evaluation*
- ▶ *Political speeches*

Test Preparation Workshop

Understanding Connotation and Denotation
Developing an understanding of denotative meanings and the power of connotation will help students perform well on standardized tests. Refer students to the sample passage on p. 184. Then, write the following sample on the board.

The word gazing as it is used in the passage most nearly means—

A not paying attention
B looking boldly at something
C looking in a prolonged and admiring way
D looking vacantly at something

Guide students to recognize that *C* is the best answer because this connotation of *gazing* fits best with the context and tone of the passage. *B* and *D* are also connotative meanings for *gazing*, but they are not appropriate meanings in this context.

Part 3 Defining an American

Eighteenth-century New England needlework
Colonial Williamsburg Foundation

The colonial victory in the Revolutionary War brought about the creation of a nation unlike any other. While the young nation was busy devising a new government and designing new currency, writers, including those in this section, tackled the task of defining what it means to be an American. The definitions that emerged include many of the characteristics that Americans still use in defining themselves today.

One-Minute Planning Guide

The selections in this section illustrate the American character that began to emerge in the eighteenth century. The excerpt from *Poor Richard's Almanack* gives practical advice on being a successful American. Abigail Adams's "Letter to Her Daughter from the New White House" illustrates both literally and figuratively that the United States was a country under construction. "Letters from an American Farmer" defines a new kind of person, an American. This section ends with an excerpt from *Roots,* a contemporary work that traces the history of Americans of African descent.

Customize for *Varying Student Needs*

When assigning the selections in this part, keep in mind these factors:

from *Poor Richard's Almanack*
- Most students will be delighted by these still-familiar aphorisms

"Letter to Her Daughter from the New White House"
- The subject of the White House under construction will appeal to most students
- Background information on designating a national capital may be helpful
- Early history of the White House and Washington, D.C. may give context to the letter

"Letters from an American Farmer"
- Vocabulary and philosophy may prove difficult to students
- Background on life in Great Britain at time the selection was written can aid comprehension

from *Roots*
- Accessible, high interest autobiographical account
- Students could benefit from background of how first Africans arrived in America.

Humanities: Art

Eighteenth-century New England needlework.

This needlework creation was made in the 1700's by a woman in New England. Help students see that the bright colors and loving detail of the work suggest the charm the creator saw in the land around her. The land is green, fertile, and abundant in both plant and animal life. The couple are happily reaping grain and picnicking. The natural scene—complete with serpent—recalls paradise in its beauty and innocence, suggesting America might be viewed as a New Eden.

Have your students link the art to the focus of Part 3, The Emerging American Identity: Defining an American, by answering the following questions:

1. According to this needlework creation, what things were important to 18th century Americans? *Sample answer: This needlework suggests that Americans valued the beauty of their land, its ability to provide for them, the animals that they encountered both wild and domestic, their homes, and their family life.*
2. Give this needlework a title appropriate to the idea of a new nation. *Sample answers: "A New Eden"; "A Day in an American Life"; "A Time to Work, A Time to Play"; "Adam and Eve in the New World."*

LESSON OBJECTIVES

1. To develop vocabulary and word identification skills
- Words With Multiple Meanings
- Using the Word Bank

2. To use a variety of reading strategies to comprehend a sermon
- Reading Strategy: Relate to Your Experiences

3. To express and support responses to the text
- Critical Thinking
- Idea Bank: Personal Narrative
- Idea Bank: Rap
- Idea Bank: Board Game
- Idea Bank: Folk Tale

4. To analyze literary elements
- Literary Focus: Aphorisms

5. To read in order to research self-selected and assigned topics
- Idea Bank: Instruction Manual

6. To plan, prepare, organize, and present literary interpretations
- Idea Bank: Oral Presentation
- Idea Bank: Magazine Article

7. To use recursive writing processes to write an Internet Page
- Guided Writing Lesson

8. To increase knowledge of the rules of grammar and usage
- Build Grammar Skills: Irregular Comparison of Adjectives and Adverbs

Test Preparation

Reading Comprehension: Recognize Cause and Effect (ATE, p. 187)
The teaching tips and sample test item in this workshop support the instruction and practice in the unit workshop:

Reading Comprehension: Recognize Cause and Effect; Predict Outcomes (SE, p. 213)

Guide for Interpreting

Featured in AUTHORS IN DEPTH Series

Benjamin Franklin

(1706–1790)

From his teen years until his retirement at forty-two, Benjamin Franklin worked as a printer. Franklin got his start as an apprentice to his brother, a Boston printer. By the time he was sixteen, he was not only printing, but writing parts of his brother's newspaper. Using the name "Silence Dogood," Franklin satirized daily life and politics in Boston. His printing career gave birth to one of Franklin's most popular and enduring contributions to American culture, *Poor Richard's Almanack*. This annual publication, which Franklin published from 1732 through 1757, contained information, observations, and advice that was very popular with readers of his day.

The "Write" Reputation Just as he had signed "Silence Dogood" to the letters he wrote for his brother's paper, Franklin created for the *Almanack* a fictitious author/editor, the chatty Richard Saunders (and his wife, Bridget). It was, however, well known that Franklin was the author. Despite the fact that he published under a pseudonym, the *Almanack* earned him a reputation as a talented writer.

Secret to Success Like most almanacs, Franklin's contained practical information about the calendar, the sun and moon, and the weather.

Poor Richard's Almanack also featured a wealth of homespun sayings and observations, many of which are still quoted today.

It was these aphorisms, with their characteristic moral overtones, that made the *Almanack* a bestseller. Franklin put an aphorism at the top or bottom of most pages of his almanacs. The wit and brevity of these sayings allowed Franklin to include many moral messages in very little space, while also entertaining his readers.

Franklin sold the almanac in 1758, and it continued publication under a different name until 1796. While *Poor Richard's Almanack* is no longer with us, the aphorisms that enlivened its pages under Franklin live on as classic bits of Americana. (For more on Benjamin Franklin, see pp. 128 and 166.)

◆ Background for Understanding

SOCIAL STUDIES: THE PROVERB TRADITION

Most of Benjamin Franklin's aphorisms are adapted from anonymous traditional or folk sayings, known as **proverbs.** Franklin, who believed that clarity and brevity were two of the most important characteristics of good prose, rewrote many proverbs, crafting short, direct, witty sayings that taught a lesson.

Proverbs are nearly as old as language itself. They have many different purposes and are used in different types of situations—to amuse, to educate, to sanction, to shame, to make a point, or to add color to a conversation.

As expressions of basic principles of folk wisdom drawn from the daily experiences of a group of people, proverbs exist in all societies. They reflect a particular culture's view of the world and convey feelings about fate, the seasons, the natural world, work and effort, love, death, and other universal experiences. These memorable bits of wisdom have survived centuries, perhaps because they reflect unchanging truths about human nature.

Prentice Hall Literature Program Resources

REINFORCE / RETEACH / EXTEND

Selection Support Pages
Build Vocabulary: Words With Multiple Meanings, p. 57
Grammar and Style: Irregular Comparison of Adjectives and Adverbs, p. 58
Reading Strategy: Relate to Your Experiences, p. 59
Literary Focus: Aphorisms, p. 60

Strategies for Diverse Student Needs, p. 12

Beyond Literature, p. 12

Formal Assessment Selection Test, pp. 61–63; Alternative Assessment, p. 12

Writing and Language Transparencies
Outline Organizer, p. 95

Resource Pro CD-ROM

Listening to Literature Audiocassettes

Literature CD-ROM

from Poor Richard's Almanack

◆ Literature and Your Life

Connect Your Experience

"No pain, no gain." "Garbage In, Garbage Out." You see sayings like these on bumper stickers, T-shirts, and billboards. Though such snippets of pop-wisdom are more likely to originate in entertainment media than an almanac, they mirror modern social values, just as Franklin's aphorisms reflect the values of colonial America.

Journal Writing Think of at least three contemporary aphorisms. What do they say about our culture? Write your answers in your journal.

Thematic Focus: Defining an American

Franklin's aphorisms were so influential that even this early United States coin was stamped "mind your business," a motto supposedly suggested by Franklin. His sayings helped shape the nation's image as a country of people who prized hard work and common sense.

◆ Literary Focus

Aphorisms

You may find that you are already familiar with many of the witty sayings, or aphorisms, from *Poor Richard's Almanack*. An **aphorism** is a short, concise statement expressing a wise or clever observation or a general truth. It usually reflects the setting and the time frame in which it was created. A variety of devices make aphorisms easy to remember. Some contain rhymes or repeated words or sounds; others use parallel structure to present contrasting ideas. The aphorism "no pain, no gain," for instance, uses rhyme, repetition, and parallel structure.

◆ Grammar and Style

Irregular Comparison of Adjectives and Adverbs

While most adjectives and adverbs use *-er* or *more/less* to form the comparative, and *-est* or *most/least* to form the superlative, some have **irregular** forms. Notice the comparative form of *well* in this sentence:

Well done is *better* than *well* said. . .

Better is the irregular comparative of the adverb *well.* If the aphorism compared a third item, the irregular superlative *best* would have been used:

. . . but *best* of all is well fed.

◆ Reading Strategy

Relate to Your Experiences

Though these eighteenth-century aphorisms may at first appear to have little relevance to your world, careful reading reveals meanings that you can **relate to your own experiences**. By definition, aphorisms—like most literature—contain observations about human nature that are just as true today as they were centuries ago. Increase your understanding of what you read by asking yourself how the meaning of each aphorism applies to experiences you've had.

◆ Build Vocabulary

Words With Multiple Meanings

The *Almanack* says, "He that lives upon hope will die fasting." In this context, *fasting* has little to do with speed. *Fasting* is the gerund formed from the verb *fast*, which means "to eat little or nothing." The adverb *fast* can also mean "firmly" or "thoroughly," as in "fast asleep."

Word Bank

Preview this list of words from the *Almanack*.

fasting
squander

Interest Grabber

Proverbs, from which Franklin's aphorisms were adapted, are familiar to all of us. Share some of the following with your students:

Haste makes waste.
No pain, no gain.
A stitch in time saves nine.

Ask students to name other proverbs or aphorisms they have heard. Write them on the chalkboard. Have students check a dictionary of quotations to check the source. How many come from Benjamin Franklin's *Poor Richard's Almanack?*

Customize for *Less Proficient Readers*

Because of their metaphoric quality, aphorisms may be difficult for less proficient readers to understand. Begin with the contemporary "Life is a box of chocolates" or use a slogan from a bumper sticker or T-shirt. Discuss the metaphoric meaning so that these students see how to draw their own comparisons as they read Franklin's aphorisms.

Customize for *AP Students*

Ask students to compare a copy of a recent issue of *The Farmer's Almanac* with a complete copy of *Poor Richard's Almanack*. (See the Internet note at the end of this selection.)

Customize for *English Language Learners*

Have students concentrate on multiple meanings of words. Ask them to choose five of Franklin's aphorisms, explain them, and give a modern application. For instance, "Fish and visitors smell in three days" includes a double meaning of "smell." Franklin does not mean that the visitors haven't bathed, but that their presence is a rotten situation and therefore "smells."

Customize for *Interpersonal Learners*

Franklin's aphorisms include advice for moral, personal, and interpersonal behavior. Ask these learners, with a partner, to pick five aphorisms which express the best guidelines for good interpersonal relationships and explain why they chose the ones they did.

Test Preparation Workshop

Reading Comprehension: Recognize Cause and Effect Because students will be required to recognize cause-and-effect relationships in standardized tests, help them practice identifying causal relationships with the following example.

Like most almanacs, Poor Richard's contained practical information about the calendar, the sun and moon, and the weather. It also contained a wealth of homespun sayings and observations, many of which are still used today. It was these aphorisms that made the almanac a bestseller.

Why was Poor Richard's a popular almanac?

A It had useful information.
B It predicted the weather.
C It contained wise sayings.
D People still read it today.

All the answer choices are true, but only choice *C* identifies the cause of the almanac's popularity as described in the passage. Warn students not to accept the first answer that appears to be true, but rather to look for the best answer to the particular question.

Develop Understanding

One-Minute Insight By providing practical wisdom through aphorisms, Benjamin Franklin teaches valuable lessons in brief and easy-to-remember sayings.

Literature CD-ROM To build background about Benjamin Franklin, use the CD-ROM *The History of American Literature*: Part 1, Disc 1, Feature 9, which focuses in part on Franklin.

▶Critical Viewing◀

❶ **Speculate** Students may speculate that *philomath* means "a lover of mathematics," since the Greek prefix *philo* means "love" and *math* is short for mathematics.

◆ Literary Focus

❷ **Aphorisms** Ask students: What device makes this aphorism easy to remember? *Repetition, rhythm, and rhyme make this aphorism easy to remember.*

◆ Critical Thinking

❸ **Connect** Ask students: Coupled with the two preceding aphorisms about friendship ("Be slow in choosing a friend, slower in changing" and "An open foe may prove a curse; but a pretended friend is worse"), what does this aphorism say about Franklin's view of friendship? *He values friendship above all else but knows that true friends are few.*

Read to Appreciate Author's Craft

Guide students to identify the characteristics that continue to make these aphorisms entertaining after two hundred years. Franklin's aphorisms are carefully crafted, stylistically pithy, and varied. Many, such as "Haste makes waste," use devices such as rhyme, alliteration, assonance, parallelism, or metaphor to make their sound and sense pleasing and memorable.

from Poor Richard's Almanack

Benjamin Franklin

Connections to World Literature, *page 1165*

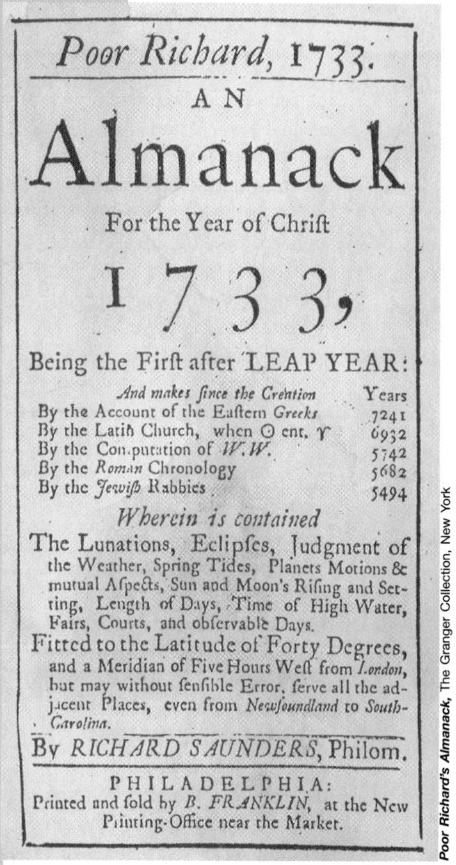
Poor Richard, 1733.

AN

Almanack

For the Year of Chrift

1733,

Being the Firft after LEAP YEAR:

And makes fince the Creation	Years
By the Account of the Eaftern *Greeks*	7241
By the Latin Church, when ☉ ent. ♈	6932
By the Computation of *W. W.*	5742
By the *Roman* Chronology	5682
By the *Jewifh* Rabbies	5494

Wherein is contained

The Lunations, Eclipfes, Judgment of the Weather, Spring Tides, Planets Motions & mutual Afpects, Sun and Moon's Rifing and Setting, Length of Days, Time of High Water, Fairs, Courts, and obfervable Days.

Fitted to the Latitude of Forty Degrees, and a Meridian of Five Hours Weft from *London*, but may without fenfible Error, ferve all the adjacent Places, even from *Newfoundland* to *South-Carolina*.

By *RICHARD SAUNDERS*, Philom.

PHILADELPHIA:
Printed and fold by *B. FRANKLIN*, at the New Printing-Office near the Market.

Poor Richard's Almanack, The Granger Collection, New York

❶ ▲ **Critical Viewing** In the byline, after Benjamin Franklin's pseudonym, Richard Saunders, is the title "Philom.," short for philomath. Use your knowledge of word roots to infer the meaning of the word philomath. **[Speculate]**

Fools make feasts, and wise men eat them.

Be slow in choosing a friend, slower in changing.

Keep thy shop, and thy shop will keep thee.

Early to bed, early to rise, makes a man healthy, wealthy, and wise. ❷

Three may keep a secret if two of them are dead.

God helps them that help themselves.

The rotten apple spoils his companions.

An open foe may prove a curse; but a pretended friend is worse.

Have you somewhat to do tomorrow, do it today.

A true friend is the best possession. ❸

A small leak will sink a great ship.

No gains without pains.

'Tis easier to prevent bad habits than to break them.

Well done is better than well said.

Humanities: Art

Cover, *Poor Richard's Almanack* by Benjamin Franklin, published annually 1733–1758.

Like most almanacs, Poor Richard's contained practical information about the calendar, the sun and moon, and the weather. It also contained a wealth of homespun sayings and observations, many of which are still used today. It was these aphorisms, with their characteristic moral overtones, that made the almanac a bestseller. Franklin sold the almanac in 1758, and it continued publication until 1796 under a different name.

Use these questions for discussion:

1. What makes the page difficult for today's audiences to read? *The letter s is printed differently.*
2. Would the information in this almanac be accurate for the area where you live? *The information is appropriate for areas adjacent to Philadelphia—from Newfoundland to South Carolina.*

4 Dost thou love life? Then do not squander time; for that's the stuff life is made of.

Write injuries in dust, benefits in marble.

A slip of the foot you may soon recover, but a slip of the tongue you may never get over.

If your head is wax, don't walk in the sun.

A good example is the best sermon.

5 Hunger is the best pickle.

Genius without education is like silver in the mine.

6 For want of a nail the shoe is lost; for want of a shoe the horse is lost; for want of a horse the rider is lost.

7 Haste makes waste.

The doors of wisdom are never shut.

Love your neighbor; yet don't pull down your hedge.

He that lives upon hope will die fasting.

◆ Build Vocabulary

squander (skwän´ dər) *v.*: Spend or use wastefully

fasting (fast´ iŋ) *v.*: Eating very little or nothing

Guide for Responding

◆ Literature and Your Life

Reader's Response Which of Franklin's aphorisms have friends or family members quoted?

Thematic Focus Which of Franklin's aphorisms express values that are still widely held in America?

Group Activity Ask your classmates to share ethnic or cultural proverbs they may have learned from family members or friends. Write them on the chalkboard and label the country of origin for each. Do any reflect the same values as Franklin's?

☑ Check Your Comprehension

1. What does Ben Franklin say is "the best possession"?
2. Identify two aphorisms that address education.
3. What advice does Franklin offer about breaking bad habits?
4. Paraphrase three of the aphorisms presented here.

Prepare and Engage

◆ Reading Strategy

4 Relate to Your Experience Ask students: How does this aphorism relate to your own life? *Students may respond that they waste too much time.*

5 Clarification Franklin is referring to the use of pickles and other relishes as appetizers, a common practice in his day.

◆ Critical Thinking

6 Ask: How does Franklin's use of humor in these aphorisms help convey his message? *Students may say that humor makes preaching palatable.*

◆ Reading Strategy

7 Relate to Your Experience In what way do Franklin's aphorisms remind you of the little sayings found in Chinese fortune cookies? *Students may respond that fortune cookies, supposedly reminiscent of Confucius' teachings, are like Franklin's aphorisms in that they often have a moral to teach.*

Reinforce and Extend

Answers

◆ Literature and Your Life

Reader's Response Student responses might include many of the aphorisms.

Thematic Connection Most of the aphorisms express timeless values.

Group Activity Students should find that aphorisms from diverse cultures express universal ideas.

☑ Check Your Comprehension

1. A true friend is a best possession.
2. Two aphorisms are "Genius without education is like silver in the mine," and "The doors of education are never shut."
3. Franklin says that it's easier to prevent bad habits than to break them.
4. Paraphrases should retain the intended meanings of the aphorisms.

Reteach

To reteach this selection, use ***Strategies for Diverse Student Needs,*** p. 12.

Beyond the Selection

FURTHER READING

Other Works About Benjamin Franklin

Benjamin Franklin as Others Saw Him, George W. Sanderlin

Miracle at Philadelphia: The Story of the Constitutional Convention, May to September 1787, Catherine D. Bowen

Benjamin Franklin: A Biography, Ronald W. Clark.

We suggest that you preview these works before recommending them to students.

INTERNET

You and your students can find additional information on the Internet.

We suggest the following site. Please note that the site may have changed from the time we published this information.

For a look at the *Old Farmer's Almanac*, visit **http://falcon.jmu.edu/~ramseyil/referenc.htm**

We *strongly recommend* that you preview the site before sending students to it.

Develop Student Writing

Answers

◆ Critical Thinking

1. The first aphorism cautions you to choose a friend carefully, then stand by them. The second aphorism advises readers to quickly forget the bad and never forget the good a person does. Each of these statements advises against rash judgments and urges deliberate, thoughtful acknowledgment of positive things.
2. Possible response: Choose your words carefully; and use your time wisely.
3. Franklin approaches life with common sense and humor. He believes in the virtues of self-reliance, self-discipline, and education.
4. Students should cite an aphorism and support their choice by explaining how it reflects a belief or value important to them.

◆ Literary Focus

1. (a) He uses rhyme, repeated words, and the same grammatical structure. Anyone can recover from a stubbed toe, but a harsh or imprudent word may inflict damage that can never be repaired. (b) He uses rhyme and repeated words and phrasing. Self-discipline increases health, wealth, and wisdom.
2. An aphorism is more effective than a statement of its meaning because it is more concise. It uses techniques that appeal to the ear and make it memorable.
3. Sample responses: Never heap too much praise on yourself or too much criticism on others. Money buys cars, but it doesn't buy happiness.

◆ Reading Strategy

Students should cite the applicable aphorism, then describe an experience or observation from their own lives and explain how it relates to the meaning of the aphorism.

◆ Build Vocabulary

1. c 2. b

Using the Word Bank

1. No 2. Yes

Guide for Responding (continued)

◆ Critical Thinking

INTERPRET

1. Explain the connection between the aphorisms "Be slow in choosing a friend, slower in changing" and "Write injuries in dust, benefits in marble." **[Connect]**
2. In your own words, state at least two recurring themes apparent in Franklin's aphorisms. **[Analyze]**
3. Based on these aphorisms, how would you describe Franklin's approach to life? **[Infer]**

APPLY

4. If you had to select one aphorism from *Poor Richard's Almanack* as a motto for your life, which would you choose and why? **[Relate]**

◆ Literary Focus

APHORISMS

Franklin uses repetition, parallelism, and rhyme to make the observations expressed in these **aphorisms** more memorable.

1. For each of the following aphorisms, identify Franklin's technique(s), then state the meaning of the aphorism:
   a. "A slip of the foot you may soon recover, but a slip of the tongue you may never get over."
   b. "Early to bed and early to rise, makes a man healthy, wealthy, and wise."
2. Explain why an aphorism has more of an impact than the simple statement of its meaning.
3. Using Franklin's techniques, write an aphorism for contemporary life.

◆ Reading Strategy

RELATE TO YOUR EXPERIENCES

If reading the aphorism "A good example is the best sermon" made you think of how your aunt's charity work inspired you to volunteer as a tutor, you were **relating to your experiences** as you read. Select an aphorism from *Poor Richard's Almanack* that struck a chord with you and explain how it relates to a situation or observation from your own life.

◆ Build Vocabulary

USING WORDS WITH MULTIPLE MEANINGS

Fast, wax, and *hedge* are three words from *Poor Richard's Almanack* that have more than one meaning.

Wax: a substance used in candles; *or* to grow larger gradually

Hedge: a fence of greenery; *or* to avoid answering directly; *or* to try to minimize loss by making counterbalancing bets or investments

In your notebook, write the synonym for the italicized word(s) in each sentence.

1. If the moon continues to *wax* in size, we will be able to read by moonlight in two days.
   (a) remain, (b) shrink, (c) grow
2. He was about to *avoid answering* when he changed his mind and replied truthfully.
   (a) fast, (b) hedge, (c) wax

USING THE WORD BANK

1. If your little brother regularly *squanders* his allowance, would he have much money saved?
2. Would a person who has been *fasting* for several days be saving money on meals?

◆ Grammar and Style

IRREGULAR COMPARISON OF ADJECTIVES AND ADVERBS

Since there are no rules for comparison of **irregular modifiers,** it's best to learn the most common ones:

good/well, better, best	*little, less, least*
bad, worse, worst	*much/many, more, most*

Writing Application Rewrite the following paragraph, substituting the appropriate adjective or adverb for the phrase in parentheses.

Benjamin Franklin, one of America's (superlative of well)-loved founding fathers, has left us with aphorisms that are far (comparative of well) known than the almanac in which they appeared. While Franklin satirized the (superlative of bad) in human nature, he also saw the (comparative of good) aspects of humankind.

◆ Grammar and Style

Writing Application

Benjamin Franklin, one of America's best-loved founding fathers, has left us with aphorisms that are far better known than the almanac in which they appeared. While Franklin satirized the worst in human nature, he also saw the better aspects of humankind.

Grammar Reinforcement

For additional instruction and practice, use the lesson in the **Language Lab CD-ROM** on Forms of Comparison and the practice pages on Degree of Comparison (p. 73) and Clear Comparisons (p. 75) in the *Writer's Solution Grammar Practice Book.*

Build Your Portfolio

Idea Bank

Writing

1. **Personal Narrative** Write an account of an episode or situation from your life that relates to one of Franklin's aphorisms. Summarize what you learned from the experience.

2. **Magazine Article** Write a how-to article on successful friendships. Include suggestions for keeping good friends. Use at least four of Franklin's aphorisms to support your points.

3. **Folk Tale** Write an original folk tale or fable illustrating an aphorism from the *Almanack*.

Speaking, Listening, and Viewing

4. **Rap** Write and perform a rap using one or more of Franklin's aphorisms. Your lyrics should illustrate the message behind the aphorism(s) you choose. **[Performing Arts Link]**

5. **Oral Presentation** Locate proverbs from around the world. Ask friends familiar with their heritage to share proverbs native to their cultures. Do you notice similar themes recurring in different cultures? Share your findings in an oral presentation. **[Social Studies Link]**

Researching and Representing

6. **Instruction Manual** Create a manual called "Poor Richard's Guide to Living Well." Refer to a complete collection of *Almanack* aphorisms. Group related aphorisms under headings, such as "Words on Running a Business" and "Making the Most of Each Day." Introduce each section with a summary of Poor Richard's advice on the topic.

7. **Board Game** Create a game based on the *Almanack.* Design game rules and a playing board. One possible approach: Make game cards labeled by subject, such as Friendship and Education.

Online Activity www.phlit.phschool.com

Guided Writing Lesson

Internet Page for Aphorisms

Imagine that you have been assigned to develop an aphorisms Web page geared to teens. Write an engaging introduction to the *Almanack* aphorisms, then create two or three links, such as "Poor Richard on Friendship," that a user could click on to view aphorisms related to a subject.

Writing Skills Focus:
Style Appropriate to Medium

To write for the Internet, select a writing **style appropriate to the medium** by considering how people get information from various media. The way in which a medium delivers news—or any information—to its audience determines its style:

- *Radio:* key facts communicated quickly in concise, vivid language
- *Television:* copy explains or supplements visual images and video footage
- *News magazine:* in-depth coverage examines many aspects of a story

As you draft your Web page, remember that the *people* getting the information and *how* they get it should determine your style.

Prewriting Use your knowledge of your audience to determine how best to present Franklin's aphorisms. Review the aphorisms, decide which links to include, name the links, then choose aphorisms to list under each.

Drafting Consider how people use the Internet—they scan quickly to decide whether a page interests them. Create an interesting and informative page.

Revising Make sure that every aspect of your writing style is geared to the fast pace of the Internet. Would you be tempted to click on these links? Rework any weak spots you identify.

Idea Bank

Customize for
Performance Levels
Following are suggestions for matching Idea Bank topics with your students' performance levels:
Less Advanced Students: 1
Average Students: 2, 4, 5, 7
More Advanced Students: 3, 6

Customize for
Learning Modalities
Following are suggestions for matching Idea Bank topics with your students' learning modalities:
Musical/Rhythmic: 4
Interpersonal: 5
Logical/Mathematical: 6
Visual/Spatial: 7

Guided Writing Lesson

For more instruction on prewriting, elaboration, and revision, see *Prentice Hall Writting and Grammar.*

Writing and Language Transparencies
Have students use the Outline Organizer, p. 95, to organize their prewriting aphorisms and links.

Writers at Work Videodisc Have students view the videodisc segment (Ch. 3) featuring Thom Harrington, Curator of the New York Transit Museum, speaking about expository writing. Ask students what pitfalls Harrington says should be avoided when writing to inform.

Play frames 23159 to 33243

Writing Lab CD-ROM
Have students complete the tutorial on Exposition. Have students follow these steps:
1. Use the Outliner to organize the elements of their Internet page.
2. Draft on the computer.
3. During revision, use the audio-annotated models demonstrating methods for changing passive voice to active voice.

ASSESSMENT OPTIONS

Formal Assessment, Selection Test, pp. 61–63, and Assessment Resources Software. The selection test is designed so that it can be easily customized to the performance levels of your students.

Alternative Assessment, p. 12, includes options for less advanced students, more advanced students, visual/spatial learners, bodily/kinesthetic learners, and interpersonal learners.

PORTFOLIO ASSESSMENT
Use the following rubrics in the ***Alternative Assessment*** booklet to assess student writing:
Personal Narrative: Narrative Based on Personal Experience Rubric, p. 111
Magazine Article: How-to/Process Explanation Rubric, p. 115
Folk Tale: Fictional Narrative Rubric, p. 110
Guided Writing Lesson: Definition/Classification Rubric, p. 114

Prepare and Engage

LESSON OBJECTIVES

1. **To develop vocabulary and word identification skills**
   - Words Origins: Etymologies
   - Using the Word Bank: Word Choice
   - Extending Word Study: Prefixes (ATE)
2. **To use a variety of reading strategies to comprehend a letter (epistle)**
   - Reading Strategy: Distinguish Between Fact and Opinion
3. **To increase knowledge of other cultures and to connect common elements across cultures**
   - Connecting Themes Across Cultures (ATE)
4. **To express and support responses to the text**
   - Critical Thinking
   - Idea Bank: Letter Reading
   - Idea Bank: American Interpretation
5. **To analyze literary elements**
   - Literary Focus: Private and Public Letters (Epistles)
6. **To read in order to research self-selected and assigned topics**
   - Idea Bank: Immigrant Interview
7. **To plan, prepare, organize, and present literary interpretations**
   - Idea Bank: Advertising Campaign
8. **To use recursive writing processes**
   - Guided Writing Lesson: Personal Letter
   - Idea Bank: Descriptive Letter
   - Idea Bank: Reflective Essay
   - Idea Bank: "Melting Pot" Epistle
9. **To increase knowledge of the rules of grammar and usage**
   - Build Grammar Skills: Using Semicolons

Test Preparation

Reading Comprehension: Cause and Effect (ATE, p. 193)
The teaching tips and sample test item in this workshop support the instruction and practice in the unit workshop:

Reading Comprehension: Recognize Cause and Effect; Predict Outcomes (SE, p. 213)

Guide for Interpreting

Abigail Smith Adams

(1744–1818)

Wife, mother, writer, first lady, revolutionary, women's rights pioneer—Abigail Smith Adams was all these and more. As the intelligent, outspoken wife of John Adams, the second president of the United States, and the mother of John Quincy Adams, the sixth president, Abigail Adams was one of the most influential American women of her time.

John Adams's political duties during and after the Revolution kept him from home for the better part of ten years. Abigail, therefore, became an avid correspondent, penning hundreds of letters to her husband and relatives, discussing everything from women's rights to her opposition to slavery. During the war, she even kept her husband posted on the movements of British troops.

When John Adams was elected president of the United States, he and Abigail became the first couple to live in the White House. This letter to her daughter, which describes their temporary home, captures the essence of life in the new nation.

Twenty-two years after Abigail Adams's death, her letters were published. Today, she is widely recognized as a pioneer of the American women's movement.

Michel-Guillaume Jean de Crèvecoeur

(1735–1813)

The first writer to compare America to a melting pot, French aristocrat Michel-Guillaume Jean de Crèvecoeur (mē shel′ gē yôm zhän də krev koer′) chronicled his experiences as a European immigrant in America. His idealistic descriptions confirmed many people's vision of America as a land of great promise.

After spending ten years traveling the colonies, Crèvecoeur married and settled on a farm in Orange County, New York, where he began writing about his experiences in America. In 1780, he sailed to London, where his *Letters From an American Farmer* was published two years later. This book, which was translated into several languages, made Crèvecoeur famous.

After visiting France, he returned to America in 1783 as a French Consul to find his farm burned, his wife killed, and his children sent to live with foster parents. When the French Revolution began in 1789, he was obliged to return to Paris. He later fled to Normandy, where he continued to write about the adoptive country he would never again see.

◆ Background for Understanding

HISTORY: CRÈVECOEUR'S AMERICA IDEALIZED

When Michel-Guillaume Jean de Crèvecoeur published *Letters From an American Farmer*, he captured the imagination of downtrodden Europeans hungry for a better life. Life in America, however, was far from idyllic, but that was not what Europeans wanted to hear.

Because the country needed hard workers, not those seeking an easy life, it is no wonder that some American leaders worried about the effects of Crèvecoeur's glowing descriptions. George Washington called the *Letters* "rather too flattering," and the wise and witty Ben Franklin responded by writing and publishing (first in France) *Advice to Such as Would Remove to America* in 1784. Franklin begins by warning that even though "there are in that country few people so miserable as the poor of Europe," neither are there many rich. "America is a land of labor," he continues, and what it needs are dedicated, skilled workers. Those interested in a life of leisure need not apply.

Prentice Hall Literature Program Resources

REINFORCE / RETEACH / EXTEND

Selection Support Pages
Build Vocabulary: Word Origins: Etymologies, p. 61
Grammar and Style: Semicolons, p. 62
Reading Strategy: Fact and Opinion, p. 63
Literary Focus: Private and Public Letters, p. 64

Strategies for Diverse Student Needs, p. 13

Beyond Literature, p. 13

Formal Assessment Selection Test, p. 64–66; Assessment Resources Software

Alternative Assessment, p. 13

Writing and Language Transparencies
Outline Organizer, p. 95

Resource Pro CD-ROM

Listening to Literature Audiocassettes

Letter to Her Daughter From the New White House
◆ *from* Letters From an American Farmer ◆

◆ Literature and Your Life

CONNECT YOUR EXPERIENCE

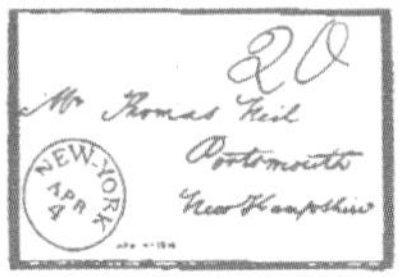

When you want to get in touch with a friend, you probably pick up the phone or send an e-mail. In our high-tech world, fewer and fewer people reach for pen and paper. Not too long ago, however, letters were the only means of communicating over distances.

Journal Writing How might your life change if letter writing were the only communication option available to you?

THEMATIC FOCUS: DEFINING AN AMERICAN

Letters were the lifeline through which early Americans sent and received personal, professional, and political information. In a country founded on free thought, letters were an important means of sharing ideas and opinions with both private and public readers. What do the letters of Crèvecoeur and Adams tell us about what it meant to be an American during our nation's early years?

◆ Build Vocabulary

WORD ORIGINS: ETYMOLOGIES

The word *extricate* comes from the Latin *extricare* meaning "disentangle"—a definition closely related to the meaning of *extricate*: set free or disengage. You can learn how words evolved by using a dictionary that shows etymologies, or word histories.

WORD BANK

Before you read, preview this list of words from the letters.

- extricate
- agues
- asylum
- penury
- despotic
- subsistence

◆ Grammar and Style

SEMICOLONS

The **semicolon** (;) joins independent clauses that have a close relationship to each other and are not already joined by a conjunction (*and, but, for, nor, or, so,* or *yet*). Both Adams and Crèvecoeur make frequent use of semicolons—with and without conjunctions:

> The American is a new man, who acts upon new principles; he must therefore entertain new ideas, and form new opinions.

◆ Literary Focus

PRIVATE AND PUBLIC LETTERS (EPISTLES)

Personal or **private letters,** like Adams's, tend to be conversational and intended only for the reader(s) to whom they are addressed. Crèvecoeur's *Letters*, on the other hand, while supposedly written by an American farmer named James to his friend Mr. F. B., are actually public letters intended for a wide audience. Called **epistles,** these works of literature are created for general publication but written in the form of personal letters.

◆ Reading Strategy

DISTINGUISH BETWEEN FACT AND OPINION

Crèvecoeur had an idealistic view of life in America, and his writing is colored by this opinion. To avoid being too easily swayed by writers, distinguish **facts**—statements that can be proven—from **opinions**—personal beliefs that cannot be proven. Look at these examples:

> *Fact:* Upstairs there is the oval room, which is designed for the drawing room . . .
>
> *Opinion:* It is a very handsome room now; but, when complete, it will be beautiful.

A good persuasive writer uses facts to provide support for his or her opinions.

Interest Grabber Inform students that the letters of Abigail Smith Adams and Michel-Guillaume Jean de Crèvecoeur provide windows through which we can catch a glimpse of early America. Divide the class into two groups—one group as an audience for Adams's letter and one group as an audience for Crèvecoeur's letter. Ask students to imagine themselves receiving Adams's letter describing the first White House or Crèvecoeur's letter describing an American. Have students in each group make a list in response to the following questions:

For Adams: What do you want to know about the new White House?

For Crèvecoeur: What do you want to learn about American life? If you were living in another country, what might make you consider moving to America?

Have students from both groups share their lists with the class. Discuss how such lists can be the basis of an informative letter.

Connecting Themes Across Cultures

Ask students to name forms of communication—such as letters, music, or poetry—which have helped cultures to define their shared values. For example, during the twentieth century, literature was used in the Soviet Union by authors such as Alexander Solzhenitsyn and Anna Akhmatova to express political dissent.

Customize for
Less Proficient Readers
Have students work in pairs to read the letters aloud. Have students alternate reading while the other summarizes what he or she has heard.

Customize for
AP Students
Although Crèvecoeur was the first to use the term "melting pot," it was popularized by Israel Zangwill in his 1908 play *The Melting Pot.* Ask these students to do a reader's theater performance of parts of the play for the class.

Test Preparation Workshop

Reading Comprehension:
Recognize Cause and Effect
Some standardized tests require students to identify relationships of cause and effect. Successful readers understand that causal relationships are sometimes signaled by transitions such as "since" or "because." Use the following example to help students identify signal words as they look for causal relationships.

> If they will. . . Let me have wood enough to keep fires, I design to be pleased. I could content myself almost anywhere three months; but surrounded with forests, can you believe that wood is not to be had because people cannot be found to cut and cart it?

Why does Abigail Adams lack firewood?

A There were no forests nearby.
B There was no one to cut the trees.
C People did not use firewood in Washington.
D Abigail Adams preferred coal fires.

Choices *A, C,* and *D* contain inaccurate information. *B* states the correct cause as it is given in the text.

Develop Understanding

One-Minute Insight This letter provides an opportunity to examine the thoughts and feelings of the first woman to occupy the White House. The beginning of the letter describes the difficulty the first lady's traveling party has in finding their way from Baltimore to Washington, a town made up at this time of nothing more than a few public buildings with crude residences widely scattered. The unfinished White House is huge but ill-equipped for easy living: there are no bells to ring for one of the thirty servants, little firewood, and no fence or yard. Mrs. Adams, however, asks her daughter to keep these negative feelings between them and to tell others only that the new White House and its city are beautiful. The first lady also shares with her daughter her active social life, including an invitation from Mrs. Washington to visit Mount Vernon.

Literature CD-ROM To build background, use *The History of American Literature:* Part 1, Disc 1, Features 5 and 7. Feature 5 focuses in part on Crèvecoeur's *Letters From an American Farmer.* Feature 7 contains information on Abigail Adams.

▶Critical Viewing◀

❶ **Speculate** Students may say that Abigail Adams would have been proud to occupy such a magnificent house. Others may say that Adams might be disappointed that construction on the house was not yet completed.

Building the First White House, N. C. Wyeth, White House Historical Association

❶ ▲ **Critical Viewing** How might Abigail Adams have reacted to this scene? **[Speculate]**

Humanities: Art

Building the First White House, 1930, by N. C. Wyeth.

Newell Convers Wyeth was a famous and prolific American illustrator. One of his first commercial illustration commissions was for the Pennsylvania Railroad to commemorate the Washington bicentennial year. On May 1, 1930, the railroad advertised that "historical posters in full color, dealing with patriotic subjects have been designed by a well-known painter." In 1971 this painting appeared on the Christmas cards sent by then-President and Mrs. Nixon.

Use these questions for discussion:

1. What details in the painting clarify the time period? *The gentlemen's wigs, hats, coats, shirts; the woman's dress; the horses and wagon; the absence of equipment like bulldozers; the workmen's appearance.*
2. What effect does the placement of the figures have on the viewer? *The figures in the foreground add a sense of drama to the scene. The two figures looking and pointing at the building draw our attention to the magnificent house on the hill.*

Letter to Her Daughter From the New White House

Abigail Adams

Washington, 21 November, 1800

My Dear Child:

I arrived here on Sunday last, and without meeting with any accident worth noticing, except losing ourselves when we left Baltimore and going eight or nine miles on the Frederick road, by which means we were obliged to go the other eight through woods, where we wandered two hours without finding a guide or the path. Fortunately, a straggling black came up with us, and we engaged him as a guide to extricate us out of our difficulty; but ❷ woods are all you see from Baltimore until you reach *the city*, which is only so in name. Here and there is a small cot, without a glass window, interspersed amongst the forests, through which you travel miles without seeing any human being. In the city there are buildings enough, if they were compact and finished, to accommodate Congress and those attached to it; but as they are, and scattered as they are, I see no great comfort for them. The river, which runs up to Alexandria,[1] is in full view of my window, and I see the vessels as they pass and repass. The ❸ house is upon a grand and superb scale, requiring about thirty servants to attend and keep the apartments in proper order, and perform the ordinary business of the house and stables; an establishment very well proportioned to the President's salary. The lighting of the apartments, from the kitchen to parlors and chambers, is a tax indeed; and the fires we are obliged to keep to secure us from daily agues is another very cheering comfort. To assist us in this great castle, and render less attendance necessary, bells are wholly wanting, not one single one being hung through the whole house, and promises are all you can obtain. This is so great an inconvenience, that I know not what to do, or how to do. ❹ The ladies from Georgetown[2] and in the city have many of them visited me. Yesterday I returned fifteen visits—but such a place as Georgetown appears—why, our Milton is beautiful.

But no comparisons—if they will put me up some bells and let me have wood enough to keep fires, I design to be pleased. I could content myself almost anywhere three months; but, surrounded with forests, can you believe that wood is not to be had because people cannot be found to cut and cart it? Briesler entered into a contract with a man to supply him with wood. A small part, a

1. **Alexandria:** City in northeastern Virginia.

2. **Georgetown:** Section of Washington, D.C.

◆ Build Vocabulary

extricate (eks´ trə kāt´) *v.*: Set free

agues (ā´ gyo͞oz) *n.*: Fits of shivering

◆ Background for Understanding

History From 1776 to 1800, when Washington, D. C., was designated as the capital, the federal government had no permanent capital. Jealousy among the states had caused a deadlock in choosing a site. Finally, via compromise, Northern politicians agreed to a Southern site in return for important legislation.

◆ Critical Thinking

❷ **Speculate** Point out that in 1800 the entire Washington area had a population of only about 8,000 people. Ask students: How might this city "which is only so in name" have compared to a city like Boston, with which Mrs. Adams was familiar? *Washington would have seemed like a rural area in comparison to Boston. Many of the amenities of a city, such as libraries and shops, would have been lacking.*

❸ **Enrichment** The White House is a Georgian mansion, designed in the classical Palladian style common in Europe in the 1700's.

◆ Critical Thinking

❹ **Compare and Contrast** Ask students: What must Adams' life have been like in Quincy, Massachusetts, compared to her new one in the unfinished White House? *Students may say that she apparently lived a more comfortable life in Quincy.*

Extending Word Study

Prefixes Call students' attention to the word *interspersed* on p. 195, and point out its prefix, *inter-*. Invite students to look up the meaning and origin of this prefix. *Latin: "among"* Have them define *interspersed* *"scattered among"*. Students can then list more words which include the prefix *inter-*, and use each in a sentence.

Block Scheduling Strategies

Consider these suggestions to take advantage of extended class time:

- Discuss the Journal Writing activity on page 193. Impress upon students the importance of letters in a time before telephones were invented.
- Have students research the history of the White House in encyclopedias or on the Internet. Then have students share the building's major milestones, such as the significant repairs made from 1948 to 1952.
- Introduce the meaning-unlocking potential (and humor) of the Build Vocabulary lesson, on page 193, by writing the following etymology on the chalkboard: *rhinoceros* < Greek: *rhinos*, nose + *keras*, horn; literally "nose-horned"; a large thick-skinned mammal with one or two upright horns on its snout.

  Ask students: If *-rrhea* is from the Greek *-rrhoia*, meaning "flow," what does *rhinorrhea* mean? *It means "a runny nose."*
- Answer the Literary Focus questions on page 200 as a class. Be sure students understand the differences between private letters and epistles.
- When students begin the Guided Writing Lesson on page 201, give them the Outline Organizer, p. 95, in ***Writing and Language Transparencies,*** to help them organize their prewriting developments.

◆ Literary Focus

❶ **Private and Public Letters (Epistles)** Elicit the following response: Only private letters could logically ask for secrecy.

◆ Reading Strategy

❷ **Distinguish Between Fact and Opinion** Have students decide which part of this sentence are fact and which are opinion. *Students should note that the only fact is that for twelve years this has been the future seat of government; all else is opinion.*

Reinforce and Extend

Answers

◆ Literature and Your Life

Reader's Response Students may have been surprised by the rural character of Washington, D. C.

Thematic Focus Adams's letter helps us understand that there were logistical as well as philosophical challenges to overcome.

☑ Check Your Comprehension

1. She calls it a city in name only, with buildings scattered in different locations. The surrounding area is mostly wooded, with just a few cottages interspersed throughout the forests, which are largely uninhabited by people.
2. The living quarters are incomplete and lack many basic conveniences. Most of the rooms are unfinished, and the main stairs have not yet been constructed. They have no fence or yard outdoors.

◆ Critical Thinking

1. It would have been inappropriate for the First Lady to make her complaints public.
2. Suggested response: She wants to find good things to like about her new home, but she is frustrated by some of the inconveniences of life outside New England.
3. The tone of Adams's letter is determined but disappointed. She probably expected more elegant accommodations. The tone of Crèvecoeur's letter is optimistic and proud.

few cords only, has he been able to get. Most of that was expended to dry the walls of the house before we came in, and yesterday the man told him it was impossible for him to procure it to be cut and carted. He has had recourse to coals; but we cannot get grates made and set. We have, indeed, come into a *new country.*

> ◆ **Literary Focus** ❶
> Why would a comment like this one be found only in a private letter, never in an epistle?

You must keep all this to yourself, and, when asked how I like it, say that I write you the situation is beautiful, which is true. The house is made habitable, but there is not a single apartment finished, and all withinside, except the plastering, has been done since Briesler came. We have not the least fence, yard, or other convenience without and the great unfinished audience room I make a drying-room of, to hang up the clothes in. The principal stairs are not up, and will not be this winter. Six chambers are made comfortable; two are occupied by the President and Mr. Shaw; two lower rooms, one for a common parlor, and one for a levee room. Upstairs there is the oval room, which is designed for the drawing room, and has the crimson furniture in it. It is a very handsome room now; but, when completed, it will be beautiful. If the twelve years, in which this place has been considered as the future seat of government had been improved, as they would have been if in New England, very many of the present inconveniences would have been removed. It is a beautiful spot, capable of every improvement, and, the more I view it, the more I am delighted with it. ❷

Since I sat down to write, I have been called down to a servant from Mount Vernon,[3] with a billet[4] from Major Custis, and a haunch of venison, and a kind, congratulatory letter from Mrs. Lewis, upon my arrival in the city, with Mrs. Washington's love, inviting me to Mount Vernon, where, health permitting, I will go before I leave this place.

Affectionately, your mother,
Abigail Adams

3. **Mount Vernon:** Home of George Washington, located in northern Virginia.
4. **billet** (bil′ it) *n.*: Brief letter.

Guide for Responding

◆ Literature and Your Life

Reader's Response What, if anything, surprised you about Adams's description of the White House and the area around Washington, D.C.?

Thematic Focus How does Adams's letter help us appreciate the challenges that faced our nation's first leaders as they strove to establish a centralized national government?

☑ Check Your Comprehension

1. How does Adams describe the city of Washington and its surroundings?
2. Describe the state of the living quarters in the White House.

◆ Critical Thinking

INTERPRET

1. Why do you think Adams tells her daughter not to share her complaints with anyone? **[Infer]**
2. How would you characterize Adams's feelings about her new home? **[Classify]**

COMPARE LITERARY WORKS

3. Note the tone in the letters by Abigail Adams and Michel-Guillame Jean de Crèvecoeur. Compare the two, noting the contrasts. How are the attitudes of the two writers different? What do you think is the basis for each one's feelings? **[Compare and Contrast]**

Analyze a Review

Jan Lewis, author of a review of Paul C. Nagel's book *The Adams Women,* makes the following observation: "Abigail Smith Adams and her daughter-in-law . . . were both intelligent, articulate and, like their President husbands, pessimistic about human potential in a democratic age."

Share this comment with students. Invite them to define *pessimism* and to discuss whether or not, based on Abigail Adams's letter to her daughter, they agree that Adams was "intelligent" and "articulate." Then have students write a journal entry in which they answer the following questions:

1. On the basis of her letter to her daughter, do you agree that Abigail Adams was "pessimistic about human potential"? Why or why not? Support your comments with examples.
2. In your opinion, why might the reviewer have considered it important to add "in a democratic age" to the remark about Adams's "pessimism"?

from

Letters From an American Farmer

Michel-Guillaume Jean de Crèvecoeur

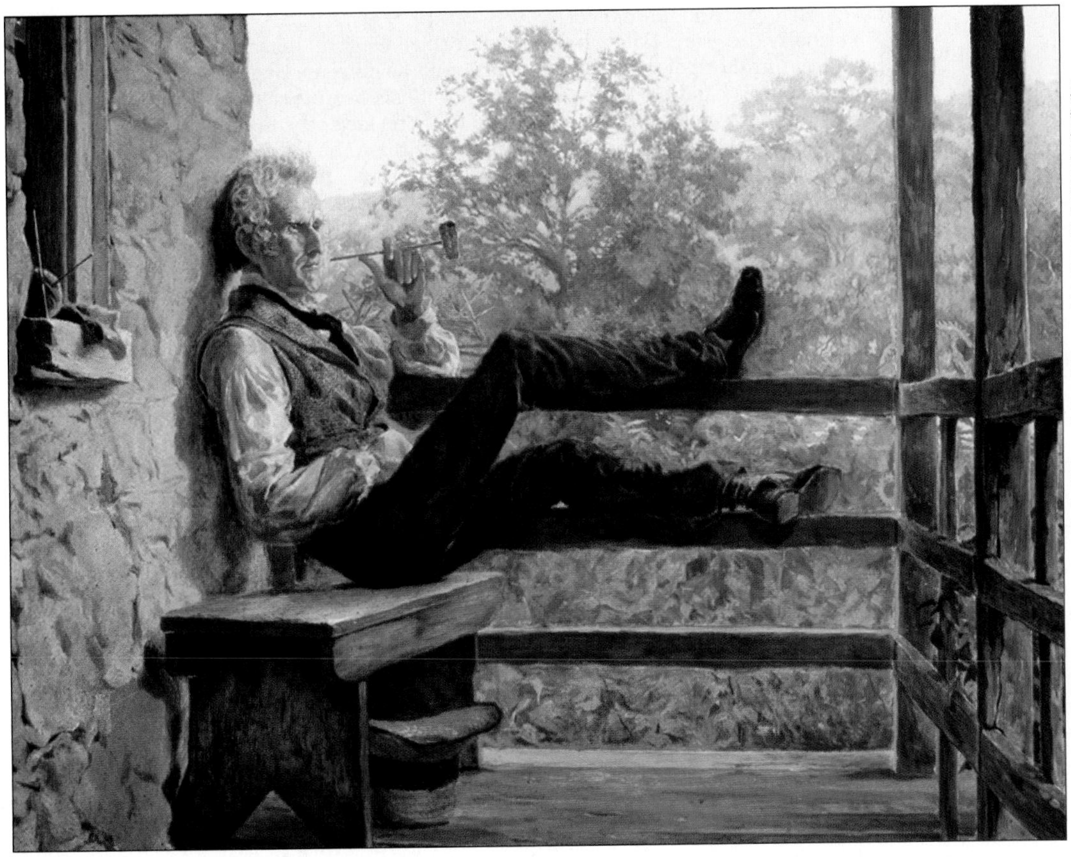

Independence (Squire Jack Porter), 1858, Frank Blackwell Mayer, National Museum of American Art, Smithsonian Institution

3 ▲ **Critical Viewing** How does this painting relate to Crèvecoeur's *Letters From an American Farmer*? **[Connect]**

Develop Understanding

One-Minute Insight

In this essay, Crèvecoeur celebrates America as the land of opportunity. He describes the experience of American immigrants, regenerated by fair laws and their own hard work. In Europe, these people were starving and unemployed; however, in America, they have prospered.

Customize for *English Language Learners*

The lengthy sentences and difficult vocabulary of Crèvecoeur's letter may prove difficult for English language learners. Ask these students to paraphrase each sentence and jot down difficult words. Review the paraphrases and word lists in class discussion.

▶Critical Viewing◀

3 **Connect** Students may note that the artist depicts a well-dressed gentleman-farmer at ease. In that respect, the painting correlates to Crèvecoeur's idyllic description of American colonists.

Connecting to Real-World Texts

To connect this selection to newspaper editorials, see p. "Where Freedom Seekers Yearn to Be Free" and Legal Immigration Must Be Curbed, Too" p. 1209–1210.

Reteach

To reteach distinguishing between fact and opinion, demonstrate with the following graphic organizer. If possible, use an actual scale and allow students to indicate their determination by placing a weight on the correct side.

Can it be proven?

Humanities: Art

Independence (Squire Jack Porter) 1858, by Frank Blackwell Mayer.

Frank Blackwell Mayer (1827–1899) was born in Baltimore and studied in Paris. Because of his realistic portrayal of subjects from everyday life, Mayer was known as a genre painter.

This painting is a portrait of Jack Porter, a prosperous farmer in western Maryland. Through the lack of action in the painting, Mayer illustrates what people want: peace and contentment in their everyday life.

Use the following questions for discussion:

1. Although this painting was not created to illustrate *Letters From an American Farmer,* how does it relate to the text? *Possible response: The painting shows a person who is at peace in his rustic environment, as are Crèvecoeur's Americans.*
2. How would you define the mood of the painting? *The mood is reflective and tranquil.*

◆ Critical Thinking

❶ **Interpreting** Pose this question: Why does Crèvecoeur compare people to plants here and elsewhere? *Students should note that he sees plants and people flourishing as a result of their environment.*

◆ Literary Focus

❷ **Private and Public Letters (Epistles)** Ask: What purpose does Crèvecoeur have in using this argument in a public letter? *Students may say that he shows Europeans the worth of colonists, who earn what they get and get what they earn.*

❸ **Clarification** The "crown" refers to the British monarchy, which Crèvecoeur sees as the protector of stability and just government.

❹ **Clarification** Although the idea of America as a "melting pot" was first expressed here, the term itself was first popularized by Israel Zangwill in his 1908 play *The Melting Pot.*

❺ **Clarification** Crèvecoeur calls Americans "the western pilgrims." In the Middle East, Mecca was known as a place of pilgrimage. By association, Crèvecoeur is suggesting that America is the new center of civilization.

❻ **Characterization** The "despotic prince," "rich abbot," and "mighty lord" are references to feudalism, the social and economic system prevailing in Western Europe during the Middle Ages.

In this great American asylum, the poor of Europe have by some means met together, and in consequence of various causes; to what purpose should they ask one another what countrymen they are? Alas, two thirds of them had no country. Can a wretch who wanders about, who works and starves, whose life is a continual scene of sore affliction or pinching penury, can that man call England or any other kingdom his country? A country that had no bread for him, whose fields procured him no harvest, who met with nothing but the frowns of the rich, the severity of the laws, with jails and punishments; who owned not a single foot of the extensive surface of this planet? No! Urged by a variety of motives, here they came. Everything has tended to regenerate them; new laws, a new mode of living, a new social system; here they are become men: in Europe they were as so many useless plants, wanting vegetative mold[1] and refreshing showers; ❶ they withered, and were mowed down by want, hunger, and war; but now by the power of transplantation, like all other plants they have taken root and flourished!

Formerly they were not numbered in any civil lists[2] of their country, except in those of the poor; here they rank as citizens. By what invisible power has this surprising metamorphosis been performed? By that of the laws and that of their industry. The laws, the indulgent ❷ laws, protect them as they arrive, stamping on them the symbol of adoption; they receive ample rewards for their labors; these accumulated rewards procure them lands; those lands confer on them the title of freemen, and to that title every benefit is affixed which men can possibly require. This is the great operation daily performed by our laws. From whence proceed these laws? From our government. Whence the government? It is derived from the original genius and ❸ strong desire of the people ratified and confirmed by the crown. . . .

What attachment can a poor European emigrant have for a country where he had nothing? The knowledge of the language, the love of a few kindred as poor as himself, were the only cords that tied him: his country is now that which gives him land, bread, protection, and consequence: *Ubi panis ibi patria*[3] is the motto of all emigrants. What then is the American, this new man? He is either a European, or the descendant of a European, hence that strange mixture of blood, which you will find in no other country. I could point out to you a family whose grandfather was an Englishman, whose wife was Dutch, whose son married a French woman, and whose present four sons have now four wives of different nations. *He* is an American, who, leaving behind him all his ancient prejudices and manners, receives new ones from the new mode of life he has embraced, the new government he obeys, and the new rank he holds. He becomes an American by being received in the broad lap of our great *Alma Mater.*[4] Here individuals of all ❹ nations are melted into a new race of men, whose labors and posterity ❺ will one day cause great changes in the world. Americans are the west-

1. **vegetative mold:** Enriched soil.
2. **civil lists:** Lists of distinguished persons.
3. ***Ubi . . . patria:*** (ü´ bē pä nis ib´ ē pä´ trē ə) "Where there is bread, there is one's fatherland" (Latin).
4. **Alma Mater** (al´ mə mä´ tər): "Fostering mother." Here, referring to America; usually used in reference to a school or college.

Cultural Connection

Immigrants Crèvecoeur's letter indicates that even in colonial times, immigrants were coming to America from a variety of countries. During the 1600's and 1700's, settlers came to the colonies from many parts of Europe, and enslaved Africans were taken to the Americas against their will.

In the 1840's a potato famine in Ireland drove one and a half million people to America's shores, and Chinese immigrants arrived in California hoping to strike it rich in the Gold Rush of 1849.

In the 1870's immigrants from Germany and Scandinavia came to the Great Plains as farmers or to the East as skilled workers. Another wave of immigrants came between 1880 and 1914.

By 1929, laws had reduced the annual quota of immigrants to 150,000. Immigration restrictions eased after World War II, however, as new prosperity made America more generous. The United States continues to be a nation of immigrants.

Ask students to discuss when and where their families first came to the United States. Have students find out what immigration was like for their families and share that information with the class.

ern pilgrims, who are carrying along with them that great mass of arts, sciences, vigor, and industry which began long since in the east; they will finish the great circle. The Americans were once scattered all over Europe: here they are incorporated into one of the finest systems of population which has ever appeared, and which will hereafter become distinct by the power of the different climates they inhabit. The American ought therefore to love this country much better than that wherein either he or his forefathers were born. Here the rewards of his industry follow with equal steps the progress of his labor; his labor is founded on the basis of nature, *self-interest;* can it want a stronger allurement? Wives and children, who before in vain demanded of him a morsel of bread, now, fat and frolicsome, gladly help their father to clear those fields whence exuberant crops are to arise to feed and to clothe them all; without any part being claimed, either by a despotic prince, a rich abbot,[5] or a mighty lord. Here religion demands but little of him; a small voluntary salary to the minister, and gratitude to God; can he refuse these? The American is a new man, who acts upon new principles; he must therefore entertain new ideas, and form new opinions. From involuntary idleness, servile dependence, penury, and useless labor, he has passed to toils of a very different nature, rewarded by ample subsistence—This is an American.

5. **abbot** *n.*: The head of a monastery.

◆ Build Vocabulary

asylum (ə sīˊ ləm) *n.*: Place of refuge
penury (penˊ yə rē) *n.*: Lack of money, property, or necessities
despotic (de spätˊ ik) *adj.*: Harsh; cruel; unjust
subsistence (səb sisˊ təns) *n.*: Means of support

Guide for Responding

◆ Literature and Your Life

Reader's Response If you were an eighteenth-century European, would this passage motivate you to relocate to the United States? Why or why not?

Thematic Focus Can Crèvecoeur's views be applied to America today? Why or why not?

☑ Check Your Comprehension

1. To what does Crèvecoeur compare impoverished Europeans before their emigration to America?
2. What are the sources of the "invisible power" responsible for transforming humble European peasants into esteemed American citizens?

◆ Critical Thinking

INTERPRET

1. To what theme does Crèvecoeur return again and again when describing life in America? **[Analyze]**
2. How would you summarize Crèvecoeur's definition of an American? **[Draw Conclusions]**

EVALUATE

3. Crèvecoeur implies that self-interest is a valuable quality because it motivates people to work harder. Does modern society commonly regard self-interest as a desirable quality? Explain your answer. **[Assess]**

Beyond the Selection

FURTHER READING

Other Works by Abigail Adams
New Letters of Abigail Adams, 1788–1801, Stewart Mitchell, ed.

Other Works by Crèvecoeur
Journey into Northern Pennsylvania and the State of New York

We suggest that you preview these works before recommending them to students.

INTERNET

Your students can find information on the following Internet sites. Please be aware that sites may have changed since we published this information.

See "Inside the White House," at **http://www.pbs.org/weta/whitehouse/whhome.htm**

To learn more about Crèvecoeur, go to **http://falcon.jmu.edu/~ramseyil/amlitfirst.htm**

We *strongly recommend* that you preview the sites before you send students to them.

◆ Critical Thinking

7 Compare and Contrast
Crèvecoeur describes Americans as people who act on new principles and entertain new ideas. How is Crèvecoeur's definition of Americans still applicable today? How is it not applicable? *Students may believe that much of Crèvecoeur's definition of Americans is still applicable today. However, students may feel that not all Americans today share in the rewards Crèvecoeur describes.*

Reinforce and Extend

Answers

◆ Literature and Your Life

Reader's Response Many students will say that Crèvecoeur writes persuasively.

Thematic Focus Students may say that many of Crèvecoeur's views can be applied to America today. However, students might feel that not everyone shares equally in the American dream.

☑ Check Your Comprehension

1. Crèvecoeur compares the Europeans to withering plants lacking fertilizer and water that are mowed down by poverty and war.
2. "New laws, a new mode of living, [and] a new social system" have regenerated the European immigrant.

◆ Critical Thinking

1. He repeatedly describes America as a place where people are able to enjoy the benefits of their own hard work.
2. Suggested response: An American is someone who has initiated a new social system through labor, industry, and self-interest.
3. Students should explain the reasoning behind their answers. Some may feel that self-interest is a characteristically American trait that motivates people to work harder and better their lives. Other may feel that too much self-interest results in a society that places individual fulfillment above the social good.

Answers

◆ Reading Strategy

1. The statement is a fact because the comments within it, such as "there is not a single apartment finished," can be checked for accuracy.
2. Suggested responses include Crèvecoeur's comment that "Formerly they were not numbered in any civil lists of their country . . . here they rank as citizens."

◆ Literary Focus

Private and Public Letters (Epistles)

1. Suggested responses: It would not contain comments or complaints she wanted to keep from the public. It would be more formally or carefully constructed.
2. The epistle form allows him to address his audience in an intimate and personal manner while supporting his views with a carefully planned argument.

◆ Grammar and Style

1. The travelers sought help finding Baltimore; the woods blocked their view of the city.
2. Six rooms were completed; two were not.
3. Adams thought she could be happy anywhere for three months; however, the wood shortage caused her distress.

Grammar Reinforcement

For additional instruction and practice, use the lesson in the **Language Lab CD-ROM** on Quotation Marks, Colons, and Semicolons and the practice page on Semicolons and Colons (p. 89) in the *Writer's Solution Grammar Practice Book.*

◆ Build Vocabulary

1. *Interspersed* can be traced back to *inter-* (meaning "among") + *spargere* (meaning "to scatter").
2. *Interspersed* means "scattered among or throughout."

Using the Word Bank: Word Choice

1. subsistence; 2. agues;
3. despotic; 4. asylum;
5. extricate; 6. penury

Guide for Responding *(continued)*

◆ Reading Strategy

Distinguish Between Fact and Opinion

While the **opinions,** or personal beliefs, Adams and Crèvecoeur express in these letters help us appreciate their points of view, it is important to distinguish their beliefs from verifiable, historical **facts.**

1. Identify the following statement as fact or opinion. Explain your reasoning. "The house is made habitable, but there is not a single apartment finished, and all withinside, except the plastering, has been done since Briesler came."

2. Identify at least one fact Crèvecoeur uses to support the following opinion. ". . . here they are become men: in Europe they were as so many useless plants . . ."

◆ Literary Focus

Private and Public Letters (Epistles)

The **private letters** of Abigail Adams provide an interesting view of life in a new nation. These letters were originally intended for her family's eyes alone. Crèvecoeur, on the other hand, reached a broad readership through **epistles**—public letters often addressed to a fictional person.

1. Name at least two ways Adams's letter would be different if written for a general audience.

2. How does the epistle form help Crèvecoeur persuade his readers to accept his ideas? Explain.

◆ Grammar and Style

Using Semicolons

The **semicolon (;)** is used in place of a conjunction to join closely related independent clauses in a compound sentence.

Practice Rewrite the following sentences, adding semicolons where they are needed:

1. The travelers sought help finding Baltimore the woods blocked their view of the city.

2. Six rooms were completed two were not.

3. Adams thought she could be happy anywhere for three months however, the wood shortage caused her distress.

◆ Build Vocabulary

Using Etymologies

Following is an *etymology*—a word history—for the word *interspersed.* Use the etymology to answer in your notebook the questions that follow.

< L *interspersus,* pp. of *interspegere* < *inter-,* among + *spargere,* to scatter

1. *Interspersed* can ultimately be traced back to what two words or word parts?

2. Based on its etymology, what is the probable meaning of *interspersed?*

Using the Word Bank: Word Choice

Review the Word Bank. Then, on your paper, write the word that best describes each situation.

1. a steady income
2. what people who live in drafty houses suffer from
3. how you might describe an evil dictator
4. the quiet privacy of your room
5. to work your way out of an argument
6. the condition in which most homeless people live

Beyond Literature

Cultural Connection

America's Immigrants Even in Crèvecoeur's time, immigrants came to America from a variety of countries. Through the 1700's, settlers came to the Thirteen Colonies from England, Germany, Holland, Ireland, Wales, Scotland, and France. At the same time, colonists from Spain settled in the Southwest, and many enslaved Africans were brought to the South as unwilling "immigrants."

During the 1800's, several great waves of immigration brought people first from Ireland (escaping the potato famine in the 1840's), then from China (hoping to strike it rich in the California Gold Rush), from northern Europe in the 1870's, and finally from southern and eastern Europe in the three decades before World War I.

Activity Where do America's immigrants come from today? Find immigration statistics for the last five years.

Research Skills Mini-Lesson

Interview

Introduce the Concept Tell students that to conduct an interview for an assignment such as the Immigrant Interview on p. 201, it is helpful to know some things in advance about the subject of the interview.

Develop Background Have students write a list of questions to ask the person they will interview. Point out that in order to come up with questions that will elicit interesting or informative responses, it is helpful to do some research in advance—in this case, about the person's country of origin.

Apply the Information Have students consult encyclopedias, maps, newspapers, magazines, and the Internet to find out their interview subject's country of origin. Have them take notes, which they can refer to as they draft their interview questions.

Assess the Outcome Evaluate students on the clarity of their questions and the thoroughness of their research. You may also wish to assess students' presentation of their interviews to the class.

Build Your Portfolio

Idea Bank

Writing

1. **Descriptive Letter** In a letter, describe your home to a friend who has never seen it. Create a picture of your home in the reader's mind.

2. **Reflective Essay** Crèvecoeur saw the United States as a land of great promise. How do you see this nation? In a brief essay, reflect on what the United States means to you.

3. **"Melting Pot" Epistle** In an epistle, celebrate the ethnic diversity found in American cities. Write with the intention of convincing the general public that cultural diversity is beneficial.

Speaking, Listening, and Viewing

4. **Letter Reading** Abigail Adams's letters provide vivid firsthand accounts of history. In a library, find a letter that captures a period of history. Read it aloud to the class and discuss what it reveals about the time in which it was written. **[Social Studies Link]**

5. **Immigrant Interview** Interview a recent immigrant to find out why and how he or she came to this country. Record your interview, then share it with your class. **[Social Studies Link]**

Researching and Representing

6. **American Interpretation** What is an American? Respond to Crèvecoeur's question in a form of your choice. Consider a poem or a photo montage to communicate your response.

7. **Advertising Campaign** Produce an advertising campaign to attract immigrants in the late eighteenth century. Draw upon the descriptions that Crèvecoeur presents in his letter. **[Media Link]**

Online Activity www.phlit.phschool.com

Guided Writing Lesson

Personal Letter

If you could write to someone from the past, what would you tell that person about modern life? Select a figure from American history who intrigues you. In a personal letter, provide an update on how an area of interest to the recipient has changed since his or her lifetime. Like a foreign pen pal, your reader lives in a different country—the country of the past—and will need help understanding your world.

Writing Skills Focus: Necessary Context/Background

When writing for an audience whose culture is different from your own, provide **necessary context and background**—the information a reader needs in order to make sense of the references you make. Don't assume that words such as *work* and *school* mean to the reader what they mean to you.

For example, Abigail Adams, a champion of women's rights, would be fascinated by advances in women's issues, such as paid maternity leave, but would need information about the changing roles of women in the family and the workplace in order to appreciate the concept.

Prewriting Decide on an appropriate subject for your letter. Outline the developments you will cover. Then decide what background information your reader will need to understand your points.

Drafting Keep in mind the person to whom you are writing as you draft your letter. Remember that this is a personal letter intended as a one-on-one form of communication between the two of you.

Revising Reread your letter and ask yourself whether the recipient would be able to understand the references you make. Have you provided context and background information necessary to someone unfamiliar with twentieth-century America?

Idea Bank

Customizing for
Performance Levels
Following are suggestions for matching Idea Bank topics with your students' performance levels:
Less Advanced Students: 1, 6
Average Students: 2, 4, 5
More Advanced Students: 3, 7

Customizing for
Learning Modalities
Following are suggestions for matching Idea Bank topics with your students' learning modalities:
Logical/Mathematical: 4
Interpersonal: 5
Intrapersonal: 6
Verbal/Linguistic: 7

Guided Writing Lesson

For more instruction on prewriting, elaboration, and revision, see *Prentice Hall Writing and Grammar.*

Writing and Language Transparencies
Have students use the Outline Organizer, p. 95, to organize their prewriting ideas.

Writers at Work Videodisc Have students view the videodisc segment (Ch. 3) featuring Thom Harrington, Curator of the New York Transit Museum, speaking about choosing a topic for exposition. Ask students how Harrington's understanding of the past helps him choose subjects to write about.

Play frames 22803 to 32243

Writing Lab CD-ROM
Have students complete the tutorial on Exposition. Have students follow these steps:
1. Use the Outliner to organize their prewriting developments and background information.
2. Draft on the computer.
3. Use the Revision checker for language variety to aid revision.

ASSESSMENT OPTIONS

Formal Assessment, Selection Test, pp. 64–66, and Assessment Resources Software. The selection test is designed so that it can be easily customized to the performance levels of your students.

Alternative Assessment, p. 13, includes options for less advanced students, more advanced students, visual/spatial learners, musical/rhythmic learners, and verbal/linguistic learners.

PORTFOLIO ASSESSMENT
Use the following rubrics in the ***Alternative Assessment*** booklet to assess student writing:
Descriptive Letter: Description Rubric, p. 112
Reflective Essay: Definition/Classification Rubric, p. 114
"Melting Pot" Epistle: Persuasion Rubric, p. 120
Guided Writing Lesson: Comparison/Contrast Rubric, p. 118

LESSON OBJECTIVES

1. To express and support responses to the text
- Critical Thinking
- Idea Bank: Journal Entry
- Idea Bank: Book Jacket

2. To read in order to research self-selected and assigned topics
- Idea Bank: Multimedia *Roots* Presentation
- Idea Bank: Cultural Heritage Display

3. To plan, prepare, organize, and present literary interpretations
- Idea Bank: Informal Debate
- Idea Bank: Director's Notes

Interest Grabber Tell students that they are about to read a passage from the book that made a lasting impression on the face of American culture—and American television—in the late 1970's. To introduce students to Alex Haley's epic tale, play your choice of scenes from the television mini-series. Afterward, ask students to discuss their impressions of what they saw. Prompt them to speculate about why the book and mini-series have had such an effect on our understanding of what it means to be American.

CONNECTIONS TO TODAY'S WORLD

from Roots
Alex Haley

Thematic Connection

THE EMERGING AMERICAN IDENTITY: DEFINING AN AMERICAN

What is an American? The works in Part 3 offer a telling look at a young nation consciously struggling with this question. At the time, neither Abigail Adams, Michel-Guillaume Jean de Crèvecoeur, nor Benjamin Franklin could have foreseen the impact that descendants of enslaved Africans would one day have on America's answer. Those writers could not have known that a book written by an African American would influence the way in which millions of Americans defined their identities.

That book, *Roots*, published in 1976, and the television mini-series of the same name, changed the nation's perception of itself as only very powerful events can. A fictionalized tale of the author Alex Haley's search for his African ancestors and the story of his family's history from their beginnings in Africa to emancipation, the book focused America's attention on the richness of the African cultural heritage. Civil rights leader Vernon Jordan called the television mini-series based on Haley's book "the single most spectacular educational experience in race relations in America."

African Americans everywhere followed Haley's example by renewing ties with their African ancestry. Thanks to a single book, the identities of millions of Americans expanded to include a new awareness of rich roots firmly planted in another time and place.

ALEX HALEY
(1921–1992)

Alex Haley spent twenty years in the Coast Guard as a journalist before deciding to become a freelance writer. His first big success came with his highly praised *The Autobiography of Malcolm X*. His greatest and best-known accomplishment, however, is *Roots: The Saga of an American Family*. The book was an immediate bestseller and within two years had won 271 awards. The television mini-series based on the book was viewed by 130 million people. About *Roots'* success, Haley said, "when you start talking about family, about lineage and ancestry, you are talking about every person on earth. We all have it; it's a great equalizer. . . . I think the book has touched a strong, subliminal chord."

Prentice Hall Literature Program Resources

REINFORCE / RETEACH / EXTEND

Selection Support Pages
Build Vocabulary: Using Descriptive Vocabulary to Set a Scene, p. 65
Thematic Connection: The Emerging American Identity: Defining an American, p. 66

Formal Assessment Selection Test, pp. 67–68, Assessment Resources Software

Resource Pro CD-ROM

Listening to Literature Audiocassettes

CONNECTIONS TO TODAY'S WORLD

from

Roots

Alex Haley

Alex Haley's search for his African roots takes him to the small village of Juffure, located in the country in western Africa now known as The Gambia. The elderly village historian honors the American visitor by relating for him the ancestral history of the Kinte clan.

The old *griot*[1] had talked for nearly two hours up to then, and perhaps fifty times the narrative had included some detail about someone whom he had named. Now after he had just named those four sons, again he appended a detail, and the interpreter translated—

1. ***griot*** (grē´ ō) *n.*: The village oral historian, generally an elderly man who recites histories of famous heroes and families on special occasions.

Develop Understanding

One-Minute Insight Franklin's American aims for moral aptitude; Adams' American concerns him- or herself with the national issues and personal challenges; and Crèvecoeur's American renounces his European heritage to join the American melting pot. Haley adds a new defining element: that of an African American whose sense of identity is firmly rooted in an African ancestry. While discovering his own particular forebear, Haley realizes his own search would be "a symbolic saga of all African-descent people." In a larger sense, his quest is symbolic of everyone's search for ancestral roots. When we define our roots, we also define ourselves as Americans.

Customize for
English Language Learners
These students may have difficulty pronouncing some of the proper nouns in the selection. To help familiarize them with unfamiliar words and pronunciations, review and define the following words in advance: Kunta, Ko, Kamby Bolongo, Juffure, Allah, Mandingo, Banjul (bän´ jo͞ol) and Dakar (də kär´). See the footnotes for additional pronunciations.

Customize for
Visual/Spatial Learners
To help these students understand the extent of Haley's search for his ancestors, use a map of Africa to point out the following: Kamby Bolongo (i.e., Gambia River, in West Africa, flowing from North Guinea, through Senegal and Gambia, into the Atlantic), Banjul (capital of Gambia, on an island in the mouth of the Gambia River), and Dakar (capital of Senegal).

Viewing and Representing Mini-Lesson

Multimedia Presentation

Introduce This mini-lesson supports the Multimedia *Roots* Presentation on p. 207.

Develop Explain to students that in a multimedia presentation, they face an interesting creative challenge. For this assignment, they can draw from an abundance of sources, including film and documentary excerpts, magazine and newspaper articles, and musical scores. Because *Roots* was so culturally influential and widely known, it received a great deal of media attention.

Apply Suggest that students solicit the help of a reference librarian to ascertain where in the library to locate the types of resources they want to find. Point out that they may find other resources through the Internet. Encourage them to look for as much material as they can find before selecting specific informational content to combine in their presentation. Also encourage them to combine different types of materials: for example, photographs or film excerpts, music, and excerpts of written texts.

Assess Assess students' presentations on the basis of their informational content, breadth, and variety, as well as the creativity with which the student has combined different media.

Thematic Connection

❶ **The Emerging American Identity: Defining an American** Ask students how growing up with this story may have affected Haley's perception of his American identity. *Students should note that Haley learned from a young age that he was descended from African ancestry; this knowledge was a big part of his identity as a person and as an African American.*

☑ Comprehension Check

❷ Have students describe in their own words what happens in this passage. *The villagers suddenly form a circle around Haley and begin to chant and dance.*

◆ Critical Thinking

❸ **Speculate** Ask students to speculate about what may have prompted the women to act in this way. *Students' speculations will vary. Some may say that the women may have considered it an honor to have the special visitor hold their babies.*

Customize for
Gifted/Talented Students
Direct students' attention to the passage beginning in the last paragraph on p. 204 and continuing to the bottom of p. 205. Have students discuss how they could communicate these circumstances through dance, art, or music. If possible, allow students to plan and present their ideas.

"About the time the King's soldiers came"—another of the *griot's* time-fixing references—"the oldest of these four sons, Kunta, went away from his village to chop wood . . . and he was never seen again. . . ." And the *griot* went on with his narrative.

❶ I sat as if I were carved of stone. My blood seemed to have congealed. This man whose lifetime had been in this back-country African village had no way in the world to know that he had just echoed what I had heard all through my boyhood years on my grandma's front porch in Henning, Tennessee . . . of an African who always had insisted that his name was "Kin-tay"; who had called a guitar a *"ko,"* and a river within the state of Virginia, "Kamby Bolongo";[2] and who had been kidnaped into slavery while not far from his village, chopping wood, to make himself a drum.

I managed to fumble from my duffelbag my basic notebook, whose first pages containing grandma's story I showed to an interpreter. After briefly reading, clearly astounded, he spoke rapidly while showing it to the old *griot*, who became agitated; he got up, exclaiming to the people, gesturing at my notebook in the interpreter's hands, and *they* all got agitated.

❷ I don't remember hearing anyone giving an order, I only recall becoming aware that those seventy-odd people had formed a wide human ring around me, moving counterclockwise, chanting softly, loudly, softly; their bodies close together, they were lifting their knees high, stamping up reddish puffs of the dust. . . .

The woman who broke from the moving circle was one of about a dozen whose infant children were within cloth slings across their backs. ❸ Her jet-black face deeply contorting, the woman came charging toward me, her bare feet slapping the earth, and snatching her baby free, she thrust it at me almost roughly, the gesture saying "Take it!" . . . and I did, clasping the baby to me. Then she snatched away her baby; and another woman was thrusting her baby, then another, and another . . . until I had embraced probably a dozen babies. I wouldn't learn until maybe a year later, from a Harvard University professor, Dr. Jerome Bruner, a scholar of such matters, "You didn't know you were participating in one of the oldest ceremonies of humankind, called 'The laying on of hands'! In their way, they were telling you 'Through this flesh, which is us, we are you, and you are us!'"

Later the men of Juffure[3] took me into their mosque[4] built of bamboo and thatch, and they prayed around me in Arabic. I remember thinking, down on my knees, "After I've found out where I came from, I can't understand a word they're saying." Later the crux of their prayer was translated for me: "Praise be to Allah for one long lost from us whom Allah has returned."

Since we had come by the river, I wanted to return by land. As I sat beside the wiry young Mandingo driver who was leaving dust pluming behind us on the hot, rough, pitted, back-country road toward Banjul, there came from somewhere into my head a staggering awareness . . . that *if* any black American could be so blessed as I had been to know only a few ancestral clues—could he or she know *who* was either the paternal or maternal African ancestor or ancestors, and about *where* that ancestor lived when taken, and finally about *when* the ancestor was taken—then only those few clues might well see that black American able to locate some wizened old black *griot* whose narrative could reveal the black American's ancestral clan, perhaps even the very village.

In my mind's eye, rather as if it were mistily being projected on a screen, I began envisioning descriptions I had read of how collectively millions of our ancestors had been enslaved. ❹ Many thousands were individually kidnaped, as my own forebear Kunta had been, but into the millions had come awake screaming in the night, dashing out into the bedlam of raided villages, which were often in flames. The captured able survivors were linked neck-by-neck with thongs into processions called "coffles," which were sometimes as much as a mile in length. I envisioned the many dying, or left to

2. **"Kamby Bolongo"** (kăm´ bē bō lôŋ´ gō): "Gambia River" in the Mandinka language of western Africa.

3. **Juffure** (jo͞o´ fo͞o rā)
4. **mosque** (măsk) *n.*: Muslim temple or place of worship.

◆ Build Vocabulary

congealed (kən jēld´) *v.*: Thickened or solidified
crux (kruks) *n.*: Essential point

Speaking, Listening, and Viewing Mini-Lesson

Informal Debate

This mini-lesson supports the Speaking, Listening, and Viewing activity in the Idea Bank on p. 207.

Introduce Explain to students that informal debates include panel discussions, in which three or four people explain and discuss their ideas on a given subject, and discussions on a given subject which are principally between two individuals.

Develop Tell students to divide into two small groups, one representing the position of Crèvecoeur and the other representing the position of Haley. Both sides should discuss in detail the views of their spokesperson, anticipate any rebuttals from his opponent, and devise strategies to refute his rebuttals. However, remind students that in this informal debate, they must base the comments of each principal debater on what they know of the views of the real individual (Crèvecoeur or Haley) he represents.

Apply After the positions of "Crèvecoeur" and "Haley" have been presented, the other team members should be invited to join in a general discussion, politely and carefully responding to one another's comments.

Assess Evaluate students on the logic, clarity, and persuasiveness of their arguments, the validity of their interpretations of each principal spokesman's views, and their willingness to listen carefully to one another.

Dance Africa, Synthia Saint James, Third World Art Exchange

5 ▲ Critical Viewing How does the artist convey the vibrancy of African dance without depicting movement? Does Haley's description of Africa convey the same feeling? [Relate]

die when they were too weak to continue the torturous march toward the coast, and those who made it to the beach were greased, shaved, probed in every orifice, often branded with sizzling irons; I envisioned them being lashed and dragged toward the longboats; their spasms of screaming and clawing with their hands into the beach, biting up great choking mouthfuls of the sand in their desperation efforts for one last hold on the Africa that had been their home; I envisioned them shoved, beaten, jerked down into slave ships' stinking holds and chained onto shelves, often packed so tightly that they had to lie on their sides like spoons in a drawer. . . . 6

My mind reeled with it all as we approached another, much larger village. Staring ahead, I realized that word of what had happened in

4 **Clarification** Explain that parties of slave traders and their henchmen sometimes raided entire villages in an effort to secure dozens of captives at a time.

▶Critical Viewing◀

5 **Relate** Students may note that the billowing forms, brilliant colors, and the way in which the figures seems to surge toward one another effectively convey the vibrancy of African dance. Haley also describes the Africans he encounters as being animated and vibrant.

◆Critical Thinking

6 **Compare** Ask students how Haley's depiction of life aboard a slave ship compares with that of Olaudah Equiano (p. 44). *The accounts are quite similar; both speak of the brutal way in which the captive were treated, and the stench and overcrowding of the ship's hold.*

Humanities: Art

Dance Africa, 1995, by Synthia Saint James.

This painting was created to promote the 1996 national tour of Dance Africa America, a North Carolina-based dance company. Each year, founding director Chuck Davis travels with his students to Africa so that they can learn the authentic African rhythms and dances which are the hallmark of the company's electrifying performances. In this painting, Davis (the central male figure) is represented in the role of *griot,*—a village historian and storyteller—the keeper of a village's folk culture.

Self-taught artist and author Synthia Saint James (b. 1949) is an internationally recognized artist whose works can be found on the covers of more than 40 books. She has created commissioned works of art for dozens of major organizations including UNICEF, and Coca-Cola. In 1997, she designed the first official Kwanzaa stamp issued by the United States Postal Service.

Use these questions to discuss the work:

1. How is the portrayal of the male figure symbolic of his role as the *griot? He unites the figures in the painting, just as the griot is the central keeper of a clan's shared history.*
2. How does this painting convey the sense of unity and joy that characterize the Africans Haley describes? *Students should note that the bright colors and figures who seem to be embracing one another echo Haley's descriptions.*

Reinforce and Extend

Customize for
Bodily/Kinesthetic Learners
Have these students develop a skit in which they act out one or more of the scenes Haley describes.

Answers

◆ ***Literature and Your Life***

Reader's Response Students may express an interest in knowing more about their daily lives and customs.

Thematic Focus It raises our awareness of the rich backgrounds from which Americans are descended.

☑ **Check Your Comprehension**

1. Haley knew his ancestor's name, the approximate area of Africa from which he came, and the time in which he was taken.
2. The fact that Kunta had disappeared while chopping wood outside the village led Haley to believe that Kunta and his Kinte ancestor were the same person.
3. (a) They were performing the ceremony known as "the laying on of hands." (b) The villagers were showing Haley that they were all descendants of the same ancestors.
4. Haley realizes that, with a few clues about their ancestors, many African Americans might be able to find their ancestral clans.

◆ Critical Thinking

1. It symbolizes his acceptance as a member of the Kinte clan.
2. (a) Haley describes the desperation of the enslaved Africans, while portraying the villagers as "buoyant, beaming" people. (b) The reader imagines how, only a few generations earlier, these same happy people were being enslaved and tormented.
3. Haley feels that his family's history is representative of what happened to millions of Africans who were brought to America in captivity.
4. He may not have been as interested in pursuing his search for his family's African roots.
5. Some may feel that the awareness of African heritage created by the book mean more than the accuracy of its contents. Others may argue that distortion diminishes the value of the work.

Juffure must have left there well before I did. The driver slowing down, I could see this village's people thronging the road ahead; they were weaving, amid their cacophony of crying out something; I stood up in the Land-Rover, waving back as they seemed grudging to open a path for the Land-Rover.

I guess we had moved a third of the way through the village when it suddenly registered in my brain what they were all crying out . . . the wizened, robed elders and younger men, the mothers and the naked tar-black children, they were all waving up at me; their expressions buoyant, beaming, all were crying out together, *"Meester Kinte! Meester Kinte!"*

Let me tell you something: I am a man. A sob hit me somewhere around my ankles; it came surging upward, and flinging my hands over my face, I was just bawling, as I hadn't since I was a baby. *"Meester Kinte!"* I just felt like I was weeping for all of history's incredible atrocities against fellowmen, which seems to be mankind's greatest flaw. . . .

Flying homeward from Dakar, I decided to write a book. My own ancestors would automatically also be a symbolic saga of all African-descent people—who are without exception the seeds of someone like Kunta who was born and grew up in some black African village, someone who was captured and chained down in one of those slave ships that sailed them across the same ocean, into some succession of plantations, and since then a struggle for freedom.

◆ Build Vocabulary

cacophony (kə käf´ ə nē) *n.*: Harsh, jarring sound

Guide for Responding

◆ Literature and Your Life

Reader's Response If you had the opportunity to learn about your own ancestors, what would you want to discover or see for yourself?

Thematic Focus How does *Roots* expand our understanding of what it means to be an American?

Journal Writing What do you already know about your ancestry, and what would you like to learn? Jot down facts about your heritage, along with questions you would like to have answered. Then list possible sources of information about your family's history, including relatives, old family photographs, and so on.

☑ Check Your Comprehension

1. Before Haley visited Juffure, what information did he have about his ancestor?
2. Which detail of the *griot's* tale convinced Haley that Kunta was the same ancestor his grandmother had described?
3. (a) Why did the African mothers hand their babies to Haley? (b) What were the villagers telling Haley through this gesture?
4. What is the "staggering awareness" that comes to Haley while traveling toward Banjul?

◆ Critical Thinking

INTERPRET

1. What does being addressed as "Meester Kinte" represent to Haley? **[Interpret]**
2. (a) Contrast Haley's portrayal of enslaved Africans with his descriptions of the Africans who greet him as he travels through Juffure and Banjul. (b) How do his descriptions of the Africans he meets in his travels make the plight of enslaved Africans seem even more tragic? **[Compare and Contrast]**
3. What does Haley mean when he writes, "My own ancestors would automatically also be a symbolic saga of all African-descent people"? **[Interpret]**

APPLY

4. If the villagers had treated Haley as an outsider rather than as a kinsman, how might his search for his heritage have been affected? **[Speculate]**

EVALUATE

5. Critics have suggested that *Roots* blurs the lines between fact and fiction, and that Haley may have presented fictional segments of the story as fact. Do you think that this blurring detracts from the book's value? Explain. **[Make a Judgment]**

Beyond the Selection

FURTHER READING

Other Works by Alex Haley

Queen: The Story of an American Family
The Autobiography of Malcolm X

Other Works With the Theme of Defining an American

Spoon River Anthology, Edgar Lee Masters
The House on Mango Street, Sandra Cisneros

We suggest that you preview these works before recommending them to students.

INTERNET

To learn more about African American heritage, we suggest visiting the following site. Please be aware, however, that sites may have changed since this information was published.

To see a Library of Congress exhibit, go to **http://lcweb.loc.gov/exhibits/african/intro.html**

We *strongly recommend* that you preview the site before you send students to it.

Thematic Connection

The Emerging American Identity: Defining an American

Today, thanks in part to the awareness generated by *Roots*, Americans tend to be more sensitive to the value of our many ethnic and cultural heritages. Though we can proudly trace our ancestry to hundreds of nations, Americans are unified by a belief in many of the same values that Crèvecoeur and Franklin professed centuries ago; we still trust in hard work, self-reliance, and democracy. We even struggle with many of the same problems Abigail Adams addressed in her lifetime of correspondence, including such national issues as education and equal rights for women and such personal challenges as keeping families united over long distances. Alex Haley has earned a place in this celebrated tradition of writers whose works help us answer the question, What is an American?

1. How do you think Alex Haley might answer the question, What is an American? Why?
2. Which of the beliefs expressed by other writers in this section do you think Haley might share? Why?

Idea Bank

Writing

1. **Journal Entry** Alex Haley describes the moment in which he realizes that he has "found" his ancestry in the village of Juffure. Imagine that you are Haley, reflecting on the events of this emotional day in your journal. Use both the excerpt and your own imagination to describe your thoughts and feelings in a journal entry.
2. **Director's Notes** As a director filming the scene in which Haley discovers his ancestral clan in Juffure, how would you want the actors to speak, move, and gesture as they recite their lines? What expressions should they wear? Write a series of notes that explain how you would like the characters to look, act, and sound at each point in the scene. **[Career Link]**
3. **Book Jacket** *Roots: The Saga of an American Family* is the fictionalized account of Haley's family history and his search for his African ancestors. The book and television mini-series raised awareness of black heritage in the 1970's. How would you convince a new generation of potential readers to buy the book? Convey the excitement and historic significance of *Roots* in a book-jacket summary that would make people want to read the book. **[Career Link]**

Speaking, Listening, and Viewing

4. **Informal Debate** Michel-Guillaume Jean de Crèvecoeur says that true Americans ought to cut their ties to their country of origin. Would Haley have shared that philosophy? Work with a small group to stage an informal debate between Haley and Crèvecoeur on the question of whether Americans should retain their ties to the lands from which their ancestors came.

Researching and Representing

5. **Multimedia *Roots* Presentation** Research the media coverage surrounding the influential 1977 *Roots* mini-series. How was it received? How did it impact the way Americans viewed their heritage? Present your findings in a narrated multimedia presentation. You might make a montage of articles about the series, play a recording of the *Roots* theme music, or show a series excerpt or interview with Haley. **[Media Link]**
6. **Cultural Heritage Display** Celebrate your own cultural heritage by creating a display. Pull together objects that capture important elements of your culture or cultures of origin. Write a paragraph explaining each of the objects. Then assemble the objects and the accompanying descriptions into an appealing visual display.

Online Activity www.phlit.phschool.com

Answers
Thematic Connection

1. Suggested responses include: An American believes that liberty and justice are the rights of all people who live in this country, regardless of their sex, race, or creed.
2. Possible response: Haley would probably have agreed with Franklin and Crèvecouer that hard work, common sense, and self-reliance are important. He probably shared Crèvecouer's belief in the value of an open-minded democracy, in which people leave behind any prejudices or preconceived notions in order to live together as Americans.

Customize for *AP Students*

Suggest that students read additional portions of *Roots* and share their insights with the class. Or suggest that they work in teams to read portions of *Queen: The Story of an American Family* about Haley's paternal ancestry, published after Haley died.

Idea Bank

Customizing for *Performance Levels*

Following are suggestions for matching Idea Bank topics with your students' performance levels:
Less Advanced Students: 1, 6
Average Students: 2, 4
More Advanced Students: 3, 5

Customizing for *Learning Modalities*

Following are suggestions for matching Idea Bank topics with your students' learning modalities:
Verbal/Linguistic: 4
Logical/Mathematical: 4
Visual/Spatial: 5, 6
Bodily/Kinesthetic: 5, 6

✓ Assessment Options

Formal Assessment, Selection Test, pp. 67–68, and Assessment Resources Software. The selection test is designed so that it can be easily customized to the performance levels of your students.

PORTFOLIO ASSESSMENT
Use the following rubrics in the ***Alternative Assessment*** booklet to assess student writing:
Journal Entry: Expression Rubric, p. 109
Director's Notes: Description Rubric, p. 112
Book Jacket: Persuasion Rubric, p. 120

Prepare and Engage

LESSON OBJECTIVES

- To use recursive writing processes to produce a multimedia presentation
- To identify and correct vague or ambiguous pronoun references
- To recognize and correctly use adverbs and adjectives

Distribute the scoring rubric for Multimedia Report (p. 122) in ***Alternative Assessment*** to show students the criteria on which their work will be evaluated. To customize the rubric to this workshop, see page 210.

Writing and Language Transparencies Present to the Writing Process Model of a Research Report (pp. 41–50)

Looking at Literature Videodisc

The Looking at Literature Videodisc includes a multimedia presentation on *The Autobiography of Benjamin Franklin.* Encourage students to watch this with an eye for technique, not content.

Chapter 3

Writing Lab CD-ROM

If your students have access to computers, you may want to have them work in the tutorial on Research. Have students follow these steps:

1. Review the interactive model of a multimedia presentation.
2. Complete a Research Profile designed to save them time while conducting research.
3. Draft on the computer.
4. Revise using Revision Checkers for unity and coherence, transitions, and sentence length.

Multimedia Presentation
Writing Process Workshop

The word **media** is the plural of *medium*—in this case, a medium of communication, a way of conveying human thoughts and feelings. Poetic writing is the original multimedia spectacle. It uses language to simulate or evoke sight, sound, touch, feeling, and thought, just as Crèvecoeur does with his captivating metaphors and images in his letter featured in this unit.

With the media of modern technology at your fingertips, you can offer more than mere verbal simulations of sights and sounds. You can dazzle your audience with the real thing: stunning full-color videos, slides, and paintings or spectacular surround-sound.

The following skills will help you produce an effective multimedia presentation.

Writing Skills Focus

- **Select a writing style appropriate** to a multimedia presentation. Your spoken text should be briefer than it would be in an entirely verbal context. (See p. 191.)
- **Provide the necessary context and background** if your listeners are unfamiliar with your topic. (See p. 201.)
- **Show, don't tell.** Since you have a variety of media at your disposal, rely more on direct sensory appeal and less on words.

This script for a multimedia presentation uses these skills.

WRITING MODEL

[VIDEOTAPE: SCENE OF CHARLIE PARKER AND DIZZY GILLESPIE] ① What you see and hear on this video is a kinescope of a TV broadcast from 1951—the heydey of bebop, a revolutionary movement in jazz. Charlie Parker on alto sax and Dizzy Gillespie on trumpet lead a quartet on the tune "Koko." ② The chordal and harmonic complexity of bebop were a challenge for talented musicians, and Parker's blizzards of improvisation astonish even now. Imagine yourself playing what you see on this sheet music, a transcription of one of Parker's solos. [HANDOUT] ③

① The directions are set off in capital letters and brackets.

② The writer uses both the visual and auditory possibilities of the video to convey important background details.

③ By using a handout of sheet music, the writer uses still another medium—print— to enhance the presentation by showing, not merely telling.

Beyond the Classroom

Career Connection

Multimedia Production The growing presence of CD-ROMs and Web sites on the Internet has led to a dramatic increase in the number of jobs that call for multimedia skills. Careers are available in software engineering, graphic design, multimedia writing, and testing. A multimedia producer's responsibilities might include selecting media, determining how elements should work together, planning the best use of available technology, and confirming that the finished product works.

Ask students to identify limitations of CD-ROMs and Web sites when compared with multimedia presentations they can deliver live to an audience. *A totally electronic presentation prohibits the use of three-dimensional objects and limits the size of text or graphics to the dimensions of the screen or monitor.* Conversely, what are some of the advantages of producing electronic over live presentations? *The audience, or user, can work through the presentation at an individual pace; and the user can replay media as many times as desired.*

Prewriting

Choose a Topic Start by coming up with a topic that interests you and for which there is multimedia material available. You might consider these topics.

Topic Ideas

- The national parks
- Joys of owning a pet
- The election process
- Skiing, scuba diving, or hiking
- Your favorite pop musicians
- New York City's theater district

Consider Possible Media Gather material through research. Your ingenuity and imagination are the only limits. You might want to consider these types of media:

- ▶ Audiotapes of music or interviews
- ▶ Videotaped interviews, films, or television programs
- ▶ Printed articles, graphs, charts, and maps
- ▶ Scale models
- ▶ Foods and plants

Drafting

Use an Outline and Flowchart Outline the information you want to include in your presentation. Next to the headings, name your multimedia resources. You might also want to create a flowchart that shows what you or another student will be saying, doing, playing, or showing at each point during your presentation. Generate a script from your flowchart, relying as little as possible on words and as much as possible on your multimedia resources. Provide the context necessary for the background of your audience.

Treat Your Presentation as a Performance Rehearse with all your items, equipment, and any co-presenters, to make sure everything works and runs smoothly. Practice making eye contact with your listeners.

APPLYING LANGUAGE SKILLS: Vague or Ambiguous Pronoun References

The antecedents of a pronoun should be clear; there should be no possibility that the pronoun refers to more than one antecedent.

Vague Pronoun Reference:

Call of the Wild is very suspenseful, which most readers enjoy.

Clear Pronoun Reference:

Call of the Wild is filled with suspense, which most readers enjoy.

Practice Revise these examples of vague pronoun references.

1. Carla is hunched over her stamp collection because it is a fascinating hobby.
2. He is an inspiring coach, and this was evident from the team's winning record.
3. The gardeners used the noisy leaf blowers early in the morning, which the neighbors disapproved of.

Writing Application Review your multimedia presentation, and eliminate any vague or confusing pronoun references.

Writer's Solution Connection
Writing Lab

For information on using on-line media sources, use the Prewriting section of the Research Writing tutorial.

Prewriting Strategy

For each of the topic ideas presented use the list of possible media to brainstorm for possible ways of obtaining such media.

Customize for
Visual/Spatial Learners

Rather than basing their presentations solely on pre-existing visual sources, these students may enjoy creating their own charts, computer-based slide shows, photographs, or drawings based on the information they uncover during their research.

Customize for
Musical/Rhythmic Learners

These students may want to choose a topic like the one featured in the writing model on page 208. Writing about a form of popular music opens up an entire world of readily accessible audio sources.

Writing Lab CD-ROM The Gathering Information section of the tutorial contains interactive instruction on using various information sources and resources including library reference materials, specific on-line services, and graphic documents such as maps, charts, and graphs.

Elaboration Strategy

Students may find it helpful to organize details of the presentation on a chart like this one. Students can add details to the presentation chart as appropriate.

Visual	Voice	Music	Props
video of Parker and Gillespie	what you see and hear on this video	supplied with video	
enlargement of music	notice on the sheet music	tape of 3 bars of music	sheet music

Applying Language Skills

Vague or Ambiguous Pronoun References

Introduce this skill by explaining to students that their audience may not fully appreciate their presentations if pronoun references are difficult to follow.

Answers

1. Carla is hunched over her stamp collection, preoccupied by her fascinating hobby.
2. He is an inspiring coach, a fact that was evident from the team's winning record.
3. The gardeners used the noisy leaf blowers early in the morning, a practice of which the neighbors disapproved.

Grammar Reinforcement

For additional instruction and practice, use the lesson on Pronouns and Antecedents in the **Language Lab CD-ROM** and practice pages on pronoun-antecedent agreement (pp. 69–72) in the *Writer's Solution Grammar Practice Book.*

Revision Strategy

Peer reviewing may be particularly helpful with this assignment, especially for those students not experienced or comfortable with performing in public.

Applying Language Skills

Adverb or Adjective? Remind students that multimedia elements should enhance, not replace, a presentation that includes proper word choice and sound grammar.

Answers

1. *Homely* is an adjective.
2. *Friendly* is an adjective.
3. *Eagerly* is an adverb.

Grammar Reinforcement

In addition to the **Language Lab CD-ROM** lesson cited in the student edition, further practice can be found on page 10 in the *Writer's Solution Grammar Practice Book.*

Reinforce and Extend

For more prewriting, elaboration, and revision strategies, see *Prentice Hall Writing and Grammar.*

Reflect on Writing

Ask students what they learned about using different types of media in their presentations. What media would they be most likely to embrace—or avoid—in the future?

APPLYING LANGUAGE SKILLS: Adverb or Adjective?

Some adjectives that end in *-ly* can easily be mistaken for adverbs. Keep in mind that adjectives modify nouns and adverbs modify verbs, adjectives, or other adverbs.

Adverb:

We arrived early. (Here early modifies the verb arrived.)

Adjective:

We caught the early train. (Here early modifies the noun train.)

Practice Identify the italicized word in each of the following items as an adjective or an adverb.

1. My sister thought that the stray dog was *homely*, but I thought he was cute.
2. The new student seemed *friendly*.
3. I devoured the book *eagerly*.

Writing Application As you draft your multimedia presentation, be sure that you have used all your *-ly* words correctly.

Writer's Solution Connection
Language Lab

For more practice, complete the Problems with Modifiers lesson.

Revising

Strike a Balance Be sure you have successfully integrated multimedia elements into your script. For example, if you rely on one slide for a long part of your presentation and then flash several more images in quick succession, you may want to rework the pacing of your presentation.

Use a Checklist After your rehearsal, go over the following points to be sure your presentation will be successful:

- Is all my equipment in proper working order?
- Have I presented the necessary background and context?
- Have I written in a concise style that does not compete with my audiovisual tools—that is, have I spent enough time showing rather than telling?

REVISION MODEL

Many of Dizzy Gillespie's compositions have become classics.
① As you listen to ② notice the unique rhythm and harmonies
This recording of "A Night in Tunisia," ~~show the qualities~~
that made bebop famous.

① The writer makes better use of the music by directing the audience's attention.
② The writer adds more specific information about the qualities of bebop

Presenting

Deliver Your Presentation Once you've finished polishing your presentation, present it to a live audience. Be sure to allow time to answer questions.

Think Big Do you think that your show is good enough to take on the road? You might start thinking bigger by moving from your classroom to a school assembly program. The next step might be a nearby school or a local club or organization that seeks out speakers on your topic. Ask the librarian at your school or in your community to help you in locating such groups.

✓ ASSESSMENT

PORTFOLIO ASSESSMENT
Use the rubric on Multimedia Report in ***Alternative Assessment*** (p. 122) to assess students' writing. Add these criteria to customize the rubric to this assignment.

	4	3	2	1
Vague or Ambiguous Pronoun Reference	The writer consistently makes accurate and clear pronoun references.	The writer makes some accurate and clear pronoun references.	The writer rarely makes accurate and clear pronoun references.	The writer makes vague or ambiguous pronoun references, making the presentation difficult to follow.
Provides Necessary Context	The writer consistently provides appropriate background information for each piece of media.	The writer provides some background information to enhance the presentation of the media.	The writer rarely provides necessary background information, instead relying on the media to convey meaning.	The writer provides unclear background information, rendering the uses of the media ineffective.

Student Success Workshop

Real-World Reading Skills: Evaluating a Writer's Motivation

Strategies for Success

Reading a news article is a very different experience from laughing through a humor column—even if the topic is the same! Why? The main reason is that the writers have very different motives: one to inform and the other to entertain. Judging a writer's motivation helps you respond to your reading.

Be Aware of Possible Motivation Most writing seeks to entertain, inform, persuade, or describe. Often, these goals overlap—a travel brochure describes a place, informs readers about its features, and persuades readers to visit. Familiarize yourself with these main writing purposes by listing some examples of each from your own recent reading.

Food for Thought
by Dave Barry

It's getting late on a school night, but I'm not letting my son go to bed yet, because there's serious work to be done.

"Robert!" I'm saying, in a firm voice. "Come to the kitchen right now and blow-dry the ant!"

We have a large ant, about the size of a mature raccoon, standing on our kitchen counter. In fact, it looks kind of like a raccoon, or possibly even a mutant lobster. We made the ant out of papier-mâché, a substance you create by mixing flour and water and newspapers together into a slimy goop that drips down and gets licked up by your dogs, who operate on the wise survival principle that you should immediately eat everything that falls onto the kitchen floor, because if it turns out not to be food, you can always throw it up later.

The ant, needless to say, is part of a Science Fair project. . . .

Recognize a Writer's Motivation To evaluate a writer's motivation, examine the topic, style, and focus of the writing. Questions like these can help:

- ▶ Who is the intended audience?
- ▶ How does the writer hope to affect or change the audience?
- ▶ What is the topic? How might the topic be related to the writer's motivation?
- ▶ What type of language does the writer use, and what does it suggest about the writer's attitude toward the subject?

Read Critically Once you recognize the writer's motivation, you can read more critically—alert to biased statements in persuasion, looking carefully for details in informative material, or relaxing to enjoy reading meant only for entertainment.

Apply the Strategies

Your brother left his newspaper on the kitchen table, open to this article. Read it and determine its writer's motivation.

1. What is the writer's motivation? How do you know?
2. Choose another motive, but keep the same topic. Rewrite the article to reflect the new motivation, adding information from your imagination if you wish.

✔ *Here are other situations in which it's important to recognize the writer's motivation:*

- ▶ Advertisements and promotional literature
- ▶ Political statements
- ▶ News articles

Introduce the Strategy

LESSON OBJECTIVES

- To evaluate the credibility of information sources, including how the writer's motivation may affect that credibility

Customize for
English Language Learners
Barry's dry wit and deadpan irony may be difficult for these students to grasp, and a line-by-line explanation of the writing style may be necessary. For example, help English language learners see the contrast that results when what starts as a formal-sounding definition of papier-mâché eventually includes the phrase "and gets licked up by your dogs." Similarly, this same long sentence includes the clause "who operate on the wise survival principle"; here Barry uses an authoritative tone and scholarly sounding words to set up an absurd conclusion to the thought. Then, at the close of the excerpt, Barry's use of the phrase "needless to say" is also ironic, directed at parents, and perhaps students, who have prior experience with preparing for a Science Fair.

Apply the Strategies

Answers

1. The writer's purpose becomes obvious only at the end of the second paragraph—the command "blow-dry the ant!" serves the same purpose as a punch line in a spoken joke, alerting the reader to the humorous intent of the piece.
2. Students' paragraphs should clearly show a different motivation from Barry's, which is to amuse the reader.

Test Preparation Workshop

Evaluating a Writer's Motivation
Standardized tests may ask students to evaluate a writer's motivation. To reinforce this skill, write this sample test item on the board:

> I have read many amusing books, but none have made me laugh out loud as often as those by Dave Barry. Barry's hysterical essays could make even the grumpiest person crack a smile. His writing is a sure-fire cure for the blues!

In this passage, the writer's motivation is to—

A inform
B persuade
C entertain
D describe

Lead students to see that the best answer is B. The writer's description of Barry's writing is clearly meant to persuade readers that Barry's work is funny.

Prepare and Engage

LESSON OBJECTIVES

- To speak clearly and effectively for a variety of purposes
- To prepare, organize, and present informative and persuasive messages

Customize for
Intrapersonal Learners
Even when they feel strongly about an issue, these students may know that they are not comfortable speaking in public. A common device used to train novice public speakers is to have them imagine that they are speaking to only one other person, with the result being that their speech takes on more natural cadences and a relaxed tone. You may want to be more patient with intrapersonal learners; that keep in mind that the first priority is for them to get in touch with the personal feelings which will motivate their speeches. Over time, and through repeated practice, they can gradually refine the techniques necessary to speaking in front of a large group.

Apply the Strategies

1. Have students use the tips in the student edition to evaluate the speeches they analyze.
2. To minimize the amount of formal research that needs to be conducted, have students take a stand that can be supported through anecdote, shared experience, or common knowledge. Have group members offer critiques during a preliminary "rehearsal" stage, not just after the final delivery.
3. Remind students that expressing their views during a public meeting is not the same as being invited to deliver a full speech. Students should keep their opinions closely on the topic or the meeting moderator may interrupt them.

Speaking, Listening, and Viewing Workshop

Delivering a Persuasive Speech

As a young adult with original ideas, you can make an important impact on the world around you. One way you can make your feelings known or influence others is by giving a persuasive speech. Use these strategies to help you:

Take a Stand First, whenever possible, address issues about which you feel strongly. You will be more persuasive if you truly believe the arguments you are presenting. Stay objective, however, in preparing your speech—verify all facts in respected sources and support all arguments with evidence.

Get Organized Introduce yourself and tell listeners why you are addressing them. State your main position early, before moving on to supporting evidence and ideas. Outline actions or positions you want the audience to take. Remember—your goal is to persuade them to act or think a certain way!

Control Your Emotions Go ahead, let your feelings show. Use gestures and tone of voice to add impact to your words. Come out from behind the podium or stand to emphasize important points, but stay in control. Listeners will be put off by overly emotional behavior.

Tips for Delivering a Persuasive Speech

✔ *If you want listeners to respond to your persuasive speech—or any speech—try these strategies:*

- Speak slowly, clearly, and loud enough to be heard at the back of the room.
- Look at the audience as much as possible. This means memorizing the main points of your speech.
- Emphasize charged words to underscore the emotional impact of your message and to sway listeners to your point of view.
- Pause during any applause. Ignore any negative comments or gestures.
- End your speech by restating your position and the actions, positions, or changes you seek from the audience.

Apply the Strategies

Complete one or more of these activities to gain experience and practice in delivering persuasive speeches.

1. View videotapes of speakers such as Martin Luther King or observe congressional leaders on C-Span. Identify and discuss how these speakers employ persuasive speaking techniques.
2. Working in a small group, develop an outline for a new speech about a contemporary issue. Take turns rehearsing and delivering the speech. Critique one another's presentations.
3. As a class, attend a public meeting at school or elsewhere in the community. During the question-and-answer period, express your views about the issues being discussed. Alternatively, you may role-play such a meeting in class.

Humanities: Performing Arts

Stage Voices Many of the elements that contribute to effective dramatic performance—timing, vocal projection, enunciation, and body language—also apply to the successful delivery of persuasive speeches. Students with a background in the performing arts, either as performers, directors or critics, may want to serve as "acting coaches" or "image consultants" to other students. Ask students with relevant performing arts experience to share stage tips with the class.
Student responses may include speak more slowly and loudly than you normally do; remember to allow time to swallow and breathe; cover the microphone if coughing or sneezing; expect to be prevented from seeing the audience clearly; conduct a sound-check of public address equipment before performing.

Test Preparation Workshop

Reading Comprehension

Recognize Cause and Effect; Predict Outcomes

Strategies for Success

The reading sections of standardized tests often require you to recognize cause-and-effect relationships and to predict probable future outcomes based on a passage's content. Use the following strategies to answer test questions on these skills:

Find the Main Cause To determine a cause-and-effect relationship in a passage, you need to find the main cause that produces a stated effect. While other causes may be stated or implied, concentrate on the cause that has the most direct influence on the outcome. For example, examine the cause-and-effect relationships in the following passage:

> The increasing growth of weeds in Cabot Lake threatens to turn it into a stagnant swamp. Ira North, a researcher for the Cabot Institute, cites an increase in phosphorus-based lawn fertilizers as the primary factor in the growth of lake weeds. "When it rains, fertilizer runs into the lake. The phosphorus reaches aquatic plants, causing them to grow rapidly. Phosphorus-laden water from washing machines and dishwashers also contributes to the problem."

What is the main cause of lake weed overgrowth in Cabot Lake?

A the fertilizing properties of phosphorus
B rainwater runoff
C lawn fertilizers
D phosphorus-laden water from dishwashers and washing machines

Answers **A, B,** and **D** all play a role in lake weed growth. **C,** however, is the "primary factor."

Predict Actions and Outcomes The most reliable predictions are those based on careful analysis of the facts. When you are asked to judge the likelihood of a particular prediction or outcome, look for supporting evidence in the text. For example, based on this paragraph, which outcome is most likely?

A Efforts will be made to limit the weed growth.
B New fertilizers will be developed.
C Available space will limit the weeds.
D Lake weed growth will continue.

Answer **D** predicts the continuance of lake weed growth, supported by the first sentence in the paragraph. The other answers are possible outcomes, but have no evidence in the text.

Apply the Strategies

Answer the questions based on this sample passage:

> At this point, more than one third of Cabot Lake is overrun by lake weeds and is unsuitable for swimming. North says that as more people build homes in the area, the use of phosphorus-based lawn fertilizers and the number of dishwashers and washing machines will increase steadily.

1 Why is one third of Cabot Lake unsuitable for swimming?
A an increased number of lawns in the area
B an overgrowth of lake weeds
C more roads, increasing rainwater runoff
D more people buying fertilizer

2 What is the most probable outcome of the development of the Cabot Lake area?
A a redesigned water-drainage system to prevent phosphorus runoff
B an increase in lake weeds over the next five years
C an improved Cabot Lake swimming area
D the passage of a law to limit fertilizer use

Correlations to Standardized Tests

The reading comprehension skills reviewed in this workshop correspond to the following standardized test sections:

SAT Critical Reading
ACT Reading

Test Preparation

Each ATE workshop in Unit 2 supports the instruction here by providing teaching suggestions and a sample test item:

- **Cause and Effect** (ATE, pp. 129, 139, 187, 193)
- **Predict Outcomes** (ATE, pp. 149, 167)

LESSON OBJECTIVES

- To analyze text structures such as compare/contrast, cause/effect, and chronological order for how they influence understanding
- To draw inferences such as conclusions, generalizations, and predictions and support them with text evidence and experience

Answers

1. (B) an overgrowth of lake weeds
2. (B) an increase in lake weed over the next five years

Test-Taking Tip

Generate an Answer Idea

On the critical reading sections of many standardized tests, students will read a long passage and then answer the test items that relate to it. They will need to form generalizations and conclusions about the information in the passage. Explain that it can be helpful to form a very general idea about what the correct answer might be. For example, question 2 in Apply the Strategies asks students to determine the probable outcome of the development of the Lake Cabot area. By glancing back to the passage, students should note that the passage indicates simply that the development will increase the use of fertilizers, dishwashers, and washing machines. As they know that these phosphorus-producing agents lead to an increase in lake weeds, students can quickly identify B as the correct answer.

Planning Instruction and Assessment

Unit Objectives

1. To read American literature written between 1800 and 1870
2. To apply strategies for reading critically to these selections
3. To analyze literary elements
4. To use a variety of strategies to read unfamiliar words and to build vocabulary
5. To learn elements of grammar, usage, and style
6. To use recursive writing processes to write in a variety of forms
7. To express and support responses to various types of texts
8. To prepare, organize, and present literary interpretations

Meeting the Objectives

With each selection, you will find instructional material and portfolio opportunities through which students can meet these objectives. You will find additional practice pages for reading strategies, literary elements, vocabulary, and grammar in the ***Selection Support*** booklet in the ***Teaching Resources*** box.

Test Preparation

The unit workshop, Reading Comprehension: Analyze Information to Make Inferences and Generalizations (SE, p. 427), is supported by teaching tips and a sample test item in the ATE workshop with each selection grouping.

- **Make Inferences and Generalizations** (ATE, pp. 227, 235, 249, 258, 275, 295, 317, 331, 363, 373, 395, 405)

The following additional workshops in the ATE give teaching tips and a sample test item for applying the skill taught in the Student Success Workshops:

- **Recognizing Modes of Persuasion** (ATE, p. 292)
- **Monitoring Reading Strategies** (ATE, p. 360)
- **Understanding Analogies** (ATE, p. 392)
- **Analyzing Reviews** (ATE, p. 425)

Niagara Falls, Thomas Chambers, Wadsworth Atheneum, Hartford, Connecticut

Humanities: Art

Niagara Falls, c. 1832–1840, by Thomas Chambers.

This view of the world-famous falls shows part of the American Falls (on the left) as well as the larger Canadian Horseshoe Falls (right).

Have your students link the art to the focus of Unit 3, *A Growing Nation*, by answering the following questions:

1. How does this painting convey the theme of a growing nation? *The painting conveys a sense of America's natural grandeur and vast reserves of energy.*
2. What does the solitary man on the rock contribute to the effect of the painting? *In one sense the man on the rock seems small in contrast to the majestic falls. However, there is also something brave and enterprising about his getting himself to this vantage point.*

UNIT 3

A Growing Nation (1800–1870)

"America is a land of wonders, in which everything is in constant motion and every change seems an improvement. . . . No natural boundary seems to be set to the efforts of man; and in his eyes what is not yet done is only what he has not yet attempted to do."

—Alexis de Tocqueville

Assessing Student Progress

The following tools are available to measure the degree to which students meet the unit objectives:

Informal Assessment

The questions on the Guide for Responding sections are a first level of response to the concepts and skills presented with the selection. Students' responses are a brief, informal measure of their grasp of the material. Their responses on this level can indicate where further instruction and practice are needed. You may then follow up with the practice pages in the ***Selection Support*** booklet.

You will find literature and reading guides in the ***Alternative Assessment*** booklet, which you may give students on an individual basis for informal assessment of their performance.

Formal Assessment

In the ***Formal Assessment*** booklet, you will find selection tests and part tests.

Selection Tests The selection tests measure comprehension and skills acquisition for each selection or group of selections.

Part Tests Each part test, which call on students to read passages of literature they have not previously seen, apply the unit skills on a broader level. The Critical Reading sections measures Unit Objectives 1, 2, and 3. The Vocabulary and Grammar sections measures Objectives 4 and 5. The Essay sections measures Objectives 1 and 6. Both the Critical Reading and Vocabulary and Grammar sections use formats similar to those found on many standardized tests, including the SAT.

Alternative Assessment

Portfolios As you review individual pieces or the collected work in students' portfolios, you will find assessment sheets available in the portfolio section of the ***Alternative Assessment*** booklet.

Scoring Rubrics You will find scoring rubrics for writing modes in the ***Alternative Assessment*** booklet. You can apply these to Guided Writing Lessons and to Writing Process Workshop lessons.

Speaking, Listening, and Viewing The ***Alternative Assessment*** booklet contains assessment sheets for speaking, listening, and viewing activities.

Learning Modalities The ***Alternative Assessment*** booklet contains activities that appeal to different learning styles. You may use these too as an alternative measurement of students' growth.

Using the Timeline

The Timeline can serve a number of instructional purposes, as follows:

Getting an Overview Use the Timeline to help students get a quick overview of themes and events of the period. This approach will benefit all students but may be especially helpful for visually oriented students, English language learners, and those less proficient in reading. (For strategies in using the Timeline as an overview, see the bottom of this page.)

Thinking Critically Questions are provided on the facing page. Use these questions to have students review the events, discuss their significance, and examine the *so what* behind the *what happened*.

Connecting to Selections Have students refer back to the Timeline when beginning to read individual selections. By consulting the Timeline regularly, they will gain a better sense of the period's chronology. In addition, they will appreciate what was occurring in the world that gave rise to these works of literature.

Projects Students can use the Timeline as a launching pad for projects like these:

- **Annotated Map** Have students use this Timeline and other sources to create an annotated map in their notebooks. This map can show the growth of America during the period 1800–1870, with dated notes indicating when each state or territory became part of the country.
- **Headline History** Have students scan the American Events section of the Timeline for ten especially newsworthy items that interest them. Then ask them to write headlines dramatizing each of these items for readers living at the time.
- **Timeline for a Martian** Have students choose ten of the most important American Events from the Timeline to summarize this period for a Martian or extraterrestrial.

Timeline
1800–1870

1800 | **1810** | **1820**

American Events

- **1803** Louisiana Purchase extends nation's territory to the Rocky Mountains.
- **1804** Lewis and Clark begin expedition exploring and mapping vast region of the West. ◀
- **1807** Robert Fulton's steamboat makes first trip from New York City to Albany.
- **1809** *A History of New York . . .* by Diedrich Knickerbocker brings recognition to Washington Irving.
- **1812** U.S. declares war on Great Britain; early battles in War of 1812 are at sea.
- **1814** Bombardment of Fort McHenry inspires Francis Scott Key to write "The Star-Spangled Banner." ▼
- **1817** William Cullen Bryant publishes early draft of "Thanatopsis" in a Boston magazine.
- **1819** Spain relinquishes claims to Florida for $5 million.

- **1820** Missouri Compromise bans slavery in parts of new territories.
- **1825** Completion and success of Erie Canal spurs canal building throughout the nation. ▶
- **1827** Edgar Allan Poe publishes *Tamerlane*, his first collection of poems.

World Events

- **1800** England: Samuel Taylor Coleridge finishes writing "Kubla Khan."
- **1804** France: Napoleon Bonaparte proclaims himself emperor. ◀
- **1804** England: William Wordsworth completes "Ode on Intimations of Immortality."
- **1805** Germany: Ludwig von Beethoven breaks formal musical conventions with Third Symphony.

- **1813** England: Jane Austen publishes *Pride and Prejudice*. ◀
- **1815** Belgium: French army under Napoleon routed at Waterloo.
- **1815** Austria: Congress of Vienna redraws map of Europe following Napoleon's downfall.
- **1818** England: Mary Wollstonecraft Shelley creates a legend with *Frankenstein*.
- **1819** England: John Keats writes "Ode to a Nightingale" and "Ode on a Grecian Urn."
- **1819** France: René Läennec invents the stethoscope. ◀

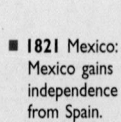

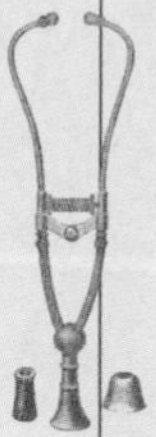

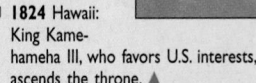

- **1821** Mexico: Mexico gains independence from Spain.
- **1824** Hawaii: King Kamehameha III, who favors U.S. interests, ascends the throne. ▲
- **1829** England: George Stephenson perfects a steam locomotive for Liverpool-Manchester Railway. ◀

Getting an Overview of the Period

Introduction To give students an overview of the period, indicate the span of dates along the top of the Timeline. How much time is covered in this unit? *Seventy years are covered, although the dates go from 1800 to 1850. Note that Timeline information for the years 1850–1870 can be found on p.430.* Indicate that the Timeline is divided into American Events on top and World Events on bottom. Have students scan the Timeline across, looking at both the American and the World Events. Finally, point out that items in the Timeline often represent beginnings, turning points, and endings. The admission of California to the Union in 1850 is an example of a turning point.

Key Events Ask students to recall the overall theme of the unit: *A Growing Nation*. Have them find one item in each group of American Events that continues this "story." *Examples include: 1803, Louisiana Purchase; 1819, Spain relinquishes claims to Florida; 1825, building of Erie Canal; 1830, first steam-driven locomotive begins service; 1845, Texas admitted to the Union; 1850, California admitted to the Union.* Then have students find items in World Events that suggest an "expanding" globe. *Examples include the exploration of Antarctica (1841) and the opening of Japan (1853).*

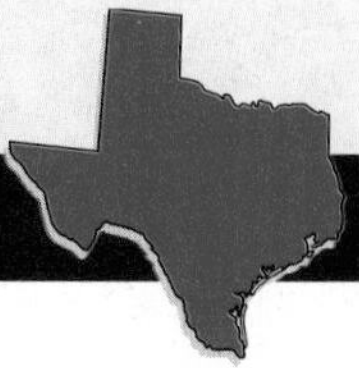

1830 1840 1850

American Events

- **1830** Tom Thumb, America's first steam-driven locomotive, begins service on Baltimore and Ohio railroad. ▲
- **1831** Cyrus McCormick invents mechanical reaper. ▶
- **1836** Battles at the Alamo and San Jacinto fought while Texas is a republic.
- **1837** Mount Holyoke, first women's college in United States, founded.

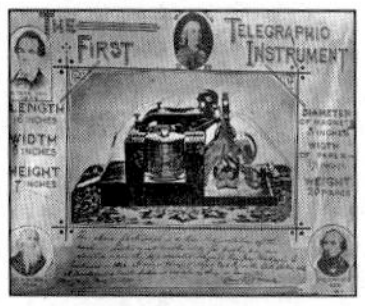

- **1837** Samuel F. B. Morse patents electromagnetic telegraph. ◀
- **1838** U.S. Army marches Cherokees of Georgia on long "Trail of Tears" to Oklahoma. ▶

- **1839** Edgar Allan Poe's "The Fall of the House of Usher" first appears in print.
- **1840** The Transcendentalist magazine, *The Dial*, begins publication.
- **1841** Ralph Waldo Emerson publishes *Essays*.
- **1842** Anesthesia first used for medical purposes.
- **1843** John Greenleaf Whittier publishes *Lays of My Home and Other Poems*.
- **1844** First telegraph message sent.
- **1845** Texas admitted to the Union. ▲
- **1846** Mexican War begins.
- **1846** Abraham Lincoln first elected to Congress.
- **1848** Mexican War ends; United States expands borders.
- **1848** California gold rush begins.
- **1848** Women's Rights Convention held in Seneca Falls, New York.
- **1850** Nathaniel Hawthorne publishes *The Scarlet Letter*.
- **1850** California admitted to the Union. ▶

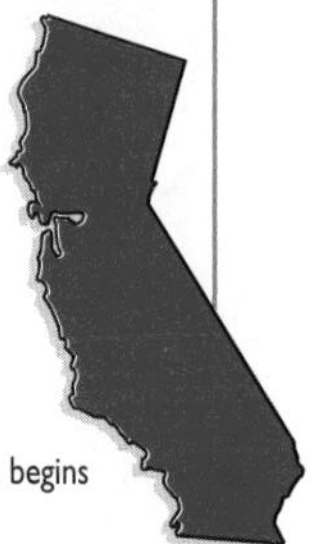

- **1851** Herman Melville publishes *Moby-Dick*.
- **1851** Nathaniel Hawthorne publishes *The House of the Seven Gables*.
- **1851** *The New York Times* begins publication.

- **1852** Harriet Beecher Stowe publishes *Uncle Tom's Cabin*. ▲
- **1853** Arizona and New Mexico purchased from Mexico.
- **1854** Henry David Thoreau publishes *Walden*.
- **1854** Republican Party organized.

World Events

- **1831** France: Victor Hugo publishes *Notre Dame de Paris*, popularly called *The Hunchback of Notre Dame*. ▲
- **1832** England: Alfred, Lord Tennyson completes "The Lady of Shalott," a poem.

- **1835** Denmark: Hans Christian Andersen publishes his first book of fairy tales. ◀
- **1837** England: Charles Dickens achieves great success with *Oliver Twist*.
- **1841** Antarctica: First explored by Englishman James Ross.
- **1842** Asia: Hong Kong becomes a British colony.
- **1844** Germany: Heinrich Heine publishes *Germany: A Winter's Tale*.
- **1845** Ireland: Famine results from failure of potato crop.
- **1847** Italy: Verdi's opera *Macbeth* first performed.
- **1847** England: Emily Brontë publishes *Wuthering Heights*.
- **1848** Belgium: Karl Marx and Friedrich Engels publish *The Communist Manifesto*.
- **1848** England: Queen's College for Women opens.
- **1850** France: Life insurance introduced.
- **1850** England: Elizabeth Barrett Browning publishes *Sonnets From the Portuguese*.
- **1850** China: Taiping Rebellion begins.
- **1851** Australia: Gold discovered in New South Wales.
- **1853** Europe: Crimean War begins.
- **1853** Japan: Ports open to trade.

◆Critical Thinking

1. (a) What event in the period 1800–1810 greatly extended America's territory? (b) In what ways would the country have been different if this event hadn't occurred? **[Hypothesize]** *(a) In 1803, the Louisiana Purchase extended the nation's territory to the Rockies. (b) Students may indicate that America would not have been such a large or powerful country without the territory and resources of this region.*
2. (a) What event in the period 1820–1830 involved slavery? (b) In what way is this event an omen of future problems? **[Infer]** *(a) In 1820, the Missouri Compromise banned slavery in parts of new territories. (b) This event foreshadows future disputes about slavery in the territories and the Civil War itself.*
3. (a) Indicate two dates that relate to the invention of the telegraph. (b) What effect did the telegraph have on communication? **[Speculate]** *(a) In 1837, Samuel F. B. Morse patented the idea for the telegraph. In 1844, the first telegraph message was sent. (b) In the era before the telephone, the telegraph offered a quick method to send messages across long distances. It was probably used for business and military affairs, as well as for brief personal messages.*
4. (a) When was "The Star-Spangled Banner" composed? (b) What is the relationship between the circumstances of its composition and its use as a national anthem? **[Analyze Cause and Effect]** *(a) It was composed in 1814. (b) It was composed during a battle in the War of 1812 and reflects the America's pride at standing up to its former colonial rulers. This sense of pride captured a national mood and propelled the song into prominence, leading to its adoption as a national anthem.*

▶Critical Viewing◀

1. What does the picture from the Lewis and Clark expedition (1804) suggest about the American West? **[Analyze]** *It indicates the vastness and great natural beauty of this region.*
2. What kind of image did Napoleon seem to have of himself (1804)? *He seemed to think of himself as a great and glorious ruler.*
3. What other type of transportation does the design of America's first steam locomotive (1830) suggest? **[Infer]** *The designers appear to have imitated the stagecoaches, an already existing form of transportation.*
4. Judging by the picture, how difficult was the Cherokees' (1838) migration to Oklahoma? **[Interpret]** *The picture indicates that Cherokees were heavily burdened with belongings, which suggests that the migration may have been difficult.*
5. What does the (1852) poster advertising a play based on *Uncle Tom's Cabin* seem to promise to theater goers? **[Speculate]** *It seems to promise a tale of peril and adventure, with two figures being menaced by dogs.*

Develop Understanding

Customize for
Less Proficient Readers
Ask less proficient learners to become experts on a particular section of *The Story of the Times* by reading it several times. Then have them devise a comprehension test on their section.

Customize for
English Language Learners
Have each of these students choose an item from A Graphic Look at the Period that they can present orally to the class.

Customize for
Interpersonal Learners
Have these students read *The Story of the Times* in pairs, one looking for negative results of the nation's expansion and one looking for positive results. Ask partners to discuss their findings with each other.

Customize for
AP Students
Challenge more advanced students to find links between this historical period and our own times. These links can take the form of interesting parallels or cause-and-effect relationships.

Answers to
A GRAPHIC LOOK

Read a Map The last region to be added to the United States was the region included in the Gadsden Purchase.

Analyze an Artifact The inscription "Peace and Friendship" and the gift of the medals suggest that Jefferson wanted peaceful relations between the United States and Native American groups.

A GRAPHIC LOOK AT THE PERIOD

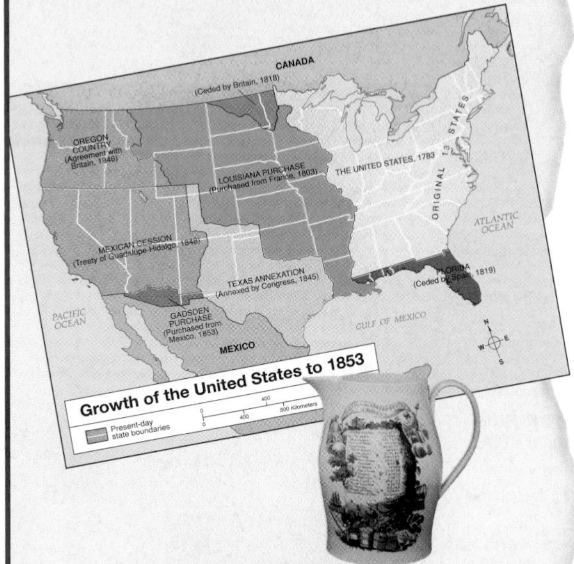

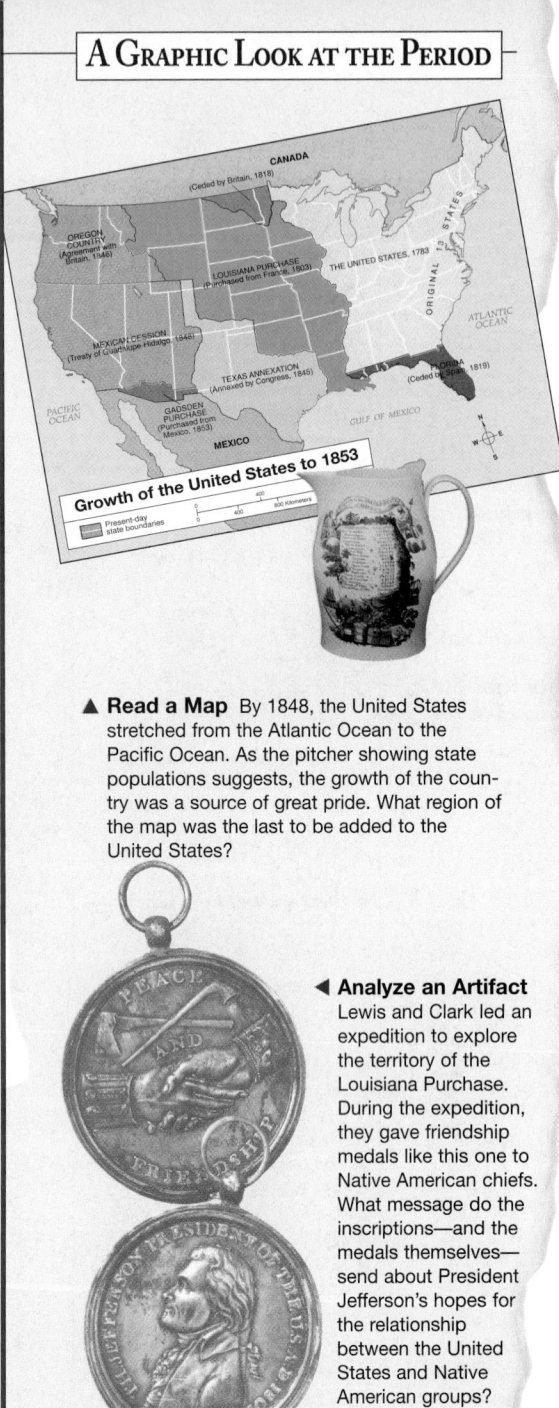

▲ **Read a Map** By 1848, the United States stretched from the Atlantic Ocean to the Pacific Ocean. As the pitcher showing state populations suggests, the growth of the country was a source of great pride. What region of the map was the last to be added to the United States?

◀ **Analyze an Artifact** Lewis and Clark led an expedition to explore the territory of the Louisiana Purchase. During the expedition, they gave friendship medals like this one to Native American chiefs. What message do the inscriptions—and the medals themselves—send about President Jefferson's hopes for the relationship between the United States and Native American groups?

The Story of the Times
1800–1870

In 1831, the Frenchman Alexis de Tocqueville, sent to report on America's prisons, ultimately wrote about something far more interesting: a bustling new nation full of individuals optimistically pursuing their destinies. His *Democracy in America* observed that Americans had "a lively faith in the perfectibility of man," believing "what appears to them today to be good may be superseded by something better tomorrow."

The bustling spirit that had enchanted De Tocqueville in 1831 would make for a turbulent "tomorrow" in the decades to come: By 1870, industrialism, explosive population and economic growth, and the Civil War had all aged the nation's spirit. American literature also matured during this time. In 1831, De Tocqueville wrote, "America has produced very few writers of distinction . . . . [The literature of England] still darts its rays into the forests of the New World." By 1870, America had produced many "writers of distinction": Irving, Cooper, Bryant, Poe, Emerson, Thoreau, Hawthorne, Melville, Dickinson, and Whitman—all of whom eventually shone their unmistakably American light into and far beyond "the forests of the New World."

Historical Background

In 1800, the United States consisted of sixteen states clustered near the east coast. In 1803, Thomas Jefferson doubled the nation's size by signing the Louisiana Purchase. The rapid growth of the nation inspired an upsurge in national pride and self-awareness.

The Growth of Democracy at Home: 1800–1840 As the nation expanded, Americans began to take more direct control of their government. The 1828 election of Andrew Jackson, "the People's President," ushered in the era of the common man, as property requirements for voting began to be eliminated. The democratic advances of the time, however, were confined

Cross-Curricular Connection: Social Studies

Old New York New York City had a population of 60,000 in 1800, making it the second largest city in the nation after Philadelphia. A decade later, it passed Philadelphia and was never again challenged for population leadership. By 1840, the population of New York City was 312,000, about the size of Philadelphia and Boston combined.

The earliest Dutch settlement on Manhattan Island had been at the very southern tip. In 1820, the built-up area extended north to 14th Street and was advancing rapidly up the island. The commercial buildings of the day were low, three or four stories at most.

Despite New York's prosperity, it was not looked upon as a cultural capital. Alexis de Tocqueville saw it as a center of "all our greatest vices, without any of those interests which counteract their baleful influence."

Ask students why New York grew so rapidly. *Students may answer that it was a major port.*

to white males. Scant political attention was paid to women, and most African Americans remained enslaved. One of the most tragic policies of this period was "Indian removal," the forced westward migration of Native Americans from confiscated tribal lands—as in the 1838 "Trail of Tears," in which 4,000 of 15,000 Cherokee perished on the trek from Georgia to Oklahoma.

Young Nation on the World Stage The War of 1812 convinced Europeans that the United States was on the world stage to stay. In the Monroe Doctrine of 1823, President James Monroe warned Europe not to intervene in the new Latin American nations. In the 1830's, the U.S. became embroiled in a conflict over the secession of Texas from Mexico; in 1836, the Mexican Army made its famous assault on the Alamo, in which every Texan defender was killed. When Texas was admitted to the Union in 1845, the resulting war with Mexico (1846–1848) ended in a U.S. victory, which added more territory to the nation, including California. Soon after, the Gold Rush of 1849 drew hundreds of thousands to this new land of promise.

The Way West and Economic Growth In a sense, the entire course of American history can be seen as a pageant rolling ever westward, as new territories opened up and transportation improved. The Erie Canal, completed in New York in 1825, set off a wave of canal building. In the 1850's, the "iron horse"—the railroad—began to dominate long-distance American travel; by 1869, rail lines linked east and west coasts.

Advances in technology spurred social change. Factories sprang up all over the Northeast. The steel plow and reaper encouraged frontier settlement by making farming practical on the vast, sod-covered grasslands. The telegraph facilitated almost instant communication across great distances. Inventor Samuel F. B. Morse's message from Washington to Baltimore in 1844 could serve as the motto for this era: "What hath God wrought!"

Winds of Change It was evident to even the most cheerful observer that the United States at mid-century faced trouble as well as bright promise. The new prosperity unleashed fierce competition, leading to the creation of factories

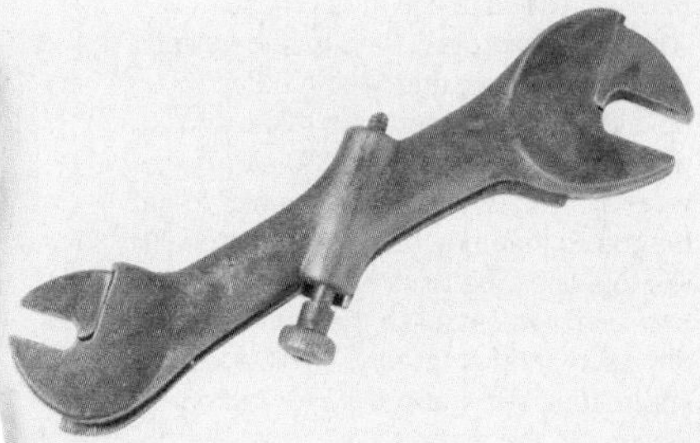

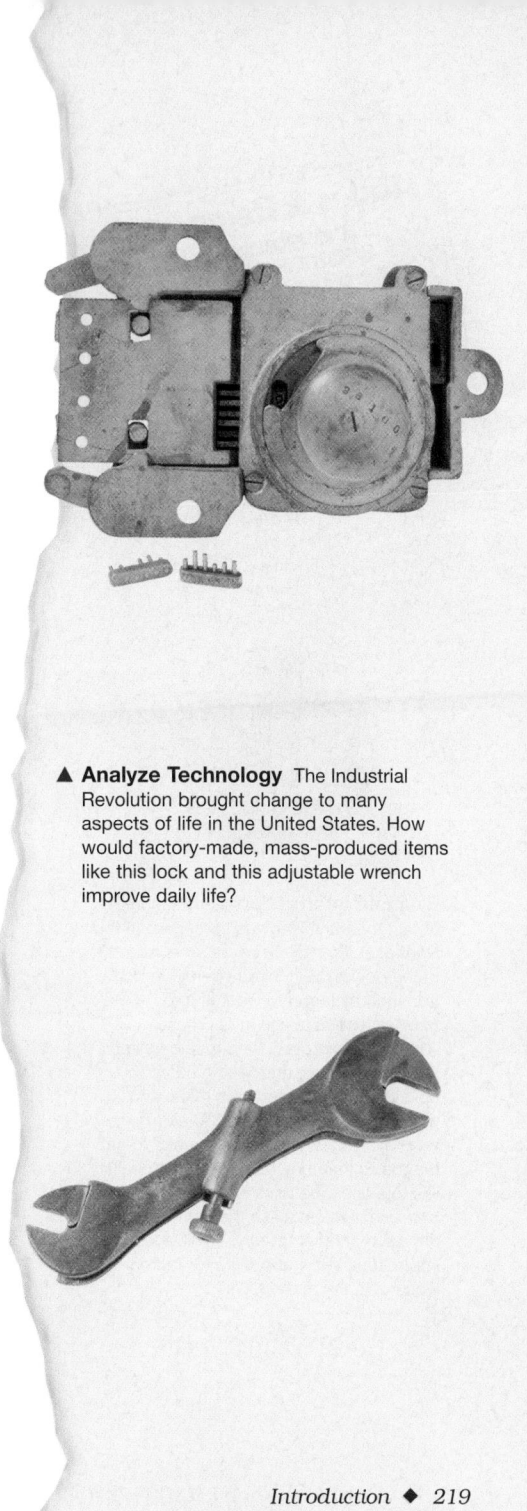

▲ **Analyze Technology** The Industrial Revolution brought change to many aspects of life in the United States. How would factory-made, mass-produced items like this lock and this adjustable wrench improve daily life?

More About the Gold Rush

James Marshall found gold at Sutter's Mill in California in January 1848. In a few days, word of the gold strike spread to San Francisco. Carpenters threw down their saws. Bakers left bread in their ovens. Schools emptied as teachers and students joined the rush to the gold fields.

The news spread outward from San Francisco. Thousands of Americans caught gold fever. People in Europe and South America joined the rush as well. More than 80,000 people made the long journey to California in 1849. They became known as forty-niners.

Connection to the Literature

- About the same time as Alexis de Tocqueville was declaring that America had produced few writers of distinction, Washington Irving was writing tales that would win him international distinction. Students can read one of those tales on page 236.
- The Louisiana Purchase was a key event of this period, and Jefferson sent Lewis and Clark to explore this new territory. Students can learn more about the Lewis and Clark expedition by reading Lewis's "Crossing the Great Divide," p. 276.

Answers to

A GRAPHIC LOOK

Analyze Technology Because they were mass-produced, these items were probably less expensive. It was therefore possible for ordinary people to buy and use them. The lock would have made it possible for people to store their goods more securely. The adjustable wrench would have made it possible for people to conveniently construct things that were more solid.

Cross-Curricular Connection: Science

Francis Lowell and American Industry

Britain's blockade of the United States during the War of 1812 provided a boost to American industries. Cut off from foreign suppliers, Americans had to produce more goods themselves.

As in Britain, advances occurred in the textile industry. A Boston merchant, Francis Cabot Lowell, had toured British textile mills. There, he saw how one factory spun thread while another wove it into cloth. Lowell wanted to combine spinning and weaving under one roof.

To finance his project, Lowell joined with several partners in 1813. They built a textile mill in Waltham, Massachusetts. The factory had all the machines needed to turn raw cotton into finished cloth. The machines were powered by water from the nearby Charles River. Lowell died in 1817, but his company continued. In time, it built an entire factory town on the Merrimack River, naming the new town after Francis Lowell. By 1836, Lowell, Massachusetts boasted more than 10,000 people.

What does this story reveal about the link between technology and national identity? *Innovation contributed to self-sufficiency and self-confidence.*

Historical Period

Comprehension Check ☑

1. What event doubled the nation's size in 1803? *The Louisiana Purchase doubled the nation's size.*
2. What era was ushered in by the election of Andrew Jackson in 1828? *The election ushered in the era of the common man.*
3. Name an important result of the war with Mexico (1846–1848). *California became part of the United States.*
4. By 1869, what development made it possible to travel relatively quickly from coast to coast? *Rail lines linked the two coasts.*
5. In what ways were women, working children, Native Americans, and African Americans excluded from the country's prosperity? *In 1840, women couldn't vote or file a lawsuit; numbers of poor children worked long hours; many Native Americans had been forcibly removed from their lands; and most African Americans were still enslaved.*

◆ Critical Thinking

1. How would America have been different if Jefferson had not made the Louisiana Purchase? **[Speculate]** *Reasonable answers include: the country may not have stretched from coast to coast, may not have had such a wealth of natural resources, and may not have become a great world power.*
2. In what ways is the story of this period the story of westward expansion? **[Support]** *The Louisiana Purchase made expansion possible. Throughout this era, settlers pressed westward and Native Americans were removed from their lands. It could be argued that the war with Mexico (1846–1848), which added to America's western territories, resulted from this expansion.*
3. What is a possible link between westward expansion and conflicts over slavery? **[Connect]** *The question of whether to have slavery in the new territories would become controversial.*

Answers to A Graphic Look

Evaluate Information These rules and regulations suggest that workdays were long and working conditions difficult. It seems that management was intolerant of any kind of informal behavior.

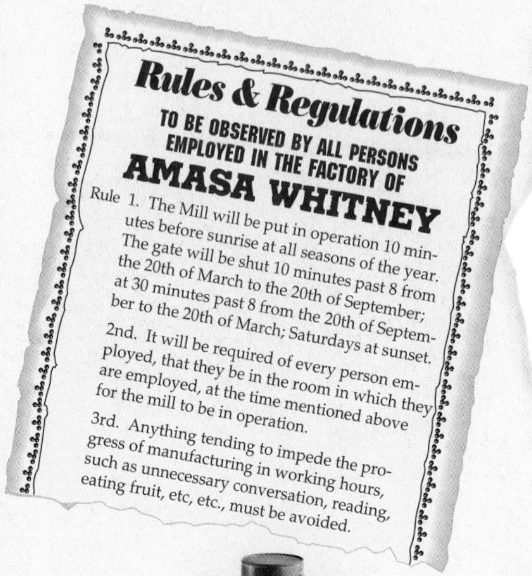

Rules & Regulations
TO BE OBSERVED BY ALL PERSONS EMPLOYED IN THE FACTORY OF
AMASA WHITNEY

Rule 1. The Mill will be put in operation 10 minutes before sunrise at all seasons of the year. The gate will be shut 10 minutes past 8 from the 20th of March to the 20th of September; at 30 minutes past 8 from the 20th of September to the 20th of March; Saturdays at sunset.

2nd. It will be required of every person employed, that they be in the room in which they are employed, at the time mentioned above for the mill to be in operation.

3rd. Anything tending to impede the progress of manufacturing in working hours, such as unnecessary conversation, reading, eating fruit, etc, etc., must be avoided.

▲ **Evaluate Information** A great number of factory and mill towns sprang up in the Northeast. Francis C. Lowell, the inventor of the power loom, hired young women from nearby farms to work in his Massachusetts textile mills. These "Lowell factory girls" lived in supervised boarding houses, attended a company-built church, followed strict rules, and worked from 5:00 A.M. to 7:30 P.M. They were allowed two half-hour breaks to eat the meals that they carried in lunch pails like this one. The rules and regulations shown above establish the working conditions in another factory. What does this information show about life for factory workers in the mid-1800's?

scarred by child labor and unsafe working conditions. In 1840, most women could not vote or file a lawsuit. The 1840's and 1850's saw an outburst of efforts promoting women's rights, notably the 1848 Seneca Falls Convention. Above all, the centuries-old institution of slavery bitterly divided the nation. The conflict between abolitionists, who opposed slavery, and the advocates of states' rights, who argued that the federal government could not bend states to its will, sharpened in the 1850's. The gathering storm finally burst into war in 1861, but it was a storm that had been building for 250 years, ever since the first slave was brought in chains to this continent.

Literature of the Period

American Literature Comes of Age Before 1800, American writers were not widely read—not even in America, but that situation soon began to change. The writers of this period would define the American voice—personal, idiosyncratic, bold—and its primary theme: the quest of the individual to define him or herself.

Romanticism Despite their unmistakable differences, the writers of the early nineteenth century—Washington Irving, James Fenimore Cooper, William Cullen Bryant, and Edgar Allan Poe—can all be described as Romantics. Romanticism is an artistic movement that dominated Europe and America during the nineteenth century. Romantic writers elevated the imagination over reason and intuition over fact. Washington Irving, the first American to be read widely overseas, made his mark with his *History of New York* (1809), which is not a dry historical record but a rollicking narrative that alters facts at will.

The Romantics reveled in nature. William Cullen Bryant is best known for his lyric poems rejoicing in the healing powers of nature. Irving's "Rip Van Winkle" and "The Legend of Sleepy Hollow" sparked an interest in his beloved Hudson River Valley. James Fenimore Cooper's four *Leatherstocking Tales* feature the exploits of Natty Bumppo in the frontier forests of upstate New York. A man of absolute moral integrity, Natty Bumppo preferred nature over civilization, establishing the pattern for countless American heroes to come.

Humanities: Music

A New American Music.

At the same time as the country was forging a new identity in literature, it was establishing its own cultural identity in the field of music as well. Among the American musicians to make important contributions during this period was Frank Johnson (1792–1844).

One of the first successful African American musicians, Johnson formed a band of flutes, clarinets, oboes, bassoons, and French horns in the 1820's. In addition to playing in the northern United States, Johnson's band traveled to England and performed for the queen.

Play for students Johnson's piece "Bonnets of Blue" on the ***Listening to Literature Audiocassettes.*** This piece is a jig, a type of music written for a lively dance of the same name. Ask these questions:

1. What is the mood of this piece? *The mood is lively and joyful.*
2. If this piece reflects the spirit of the nation, what was it like to live during this era? *It was probably a time of optimism and energy.*

Romantic writing often accented the fantastic aspects of human experience. The tortured genius Edgar Allan Poe remains popular to this day for his haunting poems and suspenseful stories whose characters, as one biographer has said, "are either grotesques or the inhabitants of another world than this."

New England Renaissance: 1840–1855 In 1837, Ralph Waldo Emerson, a former Boston minister, delivered his famous oration "The American Scholar," calling for American intellectual independence from Europe. Emerson believed that American writers should begin to interpret their own culture in new ways. As if in response to Emerson's call, an impressive burst of literary activity took place in and around Boston between 1840 and 1855. This "flowering of New England" would produce an array of great writers and enduring literature.

Transcendentalism Most, if not all, of these writers were influenced by the Transcendental philosophy originally expressed by the German Immanuel Kant. In his *Critique of Practical Reason* (1788), Kant defines the transcendental as the understanding a person gains intuitively. Closely associated with Emerson, American Transcendentalism drew on other thinkers as well: the Greek philosopher Plato, the French mathematician Pascal, the Swedish mystic and scientist Swedenborg, and the anti-materialism of Buddhist thought. The Transcendentalists believed that the most fundamental truths lie outside the experience of the senses, residing instead, as Emerson put it, in the "Over-Soul . . . a universal and benign omnipresence."

Walden The most influential expression of Transcendental philosophy came from Emerson and his younger friend and protégé, Henry David Thoreau, who withdrew from society to live by himself on the shores of Walden Pond. Thoreau begins *Walden*, his account of this experience, by writing, "When I wrote the following pages . . . I lived alone, in the woods, a mile from any neighbor, in a house which I had built myself, on the shore of Walden Pond, in Concord, Massachusetts, and earned my living by the labor of my hands only." Published in 1854, *Walden* consists

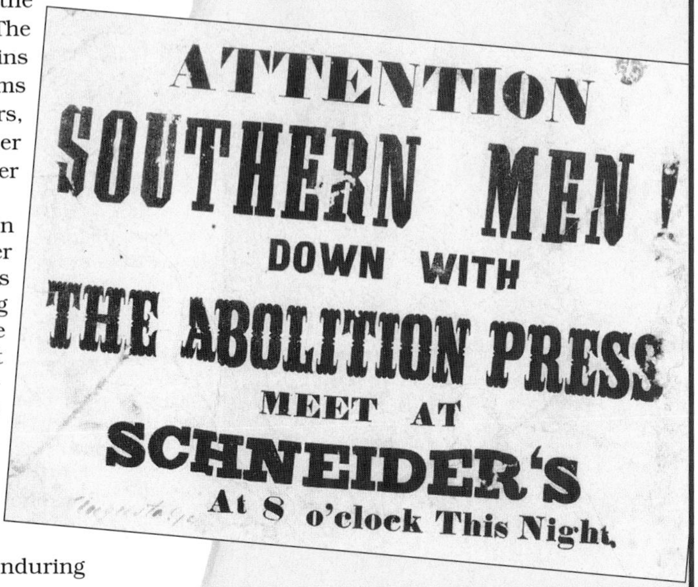

▲ **Make an Inference** Abolitionist newspapers like *The Liberator* stirred strong emotions about the issue of slavery. These broadsides, for example, announce meetings to garner support for both sides. Why would some citizens oppose slavery? Why would others oppose abolition?

More About Transcendentalism
The movement was not essentially religious, but there were religious overtones. Even though a hundred years had passed since Jonathan Edwards, a Calvinist minister in Northampton, Massachusetts, had preached that human beings can share directly in the divine light, Edwards's idea continued to exert influence in the mid-nineteenth century. More recently, William Ellery Channing, minister of the Federal Street Church, Boston, had broken with the Calvinism of his day to become the apostle of Unitarianism. His sermons and essays, promoting more tolerant religious attitudes and various social causes, reflected his own optimism and idealism. Channing helped to lay the groundwork for New England's Transcendentalism.

Connection to the Literature

- To gain a better understanding of Transcendentalism, students can read the excerpt from "Nature," p. 364, by Ralph Waldo Emerson.
- Students can read Thoreau's own description of his plan to live by Walden Pond in the excerpt from *Walden*, p. 374.

Answers to
A GRAPHIC LOOK

Make an Inference Some citizens might oppose slavery for moral reasons. Others, especially southerners, might oppose abolition because they felt it interfered with the southern economy and way of life.

Humanities: Music

American Music, New England Style.

While American literature was blossoming in New England, Lowell Mason (1792–1872) of Boston and other New England musicians were reshaping American music. Determined to bring about universal musical literacy, Mason organized the Boston Academy of Music and added music to the curriculum of Boston public schools. Mason also prompted a change in the style of American church music by emphasizing the selection of easy and solemn songs that all members of a congregation could sing in harmony. He himself wrote thousands of musical pieces, including many hymns that have remained popular.

Play Mason's hymn "Northfield" on the ***Listening to Music: The American Experience on Audio CD.***

1. What thoughts and emotions does the song express? *The song expresses joy and gratitude to God at the coming of spring.*
2. What event inspires these thoughts and emotions? *The coming of spring is the event.*

More About Melville and Hawthorne The friendship between these two great writers happened almost by accident. Melville, in his early thirties, had moved from New York City to Pittsfield in western Massachusetts, where, on a farm he called "Arrowhead," he wrote his monumental book *Moby-Dick.* It was published in 1851, a year after Hawthorne's *The Scarlet Letter* appeared. Although *Moby-Dick* would be recognized as a great work only after Melville's death, *The Scarlet Letter* achieved immediate fame in both the United States and England.

Meanwhile, Hawthorne had moved to Lenox, Massachusetts, in the Berkshires, a few miles south of Pittsfield. There he was working on the manuscript of *The House of the Seven Gables.* Melville, pessimistic about *Moby-Dick*—"the product is a final hash," he wrote, "and all my books are botches"—approached Hawthorne, seeking solace. Hawthorne may have been surprised by this adulation, but he and Melville became and remained friends.

Art Transparency Use Art Transparency 2, *Fur Traders Descending the Missouri,* to show students how American landscape painters were beginning to create a style of their own. (For more on American landscape painters, see the note below.)

Answers to

A GRAPHIC LOOK

Connect The traveling library reflects the Transcendentalists' belief in American self-reliance and the need to establish a viable culture for American, not European, realities. The museum reflects the Transcendentalists' belief that nature is a rich source of wisdom and intuitive knowledge.

▲▼ **Connect** Hoping that Americans would expand their minds as they expanded the nation, in 1839 the American Society for the Diffusion of Useful Knowledge published a traveling library, like the one above, for settlers in the West. Below is a ticket to Charles Willson Peale's museum, which he ran to teach Americans how to learn by observing nature. How do these efforts reflect Transcendentalist beliefs?

of eighteen essays about matters ranging from a battle between red and black ants to the individual's relation to society. Thoreau's observations of nature reveal his philosophy of individualism, simplicity, and passive resistance to injustice.

The Possibility of Evil Not everyone shared the Transcendentalists' optimistic views. Nathaniel Hawthorne and Herman Melville expressed the darker vision of those who, in Hawthorne's words, "burrowed into the depths of our common nature" and found the area not always shimmering, but often "dusky." Hawthorne's Puritan heritage was never far from his consciousness. His masterpiece, *The Scarlet Letter* (1850), set in Boston in the seventeenth century, deals with sin, concealed guilt, hypocrisy, and humility. In *The House of the Seven Gables*, he delves into seventeenth-century witchcraft, insanity, and a legendary curse.

Hawthorne became a kind of mentor to Melville. Depressed about the negative critical response to his novel *Moby-Dick* (1851), Melville befriended the older, more successful writer. Both men saw human life in grim terms, but their personalities were quite different. Hawthorne, despite a tendency toward solitude, was stable and self-possessed, a shrewd man without illusions. Melville, by contrast, was a man at odds with the world, a tortured and cryptic personality. For a large part of his career, he raged against his fate, much as Captain Ahab in *Moby-Dick* unleashed his fury against the white whale that had maimed him.

At Home in Amherst While Thoreau was planting beans next to Walden Pond, Emily Dickinson was growing up in the nearby town of Amherst, Massachusetts. Her startling, intensely focused poetry catapulted her into the company of the greatest American poets—although not in her lifetime. A recluse for the second half of her life, Dickinson did not write for publication, or even for her family, but rather from a personal need to wrestle with questions about death, immortality, and the soul—questions unresolved by conventional religion.

Humanities: Art

American Landscapes.

By the mid-1800's, American artists began to develop their own style. The first group to do so was called the Hudson River School because they painted landscapes of New York's Hudson River region. Two painters of this group were Thomas Cole and Asher B. Durand. In his murals, African American artist Robert S. Duncanson also reflected the style of this school.

Other American artists painted scenes of hard-working farm families and country people. George Caleb Bingham was inspired by his native Missouri. (Art Transparency 2 is a famous painting by Bingham.)

Several painters tried to capture the culture of Native Americans. George Catlin and Alfred Jacob Miller traveled to the Far West to record the daily life of Native Americans.

Have students view Asher B. Durand's *Kindred Spirits,* p. 259, and *Early Morning at Cold Spring,* p. 361. Then ask these questions:

1. What feeling about American landscapes do these two pictures convey? *They convey the lyrical beauty and, especially in* Kindred Spirits, *the inviting wildness of the landscape.*
2. Do the human figures seem dwarfed by the landscape? Why or why not? Suggested response: *The figures are small but so in harmony with the environment that they don't seem dwarfed.*

Beyond New England Meanwhile, the quintessential American poet was tramping about the countryside, laboring at odd jobs to finance his poetry. In 1855, New Yorker Walt Whitman published his groundbreaking series of poems, *Leaves of Grass*, proudly broadcasting his "barbaric yawp" from Brooklyn to the universe. Most American readers ignored the irregular forms and frank language of this revolutionary poet, but Emerson knew an American original when he saw one and praised Whitman's work. Of all the poets of the period between 1800 and 1870, Whitman would have the most lasting effect on American literature—despite the fact that the first edition of *Leaves* sold fewer than twenty copies.

Fireside Poets Those were the literary giants of the period, as singled out by twentieth-century scholars. In 1850, however, the American reading public would probably have pointed instead to four other New England writers, known as the Fireside Poets: Henry Wadsworth Longfellow, a Harvard professor and tremendously popular poet; John Greenleaf Whittier, from a hardworking Quaker farm family; James Russell Lowell, born to wealth and position; and Oliver Wendell Holmes, a poet-physician and the unofficial laureate of the group.

After the Flowering As the war clouds gathered, the great burst of creativity in the Northeast began to subside. Antislavery writers, such as Emerson, Melville, Whittier, and Lowell, strongly supported the northern effort in the Civil War. Thoreau and Hawthorne died before the war ended. Whitman worked as a nurse in the war and incorporated war poems in his later editions of *Leaves of Grass*. Dickinson ignored the war in her poetry. Oliver Wendell Holmes, energetic and cheerful, outlasted the rest of his renowned generation. He became "the last leaf upon the tree," to quote words he himself had written about Melville's grandfather, an old Revolutionary War veteran, in a poem published in 1831, when the poet and his country were still young.

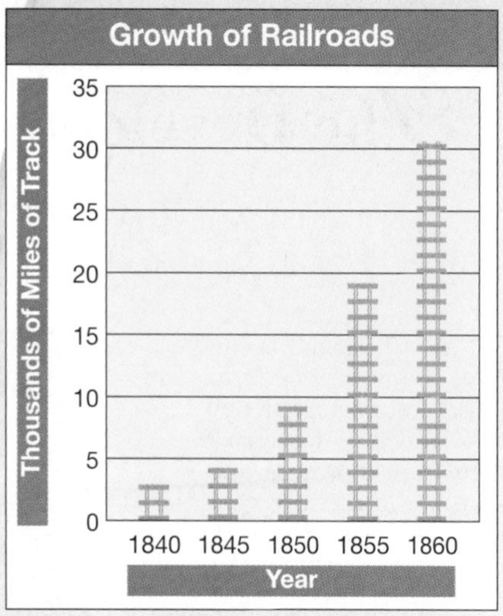

▲ **Read a Graph** Railroads expanded rapidly after 1840. Most new railroad track was laid in the North and the Midwest. According to this graph, what five-year period saw the greatest growth in railroads?

▲ **Form a Hypothesis** The railroad was a key to the growth of industry in the North. In this image, a freight train delivers ore to a foundry where it will be turned into steel. What other effects do you think the growth of the railroads had on northern life?

Literature of the Period

Comprehension Check ☑

1. What attitudes did Romantic writers have toward imagination and reason? *They elevated imagination over reason and reveled in nature.*
2. What is the New England Renaissance? *It is a burst of literary activity that took place in and around Boston during the period 1840–1855.*
3. (a) Name two famous Transcendental writers. (b) What did the Transcendentalists believe about the most fundamental truths? *Two famous Transcendentalists are Emerson and Thoreau. They believed that fundamental truths lie outside the experience of the senses.*
4. In what key way did Hawthorne and Melville differ from the Transcendentalists? *Hawthorne and Melville did not share the optimism of the Transcendentalists.*
5. (a) What is the name of the group of poets popular in 1850? (b) Which two poets were ignored at the time but have had a lasting influence on American literature? *The Fireside Poets were well known at the time. Dickinson and Whitman were only recognized later.*

◆ Critical Thinking

1. In what way is Transcendentalism a response to Puritanism? **[Connect]** *Transcendentalists were influenced by William Ellery Channing, who replaced Puritan severity with optimism and a sense of toleration.*
2. Why is *Walden* an especially meaningful book today? **[Relate]** *Thoreau's deep feeling for nature has influenced many and is related to today's environmental movement.*
3. Where did most of America's new authors live during the first part of the nineteenth century? Why? **[Analyze Causes and Effects]** *Most of the new authors lived in New England or at least on the East Coast. This may have been because the frontier did not offer opportunities for writing and culture.*

Activities

1. **Headlines and Book Jackets** Have students write four headlines that capture the key historical events of the period and book-jacket copy for two of the most important works that were published.
2. **Literary Debate** Have students role-play a debate between Emerson and Thoreau on one hand and Hawthorne and Melville on the other. Have them debate whether or not an optimistic attitude is also realistic. They can scan *The Story of the Times* for ideas.
3. **Literary Map** Ask students to design an annotated map of New England showing important literary facts of this period, including dates of authors' lives and of their works.
4. **Connect Literature, Art, and Music** Challenge students to find links among the literature, art, and music of the period. For examples of music, they can listen to selections on the ***Listening to Literature Audiocassettes,*** and they can view the period art that appears in the pages of this unit.

Answers to

A GRAPHIC LOOK

Read a Graph The five-year period 1855–1860 saw the greatest growth in railroads, with more than ten thousand miles of track added.

Form a Hypothesis Suggested response: The expansion of the railroad probably created a greater sense of mobility and unity in the North.

◆ Critical Thinking

1. Why do you think Americans are so enthusiastic about stringing initials together? **[Speculate]** *Reasonable answers include: Americans like saving time, and initials may seem faster and easier to use than the words for which they stand. Also, using initials may make it seem as if you're in on a secret or are a member of the club.*
2. What does the actual origin of the expression "O.K." suggest about the relationship between new words and politics? **[Generalize]** *The derivation suggests that new words or expressions can catch on in the excitement of a political campaign and even become more memorable than the campaign itself.*
3. Where do you think the expression "A-O.K." came from? **[Speculate]** *It may be a combination of the "A" from expressions like "A-1," meaning "the best," with the initials "O.K." The "A" means "even better than just 'O.K.'"*

Answers to Activities

1. (a) Anno Domini ("year of the Lord"; number of years after the death of Christ)/before Christ (number of years before the birth of Christ); (b) also known as; (c) grand old party (Republicans); (d) amplitude modulation/frequency modulation (in radio); (e) compact disk or certificate of deposit; (f) equal rights amendment; (g) ante meridiem (Latin for "before noon")/post meridiem (Latin for "after noon"); (h) intelligence quotient; (i) public school or postscript (for letter); (j) requiescat in pace (Latin for "rest in peace"); (k) repondez, s'il vous plait (French for "please reply"); (l) unidentified flying object.
2. Students may respond with a wide variety of initialisms. Following are some examples: (a) A.C.—alternating current; (b) ID—identification paper(s); (c) T.N.T.—trinitrotoluine; (d) C.O.D.—collect on delivery; (e) D.A.—district attorney; (f) a.w.o.l.—absent without leave; (g) F.B.I.—Federal Bureau of Investigation; (h) G.P.—general practitioner (doctor); (i) ICBM—intercontinental ballistic missile; (j) MP—military police; (k) radar—radio detecting and ranging.

The Development of American English

THE TRUTH ABOUT O.K.

by Richard Lederer

Martin Van Buren

We Americans seem to have a passion for stringing initial letters together. We use *a.m.* and *p.m.* to separate light from darkness and B.C. and A.D. to identify vast stretches of time. We may listen to a deejay or veejay on *ABC, CBS, NBC,* or *MTV* or a crusading *DA* on *CNN, NPR,* or *PBS.*

Perhaps the most widely understood American word in the world is O.K. The explanations for its origin have been as imaginative as they have been various. Some have claimed that O.K. is a version of the Chocktaw affirmative *okeh.* Others have asserted that it is short for the Greek *olla kalla* ("all good") or *Orrin Kendall* crackers or *Aux Kayes* rum, or the name of chief *Old Keokuk.*

The truth is more politically correct than any of these theories.

In the 1830's in New England, there was a craze for initialisms, in the manner of the currently popular *T.G.I.F.* and *F.Y.I.* The fad went so far as to generate letter combinations of intentional misspellings: *K.G.* for "know go," *K.Y.* for "know use," and *O.W.* for "oll wright." *O.K.* for "oll korrect" naturally followed.

Of all the loopy initialisms and misspellings of the time, *O.K.* alone survived. That's because of a presidential nickname that consolidated the letters in the national memory.

Martin Van Buren, elected our eighth president in 1836, was born in Kinderhook, New York, and, early in his political career, was dubbed "Old Kinderhook." Echoing the "Oll Korrect" initialism, *O.K.* became the rallying cry of the Old Kinderhook Club, a political organization supporting Van Buren during the 1840 campaign.

The coinage did Van Buren no good, and he was defeated in his bid for reelection. But the word honoring his name today remains what H. L. Mencken identified as "the most shining and successful Americanism ever invented."

Activities

1. In a dictionary, research what each of these initialisms stand for:
   (a) A.D./B.C.
   (b) aka
   (c) GOP
   (d) A.M./F.M.
   (e) CD
   (f) ERA
   (g) a.m./p.m.
   (h) IQ
   (i) PS
   (j) RIP
   (k) RSVP
   (l) UFO
2. Identify ten additional initialisms and the words each represents.

Cross-Curricular Connection: Social Studies

Politics and American English The initialism O.K. doesn't represent the only gift of American politics to American English. Politicians have often adapted Native American terms to provide vivid descriptions of the political process. A prime example is *powwow,* which originally meant "a priest or medicine man" and gradually evolved in meaning so that it could apply to a political conference.

The Native American term *sachem* once designated "the head of a confederation" but then came to mean "a great man." Then the Tammany Hall political organization in New York began to use the term *sachem* to designate its own political boss.

Ask students to speculate about the attraction of Native American terms for politicians. *Reasonable answers include: these terms may have been perceived as vivid, playful, and humorous.*

PART 1 *Fireside and Campfire*

Gettysburg National Military Museum

One-Minute Planning Guide

The selections in this section reflect the expansion—both literary and territorial—that characterized the nineteenth century. The "Announcement of *The Dial*" introduces students to the Transcendentalist movement. They will enjoy reading "The Devil and Tom Walker" by Washington Irving, one of the first of a new breed of purely American writers. The popular works of the Fireside Poets—Longfellow, Holmes, Lowell, and Whittier—break new ground in American literature. "Crossing the Great Divide" and "The Most Sublime Spectacle on Earth" recount the exploration of the frontier. The excerpt from *Pilgrim at Tinker Creek* invites students to parallel these nineteenth-century writers' views of nature with those of contemporary naturalist Annie Dillard.

Customize for *Varying Student Needs*

When assigning the selections in this part, keep these factors in mind:

"The Announcement of *The Dial*"
- Brief, but contains difficult language

"The Devil and Tom Walker"
- Antiquated language may challenge less proficient readers and English language learners

"A Psalm of Life"; "The Tide Rises, The Tide Falls"
- Accessible poems filled with ocean imagery

"Thanatopsis"; "Old Ironsides"; "The First Snowfall"; from *Snowbound*
- Four poems, varying in difficulty
- Challenge more advanced students to interpret "Thanatopsis"

"Crossing the Great Divide"; "The Most Sublime Spectacle on Earth"
- Vocabulary may require clarification

Humanities: Art

Untitled, by D. E. Henderson.

This "genre painting" (one that tells a story) shows a refugee family around a campfire after the Battle of Fredericksburg, Virginia, which took place during the Civil War on December 13, 1862. The defeated Union forces, which outnumbered the southern army two to one, continued to threaten Fredericksburg even after the battle. Although General Lee's Confederate troops held firm, the threat of more fighting persisted for months. The painting is a reminder of the terrible toll the Civil War took on civilians in the South, where most of the war was fought. Families fled from their homes, as farms turned into battlefields. Encourage students to imagine the hardships suffered by the women, children, and elderly man portrayed here.

Have your students answer the following questions:

1. How might a family like this one have entertained themselves around the campfire? *Students should realize that, without modern entertainment media, they would have told stories and recited poetry.*
2. What could you learn about the people in the painting from reading the books, stories, and poems they enjoyed? *The literature of the day would reveal the values and ideas that were most important to Americans at a time of tremendous growth and upheaval.*

Prepare and Engage

LESSON OBJECTIVES

1. To develop vocabulary and word identification skills
- Latin Roots: *-spect-*
- Using the Word Bank: Sentence Completions

2. To use a variety of reading strategies to comprehend an announcement
- Connect Your Experience

3. To express and support responses to the text
- Critical Thinking
- Idea Bank: Announcement Letter
- Idea Bank: Persuasive Credo
- Idea Bank: Persuasive Essay
- Idea Bank: Graphic Display

4. To analyze literary elements
- Literary Focus: Announcement
- Reading for Success

5. To read in order to research self-selected and assigned topics
- Idea Bank: Journal Review

6. To plan, prepare, organize, and present literary interpretations
- Idea Bank: Literary Reading
- Idea Bank: Panel Discussion

7. To use recursive writing processes to write a proposal for a student magazine
- Guided Writing Lesson

8. To increase knowledge of the rules of grammar and usage
- Grammar and Style: Commonly Confused Words

Test Preparation

Reading Comprehension: Make Inferences and Generalizations (ATE, p. 227)
The teaching tips and sample test item in this workshop support the instruction and practice in the unit workshop:
Reading Comprehension: Analyze Information to Make Inferences and Generalizations (SE, p. 427)

Guide for Interpreting

Margaret Fuller *(1810–1850)*

A strong individual, Margaret Fuller scorned the inferior lot of most women and urged women to develop their talents. She envisioned an equal partnership for men and women that would extend from married life to the highest ranks of government and business. She wrote, "We would have every path laid open to woman as to man."

An Influential Intellectual Fuller began her career as a teacher, first in Boston and later in Providence. She gave up teaching to conduct a series of public discussion groups for women on intellectual topics. She developed an association with Ralph Waldo Emerson and other New England writers and thinkers who were involved in a philosophical and literary movement, known as Transcendentalism, that emphasized humanity's connection to nature. When they launched their magazine *The Dial*, Fuller both edited and contributed to the publication.

Her activities attracted the attention of Horace Greeley, the editor of the New York *Tribune*, who invited her to be a columnist for his paper. Her critical pieces for the *Tribune* and her book *Woman in the Nineteenth Century* (1845) established her reputation as a social critic.

A Tragic End Fulfilling a lifelong wish, she traveled to Europe in 1846. Returning in 1850, she drowned, with her husband and son, in a shipwreck off Fire Island, New York.

Ralph Waldo Emerson *(1803–1882)*

Ralph Waldo Emerson was one of the most influential writers and philosophers of his time. The publication in 1836 of his essay "Nature" marks the beginning of Transcendentalism. Emerson, Fuller, Henry David Thoreau, and others associated with the movement formed a discussion circle known as the Transcendental Club. The group met regularly at Emerson's house in Concord, Massachusetts, to discuss their ideas related to nature, individuality, and the human spirit. (For more on Ralph Waldo Emerson, see p. 362.)

◆ Background for Understanding

LITERATURE: MARGARET FULLER AND *THE DIAL*

In the 1830's in New England, the literary and philosophical movement known as Transcendentalism took hold, with Ralph Waldo Emerson as its main spokesperson. As the movement grew, those involved in it sought a wider audience for their ideas. They decided to publish a journal, which they called *The Dial*, and chose Margaret Fuller and Ralph Waldo Emerson to be co-editors. Their choice of Fuller was both remarkable and wise—remarkable because a woman editor was unheard of, but wise because it was only through Fuller's practicality, organization, and drive that the magazine succeeded.

The Dial was to be published four times a year. After numerous delays in getting started, Fuller herself wrote several articles necessary to fill the first issue, which appeared in July 1840. In the four years that it was published, *The Dial* was instrumental in establishing the reputations of a number of authors, including Henry David Thoreau. Much of the work was done by Fuller, and after two years, she gave up the editorship because of the strain. Beset with funding problems, and without Fuller's organized leadership, the magazine lasted another two years.

Prentice Hall Literature Program Resources

REINFORCE / RETEACH / EXTEND

Selection Support Pages
Build Vocabulary: Latin Roots: *-spect-*, p. 67
Grammar and Style: Commonly Confused Words: *Principal* and *Principle*, p. 68
Reading for Success: Strategies for Reading Critically, pp. 69–70
Literary Focus: Announcement, p. 71

Strategies for Diverse Student Needs, p. 14

Beyond Literature
Career Connection: Advertising, p. 14

Formal Assessment Selection Test, pp. 72–74; Assessment Resources Software

Alternative Assessment, p. 14

Writing and Language Transparencies
Branching Transparency, p. 67

Resource Pro CD-ROM

Listening to Literature Audiocassettes

The Announcement of *The Dial*

MODEL SELECTION

◆ Literature and Your Life

Connect Your Experience

Have you ever collaborated with a group of friends on a project intended for a wider audience? Maybe you produced a play, created a newsletter, or painted a mural. Whatever your purpose, you probably got caught up in the excitement of sharing ideas and working toward a common goal. This was the spirit that produced *The Dial* in 1840.

Journal Writing Record your thoughts about the topic you'd choose if you were to produce a newsletter.

Thematic Focus: Fireside and Campfire

As adventurous pioneers moved west in the mid-nineteenth century, intellectual pioneers, such as the Transcendentalists, were exploring ideas in philosophy and literature. The Transcendentalists hoped to encourage others to change their attitudes, values, and behaviors. How can a magazine make such an impact on a nation's identity?

◆ Literary Focus

Announcement

Politicians and writers depend on announcements to publicize events or books they want to make known to the public. An **announcement** is a public notice, an official and formal declaration. The main purpose of announcements is to attract interest, but they can also serve various other goals. For example, in "The Announcement of *The Dial*," Emerson and Fuller wanted to win over their audience, build expectations about the publication, and solicit articles from writers. They also outlined the philosophy of the journal.

◆ Build Vocabulary

Latin Roots: *-spect-*

The word *circumspect*, which you will encounter in "The Announcement of *The Dial*," contains the Latin root *-spect-*, which means "to look or see." When you combine *-spect-* with *circum-*, meaning "around," you have a word that means "to look around something." In looking around something, you are acting with circumspection; that is, you are being cautious—examining all related circumstances before making a decision or judgment.

You will recognize the root in other familiar words, such as *spectacle*, *spectator*, and *inspection*.

Word Bank

Before you read, preview this list of words from the selection.

compunctions
privations
rudiments
pittance
contingent
superseding
circumspection
reiterate
inappeasable
polemics

◆ Grammar and Style

Commonly Confused Words: *Principal* and *Principle*

Principal and *principle* are words that sound alike but are spelled differently and have different meanings. ***Principal*** can be a noun or an adjective and means "first in rank, authority, or importance." ***Principle*** is always a noun and means "a basic rule or truth." Look at these sample sentences:

The *principal* cause was never discovered.

I believe in the *principle* of integrity in the face of adversity.

Look for the use of *principle* in this announcement.

Interest Grabber Ask students to form groups to talk about the kinds of new magazines they would like to see on the newsstands. Challenge each group to choose one idea for a new publication, then come up with a slogan that would entice readers to buy their magazine. Explain that Margaret Fuller and Ralph Waldo Emerson described their new publication *The Dial* by writing, "It has all things to say, and no less than all the world for its final audience." Ask students to predict the contents of such a magazine.

Customize for
Less Proficient Readers
The abstract nature of the writing will make it difficult for students to grasp its meaning in a single reading. To help less proficient readers through this very dense and demanding piece, encourage them to reread it several times, breaking down or paraphrasing difficult passages in the process. Suggest that they use a dictionary as needed.

Customize for
AP Students
Have students look for the sales pitch in the announcement. Ask them to evaluate the text to consider questions like these: What will be unique or provocative about the new publication? Who will its audience be? What topics will it cover?

Customize for
English Language Learners
Have students work in small groups with more advanced native speakers to digest the points Fuller and Emerson make. Encourage them to stop and discuss any confusing words or passages. Encourage them to keep a dictionary at hand and to paraphrase lengthy or difficult passages.

Customize for
Gifted/Talented Students
After students have read the selection, have them interpret what they have learned about Transcendentalism. Then invite them to collect more information on the subject and put together a report for the class.

Test Preparation Workshop

Make Inferences and Generalizations The reading sections of many standardized tests, including the SAT, require students to recognize implied information in a text. To teach students to make inferences from implied messages, present this sample test item:

> We do not wish to say petty or curious things, or to reiterate a few propositions in various forms, but, if we can, to give expression to that spirit which lifts men to a higher platform, restores to them the religious sentiment, brings them worthy aims and pleasures, . . .

According to this passage, the tone of *The Dial* will be—

A depressing
B uplifting
C agitated
D frivolous

Choices *A* and *D* are contradicted by the description of *The Dial* as "cheerful" and "rational." *C* is incorrect because the text claims the paper will avoid "polemics." *B* is correct.

Reading for Success

The Reading for Success page in each unit presents a set of problem-solving procedures to help readers understand authors' words and ideas on multiple levels. Good readers develop a bank of strategies from which they can draw as needed.

Unit 3 introduces strategies for reading critically. To enable students to read works of nonfiction that present a writer's ideas or philosophy, it is important that they develop a series of strategies for examining the writer's assertions. The strategies presented in this unit provide students with the tools they need to critically evaluate a work.

These strategies for reading critically are modeled with "The Announcement of *The Dial*." Each green box shows an example of the thinking process involved in applying one of these strategies.

How to Use the Reading for Success Page

- Introduce the strategies for reading critically, presenting each as a problem-solving procedure. Be sure students understand what each strategy involves and under what circumstances to apply it.
- Before students read the selection, have them preview it, looking at the annotations in the green boxes that model the strategies.
- To reinforce these strategies after students have read "The Announcement of *The Dial*," have students do the Reading for Success pages in ***Selection Support,*** pp. 69–70. These pages gives students an opportunity to read a selection and practice literal comprehension strategies by writing their own annotations.

Reading for Success

Strategies for Reading Critically

When you read a work that presents a writer's perspective or ideas on a subject, it is a good idea to read the work critically. When you read critically, you examine the writer's ideas, especially in light of his or her purpose. You also evaluate the information the writer includes (or doesn't include) as support, and you form a judgment about the validity of the work. Here are specific strategies that will help you read critically.

Draw inferences.

Writers don't always say everything they mean. Often they suggest, or imply, ideas they want their readers to grasp. You need to infer the author's larger point or message by looking beyond the details and information provided.

Recognize the author's motivation or bias.

- ▶ The author's motivation may be to persuade you, to inform you, or just to entertain you. Be aware that the writer's motivation can influence what he or she includes and how he or she chooses to present material.
- ▶ Writers often, deliberately or not, present an issue through their own bias—their point of view on a subject. Look for factors that might bias a writer's opinion. For example, the belief of Fuller and Emerson in Transcendental philosophy influenced their attitude about *The Dial.*

Evaluate the writer's main ideas or statements.

Evaluating involves making a critical judgment. You should weigh the evidence a writer brings to bear on a subject. Consider whether the examples, reasons, or illustrations used to support ideas are sound and effective.

Challenge the text.

You need not always accept what a writer says at face value. Question the author's assertions, points, portrayals, and presentation. Are characters and situations true to life? Has the writer left out information that should be considered? Is the writer's evidence appropriate and relevant?

Evaluate the writer's work.

Apply your critical judgment to the work as a whole. As you look at the work in its totality, consider questions like these: Do the statements or points follow logically? Is the material clearly organized? Are the writer's points interesting and well supported?

As you read the announcement of the publication of *The Dial,* look at the notes along the sides. These notes demonstrate how to apply the strategies to a piece of nonfiction writing.

Reading Strategies: Support and Reinforcement

Appropriate Reading Strategies Students are given a reading strategy to apply in reading each selection. In those selections that present a writer's perspective or ideas in a work of nonfiction, students are given one of these critical reading strategies. In other selections a strategy is suggested that is appropriate to the selection.

Reading Prompts To encourage application of the given reading strategy, there are occasional prompts, within green boxes, at appropriate and significant points.

In addition, there are red boxes prompting application of the Literary Focus concept and maroon boxes prompting students to connect with their lives.

Using the Boxed Annotations and Prompts The material in the green, red, and maroon boxes along the sides of selections is intended to help students apply the literary element and the reading strategy and to make a connection with their lives.

You may use the boxed material in several ways:

- Have students pause when they come to a box and respond to its prompt before they continue reading.
- Urge students to read through the selection ignoring the boxes. After they have read the selection completely, they may go back and review the selection, responding to the prompts.

MODEL

The Announcement of The Dial

Margaret Fuller and Ralph Waldo Emerson

We invite the attention of our countrymen to a new design. Probably not quite unexpected or unannounced will our Journal appear, though small pains have been taken to secure its welcome. Those, who have immediately acted in editing the present Number, cannot accuse themselves of any unbecoming forwardness in their undertaking, but rather of a backwardness, when they remember how often in many private circles the work was projected, how eagerly desired, and only postponed because no individual volunteered to combine and concentrate the freewill offerings of many cooperators. With some reluctance the present conductors of this work have yielded themselves to the wishes of their friends, finding something sacred and not to be withstood in the importunity which urged the production of a Journal in a new spirit.

> **Infer** from this reference to "private circles" that there is an audience for the journal.

❶ As they have not proposed themselves to the work, neither can they lay any the least claim to an option or determination of the spirit in which it is conceived, or to what is peculiar in the design. In that respect, they have obeyed, though with great joy, the strong current of thought and feeling, which, for a few years past, has led many sincere persons in New England to make new demands on literature, and to reprobate[1] that rigor of our conventions of religion and education which is turning us to stone, which renounces hope, which looks only backward, which asks only such a future as the past, which suspects improvement, and holds nothing so much in horror as new views and the dreams of youth. ❶

> **Challenge** this statement by noting the significant literature being written during this time period.

With these terrors the conductors of the present Journal have nothing to do,—not even so much as a word of reproach to waste. ❷ They know that there is a portion of the youth and of the adult population of this country, who have not shared them; who have in secret or in public paid their vows to truth and freedom; who love reality too well to care for names, and who live by a Faith too earnest and profound to suffer them to doubt the eternity of its object, or to shake themselves free from its authority. Under the fictions and customs which occupied others, these have explored the Necessary, the Plain, the True, the Human,—and so gained a vantage ground, which commands the history of the past and the present.

> **Recognize authors' motivation:** These are the people the writers wish to reach.

No one can converse much with different classes of society in New England, without remarking the progress of a revolution. Those who share in it have no external organization, no badge, no creed, no name. They do not vote, or print, or even meet together. They do not know each other's faces or names. They are united only in a common love of truth, and love of its work. ❸ They are of all conditions and constitutions. Of these acolytes,[2] if some are happily born and well bred, many are no doubt ill dressed, ill placed, ill made—with as many

> From the details presented, you can **infer** that this audience is large.

1. **reprobate** (rep´ rə bāt) *v.*: To reject; disapprove of; censure strongly.

2. **acolytes** (ak´ ə līts´) *n.*: Followers of a creed or belief system; also assistants to a religious order.

Block Scheduling Strategies

Consider these suggestion to take advantage of extended class time:

- Begin by having students read the biographies and Background for Understanding in the Guide for Interpreting, on p. 226.
- Introduce the Reading for Success Strategies for Reading Critically. Discuss the kinds of situations that call for critical reading. Have students preview the annotations that model the strategies. For additional practice, assign the Reading for Success pages in ***Selection Support,*** pp. 69–70.
- Play the selection on audiocassette as students follow along in their texts.
- Use the Critical Thinking questions on p. 232 to stimulate class discussion.
- Assign the Guided Writing Lesson. Review the Writing Skills Focus; then display the Branching Transparency to help students organize their Prewriting notes. Allow the last fifteen minutes of class time for peer evaluation and revision.

Develop Understanding

One-Minute Insight In this work, Margaret Fuller and Ralph Waldo Emerson announce a new magazine, *The Dial,* which purports to represent the views of the writers, artists, and philosophers known as the Transcendentalists. Using the lofty, intellectual tone characteristic of the writing style of the period, the writers aim to attract readers by emphasizing the richness of experience the contributors to the magazine will provide and by promising a voice that is authentic and broadly appealing.

Listening to Literature Audiocassettes A well-paced oral reading can make this piece more accessible. Play the audiocassette, pausing as needed to clarify or emphasize key points. Encourage students to follow along in their texts.

Customize for
Less Proficient Readers
To help these students navigate the selection, use the page on rephrasing complicated sentences in ***Strategies for Diverse Student Needs*** (p. 14).

◆ Build Vocabulary

❶ **Latin Roots: *-spect-*** Have students identify the two words in this paragraph with the root *-spect-*. Ask them to look to the prefixes of these words or use a dictionary to determine their meanings as used in the context of the selection. *respect: "reference" or "relation"; suspects: "views with suspicion or distrust"*

◆ Critical Thinking

❷ **Analyze** Ask students to explain why the writers refer to the editors of the new magazine as "conductors." *The editors, by choosing the material that will appear in the magazine, will guide readers on an intellectual and spiritual journey.*

◆ Reading for Success

❸ **Recognize the Author's Purpose or Bias** Guide students to appreciate that the authors have a deep belief in the philosophy of Transcendentalism and wish to reach out to a wide audience of like-minded people and entice them to read *The Dial.*

◆ Reading for Success

❶ Evaluate the Writer's Points or Statements Ask students to explain why they do or do not think that Transcendentalism is truly affecting "every individual." *Students may reply that Fuller and Emerson are so caught up in Transcendentalism that they mistakenly believe that everyone must feel its impact as they do.*

▶Critical Viewing◀

❷ Connect Both the announcement and the cover are reserved and quite formal. Today, the magazine would probably feature a much more colorful cover with some sort of persuasive message or a list of article titles designed to attract the interest of potential readers.

Customize for AP Students

❸ Have students analyze why the writers would make such an audacious, provocative statement about the worthiness of books. *Students may say that their intent was to rile readers, to attract their interest.*

◆ Literature and Your Life

❹ The writers imply that the pool of ideas that will fill the pages in the new magazine will be the result of interactions among friends, editors, and writers. Ask students to think about times they've been engaged in group discussions with their intimates in which they talked philosophically about ideas or their lives. Ask them if they think those experiences broadened or otherwise enriched their perspectives.

◆ Critical Thinking

❺ Interpret Ask students to explain why the Transcendentalists chose the name *The Dial* for their publication. Invite them to suggest other names they think the editors might have considered. *Students may respond that the magazine is named for a sun dial, a natural way of recording change. Guide students to see that the editors see the magazine as a means of measuring or indicating "the state of life and growth" taking place in the intellectual world.*

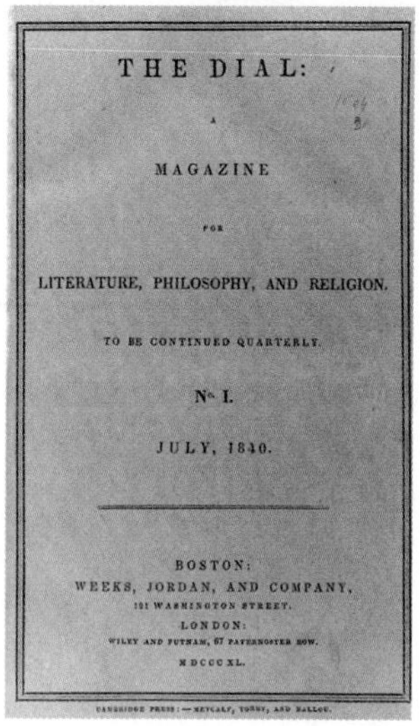
THE DIAL:
A
MAGAZINE
FOR
LITERATURE, PHILOSOPHY, AND RELIGION.
TO BE CONTINUED QUARTERLY.
No. I.
JULY, 1840.
BOSTON:
WEEKS, JORDAN, AND COMPANY,
121 WASHINGTON STREET.
LONDON:
WILEY AND PUTNAM, 67 PATERNOSTER ROW.
MDCCCXL.

◀ **Critical Viewing** How do the language of the announcement and the cover of the magazine reflect the time period in which they were written? How might the cover be designed for today's audience? **[Connect]** ❷

scars of hereditary vice as other men. Without pomp, without trumpet, in lonely and obscure places, in solitude, in servitude, in compunctions and privations, trudging beside the team in a dusty road, or drudging a hireling in other men's cornfields, schoolmasters, who teach a few children rudiments for a pittance, ministers of small parishes of the obscurer sects, lone women in dependent condition, matrons and young maidens, rich and poor, beautiful and hard-favored, without concert or proclamation of any kind, they have silently given in their several adherence to a new hope, and in all companies do signify a greater trust in the nature and resources of man, than the laws or the popular opinions will well allow.

❶ This spirit of the time is felt by every individual with some difference,—to each one casting its light upon the objects nearest to his temper and habits of thought;—to one, coming in the shape of special reforms in the state; to another, in modifications of the various callings of men, and the customs of business; to a third, opening a new scope for literature and art; to a fourth, in philosophical insight; to a fifth, in the vast solitudes of prayer. It is in every form a protest against usage, and a search for principles. In all its movements, it is peaceable, and in the very lowest marked with a triumphant success. Of course, it rouses the opposition of all which it judges and condemns, but it is too confident in its tone to comprehend an objection, and so builds no outworks for possible defense against contingent enemies. It has the step of Fate, and goes on existing like an oak or a river, because it must.

This passage reveals the **authors' bias** in support of the new philosophy.

In literature, this influence appears not yet in new books so much as in the higher tone of criticism. The antidote to all narrowness is the comparison of the record with nature, which at once shames the record and stimulates to new attempts. Whilst we look at this, we wonder how any book has been thought worthy to be preserved. There is somewhat in all life untranslatable into language. He who keeps his eye on that will write better than others, and think less of his writing, and of all writing. Every thought has a certain imprisoning as well as uplifting quality, and, in proportion to its energy on the will, refuses to become an object of intellectual contemplation. Thus what is great usually slips through our fingers, and it seems wonderful how a lifelike word ever comes to be written. If our Journal share the impulses of the time, it cannot now prescribe its own course. It cannot foretell in orderly propositions what it shall attempt. All criticism should be poetic; unpredictable; superseding, as every new thought does, all foregone thoughts, and making a new light on the whole world. Its brow is not wrinkled with circumspection, but serene, cheerful, adoring. It has all things to say, and no less than all the world for its final audience.

Challenge this statement. Do you believe that some earlier literature was worth preserving? ❸

Our plan embraces much more than criticism; were it not so, our criticism would be naught. Everything noble is directed on life, and this is. We do not wish to say pretty or curious things, or to reiterate a few propositions in varied forms, but, if we can, to give expression to that spirit which lifts men to a higher platform, restores to them the religious sentiment, brings them worthy aims and pure pleasures, purges the inward eye, makes life less desultory,[3] and, through raising men to the level of nature, takes away its melancholy

Evaluate the support for the statement that this, like everything noble, is directed on life.

3. **desultory** (des´ əl tôr´ ē) *adj.*: Random; wandering.

Cross-Curricular Connection: Social Studies

Publications for Specific Audiences It seems as though there is a newsletter, Web site, or magazine geared to every possible interest, perspective, or philosophy. Many of today's advertisers are "target-marketing" to very specific audiences that they have identified as potential consumers of their product or service. Publishers are obliging by creating publications that are tailored to highly specialized groups of readers. For instance, there are magazines written just for people who run small businesses from their homes. Companies that make home office equipment and personal computers are big advertisers in such publications.

Ask students to choose a magazine that has a clear editorial voice. For example, they might select one that is politically liberal or conservative, one that is environmentally aware, or one that has a feminist or humanitarian leaning. Have them identify the clues that indicate that publication's point of view. Ask them to look for connections between the content or readership of the magazine and the kinds of products and services advertised within it.

from the landscape, and reconciles the practical with the speculative powers.

But perhaps we are telling our little story too gravely. There are always great arguments at hand for a true action, even for the writing of a few pages. There is nothing but seems near it and prompts it,—the sphere in the ecliptic,[4] the sap in the apple tree,—every fact, every appearance seem to persuade to it.

Our means correspond with the ends we have indicated. As we wish not to multiply books, but to report life, our resources are
4 therefore not so much the pens of practiced writers, as the discourse of the living, and the portfolios which friendship has opened to us. From the beautiful recesses of private thought; from the experience and hope of spirits which are withdrawing from all old forms, and seeking in all that is new somewhat to meet their inappeasable longings; from the secret confession of genius afraid to trust itself to aught[5] but sympathy; from the conversations of fervid and mystical pietists; from tear-stained diaries of sorrow and passion; from the manuscripts of young poets; and from the records of youthful taste commenting on old works of art; we hope to draw thoughts and feelings, which being alive can impart life.

5 **Evaluate** this statement. Do you believe that thoughts can impart life?

And so with diligent hands and good intent we set down our Dial on the earth. We wish it may resemble that instrument in its celebrated happiness, that of measuring no hours but those of sunshine. Let it be one cheerful rational voice amidst the din of mourners and polemics. Or to abide by our chosen image, let it be such a Dial, not as the dead face of a clock, hardly even such as the Gnomon[6] in a garden, but rather such a Dial as in the Garden itself, in whose leaves and flowers and fruits the suddenly awakened sleeper is instantly apprised not what part of dead time, but what state of life and growth is now arrived and arriving. 5

4. **sphere in the ecliptic** (i klip´ tik): Sun's path among the stars.
5. **aught** (ôt) *n.* (archaic): Any least part; anything whatsoever.

6. **Gnomon** (nō´ män) *n.*: A sundial; an indicator of the hour by the shadow cast by an object.

◆ Build Vocabulary

compunctions (kəm puŋk´ shənz) *n.*: Anxieties; regrets
privations (prī vā´ shənz) *n.*: Loss of things previously possessed
rudiments (ro͞o´ də məntz) *n.*: Fundamental skills
pittance (pit´ əns) *n.*: Meager wage or remuneration
contingent (kən tin´ jənt) *adj.*: Unpredictable; accidental; dependent on
superseding (so͞o´ pər sēd´ iŋ) *v.*: Overriding; making outmoded
circumspection (sur´ kəm spekt´ shən) *n.*: Cautiousness; prudence
reiterate (rē it´ ə rāt´) *v.*: Repeat or state over again
inappeasable (in´ ə pē´ zə bəl) *adj.*: Unable to be quieted or calmed
polemics (pō lem´ iks) *n.*: Controversial arguments; branch of theology devoted to refuting errors

Guide for Responding

◆ Literature and Your Life

Reader's Response Would you want to read the articles announced as forthcoming in *The Dial*? Why or why not?

Thematic Focus How do the writers characterize the period in which they live? Are they hopeful or discouraged about the future of the country?

☑ Check Your Comprehension

1. Where did the idea for this journal originate? Explain.
2. Who are the participants in the "revolution" in progress? What unites them?
3. Who will write for *The Dial*? What should they write about?

Reinforce and Extend

Customize for
Interpersonal Learners
To extend learning, use the Career Connections: Advertising page in the ***Beyond Literature*** booklet of the Teacher's Resources.

Answers
◆ Literature and Your Life

Reader's Response Students should support their replies with a well-reasoned explanation.

Thematic Focus The writers see the period in which they live as mired in rigid intellectual and spiritual conventions. They are hopeful, however, that people from all walks of life "who have paid their vows to truth and freedom" will rise up to join the new philosophical movement that is transforming the country.

☑ Check Your Comprehension

1. The idea originated in "private circles" of people who, like Fuller and Emerson, shared a belief in the principles of Transcendentalism.
2. They come from every walk of life, and are united by their love of truth and their belief in the resources of man and nature.
3. "Many cooperators" will contribute, including pietists, young poets, youthful art critics, and those who are seeking a sympathetic audience or something new from life. They will write criticism of art and literature; they will also write anything that gives "expressions to that spirit which lifts men to a higher platform. . . ."

Reteach

Help students recognize author's motivation or bias by having them use a checklist like the one shown.

Is the author trying to persuade you?	___
Is only one point of view presented?	___
Is the supporting evidence valid and relevant?	___
Has information been left out?	___
Are the supporting arguments logical and clearly organized?	___

Beyond the Selection

FURTHER READING

Other Works by Margaret Fuller
Woman in the Nineteenth Century and Kindred Papers Relating to the Sphere, Condition and Duties of Woman
"Papers on Literature and Art"

We suggest that you preview these works before recommending them to students.

INTERNET

The Internet provides opportunities for students to learn more about Transcendentalism. We recommend the following site. Please be aware, however, that sites may have changed since we published this information.

For a comprehensive introduction to the life and works of Emerson, go to
http://miso.wwa.com/~jej/1emerson.html

We *strongly recommend* that you preview the site before you send students to it.

Answers

◆ Critical Thinking

Suggested responses:

1. It is characterized by a desire for newness and a love of truth and freedom.
2. It is quite appropriate because the writers imply that their intended audience are followers of Transcendentalism.
3. (a) The first refers to a common garden; "the Garden" refers to the natural world. (b) Just as a sun dial measures time, the magazine will indicate "the state of life and growth."
4. Readers are still attracted by promises of something new, different, and uplifting, and they still respond well to flattery.
5. Both try to attract audiences' attention by promising something new and eagerly anticipated. Today's media pitches, however, are far more visual and informal in tone.

◆ Reading for Success

1. Possible responses include: The individual is worthy of greater insight and vision than "the laws or the popular opinions" allow.
2. Students may respond that the claim that that magazine will lift its readers to a higher ground, restore their faith and purity, bring them pleasure and purpose in life, and raise them to the level of nature is the most unrealistic.
3. Possible responses include: "a Journal in a new spirit"; "We do not wish to say pretty or curious things, . . . but . . . to give expression to that spirit which lifts men to a higher platform . . . and, through raising men to the level of nature, takes away its melancholy from the landscape, and reconciles the practical with the speculative powers"; "Let it be one cheerful rational voice amidst the din of mourners and polemics."

Guide for Responding (continued)

◆ Critical Thinking

INTERPRET

1. What characterizes the "spirit" of the launchers of *The Dial*? **[Infer]**

2. How appropriate is the word *acolytes* (see footnote on p. 229)to describe the intended audience of *The Dial*? **[Analyze]**

3. (a) What distinction do the writers make between "a garden" and "the Garden"? (b) Why is *The Dial* an appropriate name for the new journal? **[Distinguish; Support]**

APPLY

4. Which techniques in "The Announcement of *The Dial*" would be most effective in appealing to an audience today? **[Apply]**

EXTEND

5. Compare a commercial announcing a new product or a trailer for a new film with "The Announcement of *The Dial*." What similarities and differences do you find? **[Media Link]**

◆ Reading for Success

STRATEGIES FOR READING CRITICALLY

Review the strategies for critical reading and the notes showing how to apply them. Then answer the following questions.

1. What can you infer from the announcement about the writers' belief in the individual?

2. What claim for the publication would you challenge as most unrealistic?

3. Which phrase or sentence from the announcement do you think states the purpose of *The Dial* most clearly?

◆ Literary Focus

ANNOUNCEMENT

An **announcement** informs the public about a forthcoming event. When Fuller and Emerson announce the first issue of *The Dial*, they present this information in a way that encourages potential readers to eagerly anticipate the magazine.

1. How do the writers create a sense of eager anticipation for *The Dial*?

2. List two examples that show "The Announcement of *The Dial*" flatters its audience.

◆ Build Vocabulary

USING THE LATIN ROOT ***-spect-***

Knowing that *-spect-* means "to see" can help you to decode words with this root. Explain the meaning of the following italicized words. Consult a dictionary, if necessary, to confirm your definition.

1. In *retrospect*, history is understandable as a series of causes and effects.

2. Have you *inspected* your essay for errors?

3. A conscientious effort earns the *respect* of others.

4. Don't make a *spectacle* of yourself.

USING THE WORD BANK: Sentence Completions

Complete the following sentences, filling in the blanks with appropriate words from the Word Bank.

1. He had few __?__ about deciding to work for a __?__.

2. As she easily learned the __?__ of the job, supervisors found no need to __?__ basic instructions.

3. Accustomed to __?__, he approached dubious employment offers with __?__ .

4. Fuller was __?__ in her rejection of __?__.

5. She received several tempting offers. __?__ all other offers was a bid from the *Tribune*, but her acceptance was __?__ on Emerson's approval.

◆ Grammar and Style

COMMONLY CONFUSED WORDS: *PRINCIPAL* AND *PRINCIPLE*

In "The Announcement of *The Dial*" the writers refer to the ***principles,*** or ideals, upon which their journal is founded. Don't confuse that word with ***principal,*** meaning "most important."

Practice On your paper, write the following sentences, completing them with the words *principal* and *principle*.

1. Our __?__ follows strict __?__ in running our school.

2. The __?__ result was increased sales.

3. Which __?__ apply to the decision to cancel that account?

Writing Application Write a paragraph about something in which you believe. Use both *principle* and *principal* correctly.

◆ Literary Focus

1. Suggested response: They state that the magazine has been "eagerly desired"; they promise a journal in "the new spirit"; they imply that there is a large audience that would welcome such a publication; and they propose to write about uplifting subjects.
2. It describes the audience as a special group of people who have risen to a higher "vantage ground." It states that, unlike others, this group has the vision to trust in "the nature and resources of man."

◆ Build Vocabulary

Using the Latin Root *-spect-*

Suggested responses:

1. *retrospect* means "the act of looking back"; 2. *inspected* means "looked at closely"; 3. *respect* means "the state of being regarded or looked upon with esteem"; 4. *spectacle* means "something to look at; a strange or remarkable sight"

Using the Word Bank

1. compunctions, pittance
2. rudiments, reiterate
3. privations, circumspection
4. inappeasable, polemics
5. Superseding, contingent

◆ Grammar and Style

Practice

1. principal, principles;
2. principal; 3. principles

Writing Application

Student writing should include examples of the proper use of both *principal* and *principle*.

Build Your Portfolio

Idea Bank

Writing

1. Announcement Letter Write a letter to a friend announcing a project or event. Design your letter to make the friend feel as if the project were planned especially for him or her.

2. Persuasive Credo Take a stand on an issue in which you believe strongly, and write an article that both expresses your credo, or belief, and convinces others to accept your view.

3. Persuasive Essay Like Emerson and Fuller, do you feel that reading philosophical writings can change your behavior or improve your life? In an essay, argue for or against this assertion.

Speaking, Listening, and Viewing

4. Literary Reading Prepare a reading of selections from your school's literary magazine. Organize the selections in meaningful groupings and choose classmates to read whose voices will enhance the selections. **[Performing Arts Link]**

5. Panel Discussion Research influential publications in American history, such as William Lloyd Garrison's journal *The Liberator* or Upton Sinclair's novel *The Jungle*. In a panel discussion, evaluate the extent to which such works can be credited with bringing about significant changes.

Researching and Representing

6. Journal Review Make a study of the publications at other schools. Collect samples and compare them with your school's publications. Present your report to the school's administration.

7. Graphic Display Collect articles that express exciting and well-presented ideas. Group the articles in subject areas, and arrange them into a graphic display for your classmates.

Online Activity www.phlit.phschool.com

Guided Writing Lesson

Proposal for a Student Magazine

A proposal addresses an audience for a specific purpose—to win their support for a project. Suppose you and a group of classmates want to start a student magazine at your school. Write a proposal to convince school administrators to allow you to start publishing this magazine.

Writing Skills Focus:
A Clear and Consistent Purpose

In order to persuade school administrators to allocate funds or supervision, present your case **clearly and consistently**. Notice how Fuller and Emerson present the goals for *The Dial:*

Model From the Announcement

We do not wish to say pretty or curious things, or to reiterate a few propositions in varied forms, but, if we can, to give expression to that spirit which lifts men to a higher platform . . . and, through raising men to the level of nature, takes away its melancholy from the landscape, and reconciles the practical with the speculative powers.

Prewriting Brainstorm to identify a focus for your magazine. Write your goal in one concise statement of purpose. Research the costs involved in obtaining the resources you will need. This information will demonstrate that you have thought out your proposal carefully.

Drafting State the purpose of your magazine, and support it with a philosophy. Then itemize the costs. Emphasize the need for the magazine in order to justify the expenses needed to produce it.

Revising Every fact you supply should relate to your main purpose. If necessary, add details that make the connection explicit. Ask a classmate whether your plan seems clear, consistent, and reasonable. Make changes based on feedback from your reviewer.

Idea Bank

Customizing for
Performance Levels

Following are suggestions for matching Idea Bank topics with your students' performance levels:
Less Advanced Students: 1, 4
Average Students: 2, 6, 7
More Advanced Students: 3, 5

Customizing for
Learning Modalities

Following are suggestions for matching Idea Bank topics with your students' learning modalities:
Intrapersonal: 2, 3
Musical/Rhythmic: 4
Logical/Mathematical: 5, 6
Bodily/Kinesthetic: 7

Guided Writing Lesson

Writing and Language Transparencies Use the Branching Transparency, p. 67, to help students organize their proposals. Have them write their statement of purpose in the top box, then organize supporting philosophies, evidence, and costs using the boxes and lines beneath.

For more on prewriting, elaboration, and revision, see *Prentice Hall Writing and Grammar.*

Writing Lab CD-ROM

Have students complete the tutorial on Practical and Technical Writing. Follow these steps:

1. Students can refer to the audio-annotated model of a proposal.
2. Have students use the Purpose Profile to help them clarify their purpose.
3. After students have drafted on the computer, have them use the Interactive Self-Evaluation Checklist to aid revision.

✓ ASSESSMENT OPTIONS

Formal Assessment, Selection Test, pp. 72–74, and Assessment Resources Software. The selection test is designed so that it can be easily customized to the performance levels of your students.

Alternative Assessment, p. 14, includes options for less advanced students, more advanced students, intrapersonal learners, musical/rhythmic learners, and interpersonal learners.

PORTFOLIO ASSESSMENT

Use the following rubrics in the ***Alternative Assessment*** booklet to assess student writing:
Announcement Letter: Evaluation/Review Rubric, p. 119
Persuasive Credo: Persuasion Rubric, p. 120
Persuasive Essay: Persuasion Rubric, p. 120
Guided Writing Lesson: Persuasion Rubric, p. 120

Prepare and Engage

LESSON OBJECTIVES

1. **To develop vocabulary and word identification skills**
   - Latin Prefixes: ex-
   - Using the Word Bank: Sentence Completions
   - Extending Word Study: Context Clues (ATE)
2. **To use a variety of reading strategies to comprehend a story**
   - Connect Your Experience
   - Reading Strategy: Infer Cultural Attitudes
   - Tips to Guide Reading
3. **To increase knowledge of other cultures and to connect common elements across cultures**
   - Connecting Themes Across Cultures (ATE)
   - Cultural Connection (ATE)
4. **To express and support responses to the text**
   - Critical Thinking
   - Idea Bank: Correspondence
   - Idea Bank: Revised Ending
   - Idea Bank: Enactment
   - Idea Bank: Board Game
5. **To analyze literary elements**
   - Literary Focus: Omniscient Narrator
   - Idea Bank: Analysis
6. **To read in order to research self-selected and assigned topics**
   - Idea Bank: Exhibition
   - Research Skills Mini-Lesson (ATE)
7. **To plan, prepare, organize, and present literary interpretations**
   - Idea Bank: Impromptu Speech
8. **To use recursive writing processes to write a story**
   - Guided Writing Lesson
9. **To increase knowledge of the rules of grammar and usage**
   - Grammar and Style: Adjective Clauses

Test Preparation

Reading Comprehension: Make Inferences and Generalizations (ATE, p. 235)

The teaching tips and sample test item in this workshop support the instruction and practice in the unit workshop:

Reading Comprehension: Analyze Information to Make Inferences and Generalizations (SE, p. 427)

Guide for Interpreting

Washington Irving *(1783–1859)*

Named after the first American president, Washington Irving became the first American writer to achieve an international reputation.

An American Youth Born into a wealthy family, Irving began studying law at the age of sixteen. Though he had planned to be a lawyer, he found he was more interested in travel and writing. He spent much time traveling throughout Europe and New York's Hudson Valley and reading European literature. Irving also wrote satirical essays using the pen name Jonathan Oldstyle. When Irving was twenty-four, he and his brother began publishing a magazine anonymously, *Salmagundi* (the name of a spicy appetizer), which carried humorous sketches and essays about New York society.

In 1809, he published his first major work, *A History of New York From the Beginning of the World to the End of the Dutch Dynasty,* using the pseudonym Diedrich Knickerbocker. The book, a humorous examination of New York during colonial times, was well received and made Irving famous.

Tour of Europe From 1815 to 1832, Irving lived in Europe. There he traveled extensively and learned about European customs, traditions, and folklore. Inspired by the European folk heritage, Irving created two of his most famous stories, "The Legend of Sleepy Hollow" and "Rip Van Winkle," transforming two traditional German tales into distinctly American stories set in the Hudson Valley. When Irving published these two stories in the *Sketchbook* (1820), under the pseudonymn Geoffrey Crayon, writers and critics throughout Europe and the United States responded enthusiastically.

The international success of Irving's stories marked the beginning of a distinctly American literary heritage.

A Devoted American While in Europe, Irving completed three other books, including *Tales of a Traveller,* which contains "The Devil and Tom Walker." When his patriotism was questioned because of his time abroad, Irving responded: "I am endeavoring to serve my country. Whatever I have written has been written with the feelings and published as the writing of an American. Is that renouncing my country? How else am I to serve my country—by coming home and begging an office of it: which I should not have the kind of talent or the business habits requisite to fill?—If I can do any good in this world it is with my pen." Although Irving continued to publish after returning to the United States, he is remembered mainly for a few characters he created while in Europe.

◆ Background for Understanding

LITERATURE: THE LEGEND OF FAUST

"The Devil and Tom Walker" is a variation of the Faust legend—a tale about a man who sells his soul to the Devil for earthly benefits. The legend was inspired by a real person, a wandering scholar and conjurer named Faust, who lived in early sixteenth-century Germany. *Faustbach,* the first printed version of a Faust legend, was published in 1587. That story proposed that Faust had made a pact with the Devil for knowledge and power on Earth.

Over the years, many variations of the Faust legend have appeared, including a 1604 play by English dramatist Christopher Marlowe, a two-part dramatic poem (1808, 1832) by Johann Goethe, an 1859 opera by Charles Gounod, and a 1947 novel by Thomas Mann. Each retelling involves a person who trades his soul for experience, knowledge, or treasure. Adaptations do not share the same ending—in some, the protagonist is doomed; in others, he is redeemed.

Prentice Hall Literature Program Resources

REINFORCE / RETEACH / EXTEND

Selection Support Pages
Build Vocabulary: Latin Prefixes: *ex-*, p. 72
Grammar and Style: Adjective Clauses, p. 73
Reading Strategy: Infer Cultural Attitudes, p. 74
Literary Focus: Omniscient Narrator, p. 75

Strategies for Diverse Student Needs, p. 15

Beyond Literature
Media Connection: Narrative Point of View, p. 15

Formal Assessment Selection Test, pp. 75–77; Assessment Resources Software

Alternative Assessment, p. 15

Writing and Language Transparencies
Story Map Organizer, pp. 99–101; Daily Language Practice, Week 6

Resource Pro CD-ROM

Literature CD-ROM

Listening to Literature Audiocassettes

The Devil and Tom Walker

◆ Literature and Your Life

CONNECT YOUR EXPERIENCE

In our society, it's not uncommon to see political candidates who fight to win at any cost, business executives who make money in a dishonest way, and Olympic athletes who bend the rules to get the gold. The main character in this story goes to even greater extremes to achieve his goal of great wealth: He makes a pact with the Devil—even though he knows that he will eventually have to pay for this decision.

Journal Writing Give examples of people in today's news who are driven by their need for money, power, or fame.

THEMATIC FOCUS: FIRESIDE AND CAMPFIRE

What details make this story, based on a German legend, a distinctly American tale that reflects the characteristics of its time?

◆ Literary Focus

OMNISCIENT NARRATOR

"The Devil and Tom Walker" is told not by a participant in the story but by an **omniscient** (all-knowing) **narrator** who stands outside the action and relates the thoughts and feelings of all the characters. When a story is told by an omniscient narrator, the reader is not limited to the thoughts and perspective of a single character but may know the thoughts and feelings of any character. The narrator may even comment on the events of the story.

◆ Reading Strategy

INFER CULTURAL ATTITUDES

This story reveals many of the **cultural attitudes** of the people living in New England in the 1720's. Irving doesn't tell you these attitudes directly; he suggests them through the details of the story. It's left up to you to **make inferences**, or draw conclusions, about cultural attitudes based on the details Irving provides. Look, for example, at this description of the old Indian fort:

> . . . the common people had a bad opinion of it, from the stories handed down from the time of the Indian wars; when it was asserted that the savages held incantations here, and made sacrifices to the evil spirit.

From these details, you can infer that the colonists had a suspicious attitude toward the Native Americans and a belief in the Devil.

◆ Build Vocabulary

LATIN PREFIXES: *ex-*

Tom Walker *extorts* money from people; that is, he obtains it by threat or force. The Latin prefix *ex-* means "out." The word *extort* literally means "to twist something out of someone."

WORD BANK

Before you read, preview this list of words.

avarice
usurers
extort
ostentation
parsimony

◆ Grammar and Style

ADJECTIVE CLAUSES

An **adjective clause**, also known as a relative clause, is a subordinate clause (a clause that cannot stand alone as a sentence) that modifies a noun or pronoun. Look at this example from the story:

> A miserable horse, *whose ribs were as articulate as the bars of a gridiron,* stalked about a field . . .

The words in italics are an adjective clause that modifies *horse.*

Test Preparation Workshop

Reading Comprehension: Make Inferences and Generalizations

Standardized tests such as the SAT require students to make inferences based on information in a reading passage. An inference is a reasonable guess based on facts. To help students learn to make inferences, have them answer the following sample test item.

> A miserable horse, whose ribs were as articulate as the bars of a gridiron, stalked about a field . . . and sometimes he would lean his head over the fence . . . and seem to petition deliverance from this land of famine.

According to the passage, why is the horse so miserable?

A He misses his former owner.
B He is kept in the barn all day.
C He lives in the country.
D He is starving.

The text makes no mention of any information found in choices *A, B,* and *C,* so they are incorrect. *D* is correct. The horse's ribs show, and the author describes a "land of famine," so students should infer that the horse is not well fed.

Interest Grabber Dim the lights in the classroom and read aloud the second paragraph on p. 238 of "The Devil and Tom Walker." The passage contains a detailed description of the gloomy swamp where Tom first encounters the Devil. Ask students to discuss the mood created by the description. What do they think will happen to Tom? Have students discuss their responses to the passage and make predictions about the story.

Connecting Themes Across Cultures

Stories of people who are driven by greed, power, and dishonesty are common to every culture. Sometimes these people appear as central figures in myths and legends; other times their exploits are described in historical text. For example, in the 1970s the Cambodian leader Pol Pot killed almost a third of the Cambodian population in an attempt to purge the nation of Western influences. Invite students to research other leaders who seek power and greed at the expense of others.

Customize for
Less Proficient Readers

Have students pause at key scenes in the story so that volunteers can summarize what has happened up to that point. Encourage students to jot down the main events of the story on a timeline as they read. They can use the timeline to help them complete the Guided Writing Lesson.

Customize for
AP Students

Encourage students to identify and analyze the symbols that Irving uses in his story. Have them share their observations and interpretations with the rest of the class.

Customize for
English Language Learners

The dialogue in this story includes words and expressions that are rarely used in modern conversation—for example, "Look yonder, and see how Deacon Peabody is faring." Using a two-column chart, have students jot down each unfamiliar term or expression and note what they think it might mean. Check students' understanding, clarifying as necessary.

Develop Understanding

One-Minute Insight Set in colonial Massachusetts, this story is Irving's retelling of the Faust legend. Tom Walker, faced with an opportunity to acquire wealth, makes a pact with the devil, whom he encounters in a swampy forest. Like other fictional characters who sell their souls, he obtains his heart's desire in exchange. The pact causes Walker to become even more greedy and less compassionate. Despite his tremendous wealth, Tom is just as stingy and miserly as ever. Though Tom later regrets his deal and attempts to reform his life, his efforts to save his soul are in vain; he cannot escape his terrible fate, and must pay the inevitable price of a deal with the devil. The story illustrates the tremendous extent to which people can be overcome by greed, and highlights the potentially devastating consequences of such an obsession.

Literature CD-ROM To build background on Washington Irving, use *The History of American Literature:* Part 1, Disk 1, Feature 11.

Writing and Language Transparencies Distribute a Story Map Organizer to help students track the plot of this story.

Customize for *Less Proficient Readers*
These students may have difficulty with this long selection. Help sustain interest and concentration by encouraging them to summarize paragraphs. **The Strategies for Diverse Student Needs** page for this selection offers support, p. 15.

Clarification Be sure students understand that although Irving wrote in the early nineteenth century, the events in the tale take place a hundred years earlier.

◆ Reading Strategy

❶ Infer Cultural Attitudes
Discuss with students that colonial society (publicly, at least) frowned on ill-gotten gains such as pirated treasures. Point out that to many of those religious people, the devil was assumed to be associated with all such profits.

The Devil and Tom Walker

Washington Irving

A few miles from Boston in Massachusetts, there is a deep inlet, winding several miles into the interior of the country from Charles Bay, and terminating in a thickly wooded swamp or morass. On one side of this inlet is a beautiful dark grove; on the opposite side the land rises abruptly from the water's edge into a high ridge, on which grow a few scattered oaks of great age and immense size. Under one of these gigantic trees, according to old stories, there was a great amount of treasure buried by Kidd the pirate.[1] The inlet allowed a facility to bring the money in a boat secretly and at night to the very foot of the hill; the elevation of the place permitted a good look-out to be kept that no one was at hand; while the remarkable trees formed good landmarks by which the place might easily be found again. The old stories add, moreover, that the Devil presided at the hiding of the money, and took it under his guardianship; but this it is well known he always does with buried treasure, particularly when it has been ill-gotten. ❶

1. **Kidd the pirate:** Captain William Kidd (1645–1701).

Block Scheduling Strategies

Consider these suggestions to take advantage of extended class time:

- Use the Interest Grabber (p. 235 of the teacher edition) to introduce the selection. Then have students complete the journal activity in Literature and Your Life (p. 235). Ask volunteers to share their responses.
- Introduce the Reading Strategy and any other skills you wish to emphasize. If appropriate, assign the Reading Strategy page in ***Selection Support,*** p. 74.
- After students have read the selection, have them work in discussion groups to answer the Critical Thinking questions (p. 245).
- To build skill in grammar and mechanics use the Daily Language Practice exercises for Week 6 in ***Writing and Language Transparencies.***

The Devil and Tom Walker, 1856, John Quidor, The Cleveland Museum of Art

2 ▲ Critical Viewing This painting is called *The Devil and Tom Walker*. Explain how the lighting and other elements reflect the mood of Irving's story. **[Analyze]**

Be that as it may, Kidd never returned to recover his wealth; being shortly after seized at Boston, sent out to England, and there hanged for a pirate.

3 About the year 1727, just at the time that earthquakes were prevalent in New England, and shook many tall sinners down upon their knees, there lived near this place a meager, miserly fellow, of the name of Tom Walker. He had a wife as miserly as himself: they were so miserly that they even conspired to cheat each other. Whatever the woman could lay hands on, she hid away; a hen could not cackle but she was on the alert to secure the new-laid egg. Her husband was continually prying about to detect her secret hoards, and many and fierce were the conflicts that took place about what ought to have been common property. They lived in a forlorn-looking house that stood alone, and had an air of starvation. A few straggling savin trees, emblems of sterility, grew near it; no smoke ever curled from its chimney; no traveler stopped at its door. A miserable horse, whose ribs were as articulate as the bars of a gridiron, stalked about 4

Humanities: Art

The Devil and Tom Walker, 1856, by John Quidor.

This oil painting, by American artist John Quidor (1801–1881), depicts Tom's initial meeting with the devil in the swampy forest.

Use these questions for discussion:

1. What about this painting indicates that this is not a typical chance encounter between two strangers in the woods? *Students can point to the skull on the ground and the half-clothed smiling creature holding an ax.*
2. Would this painting have been as effective if the two figures met in the middle of a sunny meadow? Why or why not? *Students should respond that the painting would not be as effective, because the gloominess of the forest setting gives the scene its sinister quality.*

Customize for *Visual/Spatial Learners*

Encourage these students to take some time to study the details in the painting. What does the painting reveal about the story's setting? What does it reveal about the main character? *Students should note that the painting highlights the dark, wooded setting where Tom Walker first meets the devil. They may also point out that the painting reveals the clothing worn during the time of the story and that Walker's physical appearance in the painting fits in with the personality faults that make him an unsympathetic character.*

▶Critical Viewing◀

2 **Analyze** The gloomy lighting and sinister setting reflect the mood of the story, particularly the scenes set in the swamp. Students may note that, while Tom is brightly lit, the Devil is in the shadows, symbolizing his association with "the dark side."

◆Critical Thinking

3 **Analyze** Why might Irving have included this detail about earthquakes? What does it suggest? *Students may reply that this detail ties the story to an actual date. Others may note that earthquakes suggest that something turbulent, disturbing, or unnatural may have been happening at that time.*

4 **Clarification** A gridiron is a grill, a framework of metal bars on which food can be cooked. Students may be more familiar with the term as it applies to a football field.

Tips to Guide Reading

Sustained Reading To help their understanding, tell students to read silently, stopping every few paragraphs to summarize what they have just read. Remind them that to summarize they should state the main idea in their own words and should include only the most important information. Suggest that students continue reading the selection using this self-monitoring strategy.

Comprehension Check ☑

Ask students to summarize what they have learned about the Walkers. *They are miserly, mean-spirited people who are too cheap even to take proper care of their own home, property, or horse.*

◆ Critical Thinking

❶ **Evaluate** Ask students if they agree with the idea that most shortcuts are ill chosen. You might point out that in this statement about the swamp, Irving echoes the Puritan ethic of valuing hard work and dismissing attempts to cut corners.

◆ Grammar and Style

❷ **Adjective Clauses** Have students identify the adjective clause in this sentence. *"which ran out like a peninsula into the deep bosom of the swamp"*

◆ Literary Focus

❸ **Omniscient Narrator** Here the narrator provides insights into contemporary feelings about the fort and its environs. The narrator also reveals colonists' attitudes toward Native Americans who inhabited the spot.

◆ Reading Strategy

❹ **Infer Cultural Attitudes** These passages reveal that the colonists thought the Native Americans to be warlike savages who practiced unholy religious ceremonies characterized by magical chants and sacrifice. The colonial Americans' attitudes reveal their lack of understanding of or respect for Native American ways and beliefs.

Extending Word Study

Context Clues Point out the word *impregnable* at the top of the second column on p. 238. Ask students to figure out its meaning from context. Tell them that sometimes they need to look in surrounding sentences for context clues. Guide students to recognize that phrases, such as "a stronghold for the Indians in their wars," "a kind of fort," and "used as a place of refuge for squaws and children" all convey that *impregnable* means "firm" or "not capable of being captured."

a field, where a thin carpet of moss, scarcely covering the ragged beds of puddingstone, tantalized and balked his hunger; and sometimes he would lean his head over the fence, look piteously at the passerby, and seem to petition deliverance from this land of famine.

The house and its inmates had altogether a bad name. Tom's wife was a tall termagant,[2] fierce of temper, loud of tongue, and strong of arm. Her voice was often heard in wordy warfare with her husband; and his face sometimes showed signs that their conflicts were not confined to words. No one ventured, however, to interfere between them. The lonely wayfarer shrunk within himself at the horrid clamor and clapperclawing;[3] eyed the den of discord askance; and hurried on his way, rejoicing, if a bachelor, in his celibacy.

One day that Tom Walker had been to a distant part of the neighborhood, he took what he considered a shortcut homeward, ❶ through the swamp. Like most shortcuts, it was an ill-chosen route. The swamp was thickly grown with great gloomy pines and hemlocks, some of them ninety feet high, which made it dark at noonday, and a retreat for all the owls of the neighborhood. It was full of pits and quagmires, partly covered with weeds and mosses, where the green surface often betrayed the traveler into a gulf of black, smothering mud; there were also dark and stagnant pools, the abodes of the tadpole, the bullfrog, and the watersnake; where the trunks of pines and hemlocks lay half-drowned, half-rotting, looking like alligators sleeping in the mire.

Tom had long been picking his way cautiously through this treacherous forest; stepping from tuft to tuft of rushes and roots, which afforded precarious footholds among deep sloughs; or pacing carefully, like a cat, along the prostrate trunks of trees; startled now and then by the sudden screaming of the bittern, or the quacking of a wild duck, rising on the wing from some solitary pool.

At length he arrived at a piece of firm ground, which ran out like a peninsula into the deep bosom of the swamp. ❷ It had been one of the strongholds of the Indians during their wars with the first colonists. Here they had thrown up a kind of fort, which they had looked upon as almost impregnable, and had used as a place of refuge for their squaws and children. Nothing remained of the old Indian fort but a few embankments, gradually sinking to the level of the surrounding earth, and already overgrown in part by oaks and other forest trees, the foliage of which formed a contrast to the dark pines and hemlocks of the swamp.

It was late in the dusk of evening when Tom Walker reached the old fort, and he paused there awhile to rest himself. Anyone but he would have felt unwilling to linger in this lonely, melancholy place, for the ❸ common people had a bad opinion of it, from the stories handed down from the time of the Indian wars; when it was asserted that the savages held incantations here, and made sacrifices to the evil spirit.

Tom Walker, however, was not a man to be troubled with any fears of the kind. He reposed himself for some time on the trunk of a fallen hemlock, listening to the boding cry of the tree toad, and delving with his walking staff into a mound of black mold at his feet. As he turned up the soil unconsciously, his staff struck against something hard. He raked it out of the vegetable mold, and lo! a cloven skull, with an Indian tomahawk buried deep in it, lay before him. The rust on the weapon showed the time that had elapsed since this deathblow had been given. It was a dreary memento of the fierce struggle that had taken place in this last foothold of the Indian warriors. ❹

> **◆ Reading Strategy** What do these sentences tell you about the **colonists' attitude** toward Native Americans?

"Humph!" said Tom Walker, as he gave it a kick to shake the dirt from it.

"Let that skull alone!" said a gruff voice. Tom lifted up his eyes, and beheld a great black man seated directly opposite him, on

2. **termagant** (tur´ mə gənt) *n.*: Quarrelsome woman.
3. **clapperclawing** (klap´ ər klô´ iŋ) *n.*: Clawing or scratching.

Cross-Curricular Connection: Social Studies

The Massachusetts Bay Colony The Puritans obtained a royal charter and established the Massachusetts Bay Colony in the Boston area in 1629. The successful colony grew and expanded into Massachusetts and Connecticut. The new settlers soon began creating the lives they wanted without interference from England. However, they had to contend with Native Americans already living in the region, whom they regarded as obstacles to progress. The Puritans and the Native Americans had lifestyles that contrasted dramatically.

Have interested students find out more about the key ways in which the Native American lifestyle differed from that of the Puritans, and about the effects of those differences. Have them find out about how the English settlers both cooperated and clashed with the Pequot and Narragansett nations.

the stump of a tree. He was exceedingly surprised, having neither heard nor seen anyone approach; and he was still more perplexed on observing, as well as the gathering gloom would permit, that the stranger was neither Negro nor Indian. It is true he was dressed in a rude half-Indian garb, and had a red belt or sash swathed round his body; but his face was neither black nor copper
5 color, but swarthy and dingy, and begrimed
6 with soot, as if he had been accustomed to toil among fires and forges. He had a shock of coarse black hair, that stood out from his head in all directions, and bore an ax on his shoulder.

He scowled for a moment at Tom with a pair of great red eyes.

"What are you doing on my grounds?" said the black man, with a hoarse growling voice.

"Your grounds!" said Tom with a sneer, "no more your grounds than mine; they belong to Deacon Peabody."

"Deacon Peabody be d—d," said the stranger, "as I flatter myself he will be, if he does not look more to his own sins and less to those of his neighbors. Look yonder, and see how Deacon Peabody is faring."

Tom looked in the direction that the stranger pointed, and beheld one of the great trees, fair and flourishing without, but rotten at the core, and saw that it had been nearly hewn through, so that the first high wind was likely to blow it down. On the bark of the tree was scored the name of Deacon Peabody, an eminent man, who had waxed wealthy by driving shrewd bargains with the
7 Indians. He now looked round, and found most of the tall trees marked with the name of some great man of the colony, and all more or less scored by the ax. The one on which he had been seated, and which had evidently just been hewn down, bore the name of Crowninshield: and he recollected a mighty rich man of that name, who made a vulgar display of wealth, which it was whispered he had acquired by buccaneering.

"He's just ready for burning!" said the black man, with a growl of triumph. "You see I am likely to have a good stock of firewood for winter."

"But what right have you," said Tom, "to cut down Deacon Peabody's timber?"

"The right of a prior claim," said the other. "This woodland belonged to me long before one of your white-faced race put foot upon the soil."

"And pray, who are you, if I may be so bold?" said Tom.

"Oh, I go by various names. I am the wild huntsman in some countries; the black miner in others. In this neighborhood I am known by the name of the black woodsman. I am he to whom the red men consecrated this spot, and in honor of whom they now and then roasted a white man, by way of sweet-smelling sacrifice. Since the red men have been exterminated by you white savages, I amuse myself by presiding at
the persecutions of Quakers and An- 8
abaptists;[4] I am the great patron and prompter of slave dealers, and the
grandmaster of the Salem witches." 9

"The upshot of all which is, that, if I mistake not," said Tom, sturdily, "you are he commonly called Old Scratch."

"The same, at your service!" replied the black man, with a half-civil nod.

Such was the opening of this interview, according to the old story; though it has almost too familiar an air to be credited. One would think that to meet with such a singular personage, in this wild, lonely place, would have shaken any man's nerves; but Tom was a hard-minded fellow, not easily daunted, and he had lived so long with a termagant wife, that he did not even fear the Devil.

It is said that after this commencement they had a long and earnest conversation together, as Tom returned homeward. The black man told him of great sums of money buried by Kidd the pirate, under the oak trees on the high ridge, not far from the morass. All

4. **Quakers and Anabaptists:** Two religious groups that were persecuted for their beliefs.

Walking stick, King Georges County, Virginia, 1846, Abby Aldrich Rockefeller Folk Art Center, Williamsburg, Virginia

Customize for
AP Students

❺ Ask students to identify the traditional symbols that mark this creature as the devil. They can, for example, point to the swarthiness, the soot from the fires of hell, and the red eyes. Have them suggest other physical features by which the devil is represented in literature and in art.

Customize for
Less Proficient Readers
English Language Learners
Visual/Spatial Learners

❻ To clarify students' understanding, ask them to draw the creature described in this passage. Use their sketches to assess their comprehension of key visual details.

❼ **Enrichment** Washington Irving is satirizing the hypocrisy of those Puritans who used their prominence to amass wealth. The early eighteenth century was a time when many colonists were beginning to replace Puritanism with a philosophy of commercialism and capitalism.

◆ Background for Understanding

❽ **History** The Quakers were an innovative religious sect. In addition to holding unorthodox views, Quakers believed in pacifism, justice, charity, and spiritual equality for all, including Native Americans. For these beliefs, they were persecuted in the Massachusetts Bay Colony, where four were executed. In Pennsylvania, however, they prospered. The Anabaptists were reformers who were persecuted for their opposition of oath taking, infant baptism, military service, and the holding of public office.

❾ **Clarification** The Salem witch trials took place in the same locale in the 1690's, scarcely thirty years before the time of this tale.

Viewing and Representing Mini-Lesson

This mini-lesson supports the Board Game activity in the Idea Bank on p. 247.

Introduce the Concept Tell students that to create a board game, they will need to consider the following: the requirements for winning, the game strategy, a complete set of directions and rules, game pieces (cards, dice, moving pieces), and the design of the game board.

Develop Background Divide students into small groups. Have each group generate ideas for their game, keeping in mind that the purpose is to teach the consequences of greed. Remind students that the game is for younger students so it should not be too complicated.

Apply the Information Tell students to jot down a basic set of rules, and draw a preliminary sketch of the board. They should assign tasks to the various members of the group. Tell students to play their game and make any necessary revisions before they present it to the class.

Assess the Outcome Assess students' work on their ability to work cooperatively, write a clear set of rules and directions, and target a young audience. You might distribute to students the Peer Assessment form for How-to/Process Explanation, p. 115 in ***Alternative Assessment.***

▶Critical Viewing◀

❶ **Support** Students should note that the teapot appears to be made of a metal such as silver or pewter, both of which were relatively rare and costly for country folk like the Walkers. You might also point out that, at that time, such an item was handcrafted, which also added to its value.

◆Critical Thinking

❷ **Speculate** Have students consider the fate of Mr. Crowninshield. Ask them if they think he, too, had dealings with Old Scratch.

◆Literary Focus

❸ **Omniscient Narrator** Point out that in this paragraph the narrator reveals both Tom's thoughts and his wife's attitudes. Ask them what they learn here about their relationship. *Students should respond that both were selfish and untrusting and that neither had any interest in pleasing the other.*

◆Literary Focus

❹ **Omniscient Narrator** The narrator reveals that Tom's wife will stop at nothing when money is at stake and that she would not hesitate to betray her husband.

---

these were under his command, and protected by his power, so that none could find them but such as propitiated his favor. These he offered to place within Tom Walker's reach, having conceived an especial kindness for him; but they were to be had only on certain conditions. What these conditions were may easily be surmised, though Tom never disclosed them publicly. They must have been very hard, for he required time to think of them, and he was not a man to stick at trifles where money was in view. When they had reached the edge of the swamp, the stranger paused— "What proof have I that all you have been telling me is true?" said Tom. "There is my signature," said the black man, pressing his finger on Tom's forehead. So saying, he turned off among the thickets of the swamp, and seemed, as Tom said, to go down, down, down, into the earth, until nothing but his head and shoulders could be seen, and so on, until he totally disappeared.

When Tom reached home, he found the black print of a finger, burnt, as it were, into his forehead, which nothing could obliterate.

❷ The first news his wife had to tell him was the sudden death of Absalom Crowninshield, the rich buccaneer. It was announced in the papers with the usual flourish, that "A great man had fallen in Israel."[5]

Tom recollected the tree which his black friend had just hewn down, and which was ready for burning, "Let the freebooter roast," said Tom, "who cares!" He now felt convinced that all he had heard and seen was no illusion. ❷

❸ He was not prone to let his wife into his confidence; but as this was an uneasy secret, he willingly shared it with her. All her <u>avarice</u> was awakened at the mention of hidden gold, and she urged her husband to comply with the black man's terms and secure what would make them wealthy for life. However Tom might have felt disposed to sell himself to the Devil, he was determined not to do so to oblige his wife; so he flatly refused, out of the mere spirit of contradiction. Many and bitter were the quarrels they had on the subject, but the more she talked, the more resolute was Tom not to be damned to please her.

❹ At length she determined to drive the bargain on her own account, and if she succeeded, to keep all the gain to herself. Being of the same fearless temper as her husband, she set off for the old Indian fort towards the close of a summer's day. She was many hours absent. When she came back, she was reserved and sullen in her replies. She spoke something of a black man, whom she had met about twilight, hewing at

❶ ▲ **Critical Viewing** On page 241, Tom Walker's wife packs up her valuables to take into the forest. Why might a teapot like this one be considered valuable? **[Support]**

Teapot, Yale University Art Gallery, New Haven

◆ Literary Focus
What does the narrator reveal about Tom's wife here?

5. **A . . . Israel:** A reference to II Samuel 3:38 in the Bible. The Puritans often called New England "Israel."

◆ Build Vocabulary

avarice (av′ ər is) *n.*: Greed

Cultural Connection

"The Devil" Across Cultures In legend and literature, from the Bible to modern fiction, the character of the devil has appeared in many guises and under many names. Examples include Beelzebub, Mephistopheles, Satan, and Lucifer, among others.

Although the devil is a Judeo-Christian creation, a pact with the devil is a common theme in the folklore of many cultures. Though evil incarnate may go by different names, most cultures have their own tales about human encounters with an embodiment of evil. For some Native Americans, evil enters this world as a creature that can change shapes and sizes at will. For example, Native American heroes from many groups have had to contend with the water monster, known as Unktehi in Nebraska and the Dakotas. Others fear No Body, the Great Rolling Head of the prairies and mountains.

Have interested students research how different cultures view evil, and read tales of confrontations between good and evil.

the root of a tall tree. He was sulky, however, and would not come to terms: she was to go again with a propitiatory offering, but what it was she forbore to say.

The next evening she set off again for the swamp, with her apron heavily laden. Tom waited and waited for her, but in vain; midnight came, but she did not make her appearance: morning, noon, night returned, but still she did not come. Tom now grew uneasy for her safety, especially as he found she had carried off in her apron the silver teapot and spoons, and every portable article of value. Another night elapsed, another morning came; but no wife. In a word, she was never heard of more.

What was her real fate nobody knows, in consequence of so many pretending to know. It is one of those facts which have become confounded by a variety of historians. Some asserted that she lost her way among the tangled mazes of the swamp, and sank into some pit or slough; others, more uncharitable, hinted that she had eloped with the household booty, and made off to
5 some other province; while others surmised that the tempter had decoyed her into a dismal quagmire, on the top of which her hat was found lying. In confirmation of this, it was said a great black man, with an ax on his shoulder, was seen late that very evening coming out of the swamp, carrying a bundle tied in a checked apron, with an air of surly triumph.

The most current and probable story, however, observes that Tom Walker grew so anxious about the fate of his wife and his property, that he set out at length to seek them both at the Indian fort. During a long summer's afternoon he searched about the gloomy place, but no wife was to be seen. He called her name repeatedly, but she was nowhere to be heard. The bittern alone responded to his voice, as he flew screaming by; or the bullfrog croaked dolefully from a neighboring pool. At length, it is said, just in the brown hour of twilight, when the owls began to hoot, and the bats to flit about, his attention was attracted by the clamor of carrion crows hovering about a cypress tree. He looked up, and beheld a bundle tied in a checked apron, and hanging in the branches of the tree, with a great vulture perched hard by, as if keeping watch upon it. He leaped with joy; for he recognized his wife's apron, and supposed it to contain the household valuables. 7

"Let us get hold of the property," said he, consolingly to himself, "and we will

6 ▶ **Critical Viewing** The narrator describes "a great vulture perched hard by" and a checked apron hanging in the tree. What do you think happened to Tom Walker's wife? **[Infer]**

Customize for
Visual/Spatial Learners

Urge these students to use the photographs on this page to help them visualize what is happening in the story. How does seeing a photograph of a vulture add to their appreciation of what Irving describes? *Students may note that the vulture's intimidating appearance adds emphasis to the disturbing turn of events in the story.*

◆ Reading Strategy

5 Infer Cultural Attitudes
Students can recognize that people gossiped then, as now. Discuss how the historians' explanations covered a wide realm of possibilities. Discuss how these explanations suggest confrontations between good and evil.

▶Critical Viewing◀

6 Infer Students can surmise that she is dead because her apron is guarded by a vulture, a symbol of death.

◆ Critical Thinking

7 Criticize Have students talk about the kind of person they think Tom Walker is. *Students may say that Walker's greed is far more consuming than love or concern for his wife. Upon seeing his wife's apron, his first reaction is joy. When he realizes that it might contain valuables, her demise no longer matters to him.*

Research Skills Mini-Lesson

Using Library Databases This mini-lesson supports the Exhibition activity in the Idea Bank on p. 247.

Introduce the Concept Tell students that they will be creating an exhibition around a variety of interpretations of the Faust legend. In gathering information for their research, they will need to consult a number of print and nonprint resources, including library databases and the Internet.

Develop Background Suggest that students begin by searching the library database for "Faust." They should also search for Faust under categories, such as drama, opera, and musicals. Explain that the library database gives them the same information as a library card catalog, but this search method is faster and yields more information.

Apply the Information After gathering a list of references from the database, have students begin checking the source materials to learn about Faust productions in other media—plays, operas, or Broadway musicals. Have them check the library for CDs or videos of these performances.

Assess the Outcome Assess students' work on their ability to use a library database to gather research information. You might have students use the Peer Assessment form for Research Report/Paper, p. 121 in ***Alternative Assessment.***

◆ Literary Focus

❶ Omniscient Narrator Students can say that the narrator makes it clear that Tom feels no grief for the loss of his wife; it is his property that he longs for.

Customize for
Less Proficient Readers
❷ Guide students to understand that here Irving points out that the devil embodies a range of bad qualities, that he is sly and manipulative.

◆ Critical Thinking

❸ Speculate Ask students to explain the one condition that "need not be mentioned." *Students can say that any deal one makes with the devil includes the condition that one's soul belongs to him. Or they might suggest that the one condition is that there's no turning back once a deal is struck.*

❹ Enrichment Point out that this opinion of slave trading does not so much reflect the mores of eighteenth-century colonists as it does the abolitionist sentiments of Washington Irving and his northern contemporaries. By 1824, antislavery attitudes were widespread and the abolitionist movement had grown strong in the Northeast.

◆ Reading Strategy

❺ Infer Cultural Attitudes Have students talk about what this discussion tells them about colonial attitudes toward brokers and usurers. *Students can say that colonists frowned on these trades, considering them the work of the devil.*

endeavor to do without the woman."

As he scrambled up the tree, the vulture spread its wide wings, and sailed off screaming into the deep shadows of the forest. Tom seized the checked apron, but woeful sight! found nothing but a heart and liver tied up in it!

Such, according to the most authentic old story, was all that was to be found of Tom's wife. She had probably attempted to deal with the black man as she had been accustomed to deal with her husband; but though a female scold is generally considered a match for the Devil, yet in this instance she appears to have had the worst of it. She must have died game, however; for it is said Tom noticed many prints of cloven feet deeply stamped about the tree, and found handfuls of hair, that looked as if they had been plucked from the coarse black shock of the woodsman. Tom knew his wife's prowess by experience. He shrugged his shoulders, as he looked at the signs of a fierce clapper-clawing. "Egad," said he to himself, "Old Scratch must have had a tough time of it!"

> **◆ Literary Focus**
> What does the narrator reveal about Tom's feelings here?

❶ Tom consoled himself for the loss of his property, with the loss of his wife, for he was a man of fortitude. He even felt something like gratitude towards the black woodsman, who, he considered, had done him a kindness. ❷ He sought, therefore, to cultivate a further acquaintance with him, but for some time without success; the old black-legs played shy, for whatever people may think, he is not always to be had for calling for: he knows how to play his cards when pretty sure of his game.

At length, it is said, when delay had whetted Tom's eagerness to the quick, and prepared him to agree to anything rather than not gain the promised treasure, he met the black man one evening in his usual woodsman's dress, with his ax on his shoulder, sauntering along the swamp, and humming a tune. He affected to receive Tom's advances with great indifference, made brief replies, and went on humming his tune.

By degrees, however, Tom brought him to business, and they began to haggle about the terms on which the former was to have the pirate's treasure. ❸ There was one condition which need not be mentioned, being generally understood in all cases where the Devil grants favors; but there were others about which, though of less importance, he was inflexibly obstinate. He insisted that the money found through his means should be employed in his service. ❹ He proposed, therefore, that Tom should employ it in the black traffic; that is to say, that he should fit out a slave ship. This, however, Tom resolutely refused: he was bad enough in all conscience, but the Devil himself could not tempt him to turn slave-trader.

Finding Tom so squeamish on this point, he did not insist upon it, but proposed, instead, ❺ that he should turn usurer; the Devil being extremely anxious for the increase of usurers, looking upon them as his peculiar[6] people.

To this no objections were made, for it was just to Tom's taste.

"You shall open a broker's shop in Boston next month," said the black man.

"I'll do it tomorrow, if you wish," said Tom Walker.

"You shall lend money at two per cent a month."

"Egad, I'll charge four!" replied Tom Walker.

"You shall extort bonds, foreclose mortgages, drive the merchant to bankruptcy—"

6. **peculiar:** Particular; special.

Beyond the Classroom

Career Connection

Loan Officer Discuss with students that although usury is still practiced illegally, the legitimate financial services industry has a useful purpose and its loan practices are strictly monitored. Banks and other institutions loan money to businesses and individuals for home mortgages, cars, tuition, renovations, and other large purchases. Rates for various loans may fluctuate within established guidelines, but are regulated by federal and state law.

Loan officers work for money-lending institutions. Their job is to determine whether applicants meet the qualifications for loans requested. For those interested in working as a loan officer, a college degree is usually helpful, though not always necessary; many loan officers start their careers as bank tellers or clerks, positions that do not generally require a college education.

Invite students to interview people who work in that capacity or in related jobs, such as mortgage broker or financial planner. Prompt students to ask what a day in their business life is like. Have them learn what loan officers look for in reviewing applicants. Encourage them to explore how different lending rates are set and what factors cause them to change.

"I'll drive him to the D——l," cried Tom Walker.

5 "You are the usurer for my money!" said the blacklegs with delight. "When will you want the rhino?"[7]

"This very night."

"Done!" said the Devil.

"Done!" said Tom Walker. So they shook hands and struck a bargain.

A few days' time saw Tom Walker seated behind his desk in a countinghouse in Boston.

His reputation for a ready-moneyed man, who would lend money out for a good consideration, soon spread abroad. Everybody remembers the time of Governor Belcher,[8] when money was particularly scarce. It was a time of paper credit. The country had been deluged with government bills; the famous Land Bank[9] had been established; there had been a rage for speculating; the people had run mad with schemes for new settlements, for building cities in the wilderness; land jobbers[10] went about with maps of grants, and townships, and El Dorados,[11] lying nobody knew where, but which everybody was ready to purchase. In a word, the great speculating fever which breaks out every now and then in the country, had raged to an alarming degree, and everybody was dreaming of making sudden fortunes from nothing. As usual the fever had subsided; the dream had gone off, and the imaginary fortunes with it; the patients were left in doleful plight, and the whole country resounded with the consequent cry of "hard times."

At this propitious time of public distress did Tom Walker set up as usurer in Boston. His door was soon thronged by customers. The needy and adventurous, the gambling speculator, the dreaming land jobber, the thriftless tradesman, the merchant with cracked credit, in short, everyone driven to raise money by desperate means and desperate sacrifices, hurried to Tom Walker.

Thus Tom was the universal friend of the needy, and acted like a "friend in need"; that 6 is to say, he always exacted good pay and good security. In proportion to the distress of the applicant was the hardness of his terms. 7 He accumulated bonds and mortgages; gradually squeezed his customers closer and closer, and sent them at length, dry as a sponge, from his door.

In this way he made money hand over hand, became a rich and mighty man, and exalted his cocked hat upon 'Change.[12] He built himself, as usual, a vast house, out of ostentation; but left the greater part of it unfinished and unfurnished, out of parsimony. He even set up a carriage in the fullness of his vainglory, though he nearly starved the horses which drew it; and as the ungreased wheels groaned and screeched on the axletrees, you would have thought you heard the souls of the poor debtors he was squeezing.

> ◆ **Reading Strategy** What can you infer about the attitudes of the day toward money? 8

As Tom waxed old, however, he grew thoughtful. Having secured the good things of this world, he began to feel anxious about those of the next. He thought with regret on the bargain he had made with his black 9 friend, and set his wits to work to cheat him out of the conditions. He became, therefore, all of a sudden, a violent churchgoer. He prayed loudly and strenuously, as if heaven

7. **rhino** (rī′nō): Slang term for money.

8. **Governor Belcher:** Jonathan Belcher, the governor of Massachusetts Bay Colony from 1730 through 1741.

9. **Land Bank:** A bank that financed transactions in real estate.

10. **land jobbers:** People who bought and sold undeveloped land.

11. **El Dorados** (el də rä′ dōz) *n.*: Places that are rich in gold or opportunity. El Dorado was a legendary country in South America sought by early Spanish explorers for its gold and precious stones.

12. **'Change:** Exchange where bankers and merchants did business.

◆ Build Vocabulary

usurers (yo͞o′ zho͞o rərz) *n.*: Moneylenders who charge very high interest

extort (eks tôrt′) *v.*: To obtain by threat or violence

ostentation (äs′ tən tā′ shən) *n.*: Boastful display

parsimony (pär′ sə mō′ nē) *n.*: Stinginess

◆ Build Vocabulary

6 Prefixes: *ex-* Have students notice the two words in this passage that begin with the prefix *ex-*. Guide them to use their grasp of the meaning of *ex-* and context clues to ascertain the meanings of the words *exacted* and *exalted*. Invite them to use a dictionary to check their answers.

Comprehension Check ☑

7 Ask students to explain the meaning of this sentence. *The more desperate the loan applicant, the more interest and security Tom demands.*

◆ Reading Strategy

8 Infer Cultural Attitudes
Students can infer that the colonists prized wealth and, if they had it, they did not mind displaying evidence of it.

Customize for *Interpersonal Learners*

9 Tom has second thoughts about the bargain he made and fears the upcoming consequences. Ask students to predict whether his efforts at religious zeal will have any effect on his future.

Beyond the Classroom

Community Connection

Help for the Needy Near the end of the story one of Tom's customers, unable to pay his debt, pleads, "My family will be ruined and brought upon the parish." Have students find out what religious and charitable institutions in your area offer help to those in need. Discuss the types of programs that are available to the homeless, the housebound or ill, the lonely, the elderly, those with special needs, etc.

Have students talk with local clergy or administrators to learn specifically what assistance churches, temples, mosques, and other charitable organizations provide to the community. Suggest that students develop their own way of helping those in need within the community; perhaps students could hold a car wash to raise funds for a local shelter or volunteer at a church soup kitchen. Interested students can do research to find out how the services that today's institutions offer compare with aid given in colonial times.

◆ Literary Focus

❶ **Omniscient Narrator** Students can say that by identifying the story as a legend, the narrator accepts no responsibility for the accuracy of its retelling and acknowledges the possibility of other interpretations.

◆ Critical Thinking

❷ **Interpret** Ask students to explain what the landjobber means when he says he will be "brought upon the parish." *He will be forced to depend on charity from the parish church in order to survive.*

❸ **Clarification** A farthing was the smallest British monetary unit, equal to about a fourth of a cent.

Customize for *AP Students*

❹ Ask students to identify the scary details in the description of Tom's capture and contrast them with those that are sardonic. *Scary: The Devil whisked him onto his saddle and galloped away in the midst of a thunderstorm; his steed struck fire from the pavement. Sardonic: The details about the whereabouts of his Bibles; the idea that he was "taken unawares"; the clerks' sticking their pens behind their ears as they watched the spectacle; his cap and gown fluttering in the wind.*

◆ Critical Thinking

❺ **Generalize** Ask students to explain the moral of the story of Tom Walker. *Some may say that people should be wary of ill-gotten wealth, or of making agreements that exact too high a price.*

were to be taken by force of lungs. Indeed, one might always tell when he had sinned most during the week, by the clamor of his Sunday devotion. The quiet Christians who had been modestly and steadfastly traveling Zionward,[13] were struck with self-reproach at seeing themselves so suddenly outstripped in their career by this new-made convert. Tom was as rigid in religious as in money matters; he was a stern supervisor and censurer of his neighbors, and seemed to think every sin entered up to their account became a credit on his own side of the page. He even talked of the expediency of reviving the persecution of Quakers and Anabaptists. In a word, Tom's zeal became as notorious as his riches.

Still, in spite of all this strenuous attention to forms, Tom had a lurking dread that the Devil, after all, would have his due. That he might not be taken unawares, therefore, it is said he always carried a small Bible in his coat pocket. He had also a great folio Bible on his countinghouse desk, and would frequently be found reading it when people called on business; on such occasions he would lay his green spectacles in the book, to mark the place, while he turned round to drive some usurious bargain.

Some say that Tom grew a little crack-brained in his old days, and that fancying his end approaching, he had his horse newly shod, saddled and bridled, and buried with his feet uppermost; because he supposed that at the last day the world would be turned upside down, in which case he should find his horse standing ready for mounting, and he was determined at the worst to give his old friend a run for it. This, however, is probably a mere old wives' fable. If he really did take such a precaution, it was totally superfluous; at least so says the authentic old legend, which closes his story in the following manner.

> **◆ Literary Focus** ❶
> How does the word *legend* distance the narrator from the story?

One hot summer afternoon in the dog days, just as a terrible black thunder-gust was coming up, Tom sat in his countinghouse in his white linen cap and India silk morning gown. He was on the point of foreclosing a mortgage, by which he would complete the ruin of an unlucky land speculator for whom he had professed the greatest friendship. The poor land jobber begged him to grant a few months' indulgence. Tom had grown testy and irritated, and refused another day.

"My family will be ruined and brought upon the parish," said the land jobber. "Charity begins at home," replied Tom; "I must take care of myself in these hard times." ❷

"You have made so much money out of me," said the speculator.

Tom lost his patience and his piety— "The Devil take me," said he, "if I have made a farthing!" ❸

Just then there were three loud knocks at the street door. He stepped out to see who was there. A black man was holding a black horse, which neighed and stamped with impatience.

"Tom, you're come for," said the black fellow, gruffly. Tom shrunk back, but too late. He had left his little Bible at the bottom of his coat pocket, and his big Bible on the desk buried under the mortgage he was about to foreclose: never was sinner taken more unawares. The black man whisked him like a child into the saddle, gave the horse the lash, and away he galloped, with Tom on his back, in the midst of the thunderstorm. ❹ The clerks stuck their pens behind their ears, and stared after him from the windows. Away went Tom Walker, dashing down the streets, his white cap bobbing up and down, his morning gown fluttering in the wind, and his steed striking fire out of the pavement at every bound. When the clerks turned to look for the black man he had disappeared.

Tom Walker never returned to foreclose the mortgage. A countryman who lived on the border of the swamp, reported that in the height of the thunder-gust he had heard a great clattering of hoofs and a howling along the road, and running to the window caught sight of a figure, such as I have described, on a horse that galloped like mad across the fields, over the hills and down into the black

13. **Zionward** (zī´ ən wôrd): Toward heaven.

Reteach

Use a visual representation like the one shown to help students understand an omniscient narrator who reveals the thoughts and feelings of many characters and presents many points of view.

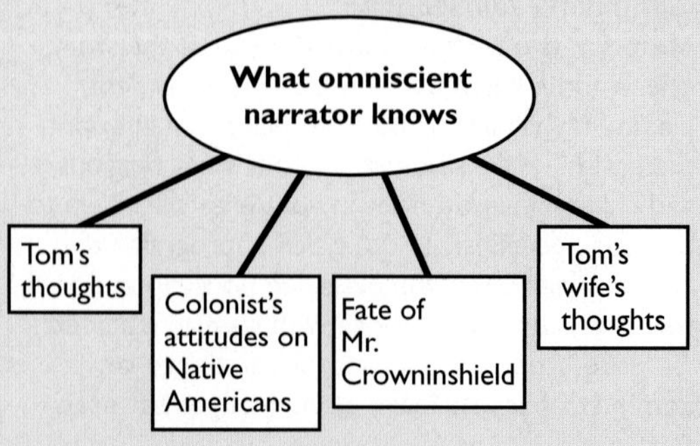

hemlock swamp towards the old Indian fort; and that shortly after a thunderbolt falling in that direction seemed to set the whole forest in a blaze.

The good people of Boston shook their heads and shrugged their shoulders, but had been so much accustomed to witches and goblins and tricks of the Devil, in all kind of shapes from the first settlement of the colony, that they were not so much horror struck as
5 might have been expected. Trustees were appointed to take charge of Tom's effects. There was nothing, however, to administer upon. On searching his coffers all his bonds and mortgages were found reduced to cinders. In place of gold and silver his iron chest was filled with chips and shavings; two skeletons lay in his stable instead of his half-starved horses, and the very next day his great house 5
took fire and was burned to the ground.

Such was the end of Tom Walker and his ill-gotten wealth. Let all griping money brokers lay this story to heart. The truth of it is not to be doubted. The very hole under the oak trees, whence he dug Kidd's money, is to be seen to this day; and the neighboring swamp and old Indian fort are often haunted in stormy nights by a figure on horseback, in morning gown and white cap, which is doubtless the troubled spirit of the usurer. In fact, the story has resolved itself into a proverb, and is the origin of that popular saying, so prevalent throughout New England, of "The Devil and Tom Walker."

Guide for Responding

◆ Literature and Your Life

Reader's Response Do you feel that Tom Walker deserves his fate? Why or why not?

Thematic Focus In what ways is this tale distinctly American?

Group Activity Stories abound in which the main character learns that an agreement he makes comes with an unexpectedly high price. With a small group, brainstorm for three other examples of characters in films who learn a similar lesson. Then contrast your choices with those of Tom Walker.

☑ Check Your Comprehension

1. Describe Tom Walker's first encounter with the Devil.
2. Explain why Tom does not, at first, agree to make a bargain with the Devil.
3. Describe Tom's reaction to the loss of his wife.
4. (a) What is the agreement that Tom Walker ultimately makes with the Devil? (b) What does he do when he begins to regret his agreement?

◆ Critical Thinking

INTERPRET

1. What does the description of their house and horse indicate about the Walkers? **[Infer]**
2. What details in the story indicate that Tom's nature remains the same although his condition changes? **[Support]**
3. (a) What does Irving mean when he says that Tom became a "*violent* churchgoer"? (b) How is Tom's approach to religion similar to his approach to financial dealings? **[Interpret]**
4. What is the lesson Irving wants his readers to learn from this story? **[Draw Conclusions]**

EVALUATE

5. Tom Walker sells his soul for money. Would he have been a more sympathetic character if he had sold his soul for knowledge? **[Evaluate]**

EXTEND

6. How might a banker respond to Irving's implication that moneylenders are greedy? What would prevent Tom Walker from having a successful moneylending business today? **[Career Link]**

Beyond the Selection

FURTHER READING

Other Works by Washington Irving

Bracebridge Hall
The Alhambra
A Chronicle of the Conquest of Granada

Other Faust Legends

Doctor Faustus, Christopher Marlowe
Doktor Faustus, Thomas Mann
The Devil and Daniel Webster, Stephen Vincent Benét

We suggest that you preview these works before recommending them to students.

INTERNET

We suggest the following Internet site to help students learn more about Washington Irving. Please be aware, however, that sites may have changed since we published this information.

To learn more about Irving and his home, a national historic landmark, go to:
http://www.hudsonvalley.org/

We *strongly recommend* that you preview the site before you send students to it.

Reinforce and Extend

Customize for
Visual/Spatial Learners
Extend these students' learning with the Media Connection page on Narrative Point of View in ***Beyond Literature*** (p. 15).

Customize for
Less Proficient Readers
These students will benefit from rereading all or parts of the story and filling in any missing elements of their story timelines. In reviewing the story, prompt students to focus on specific elements, such as cultural attitudes, Tom Walker's attitudes, or the unique position of the omniscient narrator.

Answers

◆ Literature and Your Life

Reader's Response Students will probably respond that anyone who was willing to bargain with the devil deserves his fate.

Thematic Focus Suggested responses include the following: The setting; the portrayal of the devil as a woodsman; references to Native Americans, Quakers, Anabaptists, and the Salem witches; and the evidence of Puritan influences make the story distinctly American.

☑ Check Your Comprehension

1. Tom meets the Devil in a thickly wooded swamp. The Devil offers Tom the buried treasure of Captain Kidd "on certain conditions." Tom responds that he needs time to consider the conditions.
2. Tom wants to take time to think about the terms of the bargain.
3. He is more upset at the loss of his property.
4. (a) Tom agrees to sell his soul to the Devil and to use the treasure as a moneylender in the Devil's service. (b) He begins to read the Bible and becomes a "violent churchgoer" and a religious zealot.

Answers

◆ Critical Thinking

1. The description shows that the Walkers are too miserly and mean to care for their house and field or feed their horse.
2. Suggested response: He builds a vast house, but leaves it mostly unfurnished. He almost starves his carriage horses and leaves the carriage wheels ungreased.
3. (a) He means that Tom became loud and strenuous in his observance, particularly in his repentance. (b) He becomes a stern supervisor of the spiritual accounts of his neighbors and is willing to persecute other sects, just as he harasses his debtors.
4. Suggested response: He wants them to understand that there is no real way to gain from a bargain struck for the sake of greed.
5. Students should support their responses with a well-reasoned explanation.
6. A banker would probably object to Irving's implications. Today's bankers are employees of financial institutions and do not personally profit from lending; banking and lending are carefully regulated industries.

◆ Literary Focus

1. Suggested responses include: "Tom recollected the tree which his black friend had just hewn down. . . . He now felt convinced that all he had heard and seen was no illusion." "He was not prone to let his wife into his confidence; but as this was an uneasy secret, he willingly shared it with her." "However Tom might have felt disposed to sell himself to the Devil, he was determined not to do so to oblige his wife."
2. Suggested response: The narrator states that she decided to drive a bargain with the devil and to keep all the gain for herself.

◆ Build Vocabulary

Using the Latin Prefix ex-

1. b 2. d 3. a 4. e 5. c

Using the Word Bank

1. usurers; 2. extort; 3. parsimony; 4. ostentation; 5. avarice

Guide for Responding *(continued)*

◆ Literary Focus

Omniscient Narrator

Using an **omniscient** (all-knowing) **narrator** allows a writer to reveal the thoughts and feelings of many characters, thereby presenting events from more than one point of view. In this tale, Irving uses the voice of an informed storyteller who seems to be weaving the story from various reports he has gathered over time.

1. Give three examples of Tom Walker's thoughts or perspective on a situation in the story.
2. Find one place in the story where the narrator reveals the thoughts or unspoken plans of Tom Walker's wife.

◆ Build Vocabulary

Using the Latin Prefix *ex-*

Knowing that the Latin prefix *ex-* means "out" can help you determine the meaning of words with this prefix. For example, *extort* means "to squeeze out." On a separate sheet of paper, match words on the left from the story with their definitions on the right.

1. exceed	**a.** elevate; glorify
2. exact	**b.** go beyond normal limits
3. exalt	**c.** look out; look forward
4. expedite	**d.** wring; pry out
5. expect	**e.** speed up; hasten

Using the Word Bank: Sentence Completions

On a separate sheet of paper, write the word from the Word Bank that best completes each sentence.

1. We had borrowed money from __?__ who charged an excessive rate of interest.
2. He would __?__ money by threatening to harm victims if they did not pay.
3. Her __?__ led her to refuse to send for a doctor when she was ill.
4. The house was such a model of __?__ that visitors guessed about its excessive cost.
5. A main characteristic of Mrs. Walker's personality was __?__; she always wanted more than she had.

◆ Reading Strategy

Infer Cultural Attitudes

From the dialogue, the narrator's comments about the characters, and the outcome of events, you can **make inferences,** or draw conclusions, about some of the **cultural attitudes** of the people in New England in the 1720's. What inferences about cultural attitudes can you make from each of the following passages?

1. . . . the great speculating fever which breaks out every now and then in the country, had raged to an alarming degree, and everybody was dreaming of making sudden fortunes from nothing.
2. The quiet Christians who had been modestly and steadfastly traveling Zionward, were struck with self-reproach at seeing themselves so suddenly outstripped in their career by this new-made convert.

◆ Grammar and Style

Adjective Clauses

Adjective clauses are introduced with relative pronouns: *who* or *whom, whose, which,* or *that.*

An **adjective clause** is a subordinate clause that modifies a noun or pronoun.

Practice On your paper, write the adjective clause and the word it modifies in each of these sentences.

1. At length he arrived at a piece of firm ground, which ran out like a peninsula into the . . . deep bosom of the swamp.
2. His reputation for a ready-moneyed man, who would lend money out for a good consideration, soon spread abroad.
3. She spoke something of a black man, whom she had met about twilight, hewing at the root of a tall tree.
4. He had a shock of coarse black hair, that stood out from his head in all directions, and bore an ax on his shoulder.

◆ Reading Strategy

1. This suggests a change from the Puritan ethic of hard work and modest living to belief in the values of commercialism, large profits, and consumer expansionism.
2. New Englanders prided themselves on their humble piety and religious faith.

◆ Grammar and Style

1. "which ran out like a peninsula into the . . . deep bosom of the swamp" modifies *ground*
2. "who would lend money out for a good consideration" modifies *man*
3. "whom she had met about twilight, hewing at the root of a tall tree" modifies *man*
4. "that stood out from his head in all directions" modifies *hair*

Grammar Reinforcement

For additional instruction and practice, use the page on Adjective Clauses in the *Writer's Solution Grammar Practice Book*, p. 35.

Build Your Portfolio

Idea Bank

Writing

1. Correspondence As Tom Walker, write a letter to your niece shortly before the Devil comes to take you away. In it, warn your niece about the dangers of making a pact with the Devil.

2. Revised Ending What if Tom Walker's wife had also made a bargain with the Devil? Write a new ending to the story based on this idea.

3. Analysis A critic has said, "One of Washington Irving's great gifts to prose is his ability to find humor even in the most grotesque circumstances." In an essay, identify and discuss the effect of humorous elements in this story.

Speaking, Listening, and Viewing

4. Enactment Speculate about what happens when Mrs. Walker meets the Devil. Write and enact the scenes that might have taken place between the two. **[Performing Arts Link]**

5. Impromptu Speech Deliver an unrehearsed speech about the dangers of greed. Prepare by jotting down notes on your topic. Present your speech. Avoid reading directly from your notes. After finishing, discuss the experience of extemporaneous, or ad-libbed, speaking. **[Career Link]**

Researching and Representing

6. Board Game Create a board game to teach younger students about the consequences of greed and rash decisions. Present your game to classmates. **[Art Link]**

7. Exhibition The Faust legend has inspired plays, operas, and even a Broadway musical. Research these works, and create an exhibit about what you have learned. If possible, include tape recordings, CDs, and video excerpts of some of the performances. **[Media Link]**

Online Activity www.phlit.phschool.com

Guided Writing Lesson

Updating a Story

The message of Irving's story continues to be relevant. Create an updated version of the story, set in today's world with new plot events and character details, that conveys the story's message in a way that will appeal to a contemporary audience.

Writing Skills Focus: Appropriateness for Audience

As you develop your story, focus on using language and details that today's readers will find familiar and engaging. Notice that the vocabulary and syntax in this example from "The Devil and Tom Walker," which would have appealed to readers in Irving's day, now seems dated.

Model From the Story

"And pray, who are you, if I may be so bold?" said Tom.

In your updated version of the story, you'll probably want to have Tom Walker speak in a way that will appeal more to a contemporary audience. In addition, you'll want to keep your audience's interests and background in mind as you develop details of plot and setting.

Prewriting Outline the plot of the original story. Consider the best way to update each plot event you list. For example, instead of meeting in a forest, Tom Walker might run into the Devil at the mall.

Drafting Write your story. Have your characters speak, dress, and act in a way that makes it clear the story is set in modern times. Include references to food, clothes, and shows that are currently popular.

Revising Confirm that your draft balances the original elements and new details that update it. Check to see that the conflict and the message are the same, but that you have brought the language and setting into today's world.

Idea Bank

Customizing for *Performance Levels*

Following are suggestions for matching Idea Bank topics with your students' performance levels:
Less Advanced Students: 1, 4
Average Students: 2, 6, 7
More Advanced Students: 3, 5

Customizing for *Learning Modalities*

Following are suggestions for matching Idea Bank topics with your students' learning modalities:
Bodily/Kinesthetic: 4, 6
Verbal/Linguistic: 5
Logical/Mathematical: 6
Musical/Rhythmic: 7

Guided Writing Lesson

Writing and Language Transparencies

Aid Prewriting by using the Story Map Transparency, p. 99, to help students outline the plot of the original story.

For more prewriting, elaboration, and revision strategies, see *Prentice Hall Writing and Grammar.*

Writing Lab CD-ROM

Have students complete the tutorial on Response to Literature. Have students follow these steps:

1. Refer to the Audio-Annotated Literary Model of a retelling of a literary work in the About Response to Literature section.
2. Use the Chain of Events activity to gather plot details.
3. After drafting on the computer, use the appropriate portions of the Interactive Self-Evaluation Checklist to aid revision.

✓ ASSESSMENT OPTIONS

Formal Assessment, Selection Test, pp. 75–77, and Assessment Resources Software. The selection test is designed so that it can be easily customized to the performance levels of your students.

Alternative Assessment, p. 15, includes options for less advanced students, more advanced students, visual/spatial learners, musical/rhythmic learners, and bodily/kinesthetic learners.

PORTFOLIO ASSESSMENT

Use the following rubrics in the ***Alternative Assessment*** booklet to assess student writing:
Correspondence: Expression Rubric, p. 109
Revised Ending: Fictional Narrative Rubric, p. 110
Analysis: Literary Analysis/Interpretation Rubric, p. 127
Guided Writing Lesson: Fictional Narrative Rubric, p. 110

Prepare and Engage

LESSON OBJECTIVES

1. To develop vocabulary and word identification skills
- Latin Word Roots: *-face-*
- Using the Word Bank: Context

2. To use a variety of reading strategies to comprehend poems
- Connect Your Experience
- Reading Strategy: Associate Images With Life
- Read to Interpret (ATE)

3. To increase knowledge of other cultures and to connect common elements across cultures
- Connecting Themes Across Cultures (ATE)

4. To express and support responses to the text
- Critical Thinking
- Idea Bank: Epitaph
- Idea Bank: Essay
- Idea Bank: Graphic Display

5. To analyze literary elements
- Literary Focus: Stanza Forms
- Idea Bank: Personal Response
- Idea Bank: Performance

6. To plan, prepare, organize, and present literary interpretations
- Idea Bank: Audio Presentation/Discussion
- Idea Bank: Commencement Address
- Speaking, Listening, and Viewing Mini-Lesson (ATE)

7. To use recursive writing processes to write a credo
- Guided Writing Lesson

8. To increase knowledge of the rules of grammar and usage
- Grammar and Style: Inverted Word Order

Test Preparation

Reading Comprehension: Make Inferences and Generalizations (ATE, p. 249)

The teaching tips and sample test item in this workshop support the instruction and practice in the end of the unit workshop:

Reading Comprehension: Analyze Information to Make Inferences and Generalizations (SE, p. 427)

Guide for Interpreting

Henry Wadsworth Longfellow *(1807–1882)*

Henry Wadsworth Longfellow once wrote, "Music is the universal language of mankind—poetry their universal pastime and delight." During the latter half of the nineteenth century, Longfellow's poetry certainly was a "universal pastime and delight"; his work was translated into two dozen languages and read by millions.

The Teaching Years Longfellow was born and reared in Portland, Maine. He attended Bowdoin College, where one of his classmates was Nathaniel Hawthorne. After graduating in 1825, Longfellow spent three years in Europe before returning to Bowdoin as a professor of modern languages. He left the college after five years to spend another year in Europe before accepting a position at Harvard University, where he taught for eighteen years.

Tragedy Strikes Longfellow suffered the tragic deaths of two wives. His first wife, Mary, died in Europe in 1835 from an infection following a miscarriage. Eight years later, after a long courtship, Longfellow married Frances Appleton of Boston. Their happy marriage ended tragically when Frances was fatally burned in a household accident. Longfellow's attempts to beat out the flames left him badly burned. The resulting scars prevented him from shaving, and he grew the long, flowing beard so familiar to generations of his readers.

Poet to the People Longfellow enjoyed a long and successful career as a poet, publishing his first collection of poems, *Voices in the Night*, in 1839.

> ***By writing poetry that soothed and encouraged readers, Longfellow became the first American poet to reach a wide audience and create a national interest in poetry.***

He experimented with adapting traditional European verse forms and themes to American subjects. Many of his narrative poems, such as *Evangeline* (1847), *The Song of Hiawatha* (1855), *The Courtship of Miles Standish* (1858), and "Paul Revere's Ride" (1860), gave a romanticized view of America's early history and democratic ideals.

Longfellow's poetry has been criticized for being overly optimistic and sentimental. Yet it was Longfellow's optimism and sentimentality that made him the most popular poet of his time. He became known as one of the "fireside poets," whose works were read by families gathered around the fireplace. Just as many of today's families are likely to gather around the television set to watch a favorite program, families of Longfellow's time would have spent evenings reading and discussing their favorite poems by Longfellow.

◆ Background for Understanding

LITERATURE: THE STORY BEHIND THESE POEMS

Longfellow wrote "A Psalm of Life" in 1838, after suffering through the tragic death of his first wife, Mary, coupled with the loss of the child the couple was expecting. Longfellow intended the poem as an inspiration to himself and others to overcome the misfortunes of the past and to live productively in the present.

"The Tide Rises, The Tide Falls" was penned when Longfellow was in his early seventies. The poem reveals the poet's acceptance of the inevitability of death. Gone are the youthful optimism and spirited desire to deny the power of the grave that characterize "A Psalm of Life"; the later poem is the work of a man whose life is nearing its end.

Prentice Hall Literature Program Resources

REINFORCE / RETEACH / EXTEND

Selection Support Worksheets
Build Vocabulary: Latin Word Roots: *-face-*, p. 76
Grammar and Style: Inverted Word Order, p. 77
Reading Strategy: Associate Images With Life, p. 78
Literary Focus: Stanza Forms, p. 79

Strategies for Diverse Student Needs, p. 16

Beyond Literature
Cross-Curricular Connection: Science, p. 16

Formal Assessment Selection Test, pp. 78–80; Assessment Resources Software

Alternative Assessment, p. 16

Writing and Language Transparencies
Branching Organizer, pp. 67–69

Literature CD-ROM

Listening to Literature Audiocassettes

◆ A Psalm of Life ◆
The Tide Rises, The Tide Falls

◆ Literature and Your Life

Connect Your Experience

In each stage of our lives, we want to leave a mark that will make others remember us. It could be by breaking a school scoring record in basketball, by committing acts of charity, or simply by establishing relationships that others won't soon forget. In these poems, Longfellow explores the passage of time, the fleeting nature of life, and the human desire to leave a mark on the world.

Journal Writing How would you like to be remembered?

Thematic Focus: Fireside and Campfire

As you read, think about why families of Longfellow's time might have chosen to recite poems such as these around the fireplace.

◆ Reading Strategy

Associate Images With Life

Writers often use images that take on greater meaning when we consider them as symbols of larger ideas and principles. Many of the images in these poems deal with journeys. To discover their deeper meaning, **associate the images with life** by thinking about what they mean in the broader context of the journey of life. Look, for example, at the line "The twilight darkens, the curlew calls" from "The Tide Rises, The Tide Falls." The darkening sky and evening bird signal the close of the day. In terms of life's "big picture," however, Longfellow is also foreshadowing the end of a lifetime.

◆ Grammar and Style

Inverted Word Order

To achieve a rhyme or maintain a certain rhythm, poets sometimes change the normal English sentence order of subject-verb-complement. For example, Longfellow sometimes uses **inverted word order,** reversing the subject and verb of a sentence:

...nevermore / Returns (v) the traveler (s) to the shore,

The complement—the word or group of words that completes the meaning of the predicate—can also be placed at the start of a sentence or line of poetry to achieve emphasis.

Dust (c) thou (s) art (v) ...

◆ Literary Focus

Stanza Forms

Like most traditional poets, Longfellow organized his poetry in **stanzas**—units of two or more lines arranged in a pattern of rhythm (or meter) and rhyme. Like a prose paragraph, each stanza develops a single main idea. Unlike paragraphs, however, stanzas are often a fixed length and share the same rhythm. Stanzas are commonly named according to the number of lines they contain. A two-line stanza is a **couplet;** a four-line stanza is a **quatrain;** and a five-line stanza is a **cinquain.**

As you read "A Psalm of Life" and "The Tide Rises, The Tide Falls," note which form of stanza Longfellow uses in each.

◆ Build Vocabulary

Latin Word Roots: *-face-*

In "The Tide Rises, The Tide Falls," the waves "Efface the footprints in the sands." The word *efface* contains the prefix *e-*, a form of *ex-*, meaning "out" or "without," and the Latin root *-face-*, meaning "appearance or outward aspect." To efface a footprint, then, is to remove any trace of its appearance.

Word Bank

Preview this list of words from the poems.

- bivouac
- sublime
- efface

Test Preparation Workshop

Reading Comprehension:
Make Inferences and Generalizations

Many standardized tests such as the SAT require students to make generalizations. A generalization is a broad statement based on a series of observations. After they have read "The Psalm of Life," help students practice making generalizations with this sample item:

Which of the following best describes the mood of the poem?

A pessimistic
B inspirational
C hopeless
D sentimental

A and *C* are incorrect, because the poem celebrates hope and strength in the face of adversity. The poem supports seeing the future clearly and matter-of-factly, which renders *D* incorrect. *B* is the correct choice.

Interest Grabber To help set the mood for Longfellow's poetry, ask students to close their eyes and imagine the smell of ocean air and the sound of waves washing across the sand. If possible, play a tape of ocean sounds. Then discuss why authors, poets, artists, and lyricists are so fascinated by the sea. Write the quotation "Footprints on the sands of time" on the chalkboard and tell students that they will be reading the poem in which this famous line appears.

Connecting Themes Across Cultures

Storytelling is a vital link between a culture's past and present. Oral traditions serve as a way of passing on values and preserving ideas, beliefs, and customs. The words of great philosophers and prophets of the past were first delivered orally. Invite students to recall stories or poems from other cultures and have them explain the cultural values that have been preserved through storytelling.

Customize for *Less Proficient Readers*

To help students improve their comprehension, point out examples of inverted word order, such as "nevermore/Returns the traveler to the shore." Model how to reinvert the words to make them sound more natural to the modern ear, such as *the traveler nevermore returns to the shore.*

Customize for *AP Students*

Encourage students to compare the philosophies of life Longfellow expresses in the two poems.

Customize for *English Language Learners*

Longfellow's shorter poems have long been favorites for memorization. Reciting them can provide good public speaking practice. Encourage students to recite "The Tide Rises, The Tide Falls" aloud. Students working in pairs or in small groups can deliver the poem in unison or antiphonally.

Develop Understanding

One-Minute Insight Longfellow wrote this poem after he had finally recovered from the death of his first wife. In it, he urges people to accept the idea that, despite grief, sorrow, and the inevitability of death, they should live enthusiastically, take action to make a mark on the world, and realize that strength and comfort come from the pursuit of an active, productive life.

Looking at Literature Videodisc Introduce the life and accomplishments of Henry Wadsworth Longfellow by playing Chapter 5 of the videodisc. This brief biography provides insight into his life and times. Ask students to discuss why Longfellow was such a popular literary figure.

Chapter 5

Literature CD-ROM To build background on Longfellow, use the CD-ROM *The History of American Literature:* Part 1, Disk 2, Feature 4.

◆ Reading Strategy

❶ Associate Images With Life Discuss the metaphor of tomorrow finding us "farther than today." What does the speaker mean? What is the poet's opinion of the purpose of people's actions? *Students may say that the metaphor means that each day should be a chance for people to make more progress than they did the day before; people's actions should be purposeful and forward-moving.*

◆ Critical Thinking

❷ Connect Ask students to explain how lines 14–16 relate to the idea expressed in line 13. *Each day brings us closer to inevitable death—only artistic achievements endure after we are gone.*

▶Critical Viewing◀

❸ Respond Answers will vary but should include concepts of constant change, impermanence, or transition.

A Psalm of Life

Henry Wadsworth Longfellow

Tell me not, in mournful numbers,[1]
Life is but an empty dream!—
For the soul is dead that slumbers,
And things are not what they seem.

Life is real! Life is earnest!
And the grave is not its goal:
Dust thou art, to dust returnest,
Was not spoken of the soul.

❶ Not enjoyment, and not sorrow,
Is our destined end or way;
But to act, that each tomorrow
Find us farther than today.

Art is long, and Time is fleeting,
❷ And our hearts, though stout and brave,
Still, like muffled drums, are beating
Funeral marches to the grave.

In the world's broad field of battle,
In the bivouac of Life,
Be not like dumb, driven cattle!
Be a hero in the strife!

1. **numbers:** Verses.

❸ ▲ Critical Viewing What do you associate with the image of footprints in the sand? **[Respond]**

Block Scheduling Strategies

Consider these suggestions to take advantage of extended class time:

- To introduce Longfellow, play Chapter 5 of the **Looking at Literature Videodisc/ Videotape.** Follow with a class discussion.
- Have students listen to the poems on audiocassette as they follow along in their texts. Discuss the impact of rhythm, rhyme, and repetition. Does hearing the poetry increase students' appreciation of it?
- Have students work in discussion groups to answer the Guide for Responding questions (pp. 251, 253).
- If you have access to computers, have students work in the **Writing Lab CD-ROM** to complete the Guided Writing Lesson on p. 255. You will probably want to allow two blocks or 45 to 50 minutes for students to complete all stages of the lesson.

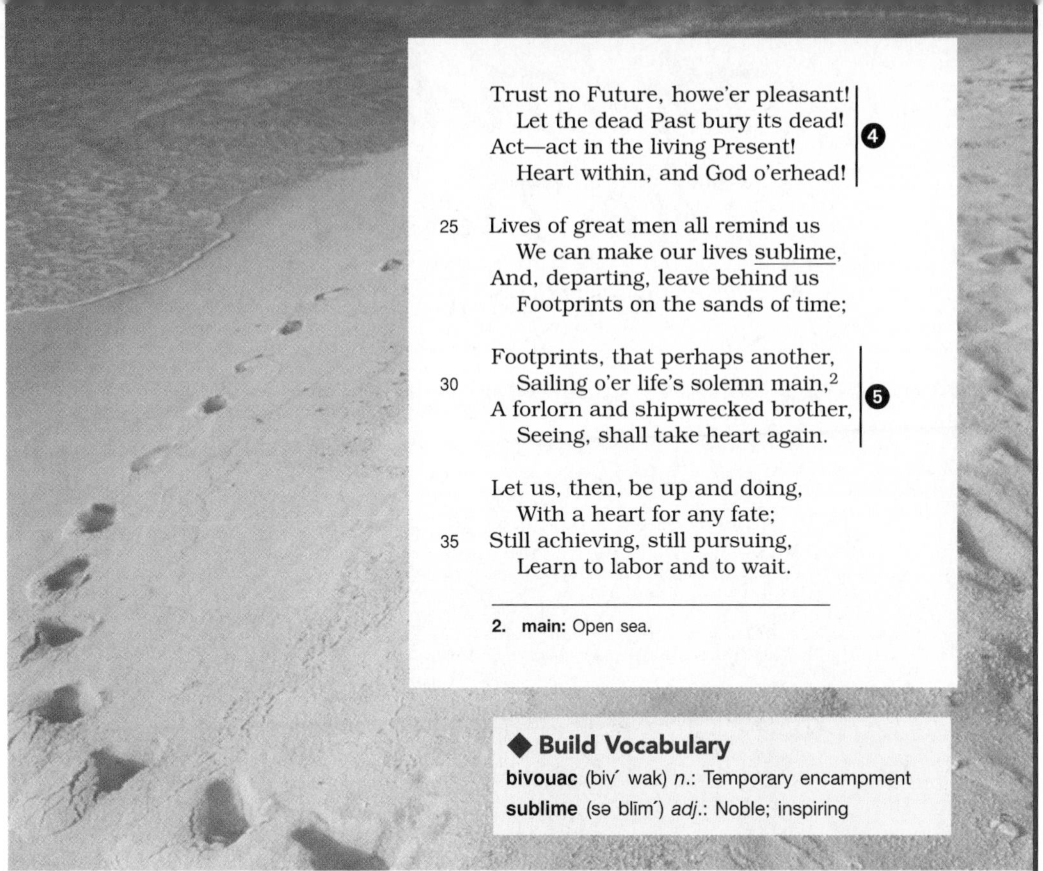

Trust no Future, howe'er pleasant!
  Let the dead Past bury its dead!
Act—act in the living Present! ❹
  Heart within, and God o'erhead!

Lives of great men all remind us
  We can make our lives sublime,
And, departing, leave behind us
  Footprints on the sands of time;

Footprints, that perhaps another,
  Sailing o'er life's solemn main,[2]
A forlorn and shipwrecked brother, ❺
  Seeing, shall take heart again.

Let us, then, be up and doing,
  With a heart for any fate;
Still achieving, still pursuing,
  Learn to labor and to wait.

---

2. main: Open sea.

◆ Build Vocabulary

bivouac (biv′ wak) *n.*: Temporary encampment
sublime (sə blīm′) *adj.*: Noble; inspiring

Guide for Responding

◆ *Literature and Your Life*

Reader's Response What "footprints" would you like to leave "on the sands of time"?

Thematic Focus What is Longfellow's idea of how a person should live?

Group Discussion The phrase "Art is long, and Time is fleeting" is a translation of a Latin motto echoed in the works of many great English poets. How do you interpret its meaning?

☑ Check Your Comprehension

1. What attitude or idea does the speaker challenge in the first two stanzas?
2. What can we learn from the "Lives of great men"?

◆ Critical Thinking

INTERPRET

1. Describe the speaker's attitude concerning individuality and self-reliance. **[Infer]**
2. According to the poem, how can our lives influence future generations? **[Interpret]**
3. Summarize the speaker's view of life. **[Draw Conclusions]**

EVALUATE

4. This poem has been criticized as trite and overly sentimental. Explain why you agree or disagree with this opinion. **[Evaluate]**

APPLY

5. What advice might the speaker give to someone suffering a personal misfortune? **[Relate]**

Speaking, Listening, and Viewing Mini-Lesson

Commencement Address

This mini-lesson supports the Speaking, Listening, and Viewing activity in the Idea Bank on p. 255.

Introduce the Concept Explain that *commencement* is the ceremony at which educational diplomas are granted. Traditionally, a noteworthy speaker delivers a commencement address to inspire graduates.

Develop Background Have students research past commencement speeches at your school or a nearby college. If possible, obtain manuscript or videotape of commencement addresses so students can understand their structure and tone.

Apply the Information Working in pairs or groups, students should summarize what they know of Longfellow's views on life. Have them imagine what Longfellow would say to students about to enter the adult world. How might he encourage them to live their lives?

Assess the Outcome Assess addresses based on authenticity and persuasiveness. You may also evaluate students' tone of voice and pace.

◆ Critical Thinking

❹ Analyze Point out to students that lines 19–24 end with exclamation marks. Ask them to explain the effect produced by this punctuation. *Students should note the sense of urgency evident in these lines; the poet is exhorting listeners to live for today and to act decisively.*

◆ Reading Strategy

❺ Associate Images With Life Discuss the sailing images in this stanza. How do these particular images fit the poet's view of life? *Students may say that sailing "life's solemn main" is as unpredictable as any kind of sailing, with risks, ups and downs, and a need for perseverance.*

Reinforce and Extend

Answers

◆ *Literature and Your Life*

Reader's Response Students should cite the personal goals they hope to achieve.

Thematic Focus He feels that people ought to live actively and make the most of the time they are given.

☑ Check Your Comprehension

1. He challenges the idea that life is an empty and meaningless journey toward the grave.
2. They teach us that we can live nobly and leave our mark on the world.

◆ Critical Thinking

1. He suggests that it is important to be an individual and not to be a passive member of the herd.
2. We can live in such away that our personal achievements give courage and inspiration to others.
3. Life is real and best lived in the here and now. We have an obligation to make something of our lives for ourselves and for those who come after us.
4. Student should support their responses with a clear explanation of their reasoning.
5. Suggested response: Don't spend your time mourning past losses or mistakes; you have to live in the present and create new meaning in your life by doing something to change the world for the better.

One-Minute Insight

The mysterious sea, with its endless cycle of tides, is the setting for this poem, which explores the idea that, though a person may die, nature is eternal. The recurring pauses, frequent repetition of words, and the refrain combine strong metrical rhythm to create a rising and falling rhythm, like the breaking of waves on the shore.

Customize for *Visual/Spatial Learners*

Encourage students to use the painting on this page to help draw them into the poem. Once they've read the poem, have them explain how the painting enhances their appreciation of it.

Listening to Literature Audiocassettes Play the reading of the poem on audiocassette to help students appreciate the hypnotic effect of its refrain.

Customize for *Less Proficient Readers*

Help students recognize metaphors with ***Strategies for Diverse Student Needs,*** p. 16.

▶Critical Viewing◀

❶ **Connect** Students may respond by citing the poem's refrain: "The tide rises, the tide falls."

Read to Interpret

As students read the poem, encourage them to look for the message behind the words. Ask students to interpret the meaning of Longfellow's images in relation to life: " the tide rises, the tide falls," "darkness," "footprints in the sand," and "the traveler." Help students understand that the sea represents life moving in cycles and that the traveler is everyone who briefly makes a difference, and then dies, leaving little or no trace. Tell students that when they read a poem to interpret, they should figure out what the poetic images represent in real life. This strategy will increase their understanding of the whole poem.

The Tide Rises, The Tide Falls

Henry Wadsworth Longfellow

***Breakers at Floodtide*, *1909*,** Frederick J. Waugh, Butler Institute of American Art, Youngstown, Ohio

❶ ▲ Critical Viewing Which lines of the poem does this painting suggest to you? **[Connect]**

Humanities: Art

Breakers at Floodtide, 1909, by Frederick Judd Waugh.

Waugh (1861–1940) was a nationally recognized painter who specialized in marinescapes. His work garnered many honors during his lifetime; he won the Carnegie International Exhibition's popular prize five consecutive years. Today, his paintings can be found in the collections of the Metropolitan Museum of Art, New York, and the National Gallery in Washington, D.C., among others.

This painting is illuminated by moonlight, which reflects on the surface of the breakers that wash over the rocky shore.

Use these questions for discussion:

1. Longfellow describes the "soft, white hands" of the waves. Compare this image to the waves Waugh paints. *Students may say that Waugh's sea is more violent and powerful.*
2. What aspects of the painting suggest death? *Students may mention the dark, cloudy sky, the emptiness of the scene, or the absence of any traces of a human presence.*

The tide rises, the tide falls.
The twilight darkens, the curlew[1] calls;
❷ Along the sea sands damp and brown
The traveler hastens toward the town,
And the tide rises, the tide falls.

Darkness settles on roofs and walls,
But the sea, the sea in the darkness calls:
❸ The little waves, with their soft, white hands,
Efface the footprints in the sands,
And the tide rises, the tide falls.

The morning breaks; the steeds in their stalls
Stamp and neigh, as the hostler[2] calls:
The day returns, but nevermore
Returns the traveler to the shore,
And the tide rises, the tide falls.

◆ Build Vocabulary

efface (ə fās′) *v.*: Erase; wipe out

1. **curlew** (kʉr′ lo͞o) *n.*: Large, long-legged wading bird whose call is associated with the evening.
2. **hostler** (häs′ lər) *n.*: Person who tends horses at an inn or stable.

Guide for Responding

◆ Literature and Your Life

Reader's Response What did you see and hear in your mind as you read this poem?

Thematic Focus What remains when we are gone from this world?

Questions for Research The ocean's rhythmic tides, vast size, and summoning horizon all occur as metaphors in poetry. What questions could you ask to learn more about the ocean in poetry? How could you research the different themes?

☑ Check Your Comprehension

1. Summarize the action of the poem.
2. What is the implied fate of the traveler?

◆ Critical Thinking

INTERPRET

1. (a) What details in the first stanza suggest that the traveler is nearing death? (b) What details in the second stanza suggest that he has died? **[Support]**
2. (a) What is the effect of the refrain, or repeated line? (b) How does the rhythm of the refrain reinforce its meaning? **[Analyze]**
3. What does the poem suggest about the relationship between humanity and nature? **[Draw Conclusions]**

EVALUATE

4. What do you think Longfellow's outlook on life and death was when he wrote "The Tide Rises, The Tide Falls"? Explain. **[Evaluate]**

COMPARE LITERARY WORKS

5. How does the philosophy of life expressed in this poem differ from that of "A Psalm of Life"? **[Compare and Contrast]**

Beyond the Selection

FURTHER READING

Other Works by Longfellow

The Song of Hiawatha
The Courtship of Miles Standish
Evangeline
"The Wreck of the Hesperus"
"Paul Revere's Ride"

We suggest that you preview these poems before recommending them to students.

INTERNET

The Internet provides opportunities for students to learn more about Henry Wadsworth Longfellow. We recommend the following site. Please be aware, however, that sites may have changed since this information was published.

For biographical information and collected poems on-line, go to **http://www.auburn.edu/~vestmon/longfellow.html**

We *strongly recommend* that you preview this site before sending students to it.

◆ Literary Focus

❷ **Stanza Forms** Have students analyze this stanza to determine its rhyme scheme and form. *AABBA; cinquain*

◆ Reading Strategy

❸ **Associate Images With Life** Discuss the meaning of the images of darkness, the sea, and footprints. *Students may say that darkness is an image of death; the sea stands for the eternity of nature; the effaced footprints represent the impermanence of life.*

Reinforce and Extend

Answers

◆ Literature and Your Life

Reader's Response Students may respond that they pictured the waves and heard them pounding the shore.

Thematic Focus The eternal chain of nature's cycles remains when we are gone.

☑ Check Your Comprehension

1. As evening falls, a traveler hurries along a beach toward the town. Overnight, the waves wash away his footprints in the sand. A new day begins, but the traveler is gone.
2. The traveler had died during the night.

◆ Critical Thinking

1. (a) The darkening of the sky and sound of the night bird suggest the ending of a life. (b) Darkness has settled and the waves have erased the footprints.
2. (a) By mirroring the repeated motion of the tide, it reminds the reader of the never-ending cycles of nature. (b) The rhythm of the refrain rises, then falls, just as the tide rises and falls.
3. Humans come and go, but the rhythms of nature endure. Man is mortal; nature is eternal.
4. Suggested response: He seems to have accepted the idea that life goes on unchanged after an individual dies.
5. Suggested response: This poem suggests that life is brief and that the world continues unchanged after we are gone. "A Psalm to Life" suggests that we can strive against death by living actively and making our mark on the world.

Answers

◆ Reading Strategy

Suggested responses:

1. Footprints are the achievements we leave behind to inspire others.
2. The solemn main is the vast and uncharted span of our lives on earth.
3. A shipwrecked brother is a fellow human who has lost his or her way in life and is left with nothing to hold onto.
4. The sea sands are the earth on which we live.
5. The sea is an image of eternal nature or of death.
6. The traveler is a person on the journey of life.

◆ Build Vocabulary

Using the Latin Root *-face-*

1. b 2. d 3. a 4. c

Using the Word Bank

1. efface; 2. bivouac; 3. sublime

◆ Literary Focus

1. (a) "A Psalm of Life" contains quatrains; lines 1 and 3, and lines 2 and 4 of each stanza rhyme. (b) "The Tide Rises, The Tide Falls" contains cinquains; lines 1, 2, and 5, and lines 3 and 4 of each stanza rhyme.
2. The eighth stanza ("Footprints, that perhaps another . . .) can only be understood when read in conjunction with the seventh stanza, which introduces the footprints described in stanza eight.
3. The use of the cinquain allows Longfellow to include the line "And the tide rises, the tide falls" in each stanza.

◆ Grammar and Style

Writing Application Writing samples should include at least two logical examples of inverted word order and should be free of major grammatical and mechanical errors.

Looking at Style

1. Complement-Verb-Subject
2. Placing the phrases *not enjoyment* and *not sorrow* at the start of the line emphasizes the meaning of the sentence.
3. Our destined end or way is not enjoyment and is not sorrow.
4. The rhythm is completely different from and no longer consistent with the rest of the poem.

Guide for Responding *(continued)*

◆ Reading Strategy

Associate Images With Life

Associating Longfellow's images, or word pictures, **with broader life** events can help you find greater meaning in these poems. Copy the chart below into your notebook. Complete it by filling in the possible meaning of each italicized image as it relates to life's journey. Feel free to offer more than one possible meaning for a particular image.

When you're finished, get together with a group of classmates and share and discuss your interpretations of the various images. How do the images contribute to the overall meaning of the two poems?

Image	How It Relates to Life
1. *Footprints* on the sands of time	
2. Sailing o'er life's *solemn main*	
3. A forlorn and *shipwrecked* brother	
4. . . . the *sea sands* damp and brown	
5. . . . *the sea*, the sea in the darkness calls	
6. Returns the *traveler* to the shore	

◆ Build Vocabulary

Using the Latin Root *-face-*

Use your knowledge of the Latin root *-face-*, meaning "appearance or outward aspect," to match each word with its definition. Write your answers in your notebook. Then use a dictionary to check your answers.

1. facade **a.** to ruin the appearance of
2. interface **b.** the front of a building
3. deface **c.** the exterior of an object
4. surface **d.** to encounter or come in contact with

Using the Word Bank: Analogies

Complete each analogy using a word from the Word Bank. Write your answers on a separate sheet of paper.

1. *Raise* is to *lower* as *inscribe* is to __?__.
2. *Hut* is to *shack* as *campsite* is to __?__.
3. *Aggravated* is to *calm* as *humble* is to __?__.

◆ Literary Focus

Stanza Forms

Longfellow uses a different **stanza form**—a unit of poetry containing a specific number of lines—in each of these poems. Consider how his choice of the number, length, and rhythm of the stanzas contributes to each poem's overall impact.

1. Describe the stanza form and rhyme pattern of (a) "A Psalm of Life" (b) "The Tide Rises, The Tide Falls."
2. With only one exception, every stanza in "A Psalm of Life" develops a separate idea and is capable of standing alone. Which stanza is dependent on the one before for its meaning?
3. How does Longfellow's choice of stanza form in "The Tide Rises, The Tide Falls" allow him to emphasize the repetition of nature's cycles?

◆ Grammar and Style

Inverted Word Order

Poetry is not the only form of writing that permits inverted word order. You can also change the structure of a prose sentence in order to emphasize a particular word or idea.

Inverted word order is a change in the normal English word order of subject-verb-complement.

Writing Application Write a paragraph, a series of stanzas, or a song describing how you'd like to leave your mark on the world. Include at least two examples of inverted word order.

Looking at Style In your notebook, answer these questions about lines 9 and 10 of "A Psalm of Life."

Not enjoyment, and not sorrow,
Is our destined end or way;

1. What word order is shown in these lines?
2. What effect does this word order have on the meaning of the lines? Explain.
3. Rewrite the lines in conventional subject-verb-complement word order.
4. What do you notice about the rhythm of these new lines when they are read aloud?

Grammar Reinforcement

For additional instruction and practice, use the lesson on Special Problems in Agreement in the Subject-Verb Agreement unit of the **Language Lab CD-ROM**.

Reteach

If students are having difficulty understanding stanza forms, have them create a chart like the one shown. Students should fill in the information for each stanza to fully understand the stanza forms in the poem.

Poem

	First Stanza	Second Stanza	Third Stanza
number of lines			
rhyming pattern			
rhythm or meter pattern			

Build Your Portfolio

Idea Bank

Writing

1. **Epitaph** Write a brief epitaph, or tribute, for Longfellow's tomb to reflect the philosophy expressed in one of the two poems you just read. Include one or two lines from the poem.
2. **Personal Response** Do we leave "Footprints on the sands of time" or does death erase all traces of our lives? In a brief paper, contrast the views presented in the two poems. With which viewpoint do you agree? Why?
3. **Essay** A German motto says: "Look not mournfully into the Past. It comes not back again. Wisely improve the Present. It is thine. Go forth to meet the shadowy Future, without fear, and with a manly heart." Write an essay explaining how "A Psalm of Life" reflects these sentiments.

Speaking, Listening, and Viewing

4. **Audio Presentation/Discussion** Play a recording of ocean sounds for the class. Then present the ideas and emotions you associate with the sea. Follow by having classmates share their associations with the ocean.
5. **Commencement Address** As Longfellow, deliver an inspirational commencement speech on how to live a worthwhile life. Base your comments on the ideas expressed in "A Psalm of Life."

Researching and Representing

6. **Performance** Listen to the beat of "The Tide Rises, The Tide Falls" as you read it aloud. Then create a piece of music or choreograph a dance to accompany the poem. **[Performing Arts Link]**
7. **Graphic Display** Create a poster displaying "A Psalm of Life" and one or more photographs or illustrations that capture the ideas expressed in the poem. **[Media Link]**

Online Activity www.phlit.phschool.com

Guided Writing Lesson

Credo

Longfellow's personal beliefs about the meaning of life and death are expressed in his poetry. Summarize your approach to life in a credo—a statement of principles or beliefs that guides your conduct. Write your credo with the goal of persuading others to adopt the same principles.

Writing Skills Focus: Persuasive Tone

A writer's tone conveys his or her attitude toward a subject. Only when it is clear that you believe in what you are saying (or writing!) can you convince others to share those beliefs. Communicate your convictions with a **persuasive tone** that is forceful and to the point. Consider the difference tone makes in these two sentences:

Neutral: Living each day to the fullest can be a worthwhile approach to life.

Persuasive: A life lived to the fullest is the only kind worth living.

Though both sentences have the same basic message, the second is more likely to influence a reader to accept the ideas being presented.

Prewriting You can't persuade others of your beliefs until they're clear in your own mind. Jot down as many of your personal beliefs as you can. Then go through the list to identify which ideas are most important. Finally, state in a sentence or two the overall outlook that ties together your various beliefs.

Drafting Start by stating your overall outlook. Then explain each of the individual beliefs that fit into this outlook. Provide examples of personal experiences that support your ideas.

Revising As you revise your credo, focus on replacing vague or weak words with more persuasive ones that will strengthen your tone.

Idea Bank

Customizing for *Performance Levels*
Following are suggestions for matching Idea Bank activities with students' performance levels:
Less Advanced Students: 1, 4
Average Students: 2, 6, 7
More Advanced Students: 3, 5

Customizing for *Learning Modalities*
Following are suggestions for matching Idea Bank activities with students' learning modalities:
Musical/Rhythmic: 4, 6
Intrapersonal: 4, 5
Verbal/Linguistic: 5
Visual/Spatial: 7

Guided Writing Lesson

Writing and Language Transparencies
Use the Branching Transparency, p. 67, to help students organize the tenets of their credo.

For more on prewriting, elaboration, and revision, see *Prentice Hall Writing and Grammar.*

Writers at Work Videodisc
Have students view the videodisc segment (Ch. 4) featuring Gasby Greely of the National Urban League to see how she persuades the public to accept the league's credo on race relations. Ask students to discuss how her insights can help them make their own credos more persuasive.

Play frames 33643 to 43235

Writing Lab CD-ROM
Have students complete the tutorial on Persuasion. Follow these steps:
1. Have student use the Keyhole Graphic Organizer to structure their credos.
2. Have students draft on computer.
3. Have students use the Persuasive Word Bins as they revise.

ASSESSMENT OPTIONS

Formal Assessment, Selection Test, pp. 78–80, and Assessment Resources Software. The selection test is designed so that it can be easily customized to the performance levels of your students.

Alternative Assessment, p. 16, includes options for less advanced students, more advanced students, visual/spatial learners, and musical/rhythmic learners.

PORTFOLIO ASSESSMENT
Use the following rubrics in the ***Alternative Assessment*** booklet to assess student writing:
Epitaph: Expression Rubric, p. 109
Personal Response: Expression Rubric, p. 109
Essay: Literary Analysis/Interpretation Rubric, p. 127
Guided Writing Lesson: Expression and Persuasion Rubrics, pp. 109 and 120

Prepare and Engage

LESSON OBJECTIVES

1. **To develop vocabulary and word identification skills**
   - Latin Word Roots: *-patr-*
   - Using the Word Bank: Antonyms or Synonyms?
2. **To use a variety of reading strategies to comprehend poetry**
   - Reading Strategy: Summarize
3. **To increase knowledge of other cultures and to connect common elements across cultures**
   - Connecting Themes Across Cultures (ATE)
4. **To express and support responses to the text**
   - Critical Thinking
   - Idea Bank: Letter
   - Idea Bank: Poem
   - Idea Bank: Graphic Display
   - Idea Bank: Dramatic Reading
5. **To analyze literary elements**
   - Literary Focus: Meter
   - Idea Bank: Poetry Critique
   - Idea Bank: Analytical Essay
6. **To plan, prepare, organize, and present literary interpretations**
   - Idea Bank: Oral Presentation
7. **To use recursive writing processes to write a précis**
   - Guided Writing Lesson
8. **To increase knowledge of the rules of grammar and usage**
   - Grammar and Style: Participles as Adjectives

Test Preparation

Reading Comprehension: Make Inferences and Generalizations (ATE, p. 258)
The teaching tips and sample test item in this workshop support the instruction and practice in the unit workshop:

Reading Comprehension: Analyze Information to Make Inferences and Generalizations (ATE, p. 427)

Guide for Interpreting

William Cullen Bryant *(1794–1878)*

As a journalist and political activist, William Cullen Bryant fought to ensure that industrialization and rapid growth did not obscure America's democratic values and principles. As a poet, Bryant helped to establish an American literary tradition by producing poems that were a match for the work of the best European poets of his day.

Bryant learned Greek and Latin from his father, a country doctor. He began writing poetry at the age of nine and wrote the first version of "Thanatopsis," his most famous poem, when he was only nineteen.

To support himself, Bryant practiced law for ten years while continuing to write poetry in his spare time. In 1825, he moved to New York City and became a journalist; by 1829, he had become editor-in-chief and part owner of the New York *Evening Post,* a newspaper. Bryant used his position to defend human rights and personal freedoms, and he was an outspoken advocate of women's rights and the abolition of slavery.

Bryant was the first American poet to win worldwide critical acclaim. His work helped establish the Romantic Movement in this country and influenced the next generation of American poets.

Oliver Wendell Holmes *(1809–1894)*

A man of many talents and interests, Oliver Wendell Holmes made important contributions to both literature and medicine. Holmes, a descendant of seventeenth-century poet Anne Bradstreet (p. 88), graduated from Harvard University, briefly studied law, then moved on to the study of medicine. After studying in Paris, he completed a medical degree at Harvard University in 1836, the same year his first collection of poetry, *Poems*, was published.

Holmes went on to have a long teaching career at Harvard, during which time he became a leading medical researcher and continued his literary pursuits. Along with James Russell Lowell, Holmes founded *The Atlantic Monthly*, in which many of his best-known poems and essays were published. His love of humorous exaggeration, colorful expressions, and quotable quotes made his essays popular with readers.

While still studying law at Harvard in 1830, Holmes wrote "Old Ironsides" to protest the planned destruction of the battleship *Constitution*, nicknamed "Old Ironsides" for its ability to withstand British attacks during the War of 1812. The poem saved the ship and earned Holmes national recognition as a poet.

James Russell Lowell *(1819–1891)*

James Russell Lowell may have been the most talented of the Fireside Poets (see Background for Understanding, p. 257). His literary career, however, was disrupted by personal tragedies, including the infant deaths of three of his four children. Following the death of his wife in 1853, the young writer lost much of his focus and was never able to match his earlier work.

Still, Lowell made many important literary contributions as a poet, editor, and critic. He published his first book of poetry, *A Year's Life,* in 1841. His literary career reached its peak in 1848 with the publication of three highly successful works—*A Fable for Critics, The Bigelow Papers,* and *The Vision of Sir Launfal*—that gained him international fame.

During the second half of his life, Lowell turned toward other interests. He wrote editorials supporting the abolition of slavery. He succeeded Longfellow as professor of languages at Harvard, and he helped found and served as the first editor of *The Atlantic Monthly.* In later years, he served as an American ambassador to Spain, then to Great Britain.

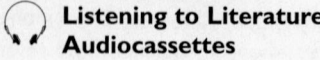

Prentice Hall Literature Program Resources

REINFORCE / RETEACH / EXTEND

Selection Support Pages
Build Vocabulary: Latin Word Roots: *-patr-,* p. 80
Grammar and Style: Participles as Adjectives, p. 81
Reading Strategy: Summarize, p. 82
Literary Focus: Meter, p. 83

Strategies for Diverse Student Needs, p. 17
Beyond Literature
Humanities Connection: Art, p. 17
Formal Assessment Selection Test, pp. 81–83; Assessment Resources Software

Alternative Assessment, p. 17
Resource Pro CD-ROM
Literature CD-ROM
Listening to Literature Audiocassettes

Thanatopsis ◆ Old Ironsides ◆ The First Snowfall ◆ *from* Snowbound

John Greenleaf Whittier *(1807–1892)*

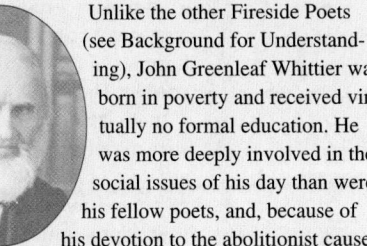

Unlike the other Fireside Poets (see Background for Understanding), John Greenleaf Whittier was born in poverty and received virtually no formal education. He was more deeply involved in the social issues of his day than were his fellow poets, and, because of his devotion to the abolitionist cause, he did not gain national prominence until after the Civil War. The son of Quakers who taught him to believe in hard work, simplicity, pacifism, religious devotion, and social justice, Whittier spent his youth working on his family's debt-ridden farm near Haverhill, Massachusetts.

As a young man, Whittier worked for antislavery newspapers, wrote a large number of antislavery poems, and became active in politics. When the Civil War ended, he focused on writing poetry. He earned national fame with the 1866 publication of *Snowbound,* which depicts the simple warmth of rural New England life.

As the way of life captured in his poetry disappeared, the popularity of Whittier's poems grew. Despite his tremendous success as a poet, he remained faithful at all times to his social and spiritual convictions.

◆ Background for Understanding

LITERATURE: THE FIRESIDE POETS—AMERICA'S FIRST GENERATION OF WRITERS

Until the third decade of the nineteenth century, America had little real literature to call its own. The Fireside Poets—Henry Wadsworth Longfellow, Oliver Wendell Holmes, James Russell Lowell, and John Greenleaf Whittier—represented a literary coming of age for the young country. This first generation of acclaimed American poets took their name from the popularity of their works, which were widely read both as fireside family entertainment and in the schoolroom, where generations of children memorized them.

The four poets—all New England born and bred—chose uniquely American settings and subjects. Their themes, meter, and imagery, however, borrowed heavily from the English tradition. Though their reliance on conservative literary styles prevented them from being truly innovative, the Fireside Poets were literary giants of their day. In their own time, and for decades afterward, they ranked as America's most read and best-loved poets.

The Four Seasons of Life, Currier & Ives

Interest Grabber Have students bring to class a recording of or lyrics to a contemporary song that has special meaning to them. Ask volunteers to share their songs. Discuss how some musical artists give voice to the concerns and ideals of an entire generation of listeners. To which musical artists do students feel such a connection? Explain to students that the poets they are about to read were to their nineteenth-century readers what recording artists are to today's audiences. These poets popularized poetry as a family entertainment long before families could turn to CDs, radio, television, movies, or other technological diversions. They expressed the values, emotions, and concerns of those who lived in the nineteenth century.

Customize for
Less Proficient Readers

To help these students better grasp the poems, invite groups to preread to identify unusual or unfamiliar words. Examples might include "the *insensible* rock," "wore *ermine too dear* for an earl," or "shook his *sage* head." Help students define the words or find synonyms for them, then read the poems to absorb their meanings.

Block Scheduling Strategies

Consider these suggestions to take advantage of extended class time:

- If you have access to technology, have students work in small groups to view and discuss the background material on Bryant, Lowell, Holmes, and Whittier on *The History of American Literature,* Part I CD-ROM.
- After students have read the poems, divide the class into four groups and have each group interpret a different poem.
- Each group should study their poet's biography (pp. 256–257), then work together to answer the Guide for Responding questions that accompany their respective poems.
- Have each group share what they have learned in a brief oral presentation. Assess the Reading Strategy skill by asking each group to summarize their assigned poem. Groups should also share their response to the Critical Viewing question.
- For additional assessment, assign your choice of the practice pages in ***Selection Support.***

Customize for
AP Students
Have students look for the use of sound devices, sensory details, figurative language, symbols, and other poetic elements. They can record examples in a journal and tell how each enhances the meaning or music of the poem or a reader's appreciation of it.

Customize for
English Language Learners
Help these students break down stanzas or lines, paraphrase, and rearrange inverted word order to get the essential meaning of the poems. It may help students to listen to the poems several times to become familiar with them and to pinpoint sections for further explication.

Guide for Interpreting *(continued)*

◆ Literature and Your Life

CONNECT YOUR EXPERIENCE

Do you find that the lyrics, approach to life, or attitudes of your favorite musical artists reflect *your* feelings, *your* concerns, and *your* views? Memorable musicians do more than strike a chord with listeners; they give voice to a generation.

Journal Writing Think about song lyrics that you find particularly meaningful, and relate them to something you've felt in your own life.

THEMATIC FOCUS: FIRESIDE AND CAMPFIRE

The works of the Fireside Poets are the early nineteenth-century equivalent of today's popular music, enjoyed by people from all walks of life. What do the themes reflected in these poems tell you about the values of the public who popularized them?

◆ Build Vocabulary

LATIN WORD ROOTS: *-patr-*

The Latin root *-patr-*, found in the word *patriarch*, comes from the Latin word *pater*, meaning "father." In *Snowbound*, "hornèd *patriarch* of the sheep" refers to the father sheep that leads the flock.

WORD BANK

Before you read, preview this list of words from the poems.

sepulcher
pensive
venerable
gloaming
ominous
querulous
patriarch

◆ Grammar and Style

PARTICIPLES AS ADJECTIVES

A **participle** is a verb form that can act as an adjective. There are two kinds of participles: **present participles,** which end in *-ing*, and **past participles,** which often end in *-ed, -d, -t,* or *-en*.

In *Snowbound,* John Greenleaf Whittier describes "A tunnel *walled* and *overlaid* / With *dazzling* crystal . . ." In these lines, *walled* and *overlaid* are past participles; *dazzling* is a present participle. All three modify "tunnel." Notice that, like adjectives, participles answer the question *what kind?* or *which one?* about the nouns and pronouns they modify.

◆ Literary Focus

METER

In poetry, a systematic arrangement of stressed (´) and unstressed (˘) syllables is called **meter.** The basic unit of meter is the **foot,** which usually consists of one stressed syllable and one or more unstressed syllables. The most frequently used foot in American and English verse is the *iamb,* which consists of one unstressed syllable followed by a stressed syllable. The type and number of feet in the lines of a poem determine its meter. A pattern of four iambs per line, as in this example from *Snowbound,* is known as **iambic tetrameter.**

Thĕ sún thăt bríef
Dĕcémbĕr dáy
Rŏse chéerlĕss óvĕr hílls
ŏf gráy

◆ Reading Strategy

SUMMARIZE

To check your understanding of what you've read, it's a good idea to **summarize** the work or parts of the work by briefly stating the main ideas and supporting details in your own words.

As you read these poems, summarize each stanza on paper or in your head. With lengthy verses, like those in "Thanatopsis" and *Snowbound,* you may find it easier to summarize after every four to six lines.

Test Preparation Workshop

Reading Comprehension:
Make Inferences and Generalizations The reading sections of standardized tests such as the SAT require students to make valid generalizations based on specific evidence in a text. Explain that faulty generalizations are not adequately supported by information found in the passage. Have students read "Old Ironsides," then ask them the following question.

Which of the following most accurately describes the ship's record of service?

A inactive
B unremarkable
C distinguished
D brief

A, B, and *D* are incorrect, because they are not supported by the text. *C* is correct. The ship survived difficult battles and won many victories at sea.

❶ Thanatopsis

William Cullen Bryant

Kindred Spirits, Asher B. Durand, New York Public Library

▶ Critical Viewing ❷ This painting pays tribute to the friendship between Bryant and landscape painter Thomas Cole. What does the painting suggest about the two men's shared interests? **[Infer]**

To him who in the love of Nature holds
Communion with her visible forms, she speaks
A various language; for his gayer hours
She has a voice of gladness, and a smile
And eloquence of beauty, and she glides

Develop Understanding

One-Minute Insight "Thanatopsis" presents the poet's musings on death and its links to nature. Nature brings joy and comfort to those who love her. When people think of death, nature teaches them that everyone and everything must die and become part of the earth again. As all of nature is intertwined, so are the bodies and spirits of all who die. Death is not to be feared or despised.

Literature CD-ROM To build background on William Cullen Bryant, use *The History of American Literature:* Part 1, Disk 1, Feature 11.

Listening to Literature Audiocassettes To help students appreciate the rhythm of Bryant's poem, have them listen to the recording of it on the audiocassettes. Have students discuss how listening to the poem enhances their appreciation of it.

Customize for
Less Proficient Readers
These students may find the poetic language of these poems challenging. Help improve their comprehension with the page on explaining poetic phrases in ***Strategies for Diverse Student Needs,*** p. 17.

❶ **Clarification** William Cullen Bryant coined this word, which he created from the Greek words *thanatos* (death) and *opsis* (vision).

▶Critical Viewing◀

❷ **Infer** Students may say that since Cole was a landscape painter, he, like Bryant, must have had deep feelings about nature. The two, standing on a rock overlooking a beautiful valley, might be sharing their views on the relationship between nature and art.

Humanities: Art

Kindred Spirits, by Asher B. Durand.

This portrait-in-nature shows artist Thomas Cole and poet William Cullen Bryant. Durand (1796–1886), Cole, and other painters were members of the Hudson River School. The once-derogatory term described painters who created scenes from nature rather than portraits or historical events, and so on. Though their contemporaries may have frowned on their choice of subject matter, the Hudson River artists' skill in portraying the wilderness helped make landscape an honorable subject in American art.

Durand, Cole, and Bryant were close friends who encouraged and supported one another's work. Use these questions for discussion:

1. What inspirations might the men have taken from this scene? *Cole may have considered painting the view; Bryant may have gleaned ideas for poems on nature or life.*
2. Why might the artist have placed the figures off to one side, rather than making them the focus of the scene? *Their positioning implies that nature takes precedence, that humans are but visitors who stand in awe of any serene spot.*

◆ Literary Focus

❶ **Meter** Point out Bryant's use of "poetic license" in these lines. He uses *list,* a short form of listen, to fit the meter he has established.

◆ Grammar and Style

❷ **Participles as Adjectives** Help students recognize that in this line the participle *beholding* still works to modify sun, even when paired with the adverb *all,* which modifies *beholding*. Guide students to find other examples of participles as adjectives, such as those in lines 31 *(resting)* and 38 *(rock-ribbed)*.

◆ Reading Strategy

❸ **Summarize** Ask students to summarize the meaning of this passage. *Students may say that it means that we return to nature when we die. They may use such phrases as "from ashes to ashes, and dust to dust."*

◆ Build Vocabulary

❹ **Word Roots: *-patr-*** Ask students to identify the patriarchs the poet describes. *They are all the fathers who came before, as far back as humans have been on Earth.*

Extending Word Study

Poetic Language In lines 8 and 14, call students' attention to Bryant's use of the words *ere* and *list* (for "listen"). These are examples of poetic language. Explain that poetic language—language used in some older, traditional poetry but not in speech—includes words such as these, which poets may include for the sake of rhyme or meter. Invite students to think of other examples of poetic language, such as *o'er* (for "over") and *e'en* (for "even").

Into his darker musings, with a mild
And healing sympathy, that steals away
Their sharpness, ere[1] he is aware. When thoughts
Of the last bitter hour come like a blight
Over thy spirit, and sad images
Of the stern agony, and shroud, and pall,
And breathless darkness, and the narrow house,[2]
Make thee to shudder, and grow sick at heart—
❶ Go forth, under the open sky, and list
To Nature's teachings, while from all around—
Earth and her waters, and the depths of air—
Comes a still voice—Yet a few days, and thee
❷ The all-beholding sun shall see no more
In all his course; nor yet in the cold ground,
Where thy pale form was laid, with many tears,
Nor in the embrace of ocean, shall exist
Thy image. Earth, that nourished thee, shall claim
Thy growth, to be resolved to earth again,
And, lost each human trace, surrendering up
❸ Thine individual being, shalt thou go
To mix forever with the elements,
To be a brother to the insensible rock
And to the sluggish clod, which the rude swain[3]
Turns with his share,[4] and treads upon. The oak
Shall send his roots abroad, and pierce thy mold.

Yet not to thine eternal resting place
Shalt thou retire alone, nor couldst thou wish
Couch[5] more magnificent. Thou shalt lie down
❹ With patriarchs of the infant world—with kings,
The powerful of the earth—the wise, the good,
Fair forms, and hoary seers of ages past,
All in one mighty sepulcher. The hills
Rock-ribbed and ancient as the sun—the vales
Stretching in pensive quietness between;
The venerable woods—rivers that move
In majesty, and the complaining brooks
That make the meadows green; and, poured round all,
Old Ocean's gray and melancholy waste—
Are but the solemn decorations all
Of the great tomb of man. The golden sun,
The planets, all the infinite host of heaven,
Are shining on the sad abodes of death,
Through the still lapse of ages. All that tread
The globe are but a handful to the tribes
That slumber in its bosom. Take the wings
Of morning,[6] pierce the Barcan[7] wilderness,
Or lose thyself in the continuous woods
Where rolls the Oregon,[8] and hears no sound,
Save his own dashings—yet the dead are there:
And millions in those solitudes, since first
The flight of years began, have laid them down

1. **ere:** Before.
2. **narrow house:** Coffin.
3. **swain:** Country youth.
4. **share:** Plowshare.
5. **couch:** Bed.
6. **Take . . . morning:** Allusion to Psalm 139:9.
7. **Barcan** (bär′ kən): Referring to Barca, a desert region in North Africa.
8. **Oregon:** River flowing between Oregon and Washington, now known as the Columbia River.

Cultural Connection

Cultural Views of Death Many cultures have looked upon death with as much interest as William Cullen Bryant does in this poem. In many ancient civilizations, death was seen as a passage to another life. The Egyptians built huge pyramids as tombs for their pharaohs and stocked them with all the comforts needed for the afterlife, including pets and servants.

The position in which the dead are buried also has significance. In some African cultures, men are buried on their right side, facing east, so the rising sun will wake them in the afterlife to hunt and farm. Women are buried facing west, so the setting sun will remind them to prepare the evening meal.

Have students from different backgrounds share details about death and burial customs in their culture. Based on the responses, compare and contrast how each culture views death.

In their last sleep—the dead reign there alone.
So shalt thou rest, and what if thou withdraw
In silence from the living, and no friend
Take note of thy departure? All that breathe
Will share thy destiny. The gay will laugh
When thou art gone, the solemn brood of care
Plod on, and each one as before will chase
His favorite phantom; yet all these shall leave
Their mirth and their employments, and shall come ❺
And make their bed with thee. As the long train
Of ages glide away, the sons of men,
The youth in life's green spring, and he who goes
In the full strength of years, matron and maid,
The speechless babe, and the gray-headed man—
Shall one by one be gathered to thy side,
By those, who in their turn shall follow them.

So live, that when thy summons comes to join
The innumerable caravan, which moves
To that mysterious realm, where each shall take
His chamber in the silent halls of death,
Thou go not, like the quarry-slave at night,
Scourged to his dungeon, but, sustained and soothed
By an unfaltering trust, approach thy grave,
Like one who wraps the drapery of his couch
About him, and lies down to pleasant dreams.

◆ Build Vocabulary

sepulcher (sep′əl kər) *n.*: Grave; tomb

pensive (pen′ siv) *adj.*: Expressing deep thoughtfulness

venerable (ven′ ər ə bəl) *adj.*: Worthy of respect

Guide for Responding

◆ Literature and Your Life

Reader's Response Did this poem make you think of nature in a new way? Explain.

Thematic Focus How does nature provide a sense of meaning to the mysteries of life and death?

Questions for Research Read about another culture and research the role of nature in that society. Is nature seen as beautiful and inviting or threatening? What are possible reasons for these beliefs? What other questions could you ask to direct your research?

☑ Check Your Comprehension

1. How does the speaker find comfort in Nature's "various language"?
2. What is the fate of the individual being?
3. In the end, who shares the individual's destiny?

◆ Critical Thinking

INTERPRET

1. The title is a composite of the Greek words *thanatos* (death) and *opsis* (a vision). Explain how the title applies to the poem. **[Connect]**
2. How would you summarize the poet's attitude toward life and death? **[Draw Conclusions]**

APPLY

3. Do you think this poem has the same impact on modern readers as it had on nineteenth-century readers? Why or why not? **[Apply]**

COMPARE LITERARY WORKS

4. What belief about death characterizes both "Thanatopsis" and "The Tide Rises, The Tide Falls" by Henry Wadsworth Longfellow? **[Synthesize]**

Beyond the Selection

FURTHER READING

Other Works by William Cullen Bryant

"To a Waterfowl"
"A Forest Hymn"
"The Battlefield"
Picturesque America: Or, The Land We Live In
Tales of Glauber-Spa

Other Works With the Theme of Death

"The First Snowfall," James Russell Lowell
"Because I could not stop for Death," Emily Dickinson
"Night on the Prairies," Walt Whitman

We suggest that you preview these works before recommending them to students.

◆ Critical Thinking

❺ **Interpret** Ask students to explain the meaning of this passage. *Though many fear death, some fear even more the idea of dying alone, with nobody to notice their passing. Bryant says that all "share thy destiny"; all will eventually die and join those already passed away.*

Reinforce and Extend

Answers

◆ Literature and Your Life

Reader's Response Students' responses should reflect new insights gained by reading the poem.

Thematic Focus In life, nature comforts and heals us. Through nature, we come to understand our place in the life cycle and how, with our deaths, our bodies return to nature.

☑ Check Your Comprehension

1. Nature can rejoice with us when we are happy and comfort us when we are sad.
2. The individual being will die, be buried, and become part of nature's elements.
3. "All that breathe"—anyone who lives—share that destiny.

◆ Critical Thinking

1. The poem is the poet's way of examining his beliefs about death and man's place in the world. In it, he conveys his own philosophy or "vision" of death: that mortal man must die in order to become part of immortal nature.
2. The poet seems to have come to terms with his place in the life cycle. He recognizes that it is his destiny to return to the earth at death so that his mortal body may in some way become part of the immortality of nature.
3. Possible response: The poem probably had more impact on nineteenth-century readers because many lived in closer contact with unspoiled nature than most modern readers, most of whom will not be buried in a natural wilderness.
4. Both poems reflect the idea that life, particularly the cycles of nature, continues after we are gone.

Develop Understanding

One-Minute Insight Written when the War of 1812 was still a living memory, this poem pays homage to the valiant role the *Constitution* played in American history. The poet pleads to let her sink at sea rather than suffer ignominious demolition.

Literature CD-ROM
To learn more about Oliver Wendell Holmes, use *The History of American Literature:* Part 1, Disk 2, Feature 2.

Enrichment Holmes was twenty-one years old when he read that the U.S. government was planning to scrap the warship U.S.S. *Constitution.* All over the country, patriots wrote letters condemning the demolition of the ship, but the government ignored them. Holmes's poem was printed in the Boston *Daily Advertiser* on September 16, 1830, and then printed and distributed on leaflets throughout the country. Public response to the poem was overwhelming; the government finally decided to preserve the ship as a national monument.

◆ Literary Focus

Meter "Old Ironsides" is composed largely of iambic feet. The lines alternate between iambic tetrameter—four feet to a line—and iambic trimeter—three feet to a line. As in most poetry, the poet occasionally varies the rhythm. For example, line 13 begins with "No more," which is a spondee—two stressed syllables.

▶Critical Viewing◀

❶ **Analyze** Students may cite lines 2–4, and lines 9–14.

◆ Grammar and Style

❷ **Participles as Adjectives** Have students identify the participle that acts as an adjective, and the noun it modifies. *tattered; ensign*

Old Ironsides

Oliver Wendell Holmes

▲ **Critical Viewing** The U.S.S. *Constitution* had not sailed on her own power in more than 116 years. To celebrate her two-hundredth birthday in July 1997, the ship sailed in Marblehead, Massachusetts. What lines from the poem still apply? **[Analyze]** ❶

❷ Ay, tear her tattered ensign down!
Long has it waved on high,
And many an eye has danced to see
That banner in the sky;
Beneath it rung the battle shout,
And burst the cannons roar;—
The meteor of the ocean air
Shall sweep the clouds no more.

Cross-Curricular Connection: Social Studies

The U.S.S. *Constitution* America has always been justifiably proud of the great ships its workers have built. Certain ships stand out as praiseworthy examples of this complex craft. The U.S.S. *Constitution,* nicknamed "Old Ironsides," is foremost among them. This forty-four-gun warship, ordered by President George Washington and completed in 1797, first won fame against Barbary pirates at Tripoli, a victory celebrated in the Marine Corps hymn. The *Constitution* is probably best remembered for its role in the War of 1812, when it outsailed British ships to win several decisive battles for the United States Navy.

Though Oliver Wendell Holmes helped win the war to save the *Constitution* from demolition, a century later it was once again in peril. The deteriorating ship was in need of major repairs. This time, America's children came to the rescue. In 1928, schoolchildren throughout the United States contributed money that they had collected to restore the ship to its original condition. The restored *Constitution* is still on display at Charlestown Navy Yard, Charlestown, Massachusetts.

❸ Her deck, once red with heroes' blood,
Where knelt the vanquished foe,
When winds were hurrying o'er the flood,
And waves were white below,
No more shall feel the victor's tread,
Or know the conquered knee;—
The harpies[1] of the shore shall pluck
The eagle of the sea!

❹ Oh, better that her shattered hulk
Should sink beneath the wave;
Her thunders shook the mighty deep,
And there should be her grave;
Nail to the mast her holy flag,
Set every threadbare sail,
And give her to the god of storms,
The lightning and the gale!

1. **harpies** (här′ pēz): In Greek mythology, hideous, filthy winged monsters with the head and trunk of a woman and the tail, legs, and talons of a bird. Here, the word refers to relentless, greedy, or grasping people.

Guide for Responding

◆ Literature and Your Life

Reader's Response If you had been alive in 1830, would this poem have inspired you to protest the demolition of *Old Ironsides*? Explain.

Thematic Focus What value do historical monuments have to American society?

☑ Check Your Comprehension

1. In the opening stanza, is the speaker agreeing that the government should "tear [the battleship *Constitution's*] tattered ensign down"? Explain.
2. What does the speaker suggest might be a more fitting end for the ship?

◆ Critical Thinking

INTERPRET

1. What did *Old Ironsides*, which Holmes calls "The eagle of the sea," represent to the poet? **[Interpret]**
2. How does the poet appeal to the American sense of patriotism? **[Analyze]**

EVALUATE

3. Is the ship or its historic role more important to the speaker? Explain. **[Make a Judgment]**

EXTEND

4. This poem aroused such protest that the ship was saved. Could a poem have such a powerful effect on the American public today? Why or why not? **[Social Studies Link]**

◆ Reading Strategy

❸ **Summarize** Have students summarize how the poet feels about the ship and the mission it once fulfilled. *He admires and respects the contributions it made in battle and regrets that it will never again carry a gallant crew or accept surrenders on its decks.*

◆ Critical Thinking

❹ **Interpret** What does the speaker suggest as an alternative to scrapping the ship? *He would rather see it go down in a storm.* Why might he consider this preferable? *He believes that to go down with all its flags flying is more dignified than being scrapped.*

Reinforce and Extend

Customize for
AP Students

Invite interested students to find out about the 200th birthday sail of the *Constitution* on July 21, 1997. That was the first time since 1881 that the nation's oldest commissioned warship sailed under its own power.

Answers

◆ Literature and Your Life

Reader's Response Students should support their responses with a well-reasoned explanation.

Thematic Focus Historical monuments remind us of our rich history.

☑ Check Your Comprehension

1. No, the speaker is being sarcastic.
2. He feels it would be better to raise its sails, nail her flag to the mast, and let it sink in a storm.

◆ Critical Thinking

1. "Old Ironsides" was to Holmes a maritime emblem of our nation.
2. He appeals to the American sense of patriotism by reminding the reader of important battles in which the ship played a key role.
3. It is the historic role of the ship that is important to Holmes. His references to the many important battles in which the ship took part are evidence that he thinks of the ship as a symbol of American liberty.
4. Possible response: Because fewer people now read poetry, a poem probably would not have as powerful an effect.

Beyond the Selection

FURTHER READING

Other Works by Oliver Wendell Holmes

"The Chambered Nautilus"
"The Wonderful One-Hoss Shay"
The Autocrat of the Breakfast Table

We suggest that you preview these works before recommending them to students.

INTERNET

To learn more about Holmes, we suggest the following sites. Please be aware, however, that sites may have changed since we published this information.

For information about "Old Ironsides," go to: **http://www.charlestown.ma.us/constitution**

For information about Holmes, go to: **http://www.tiac.net/users/eldred/owh/holmes.html**

We *strongly recommend* that you preview these sites before sending students to them.

Develop Understanding

One-Minute Insight In this poem, inspired by the death of Lowell's own child, a silent, pristine snowfall reminds a still-grieving father of the untimely loss of his young daughter some time before.

Literature CD-ROM To build background on James Russell Lowell, use *The History of American Literature:* Part 1, Disk 2, Feature 2.

Enrichment Lowell's daughter Blanche (his only child at that time) died in March 1847, when she was little more than a year old. His daughter Mabel, to whom he speaks in the poem, was born in the fall of that year. Mabel was the only one of his four children to survive infancy.

Customize for
English Language Learners
❶ Be sure students understand that the sheds do not normally have marble roofs. Here, the poet uses a metaphor to compare the smooth white layer of snow to fine, white marble.

Customize for
AP Students
❷ Guide students to identify this as a transitional stanza in the poem. Help them recognize that in these lines, the poet changes his focus from the outer landscape to the speaker's inner self.

▶Critical Viewing◀

❸ **Connect** Responses may include words such as *silence deep and white, noiseless, leaden,* and *deep.*

The First Snowfall

James Russell Lowell

Connections to World Literature, *page 1166*

The snow had begun in the gloaming,
And busily all the night
Had been heaping field and highway
With a silence deep and white.

Every pine and fir and hemlock
Wore ermine too dear for an earl
And the poorest twig on the elm tree
Was ridged inch deep with pearl.

From sheds new-roofed with Carrara[1] ❶
Came Chanticleer's[2] muffled crow
The stiff rails softened to swan's-down,
And still fluttered down the snow.

I stood and watched by the window
The noiseless work of the sky,
And the sudden flurries of snowbirds. ❷
Like brown leaves whirling by.

I thought of a mound in sweet Auburn[3]
Where a little headstone stood;

1. **Carrara** (kə rä′ rə) *n.*: Fine, white marble.
2. **Chanticleer's** (chan′ tə klirz′): Referring to a rooster.
3. **Auburn:** Mt. Auburn Cemetery in Cambridge, Massachusetts.

◀ Critical Viewing What words from the poem can describe both death and the snow in this photograph? **[Connect]** ❸

Beyond the Classroom

Community Connection

Cemetery Visit Cemeteries hold interesting clues to a community's patterns of life and death. Plan a class trip to a local cemetery, national burial ground, or mausoleum, or have students visit one of these places on their own or in groups. Discuss respectful behavior in such places. Encourage students to read the messages on the headstones or plaques and use their imaginations to infer or create family stories of the deceased. The epitaphs they read may inspire some students to conduct local research. For example, many deaths in the same year might indicate an epidemic or a natural disaster. A particularly impressive epitaph might inspire inquiries into the life and achievements of a local community leader.

How the flakes were folding it gently,
As did robins the babes in the wood.

Up spoke our own little Mabel,
Saying, "Father, who makes it snow?"
And I told of the good All-Father
Who cares for us here below.

Again I looked at the snowfall,
And thought of the leaden sky
That arched o'er our first great sorrow,
When that mound was heaped so high.

I remembered the gradual patience
❹ That fell from that cloud like snow,
Flake by flake, healing and hiding
The scar that renewed our woe.

And again to the child I whispered,
"The snow that husheth all,
Darling, the merciful Father
Alone can make it fall!"

Then, with eyes that saw not, I kissed her:
And she, kissing back, could not know
❺ That my kiss was given to her sister.
Folded close under deepening snow.

◆ Build Vocabulary

gloaming (glō´ miŋ) *n.*: Evening dusk; twilight

Guide for Responding

◆ Literature and Your Life

Reader's Response What natural events trigger personal memories for you?

Thematic Focus How do personal experiences affect the way in which we perceive natural events?

☑ Check Your Comprehension

1. Of what does the snowstorm make the speaker think?
2. (a) How does the speaker first respond to his daughter's question about the snow? (b) What does he later add to this response?
3. What does the speaker's daughter not know when he kisses her?

◆ Critical Thinking

INTERPRET

1. (a) How does the speaker imply that "our first great sorrow" is the death of his daughter? (b) Why does the snowfall remind him of her death? **[Analyze]**
2. In lines 29–36, what process is likened to the snowfall? **[Interpret]**
3. What do lines 34–36 suggest about the source of emotional healing? **[Infer]**

EXTEND

4. In the nineteenth century, infant deaths were far more common than they are today. How might the high infant mortality rate have affected the attitudes and values of the day? **[Social Studies Link]**

Beyond the Selection

FURTHER READING

Other Works by James Russell Lowell

"Auspex"
"The Vision of Sir Launfal"
"A Fable for Critics"

Other Works With the Theme of Loss

"The Raven," Edgar Allan Poe
"When Lilacs Last in the Dooryard Bloom'd," Walt Whitman

We suggest that you preview these works before recommending them to students.

INTERNET

The Internet provides opportunities for students to learn more about James Russell Lowell. We suggest the following site. Please be aware, however, that sites may have changed since this information was published. For biographical information on the poet, go to:

http://www.rodent.lib.rochester.edu/camelot/auth/lowell.htm

We *strongly recommend* that you preview this site before sending students to it.

◆ Reading Strategy

❹ **Summarize** Ask students to summarize this stanza. *Patience descended on the speaker, healing his emotional scar, just as snow fell to hide the visible "scar" of her gravesite.*

◆ Critical Thinking

❺ **Interpret** Ask students to explain how the final stanza brings together the ideas expressed in the poem. *Students may respond that, through his love and affection for his living daughter, the speaker expresses his love for the daughter he has lost.*

Reinforce and Extend

Answers

◆ Literature and Your Life

Reader's Response Students may cite thunderstorms, rainbows, or similar natural occurrences.

Thematic Focus We often associate personal experiences and the corresponding emotions with certain natural events.

☑ Check Your Comprehension

1. The snowstorm makes him think of his daughter's death and her burial place ("a mound in sweet Auburn").
2. (a) At first he answers that the "good All-Father who cares for us" makes it snow. (b) He adds that the snow hushes all; only the "merciful Father" can make it fall.
3. She does not know that his kiss is intended for his dead daughter.

◆ Critical Thinking

1. (a) He previously noted that the snowfall makes him think of a "mound . . . [w]here a little headstone stood" and later identifies the one buried as Mabel's sister. (b) Snow fell during his daughter's burial.
2. The falling snow is likened to the process of emotional healing.
3. It suggests that God is the source of the healing that eventually allows us to bury our grief.
4. Possible response: People may have been more accustomed to death, accepting it as a natural part of life. They may also have understood the fragility of life.

One-Minute Insight This narrative poem commemorates a way of life and the love that the poet's family gave him. A December snowstorm isolates a family on a New England farm. Despite extra efforts they must expend to care for their animals, keep warm, and fight off loneliness, the family relishes its cozy togetherness and the beauties of nature's artistry.

Literature CD-ROM To introduce students to John Greenleaf Whittier, use *The History of American Literature:* Part 1, Disk 2, Feature 4.

Customize for
Less Proficient Readers
To help these students digest the images and information in this lengthy poem, treat the selection in sections. You may find it helpful to divide the poem as follows:

1. Signs of the coming storm (lines 1–30)
2. Description of the storm and the family's response to it (lines 31–115)
3. Lighting a fire in the fireplace (lines 116–142)
4. Description of the outside world (lines 143–154)
5. Description of the world inside (lines 155–174)

As they read each section, have students look for different ways in which the poet appeals to the senses. They might make a graphic organizer in which they list imagery about sight, smell, sound, touch, and taste.

Customize for
Visual/Spatial Learners
The lifestyle recorded in "Snowbound" has largely disappeared. To convey a visual image of the time, bring in copies of paintings of mid-nineteenth-century America. The prints of Currier and Ives and the watercolors paintings of Winslow Homer would be among the most appropriate examples.

Old Holley House, Cos Cob, John Henry Twachtman, Cincinnati Art Museum

Humanities: Art

Old Holley House, Cos Cob, c. 1890–1900, by John Henry Twachtman.

John Henry Twachtman (1853–1902) is considered one of the best American landscape painters and was a leading American practitioner of French Impressionism. His style was innovative, especially in his use of iridescent colors and distinctive brush strokes, and in his lack of traditional form-molding shadows.

Twachtman uses soft colors in this painting. At first glance, the picture seems flat, but closer examination reveals depth and vibrancy, such as might be seen on a bright, snowy day.

Use these questions for discussion:

1. What colors does the artist use to depict the snow? Why do you think he used so many colors? *He uses shades of blue, white, gray, pink, and purple to show depth, texture, and shadow.*
2 What words from the poem also describe the picture? *Answers will vary but should include* hills of gray, white drift, glistening, dazzling crystal, snow-mist, and frost line.

from

Snowbound

John Greenleaf Whittier

A Winter Idyll ❶

The sun that brief December day
Rose cheerless over hills of gray,
And, darkly circled, gave at noon ❷
A sadder light than waning moon. ❸
Slow tracing down the thickening sky
Its mute and ominous prophecy,

◆ **Build Vocabulary**

ominous (äm´ ə nəs) *adj*.: Threatening

◀ **Critical Viewing** At the end of this poem, the speaker describes the inside of his home. Contrast that interior with the exterior of the house in this painting. **[Contrast]** ❹

Listening to Literature Audiocassettes Because Whittier uses a regular rhythm and rhyme scheme and makes frequent use of sound devices, this is an ideal poem to have your students listen to. After they've finished listening, have them discuss how the use of sound contributes to the overall impact of the poem.

❶ **Clarification** An *idyll* is a poem that describes simple, peaceful, or charming scenes or events of rural or pastoral life.

◆ Critical Thinking

❷ **Analyze** Ask students: What is the mood of the first six lines of the poem? *Students should reply that it is ominous, threatening, or gloomy.*

◆ Grammar and Style

❸ **Participles as Adjectives** Have students identify present and past participles that act as adjectives in this passage. *circled, waning, thickening*

▶ Critical Viewing ◀

❹ **Contrast** Students may say that the mood inside the speaker's home is cozy, warm, merry, and content. The painting conveys an exterior that is cold, lonely, and unwelcoming.

Research Skills Mini-Lesson

Outlining

Introduce the Concept Tell students that when they have a research assignment such as the Oral Presentation on p. 273, outlining is a useful skill.

Develop Background Point out that an outline can help students organize their presentation of information and ideas. For example, an outline of an oral presentation relating William Cullen Bryant's "vision," or perspective on life, to that of Thomas Cole and the Hudson River School might include the following main parts:

I. Introduction, stating the main idea or argument
II. Elaboration, describing:
(A) Hudson River School's
  (1) subject matter & painting style
  (2) vision of the world
(B) Cole's
  (1) subject matter & painting style
  (2) vision of the world
(C) Bryant's
  (1) subject matter & poetic style
  (2) vision of the world
III. Conclusion, persuasively summarizing the main idea.

Apply Direct students to decide ahead of time what subjects they will need to research for their oral presentation. Suggest that, after taking notes on their research, they create a simple, logical outline that helps them organize a focused comparison of works of the Hudson River School, Cole, and Bryant.

Assess Evaluate students' outlines on the basis of their clarity and logical organization.

◆ Literary Focus

❶ **Meter** Have students identify the meter Whittier uses in this poem. *He uses iambic tetrameter.* Discuss how to confirm the meter (count the number of iambs per line) and recognize exceptions, if any.

Comprehension Check ☑

❷ Ask students: What signals the coming of the snowstorm? *Students should note the following: the chill that penetrates even the warmest coat; the bitter cold that stops the blood flow in the skin of the face; and the roar and throbbing pulse of the east wind.*

◆ Critical Thinking

❸ **Analyze** What effect is created by the images in these lines? *Students should respond that the whinnying horse, clashing horns, impatiently shaking cattle, and challenging rooster crow convey the nervous unrest the animals are feeling; they sense that something powerful or unusual is coming.*

◆ Critical Thinking

❹ **Compare** Ask students to what the poet compares the movement of the snow. *He compares it to a swarm and whirl-dance.*

A portent seeming less than threat,
It sank from sight before it set.
A chill no coat, however stout,
Of homespun stuff could quite shut out,
A hard, dull bitterness of cold,
That checked, mid-vein, the circling race ❶
Of lifeblood in the sharpened face, ❷
The coming of the snowstorm told.
The wind blew east; we heard the roar
Of Ocean on his wintry shore,
And felt the strong pulse throbbing there
Beat with low rhythm our inland air.

Meanwhile we did our nightly chores—
Brought in the wood from out of doors,
Littered the stalls, and from the mows
Raked down the herd's-grass for the cows:
Heard the horse whinnying for his corn;
And, sharply clashing horn on horn,
Impatient down the stanchion[1] rows
The cattle shake their walnut bows; ❸
While, peering from his early perch
Upon the scaffold's pole of birch,
The cock his crested helmet bent
And down his querulous challenge sent.

Unwarmed by any sunset light
The gray day darkened into night,
A night made hoary with the swarm
And whirl-dance of the blinding storm, ❹
As zigzag, wavering to and fro,
Crossed and recrossed the winged snow:
And ere the early bedtime came
The white drift piled the window frame,
And through the glass the clothesline posts
Looked in like tall and sheeted ghosts.

So all night long the storm roared on:
The morning broke without a sun;
In tiny spherule[2] traced with lines
Of Nature's geometric signs,
In starry flake, and pellicle,[3]
All day the hoary meteor fell;
And, when the second morning shone,
We looked upon a world unknown,
On nothing we could call our own. ❺

1. **stanchion** (stan´ chən): Restraining device fitted around the neck of a cow to confine it to its stall.

2. **spherule** (sfer´ o͞ol): Small sphere.

3. **pellicle** (pel´ i kəl): Thin film of crystals.

◆ Build Vocabulary

querulous (kwer´ ə ləs) *adj.*: Complaining

patriarch (pā´ trē ärk´) *n.*: The father and ruler of a family or tribe

Humanities: Art

Musical "Descriptions"
Many of the wintry descriptions John Greenleaf Whittier created with words, the Italian composer Antonio Vivaldi (1678–1741) created with music. His famous *Four Seasons* concerto is rich with dynamic, tonal, and rhythmic effects. This piece, based on a cycle of four sonnets that Vivaldi himself may have written, offers musical images of spring, summer, autumn, and winter.

Play Opus 8, Number 4, "Winter," for the class. Challenge students to listen for musical illustrations of icy snow, chilling winds, and chattering teeth. Discuss the musical devices Vivaldi used to convey his imagery.

(5) Around the glistening wonder bent
The blue walls of the firmament,
No cloud above, no earth below—
A universe of sky and snow!
The old familiar sights of ours
Took marvelous shapes; strange domes and towers
Rose up where sty or corncrib stood,
Or garden wall, or belt of wood;
A smooth white mound the brush pile showed,
A fenceless drift what once was road;
The bridle post an old man sat
With loose-flung coat and high cocked hat;
The wellcurb had a Chinese roof;
And even the long sweep,[4] high aloof,
In its slant splendor, seemed to tell
Of Pisa's leaning miracle.[5]

(6) A prompt, decisive man, no breath
Our father wasted: "Boys, a path!"
(7) Well pleased (for when did farmer boy
Count such a summons less than joy?)
(8) Our buskins[6] on our feet we drew;
With mittened hands, and caps drawn low,
To guard our necks and ears from snow,
We cut the solid whiteness through.
And, where the drift was deepest, made
A tunnel walled and overlaid
With dazzling crystal: we had read
Of rare Aladdin's[7] wondrous cave,
And to our own his name we gave,
With many a wish the luck were ours
To test his lamp's supernal powers.
We reached the barn with merry din,
And roused the prisoned brutes within,
The old horse thrust his long head out,
And grave with wonder gazed about;
The cock his lusty greeting said,
And forth his speckled harem led;
The oxen lashed their tails, and hooked,
And mild reproach of hunger looked;
The hornèd patriarch of the sheep,
Like Egypt's Amun[8] roused from sleep,
Shook his sage head with gesture mute,
And emphasized with stamp of foot.

All day the gusty north wind bore
The loosening drift its breath before:
Low circling round its southern zone,
The sun through dazzling snow-mist shone.
No church bell lent its Christian tone
To the savage air, no social smoke
Curled over woods of snow-hung oak

4. **sweep:** Pole with a bucket at one end, used for raising water from a well.
5. **Pisa's leaning miracle:** Famous leaning tower of Pisa in Italy.
6. **buskins:** High-cut leather shoes or boots.
7. **Aladdin's:** Referring to Aladdin, a boy in *The Arabian Nights* who found a magic lamp and through its powers discovered a treasure in a cave.
8. **Amun:** Egyptian god with a ram's head.

Customize for *Visual/Spatial Learners*

(5) Students may better visualize the playful, stunning imagery of this passage by sketching the scene Whittier describes.

◆ Critical Thinking

(6) **Infer** Whittier captures the father's character in two lines. Based on this brief description, ask students to explain the kind of person the father is. *Students may respond that he is a person who doesn't waste time or words and that he acts quickly and decisively.*

◆ Critical Thinking

(7) **Speculate** Ask students why the boys are so excited by the father's order to make a path through the snow. *Students may say that this is not a typical farm chore; it evokes a sense of excitement and mystery and stimulates their imagination.*

◆ Reading Strategy

(8) **Summarize** Ask students to summarize the action and key details in lines 70–80. *After bundling up in boots, mittens, and caps, the boys cut through the snow with their shovels. They tunnel through the deepest drift to form a cave, which they name after Aladdin's, wishing they could have his magic lamp, as well.*

Customize for *Visual/Spatial Learners*

To help these students connect to the poetry, use the Humanities Connection: Fine Art page in the ***Beyond Literature*** booklet of the Teacher's Resources (p. 17).

Analyze Literary Criticism

In his poem "A Fable for Critics," James Russell Lowell wrote the following lines about his contemporary, John Greenleaf Whittier:

> There was ne'er a man born who had more of the swing
> Of the true lyric bard and all that kind of thing;
> And his failures arise (though he seem not to know it)
> From the very same cause that has made him a poet,—
> A fervor of mind which knows no separation
> 'Twixt simple excitement and pure inspiration. . . .
> Let his mind once get head in its favorite direction
> And the torrent of verse bursts the dams of reflection,
> While, borne with the rush of the metre along,
> The poet may chance to go right or go wrong,
> Content with the whirl and delirium of song;
> Then his grammar's not always correct, nor his rhymes,
> And he's prone to repeat his own lyrics sometimes . . . .

Share this passage with students. During a brief discussion, invite them to ask questions if there are lines or passages they don't understand. Then have them answer the following question in their journals:

Do you think Lowell's criticism of Whittier is reasonable or unreasonable? Why or why not?

Customize for
Musical Learners

❶ Encourage students to evaluate the impact of the weather-imposed solitude by identifying sound elements and sensory details in this passage. Which intensify the isolation? Which add to the mystery? *Students may cite as evidence of isolation the lack of church bells, laughter, conversation, and water sounds from the brook; mysterious sounds include the shrieking wind, moaning trees, and tapping sleet.*

Customize for
Less Proficient Readers

❷ Point out how the speaker combines images of inside and outside to create a vivid description of what the family did that evening. Help them identify words that pertain to color, texture, and temperature.

Comprehension Check ☑

❸ Ask students: What is the "mimic flame" outside? *The speaker is describing the reflection of the hearth flames in the windowpanes.*

◆ Critical Thinking

❹ **Compare** Direct students to focus on the colors the speaker mentions in this stanza and the one before. Then ask them to contrast the mood of the two stanzas, based on color imagery. *Students may say that the poet uses white, silver, and black to describe the outdoors; he uses rose, red, and gold to describe the indoors. These distinct color groups create two contrasting moods: stark, cold detachment vs. embracing warmth.*

A solitude made more intense
By dreary-voicèd elements,
The shrieking of the mindless wind,
The moaning tree boughs swaying blind,
And on the glass the unmeaning beat
Of ghostly fingertips of sleet.
Beyond the circle of our hearth
No welcome sound of toil or mirth
Unbound the spell, and testified ❶
Of human life and thought outside.
We minded that the sharpest ear
The buried brooklet could not hear,
The music of whose liquid lip
Had been to us companionship,
And, in our lonely life, had grown
To have an almost human tone.

As night drew on, and, from the crest
Of wooded knolls that ridged the west,
The sun, a snow-blown traveler, sank
From sight beneath the smothering bank,
We piled, with care, our nightly stack
Of wood against the chimney back—
The oaken log, green, huge, and thick,
And on its top the stout backstick;
The knotty forestick laid apart,
And filled between with curious art
The ragged brush; then, hovering near,
We watched the first red blaze appear, ❷
Heard the sharp crackle, caught the gleam
On whitewashed wall and sagging beam,
Until the old, rude-furnished room
Burst, flowerlike, into rosy bloom;
While radiant with a mimic flame
Outside the sparkling drift became, ❸
And through the bare-boughed lilac tree
Our own warm hearth seemed blazing free.
The crane and pendent trammels[9] showed,
The Turks' heads[10] on the andirons glowed;
While childish fancy, prompt to tell
The meaning of the miracle,
Whispered the old rhyme: *"Under the tree,*
When fire outdoors burns merrily,
There the witches are making tea."

The moon above the eastern wood
Shone at its full; the hill range stood
Transfigured in the silver flood, ❹
Its blown snows flashing cold and keen,
Dead white, save where some sharp ravine
Took shadow, or the somber green

9. **trammels** (tram′ əlz) *n.*: Adjustable pothooks hanging from the movable arm, or crane, attached to the hearth.
10. **Turks' heads:** Turbanlike knots at the top of the andirons.

Speaking, Listening, and Viewing Mini-Lesson

Dramatic Reading
This mini-lesson supports the Speaking, Listening, and Viewing activity in the Idea Bank on p. 273.

Introduce the Concept Discuss with students the distinctions between oral reading and dramatic reading: An oral reading is simply any reading out loud, but a dramatic reading includes emotional emphasis that fits the text.

Develop Background Point out that Holmes wanted his poem to stir his audiences to action. Direct students to analyze the poem to identify key phrases. Students should note which words or phrases to accentuate, which to deliver softly or reverently, and so on. Allow time for students to practice and fine-tune their interpretations for maximum effect.

Apply the Information As students take turns delivering their dramatic readings, encourage audience members to jot down evaluative notes so that they can critique the presentations afterward.

Assess the Outcome Invite open discussion on the dramatic readings. Assess each presentation's ability to move or persuade. Discuss elements that distinguished the different presentations, such pace, intensity, accent, tone, and the overall blend of these elements into a performance.

Of hemlocks turned to pitchy black
Against the whiteness at their back.
❹ For such a world and such a night
Most fitting that unwarming light,
Which only seemed where'er it fell
To make the coldness visible.

Shut in from all the world without,
We sat the clean-winged hearth[11] about,
Content to let the north wind roar
In baffled rage at pane and door,
❺ While the red logs before us beat
The frost line back with tropic heat;
And ever, when a louder blast
Shook beam and rafter as it passed,
The merrier up its roaring draft
The great throat of the chimney laughed;
The house dog on his paws outspread
Laid to the fire his drowsy head.
The cat's dark silhouette on the wall
A couchant tiger's seemed to fall:
And, for the winter fireside meet,
Between the andirons' straddling feet,
The mug of cider simmered slow,
The apples sputtered in a row,
And, close at hand, the basket stood
With nuts from brown October's wood.

11. **clean-winged hearth:** A turkey wing was used for the hearth broom.

Guide for Responding

◆ *Literature and Your Life*

Reader's Response Would you find it pleasant to be isolated, like the narrator and his family, by a powerful snowstorm? Why or why not?

Thematic Focus What effect does this strong natural event have on the residents of a rural New England farm?

☑ Check Your Comprehension

1. What weather conditions forewarn the narrator of the approaching snowstorm?

2. How long does the storm last?

3. (a) After the storm has ended, what does the narrator's father tell the boys to do? (b) How do the boys respond to the request?

◆ Critical Thinking

INTERPRET

1. What does the family's response to the storm suggest about their relationship with nature? **[Draw Conclusions]**

2. What descriptive details in lines 47–80 convey the narrator's sense of wonder upon viewing the snow-covered landscape? **[Analyze]**

3. What details in the final stanza convey a sense of warmth and security? **[Analyze]**

APPLY

4. (a) How do you think most people today would respond to the prospect of being isolated by a major snowstorm? (b) How does this response reflect the ways in which life has changed since *Snowbound* was written in 1865? **[Apply; Analyze]**

Beyond the Selection

FURTHER READING

Other Works by John Greenleaf Whittier

"Hampton Beach"
"Barbara Frietchie"
"The Barefoot Boy"

Other Works With the Theme of Winter

"The Snowstorm," Ralph Waldo Emerson
"To Build a Fire," Jack London
"The Night Is Freezing Fast," A. E. Housman

We suggest that you preview these works before recommending them to students.

INTERNET

The Internet offers additional opportunities to learn more about John Greenleaf Whittier.

For a summary of Whittier's life and a sampling of his work, we suggest the following site: **http://www.haverhill.com/library/hp12jgw.html**

Please be aware that sites may have changed since we published this information. We *strongly recommend* that you preview this site before sending students to it.

◆ Reading Strategy

❺ **Summarize** Have students summarize this passage, and tell what the speaker means by saying that the wind roars "in baffled rage." *Students may say that the family is cozy and warm inside; no matter how hard the wind blows, it cannot penetrate the house or disturb the family.*

Reinforce and Extend

Customize for
AP Students
Challenge students to compare and contrast the two winter poems: "The First Snowfall" and "Snowbound." They can focus on underlying moods or messages, sensory imagery, or any other aspects that both poems share.

Answers

◆ *Literature and Your Life*

Reader's Response Students may reply that it might be fun for a short time; others may not like the idea of being confined to their homes.

Thematic Focus The snowstorm transforms their little world as they know it and opens their eyes to the wonders of nature.

☑ Check Your Comprehension

1. There is hardly any sun to be seen, and the sky is thickening.
2. The storm begins in late afternoon, continues through the night, lasts the entire next day, and has stopped by the second morning.
3. (a) He tells them to make a path. (b) They are pleased by his request and begin eagerly.

◆ Critical Thinking

1. It suggests that they live in harmony with nature.
2. Suggested responses include the following: "No cloud above, no earth below" and "Around the glistening wonder bent/The blue walls of firmament."
3. Possible response: "Shut in from all the world without" and "the red logs before us beat/The frost line back with tropic heat."
4. Possible responses: (a) They would be anxious about not being able to get to work or run errands. (b) People today live in a hectic world where a snowbound day is considered an inconvenience.

Answers

◆ Reading Strategy

Suggested responses:

Stanza 1 Summary: One December day, the sun was very pale and faded into a dark sky before it even set. It was so icy that the cold froze our faces and, along with the roaring east wind that sounded like the ocean, warned that a storm was coming.

Stanza 2 Summary: We did our nightly chores, including bringing in wood and raking down grass for the cows, while the horses whinnied and the cattle clashed their horns in their stalls. The rooster sat at the top of the scaffold pole and crowed.

◆ Literary Focus

1. So shalt thou rest, and what if thou withdraw
   In silence from the living, and no friend
2. Her deck, once red with heroes' blood,
   Where knelt the vanquished foe

◆ Build Vocabulary

Using the Word Root *-patr-*

1. patriots; 2. paternal;
3. patrimony

Using the Word Bank: Antonyms or Synonyms

1. S 2. A 3. A 4. A 5. A
6. S 7. A 8. S

◆ Grammar and Style

Practice

1. *circled* modifies *sun*; *waning* modifies *moon*
2. *resting* modifies *place*
3. *healing* modifies *sympathy*
4. *beholding* modifies *sun*

Writing Application

Possible response: The *dazzling* snow reflected the sunlight from every *crusted* branch and *drifted* slope. As I squinted into the *chilling* wind, I could barely make out the ice-*coated* snow bank that used to be my front steps.

Grammar Reinforcement

For additional instruction and practice, use the page on Participles and Participial Phrases in the *Writer's Solution Grammar Practice Book*, p. 32.

Guide for Responding (continued)

◆ Reading Strategy

Summarize

Whenever you tell friends about the plot of the television show they missed the night before, you are using your **summarizing** skills. Imagine that, for reasons of space, the first two stanzas of "A Winter Idyll" from *Snowbound* had to be omitted from a reprinting. Write a summary of the first and second stanzas that would enable a reader to understand everything that happened before "the gray day darkened into night" at the start of the third stanza. Include the main ideas in each stanza, as well as key supporting details.

Then use a graphic organizer like this one to help you summarize "The First Snowfall." In the middle column, jot down the key details from each stanza. Review all the details you've noted. Use them to write a complete summary in the third column.

Stanza	Key Details	Summary
1		
2		

◆ Literary Focus

Meter

The poems in this group have a regular pattern of stressed and unstressed syllables known as **meter.** "Thanatopsis" is written in **iambic pentameter**—a pattern of five iambs per line—whereas "Old Ironsides" alternates lines of iambic tetrameter with lines of **iambic trimeter**—three iambs per line.

1. Copy these lines from "Thanatopsis," and mark the stressed and unstressed syllables:

   So shalt thou rest, and what if thou
   withdraw
   In silence from the living, and no friend

2. Mark the stressed and unstressed syllables in these lines from "Old Ironsides":

   Her deck, once red with heroes' blood,
   Where knelt the vanquished foe,

◆ Build Vocabulary

Using the Latin Root *-patr-*

The Latin root *-patr-*, meaning "father," can be found in many familiar words. Complete each of these sentences with one of the following words: *patrimony, patriots, paternal.*

1. People who love and loyally support their fatherland are called __?__.
2. My father's mother is my __?__ grandmother.
3. He knew the family business would come to him as part of his __?__.

Using the Word Bank: Antonyms or Synonyms?

Decide whether the words in each of the following pairs are antonyms or synonyms. On your paper, write *A* for *antonyms* and *S* for *synonyms.*

1. sepulcher, tomb
2. pensive, frivolous
3. venerable, contemptible
4. melancholy, merry
5. gloaming, sunlight
6. ominous, forbidding
7. querulous, content
8. patriarch, father

◆ Grammar and Style

Participles as Adjectives

Like adjectives, participles modify nouns or pronouns and answer the question *what kind?* or *which one?*

A **participle** is a verb form that can be used as an adjective.

Practice Identify the participle(s) in each item, along with the noun each participle modifies.

1. The sun that brief December day / Rose cheerless over hills of gray, / And, darkly circled, gave at noon / A sadder light than waning moon.
2. Yet not to thine eternal resting place / Shalt thou retire alone, . . .
3. Into his darker musings, with a mild / And healing sympathy, . . .
4. . . . Yet a few days, and thee / The all-beholding sun shall see no more / In all his course; . . .

Writing Application In your notebook, write two or three sentences describing a snow-covered landscape. Use participial forms of the following verbs as adjectives: *dazzle, coat, crust, drift, chill.*

Reteach

Students who have difficulty understanding meter may benefit from a demonstration. Write the following lines from "Old Ironsides" on the board. Scan the short and long syllables, and separate them into iambic feet, as follows:

Be neath | it rung | the bat | tle shout,
And burst | the can | nons roar.

Point out that in the first line, there are four metrical "feet," or units of meter. Because these follow a pattern of one unstressed (or "short") syllable followed by one stressed (or "long") one, each foot is called an *iamb*—so the pattern itself is called *iambic.* Depending on how many feet are in a given line, iambic poetry is described as iambic trimeter (containing three metrical feet), tetrameter (containing four feet), pentameter (containing five feet), and so on.

Build Your Portfolio

Idea Bank

Writing

1. **Letter** Imagine that you are a guest in Whittier's home during the snowstorm described in *Snowbound.* Write a letter to a friend telling about your experience. Use details from the poem to enliven your account.
2. **Poem** Write a poem that expresses your position on a political issue, just as Oliver Wendell Holmes expresses his views on preserving the *Constitution.* **[Social Studies Link]**
3. **Analytical Essay** In a brief essay, explain the symbolic role of snow and the tide as they relate to the deaths described in Lowell's "The First Snowfall" and Longfellow's "The Tide Rises, The Tide Falls" (p. 253). **[Literature Link]**

Speaking, Listening, and Viewing

4. **Dramatic Reading** Convey Holmes's patriotic fervor in a dramatic reading of "Old Ironsides." Afterward, ask your classmates to critique your reading. Did they find it moving or persuasive? **[Performing Arts Link]**
5. **Poetry Critique** Read aloud a poem by one of the Fireside Poets. Then lead a class discussion about the work. What is its theme? Is it a poem to which modern readers can relate?

Researching and Representing

6. **Oral Presentation** The painting on p. 259 depicts William Cullen Bryant and Thomas Cole. Prepare an oral presentation on Cole and the Hudson River School. In what sense can he claim kinship with Bryant? **[Art Link]**
7. **Graphic Display** Create a classroom display by mounting two or more of these poems and illustrating them with appropriate images from magazines or your own snapshots. **[Art Link]**

Online Activity www.phlit.phschool.com

Guided Writing Lesson

Précis

Put your summarizing skills to the test by writing a **précis** (prā´ sē)—a concise abridgment or brief summary of a longer work—of the selection from *Snowbound.* Include all the main ideas and key details a reader would need in order to understand what happened in the poem. Like the poem itself, your summary should have a clear beginning, middle, and end.

Writing Skills Focus: Clear Beginning, Middle, and End

Have you ever told a friend the plot of a book and started with the middle of the story? It probably wasn't the clearest summary your friend ever heard. Whether you are listening or reading, you expect information to be presented in a logical sequence. A **clear beginning, middle, and end** are especially important to a précis, which should reflect the structure or progression of the original work.

Prewriting Review *Snowbound.* For each stanza, list the main ideas and key details you will include in your précis. Select enough details to convey the feel of the poem, but not so many that your writing becomes cluttered. Can you convey a whole series of details with a single phrase or sentence?

Drafting Set the mood for the coming storm by opening your précis with a summary of the poem's opening stanza. Refer to your prewriting notes to avoid confusing the sequence of events as you draft the middle and end.

Revising Read your précis as though you were seeing it for the first time. Does it accurately reflect the phases of the storm as the narrator relates them? Have you included enough details to convey the wonder of the snowy landscape and the coziness of the farmhouse hearth?

Idea Bank

Customizing for Performance Levels

Following are suggestions for matching Idea Bank topics with your students' performance levels:
Less Advanced Students: 1, 7
Average Students: 2, 4, 6
More Advanced Students: 3, 5

Customizing for Learning Modalities

Following are suggestions for matching Idea Bank topics with your students' learning modalities:
Musical/Rhythmic: 4
Interpersonal: 5, 6
Visual/Spatial: 7

Guided Writing Lesson

Writing Lab CD-ROM

Have students complete the tutorial on Exposition. Follow these steps:

1. Refer students to the Audio-Annotated Writing Model of a summary.
2. Have students use the Timeline activity to help them organize their details.
3. Have students draft on computer.
4. Have students use the Revision Checks for Transition Words to help them revise.

ASSESSMENT OPTIONS

Formal Assessment, Selection Test, pp. 81–83, and Assessment Resources Software. The selection test is designed so that it can be easily customized to the performance levels of your students.

Alternative Assessment, p. 17, includes options for less advanced students, more advanced students, verbal/linguistic learners, intrapersonal learners, and visual/spatial learners.

PORTFOLIO ASSESSMENT

Use the following rubrics in the ***Alternative Assessment*** booklet to assess student writing:
Letter: Description Rubric, p. 112
Poem: Poetry Rubric, p. 123
Analytical Essay: Literary Analysis/Interpretation Rubric, p. 127
Guided Writing Lesson: Summary Rubric, p. 113

Prepare and Engage

LESSON OBJECTIVES

1. **To develop vocabulary and word identification skills**
   - Latin Prefixes: *multi-*
   - Using the Word Bank: Denotation
2. **To use a variety of reading strategies to comprehend nonfiction**
   - Reading Strategy: Noting Spatial Relationships
3. **To increase knowledge of other cultures and to connect common elements across cultures**
   - Connecting Themes Across Cultures (ATE)
4. **To express and support responses to the text**
   - Critical Thinking
   - Idea Bank: Travel Advertisement
   - Idea Bank: Newspaper Article
5. **To analyze literary elements**
   - Literary Focus: Description
   - Idea Bank: Abstract
6. **To read in order to research self-selected and assigned topics**
   - Idea Bank: Expedition Map
   - Idea Bank: Research Report
7. **To plan, prepare, organize, and present literary interpretations**
   - Idea Bank: Speech
   - Idea Bank: Television Documentary
8. **To use recursive writing processes to write a description**
   - Guided Writing Lesson
9. **To increase knowledge of the rules of grammar and usage**
   - Grammar and Style: Participial Phrases

Test Preparation

Reading Comprehension: Make Inferences and Generalizations (ATE, p. 275)

The teaching tips and sample test item in this workshop support the instruction and practice in the unit workshop:

Reading Comprehension: Analyze Information to Make Inferences and Generalizations (ATE, p. 427)

Guide for Interpreting

Meriwether Lewis *(1774-1809)*

Along with William Clark and a team of hearty former soldiers, Meriwether Lewis completed a two-year, 8,000-mile expedition across the uncharted territory that the United States acquired in the Louisiana Purchase. Between 1804 and 1806, Lewis and Clark traveled from St. Louis up the Missouri River to its source, then across the Rocky Mountains to the Pacific coast. When they returned to St. Louis, they brought back valuable information about the Pacific Northwest.

Lewis's efforts were sponsored by President Thomas Jefferson, who gave him and his team a rigorous assignment—map a passage to the Pacific Ocean, collect scientific information about the regions they traveled, trace the boundaries of the Louisiana territory, and claim the Oregon territory for the United States.

In preparation for his journey, Lewis spent time in Philadelphia learning about scientific classification. These skills served him well as he documented the plants, animals, and minerals he encountered during his journey. To complement Lewis's naturalist interests, Clark provided strong map skills and created detailed sketches of the regions they crossed. The men also encountered a variety of Indian nations, trading gifts and information with these natives of the frontier.

John Wesley Powell *(1834–1902)*

As a Union soldier fighting in the Civil War, John Wesley Powell lost an arm at the Battle of Shiloh. Despite this injury, Powell was the first to navigate and chart the Colorado River and the Grand Canyon.

Powell was a geologist who conducted a daring and dangerous three-month journey on the Colorado River in 1869. Financed by the Smithsonian Institution and Congress, Powell led a party of ten men and four boats. In a reflective moment before he entered the canyon, Powell described the experience ahead of him as "an unknown distance yet to run; an unknown river yet to explore." Entering the Grand Canyon by boat, the members of the expedition party faced raging rapids, towering waterfalls, and dangerously sharp rock formations. Once in the canyon, Powell's expedition party split. Those that became terrified of the river went overland at "Separation Rapids" and perished. Powell, and the others who remained on the river, survived and completed the expedition.

Powell later conducted other expeditions surveying the Rocky Mountains and the canyons of the Green River. In the 1870's, he directed a federal geographic survey of western lands in the public domain, urging the government to develop plans for using the land.

◆ Background for Understanding

HISTORY: THE LOUISIANA PURCHASE

In 1803, the United States doubled the amount of territory it controlled with a single purchase of land from the French. Looking for money to finance its wars against other European nations, France sold the land shown in red on the map to the United States for a total price of $15 million—less than three cents an acre. Known as the Louisiana Purchase, the acquisition began an era of westward expansion that lasted nearly a century.

The Louisiana Purchase

Prentice Hall Literature Program Resources

REINFORCE / RETEACH / EXTEND

Selection Support Pages
Build Vocabulary: Latin Prefixes: *multi-*, p. 84
Grammar and Style: Participial Phrases, p. 85
Reading Strategy: Spatial Relationships, p. 86
Literary Focus: Description, p. 87

Strategies for Diverse Student Needs, p. 18

Beyond Literature
Cross-Curricular Connection: Social Studies, p. 18

Formal Assessment Selection Test, pp. 84–86; Assessment Resources Software

Alternative Assessment, p. 18

Writing and Language Transparencies
Writing Process Model 2, pp. 9–12

Art Transparencies Art Transparency 7: *Storm Clouds, Maine*

Resource Pro CD-ROM

Listening to Literature Audiocassettes

Crossing the Great Divide
◆ The Most Sublime Spectacle on Earth ◆

◆ Literature and Your Life

Connect Your Experience

If you've ever had an outdoor adventure—like backpacking, mountain climbing, or white-water rafting—you know how exciting it can be to gain firsthand experiences with the beauty and power of nature. Just imagine what it would have been like to chart new territory like Meriwether Lewis and John Wesley Powell and the other adventurers who blazed a trail across the western frontier.

Thematic Focus: Fireside and Campfire

These accounts provide a firsthand view of the joys, terrors, and hardships that adventurers like Lewis and Powell experienced during their travels. How would you have reacted in their place?

◆ Literary Focus

Description

Travel writing can either be fascinating or dry as a bone. Often, description makes the difference. **Description** is writing that captures sights, sounds, smells, tastes, and physical sensations. For example, Powell vividly captures the sound of the river when he writes that "the river *thunders* in perpetual *roar*." Through descriptions, a writer can bring a scene to life in readers' minds.

As you read, use a graphic organizer like this one to record descriptive details appealing to each sense.

Sights	Sounds	Smells	Physical Sensations	Tastes

Journal Writing Picture a beautiful place. Then write a short description of it using language that captures what you see, hear, feel, or smell.

◆ Reading Strategy

Noting Spatial Relationships

When descriptions are very detailed, you can get caught up in the language and lose sight of the actual object or scene. **Noting spatial relationships** as you read can help. Pay attention to sizes, distances, and locations in space of the features being described. Use this information to form an accurate mental picture of the subject.

◆ Build Vocabulary

Latin Prefixes: *multi-*

Multi- is a common Latin prefix that means "many" or "much." For example, a *multivitamin* contains many different vitamins. Powell's selection includes the word *multitudinous,* which means "the state of being numerous."

Word Bank

Preview this list of words from the narratives.

- conspicuous
- sublime
- labyrinth
- excavated
- demarcation
- multifarious
- multitudinous

◆ Grammar and Style

Participial Phrases

In "The Most Sublime Spectacle," Powell makes frequent use of participial phrases. A **participial phrase** is a group of words that includes a participle—a verb form that modifies a noun or pronoun—and its modifiers and complements. Powell uses mostly participial phrases beginning with past participles, which usually end in *-d* or *-ed*. The participial phrase in this example modifies the noun *canyon.*

The Grand Canyon of the Colorado is a canyon *composed of many canyons.*

Test Preparation Workshop

Reading Comprehension: Make Inferences and Generalizations

Standardized tests such as the SAT may ask students to make inferences about implied information. After students read p. 277, ask them the following question:

Why does Lewis emphasize the U.S. government's "friendly disposition" toward the Indians in his meeting with them?

A He wants them to help his expedition.
B He wants to join their community.
C He wants them to join the United States.
D He wants to take their land.

B, C, and *D* are not supported by the passage. *A* is correct. Lewis explains that if the Indians help the explorers reach the Pacific Ocean and then return home, the government will provide them with many benefits.

Interest Grabber Show students a portion of the PBS *Nova* episode entitled "Rafting Through the Grand Canyon" (which includes several excerpts from John Wesley Powell's journal) or any other documentary program about the canyon. Then ask students to write a brief postcard from the Grand Canyon, describing to a friend what they have just seen. Have volunteers share their postcard messages. Ask students to discuss what it would feel like to be the first westerner to see such a sight. Explain that the journals they are about to read are the literary equivalent of postcards from the frontier of the western world.

Connecting Themes Across Cultures

Invite students to describe the experiences of explorers they know of—such as John Muir, David Livingstone, Bruce Chatwin, or individuals from their own culture who came to the United States—whose true tales of inspiration, terror, and discovery might hold people's interest around a campfire.

Customize for *Less Proficient Readers*

Help students identify familiar words used in unfamiliar ways. Examples include *affecting* (emotionally moving), *flattering* (favorable), and *prosecute* (to go forward with). Guide students to use context clues to determine the meanings in each usage.

Customize for *AP Students*

Ask students to compare these journal entries with those of the earlier explorers they read in Unit 1. They can, for example, contrast Lewis's descriptions of his interactions with the Native Americans with those Cabeza de Vaca recorded.

Connecting to Real-World Texts

To connect this selection to a historic memorandum, see "Thomas Jefferson's Commission of Meriwether Lewis," p. 1210.

Develop Understanding

One-Minute Insight Lewis kept an intermittent but very detailed, descriptive, and informative journal of his expedition. Here he describes one of the expedition's many interactions with Native Americans. It is representative of Lewis's attempts to persuade the Indians of the powers of his government and of the advantages to them of cooperating with him in his effort to reach the Pacific.

◆ Background for Understanding

History In 1804, Thomas Jefferson and his advisors knew next to nothing about the lands Lewis was to explore. For one thing, they thought there was an all-water route to the Pacific. For another, they thought Lewis might encounter mastodons. Geographically, all they knew for certain was the latitude and longitude of the mouth of the Columbia River, of St. Louis, and of the Mandan villages along the Missouri River. With so much to find out, Jefferson made choices. For example, he chose not to seek gold or silver, but was very interested in establishing trade with the Native Americans.

◆ Grammar and Style

❶ **Participial Phrases** Ask students to identify the past participial phrase in this sentence and the word it modifies. *"transported with joy"; They*

◆ Critical Thinking

❷ **Infer** Ask students: What does the reaction of the chief and other Native Americans tell you about their relationship with Lewis and his party? *They are on cordial, even affectionate, terms with one another.*

▶Critical Viewing◀

❸ **Interpret** Students can say that in the pre-photography age, detailed drawings provided the only way to present visual descriptions of the new people, places, and things Lewis encountered in his travels. The maps also provided valuable documentation of the terrain for the use of future travelers and traders.

Crossing the

August 17–20, 1805
Meriwether Lewis

Saturday, August 17th, 1805

This morning I arose very early and dispatched Drewyer and the Indian down the river. Sent Shields to hunt. I made McNeal cook the remainder of our meat which afforded a slight breakfast for ourselves and the Chief. Drewyer had been gone about 2 hours when an Indian who had straggled some little distance down the river returned and reported that the white men were coming, that he had seen them just below. They all ❶ appeared transported with joy, and ❷ the chief repeated his fraternal hug. I felt quite as much gratified at this information as the Indians appeared to be. Shortly after Capt. Clark arrived with the Interpreter Charbono, and the Indian woman, who proved to be a sister of the Chief Cameahwait. The meeting of those was really affecting, particularly between Sah-ca-ga-we-ah and an Indian woman, who had been taken prisoner at the same time with her, and who had afterwards escaped from the Minnetares and rejoined her nation. At noon the canoes arrived, and we had the satisfaction once more to find ourselves all together, with a flattering prospect of being able to obtain as many horses shortly as would enable us to prosecute our voyage by land should that by water be deemed unadvisable.

❹ We now formed our camp just below the junction of the forks on the Lard. side[1] in a level smooth bottom covered with a fine turf

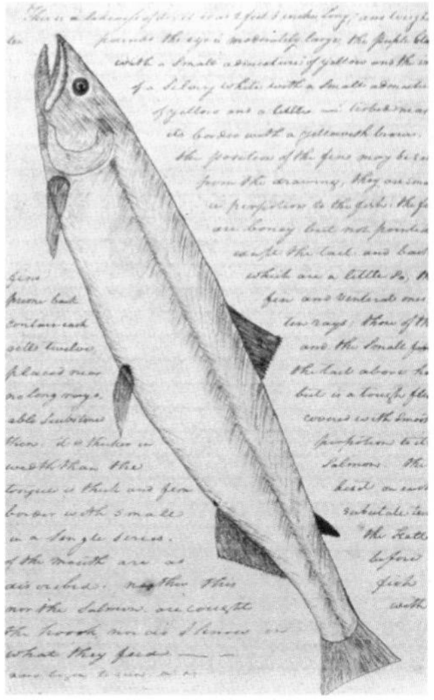

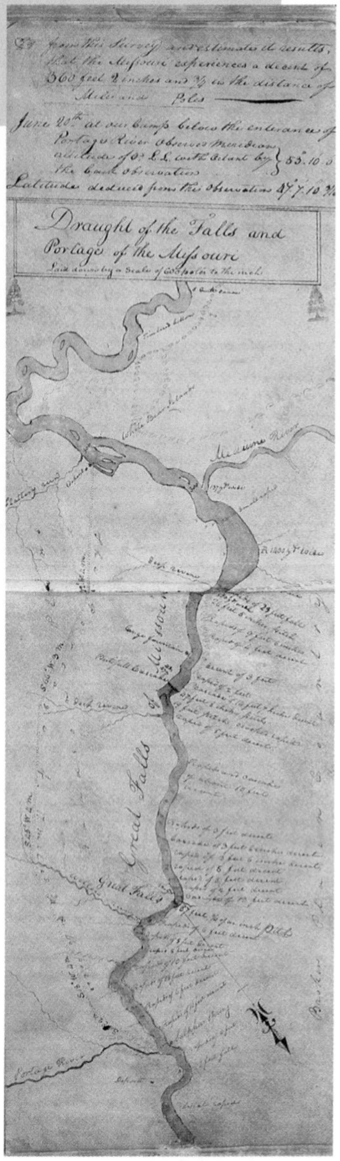

▲ ▶ **Critical Viewing** What do visuals like maps and illustrations ❸ add to the narrative of exploration accounts? **[Interpret]**

1. **Lard. side:** Abbreviation for larboard, the port side of a ship. From their perspective, they camped on the left side of the river.

Block Scheduling Strategies

Consider these suggestions to take advantage of extended class time:

- Introduce the selections using the biographies and Background for Understanding on p. 274.
- After students have read the selections, have them listen to "The Most Sublime Spectacle on Earth" on audiocassette. Discuss how Powell uses spatial relationships to enhance his descriptions.
- Have students use the Internet to gather additional information about the Lewis and Clark expedition.
- Introduce the Guided Writing Lesson (p. 283) using Writing Process Model 2: Descriptive and Observational Writing (pp. 9–12) in the ***Writing and Language Transparencies.*** Use the transparency to spark class discussion about the characteristics of an effective description. Have students look for specific examples of using transitions to show place. Volunteers can share their completed descriptions with the class.

4 of greensward. Here we unloaded our canoes and arranged our baggage on shore; formed a canopy of one of our large sails and planted some willow brush in the ground to form a shade for the Indians to sit under while we spoke to them, which we thought it best to do this evening. Accordingly about 4 P.M. we called them together and through the medium of Labuish, Charbono and Sah-ca-ga-we-ah, we communicated to them fully the objects which had brought us into this distant part of the country, in which we took care to make them a conspicuous object of our own good wishes and the care of our government. We made them sensible of their dependence on the will of our government for every species of merchandise as well for their defense and comfort; and apprised them of the strength of our government and its friendly dispositions towards them. We also gave them as a reason why we wished to penetrate the country as far as the ocean to the west of them was to examine and find out a more direct way to bring merchandise to them. That as no trade could be carried on with them before our return to our homes that it was mutually advantageous to them as well as to ourselves that they should render us such aids as they had it in their power to furnish in order to hasten our voyage and of course our return home.

Lewis and Clark With Sagagawea at the Great Falls of the Missouri, Olaf Seltzer, The Thomas Gilcrease Institute of Art, Tulsa, Oklahoma

▲ **Critical Viewing:** What does this picture suggest about the relationship among the people in it? Does the text support the suggestion? **[Infer; Support]** 5

◆ Build Vocabulary

conspicuous (kən spik′ yo͞o əs) *adj.*: Obvious; easy to see or perceive

Guide for Responding

◆ Literature and Your Life

Reader's Response What did you think of the way Lewis negotiated with the Indians? Explain.

Thematic Focus Lewis knew that one day his journal might be made public. How might this have affected his writing?

☑ Check Your Comprehension

1. Summarize the first paragraph of Lewis's account.
2. Why is Lewis so pleased at being reunited with the rest of his party?

◆ Critical Thinking

INTERPRET

1. Is Lewis being candid when he tells the Indians why the expedition is there? Explain. **[Infer]**
2. Lewis distributed gifts after negotiating with the Indians. Why might he have done this? **[Analyze]**
3. Is obtaining their help Lewis's sole interest in the Indians? Explain. **[Draw Conclusions]**

EVALUATE

4. How would you rate Lewis as a negotiator? Explain. **[Assess]**

Humanities: Art

Lewis and Clark With Sacagawea at the Great Falls of the Missouri, by Olaf Seltzer.

Olaf Seltzer (1877–1957) was a native of Denmark, where he studied art as a boy. At the age of fourteen, he emigrated to Montana with his mother. After a brief stint as a cowboy, he began working for the Great Northern Railroad. Seltzer sketched and painted in his spare time, until, at the age of forty-four, he was laid off by the railroad and began painting full time. Today he is remembered as an important western painter.

This painting depicts a scene that took place some time during the spring of 1805. Sacajawea, a Shoshone teenager, served as a guide to Lewis and Clark. The fourth figure, York, was Clark's slave and lifelong companion. Ask:

1. If you were Lewis, how might you describe the landscape in your journal entry? *Students may mention the barren, treeless, rugged landscape; the brown, rocky bluffs; and the white mesas in the distance that suggest a desertlike terrain.*
2. Speculate about what Sacajawea might be telling the men. *She may be answering a question about the navigability of the river.*

◆ Reading Strategy

4 Noting Spatial Relationships Point out the use of words, such as *below, Lard. side* (meaning *left side*) and *here,* that indicate spatial relationships.

▶Critical Viewing◀

5 Infer; Support Students should note that the figures in the painting appear to be at ease with one another. The text, which describes the explorers' friendship with and dependence on the Native Americans, mirrors the relationship in the painting.

Answers

◆ Literature and Your Life

Reader's Response Some students might observe that Lewis disguised his real motives.

Thematic Focus Students may respond that knowing his journal would be read might have inhibited Lewis, causing him to hold back anything that might seem too personal.

☑ Check Your Comprehension

1. After an apparent separation, Captain Clark and members of the expedition rejoin Captain Lewis, the chief, and the other Indians. With Clark is an Indian woman, the chief's sister, who is reunited with Sacajawea.
2. He wants to obtain enough horses to continue their voyage by land.

◆ Critical Thinking

Interpret

1. Students may say that Lewis is not being completely candid. Lewis hints at how he misled the Indians when he says that he "gave them as a reason . . . to examine and find out a more direct way to bring merchandise to them."
2. Suggested response: He distributed gifts to cement the good relations that the negotiations have achieved.
3. Based on Lewis's carefully worded explanation to the Native Americans, students should surmise that he is covering up a far more self-interested motive: He needs horses and a guide.
4. He is very persuasive in his bid to convince the Native Americans to cooperate.

Develop Understanding

One-Minute Insight In this excerpt, Powell provides a rich description of the grandeur of the Grand Canyon. He writes of its size, the many different layers and formations of rock, its colors, and its shapes. In his attempt to describe its majesty to people who have never seen anything like it, Powell admits to the inadequacy of words.

Customize for
Auditory Learners
As they listen to the audiocassette of this selection, encourage these students to close their eyes and form a mental image of what Powell describes. How does their impression compare with the painting on page 280?

Listening to Literature Audiocassettes

Customize for
Less Proficient Readers
Use p. 18 in ***Strategies for Diverse Student Needs*** to help these students develop skills in outlining main ideas and supporting details.

◆ Literary Focus

❶ **Description** Point out that, in an effort to convey the size of the canyon, Powell uses landmarks from the settled regions of the United States to describe something readers have neither seen nor imagined.

Customize for
Less Proficient Readers
❷ Help students use context clues to determine the meaning of *rill,* a small brook or rivulet. Guide them to see that a rill is "called to life" by a shower, that it is formed from a creek, and that it forms canyons "a little at each storm."

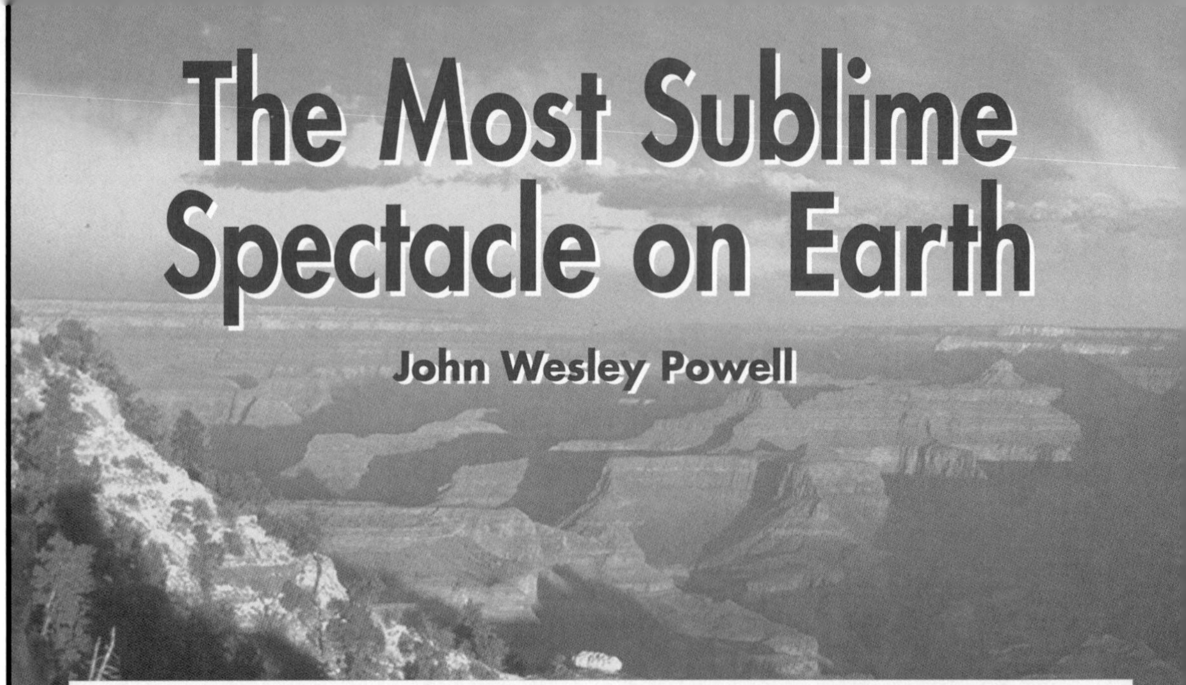

The Most Sublime Spectacle on Earth

John Wesley Powell

The Grand Canyon of the Colorado is a canyon composed of many canyons. It is a composite of thousands, of tens of thousands, of gorges. In like manner, each wall of the canyon is a composite structure, a wall composed of many walls, but never a repetition. Every one of these almost innumerable gorges is a world of beauty in itself. In the Grand Canyon there are thousands of gorges like that below Niagara Falls, and there are a thousand Yosemites. Yet all these canyons ❶ unite to form one grand canyon, the most sublime spectacle on the earth. Pluck up Mt. Washington by the roots to the level of the sea and drop it headfirst into the Grand Canyon, and the dam will not force its waters over the walls. Pluck up the Blue Ridge and hurl it into the Grand Canyon, and it will not fill it.

The carving of the Grand Canyon is the work of rains and rivers. The vast labyrinth of canyon by which the plateau region drained by the Colorado is dissected is also the work of waters. Every river has excavated its own gorge and every creek has excavated its gorge. When a shower comes in this land, the rills carve ❷ canyons—but a little at each storm; and though storms are far apart and the heavens above are cloudless for most of the days of the year, still, years are plenty in the ages, and an intermittent rill called to life by a shower can ❷ do much work in centuries of centuries.

The erosion represented in the canyons, although vast, is but a small part of the great erosion of the region, for between the cliffs blocks have been carried away far superior in magnitude to those necessary to fill the canyons. Probably there is no portion of the whole region from which there have not been more than a thousand feet degraded, and there are districts from which more than 30,000 feet of rock have been carried away. Altogether, there is a district of country more than 200,000 square miles in extent from which on the average more than 6,000 feet have been eroded. Consider a rock 200,000 square miles in extent and a mile in thickness, against which the clouds have hurled their storms and beat it into sands and the rills have carried the sands into the creeks and the creeks have carried them into the rivers and the Colorado has carried them into the sea. We think of the mountains as forming clouds about their brows, but the clouds have formed the mountains. Great continental blocks are upheaved from beneath the sea by internal geologic forces that fashion the earth. Then the wander-

Speaking, Listening, and Viewing Mini-Lesson

Speech
This mini-lesson supports the Speaking, Listening, and Viewing activity in the Idea Bank on p. 283.

Introduce the Concept Explain to students that, in order to please President Jefferson, their speeches must be respectful, friendly, and persuasive. Guide students to talk about the most effective kinds of language, gestures, and posturing to use when presenting their speeches. Explore how techniques such as smiling, making eye contact, and using words and phrases such as *together, mutual benefit, partners* and so on can create the desired impression.

Develop Background Have small groups or pairs discuss the impression Jefferson wanted to make on the Native American groups Lewis would encounter along the way. Students might also want to consider the Native Americans' thoughts about trading and dealing with the explorers.

Apply the Information Have students prepare and deliver their speeches, either to the whole class or in groups. You might tape them for later review.

Assess the Outcome Evaluate students' speeches based on their accuracy of intent and persuasiveness. Was the speech delivered in the "friendly and conciliatory manner" Jefferson requested?

ing clouds, the tempest-bearing clouds, the rainbow-decked clouds, with mighty power and with wonderful skill, carve out valleys and canyons and fashion hills and cliffs and mountains. The clouds are the artists sublime.
3

In winter some of the characteristics of the Grand Canyon are emphasized. The black gneiss[1] below, the variegated quartzite, and the green or alcove sandstone form the foundation for the mighty red wall. The banded sandstone entablature is crowned by the tower
4 limestone. In winter this is covered with snow. Seen from below, these changing elements seem to graduate into the heavens, and no plane of demarcation between wall and blue firmament[2] can be seen. The heavens constitute a portion of the facade and mount into a vast dome from wall to wall, spanning the Grand Canyon with empyrean blue. So the earth and the heavens are blended in one vast structure.

When the clouds play in the canyon, as they often do in the rainy season, another set of effects is produced. Clouds creep out of canyons and wind into other canyons. The heavens seem to be alive, not moving as move the heavens over a plain, in one direction with the wind, but following the multiplied courses of these gorges. In this manner the little clouds seem to be individualized, to have wills and souls of their own, and to be going on diverse errands—a vast assemblage of self-willed 5
clouds, faring here and there, intent upon purposes hidden in their own breasts. In the imagination the clouds belong to the sky, and when they are in the canyon the skies come down into the gorges and cling to the cliffs and lift them up to immeasurable heights, for the sky 6
must still be far away. Thus they lend infinity to the walls.

1. **gneiss** (nīs) *n.*: Coarse-grained metamorphic rock resembling granite, consisting of alternating layers of minerals such as feldspar, quartz, and mica and having a banded appearance.
2. **firmament** (fʉrm´ ə mənt) *n.*: Sky.

◆ Build Vocabulary

sublime (sə blīm´) *adj.*: Inspiring awe or admiration through grandeur or beauty

labyrinth (lab´ə rinth´) *n.*: Intricate network of winding passages; maze

excavated (eks´ kə vā tid) *v.*: Dug out; made a hole

demarcation (dē´ mär kā´ shən) *n.*: Separation

Cross-Curricular Connection: Science

The Grand Canyon Located in northwest Arizona, the Grand Canyon is nearly one mile deep, as many as eighteen miles wide, and 277 miles long.

Around six million years ago, the Colorado River began biting its way through the rock to form the Grand Canyon. The warping of the Earth's crust steepened the river's path, increasing the river's velocity and volume. The rushing water, which carried large amounts of abrasive mud, sand, and gravel, wore away the soft rock, cutting sharp, deep channels. The almost rainless climate preserved the steep pitch of the canyon walls, which would otherwise have been softened or even entirely eroded by rain wash, leaving only gentle hills behind.

The layers of rock in the canyon's walls contain a historical record of geological events. The oldest rocks at the bottom of the canyon may be as many as 4 billion years old. The canyon walls are filled with fossils, from algae and seashells in the lowest strata to trees and dinosaurs in the upper.

Customize for *AP Students*

❸ Ask students to explain what Powell means by this statement. *Students can say that the forces of nature have created this magnificent landscape.*

◆ Reading Strategy

❹ **Noting Spatial Relationships** Invite students to use the spatial relationships Powell provides to sketch what he describes here.

Comprehension Check ☑

❺ Ask students: According to this passage, how do the clouds in the canyon behave? *They seem to have minds of their own, with each going its own separate way.*

◆ Critical Thinking

❻ **Interpret** Ask students to explain what Powell means when he says the clouds "lend infinity to the walls" of the canyon? *We are used to thinking of clouds as belonging in the sky. When they drift down into the canyon, the clouds create the impression that the canyon's walls have soared into the heavens to join the sky.*

Read to Understand

Remind students that Powell is attempting a written description of a vast and constantly changing landscape that his original readers have never seen. To convey his awe-struck impressions, he invites the reader to imagine various details of geologic phenomena, sights, and sounds. Although on p. 280 he says that "language and illustration combined must fail" to convey an accurate or full impression of the Grand Canyon, he imparts information by giving readers statistics, comparisons, and detailed descriptions of colors, sounds, and movement. Suggest that students take time to picture the visual images and to "hear" the sounds the author provides, as a way to understand this information.

◆ Literature and Your Life

❶ Ask students if they have ever seen a sight so breathtaking that they could not describe it in words. Perhaps they saw a spectacular sunset or an intense lightning storm. Invite volunteers to attempt to express their impressions.

◆ Grammar and Style

❷ **Participial Phrases** Ask students to identify the participial phrase in this passage and the word it modifies. *"presented by . . . moss and lichen"; foliage*

▶Critical Viewing◀

❸ **Compare** Students may respond that the painting vividly captures the beautiful colors, forms, and unusual cloud formations Powell describes. The painting does not, however, convey the way the scene changes in different conditions, nor does it convey the "music" of the canyon's waters—both of which are important parts of Powell's written description of the Grand Canyon.

Customize for *Musical/Rhythmic Learners*

❹ These students may enhance their appreciation of this piece by listening to music composed to celebrate the Grand Canyon. For example, they can listen to *Grand Canyon Suite* by Ferdi Grofé or *Canyon Trilogy* by the Navajo-Ute flutist Carlos Nakai.

◆ Literary Focus

❺ **Description** Students can say that the Grand Canyon appeals to and can be described by senses other than sight. Those who have been there can attest to the sounds made by the water, the wind, and the canyon's creatures.

Grand Canyon With Rainbow, 1912 (detail), Thomas Moran, Fine Arts Museum of San Francisco

▲ **Critical Viewing** Compare Powell's description with the painter's interpretation of the same natural wonder. **[Compare]** ❸

❶ The wonders of the Grand Canyon cannot be adequately represented in symbols of speech, nor by speech itself. The resources of the graphic art are taxed beyond their powers in attempting to portray its features. Language and illustration combined must fail. The elements that unite to make the Grand Canyon the most sublime spectacle in nature are multifarious and exceedingly diverse. The Cyclopean forms which result from the sculpture of tempests through ages too long for man to compute, are wrought into endless details, to describe which would be a task equal in magnitude to that of describing the stars of the heavens or ❷ the multitudinous beauties of the forest with its traceries of foliage presented by oak and pine and poplar, by beech and linden and hawthorn, by tulip and lily and rose, by fern and moss and lichen. Besides the elements of form, there are elements of color, for here the colors of the heavens are rivaled by the colors of the rocks. The rainbow is not more replete with hues. But form and color do not exhaust all the divine qualities of the Grand Canyon. ❹ It is the land of music. The river thunders in perpetual roar, swelling in floors of music when the storm gods play upon the rocks and fading away in soft and low murmurs when the infinite blue of heaven is unveiled. With the melody of the great tide rising and falling, swelling and vanishing forever, other melodies are heard in the gorges of

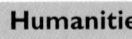

Humanities: Art

Grand Canyon With Rainbow (detail), 1912, by Thomas Moran.

Thomas Moran (1837–1926) was born in Bolton, England, but relocated with his family to the United States in 1844. Like his brother Edward under whom he studied, Moran was a landscape painter. He traveled to Yellowstone Park in 1871 and was captivated by the natural beauty of the region. Many of his paintings depict the American Southwest and Mexico. Two of his paintings of Colorado were purchased to decorate the U.S. Capitol building in Washington, D.C.

In this powerful landscape painting, Moran captures the vivid colors and awesome beauty of the Grand Canyon.

Use these questions for discussion:

1. Which passages or phrases from the selection can be used to describe this painting? *Responses may include the following: "a canyon composed of many canyons"; "the colors of the heavens are rivaled by the colors of the rocks"; "colors that vie with sunsets"; "Its colors, though many and complex at any instant, change with the ascending and declining sun."*
2. Would Powell have approved of this painting as an illustration for his journal passage? Why or why not? *Students will probably respond that he would have approved of the painting because it captures the striking colors and forms he describes in such detail.*

the lateral[3] canyons, while the waters plunge in the rapids among the rocks or leap in great cataracts. Thus the Grand Canyon is a land of song. Mountains of music swell in the rivers, hills of music billow in the creeks, and mead-
4 ows of music murmur in the rills that ripple over the rocks. Altogether it is a symphony of multitudinous melodies. All this is the music of waters. The adamant foundations of the earth have been wrought into a sublime harp, upon which the clouds of the heavens play with mighty tempests or with gentle showers.

The glories and the beauties of form, color, and sound unite in the Grand Canyon—forms unrivaled even by the mountains, colors that vie with sunsets, and sounds that span the diapason[4] from tempest to tinkling raindrop, from cataract to bubbling fountain. But more: it is a vast district of country. Were it a valley plain it would make a state. It can be seen only in parts from hour to hour and from day to day and from week to week and from month to month. A year scarcely suffices to see it all. It has infinite variety, and no part is ever duplicated. Its colors, though many and complex at any instant, change with the ascending and declining sun; lights and shadows appear and vanish with the passing clouds, and the changing seasons mark their passage in changing colors. You cannot see the Grand Canyon in one view, as if it were a changeless spectacle from which a curtain might be lifted, but to see it you have to toil from month to month through its labyrinths. It is a region more difficult to traverse than the Alps or the Himalayas, but if strength and courage are sufficient for the task, by a year's toil a concept of sublimity can be obtained never again to be equaled on the hither side of Paradise.

5 **◆ Literary Focus**
How does a reference to music strengthen the description?

3. **lateral** (lat′ ər əl) *adj.*: Of, from, or at the sides.
4. **diapason** (dī′ə pā′zən) *n.*: Entire range of a musical instrument.

◆ Build Vocabulary

multifarious (mul′ tə far′ ē əs) *adj.*: Having many parts or elements; diverse

multitudinous (mul′ tə to͞od′ ən əs) *adj.*: Numerous

Guide for Responding

◆ Literature and Your Life

Reader's Response Did you enjoy reading this piece? Why or why not?

Thematic Focus Powell says much about the Grand Canyon but almost nothing about his journey. What do you think this says about him?

☑ Check Your Comprehension

1. List four aspects of the Grand Canyon that Powell describes at length.
2. Powell describes two special visual effects that are produced seasonally. What are they?
3. To what sense besides sight does Powell appeal?

◆ Critical Thinking

INTERPRET

1. What point is Powell making when he writes that in portraying the Grand Canyon, "Language and illustration combined must fail"? **[Interpret]**
2. What do you think it meant to Powell to explore the Grand Canyon? **[Draw Conclusions]**

EVALUATE

3. How effective is Powell's description? Support your answer. **[Criticize]**

EXTEND

4. What might a painting of the Grand Canyon show that a description cannot? What can a description include that a painting cannot? **[Fine Art Link]**

Beyond the Selection

FURTHER READING

Other Works With the Theme of Exploration

Undaunted Courage, Stephen Ambrose
The Yosemite, John Muir

We suggest that you preview these works before recommending them to students.

INTERNET

The Internet provides opportunities for students to learn more about the Lewis and Clark expedition and the Grand Canyon. Please be aware, however, that these suggested sites may have changed since this information was published.

For the National Park Service Home Page for the Lewis and Clark National Historic Trail, go to **http://www.nps.gov/lecl/**

For more on the Grand Canyon, go to **hhtp://www. kaibab.org/**

We *strongly recommend* that you preview these sites before sending students to them.

Reinforce and Extend

Customize for *Logical/Mathematical Learners*
These students may enjoy looking into current ecological issues related to the Grand Canyon. Specifically, they can find out about the effects of the Glen Canyon Dam on the canyon's shoreline, fish population, and wildlife.

Enrichment To draw further connections to social studies, use p. 18 in ***Beyond Literature.***

Answers

◆ Literature and Your Life

Reader's Response Students should be prepared to offer an explanation for their responses.

Thematic Focus Possible answer: Powell was modest and didn't want to talk about himself.

☑ Check Your Comprehension

1. He describes the size, form, color, and sounds of the canyon.
2. The two effects are the blending of canyon wall into sky in the winter and the effect of clouds playing in the canyons during the rainy season.
3. He appeals to the sense of hearing.

◆ Critical Thinking

1. The details that make up the beauty of the Grand Canyon are too many and too varied for language or art to encompass.
2. Judging by his words, Powell's journey seems to have been a transcendent, almost religious experience.
3. Most students should respond that Powell does a good to excellent job of conveying the varied sights, sounds, and ever-changing qualities of life in the canyon.
4. Suggested response: A painting can capture the colors, the forms, and the play of light and shadow in a way that words cannot. A description can convey changes that take place over time, as well as the sounds that are part of the Grand Canyon experience.

Answers

◆ Reading Strategy

1. (a) The erosion of the region is greater. (b) He states one is greater than the other. He also says that the amount of soil eroded from the region is much more than the amount of soil it would take to fill the Grand Canyon.
2. Sample response: When viewed from the bottom of the canyon, the different-colored stripes on the walls become lighter and lighter until they seem to blend into the snow on the upper rim, which blends into the sky above. The sky appears to stretch from the walls of the canyon into a giant dome.

◆ Literary Focus

1. Students should choose passages that are rich in descriptive imagery.
2. He describes their campground as "a level smooth bottom covered with a fine turf of greensward."
3. Because Lewis describes little of his journey or surroundings in this passage, students should surmise that his purpose is to recount his negotiations with the Indians. Powell was probably writing with the sole purpose of conveying the canyon's grandeur.
4. Most students will probably find Powell's account more effective because of its detailed descriptions.
5. Students should be prepared to support their responses.

◆ Build Vocabulary

Using the Prefix *multi-*

Suggested responses:

1. multimillionaire: a person who is a millionaire many times over or who has many millions of dollars
2. multicultural: having or characterized by many different cultures
3. multimedia: using many different types of media, such as television, radio, print, and photography.

Using the Word Bank

1. Yes, because they are obvious.
2. Answers will depend on students' perceptions of a rainstorm.
3. Most students will probably respond in the negative; those with a sense of adventure may say "yes."
4. A bucket and a shovel are usually used to excavate a sandbox.
5. Yes, because it clearly defines and separates adjoining spaces.
6. Possible response: Yes; I like to wear many different types of clothes.
7. Yes, most anthills are occupied by dozens—even hundreds—of ants.

Guide for Responding *(continued)*

◆ Reading Strategy

NOTING SPATIAL RELATIONSHIPS

Powell's poetic yet dense descriptions in "The Most Sublime Spectacle on Earth" call for readers to carefully note **spatial relationships.** By tracking where things are and comparing them with other objects, you can see a clear, precise picture of the immense canyon that Powell describes.

1. Reread Powell's description of erosion in the Grand Canyon, noting relationships of space and size as you read. (a) Which is greater—the erosion of the canyons or the erosion of the region? (b) How do you know?
2. Describe in your own words the phenomenon of "the earth and the heavens are blended in one vast structure," which Powell describes when he talks about the walls of the Grand Canyon in winter. Include details indicating size and spatial relationships.

◆ Literary Focus

DESCRIPTION

The detailed writings of Meriwether Lewis and John Wesley Powell are both products of expeditions into uncharted western territory, but there the similarity ends. **Description**—the portrayal in words of something that can be perceived by the senses—is what sets them apart. Through his use of vivid description, Powell enables us to see and hear the Grand Canyon in all its "infinite variety." For example, Powell compares the colors of the canyon to the rainbow and the sound of the river to a melody. In contrast, while Lewis conveys much information, he doesn't create a picture that we can see.

1. Find three descriptive passages in the Powell piece. Explain what makes each effective.
2. Lewis is not as descriptive as Powell, but he does include some descriptive elements in his writing. Identify a passage in Lewis's writing that helps readers to see his camp.
3. Based on the amount of description each writer includes, what would you guess is the purpose of each piece? Why?
4. Which account did you find more effective? Why?
5. Which account did you enjoy more? Explain.

◆ Build Vocabulary

USING THE LATIN PREFIX *multi-*

Knowing that the Latin prefix *multi-* means "many" or "much," write definitions for each of the following words.

1. multimillionaire **2.** multicultural **3.** multimedia

USING THE WORD BANK: Denotation

Using your knowledge of the Word Bank, answer the following questions. Explain each answer.

1. Are *conspicuous* omissions easy to find?
2. Is a graduation day rainstorm a *sublime* experience?
3. Would you enter an unexplored *labyrinth?*
4. What tools are used to *excavate* a sandbox?
5. Is a fence a sign of *demarcation?*
6. Is your wardrobe *multifarious?*
7. Are the inhabitants of an anthill *multitudinous?*

◆ Grammar and Style

PARTICIPIAL PHRASES

A **participial phrase** is a group of words that consists of a participle—a verb form that modifies a noun or pronoun—and its complements and modifiers. Participial phrases provide an effective way to add details to descriptions.

Practice Copy the following sentences into your notebook. Underline each participial phrase, and identify the word each modifies.

1. Sights described by Powell can be seen today.
2. Lewis's expedition would not have succeeded without the woman known as Sacagawea.
3. Begun in 1804, the expedition took two years.
4. Deeply moved by what he saw, Powell produced a description both poetic and accurate.
5. Powell's description of the Grand Canyon, published years after his visit, set off a wave of tourism.

Writing Application Write a short paragraph describing something you recently witnessed. Include at least three participial phrases.

◆ Grammar and Style

Practice

1. "described by Powell" modifies *sights*
2. "known as Sacagawea" modifies *woman*
3. "Begun in 1804" modifies *expedition*
4. "deeply moved by what he saw" modifies *Powell*
5. "published years after his visit" modifies *description*

Writing Application

Paragraphs should be free of major mechanical errors and should contain at least three participial phrases.

Grammar Reinforcement

For additional instruction and practice, use the page on Participles and Participial Phrases, in the *Writer's Solution Grammar Practice Book,* p. 32.

Reteach

To reteach this selection, use ***Strategies for Diverse Student Needs,*** p. 18.

Build Your Portfolio

Idea Bank

Writing

1. **Abstract** Stripped of descriptive language, what are Powell's essential points? Write a brief summary capturing the essential details in "The Most Sublime Spectacle on Earth."

2. **Travel Advertisement** Write an advertisement for a sightseeing tour of the Grand Canyon. Create a headline and text that will entice readers to spend their next vacation exploring "the most sublime spectacle on earth." **[Career Link]**

3. **Newspaper Article** Imagine that you are a reporter on the scene with Meriwether Lewis on August 17, 1805. Write a newspaper article reporting the events of the day. **[Media Link]**

Speaking, Listening, and Viewing

4. **Speech** President Jefferson instructed Lewis to treat the Native Americans he encountered in a "friendly and conciliatory manner." Assuming the role of Lewis, deliver a speech to Native Americans that would have pleased Jefferson.

5. **Television Documentary** Make "The Most Sublime Spectacle on Earth" into a television documentary. Condense and rewrite the text into a script. Choose photographs, artwork, or music to accompany the reading of the script.

Researching and Representing

6. **Expedition Map** Lewis and Clark left St. Louis, Missouri, in April 1804. Make a map showing the route of their expedition, with important places and dates labeled. **[Social Studies Link]**

7. **Research Report** The Grand Canyon is the product of geologic forces at work over the course of eons. Write a brief research report on the canyon's geologic history. **[Science Link]**

Online Activity www.phlit.phschool.com

Guided Writing Lesson

Description of a Natural Wonder

John Wesley Powell's object of inspiration—the Grand Canyon—is one of the great natural wonders of the world. Have you ever seen a natural wonder—something so amazing that it leaves you searching for words to describe it? Choose a natural wonder that you have either observed yourself, learned about through research, or seen on film. For example, you might choose Old Faithful, a giant redwood tree, or an erupting volcano. Write a brief description of it. Keep the following tip in mind as you develop your description.

Writing Skills Focus: Use Transitions to Show Place

When writing a description, use **transitions** to show the relationship of the details you include. Following are some transitions that show relationships in space:

behind, next to, in front of, at the bottom, behind, above, below, to the right, on the left, in the north, toward the west, inside, outside, near, between.

Use such words and phrases as signposts to keep your reader oriented in space.

Prewriting Picture the natural wonder you are going to describe. Create a rough sketch of your subject, and jot down some details—sights, sounds, scents—you can use to describe it.

Drafting Decide which feature you will describe first, and continue logically—and spatially—from that point. Use your sketch to help orient yourself.

Revising Review your description to see whether it conveys a precise picture of your subject. Add or change your sensory details to make your description clearer. Also, look for places where you can add transitions to make the spatial relationships easier to follow.

ASSESSMENT OPTIONS

Formal Assessment, Selection Test, pp. 84–86, and Assessment Resources Software. The selection test is designed so that it can be easily customized to the performance levels of your students.

Alternative Assessment, p. 18, includes options for less advanced students, more advanced students, intrapersonal learners, musical/rhythmic learners, and visual/spatial learners.

PORTFOLIO ASSESSMENT

Use the following rubrics in the ***Alternative Assessment*** booklet to assess student writing:
Abstract: Summary Rubric, p. 113
Travel Advertisement: Description Rubric, p. 112
Newspaper Article: Summary Rubric, p. 113
Guided Writing Lesson: Description Rubric, p. 112

Idea Bank

Customizing for *Performance Levels*

Following are suggestions for matching Idea Bank topics with your students' performance levels:
Less Advanced Students: 1, 6
Average Students: 2, 6, 7
More Advanced Students: 3, 4, 5

Customizing for *Learning Modalities*

Following are suggestions for matching Idea Bank topics with your students' learning modalities:
Verbal/Linguistic: 4
Visual/Spatial: 5, 6
Logical/Mathematical: 6, 7

Art Transparencies As an alternative writing activity, have students describe the scene in Art Transparency 7, *Storm Clouds, Maine.*

Guided Writing Lesson

Writing and Language Transparencies Use Writing Process Model 2: Descriptive and Observational Writing, pp. 9–12, to introduce the elements of descriptive writing.

For more prewriting, elaborating, and revision strategies, see *Prentice Hall Writing and Grammar.*

Writers at Work Videodisc

Have students view the videodisc segment on Description (Ch. 1) featuring Poet Laureate Rita Dove to see how she captures the details that bring her works alive. Have students discuss how her approach to language can help them find the words to convey the awesome power of a natural wonder.

Play frames 335 to 10985

Writing Lab CD-ROM

Have students complete the tutorial on Description. Follow these steps:

1. Have students use the Cluster Diagram to help them organize.
2. After drafting on the computer, use the Word Bins for Sensory Words and Places to aid revision.

Prepare and Engage

LESSON OBJECTIVES

1. **To express and support responses to the text**
   - Critical Thinking
   - Folk Ballad
2. **To plan, prepare, organize, and present literary interpretations**
   - Idea Bank: Music Critique
3. **To use recursive writing processes**
   - Idea Bank: Comparison-and-Contrast Essay
   - Idea Bank: Description
   - Idea Bank: Nature Journal

Interest Grabber Plan an "eyes-on" experiment to test students' observation skill. Have an unannounced visitor enter the room, briefly say or do something, and leave. Ask students to record everything they saw: the guest's clothing; what he or she did, touched, said; the length of the visit; and so on. As students share observations, which may vary, focus on the idea of active seeing. Explain that, in the excerpt they are about to read, author Annie Dillard will open their eyes to a new way of really seeing the world around them.

CONNECTIONS TO TODAY'S WORLD

from Seeing

Annie Dillard

Thematic Connection

FIRESIDE AND CAMPFIRE: VIEWS OF NATURE

The world of nature takes on a different meaning for just about every person. Henry Wadsworth Longfellow looked at the eternal flow of the ocean's tides and saw a reminder of our mortality. William Cullen Bryant found comfort in nature's never-ending cycle of life and death. For James Russell Lowell, snow symbolized emotional healing, while Whittier saw a force with the power to transform the landscape. John Wesley Powell encountered awesome majesty. What do you see?

A NEW PERSPECTIVE

In an effort to find new ways of viewing nature, contemporary writer and naturalist Annie Dillard lived for a year in a small cabin next to Tinker Creek in the Blue Ridge Mountains of Virginia, with her only companion—a goldfish named Ellery Channing. She described her life and thoughts there in the award-winning book *Pilgrim at Tinker Creek*, published in 1974, from which this excerpt is taken. As "Seeing" reveals, Dillard's experiences in the Virginia wilderness reshaped her way of viewing nature and led her to find underlying meaning in her observations of trees, water, animals, and the changing seasons.

As you read, use a Venn diagram like the one below to compare and contrast Dillard's views of nature with those of one of the other writers in this section.

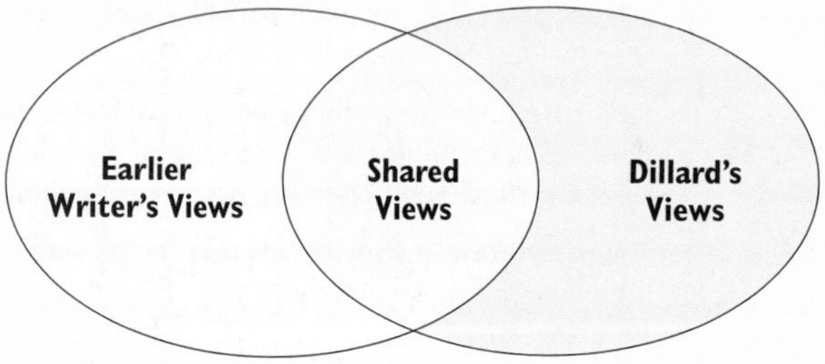

ANNIE DILLARD
(1945–)

As a child in Pittsburgh, Pennsylvania, Annie Dillard loved reading, drawing, and observing the natural world. She attended Hollins College in Roanoke, Virginia, and graduated with a B.A. and later an M.A. in English. Her exploration of a Virginia valley during her years at Hollins led to the publication of *Pilgrim at Tinker Creek* (1974), which won the Pulitzer Prize for Nonfiction in 1975. A few years later, on an island in the Puget Sound, she wrote *Holy the Firm* (1978), a meditation on the ultimate meaning of life.

In her essays, poetry, and fiction, Dillard accurately and vividly records the natural world, seeking its spiritual meanings. Her books include *An American Childhood* (1987), *The Writing Life* (1989), *Living by Fiction* (1982), *Teaching a Stone to Talk* (1982), and a novel, *The Living* (1992).

Prentice Hall Literature Program Resources

REINFORCE / RETEACH / EXTEND

Selection Support Pages
Build Vocabulary: Using Scientific Vocabulary, p. 88
Thematic Connection: Views of Nature, p. 89

Formal Assessment Selection Test, pp. 87–88; Assessment Resources Software

Resource Pro CD-ROM

Listening to Literature Audiocassettes

from

Pilgrim *at* Tinker Creek

Annie Dillard

Seeing

CONNECTIONS TO TODAY'S WORLD

When I was six or seven years old, growing up in Pittsburgh, I used to take a precious penny of my own and hide it for someone else to find. It was a curious compulsion; sadly, I've never been seized by it since. For some reason I always "hid" the penny along the same stretch of sidewalk up the street. I would cradle it at the roots of a sycamore, say, or in a hole left by a chipped-off piece of sidewalk. Then I would take a piece of chalk and, starting at either end of the block, draw huge arrows leading up to the penny from both directions. After I learned to write I labeled the arrows: SURPRISE AHEAD or MONEY THIS WAY. I was greatly excited, during all this arrow drawing, at the thought of the first lucky passerby who would receive in this way, regardless of merit, a free gift from the universe. But I never lurked about, I would go straight home and not give the matter another thought until, some months later, I would be gripped by the impulse to hide another penny.

It is still the first week in January, and I've got great plans. I've been thinking about seeing. There are lots of things to see, unwrapped gifts and free surprises. The world is fairly studded and strewn with pennies cast broadside from a generous hand. But—and this is the point—who gets excited by a mere penny? If you follow one arrow, if you crouch motionless on a bank to watch a tremulous ripple thrill on the water and are rewarded by the sight of a muskrat kit paddling from its den, will you count that sight a chip of copper only, and go your rueful way? It is dire poverty indeed when a man is so malnourished and fatigued that he won't stoop to pick up a penny. But if you cultivate a healthy poverty and simplicity, so that finding a penny will literally make your day, then, since the world is in fact planted in pennies, you have with your poverty bought a lifetime of days. It is that simple. What you see is what you get. ❶

I used to be able to see flying insects in the air. I'd look ahead and see, not the row of hemlocks across the road, but the air in front of it. My eyes would focus along that column of air, picking out flying insects. But I lost interest, I guess, for I dropped the habit. Now I can see birds. Probably some people can look at the grass at their feet and discover all the crawling creatures. I would like to know grasses and sedges—and care. Then my least journey into the world would be a field trip, a series of happy recognitions. Thoreau, in an expansive mood, exulted, "What a rich book might be made about buds, including, perhaps, sprouts!" It would be nice to think so. I cherish mental images of three perfectly happy people. One collects stones. Another—an Englishman, say—watches clouds. The third lives on a coast and collects drops of seawater, which he examines microscopically and mounts. But I don't see what the specialist sees, and so I cut myself off, not only from the total picture, but from the various forms of happiness.

Unfortunately, nature is very much a now-you-see-it, now-you-don't affair. A fish flashes, then dissolves in the water, before my eyes like so much salt. Deer apparently ascend bodily into heaven; the brightest oriole fades into leaves. These disappearances stun me into stillness and concentration; they say of nature that

Cross-Curricular Connection: Science

The SETI Program Dillard describes her experiences with heightened awareness. For decades, astronomers have been carefully looking and listening for signs of life beyond Earth. Massive radio antennae and receivers have been scanning the heavens in search of radio signals from other solar systems. These efforts, resulted in the creation of the Search for Extraterrestrial Intelligence or SETI. The program was formally adopted by NASA in 1988; observations officially began in 1992. However, these radio messages, if they do exist, may not be readily apparent, even to highly trained and motivated scientists. When receivers failed to detect any signals, Congress terminated funding in 1993.

Today, SETI continues as a nonprofit organization. Invite students to learn more about its experiments, and why scientists feel that the "window of opportunity" may soon close. (Growing radio interference will soon compromise the ability to detect weak signals.) Students interested in learning more can contact the SETI Institute Home Page at **http://www.seti-inst.edu/** Preview this page carefully before sending students to it.

Connections to Today's World

Just as her nineteenth-century counterparts did, contemporary writer and naturalist Annie Dillard finds comfort and endless joys in nature. Margaret Fuller and Ralph Waldo Emerson communed with nature; Longfellow found an analogy for life in the ocean waves; and Bryant, Lowell, and Whittier explored the connection between humanity and the natural world. Dillard carries on their legacy, while teaching us something new about how to "see" and appreciate nature's gifts in our increasingly complex modern world.

Develop Understanding

One-Minute Insight

Dillard explores the mystery of vision, based on keen observations of her environment. She examines the roles that expectation, interest, and expertise play in helping one to fully see what awaits discovery. Only when we learn to "cultivate a healthy poverty and simplicity" will our eyes be opened to the wonderful gifts of nature that surround us.

Customize for *English Language Learners*

This piece discusses many different birds, insects, and animals whose names may be unfamiliar to these students. They include fish, deer, blackbirds, ducks, zebras, caterpillars, field mice, monarch butterflies, squirrels, bullfrogs, horses, goldfish, and snakes. To help students connect these creatures with their proper English names, display a photograph of each, using an encyclopedia or nature book.

Customize for *Less Proficient Readers*

❶ This passage provides the essence of the piece. Help these students grasp this key point by asking them to analyze the meaning of the phrases "healthy poverty and simplicity," "world planted in pennies," and "bought a lifetime of days." *Students may say that Dillard believes that if you free yourself from materialistic goals, the most simple gift becomes precious and gives your life a richness you never imagined.*

Thematic Connection

1 Fireside and Campfire: Views of Nature Discuss with students why this anecdote is so surprising to the author. Why do characteristics of nature take us by surprise? *Students may say that nature's wonders are often hidden from casual view, but that if one sets aside other distractions and focuses on seeking the hidden, on looking beyond the obvious, there can be amazing rewards to behold.*

Thematic Connection

2 Fireside and Campfire: Views of Nature This passage restates the author's idea that the ability to see is more than a simple matter of vision. What other senses, traits, or qualities do people use to see nature's minutiae? *Students may say that seeing depends on being observant, keeping an open mind, actively looking for what is, by nature, hidden from perfunctory view.*

◆ Critical Thinking

3 Analyze What is ironic about the book's instruction on finding a caterpillar? *Students should realize that caterpillar droppings are even smaller and—for most people—harder to see than caterpillars themselves.*

◆ *Literature and Your Life*

4 Ask students if they, like Dillard, have ever had the experience of not being able to "see" something that was right before their eyes. What was it? What prevented them from recognizing it? Ask volunteers to share the circumstances.

it conceals with a grand nonchalance, and they say of vision that it is a deliberate gift, the revelation of a dancer who for my eyes only flings away her seven veils. For nature does reveal as well as conceal: now you don't see it, now you do. For a week last September, migrating red-winged blackbirds were feeding heavily down by the creek at the back of the house. One day I went out to investigate the racket; I walked up to a tree, an Osage orange, and a hundred birds flew away. They simply materialized out of the tree. I saw a tree, then a whisk of color, then a tree again. I walked closer, and another hundred blackbirds took flight. Not a branch, not a twig budged: the birds were apparently weightless as well as invisible. Or it was as if the leaves of the Osage orange had been freed from a spell
1 in the form of red-winged blackbirds: they flew from the tree, caught my eye in the sky, and vanished. When I looked again at the tree, the leaves had reassembled as if nothing had happened. Finally I walked directly to the trunk of the tree, and a final hundred, the real diehards, appeared, spread, and vanished. How could so many hide in the tree without my seeing them? The Osage orange, unruffled, looked just as it had looked from the house, when three hundred red-winged blackbirds cried from its crown. I looked downstream where they flew, and they were gone. Searching, I couldn't spot one. I wandered downstream to force them to play their hand, but they'd crossed the creek and scattered. One show to a customer. These appearances catch at my throat; they are the free gifts, the bright coppers at the roots of trees.

It's all a matter of keeping my eyes open. Nature is like one of those line drawings of a
2 tree that are puzzles for children: Can you find hidden in the leaves a duck, a house, a boy, a bucket, a zebra, and a boot? Specialists can find the most incredibly well-hidden things. A book I read when I was young recommended an easy way to find caterpillars to rear: you simply find
3 some fresh caterpillar droppings, look up, and there's your caterpillar. Most recently an author advised me to set my mind at ease about those piles of cut stems on the ground in grassy fields. Field mice make them; they cut the grass down by degrees to reach the seeds at the head. It seems that when the grass is tightly packed, as in a field of ripe grain, the blade won't topple at a single cut through the stem; instead the cut stem simply drops vertically, held in the crush of grain. The mouse severs the bottom again and again, the stem keeps dropping an inch at a time, and finally the head is low enough for the mouse to reach the seeds. Meanwhile, the mouse is positively littering the field with its little piles of cut stems, into which, presumably, the author of the book is constantly stumbling.

If I can't see these minutiae,[1] I still try to keep my eyes open. I'm always on the lookout for ant lion traps in sandy soil, monarch pupae near milkweed, skipper larvae in locust leaves. These things are utterly common, and I've not seen one. I bang on hollow trees near water, but so far no flying squirrels have appeared. In flat country I watch every sunset in hopes of seeing the green ray. The green ray is a seldom-seen streak of light that rises from the sun like a spurting fountain at the moment of sunset; it throbs into the sky for two seconds and disappears. One more reason to keep my eyes open. A photography professor at the University of Florida just happened to see a bird die in mid-flight; it jerked, died, dropped, and smashed on the ground. I squint at the wind because I read Stewart Edward White: "I have always maintained that if you looked closely enough you could *see* the wind—the dim, hardly-made-out, fine débris fleeing high in the air." White was an excellent observer, and devoted an entire chapter of *The Mountains* to the subject of seeing deer: "As soon as you can forget the naturally obvious and construct an artificial obvious, then you too will see deer."

But the artificial obvious is hard to see. My eyes account for less than one percent of the weight of my head; I'm bony and dense; I *see* what I expect. I once spent a full three minutes looking at a bullfrog that was so unexpectedly large I couldn't see it even though a dozen en- 4
thusiastic campers were shouting directions. Finally I asked, "What color am I looking for?" and a fellow said, "Green." When at last I picked out the frog, I saw what painters are up against: the thing wasn't green at all, but the color of wet hickory bark.

The lover can see, and the knowledgeable. I visited an aunt and uncle at a quarter-horse ranch in Cody, Wyoming. I couldn't do much of

1. **minutiae** (mi noo͞´ shē ī) *n.*: Small or relatively unimportant details.

Beyond the Classroom

Workplace Skill

Keen Senses Many jobs demand a sharp eye for detail. Some of these include proofreader, quality control inspector, and lab technician. Other jobs demand a sharpness of other senses, such as a keen nose for a perfumer or cheese maker, sharp ears for a recording technician or translator, a heightened sense of touch for a surgeon or physical therapist, and a sophisticated palate for a food critic or chef. Have students brainstorm for a list of jobs that demand keen senses. You may want to divide students into five groups and assign a different sense to each.

Students can conduct research or interview people who hold such jobs to find out how they prepare, whether they believe they can train themselves to sharpen their senses, or how they learn to differentiate among stimuli that most people would not perceive.

anything useful, but I could, I thought, draw. So as we all sat around the kitchen table after supper, I produced a sheet of paper and drew a horse. "That's one lame horse," my aunt volunteered. The rest of the family joined in: "Only place to saddle that one is his neck"; "Looks like we better shoot the poor thing, on account of those terrible growths." Meekly, I slid the pencil and paper down the table. Everyone in that family, including my three cousins, could draw a horse. Beautifully. When the paper came back, it looked as though five shining, real quarter horses had been corraled by mistake with a papier-mâché moose; the real horses seemed to gaze at the monster with a steady, puzzled air. I stay away from horses now, but I can do a creditable goldfish. The point is that I just don't know what the lover knows; I just can't see the artificial obvious that those in the know construct. The herpetologist[2] asks the native, "Are there snakes in the ravine?" "Nosir." And the herpetologist comes
5 home with, yessir, three bags full. Are there butterflies on that mountain? Are the bluets in bloom, are there arrowheads here, or fossil shells in the shale?

Peeping through my keyhole, I see within the range of only about 30 percent of the light that comes from the sun; the rest is infrared and some little ultraviolet, perfectly apparent to many animals, but invisible to me. A nightmare network of ganglia,[3] charged and firing without my knowledge, cuts and splices what I do see, editing it for my brain. Donald E. Carr points out that the sense impressions of one-celled animals are not edited for the brain: 6
"This is philosophically interesting in a rather mournful way, since it means that only the simplest animals perceive the universe as it is."

A fog that won't burn away drifts and flows across my field of vision. When you see fog move against a backdrop of deep pines, you see not the fog itself but streaks of clearness floating across the air in dark shreds. So I see only tatters of clearness through a pervading obscurity. I can't distinguish the fog from the overcast sky; I can't be sure if the light is direct or reflected. Everywhere darkness and the presence of the unseen appalls. We estimate now that only one atom dances alone in every cubic meter of intergalactic space. I blink and squint. What planet or power yanks Halley's Comet out of orbit? We haven't seen that force yet; it's a question of distance, density, and the pallor of reflected light. We rock, cradled in the swaddling band of darkness. Even the simple darkness of night whispers suggestions to the mind.

---

2. **herpetologist** (hʉr′ pə täl′ ə jəst): One who practices the study of reptiles and amphibians.

3. **ganglia** (gaŋ′ glē ə): Masses of nerve cells that serve as centers from which nerve impulses are transmitted.

CONNECTIONS TO TODAY'S WORLD

Guide for Responding

◆ Literature and Your Life

Reader's Response What "unwrapped gifts and free surprises" have you received from nature?

Thematic Focus Why do we overlook the "bright coppers" in a world "planted with pennies"?

Journal Writing Take a few moments to observe something you see every day—your own hand, your bookbag, the bracelet on your wrist. Then write a detailed description of it. What do you really see? What have you never noticed before?

☑ Check Your Comprehension

1. Why did Dillard "hide" pennies as a child?
2. What does the author mean when she comments that she would "like to know grasses and sedges—and care"?
3. Why couldn't Dillard see the bullfrog that campers were pointing out to her?

Beyond the Selection

FURTHER READING

Other Works by Annie Dillard

An American Childhood
The Writing Life
Tickets for a Prayer Wheel
Teaching a Stone to Talk

We suggest that you preview these works before recommending them to students.

INTERNET

The Internet provides opportunities for students to learn more about Annie Dillard and her writing. Please be aware, however, that these sites may have changed since this information was published.

For an article about Dillard, go to **http://www.seattletimes.com/extra/browse/html/dill092496.htm**

For a poem by Dillard, visit **http://www.theatlantic.com/atlweb/poetry/atlpoets/dill9409.htm**

We *strongly recommend* that you preview these sites before sending students to them.

Thematic Connection

5 Fireside and Campfire: Views of Nature Discuss the point Dillard makes by posing all these questions. *Students may say that the questions suggest that there's always something more to ask and something more to see if one knows what to look for.*

Customize for
Logical/Mathematical Learners

6 Ask students what conclusions they can draw from this quotation. *Students may say that perception is subjective: What you get from it is colored by what you bring to it. One-celled animals, however, cannot edit anything out, so they get the full impact of what they perceive, but they have no ability to synthesize or interpret as higher-level creatures can. The mystery is that a one-celled animal experiences fully, but cannot go any farther with those perceptions. Complex creatures, like humans, cloud their perceptions with preconceived ideas or other mental distractions.*

Reinforce and Extend

Customize for
Less Proficient Readers

These students will benefit from rereading all or part of the essay. In reviewing it, students should try to link the meaning of Dillard's anecdotes with her philosophical questions about perception.

Answers

◆ Literature and Your Life

Reader's Response Students' responses might include a beautiful sunset or breathtaking view—some unexpected but wonderful sight or event.

Thematic Focus We lack the "healthy poverty and simplicity" required to appreciate them.

☑ Check Your Comprehension

1. She took pleasure in giving a stranger an unexpected gift.
2. If she could recognize and take pleasure in something as simple as the grass, she would find happiness every time she stepped outdoors.
3. She was looking only for what she expected to see; the bullfrog was so much larger than normal that it didn't register in her mind.

Answers

◆ Critical Thinking

1. She is making the point that we really see only what we really love. Her cousins can draw horses beautifully because they have observed everything about the animals they love.
2. We are prevented from seeing most of what surrounds us; only small bits of the world are truly visible to us.
3. (a) Suggested response: She would suggest that they keep their minds and eyes open to the possibility of seeing other than what they expect to see. (b) We cannot change the eye's limited ability to perceive light or the way our brains "edit" visual signals.
4. Students may reply that the passage succeeds in affecting the way readers see by opening their eyes to a range of sights and experiences often overlooked.
5. Students should relate the idea to a subject or hobby they enjoy.

Thematic Connection

1. Dillard sees a series of free and wonderful gifts.
2. Suggested response: We cannot see because we don't know or care enough about most things to notice them as they really are.
3. Their knowledge or love of particular aspects of nature allows some people to see the things about which they care most; they are able to construct an "artificial obvious" by expecting to see the unexpected.
4. Students should offer evidence to justify their responses.

Idea Bank

Customizing for
Performance Levels

Following are suggestions for matching Idea Bank activities with performance levels:
Less Advanced Students: 1, 5
Average Students: 2, 4
More Advanced Students: 3

Customizing for
Learning Modalities

Following are suggestions for matching Idea Bank activities with learning modalities:
Musical/Rhythmic: 4
Visual/Spatial: 5

◆ Critical Thinking

Interpret

1. Why does Dillard tell a story of her cousins' ability to draw horses? **[Connect]**
2. Explain how the image of "streaks of clearness" in a fog symbolizes, or represents, our vision of the world in which we live. **[Support]**
3. (a) How might Dillard advise someone to improve his or her ability to see? (b) What is beyond our power to change? **[Draw Conclusions]**

Evaluate

4. Could this passage influence the way a reader sees and appreciates the world? Explain. **[Assess]**

Apply

5. Apply the idea "The lover can see, and the knowledgeable" to your own life. How do you see and experience differently those things in which you take a special interest? **[Apply]**

Thematic Connection

What Do We See in Nature?

After reading "Seeing," you may have been struck by how much you've probably missed in the world around you. Dillard shows us that, for those who are willing to educate their minds and eyes, there is always more to see and appreciate in nature than in any manufactured form of entertainment. The more attention we give to our natural surroundings, the greater the rewards for our efforts.

1. What does Dillard see when she looks at nature?
2. According to "Seeing," why are we unable to see much of what surrounds us in nature?
3. What enables some people to see things in nature that go unnoticed by others?
4. Name two poems in Part 1 in which the speakers share the appreciation of nature expressed in "Seeing." Explain your choices.

Idea Bank

Writing

1. **Folk Ballad** Write the lyrics to a folk ballad that commemorates the year that Dillard spent communing with nature in the mountains of Virginia. Your ballad should include a refrain, or group of repeated lines. **[Music Link]**
2. **Description** Have you ever received an "unwrapped gift" from nature? Describe in detail what you saw and why it was special to you. Include an explanation of the emotional impact of the experience.
3. **Comparison-and-Contrast Essay** How is Annie Dillard connected to the literary tradition of the nineteenth-century writers featured in this section? Compare and contrast Dillard's view of the natural world with that of the Part 1 writer with whom you feel she has the most in common. Support your ideas with examples from the selections.

Speaking, Listening, and Viewing

4. **Music Critique** Most of us hear the way we see; we miss the details. Select a familiar song or piece of music and listen to it repeatedly until you begin to hear its subtleties. For instance, you might distinguish the bass line from the melody, gain new insight into the lyrics, or detect a change in rhythm that you never noticed before. Play the music for the class, share your insights, and then play the music again. Were your classmates able to hear what you heard? **[Music Link]**

Researching and Representing

5. **Nature Journal** Spend five minutes sitting quietly and observing nature. What do you see? What small changes and movements do you notice? Record your detailed impressions in a journal entry. Continue recording your observations over the course of three or four days. Then write a paragraph summarizing what you learned from the experience. You may wish to illustrate your journal entries. **[Science Link; Art Link]**

Online Activity www.phlit.phschool.com

ASSESSMENT OPTIONS

Formal Assessment, Selection Test, pp. 87–88, and Assessment Resources Software. The selection test is designed so that it can be easily customized to the performance levels of your students.

PORTFOLIO ASSESSMENT

Use the following rubrics in the ***Alternative Assessment*** booklet to assess student writing:
Folk Ballad: Poetry Rubric, p. 123
Description: Description Rubric, p. 112
Comparison-and-Contrast Essay: Comparison/Contrast Rubric, p. 118

Writing Process Workshop

Travel Brochure

The foreign, the strange, and the exotic have always exerted a powerful pull on the human imagination. Reading about the adventurous wanderings of John Wesley Powell and Meriwether Lewis, do you find yourself yearning to explore some unknown part of the world or wanting to share your observations of a place you've visited? Choose a place that you've visited or would like to explore, and create a travel brochure filled with vivid descriptions to entice your audience to visit that place.

The following skills, introduced in this section's Guided Writing Lessons, will help you create your travel brochure.

Writing Skills Focus

- **Use language that is appropriate for your audience** to communicate your message effectively. (See p. 247.)
- **Adopt a persuasive tone** that will entice your readers to visit the destination. (See p. 255.)
- **A clear beginning, middle, and end** are crucial in conveying an accurate picture to your readers. (See p. 273.)
- **Use transitional words** to connect your details. (See p. 283.)

Notice how John Wesley Powell uses these skills in his description of the Grand Canyon.

Model From Literature

from *The Most Sublime Spectacle on Earth*
by John Wesley Powell

The glories and the beauties of form, color, and sound unite in the Grand Canyon ① —forms unrivaled even by the mountains, colors that vie with sunsets, and sounds that span the diapason from tempest to tinkling raindrop, from cataract to bubbling fountain. But more: ② it is a vast district of country. Were it a valley plain it would make a state.

① Powell's soaring prose carries great conviction, persuading the reader of the greatness of what he is describing.

② Words like "span," "from," "to," and "more" show a shift in place and carry the reader from image to image.

Prepare and Engage

Lesson Objectives

- To use recursive writing processes to write a travel brochure
- To compose increasingly more involved sentences that contain appositives and figurative language

Establish Writing Guidelines
Distribute the scoring rubric for Description (p. 112 in the ***Alternative Assessment*** booklet) to show students the criteria on which their work will be evaluated. See the suggestions on p. 291 for customizing the rubric to this workshop.

Refer students to the Writing Handbook, p. 1192, for instruction in the writing process, and p. 1194 for further information on descriptive writing. You may also want to present the Writing Process Model of Descriptive and Observational Writing from the ***Writing and Language Transparencies.***

Connect to Literature
Meriwether Lewis (p. 276), John Wesley Powell (p. 278), and Annie Dillard (p. 285) provide models of the key elements of description.

Writers at Work Videodisc
Play the segment featuring Rita Dove (Ch. 1). Ask students how Dove's notion that details "re-create a world" can help them choose details to use in their brochure.

Play frames 335 to 10985

Writing Lab CD-ROM
You may want to have students use the tutorial on Description. Have students follow these steps:

1. Review the interactive model of a travel brochure.
2. Use the Sensory Word Bins.
3. Draft on the computer.
4. Use the Self-Evaluation Checklist to help revise.

Cross-Curricular Connection: Science

Eco-Tourism In recent years the industry of "eco-tourism" has gone through explosive growth around the globe. Both established and new tour operators create guided itineraries that educate travelers about an area's wildlife, ecosystems, and potential threats to a region. Encourage interested students to conduct research—both on a region's environment and its eco-aware tour providers. Questions such as the following may help them to give their brochures an eco-tourist slant.

1. What are some the unique flora and fauna that visitors will be able to view in unspoiled settings?
2. Are there any particularly endangered species to be appreciated, or others that are making an inspiring comeback?
3. How will the tour ensure that visitors to the area will not inadvertently contribute to its degradation?
4. Is there an opportunity for visitors to engage directly in activities that support environmental concerns, such as planting trees, cataloging migrating bird species, or restoring a shoreline to its pristine state?

Prewriting Strategy

Help students prepare for the brainstorming activity on sensory language by having them first consider the broad categories that their words might relate to: food and recreation; culture; lodging; weather and climate; seasonal activities or events; cost and convenience. Suggest that they record their ideas in a chart like the one shown.

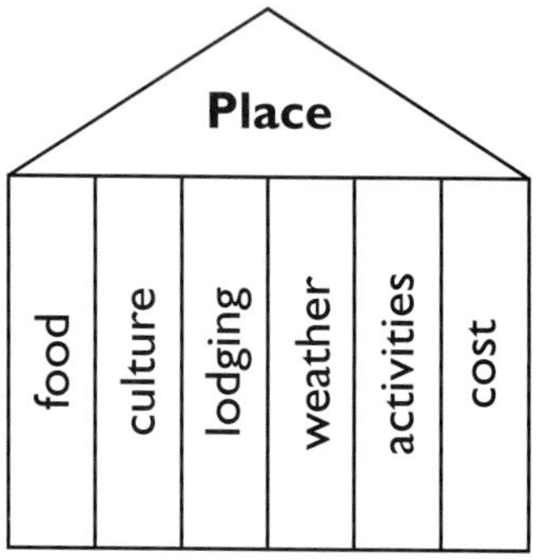

Customize for *Verbal/Linguistic Learners*

Have these students add authenticity and color to their brochures with the appropriate inclusion of local terms, idioms, and expressions. If these phrases contain foreign words, remind students to use italics or, if they are defining them, quotation marks.

Writing Lab CD-ROM

Have students use the Note Card Activity that appears in the Gathering Details section of the tutorial. Students can use this organizing tool to gather details for their brochures.

Elaboration Strategy

In addition to using spatial transitional words, students can supply specific details about an area with geographic, ecological, and geological terms. They can use words that indicate specific physical features such as *peninsula* or *reef*, compass directions, and specific references to altitude or air temperature.

Applying Language Skills: Appositives

An **appositive** is a noun or a noun phrase that generally follows another noun or pronoun to identify or provide extra information about it. The appositives below are underlined:

Grier and Ericka, <u>my new friends</u>, speak fluent Japanese.

Their band, <u>Ichi Ban</u>, played at the last school dance.

Because they can be used to combine sentences that contain related information, appositives are a cure for a dull style.

Practice On your paper, combine each set of sentences using appositives.

1. (a) Take a scenic evening boat ride through Paris.
   (b) Paris is "the City of Lights."
2. (a) Chocolate crepes are sold on the street.
   (b) Crepes are Parisian fast-food.

Writing Application Revise your travel brochure, using appositives to combine choppy sentences.

Writer's Solution Connection
Writing Lab

To help you gather sensory details, use the Sensory Word Bin in this tutorial on Descriptions.

Prewriting

Choose a Topic Consider the places that have captured your imagination—places you've read about, seen in the movies, or actually visited. Make a list of those that interest you most. Then choose one as the subject for your travel brochure. If you choose a place you haven't visited, you'll need to conduct research to gather details about it.

Topic Ideas

- Paris, London, Venice, Moscow, Nairobi, or another foreign city
- The fictional city where your favorite television drama is set
- Your hometown

Use a Sensory Language Chart To make your brochure as persuasive as possible, use vivid language that appeals to the reader's senses. To help you do so, create a chart with five columns. Then brainstorm for words that appeal to each of the five senses. The following chart lists a few words that might help you get started.

Sounds	Sights	Smells	Tastes	Physical Sensations
roaring	glowing	aromatic	savory	smooth
blaring	mountainous	spicy	buttery	warm
buzzing	panoramic	fresh	fruity	pillow soft
pounding	colorful	flowery	zesty	balmy

Drafting

Organize Your Brochure A travel brochure presents details relating to culture, architecture, music, food, and scenic features. Focus on the most appealing aspects of your locale, and decide on a clear organization. You might want to use a spatial order, describing the place in the form of a walking or driving tour.

Use Transitional Words Make use of key transitional words to show shifts in spatial order as you move from place to place in your brochure. Words like *behind, next to, on top of, below, left, north, in the center, background,* and *within* will keep your description clear.

Applying Language Skills

Appositives To introduce this language skill, explain that appositives represent a highly efficient way to deliver information to readers. Remind students that a brochure should present facts concisely to pique readers' interest. However, it should not provide the comprehensive treatment one might expect from an expository essay on the same topic.

Answers

1. Take a scenic evening boat ride through Paris, "the City of Lights."
2. Chocolate crepes, a Parisian fast food, are sold on the street.

Grammar Reinforcement

For additional instruction and practice, refer students to the **Language Lab CD-ROM** lesson Recognizing and Using Phrases, and the *Sourcebook* lesson on Using Appositives Correctly (p. 27).

Include Visuals to Bring a Place to Life Whenever possible, let a location sell itself. If a map, photograph, or a piece of fine art will convey the "feel" of a city, be sure to include it.

Revising

Sharpen Your Language Read over your brochure as if you were seeing it for the first time. Focus on finding any parts that could be made more clear. Look for unnecessary details to eliminate, and find places where you might need to add details to enhance your descriptions.

Polish Your Organization Ask a classmate to read your brochure. If your writing confuses a peer reviewer, it will probably confuse others. You may want to add subheads to help make your organizational plan more appealing.

Revision Model

Robert's Grove in Belize offers every modern convenience, ① , yet You'll feel transported to another time and place ② by the beautiful Spanish colonial decor featuring carved colonial furniture, Mexican tile floors, ceiling fans, Guatemalan fabrics and rugs, and fine art from around the world.

① The use of the transitional word "yet" makes the contrast more effective.

② The addition of vivid, specific language makes the description far more persuasive.

Publishing

Create a Multimedia Anthology Working with other students, select travel brochures that have visual appeal. Gather photographs, art, illustrations, and musical accompaniment for each piece. If possible, videotape the visuals with an audio voice-over. Make the recordings available in your classroom, computer lab, or school library for others to share.

Hold a Travel Fair Get together with classmates to present a "Fantastic Destinations" travel fair. Using your travel brochures as the centerpiece, create booths that advertise each location you've described. To make the fair entertaining as well as educational, you might want to provide traditional music and food at each booth.

Applying Language Skills: Figurative Language

Figurative language is writing or speech not meant to be taken literally. Writers use figurative language to express ideas in vivid and imaginative ways. Two of the most common figures of speech are metaphors (implied comparisons of unlike things without using *like* or *as*) and similes (direct comparisons of unlike things using *like* or *as*).

Simile:
He had biceps like iron.

Metaphor:
He flexed his iron biceps.

Practice On your paper, use the suggested comparisons to revise these sentences:

1. Crowds filled the arena. [compare crowds to swarms of bees]

2. The airport was confusing. [compare airport to a maze]

Writing Application Look for places in your travel brochure where metaphors or similes would bring life to your description.

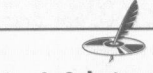

Writer's Solution Connection
Writing Lab

For more practice with figurative language, see the Prewriting section of the tutorial on Description.

Revision Strategy

As students revise to sharpen their language, have them check to see whether they have used words that fit their intended audience. Ask students to revise or define terms that may be unfamiliar to readers.

Writing Lab CD-ROM

The Revising and Editing section includes interactive student models that illustrate the revising and proofreading processes.

Publishing

To enhance either a multimedia anthology or a travel fair, inform students that pamphlets and videotapes are typically available through a region's Department or Ministry of Tourism.

Applying Language Skills

Figurative Language

Answers

1. Frenetic crowds filled the arena like swarms of bees in a honeycomb.
2. The airport was a veritable maze for the confused travelers.

Further instruction on figurative language can be found in the *Sourcebook* (p. 184).

Reinforce and Extend

Reflect on Writing Ask students how the process has increased their interest in the place they wrote about.

Prentice Hall Writing and Grammar For more prewriting, elaboration, and revision stategies, see *Prentice Hall Writing and Grammar.*

✓ ASSESSMENT		4	3	2	1
PORTFOLIO ASSESSMENT Use the rubric on Description in ***Alternative Assessment*** (p. 112) to assess students' writing. Add these criteria to customize the rubric to this assignment.	**Using Appropriate Language**	The writer consistently uses language that is appropriate to the intended audience, making the brochure informative.	For the most part the writer uses appropriate language that helps communicate the brochure's basic message.	The writer seems to have trouble determining what constitutes appropriate language for the intended audience.	The writer consistently uses inappropriate language that is too simplistic or too specialized for the intended audience.
	Figurative Language	The writer consistently uses figurative language in ways that are both appropriate and effective.	The writer includes figurative language that is occasionally effective.	The writer includes figurative language that at times impedes the sense of the brochure.	The writer includes figurative language that does not make sense, or avoids using it.

Prepare and Engage

LESSON OBJECTIVES

- To read critically to evaluate texts and the authority of sources, recognizing logical, deceptive, and/or faulty modes of persuasion

Customize for
Interpersonal Learners
Have students name controversial issues in the news. Choose one for an informal debate, with a pair of students representing each side. The debaters must do research to gather facts, anticipate likely arguments from opponents, and develop logical arguments. Together, set time limits and rules for the debate: first speaker, second speaker, rebuttals, and so on.

Apply the Strategies

Answers

1. The company's main arguments, or selling points, are free calls on nights and weekends and a free phone. To receive free calls, you must sign up for a PhoneSoft cellular phone. To receive the free phone, you must purchase a one-year CallAll plan.
2. The supporting information seems vague and weak. More details are needed about exact costs, since "standard rates" apply during weekdays. The cost of the CallAll plan is also missing.
3. The offer does seem too good to be true. No mention is made about whether you can send free calls on nights and weekends. And the word *lease* seems misleading—why is it called *leased* if it's free? Finally, the CallAll plan is not explained—it could be complicated and expensive.

Student Success Workshop

Real-World Reading Skills

Recognizing Modes of Persuasion

Strategies for Success

Whenever you read an advertisement, an editorial, or a position paper, you're reading a persuasive text. Persuasive texts are everywhere—billboards, magazines, brochures, and TV. Even when you rent movies, you're being persuaded. Text on the video box, such as "This summer's best film!" is meant to persuade you to rent the movie. Recognizing modes of persuasion will help you become a more critical reader.

See If the Argument Is Supported When you encounter a persuasive message, see if the argument is well supported. For example, a college brochure might say, "You can choose from an abundance of courses at University State College. University State offers more than 300 different courses each semester." The brochure supports its claim that the university has an abundance of courses by giving the number they offer.

Search for Facts Have you ever read about a fantastic offer and wondered if it's too good to be true? Deceptive persuasion tries to entice you to buy a product or service or to support a position with untruths or half-truths. Search for the facts, and be on the lookout for missing information, vague statements, and partial truths. Ask yourself questions about information not mentioned. If it's not there, it may be that the writer doesn't want you to think about it!

Recognize False Conclusions To persuade you, writers sometimes use faulty modes of persuasion. For example, you might read a campaign flyer that states, "If you elect Carol Wright, unemployment in Simsville will vanish." This statement draws a false conclusion. The statement oversimplifies a situation by implying that unemployment can be controlled, and even ended, by electing a certain person. It also offers no details about how the candidate plans to end unemployment. When you read persuasive texts, notice oversimplifications and false conclusions. Make decisions based on facts.

Apply the Strategies

Read this advertisement carefully. Keep in mind what you've learned about different types of persuasion. Then answer the questions.

> **YOUR LUCKY MONTH!**
> By signing up for a **PhoneSoft** cellular phone today, you can receive free calls on nights and weekends. Standard rates apply M–F, 7 A.M.–7 P.M. Additionally, purchase our one-year **CallAll** call plan and we'll lease you a **PhoneSoft** phone. Call now for a **FREE** phone and **FREE** calling!

1. What are the main arguments? Write down the ways they are supported.
2. Is the supporting information vague or incomplete? Write down any additional details that could have been provided.
3. Is the offer too good to be true? Write down any misleading information.

Think about modes of persuasion the next time you're in these situations:

- *Watching a political debate*
- *Buying merchandise online*
- *Joining a club or an organization*
- *Planning which movie to see*

Test Preparation Workshop

Reading Comprehension:
Recognizing Modes of Persuasion
Standardized tests require students to use critical reasoning skills to recognize modes of persuasion. Display the following sample test item:

> The town of Medville is considering installing video cameras on school buses. Which of the following statements offers the most convincing support for surveillance equipment on school buses?

A Surveillance cameras on buses in nearby Fallstown have cut vandalism costs by two-thirds.
B Rides will become safer and quieter if students are being videotaped.
C Cameras are not an invasion of privacy if they are posted in public places.
D Video cameras cost about $1,000 each.

Students should explain why A is the correct answer: It is the only choice that gives factual support for the positive effects of installing cameras.

PART 2 *Shadows of the Imagination*

Mysterious Night, ca. 1895, Daingerfield, Morris Museum of Art, Georgia

Humanities: Art

Mysterious Night, c. 1895, by Elliott Daingerfield.

Encourage students to use their imaginations to fill in the circumstances of this shadowy watercolor painting. The white shape on the right may be the roof of a small structure; someone may be standing under it. There seems to be a fence around the bright area in the middle of the painting—it could be a pond reflecting the moonlight. Ask students what they see in this painting, and generate a list of possibilities on the board for students to compile situations from. Then use these questions to spark discussion.

1. Imagine that a person lurks underneath the white shape on the right. Make up a story idea explaining what he or she is doing out on this foggy night. *Sample answer: He is waiting to meet someone who has the other half of a treasure map.*
2. Describe the mood of this painting. What details and elements contribute most to this mood? *The mood of the painting is mysterious, haunting, ominous. Details that contribute to the mood include the fog or mist; the large, shadowy tree; the pool of light in the middle of the painting.*

One-Minute Planning Guide

The selections in this section deal with the ominous side of human emotions. Here we find characters who are tortured individuals ruled by the menacing shadows of their imaginations. "The Fall of the House of Usher" introduces us to Roderick Usher, a physically deteriorating person who knows he is losing his mind and tries anything, including burying his twin sister alive, to escape death. In "The Raven," Poe presents a man whose grief for his deceased beloved knows no bounds. His wounded psyche proves far too fragile to survive the shattering blows of the single negative word uttered repeatedly by an uninvited feathered friend. The next selection provides a close-up look at obsession at its most dangerous. In an excerpt from the novel *Moby-Dick,* Captain Ahab, a captain of a whaling vessel, is driven by his darker side to accomplish revenge at all costs, including the lives of most of his crew and himself. Part 2 ends with "Where *Is* Here?" a story about a tortured soul who visits his childhood home. The visit is both unusual and painful because of deep, dark secrets in the shadows of the past.

Customize for *Varying Student Needs*

When assigning the selections in this part, keep in mind these factors:

"The Fall of the House of Usher"
- Less proficient readers might have difficulty with Poe's long sentences.

"The Raven"
- Less proficient readers may need help with some of the obscure words and unique sentence constructions.

"The Minister's Black Veil"
- Background information about symbolism will aid understanding of this piece.
- Difficult vocabulary may cause problems for less proficient readers.

From *Moby-Dick*
- English language learners may have difficulty with Captan Ahab's thick dialect.

"Where *Is* Here?"
- This tale of the unknown will capture students' interest.
- Less proficient readers will need help finding the clues to the stranger's secret past.

Prepare and Engage

LESSON OBJECTIVES

1. **To develop vocabulary and word identification skills**
   - Latin Word Roots: *-voc-*
   - Using the Word Bank: Synonyms or Antonyms?
   - Extending Word Study: Word Origins
2. **To use a variety of reading strategies to comprehend a short story**
   - Connect Your Experience
   - Reading Strategy: Break Down Long Sentences
   - Tips to Guide Reading
3. **To read for different purposes in varied sources, including American literature**
   - Background for Understanding: Literature
4. **To express and support responses to the text**
   - Critical Thinking
   - Analyze Literary Criticism (ATE)
   - Idea Bank: Obituary
   - Idea Bank: Essay
   - Idea Bank: Movie Analysis
5. **To analyze literary elements**
   - Literary Focus: Single Effect
   - Idea Bank: Letter
6. **To read in order to research self-selected and assigned topics**
   - Idea Bank: Report
   - Research Skills Mini-Lesson (ATE)
7. **To plan, prepare, organize, and present literary interpretations**
   - Idea Bank: Dramatic Reading
   - Speaking, Listening, and Viewing Mini-Lesson (ATE)
   - Viewing and Representing Mini-Lesson (ATE)
8. **To use recursive writing processes to write an introduction to a radio show**
   - Guided Writing Lesson
9. **To increase knowledge of the rules of grammar and usage**
   - Grammar and Style: Coordinate Adjectives

Test Preparation

Reading Comprehension: Make Inferences and Generalizations (ATE p. 295)

The teaching tips and sample test item in this workshop support the instruction and practice in the unit workshop:

Reading Comprehension: Analyze Information to Make Inferences and Generalizations (SE p. 427)

Guide for Interpreting

Featured in AUTHORS IN DEPTH Series

Edgar Allan Poe

(1809–1849)

When Edgar Allan Poe died, Rufus Griswold wrote a slanderous obituary of the eccentric writer. He claimed that Poe had been expelled from college, that he had neither good friends nor good qualities, and that he committed unparalleled plagiarism. Suspicious of this unconventional obituary, some have speculated that Poe orchestrated the death notice himself to keep his name alive.

Poe's own life was almost as dark and dismal as the fiction he produced.

A Troubled Childhood Poe was born in Boston in 1809, the son of impoverished traveling actors. Shortly after Poe's birth, his father deserted the family; a year later, his mother died. Young Edgar was taken in—though never formally adopted—by the family of John Allan, a wealthy Virginia merchant. The Allans provided for Poe's education; however, when his stepfather refused to pay Poe's large gambling debts at the University of Virginia, the young man was forced to leave the school.

Building a Literary Career In 1827, after joining the army under an assumed name, Poe published his first volume of poetry, *Tamerlane and Other Poems.* Two years later, he published a second volume, *Al Aaraaf.* In 1830, John Allan helped Poe win an appointment to the Military Academy at West Point. Within a year, Poe was expelled for academic violations, and his dismissal resulted in an irreparable break with his stepfather.

An Unhappy Ending During the second half of his short life, Poe pursued a literary career in New York, Richmond, Philadelphia, and Baltimore, barely supporting himself by writing and working as an editor for several magazines. After a third volume of poetry, *Poems* (1831), failed to bring him money or acclaim, he turned to fiction and literary criticism. Five of his short stories were published in newspapers in 1832, and in 1838 he published his only novel, *The Narrative of Arthur Gordon Pym.* Though his short stories gained him some recognition and his poem "The Raven" (1845) was greeted with enthusiasm, he could never escape from poverty. In 1849, two years after the death of his beloved wife, Virginia, Poe died in Baltimore alone and unhappy.

A Legacy In the years since his death, Poe's work has been a magnet for attention. Poe is widely known as the inventor of the detective story, and his psychological thrillers have been imitated by scores of modern writers. Some scholars have harshly criticized Poe's writing; others have celebrated his use of vivid imagery and sound effects and his tireless exploration of altered mental states and the dark side of human nature. Despite Poe's uncertain status among critics, however, his work has remained extremely popular among generations of American readers.

◆ Background for Understanding

LITERATURE: POE AS AN EDITOR

In 1839, Poe lived in Philadelphia and became co-editor of *Burton's Gentleman's Magazine*, a journal that published essays, fiction, reviews, and poems, as well as various articles on sailing, hunting, and cricket. Poe's articles ran the gamut of topics. He explained the parallel bars, mused about the mysteries of Stonehenge, and reviewed more than eighty books on a variety of topics.

It was in this magazine that Poe first published "The Fall of the House of Usher" in 1839.

Prentice Hall Literature Program Resources

REINFORCE / RETEACH / EXTEND

Selection Support Worksheets
Build Vocabulary: Latin Word Roots: *-voc-*, p. 90
Grammar and Style: Coordinate Adjectives, p. 91
Reading Strategy: Break Down Long Sentences, p. 92
Literary Focus: Single Effect, p. 93

Strategies for Diverse Student Needs, p. 19

Beyond Literature Media Connection: Film Versions of Poe Stories, p. 19

Formal Assessment Selection Test, pp. 93–95; Assessment Resources Software

Alternative Assessment, p. 19

Writing and Language Transparencies
Branching Organizer, p. 67
Daily Language Practice, Week 7

Resource Pro CD-ROM

Listening to Literature Audiocassettes

The Fall of the House of Usher
◆ The Raven ◆

◆ *Literature and Your Life*

CONNECT YOUR EXPERIENCE

It's natural to feel anxiety. We're all familiar with the trembling hand or the fluttering stomach that can accompany a dreaded event. In extreme circumstances, however, "nerves" can become a destructive part of a person's personality. Stress can even lead to emotional breakdowns, as is the case for characters in both the poem and the story that follow.

Journal Writing Write a paragraph about some event or situation that makes you feel nervous. In your opinion, is there any difference between nervousness and fear?

THEMATIC FOCUS: SHADOWS OF THE IMAGINATION

Edgar Allan Poe was fascinated by the dark reaches the imagination can inhabit when a person is under great stress. How do shadows of the *reader's* imagination contribute to the atmosphere of terror in the following story and poem?

◆ Reading Strategy

BREAK DOWN LONG SENTENCES

Long, complicated sentences can challenge a reader's understanding. By **breaking down a long sentence** into logical parts and analyzing the relationship of these parts, a reader can clarify the author's meaning. Look for a sentence's core: its subject and its predicate. You can find further clues to the structure of a sentence in punctuation, conjunctions, and modifying words. Pare away Poe's decorative language. While descriptive details can intensify mood, they may not be central to the meaning of the sentence.

◆ Literary Focus

SINGLE EFFECT

Poe was the first writer to define the short story as a distinct literary genre and to argue that it deserved the same status as a poem or novel. In Poe's definition (which appeared in his review of Hawthorne's *Twice-Told Tales*), he asserted that a story should be constructed to achieve "a certain unique or **single effect**." He believed that every character, incident, and detail in a story should contribute to this effect. Poe said that if a writer's "very initial sentence tend not to the outbringing of this effect, then he has failed in his first step."

◆ Build Vocabulary

LATIN WORD ROOTS: *-voc-*

Poe uses the word *equivocal* to describe the naming of the "House of Usher." This word contains the Latin root *-voc-*, meaning "voice." In *equivocal*, the root is joined by the word form *-equi-*, meaning "equal." *Equivocal* can be defined as "equal voices" or "having two or more interpretations."

WORD BANK

Before you read, preview this list of words from the selections.

importunate
munificent
equivocal
appellation
specious
anomalous
sentience
obeisance
craven

◆ Grammar and Style

COORDINATE ADJECTIVES

Poe uses adjectives to infuse his writing with mood and atmosphere. When two or more adjectives precede a noun, they may be either coordinate or not coordinate. **Coordinate adjectives** modify the same noun to an equal degree and are separated by commas. Adjectives that are not coordinate do not need a comma between them.

Coordinate: a *dull, dark,* and *soundless* day

Not Coordinate: a *gloomy young* man (*gloomy* modifies *young man*)

Test Preparation Workshop

Reading Comprehension: Make Inferences and Generalizations

Many standardized tests, including the SAT, require students to make inferences—to fill in information not stated by the author—about written texts. Students can practice making inferences by completing the following exercise:

> While he spoke, the lady Madeline . . . passed through a remote portion of the apartment, and without having noticed my presence, disappeared. I regarded her with an utter astonishment not unmingled with dread . . .

In this passage, Madeline most resembles—

A a movie star
B a ghost
C a dancer
D a servant

A and *D* are incorrect. Madeline silently enters, then "disappears," causing a feeling of dread in the speaker. *B* is correct.

Interest Grabber Students will find the odd deterioration of Roderick Usher and the fall into madness of the speaker in "The Raven" shrouded in as much mystery and eerieness as any psychological thriller they may have seen. Hook students' interest in Poe by writing the following passages on the chalkboard:

> "There was an iciness, a sinking, a sickening of the heart—an unredeemed dreariness of thought . . ."

> "Having deposited our mournful burden . . . within this region of horror, we partially turned aside the yet unscrewed lid of the coffin, and looked upon the face of the tenant."

> "Deep into that darkness peering, long I stood there wondering, fearing/doubting, dreaming dreams no mortal ever dared to dream before . . ."

Have students use the passages to make predictions about the story and poem.

Customize for
Less Proficient Readers

To help students through the challenging language and sentence structure of the story and poem, you might have students read in small groups to break apart passages or stanzas to enhance comprehension.

Customize for
AP Students

Poe used the first-person voice in both pieces in this selection. Challenge students to analyze the impact of this choice.

Customize for
English Language Learners

Students can gain a great deal from simply hearing the recording of Poe's story and poem. Even if they miss individual words or images, the eerie, creepy, unsettling feelings Poe creates will become apparent to them. Students can follow along in their text as they listen to the recording of the selection. Feel free to repeat passages as needed to enhance understanding.

Listening to Literature Audiocassettes

Develop Understanding

One-Minute Insight

In Poe's classic tale into the inner reaches of a decaying mind, the narrator honors a request from a boyhood friend to visit him during an oppressive illness. The narrator arrives at the remote, gloomy Usher mansion, where he finds Roderick in poor health, both physically and mentally. Usher knows his mind is disintegrating. He tries to destroy his twin sister, who is in reality, a part of him, because he thinks that her removal might end his torment. Yet he also realizes that once she dies, he'll die too. So he tries to bury her alive. This despicable act hastens his final descent into madness and the end of the Usher family forever.

Customize for
Less Proficient Readers
Distribute the Sequence Events page in ***Strategies for Diverse Student Needs,*** p. 19 to help these students track the action of this story.

▶Critical Viewing◀

❶ **Analyze** Dim colors, gnarled, bare trees, swampy water, and cloudy skies create a gloomy and foreboding mood. The painter conveys the dreariness of the area; the decaying trees; the depressing house with its vacant, eyelike windows; and the pervasive feeling of melancholy the House of Usher evokes.

Tips to Guide Reading

Summarizing Have students stop reading at various points to summarize the main ideas and to ask questions. If the text is a short story, summarizing includes identifying the characters, setting, and plot. Have students pair off for "buddy reading" and decide where they will stop in the text to summarize and discuss their questions. After reading silently, students should write their summary statements and questions independently, then have a discussion with their reading buddies. Discussing the text and checking facts helps students focus on the main ideas and clarify their understandings.

" I at length...," Edgar Allan Poe's *Tales of Mystery and Imagination*, Arthur Rackham, The New York Public Library

❶ ▲ **Critical Viewing** How do the shapes and colors contribute to the mood of this painting? What details of the story's opening paragraph does the painter convey? **[Analyze]**

Humanities: Art

"I at length . . ." Edgar Allan Poe's Tales of Mystery and Imagination, 1935, by Arthur Rackham.

London-born Arthur Rackham (1867–1936) was one of the best-known illustrators of his day; his work is still familiar to millions of readers. Some of his most famous works were his illustrations for *Grimm's Fairy Tales* (1900) and sumptuous limited editions of German legends and Christmas stories. His imaginative, fanciful style was well suited to whimsical, grotesque, and gruesome subjects. For example, this illustration for *The Fall of the House of Usher* dramatically captures the tortured mood of the story through Rackham's use of form and color.

Use these questions for discussion:

1. How does Rackham's rendition of this scene compare with the image Poe creates? *Students may say that the scene is gloomy, remote, and eerie, like Poe describes it.*
2. Rackham's trees often had gnarled, twisted, or misshapen trunks. How does this style work in this scene? *Students may say that the trees forebode death and distortion.*

The Fall of the House of Usher

Edgar Allan Poe

Connections to World Literature, *page 1168*

2 Son Coeur est un luth suspendu:
Sitôt qu'on le touche il résonne.[1]

During the whole of a dull dark, and soundless day in the autumn of the year, when the clouds hung oppressively low in the heavens, I had been passing alone, on horseback, through a singularly dreary tract of country, and at length found myself, as the shades of evening drew on, within view of the melancholy House of Usher. I know not how it was—but, with the first glimpse of the building, a sense of insufferable gloom pervaded my spirit. I say insufferable; for the feeling was unrelieved by any of that half-pleasurable, because poetic, sentiment, with which the mind usually receives even the sternest natural images of the desolate or terrible. I looked upon the scene before me—upon the mere house, and the simple landscape features of the domain—upon the bleak walls—upon the vacant eyelike windows—upon a few rank sedges[2]—and upon a few white trunks of decayed trees—with an utter depression of soul, which I can compare to no earthly sensation more properly than to the afterdream of the reveler upon opium—the bitter lapse into everyday life—the hideous dropping off of the veil. There was an iciness, a sinking, a sickening of the heart—an unredeemed dreariness of thought which no goading of the imagination could torture into aught[3] of the sublime. What was it—I paused to think—what was it that so unnerved me in the contemplation of the House of Usher? It was a mystery all insoluble; nor could I grapple with the shadowy fancies that crowded upon me as I pondered. I was forced to fall back upon the unsatisfactory conclusion, that while, beyond doubt, there *are* combinations of very simple natural objects which have the power of thus affecting us, still the analysis of this power lies among considerations beyond our depth. It was possible, I reflected, that a mere different arrangement of the particulars of the scene, of the details of the picture, would be sufficient to modify, or perhaps to annihilate its capacity for sorrowful impression; and, acting upon this idea, I reined my horse to the precipitous brink of a black and lurid tarn[4] that lay in unruffled luster by the dwelling, and gazed down—but with a shudder even more thrilling than before—upon the remodeled and inverted images of the gray sedge, and the ghastly tree stems, and the vacant and eyelike windows.

> ◆ Literary Focus
> What "single effect" does Poe create in the first sentence?

Nevertheless, in this mansion of gloom I now proposed to myself a sojourn of some weeks. Its proprietor, Roderick Usher, had been one of my boon companions in boyhood; but many years had elapsed since our last meeting. A letter, however, had lately reached me in a distant part of the country—a letter from him—which,

1. **Son . . . résonne:** "His heart is a suspended lute: as one touches it, it resounds." From "Le Rufus" by Pierre Jean de Béranger (1780–1857).
2. **sedges** (sej´ iz) *n.*: Grasslike plants.
3. **aught** (ôt): Anything.
4. **tarn** (tärn) *n.*: Small lake.

Customize for *AP Students*

2 Have students speculate why Poe opens the story with this French couplet. Ask them why they think Poe chose this particular quotation. *Students may say that Poe admired "Le Rufus" and/or Pierre Jean de Béranger or that he found the quotation moving or pertinent to the tale he wanted to tell.*

◆ Literary Focus

3 **Single Effect** The first sentence establishes the single effect of the gloominess of the setting of the story.

◆ Literary Focus

4 **Single Effect** Guide students to appreciate how the entire introduction sets the scene, much like opening shots in a film do. Poe wants to draw readers to the House of Usher and evoke the unsettling and melancholy mood he will maintain throughout the story.

Customize for *Intrapersonal Learners*

5 Point out to students that despite all the gloom the opening passages forebode, the narrator plans to stick to his decision to stay for some weeks. Have groups of students discuss why he might have made this choice. What might happen during the visit? *Students may say that he feels a loyalty to his old friend, that he doesn't want to let the gloom frighten him away, or that his curiosity impels him to go on.*

6 **Clarification** The use of *boon* here, as in "boon companions" is archaic. Its meaning comes from the French word *bon*, which means good.

Block Scheduling Strategies

Consider these suggestions to take advantage of extended class time:

- To provide students with grammar and usage practice relevant to the selections, use the Daily Language Practice for Week 7.
- Introduce the concept of single effect. Have students read the Literary Focus on p. 295. After students have read the story and the poem, have them answer the Reading Focus questions on p. 314. You may follow up with the Literary Focus page in ***Selection Support,*** p. 93.
- Play for students all or parts of the story and poem on the Listening to Literature Audiocassettes. Have students discuss the feelings Poe evokes. In what ways does listening to the selections add to students' appreciation of them?
- To learn more about Poe's tragic life and its influences on what he wrote, have students research Poe in the library or on the Internet either before or after they read.
- Have students work in discussion groups to answer the Critical Thinking questions (pp. 308, 313).
- Before students begin the Guided Writing Lesson (p. 315), have a class discussion on dramatic effect. Have students look for examples of vivid details that would suit a dramatic reading for radio.

◆ Reading Strategy

❶ Break Down Long Sentences This is a good example of a lengthy sentence that is difficult to comprehend at first, but can be understood if it's broken down into smaller parts and paraphrased. For instance, students might restate the sentence like this: "It was how he asked — how intensely he pleaded—that left me no choice. I felt I had to come right away once I got his unique request."

◆ Reading Strategy

❷ Break Down Long Sentences Students may say that the narrator knew that the Usher family has long been known for its generosity to others and its keen interest in the finer points of art and music.

Thematic Focus

❸ Shadows of the Imagination The narrator's observations add to a growing sense of terror. He ascribes to the house and property a devilish, sinister affect. Discuss with students Poe's idea that people are suggestible and that anxieties can so prey on the mind that they grow into obsessions.

◆ Literary Focus

❹ Single Effect Help students notice the single effect Poe achieves in this passage. He describes the house as an old, decaying entity. Its "barely perceptible fissure" suggests a trait or quirk that will become destructive. Discuss how Poe repeatedly emphasizes the isolation of the house from its surroundings. Ask students what these clues may say about the inhabitants the narrator will soon encounter.

in its wildly importunate nature, had admitted of no other than a personal reply. The MS[5] gave evidence of nervous agitation. The writer spoke of acute bodily illness—of a mental disorder which oppressed him—and of an earnest desire to see me, as his best and indeed his only personal friend, with a view of attempting, by the cheerfulness of my society, some alleviation of his malady. ❶ It was the manner in which all this, and much more, was said—it was the apparent *heart* that went with his request—which allowed me no room for hesitation; and I accordingly obeyed forthwith what I still considered a very singular summons.

❷ Although, as boys, we had been even intimate associates, yet I really knew little of my friend. His reserve had been always excessive and habitual. I was aware, however, that his very ancient family had been noted, time out of mind, for a peculiar sensibility of temperament, displaying itself, through long ages, in many works of exalted art, and manifested, of late, in repeated deeds of munificent yet unobtrusive charity, as well as in a passionate devotion to the intricacies, perhaps even more than to the orthodox and easily recognizable beauties, of musical science.

> ◆ **Reading Strategy**
> What is the core of this sentence?

I had learned, too, the very remarkable fact, that the stem of the Usher race, all time-honored as it was, had put forth, at no period, any enduring branch: in other words, that the entire family lay in the direct line of descent, and had always, with very trifling and very temporary variations, so lain. It was this deficiency, I considered, while running over in thought the perfect keeping of the character of the premises with the accredited character of the people, and while speculating upon the possible influence which the one, in the long lapse of centuries, might have exercised upon the other—it was this deficiency, perhaps of collateral issue,[6] and the consequent undeviating transmission, from sire to son, of the patrimony[7] with the name, which had, at length, so identified the two as to merge the original title of the estate in the quaint and equivocal appellation of the "House of Usher"—an appellation which seemed to include, in the minds of the peasantry who used it, both the family and the family mansion.

I have said that the sole effect of my somewhat childish experiment—that of looking down within the tarn—had been to deepen the first singular impression. There can be no doubt that the consciousness of the rapid increase of my superstition—for why should I not so term it?—served mainly to accelerate the increase itself. Such, I have long known, is the paradoxical law of all sentiments having terror as a basis. And it might have been for this reason only, that, when I again uplifted my eyes to the house itself, from its image in the pool, there grew in my mind a strange fancy—a fancy so ridiculous, indeed, that I but ❸ mention it to show the vivid force of the sensations which oppressed me. I had so worked upon my imagination as really to believe that about the whole mansion and domain there hung an atmosphere peculiar to themselves and their immediate vicinity—an atmosphere which had no affinity with the air of heaven, but which had reeked up from the decayed trees, and the gray wall, and the silent tarn—a pestilent and mystic vapor, dull, sluggish, faintly discernible and leaden-hued.

Shaking off from my spirit what *must* have been a dream, I scanned more narrowly the real aspect of the building. Its principal feature seemed to be that of an excessive antiquity. The discoloration of ages had been great. Minute fungi overspread the whole exterior, hanging in ❹ a fine tangled web-work from the eaves. Yet all this was apart from any extraordinary dilapidation. No portion of the masonry had fallen; and there appeared to be a wild inconsistency between its still perfect adaptation of parts, and the crumbling condition of the individual

5. **MS.** *abbr.*: Manuscript.
6. **collateral issue** (kə lat′ ər əl): Descended from the same ancestors but in a different line.
7. **patrimony** (pat′ rə mō′ nē) *n.*: Property inherited from one's father.

◆ Build Vocabulary

importunate (im pôr′ chə nit) *adj.*: Insistent

munificent (myo͞o nif′ ə sənt) *adj*: Generous

equivocal (i kwiv′ ə kəl) *adj*: Having more than one possible interpretation; uncertain

appellation (ap′ ə lā′ shən) *n.*: Name or title

specious (spē′ shəs) *adj.*: Seeming to be good or sound without actually being so

Viewing and Representing Mini-Lesson

Set Design
This mini-Lesson supports the Researching and Representing activity in the Idea Bank on p. 315.

Introduce the Concept Explain to students that their set design should be based on details from the story.

Develop the Background Call on students to read aloud a passage describing the mansion. Have listeners describe the images they see and identify the descriptive words that evoke those images. Suggest that students list the words and phrases Poe uses to describe the mansion, for example, the "ebon blackness of the floors."

Apply the Information Ask students how they will use the descriptive details to create a set design. How would they use props, lighting, and scenery to create the atmosphere? Students may work in small groups to plan the set design and choose the type of representation they will use.

Assess the Outcome Evaluate students on their ability to create a set design that reflects the story description.

stones. In this there was much that reminded me of the specious totality of old woodwork which has rotted for long years in some neglected vault, with no disturbance from the breath of the external air. Beyond this indica- ❹ tion of extensive decay, however, the fabric gave little token of instability. Perhaps the eye of a scrutinizing observer might have discovered a barely perceptible fissure, which, extending from the roof of the building in front, made its way down the wall in a zigzag direction, until it became lost in the sullen waters of the tarn.

Noticing these things, I rode over a short causeway to the house. A servant in waiting took my horse, and I entered the Gothic[8] archway of the hall. A valet, of stealthy step, then conducted me, in silence, through many dark and intricate passages in my progress to the *studio* of his master. Much that I encountered on the way contributed, I know not how, to heighten the vague sentiments of which I have already spoken. While the objects around me—while the carvings of the ceilings, the somber tapestries of the walls, the ebon blackness of the floors, and the phantasmagoric[9] armorial ❺ trophies which rattled as I strode, were but matters to which, or to such as which, I had been accustomed from my infancy—while I hesitated not to acknowledge how familiar was all this—I still wondered to find how unfamiliar were the fancies which ordinary images were stirring up. On one of the staircases, I met the physician of the family. His countenance, I thought, wore a mingled expression of low cunning and perplexity. He accosted me with trepidation and passed on. The valet now threw open a door and ushered me into the presence of his master.

The room in which I found myself was very large and lofty. The windows were long, narrow, and pointed, and at so vast a distance from the black oaken floor as to be altogether inaccessible from within. Feeble gleams of encrimsoned ❻ light made their way through the trellised panes, and served to render sufficiently distinct the more prominent objects around; the eye, however, struggled in vain to reach the remoter angles of the chamber, or the recesses of the vaulted and fretted[10] ceiling. Dark draperies hung upon the walls. The general furniture was profuse, comfortless, antique, and tattered. Many books and musical instruments lay scat- ❻ tered about, but failed to give any vitality to the scene. I felt that I breathed an atmosphere of sorrow. An air of stern, deep, and irredeemable gloom hung over and pervaded all.

Upon my entrance, Usher arose from a sofa on which he had been lying at full length, and greeted me with a vivacious warmth which had much in it, I at first thought, of an overdone ❼ cordiality—of the constrained effort of the *ennuyé*[11] man of the world. A glance, however, at his countenance convinced me of his perfect sincerity. We sat down; and for some moments, while he spoke not, I gazed upon him with a feeling half of pity, half of awe. Surely, man had never before so terribly altered, in so brief a period, as had Roderick Usher! It was with difficulty that I could bring myself to admit the identity of the wan being before me with the companion of my early boyhood. Yet the character of his face had been at all times remarkable. A cadaverousness of complexion; an eye large, liquid, and luminous beyond comparison; lips somewhat thin and very pallid, but of a surpassingly beautiful curve; a nose of a delicate Hebrew model, but with a breadth of nostril unusual in similar formations; a finely molded chin, speaking, in its want of prominence, of a want of moral energy; hair of a more than weblike softness and tenuity—these features, with an inordinate expansion above the regions of the temple, made up ❽ altogether a countenance not easily to be forgotten. And now in the mere exaggeration of the prevailing character of these features, and of the expression they were wont to convey, lay so much of change that I doubted to whom I spoke. The now ghastly pallor of the skin, and the now miraculous luster of the eye, above all things startled and even awed me. The silken hair, too, had been suffered to grow all unheeded, and as, in its wild gossamer texture, it floated rather than fell about the face, I could

8. **Gothic:** High and ornate.
9. **phantasmagoric** (fan taz´ mə gôr´ ik) adj.: Fantastic or dreamlike.
10. **fretted** (fret´ id) *v.:* Ornamented with a pattern of small straight intersecting bars.
11. ***ennuyé*** (än´ wē ā´) *adj.:* Bored (French).

Customize for
Less Proficient Readers

❺ Help students infer the kind of background or upbringing the narrator had, based on his comments and observations. *Students may notice the narrator's awareness of and familiarity with the objects of wealth and finery, to which "[he] had been accustomed from [his] infancy." They can conclude that he had been raised around wealth.*

◆ Build Grammar Skills

❻ **Coordinate Adjectives** Invite students to look for examples in this passage of coordinate adjectives. Have them apply the "order test" (explained on page 314) to verify whether the adjectives are coordinate.

◆ Reading Strategy

❼ **Break Down Long Sentences** Have students break down this long sentence to interpret its meaning. Students may break the sentence into parts like these: *Usher, who had been lying on the sofa, got up to greet me; his warmth seemed a little forced at first.*

◆ Literary Focus

❽ **Single Effect** Have students find parallels between the descriptions of Roderick Usher and those of the house. This is another manifestation of Poe's use of single effect. For example, Usher's weblike hair is like the tangled web-work of fungi on the house; the ghastly pallor of his skin is like the bleak walls.

Customize for
Gifted/Talented Students

Students may be challenged to write dialogue for the scene on this page between the speaker and Roderick Usher. Suggest that students reread the text several times to develop dialogue that reveals the characters' personalities and emotions as described in the narrative. Allow interested students to perform their dialogue for the class.

Cross-Curricular Connection: Art

The Gothic Style Have students learn the characteristics of Gothic architecture—as found in cathedrals of Europe between the twelfth and sixteenth centuries—such as interior pillars, side aisles, radiating chapels, soaring ceilings, flying buttresses, and luminous windows. Display pictures of famous Gothic structures, such as the Cathedrals of Notre Dame (Paris), Chartres, Reims, and Amiens in France; Salisbury, Gloucester, and Canterbury Cathedrals and Westminster Abbey (London) in England; the Cathedrals of Avila, Barcelona, Toledo, and Palma da Majorca in Spain; Santa Croce (Florence) and Milan Cathedral in Italy; and Town Hall in Brussels, Belgium. Discuss how these structures affect people who approach or enter them. Link their responses to Poe's work.

Artistic students may want to present their own Gothic-style paintings or designs for stained-glass windows.

Thematic Focus

❶ Shadows of the Imagination Most people associate sensory experiences with pleasure and a sense of opening one's perceptions of the world. But Roderick Usher's senses betray him, causing him to retreat into near madness. For more, see the Reinforce and Extend note, p. 308.

◆ Literary Focus

❷ Single Effect Discuss Usher's mental state and how it relates to the house. *Students may say that his peculiarities have taken over, as if the house itself has caused it. Usher suggests that the house's physical condition has influenced his mental condition.*

Extending Word Study

Word Origins Have students research the origin of *Arabesque* in a dictionary or book of etymology (*arabus,* Latin) and make a list of other words with the same origin. Then have students map the words to show how word origin connects them. This map may be completed by students.

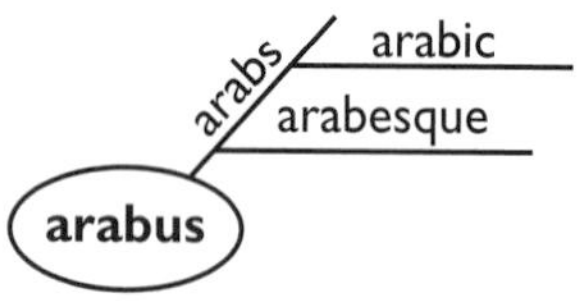

not, even with effort, connect its Arabesque[12] expression with any idea of simple humanity.

In the manner of my friend I was at once struck with an incoherence—an inconsistency; and I soon found this to arise from a series of feeble and futile struggles to overcome an habitual trepidancy—an excessive nervous agitation. For something of this nature I had indeed been prepared, no less by his letter than by reminiscences of certain boyish traits, and by conclusions deduced from his peculiar physical conformation and temperament. His action was alternately vivacious and sullen. His voice varied rapidly from a tremulous indecision (when the animal spirits seemed utterly in abeyance) to that species of energetic concision—that abrupt, weighty, unhurried, and hollow-sounding enunciation—that leaden, self-balanced, and perfectly modulated guttural utterance, which may be observed in the lost drunkard, or the irreclaimable eater of opium, during the periods of his most intense excitement.

It was thus that he spoke of the object of my visit, of his earnest desire to see me, and of the solace he expected me to afford him. He entered, at some length, into what he conceived to be the nature of his malady. It was, he said, a constitutional and a family evil and one for which he despaired to find a remedy—a mere nervous affection,[13] he immediately added, which would undoubtedly soon pass off. It displayed itself in a host of unnatural sensations. Some of these, as he detailed them, interested and bewildered me; although, perhaps, the terms and the general manner of their narration had their weight. He suffered much from a morbid acuteness of the senses; the most insipid food was alone endurable; he could wear only garments of certain texture; the odors of all flowers were oppressive; his eyes were tortured by even a faint light; and there were but peculiar sounds, and these from stringed instruments, which did not inspire him with horror. ❶

To an <u>anomalous</u> species of terror I found him a bounden slave. "I shall perish," said he, "I *must* perish in this deplorable folly. Thus, thus, and not otherwise, shall I be lost. I dread the events of the future, not in themselves, but in their results. I shudder at the thought of any, even the most trivial, incident, which may operate upon this intolerable agitation of soul. I have, indeed, no abhorrence of danger, except in its absolute effect—in terror. In this unnerved, in this pitiable, condition I feel that the period will sooner or later arrive when I must abandon life and reason together, in some struggle with the grim phantasm, FEAR."

I learned, moreover, at intervals, and through broken and equivocal hints, another singular feature of his mental condition. He was enchained by certain superstitious impressions in regard to the dwelling which he tenanted, and whence, for many years, he had never ventured forth—in regard to an influence whose supposititious[14] force was conveyed in terms too shadowy here to be restated—an influence which some peculiarities in the mere form and substance of his family mansion had, by dint of long sufferance, he said, obtained over his spirit—an effect which the physique of the gray walls and turrets, and of the dim tarn into which they all looked down, had at length, brought about upon the morale of his existence. ❷

He admitted, however, although with hesitation, that much of the peculiar gloom which thus afflicted him could be traced to a more natural and far more palpable origin—to the severe and long-continued illness—indeed to the evidently approaching dissolution—of a tenderly beloved sister, his sole companion for long years, his last and only relative on earth. "Her decease," he said, with a bitterness which I can never forget, "would leave him (him, the hopeless and the frail) the last of the ancient race of the Ushers." While he spoke, the lady Madeline (for so was she called) passed through a remote portion of the apartment, and, without having noticed my presence, disappeared. I regarded her with an utter astonishment not unmingled with dread; and yet I found it impossible to account for such feelings. A sensation of stupor oppressed me as my eyes

12. **Arabesque** (ar´ ə besk´) *adj.*: Of complex and elaborate design.
13. **affection:** Affliction.
14. **supposititious** (sə päz´ ə tish´ əs) *adj.*: Supposed.

◆ Build Vocabulary

anomalous (ə näm´ ə ləs) *adj*: Abnormal

Analyze Literary Criticism

The French poet Charles Baudelaire first read Poe in translation in 1847. Seeing the American as both an outlaw and a hero, Baudelaire set out to promote Poe's genius in French literary circles. In an essay in the *Paris Review,* published in 1852, Baudelaire offered this assessment:

"Poe usually suppresses the minor details or gives them a minimal value. Because of this harsh severity, the generating idea is more evident and the subject stands out vividly against the bare background. In Poe's books the style is condensed, tightly linked. The ill will or laziness of the reader cannot slip through the mesh of this logically woven net. All ideas, like obedient arrows, fly to the same target."

Read aloud Baudelaire's critique and work with students to paraphrase it. Then have students discuss these questions:

1. Does Poe "suppress the minor details"? Explain. Which ones might he have suppressed in "The Fall of the House of Usher"?
2. Do you agree that "all arrows fly to the same target" in Poe's story? What is the target?

followed her retreating steps. When a door, at length, closed upon her, my glance sought instinctively and eagerly the countenance of the brother; but he had buried his face in his hands, and I could only perceive that a far more than ordinary wanness had overspread the emaciated fingers through which trickled many passionate tears.

The disease of the lady Madeline had long baffled the skill of her physicians. A settled apathy, a gradual wasting away of the person, and frequent although transient affections of a partially cataleptical[15] character were the unusual diagnosis. Hitherto she had steadily borne up against the pressure of her malady, and had not betaken herself finally to bed; but on the closing in of the evening of my arrival at the house, she succumbed (as her brother told me at night with inexpressible agitation) to the prostrating power of the destroyer; and I learned that the glimpse I had obtained of her person would thus probably be the last I should obtain—that the lady, at least while living, would be seen by me no more.

> ◆ **Literary Focus**
> 3 How does Madeline's surrender on this night contribute to a single effect?

For several days ensuing, her name was unmentioned by either Usher or myself; and during this period I was busied in earnest endeavors to alleviate the melancholy of my friend. We painted and read together, or I listened, as if in a dream, to the wild improvisations of his speaking guitar. And thus, as a closer and still closer intimacy admitted me more unreservedly into the recesses of his spirit, the more bitterly
4 did I perceive the futility of all attempt at cheer-
5 ing a mind from which darkness, as if an inherent positive quality, poured forth upon all objects of the moral and physical universe in one unceasing radiation of gloom.

I shall ever bear about me a memory of the many solemn hours I thus spent alone with the master of the House of Usher. Yet I should fail in any attempt to convey an idea of the exact character of the studies, or of the occupations, in which he involved me, or led me the way. An excited and highly distempered ideality[16] threw a sulfureous[17] luster over all. His long improvised dirges will ring forever in my ears. Among other things, I hold painfully in mind a certain singular perversion and amplification of the wild air of the last waltz of von Weber.[18] From the paintings over which his elaborate fancy brooded, and which grew, touch by touch, into vaguenesses at which I shuddered the more thrillingly, because I shuddered knowing not why—from these paintings (vivid as their images now are before me) I would in vain endeavor to educe more than a small portion which should lie within the compass of merely written words. By the utter simplicity, by the nakedness of his designs, he arrested and overawed attention. If ever mortal painted an idea, that mortal was Roderick Usher. For me at least, in the circumstances then surrounding me, there arose out of the pure abstractions which the hypochondriac contrived to throw upon his canvas, an intensity of intolerable awe, no shadow of which felt I ever yet in the contemplation of the certainly glowing yet too concrete reveries of Fuseli.[19]

One of the phantasmagoric conceptions of my friend, partaking not so rigidly of the spirit of abstraction, may be shadowed forth, although feebly, in words. A small picture presented the interior of an immensely long and rectangular vault or tunnel, with low walls, smooth, white and without interruption or device. Certain accessory points of the design served well to convey the idea that this excavation lay at an 6
exceeding depth below the surface of the earth. No outlet was observed in any portion of its vast extent, and no torch or other artificial source of light was discernible; yet a flood of intense rays rolled throughout, and bathed the whole in a ghastly and inappropriate splendor.

I have just spoken of that morbid condition of the auditory nerve which rendered all music intolerable to the sufferer, with the exception of

15. **cataleptical** (kat′ əl ep′ tik əl) *adj.*: In a state in which consciousness and feeling are suddenly and temporarily lost and the muscles become rigid.

16. **ideality** (ī dē al′ i tē) *n.*: Something that is ideal and has no reality.
17. **sulfureous** (sul fyo͞or′ ē əs) *adj.*: Greenish-yellow.
18. **von Weber** (fôn vā′ bər): Karl Maria von Weber (1786–1826), a German Romantic composer.
19. **Fuseli** (fo͞o ze′ lē): Johann Hinrich Fuseli (1742–1825), Swiss-born painter who lived in England and was noted for his work in the supernatural.

◆ Literary Focus

3 Single Effect Students may say that her mysterious passing adds to the foreboding and gives the narrator more cause for anxiety.

Customize for
Interpersonal Learners

4 Have students discuss the narrator's conclusion about Roderick Usher—that he's so deeply rooted in gloom that no amount of friendship or anything else that might take place between them could cheer him up. *Students may say that a person so fraught with emotional turmoil is unlikely to change even with the attentions of a devoted friend.*

◆ Literature and Your Life

5 Ask students if they have ever tried to help a friend who was so depressed or upset that they did not know what to do to bring the person hope. Ask what they might decide to do if they were the narrator.

Customize for
Visual/Artistic Learners

6 Have students visualize this painting and tell what they think it represents. *Students will probably say it is a tomb or burial crypt.*

Humanities: Music

Romantic Music Poe mentions the music of German Romantic composer Carl Maria von Weber (1786–1826). Play excerpts of his work, such as the overtures from his operas *Der Freischütz* and *Oberon*. Tell students that von Weber had a great influence on later Romantic composers, much like Poe had on writers who followed him. Or you might play the works of other Romantic composers such as Chopin, Liszt, Schumann, and Berlioz. Have students respond to the moods evoked by these pieces. Ask students: Does Romantic music seem to evoke a strong emotional response? *Students may respond that the melodious and at times poignant aspects of much of Romantic music do seem to elicit a strong emotional response.*

◆ Background for Understanding

❶ **History** Tell students that "The Haunted Palace" was published five months before it appeared in Poe's story. It's possible that the poem inspired the tale. In one of his letters, Poe says that the palace in the poem's title symbolizes the human mind: "... by the Haunted Palace I mean to imply a mind haunted by phantoms—a disordered brain." Invite students to use this detail to interpret the poem and then relate its meaning to the theme of the story.

◆ Literary Focus

❷ **Single Effect** Guide students to notice ways in which the poem within the story evokes the same feelings as the story itself, contributing to a single effect. For example, students may say that the reference to a lute (stanza III) echoes the opening French couplet, or that the words "But evil things, in robes of sorrow, / Assailed the monarch's high estate" (stanza V) reflect the eerie mood at the Usher mansion.

Customize for *Musical/Rhythmic Learners*

❸ These students might gain greater appreciation of "The Haunted Palace" if they accompany the words with music, as was done by Usher. Students may either sing the piece to a melody they know or recite the piece accompanied by a recording of appropriate—melancholy or softly moody—background music. Classmates can evaluate whether the music enhanced the mood of the words.

certain effects of stringed instruments. It was, perhaps, the narrow limits to which he thus confined himself upon the guitar which gave birth, in great measure, to the fantastic character of his performances. But the fervid facility of his impromptus could not be so accounted for. They must have been, and were, in the notes, as well as in the words of his wild fantasias (for he not unfrequently accompanied himself with rhymed verbal improvisations), the result of that intense mental collectedness and concentration to which I have previously alluded as observable only in particular moments of the highest artificial excitement. The words of one of these rhapsodies I have easily remembered. I was, perhaps, the more forcibly impressed with it as he gave it because, in the under or mystic current of its meaning, I fancied that I perceived, and for the first time, a full consciousness on the part of Usher of the tottering of his lofty reason upon her throne. The verses, which were entitled "The Haunted Palace," ran very nearly, if not accurately, thus:

I

In the greenest of our valleys,
By good angels tenanted,
Once a fair and stately palace—
Radiant palace—reared its head.
In the monarch Thought's dominion—
It stood there!
❶ *Never seraph*[20] *spread a pinion*
❷ *Over fabric half so fair.*

II

Banners yellow, glorious, golden,
On its roof did float and flow
(This—all this—was in the olden
Time long ago)
And every gentle air that dallied,
In that sweet day,
Along the ramparts plumed and pallid,
A winged odor went away.

III

Wanderers in that happy valley
Through two luminous windows saw
Spirits moving musically
To a lute's well-tunéd law;
Round about a throne, where sitting
(Porphyrogene!)[21]
In state his glory well befitting,
The ruler of the realm was seen.

IV

And all with pearl and ruby glowing
Was the fair palace door,
Through which came flowing, flowing, flowing
And sparkling evermore,
A troop of Echoes whose sweet duty
Was but to sing,
In voices of surpassing beauty,
The wit and wisdom of their king.

V

But evil things, in robes of sorrow,
Assailed the monarch's high estate;
(Ah, let us mourn, for never morrow
Shall dawn upon him, desolate!)
And, round about his home, the glory
That blushed and bloomed
Is but a dim-remembered story
Of the old time entombed.

VI

And travelers now within that valley,
Through the red-litten[22] *windows see*
Vast forms that move fantastically
To a discordant melody;
While, like a rapid ghastly river,
Through the pale door,
A hideous throng rush out forever,
And laugh—but smile no more.

I well remember that suggestions arising from this ballad led us into a train of thought wherein there became manifest an opinion of

20. **seraph** (ser´ əf): Angel.

21. **Porphyrogene** (pôr fər ō jēn´): Born to royalty or "the purple."

22. ***litten:*** Lighted.

Research Skills Mini-Lesson

Resources for Literary Research

This mini-lesson supports the Report activity in the Idea Bank on p. 315.

Introduce the Concept Explain to students that in order to write a report about the Gothic novel, they will need to use literary resources. Have students brainstorm for ideas about what they want to find out, how they might find resources, and the ways in which they will conduct their research. Ideas should include using the library, the Internet, and other print and nonprint resources.

Develop the Background Have students generate a list of questions related to the history of the Gothic novel, for example: How did the Gothic novel begin and where? Who were the first authors and how did this genre grow in Europe and the United States? What Gothic novels are still popular?

Apply the Information Suggest that students gather information in an outline and include dates that mark important works. Remind students to record the sources of their information, including the Internet. Have students present their outlines and summaries to the class.

Assess the Outcome Evaluate students' ability to find resources and to present a complete report. You might use the Scoring Rubric: Research Report/Paper on p. 121 of ***Alternative Assessment.***

Usher's which I mention not so much on account of its novelty (for other men have thought thus), as on account of the pertinacity with which he maintained it. This opinion, in its general form, was that of the sentience of all vegetable things. But, in his disordered fancy
4 the idea had assumed a more daring character, and trespassed, under certain conditions, upon the kingdom of inorganization.[23] I lack words to express the full extent, or the earnest abandon of his persuasion. The belief, however, was connected (as I have previously hinted) with the gray stones of the home of his forefathers. The conditions of the sentience had been here, he imagined, fulfilled in the method of collocation of these stones—in the order of their arrangement, as well as in that of the many fungi which overspread them, and of the decayed trees which stood around—above all, in the long undisturbed endurance of this arrangement, and in its reduplication in the still waters of the tarn.
5 Its evidence—the evidence of the sentience—was to be seen, he said (and I here started as he spoke), in the gradual yet certain condensation of an atmosphere of their own about the waters and the walls. The result was discoverable, he added, in that silent yet importunate and terrible influence which for centuries had molded the destinies of his family, and which made him what I now saw him—what he was. Such opinions need no comment, and I will make none.

Our books—the books which, for years, had formed no small portion of the mental existence of the invalid—were, as might be supposed, in strict keeping with this character of phantasm. We pored together over such works as the *Ververt et Chartreuse*[24] of Gresset; the *Belphegor* of Machiavelli; the *Heaven and Hell* of Swedenborg; the *Subterranean Voyage of Nicholas Klimm* by Holberg; the *Chiromancy* of Robert Flud, of Jean D'Indaginé and of De la Chambre; the *Journey into the Blue Distance* of Tieck; and the *City of the Sun* of Campanella. One favorite volume was a small octavo edition of the *Direc-*
6 *torium Inquisitorium*, by the Dominican Eymeric de Gironne; and there were passages in Pomponius Mela, about the old African Stayrs and Œgipans, over which Usher would sit dreaming for hours. His chief delight, however, was found in the perusal of an exceedingly rare and curious book in quarto Gothic—the manual of a forgotten church—the *Vigilae Mortuorum secundum Chorum Ecclesiae Maguntinae*. 6

I could not help thinking of the wild ritual of this work, and of its probable influence upon the hypochondriac, when, one evening, having informed me abruptly that the lady Madeline was no more, he stated his intention of preserving her corpse for a fortnight (previously to its final interment), in one of the numerous vaults within the main walls of the building. 7 The worldly reason, however, assigned for this singular proceeding, was one which I did not feel at liberty to dispute. The brother had been led to his resolution (so he told me) by consideration of the unusual character of the malady of the deceased, of certain obtrusive and eager inquiries on the part of her medical men, and of the remote and exposed situation of the burial ground of the family. I will not deny that when I called to mind the sinister countenance of the person whom I met upon the staircase, on the day of my arrival at the house, I had no desire to oppose what I regarded as at best but a harmless, and by no means an unnatural precaution.

At the request of Usher, I personally aided him in the arrangements for the temporary entombment. The body having been encoffined, we two alone bore it to its rest. The vault in which we placed it (and which had been so long unopened that our torches, half smothered in its oppressive atmosphere, gave us little opportunity for investigation) was small, damp, and entirely without means of admission for light; lying, at great depth, immediately beneath that portion of the building in which was my own sleeping apartment. 8 It had been used, apparently, in remote feudal times, for the worst purposes of a donjon-keep, and, in later days, as a place of deposit for powder, or some other highly combustible substance, as a portion of

> **◆ Reading Strategy**
> Clarify the main idea of this sentence.

23. **inorganization** (in´ ôr gə ni zā´ shən) *n.*: Inanimate objects.
24. ***Ververt et Chartreuse*, etc.:** All the books listed deal with magic or mysticism.

◆ Build Vocabulary
sentience (sen´ shəns) *n.*: Capacity of feeling

◆ Reading Strategy

4 Break Down Long Sentences Students may restate the meaning like this: *Usher's disordered beliefs that inanimate objects could have a capacity for feeling was becoming an obsession to him.*

◆ Literary Focus

5 Single Effect Ask students to explain what the narrator realizes here that startles him. *He realizes that Roderick, like the Usher house itself, is in a state of decay.*

◆ Background for Understanding

6 Literature An octavo edition is a book whose page size is six by nine inches. A quarto Gothic book has a page size of about nine by twelve inches; the words appear in Gothic type.

7 Clarification Be sure students know that a *fortnight* is two weeks.

◆ Reading Strategy

8 Break Down Long Sentences Students may say the main idea is that the small, damp, dark vault where Madeline's body was to be temporarily entombed had been unused for so long that it was musty and dank. It was located deep beneath the part of the house where the narrator was staying.

Humanities: Film

The vivid images in Edgar Allan Poe's stories and poems and the macabre, gruesome, and chilling themes he explored make them appealing to adapt for film, some more than once. Films based on Poe's works include *The Raven* (1935, 1963), *The Tell-Tale Heart* (1963), *The Fall of the House of Usher* (1982), *The House of Usher* (1960), *Murders in the Rue Morgue* (1932, 1971, 1986), *The Masque of the Red Death* (1964, 1989), and *The Pit and the Pendulum* (1961). Have interested students read the original poem or tale, then watch the film adaptation of it. Have them write a critical essay that analyzes the strengths and weaknesses of both versions.

◆ Critical Thinking

❶ **Speculate** Have students describe the change that has come over Roderick Usher since his sister's death, and speculate what may have caused this deterioration. *Students may say that grief has overwhelmed him, that he has lost his will to live, that his twin's death has made him fear for his own life, or that he has harbored a terrible secret that has tormented him.*

◆ Critical Thinking

❷ **Analyze Causes and Effects** The narrator says that Roderick's condition is beginning to infect him. Ask students: How can someone's emotional state become similar to someone else's? *Students might say that being with someone for a number of days could influence emotional state. For example, a usually happy person who spends a long visit with an unhappy friend might begin to feel sad because of the negative stimulus of the friend.*

◆ Literary Focus

❸ **Single Effect** As the narrator is overcome by a feeling of horror, he begins pacing the floor to and fro. Ask students: How does such pacing enhance the effect of horror? *Students may say that rapidly pacing the floor to and fro is an activity that someone who is mentally unbalanced might do. The pacing of the narrator shows that he too might be falling victim to the atmosphere of horror in the house of Usher.*

its floor, and the whole interior of a long archway through which we reached it, were carefully sheathed with copper. The door, of massive iron, had been, also, similarly protected. Its immense weight caused an unusually sharp, grating sound, as it moved upon its hinges.

Having deposited our mournful burden upon trestles within this region of horror, we partially turned aside the yet unscrewed lid of the coffin, and looked upon the face of the tenant. A striking similitude between the brother and sister now first arrested my attention; and Usher, divining, perhaps, my thoughts, murmured out some few words from which I learned that the deceased and himself had been twins, and that sympathies of a scarcely intelligible nature had always existed between them. Our glances, however, rested not long upon the dead—for we could not regard her unawed. The disease which had thus entombed the lady in the maturity of youth, had left, as usual in all maladies of a strictly cataleptical character, the mockery of a faint blush upon the bosom and the face, and that suspiciously lingering smile upon the lip which is so terrible in death. We replaced and screwed down the lid, and, having secured the door of iron, made our way, with toil, into the scarcely less gloomy apartments of the upper portion of the house.

❶ And now, some days of bitter grief having elapsed, an observable change came over the features of the mental disorder of my friend. His ordinary manner had vanished. His ordinary occupations were neglected or forgotten. He roamed from chamber to chamber with hurried, unequal, and object-less step. The pallor of his countenance had assumed, if possible, a more ghastly hue—but the luminousness of his eye had utterly gone out. The once occasional huskiness of his tone was heard no more; and a tremulous quaver, as if of extreme terror, habitually characterized his utterance. There were times, indeed, when I thought his unceasingly agitated mind was laboring with some oppressive secret, to divulge which he struggled for the necessary courage. At times, again, I was obliged to resolve all into the mere inexplicable vagaries[25] of madness, for I beheld him gazing upon vacancy for long hours, in an attitude of the profoundest attention, as if listening to some imaginary sound. ❷ It was no wonder that his condition terrified—that it infected me. I felt creeping upon me, by slow yet uncertain degrees, the wild influences of his own fantastic yet impressive superstitions.

It was, especially, upon retiring to bed late in the night of the seventh or eighth day after the placing of the lady Madeline within the donjon, that I experienced the full power of such feelings. Sleep came not near my couch—while the hours waned and waned away. I struggled to reason off the nervousness which had dominion over me. I endeavored to believe that much, if not all of what I felt, was due to the bewildering influence of the gloomy furniture of the room—of the dark and tattered draperies, which, tortured into motion by the breath of a rising tempest, swayed fitfully to and fro upon the walls, and rustled uneasily about the decorations of the bed. But my efforts were fruitless. An irrepressible tremor gradually pervaded my frame; and, at length, there sat upon my very heart an incubus[26] of utterly causeless alarm. Shaking this off with a gasp and a struggle, I uplifted myself upon the pillows, and, peering earnestly within the intense darkness of the chamber, hearkened—I know not why, except that an instinctive spirit prompted me—to certain low and indefinite sounds which came, through the pauses of the storm, at long intervals, I knew not whence. ❸ Overpowered by an intense sentiment of horror, unaccountable yet unendurable, I threw on my clothes with haste (for I felt that I should sleep no more during the night), and endeavored to arouse myself from the pitiable condition into which I had fallen by pacing rapidly to and fro through the apartment.

I had taken but few turns in this manner, when a light step on an adjoining staircase arrested my attention. I presently recognized it as that of Usher. In an instant afterward he rapped, with a gentle touch, at my door, and entered, bearing a lamp. His countenance was, as usual, cadaverously wan—but, moreover, there was a species of mad hilarity in his eyes—an evidently

25. vagaries (vā ger´ ēz) *n.*: Odd, unexpected actions or notions.

26. incubus (iŋ´ kyə bəs) *n.*: Something nightmarishly burdensome.

Beyond the Classroom

Career Connection

Literary Critic A literary critic reads, evaluates, analyzes, and comments on literature for both general and specialized audiences. He or she does so on-line, in magazines or newspapers, or in professional journals. Have students read some literary criticism about Edgar Allan Poe's "The Fall of the House of Usher" or "The Raven" to get a better grasp of a critic's objectives and style of writing. Tell students that literary critics usually support their opinions—whether positive or negative—about a work being reviewed with citations from that work. Have students brainstorm for a list of traits that a literary critic should possess to do a good job. Students who have an interest in this field might submit their own literary reviews to the school newspaper.

restrained hysteria in his whole demeanor. His air appalled me—but anything was preferable to the solitude which I had so long endured, and I even welcomed his presence as a relief.

"And you have not seen it?" he said abruptly, after having stared about him for some moments in silence—"you have not then seen it?—but,
4 stay! you shall." Thus speaking, and having carefully shaded his lamp, he hurried to one of the casements, and threw it freely open to the storm.

The impetuous fury of the entering gust nearly lifted us from our feet. It was, indeed, a tempestuous yet sternly beautiful night, and one wildly singular in its terror and its beauty.
5 A whirlwind had apparently collected its force in our vicinity; for there were frequent and violent alterations in the direction of the wind; and the exceeding density of the clouds (which hung so low as to press upon the turrets of the house) did not prevent our perceiving the lifelike velocity with which they flew careering from all points against each other, without passing away into the distance. I say that even their exceeding density did not prevent our perceiving this—yet we had no glimpse of the moon or stars, nor was there any flashing forth of the lightning. But the under surfaces of the huge masses of agitated vapor, as well as all terrestrial objects immediately around us, were glowing in the unnatural light of a faintly luminous and distinctly visible gaseous exhalation which hung about and enshrouded the mansion.

6 ◆ **Literary Focus** How does the description of the storm contribute to the growing sense of terror?

"You must not—you shall not behold this!" said I, shuddering, to Usher, as I led him, with a gentle violence, from the window to a seat. "These appearances, which bewilder you, are merely electrical phenomena not uncommon—or it may be that they have their ghastly origin in the rank miasma[27] of the tarn. Let us close this casement:—the air is chilling and dangerous to your frame. Here is one of your favorite romances. I will read, and you shall listen:—and so we will pass away this terrible night together."

The antique volume which I had taken up was the *Mad Trist* of Sir Launcelot Canning;[28] but I had called it a favorite of Usher's more in sad jest than in earnest; for, in truth, there is little in its uncouth and unimaginative prolixity which could have had interest for the lofty and spiritual 7 ideality of my friend. It was, however, the only book immediately at hand; and I indulged a vague hope that the excitement which now agitated the hypochondriac, might find relief (for the history of mental disorder is full of similar anomalies) even in the extremeness of the folly which I should read. Could I have judged, indeed, by the wild overstrained air of vivacity with which he hearkened, or apparently hearkened, to the words of the tale, I might well have congratulated myself upon the success of my design.

I had arrived at that well-known portion of the story where Ethelred, the hero of the Trist, having sought in vain for peaceable admission into the dwelling of the hermit, proceeds to make good an entrance by force. Here, it will be remembered, the words of the narrative run thus:

"And Ethelred, who was by nature of a doughty heart, and who was now mighty withal, on account of the powerfulness of the wine which he had drunken, waited no longer to hold parley with the hermit, who, in sooth, was of an obstinate and maliceful turn, but feeling the rain upon his shoulders, and fearing the rising of the tempest, uplifted his mace outright, and, with blows, made quickly room in the plankings of the door for his gauntleted hand; and now pulling therewith sturdily, he so cracked, and ripped, and tore all asunder, that the noise of the dry and hollow-sounding wood alarumed 8
and reverberated throughout the forest."

At the termination of this sentence I started and, for a moment, paused; for it appeared to me (although I at once concluded that my excited fancy had deceived me)—it appeared to me that, from some very remote portion of the mansion, there came, indistinctly to my ears, which might have been, in its exact similarity of character, the echo (but a stifled and dull one certainly) of the very cracking and ripping sound which Sir Launcelot had so particularly described. It was, beyond doubt, the coincidence alone which had arrested my attention; for, amid

27. **miasma** (mī az´ mə) *n.*: Unwholesome atmosphere.

28. ***Mad Trist* of Sir Launcelot Canning:** Fictional book and author.

Customize for
Less Proficient Readers

4 Have students infer what Usher means by his question. Encourage responses that support Poe's principle of single effect. *Students may say that "it" is the ghost of his sister, evil spirits of inanimate objects around the house, or a sinister force of nature that will bring destruction.*

5 **Enrichment** Tell students that whirlpools and whirlwinds are recurring symbols in Poe stories. Since they draw things toward their center, they stand for destructive collapse. Poe believed that the universe was destined to collapse in on itself. In fact, he wrote about his theories of cosmology in his book *Eureka*. His ideas about the origin and end of the universe are remarkable because they anticipated by more than a century today's Big Bang theory.

◆ Literary Focus

6 **Single Effect** Students may say that Poe describes the storm with many of the same words he has used to describe the mansion and Roderick Usher himself, such as *agitated, unnatural, luminous, ghastly, rank, chilling,* and *dangerous.*

Customize for
Verbal/Linguistic Learners

7 Tell students that a prolixity is something long-winded and drawn out, so wordy as to be tiresome. Some critics have accused Poe of this fault. Ask students whether they agree or disagree with this charge.

◆ Literary Focus

8 **Single Effect** Discuss with students how this passage from the *Mad Trist* relates to the events of the story. Guide them to notice parallels between Roderick's behavior, the gloom of the house, and Ethelred's change in character, the rising tempest, hollow-sounding wood, and crackling, ripping sounds.

Cultural Connection

Dragons In this tale, Poe describes a dragon slain by Ethelred in the story within a story. Dragons are imaginary creatures that appear in myths and legends of many cultures. But not all dragons are alike. Dragons in Chinese and Japanese cultures symbolize wisdom, power, and the mysteries of the universe. They possess courage, impart knowledge, and are thought to be fabulously rich. Their strength explains forces of nature such as lightning and wind.

Unlike the benevolent eastern dragon, the western dragon is unmercifully evil. This dragon has a hideous, scaly body with angular wings. Its breath is so foul that the stench alone can kill, or the blast of red-hot fire from its gaping mouth can! Western legends place dragons in many habitats. Most live in caves or under ground in tunnels, cellars, or wells. Some live above ground in trees, fields, or mountains. Like eastern dragons, some western dragons live in or near lakes, rivers, swamps, or oceans.

Have students make a graphic organizer to compare and contrast characteristics of eastern and western dragons.

◆ Literary Focus

1 Single Effect Students may cite the narrator's feeling of wild amazement, the harsh, protracted, and unusual grating sounds, the unnatural shrieks, the oppression, and the conflicting sensations of wonder and terror.

◆ Critical Thinking

2 Infer Ask students: Based upon this description, what can you infer about the condition of Roderick? What details lead you to this conclusion? *The trembling lips, slumped head, rigid opening of the eye, and the constant rocking of Roderick attest to a seriously deteriorated physical and emotional condition. He seems to be withdrawing from the world of reality and into a world of his own.*

3 Enrichment Point out to students that Poe is using the narrative of Sir Launcelot—the story within the story—to parallel and even foretell events that take place within the house of Usher. In this passage, the metallic sound of the crashing shield in the narrative parallels a metallic reverberation in the house.

◆ Critical Thinking

4 Predict Ask students to predict what message will be revealed in the "hideous import of his words." *Students may say that Roderick will reveal why he is so disturbed.*

the rattling of the sashes of the casements, and the ordinary commingled noises of the still increasing storm, the sound, itself, had nothing, surely, which should have interested or disturbed me. I continued the story:

"But the good champion Ethelred, now entering within the door, was sore enraged and amazed to perceive no signal of the maliceful hermit; but, in the stead thereof, a dragon of a scaly and prodigious demeanor, and of a fiery tongue, which sate in guard before a palace of gold, with a floor of silver; and upon the wall there hung a shield of shining brass with this legend enwritten—

Who entereth herein, a conqueror
hath bin;
Who slayeth the dragon, the shield
he shall win.

And Ethelred uplifted his mace, and struck upon the head of the dragon, which fell before him, and gave up his pasty breath, with a shriek so horrid and harsh, and withal so piercing, that Ethelred had fain to close his ears with his hands against the dreadful noise of it, the like whereof was never before heard."

Here again I paused abruptly, and now with a feeling of wild amazement—for there could be no doubt whatever that, in this instance, I did actually hear (although from what direction it proceeded I found it impossible to say) a low and apparently distant, but harsh, protracted, and most unusual screaming or grating sound—the exact counterpart of what my fancy had already conjured up for the dragon's unnatural shriek as described by the romancer.

1 **◆ Literary Focus** Which words and details from this description add to the single effect?

Oppressed, as I certainly was, upon the extraordinary coincidence, by a thousand conflicting sensations, in which wonder and extreme terror were predominant, I still retained sufficient presence of mind to avoid exciting, by an observation, the sensitive nervousness of my companion. I was by no means certain that he had noticed the sounds in question; although, assuredly, a strange alteration had, during the last few minutes, taken place in his demeanor. From a position fronting my own, he had gradually brought round his chair; so as to sit with his face to the door of the chamber; and thus I could but partially perceive his features, although I saw that his lips trembled as if he were murmuring inaudibly. His head had dropped upon his breast—yet I knew that he was not asleep, from the wide and rigid opening of the eye as I caught a glance of it in profile. The motion of his body, too, was at variance with this idea—for he rocked from side to side with a gentle yet constant and uniform sway. Having rapidly taken notice of all this, I resumed the narrative of Sir Launcelot, which thus proceeded: 2

"And now, the champion, having escaped from the terrible fury of the dragon, bethinking himself of the brazen shield, and of the breaking up of the enchantment which was upon it, removed the carcass from out of the way before him, and approached valorously over the silver pavement of the castle to where the shield was upon the wall; which in sooth tarried not for his full coming, but fell down at his feet upon the silver floor, with a mighty great and terrible ringing sound."

No sooner had these syllables passed my lips, than—as if a shield of brass had indeed, at the moment, fallen heavily upon a floor of silver—I became aware of a distinct, hollow, metallic, and clangorous, yet apparently muffled, reverberation. Completely unnerved, 3 I leaped to my feet; but the measured rocking movement of Usher was undisturbed. I rushed to the chair in which he sat. His eyes were bent fixedly before him, and throughout his whole countenance there reigned a stony rigidity. But, as I placed my hand upon his shoulder, there came a strong shudder over his whole person; a sickly smile quivered about his lips; and I saw that he spoke in a low, hurried, and 4 gibbering murmur, as if unconscious of my presence. Bending closely over him I at length drank in the hideous import of his words.

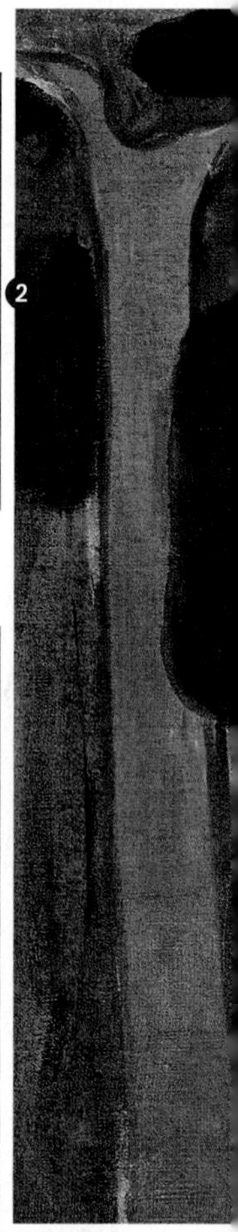

Beyond the Classroom

Community Connection

Haunted Houses Some communities set up a "haunted house" at Halloween or Mardi Gras time. These haunted houses are full of props, sound effects, and details meant to "safely" scare visitors. By contrast, some communities have "real" haunted houses. These may be old houses whose former occupants' lives or deaths gave rise to eerie legends. Have interested students research your community for old houses that people say are haunted, or for sites where unexplained events are said to have occurred. Students could prepare a local guidebook of these locations.

Separation, 1896, Edvard Munch, Munch Museet, Oslo, Norway

5 ▲ Critical Viewing How does the painting convey the same unnatural sense of terror Poe creates in the story? **[Analyze]**

6 "Not hear it?—yes, I hear it, and have heard it. Long—long—long—many minutes, many hours, many days, have I heard it—yet I dared not—oh, pity me, miserable wretch that I am!—I dared not—I *dared* not speak! *We have put her living in the tomb!* Said I not that my senses were acute? I *now* tell you that I heard her first feeble movement in the hollow coffin. I heard them—many, many days ago—yet I dared not—*I dared not speak!* and now—tonight—Ethelred—ha! ha!—the breaking of the hermit's door, and the death cry of the dragon, and the clangor of the shield—say, rather, the rending of her coffin, and the grating of the iron hinges of her prison, and her struggles within the coppered archway of the vault! Oh! wither shall I fly? Will she not be here anon? Is she not hurrying to upbraid me for my haste? Have I not heard her footstep on the stair? Do I not distinguish that heavy and horrible beating of her heart? Madman!"—here he sprang furiously to his feet, and shrieked out his syllables, as if in the effort he were giving up his soul—"*Madman! I tell you that she now stands without the door!*" 7

▶Critical Viewing◀

5 Analyze The painting shows two people. One of them seems to have a troubled expression. The other appears to be a faceless ghost. Perhaps the first person has just had an encounter with the ghost. In any case, the composition of this painting conveys a sense of terror.

◆Critical Thinking

6 Draw Conclusions Ask students why Roderick was unable to speak out if he so desperately feared that he had buried his sister alive. *Students may say that Roderick felt guilty about what he'd done but feared exposing the gruesome act to his one friend, or that he feared terrible retribution.*

◆Critical Thinking

7 Draw Conclusions Ask students if they think Madeline is really just outside the door or, if instead, Roderick's statement is the irrational utterance of someone gone mad.

Humanities: Art

Separation, 1896, Edvard Munch.

Edvard Munch (1863–1944) was a painter and graphic artist who studied in Paris as well as in his native Norway. Munch's complex psychological style is considered one of the earliest manifestations of Expressionism, a movement in art marked by the use of symbols and images distorted to give expression to emotion and inner experience. Like Poe, Munch's identity as an artist came from his obsession with depression, fear, and death; his exploration of these dark themes infused his art with a harrowing power.

Like so many of Munch's works, *Separation* focuses on the emotional effects of a situation. The dark colors and drawn expression of the person in the foreground create a mood of despair. The flowing dress and hair of the woman are ethereal, emphasizing her isolation from others and from the dark forces around her.

Use these questions for discussion:

1. How does the artist create contrast in the painting? *Students may note that one person is dressed in dark clothes and is stationary. The other figure's dress is light, she is in motion, and her face and fingers are only suggested. They may also point out the contrasting settings in the painting.*
2. In what ways is the image related to Poe's tale? *Roderick Usher is a man in despair; his sister Madeline is isolated by illness. The story describes their "separation."*

Customize for
Less Proficient Readers

❶ Help students summarize what happens here, and what it means. *The huge old doors mysteriously fly open to reveal Madeline, who is gaunt and bloody from her ordeal. With her last gasp, she lunges forward to choke her brother, thus delivering the retribution he so feared.*

Customize for
Visual/Spatial Learners

❷ Have students compare the description of the house from the beginning of the tale to its description at the end to identify another example of single effect. *Students may cite the unusual gleam, the vast house standing alone in shadow, the fissure, the sinister tarn, and the sullen silence at its final destruction.*

As if in the superhuman energy of his utterance there had been found the potency of a spell, the huge antique panels to which the speaker pointed threw slowly back, upon the instant, their ponderous and ebony jaws. It was the work of the rushing gust—but then without those doors there *did* stand the lofty and enshrouded figure of the lady Madeline of Usher. ❶ There was blood upon her white robes, and the evidence of some bitter struggle upon every portion of her emaciated frame. For a moment she remained trembling and reeling to and fro upon the threshold—then, with a low moaning cry, fell heavily inward upon the person of her brother, and in her violent and now final death agonies, bore him to the floor a corpse, and a victim to the terrors he had anticipated.

From that chamber, and from that mansion, I fled aghast. The storm was still abroad in all its wrath as I found myself crossing the old causeway. Suddenly there shot along the path a wild light, and I turned to see whence a gleam so unusual could have issued; for the vast house and its shadows were alone behind me. The radiance was that of the full, setting, and blood-red moon, which now shone vividly through that once barely discernible fissure, of which I have before spoken as extending from the roof of the building, in a zigzag direction, to ❷ the base. While I gazed, this fissure rapidly widened—there came a fierce breath of the whirlwind—the entire orb of the satellite burst at once upon my sight—my brain reeled as I saw the mighty walls rushing asunder—there was a long tumultuous shouting sound like the voice of a thousand waters—and the deep and dank tarn at my feet closed sullenly and silently over the fragments of the "*House of Usher*."

Guide for Responding

◆ Literature and Your Life

Reader's Response What images from the story linger in your mind? Why?

Thematic Focus In this story, the narrator barely escapes being drawn into Roderick's fantasy world. Were you drawn into the fantasy world of the story? What was the effect of the story upon your imagination? Explain.

☑ Check Your Comprehension

1. Why has the narrator come to the Usher house?
2. When the narrator meets Usher, what startles him most about Usher's appearance and behavior?
3. To what is Usher a "bounden slave"?
4. What opinion does Usher offer following his performance of "The Haunted Palace"?
5. What does the narrator find striking about Madeline's dead body?
6. (a) What noises does the narrator hear in the midst of reading the *Mad Tryst?* (b) How does Usher explain these noises? (c) What happens immediately after Usher finishes his explanation?

◆ Critical Thinking

INTERPRET

1. How is the appearance of the interior of the house of Usher related to Usher's appearance and to the condition of his mind? **[Connect]**
2. Critics have argued that Madeline and Roderick are actually physical and mental components of the same being. What evidence is there in the story to support this claim? **[Support]**
3. What is the significance of the fact that, rather than helping Usher, the narrator finds himself infected by Usher's condition? **[Analyze]**
4. What message does this story convey about the importance of maintaining contact with the outside world? Support your answer. **[Draw Conclusions]**

EVALUATE

5. Poe's story may suggest that the human imagination is capable of producing false perceptions of reality. Do you agree with this suggestion? Why or why not? **[Evaluate]**

COMPARE LITERARY WORKS

6. Compare this story with Irving's "The Devil and Tom Walker" (p. 236). How does each address the dark side of human experience? **[Compare]**

Reinforce and Extend

Answers

◆ Literature and Your Life

Reader's Response Students may cite many images of horror that linger in the mind.

Thematic Focus Students may say that they *were* drawn into the fantasy world. The unbroken span of terror in this story may have made students imagine the frightening scene all too clearly.

☑ Check Your Comprehension

1. He arrives in response to a compelling letter from his boyhood friend.
2. He is startled by the degree of change in his friend's appearance, especially "the pallor of the skin, and the now miraculous luster of the eye. . . ."
3. Usher is filled with terror and fear.
4. Usher expresses his belief in the human quality of matter and his conviction that the house and its surroundings are themselves alive.
5. The corpse seems to have color in the cheeks as if alive.
6. (a)The narrator hears a metallic reverberation. (b) Usher explains that his sister is making the noises. (c) A door opens, Madeline collapses into Usher's arms, and they both fall dead.

◆ Critical Thinking

1. Like Usher's physical appearance, the house is in a state of decay; like his mind, it is sorrowful and gloomy.
2. Suggested response: Roderick seems always to know what Madeline is experiencing, especially when she is entombed; he does not attempt to rescue her because he knows they are both doomed; he mentions the extremely intuitive feelings that have always been between them.
3. It indicates that when a person is isolated from the real world, he or she can become infected by another person's psychological maladies.
4. The story conveys the message that maintaining contact with the outside world is important for maintaining sanity. Students can cite Roderick's condition as support.
5. Suggested response: Yes, the imagination can produce false perceptions of reality because the imagination can be altered by many internal and external factors.
6. In "The Devil and Tom Walker," people are willing to bargain with the devil for personal gain. In "The Fall of the House of Usher," Roderick leads such a fearful existence that he refuses to help his dying sister.

the Raven

Edgar Allan Poe

❶ Once upon a midnight dreary, while I pondered, weak and weary,
Over many a quaint and curious volume of forgotten lore—
While I nodded, nearly napping, suddenly there came a tapping,
As of some one gently rapping, rapping at my chamber door.
❷ "'Tis some visitor," I muttered, "tapping at my chamber door—
Only this, and nothing more."

Cultural Connection

Ravens Point out that when Edgar Allan Poe wrote this poem, he drew from a long tradition that viewed the raven as a bird of ill omen. Yet in some cultures, the raven enjoys a more positive image. In the Bible, ravens fed the prophet Elijah in the desert; Christian art depicts them as symbols of God's providence. When Vikings were lost at sea, they would set a raven free from their ship. The raven would fly toward land, thus directing the ship. The Vikings prized ravens highly and featured them on their flags.

Discuss with students the symbolic meanings, both positive and negative, of ravens and other birds in various cultures. You might speak of such birds as the albatross, bluebird, crow, nightingale, owl, and parrot. Individual students can be assigned to research the symbolism of one type of bird and report their findings to the class.

Develop Understanding

One-Minute Insight On one level, "The Raven" tells of a man who grieves for his lost love, Lenore. A mysterious talking raven appears at the speaker's door, prompting him to ask it questions about Lenore. The raven responds to each question—including the question of whether he will ever see Lenore again in the afterlife—with one word only, "Nevermore," leaving the man broken and devoid of hope. On another level, the poem explores how grief and loneliness can turn to madness. Poe evokes a mind going to pieces, even watching itself in the process.

◆ Background for Understanding

Literature Poets use sound devices, such as alliteration, assonance, consonance, repetition, internal rhyme, and onomatopoeia, to give a musical quality to their writing. Sound devices please the ear and reinforce meaning by emphasizing key sounds, ideas, words, or images. Poe's use of all these devices in "The Raven" creates a hypnotic effect that draws us into the speaker's irrational world. As a result, Poe persuades us temporarily to abandon our notion of reality to accept the speaker's demented vision.

Literature CD-ROM To build background, use the CD-ROM *The History of American Literature:* Part I, Disk 2, Feature 6, a part of which focuses on "The Raven" by Poe.

◆ Critical Thinking

❶ **Infer** Help students to infer from the clues in just these two lines what kind of person the speaker is. *Students may say that he is a weak, weary, lonely man who loses himself in old books.*

Thematic Focus

❷ **Shadows of the Imagination** Point out how, by saying "Only this and nothing more," the speaker tries to convince himself that the tapping is a sound he can explain rationally. Remind students, however, that since the poet is Poe, they should expect an explanation that is more sinister or mysterious.

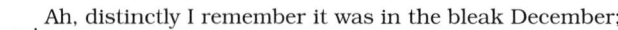

◆ Critical Thinking

❶ **Interpret** Ask students to explain the meaning of the "ghost" in this line. *Students may say that the "ghost" is the glow the dying fire casts upon the floor; symbolically, it may represent one last spark of sanity in the speaker's mind.*

❷ **Enrichment** In his work, Poe often depicts the death of a beautiful, young woman. He considered this to be the ultimate tragic theme, perhaps because of his wife's fragile health or his mother's early death.

◆ Build Grammar Skills

❸ **Coordinate Adjectives** Point out the coordinate adjectives in this line: *silken, sad, uncertain.* Guide students to identify other examples throughout the poem.

Customize for *Musical/Rhythmic Learners*

❹ Have students identify examples of Poe's use of assonance, consonance, and alliteration in lines 37–38. Discuss the musical effect these devices create. *The repetition of vowel sounds in the words* flung, shutter, *and* flutter *is an example of assonance. The repetition of consonant sounds in the accented syllables of the words* shutter, flirt, *and* flutter *is an example of consonance. The repetitions of initial consonant sounds in the words* when *and* with, flirt *and* flutter *are examples of alliteration. These devices give the poem a driving rhythm with a musical flair.*

Ah, distinctly I remember it was in the bleak December;
❶ And each separate dying ember wrought its ghost upon the floor.
Eagerly I wished the morrow;—vainly I had sought to borrow
From my books surcease[1] of sorrow—sorrow for the lost Lenore—
❷ For the rare and radiant maiden whom the angels name Lenore—
Nameless *here* for evermore.

❸ And the silken, sad, uncertain rustling of each purple curtain
Thrilled me—filled me with fantastic terrors never felt before;
So that now, to still the beating of my heart, I stood repeating
"'Tis some visitor entreating entrance at my chamber door—
Some late visitor entreating entrance at my chamber door;—
This it is and nothing more."

Presently my soul grew stronger; hesitating then no longer,
"Sir," said I, "or Madam, truly your forgiveness I implore;
But the fact is I was napping, and so gently you came rapping,
And so faintly you came tapping, tapping at my chamber door,
That I scarce was sure I heard you"—here I opened wide the door;—
Darkness there and nothing more.

Deep into that darkness peering, long I stood there wondering, fearing,
Doubting, dreaming dreams no mortal ever dared to dream before;
But the silence was unbroken, and the stillness gave no token,
And the only word there spoken was the whispered word, "Lenore?"
This I whispered, and an echo murmured back the word, "Lenore!"
Merely this and nothing more.

Back then into the chamber turning, all my soul within me burning,
Soon again I heard a tapping somewhat louder than before.
"Surely," said I, "surely that is something at my window lattice;
Let me see, then, what thereat is, and this mystery explore—
Let my heart be still a moment and this mystery explore;—
'Tis the wind and nothing more!"

❹ Open here I flung the shutter, when, with many a flirt and flutter,
In there stepped a stately Raven of the saintly days of yore;
Not the least obeisance made he; not a minute stopped or stayed he;
But, with mien of lord or lady, perched above my chamber door—
Perched upon a bust of Pallas[2] just above my chamber door—
Perched, and sat, and nothing more.

1. **surcease** (sur sēs´): End.
2. **Pallas** (pal´ əs): Pallas Athena, the ancient Greek goddess of wisdom.

◆ Build Vocabulary

obeisance (ō bā´ səns) *n.*: Gesture of respect
craven (krā´ vən) *adj.*: Very cowardly

Speaking, Listening, and Viewing Mini-Lesson

Movie Analysis

This mini-lesson supports the Speaking, Listening, and Viewing activity in the Idea Bank on p. 315.

Introduce the Concept Have students name horror films they have seen. As you list titles on the chalkboard, invite students to briefly evaluate how well each film created suspense and fear.

Develop Background Divide the class into groups. Have groups brainstorm for a list of techniques filmmakers use to create fear. Some examples include the use of eerie background music, sound and visual effects, camera angles, and editing techniques that add to the tension. Have the group select a film to see and analyze together. Encourage students to take notes as they watch.

Apply the Information Have groups compare their list of film techniques with what they actually saw in the film they watched. Have them speculate about which elements could have derived from Poe and which are later innovations.

Assess the Outcome After groups share their reports with the class, use the following criteria to evaluate each report: (1) Variety of horror techniques found in films. (2) Appropriateness and logic of comparisons made between Poe's techniques and film's techniques. (3) Logical order of information presented.

The Raven, Edmund Dulac

▲ **Critical Viewing** Explain the effect produced by the lines and shading of this drawing. Does the mood of the illustration match that of the poem? Explain. **[Assess]** ❺

Then this ebony bird beguiling[3] my sad fancy into smiling,
By the grave and stern decorum of the countenance[4] it wore,
"Though thy crest be shorn and shaven, thou," I said, "art sure no craven,
Ghastly grim and ancient Raven wandering from the Nightly shore—
Tell me what thy lordly name is on the Night's Plutonian[5] shore!"
Quoth the Raven, "Nevermore."

Much I marveled this ungainly fowl to hear discourse so plainly,
Though its answer little meaning—little relevancy bore;
For we cannot help agreeing that no living human being
Ever yet was blessed with seeing bird above his chamber door—
Bird or beast upon the sculptured bust above his chamber door,
With such name as "Nevermore." ❻

3. **beguiling** (bi gil′ iŋ) *part.*: Charming.
4. **countenance** (koun′ tə nəns) *n.*: Facial expression.
5. **Plutonian** (plo͞o tō′ nē ən) *adj.*: Like the underworld or infernal regions. Refers to Pluto, Greek and Roman god of the underworld.

Clarification The version of "The Raven" printed here is from Poe's *The Raven and Other Poems* (November, 1845). Other earlier versions exist.

▶Critical Viewing◀

❺ **Assess** Suggested response: The lines going at many angles convey the feeling of chaos or frenzy. The shading lets the raven stand out from the vortex-like background at the same time it is clearly part of it. The mood of the illustration, that of frenzy or lurking evil, clearly matches that of the poem.

◆ Literary Focus

❻ **Single Effect** Guide students to notice that in this passage, the speaker begins to comment upon conversing with the bird as if such conversation were a common occurrence. This action signals readers to start to worry for the speaker's stability.

Humanities: Art

The Raven, 1845, by Edmund Dulac.

This picture of the raven features bold lines that give the raven a frenzied or disheveled quality while at the same time symbolically evoking a troubled or discordant mind.

Use these questions for discussion:

1. What images from the poem does the artist evoke? *Students may say that the raven sits on a bust, its open mouth suggesting speech; its ruffled appearance fits the line about the "ungainly fowl"; the brightness behind it recalls "lamp-light o'er him streaming."*
2. Why is the raven off-center? *Students may say that the unbalanced scene suggests the speaker's unbalanced mind.*

◆ Literary Focus

❶ **Single Effect** Ask students to explain the meaning of the Raven's answer to the speaker. *Students may say that the bird's response of "Nevermore" means that the Raven will never leave the speaker.*

◆ Literary Focus

❷ **Single Effect** Point out the mood transition in this passage. Now the speaker begins to contemplate the bird. He notices ominous details but, still longing for Lenore, he hopes that the bird can bring him some measure of solace.

◆ Reading Strategy

❸ **Break Down Long Sentences** Help students restate what the speaker is saying to the Raven here. *The speaker begs the bird for a way to help him heal his pain over the loss of Lenore.*

◆ Critical Thinking

❹ **Interpret** Help students restate the two questions the speaker asks the Raven in this passage. *The speaker asks, "Will I be reunited with Lenore in heaven?" and "Will you please go away?"*

◆ Critical Thinking

❺ **Draw Conclusions** Ask students what the Raven symbolizes. *Students may say that it represents death, loss, madness, a lost soul, or hopelessness.*

But the Raven, sitting lonely on the placid bust, spoke only
That one word, as if his soul in that one word he did outpour.
Nothing farther than he uttered—not a feather then he fluttered—
Till I scarcely more than muttered, "Other friends have flown before—
❶ On the morrow *he* will leave me, as my Hopes have flown before."
Then the bird said, "Nevermore."

Startled at the stillness broken by reply so aptly spoken,
"Doubtless," said I, "what it utters is its only stock and store
Caught from some unhappy master whom unmerciful Disaster
Followed fast and followed faster till his songs one burden bore—
Till the dirges of his Hope that melancholy burden bore
Of 'Never—nevermore.'"

But the Raven still beguiling my sad fancy into smiling,
Straight I wheeled a cushioned seat in front of bird, and bust and door;
Then, upon the velvet sinking, I betook myself to linking
Fancy unto fancy, thinking what this ominous[6] bird of yore—
What this grim, ungainly, ghastly, gaunt, and ominous bird of yore
Meant in croaking "Nevermore."
❷

This I sat engaged in guessing, but no syllable expressing
To the fowl whose fiery eyes now burned into my bosom's core;
This and more I sat divining, with my head at ease reclining
On the cushion's velvet lining that the lamp-light gloated o'er,
But whose velvet-violet lining with the lamp-light gloating o'er,
She shall press, ah, nevermore!

Then, methought, the air grew denser, perfumed from an unseen censer
Swung by seraphim whose foot-falls tinkled on the tufted floor.
"Wretch," I cried, "thy God hath lent thee—by these angels he hath sent thee
Respite—respite and nepenthe[7] from thy memories of Lenore;
Quaff, oh quaff this kind nepenthe and forget this lost Lenore!"
Quoth the Raven, "Nevermore."

"Prophet!" said I, "thing of evil!—prophet still, if bird or devil!—
Whether Tempter sent, or whether tempest tossed thee here ashore,
Desolate yet all undaunted, on this desert land enchanted—
On this home by Horror haunted—tell me truly, I implore—
❸ Is there—*is* there balm in Gilead?[8]—tell me—tell me, I implore!"
Quoth the Raven, "Nevermore."

6. **ominous** (äm´ ə nəs) *adj.*: Threatening; sinister.
7. **nepenthe** (ni pen´ thē) *n.*: Drug that the ancient Greeks believed could relieve sorrow.
8. **balm in Gilead** (gil´ ē əd): In the Bible, a healing ointment made in Gilead, a region of ancient Palestine.

Reteach

Break Down Long Sentences

To aid students' understanding, suggest that they break down long sentences into phrases that tell about the key ideas: who, what, and why. Using this visual device will help students focus on the ideas for restatement:

Who?	
Did What?	
How?	

Explain that by separating out the nonessential information or details, students can restate a passage in their own words. To segment the sentence or passage, students write: *Who* (tells what the sentence is about); *Did What* (describes the action); and *How* or *Why* (gives only important details).
Have students use the device to break down the passage on p. 312, lines 67–78, into phrases or segments of information. Then have students summarize the text in their own words.

"Prophet!" said I, "thing of evil!—prophet still, if bird or devil!
By that Heaven that bends above us—by that God we both adore—
Tell this soul with sorrow laden if, within the distant Aidenn,[9]
It shall clasp a sainted maiden whom the angels name Lenore—
Clasp a rare and radiant maiden whom the angels name Lenore."
Quoth the Raven, "Nevermore." 4

"Be that word our sign of parting, bird or fiend!" I shrieked, upstarting—
"Get thee back into the tempest and the Night's Plutonian shore!
Leave no black plume as a token of that lie thy soul hath spoken!
Leave my loneliness unbroken!—quit the bust above my door!
Take thy beak from out my heart, and take thy form from off my door!"
Quoth the Raven, "Nevermore."

And the Raven, never flitting, still is sitting, *still* is sitting
On the pallid bust of Pallas just above my chamber door;
And his eyes have all the seeming of a demon's that is dreaming; 5
And the lamp-light o'er him streaming throws his shadow on the floor;
And my soul from out that shadow that lies floating on the floor
Shall be lifted—nevermore!

---

9. **Aidenn** (ā´ den): Arabic for Eden or heaven.

Guide for Responding

◆ Literature and Your Life

Reader's Response What are your impressions of the poem's speaker? Explain.

Thematic Focus What does the poem say about the dark power of the imagination?

Class Discussion "The Raven" has been popular for well over one hundred years. Explain why you think the poem does or does not merit this continued attention.

☑ Check Your Comprehension

1. How does the speaker respond to the noise he hears?

2. What does the speaker of "The Raven" want to forget?

3. (a) What does the speaker ask the raven? (b) What is the response? (c) What does the speaker order the raven to do?

◆ Critical Thinking

INTERPRET

1. (a) During the course of "The Raven," what changes occur in the speaker's attitude toward the bird? (b) What brings about each change? (c) What does the raven finally come to represent? **[Analyze]**

2. How does the speaker's emotional state change during the poem? (b) How are these changes related to the changes in his attitude toward the raven? **[Connect]**

3. How is the word *nevermore* related to the speaker's emotional state at the end of the poem? **[Interpret]**

APPLY

4. How might a psychologist explain the speaker's experience? **[Synthesize]**

Beyond the Selection

FURTHER READING

Other Works by Edgar Allan Poe

"The Black Cat"
"The Pit and the Pendulum"
"The Bells"
"The Cask of Amontillado"

We suggest that you preview these works before recommending them to students.

INTERNET

The Internet provides opportunities to learn more about Poe. We suggest the following sites. Please be aware, however, that the sites may have changed from the time we published this information.

Two comprehensive Poe sites are **http://raven.ubalt.edu/features/poe/** and **http://.ezonline.com/dcle/poe.html**

We *strongly recommend* that you preview the sites before you send students to them.

Reinforce and Extend

Answers

◆ Literature and Your Life

Reader's Response Students may feel that the speaker is a lonely, grief-stricken, and mentally unbalanced individual.

Thematic Focus Suggested response: Though the speaker does not imagine the bird itself, his imagination runs wild, and his madness eventually overtakes him as the bird utters its three-syllable message.

☑ Check Your Comprehension

1. At first the speaker, thinking the noise is a visitor rapping at the door, casually opens the door.
2. He wants to forget his sorrow at the loss of his beloved Lenore.
3. (a) He asks who the raven is, if there is balm in Gilead, and if he shall be reunited with Lenore in heaven. (b) Its response is "Nevermore." (c) He orders the raven to leave.

◆ Critical Thinking

1. (a) At first he is amused; then he marvels that the bird can speak; he tries to figure out its meaning; he begins to believe that the bird is an omen from heaven; then he thinks it is evil; he finally becomes angry and orders the bird to leave. (b) The bird's repetition of the word *nevermore* in response to questions causes these changes. (c) It represents the speaker's permanent state of madness.
2. (a) The speaker's emotional state varies among agitation, sadness, anger, and desperation. (b) The speaker's emotions are directly related to his attitude toward the raven. For example, when the speaker believes the raven to be evil, he becomes angry.
3. At the end of the poem, the speaker is desperately unhappy because the raven answers "Nevermore" to key questions that mean everything to the speaker.
4. A psychologist might say that the speaker is irrationally believing something untrue, that the raven understands the questions it is being asked.

Answers

◆ Reading Strategy

1. The subjects are *I, I.* The predicates are *was obliged, beheld.* Sometimes I thought that everything was just the quirks of insanity, because I saw him looking at emptiness for hours in wrapped attention, as if listening to an imaginary sound.
2. Students' paraphrases need not follow same grammatical structures of the original sentences.

◆ Build Vocabulary

1. vocal—"uttered or produced by the *voice*"
2. equivocate—"to *voice* vague terms to deceive or mislead"
3. vociferous—"using a loud or vehement *voice* in making one's feelings known"
4. vocation—"a call, or *voice;* summons; or impulsion to enter a certain career"

Using the Word Bank

1. antonyms; 2. synonyms;
3. synonyms; 4. synonyms;
5. antonyms; 6. synonyms
7. synonyms; 8. antonyms

◆ Literary Focus

1. (a) The description of the House of Usher gives the story an ominous start and establishes a mood of gloom and bleakness. (b) The storms reinforce the growing terror inside the house. (c) Madeline's appearance embodies the final terror for Roderick and for many people: the fear of being buried alive.
2. (a) The growing loudness emphasizes an increasingly acute sensitivity to sensory stimuli. (b) The speaker is attaching irrational significance to the raven. (c) The speaker is now attributing expression to the bird's eyes.

◆ Grammar and Style

1. Correct
2. He gazed longingly at the clear, placid lake.
3. She marveled at the low, smooth, white walls of the tunnel.
4. Correct
5. As the dry, hollow-sounding wood splintered and crashed, the horrible noise reverberated throughout the forest.

Guide for Responding *(continued)*

◆ Reading Strategy

Break Down Long Sentences

By **breaking down a long sentence** into logical parts, you can unlock the meaning at its core.

1. Identify the subject(s) and predicate(s) in the sentence below. Then restate it in your own words.

> At times, again, I was obliged to resolve all into the mere inexplicable vagaries of madness, for I beheld him gazing upon vacancy for long hours, in an attitude of the profoundest attention, as if listening to some imaginary sound.

2. Find another long sentence in Poe's story. Identify its subject(s) and predicate(s), and restate it in your own words.

◆ Build Vocabulary

Using the Latin Root *-voc-*

The Latin root *-voc-* derives from the Latin word *vox*, meaning "voice." Explain how the root influences each of the following words.

1. vocal **2.** equivocate **3.** vociferous **4.** vocation

Using the Word Bank: Synonyms or Antonyms?

Identify each pair as synonyms or antonyms.

1. anomalous, normal
2. appellation, title
3. craven, weak
4. equivocal, ambiguous
5. importunate, yielding
6. munificent, charitable
7. obeisance, reverence
8. specious, sound

Beyond Literature

Media Connection

Hitchcock and the Gothic Tradition

"At sixteen I discovered the work of Edgar Allan Poe," recalled Alfred Hitchcock (1899–1980), the great director of horror and suspense films. Hitchcock won fame for thrillers as eerie and frightening as Poe's tales. Borrowing from the Gothic tradition and adding film techniques of lighting and sound, Hitchcock created suspense classics such as *Rebecca* (1940) and *Psycho* (1960). What cinematic elements can help create a movie that is scarier than the written story that inspired it?

◆ Literary Focus

Single Effect

In his definition of a short story, Poe asserted that a story should be constructed to achieve a **single effect,** to which every word, detail, character, and incident in a story should contribute. While the theory was originally developed for stories, Poe also applied it to poetry.

1. Explain how the following events or details contribute to the effect of a growing sense of terror in "The Fall of the House of Usher."
a. the description of the house of Usher
b. storms and other natural phenomena
c. Madeline's appearance at the end of the story

2. Explain how the following details contribute to the sense of a deteriorating emotional state in "The Raven."
a. the growing loudness of a tapping (line 32)
b. a raven is a bird of ill omen (line 70)
c. the raven's fiery eyes (line 74)

◆ Grammar and Style

Coordinate Adjectives

To determine whether adjectives are coordinate, switch their order. If the sentence still makes sense, the adjectives are coordinate. **Coordinate adjectives** should always be separated by commas.

> **Coordinate adjectives** are adjectives of equal rank that separately modify the noun they precede.

Practice On your paper, insert commas where they are necessary in the following sentences. If a sentence needs no commas, write *Correct.*

1. I was his only personal friend.
2. He gazed longingly at the clear placid lake.
3. She marveled at the low smooth white walls of the tunnel.
4. The guests noticed her wild theatrical manner.
5. As the dry hollow-sounding wood splintered and crashed, the horrible noise reverberated throughout the forest.

Grammar Reinforcement

For additional instruction and practice, use the lesson in the **Language Lab CD-ROM** on Commas and the practice pages on Commas (pp. 86–88) in the *Writer's Solution Grammar Practice Book.*

Build Your Portfolio

Idea Bank

Writing

1. Letter Write a letter to a film student explaining why you think he or she would benefit from analyzing the suspenseful works of Poe.

2. Obituary Elaborate on details from the story to write an obituary of Roderick Usher. Include the circumstances of his death, a brief biography, and information about the funeral arrangements.

3. Essay Poe stated, "A poem, in my opinion, is opposed to a work of science by having, for its *immediate* object, pleasure, not truth. . . ." Using "The Raven" as evidence, write a response to this provocative statement.

Speaking, Listening, and Viewing

4. Dramatic Reading Present a dramatic reading of "The Raven" that captures the poem's building tension and brings to life its unique rhymes and rhythms. Rehearse before delivering your reading. **[Performing Arts Link]**

5. Movie Analysis Watch a contemporary horror film and analyze the techniques used to produce suspense and fear. How do they compare with Poe's? Poll your classmates to see if print or film is a better medium for horror. **[Media Link]**

Researching and Representing

6. Report Research the Gothic novel in Europe and America, and write a report in which you summarize the important works in this genre.

7. Set Design Design the set for a local stage production of "The Fall of the House of Usher." Reread Poe's description of the "mansion of doom"; then draw a picture, create a model, or describe in detail the set you would use. **[Performing Arts Link]**

Online Activity www.phlit.phschool.com

Guided Writing Lesson

Introduction to a Radio Show

The works of Edgar Allan Poe are remarkable for their vivid dramatic effects. Choose "The Raven" or "The Fall of the House of Usher," and think about how you would introduce a dramatic reading of it on the radio. Your goal is to set the stage for listeners who are far removed from the worlds of Poe's work. Your introduction should both capture the interest of listeners and provide any background information they might need.

Writing Skills Focus: Appropriateness for Medium

In preparing an effective introduction to a radio presentation, keep in mind that your writing must be **appropriate for the medium.** Follow these tips:

- Use sound effects to establish the atmosphere you desire for your *listeners*, who are unable to see characters, actions, settings, or lighting.
- Write sentences that are clear and to the point for a radio audience, which has no "second chance" to understand your words and ideas.

Prewriting Begin by rereading the Poe selection you've chosen to introduce. Jot down words or phrases that might help to prepare a listener for the work. Add your own explanatory notes and possible sound effects. Finally, organize your notes in a way that will lead to an effective introduction.

Drafting Orient listeners by identifying or clarifying obscure or difficult elements of the work, such as a theme or setting. Don't reveal important plot details or ruin the suspense that so delights an audience. Refer to your prewriting notes as you draft.

Revising Read aloud your introduction, listening to how it sounds. Where appropriate, simplify sentences to make them clearer. Change long, winding sentences to shorter ones.

Idea Bank

Customizing for Performance Levels

Following are suggestions for matching Idea Bank topics with your students' performance levels:
Less Advanced Students: 1
Average Students: 2, 4, 6, 7
More Advanced Students: 3, 5

Customizing for Learning Modalities

Following are suggestions for matching Idea Bank topics with your students' learning modalities:
Musical/Rhythmic: 4
Logical/Mathematical: 5
Verbal/Linguistic: 6
Visual/Spatial: 7

Guided Writing Lesson

Writing Process Transparencies

Have students use the Outline Organizer in ***Writing and Language Transparencies,*** p. 95, to organize their prewriting notes.

For more prewriting, elaboration, and revision strategies, see *Prentice Hall Writing and Grammar.*

Writing Lab CD-ROM

Have students complete the tutorial on Response to Literature. Follow these steps:

1. Have students use the Audience Profile to gear writing toward the audience.
2. Have students draft on computer.
3. Have students use the Self-Evaluation Checklist to help them revise.

ASSESSMENT OPTIONS

Formal Assessment, Selection Test, pp. 93–95, and Assessment Resources Software. The selection test is designed so that it can be easily customized to the performance levels of your students.

Alternative Assessment, p. 19, includes options for less advanced students, more advanced students, visual/spatial learners, musical/rhythmic learners, and verbal/linguistic learners.

PORTFOLIO ASSESSMENT

Use the following rubrics in the ***Alternative Assessment*** booklet to assess student writing:
Letter: Persuasion Rubric, p. 120
Obituary: Summary Rubric, p. 113
Essay: Literary Analysis/Interpretation, p. 127
Guided Writing Lesson: Response to Literature Rubric, p. 125

Prepare and Engage

LESSON OBJECTIVES

1. **To develop vocabulary and word identification skills**
   - Latin Word Roots: *-equi-*
   - Using the Word Bank: Synonyms
2. **To use a variety of reading strategies to comprehend a short story**
   - Reading Strategy: Evaluate the Author's Messages
   - Background for Understanding
   - Connect Your Experience
   - Read to Appreciate Author's Craft (ATE)
3. **To increase knowledge of other cultures and to connect common elements across cultures**
   - Connecting Themes Across Cultures (ATE)
4. **To express and support responses to the text**
   - Critical Thinking Questions
   - Idea Bank: Essay
   - Idea Bank: Debate
   - Idea Bank: Reading Report
5. **To analyze literary elements**
   - Literary Focus: Allegory
   - Idea Bank: Letter
   - Idea Bank: Memo
6. **To read in order to research self-selected and assigned topics**
   - Research Skills Mini-Lesson (ATE)
   - Cultural Connection (ATE)
7. **To plan, prepare, organize, and present literary interpretations**
   - Idea Bank: Soundtrack
   - Idea Bank: Illustrations
   - Researching and Representing Mini-Lesson (ATE)
8. **To use recursive writing processes to write a response**
   - Guided Writing Lesson
9. **To increase knowledge of the rules of grammar and usage**
   - Grammar and Style: Varying Sentence Openers

Test Preparation

Reading Comprehension: Make Inferences and Generalizations (ATE, p. 317)

The teaching tips and sample test item in this workshop support the instruction and practice in the unit workshop:

Reading Comprehension: Analyze Information to Make Inferences and Generalizations (SE, p. 427)

Guide for Interpreting

Nathaniel Hawthorne

(1804–1864)

Although he lived in a time when many intellectuals embraced the power of the human spirit, Nathaniel Hawthorne found it impossible to adopt an optimistic world view. He believed that evil was a dominant force in the world, and his fiction expresses a gloomy vision of human affairs.

Inherited Guilt Born in Salem, Massachusetts, Hawthorne was descended from a prominent Puritan family. One of Hawthorne's ancestors was a Puritan judge who played a key role in the Salem witchcraft trials. Another ancestor was a judge known for his persecution of Quakers.

> ***Both Hawthorne's character and his focus as a writer were shaped by a sense of inherited guilt.***

Hawthorne was haunted by the intolerance and cruelty of these ancestors, even though he wasn't a Puritan and was born 112 years after the Salem witchcraft trials.

The Long Seclusion After graduation from Maine's Bowdoin College in 1825, Hawthorne secluded himself at his mother's house in Salem and wrote a novel, *Fanshawe.* Soon after the book's anonymous publication in 1828, the young author was seized by shame and abruptly burned most available copies of it. During the nine years that followed, Hawthorne single-mindedly honed his writing skills, while remaining in seclusion at his mother's house for a period of twelve years. In 1837, he published *Twice-Told Tales,* a story collection. At that point, he ended what he termed his self-imposed isolation and moved out of his mother's house. In 1842, Hawthorne married Sophia Peabody and moved to Concord, Massachusetts, where Ralph Waldo Emerson lived. During his years in Concord, Hawthorne befriended both Emerson and Henry David Thoreau—two men whose upbeat spiritual philosophy drastically opposed his. Hawthorne published a second collection of stories, *Mosses From an Old Manse* (1846), and saw the birth of his first daughter, Una.

Man of Letters When he was appointed surveyor at the Salem customhouse, Hawthorne moved with his family back to his birthplace. In 1850, he published his masterpiece, *The Scarlet Letter,* a powerful novel about sin and guilt among early Puritans. The book earned him international fame. He soon wrote two more novels, *The House of the Seven Gables* (1851) and *The Blithedale Romance* (1852).

When his college friend Franklin Pierce became president, Hawthorne was made the American consul at Liverpool, England. He spent several years in England and traveled through Italy before returning to Massachusetts. He used his Italian experiences in the novel *The Marble Faun* (1860). Hawthorne died four years later, leaving four unfinished novels among his belongings.

◆ Background for Understanding

HISTORY: THE WORLD OF HAWTHORNE'S PURITAN ANCESTORS

This story reflects Hawthorne's deep awareness of his Puritan ancestry. The story is set in the 1600's, a time when the Puritans dominated New England. The Puritans lived stern, simple lives and emphasized hard work and religious devotion. They believed that only certain people were predestined by God to go to heaven. This belief led Puritans to search their souls continually for signs of grace.

The Puritans were intolerant of those who lived lives that didn't conform to their ways. People who behaved unusually were often believed to be controlled by evil forces. This attitude contributed to the Salem witchcraft trials of 1692, when at least twenty accused witches were executed.

Prentice Hall Literature Program Resources

REINFORCE / RETEACH / EXTEND

Selection Support Pages
Build Vocabulary: Latin Word Roots: *-equi-*, p. 94
Grammar and Style: Varying Sentence Openers, p. 95
Reading Strategy: Evaluate the Author's Messages, p. 96
Literary Focus: Allegory, p. 97

Strategies for Diverse Student Needs, p. 20

Beyond Literature
Cross-Curricular Connection: Art, p. 20

Formal Assessment Selection Test, pp. 96–98; Assessment Resources Software

Alternative Assessment, p. 20

Writing and Language Transparencies
Cubing Organizer, p. 71

Resource Pro CD-ROM

Listening to Literature Audiocassettes

Literature CD-ROM

The Minister's Black Veil

◆ Literature and Your Life

Connect Your Experience

When kept over a period of time, a secret can grow increasingly mysterious, important, or even menacing. People can become consumed by a desire to learn the secret and will draw their own conclusions if the secret isn't revealed. In "The Minister's Black Veil," a Puritan parson keeps a secret from an entire village for many years.

Journal Writing Recall a time when you or someone you know kept an important secret. Write about how others reacted and the time it took before the secret was revealed.

Thematic Focus: Shadows of the Imagination

This story takes place in a gloomy world inhabited by people haunted by guilt. What role does imagination play in the story?

◆ Build Vocabulary

Latin Word Roots: *-equi-*

The Latin root *-equi-* means "equal" or "plain." The spelling of the root changes slightly in the word *iniquity*, which Hawthorne uses to describe the evil thoughts of parishioners. The word's meaning—"sin or gross injustice"—comes from the combination of the root *-equi-* and the prefix *in-* ("not").

Word Bank

Preview this list of words from the story.

venerable
iniquity
indecorous
ostentatious
sagacious
vagary
tremulous
waggery
impertinent
obstinacy

◆ Grammar and Style

Varying Sentence Openers

In Hawthorne's story, each sentence flows smoothly into the next sentence. This chart shows just a few of the **varied sentence openers** that he uses.

Sentence Openers	
Article/Subject/Verb	The old people . . . came stooping along the street.
Participial Phrase	Swathed about his forehead, . . . Mr. Hooper had on a black veil.
Transitional Phrase	At the close of the services, the people hurried out . . .

◆ Literary Focus

Allegory

An **allegory** is a work of literature in which events, characters, and details of setting have a symbolic meaning. For example, a character in an allegory may personify a single human trait, such as jealousy, greed, or compassion. Allegories are used to teach or explain moral principles and universal truths.

◆ Reading Strategy

Evaluate the Author's Messages

A good piece of literature not only can entertain us but can also challenge us to consider new points of view or outlooks on life. Through the portrayal of characters, settings, and events, writers often convey a message about life that reflects their view of the world. In "The Minister's Black Veil," for example, Hawthorne conveys a message closely tied to his dark view of human nature.

Use the details in the story to interpret Hawthorne's message. Then **evaluate the author's message** by weighing it against your own experiences and beliefs. Ask yourself: In what ways do I agree with the points Hawthorne is making? In what ways do I disagree?

Interest Grabber Write the following quotation on the chalkboard:

"But what has good Parson Hooper got upon his face?" cried the sexton in astonishment.

When Parson Hooper appears one day wearing a black veil, it causes quite a stir among his congregation. Have students imagine that someone they know unexpectedly appears wearing a mask. Ask them to predict how they would react. What would they want to ask?

Connecting Themes Across Cultures

Explain to students that our imaginative thoughts must come from what we know. Because of this, imaginations differ cross-culturally just as much as any other cultural aspect. For example, the myths of different cultures tell many of the same stories, but with very different details. Read several myths about a similar topic to students and discuss the similarities and differences with them as reflections of cultural imagination.

Customize for *Less Proficient Readers*

Set the tone of this story by discussing the use of a mask as a literary device. For instance, talk about how the mask Batman wears is a symbol of mystery and power, or how the one worn by the phantom in *The Phantom of the Opera* is symbolic of isolation and self-loathing.

Customize for *AP Students*

Tell students that Hawthorne's writing reflected his preoccupation with the superstitions and cruelty of his Puritan ancestors. Ask them to analyze examples of this in the story, as well as character flaws on which the story turns. Then point out that along with Herman Melville, Hawthorne exemplified the literary movement known as Anti-Transcendentalism. These writers wrote with an awareness of human flaws. Ask students to keep this author's grim views in mind when they read the works of the Transcendentalists Emerson and Thoreau later in this unit.

Test Preparation Workshop

Reading Comprehension: Make Inferences and Generalizations

Standardized tests such as the SAT require students to make generalizations—that is, general statements based on specific information from the written passage. A generalization is a general idea that is supported by textual evidence. Use the following sample question about Hawthorne's story to show students how to make generalizations about a written text:

What effect does the appearance of Minister Hooper's black veil have on his congregation?

A They are afraid and confused.
B They are indifferent.
C They are quietly supportive.
D They are angry and violent.

Choices *B*, *C*, and *D* contain information not found in the text. *A* is correct. The veil is mysterious and makes Mr. Hooper appear more serious and powerful.

Develop Understanding

One-Minute Insight In this allegory, Mr. Hooper, a highly respected minister in a small Puritan community, suddenly appears wearing a black veil, a mask he vows never to remove. The veil has a powerful, gloomy effect on his parishioners; they are stunned, so much so that they cannot ask him directly why he wears it. Even his fiancée turns from him. The veil's symbolic meaning—an emblem and constant reminder of secret sins—is revealed through the remarks and actions of Hooper's parishioners and in his own deathbed explanation.

Customize for
Less Proficient Readers
Help improve students' comprehension with the Analyze Characters' Behavior page in ***Strategies for Diverse Student Needs,*** p. 20.

◆ Grammar and Style

❶ Varying Sentence Openers
Point out to students that the first four sentences of this excerpt begin with the same element, a subject of a sentence. Ask students what effect beginning the fifth sentence with a different opening—the adverbial clause "when the throng had mostly streamed into the porch"—has on the reader. *Students may say that the different opening makes the reader pause and take note, focusing particular attention on the content of the fifth sentence.*

The Minister's Black Veil

NATHANIEL HAWTHORNE

A PARABLE

❶ The sexton[1] stood in the porch of Milford meetinghouse, pulling busily at the bell rope. The old people of the village came stooping along the street. Children, with bright faces, tripped merrily beside their parents, or mimicked a graver gait, in the conscious dignity of their Sunday clothes. Spruce bachelors looked sidelong at the pretty maidens, and fancied that the Sabbath sunshine made them prettier than on weekdays. When the throng had mostly streamed into the porch, the sexton began to toll the bell, keeping his eye on the Reverend Mr. Hooper's door. The first glimpse of the clergyman's figure was the signal for the bell to cease its summons.

"But what has good Parson Hooper got upon his face?" cried the sexton in astonishment.

All within hearing immediately turned about, and beheld the semblance of Mr. Hooper, pacing slowly his meditative way towards the meetinghouse. With one accord they started, expressing more wonder than if some strange minister were coming to dust the cushions of Mr. Hooper's pulpit.

"Are you sure it is our parson?" inquired Goodman[2] Gray of the sexton.

"Of a certainty it is good Mr. Hooper," replied the sexton. "He was to have exchanged pulpits with Parson Shute, of Westbury; but Parson Shute sent to excuse himself yesterday, being to preach a funeral sermon."

The cause of so much amazement may appear sufficiently slight. Mr. Hooper, a gentlemanly person, of about thirty, though still a bachelor, was dressed with due clerical neatness, as if a careful wife had starched his band, and brushed the weekly dust from his Sunday's garb. There was but one thing remarkable in his appearance. Swathed about his forehead, and hanging down over his face, so low as to be shaken by his breath, Mr. Hooper had on a black veil. On a nearer view it seemed to consist of two folds of crape,[3] which entirely concealed his features, except the mouth and chin, but probably did not intercept his sight, further than to give a darkened aspect to all living and inanimate things. With this gloomy shade before him, good Mr. Hooper walked onward, at a slow and quiet pace, stooping somewhat, and looking on the ground, as is customary with abstracted men, yet nodding kindly to those of his parishioners who still waited on the ❷

1. **sexton** (seks´ tən) *n.*: Person in charge of the maintenance of a church.
2. **Goodman:** Title of respect similar to "Mister."
3. **crape** (krāp) *n.*: Piece of black cloth worn as a sign of mourning.

Block Scheduling Strategies

Consider these suggestions to take advantage of extended class time:

- To give students background on the author and the period during which he wrote, have them view *The History of American Literature:* Part 1, Disc 2, Feature 2 on the **Literature CD-ROM.** This feature focuses in part on Nathaniel Hawthorne. Discuss the influence of Hawthorne's sense of inherited guilt on his writings.
- You may wish to have students gain greater insight into Hawthorne and his writings by having students research Hawthorne in reference works or on the Internet either before or after they read.
- Introduce the allegory. Have students read the Literary Focus on p. 317. After students read the story, have them answer the Literary Focus questions on p. 328. You may follow this up with the Literary Focus page in ***Selection Support,*** p. 97.
- Have students work in discussion groups to answer the Critical Thinking questions on p. 327.
- Before students begin the writing Guided Writing Lesson on p. 329, hold a class discussion on using quotations to cite precise details. Guide students to look for specific parts of the story that made a strong impression on them.

Winter Sunday in Norway, Maine, Unidentified artist, New York State Historical Association, Cooperstown

3 ▲ **Critical Viewing** Identify the elements or details of this painting that correspond to those in Hawthorne's story. **[Connect]**

2 meetinghouse steps. But so wonderstruck were they that his greeting hardly met with a return.

"I can't really feel as if good Mr. Hooper's face was behind that piece of crape," said the sexton.

"I don't like it," muttered an old woman, as she hobbled into the meetinghouse. "He has changed himself into something awful, only by
4 hiding his face."

"Our parson has gone mad!" cried Goodman Gray, following him across the threshold.

A rumor of some unaccountable phenomenon had preceded Mr. Hooper into the meetinghouse, and set all the congregation astir. Few could refrain from twisting their heads towards the door; many stood upright, and turned directly about; while several little boys clambered upon the seats, and came down again with a terrible racket. There was a general bustle, a rustling of the women's gowns and shuffling of the men's feet, greatly at variance 4
with that hushed repose which should attend the entrance of the minister. But Mr. Hooper appeared not to notice the perturbation of his people. He entered with an almost noiseless step, bent his head mildly to the pews on each side, and bowed as he passed his oldest parishioner, a white-haired great-grandsire, who occupied an armchair in the center of the aisle. It was strange to observe how slowly this

◆ Literary Focus

2 Allegory The veil, which gives a "darkened aspect to all living and inanimate things," is a symbol. Have students describe the impact it creates. Ask them to predict why the minister wears it and what it may signify. *The veil shocks most of the congregation. Students might predict from the context of the story that the veil has some religious significance.*

▶Critical Viewing◀

3 Connect Students can point to the painting's cold, dark, gray, gloomy setting as well as to the stiff, uniform appearance of the people.

◆ Reading Strategy

4 Evaluate the Author's Messages Draw students' attention to the strong reactions, both verbal and physical, that the people have toward the veil. Ask them what these reactions reveal about Hooper's parishioners. *They reveal their inability to accept change or to tolerate differences.*

Literature CD-ROM To provide students with background on the author and the period during which he wrote, have them view *The History of American Literature:* Part 1, Disc 2, Feature 2 on the **Literature CD-ROM.** This feature focuses in part on Nathaniel Hawthorne.

Read to Appreciate Author's Craft

Hawthorne's focus on the superstitious character of the Puritans provides much of the mystery and tension in his stories. Guide students to recognize the elements of tension Hawthorne uses to build suspense throughout "The Minister's Black Veil." Have them point out some examples of the mysterious and dark aspects in his writing. Remind students that mystery is created both by description and by space, that is, by deliberately leaving out information. Encourage students to identify both types in this story.

Humanities: Art

Winter Sunday in Norway, Maine, artist unidentified.

This painting is by an anonymous folk artist. Folk artists provide a link between the past and the present by reflecting American social history. Folk art paintings offer an intimate view of America through the eyes of common people—unsophisticated, homey, emotional, and nonintellectual. Unschooled yet charming, folk art incorporates common scenes and materials, native designs, and artisanship.

Use these questions for discussion:

1. How would you describe the mood of this scene? *Students may say that it is a dreary, somber, winter day in a small town where the church plays a prominent role. Students may notice that the insides of the church and houses are as colorless as the bleak landscape.*
2. What seems to be missing from this scene? *Students may notice that no smoke comes from the chimneys and that there appears to be a lack of warmth inside and out.*

◆ Literary Focus

1 Allegory Although they are unlikely at this time to know precisely what the veil symbolizes, students might respond that since it's a mask, it is probably concealing something, representing a secret of some kind.

◆ Critical Thinking

2 Analyze Help students see the link between Hooper's wearing of the veil and the force of his sermon. Guide them to appreciate the unexpected impact of the oratory by noting the descriptions of the parishioners' reactions. Point out that although the congregation recognizes that Mr. Hooper is the same man he was before, they now feel his message much more powerfully.

◆ Grammar and Style

3 Varying Sentence Openers Guide students to notice that the first sentence in this passage begins with a transitional phrase, "At the close of the services," while the next sentence begins with a subject, "some." Point out that varying the sentence opening does more here than merely make the passage less monotonous. Beginning the first sentence with the transitional phrase highlights the time at this point of the story.

◆ Reading Strategy

4 Evaluate the Author's Messages Have students describe the parishioners' attitudes toward the "new" minister Hooper. Ask them to identify the charge Hawthorne levies here against these Puritans. *Students may say that the author charges them with being too quick to judge a man they have long known and respected, simply because his appearance has changed and they don't know why.*

---

venerable man became conscious of something singular in the appearance of his pastor. He seemed not fully to partake of the prevailing wonder, till Mr. Hooper had ascended the stairs, and showed himself in the pulpit, face to face with his congregation, except for the black veil. That mysterious emblem was never once withdrawn. It shook with his measured breath, as he gave out the psalm; it threw its obscurity between him and the holy page, as he read the Scriptures; and while he prayed, the veil lay heavily on his uplifted countenance. Did he seek to hide it from the dread Being whom he was addressing?

> **◆ Literary Focus** 1
> Here is the first suggestion that the veil is a symbol. What might the veil symbolize?

Such was the effect of this simple piece of crape, that more than one woman of delicate nerves was forced to leave the meetinghouse. Yet perhaps the palefaced congregation was almost as fearful a sight to the minister, as his black veil to them.

Mr. Hooper had the reputation of a good preacher, but not an energetic one: he strove to win his people heavenward by mild, persuasive influences, rather than to drive them thither by the thunders of the Word. The sermon which he now delivered was marked by the same characteristics of style and manner as the general series of his pulpit oratory. But there was something, either in the sentiment of the discourse itself, or in the imagination of the auditors, which made it greatly the most powerful effort that they had ever heard from their pastor's lips. It was tinged, rather more darkly 2 than usual, with the gentle gloom of Mr. Hooper's temperament. The subject had reference to secret sin, and those sad mysteries which we hide from our nearest and dearest, and would fain conceal from our own consciousness, even forgetting that the Omniscient[4] can detect them. A subtle power was breathed into his words. Each member of the congregation, the most innocent girl, and the man of hardened breast, felt as if the preacher had crept upon them, behind his awful veil, and discovered their hoarded iniquity of deed or thought. Many spread their clasped hands on their bosoms. There was nothing terrible in what Mr. Hooper said, at least, no violence; and yet, with every tremor of his melancholy voice, the hearers quaked. An unsought pathos came 2 hand in hand with awe. So sensible were the audience of some unwonted attribute in their minister, that they longed for a breath of wind to blow aside the veil, almost believing that a stranger's visage would be discovered, though the form, gesture, and voice were those of Mr. Hooper.

At the close of the services, the people hurried out with indecorous confusion, eager to communicate their pent-up amazement, and conscious of lighter spirits the moment they lost sight of the black veil. Some gathered in little circles, huddled closely together, with their 3 mouths all whispering in the center; some went homeward alone, wrapt in silent meditation; some talked loudly, and profaned the Sabbath day with ostentatious laughter. A few shook their sagacious heads, intimating that they could penetrate the mystery; while one or two affirmed that there was no mystery at all, but only that Mr. Hooper's eyes were so weakened by the midnight lamp, as to require a shade. After a brief interval, forth came good Mr. Hooper also, in the rear of his flock. Turning his veiled face from one group to another, he paid due reverence to the hoary heads, saluted the middle-aged with kind dignity as their friend and spiritual guide, greeted the young with mingled authority and love, and laid his hands on the little children's heads to bless them. Such was always his custom on the Sabbath day. Strange and bewildered looks repaid 4 him for his courtesy. None, as on former occasions, aspired to the honor of walking by their pastor's side. Old Squire Saunders, doubtless by an accidental lapse of memory, neglected to invite Mr. Hooper to his table, where the good clergyman had been wont to bless the food, almost every Sunday since his settlement. He returned, therefore, to the parsonage, and, at the moment of closing the door, was observed to look back upon the people, all of whom had their eyes fixed upon the minister. A sad smile

4. **Omniscient** (äm nish′ ənt): All-knowing God.

Research Skills Mini-Lesson

Taking Notes

Introduce the Concept Tell students that when they conduct research for an assignment, such as the Cultural Connection about veils on p. 321 (ATE), taking effective notes is very important.

Develop Background Have students locate at least three sources of information. Suggest that they search for information in periodicals, academic journals, and library databases such as the *Sociofile Index*.

Apply Tell students to be deliberate about their note taking. Remind them to stick to the topic at hand and to skim the text looking for information specific to their research. Using note cards, have students take notes in different styles to see what works best. Have them try taking notes in complete sentences, phrases, and groupings of words. Whatever method they choose, they should keep their notes organized.

Assess Evaluate students on their note-taking skills: gathering, sorting, and organizing pertinent information. See the Scoring Rubric for a Research Report/Paper on p. 121 of ***Alternative Assessment***.

gleamed faintly from beneath the black veil, and flickered about his mouth, glimmering as he disappeared.

"How strange," said a lady, "that a simple black veil, such as any woman might wear on her bonnet, should become such a terrible thing on Mr. Hooper's face!"

"Something must surely be amiss with Mr. Hooper's intellects," observed her husband, the physician of the village. "But the strangest part of the affair is the effect of this vagary, even on a sober-minded man like myself. The black veil, though it covers only our pastor's face,
5 throws its influence over his whole person, and makes him ghostlike from head to foot. Do you not feel it so?"

"Truly do I," replied the lady; "and I would not be alone with him for the world. I wonder he is not afraid to be alone with himself!"

"Men sometimes are so," said her husband.

The afternoon service was attended with similar circumstances. At its conclusion, the bell tolled for the funeral of a young lady. The relatives and friends were assembled in the house, and the more distant acquaintances stood about the door, speaking of the good qualities of the deceased, when their talk was interrupted by the appearance of Mr. Hooper, still covered with his black veil. It was now an appropriate emblem. The clergyman stepped into the room where the corpse was laid, and bent over the coffin, to take a last farewell of his deceased parishioner. As he stooped, the veil hung straight down from his forehead, so
6 that, if her eyelids had not been closed forever, the dead maiden might have seen his face. Could Mr. Hooper be fearful of her glance, that he so hastily caught back the black veil? A person who watched the interview between the dead and living, scrupled not to affirm, that, at the instant when the clergyman's features were disclosed, the corpse had slightly shuddered, rustling the shroud and muslin cap, though the countenance retained the composure of death. A superstitious old woman was the only witness of this prodigy. From the coffin Mr. Hooper passed into the chamber of the mourners, and thence to the head of the staircase; to make the funeral prayer. It was a tender and heart-dissolving prayer, full of sorrow, yet so imbued with celestial hopes, that the music of a heavenly harp, swept by the fingers of the dead, seemed faintly to be heard among the saddest accents of the minister. The people trembled, though they but darkly understood him when he prayed that they, and himself, and all of mortal race, might be ready, as he trusted this young maiden had been, for the dreadful hour that should snatch the veil from their faces. The bearers went heavily forth, and the mourners followed, saddening all the street, with the dead before them, and Mr. Hooper in his black veil behind.

"Why do you look back?" said one in the procession to his partner.

"I had a fancy," replied she, "that the minister and the maiden's spirit were walking hand 7
in hand."

"And so had I, at the same moment," said the other.

That night, the handsomest couple in Milford village were to be joined in wedlock. Though reckoned a melancholy man, Mr. Hooper had a placid cheerfulness for such occasions, which often excited a sympathetic smile where livelier merriment would have been thrown away. There was no quality of his disposition which made him more beloved than this. The company at the wedding awaited his arrival with impatience, trusting that the strange awe, which had gathered over him throughout the day, would now be dispelled. But such was not the result. When Mr. Hooper came, the first thing that their eyes rested on
was the same horrible black veil, which had 8
added deeper gloom to the funeral, and could portend nothing but evil to the wedding. Such

◆ Build Vocabulary

venerable (ven′ ər ə bəl) *adj.*: Commanding respect

iniquity (in ik′ wə tē) *n.*: Sin

indecorous (in dek′ ər əs) *adj.*: Improper

ostentatious (äs′ tən tā′ shəs) *adj*: Intended to attract notice

sagacious (sə gā′ shəs) *adj.*: Shrewd

vagary (və ger′ ē) *n.*: Unpredictable occurrence

◆ Literary Focus

5 Allegory Here, in the comments of two parishioners, Hawthorne gives readers another hint about why the minister has chosen to wear the veil. Guide students to note the other hints throughout the story and to evaluate the credibility of each.

◆ Critical Thinking

6 Make Inferences Discuss with students the suggestion in this passage that Hooper's wearing of the veil might be in some way connected to the death of the maiden.

Thematic Focus

7 Shadows of the Imagination Ask students to discuss whether this suspicion supports a link between Mr. Hooper's wearing of the veil and the maiden's death. *Sample response: The mourners are only gossiping, and the remarks are pure speculation. Hawthorne may be alluding to the Salem witch trials, in which innocent people were condemned by the specious and hysterical testimony of neighbors.*

◆ Critical Thinking

8 Compare and Contrast Ask students: Why might the foreboding effect of the black veil be more intense at the wedding than at the funeral? *Suggested response: People expect such dismal attire, as well as sadness, at a funeral. A wedding, however, is ordinarily a time of joy. Therefore, the appearance of the minister wearing a black veil at such a joyous occasion makes the veil even more foreboding than at the funeral.*

Cultural Connection

Veils A veil is a garment that can be defined as "a piece of light fabric, as of net or gauze, worn especially by women over the face or head or draped from a hat to conceal, protect, or enhance the face." Traditionally, veils have been worn for a variety of reasons in different cultures. They are worn at weddings, funerals, and other religious ceremonies. People may wear veils to express modesty or mourning.

Have students do research to find out more about why, when, how, and by whom veils are worn in different cultures. When students complete their research, they may share their findings with their classmates during a class discussion on veils.

◆ Background for Understanding

❶ In Hawthorne's short story "The Wedding Knell," an elderly twice-widowed woman hears a death knell as she enters the church to marry her childhood sweetheart. He soon appears at the wedding in a shroud. They marry anyway, knowing that death is not far off.

◆ Reading Strategy

❷ **Evaluate the Author's Messages** Have students interpret why the minister recoils at the sight of his own veil. *Hooper probably realizes that darkness is always present, even at an event as joyous as a wedding.*

Customize for *English Language Learners*

❸ Help these students understand what this sentence means: that none of the busybodies in the parish could ask him a plain question, even though it was on all their minds.

◆ Reading Strategy

❹ **Evaluate the Author's Messages** Have students explain why the committee fails to pose the question they set out to ask. Have them explain what Hawthorne is saying here about human nature. *Suggested response: The author believes that people are reluctant to ask a question when they fear the answer.*

was its immediate effect on the guests that a cloud seemed to have rolled duskily from beneath the black crape, and dimmed the light of the candles. The bridal pair stood up before the minister. But the bride's cold fingers quivered in the tremulous hand of the bridegroom, and her deathlike paleness caused a whisper that the maiden who had been buried a few hours before was come from her grave to be married. ❶ If ever another wedding were so dismal, it was that famous one where they tolled the wedding knell.[5] After performing the ceremony, Mr. Hooper raised a glass of wine to his lips, wishing happiness to the new-married couple in a strain of mild pleasantry that ought to have brightened the features of the guests, like a ❷ cheerful gleam from the hearth. At that instant, catching a glimpse of his figure in the looking glass, the black veil involved his own spirit in the horror with which it overwhelmed all others. His frame shuddered, his lips grew white, he spilt the untasted wine upon the carpet, and rushed forth into the darkness. For the Earth, too, had on her Black Veil.

The next day, the whole village of Milford talked of little else than Parson Hooper's black veil. That, and the mystery concealed behind it, supplied a topic for discussion between acquaintances meeting in the street, and good women gossiping at their open windows. It was the first item of news that the tavernkeeper told to his guests. The children babbled of it on their way to school. One imitative little imp covered his face with an old black handkerchief, thereby so affrighting his playmates that the panic seized himself, and he well nigh lost his wits by his own waggery.

❸ It was remarkable that of all the busybodies and impertinent people in the parish, not one ventured to put the plain question to Mr. Hooper, wherefore he did this thing. Hitherto, whenever there appeared the slightest call for such interference, he had never lacked advisers, nor shown himself averse to be guided by their judgment. If he erred at all, it was by so painful a degree of self-distrust that even the mildest censure would lead him to consider an indifferent action as a crime. Yet, though so well acquainted with this amiable weakness, no individual among his parishioners chose to make the black veil a subject of friendly remonstrance. ❹ There was a feeling of dread, neither plainly confessed nor carefully concealed, which caused each to shift the responsibility upon another, till at length it was found expedient to send a deputation of the church, in order to deal with Mr. Hooper about the mystery, before it should grow into a scandal. Never did an embassy so ill discharge its duties. The minister received them with friendly courtesy, but became silent, after they were seated, leaving to his visitors the whole burden of introducing their important business. The topic, it might be supposed, was obvious enough. There was the black veil swathed round Mr. Hooper's forehead, and concealing every feature above his placid mouth, on which, at times, they could perceive the glimmering of a melancholy smile. But that piece of crape, to their imagination, seemed to hang down before his heart, the symbol of a fearful secret between him and them. Were the veil but cast aside, they might speak freely of it, but not till then. Thus they sat a considerable time, speechless, confused, and shrinking uneasily from Mr. Hooper's eye, which they felt to be fixed upon them with an invisible glance. Finally, the deputies returned abashed to their constituents, pronouncing the matter too weighty to be handled, except by a council of the churches, if, indeed, it might not require a general synod.[6]

But there was one person in the village unappalled by the awe with which the black veil had impressed all beside herself. When the deputies returned without an explanation, or even venturing to demand one, she, with the calm energy of her character, determined to chase away the strange cloud that appeared to be settling round Mr. Hooper, every moment more darkly than before. As his plighted wife,[7]

5. **If . . . knell:** Reference to Hawthorne's short story "The Wedding Knell." A knell is the slow ringing of a bell, as at a funeral.

6. **synod** (sin´ əd) *n.*: High governing body in certain Christian churches.

7. **plighted wife:** Fiancée.

Beyond the Classroom

Career Connection

The Clergy Mr. Hooper is a central figure in his community, like members of the clergy, such as ministers, rabbis, and priests are apt to be. In addition to offering religious instruction and counseling to their congregations, the clergy preside over weddings, funerals, and other rites of passage. Many are involved in education and social service. Today, as in Hooper's time, a minister is a public figure whose words and actions are observed by all.

Have students interview members of the clergy in your area to find out how they view the breadth of their responsibilities. Students might ask them how they interact with their congregation and with the community. Students can compare notes to identify characteristics that effective clergy share, and to get a better understanding of their leadership roles.

it should be her privilege to know what the black veil concealed. At the minister's first visit, therefore, she entered upon the subject with a direct simplicity, which made the task easier both for him and her. After he had seated himself, she fixed her eyes steadfastly upon the veil, but could discern nothing of the dreadful gloom that had so overawed the multitude: it was but
5 a double fold of crape, hanging down from his forehead to his mouth, and slightly stirring with his breath.

"No," said she aloud, and smiling, "there is nothing terrible in this piece of crape, except that it hides a face which I am always glad to look upon. Come, good sir, let the sun shine from behind the cloud. First lay aside your black veil; then tell me why you put it on."

Mr. Hooper's smile glimmered faintly.

"There is an hour to come," said he, "when all of us shall cast aside our veils. Take it not amiss, beloved friend, if I wear this piece of crape till then."

"Your words are a mystery, too," returned the young lady. "Take away the veil from them, at least."

"Elizabeth, I will," said he, "so far as my vow may suffer me. Know, then, this veil is a type and a symbol, and I am bound to wear it ever, both in light and darkness, in solitude and before the gaze of multitudes, and as with strangers, so with my familiar friends. No mortal eye will see it withdrawn. This dismal shade must separate me from the world: even you, Elizabeth, can never come behind it!"

"What grievous affliction hath befallen you," she earnestly inquired, "that you should thus darken your eyes forever?"

"If it be a sign of mourning," replied Mr. Hooper, "I, perhaps, like most other mortals, have sorrows dark enough to be typified by a black veil."

"But what if the world will not believe that it is the type of an innocent sorrow?" urged Elizabeth. "Beloved and respected as you are, there may be whispers that you hide your face under
6 the consciousness of secret sin. For the sake of your holy office, do away this scandal!"

The color rose into her cheeks as she intimated the nature of the rumors that were already abroad in the village. But Mr. Hooper's mildness did not forsake him. He even smiled again—that same sad smile, which always appeared like a faint glimmering of light, proceeding from the obscurity beneath the veil.

"If I hide my face for sorrow, there is cause enough," he merely replied; "and if I cover it for 7
secret sin, what mortal might not do the same?"

And with this gentle, but unconquerable obstinacy did he resist all her entreaties. At length Elizabeth sat silent. For a few moments she appeared lost in thought, considering, probably, what new methods might be tried to withdraw her lover from so dark a fantasy, which, if it had no other meaning, was perhaps a symptom of mental disease. Though of a firmer character than his own, the tears rolled down her cheeks. But in an instant, as it were, a new feeling took the place of sorrow: her eyes were fixed insensibly on the black veil, when, like a sudden twilight in the air, its terrors fell around her. She arose, and stood trembling 8
before him.

"And do you feel it then, at last?" said he mournfully.

She made no reply, but covered her eyes with her hand, and turned to leave the room. He rushed forward and caught her arm.

"Have patience with me, Elizabeth!" cried he, passionately. "Do not desert me, though this veil must be between us here on earth. Be mine, and hereafter there shall be no veil over my face, no darkness between our souls! It is but a mortal veil—it is not for eternity! O! you know not how lonely I am, and how frightened, to be alone behind my black veil. Do not leave me in this miserable obscurity forever!"

"Lift the veil but once, and look me in the face," said she.

◆ Build Vocabulary

tremulous (trem´ yo͞o ləs) *adj.*: Characterized by trembling

waggery (wag´ ər ē) *n.*: Mischievous humor

impertinent (im pʉr´ tən ənt) *adj.*: Not showing proper respect

obstinacy (äb´ stə nə sē) *n.*: Stubbornness

Customize for
Interpersonal Learners

❺ Have students discuss why Elizabeth is perturbed by the veil. *Students may suggest that it conceals a mystery between them, perhaps for the first time.*

◆ Critical Thinking

❻ **Interpret** Ask students: On what grounds does Elizabeth appeal to him to remove the veil? *She appeals to him on the grounds that some people may believe he is hiding a secret sin. She fears that a scandal might result.*

◆ Reading Strategy

❼ **Evaluate the Author's Messages** Have students summarize Hooper's reasons for wearing the veil. Ask them to explain what his responses say about Hawthorne's view of humanity. *Students may say that Hawthorne believes that people everywhere know sorrow, but more importantly, that they live burdened with secret sins.*

Thematic Focus

❽ **Shadows of the Imagination** Ask students to explain why Elizabeth is suddenly afraid. Ask them to suggest what she might be imagining. *Sample response: Elizabeth is disheartened with Hooper's unexpected response; she fears he doesn't trust her or that he may be insane; she realizes that the end of their relationship is at hand.*

Viewing and Representing Mini-Lesson

Illustrations

This mini-lesson supports the Researching and Representing activity on p. 329.

Introduce the Concept Students should be familiar with story illustrations. Show them several examples of different illustrative styles to help prompt ideas.

Develop Background Have students discuss different ideas for illustrations. Guide them to think about issues such as degrees of realism and the balance between general and specific scenes. Most importantly, the illustrations should express an interpretation of the story.

Apply Have students create a series of illustrations to accompany the story.

Assess the Outcome Assess students on their abilities to explain their interpretations. Students should state their reasoning process behind their illustrations.

◆ Reading Strategy

❶ **Evaluate the Author's Messages** Hawthorne's pessimistic view of human nature shows itself in this passage. Marital bliss is denied the minister and his fiancée because of the minister's refusal to provide a straight answer about the veil. Thus, a "material emblem" destroys happiness. Perhaps Hawthorne is suggesting that true happiness is impossible in this imperfect material world.

◆ Critical Thinking

❷ **Speculate** Guide students to understand that when Elizabeth rejects Hooper, the story reaches a turning point. There will be no more attempts to discover the secret the veil supposedly hides. Ask students to predict what may happen to Hooper from here on. *Students may say that Hooper will now lead a very lonely life.*

◆ Literature and Your Life

❸ Ask students to tell what they think Hooper's reasons are for wearing the veil. Ask them to imagine what they might think if someone in their circle began behaving in a new and unexplained manner. *Students might believe Hooper is wearing the veil to conceal a sin or to remind people that death comes to all. Students might anticipate feeling bewildered or surprised if someone they knew began behaving differently.*

◆ Literary Focus

❹ **Allegory** Students may say that Hawthorne believes that sinfulness is the normal human condition, as natural as the wind.

◆ Critical Thinking

❺ **Analyze Causes and Effects** Discuss why the black veil made Mr. Hooper "a very efficient clergyman." Guide students to understand the effect the veiled minister had upon people with serious sins. People who agonized over their sins could more easily present themselves before a veiled minister and, thus, could more easily face their own sins.

"Never! It cannot be!" replied Mr. Hooper.

"Then farewell!" said Elizabeth.

❶ ❷ She withdrew her arm from his grasp, and slowly departed, pausing at the door, to give one long shuddering gaze, that seemed almost to penetrate the mystery of the black veil. But, even amid his grief, Mr. Hooper smiled to think that only a material emblem had separated him from happiness, though the horrors, which it shadowed forth, must be drawn darkly between the fondest of lovers.

> **◆ Reading Strategy**
> How might this passage relate to Hawthorne's message?

From that time no attempts were made to remove Mr. Hooper's black veil, or, by a direct appeal, to discover the secret which it was supposed to hide. By persons who claimed a superiority to popular prejudice, it was reckoned merely an eccentric whim, such as often mingles with the sober actions of men otherwise rational, and tinges them all with its own semblance of insanity. But with the multitude, good Mr. Hooper was irreparably a bugbear.[8] He could not walk the street with any peace of mind, so conscious was he that the gentle and timid would turn aside to avoid him, and that others would make it a point of hardihood to throw themselves in his way. The impertinence of the latter class compelled him to give up his customary walk at sunset to the burial ground; for when he leaned pensively over the gate, there would always be faces behind the gravestones, peeping at his black veil. A fable went the rounds that the stare of the dead people drove him thence. It grieved him, to the very depth of his kind heart, to observe how the children fled from his approach, breaking up their merriest sports, while his melancholy figure was yet afar off. Their instinctive dread caused him to feel more strongly than aught else, that a preternatural[9] horror was interwoven with the threads of the black crape. In truth, his own antipathy to the veil was known to be so great that he never willingly passed before a mirror, nor stooped to drink at a still fountain, lest, in its peaceful bosom, he should be affrighted by himself. This was what gave plausibility to the whispers, that Mr. Hooper's conscience tortured him for some great crime too horrible to be entirely concealed, or otherwise than so obscurely intimated. Thus, from beneath the black veil, there rolled a cloud into the sunshine, an ambiguity of sin or sorrow, which enveloped the poor minister, so that love or sympathy could never reach him. ❸ It was said that ghost and fiend consorted with him there. With self-shudderings and outward terrors, he walked continually in its shadow, groping darkly within his own soul or gazing through a medium that saddened the whole world. Even the lawless wind, it was believed, respected his dreadful secret, and never blew aside the veil. But still good Mr. Hooper sadly smiled at the pale visages of the worldly throng as he passed by. ❹

> **◆ Literary Focus**
> Why is it significant that nature respects his veil?

Among all its bad influences, the black veil had the one desirable effect, of making its wearer a very efficient clergyman. By the aid of his mysterious emblem—for there was no other apparent cause—he became a man of awful power over souls that were in agony for sin. His converts always regarded him with a dread peculiar to themselves, affirming, though but figuratively, that, before he brought them to celestial light, they had been with him behind the black veil. Its gloom, indeed, enabled him ❺ to sympathize with all dark affections. Dying sinners cried aloud for Mr. Hooper, and would not yield their breath till he appeared; though ever, as he stooped to whisper consolation, they shuddered at the veiled face so near their own. Such were the terrors of the black veil, even when Death had bared his visage! Strangers came long distances to attend service at his church, with the mere idle purpose of gazing at his figure, because it was forbidden them to behold his face. But many were made to quake ere they departed! Once, during Governor Belcher's[10] administration, Mr. Hooper was appointed to preach the election sermon. Covered

8. **bugbear** *n.*: Something causing needless fear.
9. **preternatural** (prēt′ ər năch′ ər əl) *adj.*: Supernatural.

10. **Governor Belcher:** Jonathan Belcher (1682–1757), the royal governor of the Massachusetts Bay Colony, from 1730 to 1741.

Speaking, Listening, and Viewing Mini-Lesson

Debate

This mini-lesson supports activity 4, p. 329.

Introduce the Concept Have students determine the exact focus of their debate. Once students have decided on the topic, have them form debating teams.

Develop Background If students plan to debate a broad topic, they'll need to conduct research to support their viewpoint. History provides ample evidence for and against the rights and responsibilities of leaders.

Apply the Information Decide on a format and rules for the debate. You may wish to hold several debates in which two teams contest each other while the rest of the class acts as the audience.

Assess the Outcome Evaluate each students on their knowledge of pertinent facts, the logical presentation of argument, and the effective response to questions and objections.

Cemetery, Peter McIntyre, Courtesy of the artist

6 ▲ **Critical Viewing** Describe the atmosphere in this painting. What has the artist done to create this atmosphere? **[Identify; Support]**

with his black veil, he stood before the chief magistrate, the council, and the representatives, and wrought so deep an impression that the legislative measures of that year were characterized by all the gloom and piety of our earliest ancestral sway.

In this manner Mr. Hooper spent a long life, irreproachable in outward act, yet shrouded in dismal suspicions; kind and loving, though unloved, and dimly feared; a man apart from 7

▶Critical Viewing◀

6 Identify; Support Students may say that the artist has created a gloomy atmosphere in which death and dying hover menacingly over a sleepy village. The artist has used composition, color, and contrast to create this atmosphere. In the background, for example, the village sits in a faint haze, as if peaceful and innocent. But in the foreground, the overgrown cemetery sits dark and large on the hill beneath a dominating, foreboding, dying tree.

◆Critical Thinking

7 Draw Conclusions Ask students: How has the veil isolated the minister? Would his calling alone have isolated him? *Students will probably say that the veil has isolated the minister by making him appear markedly different from other people, even frightening. The minister's calling alone probably would not have isolated him. In fact, his good nature might have attracted people to him.*

Customize for *Visual/Spatial Learners*

Invite these students to create a picture that evokes the eerie atmosphere of this story. Have the students draw or paint the minister meeting a stranger by chance along a road. Make sure that the minister is wearing his veil and that the expression on the face of the stranger is clearly visible. Remind students to decide what emotion the stranger will feel when confronted by the veiled minister: Will he or she display fear, surprise, curiosity, or terror?

Humanities: Art

Cemetery, 1970, by Peter McIntyre.

Peter McIntyre (1910–) was born in New Zealand. He studied art in London, where he became involved in illustrating books and magazines and in stage design. He was an "Official War Artist" during World War II. He served in that capacity in Greece, Crete, North Africa, and Italy. *Cemetery* was completed during a trip to the United States and published in the book *Peter McIntyre's West.*

Use these questions for discussion:

1. How do you think the artist's perspective and his feelings about this place suggest that he tried for more than photographic likeness? *Students may point to the vivid contrast between the menacing, overgrown, disorderly graveyard with its huge half-dead portentous tree and the serene village in the background, and say that the artist creates the impression that there may be something ominous in the town's past, or perhaps in its future.*
2. Do you think this picture is an appropriate illustration for this story? Why or why not? *Students who say yes will point out that the dismal scene is appropriate for the atmosphere of the story. Students who say no might point out that a picture showing a member of the clergy or a church would be more appropriate.*

Customize for
English Language Learners

❶ Guide these students to understand the meaning of this passage: that Mr. Hooper is about to die.

◆ Critical Thinking

❷ **Infer** Ask students to explain what Elizabeth's lifelong faithfulness, without marriage, to Mr. Hooper says about her character. *Students may say that Elizabeth did not trust Hooper enough to marry him, but she loved and respected him enough to offer him her lifelong support and friendship.*

◆ Literary Focus

❸ **Allegory** Guide students to note that Minister Clark refers to another symbolic veil—the one that separates life from death.

Reteach

Students may have difficulty identifying allegorical elements. Explain to them that story elements have symbolic meaning in allegory. This symbolism may be about a general topic, or it may specifically parallel a real event or specific situation. To help students recognize allegory in "The Minister's Black Veil," create a chart, listing the allegorical elements in the story and their symbolic meanings. Fill in one example on the chart. Then, in class discussion, ask for suggestions, listing the different symbolic relationships that make this story an allegory.

bride, bridegroom	
children	
corpse	

men, shunned in their health and joy, but ever summoned to their aid in mortal anguish. As years wore on, shedding their snows above his sable veil, he acquired a name throughout the New England churches, and they called him Father Hooper. Nearly all his parishioners, who were of mature age when he was settled, had been borne away by many a funeral: he had one congregation in the church, and a more crowded one in the churchyard; and having wrought so late into the evening, and done his
❶ work so well, it was now good Father Hooper's turn to rest.

Several persons were visible by the shaded candlelight, in the death chamber of the old clergyman. Natural connections[11] he had none. But there was the decorously grave, though unmoved physician, seeking only to mitigate the last pangs of the patient whom he could not save. There were the deacons, and other eminently pious members of his church. There, also, was the Reverend Mr. Clark, of Westbury, a young and zealous divine, who had ridden in haste to pray by the bedside of the expiring minister. There was the nurse, no hired handmaiden of death, but one whose calm affection
❷ had endured thus long in secrecy, in solitude, amid the chill of age, and would not perish, even at the dying hour. Who, but Elizabeth! And there lay the hoary head of good Father Hooper upon the death pillow, with the black veil still swathed about his brow, and reaching down over his face, so that each more difficult gasp of his faint breath caused it to stir. All through life that piece of crape had hung between him and the world: it had separated him from cheerful brotherhood and woman's love, and kept him in that saddest of all prisons, his own heart; and still it lay upon his face, as if to deepen the gloom of his darksome chamber, and shade him from the sunshine of eternity.

For some time previous, his mind had been confused, wavering doubtfully between the past and the present, and hovering forward, as it were, at intervals, into the indistinctness of the world to come. There had been feverish turns, which tossed him from side to side, and wore away what little strength he had. But in his most convulsive struggles, and in the wildest vagaries of his intellect, when no other thought retained its sober influence, he still showed an awful solicitude lest the black veil should slip aside. Even if his bewildered soul could have forgotten, there was a faithful woman at his pillow, who, with averted eyes, would have covered that aged face, which she had last beheld in the comeliness of manhood. At length the death-stricken old man lay quietly in the torpor of mental and bodily exhaustion, with an imperceptible pulse, and breath that grew fainter and fainter, except when a long, deep, and irregular inspiration seemed to prelude the flight of his spirit.

The minister of Westbury approached the bedside.

"Venerable Father Hooper," said he, "the moment of your release is at hand. Are you ready for the lifting of the veil that shuts in time from eternity?"

Father Hooper at first replied merely by a feeble motion of his head; then, apprehensive, perhaps, that his meaning might be doubtful, he exerted himself to speak.

"Yea," said he, in faint accents, "my soul hath a patient weariness until that veil be lifted."

"And is it fitting," resumed the Reverend Mr. ❸
Clark, "that a man so given to prayer, of such a blameless example, holy in deed and thought, so far as mortal judgment may pronounce; is it fitting that a father in the church should leave a shadow on his memory, that may seem to blacken a life so pure? I pray you, my venerable brother, let not this thing be! Suffer us to be gladdened by your triumphant aspect as you go to your reward. Before the veil of eternity be lifted, let me cast aside this black veil from your face!"

And thus speaking, the Reverend Mr. Clark bent forward to reveal the mystery of so many years. But, exerting a sudden energy, that made all the beholders stand aghast, Father Hooper snatched both his hands from beneath the bedclothes, and pressed them strongly on the black veil, resolute to struggle, if the minister of Westbury would contend with a dying man.

11. natural connections: Relatives.

"Never!" cried the veiled clergyman. "On earth, never!"

"Dark old man!" exclaimed the affrighted minister, "with what horrible crime upon your soul are you now passing to the judgment?"

Father Hooper's breath heaved; it rattled in his throat; but, with a mighty effort, grasping forward with his hands, he caught hold of life, and held it back till he should speak. He even raised himself in bed; and there he sat, shivering with the arms of death around him, while the black veil hung down, awful, at that last moment, in the gathered terrors of a lifetime. And yet the faint, sad smile, so often there, now seemed to glimmer from its obscurity, and linger on Father Hooper's lips.

4 "Why do you tremble at me alone?" cried he, turning his veiled face round the circle of pale spectators. "Tremble also at each other! Have men avoided me, and women shown no pity, and children screamed and fled, only for my black veil? What, but the mystery which it obscurely typifies, has made this piece of crape so awful? When the friend shows his inmost heart to his friend; the lover to his best beloved; when man does not vainly shrink from the eye of his Creator, loathsomely treasuring up the secret of his sin; then deem me a monster, for the symbol beneath which I have lived, and die! I look around me, and, lo! on every visage a Black Veil!" 4

While his auditors shrank from one another, in mutual affright, Father Hooper fell back upon his pillow, a veiled corpse, with a faint smile lingering on the lips. Still veiled, they laid him in his coffin, and a veiled corpse they bore him to the grave. The grass of many years has sprung up and withered on that grave, the burial stone is moss-grown, and good Mr. Hooper's face is dust; but awful is still the thought that it moldered beneath the Black Veil!

Guide for Responding

◆ Literature and Your Life

Reader's Response If you were a member of the congregation, how would you have reacted to the black veil?

Thematic Focus How does Parson Hooper use the imaginations of his parishioners to convey a religious message?

☑ Check Your Comprehension

1. How do the parishioners first react to the minister's veil?
2. (a) What is different about Parson Hooper's sermon on the first day he wears the veil? (b) What is the sermon's subject?
3. What is the veil's "one desirable effect"?
4. (a) What happens when Reverend Clark tries to remove the veil? (b) What does Parson Hooper suggest that makes the veil so awful?

◆ Critical Thinking

INTERPRET

1. (a) Explain how the veil affects Parson Hooper's perception of the world. (b) In what way does it isolate him? (c) Why does it make him a more effective minister? **[Analyze]**
2. What does Parson Hooper mean when he tells Elizabeth, "There is an hour to come . . . when all of us shall cast aside our veils"? **[Interpret]**
3. Why does the veil have such a powerful effect on people? **[Analyze]**
4. Why do you think Hawthorne does not reveal the reason Parson Hooper begins wearing the veil? **[Draw Conclusion]**

APPLY

5. This story involves characters who live very differently from the way we live today. What messages does the story convey that can be applied to today's world? **[Apply]**

Beyond the Selection

FURTHER READING

Other Works by Nathaniel Hawthorne

The Scarlet Letter
The House of the Seven Gables
The Marble Faun

Other Works About Hypocrisy

The Crucible, Arthur Miller
"We Wear the Mask," Paul Laurence Dunbar
"Hawthorne," Robert Lowell

We suggest that you preview these works before recommending them to students.

INTERNET

You and your students may find additional information about Nathaniel Hawthorne on the Internet. We suggest the following site. Please be aware, however, that the site may have changed from the time we published this information.

For Hawthorne biographical information, a list of works, criticism, and an audio page, go to **http://www.tiac.net/users/eldred/toc.html#nh**

We *strongly recommend* that you preview the site before you send students to it.

◆ Reading Strategy

4 Evaluate the Author's Messages Ask students to tell what the meaning of the veil is, based on Mr. Hooper's deathbed speech. *Students may say that the veil represents the secret sins of which all are guilty.*

Reinforce and Extend

Answers

◆ Literature and Your Life

Reader's Response Some students may say that they would have reacted to the veil with fear or shock. Others may say they wouldn't have been bothered by the veil.

Thematic Focus Suggested Response: Parson Hooper senses that allowing people to *imagine* his reason for wearing the veil will lead them to think about their own shortcomings and sins.

☑ Check Your Comprehension

1. They are "wonderstruck" and perturbed.
2. (a) His sermon is more powerful than usual. (b) Its subject is secret sin.
3. It makes him a very efficient clergyman.
4. (a) Mr. Hooper refuses to remove it "on earth." (b) People are terrified by it because it symbolizes their secret sins.

◆ Critical Thinking

1. (a) It darkens his own view of the world. (b) It creates a barrier in human relations. (c) It gives him power over those grappling with sin and, at the same time, enables him to sympathize with sinners.
2. He means that our true natures will be exposed when our judgment day comes.
3. It has a powerful effect on people because it reminds them of their secret sins.
4. By not revealing the reason, he creates ambiguity and forces the reader to interpret the reason by examining the evidence in the story.
5. The story conveys several messages applicable to today's world: (1) People should not judge others or jump to conclusions about others. (2) No one is perfect. (3) One's right to privacy should be respected.

Answers

◆ Literary Focus

1. Suggested response: The maiden's corpse represents death, the unknown, and eternity—hinting that the veil may be the barrier between earthly existence and the afterlife. The bride and bridegroom represent youth, hope, and romantic love—hinting that the veil may mean that even young lovers may hide sins from each other. The various children represent innocence and purity—hinting that the veil may mean sin that will shroud their lives after their days of innocence are over.
2. Suggested response: The moral lesson might be that because everyone is a sinner, no one should harshly judge anyone else.

◆ Build Vocabulary

Using the Word Root *-equi-*

1. equidistant; 2. equate;
3. equilibrium; 4. equivalent

Using the Word Bank

1. f 2. c 3. i 4. g 5. a 6. e
7. b 8. j 9. h 10. d

◆ Reading Strategy

1. (a) The reactions may suggest that it is human nature to jump to false conclusions. (b) Students' responses should follow logically from the suggestion about human nature.
2. (a) Perhaps the message is that the people are afraid to see their own sinfulness. (b) Student responses should include logical arguments.

◆ Grammar and Style

Looking at Style Answers should include the following: (1) two paragraphs from the selection; (2) a list of the types of openers of the sentences; (3) rewritten paragraphs, each with sentences containing the same type of opener; (4) an explanation of the ineffectiveness of the rewritten paragraphs.

Guide for Responding *(continued)*

◆ Literary Focus

ALLEGORY

An **allegory** is a literary work in which characters, events, details of setting, and other story elements have a symbolic meaning. For example, the minister's veil in Hawthorne's story is a symbol of the secret sins of all humanity.

1. Find three details or events in the story that hint at the veil's symbolic meaning. Explain the meaning of each of these symbols.
2. Through the use of symbols such as the minister's veil, allegories teach a moral lesson. What is the moral lesson that Hawthorne's story teaches? Support your answer.

◆ Build Vocabulary

USING THE LATIN ROOT *-equi-*

The Latin root *-equi-* means "equal." Using your knowledge of this root, complete the following sentences using the words below.

equidistant equivalent
equate equilibrium

1. The rest area was __?__ between the towns of Bath and Brunswick.
2. Clearly the dog had begun to __?__ the small kitchen cupboard with a tasty reward.
3. Despite gale-force winds, the sailor never lost her __?__.
4. I handed over a $20 bill and asked for the __?__ in Japanese currency.

USING THE WORD BANK: Synonyms

On a separate sheet of paper, write the letter of the best synonym for each numbered word.

1. venerable	**a.** perceptive
2. iniquity	**b.** agitated
3. indecorous	**c.** wickedness
4. ostentatious	**d.** inflexibility
5. sagacious	**e.** oddity
6. vagary	**f.** respected
7. tremulous	**g.** showy
8. waggery	**h.** discourteous
9. impertinent	**i.** vulgar
10. obstinacy	**j.** jocularity

◆ Reading Strategy

EVALUATE THE AUTHOR'S MESSAGES

In stories such as "The Minister's Black Veil," Hawthorne conveys messages that reflect his dark view of the world. By drawing on your own experiences, you can **evaluate the messages** he conveys and decide whether or not you agree with the messages and consider what, if anything, you can learn from the stories.

1. (a) What does the way the other characters react to Parson Hooper suggest about human nature? (b) Based on your own experience, do you agree with this suggestion about human nature? Explain.
2. (a) What message is conveyed through the parishioners' inability to grasp the meaning of the veil? Support your answer. (b) Do you agree with this message? Why or why not?

◆ Grammar and Style

VARYING SENTENCE OPENERS

By **varying the sentence openers** he uses, Hawthorne helps readers flow from detail to detail and event to event. For example, some sentences begin with an article followed by the subject and verb; others begin with transitions. Look at this example from the story:

> *That night*, the handsomest couple in Milford village were to be joined in wedlock. *Though reckoned a melancholy man*, Mr. Hooper had a placid cheerfulness for such occasions, which often excited a sympathetic smile where livelier merriment would have been thrown away. *There was* no quality of his disposition which made him more beloved than this.

Looking at Style Review the story, and find two paragraphs that contain at least three types of sentence openers. Copy the paragraphs into your notebook. Using the Grammar and Mechanics Handbook on page 1197 for help, identify the type of opener used in each sentence. Then rewrite the two paragraphs so that all of the sentences have the same type of opener. Finally, explain why the rewritten paragraphs are less effective than the original ones.

Grammar Reinforcement

For additional instruction and practice, use the lesson in the **Language Lab CD-ROM** on Varying Sentence Structure and the practice pages on Improving Your Sentences (pp. 110–112) in the *Writer's Solution Grammar Practice Book.*

Build Your Portfolio

Idea Bank

Writing

1. Letter As Elizabeth, write a personal letter in which you appeal to your fiancé to remove his black veil. Capture Elizabeth's directness, as well as her deep love for her fiancé.

2. Memo to New Ministers The narrator comments, "perhaps the palefaced congregation was almost as fearful a sight to the minister, as his black veil to them." As Parson Hooper, write a memo to future ministers, telling what to expect and giving advice about how to prepare to face a congregation for the first time. **[Career Link]**

3. Essay Did Hawthorne have a negative attitude toward the Puritans? Explore your response in an essay, using examples from the story.

Speaking, Listening, and Viewing

4. Debate Parson Hooper is a religious leader commanding the utmost respect. His action throws the village into confusion and anxiety. Stage a debate on whether a leader has the right to take such an action. **[Social Studies Link]**

5. Soundtrack Select an excerpt of this story for an oral reading. Choose an appropriate piece of music to accompany your reading. Present your reading with the music to the class. **[Music Link]**

Researching and Representing

6. Reading Report Read "The Wedding Knell"—another story in *Twice-Told Tales*. Compare and contrast it with "The Minister's Black Veil." Then prepare and deliver an oral presentation in which you discuss the two stories.

7. Illustrations Create a series of drawings or paintings to illustrate the story. Focus on capturing the mood of each scene. **[Art Link]**

Online Activity www.phlit.phschool.com

Guided Writing Lesson

Response to a Short Story

Some aspect of this odd and ambiguous story probably made a distinct impression on you. Perhaps you were fascinated by the spectacle of the veil or upset by Parson Hooper's (or the villagers') behavior. Write a short paper in which you present your response to an element of the story that made an especially strong impression on you. Support your response with specific details from the story.

Writing Skills Focus: Precise Details

Often, the most effective way to cite **details** from a literary work is to use brief or extended word-for-word quotations. For example, if you wanted to capture the parishioners' reaction to Parson Hooper, you might include this quotation:

> In this manner, Mr. Hooper spent a long life, irreproachable in outward act, yet shrouded in dismal suspicions; . . .

If you wanted to include a description of the veil, on the other hand, you might simply quote a couple of words from the story:

> The Parson's veil, which Hawthorne describes as a "gloomy shade," conceals his entire face except for his chin and mouth.

Prewriting Review the story, and jot down your thoughts and feelings about the characters, setting, plot, and symbols. Choose one element to which you have an especially strong reaction. Then find passages and other details that you can use to help you explain your reactions.

Drafting In an introductory paragraph, identify the element of the story on which you're focusing and explain your reaction to it. Then provide an explanation of the role of this element in the story, citing the passage and other details for support. Follow with a more detailed description of your reactions.

Revising Is your reaction to the story clear? Do you include enough passages and details from the story? Make revisions to strengthen your response.

ASSESSMENT OPTIONS

Formal Assessment, Selection Test, pp. 96–98, and Assessment Resources Software. The selection test is designed so that it can be easily customized to the performance levels of your students.

Alternative Assessment, p. 20, includes options for less advanced students, more advanced students, visual/spatial learners, bodily/kinesthetic learners, musical/rhythmic learners, and verbal/linguistic learners.

PORTFOLIO ASSESSMENT
Use the following rubrics in the ***Alternative Assessment*** booklet to assess student writing:
Letter: Persuasion Rubric, p. 120
Memo to New Ministers: How-to/Process Explanation Rubric, p. 115
Essay: Literary Analysis/Interpretation, p. 127
Guided Writing Lesson: Response to Literature Rubric, p. 125

Idea Bank

Customizing for
Performance Levels
Following are suggestions for matching Idea Bank topics with your students' performance levels:
Less Advanced Students: 1, 5
Average Students: 2, 4, 7
More Advanced Students: 3, 6

Customizing for
Learning Modalities
Following are suggestions for matching Idea Bank topics with your students' learning modalities:
Interpersonal: 4
Musical/Rhythmic: 5
Logical/Mathematical: 6
Visual/Spatial: 7

Guided Writing Lesson

Have students use the Cubing Organizer in ***Writing and Language Transparencies,*** p. 71, to organize their prewriting details.

For more prewriting, elaboration, and revision strategies, see *Prentice Hall Writing and Grammar.*

Writers at Work Videodisc Have students view the videodisc segment (Ch. 7) featuring literary agent Theresa Parks speaking about starting a draft of a response to literature. Ask students what it means to "start out with a bang."

Play frames 26321 to 29738

Writing Lab CD-ROM
Have students complete the tutorial on Response to Literature. Follow these steps:

1. To help gather details have students use one of the activities, such as the Character Personality Profile.
2. Have students draft on computer.
3. Use the Interactive Self-Evaluation Checklist to aid revision.

Prepare and Engage

LESSON OBJECTIVES

1. **To develop vocabulary and word identification skills**
   - Latin Prefixes: *mal-*
   - Using the Word Bank: Sentence Completions
   - Extending Word Study
2. **To use a variety of reading strategies to comprehend nonfiction**
   - Connect Your Experience
   - Reading Strategy: Recognize Symbols
3. **To increase knowledge of other cultures and to connect common elements across cultures**
   - Idea Bank: Report
4. **To express and support responses to the text**
   - Critical Thinking
   - Idea Bank: Character Sketch
   - Idea Bank: Eulogy
   - Idea Bank: Readers Theater
5. **To analyze literary elements**
   - Literary Focus: Symbol
6. **To read in order to research self-selected and assigned topics**
   - Idea Bank: Model
7. **To plan, prepare, organize, and present literary interpretations**
   - Idea Bank: Essay
8. **To use recursive writing processes to write a dramatic scene**
   - Guided Writing Lesson
9. **To increase knowledge of the rules of grammar and usage**
   - Grammar and Style: Agreement With Collective Nouns

Test Preparation

Reading Comprehension: Make Inferences and Generalizations (ATE, p. 331)
The teaching tips and sample test item in this workshop support the instruction and practice in the unit workshop:

Reading Comprehension: Analyze Information to Make Inferences and Generalizations (SE, p. 427)

Guide for Interpreting

Herman Melville *(1819–1891)*

Deemed by his father to be "backward in speech and somewhat slow in comprehension" as a youth, Herman Melville is now widely considered one of America's greatest novelists.

Melville was born in New York City, the son of a wealthy merchant. His family's financial situation changed drastically in 1830, however, when his father's import business failed. Two years later his father died, leaving the family in debt. Forced to leave school, Melville spent the rest of his childhood working as a clerk, a farmhand, and a teacher to help support his family.

Whaling in the South Pacific Melville became a sailor at the age of nineteen and spent several years working on whaling ships and exploring the South Pacific. After returning to the United States in 1844, he began his career as a writer, using his adventures in the South Seas as material for his fiction. He quickly produced two popular and financially successful novels, *Typee* (1846) and *Omoo* (1847), both set in the Pacific islands. His third novel, *Mardi* (1849), was considerably more abstract and symbolic. When readers rejected the book and his fame began to fade, Melville grew increasingly melancholy. He continued writing, however, turning out two more novels, *Redburn* (1849) and *White-Jacket* (1850), over the next two years.

Writing in the Berkshires Using the profits from his popular novels, Melville bought a farm in Massachusetts, where he befriended Nathaniel Hawthorne, who lived nearby. Encouraged by Hawthorne's interest and influenced by his reading of Shakespeare, Melville began producing deeper and more sophisticated works. In 1851, he published his masterpiece, *Moby-Dick*, under the title *The Whale*. *Moby-Dick* is a novel with several layers of meaning. On the surface, it is the story of the fateful voyage of a whaling ship. On another level, it is the story of a bitter man's quest for vengeance and truth. On still another level, it is a philosophical examination of humanity's relationship to the natural world.

Unable to appreciate the novel's depth, nineteenth-century readers responded unfavorably to *Moby-Dick*. Audiences also rejected his next two novels, *Pierre* (1852) and *The Confidence Man* (1857). As a result, Melville fell into debt and was forced to accept a job as an inspector at a New York customshouse.

Disillusioned and bitter, Melville turned away from writing fiction during the latter part of his life. He produced only a handful of short stories and the powerful novella *Billy Budd*. Melville died unappreciated and unnoticed in 1891. In the 1920's, however, his novels and tales were rediscovered and hailed by scholars. Today, *Moby-Dick* is widely regarded as one of the finest novels in all of American literature.

◆ Background for Understanding

LITERATURE: MELVILLE'S SOUTH PACIFIC INSPIRATION

Melville's whaling career in the South Pacific provided him with rich material for his writing. While working aboard the whaling ship *Acushnet*, he often heard stories about an elusive, monstrous white whale known as "Mocha Dick," or "Moby Dick." Melville expanded this legend—adding his knowledge of the day-to-day workings of a whaling vessel—into his best-known work, *Moby-Dick*.

When the *Acushnet* rounded Cape Horn and crossed the Pacific to the Marquesas Islands in 1842, Melville deserted the ship and headed inland. There, he encountered the Typees, an island tribe rumored to be cannibals. To Melville's surprise, the people were peaceful and generous. He was to use this experience later as the basis for his 1846 novel *Typee*.

Prentice Hall Literature Program Resources

REINFORCE / RETEACH / EXTEND

Selection Support Pages
Build Vocabulary: Latin Prefixes: *mal-*, p. 98
Grammar and Style: Agreement With Collective Nouns, p. 99
Reading Strategy: Recognize Symbols, p. 100
Literary Focus: Symbol, p. 101

Strategies for Diverse Student Needs, p. 21

Beyond Literature
Cross-Curricular Connection: Art, p. 21

Formal Assessment Selection Test, pp. 99–101; Assessment Resources Software

Alternative Assessment, p. 21

Writing and Language Transparencies
Outline, p. 95

Resource Pro CD-ROM

Listening to Literature Audiocassettes

Literature CD-ROM

from Moby-Dick

◆ Literature and Your Life

CONNECT YOUR EXPERIENCE

You may remember a time when you needed to focus all your attention on some complicated or daunting task. Some situations demand intense concentration. However, as this selection illustrates, it is possible to focus *too* much on a problem, an idea, or a goal. Such an obsession can produce a sense of isolation and anxiety.

Journal Writing List some of the warning signs indicating that a personal interest may be turning into an obsession.

THEMATIC FOCUS: SHADOWS OF THE IMAGINATION

Melville focuses on the grim, shadowy imagination of Captain Ahab. What is Melville saying about nature, humanity, and life?

◆ Literary Focus

SYMBOL

A **symbol** is a person, place, or thing that has a meaning in itself and also represents something larger. For example, a flag symbolizes the character and values of a country. The white whale of Melville's *Moby-Dick* is an extremely complex symbol. Only by examining every meaning suggested by its appearance and behavior does one understand that ultimately the whale represents everything contradictory, inexplicable, and uncontrollable in nature. Like nature, Moby-Dick is massive, threatening, and awe-inspiring, yet beautiful; and though it seems unpredictable and mindless, the whale is controlled by natural laws. Like nature itself, Moby-Dick seems immortal and indifferent to human mortality.

◆ Grammar and Style

AGREEMENT WITH COLLECTIVE NOUNS

Collective nouns—such as *class, team*, or *flock*—refer to a group of people or things. They can be either singular or plural depending on the meaning you wish them to have. Verbs must agree in number with the meaning of the collective noun. In the first example, *company* refers to each group member; thus, the plural verb *were* is necessary. In the second example, *company* refers to a unit and takes the singular verb *consists*.

When the entire ship's *company were* assembled, . . .
The *company consists* of 150 sailors.

◆ Reading Strategy

RECOGNIZE SYMBOLS

To **recognize symbols,** look for characters, places, or objects that are stressed, mentioned repeatly, or connected by the narrator or characters to larger concepts or idea. For example, Ahab's description of Moby-Dick in this passage makes it clear that the whale has a symbolic meaning: "All visible objects, man, are but as pasteboard masks. . . . If man will strike, strike through the mask! How can the prisoner reach outside except by thrusting through the wall? To me, the white whale is that wall, shoved near to me. Sometimes I think there's naught beyond." From Ahab's description, you might guess that Moby-Dick symbolizes things that are beyond our reach or control.

◆ Build Vocabulary

LATIN PREFIXES: *mal-*

Melville's narrator speaks of "maledictions against the white whale." The word *malediction* contains the Latin prefix *mal-*, which means "bad" or "badly." Based on this prefix and the word's context, what do you think *malediction* means?

WORD BANK

Preview these words from the story.

inscrutable
maledictions
prescient
pertinaciously

Interest Grabber Ahab says, "Death to Moby-Dick! God hunt us all, if we do not hunt Moby-Dick to his death!" Read this quotation to students, telling them that Ahab is a man obsessed. Discuss the concept of obsession. Then have students think of people or fictional characters they know who have worked intensely to reach a goal. Mention people like Midori, Tiger Woods, and Gary Kasparov, as well as world-class ice skaters, gymnasts, and others whose intense, single-minded efforts began at an early age. Have students discuss whether they see a distinction between concentrated effort and obsession. Ask whether they think it takes obsession to reach lofty goals.

Customize for
Less Proficient Readers
To help these students through this difficult work, have them read in groups. Do frequent comprehension checks—as often as each paragraph —to ensure that students are following the story. Guide students to keep a dictionary at hand and reread passages as often as necessary.

Customize for
AP Students
Guide students to look for examples of how the different characters on the *Pequod* view the adventure from their own perspectives. For example, the first mate, Starbuck, offers a literal interpretation of the journey. Point out that the sailors' different views help establish layers of symbolism and contribute to the complexity of the story.

Customize for
English Language Learners
Provide students with visual aids that can help them understand more about whaling and life on whaling ships. Display illustrations of whales, whaling ships, harpoons, and whalers in action.

Test Preparation Workshop

Reading Comprehension: Make Inferences and Generalizations
Standardized tests require students to make generalizations about a written passage. Use this sample test item:

> . . . to and fro he paced his old rounds, upon planks so familiar to his tread, that they were all over dented, like geological stones, with the peculiar mark of his walk. Did you fixedly gaze, too, upon that ribbed and dented brow; there also, you would see still stranger footprints,—the footprints of his one unsleeping, ever-pacing thought.

Based on this passage, which of the following best describes Ahab?

A rational and energetic
B calm and powerful
C reverent and self-effacing
D tormented and obsessed

A, B, and *C* are not supported by the text. Ahab's pacing shows that he is obsessed with Moby-Dick and tormented by the attack that cost him his leg.

Develop Understanding

One-Minute Insight Widely regarded as one of the finest American novels ever written, *Moby-Dick* expresses the view that, despite people's desire to do so, they will never be able to completely understand or control nature. "The Quarter-Deck" is one of the key chapters in the novel. Here, Ahab first becomes the novel's dominant character; his vengeful, obsessive personality is revealed, as is his conflict with Moby-Dick. At this turning point, readers and sailors alike learn the true purpose of the *Pequod's* voyage. "The Chase—Third Day" is the book's last chapter. The novel reaches its climax with the final catastrophic contest with Moby-Dick.

Customize for
Intrapersonal Learners
To promote active reading, invite students to keep a reader's response journal as they read. Guide them to focus their observations on Ahab's obsession with revenge and with Starbuck's responses. Encourage them to record their own opinions of Ahab's quest and the reactions of the other sailors.

◆ Background for Understanding

❶ Inform students that in Melville's day, the captain of a ship had unlimited authority. All aboard ship knew this. Failing to follow orders brought harsh and perhaps arbitrary punishment, and most crew members were careful not to challenge the captain directly.

◆ Reading Strategy

❷ **Recognize Symbols** Have students notice that in this paragraph, Melville moves from a literal description of footprints to one that is figurative.

from MOBY-DICK

Herman Melville

Moby-Dick is the story of a man's obsession with the dangerous and mysterious white whale that years before had taken off one of his legs. The man, Captain Ahab, guides the Pequod, *a whaling ship, and its crew in relentless pursuit of this whale, Moby-Dick. Among the more important members of the crew are Starbuck, the first mate; Stubb, the second mate; Flask, the third mate; Queequeg, Tashtego, and Daggoo, the harpooners; and Ishmael, the young sailor who narrates the book.*

When the crew signed aboard the Pequod, *the voyage was to be nothing more than a business venture. However, in the following excerpt early in the voyage, Ahab makes clear to the crew that his purpose is to seek revenge against Moby-Dick.*

from The Quarter-Deck

❶ One morning shortly after breakfast, Ahab, as was his wont, ascended the cabin gangway to the deck. There most sea captains usually walk at that hour, as country gentlemen, after the same meal, take a few turns in the garden.

❷ Soon his steady, ivory stride was heard, as to and fro he paced his old rounds, upon planks so familiar to his tread, that they were all over dented, like geological stones, with the peculiar mark of his walk. Did you fixedly gaze, too, upon that ribbed and dented brow; there also, you would see still stranger footprints—the footprints of his one unsleeping, ever-pacing thought.

But on the occasion in question, those dents looked deeper, even as his nervous step that morning left a deeper mark. And, so full of his thought was Ahab, that at every uniform turn that he made, now at the mainmast and now at the binnacle,[1] you could almost see that thought turn in him as he turned, and pace in

1. **binnacle** (bin′ ə kəl) *n.*: Case enclosing a ship's compass.

◆ Background for Understanding

Literature *Moby-Dick* is a long and complex novel that can be thought of in five parts. In the first part, we meet Ishmael, who tells the story, and learn of his relationship with the harpooner Queequeg. The chapter "The Quarter-Deck" appears in the next part of the book, the section that develops the character of Ahab and the conflict between Ahab and Moby-Dick. "The Chase—Third Day" is the last chapter of the fifth and final part, in which Melville focuses on the search for and confrontation with the great whale. Parts three and four are about the business of the *Pequod* and about whales and whaling. In the one-page epilogue, Ishmael tells how he survived to tell his tale: He was rescued by another ship, the *Rachel*, "that in her retracing search after her missing children, only found another orphan."

him as he paced; so completely possessing him, indeed, that it all but seemed the inward mold of every outer movement.

3 "D'ye mark him, Flask?" whispered Stubb; "the chick that's in him pecks the shell. 'Twill soon be out."

The hours wore on—Ahab now shut up within his cabin; anon, pacing the deck, with the same intense bigotry of purpose[2] in his aspect.

4 It drew near the close of day. Suddenly he came to a halt by the bulwarks, and inserting his bone leg into the auger hole there, and with one hand grasping a shroud, he ordered Starbuck to send everybody aft.

"Sir!" said the mate, astonished at an order seldom or never given on shipboard except in some extraordinary case.

"Send everybody aft," repeated Ahab. "Mastheads, there! come down!"

5 When the entire ship's company were assembled, and with curious and not wholly unapprehensive faces, were eyeing him, for he looked not unlike the weather horizon when a storm is coming up, Ahab, after rapidly glancing over the bulwarks, and then darting his eyes among the crew, started from his standpoint; and as though not a soul were nigh him resumed his heavy turns upon the deck. With bent head and half-slouched hat he continued to pace, unmindful of the wondering whispering among the men; till Stubb cautiously whispered to Flask, that Ahab must have summoned them there for the purpose of witnessing a pedestrian feat. But this did not last long. Vehemently pausing, he cried:

"What do ye do when ye see a whale, men?"

"Sing out for him!" was the impulsive rejoinder from a score of clubbed voices.

"Good!" cried Ahab, with a wild approval in his tones; observing the hearty animation into which his unexpected question had so magnetically thrown them.

"And what do ye next, men?"

"Lower away, and after him!"

"And what tune is it ye pull to, men?"

"A dead whale or a stove[3] boat!"

More and more strangely and fiercely glad and approving, grew the countenance of the old man at every shout; while the mariners began to gaze curiously at each other, as if marveling how it was that they themselves became so excited at such seemingly purposeless questions.

But, they were all eagerness again, as Ahab, now half-revolving in his pivot hole, with one hand reaching high up a shroud,[4] and tightly, almost convulsively grasping it, addressed them thus:

"All ye mastheaders have before now heard me give orders about a white whale. Look ye! d'ye see this Spanish ounce of gold?"—holding up a broad bright coin to the sun—"it is a sixteen-dollar piece, men. D'ye see it? Mr. Starbuck, hand me yon topmaul."

While the mate was getting the hammer, Ahab, without speaking, was slowly rubbing the gold piece against the skirts of his jacket, as if to heighten its luster, and without using any words was meanwhile lowly humming to himself, producing a sound so strangely muffled and inarticulate that it seemed the mechanical humming of the wheels of his vitality in him.

Receiving the topmaul from Starbuck, he advanced towards the mainmast with the hammer uplifted in one hand, exhibiting the gold with the other, and with a high raised voice exclaiming: "Whosoever of ye raises me a white-headed whale with a wrinkled brow and a crooked jaw; whosoever of ye raises me that white-headed whale, with three holes punctured in his starboard fluke[5]—look ye, whosoever of ye raises me that same white whale, he shall have this gold ounce, my boys!" 6

"Huzza! huzza!" cried the seamen, as with swinging tarpaulins they hailed the act of nailing the gold to the mast.

"It's a white whale, I say," resumed Ahab, as he threw down the topmaul: "a white whale. Skin your eyes for him, men; look sharp for white water; if ye see but a bubble, sing out."

All this while Tashtego, Daggoo, and Queequeg had looked on with even more intense interest and surprise than the rest, and at the mention of the wrinkled brow and crooked jaw they had started as if each was separately touched by some specific recollection.

"Captain Ahab," said Tashtego, "that white whale must be the same that some call

---

2. **bigotry of purpose:** Complete single-mindedness.
3. **stove** *v.*: Broken; smashed.
4. **shroud** *n.*: Set of ropes from a ship's side to the masthead.
5. **starboard fluke** (flo͞ok) *n.*: Right half of a whale's tail.

Literature CD-ROM To build background, use the CD-ROM *The History of American Literature:* Part 1, Disc 2, Features 7, 8. A portion of Feature 7 focuses upon Herman Melville, while part of Feature 8 focuses upon both Herman Melville and *Moby-Dick.*

Customize for
English Language Learners

3 Make sure these students understand the image in Stubb's remark; he states that an idea that has been troubling Ahab is beginning to come out into the open.

◆ Reading Strategy

4 **Recognize Symbols** Guide students to see that when Ahab's leg fills in the auger hole, it symbolizes plugging the whale's blowhole, thereby suffocating the creature.

5 **Clarification** Discuss with students why the men are curious and apprehensive. The reasons include the fact that it is unusual for the men to be gathered on this deck. The men are also wary of Ahab's peculiar behavior; he paces about as if not noticing them.

◆ Reading Strategy

6 **Recognize Symbols** Discuss the significance of the gold coin nailed to the main mast. Help students understand that it serves not only as a reminder of a forthcoming reward, but also as a beacon, always there, to guide them on their search as it reflects the sun's rays.

Block Scheduling Strategies

Consider these suggestions to take advantage of extended class time:

- Grab your students' interest by playing one of the final scenes from the movie *Jaws.* Explain to them that long before *Jaws* was produced, Herman Melville wrote the masterpiece from which they're about to read, telling about a life-and-death struggle against another powerful creature of the sea, a great white whale.
- Challenge your students to review the complete novel and to find other climactic sections. Encourage them to read aloud these sections, and to use them to stimulate class discussion.
- If you decide to assign any of the projects or Speaking, Listening, and Viewing activities in the Idea Bank, allow time for students to make their presentations.
- If your students have access to computers, have them work in the **Writing Lab CD-ROM** to complete the Guided Writing Lesson. Use the suggestions on p. 347 to structure students' time on the CD-ROM.

❶ **Clarification** Tashtego is called "the Gay-Header" because he hails from Gay Head, Massachusetts.

Customize for
Less Proficient Readers
❷ To help these students comprehend the text, have them list and discuss the physical traits that Ahab and the crew members say distinguish Moby-Dick from other whales.

▶Critical Viewing◀

❸ **Evaluate** Students may make the following observations about the portrait. They may say that the image, showing Ahab as if deep in thought, captures his obsessive attitude about the whale Moby-Dick. Others might say that Ahab's apparently detached attitude creates a foreboding or frightening mood. They might say that the dark shadows in the picture contribute to this mood. They may also say that Ahab has his eyes closed, implying that he is going into this quest blindly, oblivious to all outside his mind.

◆ Background for Understanding

❹ **History** Discuss why Ahab's command would surprise the crew. Point out that sailors on a whaler signed on for a share of the net profits. Although some probably hoped for adventure, most sailors simply desired to capture as many whales as possible so they could bring back and sell the valuable whale oil, whalebone, and other whale byproducts. So it would be understandable if Ahab's crew were to show reluctance to chase only one whale.

Customize for
Less Proficient Readers
Help improve students' comprehension with the Identify Chain of Events page in ***Strategies for Diverse Student Needs,*** p. 21.

Captain Ahab on the Deck of the Pequod, Rockwell Kent

◀ **Critical Viewing** How does this portrait of Ahab compare or contrast with your mental image of him? **[Evaluate]** ❸

Moby-Dick."

"Moby-Dick?" shouted Ahab. "Do ye know the white whale then, Tash?"

❶ "Does he fantail[6] a little curious, sir, before he goes down?" said the Gay-Header deliberately.

❷ "And has he a curious spout, too," said Daggoo, "very bushy, even for a parmacetty,[7] and mighty quick, Captain Ahab?"

"And he have one, two, tree—oh! good many iron in him hide, too, Captain," cried Queequeg disjointedly, "all twiske-tee betwisk, like him—him—" faltering hard for a word, and screwing his hand round and round as though uncorking a bottle—"like him—him—"

"Corkscrew!" cried Ahab, "aye, Queequeg, the harpoons lie all twisted and wrenched in him; aye, Daggoo, his spout is a big one, like a whole shock of wheat, and white as a pile of our Nantucket wool after the great annual sheepshearing; aye, Tashtego, and he fantails like a split jib in a squall. Death and devils! men, it is Moby-Dick ye have seen—Moby-Dick—Moby-Dick!" ❷

"Captain Ahab," said Starbuck, who, with Stubb and Flask, had thus far been eyeing his superior with increasing surprise, but at last seemed struck with a thought which somewhat explained all the wonder. "Captain Ahab, I have heard of Moby-Dick—but it was not Moby-Dick that took off thy leg?"

"Who told thee that?" cried Ahab; then pausing, "Aye, Starbuck; aye, my hearties all round; it was Moby-Dick that dismasted me; Moby-Dick that brought me to this dead stump I stand on now. Aye, aye," he shouted with a terrific, loud, animal sob, like that of a heart-stricken moose; "Aye, aye! it was that accursed white whale that razeed me; made a poor pegging lubber[8] for me forever and a day!" ❹ Then tossing both arms, with measureless imprecations he shouted out: "Aye, aye! and I'll chase him round Good Hope, and round the Horn, and round the Norway Maelstrom, and round perdition's flames before I give him up. And this is what ye have shipped for, men! to chase that white whale on both sides of land, and over all sides of earth, till he spouts black blood and rolls fin out. What say ye, men, will ye splice hands on it, now? I think ye do look brave."

"Aye, aye!" shouted the harpooneers and seamen, running closer to the excited old man: "A sharp eye for the white whale; a sharp lance for Moby-Dick!"

"God bless ye," he seemed to half sob and half shout. "God bless ye, men. Steward! go

6. **fantail** *v.:* To spread the tail like a fan.
7. **parmacetty** (pär′ mə set′ ē) *n.:* Dialect for spermaceti, a waxy substance taken from a sperm whale's head and used to make candles.
8. **lubber** (lub′ ər) *n.:* Slow, clumsy person.

Cross-Curricular Connection: Social Studies

Nineteenth-Century Seaports The *Pequod* sails from the island of Nantucket, which is situated in the Atlantic, off the southern coast of Massachusetts, about twenty miles south of Cape Cod and just east and south of Martha's Vineyard. In the late 1700's and early 1800's, it was one of the world's major whaling centers. At one time, well over 100 whaling ships used the island as their main port. In the mid-nineteenth century, the whaling industry began to decline and the island developed its other resources.

Invite students to research on the Internet and elsewhere to discover where one can find restored seaports to visit that include whaling ships, tools, and other objects associated with the whaling industry. Have students create a list of sites and plan an itinerary for a visit to one or more of them. Students can send for brochures to help finalize their plans.

draw the great measure of grog. But what's this long face about, Mr. Starbuck; wilt thou not chase the white whale? art not game for Moby-Dick?"

❺ "I am game for his crooked jaw, and for the jaws of Death too, Captain Ahab, if it fairly comes in the way of the business we follow; but I came here to hunt whales, not my commander's vengeance. How many barrels will thy vengeance yield thee even if thou gettest it, Captain Ahab? it will not fetch thee much in our Nantucket market."

"Nantucket market! Hoot! But come closer, Starbuck; thou requirest a little lower layer. If money's to be the measurer, man, and the accountants have computed their great counting-house the globe, by girdling it with guineas, one to every three parts of an inch; then, let me tell thee, that my vengeance will fetch a great premium *here!*"

"He smites his chest," whispered Stubb, "what's that for? methinks it rings most vast, but hollow."

❻ "Vengeance on a dumb brute!" cried Starbuck, "that simply smote thee from blindest instinct! Madness! To be enraged with a dumb thing, Captain Ahab, seems blasphemous."

"Hark ye yet again—the little lower layer. All visible objects, man, are but as pasteboard masks. But in each event—in the living act, the undoubted deed—there, some unknown but still reasoning thing puts forth the moldings of its features from behind the unreasoning mask. If man will strike, strike through the mask! How can the prisoner reach outside except by thrusting through the wall? To me, the white whale is that wall, shoved near to me. Sometimes I think there's naught beyond. But 'tis enough. He tasks me; he heaps me; I see in him outrageous strength, with an inscrutable malice sinewing it. That inscrutable thing is chiefly what I hate; and be the white whale agent, or be the white whale principal, I will wreak that hate upon him. Talk not to me of blasphemy, man; I'd strike the sun if it insulted me. For could the sun do that, then could I do the other; since there is ever a sort of fair play herein, jealousy presiding over all creations. But not my master, man, is even that fair play. Who's over me? Truth hath no confines. Take off thine eye! more intolerable than fiends' glarings is a doltish stare! So, so; thou reddenest and palest; my heat has melted thee to anger-glow. But look ye, Starbuck, what is said in heat, that thing unsays itself. There are men from whom warm words are small indignity. I meant not to incense thee. Let it go. Look! see yonder Turkish cheeks of spotted tawn—living, breathing pictures painted by the sun. The pagan leopards—the unrecking and unworshiping things, that live, and seek, and give no reasons for the torrid life they feel! The crew, man, the crew! Are they not one and all with Ahab, in this matter of the whale? See Stubb! he laughs! See yonder Chilean! he snorts to think of it. Stand up amid the general hurricane, thy one tossed sapling cannot, Starbuck! And what is it? Reckon it. 'Tis but to help strike a fin; no wondrous feat for Starbuck. What is it more? From this one poor hunt, then, the best lance out of all Nantucket, surely he will not hang back, when every foremasthand has clutched a whetstone. Ah! constrainings seize thee; I see! the billow lifts thee! Speak, but speak!—Aye, aye! thy silence, then, that voices thee. *(Aside)* Something shot from my dilated nostrils, he has inhaled it in his lungs. Starbuck now is mine; cannot oppose me now, without rebellion." ❽ ❾

> ❼ ◆ **Literary Focus**
> What insights into the whale's symbolic meaning can you gain from a close reading of this passage?

"God keep me!—keep us all!" murmured Starbuck, lowly.

But in his joy at the enchanted, tacit acquiescence of the mate, Ahab did not hear his foreboding invocation; nor yet the low laugh from the hold; nor yet the presaging vibrations of the winds in the cordage; nor yet the hollow flap of the sails against the masts, as for a moment their hearts sank in. For again Starbuck's downcast eyes lighted up with the stubbornness of life; the subterranean laugh died away; the winds blew on; the sails filled out; the ship heaved and rolled as before. Ah, ye admonitions and warnings! why stay ye not when ye come? But rather are ye predictions than warnings,

◆ Build Vocabulary

inscrutable (in skro͞ot′ ə bəl) *adj.*: Not able to be easily understood

Cultural Connection

Pre-Hunt Rituals Ahab gathers his crew on the quarter-deck to begin the hunt for Moby-Dick. The gathering has ceremonial aspects that echo the tradition of centuries of pre-hunt rituals. Tell students that ever since the earliest identifiable Americans, the *Clovis* people, drummed and sang to address the animal spirits before a hunt, Native Americans have believed in the power of ritual to aid their success. For example, before buffalo hunts, the Blackfeet and other Plains Indians held celebrations in which they prayed, danced, sang, smoked, and made offerings to ensure that the animals would come near enough to be taken.

Have students find out more about pre-hunt rituals in North America or elsewhere. Have them look for similarities and differences among them. Invite students to make class presentations of their findings.

◆ Critical Thinking

❺ **Evaluate** Ask students to tell what they think about Starbuck from his misgivings stated here. *Students may say that Starbuck is practical and down to earth; that he sees in the captain's quest a loss of income.*

Comprehension Check ☑

❻ How does Starbuck view Ahab's obsession? *Starbuck views the obsession as madness because animal instinct, not deliberate reason on the part of the whale, caused Ahab's injury.*

◆ Literary Focus

❼ **Recognize Symbols** Students may say that Ahab feels imprisoned by the idea of Moby-Dick, and that killing the whale symbolizes escape from the bondage of his obsession.

Customize for *AP Students*

❽ Point out that Ahab could be described as suffering from what the Greeks called *hubris,* or excessive pride. Students may know that this excessive pride is a common characteristic of tragic heroes.

Customize for *Interpersonal Learners*

❾ Have students notice how Ahab uses the group dynamic to press Starbuck to conform. Discuss that Ahab knows that his first mate can't object without risking a charge of mutiny. Then ask students if they think Ahab has truly won over Starbuck. *Students may reply that Starbuck has not been convinced by Ahab, and that the captain simply has used his authority to keep his first mate from challenging him.*

Tips to Guide Reading

Sustained Reading *Moby-Dick* is a huge novel, and when read in its entirety, the characters grow before the reader's eyes into fullness. In excerpts like this selection, students may need help delineating the characters. Have students read silently for sustained periods, pausing to note any fragments of dialogue that seem important or suggestive about the speaker's character.

◆ Reading Strategy

❶ **Recognize Symbols** Discuss the events, actions, and images in this passage. They may cite Starbuck's "foreboding invocation" that foreshadows danger, as well as "low laugh from the hold . . . vibrations of the winds in the cordage . . . hollow flap of the sails . . . bloodshot eyes of the prairie wolves . . . snare of the Indian." Guide students to note that Ahab ignores them all.

◆ Build Grammar Skills

❷ **Agreement With Collective Nouns** Have students notice in this sentence the agreement between the verb *drink* and the collective noun *crew*. The noun *crew* refers to each crew member, so the plural verb form *drink* is correct.

◆ Literary Focus

❸ **Symbols** Guide students to recognize that this ceremony has a ritual aspect to it that is symbolic of pre-hunt or pre-battle rites. For more information, see the Cultural Connection on p. 335 of the teacher edition.

Customize for *Visual/Spatial Learners*

❹ Have students visualize or model what the harpooners are doing here and what Ahab has in mind for them. *They are removing the iron part of their harpoons to use as cups, which Ahab will fill with drink.*

◆ Literary Focus

❺ **Symbols** Students may respond that the drinking from the "chalices" is reminiscent of parts of many religious rituals in which people drink wine or holy water to sanctify a blessing or rite.

Extending Word Study

Specialized Dictionaries To fully clarify the meaning of certain specialized words, such as *capstan*, have students try to find a dictionary of nautical or sailing terms.

ye shadows! Yet not so much predictions from without, as verifications of the foregoing things within. For with little external to constrain us, the innermost necessities in our being, these still drive us on.

"The measure! the measure!" cried Ahab.

Receiving the brimming pewter, and turning to the harpooneers, he ordered them to produce their weapons. Then ranging them ❶ before him near the capstan,[9] with their harpoons in their hands, while his three mates stood at his side with their lances, and the rest of the ship's company formed a circle round the group; he stood for an instant searchingly eyeing every man of his crew. But those wild eyes met his, as the bloodshot eyes of the prairie wolves meet the eye of their leader, ere he rushes on at their head in the trail of the bison; but, alas! only to fall into the hidden snare of the Indian.

"Drink and pass!" he cried, handing the heavy charged flagon to the nearest seamen. ❷ "The crew alone now drink. Round with it, round! Short drafts—long swallows, men; 'tis hot as Satan's hoof. So, so; it goes round excellently. It spiralizes in ye; forks out at the serpent-snapping eye. Well done; almost drained. That way it went, this way it comes. Hand it me—here's a hollow! Men, ye seem the years; so brimming life is gulped and gone. Steward, refill!

"Attend now, my braves. I have mustered ye all round this capstan; and ye mates, flank me with your lances; and ye harpooneers, stand there with your irons; and ye, stout mariners, ring me in, that I may in some sort revive a noble custom of my fishermen fathers before me. ❸ O men, you will yet see that—Ha! boy, come back? bad pennies come not sooner. Hand it me. Why, now, this pewter had run brimming again, wer't not thou St. Vitus' imp[10]—away, thou ague![11]

"Advance, ye mates! cross your lances full before me. Well done! Let me touch the axis." So saying, with extended arm, he grasped the three level, radiating lances at their crossed center; while so doing, suddenly and nervously twitched them; meanwhile glancing intently from Starbuck to Stubb; from Stubb to Flask. It seemed as though, by some nameless, interior volition, he would fain have shocked into them the same fiery emotion accumulated ❸ within the Leyden jar[12] of his own magnetic life. The three mates quailed before his strong, sustained, and mystic aspect. Stubb and Flask looked sideways from him; the honest eye of Starbuck fell downright.

"In vain!" cried Ahab; "but, maybe, 'tis well. For did ye three but once take the full-forced shock, then mine own electric thing, *that* had perhaps expired from out me. Perchance, too, it would have dropped ye dead. Perchance ye need it not. Down lances! And now, ye mates, I do appoint ye three cupbearers to my three pagan kinsmen there—yon three most honorable gentlemen and noblemen, my valiant harpooneers. Disdain the task? What, when the great Pope washes the feet of beggars, using his tiara for ewer? Oh, my sweet cardinals! your own condescension, that shall bend ye to it. I do not order ye; ye will it. Cut your seizings and draw the poles, ye harpooneers!"

Silently obeying the order, the three harpooneers now stood with the detached iron part ❹ of their harpoons, some three feet long, held, barbs up, before him.

"Stab me not with that keen steel! Cant them; cant them over! know ye not the goblet end? Turn up the socket! So, so; now, ye cupbearers, advance. The irons! take them; hold ❺ them while I fill!" Forthwith, slowly going from one officer to the other, he brimmed the harpoon sockets with the fiery waters from the pewter.

> **◆ Literary Focus**
> How do these details suggest that the harpooners' actions have a symbolic meaning?

"Now, three to three, ye stand. Commend the murderous chalices! Bestow them, ye who are now made parties to this indissoluble league. Ha! Starbuck! but the deed is done! Yon ratifying sun now waits to sit upon it. Drink, ye harpooneers! drink and swear, ye men that man the deathful whaleboat's bow—Death to Moby-Dick! God hunt us all, if we do not hunt Moby-

---

9. **capstan** (kap´ sten) *n.*: Large cylinder, turned by hand, around which cables are wound.

10. **St. Vitus' imp:** Offspring of St. Vitus, the patron saint of people stricken with the nervous disorder chorea, which is characterized by irregular, jerking movements.

11. **ague** (ā´ gyōō) *n.*: A chill or fit of shivering.

12. **Leyden** (līd´ ən) **jar** *n.*: Glass jar coated inside and out with tinfoil and having a metal rod connected to the inner lining; used to condense static electricity.

Analyze a Movie Review

Melville's tale of the great white whale has all the elements of a blockbuster movie. There are compelling characters, exotic locations, and one of the largest movie villains imaginable. No wonder then, that filmmakers have tried a number of times to bring *Moby-Dick* to screen.

One of the best attempts was made by director John Huston, who cast Gregory Peck as Ahab in the 1956 film *Moby Dick*. With a famous leading man, a great director, and the most famous American novel providing the plot, the movie looked to be a classic. Was it? Reviewer Larry Rudner hedges: "Although Huston does not succeed in capturing all the nuances of Melville's novel, he does effectively focus on the central character of Ahab. . . .[the movie] will stand as a well-crafted attempt" to bring the novel to life.

Ask students what characteristics the director should have focused on to portray Ahab. If possibvle, have students view the film, then ask:

What nuances did the director fail to translate from the book into the movie?

Dick to his death!" The long, barbed steel goblets were lifted; and to cries and maledictions against the white whale, the spirits were simultaneously quaffed down with a hiss. Starbuck paled, and turned, and shivered. Once more, and finally, the replenished pewter went the rounds among the frantic crew; when, waving his free hand to them, they all dispersed; and Ahab retired within his cabin.

6 *After Moby-Dick has been sighted in the Pacific Ocean, the* Pequod's *boats pursue the whale for two days. One of the boats has been sunk, and Ahab's ivory leg has been broken off. However, as the next day dawns, the chase continues.*

The Chase—Third Day

The morning of the third day dawned fair and fresh, and once more the solitary night man at the foremasthead was relieved by crowds of the daylight lookouts, who dotted every mast and almost every spar.

"D'ye see him?" cried Ahab; but the whale was not yet in sight.

"In his infallible wake, though; but follow that wake, that's all. Helm there; steady, as thou goest, and hast been going. What a lovely day again! were it a new-made world, and made for a summerhouse to the angels, and this morning the first of its throwing open to them, a fairer day could not dawn upon that world. Here's food for thought, had Ahab time to think; but Ahab never thinks; he only feels, feels, feels; that's tingling enough for mortal man! to think's audacity. God only has that right and privilege. Thinking is, or ought to be, a coolness and a calmness; and our poor hearts throb, and our poor brains beat too much for that. And yet, I've sometimes thought my brain was very calm—frozen calm, this old skull cracks so, like a glass in which the contents turned to ice, and shiver it. And still this hair is growing now; this moment growing, and heat must breed it; but no, it's like that sort of common grass that will grow anywhere, between the earthy clefts of Greenland ice or in Vesuvius lava. How the wild winds blow it; they whip it about me as the torn shreds of split sails lash the tossed ship they cling to. A vile wind that has no doubt blown ere this through prison corridors and cells, and wards of hospitals, and ventilated them, and now comes blowing hither as innocent as fleeces.[13] Out upon it!—it's tainted. Were I the wind, I'd blow no more on such a wicked, miserable world. I'd crawl somewhere to a cave, and slink there. And yet, 'tis a noble and heroic thing, the wind! who ever conquered it? In every fight it has the last and bitterest blow. Run tilting at it, and you but run through it. 7 Ha! a coward wind that strikes stark-naked men, but will not stand to receive a single blow. Even Ahab is a braver thing—a nobler thing than *that.* Would now the wind but had a body but all the things that most exasperate and outrage mortal man, all these things are bodiless, but only bodiless as objects, not as agents. There's a most special, a most cunning, oh, a most malicious difference! And yet, 8 I say again, and swear it now, that there's something all glorious and gracious in the wind. These warm trade winds, at least, that in the clear heavens blow straight on, in strong and steadfast, vigorous mildness; and veer not from their mark, however the baser currents of the sea may turn and tack, and mightiest Mississippis of the land swift and swerve about, uncertain where to go at last. And by the eternal poles! these same trades that so directly blow my good ship on; these trades, or something like them—something so unchangeable, and full as strong, blow my keeled soul along! To it! Aloft there! What d'ye see?"

"Nothing, sir."

"Nothing! and noon at hand! The doubloon[14] goes a-begging! See the sun! Aye, aye, it must be so. I've oversailed him. How, got the start? Aye, he's chasing me now; not 9 I, him—that's bad; I might have known it, too. Fool! the lines—the harpoons he's towing.

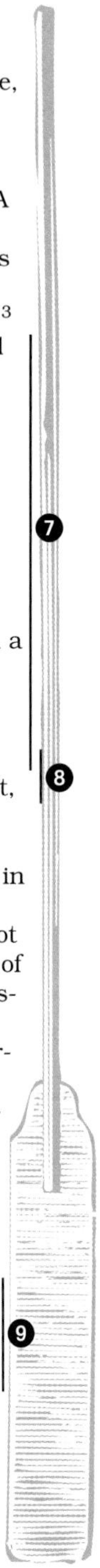

◆ **Build Vocabulary**

maledictions (mal´ ə dik´ shənz) *n.:* Curses

13. fleeces (flēs´ əz) *n.:* Sheep.

14. doubloon (du blo͞on´) *n.:* Old Spanish gold coin. (Ahab offered it as a reward to the first man to spot the whale.)

6 Clarification Tell students that this is the final chapter of the novel. Then point out that in whaling, while the ship stands ready to process the caught whale, the actual hunting is done by harpooners from smaller boats that the sailors row.

◆ Critical Thinking

7 Analyze Discuss how this passage clearly expresses Ahab's negative view of the world. Guide students to understand that the wind is another natural enemy that Ahab cannot control, an enemy even harder to conquer than Moby-Dick.

◆ Build Vocabulary

8 Prefixes: *mal-* Point out the prefix *mal-* in the word *malicious.* Explain how the meaning of *mal-,* "bad or badly," contributes to the meaning of *malicious.* Tell students that *malicious,* meaning "ill-willed," comes from the word *malice,* which means "ill will."

Thematic Focus

9 Shadows of the Imagination Ask students if they think that Ahab is correct in stating that Moby-Dick is now chasing him. *Students may say that Ahab imagines this, that it is very unlikely that the whale would stalk the boat.*

Cross-Curricular Connection: Science

Whales Whales have been in existence for over 10 million years. Not only are whales among the world's most ancient and intelligent animals; they are also the largest—the blue whale is heavier and longer than any dinosaur was. Invite students to find out more about these amazing mammals. They can find interesting information by answering questions like these:

1. How do whales keep warm? How deep do they dive?
2. How does the way whales swim differ from the way fish do? How far do they swim?
3. What is the world whale population today? Are they in danger of extinction?
4. What are the differences between whales, porpoises, and dolphins?
5. How do whales communicate with one another?

Invite students to share their findings.

Customize for
Visual/Spatial Learners
Encourage these students to use this and other illustrations accompanying the selection to help them picture the action. Have them list key details that they find in the illustrations that add to what they find in the text. Then have them share the details on their lists with other students.

▶Critical Viewing◀

❶ **Infer** Students may infer that the whale pictured is huge. Their inference might be based on the proximity of three small whales. If these are swimming in the vicinity of the large one, then it is indeed enormous.

Moby-Dick, Rockwell Kent

▲ Critical Viewing Draw an inference about the size of the whale pictured. On what details do you base your inference? **[Infer]** ❶

Humanities: Art

Moby-Dick, 1930, by Rockwell Kent.

Rockwell Kent made many pen-and-ink drawings, including those that appear in this selection, for the 1930 Lakeside Press edition of *Moby-Dick,* published by Random House, Chicago. Kent was a painter, printmaker, author, illustrator, explorer, and political activist.

Throughout his life, Kent tested his devotion to nature. He spent extended time in some of the Earth's coldest and most remote, severe environments. Kent captured these experiences in his drawings, paintings, illustrations, and prints in some of the most authentic evocations of nature's power in twentieth-century art.

Use this question for discussion: Study Kent's drawings on pp. 334, 338, and 341. What evidence of symbolism can you find? *Responses may include the island aimed directly at Ahab's face in the first drawing. This island can represent the great whale setting its sights on him. In the second drawing they may cite the small whales fleeing Moby-Dick as the giant surfaces. The act of surfacing might represent the destiny of the whale in this novel. In the last drawing, although the whale is largely out of sight, students may say that it was responsible for the chaos and destruction portrayed. This might be symbolic of the awesome power of nature.*

Aye, aye, I have run him by last night. About! about! Come down, all of ye, but the regular lookouts! Man the braces!"

Steering as she had done, the wind had been somewhat on the Pequod's quarter, so that now being pointed in the reverse direction, the braced ship sailed hard upon the breeze as she rechurned the cream in her own white wake.

❷ "Against the wind he now steers for the open jaw," murmured Starbuck to himself, as he coiled the new-hauled main brace upon the rail. "God keep us, but already my bones feel damp within me, and from the inside wet my flesh. I misdoubt me that I disobey my God in obeying him!"

"Stand by to sway me up!" cried Ahab, advancing to the hempen basket.[15] "We should meet him soon."

"Aye, aye, sir," and straightway Starbuck did Ahab's bidding, and once more Ahab swung on high.

A whole hour now passed; gold-beaten out to ages. Time itself now held long breaths with keen suspense. But at last, some three points off the weather bow, Ahab descried the spout again, and instantly from the three mastheads three shrieks went up as if the tongues of fire had voiced it.

❸ "Forehead to forehead I meet thee, this third time, Moby-Dick! On deck there!—brace sharper up; crowd her into the wind's eye. He's too far off to lower yet, Mr. Starbuck. The sails shake! Stand over that helmsman with a top-maul! So, so; he travels fast, and I must down. But let me have one more good round look aloft here at the sea; there's time for that. An old, old sight, and yet somehow so young; aye, and not changed a wink since I first saw it, a boy, from the sand hills of Nantucket! The same!—the same!—the same to Noah as to me. There's a soft shower to leeward. Such lovely leewardings! They must lead somewhere—to something else than common land, more palmy than the palms. Leeward! the white whale goes that way; look to windward, then; the better if the bitterer quarter. But good-bye, good-bye, old masthead! What's this?—green? aye, tiny mosses in these warped cracks. No such green weather stains on Ahab's head! There's the difference now between man's old age and matter's. But aye, old mast, we both grow old together; sound in our hulls, though, are we not, my ship? Aye, minus a leg, that's all. By heaven this dead wood has the better of my live flesh every way. I can't compare with it; and I've known some ships made of dead trees outlast the lives of men made of the most vital stuff of vital fathers. What's that he said? he should still go before me, my pilot; and yet to be seen again? But where? Will I have eyes at the bottom of the sea, supposing I descend those endless stairs? and all night I've been sailing from him, wherever he did sink to. Aye, aye, like many more thou told'st direful truth as touching thyself, O Parsee; but, Ahab, there thy shot fell short. Good-bye, masthead—keep a good eye upon the whale, the while I'm gone. We'll talk tomorrow, nay, tonight, when the white whale lies down there, tied by head and tail."

> ◆ **Literary Focus**
> What symbolic meaning can you detect in the comparison between Ahab and the mast? ❹

❺

He gave the word; and still gazing round him, was steadily lowered through the cloven blue air to the deck.

In due time the boats were lowered; but as standing in his shallop's stern, Ahab just hovered upon the point of the descent, he waved to the mate—who held one of the tackle ropes on deck—and bade him pause.

"Starbuck!"

"Sir?"

"For the third time my soul's ship starts upon this voyage, Starbuck."

"Aye, sir, thou wilt have it so."

"Some ships sail from their ports, and ever afterwards are missing, Starbuck!"

"Truth, sir: saddest truth."

"Some men die at ebb tide; some at low water; some at the full of the flood—and I feel now like a billow that's all one crested comb, Starbuck. I am old—shake hands with me, man." ❻ ❼

Their hands met; their eyes fastened; Starbuck's tears the glue.

"Oh, my captain, my captain!—noble heart—go not—go not!—see, it's a brave man that weeps; how great the agony of the persuasion then!"

15. **hempen basket:** Rope basket. (The basket was constructed earlier by Ahab, so that he could be raised, by means of a pulley device, to the top of the mainmast.)

◆ Critical Thinking

❷ Explain Ask students to explain why Starbuck is tormented by the idea of following Ahab's command. *Students may say that Starbuck believes that Ahab is going to get them all killed.*

◆ Reading Strategy

❸ Recognize Symbols Discuss with students the possible symbolism in this sentence. Explain that the number three is often symbolic. This is the third day, and Ahab is meeting Moby-Dick for the third time.

◆ Literary Focus

❹ Symbol Students may say that to Ahab the mast represents his resolve in his quest for Moby-Dick. The mast stands alone, tall, firm, and long-lasting, as he does in his single-mindedness.

❺ Clarification Parsee is a Persian sailor who disappeared in the previous chapter. Earlier in the book, a prediction was made that Parsee would die before Ahab, but that Ahab would see him once more before his own death.

◆ Reading Strategy

❻ Recognize Symbols Once again the number three is mentioned. Discuss with students the possible symbolism of the number three.

◆ Critical Thinking

❼ Analyze Ask students to explain what is happening in this exchange between Ahab and Starbuck. *Students may respond that Ahab expresses fear and apprehension prior to this, his next attempt to kill Moby-Dick, and that Starbuck makes one last futile effort to persuade him to forgo the quest. They may note that by pleading with Ahab to cease, Starbuck "tears the glue" between them.*

Viewing and Representing Mini-Lesson

Model

Introduce the Concept This mini-lesson supports the Researching and Representing activity in the Idea Bank, p. 347.

Develop Students preparing to create a model harpoon will need to research what the harpoon should look like. Students should strive for authenticity in their models.

Apply Suggest that students begin by researching whaling in general, and focus in on the use of the harpoon. They will find, for instance, that the harpoon was one of several spearlike weapons thrown by whalers at the whales. Students should also note the differences among harpoons from various times and places. Did Nantucket whalers use harpoons different from those used by whalers elsewhere or at other times? As students progress in their research, have them collect the images that will guide them in their project.

Assess Evaluate students on the usefulness of the images they collect in showing what the final model will look like.

◆ Reading Strategy

❶ Recognize Symbols Guide students to see the symbolism in the form of sharks that appear for the hunt and then follow Ahab's boat. The sharks separate Ahab further from his crew. They suggest that the pursuit is folly, and doomed. They add an extra element of danger; they are harbingers of death.

◆ Literary Focus

❷ Symbol Three is a traditional symbol echoing the trinity in Christian belief. The third number often represents finality. Many images in *Moby-Dick* appear in threes. Point out that Starbuck, usually the voice of practicality, now recognizes the grim meaning of the chase having three days, of which they are now in the third—and final one.

Customize for
Less Proficient Readers

❸ This paragraph begins the dramatic final clash with Moby-Dick. Encourage these students to pause here to picture the sudden appearance of the whale and its powerful movements. Have them imagine the spray, the sounds, and the changing shapes and textures of the surface of the water as the giant emerges from and then dives back into the depths. You might encourage these students to draw their own illustration of this dramatic passage.

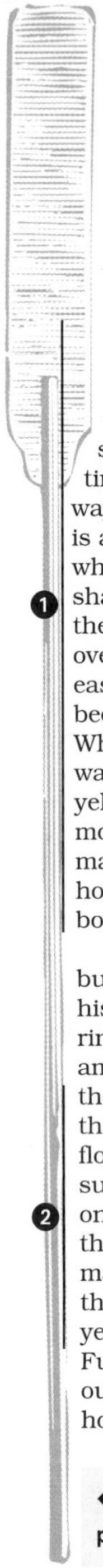

"Lower away!"—cried Ahab, tossing the mate's arm from him. "Stand by the crew!"

In an instant the boat was pulling round close under the stern.

"The sharks! the sharks!" cried a voice from the low cabin window there; "O master, my master, come back!"

But Ahab heard nothing; for his own voice was high-lifted then; and the boat leaped on.

Yet the voice spake true; for scarce had he pushed from the ship, when numbers of sharks, seemingly rising from out the dark waters beneath the hull, maliciously snapped at the blades of the oars, every time they dipped in the water; and in this way accompanied the boat with their bites. It is a thing not uncommonly happening to the whaleboats in those swarming seas; the ❶ sharks at times apparently following them in the same prescient way that vultures hover over the banners of marching regiments in the east. But these were the first sharks that had been observed by the *Pequod* since the White Whale had been first descried; and whether it was that Ahab's crew were all such tiger-yellow barbarians, and therefore their flesh more musky to the senses of the sharks—a matter sometimes well known to affect them—however it was, they seemed to follow that one boat without molesting the others.

"Heart of wrought steel!" murmured Starbuck gazing over the side, and following with his eyes the receding boat—"canst thou yet ring boldly to that sight?—lowering thy keel among ravening sharks, and followed by them, open-mouthed to the chase; and this the critical third day?—For when three days flow together in one continuous intense pursuit; be sure the first is the morning, the sec- ❷ ond the noon, and the third the evening and the end of that thing—be that end what it may. Oh! my God! what is this that shoots through me, and leaves me so deadly calm, yet expectant—fixed at the top of a shudder! Future things swim before me, as in empty outlines and skeletons; all the past is somehow grown dim. Mary, girl; thou fadest in pale glories behind me; boy! I seem to see but thy eyes grown wondrous blue.[16] Strangest problems of life seem clearing; but clouds sweep between—Is my journey's end coming? My legs feel faint; like his who has footed it all day. Feel thy heart—beats it yet? Stir thyself, Starbuck!—stave it off—move, move! speak aloud!—Masthead there! See ye my boy's hand on the hill?—Crazed—aloft there!—keep thy keenest eye upon the boats—mark well the whale!—Ho! again!—drive off that hawk! see! he pecks—he tears the vane"—pointing to the red flag flying at the maintruck—"Ha, he soars away with it!—Where's the old man now? see'st thou that sight, oh Ahab!—shudder, shudder!"

The boats had not gone very far, when by a signal from the mastheads—a downward pointed arm, Ahab knew that the whale had sounded; but intending to be near him at the next rising, he held on his way a little sideways from the vessel; the becharmed crew maintaining the profoundest silence, as the head-beat waves hammered and hammered against the opposing bow.

"Drive, drive in your nails, oh ye waves! to their uttermost heads drive them in! ye but strike a thing without a lid; and no coffin and no hearse can be mine:—and hemp only can kill me! Ha! ha!"

Suddenly the waters around them slowly swelled in broad circles; then quickly upheaved, as if sideways sliding from a submerged berg of ice, swiftly rising to the surface. A low rumbling sound was heard; a subterraneous hum; and then all held their breaths; as bedraggled with trailing ropes, and harpoons, and lances, a vast form shot lengthwise, but ❸ obliquely from the sea. Shrouded in a thin drooping veil of mist, it hovered for a moment in the rainbowed air; and then fell swamping back into the deep. Crushed thirty feet upwards, the waters flashed for an instant like heaps of fountains, then brokenly sank in a shower of flakes, leaving the circling surface creamed like new milk round the marble trunk of the whale.

"Give way!" cried Ahab to the oarsmen, and the boats darted forward to the attack; but maddened by yesterday's fresh irons that corroded in him, Moby-Dick seemed combinedly

◆ Build Vocabulary

prescient (presh´ ənt) *adj.*: Having foreknowledge

16. **Mary . . . blue:** Reference to Starbuck's wife and son.

Humanities: Music

Some people, scientists and musicians alike, are fascinated by the mysterious, mournful, musical sounds whales make as they communicate with one another. Their groans, yips, and wails can carry many miles through the water. The humpback whales, in particular, are skillful performers. Each male sings its own unique song, which can last for up to thirty-five minutes. He sings it over and over again.

Obtain recordings of whale songs to play for students. For example, on the Judy Collins album *Whales and Nightingales,* the traditional sea song "Farewell to Tarwathie" incorporates melodies of the humpback whale. Invite students to freewrite in response to the sounds they hear.

Moby-Dick, Rockwell Kent

◀ **Critical Viewing** What details from *Moby-Dick* did the artist probably use to create this illustration? **[Hypothesize]** ❹

possessed by all the angels that fell from heaven. The wide tiers of welded tendons overspreading his broad white forehead, beneath the transparent skin, looked knitted together; as head on, he came churning his tail among the boats; and once more flailed them apart; spilling out the irons and lances from the two mates' boats, and dashing in one side of the upper part of their bows, but leaving Ahab's almost without a scar.

While Daggoo and Queequeg were stopping the strained planks; and as the whale swimming out from them, turned, and showed one entire flank as he shot by them again; at that moment a quick cry went up. Lashed round and round to the fish's back; pinioned in the turns upon turns in which, during the past night, the whale had reeled the involutions of the lines around him, the half-torn body of the Parsee was seen; his sable raiment frayed to shreds; his distended eyes turned full upon old Ahab.

The harpoon dropped from his hand.

"Befooled, befooled!"—drawing in a long lean breath—"Aye, Parsee! I see thee again—Aye, and thou goest before; and this, this then is the hearse that thou didst promise. But I hold thee to the last letter of thy word. Where is the second hearse? Away, mates, to the ship! those boats are useless now; repair them if ye can in time, and return to me; if not, Ahab is enough to die—Down, men! the first thing that but offers to jump from this boat I stand in, that thing I harpoon. Ye are not other men, but my arms and my legs; and so obey me—Where's the whale? gone down again?"

◆ *Literature and Your Life*

Have you ever pursued a goal with Ahab's desperate persistence? ❺

But he looked too nigh the boat; for as if bent upon escaping with the corpse he bore, and as if the particular place of the last encounter had been but a stage in his leeward voyage, Moby-Dick was now again steadily swimming forward; and had almost passed the ship—which thus far had been sailing in the contrary direction to him, though for the present her headway had been stopped. He seemed swimming with his utmost velocity, and now only intent upon pursuing his own straight path in the sea.

"Oh! Ahab," cried Starbuck, "not too late is ❻

▶Critical Viewing◀

❹ **Hypothesize** Students may respond that the artist used many details from *Moby-Dick* to create this illustration, among them the descriptions of the boats, harpoons, and lines and the descriptions of the size, speed, and power of Moby-Dick as the whale dives and surfaces.

◆ *Literature and Your Life*

❺ Encourage students to discuss what is important to them. Students might mention such goals as trying to get A's in all of their subjects; practicing to make the school band or a school sports team; giving their all in pursuing a hobby such as painting or model railroading; or trying to convince their parents that a cat, a dog, or a hamster would make a fine addition to the household.

Thematic Focus

❻ **Shadows of the Imagination** Here, again, Starbuck is the voice of reason, pointing out that Moby-Dick only wants to swim away. But Ahab's obsession won't let him stop his quest.

Beyond the Classroom

Career Connection

Cetologist or Oceanographer Cetology is the branch of zoology that deals with whales. Oceanography is the study of the environment in the oceans, including analysis of the water, ocean depths, sea beds, animals, and plants.

Invite interested students to look into the kinds of work scientists at the cutting edge of these branches of science are currently doing. To find out today's cetology or oceanography issues, students can research the Internet, books, scientific journals, or magazines like *Nature* or *Natural History.* Students can even interview scientists who are doing research in either field. Suggest that students get started on their research by talking with their science teacher about the best research paths to follow.

◆ Critical Thinking

1 Speculate Note that the narrator suggests that Moby-Dick may be giving up the fight. Ask students what they think will happen next. *Students might respond that because of what has happened up to this point, the fight with Moby-Dick is far from over. In fact, catastrophe may yet result.*

Customize for *AP Students*

2 Guide these students to appreciate that the action is becoming increasingly kaleidoscopic. Have them notice that readers now catch only brief bits of the action, much as a sailor at the scene would do in the midst of the chaos of battle.

Customize for *Bodily/Kinesthetic Learners*

These students might enjoy acting out part of the exciting action of this chapter. Guide students to rehearse lines and actions before performing their scene for the class. If possible, have students include props to make their performance more realistic.

it, even now, the third day, to desist. See! Moby-Dick seeks thee not. It is thou, thou, that madly seekest him!"

Setting sail to the rising wind, the lonely boat was swiftly impelled to leeward, by both oars and canvas. And at last when Ahab was sliding by the vessel, so near as plainly to distinguish Starbuck's face as he leaned over the rail, he hailed him to turn the vessel about, and follow him, not too swiftly, at a judicious interval. Glancing upwards he saw Tashtego, Queequeg, and Daggoo, eagerly mounting to the three mastheads; while the oarsmen were rocking in the two staved boats which had just been hoisted to the side, and were busily at work in repairing them, one after the other, through the portholes, as he sped, he also caught flying glimpses of Stubb and Flask, busying themselves on deck among bundles of new irons and lances. As he saw all this; as he heard the hammers in the broken boats; far other hammers seemed driving a nail into his heart. But he rallied. And now marking that the vane or flag was gone from the main masthead, he shouted to Tashtego, who had just gained that perch, to descend again for another flag, and a hammer and nails, and so nail it to the mast.

Whether fagged by the three days' running chase, and the resistance to his swimming in the knotted hamper he bore; or whether it was some latent deceitfulness and malice in him: [1] whichever was true, the White Whale's way now began to abate, as it seemed, from the boat so rapidly nearing him once more; though indeed the whale's last start had not been so long a one as before. And still as Ahab glided over the waves the unpitying sharks accompanied him; and so pertinaciously stuck to the boat; and so continually bit at the plying oars, that the blades became jagged and crunched, and left small splinters in the sea, at almost every dip.

"Heed them not! those teeth but give new rowlocks to your oars. Pull on! 'tis the better rest, the sharks' jaw than the yielding water."

"But at every bite, sir, the thin blades grow smaller and smaller!"

"They will last long enough! pull on!—But who can tell"—he muttered—"whether these sharks swim to feast on the whale or on Ahab?—But pull on! Aye, all alive, now—we near him. The helm! take the helm! let me pass"—and so saying, two of the oarsmen helped him forward to the bows of the still flying boat.

At length as the craft was cast to one side, and ran ranging along with the White Whale's flank, he seemed strangely oblivious of its advance—as the whale sometimes will—and Ahab was fairly within the smoky mountain mist, which, thrown off from the whale's spout, curled round his great Monadnock[17] hump; he was even thus close to him; when, with body arched back, and both arms lengthwise highlifted to the poise, he darted his fierce iron, and his far fiercer curse into the hated whale. As both steel and curse sank to the socket, as if sucked into a morass, Moby-Dick sidewise writhed; spasmodically rolled his nigh flank [2] against the bow, and, without staving a hole in it, so suddenly canted the boat over, that had it not been for the elevated part of the gunwale to which he then clung, Ahab would once more have been tossed into the sea. As it was, three of the oarsmen—who foreknew not the precise instant of the dart, and were therefore unprepared for its effects—these were flung out; but so fell, that, in an instant two of them clutched the gunwale again, and rising to its level on a combing wave, hurled themselves bodily inboard again; the third man helplessly dropping astern, but still afloat and swimming.

Almost simultaneously, with a mighty volition of ungraduated, instantaneous swiftness, the White Whale darted through the weltering sea. But when Ahab cried out to the steersman to take new turns with the line, and hold it so; and commanded the crew to turn round on their seats, and tow the boat up to the mark; the moment the treacherous line felt that double strain and tug, it snapped in the empty air!

"What breaks in me? Some sinew cracks!—'tis whole again; oars! oars! Burst in upon him!"

Hearing the tremendous rush of the sea-

17. **Monadnock** (mə nad′ näk): Mountain in New Hampshire.

◆ Build Vocabulary

pertinaciously (pʉr′ tə nā′ shəs lē) *adv.:* Holding firmly to some purpose

Speaking, Listening, and Viewing Mini-Lesson

Readers Theatre

This mini-lesson supports the Speaking, Listening, and Viewing activity in the Idea Bank on p. 347.

Introduce the Concept Divide students into performance groups. Students can read more than one role and one or more students can share the role of Ishmael, the narrator.

Develop Background Ask groups to choose places in the text to begin and end the scene. Encourage groups to work together to decide how each role should be read, and who will read. Allow groups to rehearse the reading until they are satisfied with their performance.

Apply the Information Have groups perform their readings for the class. You may want to invite other classes, or videotape the performances for later viewing.

Assess the Outcome Discuss with students how giving and listening to oral interpretations of the pre-hunt scene helped them to better understand its meaning or to appreciate Melville's writing skill. Evaluate the performances on the following criteria: appropriate dramatic expression, fluency of reading, clarity, and enunciation.

3 

 3

crashing boat, the whale wheeled round to present his blank forehead at bay; but in that evolution, catching sight of the nearing black hull of the ship; seemingly seeing in it the source of all his persecutions; bethinking it—it may be—a larger and nobler foe; of a sudden, he bore down upon its advancing prow, smiting his jaws amid fiery showers of foam.

Ahab staggered; his hand smote his forehead. "I grow blind; hands! stretch out before me that I may yet grope my way. Is't night?"

"The whale! The ship!" cried the cringing oarsmen.

"Oars! oars! Slope downwards to thy depths. O sea that ere it be forever too late, Ahab may slide this last, last time upon his mark! I see:
4 the ship! the ship! Dash on, my men! will ye not save my ship?"

But as the oarsmen violently forced their boat through the sledge-hammering seas, the before whale-smitten bow-ends of two planks burst through, and in an instant almost, the temporarily disabled boat lay nearly level with the waves; its half-wading, splashing crew, trying hard to stop the gap and bale out the pouring water.

Meantime, for that one beholding instant, Tashtego's masthead hammer remained suspended in his hand; and the red flag, half wrapping him as with a plaid, then streamed itself straight out from him, as his own forward-flowing heart; while Starbuck and Stubb, standing upon the bowsprit beneath, caught sight of the down-coming monster just as soon as he.

"The whale, the whale! Up helm, up helm! Oh, all ye sweet powers of air, now hug me close! Let not Starbuck die, if die he must, in a woman's fainting fit. Up helm I say—ye fools, the jaw! the jaw! Is this the end of all my bursting prayers? all my lifelong fideli- 5
ties? Oh, Ahab, Ahab, lo, thy work. Steady! helmsman, steady. Nay, nay! Up helm again! He turns to meet us! Oh, his unappeasable brow drives on towards one, whose duty

3 Clarification Tell students that these photos are stills from the climactic scene of the 1956 film version of *Moby-Dick*. Gregory Peck, as Ahab, is the harpooner.

◆ Critical Thinking

4 Draw Conclusions This is the first time that Ahab seems concerned with the welfare of his ship. Ask students: Why does Ahab suddenly care about saving his ship when he never seemed to care about the ship before this moment? *Students may say that because the ship is now in imminent danger, Ahab finally realizes the gravity of the situation.*

◆ Critical Thinking

5 Evaluate Ask students to explain what Starbuck is concerned with at this desperate moment. *Students may say that Starbuck's chief concern is not to die in a cowardly fashion, one unbecoming to such a proud and able sailor as himself.*

Cross-Curricular Connection: Ecology

Whaling A decade after *Moby-Dick* was published, a Norwegian whaling captain developed two inventions that revolutionized the whaling industry. One was a new harpoon tipped with an exploding bomb to kill whales more quickly; the other was a faster, steam-powered whaling boat. As a result, more whales were killed in the first forty years of the twentieth century than in the four preceding centuries.

For humanitarian reasons, many nations, including the United States, Canada, and most of Europe, have stopped hunting whales. Japan and the former Soviet Union still hunt, although international pressure to outlaw whaling increases each year. Have students find out what whale products are used today and the size of the world's whale population. Ask them to give and support their opinion on whether or not to end whaling.

◆ **Literary Focus**

❶ **Symbols** Details that students may point to include the whale's "swift vengeance" and the "eternal malice [of] his whole aspect."

◆ **Literary Focus**

❷ **Symbols** Have students notice that the symbols of death mount and continue to the end. Here, Ahab refers to the boats as hearses.

Customize for
Less Proficient Readers

❸ Help students understand how Ahab dies. Guide them to see that he is caught around the neck by the harpoon line and jerked from the boat. He dies throwing a harpoon into a fleeing Moby-Dick.

Customize for
AP Students

❹ Ask students to assess what this final paragraph indicates about the relationship between human beings and nature. *Students may respond that nature endures in the face of human mortality and is indifferent to human suffering.*

tells him he cannot depart. My God, stand by me now!"

"Stand not by me, but stand under me, whoever you are that will now help Stubb; for Stubb, too, sticks here. I grin at thee, thou grinning whale ! Who ever helped Stubb, or kept Stubb awake, but Stubb's own unwinking eye? And now poor Stubb goes to bed upon a mattress that is all too soft; would it were stuffed with brushwood! I grin at thee, thou grinning whale! Look ye, sun, moon, and stars! I call ye assassins of as good a fellow as ever spouted up his ghost. For all that, I would yet ring glasses with thee, would ye but hand the cup! Oh, oh! oh, oh! thou grinning whale, but there'll be plenty of gulping soon! Why fly ye not, O Ahab! For me, off shoes and jacket to it; let Stubb die in his drawers! A most moldy and oversalted death, though—cherries! cherries! cherries! Oh, Flask, for one red cherry ere we die!"

"Cherries? I only wish that we were where they grow. Oh, Stubb, I hope my poor mother's drawn my part-pay ere this; if not, few coppers will now come to her, for the voyage is up."

❶ From the ship's bows, nearly all the seamen now hung inactive; hammers, bits of plank, lances, and harpoons, mechanically retained in their hands, just as they had darted from their various employments; all their enchanted eyes intent upon the whale, which from side to side strangely vibrating his predestinating head, sent a broad band of overspreading semicircular foam before him as he rushed. Retribution, swift vengeance, eternal malice were in his whole aspect, and spite of all that mortal man could do, the solid white buttress of his forehead smote the ship's starboard bow, till men and timbers reeled. Some fell flat upon their faces. Like dislodged trucks, the heads of the harpooneers aloft shook on their bull-like necks. Through the breach, they heard the waters pour, as mountain torrents down a flume.

> ◆ **Literary Focus**
> What details in this paragraph suggest that the whale has become a symbol of retribution?

❷ "The ship! The hearse!—the second hearse!" cried Ahab from the boat; "its wood could only be American!"

Diving beneath the settling ship, the whale ran quivering along its keel; but turning under water, swiftly shot to the surface again, far off the other bow, but within a few yards of Ahab's boat, where, for a time, he lay quiescent.

"I turn my body from the sun. What ho, Tashtego! let me hear thy hammer. Oh! ye three unsurrendered spires of mine; thou uncracked keel; and only god-bullied hull; thou firm deck, and haughty helm, and Polepointed prow—death-glorious ship! must ye then perish, and without me? Am I cut off from the last fond pride of meanest shipwrecked captains? Oh, lonely death on lonely life! Oh, now I feel my topmost greatness lies in my topmost grief. Ho, ho! from all your furthest bounds, pour ye now in, ye bold billows of my whole foregone life, and top this one piled comber of my death! Towards thee I roll, thou all-destroying but unconquering whale; to the last I grapple with thee; from hell's heart I stab at thee; for hate's sake I spit my last breath at thee. Sink all coffins and all hearses to one common pool! and since neither can be mine, let me then tow to pieces, while still chasing thee, though tied to thee, thou damned whale! *Thus*, I give up the spear!"

The harpoon was darted; the stricken whale flew forward; with igniting velocity the line ran through the groove;—ran foul. Ahab stooped to clear it; he did clear it; but the flying turn caught him round the neck, and voicelessly as Turkish mutes bowstring their victim, he was shot out of the boat, ere the crew knew he was gone. Next instant, the heavy eye splice in the rope's final end flew out of the stark-empty tub, knocked down an oarsman, and smiting the sea, disappeared in its depths. ❸

For an instant, the tranced boat's crew stood still; then turned. "The ship? Great God, where is the ship?" Soon they through dim, bewildering mediums saw her sidelong fading phantom, as in the gaseous fata morgana,[18] only the uppermost masts out of water: while fixed by infatuation, or fidelity, or fate, to their once lofty perches, the pagan harpooneers still maintained their sinking lookouts on the sea. And now, concentric circles seized the lone boat itself, and all its crew, and each floating oar, and every lance pole, and spinning, animate and inanimate, all round and round in one vortex, carried the smallest chip of the *Pequod* out of sight.

18. **fata morgana** (fät′ ə môr gän′ ə) *n.*: Mirage seen at sea.

Reteach

Remind students that symbols are items that represent larger concepts or ideas. Use a graphic organizer like the one shown to reteach symbol.

The central symbol of Melville's novel is the whale, Moby-Dick. Mellville builds symbolism partly by telling the stories of the whale's enormous power and capacity for destruction. The foremost representation of this destructiveness is Ahab's missing limb.

Ahab himself articulates the symbolic nature of the great whale in a conversation with Starbuck: "I see in him outrageous strength, with an inscrutable malice sinewing it."

Symbol	Concept/Idea
Moby Dick	Cruelty and destructiveness in nature
Ahab's ivory leg	The toll of nature on man

But as the last whelmings intermixingly poured themselves over the sunken head of the Indian at the mainmast, leaving a few inches of the erect spar yet visible, together with long streaming yards of the flag, which calmly undulated, with ironical coincidings, over the destroying billows they almost touched—at that instant, a red arm and a hammer hovered backwardly uplifted in the open air, in the act of nailing the flag faster and yet faster to the subsiding spar. A sky hawk that tauntingly had followed the main-truck downwards from its natural home among the stars, pecking at the flag, and incommoding Tashtego there: this bird now chanced to intercept its broad fluttering wing between the hammer and the wood: and simultaneously feeling that ethereal thrill, the submerged savage beneath, in his deathgasp, kept his hammer frozen there: and so the bird of heaven, with archangelic shrieks, and his imperial beak thrust upwards, and his whole captive form folded in the flag of Ahab, went down with his ship, which, like Satan, would not sink to hell till she had dragged a living part of heaven along with her, and helmeted herself with it.

Now small fowls flew screaming over the yet yawning gulf; a sullen white surf beat against its steep sides; then all collapsed, and the great shroud of the sea rolled on as it rolled five thousand years ago. 4

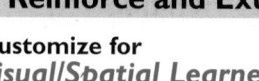

Reinforce and Extend

Customize for
Visual/Spatial Learners
Students may enjoy seeing the 1956 film version of *Moby-Dick* to compare its presentation of the quarter-deck scene and the climax with the mental images they formed from Melville's words. Students may also enjoy seeing *Jaws,* the 1975 film by Steven Spielberg, which also deals with a man's fatal obsession with a deadly creature of the sea.

Answers

◆ *Literature and Your Life*

Reader's Response Students should support their opinions with details from the selection.

Thematic Focus Suggested response: Imagination plays a key role. Ahab's past experiences with Moby-Dick play on his imagination in a powerful and distorted way. His imagination tends to run wild, and it leads him to behave irrationally.

☑ **Check Your Comprehension**

1. Ahab offers a Spanish coin made of one ounce of gold.
2. (a) Moby-Dick bit off Ahab's leg, and Ahab sees the whale as a symbol of power and malice. (b) Starbuck sees the obsession as vengeance against a dumb animal.
3. (a) He says that for the third time his soul's ship starts on the voyage. (b) Sharks follow his boat.
4. Ahab is caught by the fouled harpoon line and is shot out of the boat and disappears; with the harpoon in him, Moby-Dick disappears; the *Pequod* sinks.

(Answers continue on p. 346)

Guide for Responding

◆ *Literature and Your Life*

Reader's Response How do you feel about the fate of Ahab and his crew? Explain.

Thematic Focus Do you admire, despise, or pity Captain Ahab? What role does the imagination play in Ahab's quest for Moby-Dick? Explain.

Journal Writing Review Melville's last paragraph to discover his attitude about the relationship between humanity and nature. In a journal entry, state the writer's view and your own feelings.

☑ Check Your Comprehension

1. What does Ahab offer to the man who spots Moby-Dick?
2. (a) Why is Ahab obsessed with killing Moby-Dick? (b) How does Starbuck interpret Ahab's obsession?
3. (a) Just before his whaleboat is lowered into the water, what does Ahab tell Starbuck? (b) What follows Ahab's boat as it pulls away from the ship?
4. What happens to Ahab, Moby-Dick, and the *Pequod* at the end?

◆ Critical Thinking

INTERPRET

1. (a) What does Ahab's obsession with Moby-Dick reveal about his character? (b) In what ways is Starbuck different from Ahab? **[Infer; Contrast]**
2. (a) Why does Starbuck obey Ahab though he disagrees with him? (b) Why does the crew join Ahab's quest without hesitation? **[Interpret]**
3. What do Ahab's comments about the wind at the start of "The Chase—Third Day" suggest about his attitude toward nature? **[Interpret]**
4. (a) What omens appear as Ahab's whaleboat pulls away from the ship and when Moby-Dick surfaces? (b) How does Ahab respond to these omens? **[Analyze]**
5. What is the significance of the fact that Moby-Dick seems "strangely oblivious" to the advance of Ahab's boat? **[Interpret]**

EVALUATE

6. Ahab believes people are guided by instinct and intuition rather than by reason. Explain why you believe his view is valid or flawed. **[Evaluate]**

EXTEND

7. (a) How can obsession with a goal affect a person's ability to reach that goal? (b) What goals are people obsessed with today? **[Health Link]**

Beyond the Selection

FURTHER READING

Other Works by Herman Melville
Typee
Bartleby the Scrivener
Benito Cereno

Other Works About Obsession or Revenge
"The Cask of Amontillado," Edgar Allan Poe
Jaws, Peter Benchley
Of Human Bondage, Somerset Maugham

We suggest that you preview these works before recommending them to students.

INTERNET

You and your students may find additional information about Herman Melville on the Internet. We suggest the following site. Please be aware, however, that the site may have changed from the time we published this information.

For information on Melville, a list of his works, literary criticism, and links to literature, whaling, and sailing, go to **http://www.melville.org/**

We *strongly recommend* that you preview the site before you send students to it.

Answers *(continued from p. 345)*

◆ Critical Thinking

1. (a) It reveals that he is a stubborn, angry, and bitter man. (b) Starbuck is practical and realistic and is disturbed by Ahab's obsession.
2. (a) Suggested response: Perhaps Starbuck obeys him simply because Ahab is the captain, or perhaps he still admires Ahab's courage. (b) Suggested response: Crew members are moved by Ahab's speech and lured by the offer of a reward.
3. They indicate that he sees nature as being uncontrollable, unexplainable, and filled with contradictions.
4. (a) Sharks appear, and Starbuck sees visions of his family. Parsee's body is seen lashed to Moby-Dick. (b) Ahab says that the last part of the omen has not been seen, and he continues to pursue Moby-Dick.
5. It indicates that Moby-Dick is merely a creature following its instincts rather than the evil, scheming creature that Ahab believes it to be.
6. Students should support their opinions with evidence from the selection.
7. Suggested response: (a) Obsession can strengthen the effort to reach the goal, but it can also blind people to reality. (b) Many people are obsessed with attaining financial prosperity, and others focus on getting political power.

◆ Literary Focus

1. Suggested response: Given the fact that he narrates the tale, Ishmael may represent the artist in society.
2. Suggested response: The ship's voyage symbolizes humanity's efforts to explain and control nature.
3. Suggested response: The journey points out that—despite their desire to do so—people will never be able to completely understand or control nature and that nature will remain powerful, eternal, and indifferent.

◆ Grammar and Style

1. Collective Noun = crew; Verb = line up.
2. Collective Noun = team; Verb = draws
3. Collective Noun = crew; Verb = is
4. Collective Noun = flock; Verb = glides
5. Collective Noun = crowd; Verb = gathers

◆ Reading Strategy

1. One example might be "There's a soft shower to leeward. Such lovely leewardings! They must lead somewhere—to something else than common land, more palmy than the palms. Leeward! the white whale goes that way; look to windward, then. . . ."
2. One example might be ". . . it was Moby-Dick that dismasted me; Moby-Dick that brought me to this dead stump I stand on now. . . ."
3. Students may mention Moby-Dick's disappearance—but not death—at the end of the fight with Ahab.

◆ Build Vocabulary

Using the Latin Prefix *mal-*

1. d 2. c 3. e 4. b 5. a

Using the Word Bank

1. pertinaciously; 2. prescient; 3. inscrutable; 4. maledictions

Guide for Responding *(continued)*

◆ Literary Focus

Symbol

A **symbol** is a person, place, or thing that has a meaning in itself and also represents something larger than itself. For instance, the fact that the crew of the *Pequod* includes representatives from many of the world's races and cultures indicates that the crew is more than just a collection of people. It may symbolize humanity itself.

1. Explain the possible symbolic meaning of Ishmael in *Moby-Dick*.
2. Given the fact that the crew of the *Pequod* symbolizes humanity and that Moby-Dick symbolizes everything in nature that is paradoxical, unexplainable, and uncontrollable, what do you think the ship's voyage symbolizes?
3. Considering the journey's symbolic meaning and outcome, speculate about the novel's theme, or central idea.

◆ Grammar and Style

Agreement With Collective Nouns

A collective noun may be either singular or plural, depending on whether the group it names is seen as a unit or as a collection of individuals. The verb must agree with the intended meaning.

A **collective noun** names a group of persons or things.

Practice Identify the collective noun in each sentence. Then choose the verb form that agrees with each collective noun.

1. The crew (lines, line) up along the railing of the ship.
2. A team of horses (draws, draw) the carriage.
3. The crew (is, are) composed of fine, upstanding men and women.
4. A flock of gulls (glide, glides) over the ship.
5. A crowd (gathers, gather) near the site of the accident.

◆ Reading Strategy

Recognize Symbols

You can **recognize symbols** by noticing an author's effort to connect a place, thing, or character with some larger concept or value. Melville's elaborate description of Moby-Dick suggests that the whale has many facets of symbolic meaning. Find events or descriptions in the text of *Moby-Dick* that demonstrate each of the following aspects of the whale's symbolism.

1. nature's beauty
2. nature's power and destructiveness
3. nature's immortality

◆ Build Vocabulary

Using the Latin Prefix *mal-*

The Latin prefix *mal-* means "bad" or "badly." Each of the words in the left column contains this prefix. In your notebook, write the letter of the definition that matches each of these words. Refer to a dictionary if you need help.

1. malcontent	a. active ill will
2. malevolent	b. causing or likely to cause death
3. malign	c. wishing harm to others
4. malignant	d. dissatisfied
5. malice	e. to slander

Using the Word Bank: Sentence Completions

On your paper, write the word that best completes each sentence.

inscrutable maledictions prescient pertinaciously

1. They __?__ continued to believe in my innocence of the crime.
2. We marveled at the child's __?__ comment; the rain poured down on us just as she said it would.
3. The woman's behavior was odd, and her intentions were __?__.
4. The deposed dictator was greeted with __?__ from the crowd.

Build Your Portfolio

Idea Bank

Writing

1. Eulogy Write the eulogy that Ishmael might have delivered at a memorial service for his shipmates.

2. Character Sketch Ahab, the protagonist of *Moby-Dick*, has become one of the most famous characters in all of American literature. Write a character sketch in which you concisely describe Ahab's personality and behavior.

3. Essay Write an essay in which you discuss how the theme of *Moby-Dick* is revealed through Melville's symbolism. Discuss two or three symbols, defining each symbol in your own words.

Speaking, Listening, and Viewing

4. Monologue Take the part of Ishmael and retell the tale of his experience aboard the doomed *Pequod* to a crowd of whalemen. Use the selection to help you duplicate Ishmael's unique tone and outlook. **[Performing Arts Link]**

5. Readers Theatre With a group of your classmates, take the parts of Ahab, Stubb, Starbuck, Flask, Tashtego, Daggoo, Queequeg, other sailors, and a narrator, and dramatize the scene in which Ahab exhorts his crew to hunt Moby-Dick. **[Performing Arts Link]**

Researching and Representing

6. Model Research the harpoon, the special tool the crew used to hunt Moby-Dick. Then make a scale model of a whaling harpoon, using wood, wire, or clay. **[Art Link]**

7. Report Find out which species of whales face possible extinction today and what efforts are being made to save them. Present your findings in a brief oral or written report. **[Science Link]**

Online Activity www.phlit.phschool.com

Guided Writing Lesson

A Dramatic Scene

Because they are meant to be seen and not read, dramas must convey character, establish and resolve conflict, and develop plot through dialogue and physical actions. Choose a scene from *Moby-Dick*, and adapt it as a dramatic scene for the stage. As you develop your scene, use dialogue that sounds natural.

Writing Skills Focus: Realistic Dialogue

One of the keys to an effective drama is **realistic dialogue**—dialogue that sounds like natural speech. People often use contractions and speak in incomplete sentences. In addition, many people use slang expressions or speak in a way that is grammatically incorrect. As you write dialogue, check to see that it sounds natural by pausing to read it aloud. Revise passages that seem stiff or unnatural. In addition, make sure that the dialogue you've written is appropriate for each character's background and level of education.

Prewriting Choose a scene that would be effective in a stage setting. Make some notes about the characters' behavior and the conflict in the scene. Outline the scene's natural beginning, middle, and end; pinpoint any physical actions that occur.

Drafting Use some of Melville's dialogue in your scene, but modernize the language for a contemporary audience. You may also transform important descriptive passages into speeches for one or more characters. Remember to include written stage directions (in parentheses) that clarify characters' actions, tone of voice, and position on stage.

Revising Perform your scene with a classmate. Listen carefully to the dialogue. Notice places where it seems unnatural. Revise these sections. Then look for places where you need to add stage directions.

Idea Bank

Customizing for Performance Levels
Following are suggestions for matching Idea Bank topics with your students' performance levels:
Less Advanced Students: 1, 6
Average Students: 2, 5, 7
More Advanced Students: 3, 4

Customizing for Learning Modalities
Following are suggestions for matching Idea Bank topics with your students' learning modalities:
Musical/Rhythmic: 4
Interpersonal: 5
Bodily/Kinesthetic: 6
Logical/Mathematical: 7

Guided Writing Lesson

Refer students to the Writing Handbook, p. 1192, for instruction on the writing process, and p. 1195 for further information on creative writing.

Writing and Language Transparencies Have students use the Outline Organizer, p. 95, to outline their scenes.

Writing Lab CD-ROM
Have students complete the tutorial on Creative Writing. Follow these steps:

1. To help develop characterization through dialogue, use the video clips about gathering details for drama.
2. Have students draft on computer.
3. Have students use the Self-Evaluation Checklist to aid revision.

✓ ASSESSMENT OPTIONS

Formal Assessment, Selection Test, pp. 99–101, and Assessment Resources Software. The selection test is designed so that it can be easily customized to the performance levels of your students.

Alternative Assessment, p. 21, includes options for less advanced students, more advanced students, bodily/kinesthetic learners, verbal/linguistic learners, and visual/spatial learners.

PORTFOLIO ASSESSMENT
Use the following rubrics in the ***Alternative Assessment*** booklet to assess student writing:
Eulogy: Summary Rubric, p. 113
Character Sketch: Description Rubric, p. 112
Essay: Literary Analysis/Interpretation Rubric, p. 127
Guided Writing Lesson: Drama Rubric, p. 124

Prepare and Engage

LESSON OBJECTIVES

1. **To express and support responses to the text**
   - Critical Thinking
   - Idea Bank: Diary Entry
   - Idea Bank: Radio Presentation
2. **To analyze literary elements**
   - Idea Bank: Essay
3. **To read in order to research self-selected and assigned topics**
   - Idea Bank: Floor Plans
   - Questions for Research
4. **To plan, prepare, organize, and present literary interpretations**
   - Idea Bank: Comparison and Contrast

Connections to Today's World

Edgar Allan Poe, Nathaniel Hawthorne, and Herman Melville often presented characters who were atypical in emotional terms. They carried with them the extra baggage of fear, obsession, or guilt. They often met with catastrophe driven by their uncommon emotional makeup. The shadows of their imaginations were dark and mysterious, as are the shadows of the imagination of a stranger you'll meet in "Where *Is* Here?" a contemporary story by Joyce Carol Oates. What is the mysterious secret of the stranger?

CONNECTIONS TO TODAY'S WORLD

Where *Is* Here?

Joyce Carol Oates

Thematic Connection

SHADOWS OF THE IMAGINATION

Edgar Allan Poe, Nathaniel Hawthorne, and Herman Melville are towering figures in American literature. They were fascinated by the ways in which human beings behave in extreme situations, and each often portrayed characters acting in disturbing or extraordinary ways because of an internal conflict or a crisis. Using their powerful imaginations, these writers transformed realistic details of daily human life into ambiguous, shadowy, and precarious worlds.

In Edgar Allan Poe's work, for instance, gloomy heroes like Roderick Usher languish as their mental equilibrium teeters and the outside world—which once seemed orderly and healthful—collapses. Many of Nathaniel Hawthorne's characters have some secret, shadowy knowledge that leads them to behave in unsettling and unaccountable ways; often Hawthorne focuses on the odd ways human beings think and act when they are struggling with dark emotions such as guilt. One of Herman Melville's finest fictional creations, Captain Ahab, is a man who suffers an episode of violence and then proves unable to stop chasing the shadows of his own diseased imagination.

MODERN GOTHIC

In the twentieth century, only a few American writers have been inclined to embrace or evoke the dusky themes, characters, and atmospheres that stamped the work of their Romantic forebears. One of these writers is Joyce Carol Oates.

Many of Oates's novels and stories concern individuals whose ordinary lives are suddenly upset by mysterious forces beyond their control. Much of the suspense and emotional power in Oates's fiction can be traced to her depiction of common people who seem powerless to save their identities from alteration or destruction by some shadowy force.

JOYCE CAROL OATES (1938–)

In her short stories, novels, poems, and plays, Joyce Carol Oates delves into the human mind. Her work often focuses on characters who are disturbed or who are searching anxiously for their identities.

Oates grew up in a tiny town on the Erie Canal, and her earliest stories and first novel are accounts of life in Erie County. Oates's fictional Eden County is elaborately conceived and populated with inhabitants who turn up in various ways from story to story. Eden County is not the paradise its name implies; in fact, it can be insufferable to its inhabitants. It has been suggested that Oates may have chosen the name to remind readers just how much human beings have lost.

Prentice Hall Literature Program Resources

REINFORCE / RETEACH / EXTEND

Selection Support Worksheets
Build Vocabulary: Using Vocabulary to Set a Mood, p. 102
Thematic Connection: Shadows of the Imagination, p. 103

Formal Assessment Selection Test, pp. 102–103; Assessment Resources Software

Listening to Literature Audiocassettes

Literature CD-ROM

Where Is Here?

Joyce Carol Oates

For years they had lived without incident in their house in a quiet residential neighborhood when, one November evening at dusk, the doorbell rang, and the father went to answer it, and there on his doorstep stood a man he had never seen before. The stranger apologized for disturbing him at what was probably the dinner hour and explained that he'd once lived in the house— "I mean, I was a child in this house"—and since he was in the city on business he thought he would drop by. He had not seen the house since January 1949 when he'd been eleven years old and his widowed mother had sold it and moved away but, he said, he thought of it often, dreamt of it often, and never more powerfully than in recent months. The father said, "Would you like to come inside for a few minutes and look around?" The stranger hesitated, then said firmly, "I think I'll just poke around outside for a while, if you don't mind. That might be sufficient." He was in his late forties, the father's approximate age. He wore a dark suit, conservatively cut; he was hatless, with thin silver-tipped neatly combed hair; a plain, sober, intelligent face and frowning eyes. The father, reserved by nature, but genial and even gregarious when taken unaware, said amiably, "Of course we don't mind. But I'm afraid many things have changed since 1949."

So, in the chill, damp, deepening dusk, the stranger wandered around the property while the mother set the dining room table and the father peered covertly out the window. The children were upstairs in their rooms. "Where is he now?" the mother asked. "He just went into the garage," the father said. "The garage! What does he want in there!" the mother said uneasily. "Maybe you'd better go out there with him." "He wouldn't want anyone with him," the father said. He moved stealthily to another window, peering through the curtains. A moment passed in silence. The mother, paused in the act of setting down plates, neatly folded paper napkins, and stainless-steel cutlery, said impatiently, "And where is he now? I don't like this." The father said, "Now he's coming out of the garage," and stepped back hastily from the window. "Is he going now?" the mother asked. "I wish I'd answered the door." The father watched for a moment in silence then said, ❶

◆ Build Vocabulary

genial (jēn´ yəl) *adj.*: Cheerful; friendly

gregarious (grə ger´ ē əs) *adj.*: Sociable

covertly (kō vərt´ lē) *adv.*: Secretly; surreptitiously

Develop Understanding

Interest Grabber

Write this quotation on the chalkboard: "... at dusk, the doorbell rang, and the father went to answer it, and there on his doorstep stood a man he had never seen before ... [who] explained that he'd once lived in the house ..."

Have students imagine themselves in that situation. Ask what they would do if they were the father or the stranger. After discussion, have students make predictions about the story.

One-Minute Insight

A stranger rings a family's doorbell one night, asking to see their home, where he'd once lived as a chld. Not wanting to be rude, the owners reluctantly invite him in. The man moves from room to room, offering odd comments, noting uneasy coincidences, and making everyone feel anxious. The more he says, the more the family realizes that he's no ordinary visitor. They come to grasp their unexplainable link to terrible events of his past.

Customize for
English Language Learners
Oates uses architectural terms that students may not know, such as *mantel, fanlight,* and *leaded panes.* Display pictures of these features to help students form mental images of the house.

Customize for
Intrapersonal Learners
Have students look for details that convey tension or fear. Urge them to identify with the characters by asking questions like *How would I feel? What would I do? What would I say?* Students can jot down answers in a reader's response log.

◆ Critical Thinking

❶ **Analyze** Ask students how Joyce Carol Oates builds suspense and foreshadows danger in this passage. *Students may note the gloomy setting and the parents' anxiety as they stealthily spy on the stranger while he moves from place to place on the property.*

Cultural Connection

Visiting Etiquette In this story, the occupants of the house reluctantly invite a stranger into their home because they do not wish to appear rude or cruel. Ideas of hospitality vary from culture to culture. In some cultures, guests are expected to bring gifts to honor their hosts, while in other cultures, the reverse is true. Some cultures consider it dishonorable *not* to offer hospitality, even to total strangers or enemies. Encourage students to investigate customs of hospitality to strangers in their own or other cultures. You might compile the results as an informal guidebook for tourists.

▶Critical Viewing◀

1 Analyze The dark shadows across the side of the house, in contrast with the illumination of a portion of the house, add a sense of mystery or foreboding. The almost opaque quality of the lawn and the areas above and alongside the house create a fearful atmosphere. Because the surroundings are shrouded in darkness, the viewer can imagine all sorts of dangers lurking behind the house.

Customize for
Gifted/Talented Students

The stranger who visits the home begins his exploration by looking into the garage and around the backyard. As the father notes at the time, the stranger seems to have a slight limp. Have students revise the story line from this point so that it explains the limp.

▶ Critical Viewing
1 How does this photograph lend an air of mystery—even menace—to an ordinary house? **[Analyze]**

Beyond the Classroom

Career Connection

Realtor A real estate broker is a person who helps people buy and sell land, houses, or apartments. Most real estate brokers tour available properties to become acquainted with their features. Some obtain knowledge of the history of the property or of previous occupants. Many use computer databases to match interested buyers with available homes. Real estate brokers often have keys so they can get into houses or apartments when the occupants are away, or when a property is vacant. Invite a real estate broker to address the class about safety and security issues they face by having access to so many homes. Students might ask them how or if they screen buyers and how they protect the rights of the people whose homes they show to potential buyers.

Summer Nights, #18, 1985, Robert Adams, Museum of Modern Art

CONNECTIONS TO TODAY'S WORLD

"He's headed into the backyard." "Doing what?" the mother asked. "Not *doing* anything, just walking," the father said. "He seems to have a slight limp." "Is he an older man?" the mother asked. "I didn't notice," the father confessed. "Isn't that just like you!" the mother said.

2 She went on worriedly, "He could be anyone, after all. Any kind of thief, or mentally disturbed person, or even a murderer. Ringing our doorbell like that with no warning and you don't even know what he looks like!"

The father had moved to another window and stood quietly watching, his cheek pressed against the glass. "He's gone down to the old swings. I hope he won't sit in one of them, for memory's sake, and try to swing—the posts are rotted almost through." The mother drew breath to speak but sighed instead, as if a powerful current of feeling had surged through her. The father was saying, "Is it possible he remembers those swings from his childhood? I can't believe they're actually that old." The mother said vaguely, "They were old when we bought the house." The father said, "But we're talking about forty years or more, and that's a long time." The mother sighed again, involuntarily. "Poor man!" she murmured. She was standing before her table but no longer seeing it. In her hand were objects—forks, knives,
3 spoons—she could not have named. She said, "We can't bar the door against him. That would be cruel." The father said, "What? No one has barred any door against anyone." "Put yourself in his place," the mother said. "He told me he didn't *want* to come inside," the father said. "Oh—isn't that just like you!" the mother said in exasperation.

Without a further word she went to the back door and called out for the stranger to come inside, if he wanted, when he had finished looking around outside.

4 They introduced themselves rather shyly, giving names, and forgetting names, in the confusion of the moment. The stranger's handshake was cool and damp and tentative. He was smiling hard, blinking moisture from his eyes; it was clear that entering his childhood home was enormously exciting yet intimidating to him.

◆ Critical Thinking

2 Speculate Ask students: Based upon this paragraph, what do you think will happen next in the story? *Some students may say that something tragic, such as a robbery or kidnapping, might occur. Others might say that just because the mother expresses fears of what might happen does not mean anything bad actually will happen.*

◆ Critical Thinking

3 Draw Conclusions Discuss this apparent about-face by the mother. The mother had previously said that the stranger could be "any kind of thief, or mentally disturbed person, or even a murderer." Now the mother says that barring the door to the stranger "would be cruel." She even calls out to the stranger to come inside the house. Ask students why the mother reverses her opinion. *Some students may say that she simply thought things over and changed her mind. Others may say that something strange or sinister may be happening.*

Thematic Connection

4 Shadows of the Imagination Discuss with students whether the stranger's behavior is odd or rational. Point out the many shifts he makes as he speaks. What does the author want readers to think? *Students may say that the stranger tries to act normally, but he is agitated about something. Oates wants us to feel put off by him.*

Research Skills Mini-Lesson

Using Text Organizers

Introduce the Concept When students work on the project suggested as part of the Cultural Connection on p. 349, they will find that appropriate use of text organizers can help in locating and categorizing information as they do their research.

Develop Background Point out that text organizers include all the elements of a text that highlight the basic structure or organization of the text. Thus, chapter titles, heads and subheads, and any overviews or outline of the text are all text organizers.

Apply the Information When students begin to research the topic of hospitality as an aspect of culture, they should use text organizers to improve the efficiency of their search. For instance, they may find excellent information in a book that treats a particular culture in a general way. Using text organizers, students should see that much of the book would not be helpful, but that certain sections will speak directly to their topic. Have students make an outline of such a book, highlighting the places where the text is useful.

Assess the Outcome Evaluate students on the clarity of their outline and the value of the information it displays for the research project detailed on p. 349.

◆ Critical Thinking

❶ **Speculate** Have students speculate why the parents feel uncomfortable allowing the stranger to see their basement. *Students may say that a dusty basement is no place to take a guest; that the basement holds family mementos or piles of junk they wouldn't want a stranger to see; or that they're too suspicious of the man to go there with him.*

Comprehension Check ☑

❷ Ask students to summarize the coincidences the stranger has noted thus far. *Students should cite the same number of children in both families; that both families used the same seats at the table; and that the stranger, when he lived there, was the same age as their son is now.*

Thematic Connection

❸ **Shadows of the Imagination** Guide students to notice how the eerieness escalates here. *Students may say that the stranger now limps, he tests objects for materiality, as if he can't believe they are real, he mentions a stain that the current residents have never seen.*

CONNECTIONS TO TODAY'S WORLD

Repeatedly he said, "It's so nice of you to invite me in—I truly hate to disturb you—I'm really so grateful, and so—" But the perfect word eluded him. As he spoke his eyes darted about the kitchen almost like eyes out of control. He stood in an odd stiff posture, hands gripping the lapels of his suit as if he meant to crush them. The mother, meaning to break the awkward silence, spoke warmly of their satisfaction with the house and with the neighborhood, and the father concurred, but the stranger listened only politely, and continued to stare, and stare hard. Finally he said that the kitchen had been so changed—"so modernized"—he almost didn't recognize it. The floor tile, the size of the windows, something about the position of the cupboards—all were different. But the sink was in the same place, of course; and the refrigerator and stove; and the door leading down to the basement—"That *is* the door leading down to the basement, isn't it?" He spoke strangely, staring at the door. For a moment it appeared he might ask to be shown the basement but the moment passed, fortunately—this was not a part of their house the father and mother would have been comfortable showing to a stranger. ❶

Finally, making an effort to smile, the stranger said, "Your kitchen is so—pleasant." He paused. For a moment it seemed he had nothing further to say. Then, "A—controlled sort of place. My mother—When we lived here—" His words trailed off into a dreamy silence and the mother and father glanced at each other with carefully neutral expressions.

On the windowsill above the sink were several lushly blooming African violet plants in ceramic pots and these the stranger made a show of admiring. Impulsively he leaned over to sniff the flowers— "Lovely!"—though African violets have no smell. As if embarrassed he said, "Mother too had plants on this windowsill but I don't recall them ever blooming."

The mother said tactfully, "Oh they were probably the kind that don't bloom—like ivy."

In the next room, the dining room, the stranger appeared to be even more deeply moved. For some time he stood staring, wordless. With fastidious slowness he turned on his heel, blinking, and frowning, and tugging at his lower lip in a rough gesture that must have hurt. Finally, as if remembering the presence of his hosts, and the necessity for some display of civility, the stranger expressed his admiration for the attractiveness of the room, and its coziness. He'd remembered it as cavernous, with a ceiling twice as high. "And dark most of the time," he said wonderingly. "Dark by day, dark by night." The mother turned the lights of the little brass chandelier to their fullest: shadows were dispersed like ragged ghosts and the cut-glass fruit bowl at the center of the table glowed like an exquisite multifaceted jewel. The stranger exclaimed in surprise. He'd extracted a handkerchief from his pocket and was dabbing carefully at his face, where beads of perspiration shone. He said, as if thinking aloud, still wonderingly, "My father was a unique man. Everyone who knew him admired him. He sat *here*," he said, gingerly touching the chair that was in fact the father's chair, at one end of the table. "And Mother sat *there*," he said, merely pointing. "I don't recall my own place or my sister's but I suppose it doesn't matter. . . . I see you have four place settings, Mrs. . . .? Two children, I suppose?" "A boy eleven, and a girl thirteen," the mother said. The stranger stared not at her but at the table, smiling. "And so too *we* were—I mean, there were two of us: my sister and me." ❷

The mother said, as if not knowing what else to say, "Are you—close?"

The stranger shrugged, distractedly rather than rudely, and moved on to the living room.

This room, cozily lit as well, was the most carefully furnished room in the house. Deep-piled wall-to-wall carpeting in hunter green, cheerful chintz drapes, a sofa and matching chairs in nubby heather green, framed reproductions of classic works of art, a gleaming gilt-framed mirror over the fireplace: wasn't the living room impressive as a display in a furniture store? But the stranger said nothing at first. Indeed, his eyes narrowed sharply as if he were confronted with a disagreeable spectacle. He whispered, "Here too! Here too!"

He went to the fireplace, walking, now, with a decided limp; he drew his fingers with excruciating slowness along the mantel as if testing its materiality. For some time he merely stood, and stared, and listened. He tapped a section of wall with his knuckles—"There used to be a large water stain here, like a shadow." ❸

Cross-Curricular Connection: Math

The Mathematic Concept of Infinity The stranger in this story tries to draw a geometric figure that represents infinity. (See p. 354 of the story.) Students can use geometric figures to explore the concept of infinity. Those with access to Logo or similar computer software can try making recursive designs that appear to go on forever. Others can set up a series of mirrors to see how angles of reflection make figures seem to go on infinitely. Students can examine kaleidoscopes, spirographs, or other objects that use geometric designs to suggest infinity. Consult a geometry teacher for ideas on how students can explore this concept.

3 "Was there?" murmured the father out of politeness, and "Was there!" murmured the mother. Of course, neither had ever seen a water stain there.

Then, noticing the window seat, the stranger uttered a soft surprised cry, and went to sit in it. He appeared delighted: hugging his knees like a child trying to make himself smaller. "This was one of my happy places! At least when Father wasn't home. I'd hide away here for hours, reading, daydreaming, staring out the window! Sometimes Mother would join me, if she was in the mood, and we'd plot together—oh, all sorts of fantastical things!" The stranger remained sitting in the window seat for so long, tears shining in his eyes, that the father and mother almost feared he'd forgotten them. He was stroking the velvet fabric of the cushioned seat, gropingly touching the leaded windowpanes. Wordlessly, the father and mother exchanged a glance: who was this man, and how could they tactfully get rid of him? The father made a face signaling impatience and the mother shook her head without seeming to move it. For they couldn't be rude to a guest in their house.

The stranger was saying in a slow, dazed voice, "It all comes back to me now. How could I have forgotten! Mother used to read to me, and tell me stories, and ask me riddles I couldn't answer. 'What creature walks on four legs in the morning, two legs at midday, three legs in the evening?' 'What is round, and flat, measuring mere inches in one direction, and infinity in the other?' 'Out of what does our life arise? Out of what does our consciousness arise? Why are we here? Where *is* here?' " 4

The father and mother were perplexed by these strange words and hardly knew how to respond. The mother said uncertainly, "Our daughter used to like to sit here too, when she was younger. It *is* a lovely place." The father said with surprising passion, "I hate riddles—they're moronic some of the time and obscure the rest of the time." He spoke with such uncharacteristic rudeness, the mother looked at him in surprise.

5 Hurriedly she said, "Is your mother still living, Mr. . . .?" "Oh no. Not at all," the stranger said, rising abruptly from the window seat, and looking at the mother as if she had said something mildly preposterous. "I'm sorry," the mother said. "Please don't be," the stranger said. "We've all been dead—*they've* all been dead—a long time."

The stranger's cheeks were deeply flushed as if with anger and his breath was quickened and audible.

6 The visit might have ended at this point but so clearly did the stranger expect to continue on upstairs, so purposefully, indeed almost defiantly, did he limp his way to the stairs, neither the father nor the mother knew how to dissuade him. It was as if a force of nature, benign at the outset, now uncontrollable, had swept its way into their house! The mother followed after him saying nervously, "I'm not sure what condition the rooms are in, upstairs. The children's rooms especially—" The stranger muttered that he did not care in the slightest about the condition of the household and continued on up without a backward glance.

The father, his face burning with resentment and his heart accelerating as if in preparation for combat, had no choice but to follow the stranger and the mother up the stairs. He was flexing and unflexing his fingers as if to rid them of stiffness.

On the landing, the stranger halted abruptly to examine a stained-glass fanlight—"My God, I haven't thought of this in years!" He spoke excitedly of how, on tiptoe, he used to stand and peek out through the diamonds of colored glass, red, blue, green, golden yellow: seeing with amazement the world outside so *altered*. "After such a lesson it's hard to take the world on its own terms, isn't it?" he asked. The father asked, annoyed, "On what terms should it be taken, then?" The stranger replied, regarding him levelly, with a just perceptible degree of disdain, "Why, none at all."

7 It was the son's room—by coincidence, the stranger's old room—the stranger most wanted to see. Other rooms on the second floor, the "master" bedroom in particular, he decidedly did not want to see. As he spoke of it, his mouth twisted as if he had been offered something repulsive to eat.

The mother hurried on ahead to warn the boy and to straighten up his room a bit. No one had expected a visitor this evening! "So you have two children," the stranger murmured, looking at the father with a small quizzical smile. "Why?" The father stared at him as if he hadn't heard correctly. "'Why'? " he asked. "Yes. *Why?*" the stranger repeated. They looked

CONNECTIONS TO TODAY'S WORLD

4 Clarification The first riddle the stranger recites is the classic "Riddle of the Sphinx." The answer is man: He crawls on all fours as a baby in the morning of life, he walks upright in the midday of life, and he walks with a cane (the third leg) in the evening, or end of life. The answer to the second riddle may be a watch, which measures but a few inches in size but measures time endlessly. The other questions concern mysteries of life that philosophers have argued for ages.

Thematic Connection

5 Shadows of the Imagination
Ask students what they think about the stranger now. *Students may say that he is the ghost of the boy who once lived—and died—in the house.*

◆ Critical Thinking

6 Analyze Guide students to realize that the level of weirdness rises again at this point. The stranger is now out of control; he ignores his host; he mutters and rushes around the house at will. Ask students who they think the stranger is.

Thematic Connection

7 Shadows of the Imagination
Challenge students to infer the relationship between the stranger and his parents, or what may have happened to them. *Students may say that the stranger is the ghost of an eleven-year-old boy who may have killed his parents or may have been killed by them.*

Analyze an Author's Comment

Joyce Carol Oates has become one of the nation's most productive and respected literary figures. She was one of the youngest writers ever to win the National Book Award, which she received for her novel *Them,* and she has won dozens of other awards, fellowships, and tributes for her work.

Two recurring themes that critics have noted in Oates's writing are the violence that underpins much of her fiction, and the melancholy that is often present in he characters. Oates herself has commented on this, saying "A melancholy vision, a 'tragic' vision is inevitable . . . Uplifting endings and resolutely cheery world views are appropriate to television commercials but insulting elsewhere. It is not only wicked to pretend otherwise; it is futile."

Have students answer these questions in their journals.

1. As you were reading, was there a point at which you thought the story might take a more violent path?
2. In what ways does the story exemplify Oates' desire to avoid unrealistic cheerfulness?

◆ Critical Thinking

❶ **Infer** Have students infer in this passage what the stranger could mean by asking such an unexpected and startling question. *Students may infer that the stranger believes his parents did not love him, so he wonders why parents have children at all.*

◆ Critical Thinking

❷ **Draw Conclusions** In this passage, the stranger continues his habit of "testing materiality," rapping the window glass and noting the ceiling overhead. Ask students: Why is the stranger astonished by material things such as windows, walls, and ceilings? *Students may say that the stranger is no longer a part of the material world. He is a ghost to whom the material world is now foreign.*

Thematic Connection

❸ **Shadows of the Imagination** Have students connect this unexpected twist to details revealed earlier in the story. Ask them what threads come together here, and what may have happened in this house. *Students may say that the father's aversion to riddles echoes the stranger's feelings when he was a boy, suggesting a mysterious link between the father and the stranger. Perhaps the father represents the stranger as the man he never became because he died as a child. Perhaps the stranger's father tormented him with mathematical riddles that were beyond him, to the point where the boy, in a rage, killed his father, or the angry father killed his son.*

CONNECTIONS TO TODAY'S WORLD

❶ at each other for a long strained moment, then the stranger said quickly, "But you love them—of course." The father controlled his temper and said, biting off his words, "Of course."

"Of course, of course," the stranger murmured, tugging at his necktie and loosening his collar, "otherwise it would all come to an end." The two men were of approximately the same height but the father was heavier in the shoulders and torso; his hair had thinned more severely so that the scalp of the crown was exposed, flushed, damp with perspiration, sullenly alight.

❷ With a stiff avuncular formality the stranger shook the son's hand. "So this is your room, now! So you live here, now!" he murmured, as if the fact were an astonishment. Not used to shaking hands, the boy was stricken with shyness and cast his eyes down. The stranger limped past him, staring. "The same!—the same!—walls, ceiling, floor—window—" He drew his fingers slowly along the windowsill; around the frame; rapped the glass, as if, again, testing materiality; stooped to look outside—but it was night, and nothing but his reflection bobbed in the glass, ghostly and insubstantial. He groped against the walls, he opened the closet door before the mother could protest, he sat heavily on the boy's bed, the springs creaking beneath him. He was panting, red-faced, dazed. "And the ceiling overhead," he whispered. He nodded slowly and repeatedly, smiling. "And the floor beneath. That is what *is*."

He took out his handkerchief again and fastidiously wiped his face. He made a visible effort to compose himself.

The father, in the doorway, cleared his throat and said, "I'm afraid it's getting late—it's almost six."

The mother said, "Oh yes I'm afraid— I'm afraid it *is* getting late. There's dinner, and the children have their homework—"

The stranger got to his feet. At his full height he stood for a precarious moment swaying, as if the blood had drained from his head and he was in danger of fainting. But he steadied himself with a hand against the slanted dormer ceiling. He said, "Oh yes!—I know!—I've disturbed you terribly!—you've been so *kind*." ❸ It seemed, surely, as if the stranger *must* leave now, but, as chance had it, he happened to spy, on the boy's desk, an opened mathematics textbook and several smudged sheets of paper, and impulsively offered to show the boy a mathematical riddle—"You can take it to school tomorrow and surprise your teacher!"

So, out of dutiful politeness, the son sat down at his desk and the stranger leaned familiarly over him, demonstrating adroitly with a ruler and a pencil how "what we call 'infinity' " can be contained within a small geometrical figure on a sheet of paper. "First you draw a square; then you draw a triangle to fit inside the square; then you draw a second triangle, and a third, and a fourth, each to fit inside the square, but without their points coinciding, and as you continue—here, son, I'll show you—give me your hand, and I'll show you—the border of the triangles' common outline gets more complex and measures larger, and larger, and larger—and soon you'll need a magnifying glass to see the details, and then you'll need a microscope, and so on and so forth, forever, laying triangles neatly down to fit inside the original square *without their points coinciding*—!" The stranger spoke with increasing fervor; spittle gleamed in the corners of his mouth. The son stared at the geometrical shapes rapidly materializing on the sheet of paper before him with no seeming comprehension but with a rapt staring fascination as if he dared not look away.

After several minutes of this the father came abruptly forward and dropped his hand on the stranger's shoulder. "The visit is over," he said calmly. It was the first time since they'd shaken hands that the two men had touched, and the touch had a galvanic effect upon the stranger: he dropped ruler and pencil at once, froze in his stooped posture, burst into frightened tears.

Now the visit truly was over; the stranger, at last, *was* leaving, having wiped away his tears and made a stoical effort to compose himself; but on the doorstep, to the father's astonishment, he made a final, preposterous appeal—he wanted to see the basement. "Just to sit on the stairs?

◆ Build Vocabulary

avuncular (ə vuŋ´ kyo͞o lər) *adj.*: Having traits considered typical of uncles: jolly, indulgent, stodgy

galvanic (gal van´ ik) *adj.*: Startling; stimulating as if by electric current

Viewing and Representing Mini-Lesson

Introduce the Concept This mini-lesson supports the Floor Plans activity found in the Idea Bank on p. 356. It is designed to familiarize students with the basic "language" of floor plans.

Develop Background If possible obtain and present to students an actual set of architect's floor plans. Have them read the plans closely enough to note where familiar rooms or other places are in the plan. Have them note, too, how stairs, closets, doors, and various kinds of walls are rendered.

Apply the Information Before attempting the Floor Plans activity on p. 356, have students practice their ability to draw floor plans by drawing some of the basic architectural elements on paper as an architect would. Have them execute such basic features as stairs, walls, and doors.

Assess the Outcome Evaluate students on their ability to recreate architect's drawings of standard building elements faithfully.

In the dark? For a few quiet minutes? And you could close the door and forget me, you and your family could have your dinner and—"

The stranger was begging but the father was resolute. Without raising his voice he said, "No. *The visit is over.*"

He shut the door, and locked it.

Locked it! His hands were shaking and his heart beat angrily.

He watched the stranger walk away—out to the sidewalk, out to the street, disappearing in the darkness. Had the streetlights gone out?

Behind the father the mother stood apologetic and defensive, wringing her hands in a classic stance. "Wasn't that sad! Wasn't that—*sad!* But we had no choice but to let him in, it was the only decent thing to do." The father pushed past her without comment. In the living room he saw that the lights were flickering as if on the brink of going out; the patterned wallpaper seemed drained of color; a shadow lay upon it shaped like a bulbous cloud or growth. Even the robust green of the carpeting looked faded. Or was it an optical illusion? Everywhere the father looked, a pulse beat mute with rage. "*I* wasn't the one who opened the door to that man in the first place," the mother said, coming up behind the father and touching his arm. Without seeming to know what he did the father violently jerked his arm and thrust her away.

"Shut up. We'll forget it," he said.

"But—"

"*We'll forget it.*"

The mother entered the kitchen walking slowly as if she'd been struck a blow. In fact, a bruise the size of a pear would materialize on her forearm by morning. When she reached out to steady herself she misjudged the distance of the door frame—or did the door frame recede an inch or two—and nearly lost her balance.

In the kitchen the lights were dim and an odor of sourish smoke, subtle but unmistakable, made her nostrils pinch.

She slammed open the oven door. Grabbed a pair of pot holders with insulated linings. "*I* wasn't the one, . . ." she cried, panting, "and you know it."

CONNECTIONS TO TODAY'S WORLD ❹

Guide for Responding

◆ Literature and Your Life

Reader's Response Would you have reacted or behaved differently from the father and mother in the story? Why or why not?

Thematic Focus In what sense does this story explore the shadows of the imagination?

Questions for Research What makes a good suspense movie? Could this story be one? Ask questions relevant to suspense in movies. What resources could you use to research which suspense techniques work or fail?

☑ Check Your Comprehension

1. According to the stranger, when was the last time he saw the house?
2. How does the stranger react when the father tells him, "The visit is over"?
3. How do the rooms of the house seem changed after the stranger's visit?

◆ Critical Thinking

INTERPRET

1. How would you describe the characters of the father and mother in the story? **[Infer]**
2. What does the stranger do that makes the family uncomfortable or anxious? **[Analyze]**
3. How does the mother's attitude toward the stranger change? **[Connect]**
4. What details in the story suggest that the stranger's visit is some kind of bizarre, unnatural event? **[Interpret]**

EVALUATE

5. How well does Oates maintain suspense in the story? Explain. **[Evaluate]**

EXTEND

6. What advice might a police officer provide the couple after their experience? **[Career Link]**

Beyond the Selection

FURTHER READING

Other Works by Joyce Carol Oates

Bellefleur

Them

"Journey"

We suggest that you preview these works before recommending them to students.

INTERNET

You and your students may find additional information about Joyce Carol Oates on the Internet. We suggest the following site. Please be aware, however, that the site may have changed from the time we published this information.

Students can visit the Home Page of Joyce Carol Oates at **http://www.storm.usfca.edu/fac-staff/southerr/jco.html**

We *strongly recommend* that you preview the site before you send students to it.

Thematic Connection

❹ Shadows of the Imagination

Discuss how the lines blur between past and present and between reality and imagination. Ask students to develop an explanation of the characters now, based on the ending.

Students may say that the father killed his son (or vice versa); the boy's mother may have been made to take the blame, as echoed in the words of the modern mother: "I wasn't the one . . . and you know it." Or the boy may have killed both his parents, and his mother's last words were echoed by the modern mother.

Reinforce and Extend

Customize for
Less Proficient Readers

These students will benefit from rereading all or part of the story. In reviewing, students should focus on their best interpretation to see whether it fits the details.

Answers

◆ Literature and Your Life

Reader's Response Students should support their responses with allusions to the story.

Thematic Focus Sample response: This story concerns a mysterious, shadowy figure who is very uncomfortable discussing his life and past; some of his words and actions are ambiguous or unexplained, and after his visit, the mother and father of the house are left feeling violated and confused.

☑ Check Your Comprehension

1. He last saw the house in 1949, when he was eleven.
2. He cries, composes himself, then begs to be able to see the basement.
3. The rooms seem faded, dim, and shadowy.

(Answers continue on p. 356)

Answers

◆ Critical Thinking

1. Suggested response: They are "ordinary," unassuming citizens; both are proud and protective of their children and their home.
2. Suggested response: He asks personal questions and unsettling questions; he reveals odd bits of information about his own shadowy past; his behavior is intense, emotional, yet isolated and strange.
3. At first she is frightened by him; next, she pities him; then, she is interested in him; finally, she is annoyed by him.
4. Details include the stranger's slip of the tongue ("We've all been dead—*they've* all been dead . . .") and the physical changes in the house after he has left the premises.
5. Possible answer: Oates maintains suspense quite well. One of the chief ways in which she does so is by not saying at the beginning of the story just who the stranger is.
6. Sample response: A police officer might advise the couple to keep their doors locked and never to let a stranger inside the house.

Thematic Connection

1. Suggested response: Mystery plays a vital role in "Where *Is* Here?" The central mystery is the identification of the stranger.
2. Suggested response: Parson Hooper and the stranger are powerful because of the knowledge they hold from others.

Idea Bank

Customizing for *Performance Levels*

Following are suggestions for matching Idea Bank topics with your students' performance levels:
Less Advanced Students: 1
Average Students: 2, 4
More Advanced Students: 3, 5

Customizing for *Learning Modalities*

Following are suggestions for matching Idea Bank topics with your students' learning modalities:
Intrapersonal: 1
Verbal/Linguistic: 2
Logical/Mathematical: 3
Musical/Rhythmic: 4
Visual/Spatial: 5

Thematic Connection

SHADOWS OF THE IMAGINATION

The fiction of Poe, Hawthorne, and Melville is filled with shadowy characters, gloomy settings, and often tragic events. Similarly, Oates's story centers on a mysterious character whose actions and appearance contribute to the story's gloomy mood, or atmosphere.

1. Mystery plays an important role in the works of Poe, Hawthorne, and Melville. What is the role of mystery in Oates's story?
2. Compare Parson Hooper in "The Minister's Black Veil" and the stranger in "Where *Is* Here?" In what sense are they the most powerful figures in their respective stories? What role does imagination play in their power?

Idea Bank

Writing

1. **Diary Entry** How would either the husband or the wife describe the experience with the mysterious stranger? Assuming the role of one of the two characters, write a diary entry describing the stranger's visit and presenting your reactions to it.
2. **Comparison and Contrast** Both the villagers of Hawthorne's Milford in "The Minister's Black Veil" and the mother and father in Oates's "quiet residential neighborhood" are unnerved by the sudden appearance of something strange and mysterious. Write a short paper comparing and contrasting the reactions of the husband and wife with those of the townspeople.
3. **Essay** In "The Minister's Black Veil," Hawthorne uses many unnamed characters—*the sexton, the physician,* and *the bridegroom*—who are less developed than the central character, Parson Hooper. Similarly, Oates calls her characters *the father, the mother,* and *the stranger.* In an essay, discuss why Hawthorne and Oates may have chosen to leave these characters nameless.

Speaking, Listening, and Viewing

4. **Radio Presentation** Both "Where *Is* Here?" and "The Raven" contain elements of mystery and suspense—qualities that make both works good candidates for chilling dramatic readings. With a small group of classmates, prepare dramatic readings of these two works, as if they were being paired on a radio broadcast. Discuss whether you wish to use sound effects or music in either work. Then rehearse the readings and record them for your classmates. **[Performing Arts Link]**

Researching and Representing

5. **Floor Plans** The houses that figure centrally in "The Fall of the House of Usher" and "Where *Is* Here?" are radically different from each other. Review the two stories and jot down facts, details, and descriptions of these two structures. Then make labeled architect's diagrams of the floor plans of each house. **[Art Link; Math Link]**

Online Activity www.phlit.phschool.com

✓ ASSESSMENT OPTIONS

Formal Assessment, Selection Test, pp. 102–103, and Assessment Resources Software. The selection test is designed so that it can be easily customized to the performance levels of your students.

PORTFOLIO ASSESSMENT

Use the following rubrics in the ***Alternative Assessment*** booklet to assess student writing:
Diary Entry: Fictional Narrative Rubric, p. 110
Comparison and Contrast: Comparison/Contrast Rubric, p. 118
Essay: Literary Analysis/Interpretation Rubric, p. 127

Writing Process Workshop

Video Script

All day long, our eyes are awash in images from the mass media—from computer screens to the movies to television to advertising billboards. With all these polished images, it is easy to forget that the final product is only the tip of an iceberg: Hidden from the eye is a long process of careful planning and scripting.

Holding and pointing a video camera is easy, but did you ever try to craft a video script complete with story, dialogue, stage directions, and technical actions? Here's your chance to plan and create a video script for a drama, comedy, or documentary. Strive for visual images as sharp and memorable as the verbal ones you found in this unit in the works of Poe and Melville. The following skills, introduced in this section's Guided Writing Lessons, will help you to create your video script.

Writing Skills Focus

- ▶ **Use a style that is appropriate for your medium** and your type of project—depending on whether it is a drama, comedy, or documentary. You'll probably want to rely as much on visual images as dialogue. (See p. 315.)
- ▶ **Use precise details,** both visual and verbal, to create a vivid impression of the characters, setting, and events. (See p. 329.)
- ▶ **Use realistic dialogue** to enhance the impact of a fictional drama or comedy. (See p. 347.)

The following scene from Melville's *Moby-Dick* has been adapted as a video script.

Model

[CLOSEUP of Ahab on deck addressing the sailors] ①
AHAB: "What do ye do when ye see a whale, men?"
[WIDE SHOT of sailors on deck]
SAILORS: Sing out for him! [the sailors cry out enthusiastically, some raising harpoons above their heads] ②
[SHOT behind Ahab facing sailors]
AHAB: "Good!" [with a wild approval in his tones; observing the hearty animation into which his unexpected question had so magnetically thrown the men] ③

① *The explicit camera directions indicate the visual images to be presented.*

② *The dialogue is realistic for the time when it takes place.*

③ *Precise details in these stage directions vividly capture the sailors' attitudes.*

Prepare and Engage

LESSON OBJECTIVES

- To use recursive writing processes to write a video script
- To recognize appropriate sentence construction, eliminating unnecessary words

Establish Writing Guidelines To make students aware of some of the criteria on which their work will be evaluated, distribute the scoring rubrics for Drama (p. 124 in ***Alternative Assessment***). See the suggestions on p. 359 for customizing these rubrics to this workshop.

Refer students to the Writing Handbook, p. 1192, for instruction in the writing process, and p. 1195 for information on creative writing. You may also want to present to the class the Story Map Graphic Organizer (pp. 99–101) from the ***Writing and Language Transparencies.***

Connect to Literature To familiarize students with the conventions of stage directions and dramatic dialogue, review sections of Arthur Miller's *The Crucible* (p. 1089) as needed.

Writing Lab CD-ROM
If your students have access to computers, you may want to have them work in the tutorial on Creative Writing. Have students follow these steps:

1. Review the audio-annotated model of a video script.
2. View the video clips about gathering details for drama.
3. Draft on the computer.
4. Respond to a Self-Evaluation Checklist to help judge the effectiveness of their video scripts.

Beyond the Classroom

Career Connection

Script Writing Students may be familiar with the art of script writing from movies, television, and the theater. A career as a script writer can encompass these markets and others that require a grasp of basic script format. With increasing frequency, companies use videos for public relations purposes, to train employees, and to lure and inform potential investors. Explain that though writing scripts does not require a formal degree or intensive training, production experience in areas like directing, acting, or editing may be helpful. Ask students why this might be true. *Responses might include that experience in these roles, in which one is the intended audience for a script, might lend a writer a better sense of what sort of information to include in scripts—and what not to.*

Develop Student Writing

Prewriting Strategy
Students can annotate their lists of specific details to indicate whether items should be shown directly or conveyed better through voice-over or dialogue. You may also want to point out that scripts often contain a third way of providing information: Subtitles can superimpose text over a shot for the audience to read simultaneously. Such text typically establishes the setting, time, or other basic information.

Customize for
Visual/Spatial Learners
Encourage these students to develop storyboards—sketchlike illustrations with explanatory captions—to help them organize their ideas visually.

Customize for
Bodily/Kinesthetic Learners
Encourage these students to move around the actual set of their videos. This way, they can get a feel for the action to be captured on camera. For example, students can stride about like lawyers in a courtroom drama, or strike poses the band members might in a music video. Bodily/kinesthetic learners can jot down what they learn by observing their own gestures and pacing, and then incorporate these findings into their scripts.

Writing Lab CD-ROM
Students may benefit from completing the activities in the Considering Audience and Purpose sections of the tutorial.

Elaboration Strategy
When creating realistic dialogue, students may find it helpful to say lines aloud. By paying close attention to the way they "perform" the text, writers can get ideas for adding pauses and physical gestures. Encourage students to eliminate lines that do not sound natural.

Revision Strategy
Have students conduct mini-rehearsals of their scripts to aid in the revision process. Student actors can read directly from the scripts. This type of live reading is often used by professional screen writers to gauge the effectiveness of their work.

Applying Language Skills: Eliminating Unnecessary Words

Students sometimes overwrite, using too many words or an unnecessarily flowery tone. The most impressive prose, however, is simple and direct. Eliminate overwriting by condensing clauses to phrases and phrases to single words.

Wordy:
My father, who is a surgeon, has nerves of steel.

Better:
My father, a surgeon, has nerves of steel.

Practice Revise these wordy sentences.

1. On our walk, we reveled in a flurry of leaves that were falling.
2. Jorge, who is my friend, excels in soccer.

Writing Application Review your script, and pare down any bloated sentences.

Writer's Solution Connection
Language Lab
For more practice with editing unnecessary words, see the Writing Style lesson in the Language Lab.

Prewriting

Choose a Topic Your video script can be a work of fiction that springs from a combination of imagination and experience or a documentary based on an issue that concerns you. The key to finding a topic is choosing one that has meaning to you. Consider the topic ideas listed here or choose one of your own:

Topic Ideas
- Music video script
- Hiking in the wilderness
- A threat to the local environment (factory waste, an incinerator, overdevelopment)
- Contemporary styles in dress and fashion
- A fictional drama about conflict—betrayal by a friend, facing disease or natural disaster, a battle with conscience
- A courtroom drama

Use Specific Details Specific details are critical in bringing your script to life. If your script involves a fictional character, for example, don't scrimp on specifics of speech patterns, dress, outward mannerisms, or tone of voice. Likewise, a documentary achieves its impact by *showing*, not merely *telling*: a polluted river, the features of Thoreau's cabin, a personal interview with a role model, and so on.

Drafting

Create Realistic Dialogue Realistic dialogue is essential to making a teleplay come alive for your audience. Remember that people often speak in incomplete sentences and use contractions and slang expressions. As you write your dialogue, pause after each exchange and ask yourself: Can I imagine two people I know saying these things or do their words seem stilted and contrived? Here's one case where everyday speech, even slang, might be a more reliable guide than standard English.

Indicate Stage and/or Camera Directions Technical instructions are critical to a drama or documentary. Use clear and concise language in this portion of the text. You can recommend the actors' delivery, settings, costumes, and stage movements, as well as indicating camera angles. Be specific: This is your chance to communicate your vision.

Applying Language Skills
Eliminating Unnecessary Words Introduce this skill by explaining that in an effective video or film, footage is edited so that extraneous or low-impact segments are cut. The same philosophy must be followed when revising the script. Without careful editing, the high-energy visuals may be supported by slow-moving or heavy-sounding text. Point out that one advantage of scripts over other types of writing is that the writer can use images to convey information that otherwise might rely exclusively on words.

Answers
1. On our walk we reveled in a flurry of falling leaves.
2. My friend Jorge excels in soccer.

Revising

Use a Checklist Go back to the Writing Skills Focus on the first page of the lesson and use the items as part of a checklist to evaluate and revise your script.

- ▶ Is my language appropriate to the video medium and to my project?
- ▶ Have I provided enough precise details, both visual and verbal, to make the script come alive for the viewer?
- ▶ If my project is a fictional drama, have I checked the dialogue to make sure that it sounds natural?

Add to Stage and/or Camera Direction Sometimes adding a few words to your camera or stage directions can make all the difference. Look at this example:

REVISION MODEL

TASHTEGO: Captain Ahab, that white whale must be the same that some call Moby-Dick.

① [shouting]
AHAB: Moby-Dick? Do ye know the white whale, then, Tash?

① By adding this direction, the writer makes Ahab's emotions clear to both the reader and the actor.

Publishing

Videotape Your Script Share your work with an audience by capturing it on videotape. Follow these suggestions to successfully record your production:

- ▶ Use the stage directions to direct actors, set designers, and camera operators.
- ▶ Rehearse each scene in your script. Plan and practice where actors will stand, how they will move, and where the camera will be in each scene. Run through the action a few times before filming.
- ▶ Take advantage of the portability of the video camera, but don't take the technology for granted. Make sure that the audio and video are being recorded correctly.

APPLYING LANGUAGE SKILLS: Spoken vs. Written Language

In your script, be sensitive to the differences between written English and spoken English. Spoken language allows a wider range of informal expressions and may contradict the rules of grammar. Here's an example:

Written:
Jamie, whom I met at the theater, wishes to be an actor.

Spoken:
Jamie, who I met at the theater, wants to be an actor.

Although grammatically correct, "whom" is so rare in everyday speech that it makes the dialogue sound stilted.

Practice Rewrite these sentences in less formal spoken English.

1. I grew utterly exasperated at his obstinacy.
2. The quality of which I speak is self-esteem.

Writing Application Check that the dialogue in your script sounds natural and believable.

Writer's Solution Connection Writing Lab

To help you write your video script, use the instruction and activities in the tutorial on Creative Writing.

Writing Lab CD-ROM
A Revision Checker for Vague Adjectives in the Revising and Editing section of the tutorial can help students ensure that their scripts use precise details.

Publishing

Reassure students that it's normal for unanticipated issues to arise while videotaping their scripts. These might include the logistical limitations of a set or circumstances relating to budget and weather. Even under ideal conditions, a script is a flexible document to be used actively. Ultimately the public will judge a script by the finished product—the actual video.

Applying Language Skills

Spoken vs. Written English
Explain to students that the effective use of spoken English conventions will make their scripts more engaging for the audience.

Answers
1. I got frustrated with his stubbornness.
2. I'm talking about self-esteem.

For additional instruction, refer to the **Writing Lab CD-ROM** section on Using Dialogue to Develop Character.

Reinforce and Extend

Prentice Hall Writing and Grammar For more prewriting, elaboration, and revision strategies, see *Prentice Hall Writing and Grammar.*

✓ ASSESSMENT

PORTFOLIO ASSESSMENT
Use the rubric on drama in ***Alternative Assessment*** (p. 124) to assess students' writing. Add the following criteria to further customize the rubrics to this assignment.

	4	3	2	1
Eliminating Unnecessary Words	The writer's style is simple and direct, giving the impression that "each word counts."	For the most part the writer keeps the script free of unnecessary words.	The writer frequently overwrites, not shortening clauses and phrases to single words.	The writer consistently uses unnecessary words, lending the script an unappealing flowery tone.
Spoken vs. Written Language	The writer makes effective use of informal expressions and other examples of spoken language.	The writer uses the conventions of spoken language to enhance dialogue and voice-over narration.	The writer effectively makes use of informal expressions and other examples of spoken language.	The writer consistently relies on the conventions of written language, lending much of the script a stilted, formal tone.

Prepare and Engage

LESSON OBJECTIVES

- To monitor one's own reading strategies and make modifications when understanding breaks down, such as by rereading, using resources, and questioning

Customize for
Bodily/ Kinesthetic Learners
A motor activity, such as underlining, note taking, and writing margin comments, can help students stay involved with a text. Less experienced learners often need practice in highlighting or underlining; the tendency is to overmark. Small groups may read informational text silently, highlight main ideas, and then compare their judgments of what is essential information.

Apply the Strategies

Answers

1. A dictionary might be used to check the meaning of *motion* in the context of this letter.
2. A question such as, "Why does the writer mention God twice?" could lead to an understanding of the letter writer's argument. The writer wants his marriage proposal to be accepted since it is a sign of God's will.
3. The paragraph beginning "1st" is made of a sentence with more than 75 words in it. A helpful strategy for understanding the long, archaic text is to reread slowly, breaking apart the sentence into clauses and phrases. The main point, paraphrased, is that the writer believes that his strong feelings for someone after a short meeting must be a sign from God.

Student Success Workshop

Real-World Reading Skills — Monitoring Reading Strategies

Strategies for Success

In your reading, you may come across a passage or section that you find confusing or complex. When this happens, notice the way you read. Identify your reading strategies and be prepared to try others when one doesn't work. Break down, review, and research parts of what you've read, so that you understand it better.

Start Over Don't be surprised if you find it necessary to reread some passages or individual sentences. Read the entire text once for its general meaning, and then go back and reread it more carefully a second time. Pay attention to the organization of the text. This will help you understand the relationship of ideas in the text. Be sure to note any titles or section headings. Also, look for footnotes, illustrations, or captions that might help direct your understanding.

Use Resources When your understanding breaks down, turn to resources for clarification. Some, such as introductions and glossaries, can often be found right in the book you're reading. In other instances, you may need to consult an outside resource, such as a dictionary, atlas, or encyclopedia. For example, if you were reading about an event in another country, you might want to consult an atlas to help you envision that country's location and geography.

Ask Questions As you reread a text, write down any questions that come to mind. Writing down questions helps you think through the problem, and as you discover answers, you will gain a fuller understanding of what you've read. Many times, as you reread and continue reading, the answers to your questions will be found in the text.

Apply the Strategies

Monitor your reading strategies as you read this excerpt from a letter. Then, answer the questions that follow.

> *Malden March 23, 1691*
>
> *I make bold to spread before you these following considerations, which possibly may help to clear up your way before you return an answer unto the motion I have made to you. I hope you will take them in good part, and ponder them seriously.*
>
> *1st. I have a great persuasion that the motion is of God, for diverse reasons: [such] as, first, that I should get a little acquaintance with you by a short and transient visit, having been altogether a stranger to you before, and that so little acquaintance should leave such an impression behind it as neither length of time, distance of place, nor any other objects could wear off, but that my thoughts and heart have been toward you ever since.*
>
> *2ly. That upon serious, earnest, and frequent seeking of God for guidance and direction in so weighty a matter, my thoughts have still been determined unto and fixed upon yourself as the most suitable person for me. . . .*

1. What resources did you consult to help clarify your understanding?
2. How did the questions you wrote down assist you in understanding your reading?
3. Which section was the most difficult to understand? What strategies helped?

✔ *Here are some situations in which to monitor your reading strategies:*
- ▶ Reading a novel with many characters and settings
- ▶ Reviewing a set of involved directions
- ▶ Reading legal documents, such as contracts

Test Preparation Workshop

Reading Comprehension: Monitoring Reading Strategies
Students should keep in mind that most reading passages on standardized tests are followed by a question about the main idea. Recommend that students first read the whole passage at a normal-to-fast rate to get the main idea. Then the best monitoring strategy to use is scanning for specific information in the test questions.

Display this test item:

According to "Strategies for Success" on this page, you should use an atlas when—

A you look for footnotes and captions
B resources exist in the book you are reading
C the glossary lacks the definition you need
D a text description of a region could be clarified by a map

Discuss where in the text students looked for answers to a question about an atlas. A volunteer can demonstrate scanning the paragraphs to find mention of an atlas in the section "Use Resources" and then choosing the correct answer, D.

PART 3

The Human Spirit and the Natural World

Early Morning at Cold Spring, 1850, Asher B. Durand, Montclair Art Museum, Montclair, New Jersey

By the mid-1800's, The United States had firmly established itself as a nation. Inspired by the words and actions of writers in this section, the nation embraced a belief in individuality and an awareness of the vastness and beauty of nature.

One-Minute Planning Guide

The section introduces students to two of the most influential writers of the nineteenth century. Ralph Waldo Emerson and Henry David Thoreau helped define the American character by inspiring people to turn to nature in order to better understand both themselves and the universal truths. Students may be surprised to find that they share many of Emerson's views on nature and individuality expressed in *Nature* and "Self-Reliance." "The Snowstorm" and "Concord Hymn" reveal the poetic—and perhaps more accessible—side of Emerson's literary talent. Thoreau's views on how to live a productive life in *Walden* may intrigue students. Encourage them to evaluate the validity of his comments on government in *Civil Disobedience*. Connections to Today's World looks at how contemporary society interacts with the natural world.

Customize for *Varying Student Needs*

from *Nature*; from "Self-Reliance"; "The Snowstorm"; "Concord Hymn"

- Students may be challenged by the abstract concepts in the two essays.
- Personification and strong imagery bring "The Snowstorm" to life.

from *Walden*; from *Civil Disobedience*

- Most readers will be challenged by these essay excerpts.
- Less proficient readers and English language learners may need help breaking down lengthy sentences.
- Students can relate Thoreau's ideas on government in *Civil Disobedience* to contemporary views.

"Gardening"; "Hammer and a Nail"

- Accessible, contemporary narrative essay and song lyrics

Humanities: Art

Early Morning at Cold Spring, 1850, by Asher B. Durand.

One of the founders of the Hudson River School of painting, Asher Durand (1796–1886) began his career as an engraver, reproducing paintings by others and engraving banknotes; in fact, U.S. currency incorporates a number of the designs he developed. In his middle age, Durand turned to landscape painting and became one of the leaders of a group of northeastern artists who painted scenes from the Hudson River, Adirondack Mountains, and New England. Cold Spring is a city north of New York City along the Hudson River, a favorite area of Durand and his colleagues.

Have students link the art to the theme of Part 3, The Human Spirit and the Natural World, by answering these questions:

1. Why might the artist have painted solitary man, rather than a group of people, in such a setting? *He probably wanted to portray an individual quietly contemplating the beauty of the landscape.*
2. What does the human figure add to this tranquil landscape painting? *The figure adds a human dimension—it represents the human mind responding to or interacting with the beauty of nature.* Would you prefer the painting without it? Why or why not? *Some students might argue that nature should be enjoyed for its own sake; others may respond that by imagining what the man feels, the viewer's appreciation for the scene grows.*

LESSON OBJECTIVES

1. **To develop vocabulary and word identification skills**
   - Latin Word Roots: *-radi-*
   - Using the Word Bank: Antonyms or Synonyms?
2. **To use a variety of reading strategies to comprehend nonfiction**
   - Connect Your Experience
   - Reading Strategy: Challenge the Text
3. **To increase knowledge of other cultures and to connect common elements across cultures**
   - Connecting Themes Across Cultures
   - Idea Bank: Research
4. **To express and support responses to the text**
   - Critical Thinking
   - Idea Bank: Poem
   - Idea Bank: Advertisement
   - Idea Bank: Public-Service Announcement
5. **To analyze literary elements**
   - Literary Focus: Transcendentalism
   - Idea Bank: Critical Evaluation
6. **To read in order to research self-selected and assigned topics**
   - Idea Bank: Analysis
7. **To plan, prepare, organize, and present literary interpretations**
   - Idea Bank: Art
8. **To use recursive writing processes to write a letter to the editor**
   - Guided Writing Lesson
9. **To increase knowledge of the rules of grammar and usage**
   - Grammar and Style: Varying Sentence Length

Test Preparation

Reading Comprehension: Make Inferences and Generalizations (ATE, p. 363)
The teaching tips and sample test item in this workshop support the instruction and practice in the unit workshop:
Reading Comprehension: Analyze Information to Make Inferences and Generalizations (SE, p. 427)

Guide for Interpreting

Ralph Waldo Emerson

(1803–1882)

Individuality, independence, and an appreciation for the wonders of nature—these are just a few of the principles that Ralph Waldo Emerson helped to ingrain in our nation's identity. Although his ideas were sometimes considered controversial, he had a tremendous influence on the young people of his time, and his beliefs have continued to inspire people to this day.

Throughout his life, Emerson's mind was constantly in motion, generating new ideas and defining and redefining his view of the world. His natural eloquence in expressing these ideas—in essays, lectures, and poetry—makes him one of the most quoted writers in American literature.

A New England Childhood The son of a Unitarian minister, Emerson was born in Boston. When Emerson was eight, his father died. The boy turned to a brilliant and eccentric aunt, Mary Moody Emerson, who encouraged his independent thinking. At fourteen, Emerson entered Harvard, where he began the journal he was to keep all his life. After postgraduate studies at Harvard Divinity School, he became pastor of the Second Church of Boston.

Finding His Niche Emerson's career as a minister was short-lived. Grief-stricken at the death of his young wife, and dissatisfied with what he saw as the spiritual restrictions in Unitarianism, Emerson resigned after three years. He then went to Europe, where he met the English writers Thomas Carlyle, Samuel Taylor Coleridge, and William Wordsworth. On his return to the United States, Emerson settled in Concord, Massachusetts. He married again and began his lifelong career of writing and lecturing.

An Independent Thinker Emerson was a soft-spoken man, given to neither physical nor emotional excess.

> ***Beneath Emerson's calm, sober demeanor existed a restless, highly individualistic mind that resisted conformity.***

"Good men," he once wrote, "must not obey the laws too well."

Emerson first achieved national fame in 1841, when he published *Essays,* a collection based on material from his journals and lectures. He went on to publish several more volumes of essays, including *Essays, Second Volume* (1844), *Representative Men* (1849), and *The Conduct of Life* (1860).

Though Emerson was known mostly for his essays and lectures, he considered himself primarily a poet. "I am born a poet," he once wrote, "of a low class without doubt, yet a poet. That is my nature and my vocation." He published two successful volumes of poetry, *Poems* (1847) and *May-Day and Other Pieces* (1867). Like his essays, Emerson's poems express his beliefs in individuality and in humanity's spiritual connection to nature.

◆ Background for Understanding

PHILOSOPHY: EMERSON AND THE TRANSCENDENTAL CLUB

During the 1830's and 1840's, Emerson and a small group of like-minded intellectual friends gathered regularly in his study to discuss philosophy, religion, and literature. Among them were Emerson's protégé, Henry David Thoreau, as well as educator Bronson Alcott, feminist writer Margaret Fuller, and ex-clergyman and author George Ripley. The group, known as the Transcendental Club, developed a philosophical system that stressed intuition, individuality, and self-reliance.

In 1836, Emerson published "Nature," a lengthy essay that became the Transcendental Club's unofficial statement of belief. (For more on the Transcendentalists, see p. 221.)

Prentice Hall Literature Program Resources

REINFORCE / RETEACH / EXTEND

Selection Support Pages
Build Vocabulary: Latin Word Roots: *-radi-*, p. 104
Grammar and Style: Varying Sentence Length, p. 105
Reading Strategy: Challenge the Text, p. 106
Literary Focus: Transcendentalism, p. 107

Strategies for Diverse Student Needs, Identifying Key Ideas, p. 22

Beyond Literature
Community Connection, Local Landmarks, p. 22

Formal Assessment Selection Test, pp. 107–109; Assessment Resources Software

Alternative Assessment, p. 22

Writing and Language Transparencies
Writing Process Model: Persuasive Essay, pp. 33–36

Resource Pro CD-ROM

Listening to Literature Audiocassettes

from Nature ◆ *from* Self-Reliance ◆ The Snowstorm ◆ Concord Hymn

◆ Literature and Your Life

CONNECT YOUR EXPERIENCE

"Be true to yourself." "Follow your dream." Do these words sound familiar? Most of us have faced the choices these sentiments address: whether to conform to what's expected or to step out of the crowd and follow our own judgment. In "Self-Reliance," Emerson states his views on the matter in uncompromising terms, coming down squarely in favor of nonconformity.

Journal Writing Describe a time when you had to choose whether to follow others or to blaze your own trail.

THEMATIC FOCUS: THE HUMAN SPIRIT AND THE NATURAL WORLD

Emerson found spirituality and profound meaning in nature. How can a study of the natural world reveal the human spirit?

◆ Reading Strategy

CHALLENGE THE TEXT

When you read a work that presents an individual's ideas, don't simply accept the ideas, challenge them. To **challenge a text** simply means to question the author's assertions and reasoning. In "Self-Reliance," for example, Emerson states: "Whoso would be a man must be a nonconformist." Look for how he backs up this statement. Compare the evidence he offers with what you already know through personal experience or other reading. Then decide whether you agree with Emerson.

◆ Literary Focus

TRANSCENDENTALISM

Transcendentalism was an intellectual movement founded by Emerson that affected most of the writers of his day. The Transcendentalists believed that the human senses can know only physical reality. To the Transcendentalists, the fundamental truths of existence lay outside the reach of the senses and could be grasped only through intuition. As a result, the Transcendentalists focused their attention on the human spirit. They also had a deep interest in the natural world and its relationship to humanity. Through the careful observation of nature, they believed that the human spirit is reflected in the natural world. This led them to the conclusion that formed the heart of their beliefs: All forms of being—God, nature, and humanity—are spiritually united through a shared universal soul, or Over-Soul.

◆ Grammar and Style

VARY SENTENCE LENGTH

Good writers vary the length of their sentences to help sustain the reader's interest and to establish rhythm. Notice in this passage from "Nature" how Emerson follows a long sentence with a short one:

> Crossing a bare common, in snow puddles, at twilight, under a clouded sky, without having in my thoughts any occurrence of special good fortune, I have enjoyed a perfect exhilaration. I am glad to the brink of fear.

◆ Build Vocabulary

LATIN WORD ROOTS: *-radi-*

The Latin root *-radi-* means "spoke" or "ray." This root contributes to the meaning of *radiant*—"shining brightly" or "giving off rays of light"—a word that you'll find in "The Snowstorm." What other words can you think of that contain the Latin root *-radi-*?

WORD BANK

Before you read, preview this list of words.

- blithe
- connate
- chaos
- aversion
- suffrage
- divines
- radiant
- tumultuous
- bastions

Test Preparation Workshop

Reading Comprehension: Make Inferences and Generalizations The reading sections of standardized tests like the SAT require students to make inferences that are drawn from implied information in written texts. For example, students might be asked to recognize implied messages found in poetry.

According to the third stanza of "Concord Hymn," what is the purpose of the monument?

A to remember the sacrifices made by Revolutionary War soldiers
B to add support to the crumbling Lexington bridge
C to commemorate the British soldiers who died in the American Revolution
D to direct visitors to the towns of Lexington and Concord

The last three answers contain incorrect information. *A* is supported by the lines "That memory may their deed redeem, / When, like our sires, our sons are gone."

Interest Grabber In his writings, Emerson touches on an issue that is especially relevant to high-school students: conformity. Write the word *conformity* on the chalkboard. Create a two-column chart with the headings Advantages and Disadvantages. Then have the class brainstorm for a list of as many advantages and disadvantages of conformity as they can think of. Take a vote to see if students think that the advantages of conformity outweigh the disadvantages, or vice versa. Tell students that the writer whose works they're about to read is one of history's greatest champions of nonconformity.

Connecting Themes Across Cultures

Point out that several cultures have founded movements based on ideas similar to Emerson's. For example, Buddhist monks of Tibet, China, and India seek a greater connection to the world around them through meditation. Ask students to explain the appeal of Emerson's philosophy. How can people across cultures find connections between nature and the human spirit?

Customize for *Less Proficient Readers*

Have students read the essays in pairs or small groups, pausing at the end of each paragraph to identify the sentence that best sums up its meaning. Students should then try to restate the meaning of each topic sentence in their own words. Circulate through the class to check on the progress of the groups or pairs and clarify any misinterpretations.

Customize for *AP Students*

These students may be intrigued by Emerson's ideas. Encourage them to continue their exploration of Emerson by finding other essays in the library and sharing what they learn from these essays with their classmates.

Connecting to World Literature

To connect Emerson's writing to a world literature selection, see p. 1186.

Develop Understanding

One-Minute Insight In this excerpt from his book *Nature*, Emerson expresses his belief that the meaning of existence can be found by exploring the natural world. He describes how through an exploration of nature he has discovered that he is spiritually connected with the universe, with God, and with every living thing. This discovery is conveyed in the lines "I become a transparent eyeball; I am nothing; I see all; the currents of the Universal Being circulate through me, I am part or parcel of God."

◆ Background for Understanding

Inform students that *Nature* was a small, ninety-six-page book that Emerson published anonymously in Boston. It predated *The Dial* by four years. Almost everything Emerson wrote after *Nature* amplified or extended the ideas that appeared in it. The excerpts here come from the end of the first of seven sections, which is itself entitled "Nature."

◆ Literary Focus

❶ **Transcendentalism** Ask students to explain how the ideas presented in this passage reflect the beliefs of the Transcendentalists. *Students should respond that the passage suggests that in the natural environment of the woods people can more easily discover themselves and recognize universal truths.*

◆ Grammar and Style

❷ **Varying Sentence Length** Ask students: What effect does Emerson create by following three longer sentences with a short one? *Students should note that the shorter sentence stands out from the others, calling attention to the impact of the experience on Emerson.*

◆ Reading Strategy

❸ **Challenge the Text** Have students discuss whether Emerson supports his contention here that nature and humanity are spiritually connected. *Some students may say that Emerson's descriptions here sound more fanciful than factual.*

from

Nature

Ralph Waldo Emerson

Connections to World Literature, *page 1172*

Nature is a setting that fits equally well a comic or a mourning piece. In good health, the air is a cordial of incredible virtue. Crossing a bare common,[1] in snow puddles, at twilight, under a clouded sky, without having in my thoughts any occurrence of special good fortune, I have enjoyed a perfect exhilaration. I am glad to the brink of fear. In the woods, too, a man casts off his years, as the snake his slough, and at what period soever of life is always a child. In the woods is perpetual youth. Within these plantations of God, a decorum and sanctity reign, a perennial festival is dressed, and the guest sees not how he should tire of them in a thousand years. ❶ In the woods, we return to reason and faith. There I feel that nothing can befall me in life—no disgrace, no calamity (leaving me my eyes), which nature cannot repair. Standing on the bare ground—my head bathed by the blithe air and uplifted into infinite space—all mean egotism vanishes. I become a transparent eyeball; I am nothing; I see all; the currents of the Universal Being circulate through me; I am part or parcel of God. The name of the nearest friend sounds then foreign and accidental: to be brothers, to be acquaintances, master or servant, is then a trifle and a disturbance. I am the lover of uncontained and immortal beauty. In the wilderness, I find something more dear and connate than in the streets or villages. In the tranquil landscape, and especially in the distant line of the horizon, man beholds somewhat as beautiful as his own nature.

The greatest delight which the fields and woods minister is the suggestion of an occult relation between man and the vegetable. I am not alone and unacknowledged. ❷ They nod to me, and I to them. The waving of the boughs in the storm is new to me and old. It takes me by surprise, and yet is not unknown. ❸ Its effect is like that of a higher thought or a better emotion coming over me, when I deemed I was thinking justly or doing right.

Yet it is certain that the power to produce this delight does not reside in nature, but in man, or in a harmony of both. It is necessary to use these pleasures with great temperance. For nature is not always tricked[2] in holiday attire, but the same scene which yesterday breathed perfume and glittered as for the frolic of the nymphs is overspread with melancholy today. Nature always wears the colors of the spirit. To a man laboring under calamity, the heat of his

1. **common** *n.*: Piece of open public land.

2. **tricked** *v.*: Dressed.

◆ Build Vocabulary

blithe (blīth) *adj.*: Carefree

connate (kän′ āt) *adj.*: Existing naturally; innate

Block Scheduling Strategies

Consider these suggestions to take advantage of extended class time:

- If you have access to computers, have groups of students explore the information on Emerson and the Transcendentalists on the *The History of American Literature:* Part 1, Disk 2, Feature 2 in the **Literature CD-ROM Library.**
- Have students listen to Emerson's poems on the **Listening to Literature Audiocassettes.** Follow with a discussion of the differences between reading and listening to poetry.
- Divide students into discussion groups to respond to the Literature and Your Life and Critical Thinking questions following each selection. Have the discussion groups share their responses with the rest of the class, and use the responses as a springboard for class discussion.

Sunset, Frederick E. Church, Munson-Williams-Proctor Institute Museum of Art, Utica, New York

own fire hath sadness in it. Then there is a kind of contempt of the landscape felt by him who has just lost by death a dear friend. The sky is less grand as it shuts down over less worth in the population.

▲ **Critical Viewing** Emerson says that nature often allows us to become transparent eyeballs, seeing all, but detaching from the business of the world. How does this image reinforce his statement? **[Support]** 4

Guide for Responding

◆ Literature and Your Life

Reader's Response Which of your experiences have made you "glad to the brink of fear"?

Thematic Focus Do you find any evidence of Emerson's reverence for nature in American culture today? Explain.

☑ Check Your Comprehension

1. According to Emerson, where can we "return to reason and faith"?
2. What happens to Emerson when he stands with his head "uplifted into infinite space"?
3. What is the "greatest delight which the fields and woods minister"?

◆ Critical Thinking

INTERPRET

1. What does Emerson mean when he says that in the woods "a man casts off his years"? **[Analyze]**
2. What does Emerson mean when he describes himself as a "transparent eyeball"? **[Interpret]**
3. Find evidence in this essay to support the Transcendentalist belief in the unity of the human spirit and the natural world. **[Support]**

EVALUATE

4. How persuasive is Emerson? Explain why you do or do not accept his ideas about nature. **[Assess]**

EXTEND

5. In what ways is Emerson's attitude toward nature different from that of a scientist? **[Science Link]**

▶Critical Viewing◀

4 Support Students may refer to the painting's serenity, its apparent meshing of land and heavens, the reflection of the landscape in the water, and the complete absence of any traces of humankind.

Reinforce and Extend

Answers

Reader's Response Students' responses will be very personal, reflecting strong emotional reactions to joyful events.

Thematic Focus Some students may say that the urbanization of much of the American landscape shows that we no longer revere nature. Other students may respond that the growth of the environmental movement and the popularity of recreational activities such as hiking, camping, and gardening prove that Americans still value nature.

☑ Check Your Comprehension

1. We return to reason and faith in the woods.
2. His "mean egotism" vanishes; he becomes part of the universe.
3. It is the mysterious relationship between man and the plant world.

◆ Critical Thinking

1. People feel a childlike wonder in the presence of nature.
2. He himself is no longer important; he feels spiritually united with all forms of being.
3. Responses include: We find nature strange and surprising, yet familiar at the same time. Our ability to delight in nature comes neither from nature nor from man, but from the harmony of the two. The landscape always reflects the mood of its viewer.
4. Students' responses should be well reasoned and supported by their evaluation of Emerson's ideas.
5. Suggested response: A scientist would analyze nature to learn how it works; Emerson is more interested in his intuitive relationship to nature.

Humanities: Art

Sunset, 1856, by Frederic E. Church.

Frederic Church (1826–1900) was born in Connecticut. At sixteen, he became the only student of Thomas Cole, one of the leaders of a group of artists known as the Hudson River School. Church eventually went on to become a key member of that group. His work reveals his deep love of nature and his belief that painting should depict the natural world in a grand way. Draw students' attention to how this painting glows with the vibrancy of nature at the most colorful moment of the day. Have them compare Church's depiction of sunset with images of sunsets that stand out in their memories.

Use this question for further discussion:

Is this painting an appropriate illustration for Emerson's essay? Why or why not? *Some students will say that the painting is appropriate because it portrays the enduring grandeur of nature. Other students may remark that it would have been more appropriate to use a painting that portrayed a person appreciating a beautiful view of nature.*

Develop Understanding

One-Minute Insight

In this essay, which echoes a theme common to many of Emerson's speeches, Emerson exhorts readers to avoid blindly conforming to the ideas and behavior dictated by society or peers. He instead urges people to think and act independently.

Customize for
Less Proficient Readers
Encourage these students to look closely at the first sentence of each paragraph. These sentences essentially serve as an outline of the key points in the essay. By grasping the ideas in these sentences, students will be well on their way to identifying Emerson's main ideas.

Customize for
AP Students
Challenge your more advanced students to come up with reasons why self-reliance would have been an especially essential quality for people to possess during Emerson's day. *Students might point out that a majority of Americans lived on farms far from established towns and cities; such a rural and often isolated existence demanded self-reliance.*

◆ Reading Strategy

❶ **Challenge the Text** Ask students whether they agree that every person comes to these realizations. *Students are likely to respond that many people do not ever arrive at such realizations. Many people spend their whole lives conforming to expectations without thinking about it.*

◆ Literature and Your Life

❷ Ask students whether they agree with Emerson's assertion that only one's best efforts will bring satisfaction. Have them describe how their own experiences have or have not borne this out. *Students may respond that they feel satisfied when they do well, even if they have not put out their best efforts.*

◆ Reading Strategy

❸ **Challenge the Text** Students may agree with Emerson that society, by definition, breeds conformity. Or they may believe that there's room within it for self-reliance and individuality. Guide them to support their views with examples.

from

Self-Reliance

Ralph Waldo Emerson

There is a time in every man's education when he arrives at the conviction that envy is ignorance; that imitation is suicide; that he must take himself for better, for worse, as his portion; that though the wide universe is full of good, no kernel of nourishing corn can come to him but through his toil bestowed on that plot of ground which is given to him to till. The power which resides in him is new in nature, and none but he knows what that is which he can do, nor does he know until he has tried. ❶ Not for nothing one face, one character, one fact makes much impression on him, and another none. This sculpture in the memory is not without preestablished harmony. The eye was placed where one ray should fall, that it might testify of that particular ray. We but half express ourselves, and are ashamed of that divine idea which each of us represents. It may be safely trusted as proportionate and of good issues, so it be faithfully imparted, but God will not have his work made manifest by cowards. ❷ A man is relieved and gay when he has put his heart into his work and done his best; but what he has said or done otherwise, shall give him no peace. It is a deliverance which does not deliver. In the attempt his genius deserts him; no muse befriends; no invention, no hope.

Trust thyself: every heart vibrates to that iron string. Accept the place the divine providence has found for you; the society of your contemporaries, the connection of events. Great men have always done so and confided themselves childlike to the genius of their age, betraying their perception that the absolutely trustworthy was stirring at their heart, working through their hands, predominating in all their being. And we are now men, and must accept in the highest mind the same transcendent destiny; and not minors and invalids in a protected corner, but guides, redeemers, and benefactors. Obeying the Almighty effort and advancing on Chaos and the Dark. . . .

❸ Society everywhere is in conspiracy against the manhood of every one of its members. Society is a joint-stock company in which the members agree for the better securing of his bread to each shareholder, to surrender the liberty and culture of the eater. The virtue in most request is conformity. Self-reliance is its aversion. It loves not realities and creators, but names and customs.

> ◆ Reading Strategy
> **Challenge** this statement. Do you agree with Emerson?

Whoso would be a man must be a nonconformist. He who would gather immortal

Cross-Curricular Connection: Social Studies

Emerson's Abolitionist Views After the passage of the Fugitive Slave Act, which required people to return runaway slaves to the owners, Emerson became an active and vocal abolitionist. He remarked that anyone building a house should include space in it for fugitive slaves. Prompt students to discuss how Emerson's position on slavery relates to his statement in this essay that "Nothing is at last sacred but the integrity of your own mind."

Encourage interested students to find out more about the details of the Fugitive Slave Act and the Compromise of 1850 of which it was part. Have them research how the abolitionists responded to the law. Invite students to share any poignant incidents and anecdotes they come across.

palms must not be hindered by the name of goodness, but must explore if it be goodness. Nothing is at last sacred but the integrity of your own mind. Absolve you to yourself, and you shall have the suffrage of the world. . . .

4 A foolish consistency is the hobgoblin of little minds, adored by little statesmen and philosophers and divines. With consistency a great soul has simply nothing to do. He may as well concern himself with his shadow on the wall. 5 Speak what you think now in hard words and tomorrow speak what tomorrow thinks in hard words again, though it contradict everything you said today. "Ah, so you shall be sure to be misunderstood?"—is it so bad, then, to be misunderstood? Pythagoras was misunderstood, and Socrates, and Jesus, and Luther, and Copernicus, and Galileo, and Newton,[1] and every pure and wise spirit that ever took flesh. To be great is to be misunderstood. . . .

1. **Pythagoras . . . Newton:** Individuals who made major contributions to scientific, philosophical, or religious thinking.

◆ Build Vocabulary

Chaos (kā´ äs) *n.*: Disorder of formless matter and infinite space, supposed to have existed before the ordered universe

aversion (ə vʉr´ zhən) *n.*: Object arousing an intense or definite dislike

suffrage (suf´ rij) *n.*: Vote or voting

divines (də vīnz´) *n.*: Clergy

Guide for Responding

◆ Literature and Your Life

Reader's Response Which of Emerson's statements, if any, would you choose as a guideline for personal conduct? Explain.

Thematic Focus Transcendentalism is a uniquely American philosophy. What aspects of today's American culture reflect Emerson's belief in self-reliance?

Group Discussion Conforming to society's expectations can have its advantages and disadvantages, as can nonconformity. In small groups, discuss and list the pros and cons of each.

☑ Check Your Comprehension

1. According to the first paragraph, what conviction does every person eventually adopt?
2. How does Emerson describe society?
3. What is Emerson's view of consistency?

◆ Critical Thinking

INTERPRET

1. According to Emerson, why should people trust themselves? **[Analyze]**
2. How does Emerson believe people should be affected by the way others perceive them? **[Interpret]**
3. How does Emerson support his claim that "to be great is to be misunderstood"? **[Support]**

EVALUATE

4. Based on this essay, what is your assessment of Emerson's character? **[Assess]**

COMPARE LITERARY WORKS

5. Compare themes in Benjamin Franklin's writings with those in "Self-Reliance." Do you think Franklin would agree or disagree with Emerson's message? **[Compare]**

Reteach

In our fast-paced, mechanical society, students may have trouble understanding the basis of Transcendentalism. Explain that this philosophy centers on the sense of spirituality gained from a connectedness to the surrounding world. One way to achieve this is to reduce the unnecessary clutter in one's life, striving for simplicity and a return to the basics. Create activities that encourage students to experience life in a more direct sense. For example, you could have them walk to a destination rather than ride in a car. They could also hand-write their assignments rather than type them on a computer. Encourage students to help cook dinner or begin a craft. All these exercises will help them regain a transcendental connection to daily life.

◆ Critical Thinking

4 Assess Ask students if they have ever heard this statement. Discuss what it means, informing students that a hobgoblin is a frightening apparition. Point out that this statement is often misquoted—the first two words are omitted. Ask students to evaluate how the omission of those two words changes Emerson's meaning. *Students should respond that Emerson's original statement suggests that rigid consistency is bad. Without the first two words, the saying implies that consistency of any kind is bad.*

◆ Reading Strategy

5 Challenge the Text Tell students that what Emerson describes here is what we today might call "waffling." Ask students to tell what they think about his idea of the acceptability of self-contradiction. *Students may respond that it's acceptable to change one's mind if the change results from an ongoing process of education.*

Reinforce and Extend

Answers

Reader's Response Students' responses should reflect a careful reading of the essay.

Thematic Focus Students may cite our society's tendency to admire "self-made" people.

☑ Check Your Comprehension

1. Every person comes to accept who he or she is.
2. Emerson compares society to a joint-stock company, which conspires against individual self-reliance.
3. He feels that it restricts the freedom of great minds.

◆ Critical Thinking

1. People must trust in themselves because each of us has a part of the divine idea within.
2. People should not care how others perceive them.
3. He points out that some of the greatest people who've ever lived were misunderstood.
4. Students should back up their answers with details from the essay.
5. Students should support their answers with details from Franklin's writing.

Develop Understanding

One-Minute Insight In "The Snowstorm" Emerson develops an extended metaphor in which he compares nature's force during a snowstorm to an architect crafting a building. The poem conveys the message that nature is capable of creating works of amazing beauty that parallel or surpass those that any people can produce.

Comprehension Check ☑

❶ Who is the "he" referred to in these lines? *Students should respond that "he" refers to the north wind.*

Customize for ***Less Proficient Readers***

❷ Guide students to understand that the snowstorm, by coating manufactured structures, has created the illusion that it has formed from snow in a single night buildings that would take people years to build.

◆ Literary Focus

Transcendentalism Ask students to explain how this poem reflects the attitudes of Transcendentalists. *Students may say that nature, like humans, has a creative force. They may say that nature's creativity parallels that of humans.*

Customize for ***AP Students***

Invite students to compare Emerson's view of a snowstorm to that of John Greenleaf Whittier in his poem *Snowbound* (p. 266).

Customize for ***Less Proficient Readers***

To help these students paraphrase Emerson's poetry, use the ***Strategies for Diverse Student Needs*** page, Reword Author's Ideas (p. 22).

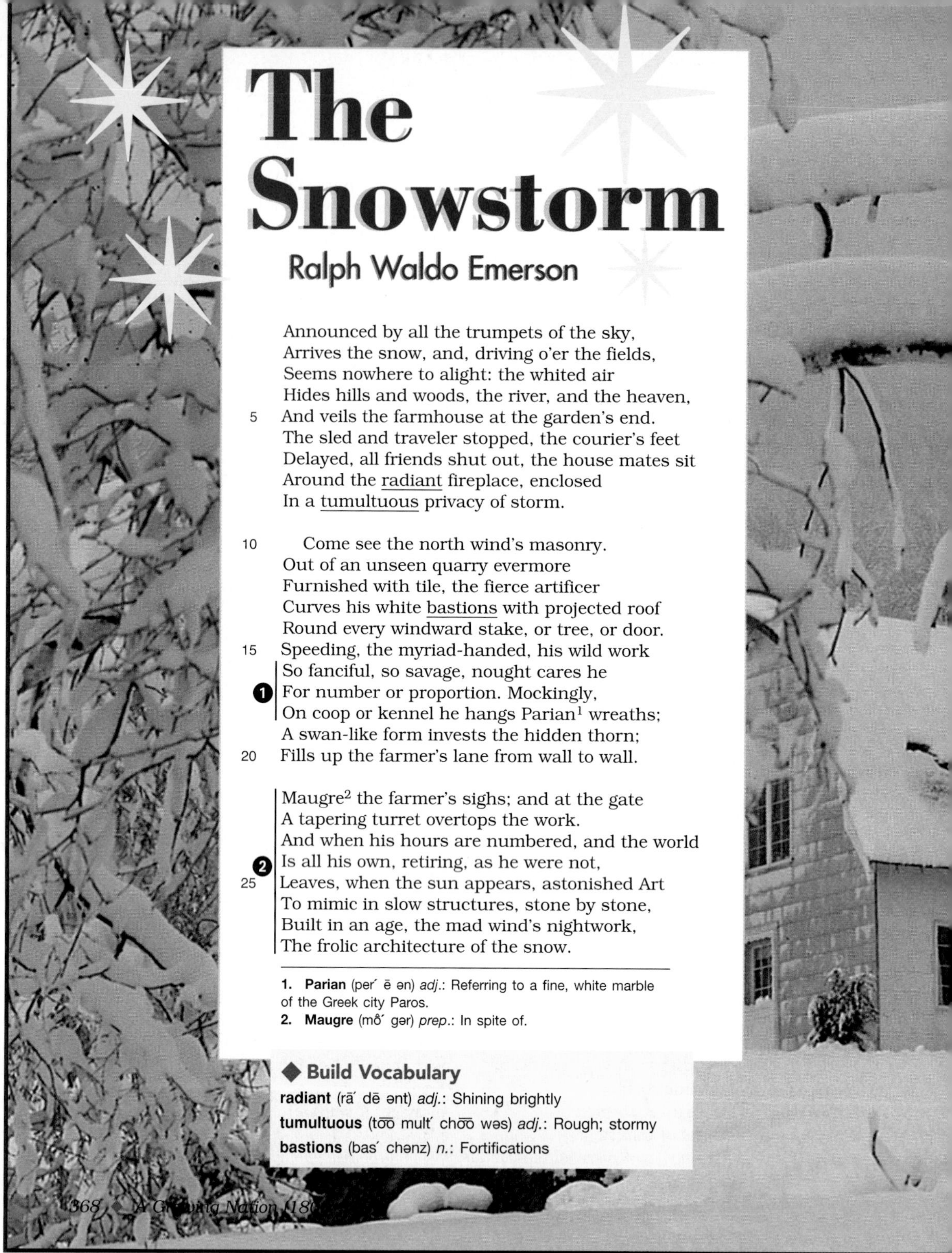

The Snowstorm

Ralph Waldo Emerson

Announced by all the trumpets of the sky,
Arrives the snow, and, driving o'er the fields,
Seems nowhere to alight: the whited air
Hides hills and woods, the river, and the heaven,
And veils the farmhouse at the garden's end.
The sled and traveler stopped, the courier's feet
Delayed, all friends shut out, the house mates sit
Around the radiant fireplace, enclosed
In a tumultuous privacy of storm.

Come see the north wind's masonry.
Out of an unseen quarry evermore
Furnished with tile, the fierce artificer
Curves his white bastions with projected roof
Round every windward stake, or tree, or door.
Speeding, the myriad-handed, his wild work
So fanciful, so savage, nought cares he
❶ For number or proportion. Mockingly,
On coop or kennel he hangs Parian[1] wreaths;
A swan-like form invests the hidden thorn;
Fills up the farmer's lane from wall to wall.

Maugre[2] the farmer's sighs; and at the gate
A tapering turret overtops the work.
And when his hours are numbered, and the world
❷ Is all his own, retiring, as he were not,
Leaves, when the sun appears, astonished Art
To mimic in slow structures, stone by stone,
Built in an age, the mad wind's nightwork,
The frolic architecture of the snow.

1. **Parian** (per´ ē ən) *adj.*: Referring to a fine, white marble of the Greek city Paros.
2. **Maugre** (mô´ gər) *prep.*: In spite of.

◆ Build Vocabulary

radiant (rā´ dē ənt) *adj.*: Shining brightly

tumultuous (to͞o mult´ cho͞o wəs) *adj.*: Rough; stormy

bastions (bas´ chənz) *n.*: Fortifications

Humanities: Art

Minute Man, 1871–1875, by Daniel Chester French.

Daniel Chester French completed this commemorative statue (p. 369) for the centennial of the American Revolution. The project was funded by a Concord resident who wished to memorialize the spot where Americans fell. The Minute Man was cast using bronze from condemned Civil War cannons. Emerson, a member of the committee that requested the work, praised the statue at its unveiling.

Guide students to notice the position of the soldier's feet and the plow on which his hand rests. Then use these questions for discussion:

1. What is the significance of the minuteman's firm grip on the plow? *It symbolizes that he is a peaceful farmer who took up a rifle because his land and freedom were threatened.*
2. Why do you think French placed the minuteman's right foot in a raised position? *It shows that the soldier is ready to leave his work in the field to join the impending fight.*

▲ **Critical Viewing** This poem was written for the unveiling of this monument commemorating the minutemen, who fought the British at Lexington and Concord, Massachusetts, in April 1775. How does the sculpture communicate the emotions of the poem? **[Connect]** ❹

Concord Hymn

Sung at the Completion of the Battle Monument, April 19, 1836

Ralph Waldo Emerson

By the rude[1] bridge that arched the flood,
  Their flag to April's breeze unfurled,
Here once the embattled farmers stood,
  And fired the shot heard round the world.

The foe long since in silence slept;
  Alike the conqueror silent sleeps;
And Time the ruined bridge has swept
  Down the dark stream which seaward creeps.

On this green bank, by this soft stream,
  We set today a votive[2] stone;
That memory may their deed redeem,
  When, like our sires, our sons are gone.

Spirit, that made those heroes dare
  To die, and leave their children free,
Bid Time and Nature gently spare
  The shaft we raise to them and thee. ❸

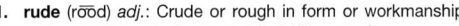

1. **rude** (ro͞od) *adj.*: Crude or rough in form or workmanship.
2. **votive** (vōt′iv) *adj.*: Dedicated in fulfillment of a vow or pledge.

Guide for Responding

◆ Literature and Your Life

Reader's Response Do you think it is important to build war monuments? Why or why not?

Thematic Focus What beliefs and values does the poet convey in these poems?

☑ Check Your Comprehension

1. Summarize the action of "The Snowstorm."
2. (a) In "Concord Hymn," what event took place by the "rude bridge"? (b) What has since happened to the bridge?
3. According to "Concord Hymn," what may redeem the farmers' deeds?

◆ Critical Thinking

INTERPRET

1. In "The Snowstorm," Emerson compares the storm and an artist at work. How does he develop this comparison in the poem? **[Analyze]**
2. What element in "The Snowstorm" expresses Emerson's belief in a spiritual unity betwen humanity and nature? Explain. **[Support]**
3. In "Concord Hymn," what is Emerson's attitude toward the minutemen? Explain. **[Infer]**

EXTEND

4. Having read both his essays and his poetry, where do you think Emerson's greater talent lies? Explain. **[Literature Link]**

One-Minute Insight

In this poem, Emerson celebrates the bravery of the minutemen who fought at Lexington and Concord. The poem conveys the message that people who make great sacrifices for noble causes such as freedom will never be forgotten.

◆ Background for Understanding

History In April 1775, a British military force went to confiscate colonial arms they knew was stockpiled in Concord, Massachusetts. Along the way, they were confronted at dawn, April 19, by a small group of militia on the Lexington green. The British dispersed the Americans, killing ten, and then moved on to Concord, five miles away. There, they were met by a larger contingent of militia, who attacked them at the North Bridge. At this spot, the first British blood of the Revolution was spilled. The British retreated to Boston. On the way, they were repeatedly attacked by thousands of American militia.

Customize for
Less Proficient Readers

❸ Help these students paraphrase the wish that Emerson expresses in this stanza. *Emerson asks the same Creator or Spirit who inspired the bravery of the minutemen to command time and nature to spare the monument from the ravages of time and weather.*

▶Critical Viewing◀

❹ **Connect** Students should note that, like the poem, the statue captures the bravery and devotion of the minutemen.

Reinforce and Extend

Enrichment To spark student interest in the memorials in your area, use the Community Connection: Local Landmarks page in ***Beyond Literature*** (p. 22).

Answers

Reader's Response Most students will probably feel that it is important to honor war heroes.

Thematic Focus He expresses his respect for bravery and sacrifice.

(Answers continue on p. 370)

Beyond the Selection

FURTHER READING

Other Works by Ralph Waldo Emerson

Essays: "The Over-Soul," "The American Scholar," "The Conduct of Life"

The Complete Works of Ralph Waldo Emerson, Edward W. Emerson, ed.

The Letters of Ralph Waldo Emerson, Ralph L. Rusk, ed.

INTERNET

You can find additional information about Emerson on the Internet. Please be aware, however, that the site may have changed since this information was published.

For a comprehensive Ralph Waldo Emerson page with links to other sites and information on Transcendentalism, go to **http://miso.wwa.com/~jej/1emerson.html**

We *strongly recommend* that you preview the site before you send students to it.

Answers *(continued from p. 369)*

◆ Critical Thinking

1. The north wind is described as an artificer who has carved, formed, and hung shapes. The wind leaves overnight work that mimics human architectural efforts that took ages to create.
2. The poem personifies nature as an "artificer" who creates architecture that mimics our own, underscoring Emerson's belief that humans can find a parallel to their own creative force in nature.
3. Suggested response: Emerson seems reverent toward the minutemen and grateful for their courage.
4. Students should support their responses with their evaluations of Emerson's strengths and weaknesses as both an essayist and poet.

◆ Reading Strategy

1. Emerson claims that only small-minded people are strictly consistent; people with great minds speak their opinions, even if they change with time. Inconsistency will make you misunderstood, just as the greatest and wisest people in history have been misunderstood.
2. Sample responses: People who are inconsistent don't take the time to think before they speak. People who are misunderstood are not necessarily great; they may just lack the ability to explain themselves clearly.
3. Students should explain the reasoning behind their responses.

◆ Literary Focus

Suggested responses:

1. The Transcendentalists had a deep love for nature and a deep interest in humanity's relationship with nature. Emerson says that nature has the power to fill him with great joy and to experience child-like wonder. He also expresses the belief that nature reflects our personal moods.
2. "I become a transparent eyeball; I am nothing; I see all; the currents of the Universal Being circulate through me; I am part and parcel of God." "The greatest delight which fields and woods minister is the suggestion of an occult relation between man and the vegetable. I am not alone and unacknowledged."
3. The Transcendentalists believed that since real truths cannot be found in physical reality, you have to trust what your intuition tells you, even if it changes from day to day.

Guide for Responding *(continued)*

◆ Reading Strategy

Challenge the Text

In "Nature" and "Self-Reliance," you encountered the opinions of one of the most individualistic men of nineteenth-century letters. By **challenging the text,** or questioning his assertions, you can reach an informed decision about whether or not you agree with the ideas he presents.

Look at this assertion from "Self-Reliance": "A foolish consistency is the hobgoblin of little minds. . . ." Challenge the assertion by answering these questions.

1. What evidence does Emerson provide to support his position?
2. Offer two arguments against this statement.
3. After weighing both sides of this controversial statement, explain whether you agree with it. Support your answer.

◆ Literary Focus

Transcendentalism

Emerson's writings introduce readers to **Transcendentalism**, the intellectual movement that asserted that knowledge of fundamental reality was beyond the reach of a person's limited senses and was derived through intuition rather than sensory experience. Transcendentalists focused on the human spirit, the spiritual relationship between humanity and nature, and an optimistic belief in human potential. At the core of their philosophy was the belief that all forms of being are spiritually united through a shared universal soul, or Over-Soul.

1. What does "Nature" reveal about the Transcendentalists' attitude toward nature? Support your answers with specific examples from the text.
2. Find two passages in "Nature" that express the Transcendentalists' belief in the Over-Soul.
3. Toward the end of "Self-Reliance," Emerson writes: "Speak what you think now in hard words and tomorrow speak what tomorrow thinks in hard words again, though it contradict everything you said today." Explain how this statement reflects the Transcendentalist belief in the importance of intuition.

◆ Build Vocabulary

Using the Latin Root *-radi-*

The Latin root *-radi-* means "spoke" or "ray." Knowing this, write a definition for each of these words.

1. radiator
2. radiation
3. radical
4. radiology
5. radio

Using the Word Bank: Antonyms or Synonyms?

Read the following word pairs. In your notebook, label each pair *A* for *antonyms*, or *S* for *synonyms*.

1. chaos, order
2. aversion, repugnance
3. suffrage, vote
4. divines, ministers
5. blithe, anxious
6. connate, acquired
7. radiant, luminous
8. tumultuous, serene
9. bastions, bulwarks

◆ Grammar and Style

Varying Sentence Length

In "Nature" and "Self-Reliance," Emerson often follows a very long sentence with one or more short ones. If he had relied entirely on long sentences, he could easily have lost the reader's interest or made his writing difficult to follow. On the other hand, if he'd relied mainly on short sentences, his writing would have been choppy. By varying the length of his sentences, he makes his writing lively and engaging. In addition, you may notice that he often uses a short sentence to clarify or emphasize ideas he's expressed in the longer sentence preceding it.

Looking at Style Find three passages from Emerson's essays in which he varies the length of his sentences. Explain the effect of the sentence variation in each passage.

Writing Application Rewrite the following passage to create more sentence variety.

Like Emerson, I love nature. I enjoy taking long walks. Most often, I walk in a forest near my house. The ground is covered with pine needles. I usually take a path that leads to a waterfall. When I reach the waterfall, I take time to reflect on events in my life.

◆ Build Vocabulary

Using the Latin Root *-radi-*

Sample responses:

1. A radiator projects heat into a room.
2. Radiation is the emission of energy as rays or waves.
3. A person or idea is radical if it is outside the norm.
4. Radiology is the medical use of X-rays.
5. A radio receives waves from a transmitter and converts them into sound which radiates from its speakers.

Using the Word Bank

1. A 2. S 3. S 4. S 5. A
6. A 7. S 8. A 9. S

◆ Grammar and Style

Looking at Style Students should identify passages in which sentence length varies by at least ten words.

Writing Application

Sample response: Like Emerson, I love nature. I enjoy taking long walks, most often in the forest near my house. The ground is covered with pine needles. I usually take a path that leads to a waterfall, where I take time to reflect on events in my life.

Build Your Portfolio

Idea Bank

Writing

1. Poem About Nature Write a poem that expresses experiences, sensations, or emotions you have had in connection with nature.

2. Advertisement Suppose you wanted to form a group similar to the Transcendentalist Club. How would you attract members? In an advertisement, inform and persuade people to join.

3. Critical Evaluation Write an essay summarizing "Self-Reliance" and stating your opinion of its ideas and the way in which these ideas are expressed. Back up your opinion with examples.

Speaking, Listening, and Viewing

4. Public-Service Announcement Drawing from Emerson's words and ideas, create a public-service announcement encouraging people to resist conformity. Record your announcement and share it with the class. **[Media Link]**

5. Analysis Many art movements arose from an artist's nonconformity. In an art history book, find an artist whose work differs from the mainstream. Describe how his or her work is unique. **[Art Link; Music Link; Performing Arts Link]**

Researching and Representing

6. Art Illustrate a vivid phrase from "Nature" in any way you choose. Draw a picture, find a piece of music, or create and perform a dance. **[Art Link; Music Link; Performing Arts Link]**

7. Research According to Emerson, the misunderstood individual joins the ranks of Pythagoras, Socrates, Jesus, Joan of Arc, Martin Luther, Copernicus, Galileo, and Newton. Research one of these "great souls" to learn how or why the person was misunderstood. Share your findings with your classmates. **[Social Studies Link]**

Online Activity www.phlit.phschool.com

Guided Writing Lesson

Letter to the Editor

If Emerson were alive today, he would probably be a dedicated conservationist. Choose a current environmental issue, and decide where you stand on it. Write a letter to the editor of a local newspaper expressing your opinion and defending it with reasons, facts, or examples. The more personal your examples are, the more persuasive your letter will be.

Writing Skills Focus: Elaboration to Make Writing Personal

One way to **elaborate** on, or develop, the ideas in a piece of writing is to share personal experiences or observations. For example, if you're writing about pollution in a local lake, you might describe how you used to swim at the lake as a child, and point out that on a recent visit you noticed that no one swims there anymore. Sharing such experiences not only helps make your writing convincing by demonstrating your firsthand knowledge, but it also helps to establish a personal connection to your readers.

Prewriting Make a list of the main points you want to make. Jot down personal experiences and obserations you can use to support each point. In addition, you may want to gather other facts and statistics you can use for support.

Drafting Start your letter by stating your main points up front. Then support your points by presenting your experiences and observations, along with any facts and statistics you've gathered. Throughout your letter, be as direct and to the point as possible.

Revising Have a classmate read your letter and suggest ways to make it more personal, direct, and convincing.

✓ ASSESSMENT OPTIONS

Formal Assessment, Selection Test, pp. 107–109, and Assessment Resources Software. The selection test is designed so that it can be easily customized to the performance levels of your students.

Alternative Assessment, p. 22, includes options for less advanced students, more advanced students, intrapersonal learners, visual/spatial learners, and interpersonal learners.

PORTFOLIO ASSESSMENT
Use the following rubrics in the ***Alternative Assessment*** booklet to assess student writing:
Poem About Nature: Poetry Rubric, p. 123
Advertisement: Persuasion Rubric, p. 120
Critical Evaluation: Response to Literature Rubric, p. 125
Guided Writing Lesson: Letter to the Editor, Persuasion Rubric, p. 120

Idea Bank

Customizing for
Performance Levels
Following are suggestions for matching Idea Bank topics with your students' performance levels:
Less Advanced Students: 1, 6
Average Students: 2, 4, 7
More Advanced Students: 3, 5

Customizing for
Learning Modalities
Following are suggestions for matching Idea Bank topics with your students' learning modalities:
Verbal/Linguistic: 4, 5
Interpersonal: 5
Intrapersonal: 6
Visual/Spatial: 6
Logical/Mathematical: 5, 7

Guided Writing Lesson

Writing and Language Transparencies To help students develop an understanding of the key elements of persuasion, display and discuss the various stages of the Writing Process Model: Persuasive Essay, pp. 33–36.

For more prewriting, elaboration, and revision strategies, see *Prentice Hall Writing and Grammar.*

Writers at Work Videodisc
Have students view the videodisc segment (Ch. 4) featuring Gasby Greely, vice president of communications for the National Urban League, to see how she approaches the challenges of persuading her audience. Prompt students to discuss how Greely organizes her ideas before she begins to write. How might her approach help them organize their own letters?

Play frames 22513 to 31258

Writing Lab CD-ROM
Have students complete the tutorial on Persuasion. Follow these steps:
1. Have students use the Pros and Cons chart to help them gather evidence to use in their letters.
2. Have students draft on computer.
3. Have students use the Persuasive Word Bins to strengthen word choice as they revise.

LESSON OBJECTIVES

1. **To develop vocabulary and word identification skills**
   - Latin Roots: *-flu-*
   - Using the Word Bank: Synonyms
2. **To use a variety of reading strategies to comprehend nonfiction**
   - Reading Strategy: Evaluate the Writer's Statement of Philosophy
3. **To increase knowledge of other cultures and to connect common elements across cultures**
   - Connecting Themes Across Cultures (ATE)
4. **To express and support responses to the text**
   - Critical Thinking
   - Idea Bank: Letter to the Editor
   - Idea Bank: Debate
   - Idea Bank: Television Script
5. **To analyze literary elements**
   - Literary Focus: Style
   - Idea Bank: Comparison-and-Contrast Essay
6. **To read in order to research self-selected and assigned topics**
   - Idea Bank: Report
   - Idea Bank: Walden Pond Research
7. **To use recursive writing processes to write a persuasive essay**
   - Guided Writing Lesson: Persuasive Essay
8. **To increase knowledge of the rules of grammar and usage**
   - Grammar and Style: Infinitives and Infinitive Phrases

Test Preparation

Reading Comprehension: Make Inferences and Generalizations (ATE, p. 373)
The teaching tips and sample test item in this workshop support the instruction and practice in the unit workshop:
Reading Comprehension: Analyze Information to Make Inferences and Generalizations (SE, p. 427)

Guide for Interpreting

Henry David Thoreau
(1817–1862)

From the time he was a child, Henry David Thoreau was known by his Concord, Massachusetts, neighbors as an eccentric. He rarely followed rules. He was independent, strong willed, and not very dedicated to his studies, but his mother's love of nature and her own drive convinced him to pursue an education. Thoreau went to Concord Academy, a college preparatory school, and five years later he enrolled at Harvard, where he pursued his studies in his own unique style.

Although Harvard University's code called for students to wear black, Thoreau wore green.

Questioning Authority Thoreau always questioned the rules that were presented to him. When his objection to corporal punishment forced him to quit his first teaching job, Thoreau and his older brother John opened their own school in Concord. The school was quite successful, but they had to close it when John became ill.

In 1842, Thoreau moved into the house of another famous Concord resident, Ralph Waldo Emerson. He lived there for two years, performing odd jobs to pay for his room and board. While there, Thoreau was fascinated by Emerson's Transcendentalist beliefs, and soon Thoreau became Emerson's close friend and devoted disciple.

Deciding not to go back to teaching and refusing to pursue another career, Thoreau dedicated himself to testing the Transcendentalist philosophy through experience. By simplifying his needs, Thoreau was able to devote the rest of his life to exploring and writing about the spiritual relationship between humanity and nature and supporting his political and social beliefs.

On Walden Pond For two years (1845–1847) Thoreau lived alone in a cabin he built himself at Walden Pond outside of Concord. Thoreau's experiences during this period provided him with the material for his masterwork, *Walden* (1854). Condensing his experiences at Walden Pond into one year, Thoreau used the four seasons as a structural framework for the book.

A unique blend of natural observation, social criticism, and philosophical insight, *Walden* is now generally regarded as the supreme work of Transcendentalist literature.

Carefully and deliberately crafted, Thoreau's work reflects the economy for which he strove throughout his life and about which he wrote in *Walden*.

When Henry David Thoreau died of tuberculosis at the age of forty-four, his work had received little recognition. However, his reputation has steadily grown since his death. His work has inspired writers, environmentalists, and social and political leaders. It has made generations of readers aware of the possibilities of the human spirit and the limitations of society.

◆ Background for Understanding

HISTORY: THOREAU AND THE MEXICAN WAR

The Mexican War was a conflict between Mexico and the United States that took place from 1846 to 1848. The war was caused by a dispute over the boundary between Texas and Mexico, as well as Mexico's refusal to discuss selling California and New Mexico to the United States. Believing that President Polk had intentionally provoked the conflict before having congressional approval, Thoreau and many other Americans strongly objected to the war. To demonstrate his disapproval, Thoreau refused to pay his taxes and was forced to spend a night in jail for his convictions. After that experience, Thoreau wrote "Civil Disobedience," urging people to resist governmental policies with which they disagree.

Prentice Hall Literature Program Resources

REINFORCE / RETEACH / EXTEND

Selection Support Pages
Build Vocabulary: Latin Roots: *-flu-*, p. 108
Grammar and Style: Infinitives and Infinitive Phrases, p. 109
Reading Strategy: Evaluate the Writer's Statement of Philosophy, p. 110
Literary Focus: Style, p. 111

Strategies for Diverse Student Needs, p. 23

Beyond Literature
Cross-Curricular Connection: Social Studies, p. 23

Formal Assessment Selection Test, pp. 110–111; Assessment Resources Software

Alternative Assessment, p. 23

Writing and Language Transparencies
Writing Process Models: Persuasive Essay, pp. 33–36

Resource Pro CD-ROM

Listening to Literature Audiocassettes

from Walden ◆ from Civil Disobedience

◆ Literature and Your Life

Connect Your Experience

In today's world, we rely on countless modern conveniences—cellular phones, computers, televisions. Not long ago, all of these things existed only in the imagination. Although most of us don't ever think about it, some people wonder whether technological advances have really made life better—or just more complicated.

Thematic Focus: The Human Spirit and the Natural World

The time in which Thoreau lived was also an age in which modernization was bringing about rapid change. As the experiences described in *Walden* reveal, Thoreau believed that people needed to simplify their lives and rekindle their connection with nature.

Journal Writing Explain what you think it would be like to live in the woods without modern conveniences.

◆ Literary Focus

Style

Style refers to the manner in which a writer puts his or her thoughts into words. In *Walden*, Thoreau's style is closely related to his purpose, which is to encourage us to examine the way we live and think. To achieve his purpose, Thoreau constructs paragraphs so that the sentences build to a climax.

Like Emerson, who admired Thoreau's style, most contemporary readers and critics are struck by the strength and vigor of Thoreau's writing. Within his most effective paragraphs, the sentences build to create an effect that can be compared to a hammer driving a nail into wood.

◆ Grammar and Style

Infinitives and Infinitive Phrases

Infinitive phrases combine an **infinitive** (the basic form of the verb preceded by the word *to*) and its complements and modifiers. Infinitive phrases function as nouns, adjectives, or adverbs.

Noun: I dearly love *to talk.* [functions as object of the verb *love*]

Adjective: It seemed to me that I had several more lives *to live.* [modifies the noun *lives*]

Adverb: This was an airy . . . cabin, fit *to entertain a traveling god.* [modifies the participle *fit*]

◆ Reading Strategy

Evaluate the Writer's Statement of Philosophy

Thoreau wrote to educate himself and his audience. He outlined a philosophy, a system of beliefs and values, that guided his life and actions. As a reader, you are not bound to accept everything you see in print. In fact, when reading essays like those of philosophers, you should **evaluate the writer's philosophy.** To do this, pay special attention to the proof or support the writer provides to back up his or her outlook. Compare the writer's ideas and supporting details with your own experiences.

◆ Build Vocabulary

Latin Roots: *-flu-*

Thoreau uses the word *superfluous* to describe things that are unnecessary. The Latin root *-flu-*, found in words like *fluid, fluent,* and *influence*, means "flow." The word *superfluous* means "overflowing" or "exceeding what is sufficient."

Word Bank

Before you read, preview this list of words from the selections.

dilapidated
sublime
superfluous
evitable
magnanimity
expedient
posterity
alacrity

Test Preparation Workshop

Reading Comprehension: Make Inferences and Generalizations Many standardized tests specify that students make generalizations drawn from evidence presented in the text. To help students practice making generalizations, have them complete this sample test item:

> I heartily accept the motto, "That government is best which governs least"; and I should like to see it acted up to more rapidly and systematically.

Based on this statement, Thoreau probably believes that—

A governments should be more involved in the lives of the people.
B people could do more if governments did less.
C the American people need help from the government to improve the country.
D government should be abolished.

B is the most accurate generalization, because it is based on details from the passage.

Interest Grabber Share with students the following quotation from Thoreau: "I went to the woods because I wished to live deliberately, to front only the essential facts of life." Have students imagine that they are about to spend a stretch of time alone in the wilderness. Ask them to tell what essentials they would bring with them other than the necessities associated with food and shelter. Prompt them to predict what the experience would be like, physically, emotionally, and spiritually. Invite students who have spent any time in wilderness areas to tell about it. Explain that the works they are about to read are drawn from the ideas and philosophies Thoreau developed while voluntarily living a life of rustic isolation.

Customize for
Less Proficient Readers

Students may find the lengthy sentences, figurative language, and nineteenth-century diction to be challenging. To help them overcome these obstacles, have them listen to the selections on audiocassette as they follow along in their texts. Pause periodically to help them paraphrase passages and break long sentences down into logical parts.

Customize for
AP Students

Guide students to be on the lookout for passages in which Thoreau uses fresh metaphors and poetic images to support his philosophy. Have them note the images and metaphors that stand out for them, and explain how the images and metaphors contribute to the effectiveness of Thoreau's essay. Why would the essay have been much less effective if Thoreau had not used figurative language?

Customize for
English Language Learners

The difficult language in these selections will challenge English language learners. Before having them read the selections, preview the vocabulary words, and work with them to develop sentences using each of the words. To provide more support, you may want to have students listen to one or both of the selections on audiocassette.

Develop Understanding

One-Minute Insight *Walden* was published in 1854, seven years after Thoreau's two-year residence at Walden Pond. During the intervening years, Thoreau reflected upon and revised the journals he had kept at Walden. A celebration of life and nature, *Walden* presents Thoreau's views on society and his philosophy of life. In sections that follow, Thoreau expresses the belief that society has become too complicated and fast-paced and that people should do everything possible to simplify their lives. He also stresses the need to resist conformity and to follow our own inner voices, and he suggests that by doing so people can experience a spiritual awakening.

Looking at Literature Videodisc To provide students with a preview of the ideas expressed in *Walden*, play Chapter Six of the videodisc. Then ask students how the setting and living conditions at Walden may have influenced Thoreau's thinking.

Chapter 6

Literature CD-ROM To build further background on Thoreau, have students explore *The History of American Literature:* Part 1, Disk 2, Features 2 and 3.

❶ **Clarification** This excerpt is from the second of the eighteen chapters that make up *Walden.*

◆ Reading Strategy

❷ **Evaluate the Writer's Statement of Philosophy** Ask: What does this passage reveal about Thoreau's outlook? *It reveals that the home, not the village, is central to Thoreau.*

Customize for *Gifted/Talented Students* Challenge students to deduce the implications of Thoreau's comment that "a man is rich in proportion to the number of things which he can afford to let alone." Do they agree or disagree with Thoreau?

from

Walden

Henry David Thoreau

❶ *from* Where I Lived, and What I Lived For

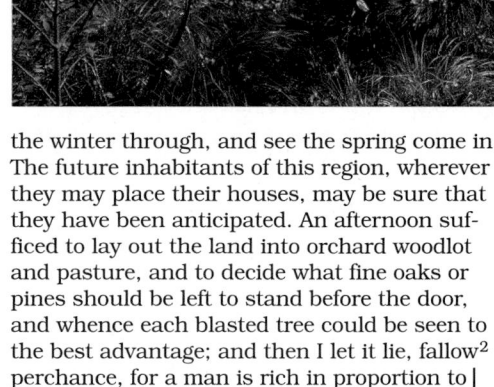

At a certain season of our life we are accustomed to consider every spot as the possible site of a house. I have thus surveyed the country on every side within a dozen miles of where I live. In imagination I have bought all the farms in succession, for all were to be bought, and I knew their price. I walked over each farmer's premises, tasted his wild apples, discoursed on husbandry[1] with him, took his farm at his price, at any price, mortgaging it to him in my mind; even put a higher price on it—took everything but a deed of it—took his word for his deed, for I dearly love to talk—cultivated it, and him too to some extent, I trust, and withdrew when I had enjoyed it long enough, leaving him to carry it on. This experience entitled me to be regarded as a sort of real-estate broker by my friends. Wherever I sat, there I might live, and the landscape radiated from me accordingly. What is a house but a *sedes*, a seat?—better if a country seat. ❷ I discovered many a site for a house not likely to be soon improved, which some might have thought too far from the village, but to my eyes the village was too far from it. Well, there might I live, I said; and there I did live, for an hour, a summer and a winter life; saw how I could let the years run off, buffet the winter through, and see the spring come in. The future inhabitants of this region, wherever they may place their houses, may be sure that they have been anticipated. An afternoon sufficed to lay out the land into orchard woodlot and pasture, and to decide what fine oaks or pines should be left to stand before the door, and whence each blasted tree could be seen to the best advantage; and then I let it lie, fallow[2] perchance, for a man is rich in proportion to the number of things which he can afford to let alone. ❸

My imagination carried me so far that I even had the refusal of several farms—the refusal was all I wanted—but I never got my fingers burned by actual possession. The nearest that I came to actual possession was when I bought the Hollowell Place, and had begun to sort my seeds, and collected materials with which to make a wheelbarrow to carry it on or off with; but before the owner gave me a deed of it, his wife—every man has such a wife—changed her mind and wished to keep it, and he offered me ten dollars to release him. Now, to speak the truth, I had but ten cents in the world, and it surpassed my arithmetic to tell, if I was that

1. **husbandry** (huz´ bən drē) *n.*: Farming.

2. **fallow** (fal´ ō) *adj.*: Left uncultivated or unplanted.

From J. Lyndon Shanley, ed., *Walden: The Writings of Henry D. Thoreau.* Copyright © 1971 by Princeton University Press. Excerpts, pp. 81–98 and 320–333, reprinted with permission of Princeton University Press.

Block Scheduling Strategies

Consider these suggestions to take advantage of extended class time:

- Build background and engage student interest by playing the segment on Thoreau and Walden on the **Looking at Literature Videodisc** (Ch. 6).
- Read the selections aloud, with students taking turns reading. Pause to clarify the meaning of difficult words.
- Have students work in small groups to identify the key elements of Thoreau's writing style.
- Follow with a class discussion in which the groups share their conclusions.
- As an extension activity, have students write a paragraph modeled on Thoreau's style. Encourage students students to share their paragraphs.
- Allow time for students to research Thoreau or Walden Pond on the Internet (see the Internet note on p. 381 for suggested Web sites). They can use the information to help them complete the Television Script or Walden Pond Research activities in the Idea Bank (p. 383).

◀ Critical Viewing Based on this picture, what do you think it would be like to live at Walden Pond? **[Speculate]** ❹

man who had ten cents, or who had a farm, or ten dollars, or all together. However, I let him keep the ten dollars and the farm too, for I had carried it far enough; or rather, to be generous, I sold him the farm for just what I gave for it, and, as he was not a rich man, made him a present of ten dollars, and still had my ten cents, and seeds, and materials for a wheelbarrow left. I found thus that I had been a rich man without any damage to my poverty. But I retained the landscape, and I have since annually carried off what it yielded without a wheelbarrow. With respect to landscapes:

> "I am monarch of all I *survey*,
> My right there is none to dispute."[3]

I have frequently seen a poet withdraw, having enjoyed the most valuable part of a farm, while the crusty farmer supposed that he had got a few wild apples only. Why, the owner does not know it for many years when a poet has put
❺ his farm in rhyme, the most admirable kind of invisible fence, has fairly impounded it, milked it, skimmed it, and got all the cream, and left the farmer only the skimmed milk.

The real attractions of the Hollowell farm, to me, were: its complete retirement, being about two miles from the village, half a mile from the nearest neighbor, and separated from the highway by a broad field; its bounding on the river, which the owner said protected it by its fogs from frosts in the spring, though that was nothing to me; the gray color and ruinous state of the house and barn, and the dilapidated fences, which put such an interval between me and the last occupant; the hollow and lichen-covered apple trees, gnawed by rabbits, showing what kind of neighbors I should have; but above all, the recollection I had of it from my earliest voyages up the river, when the house was concealed behind a dense grove of red maples, through which I heard the house-dog bark. I ❻
was in haste to buy it, before the proprietor finished getting out some rocks, cutting down the hollow apple trees, and grubbing up some young birches which had sprung up in the pasture, or, in short, had made any more of his improvements. To enjoy these advantages I was ready to carry it on; like Atlas,[4] to take the world on my shoulders—I never heard what compensation he received for that—and do all those things which had no other motive or excuse but that I might pay for it and be unmolested in my possession of it; for I knew all the while that it would yield the most abundant crop of the kind I wanted if I could only afford to let it alone. But it turned out as I have said.

All that I could say, then, with respect to farming on a large scale (I have always cultivated a garden) was that I had had my seeds ❼
ready. Many think that seeds improve with age. I have no doubt that time discriminates between the good and the bad; and when at last I shall plant, I shall be less likely to be disappointed. But I would say to my fellows, once for all, As long as possible live free and uncommit- ❽
ted. It makes but little difference whether you are committed to a farm or the county jail.

3. **"I . . . dispute":** From William Cowper's *Verses Supposed to Be Written by Alexander Selkirk*.

4. **Atlas** (at′ ləs): From Greek mythology, a Titan who supported the heavens on his shoulders.

◆ Build Vocabulary

dilapidated (di lap′ ə dā tid) *adj.*: In disrepair

◆ Reading Strategy

❸ **Evaluate the Writer's Statement of Philosophy** Discuss the meaning of this statement. Lead students to see that Thoreau is asserting that the fewer encumbrances there are on one's life, the richer and freer that life will be. How do students react to this outlook? *Given today's emphasis on material possessions, students may have a different outlook from Thoreau's. If students express disagreement, encourage them to cite evidence to back up their position.*

▶Critical Viewing◀

❹ **Speculate** Students may respond that it must have been beautiful, yet isolated. Others may say that it would be boring to live so far from society and modern conveniences.

◆ Critical Thinking

❺ **Interpret** Have students interpret the meaning of Thoreau's anecdote. *Students may say that Thoreau means that one needn't farm a piece of land to extract richness from it.*

Customize for
Less Proficient Readers

❻ Lead less proficient readers toward an understanding of the central point of this lengthy paragraph: Thoreau considers an ideal property one that is isolated and in a natural, "unimproved" condition.

◆ Literature and Your Life

❼ Thoreau says, "time discriminates between the good and the bad." What evidence can students come up with from their own lives to either support or refute Thoreau's position? *Students may share a variety of responses, ranging from whether the popularity of a rock band lasts over time to which of the plants in a garden will survive.*

◆ Reading Strategy

❽ **Evaluate the Writer's Statement of Philosophy** Ask students to explain what Thoreau means when he comments that it makes little difference whether one is on a farm or in a jail. *Students should respond that Thoreau believes that once you make a commitment to something—even to caring for a farm—you have lost your freedom as completely as a person in a prison.*

Cross-Curricular Connection: Social Studies

Touring Walden Pond Today, tourists come from all over the world to visit Walden Pond. Some are drawn by the natural beauty of the place; others by its literary and historical significance. The pond and the surrounding forestland is now a public park preserve, the Walden Pond State Reservation. There are guided walks along the many pathways surrounding the pond, and visitors are welcome to swim, boat, picnic, and hike. During the summer months, large numbers of people from the area around Walden Pond go to the state park Pond to sunbathe on public beaches.

A re-creation of Thoreau's cabin stands a few dozen feet from the site of his original home. In a tradition begun decades ago, visitors still leave rocks and notes to Thoreau piled on the site. Above the house site, the stumps of some of the 400 white pines Thoreau planted can still be seen; they were wiped out by the great hurricane of 1938.

◆ Grammar and Style

❶ Infinitives and Infinitive Phrases Ask students to identify examples of infinitives and infinitive phrases in this passage and to determine how each functions. *Following are the examples in this passage: "to write an ode to dejection," which functions as an object of the verb propose; "to brag as lustily as chanticleer in the morning," which functions as the object of the verb propose; and "to wake my neighbors up," which functions as an adverb modifying to brag.*

◆ Reading Strategy

❷ Evaluate the Writer's Statement of Philosophy Lead students to recognize that this paragraph is a statement of Thoreau's purpose in going to live at Walden Pond. Encourage students to restate Thoreau's purpose in their own words. *Students may paraphrase the passage as follows: Thoreau went to live at Walden to experience what it was like to live a simple, deliberate life. He wished to immerse himself in the experience of living in the woods, focusing all of his energy on drawing meaning from the experience.*

◆ Literary Focus

❸ Style Discuss with students the style in which this paragraph is written. Lead them to see that with each sentence Thoreau drives home the point he makes in the opening sentence. Also point out the poetic rhythm of Thoreau's writing.

Enrichment The beliefs that Thoreau expresses in these passages are echoed in the theme of the film *Dead Poets Society*. As an enrichment activity, you may wish to show portions of this film, or have students view it on their own. Be aware, however, that the film does address some sensitive issues, including teen suicide. Preview the film to decide whether you feel it is appropriate for your students.

Old Cato,[5] whose "De Re Rustica" is my "Cultivator," says, and the only translation I have seen makes sheer nonsense of the passage, "When you think of getting a farm, turn it thus in your mind, not to buy greedily; nor spare your pains to look at it, and do not think it enough to go round it once. The oftener you go there the more it will please you, if it is good." I think I shall not buy greedily, but go round and round it as long as I live, and be buried in it first, that it may please me the more at last. . . .

I do not propose to write an ode to dejection, but to brag as lustily as chanticleer[6] in the
❶ morning, standing on his roost, if only to wake my neighbors up.

When first I took up my abode in the woods, that is, began to spend my nights as well as days there, which, by accident, was on Independence Day, or the fourth of July, 1845, my house was not finished for winter, but was merely a defense against the rain, without plastering or chimney, the walls being of rough weatherstained boards, with wide chinks, which made it cool at night. The upright white hewn studs and freshly planed door and window casings gave it a clean and airy look, especially in the morning, when its timbers were saturated with dew, so that I fancied that by noon some sweet gum would exude from them. To my imagination it retained throughout the day more or less of this auroral[7] character, reminding me of a certain house on a mountain which I had visited the year before. This was an airy and unplastered cabin, fit to entertain a traveling god, and where a goddess might trail her garments. The winds which passed over my dwelling were such as sweep over the ridges of mountains, bearing the broken strains, or celestial parts only, of terrestrial music. The morning wind forever blows, the poem of creation is uninterrupted; but few are the ears that hear it. Olympus[8] is but the outside of the earth everywhere. . . .

I went to the woods because I wished to live deliberately, to front only the essential facts of life, and see if I could not learn what it had to teach, and not, when I came to die, discover that I had not lived. I did not wish to live what was not life, living is so dear; nor did I wish to practice resignation, unless it was quite necessary. I wanted to live deep and suck out all the marrow of life, to live so sturdily and Spartanlike[9] as to put to rout all that was not life, to cut a broad ❷
swath and shave close, to drive life into a corner, ❸
and reduce it to its lowest terms, and, if it proved to be mean, why then to get the whole and genuine meanness of it, and publish its meanness to the world; or if it were <u>sublime</u>, to know it by experience, and be able to give a true account of it in my next excursion. For most men, it appears to me, are in a strange uncertainty about it, whether it is of the devil or of God, and have *somewhat hastily* concluded that it is the chief end of man here to "glorify God and enjoy him forever."[10]

Still we live meanly, like ants; though the fable tells us that we were long ago changed into men; like pygmies we fight with cranes:[11] it is error upon error, and clout upon clout, and our best virtue has for its occasion a <u>superfluous</u> and <u>evitable</u> wretchedness. Our life is frittered away by detail. An honest man has hardly need to count more than his ten fingers, or in extreme cases he may add his ten toes, and lump the rest. Simplicity, simplicity, simplicity! I say, let your affairs be as two or three, and not a hundred or a thousand; instead of a million count half a dozen, and keep your accounts on your thumbnail. In the midst of this chopping sea of civilized life, such are the clouds and storms and quicksands and thousand-and-one items to be

5. **Old Cato:** Roman statesman (234–149 B.C.). "De Re Rustica" is Latin for "Of Things Rustic."
6. **Chanticleer** (chan´ tə klir´) *n.*: Rooster.
7. **auroral** (ô rôr´ əl) *adj.*: Resembling the dawn.
8. **Olympus** (ō lim´ pəs): In Greek mythology, the home of the gods.
9. **Spartanlike:** Like the people of Sparta, an ancient Greek state whose citizens were known to be hardy, stoical, simple, and highly disciplined.
10. **"glorify . . . forever":** The answer to the question "What is the chief end of man?" in the Westminster catechism.
11. **like . . . cranes:** In the *Iliad*, the Trojans are compared to cranes fighting against pygmies.

Cross-Curricular Connection: Science

Geology The creation of Walden Pond began nearly 12,000 years ago when the glacier that covered New England began to retreat. As it slowly melted, one huge block of ice remained behind on the site that is now Walden Pond. Streams of melted water began running southward from the main glacier, bringing with them sand and gravel that had become embedded in the giant iceberg as it scraped across the land. Deposits of this gravelly sediment built up around the base of the detached ice block; when the block melted, a steep-side, water-filled basin, roughly 100 feet deep, remained.

Walden Pond is noteworthy for more than its famous resident. Unlike nearby ponds, whose water levels tend to rise and recede dramatically, the water level of Walden Pond changes little. Walden's water also remains pure and clear while the quality of the water in other ponds fluctuates. *(Continued on p. 377)*

allowed for, that a man has to live, if he would not founder and go to the bottom and not make his port at all, by dead reckoning,[12] and he must be a great calculator indeed who succeeds. Simplify, simplify. Instead of three meals a day,
❹ if it be necessary eat but one; instead of a hundred dishes, five; and reduce other things in proportion. Our life is like a German Confederacy,[13] made up of petty states, with its boundary
❺ ary forever fluctuating,so that even a German cannot tell you how it is bounded at any moment. The nation itself, with all its so-called internal improvements, which, by the way, are all external and superficial, is just such an unwieldy and overgrown establishment, cluttered with furniture and tripped up by its own traps, ruined by luxury and heedless expense, by want of calculation and a worthy aim, as the million households in the land; and the only cure for it as for them is in a rigid economy, a stern and more than Spartan simplicity of life and elevation of purpose. It lives too fast. Men think that it is essential that the *Nation* have commerce, and export ice, and talk through a telegraph, and ride thirty miles an hour, without a doubt, whether *they* do or not; but whether we should live like baboons or like men, is a little uncertain. If we do not get out sleepers,[14] and forge
❻ rails, and devote days and nights to the work, but go to tinkering upon our *lives* to improve *them*, who will build railroads? And if railroads are not built, how shall we get to heaven in season? But if we stay at home and mind our business, who will want railroads? We do not ride on the railroad; it rides upon us. . . .

Time is but the stream I go a-fishing in. I drink at it; but while I drink I see the sandy bottom and detect how shallow it is. Its thin current slides away, but eternity remains. I would drink deeper; fish in the sky, whose bottom is pebbly with stars. I cannot count one. I know not the first letter of the alphabet. I have always been regretting that I was not as wise as the day I was born. The intellect is a cleaver; it discerns and rifts its way into the secret of things. I do not wish to be any more busy with my hands than is necessary. My head is hands and feet. I feel all my best faculties concentrated in it. My instinct tells me that my head is ❼
an organ for burrowing, as some creatures use their snout and forepaws, and with it I would mine and burrow my way through these hills. I think that the richest vein is somewhere hereabouts; so by the divining rod[15] and thin rising vapors I judge; and here I will begin to mine. . . .

from The Conclusion

I left the woods for as good a reason as I went there. Perhaps it seemed to me that I had several more lives to live, and could not spare any more time for that one. It is remarkable how easily and insensibly we fall into a particular route, and make a beaten track for ourselves. I ❽
had not lived there a week before my feet wore a path from my door to the pondside; and though it is five or six years since I trod it, it is still quite distinct. It is true, I fear that others may have fallen into it, and so helped to keep it open. The surface of the earth is soft and impressible by the feet of men; and so with the paths which the mind travels. How worn and dusty, then, must be the highways of the world, how deep the ruts of tradition and conformity! I did not wish to take a cabin passage, but rather to go before the mast and on the deck of the world, for there I could best see the moonlight amid the mountains. I do not wish to go below now.

I learned this, at least, by my experiment; that if one advances confidently in the direction

12. **dead reckoning:** Navigating without the assistance of stars.
13. **German Confederacy:** At the time, Germany was a loose union of thirty-eight independent states, with no common government.
14. **sleepers** (slē´ pərz) *n.*: Ties supporting railroad tracks.
15. **divining rod:** A forked branch or stick alleged to reveal underground water or minerals.

◆ Build Vocabulary

sublime (sə blīm´) *adj.*: Noble; majestic

superfluous (so͞o pur´ flo͞o wəs) *adj.*: Excessive; not necessary

evitable (ev´ ə tə bəl) *adj.*: Avoidable

◆ Literary Focus

❹ **Style** Help students see that Thoreau uses repetition and presents a series of examples to build to a climactic point stated in the final sentence: Unfortunately, technology and regulations rule people, not the other way around.

◆ Build Vocabulary

❺ **Word Roots: *-flu-*** Ask students to use the meaning of the word root *-flu-* to help them determine the meaning of the word *fluctuating.* *Accept answers that reflect the meaning of the root, such as "flowing back and forth."*

◆ Reading Strategy

❻ **Evaluate the Writer's Statement of Philosophy** Encourage students to summarize Thoreau's attitude toward progress. Do they agree with his attitude? Why or why not? *Students should respond that Thoreau believes that progress distracts people from the worthier pursuit of self-betterment; progress controls people, rather than the other way around. Students may say that they disagree with Thoreau and feel that progress is essential to bettering the quality of life.*

◆ Reading Strategy

❼ **Evaluate the Writer's Statement of Philosophy** Guide students to see that this passage summarizes Thoreau's Transcendentalist philosophy. Thoreau is stressing intuition over intellect. Have students respond to his description of the intellect as a cleaver that cuts to the heart of ideas, much like snouts and forepaws burrow into the earth.

Customize for
Less Proficient Readers

❽ Review with these students the reasons why Thoreau came to Walden Pond. If necessary, have them reread the paragraph on p. 376 in which Thoreau states his purpose for coming to Walden. Stress to students that whenever a writer makes a connection, as Thoreau does in this paragraph, it's helpful to review the portion of the text to which the connection is being made.

Cross-Curricular Connection: Science

(continued)

Science holds the key to explaining Walden's mysteries. Because its banks are composed of permeable sands that quickly absorb water, draining rainwater does not rush down its banks, washing dirt and debris into the pond. With no shoreline development or tributary streams, there is nothing to spoil the water quality. The stable water level can also be explained: Walden intersects a water table, so its levels are relatively unaffected by short-term wet and dry spells.

Customize for
Less Proficient Readers

❶ Help these students figure out the meaning of the apparent contradictions in this passage and lead them to an understanding of the metaphor "castles in the air." Guide them to understand that Thoreau is urging people to simplify their lives, to dream, and then to follow their dreams by building the foundations for them.

◆ *Literature and Your Life*

❷ Point out that the image of hearing a different drummer has become part of our common lexicon. Ask students to share how in their lives they have exemplified the experience of marching to "a different drummer."

◆ Critical Thinking

❸ **Speculate** Point out that Thoreau had a very casual, romantic view of poverty. Tell students that although not wealthy, he did have a Harvard education and the family pencil business to fall back upon. Ask students if they think Thoreau would give the same advice about poverty today. *Some students may respond that Thoreau's views might be different today, since we live in a world where most poverty-stricken Americans cannot live off the land as he did. Most poor people today live in cities where poverty lacks the rustic simplicity Thoreau is fond of praising.*

◆ Reading Strategy

❹ **Evaluate the Writer's Statement of Philosophy**
Students may or may not be convinced that poverty is preferable to wealth. Remind them that Thoreau never experienced abject, desperate poverty himself. Talk about whether his views were elitist.

of his dreams, and endeavors to live the life which he has imagined, he will meet with a success unexpected in common hours. He will put some things behind, will pass an invisible boundary; new, universal, and more liberal laws will begin to establish themselves around and within him; or the old laws be expanded, and interpreted in his favor in a more liberal sense, and he will live with the license of a higher order of beings. In proportion as he simplifies his life, the laws of the universe will appear less complex, and solitude will not be solitude, nor ❶ poverty poverty, nor weakness weakness. If you have built castles in the air, your work need not be lost; that is where they should be. Now put the foundations under them. . . .

Why should we be in such desperate haste to succeed, and in such desperate enterprises? ❷ If a man does not keep pace with his companions, perhaps it is because he hears a different drummer. Let him step to the music which he hears, however measured or far away. It is not important that he should mature as soon as an apple tree or an oak. Shall he turn his spring into summer? If the condition of things which we were made for is not yet, what were any reality which we can substitute? We will not be shipwrecked on a vain reality. Shall we with pains erect a heaven of blue glass over ourselves, though when it is done we shall be sure to gaze still at the true ethereal heaven far above, as if the former were not? . . .

However mean your life is, meet it and live it; do not shun it and call it hard names. It is not so bad as you are. It looks poorest when you are richest. The faultfinder will find faults even in paradise. Love your life, poor as it is. You may perhaps have some pleasant, thrilling, glorious hours, even in a poorhouse. The setting sun is reflected from the windows of the almshouse[16] as brightly as from the rich man's abode; the snow melts before its door as early in the spring. I do not see but a quiet mind may live as contentedly there, and have as cheering thoughts, as in a palace. The town's poor seem to me often to live the most independent lives of any. Maybe they are simply great enough to receive without misgiving. Most think that they are above being supported by the town; but it oftener happens that they are not above supporting themselves by dishonest means, which should be more disreputable. Cultivate poverty like a garden herb, like sage. Do not trouble ❸ yourself much to get new things, whether clothes or friends. Turn the old; return to them. Things do not change; we change. Sell your clothes and keep your thoughts. God will see that you do not want society. ❹ If I were confined to a corner of a garret[17] all my days, like a spider, the world would be just as large to me while I had my thoughts about me. The philosopher said: "From an army of three divisions one can take away its general, and put it in disorder; from the man the most abject and vulgar one cannot take away his thought." Do not seek so anxiously to be developed, to subject yourself to many influences to be played on; it is all dissipation. Humility like darkness reveals the heavenly lights. The shadows of poverty and meanness gather around us, "and lo! creation widens to our view."[18] We are often reminded that if there were bestowed on us the wealth of Croesus,[19] our aims must still be the same, and our means essentially the same. Moreover, if you are restricted in your range by poverty, if you cannot buy books and newspapers, for instance, you are but confined to the most significant and vital experiences; you are compelled to deal with the material which yields the most sugar and the most starch. It is life near the bone where it is sweetest. You are defended from being a trifler. No man loses ever on a lower level by magnanimity on a higher. Superfluous wealth can buy superfluities only. Money is not required to buy one necessary of the soul. . . .

> **◆ Reading Strategy**
> Thoreau has strong opinions about how people should live. Has he convinced you?

16. **almshouse** *n.*: Home for people too poor to support themselves.

17. **garret** (gar′ it) *n.*: Attic.
18. **"and . . . view":** From the sonnet "To Night" by British poet Joseph Blanco White (1775–1841).
19. **Croesus** (krē′ səs): King of Lydia (d. 546 B.C.), believed to be the wealthiest person of his time.

Speaking, Listening, and Viewing Mini-Lesson

Television Script
This mini-lesson supports a Speaking, Listening, and Viewing activity in the Idea Bank on p. 383.

Introduce the Concept Explain that before any television drama or situation comedy is aired, it is carefully scripted. Set design, stage directions, camera angles, and special effects are all described in the television script.

Develop Background Tell students that while at Walden, Thoreau was arrested in July 1846 for refusing to pay the poll tax of $1.50, which he had not paid in four years as a protest against slavery. When the United States invaded Mexico in 1846, Thoreau urged people to join him in a "peaceable revolution" by not paying taxes. He stayed in jail just one night before an anonymous friend paid his taxes for him.

Apply the Information Break students into groups and have group members share the task of reviewing the selections to gather ideas for dialogue and directions. Have students write their scripts and read or act them out for the class.

Assess the Outcome Have students assess their own scripts. Was the dialogue consistent with what they have learned about Thoreau's ideas and principles?

The life in us is like the water in the river. It may rise this year higher than man has ever known it, and flood the parched uplands; even this may be the eventful year, which will drown out all our muskrats. It was not always dry land where we dwell. I see far inland the banks which the stream anciently washed, before science began to record its freshets. Everyone has heard the story which has gone the rounds of New England, of a strong and beautiful bug which came out of the dry leaf of an old table of apple-tree wood, which had stood in a farmer's kitchen for sixty years, first in Connecticut, and afterward in Massachusetts—from an egg deposited in the living tree many years earlier still, as appeared by counting the annual layers beyond it; which was heard gnawing out for several weeks, hatched perchance by the heat of an urn. Who does not feel his faith in a resurrection and immortality strengthened by hearing of this? Who knows what beautiful and winged life, whose egg has been buried for ages under many concentric layers of woodenness in the dead dry life of society, deposited at first in the alburnum[20] of the green and living tree, which has been gradually converted into the semblance of its well-seasoned tomb—heard perchance gnawing out now for years by the astonished family of man, as they sat round the festive board—may unexpectedly come forth from amidst society's most trivial and handselled furniture, to enjoy its perfect summer life at last!

I do not say that John or Jonathan[21] will realize all this; but such is the character of that morrow which mere lapse of time can never make to dawn. The light which puts out our eyes is darkness to us. Only that day dawns to which we are awake. There is more day to dawn. The sun is but a morning star. ❺

20. **alburnum** (al bur′ nəm) *n.*: Soft wood between the bark and the heartwood, where water is conducted.
21. **John or Jonathan:** Average person.

◆ Build Vocabulary

magnanimity (mag′ nə nim′ ə tē) *n.*: Generosity

Guide for Responding

◆ Literature and Your Life

Reader's Response From your point of view, what would be the advantages and disadvantages of spending two solitary years in a natural setting?

Thematic Focus What might Thoreau think of today's fast-paced society? What specific things in your life might especially concern him?

☑ Check Your Comprehension

1. What does Thoreau imagine doing?
2. (a) Why does Thoreau go to live in the woods? (b) Why does he eventually leave?
3. What does he learn from his "experiment"?
4. What advice does Thoreau offer to those who live in poverty?

◆ Critical Thinking

INTERPRET

1. What does Thoreau mean by his comment: "It makes but little difference whether you are committed to a farm or the county jail"? **[Analyze]**
2. In your own words, describe Thoreau's attitude toward individuality and conformity. **[Interpret]**
3. Why, according to Thoreau, are people better off being poor than wealthy? **[Support]**

APPLY

4. Explain why you either do or do not believe that it would be possible for Thoreau to conduct his "experiment" in today's society. **[Hypothesize]**

EXTEND

5. Today's travel agencies and vacation planners design vacations for people who want to get back to nature. Why is such a trip appealing? **[Career Link]**

Cultural Connection

Gandhi Thoreau's beliefs have influenced people throughout the world in the decades since his death. For example, his concept of civil disobedience, which is vividly described in the selection that follows, greatly influenced Indian leader Mohandas Karamchand Gandhi in his campaign against British rule in his homeland. Drawing on Thoreau's ideas, Gandhi formulated his philosophy of *Satyagraha* ("The Devotion to Truth" in Sanskrit, an ancient Indian language) in 1906. Guided by this philosophy, Gandhi called for massive boycotts of British goods and British-run institutions in India that treated Indians unfairly. Thousands of Gandhi's supporters and Gandhi himself repeatedly went to prison without resistance. When India won its independence in 1947, it was largely due to Gandhi's nonviolent protests.

Interested students can conduct research to find out more about Gandhi and learn how he influenced Martin Luther King, Jr.'s, leadership of the civil rights movement in the United States.

◆ Literary Focus

❺ **Style** Point out that this paragraph is typical of Thoreau's style; its sentences build up to the final striking image of the sun as "but a morning star."

Reinforce and Extend

Customize for
AP Students

Point out Thoreau's use of figurative language in "The Conclusion." For example, list or ask these students to list some of the metaphors that Thoreau uses for life. *He compares life to a road or path, a ship, a parade, a bone, a river, a day, and the seasons of the year.*

Answers

◆ Literature and Your Life

Reader's Response Advantages include having a chance to get an intimate view of nature. Disadvantages include being separated from family, friends, and modern conveniences.

Thematic Focus Possible response: Thoreau would be concerned with how little time we spend reflecting on our lives and on nature. He might feel that we are too closely controlled by material possessions.

☑ Check Your Comprehension

1. He imagines buying and living on many different farms.
2. (a) He wants to "live deliberately." (b) He fears falling into a routine.
3. Possible response: He learns that "if one advances confidently in the direction of his dreams, and endeavors to live the life he has imagined, he will meet with a success unexpected in common hours."
4. They should love life and find the best in it.

◆ Critical Thinking

1. Living in either place puts constraints on your liberty.
2. He believes that people should resist conformity and assert their individuality.
3. Wealth demands attention to the nonessential details of life.
4. Students may feel that today life is simply too complex to allow such an experiment.
5. Suggested response: Many people live urban or suburban lives and don't often have the opportunity to experience nature.

Develop Understanding

One-Minute Insight This selection is excerpted from a long essay, about twenty pages in length, in which Thoreau advocates civil disobedience—the deliberate and public refusal to obey laws that violate one's personal principles. In the portions included here, Thoreau expresses his belief that government has been no more than an impediment to the productivity and achievements of the American people. Philosophically, he stands opposed to government. Practically, he urges readers to try to make a better government, one that would command respect.

▶Critical Viewing◀

❶ **Support** Students should respond that the motto "Don't tread on me" reflects Thoreau's attitude toward government: He believes that a government that steps on the rights or freedoms of its people can expect them to retaliate with civil disobedience.

◆Critical Thinking

❷ **Connect** Ask students which groups today would be most likely to agree or disagree with these statements. *Students may say that conservative groups would applaud smaller government and that liberal, social-minded groups would wish for a more active government.*

◆Critical Thinking

❸ **Generalize** Have students debate whether it is possible today for a few influential politicians, military leaders, or business moguls to use the government as their tool.

from CIVIL DISOBEDIENCE

Henry David Thoreau

❶ ▲ **Critical Viewing** This flag, which dates back to 1775, displays the motto adopted by the American colonies. What makes the flag an appropriate illustration for this work? **[Support]**

I heartily accept the motto, "That government is best which governs least";[1] and I should like to see it acted up to more rapidly and systematically. Carried out, it finally amounts ❷ to this, which also I believe: "That government is best which governs not at all"; and when men are prepared for it, that will be the kind of government which they will have. Government is at best but an expedient; but most governments are usually, and all governments are sometimes, inexpedient. The objections which have been brought against a standing army, and they are many and weighty, and deserve to prevail, may also at last be brought against a standing government. The standing army is only an arm of the standing government. The government itself, which is only the mode which the people have chosen to execute their will, is equally liable to be abused and perverted before the people can act through it. Witness the present Mexican war, the work of comparatively a few individuals using the standing government ❸ as their tool; for in the outset, the people would not have consented to this measure.

This American government—what is it but

1. **"That . . . least":** The motto of the *United States Magazine and Democratic Review*, a literary-political journal.

Beyond the Classroom

Community Connection

Participating in Government Discuss whether government is, as Thoreau contends, an impediment to our freedoms and progress, or whether citizens can improve their local, state, and federal governments by exercising their right to participate. Explain that citizens have many opportunities to make our voices heard, particularly on the local level. Discuss the following ways groups and individuals can influence public policy. Ask students to add their own suggestions to this list:

- Write a letter to a civic leader
- Organize or sign a petition
- Submit a letter to the editor of a local paper
- Speak out at a town meeting
- Exercise the right to vote

Have students think about their own responses to governmental issues. Ask them if they have ever signed a petition or written a letter voicing their feelings on a particular issue. Have students share their experiences and discuss their views on what roles and responsibilities individuals have as citizens in a democracy.

a tradition, though a recent one, endeavoring to transmit itself unimpaired to posterity, but each instant losing some of its integrity? It has not the vitality and force of a single living man; for a single man can bend it to his will. It is a sort of wooden gun to the people themselves; and, if ever they should use it in earnest as a real one against each other, it will surely split. But it is not the less necessary for this; for the people must have some complicated machinery or other, and hear its din, to satisfy that idea of government which they have. Governments show thus how successfully men can be imposed on, even impose on themselves, for their own advantage. It is excellent, we must all allow; yet this government never of itself furthered any enterprise, but by the alacrity with which it got out of its way. *It* does not keep the

4 country free. *It* does not settle the West. *It* does not educate. The character inherent in the American people has done all that has been accomplished; and it would have done somewhat more, if the government had not sometimes got in its way. For government is an expedient by which men would fain succeed in letting one another alone; and, as has been said, when it is most expedient, the governed are most let alone by it. Trade and commerce, if they were not made of India rubber,[2] would never manage to bounce over the obstacles which legislators are continually putting in their way; and, if one were to judge these men wholly by the effects of their actions, and not partly by their intentions, they would deserve to be classed and punished with those mischievous persons who put obstructions on the railroads.

But, to speak practically and as a citizen, unlike those who call themselves no government men, I ask for, not at once no government, but *at once* a better government. Let every man make known what kind of government would command his respect, and that will be one step toward obtaining it. . . . 5

2. **India rubber:** A form of crude rubber.

◆ Build Vocabulary

expedient (ik spē´ dē ənt) *n.*: Resource

posterity (päs ter´ ə tē) *n.*: All succeeding generations

alacrity (ə lak´ rə tē) *n.*: Speed

Guide for Responding

◆ Literature and Your Life

Reader's Response What kind of government commands your respect? Why?

Thematic Focus Does Thoreau's philosophy of government agree or conflict with the Transcendentalist belief in the human spirit and the natural world? Explain.

Group Discussion Discuss Thoreau's ideas about the role of government. Then list five things he would think government should do and five things he would think a government should not do.

☑ Check Your Comprehension

1. What motto does Thoreau heartily accept?
2. How does Thoreau suggest people can contribute to improving the government?

◆ Critical Thinking

INTERPRET

1. Whom does Thoreau suggest is responsible for the Mexican War? **[Infer]**
2. Why does Thoreau think that a small handful of individuals can get away with perverting the government? **[Analyze]**
3. According to Thoreau, when will Americans get the best possible kind of government? **[Draw Conclusions]**

EVALUATE

4. Does Thoreau present a convincing argument for opposing a government policy of which one does not approve? **[Evaluate]**

APPLY

5. Thoreau says "if ever [the people] should use [the government] in earnest as a real [gun] against each other, it will surely split." Use your knowledge of history to judge this statement. **[Social Studies Link]**

Beyond the Selection

FURTHER READING

Other Works by Thoreau

A Week on the Concord and Merrimack Rivers
The Maine Woods
"Slavery in Massachusetts"

We suggest that you preview these works before recommending them to students.

INTERNET

You and your students may find additional information about Thoreau and Walden Pond on the Internet. We suggest the following sites. Please be aware, however, that sites may have changed since we published this information.

To learn more about the world of Henry David Thoreau, go to **http://umsa.umd.edu/thoreau/**

For information about Walden Pond State Reservation and Thoreau's life at Walden, go to **http://www.tiac.net/users/morganti/walden.htm**

We *strongly recommend* that you preview the sites before you send students to them.

◆ Reading Strategy

4 Evaluate the Writer's Statement of Philosophy Guide students to understand that here Thoreau credits the people, not the government, for the development of the country. Have students debate this point of view. *Some may say that Thoreau's views reflect our nation's early history, when determined individuals carved their own way in the American wilderness. Today's complex domestic and international affairs require a larger, more active government structure.*

◆ Critical Thinking

5 Infer Ask students what type of government they believe Thoreau wants. *Students can surmise that he wants one that furthers the aspirations and efforts of the individual.*

Reinforce and Extend

Answers

◆ Literature and Your Life

Reader's Response Students should explain the reasoning behind their opinions.

Thematic Focus Students may note that Thoreau's views of government fit in with the Transcendentalist belief in individuality and personal freedom.

☑ Check Your Comprehension

1. "That government is best which governs least."
2. They can express their opinions concerning the type of government they want.

◆ Critical Thinking

1. He suggests that the war is the work of a few individuals who use the government as their tool.
2. Thoreau believes that government has no vitality of its own and can be bent to the will of individuals.
3. Americans will get the best possible government when they express their opinions on the type of government that would command their respect.
4. Students should support their responses with an evaluation of Thoreau's arguments.
5. Students may cite the South's secession from the Union over slavery issues and the resulting Civil War to support Thoreau's statement.

Answers

◆ Reading Strategy

1. (a) He claims that we fritter away our lives in details that distract us from the real living. (b) Sample response: The details of living add richness and variety to our lives. (c) Students should defend their responses.
2. (a) He contends that government is too easily perverted by a few individuals, and that government itself never did anything to further the country. (b) Students should explain the reasoning behind their responses.

◆ Literary Focus

1. (a) He begins with a simile about ants and proceeds to a statement about detail. Then he urges simplicity and gives examples about simplifying individual lives. He then makes another comparison and launches an attack on the complexities of progress. (b) The paragraph that begins "However mean your life is" on p. 378 also builds to a single sentence that expresses the meaning of the entire paragraph.
2. Suggested responses include the first paragraph from "The Conclusion."

◆ Build Vocabulary

Using the Word Root *-flu-*
1. b 2. a 3. c

Using the Word Bank:
1. b 2. a 3. b 4. a
5. b 6. a 7. a 8. b

◆ Grammar and Style

Suggested responses include to live deliberately (noun); to front only the essential facts of life (noun); [to] see if I could not learn (noun); to teach (noun); to die (adverb); [to] discover that I had not lived (noun); to live what was not life (noun); to practice resignation (noun); to live deep (noun); [to] suck out all the marrow of life (noun); to live so sturdily and Spartanlike (noun); to put (adverb); to cut a broad swath (noun); [to] shave close (noun); to drive life into a corner (noun); [to] reduce it to its lowest terms (noun); to be mean (adjective); to get the whole and genuine meanness of it (noun); [to] publish its meanness to the world (noun); to know it by experience (noun); to be able (noun); to give a true account of it (noun); to "glorify God (noun); [to] enjoy him forever" (noun).

Writing Application

Possible responses include
1. to find a simpler life.
2. to follow his example.
3. from which to fish and [to] drink or to fish and [to] drink from.

Grammar Reinforcement

For additional instruction and practice, use the practice page on infinitives and infinitive clauses in the *Writer's Solution Grammar Practice Book* (p. 34).

Reteach

To reteach this selection, use ***Strategies for Diverse Student Needs,*** p. 23.

Guide for Responding *(continued)*

◆ Reading Strategy

Evaluate the Writer's Statement of Philosophy

Evaluate a writer's ideas and arguments by weighing them against your own knowledge.

1. Thoreau writes that people should simplify their lives. (a) What support for this belief does he provide? (b) How could you argue against this idea? (c) Is his argument convincing? Explain.

2. (a) How does Thoreau support his contention that "That government is best which governs not at all"? (b) Do you agree with Thoreau? Explain.

◆ Literary Focus

Style

The way a writer puts thoughts into words is called **style**. Thoreau's style is characterized by his continual reinforcement of his ideas. Some critics argue that Thoreau overstates his points. Thoreau, however, felt that it was impossible to overstate the truth about human potential. He deliberately repeated his main ideas to reinforce his message.

1. (a) How does the paragraph in *Walden* on simplicity demonstrate Thoreau's tendency to make sentences build to a climax? (b) Find one other paragraph that is structured in this manner.

2. Thoreau often starts a paragraph by discussing specific incidents or examples. He then applies them to a larger truth. Find one such paragraph.

Beyond Literature

Cultural Connection

Civil Disobedience Thoreau was not the only advocate of civil disobedience. In the twentieth century, Mohandas Gandhi used forms of nonviolent civil disobedience in his commitment to justice and peace. He first worked for the rights of Indian immigrants in South Africa. Upon his return to India, Gandhi focused on forms of peaceful civil disobedience as he fought for India's independence from Britain. His strong example later inspired Martin Luther King, Jr. Debate this type of protest with your classmates.

◆ Build Vocabulary

Using the Latin Root *-flu-*

The Latin root *-flu-*, found in *fluency* and *influence*, means "flow." Match each of the following words containing the Latin root *-flu-* with its definition. Check your answers in a dictionary.

a. affluence **b.** confluence **c.** fluent

1. a flowing together; for example, the flowing together of two or more streams
2. wealth; an abundant flow; prosperity
3. effortlessly smooth; flowing

Using the Word Bank: Synonyms

On your paper, write the word or phrase whose meaning is closer to that of the first word.

1. dilapidated: (a) depressed, (b) in disrepair
2. sublime: (a) majestic, (b) filthy
3. superfluous: (a) superb, (b) unnecessary
4. evitable: (a) avoidable, (b) evident
5. magnanimity: (a) spontaneity, (b) kindness
6. expedient: (a) resource, (b) expense
7. posterity: (a) succeeding generations, (b) previous generations
8. alacrity: (a) awareness, (b) readiness

◆ Grammar and Style

Infinitives and Infinitive Phrases

Thoreau makes frequent use of infinitives and infinitive phrases to explain his beliefs and the motives for his actions.

An **infinitive** is a form of a verb that generally appears with the word *to* and acts as a noun, adjective, or adverb. **Infinitive phrases** contain an infinitive and its complements.

Practice Find at least six infinitives or infinitive phrases in the paragraph on p. 376 that begins "I went to the woods . . ." Identify the function of the infinitive in each.

Writing Application

Complete these sentences by adding infinitive phrases.

1. Thoreau went to Walden Pond hoping __?__ .
2. Thoreau wants us __?__ .
3. Thoreau says that time is merely a stream __?__ .

Build Your Portfolio

Idea Bank

Writing

1. **Letter to the Editor** How well do Thoreau's philosophies apply today? Write a letter to the editor of a newspaper, promoting the idea that people should simplify their lives.

2. **Report** Thoreau spent a night in jail to protest the Mexican War. In a report, explain the causes and results of the war and the response by United States citizens. **[Social Studies Link]**

3. **Comparison-and-Contrast Essay** Write an essay in which you compare and contrast the beliefs of Emerson and Thoreau, using passages and details from their writings for support.

Speaking, Listening, and Viewing

4. **Television Script** It is said that when Thoreau was in jail, Emerson came to see him and asked, "Henry, what are you doing in there?" to which Thoreau replied, "Waldo, what are you doing out there?" Using ideas from the essays, write a script for a scene depicting this famous meeting. **[Media Link]**

5. **Debate** Stage a debate to argue the pros and cons of civil disobedience as a form of protest. **[Social Studies Link]**

Researching and Representing

6. **Walden Pond Research** Conduct research to find out what Walden Pond is like now. If possible, gather photographs of the area. Share your findings with the class. Follow with a discussion of how Walden Pond has changed since Thoreau's day.

7. **Nature Journal** Make several visits to an area close to you—a park, forest, or seashore—where you can observe nature. Record your observations in a nature journal to share with classmates. **[Science Link]**

Online Activity www.phlit.phschool.com

Guided Writing Lesson

Persuasive Essay

Thoreau writes persuasively on subjects about which he has strong feelings. Choose an issue of importance to you. Then write an essay persuading others to accept your position and take an action. Use a cause-and-effect organization to show your audience the consequences of action—or inaction.

Writing Skills Focus: Cause-and-Effect Organization

To argue why or how something happened or will happen, connect ideas by using a **cause-and-effect organization**. Follow either of these two approaches:

- State a cause—evidence that something has happened or will happen—followed by the effects that have resulted or will result from that cause.
- Alternatively, state a series of related effects, and then state the cause that shows your evidence is or will be responsible for those effects.

Prewriting Think about the main idea you want to convey and the kinds of evidence you will need to support it. To help you gather evidence of causes and effects, use a chart like the following:

Topic: ______________________________

Causes	Effects

Drafting State your position clearly in an introduction. Develop each point you wish to make in a separate paragraph, and organize your points in a logical order. Refer to your list of causes and effects to help you develop your argument.

Revising Reread your draft, adding details as necessary to sharpen your argument and clarify all cause-and-effect relationships.

✓ ASSESSMENT OPTIONS

Formal Assessment, Selection Test, pp. 110–112, and Assessment Resources Software. The selection test is designed so that it can be easily customized to the performance levels of your students.

Alternative Assessment, p. 23, includes options for less advanced students, more advanced students, visual/spatial learners, and bodily/kinesthetic learners.

PORTFOLIO ASSESSMENT
Use the following rubrics in the ***Alternative Assessment*** booklet to assess student writing:
Letter to the Editor: Persuasion Rubric, p. 120
Report: Research Report/Paper Rubric, p. 121
Compare and Contrast Essay: Comparison/Contrast Rubric, p. 118
Guided Writing Lesson: Persuasion Rubric, p. 120

Idea Bank

Customizing for
Performance Levels
Following are suggestions for matching Idea Bank topics with your students' performance levels:
Less Advanced Students: 1, 6
Average Students: 2, 4, 7
More Advanced Students: 3, 5

Customizing for
Learning Modalities
Following are suggestions for matching Idea Bank topics with your students' learning modalities:
Verbal/Linguistic: 4, 5, 6
Logical/Mathematical: 5
Body/Kinesthetic: 7

Guided Writing Lesson

Writing and Language Transparencies Use the Writing Process Model 6: Persuasive Essay, pp. 33–36, to model persuasive writing. Then use the Cause-and-Effect Transparency, p. 91, to help students organize their Prewriting notes.

For more prewriting, elaboration, and revision strategies, see *Prentice Hall Writing and Grammar.*

Writing Lab CD-ROM
Have students complete the tutorial on Persuasion. Follow these steps:
1. Refer students to the model of a persuasive essay and the Evaluation Guidelines.
2. Have students look through the Inspirations for Persuasion to help them come up with a topic idea.
3. Use the example of cause-and-effect organization and the Chain-of-Events graphic organizer to help students with Prewriting.
4. Have students draft on computer.
5. Have students use the Self-Evaluation Checklist to help them revise.

LESSON OBJECTIVES

1. **To express and support responses to the text**
   - Critical Thinking
   - Idea Bank: Drawing
   - Idea Bank: Critique
2. **To analyze literary elements**
   - Idea Bank: Music Analysis
3. **To use recursive writing processes**
   - Idea Bank: Personal Anecdote
   - Idea Bank: Grant Proposal

Interest Grabber In the song "Hammer and a Nail," Emily Saliers observes, "The sweetest part is acting after making a decision." Others claim that half the joy of a task is figuring out how to do it, that all the fun is in the chase, or that process is more satisfying than product. Have student groups debate these ideas. Encourage students to share any experiences they may have had that support or refute these notions.

Customize for
English Language Learners
Bailey White's personal anecdote mentions many gardening tools and activities, as well as the names of dozens of plants. Display captioned photos from gardening books, catalogs, and magazines to help students form mental pictures of the tools, plants, and processes she describes.

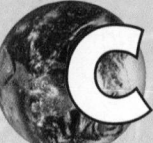

CONNECTIONS TO TODAY'S WORLD

Gardening
Bailey White

Hammer and a Nail
Emily Saliers

Thematic Connection

THE HUMAN SPIRIT AND THE NATURAL WORLD

When was the last time you strolled through a meadow or hiked in a forest? The untouched natural landscapes that gave so much joy and meaning to the lives of Emerson and Thoreau are not as accessible today as they were in the nineteenth century. Even if they were, most Americans don't have the leisure time to commune with nature on the shores of a pond as did Thoreau or take the twilight rambles that Emerson describes in "Nature."

So how do we make the universal connection that these writers found in the unspoiled wilderness? Where do we turn to find the greater meaning that Emerson and Thoreau saw reflected in the wonder of a snowstorm or the beauty of a sunset?

SIMPLICITY, SIMPLICITY, SIMPLICITY!

"Getting back to nature" and "getting back to basics" have become catch phrases for everything from weekend camping trips to the decision to trade big-city life for small-town living. The implication is that nature, or something of unifying and enduring value, has been lost or left behind, and we must find our way back to it.

This need to return to "the simpler things in life" drives millions to spend their weekends working in the garden or puttering with tools. This kind of work can become a pleasure in and of itself. In her humorous essay "Gardening," Bailey White discovers the satisfaction that comes from working the land. In the song "Hammer and a Nail," Emily Saliers, of the modern folk duo Indigo Girls, writes of the liberating effect of taking shovel and hammer in hand—both literally and figuratively. These contemporary works celebrate a sense of well-being that closely resembles the simple pleasures that Emerson and Thoreau found in nature.

BAILEY WHITE
(1950–)

Until the summer of 1993, Bailey White was little known outside her hometown of Thomasville, Georgia, where she taught first grade at the local elementary school. As a commentator for National Public Radio, White had earned a loyal audience with her sketches about rural southern life. With the publication of her first book, however, White became, to her own surprise, a best-selling author. The success of *Mama Makes Up Her Mind* hasn't changed White at all; she's still a homebody who appreciates life's simple pleasures.

EMILY SALIERS
(1963–)

Emily Saliers was in the sixth grade when her family moved from New Haven, Connecticut, to Decatur, Georgia, where she met musical partner Amy Ray. Today, this duo, which records under the name the Indigo Girls, is known for its gutsy yet spiritual brand of contemporary folk music. Saliers and Ray—both singers, songwriters, and guitarists—began performing while still in high school. In 1989, the Indigo Girls released their first recording with a major label. The album, also called "Indigo Girls," won a Grammy Award. The duo has been recording and performing ever since.

Prentice Hall Literature Program Resources

REINFORCE / RETEACH / EXTEND

Selection Support Pages
Build Vocabulary: Using Horticultural Vocabulary, p. 112
Thematic Connection: The Human Spirit and the Natural World, p. 113

Formal Assessment Selection Test, pp. 113–114; Assessment Resources Software

Resource Pro CD-ROM

Listening to Literature Audiocassettes

Gardening

BAILEY WHITE

CONNECTIONS TO TODAY'S WORLD

About six years ago, like so many romantic gardening fools, I fell for it: the wildflower meadow. I don't know whether it was the pictures on the seed packets, or the vision I had of myself, dressed all in white, strolling through an endless vista of poppies and daisies.

"A garden in a can," the seed catalogs said. The pictures showed a scene of rolling hills and dales, an area about the size of Georgia and Alabama combined, covered solid as far as the eye could see with billowing drifts of lupine and phlox.

But I wasn't born yesterday. I had been tricked by those pictures before. I come from down south, where
1 vegetation does not know its place. Honeysuckle can work through cracks in your walls and strangle you while you sleep. Kudzu can completely shroud a house and a car parked in the yard in one growing season. Wisteria can lift a building off its foundation, and certain terrifying mints spread so rapidly that just the thought of them on a summer night can make your hair stand on end.

I knew what Lady Bird Johnson[1] was talking about when she gave the wildflower romantics a look and said, "You can't just scatter the seeds around as if you were feeding chickens." Even the more responsible plant catalogs, in their offer of wildflower seed mixes for the various regions of the country admitted, "We have not been able to develop
2 a mixture suitable for Zone 9." So I knew it wouldn't be easy.

But it's hard to squash a romantic. I made a plan. I would prepare my ground, about a half acre, and plant the wildflowers in rows. I would keep the weeds out for five years, by cultivating between the rows with a push plow and a hoe, and weeding by hand within each row. By the end of those five years, I figured I would have eliminated any perennial weeds and weed seeds. Then the garden would be on its own. The wildflowers would spread, eventually taking up the spaces between the rows, and I would get out my white dress and begin my leisurely strolls.

My garden's first spring: the seeds arrived. I planted by hand. The rows, neatly set out with stakes and string, seemed endless. I crawled up and down and up and down every afternoon examining each seedling as it sprouted. Was this spotted spurge or sweet Annie? Red-root pigweed or showy primrose? I recognized most of our common weeds and tweaked them out.

After every rain I hoed between the rows. My hands got hard and callused. They took on the curve of the hoe handle so that everywhere I went, I looked as if I were gripping a ghostly hoe.

The first summer, my annual plants bloomed. The *Coreopsis tinctoria* was spectacular, a glowing red, and the cosmos was shoulder high. Its lavender petals brushed my face as I scritched and scritched up and down each row. I loved the sight of the clean brown earth stretching away from the blade of my hoe. On my

1. **Lady Bird Johnson:** First Lady and wife of Lyndon Baines Johnson, 36th president of the United States.

Cross-Curricular Connection: Science

Gardening Without Soil Hydroponics, also known as soilless agriculture, was developed more than 100 years ago, but it's grown in popularity in recent years. Today, even home gardeners can purchase hydroponic systems that allow them to grow a wide variety of plants, including flowers and vegetables, in self-contained indoor gardens.

The word *hydroponics* comes from the Greek *hydro* meaning "water" and *ponos* meaning "labor." Plants normally obtain the nutrients they need to grow from the soil. In hydroponics, plants are cultivated in nutrient-enriched water. The plants are grown in a watertight bed or bench, and a liquid fertilizer solution is pumped through the system regularly, providing the plants with all the nutrients they need to grow.

There are two basic types of hydroponics. In water culture, plants are supported from above with their roots suspended in water. In aggregate culture, the roots are anchored in a small amount of substrate material, such as course sand or gravel.

Students can use the Internet or library resources to learn more about how hydroponics is used in commercial and amateur gardening.

Develop Understanding

Connections to Today's World

Although few people in today's world would choose to seclude themselves in a cabin in the woods as Thoreau did, many people are attracted by Thoreau's belief in simplicity and in the need to establish a connection to nature. People act on these ideas through adventure travel expeditions, by moving away from the city into the country, or simply by engaging in an outdoor activity such as gardening. The two selections included in this feature capture the attraction of such pursuits.

One-Minute Insight

In this humorous personal anecdote, the author shares the wild notion that prompted her to create a wildflower meadow. Though she knew it would be a long, difficult task, she was inspired by the romantic image of herself, clad in a white dress, strolling through drifts of flowers. As the garden takes shape, however, her romantic vision fades, leaving the author with the realization that it is the work of gardening, not its final result, that she most enjoys.

Customize for *AP Students*

As students read, ask them to note differences in tone and writing style between Bailey White and the Transcendentalist writers Emerson and Thoreau.

Customize for *Less Proficient Readers*

1 Help students recognize White's wit in this passage. She uses exaggeration, self-deprecation, and idiomatic language to convey her points. Guide students to look for other examples of her humorous writing style.

2 **Clarification** Most seed packages provide a simple map of the United States that shows various growing regions. Each region, or zone, is assigned a number based upon the length of its growing season, average daytime temperature, rainfall, and other key factors. Savvy gardeners select seeds or plants cultivated to do well in their particular zone.

❶ **Clarification** Explain to students that annuals are plants that generally live only one year or growing season. Biennials, which live for two years, generally bloom in their second year. Perennials return year after year.

◆ Critical Thinking

❷ **Interpret** Ask students what the white dress symbolizes for the author. *It is a symbol of the pleasure she will enjoy when her garden is finally finished.*

Thematic Connection

❸ **The Human Spirit and the Natural World** Ask students what the author now realizes about her romantic idea of nature and the realities of it. *Students may say that she now realizes that the joy in gardening is working the soil, not strolling through a picture postcard scene.*

◆ Critical Thinking

❹ **Analyze** Why might White be particularly attracted to "intensive gardening"? *An intensive garden is never finished.*

◆ Critical Thinking

❺ **Compare** Have students compare this idea with the main idea Bailey White expresses in her piece. *Students may say that like White, Saliers learned that it is better to do something than fantasize about it, and that once you begin to act, life becomes the sum of those actions.*

Thematic Connection

❻ **The Human Spirit and the Natural World** Have students paraphrase the views expressed in these lines. *Students may say that she realizes it's wrong to think that the actions of one person won't make a difference; that each person belongs to a larger community and, as such, is responsible for doing whatever she can to help.*

hands and knees I weeded between plants. My knees ached, but the smell down there was nice, damp ground and bruised artemisia. I developed a gardener's stoop and a horticulturist's[2] squint.

That first winter, I could relax only a little. Bermuda grass can establish itself during a winter and get away from you the following spring. So every evening at dusk, I would stalk up and down my garden like a demented wraith, peering at the ground for each loathed blue-green blade, my cloak billowing in the wind and my scarf snagging on the bare gray branches of last summer's sunflowers.

At night, I would lie in my bed under the quilt listening to the wind outside and pinching and sniffing the little bunches of sweet Annie I had harvested and dried in July. I dreamed of that summer, only four years away now, when the garden would be finished. My white dress would be linen, I decided.

The second summer was very fine. Some of ❶ the annuals had reseeded, and the perennials and biennials bloomed for the first time. But I had a real problem with something called Old Horrible Snakeroot, one of the terrifying mints, creeping in around the edges. Every afternoon, dressed in a wide straw hat, big boots, and little else, and pouring sweat, I violently hoed the perimeter of my garden. I wore out my first hoe that year with sharpening the blade, and the handles of my Little Gem cultivator became as smooth as ivory.

During the third and fourth years the rows began to close in. There were great irregular patches of gaillardia spanning several rows, with Queen Anne's lace and moss verbena weaving themselves among clumps of black-eyed Susans. When I stood up to ease my back and looked across the garden, I could see that it was truly as beautiful as the picture in the Park's seed catalog. I wiped the sweat out of my eyes and washed my face in the watering ❷ can. My white linen dress would have lace.

The fifth summer, I had to go to the doctor about my knees. "You've got to quit squatting down," he told me.

"I can't quit squatting down," I said. "I've got a garden." He sighed and gave me a pair of elastic bandages.

I had a problem with thistles that year. The seeds must have blown in from somewhere. I wore gloves to pull them out, and every time I took out a thistle, I would transplant a wildflower in its place. Every one of the transplants thrived and multiplied, and by the end of that summer, there was not a spot of bare ground for a weed seed to settle in. My garden was complete.

That winter I bought the linen and the lace and sewed my white dress.

In March I went out to the garden. The linaria was the first thing to bloom. I knew it would be. I knew that a week later the verbena would show up, then the shasta daisies and the gaillardia—a clump here, here, and here. In midsummer the Queen Anne's lace would begin to bloom. I knew exactly how it would be. I knew the name of every plant. I could recognize each one even before it got its true leaves.

I sighted down the length of the garden. There was no trace of the neat rows I had worked and worked for all those years. The garden had taken over itself, just as I had planned.

I walked back to the house. I looked at my soft, limp hands. I looked at my white linen dress, with lace. It seemed like the stupidest thing I had ever thought up. "The fact is," ❸ I said to myself, "I want something to hoe." ❹

I've started reading about intensive gardening. It involves double digging and raised beds. Every season you pull out the old plants and put in new ones. It's a garden that never gets finished.

I gave the white dress to my sister, Louise. Sometimes she comes for a visit and strolls in the wildflower meadow. She ooohs and aaahs and brings her friends to see it. They pick armloads of flowers. I sit on the edge and draw diagrams of my next season's garden in the raised beds. I'm learning about companion planting.

In the wildflower meadow, the Queen Anne's lace waves its filigree heads over the marsh pinks, and the sweet alyssum tucks up neatly around the clumps of painted daisies. But I hardly notice. I've got a new garden now.

2. **horticulturist's:** Belonging or pertaining to someone who practices the art and science of growing flowers, fruits, vegetables, and shrubs.

◆ Build Vocabulary

filigree (fil′ i grē′) *adj.*: Resembling delicate, lacelike ornamental work of intertwined gold or silver wires

Beyond the Classroom

Career Connection

Landscape Architect Just as an architect designs and builds structures, a landscape architect designs and installs gardens, ponds, and other elements of an outdoor landscape, such as watering systems, garden and shrubbery maintenance programs, and so on. Successful landscape architects mix a love of nature with a thorough knowledge of the characteristics of plants, soils, grasses, shrubs, and trees, and an artistic understanding of design, shape, and balance.

Interested students can interview local landscape architects to find out how they create plans, determine budgets, schedule planting and maintenance, and weigh key factors such as growing season, light, and drainage. Ask students to share their findings with the class.

HAMMER AND A NAIL

Words and Music by Emily Saliers

CONNECTIONS TO TODAY'S WORLD

Clearing webs from the hovel
A blistered hand on the handle of a shovel
I've been diggin too deep, I always do.
I see my face on the surface
I look a lot like Narcissus[1]
A dark abyss of an emptiness
Standing on the edge of a drowning blue

I look behind my ears for the green
Even my sweat smells clean
Glare off the white hurts my eyes
Gotta get out of bed get a hammer and a nail
Learn how to use my hands not just my head
I think myself into jail
Now I know a refuge never grows
From a chin in a hand in a thoughtful pose
Gotta tend the earth if you want a rose

I had a lot of good intentions
Sit around for fifty years and then collect a pension
Started seeing the road to hell and just where it starts
But my life is more than a vision
The sweetest part is acting after making a decision 5
Started seeing the whole as a sum of its parts.

My life is part of the global life
I'd found myself becoming more immobile
When I'd think a little girl in the world can't do anything 6
A distant nation my community
A street person my responsibility
If I have a care in the world I have a gift to bring

◆ **Build Vocabulary**

hovel (huv´ əl) *n.:* Low, open storage shed; hut

abyss (ə bis´) *n.:* Bottomless gulf; immeasurable depth

1. **Narcissus** (när sis´ əs): In Greek mythology, a beautiful youth who pines away for love of his own reflection in the pool of a spring and is changed into a flower.

"Hammer and a Nail" words and music by Emily Saliers. Copyright © 1990 EMI VIRGIN SONGS, INC. and GODHAP MUSIC. All rights controlled and administered by EMI VIRGIN SONGS, INC. All rights reserved. International Copyright secured. Used by permission.

Guide for Responding

◆ Literature and Your Life

Reader's Response Which ideas in these selections reflect ideas with which you agree? Explain.

Thematic Focus How does taking action or "making things happen" give you a sense of purpose in life?

☑ Check Your Comprehension

1. (a) At the end of "Gardening," how does White feel about her garden? (b) On what is she focused?
2. What does the singer in "Hammer" want to learn?
3. What do the lyrics refer to as the "sweetest part" of life?

Develop Understanding

One-Minute Insight These lyrics explore the idea that physical, active work is as important as mind work. Overanalyzing can paralyze a person; therefore, it's better to act so you can benefit from life's experiences and share your gifts.

Customize for
ESL Students
Help students grasp the meaning of the metaphors in these lyrics, such as "digging too deep" or "I think myself into jail."

Reinforce and Extend

Customize for
Musical/Rhythmic Learners
Have these students listen to a recording of the song "Hammer and a Nail" from the CD *nomads. indians. saints.* Challenge them to imagine the kind of person who might be inspired by hearing this song.

Answers

◆ ***Literature and Your Life***

Reader's Response Students who take pride in doing something well may agree with the idea that work can be rewarding in and of itself.

Thematic Focus Students may respond that taking action helps people feel empowered and productive.

☑ Check Your Comprehension

1. (a) She is not interested in the garden because there's nothing left to do to it; it is complete. (b) She is learning about new, intensive forms of gardening.
2. She wants to learn how to use her hand instead of just her head.
3. Acting after making a decision is described as the sweetest part of life.

Beyond the Selection

FURTHER READING

Other Works by Bailey White

Mama Makes Up Her Mind

Sleeping at the Starlight Motel and Other Adventures on the Way Back Home

Other Songs by the Indigo Girls

"Closer to Fine"

"Galileo"

We suggest that you preview these works before recommending them to students.

INTERNET

The Internet provides opportunities for students to learn more at the following Web sites. Be aware that sites may have changed since this information was published.

For an index of Indigo Girls links, go to **http://www.sky.net/~eml/indigo.html**

To find Bailey White's radio scripts, use her name in a search at **http://www.npr.org/**

We *strongly recommend* that you preview sites before you send students to them.

Answers
◆ Critical Thinking

1. Though she had long anticipated the pleasure of wearing her white dress, when the time comes to wear it, she no longer likes it. In the same way, she thinks that she will enjoy completing her garden, only to find that the finished garden doesn't satisfy her; it was the challenge that she really enjoyed.
2. Both works focus on the satisfaction that comes from physical work.
3. Suggested response: A "meaningful life" is productive and filled with worthwhile physical activities; it is a life of doing, not dreaming.
4. Possible response: They might recommend volunteering to plant a community garden.
5. Both works express the idea that hard work can be very rewarding.

Thematic Connection

1. Suggested response: White sees nature as something that needs to be kept in check and carefully tended in order to produce the desired effect. Emerson and Thoreau accept nature as they find it: wild, overgrown, and untouched by human beings.
2. Suggested responses include: "Learn how to use my hands, not just my head/I think myself into a jail," "But my life is more than a vision/The sweetest part is acting after making a decision/I start seeing the whole as a sum of its parts."

Idea Bank

Customizing for *Performance Levels*

Following are suggestions for matching Idea Bank topics with your students' performance levels:
Less Advanced Students: 1, 5
Average Students: 2, 4
More Advanced Students: 3

Customizing for *Learning Modalities*

Following are suggestions for matching Idea Bank topics with your students' learning modalities:
Intrapersonal: 1
Musical/Rhythmic: 4
Visual/Spatial: 5

◆ Critical Thinking

INTERPRET

1. In "Gardening," how do the writer's feelings about the white dress reflect her changing ideas about what she expects to receive from her garden? **[Connect]**
2. Explain values expressed in both "Gardening" and "Hammer and a Nail."

APPLY

3. How might White or Saliers define a "meaningful life"? **[Generalize]**

EXTEND

4. What activities in your hometown might both White and Saliers suggest to people who feel "out of touch" with nature? **[Community Link]**

COMPARE LITERARY WORKS

5. Explain and compare values expressed in both "Gardening" and "Hammer and a Nail." **[Compare and Contrast]**

Thematic Connection

THE HUMAN SPIRIT AND THE NATURAL WORLD

Spending time out of doors on a beautiful summer day, walking through a rolling park or picturesque garden, even doing yard work—activities like these lift our spirits in a unique way. This kind of day-to-day contact with nature was once a way of life in this country.

Today, these experiences are fewer and farther between for millions of Americans who spend their days confined in offices and factories—often without so much as a glimpse of blue sky or green grass. This enforced separation may increase nature's power to affect and restore the human spirit.

1. How does White's approach to nature differ from that of Emerson and Thoreau?
2. What details from "Hammer and a Nail" express the idea that working with one's hands can inspire the human spirit to better things?

Idea Bank

Writing

1. **Personal Anecdote** Have you ever made something with your own hands? Perhaps you baked a cake or built something in woodworking shop. Write an anecdote, or story, about such an experience. What part of the experience was most satisfying? What did you learn?
2. **Grant Proposal** Imagine that a group from your school is applying for a grant to develop a community garden. Write a proposal that explains your plans for an empty lot and why you feel it is important. Base your argument on the ideas expressed in the works of Emerson, Thoreau, White, and Saliers. **[Community Link]**
3. **Critique** In *Walden,* Thoreau writes, "I do not wish to be any more busy with my hands than is necessary." What might Thoreau have thought of the years White worked at creating something that was meant to look as though it had occurred naturally? From the viewpoint of Thoreau, write a critique of "Gardening" or "Hammer and a Nail."

Speaking, Listening, and Viewing

4. **Music Analysis** Listen to a recording of the song "Hammer and a Nail" from the album *nomads. indians. saints.* by the Indigo Girls. Did anything strike you that you hadn't noticed from reading the lyrics? Was the emotional tone what you expected? Jot down your answers in your journal. **[Music Link]**

Researching and Representing

5. **Drawing** Reread the passages in which White describes herself at work in her garden. Then, using charcoals or watercolors, draw or paint a scene depicting White in her wildflower meadow. **[Art Link]**

Online Activity www.phlit.phschool.com

✓ ASSESSMENT OPTIONS

Formal Assessment, Selection Test, pp. 113–114, and Assessment Resources Software. The selection test is designed so that it can be easily customized to the performance levels of your students.

PORTFOLIO ASSESSMENT

Use the following rubrics in the ***Alternative Assessment*** booklet to assess student writing:
Personal Anecdote: Expression, p. 109
Grant Proposal: Persuasion Rubric, p. 120
Critique: Critical Review Rubric, p. 126

Writing Process Workshop

Reflective Essay

What does thought add to an experience? Reflecting on an event can help you realize its importance or uncover attitudes and values you may not have known you had. Emerson and Thoreau spent a great deal of time analyzing and reflecting on their experiences; this helped them develop and refine their philosophies.

In a **reflective essay**, a writer describes personal experiences or pivotal events and conveys his or her feelings about these events or experiences. Often, the writer reflects on the meaning or significance of the experience being described, as Emerson and Thoreau do in the pieces you have read in this section. Think about a meaningful event in your own life, and write a reflective essay that describes the event and explains its significance to you.

The following skills will help you write your reflective essay:

Writing Skills Focus

- ▶ **Use specific examples** when describing the experience and explaining its impact. Be as specific as possible so your readers will be able to share your experience.
- ▶ **Write with a personal tone** to give your essay an authentic, heartfelt quality. (See p. 371.)

Thoreau uses these skills as he reflects on the busy lives he sees in nineteenth-century America.

MODEL FROM LITERATURE

from *Walden* by Henry David Thoreau

. . . Our life is frittered away by detail. An honest man has hardly need to count more than his ten fingers, or in extreme cases he may add his ten toes, and lump the rest. Simplicity, simplicity, simplicity! I say, ① let your affairs be as two or three, and not a hundred or a thousand; instead of a million count half a dozen, and keep your accounts on your thumbnail. ②

① Thoreau's use of the first-person pronoun helps to give his reflection a personal tone.

② Thoreau clearly expresses his position regarding how people should approach life.

Prepare and Engage

LESSON OBJECTIVES

- To use recursive writing processes to write a reflective essay
- To recognize appropriate sentence construction, including correct use of precise nouns
- To recognize appropriate sentence construction, including correct use of pronoun case

Establish Writing Guidelines Distribute the scoring rubrics in ***Alternative Assessment*** for Description and Expression (pp. 104 and 112) to make students aware of the criteria on which their work will be evaluated. For suggestions on how you can customize these rubrics to this workshop see p. 391.

Refer students to the Writing Handbook, p. 1192, for instruction in the writing process, and p. 1194 for further information on descriptive writing. You may also want to present the Writing Process Model of a Reflective Essay (pp. 5–8) in ***Writing and Language Transparencies***.

Connect to Literature You may want to have students look at Thoreau's *Walden* (p. 374) and "Straw Into Gold" by Sandra Cisneros (p. 1006).

Writers at Work Videodisc
To introduce the elements of description, play the videodisc segment featuring poet and novelist, Rita Dove (Ch. 1).

Play frames 335 to 10985

Writing Lab If your students have access to computers, you may want to have them work in the tutorial on Description. Have students follow these steps:

1. Review the interactive model of a reflective essay.
2. Use the Word Bins to gather details.
3. Draft their essays on the computer.
4. Use Revision Checkers to identify vague or overused adjectives.

Cross-Curricular Connection: Social Studies

Throughout history and across the world's many cultures, reflective essays have come to function as the key touchstones for major philosophies. In the Western "Age of Enlightenment," reflective essays often became the basis for later political movements. In Japan, the reflective essays of the educated samurai often became handbooks for new generations of leaders to follow. When Thoreau wrote *Walden,* a work based on the experiences of a specific period in his life and his reflections on them, he probably never imagined the lasting impact his writing would have on his culture. Challenge students to come up with similar examples from their knowledge of social studies.

Ask students what philosophies their reflective essays explore. Ask students to imagine that people from another time or culture were to read the class's essay. These readers could make inferences about contemporary life and values. Ask students what future readers might learn from their reflections. Have students bear this idea in mind to lend greater depth to their writing.

Develop Student Writing

Prewriting Strategy
For additional practice on considering audience and purpose, have students conduct the same audience-purpose-language analysis as illustrated in the chart for each of the topic ideas provided in the student edition.

Customize for
Intrapersonal Learners
You may need to clarify for these students the difference between writing reflective essays and other personal forms such as journal writing. Consider pairing intrapersonal learners with interpersonal learners to help them verbally articulate their topics and writing purposes before beginning to draft. This process should help ensure that they transform personal material into a form that is accessible to a wide audience.

Writing Lab CD-ROM The Drafting section of the tutorial contains several useful interactive models that can help students with their reflective essays. Direct students to models of tone, point-of-view, and figurative language.

Elaboration Strategy
The process of writing is one of self-discovery. While drafting their reflective essays, students may notice that new ideas surface as a result of their focused introspection. Encourage students to capture these thoughts as they occur, either incorporating them into their existing organization or taking notes that they can work into their drafts when revising.

Revision Strategy
Have students reenter their writing and use highlighter pens to mark vague nouns that should be replaced with more specific and precise ones.

Applying Language Skills: Precise Nouns

Good writers avoid general, abstract nouns and instead choose specific, precise nouns to make their writing clearer and more interesting. These sentences demonstrate the difference:

General:
I drove my car to a restaurant.

Precise:
I drove my convertible to the pizza parlor.

Practice Make the general nouns in these sentences more precise.

1. The trees on the road were bending during the storm.
2. The surface was wet after I spilled the liquid.
3. I saw the book at a store.

Writing Application As you draft your reflective essay, be sure that your nouns are as specific and precise as possible.

Writer's Solution Connection
Writing Lab

To help you gather precise nouns for your reflective essay, use the Sensory Word Bin activities in the Writing Lab tutorial on Description.

Prewriting

Choose a Topic Look through your possessions to find objects that relate to specific memories or important periods from your childhood: perhaps an old collection of dolls or a shoebox of baseball cards. Jot down your thoughts in a notebook, and then review the notes to find a topic. You might also consider one of the following topics:

Topic Ideas
- Nature (a favorite place or an occurrence like a thunderstorm)
- Being a teenager
- Dance
- The importance of the telephone or e-mail in your life
- A work of art—music, theater, film, painting—that influenced you

Consider Your Audience and Purpose For whom are your reflections intended, and what is your purpose? Your choice of words and details will be shaped to a large extent by who is reading your work and what you want to convey to them. Look at these examples:

Topic: The Uncertainties of Adolescence

Audience:	Purpose:	Language:
Peers	Share feelings	Informal
Adults	Plea for greater understanding	More formal
Children	Offer cautionary advice	Simple

Drafting

Organize Your Reflections When you write your essay, take the time to develop a clear organization. Most likely, you'll want to organize your details either in the order in which they happened or by order of importance.

Applying Language Skills
Precise Nouns Introduce this skill by explaining to students that the use of precise nouns helps descriptive writing move away from the generic and the abstract—as illustrated by the "general" sentence—and towards the particular and the personal.

Answers
Possible responses:

1. The palm trees on the interstate median were bending during the summer downpour.
2. The table top was wet after I spilled the can of soda.
3. I saw the paperback at a drugstore.

Grammar Reinforcement

For additional instruction and practice, refer to the lesson on Writing with Nouns and Verbs in the **Language Lab CD-ROM** and the *Sourcebook* lesson on Using Precise Nouns (p. 26).

Revising

Replace Vague Words Don't view your revision as a chore; greet it as an opportunity or a challenge. Focus on finding parts of your reflection that could be clearer; see where you might add clarifying details or vivid verbs to strengthen weak or vague words. For example, replace "good" with stronger words, such as "exciting," "critical," and "revealing."

Make Your Writing More Personal Look for places in your essay that could benefit from a personal touch. Make stiff words informal, and make your opening and closing paragraphs friendly in tone.

Revision Model

When I signed up for acting class, I heard ~~the usual objections~~ ① a chorus of discouragement from friends and family. But then I remembered Thoreau's inspiring advice to advance "confidently in the direction of one's dreams." ② It was time, I realized, to step to the music that I hear.

① The writer enlivens the sentence with more vivid, concrete language.

② The added sentence creates a more urgent, personal tone.

Publishing

Prepare a Bulletin Board Display A classroom, hall, or library bulletin board offers an excellent place to display your writing.

- Choose illustrations from magazines or prepare artwork to accompany your piece.
- Choose attractive background colors and designs, and arrange the illustrations dramatically. It might be helpful to design the arrangement on paper before setting up the actual display.

Stage a Round Table Discussion With a group of classmates, hold a meeting to share your reflective essays. Read each essay aloud, and then offer each student feedback. To conclude the discussion, look for similarities among all essays.

Applying Language Skills: Pronoun Case

Personal pronouns have different subject and object forms, or cases, that reflect how they are used in the sentence.

Subjective Case:

She is delighted.

The first-prize winner is she.

Objective Case:

Tyrone handed the letter to him.

Tyrone handed him the letter.

The letter mentioned him.

Practice On your paper, circle the correct choice in each item.

1. My friend and (me/I) made the wrong turn.
2. Antonio gave a lift to (he/him) and Terry.
3. The ending was too intense for Olivia and (she/her) to watch.

Writing Application Review your reflective essay, and be sure that all your personal pronouns are in the correct case.

Writer's Solution Connection
Language Lab

For more practice, complete the Language Lab lesson on Pronoun Case.

Writing Lab CD-ROM The Revising and Editing section includes word bins that students can use to strengthen their essays.

Publishing

If the class chooses to display its work, keep in mind the personal nature of the reflective essays: Some students may not be comfortable with so public an audience. Discuss possible alternatives with these students.

Applying Language Skills

Pronoun Case

Reflective essays feature the heavy use of the first person pronoun in both subjective and objective cases. Have students tally the number of times they use the words *I* and *me*. Explain that it is imperative that they use these forms—and the cases of other pronouns—correctly.

Answers

1. I; 2. him; 3. her

Grammar Reinforcement

More practice can be found on p. 62 in the *Writer's Solution Grammar Practice Book.*

Reinforce and Extend

Review the Writing Guidelines Students can review the characteristics of a reflective essay and come up with additional criteria based on what they learned.

Prentice Hall Writing and Grammar For more prewriting, elaboration, and revision strategies, see *Prentice Hall Writing and Grammar.*

ASSESSMENT

PORTFOLIO ASSESSMENT

Use the rubric on Expression and Description in the ***Alternative Assessment*** booklet (p.109 and p. 112) to assess students' writing. Add these criteria to customize the rubrics to this assignment.

	4	3	2	1
Precise Nouns	The writer consistently uses precise nouns instead of general nouns.	The writer uses some general nouns instead of precise nouns.	The writer uses more general nouns than precise nouns.	The writer consistently uses general nouns, lending the descriptions a generic tone.
Personal Tone	The writer gives the essay a heartfelt, personal tone.	The writer gives a friendly tone to the opening or closing paragraphs, but is not informal throughout.	The writer rarely uses a personal tone in the essay.	The writer uses stiff, formal language and an impersonal tone.

Prepare and Engage

LESSON OBJECTIVES

- To acquire an extensive vocabulary through reading and systematic word study, including reading and understanding analogies

Customize for
English Language Students
Encourage students to say a complete sentence using the first pair of words in each analogy. Their sentence should describe the meaning relationship between the words. Examples: *The heart is inside the body; the heart pumps blood through the body; the heart makes the body work.* Then they can say analogous sentences using the second pair. Examples: *An engine is inside a car; an engine powers a car; an engine makes a car run.*

Apply the Strategies

Answers

1. Part-whole: The goal is part of a soccer field; the end zone is part of a football field.
2. Type of: A Labrador is a type of dog; a Siamese is a type of cat.
3. The words are antonyms.
4. The words are synonyms.
5. Part-whole: A brick is part of a wall; a person is part of a community.

1. (B) catastrophe
2. (A) word
3. (C) author
4. (C) bee

Student Success Workshop

Vocabulary Development — Understanding Analogies

Strategies for Success

An analogy makes a comparison between two different things on the basis of some similarity between them. Since writers often use analogies to make a point, recognizing analogies can help you understand what you are reading. Identifying the comparisons within analogies can help expand your vocabulary by putting new words into context. Understanding analogies is also important because many standardized tests include them.

Analogies on Tests In the kind of analogy found in standardized tests, a comparison is made between two pairs of words. The relationship between the words in the first pair is similar to the relationship between the words in the second pair. For instance, in the analogy *the heart is to the body as an engine is to a car,* the relationship between *heart* and *body* is similar to the relationship between *engine* and *car.* The heart makes the body run, while an engine makes a car run. Often, especially on standardized tests, analogies are expressed as formulas:

HEART : BODY :: ENGINE : CAR

Relationships in Analogies There are many kinds of relationships in analogies. Recognizing the relationships is the key to understanding them. Some analogies show pairs of synonyms, and some show antonyms. Others are descriptive in nature: They show how one thing is a type of another. You may also encounter analogies that show the relationship between an item and its function or between a part and its whole. For example, the wing of a bird is analogous to the wing of an insect by function. The analogy TIBET : ASIA :: GHANA : AFRICA expresses a part-to-whole relationship.

Apply the Strategies

Determine the type of relationship in each of the following analogies:

1. GOAL : SOCCER :: END ZONE : FOOTBALL
2. LABRADOR : DOG :: SIAMESE : CAT
3. *Certain* is to *doubtful* as *optimistic* is to *pessimistic.*
4. *Frigid* is to *cold* as *steamy* is to *warm.*
5. BRICK : WALL :: PERSON : COMMUNITY

Choose the word that best completes each of these analogies:

1. MISDEMEANOR : FELONY :: MISHAP :
   A OCCURRENCE **C** PROSPERITY
   B CATASTROPHE **D** SUCCESS
2. AMINO ACID : PROTEIN :: LETTER :
   A WORD **C** SPELLING
   B ENVELOPE **D** FRIEND
3. ABRAHAM LINCOLN : PRESIDENT :: MARK TWAIN :
   A SENATOR **C** AUTHOR
   B MAN **D** VICE PRESIDENT
4. WISDOM : OWL :: INDUSTRIOUSNESS :
   A SNAKE **C** BEE
   B DOG **D** DRAGON

Here are situations in which you might need to understand the comparisons made in analogies:

- *Reading a complex article or novel*
- *Understanding a clever joke or pun*
- *Figuring out a crossword puzzle or word game*

Test Preparation Workshop

Reading Comprehension:
Understanding Analogies On standardized tests such as the SAT, a pair of items is given and test takers must choose the analogous pair. Offer this example:

CROWBAR : PRY

A pulley : tool
B weight : heavy
C hit : hammer
D brush : paint

Students may state the relationship between CROWBAR and PRY as "tool and function"—"the function of a crowbar is to pry." Looking for an analogous pair, they will find that the only one that works is "the function of a brush is to paint"—choice *D*. Point out the reversed relationship in choice *C*, which sometimes occurs on test items. Also discuss how mismatched parts of speech are clues to an incorrect choice (the noun/adjective pair in choice *B* does not match the noun/verb pair in the stem).

PART 4 # *Looking at Literary Forms:* *Poetry*

Walden Pond Revisited, 1942, N.C. Wyeth, Brandywine River Museum

As the nation's boundaries pushed west in the nineteenth century, writers were pioneering new styles of poetry. Walt Whitman abandoned traditional poetic forms in favor of free verse. Emily Dickinson combined striking languages and a highly imaginative view of the world. Together, these two influential poets set the stage for a new American poetry.

One-Minute Planning Guide

The selections in this section reveal the range of two of the nation's most famous poets. Emily Dickinson's poetry explores the vast inner landscape. "The Brain—is wider than the Sky—" asserts that the human soul can encompass all things in the natural world and an individual identity. In "Because I could not stop for Death—" and "I heard a Fly buzz—when I died—," the poet describes the somber journey from life to death. Rich in imagery and symbolism and innovative in its form, Dickinson's poetry has been celebrated and emulated long after the poet's death. Similarly, Walt Whitman broke the conventions of the poetry of his time. Whitman's strong belief in the connection between humanity and nature as well as his unique catalog style are evident in the excerpt from "Song of Myself" and "I Hear America Singing."

Customize for ***Varying Student Needs***

When assigning the selection in this part, keep these factors in mind.

Emily Dickinson's poetry

- Vivid imagery may make "Because I could not stop for Death—" and "I heard a Fly buzz—when I died—" the most accessible for less proficient readers.
- The subject matter and language of "The Soul selects her own Society—" makes it challenging.

Walt Whitman's poetry

- "I Hear America Singing" is an accessible celebration of the variety of workers in America.
- Less proficient readers may need to read From "Preface to the 1855 Edition of *Leaves of Grass*" and From "Song of Myself" in sections.

"I, Too"; "To Walt Whitman"

- Contemporary poets reflect on Whitman's legacy.

Humanities: Art

Walden Pond Revisited, 1942, by N.C. Wyeth.

Newell Convers Wyeth (1882–1945) was the premiere book illustrator of his day. Born in Needham, Massachusetts, Wyeth knew early on that he wanted to be an artist, and so he studied with the great American illustrator Howard Pyle, often visiting Pyle at his home in Chadds Ford, Pennsylvania. Wyeth eventually settled his family in this beautiful area.

This painting, a mixture of egg-based tempera and other media, is somewhat surrealistic in its style. Wyeth renders various natural elements in careful detail, but the unnaturally crowded composition and dramatic lighting of the painting suggest a kind of dreamscape. Painted a century after Thoreau's historic sojourn at Walden Pond, this work reveres the writer as a kind of philosopher saint, setting him in an idealized landscape. Ask:

1. If a photograph is comparable to prose, in what ways might this painting be comparable to poetry? *It is not realistic, it includes imaginative elements, and it is full of vivid images dramatically highlighted.*
2. Based on this painting, what would you say Wyeth felt about Thoreau, and what elements in the painting lead you to this idea? *Wyeth seems to admire Thoreau, and this admiration is conveyed by the halo-like light that surrounds the writer.*

Prepare and Engage

LESSON OBJECTIVES

1. To develop vocabulary and word identification skills
- Latin Roots: *-finis-*
- Using the Word Bank: Synonyms

2. To use a variety of reading strategies to comprehend poetry
- Connect Your Experience
- Reading Strategy: Analyze Images

3. To read for different purposes in varied sources, including American literature
- Background for Understanding: Literature

4. To express and support responses to the text
- Critical Thinking
- Idea Bank: Editor's Letter
- Idea Bank: Critical Response
- Idea Bank: Painting

5. To analyze literary elements
- Literary Focus: Slant Rhyme

6. To read in order to research self-selected and assigned topics
- Idea Bank: Report

7. To plan, prepare, organize, and present literary interpretations
- Speaking, Listening, and Viewing Mini-Lesson (ATE)
- Idea Bank: Oral Interpretation
- Idea Bank: Musical Interpretation

8. To use recursive writing processes to write a letter to an author
- Guided Writing Lesson

9. To increase knowledge of the rules of grammar and usage
- Grammar and Style: Gerunds

Test Preparation

Reading Comprehension: Make Inferences and Generalizations (ATE, p. 395)
The teaching tips and sample test item in this workshop support the instruction and practice in the unit workshop:
Reading Comprehension: Analyze Information to Make Inferences and Generalizations (SE, p. 427)

Guide for Interpreting

Emily Dickinson *(1830–1886)*

Of the 1,775 poems Emily Dickinson wrote during her lifetime, only seven were published before her death—and these few appeared anonymously. Dickinson was a private person who was extremely reluctant to reveal herself (or her work) to the world. As a result, few people outside her family and a few friends knew of her poetic genius. Today, however, she is widely regarded as one of the greatest American poets.

A Life Apart Dickinson was born in Amherst, Massachusetts, the daughter of a prominent lawyer. As a child, she was energetic and enjoyed the tasks of daily life—cooking, sewing, playing with friends, winter sports, even studying at a boarding school. Her childhood seemed normal in many respects. However, as an adult she became increasingly isolated. Though she traveled as a young woman to Boston, Washington, D.C., and Philadelphia to visit friends, she rarely left her small valley town as she grew older. In fact, during the last ten years of her life, she refused to leave even her house and garden.

Dickinson's circle of friends grew smaller and smaller, and she communicated with the few that remained mainly through notes and fragments of poems.

Her Talent Is Recognized Though she chose to live most of her life in virtual isolation, Emily Dickinson was a remarkably energetic, intense person. She possessed a clear sense of purpose and devoted most of her time to writing poetry. Yet because she shared her work with few people, she sometimes doubted her abilities. In 1862, she sent four poems to Thomas Wentworth Higginson, an influential literary critic, and asked him to tell her whether her verse was "alive."

Like the editors who first published her work after her death, Higginson sought to change her unconventional style—her eccentric use of punctuation and irregular meter and rhyme. He did not understand that she had crafted her poetry with great precision and that her unique style was an important element of it. Still, he did recognize her talent and encouraged her to keep writing.

Her Final Years In the last several years of her life, Dickinson dressed only in white and would not allow neighbors or strangers to see her. Her reluctance to interact with people grew so extreme that, despite failing health, she permitted her doctor to examine her only from a distance.

In 1886, after fighting illness for two years, she died in the same house in which she had been born. After her death, her sister Lavinia discovered packets of poems in the drawers of Emily's dresser. Her first books of verse were published four years later.

◆ Background for Understanding

LITERATURE: DICKINSON'S TALENT IS DISCOVERED

The extent of Emily Dickinson's gift was not generally recognized until 1955, when a complete, unedited edition of her poems was published under the guidance of Thomas H. Johnson. Viewing her work in its original form, writers and critics could see that Dickinson was utterly unlike other poets of her era. For the first time, her poetry was appreciated for its unique style, concrete imagery, and simple but forceful language. Dickinson's work is often compared with that of the modern poets, and she is now acknowledged as a visionary who was far ahead of her time.

Prentice Hall Literature Program Resources

REINFORCE / RETEACH / EXTEND

Selection Support Pages
Build Vocabulary: Latin Roots: *-finis-*, p. 114
Grammar/Style: Gerunds, p. 115
Reading Strategy: Analyze Images, p. 116
Literary Focus: Slant Rhyme, p. 117

Strategies for Diverse Student Needs, p. 24

Beyond Literature
Cross-Curricular Connection: Art, p. 24

Formal Assessment Selection Test, pp. 118–120; Assessment Resources Software

Alternative Assessment, p. 24

Writing and Language Transparencies
Outline Organizer, pp. 95–97
Daily Language Practice, Week 11

Literature CD-ROM

Resource Pro CD-ROM

Emily Dickinson's Poetry

◆ Literature and Your Life

Connect Your Experience

Although you may not often speak your most private thoughts about life's "big topics," you probably have many ideas and feelings about them. In the following poems, Emily Dickinson shines light on shadowy "private" thoughts and ideas about several vast or abstract topics—society, death, solitude, consciousness, and the soul.

Journal Writing Choose one of these abstract topics and quickly write your immediate thoughts about it. Use your initial reaction to help you approach Dickinson's poetry.

Thematic Focus: The Human Spirit and the Natural World

As a truly American literature emerged, some of it reflected the nation's vitality and open spaces. A few writers, however, chose to examine details of personal, domestic, or spiritual life in the young nation. How does Dickinson illuminate her own inner landscape?

◆ Build Vocabulary

Latin Roots: *-finis-*

In "There is a solitude of space," you'll find the words *finite* and *infinity,* both of which contain the Latin root *-finis-,* meaning "end" or "limit." A finite entity is limited in time or space; infinity is limitless.

Word Bank

As you read these selections, you will encounter the words on this list. Preview the list before you read.

cornice
surmised
oppresses
finite
infinity

◆ Literary Focus

Slant Rhyme

Poets use rhyme to create pleasant musical sounds and to unify groups of lines or stanzas. **Exact rhyme** occurs when two words have identical sounds in their final accented syllables. However, in a **slant rhyme,** the final sounds are similar but not identical. *Glove-above* is an exact rhyme, but *glove-prove* is a slant rhyme.

Dickinson uses both exact and slant rhyme in her poetry. Her independence from strict rhyme keeps her verses surprising.

◆ Grammar and Style

Gerunds

A **gerund** is a verb form that ends in *-ing* and is used as a noun. Like nouns, they function in sentences as subjects, complements (such as direct objects and subject complements), and objects of prepositions. In the following passage, Dickinson uses the gerund *meanings:*

We can find no scar,
But internal difference,
Where the Meanings,
are—

◆ Reading Strategy

Analyze Images

Poets often link abstract concepts such as love, life, death, and spirituality to concrete images, or word pictures. In "Because I could not stop for Death—" Dickinson uses an image of a carriage ride to capture the experience of death. It is important to **analyze** what the author is conveying through the choice of each **image**.

Complete a chart like this one to help you.

Image	Abstract Idea
Carriage, slow journey	Death
Schoolchildren, grain, sunset	Life
House, roof below ground	Eternity

Test Preparation Workshop

Reading Comprehension: Make Inferences and Generalizations The reading sections of many standardized tests, including the SAT, require students to make inferences. Explain to students that making inferences will help them understand poetry because poets often leave much of their message unstated. Use the following example to help students make inferences about "There's a certain Slant of light," on p. 399:

Which of the following best describes the effect of the light?

A overwhelming
B uplifting
C encouraging
D energizing

The last three answers cannot be supported by details from the text. The light is oppressive and feels heavy, so A is the best choice.

Interest Grabber

Many of Emily Dickinson's poems deal with the abstract concept of solitude. Ask students to consider their personal reactions to the word *alone*. Each student should list the five words that come immediately to mind. Then elicit answers from each student. As you write responses on the chalkboard, ask the class to classify each response as positive or negative. When you have collected at least one response from every student, ask students to determine whether the word *alone* has a more positive or negative connotation. Ask students to consider both sides—independence and isolation—as they approach Emily Dickinson's poetry.

Customize for *Less Proficient Readers*

The poems in this grouping are rich with imagery. To prepare students to recognize Dickinson's techniques, review examples of figurative language, such as simile, metaphor, and personification. These students may also benefit from the ***Strategies for Diverse Student Needs*** page on forming mental pictures (p. 24).

Customize for *AP Students*

Emily Dickinson's words may seem straightforward, yet they conceal metaphors and hidden messages. Challenge students to read the poems on more than one level to find the meanings behind the simple words. Hearing the poems several times can also help students identify meaning.

Listening to Literature Audiocassettes

Customize for *English Language Learners*

The words in these poems may be easy to decode, but the imagery and symbolism are less apparent. Encourage students to sketch visual images to help them ascertain the symbolic meaning, or use reader's response logs to record some of their reactions to the poems.

Customize for *Interpersonal Learners*

Some students may have trouble imagining or respecting Dickinson's choice of a solitary life. Help them consider the benefits of contemplative time.

Develop Understanding

One-Minute Insight The first poem describes the final moments between life and death. A fly, an almost trivial symbol of life, is what the speaker is most aware of before death. In the second poem, Dickinson captures the inevitability of death and suggests a belief in an eternal afterlife through the personification of Death as a coach driver who carries people toward their ultimate resting places.

Customize for
AP Students

❶ Discuss the circumstances in which a person might become aware of the sound of a fly. What might a fly represent? *One hears the small sound of a fly when there is silence or when one is aware of only the nearest sound; a fly can stand for death and decay.*

▶Critical Viewing◀

❷ **Support** Both the image and the poem convey a stillness. There appears to be no life in the room. The chairs and lamps are placed symmetrically around the mirror. The curtains do not move; this detail reinforces the "Stillness."

◆ Literary Focus

❸ **Slant Rhyme** Point out the poet's use of slant rhyme in this ABCB stanza: *Room* and *Storm* do not precisely echo. The next two stanzas also use slant rhyme. However, the last stanza uses complete rhyme, perhaps suggesting that death is a kind of perfection or completeness.

◆ Reading Strategy

❹ **Analyze Images** Ask students to explain the meaning of the images in the final stanza. *The "uncertain stumbling Buzz" is the faltering life force. "the Windows failed" means that the speaker's eyes closed for the last time so that she "could not see," which means that she died.*

◆ Reading Strategy

❺ **Assess** What does the final dash convey? *The dash suggests a fading away.* How would the poem be different if the final punctuation were a period? *A period might have made the death more concrete and final.*

❶ *I heard a Fly buzz—when I died—*

Emily Dickinson

Room With a Balcony, Adolph von Menzel, Staatliche Museen Preubischer Kulturbesitz Nationgalerie, Berlin

◀ **Critical Viewing** Why is this an appropriate illustration for Dickinson's poem? **[Support]** ❷

❸ I heard a Fly buzz—when I died—
The Stillness in the Room
Was like the Stillness in the Air—
Between the Heaves of Storm—

The Eyes around—had wrung them dry—
And Breaths were gathering firm
For that last Onset—when the King
Be witnessed—in the Room—

I willed my Keepsakes—Signed away
What portion of me be
Assignable—and then it was
There interposed a Fly—

With Blue—uncertain stumbling Buzz—
❹ Between the light—and me—
❺ And then the Windows failed—and then
I could not see to see—

Block Scheduling Strategies

Consider these suggestions to take advantage of extended class time:

- Have students take turns reading aloud the poems, or have students listen to one or more of the audiocassette recordings of the poems.
- After students have read or listened to the poems, divide the class into small groups and assign each group a different poem. Students can use the chart presented on p. 395 to analyze the poem and then share their interpretation with the class.
- Use the Daily Language Practice sentences for Week 11 in the ***Writing and Language Transparencies.*** You may display the practice sentences on an overhead projector and have students write them correctly, or you may dictate the sentences to the students.
- Use the outline organizer on pp. 95–97 in the ***Writing and Language Transparencies*** to help students prepare for the Guided Writing Lesson. Students can work alone or in pairs to complete the assignment.

Because I could not stop for Death—

Emily Dickinson

Because I could not stop for Death—
He kindly stopped for me—
The Carriage held but just Ourselves—
And Immortality.

We slowly drove—He knew no haste
And I had put away
My labor and my leisure too,
For his Civility—

We passed the School, where Children strove
At Recess—in the Ring—
We passed the Fields of Gazing Grain—
We passed the Setting Sun—

Or rather—He passed Us—
6 The Dews drew quivering and chill—
For only Gossamer,[1] my Gown—
My Tippet[2]—only Tulle[3]—

We paused before a House that seemed
A Swelling of the Ground—
The Roof was scarcely visible—
The Cornice—in the Ground—

Since then—'tis Centuries—and yet
Feels shorter than the Day
I first surmised the Horses Heads
Were toward Eternity—

1. **Gossamer:** Very thin, soft, filmy cloth.
2. **Tippet:** Scarflike garment worn over the shoulders and hanging down in front.
3. **Tulle** (to͞ol) *n.*: Thin, fine netting used for scarves.

◆ Build Vocabulary

Cornice (kôr´ nis) *n.*: Projecting decorative molding along the top of a building

surmised (sər mīzd´) *v.*: Guessed

Guide for Responding

◆ Literature and Your Life

Reader's Response How did the images and ideas in these poems make you feel?

Thematic Focus In "Because I could not stop for Death—" how does Dickinson use images of nature to convey her speaker's inner landscape?

☑ Check Your Comprehension

1. In "I heard a Fly buzz—when I died—" what three sounds does the speaker note?
2. (a) Why does Death stop for the speaker of "Because I could not stop for Death—"? (b) What is in the carriage?
3. How much time has passed since Death stopped for the speaker?

◆ Critical Thinking

INTERPRET

1. (a) How can you tell that the speaker of "I heard a Fly buzz—when I died—" has prepared herself for death? (b) What happens in the poem's last moment? **[Support; Analyze]**
2. What statement about dying do you think Dickinson makes in this poem? **[Draw Conclusions]**
3. (a) How is Death characterized in the first two stanzas of "Because I could not stop for Death—"? (b) In what sense is this characterization ironic? **[Analyze]**
4. (a) What is the significance of the carriage's passing "the School," "the Fields," and "the Setting Sun"? (b) What does the "House" in stanza five represent? **[Interpret]**

APPLY

5. Why do you think Emily Dickinson is so interested in death? **[Hypothesize]**

COMPARE LITERARY WORKS

5. Contrast Dickinson's tones in "I heard a Fly buzz—when I died—" and "Because I could not stop for Death—." Although both poems speak about death, how are they different? **[Contrast]**

◆ Background for Understanding

Literature Explain that Emily Dickinson did not give titles to her poems, so an editorial decision was later made to use the first lines as titles. In some scholarly editions, the poems are numbered.

Customize for
Verbal/Linguistic Learners
6 Ask students to explain how the speaker's attitude toward death changes in this stanza. *The speaker's focus shifts from the external world to the internal; in earlier stanzas, the speaker noticed the townspeople and nature but now acknowledges her own coldness and vulnerability.*

Reinforce and Extend

Answers

◆ Literature and Your Life

Reader's Response Some students may indicate that the poems elicited feelings of isolation or stillness.

Thematic Focus Dickinson uses images such as fields, the setting sun, and dews to describe stages of life.

☑ Check Your Comprehension

1. The speaker notes a fly's buzz, stillness, and breath.
2. (a) It is time for her to die. (b) Death's carriage holds the speaker, Death, and Immortality.
3. It has been centuries since Death stopped for the speaker.

◆ Critical Thinking

1. (a) She willed away her keepsakes. (b) The speaker hears the fly buzz as she loses consciousness.
2. Students may say she shows that death is an everyday event or points out that the experience does not match people's expectations.
3. (a) Death is portrayed as a kindly, calm, patient figure. (b) Possible response: Death is usually personified in negative terms.
4. (a) These details could represent the stages of life. (b) The "House" represents a grave.
5. Possible response: As a recluse, she did not seem to be involved in life; this may be why she wrote so frequently about death.
6. Possible response: The first poem creates a feeling of quiet anticipation, the second a feeling of finality.

Humanities: Art

Room With a Balcony, 1845, by Adolph von Menzel.

Adolph von Menzel (1815–1905) was a German illustrator and painter. He took over his father's lithography business in 1832, which initiated his long career as an illustrator. His work was distinguished by expressiveness, accurate detail, and the use of light and shade for subtle effects.

Use these questions for discussion:

1. What unusual detail does the mirror reveal? *The mirror shows a sofa and painting that are no longer in the room, but whose former presence is suggested by shadows.*
2. What is the impact of the open window? *It suggests that something or someone may have just entered or left the room.*

For further humanities instruction, use the Cross-Curricular Connection: Art page in ***Beyond Literature,*** p. 24.

Develop Understanding

One-Minute Insight The first poem conveys the sense of pain that comes from parting with a loved one. The second poem asserts the speaker's decision to live in isolation, stressing a belief in a soulmate, even when that mate is loneliness itself. The third poem describes an unbearable hurt that fills the soul. It can come and go with certain times of day, but it always reminds us of mortality.

◆ Critical Thinking

❶ **Interpret** Discuss what the poet may mean by saying that "life closed twice before its close." *Twice in her life events happened that felt as final and painful as death. Perhaps she alludes to the death of a loved one or to a failed relationship.*

Customize for
Less Proficient Students

❷ Point out the gerund in line 7 *parting* and identify it as the subject of the sentence. Then help students grasp the meaning of these final lines. *Students may say that parting, or death, is all we know of heaven because we remain on Earth when our loved ones pass on; yet it is all we need of hell because no hell could be as painful as losing someone deeply beloved.*

◆ Critical Thinking

❸ **Interpret** Discuss the central meaning of this poem, and have students restate it in their own words. *Students may paraphrase the poem like this: Each of us chooses our soulmate, and once we choose, nothing can dissuade us.* Ask them to describe the kind of person the speaker is. *The speaker, who is proud, defiant, and solitary, may have chosen herself as her soulmate.*

My life closed twice before its close—

Emily Dickinson

Connections to World Literature, *page 1174*

My life closed twice before its close— ❶
It yet remains to see
If Immortality unveil
A third event to me.

So huge, so hopeless to conceive
As these that twice befell.
Parting is all we know of heaven. ❷
And all we need of hell.

The Soul selects her own Society—

Emily Dickinson

The Soul selects her own Society—
Then—shuts the Door—
To her divine Majority—
Present no more—

Unmoved—she notes the Chariots—pausing—
At her low Gate—
Unmoved—an Emperor be kneeling
Upon her Mat—

I've known her—from an ample nation—
Choose One—
Then—close the Valves of her attention—
Like Stone— ❸

Speaking, Listening, and Viewing Mini-Lesson

Musical Interpretation

This mini-lesson supports activity 5, p. 403.

Introduce Play several examples of music—commercial jingles, popular songs, or classical—and ask students to identify the mood of each one. Remind students that a song lyric is a form of poetry. When music is added, its rhythms, harmonies, or key can reinforce the mood of the lyrics.

Develop Many poets' works have been set to music. For the Broadway show *Cats*, composer Andrew Lloyd Weber set the lyrics of some T. S. Eliot poems to music.

Apply Have students read the poem aloud to get a feel for its rhythms. Students should choose or compose a melodic line that works with the main images of the poem.

Assess Have students perform or play a tape of their musical interpretation for classmates. Invite evaluations of the music based on clarity, suitability of the musical style to the mood of the poem, and presentation.

There's a certain *Slant* of light,

Emily Dickinson

❹ There's a certain Slant of light,
Winter Afternoons—
That oppresses, like the Heft
Of Cathedral Tunes—

Heavenly Hurt, it gives us—
We can find no scar,
❺ But internal difference,
Where the Meanings, are—

None may teach it—Any—
'Tis the Seal Despair—
An imperial affliction
Sent us of the Air—

When it comes, the Landscape listens—
Shadows—hold their breath—
When it goes, 'tis like the Distance
On the look of Death—

◆ Build Vocabulary

oppresses (ə presˊ əz) *v.*: Weighs heavily on the mind

Guide for Responding

◆ *Literature and Your Life*

Reader's Response Which do you prefer—the light of the morning, afternoon, or evening? Why?

Thematic Focus How does "My life closed twice before its close—" relate details of personal history to ideas about eternity?

☑ Check Your Comprehension

1. According to the speaker of "My life closed twice before its close—" what were "huge" and "hopeless to conceive"?
2. In "The Soul selects her own Society—" what leaves the soul "unmoved"?
3. According to the speaker of "There's a certain Slant of light," how does "a certain Slant of light" affect people?

◆ Critical Thinking

INTERPRET

1. (a) In "My life closed twice before its close—" what event could have caused the speaker's life to close "twice before its close"? (b) Which line holds a clue to the nature of the events "that twice befell"? (c) What is the third event to which the speaker refers? (d) How are the three events related? **[Analyze; Interpret; Connect]**
2. (a) In "The Soul selects her own Society —" what is the soul's "divine Majority"? (b) How many people make up the soul's "Society"? **[Interpret]**
3. (a) What mood is created by the "Slant of light"? (b) What does this light seem to represent to the speaker? **[Analyze; Interpret]**

APPLY

4. You probably don't limit your companions to a "society" of one; you might choose a variety of different "societies." What do these variations indicate about your nature? **[Apply]**

◆ Critical Thinking

❹ **Interpret** What words contribute to the mood of the first stanza? *Winter, oppresses, and heft suggest a somber, heavy, and dark mood.*

◆ Critical Thinking

❺ **Analyze** What might be the meaning of lines 7–8? *Once this feeling comes over the speaker, it creates a dissonance in the way she sees the world.*

Reinforce and Extend

Answers

◆ *Literature and Your Life*

Reader's Response Students should provide support for their responses.

Thematic Focus The speaker connects life experiences of loss to her expectations of heaven and hell.

☑ Check Your Comprehension

1. The speaker anticipates but cannot imagine a third tragic event still to come.
2. Chariots and emperors leave the soul unmoved.
3. It oppresses them.

◆ Critical Thinking

1. (a) The speaker has grieved the loss of two loved ones. (b) Line 7 reveals a clue. (c) The third event is her own death. (d) They are all kinds of parting.
2. (a) Possible response: It is the person or people the soul has chosen. (b) The soul's society may actually consist of one other person.
3. (a) It creates a mood of despair. (b) It symbolizes death.
4. Possible response: The fact that people select a variety of "societies" indicates that the human race is a very diverse group.

Cross-Curricular Connection: Science

Seasonal Affective Disorder In "There's a certain Slant of light," Emily Dickinson describes a medical condition unknown to her and the doctors of her time. In the nineteenth century a person who felt lethargic and depressed during the winter months would simply be resigned to the fact that he or she had "cabin fever." However, in recent years, doctors have diagnosed this depression as a treatable mood disorder that stems from a lack of sunlight. The major symptoms of this condition, called Seasonal Affective Disorder (SAD), are depression, low energy, and weight gain.

SAD is more prevalent in the northern part of the hemisphere, where winter days are short and temperatures are low. For example, compared to those living in Florida or Hawaii, people in Washington State, Canada, and Alaska are at higher risk.

SAD can be treated with sun lamps, which help restore the body's hormone balance. Sessions as short as thirty minutes a day can help reduce symptoms of this illness. People with milder symptoms can help themselves by spending more time outdoors and exercising regularly in the winter.

Ask students how winter affects them. Have groups brainstorm for a list of wintry images and the feelings students associate with them.

Develop Understanding

One-Minute Insight In the first poem, Dickinson says that the strongest solitude is the solitude of inner loneliness. The second contrasts the brain, as a metaphor for the soul, with the sky, the sea, and God to arrive at the notion that the human soul is infinite. The third poem suggests that comparison and contrast are pointedly useful ways to learn; we can only learn things by recognizing their absence.

▶Critical Viewing◀

❶ **Respond** Students may cite general feelings of serenity, beauty, awe, or solemnity.

Customize for
Less Proficient Readers
❷ Help students to paraphrase the poem. The words *these/Society* may provide a helpful key to the poet's meaning. Point out that the poet names several solitudes (of space, of sea, and of death) and then compares all of these to the soul who has chosen to be alone. Guide students to notice that the speaker feels that the most profound solitude is the solitude of inner loneliness.

◆Critical Thinking

❸ **Interpret** What is meant by the apparent contradiction "*Finite Infinity*"? *Profound privacy of the soul is finite because eventually death ends even that solitude.*

◆Reading Strategy

❹ **Analyze Images** The human brain is physically tiny compared to the sky. Discuss the effect of this surprising comparison in the first stanza.

Customize for
English Language Learners
❺ Help students realize that the poet uses the brain as a metaphor for the human soul. Point out that in the last stanza, the speaker compares the brain with God. She says it is "just the weight of God," as if the brain (or soul) is a part of God and God a part of it, just as syllable and sound are so totally intertwined that it is hard to separate one from the other.

Twilight in the Wilderness, Frederick E. Church, The Cleveland Museum of Art

❶ ▲ **Critical Viewing** What feelings are evoked by the sweep of sky, mountains, and water in this painting? **[Respond]**

There is a solitude of space

Emily Dickinson

There is a solitude of space
A solitude of sea
A solitude of death, but these
❷ Society shall be
❸ Compared with that profounder site
That polar privacy
A soul admitted to itself—
Finite Infinity.

◆ Build Vocabulary

Finite (fī′ nīt) *adj.*: Having measurable or definable limits

Infinity (in fin′ i tē) *n.*: Endless or unlimited space, time, or distance

The Brain—is wider than the Sky—

Emily Dickinson

The Brain—is wider than the Sky—
For—put them side by side—
The one the other will contain
With ease—and You—beside— ❹

The Brain is deeper than the sea—
For—hold them—Blue to Blue—
The one the other will absorb—
As Sponges—Buckets—do—

The Brain is just the weight of God—
For—Heft them—Pound for Pound—
And they will differ—if they do—
As Syllable from Sound— ❺

Humanities: Art

Twilight in the Wilderness, 1860, by Frederic Edwin Church.

American painter Frederic Church (1826–1900) was a leading member of the Hudson River School of landscape painting. His early works, including *Twilight in the Wilderness,* are panoramic compositions with emphatic visual effects. Some critics call this work Church's finest sunset painting.

Use these questions for discussion:

1. How does Church use color for dramatic effect? *Students may say that bold contrasts between the near and far mountains and between the distant horizon and the sky overhead suggest vastness and idealized natural beauty.*
2. How does this painting suit both "There is a solitude of space" and "The Brain—is wider than the Sky—"? *Students may say that Church's expansive view echoes the vast solitude Dickinson describes in the first poem and demonstrates the vastness of the sky central to the second poem.*

Water, is taught by thirst.

Emily Dickinson

Water, is taught by thirst.
Land—by the Oceans passed.
Transport[1]—by throe[2]—
Peace—by its battles told—
Love, by Memorial Mold[3]—
6 Birds, by the Snow.

1. **Transport:** Ecstasy; rapture.
2. **throe:** Spasm or pang of pain.
3. **Memorial Mold:** Memorial grounds or cemetery.

Guide for Responding

◆ Literature and Your Life

Reader's Response Do you think it is a good idea for people to seek solitude? Why or why not?

Thematic Focus In "The Brain—is wider than the Sky—" what meaning does the speaker deduce from the comparison between an outer and inner landscape?

☑ Check Your Comprehension

1. In "There is a solitude of space," what three things does the speaker compare to "polar privacy"?
2. In"The Brain—is wider than the Sky—" what three things does the speaker compare or contrast to the human brain?
3. In "Water, is taught by thirst," what is the relationship between each line's first word and the following words?

◆ Critical Thinking

INTERPRET

1. In "There is a solitude of space," how does the solitude of a "soul admitted to itself" differ from the solitude of space, sea, and death? **[Contrast]**
2. In "The Brain—is wider than the Sky—" Dickinson makes three figurative comparisons. Explain in your own words how the human brain can "contain with ease" both the sky and one's self.
3. How would you state the theme or message of "Water, is taught by thirst." in a single sentence? **[Interpret]**

APPLY

4. Identify two or three situations or examples from everyday life that demonstrate the theme of "Water, is taught by thirst." **[Relate]**

Beyond the Selection

FURTHER READING

Other Works by Emily Dickinson
"I never saw a Moor—"
"The Bustle in a House"
"Success is counted sweetest"

Other Works With the Theme of Solitude
"The Mortgaged Heart," Carson McCullers
Walden, Henry David Thoreau
Desert Solitaire, Edward Abbey

We suggest that you preview these works before recommending them to students.

INTERNET

You may find additional information on the Internet. We suggest the following sites. Please be aware that sites may have changed since we published this information.

Two comprehensive Dickinson sites are **http://www/planet.net/pkrisxle/emily/dickinson.html** and **http://english.cla.umn.edu/Courseweb/1017/EmilyDickinson/home**

We *strongly recommend* that you preview the sites before you send students to them.

◆ Critical Thinking

6 Analyze Challenge students to explain the meaning of the last line. *Students may say that fallen snow is cold, still, and lifeless, while birds are vibrant, lively, and can move where they want. Students may also note that the whiteness of snow may help make birds more visible.*

Reinforce and Extend

Customize for
Less Proficient Readers
These students will benefit from rereading any or all of the poems. When they do, encourage them to focus on understanding the poet's use of imagery and symbolism to express the deeper meaning in each poem.

Answers

◆ Literature and Your Life

Reader's Response Students should support their opinion.

Thematic Focus Possible response: The speaker believes that human consciousness is more deep and vast than the sky.

☑ Check Your Comprehension

1. Privacy is compared to the solitudes of space, sea, and death.
2. The speaker compares the brain to the sky, the sea, and the weight of God.
3. In each line, the speaker states the first word is learned from the words that follow.

◆ Critical Thinking

1. While the solitude of a "soul admitted to itself" cannot be shared, the other solitudes can.
2. Possible response: The brain can comprehend or conceive the idea of the sky—even in its infinity—as well as the idea of self.
3. Possible responses: One knows a thing by its absence, its opposite, or by need. Things have meaning only with context.
4. Possible responses: The absence of a friend makes one see his or her value. The lack of money reveals its power.

Answers

◆ Reading Strategy

1. She uses the image of a house below ground.
2. The fly buzz suggests the moment of death is calm and silent.
3. (a) Each line of the poem presents an image. (b) Each stanza of the poem presents an image. (c) These images compare abstract ideas to concrete objects.

◆ Build Vocabulary

Using the Latin Root *-finis-*

1. Finish means end.
2. Confine means to limit an action.
3. Final means the end product.

Using the Word Bank

1. a 2. b 3. a 4. c 5. c

◆ Literary Focus

1. Two other slant rhymes are *society-majority* and *gate-mat.*
2. *Me, away,* and *day* are slant rhymes for these words.
3. *Room-storm* and *be-fly* are slant rhymes because they have similar but not identical vowel sounds.

◆ Grammar and Style

Practice

1. *Swelling* is a predicate nominative.
2. *Writing* is a subject.
3. *Parting* is a subject.
4. *Cooking* and *reading* are objects of the preposition *among.*
5. *Traveling* is a direct object.

Writing Application Students should identify the gerunds in their paragraphs. Possible response: I love to spend time *sewing. Choosing* a pattern and actually *creating* something to wear can be rewarding. I like *seeing* the smile on a friend's face when I give her a gift I've made.

Grammar Reinforcement

For additional instruction and practice, use the practice page on Gerunds and Gerund Phrases in *Writer's Solution Grammar Practice Book* (p. 33).

Guide for Responding (continued)

◆ Reading Strategy

ANALYZE IMAGES

The ability to **analyze images** allows you to understand and appreciate poetry and other types of literature more deeply. When you come across each image, look to see if it is connected to a larger idea. Analyze the meaning conveyed through the image and the associated idea.

For example, in "Because I could not stop for Death—" Dickinson describes the speaker riding with Death and Immortality in a carriage drawn by horses headed toward "Eternity." This image suggests that the speaker is describing her own death.

1. What does Dickinson use to describe a grave site in "Because I could not stop for Death—"?

2. In "I heard a Fly buzz—when I died—" what does the image of a fly in a still room suggest about the moment of death?

3. (a) Identify two images in "Water, is taught by thirst." (b) Identify two images in "The Brain—is wider than the Sky—." (c) How do these images help the speaker communicate an idea?

◆ Build Vocabulary

USING THE LATIN ROOT *-finis-*

The words *finite* and *infinity* derive from the Latin root *-finis-*, meaning "end" or "limit." Explain how the meaning of the root *-finis-* relates to the meaning of each of the following words.

1. finish **2.** confine **3.** final

USING THE WORD BANK: Synonyms

Identify the word whose meaning is most nearly the same as that of the first word in each item.

1. cornice: (a) ledge, (b) corner, (c) spire

2. surmised: (a) explained, (b) determined, (c) reduced

3. oppresses: (a) inhibits, (b) obliges, (c) judges

4. finite: (a) heavenly, (b) endless, (c) limited

5. infinity: (a) mystery, (b) multitude, (c) endlessness

◆ Literary Focus

SLANT RHYME

A **slant rhyme** occurs when two or more words have similar (but not identical) vowel sounds. For instance, in "The Soul selects her own Society—" Emily Dickinson uses the slant rhyme *one-stone.*

1. What two other slant rhymes appear in "The Soul selects her own Society—"?

2. In "Because I could not stop for Death—," what three words does Dickinson use to create slant rhymes for *immortality, civility,* and *eternity*?

3. In "I heard a Fly buzz—" Dickinson rhymes the words *room* and *storm, be* and *fly,* and *me* and *see.* Which are slant rhymes, and why?

◆ Grammar and Style

GERUNDS

Because gerunds function as nouns, they can appear in sentences as subjects, direct objects, predicate nominatives, and objects of prepositions.

Gerunds are verb forms that end in *-ing* and are used as nouns.

Subject: *Writing* requires discipline.
Direct Object: Dickinson left her *writing* in her dresser.
Object of Preposition: She learned about *writing* by *practicing.*

Practice Each of these sentences contains at least one gerund. Write each gerund on your paper. Tell how it is used in its sentence.

1. We paused before a House that seemed / A Swelling of the Ground—.

2. Writing was Emily Dickinson's greatest passion.

3. Parting is all we know of heaven. / And all we need of hell.

4. Among Dickinson's favorite activities were cooking and reading.

5. Dickinson avoided traveling great distances.

Writing Application Write a paragraph to describe an interest or hobby—skiing or painting, for example. Include at least three gerunds.

Reteach

Use a concept map or web to show students how abstract concepts can be linked to concrete images in poetry and literature. Explain that by analyzing the images, a reader learns what the author is conveying.

Have students analyze the images in "There is a solitude of space" by Dickinson. Using a visual like the one shown, help students link abstract words to concrete images, then tell what is being compared.

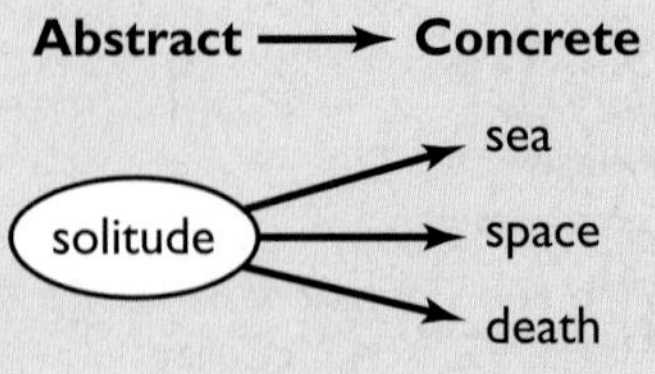

Build Your Portfolio

Idea Bank

Writing

1. Poem Emily Dickinson wrote poetry that addressed timeless themes. Write a poem using images that convey your thoughts about a universal theme, such as happiness, time, or family.

2. Editor's Letter Imagine that you are an editor of a nineteenth-century literary journal. In a letter to Dickinson, comment on two or three of her poems and ask questions about the work.

3. Critical Response A critic has stated that Dickinson's poetry "is exploration on a variety of levels of the ultimate meaning of life itself and equally important of the depths and heights of her own inner nature." Write an essay supporting this statement with evidence from the poems.

Speaking, Listening, and Viewing

4. Oral Interpretation Choose three Dickinson poems to read aloud. Consider the meaning of each idea, image, and punctuation mark. Convey your understanding of the works in a reading for the class. **[Performing Arts Link]**

5. Musical Interpretation Set a Dickinson poem to music. Consider the poem's use of rhythm and its overall tone, and choose or write music that suits the mood. **[Music Link]**

Researching and Representing

6. Painting Dickinson communicates her ideas through strong images and comparison. Depict one of Dickinson's literary images in a drawing or painting. Try to capture or convey the content of Dickinson's imagery. **[Art Link]**

7. Report Dickinson was close to her brother Austin. Research him and their relationship. Present your findings in a written report.

Online Activity www.phlit.phschool.com

Guided Writing Lesson

Letter to an Author

Dickinson's poetry may have stirred your emotions, challenged you to think about an idea or aspect of existence, or helped you better understand yourself. Imagine that Dickinson is still alive. Write a letter to the poet in which you express your reactions to her verses. Be sure to use a clear organization in presenting your ideas.

Writing Skills Focus: Clear and Logical Organization

An effective letter—whether it is addressed to a friend, an author, or a business associate—contains ideas that are not only well expressed, but also **organized clearly and logically**.

Open your letter with an explanation of your reason for writing.

- Develop each important idea in a separate paragraph, and support it with examples.
- Use transitions to carry the reader from one paragraph to the next.
- Summarize your ideas or reactions in a conclusion that leaves the reader with some memorable reflection, opinion, or piece of information.

Prewriting Select a single poem or group of two or three on which to focus. Jot down some thoughts and feelings about the poetry and how it affected you. Boil down your reactions to three or four important points; then consider how your notes support each idea.

Drafting Open your letter with an explanation of why you are writing. Then develop and support each important idea in a separate paragraph.

Revising Ask yourself how Dickinson might react to your letter. Are your tone and word choice appropriate? Make sure that your thoughts are conveyed in a clear and logical way, with appropriate transitions between each paragraph.

Idea Bank

Customizing for
Performance Levels
Following are suggestions for matching Idea Bank topics with your student's performance levels:
Less Advanced Students: 1, 6
Average Students: 2, 4, 5
More Advanced Students: 3, 7

Customizing for
Learning Modalities
Following are suggestions for matching Idea Bank topics with your students' learning modalities:
Musical/Rhythmic: 4, 5
Visual/Spatial: 6

Guided Writing Lesson

For more prewriting, elaboration, and revision strategies, see *Prentice Hall Writing and Grammar.*

Writers at Work Videodisc
Share the videodisc segment on Response to Literature which features literary agent Theresa Parks. As an agent, Parks frequently writes letters to authors about their works.

Play frames 22513 to 31258

Writing Lab CD-ROM
Have students complete the tutorial on Response to Literature. Follow these steps:

1. Have students use the Sunburst Diagram to help them organize their details.
2. To reinforce a clear and logical organization, use the models of a structured response. Have students draft on the computer.
3. Use the Self-Evaluation Checklist to aid revision and editing.

ASSESSMENT OPTIONS

Formal Assessment, Selection Test, pp. 118–120, and Assessment Resources Software. The selection test is designed so that it can be easily customized to the performance levels of your students.

Alternative Assessment, p. 24, includes options for less advanced students, more advanced students, visual/spatial learners, musical/rhythmic learners, and intrapersonal learners.

PORTFOLIO ASSESSMENT
Use the following rubrics in the ***Alternative Assessment*** booklet to assess student writing:
Poem: Poetry Rubric, p. 123
Editor's Letter: Response to Literature Rubric, p. 125
Critical Response: Response to Literature Rubric, p. 125
Guided Writing Lesson: Response to Literature Rubric, p. 125

Prepare and Engage

LESSON OBJECTIVES

1. **To develop vocabulary and word identification skills**
   - Latin Roots: *-fus-*
   - Using the Word Bank: Denotations
2. **To use a variety of reading strategies to comprehend a poem**
   - Connect Your Experience
   - Reading Strategy: Infer the Poet's Attitude
   - Background for Understanding
3. **To increase knowledge of other cultures and to connect common elements across cultures**
   - Connecting Themes Across Cultures (ATE)
4. **To express and support responses to the text**
   - Critical Thinking
   - Idea Bank: Speculative Essay
   - Idea Bank: Inscription
   - Idea Bank: Poem
   - Idea Bank: Collage
   - Idea Bank: Graphic Display
5. **To analyze literary elements**
   - Compare Literary Works
   - Literary Focus: Free Verse
6. **To read in order to research self-selected and assigned topics**
   - Idea Bank: Report
7. **To plan, prepare, organize, and present literary interpretations**
   - Idea Bank: Oral Interpretation
8. **To use recursive writing processes to imitate an author's style**
   - Guided Writing Lesson
9. **To increase knowledge of the rules of grammar and usage**
   - Grammar and Style: Pronoun and Antecedent Agreement

Test Preparation

Reading Comprehension: Make Inferences and Generalizations (ATE, p. 405)
The teaching tips and sample test item in this workshop support the instruction and practice in the unit workshop:
Reading Comprehension: Analyze Information to Make Inferences and Generalizations (SE, p. 427)

Guide for Interpreting

Featured in AUTHORS IN DEPTH Series

Walt Whitman
(1819–1892)

Walt Whitman was harshly denounced for his first volume of poetry. Yet in the following decades, his poems gained popularity, and he became famous as "the Good Gray Poet" and "the Bard of Democracy." In his later years, Whitman was admired by writers and intellectuals on both sides of the Atlantic. Today, he is widely recognized as one of the greatest and most influential poets the United States has ever produced.

The Poet at Work Whitman was born on Long Island and raised in Brooklyn, New York. He trained to be a printer and spent his early years alternating between printing jobs and newspaper writing. At age twenty-seven, he became the editor of the Brooklyn *Eagle*, a respected newspaper. After the newspaper's ownership dismissed him in 1848 because of his opposition to slavery, Whitman traveled across the country to New Orleans, observing the diversity of America's landscapes and people.

Whitman soon returned to New York City, however, and in 1850 quit journalism to devote his energy to writing poetry. Five years later, when the first edition of *Leaves of Grass* was published, critics attacked Whitman's subject matter and abandonment of traditional poetic devices such as rhyme and meter. Noted poet John Greenleaf Whittier hated Whitman's poems so much that he hurled his copy of *Leaves of Grass* into the fireplace. Ralph Waldo Emerson, on the other hand, responded with great enthusiasm, remarking that the collection was "the most extraordinary piece of wit and wisdom that America has yet contributed."

The Bard of Democracy Though Whitman did publish other works in the course of his career, his life's work proved to be *Leaves of Grass*, which he continually revised, reshaped, and expanded until his death in 1892. He viewed the volume as a single long poem that expressed his evolving vision of the world. Using his poetry to convey his passionate belief in democracy, equality, and the spiritual unity of all forms of life, he celebrated the potential of the human spirit. Though Whitman's philosophy grew out of the ideas of the Transcendentalists, his poetry was mainly shaped by his ability to absorb and comprehend everything he observed. From its first appearance as twelve unsigned and untitled poems in 1855, *Leaves of Grass* grew to include 383 poems in its final, "death-bed" edition (1892). The collection captures the diversity of the American people and conveys the energy and intensity of all forms of life. In the century since Whitman's death, *Leaves of Grass* has become one of the most highly regarded collections of poetry ever written.

◆ Background for Understanding

LITERATURE: PRAISE FOR WHITMAN'S WORK

In his lifetime, Whitman's poetry provoked both glowing reviews and fiercely negative reactions. After receiving his complimentary copy of *Leaves of Grass*, Ralph Waldo Emerson had abundant praise for the poet. In a letter to Whitman, he said:

. . . I give you joy of your free and brave thought. I have great joy in it. I find incomparable things said incomparably well, as they must be. I find the courage of treatment, which so delights me, and which large perception only can inspire. I greet you at the beginning of a great career. . . .

Prentice Hall Literature Program Resources

REINFORCE / RETEACH / EXTEND

Selection Support Pages
Build Vocabulary: Latin Roots: *-fus-*, p. 118
Grammar: Pronoun-Antecedent Agreement, p. 119
Reading Strategy: Infer the Poet's Attitude, p. 120
Literary Focus: Free Verse, p. 121

Strategies for Diverse Student Needs, p. 25

Beyond Literature
Cross-Curricular Connection: Science, p. 25

Formal Assessment Selection Test, pp. 121–123; Assessment Resources Software

Alternative Assessment, p. 25

Daily Language Practice, Week 17

Art Transparencies, Transparency 19, *Builders in the City*, p. 79

Resource Pro CD-ROM

Literature CD-ROM *History of American Literature*: Part 1, Disk 2, Feature 5

Listening to Literature Audiocassettes

Walt Whitman's Poetry

◆ Literature and Your Life

CONNECT YOUR EXPERIENCE

You probably learn something new about yourself, your world, or life in general almost every day. You may not even be aware of all you're learning. As you'll discover in these poems, Walt Whitman devoted his life to making new discoveries and reaching new understandings.

Journal Writing Write a brief journal entry in which you describe an important exploration you have made.

THEMATIC FOCUS: THE HUMAN SPIRIT AND THE NATURAL WORLD

Like many writers of his day, Whitman's self-exploration led him to look at his relationship to the natural world. In what ways, if any, does the world of nature shape your view of yourself?

◆ Literary Focus

FREE VERSE

In contrast to verse written in iambic pentameter or other fixed patterns, **free verse** is poetry that has irregular meter and line length. Free verse is designed to re-create the rising and falling cadences of natural speech. A writer of free verse uses whatever rhythms and line lengths are appropriate to what he or she is saying.

Though free verse is as old as the Psalms in the Bible, it was not widely used until the twentieth century. Whitman was the first American poet to write free verse—the perfect form for this individualist: It allowed him to express himself without formal restraints.

◆ Reading Strategy

INFER THE POET'S ATTITUDE

You can **infer a poet's attitude** toward a subject by examining his or her choice of words and details. Look at this passage from Whitman's "Song of Myself":

> I am there, I help, I came stretch'd atop of the load, / I felt its soft jolts, one leg reclined on the other, / I jump from the crossbeams and seize the clover and timothy, / And roll head over heels . . .

From these words and images—*reclined, jump, seize,* and *roll head over heels*—you can infer that he is invigorated by rural life.

As you read, note key words and images and the attitudes they suggest.

◆ Build Vocabulary

LATIN ROOTS: *-fus-*

In "Song of Myself," Whitman writes, "I effuse my flesh in eddies, and drift it in lacy jags." The word *effuse* is based on the Latin root *-fus-*, meaning "pour." The prefix *e-* means "out" or "away." By combining the meanings, you can see how *effuse* has come to mean "pour" or "spread out."

WORD BANK

Before you read, preview these words from Whitman's works.

abeyance
effuse

◆ Grammar and Style

PRONOUN AND ANTECEDENT AGREEMENT

A **pronoun** must **agree** in number (singular or plural) and gender (masculine, feminine, or neuter) with its **antecedent**—the word to which it refers. In the following line from "I Hear America Singing," the pronouns *he* and *his* (masculine, singular) agree with the antecedent *shoemaker* (also masculine, singular):

> The *shoemaker* singing as *he* sits on *his* bench.

Interest Grabber Walt Whitman's poetry celebrated his vision of the United States. Brainstorm with students for images or metaphors for a poem about America by completing this line:

America is _____ .

Students may suggest ideas such as "America is energy," "America is a struggle for freedom," "America is another chance," and so on. List the variety of responses; then examine them for both positive and negative images and examples of the dignity, intensity, diversity, and democracy that Whitman evoked in his poetry.

Connecting Themes Across Cultures

Ask students to recall literature from other cultures that emphasizes humans' connection with the natural world. They might mention Native American legends, English poetry of the Romantic Period, and Japanese haiku. As they read Whitman, have them notice how his attitude toward nature is similar to and different from the attitudes expressed in the literature of the cultures they mentioned.

Customize for
Less Proficient Readers

To help students through these pieces, guide them to break down sentences to find the subject or main idea. It can also help students to follow along in their text as they listen to the recorded selections.

Listening to Literature Audiocassettes

Customize for
AP Students

Whitman rejected the restrictive poetic elements of meter, rhyme, and pattern to pioneer his style of free verse, but he did not resist all traditional poetic devices. Have students analyze his use of inverse word order, assonance, alliteration, personification, onomatopoeia, repetition, and other poetic devices. Discuss how Whitman's use of these elements adds power to his style.

Test Preparation Workshop

Reading Comprehension: Make Inferences and Generalizations Many standardized tests such as the SAT require students to make inferences about a written passage. Explain that sometimes inferences need to be drawn concerning an author's point of view, opinions, or attitudes. Have students read "I Hear America Singing" on p. 413, then ask them the following question:

What is the poet's attitude toward the American workers about whom he writes?

A uncertain
B celebratory
C dismissive
D somber

The poet emphatically proclaims his support of the laborers. Thus, *A, C,* and *D* cannot be correct. The best choice is *B.*

Develop Understanding

One-Minute Insight In this preface to his historic 1855 Edition of *Leaves of Grass,* Whitman says that America has never been static. It is an ever-growing nation of people, ideas, and beliefs that evolve as the nation itself changes. Americans perceive that old ways are passing and strong new ways approaching. Whitman comments that the United States is a great poem, a nation characterized by activity, diversity, and the gifts of its rich natural bounties.

◆ Background for Understanding

❶ **Literature** These are the first two paragraphs of a long essay that appeared in the first edition of *Leaves of Grass*. In the preface, Whitman discusses his purposes for writing and his poetic vision. He ends the full preface with a prophetic statement: "The proof of a poet is that his country absorbs him as affectionately as he has absorbed it."

Customize for
Less Proficient Readers
❷ Help students interpret the ideas separated by ellipses by modeling how to insert a missing subject or verb to clarify meaning. For example, "[America] accepts the lesson with calmness . . ." or "[perceives] that it was fittest for its days."

◆ Reading Strategy

❸ **Infer the Poet's Attitude** Discuss Whitman's attitudes toward change, the past, and the future. How does he explain that the past is part of the future? *Students may respond that Whitman says that what came before passes to each new generation and will continue to do so.*

◆ Critical Thinking

❹ **Interpret** Ask students to explain what Whitman means by saying that Americans have the "fullest poetical nature." *Students may say that Whitman finds America and Americans to be so rich with vitality, action, and growth that they offer a poet an endless kaleidoscope of ideas.*

❶ *from* Preface to the 1855 Edition of Leaves of Grass

Walt Whitman

America does not repel the past or what it has produced under its forms or amid other politics or the idea of castes or the old religions . . . . accepts the lesson with calmness . . . is not so impatient as has been supposed that the slough still sticks to opinions and manners and literature while the life ❷ which served its requirements has passed into the ❸ new life of the new forms . . . perceives that the corpse is slowly borne from the eating and sleeping rooms of the house . . . perceives that it waits a little while in the door . . . that it was fittest for its days . . . that its action has descended to the stalwart and well-shaped heir who approaches . . . and that he shall be fittest for his days.

The Americans of all nations at any time upon ❹ the earth have probably the fullest poetical nature. The United States themselves are essentially the greatest poem. In the history of the earth hitherto the largest and most stirring appear tame and orderly to their ampler largeness and stir. Here ❺ at last is something in the doings of man that

Block Scheduling Strategies

Consider these suggestions to take advantage of extended class time:

- If you have access to computers, have your students work in small groups to view the material on Whitman on *The History of American Literature,* Part I, on the Literature CD-ROM.
- Have students listen to some or all of the poetry selections on audiocassette as they follow along. Can they hear the rhythms of natural speech in Whitman's verse?
- As a class, discuss the Critical Thinking questions (pp. 407, 412, 413, and 415).
- Using the Speaking, Listening, and Viewing Mini-Lesson on p. 411, have students complete the Oral Interpretation in the Idea Bank. Allow time for students to assess one another's interpretations.
- Assign the Daily Language Practice sentences for Week 17. Display the transparency in ***Writing and Language Transparencies,*** p. 124, or dictate them.

corresponds with the broadcast doings of the day and night. Here is not merely a nation but a teeming nation of nations. Here is action untied from strings necessarily blind to particulars and details magnificently moving in vast masses. Here is the hospitality which forever indicates heroes. . . . Here are the roughs and beards and space and ruggedness and nonchalance that the soul loves. Here the performance disdaining the trivial unapproached in the tremendous audacity of its crowds and groupings and the push of its perspective spreads with crampless and flowing breadth and showers its prolific and splendid extravagance. One sees it must indeed own the riches of the summer and winter, and need never be bankrupt while corn grows from the ground or the orchards drop apples or the bays contain fish or men beget children upon women. . . . ❺

Guide for Responding

◆ Literature and Your Life

Reader's Response Do you think that Whitman's characterization of the United States is still accurate? Why or why not?

Thematic Focus What is unusual or original about the idea of the United States as a poem?

Group Discussion With a small group, develop your definition of America. Provide examples to clarify your definition.

☑ Check Your Comprehension

1. What theme or subject does the speaker address in the first paragraph?
2. According to the speaker, what is the greatest of all poems?

◆ Critical Thinking

INTERPRET

1. What is Whitman's view of the past? **[Interpret]**
2. What is the meaning of Whitman's notion that the United States "is not merely a nation but a teeming nation of nations"? **[Interpret]**
3. In your own words, describe the poet's attitude toward the United States. **[Interpret]**

COMPARE LITERARY WORKS

4. What parallels can you draw between Whitman's ideas about the United States and those expressed by Michel-Guillaume Jean de Crèvecoeur in *Letters From an American Farmer* on p. 197? **[Synthesize]**

Beyond the Classroom

Career Connection

Journalist/Travel Writer During his life, Walt Whitman worked as a journalist. His sharp ears and eyes and deep appreciation of America inspired some of the poet's most impassioned works. Have students identify modern-day journalists, such as Charles Osgood or Dave Barry, who specialize in sharing off-the-beaten-path views of American people, places, and practices. Discuss the qualities this kind of writer should possess, such as a spirit of adventure, an appreciation for diversity, and a love of people. Strong oral and written communications skills are also crucial. Students can also read off-beat travel writing, such as *North Carolina Curiosities* by Jerry Bledsoe or *Great Plains* by Ian Frazier, to get a feel for the unique perspective a clever journalist or travel writer can share.

We suggest that you preview these works before recommending them to students.

Customize for
ESL Students

❺ Be sure students understand that when Whitman repeats *Here,* he means here in America or the United States. The growing nation bursting with vitality exhilarates Whitman. He sees America as a land expansive and generous enough to provide opportunities for everyone.

Customize for
Less Proficient Readers

To help these students interpret Whitman's ideas, use the Identify Themes page in ***Strategies for Diverse Student Needs,*** p. 25.

Reinforce and Extend

Answers

◆ Literature and Your Life

Reader's Response Students should support their responses with evidence.

Thematic Focus Students may observe that it is unusual to characterize a poem as anything other than a highly organized group of words on a page. Whitman's image seems to replace lines with states and words with human beings.

☑ Check Your Comprehension

1. Suggested response: The speaker addresses the subject of the past.
2. According to the speaker, "the United States themselves are essentially the greatest poem."

◆ Critical Thinking

Suggested responses:

1. He embraces the lessons of the past.
2. In this line Whitman refers to the cultural diversity of the American people.
3. The poet has a tremendous amount of love and respect for the country.
4. Both writers view the United States as a country that welcomes people of different backgrounds, and both consider the land to be a rich source of food and plenty.

Develop Understanding

One-Minute Insight In these sections from "Song of Myself," the poet gives his evolving vision of life through the perspective of a vast set of encounters and observations. Its tone is optimistic, exuberant, and energetic; its subject, the poet himself. Yet it reaches beyond individual experience to all humankind. Whitman conveys his belief in the limitless potential of the human spirit to embrace the world and grow from everything it experiences.

◆ Background for Understanding

Literature Literary scholar James E. Miller, Jr., characterizes "Song of Myself" as a drama in which the poet is the main character. The complete work has fifty-two numbered sections that can be seen as acts in the play. Sections 1–5 set up the poet's entry into a mystical state. Sections 6–16 portray the poet's awakening of self followed by a purification of self in sections 17–32. Sections 33–37 offer illumination of the soul, while sections 38–40 emphasize unity through faith, love, and perception. Sections 50–52 conclude the work as the poet emerges from the mystical state.

▶Critical Viewing◀

❶ **Infer; Support** Students may respond that Whitman looks like a rugged free spirit who shuns the formal dress of his time for simple clothing that suits his wandering.

◆ Critical Thinking

❷ **Connect** Ask students to link Whitman's idea expressed here with the Transcendentalist view of unity. *Students may say that Whitman, like Emerson and Thoreau, suggests that intuition and conscience transcend experience and are thus better guides to truth than is logic. He believes in a unity of life and in divinity in nature and in all people, including himself.*

from

Song of Myself

Walt Whitman

◀ **Critical Viewing** This illustration depicts Walt Whitman as a young man. What can you conclude about his attitudes and personality from this picture? How are they reflected in this poem? **[Infer; Support]** ❶

1

I celebrate myself, and sing myself,
And what I assume you shall assume,
For every atom belonging to me as good belongs to you.

I loaf and invite my soul,
I lean and loaf at my ease observing a spear of summer grass.

My tongue, every atom of my blood, formed from this soil, this air,
❷ Born here of parents born here from parents the same, and their
❸ parents the same,
I, now thirty-seven years old in perfect health begin,
Hoping to cease not till death.

Creeds and schools in abeyance,
Retiring back a while sufficed at what they are, but never forgotten,
I harbor for good or bad, I permit to speak at every hazard,
Nature without check with original energy.

◆ Reading Strategy

❸ **Infer the Poet's Attitude** Discuss Whitman's exuberant desire to be totally alive and to experience all he possibly can. Although students may not consider thirty-seven a youthful age, Whitman sets out with all the wide-eyed enthusiasm of a young man about to go forth into the world for the first time.

6

A child said *What is the grass?* fetching it to me with full hands,
How could I answer the child? I do not know what it is any more than he.

I guess it must be the flag of my disposition, out of hopeful green stuff woven. ❹

Or I guess it is the handkerchief of the Lord,
A scented gift and remembrancer[1] designedly dropped,
Bearing the owner's name someway in the corners, that we may see and remark, and say *Whose?*

. . .

What do you think has become of the young and old men?
And what do you think has become of the women and children?

They are alive and well somewhere,
The smallest sprout shows there is really no death,
And if ever there was it led forward life, and does not wait at the end to arrest it, ❺
And ceas'd the moment life appear'd.
All goes onward and outward, nothing collapses,
And to die is different from what anyone supposed, and luckier.

9

The big doors of the country barn stand open and ready,
The dried grass of the harvest-time loads the slow-drawn wagon.
The clear light plays on the brown gray and green intertinged,
The armfuls are pack'd to the sagging mow. ❻

I am there, I help, I came stretch'd atop of the load,
I felt its soft jolts, one leg reclined on the other,
I jump from the crossbeams and seize the clover and timothy,
And roll head over heels and tangle my hair full of wisps.

14

The wild gander leads his flock through the cool night,
Ya-honk he says, and sounds it down to me like an invitation,
The pert may suppose it meaningless, but I listening close,
Find its purpose and place up there toward the wintry sky.

---

1. remembrancer: Reminder.

◆ Build Vocabulary

abeyance (ə bā′ əns) *n.*: Temporary suspension

◆ Reading Strategy

❹ **Infer the Poet's Attitude** In this passage the speaker looks at the grass with a child. He sees it as "hopeful green stuff," which is the "flag" of his disposition and the "handkerchief of the Lord." Discuss how these images communicate Whitman's optimism about life. *Students may describe the grass as a carpet that beckons, a gift of nature that lures the speaker to go forth; its greenness may represent innocence and inexperience.*

Customize for *AP Students*

❺ Tell students that the ellipses dots between lines 6–7 represent lines that have not been included here. In one such line, the poet likens grass to "the beautiful uncut hair of graves." Then challenge students to compare the ideas in lines 7–14 with those William Cullen Bryant explored in "Thanatopsis" (p. 259). *Students may say that both poets believe in an interconnectedness between life and death.*

Comprehension Check ☑

❻ Ask students to summarize in their own words the action described in these lines from section 9. *A wagon carries a heavy load of harvest hay. Workers pack it into the loft of the barn. The speaker arrives atop the wagon hayload, then jumps through the barn loft, rolling in the hay.*

Art Transparency After students have read "I Hear America Singing," challenge them to list as many "singing" references in the poem as they can. Emphasize that Whitman referred to everyday people, pursuing everyday activities. Then display Art Transparency 12, pointing out the "everyday" look of the scene, the "slice of life" character of the sculpture. Remind students that according to Whitman, everyone has "strong melodious songs" that belong "to him or her and to none else." Invite students to speculate about the "song" that this bowler could be singing.

Cross-Curricular Connection: Social Studies

Farming in Today's America The largely agrarian society in which Walt Whitman lived for most of his life has almost disappeared from today's America. Although some Americans still live in rural areas, few still operate farms; those who do, work in vastly different ways from the way they did in the nineteenth century.

Farming—the sowing, tending, and harvesting of crops—is now largely mechanized. In 1992, 100 years after Whitman's death, only 7 percent of rural residents lived on farms.

Have students research population trends in America over the past century. They should consider such issues as changes in the percentage of people who live in urban, suburban, and rural areas; changes in the number of active family farms; variations in population density; and so on. Students can share their findings orally, accompanied by graphs, tables, or charts.

◆ Critical Thinking

❶ **Interpret** Ask students what the poet means when he says that he sees in the animals and in himself "the same old law." *Students may say that he refers to the immutable laws of nature and its never-ending cycles.*

◆ *Literature and Your Life*

❷ Ask students what other outdoor activities or forms of labor offer "vast returns." Can a nine-to-five person, working indoors, reap such returns? Encourage students to share their personal responses to these questions.

Thematic Focus

❸ **The Human Spirit and the Natural World** Help students understand the meaning of this section so they can identify the missing antecedents for *These*, *they*, and *this*. Guide them to consider Whitman's personal connections to nature as they speculate about what the poet may have been referring to. *Students should realize that these pronouns refer to eternal truths and spiritual bonds that link humanity and nature.*

Comprehension Check ☑

❹ Ask students: Whom is the speaker addressing in lines 3–6? *Students may say that the speaker addresses a supreme being or the vast universe itself.*

❺ **Clarification** Discuss the double meaning of the "I" of this passage: It refers to the speaker as well as to the developing nation he captures in his poetry. Both are full of growing pains and contradictions, but the poet cherishes the richness forged by those contradictions in himself and in the nation he so admires.

The sharp-hoof'd moose of the north, the cat on the house-sill,
 the chickadee, the prairie dog,
❶ The litter of the grunting sow as they tug at her teats,
The brood of the turkey hen and she with her half-spread wings,
I see in them and myself the same old law.

The press of my foot to the earth springs a hundred affections,
They scorn the best I can do to relate them.

I am enamor'd of growing outdoors,
Of men that live among cattle or taste of the ocean or woods,
Of the builders and steerers of ships and the wielders of axes and
 mauls, and the drivers of horses,
I can eat and sleep with them week in and week out.

❷
What is commonest, cheapest, nearest, easiest, is Me,
Me going in for my chances, spending for vast returns,
Adorning myself to bestow myself on the first that will take me,
Not asking the sky to come down to my good will,
Scattering it freely forever.

17

These are really the thoughts of all men in all ages and lands,
 they are not original with me,
If they are not yours as much as mine they are nothing, or next
 to nothing,
❸ If they are not the riddle and the untying of the riddle they are
 nothing,
If they are not just as close as they are distant they are nothing.
This is the grass that grows wherever the land is and the water is,
This is the common air that bathes the globe.

51

The past and present wilt—I have fill'd them, emptied them,
And proceed to fill my next fold of the future.

Listener up there! what have you to confide to me?
❹ Look in my face while I snuff the sidle of evening,[2]
(Talk honestly, no one else hears you, and I stay only a minute
 longer.)

Do I contradict myself?
❺ Very well then I contradict myself,
(I am large, I contain multitudes.)

---

2. snuff . . . evening: Put out the hesitant last light of day, which is moving sideways across the sky.

Cultural Connection

Taosim Walt Whitman found much inspiration in Asian philosophy and thought. Whitman believed in the sacredness of the self and in placing the individual above society, ideas that echo the beliefs of the Chinese religion of Taoism. Tao, or the Way, is the central force that makes each thing in the universe unique but also brings everything together in a whole that is reality. Taoist poetry, like Whitman's, shows a love of the beauty of nature and the importance of living one's life in harmony with it. Whitman also espoused the belief in a spiritual unity that connects all things. Such universal philosophy gives Whitman's poetry broad appeal.

Invite interested students to learn more about the principles of Taoism. They can use their research to complete the Report activity in the Idea Bank (p. 417), which asks them to examine the similarities between Taoist philosophy and poetry and Whitman's poetry. They may wish to read *The Way of Life According to Laotzu*, which forms the basis of Taoism.

I concentrate toward them that are nigh,[3] I wait on the door-slab.

Who has done his day's work? who will soonest be through with his supper?
Who wishes to walk with me?

Will you speak before I am gone? will you prove already too late?

52

The spotted hawk swoops by and accuses me, he complains of my gab and my loitering.

I too am not a bit tamed, I too am untranslatable,
I sound my barbaric yawp over the roofs of the world. **6**

The last scud[4] of day holds back for me,
It flings my likeness after the rest and true as any on the shadow'd wilds,
It coaxes me to the vapor and the dusk.

I depart as air, I shake my white locks at the runaway sun,
I effuse my flesh in eddies, and drift it in lacy jags.

I bequeath myself to the dirt to grow from the grass I love,
If you want me again look for me under your boot soles. **7**

You will hardly know who I am or what I mean,
But I shall be good health to you nevertheless,
And filter and fiber your blood.

Failing to fetch me at first keep encouraged,
Missing me one place search another,
I stop somewhere waiting for you.

---

3. **nigh:** Near.
4. **scud:** Low, dark, wind-driven clouds.

◆ Build Vocabulary

effuse (e fyo͞oz´) v.: Spread out; diffuse

◆ Reading Strategy

6 Infer the Poet's Attitude Ask students to infer how the poet feels about himself and his view of life. *Students may say that he bursts to share his ideas with the world; he is a jumble of energy who looks forward to the freedom to, in the words of Thoreau, "live deep and suck out all the marrow from life."*

◆ Critical Thinking

7 Synthesize The speaker bequeaths himself "to the dirt." How does this take the grass and him full cycle? *Students may say that he began the poem speculating about the meaning of the grass; by bequeathing himself to it, he echoes the biblical idea of "ashes to ashes, dust to dust"—in the eternal circle of life, he will become one with the earth.*

◆ Background for Understanding

Literature Whitman clearly stated his goals as a poet in an 1856 letter to Ralph Waldo Emerson. He wrote, "Swiftly, on limitless foundations, the United States too are founding a literature. It is all as well done, in my opinion, as could be practicable. Each element here is in condition. Every day I go among the people of Manhattan Island, Brooklyn, and other cities, and among the young men, to discover the spirit of them, and to refresh myself. These are to be attended to; I am myself more drawn here than to those authors, publishers, importations, reprints, and so forth. . . . In poems, the young men of The States shall be represented, for they out-rival the best of the rest of the earth."

Speaking, Listening, and Viewing Mini-Lesson

Oral Interpretation

This mini-lesson supports the Speaking, Listening, and Viewing activity on p. 417.

Introduce the Concept Discuss the importance of speaking and hearing poetry as well as reading it. Talk about how reading a poem aloud can help reveal its musicality and rhythm.

Develop Background Tell students that effective oral interpretation of a poem depends on the presenter's ability to:

- capture the mood and melody of the poem—the way lines rise and fall with the intonations of natural speech,
- accentuate key words,
- reflect the poet's ideas, and
- bring drama to the reading.

Apply the Information Have pairs of students select two or three poems or stanzas that are meaningful to them. Students should discuss how best to interpret the poems, then rehearse and refine their presentations. Partners can take turns presenting and coaching each other. Students may find it helpful to tape-record their practices so that they can analyze the musicality of the interpretation and revise it as needed.

Assess the Outcome Have peers evaluate the effectiveness of the interpretations, judge how well presenters put forth Whitman's essential message, and explain how the presentations broadened their appreciation of the poems.

Reinforce and Extend

Answers

◆ Literature and Your Life

Reader's Response Students' responses will reflect their attitudes toward life.

Thematic Focus Students may mention images such as "big doors of the country barn stand open and ready," "men that live among cattle or taste of the ocean or woods," and "the builders and steerers of ships and the wielders of axes and mauls," etc.

☑ Check Your Comprehension

1. The dead "are alive and well somewhere" in nature.
2. In lines 1–4 the speaker notes that some people would find a gander's honk meaningless, whereas he hears "an invitation."
3. The speaker suggests that he will be "somewhere waiting."

◆ Critical Thinking

1. (a) He views himself and nature as one. (b) He views himself and other human beings as equal partners.
2. He feels that there really is no death.
3. Suggested response: Whitman notes that grass grows everywhere and that air "bathes" the whole world; he links these images to the "thoughts of all men in all ages and lands."
4. The "listener" he addresses may be God or Nature.
5. Students should support their responses with a careful evaluation of Whitman's poetic ideas.
6. Students should compare and contrast their own attitudes with those of Whitman.

Guide for Responding

◆ Literature and Your Life

Reader's Response Which of the ideas expressed in "Song of Myself" do you find most—and least—appealing?

Thematic Focus Which images in "Song of Myself"show that the United States was expanding and maturing?

Journal Writing If you were to celebrate yourself in a poem, what qualities and self-realizations would you include? Jot down your ideas in your journal.

☑ Check Your Comprehension

1. According to the speaker, where do the dead reside?
2. In which lines of section 14 does the speaker distinguish himself from people with less sensitivity to the natural world?
3. In section 52, what does the speaker suggest will happen to his spirit and message when he is gone?

◆ Critical Thinking

INTERPRET

1. (a) In section 1, what is the speaker's conception of his relationship with nature? (b) How does he view the relationship between himself and other people? **[Analyze]**
2. What do lines 6–14 of section 6 reveal about the speaker's attitude toward death? **[Infer]**
3. How do the images of grass and air in section 17 convey a belief in the spiritual unity of all natural forms? **[Support]**
4. In section 51, whom do you think the speaker is addressing? **[Infer]**

EVALUATE

5. In section 52, Whitman proudly characterizes his poetry as "barbaric yawp." How would you describe and evaluate his work? **[Assess]**

APPLY

6. In what ways is your own attitude toward nature similar to or different from the attitude conveyed in "Song of Myself"? **[Relate]**

The Reaper, Louis C. Tiffany, National Academy of Design, New York City

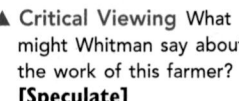

▲ Critical Viewing What might Whitman say about the work of this farmer? **[Speculate]** 3

Humanities: Art

The Reaper, 1881, by Louis C. Tiffany.

Louis Comfort Tiffany (1848–1933), son of famous jeweler Charles Lewis Tiffany, was a painter, craftsman, philanthropist, decorator, and designer. Though he is perhaps best known for his work in decorative glass—he originated the formula for Favrile glass—Tiffany was also an accomplished painter. He trained with several great artists of his day, and he painted in both oil and watercolor.

This oil-on-canvas painting celebrates the harvest. The farmhand stands surrounded by grain in the midst of the field, sharpening his blade in preparation for harvesting.

Use the following question for discussion: What parallels can you draw between the artists' and the poets' attitudes toward their subjects? *Both men seem to have admired and respected those who earned their livings through manual labor.*

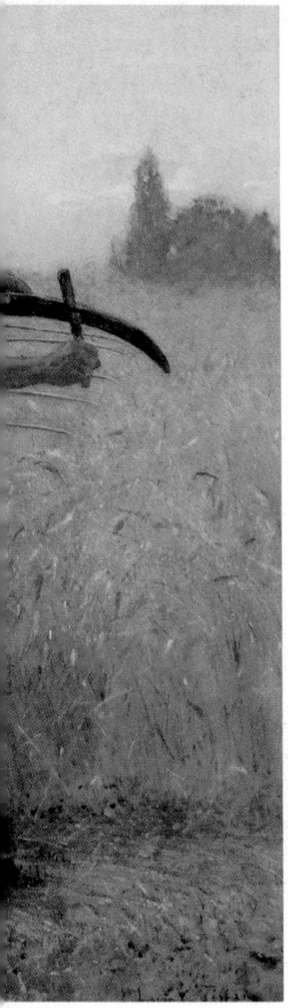

I Hear America Singing

Walt Whitman

I hear America singing, the varied carols I hear,
Those of mechanics, each one singing his as it should be blithe and strong,
The carpenter singing his as he measures his plank or beam,
The mason singing his as he makes ready for work, or leaves off work,
The boatman singing what belongs to him in his boat, the deckhand singing on the steamboat deck,
The shoemaker singing as he sits on his bench, the hatter[1] ❶
singing as he stands, ❷
The wood-cutter's song, the ploughboy's on his way in the morning, or at noon intermission or at sundown,
The delicious singing of the mother, or of the young wife at work, or of the girl sewing or washing,
Each singing what belongs to him or her and to none else,
The day what belongs to the day—at night the party of young fellows, robust, friendly,
Singing with open mouths their strong melodious songs.

1. **hatter:** Person who makes, sells, or cleans hats.

Guide for Responding

◆ Literature and Your Life

Reader's Response If Whitman were to write this poem today, how might he change it? Do you think his message would be the same?

Thematic Focus How does Whitman celebrate the originality of American laborers?

☑ Check Your Comprehension

1. What "belongs to" each worker?
2. What are the speaker's associations with daytime and with night?

◆ Critical Thinking

INTERPRET

1. (a) How would you characterize this poem's mood? (b) In what way is this mood apt for a poem written in the mid-1800's? **[Analyze]**
2. How does the poem's form—free verse and parallel structures—support Whitman's ideas about work? Explain. **[Assess]**

EXTEND

3. Which voices (or careers) would you add to this poem to reflect modern society? **[Career Link]**

Develop Understanding

One-Minute Insight This poem celebrates Whitman's joyous view of the indomitable American spirit. People distinguish themselves by righteous hard work, take pride in tasks that build the future, and demonstrate an exuberance of skill and purpose that makes each of them a vibrant contributor to the spirit of a proud nation.

◆ Reading Strategy

❶ **Infer the Poet's Attitude** Have students respond to the feeling Whitman creates in these lines. Discuss Whitman's attitude toward physical labor. *Students may say that he found inspiration, energy, and purity in it.*

◆ Critical Thinking

❷ **Classify/Analyze** Ask students to look closely at the types of laborers Whitman celebrates. What do they have in common? *All are physical laborers.* Which types of workers are notably absent? *Whitman does not mention the "white-collar" workers of his day—clerks, bankers, lawyers, etc.*

▶Critical Viewing◀

❸ **Speculate** Whitman would probably praise the merits of physical labor done in the great outdoors.

Reinforce and Extend

Answers

◆ Literature and Your Life

Reader's Response Students should note that Whitman might change certain occupations to reflect a society that is more advanced industrially and technologically.

Thematic Focus He describes the unique work each contributes as a collection of varied carols, with each worker singing "what belongs to him or her and to none else."

☑ Check Your Comprehension

1. Each worker "owns" his or her labor.
2. He associates day with work and night with rest and recreation.

◆ Critical Thinking

Suggested responses:

1. (a) The mood is vibrant, hearty, and proud. (b) In the mid-nineteenth century, the nation was still young and idealistic. The mood in Whitman's poem reflects this youth.
2. Whitman is cataloging a wide variety of American workers, all of whom contribute to the varied carols of America. Free verse supports the uniqueness and originality Whitman seeks to emphasize, while parallel structures underscore the rhetorical, list-oriented quality of Whitman's expression.
3. Students may mention the voices of workers involved with various forms of technology, electronics, and service, as well as those involved in modern-day forms of manual labor, such as construction workers, plumbers, painters, etc.

One-Minute Insight Watching a spider spin its thread, the speaker in "A Noiseless Patient Spider" compares the insect to his soul. Like the spider, he stands in oceans of space, throwing out threads, seeking connections with the universe. "By the Bivouac's Fitful Flame" contrasts a sentry's physical surroundings in an army camp with the procession of "tender and wondrous thoughts" of life, love, home, family, and friends that carry him back to the life left behind.

Customize for
Musical/Rhythmic Learners
❶ Have students read this poem aloud to listen for poetic devices such as alliteration, assonance, consonance, and repetition.

Thematic Focus

❷ **The Human Spirit and the Natural World** How does this poem emphasize Whitman's close ties to nature? *Students should note that only a lover of nature would note the parallels between his soul and a common insect.*

◆ Reading Strategy

❸ **Infer the Poet's Attitude** Talk with students about the tender yet conflicting feelings the speaker expresses: wistful longing, fear, regret, hope. Have them infer how Whitman felt about war. *Whitman saw war the way he saw most other things: full of uncertainties and contradictions.*

◆ Literary Focus

❹ **Free Verse** Point out that, though the poem is written in free verse, the first and last lines are the same, and the word *procession* is repeated three times. Discuss how this repetition affects the mood and meaning of the poem. *Repetition creates unity by bringing the poem full circle. The repetition of* procession *also suggests the movement of the sentry at his post.*

A Noiseless Patient Spider

Walt Whitman

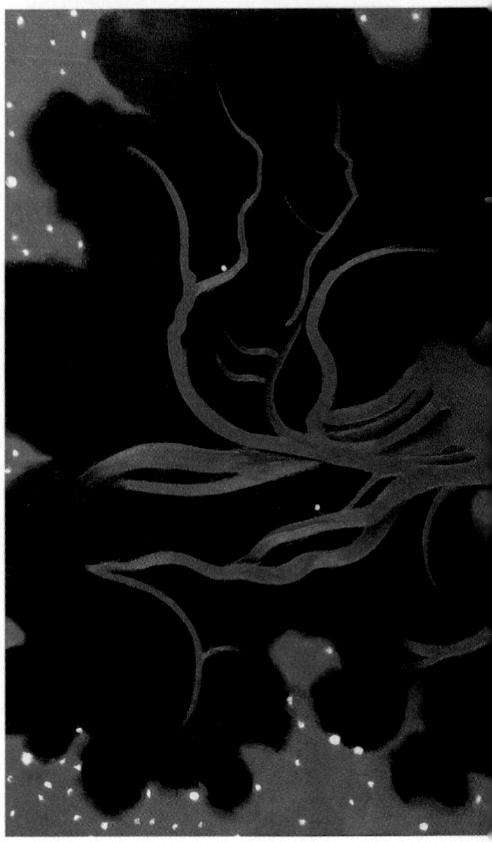

A noiseless patient spider,
I mark'd where on a little promontory it stood isolated,
Mark'd how to explore the vacant vast surrounding,
It launch'd forth filament, filament, filament, out of itself,
Ever unreeling them, ever tirelessly speeding them. ❶

❷ And you O my soul where you stand,
Surrounded, detached, in measureless oceans of space,
Ceaselessly musing, venturing, throwing, seeking the spheres to connect them,
Till the bridge you will need be form'd, till the ductile anchor hold,
Till the gossamer thread you fling catch somewhere, O my soul.

By the Bivouac's Fitful Flame

Walt Whitman

By the bivouac's[1] fitful flame,
A procession winding around me, solemn and sweet and slow—but first I note,
The tents of the sleeping army, the fields' and woods' dim outline,
The darkness lit by spots of kindled fire, the silence,
Like a phantom far or near an occasional figure moving,
The shrubs and trees, (as I lift my eyes they seem to be stealthily watching me,)
While wind in procession thoughts, O tender and wondrous thoughts,
Of life and death, of home and the past and loved, and of those that are far away;
A solemn and slow procession there as I sit on the ground,
By the bivouac's fitful flame.

1. **bivouac** (biv′ wak′) *n.*: Night guard to prevent surprise attacks.

Humanities: Art

The Lawrence Tree, 1929, by Georgia O'Keeffe.

Georgia O'Keeffe (1887–1985) knew by the age of ten that she wanted to be an artist. The realization that she could say things with color and shape that she could not say any other way led her to create the strikingly powerful paintings for which she is so well remembered.

About *The Lawrence Tree*, O'Keeffe wrote: "I spent several weeks up at the Lawrence ranch that summer [1929]. There was a long weathered carpenter's bench under the tall tree in front of the little old house that Lawrence had lived in there. I often lay on that bench looking up into that tree—past the trunk and up into the branches. It was particularly fine at night with the stars above the trees." O'Keeffe reveals her very personal experience through this painting.

Use this question for discussion:

What is O'Keeffe saying about nature in this work? *Students may say that her message is that nature is lofty and that its grandness and majesty dwarf people on Earth.*

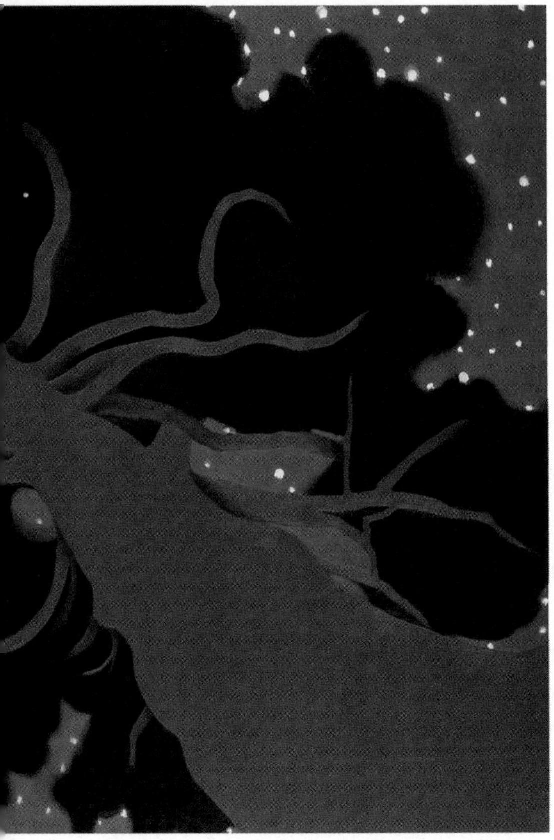

The Lawrence Tree, 1929, Georgia O'Keeffe, Wadsworth Atheneum, Hartford

WHEN I HEARD THE LEARN'D ASTRONOMER

Walt Whitman

When I heard the learn'd astronomer,
When the proofs, the figures, were ranged in columns before me,
When I was shown the charts and diagrams, to add, divide and measure them,
When I sitting heard the astronomer where he lectured with much applause in the lecture room, ⑤
How soon unaccountable I became tired and sick,
Till rising and gliding out I wander'd off by myself,
In the mystical moist night air, and from time to time,
Look'd up in perfect silence at the stars.

◀ Critical Viewing How does the artist's viewpoint in this painting compare with Whitman's in "When I Heard the Learn'd Astronomer"? **[Connect]** ⑥

Guide for Responding

◆ *Literature and Your Life*

Reader's Response To which of these poems do you relate most strongly? Why?

Thematic Focus How do the speakers of these poems demonstrate individuality or originality?

☑ Check Your Comprehension

1. In "A Noiseless Patient Spider," why does the spider "tirelessly" spin out filament?
2. What actions are performed by the speaker of "When I Heard the Learn'd Astronomer"?

◆ Critical Thinking

INTERPRET

1. (a) In "A Noiseless Patient Spider," how is the speaker's soul similar to the spider? (b) In what sense is his soul's "venturing" different from the spider's exploration? **[Support; Analyze]**
2. (a) In "Astronomer," how are the speaker's and the astronomer's attitudes toward the stars different? (b) How would you express the poem's theme? **[Compare and Contrast; Interpret]**
3. (a) Where is the speaker in "By the Bivouac's Fitful Flame"? (b) Explain the procession to which he refers. **[Infer; Interpret]**

Beyond the Selection

FURTHER READING

Other Works by Walt Whitman
"Beat! Beat! Drums!"
"When Lilacs Last in the Dooryard Bloom'd"
"Poets to Come"
Leaves of Grass

Other Works About Walt Whitman
Walt Whitman: The Making of the Poet, Paul Zweig

We suggest that you preview these works before recommending them to students.

INTERNET

You can find information about Whitman at these suggested Internet sites. Please be aware that sites may have changed since this information was published.

Two comprehensive Whitman sites are **http://lcweb2.loc.gov/ammem/wwhome.html** and **http://jefferson.village.Virginia.EDU/Whitman**

We *strongly recommend* that you preview the site before you send students to it.

Develop Understanding

One-Minute Insight In this poem, the speaker reveals that he prefers imagining and experiencing the mystery of the stars to knowing the precise scientific facts an expert scientist can teach.

◆ Reading Strategy

⑤ Infer the Poet's Attitude Ask students to explain the poet's attitude toward "book learning" versus empirical or "hands-on" learning. *The poet places greater value on the experience of seeing and feeling the grandeur and mystery of the stars than he does on any objective mathematical or scientific knowledge of astronomy.*

▶Critical Viewing◀

⑥ Connect Both the artist and the poet view the stars with the awe as they gaze upward at the canopy of the night sky. From such an angle, the viewer seems small and insignificant, while the stars appear very distant and mysterious.

Reinforce and Extend

Answers

◆ *Literature and Your Life*

Reader's Response Students should be prepared to explain their responses.

Thematic Focus Students may note that the speaker of "Spider" creates an unusual analogy when he compares his soul to "a noiseless patient spider." The speaker of "Bivouac" creates his own world of memories and remembrances of beloved people and places. In "Astronomer," the speaker shuns the conventional, scientific approach to the stars, viewing them instead as a mysterious, natural wonder.

☑ Check Your Comprehension

1. It spins filament to create a kind of bridge to another surface.
2. He listens to an astronomer, wanders outdoors, and looks at the stars.

(Answers continue on p. 416)

Answers *(continued from p. 415)*

◆ Critical Thinking

1. (a) Both the speaker's soul and the spider are poised in isolation, and both seek to explore and connect themselves with aspects of the greater world. (b) The speaker describes the spider's exploration as purely physical, whereas his own soul's journey is spiritual.
2. (a) The speaker is attracted by the beauty and mystery of the heavens, whereas the scientist views the stars as a subject for scientific study. (b) The poem suggests that one does not need formal knowledge of a thing to enjoy a spiritual connection to it.
3. (a) He is in a military encampment. (b) As he looks out upon the shadowy, silent forms of wartime at night, he thinks about life, death, and his own home and loved ones.

◆ Reading Strategy

1. (a) Whitman seems to distrust or downplay the importance of the astronomer's scientific study of the stars. (b) Whitman prefers the beauty and mystery of the stars to the scientific understanding of them.
2. Suggested responses include *to add, divide, and measure them; sitting; tired and sick; rising and gliding; the mystical moist night air;* and *in perfect silence.*
3. Whitman values physical labor; he seems to exult in the work and the workers he observes.
4. Students may cite Whitman's belief that the spirit does not die after bodily death expressed in lines 7–14 of Section 6 in "Song of Myself."

◆ Literary Focus

1. The use of free verse emphasizes Whitman's free, unconventional, and unconfined approach to the wonders of nature.
2. Free verse is an ideal form for expressing rebellion; like the speaker in the poem, free verse bucks convention and objectivity.
3. In this poem, Whitman celebrates the American individual at work, and all of these people are "common laborers." Free verse is appropriate for such a poem because it allows him to use common, everyday language instead of literary language to describe these people. Whitman's use of free verse reflects his belief in freedom, democracy, and individuality.

Guide for Responding *(continued)*

◆ Reading Strategy

Infer the Poet's Attitude

By making **inferences,** you can gain insight into Whitman's feelings and beliefs about his subjects. To help you do this, carefully consider the writers subjects, details, and word choice.

1. In "When I Heard the Learn'd Astronomer," how would you describe Whitman's attitude toward (a) the astronomer and (b) the stars themselves?
2. Name at least five descriptive words or phrases in "When I Heard the Learn'd Astronomer" that help you infer the contrast between Whitman's attitude toward the science of astronomy and his feelings about the stars.
3. Use the catalog, or list, of workers in "I Hear America Singing" to determine Whitman's attitude toward labor.
4. Find a passage from another Whitman poem that conveys his attitude or belief about something. Explain what the passage reveals.

◆ Literary Focus

Free Verse

At the beginning of "A Noiseless Patient Spider," Walt Whitman uses lines of different lengths and meters:

A noiseless patient spider,
I mark'd where on a little promontory
it stood isolated, . . .

This is an example of **free verse**—poetry that has irregular meter and line length. Whitman's use of free verse reflects his belief in freedom, democracy, and individuality.

1. "Song of Myself" is an exploration of the speaker's relationship with the world that surrounds him. How does free verse allow the poet to express these ideas more freely?
2. Whitman rebels against a scientific interpretation of the wonders of nature in "When I Heard the Learn'd Astronomer." Why is free verse an appropriate form for the poem?
3. How does "I Hear America Singing" represent a perfect marriage of form and theme?

◆ Build Vocabulary

Using the Latin Root *-fus-*

The Latin root *-fus-* means "pour." Each of the words in the left column is based on this root. On your paper, match each word with its definition in the right column.

1. profusion	**a.** rich or lavish supply
2. infuse	**b.** dispersed
3. effusive	**c.** gushing
4. diffuse	**d.** fill

Using the Word Bank: Denotations

Answer the following questions on your paper. Be prepared to explain your answer.

1. If a judge hands down a ruling in *abeyance* of a particular law, is she enforcing that law?
2. Does light that *effuses* from a lamp spread softly through a room or shine in a sharply focused beam?

◆ Grammar and Style

Pronoun and Antecedent Agreement

When the word to which a pronoun refers is a singular indefinite pronoun—a word like *each* or *someone*—a writer must refer to it with singular pronouns. Notice that Whitman uses *him* or *her* (singular)—not *their* (plural)—to refer to *each* in the following line: "*Each* singing what belongs to *him* or *her* and to none else."

A **pronoun** must agree in number and gender with its antecedent.

Practice In your notebook, write the correct pronoun for each sentence. Then write the antecedent to which the pronoun refers.

1. The turkey hen awoke, and then (she, it) stepped toward the door of the cage.
2. The woman and child opened (his, their) books and began to sing.
3. Life has (its, their) challenges and gratifications.
4. The shoemaker went on (their, his) lunch break.
5. All of the laborers received a pay increase after (he, they) made requests to the company boss.

◆ Build Vocabulary

Using the Latin Root *-fus-*

1. a 2. d 3. c 4. b

Using the Word Bank

1. No, because her ruling temporarily overturns the law.
2. Light that effuses spreads out through the room.

◆ Grammar and Style

1. she, *the turkey hen*
2. their, *the woman and child*
3. its, *life*
4. his, *shoemaker*
5. they, *the laborers*

Grammar Reinforcement

For additional instruction and practice, use the Pronouns and Antecedents lesson in the Nouns and Pronouns unit of the **Language Lab CD-ROM,** and the pages on Pronoun and Antecedent Agreement in the *Writer's Solution Grammar Practice Book,* pp. 69–70.

Build Your Portfolio

Idea Bank

Writing

1. Inscription It is 1892 and you are attending a book-signing for the final edition of *Leaves of Grass*. What might the poet write in your copy? Write an inscription that he addresses to you.

2. Poem Write a poem in free verse expressing your connection with an element of nature, such as the ocean, the sun, or the moon. Choose and arrange words to approximate natural speech.

3. Speculative Essay Whitman revised *Leaves of Grass* many times. He called it an attempt to put a human being on record. Why did he choose to revise this "attempt" rather than write brand-new books? Explore this question in an essay.

Speaking, Listening, and Viewing

4. Collage Whitman's poems capture the United States at the dawning of the Industrial Age. Look through magazines and create a collage that captures the country's essence today. How do the collage themes compare to Whitman's poems?

5. Oral Interpretation Rehearse and make an oral presentation of two or three of Whitman's lyrics. Use voice tone and volume, as well as your sense of rhythm, to achieve musicality in your delivery. **[Performing Arts Link]**

Researching and Representing

6. Graphic Display Work with a group to create a mural illustrating all twelve of the workers described in "I Hear America Singing." **[Art Link]**

7. Report Whitman's poems have much in common with Eastern thought. Research the Chinese religion of Taoism. In a report, examine the similarities between Taoist philosophy and poetry and Whitman's ideas. **[Social Studies Link]**

Online Activity www.phlit.phschool.com

Guided Writing Lesson

Imitation of an Author's Style

Walt Whitman is acclaimed not only for the ideas in his poems, but also for his original style. Write a poem in which you imitate Whitman's typical way of writing. Choose several elements of Whitman's style —his word choice, tone, degree of formality, figurative language, rhythm, use of lists, and organization— and use them throughout your poem.

Writing Skills Focus: Consistent Style

Whenever you write, make sure that the style in which you write remains the same from start to finish. For example, if you begin in a very informal style, don't switch to more formal language and structures; maintain a **consistent style** from start to finish.

Prewriting Reread Whitman's poems and note which elements of his style you will imitate. Decide on a "Whitmanesque" topic, and review the characteristics of free verse. Make a list or cluster diagram of sensory details to record images or details related to your topic.

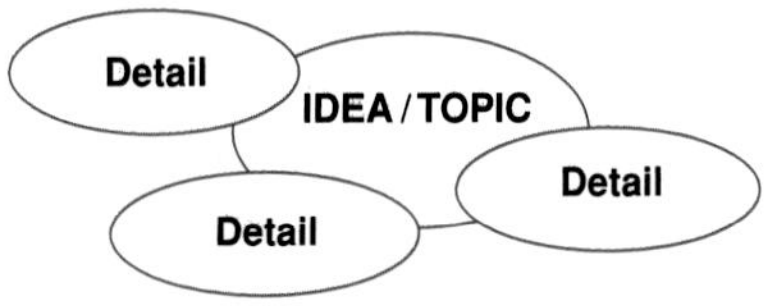

Drafting As you write, maintain a consistent style and tone—whether it is exuberant, reflective, or full of wonder—and let the meaning of what you are saying determine the lengths of lines and stanzas.

Revising Read your poem aloud many times as you revise it. Do you hear the natural rhythm of speech in Whitman's poems, or do you hear unnatural rhythms or formal grammatical structures?

✓ ASSESSMENT OPTIONS

Formal Assessment, Selection Test, pp. 121–123, and Assessment Resources Software. The selection test is designed so that it can be easily customized to the performance levels of your students.

Alternative Assessment, p. 25, includes options for less advanced students, more advanced students, visual/spatial learners, intrapersonal learners, interpersonal learners, and verbal/linguistic learners.

PORTFOLIO ASSESSMENT

Use the following rubrics in the ***Alternative Assessment*** booklet to assess student writing:
Inscription: Expression Rubric, p. 109
Poem: Poetry Rubric, p. 123
Speculative Essay: Cause-Effect Rubric, p. 117
Guided Writing Lesson: Poetry Rubric, p. 123

Idea Bank

Customizing for *Performance Levels*
Following are suggestions for matching Idea Bank activities with students' performance levels:
Less Advanced Students: 1, 6
Average Students: 2, 5
More Advanced Students: 3, 4, 7

Customizing for *Learning Modalities*
Following are suggestions for matching Idea Bank activities with students' learning modalities:
Verbal/Linguistic: 5
Musical/Rhythmic: 5
Visual/Spatial: 6
Logical/Mathematical: 7

Guided Writing Lesson

For more prewriting, elaboration and revision strategies, see *Prentice Hall Writing and Grammar.*

Art Transparencies Students may find inspiration for their poems in Art Transparency 19, *Builders in the City*, p. 79.

Writers at Work Videodisc
Have students view the videodisc segment on Creative Writing (Ch. 6) featuring Latino poet Martín Espada to see how he comes up with ideas and shapes them into poetry. Have students discuss what it takes to turn personal experiences, ideas, and questions into "the stuff of poetry."

Play frames 14950 to 17080

Writing Lab CD-ROM
Have students complete the tutorial on Creative Writing. Follow these steps:

1. Refer students to the Literary Model of an imitation of an author's style in About Creative Writing.
2. Students can use the Inspirations for Creative Writing to decide on a topic.
3. After students have drafted on the computer, they can use the Interactive Self-Evaluation Checklist for poetry to aid revision.

LESSON OBJECTIVES

1. **To increase knowledge of other cultures and to connect common elements across cultures**
   - Thematic Connection
2. **To express and support responses to the text**
   - Critical Thinking Questions
   - Idea Bank: Letter
   - Idea Bank: Poetic Response
   - Idea Bank: Diptych
3. **To analyze literary elements**
   - Compare Literary Works
   - Literary Connection
   - Idea Bank: Comparison-and-Contrast Essay
   - Idea Bank: Group Discussion

Connections to Today's World

The poetry of Walt Whitman and Emily Dickinson captured the America of their time. Distinctly different in topics and style from earlier European poetry, the poetry of the two poets established a truly unique American voice.

The American voice continues to change, as additional subject matter and cultures add to the diversity of American poetry. The poetry of Langston Hughes and Angela de Hoyos enriches the modern American voice by adding the African American and Hispanic American harmonies of poetic style and thought in unique, contemporary fashion.

CONNECTIONS TO TODAY'S WORLD

I, Too
Langston Hughes

To Walt Whitman
Angela de Hoyos

Thematic Connection

THE EMERGENCE OF AN AMERICAN VOICE

Walt Whitman and Emily Dickinson were two of the poets most responsible for establishing a distinctly American poetic voice. The American poets who preceded them were all heavily influenced by the styles and themes of British poets of the time. Whitman and Dickinson, on the other hand, produced poetry that was fresh and original. Different in style and content from the work of any earlier poet, Whitman's poetry embodies the freedom that characterizes the American spirit and captures the immensity of the American landscape. Dickinson's poetry is filled with stylistic innovations and has a highly personal quality that parallels the American emphasis on individuality.

The America that Walt Whitman celebrated in his poetry has grown increasingly diverse. The growing diversity has once again expanded the boundaries of American literature, introducing readers to the traditions and issues of the myriad of cultures represented in our population. Like Whitman and Dickinson, Langston Hughes helped establish a new American literature. He and a group of other African American poets associated with an artistic movement known as the Harlem Renaissance (see page 838) produced musical verse that captured the African American experience during the first half of this century. More recently, Angela de Hoyos and a growing number of Hispanic American poets have brought the rhythms of the Spanish language to American literature and captured the experiences of people descended from various Latin American cultures. In the two poems that follow, Hughes and de Hoyos offer their modifications to Walt Whitman's vision of what it means to be an American.

Literary Connection

POETRY

Dickinson and Whitman started the movement toward a uniquely American poetry, but they certainly were not the last innovative American poets. Twentieth-century poets such as Langston Hughes and Angela de Hoyos continue to experiment with poetic form. These poems by Hughes and de Hoyos—written in free verse—reflect the influence of Whitman and Dickinson.

Featured in AUTHORS IN DEPTH Series

LANGSTON HUGHES (1902–1967)

Langston Hughes emerged from the Harlem Renaissance as the most prolific and successful African American writer. Hughes published several volumes of poetry. In these works he experimented with a variety of forms and techniques and often tried to re-create the rhythms of contemporary jazz. (For more information on Hughes, see page 838.)

ANGELA DE HOYOS (1945–)

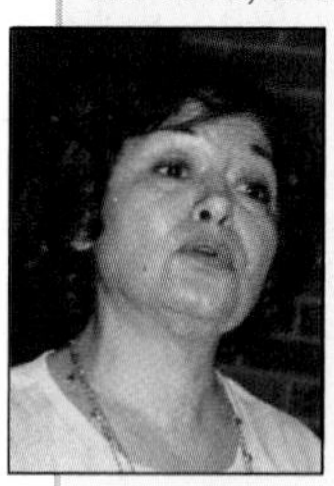

Angela de Hoyos has emerged as a voice of her times, celebrating her heritage and knowledge of what it means to live in a world of diversity. De Hoyos first published poetry in high school, and by her early twenties, she had published poetry in literary journals. Between 1969 and 1975, de Hoyos studied, wrote, and established her reputation through readings at Mexican American gatherings in the Southwest. She has published five collections of poetry.

Prentice Hall Literature Program Resources

REINFORCE / RETEACH / EXTEND

Selection Support Worksheets Thematic Connection: The Emergence of an American Voice, p. 122

Formal Assessment Selection Test, pp. 124–125; Assessment Resources Software

Listening to Literature Audiocassettes

Literature CD-ROM *The History of American Literature*: Part 2, Disk 1, Feature 4

I, Too

Langston Hughes

CONNECTIONS TO TODAY'S WORLD

Nobody Around Here Calls Me Citizen, 1943, Robert Gwathmey, University of Minnesota, © Estate Robert Gwathmey/Licensed by VAGA, New York, NY

I, too, sing America.

I am the darker brother.
They send me to eat in the kitchen
When company comes,
But I laugh,
And eat well,
And grow strong.

Tomorrow,
I'll be at the table
When company comes.
Nobody'll dare
Say to me,
"Eat in the kitchen,"
Then.

Besides,
They'll see how beautiful I am
And be ashamed—

I, too, am America.

▲ Critical Viewing Which image in this painting better illustrates the sentiments of this poem—the man or the lion? Explain. **[Make a Decision]** ❶

Humanities: Art

Nobody Around Here Calls Me Citizen, 1943, by Robert Gwathmey.

Robert Gwathmey (1903–1988), the artist who painted this picture, was born in Richmond, Virginia.

Use the following questions for discussion:

1. Why did the artist include the large numeral 2 near the center of the work? *The artist may suggest that African Americans are often seen as second-class citizens, or that they have two sides to them: One is the side they reveal, the other is the inner spirit, which is hidden.*
2. Compare the facial expressions of the man and the lion. What message does this contrast convey? *Students may say that the man seems dejected, distant, and worn out, while the lion seems aggressive, focused, and ready to attack. The artist may be suggesting that the world sees the passive and sad side of the black man but in his soul, represented by the lion, he is defiant and angry.*

Develop Understanding

Interest Grabber Write the line "I, too, sing America" on the chalkboard. Say that it is the opening of a poem written in response to Whitman by someone who felt left out of Whitman's America. Have students predict the tone of poems written by minority poets responding to Whitman.

One-Minute Insight Both poems in this grouping attempt to expand Walt Whitman's views of America by highlighting cultures that were underrepresented in his works. Langston Hughes celebrates the American part of African American culture, while Angela de Hoyos reminds Whitman of the special songs that Native American people have to sing of their American experience.

Customize for
Less Proficient Readers
It may help students to paraphrase the essence of the poem in their own words. *"You can't ignore me any more. I'm part of America, too. You should be ashamed for trying to exclude me. Just open your eyes to my beauty."*

Literature CD-ROM To build background, use the CD-ROM *The History of American Literature*: Part 2, Disc 1, Feature 4. A portion of this feature focuses upon Langston Hughes.

▶Critical Viewing◀

❶ **Make a Decision** Sample response: The lion better illustrates the sentiments of the poem because, like a lion roaring, the poet is boldly stating the message that black Americans deserve to be equal members of American society.

To Walt Whitman

Angela de Hoyos

hey man, my brother
world-poet
prophet democratic
here's a guitar
for you
—a chicana guitar—
so you can spill out a song
for the open road
big enough for my people
—my Native Amerindian race
that I can't seem to find
in your poems

▶ Critical Viewing
❶ How does the mood of this painting compare with that of the poem? Explain. **[Assess]**

Mandolin, Rosa Ibarra

Guide for Responding

◆ *Literature and Your Life*

Reader's Response To which poem do you have a stronger response? Why?

Thematic Focus How do these two poems reflect the idea of emerging American voices?

☑ Check Your Comprehension

1. (a) What causes the speaker in "I, Too" to be banished to the kitchen? (b) According to the speaker, what changes will occur in the future?
2. Why does the speaker of "To Walt Whitman" offer a gift to the famous poet?

◆ Critical Thinking

INTERPRET

1. (a) To what or whom does the first line of "I, Too" allude? (b) To whom does *they* refer? **[Interpret]**
2. What is the significance of the actions the speaker names in lines 5–7 of "I, Too"? **[Infer]**
3. Summarize the attitude of the speaker of "To Walt Whitman" toward Whitman. **[Analyze]**

COMPARE LITERARY WORKS

4. How do "I, Too" and "To Walt Whitman" expand the message about America that Whitman conveys in his poetry? **[Synthesize]**

▶Critical Viewing◀

❶ **Assess** While the mood of the painting is tranquil, melancholy, and traditional, the mood of the poem is dynamic and contemporary.

Reinforce and Extend

Answers

◆ *Literature and Your Life*

Reader's Response Student responses should indicate an understanding of the poems' meanings.

Thematic Focus Suggested response: The speakers of these two poems are members of ethnic groups that have historically been polarized in American society. However, in recent years some literary voices such as theirs have emerged into the mainstream of this society.

☑ Check Your Comprehension

1. (a) The speaker is ordered to eat in the kitchen "When company comes." (b) The speaker will be allowed to eat with the visitors, and his oppressors will see his beauty and feel shame for their former actions.
2. The speaker gives Whitman a guitar so that he "can spill out a song/for the open road/big enough for my people."

◆ Critical Thinking

1. Suggested response: (a) The first line alludes to Walt Whitman and his poems "I Hear America Singing" and "Song of Myself." (b) The pronoun *they* refers to white people or to employers and others who have power over the speaker.
2. Suggested response: Rather than resigning himself to ignominy and defeat, the speaker takes care of himself—both emotionally and physically—and so prepares himself to triumph over his oppressors.
3. Suggested response: The speaker seems to respect Whitman; yet in the last lines, she challenges him to live up to his reputation as "the democratic bard."
4. The poems expand Whitman's message about America by adding the voices of additional American cultures to poetry.

Beyond the Selection

FURTHER READING

Other Works by Langston Hughes
"The Negro Speaks of Rivers"
"Harlem"
Big Sea

Other Works by Angela de Hoyos
Dedicatorias

We suggest that you preview these works before recommending them to students.

INTERNET

You can find additional information about Langston Hughes and the Harlem Renaissance on the Internet. We suggest the following site. Please be aware that sites may have changed from the time we published this information.

For information on Langston Hughes and his works, visit **http://www.cwrl.utexas.edu/~mmaynard/Hughes/hughes/htm**

We *strongly recommend* that you preview the site before you send students to it.

Thematic Connection

The Emergence of an American Voice

Since the nineteenth century, writers with new vantage points have continued to change the face of American literature. Poets such as Langston Hughes and Angela de Hoyos, for example, have sought to challenge conventional notions about which topics (and which people) are appropriate for serious poetry.

1. Compare the speaker's declaration of his own beauty in Hughes's "I, Too" with the opening verses of Walt Whitman's "Song of Myself." How are the two speakers alike? How are their circumstances different?
2. Angela de Hoyos's speaker in "To Walt Whitman" offers a challenge or reproach to Whitman. What would de Hoyos like to have added to or changed about Whitman's portrayal of America?

Literary Connection

Poetry

The unique sensibilities of Walt Whitman and Emily Dickinson—as well as their arresting ideas about poetic form—signaled that America was developing a literary culture distinct from Europe's.

1. How might the effect of either of the poems presented here be different if the writer had used rhyming stanzas?
2. How do "To Walt Whitman" and "I, Too" reflect the changes in the American literary voice since the time of Dickinson and Whitman?

Idea Bank

Writing

1. **Letter** Both Langston Hughes and Angela de Hoyos chose to "answer" Walt Whitman in their own poems. Imagine that the "Good Gray Poet" was able to read these responses to his work. As Whitman, write a letter to either Hughes or de Hoyos in which you respond to his or her poem.
2. **Comparison-and-Contrast Essay** Write a short essay comparing these two poems. Point out similarities and differences in subject matter, theme, style, and word choice.
3. **Poetic Response** Both these poems are direct responses to specific Whitman poems and echo lines from the original poetry. Follow this example by writing your own poetic response to one of Dickinson's or Whitman's poems. Your poem should be similar in style to the original poem and should echo one or more of its lines.

Speaking, Listening, and Viewing

4. **Group Discussion** Both Dickinson and Whitman were stylistic innovators. Whitman's use of free verse led the way for innumerable twentieth-century poets to express their views of the world. Analyze the writing styles of Dickinson, Whitman, Hughes, and de Hoyos. Then select a poem from each writer's work that you believe represents his or her style. Read the four poems aloud for the class; then lead a discussion comparing these poets' use of language.

Researching and Representing

5. **Diptych** The word *diptych* (dip′ tik′) comes from an ancient Greek word for a writing tablet made of two hinged pieces. Today the term refers to a picture painted on two hinged canvases or pages. Paint or draw a diptych that evokes or conveys the connection between two poems—one by Whitman and one by Hughes or de Hoyos. **[Art Link]**

Online Activity www.phlit.phschool.com

ASSESSMENT OPTIONS

Formal Assessment, Selection Test, pp. 124–125, and Assessment Resources Software. The selection test is designed so that it can be easily customized to the performance levels of your students.

PORTFOLIO ASSESSMENT

Use the following rubrics in the ***Alternative Assessment*** booklet to assess student writing:
Letter: Response to Literature Rubric, p. 125
Compare-and-Contrast Essay: Comparison/Contrast Rubric, p. 118
Poetic Response: Poetry Rubric, p. 123

Answers

Thematic Connection

1. Suggested response: Hughes's speaker declares his strength and beauty; although Whitman's speaker never explicitly claims to be beautiful, the opening lines of "Song of Myself" are infused with the belief that the speaker is filled with goodness and health. Neither speaker is arrogant about claiming to be beautiful. Rather, their declarations are made to establish their individuality and value as people. Whitman's speaker, however, is confident and secure in his sense of belonging and acceptance, something Hughes's speaker hopes one day to attain.
2. Angela de Hoyos would like to have added to Whitman's portrayal of America the voices of the people of America who traditionally have not been included in the cultural landscape of American poetry.

Literary Connection

1. Sample response: The use of rhyming stanzas may have subordinated the poems' messages in relation to poetic form.
2. Sample response: Since the time of Dickinson and Whitman, the American literary voice has spoken of diverse cultures that make up America, as do these two poems.

Idea Bank

Customizing for
Performance Levels

Following are suggestions for matching Idea Bank topics with your students' performance levels:
Less Advanced Students: 1
Average Students: 2, 5
More Advanced Students: 3, 4

Customizing for
Learning Modalities

Following are suggestions for matching Idea Bank topics with your students' learning modalities:
Verbal/Linguistic: 1, 3
Logical/Mathematical: 2, 4
Visual/Spatial: 5

Prepare and Engage

LESSON OBJECTIVES

- To use recursive writing processes to write a critical evaluation
- To understand the conventions and mechanics of written English, including the correct use of quotation marks

Distribute the scoring rubric for Critical Review (p. 126 in ***Alternative Assessment***) to make students aware of the criteria on which their work will be evaluated. See the suggestions on p. 424 for customizing the rubric to this workshop.

Refer students to the Writing Handbook, p. 1192, for instruction in the writing process, and p. 1196 for further information on writing a Response to Literature. Present the Writing Process Model for Interpreting a Work of Literature (pp. 37–40) in ***Writing and Language Transparencies***.

Writers at Work Videodisc
To show how literary agent Theresa Park uses the methods of critical evaluation as part of her job, play the videodisc segment on Response to Literature (Ch. 7).

Play frames 22209 to 31154

Writing Lab CD-ROM
If your students have access to computers, use the tutorial on Responding to Literature. Have students follow these steps:

1. Explore the Response Wheels to see combinations of literary elements and response methods.
2. Draft on the computer.
3. Use the Evaluation Word Bin to select precise adverbs and adjectives for a literary response.

Critical Evaluation — Writing Process Workshop

Without even realizing it, you probably evaluate each piece of literature that you read. You might decide whether a novel you've just read is worth recommending to friends or whether a poem has a special meaning that makes you want to read other works by that poet. When you write your own **critical evaluation,** you simply capture your opinion of a literary work on paper. Your evaluation doesn't have to be positive, but you do have to back up your opinions with passages and details from the piece.

Choose an author or poem that interests you, and write a critical evaluation of the work. The following skills will help you write your critical evaluation:

Writing Skills Focus

- **Follow a clear and logical organization.** Discuss one aspect of the work in each paragraph, and arrange the paragraphs in an order that makes sense. (See p. 403.)
- **Use specific examples** from the work to thoroughly back up your opinion.
- **Use a consistent style.** For example, if you begin with a serious tone and formal language, stick with it. (See p. 417.)

This model uses these skills to create an effective and clear evaluation of Walt Whitman's style.

① The writer begins with a clear statement of her point of view regarding Whitman's poem.

② The writer follows with specific examples to support her opinion.

WRITING MODEL

Walt Whitman's poem "I Hear America Singing" is an inspirational catalog of the many workers who bring life and pride to their jobs. ① Through his signature listings, Whitman celebrates the usually unsung. Whitman starts with the carpenter, "singing as he measures his plank or beam."② In this poem, he names mechanics, masons, and other working class laborers, calling out and acknowledging the importance of the contribution each one makes.

Beyond the Classroom

Workplace Skills Connection

Written Evaluations The skills relevant to critical evaluations—using a clear organization for opinions that are carefully supported by specific examples—are also necessary in many workplace contexts. On a regular basis managers must write detailed performance appraisals of the employees who report to them. At other times internal project proposals may require a formal, written evaluation. Explain that subjective opinions are appropriate in workplace evaluations as long as they are supported by references to observable or verifiable data. Ask students how writing such evaluations might differ from writing critical responses to literature. *Students may respond that the tone of workplace evaluations must always be formal, avoiding playful or lyrical language. Workplace appraisals usually do not include reference to earlier works, nor do they attempt to place the item being evaluated within a biographical or historical context. Finally, workplace evaluations might be required to follow a format and organization dictated by management.*

Prewriting

Choose a Topic Because they're fresh in your mind, you may want to write an evaluation of one of the poems you've just read in this section. As an alternative, you can search your memory to recall other literary works that have evoked an especially strong reaction—either positive or negative—in you.

Use Your Journal to Get Started Once you've chosen a literary work to write about, quickly write down your thoughts and impressions about that work. This process will help you sort through your feelings about the work and pinpoint what it was about the work that evoked these feelings.

Review the Work In a critical evaluation, it isn't enough to simply state your opinion about a work—you have to back up your opinion. As a result, it's essential to review the work you've chosen to refresh your memory and to gather details to back up your opinion. You might want to use note cards to record passages and details you identify. Look at this example:

Opinion: Whitman vividly captures the unique importance of work to each person.

Support: "Each singing what belongs to him or her and to none else," I Hear America Singing, line 9

Organize Your Ideas Arrange your note cards into groups, with each group focusing on one of your opinions or on a single aspect of the work.

Drafting

Follow a Clear Organization The best way to organize your evaluation is to follow the classic sequence of thesis-body-conclusion: stating your main idea clearly in your introduction, developing it with specific examples in the body, and clinching it with a persuasive restatement in your conclusion. Focus each of your body paragraphs on a single main point.

APPLYING LANGUAGE SKILLS: Quotations and Quotation Marks

Use quotation marks to set off direct quotations from literary works. Commas and periods go inside the final quotation marks, colons and semicolons go outside.

Poe opens his poem, "Once upon a midnight dreary."

"I celebrate myself, and sing myself": surely this is among the most famous lines in American poetry.

When a question mark or exclamation point is part of the quotation, place it inside the final closing quotation marks; otherwise, place it outside:

The poet asks, "Was it a dream?"

Why does the poet ask if it was "a dream"?

Writing Application As you revise your critical evaluation, check that you are using quotation marks correctly.

Writer's Solution Connection
Language Lab

For more practice with quotation marks, see the Language Lab lesson on Semicolons, Colons, and Quotation Marks in the Punctuation unit.

Develop Student Writing

Prewriting Strategy

When choosing a topic for their critical evaluations, students may wonder whether they should select a work with which they are already familiar. Advise students that reviewing the work is apt to be a time-consuming task, so it may best to choose a work they have already read, or select a brief work that is new to them. If students review a long work they have not read, remind them to budget their time accordingly.

Customize for
English Language Learners
Students may feel uncomfortable being critical about a work written in a language that they themselves are still learning. Guide English language learners to choose a work with an appropriate vocabulary level, and encourage them to review the work with a dictionary at hand. Native speakers can help them with idiomatic or slang expressions that appear in dialogue or in first-person narratives with a conversational tone.

Writing Lab CD-ROM
The Gathering Details section of the tutorial includes several activities to help students during the Prewriting stage. Direct students to the Chain of Events chart, Sunburst, or Venn Diagrams to help gather specific information and ideas.

Elaboration Strategy

While pulling quotes from the text to support their opinions, students may come across interesting aspects of the work that they missed earlier. Encourage these students to be selective about adding further observations, making sure they do not disrupt the organization they have already decided upon. Points that support the writer's central concerns should be noted for inclusion during the revision process.

Applying Language Skills

Quotation and Quotation Marks To introduce this skill, stress the importance of providing specific examples to support a critical evaluation. Explain that punctuation can change the meaning of a sentence. When quoting sources, students must accurately identify the start and end of an author's words.

Writing Application
When reviewing student writing for the correct use of quotations and quotation marks, you may want to ask students to make a copy of the literary work available to you. In addition, look for dashes, ellipses, and other marks that may be used in conjunction with direct quotations.

Grammar Reinforcement

In addition to the **Language Lab CD-ROM** lesson cited in the student edition, refer students to the *Sourcebook* lesson on p. 226 and practice page 90 in the *Writer's Solution Grammar Practice Book.*

Revision Strategy

To supplement the checklist add the following questions:

- Have I devoted too much of the evaluation to summarizing the work, and not enough space to analysis?
- Have I quoted too much or too little from the work? Are direct quotations too brief to support my points?

Applying Language Skills

Indirect and Direct Quotations
Explain that paraphrasing is an efficient way of summarizing aspects of a literary work—but readers need to know when the words are the author's.

Answers

1. correct
2. Pascal wrote, "Man is a reed, but a thinking reed."

Grammar Reinforcement

For additional instruction, use the **Language Lab CD-ROM** lesson Quotation Marks, Colons, Semicolons and p. 90 in the *Writer's Solution Grammar Practice Book.*

Reinforce and Extend

Review the Writing Guidelines
After students have completed the assignment, review the characteristics of a critical evaluation, and ask them to come up with additional criteria based on what they learned through writing.

Prentice Hall Writing and Grammar For more prewriting, elaboration, and revision strategies, see *Prentice Hall Writing and Grammar.*

Applying Language Skills: Indirect and Direct Quotations

When you use a **direct quotation**, you repeat someone else's words exactly. When you use an **indirect quotation**, you paraphrase, or restate, someone else's words.

Indirect:

The critic wrote that Emily Dickinson was the greatest American poet.

Direct:

The critic wrote, "Emily Dickinson was the greatest American poet."

Practice Decide whether each sentence makes a direct or indirect quotation. Then add quotation marks as needed.

1. The writer said that citizens should be concerned.
2. Pascal wrote Man is a reed, but a thinking reed.

Writing Application Check that you have used proper punctuation for direct and indirect quotations.

Writer's Solution Connection
Writing Lab

For additional instruction and support in all stages of the writing process, use the models and activities in the tutorial on Response to Literature.

Back Up Your Opinions Throughout your evaluation, cite details and passages from the literary work to support your opinions. For example, if you say that a poem has musical qualities, quote passages that contain sound devices such as rhyme and alliteration.

Revising

Use a Checklist Go back to the Writing Skills Focus on page 422, and use the items as a checklist to evaluate and revise your evaluation.

- ▶ Have I followed a clear and logical organization throughout the evaluation? What can I do to improve the organization?
- ▶ Are my key ideas thoroughly supported with specific examples from the text? What additional support can I include?
- ▶ Have I maintained a consistent writing style that is appropriate to my topic? How can I refine my style?

Revision Model

① the "varied carols" of
By outlining ^ the American working landscape, Whitman creates poetry that inspires.

① The writer strengthens the conclusion with a quotation to illustrate the point.

Publishing

Create a Class Literary Magazine As a group project, gather the critical evaluations of several class members into a class literary magazine. Include a cover, title, and table of contents; artistically talented students might also create illustrations to accompany the pieces.

Publish On-line To reach a wide audience, consider publishing your response on-line. You might post your work to an on-line bulletin board, a student magazine, or a Web site devoted to the writer you discuss.

✓ ASSESSMENT

PORTFOLIO ASSESSMENT		4	3	2	1
Use the rubric on Critical Review in ***Alternative Assessment*** (p. 126) to assess students' writing. Add these criteria to customize the rubric to this assignment.	**Quotation Marks**	Quotation marks are used consistently and correctly.	Quotation marks are almost always used correctly.	There are significant errors in the use of quotation marks.	Quotation marks are rarely used correctly.
	Summarizes the Literary Work	The summary concisely covers the points necessary to understanding the evaluation.	The summary gives adequate information to understand the evaluation.	The summary lacks some information needed to understand the evaluations.	The summary is inadequate or is not included.

Student Success Workshop

Real-World Reading Skills

Analyzing Reviews of Literature, Film, and Performance

Strategies for Success

Everyone responds to literature and other media—such as film, theater, and dance—in different ways. A response is subjective; that is, particular to an individual. Even so, a reviewer must support his or her evaluation with details and examples from the work itself. Reading a review of a book or a play can add to your understanding of the work and give you a new appreciation for it. Analyzing a review helps you evaluate your own response.

Analyzing Film and Performance Reviews If you read reviews of films or plays, what makes you decide whether or not to see the film or drama? To analyze a review of a film or performance, first identify the reviewer's criteria. What does the reviewer consider a good performance? Are there details and examples from the film or performance that support the reviewer's judgment? Do you have the same criteria as the reviewer? For example, a reviewer may expect a film to be believable, while you are willing to suspend disbelief for an exciting plot.

Analyzing Literature Reviews When reading a literature review, notice whether the reviewer analyzes literary elements. Is there a discussion of the writer's tone, themes, organization, or conclusions? Does the reviewer point out how the writer's style and word choice affect the text's content? Ask questions like these as you analyze a review. Also, be sure a reviewer supports his or her judgment with examples from the text. The examples and the review should enhance your understanding of the text.

Apply the Strategies

Analyze this review, and compare your own responses to the excerpt on p. 285. Then answer the questions that follow.

> Do not be put off by the absence of characters and dialogue in Annie Dillard's personal narrative, *Pilgrim at Tinker Creek*. This is a book about seeing, and the importance of seeing, not speaking. Dillard systematically shares with the reader truthful and intimate observations of animals and insects, using flowing prose and fresh figurative language.
>
> No matter how quiet we are, the muskrats stay hidden. Maybe they sense the tense hum of consciousness, the buzz from two human beings who in silence cannot help but be aware of each other, and so of themselves.
>
> Throughout the book, Dillard uses nature and human knowledge to explore a greater theme: the existence of good and evil in the world and the nature of its creator.

1. Explain why the reviewer's argument is or is not valid by answering the following questions: What literary elements are discussed in this review? What supporting details are given for the writer's opinion?
2. Write a review of the excerpt from *Pilgrim at Tinker Creek* on page 285, and compare it to this one. List the similarities and differences.
3. In the arts section of a newspaper, find a review of a film or performance, preferably one you have seen. Analyze the review, using the strategies in this workshop.

✔ *Here are some other situations in which you might analyze reviews:*
- Deciding whether or not to buy a CD
- Choosing a restaurant
- Selecting what brand of television to buy

Test Preparation Workshop

Analyzing Reviews

Some critical reading questions on standardized tests measure students' ability to judge the strengths and weaknesses of a critical argument. Display this test item:

A book reviewer says: "The plot of this mystery is unoriginal." Which statement offers the best support for that opinion?

A The detective learns who the murderer is on page 55, and the ending becomes obvious.

B The writing is imaginative and startling.

C The plot revolves around a crime committed one hundred years earlier.

D The characters are vivid and compelling.

Have students explain why A is the correct answer: It offers the reviewer's reason for the stated opinion. Students should recognize that choice *B* is irrelevant, and choices *C* and *D* do not offer logical support for the opinion.

Prepare and Engage

LESSON OBJECTIVES

- To analyze written reviews of literature, film, and performance to compare with his/her own responses

Customize for
AP Students

Together, students may choose a film, book, or performance of interest. Have them use Internet sources and databases for periodicals and newspapers to find at least two reviews of the same work. After reading and discussion, they may categorize the reviews based on scales they devise: favorable/unfavorable, clear support/vague support, precise word choice/extreme language, and so on.

Apply the Strategies

Answers

1. The reviewer is impressed by the author's use of language, the "flowing prose" and the "fresh figurative language." The quotation supports the reviewer's argument. The reviewer also notes possible themes—the importance of seeing in silence, and the nature of good and evil. The quotation explains what the reviewer means about the significance of silence. The reviewer's reason for thinking that the book is about good and evil, however, is not supported with explicit details.
2. Students may focus on literary elements or techniques that have captured their attention. In their comparison to the workshop review, they may note similarities and/or differences in text organization and in explanations of the author's ideas.
3. In students' analyses, they should note the criteria that the reviewer used and tell why they think the criteria are or are not valid.

Prepare and Engage

LESSON OBJECTIVES

- To speak clearly and effectively for a variety of purposes

Establish a real-world context for this workshop's strategies by asking students to share examples of prior occasions that involved an interview. Ask, what were some problems you encountered? *Student responses may include that their nervousness rendered their preparation useless, that the interviewer asked "trick" questions, or that they had nothing interesting to say.* In contrast, what are some actual or expected positive aspects of the interview process? *Responses may include that it can provide students with valuable information about a college or a job prospect, that they become less anxious as the interview progresses, that the interviewer can be talked to like a "regular person."* Conclude your introduction by explaining that this workshop may minimize the unpleasant aspects of interviewing so that students can communicate effectively.

Apply the Strategies

Customize for
Interpersonal Learners
These students may enjoy modeling the strategies with you in front of the class. As a basis for these mock interviews, pretend that they involve an institution and position with which both parties are familiar—such as a teaching assistant at your school.

1. Tell students that this situation arises in almost every interview. Inform students that the trick is to provide a bridge between the "never-tried" experience and an impressive accomplishment in their past.
2. Advise students to think about the aspects of the job or college that appealed to them, and to ask a specific question that showed that they had "done their homework." This places the interviewer in the position of "selling" the college or company to them.
3. Sample respons: "I'd like to know if there is any aspect of my achievements that I should clarify. I feel strongly about this college/job and I'd like to take whatever steps are necessary for my success."

Speaking, Listening, and Viewing Workshop

Handling a College or Job Interview

An interview is just an informal chat, a chance to say hello, right? Think again. Sometimes your interview is the deciding factor in getting a job or securing college admission.

Do Some Homework Both you and the interviewer have certain goals for your conversation. If possible, learn about your interviewer's focus—and any biases he or she may have—before the interview. Identify your own goals as well. What do you want to know about this job or college? Make a list of key questions.

Listen . . . and Respond Answer the questions you are asked—even if they are different from those you expected. If you can't answer, try to address the question topic from another angle. Present your own inquiries at the appropriate time, and listen thoughtfully for the information you seek.

Value the Interviewer's Time Give concise answers, and stay on the subject. Always thank your interviewer for his or her time, in person at the close of the interview and later with a note.

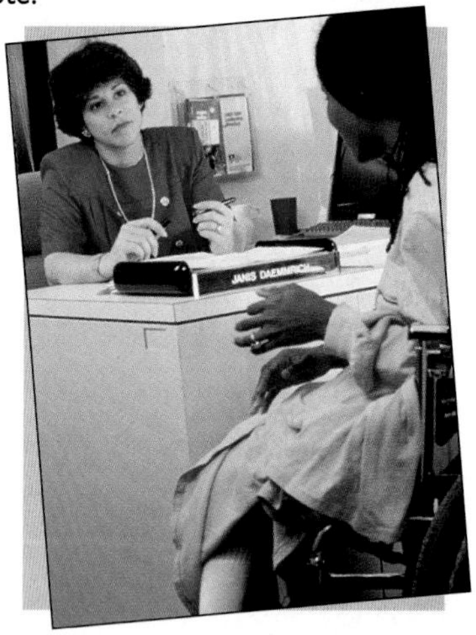

Tips for Handling College or Job Interviews

If you want to secure your success with a great interview, follow these strategies:

- Make eye contact with the interviewer.
- Be courteous and respectful.
- Develop replies as you did questions—avoid giving yes or no answers in favor of greater depth.
- Focus on what you can offer the school or business.
- Relax. It's okay to make a small joke or express your enthusiasm appropriately.

Apply the Strategies

You're at a college or job interview. Consider carefully, and respond to each of the following situations.

1. The interviewer asks you to describe your experience with a skill you have never tried. What might you say?
2. After introducing herself, the interviewer sits back and waits for you to speak. Develop some questions to jump-start the interview.
3. As the meeting progresses, your interest in the job or school increases. How might you express your enthusiasm appropriately to the interviewer? Role-play some ideas with a partner.

Beyond the Classroom

Human Resources Administrator Many companies have Human Resources departments whose job it is to fill open positions within the company. Often such "HR" representatives serve as the "first hurdle" for applicants as they screen prospects so that management need only interview those that show the most potential.

Encourage interested students to contact Human Resources personnel who work at the company of a family member or adult friend to find out the necessary qualifications and educational requirements for this career. Point out that the tips for handling interviews in the student edition can easily be adapted to serve as a checklist for interviewers: Does the applicant maintain eye contact with me? Does the applicant provide in-depth answers, or simple "yes or no" responses? Ask students to brainstorm other items that might appear on an interviewer's checklist. *Responses might include: Did the applicant arrive on time for the interview? Does the applicant show a thorough knowledge of the company or college? Is the applicant confident about his or her accomplishments and potential?*

Test Preparation Workshop

Reading Comprehension

Analyze Information to Make Inferences and Generalizations

Strategies for Success

The reading sections of standardized tests often require you to read a passage of fiction and draw inferences and generalizations about the passage's plot, setting, characters, and mood. The following strategies will help you answer such test questions:

Draw Inferences A test may ask about something not stated directly in the passage. To infer is to read between the lines, recognizing the implied message. Examine the passage for clues. For example, you might be asked to infer the conflict that forms the plot in this passage:

> A weak rain drizzled outside the cabin, and Dan sat at the kitchen table, trying to gather courage. The idea of quitting his new job nearly filled him with fear. He thought of returning home to the wilds of Oregon would help. But as the thunder boomed outside, he tried in vain to overcome his worries. He was simply too afraid of failure to quit—even if he disliked his new boss and felt indifferent toward his co-workers. The courage he had mustered to come here slowly evaporated, and Dan realized sadly that he would just return to work on Monday.

In this passage, Dan's main conflict is with

A the wilds of Oregon.
B himself.
C his new boss.
D his co-workers.

Answer **A** tells where Dan feels at home. **C** and **D** may be reasons to quit but are not his direct conflict. **B** is correct. Dan struggles with fears of failure and future uncertainty if he quits his job.

Make Generalizations A generalization is a general statement based on specific evidence. For example, which of the following best describes the mood of the passage?

A rainy
B confident
C indifferent
D bleak

Answer **A** describes setting, not mood. Dan's fears prove **B** incorrect. **C** is wrong as well; Dan is focused on the problem at hand. The descriptions in the passage produce a bleak mood. **D** is correct.

Apply the Strategies

Read this passage, and answer the questions that follow:

> Ellen's plan to garden on the dusty plot of Oklahoma clay didn't surprise anyone. When the rain rotted her tomato sprouts, she simply planted more. When the deer nibbled her corn, she built a strong fence around the garden bed. When the summer skies withheld rain, she lugged bucketsful of water from a nearby spring. And when the town amateur gardening contest gave out blue ribbons, Ellen won them all.

1 Which of the following most accurately describes Ellen?

A talented
B lucky
C determined
D strong

2 Which of the following most accurately describes the setting?

A spring in Oklahoma
B Ellen's garden
C a town gardening exhibit
D a commercial farm

Correlations to Standardized Tests

The reading comprehension skills reviewed in this workshop correspond to the following standardized test sections:

SAT Critical Reading
ACT Reading

Test Preparation

Each ATE workshop in Unit 3 supports the instruction here by providing teaching suggestions and a sample test item:

- **Make Inferences and Generalizations** (ATE, pp. 227, 235, 249, 258, 275, 295, 317, 331, 363, 373, 395, 405)

LESSON OBJECTIVES

- To comprehend selections using a variety of strategies, drawing inferences such as conclusions, generalizations, and predictions and supporting them with text evidence and experience

Answers

1. (C) determined
2. (B) Ellen's garden

Test-Taking Tip

Read All Answer Choices

Remind students that working speedily on a test does not mean working hastily—it is important to read through all the answer choices, even if the first one seems correct.

Have students reread question 1 in this workshop: "Which of the following most accurately describes Ellen?" Point out that answer *A* might seem correct—Ellen is a talented gardener. But the passage is mostly about how Ellen persists even when things go wrong, so answer *C*, "determined," is the better choice.

Planning Instruction and Assessment

Unit Objectives

1. To read selections from American literature written during the period (1850–1914)
2. To apply a variety of reading strategies, particularly interactive reading strategies, appropriate for reading these selections
3. To analyze literary elements
4. To use a variety of strategies to read unfamiliar words and to build vocabulary
5. To learn elements of grammar, usage, and style
6. To use recursive writing processes to write in a variety of forms
7. To prepare, organize, and present literary interpretations

Meeting the Objectives

With each selection, you will find instructional material and portfolio opportunities through which students can meet these objectives. Further, you will find additional practice pages for reading strategies, literary elements, vocabulary, and grammar in the ***Selection Support*** booklet in the ***Teaching Resources*** box.

Test Preparation

The unit workshop, **Reading Comprehension: Using Context** (SE, p. 631)is supported by teaching tips and a sample test item in the ATE workshop with each selection grouping.

- **Context** (ATE, pp. 441, 451, 457, 467, 479, 495, 519, 533, 545, 555, 569, 591, 599, 605, 613)

The following additional workshops in the ATE give teaching tips and a sample test item for applying the skill taught in the Student Success Workshops.

- **Using Visuals** (ATE, p. 492)
- **Recognizing Forms of Propaganda** (ATE, p. 516)
- **Evaluating Information Sources** (ATE, p. 588)

Detail of Battle of Cedar Creek (partial study for larger painting), Julian Scott, Historical Society of Plainfield, New Jersey

Humanities: Art

Detail of Battle of Cedar Creek by Julian Scott.

The Battle of Cedar Creek (near Middletown, Virginia) was fought in October 1864. While their commander, General Philip Sheridan, was at a meeting in Washington, the Union army was surprised by a Confederate attack.

Have students use what they see in the painting to speculate about the impression of war this painter intended to create. *Reasonable answers include: Given the fact that smoke and shadows make it hard to see clearly, the painter seems to focus more on the small moments of war and the confusion of battle than on the heroism or excitement of fighting. Many soldiers seem to turn away from the actual front line, tending to other matters.*

What elements or details in this painting suggest what the two sides have in common? *The smoke and shadows that make it hard to see make the two sides blend together, as does the fact that men in blue and men in gray seem to be mingling.*

UNIT 4

Division, Reconciliation, and Expansion (1850–1914)

"If we do not make common cause to save the good old ship of the Union on this voyage, nobody will have a chance to pilot her on another voyage."

—Abraham Lincoln,
President of the United States of America, February 15, 1861

"I worked night and day for twelve years to prevent the war, but I could not. The North was mad and blind, would not let us govern ourselves, and so the war came. Now it must go on until the last man of this generation falls in his tracks and his children seize his musket and fight our battles."

—Jefferson Davis,
President of the Confederate States of America, July 17, 1864

Assessing Student Progress

The following tools are available to measure the degree to which students meet the unit objectives:

Informal Assessment

The questions in the Guide for Responding sections are a first level of response to the concepts and skills presented with the selection. Students' responses are a brief informal measure of their grasp of the material. Their responses on this level can indicate where further instruction and practice are needed. You may then follow up with the practice pages in the ***Selection Support*** booklet.

You will find literature and reading guides in the ***Alternative Assessment*** booklet, which you may give students on an individual basis for informal assessment of their performance.

Formal Assessment

In the ***Formal Assessment*** booklet, you will find selection tests and part tests.

Selection Tests The selection tests measure comprehension and skills acquisition for each selection or group of selections.

Part Tests Each part test, which calls on students to read a passage of literature they have not previously seen, applies the unit skills on a broader level. The Critical Reading section measures Unit Objectives 1, 2, and 3. The Vocabulary and Grammar section measures Objectives 4 and 5. The Essay section measures Objectives 1 and 6. Both the Critical Reading and Vocabulary and Grammar sections use formats similar to those found on many standardized tests, including the SAT.

Alternative Assessment

Portfolios As you review individual pieces or the collected work in students' portfolios, you will find assessment sheets available in the portfolio section of the ***Alternative Assessment*** booklet.

Scoring Rubrics You will find scoring rubrics for writing modes in the ***Alternative Assessment*** booklet. You can apply these to Guided Writing Lessons and to Writing Process Workshop lessons.

Speaking, Listening, and Viewing The ***Alternative Assessment*** booklet contains assessment sheets for speaking, listening, and viewing activities.

Learning Modalities The ***Alternative Assessment*** booklet contains activities that appeal to different learning styles. You may use these too as an alternative measurement of students' growth.

Using the Timeline

The Timeline can serve a number of instructional purposes, as follows:

Getting an Overview Use the Timeline to help students get a quick overview of themes and events of the period. This approach will benefit all students but may be especially helpful for visually oriented students, English language learners, and those less proficient in reading. (For strategies in using the Timeline as an overview, see the bottom of this page.)

Thinking Critically Questions are provided on the facing page. Use these questions to have students review the events, discuss their significance, and examine the *so what* behind the *what happened.*

Connecting to Selections Have students refer back to the Timeline when beginning to read individual selections. By consulting the Timeline regularly, they will gain a better sense of the period's chronology. In addition, they will appreciate what was occurring in the world that gave rise to these works of literature.

Projects Students can use the Timeline as a launching pad for projects like these:

- **Cause-and-Effect Connections** Have students scan the Timeline and speculate about cause-and-effect connections among events. They may want to diagram these links using the Cause-and-Effect Organizer, p. 91, in the ***Writing and Language Transparencies.***
- **Additional Illustrations** Have students search for additional illustrations for items in the Timeline. They can find such illustrations in biographies of the figures mentioned in the Timeline, encyclopedias, books on American history, and books on the history of technology. Students should be prepared to justify each new illustration they suggest.

Timeline

1850 – 1914

1850 | 1860 | 1870

American Events

- **1852** Harriet Beecher Stowe's *Uncle Tom's Cabin* becomes an instant bestseller.
- **1855** Walt Whitman publishes first edition of *Leaves of Grass.*
- **1855** *My Bondage and My Freedom,* Frederick Douglass's second autobiography makes its appearance. ▶
- **1858** Oliver Wendell Holmes publishes *The Autocrat of the Breakfast-Table.*
- **1858** Lincoln-Douglas debates help make Abraham Lincoln a national figure.
- **1859** John Brown, an abolitionist, leads a raid on federal arsenal at Harpers Ferry, Virginia; he is hanged for treason. ▲
- **1859** The Supreme Court supports slave owners in the Dred Scott decision.

- **1860** Essays by Ralph Waldo Emerson published as *The Conduct of Life.*
- **1860** Republican Abraham Lincoln is elected United States president.
- **1860** South Carolina secedes from the Union.
- **1860** Civil War begins in April with firing on Fort Sumter.
- **1861** Lincoln inaugurated in March.
- **1862** Julia Ward Howe writes "The Battle Hymn of the Republic."
- **1862** Major battles are fought at Shiloh, Antietam, and Fredericksburg.
- **1863** After Antietam, Lincoln issues the Emancipation Proclamation.
- **1863** Union forces lose at Chancellorsville but win at Gettysburg and Vicksburg.
- **1864** Lincoln wins reelection. ▶
- **1865** President Lincoln is assassinated.
- **1865** The 13th Amendment abolishes slavery.
- **1865** General Robert E. Lee surrenders to General Ulysses S. Grant at Appomattox. ▶
- **1869** The Wyoming and Utah territories grant women the right to vote.

- **1870** Bret Harte publishes *The Luck of Roaring Camp and Other Stories.*
- **1876** Baseball's National League founded.
- **1876** Republican Rutherford B. Hayes wins the presidential election despite losing the popular vote.
- **1876** Mark Twain publishes *The Adventures of Tom Sawyer.* ▲
- **1877** The Compromise of 1877 ends military occupation of the South.
- **1877** Thomas Edison patents the phonograph.

World Events

- **1855** England: Alfred, Lord Tennyson publishes his long poem *Maud.*
- **1857** France: Gustave Flaubert completes *Madame Bovary,* a classic novel of realism.
- **1859** England: Charles Dickens adds to his fame with *A Tale of Two Cities.*
- **1859** England: Charles Darwin introduces theory of evolution in *The Origin of Species.* ◀

- **1861** England: George Eliot (Mary Ann Evans) publishes her popular novel *Silas Marner.*
- **1862** France: Louis Pasteur proposes modern germ theory of disease.
- **1863** Mexico: French occupy Mexico City and establish Maximilian as emperor of Mexico.
- **1864** England: *Dramatis Personae* by Robert Browning appears.
- **1865** England: Lewis Carroll completes *Alice's Adventures in Wonderland.*
- **1865** Germany: Karl Benz builds first automobile powered by the internal-combustion engine.
- **1869** France: Jules Verne publishes *Twenty Thousand Leagues Under the Sea.*
- **1872** Russia: Leo Tolstoy publishes *War and Peace.*
- **1874** France: Claude Monet gathers Impressionist painters for first exhibition.
- **1877** England: First tennis championship held at Wimbledon. ▼
- **1879** Norway: Henrick Ibsen writes *A Doll's House.*

Getting an Overview of the Period

Introduction To give students an overview of the period, indicate the span of dates in the title of the Timeline. *A period of 64 years is covered.* Into what units is this period divided? *It is divided into ten-year units.* Next, point out that the Timeline is divided into American Events (on top) and World Events (on bottom). Have them scan the Timeline, looking both at the American Events and the World Events. Finally, point out that the events in the Timeline often represent beginnings, turning points, and endings (for example, 1860 marks the beginning of the Civil War).

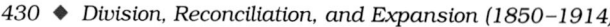

Key Events Have students identify key events related to division, reconciliation, and expansion. *Reasonable answers include: division—Civil War begins (1860), major Civil War battles fought (1862); reconciliation—Compromise of 1877 ends military occupation of South; expansion—last major battle between U.S. troops and Native Americans (1890), Boston and Chicago linked by telephone (1893).* What are two key scientific developments that occurred in the world during this time? *Darwin introduced the theory of evolution (1859) and Pasteur introduced the germ theory of disease (1862).*

1880 | 1890 | 1900

American Events

- **1883** Railroads adopt standard time zones.
- **1883** The Brooklyn Bridge is opened.
- **1884** Mark Twain publishes *The Adventures of Huckleberry Finn.*

- **1886** Statue of Liberty dedicated in New York Harbor. ▲

- **1888** Great mid-March blizzard in eastern United States piles 30-foot drifts in New York's Herald Square. ◀
- **1890** Last major battle between U.S. troops and Native Americans fought at Wounded Knee, South Dakota.
- **1890** Daughters of the American Revolution founded in Washington.
- **1893** Boston and Chicago are linked by long-distance telephone.
- **1893** Ambrose Bierce publishes *Can Such Things Be?*
- **1894** Kate Chopin's *Bayou Folk* published.
- **1895** Stephen Crane publishes *The Red Badge of Courage.*
- **1895** First professional football game played in Latrobe, Pennsylvania.
- **1896** Paul Laurence Dunbar publishes *Lyrics of Lowly Life.*
- **1896** *The Country of the Pointed Firs,* Sarah Orne Jewett's masterpiece, appears.
- **1901** President William McKinley shot in Buffalo; succeeded by Theodore Roosevelt.
- **1903** Jack London publishes *The Call of the Wild.*
- **1903** Boston Red Sox and Pittsburgh Pirates play in first World Series.
- **1903** Wright Brothers stay aloft for 582 feet in their airplane at Kitty Hawk, North Carolina. ▲
- **1905** Willa Cather publishes *The Troll Garden.*
- **1905** Edith Wharton's *The House of Mirth* appears.
- **1908** Henry Ford builds his first car. ▼

- **1909** National Association for the Advancement of Colored People (NAACP) founded.

World Events

- **1881** French scientist Louis Pasteur administers the first successful rabies vaccination. ▶
- **1884** Russia: Leo Tolstoy completes *The Death of Ivan Ilyich.*
- **1886** England: Thomas Hardy publishes *The Mayor of Casterbridge.*
- **1891** England: Thomas Hardy publishes *Tess of the D'Urbervilles.*
- **1894** Sino-Japanese War breaks out; Japanese army easily defeats Chinese.
- **1895** Germany: Wilhelm Roentgen discovers X-rays.
- **1898** France: Pierre and Marie Curie discover radium and polonium.
- **1901** Italy: First transatlantic radio telegraphic message is achieved by Marconi.
- **1903** Spain: Pablo Picasso paints *The Old Guitarist.*

- **1904** Russo-Japanese War begins.
- **1905** Germany: Albert Einstein proposes his relativity theory. ◀
- **1908** Italy: Earthquake in Calabria and Sicily: 150,000 killed.

▶Critical Viewing◀

1. What does John Brown's picture (1859) suggest about his character? **[Infer]** *The picture suggests that he was intense and forceful.*
2. Who do you think are the men standing near General Grant (1865) at Appomattox? **[Infer]** *They might be fellow generals or Grant's aides.*
3. What are some details in the picture of the Statue of Liberty (1886) suggesting that its dedication was a festive occasion? **[Analyze]** *The sky seems to be filled with fireworks in honor of the occasion, and there are many ships in the harbor.*
4. In what ways is Henry Ford's first car (1908) similar to and different from cars of today? **[Compare and Contrast]** *Ford's first car is similar to today's cars in that it has four tires, a steering wheel, and front and back seats. It is different in that it seems to be open with only a canopy for a covering. Also, it is more vertical and less sleek than today's cars.*

◆Critical Thinking

1. (a) Name two American events during the decade 1850–1860 that relate to the conflict over slavery. *In 1858, the Lincoln-Douglas debates made Lincoln a national figure. In 1859 the Supreme Court supported slave owners in the Dred Scott decision.* (b) Explain how these events might have set the stage for the Civil War. **[Speculate]** *The debates made it possible for Lincoln to pursue and win the presidency, thereby provoking the Civil War. The Supreme Court decision may have made abolitionists even more determined to do away with slavery.*
2. (a) What key Civil War events occurred in 1863? *Lincoln issued the Emancipation Proclamation, and the Union forces lost at Chancellorsville but won at Gettysburg and Vicksburg.* (b) What do these events suggest about the course of the war? **[Infer]** *The two Union victories suggest that the Union was beginning to win the war.*
3. (a) Looking at both American and World Events, name two key sporting events that occurred during the decade 1870–1880. *In 1876, baseball's National League was founded, and in 1877, the first tennis championship was held at Wimbledon.* (b) What is the importance of these events for us today? **[Relate]** *Baseball and the National League are still going strong, and tennis championships are still held at Wimbledon.*
4. (a) What important battle was fought in America in 1890? *The last major battle between U.S. troops and Native Americans was fought at Wounded Knee, South Dakota.* (b) In what way did this battle suggest that the frontier period was ending? **[Interpret]** *The battle indicates that Native Americans were no longer in a position to oppose settlers, as they had during the period of the expanding frontier.*
5. (a) Name two developments in transportation that occurred in the first decade of the twentieth century. *In 1903, the Wright brothers flew an airplane, and in 1908, Henry Ford built his first automobile.* (b) In what way did these beginnings have dramatic effects? **[Connect]** *These two events led to the America of today, with its extensive system of roads and its skies filled with air traffic.*

Develop Understanding

Customize for
Less Proficient Readers
Have students read the heads and subheads in *The Story of the Times.* Then have them make connections with the subheads under Historical Background and those under Literature of the Period. For example, "The Union Is Dissolved," p. 433, suggests the war that gave rise to "Wartime Voices," p. 436.

Customize for
English Language Learners
Have these students use A Graphic Look at the Period, without the questions, to gain a better understanding of the unit's key themes: division, reconciliation, and expansion. For example, have them use the photographs on pp. 432–433 to speculate about the nature of the Civil War.

Customize for
Bodily/Kinesthetic Learners
Students with a kinesthetic orientation will benefit by creating *tableaux vivant*—representations of dramatic scenes by a person or group posing silently without moving—to illustrate *The Story of the Times*. These might include such scenes as the trial of John Brown or the completion of the transcontinental railroad.

Customize for
AP Students
Ask AP Students to read *The Story of the Times* and note key ways in which the national identity changed during this period.

Answers to
A Graphic Look

Analyze a Primary Source
Citizens of South Carolina may have reacted with a feeling of liberation but also with a sense of concern about a possible conflict. *They might ask about a new government, new currency, or about their personal safety.*

Support a Hypothesis The soldier brought his wife and children with him, and his wife appears to be doing the wash. The whole family seems to be living in the tent that is just behind the wife.

A Graphic Look at the Period

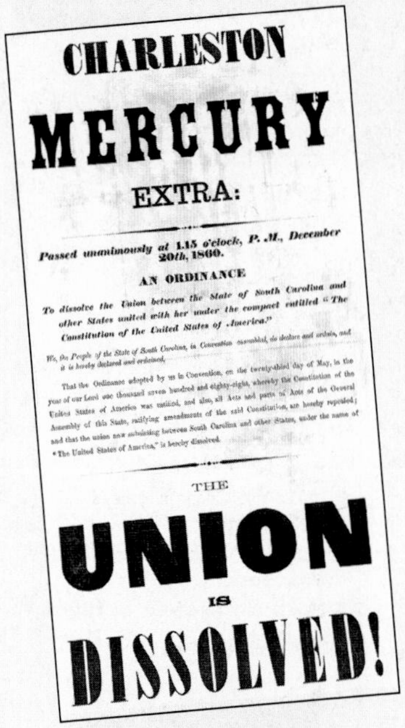
CHARLESTON
MERCURY
EXTRA:

Passed unanimously at 1.15 o'clock, P. M., December 20th, 1860.

AN ORDINANCE

To dissolve the Union between the State of South Carolina and other States united with her under the compact entitled "The Constitution of the United States of America."

We, the People of the State of South Carolina, in Convention assembled, do declare and ordain, and it is hereby declared and ordained,

That the Ordinance adopted by us in Convention, on the twenty-third day of May, in the year of our Lord one thousand seven hundred and eighty-eight, whereby the Constitution of the United States of America was ratified, and also, all Acts and parts of Acts of the General Assembly of this State, ratifying amendments of the said Constitution, are hereby repealed; and that the union now subsisting between South Carolina and other States, under the name of "The United States of America," is hereby dissolved.

THE
UNION
IS
DISSOLVED!

▲ **Analyze a Primary Source** This broadside announced the news of South Carolina's decision to secede from the Union. How might you have reacted to this poster if you were a citizen of this state? What questions would you have asked? Why?

▲ **Support a Hypothesis** What evidence is there to suggest that this Pennsylvania soldier and his family tried to continue normal life even while encamped?

The Story of the Times
1850 – 1914

The years between 1850 and 1914 witnessed a transformation of the United States. During those years, America changed from a decentralized, mostly agricultural nation to the modern industrial nation that we know today. This transformation began with the Civil War. The Civil War era was a time of intense conflict. Americans took up arms against other Americans to determine which should prevail: North or South? freedom or slavery? the federal Union or states' rights? The North won, the Union held, and slavery was abolished, but at a devastating cost to the nation.

Historical Background

Prelude to War Disagreements over slavery were nothing new, but the controversy was rekindled in 1850 by passage of the Fugitive Slave Act. It required all citizens—of free states as well as slave states—to help catch runaway slaves. Southerners saw the law as just; northerners, as an outrage.

The expansion of slavery into the West was hotly contested. When, in 1854, the Kansas-Nebraska Act opened up a vast area of previously free western land to slavery, the argument became a fight. "We will engage in competition for the virgin soil of Kansas," a senator from New York insisted. The "competition" turned Kansas into a bloody battleground.

Just as it dominated politics and preoccupied the nation, the controversy over slavery influenced the literature of the day—and in one classic case, literature fueled the controversy. Harriet Beecher Stowe's novel *Uncle Tom's Cabin,* published in 1852, vividly depicted the cruelty of slavery. The book became a powerful antislavery weapon, selling more than 300,000 copies within a year. Its impact was such that within three years no fewer than thirty southern novels came out attempting to counter its influence.

The deep national division intensified in 1859 when a group of antislavery extremists raided a

Cross-Curricular Connection: Social Studies

The North and the South The North and South had developed along different economic lines. In the North, commerce, not cotton, was king. The Industrial Revolution and cheap transportation had helped turn northern towns and cities into centers of bustling activity. Education, banking, science, and reform movements—all were topics of interest and concern. Immigration, too, was changing the face of the North. A rising tide of Irish and Germans, among others, were seeking a new life in northern cities.

The South, by contrast, was a slower-paced region of plantations and small farms. There were cities, to be sure, but the area was most truly defined by its cotton plantations. Sugar, rice, and tobacco were also important crops. The march of technological progress, with its social issues and problems, had little impact on the prewar South.

What do these differences suggest about the outcome of a war between these regions? *The North, with its greater population and more developed industry, would probably win the war.*

federal arsenal. Led by John Brown, the group had intended to provoke an armed slave revolt. The attempt failed, and Brown was executed for treason, but this only fed the controversy which now threatened to escalate out of control.

The Union Is Dissolved The conflict between North and South came to a head when Abraham Lincoln was elected in 1860. Lincoln represented the newly formed Republican party, which had dedicated itself to halting the spread of slavery. South Carolina had threatened to secede if Lincoln was elected, and in December it did so. Six states followed South Carolina out of the Union. In February 1861, the secessionist states established the Confederate States of America.

Fighting began on April 11, 1861, when Confederate artillery fired on Union troops holding Fort Sumter, in Charleston Harbor. Many on both sides anticipated a short war ending in victory. No one could know what lay ahead—the carnage of Antietam, where 23,000 men fell in a single day; the deprivation of the seige of Vicksburg, where people survived by eating dogs and rats; the wholesale destruction of Georgia, when Union general William T. Sherman's troops marched to the sea. In fact, the devastating war would last four long years.

By the time Confederate general Robert E. Lee surrendered to Union general Ulysses S. Grant in the spring of 1865, more than 620,000 soldiers had lost their lives. Nearly that number had been wounded. The South lay in ruins, its cities razed, its farms and plantations destroyed.

An Expanding America If conflict characterized the Civil War years, change—on an astonishing scale—characterized the period that followed. Over the next fifty years, physical expansion and industrialization transformed our landscape, economy, society, and identity.

The Homestead Act of 1862 promised 160 acres of land to anyone who would farm it for five years. This shifted the westward movement into high gear. Half a million farmers, including tens of thousands of emancipated African Americans, staked claims on the Great Plains. Miners went west by the thousands, lured by the prospect of striking it rich in gold. Still others moved west to become cattle ranchers. Westward expansion was

▲ **Compare and Contrast** Robert E. Lee (left) and Ulysses S. Grant (right) were the military leaders of the Confederacy and the Union, respectively. What can you infer about their different personalities and backgrounds by comparing and contrasting their posture and dress?

▲ **Link Past to Present** This picture shows a young Confederate soldier, Private Edwin Jennison. Most of the soldiers in both armies were between the ages of 18 and 21. Some were even younger. What problems do you think a 16-year-old would face? Could a 16-year-old serve in the army today? Explain.

Connection to the Literature

- In "An Episode of War" by Stephen Crane, p. 443, and "Willie Has Gone to the War," p. 447, students will encounter a realistic and a somewhat sentimental view (respectively) of the Civil War.
- The spirituals "Swing Low, Sweet Chariot," p. 452, and "Go Down, Moses," p. 453, will help students better understand the situation and aspirations of enslaved African Americans.
- In the excerpt from *My Bondage and My Freedom,* p. 458, students will learn about slavery from the first-person account of Frederick Douglass.

More About African Americans in the Civil War The Civil War was the first American war in which black troops fought in large numbers. By the end of the war, there were some 180,000 black soldiers in more than a hundred Union regiments. On the Confederate side, both slaves and free blacks accompanied the army as cooks, teamsters, and laborers.

Answers to

A GRAPHIC LOOK

Compare and Contrast Lee's upright posture suggests that he is more formal than Grant, who leans informally against a tree. Also, Lee looks more aristocratic than Grant.

Link Past to Present A sixteen-year-old might become very homesick and might be shocked by the realities of wartime life. Today one would have to be at least eighteen to serve in the armed forces.

Cross-Curricular Connection: Science

Ironclad Ships in the Civil War The South desperately needed a way to break the Union blockade of its ports. One method it tried was the ironclad ship. Confederates covered the *Merrimack,* an abandoned Union ship, with iron plates 4 inches thick and sent it into battle against the Union navy. On March 8, 1862, the Merrimack sank one Union ship, drove another aground, and forced a third to surrender. Their cannonballs bounced harmlessly off the *Merrimack's* metal skin.

The Union countered with its own ironclads. One of these, the *Monitor,* struck back at the *Merrimack* in the waters off Hampton Roads, Virginia. The Confederate ship had more firepower, but the *Monitor* maneuvered more easily. In the end, neither ship seriously damaged the other, and both withdrew.

Ironclad ships changed naval warfare. Both sides rushed to build more of them. However, the South never mounted a serious attack against the Union navy. The Union blockade held.

What later advances in naval warfare do the ironclads foreshadow? *They foreshadow such later developments in naval warfare as the battleship.*

More About Women on the Plains People had to be strong to survive the hardships of life on the Great Plains. With few stores, women made clothing, quilts, soap, candles, and other goods by hand. They also had to cook and preserve all the food needed through the long winter.

Women had many other duties. They educated the children. With no doctors nearby, they treated the sick and injured. Women also helped with the planting and harvesting. When needed, they helped build sod houses.

More About the Disappearing Frontier As farmers spread across the Plains, fewer areas remained to be settled. The last major land rush took place in Oklahoma in 1889. Late in April 1889, as many as 100,000 land seekers lined up at the Oklahoma border. The government had announced that farmers could claim free homesteads in Oklahoma. Claims, however, could not be staked until noon on April 22. As the "boomers" charged into Oklahoma, they found to their surprise that others were already there. "Sooners" had sneaked into Oklahoma and staked out much of the best land.

The 1890 census reported that the United States no longer had a frontier. For 100 years, the frontier had absorbed immigrants, adventurers, and city folks. Now the frontier was closed.

Answers to A GRAPHIC LOOK

Respond to a Photograph Appropriate adjectives might include: *complete, fearful, extensive,* and *tremendous.*

Analyze a Situation As the picture suggests, the West offered African Americans the hope of owning their own house and land and of living in freedom.

▲ **Respond to a Photograph** This 1865 photograph shows the effects of the war on southern cities. What adjectives would you use to describe the destruction?

▼ **Analyze a Situation** For African Americans, the West offered the hope of freedom. Here the Shores family poses in front of their Nebraska sod house. What opportunities might the West offer African Americans that the East did not?

boosted by completion of the first transcontinental railroad in 1868. As the national railroads grew, the covered wagon—symbol of the American pioneer—was replaced by the railroad as the main means of transportation.

The Disappearing Frontier By 1890, the frontier as Americans had known it for centuries had ceased to exist. The steady influx of settlers, the burgeoning railroads, the growth of mining and cattle ranching—all had combined to transform the West. Gone were the great herds of buffalo. Gone was the expanse of open range. In its place was an enormous patchwork of plowed fields and grazing lands, separated by miles of barbed wire fencing.

Gone, too, were the Indian nations, many of which had depended on the buffalo for survival. By 1890, virtually all the Native Americans in the West had been forced from their land. Decades of fierce and bloody resistance had ultimately proved futile. "I am tired of fighting," Chief Joseph of the Nez Percé reportedly said after being hunted down by the United States Army in 1877. Like others before them, Chief Joseph and his people were sent to live in Indian Territory, in what is now Oklahoma. However, even Indian Territory, which Congress had set aside in 1834, was not safe from white encroachment. In 1889, unassigned land in Indian Territory was opened up to settlers.

The frontier may have disappeared, but its legacy lived on in a rich western folk tradition. Larger-than-life folk heros like Pecos Bill were celebrated in tall tales and legends. The frontier survived, too, in the songs of the sod busters and railroad workers, cowpokes, and miners.

A Changing American Society With the introduction of electricity in the 1880's, the second Industrial Revolution began in earnest. Electricity replaced steam power in many manufacturing industries. The now familiar trappings of modern life began to make their appearance: the electric light, telephone, automobile, motion picture, phonograph. The mass production of consumer goods sparked the rise of an important new medium: advertising. Skyscrapers, department stores, and mass transportation

Humanities: Music

Railroad Songs.
Play for students the song "Drill, Ye Tarriers" on the **Listening to Music: The American Experience Audio CD.** Tell students that during the mid- and late 1800's, millions of European immigrants flooded into the United States, bringing their work songs with them and creating new work songs for the new conditions they faced.

These songs generally were of anonymous authorship. "Drill, Ye Tarriers" is such a song, created by Irish workers building America's railroads. Irish workers were sometimes called "terriers" because their stubby red beards looked like terriers' coats, hence the name of the song (*tarriers* is an Irish adaptation of *terrier*).

You might use the following questions to discuss the music.

1. Describe the mood of this song. *The song is both brisk and grim as it drives forward, imitating the rhythm of railroad work.*
2. Which elements of the song contribute to this mood? *The rhythm drives along in a brisk way, and the words reflect the grim realities involved in working on the railroad.*

became part of city life—as did noise, traffic jams, air pollution, crime, and slums.

The country's industrial and urban growth were both fueled by immigration. Between 1865 and 1915, 25 million people came to the United States seeking freedom and economic opportunity. (By comparison, the population of the entire nation at the end of the Civil War was 31.5 million.) Most, though not all, of the newcomers settled in cities. In the same period, millions of Americans left farms and small towns and moved to the cities seeking work. This influx swelled urban populations and provided an inexhaustible supply of cheap labor for industry.

The industrial boom of the late nineteenth century created new extremes of wealth and poverty. The wages of industrial workers were so low that a single worker, or even two, often could not support a family. Child labor became the norm among the poor working class. Immigrant families often lived in small, dark, unventilated apartments with no toilet. In these conditions, disease was rampant.

Meanwhile, a relative handful of men—the owners of big industrial corporations—made fortunes and lived like royalty. Their ostentatious displays of wealth led Mark Twain to dub this period "The Gilded Age," implying a thin veneer of glitter over something of poor quality.

Indeed, just beneath the nation's prosperity, discontentment grew. Women, African Americans, and workers agitated for changes in their social, economic, and political status. Women still did not have the vote; most African Americans, despite emancipation, were hardly better off in 1914 than they had been in 1850; labor reform was desperately needed. Bitter struggles erupted between emerging workers' unions and management.

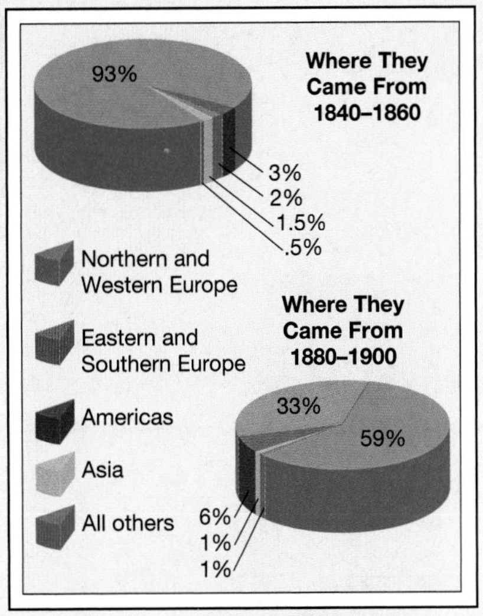

▲ **Interpret a Pattern** Most new immigrants settled in cities. Use these charts to summarize the changing pattern of immigration in the late 1800's. Where did most immigrants come from between 1840 and 1860? 1880 and 1900?

▼ **Read a Graph** The ups and downs of the economy were felt more sharply as the nation industrialized and more people worked for wages. Which years were the most prosperous? In which years did severe depression strike?

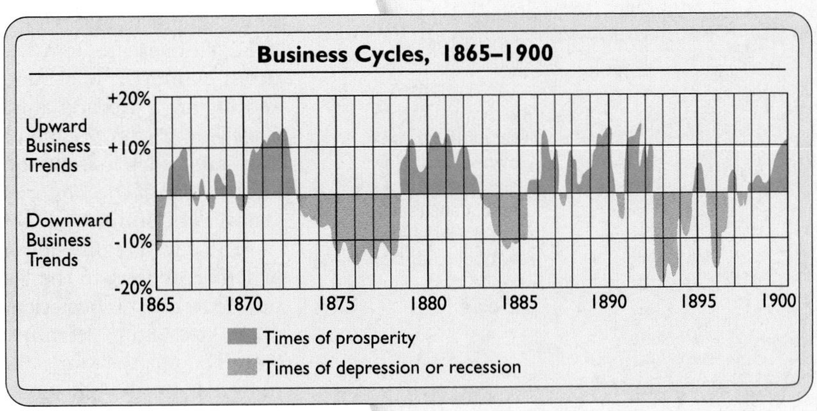

Historical Background

Comprehension Check ☑

1. What major transformation did America undergo in the years between 1850 and 1914? *It changed from a mostly agricultural nation to the urban, industrial nation that we know.*
2. Name the event that brought the conflict between North and South to a head. *The election of Abraham Lincoln as President brought the conflict to a head.*
3. In what way did the Civil War surprise both sides? *It was longer and more costly than either side anticipated.*
4. What three factors combined to transform the West in the years after the Civil War? *These were the influx of settlers, the burgeoning railroads, and the growth of mining and cattle ranching.*
5. Why did Twain call the late 1800's "The Gilded Age"? *A few powerful men displayed their wealth, but underneath this veneer, people were in need.*

◆ Critical Thinking

1. Why is the Civil War sometimes called the first modern war? **[Support]** *It resulted in many casualties and caused great destruction in civilian areas.*
2. If America had been a smaller country, without a frontier, how might its history have been different? **[Speculate]** *Reasonable answers include: It might have been urbanized more quickly. However, it might not have attracted as many immigrants.*
3. What were drawbacks to America's industrialization and expansion? **[Analyze]** *Drawbacks included mistreatment of Native Americans and poverty among African Americans and immigrants.*

Answers to A Graphic Look

Interpret a Pattern In both periods, most immigrants came from Northern and Western Europe; however, in the period 1880 to 1900, a large minority also were coming from Eastern and Southern Europe.

Read a Graph Among the most prosperous years were 1872, 1881, 1886, 1890, 1891, and 1900. Severe depression struck in 1865, 1876–1878, 1884, 1893, and 1896.

Humanities: Music

Songs Related to the Civil War.

Play for students "Willie Has Gone to War" by Stephen Foster and renditions of the spirituals "Swing Low, Sweet Chariot" and "Go Down, Moses," from the **Listening to Music: The American Experience Audio CD.**

Tell them that among the many moving songs about the Civil War is Stephen Foster's (1826–1864) "Willie Has Gone to War," a ballad expressing the anxiety of a young woman whose loved one has gone to fight in the war.

Explain to students that spirituals were created among groups of enslaved African Americans and that singers customarily embellish on the words and melody of spirituals. Consequently, each rendition is unique.

Ask students how all three songs throw new light on the Civil War. *Students may respond that the spirituals reveal the deep feeling with which African Americans yearned for freedom and that Foster's song discloses the personal sadness caused by wartime separations.*

More About Wartime Voices
Perhaps surprisingly, Lincoln's two most able commanders—Ulysses S. Grant and William T. Sherman—produced memoirs that are still regarded as models of their kind. In fact, the quality of the writing done by high-ranking officers on both sides is remarkable.

A great many patriotic songs were written and sung during the war. Among the most popular ones in the North were "The Battle Cry of Freedom" and "Tenting Tonight on the Old Campground." The most famous Union song of all is probably Julia Ward Howe's stirring "The Battle Hymn of the Republic." Among southerners, "The Bonnie Blue Flag" and "The Yellow Rose of Texas" were favorites, as was the well-known "Dixie."

Literature CD-ROM To build background, use the **CD-ROM** *The History of American Literature:* Part 1, Disk 2, Feature 9, which contains information on Mark Twain, Realism, and Bret Harte.

Answers to
A GRAPHIC LOOK

(from page 436)

Read a Map The Chisolm Trail ended in Abilene. The Goodnight-Loving Trail ended in Cheyenne. Cattle trails tend to end at prominent railroad stations, so that cattle could be easily transported. Mining centers are often, but not always, close to railroad lines. This would make it easier to transport the ore.

Analyze a Primary Source
Native Americans tended to believe that land couldn't be owned privately. It is logical to assume that they would be horrified by barbed wire, which separated land into protected, small, private holdings.

(from page 437)

Interpret an Illustration The ability to create a steel frame, which carried the weight of the building, seems to have made taller buildings possible.

Draw a Conclusion The chart suggests that as the country grew and industrialized, new inventions increased dramatically—especially between 1865 and 1870, 1880 and 1885, and 1885 and 1890—but at a gradually slowing rate of increase.

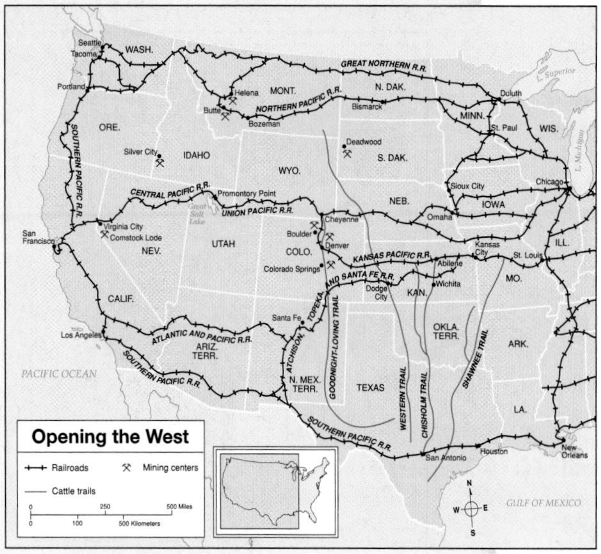

▲ **Read a Map** Railroads, mining, and cattle grazing helped open the Great Plains for later settlement, as indicated on this map. Which cattle trail ended in Abilene? In Cheyenne? What relationships do you see between railroads and cattle trails? Railroads and mining centers?

◀ **Analyze a Primary Source** Barbed wire fencing was introduced in the 1870's. Barbed wire was used to separate privately owned land. How might Native Americans react to this physical and symbolic addition to the landscape? Explain.

Literature of the Period

Wartime Voices Thousands of diaries, letters, journals, and speeches were produced during the war, providing a richly detailed and moving record of what Americans—from the lowliest private to General Lee himself experienced. The 400,000-word diary of Mary Chesnut, the wife of a high-ranking Confederate officer, is a notable example of the extraordinary literary output of the Civil War years.

One of the greatest masters of the language at mid-century was President Lincoln. His speeches and letters are models of clarity and eloquence. His Gettysburg Address, a mere ten sentences in length, has become a classic expression of the meaning of American democracy.

Lincoln guided the nation through the worst crisis in its history. At the end, however, he did not have the chance to reconstruct the Union. Just days after Lee's surrender, Lincoln was assassinated. He died on April 15, 1865. The nation, war-torn and weary, would have to face the daunting tasks of reconciliation and reconstruction without him.

Frontier Voices As America expanded westward, so, too, did America's literature. In this period, for the first time, a number of writers represented the Midwest and the Far West. Some, like Bret Harte and Willa Cather, were born in the East or South but later moved West. As a young man, Harte moved from New York to California. Cather moved from Virginia to Nebraska as a child. One of the greatest writers in all of American literature—Mark Twain—grew up in Hannibal, Missouri, but traveled widely, settling in a Nevada mining town during the Civil War. Twain drew on the colorful language and outsized sensibility of the West for his first short story, "The Notorious Jumping Frog of Calaveras County."

The harsh reality of frontier life coupled with artists' reactions to the Civil War gave rise to a new movement in American literature called Realism. Realism in literature began after the Civil War. Though the war's outcome had given the nation a hard-won sense of unity, the war's

Humanities: Literature

Whitman in the Civil War.
A northern poet who wrote about the war unforgettably was Walt Whitman, one of the giants of American literature. A New Yorker, Whitman worked as a journalist and editor of various newspapers, including *The Brooklyn Eagle*.

After the Civil War broke out, Whitman's younger brother George enlisted in the Union army. When George was wounded at the Battle of Fredericksburg, Whitman went to Virginia to care for him. He remained in Washington, D.C., for the rest of the war, working as a volunteer in military hospitals. Out of this experience came such masterful poems as "Cavalry Crossing a Ford," "By the Bivouac's Fitful Flame," and "Beat! Beat! Drums!"

Upon the assassination of Lincoln, Whitman wrote the much-quoted "O Captain! My Captain" and the classic elegy "When Lilacs Last in the Dooryard Bloom'd."

Ask students how Whitman, a noncombatant, could have written so vividly about Civil War scenes. *Students may respond that the poet's contact with wounded soldiers may have given him a strong sense of what the war was like.*

enormous cost in human life had shattered the nation's idealism. Young writers turned away from the Romanticism that was popular before the war. Instead, writers began to focus on portraying "real life" as ordinary people lived it and attempted to show characters and events in an honest, objective, almost factual way. Willa Cather, for example, was a Realist noted for her unflinching portrayal of the loneliness and cultural isolation of life on the prairie. In "A Wagner Matinée," she contrasts this isolation with the cultural richness of an eastern city.

An important literary offshoot of Realism was Naturalism. Naturalist writers also depicted real people in real situations, but they believed that forces larger than the individual—nature, fate, heredity—shaped individual destiny. Jack London, for example, set much of his fiction in Alaska, where the environment was cruel and unforgiving. The theme of human endurance in the face of overwhelming natural forces pervades his fiction, including "To Build a Fire."

If the reality these writers depicted seemed always to be a harsh one, it was because hardship influenced their artistic vision. It was a vision rooted in war, in the frontier, and, increasingly, in America's growing cities.

Literature of Discontent The social ills that grew out of industrialization came under the sharp eye and pen of many talented writers of the day. Kate Chopin's writing, for example, explored women's desire for equality and independence. The Naturalists saw industrialization as a force against which individuals were powerless. Stephen Crane, a leader of the Naturalist movement, took this view in his first novel, *Maggie: A Girl of the Streets,* a realistic depiction of life in New York City's slums. Poets, too, captured a growing sense of dissatisfaction. Paul Laurence Dunbar's "We Wear the Mask" revealed the alienation of African Americans who smile in white society to mask despair.

By 1914, America had grown up; in a sense, American literature had, too. The Civil War, the closing of the frontier, and industrialization had brought about a loss of innocence, a shift from idealism to pragmatism in the American character. In their rejection of Romanticism and embrace of Realism, American writers reflected this change.

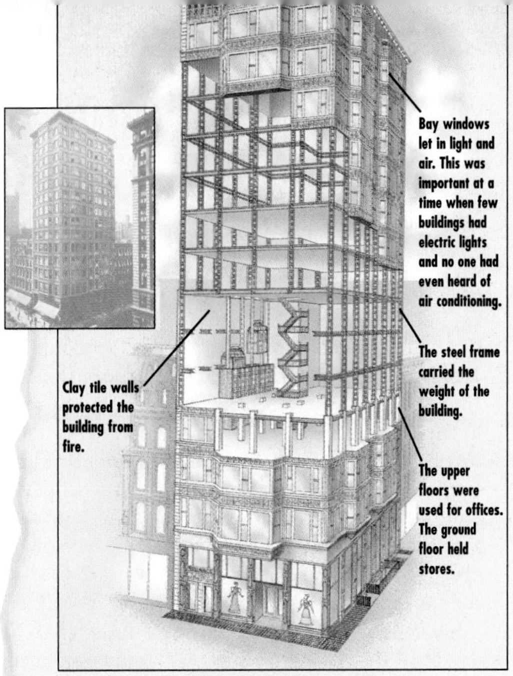

Bay windows let in light and air. This was important at a time when few buildings had electric lights and no one had even heard of air conditioning.
The steel frame carried the weight of the building.
Clay tile walls protected the building from fire.
The upper floors were used for offices. The ground floor held stores.

▲ **Interpret an Illustration** As people crowded into American cities, architects began building up instead of out. When the Reliance Building in Chicago was built in the 1890's, its sixteen stories made it a "skyscraper." According to this illustration, what new technology of the period made buildings of more than six stories possible?

United States Patents Issued 1861– 1900

Five-Year Periods	Number of Patents
1861–1865	20,725
1866–1870	58,734
1871–1875	60,976
1876–1880	64,462
1881–1885	97,156
1886–1890	110,358
1891–1895	108,420
1896–1900	112,188

▲ **Draw a Conclusion** What does this chart suggest about the relationship between new inventions and the growth of the country?

Literature of the Period

Comprehension Check ☑

1. What sources provide a detailed record of the Civil War from the perspective of those who experienced it? *Thousands of diaries, letters, journals, and speeches provide such a record.*
2. What are two qualities that make Lincoln's speeches and letters so memorable? *They are models of clarity and eloquence.*
3. Indicate the region of the country that influenced Mark Twain's colorful language and use of humorous exaggeration. *That region was the West.*
4. (a) What event turned American writers toward Realism? *The Civil War turned writers toward Realism.* (b) What is Realism? *Writers in this movement described the lives of ordinary people in an honest, objective way.*
5. (a) Which literary movement was an important offshoot of Realism? *Naturalism was an offshoot of Realism.* (b) What did writers in this new movement attempt to do? *Writers in this new movement showed how forces like nature, heredity, and fate shaped individuals.*

◆ Critical Thinking

1. How does the saying "Less is more" relate to Lincoln's Gettysburg Address? **[Connect]** *The speech supports the saying. It shows how a brief address, if eloquently written, can be more memorable than a long speech.*
2. What accounts for the fact that the most famous Western writers were born in other regions? **[Speculate]** *Reasonable answers include: The expanding frontier attracted people of adventurous spirit, no matter where they were born. Also, people drawn to the West from elsewhere may have had a special love for the region that inspired them to write about it.*
3. In what ways did literary movements like Realism and Naturalism suggest that the country was "growing up"? **[Analyze Causes and Effects]** *Reasonable answers include: These two literary movements were reactions to a national crisis, the Civil War, and to the rapid urbanization and industrialization of the country. In the sense that these movements tried to take account of some problems and grim realities, they can be said to reflect a process of "growing up."*

Activities

1. **Technology Bazaar** Set up a technology bazaar, in which students use information from The Story of the Times and A Graphic Look at the Period to "sell" such technology as railroads, barbed wire, and skyscrapers.
2. **Panels of Writers** Give students the choice of being a Romantic, a Realist, or a Naturalist writer. Then form panels that reflect each of these three schools. Ask students to discuss the history of the period from the perspective of their "school."
3. **Veteran's Monologue** Have students role-play a Civil War veteran telling his or her grandchildren what it was like to fight in the war as a mere teenager.
4. **A National Sketchbook** Have students draw a series of sketches to illustrate some key events and themes described in *The Story of the Times:* John Brown's raid, a Civil War battle, Lincoln's assassination, westward expansion, immigration, and the advance of technology.

◆ Critical Thinking

1. Why was it important that Twain "captured the everyday speech of characters"? **[Speculate]** *If a country's literature is to express its life, then books ought to talk the way people do.*
2. What did Twain mean by his observation about American English compared with British English? **[Interpret]** *Twain meant that Americans would now influence the future development of the English language even more than Britons would.*
3. Why do you think Twain favored short words over long ones? **[Speculate]** *He seems to have felt that long words were pretentious, flowery, misleading, dishonest, and perhaps more European than American.*

▶Critical Viewing◀

Look at the picture of Twain on this page. Does he look the way he sounds in the quotations? **[Connect]** *Obviously, there is no "correct" answer, but students may say that Twain looks like a down-to-earth, no-nonsense guy, and these are qualities reflected in the quotations.*

Answers to Activities

1. Before students begin the discussion, be sure that they understand the quotation. Its gist is that dialects are universal. Define the word *dialect* for students, or help them to define it for themselves: the form or variety of a spoken language peculiar to a region, social group, or occupational group.
2. Be sure students understand the quotation they choose.
3. Students should show how the passage exemplifies the down-to-earth directness of Twain's style ("like water").

*T*he Development of American English

MARK TWAIN AND THE AMERICAN LANGUAGE

by Richard Lederer

American literature comes of age
On February 18, 1885, thirty thousand copies of Mark Twain's *The Adventures of Huckleberry Finn* were released in the United States. The novel turned out to be Twain's masterpiece, and it changed the direction of American letters. Twain captured the everyday speech of characters, instead of the more formal, standard English that writers before him used. In *The Adventures of Huckleberry Finn,* Twain used seven distinct dialects to reflect the speech patterns of various characters, and he also became the first important author to show the freshness and vitality of the new American idiom in narrative as well as in dialogue. Just as Geoffrey Chaucer's *The Canterbury Tales* is the first significant work written in English, *Huckleberry Finn* is the first novel of world rank to be written entirely in American.

Readin', Writin', and Twain
Twain held strong opinions about a passel of subjects, and he possessed the gift of being able to state these views in memorable ways: "It's better to keep your mouth shut and appear stupid than to open it and remove all doubt"; "Be careful about reading health books. You may die of a misprint."

Twain also had a lot to say about style, literature, and the American language that he, more than any other writer, helped to shape:

▶ *On American English, compared with British English:* The property has gone into the hands of a joint stock company, and we own the bulk of the shares.

▶ *On dialects:* I have traveled more than anyone else, and I have noticed that even the angels speak English with an accent.

▶ *On choosing words:* The difference between the almost right word and the right word is really a large matter—'tis the difference between the lightning-bug and the lightning.

▶ *On style* (in a letter to a twelve-year-old boy): I notice that you use plain, simple language, short words, and brief sentences. That is the way to write English—it is the modern way and the best way. Stick to it; and don't let fluff and flowers and verbosity creep in.

▶ *On being concise:* A successful book is not made of what is in it, but what is left out of it.

▶ *On using short words:* I never write metropolis for seven cents when I can get the same for city. I never write

policeman because I can get the same for cop.

▶ *On reading:* The man who does not read good books has no advantage over the man who can't read them.

Activities

1. With a group, discuss Twain's statement on dialects, above. In your discussion, include some of the outstanding characteristics of the dialect that you speak.
2. Use one of Mark Twain's statements about writing or language, above, as the thesis for an essay or discussion on the subject.
3. In 1885, Twain wrote in his notebook, "My works are like water. The works of the great masters are like wine. But everyone drinks water." Choose a passage from one of Twain's stories or essays, and show how that passage exemplifies the author's philosophy of style.

More of Twain's Wit and Wisdom

You may want to have students use one of these passages to answer question 3, above:

Soap and education are not as sudden as a massacre, but they are more deadly in the long run.
—*The Facts Concerning the Recent Resignation*

Work consists of whatever a body is obliged to do . . . Play consists of whatever a body is not obliged to do.
—*The Adventures of Tom Sawyer*

Hain't we got all the fools in town on our side? And ain't that a big enough majority in every town?
—*The Adventures of Huckleberry Finn*

War talk by men who have been in a war is always interesting; whereas moon talk by a poet who has not been in the moon is likely to be dull.
—*Life on the Mississippi*

The reports of my death are greatly exaggerated.
—Cable from London, 1897

PART 1 *A Nation Divided*

Fight for the Standard, Wadsworth Atheneum, Hartford, Connecticut

Possibly the most painful chapter in our nation's history, the Civil War era left a lasting imprint on our nation's identity. Although at the time, the war tore our nation apart, the legacy that it left behind is the country's ability to survive in the face of tremendous adversity.

One-Minute Planning Guide

The selections in this section show the many faces of a nation divided. Stephen Crane's "An Episode of War" and the accompanying ballad portray the two fronts of warfare: the battle-front and the homefront. The spirituals and Frederick Douglass excerpt provide a candid look at the divisive issue of slavery. "An Occurrence at Owl Creek Bridge" will have students debating whether all is really fair in love and war. Two of the war's greatest figures—Abraham Lincoln and Robert E. Lee—reveal in their own words the issues at the heart of the Civil War. "For What It's Worth," a protest song from the Vietnam War era, provides a more contemporary portrait of division within the nation.

Customize for *Varying Student Needs*

When assigning the selections in this part, keep in mind these factors:

"An Episode of War"; "Willie Has Gone to the War"
- A haunting short story paired with a sentimental Civil War ballad

"Swing Low, Sweet Chariot"; "Go Down, Moses"
- Spirituals with accessible lyrics

from *My Bondage and My Freedom*
- Autobiographical excerpt
- Lengthy sentences may challenge less proficient readers.

"An Occurrence at Owl Creek Bridge"
- High interest story with surprise plot twist and shifting time frame

"The Gettysburg Address"; "Second Inaugural Address"; "Letter to His Son"
- Formal diction and abstract concepts may challenge less proficient readers.

"For What It's Worth"
- Contemporary protest song

Humanities: Art

Fight for the Standard.
In old-fashioned warfare, capturing the opponents' flag was meant to throw the other side into despair and confusion. Help students see that this traditional painting seems posed for dramatic effect, with two cavalrymen emerging from smoky background to battle. Point out that the Confederate soldier who grabs the Union flag is about to be mortally wounded by the Union soldier on the white horse.

Have your students link the painting to the theme "A Nation Divided" by answering the following questions:

1. Do you think the painter favored one side over the other in this painting? What leads you to that impression? *Some students will say that the balance of the composition—two figures of equal size centrally positioned, the Southerner grabbing the Northerner's flag, the Northerner piercing the Southerner's chest—projects a balanced view of the fight. Others may point to details that favor the Northerner—he rides a white horse, his face and not the Southerner's is visible, and he is about to win.*
2. Does this artist create a romanticized or realistic view of war? Explain. *Details like the excitement of hand-to-hand mortal combat, the beautiful horses, and the almost knightly sabers support a romanticized view of warfare. The Southerner's imminent death reflects a realistic view.*

LESSON OBJECTIVES

1. **To develop vocabulary and word identification skills**
   - Latin Word Roots: *-greg-*
   - Using the Word Bank: Analogies
2. **To use a variety of reading strategies to comprehend nonfiction**
   - Connect Your Experience
   - Reading for Success: Interative Reading Strategies
3. **To increase knowledge of other cultures and to connect common elements across cultures**
   - Connecting Themes Across Cultures (ATE)
4. **To express and support responses to the text**
   - Critical Thinking
   - Idea Bank: Letter
   - Idea Bank: Enactment
5. **To analyze literary elements**
   - Literary Focus: Realism and Naturalism
6. **To read in order to research self-selected and assigned topics**
   - Idea Bank: Editorial
   - Idea Bank: Music Performance
   - Idea Bank: Oral Presentation on Civil War Heroines
7. **To plan, prepare, organize, and present literary interpretations**
   - Idea Bank: Definition Essay
8. **To use recursive writing processes to write a field report**
   - Guided Writing Lesson
9. **To increase knowledge of the rules of grammar and usage**
   - Grammar and Style: Correct Use of *Like* and *As*

Test Preparation

Reading Comprehension: Context (ATE, p. 441)
The teaching tips and sample test item in this workshop support the instruction and practice in the unit workshop:
Reading Comprehension: Using Context (SE, p. 631)

Guide for Interpreting

Stephen Crane *(1871–1900)*

Stephen Crane hadn't even been born when the last battle of the American Civil War was fought, yet he is best remembered for his compelling depiction of the conflict. During his tragically brief life, Crane established himself as both a leader of the Naturalist movement and one of the greatest writers of his time.

Early in his career, Crane worked as a newspaper writer in New York City. His experiences there inspired his first novel, *Maggie: A Girl of the Streets* (1893). Its grimly realistic portrayal of life in the city's slums was so frank and shocking that Crane was unable to find a publisher, so he printed the book at his own expense.

His second novel, published in 1895, was *The Red Badge of Courage: An Episode of the American Civil War.* A psychological exploration of a young soldier's mental and emotional reactions under enemy fire, the wildly successful novel earned international acclaim for the twenty-four-year-old. Though Crane had never experienced military combat, he interviewed Civil War veterans and studied photographs, battle plans, and biographical accounts before writing the realistic battle scenes.

Crane later viewed war firsthand when he served as a newspaper correspondent during the Greco-Turkish War in 1897 and the Spanish-American War in 1898. His war experiences provided material for a collection of poetry, *War Is Kind* (1899), but they took their toll on his health. He died of tuberculosis at the age of twenty-eight.

Stephen Foster *(1826–1864)*

The popular minstrel songs and sentimental ballads written by Stephen Foster earned him an honored place in American music. He composed about 200 works in his rather short lifetime, including such classics as "The Old Folks at Home" (popularly known as "Way Down Upon the Swanee River"), "Camptown Races," "Oh! Susanna," and "My Old Kentucky Home." Foster wrote the words as well as the music to most of his songs, though he collaborated with lyricist George Cooper on the Civil War ballad "Willie Has Gone to the War."

◆ Background for Understanding

HISTORICAL CONTEXT: THE BLOODY LEGACY OF THE AMERICAN CIVIL WAR

Both this short story and this song were inspired by the American Civil War, the bloodiest war in American history. The conflict claimed the lives of 600,000 soldiers—more American casualties than the total of all other wars in which the United States has fought. Hundreds of thousands more were left maimed by battle wounds and crude medical care.

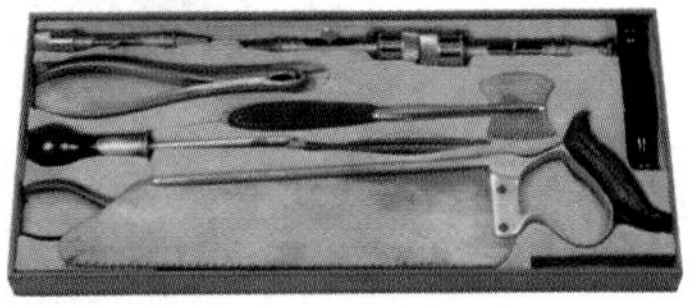

© Museum of the Confederacy, Richmond, Virginia

As you read "An Episode of War," keep in mind that amputation was routine treatment for injured limbs. A wounded soldier knew that he risked losing his injured arm or leg to a surgeon's saw, like those in this Civil War medical kit.

When the war began, neither side was prepared to care for the wounded. There were no ambulances to transport them from the battlefield, no medical corps to treat them, no medicines, no nursing staff. Barns, warehouses, and schools were converted into makeshift hospitals, like the one described in this story. The conditions were terrible. Even a minor injury was liable to result in death, most often from disease; twice as many Civil War soldiers died of infections than of combat wounds.

Prentice Hall Literature Program Resources

REINFORCE / RETEACH / EXTEND

Selection Support Pages
Build Vocabulary: Word Roots: *-greg-*, p.123
Grammar and Style: Use of *Like* and *As*, p. 124
Reading for Success: Interactive Reading, pp. 125–126
Literary Focus: Realism and Naturalism, p. 127

Strategies for Diverse Student Needs, p. 26

Beyond Literature
Humanities Connection: Photography, p. 26

Formal Assessment Selection Test, pp. 129–131; Assessment Resources Software

Alternative Assessment, p. 26

Writing and Language Transparencies
Writing Process Model: Description, pp. 9–12

Resource Pro CD-ROM

Listening to Literature Audiocassettes

Literature CD-ROM

◆ An Episode of War ◆
Willie Has Gone to the War

MODEL SELECTION

◆ Literature and Your Life

CONNECT YOUR EXPERIENCE

Being "in control" of a situation and making responsible decisions help to make you feel in command of your life. Often, however, you don't have control over the situations—good and bad—that life presents. Do you imagine that the soldiers who fought in the Civil War felt as if they were in control of their destinies?

Journal Writing Has a chance event ever had an effect on your life? Write about the experience and its impact.

THEMATIC FOCUS: A NATION DIVIDED

Stephen Crane was a proponent of Naturalism, which holds that all humanity is driven by the winds of chance, with human suffering the only certainty. Stephen Foster was a popular musician. As you read the two selections, ask yourself: How do these works reflect a difference in attitude toward the "glories" of war?

◆ Build Vocabulary

LATIN WORD ROOTS: *-greg-*

Crane describes a group of men and horses pulling cannons as an "aggregation of wheels, levers, and motors." The word *aggregation* contains the Latin root *-greg-*, meaning "herd" or "flock." An *aggregation* is a group of people or things considered as a whole.

WORD BANK

Preview these words from the selections.

precipitate
aggregation
inscrutable
disdainfully
glade

◆ Grammar and Style

CORRECT USE OF *LIKE* AND *AS*

Although *like* and *as, as if,* and *as though* are often used interchangeably, they actually serve different purposes. ***As, as if,*** and ***as though*** are subordinating conjunctions that introduce subordinating—or less important—ideas. ***Like*** is a preposition; it takes a noun or pronoun as its object and introduces a prepositional phrase. Notice the difference between these examples from "An Episode of War":

[The lieutenant] looked quickly at a man near him *as if he suspected it was a case of personal assault.*

He had winced *like a man stung . . .*

◆ Literary Focus

REALISM AND NATURALISM

"An Episode of War" is a harsh tale of how a chance event forever changes the life of a Civil War officer. The story is characteristic of two new literary movements that sprang up in reaction to Romanticism—an earlier nineteenth-century literary movement that stressed emotion, imagination, and an appreciation of nature. The first movement, **Realism**, sought to portray real life as faithfully and accurately as possible. Realists focused on ordinary people faced with the harsh realities of everyday life—a far cry from the improbable situations and optimistic vision of the world typical of Romanticism.

From the Realism movement grew **Naturalism**, which also focused on truthfully portraying the lives of ordinary people. Naturalists, however, believed that a person's fate is determined by environment, heredity, and chance. As a result, they often depicted characters whose lives were shaped by forces they could neither understand nor control, but endured with strength and dignity, thereby affirming the significance of their existence.

Interest Grabber To engage students' interest, play the scene from the 1993 film *Gettysburg* in which General Longstreet visits General Hood, who is recovering from an amputation in a Confederate field hospital. Use this scene, which is in the beginning of Part 2 (after the fight on Little Round Top) to help students gain an appreciation of the conditions in a Civil War field hospital. Invite them to give their reactions to what they see. Then tell them that they are about to read a story about an injured soldier's journey toward such a place.

Customize for
Less Proficient Readers
Work with these students to help them utilize the Reading for Success Strategies. Before they read, check their understanding of each of the Reading for Success strategies on p. 442. Then guide them through the process of using the reading prompts that appear in Crane's story.

Customize for
AP Students
According to the Naturalists, a person's fate is determined by environment, heredity, and chance. Have students look for examples in Crane's story that support the view that people's lives are shaped by forces they can neither understand nor control.

Customize for
English Language Learners
Crane uses many vivid verbs that may be unfamiliar to students acquiring English. Help students by providing synonyms or by acting out some of these words, such as *wince, sheathe, berate,* and *gesticulate.*

Test Preparation Workshop

Reading Comprehension: Context The reading sections of standardized reading tests require students to use context to determine the meaning of figurative language. Remind students that the words surrounding the targeted expression can provide clues to its meaning. Use the following sample test item to demonstrate.

But at this instant the men, the spectators, awoke from their stone-like poses and crowded forward sympathetically.

In this passage, "awoke from their stone-like poses" most nearly means?

A Got off their stone beds.
B Moved suddenly after being still.
C Got up to look at statues.
D Posed for a sculpture.

The men, referred to as impassive "spectators," were like "stone" until they "awoke" and roused themselves from their stupor. Context clues support B.

Reading for Success

The Reading for Success page in each unit presents a set of problem-solving procedures to help readers understand authors' words and ideas on multiple levels. Good readers develop a bank of strategies from which they can draw as needed.

Unit 4 introduces strategies for interactive reading. It is important for students to realize that reading a piece of literature is a two-way street: the more they contribute to the process, the more they will gain from it. These interactive strategies give readers a series of practical launching points to help them become more emotionally and intellectually involved in the works they read. They will learn that the knowledge and ideas they bring to a work can greatly enhance their reading experience.

These strategies for interactive reading are modeled with "An Episode of War." Each green box shows an example of the thinking process involved in applying one of these strategies.

How to Use the Reading for Success Page

- Introduce the interactive reading strategies, presenting each as a means of getting more from the reading experience. Be sure students understand what each strategy involves and under what circumstances to apply it.
- Before students read the story, have them preview it, looking at the annotations in the green boxes that model the strategies.
- To reinforce these strategies after students have read "An Episode of War," have students complete the Reading for Success pages in ***Selection Support,*** pp. 125–126. These pages give students an opportunity to read a selection and practice interactive strategies by writing their own annotations.

Reading for Success

Interactive Reading Strategies

Interactive is a term that applies to more than video games and computer technology. It also describes a way to approach your reading. Your experiences and knowledge actively affect the way you understand a piece of literature. The more you bring to your reading, the more you'll get from it. Use these strategies to help you.

Use prior background knowledge.

As you read, keep in mind what you already know about the subject—in this case, the Civil War. Use that knowledge to make connections with what the author is saying.

Question.

Ask questions about important ideas in the text. List ideas you'd like to clarify or topics about which you would like to learn. Then search the text for answers to your questions.

Predict.

Using information from the text—details, dialogue, facts—make predictions about what will happen. Confirm or revise predictions as you gain new information or understanding from your reading.

Clarify details and information.

Focus on sections that seem confusing or unclear, and use questioning to identify the source of your confusion.

- Draw on your prior background knowledge to place information in context.
- Reread an earlier passage for information you may have missed.
- Organize information visually. Setting details, for example, may be clearer if you draw them, and relationships among characters might be understood if you represented them in a graphic organizer.
- Read ahead. Your confusion may be clarified by text read later on.

Connect literature to historical contexts.

Consider the social and political climate surrounding a piece of writing as part of its setting and context. Determine how the attitudes of both writer and characters reflect the ideas of their day.

Respond to the text.

Reflect on what you have read. Do you agree with the characters' ideas or actions? How might you behave in the same situation?

As you read "An Episode of War," look at the notes along the sides. They demonstrate how to apply these strategies to your reading.

Reading Strategies: Support and Reinforcement

Appropriate Reading Strategies Students are given a reading strategy to apply in reading each selection. Where appropriate, one of these interactive reading strategies will be applied. In other selections a strategy is suggested that is applicable to the selection.

Reading Prompts To encourage application of the given reading strategy, there are occasional prompts, within green boxes, at appropriate and significant points.

In addition, there are red boxes prompting application of the Literary Focus concept and maroon boxes prompting students to connect with their lives.

Using the Boxed Annotations and Prompts

The material in the green, red, and maroon boxes along the sides of selections is intended to help students apply the literary element and the reading strategy and to make a connection with their lives.

You may use the boxed material in several ways:

- Have students pause when they come to a box and respond to its prompt before they continue reading.
- Urge students to read through the selection ignoring the boxes. After they have read the selection completely, they may go back and review the selection, responding to the prompts.

MODEL

An Episode of War

Stephen Crane

The lieutenant's rubber blanket lay on the ground, and upon it he had poured the company's supply of coffee. Corporals and other representatives of the grimy and hot-throated men who lined the breast-work[1] had come for each squad's portion.

The lieutenant was frowning and serious at this task of division. His lips pursed as he drew with his sword various crevices in the heap, until brown squares of coffee, astoundingly equal in size, appeared on the blanket. He was on the verge of a great triumph in mathematics, and the corporals were thronging forward, each to reap a little square, when suddenly the lieutenant cried out and looked quickly at a man ❶ near him as if he suspected it was a case of personal assault. The others cried out also when they saw blood upon the lieutenant's sleeve. ❶

He had winced like a man stung, swayed dangerously, and then straightened. The sound of his hoarse breathing was plainly audible. He looked sadly, mystically, over the breast-work at the green face of a wood, where now were many little puffs of white smoke. ❷ During this moment the men about him gazed statuelike and silent, astonished and awed by this catastrophe which happened when catastrophes were not expected—when they had leisure to observe it.

As the lieutenant stared at the wood, they too swung their heads, so that for another instant all hands, still silent, contemplated the distant forest as if their minds were fixed upon the mystery of a bullet's journey. ❸

1. **breast-work:** Low wall put up quickly as a defense in battle.

▼ **Critical Viewing** This is an actual photograph of a temporary Civil War hospital. Do you think that soldiers received quality treatment there? On what details do you base your answer? **[Assess]** ❹

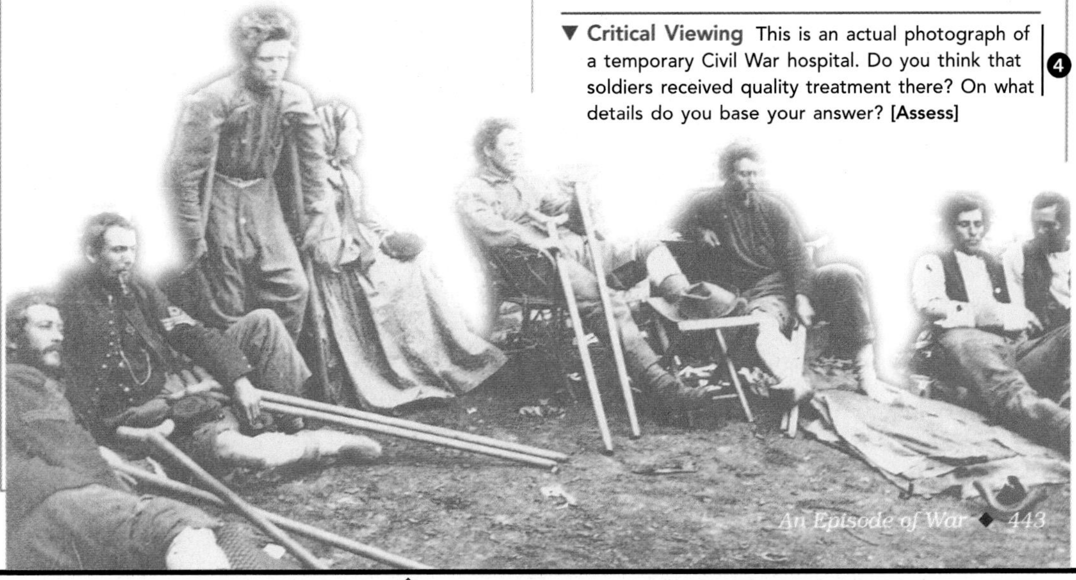

Develop Understanding

One-Minute Insight This stark account of how a Civil War lieutenant loses his arm to amputation is detached and impersonal, yet hauntingly moving. The lieutenant is rationing coffee when a stray bullet hits his arm, changing his life forever. So begins his dreamlike journey toward the field hospital. Though the nameless lieutenant appears numb, the reader can imagine his dread as he anticipates the "treatment" he will receive. Despite his protests and the doctor's false assurances, the lieutenant loses his arm in just another "episode of war." Through his depiction of this gripping sequence of events, Crane conveys an important message about the tragedy of war and the helplessness of those caught up in the fighting.

Comprehension Check ☑

❶ Ask students to explain what has just happened to the lieutenant. *He was shot in the arm.*

◆ Reading for Success

❷ **Clarify Details** Point out that the "little puffs of white smoke" are the result of gunfire coming from the opposing army.

◆ Grammar and Style

❸ **Correct Use of *Like* and *As*** Point out the use of the subordinating conjunction *as if* to connect the main clause and the subordinate clause in this sentence.

▶Critical Viewing◀

❹ **Assess** Students may say that the soldiers' facial expressions and the manner in which the soldiers lie about in crowded and unsanitary conditions indicate that they were not getting quality treatment.

Customize for *Gifted/Talented Students*

Stephen Crane opens this selection with a portrait of life in camp in a lull just before shooting breaks out. Have students draw or create a tableau based on Crane's description here, that captures the ordinariness of camp life.

Block Scheduling Strategies

Consider these suggestions to take advantage of extended class time:

- If you have access to computers, have students work either in small groups or as a whole class to view the multimedia feature (Feature 11) on Stephen Crane and his works on the *History of American Literature*, Part 1 **Literature CD-ROM**.
- Extend students background knowledge of the Civil War by showing them portions of Ken Burns's documentary on the Civil War.
- After students have read the selections, have them choose from among the Speaking, Listening, and Viewing activities and projects in the Idea Bank (p. 449). Allow class time for students to present their projects. Follow each presentation with class discussion.
- To help students apply the interactive reading strategies, have students create their own annotated model selections using the Reading for Success selection pages (pp. 125–126) in the ***Selection Support*** booklet in the Teaching Resources.

Customize for
Bodily/Kinesthetic Learners
Help these students picture the lieutenant's maneuvers with his sword by asking them to act out his movements. Do they understand why his wounded arm made him so awkward?

Customize for
Visual/Spatial Learners
Encourage these students to use the photographs and art on pp. 443, 444, and 446 to help them picture the setting, characters, and events in the story. Make sure they are aware that the photographs on pages 443 and 444 depict real soldiers who fought in the war. Have students discuss how the photographs add to the details that Crane provides in his story. You may also wish to have a more general discussion about the differences between written and visual records of historic events. What do photographs offer that text accounts cannot? What can text records offer that photographs do not? *Photographs can capture visual details more thoroughly and precisely than textual descriptions. However, written accounts—especially first-person accounts written by those who participated in the events—can more effectively capture the feelings of the people involved.*

▶Critical Viewing◀

❶ **Assess** Like the men in the story, this soldier appears to stand next to his wounded comrade without touching him. You may wish to point out, however, that this type of behavior was not necessarily the standard. Soldiers generally helped the wounded—even enemy causalities—whenever possible.

◆Reading for Success

❷ **Connect Literature to Historical Context** Inform students that Civil War officers, for the most part, were Victorian gentlemen who had romantic notions of war and battle. To some, a wound was a sign of bravery and glory. Tell students that as the bloody war raged on, this notion began to lose its appeal.

◀ Critical Viewing
How does this photograph correspond with Crane's description of the wounded lieutenant being helped by his men? **[Connect]** ❶

The officer had, of course, been compelled to take his sword into his left hand. He did not hold it by the hilt. He gripped it at the middle of the blade, awkwardly. Turning his eyes from the hostile wood, he looked at the sword as he held it there, and seemed puzzled as to what to do with it, where to put it. In short, this weapon had of a sudden become a strange thing to him. He looked at it in a kind of stupefaction, as if he had been endowed with a trident, a sceptre,[2] or a spade.

Use prior background knowledge about the military to understand the soldier's dilemma: Many weapons are held in the right hand.

Finally he tried to sheathe it. To sheathe a sword held by the left hand, at the middle of the blade, in a scabbard hung at the left hip, is a feat worthy of a sawdust ring.[3] This wounded officer engaged in a desperate struggle with the sword and the wobbling scabbard, and during the time of it breathed like a wrestler.

Clarify this awkward movement by "seeing" it in your mind.

2. **a trident, a sceptre** (trīd′ ənt; sep′ tər): Three-pronged spear; decorated ornamental rod or staff symbolizing royal authority.
3. **sawdust ring:** Ring in which circus acts are performed.

But at this instant the men, the spectators, awoke from their stone-like poses and crowded forward sympathetically. The orderly-sergeant took the sword and tenderly placed it in the scabbard. At the time, he leaned nervously backward, and did not allow even his finger to brush the body of the lieutenant. A wound gives strange dignity to him who bears it. Well men shy from his new and terrible majesty. It is as if the wounded man's hand is upon the curtain which hangs before the revelations of all existence—the meaning of ants, potentates,[4] wars, cities, sunshine, snow, a feather dropped from a bird's wing; and the power of it sheds radiance upon a bloody form, and makes the other men understand sometimes that they are little. His comrades look at him with large eyes thoughtfully. Moreover, they fear vaguely that the weight ❷

4. **potentates** (pōt′ ən tāts): *n.*: Rulers; powerful people.

◆ Build Vocabulary

precipitate (prē sip′ ə tāt′) *v.*: Cause to happen before expected or desired
aggregation (ag′ grə gā′ shən) *n.*: Group or mass of distinct objects or individuals
inscrutable (in skro͞ot′ ə bəl) *adj.*: Impossible to see; completely obscure or mysterious

Beyond the Classroom

Career Connection
Photojournalist The work of photographers such as Mathew Brady (whose work appears on pp. 443 and 444) and Alexander Gardner brought the horrors of Civil War into the parlors of American. Like their earlier counterparts, today's photojournalists capture news events or explore timely issues through pictures, rather than words. Some work as staff photographers for newspapers and magazines; most work as freelancers. They may be hired by the assignment, or they may sell their photographs to individual publications or to photo services that distribute them to subscribers.

Invite students to discuss the idea of working as a photojournalist. Ask them to talk about the kinds of events they would most like to cover. Would they prefer to work as staff or freelance photographers? Why? Suggest that they contact modern-day photojournalists to find out more about the nature of their jobs and the history of and developments in their field.

Question the men's fearful reaction. The soldier's wound may remind them of the life-threatening dangers of the war.

of a finger upon him might send him headlong, precipitate the tragedy, hurl him at once into the dim, grey unknown. And so the orderly-sergeant, while sheathing the sword, leaned nervously backward.

There were others who proffered assistance. One timidly presented his shoulder and asked the lieutenant if he cared to lean upon it, but the latter waved him away mournfully. He wore the look of one who knows he is the victim of a terrible disease and understands his helplessness. He again stared over the breast-work at the forest, and then, turning, went slowly rearward. He held his right wrist tenderly in his left hand as if the wounded arm was made of very brittle glass.

Use your knowledge of the historical context to realize the potential outcomes of injury during the Civil War—among them, death and amputation.

And the men in silence stared at the wood, then at the departing lieutenant; then at the wood, then at the lieutenant.

❸ As the wounded officer passed from the line of battle, he was enabled to see many things which as a participant in the fight were unknown to him. He saw a general on a black horse gazing over the lines of blue infantry at the green woods which veiled his problems. An aide galloped furiously, dragged his horse suddenly to a halt, saluted, and presented a paper. It was, for a wonder, precisely like a historical painting.

To the rear of the general and his staff a group, composed of a bugler, two or three orderlies, and the bearer of the corps standard,[5] all upon maniacal horses, were working like slaves to hold their ground, preserve their respectful interval, while the shells boomed in the air about them, and caused their chargers to make furious quivering leaps.

❹ A battery, a tumultuous and shining mass, was swirling toward the right. The wild thud of hoofs, the cries of the riders shouting blame and praise, menace and encouragement, and, last, the roar of the wheels, the slant of the glistening guns, brought the lieutenant to an intent pause. The battery swept in curves that stirred the heart; it made halts as dramatic as the crash of a wave on the rocks, and when it fled onward this aggregation of wheels, levers, motors had a beautiful unity, as if it were a missile. The sound of it was a war-chorus that reached into the depths of man's emotion. ❹

The lieutenant, still holding his arm as if it were of glass, stood watching this battery until all detail of it was lost, save the figures of the riders, which rose and fell and waved lashes over the black mass.

Later, he turned his eyes toward the battle, where the shooting sometimes crackled like bush-fires, sometimes sputtered with exasperating irregularity, and sometimes reverberated like the thunder. He saw the smoke rolling upward and saw crowds of men who ran and cheered, or stood and blazed away at the inscrutable distance.

Note the soldier's detachment from the rest of the battle scene. **Read ahead** to find details about his thoughts and feelings.

He came upon some stragglers, and they told him how to find the field hospital. They described its exact location. In fact, these men, no longer having part in the battle, knew more of it than others. They told the performance of every corps, every division, the opinion of every general. The lieutenant, carrying his wounded arm rearward, looked upon them with wonder. ❺

At the roadside a brigade was making coffee and buzzing with talk like a girls' boarding-school. Several officers came out to him and inquired concerning things of which he knew nothing. One, seeing his arm, began to scold. "Why, man, that's no way to do. You want to fix that thing." He appropriated the lieutenant and the lieutenant's wound. He cut the sleeve and laid bare the arm, every nerve of which softly fluttered under his touch. He bound his handkerchief over the wound, scolding away in the meantime. His tone allowed one to think that he was in the habit of being wounded every day. The lieutenant hung his head, feeling, in this presence, that he did not know how to be correctly wounded.

Use the vivid details of this sentence to **respond** to the soldier's situation. You may find you understand the pain he must be feeling.

5. **corps standard** (kôr): Flag or banner representing a military unit.

◆ Background for Understanding

❸ **History** Tell students that Civil War battles were often large affairs that took place over miles of terrain. Most soldiers knew very little of the battle as a whole; they knew only about the action taking place in their immediate vicinity.

❹ **Clarification** Explain that a "battery" is a set of four or six guns, each with a crew of several men. Teams of horses pulled the guns and the caissons (a wagon designed to hold ammunition) to wherever they were needed on the battlefield.

◆ Reading for Success

❺ **Question** Ask students to explain why the stragglers might have known more about the battle than the lieutenant did. Was their information reliable? *Students may say that if the stragglers represented men from several regiments, then they certainly had seen more of the fight than the lieutenant had. They may suggest that these men were as likely as not to pass on inaccurate or incomplete information and they probably knew nothing of what the generals were thinking.*

Humanities: Art

Photography The Civil War was the first war to be captured in photographs. Due to the limitations of the photographic process at that time, photographers very rarely captured action or battle scenes. They took pictures of events behind the scenes or photographed the carnage that remained after battle. Have students contrast the photographs that appear with this story with photographs they've seen of later wars.

Follow up with the Humanities Connection: Photography page in ***Beyond Literature,*** (p. 26).

Speaking, Listening, and Viewing Mini-Lesson

Music Performance

This mini-lesson supports the Speaking, Listening, and Viewing activity in the Idea Bank on p. 449.

Introduce the Concept In this activity, students will research and then listen to or perform a Civil War era song.

Develop Background Civil War soldiers sang all the time, leaving us with a wealth of songs and music. Many have been recorded and are available as tapes, CDs, and videos. Two albums that attempt to authentically re-create the music of the Civil War period are the *Original Soundtrack Recording: The Civil War,* produced by Ken Burns and John Colby, and *The Blue and Gray in Black and White,* by Sparky and Rhonda Rucker.

Apply the Information Once students have selected and researched their songs, allow time for presentations. Ask students to introduce their songs and then play or sing them for the class. If they have found more than one version invite them to play each one and to discuss with classmates which version seems most authentic.

Assess the Outcome Consider how thoughtfully students chose their song. How much background did they present? Did they listen carefully to other presentations and participate fully in discussions?

◆ Literary Focus

❶ **Realism and Naturalism** Ask students: How does the depiction of war in this passage exemplify a Realist approach? *The passage depicts the grim, everyday details of war—ordinary soldiers caught up in chaos and death far from the "glories" of the battlefield.*

◆ Reading for Success

❷ **Predict** Students may predict that both the doctor and the lieutenant know full well that amputation was the treatment for bullet wounds that shattered limbs, and that this grim procedure was surely in store for the officer.

◆ Reading for Success

❸ **Use Prior Background Knowledge** Students should understand that the lieutenant had seen people in situations far worse than his during the war, which was continuing in his absence. He may have been ashamed at having to leave his men for the comfort of home and family, knowing that many officers stayed in service or quickly returned to it despite wounds or loss of limbs.

▶Critical Viewing◀

❹ **Contrast** Students may say that the eager young volunteers soon came to understand all too well that "glory on the battlefield" was not to be. They may say that soldiers quickly discovered that war was a terrifying and horrifying experience, not the great adventure they had imagined it to be.

Humanities: Music

In the wealth of songs that Stephen Foster composed lie the beginnings of popular music, of jazz melodies based on folk tunes, even the first hints of the music of American musical theater. He was strongly influenced both by the Anglo-Irish folk tradition and by the music and speech of African Americans. Foster drew on these influences to create the distinctly American song. Obtain a copy of *American Dreamer: Songs of Stephen Foster*. Invite students to listen to these songs and to note the rich melodies and variety of emotions they evoke.

❶ The low white tents of the hospital were grouped around an old schoolhouse. There was here a singular commotion. In the foreground two ambulances interlocked wheels in the deep mud. The drivers were tossing the blame of it back and forth, gesticulating and berating, while from the ambulances, both crammed with wounded, there came an occasional groan. An interminable crowd of bandaged men were coming and going. Great numbers sat under the trees nursing heads or arms or legs. There was a dispute of some kind raging on the steps of the schoolhouse. Sitting with his back against a tree a man with a face as grey as a new army blanket was serenely smoking a corncob pipe. The lieutenant wished to rush forward and inform him that he was dying.

A busy surgeon was passing near the lieutenant. "Good-morning," he said, with a friendly smile. Then he caught sight of the lieutenant's arm, and his face at once changed. "Well, let's have a look at it." He seemed possessed suddenly of a great contempt for the lieutenant. This wound evidently placed the latter on a very low social plane. The doctor cried out impatiently, "What mutton-head had tied it up that way anyhow?" The lieutenant answered, "Oh, a man."

When the wound was disclosed the doctor fingered it disdainfully. "Humph," he said. "You come along with me and I'll 'tend to you." His voice contained the same scorn as if he were saying: "You will have to go to jail."

❷ The lieutenant had been very meek, but now his face flushed, and he looked into the doctor's eyes. "I guess I won't have it amputated," he said.

"Nonsense, man! Nonsense! Nonsense!" cried the doctor. "Come along, now. I won't amputate it. Come along. Don't be a baby."

> Do you believe the doctor? **Predict** what will happen to the lieutenant.

"Let go of me," said the lieutenant, holding back wrathfully, his glance fixed upon the door of the old schoolhouse, as sinister to him as the portals of death.

❸ And this is the story of how the lieutenant lost his arm. When he reached home, his sisters, his mother, his wife, sobbed for a long time at the sight of the flat sleeve. "Oh, well," he said, standing shamefaced amid these tears, "I don't suppose it matters so much as all that."

Young Soldier: Separate Study of a Soldier Giving Water to a Wounded Companion, 1861, Winslow Homer, Cooper-Hewitt, National Museum of Design, Smithsonian Institution

▲ **Critical Viewing** This teenaged Union soldier may have enlisted in the army in hopes of finding glory on the battlefield. How does "An Episode of War" contrast with this sentiment? **[Contrast]** ❹

◆ Build Vocabulary

disdainfully (dis dān´ fəl ē) *adv.*: Showing scorn or contempt

Humanities: Art

Young Soldier by Winslow Homer.

Homer (1836–1910), considered one of the greatest painters of the nineteenth century, is best known for his watercolors. His first claim to fame, however, came as an illustrator. After an apprenticeship to a lithographer, he worked as a freelance illustrator for such publications as *Harper's Weekly*. During the Civil War, he abandoned this lucrative career to serve as an artist for the Army of the Potomac. His work, mostly drawings and oil sketches done at or near the front lines and in the encampments, was superior to the lifeless depictions of other wartime illustrators. His renderings were works of art—unsentimental images of the fear and despair that permeated the life of the Civil War soldier.

This poignant drawing of a young Union soldier reveals Homer's sensitivity to the shyness and bewilderment felt by a young boy who suddenly finds himself thrust into a frightening man's world. Have students compare and contrast what a drawing such as this one can offer with what a painting offers to the viewer.

Willie Has Gone to the War

Words by George Cooper   Music by Stephen Foster

The blue bird is singing his lay,[1]
To all the sweet flow'rs of the dale,
The wild bee is roaming at play,
And soft is the sigh of the gale;
I stray by the brookside alone,
Where oft we have wander'd before,
And weep for my lov'd one, my own,
My Willie has gone to the war!

Willie has gone to the war, Willie,
Willie my lov'd one, my own;
Willie has gone to the war, Willie,
Willie my lov'd one is gone!

'Twas here, where the lily bells grow,
I last saw his noble young face,
And now while he's gone to the foe,
Oh! dearly I love the old place;
The whispering waters repeat
The name that I love o'er and o'er,
And daisies that nod at my feet,
Say Willie has gone to the war!

Willie has gone to the war, Willie,
Willie my lov'd one, my own;
Willie has gone to the war, Willie,
Willie my lov'd one is gone!

The leaves of the forest will fade,
The roses will wither and die,
But spring to our home in the glade,
On fairy like pinions[2] will fly;
And still I will hopefully wait
The day when these battles are o'er,
And pine like a bird for its mate,
Till Willie comes home from the war!

Willie has gone to the war, Willie,
Willie my lov'd one, my own;
Willie has gone to the war, Willie,
Willie my lov'd one is gone!

1. **lay** *n.*: Song or melody.
2. **pinions** (pin´ yənz) *n.*: Antiquated term meaning "wings."

◆ **Build Vocabulary**

glade (glād) *n.*: Open space in a wood or forest

Guide for Responding

◆ Literature and Your Life

Reader's Response Which aspects of "An Episode of War" did you find particularly tragic or unsettling? Explain.

Thematic Focus How does the portrayal of the Civil War in the story differ in perspective or point of view from the song?

☑ Check Your Comprehension

1. Give two reasons that the lieutenant's comrades "look at him with large eyes thoughtfully" but will not touch him in "An Episode of War."
2. In "An Episode of War," what treatment does the doctor ultimately administer to the lieutenant's wounded arm?
3. Why is the brook special to the speaker in "Willie Has Gone to the War"?

◆ Critical Thinking

INTERPRET

1. How does the way in which the lieutenant is wounded in "An Episode of War" make him a sympathetic character? **[Analyze]**
2. In "An Episode of War," the lieutenant walks with the detached air of a man watching someone else's nightmare unfold. What accounts for his numb state? **[Infer]**
3. Name three ways in which "An Episode of War" suggests that the lieutenant is seen by both himself and others as separate from, and somehow less a human being than, the uninjured people he encounters. **[Support]**
4. How does "Willie Has Gone to the War" romanticize the monotony and anguish of waiting for a soldier to return from war? **[Analyze]**

APPLY

5. According to the Naturalists, humans are weak and ineffectual beings at the mercy of deterministic forces. Defend this statement using examples from "An Episode of War." **[Defend]**

Develop Understanding

One-Minute Insight Using a stanza and chorus format, lyricist George Cooper and composer Stephen Foster created this Civil War ballad that romanticizes the idea of waiting for a loved one to return from war.

Reinforce and Extend

Customize for *Musical/Rhythmic Learners*
Ask students to write song lyrics or lyrics and music for a song Willie might sing back to the person who misses him. Or, ask them to write a song about the effects of chance events on their lives. Invite interested students to sing their songs to the class.

Answers

Reader's Response Students may be disturbed by the soldiers' and the doctor's attitude toward the wounded lieutenant or by the amputation itself.

Thematic Focus Unlike the song, which reflects the romanticized vision of war cherished by those at home, the story reflects the harsh realities experienced by the soldiers who fought the war.

☑ Check Your Comprehension

1. They do not touch him out of respect for his "new and terrible majesty." They are also afraid that even a light touch could hasten his death.
2. He amputates his arm.
3. She and Willie often walked there together, and it was there that they said good-bye.

(Answers continue on p. 448)

Reteach

To reteach Realism and Naturalism, use a Venn diagram to help students identify the common ground between the two and the differentiating philosophy of Naturalism. You might also use a branching illustration to show the common "stem" of portraying realistic, ordinary people, and then note the defining characteristics of each movement on the "branches."

Beyond the Selection

FURTHER READING

Other Works by Stephen Crane

Maggie: A Girl of the Streets
The Red Badge of Courage
The Little Regiment
"The Open Boat"

We suggest that you preview these works before recommending them to students.

INTERNET

You can find additional information about Stephen Crane on the Internet. We suggest the following site, which provides biographical information, sound clips of readings from Crane's works, and links to other Crane materials on the Internet:

http://www.cwrl.utexas.edu/~mmaynard/Crane/crane.html

Be aware that sites may have changed from the time we published this information. We *strongly recommend* that you preview the site.

Guide for Responding (continued)

◆ Reading for Success

INTERACTIVE READING STRATEGIES

As you read, you used a series of interactive strategies that rely on your personal involvement, experiences, and knowledge to help you get the most from your reading. Consider the doctor's promise not to amputate, and answer these questions.

1. Drawing upon your background knowledge of Civil War medical practices, why do you think the doctor made such a promise?
2. What was your response to this promise?
3. How does the final paragraph of the story help you to clarify the doctor's actual intent?

◆ Grammar and Style

CORRECT USE OF *LIKE* AND *AS*

The subordinating conjunction *as* sometimes introduces elliptical clauses in which all or part of the verb is omitted but understood. The omitted part of the verb is shown in brackets:

> **Like** is a preposition. **As, as if**, and **as though** are subordinating conjunctions used to introduce a subordinate clause.

He hesitated to follow the doctor, as any soldier would [hesitate].

Do not use *like* in place of *as*.

Practice On your paper, write the following sentences, correcting any errors in the use of *like, as, as if,* or *as though*. If a sentence contains no errors, write "correct."

1. The lieutenant divided the coffee evenly, just like he promised he would.
2. He staggered as though weak with fatigue.
3. The men stood as stones, frightened like they had never seen a man wounded in battle.
4. The lieutenant stumbled toward the field hospital as if a man in a trance.
5. Like any wounded man, he dwelled on the possibility of amputation.

◆ Literary Focus

REALISM AND NATURALISM

"An Episode of War" includes elements of both **Realism,** a literary movement that emphasized the faithful and accurate portrayal of ordinary life, and **Naturalism,** which generally portrayed people as being manipulated by forces beyond their control.

1. How does the fact that the lieutenant is rationing coffee at the time of his shooting contribute to the realistic quality of "An Episode of War"?
2. How can the same situation be used to support the assertion that this story is distinctly Naturalistic?
3. Give two examples of how the lieutenant exhibits the quiet, courageous endurance typical of characters in Naturalist works.
4. How would you refute the statement that "Willie Has Gone to the War" reflects Realism? Cite examples from the lyrics to support your argument.

◆ Build Vocabulary

USING THE LATIN ROOT ***-greg-***

Knowing that *-greg-* means "herd" or "flock" will help you remember that a *congregation* is a "group" and a *gregarious* person enjoys being part of a crowd.

Copy the paragraph below, filling in the blanks with the appropriate words from the following list.

aggregate gregarious congregated

The wounded soldiers __?__ on the steps, waiting to see the doctor. They were silent, except for one __?__ private who described his injury to everyone. In the __?__, a nearby orderly reflected, wounded men are a quiet bunch, but there is always an exception.

USING THE WORD BANK: Analogies

Copy these analogies, and complete each one with the appropriate word from the Word Bank.

1. *Quickly* is to *rapidly* as __?__ is to *scornfully*.
2. *Hidden* is to *revealed* as __?__ is to *obvious*.
3. *Brook* is to *stream* as __?__ is to *meadow*.
4. *Laugh* is to *cry* as __?__ is to *delay*.
5. *Sum* is to *parts* as __?__ is to *individual*.

Answers *(continued from p. 447)*

◆ Critical Thinking

1. Because the lieutenant is wounded while working at a task as humble and ordinary as rationing coffee, his wound seems especially unjust.
2. He is already dreading the horror of losing his arm.
3. Suggested responses: He observes things as though from a great distance, and looks at others "with wonder." The doctor treats the lieutenant with contempt once he realizes he is injured. He tries to downplay the importance of his injury. His empty sleeve is a lifelong reminder of how he is now different from other people.
4. The song is idealized and sentimental; it doesn't portray the hardships of life for the women left at home.
5. Suggested response: The nameless lieutenant symbolizes the unfortunate Everyman, helpless to prevent his injury, sheathe his own sword, or avoid amputation. He is wounded by chance, then swept toward a fate he is powerless to escape. His horrible experience is just one more in a string of such tragedies that humanity is powerless to avoid; it is just "an episode of war."

◆ Reading for Success

1. It was probably the only way to get the lieutenant to agree to be treated by the doctor.
2. Students may say that they didn't believe the doctor, or that they were outraged to learn that he lied.
3. The narrator announces that "this is the story of how the lieutenant lost his arm."

◆ Grammar and Style

1. The lieutenant divided the coffee evenly, just as he promised he would.
2. Correct
3. The men stood like stones, frightened as though they had never seen a man wounded in battle.
4. The lieutenant stumbled toward the field hospital like a man in a trance.
5. Correct.

◆ Literary Focus

1. Soldiers did not spend all their time fighting glorious battles; much of their day was occupied with everyday tasks.
2. The lieutenant is not in a situation where he expects to be wounded. It is a random bullet—the type of chance event characteristic of Naturalist literature—that changes his life forever.
3. He submits to the doctor, even when he suspects his worst fear is about to be made real. He downplays how much he has been traumatized by the amputation so his family won't be too upset.
4. The ballad is a sentimental depiction of a woman whose longing for her loved one is reflected in idealized nature ("The whispering waters repeat / The name that I love o'er and o'er"). There is no depiction of the hardships that faced the women left alone to run homes and businesses.

◆ Build Vocabulary

Using the Latin Root *-greg-*
The wounded soldiers *congregated* on the steps . . . They were silent, except for one *gregarious* private . . . In the *aggregate*, . . .

Using the Word Bank
1. disdainfully; 2. inscrutable; 3. glade; 4. precipitate; 5. aggregation

Build Your Portfolio

Idea Bank

Writing

1. Letter As the lieutenant, write a letter to your wife explaining how you lost your arm.

2. Editorial During the Civil War, infections spread by a lack of basic sanitary procedures killed more soldiers than combat wounds did. Write a newspaper editorial exposing disease and poor sanitary conditions as the biggest killers of the war.

3. Definition Essay What events in this story reflect the belief that humankind is helpless in the face of events it cannot control? In an essay, use "An Episode of War" to define Naturalism.

Speaking, Listening, and Viewing

4. Enactment Imagine what took place when the lieutenant awoke from surgery to find that his arm had been amputated. Work with a small group to dramatize your interpretation of the scene. **[Performing Arts Link]**

5. Music Performance The Civil War inspired hundreds of songs. Among the most familiar are "Battle Hymn of the Republic" and "Dixie." Select one such Civil War song, give some background on its origins, then perform or play a recording of the song for the class. **[Music Link]**

Researching and Representing

6. Soldier's Scrapbook Create a scrapbook documenting the experiences of an imaginary Civil War soldier. Include photocopied photographs from history and Civil War books, and write brief captions for each. **[Social Studies Link; Art Link]**

7. Oral Presentation on Civil War Heroines Research Dorothea Dix, Dr. Elizabeth Blackwell, Clara Barton, or another Civil War heroine. Share your findings in an oral presentation.

Online Activity www.phlit.phschool.com

Guided Writing Lesson

Field Report on Hospital Conditions

Imagine that the lieutenant serves under a colonel who wants to know why so many of his soldiers are dying from minor wounds. Writing as the lieutenant, provide the colonel with a report on the treatment you received and the problems you observed during your stay at the army hospital.

Writing Skills Focus: Precise Details

To make your report—or any piece of writing—more vivid and complete, **include precise details** to support your ideas and opinions. Simply stating that the wounded soldiers are neglected, for example, wouldn't give the colonel enough information to solve problems. Adding precise details provides a more complete picture of hospital conditions.

Model

The wounded often lie on filthy beds and floors for hours and even days at a time without being fed, bathed or treated.

Prewriting Scan the Background for Understanding on p. 440 and the photograph on p. 443 to help you develop a list of issues for your report. Jot down the precise details you will use to support each issue. Consult a Civil War reference book if you feel that you need more information.

Drafting After an introduction in which you state the purpose of your report, present each issue and supporting details in a separate paragraph. Then, summarize the main points of your report in the conclusion. Remember to use formal language.

Revising Reread your report, checking to see that you have presented your points in a logical order and with sufficient supporting details. Ask yourself what you can do to improve your organization and what information might strengthen or clarify your writing.

✓ ASSESSMENT OPTIONS

Formal Assessment, Selection Test, pp. 129–131, and Assessment Resources Software. The selection test is designed so that it can be easily customized to the performance levels of your students.

Alternative Assessment, p. 26, includes options for less advanced students, more advanced students, musical/rhythmic learners, verbal/linguistic learners, and bodily/kinesthetic learners.

PORTFOLIO ASSESSMENT
Use the following rubrics in the ***Alternative Assessment*** booklet to assess student writing:
Letter: Narrative Based on Personal Experience Rubric, p. 111
Editorial: Cause-Effect Rubric, p. 117
Definition Essay: Definition/Classification Rubric, p. 114
Guided Writing Lesson: Description Rubric, p. 112

Idea Bank

Customizing for
Performance Levels
Following are suggestions for matching Idea Bank topics with your students' performance levels:
Less Advanced Students: 1, 4
Average Students: 2, 5, 7
More Advanced Students: 3, 6

Customizing for
Learning Modalities
Following are suggestions for matching Idea Bank topics with your students' learning modalities:
Body/Kinesthetic: 4
Musical/Rhythmic: 5
Visual/Spatial: 6
Verbal/Linguistic: 7

Guided Writing Lesson

For more prewriting, elaboration, and revision strategies, see *Prentice Hall Writing and Grammar.*

Writing and Language Transparencies Use Writing Process Model 2: Descriptive and Observational Writing, pp. 9–12, to show students how the addition of details can strengthen the observations they will relate in their field reports.

Writers at Work Videodisc
Have students view the videodisc segment on Exposition (Ch. 3) featuring museum curator Thom Harrington to learn his ideas about writing to inform. What do students think of his idea of using an outline to organize ideas?

Play frames 23159 to 33243

Writing Lab CD-ROM
Have students complete the tutorial on Exposition. Follow these steps:
1. Use the Note Cards Activities to help students organize.
2. Refer students to the Transition Word Bin to aid in drafting.
3. After students have drafted on the computer, have them use one of the Interactive Self-Evaluation Checklists to aid revision.

Prepare and Engage

LESSON OBJECTIVES

1. **To develop vocabulary and word identification skills**
   - Latin Word Roots: *-press-*
   - Using the Word Bank: Antonyms
2. **To use a variety of reading strategies to comprehend songs**
   - Connect Your Experience
   - Reading Strategy: Listen
3. **To increase knowledge of other cultures and to connect common elements across cultures**
   - Connecting Themes Across Cultures
   - Idea Bank: Map
4. **To express and support responses to the text**
   - Critical Thinking
   - Idea Bank: Letter
   - Idea Bank: Original Spiritual
   - Idea Bank: Choral Reading
5. **To analyze literary elements**
   - Literary Focus: Refrain
6. **To read in order to research self-selected and assigned topics**
   - Idea Bank: Music Appreciation
7. **To plan, prepare, organize, and present literary interpretations**
   - Idea Bank: Reflective Essay
   - Idea Bank: Logo
8. **To use recursive writing processes to write a song to support a cause**
   - Guided Writing Lesson
9. **To increase knowledge of the rules of grammar and usage**
   - Grammar and Style: Direct Address

Test Preparation

Reading Comprehension: Context (ATE, p. 451)
The teaching tips and sample test item in this workshop support the instruction and practice in the unit workshop:
Reading Comprehension: Using Context (SE, p. 631)

Guide for Interpreting

Spirituals

Spirituals are folk songs that originated among enslaved African Americans. The songs served as an important means of communication and a way of expressing the desire for freedom and religious salvation. At the same time, the songs helped to replace lost African religious traditions and allowed men and women to maintain a connection to their musical heritage.

Plantation owners, fearing discontent among their slaves, encouraged field hands to sing while they picked cotton or sugar, reasoning that people who were busy singing could not plot escape or rebellion. The slaves, however, found ways to benefit from singing. Their songs provided an outlet for the grief and frustration they often kept bottled up inside. Spirituals also fostered a sense of personal self-worth by portraying slaves as innocents of a mighty God, deserving of a heavenly reward for their earthly labors. By grafting African styles and rhythms onto Christian hymns, enslaved Africans managed to hold on to part of their heritage. In addition, the language in some songs provided a means to communicate forbidden thoughts and feelings.

A Double Message Many spirituals had a double meaning. References to figures and events in the Bible were a kind of code for the slaves' own experience. Slaves identified with the ancient Israelites, who had once been the slaves of the Egyptians. Singing about the Israelites was a safe way to voice their own yearning for liberty. One work song did more than just express discontent; it gave directions for escape: In "Follow the Drinking Gourd," fugitive slaves were advised to follow the Big Dipper north to freedom.

◆ Background for Understanding

History: Harriet Tubman and the Underground Railroad

Africans first came to this country as slaves in 1619. After 1808, the slave trade was banned, but slavery remained legal. In response to slave rebellions in the 1820's and 1830's, many southern states enacted tough new laws. In the years before the Civil War, deprived of nearly all their rights under these laws, many enslaved Africans ran away. They were hidden and transported by the Underground Railroad, a secret network of activists dedicated to helping fugitives reach freedom in the northern states and in Canada.

One of those activists was Harriet Tubman, called the Moses of her people. In the Old Testament, Moses led the Israelites out of their captivity in Egypt. Harriet Tubman followed his example in the years before the Civil War. Born a slave around 1820, she eventually escaped to the North along the Underground Railroad. She then risked her life to go back and rescue her family. Driven by the desire to help others still oppressed, this quick-witted and courageous woman returned to the South again and again to rescue other enslaved Africans who were desperate for a life of liberty. Tubman, standing at the left, posed for this photograph with just a few of the more than 300 people she led to freedom. The spiritual "Go Down, Moses" most likely refers to Tubman as well as to the Moses of the Bible.

Prentice Hall Literature Program Resources

REINFORCE / RETEACH / EXTEND

Selection Support Pages
Build Vocabulary: Latin Word Roots: *-press-*, p. 128
Grammar and Style: Direct Address, p. 129
Reading Strategy: Listen, p. 130
Literary Focus: Refrain, p. 131

Strategies for Diverse Student Needs, p. 27

Beyond Literature
Cross-Curricular Connection: Social Studies, p. 27

Formal Assessment Selection Test, pp. 132–134; Assessment Resources Software

Alternative Assessment, p. 27

Resource Pro CD-ROM

Listening to Music: The American Experience Audio CD

Swing Low, Sweet Chariot ◆ Go Down, Moses ◆

◆ Literature and Your Life

Connect Your Experience

Songs have an amazing power to sway our emotions. They can soothe us when we're feeling sad, or bring back memories or special people or places. As is the case with the two songs you're about to read, songs can even help people endure great hardships.

Journal Writing Discuss one or two songs that have an especially strong emotional impact on you.

Thematic Focus: A Nation Divided

In these two spirituals, you will hear the singers' pain, their yearning for freedom, and their rage against slavery. These songs bring to life the emotional impact of an issue that divided our nation for decades and played a key role in causing the Civil War.

◆ Build Vocabulary

Latin Word Roots: *-press-*

In "Go Down, Moses," the people of Israel are described as *oppressed*. The Latin root *-press-* means "push." If you weren't sure of the meaning of *oppressed* but knew the root *-press-*, you might still determine that the Israelites were pushed or kept down in some way.

Word Bank

Preview these words from the spirituals.

oppressed
smite

◆ Grammar and Style

Direct Address

In both spirituals, the speaker creates a dramatic effect by using **direct address** in the opening lines. When a speaker directly addresses someone or something by name, the name is set off by one or more commas, depending on its position in the sentence. Look at these examples.

Swing low, sweet chariot,
Coming for to carry me home.

Go down, Moses,
Way down in Egypt land.

The use of direct address adds to the emotional intensity of these songs.

◆ Literary Focus

Refrain

If you're searching for the meaning of a song or poem, you'll often find it in the **refrain**—a word, phrase, line, or group of lines repeated at regular intervals throughout the work. Most spirituals, including these, contain at least one refrain. It emphasizes the most important ideas and helps establish the rhythm of the song. A chorus usually sang the refrain of a spiritual, with a soloist singing the other words. This back-and-forth pattern resembles the African tradition known as "call and response." Soloists often improvised, creating new lyrics as they sang. Refrains, however, seldom changed.

◆ Reading Strategy

Listen

Since songs are created for the ear, not the eye, **listening** is an especially important skill for appreciating lyrics. Read each spiritual aloud, listening to its rhythm. Also pay attention to rhymes and other repeated sounds. For example, the opening line in "Go Down, Moses" contains three stressed syllables in a row. Often, the rhythms and sounds of a song suggest a mood. What mood do these three strong consecutive sounds create? What mood do you sense as you listen to these spirituals?

Interest Grabber The best way to engage students' interest in the spirituals is by having them listen to them. Play the recordings of "Go Down, Moses" and "Swing Low, Sweet Chariot" on the **Listening to Music: The American Experience Audio CD.** As students listen, have them focus more on the sound of the spirituals than on the meaning. Follow with a discussion of why spirituals may have remained popular for so long. With whom are they most likely to be popular? Why? Why have they influenced other types of music? After you've completed the discussion, have students read the spirituals.

Listening to Music: The American Experience Audio CD

Connecting Themes Across Cultures

The United States has faced divisive issues throughout its history, though never in a more severe form than the Civil War. Still, while our nation holds within itself stinging divisions, it is also a place of the most remarkable unities. The spiritual "Go Down, Moses," for instance, is distilled from the combined experiences of three cultures: African, British, and Hebrew. Discuss with students other musical forms, such as Blues and rock-a-billy, that have several cultural influences.

Customize for
Less Proficient Readers

Guide these students to understand the underlying meaning of important lines and details in the spirituals. For example, help them to see the that the line "Coming for to carry me home" referred not only to the hope of freedom in heaven, but also to the chance at freedom by escaping on the underground railroad.

Customize for
AP Students

Encourage these students to extend their appreciation of spirituals by considering connections between the spirituals and some of today's popular music. Have them share their conclusions with the class.

Test Preparation Workshop

Reading Comprehension:
Context Clues Many standardized tests require students to use context clues to determine the meaning of unfamiliar words. Use the following sample test item to give students practice in this skill.

. . . bold Moses said,
"Let my people go;
If not I'll smite your first-born dead
Let my people go."

In this passage, smite most nearly means—

A build
B strike
C cure
D affect

From the context of the passage, students should be able to determine that *smite* means a violent, destructive action. Even if they are not certain of the meaning of *strike,* students should recognize that none of the other choices fits this defininition. Guide students to recognize that B is the correct answer.

Develop Understanding

One-Minute Insight This spiritual, constructed around the refrain "Coming for to carry me home," expresses both a desire for eternal salvation in heaven and a longing for freedom from slavery. The "sweet chariot" and the "band of angels" referred to in spiritual are symbols for the underground railroad.

◆ Background for Understanding

In his autobiography, former slave Frederick Douglass explained why enslaved Africans sang spirituals as they worked: "Slaves are generally expected to sing as well as to work. A silent slave is not liked by masters or overseers. . . . The remark is not unfrequently made, that slaves are the most contented and happy laborers in the world. They dance and sing, and make all manner of joyful noise—so they do; but it is a great mistake to suppose them happy because they sing. The songs of the slave represent the sorrows rather than the joys, of his heart; and he is relieved by them, only as an aching heart is relieved by its tears."

◆ Background for Understanding

"Swing Low, Sweet Chariot" is based on an Old Testament story in which Elijah flew to heaven in a fiery chariot.

▶Critical Viewing◀

❶ **Infer** From the clothing of the escaped slaves you can infer that they had difficult lives and few material possessions.

◆ Literary Focus

❷ **Refrain** Have students identify the refrains in this piece. Which refrain is predominant? *Coming for to carry me home.* How does the refrain emphasize the speaker's yearning, and what is that yearning? *Repetition emphasizes steady hope or belief that release will come; the speaker yearns for escape, by being set free or by dying and going to heaven.*

Swing Low, Sweet Chariot

Spiritual

▲ **Critical Viewing** Looking at the clothing of the escaped slaves in this photograph, what can you infer about their lives as fugitives? **[Infer]** ❶

Swing low, sweet chariot,
Coming for to carry me home,
Swing low, sweet chariot,
Coming for to carry me home.

I looked over Jordan[1] and what did I see
Coming for to carry me home,
A band of angels coming after me,
Coming for to carry me home.

❷

If you get there before I do,
Coming for to carry me home,
Tell all my friends I'm coming too,
Coming for to carry me home.

Swing low, sweet chariot,
Coming for to carry me home,
Swing low, sweet chariot,
Coming for to carry me home.

1. **Jordan:** River of the Near East that flows from the Lebanon Mountains through the Sea of Galilee to the Dead Sea. Many spirituals use the phrase "crossing over Jordan" as a metaphor for crossing the Ohio River to freedom or going to heaven.

Block Scheduling Strategies

Consider these suggestions to take advantage of extended class time:

- As a homework assignment, have students gather information about the Underground Railroad. Have them share this information to help create a context for the spirituals.
- Play the recordings of the spirituals on the **Listening to Music: The American Experience Audio CD.** Follow with a class discussion about how listening to the spirituals affects students appreciation for them.
- Have students learn more about spirituals by conducting research in the library or on the Internet before or after they read or listen to the selections.
- Have students complete the Idea Bank activity on music appreciation on p. 455. Allow time for a class discussion of the musical pieces that students share.
- Extend student knowledge of the message in Spirituals by having them complete the ***Beyond the Literature*** activity sheet (p. 27).

Go Down, Moses

Spiritual

Go down, Moses,
Way down in Egypt land
Tell old Pharaoh
To let my people go.

When Israel was in Egypt land
Let my people go
Oppressed so hard they could not stand
Let my people go.

Go down, Moses,
Way down in Egypt land [3]
Tell old Pharaoh [4]
"Let my people go."

"Thus saith the Lord," bold Moses said,
"Let my people go;
If not I'll smite your first-born dead
Let my people go."

Go down, Moses,
Way down in Egypt land,
Tell old Pharaoh,
"Let my people go!"

◆ **Build Vocabulary**

oppressed (ə prest′) *v.*: Kept down by cruel or unjust power or authority

smite (smīt) *v.*: To kill by a powerful blow

Guide for Responding

◆ Literature and Your Life

Reader's Response Think about the spirituals you just read. If you were a slave, which do you think would better express your feelings? Why?

Thematic Response How do spirituals soothe the feelings of longing, sadness, and injustice they express?

☑ Check Your Comprehension

1. In "Swing Low, Sweet Chariot," who is coming over Jordan to carry the speaker home?
2. According to Moses, with what punishment does the Lord threaten the Egyptians if they refuse to free the Israelites?

◆ Critical Thinking

INTERPRET

1. If "Swing Low . . ." is an expression of the slaves' desire for escape, explain what each of these represents: (a) chariot, (b) home, (c) band of angels. **[Interpret]**
2. In the comparison of America with ancient Egypt in "Go Down, Moses," whom does the old Pharaoh represent? **[Interpret]**
3. Compare the mood of "Go Down, Moses," with that of "Swing Low, Sweet Chariot." **[Compare]**

EVALUATE

4. Explain the effectiveness of the mix of formal and informal language in "Go Down, Moses." **[Evaluate]**

Beyond the Selection

FURTHER READING

Works About Spirituals

The Treasury of Negro Spirituals, Herbert Arthur Chambers

Walk Together Children, Ashley Bryan

Black Song: The Forge and the Flame: The Story of How the Afro-American Spiritual Was Hammered Out, John Lovell

We recommend that you preview these books before suggesting them to students.

INTERNET

You and your students may find additional information on the Internet. We suggest the following site. Please be aware, however, that sites may have changed since we published this information.

For a comprehensive treatment of African American literature and history, go to: **http://falcon.jmu.edu/~ramseyil/afroamer.htm**

We *strongly recommend* that you preview the site before you send students to it.

One-Minute Insight These lyrics refer to the Biblical account of Moses leading the Hebrews, who had been enslaved by the Pharaoh of Egypt, out of bondage. Here, the Pharaoh is a metaphor for any slaveholder, the Israelites are the slaves, Moses is a redeemer or savior, and Egypt represents the American South.

◆ Reading Strategy

Listen Play the **Listening to Music: The American Experience Audio CD** version of this spiritual. Encourage students to listen actively to hear rhythmic and melodic emphasis and to identify refrain and call-and-response lines.

◆ Literary Focus

[3] Refrain Have students identify the refrain, and explain how they can recognize it. *The refrain is found in the first four lines, and again in lines 8–12 and in lines 16–20; this is the refrain because it is the part that repeats.*

Customize for *ESL Students*

[4] Be sure students know the meaning of the archaic verb *saith* (says).

Reinforce and Extend

Customize for *AP Students*

Moses does not just "tell old Pharaoh" to let his people go; he threatens that the Lord will "smite" Pharaoh's first-born. Can nonviolent methods be used to end oppression, or is violence an inevitable result? Challenge students to debate this issue, using their knowledge of oppression in any historical time.

Answers

◆ Literature and Your Life

Reader's Response Students should support their answers with details from the spiritual they choose.

Thematic Response Possible response: The songs offer the hope of freedom.

☑ Check Your Comprehension

1. "A band of angels" is coming to carry the speaker home.
2. He will smite their "first-born."

(Answers continue on p. 454)

Answers *(continued from p. 453)*

◆ Critical Thinking

1. (a) It symbolizes death or the underground railroad. (b) Home represents heaven or freedom. (c) The angels are conductors on the underground railroad.
2. The old Pharaoh represents slave-owners or the governments that support slavery.
3. "Go Down, Moses" is firmly determined in mood, while "Swing Low" is calmer and more melancholy; it expresses longing, rather than a demand, for freedom.
4. The song uses both informal language, such as "Way down in Egypt land" and "old Pharaoh," and formal language, such as "saith," and "smite." Students may find this an effective way to differentiate between the speaker's own voice and that of Moses. The use of formal language also lends even greater authority to the Biblical demand for freedom.

◆ Reading Strategy

1. Suggested response: In both songs, the refrain, which is repeated many times, is a clear statement of the theme. Rhyme is used to frame the refrains and reinforce the meaning of the lines in between the refrains. The rhythms support the messages by drawing readers into the songs.
2. The soloist would probably have sung the verses, which tell the story. The refrains would have been sung by a chorus as a way of reinforcing the main theme of the song.

◆ Literary Focus

1. (a) The entire first stanza is a refrain that appears twice in "Swing Low, Sweet Chariot." The line "Coming for to carry me home" is also used as a refrain. (b) The entire first stanza is a refrain that appears three times in the song. The line "let my people go" is also a refrain.
2. The refrain "let my people go" expresses the slaves' desire for freedom, which is the main idea of the song.

Reteach

To reteach this selection, use ***Strategies for Diverse Student Needs,*** p. 27.

Guide for Responding (continued)

◆ Reading Strategy

Listen

Listening to the sounds and rhythms of "Swing Low, Sweet Chariot" and "Go Down, Moses" as you read helps you to gain more insight into the songs.

1. Explain how each of the songs uses rhythm, rhyme, and repetition to reinforce meaning.
2. In each song, which lines might have been sung by a soloist and which by the chorus? Why?

◆ Literary Focus

Refrain

Both "Swing Low, Sweet Chariot" and "Go Down, Moses" use **refrains** to express the speaker's deepest yearnings. Sometimes the refrain is a single repeated line; at other times, the refrain is an entire stanza. Each time the refrain is repeated, the image or emotion it contains gathers force.

1. List all the refrains, both lines and entire stanzas, in (a) "Swing Low . . ." and (b) "Go Down . . ."
2. What idea or message is emphasized through the single-line refrain in "Go Down, Moses"?

◆ Build Vocabulary

Using the Latin Root *-press-*

Copy the following sentences into your notebook, filling in the blanks with an appropriate word consisting of the Latin root *-press-*, meaning "push," and one of the prefixes defined below.

com- ("together") *re-* ("back")
de- ("down") *im-* ("into")

1. ___?___ the metal seal on the hot wax to make your mark.
2. Watch as I ___?___ the paper into a tight ball.
3. If you ___?___ that button, a buzzer will go off.
4. The enthusiastic fans weren't able to ___?___ their squeals.

Using the Word Bank: Antonyms

On your paper, write the word that is the closest antonym, or opposite, of the first word.

1. oppressed: (a) crushed, (b) assisted, (c) punished, (d) ignored
2. smite: (a) hit, (b) question, (c) criticize, (d) caress

◆ Grammar and Style

Direct Address

> In **direct address**, commas are used to set off the name of the person or thing being addressed by the speaker.

When you use direct address, put a comma after the name if it comes first in the sentence, before the name if it comes at the end of the sentence, and both before and after the name if it comes in the middle of the sentence.

Practice On your paper, copy the following sentences. Underline the noun or noun phrase of direct address, and add punctuation where necessary.

1. Selena, sing slowly and with great feeling.
2. The choir performed beautifully Ms. Phipps.
3. I think, choir members that you need to stand straighter.
4. Everyone agrees Joe that you have a great voice.

Writing Application Rewrite each sentence, inserting the noun of direct address in the part of the sentence indicated. Insert commas where necessary.

1. Sing the refrain as if you really mean it. (sopranos—beginning of sentence)
2. Do you plan to join the senior choir? (Nathan—end of sentence)
3. Before you begin the first verse take a deep breath. (students—middle of sentence)

Beyond Literature

Cultural Connection

West African Music While Europeans developed music centered on variations of pitch, many African cultures created music based on drums and rhythms. Different tones are produced by a variety of drum sizes and shapes as well as hand positions. The music can be quite complex, and it is not uncommon for six or seven drummers to play in different time signatures, which they weave together to create intricate, musical patterns. Listen to selections of African drumming and see if your ears can pick out the different drummers and rhythms. **[Music Link]**

◆ Build Vocabulary

Using the Latin Root *-press-*

1. impress; 2. compress; 3. depress; 4. repress

Using the Word Bank

1. b 2. d

◆ Grammar and Style

Practice

1. Selena, sing slowly and with great feeling.
2. The choir performed beautifully, Ms. Phipps.
3. I think, choir members, that you need to stand straighter.
4. Everyone agrees, Joe, that you have a great voice.

Writing Application

1. Sopranos, sing the refrain as if you really mean it.
2. Do you plan to join the choir, Nathan?
3. Before you begin the first verse, students, take a deep breath.

Grammar Reinforcement

For additional practice, use the page on Commas in the *Grammar Practice Book,* p. 87.

Beyond Literature

Students may draw connections to the music of certain rhythm and blues performers, such as Whitney Houston.

Build Your Portfolio

Idea Bank

Writing

1. Letter Think of a contemporary performer (from country, rap, rock, or jazz) with the potential to perform spirituals in an interesting new way. Write to the artist, proposing that he or she record this type of music, and explain why.

2. Original Spiritual Write your own spiritual, using refrains to emphasize an important idea.

3. Reflective Essay Imagine that you are a free person living in the South before the Civil War. You hear these spirituals and, for the first time, really pay attention to the lyrics. In a reflective essay, analyze what the songs have taught you about the realities of slavery.

Speaking, Listening, and Viewing

4. Choral Reading With a small group, read a spiritual aloud in call-and-response format, with one student calling out the verses and the rest answering with the refrains. Each "soloist" should create at least one new verse. **[Performing Arts Link]**

5. Music Appreciation Find contemporary recordings of spirituals in a library's gospel music collection. Play several for the class; then compare the songs' messages and images with the spirituals you just studied. **[Music Link]**

Researching and Representing

6. Map In an on-line or printed historical atlas, find a map showing ancient Palestine, the river Jordan, and ancient Egypt. Make a copy of the map; then label each location with a caption that explains how it relates to these spirituals. **[Social Studies Link]**

7. Logo Design a logo for the Underground Railroad. Use words or images from the spirituals to symbolize the organization's mission. **[Art Link]**

Online Activity www.phlit.phschool.com

Guided Writing Lesson

Song to Support a Cause

"Go Down, Moses" is a plea for freedom from slavery based on the Old Testament story of Moses' demand of freedom for the Israelites. Over the years, songwriters have written lyrics urging everything from an end to war to a cure for world hunger. Write a song in support of a cause about which you feel strongly. Use repetition to emphasize your most important ideas.

Writing Skills Focus: Effective Repetition

The use of the same word, phrase, or sound more than once to create an effect or emphasize a point is known as **effective repetition.** Don't repeat just any word or phrase; rather, repeat images or statements that communicate your main idea. In "Swing Low, Sweet Chariot," for example, the speaker uses the word *home*—a word with deep emotional connotations—a total of eight times in sixteen lines.

Prewriting Choose a cause in which you believe. Jot down several good reasons for supporting the cause, then select one or two that appeal directly to the emotions. Brainstorm for words and images that capture these ideas and feelings.

Drafting Write at least two verses and a refrain.

Verses: State your cause and build support for it.
Refrain: Use emotional words and/or powerful images to get to the heart of the issue.

Build the intensity of your message by repeating the key words and phrases you identified while brainstorming in the prewriting phase.

Revising Read your song aloud as though seeing it for the first time. Is your message strong and clear? Does your use of repetition emphasize the main idea?

Idea Bank

Customizing for *Performance Levels*
Following are suggestions for matching Idea Bank topics with your students' performance levels:
Less Advanced Students: 1, 4
Average Students: 2, 5, 7
More Advanced Students: 3, 6

Customizing for *Learning Modalities*
Following are suggestions for matching Idea Bank topics with your students' learning modalities:
Visual/Spatial: 6, 7
Musical/Rhythmic: 4, 5
Interpersonal: 4

Guided Writing Lesson

For more prewriting, elaboration, and revision strategies, see *Prentice Hall Writing and Grammar.*

Writers at Work Videodisc
Have students view the videodisc segment on Creative Writing featuring poet Martín Espada (Ch. 6). In this segment Espada explains the process he uses to write poetry. Discuss the similarities between poems and songs, and encourage students to point out techniques that he uses that can help them write their songs.

Play frames 14950 to 17080

Writing Lab CD-ROM
Have students work in the tutorial on Creative Writing as they write their songs. Have students follow these steps:

1. Use the Word Bins in the Gathering Details section to select words and details to use in their poems.
2. Refer to the interactive literary models illustrating the use of poetic sound devices.
3. After students have drafted on the computer, have them use the Self-Evaluation Checklist for poetry to aid in revision.

ASSESSMENT OPTIONS

Formal Assessment, Selection Test, pp. 132–134, and Assessment Resources Software. The selection test is designed so that it can be easily customized to the performance levels of your students.

Alternative Assessment, p. 27, includes options for less advanced students, more advanced students, musical/rhythmic learners, interpersonal learners, and verbal/linguistic learners.

PORTFOLIO ASSESSMENT
Use the following rubrics in the ***Alternative Assessment*** booklet to assess student writing:
Letter: Persuasion Rubric, p. 120
Original Spiritual: Poetry Rubric, p. 123
Reflective Essay: Expression Rubric, p. 109
Guided Writing Lesson: Poetry Rubric, p. 123

Prepare and Engage

LESSON OBJECTIVES

1. **To develop vocabulary and word identification skills**
   - Latin Word Roots: *-bene-*
   - Using the Word Bank: Sentence Completions
2. **To use a variety of reading strategies to comprehend nonfiction**
   - Connect Your Experience
   - Reading Strategy: Establish a Purpose
3. **To increase knowledge of other cultures and to connect common elements across cultures**
   - Background for Understanding
4. **To express and support responses to the text**
   - Critical Thinking
   - Idea Bank: Diary Entry
   - Idea Bank: New Version
   - Idea Bank: Dramatic Dialogue
5. **To analyze literary elements**
   - Literary Focus: Autobiography
6. **To read in order to research self-selected and assigned topics**
   - Idea Bank: Oral Interpretation
7. **To plan, prepare, organize, and present literary interpretations**
   - Idea Bank: Essay
   - Idea Bank: Interpretive Dance
   - Idea Bank: Graphic Display
8. **To use recursive writing processes to write a college admissions essay**
   - Guided Writing Lesson
9. **To increase knowledge of the rules of grammar and usage**
   - Grammar and Style: Correlative Conjunctions

Test Preparation

Reading Comprehension: Context (ATE, p. 457)
The teaching tips and sample test item in this workshop support the instruction and practice in the unit workshop:

Reading Comprehension: Using Context (SE, p. 631)

Guide for Interpreting

Frederick Douglass
(1818–1895)

Frederick Douglass rose out of slavery to become one of the most gifted writers and orators of his time. Using these talents, he dedicated his life to fighting for the abolition of slavery and for civil rights. Douglass's life served as an inspiration and example for both blacks and whites throughout the country.

Early Years Douglass was born on a Maryland plantation. It is believed that his name at birth was Frederick Augustus Bailey. At the age of eight, he was sent as a slave to the Baltimore home of the Auld family, where he learned to read and write, at first with the encouragement of Mrs. Auld and later despite her objections. Learning soon became an unquenchable thirst for the boy.

Douglass often traded biscuits for reading lessons with his playmates.

His reading fueled a quest for freedom. At age twenty-one he escaped to Massachusetts, a free state, and took the surname Douglass to avoid arrest as a fugitive.

A Public Life Despite his fear of being arrested, Douglass delivered a tremendously powerful and moving debut speech at the 1841 convention of an abolitionist organization. He then spent the next four years lecturing against slavery and arguing for the need for civil rights for all people.

Rumors spread that a man of such eloquence could not possibly have been a slave. In response, Douglass published his first autobiography, *Narrative of the Life of Frederick Douglass, an American Slave, Written By Himself* (1845). He then fled to England, where he spent years trying to gain British support for the abolitionist movement. After English friends raised money to buy his freedom, Douglass returned to the United States, established a newspaper for African Americans, and resumed lecturing. In 1855, he published *My Bondage and My Freedom,* an updated version of his autobiography.

During the Civil War, Douglass helped recruit African American soldiers for the Union army. After slavery was abolished, he fought vigorously for civil rights for African Americans. He became a consultant to President Lincoln and held several government positions, including United States minister to Haiti.

◆ Background for Understanding

CULTURE: THE INFLUENCE OF FREDERICK DOUGLASS

Frederick Douglass was perhaps the most prominent African American leader of the nineteenth century, and his influence is still felt. As a crusader for human rights, Douglass served as a role model for African American leaders such as Booker T. Washington and W.E.B. DuBois. In our own era, the civil rights movement has drawn inspiration from Douglass, who opposed segregation decades before other voices of objection were raised. As a young man, he protested segregated seating on trains by sitting in cars reserved for whites until the authorities forcibly removed him. Later, he fought job discrimination against African Americans and protested segregation in schools.

Douglass did not limit himself to fighting for the civil rights of African Americans. He also helped women in their battle to win the vote. Because he did not segregate his causes, Douglass is a model for all those who struggle against injustice.

Many American writers have paid tribute to Douglass in their works. Two of those works are included in this book: Paul Laurence Dunbar's poem "Douglass" on p. 600 and Robert Hayden's poem "Frederick Douglass" on p. 1053.

Prentice Hall Literature Program Resources

REINFORCE / RETEACH / EXTEND

Selection Support Pages
Build Vocabulary: Latin Roots: *-bene-*, p. 132
Grammar/Style: Correlative Conjunctions, p. 133
Reading Strategy: Set a Purpose, p. 134
Literary Focus: Autobiography, p. 135

Strategies for Diverse Student Needs, p. 28
Beyond Literature, p. 28
Formal Assessment Selection Test, pp. 135–137; Assessment Resources Software
Alternative Assessment, p. 28

Writing and Language Transparencies
Cubing Organizer, pp. 71–73
Resource Pro CD-ROM
Literature CD-ROM
Listening to Literature Audiocassettes

from My Bondage and My Freedom

◆ Literature and Your Life

Connect Your Experience

Can you remember your pride and excitement as you learned to read by yourself? Imagine another person denying your right to read just as you were discovering what it meant to learn. If you were enslaved like Frederick Douglass, you would have no choice but to submit (or at least appear to submit) to your owner's wishes.

Journal Writing Briefly discuss whether you believe that education is a privilege or an undeniable right.

Thematic Focus: A Nation Divided

Douglass's autobiography presents a powerful argument against slavery—a major cause of the Civil War. Few issues have more dramatically torn apart our nation. As you read, consider both the political and personal divisions caused by this issue.

◆ Literary Focus

Autobiography

An **autobiography** is a person's written account of his or her own life, focusing on the events the author considers most significant. Because the writer's life is presented as he or she views it, the portrayal of people and events is colored by the author's feelings and beliefs. In fact, some of the writer's attitudes and beliefs may be directly stated. Usually, the writers of autobiographies believe that their lives are interesting or important or can in some way serve as examples for others. Frederick Douglass, for instance, wrote his autobiography because he believed that his life proved that blacks were no less perceptive, intelligent, and capable than whites.

◆ Grammar and Style

Correlative Conjunctions

Douglass writes of Mrs. Auld that "the good lady had *not only* ceased to instruct me, herself, *but* had set her face as a flint against my learning to read by any means." The italicized words in the passage are **correlative conjunctions**—pairs of connecting words that link ideas. The words *not only* and *but* show the relationship between the two actions in the sentence. Here are some common correlative conjunctions, which are usually used in pairs.

either . . . or   *neither . . . nor*   *whether . . . or*
not only . . . but (also)   *just as . . . so*

◆ Reading Strategy

Establish a Purpose

Establishing a purpose for reading helps you get more from a work by giving you an idea or a concept on which to focus. Read this section from Douglass's autobiography with the purpose of learning about the author's special qualities and expanding your understanding of what it was like to be a slave. Record appropriate details in a chart like this one.

Douglass's Character Traits	Details About Slavery

◆ Build Vocabulary

Latin Roots: *-bene-*

Frederick Douglass describes his owner, Mrs. Auld, as a *benevolent* woman. The Latin root *-bene-* means "well" or "good." Other words containing this root—*benefit, benediction,* and *benefactor*—all relate in some way to the concept of goodness.

Word Bank

Preview this list of words from *My Bondage and My Freedom.*

congenial
benevolent
stringency
depravity
consternation
redolent

Interest Grabber Engage students' interest by sharing one of Douglass's paradoxes—that both slaves and slaveholders were victims of slavery. Have students react to this idea. How can slaveholders be perceived as victims of slavery? Have students speculate about what evidence Douglass might offer to support his point. Then have them read the selection to find out. When they've finished reading, have a follow-up discussion in which students explain whether their views were in any way changed by Douglass's writing.

Customize for *Less Proficient Readers*
Douglass makes frequent use of long sentences that may pose a challenge for less proficient readers. Help these students to break down the long sentences by identifying the core of each sentence—the subject and the verb—then looking at how the other groups of words in the sentence relate to the subject and verb.

Customize for *AP Students*
To better appreciate the impact of this autobiography, students can read a portion of a biography of Douglass, such as the one by William S. McFeely, to compare and contrast its retelling of the events described in this excerpt with Douglass's presentation.

Customize for *English Language Learners*
Help students use context clues and a dictionary to decode the meanings of familiar words such as *marked, checked,* and *waxed,* used here in less familiar ways.

Customize for *Interpersonal Learners*
Douglass wrote that his mistress was a "most kind and tenderhearted woman. . . ." Have students discuss whether it was indeed possible for a slave owner to have been a "good" person or, more broadly, whether it is possible for a "good" person to do "bad" things.

Test Preparation Workshop

Reading Comprehension: Context Many standardized tests require students to use context to determine the appropriate meaning of a multiple-meaning word. Use the following sample test item to give students practice in this skill.

> I was compelled to resort to indirections by no means congenial to my nature, and which were really humiliating to me.

In this passage, congenial most nearly means—

A friendly
B sympathetic
C kindred
D suited

The word *humiliating* gives a context that the indirections are not suited to the speaker's nature or temperament. Although the other choices are also definitions of *congenial,* D is the appropriate meaning in the context of this passage.

Develop Understanding

One-Minute Insight In this excerpt from his second autobiography, Douglass tries to show that slavery corrupted, dehumanized, and victimized everyone—including slaveholders. The passage describes how his master's kind wife, Mrs. Auld, feels compelled to abandon her efforts to educate young Frederick. Convinced by her husband that slavery and education are incompatible, she attempts to block any learning opportunities for the young boy—even though such hard-heartedness goes against her nature. Douglass continues to learn from his white playmates, trading biscuits for lessons. Influenced by the ideas to which he is exposed through his reading, Douglass becomes consumed by his constant yearning for freedom and thoughts about the oppression of slavery. He grows to hate the institution of slavery, which has made enemies of him and his mistress, who might otherwise have been friends.

Read to Be Informed

Point out to students that being informed is one of the basic purposes of reading. When Mrs. Auld tried to prevent Frederick Douglass from learning to read, he likened it to being shut up "in mental darkness." These memoirs by Douglass are especially valuable for students learning about the crucial issues of slavery, race, and freedom in the nineteenth century. Douglass was not only articulate and passionate, but experienced both slavery and freedom during his life, giving him great perspective on these issues.

Literature CD-ROM Use *The History of American Literature:* Part 1, Disk 2, Feature 4, which contains a segment on Frederick Douglass, to introduce students to this influential author and abolitionist.

▶Critical Viewing◀

❶ **Interpret** Students may say that the light shining on this man reading in a dark chamber symbolizes the beacon of knowledge, an awakening of understanding, or a glimmer or hope.

from My Bondage *and* My Freedom

Frederick Douglass

The Chimney Corner, 1863, Eastman Johnson, Munson-Williams-Proctor Institute Museum of Art, Utica, New York

❶ ▶ **Critical Viewing** What is symbolized by the light shining on the reader? **[Interpret]**

❷ I lived in the family of Master Hugh, at Baltimore, seven years, during which time—as the almanac makers say of the weather—my condition was variable. The most interesting feature of my history here, was my learning to read and write, under somewhat marked disadvantages. In attaining this knowledge, I was compelled to resort

Block Scheduling Strategies

Consider these suggestions to take advantage of extended class time:

- Have students read the biography (p. 456) and Literature and Your Life sections (p. 457) and complete the Journal Writing activity. Encourage volunteers to share their responses.
- Pause to review the Critical Viewing questions as students read the selection. They can work in discussion groups to answer the Critical Thinking questions (p. 464).
- Use the Daily Language Practice sentences for Week 13 in the Teaching Resources and ***Writing and Language Transparencies*** (p. 120). Display the sentences on the transparency and have students correct them, or dictate the sentences.
- Assign an Idea Bank writing activity (p. 465), or use an activity from ***Alternative Assessment*** (p. 28) for students with varying learning modalities.

to indirections by no means congenial to my nature, and which were really humiliating to me. My mistress—who had begun to teach
3 me—was suddenly checked in her benevolent design, by the strong advice of her husband. In faithful compliance with this advice, the good lady had not only ceased to instruct me, herself, but had set her face as a flint against my learning to read by any means. It is due, however, to my mistress to say, that she did not adopt this course in all its stringency at the first. She either thought it unnecessary, or she lacked the depravity indispensable to shutting me up in mental darkness. It was, at least, necessary for her to have some training, and some hardening, in the exercise of the slaveholder's prerogative, to make her equal to forgetting my human nature and character, and
4 to treating me as a thing destitute of a moral or an intellectual nature. Mrs. Auld—my mistress—was, as I have said, a most kind and tenderhearted woman; and, in the humanity of her heart, and the simplicity of her mind, she set out, when I first went to live with her, to treat me as she supposed one human being ought to treat another.

It is easy to see, that, in entering upon the duties of a slaveholder, some little experience is needed. Nature has done almost nothing to prepare men and women to be either slaves or
5 slaveholders. Nothing but rigid training, long persisted in, can perfect the character of the one or the other. One cannot easily forget to love freedom; and it is as hard to cease to respect that natural love in our fellow creatures. On entering upon the career of a slaveholding mistress, Mrs. Auld was singularly deficient; nature, which fits nobody for such an office, had done less for her than any lady I had known. It was no easy matter to induce her to think and to feel that the curly-headed boy, who stood by her side, and even leaned on her lap; who was loved by little Tommy, and who loved little Tommy in turn; sustained to her only the relation of a chattel. I was *more* than that, and she felt me to be more than that. I could talk and sing; I could laugh and weep; I could reason and remember; I could love and 6
hate. I was human, and she, dear lady, knew and felt me to be so. How could she, then, treat me as a brute, without a mighty struggle with all the noble powers of her own soul. That struggle came, and the will and power of the husband was victorious. Her noble soul was overthrown; but, he that overthrew it did not, himself, escape the consequences. He, not less than the other parties, was injured in his domestic peace by the fall.

When I went into their family, it was the abode of happiness and contentment. The mistress of the house was a model of affection and tenderness. Her fervent piety and watchful uprightness made it impossible to see her without thinking and feeling—"that woman is a Christian." There was no sorrow nor suffering for which she had not a tear, and there was no innocent joy for which she did not a smile. She had bread for the hungry, clothes for the naked, and comfort for every mourner that came within her reach. Slavery soon proved its ability to divest her of these excellent qualities, and her home of its early happiness. Conscience cannot stand

◆ Literary Focus
Douglass blames slavery, rather than Mrs. Auld, for the changes that take place in the household. What does this tell you about him? 7

◆ Build Vocabulary

congenial (kən jēn´ yəl) *adj.*: Agreeable
benevolent (bə nev´ ə lənt) *adj.*: Kindly; charitable
stringency (strin´ jən sē) *n.*: Strictness; severity
depravity (di prav´ ə tē) *n.*: Corruption; wickedness

Humanities: Art

The Chimney Corner, 1863, by Eastman Johnson.

Eastman Johnson (1824–1906) was the son of a wealthy Maine politician. He studied art in Germany, Holland, and France, and returned to the United States well-trained in genre painting. He painted portraits of some of the most notable Americans of his time, including John Quincy Adams and Henry Wadsworth Longfellow. During the Civil War, he used his talents to record events.

Use these questions for discussion:

1. Do you think this man is a slave? Explain. *Students may say that since the painting dates from 1863, the man may be a slave who, by the look of his clothing, works in the house. Perhaps he has found a moment of privacy in a remote part of the house to sneak a few moments of reading. If he is not a slave, he is probably a house servant who was not discouraged from reading.*
2. How would you describe the mood of the painting? *Students may say that the dark, uncomfortable corner provides a sense of calm and tranquility as the man is quietly engrossed in his reading, despite the meanness of his surroundings.*

❷ **Clarification** Frederick Bailey was born on the Eastern Shore, on land facing west toward Chesapeake Bay. His first owner was Aaron Anthony, who worked for the wealthy planter Edward Lloyd. Before his years with Sophie and Hugh Auld in Baltimore, Frederick lived on Lloyd's plantation. At fifteen, Douglass was sent by Hugh Auld to St. Michaels on the Eastern Shore to work for Thomas Auld. There, he was hired out as a laborer to a number of farmers, and there he first attempted to escape his bondage. At twenty-one he took the name Douglass.

◆ Build Vocabulary

❸ **Latin Roots: *-bene-*** Have students discuss how knowing the word root *-bene-* can help them understand this sentence—even if they are unfamiliar with the word *benevolent.* *Students should point out that simply by substituting the word* good *for* benevolent *they can understand the sentence.*

◆ Reading Strategy

❹ **Set a Purpose** Discuss with students what Douglass is expressing about slave owners in general and his mistress in particular. Guide them to see that he says that the wickedness and corruption required of slave owners needs to be taught, particularly if a person is tenderhearted. Douglass states that it is not natural to deprive one of human dignity, that that kind of cruelty requires training.

◆ Literary Focus

❺ **Autobiography** Discuss Douglass's point about slavery: it is as unnatural to be a slaveholder as it is to be a slave; just as it is natural to want the right of freedom, it is unnatural to deny that right to others.

❻ **Clarification** Help students put this remarkable statement into historical perspective. In 1825, many whites in the North and in the South, in their ignorance, did not believe that blacks were human. Through her experience with Frederick, Mrs. Auld learned the truth.

◆ Literary Focus

❼ **Autobiography** Students may respond that Douglass essentially had a positive view of human nature. They may say that he blamed the institution of slavery rather than individuals for its evils.

Customize for
Visual/Spatial Learners
Have these students use the painting on this page to help them picture the story's setting in their mind. Ask: What does the painting reveal about the lives of plantation owners? *The painting reveals that the plantation owners were wealthy and enjoyed personal luxuries, including large, beautiful homes.*

▶Critical Viewing◀

❶ **Contrast** Suggested response: The painting suggests that plantation owners lived lives of luxury that contrasted sharply with the experiences of the slaves.

◆ Literary Focus

❷ **Autobiography** Guide students to appreciate Douglass's views on the intrinsic right of an individual to acquire knowledge and on the negative effects of denying a person that right. Invite students to discuss why the Aulds' decision regarding his education placed them in a "condition" Douglass viewed as worse than his own. *Many students will probably disagree with Douglass's point of view, pointing out that while the Aulds may have had repressed feelings of guilt, they had the advantages of education, freedom, and material possessions.*

◆ Build Vocabulary

❸ **Latin Root: *-bene-*** Students can use their understanding of the meaning of *-bene-* to figure out that *benevolence* in this context means "the disposition to do good." Douglass believed that by "arresting the benevolence that would have enlightened my young mind," the Aulds went against nature and suffered as a result.

A Home on the Mississippi, Currier & Ives, The Museum of the City of New York

❶ ▲ Critical Viewing How does this idealized picture of plantation life contrast with Douglass's experiences as an enslaved African American? **[Contrast]**

much violence. Once thoroughly broken down, *who* is he that can repair the damage? It may be broken toward the slave, on Sunday, and toward the master on Monday. It cannot endure such shocks. It must stand entire, or it does not stand at all. If my condition waxed bad, that of the family waxed not better. The first step, in the wrong direction, was the violence done to nature and to conscience, in arresting
❷ the benevolence that would have enlightened
❸ my young mind. In ceasing to instruct me, she must begin to justify herself *to* herself; and, once consenting to take sides in such a debate, she was riveted to her position. One needs very little knowledge of moral philosophy, to see *where* my mistress now landed. She finally be- ❷
came even more violent in her opposition to my ❸
learning to read, than was her husband himself. She was not satisfied with simply doing as *well* as her husband had commanded her, but seemed resolved to better his instruction. Nothing appeared to make my poor mistress—after her turning toward the downward path—more angry, than seeing me, seated in some nook or corner, quietly reading a book or a newspaper. I have had her rush at me, with the utmost fury, and snatch from my hand such newspaper or book, with something of the wrath

Humanities: Art

A Home on the Mississippi, 1871, by Currier and Ives.

Nathaniel Currier (1813–1888) and James Ives (1824–1895) started the firm of Currier and Ives in 1857 to commercially produce countless lithographic chronicles of nineteenth-century American life. Hand-colored scenes like this one were immensely popular with the American public. People obtained them by mail order, from traveling salespeople, and from the shop in New York City. A favorite Currier and Ives theme was the homes. *A Home on the Mississippi* was reproduced more than 3.5 billion times on the label of a popular beverage. The scene is filled with typical Southern atmosphere accentuated by the gracious verandah on the house and the Spanish moss hanging from the trees.

Use these questions for discussion:

1. What impression of Southern living does this print convey? *Students may say that it suggests a calm, genteel, leisurely lifestyle.*
2. Do you think this view of the South matches Frederick Douglass's? Explain. *Students may say that it does in that it shows the Southern gentry riding in elegant carriages while the slaves walk along the side of the road or stand outside the fences.*

and consternation which a traitor might be supposed to feel on being discovered in a plot by some dangerous spy.

Mrs. Auld was an apt woman, and the advice of her husband, and her own experience, soon demonstrated, to her entire satisfaction, that education and slavery are incompatible with each other. When this conviction was thoroughly established, I was most narrowly watched in all my movements. If I remained in a separate room from the family for any considerable length of time, I was sure to be suspected of having a book, and was at once called upon to give an account of myself. All this, however, was entirely *too late*. The first, and never to be retracted, step had been taken. In teaching me the alphabet, in the days of her
4 simplicity and kindness, my mistress had given me the "inch," and now, no ordinary precaution could prevent me from taking the "ell."[1]

Seized with a determination to learn to read, at any cost, I hit upon many expedients to accomplish the desired end. The plea which I mainly adopted, and the one by which I was most successful, was that of using my young white playmates, with whom I met in the street, as teachers. I used to carry, almost constantly, a copy of Webster's spelling book in my pocket;
5 and, when sent on errands, or when play time was allowed me, I would step, with my young friends, aside, and take a lesson in spelling. I generally paid my *tuition fee* to the boys, with bread, which I also carried in my pocket. For a single biscuit, any of my hungry little comrades would give me a lesson more valuable to me than bread. Not everyone, however, demanded this consideration, for there were those who took pleasure in teaching me, whenever I had a chance to be taught by them. I am strongly tempted to give the names of two or three of
those little boys, as a slight testimonial of the 5
gratitude and affection

I bear them, but prudence forbids; not that it
would injure me, but it might, possibly, embar- 6
rass them; for it is almost an unpardonable offense to do anything, directly or indirectly, to promote a slave's freedom, in a slave state. It is enough to say, of my warm-hearted little play fellows, that they lived on Philpot Street, very near Durgin & Bailey's shipyard.

Although slavery was a delicate subject, and very cautiously talked about among grownup people in Maryland, I frequently talked about it—and that very freely—with the white boys. I would, sometimes, say to them, while seated on a curbstone or a cellar door, "I wish I could be free, as you will be when you get to be men." "You will be free, you know, as soon as you are twenty-one, and can go where you like, but I
am a slave for life. Have I not as good a right to 7
be free as you have?" Words like these, I observed, always troubled them; and I had no 8
small satisfaction in wringing from the boys, occasionally, that fresh and bitter condemnation of slavery, that springs from nature, unseared and unperverted.[2] Of all consciences let me have those to deal with which have not been bewildered by the cares of life. I do not remember ever to have met with a *boy*, while I was in slavery, who defended the slave system; but I have often had boys to console me, with the hope that something would yet occur, by

1. **ell** *n.*: Former English measure of length, equal to forty-five inches.

2. **unperverted** (un′ pər vurt′ id) *adj.*: Uncorrupted; pure.

◆ Build Vocabulary

consternation (kän′ stər nā′ shən) *n.*: Great fear or shock that makes one feel helpless or bewildered

Cultural Connection

Slavery in History Slavery neither began nor ended with Southern plantation owners. In existence since ancient times, slavery originated with conquest; it was the fate that awaited the conquered. Slave markets existed by the time of the first Babylonian empire, more than three thousand years ago. Sadly, slavery continues to exist in parts of the world even today.

Students have read about one slave's reaction to his circumstances. Invite them to look into how some others have responded. They might, for instance, obtain a copy of a Haggadah (the narrative of the Exodus from Egypt that is read every year at the Jewish festival of Passover) to read about what the slave Nachshon did to get his freedom. Or, they can research one of the several slave revolts in America; in particular, they can find out about the only sustained revolt in American history, the 1831 rebellion led by Nat Turner.

◆ Critical Thinking

4 Interpret/Support Invite students to explain the meaning of the expression, "Give [him] an inch and [he'll] take a mile," and to support their definitions with examples. Then point out that this saying summarizes Mr. Auld's fear regarding the potential results of Douglass's education. Auld once said that if Frederick learned to read ". . . there would be no keeping him. . . . If you learn him how to read, he'll want to know how to write; and this accomplished, he'll be running away with himself."

◆ Literary Focus

5 Autobiography Here, after illustrating the incompatibility of education and slavery, Douglass emphasizes his own strong desire to educate himself. Guide students to appreciate his efforts to continue on the road to knowledge in spite of the obstacles the Aulds placed in his path.

◆ Grammar and Style

6 Correlative Conjunctions Guide students to recognize that Douglass uses the correlative conjunctions *not that . . . but* to show the relationship between his gratitude toward the boys for helping in his education, and his reluctance to embarrass them for it.

◆ Literary Focus

7 Autobiography Have students summarize the view of slavery that Douglass presents here. *Students may say that here he points out that even children can see the perversity of slavery, that in their innocence, they have not yet adopted the attitudes of slaveholders.*

8 Enrichment Remind students that Maryland was not one of the states that seceded from the United States to join the Confederacy. Point out that although slavery was present in Maryland, it was not as prevalent as it was in the states of the deep South.

Customize for
Less Proficient Readers

❶ In this long paragraph, Douglass presents one of the key ideas of this selection: that reading the *Columbian Orator* caused him to develop an overpowering desire for freedom. This point is made toward the middle of the paragraph, and it is restated and reinforced in the sentences that follow. Guide less proficient readers in identifying the main idea and noting the ways in which Douglass develops and supports it.

◆ Literary Focus

❷ **Autobiography** Students may say that reading this book unequivocally led Douglass to recognize his plight and awakened in him a strong, continual desire for liberty.

◆ Literary Focus

❸ **Autobiography** Guide students to appreciate the extent of Douglass's torment at this turning point in his life: he has gained a fuller understanding of the incompatibility between his desires and his predicament.

Customize for
English Language Learners

❹ Clarify the meaning of the term *Nature* for students, by pointing out that here it means "human nature," the qualities all human beings share.

which I might be made free. Over and over again, they have told me, that "they believed *I* had as good a right to be free as *they* had"; and that "they did not believe God ever made any-one to be a slave." The reader will easily see, that such little conversations with my play fellows, had no tendency to weaken my love of liberty, nor to render me contented with my condition as a slave.

❶ When I was about thirteen years old, and had succeeded in learning to read, every increase of knowledge, especially respecting the free states, added something to the almost intolerable burden of the thought—"I am a slave for life." To my bondage I saw no end. It was a terrible reality, and I shall never be able to tell how sadly that thought chafed my young spirit. Fortunately, or unfortunately, about this time in my life, I had made enough money to buy what was then a very popular schoolbook, the *Columbian Orator.* I bought this addition to my library, of Mr. Knight, on Thames street, Fell's Point, Baltimore, and paid him fifty cents for it. I was first led to buy this book, by hearing some little boys say they were going to learn some little pieces out of it for the Exhibition.This volume was, indeed, a rich treasure, and every opportunity afforded me, for a time, was spent in diligently perusing it . . . The dialogue and the speeches were all redolent of the principles of liberty, and poured floods of light on the nature and character of slavery. As I read, behold! the very discontent so graphically predicted by Master Hugh, had already come upon me. I was no longer the light-hearted, gleesome boy, full of mirth and play, as when I landed first at Baltimore. Knowledge had come . . . This knowledge opened my eyes to the horrible pit, and revealed the teeth of the frightful dragon that was ready to pounce upon me, but it opened no way for my escape. I have often wished myself a beast, or a bird—anything, rather than a slave. I was wretched and gloomy, beyond my ability to describe. I was too thoughtful to be happy. It was this everlasting thinking which distressed and tormented me; and yet there was no getting rid of the subject of my thoughts. All nature was redolent of it. Once awakened by the silver trump[3] of knowledge, ❷
my spirit was roused to eternal wakefulness. ❸
Liberty! the inestimable birthright of every man, had, for me, converted every object into an asserter of this great right. It was heard in every sound, and beheld in every object. It was ever present, to torment me with a sense of my wretched condition. The more beautiful and charming were the smiles of nature, the more horrible and desolate was my condition. I saw nothing without seeing it, and I heard nothing without hearing it. I do not exaggerate, when I say, that it looked from every star, smiled in every calm, breathed in every wind, and moved in every storm.

◆ Literary Focus
How does reading this book become a turning point in Douglass's life?

I have no doubt that my state of mind had something to do with the change in the treatment adopted, by my once kind mistress toward me. I can easily believe, that my leaden, downcast, and discontented look, was very offensive to her. Poor lady! She did not know my

◆ Build Vocabulary
redolent (red´ əl ənt) *adj.*: Suggestive

3. **trump:** Trumpet.

Speaking, Listening, and Viewing Mini-Lesson

Dramatic Dialogue
This mini-lesson supports the Speaking, Listening, and Viewing activity in the Idea Bank on p. 465.

Introduce the Concept Review with students the nature of the interaction between Douglass and his young friends, and the ways in which he learned from them.

Develop Background To prepare for the dialogue, students should find out more about Douglass's views on issues other than slavery. Remind them that he became a figure of national prominence who spoke up passionately and eloquently on major social issues. Students should establish what his ideas were on black soldiers, on equality and citizenship for black Americans, and on women's rights. Have students agree on what views on social issues Douglass's friends might have had as adults. Remind them that Maryland, although it had its share of Southern sympathizers, was not part of the Confederacy.

Apply the Information Have students write, practice, and then perform the dialogues for the class. You may wish to have "Douglass" talk about issues with *more* than one former friend, each of whom can present a point of view that differs from Douglass's.

Assess the Outcome Ask the audience to assess whether the portrayals accurately represent the views Douglass and his friends were likely to have held.

trouble, and I dared not tell her. Could I have freely made her acquainted with the real state of my mind, and given her the reasons therefor, it might have been well for both of us. Her abuse of me fell upon me like the blows of the false prophet upon his ass; she did not know that an *angel* stood in the way;[4] and—such is the relation of master and slave—I could not
4 tell her. Nature had made us *friends*; slavery made us *enemies*. My interests were in a direction opposite to hers, and we both had our private thoughts and plans. She aimed to keep me ignorant; and I resolved to know, although knowledge only increased my discontent. My feelings were not the result of any marked cruelty in the treatment I received; they sprung from the consideration of my being a slave at all. It was *slavery*—not its mere *incidents*—that I hated. I had been cheated. I saw through the attempt to keep me in ignorance . . . The feeding and clothing me well, could not atone for taking my liberty from me. The smiles of my mistress could not remove the deep sorrow that dwelt in my young bosom. Indeed, these, in time, came only to deepen my sorrow. She had changed; and the reader will see that I had changed, too. We were both victims to the same overshadowing evil—*she*, as mistress, *I*, as slave. I will not censure her harshly; she cannot censure me, for she knows I speak but the truth, and have acted in my opposition to slavery, just as she herself would have acted, in a reverse of circumstances.

◆ Reading Strategy Reread this final paragraph and explain why Douglass doesn't blame Mrs. Auld for the way she treated him. 5

4. **blows . . . the way:** Allusion to a biblical tale (Numbers 22: 21–35) about an ass that cannot move, though she is beaten by her master, because her path is blocked by an angel.

Guide for Responding

◆ Literature and Your Life

Reader's Response Do you think it is possible to be a benevolent slaveholder? Why or why not?

Thematic Focus How does slavery make victims of both slaves and slaveholders?

Group Poll Conduct a quick poll to determine whether fellow students agree or disagree that slavery and education are incompatible. Prompt respondents with opposing viewpoints to explain their reasoning.

☑ Check Your Comprehension

1. Why does Douglass live with the Auld family?
2. How does he learn to read?
3. Describe the changes in Mrs. Auld's behavior toward young Douglass.
4. What is responsible for his transformation from a "light-hearted" boy to a "wretched and gloomy" one?
5. What is it that Douglass says "looked from every star, smiled in every calm, breathed in every wind, and moved in every storm"?

◆ Reading Strategy

5 **Set a Purpose** Students may respond that Douglass blames not individuals, but rather the institution of slavery, for the suffering of the slaves and the actions of the slaveholders.

Reinforce and Extend

◆ Critical Thinking

Extend Douglass sings the praises of education and stresses the value of learning. To introduce students to a profession in education, use the Career Connection: Teaching page in ***Beyond Literature*** (p. 28).

Customize for
AP Students
Students may enjoy reading Douglass's first autobiography, *Narrative of the Life of Frederick Douglass*. Invite them to compare its version of the Baltimore years with Douglass's description of that period here.

Answers

◆ Literature and Your Life

Reader's Response Students should offer solid reasons to back up their point of view.

Thematic Focus Possible response: Slaves suffer from a lack of freedom; slaveholders are forced to go against their nature.

☑ Check Your Comprehension

1. He is enslaved by them.
2. He is first taught by Mrs. Auld and later by young white playmates.
3. After her husband insisted that she stop teaching him, Mrs. Auld became outraged whenever she saw Frederick with a book.
4. He read a book about liberty and realized that he could no longer live without it.
5. Liberty was everywhere.

Beyond the Selection

FURTHER READING

Other Works by Frederick Douglass

Narrative of the Life of Frederick Douglass, an American Slave, Written By Himself, 1845

"Speech at the Civil Rights Mass Meeting," 1883, Washington, DC

Other Works About Frederick Douglass

Frederick Douglass, William S. McFeely

Frederick Douglass, A Biography, Philip S. Foner

We suggest that you preview these works before recommending them to students.

INTERNET

To learn more, you and your students can visit the following Web pages. Please be aware that sites may have changed since this information was published.

To read his autobiography, go to **http://downwithopp.com/lit/douglass**

Learn about the Frederick Douglass National Historic Site, at **http://www.nps.gov/frdo/freddoug.html**

We *strongly recommend* that you preview the sites before you send students to them.

Guide for Responding (continued)

◆ Critical Thinking

INTERPRET

1. How does Douglass's experience prove his mistress's belief that education and slavery are incompatible? **[Support]**

2. Why do you think that the white children's attitude toward slavery is different from that of their parents? **[Analyze]**

EVALUATE

3. How effectively does Douglass support his view that slaveholders, as well as slaves, are victims of slavery? Explain. **[Assess]**

APPLY

4. Mahatma Gandhi wrote, "The moment the slave resolves that he will no longer be a slave, his fetters fall." Based on the selection, explain whether or not you feel Douglass was free even while in bondage. **[Apply]**

◆ Reading Strategy

ESTABLISH A PURPOSE FOR READING

Before you read from *My Bondage and My Freedom*, you **established the purpose** of learning more about Douglass's special qualities and expanding your understanding of slavery.

1. Which of Douglass's special qualities are conveyed through this section of his autobiography? Explain.

2. How did reading this section add to your understanding of the effects of slavery?

◆ Literary Focus

AUTOBIOGRAPHY

The portrayal of people and events in an **autobiography** is colored by the author's personal feelings, views, and purpose in writing. Douglass intended that his autobiography be both an inspiration to others and a condemnation of slavery.

1. How do the tone and style of this selection support Douglass's desire to serve as a model?

2. Douglass is well cared for as a slave. How, then, does he go about making his case against slavery?

3. How do you think this account would be different if it had been written by Mrs. Auld?

◆ Build Vocabulary

USING THE LATIN ROOT ***-bene-***

Define each of the following words, incorporating the meaning of the Latin root *-bene-* ("well" or "good") into your definition. If necessary, use a dictionary for help.

1. benefit **2.** benefactor **3.** benediction

USING THE WORD BANK: Sentence Completions

Copy this passage into your notebook, filling the blanks with appropriate Word Bank words.

I could see my neighbor scowling with a look of __?__. Usually she wore a __?__ expression, so I knew something was wrong. Her yard was usually __?__ with the fragrance of roses, which she was __?__ enough to share with me. The bushes were cut down to the ground! I was stunned at the __?__ of the deed. I could understand the __?__ of her message as she tacked up a KEEP OUT sign.

◆ Grammar and Style

CORRELATIVE CONJUNCTIONS

Correlative conjunctions are used to connect similar kinds of words and word groups that are grammatically alike, such as the underlined words in this example.

Not only ***my body,*** *but also* ***my soul*** was bound by slavery.

Practice For each item, add a pair of correlative conjunctions from the italicized list to create a logical sentence.

either. . .or; neither. . .nor; whether. . .or; not only. . .but (also); just as. . .so

1. __?__ slave __?__ mistress was truly free.

2. __?__ Maryland __?__ Mississippi and Tennessee were slave states.

3. __?__ a slave __?__ a slaveholder, all people are harmed by slavery.

4. __?__ Douglass worked to abolish slavery, __?__ did the Grimké sisters and Sojourner Truth.

Writing Application Write an original sentence using each of the five pairs of correlative conjunctions listed in the previous activity.

Answers

◆ Critical Thinking

1. Through his education and reading, Douglass is exposed to ideas, such as the right to liberty, that make his slavery that much more unbearable for him. From the time he first begins to read on his own, he resolves to seek freedom.
2. They have not yet learned to be slaveholders.
3. Students should support their responses with details from the text.
4. Some students may observe that, in one sense, Douglass was free because he realized his self-worth. This awareness led him to seek actual freedom. Many other students will respond that Douglass was not free while still in bondage.

◆ Reading Strategy

1. Suggested response: It reveals his intelligence, his persistence, and ingenuity.
2. Students should support their answers with details from the text.

◆ Literary Focus

1. Douglass's straightforward yet eloquent telling of his life's story reflects his intelligence and his ability to understand human nature at its best and worst, without being judgmental. It illustrates that African Americans of Douglass's time were capable of achieving great things when given the opportunity.
2. He uses his relationship with his mistress as an example of the many ways in which slavery forces people to betray their natural tendencies: hers toward kindness, and his toward liberty.
3. Possible response: She would have denied any change in her personality and would have seen her actions as proper.

◆ Build Vocabulary

Using the Latin Root *-bene-*

1. a positive effect
2. someone who does good things for someone or something
3. a blessing

Using the Word Bank

consternation; congenial; redolent; benevolent; depravity; stringency

◆ Grammar and Style

Practice

1. neither . . . nor
2. not only . . . but also
3. whether . . . or
4. just as . . . so

Writing Application

Check to see that students have used correlative conjunctions in proper pairs.

Grammar Reinforcement

For additional instruction and practice use the page on conjunctions in the *Writer's Solution Grammar Practice Book*, p. 13.

Reteach

To reteach the definition of autobiography and to help students understand how it is similar to and different from other forms of writing, have groups of students create Venn diagrams or other types of charts in which they compare autobiography and one other literary form such as short story, biography, or poetry. Each group should compare a different literary form.

Build Your Portfolio

Idea Bank

Writing

1. Diary Entry Once Mrs. Auld was persuaded to prevent Douglass from reading, she took her position to extremes. Write a diary entry in which she justifies "herself *to* herself."

2. New Version Imagine that one of the boys who helped teach Douglass to read were to write his own life story. Tell the story of the reading lessons as they might appear in his autobiography.

3. Essay Slavery not only divided the nation; Douglass suggests that it also divided people from one another and from the better aspects of their own natures. Explore this idea in an essay, supported with examples from the selection.

Speaking, Listening, and Viewing

4. Dramatic Dialogue Imagine that one of the boys who helped teach Douglass to read were to meet him again years later. With a partner, prepare and perform a dialogue between the two men. **[Performing Arts Link]**

5. Oral Interpretation Select a passage from this selection or another of Douglass's writings and speeches. Present the excerpt as Douglass might have read it to an audience of abolitionist sympathizers. **[Social Studies Link]**

Researching and Representing

6. Interpretive Dance Create an interpretive dance that conveys Douglass's feelings about slavery. Select background music to accompany your dance. **[Performing Arts Link; Music Link]**

7. Graphic Display Using words and pictures from magazines, newspapers, photographs, and other sources, make a collage that expresses the importance of literacy. **[Art Link]**

Online Activity www.phlit.phschool.com

Guided Writing Lesson

College Admissions Essay

A college application often requires you to write about an experience that helped to make you the person you are today. Think about a key event from your life, and write an essay describing it and explaining how it affected you. Keep the following in mind as you develop your essay.

Writing Skills Focus: Clear and Logical Organization

A **clear and logical organization** will make your essay easy for your audience to follow. Start with a paragraph in which you introduce the experience you plan to describe, and explain why you're writing about it. Then write a series of body paragraphs describing the details of the experience in chronological order. Conclude with a paragraph that sums up the impact that the experience has had on you.

Prewriting Outline the details of the event, and describe how it affected you. You might use a chart similar to the following to organize your details.

Event:				
Who	What	Where	When	Effect It Had on Me

Drafting Using the details you've gathered, write a draft of your essay. Focus on using precise words that capture your experience as vividly as possible. Use transition words to connect your ideas.

Revising Ask a friend to read your essay aloud as you listen. Are your ideas related? Do they flow logically from one paragraph to the next? Is it clear how this event made you the person you are today?

Idea Bank

Customizing for *Performance Levels*

Following are suggestions for matching Idea Bank topics with your students' performance levels:
Less Advanced Students: 1, 4, 7
Average Students: 2, 5, 6
More Advanced Students: 3, 5

Customizing for *Learning Modalities*

Following are suggestions for matching Idea Bank topics with your students' learning modalities:
Interpersonal: 4
Musical/Rhythmic: 5, 6
Bodily/Kinesthetic: 6
Visual/Spatial: 7

Guided Writing Lesson

For more prewriting, elaboration, and revision, see *Prentice Hall Writing and Grammar.*

Writing and Language Transparencies Display the Cubing Transparency, p. 71, to help students analyze the effect of the experience they plan to write about in their essays.

Writing Lab CD-ROM
Have students work in the tutorial on Practical and Technical Writing to complete all or part of their essays. Follow these steps:

1. Have students complete an audience profile in the Considering Audience and Purpose section.
2. Encourage students to use the Cluster Diagram in the Gathering Details section to organize their ideas.
3. Have them draft on computer.
4. Direct students to use the Revision Checkers in the Revising and Editing section to help them revise.

✓ ASSESSMENT OPTIONS

Formal Assessment, Selection Test, pp. 135–137, and Assessment Resources Software. The selection test is designed so that it can be easily customized to the performance levels of your students.

Alternative Assessment, p. 28, includes options for less advanced students, more advanced students, verbal/linguistic learners, interpersonal learners, and musical/rhythmic learners.

PORTFOLIO ASSESSMENT
Use the following rubrics in the ***Alternative Assessment*** booklet to assess student writing:
Diary Entry: Expression Rubric, p. 109
New Version: Fictional Narrative Rubric, p. 110
Essay: Cause-Effect Rubric, p. 117
Guided Writing Lesson: Cause-Effect Rubric, p. 117

Prepare and Engage

LESSON OBJECTIVES

1. **To develop vocabulary and word identification skills**
   - Latin Word Roots: *-sum-*
   - Using the Word Bank: Context
   - Extending Word Study: Dictionary/Glossary (ATE)
2. **To use a variety of reading strategies to comprehend nonfiction**
   - Connect Your Experience
   - Reading Strategy: Chronological Order
   - Tips to Guide Reading (ATE)
3. **To increase knowledge of other cultures and to connect common elements across cultures**
   - Connecting Themes Across Cultures (ATE)
   - Cultural Connection (ATE)
4. **To express and support responses to the text**
   - Critical Thinking
   - Idea Bank: Spoken Review
   - Speaking, Listening, and Viewing Mini-Lesson (ATE)
   - Analyze Literary Criticism (ATE)
5. **To analyze literary elements**
   - Literary Focus: Point of View
   - Viewing and Representing Mini-Lesson (ATE)
   - Idea Bank: Critical Essay
6. **To read in order to research self-selected and assigned topics**
   - Idea Bank: Oral Presentation
   - Idea Bank: Museum Exhibit
   - Research Skills Mini-Lesson (ATE)
7. **To plan, prepare, organize, and present literary interpretations**
   - Idea Bank: Farewell Letter
   - Idea Bank: Prequel
8. **To use recursive writing processes to write a fictional news article**
   - Guided Writing Lesson
9. **To increase knowledge of the rules of grammar and usage**
   - Grammar and Style: Semicolons in Compound Sentences

Test Preparation

Reading Comprehension: Using Context (ATE, p. 467)
The teaching tips and sample test item in this workshop support the instruction and practice in the unit workshop:
Reading Comprehension: Using Context (SE, p. 631)

Guide for Interpreting

Ambrose Bierce *(1842–1914?)*

Ambrose Bierce's writing and philosophy of life were shaped by his career as a Union officer in the Civil War. The poverty in which he was raised fostered Bierce's unsentimental, pessimistic view of the world; the brutality he saw during the war cemented his cynicism.

Writing that harped on themes of cruelty and death earned Ambrose Bierce the nickname "Bitter Bierce."

A Civil War Soldier Bierce was born in Ohio and raised on a farm in Indiana. Having educated himself by reading his father's books, he left the farm while in his teens to attend a military academy in Kentucky. When the Civil War broke out, he enlisted in the Union army. He fought in several important battles, rose from private to major, and won many awards for bravery. Toward the end of the war, he was seriously wounded, but he returned to battle a few months later.

Poisoned Pen After the war, Bierce settled in San Francisco as a journalist. His column, the "Prattler," which appeared in *The Argonaut* (1877–1879), the *Wasp* (1880–1886), and the *San Francisco Sunday Examiner* (1887–1896), mixed political and social satire, literary reviews, and gossip. The broodingly handsome writer was dubbed "the wickedest man in San Francisco" for his cynical and often malicious commentary. Though his journalistic barbs angered many key political and business figures, Bierce's dark reputation only added to his personal popularity. He was a magnetic figure who charmed those around him despite the malice of his words.

Though Bierce published many of his finest short stories in his column, he decided in the early 1890's to publish his collected short stories in two volumes, entitled *Tales of Soldiers and Civilians* (1891) and *Can Such Things Be?* (1893). The concise, carefully plotted stories in these collections, set for the most part during the Civil War, capture the cruelty and futility of war and the indifference of death. His pessimism is also reflected in *The Devil's Dictionary* (1906), a book of humorous and cynical definitions.

The Perfect Cynic Writer George Sterling wrote of Bierce, his longtime friend, that he "never troubled to conceal his justifiable contempt of humanity. . . . Bierce was a 'perfectionist,' a quality that in his case led to an intolerance involving merciless cruelty. He demanded in all others, men or women, the same ethical virtues that he found essential to his own manner of life. . . . To deviate from his point of view, indeed, to disagree with him even in slight particulars, was the unpardonable sin."

Though professionally successful, Bierce found little happiness in a world where so few people met his expectations. His marriage ended in divorce, and both of his sons died at an early age. In 1913, at age 71, the lonely writer traveled to Mexico, a country in the midst of a bloody civil war. To this day, his fate is unknown.

◆ Background for Understanding

HISTORY: THE CIVIL WAR

The senseless violence, death, and destruction Ambrose Bierce witnessed during the American Civil War (1861–1865) convinced him that war was terrible and futile. He set much of his best fiction, including this story, against the backdrop of this divisive war in which the agricultural South, whose economy was based on slavery, battled the more industrialized North. Fought mostly in the South, the war caused hundreds of thousands of casualties on both sides. Yet because the North had more than twice the amount of railroad track, more than twice the population, and five times as many factories, many have argued that the North's victory was assured from the beginning.

Prentice Hall Literature Program Resources

REINFORCE / RETEACH / EXTEND

Selection Support Worksheets
Build Vocabulary: Word Roots: *-sum-*, p. 136
Grammar and Style: Semicolons, p. 137
Reading Strategy: Sequence of Events, p. 138
Literary Focus: Point of View, p. 139

Strategies for Diverse Student Needs, p. 29

Beyond Literature
Community Connection: The Legal System, p. 29

Formal Assessment Selection Test, pp. 138–140; Assessment Resources Software

Alternative Assessment, p. 29

Writing and Language Transparencies
Branching Organizer, pp. 67–69

Resource Pro CD-ROM

Listening to Literature Audiocassettes

An Occurrence at Owl Creek Bridge

◆ Literature and Your Life

Connect Your Experience

"All's fair in love and war." This phrase has been used to excuse everything from trivial lies to wide-scale atrocities. Though you've heard the words countless times, you've probably never given them much thought. Do you think that there are times when the rules of the game are no rules at all? How do you define those times?

Journal Writing In a journal entry, write about an experience from literature or your own life where the phrase "all's fair in love and war" might explain or justify certain actions.

Thematic Focus: A Nation Divided

In "An Occurrence at Owl Creek Bridge," a civilian who believes that all's fair in love and war finds himself in a life-threatening situation. Does war justify actions that would be deemed unfair in times of peace?

◆ Build Vocabulary

Latin Word Roots: *-sum-*

You may not know what it means to be "*summarily* hanged." You do know, however, that *summary* suggests a brief, general idea. Likewise, *summarily* describes an action taken hastily or promptly, without attention to detail. These words derive from the Latin root *-sum-* or *-summ-*, meaning "highest," as in a *summary* of high points or the *summit*, or peak, of a mountain.

Word Bank

Preview this list of words from the story.

- etiquette
- deference
- imperious
- dictum
- summarily
- effaced
- oscillation
- apprised
- malign
- ineffable

◆ Grammar and Style

Semicolons in Compound Sentences

Bierce frequently forms **compound sentences** by linking independent clauses—clauses that can stand alone as sentences—with a **semicolon** rather than a conjunction. This style emphasizes the connection between the ideas in the clauses. Look at this example:

They hurt his ear like the thrust of a knife; he feared he would shriek.

The pattern of short clauses creates a rhythm of gunfire, shooting out facts and eliminating excess descriptions.

◆ Literary Focus

Point of View

In "An Occurrence at Owl Creek Bridge," Bierce uses his main character's warped perception of time to distort reality. The way that you perceive time in a story may depend on the **point of view**—or vantage point from which it is told. In stories told from an objective point of view, you follow the action without understanding each character's thoughts about the events. In stories told from the third-person limited point of view, the narrator relates the inner thoughts and feelings of one character. In this story, Bierce uses both an objective and a third-person limited point of view. As he shifts from one to the other, the emotional tone and sense of time may change as well.

◆ Reading Strategy

Chronological Order

In many stories, including Bierce's, events are not presented in the order in which they occurred. Instead, the action jumps backward or forward in time. As you read, you have to reorder events. This process will help you see the true **chronological order.** Pay attention to the order and time duration of events in this story. To help you, create a timeline of story events, and note the amount of time you estimate each event takes.

Test Preparation Workshop

Reading Comprehension:
Context Many standardized tests ask students to determine the meaning of words in a variety of texts. Use the following sample item to teach students how to use context clues to determine the meanings of specialized terms.

> The two private soldiers stepped aside and each drew away the plank upon which he had been standing. The sergeant turned to the captain, saluted and placed himself immediately behind that officer.

Which order shows the soldiers ranked from lowest to highest?

A captain, sergeant, private
B sergeant, private, captain
C private, sergeant, captain
D private, captain, sergeant

Encourage students to identify the interactions between the soldiers that indicate the ranks. The privates perform duties, the sergeant salutes the captain, and the captain is an officer. The correct answer is C.

Interest Grabber Play the opening scene of the video *An Occurrence at Owl Creek Bridge.* Pause the video after the noose is placed around the civilian's neck. Have students discuss possible reasons the man is in this situation. Then, tell students to read the story to discover the man's fate. For an alternative, see the Interest Grabber Video in the **Literary Focus and Reading Strategy Kit**.

Connecting Themes Across Cultures

Have students identify civil wars that have divided nations around the world in the past century, and the effects these wars have had on civilians.

Customize for *Less Proficient Readers*

The shifts in time in Bierce's story may prove to be a challenge for these students. To help them keep track of events, have them create a timeline in which they chart the events in the order in which they happened. Encourage them to be as specific as possible when noting the time at which each event occurs.

Customize for *AP Students*

Guide students to look for the contradictory descriptions Bierce carefully inserts to introduce a sense of uncertainty. For instance, they can note the different ways in which he describes time passed, movements, and sounds.

Customize for *English Language Learners*

Students may be unfamiliar with the terms used to identify the officers on the bridge. Inform them that according to the military chain of command, a *sergeant* would take orders from a *lieutenant* who, in turn, takes his orders from a *captain.* The sentinels were most likely *privates.*

Customize for *Body/Kinesthetic Learners*

Students may be better able to imagine what happens on the bridge if they act out the positions, stances, and actions of the soldiers standing by the condemned man.

Develop Understanding

One-Minute Insight Ambrose Bierce creates a compelling depiction of the Civil War hanging of a Southern planter who attempts an act of sabotage. Bierce explores the rapid movement of people's thoughts in the moments before death and the way in which people's sense of time can become distorted in certain situations. As the character, Peyton Farquhar, falls toward his death, he imagines that the rope has broken and set him free. Farquhar then imagines himself falling in the stream below, swimming to safety, and returning home. Unaware that the events are taking place in Farquhar's imagination, the reader is surprised by the story's abrupt ending, when Farquhar's thoughts suddenly stop, and Bierce describes Farquhar's dead body swinging "gently from side to side beneath the timbers of the Owl Creek bridge."

Tips to Guide Reading

Sustained Reading Suggest to students that while reading independently, they use sticky notes to mark any passages that have confusing ideas or vocabulary and continue reading. Reading further may clarify points. If not, students can use the sticky notes to return to these pages and ask questions during a class discussion.

Customize for
Less Proficient Readers
Help these students track the story's action with the Plot a Story Map page in ***Strategies for Diverse Student Needs*** (p. 29).

◆ Background for Understanding

❶ **History** In early April 1862, Union troops were headed toward Corinth—an Alabama town that was strategically important because two key railroads crossed at that point. On their journey, the Union soldiers collided with Confederate troops at the bloody battle of Shiloh, in Tennessee. Owl Creek is the stream that runs through the Shiloh Battlefield. Soon after Shiloh, a Federal army occupied and then defended Corinth. They held the town until it was no longer strategically important.

Connections to World Literature, *page 1176*

❶
An Occurrence at OWL CREEK BRIDGE

Ambrose Bierce

I

❷ A man stood upon a railroad bridge in northern Alabama, looking down into the swift water twenty feet below. The man's hands were behind his back, the wrists bound with a cord. A rope closely encircled his neck. It was attached to a stout cross timber above his head and the slack fell to the level of his knees. Some loose boards laid upon the sleepers supporting the metals of the railway supplied a footing for him and his executioners—two private soldiers of the Federal army, directed by a sergeant who in civil life may have been a deputy sheriff. At a short remove upon the same temporary platform was an officer in the uniform of his rank, armed. He was a captain. A sentinel at each end of the bridge stood with his rifle in the position known as "support," that is to say, vertical in front of the left shoulder, the hammer resting on the forearm thrown straight across the chest—a formal and unnatural position, enforcing an erect carriage of the body. It did not appear to be the duty of these two men to know what was occurring at the center of the bridge; they merely blockaded the two ends of the foot planking that traversed it.

❸ **◆ Literary Focus**
What clues allow you to identify the point of view from which this passage is told?

Beyond one of the sentinels nobody was in sight; the railroad ran straight away into a forest for a hundred yards, then, curving, was lost to view. Doubtless there was an outpost farther along. The other bank of the stream was open ground—a gentle acclivity[1] topped with a stockade of vertical tree trunks, loopholed for rifles, with a single embrasure through which protruded the muzzle of a brass cannon commanding the bridge. Midway of the slope between bridge and fort were the spectators—a single company of infantry in line, at "parade rest," the butts of the rifles on the ground, the barrels inclining slightly backward against the right shoulder, the hands crossed upon the stock. A lieutenant stood at the right of the line, the point of his sword upon the ground, his left hand resting upon his right. Excepting the

1. **acclivity** (ə kliv´ ə tē) *n.*: Upward slope.

Block Scheduling Strategies

Consider these suggestions to take advantage of extended class time:

- Because this story contains many difficult vocabulary words, you may want to have students complete the Build Vocabulary Practice Sheet (p. 136) in the ***Selection Support*** booklet prior to reading.
- Have students listen to all or part of the selection on audiocassette. Have them discuss where or whether they identify changes in the narrator's point of view. Does listening to the story add to their appreciation of it?
- Have students research the writings of Ambrose Bierce on the Internet either before or after they read.
- Have students work in discussion groups to answer the Critical Thinking questions (p. 475).
- Have students complete the Guided Writing Lesson (p. 477). Before they begin, have a class discussion on the correct tone to use when writing a news story. Have students browse through a newspaper or news magazine to find specific examples of objective tone.

group of four at the center of the bridge, not a man moved. The company faced the bridge, staring stonily, motionless. The sentinels, facing the banks of the stream, might have been statues to adorn the bridge. The captain stood with folded arms, silent, observing the work of his subordinates, but making no sign. Death is a dignitary who when he comes announced is to be received with formal manifestations of respect, even by those most familiar with him. In the code of military etiquette silence and fixity are forms of deference.

The man who was engaged in being hanged was apparently about thirty-five years of age. He was a civilian, if one might judge from his
❹ habit, which was that of a planter. His features were good—a straight nose, firm mouth,
❺ broad forehead, from which his long, dark hair was combed straight back, falling behind his ears to the collar of his well-fitting frock coat. He wore a mustache and pointed beard, but no whiskers; his eyes were large and dark gray, and had a kindly expression which one would hardly have expected in one whose neck was in the hemp. Evidently this was no vulgar assassin. The liberal military code makes provision for hanging many kinds of persons, and gentlemen are not excluded.

The preparations being complete, the two private soldiers stepped aside and each drew away the plank upon which he had been
❻ standing. The sergeant turned to the captain, saluted and placed himself immediately behind that officer, who in turn moved apart one pace. These movements left the condemned man and the sergeant standing on the two ends of the same plank, which spanned three of the crossties of the bridge. The end upon which the civilian stood almost, but not quite, reached a fourth. This plank had been held in ❻
place by the weight of the captain; it was now held by that of the sergeant. At a signal from the former the latter would step aside, the plank would tilt and the condemned man go down between two ties. The arrangement commended itself to his judgment as simple and effective. His face had not been covered nor his eyes bandaged. He looked a moment at his "unsteadfast footing," then let his gaze wander to the swirling water of the stream racing madly beneath his feet. A piece of dancing driftwood caught his attention and his eyes ❼
followed it down the current. How slowly it appeared to move! What a sluggish stream!

He closed his eyes in order to fix his last thoughts upon his wife and children. The water, touched to gold by the early sun, the brooding mists under the banks at some distance down the stream, the fort, the soldiers, the piece of drift—all had distracted him. And now he became conscious of a new

◆ Build Vocabulary

etiquette (et′ i kit) *n.*: Appropriate behavior and ceremonies

deference (def′ ər əns) *n.*: Respect; courtesy; regard

◆ Critical Thinking

❷ **Interpret** Ask students why Bierce may have chosen to conceal the identity of the condemned man. *Students may suggest that Bierce chose not to reveal the condemned man's identity to capture the cold, impersonal nature of executions during wartime.*

◆ Literary Focus

❸ **Point of View** Students may say that the narrator's detached, yet detailed description of the people on the bridge, indicates a third-person objective point of view.

◆ Critical Thinking

❹ **Analyze** Ask students: Why does Bierce personify death as a "dignitary"? *Students may suggest that Bierce personifies death to tie an abstract, distant concept to something that readers will find familiar.*

❺ **Clarification** During the Civil War, executions were always carried out according to strict military code. In that war, as in most others, civilian attempts at sabotage were treated harshly; the culprits were immediately hanged or shot. Saboteurs knew the extreme penalty for their deeds.

Customize for
Less Proficient Readers

❻ Students may need to reread this passage or act it out in order to understand the procedure for hanging the man.

Customize for
AP Students

❼ Students should note that Bierce describes the water as *swirling* and *racing,* and then as *sluggish*. These apparent contradictions hint that things may not be what they seem, that the man's perceptions may not be altogether reliable.

Viewing and Representing Mini-Lesson

This mini-lesson will extend students' appreciation of the narrative technique of the story by having them explore how a changing point of view might be represented on video.

Introduce the Concept Remind students that the point of view in the story shifts from objective to third person limited. Bierce highlights the difference by focusing on minute sensory details to show Farquhar's perceptions. In the objective point of view, he focuses on actions and events.

Develop Background Have students work in groups to identify the details they would use to show the changing viewpoint in a video version. Ask them also to consider different types of shots, such as close-ups, or panning across a scene.

Apply the Information Have students sketch a series of storyboards. Encourage them to include notes on the angle or depth of the shot.

Assess the Outcome Assess students' work on the number and accuracy of details from the story and effectiveness with which they show a change in viewpoint.

Extending Word Study

Dictionary/Glossary Have students use the Vocabulary Access Guide to find *ineffable*, which appears in this selection on p. 475 and on p. 101, in "Sinners in the Hands of an Angry God." Have students compare the usage and definition in this story and in the sermon. Then have students rewrite the sentences in which the words are used, supplying an appropriate synonym for each use.

◆ Literary Focus

❶ Point of View Students may point to the phrase *Now he became conscious* as a clear indication that the point of view has shifted to third-person limited. This shift allows the writer to introduce the man's thoughts and emotions.

◆ Critical Thinking

❷ Make Connections Guide students to notice the man's over-acute senses: A watch's ticking sounds to him like *the stroke of a blacksmith's hammer upon the anvil.* Ask students to explain what this tells them about him. *Students may not trust Farquhar's perceptions of things.* Ask them to compare the man's heightened awareness of sound with that of other characters in stories and poems in this textbook. *Students may recall the speaker in Emily Dickinson's poem "I heard a Fly Buzz—when I died—" or to Roderick's ability to hear his sister in "The Fall of the House of Usher."*

◆ Reading Strategy

❸ Sequence of Events Help students clarify the action of this passage. The captain has signaled the sergeant, who steps off the plank. With the sergeant's weight off it, the plank will tilt and consequently send the man tumbling to his death by hanging.

❹ Clarification In the Civil War, Confederate soldiers generally wore gray or brown uniforms. The Federal army uniform was blue.

Read to Interpret

Bierce is known for having a cynical, pessimistic view of the world. His short stories about the Civil War capture the cruelty and futility of the war. Help students identify these views in "An Occurrence at Owl Creek Bridge." Draw their attention to the unsentimental first section, in which Farquhar's fate is laid out. In the second section, readers discover Farquhar's daring plan, which has obviously failed, since he is to be hung from the very bridge he planned to destroy. In the third section, it at first appears that Farquhar escapes. Even in his apparent escape, however, he is carried along by a current, with no control over his own fate. In the end, it is revealed that Farquhar has in fact died futilely, having accomplished nothing.

> **◆ Literary Focus**
> What phrase indicates that the point of view has shifted from objective to third-person limited? Why?

❶ disturbance. Striking through the thought of his dear ones was a sound which he could neither ignore nor understand, a sharp, distinct, metallic percussion like the stroke of a blacksmith's hammer upon the anvil; it had the same ringing quality. He wondered what it was, and whether immeasurably distant or near by—it seemed both. Its recurrence was regular, but as slow as the tolling of a death knell. ❷ He awaited each stroke with impatience and—he knew not why—apprehension. The intervals of silence grew progressively longer; the delays became maddening. With their greater infrequency the sounds increased in strength and sharpness. They hurt his ear like the thrust of a knife; he feared he would shriek. What he heard was the ticking of his watch.

He unclosed his eyes and saw again the water below him. "If I could free my hands," he thought, "I might throw off the noose and spring into the stream. By diving I could evade the bullets and, swimming vigorously, reach the bank, take to the woods and get away home. My home, thank God, is as yet outside their lines; my wife and little ones are still beyond the invader's farthest advance."

As these thoughts, which have here to be set down in words, were flashed into the ❸ doomed man's brain rather than evolved from it the captain nodded to the sergeant. The sergeant stepped aside.

II

Peyton Farquhar was a well-to-do planter, of an old and highly respected Alabama family. Being a slave owner and like other slave owners a politician he was naturally an original secessionist and ardently devoted to the Southern cause. Circumstances of an imperious nature, which it is unnecessary to relate here, had prevented him from taking service with the gallant army that had fought the disastrous campaigns ending with the fall of Corinth,[2] and he chafed under the inglorious restraint, longing for the release of his energies, the larger life of the soldier, the opportunity for distinction. That opportunity, he felt, would come, as it comes to all in war time. Meanwhile he did what he could. No service was too humble for him to perform in aid of the South, no adventure too perilous for him to undertake if consistent with the character of a civilian who was at heart a soldier, and who in good faith and without too much qualification assented to at least a part of the frankly villainous dictum that all is fair in love and war.

One evening while Farquhar and his wife were sitting on a rustic bench near the entrance to his grounds, a gray-clad soldier rode up to the gate and asked for a drink of water. ❹ Mrs. Farquhar was only too happy to serve him with her own white hands. While she was fetching the water her husband approached the dusty horseman and inquired eagerly for news from the front.

"The Yanks are repairing the railroads," said the man, "and are getting ready for another advance. They have reached the Owl Creek bridge, put it in order and built a stockade on the north bank. The commandant has issued an order, which is posted everywhere, declaring that any civilian caught interfering with the railroad, its bridges, tunnels or trains will be summarily hanged. I saw the order."

"How far is it to the Owl Creek bridge?" Farquhar asked.

"About thirty miles."

"Is there no force on this side the creek?"

"Only a picket post[3] half a mile out, on the railroad, and a single sentinel at this end of the bridge."

"Suppose a man—a civilian and student of hanging—should elude the picket post and

---

2. **Corinth:** Mississippi town that was the site of an 1862 Civil War battle.

3. **picket post:** Troops sent ahead with news of a surprise attack.

◆ Build Vocabulary

imperious (im pir´ ē əs) *adj.:* Urgent; imperative

dictum (dik´ təm) *n.:* Formal statement of fact or opinion

summarily (sə mer´ ə lē) *adv.:* Promptly and without formality

Research Skills Mini-Lesson

Note Cards

Introduce the Concept Tell students that when they conduct research for an assignment such as the Fictional News Article on p. 477, a good way to record information is to create note cards.

Develop Background Have students locate at least three sources of information. Suggest that they consult some of the following: *The Reader's Guide to Periodical Literature*; The new York Times Index; vertical files of pamphlets, booklets, and government publications; and Internet search engines, such as the Yahoo Directory and the Webcrawler.

Apply the Information Tell students to use their sources to create six note cards, each containing a separate item of information. Students may find it helpful to label the tops of the cards to help identify the information later. Remind students to record all direct quotations accurately and to note the source of each piece of information. Have students group the note cards by subtopic.

Assess the Outcome Evaluate students on their ability to locate different sources, and to accurately record individual items of information on note cards.

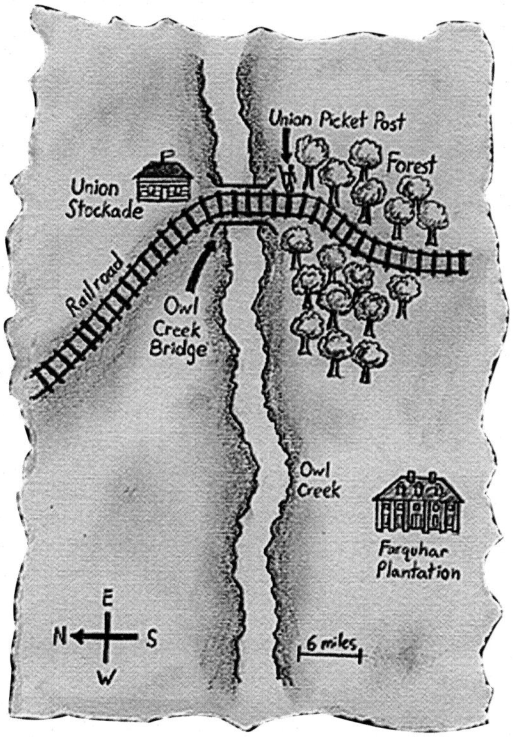

5 ▲ **Critical Viewing** How does the map reveal why the bridge was so important to the Union army? **[Interpret]**

perhaps get the better of the sentinel," said Farquhar, smiling, "what could he accomplish?"

The soldier reflected. "I was there a month ago," he replied. "I observed that the flood of last winter had lodged a great quantity of driftwood against the wooden pier at this end of the bridge. It is now dry and would burn like tow."[4]

6 ◆ **Reading Strategy** Does this scene take place before or after the opening scene at the bridge? What clues help you identify the sequence of events?

7 The lady had now brought the water, which the soldier drank. He thanked her ceremoniously, bowed to her husband and rode away. An hour later, after nightfall, he repassed the plantation, going northward in the direction from which he had come. He was a Federal scout. 7

4. **tow** (tō) *n.*: Coarse, broken fibers of hemp or flax before spinning.

III

As Peyton Farquhar fell straight downward through the bridge he lost consciousness and was as one already dead. From this state he was awakened—ages later, it seemed to him—by the pain of a sharp pressure upon his throat, followed by a sense of suffocation. Keen, poignant agonies seemed to shoot from his neck downward through every fiber of his body and limbs. These pains appeared to flash along well-defined lines of ramification[5] and to beat with an inconceivably rapid periodicity. They seemed like streams of pulsating fire heating him to an intolerable temperature. As to his head, he was conscious of nothing but a feeling of fullness—of congestion. These sensations were unaccompanied by thought. The intellectual part of his nature was already effaced: he had power only to feel, and feeling was torment. He was conscious of motion. Encompassed in a luminous cloud, of which he was now merely the fiery heart, without material substance, he swung through unthinkable arcs of oscillation, like a vast pendulum. Then all at once, with terrible suddenness, the light about him shot upward with the noise of a loud plash; a frightful roaring was in his ears, and all was cold and dark. The power of thought was restored; he knew that the rope

◆ **Reading Strategy** Describe the shift in time that occurs between sections II and III. What is the impact of this shift? 8 9

5. **flash along well-defined lines of ramification:** Spread out quickly along branches from a central point.

◆ Build Vocabulary

effaced (ə fāsd′) *adj.:* Erased; wiped out

oscillation (äs′ ə lā′ shən) *n.:* Act of swinging or moving regularly back and forth

▶Critical Viewing◀

5 **Interpret** Students should note that this bridge supported railroad tracks. Since trains were critical to the movement of troops and supplies, either side would have wanted control of this bridge. However, the Union would be especially concerned about maintaining access because a stockade was within miles of the river.

◆ Reading Strategy

6 **Sequence of Events** Students should recognize that this scene takes place before the opening scene. A reference to driftwood connects this scene to the one on the bridge. Students may say that here the reader learns what generated Farquhar's interest in the bridge and suggests the reason for his hanging.

Customize for *Less Proficient Readers*

7 Help students understand what has happened by pointing out that the scout piqued Farquhar's interest and planted an idea. Farquhar considered burning the bridge; the scout brought news of this possibility to the soldiers' attention. Guide them to understand, as they begin to read Part III, that Farquhar's capture is a result of the scout's trickery.

◆ Reading Strategy

8 **Sequence of Events** Students may respond that the scene shifts abruptly to the present. They should note that they immediately come to appreciate the sequence of events which brought Farquhar his fate: standing on the bridge with a noose around his neck.

◆ Literary Focus

9 **Point of View** Guide students to see that for this sequence, the narrator's point of view has shifted from third-person objective to third-person limited to describe events as perceived by Farquhar.

Beyond the Classroom

Career Connection

Engineering During the Civil War, armies regularly blew up bridges and destroyed tracks to set back the pursuing armies. Civil engineers rapidly put them back together again. Clever and competent civil engineers were indispensable during that conflict. Today, strong mathematic minds can find work in several different engineering fields. Share these distinctions with students:

- ***Civil engineers*** plan and implement municipal projects such as highway and airport runway design and storm water management.
- ***Mechanical engineers*** plan the design of engines and machinery such as elevators, water-sprinkler systems, and irrigation plans.
- ***Electrical engineers*** design power systems, lighting of bridges and stadiums, and the electrical components of radio, television, and Internet systems.
- ***Aeronautical engineers*** design domestic aircraft, helicopters, and spacecraft.

Have interested students find out more about the work of engineers today.

◆ Grammar and Style

1 Semicolons in Compound Sentences Point out that the three sentences in succession are compound sentences in which semicolons link closely related independent clauses. Ask students to evaluate the emotional effect of these sentences. *They create a detached, rapid-fire, frightening account of the hanging.*

Customize for *AP Students*

2 Students may enjoy reading Edgar Allan Poe's short story "The Tell-Tale Heart" to appreciate another striking example of a character who is "preternaturally keen and alert." The Poe character hears "all things in heaven and hell."

Customize for *ESL Students*

3 The term *report* is one of several examples in this story of a familiar word used in an unfamiliar way. *Habit, sleepers,* and *bank* are others. Guide students to use context clues to ascertain the meanings or to consult a dictionary.

Tips to Guide Reading

Sustained Reading Point out to students that the numbered sections of this story provide a natural point at which to pause and think about what they have read so far. Pausing to think about what questions have been answered, what new questions have come up, and how events are fitting together will help them comprehend new information as they read forward. In this story, particularly, encourage students to think about the sequence of events. Some students may choose to jot down events on a timeline as they read.

had broken and he had fallen into the stream. There was no additional strangulation; the noose about his neck was already suffocating him and kept the water from his lungs. To die of hanging at the bottom of a river!—the idea seemed to him ludicrous. He opened his eyes in the darkness and saw above him a gleam of light, but how distant, how inaccessible! He was still sinking, for the light became fainter and fainter until it was a mere glimmer. Then it began to grow and brighten, and he knew that he was rising toward the surface—knew it with reluctance, for he was now very comfortable. "To be hanged and drowned," he thought, "that is not so bad; but I do not wish to be shot. No; I will not be shot; that is not fair."

He was not conscious of an effort, but a sharp pain in his wrist apprised him that he was trying to free his hands. He gave the struggle his attention, as an idler might observe the feat of a juggler, without interest in the outcome. What splendid effort!—what magnificent, what superhuman strength! Ah, that was a fine endeavor! Bravo! The cord fell away; his arms parted and floated upward, the hands dimly seen on each side in the growing light. He watched them with a new interest as first one and then the other pounced upon the noose at his neck. They tore it away and thrust it fiercely aside, its undulations resembling those of a watersnake. "Put it back, put it back!" He thought he shouted these words to his hands, for the undoing of the noose had been succeeded by the direst pang that he had yet experienced. His neck ached horribly; his brain was on fire; his heart, which had been fluttering faintly, gave a great leap, trying to force itself out at his mouth. His whole body was racked and wrenched with an insupportable anguish! But his disobedient hands gave no heed to the command. They beat the water vigorously with quick, downward strokes, forcing him to the surface. He felt his head emerge; his eyes were blinded by the sunlight; his chest expanded convulsively, and with a supreme and crowning agony his lungs engulfed a great draft of air, which instantly he expelled in a shriek!

He was now in full possession of his physical senses. They were, indeed, preternaturally[6] keen and alert. Something in the awful disturbance of his organic system had so exalted and refined them that they made record of things never before perceived. He felt the ripples upon his face and heard their separate sounds as they struck. He looked at the forest on the bank of the stream, saw the individual trees, the leaves and the veining of each leaf—saw the very insects upon them: the locusts, the brilliant-bodied flies, the gray spiders stretching their webs from twig to twig. He noted the prismatic colors in all the dewdrops upon a million blades of grass. The humming of the gnats that danced above the eddies of the stream, the beating of the dragonflies' wings, the strokes of the water spiders' legs, like oars which had lifted their boat—all these made audible music. A fish slid along beneath his eyes and he heard the rush of its body parting the water.

He had come to the surface facing down the stream; in a moment the visible world seemed to wheel slowly round, himself the pivotal point, and he saw the bridge, the fort, the soldiers upon the bridge, the captain, the sergeant, the two privates, his executioners. They were in silhouette against the blue sky. They shouted and gesticulated, pointing at him. The captain had drawn his pistol, but did not fire; the others were unarmed. Their movements were grotesque and horrible, their forms gigantic.

Suddenly he heard a sharp report and something struck the water smartly within a few inches of his head, spattering his face with spray. He heard a second report, and saw one of the sentinels with his rifle at his shoulder, a light cloud of blue smoke rising from the muzzle. The man in the water saw the eye of the man on the bridge gazing into his own through the sights of the rifle. He observed that it was a gray eye and remembered having read that gray eyes were keenest, and that all famous marksmen had them. Nevertheless,

◆ Build Vocabulary

apprised (ə prīzd′) *v.:* Informed; notified

6. **preternaturally** (prēt′ ər nach′ ər əl ē) *adv.:* Abnormally; extraordinarily.

Analyze Literary Criticism

Ernest Hopkins, author of several articles on the subject, claims that Bierce's general philosophy was a "realistic, pessimistic, hard-boiled attitude toward life. This first-hand approach made him rather difficult to work with, no doubt, but it did make his writings refreshingly original and does so today—to read Bierce is to enter a different world." Read Hopkins's evaluation of Bierce's work to students. Then, have students discuss whether or not they agree with his statements. Have students write a journal entry in which they answer the following questions:

1. Do you find "An Occurrence at Owl Creek Bridge" refreshingly original? Why or why not? *Students may cite the structure and the ending as original. Others may feel that, compared to contemporary writing, this story is not original.*
2. Do you think the story reflects a pessimistic attitude toward life? Why or why not? *Most students will agree that the story's conclusion shows a pessimistic attitude toward life.*

Students can incorporate their journal entries into the Critical Essay or Spoken Review on p. 477.

◆ Literary Focus
How do you know that this passage is told from a third-person limited point of view? ❹

this one had missed.

A counterswirl had caught Farquhar and turned him half round; he was again looking into the forest on the bank opposite the fort. The sound of a clear, high voice in a monotonous singsong now rang out behind him and came across the water with a distinctness that pierced and subdued all other sounds, even the beating of the ripples in his ears. Although no soldier, he had frequented camps enough to know the dread significance of that deliberate, drawling, aspirated chant; the lieutenant on shore was taking a part in the morning's work. How coldly and pitilessly—with what an even, calm intonation, presaging,[7] and enforcing tranquillity in the men—with what accurately measured intervals fell those cruel words:

"Attention, company! . . . Shoulder arms! . . . Ready! . . . Aim! . . . Fire!"

Farquhar dived—dived as deeply as he could. The water roared in his ears like the voice of Niagara, yet he heard the dulled thunder of the volley and, rising again toward the surface, met shining bits of metal, singularly flattened, oscillating slowly downward. Some of them touched him on the face and hands, then fell away, continuing their descent. One lodged between his collar and neck; it was uncomfortably warm and he snatched it out.

As he rose to the surface, gasping for breath, he saw that he had been a long time under water; he was perceptibly farther down stream—nearer to safety. ❺ The soldiers had almost finished reloading; the metal ramrods flashed all at once in the sunshine as they were drawn from the barrels, turned in the air, and thrust into their sockets. The two sentinels fired again, independently and ineffectually. ❻

7. **presaging** (prē sāj′ iŋ): Predicting; warning.

▼ **Critical Viewing** What potential obstacles to Farquhar's escape are presented by the stream bank? **[Analyze]** ❼

◆ Literary Focus

❹ **Point of View** Students may cite the presentation of Farquhar's inner thoughts and observations.

Customize for
AP Students

❺ After completing the story, you may want to have your more advanced students go back through the story and look for clues which show what was actually happening to Farquhar as he was imagining his escape. In this passage, for example, he may have in reality been gasping for breath at this point in the story.

◆ Background for Understanding

❻ **History** Inform students that in 1862, soldiers fired muzzle-loading rifles. A capable soldier could get off just two shots per minute. When the men on the bridge fired all at once, Farquhar had about thirty seconds of safety between shots.

▶Critical Viewing◀

❼ **Analyze** Students may say that the stream bank appears to afford little firm footing and the dense undergrowth could inhibit movement.

Cultural Connection

Community Connection

Civil War Sites The Civil War was fought in thousands of places all over the country. Have students find out about ways that the war affected the area in which you live. Guide their exploration with the following questions:

- Were any battles fought in your community, region, or state?
- What roads or railroads were built at the time?
- What historical structures were destroyed?
- Which factories were built then or were quickly retooled to make ammunition or clothing? Which buildings became temporary hospitals?
- After which leaders and generals were streets or schools named?

Have students share findings with the class.

❶ **Clarification** Point out that since light travels faster than sound, Farquhar would hear the sound of the gunfire *after* he saw the visual evidence of the shots fired.

◆ Critical Thinking

❷ **Speculate** Once students have finished reading the story, refer them to Bierce's description of the forest here, and ask them how it foreshadows the conclusion. *Students may say that the forest is enchanting, that it takes on a heavenly quality. They may say that it gives the reader a solid clue that things are not as they appear.*

◆ Critical Thinking

❸ **Interpret** Everything in his surroundings seems unfamiliar to Farquhar. Ask students to predict what this may mean, or have them refer back to this passage after they've read the conclusion. *Students will probably comment that the walk is more dreamlike than real. This is suggested by the fact that the surroundings seem unfamiliar, the journey seems endless, and the path seems untraveled.*

◆ Reading Strategy

❹ **Sequence of Events** Guide students to note the present tense here, as Bierce brings us to real time in Farquhar's life, and to his imminent death.

◆ Reading Strategy

❺ **Point of View** Students can say that only a moment or two separates the last paragraph from the opening scene since, when first encountered, Farquhar already had a rope around his neck.

The hunted man saw all this over his shoulder; he was now swimming vigorously with the current. His brain was as energetic as his arms and legs; he thought with the rapidity of lightning.

"The officer," he reasoned, "will not make that martinet's[8] error a second time. It is as easy to dodge a volley as a single shot. He has probably already given the command to fire at will. God help me, I cannot dodge them all!"

An appalling plash within two yards of him was followed by a loud, rushing sound, *diminuendo*,[9] which seemed to travel back through the air to the fort and died in an explosion which stirred the very river to its deeps! A rising sheet of water curved over him, fell down upon him, blinded him, strangled him! The cannon had taken a hand in the game. As he shook his head free from the commotion of the smitten water he heard the deflected shot humming through the air ahead, and in an instant it was cracking and smashing the branches in the forest beyond.

"They will not do that again," he thought; "the next time they will use a charge of grape[10]. ❶ I must keep my eye upon the gun; the smoke will apprise me—the report arrives too late; it lags behind the missile. That is a good gun."

Suddenly he felt himself whirled round and round—spinning like a top. The water, the banks, the forests, the now distant bridge, fort and men—all were commingled and blurred. Objects were represented by their colors only; circular horizontal streaks of color—that was all he saw. He had been caught in a vortex and was being whirled on with a velocity of advance and gyration that made him giddy and sick. In a few moments he was flung upon the gravel at the foot of the left bank of the stream—the southern bank—and behind a projecting point which concealed him from his enemies. The sudden arrest of his motion, the abrasion of one of his hands on the gravel, restored him, and he wept with delight. He dug his fingers into the sand, threw it over himself in handfuls and audibly blessed it. It looked like diamonds, rubies, emeralds; he could think of nothing beautiful which it did not resemble. The trees upon the bank were giant garden plants; he noted a definite order in their arrangement, inhaled the fragrance of ❷ their blooms. A strange, roseate[11] light shone through the spaces among their trunks and the wind made in their branches the music of aeolian harps.[12] He had no wish to perfect his escape—was content to remain in that enchanting spot until retaken.

A whiz and rattle of grapeshot among the branches high above his head roused him from his dream. The baffled cannoneer had fired him a random farewell. He sprang to his feet, rushed up the sloping bank, and plunged into the forest.

All that day he traveled, laying his course by the rounding sun. The forest seemed interminable; nowhere did he discover a break in it, not even a woodman's road. He had not known that he lived in so wild a region. There was something uncanny in the revelation.

By night fall he was fatigued, footsore, famishing. The thought of his wife and children urged him on. At last he found a road which led him in what he knew to be the right direction. It was as wide and straight as a city street, yet it seemed untraveled. No fields bordered it, no dwelling anywhere. ❸ Not so much as the barking of a dog suggested human habitation. The black bodies of the trees formed a straight wall on both sides, terminating on the horizon in a point, like a diagram in a lesson in perspective. Overhead, as he looked up through this rift in the wood, shone great golden stars looking unfamiliar and grouped in strange constellations. He was sure they were arranged in some order which had a secret and malign significance. The wood on either side was full of singular noises, among which—once, twice, and again, he distinctly heard whispers in an unknown tongue.

His neck was in pain and lifting his hand to it he found it horribly swollen. He knew that it

---

8. **martinet** (märt′ ən et′): Strict military disciplinarian.
9. ***diminuendo*** (də min′ yoo͞ en′ dō): Musical term used to describe a gradual reduction in volume.
10. **charge of grape:** Cluster of small iron balls—"grape shot"—that disperse once fired from a cannon.

11. **roseate** (rō′ zē it) *adj.*: Rose-colored.
12. **aeolian** (ē ō′ lē ən) **harps:** Stringed instruments that produce music when played by the wind. In Greek mythology, Aeolus is the god of the winds.

Speaking, Listening, and Viewing Mini-Lesson

Spoken Review

This mini-lesson supports the Speaking, Listening, and Viewing activity in the Idea Bank on p. 477.

Introduce the Concept Students may be familiar with movie reviews that often appear on local news programs on television or radio. Share examples of these with students to establish the tone and format of the presentations.

Develop Background Emphasize that students should give their opinions freely but should be prepared to summarize key plot elements and support their views with reasons.

Apply the Information Hold radio shows. Guide the audience to be respectful of the guests.

Assess the Outcome Evaluate students on their ability to organize and deliver a thoughtful review. Your assessment should take appropriate language, tone, and pacing into account.

had a circle of black where the rope had bruised it. His eyes felt congested: he could no longer close them. His tongue was swollen with thirst; he relieved its fever by thrusting it forward from between his teeth into the cold air. How softly the turf had carpeted the untraveled avenue—he could no longer feel the roadway beneath his feet!

4 Doubtless, despite his suffering, he had fallen asleep while walking, for now he sees another scene—perhaps he has merely recovered from a delirium. He stands at the gate of his own home. All is as he left it, and all bright and beautiful in the morning sunshine. He must have traveled the entire night. As he pushes open the gate and passes up the wide white walk, he sees a flutter of female garments: his wife, looking fresh and cool and sweet, steps down from the veranda to meet him. At the bottom of the steps she stands waiting, with a smile of ineffable joy, an attitude of matchless grace and dignity. Ah, how beautiful she is! He springs forward with extended arms. As he is about to clasp her he feels a stunning blow upon the back of the neck; a blinding white light blazes all about him with a sound like the shock of a cannon—then all is darkness and silence! 4

Peyton Farquhar was dead; his body, with a broken neck, swung gently from side to side beneath the timbers of the Owl Creek bridge.

> **◆ Reading Strategy** 5
> How much time has passed from the opening scene until this last paragraph? How do you know?

> **◆ Build Vocabulary**
> **malign** (mə līn′) *adj.*: Malicious; very harmful
> **ineffable** (in ef′ə bəl) *adj.*: Too overwhelming to be described in words

Guide for Responding

◆ Literature and Your Life

Reader's Response What emotions did the story's ending evoke? Why?

Thematic Focus Is Farquhar's death a fair one? Why or why not?

Class Poll Farquhar knew in advance that death was the penalty for tampering with the bridge. Is his fate therefore justified? Using this question, conduct a quick poll of classmates.

☑ Check Your Comprehension

1. Which pieces of information about Farquhar's background explain why he would risk his life on such a dangerous mission?
2. (a) What do Farquhar and his wife learn from the visitor? (b) What do you learn about the visitor after he leaves the couple?
3. What is Farquhar's fate?

◆ Critical Thinking

INTERPRET

1. In Part I, Bierce reveals little about the condemned man and the reason for his hanging. How do these omissions create suspense? **[Analyze]**
2. (a) In what ways are Farquhar's perceptions of time and motion distorted as he waits to be hanged? (b) What causes this distortion? **[Support; Interpret]**
3. Bierce creates contrasts between reality and fantasy in this story. What details suggest that Farquhar's escape occurs in his mind? **[Distinguish]**
4. How does the contrast between real and imagined time help prepare you for the ending of the story? **[Compare and Contrast]**

EVALUATE

5. Explain whether you think that the portrayal of Farquhar's final thoughts is realistic. **[Evaluate]**

EXTEND

6. Why were railroad bridges like the one at Owl Creek such an important target during the Civil War? **[Social Studies Link]**

Beyond the Selection

FURTHER READING

Other Works by Ambrose Bierce

Tales of Soldiers and Civilians
Can Such Things Be?
Devil's Dictionary

Other Fiction About the Civil War

The Red Badge of Courage, Stephen Crane
The Killer Angels, Michale Shaara

We suggest that you preview these works before recommending them to students.

INTERNET

You and your students may find additional information about Ambrose Bierce on the Internet. We suggest the following site. Please be aware, however, that sites may have changed since this information was published.

For a biography and bibliography related to Bierce, go to: **http://www.creative.net/~alang/lit/horror/bierce.sht**

We *strongly recommend* that you preview sites before you send students to them.

Reinforce and Extend

Customize for
Less Proficient Readers
Once students know how the story ends, they can go back and read it again. The second time, they can look for clues as to what is real and what is in Farquhar's imagination.

Answers

◆ Literature and Your Life

Reader's Response Most students will probably say that they were shocked by the story's ending.

Thematic Focus Most students will probably say that he did not deserve to die.

☑ Check Your Comprehension

1. Possible answers: He is a slave owner. He is wealthy. He admires soldiers.
2. (a) They learn that the Union army is repairing the railroad at the Owl Creek Bridge and preparing to advance. (b) He is a Union soldier.
3. He dies.

◆ Critical Thinking

1. They make the reader want to read on to learn more about the man.
2. (a) Things seem to be going in slow motion; even sounds are elongated. (b) Suggested answer: His perceptions are distorted by his fear and his awareness of his fate.
3. Answers include: The narrator says that he "was one already dead" and the he experienced a "sense of suffocation."
4. Possible answer: The contrast between the real and the imagined raises the possibility in the reader's mind that maybe Farquhar hasn't really escaped.
5. Many students will respond that the portrayal of his final thoughts is realistic because it seems likely that someone who knows he is about to die would lapse into a dreamlike state.
6. Suggested response: They provide the means for armies to safely and efficiently cross bodies of water.

Answers

◆ Reading Strategy

1. The encounter comes first.
2. A few minutes elapse.
3. The ending makes it clear that the events have taken place over just a matter of seconds, rather than hours.

◆ Build Vocabulary

Using the Word Root *-sum-*

1. true; 2. true; 3. false; 4. false

Using the Word Bank

1. etiquette, deference, summarily, dictum,
2. malign, ineffable
3. apprised, imperious, effaced
4. oscillation

◆ Literary Focus

1. It allows Bierce to delve into Farquhar's thoughts while still depicting his death.
2. (a) He uses an objective point of view at the beginning and at the end. (b) His use of this point of view in these two sections frames the parts of the story that portray Farquhar's inner thoughts.
3. The abrupt shift surprises the reader and emphasizes the finality of Farquhar's death.

◆ Grammar and Style

Possible answers: Peyton Farquhar desperately surveyed the landscape; thoughts of escape rushed through his mind.

Peyton Farquhar dropped from the bridge into the stream below; the shock of the cold water jolted his senses.

The silent, interminable moment finally ended; a thunderous roar shattered the calm.

Grammar Reinforcement

For additional instruction and practice, use the lesson on Capitalization and Punctuation in the **Language Lab CD-ROM,** and the page on Semicolons and Colons (p. 89) in the *Writer's Solution Grammar Practice Book.*

Guide for Responding *(continued)*

◆ Reading Strategy

Chronological Order

Because the events in this story aren't presented in **chronological order,** you have to piece together the sequence of events in order to follow the action.

1. Which takes place first: Farquhar's encounter with the Federal scout or his preoccupation with the ticking of his watch?
2. How much real time do you estimate elapses from the opening to the closing scene of the story?
3. How did the story's ending change your initial perception of the sequence and duration of the story's events?

◆ Build Vocabulary

Using the Latin Root *-sum-*

The Latin root *-sum-* means "highest" and denotes authority. Use your understanding of this root to decide whether each of the following statements is true or false. Write your answers in your notebook.

1. A painter of *consummate* artistry is among the most skilled at his or her craft.
2. Dialing 911 is a fast way to *summon* the police.
3. A *summation* covers every detail of an argument.
4. A *summons* is a casual invitation to visit a courtroom.

Using the Word Bank: Connotations

Review the vocabulary words in the Word Bank; then use them to answer these questions in your notebook.

1. Which four words best relate to a book entitled *Lady Windmere's Authoritative Guide to Manners for Servants?*
2. Which two words best relate to an unspeakably vicious comment?
3. Which three words best relate to a court clerk who hastily interrupts a judge to inform her that audiotaped evidence had been accidentally erased?
4. Which word relates to a table fan that revolves to cool an entire room?

◆ Literary Focus

Point of View

The **point of view,** or vantage point from which this story is narrated, changes several times. An objective point of view provides a detached description of the opening scene at Owl Creek bridge. Then, a shift to the third-person limited point of view allows readers to share Farquhar's thoughts and emotions.

1. How is the limited point of view effective where it is used?
2. (a) In which parts of the story does Bierce use the objective point of view? (b) What effect does it create?
3. What is the effect of the shift in point of view in the last paragraph of the story?

◆ Grammar and Style

Semicolons in Compound Sentences

Compound sentences can be formed by joining two closely related independent clauses with a **semicolon.**

The pattern of short clauses connected by semicolons in this story often creates a rapid-fire rhythm. Notice how Bierce makes greater use of this style in parts of the story that are cold and objective but abandons it in other parts.

Compound sentences can be formed by joining two closely related independent clauses with a **semicolon.**

Writing Application Choose from among the following clauses to create three compound sentences. Use semicolons to join clauses that make meaningful, powerful sentences.

1. Thoughts of escape rushed through his mind.
2. Peyton Farquhar dropped from the bridge to the stream below.
3. The silent, interminable moment finally ended.
4. The shock of the cold water jolted his senses.
5. A thunderous roar shattered the calm.
6. Peyton Farquhar desperately surveyed the landscape.

Reteach

Students who have difficulty understanding the literary concept of point of view and how it changes during this story may benefit from a visual demonstration. Cut out two large circles of the same size. On one, draw a diagram and label it in the same way as the one shown. In the center of the other circle, cut a hole the same size as the center circle on the diagram. Do not write anything on the circle with the hole in it. Show how the scope of a reader's view changes by laying the same hole over the diagram. Students should note that they can see only what happens. This represents the objective point of view. When the covering circle is removed, Farquhar's thoughts and feelings are revealed. This represents the limited third-person point of view.

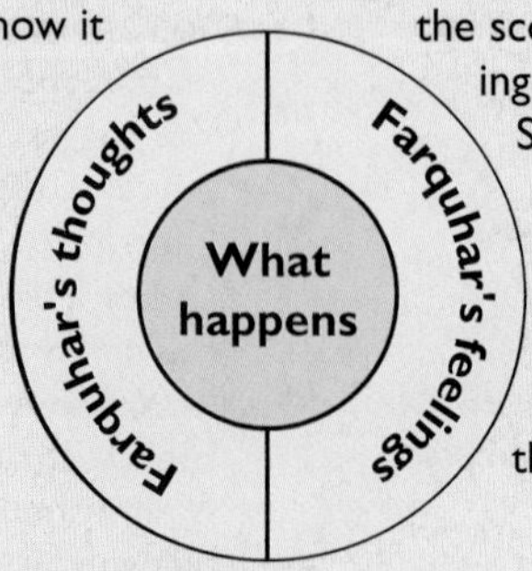

Build Your Portfolio

Idea Bank

Writing

1. **Farewell Letter** Imagine that Farquhar has been allowed to communicate his fate to his wife. Compose his message to her. Be true to Farquhar's character as a loyal southern gentleman.

2. **Prequel** How was Farquhar captured? Did the soldiers dread or anticipate his hanging? Write a narrative of the events leading up to the hanging.

3. **Critical Essay** Bierce was one of the first writers to use stream of consciousness—a style that imitates the natural flow of thoughts, images, and feelings. In an essay, explain how this technique makes the story more dramatic. Use details from the narrative to support your ideas.

Speaking, Listening, and Viewing

4. **Viewing** When the rope snaps and Farquhar begins his escape, he notices a new acuteness in his senses. Pay attention to your viewing for a week, observing every detail around you. Write in your journal about the experience.

5. **Oral Presentation** Ask a librarian to help you find a science article about the perception of time. Summarize it—and its connection to this story—for your classmates. **[Science Link]**

Researching and Representing

6. **Chart** Use the map on p. 471 to estimate how long it would have taken Farquhar to reach the bridge, destroy it, and return. Include key information, such as Farquhar's mode of travel (on horse or foot) and rate of speed. **[Mathematics Link]**

7. **Graphic Display** Gather photographs and visuals related to the Civil War. Write captions for the images. Then put everything together to create a museum exhibit about the war.

Online Activity www.phlit.phschool.com

Guided Writing Lesson

Fictional News Article

Bierce's story underscores the horrible way in which war can impact individuals. Write a news article that reports the effects of a contemporary civil war on civilians. Remember that news writing must be impartial; use a tone like the one in the opening and closing paragraphs of Bierce's story.

Writing Skills Focus: Objective Tone

An objective tone can be described as the lack of any detectable attitude. Writing in the objective tone is unbiased and reveals no hint of the writer's value judgments toward the subject. For example, Bierce's initial description of Farquhar betrays neither sympathy nor contempt for the character.

Model From the Story

The man who was engaged in being hanged was apparently about thirty-five years of age. He was a civilian, if one might judge from his habit, which was that of a planter. His features were good. . . . He wore a mustache and pointed beard, but no whiskers. . . .

News reporting should maintain an objective tone, even if the subject is emotionally charged.

Prewriting Scan newspapers or magazines or listen to television news reports to find a contemporary civil war to write about. Gather information to provide a balanced, factual background on the conflict.

Drafting Open with a statement that answers as many of the *who, what, where, when, why,* and *how* questions as possible. Without injecting your own judgments, describe the events and their effects on civilians. Remain objective; include facts other than those that favor your own opinion.

Revising How does your article compare with reports you might find in the international news pages of a newspaper? Is your reporting as unbiased?

Idea Bank

Customizing for
Performance Levels

Following are suggestions for matching Idea Bank topics with your students' performance levels:
Less Advanced Students: 1, 4
Average Students: 2, 6
More Advanced Students: 3, 5, 7

Customizing for
Learning Modalities

Following are suggestions for matching Idea Bank topics with your students' learning modalities:
Visual/Linguistic: 4, 5
Logical/Mathematical: 5, 6
Visual/Spatial: 7

Guided Writing Lesson

For more instruction on prewriting, elaboration, and revision, see *Prentice Hall Writing and Grammar.*

Writing and Language Transparencies Have students use the Branching Organizer, pp. 67–69 to help students gather details for their articles.

Writing Lab CD-ROM
Have students complete the tutorial on Narration. Follow these steps:

1. Encourage students to complete an Audience Profile.
2. Have students use a Story Line Diagram to chart out their plot events.
3. After students draft on computer, they can use the Language Variety Checker to aid revisions.

ASSESSMENT OPTIONS

Formal Assessment, Selection Test, pp. 138–140, and Assessment Resources Software. The selection test is designed so that it can be easily customized to the performance levels of your students.

Alternative Assessment, p. 29, includes options for less advanced students, more advanced students, intrapersonal learners, interpersonal learners, and visual/spatial learners.

PORTFOLIO ASSESSMENT
Use the following rubrics in the ***Alternative Assessment*** booklet to assess student writing:
Farewell Letter: Expression, p. 109
Prequel: Fictional Narrative Rubric, p. 110
Essay on Stream of Consciousness: Literary Analysis Rubric, p. 127
Guided Writing Lesson: Fictional Narrative Rubric, p. 110

LESSON OBJECTIVES

1. **To develop vocabulary and word identification skills**
   - Greek Word Roots: *-archy-*
   - Using the Word Bank: Synonyms
2. **To use a variety of reading strategies to comprehend an historical document**
   - Connect Your Experience
   - Reading Strategy: Use Background Knowledge
   - Background for Understanding: History
3. **To express and support responses to the text**
   - Critical Thinking
   - Idea Bank: Letter of Response
   - Idea Bank: Diary Entry
   - Idea Bank: Newspaper Column
4. **To analyze literary elements**
   - Literary Focus: Diction
5. **To read in order to research self-selected and assigned topics**
   - Idea Bank: Graphic Display
   - Idea Bank: Web Site
6. **To plan, prepare, organize, and present literary interpretations**
   - Idea Bank: Reenactment
   - Idea Bank: Mock Court
7. **To use recursive writing processes to write a research query**
   - Guided Writing Lesson
9. **To increase knowledge of the rules of grammar and usage**
   - Grammar and Style: Parallel Structure

Test Preparation

Reading Comprehension: Context (ATE, p. 479)
The teaching tips and sample test item in this workshop support the instruction and practice in the unit workshop:
Reading Comprehension: Using Context (SE, p. 631)

Guide for Interpreting

Abraham Lincoln *(1809–1865)*

Serving as president during one of the most tragic periods in American history, Abraham Lincoln fought to reunite a nation torn apart by war. His courage, strength, and dedication in the face of an overwhelming national crisis have made him one of the most admired and respected American presidents.

A man of humble origins, Lincoln developed an early interest in politics. He served in the Illinois state legislature and the United States Congress, where he earned a reputation as a champion of emancipation. In 1858, he ran for the United States Senate against Stephen Douglas. Lincoln lost the election, but his heated debates with Douglas brought him national recognition and helped him win the presidency in 1860.

Shortly after his election, the Civil War erupted. Throughout the war, Lincoln showed great strength and courage. He also demonstrated his gift for oratory. He was invited to make "a few appropriate remarks" in November 1863 for a dedication of the Gettysburg battlefield as a national cemetery. The world has long remembered what he said there.

Robert E. Lee *(1807–1870)*

The job of commanding the Confederate army during the Civil War wasn't one that Robert E. Lee wanted. As the dispute over slavery grew, Lee was torn. He believed in the Union, he opposed both slavery and secession, and he was regarded as one of the finest military leaders in the United States Army. When President Lincoln offered him command of the Union forces, however, Lee refused to lead an army against his native state and resigned from the army, vowing to fight only in defense of Virginia.

Unlike many Confederate leaders, Lee had no illusions about the South's power. Serving initially as commander of the army of northern Virginia and later of all the Confederate armies, he expected the widespread bloodshed and destruction caused by the war. He was an extraordinary military leader whose accomplishments and personal integrity in the face of overwhelming odds inspired great loyalty in both soldiers and civilians.

On the eve of resigning his U.S. Army commission, Lee explored his divided loyalties in "Letter to His Son."

◆ Background for Understanding

History: Lincoln Prepares to Speak at Gettysburg

The battle of Gettysburg, Pennsylvania, fought in July 1863, was an important Union victory and marked a turning point in the war. More than 51,000 soldiers were injured in the battle. On November 19, 1863, a military cemetery on the battlefield was dedicated. Unsure of President Lincoln's availability, the dedication organizers slated him as a secondary speaker, asking him to make only "a few appropriate remarks." In drafting that brief address, Lincoln wanted to lead the 15,000 American citizens at the cemetery dedication through an emotional final rite of passage. He also needed to gain continuing support for a bloody conflict that was far from won.

Stories abound regarding Lincoln's drafting of the speech: He wrote it the week before; he wrote it the night before; he wrote it on the train; he wrote it on a piece of scrap paper. Certainly, he was still revising even as he spoke, adding the phrase "under God" to describe the nation. An experienced speaker, Lincoln probably anticipated the positive effect this suggestion of divine approval of the United States and its goals of freedom would have on the audience.

Prentice Hall Literature Program Resources

REINFORCE / RETEACH / EXTEND

Selection Support Worksheets
Build Vocabulary: Greek Word Roots: *-archy-*, p. 140
Grammar and Style: Parallel Structure, p. 141
Reading Strategy: Use Prior Knowledge, p. 142
Literary Focus: Diction, p. 143

Strategies for Diverse Student Needs, Summarize Main Idea, p. 30

Beyond Literature Cross-Curricular Connection: Music, p. 30

Formal Assessment Selection Test, pp. 141–143; Assessment Resources Software

Alternative Assessment, p. 30

Resource Pro CD-ROM

The Gettysburg Address ◆ Second Inaugural Address ◆ Letter to His Son ◆

◆ Literature and Your Life

Connect Your Experience

Divided loyalties like Robert E. Lee's were common in a time when many felt more closely tied to their home state than to the nation. Divided loyalties are still common, though the choices are different. Friends with opposing priorities, commitments at school and work—all can become forces in a tug of war for your loyalty.

Journal Writing Describe a situation—in your life, a film or book, or recent public events—where divided loyalties required a difficult choice. Explore how the decision was made.

Thematic Focus: A Nation Divided

The right words can often overcome division. In the "Second Inaugural Address," President Lincoln sought to heal a torn nation. How can a moving description of common beliefs and goals encourage enemies to set aside their differences?

◆ Build Vocabulary

Greek Word Roots: *-archy-*

The word *anarchy* in "Letter to His Son" derives from the Greek root *-archy-*, meaning "rule" or "government." In combination with the prefix *an-*, meaning "without," you can guess that *anarchy* means "without government."

Word Bank

Preview this list of words from the selections.

- consecrate
- hallow
- deprecated
- insurgents
- discern
- scourge
- malice
- anarchy
- redress

◆ Grammar and Style

Parallel Structure

Lincoln uses **parallel structure**—the expression of similar ideas in similar form—to emphasize his important ideas. For example, these phrases from his "Second Inaugural Address" make such an impression that the words remain among Lincoln's most memorable:

> With malice toward none; with charity for all;
> with firmness in the right . . .

Each phrase is an introductory prepositional phrase containing the preposition "with." You will find many other examples of parallel structure in Lincoln's two speeches. Note how they linger in your memory.

◆ Literary Focus

Diction

You'll notice that Lee's **diction**—or word choice—in writing to his son was more informal than that of President Lincoln in drafting a public speech. Word choice—formal or informal, concrete or abstract—gives a writer's voice its unique quality. For example, Lee's phrase, *"I see that four states have declared themselves out of the Union . . ."* is more personal and informal than Lincoln's statement, *"insurgent agents were . . . seeking to dissol[v]e the Union, and divide effects, by negotiation."* Notice how each writer's diction reflects his audience and purpose.

◆ Reading Strategy

Use Background Knowledge

Reading a historical document without understanding its historical context is like viewing a sequel before the original film: You may grasp the basic story, but you'll miss much of the underlying meaning. As you read, **use prior background knowledge** of the Civil War to help you analyze ideas, actions, and decisions in context. For example, you already know that Lee felt more closely allied to his home state than to the nation. Use this knowledge to understand the decisions he presents in his letter.

Test Preparation Workshop

Reading Comprehension: Context Many standardized tests require students to use context clues such as synonyms and antonyms to determine the meanings of unfamiliar words. Write the following passage from p. 481 on the chalkboard, then ask students the question that follows.

> Both parties deprecated war; but one of them would *make* war rather than let the nation survive; and the other would *accept* war rather than let it perish.

In this passage, the word perish means—

A flourish
B compromise
C expand
D die

The parallel construction of the sentence—"let the nation *survive* / rather than let it *perish*"—combined with the use of "rather," which means *to the contrary,* or *instead,* suggests that perish means the opposite of survive. D is the correct answer.

Interest Grabber If you can obtain a taped version of Ward and Burns's documentary, *The Civil War,* show students a sampling of the carnage and destruction that the war created. Tell students that the selections presented here address the turmoil created by a war between the states. Ask students to discuss the ways that a civil war is more devastating than a war with an external enemy.

◆ Background for Understanding

History Explain that the three selections in this grouping were written at radically different moments during the conflict. Lee's letter was written as the Civil War was first erupting. Lincoln's "Gettysburg Address" was written after two years of bitter fighting. Lincoln's second inaugural address was written as the war was nearing an end, when a Union victory was now assured. By the end, both sides had suffered wounds that would not heal for generations. Have students discuss each occasion and how the public and the leaders of both the North and the South might have felt at the time.

Customize for *Less Proficient Readers*
Although the selections are brief, they contain difficult vocabulary and long sentences. To help these readers meet these challenges, preview the vocabulary words. You might also distribute the Summarize Main Idea page in ***Strategies for Diverse Student Needs*** (p. 30).

Customize for *English Language Learners*
To help these students grasp the meaning of the selections, have them listen to the recordings of the selections on audiotape as they follow along in their texts.

Listening to Literature Audiocassettes

Customize for *AP Students*
The Gettysburg Address was greatly influenced by Greek funeral oratory. Invite interested students to research the style and rhetoric of the ancient speeches and to look for examples of it in the Gettysburg Address.

Develop Understanding

One-Minute Insight Lincoln's short but powerful Gettysburg Address places one specific battle of the Civil War into the historical context of the American fight for freedom. Lincoln asserts that the civil war is a test of the ideals for which colonials fought in 1776. In an attempt to give direction to his divided country, Lincoln urged Americans to devote themselves to the task begun by the honored dead—to preserve freedom for *all* Americans.

▶Critical Viewing◀

❶ **Analyze** Students may say that it depicts Lincoln's intensity, confidence, and sincerity.

❷ **Clarification** "Four score and seven years" is 87 years. Eighty-seven years before 1863 was the year 1776, the year the Declaration of Independence was signed.

◆ Literary Focus

❸ **Diction** Have students discuss the effect of using the words "four score and seven years." *Students should note that these words add to the eloquence of his speech.*

Customize for
English Language Learners
❹ Guide these students to understand that the phrase "last full measure of devotion" is a reference to the fact that the men died in battle.

◆ Reading Strategy

❺ **Use Background Knowledge** Students may understand that here Lincoln refers to the Declaration of Independence, which demanded freedom for all. He implies that America should look to promote the views of that document rather than the Constitution, which did not recognize the rights of all people.

◆ Grammar and Style

❻ **Parallel Structure** Point to Lincoln's repeated use of "that." What is the effect of this repetition? *Using the parallel structure helps Lincoln to drive home each individual point.*

The Gettysburg Address

Abraham Lincoln — November 19, 1863

Abraham Lincoln's Address at the Dedication of the Gettysburg National Cemetery, 19 November 1863

◀ **Critical Viewing** What personal qualities of President Lincoln are conveyed through this illustration of his delivery of "The Gettysburg Address"? **[Analyze]** ❶

❷ ❸ Four score and seven years ago our fathers brought forth on this continent a new nation, conceived in Liberty, and dedicated to the proposition that all men are created equal.

Now we are engaged in a great civil war, testing whether that nation, or any nation so conceived and so dedicated, can long endure. We are met on a great battle-field of that war. We have come to dedicate a portion of that field, as a final resting place for those who here gave their lives that that nation might live. It is altogether fitting and proper that we should do this.

But, in a larger sense, we cannot dedicate—we cannot consecrate—we cannot hallow—this ground. The brave men, living and dead, who struggled here, have consecrated it, far above our poor power to add or detract. The world will little note, nor long remember what we say here, but it can never forget what they did here. It is for us the living, rather, to be dedicated here to the unfinished work which they who fought here have thus far so nobly advanced. It is rather for us to be here dedicated to the great task remaining before us—that from these honored dead we take increased devotion to that cause for which they gave the last full measure of devotion—that we here highly resolve that these ❹ dead shall not have died in vain—that this ❺ nation, under God, shall have a new birth of ❻ freedom—and that government of the people, by the people, for the people, shall not perish from the earth.

◆ Build Vocabulary

consecrate (kän′ sə krāt′) *v.*: Cause to be revered or honored

hallow (hal′ ō) *v.*: Honor as sacred

Block Scheduling Strategies

Consider these suggestions to take advantage of extended class time:

- Have students complete the journal activity in Literature and Your Life (p. 478) and discuss their entries in small groups.
- Have students listen to all or part of the selections on audiotape. Have them discuss whether listening to the selections adds to their appreciation of the issues and ideas they embrace.
- Have students research the writings of Lincoln and Lee on the Internet either before or after they read.
- Using Speaking, Listening, and Viewing Activity 5, allow time for students to prepare and present a mock court case.
- Have students complete the Guided Writing Lesson (p. 485). Before they begin, hold a class discussion on understanding audience and purpose so that students can choose language that will be appropriate and effective. Have students look for specific examples of how Lincoln and Lee show their understanding of their audiences.

Second Inaugural Address

Abraham Lincoln — March 4, 1865

At this second appearing to take the oath of the presidential office, there is less occa- (7) sion for an extended address than there was at the first. Then a statement, somewhat in detail, of a course to be pursued, seemed fitting and proper. Now, at the expiration of four years, during which public declarations have been constantly called forth on every point and phase of the great contest which still absorbs the attention, and engrosses the energies of the nation, little that is new could be presented. The progress of our arms, upon which all else chiefly depends, is as well known to the public as to myself; and it is, I (8) trust, reasonably satisfactory and encouraging to all. With high hope for the future, no prediction in regard to it is ventured.

On the occasion corresponding to this four years ago, all thoughts were anxiously directed to an impending civil war. All dreaded it—all sought to avert it. While the inaugural address was being delivered from this place, devoted altogether to *saving* the Union without war, insurgent agents were (9) in the city seeking to *destroy* it without war—seeking to dissol[v]e the Union, and divide effects, by negotiation. Both parties deprecated war; but one of them would *make* war rather than let the nation survive; and the other would *accept* war rather than let it perish. And the war came.

One eighth of the whole population were colored slaves, not distributed generally over the Union, but localized in the Southern part of it. These slaves constituted a peculiar and powerful interest. All knew that this interest was, somehow, the cause of the war. To strengthen, perpetuate, and extend (9) this interest was the object for which the insurgents would rend the Union, even by war; while the government claimed no right to do more than to restrict the territorial enlargement of it. Neither party expected for the war, the magnitude, or the duration, which it has already attained. Neither anticipated that the *cause* of the conflict might cease with, or even before, the conflict itself (10) should cease. Each looked for an easier triumph, and a result less fundamental and astounding. Both read the same Bible, and pray to the same God; and each invokes His aid against the other. It may seem strange that any men should dare to ask a just God's assistance in wringing their bread from the sweat of other men's faces; but let us judge not that we be not judged. The prayers of both could not be answered; that of neither has been answered fully. The Almighty has his own purposes. "Woe unto the world because of offences! for it must

◆ Build Vocabulary

deprecated (dep´ rə kāt´ id) *v.*: Expressed disapproval of; pleaded against

insurgents (in sur´ jənts) *n.*: Rebels; those who revolt against established authority

One-Minute Insight

In his Second Inaugural Address, given a month before his death, Lincoln recalled the issues that faced the country four years earlier, acknowledged slavery as the real cause of the ongoing war, and lamented the tragedy of the war. He expressed hope for the end of that war and urged Americans to strive for a lasting peace.

◆ Reading Strategy

7 Use Background Knowledge Students may know that the President and Vice-President are sworn into office in an inauguration ceremony, and that this ceremony is the occasion of the President's inaugural address. They may know that the Twentieth Amendment to the Constitution, ratified in 1933, set the terms of Pres-ident and Vice-President to begin on January 20. Lincoln gave his first inaugural address on March 4, 1861, and his second, exactly four years later.

◆ Literary Focus

8 Diction Students should notice that Lincoln, clearly and succinctly, gives his audience credit for keeping up-to-date on current affairs and the war effort.

◆ Background for Understanding

9 History Inform students that when Lincoln was elected, the country had a population of about 31 million, of which 9 million lived in southern states. Of that 9 million, 4 million were slaves. By the time of his first inauguration, seven states had already seceded and others were on the verge of joining them in the recently formed Confederacy.

◆ Build Grammar Skills

10 Parallel Structure Guide students to notice the way Lincoln used parallel structure to link the ideas in these sentences. Point out the effectiveness of beginning the sentences with *Neither . . . , Neither . . . , Each . . . ,* and *Both. . . .*

Humanities: Art

Abraham Lincoln's Address at the Dedication of the Gettysburg National Cemetery, 19 November 1863, by Arthur Ignatius Keller.

Arthur Ignatius Keller (1886–1924) began his career as an illustrator for the *New York Herald* and then went on to illustrate for several other magazines and many books.

In this illustration, Keller provides an almost photographic depiction of the famous event. He vividly portrays Lincoln's sincerity and leadership qualities. The attentiveness of the large audience to Lincoln's speech is effectively portrayed here. Use these questions for discussion:

1. Why do you think the artist used this platform view of the scene? *Students may say that this angle shows the size of the audience and their rapt attention to the speech.*
2. Why do you think there are no photos of Lincoln in the act of giving his famous address? *Students may propose that due to the limitations of the photographic process then and the brevity of the speech, there wasn't time for a photographer to set up and take the picture.*

◆ Literary Focus

❶ **Diction** Here again Lincoln demonstrates a solid understanding of what his audience thinks and feels. Ask students to explain how his words show this. *Students may notice that Lincoln recognizes the suffering people have endured and the losses they have experienced. In keeping with the times, Lincoln invokes religious sentiments and appeals for divine inspiration.*

One-Minute Insight

In this letter Robert E. Lee, addresses the difficult decision he faced as the country approached a war that would pit the states against each other. Lee, the most respected officer in the United States Army, explains that despite his strong belief in the Constitution and in preserving the Union, his strongest loyalty is to his home state of Virginia, and he shows his willingness to take up arms to defend his state. The letter powerfully illustrates Lee's dignity, loyalty, and bravery.

◆ Background for Understanding

❷ **History** Just four days before Lee wrote this letter, Georgia seceded from the United States, joining South Carolina, Mississippi, Florida, and Alabama. Virginia seceded in April 1861.

◆ Reading Strategy

❸ **Use Background Knowledge** Students can use their knowledge of causes of the Civil War to understand that Lee is referring to the Southerners' fear that the election of Lincoln could lead to the abolition of slavery and, in a larger sense, to an infringement on the principle of states' rights.

◆ Literary Focus

❹ **Diction** Students can note Lee's formal tone, his regrets, and his deep respect for his state and its rights. They can appreciate that he tries to reassure his son that he shares his views about protecting their common interests. You may wish to clarify that, as a trained military leader, Lee would not actually "draw [his] sword," but would lead an army into battle.

needs be that offences come; but woe to that man by whom the offence cometh!"[1] If we shall suppose that American Slavery is one of those offences which, in the providence of God,[2] must needs come, but which, having continued through His appointed time, He now wills to remove, and that He gives to both North and South, this terrible war, as the woe due to those by whom the offence came, shall we discern therein any departure from those divine attributes which the believers in a Living God always ascribe to Him? ❶ Fondly do we hope—fervently do we pray—that this mighty scourge of war may speedily pass away. Yet, if God wills that it continue, until all the wealth piled by the bond-man's two hundred and fifty years of unrequited toil shall be sunk, and until every drop of blood drawn with the lash, shall be paid by another drawn with the sword, as was said three thousand years ago, so still it must be said "the judgments of the Lord, are true and righteous altogether."[3]

With malice toward none; with charity for all; with firmness in the right, as God gives us to see the right, let us strive on to finish the work we are in; to bind up the nation's wounds; to care for him who shall have borne the battle, and for his widow, and his orphan—to do all which may achieve and cherish a just and lasting peace, among ourselves, and with all nations. ❶

1. **"Woe unto the world . . . offence cometh":** From Matthew 18:7 of the King James Version of the Bible.
2. **providence of God:** Benevolent care or wise guidance of God.
3. **"The judgments . . . altogether":** From Psalm 19:9.

◆ Build Vocabulary

discern (di surn´) *v.*: Receive or recognize; make out clearly

scourge (skurj) *n.*: Cause of serious trouble or affliction

malice (mal´ is) *n.*: Ill will; spite

❷ Letter to His Son

Robert E. Lee

January 23, 1861

I received Everett's[1] *Life of Washington* which you sent me, and enjoyed its perusal. How his spirit would be grieved could he see the wreck of his mighty labors! I will not, however, permit myself to believe, until all ground of hope is gone, that the fruit of his noble deeds will be destroyed, and that his precious advice and virtuous example will so soon be forgotten by his countrymen. As far as I can judge by the papers, we are between a state of anarchy and civil war. May God avert both of these evils from us! I fear that mankind will not for years be sufficiently Christianized to bear the absence of restraint and force. I see that four states[2] have declared themselves out of the Union; four more will apparently follow their example. Then, if the border states are brought into the gulf of revolution, one half of the country will be arrayed against the other. I must try and be patient and await the end, for I can do nothing to hasten or retard it.

The South, in my opinion, has been aggrieved by the acts of the North, as you say. I feel the aggression and am willing to take every proper step for redress. It is the principle I contend for, not individual or private benefit. ❸ As an American citizen, I take great pride in my country, her prosperity and institutions, and would defend any state if her

1. **Everett's:** Referring to Edward Everett (1789–1865), an American scholar and orator who made a long speech at Gettysburg before Lincoln delivered his famous address.
2. **four states:** South Carolina, Mississippi, Florida, and Alabama.

Humanities: Music

At the outbreak of World War II, American composer Aaron Copland (1900–1990) received a letter from conductor Andre Kostalanetz, who asked him to contribute to a "musical portrait gallery of great Americans." In response, Copland chose Abraham Lincoln as his subject. "A Lincoln Portrait" blends original music with familiar American folk tunes to accompany a spare and dramatic script based on Lincoln's own words. Invite students to listen to a recording of the piece and respond to it. A fine current recording is the 1993 Delos version featuring the Seattle Symphony and the commanding voice of James Earl Jones.

rights were invaded. But I can anticipate no greater calamity for the country than a dissolution of the Union. It would be an accumulation of all the evils we complain of, and I am willing to sacrifice everything but honor for its preservation. I hope, therefore, that all constitutional means will be exhausted before there is a resort to force. Secession is nothing but revolution. The framers of our Constitution never exhausted so much labor, wisdom, and forbearance in its formation, and surrounded it with so many guards and securities, if it was intended to be broken by every member of the Confederacy at will. It was intended for "perpetual union," so expressed in the preamble, and for the establishment of a government, not a compact, which can only be dissolved by revolution or the consent of all the people in convention assembled. It is idle to talk of secession. Anarchy would have been established, and not a government, by Washington, Hamilton, Jefferson, Madison, and the other patriots of the Revolution. . . . Still, a Union that can only be maintained by swords and bayonets, and in which strife and civil war are to take the place of brotherly love and kindness, has no charm for me. I shall mourn for my country and for the welfare and progress of mankind. If the Union is dissolved, and the government disrupted, I shall return to my native state and share the miseries of my people; and, save in defense, will draw my sword on none. 4

◆ **Build Vocabulary**

anarchy (an´ ər kē) *n.*: Absence of government

redress (ri´ dres) *n.*: Atonement; rectification

Guide for Responding

◆ *Literature and Your Life*

Reader's Response What do you think are the most memorable phrases in Lincoln's speeches?

Thematic Focus (a) How does Lincoln use language to soothe and heal his listeners' hearts? (b) Does Lee's aversion to a Union "maintained by swords" justify his decision to place the preservation of Virginia over the preservation of the union?

Journal Entry After the Civil War, Robert E. Lee applied for a complete pardon of his role in leading the Confederate forces against the Union army. If you were a member of Congress, would you have voted to grant it? Why or why not? Explore your answers in a brief journal entry.

☑ Check Your Comprehension

1. Briefly describe the occasion on which each of these two Lincoln speeches was delivered.
2. What views about slavery does Lincoln express in these speeches?
3. What choice was Lee considering in his letter?
4. How does Lee define secession?

◆ Critical Thinking

INTERPRET

1. (a) Beyond dedicating the battlefield cemetery, what was Lincoln's main purpose in "The Gettysburg Address"? (b) What was his main purpose in the "Second Inaugural Address"? **[Infer]**
2. Lincoln closed both speeches by describing his visions of the nation's eventual rebirth. Considering his purpose, why is this an effective way to structure both speeches? **[Connect]**
3. How does Lincoln attempt to reconcile or reach out to both the North and the South in his speeches? **[Analyze]**
4. In your own words, explain Robert E. Lee's argument against secession. **[Relate]**
5. How does Lee link his acknowledgment of his son's gift to his argument? **[Connect]**
6. What qualities did Lee and Lincoln share? **[Connect]**

APPLY

7. How are Lincoln's speeches different from modern presidential addresses? **[Relate]**

Beyond the Selection

FURTHER READING

Other Works by or About Lincoln

The Collected Works of Abraham Lincoln (9 volumes), Basler, Pratt, and Dunlap, eds.

With Malice Toward None, Stephen B.Oates

Lincoln, David Herbert Donald

Other Works by or About Lee

R. E. Lee, Douglas Southall Freeman (4 volumes)

Lee's Dispatches, Douglas Southall Freeman, ed.

We suggest that you preview these works before recommending them to students.

INTERNET

You may find additional information about Lincoln and Lee on the Internet. We suggest the following site. Please be aware, however, that sites may have changed since this information was published.

Visit the U.S. Civil War Center at **http://www.cwc.lsu.edu/index.htm**

We *strongly recommend* that you preview the sites before you send students to them.

Reinforce and Extend

Customize for *Musical/Rhythmic Learners*

Like Lincoln's moving speeches, the lyrics of popular songs can also bring the cry for peace to large audiences. Ask these students to explain why popular music is a powerful tool for political ends. Follow up with the Cross-Curricular Connection: Music page in ***Beyond Literature*** (p. 30).

Answers

◆ *Literature and Your Life*

Reader's Response Students should support their answers with clear reasons.

Thematic Focus (a) Possible response: He uses elegant phrases like "four score and seven years ago," and biblical language. (b) Students should support their answers with clear reasons.

☑ **Check Your Comprehension**

1. The first was delivered after the Battle of Gettysburg; the second was delivered toward the end of the war, after he'd been reelected.
2. He expresses opposition to slavery.
3. He is considering whether to side with the Union or with his home state.
4. "Secession is nothing but revolution."

◆ **Critical Thinking**

1. (a) His purpose is to rally the American public around the cause of winning the war. (b) His purpose is to lead people to recognize the need to heal the nation's wounds.
2. This is an effective way of ending the speeches because his purpose is to rally the nation behind the idea of regaining national unity.
3. He suggests that the continuation of the war is God's will and that citizens must work together to pray that the "scourge" will pass.
4. He argues that secession conflicts with the goals of the Constitution.
5. His son had given him a biography of Washington. Lee asserts that Washington would be upset if he knew that the Union he worked so hard to create would soon be destroyed.
6. Suggested answer: Both are dignified, thoughtful, and courageous.
7. Possible answer: Today's addresses are longer and less eloquent.

Answers

◆ Reading Strategy

1. He was asked only to "make a few appropriate remarks."
2. As president, he wanted to see the nation survive. He did not want those who had died to have sacrificed their lives in vain.
3. Suggested response: He did so because both sides shared the same religious beliefs.
4. Having served in the United States military for years and having descended from generations of loyal Americans, Lee had strong ties to the Union.

◆ Build Vocabulary

Using the Greek Word Root *-archy-*

1. government with one ruler
2. a family or culture in which the father has ultimate authority
3. a government in which a select few have power

Using the Word Bank

1. b 2. a 3. a 4. c 5. b 6. a 7. c 8. c 9. a

◆ Literary Focus

1. Possible response: "Now, at the expiration of four years . . ."; "Both parties deprecated war . . ."
2. Possible response: "I received Everett's *Life of Washington,* which you sent me, and enjoyed its perusal . . ."; "a Union that can only be maintained by swords and bayonets, . . . has no charm for me."
3. Lincoln's address is intended for a general audience; Lee's writing is intended only for his son.

◆ Grammar and Style

Practice

2. adverb + do we + verb
3. until + adjective + direct object + verb + prepositional phrase
4. all + verb phrase + it

Writing Application

Check student responses for faulty parallelism.

Guide for Responding (continued)

◆ Reading Strategy

USE BACKGROUND KNOWLEDGE

Although the pieces by Lincoln and Lee reveal important information about events connected to the Civil War, it's not possible to completely understand and appreciate the selections without having some **prior background knowledge** of the Civil War era. One way to build on your prior knowledge before reading any literary work is to look at background information related to the subject. Add to your background about the Civil War by reviewing the biographies and Background for Understanding on p. 478. Then answer each question that follows.

1. Why did President Lincoln write such a short speech for his address at Gettysburg?
2. Why did Lincoln connect the honoring of the Gettysburg dead with the goal of continuing the war toward a Union victory?
3. In the "Second Inaugural Address," why did Lincoln suggest that both the war and an end to slavery were God's wish?
4. Why was Lee so opposed to secession?

◆ Build Vocabulary

USING THE GREEK ROOT *-archy-*

Each of the following words contains the Greek root *-archy-*, meaning "rule" or "government." Use your knowledge of the root and the supplied definitions to write a definition for each word on your paper.

1. monarchy (*mono* = single; one)
2. patriarchy (*patri* = father)
3. oligarchy (*olig* = few)

USING THE WORD BANK: Synonyms

In your notebook, write the letter of the word or phrase that is the best synonym for the first word.

1. consecrate: (a) destroy, (b) bless, (c) join together
2. hallow: (a) honor, (b) greet, (c) enlarge
3. deprecated: (a) condemned, (b) proved, (c) sensed
4. insurgents: (a) patriots, (b) loyal citizens, (c) rebels
5. discern: (a) overlook, (b) understand, (c) disregard
6. scourge: (a) punishment, (b) reward, (c) desire
7. malice: (a) forgiveness, (b) kindness, (c) ill will
8. anarchy: (a) leadership, (b) order, (c) chaos
9. redress: (a) atonement, (b) fear, (c) disturbance

◆ Literary Focus

DICTION

Diction refers to a writer's choice of words. President Lincoln used formal words and phrases to lend elegance and importance to his speeches. General Lee's less formal language creates a more intimate and personal feeling in his letter. Each writer used language that was appropriate to his subject, audience, occasion, and literary form.

1. Find two examples of formal diction in the "Second Inaugural Address."
2. Find two examples of informal, personal diction in Lee's "Letter to His Son."
3. Why is each writer's diction appropriate?

◆ Grammar and Style

PARALLEL STRUCTURE

When President Lincoln told the crowd at Gettysburg, "we cannot dedicate—we cannot consecrate—we cannot hallow—this ground," he was using **parallel structure** to dramatize his point.

Parallel structure is the repeated use of similar ideas expressed in a similar grammatical form.

Practice In your notebook, identify the parallel structures in each of the following examples from Lincoln's speeches. The first one is done for you.

1. . . . we cannot dedicate—we cannot consecrate—we cannot hallow—this ground
Parallel structure: *we cannot* + verb
2. Fondly do we hope—fervently do we pray—that this mighty scourge . . .
3. . . . until all the wealth piled by the bond-man's . . . and until every drop of blood drawn with the lash . . .
4. All dreaded it—all sought to avert it.

Writing Application Rewrite a sentence from "Letter to His Son" using parallel structure to emphasize Lee's ideas.

Reteach

To reteach diction, have students think about a time they listened to a politician's speech. Was the speech formal or informal and how do they know? Were the words precise and eloquent or were they more like everyday conversations? Have students discuss the characteristics of a formal speech such as one made in Congress. Compare this to a speech given by a softball team captain at a fundraiser. To help students recognize differences in diction, have them think of formal and informal words and phrases to add to the chart. Then have students use the words in two short speeches to compare the diction.

DICTION

Formal	Informal
1. My fellow Senators	1. Hi folks!
2. cannot	2. can't
3.	3.
4.	4.

Build Your Portfolio

Idea Bank

Writing

1. **Letter of Response** Assume the role of Lee's son and write an informal letter in which you respond to the ideas in your father's letter. **[Social Studies Link]**

2. **Diary Entry** It is the eve of the address at Gettysburg. Writing as Lincoln, describe the message you are striving to convey in the still-unfinished speech. How do you want it to be remembered?

3. **Newspaper Column** Writing as a journalist covering "The Gettysburg Address," react to the speech in a column. Do you agree with Lincoln, who thought the speech a failure, or with fellow speaker Edward Everett, who greatly admired it? Support your ideas with examples. **[Career Link]**

Speaking, Listening, and Viewing

4. **Reenactment** With a partner, brainstorm about what might have occurred when President Lincoln asked Lee to lead the Union army. Reenact the situation for the class. **[Career Link]**

5. **Mock Court** Stage a mock Supreme Court hearing in which students argue for or against a state's right to secede from the Union. After hearing "lawyers'" arguments, each "judge" should render an opinion. **[Social Studies Link]**

Researching and Representing

6. **Graphic Display** Copy photographs or drawings of the Battle of Gettysburg from library or Internet sources. Combine them with text to create a collage. **[Art Link]**

7. **Web Site** Develop a plan for an Internet Web site providing information and images related to the Civil War. Create a flowchart that illustrates the links you'll include in your site. **[Media Link; Technology Link]**

Online Activity www.phlit.phschool.com

Guided Writing Lesson

Research Query

Choose an aspect of Civil War history that interests you, and write a research query, or letter of request, to gather information about it. Address your request to one of the many organizations, libraries, or historical societies that focus on this period of American history. Make your letter effective by using language and format appropriate to a business letter.

Writing Skills Focus: Appropriate Language for Purpose

Appropriate language ensures that readers understand your request and feel that their efforts are appreciated. Use courteous and formal language. Spell out organization names, choose concise words and phrases, and structure your sentences formally.

Prewriting Identify an organization or individual who can provide the data you want. To help you do so, search the Internet, computer databases, or library sources such as the *United States Government Manual* and the *Washington Information Directory*. Ask relevant questions to start your research: What information do I want? Who is the best person to query? How can I narrow my query to elicit the most useful response?

Drafting Begin the letter with your own address, the date, an address containing the name and address of your recipient, and a salutation. In the body of the letter, state your request clearly and briefly. Then thank the recipient, sign the letter, and type or print your name below your signature.

Revising Read your letter aloud, making sure that you have used respectful language appropriate to your audience and purpose and that you've clearly indicated the information you're seeking. In addition, verify that names of people, places, and organizations are spelled correctly.

Idea Bank

Customizing for *Performance Levels*

Following are suggestions for matching Idea Bank topics with your students' performance levels:
Less Advanced Students: 1, 6
Average Students: 2, 4, 6
More Advanced Students: 3, 5, 7

Customizing for *Learning Modalities*

Following are suggestions for matching Idea Bank topics with your students' learning modalities:
Interpersonal: 4, 5
Visual/Spatial: 6, 7
Logical/Mathematical: 5, 7

Guided Writing Lesson

For more instruction on prewriting, elaboration, and revision, see *Prentice Hall Writing and Grammar.*

Writers at Work Videodisc

To introduce students to research techniques, show the videodisc segment on Research Writing (Ch. 5) featuring music writer Gillian Gaar. Have students discuss which of Gaar's techniques they can apply when conducting their own research.

Play frames 3 to 9643

Writing Lab CD-ROM

Have students complete the tutorial on Practical and Technical Writing. Follow these steps:

1. Have students complete an Audience Profile.
2. Have students draft their letters in the Letter Shell.
3. Have students use the Interactive Self-Evaluation Checklist to help them revise.

ASSESSMENT OPTIONS

Formal Assessment, Selection Test, pp. 141–143, and Assessment Resources Software. The selection test is designed so that it can be easily customized to the performance levels of your students.

Alternative Assessment, p. 30, includes options for less advanced students, more advanced students, musical/rhythmic learners, visual/spatial learners and interpersonal learners.

PORTFOLIO ASSESSMENT

Use the following rubrics in the ***Alternative Assessment*** booklet to assess student writing:
Letter of Response: Expression Rubric, p. 109
Diary Entry: Expression Rubric, p. 109
Newspaper Column: Persuasion Rubric, p. 120
Guided Writing Lesson: Business Letter Rubric, p. 128

Prepare and Engage

LESSON OBJECTIVES

1. **To read for different purposes in varied sources, including American literature**
   - Thematic Connection
2. **To express and support responses to the text**
   - Critical Thinking
   - Idea Bank: Evaluation
3. **To write in a variety of forms**
   - Idea Bank: Updated Lyrics
4. **To read in order to research self-selected and assigned topics**
   - Questions for Research
   - Idea Bank: Graphics Display
5. **To plan, prepare, organize, and present literary interpretations**
   - Idea Bank: Interpretation
   - Idea Bank: Interview/Group Discussion

Interest Grabber As a homework assignment, have students gather photographs, musical recordings, video footage, and other materials relating to the Vietnam War and the protest movements of the 1960's. Have students share the materials they bring in and use the materials as a springboard for a class discussion about what it was like to live through the 1960's. Follow the discussion by having students read and/or listen to the song (if you can obtain a recording of it) and relate it to what they've learned through the discussion.

Customize for *English Language Learners*
This song uses some slang terms of the sixties, such as "going down" *(happening)* and "the man" *(power figure, such as a police officer or FBI agent)*. Review these terms in advance to help language learners better understand the lyrics.

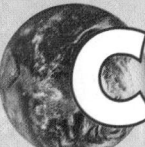

CONNECTIONS TO TODAY'S WORLD

For What It's Worth
Stephen A. Stills

Thematic Connection

A NATION DIVIDED

The 1860's was a decade of great turmoil for our young nation, which found itself torn by a Civil War that arose from fundamental disagreements between North and South over many issues, including slavery. A century later, the United States was again torn by civil strife, with the Vietnam War and civil rights at the heart of the unrest. Protests were seemingly an everyday occurrence in the 1960's, and the nation once again found itself divided.

Just as the Civil War inspired memorable and enduring songs, the upheavals of the 1960's unleashed an outpouring of protest songs that quickly became an important means of expressing the ideas and feelings of a new generation. For young people openly challenging conventional attitudes and politics, music was more than just a form of entertainment; it was a means of social and political criticism. "For What It's Worth," written by folk-rock singer Stephen Stills, is characteristic of the era that produced such classics as "Where Have All the Flowers Gone?" and "Blowing in the Wind."

STEPHEN A. STILLS
(1945–)

Though a Dallas, Texas, native, double Rock & Roll Hall of Fame inductee Stephen Stills first made his mark on New York's music scene in the mid-1960's. The multi-talented songwriter, vocalist, and musician then moved to Los Angeles in 1966, where he invited fellow musicians Richie Furay and Neil Young to form Buffalo Springfield. Though the band stayed together only two years, Stills wrote one of his most famous songs, "For What It's Worth," for Buffalo Springfield. The song captured the mood of unrest and disenchantment characteristic of the late sixties.

Prentice Hall Literature Program Resources

REINFORCE / RETEACH / EXTEND

Selection Support Worksheets
Thematic Connection: A Nation Divided, p. 144

Formal Assessment Selection Test, pp. 144–145; Assessment Resources Software

Resource Pro CD-ROM

FOR WHAT IT'S WORTH

Words and Music by Stephen A. Stills

There's something happening here
What it is ain't exactly clear
There's a man with a gun over there
Telling me I got to beware
(1) I think it's time we stop, children,
what's that sound
Everybody look what's going down

(2) There's battle lines being drawn
Nobody's right if everybody's wrong
Young people speaking their minds
Getting so much resistance from behind

I think it's time we stop, hey,
what's that sound
Everybody look what's going down

(3) What a field-day for the heat[1]
A thousand people in the street
Singing songs and carrying signs
Mostly say, hooray for our side

It's time we stop, hey, what's that sound
Everybody look what's going down

Paranoia strikes deep
Into your life it will creep
It starts when you're always afraid
You step out of line,
the man come and take you away

We better stop, hey, what's that sound
Everybody look what's going down
Stop, hey, what's that sound
Everybody look what's going down
Stop, now, what's that sound
Everybody look what's going down
Stop, children, what's that sound
Everybody look what's going down

1. **the heat:** Slang term for police or law enforcement.

◆ Build Vocabulary

Paranoia (par′ ə noi′ ə) *n.*: Mental disorder characterized by delusions, especially of persecution

Guide for Responding

◆ Literature and Your Life

Reader's Response Is this song, which was written three decades ago, relevant to your world? Why or why not?

Thematic Focus How does this song reflect the social unrest that characterized the late 1960's?

Questions for Research This song offers insights into the psychology of group movements, such as people's motives and the role of fear. Examine the lyrics again and write questions that could guide your research about this topic.

☑ Check Your Comprehension

1. What is being described in lines 13–16?
2. According to lines 19–22, what happens to those who openly disagree with the establishment?

◆ Critical Thinking

INTERPRET

1. In lines 3–4, the "man with a gun" who warns the speaker to beware is not a criminal but a military or law enforcement officer. How does this shed new light on your understanding of the chorus? **[Interpret]**
2. According to lines 19–22, what effect do social problems eventually have on individuals? **[Analyze]**
3. What does line 16 imply about the protesters in the streets? **[Infer]**

EVALUATE

4. Is the reference to "battle lines" in line 7 literal or figurative? Explain your reasoning. **[Make a Judgment]**

APPLY

5. Based on these lyrics, how would you characterize the relationship between young people—many of whom shared the point of view presented in this song—and authority figures during the 1960's? Explain. **[Synthesize]**

CONNECTIONS TO TODAY'S WORLD

Beyond the Selection

FURTHER READING

Other Songs by Stephen Stills

"Suite: Judy Blue Eyes"
"We Are Not Helpless"
"Wooden Ships"

Other Protest Songs

"Born in the U.S.A.," Bruce Springsteen
"Biko," Peter Gabriel

We suggest that you preview these works before recommending them to students.

INTERNET

You and your students may find additional information about Stephen Stills on the Internet. We suggest the following site. Please be aware, however, that sites may have changed since this information was published.

For general information about Stephen Stills and his body of work, visit **http://www.gate.net/~masterv/other/stills.html**

We *strongly recommend* that you preview the site before you send students to it.

Develop Understanding

Connections to Today's World

Use this song as the basis for a discussion of the similarities and differences between the divisions in society during the 1960's and those that occurred during the Civil War.

One-Minute Insight

This classic protest song captures the divisions in society in the 1960's. At the time, the major divisions occurred between those who supported the Vietnam War and those who protested against it. The speaker of this song represents the voice of the peace protesters.

Thematic Connection

(1) A Nation Divided Ask students to identify the "sound" that the speaker refers to in this lyric. *Students may say that it is the sound of war, against which the speaker believes it is necessary to protest.*

◆ Critical Thinking

(2) Interpret Discuss with students what the speaker is saying in this stanza. *Students may respond that the speaker sees people choosing the side to support in the emerging protest against the war in Vietnam; that "Nobody's right if everybody's wrong" means that the majority can make a moral or ethical mistake, or "might doesn't make right"; and that the youth protest with little or no support from their elders.*

Thematic Connection

(3) A Nation Divided Draw students' attention to the conflict be-tween the "heat"—the police or the establishment—and the protesters.

Reinforce and Extend

Answers

◆ Literature and Your Life

Reader's Response Students may respond that the song is not relevant, since the nation is not divided as it was during the 1960's.

(Answers continue on p. 488)

Answers

Thematic Focus The song captures the divisions between protesters and the establishment.

Check Your Comprehension

1. A protest is being described.
2. They get arrested.

◆ Critical Thinking

1. Suggested response: It reveals that the song is about societal divisions.
2. People can become paranoid.
3. They are enjoying the conflict of protest.
4. It is both literal and figurative. The sides are divided in terms of ideas, but there is an indication of violence between the two sides.
5. The two sides were divided.

Thematic Connection

1. He is protesting authority's right to set policy, and he is trying to urge others to protest.
2. "For What It's Worth" focuses on unifying people against the war. The spirituals focused on unifying enslaved Africans in the cause of achieving freedom.
3. (a) Through its portrayal of events, "An Episode of War" protests war as being random and destructive. (b) By showing the death of a civilian, "An Occurrence at Owl Creek Bridge" can also be seen as a protest against the cruelty of war.

Idea Bank

Customizing for *Performance Levels*

Following are suggestions for matching Idea Bank topics with your students' performance levels:
Less Advanced Students: 1, 5
Average Students: 2, 4, 5
More Advanced Students: 3, 4

Customizing for *Learning Modalities*

Following are suggestions for matching Idea Bank topics with your students' learning modalities:
Interpersonal: 4
Visual/Spatial: 5

Thematic Connection

A Nation Divided

The theme of protest is found throughout American history—from the days of the early colonists to the present. Because the right to free speech is protected by our Constitution, Americans have always been able to voice their beliefs and opinions openly. In the 1960's, in particular, musical artists used their place in the media spotlight to take a high-profile stand on issues of concern to their young listeners. Like other protest songs of its day, "For What It's Worth" reached a wide audience of radio listeners, record buyers, and concertgoers, who quickly adopted it as an anthem for the political and antiwar demonstrations of the late sixties.

1. Though "For What It's Worth" never takes a direct stand on a particular issue, it is clearly a protest song. What is Stills protesting, and what action is he trying to bring about on the part of his listeners?
2. How would you make the case for classifying spirituals, such as "Go Down, Moses," as protest songs of the Civil War era?
3. It can be argued that the following works from Part 1 were written as forms of protest. For each of the following selections, explain what is being protested and how the writer conveys his or her opposition. (a) "An Episode of War" (b) "An Occurrence at Owl Creek Bridge."

Idea Bank

Writing

1. **Updated Lyrics** Think about the social, environmental, and political issues of concern to you, your friends, and your classmates. Select one or two and use them as the focus of a modern version of "For What It's Worth." Rewrite the stanzas so that they reflect contemporary events and viewpoints. **[Performing Arts Link]**
2. **Interpretation** Review some of the specific events of the 1960's in an encyclopedia or history text. Write an interpretation of "For What It's Worth" that relates Stills's lyrics to specific events. Explain how you made the connection between the song lyrics and the events. **[Social Studies Link]**
3. **Evaluation** Musical artists continue to use their fame and their songs as a platform for social commentary and protest. How effective is popular music as a means of generating awareness and social change? Explore your response in a essay in which you support your points with examples from real life. **[Music Link]**

Speaking, Listening, and Viewing

4. **Interview/Group Discussion** Interview a parent, relative, family friend, or teacher who remembers the protest era of the 1960's. Prepare a series of questions about the changes taking place in society at that time, the issues and events that concerned young people, the prevalent philosophies and attitudes, and the ways in which people expressed their opposition. Tape-record or videotape your interview, and share it with the class. Afterward, lead a discussion of your classmates' responses to the interview. **[Social Studies Link]**

Researching and Representing

5. **Graphic Display** In the graphic medium of your choice (painting, collage, poster, or video montage), illustrate the theme "A Nation Divided" as it relates to the Civil War era, the 1960's, or a combination of the two. The finished work should illustrate both the issues at the heart of the division and their effect on the country. **[Art Link]**

Online Activity www.phlit.phschool.com

ASSESSMENT OPTIONS

Formal Assessment, Selection Test, pp. 144–145, and Assessment Resources Software. The selection test is designed so that it can be easily customized to the performance levels of your students.

PORTFOLIO ASSESSMENT

Use the following rubrics in the ***Alternative Assessment*** booklet to assess student writing:
Updated Lyrics: Poetry Rubric, p. 123
Interpretation: Literary Analysis/Interpretation Rubric, p. 127
Evaluation: Evaluation Rubric, p. 119

Writing Process Workshop

Problem-and-Solution Essay

It is one thing to identify a problem, but quite another to find a workable solution. The works in this section by Lincoln, Lee, and Chief Joseph all present solutions to significant problems: Lincoln, on how best to honor the sacrifices of the Union dead; Lee, on implementing constitutional measures as an alternative to civil war; and Chief Joseph, on resignation as the only possible response to further incursions by white settlers. In each case, the writer, after clearly identifying a problem, explains his strategy and gives the steps necessary for a solution. Follow their example by writing an essay in which you outline solutions to a problem in today's world that concerns you.

The following skills will help you write your essay:

Writing Skills Focus

- **Use precise details** to ensure that readers have a clear understanding of both the problem and solutions. (See p. 449.)
- **Maintain an objective tone** so that your readers trust the soundness of your solutions. (See p. 477.)
- **Organize your thoughts clearly and logically** so that your readers aren't lost in a maze of vaguely stated problems and half-thought-out answers. (See p. 465.)

Robert E. Lee's "Letter to His Son" demonstrates many of these skills:

MODEL FROM LITERATURE

[The dissolution of the Union] would be an accumulation of all the evils we complain of, and I am willing to sacrifice everything but honor for its preservation. ① I hope, therefore, that all constitutional means will be exhausted before there is a resort to force. ② Secession is nothing but revolution. The framers of our Constitution never exhausted so much labor, wisdom, and forbearance in its formation, and surrounded it with so many guards and securities, ③ if it was intended to be broken by every member of the Confederacy at will. ④

① ② The brief statement of the problem and the simple solution suggested make the writer's organization clear.

③ Information on constitutional safeguards adds force to his suggested solution.

④ Despite his southern roots, Lee maintains objectivity by recognizing the importance of constitutional measures.

Prepare and Engage

LESSON OBJECTIVES

- To use recursive writing processes to write a problem-solution essay
- To recognize and appropriately use active and passive voice
- To recognize and avoid logical fallacies

Distribute the scoring rubric for Problem-Solution in ***Alternative Assessment*** to make students aware of the criteria on which their work will be evaluated. (p. 116). For suggestions on customizing the rubric to this workshop, see page 491.

You may also want to present the Problem/Solution Graphic Organizer from the ***Writing and Language Transparencies.***

Writers at Work Videodisc

To introduce the elements of expository writing, play the videodisc segment featuring curator Thom Harrington (Ch. 3).

Play frames 23159 to 33243

Writing Lab CD-ROM

If your students have access to computers, you may want to have them use the tutorial on Exposition. Have students follow these steps:

1. Complete an interactive questionnaire designed to help them gather details for a problem-and-solution essay.
2. Draft on the computer.
3. Use the Self-Evaluation Checklist to help them revise their essays.

Cross-Curricular Connection: Science

Problems and Solutions in Science Professional scientific journals and science magazines geared toward the lay reader publish pieces that outline important problems and offer innovative solutions. Sometimes these articles are about a problem in methodology—how scientists go about conducting research or evaluating its results. At other times they take a real-world situation such as global warming, species depletion, or disease control and suggest steps that the scientific community, government, and regular citizens can take to help. Encourage interested students to choose a scientific topic for their problem-and-solution essays, while limiting themselves to one that does not require extensive original experimentation or expertise. Ask students what type of visual aids they might include with their essays to clarify issues for readers. *Responses might include using graphs, charts, and tables of figures or statistics, photographs of the problem, or an illustration (often called an "artist's conception") of the proposed solution.*

Develop Student Writing

Prewriting Strategy
Have students use a looping strategy to narrow and focus their topics. Allow time for students to freewrite about a general problem of their choice such as "pollution." After five minutes of freewriting, have students identify the main concern in their writing and "loop" it. (For example, "litter.") This becomes the new topic about which students will freewrite for another five minutes, looping the idea that concerns them most and writing again. Students can continue the looping process until they feel they have sufficiently narrowed the problem.

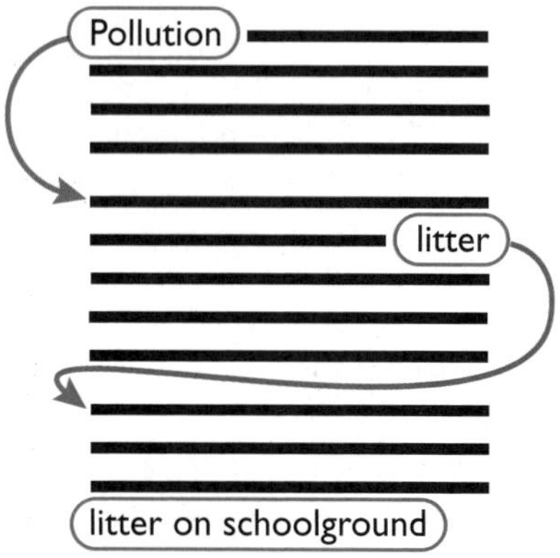

Customize for
Logical/Mathematical Learners
These students can enhance their essays by using numerical data to illustrate the scope of the problem they choose to write about. Advise logical/mathematical learners to restrict original work to conducting simple mathematical operations such as projecting a current situation into the future.

Customize for
Interpersonal Learners
These learners may benefit from interviewing others either by phone or face-to-face to gather details for their essays. They can also discuss their proposed solution with professionals who work in areas related to their topics.

Writing Lab CD-ROM
The Organizing Details section of the tutorial contains a Note Cards Activity and an Outliner that students can use to organize the information they have gathered.

Applying Language Skills: Active and Passive Voice

A verb is in the **active voice** when the subject of a sentence performs the action *(I hired the clerk)*. A verb is in the **passive voice** when the subject of a sentence receives an action—that is, when something is done to the subject *(The clerk was hired by me)*.

Usually, the passive voice makes writing seem dull and plodding. Try to maintain the active voice.

Practice On your paper, rewrite each of these sentences in the active voice.

1. Success was attained by Bob by sheer hard work.
2. Training was offered to freshmen by the coach.
3. The secret map was contained in a jewel box under the bed.

Writing Application As you draft your essay, avoid using passive constructions. Rewrite sentences in the passive voice so that the subject performs, rather than receives, the action of the verb.

Writer's Solution Connection
Language Lab
For more practice with active and passive voice, complete the Language Lab lesson on Strengthening Sentences.

Prewriting

Choose a Topic With a group of your classmates, brainstorm for a list of problems that affect you or the people around you. After you've created a broad list, discuss ideas for solving each of these problems. Review your notes for possible writing topics, or consider choosing one of the following ideas.

Topic Ideas
- The rising cost of movie tickets
- Pollution
- Slowing the aging process
- A dangerous local intersection

Gather Details Before you can make problems and solutions clear to the reader, you'll need to clarify them for yourself. Consider the following questions:
- What does your audience know about your topic?
- What insights do you bring that will help others understand your topic better?
- How does the situation present a problem? Whom does the problem affect, and how does it affect him or her?
- Is there just one problem or are there several related problems that need to be solved?
- How is your topic important, unique, or special?

Drafting

Identify the Problem Start your essay with a clear explanation of the problem you're addressing. Offer background information that shows why the problem exists and how it affects people.

Outline the Steps of Your Solution Don't assume that your readers can take a vague suggestion and solve a complex problem. Make the path to solution clear. For example, if you are writing about ways to slow the aging process, it is not enough to mention eating a healthy diet and exercising; rather, you should give information about which foods to eat and the amount and types of exercise recommended for a particular age group.

Elaboration Strategy
Remind students to include examples and illustrations of the benefits of the solution they propose.

Applying Language Skills
Active and Passive Voice Tell students that the active voice will make their problem-and-solution essays more lively. Because they sometimes address abstract ideas, these esssays can push writers into an overuse of the passive voice. For example, when referencing concepts such as "pollution," "costs," writers, must resist the temptation to make those ideas the subjects of their sentences instead of the objects.

Answers
1. Bob attained success by sheer hard work.
2. The coach offered training to freshmen.
3. The jewel box under the bed contained the secret map.

Grammar Reinforcement

For additional instruction and practice, refer students to the **Language Lab CD-ROM** lesson Strengthening Sentences, and the *Sourcebook* lesson on Active and Passive Voice (p. 57).

Remain Objective Your credibility hinges on your ability to maintain an even, objective approach. If you write without anger or emotion, you'll inspire the confidence that your solutions are the result of careful, logical reflection.

Revision Model

① The toll for the past year is sobering: six accidents, five injuries, three fatalities.

The intersection is a major hazard. ^ A traffic light would be well worth the safety gained for our community.

② —in equipment, employees, and traffic delays—

To implement this, the cost ^ would be small compared to the benefits of a safer town.

① The writer elaborates with specific, objective information.

② The writer organizes the costs and will use this sentence as the outline for the essay.

Revising

Use a Peer Reviewer Have a classmate read your essay and comment on its logic, clarity, and objectivity. Ask your reviewer to suggest places where you might give more information. After making revisions based on your reviewer's comments, proofread your essay to be sure the grammar, spelling, and punctuation are correct.

Publishing

- **Give an Informative Speech to Your Class** A good way to share your essay is to give a class presentation. To prepare, practice reading your essay several times, either in front of a mirror or to a friend. Also, assemble any appropriate charts, diagrams, or maps. When you deliver your speech, remember to speak clearly and make eye contact with your audience.
- **Submit Your Essay for Publication** If your essay concerns an issue of importance to your classmates or community, consider submitting it to your school or local newspaper. Enclose a cover letter stating your reasons for wanting your essay to be published. Also, include your name, address, and phone number, in case the editor needs to contact you.

Applying Language Skills: Avoiding Logical Fallacies

Fallacies are illogical conclusions based on unproven assumptions. Avoid these types of faulty logic:

Circular reasoning—restating the same argument in other words

Example: Neil is the richest because he has the most money.

Improved: Neil is the richest because he invested wisely.

Overgeneralization—a statement that is too broad for the evidence that backs it up

Example: Vegetarians are healthier and live longer.

Improved: Scientists found that vegetarians in a controlled study had fewer illnesses and longer lives.

Practice On your paper, identify the logical fallacies in the following statements.

1. People with hobbies are happier than those without.
2. Ann is the best student because she gets the best grades.

Writing Application Review your essay, and weed out any overgeneralizations or circular reasoning.

Writer's Solution Connection Writing Lab

For more information about logical fallacies, see the Drafting section of the Writing Lab Persuasion tutorial.

Revision

Writing Lab CD-ROM

The Revising and Editing section includes interactive instruction on citing sources. Students can select passages to learn methods of crediting sources by using footnotes, citations within text, and direct quotations.

Publishing

If students choose to deliver informative speeches, have them consider using a "before" and "after" organization to dramatize the impact of their solutions.

Applying Language Skills

Avoiding Logical Fallacies

Warn students that writers' attempts to use logic sometimes backfire.

Answers

1. overgeneralization
2. circular reasoning

Grammar Reinforcement

For additional instruction and practice on logical fallacies, refer to the Avoiding Faulty Logic lesson in the *Sourcebook* (p. 119) and practice page 117 in the *Writer's Solution Grammar Practice Book.*

Reinforce and Extend

Prentice Hall Writing and Grammar For more instruction on prewriting, elaboration, and revision, see *Prentice Hall Writing and Grammar.*

Reflect on Writing To extend the assignment, have students discuss what they might realistically do to help fight the problems they wrote about.

✓ Assessment

PORTFOLIO ASSESSMENT		4	3	2	1
Use the rubric on Problem-Solution in ***Alternative Assessment*** (p. 116) to assess student writing. Add these criteria to customize the rubric to this assignment.	**Active Voice**	The writer consistently uses active voice.	The writer uses a mixture of active and passive voice.	The writer uses active voice in only a few cases where it would be appropriate.	The writer consistently uses passive voice.
	Avoids Logical Fallacies	The writer consistently uses sound logic, contributing to the effectiveness of the essay's analysis.	The writer makes some questionable moves in logic.	The writer includes several logical fallacies in advancing the solution.	The writer's proposed solution is founded on one or more logical fallacies, severely undermining credibility.

Prepare and Engage

LESSON OBJECTIVES

- To identify main ideas and their supporting details
- To draw inferences and support them from the text

Customize for
English Language Learners
Use graphic images to demonstrate for these students abstract concepts such as *years, greater than, less than, similar,* and *different.*

Customize for
Logical/Mathematical Learners
Allow students to use graphic organizers as a prompt when summarizing, explaining, or analyzing. Encourage students to take notes graphically whenever appropriate.

Apply the Strategies

Answers

1. Students may choose to use a chart to represent the number of parks visited and miles traveled. They may also use a graph to compare the travels in the Southwest and the Northwest.
2. Students will probably suggest that the chart allows them to include the greatest amount and variety of information from this sample. For other types of information, another organizer would work as well or better.

Student Success Workshop

Real-World Reading Skills

Constructing Graphic Devices for Reading Comprehension

Strategies for Success

Constructing graphic organizers can help you understand a text. Graphic organizers are visual aids that arrange and clarify information. As you read, use text descriptions and organization to construct a graphic organizer to help you see the relationships among the ideas in the text.

Graphic Organizers Graphic organizers come in many forms. The following are examples:

- ▶ **Graphs** organize information for comparison. For example, a graph might compare graduation rates among schools.
- ▶ **Charts** show information at a glance. For instance, after reading an article about a political candidate, you may construct a chart showing his or her voting record.
- ▶ **Diagrams** can show parts or functions of an object or a system, or relationships between ideas, as in a Venn diagram. A Venn diagram is two overlapping circles, which lets you show similarities and differences between two items.

Timelines Timelines are a type of chart that can help you keep track of events and be aware of cause-and-effect relationships in a span of time.

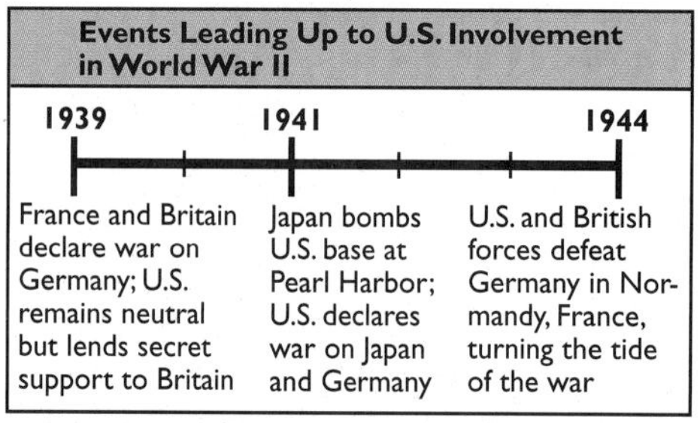
Events Leading Up to U.S. Involvement in World War II
1939
1941
1944
France and Britain declare war on Germany; U.S. remains neutral but lends secret support to Britain
Japan bombs U.S. base at Pearl Harbor; U.S. declares war on Japan and Germany
U.S. and British forces defeat Germany in Normandy, France, turning the tide of the war

Story Maps Story maps outline the events in a story. They can take many forms, helping you track people, problems, solutions, and events.

Title: A Year of Champions
Author: Susan Willis
Character: Ellen Lee
Setting: Collins High School swim team
Plot Events:
1. Ellen wants to be a champion swimmer, but the coach says she isn't strong enough to make the team.
2. Ellen trains on her own and wins the city amateur meet.
3. The coach invites her to join the team, but she decides she'd rather swim for fun than compete.

Apply the Strategies

Read this paragraph, and follow the instructions:

Every year for the past five years, Raymond's parents have taken him and his three younger brothers and two older sisters on a tour of one of America's national parks. So far they've visited two parks in the Southwest and three in the Northwest. Their travels have taken them an average of 1,500 miles each summer. This summer they plan to travel 2,000 miles, visiting the East Coast.

1. Select either a graph or a chart to represent some of this information visually.
2. Explain why you chose that graphic organizer. Would another one have worked?

✔ *Constructing graphic organizers can help you do the following:*
- ▶ *Recognize a cause-and-effect connection between events in a news article*
- ▶ *Track data in a scientific article*

Test Preparation Workshop

Using Visuals
Many standardized tests require students to interpret graphs, charts, diagrams, and tables. Use the following sample to demonstrate.

According to the timeline of events leading up to U.S. involvement in World War II, how many years was the United States officially at war with Germany before defeating Germany at Normandy?

A Five
B Thirty-nine
C Three
D Forty-four

Students should be able to use the information on the timeline to determine that the United States declared war in 1941 and that Germany was defeated at Normandy in 1944, making C the correct answer.

PART 2 Focus on Literary Forms: Diaries, Journals, and Letters

Newspapers in the Trenches '64, William Sheppard, Museum of the Confederacy, Richmond, Virginia

The Civil War was one of the most painful chapters of American history. The diaries, letters, and journals in this section tell the story of the tragic conflict between the states, allowing readers to experience the events through the eyes of people who experienced them firsthand.

Humanities: Art

Newspapers in the Trenches '64 by William Ludwell Sheppard.

This work shows another side of the war—the human faces of the men who, between battles, turned from soldiers into letter writers, journal keepers, and sharers of news.

Have your students link the painting to the focus of Part 2 (Diaries, Journals, and Letters) by answering the following questions:

1. How does the artist communicate the fact that reading a newspaper is a special event for the soldiers? *They are gathered attentively around the single soldier who is holding a newspaper and they appear eager to hear the latest news.*
2. Why might letters, journals, diaries, and newspapers have been so important to Civil War soldiers? *Besides being a diversion, reading and writing were a means of contact with the world outside the trenches; writing also helped them preserve a sense of their own individuality and humanity and gave them some hope of living on in some form, even if they died in battle.*

One-Minute Planning Guide

The firsthand accounts in Part 2 tell the story of the Civil War and its aftermath in the words of those who experienced it, both on and off the battlefield. In her journal, southern gentlewoman Mary Chesnut describes the attack on Fort Sumter. The accounts of Warren Lee Goss, Randolph McKim, and Stonewall Jackson provide three perspectives on the war from the soldiers who fought it. "Reaction to the Emancipation Proclamation," shows how the African American community responded to Lincoln's momentous proclamation, while Soujourner Truth's account demonstrates how much was still to be done in the fight for equality. Journalist Molly Moore's account of the 1991 Gulf War takes a behind-the-scenes look at the media's role in reporting—and shaping our perceptions of—modern warfare.

Customize for *Varying Student Needs*

When assigning selections in this part, keep in mind the following factors:

from *Mary Chesnut's Civil War*
- Southern woman recounts her reaction to attack on Fort Sumter

"Recollections of a Private"
- Brief, accessible account contrasts a soldier's expectation with the realities of military life

"A Confederate Account of the Battle of Gettysburg" and "An Account of the Battle of Bull Run"
- Brief, personal accounts of battles

"Reaction to the Emancipation Proclamation" and "An Account of an Experience With Discrimination"
- African American perspective on struggle for equality under the law

"Gulf War Journal"
- Contemporary journalist's firsthand account of Gulf War

LESSON OBJECTIVES

1. **To develop vocabulary and word identification skills**
   - Latin Prefixes: *ob-*
   - Using the Word Bank: Sentence Completions
   - Extending Word Study: Connotations
2. **To use a variety of reading strategies to comprehend historical documents**
   - Connect Your Experience
   - Reading Strategy: Distinguish Fact From Opinion
   - Background for Understanding
3. **To express and support responses to the text**
   - Critical Thinking
   - Idea Bank: Summary
4. **To analyze literary elements**
   - Literary Focus: Diaries, Journals, and Letters
5. **To read in order to research self-selected and assigned topics**
   - Questions for Research
   - Idea Bank: Viewing
   - Idea Bank: Timeline
   - Idea Bank: Model/Map
   - Viewing and Representing Mini-Lesson (ATE)
6. **To plan, prepare, organize, and present literary interpretations**
   - Idea Bank: Dramatic Reading
7. **To write in a variety of forms**
   - Idea Bank: Book Jacket
   - Idea Bank: Reflective Essay
8. **To use recursive writing processes to write a firsthand biography**
   - Guided Writing Lesson
9. **To increase knowledge of the rules of grammar and usage**
   - Grammar and Style: Capitalization of Proper Nouns

Test Preparation

Reading Comprehension: Context (ATE, p. 495)

The teaching tips and sample test item in this workshop support the instruction and practice in the unit workshop:

Reading Comprehension: Using Context (SE, p. 631)

Guide for Interpreting

Civil War Voices

The Civil War was one of the most painful chapters of American history, touching the lives of millions of soldiers and civilians. The following diaries, journals, and letters tell the story of the war through the eyes of just a few of those whose lives were affected by it.

No one was hurt when the opening shots of the war were fired on Fort Sumter on April 12, 1860, but **Mary Boykin Chesnut** (1823–1886) seems to have sensed the carnage to come. The daughter of a cotton plantation owner and United States senator, Mary Boykin was raised in an aristocratic family in Charleston, South Carolina. At the age of seventeen, she married James Chesnut, Jr., a wealthy lawyer and future senator. Her journal entries convey the mingled optimism and dread that marked the opening days of the Civil War.

Men hurried to enlist in what most believed would be a swift and glorious war. Some young men, as we learn from the account of Union soldier **Warren Lee Goss,** saw the military as an opportunity for respect and advancement. The harsh realities of the training camp and battlefield soon taught soldiers on both sides that lives and limbs were the price of glory. The cost was especially high at the Battle of Gettysburg—a stunning defeat for Confederate general Robert E. Lee. In his diary, Confederate soldier **Randolph McKim** recounts the bravery of companions, many of whom were among the 51,000 killed or wounded at Gettysburg.

Confederate general and military strategist **Thomas Jonathan "Stonewall" Jackson** (1824–1863) earned his nickname early in the war for his steadiness and determination during the Battle of Bull Run in 1861. Jackson, who recounted the battle in a letter to his wife, died two years after his great victory; he was accidentally shot by his own troops and died of complications.

The Emancipation Proclamation, issued by President Lincoln on September 22, 1862, changed the purpose of the war. By declaring that all slaves would be freed on January 1, 1863, the Proclamation made the conflict into a war to end slavery, as well as a war to restore the Union. **Reverend Henry M. Turner**, a free-born African American who lived in Washington, D.C., recounts his community's reaction to the news.

When the war ended in 1865, abolitionist **Sojourner Truth** (1797–1883) had only begun to battle discrimination. A preacher and former slave, Truth is also recognized as an advocate of women's rights, temperance, and workplace and prison reform.

◆ Background for Understanding

MEDIA: THE PAST COMES TO LIFE IN *THE CIVIL WAR*

For five nights in early October 1990, Americans sat riveted by a public-television documentary called *The Civil War*. This unexpected hit, which garnered the highest rating of any series in PBS history, presented the story of the war as it had never been told: in the words of those who had lived it. In the course of creating *The Civil War*, filmmaker Ken Burns worked with 2,500 first-person quotations and 16,000 original photographs.

America's fascination with the series is a testament to the power of firsthand accounts to engage and move us. In the companion book, Burns explains how ordinary people captured the many facets of the war as no historian ever could.

"The America that went to war in 1861 was perhaps the most literate nation on earth. Soldiers at the front and civilians at home left an astonishingly rich and moving record of what they saw and felt . . . descriptions, reflections, opinions, cries of outrage, cynicism, sorrow, laughter and triumph . . . hundreds of voices from across the spectrum of American experience, men and women whose lives were touched or destroyed or permanently changed by the war."

Prentice Hall Literature Program Resources

REINFORCE / RETEACH / EXTEND

Selection Support Pages
Build Vocabulary: Prefixes: *ob-*, p. 145
Grammar and Style: Capitalization of Proper Nouns, p. 146
Reading Strategy: Distinguish Fact From Opinion, p. 147
Literary Focus: Diaries, Journals, Letters, p. 148

Strategies for Diverse Student Needs, p. 31

Beyond Literature
Humanities Connection: Journals, p. 31

Formal Assessment Selection Test, pp. 150–152; Assessment Resources Software

Alternative Assessment, p. 31

Resource Pro CD-ROM

Listening to Literature Audiocassettes

Civil War Diaries, Journals, and Letters

◆ Literature and Your Life

Connect Your Experience

In today's world, you can learn about key events almost instantly. You can see news footage that captures the sights and sounds of an event, and hear interviews in which the people involved describe what happened and share their feelings. The Civil War took place long before television cameras were invented, however, so the best way to learn about the war and share the experiences of those involved is through letters, journals, diaries, and photographs.

Thematic Focus: Division, War, and Reconciliation

What insights about the Civil War do these letters, diaries, and journals provide that aren't captured in most history books?

Journal Writing Describe what you already know about the impact of the Civil War on people's lives. When you've finished reading, note any additional insights you've gathered.

◆ Build Vocabulary

Latin Prefixes: *ob-*

Mary Chesnut uses the word *obstinate* to describe the Union commander's response to a Confederate attack. The word *obstinate* comes from a combination of the Latin prefix *ob-*, meaning "against," and a form of the Latin root *-stare-*, meaning "stand." The adjective describes the commander's stubborn refusal to surrender.

Word Bank

Preview this list of words from the selections.

capitulate
audaciously
foreboding
obstinate
imprecations
serenity

◆ Grammar and Style

Capitalization of Proper Nouns

Proper nouns—nouns that name particular persons, places, things, or ideas—should begin with a capital letter. If a proper noun consists of two or more words, capitalize each with the exception of articles, coordinating conjunctions, and prepositions of fewer than four letters. Randolph McKim, for instance, uses capitalized proper nouns throughout his account: They include titles used before or in place of a name *(General Ewell)*, particular places *(Culp's Hill)*, and the names of specific regiments *(Second Maryland)*.

◆ Literary Focus

Diaries, Journals, and Letters

Diaries and **journals** are personal records of events, thoughts, feelings, and observations. Written on a day-to-day basis, they allow people to record immediate responses to experiences. Because diaries and journals are generally kept for personal use, they are usually written in an informal style that captures the writer's ideas and emotions. Similarly, a personal **letter** is written without the intention of publication. Yet because it is written to another person, it is not entirely private writing.

◆ Reading Strategy

Distinguish Fact from Opinion

A fact is a statement that can be proven true; an opinion is a personal judgment that cannot be proved. As you read, **distinguish facts from opinions** by asking yourself whether a statement can be proved or only reflects the writer's bias. Consider this statement by Chesnut:

> Lincoln or Seward have made such silly advances and then far sillier drawings back.

While it is a fact that Union forces made advances and then drew back, the characterization of these actions as "silly" makes this a statement of opinion.

Interest Grabber The words of actual witnesses to history are often more powerful than those of any secondhand account. Ask students to bring to class any firsthand accounts of historic events that may be in their family's possession, such as a letter from a grandfather who fought in World War II, or a diary entry recounting President Kennedy's assassination. Once students have shared their accounts, review the Background for Understanding (p. 494). To help students better appreciate the power of firsthand accounts, show an excerpt from *The Civil War* series, or display the companion book. Then explain that the diaries, journals, and letter they are about to read were written by people from different walks of life, each of whom offered a unique perspective on the events surrounding the Civil War.

Connecting Themes Across Cultures

Across cultures and throughout history, the effects of war on individuals have been recorded in personal letters, diaries, and journals. Point out that one of the most famous diaries kept during a war is *Diary of a Young Girl*, the diary of Anne Frank. Ask students what they have learned about the human sacrifices of war in other cultures from published diaries and letters they have read.

Customize for
Less Proficient Readers

To help students through these diaries, letters and journal entries, suggest that partners paraphrase complex passages. Have them focus in particular on those passages filled with terminology peculiar to that time or those that contain military terms, such as *battery, works, flank fire,* and *brigade*.

Customize for
AP Students

Guide students to read "between the lines" as they read the selections in this grouping, looking for evidence of each writer's emotions, fear, passion, and anger. Encourage them to analyze the perspective of and influences on each writer.

Test Preparation Workshop

Reading Comprehension: Context Many standardized tests require students to use context clues to determine the meaning of unfamiliar words. Use this sample test item to give students practice in this skill.

> With a nervous tremor convulsing my system, and my heart thumping like muffled drumbeats, I stood before the door of the recruiting office.

In this passage, the word convulsing most nearly means—

A shaking
B settling
C straightening
D deadening

There is no contextual support for the last three answers. A "tremor" is a trembling motion. The overall context—the nervousness, the thumping heart—suggests agitation. A is correct.

Develop Understanding

One-Minute Insight Mary Chesnut, who was both on the scene and privy to the actions and reactions of higher-ups in the Confederacy, started keeping a diary as the tension mounted in Charleston. In these entries, she provides readers with a vivid picture of the chaos and excitement accompanying the dizzying events during the days leading up to the bombardment of Fort Sumter.

◆ Background for Understanding

History South Carolina had seceded from the Union on December 20, 1860, and demanded all the federal property within the state. Federal Major Robert Anderson resisted the surrender of Fort Sumter, a fortification on an island in Charleston Harbor. On April 6, President Lincoln notified the governor of South Carolina that a ship would be bringing provisions to the fort. In response, the Confederacy decided to attack before relief arrived.

Coincidentally, while an artillery instructor at West Point, Major Anderson taught Pierre Gustave Toutant Beauregard, the Confederate brigadier general in charge of the batteries that fired on Fort Sumter.

Customize for
Less Proficient Readers
To help students track the sequence of events in these accounts, use the Chain of Events page in ***Strategies for Diverse Student Needs,*** (p. 31).

◆ Critical Thinking

❶ **Analyze** Ask students what might have prompted Mrs. Hayne to make such a comment. What do her words tell the reader about the Charlestonians' attitude toward the impending battle? *They are confident that they will win a victory over the Union troops at Fort Sumter.*

◆ Reading Strategy

❷ **Distinguish Fact From Opinion** Students should recognize that here Mary Chesnut gives her opinion; she could not have known all the facts that governed Anderson's actions or, very much about military strategy.

Connections to World Literature, *page 1180*

from

Mary Chesnut's Civil War

Mary Chesnut

In the early days of April 1861, the nation held its collective breath as the tension between North and South mounted steadily. On April 12, the opening shots of the Civil War were fired on Fort Sumter, a Union military post in Charleston, South Carolina, as the city's citizens watched from their rooftops. Mary Chesnut captured the emotional upheaval of the time in her journal.

April 7, 1861. Today things seem to have settled down a little.

One can but hope still. Lincoln or Seward[1] have made such silly advances and then far sillier drawings back. There may be a chance for peace, after all.

Things are happening so fast.

My husband has been made an aide-de-camp[2] of General Beauregard.

Three hours ago we were quietly packing to go home. The convention has adjourned.

Now he tells me the attack upon Fort Sumter[3] may begin tonight. Depends upon Anderson and the fleet outside. The *Herald* says that this show of war outside of the bar is intended for Texas.

John Manning came in with his sword and red sash. Pleased as a boy to be on Beauregard's staff while the row goes on. He has gone with Wigfall to Captain Hartstene with instructions.

Mr. Chesnut is finishing a report he had to make to the convention.

Mrs. Hayne called. She had, she said, "but one feeling, pity for those who are not here." ❶

Jack Preston, Willie Alston—"the take-life-easys," as they are called—with John Green, "the big brave," have gone down to the island—volunteered as privates.

Seven hundred men were sent over. Ammunition wagons rumbling along the streets all night. Anderson burning blue lights—signs and signals for the fleet outside, I suppose.

Today at dinner there was no allusion to things as they stand in Charleston Harbor. There was an undercurrent of intense excitement. There could not have been a more brilliant circle. In addition to our usual quartet (Judge Withers, Langdon Cheves, and Trescot) our two governors dined with us, Means and Manning.

These men all talked so delightfully. For once in my life I listened.

That over, business began. In earnest, Governor Means rummaged a sword and red sash from somewhere and brought it for Colonel Chesnut, who has gone to demand the surrender of Fort Sumter.

And now, patience—we must wait.

Why did that green goose Anderson go into Fort Sumter? Then everything began to go wrong.

Now they have intercepted a letter from him, urging them to let him surrender. He paints the horrors likely to ensue if they will not. ❷

He ought to have thought of all that before he put his head in the hole.

April 12, 1861. Anderson will not capitulate.

Yesterday was the merriest, maddest dinner we have had yet. Men were more audaciously wise and witty. We had an unspoken foreboding it was to be our last pleasant

1. **Seward:** William Henry Seward (1801–1872), U.S. Secretary of State from 1861 through 1869.
2. **aide-de-camp** (ād′ də kamp′) *n.*: Officer serving as assistant and confidential secretary to a superior.
3. **Fort Sumter:** Fort in Charleston Harbor, South Carolina. At the time, the fort was occupied by Union troops commanded by Major Robert Anderson.

From *Mary Chesnut's Civil War*, edited by C. Vann Woodward. Copyright © 1981 by C. Vann Woodward, Sally Bland Metts, Barbara G. Carpenter, Sally Bland Johnson, and Katherine W. Herbert. All rights reserved. Reprinted by permission of the publisher, Yale University Press.

Block Scheduling Strategies

Consider these suggestions to take advantage of extended class time:

- If you have access to technology, build background for the selections by working with your students to research the Civil War on the Internet. Consider going to the site suggested on p. 503.
- Hold a class discussion in which you compare and contrast the various points of view presented in these selections. How do the selections work together to present a complete story of the war?
- Have students work in small groups to complete the Literary Focus and Reading Strategy sections of the Guide for Responding (p. 504). Have the groups share their responses, and use the responses to stimulate class discussion.
- Allow class time for students to work through the stages of the Guided Writing Lesson (p. 505). Pair students with peer reviewers to assess each other's work, using the rubric for narratives based on personal experiences in the ***Formal Assessment*** booklet (p. 111).

meeting. Mr. Miles dined with us today. Mrs. Henry King rushed in: "The news, I come for the latest news—all of the men of the King family are on the island"—of which fact she seemed proud.

❸ While she was here, our peace negotiator—or envoy—came in. That is, Mr. Chesnut returned—his interview with Colonel Anderson had been deeply interesting—but was not inclined to be communicative, wanted his dinner. Felt for Anderson. Had telegraphed to President Davis[4] for instructions.

What answer to give Anderson, etc., etc. He has gone back to Fort Sumter with additional instructions.

When they were about to leave the wharf, A. H. Boykin sprang into the boat, in great excitement; thought himself ill-used. A likelihood of fighting—and he to be left behind!

I do not pretend to go to sleep. How can I? If Anderson does not accept terms—at four—the orders are—he shall be fired upon.

❹ I count four—St. Michael chimes. I begin to hope. At half-past four, the heavy booming of a cannon.

I sprang out of bed. And on my knees—prostrate—I prayed as I never prayed before.

There was a sound of stir all over the house—pattering of feet in the corridor—all seemed hurrying one way. I put on my double gown and a shawl and went, too. It was to the housetop.

The shells were bursting. In the dark I heard a man say "waste of ammunition."

I knew my husband was rowing about in a boat somewhere in that dark bay. And that the shells were roofing it over—bursting toward the fort. If Anderson was obstinate—he was to order the forts on our side to open fire. Certainly fire had begun. The regular roar of the cannon—there it was. And who could tell what each volley accomplished of death and destruction.

The women were wild, there on the housetop. Prayers from the women and imprecations from the men, and then a shell would light up the scene. Tonight, they say, the forces are to attempt to land.

The *Harriet Lane*[5] had her wheelhouse[6] smashed and put back to sea. ❺

We watched up there—everybody wondered. Fort Sumter did not fire a shot.

Today Miles and Manning, colonels now—aides to Beauregard—dined with us. The latter hoped I would keep the peace. I give him only good words, for he was to be under fire all day and night, in the bay carrying orders, etc.

Last night—or this morning truly—up on the housetop I was so weak and weary I sat down on something that looked like a black stool.

"Get up, you foolish woman—your dress is on fire," cried a man. And he put me out.

It was a chimney, and the sparks caught my clothes. Susan Preston and Mr. Venable then came up. But my fire had been extinguished before it broke out into a regular blaze. ❻

Do you know, after all that noise and our tears and prayers, nobody has been hurt. Sound and fury, signifying nothing.[7] A delusion and a snare. . . .

Somebody came in just now and reported Colonel Chesnut asleep on the sofa in General Beauregard's room. After two such nights he must be so tired as to be able to sleep anywhere. . . .

April 13, 1861. Nobody hurt, after all. How gay we were last night.

Reaction after the dread of all the slaughter we thought those dreadful cannons were making such a noise in doing.

Not even a battery[8] the worse for wear.

4. **President Davis:** Jefferson Davis (1808–1889), president of the Confederacy (1861–1865).

5. **The *Harriet Lane*:** Federal steamer that had brought provisions to Fort Sumter.

6. **wheelhouse** *n.*: Enclosed place on the upper deck of a ship, in which the helmsman stands while steering.

7. **Sound . . . nothing:** From Shakespeare's *Macbeth,* Act V, Scene v, lines 27–28. Macbeth is contemplating the significance of life and death after learning of his wife's death.

8. **battery** *n.*: Artillery unit.

◆ Build Vocabulary

capitulate (kə pich´ ə lāt´) *v.*: Surrender conditionally
audaciously (ô dā´ shəs lē) *adv.*: Boldly or daringly
foreboding (fôr bōd´ iŋ) *n.*: Presentiment
obstinate (äb´ stə nit) *adj.*: Stubborn
imprecations (im´ prə kā´ shənz) *n.*: Curses

◆ Literary Focus

❸ Diaries, Journals, and Letters Point out the writer's informal style of using fragments and incomplete sentences. These indicate that this is a diary entry not necessarily intended for publication.

◆ Critical Thinking

❹ Speculate Ask students to explain what they think Mary Chesnut prays for as she hears the cannon. *Students may say that she prays for her husband's safety, for the safety of the Confederate soldiers or for those men being shelled in the fort, or for what she fears lies ahead for everyone.*

◆ Grammar and Style

❺ Capitalization of Proper Nouns Point out that, because it is the name of a ship, *Harriet Lane* is capitalized and italicized.

◆ Background for Understanding

❻ History Explain to students that, in past centuries, it was not uncommon for a woman's skirts to catch fire. Spreading hoop skirts and open hearths were a deadly combination that left thousands of women badly—even fatally—injured.

Customize for
Intrapersonal Learners
To help these students appreciate the value of journals, use the Humanities Connection: Journals page in ***Beyond Literature.***

Extending Word Study

Connotations Ask students to reread the passage with *imprecations* and explain why the word *prayers* in the text is a clue to the meaning. Remind students that a connotation refers to the ideas a word suggests. Why did the author use *imprecations* instead of *curses?* Would the text have a different effect if *curses* were used in place of *imprecations?* Point out that the longer, more Latinate *imprecations* has a more formal and genteel sound than curses. Have students look at the connotations of *capitulate, audaciously, foreboding,* and *obstinate* on this page and substitute other words. How would different words affect the meaning or impact of the text?

Cross-Curricular Connection: Social Studies

Women's Roles in Wartime While men fought the Civil War on the battlefield, women fought it at home in several crucial ways. Many women single-handedly ran family businesses, farms, and plantations while their husbands and sons were away. Women from both the North and South worked in factories, hospitals, and in relief efforts. Some sewed uniforms at home; others functioned as spies. Hundreds even disguised themselves as men and joined the ranks.

Invite students to find out more about the role of women during the war. For instance, they can research the work of Dorothea Dix and of Clara Barton, the "angel of the battlefield." They can learn about the efforts of Mary Livermore and Mary Ann Bickerdyke for the Sanitary Commission. They can find out about Sally Tompkins and the hospital she ran in Richmond, Virginia, and of organizations such as the Women's Central Association of Relief. Some might find it interesting to look into the espionage work of Belle Boyd, Elizabeth Van Lew, or Rose Greenhow. Encourage them to share their findings with the class.

Customize for
Visual/Spatial Learners
Encourage these students to study the details in the artwork, which is closely connected to Chesnut's text. Have them consider these questions: What does the artwork reveal about the battle for Fort Sumter? What does the artwork reveal about the city of Charleston at the time of the battle? What does it reveal about the attitude of those living in Charleston toward the events that were taking place? *The fact that Fort Sumter is burning suggests that the Southerners were in the process of winning a decisive victory. The buildings in the artwork and the clothing worn by the people suggest that Charleston was a thriving cosmopolitan city. The number of people on the rooftops and their body language indicate that the people of Charleston were engrossed by the conflict and were concerned about where the fighting might lead.*

▶Critical Viewing◀

❶ **Analyze** Most of the women seem to be quite upset by the shelling and are trying to console one another. A number of them appear to be in a state of collapse.

◆Reading Strategy

❷ **Distinguish Fact From Opinion** Guide students to notice how hard Mary Chesnut had to work to separate fact from opinion, just to make sense of what was happening. Have students compare the circumstances she faced with the quality and extent of news reports today when there is a "late-breaking" story.

Connecting to World Literature

To connect this selection to world literature, see "The Eruption of Vesuvius," p. 1188.

Bombardment of Sumter, Harper's Weekly, 1861

▲ Critical Viewing How do the figures in this painting seem to be reacting to the bombing of Fort Sumter? **[Analyze]** ❶

Fort Sumter has been on fire. He has not yet silenced any of our guns. So the aides—still with swords and red sashes by way of uniform—tell us.

But the sound of those guns makes regular meals impossible. None of us go to table. But tea trays pervade the corridors, going everywhere.

Some of the anxious hearts lie on their beds and moan in solitary misery. Mrs. Wigfall and I solace ourselves with tea in my room.

These women have all a satisfying faith.

April 15, 1861. I did not know that one could live such days of excitement.

They called, "Come out—there is a crowd coming."

A mob indeed, but it was headed by Colonels Chesnut and Manning.

The crowd was shouting and showing these two as messengers of good news. They were escorted to Beauregard's headquarters. Fort Sumter had surrendered.

Those up on the housetop shouted to us, "The fort is on fire." That had been the story once or twice before.

When we had calmed down, Colonel Chesnut, who had taken it all quietly enough—if anything, more unruffled than usual in his serenity—told us how the surrender came about.

Wigfall was with them on Morris Island when he saw the fire in the fort, jumped in a little boat and, with his handkerchief as a white flag, rowed over to Fort Sumter. Wigfall went in through a porthole.

When Colonel Chesnut arrived shortly after and was received by the regular entrance, Colonel Anderson told him he had need to pick his way warily, for it was all mined.

As far as I can make out, the fort surrendered to Wigfall.

But it is all confusion. Our flag is flying there. Fire engines have been sent to put out the fire. ❷

Everybody tells you half of something and then rushes off to tell something else or to hear the last news. . . .

◆ Build Vocabulary

serenity (sə renˊ ə tē) *n.*: Calmness

Humanities: Art

Bombardment of Fort Sumter, 1861.

This wood engraving was done by an unknown artist for *Harper's Weekly* (May 4, 1861, edition). *Harper's Weekly* was one of the two major Northern illustrated newspapers that provided on-the-spot coverage of the Civil War. Correspondents and artists were dispatched by the paper to war zones to provide a steady flow of written and pictorial information for publication. Although the process of photography was in existence at this time, there was as yet no method for reproducing photographs in a newspaper. On-the-scene drawings were the means by which events of the war were visually recorded for the public. These drawings were sent to the newspaper, where a skilled artisan engraved the image into a block of wood that was inked and pressed onto paper to transfer the image.

Use these questions for discussion:

1. What details correspond to those in Mary Chesnut's account? *Chesnut describes the women as being "wild" as they watched from the rooftops.*
2. Do you think a photograph of the same scene would have been more or less effective than the drawing? Explain. *Students might note that a photograph captures only a single moment, while an artist is free to include a series of events that may have happened over a period of time.*

Recollections of a Private

Warren Lee Goss

In the weeks that followed the attack on Fort Sumter, thousands of men on both sides volunteered to fight. Among the early enlistees was Warren Lee Goss of Massachusetts.

"Cold chills" ran up and down my back as I got out of bed after the sleepless night, and shaved preparatory to other desperate deeds of valor. I was twenty years of age, and when anything unusual was to be done, like fighting or courting, I shaved.

With a nervous tremor convulsing my system, and my heart thumping like muffled
❸ drumbeats, I stood before the door of the recruiting office, and before turning the knob to
❹ enter read and reread the advertisement for recruits posted thereon, until I knew all its peculiarities. The promised chances for "travel and promotion" seemed good, and I thought I might have made a mistake in considering war so serious after all. "Chances for travel!" I must confess now, after four years of soldiering, that the "chances for travel" were no myth; but "promotion" was a little uncertain and slow.

I was in no hurry to open the door. Though determined to enlist, I was half inclined to put it off awhile; I had a fluctuation of desires; I was fainthearted and brave; I wanted to enlist, and yet—Here I turned the knob, and was relieved. . . .

My first uniform was a bad fit: My trousers
❺ were too long by three or four inches; the flan-
❻ nel shirt was coarse and unpleasant, too large at the neck and too short elsewhere. The forage cap[1] was an ungainly bag with pasteboard top and leather visor; the blouse was the only part which seemed decent; while the overcoat made me feel like a little nubbin of corn in a large ❺
preponderance of husk. Nothing except "Vir- ❻
ginia mud" ever took down my ideas of military pomp quite so low.

After enlisting I did not seem of so much consequence as I had expected. There was not so much excitement on account of my military appearance as I deemed justly my due. I was taught my facings, and at the time I thought the drillmaster needlessly fussy about shouldering, ordering, and presenting arms. At this time men were often drilled in company and regimental evolutions long before they learned the manual of arms, because of the difficulty of obtaining muskets. These we obtained at an ❼
early day, but we would willingly have resigned them after carrying them a few hours. The musket, after an hour's drill, seemed heavier and less ornamental than it had looked to be.

The first day I went out to drill, getting tired of doing the same things over and over, I said to the drill sergeant: "Let's stop this fooling and go over to the grocery." His only reply was addressed to a corporal: "Corporal, take this man ❽
out and drill him"; and the corporal did! I found that suggestions were not so well appreciated in the army as in private life, and that no wisdom was equal to a drillmaster's "Right face," "Left wheel," and "Right, oblique, march." It takes a raw recruit some time to learn that he is not to think or suggest, but obey. Some never do learn. I acquired it at last, in humility and mud, but it was tough. Yet I doubt if my patriotism, during my first three weeks' drill, was quite knee high. Drilling looks easy to a spectator, but it isn't. After a time I had cut down my uniform so that I could see out of it, and had conquered the drill sufficiently to see through it. Then the word came: on to Washington! . . .

1. **forage cap:** Cap worn by infantry soldiers.

One-Minute Insight In this journal entry, a recent Union recruit describes the reality of the drudgery of camp life for enlisted men: mud, drill, and more drill. His observations contrast sharply with the expectations that he and many other recruits had when they enlisted.

◆ Literature and Your Life

❸ Ask students if they have ever experienced a physical reaction to nervousness or excitement like the one described here. Have volunteers describe the sensation in their own words.

Customize for
Less Proficient Readers

❹ Guide students to use context clues to understand what the writer meant by *peculiarities,* since the word has a different meaning today. Help students understand that, in this case, *peculiarities* means "particulars or specifics." Today, peculiarity is generally defined as *strangeness.*

◆ Literary Focus

❺ **Diaries, Journals, and Letters** Students can appreciate the self-effacing description of the clothing Goss gives. Guide them to see that he blends fact and opinion here and elsewhere in this recollection.

Customize for
English Language Learners

❻ Refer to the lithograph on page 501 to illustrate the articles of clothing described in this passage. Provide concrete examples to clarify descriptive elements like *flannel, coarse, too large, too short,* and *too long.*

◆ Build Vocabulary

❼ **Latin Prefixes: *ob-*** Point out that the word *obtaining* contains the Latin prefix *ob-*. What word in the next paragraph also contains the prefix? *The word is* oblique.

◆ Grammar and Style

❽ **Capitalization of Proper Nouns** Explain to students that *corporal* is not capitalized here because it is not part of a proper name. Tell them that *corporal* would be capitalized if it were part of a proper name, as in "Corporal Miller."

Humanities: Music

War-time Music In 1862, abolitionist and suffragist Julia Ward Howe wrote "The Battle Hymn of the Republic" and sold it to the *Atlantic Monthly*. Union soldiers sang this song nonstop. In fact, music was ever present during the Civil War. Robert E. Lee said that he didn't believe there could be an army without music. Drumbeats spurred soldiers into battle, and regimental bands raised the spirits of marching soldiers and entertained at reviews and parades. During the lengthy and lonely encampments, soldiers sang both patriotic songs and sentimental ones.

There is a wide selection of music available that sprang from or became associated with the Civil War. Have students find out what the armies sang and listened to, North and South, and have them listen to it themselves. Invite them to learn more about the origin of some songs.

One-Minute Insight In this diary entry, Confederate soldier Randolph McKim describes the futile and bloody attempts of his regiment and others to capture Culp's Hill, the extreme right of the Federal position.

◆ Grammar and Style

❶ Capitalization of Proper Names Have students notice that full names of the regiments are capitalized.

◆ Reading Strategy

❷ Distinguish Fact From Opinion Guide students to understand that this is McKim's opinion, even though it may have been a well-informed one gained from firsthand experience.

❸ Clarification McKim correctly observes that, like Pickett's disastrous attack, the attack in which he participated was not sufficiently supported by artillery nor were its flanks, or sides, protected from enfilading fire.

A Confederate Account of the Battle of Gettysburg

Randolph McKim

From July 1 to July 3, 1863, Union and Confederate troops fought near the small town of Gettysburg, Pennsylvania. After Union troops gained control of the hills surrounding the town, the Confederate troops commanded by Robert E. Lee launched a risky attack on the strongest Union position. When the attack failed, the Confederate troops were forced to retreat at a great cost of lives. The battle, the first in which troops commanded by Lee were defeated, marked a turning point in the war. In a diary entry, Confederate soldier Randolph McKim described the final day of the battle.

Then came General Ewell's order to assume the offensive and assail the crest of Culp's Hill, on our right. . . . The works to be stormed ran almost at right angles to those we occupied. Moreover, there was a double line of entrenchments, one above the other, and each filled with troops. In moving to the attack we were exposed to enfilading fire[1] from the woods on our left flank, besides the double line of fire which we had to face in front, and a battery of artillery posted on a hill to our left rear opened upon us at short range. . . .

❶ On swept the gallant little brigade, the Third North Carolina on the right of the line, next the Second Maryland, then the three Virginia regiments (10th, 23d, and 37th), with the First North Carolina on the extreme left. Its ranks had been sadly thinned, and its energies greatly depleted by those six fearful hours of battle that morning; but its nerve and spirit were undiminished. Soon, however, the left and center were checked and then repulsed, probably by the severe flank fire from the woods; and the small remnant of the Third North Carolina, with the stronger Second Maryland (I do not recall the banners of any other regiment), were far in advance of the rest of the line. On they pressed to within about twenty or thirty paces of the works—a small but gallant band of heroes daring to attempt what could not be done by flesh and blood. ❷

The end soon came. We were beaten back to the line from which we had advanced with terrible loss, and in much confusion, but the enemy did not make a countercharge. By the strenuous efforts of the officers of the line and of the staff, order was restored, and we re-formed in the breastworks[2] from which we had emerged, there to be again exposed to an artillery fire exceeding in violence that of the early morning. It remains only to say that, like Pickett's men[3] later in the day, this single brigade was hurled unsupported against the enemy's works. ❸ Daniel's brigade remained in the breastworks during and after the charge, and neither from that command nor from any other had we any support. Of course it is to be presumed that General Daniel acted in obedience to orders. We remained in this breastwork after the charge about an hour before we finally abandoned the Federal entrenchments and retired to the foot of the hill.

1. **enfilading** (en´ fə lād iŋ) **fire:** Gunfire directed along the length of a column or line of troops.

2. **breastworks:** Low walls put up quickly as a defense in battle.

3. **Pickett's men:** General George Pickett was a Confederate officer who led the unsuccessful attack on the Union position.

Viewing and Representing Mini-Lesson

Timeline
This mini-lesson supports the Timeline activity in the Idea Bank on p. 505.

Introduce the Concept Explain that a timeline is graphic device for organizing events in chronological order and showing the connection between the events.

Develop Background Have students brainstorm some of the events leading up to the Civil War. Discuss the amount of time between events. How will the timeline mark the dates of these events? Tell students that a timeline can include brief information to explain the events. Have students discuss possible formats for the timeline and the kinds and amounts of information to be included. Students may want to review some timelines for ideas.

Apply the Information Suggest that students use note cards to record the events of the Civil War. Remind students that the timeline should be a visual representation of the key events in chronological order.

Assess the Outcome Evaluate students on their ability to create an accurate and complete timeline of the events leading to the Civil War. You may want to use the Scoring Rubric for Research Report/Paper on p. 121 in ***Alternative Assessment.***

An Account of the Battle of Bull Run

Stonewall Jackson

In this letter to his wife, Confederate General Thomas "Stonewall" Jackson recounts the first southern victory of the war: a battle fought in July 1861, outside Washington, D.C., near a small stream named Bull Run.

Stonewall Jackson at Bull Run

4 ▲ **Critical Viewing** How does the artist's depiction of Jackson enable the viewer to immediately distinguish the general from the officers and soldiers who surround him? **[Analyze]**

My precious pet,

Yesterday we fought a great battle and gained a great victory, for which all the glory is due to God alone. Although under a heavy fire for several continuous hours, I received only one wound, the breaking of the longest finger of my left hand; but the doctor says the finger can be saved. It was broken about midway between the hand and knuckle, the ball passing on the side next [to] the forefinger. Had it struck the center, I should have lost the finger. My horse was wounded, but not killed. Your coat got an ugly wound near the hip, but my servant, who is very handy, has so far repaired it that it doesn't show very much. My preservation was entirely due, as was the glorious victory, to our God, to whom be all the honor, praise and glory. The battle was the hardest that I have ever been in, but not near so hot in its fire. I commanded the center more particularly, though one of my regiments extended to the right for some distance. There were other commanders on my right and left. Whilst great credit is due to other parts of our gallant army, God made my brigade more instrumental than any other in repulsing the main attack. This is for your information only—say nothing about it. Let others speak praise, not myself. 5

One-Minute Insight Stonewall Jackson writes to his wife to inform her that he has been in a great and successful battle. He and his command performed admirably and he has emerged with no more than a broken finger. He credits God with providing for his own safety and the achievements of his troops. The letter reveals Jackson's bravery, modesty, and religious devotion.

◆ Background for Understanding

History Jackson's stand at Bull Run is the reason for his nickname, Stonewall. He held his line against overwhelming odds, bringing about an unexpected Confederate victory. His repeated references to God's hand in the victory reflect his religious fervor, which his detractors mocked with another nickname, Deacon Jackson.

Ironically, Jackson, a master tactician, died as an indirect result of a careless error. Returning at dusk after a daring and successful maneuver, he was accidentally shot by his own men. His arm was amputated, complications resulted, and he died two weeks later.

▶Critical Viewing◀

4 Analyze Students may respond that Jackson's confident, composed posture in the heat of battle, his elegant full officer's dress, and his flamboyant hat mark him as the officer in charge.

◆ Literary Focus

5 Diaries, Journals, and Letters Ask students to describe what they learn about Jackson from this letter. *Students may say that he is proud and confident, but not boastful, and that he holds strong religious beliefs.*

Humanities: Art

Stonewall Jackson at Bull Run, c. 1900, by H. A. Ogden.

Henry Alexander Ogden was an illustrator who specialized in military subjects. This image was created approximately forty years after the Battle of Bull Run actually took place. Ogden drew the original illustration, which was then made into the lithograph that appears on this page.

Lithography is a 200-year-old method of reproducing pictures. In the process, the artist draws on a specially prepared stone or metal plate with a greasy crayon. After the plate is soaked in water, it is covered with ink that sticks to the crayon but not the wet surface. Then the artist presses the paper to the plate to receive the ink. The artist applies color by hand after lifting the print off the stone.

Use the following questions for discussion:

1. Based on both this illustration and his letter, what can you infer about Jackson's personality in times of crisis? *He seems calm and in control, even in the midst of battle.*
2. Reread Jackson's description of the battle, and explain how it differs from the illustration. *Students should note that Jackson mentions his horse, suggesting that he commanded his troops from horseback, rather than on foot. He also speaks of having actively led the central regiment in battle, while he appears to be removed from the worst of the fighting in the illustration.*

One-Minute Insight Reverend Henry M. Turner uses an effusive tone to describe the exciting experience of being among the exhilarated crowd clamoring to read the Emancipation Proclamation when it was hot off the presses.

▶Critical Viewing◀

1 Connect Students may respond that the rapt attention the readers and listeners display is representative of the scene described by Reverend Turner.

2 Clarification Remind students that at that time in American history, African Americans were commonly referred to as "colored people."

◆ Grammar and Style

3 Capitalization of Proper Nouns Point out to students that the word "president" is capitalized in the first instance because it is a title, and in the second instance because it refers to a particular chief executive, Lincoln.

◆ Reading Strategy

4 Distinguish Fact From Opinion Students may recognize that Reverend Turner's euphoric conclusion, however forceful, is pure opinion.

Reteach

Distinguish Fact from Opinion

To reteach fact and opinon, draw the diagram shown here on the chalkboard. Have students provide examples in each category. Then, have students suggest other categories of fact and opinion.

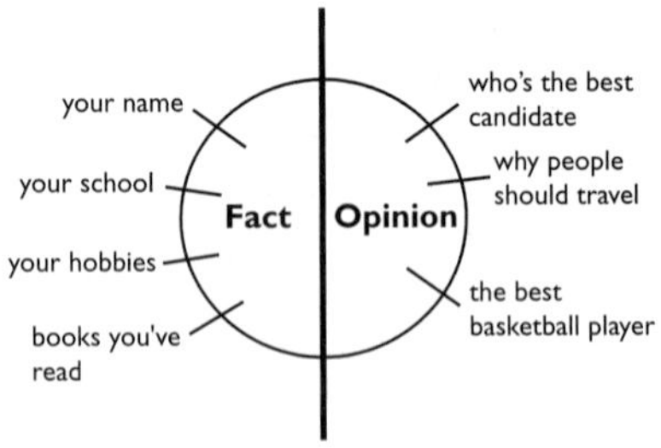

Reaction to the Emancipation Proclamation

Reverend Henry M. Turner

Reading the Emancipation Proclamation, Artist unknown

▲ **Critical Viewing** How does this illustration relate to Reverend Turner's account? **[Connect]** 1

On September 22, 1862, President Lincoln issued the Emancipation Proclamation, declaring that all slaves in states still in rebellion would be free as of January 1, 1863. Because those states were not under Union control at the time, no slaves were actually set free that day. The Proclamation, however, was a powerful symbol of hope for those still in slavery and inspired a wave of Union support from free African Americans. In this account, Reverend Henry M. Turner, a free-born African American living in Washington, D.C., describes his people's reaction to the news of the Proclamation.

Seeing such a multitude of people in and around my church, I hurriedly sent up to the office of the first paper in which the proclamation of freedom could be printed, known as the *Evening Star*, and squeezed myself through the dense crowd that was waiting for the paper. The first sheet run off with the proclamation in it was grabbed for by three of us, but some active young man got possession of it and fled. The next sheet was grabbed for by several, and was torn into tatters. The third sheet from the press was grabbed for by several, but I succeeded in procuring so much of it as contained the proclamation, and off I went for life and death. Down Pennsylvania Avenue I ran as for my life, and when the people saw me coming with the paper in my hand they raised a shouting cheer that was almost deafening. As many as could get around me lifted me to a great platform, and I started to read the proclamation. I had run the best end of a mile, I was out of breath, and could not read. Mr. Hinton, to whom I handed the paper, read it with great force and clearness. While he was reading every kind of demonstration and gesticulation was going on. Men squealed, women fainted, dogs barked, white and colored people shook hands, songs were sung, and by this time 2 cannons began to fire at the navy yard, and follow in the wake of the roar that had for some time been going on behind the White House. . . . Great processions of colored and white men marched to and fro and passed in front of the White House and congratulated President Lincoln on his proclamation. The President 3 came to the window and made responsive bows, and thousands told him, if he would come out of that palace, they would hug him to death. . . . It was indeed a time of times, and nothing like it will ever be seen again in this life. 4

Humanities: Art

Reading the Emancipation Proclamation, 1865, Anonymous.

This lithograph is a dramatization of an event that must have occurred countless times in the South in 1863, the year the Emancipation Proclamation was issued. Created by an artist whose name is lost to history, the lithograph shows a Union Soldier reading the proclamation to African Americans living in a cabin in the South. Although the artist may have been overly sentimental in this depiction, the proclamation must have inspired an intense emotional reaction.

Use these questions for discussion:

1. How does the artist create a sense of drama? *Students may note how a burning torch is held over the soldier, lighting both the proclamation and the dramatic figure of the kneeling woman dressed in white.*
2. What emotions do the people in the picture exhibit? *The soldier has the undivided attention of the listeners. Their faces, gestures, and body language appear to express relief, amazement, awe, and excitement.*

An Account of an Experience With Discrimination

Sojourner Truth

Although the Civil War brought an end to slavery, the struggle against racial discrimination was just beginning. In the following letter, written on October 1, 1865, Sojourner Truth describes an encounter with racism.

A few weeks ago I was in company with my friend Josephine S. Griffing, when the conductor of a streetcar refused to stop his car for me, although [I was] closely following Josephine and holding on to the iron rail. They dragged me a number of yards before she succeeded in stopping them. She reported the conductor to the president of the City Railway, who dismissed him at once, and told me to take the number of the car whenever I was mistreated by a conductor or driver. On the 13th I had occasion to go for necessities for the patients in the Freedmen's Hospital where I have been doing and advising for a number of months. I thought now I would get a ride without trouble as I was in company with another friend, Laura S. Haviland of Michigan. As I ascended the platform of the car, the conductor pushed me, saying "Go back—get off here." I told him I was not going off, then "I'll put you off" said he furiously, clenching my right arm with both hands, using such violence that he seemed about to succeed, when Mrs. Haviland told him he was not going to put me off. "Does she belong to you?" said he in a hurried angry tone. she replied, "She does not belong to me, but she belongs to humanity." The number of the car was noted, and conductor dismissed at once upon the report to the president, who advised his arrest for assault and battery as my shoulder was sprained by his effort to put me off. Accordingly I had him arrested and the case tried before Justice Thompson. My shoulder was very lame and swollen, but is better. It is hard for the old slaveholding spirit to die. But die it must. . . .

Guide for Responding

◆ Literature and Your Life

Reader's Response In the early days of the Civil War, would you have volunteered to fight? Why or why not?

Thematic Focus In what ways have these selections added to your understanding of the Civil War?

Questions for Research Did any Southerners oppose slavery? Did Northerners support it? Refine these questions to begin research.

☑ Check Your Comprehension

1. What events does Mary Chesnut describe in her diary entries?
2. Summarize the events described in the accounts of the three soldiers.
3. What is the reaction to the Emancipation Proclamation among the members of Reverend Turner's audience?

◆ Critical Thinking

INTERPRET

1. What does Mary Chesnut's diary reveal about her attitude toward the war? **[Interpret]**
2. How do Private Goss's attitudes and expectations change after he has enlisted? **[Analyze]**
3. How would you describe the tone of (a) Randolph McKim's and (b) Stonewall Jackson's accounts? **[Analyze]**
4. Why did the Emancipation Proclamation have such an emotional effect on African Americans who were already free? **[Speculate]**
5. Given that Truth assumed she could ride a streetcar "without trouble as I was in company with" Laura S. Haviland, what can you reasonably infer about Haviland? **[Infer]**

APPLY

6. How might Chesnut's diary have been different if she had been from the North? **[Modify]**

COMPARE LITERARY WORKS

7. Contrast the different tones of Sojourner Truth and Henry Turner. Speculate why they might be different. **[Compare and Contrast]**

Beyond the Selection

FURTHER READING

Other Firsthand Accounts of the Civil War

For Cause & Comrades: Why Men Fought in the Civil War, James M. McPherson
The Life of Johnny Reb, Bell I. Wiley
The Life of Billy Yank, Bell I. Wiley

INTERNET

To learn more about the life and times of these diarists, we suggest the following sites. Please be aware, however, that sites may have changed since

For battlefield maps, see
http://icorps.com/gburgmap.jpg

To read the speech given by Sojourner Truth at the 1851 Woman's Convention in Akron, Ohio, go to
http://pacific.discover.net/~dansyr/truth.html

We *strongly recommend* that you preview the sites before you send students to them.

One-Minute Insight Sojourner Truth describes her proactive responses to acts of racial discrimination on a streetcar.

Reinforce and Extend

Customize for
AP Students
To get a richer appreciation of the common soldier's experience in the Civil War, historians rely heavily on regimental histories and individual memoirs. Students interested in getting these firsthand insights may enjoy reading the published histories of the First Minnesota or of the Iron Brigade. Or they may enjoy *All For The Union: The Civil War Diary and Letters of Elisha Hunt Rhodes.*

Answers

◆ Literature and Your Life

Reader's Response Students should explain the reasoning behind their responses.

Thematic Focus Student responses should reflect a new awareness of the impact of the war on the lives of individuals.

☑ Check Your Comprehension

1. She describes the events surrounding the firing on Fort Sumter by Confederate troops.
2. Goss describes his enlistment and training as a Union soldier. McKim recounts how his brigade attempted to charge Culp's Hill and was beaten back. Jackson relates his victory at Bull Run.
3. The proclamation is received with jubilation, relief, and gratitude.

◆ Critical Thinking

1. She thinks the South has no choice but to fight, but she is afraid of the war's consequences.
2. Suggested response: Before enlisting he imagined himself looking impressive and exciting in uniform; after enlistment he develops a more realistic and humble image of himself.
3. (a) McKim's tone might be described as proud and slightly fatalistic; (b) Jackson's might be described as straightforward and humble.

(Answers continue on p. 504)

Guide for Responding (continued)

◆ Literary Focus

Diaries, Journals, and Letters

These **diaries, journals,** and **letters** describe Civil War events and people, as well as the writers' personal responses to them.

1. Many of Mary Chesnut's descriptions are colored by her dislike for the war. Give at least two examples that indicate this dislike.

2. Stonewall Jackson's letter is intended for his wife alone. Find three examples of details or ideas that Jackson probably would have omitted from an account intended for publication.

3. What does Sojourner Truth's letter reveal about her own personality?

◆ Build Vocabulary

Using the Latin Prefix *ob-*

Use your understanding of the Latin prefix *ob-*, meaning "against," to match each of the following situations to the word that most closely relates to it.

a. obstruction *(n.)* **b.** obscure *(v.)* **c.** object *(v.)*

1. voice opposition in the courtroom

2. a fallen tree blocking the road

3. cloud an issue with confusing arguments

Using the Word Bank: Sentence Completions

Write each of the following sentences on your paper, filling in the blanks with an appropriate word from the Word Bank.

1. When the rifle jammed, the soldier muttered __?__ at his bad luck.

2. There was no __?__ to be found in the troubled hearts and minds of soldiers and civilians.

3. As enemy shells exploded in the distance, a sense of __?__ hung over the camp like fog.

4. Despite the overwhelming odds facing his brigade, the general refused to __?__.

5. What one person would call __?__, another person might call courageous.

6. After midnight, the spies crept __?__ close to the enemy's encampment.

◆ Reading Strategy

Distinguish Fact From Opinion

By reading carefully and asking yourself whether certain assertions can be verified, you can **distinguish fact from opinion.** Each of the following sentences contains elements of fact and opinion. Identify the facts and opinions in each.

1. [Goss:] The forage cap was an ungainly bag with pasteboard top and leather visor; the blouse was the only part which seemed decent; while the overcoat made me feel like a little nubbin of corn in a large preponderance of husk.

2. [Jackson:] Your coat got an ugly wound near the hip, but my servant, who is very handy, has so far repaired it that it doesn't show very much.

3. [Turner:] Mr. Hinton, to whom I handed the paper, read it with great force and clearness.

◆ Grammar and Style

Capitalization of Proper Nouns

The name of a street, road, town, city, county, or state is considered a **proper noun** and should begin with a **capital letter**. Directional words (east, west, and so on) that are part of the name of a place should also begin with a capital; for example, **N**orth **D**akota.

Practice Rewrite these sentences from the selections, correcting any errors in capitalization.

1. The *herald* says that this show of war outside of the bar is intended for texas.

2. On swept the gallant little brigade, the third north Carolina on the right of the line, next the second maryland, then the three virginia regiments (10th, 23d, and 37th), with the first north carolina on the extreme left.

3. Down Pennsylvania avenue I ran as for my life, and when the People saw me coming with the paper in my hand they raised a shouting cheer that was almost deafening.

4. Accordingly I had him arrested and the Case tried before justice Thompson.

Answers *(continued from p. 503)*

4. Suggested response: It represented an official recognition of African Americans' right to live freely and symbolized the beginning of a new era in United States history.
5. One can infer that Laura Haviland was white.
6. Suggested response: She probably would have dreaded the shelling even more, and would have seen the Union soldiers who defended Fort Sumter as heroes.
7. Possible response: Rev. Turner's tone is one of excitement and hope while Sojourner Truth's tone reflects the pain of discrimination.

◆ Literary Focus

1. Suggested responses include: When the deadline passes without drawing gunfire on Fort Sumter, she writes, "I begin to hope [that there will be no fighting]." She could not sleep beforehand and is so distracted by the prospect of the war that she accidentally set herself on fire. She comments that the sound of the guns makes regular meals and social activities impossible. Her quotation of *Macbeth* also expresses her feelings.
2. Suggested response: He would have omitted the salutation to his wife, the details about the wound to his finger, about damage to his coat, and about his brigade being central to the Confederate success in the battle.
3. It reveals that she is a strong, determined woman who will not allow herself to be intimidated.

◆ Build Vocabulary

Using the Latin Prefix *ob-*

1. c 2. a 3. b

Using the Word Bank

1. imprecations; 2. serenity; 3. foreboding; 4. capitulate; 5. obstinate; 6. audaciously

◆ Reading Strategy

1. Facts: The forage cap had a pasteboard top and leather visor. Opinions: The forage cap was "an ungainly bag"; the blouse "was the only part which seemed decent"; and the coat made him feel like a small ear of corn lost in its husk.
2. Facts: Jackson's coat was damaged near the hip; his servant repaired it. Opinions: The word *ugly* and the statement that the repair "doesn't show very much."
3. Facts: Rev. Turner handed the paper to Mr. Hinton, who read it. Opinion: It was read with "great force and clearness."

◆ Grammar and Style

1. *Herald*, Texas
2. the Third North Carolina, the Second Maryland, the three Virginia regiments, the First North Carolina
3. Pennsylvania Avenue, the people
4. the case, Justice Thompson

Grammar Reinforcement

For additional instruction and practice, use the lesson on Types of Nouns in the Nouns and Pronouns unit of the **Language Lab CD-ROM** and the pages on Capitalization, pp. 81–82, in the *Writer's Solution Grammar Practice Book.*

Build Your Portfolio

Idea Bank

Writing

1. **Summary** Write a factual summary of the events described in the excerpt from *Mary Chesnut's Civil War.* Use transitions to link ideas and indicate the time order of events.
2. **Book Jacket** Persuade readers to buy a book of Civil War diary and journal entries and letters by writing a book jacket explaining the unique perspective of the war offered in these accounts.
3. **Reflective Essay** Today, few take the time to correspond or keep a journal. How is this a loss? In an essay, explore the personal benefits and historical value of engaging in this type of writing. Use these selections to illustrate your points.

Speaking, Listening, and Viewing

4. **Viewing** Examine pictures of weapons used in the Civil War and compare them with weapons used in wars today. What different impressions of war do the images convey? Poll classmates about what impressions the images give them. **[Performing Arts Link]**
5. **Dramatic Reading** Rev. Turner recounts the emotional impact created by the Emancipation Proclamation. Deliver a dramatic reading of the document, accompanied by music that conveys the tone of your interpretation. **[Music Link]**

Researching and Representing

6. **Timeline** By the time Lincoln was inaugurated, seven states had seceded. Research the 1860 presidential election to learn what Lincoln's victory meant to the South. Create a timeline of events leading to the Civil War. **[Social Studies Link]**
7. **Model/Map** Work in a small group to research the Battle of Gettysburg. Create a model or map of the battlefield. Identify the locations of key events with explanatory captions. **[Social Studies Link]**

Online Activity www.phlit.phschool.com

Guided Writing Lesson

Firsthand Biography

Do you know someone personally whose accomplishments or experiences are noteworthy? Recount the events of his or her life in a firsthand biography that reflects your perspective on the individual. This brief but revealing profile should include some description of the person, as well as biographical information and your impressions of his or her achievements and personality. Bring your subject to life with action-packed verbs that engage readers.

Writing Skills Focus: Vivid Verbs

Strong, precise verbs, called **vivid verbs**, add liveliness to writing. They name specific actions that help readers envision the events being recounted. This passage from Goss's "Recollections of a Private," for example, would not be nearly as effective if it simply stated that Goss "was nervous." Vivid verbs, however, bring to life his experience as he prepared to enlist in the army.

Model From Private Goss's Account

With a nervous tremor *convulsing* my system, and my heart *thumping* like muffled drumbeats . . .

Prewriting Make a list of your subject's accomplishments or experiences and his or her personal qualities—character, appearance, behavior, and so on. If possible, interview your subject to gather specific biographical information. Then decide which details best reveal your perspective on your subject.

Drafting Focus on the most telling facts, details, and anecdotes. Consider using quotations or dialogue to convey your subject's personality. Keep your writing lively by using vivid verbs.

Revising Compare your draft with your prewriting list. Did you capture the subject as you perceive him or her? Which details should you add? Which seem unnecessary? Where can you replace dull verb choices with vivid verbs?

✓ ASSESSMENT OPTIONS

Formal Assessment, Selection Test, pp. 150–152, and Assessment Resources Software. The selection test is designed so that it can be easily customized to the performance levels of your students.

Alternative Assessment, p. 31, includes options for less advanced students, more advanced students, interpersonal learners, musical/rhythmic learners, and visual/spatial learners.

PORTFOLIO ASSESSMENT

Use the following rubrics in the ***Alternative Assessment*** booklet to assess student writing:
Summary: Summary Rubric, p. 113
Book Jacket: Persuasion Rubric, p. 120
Reflective Essay: Expression Rubric, p. 109
Guided Writing Lesson: Narrative Based on Personal Experience Rubric, p. 111

Idea Bank

Customizing for *Performance Levels*

Following are suggestions for matching Idea Bank topics with your students' performance levels:
Less Advanced Students: 1, 4
Average Students: 2, 5, 7
More Advanced Students: 3, 6

Customizing for *Learning Modalities*

Following are suggestions for matching Idea Bank topics with your students' learning modalities:
Verbal/Linguistic: 4
Musical/Rhythmic: 5
Logical/Mathematical: 6
Visual/Spatial: 7

Guided Writing Lesson

For more prewriting, elaboration, and revision strategies, see *Prentice Hall Writing and Grammar.*

Writers at Work Videodisc

Have students view the videodisc segment (Ch. 2) featuring Native American writer N. Scott Momaday to learn the Pulitzer Prize-winning author's thoughts on the rules of narration. Ask students to discuss which of these rules might apply to their firsthand biographies.

Play frames 14950 to 17080

Writing Lab CD-ROM

Have students complete the tutorial on Narration. Follow these steps:

1. Have students focus their writing by completing a Purpose Profile.
2. Have students gather details using the Character Trait Word Bin either before or after they have drafted on the computer.
3. Students who have trouble punctuating dialogue can use the interactive instruction in the Revising and Editing section to aid revision.

LESSON OBJECTIVES

1. **To develop vocabulary and word identification skills**
   - Critical Thinking
   - Idea Bank: Telegram
   - Idea Bank: Critical Essay
2. **To analyze literary elements**
   - Thematic Connection
   - Literary Connection
3. **To read in order to research self-selected and assigned topics**
   - Idea Bank: Poster
4. **To plan, prepare, organize, and present literary interpretations**
   - Idea Bank: News Story
   - Idea Bank: Debate

Interest Grabber Have groups of students gather video footage of the Gulf War. Have them show highlights to the class. Follow with a discussion of the differences between seeing these events on TV and experiencing them firsthand. Tell students that they're about to read a firsthand account.

Customize for
English Language Learners
Less Proficient Readers
Help these students comprehend journalistic jargon, such as *pool, zones,* and *squeezed . . . for details.* Explain political and military terms they may not know, such as *coalition of nations* or *collateral damage.*

Customize for
Visual/Spatial Learners
Display a map of the Persian Gulf region to help students locate key places mentioned in this piece: Saudi Arabia, Dhahran, Kuwait, Iraq, Baghdad, and the Red Sea. Keep the map available as students read.

CONNECTIONS TO TODAY'S WORLD

Gulf War Journal *from* A Woman at War

Molly Moore

Literary Connection

WAR DIARIES, JOURNALS, AND LETTERS

The letters and diary and journal entries in Part 2 tell the story of the Civil War as seen through the eyes of people who experienced it firsthand. Through these intimate literary forms, each of these eyewitnesses—none of whom was a professional writer—presents a personal view of the events of the time.

In her book *A Woman at War*, journalist Molly Moore records her impressions of a modern conflict, the Persian Gulf War between Iraq and a coalition of forces led by the United States. Although Moore, as a newspaper reporter, usually writes objective news stories, this personal account of her experiences as a witness to history makes exciting reading. In this excerpt, she relates her story behind the news story—what it was like to cover the Persian Gulf War from the military zone. Like the personal accounts you have already read, Moore's narrative reveals a human side to war.

Thematic Connection

REVEALING THE HIDDEN FACES OF WAR

The Civil War was a long, bloody conflict that tore the nation apart. Those living outside the war zone, however, never fully comprehended the horror and devastation wrought by the war. Communication was limited and slow. Newspapers, where available, were a key source of information, but the news they contained was often days old. The only way to really understand the impact of the war was to live through it.

In the late 1960's, Americans experienced their first "living-room war" as violent, disturbing footage of the Vietnam War flashed across television screens every evening. The 1991 Persian Gulf War was a full-scale media event that unfolded in real time before the eyes of millions worldwide who watched round-the-clock coverage on satellite and cable news stations. Though viewers were able to "experience" war as never before, there is still something unique and compelling about a personal account by an eyewitness near the action, as journalist Molly Moore was in Saudi Arabia during the Gulf War.

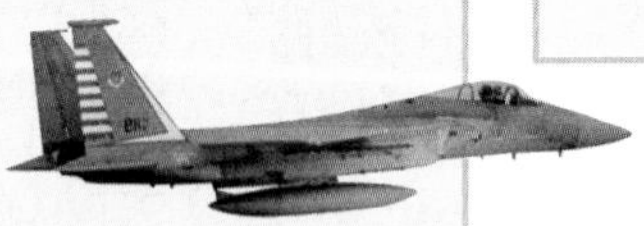

MOLLY MOORE
(1956–)

Molly Moore has worked for *The Washington Post* since 1981, covering local and state government; the Pentagon (for five years, including the Gulf War); and as a foreign correspondent in South Asia, covering India, Pakistan, Afghanistan, Bangladesh, Nepal, Bhutan and Sri Lanka. She is currently a foreign correspondent based in Mexico City.

Moore says she wrote *A Woman at War* because she came away from the Gulf War believing that most of the world had seen only the television version that was portrayed as a quick and effortless victory by the American armed forces. "That was not the war I witnessed as I accompanied the commanding Marine general on the front lines as he led his troops into Kuwait. There was nothing easy about the ground war. It was a war fraught with mistakes, miscalculations, and human frailty, a war in which each tent and every foxhole was a private battlefield of anguish and emotion."

Prentice Hall Literature Program Resources

REINFORCE / RETEACH / EXTEND

Selection Support Pages
Build Vocabulary: Military Jargon, p. 149
Thematic Connections: Revealing the Hidden Faces of War, p. 150

Formal Assessment Selection Test, pp. 153–154; Assessment Resources Software

Resource Pro CD-ROM

Gulf War Journal *from* A Woman at War

Molly Moore

1 ▲ **Critical Viewing** Speculate about the events leading up to this photograph taken outside the Dhahran International Hotel. What might the camera operator have been doing that caused the Saudi Arabian security guard to intervene? **[Speculate]**

2 *In August 1990, Iraqi troops under the command of dictator Saddam Hussein invaded neighboring Kuwait, a tiny oil-rich nation on the Persian Gulf. Despite economic sanctions and repeated demands by the United Nations Security Council, Iraq refused to withdraw from Kuwait. In late November 1990, the Council presented the invaders with an ultimatum: leave Kuwait by January 15, 1991, or a coalition of nations, including the United States, would use "all necessary means" to remove Iraqi troops from Kuwait. Iraq ignored the threat. Early on the morning of January 17, 1991, coalition forces began bombing Iraqi targets, marking the official launch of the Persian Gulf War, also known as Operation Desert Storm. Hundreds of reporters, Molly Moore among them, were gathered at the Dhahran International Hotel in Dhahran, Saudi Arabia, when the airstrike began.*

A thunderous roar jarred me out of a light sleep. The hotel windows rattled and the entire building shook. I recognized the sound almost instantly: The U.S. Air Force's 1st Tactical Fighter Wing was taking off outside my window. The fighter jets normally took off in pairs, seldom more than six at a time. But this was a massive, continuous wave of noise as a dozen or more of the F-15 Eagle fighters fired their afterburners and sped into the night sky. It could mean only one thing: The war had started. I glanced at my watch. It was 1:45 a.m.

Almost simultaneously I heard dozens of

Develop Understanding

Connections to Today's World

This selection provides an excellent opportunity for contrasting the events of the Civil War with more recent wars such as the Persian Gulf War. As students read, have them focus on making the following comparisons between the Persian Gulf War and the Civil War: differences in how the wars were fought; differences in how the public received information about the events; differences in how the nation reacted to the two wars; similarities and differences in the emotions experienced by those involved in the events.

One-Minute Insight

This piece blends the objective reporting style of a seasoned military correspondent at the brink of war with the human reactions of a person suddenly put in a life-threatening situation. The author provides a glimpse into the chaotic life of a war reporter racing to do her job in the face of fear, confusion, technical problems, and ethical questions.

▶Critical Viewing◀

1 **Speculate** Students may say that he was filming something he was not allowed to film. They may suggest that the men in the background could have been Saudi dignitaries.

◆ *Literature and Your Life*

2 Ask students whether they have any personal recollections of the Persian Gulf War in 1991. They may have had family members or friends who were involved in Operation Desert Storm, at home or abroad, or who lived or worked in the area at that time. Do any students recall seeing or reading news coverage of the event? Invite volunteers to share their memories.

Block Scheduling Strategies

Consider these suggestions to take advantage of extended class time:

- Following the suggestions in the Interest Grabber note on p. 506, allow class time for groups of students to show video footage of the Persian Gulf War. Follow with a class discussion.
- Either before or after students read the selection, have small groups research the Gulf War on the Internet. Allow time for the groups to share their findings with the rest of the class.
- After students have finished reading, hold a class discussion in which you compare and contrast Molly Moore's journal entry with the accounts of the Civil War on pp. 496–503. You can use the questions in the Literary Connection and Thematic Connection sections on p. 512 to guide the discussion.
- Have groups of students hold debates on the rights and responsibilities of the press during wartime (assignment 4 in the Idea Bank, p. 512).

▶Critical Viewing◀

❶ **Hypothesize** This location adds a sense of immediacy and drama to the report—falsely creating a sense that the reporter is on the front lines in the middle of the action.

❷ **Clarification** Explain to students that major newspapers like *The Washington Post* have different departments, with editors in charge of the articles for those departments. The "foreign desk" refers to the staff that edits articles about foreign affairs. Other departments might include the national desk, sports desk, local desk, science desk, and so on.

▶Critical Viewing◀

❸ **Compare** Have students compare the polished news reports they typically see or read with the chaotic moments the journalist experiences behind the scenes. *Students should note that most news reports are delivered with a sense of calm and authority that contrasts with the chaos described here.* Discuss why "the enormity of the moment and the uncertainty of its consequences" must have felt so overwhelming. *Students may say that when a long-awaited event finally happens, the fears of the unknown outcome become very real.*

❶ ▲ **Critical Viewing** These journalists are presenting their report from atop a tank. Why might the journalists have chosen this location for filming? **[Hypothesize]**

footsteps pounding down the hallways outside my door. The telephone rang. It was my *Washington Post* colleague in the room across the hall.

"It's started," said Guy Gugliotta, a seasoned foreign correspondant who'd been sent to Saudi Arabia to relieve me when I'd returned to Washington in December.

"I just heard the planes take off," I replied, collecting notebooks and a pen from the small desk in my room.

❷ "We just got the first pool report[1] from another air base up north," Gugliotta said. "I'm calling the foreign desk now."

"I'll be upstairs," I told him. "See you there."

❸ I joined the mob surging up the steps to the military's Joint Information Bureau on the third floor of the hotel. Despite the months of waiting and speculation and the more than one hundred stories I'd written dissecting Operation Desert Shield, the enormity of the moment and the uncertainty of its consequences were almost overwhelming.

So much for "military disinformation." More than three hundred reporters now jammed the Dhahran International's opulent third-floor ballroom, which had been converted into large pressrooms. Reporters squeezed the public affairs officers for details and snatched copies of the media pool reports as soon as they were dictated by the pool of reporters assigned to an air base northwest of Dhahran.

Gugliotta joined me after giving the *Post* the meager information he had from the first pool report. "There's nothing coming out of Washington," he said. "Nobody has announced anything. Cheney[2] is supposed to make a statement later tonight."

An ABC *Nightline* reporter thrust a microphone into my face. "How do you feel about the information the military is providing about the war?"

1. **pool report:** During the Persian Gulf War, firsthand information was compiled, or pooled, in reports that then were released to all of the media organizations covering the war.

2. **Cheney** (chā´ nē): U.S. Secretary of Defense Richard Cheney.

Beyond the Classroom

Career Connection

News Journalist The field of news journalism offers professional writers the opportunity to report on newsworthy events on the local, national, and international levels. From parades and town meetings to politics, finance, and war, the news media deliver information on a broad range of topics each day. Journalists may write for newspapers, news magazines, or news services, or they may broadcast their reports via radio, television, or cable news programming.

Within the field of news journalism, the training requirements are as varied as the career options. While many journalists enter the job market with a liberal arts degree, others pursue specialized degrees at universities with schools of journalism. Internships with local newspapers and radio and television stations provide potential young news journalists with valuable, hands-on job experience.

I was tempted to say, "What information?" It's always a sure sign that there isn't any real information when reporters start interviewing each other.

"The only information we've gotten so far has been from the reporters on one of the pools," I replied. "At least that worked pretty well. Reporters were at the base where some of the first planes took off and they managed to get to a telephone to dictate a story before Washington even admitted the war had started."

Suddenly an ear-piercing siren wailed through the building.

"What is that?" I shouted to Gugliotta.

"Bomb shelter, get down to the bomb shelter," he yelled.

I followed the herd. As I sprinted down the stairs I noticed the signs that had been added since I'd left six weeks earlier: "To the shelters," with arrows pointing the way.

Almost six hundred hotel guests and staff spilled down the stairwells in near panic. Had the Iraqis launched a counterattack? Were they roaring down the coastal highway toward Dhahran? Had Saddam Hussein fired Scud missiles at us? We'd known since August that the hotel was in a prime target zone. It sat beside the most active military airfield in Saudi Arabia.

In the basement, frantic hotel employees tried to guide the frenzied crowd into half a
❹ dozen rooms, including the kitchen. Above the din, Philip Congdon, a former officer of the British special forces, who had been hired as the hotel's defense consultant, threatened, "Sit down or you will be tried!"

I was in a group that was shoved into the kitchen and ordered to lie on the floor. We were surrounded by large plate-glass windows. An explosion would send shards ripping through the air. I crawled beneath a large steel table, thinking it might protect me from flying glass.

"Everyone please sit down and put on your gas masks," directed Congdon, a wiry man who looked to be in his early fifties. Even when giving frightening directives, Congdon had one of those self-assured voices that could calm a hysterical mob.

❺ The people around me were pulling gas masks over their faces. I panicked. I had no mask. *The Washington Post*'s chemical protection suits had not yet arrived from British Aerospace in London even though we'd ordered them almost two months earlier.

"I don't have a mask," I called in a strained voice to Congdon. He looked at me with exasperation. "Just sit down, I'll get you something," he said impatiently.

Moments later he returned with a crude, spongy contraption that looked somewhat like a surgical mask and covered only my nose and mouth. I slipped it on, knowing it would merely postpone death a microsecond. I sat on the gritty kitchen floor, surrounded by slimy, rotting tomato halves and colleagues in full-face masks. If I could smell the stench of the tomatoes on the floor and the spoiled chicken parts on the counter above me, I figured chemical particles would have no trouble penetrating my pathetic mask.

The information vacuum was almost unbearable. We knew nothing about what was going on at the air base outside our windows or the world outside Saudi Arabia. The siren continued its annoying wail.

Someone pulled out a shortwave radio.

". . . In the event of an attack, there is likely to be a reprisal," the crackly voice said. "There is no reaction from the Iraqi side yet."

I breathed a little easier.

At 3:50 a.m., about thirty minutes after the siren sounded, the hotel security chief called an all clear, the signal that we could remove our gas masks and leave the basement shelter. The civil defense alert had been called because of uncertainty about how the Iraqi military would react to the first bombs dropped on Baghdad. As we pushed our way into the ❻
crowded corridors, Congdon warned, "You should be aware that the early stage of an offensive is the most likely time for an attack on Dhahran."

As soon as we were released from our temporary captivity, the JIB began activating emergency media pools in an effort to get reporters across the street to the air base, where pilots would soon be returning with tales of the first bombing runs. The reporters who would serve on these quick-reaction pools had been

Thematic Connection

❹ Revealing the Hidden Faces of War During the Civil War, journalists were usually not in immediate danger. They would travel with the commander's staff, well behind the firing lines. Photographers and artists did their work before or after battles. The group at the Dhahran International Hotel, however, were in "a prime target zone." The group included reporters, photographers, guests, tourists, hotel workers, and others who just happened to be there at that time. Encourage students to compare the descriptions of this scene to the descriptions of fear and chaos expressed by Mary Chesnut and Randolph McKim.

❺ Clarification Explain that during the Persian Gulf War there was fear that the Iraqis would use invisible chemical or biological weapons, such as nerve gas, against Allied forces.

❻ Clarification Baghdad, the capital of Iraq, is located near the center of the country on the Tigris River.

Cross-Curricular Connection: Social Studies

Technology and the News Major newspapers cover stories that break all over the world. How do they accomplish this? Advances in technology have transformed the way news is gathered, reported, and delivered to our nation's newspapers and newsmagazines. Digital phones, satellite links, computer modems, the Internet, and even e-mail now make it possible for reporters to file stories in seconds from virtually anywhere in the world. Photographs, which once took hours, even days, to develop, print, and ship, are now digitized and transmitted electronically. Computer desktop publishing programs give publications the speed and flexibility to make last-minute changes and additions that were once difficult, if not impossible, to make.

Have each interested student research one of the many ways in which newspapers report, photograph, and transmit news from all corners of the globe so that articles are accurate, prompt, and compelling. They can combine their findings with those of other students to present a multifaceted group presentation.

Thematic Connection

❶ Revealing the Hidden Faces of War Discuss the difference in journalism during this war and the Civil War. While it took days, perhaps weeks, for news of the Civil War to make its way to the anxious public, the Persian Gulf War practically unfolded in the world's living rooms. Not only do technological advances today let journalists speed their stories almost instantly to any part of the world, the standards of quality reporting are more strict than they were in the nineteenth century. Then, it took days for "true facts" to become available; early stories were often filled with errors and inaccuracies, some of which remained uncorrected. Journalists, then as now, had jobs to do, so they submitted reports with whatever details they gathered.

▶Critical Viewing◀

❷ Speculate Due to the sophistication of today's computer-guided weaponry, the military can launch attacks from great distances. Today's soldiers may fight an entire war without ever confronting enemy troops.

Thematic Connection

❸ Revealing the Hidden Faces of War In the Civil War, many ordinary soldiers and citizens wrote about their experiences. These writings describe a broad range of human emotions, including pride, fear, revulsion, and loneliness. Discuss the impact of reading a firsthand observation, especially from someone who does a dangerous and possibly deadly job. Human nature intervenes so that even a brave fighter pilot acknowledges fear amidst his duty.

selected days earlier after acrimonious debates among feuding news organizations. Now, the public affairs officers couldn't find the *New York Times* reporter assigned to the pool. Guy Gugliotta volunteered to take his place. As he collected his sleeping bag and rucksack, ❶ Gugliotta rattled off the instructions for operating the satellite telephone the *Post* had leased for our war coverage. For a $53,000 leasing fee, we could have instant communications to Washington from anywhere on the battlefield, including the roof of the Dhahran International Hotel, where the high-tech contraption now sat.

Within the last hour, a convoy of humvees[3] with machine guns mounted on their roofs had formed a tight ring around the front of the hotel.

I began piecing together the details. At 1:30 a.m., the guided-missile cruiser USS *San Jacinto*, stationed in the Red Sea, had fired the opening shot of the war: a 1.6 ton, twenty-foot-long Tomahawk cruise missile aimed at downtown Baghdad. Minutes later fighter planes based across the street from our hotel, as well as warplanes from bases across the Arabian Peninsula, roared into the sky toward Iraq.

Pool reports from reporters interviewing pilots began trickling into the JIB.

3. **humvees:** Large, rugged military vehicles known as High Mobility Multi-Purpose Wheeled Vehicles. The term *humvee* is derived from the acronym HMMWV.

▼ **Critical Viewing** How did computer-guided missiles such as the one in this photograph change the nature of combat? **[Speculate]** ❷

Beyond the Classroom

Workplace Skills Connection

Networking Have students ever wondered how reporters get their information? How do these writers "get the scoop" on stories that no one else is reporting? One way journalists get the news as it breaks is by working hard to cultivate networks of friends, acquaintances, and other well-placed sources who can provide pertinent information. Successful journalists must be good listeners; they must also be able to record and recall information accurately, and use good judgment, often with little or no time to spare.

Have students think of other work environments in which the ability to build and rely on a network of contacts is a useful skill. Examples might include police or detective work, social work, real estate, public relations, or scientific research.

"Baghdad lit up like a Christmas tree," Air Force colonel George Walton told reporters as he climbed out of his F-4G Wild Weasel electronic warfare jet.

"It was the scariest thing I've ever done," Lieutenant Ian Long, a British Tornado pilot, recounted. "Some tracers came off the target[4] down our left-hand side. We tried to avoid that by going right. On our right-hand side was a
3 mass of white explosions, and yellow explosions that looked like flak.[5] You're frightened of failure, you're frightened of dying. You're flying as low as you dare, but high enough to get the weapons off. As the bombs come off, you just run . . . "

I tried to telephone the new details to the *Post.* I dialed and redialed and redialed. The hotel's switchboard was jammed. I raced to the roof of the hotel. Since I had last been there six weeks earlier, it had become a jungle of satellite dishes, talk-show sets, and camera tripods. The hotel employees called it "Little Hollywood." Wires and electrical cords were coiled and stretched in every direction like a giant plate of spaghetti. It was dark and starting to mist.

I found the *Post* satellite telephone, a midget beside the monster network dishes. Its collapsible dish was about the size of a large umbrella. I pulled out my scribbled instructions and read them in the beam of my flashlight.

"Turn the generator on. The choke is on the back. Give pull one jerk. Adjust the choke." It operated like a lawn mower. Unlike a lawn mower, it started on the first try.

I switched on the telephone, encased in a metal box that looked like a large suitcase, and punched numbers on a keypad until "Indian"—as in Indian Ocean—appeared on a digital readout. I pressed the keypad again to find the designated satellite shore station at Perth, Australia. I dialed a code and *The Washington Post* foreign desk number. I heard three rings. "Foreign desk," said the perfectly clear voice on the other end of the telephone.

4. **"Some tracers . . . target:** The Iraqi military bases targeted for bombing responded by firing tracers, ammunition that traces its own course with a visible trail of smoke or fire.
5. **flak** (flak): Antiaircraft gunfire.

Guide for Responding

◆ Literature and Your Life

Reader's Response If you had been in Moore's place, would you have been exhilarated or terrified by the experiences described in this excerpt? Explain.

Thematic Focus How does this passage provide a subjective look at the process of objectively reporting a war?

☑ Check Your Comprehension

1. Why do the author and her colleagues rush to the Joint Information Bureau?
2. Why are the journalists at the Dhahran International Hotel at risk of injury?
3. Why is the civil defense alert called?

◆ Critical Thinking

INTERPRET

1. Given that the Dhahran International Hotel is located in a "prime target zone," why do you think journalists are willing to stay there? **[Infer]**
2. Why is an attack on "the most active military airfield in Saudi Arabia" a real possibility? **[Analyze]**

APPLY

3. Why do you think the author straps on the "pathetic mask," if she knows it will "merely postpone death a microsecond"? **[Speculate]**

EXTEND

4. Based on this journal passage, what personal qualities do you think are necessary for a career as a war correspondent for a newspaper, magazine, or broadcast company? **[Career Link]**

Reinforce and Extend

Customize for
AP Students
Challenge students to read news articles of the time to compare the early coverage of Operation Desert Storm with Molly Moore's account.

Answers

◆ Literature and Your Life

Reader's Response Students should support their responses with well-reasoned explanations.

Thematic Focus Because it is told from the personal perspective of a reporter, the reader is given a "behind-the-scenes" look at what goes into the job of gathering news.

☑ Check Your Comprehension

1. After hearing fighter planes take off, they want to collect information from public affairs officers and the "pool reporters."
2. The hotel is located next to an active air base.
3. U. S. planes bombed Baghdad, and an Iraqi reprisal is possible.

◆ Critical Thinking

1. Suggested response: Despite the obvious dangers, they must feel that being close to the action will give them a better opportunity to gather information for their stories.
2. U.S. war planes have dropped bombs on downtown Baghdad. In response, the Iraqi government could order bombing of American strongholds, such as the airfield next to the Dhahran International Hotel.
3. She is near panic, and she probably feels that even limited protection is better than none.
4. Suggested response: War correspondents must have the ability to stay calm and collected in the face of danger.

Beyond the Selection

FURTHER READING

Other Observations of the Persian Gulf and Civil Wars

Hotel Warriors: Covering the Gulf War, John J. Fialka
Ironclaw: A Navy Carrier Pilot's War Experience, Sherman Baldwin
Recollections of the Civil War, Charles A. Dana
Dispatches, Michael Herr

We suggest that you preview these works before recommending them to students.

INTERNET

You can get additional information about the Gulf War on the Internet. We suggest the following site, which includes maps, photographs, commentary, and a chronology of events:
http://www.pbs.org/wgbh/pages/frontline/gulf/index.html

Please be aware that the site may have changed since this information was published. We *strongly recommend* that you preview the site before you send students to it.

Answers
Literary Connection

1. As a reporter, Moore has the high-profile and often high-risk job of gathering the news where it happens—in the war zone. Most women of the Civil War era played important supporting roles, but they were usually more removed from the battlefront.
2. Moore's account is full of references to modern military and communications technology, such as jets, cruise missiles, humvees, machine guns, telephones, satellites, microphones, and shortwave radios.

Thematic Connection

1. Mary Chesnut gets her information from personal observation, her husband, the newspaper, and various acquaintances. Molly Moore gets her information from personal observation, her colleagues, and official announcements.
2. Molly Moore's situation in the Dhahran International Hotel more closely resembles the situation of Randolph McKim. Both are on—or perilously near—a battlefield or military target. Mary Chesnut writes from the relative safety of her own home, far from Charleston Harbor.

Idea Bank

Customizing for
Performance Levels
Following are suggestions for matching Idea Bank topics with your students' performance levels:
Less Advanced Students: 1
Average Students: 2, 5
More Advanced Students: 3, 4

Customizing for
Learning Modalities
Following are suggestions for matching Idea Bank topics with your students' learning modalities:
Logical/Mathematical: 4, 5
Visual/Spatial: 5

Literary Connection

Twentieth-Century Diaries, Journals, and Letters

Through Civil War letters and journals, you get a "behind the scenes" look at the individuals who were caught up in the war's dramatic events. Similarly, Molly Moore, in her journal of Gulf War experiences, gives readers a glimpse of what daily life was like for the journalists who sent news reports home from the battlefield.

1. How does Molly Moore's role in the war contrast with that of women during the Civil War?
2. What other details of Molly Moore's account confirm that it was written in the 1990's and not the 1860's?

Thematic Connection

Revealing the Hidden Faces of War

"Official" information about the Civil War was hard to obtain. However, in our own time, information about war is instantly accessible to people far from the battlefields. Sophisticated media technology allows civilians to "witness" the sights, sounds, and harsh realities of conflicts taking place around the globe.

1. Compare and contrast the way Mary Chesnut and Molly Moore get information about the wars.
2. Does Molly Moore's situation in the Dhahran International Hotel more closely resemble the situation of Mary Chesnut or of Randolph McKim? Explain your answer.

Idea Bank

Writing

1. **Telegram** None of the six accounts of the Civil War in Part 2 is written by a journalist. Imagine that you are Molly Moore observing the Battle of Gettysburg firsthand. Compose a telegram to your editor at a Washington newspaper, in which you give information about what you have witnessed. **[Social Studies Link]**
2. **News Story** As a professional journalist, Molly Moore writes objective, factual stories for publication in *The Washington Post.* Write a news story such as Moore might have written about the war-related events described in this journal excerpt. **[Career Link]**
3. **Critical Essay** The accounts in Part 2 offer a personal glimpse of the excitement and confusion that often surround dramatic historic events. Good journalism, however, dictates that news accounts be factually accurate and unbiased. Write an essay in which you discuss the historical value of each type of account—personal/subjective journals and letters versus objective news reports—using the selections in Part 2 as well as your own knowledge of news media to support your points. **[Social Studies Link]**

Speaking, Listening, and Viewing

4. **Debate** In times of war, soldiers' lives often depend on how well military secrets are kept. In a democracy, though, the public has the right to know what policies the government is pursuing—in war as well as in peace. When does the press cross the line between keeping citizens informed and endangering national security? With a group of classmates, organize and stage a debate about the rights and responsibilities of the press during wartime. **[Social Studies Link]**

Researching and Representing

5. **Poster** The Civil War and the Persian Gulf War were dramatically different wars in almost every way: why, where, and how they were fought. Research both the American Civil War and the Persian Gulf War. Use your research and your knowledge of the selections to create a poster that compares and contrasts the two wars. Use both words and pictures to show the contrast in at least four areas, such as location, American casualties, weaponry, technology, news coverage, and so on. **[Social Studies Link; Art Link]**

Online Activity www.phlit.phschool.com

ASSESSMENT OPTIONS

Formal Assessment, Selection Test, pp. 153–154, and Assessment Resources Software. The selection test is designed so that it can be easily customized to the performance levels of your students.

PORTFOLIO ASSESSMENT
Use the following rubrics in the ***Alternative Assessment*** booklet to assess student writing:
Telegram: Description Rubric, p. 112
News Story: Description Rubric, p. 112
Critical Essay: Literary Analysis/Interpretation Rubric, p. 127

Writing Process Workshop — Historical Narrative

In this section, you saw how a historical event such as the Civil War can be brought to life through the stories of people who lived through it. Stories that capture or re-create significant events from the past are called historical narratives. Historical narratives can be true stories told from the point of view of people who lived through the events, or they can be written by historians or even fiction writers who piece together events through research. The following skills will help you write your own historical narrative:

Writing Skills Focus

- **Use vivid verbs** to capture the action as clearly and precisely as possible. (See p. 505.)
- **Establish a mood** that is appropriate to the event you are describing.
- **Show, don't tell.** Instead of simply telling what happened, focus on bringing the event to life through dialogue and vivid descriptions of the action.

Warren Lee Goss uses all of these skills to bring his wartime experiences to life.

MODEL FROM LITERATURE

from "Recollections of a Private"
by Warren Lee Goss

"Cold chills" ran up and down my back as I got out of bed after the sleepless night, ① and shaved preparatory to other desperate deeds of valor. I was twenty years of age, and when anything unusual was to be done, like fighting or courting, I shaved.

With a nervous tremor convulsing my system, and my heart thumping ② like muffled drumbeats, ③ I stood before the door of the recruiting office. . . ."

① *Goss creates a chilling, suspenseful mood.*
② *Words like "convulsing" and "thumping" create a vivid picture of the action.*
③ *Instead of just telling the reader "I was so nervous," Goss re-creates his feelings for readers through a detailed description.*

Prepare and Engage

LESSON OBJECTIVES

- To use recursive writing processes to write a historical narrative
- To recognize and correct shifts in tense
- To recognize and use correct punctuation

To make students aware of some of the criteria on which their work will be evaluated, distribute the scoring rubric for Fictional Narrative in ***Alternative Assessment*** (p. 110). See the suggestions on page 515 for customizing the rubric to this workshop.

Refer students to the Writing Handbook, page 1192, for instruction in the writing process, and page 1194 for further information on narrative writing.

Writers at Work Videodisc
To introduce students to key elements of narrative writing, play the videodisc segment on Narration featuring Pulitzer Prize-winning novelist and poet N. Scott Momaday (Ch. 2).

Play frames 14950 to 17080

Writing Lab CD-ROM
If your students have access to computers, you may want to have them work in the tutorial on Narration to complete all or part of their historical narratives. Have students follow these steps:

1. Use the Story Line Diagram, an organizing tool that shapes main events into a plot.
2. Draft their historical narratives on the computer.
3. Respond to an interactive Self-Evaluation Checklist to help them judge the effectiveness of their historical narratives.

Humanities: Film

Bringing History to Life Books, feature films, and made-for-television movies are contemporary examples of historical fiction.

Point out that writers of historical fiction base their stories on actual events but must create dialogue since there is usually no complete record of individual's thoughts and ideas. In addition, writers may create characters or condense several real people into one character to maintain the accessibility or interest level of the story.

Ask students to discuss films or books they know that fit this genre. *Students may suggest television movies like* "The Tuskegee Airmen" *about an African American fighting squadron during World War II and* "The Soul of the Game" *about Negro League baseball; feature films like* Titanic *about the doomed oceanliner and* A League of Their Own *about the professional women's baseball league. The novel* The Autobiography of Miss Jane Pittman *is another example of historical narrative.*

Develop Student Writing

Prewriting Strategy

To help students focus their narratives, use a pentad like the one shown here. After students have filled out the points, have them draw a triangle between the three points they find most compelling. Although they will include the details from all the points, the triangle will be the focus of their narrative.

Customize for
Visual/Spatial Learners

A great way to learn about the daily life of those who lived in the past is to view paintings from that time period, either in museums or in art history books. Watching movies can also help students gather details related to dress and dialect. However, point out that Hollywood can sometimes glamorize or exaggerate the past, sacrificing an historically accurate picture.

Elaboration Strategy

Encourage students to reveal character traits through dialogue and actions rather than direct statements.

Writing Lab CD-ROM

Students may benefit from reviewing audio-annotated literary models of settings with different moods in the Developing Narrative Elements section of the tutorial. Students can see examples of how the choice of details creates a specific mood.

Applying Language Skills

Avoiding Shifts in Tense Writers of historical narratives must keep the action in the past. While students may have little difficulty with the simple past tense, you may need to focus instruction on past perfect forms. Encourage students to imagine a time line with the different events plotted on it. This graphic aid can help them determine which past events occurred prior to other events that are also in the past.

APPLYING LANGUAGE SKILLS: Avoiding Shifts in Tense

When writing a narrative, it's important to be careful to avoid shifts in verb tense. For example, if you are writing in the past tense, be careful not to shift into the present.

Incorrect: The private waited as the enemy approached. He is nervous.

Correct: The private waited as the enemy approached. He was nervous.

Practice Identify and correct shifts in verb tense in the following items. Indicate if any are correct as written.

1. My mom walked in. She's amazed to see how clean my room was.
2. All of our energy had drained out of us by the time the game began. There was little chance we'd win.
3. Everyone is laughing as the circus clown ran through the audience.

Writing Application As you draft your narrative, be careful to avoid shifts in tense.

Writer's Solution Connection
Writing Lab

Use the Character Trait Word Bin and the Setting Profile in the Narration tutorial to develop these elements.

Prewriting

Choose a Topic Think of family members, neighbors, and family friends who have had interesting experiences. Interview one or more of them and ask them about their experiences or their memories of historical events. Review the information you've gathered, and choose an event that you think will make an interesting topic. As an alternative, you might consider one of the topic ideas listed here.

Topic Ideas

- The Califonia gold rush
- A record-breaking sports event
- The discovery of a cure for a disease
- A political scandal

Gather Information If you've chosen a topic from the distant past, you will have to conduct library research to learn more about it. Search computer databases for information using key words about your topic. Good nonfiction books and journal articles about your topic or original news stories from the period will provide you with the kinds of details you need to write a lively and interesting historical narrative. If your topic is from the recent past, search the Internet for facts you might not find elsewhere and consider conducting personal interviews with people who remember the events about which you are writing.

Drafting

Start Your Narrative A historical narrative, like any other story, should have one or more characters, a setting, and a clear sequence of events. Use one of those elements to grab your readers' attention.

- Begin with a vivid description of the setting (Example: a quiet laboratory or a noisy, crowded stadium).
- Introduce one of the characters with a catchy bit of dialogue (Example: a politician's comments to a reporter).
- Jump right into a high point of the action (Example: the moment a character first strikes gold).

Develop Characters and Setting Drawing from the information you gathered through research, create well-developed characters and a vivid setting. Include details of setting that will give readers a clear picture of time and place of the action. Remember that your setting is most likely very different from the settings with which readers are familiar.

Answers

1. My mom walked in. She was amazed to see how clean my room was.
2. *Correct as is.*
3. Everyone was laughing as the circus clown ran through the audience.

Grammar Reinforcement

For additional instruction and practice, refer students to the Correct and Effective Verbs lesson in the **Language Lab CD-ROM** and practice (p. 57) in the *Writer's Solution Grammar Practice Book.*

Revising

Use a Checklist Go back to the Writing Skills Focus on the first page of the lesson and use the items as a checklist to evaluate and revise your historical narrative.

- ▶ Have you created a mood that is appropriate to your subject? Is it suspenseful, comic, serious, tragic, or exciting? *Look for places where you can add or change details to enhance the mood of your narrative.*
- ▶ Have you used vivid verbs that bring each action to life? *Replace any dull or vague verbs with precise, vivid ones. For example, you might replace the verb "ran" with the more precise verb "sprinted."*
- ▶ Have you shown the action rather than merely telling about it? *Look for places where you can create a more detailed picture of the action by adding dialogue or vivid descriptive details.*

Revision Model

Before she finished milking the cows, Sarah ~~checked her watch~~ ① noticed the sun setting and wondered when Jonah would return from market. He had been gone for four days, and the journey ~~was~~ usually ~~shorter.~~ ② took only three.

① The writer edits out details that do not match the setting.

② This information clarifies the narrative's conflict.

Publishing

Illustrate Your Narrative Illustrations can give your narrative a polished, professional appearance. Aside from embellishing your writing, illustrations can set a mood or help your readers visualize characters, settings, and events. If you like to draw, you might enjoy creating portraits of the characters or bringing major scenes to life through your artwork.

Publish a Class Anthology Collect the finished narratives, and assemble them into an anthology. Bind them together with a table of contents and illustrations. If you have access to a desktop publishing program, reformat the narratives to give your anthology a unified look. Make several copies of your anthology to distribute to other classrooms or the school library.

Applying Language Skills: Punctuating Dialogue

Observe these punctuation rules when writing dialogue:

- Use a comma inside the closing quotation marks when a remark comes before the speaker tag:

  "I'm going out," my brother shouted.

- Use a comma before the opening quotation marks when a quoted statement comes after the speaker tag:

  He then added, "Come along!"

- When a speaker tag interrupts a direct quotation, use commas to set off the two parts of the quotation.

  "I would love to," I responded, "but I have to study for a test."

Practice Correct punctuation errors in the following items.

1. The porter shouted "All aboard!"
2. "Why" he asked "is there a chase in every movie?"
3. "That trail is the most scenic" the guide said.

Writing Application As you review your narrative, check to be sure all dialogue is punctuated correctly.

Writer's Solution Connection
Writing Lab

For more on punctuating dialogue, see the Proofreading section of the Writing Lab Narration tutorial.

Revision Strategy

Encourage students to meet in writing groups and discuss ways of improving the clarity, detail, or realism or their work.

Writing Lab CD-ROM

The Revising and Editing section of the Narration tutorial includes tools to check for transitions, language variety, and sentence length.

Publishing

Illustrated narratives and class anthologies can be donated to a library, tourism bureau, or historical society.

Applying Language Skills

Punctuating Dialogue Explain that dialogue won't flow if readers need to stop to make sense of the mechanics involved. When dialogue is punctuated correctly, readers should not even notice its punctuation.

Answers

1. The porter shouted, "All aboard!"
2. "Why," he asked, "is there a chase in every movie?"
3. "That trail is the most scenic," the guide said.

Grammar Reinforcement

For additional instruction and practice, refer to the **Language Lab CD-ROM** lesson on Quotation Marks, Colons, and Semicolons.

Reinforce and Extend

Prentice Hall Writing and Grammar For more prewriting, elaboration, and revision strategies, see *Prentice Hall Writing and Grammar.*

✓ ASSESSMENT

PORTFOLIO ASSESSMENT Use the rubrics on fictional narratives in ***Alternative Assessment*** booklet (p. 110) to assess students' writing. Add the following criteria to further customize the rubric to this assignment.

	4	3	2	1
Establishing Mood	The writer effectively creates and sustains a memorable mood for the entire narrative.	The writer sustains a mood for most of the narrative.	The writer rarely establishes any mood in the course of the narrative.	The writer avoids establishing any mood, or attempts to do so are ineffective or unclear.
Punctuating Dialogue	The writer consistently punctuates various types of dialogue correctly.	The writer punctuates some types of dialogue correctly, but makes errors with certain positions of dialogue within sentences.	The writer rarely punctuates dialogue correctly.	The writer consistently makes errors in punctuating dialogue.

Prepare and Engage

LESSON OBJECTIVES

- To locate information on the Internet
- To recognize bias and propaganda

Customize for
Logical/Mathematical Learners
Challenge these students to look for information that is omitted from the screen shot in the student edition. Ask, what is missing that might serve to make this Steinbeck Home Page more credible? Logical/Mathematical learners may point out that the name of the author of the brief biographical text is not included. Furthermore, no information is given about the funding or mailing address of this "institute." Not only is this information missing, but there are no links to other pages that might include it (e.g., "Click here to find out more about . . .").

Customize for
Visual/Spatial Learners
These students might enjoy sketching an alternate design for this Web page that allows for more space to cite sources and thus improve its credibility. For example, the sources cited for the biography might be listed on a separate page that contains source information for all facts presented on the entire site. Also, the word "members" could be color-coded to provide a link to a list of profiles of the institute members.

Apply the Strategies

Answers

1. The following credentials support this source: the Home Page is credited to an institute dedicated to Steinbeck Studies; the entry is written by a former English professor at Stanford; and the details are cited as being from *Benet's Reader Encyclopedia* and the *Encyclopedia Britannica*.
2. The information is probably reliable because the source has valid credentials. It may not be completely objective becaue it is the Home Page of Steinbeck aficionados; it may be biased against including information that is unflattering to the writer.

Student Success Workshop

Real-World Reading Skills: Locating Information on the Internet

Strategies for Success

Sports scores, articles, discussions, games, images, and more travel the Internet every second. When you locate information on the Internet, you must determine what is useful or reliable and what is not.

Internet Sources There are many indexes and directories organized by subject to help you locate information on the Internet, including Yahoo!, the World Wide Web Virtual Library, and the Webcrawler. These help you find direct links to information related to your topic.

Question the Source All Internet sources are not created equal. Anyone with a computer and an Internet linkup can transmit data or create a Home Page. Complete your own review process to determine the reliability of the information.

Sort the Information To evaluate Internet data, examine its content and format. Questions like these can help:

- ▶ What is the source of the information—a respected publisher or organization, a discussion group, or an individual's Home Page? Are original sources provided?
- ▶ Does the source have credentials—such as experience in the subject area or affiliation with a recognized organization?
- ▶ Is the source objective, or is the organization or individual seeking to persuade you to think or act in a certain way?
- ▶ Is the information up to date?

Take Action If the source seems reliable, review the information to determine whether it's appropriate. Are statements supported by evidence? Verify information in at least one—and preferably two—additional sources.

Apply the Strategies

As a fan of John Steinbeck, you want to learn more about him. A friend referred you to this Steinbeck Home Page. Evaluate its reliability.

1. What credentials support this source?
2. Would you consider the information reliable? Objective? Why or why not?

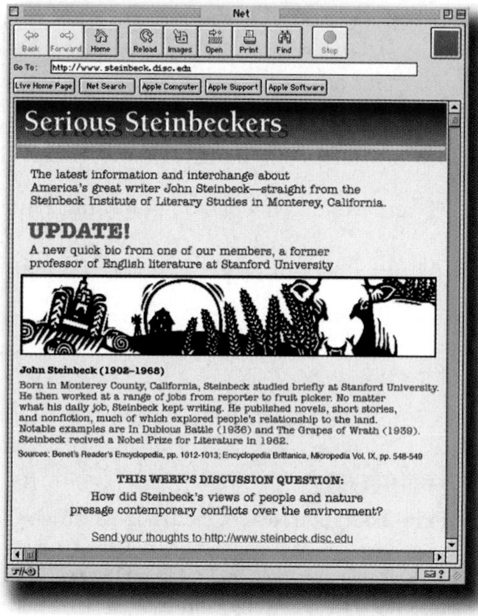

✔ *You should evaluate Internet information when doing the following:*

- ▶ *Conducting research for a project*
- ▶ *Finding information on hobbies and special interests*
- ▶ *Comparing products and services*

Test Preparation Workshop

Recognize Forms of Propaganda
Many standardized tests require students to identify bias and propaganda. Use the following sample test item to give students practice in this skill.

Steinbeck is the most important American writer of this century. His Nobel Prize-winning novel "The Grapes of Wrath" is a favorite of anyone who knows anything about American literature.

The writer tries to convince the reader of Steinbeck's superiority by—

A suggesting that to disagree means the reader doesn't know American literature
B suggesting that Steinbeck won the Nobel Prize
C suggesting that Steinbeck wrote a novel
D suggesting that Steinbeck is an American author

The writer uses a reader's fear of appearing uninformed about American literature to discourage disagreement. The correct answer is A.

Part 3 # *Forging New Frontiers*

The Old Stage Coach of the Plains, Frederic Remington, Amon Carter Museum, Fort Worth, Texas

Humanities: Art

The Old Stage Coach of the Plains, Frederic Remington.

Remington (1861–1909) was a New Yorker who fell in love with the West after a trip to Montana; he continued to live in the East but traveled extensively throughoutout the West and became known for lively paintings that captured the spirit of the American frontier. Remington's earlier paintings are full of precise detail, but his later work focused on communicating emotion.

Have your students link the painting to the focus of this part (Forging New Frontiers) by answering the following questions:

1. What ideas does Remington convey by focusing more on the horses than on the coach and its passengers? *Sample answer: Remington suggests the power and physical effort needed to transport people and settle the West.*
2. How does the twilight help to convey a mood? *Since the travellers are moving at night, the painting suggests that life on the frontier is one of endlessness or exhaustion.*

One-Minute Planning Guide

The selections in this section capture the flavor of frontier life in the Old West, a unique time and place in American history. The hilarious narrative of "The Notorious Jumping Frog of Calaveras County" takes students deep into the American frontier. "The Outcasts of Poker Flat" presents an entirely different aspect of frontier life—its singular system of justice. "Heading West" is an excerpt from a diary of a woman who, along with her husband, leaves the comfortable East to move to a community in the Kansas frontier. "I Will Fight No More Forever" is Native American Chief Joseph's poignant surrender speech in which he relates the tragic plight of his people, who are scattered, dead, or starving because of battles with the United States Army. The classic story "To Build a Fire" pits the brutal cold of the Yukon against a foolish traveler. This section also features folklore of the American West; "Pecos Bill Becomes a Coyote," "The Legend of Gregorio Cortez," and "The Streets of Laredo" present a more romanticized view of the frontier. Part 3 ends with an excerpt from *Lonesome Dove,* a contemporary work that presents another idealized picture of the Old West.

Customize for *Varying Student Needs*

When assigning the selections in this part, keep in mind these factors:

"The Notorious Jumping Frog of Calaveras County"
- A very engaging humorous tall tale
- English language learners may need help with the unique dialect.

"The Outcasts of Poker Flat"
- Engaging story of western justice and survival

"Heading West"
- Clear juxtaposition of expectations and reality as experienced by the pioneers

"I Will Fight No More Forever"
- Poignant and very brief surrender speech
- Challenge more advanced students to contrast contemporary portrayals of Native Americans with the impression made here.

"To Build a Fire"
- High-interest story of a battle for survival against nature

Prepare and Engage

LESSON OBJECTIVES

1. **To develop vocabulary and word identification skills**
   - Greek Prefixes: *mono-*
   - Using the Word Bank: Antonyms
2. **To use a variety of reading strategies to comprehend a short story**
   - Connect Your Experience
   - Background for Understanding
3. **To express and support responses to the text**
   - Critical Thinking
   - Idea Bank: Cartoon
   - Idea Bank: Obituary
   - Idea Bank: Analytic Essay
   - Idea Bank: Illustration
4. **To analyze literary elements**
   - Literary Focus: Humor
   - Compare Literary Works
   - Reading Strategy: Understand Regional Dialect
5. **To read in order to research self-selected and assigned topics**
   - Research Skills Mini-Lesson (ATE)
   - Questions for Research
   - Idea Bank: Interview
   - Idea Bank: Multimedia Presentation
6. **To plan, prepare, organize, and present literary interpretations**
   - Idea Bank: Oral Interpretation
7. **To use recursive writing processes to write a humorous anecdote**
   - Guided Writing Lesson
8. **To increase knowledge of the rules of grammar and usage**
   - Grammar and Style: Double Negatives

Test Preparation

Reading Comprehension: Context (ATE, p. 519)
The teaching tips and sample test item in this workshop support the instruction and practice in the unit workshop:
Reading Comprehension: Using Context: (SE, p. 631)

Guide for Interpreting

Featured in AUTHORS IN DEPTH Series

Mark Twain *(1835–1910)*

Although Mark Twain is widely regarded as one of the greatest American writers, the world-renowned author once indicated that he would have preferred to spend his life as a famous Mississippi riverboat pilot. Though the comment was probably not entirely serious, Twain so loved life on the river that as a young man, he did in fact work as a riverboat pilot for several years. His childhood on the banks of the Mississippi fostered more than a love of riverboats—it also became the basis for many of his most famous works, including *The Adventures of Tom Sawyer* (1876) and *The Adventures of Huckleberry Finn* (1884).

Life on the River Twain, whose real name is Samuel Langhorne Clemens, felt so closely tied to the Mississippi River that he even took his pen name, Mark Twain, from a river man's call meaning "two fathoms deep," indicating that the river is deep enough for a boat to pass safely. He grew up in the Mississippi River town of Hannibal, Missouri. When he was eleven, his father died, and he left school to become a printer's apprentice. He worked as a printer in a number of different cities before deciding at age twenty-one to pursue a career as a riverboat pilot.

A Traveling Man When the Civil War closed traffic on the Mississippi, Twain went west to Nevada. There he worked as a journalist and lecturer, developing the entertaining writing style that made him famous. In 1865, when he published "The Notorious Jumping Frog of Calaveras County," his version of a tall tale he heard in a mining camp, Twain became an international celebrity.

Following the publication of *The Innocents Abroad* (1869), a successful book of humorous travel letters, Twain moved to Hartford, Connecticut, where he was to make his home for the rest of his life. There he began using his past experiences as raw material for his books. He drew on his travels in the western mining region for *Roughing It* (1872) and turned his childhood experiences on the Mississippi into *The Adventures of Tom Sawyer, Life on the Mississippi,* and *The Adventures of Huckleberry Finn.* The latter title in particular so greatly influenced other writers that Ernest Hemingway praised it with these words:

> ***"All modern American literature comes from one book by Mark Twain called* Huckleberry Finn.*"***

Twain traveled widely throughout his career, and his adventures abroad were fuel for a number of books. After living in Europe for several years, he returned home with his family. Following the death of his wife and three of their four children, Twain's writing depicted an increasingly pessimistic view of society and human nature. His work, however, continued to display the same masterful command of language that had already established him as one of America's finest fiction writers.

◆ Background for Understanding

HISTORY: TWAIN WITNESSES AMERICA'S WESTWARD EXPANSION

Twain was an eyewitness to the nineteenth-century expansion of the western frontier. He was a young man when wagon trains left his home state to cross the prairies on the Oregon Trail, and he later saw the transcontinental railroad built. He traveled throughout the rapidly expanding nation, working first on the Mississippi, then in the West, before settling in Connecticut. The rich variety of people and places he observed are reflected in the setting, characters, and dialogue of his uniquely American literature. Twain was working as a gold prospector in California when he heard the story that became "The Notorious Jumping Frog of Calaveras County."

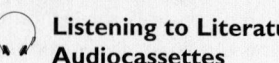

Prentice Hall Literature Program Resources

REINFORCE / RETEACH / EXTEND

Selection Support Pages
Build Vocabulary: Prefixes: *mono-*, p. 151
Grammar and Style: Double Negatives, p. 152
Reading Strategy: Regional Dialect, p. 153
Literary Focus: Humor, p. 154

Strategies for Diverse Student Needs, p. 32

Beyond Literature Workplace Skills: Jargon, p. 32

Formal Assessment Selection Test, pp. 158–160; Assessment Resources Software

Alternative Assessment, p. 32

Writing and Language Transparencies
Writing Process Model 3, pp. 13–16

Resource Pro CD-ROM

Listening to Literature Audiocassettes

Literature CD-ROM

◆ The Boys' Ambition *from* Life on the Mississippi ◆ The Notorious Jumping Frog of Calaveras County

◆ *Literature and Your Life*

Connect Your Experience

Today, the world is changing rapidly through almost daily advancements in technology. During Mark Twain's day, America was also changing at a fast pace—although perhaps not as rapidly as today—as advances in transportation helped settlers venture across the ever-expanding frontier. As these stories illustrate, no writer better captured the flavor of life on the new frontier than Twain.

Journal Writing Jot down your impressions of American frontier life, and explain whether or not you think you would have thrived on the frontier.

Thematic Focus: Forging New Frontiers

As you read, notice what the stories reveal about life on the developing frontier, and compare frontier life to life in today's world.

◆ Build Vocabulary

Greek Prefixes: *mono-*

Simon Wheeler from "The Notorious Jumping Frog of Calaversas County" is described as a *monotonous* storyteller. Knowing that the Greek prefix *mono-* means "alone," "single," or "one," you might guess that a monotonous storyteller is someone who drones on without varying his or her tone and pace. You'd be close to the actual meaning of the word: "tiresome because unvarying."

Word Bank

Preview this list of words from the selections.

- transient
- prodigious
- eminence
- garrulous
- conjectured
- monotonous
- interminable
- ornery

◆ Grammar and Style

Double Negatives

To capture how people from certain regions speak, writers like Mark Twain sometimes have their characters use **double negatives**—two words with negative meanings when only one is needed. Double negatives are not acceptable in standard English.

Nonstandard: . . . he didn't have no idea what the matter was

Standard: . . . he had no idea what the matter was
. . . he didn't have any idea what the matter was

Some negative words to watch for are *no, none, never, nobody, not* (and *-n't*), *no one, nothing, nowhere, neither, barely, scarcely,* and *hardly*.

◆ Literary Focus

Humor

"The Notorious Jumping Frog of Calaveras County" has become a classic humorous tale. **Humor** is writing intended to evoke laughter. Humorists use a variety of techniques to make their work amusing. Many western humorists of the 1800's, including Mark Twain, exaggerate and embellish certain incidents and details to such an extent that they become comical. Often these incidents are related by a narrator or storyteller in a very serious tone. This tone makes the story even funnier by creating the impression that the storyteller is unaware of the ridiculousness of what he or she is describing.

◆ Reading Strategy

Understand Regional Dialect

Much of the humor in Twain's writing comes not just from exaggeration and embellishment, but also from the language he uses. Twain was a master at using **regional dialect**—language specific to a particular region. You may not at first recognize the words that some of the characters use. By sounding out these words, however, you'll discover that they represent regional pronunciations of words with which you're familiar.

Interest Grabber Tell students that Mark Twain was a writer who used exaggeration, embellishment, regional dialect, and—as in the preceding example—boyhood recollections to make his stories humorous. Then ask students to brainstorm for a list of different kinds of humor that they enjoy—such as humorous stories, jokes, or riddles—inviting students to come up with examples for each category. Ask them to distinguish between spoken humor and humor meant to be read, and have them describe what it is about written humor that makes them laugh. Then invite them to enjoy two selections by an eminent American writer and humorist, Mark Twain.

Customize for
Less Proficient Readers
Mark Twain's work is characterized by regional dialect and expressions. Help readers to understand the meanings of words and expressions that are likely to be unfamiliar to them, such as *feller, considable better* or *suffering to try.*

Customize for
AP Students
Guide students to look for examples of Twain's humor that, although written a century ago, are still fresh and funny today. Students can compare his sense of humor with that of today's witty storytellers. Who among today's comedy writers is most like Mark Twain?

Customize for
English Language Learners
Help students figure out the meanings of the many compound words Twain uses, like *steamboatman, pilothouse, paddleboxes,* and *deckhand.* Students can break these words apart to determine meaning.

Test Preparation Workshop

Reading Comprehension: Context Many standardized reading tests require students to use contextual analysis to determine the meaning of figurative expressions. Remind students that the context may extend to sentences before or after the targeted word. Use the following sample test item to demonstrate.

> I went meekly aboard a few of the boats that lay <u>packed together like sardines</u> at the the long St. Louis wharf, and very humbly inquired for the pilots, but got only a cold shoulder and short words from mates and clerks.

In this passage, the expression <u>packed together like sardines</u> means—

A The boats were docked close together in a row.
B The boats had been fishing for sardines.
C The boats were made of metal like tins for sardines.
D The boats were packed with passengers.

A is the correct answer.

One-Minute Insight With charm and wit, Mark Twain gives an insightful look into the hopes and ambitions of a boy growing up in a town along the Mississippi River. The boy dreams of becoming a steamboatman working on one of the great riverboats on the majestic river. His desire for the opportunities and prestige the job affords, his envy of a boy who already has such a job, and the contrast he sees between the dullness of the small town and the adventures promised on the river provide a rich bounty of humorous situations and descriptions.

Customize for
Musical/Rhythmic and Verbal/Linguistic Learners
Invite students to listen to the audiocassette recordings of these stories to hear and appreciate the cadences, the colloquial expressions and pronunciations, the understatements, and the exaggerations that all contribute to create the humorous effect Twain seeks.

Enrichment Emphasize the importance of riverboat trade to the economy around the river. In an age without television or radio, the boats were also an important link between river communities and the rest of the world. Set the mood for this story by bringing in pictures of and literature about riverboats. If possible, include information about the routes the boats traveled and the types of entertainment on board. Ask students: In what ways were the boats like modern ocean liners?

▶Critical Viewing◀

❶ Analyze Students may say that the majestic portrayal of the steamboat and the group of boys waving energetically convey the excitement of the steamboat's arrival.

Art Transparency After students read Twain's biography on p. 518, display Art Transparency 4, *Deck Life on the* Paragon, to generate discussion about why Twain might have found living and working on a boat appealing.

▼ **Critical Viewing** How does the painting convey the excitement generated by the arrival of a steamboat? **[Analyze]** ❶

Paddle Steamboat Mississippi, Shelburne Museum, Shelburne, Vermont

Block Scheduling Strategies

Consider these suggestions to take advantage of extended class time:

- To introduce the era in which these selections take place, discuss the Background for Understanding on p. 518. Stress nineteenth-century advances in transportation, especially the riverboat and the railroad.
- If students have access to computers, introduce Mark Twain with ***The History of American Literature CD-ROM.***
- Introduce students to regional dialects by discussing the Reading Strategy on p. 519. For reinforcement, have students complete the ***Se-lection Support*** page on regional dialect, p. 153.
- Have students work in small groups to answer the Critical Thinking questions on pp. 524 and 530.
- Assign the Guided Writing Lesson on p. 531. Allow time for students to present their humorous anecdotes to the class.

from Life on the Mississippi

Mark Twain

The Boys' Ambition

When I was a boy, there was but one permanent ambition among my comrades in our village[1] on the west bank of the Mississippi River. That was, to be a steamboatman. We had transient ambitions of other sorts, but they were only transient.

When a circus came and went, it left us all burning to become clowns; the first Negro minstrel show that came to our section left us 2
all suffering to try that kind of life; now and then we had a hope that if we lived and were good, God would permit us to be pirates. These ambitions faded out, each in its turn; but the ambition to be a steamboatman always remained.

Once a day a cheap, gaudy packet[2] arrived upward from St. Louis, and another downward from Keokuk.[3] 3
Before these events, the day was glorious with expectancy; after them, the day was a dead and empty thing. Not only the boys, but the whole village, felt this. After all these years I can picture that old time to myself now, just as it was then: the white town drowsing in the sunshine of a summer's morning; the streets empty, or pretty nearly so; one or two clerks sitting in front of the Water Street stores, with their splint-bottomed chairs tilted back against the wall,

1. **our village:** Hannibal, Missouri.
2. **packet** *n.*: Boat that travels a regular route, carrying passengers, freight, and mail.
3. **Keokuk** (kē′ ə kuk′): Town in southeastern Iowa.

◆ Build Vocabulary

transient (tran′ zē ənt) *adj.*: Not permanent

Humanities: Art

Paddle Steamboat *Mississippi.*

This oil on canvas provides a visual record of a steamboat plying the Mississippi and of what the river banks looked like at the time Mark Twain was writing. The size of the boats in contrast to the houses on land suggests the grandeur and royalty of these vessels.

Use this question for discussion:

1. What was it about steamboats that excited people like the young Mark Twain and the boys in the painting? *Students may say that the steamboats offered a way out of small-town life and promised travel, adventure, and a sophisticated, modern life.*

◆ Literature and Your Life

2 Ask students to think back to their earlier childhood days and to their own transient ambitions. Invite them to share some of the reasons they longed for those particular jobs and to describe what happened to change their minds or their plans.

Customize for
Visual/Spatial Learners

3 Encourage students to obtain and examine a map showing the Mississippi River and the states of Missouri, Indiana, Nebraska, and Iowa. Students can get their bearings by locating Hannibal, Keokuk, and St. Louis.

Enrichment *Life on the Mississippi* was published in 1883. Considered second only to *Huckleberry Finn* (1885) in literary quality, *Life on the Mississippi* grew out of a series of articles about Mississippi River piloting that Twain wrote for the *Atlantic Monthly* in 1875. The first half of the book tells how Twain became a pilot and relates his experiences learning about the river. The second half tells about the author's 1882 trip down the river and his visit to his home in Hannibal, Missouri.

Life on the Mississippi offers an outstanding description of the profession of steamboat piloting. The steamboat and the job of pilot are seen through the eyes of a boy who romanticizes and glamorizes whatever is foreign to his limited experience. At the same time, however, the reader gets a second point of view: the older narrator looks back on his boyhood, and gently mocks his own innocence.

Customize for
Gifted/Talented Students

Have student jot notes and create storyboards or sketches to demonstrate how they would capture the mood of Twain's opening lines in the opening scene of a video. Encourage students to suggest sound effects and camera effects as well as the actual images to be filmed.

◆ Literary Focus

❶ **Humor** All the details contribute to the sleepy appearance of the town prior to the arrival of the steamboat and contrast with the bustle and excitement in the awakening that greets the boat's appearance.

◆ Reading Strategy

❷ **Understand Regional Dialect** Help students appreciate how the words "S-t-e-a-m-boat a-comin'!" add realism and life to the story. Ask students: How would the words "Steamboat coming!" change the effect of the event being described? *Students may say that the effect would be to deaden the event and take away the vision of the drayman in the mind's eye of the reader.*

▶Critical Viewing◀

❸ **Infer** Students may suggest that the Mississippi River served as a highway, a wide thoroughfare for shipping goods, such as tobacco and cotton, and for receiving needed supplies. Goods shipped downriver to the port of New Orleans could go from there to the east coast and to Europe, as could those shipped to the river cities of Memphis, Vicksburg, and St. Louis, which were railroad centers.

chins on breasts, hats slouched over their faces, asleep—with shingle shavings enough around to show what broke them down; a sow and a litter of pigs loafing along the sidewalk, doing a good business in watermelon rinds and seeds; two or three lonely little freight piles scattered about the levee;[4] a pile of skids[5] on the slope of the stone-paved wharf, and the fragrant town drunkard asleep in the shadow of them; two or three wood flats[6] at the head of the wharf, but nobody to listen to the peaceful lapping of the wavelets against them; the great Mississippi, the majestic, the magnificent Mississippi, rolling its mile-wide tide along, shining in the sun; the dense forest away on the other side; the point above the town, and the point below, bounding the river-glimpse and turning it into a sort of sea, and withal a very still and brilliant and lonely one. Presently a film of dark smoke appears above one of those remote points; instantly a Negro drayman,[7] famous for his quick eye and prodigious voice, lifts up the cry, "S-t-e-a-m-boat a-comin'!" and the scene changes! The town drunkard stirs, the clerks wake up, a furious clatter of drays follows, every house and store pours out a human contribution, and all in a twinkling the dead town is alive and moving. Drays, carts, men, boys, all go hurrying from many quarters to a common center, the wharf. Assembled there, the people fasten their eyes upon the coming boat as upon a wonder they are seeing for the first time. And the boat *is* rather a handsome sight, too. She is long and sharp and trim and pretty; she has two tall, fancy-topped chimneys, with a gilded device of some kind swung between them; a fanciful pilothouse, all glass

> **◆ Literary Focus** ❶ Notice how the detail about the pigs adds humor to the piece. How do the other details contribute to describing the setting?

Plantations on the Mississippi River, map from Natchez to New Orleans, 1858 (Norman Chart), Historic New Orleans Collection

▲ Critical Viewing This map shows the location of plantation lands on the banks of the Mississippi. Why might the river have been a desirable location for plantations, as well as for towns? **[Infer]** ❸

4. **levee** (lev´ ē) *n.*: Landing place along the bank of a river.
5. **skids** *n.*: Low, movable wooden platforms.
6. **flats** *n.*: Small, flat-bottomed boats.
7. **drayman** (drā´ mən) *n.*: Driver of a dray, a low cart with detachable sides.

Research Skills Mini-Lesson

Citing Sources

Introduce the Concept Tell students that for most research papers and projects, they will need to cite the sources they used for information.

Develop the Background Tell students there are two main styles for citing sources. One is the Modern Language Association (MLA) style. The other is the American Psychological Association (APA) style. Guidelines for both can be found in most writing handbooks. The type of paper they are writing will usually determine which they use on any given project. Show two examples like the ones here.

MLA

Nyberg, David. The Vanished Truth: Truth Telling and Deceiving in Ordinary Life. Chicago: U of Chicago P, 1993.

APA

Goleman, D. (1995). Emotional intelligence: Why it can matter more than IQ. New York: Bantam.

Apply the Information Have students choose three different types of sources containing information on Mark Twain. (For example, a book with one author, a book with two authors, and a magazine article.) Tell students to write two citations for each source, one in each style.

Assess the Outcome Evaluate students' accuracy in using each style for each type of note.

and gingerbread, perched on top of the texas deck[8] behind them; the paddleboxes are gorgeous with a picture or with gilded rays above the boat's name; the boiler deck, the hurricane deck, and the texas deck are fenced and ornamented with clean white railings; there is a flag gallantly flying from the jackstaff;[9] the furnace doors are open and the fires glaring bravely; the upper decks are black with passengers; the captain stands by the big bell, calm, imposing, the envy of all; [4] great volumes of the blackest smoke are rolling and tumbling out of the chimneys—a husbanded grandeur created with a bit of pitch pine just before arriving at a town; the crew are grouped on the forecastle;[10] the broad stage is run far out over the port bow, and an envied deckhand stands picturesquely on the end of it with a coil of rope in his hand; the pent steam is screaming through the gauge cocks; the captain lifts his hand, a bell rings, the wheels stop; then they turn back, churning the water to foam, and the steamer is at rest. Then such a scramble as there is to get aboard, and to get ashore, and to take in freight and to discharge freight, all at one and the same time; and such a yelling and cursing as the mates facilitate it all with! Ten minutes later the steamer is under way again, with no flag on the jackstaff and no black smoke issuing from the chimneys. After ten more minutes the town is dead again, and the town drunkard asleep by the skids once more.

[5] My father was a justice of the peace, and I supposed he possessed the power of life and death over all men and could hang anybody that offended him. This was distinction enough for me as a general thing; but the desire to be a steamboatman kept intruding, nevertheless. [6] I first wanted to be a cabin boy, so that I could come out with a white apron on and shake a tablecloth over the side, where all my old comrades could see me; later I thought I would rather be the deckhand who stood on the end of the stage plank with the coil of rope in his hand, because he was particularly conspicuous. But these were only daydreams—they were too heavenly to be contemplated as real possibilities. By and by one of our boys went away. [7] He was not heard of for a long time. At last he turned up as apprentice engineer or striker on a steamboat. This thing shook the bottom out of all my Sunday-school teachings. That boy had been notoriously worldly, and I just the reverse; yet he was exalted to this <u>eminence,</u> and I left in obscurity and misery. There was nothing generous about this fellow in his greatness. He would always manage to have a rusty bolt to scrub while his boat tarried at our town, and he would sit on the inside guard and scrub it, where we could all see him and envy him and loathe him. And whenever his boat was laid up he would come home and swell around the town in his blackest and greasiest clothes, so that nobody could help remembering that he was a steamboatman; and he used all sorts of steamboat technicalities in his talk, as if he were so used to them that he forgot common people could not understand them. He would speak of the labboard[11] side of a horse in an easy, natural way that would make one wish he was dead. And he was always talking about "St. Looey" like an old citizen; he would refer casually to occasions when he "was coming down Fourth Street," or when he was "passing by the Planter's House," or when there was a fire and he took a turn on the brakes of "the old Big Missouri"; and then he would go on and lie about how many towns the size of ours were burned down there that day. Two or three of the boys had long been persons of consideration among us because they had been to St. Louis once and had a vague general knowledge of its wonders, but the day of their glory was over now. They lapsed into a humble silence, and

> **◆ Reading Strategy** [8]
> What does the apprentice engineer's use of riverboat jargon reveal about him?

8. **texas deck:** Deck adjoining the officers' cabins, the largest cabins on the ship.
9. **jackstaff** (jak′ staf) *n.*: Small staff at the bow of a ship for flying flags.
10. **forecastle:** (fōk′ səl) *n.*: Front part of the upper deck.

11. **labboard** (lab′ ərd): Larboard, the left-hand side of a ship.

◆ Build Vocabulary

prodigious (prə dij′ əs) *adj.*: Of great power or size
eminence (em′ ə nəns) *n.*: Greatness; celebrity

◆ Critical Thinking

4 Draw Conclusions Point out that "husbanded grandeur" refers to a deliberately created effect. Tell students that pitch pine is wood from the heart of a pine tree, and that it is heavily saturated with pitch, burns quickly, and emits large amounts of black smoke. Ask students: Why would the crew want to create a special effect with black smoke? *A visible smoke might suggest harder or more important work.*

◆ Literary Focus

5 Humor Have students notice the transition to a personal voice here as Twain applies his detached, self-deprecating sense of humor to this description of his father's position and powers.

◆ Literary Focus

6 Humor Note the way Twain makes ordinary duties—shaking out a tablecloth and holding a rope—seem exalted and important. Ask students: How do these details add to the humor of his narrative? *These details illustrate how an inexperienced child can jump to erroneous—and comical—conclusions about what is important or prestigious.*

◆ Literary Focus

7 Humor Students should appreciate how Twain uses exaggeration in a comical way here to compare the "obscurity" of the boy with the "eminence" of the apprentice.

◆ Reading Strategy

8 Understand Regional Dialect Some students may say that the apprentice uses jargon to establish the celebrity of his position before his envious former peers. Others might say he does so to cloak his insecurities about what he truly knows about his position on the ship—it is by no means an eminent one.

Customize for
Verbal/Linguistic Learners
To extend these students' understanding of specialized vocabulary, use the Workplace Skills: Jargon page in ***Beyond Literature,*** (p. 32).

Cross-Curricular Connection: Social Studies

The Age of Steam By the early nineteenth century, steamboats were regularly carrying cargo upstream on the Mississippi and Ohio rivers. The boats were essential to the economy of towns along these rivers, linking them to each other and to the rest of the world. Until the 1850's, when railroad development grew rapidly in the West, steamboats carried more freight than trains.

Have students research to find out about life on, and associated with, the great riverboats. Among other things, they can find out about routes, available jobs, and on-board entertainment. Have them look into how large the boats were, how fast they traveled, and how many there were. Students can also learn about tours and trips, such as Civil War excursions, that can be enjoyed on modern-day riverboats. They can write for brochures. Invite students to share the information they compile.

◆ Critical Thinking

❶ **Analyze** Ask students to explain whether they think the apprentice's riches are really as wonderful as they seemed to Twain at the time. Ask them what they think life really must have been like for a young apprentice on a riverboat. *Students may suggest that although the possessions may have appeared as riches to a boy, they were not, and that the life of an apprentice was probably hard, tedious, low paying, and of low status aboard ship.*

◆ Literary Focus

❷ **Humor** Guide students to recognize that here Twain satirizes the dismal safety record of steamboats, which "blew up" with regularity at that time. Have them note the very modern form of humor with which he expresses the boy's view of the wounded apprentice, the "undeserving reptile."

Reinforce and Extend

Customize for
AP Students
Inform students that Twain actually did become a riverboat pilot. Suggest that they read and compare other excerpts from *Life On the Mississippi* to learn more about that phase of the writer's life.

Answers

◆ *Literature and Your Life*

Reader's Response Students' responses should be supported by details from the selection.

Thematic Focus Twain's ambition to travel to different places as captain of a steamboat reflects the American desire for expansion and adventure.

☑ **Check Your Comprehension**

1. They all want to be steamboat men.
2. They all stop to greet the boat as it arrives.
3. (a) The boat blows up. (b) At first, thinking the apprentice had been killed, the boys are pacified. Upon learning he is alive, they are resentful.

◆ Critical Thinking

1. Twain's description of the town suggests it is a sleepy place where not much happens. The arrival of the steamboat causes the only excitement.
2. He describes the steamboat in glowing terms.
3. The other boys are resentful of his influence and envious at the same time.
4. Possible response: Twain's love for the Mississippi River led him to eloquently describe the river, its towns, and its people. His love led him to use regional dialect in his writing to bring the people of the area to life.
5. Sample response: A career as a commercial jetliner pilot or as an astronaut are probably comparable in romance and adventure. Both careers involve soaring far above the Earth and visiting new or exotic places.

---

learned to disappear when the ruthless cub engineer approached. This fellow had money, too, and hair oil. Also an ignorant silver watch and a showy brass watch chain. He wore a leather ❶ belt and used no suspenders. If ever a youth was cordially admired and hated by his comrades, this one was. No girl could withstand his charms. He cut out every boy in the village. When his boat blew up at last, it diffused a tranquil contentment among us such as we had not known for months. But when he came home the next week, alive, renowned, and ❷ appeared in church all battered up and bandaged, a shining hero, stared at and wondered over by everybody, it seemed to us that the partiality of Providence for an undeserving reptile had reached a point where it was open to criticism.

This creature's career could produce but one result, and it speedily followed. Boy after boy managed to get on the river. The minister's son became an engineer. The doctor's and the postmaster's sons became mud clerks; the wholesale liquor dealer's son became a barkeeper on a boat; four sons of the chief merchant, and two sons of the county judge, became pilots. Pilot was the grandest position of all. The pilot, even in those days of trivial wages, had a princely salary—from a hundred and fifty to two hundred and fifty dollars a month, and no board to pay. Two months of his wages would pay a preacher's salary for a year. Now some of us were left disconsolate. We could not get on the river—at least our parents would not let us.

So by and by I ran away. I said I never would come home again till I was a pilot and could come in glory. But somehow I could not manage it. I went meekly aboard a few of the boats that lay packed together like sardines at the long St. Louis wharf, and very humbly inquired for the pilots, but got only a cold shoulder and short words from mates and clerks. I had to make the best of this sort of treatment for the time being, but I had comforting daydreams of a future when I should be a great and honored pilot, with plenty of money, and could kill some of these mates and clerks and pay for them.

Guide for Responding

◆ *Literature and Your Life*

Reader's Response Would working on a riverboat appeal to you? Explain why or why not.

Thematic Focus How does Twain's childhood ambition reflect the American desire for expansion and adventure that gave rise to the settlement of new frontiers?

Journal Writing Suppose you lived in Mark Twain's time. Record your ideas about what types of work opportunities might have intrigued you.

☑ **Check Your Comprehension**

1. What is the one permanent ambition of Twain and his boyhood friends?
2. How do the people of Hannibal respond to the arrival of the steamboat?
3. (a) What happens to the young apprentice engineer's boat? (b) How do the other boys respond?

◆ Critical Thinking

INTERPRET

1. What impression is conveyed by Twain's description of the town and its response to the arrival of the steamboat? **[Interpret]**
2. How does Twain's description of the steamboat reflect his boyhood desire to work on a steamboat? **[Analyze]**
3. How would you describe the attitude of the other boys toward the apprentice engineer? **[Infer]**

APPLY

4. How do you think Twain's love for the Mississippi River contributed to his success as a writer? **[Synthesize]**

EXTEND

5. What career today might be comparable in romance and adventure to being a riverboat pilot in the 1800's? Explain your answer. **[Career Link]**

The Notorious Jumping Frog of Calaveras County ❸

Mark Twain

Mark Twain (Samuel L. Clemens) Riding the Celebrated Jumping Frog

❹ ▲ **Critical Viewing** Do you think Mark Twain would have been amused or offended by this caricature of himself? Explain. **[Make a Judgment]**

In compliance with the request of a friend of mine, who wrote me from the East, I called on good-natured, garrulous old Simon Wheeler, and inquired after my friend's friend, Leonidas W. Smiley, as requested to do, and I hereunto append the result. I have a lurking suspicion that *Leonidas W.* Smiley is a myth; that my friend never knew such a personage: and that he only conjectured that if I asked old Wheeler about him, it would remind him of his infamous *Jim* Smiley, and he would go to work and bore me to death with some exasperating reminiscence of him as long and as tedious as it should be useless to me. If that was the design, it succeeded. ❺

I found Simon Wheeler dozing comfortably by the barroom stove of the dilapidated tavern in the decayed mining camp of Angel's, and I noticed that he was fat and baldheaded, and had an expression of winning gentleness and simplicity upon his tranquil countenance. He roused up, and gave me good day. I told him a friend of mine had commissioned me to make some inquiries about a cherished companion of his boyhood named *Leonidas W.* Smiley—*Rev. Leonidas W.* Smiley, a young minister of the Gospel, who he had heard was at one time a resident of Angel's Camp. I added that if Mr. Wheeler could tell me anything about this Rev. Leonidas W. Smiley, I would feel under many obligations to him.

Simon Wheeler backed me into a corner and blockaded me there with his chair, and then sat down and reeled off the monotonous narrative which follows this paragraph. He never smiled, he never frowned, he never changed his voice from the gentle-flowing key to which he tuned his initial sentence, he never betrayed the slightest suspicion of enthusiasm; but all through the interminable narrative there ran a vein of impressive earnestness and sincerity, which showed me plainly that, so far from his ❻

◆ Build Vocabulary

garrulous (gar´ ə ləs) *adj.*: Talking too much

conjectured (kən jek´ chərd) *v.*: Guessed

monotonous (mə nät´ ən əs) *adj.*: Tiresome because unvarying

interminable (in tʉr´ mi nə bəl) *adj.*: Seeming to last forever

Develop Understanding

One-Minute Insight

According to one of Mark Twain's biographers, Twain first heard the story that would become this one while in the bar of a rundown tavern in Angel's Camp, California. Like the storyteller in that bar, Twain's narrator, Simon Wheeler, spins a funny, improbable yarn about the exploits of a betting man. Wheeler tells his tale of dogfights and frog-jumping contests with no suspicion of humor, but with a heavy dose of colorful regional dialect.

Customize for *Less Proficient Readers*

These students may benefit from the Recognize Humor page in ***Strategies for Diverse Student Needs,*** (p. 32).

❸ **Clarification** Inform students that Calaveras County is a real place; it is located in central California, southeast of Sacramento, northeast of Modesto. It borders Tuolomne County to the east, home of Yosemite National Park.

▶Critical Viewing◀

❹ **Make a Judgment** Students may say that Twain, as a writer who knew the effectiveness of exaggeration, would have enjoyed the humor in this caricature, particularly the deadpan expression on his face and the exaggerated leap the frog makes.

Customize for *Less Proficient Readers*

❺ Help students understand the premise of the story as set forth in the opening paragraph. Point out that Twain knows that he might be the target of his friend's prank. As needed, have students refer back to this opening when they have finished reading the story.

◆ Literary Focus

❻ **Humor** Point out the use of the term "blockaded" as another example of Twain's rich use of language to create exaggeration and humor. "Blockaded" is a verb usually reserved for war-time activities.

Humanities: Art

Mark Twain Riding the Celebrated Jumping Frog, [1872], by Frederick Waddy.

A caricature is a drawing made to satirize or poke fun at someone by exaggerating certain features so that the person looks ridiculous, yet recognizable. Waddy was an English caricaturist, whose humorous drawings were reproduced as wood engravings in the *Illustrated London News.* Authors and other famous figures were his favorite subjects. His work is characterized by large heads and tiny bodies.

Use these questions for discussion:

1. What aspects of Twain does Waddy poke fun at in this drawing? *Students may say that the artist lampoons the idea that such a respected writer would choose such a foolish topic for his efforts; or that Twain's fame would ride on something so silly as a jumping frog.*
2. What is your opinion of this caricature? Is it fitting? Good humored? Explain. *Students' responses should reflect knowledge of Twain as both a great writer and a noted humorist.*

Literature CD-ROM To build background, use the CD-ROM *The History of American Literature:* Part 1, Disc 2 Feature 9. This segment focuses in part on Mark Twain and on "The Celebrated Jumping Frog of Calaveras County."

◆ Reading Strategy

(1) Understand Regional Dialect Guide students to recognize the transition here. As Wheeler's tale begins, the language shifts from the formal language of the narrator to the colloquial language of the storyteller.

◆ Critical Thinking

(2) Analyze Ask students to explain how Twain manages to develop two characters at the same time in this passage. *Twain creates a unique storyteller with idiosyncrasies of his own. As readers make inferences about the kind of man Simon Wheeler is, Wheeler describes Jim Smiley.*

◆ Reading Strategy

(3) Understand Regional Dialect Have students read "Thish-yer" aloud to appreciate that this unusually-spelled word is Twain's way of informing the reader what "This here" sounds like when Wheeler says it. Guide students to look for other examples of this technique.

Read to Be Entertained

Humor can be the driving force of a story. It can also be subtle and coy, teasing the reader just enough to lighten the mood of the story or to break up a long narrative paragraph. Either way, humor provides added enjoyment when reading. Help students recognize the humorous elements in Twain's writing, from his creation of unique characters to his deadpan delivery of absurd statements. Reading to be entertained is a valid purpose for reading, and many books are written for entertainment. Encourage students to read to be entertained, looking for the humorous elements in Twain's writing

imagining that there was anything ridiculous or funny about his story, he regarded it as a really important matter, and admired its two heroes as men of transcendent genius in *finesse*. I let him go on in his own way, and never interrupted him once.

"Rev. Leonidas W. H'm, Reverend Le— well, there was a feller here once by the name of *Jim* Smiley, in the winter of '49—or maybe it was the spring of '50—I don't recollect exactly, somehow, though what makes me think it was one or the other is because I remember the big flume[1] warn't finished when he first come to the camp; but anyway, he was the curiousest man about always betting on anything that turned up you ever see, if he could get anybody to bet on the other side; and if he couldn't he'd change sides. Any way that suited the other man would suit *him*—any way just so's he got a bet, *he* was satisfied. But still he was lucky, uncommon lucky; he most always come out winner. He was always ready and laying for a chance; there couldn't be no solit'ry thing men-
(1) tioned but that feller'd offer to bet on it, and
(2) take ary side you please, as I was just telling you. If there was a horse race, you'd find him flush or you'd find him busted at the end of it; if there was a dogfight, he'd bet on it; if there was a cat fight, he'd bet on it; if there was a chicken fight, he'd bet on it; why, if there was two birds setting on a fence, he would bet you which one would fly first; or if there was a camp meeting,[2] he would be there reg'lar to bet on Parson Walker, which he judged to be the best exhorter about here and so he was too, and a good man. If he even see a straddle bug[3] start to go anywheres, he would bet you how long it would take him to get to—to wherever he was going to, and if you took him up, he would foller that straddle bug to Mexico but what he would find out where he was bound for and how long he was on the road. Lots of the boys here has seen that Smiley, and can tell you about him. Why, it never made no difference to *him*—he'd bet on *any* thing—the dangdest feller. Parson Walker's wife laid very sick once, for a good while, and it seemed as if they warn't going to save her; but one morning he come in, and Smiley up and asked him how she was,
and he said she was considable better—thank (1)
the Lord for his inf'nite mercy—and coming on (2)
so smart that with the blessing of Prov'dence she'd get well yet; and Smiley, before he thought, says, 'Well, I'll resk two-and-a-half she don't anyway.'

Thish-yer Smiley had a mare—the boys called (3)
her the fifteen-minute nag, but that was only in fun, you know, because of course she was faster than that—and he used to win money on that horse, for all she was so slow and always had the asthma, or the distemper, or the consumption, or something of that kind. They used to give her two or three hundred yards start, and then pass her under way; but always at the fag end[4] of the race she'd get excited and desperate like, and come cavorting and straddling up, and scattering her legs around limber, sometimes in the air, and sometimes out to one side among the fences, and kicking up m-o-r-e dust and raising m-o-r-e racket with her coughing and sneezing and blowing her nose—and *always* fetch up at the stand just about a neck ahead, as near as you could cipher it down.

And he had a little small bull-pup, that to look at him you'd think he warn't worth a cent but to set around and look ornery and lay for a chance to steal something. But as soon as money was up on him he was a different dog; his under-jaw'd begin to stick out like the fo'castle[5] of a steamboat, and his teeth would uncover and shine like the furnaces. And a dog might tackle him and bullyrag him, and bite him, and throw him over his shoulder two or three times, and Andrew Jackson—which was the name of the pup—Andrew Jackson would never let on but what *he* was satisfied, and hadn't expected nothing else—and the bets being doubled and doubled on the other side all the time, till the money was all up; and then all of a sudden he would grab that other dog jest

1. **flume** (flo͞om) *n.*: Artificial channel for carrying water to provide power and transport objects.
2. **camp meeting:** Religious gathering at the mining camp.
3. **straddle bug:** Insect with long legs.
4. **fag end:** Last part.
5. **fo'castle** (fōk′ səl) *n.*: Forecastle; the forward part of the upper deck.

◆ Build Vocabulary

ornery (ôr′ nər ē) *adj.*: Having a mean disposition

Beyond the Classroom

Community Connection

Calaveras County Fair and Jumping Frog Jubilee Every spring, on the Calaveras Fairgrounds in Angel's Camp, California, there is a fair and a reenactment of Twain's celebrated contest. The contest annually attracts people from all over the world who bring more than 3,000 frogs. Invite students to find out more about the history of, and records associated with, this "Olympics" of frog jumping. Students can find out how to enter the contest and what kind of jump it would take to win. They can get information by writing to the 39th District Agricultural Association, Box 489, S. Highway 49, Angels Camp, CA 95222.

4 ▲ **Critical Viewing** Which moment of the story is depicted in this illustration? **[Connect]**

by the j'int of his hind leg and freeze to it—not chaw, you understand, but only just grip and hang on till they throwed up the sponge, if it was a year. Smiley always come out winner on that pup, till he harnessed a dog once that didn't have no hind legs, because they'd been sawed off in a circular saw, and when the thing had gone along far enough, and the money was all up, and he come to make a snatch for his pet holt,[6] he see in a minute how he'd been imposed on, and how the other dog had him in the door, so to speak, and he 'peared surprised, and then he looked sorter discouraged-like, and didn't try no more to win the fight, and so he got shucked out bad. He give Smiley a look, as much as to say his heart was broke, and it was *his* fault, for putting up a dog that hadn't no hind legs for him to take holt of, which was his main dependence in a fight, and then he limped off a piece and laid down and died. It was a good pup, was that Andrew Jackson, and would have made a name for hisself if he'd lived, for the stuff was in him and he had genius—I know it, because he hadn't no opportunities to speak of, and it don't stand to reason that a dog could make such a fight as he could under them circumstances if he hadn't no talent. It always makes me feel sorry when I think of that last fight of his'n, and the way it turned out. 6

5 **◆ Reading Strategy** How would you rephrase this section in standard English? How does the use of dialect create humor?

6

Well, thish-yer Smiley had rat terriers,[7] and chicken cocks,[8] and tomcats and all them kind of things, till you couldn't rest, and you couldn't fetch nothing for him to bet on but he'd match you. He ketched a frog one day, and took him home, and said he cal'lated to educate him; and

6. **holt:** Hold.

7. **rat terriers:** Dogs skilled in catching rats.
8. **chicken cocks:** Roosters trained to fight.

▶Critical Viewing◀

4 Connect Students may say that the illustration shows the defeat of Dan'l by the stranger's frog.

◆ Reading Strategy

5 Understand Regional Dialect Students may rephrase as follows: In each of his fights, Andrew Jackson would appear to be losing until all bettors placed more and more money on the other dog. Then he would win the fight simply by gripping one of the other dog's hind legs. But one time, Andrew Jackson fought a dog without any hind legs and, with no leg to grip, lost the bout.

The use of dialect creates humor by animating the speech and by adding flamboyance and authenticity to the speaker.

◆ Grammar and Style

6 Double Negatives Have students identify the four sets of double negatives in this passage. *They are: didn't try no more; hadn't no hind legs; hadn't no opportunities; and hadn't no talent.* Ask them to restate these in correct grammatical form. *Corrections are: didn't try any more; had no hind legs; had no opportunities; had no talent.*

Enrichment Mark Twain often continued working on his stories after they were published. For example, on November 18, 1865, his story "The Celebrated Jumping Frog of Calaveras county" was published in *The Saturday Press.* Twain revised this story later that same year, again in 1867, then in 1872, and published it in its final form in 1875. Twain's final choice of title was "The Notorious Jumping Frog of Calaveras County."

According to Twain scholar Walter Blair, "Twain's enthusiasm about this story varied; but his characterization of it in 1869 as 'the best humorous sketch America has produced' and his extensive revision before he printed it in its final form in 1875 attest to his belief that it merited painstaking care."

Analyze Literary Criticism

When describing the publication history of Twain's "The Notorious Jumping Frog of Calaveras County," James D. Wilson cites Marie-Therese Blanc who considered Twain to be a purveyor "of a crude, 'western' humor that lacked the refinement of a regionalist like Bret Harte," whom she admired. This opinions stands in stark contrast to those who consider Twain's character description and use of dialect to be the work of a genius. Read this description of Twain's work to students.

Have them respond to the following questions in a journal entry:

1. Do you feel Twain's humor is crude and unrefined or carefully and deliberately crafted? Why?
2. Find several examples from the text to support your answer above.

Students can use their journal entries as a starting point for the Analytic Essay in the Idea Bank on p. 531.

◆ Literary Focus

❶ **Humor** The embellishments provide hilarious verbal images that exaggerate the abilities of the frog. Among the embellishments that add to the comical effect are the following: talking about the frog as being educated, describing the frog whirling through the air like a doughnut, having the frog land flatfooted and all right like a cat, speaking of the frog catching flies and then scratching the side of its head indifferently.

◆ Literary Focus

❷ **Humor** Ask students to point out Twain's humor in this passage. *Students can appreciate the absurd idea that a frog can be "modest and straightfor'ard," and that the storyteller presents the notion in all seriousness.*

◆ Background for Understanding

❸ **History** Explain to students that forty dollars was a great deal of money at that time, perhaps equal to a month's wages.

◆ Critical Thinking

❹ **Predict** Ask students if they think the stranger is as naive as he seems to be. *Many students will say that the stranger is smarter that he appears.* Ask them to predict the outcome of the contest. *They will guess that the size of the bet is an indication that the stranger is hiding something that will affect the result of the contest.*

◆ Literary Focus

❺ **Humor** Point out to students how the exaggeration in the two similes presented here adds humor. In one simile, Dan'l moves his shoulders "like a Frenchman." In the other simile, the frog is planted "as solid as a church."

so he never done nothing for three months but set in his back yard and learn that frog to jump. And you bet you he *did* learn him, too. He'd give him a little punch behind, and the next minute you'd see that frog whirling in the air like a doughnut—see him turn one summerset, or maybe a couple, if he got a good start, and come down flatfooted and all right, like a cat. He got him up so in the matter of ketching flies, and kep' him in practice so constant, that he'd nail a fly every time as fur as he could see him. Smiley said all a frog wanted was education, and he could do 'most anything—and I believe him. Why, I've seen him set Dan'l Webster down here on this floor—Dan'l Webster was the name of the frog—and sing out, "Flies, Dan'l, flies!" and quicker'n you could wink he'd spring straight up and snake a fly off'n the counter there, and flop down on the floor ag'in as solid as a gob of mud, and fall to scratching the side of his head with his hind foot as indifferent as if he hadn't no idea he'd been doin' any more'n any frog might do. You never see a frog so modest and straightfor'ard as he was, for all he was so gifted. And when it come to fair and square jumping on a dead level, he could get over more ground at one straddle than any animal of his breed you ever see. Jumping on a dead level was his strong suit, you understand; and when it come to that, Smiley would ante up money on him as long as he had a red.[9] Smiley was monstrous proud of his frog, and well he might be, for fellers that had traveled and been everywheres all said he laid over any frog that ever *they* see.

> ◆ **Literary Focus** How do these embellishments heighten the comical effect of this passage?

Well, Smiley kep' the beast in a little lattice box, and he used to fetch him downtown sometimes and lay for a bet. One day a feller—a stranger in the camp, he was—come acrost him with his box, and says:

'What might it be that you've got in the box?'

And Smiley says, sorter indifferent-like, 'It might be a parrot, or it might be a canary, maybe, but it ain't—it's only just a frog.'

And the feller took it, and looked at it careful, and turned it round this way and that, and says, 'H'm—so 'tis. Well, what's *he* good for?'

'Well,' Smiley says, easy and careless, 'he's good enough for *one* thing, I should judge—he can outjump any frog in Calaveras county.'

The feller took the box again, and took another long, particular look, and give it back to Smiley, and says, very deliberate, 'Well,' he says, 'I don't see no p'ints about that frog that's any better'n any other frog.'

'Maybe you don't,' Smiley says. 'Maybe you understand frogs and maybe you don't understand 'em; maybe you've had experience, and maybe you ain't only a amature, as it were. Anyways, I've got *my* opinion, and I'll resk forty dollars that he can outjump any frog in Calaveras county.'

And the feller studied a minute, and then says, kinder sad like, 'Well, I'm only a stranger here, and I ain't got no frog; but if I had a frog, I'd bet you.'

And then Smiley says, 'That's all right—that's all right—if you'll hold my box a minute, I'll go and get you a frog.' And so the feller took the box, and put up his forty dollars along with Smiley's, and set down to wait.

So he set there a good while thinking and thinking to hisself, and then he got the frog out and prized his mouth open and took a teaspoon and filled him full of quailshot[10] —filled him pretty near up to his chin—and set him on the floor. Smiley he went to the swamp and slopped around in the mud for a long time, and finally he ketched a frog, and fetched him in, and give him to this feller, and says:

'Now, if you're ready, set him alongside of Dan'l, with his forepaws just even with Dan'l's, and I'll give the word.' Then he says, 'One—two—three—*git!*' and him and the feller touched up the frogs from behind, and the new frog hopped off lively, but Dan'l give a heave, and hysted up his shoulders—so—like a Frenchman, but it warn't no use—he couldn't budge; he was planted as solid as a church, and he couldn't no more stir than if he was anchored out. Smiley was a good deal surprised, and he was disgusted too, but he didn't have no idea what the matter was, of course.

9. **a red:** Red cent; colloquial expression for "any money at all."

10. **quailshot:** Small lead pellets used for shooting quail.

Speaking, Listening, and Viewing Mini-Lesson

Oral Interpretation

This mini-lesson supports the Speaking, Listening, and Viewing activity in the Idea Bank on p. 531.

Introduce the Concept In this activity students will role-play part of the "Jumping Frog" story. Explain that a deadpan delivery is one that involves little or no emotion on the part of the speaker. A deadpan delivery heightens humor by contrasting it with seriousness.

Develop Background Have students discuss the importance of comedic delivery—the presentation may have more impact than the writing. They can brainstorm for a list of present-day comedians, such as Bob Newhart, who use this approach; many TV sitcoms usually have at least one character who consistently delivers humorous lines in complete deadpan. Students may benefit by studying this approach. Some may find it useful to tape themselves and then listen to hear if they are getting the effect they seek. Challenge students to try to capture Wheeler's dialect.

Apply the Information Have partners choose their scene, practice it, and then present it to the class.

Assess the Outcome You may wish to have the whole class evaluate students' performances. To provide students with assessment criteria, use the Peer Assessment: Oral Interpretation page in ***Alternative Assessment,*** p. 134.

The feller took the money and started away; and when he was going out at the door, he sorter jerked his thumb over his shoulder—so—at Dan'l, and says again, very deliberate, 'Well,' he says, '*I* don't see no p'ints about that frog that's any better'n any other frog.'

Smiley he stood scratching his head and looking down at Dan'l a long time, and at last he says, 'I do wonder what in the nation that frog throw'd off for—I wonder if there ain't something the matter with him—he 'pears to look mighty baggy, somehow.' And he ketched Dan'l by the nap of the neck, and hefted him, and says, 'Why blame my cats if he don't weigh five pound!' and turned him upside down and he belched out a double handful of shot. And then he see how it was, and he was the maddest man—he set the frog down and took out after that feller, but he never ketched him. And—"

Here Simon Wheeler heard his name called from the front yard, and got up to see what was wanted. And turning to me as he moved away, he said: "Just set where you are, stranger, and rest easy—I ain't going to be gone a second."

But, by your leave, I did not think that a continuation of the history of the enterprising vagabond *Jim* Smiley would be likely to afford me much information concerning the Rev. *Leonidas W.* Smiley, and so I started away. ❻

At the door I met the sociable Wheeler returning, and he buttonholed me and recommenced:

"Well, thish-yer Smiley had a yaller one-eyed cow that didn't have no tail, only just a short stump like a bannanner, and—"

However, lacking both time and inclination, I did not wait to hear about the afflicted cow, but took my leave.

> ◆ *Literature and Your Life*
> If you were the narrator, what would you have done at this point? Explain. ❼

Guide for Understanding

◆ *Literature and Your Life*

Reader's Response If Mark Twain were a stand-up comic today, would you want to see him perform? Why or why not?

Thematic Focus Telling tall tales was a common form of entertainment on the western frontier. What does this tale suggest about the setting and characters of the developing West?

Questions for Research Look at the elements comprising Twain's humor and his use of regional dialect. What questions could you ask to research one of these topics?

☑ Check Your Comprehension

1. What prompts Simon Wheeler to tell the story of Jim Smiley?
2. What was Jim Smiley's response to any event?
3. Why was Smiley so proud of his frog?
4. How did the stranger outwit Smiley?

◆ Critical Thinking

INTERPRET

1. Why had the narrator's friend suggested he ask Wheeler about Leonidas Smiley? Explain. **[Infer]**
2. Based on the way they use language, compare the personality of the anonymous narrator with that of Simon Wheeler. **[Compare and Contrast]**
3. Why did Twain have Wheeler, rather than the narrator, relay the story of Jim Smiley? **[Draw Conclusions]**

EVALUATE

4. Does "The Notorious Jumping Frog . . ." succeed in conveying the character of Simon Wheeler as effectively as it conveys the character of Jim Smiley, the subject of the tale? Explain. **[Evaluate]**

COMPARE LITERARY WORKS

5. Notice the different styles of humor in these two selections. Could they be successfully switched? Explain. **[Compare and Contrast]**

◆ Critical Thinking

❻ **Analyze** Ask students to interpret this passage. *Although the narrator got to hear an interesting story, it was about the wrong Smiley!*

◆ *Literature and Your Life*

❼ Some students may say that they would have remained to hear another entertaining tale.

Reinforce and Extend

Customize for
Interpersonal Learners
Have students recall favorite funny stories, involving exaggeration and embellishment, that are retold by family members. Invite them to explain the accounts and compare their knowledge of what actually happened to the way it is rendered in those tales intended to amuse.

Answers
◆ *Literature and Your Life*

Reader's Response You may wish to have students listen to Hal Holbrook's *Mark Twain Tonight* to appreciate the kind of verbal humor that was characteristic of Twain.

Thematic Focus The tale suggests that the setting is rugged and the characters were unique individuals.

☑ Check Your Comprehension

1. The narrator's friend suggests that he ask about a friend with the same last name.
2. He would bet on anything and everything.
3. He was proud because he had taught the frog to be a champion jumper.
4. He lured him outside and loaded Smiley's frog with quailshot.

(Answers continue on p. 530)

Reteach

To reteach regional dialect, play the audiocassette recording so student's can listen to the effects of dialect.

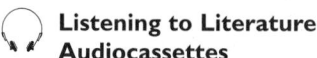

Listening to Literature Audiocassettes

Beyond the Selection

FURTHER READING

Other Works by Mark Twain
The Adventures of Tom Sawyer
The Adventures of Huckleberry Finn

Other Works About Humor in the American West
Davy Crockett's Dream, Davy Crockett
Little Big Man, Thomas Berger

We suggest that you preview these works before recommending them to students.

INTERNET

You may find additional information about Twain on the Internet. We suggest the following site. Please be aware, however, that sites may have changed from the time we published this information.

To visit the Mark Twain project at UC Berkeley, go to **http://library.berkeley.edu/BANC/MTP**

We *strongly recommend* that you preview the sites before you send students to them.

Guide for Responding (continued)

◆ Reading Strategy

Understand Regional Dialect

The **regional dialect** you encountered in these stories can both amuse and confuse readers. Some regional expressions may be unfamiliar, and certain words may not be spelled as they are in standard English. However, by reading aloud to yourself, you can usually decipher the meaning of the passages and better appreciate their comic effect. In your own words, explain the meaning of each of the following excerpts.

1. "... he 'peared surprised, and then he looked sorter discouraged-like, and didn't try no more to win the fight, and so he got shucked out bad."
2. "He got him up so in the matter of ketching flies, and kep' him in practice so constant, that he'd nail a fly every time as fur as he could see him."
3. "Well, thish-yer Smiley had a yaller one-eyed cow that didn't have no tail, only just a short stump like a bannanner ..."

◆ Build Vocabulary

Using the Greek Prefix *mono-*

The Greek prefix *mono-* means "alone" or "single." Add the prefix *mono-* to each of these word roots. Use your understanding of the prefix along with the definition of the root to tell the meaning of the new word.

1. *theism* = belief in god
2. *logue* = speaking
3. *lith* = stone
4. *chrome* = color

Using the Word Bank: Antonyms

Write the letter of the word in the right column that is the best antonym of the Word Bank word in the left column.

1. transient	**a.** varied
2. prodigious	**b.** meager
3. eminence	**c.** quiet
4. garrulous	**d.** permanent
5. conjectured	**e.** kind
6. monotonous	**f.** verified
7. interminable	**g.** obscurity
8. ornery	**h.** brief

◆ Literary Focus

Humor

Twain uses a broad range of techniques, including exaggeration, embellishment, and regional dialect, to amuse and entertain readers. "The Notorious Jumping Frog" is a particularly good example of Twain's special brand of **humor**, though there are plenty of amusing details and tongue-in-cheek observations to be found in "The Boys' Ambition," as well.

1. In "The Boys' Ambition," Twain daydreams about the "heavenly" steamboat duties of shaking out a tablecloth or holding a rope. How does his description of these everyday activities add to the humor of his narrative?
2. Find at least two examples of exaggeration in "The Notorious Jumping Frog," and explain why each is amusing.
3. Why would "The Notorious Jumping Frog" be less effective if Wheeler spoke in standard English?

◆ Grammar and Style

Double Negatives

The use of **double negatives**—two negative words in a sentence where only one is needed—can change the intended meaning of a sentence; in effect, the words cancel each other out. Pay special attention to the words *neither, barely, scarcely*, and *hardly*. It is easy to forget that they are negative words and should not be combined with another negative word.

Looking at Style Explain how Simon Wheeler's frequent use of double negatives fits his character and contributes to the story's humor.

Writing Application In your notebook, rewrite the following sentences from the story, revising them as necessary to eliminate double negatives.

1. Why, it never made no difference to him....
2. ... you couldn't fetch nothing for him to bet on but he'd match you.
3. ... maybe you've had experience and maybe you ain't only a amature.
4. ... it warn't no use—he couldn't budge.

Answers (continued from p. 529)

◆ Critical Thinking

1. He probably hoped Wheeler would tell the story of Jim Smiley.
2. The narrator is formal, humorless and impatient. Wheeler is slow, talkative, and "laid back."
3. Wheeler's style of speaking is humorous and better suited to telling a long, drawn-out tale.
4. Suggested response: The story does succeed in conveying the character of Simon Wheeler. By relating the mannerisms and the dialect of Wheeler, Twain gives us a portrait of Wheeler in words.
5. Possible response: No, they could not be switched. "The Boys' Ambition" is a reminiscent narrative with subtle, mature humor, while the "The Notorious Jumping Frog" is a story centered on the bizarrely humorous characters of Twain.

◆ Reading Strategy

1. He appeared surprised and discouraged. He didn't try to win anymore and was badly fooled.
2. He trained him so well in catching flies, that he would always catch any fly that he could see.
3. Smiley had a yellow one-eyed cow that had no tail, just a short stump like a banana.

◆ Build Vocabulary

Using the Greek Prefix *mono-*

1. monotheism = belief in one God
2. monologue = speech given by one person
3. monolith = a single giant stone
4. monochrome = something of one color

Using the Word Bank

1. d 2. b 3. g 4. c 5. f 6. a 7. h 8. e

◆ Literary Focus

1. Twain's description adds humor by showing through contrast how foolish some of his ambitions were as a child.
2. One example of exaggeration is the frog whirling in the air, doing one or two somersaults, and landing like a cat. Another example is the frog leaping upward on command to catch flies. Each example is amusing because it attributes to frogs activities that most frogs probably wouldn't do.
3. The story would by less effective because the humor of Wheeler's dialect would be lost.

◆ Grammar and Style

Looking at Style

Wheeler's use of double negatives shows him to be a rugged frontiersman, and it adds to the humor by adding extra flair to the story.

Writing Application

1. Why, it never made any difference to him....
2. ...you couldn't fetch anything for him to bet on but he'd match you.
3. ...maybe you've had experience and maybe you are only an amateur.
4. ...it wasn't any use—he couldn't budge.

Grammar Reinforcement

For additional instruction and practice, use the lesson in the **Language Lab CD-ROM** on Problems With Modifiers and the practice pages on Negative Sentences (pp. 78–79) in the *Writer's Solution Grammar and Practice Book*.

Build Your Portfolio

Idea Bank

Writing

1. Cartoon Develop one of the shorter anecdotes in Simon Wheeler's tale into a cartoon strip. Create a caption and an illustration for each frame.

2. Obituary Write a newspaper obituary for the famous jumping frog, Dan'l Webster, in which you relate his accomplishments. Use exaggeration to make it funny.

3. Analytic Essay Mark Twain wrote, "The humorous story may be spun out to great length, and may wander around as much as it pleases, and arrive nowhere in particular. . . . [It] is told gravely; the teller does his best to conceal the fact that he even dimly suspects there is anything funny about it." In an essay, discuss how these techniques were applied to "Jumping Frog."

Speaking, Listening, and Viewing

4. Interview Prepare a list of questions about a career that interests you. Then interview someone in the field to obtain answers. Present your findings to the class. **[Career Link]**

5. Oral Interpretation Much of the humor in "Jumping Frog" is in the speaker's deadpan delivery. With a partner, practice a part of the story and role-play the characters, Simon Wheeler and the narrator. **[Performing Arts Link]**

Researching and Representing

6. Multimedia Presentation Create a multimedia report on Mississippi riverboats. Use text, visual images, and video or audio clips to convey the sights and sounds of nineteenth-century riverboat life. **[Social Studies Link]**

7. Illustration Select a scene from either work and illustrate it. Include an extended caption describing the events depicted. **[Art Link]**

Online Activity www.phlit.phschool.com

Guided Writing Lesson

Humorous Anecdote

Choose a funny event that you have heard about or that happened to you. Then develop it into an amusing anecdote. Create humor by making the characters amusing and by using exaggeration where appropriate. Also keep the following in mind:

Writing Skills Focus: Elaboration for Vividness

As you develop your anecdote, **elaborate for vividness** by adding details that make the events come alive. Elaboration can take the form of sensory details, unexpected comparisons, or restatements. Twain brings Simon Wheeler to life by filling his dialogue with a stream of unexpected details, asides, and comparisons.

Model From the Story

Thish-yer Smiley had a mare—the boys called her the fifteen-minute nag, but that was only in fun, you know, because of course she was faster than that—and he used to win money on that horse, for all she was so slow and always had the asthma, or the distemper, or the consumption, or something of that kind.

Prewriting Select an event on which to base your humorous anecdote. Then, in a web like this one, note details that will make the story funny.

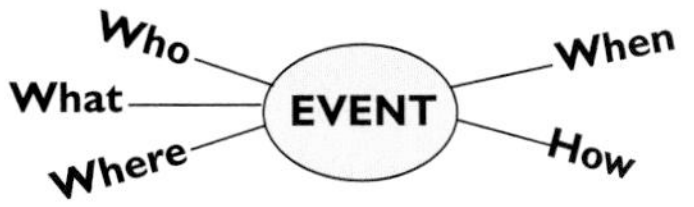

Drafting Use your completed word web to help you write a draft of your anecdote. Include unusual comparisons and sensory details that will make the characters and events especially vivid.

Revising Use these questions to guide your revision: Is the sequence of events clear? How can I make the characters more humorous? How effectively have I used exaggeration?

ASSESSMENT OPTIONS

Formal Assessment, Selection Test, pp. 158–160, and Assessment Resources Software. The selection test is designed so that it can be easily customized to the performance levels of your students.

Alternative Assessment, p. 32, includes options for less advanced students, more advanced students, visual/spatial learners, verbal/linguistic learners, and musical/rhythmic learners.

PORTFOLIO ASSESSMENT

Use the following rubrics in the ***Alternative Assessment*** booklet to assess student writing:
Cartoon: Fictional Narrative Rubric, p. 110
Obituary: Summary Rubric, p. 113
Analytic Essay: Literary Analysis/Interpretation Rubric, p. 127
Guided Writing Lesson: Fictional Narrative Rubric, p. 110

Idea Bank

Customizing for *Performance Levels*

Following are suggestions for matching Idea Bank topics with your students' performance levels:
Less Advanced Students: 1
Average Students: 2, 4, 5, 7
More Advanced Students: 3, 6

Customizing for *Learning Modalities*

Following are suggestions for matching Idea Bank topics with your students' learning modalities:
Interpersonal: 4
Bodily/Kinesthetic: 5
Visual/Spatial: 6, 7

Guided Writing Lesson

For more instruction on prewriting, elaboration, and revision, see *Prentice Hall Writing and Grammer.*

Writing and Language Transparencies Use Writing Process Model 3: Personal Narrative, pp. 13–16, to guide students in writing their humorous anecdotes.

Writers at Work Videodisc
Have students view the videodisc segment (Ch. 2) featuring novelist, poet, and essayist N. Scott Momaday speaking about choosing a topic for a narrative. Ask students how discussing something with a person or listening to music can trigger a writing idea.

Play frames 11644 to 20980

Writing Lab CD-ROM
Have students complete the tutorial on Narration. Follow these steps:

1. Have students use the Character Trait Word Bin to help develop characters.
2. Have students draft on the computer.
3. Refer students to the Tips on Making Dialogue More Realistic to help them revise dialogue.

Prepare and Engage

LESSON OBJECTIVES

1. To develop vocabulary and word identification skills
- Latin Word Roots: *-bel-*
- Using the Word Bank: Synonyms
- Extending Word Study: Latin Roots (ATE)

2. To use a variety of reading strategies to comprehend a story
- Connect Your Experience
- Reading Strategy: Question the Text
- Tips to Guide Reading

3. To increase knowledge of other cultures and to connect common elements across cultures
- Connecting Themes Across Cultures (ATE)
- Cultural Connection (ATE)

4. To express and support responses to the text
- Critical Thinking
- Idea Bank: Newspaper Editorial
- Analyze Literary Criticism: (ATE)
- Idea Bank: Review

5. To analyze literary elements
- Literary Focus: Regionalism
- Idea Bank: Visitor's Guide

6. To read in order to research self-selected and assigned topics
- Idea Bank: Boom Towns
- Idea Bank: In Search of Gold
- Research Skills Mini-Lesson (ATE)

7. To plan, prepare, organize, and present literary interpretations
- Idea Bank: Literary Discussion
- Idea Bank: Eulogy
- Speaking Listening, and Viewing Mini-Lesson (ATE)

8. To use recursive writing processes to write a description of a place
- Guided Writing Lesson

9. To increase knowledge of the rules of grammar and usage
- Coordinating Conjunctions

Test Preparation

Reading Comprehension: Context (ATE, p. 533)
The teaching tips and sample test item in this workshop support the instruction and practice in the unit workshop:
Reading Comprehension: Using Context (SE, p. 631)

Guide for Interpreting

Bret Harte *(1836–1902)*

A literary pioneer, Bret Harte played a key role in creating a vivid, lasting portrait of the Old West. His stories, filled with picturesque characters and colorful dialogue, provided much of post-Civil War America with its first glimpse of western life and established the Old West as a popular fictional setting.

In many ways, the roots of the Hollywood western can be traced back to Harte's tales.

Heading West Harte was born and raised in Albany, New York. In 1854, when he was eighteen, he traveled to California, a land undergoing a turbulent period of rapid growth due to the discovery of gold in 1848. During his first few years in California, Harte worked as a schoolteacher, messenger, clerk, and prospector. While Harte's life seemed to have little direction at the time, his observations of the rugged, often violent life in the mining camps and the towns and cities of the new frontier provided him with the inspiration for his most successful short stories.

A Career of Ups and Downs After working as a typesetter and writer for two California periodicals and publishing two books of verse, *Outcroppings* (1865) and *The Last Galleon* (1867), Harte became the editor in 1868 of the *Overland Monthly*. When he published his story "The Luck of Roaring Camp" in the magazine's second issue, he immediately became famous. The American public, eager to learn about life in the new frontier, responded to the story with enthusiasm. Over the next two years, Harte published "The Outcasts of Poker Flat" and other stories about life in the frontier, and his popularity grew at a rapid pace.

Following the publication of *The Luck of Roaring Camp and Other Sketches* in 1870, Harte's popularity reached its peak. In 1871, *The Atlantic Monthly,* a distinguished literary magazine, contracted to pay Harte the large sum of $10,000 for any twelve sketches or stories he contributed over the next year. Harte returned to the East to fulfill his contract, but the stories he wrote were flat and disappointing compared with his earlier work. His celebrity waned almost as quickly as it had grown.

A Political Appointment Harte continued to publish stories, short novels, and plays during the next twenty years, but most of his later work was unsuccessful. Some friends helped him land a diplomatic post, however, and from 1878 to 1885, Harte served as a United States consul in Germany and Scotland. He retired to London for the remainder of his life.

◆ Background for Understanding

LITERATURE: THE REAL MR. OAKHURST

Mr. Oakhurst, a gambler and the main character of "The Outcasts of Poker Flat," is a generous, genial man who is seemingly nonchalant in the face of danger. As you read the story, you may wonder how true-to-life Mr. Oakhurst is.

Harte's biographer, Henry Childs Merwin, described a gambler named Lucky Bill who demonstrated traits similar to Mr. Oakhurst's. According to Merwin, "Lucky Bill was noted for his generosity, and, though finally hanged by a vigilance committee, he made a 'good end,' for, on the scaffold, he exhorted his son who was among the spectators, to avoid bad company, to keep away from saloons, and to lead an industrious and honest life."

Prentice Hall Literature Program Resources

REINFORCE / RETEACH / EXTEND

Selection Support Pages
Build Vocabulary: Word Roots: *-bel-*, p. 155
Grammar and Style: Coordinating Conjunctions in Compound Sentences, p. 156
Reading Strategy: Question the Text, p. 157
Literary Focus: Regionalism, p. 158

Strategies for Diverse Student Needs, p. 33

Beyond Literature Cross-Curricular Connection: Social Studies, p. 33

Formal Assessment Selection Test, pp. 161–163; Assessment Resources Software

Alternative Assessment, p. 33

Writing and Language Transparencies
Cubing Organizer, p. 71

Resource Pro CD-ROM

Listening to Literature Audiocassettes

Literature CD-ROM

The Outcasts of Poker Flat

◆ Literature and Your Life

Connect Your Experience

The "outcasts" in Bret Harte's story are tested by circumstances. Think of a time you—or someone you know—used the words, "It was a real test of character." What was the situation? What qualities did it bring out in the people involved?

Thematic Focus: Forging New Frontiers

Stories of the Old West have endured in popularity. As you read, think about the qualities of frontier life depicted in this story that make the Old West so interesting to modern readers.

Journal Writing List some the characteristics that you associate with a western hero.

◆ Literary Focus

Regionalism

Bret Harte's early stories about frontier life helped to fuel a new literary movement known as **Regionalism**—a movement in which writers attempted to capture the "local color" of a region by accurately depicting the distinctive qualities of its people and its physical environment. The interest in regional literature was driven by the fact that during the mid- to late-1800's, the country was expanding at a rapid pace—both in population and in geographical area. Yet, there were then few ways for people to learn about life in regions other than their own—photography had just been developed and television was still decades away from becoming a reality. However, stories like "The Outcasts of Poker Flat" painted a vivid and engaging portrait of what life was like in the far reaches of the land.

◆ Grammar and Style

Coordinating Conjunctions in Compound Sentences

Coordinating conjunctions—*and, or, but, nor, for, so,* and *yet*—connect words or phrases of equal weight. In compound sentences, they connect two or more independent clauses to form a single sentence. They also indicate the relationship between the ideas expressed. In this example, *but* indicates a contrast:

Tommy, you're a good little man, *but* you can't gamble worth a cent.

◆ Reading Strategy

Question the Text

When you read any piece of literature—from an essay to a short story—**question the text.** Ask yourself, What's happening? What's the author's purpose here? What is the motive for this character's action? Will this idea be further developed? Consider this description of the place known as Poker Flat:

> There was a Sabbath lull in the air which, in a settlement unused to Sabbath influences, looked ominous.

Here you might ask yourself, Where will this ominous mood lead? What makes Poker Flat a place of doubtful virtue? Look for answers to these and other questions as you read.

◆ Build Vocabulary

Latin Word Roots: *-bel-*

In this story, a character is described as being "in a *bellicose* state." You might already be familiar with the word *belligerent,* which also contains the root *-bel-* and which is close in meaning. The Latin root *-bel-* means "war." Both *belligerent* and *bellicose* mean "warlike" or "ready to fight or quarrel."

Word Bank

Preview this list of words from the story.

- expatriated
- anathema
- bellicose
- recumbent
- equanimity
- vociferation
- vituperative
- querulous

Test Preparation Workshop

Reading Comprehension: Context Many standardized tests require students to use context to determine the meaning of unfamiliar words. Use the following sample test item to give students practice in this skill.

> But even this act did not draw the group into any closer sympathy. . . . Mother Shipton eyed the possessor of "Five Spot" with malevolence, and Uncle Billy included the whole party in one sweeping anathema.
>
> In this passage, malevolence means—

A sympathy
B contentment
C hatred
D mellowness

The *but* at the beginning of the passage indicates that sympathy is in contrast to malevolence. The *and* before Uncle Billy's reaction indicates that *anathema* is similar to *malevolence.* These context clues should lead students to discover that the correct response is *C.*

Interest Grabber Discuss the idea that people as well as characters in fiction may not be as they appear at first impression. Point out, for example, that students must know seemingly tough characters who inevitably show they have a heart of gold, or weak ones who show they have an unexpected inner strength during a crisis. Have students think about and suggest a list of fictional characters from short stories, books, movies, and television who turn out to be different than their initial impression would suggest. Guide students to pay attention to how their views of the different characters in this story change as they read.

Connecting Themes Across Cultures

There are few new frontiers left to explore on Earth, but countries around the world are forging new frontiers in space. Joint space ventures have brought people from different cultures together. For example, a number of United States astronauts joined cosmonauts on the Russian space station *Mir.* Invite students to research the International Space Station and other joint space projects that bring people of different cultures together.

Customize for *Less Proficient Readers*

This story contains an abundance of lengthy and potentially confusing compound sentences. To help students better understand them, suggest that they break apart the sentences as they read. Guide them to use coordinating conjunctions to help them understand the connection between the ideas.

Customize for *AP Students*

Students are likely to make observations and inferences as they read, and also to formulate questions as they try to grasp characters' motivations as well as twists in the story line. Suggest that they keep a reader's response journal to jot down their inferences and predictions, to record their answers to their questions, or to note which of the questions remain unanswered. Students can compare notes.

Develop Understanding

One-Minute Insight

In a regenerative effort, the mining town of Poker Flat has been ridding itself of unsavory characters. The gambler John Oakhurst and three other outcasts attempt to make their way to the more hospitable camp of Sandy Bar. A snowstorm stops them in their tracks and links them with two innocents heading in the opposite direction. As the story of survival unfolds, readers come to understand each of the characters in a new light. The character's experiences force readers to explore the larger issues of weakness and strength, charity and greed, and life and death.

Customize for
Interpersonal Learners
Guide students to notice the composition of characters in the group of outcasts, and how each contributes to the group dynamics. Compare this collection with the traditional make-up of groups in disaster movies. Discuss that these groups routinely include an intrepid male leader, a young innocent, a corrupt old man, a tough, worldly woman, and an untrustworthy young drifter.

◆ Literary Focus

1 Regionalism Ask students what this passage suggests about characteristics of this mining camp. *The camp was small and corrupt, that it had allowed gambling, and that life there was volatile and could quickly change.*

2 Clarification Guide students to understand that a "Sabbath lull" refers to a time of quiet and calm, such as one would expect on a day of religious observance and rest. A gambler would be wary to awake to find a "Sabbath lull in the air. . . ."

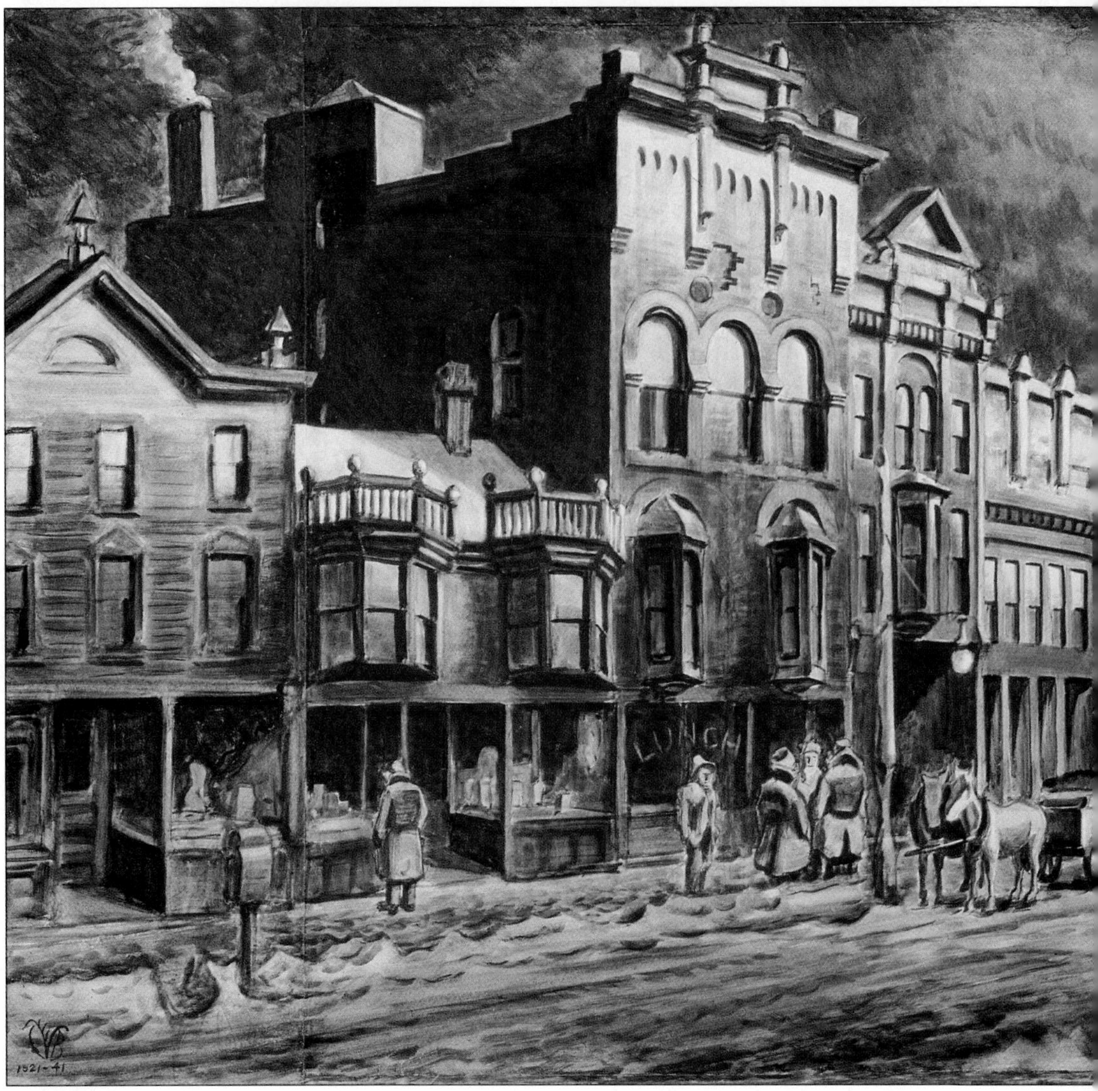

Edge of Town, Charles Burchfield, The Nelson-Atkins Museum of Art, Kansas City, Missouri

As Mr. John Oakhurst, gambler, stepped into the main street of Poker Flat on the morning of the twenty-third of November, 1850,
1 he was conscious of a change in
2 its moral atmosphere since the preceding night. Two or three men, conversing earnestly together, ceased as he approached, and exchanged significant glances. There was a Sabbath lull in the air which, in a settlement unused to Sabbath influences, looked ominous.

Mr. Oakhurst's calm, handsome face betrayed small concern in these indications. Whether he was conscious of any predisposing cause was another question. "I reckon they're after somebody," he reflected; "likely it's me." He returned to his pocket the handkerchief with which he had been whipping away the red dust of Poker Flat from his neat boots, and quietly discharged his mind of any further conjecture.

In point of fact, Poker Flat was "after somebody." It had lately suffered the loss of several 4

Block Scheduling Strategies

Consider these suggestions to take advantage of extended class time:

- Introduce Regionalism to students by discussing with them the Literary Focus section (p. 533). Brainstorm for attributes of the Old West that students are familiar with through other reading and movies.
- Have students discuss ways in which the story reveals elements of that part of California characterized by lawless mining towns like Poker Flat and their colorful characters.
- Help students to become active readers by discussing with them the Reading Strategy (p. 533). You may want to model the questions you would ask yourself while reading the first couple of paragraphs of the selection.
- Use the Cross-Curricular Connection: Science note on p. 539 of the ATE. To help students explore the idea of living in tight spaces with strangers, place them in small groups and ask them to imagine such a situation. After each group devises a list of "ground rules" they might establish to keep the peace, compare lists as a class.
- Assign the Guided Writing Lesson (p. 543). Before students begin, have a discussion on using precise details to make descriptions true-to-life. Have students look for specific examples of the author's use of precise images and details to capture the look and feel of events and places in the story.

The Outcasts of Poker Flat

Bret Harte

3 ▲ **Critical Viewing** How does the mood of this painting echo the mood of the story's opening paragraphs? **[Compare]**

thousand dollars, two valuable horses, and a prominent citizen. It was experiencing a spasm of virtuous reaction, quite as lawless and ungovernable as any of the acts that had provoked it. A secret committee had determined to rid the town of all improper persons. This was done permanently in regard of two men who were then hanging from the boughs of a sycamore in the gulch, and temporarily in the banishment of certain other objectionable characters. I regret to say that some of these were ladies. It is but due to the sex, however, to state that their impropriety was professional, and it was only in such easily established standards of evil that Poker Flat ventured to sit in judgment. 4

Mr. Oakhurst was right in supposing that he was included in this category. A few of the committee had urged hanging him as a possible example, and a sure method of reimbursing themselves from his pockets of the sums he had won from them. "It's agin justice," said Jim Wheeler, "to let this yer young man from Roaring Camp—an entire stranger—carry away our money." But a crude sentiment of equity residing in the breasts of those who had been fortunate enough to win from Mr. Oakhurst overruled this narrower local prejudice. 5 6

◆ **Literary Focus** What does this passage reveal about some of the inhabitants of Poker Flat?

Mr. Oakhurst received his sentence with philosophic calmness, none the less coolly that

▶Critical Viewing◀

❸ **Compare** The mood of the painting accurately echoes the mood of the opening paragraphs. The painting shows a small western town that is quite still except for the few people milling in the street. The daylight upon the buildings is eerie and the dark clouds are ominous. The scene evokes calm but also a sense of foreboding.

◆Literary Focus

❹ **Regionalism** Point out to students that this passage provides both a glimpse of life in a lawless frontier town and a good indication of what constituted frontier justice. It suggests that gambling, thievery, and prostitution were present in these towns and that violent vigilantism was the response to them.

◆Reading Strategy

❺ **Question the Text** Tell students that they should question why Oakhurst was not hanged, as "a few of the committee had urged." *Students can recognize that Oakhurst escaped the noose because one faction in town, those who won from him, overruled another, those from whom he profited.* Ask students whether a smart gambler like Oakhurst would make a point of losing occasionally, so that he might have allies when he needed them.

◆Literary Focus

❻ **Regionalism** Students may say that some inhabitants' actions were governed by greed—if they had lost money, they would hang a gambler; if they had won money, they would not.

Tips to Guide Reading

Shared Reading To get students started reading "The Outcasts of Poker Flat," pick a volunteer to read the first several paragraphs aloud while students follow in their texts. Afterward, answer any questions that students might have. Then have students read the rest of the selection silently. Suggest that they note any difficult lines or passages to discuss later on.

Humanities: Art

Edge of Town by Charles Burchfield.

Charles Burchfield (1893–1967) studied at the Cleveland Art Institute, where he developed his poetic and introspective painting style. This work, the last of Burchfield's "main street" paintings, provides a view of a small-town street on a bleak winter day. It demonstrates that Burchfield did not relinquish his intense fascination with the forces of nature even when painting a human scene.

Use these questions for discussion:

1. How does the artist create a scene filled with mystery and tension? *The buildings glow with a dull light that is in eerie contrast to the stormy sky. The static figures are more like elements of the landscape than people.*
2. Why is this painting an appropriate illustration for this story? *Students may say that the painting is appropriate because it depicts a small western town with an ominous undercurrent.*

Customize for
Logical/Mathematical Learners

❶ Emphasize the principle that in games of chance, the gambling institution, known as the "house," usually has the mathematical advantage, and therefore the greater probability of winning. Tell them that although the degree to which the odds favor the house may differ from game to game, in poker they usually favor the house. A gambler like Oakhurst must know the precise advantage the dealer has.

◆ Reading Strategy

❷ **Question the Text** Ask students to describe Oakhurst's view of life. *Students may say that he believes that luck is the key factor in determining the direction one's life will take. They may guess that, as a gambler, he always plays the odds, calculates the probability of events occurring, and always responds in a way that will give him the best chance of success. They may say that when Oakhurst says that he "recognized the usual percentage . . ." he means that he knows when to accept defeat—to fold his cards.* Ask them whom he is referring to here as the "dealer." *They may say that the "dealer" Oakhurst refers to is God, or fate.*

❸ **Clarification** Explain the meaning of this sentence. Guide students to understand that Sandy Bar is another mining town across the mountains. Since it is still all right to be a gambler or to engage in other unsavory practices there, Sandy Bar is a place where the outcasts would be welcome.

◆ Literary Focus

❹ **Regionalism** In the Old West, travel could be quite difficult. This passage reveals that massive mountain ranges, such as the Sierra Nevada, had few good trails. Crossing the mountains took much time, and sudden shifts in weather or a slip along the edge of a steep cliff could have disastrous consequences.

he was aware of the hesitation of his judges. He was too much of a gambler not to accept Fate. ❶ With him life was at best an uncertain game, ❷ and he recognized the usual percentage in favor of the dealer.

A body of armed men accompanied the deported wickedness of Poker Flat to the outskirts of the settlement. Besides Mr. Oakhurst, who was known to be a coolly desperate man, and for whose intimidation the armed escort was intended, the expatriated party consisted of a young woman familiarly known as the "Duchess"; another, who had won the title of "Mother Shipton";[1] and "Uncle Billy," a suspected sluice robber[2] and confirmed drunkard. The cavalcade provoked no comments from the spectators, nor was any word uttered by the escort. Only, when the gulch which marked the uttermost limit of Poker Flat was reached, the leader spoke briefly and to the point. The exiles were forbidden to return at the peril of their lives.

As the escort disappeared, their pent-up feelings found vent in a few hysterical tears from the Duchess, some bad language from Mother Shipton, and a Parthian volley of expletives[3] from Uncle Billy. The philosophic Oakhurst alone remained silent. He listened calmly to Mother Shipton's desire to cut somebody's heart out, to the repeated statements of the Duchess that she would die in the road, and to the alarming oaths that seemed to be bumped out of Uncle Billy as he rode forward. With the easy good humor characteristic of his class, he insisted upon exchanging his own riding horse, "Five Spot," for the sorry mule which the Duchess rode. But even this act did not draw the party into any closer sympathy. The young woman readjusted her somewhat draggled plumes with a feeble, faded coquetry; Mother Shipton eyed the possessor of "Five Spot" with malevolence, and Uncle Billy included the whole party in one sweeping anathema.

The road to Sandy Bar—a camp that, not having as yet experienced the regenerating influences of Poker Flat, consequently seemed ❸ to offer some invitation to the emigrants—lay over a steep mountain range. It was distant a day's severe travel. In that advanced season, the party soon passed out of the moist, temperate regions of the foothills into the dry, cold, bracing air of the Sierras.[4] The trail was narrow and difficult. At noon the Duchess, rolling out of her saddle upon the ground, declared her intention of going no farther, and the party halted.

◆ Literary Focus
What does this passage reveal about difficulties related to travel in the Old West? ❹

The spot was singularly wild and impressive. A wooded amphitheater, surrounded on three sides by precipitous cliffs of naked granite, sloped gently toward the crest of another precipice that overlooked the valley. It was, undoubtedly, the most suitable spot for a camp, had camping been advisable. But Mr. Oakhurst knew that scarcely half the journey to Sandy Bar was accomplished, and the party were not equipped or provisioned for delay. This fact he pointed out to his companions curtly, with a philosophic commentary on the folly of "throwing up their hand before the game was played out." But they were furnished with liquor, which in this emergency stood them in place of food, fuel, rest, and prescience. In spite of his remonstrances, it was not long before they were more or less under its influence. Uncle Billy passed rapidly from a bellicose state into one of stupor, the Duchess became maudlin, and Mother Shipton snored. Mr. Oakhurst alone remained erect, leaning against a rock calmly surveying them.

1. **"Mother Shipton":** English woman who lived in the sixteenth century and was suspected of being a witch.
2. **sluice robber:** Person who steals gold from sluices—long troughs used for sifting gold.
3. **Parthian . . . expletives:** Hostile remarks made while leaving. The Parthians were an ancient society whose cavalrymen usually shot at the enemy while retreating or pretending to retreat.
4. **Sierras** (sē er´ əz): Mountains in eastern California, also called the Sierra Nevadas.

◆ Build Vocabulary

expatriated (eks pā´ trē āt´ id) *adj.*: Deported; driven from one's native land

anathema (ə nath´ ə mə) *n.*: Curse

bellicose (bel´ ə kōs) *adj.*: Quarrelsome

recumbent (ri kum´ bənt) *adj.*: Resting

equanimity (ek´ wə nim ə tē) *n.*: Composure

Analyze a Film Review

"The Outcast of Poker Flat" was made into a movie in the late 1930's. At that time, cinematography was a new science and special effects, as audiences know them today, did not exist. Here is a review of the movie as it appeared in *Time* magazine:

"Though skimpily produced, it invokes with a fidelity unusual in a double-biller the wild land and rugged times in which its scene is laid, and the nostalgic charm of the Harte stories. Its worst fault is the failure of explicitness in the last sequence, leaving the audience completely fuddled."

Have students write a journal entry in which they answer the following questions:

1. Do you agree with the reviewer that there is a nostalgic charm to Harte's story? Why or why not? *Students might say yes because of regional descriptions of an earlier era in the West.*
2. The reviewer considers the last scenes in the movie to be strained and unnatural. Do you think that the end of the original story is believable and a logical resolution? Why or why not? *Students might say that the ending of the story is a believable resolution of the conflict.*

5 Mr. Oakhurst did not drink. It interfered with a profession which required coolness, impassiveness, and presence of mind, and, in his own language, he "couldn't afford it." As he gazed at his recumbent fellow exiles, the loneliness begotten of his pariah trade, his habits of life, his very vices, for the first time seriously oppressed him. He bestirred himself in dusting his black clothes, washing his hands and face, and other acts characteristic of his studiously neat habits, and for a moment forgot his annoyance. The thought of deserting his weaker and more pitiable companions never perhaps occurred to him. Yet he could not help feeling the want of that excitement which singularly enough, was most conducive to that calm equanimity for which he was notorious. He looked at the gloomy walls that rose a thousand feet sheer above the circling pines around him; at the sky, ominously clouded; at the valley below, already deepening into shadow. And, doing so, suddenly he heard his own name called.

6 A horseman slowly ascended the trail. In the fresh, open face of the newcomer Mr. Oakhurst recognized Tom Simson, otherwise known as the "Innocent" of Sandy Bar. He had met him some months before over a "little game," and had, with perfect equanimity, won the entire fortune—amounting to some forty dollars—of that guileless youth. After the game was finished, Mr. Oakhurst drew the youthful speculator behind the door and thus addressed him: "Tommy, you're a good little man, but you can't gamble worth a cent. Don't try it over again." He then handed him his money back, pushed him gently from the room, and so made a devoted slave of Tom Simson.

There was a remembrance of this in his boyish and enthusiastic greeting of Mr. Oakhurst. He had started, he said, to go to Poker Flat to seek his fortune. "Alone?" No, not exactly alone; in fact (a giggle), he had run away with Piney Woods. Didn't Mr. Oakhurst remember Piney? She that used to wait on the table at the Temperance House? They had been engaged a long time, but old Jake Woods had objected, and so they had run away, and were going to Poker Flat to be married, and here they were. And they were tired out, and how lucky it was they had found a place to camp and company. All this the Innocent delivered rapidly, while Piney, a stout, comely damsel of fifteen, emerged from behind the pine tree, where she had been blushing unseen, and rode to the side of her lover.

Mr. Oakhurst seldom troubled himself with sentiment, still less with propriety; but he had a vague idea that the situation was not fortunate. He retained, however, his presence of mind sufficiently to kick Uncle Billy, who was about to say something, and Uncle Billy was sober enough to recognize in Mr. Oakhurst's kick a superior power that would not bear trifling. He then endeavored to dissuade Tom Simson from delaying further, but in vain. He even pointed out the fact that there was no provision, nor means of making a camp. But, unluckily, the Innocent met this objection by assuring the party that he was provided with an extra mule loaded with provisions and by the discovery of a rude attempt at a log house near the trail. "Piney can stay with Mrs. Oakhurst," said the Innocent, pointing to the Duchess, "and I can shift for myself."

Nothing but Mr. Oakhurst's admonishing foot saved Uncle Billy from bursting into a roar of laughter. As it was, he felt compelled to retire up the canyon until he could recover his gravity. There he confided the joke to the tall pine trees, with many slaps of his leg, contortions of his face, and the usual profanity. But when he returned to the party, he found them seated by a fire—for the air had grown strangely chill and the sky overcast—in apparently amicable conversation. Piney was actually talking in an impulsive, girlish fashion to the Duchess, who was listening with an interest 7
and animation she had not shown for many days. The Innocent was holding forth, apparently with equal effect, to Mr. Oakhurst and Mother Shipton, who was actually relaxing into amiability. "Is this yer a d——d picnic?" said Uncle Billy with inward scorn as he surveyed the sylvan[5] group, the glancing firelight, and the tethered animals in the foreground. Suddenly an idea mingled with the alcoholic fumes that disturbed his brain. It was apparently of a jocular nature, for he felt impelled to slap his leg again and cram his fist into his mouth.

As the shadows crept slowly up the mountain, a slight breeze rocked the tops of the pine

5. **sylvan:** (sil′ vən) *adj.*: Characteristic of the forest.

◆ Critical Thinking

5 Analyze Have students revisit their assessment of Mr. Oakhurst again, now that they know him a bit better. Ask them to identify any paradoxes in his personality and speculate on why he became a gambler. *Students may say that although he thrives on excitement such as he might find in a card game, Oakhurst has the bearing of someone who never gambles, who always relies on cool, dispassionate reason, who likes to be in control. They may say that his composure and calm personality, combined with his belief in the significance of luck and in the inevitability of fate, ideally suit him to his chosen profession.*

◆ Reading Strategy

6 Question the Text Ask students to suggest possible reasons that would explain why Oakhurst returned Simson's money. *Students may suggest that the gambler did not like taking advantage of innocents or that he felt paternalistic toward the young man. Others may say that Oakhurst sought an ally in dangerous times.*

◆ Reading Strategy

7 Question the Text Ask students to tell what is so funny to Uncle Billy. Ask them speculate about why Billy slaps his leg a second time. *Students may say that Billy finds humor in Simson's complete ignorance of what awaits him in Poker Flat and of the predicament of the outcasts. They may speculate that when Billy sees the pack animals, he gets the idea to take them.*

Extending Word Study

Latin Root *-cumb-* Point out the word *recumbent* at the top of page 537. Have students consult a dictionary to discover the meaning of the words *recumbent* and *incumbent*. Explain that both words have the same Latin root *-cumb-*. Tell students to write the meaning of this root. *The word root -cumb- means "lie down," "recline," and "lean." An incumbent is someone who holds—reclines in—an office.*

Cultural Connection

Outcasts Inform students that individuals have been rejected from societies from the earliest times for such diverse reasons as their religious beliefs or their antisocial behavior. About five hundred years ago, Jews were forced to leave Spain unless they converted to Catholicism. Great Britain shipped criminals to Australia, where they eventually helped to develop that country. Until 1950, India's rigid caste system forced an entire class of people, called Untouchables, to live a life of poverty and begging.

Have students research a group of people who were considered outcasts of society. Students' research should attempt to provide the following: the reasons why the people were made outcasts, a description of the daily lives of the outcasts and, in the cases in which the outcasts were not criminals, why the injustice of exclusion was allowed to occur. Invite students to report their findings to the class.

◆ Reading Strategy

❶ **Question the Text** Students can guess that Uncle Billy left with the mules. They may reach this conclusion knowing Billy's reputation for thievery. They may point to the fact that on the previous evening, he noticed the animals and slapped his leg and crammed his fist into his mouth, as if to conceal a revelation.

◆ Grammar and Style

❷ **Coordinating Conjunctions in Compound Sentences** Have students name the coordinating conjunction *(and)* in Mr. Oakhurst's sentence. Point out that a comma precedes *and* because the conjunction joins two independent clauses.

◆ Critical Thinking

❸ **Evaluate** Ask students to discuss whether Simson's analysis of the situation is accurate. *Students may say that since it's winter and the group is encamped high in the mountains, it is very unlikely that the snow will melt any time soon. They may say that Simson has no idea of the danger they are in.*

◆ Literary Focus

❹ **Regionalism** Ask students: What characteristic western phrase does Piney use, and what does it mean? *The phrase is* I reckon, *which means "I figure," "I suppose," or "I regard as being."*

trees, and moaned through their long and gloomy aisles. The ruined cabin, patched and covered with pine boughs, was set apart for the ladies. As the lovers parted, they unaffectedly exchanged a kiss, so honest and sincere that it might have been heard above the swaying pines. The frail Duchess and the malevolent Mother Shipton were probably too stunned to remark upon this last evidence of simplicity, and so turned without a word to the hut. The fire was replenished, the men lay down before the door, and in a few minutes were asleep.

Mr. Oakhurst was a light sleeper. Toward morning he awoke benumbed and cold. As he stirred the dying fire, the wind, which was now blowing strongly, brought to his cheek that which caused the blood to leave it—snow!

He started to his feet with the intention of awakening the sleepers, for there was no time to lose. But turning to where Uncle Billy had been lying, he found him gone. A suspicion leaped to his brain and a curse to his lips. He ran to the spot where the mules had been tethered; they were no longer there. The tracks were already rapidly disappearing in the snow.

> ❶ **◆ Reading Strategy**
> What is the meaning behind Uncle Billy's disappearance? Identify one or more clues that point to the answer.

The momentary excitement brought Mr. Oakhurst back to the fire with his usual calm. He did not waken the sleepers. The Innocent slumbered peacefully, with a smile on his good-humored, freckled face; the virgin Piney slept beside her frailer sisters as sweetly as though attended by celestial guardians; and Mr. Oakhurst, drawing his blanket over his shoulders, stroked his mustaches and waited for the dawn. It came slowly in a whirling mist of snowflakes that dazzled and confused the eye. What could be seen of the landscape appeared magically changed. He looked over the valley, and summed up the present and future in two words—"snowed in!"

A careful inventory of the provisions, which, fortunately for the party, had been stored within the hut and so escaped the felonious fingers of Uncle Billy, disclosed the fact that with care and prudence they might last ten days longer. "That is," said Mr. Oakhurst, sotto voce[6] to the Innocent, "if you're willing to board us. If you ain't—and perhaps you'd better not—you can wait till Uncle Billy gets back with provisions." For some occult reason, Mr. Oakhurst could not bring himself to disclose Uncle Billy's rascality, and so offered the hypothesis that he had wandered from the camp and had accidentally stampeded the animals. He dropped a warning to the Duchess and Mother Shipton, who of course knew the facts of their associate's defection. "They'll find out the truth about us *all* when they find out anything," he added, significantly, "and there's no good frightening them now." ❷

Tom Simson not only put all his worldly store at the disposal of Mr. Oakhurst, but seemed to enjoy the prospect of their enforced seclusion. "We'll have a good camp for a week, and then the snow'll melt, and we'll all go back together." ❸ The cheerful gaiety of the young man, and Mr. Oakhurst's calm, infected the others. The Innocent with the aid of pine boughs extemporized a thatch for the roofless cabin, and the Duchess directed Piney in the rearrangement of the interior with a taste and tact that opened the blue eyes of that provincial maiden to their fullest extent. "I reckon now you're used to fine things at Poker Flat," said Piney. ❹ The Duchess turned away sharply to conceal something that reddened her cheek through its professional tint, and Mother Shipton requested Piney not to "chatter." But when Mr. Oakhurst returned from a weary search for the trail, he heard the sound of happy laughter echoed from the rocks. He stopped in some alarm, and his thoughts first naturally reverted to the whisky, which he had prudently cached.[7] "And yet it don't somehow sound like whisky," said the gambler. It was not until he caught sight of the blazing fire through the still-blinding storm and the group around it that he settled to the conviction that it was "square fun."

Whether Mr. Oakhurst had cached his cards with the whisky as something debarred the free access of the community, I cannot say. It was certain that, in Mother Shipton's words, he "didn't say cards once" during that evening. Haply the time was beguiled by an accordion, produced somewhat ostentatiously by Tom Simson from his pack. Notwithstanding some

6. **sotto voce** (sät´ ō vō´ chē): In an undertone.

7. **cached** (kasht) *v.*: Hidden.

difficulties attending the manipulation of this instrument, Piney Woods managed to pluck several reluctant melodies from its keys, to an accompaniment by the Innocent on a pair of bone castanets. But the crowning festivity of the evening was reached in a rude camp-meeting hymn, which the lovers, joining hands, sang with great earnestness and vociferation. I fear that a certain defiant tone and Covenanter's[8] swing to its chorus, rather than any devotional quality, caused it speedily to infect the others, who at last joined in the refrain:

> **◆ Literary Focus**
> 5 What aspects of "local color" does this passage convey?

"I'm proud to live in the
service of the Lord,
And I'm bound to die in
His army."[9]

The pines rocked, the storm eddied and whirled above the miserable group, and the flames of their altar leaped heavenward as if in token of the vow.

At midnight the storm abated, the rolling clouds parted, and the stars glittered keenly above the sleeping camp. Mr. Oakhurst, whose professional habits had enabled him to live on the smallest possible amount of sleep, in dividing the watch with Tom Simson somehow managed to take upon himself the greater part of that duty. He excused himself to the Innocent by saying that he had "often been a week without sleep." "Doing what?" asked Tom. "Poker!" replied Oakhurst, sententiously; "when a man gets a streak of luck, he don't get tired. The luck gives in first. Luck," continued the gambler, reflectively, "is a mighty queer thing. All you know about it for certain is that it's bound to change. And it's finding out when it's going to change that makes you. We've had a streak of bad luck since we left Poker Flat—you come along, and
6 slap you get into it, too. If you can hold your cards right along you're all right. For," added the gambler, with cheerful irrelevance,

" 'I'm proud to live in the service
of the Lord,
And I'm bound to die in
His army.' " 6

The third day came, and the sun, looking through the white-curtained valley, saw the outcasts divide their slowly decreasing store of provisions for the morning meal. It was one of the peculiarities of that mountain climate that its rays diffused a kindly warmth over the wintry landscape, as if in regretful commiseration of the past. 7 But it revealed drift on drift of snow piled high around the hut—a hopeless, uncharted, trackless sea of white lying below the rocky shores to which the castaways still clung. Through the marvelously clear air the smoke of the pastoral village of Poker Flat rose miles away. Mother Shipton saw it, and from a remote pinnacle of her rocky fastness hurled in that direction a final malediction. It was her last vituperative attempt, and perhaps for that reason was invested with a certain degree of sublimity. It did her good, she privately informed the Duchess. "Just you go out there and cuss, and see." She then set herself to the task of amusing "the child," as she and the Duchess were pleased to call Piney. Piney was no chicken, but it was a soothing and original theory of the pair thus to account for the fact that she didn't swear and wasn't improper.

When night crept up again through the gorges, the reedy notes of the accordion rose and fell in fitful spasms and long-drawn gasps by the flickering campfire. But music failed to fill entirely the aching void left by insufficient food, and a new diversion was proposed by Piney—storytelling. Neither Mr. Oakhurst nor his female companions caring to relate their personal experiences, this plan would have failed too but for the Innocent. Some months before he had chanced upon a stray copy of Mr. Pope's[10] ingenious translation of the *Iliad*.[11] He now proposed to narrate the principal incidents

8. **Covenanter's** (kuv´ ə nan´ tərz): Seventeenth-century Scottish Presbyterians who resisted the rule of the Church of England.
9. **"I'm . . . army:** Lines from the early American spiritual "Service of the Lord."

10. **Mr. Pope:** English poet Alexander Pope (1688–1744).
11. **Iliad** (il´ ē əd): Greek epic poem written by Homer that tells the story of the Trojan War.

◆ Build Vocabulary

vociferation (vō sif´ ər ā´ shən) *n.*: Loud or vehement shouting

vituperative (vī to͞o´ pər ə tiv) *adj.*: Spoken abusively

◆ Literary Focus

5 Regionalism Students may say that the outcasts unite in singing hymns. They may know that in the nineteenth century many Americans had strong religious beliefs, and that even for people living in the most chaotic and wildest parts of the country, religion was a common denominator.

◆ Reading Strategy

6 Question the Text Ask students to describe Oakhurst's view on luck and on fate, as expressed here. Ask them to explain what the song he repeats portends for the future of the group. *Students may say that Oakhurst believes in luck, and thinks that his is running out. They may say that he assumes the group is in deep danger of not surviving their predicament and calmly accepts his fate.*

◆ Critical Thinking

7 Predict Ask students: What do you predict will happen to the snowbound group? *Some students will say that the group will die in the snow. Others will say that the group will find a way out of the snowy mountains or be rescued.*

Literature CD-ROM To build background and enhance students' reading of the story, use the CD-ROM *The History of American Literature:* Part 1, Disc 2, Feature 9, which focuses in part on Bret Harte and the West.

Reteach

Students who are having difficulty understanding the Literary Focus on regionalism may benefit from a visual representation such as the following.

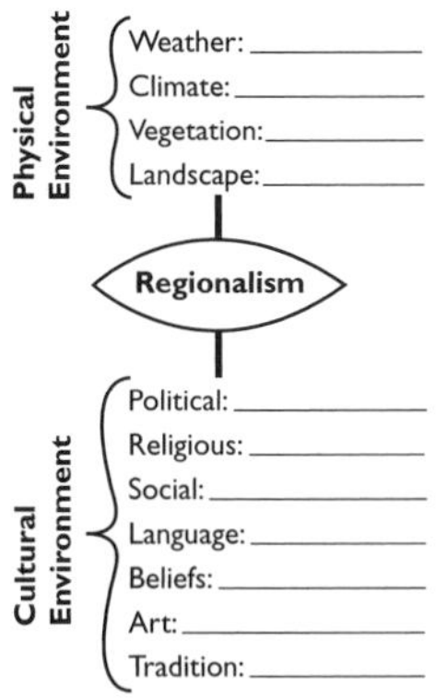

Students should note that physical and culture characteristics help define a region. To help them understand the concept, have them fill in the categories with details from the story.

Cross-Curricular Connection: Social Studies

Close Quarters In *The Outcasts of Poker Flat,* several strangers or near-strangers are forced to camp together for a while. How well people will do living with others in cramped conditions for long periods of time is an issue that NASA and astronauts face today when planning and executing space missions. Ask students to imagine, for example, what it would be like to live in a spaceship on a mission to Mars. The trip would take many months and would require that a group of people live and work together in very tight quarters.

Ask students to discuss what they think would be easy, difficult, or impossible about that experience or one like it. Have them talk about who would survive best in tight quarters. Ask them if they would be willing to try such an adventure themselves.

◆ Literature and Your Life

❶ Here, the outcasts enjoy storytelling around a campfire. Ask students to explain, from experience perhaps, what effects such an activity can have. Ask them to tell what purpose the activity serves here. *Students may say that campfire storytelling, in its ability to entertain, amuse, and even inspire, can bring a group closer together. They may say that here, it helps the outcasts temporarily forget their plight and think of the feats of gods and warriors.*

▶Critical Viewing◀

❷ **Compare and Contrast** The photograph illustrates enormous mountains like those that surround the group. The snow in the photograph also indicates a wintry scene. However, the image does not illustrate snow of considerable depth. The photograph does not present the hopelessly snowbound condition in which the group finds themselves.

◆ Reading Strategy

❸ **Question the Text** Ask students to tell what Mother Shipton has done. Ask them to explain why she did it and what this action reveals about her. *Students may say that Mrs. Shipton had been starving herself, but keeping her share of the food for Piney to have so she might survive. They may surmise that underneath her coarse, hard-hearted exterior, the old woman had a soft heart, that she was taken by the girl's purity and innocence.* Ask students to explain why Harte might have included this event in the story. *Mother Shipton's death underscores the severity of the group's situation.*

◀ **Critical Viewing** Compare and contrast this photograph with the group's wintry surroundings. **[Compare and Contrast]** ❷

❶ of that poem—having thoroughly mastered the argument and fairly forgotten the words—in the current vernacular of Sandy Bar. And so for the rest of that night the Homeric demigods again walked the earth. Trojan bully and wily Greek wrestled in the winds, and the great pines in the canyon seemed to bow to the wrath of the son of Peleus.[12] Mr. Oakhurst listened with quiet satisfaction. Most especially was he interested in the fate of "Ash-heels," as the Innocent persisted in denominating the "swift-footed Achilles."

So with small food and much of Homer and the accordion, a week passed over the heads of the outcasts. The sun again forsook them, and again from leaden skies the snowflakes were sifted over the land. Day by day closer around them drew the snowy circle, until at last they looked from their prison over drifted walls of dazzling white that towered twenty feet above their heads. It became more and more difficult to replenish their fires, even from the fallen trees beside them, now half-hidden in the drifts. And yet no one complained. The lovers turned from the dreary prospect and looked into each other's eyes, and were happy. Mr. Oakhurst settled himself coolly to the losing game before him. The Duchess, more cheerful than she had been, assumed the care of Piney. Only Mother Shipton—once the strongest of the party—seemed to sicken and fade. At midnight on the tenth day she called Oakhurst to her side. "I'm going," she said, in a voice of querulous weakness, "but don't say anything about it. Don't waken the kids. Take the bundle from under my head and open it." Mr. ❸ Oakhurst did so. It contained Mother Shipton's rations for the last week, untouched. "Give 'em to the child," she said, pointing to the sleeping Piney. "You've starved yourself," said the gambler. "That's what they call it," said the woman, querulously, as she lay down again and, turning her face to the wall, passed quietly away.

The accordion and the bones were put aside that day, and Homer was forgotten. When the body of Mother Shipton had been committed to the snow, Mr. Oakhurst took the Innocent aside, and showed him a pair of snowshoes, which he had fashioned from the old pack saddle. "There's one chance in a hundred to save her yet," he said, pointing to Piney; "but it's there," he added, pointing toward Poker Flat. "If you can reach there in two days she's safe." "And you?" asked Tom Simson. "I'll stay here," was the curt reply.

The lovers parted with a long embrace. "You are not going, too?" said the Duchess as she saw Mr. Oakhurst apparently waiting to accompany him. "As far as the canyon," he replied. He turned suddenly, and kissed the Duchess, leaving her pallid face aflame and her trembling limbs rigid with amazement.

12. **son of Peleus** (pē′ lē əs): Achilles (ə kil′ ēz), the Greek warrior hero in the *Iliad*.

◆ Build Vocabulary

querulous (kwer′ ə ləs) *adj.*: Inclined to find fault

Speaking, Listening, and Viewing Mini-Lesson

Eulogy

This mini-lesson supports the Speaking, Listening, and Viewing activity in the Idea Bank on p. 543.

Introduce the Concept Tell students that a eulogy is a speech written in praise of a person who has recently died. Generally, because they are meant to assuage survivors, eulogies call out the best parts of a person's life and character.

Develop Background Have students review the events and interactions between Tom Simson and Mr. Oakhurst that would have colored their relationship and the Innocent's most recent view of the gambler. Have them discuss aspects of Oakhurst's personality that Simson would recognize and appreciate. Guide students to consider the limitations on Simson's eloquence as well as his intentions to present Oakhurst in the best light.

Apply the Information Have students plan, write, practice, and deliver their eulogies. Urge them, when making their presentations, to be mindful of the solemnity the situation demands.

Assess the Outcome When you evaluate students' efforts, focus on whether they accurately captured in their eulogies what Simson would have said on Oakhurst's behalf, both in content and style: Was the content of the eulogy appropriate? Was the content logically organized? Was the eulogy delivered in a respectful tone? Did the eulogy evoke an emotional response?

Night came, but not Mr. Oakhurst. It brought the storm again and the whirling snow. Then the Duchess, feeding the fire, found that someone had quietly piled beside the hut enough fuel to last a few days longer. The tears rose to her eyes, but she hid them from Piney.

The women slept but little. In the morning, looking into each other's faces, they read their fate. Neither spoke; but Piney, accepting the position of the stronger, drew near and placed her arm around the Duchess's waist. They kept this attitude for the rest of the day. That night the storm reached its greatest fury, and, rending asunder the protecting pines, invaded the very hut.

Toward morning they found themselves unable to feed the fire, which gradually died away. As the embers slowly blackened, the Duchess crept closer to Piney, and broke the silence of many hours: "Piney, can you pray?" "No, dear," said Piney, simply. The Duchess, without knowing exactly why, felt relieved, and, putting her head upon Piney's shoulder, spoke no more. And so reclining, the younger and purer pillowing the head of her soiled sister upon her virgin breast, they fell asleep.

The wind lulled as if it feared to waken them. Feathery drifts of snow, shaken from the long pine boughs, flew like white-winged birds, and settled about them as they slept. The moon through the rifted clouds looked down upon
4 what had been the camp. But all human stain, all trace of earthly travail, was hidden beneath the spotless mantle mercifully flung from above. 4

They slept all that day and the next, nor did they waken when voices and footsteps broke the silence of the camp. And when pitying fingers brushed the snow from their wan faces, you could scarcely have told from the equal peace that dwelt upon them which was she that had sinned. Even the law of Poker Flat recognized this, and turned away, leaving them still locked in each other's arms. 5

But at the head of the gulch, on one of the largest pine trees, they found the deuce of clubs pinned to the bark with a bowie knife. It bore the following, written in pencil, in a firm hand:

BENEATH THIS TREE
LIES THE BODY
OF
JOHN OAKHURST,
WHO STRUCK A STREAK OF BAD LUCK
ON THE 23D OF NOVEMBER, 1850
AND
HANDED IN HIS CHECKS
ON THE 7TH DECEMBER, 1850.

And pulseless and cold, with a Derringer[13] by his side and a bullet in his heart, though still calm as in life, beneath the snow lay he who was at once the strongest and yet the weakest of the outcasts of Poker Flat.

13. **Derringer:** Small pistol.

Guide for Responding

◆ Literature and Your Life

Reader's Response Which character did you admire the most? Why?

Thematic Focus Would you like to be transported back in time to the western frontier that Harte depicts? Why or why not?

Group Discussion As a group, brainstorm for two lists: one showing the traits you associate with heroes from movie and television westerns, and one showing traits you found in Mr. Oakhurst. Compare and discuss the two lists. Do the similarities outweigh the differences?

☑ Check Your Comprehension

1. At the opening of the story, what has the secret committee of Poker Flat decided?
2. Who joins the outcasts at their camp?
3. What does Mr. Oakhurst discover when he awakens after his first night at the camp?
4. What does Mother Shipton do with her rations?
5. What does the rescue party discover?

Beyond the Selection

FURTHER READING

Other Works by Bret Harte

"The Luck of Roaring Camp"
Outcroppings
The Lost Galleon

Other Works About Life in the Old West

Lonesome Dove, Larry McMurtry
Angle of Repose, Wallace Stegner
Centennial, James Michener

We suggest that you preview these works before recommending them to students.

INTERNET

You and your students may find additional information about the California Gold Rush on the Internet. We suggest the following site. Please be aware, however, that the site may have changed from the time we published this information.

For information on the Gold Rush, go to **http://www.sfmuseum.org/hist6/masonrpt.html**

We *strongly recommend* that you preview the site before you send students to it.

◆ Reading Strategy

4 Question the Text Discuss the symbolism of the "spotless mantle" that covered the outcasts. Guide students to see that under that layer of snow, both the innocents and the sinners reach the same peaceful state.

◆ Critical Thinking

5 Analyze Ask students to tell what is ironic about the reaction of the law of Poker Flat. *Students may respond that the irony lies in that it was the callous and arbitrary decisions of the town law that caused this tragedy to happen. Here, the law is unable to distinguish the sinner from the innocent.*

Reinforce and Extend

Customize for
AP Students
Invite students to compare the views of fate and death expressed in this story with views expressed in other selections they may have read, such as in the works of Irving, Hawthorne, Melville, Dickinson, Bierce, and Poe.

Answers

◆ Literature and Your Life

Reader's Response Many students are likely to name Mr. Oakhurst, because he proved to be coolheaded and compassionate. Some might name Mother Shipton, because she sacrificed her own life to save Piney's.

Thematic Focus Students who say "yes" are likely to cite the adventures associated with frontier life. Students who say "no" are likely to cite the dangers.

☑ Check Your Comprehension

1. They have decided to rid the town of improper persons by hanging two and banishing several others.
2. Tom Simson and Piney Woods, who are running away in order to get married, join the outcasts.
3. He discovers that Uncle Billy has disappeared, along with the mules.
4. She stores her rations, starving herself in order to leave them to Piney.
5. They find the frozen bodies of Piney and the Duchess, the farewell note, and the body of Mr. Oakhurst, who has shot himself in the heart.

Guide for Understanding *(continued)*

◆ Critical Thinking

INTERPRET

1. What motivates the committee to take action against Mr. Oakhurst? **[Infer]**

2. What effect do Tom and Piney have on all the outcasts except Uncle Billy? Why? **[Analyze]**

3. What does Harte mean in writing that Oakhurst "was at once the strongest and yet the weakest of the outcasts of Poker Flat"? **[Interpret]**

4. What is contradictory about the identity of the "good guys" and the "bad guys" in this tale? **[Interpret]**

APPLY

5. Though the characters in this story have little in common, they band together. Why might people tend to draw together in life? **[Generalize]**

EXTEND

6. Based on the story, what conclusions can you draw about law in settlements that sprang up during the Gold Rush? **[Social Studies Link]**

◆ Literary Focus

REGIONALISM

Harte's portrait of Poker Flat and its outcasts is an example of **Regionalism,** which attempts to capture the "local color" of an area.

1. Find a passage in which Harte describes the physical environment. What specific details help you picture the California landscape?

2. Find three examples of distinctly western speech.

◆ Reading Strategy

QUESTION THE TEXT

If you **question** important ideas, plot developments, and the author's purpose in a text, you can get more out of your reading. Review this passage:

> There was a Sabbath lull in the air which, in a settlement unused to Sabbath influences, looked ominous.

1. What turned out to be the cause of the ominous lull in the air?

2. Cite a passage that helped you determine the cause.

◆ Grammar and Style

COORDINATING CONJUNCTIONS IN COMPOUND SENTENCES

Place a comma before a **coordinating conjunction** that joins the independent clauses in a compound sentence.

In compound sentences, **coordinating conjunctions** —*and, or, but, nor, for, so,* and *yet*— connect two or more independent clauses to form a single sentence.

Writing Application In your notebook, combine each pair of sentences to form a compound sentence. Use the coordinating conjunction given in parentheses.

1. She felt he wasn't joking. She continued to laugh. (*yet*)

2. He raced to the gate. The plane was about to depart. (*for*)

3. Vitamins can be good supplements. They are no substitute for a healthy diet. (*but*)

◆ Build Vocabulary

USING THE LATIN ROOT *-bel-*

On your paper, write the letter of the item that best defines the italicized word in each sentence.

a. quick to pick a fight **b.** an instance of resistance

1. The *rebellion* known as the Boston Tea Party was the result of opposition to British taxation.

2. He must control his rage and not be so *bellicose*.

USING THE WORD BANK: Synonyms

On your paper, write the letter of the word whose meaning is closest to that of the first word.

1. expatriated: (a) honored, (b) ignored, (c) expelled

2. anathema: (a) curse, (b) riddle, (c) chant

3. bellicose: (a) strong, (b) quarrelsome, (c) beautiful

4. recumbent: (a) full, (b) reclining, (c) unnecessary

5. equanimity: (a) fairness, (b) precision, (c) serenity

6. vociferation: (a) uncertainty, (b) loudness, (c) cleverness

7. vituperative: (a) scolding, (b) healthful, (c) complex

8. querulous: (a) trustworthy, (b) mysterious, (c) disagreeable

Answers

◆ Critical Thinking

1. Some of the secret committee's members are motivated because they had lost money to Mr. Oakhurst while gambling with him.
2. They make the outcasts feel protective toward them, and they also lift the outcasts' spirits. Tom and Piney are young, openhearted, and naive; these qualities bring out tenderness in the others.
3. He was the strongest in that he squarely faced the hopelessness of the group's situation; he was also the only one who actively took measures that would increase their chances of survival. He was the weakest in that he "handed in his checks" rather than see the "losing game" through to the end.
4. Those in the secret committee hold themselves up as virtuous citizens who have the right to dispense justice as they see fit. Their righteous actions, however, lead to the death of three "outcasts." The outcasts, on the other hand, are supposedly wicked people. Yet all except Uncle Billy show a spirit of compassion and self-sacrifice while stranded in the mountains.
5. Students may cite natural disasters, such as hurricanes and floods, and situations in which people unite in the name of a social, political, or environmental cause.
6. Students may conclude that citizens sometimes took the law into their own hands and that justice was sometimes arbitrary and harsh.

◆ Literary Focus

1. Sample response: Students may cite the paragraph on page 536 beginning "The road to Sandy Bar . . ."; details include "steep mountain range," "day's severe travel," "moist, temperate regions," "cold, bracing air," and "narrow and difficult." They may also cite the subsequent paragraph; details include "wooded amphitheater," "precipitous cliffs," and "naked granite."
2. Possibilities include: "I reckon they're after somebody . . ."; "If you ain't . . ."; ". . . slap you get into it, too"—Oakhurst; "I reckon now . . ." —Piney; "Just you go out there and cuss . . ."—Mother Shipton.

◆ Reading Strategy

1. The secret committee's decision to "clean up" the town turned out to be the cause.
2. Students should cite the story's third paragraph, particularly the first five sentences.

◆ Grammar and Style

1. She felt he wasn't joking, yet she continued to laugh.
2. He raced to the gate, for the plane was about to depart.
3. Vitamins can be good supplements, but they are no substitute for a healthy diet.

◆ Build Vocabulary

Using the Latin Root *-bel-*

1. b 2. a

Using the Word Bank

1. c 2. a 3. b 4. b 5. c
6. b 7. a 8. c

Build Your Portfolio

Idea Bank

Writing

1. Visitor's Guide Create a visitor's guide to the three main sites in the story: Poker Flat, Sandy Bar, and the slope where the outcasts become stranded. Briefly describe each site, and explain its significance in the story.

2. Review Write a critical review of the story to appear in a magazine targeted at fans of westerns. Present and support your opinion of the story.

3. Newspaper Editorial Put yourself in the place of the editor of a newspaper serving Poker Flat and several other frontier camps. Write an editorial about the outcasts and their fate.

Speaking, Listening, and Viewing

4. Literary Discussion With a classmate, prepare and act out a dialogue in which two friends living in the East in 1870 discuss their reactions to frontier life as depicted in "The Outcasts of Poker Flat." **[Social Studies Link]**

5. Eulogy As Tom Simson, the only survivor of the stranded group, prepare and deliver a eulogy—a speech in honor of someone who has died—for Mr. Oakhurst. **[Performing Arts Link]**

Researching and Representing

6. Boom Towns Research Helena, Montana; San Francisco, California; or Denver, Colorado. Then write a brief history of one of the cities, including a discussion of the role that the discovery of gold played in its founding. **[Social Studies Link]**

7. In Search of Gold Use library databases or the Internet to learn about prospecting and mining. Then give a brief oral report in which you identify the main steps in each of these processes. **[Science Link]**

Online Activity www.phlit.phschool.com

Guided Writing Lesson

Description of a Place

Bret Harte's stories transported readers to the rugged landscapes and rough, dusty settlements of the western frontier. Think of a place you would like to share with others; then write a description that will make your readers feel as though they've been there themselves.

Writing Skills Focus: Precise Details

Use **precise details**—details that deliver concrete information—to make your description of a place as true-to-life as possible. Notice, for example, that Bret Harte does not simply mention the *dust* or *trees* around Poker Flat, he also supplies precise images: the *red* dust, the *sycamore*, the *pines*. Notice Harte's use of the precise details:

Model From the Story

A wooded amphitheater, surrounded on three sides by precipitous cliffs of naked granite, sloped gently toward the crest of another precipice. . . .

Try to capture the look and feel of a place you know well by zooming in on precise details.

Prewriting Revisit in your mind the place you have chosen. Jot down some words that describe its distinctive atmosphere or qualities. Then note the specific physical features that help to produce this atmosphere.

Drafting Identify your place early in your description so that readers can get their bearings. Use the precise details you gathered in the prewriting stage to build up a sense of its physical reality as well as to reveal its "personality."

Revising Reread your description from the point of view of someone who has never been to the place it presents. Have you overlooked any essential details? Is there anything you can do to make the details you included more vivid and more precise?

ASSESSMENT OPTIONS

Formal Assessment, Selection Test, pp. 161–163, and Assessment Resources Software. The selection test is designed so that it can be easily customized to the performance levels of your students.

Alternative Assessment, p. 33, includes options for less advanced students, more advanced students, visual/spatial learners, interpersonal learners, and intrapersonal learners.

PORTFOLIO ASSESSMENT

Use the following rubrics in the ***Alternative Assessment*** booklet to assess student writing:
Visitor's Guide: Description Rubric, p. 112
Review: Evaluation/Review Rubric, p. 119
Newspaper Editorial: Cause-Effect Rubric, p. 117
Guided Writing Lesson: Description Rubric, p. 112

Idea Bank

Customizing for
Performance Levels

Following are suggestions for matching Idea Bank topics with your students' performance levels:
Less Advanced Students: 1
Average Students: 2, 4, 5, 7
More Advanced Students: 3, 6

Customizing for
Learning Modalities

Following are suggestions for matching Idea Bank topics with your students' learning modalities:
Bodily/Kinesthetic: 4
Verbal/Linguistic: 5, 6
Logical/Mathematical: 7

Guided Writing Lesson

For more instruction on prewriting, elaboration, and revision, see *Prentice Hall Writing and Grammar.*

Writing and Language Transparencies Have students use the Cubing Organizer, p. 71, to organize different kinds of details that describe a place.

Writers at Work Videodisc
Have students view the videodisc segment (Ch. 1) featuring poet and novelist Rita Dove speaking about description. Ask students what Dove means by details that "will re-create a world."

Play frames 335 to 10985

Writing Lab CD-ROM
Have students complete the tutorial on Description. Follow these steps:

1. Have students use the Word Bins to choose sensory details, places, and modifiers to enhance descriptions.
2. Have students use the slide show on drafting to see how to structure a descriptive piece.
3. Have students use the revision checkers to aid revision.

Prepare and Engage

LESSON OBJECTIVES

1. **To develop vocabulary and word identification skills**
   - Words From Latin: *terra firma*
   - Using the Word Bank: Word Choice
2. **To use a variety of reading strategies to comprehend a diary and a speech**
   - Connect Your Experience
   - Reading Strategy: Respond
   - Read to Discover Models for Writing (ATE)
3. **To increase knowledge of other cultures and to connect common elements across cultures**
   - Connecting Themes Across Cultures (ATE)
   - Background for Understanding
4. **To express and support responses to the text**
   - Critical Thinking
   - Idea Bank: Poem
   - Idea Bank: Character Sketch
   - Idea Bank: Viewing
   - Idea Bank: Brochure
   - Idea Bank: Quilt
   - Idea Bank: Speech
5. **To analyze literary elements**
   - Literary Focus: Tone
6. **To plan, prepare, organize, and present literary interpretations**
   - Idea Bank: Oral Interpretation
   - Speaking, Listening, and Viewing Mini-Lesson (ATE)
7. **To use recursive writing processes to write a position paper on development**
   - Guided Writing Lesson
8. **To increase knowledge of the rules of grammar and usage**
   - Grammar and Style: Sentence Fragments

Test Preparation

Reading Comprehension: Context (ATE, p. 545)

The teaching tips and sample test item in this workshop support the instruction and practice in the unit workshop:

Reading Comprehension: Using Context (SE, p. 631)

Guide for Interpreting

Chief Joseph *(1840–1904)*

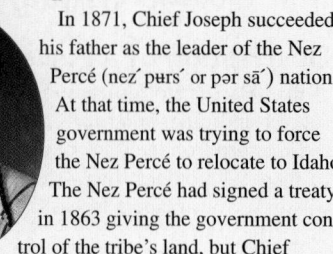

In 1871, Chief Joseph succeeded his father as the leader of the Nez Percé (nez′ pʉrs′ or pər sā′) nation. At that time, the United States government was trying to force the Nez Percé to relocate to Idaho. The Nez Percé had signed a treaty in 1863 giving the government control of the tribe's land, but Chief Joseph felt that the treaty was illegal and refused to recognize it.

A Reluctant Warrior In 1877, the dispute between the Nez Percé and the United States government erupted into war. Chief Joseph, hoping to join forces with the Sioux, led his people on a long march through Idaho and Montana, during which the outnumbered Nez Percé frequently clashed with federal troops.

The Bitter End By October 1877, the Nez Percé were cold, starving, and scattered. Chief Joseph accepted reasonable terms of surrender, which the United States government failed to honor. Instead, the Nez Percé were sent to a barren Oklahoma territory where many of them became ill and died.

The speech in which Chief Joseph finally accepted defeat contains some of the most achingly sad and beautiful words ever spoken. Because of the widespread attention his words received, Chief Joseph became for many a symbol of the Nez Percé and their tragic plight.

Miriam Davis Colt *(1815–c.1900)*

Miriam Davis Colt was one of a quarter of a million Americans who traveled across the United States in the mid-1800's to forge a new frontier. These pioneers knew they were making history, and hundreds of them kept diaries to send to relatives back east or to pass down to their children.

The Women's Perspective Usually, the pioneer men, filled with a sense of destiny and excitement, made the decision to sell their homes and move their families west. The women's diaries, however, reveal a different point of view. Many women describe their anguish at leaving home, their struggle to maintain some sort of domestic comfort in the harsh conditions, and their fear of the dangers that lay ahead.

A Vision of the Future The women, nevertheless, did share their husbands' belief that they were building a better future for their children. The path to that future might be hard, but it was also filled with moments of sudden beauty, like the "crab-apple trees . . . blooming in sheets of whiteness" that Colt saw by the side of a Kansas road as she and her family traveled toward a new life in a "city" established by a group of vegetarians. Her family was one of many that invested money in the creation of this new settlement, where they hoped to live with people "whose tastes and habits" would coincide with their own.

◆ Background for Understanding

CULTURE: THIS LAND IS WHOSE LAND?

"The earth is the mother of all people, and all people should have equal rights upon it." Chief Joseph's words express the point of view of Native Americans, who saw themselves as using land but never owning it. Because they were a culture of hunters, the Nez Percé ranged over a vast territory. Settlers like Miriam Davis Colt, however, were farmers, and they had a very different view of the land. They wanted individual plots to cultivate, and they considered the land they settled as their own. These opposing viewpoints were a source of ongoing strife in frontier America.

Prentice Hall Literature Program Resources

REINFORCE / RETEACH / EXTEND

Selection Support Pages
Build Vocabulary: Words From Latin: *Terra Firma,* p. 159
Grammar and Style: Sentence Fragments, p. 160
Reading Strategy: Respond, p. 161
Literary Focus: Tone, p. 162

Strategies for Diverse Student Needs, p. 34

Beyond Literature
Cross-Curricular Connection: Social Studies, p. 34

Formal Assessment Selection Test, pp. 164–166; Assessment Resources Software

Alternative Assessment, p. 34

Writing and Language Transparencies
Argument Organizer, p. 75–77

Resource Pro CD-ROM
"Heading West," "I Will Fight No More Forever"

Listening to Literature Audiocassettes

Art Transparencies
Art Transparency 1: *Kiowa Apache,* p. 7

Heading West ◆ I Will Fight No More Forever

◆ *Literature and Your Life*

CONNECT YOUR EXPERIENCE

For very different reasons, both Chief Joseph and Miriam Davis Colt had to say goodbye to the places they called home. Think about how you would feel if you suddenly had to leave everything that you loved, with no possibility of ever returning.

THEMATIC FOCUS: FORGING NEW FRONTIERS

Saying goodbye to one home and one way of life means standing on the frontier of a new world. As you read these selections, consider how Chief Joseph and Miriam Davis Colt felt on the frontier of a new existence. How and why did their emotions differ?

Journal Writing If you could take only a few possessions to a new home, what would they be? List them in your journal.

◆ Build Vocabulary

WORDS FROM LATIN: *TERRA FIRMA*

In "Heading West," you'll find *terra firma*, a Latin term meaning "solid ground." If you encounter an unfamiliar Latin word or phrase when reading, you can often find its meaning in a dictionary.

WORD BANK

Preview this list of words before you read.

genial
pervading
terra firma
emigrants
profusion
depredations
nonplused

◆ Grammar and Style

SENTENCE FRAGMENTS

The early entries in Miriam Colt's diary are written in complete sentences, whereas many of the later entries contain **sentence fragments**—incomplete sentences that may lack either a subject or a verb. As Colt heads west, she begins dropping the subjects of her sentences as a form of shorthand—an effort to hurriedly record her impressions during her few quiet moments. In polished writing, however, fragments are not acceptable. Use only complete sentences, which contain a subject and a verb.

Sentence Fragment: Have been on the cars again since yesterday morning. (no subject)

Complete Sentence: We have been on the cars again since yesterday morning. (subject, *We*, has been added)

◆ Literary Focus

TONE

A writer's attitude toward his or her subject, characters, or audience comes through in the **tone** of a work. As you read, pay careful attention to tone, just as you would when listening to a speaker. The tone of a nonfiction work is established by the writer's use of descriptive words and choice of details. The tone of "I Will Fight No More Forever" clearly reflects the desolate situation in which the speech was made. Different entries in "Heading West" have different tones, depending on Miriam Davis Colt's feelings when she wrote them.

◆ Reading Strategy

RESPOND

As you read "I Will Fight No More Forever" and "Heading West," pay close attention to your personal responses. What emotions do you feel? What images do you see? What words and phrases have the most striking effects on you? You will get much more from your reading when you take the time to note how you **respond** to a piece of literature. Both of the selections you are about to read describe life-changing situations, the kind that are sure to evoke responses that will affect your understanding and appreciation of the works.

Interest Grabber Propose a hypothetical new law to the class: by the time all young people turn eighteen, they must leave America to relocate elsewhere. Have students form groups to discuss how they would respond to this directive. What would they do? Where would they go? With whom and how would they travel? What would they bring with them? How would they bid farewell to friends and family? After the discussion, tell students that they will read about two people who left home for very different reasons: Miriam Davis Colt's family left their upstate New York home by choice to live on a prairie commune, while Chief Joseph and his people were forced off their land.

Customize for
Less Proficient Readers
These students may benefit from completing the page on using a chain of events organizer, p. 34 in ***Strategies for Diverse Student Needs***. This strategy can help them better comprehend the events related in "Heading West."

Customize for
AP Students
Encourage students to compare and contrast Miriam Davis Colt's journal entries with any others they have read. Also guide them to look for ways the entries written by women are different from and similar to those written by men.

Customize for
English Language Learners
The many sentence fragments in the first selection may confuse students. Help them to identify the missing subjects or verbs. If helpful, guide them to restate the fragments as complete sentences.

Customize for
Visual/Spatial Learners
These students may wish to sketch scenes described by Miriam Davis Colt or to make portraits of her or of Chief Joseph. Each portrait should reflect the tone of what the subject of the portrait has written.

Test Preparation Workshop

Reading Comprehension:
Context The reading sections of many standardized tests require students to use context clues such as definitions and explanations to determine the meanings of unfamiliar words and phrases. Write the following passage from p. 550 on the chalkboard. Then use the following exercise to help them use context clues to identify the correct definition.

> In the large tent here is a cook stove—they have supper prepared for us; it consists of hominy, soft Johnny cake (or corn bread, as it is called here), stewed apple, and tea.

According to information found in this passage, what is "Johnny Cake"?

A apple cake
B corn bread
C hominy
D tea cake

B is the correct answer, because it contains the explanation found in the parenthetical phrase: "Johnny Cake (or corn bread, as it is called here)."

Develop Understanding

One-Minute Insight Miriam Davis Colt and her family are among a group of families making the trip to join a commune of vegetarians in the Kansas territory. Her journal entries describe what she saw, felt, and experienced en route and upon arrival.

◆ Background for Understanding

History When students think of a pioneer excursion westward, they may imagine a long and treacherous one across the heartland, the plains, and the mountains, to reach California or Oregon. Point out that in 1856, Kansas was considered by Americans to be in the far "West." Many emigrants had as their final destination the then western states of Iowa, Illinois, Michigan, Wisconsin, and Minnesota, or the territories of Kansas, Nebraska, and the Dakotas.

▶Critical Viewing◀

❶ **Analyze** Students may say that it is surprising that despite being in the wilderness, the family still eats lunch graciously on a white tablecloth.

◆ Literary Focus

❷ **Tone** Ask students: What is the tone of this entry? *Students should recognize the hopeful, optimistic tone of this passage. They may guess that the author is trying to convince herself of the strengths of their plan.*

◆ Literary Focus

❸ **Tone** Have students contrast the tone of this passage with that of the author's entries for January 15. *They may find the tone of this passage more poignant and religious. Miriam Davis Colt expects to see her mother next in the afterlife.*

HEADING WEST

Miriam Davis Colt

Emigrants stopping to lunch on a white tablecloth in Greenwood County, Kansas State Historical Society

❶ ▲ **Critical Viewing** Which details of this photograph of pioneers stopping for lunch seem surprising or out of place? **[Analyze]**

❷ **January 5th, 1856.** We are going to Kansas. The Vegetarian Company that has been forming for many months, has finally organized, formed its constitution, elected its directors, and is making all necessary preparations for the spring settlement. . . . We can have, I think, good faith to believe, that our directors will fulfill on their part; and we, as settlers of a new country, by going in a company will escape the hardships attendant on families going in singly, and at once find ourselves surrounded by improving society in a young and flourishing city. It will be better for ourselves pecuniarily,[1] and better in the future for our children.

My husband has long been a practical vegetarian, and we expect much from living in such a genial clime, where fruit is so quickly grown, and with people whose tastes and habits will coincide with our own. ❷

January 15th. We are making every necessary preparation for our journey, and our home in Kansas. My husband has sold his farm, purchased shares in the company, sent his money as directed by H.S. Clubb. . . . I am very busy in repairing all of our clothing, looking over bags of pieces, tearing off and reducing down, bringing everything into as small a compass as possible, so that we shall have no unnecessary baggage.

April 15th. Have been here in West Stockholm, at my brother's, since Friday last. Have visited Mother very hard, for, in all probability, ❸

1. **pecuniarily** (pi kyo͞o´ nē er´ i lē) *adv.*: Financially.

◆ Build Vocabulary

genial (jēn´ yəl) *adj.*: Promoting life and growth

Block Scheduling Strategies

Consider these suggestions to take advantage of extended class time:

- To build background for "I Will Fight No More Forever," discuss Art Transparency 1: *Kiowa Apache,* p. 7, in ***Art Transparencies***. Contrast the pride of this portrait with the hopelessness of Chief Joseph.
- Have students research the pioneer experience and that of Chief Joseph and the Nez Percé on the Internet before or after they read.
- Introduce the concept of literary tone by discussing the Literary Focus section (p. 545). After they read the selections, have students complete the Literary Focus questions on p. 552.
- Play the audiocassette recordings of one or both selections. Discuss which selection is more effective when heard.
- Form discussion groups in which students can answer the Critical Thinking questions (pp. 550 and 552).
- Assign the Guided Writing Lesson (p. 553). Before students begin, discuss how to make a piece of persuasive writing coherent by organizing ideas logically. Have students identify specific examples of how Chief Joseph uses repetition of both terms and structure to emphasize his key points.

3 it is the last visit we shall have until we meet where parting never comes—believe we have said everything we can think of to say.

4 **April 16th.** Antwerp, N.Y. Bade our friends good bye, in Potsdam, this morning, at the early hour of two o'clock.

April 22nd. Have been on the cars[2] again since yesterday morning. Last night was a lovely moonlit night, a night of thought, as we sped almost with lightning speed, along in the moonlight, past the rail fences.

5 Found ourselves in this miserable hotel before we knew it. Miserable fare—herring boiled with cabbage—miserable, dirty beds, and an odor pervading the house that is not at all agreeable. Mistress gone.

April 23rd. On board streamer "Cataract," bound for Kansas City.

April 24th. A hot summer day. The men in our company are out in the city, purchasing wagons and farming implements, to take along on the steamer up to Kansas City.

April 28th. The steamer struck a "snag" last night; gave us a terrible jar; tore off a part of the kitchen; ladies much frightened. Willie is not very well; the water is bad; it affects all strangers.

April 30th. Here we are, at Kansas City, all safely again on terra firma. Hasten to the hotel—find it very much crowded. Go up, up, up, and upstairs to our lodging rooms.

6 **May 1st.** Take a walk out onto the levee—view the city, and see that it takes but a few buildings in this western world to make a city. The houses and shops stand along on the levee, extending back into the hillsides. The narrow street is literally filled with huge merchandise wagons bound for Santa Fe. The power attached to these wagons is seven or eight and sometimes nine pair of long-eared mules, or as many pair of oxen, with a Mexican driver who wields a whip long enough to reach the foremost pair, and who does not hesitate to use it with severity, and a noise, too.

Large droves of cattle are driven into town to be sold to emigrants, who like us, are going into the Territory. Our husbands are all out today buying oxen, provisions and cooking utensils for our ox-wagon journey into the Territory.

This is the anniversary of my wedding-day, and as I review the past pleasant years as they have passed, one after an other, until they now number eleven, a shadow comes over me, as I try to look away into the future and ask, "What is my destiny?"

Ah! away with all these shadowings. We shall be very busy this year in making our home comfortable, so that no time can be spared for that dreaded disease, "home-sick ness," to take hold of us, and we mean to obey physical laws,[3] thereby securing to ourselves strength of body and vigor of mind.

> ◆ *Literature and Your Life*
>
> Do you ever feel fearful when you try to imagine your future? How do you try to reassure yourself when you get nervous about your "destiny"? 7

May 2nd. A lovely day. Our husbands are loading the ox-wagons. . . . Women and children walk along up the hill out of this "Great City," wait under a tree—what a beautiful country is spread out before us! Will our Kansas scenery equal this . . .?

One mile from the city, and Dr. Thorn has broke his wagon tongue;[4] it must be sent back 8 to Kansas City to be mended. Fires kindled—women cooking—supper eaten sitting round on logs, stones and wagon tongues. This I am sure is a "pic-nic." We expect "pic-nic" now all the time. We are shaded by the horse-chestnut,

2. **cars:** Train cars.

3. **physical laws:** Community's by-laws that dictated members abstain from alcohol and meat.

4. **wagon tongue:** Harnessing pole attached to the front axle of a horse-drawn vehicle.

◆ Build Vocabulary

pervading (pər vād iŋ) *adj.*: Spreading throughout

terra firma (ter´ ə fur´ mə) *n.*: Firm earth; solid ground (Latin)

emigrants (em´ i grəntz) *n.*: People who leave one area to move to another

Customize for
Visual/Spatial Learners

4 Have students locate Potsdam and Antwerp on a map of New York. Suggest that they follow the family's route west by locating the other places the author mentions, such as Kansas City, Westport, and the Little Osage River.

◆ Grammar and Style

5 **Sentence Fragments** Guide students to notice that the author uses only fragments to describe this hotel stay. Students may suggest that she does so in order not to dwell any longer than she has to on this unpleasant experience.

▶Critical Thinking◀

6 **Infer** Ask students what they can infer from this statement about Kansas City during the frontier era. *From this statement, readers can infer that Kansas City was little more than a small town during the mid-nineteenth century.*

◆ *Literature and Your Life*

7 Students may say they sometimes feel anxious about their future, perhaps wondering about what they will do for a living when they are adults. They may reassure themselves with the thought that as long as they study hard in school, they will be ready for any career in the future.

▶Critical Thinking◀

8 **Compare and Contrast** Ask students: What are some of the difficulties nineteenth-century pioneer travelers faced that made traveling more difficult than today? *Sample response: The pioneers had to depend upon oxen and other animals for power. Such animals had to be fed and cared for. Wagons traveled slowly and often needed repairs. Roads in some areas were little more than dirt trails.*

Humanities: Film

Hollywood Goes West Hollywood has chronicled much of the American experience; the settlement of the West is no exception. For a well-made film that offers a woman's perspective on what it was like to survive the rigors of frontier life, students can view *Heartland* (1979; Richard Pierce, director). The film was based on the actual diaries of a frontierswoman.

For another perspective on life on the frontier based on the actual diaries of a frontier—that of the immigrant—students can see *The New Land* (1972; Jan Troell, director), which is the sequel to *The Emigrants* (1971).

For an entirely different look at the way west, one from the Depression era of the twentieth century, students can watch *The Grapes of Wrath*, directed by John Ford. This 1940 film masterpiece based on the Steinbeck novel depicts a desperate trip from Oklahoma's dust bowl to disappointment in migrant camps in the valleys of California.

◆ Background for Understanding

❶ **History** According to the Kansas-Nebraska Act of 1854, settlers in these two territories were to determine for themselves whether the territories would be slave or free. Hostilities between bands of pro-slavery and anti-slavery settlers erupted. Pro-slavery southerners, known as "border ruffians" entered the state and sacked the anti-slavery town of Lawrence, Kansas. In response, John Brown and his sons slaughtered five pro-slavery settlers along Pottawatomie Creek. The violence in "Bleeding Kansas" continued into 1861. Miriam Davis Colt's family entered Kansas during this time of bloodshed and chaos.

◆ Literary Focus

❷ **Tone** Students should note that Miriam Davis Colt's attitude toward the border ruffians is one of disdain. They might say that she fears the violence these thugs might commit.

◆ Reading Strategy

❸ **Respond** Miriam Davis Colt tries to put a positive spin on this latest disaster by focusing on the sweetness of the crabapple trees. Ask them how they think they themselves would hold up under such trying circumstances.

◆ Reading Strategy

❹ **Respond** Have students respond to the image of a refined, sophisticated easterner miserably confronting her likely future as a frontierswoman. Have them imagine how she must have felt.

sweet walnut, and spreading oak; flowers blooming at our feet, and grasshoppers in profusion hopping in every direction. This is summer time.

May 3rd. The women and children, who slept in their wagons last night, got a good drenching from the heavy shower. It was fortunate for mother, sister, myself and children, that lodgings were found for us in a house. My husband said not a rain drop found him; he had the whole wagon to himself, besides all of our Indian blankets. Father, it seems, fell back a little and found a place to camp in a tavern (not a hotel), where he fell in with the scores of Georgians ❶ who loaded a steamer and came up the river the same time that we did. He said he had to be very shrewd indeed not to have them find out that he was a "Free States"[5] man. These Bandits have been sent in here, and will commit all sorts of depredations on the Free State settlers, and no doubt commit many a bloody murder. ❷

> **◆ Literary Focus**
> What is Colt's tone as she discusses the Georgians who have come up river at the same time as her party?

Have passed Westport, the foothold for Border-Ruffianism. The town looks new, but the hue is dingy. Our drivers used their goads to hurry up the oxen's heavy tread, for we felt somewhat afraid, for we learned the Georgians had centered here. Here, too, came in the Santa Fe and Indian trade—so here may be seen the huge Mexican wagon, stubborn mule, swarthy driver with his goad-like whip, and the red man of the prairie on his fleet Indian pony, laden with dried meat, furs, and buffalo robes.

"What! fast in the mud, and with our wagon tongue broke?" "Why yes, to be sure." So a long time is spent before my husband and Dr. House can put our vehicle in moving order again. Meanwhile, we women folks and children must sit quietly in the wagon to keep ❸ out of the rain—lunch on soda biscuit, look at the deep, black mud in which our wagon is set, and inhale the sweet odor that comes from the blossoms of the crab-apple trees that are blooming in sheets of whiteness along the roadside. . . .

5. **"Free States":** Free Soil movement; a group whose goal was to keep slavery out of the western territories.

May 6th. Dined on the prairie, and gathered flowers, while our tired beasts filled themselves with the fresh, green grass. . . . Have driven 18 miles to-day . . . so here we are, all huddled into this little house 12 by 16—cook supper over the fire . . . fill the one bed lengthwise and crosswise; the family of the house take to the trundle-bed,[6] while the floor is covered . . . with men, women and children, rolled in Indian blankets like silk worms in cocoons.

May 11th. "Made" but a few miles yesterday. Forded the Little Osage; the last river, they say, we have to ford . . . our "noble lords" complained of the great weight of the wagons. . . . That our wagon is heavily loaded, have only to make a minute of what we have stowed away in it—eight trunks, one valise, three carpet bags, a box of soda crackers, 200 lbs. flour, 100 lbs. corn meal, a few lbs. of sugar, rice, dried apple, one washtub of little trees, utensils for cooking, and two provision boxes—say nothing of mother, a good fat sister, self, and two children, who ride through the rivers. . . .

At nightfall came to a log-cabin at the edge of the wood, and inquired of the "Lord of the Castle" if some of the women and children could take shelter under his roof for the night; the masculine number and whichever of the women that chose, couching in the wagons and under them. He said we could. His lady, who was away, presently came, with bare feet, and ❹ a white sack twisted up and thrown over her shoulder, with a few quarts of corn meal in the end that hung down her back. I said to myself—"Is that what I have got to come to?" She seemed pleased to have company—allowed us the first chance of the broad, Dutch-backed fireplace with its earthy hearth, and without pot hooks or trammels,[7] to make ready our simple evening repast. . . .

6. **trundle-bed:** Low, portable bed that can be stored beneath a larger bed.
7. **trammels** (tram′ əlz) *n.*: Devices for hanging several pothooks in a fireplace.

◆ Build Vocabulary

profusion (prō fyo͞o′ zhən) *n.*: Abundance; rich supply

depredations (dep′ rə dā′ shənz) *n.*: Acts of robbing or plundering

Beyond the Classroom

Workplace Skill

Adaptability v. Specialization Pioneers had to be skilled at a wide variety of tasks, so they could do all the work that needed to be done on the trail. In today's working world some people, such as farmers, building superintendants, and owners of small businesses, need to know all aspects of their business to do any task as need arises. Other workers may be called upon only to perform a narrow range of tasks. A video post-production editor and a telephone operator are two examples.

Ask students to make a chart in which they list in one category all jobs that require a broad range of skills and in another, jobs that require command of but a few. Have students compare charts and explain their choices when there are differences of opinion. Some students may have more success if they create additional categories, so they can place jobs that don't quite fit in either of the two. Which kinds of jobs are more appealing to students?

Covered wagons on Main Street in Ottawa, Kansas, 1866, Kansas State Historical Society

5 ▲ **Critical Viewing** This 1866 photograph shows covered wagons on Main Street in Ottawa, Kansas. How does the diary suggest that towns like this one were important to the wagon trains of settlers traveling westward? **[Draw Conclusions]**

Are now [May 11th] crossing the 20 mile prairie, no roads—Think Mrs. Voorhees will get walking enough crossing this prairie. She is quite a pedestrian, surely, for she has walked every bit of the way in, so far, from Kansas City, almost 100 miles.

Arrive at Elm Creek—no house to lodge in tonight—campfire kindled—supper cooked, and partaken of with a keen relish, sitting in family groups around the "great big" fire. Some will sleep in wagons, others under the canopy of the blue vault of Heaven. The young men have built some shady little bowers of the green boughs; they are looking very cosily under them, wrapped in their white Indian blankets.

6 We ladies, or rather, "emigrant women," are having a chat around the camp-fire—the bright stars are looking down upon us—we wonder if we shall be neighbors to each other in the great "Octagon City. . . ." 6

May 12th. Full of hope, as we leave the smoking embers of our camp-fire this morning. 7 Expect tonight to arrive at our new home.

It begins to rain, rain, rain, like a shower; we move slowly on, from high prairie, around the deep ravine—are in sight of the timber that skirts the Neosho river. Have sent three men in advance to announce our coming; are looking for our Secretary, (Henry S. Clubb) with an escort to welcome us into the embryo city. If the booming of cannon is not heard at our approach, shall expect a salute from the firing of Sharp's rifles, certainly.

No escort is seen! no salute is heard! We move slowly and drippingly into town just at nightfall—feeling not a little nonplused on learning that our worthy, or unworthy

◆ Build Vocabulary

nonplused (nän′ plüsd′) *adj.*: Bewildered; perplexed

▶Critical Viewing◀

5 Draw Conclusions Students may conclude that in these frontier towns, travelers could resupply, perhaps get medical help or get their wagons fixed, and speak with others to learn about what they would face in the miles ahead. Here, travelers might get to sleep under a roof, or might meet and join a group heading back east.

◆ Critical Thinking

6 Draw Conclusions Ask students: What does the term "Octagon City" indicate about the type of destination Miriam Davis Colt expects to find? *Sample response: Colt probably believes that the destination of the pioneers will be a bustling settlement with many families living in houses and with amenities such as stores in which to purchase household items and blacksmith shops at which wagons and farm implements can be repaired.*

◆ Literary Focus

7 Tone Ask students what they can learn about the author's character by analyzing the tone of this passage. *Students can appreciate that despite all she and her family have been through, and despite the fact that little has measured up to her expectations thus far, Miriam Davis Colt remains filled with undiminished optimism. She still has great hopes for her new home.*

Read to Discover Models for Writing

Guide students to notice the style that Miriam Colt uses in her diary. Point out that this is a first-person narrative, that it's arranged chronologically by month and date, and that it contains sentence fragments as well as complete sentences. Students should also notice that Colt's writing style changes from entry to entry. In different places, she writes to provide factual information, to describe her surroundings, and to make personal reflections. Have students find examples of these writing elements. Then suggest that they use what they've learned from this diary as a model for their own journal writing.

Viewing and Representing Mini-Lesson

This mini-lesson supports the Brochure activity in the Idea Bank on p. 553.

Introduce the Concept Tell students that to create a brochure to convince settlers to join the Colt community, they will need to develop persuasive arguments. Suggest that students use an atlas to find information about the weather, climate, physical landscape, and vegetation in the region where the Colts live. Tell them to collect attractive photographs of the area.

Develop Background Have students brainstorm for ideas about their vegetarian community. Have them determine their community's location, goals, conditions for joining, financial considerations, and living philosophy before they begin the brochure.

Apply the Information After outlining the basic structure of the community, have students use persuasive techniques in their brochure to entice settlers, such as attractive visuals, sound reasons, catchy phrases and sayings, and so on.

Assess the Outcome Assess students' work on their ability to produce a marketing brochure with attractive visuals and persuasive copy.

◆ Reading Strategy

1 Respond Some students may respond that the dismal conditions are consistent with the conditions the travelers have experienced throughout the journey; therefore, however disappointing, they should have come as no surprise.

Reinforce and Extend

◆ Critical Thinking

Analyze Ask students what Colt's reactions to her new "home" tells them about the nature of the information people in the East had about life in the West at that time. *Students can suggest that many had inaccurate or incomplete information, or that expectations were unrealistic.*

Answers

◆ Literature and Your Life

Reader's Response Students should discuss their aptitude for pioneer life.

Thematic Focus Students might say that the unknown is attractive because it offers adventure, mystery, and excitement, but that it is frightening because it might contain danger and disappointment as well.

☑ Check Your Comprehension

1. She expects a financially better life for herself, a better future for her children, and an "improving" society of other vegetarians.
2. The modes of transportation are train, steamer, and wagon.
3. They left because the directors of the Vegetarian Company failed to build the mills they received money to construct.

◆ Critical Thinking

1. (a) She seems shocked by or disapproving of the woman's appearance. (b) Colt fears that she will become just as unkempt.
2. Instead of a thriving community of homes, Colt finds a makeshift settlement of a few tents and one poorly constructed log cabin.
3. Students may say that the Colts were naive to hand money over to the Vegetarian Company with no way of overseeing or controlling its direction.
4. Suggested response: Successful pioneers had to be courageous, flexible, adaptable, and dedicated.

Secretary was out walking in the rain with his *dear* wife. We leave our wagons and make our way to the large camp-fire. It is surrounded by men and women cooking their suppers—while others are busy close by, grinding their hominy[8] in hand mills.

Look around, and see the grounds all around the camp-fire are covered with tents, in which the families are staying. Not a house is to be seen. In the large tent here is a cook stove—they have supper prepared for us; it consists of hominy, soft Johnny cake (or corn bread, as it is called here), stewed apple, and tea. We eat what is set before us, "asking no questions for conscience' sake."

> **◆ Reading Strategy**
> 1 How do you respond to the description of the travelers' arrival in their new home? Do you share their surprise and disappointment? Why or why not?

The ladies tell us they are sorry to see us come to this place; which shows us that all is not right. Are too weary to question, but with hope depressed go to our lodgings, which we find around in the tents, and in our wagons.

May 13th. Can anyone imagine our disappointment this morning, on learning from this and that member, that no mills have been built; that the directors, after receiving our money to build mills, have not fulfilled the trust reposed in them, and that in consequence, some families have already left the settlement . . . ?

As it is, we find the families, some living in tents of cloth, some of cloth and green bark just peeled from the trees, and some wholly of green barn, stuck up on the damp ground, without floors or fires. Only two stoves in the company. . . .

We see that the city grounds, which have been surveyed . . . contain only one log cabin, 16 by 16, muddled between the logs on the inside, instead of on the outside; neither door nor window; the roof covered with "shakes" (western shingles), split out of oak I should think, 3 ½ feet in length, and about as wide as a sheet of fools cap paper.[9]

8. **hominy** (häm´ ə nē) *n.*: Dry corn, usually ground and boiled for food.

9. **fools cap paper:** Writing paper usually measuring 13 by 16 inches.

Guide for Responding

◆ Literature and Your Life

Reader's Response Would you have had the courage and determination to leave your home and family to become a pioneer?

Thematic Focus How was the promise of a new life in the West both attractive and frightening for Colt and thousands like her?

Journal Writing If you could move to a new home anywhere in the world, where would it be? How do you imagine your life would be different?

☑ Check Your Comprehension

1. List two ways in which Miriam Davis Colt expects her new way of life to be an improvement from her life in New York.
2. What are the three modes of transportation required to reach the Octagon City settlement?
3. Why have some families already left the settlement by the time Colt and her family arrive?

◆ Critical Thinking

INTERPRET

1. (a) What does Colt think of the appearance of the settler woman who appears with bare feet and a sack flung over her back? (b) What does this settler woman suggest to Colt about her own future? **[Infer; Interpret]**
2. How does Colt's expectation about life at Octagon City compare with the realities? **[Compare and Contrast]**

EVALUATE

3. Were Colt and her husband too naive and trusting in making their plans? Explain. **[Assess]**

APPLY

4. Based on Colt's experiences, explain which character traits you feel were necessary to being a successful pioneer. **[Synthesize]**

Speaking, Listening, and Viewing Mini-Lesson

Oral Interpretation

This mini-lesson supports the Speaking, Listening, and Viewing activity in the Idea Bank on p. 553.

Introduce the Concept To recite a speech is not only to say the words aloud, but to say them with feeling and with regard for the audience.

Develop Background Have groups of students find out more about the tragic experiences of the Nez Percé. Groups can discuss how to best capture Chief Joseph's passion and resignation. Groups can audition members to select the one who will deliver the speech.

Apply the Information Have one member of a group introduce the speech by providing background information on the plight of the Nez Percé. Then have the speaker give the dramatic presentation of Chief Joseph's words.

Assess the Outcome Look for how well speakers' presentations capture Chief Joseph's sadness, resignation, and dignity. Students can evaluate their classmates' presentations by using the Peer Assessment: Oral Interpretaion Rubric in ***Alternative Assessment,*** p. 134.

❷ I Will Fight No More Forever

Chief Joseph

❸ Tell General Howard I know his heart. What he told me before, I have in my heart. I am tired of fighting. Our chiefs are killed. Looking Glass is dead. Toohoolhoolzote is dead. The old men are all dead. It is the young men who say yes and no. He who led on the young men is dead. It is cold and we have no blankets. The little children are freezing to death. My people, some of them, have run away to the hills and have no blankets, no food; no one knows where they are—perhaps freezing to death. I want to have time to look for my children and see how many I can find. Maybe I shall find them among the dead. Hear me, my chiefs. I am tired; my heart is sick and sad. From where the sun now stands I will fight no more forever.

Guide for Responding

◆ Literature and Your Life

Reader's Response In the opening to his speech, Chief Joseph speaks of knowing his enemy's heart and having the general's words in his heart. Have you ever felt as if you knew something with your heart rather than with your head? What is the difference?

Thematic Focus Chief Joseph stands on the brink of a new and unpromising life. What are his limited hopes for the future?

Questions for Research Read about one Native American tribe. Ask relevant questions about the people and their lifestyle to focus your research on a specific aspect of their culture.

☑ Check Your Comprehension

1. At the time of Chief Joseph's surrender, what has happened to the other chiefs of the Nez Percé?
2. Why is it urgent that Chief Joseph get immediate help for his people?

◆ Critical Thinking

INTERPRET

1. Based on this speech, how would you describe Chief Joseph's relationship to his people? Explain. **[Infer]**
2. Although Chief Joseph delivered his speech to notify federal troops of his tribe's surrender, the speech had another, equally important purpose. What was that purpose? **[Interpret]**

EVALUATE

3. Would Chief Joseph's speech have been more or less effective if it had contained longer, more detailed explanations of the reasons for his decision to surrender? Explain your answer. **[Evaluate]**

COMPARE LITERARY WORKS

4. Both Colt and Chief Joseph face survival struggles and disappointments as they work for what they feel is right; however, their conflicts differ greatly. Compare the conflicts of Colt and Chief Joseph. **[Compare and Contrast]**

Develop Understanding

One-Minute Insight In this speech, a weary and demoralized Chief Joseph, speaking for a people in desperate straights, decides to stop forever his losing fight with the pursuing United States Army.

Art Transparencies To build background, use Art Transparency 1: *Kiowa Apache* in ***Art Transparencies***, p. 7. The portrait, by Native American artist John Nieto (b. 1936), conveys dignity, determination, and power. Point out to students that the selection they are about to read is about a Native American tribe, the Nez Percé, that felt not pride but despair, after having been beaten and dispersed in battles with the United States Army. Poignantly, Chief Joseph expresses the plight of his people.

Customize for
Less Proficient Readers
❷ Paraphrase the title so students understand that it means that Chief Joseph will never fight again.

❸ **Enrichment** General Oliver Howard was a corps commander in the Federal Army during the Civil War. Immediately after the war, he was reassigned to the Western states and territories to protect American settlers and to deal with the resettlement of Native Americans.

Reinforce and Extend

Answers

◆ Literature and Your Life

Reader's Response Students should describe in terms of their own experience the difference between knowing something intellectually and knowing something emotionally or intuitively.

Thematic Focus He hopes to find his children, even though he fears that they may be dead.

☑ Check Your Comprehension

1. The other chiefs have been killed.
2. It is winter and his people are starving and freezing to death.

(Answers continue on p. 552)

Beyond the Selection

FURTHER READING

Other Works About the West

Pioneer Women: Voices From the Kansas Frontier, Joanna L. Stratton

Women and Their Families on the Overland Trail 1846–1867, J. M. Faragher and C. Stansell

Bury My Heart at Wounded Knee: An Indian History of the American West, Dee Brown

We suggest that you preview these works before recommending them to students.

INTERNET

To learn more about Chief Joseph and the Nez Percé, we suggest the following Internet site. Please be aware, however, that the site may have changed since this information was published.

To see an excerpt from the "Historical Gazette" of 1877 that describes Joseph's surrender, go to **http://www.aracnet.com/~histgaz/hgv2n8.htm**

We *strongly recommend* that you preview the site.

Answers *(continued from p. 551)*

◆ Critical Thinking

1. Chief Joseph is like a father to his people. He cannot bear to see them suffering and dying.
2. His purpose was to build awareness of his people's plight.
3. Students might say that a longer speech would have been less effective because more details might have obscured the simple power of the speech.
4. Colt faces external conflicts as she acts in accordance with her beliefs. Chief Joseph faces internal conflicts as he accepts conditions he does not agree with.

◆ Reading Strategy

Students should cite passages that evoke emotions. Students' descriptions of their responses should be appropriate for the passages cited.

◆ Literary Focus

1. (a) The overall tone of Chief Joseph's surrender is one of complete resignation to his fate. (b) He describes his own exhaustion and the desperation of his people's plight and conveys his understanding of the enemy's position.
2. Examples of an upbeat tone include Colt's first entry, describing her family's goals; the beginning of the April 22 entry, describing the lovely moonlit journey by train; and the May 2 description of the "pic-nic."
3. Examples of a negative tone include her April 22 description of the "miserable hotel," her description of the Georgian "Bandits," and her subdued reaction when she actually arrives in "Octagon City."

Beyond Literature
Suggested response: People moved west in search of free land, opportunities, and a better life.

Guide for Responding (continued)

◆ Reading Strategy

Respond

As you read, you paid close attention to how you felt about the people and the events in the selections. Did the way in which you **responded** to a work affect your appreciation of it?

For each selection, cite one passage that affected you strongly, and describe your response to it.

◆ Literary Focus

Tone

To fully understand the meaning of a literary work, you must appreciate the **tone,** or attitude, the writer wishes to convey. Chief Joseph's simple language and delivery establishes a tone that communicates more than the message contained in the words alone. The journal entries of Miriam Davis Colt are not an objective telling of her experiences; the tone of her writing reveals her attitudes about the people and situations she encounters.

1. A military leader might adopt many tones when admitting defeat. (a) What is the overall tone of Chief Joseph's surrender? (b) What contributes to this tone?
2. Find two examples of an upbeat, positive tone in Miriam Davis Colt's diary entries.
3. Find two examples of a negative tone in "Heading West."

Beyond Literature

History Connection

Moving West The pioneers who flocked to the Oregon Country and California in the 1840's and 1850's faced great difficulties. The trip through the Rocky Mountains could last up to six months, and life on the trail was difficult and dangerous. Sickness—cholera and other diseases—not only wiped out entire wagon trains, but devastated the Native American communities along the routes. Why did so many people emigrate to the West despite the dangers?

◆ Build Vocabulary

Using the Latin Term *Terra Firma*

Follow the directions for each item by writing a sentence that contains the Latin term *terra firma,* meaning "firm earth" or "solid ground."

1. Describe the Pilgrims landing on Plymouth Rock after months at sea in a tiny boat.
2. Describe a hot-air balloon safely touching down after a rough flight.

Using the Word Bank: Word Choice

Select the word from the Word Bank that best describes or relates to each "situation."

1. People who left America to live in another country
2. Acts committed by hostile invading troops
3. The personality of a pleasant host
4. The scents in a perfume shop
5. A buffet of more than fifty desserts
6. An auto mechanic perplexed by a car he is unable to fix

◆ Grammar and Style

Sentence Fragments

Though they are an effective way to lend a sense or urgency or immediacy to a piece of writing, **sentence fragments** are not acceptable in formal English.

A **sentence fragment** is a part of a sentence used in place of a complete sentence. It may lack a subject, a predicate, or both.

Practice Read these passages from "Heading West." If a sentence is complete, write "correct" on your paper; if it is incomplete, write "fragment." Rewrite each fragment as a complete sentence.

1. A hot summer day.
2. Have been here in West Stockholm, at my brother's, since Friday last.
3. Hasten to the hotel—find it very much crowded.

Looking at Style Miriam Davis Colt uses many sentence fragments in her writing. As a reader, evaluate the effect of that style on your understanding of her experiences.

◆ Build Vocabulary

Using the Latin Term *Terra Firma*

1. After their voyage, the Pilgrims were glad to be on *terra firma.*
2. The balloon's basket jolted violently as it struck *terra firma.*

Using the Word Bank

1. emigrants 2. depredations
3. genial 4. pervading
5. profusion 6. nonplused

◆ Grammar and Style

Practice

1. fragment; sample rewrite: "It was a hot summer day."
2. fragment; sample rewrite: "I have been here in West Stockholm, at my brother's, since Friday last."
3. fragment; sample rewrite: "We hasten to the hotel and find it very much crowded."

Looking at Style
Students may respond that the use of fragments gives her experiences a sense of urgency or immediacy.

Grammar Reinforcement

For additional instruction and practice, use the Fragments and Run-on Sentences lesson in the **Language Lab CD-ROM,** and the practice pages on Fragments and Run-ons, pp. 45–46, in the *Writer's Solution Grammar Practice Book.*

Reteach

To reteach this selection, use *Strategies for Diverse Student Needs,* p. 34

Build Your Portfolio

Idea Bank

Writing

1. Poem Write a poem using the refrain "I will fight no more forever." The subject may be a historic, contemporary, or personal conflict.

2. Character Sketch Describe the characteristics of Miriam Davis Colt's personality, and explain how you inferred them from the actions and comments recorded in her diary.

3. Speech Write a speech in which you express your thoughts on an issue or current event that interests you. Strive for the simplicity of language that makes Chief Joseph's speech so effective. **[Social Studies Link]**

Speaking, Listening, and Viewing

4. Oral Interpretation Chief Joseph's speech so moved the officers present that they were unable to speak. Recite the speech for the class as you imagine Chief Joseph did. **[Performing Arts Link]**

5. Viewing The United States government relocated the Nez Percé from the Northwest to Oklahoma. Looking at photos of the terrain of these two places, draw conclusions about the different lifestyles needed for each. Was it a fair move? Why or why not? Using photos, present your conclusions to your class.

Researching and Representing

6. Brochure Write and produce a marketing brochure to attract members to the vegetarian community the Colts joined. Describe its goals, location, attitudes, and practices. **[Career Link]**

7. Quilt Use colored pencils or markers to draw a design for a story quilt that Miriam Davis Colt might have made to commemorate her trip. Each square should represent a different step on the journey. **[Art Link]**

Online Activity www.phlit.phschool.com

Guided Writing Lesson

Position Paper on Development

The great open stretches of frontier land where both Chief Joseph and Miriam Davis Colt made their homes are increasingly rare today. Imagine that you live in a community whose only undeveloped section of land is about to be turned into a shopping mall. The mall would be a boost to the local economy, but it would also mean the loss of a beautiful stretch of land. Support or oppose the planned development in a position paper—a formal piece of writing that argues one side of a controversial issue. Your readers will grasp your point quickly if you present a coherent argument.

Writing Skills Focus: Coherence

A position paper must have **coherence** in order to be persuasive. In a coherent piece of writing, ideas are logically organized and clearly explained. Here are tips for writing coherently:

- Pick an organizational method (for example, chronological order, comparison and contrast, or cause and effect) and use it consistently.
- Use transition words to show relationships.
- Use specific rather than vague terminology.
- Repeat words and grammatical structures to emphasize important points.

Prewriting List the reasons you support or oppose the project, along with facts to back up your reasons.

Drafting Begin your paper with a clear statement of your position. Then give the reasons for your stand. Follow up with specific details to support your case, and end with a persuasive conclusion.

Revising Check your paper for coherence. Does your argument proceed logically and flow smoothly from one paragraph to the next? Do you provide convincing reasons and back up opinions with facts?

Idea Bank

Customizing for *Performance Levels*
Following are suggestions for matching Idea Bank topics with your students' performance levels:
Less Advanced Students: 1, 4
Average Students: 2, 6, 7
More Advanced Students: 3, 5

Customizing for *Learning Modalities*
Following are suggestions for matching Idea Bank topics with your students' learning modalities:
Musical/Rhythmic: 4
Interpersonal: 5
Logical/Mathematical: 6
Visual/Spatial: 7

Guided Writing Lesson

For more instruction on prewriting, elaboration, and revision, see *Prentice Hall Writing and Grammar.*

Writing and Language Transparencies Have students use the Argument Organizer, p. 75, to organize their argument.

Writers at Work Videodisc
Have students view the videodisc segment (Ch. 4) featuring M. Gasby Greely, the Vice President of Communications for the National Urban League, to learn how she approaches persuasive writing. Ask students to discuss how Greely's organizational techniques can help them develop their position papers.

Play frames 33643 to 43235

Writing Lab CD-ROM
Have students complete the tutorial on Persuasion. Follow these steps:

1. Use the Interactive Instruction on Deciding What Type of Organization to Use.
2. Have students draft on the computer.
3. Use the Interactive Self-Evaluation Checklist to aid revision.

✓ ASSESSMENT OPTIONS

Formal Assessment, Selection Test, pp. 164–166, and Assessment Resources Software. The selection test is designed so that it can be easily customized to the performance levels of your students.

Alternative Assessment, p. 34, includes options for less advanced students, more advanced students, visual/spatial learners, bodily/kinesthetic learners, and verbal/linguistic learners.

PORTFOLIO ASSESSMENT
Use the following rubrics in the ***Alternative Assessment*** booklet to assess student writing:
Poem: Poetry Rubric, p. 123
Character Sketch: Description Rubric, p. 112
Speech: Expression Rubric, p. 109
Guided Writing Lesson: Persuasion Rubric, p. 120

Prepare and Engage

LESSON OBJECTIVES

1. **To develop vocabulary and word identification skills**
   - Latin Roots: *-ject-*
   - Using the Word Bank: Sentence Completions
2. **To use a variety of reading strategies to comprehend fiction**
   - Reading Strategy: Predict
3. **To increase knowledge of other cultures and to connect common elements across cultures**
   - Connecting Themes Across Cultures (ATE)
4. **To express and support responses to the text**
   - Critical Thinking
   - Idea Bank: Enactment
   - Idea Bank: Oral Storytelling
   - Idea Bank: Diary Entry
   - Idea Bank: Sequel
5. **To analyze literary elements**
   - Literary Focus: Conflict
   - Idea Bank: Character Analysis
6. **To read in order to research self-selected and assigned topics**
   - Idea Bank: Graphic Display
   - Idea Bank: Pamphlet
7. **To use recursive writing processes to write a literary analysis**
   - Guided Writing Lesson
8. **To increase knowledge of the rules of grammar and usage**
   - Grammar and Style: Adverb Clauses

Test Preparation

Reading Comprehension: Context (ATE, p. 555)
The teaching tips and sample test item in this workshop support the instruction and practice in the unit workshop:
Reading Comprehension: Using Context (ATE, p. 631)

Guide for Interpreting

Jack London *(1876–1917)*

Jack London had endured more hardships by the age of twenty-one than most people experience in a lifetime. His struggles developed in him a sympathy for the working class and a lasting dislike of drudgery and provided inspiration for his career as a writer.

Difficult Beginnings London grew up in San Francisco in extreme poverty. At an early age, he left school and supported himself through a succession of unskilled jobs—working as a paper boy, in bowling alleys, on ice wagons, and in canneries and mills. Despite working long hours at these jobs, London was able to read constantly, borrowing travel and adventure books from the library.

The books London read inspired him to travel, and his job experiences led him to become active in fighting for the rights of workers. He sailed to Japan on a sealing expedition and joined a cross-country protest march with a group of unemployed workers. After being arrested for vagrancy near Buffalo, New York, London decided to educate himself and reshape his life. He quickly completed high school and entered the University of California.

After only one semester, however, the lure of fortune and adventure proved irresistible. London abandoned his studies and traveled to the Alaskan Yukon in 1897 in search of gold. Although he was unsuccessful as a miner, London's experiences in Alaska taught him about the human desire for wealth and power and about humankind's inability to control the forces of nature. While in Alaska, London also absorbed memories and stories that would make his name known one hundred years later.

A Writing Life Once back in California, London became determined to earn a living as a writer. He rented a typewriter and worked up to fifteen hours a day, spinning his Alaskan adventures into short stories and novels.

According to legend, London's stack of rejection slips from publishers grew to five feet in height!

Even so, London persevered. In 1903, he earned national fame when he published the popular novel *The Call of the Wild*. He soon became the highest paid and most industrious writer in the country. During his career, he produced more than fifty books and earned more than a million dollars. Several of his novels, including *The Call of the Wild* (1903), *The Sea-Wolf* (1904), and *White Fang* (1906), have become American classics. His best works depict a person's struggle for survival against the powerful forces of nature. "To Build a Fire," for example, tells the story of a man's fight to survive the harsh cold of the Alaskan winter.

◆ Background for Understanding

History: London and the Gold Rush

The United States Secretary of State William Seward purchased Alaska from Russia in 1867 for two cents an acre. Many Americans, believing it to be nothing but a frozen barren wasteland, called the purchase "Seward's Folly."

In 1896 the discovery of a rich lode of gold in the Yukon, part of the Arctic wilderness, led to the Klondike stampede of 1897–1898. Thousands of prospectors headed for the frozen north, lured by the promise of quick riches from gold and other natural resources.

Jack London was among the first of these prospectors. He may have searched for more than gold, however. London once commented, "True, the new territory was mostly barren; but its several hundred thousand square miles of frigidity at least gave breathing space to those who else would have suffocated at home."

Prentice Hall Literature Program Resources

REINFORCE / RETEACH / EXTEND

Selection Support Pages
Build Vocabulary: Word Roots: *-ject-*, p. 163
Grammar and Style: Adverb Clauses, p. 164
Reading Strategy: Predict, p. 165
Literary Focus: Conflict, p. 166

Strategies for Diverse Student Needs, p. 35

Beyond Literature
Media Connection: Film, p. 35

Formal Assessment Selection Test, pp. 167–169; Assessment Resources Software

Alternative Assessment, p. 35

Writing and Language Transparencies
Interpreting a Work of Literature, pp. 37–40

Resource Pro CD-ROM

Listening to Literature Audiocassettes

Literature CD-ROM

To Build a Fire

◆ *Literature and Your Life*

Connect Your Experience

Some people enjoy pushing themselves to their physical limits through sports such as rock climbing and sky diving. In some cases, as in this story, people push themselves to such extremes that they actually place their lives in jeopardy.

Journal Writing Describe a time when you endured extreme weather or engaged in a physically demanding activity.

Thematic Focus: Forging New Frontiers

Jack London, along with thousands of other prospectors, helped establish the Alaskan frontier. Like the main character of "To Build a Fire," they were drawn to a brutal setting by the lure of gold. What qualities are key to survival in this frozen frontier?

◆ Reading Strategy

Predict

The main character in this story fails to notice signs of danger and take proper precautions. A more alert person might have anticipated the dangers. As a reader, you too can anticipate, or **predict,** what will happen by taking note of clues that hint at later events. The clues in this story include the repeated references to the frigid temperatures and the man's determination to reach his goal. As you read, use a chart like this to note clues and record your predictions. Revise your predictions as you encounter new information.

As you read, take note of clues and chart your own predictions.

Clues	Prediction	Outcome

◆ Grammar and Style

Adverb Clauses

"Day had broken cold and gray, exceedingly cold and gray, *when the man turned aside from the main Yukon trail* . . . There was no sun nor hint of sun, *though there was not a cloud in the sky.*" The italicized portions of this passage from the story are adverb clauses. An **adverb clause** is a subordinate clause—a group of words with a subject and a verb that cannot stand by itself as a sentence—that describes *how, when, where, why, under what circumstances,* and *to what extent* an action occurs. The first adverb clause tells when the action occurred; the second tells under what circumstances.

◆ Literary Focus

Conflict

With only a dog for company, an unnamed man struggles to survive in the frigid Alaskan wilderness. This man is in the throes of a **conflict,** a struggle between two opposing forces. Conflicts may be **external**—between a character and an outside force such as nature or another person—or **internal**—a struggle within an individual. A character's struggle to resolve these conflicts forms the basis for the plot of a literary work. As you read, identify the conflicting forces at work in "To Build a Fire."

◆ Build Vocabulary

Latin Roots: *-ject-*

The main character in this story *rejects* an old-timer's advice not to travel alone and fails to *conjecture* about the consequences. The Latin root *-ject-* means "to throw." When you *conjecture,* you throw out a guess. If you *reject* an idea, you throw it back. What other words do you know that contain the root *-ject-?*

Word Bank

Preview this list of words before you read the story.

conjectural
unwonted
conflagration
peremptorily

Test Preparation Workshop

Reading Comprehension: Context Many standardized tests require students to use contextual analysis to determine the meanings of words and phrases they don't know. Use the following sample test item to demonstrate.

> Fifty degrees below zero meant eighty-odd degrees of frost. Such fact . . . did not lead him to meditate upon his <u>frailty as a creature of temperature</u>, and upon man's frailty in general, able only to live within certain narrow limits of heat and cold.

In this passage, the phrase <u>frailty as a creature of temperature</u> means—

A Humans can be adversely affected by extreme temperatures.
B Humans are frail when they have a temperature.
C Humans can survive in the cold.
D Even frail humans can withstand extreme temperatures.

The last part of the sentence gives context clues that show A is the correct answer.

Interest Grabber Draw students into the story by using the following description:

"Day had broken, cold and gray. . . . There was no sun nor hint of sun. . . . The Yukon lay a mile wide and hidden under three feet of ice. On top of this ice was as many feet of snow. North and South, as far as he could see, it was unbroken white . . . Undoubtably it was colder than fifty degrees below zero. . . ."

Encourage students to speculate about what might happen to a person who sets out alone on a day-long journey on foot in such conditions.

Connecting Themes Across Cultures

Ask students to cite examples of other "frontiers" around the world that have been "forged" by foreign prospectors, traders, adventurers, soldiers, or pioneers in quest of land or fortune.

Customize for *Less Proficient Readers*

These students will be challenged by the fact that London's story contains no dialogue and consists mainly of long passages filled with detailed descriptions. To help the students overcome these obstacles, encourage them to pause at the end of each paragraph to jot down the key descriptive details that it contains.

Customize for *AP Students*

Challenge these students to place this selection in an appropriate historical and literary context by identifying how it illustrates the key characteristics of Naturalism, a late nineteenth century literary movement that stressed the idea that people's lives are shaped by forces of society and nature beyond their control.

Customize for *English Language Learners*

Help students to understand language specific to the Arctic weather and landscape, such as *cold snap, husky, timber jam, ice muzzle, freeze-up,* and so on.

Develop Understanding

One-Minute Insight Along the Yukon River in the frozen northern wilderness, an inexperienced but confident prospector and his work dog make a long and dangerous journey on foot toward a camp. The temperature is far colder than the man thinks, too cold for a solitary walk. That is his first mistake. His second mistake—building a fire in the wrong spot—proves fatal. Though nature is the antagonist of this tale, the man's own false sense of confident invulnerability contributes to his downfall. The dog, who has sensed the danger of their predicament from the start, stays with the man until the very end. Then its instincts direct it on toward the camp, where other food and fire providers are to be found.

❶ **Clarification** Explain to students that in the Arctic, there is a period of time during the winter when the sun never rises above the horizon. Conversely, there are periods in the summer when the sun never sets.

Customize for
Visual/Spatial Learners
❷ It would be helpful to provide these students with a map of Alaska and of the Yukon Territory so that they can get their bearings. They can see how far north the man was and note the remoteness of the region.

◆ Reading Strategy

❸ **Predict** Point out that here London presents a picture of the man and his limitations. Ask students to predict how his lack of imagination might prove harmful to him in the extreme conditions of this frozen land. *Students may predict that the unimaginative man may be challenged by events that he does not foresee.*

◆ Literary Focus

❹ **Conflict** Have students discuss what the details here suggest about the most likely resolution of a conflict between the man and the extreme forces of nature that now confront him. *Students should point to London's mention of "man's frailty" as an indication that nature will almost certainly win out in such a conflict.*

To Build a Fire

Jack London

Connections to World Literature, *page 1183*

Day had broken cold and gray, exceedingly cold and gray, when the man turned aside from the main Yukon[1] trail and climbed the high earth-bank, where a dim and little-traveled trail led eastward through the fat spruce timberland. It was a steep bank, and he paused for breath at the top, excusing the act to himself by looking at his watch. It was nine o'clock. There was no sun nor hint of sun, though there was not a cloud in the sky. It was a clear day, and yet there seemed an intangible pall over the face of things, a subtle gloom that made the day dark, and that was due to the absence of
❶ sun. This fact did not worry the man. He was used to the lack of sun. It had been days since he had seen the sun, and he knew that a few more days must pass before that cheerful orb, due south, would just peep above the skyline and dip immediately from view.

The man flung a look back along the way he had come. The Yukon lay a mile wide and hidden under three feet of ice. On top of this ice were as many feet of snow. It was all pure white, rolling in gentle undulations where the
❷ ice jams of the freeze-up had formed. North and south, as far as his eye could see, it was unbroken white, save for a dark hairline that curved and twisted from around the spruce-covered island to the south, and that curved and twisted away into the north, where it disappeared behind another spruce-covered island. This dark hairline was the trail—the main trail—that led south five hundred miles to the Chilcoot Pass, Dyea,[2] and salt water; and that led north seventy miles to Dawson, and still on ❷
to the north a thousand miles to Nulato,[3] and finally to St. Michael on Bering Sea, a thousand miles and half a thousand more.

But all this—the mysterious, far-reaching hairline trail, the absence of sun from the sky, the tremendous cold, and the strangeness and weirdness of it all—no impression on the man. It was not because he was long used to it. He was a newcomer in the land, a *chechaquo*,[4] and this was his first winter. The trouble with him was that he was without imagination. He was quick and alert in the things of life, but only in the things, and not in the significances. Fifty degrees below zero meant eighty-odd degrees of frost. Such fact impressed him as being cold ❸
and uncomfortable, and that was all. It did not ❹
lead him to meditate upon his frailty as a creature of temperature, and upon man's frailty in general, able only to live within certain narrow limits of heat and cold; and from there on it did not lead him to the conjectural field of immortality and man's place in the universe. Fifty

1. **Yukon** (yo͞o´ kän): Territory in northwestern Canada, east of Alaska; also, a river.

2. **Dyea** (dī´ ā): Former town in Alaska at the start of the Yukon trail.

3. **Dawson . . . Nulato:** Former gold-mining villages in the Yukon.

4. ***chechaquo*** (chē chä´ kwō): Slang for newcomer.

Block Scheduling Strategies

Consider these suggestions to take advantage of extended class time:

- Read the story as a class in sections, with students taking turns reading aloud. Pause every couple of pages to have students share their reactions to the man's behavior and to make predictions about what will happen to him.
- Have students research Jack London or the Yukon Gold Rush on the Internet before or after they read. Ask students to share their findings. Would they, like London, have been willing to take on the risks of life in the Yukon for the sake of a chance at gold?
- Allow class time for students to practice, prepare, and present the Oral Storytelling project in the Idea Bank, p. 567.
- Display and discuss the model transparencies of a literary analysis (pp. 37–40) in the ***Writing and Language Transparencies*** prior to having students complete the Mini-Lesson (p. 567).

degrees below zero stood for a bite of frost that hurt and that must be guarded against by the use of mittens, earflaps, warm moccasins, and
3 thick socks. Fifty degrees below zero was to
4 him just precisely fifty degrees below zero. That there should be anything more to it than that was a thought that never entered his head.

As he turned to go on, he spat speculatively. There was a sharp, explosive crackle that startled him. He spat again. And again, in the air, before it could fall to the snow, the spittle crackled. He knew that at fifty below spittle crackled on the snow, but this spittle had crackled in the air. Undoubtedly it was colder than fifty below—how much colder he did not know. But the temperature did not matter. He was bound for the old claim on the left fork of Henderson Creek, where the boys were already. They had come over across the divide from the Indian Creek country, while he had come the roundabout way to take a look at the possibilities of getting out logs in the spring from the islands in the Yukon. He would be in to camp by six o'clock; a bit after dark, it was true, but the boys would be there, a fire would be going, and a hot supper would be ready. As for lunch, he pressed his hand against the protruding bundle under his jacket. It was also under his shirt, wrapped up in a handkerchief and lying against the naked skin. It was the only way to keep the bis-
6 cuits from freezing. He smiled agreeably to him-
7 self as he thought of those biscuits, each cut open and sopped in bacon grease, and each enclosing a generous slice of fried bacon.

5
> **◆ Literary Focus**
> The great elaboration on the cold points out the central conflict in this story. With what or whom is the man in conflict?

He plunged in among the big spruce trees. The trail was faint. A foot of snow had fallen since the last sled had passed over, and he was glad he was without a sled, traveling light. In fact, he carried nothing but the lunch wrapped in the handkerchief. He was surprised, however, at the cold. It certainly was cold, he concluded, as he rubbed his numb nose and cheekbones with his mittened hand. He was a warm-whiskered man, but the hair on his face did not protect the high cheekbones and the eager nose that thrust itself aggressively into the frosty air.

At the man's heels trotted a dog, a big native husky, the proper wolf dog, gray-coated and without any visible or temperamental difference from its brother, the wild wolf. The animal was depressed by the tremendous cold. It knew that it was no time for traveling. Its instinct told it a truer tale than was told to the man by the man's judgment. In reality, it was not merely colder than fifty below zero; it was colder than sixty below, than seventy below. It was seventy-five below zero. Since the freezing point is thirty-two above zero, it meant that one hundred and seven degrees of frost obtained. The dog did not know anything about 8
thermometers. Possibly in its brain there was no sharp consciousness of a condition of very cold such as was in the man's brain. But the brute had its instinct. It experienced a vague but menacing apprehension that subdued it and made it slink along at the man's heels, and that made it question eagerly every unwonted movement of the man as if expecting him to go into camp or to seek shelter somewhere and build a fire. The dog had learned fire, and it wanted fire, or else to burrow under the snow and cuddle its warmth away from the air.

The frozen moisture of its breathing had settled on its fur in a fine powder of frost, and especially were its jowls, muzzle, and eyelashes whitened by its crystalled breath. The man's red beard and mustache were likewise frosted, but more solidly, the deposit taking the form of ice and increasing with every warm, moist breath he exhaled. Also, the man was chewing tobacco, and the muzzle of ice held his lips so rigidly that he was unable to clear his chin when he expelled the juice. The result was that a crystal beard of the color and solidity of amber was increasing its length on his chin. If he fell down it would shatter itself, like glass, into brittle fragments. But he did not mind the appendage. It was the penalty all tobacco-chewers paid in that country, and he had been out before in two cold snaps. They had not been so cold as this, he knew, but by

◆ Build Vocabulary

conjectural (kən jek´ chər əl) *adj.*: Based on guesswork

unwonted (un wän´ tid) *adj.*: Unusual; unfamiliar

◆ Literary Focus

5 Conflict Students may say that the man is in conflict not only with the forces of extreme weather conditions, but with the limits of his own perceptions.

◆ Critical Thinking

6 Support Have students explain how the characterization of the man demonstrates that he lacks imagination. *Students should point out that he doesn't account for the possibility of any snags that might delay his arrival, that he is traveling too light for such a dangerous trip, and that he isn't concerned with the faintness of the trail.*

◆ Critical Thinking

7 Support Have students speculate about why London points out that the freezing point is thirty-two above zero—even though readers will almost certainly be aware of this information. *London does so to create a point of comparison that helps to emphasize the severity of the cold.*

◆ Reading Strategy

8 Predict Point out to students that the dog's basic instincts tell it what the man has yet to conclude: that it is too dangerously cold to be traveling. Based on the dog's apprehensions, ask students to predict whether the man or the dog will prove to be correct in his assumptions about the safety of traveling under such conditions. *Students' responses will vary, but it is likely that many will side with the instincts of the animal.*

Tips to Guide Reading

Sustained Reading Encourage students to sustain their reading, trying to avoid pausing or letting their attention wander. To keep their attention from wandering, emphasize the importance of finding a quiet, well-lighted place to read, where they may sit comfortably (but not so comfortably that they are apt to fall asleep), without distractions. Emphasize that by sustaining their reading, students will get the fullest experience from reading this story—experiencing its events almost as though they are "there."

Research Skills Mini-Lesson

Using Museums for Research

Introduce the Concept Tell students that museums can help them conduct research for activities such as the Cultural Connection on p. 559 and the Graphic Display in the Idea Bank on p. 567.

Develop the Information Explain that natural history museums often include interesting displays of many different kinds—including dioramas, diagrams, artifact exhibits, reproductions and representations of various kinds, and videofilm.

Apply the Information Tell students to visit a local or regional natural history museum, if one is available, and to take notes on information they find. If a local or regional museum is not nearby, point out that the Internet offers access to virtual museums. Suggest that students begin by searching for Canadian or Alaskan museums, such as the Museum of Anthropology at the University of British Columbia in Vancouver.

Assess the Outcome Assess students' findings on the basis of their informational relevance and specificity.

Customize for *Logical/Mathematical Learners*

❶ Ask these students to explain whether the man's calculations make sense. *Students may point out that 4 miles an hour is a very quick walking pace, and one that he is unlikely to be able to keep up for very long in the snow.*

◆ Reading Strategy

❷ **Predict** Ask students to tell whether they believe the man will reach camp as he plans, now that he is traveling on an unused trail. *Unlike the man, students may recognize that the trail has been unused for a reason, that perhaps it is too dangerous to travel on now. They may predict that he won't arrive as planned.*

◆ Reading Strategy

❸ **Predict** Students might predict that the man will be severely frostbitten by the extreme cold.

▶Critical Viewing◀

❹ **Analyze** Students may choose several descriptive words or passages from the story to describe the scene. The following are examples: intangible pall over the face of things; subtle gloom; gentle undulations; dark hairline; spruce-covered island; silent creek; arctic winter.

the spirit thermometer[5] at Sixty Mile he knew they had been registered at fifty below and at fifty-five.

He held on through the level stretch of woods for several miles, crossed a wide flat, and dropped down a bank to the frozen bed of a small stream. This was Henderson Creek, and he knew he was ten miles from the forks. He looked at his watch. It was ten o'clock. He was ❶ making four miles an hour, and he calculated that he would arrive at the forks at half past twelve. He decided to celebrate that event by eating his lunch there.

The dog dropped in again at his heels, with a tail drooping discouragement, as the man swung along the creek bed. The furrow of the old sled trail was plainly visible, but a dozen inches of snow covered the marks of the last runners. In a month no man had come up or down that silent creek. The man held steadily on. He was not much given to thinking, and ❷ just then particularly he had nothing to think about save that he would eat lunch at the forks and that at six o'clock he would be in camp with the boys. There was nobody to talk to; and, had there been, speech would have been impossible because of the ice-muzzle on his mouth. So he continued monotonously to chew tobacco and to increase the length of his amber beard.

Once in a while the thought reiterated itself that it was very cold and that he had never experienced such cold. As he walked along he rubbed his cheekbones and nose with the back of his mittened hand. He did this automatically, now and again changing hands. But rub as he would, the instant he stopped his cheekbones went numb, and the following instant the end of his nose went numb. He was sure to frost his cheeks; he knew that, and experienced a pang of regret that he had not devised a nose strap of the sort Bud wore in cold snaps. Such a strap passed across the cheeks, as well, and saved them. But it didn't matter much, after all. What were frosted cheeks? A bit painful, that was all: they were never serious.

❸ **◆ Reading Strategy** Based on this passage, what can you predict might happen?

▲ **Critical Viewing** Which words or passages from the story could be used to describe this scene? **[Analyze]** ❹

Empty as the man's mind was of thoughts, he was keenly observant, and he noticed the changes in the creek, the curves and bends and timber jams, and always he sharply noted where he placed his feet. Once, coming around a bend, he shied abruptly, like a startled horse, curved away from the place where he had been walking, and retreated several paces back along the trail. The creek he knew was frozen clear to the bottom—no creek could contain water in that arctic winter—but he knew also that there were springs that bubbled out from the hillsides and ran along under the snow and on top the ice of the creek. He knew that the coldest snaps never froze these springs, and he knew likewise their danger. They were traps. They hid pools of water under the snow that might be three inches deep, or three feet. Sometimes a skin of ice half an inch thick covered them, and in turn was covered by the snow. Sometimes there were alternate layers of water and ice skin, so that when one broke through he kept on breaking through for a while, sometimes wetting himself to the waist.

That was why he had shied in such panic. He had felt the give under his feet and heard the

5. **spirit thermometer:** Thermometer containing alcohol; used in extreme cold.

Cross-Curricular Connection: Science

Dangers of Cold Weather Discuss with students how the rising popularity of winter outdoor activities has led to a rise in cold-weather accidents. Frostbite is one result of prolonged exposure to extremely low temperatures, and so is hypothermia, or sub-normal body temperature. The most obvious signs of frostbite are progressive, painful loss of feeling (usually beginning in vulnerable areas, such as the hands, feet, and face) leading to numbness, skin discoloration, and then loss of function. Students can find out about the effects of hypothermia by following what happens to the man in the story. They can notice his difficulty moving, his confusion, his drowsiness, and his eventual death.

Ask students to find out about precautions people who plan to spend time in sub-freezing temperatures can take to prevent these severe problems. Have them learn what first-aid steps to follow if frostbite or hypothermia occurs. They can use this information to complete the Pamphlet project in the Idea Bank (p. 567).

crackle of a snow-hidden ice skin. And to get his feet wet in such a temperature meant trouble and danger. At the very least it meant delay, for he would be forced to stop and build a fire, and
5 under its protection to bare his feet while he
6 dried his socks and moccasins. He stood and studied the creek bed and its banks, and decided that the flow of water came from the right. He reflected awhile, rubbing his nose and cheeks, then skirted to the left, stepping gingerly and testing the footing for each step. Once clear of the danger, he took a fresh chew of tobacco and swung along at his four-mile gait.

> ◆ **Literary Focus**
> Until now, the man has struggled with the frigid air temperature. What other element of conflict is introduced here?

In the course of the next two hours he came upon several similar traps. Usually the snow above the hidden pools had a sunken, candied appearance that advertised the danger. Once again, however, he had a close call; and once, suspecting danger, he compelled the dog to go on in front. The dog did not want to go. It hung back until the man shoved it forward, and then it went quickly across the white, unbroken surface. Suddenly it broke through, floundered to one side, and got away to firmer footing. It had wet its forefeet and legs, and almost immediately the water that clung to it turned to ice.
7 It made quick efforts to lick the ice off its legs, then dropped down in the snow and began to bite out the ice that had formed between the toes. This was a matter of instinct. To permit the ice to remain would mean sore feet. It did not know this. It merely obeyed the mysterious prompting that arose from the deep crypts of its being. But the man knew, having achieved a judgment on the subject, and he removed the mitten from his right hand and helped tear out the ice particles. He did not expose his fingers more than a minute, and was astonished at the swift numbness that smote them. It certainly was cold. He pulled on the mitten hastily, and beat the hand savagely across his chest.

At twelve o'clock the day was at its brightest.
8 Yet the sun was too far south on its winter journey to clear the horizon. The bulge of the earth intervened between it and Henderson
Creek, where the man walked under a clear 8
sky at noon and cast no shadow. At half-past twelve, to the minute, he arrived at the forks of the creek. He was pleased at the speed he had made. If he kept it up, he would certainly be with the boys by six. He unbuttoned his jacket and shirt and drew forth his lunch. The action consumed no more than a quarter of a minute, yet in that brief moment the numbness laid hold of the exposed fingers. He did not put the mitten on, but, instead, struck the fingers a dozen sharp smashes against his leg. Then he sat down on a snow-covered log to eat. The sting that followed upon the striking of his fingers against his leg ceased so quickly that he was startled. He had had no chance to take a bite of biscuit. He struck the fingers repeatedly and returned them to the mitten, baring the other hand for the purpose of eating. He tried to take a mouthful, but the ice muzzle prevented. He had forgotten to build a fire and thaw out. He chuckled at his foolishness, and as he chuckled he noted the numbness creeping into the exposed fingers. Also, he noted that the stinging which had first come to his toes when he sat down was already passing away. He wondered whether the toes were warm or numb. He moved them inside the
moccasins and decided that they were numb. 9

He pulled the mitten on hurriedly and stood up. He was a bit frightened. He stamped up and down until the stinging returned into the feet. It certainly was cold, was his thought. That man from Sulphur Creek had spoken the truth when telling how cold it sometimes got in the country. And he had laughed at him at the time! That showed one must not be too sure of things. There was no mistake about it, it *was* cold. He strode up and down, stamping his feet and threshing his arms, until reassured by the returning warmth. Then he got out matches and proceeded to make a fire. From the undergrowth, where high water of the previous spring had lodged a supply of seasoned twigs, he got his firewood. Working carefully from a small beginning, he soon had a roaring fire, over which he thawed the ice from his face and in the protection of which he ate his biscuits. For the moment the cold of space was outwitted.

◆ Literary Focus

5 Conflict Students can recognize that now the man faces the danger of hidden traps in the landscape, such as hidden pockets of water. These hidden traps place the man at an even greater disadvantage in his struggle against the harsh environment.

◆ Critical Thinking

6 Connect Ask students to identify the implications of a delay in the man's journey. Remind them that even without a delay he expects to arrive after dark. *Students should recognize that even a small delay is likely to spell disaster for the man, given the fact that he has allowed no margin for error in planning his journey.*

◆ Critical Thinking

7 Evaluate Guide students to recognize the boundaries of the man's relationship with his dog: it is his worker and he uses it as a tool. Here he uses the animal to find out whether a snow-hidden trap lies ahead.

◆ Literary Focus

8 Conflict Guide students to appreciate the symbolism in the idea that the man casts no shadow. They may understand it to mean that he has no presence there and shouldn't be there at all, or that he is marked for death and, like one already dead, no longer exists in the physical world.

◆ Reading Strategy

9 Predict Guide students to notice the shift in the man's attitude in this passage. At first, he laughs at his foolishness. Then he suddenly thinks his predicament is dangerous and becomes fearful.

◆ Critical Thinking

❶ Analyze Ask students: How has the narrator prepared us for this possibility and what it might mean? *Students should respond that the narrator has already detailed the great danger presented by water in such an environment. He has also explained that stepping in water would require a traveler to stop and build a fire, or risk freezing to death.*

◆ Grammar and Style

❷ Adverb Clauses Ask students to identify the adverb clause in this sentence and the question it answers. *The adverb clause is ". . . before he floundered out to the firm crust." It answers the question: When?*

◆ Literary Focus

❸ Conflict Discuss with students that the man has lost all sense of frivolity, that he is intensely focused on doing what he knows he must do to survive. How does the change in the man's attitude relate to a heightening of the story's central conflict? *Students can see that he has become more humble about his human limitations and respectful of the powers of nature. This change occurs because he is becoming perilously close to losing his struggle against the powerful forces of nature.*

The dog took satisfaction in the fire, stretching out close enough for warmth and far enough away to escape being singed.

When the man had finished, he filled his pipe and took his comfortable time over a smoke. Then he pulled on his mittens, settled the earflaps of his cap firmly about his ears, and took the creek trail up the left fork. The dog was disappointed and yearned back toward the fire. This man did not know cold. Possibly all the generations of his ancestry had been ignorant of cold, of real cold, of cold one hundred and seven degrees below freezing point. But the dog knew; all its ancestry knew, and it had inherited the knowledge. And it knew that it was not good to walk abroad in such fearful cold. It was the time to lie snug in a hole in the snow and wait for a curtain of cloud to be drawn across the face of outer space whence this cold came. On the other hand, there was no keen intimacy between the dog and the man. The one was the toil slave of the other, and the only caresses it had ever received were the caresses of the whiplash and of harsh and menacing throat sounds that threatened the whiplash. So the dog made no effort to communicate its apprehension to the man. It was not concerned in the welfare of the man; it was for its own sake that it yearned back toward the fire. But the man whistled, and spoke to it with the sound of whiplashes, and the dog swung in at the man's heels and followed after.

The man took a chew of tobacco and proceeded to start a new amber beard. Also, his moist breath quickly powdered with white his mustache, eyebrows, and lashes. There did not seem to be so many springs on the left fork of the Henderson, and for half an hour the man saw no signs of any. And then it happened. At a place where there were no signs, where the soft, ❶ unbroken snow seemed to advertise solidity beneath, the man broke through. It was not deep. ❷ He wet himself halfway to the knees before he floundered out to the firm crust.

He was angry, and cursed his luck aloud. He had hoped to get into camp with the boys at six o'clock, and this would delay him an hour, for he would have to build a fire and dry out his footgear. This was imperative at that low temperature—he knew that much; and he turned aside to the bank, which he climbed. On top, tangled in the underbrush about the trunks of several small spruce trees, was a high-water deposit of dry firewood—sticks and twigs, principally, but also larger portions of seasoned branches and fine, dry, last year's grasses. He threw down several large pieces on top of the snow. This served for a foundation and prevented the young flame from drowning itself in the snow it otherwise would melt. The flame he got by touching a match to a small shred of birch bark that he took from his pocket. This burned even more readily than paper. Placing it on the foundation, he fed the young flame with wisps of dry grass and with the tiniest dry twigs.

He worked slowly and carefully, keenly aware of his danger. Gradually, as the flame grew stronger, he increased the size of the twigs with which he fed it. He squatted in the snow, pulling the twigs out from their entanglement in the brush and feeding directly to the flame. He knew there must be no failure. When it is seventy-five below zero, a man must not fail in his ❸ first attempt to build a fire—that is, if his feet are wet. If his feet are dry, and he fails, he can run along the trail for half a mile and restore his circulation. But the circulation of wet and freezing feet cannot be restored by running when it is seventy-five below. No matter how fast he runs, the wet feet will freeze the harder.

All this the man knew. The old-timer on Sulphur Creek had told him about it the previous fall, and now he was appreciating the advice. Already all sensation had gone out of his feet. To build the fire he had been forced to remove his mittens, and the fingers had quickly gone numb. His pace of four miles an hour had kept his heart pumping blood to the surface of his body and to all the extremities. But the instant he stopped, the action of the pump eased down. The cold of space smote the unprotected tip of the planet, and he, being on that unprotected tip, received the full force of the blow. The blood of his body recoiled before it. The blood was alive, like the dog, and like the dog it wanted to hide away and cover itself up from the fearful cold. So long as he walked four miles an hour, he pumped that blood, willy-nilly, to the surface; but now it ebbed away and sank down

---

Viewing and Representing Mini-Lesson

Pamphlet

This mini-lesson supports the Researching and Representing activity in the Idea Bank on p. 567.

Introduce the Concept Explain to students that a pamphlet is a small booklet or brochure that presents general information on a topic. This information is presented in various formats, which may include short paragraphs of text, lists, boxed information, and illustrations such as maps, diagrams, charts, photographs, detailed drawings, or decorative art. Because the pamphlet offers condensed information, it usually gives readers only the most important or useful facts, guidelines, or details on the topic.

Develop Background Have students work in pairs to research the causes, symptoms, and recommended treatment of hypothermia. Discuss with students how they might visually highlight important information such as emergency phone numbers.

Apply the Information Partners can decide how to combine and illustrate the most important points, guidelines, and tips for avoiding, detecting, and treating hypothermia. If students have access to a computer with a scanner, encourage them to design and publish their pamphlets electronically, making them as readable and visually interesting as possible.

Assess the Outcome Assess students' pamphlets on the basis of the effectiveness of their presentation of information.

into the recesses of his body. The extremities were the first to feel its absence. His wet feet froze the faster, and his exposed fingers numbed the faster, though they had not yet begun to freeze. Nose and cheeks were already freezing, while the skin of all his body chilled as it lost its blood.

But he was safe. Toes and nose and cheeks would be only touched by the frost, for the fire was beginning to burn with strength. He was feeding it with twigs the size of his finger. In another minute he would be able to feed it with branches the size of his wrist, and then he could remove his wet foot-gear, and, while it dried, he could keep his naked feet warm by the fire, rubbing them at first, of course, with snow. The fire was a success. He was safe. He remembered the advice of the old-timer on Sulphur Creek, and smiled. The old-timer had been very serious in laying down the law that no man must travel alone in the Klondike after
4 fifty below. Well, here he was; he had had the accident; he was alone; and he had saved himself. Those old-timers were rather womanish, some of them, he thought. All a man had to do was to keep his head, and he was all right. Any man who was a man could travel alone. But it was surprising, the rapidity with which his cheeks and nose were freezing. And he had not thought his fingers could go lifeless in so short a time. Lifeless they were, for he could scarcely make them move together to grip a twig, and they seemed remote from his body and from him. When he touched a twig, he had to look and see whether or not he had hold of it. The wires were pretty well down between him and his finger ends.

5 **◆ Reading Strategy**
Has the man saved himself? What do you predict will happen?

All of which counted for little. There was the fire, snapping and crackling and promising life with every dancing flame. He started to untie his moccasins. They were coated with ice; the thick German socks were like sheaths of iron halfway to the knees; and the moccasin strings were like rods of steel all twisted and knotted as by some conflagration. For a moment he tugged with his numb fingers, then, realizing the folly of it, he drew his sheath-knife.

But before he could cut the strings, it happened. It was his own fault or, rather, his mistake. He should not have built the fire under the spruce tree. He should have built it in the open. But it had been easier to pull the twigs from the brush and drop them directly on the fire. Now the tree under which he had done this carried a weight of snow on its boughs. No wind had blown for weeks, and each bough was fully freighted. Each time he had pulled a twig he had communicated a slight agitation to 6
the tree—an imperceptible agitation, so far as he was concerned, but an agitation sufficient to bring about the disaster. High up in the tree one bough capsized its load of snow. This fell on the boughs beneath, capsizing them. This process continued, spreading out and involving the whole tree. It grew like an avalanche, and it descended without warning upon the man and the fire, and the fire was blotted out! Where it had burned was a mantle of fresh and disordered snow.

The man was shocked. It was as though he had just heard his own sentence of death. For a moment he sat and stared at the spot where the fire had been. Then he grew very calm. Perhaps the old-timer on Sulphur Creek was right. If he had only had a trail mate he would have been in no danger now. The trail mate could have built the fire. Well, it was up to him to build the fire over again, and this second time there must be no failure. Even if he succeeded, he would most likely lose some toes. His feet must be badly frozen by now, and there would be some time before the second fire was ready.

Such were his thoughts, but he did not sit and think them. He was busy all the time they were passing through his mind. He made a new foundation for a fire, this time in the open, where no treacherous tree could blot it out. Next, he gathered dry grasses and tiny twigs from the high-water flotsam. He could not bring his fingers together to pull them out, but he was able to gather them by the handful. In

◆ Build Vocabulary

conflagration (kän′ flə grā′ shən) *n.*: Big, destructive fire

◆ Critical Thinking

4 Analyze Talk with students about the man's reaction to having saved himself. Ask them if they think he is being cocky or overconfident. *Some may respond that he is being cocky, but others may suggest that he is a man who is all alone, deep in the wilderness, and simply talks to himself to keep his spirits up, much like anyone might do in similar circumstances.*

◆ Reading Strategy

5 Predict Students' predictions will vary. Some may say that danger seems to find people when they least expect it, and that now is such a time for the man who is busy feeling proud of himself and perhaps vulnerable to carelessness.

◆ Reading Strategy

6 Predict Ask students to tell whether they saw this accident coming. Have them provide details to back up their predictions. *Most students will have been caught by surprise, but they are likely to have expected some type of disaster to have occurred.*

Cross-Curricular Connection: Social Studies

The Race to the South Pole Inform students that the deadly situation presented in *To Build a Fire* has many parallels in real-life explorations of the Arctic regions. Relate the story of the race to the South Pole, in which British explorer Robert Falcon Scott and Norwegian explorer Roald Amundsen competed to see which would be the first to lead an exploration party to the newly-charted pole. Their goal: to reach the South Pole in 1910. When Amundsen and his party finally arrived in December 1911, they were the first to set foot in the fabled South Pole. Traveling by sled, Scott and four others reached the spot in January 1912, only to find that Amundsen's party had beaten them to their goal. By March, Scott and his party were dead, victims of illness, extreme weather conditions, and a shortage of supplies.

Get students' reactions to the tragic competition. Ask them if they themselves would have joined one of the those expeditions of discovery had they had the opportunity to do so. Encourage interested students to research the details of the race to the pole and to share their findings with the class.

◆ *Literature and Your Life*

❶ Ask students who own dogs to respond to London's description of the dog's reaction here, and to other perceptions about the animal's instinctive behavior and actions. Ask them whether they think the description is on target. *Students may be impressed with London's astute understanding of canine behavior.*

◆ Literary Focus

❷ **Conflict** Students can note that the man now feels the initial pangs of panic; with each mishap, his attitude has changed. Overconfident at first, he begins to laugh at his errors, then to appreciate his limitations and, now, to experience real concern.

▶Critical Viewing◀

❸ **Infer; Relate** Students may say that the husky's eyes indicate an intense focus or alertness, one that is unfettered by any sense of imagination or other distraction. Some may detect intelligence, wisdom, or signs of the survival instinct that guides the actions of the husky in the story.

◆ *Literature and Your Life*

❹ Ask students to imagine the man's frustration after all his painstaking efforts come to nothing. Have students reflect on situations from their own lives when something beyond their control foiled their best efforts. How did they feel?

this way he got many rotten twigs and bits of green moss that were undesirable, but it was the best he could do. He worked methodically, even collecting an armful of the larger branches to be used later when the fire gathered strength. And all the while the dog sat and ❶ watched him, a certain yearning wistfulness in its eyes, for it looked upon him as the fire provider, and the fire was slow in coming.

When all was ready, the man reached in his pocket for a second piece of birch bark. He knew the bark was there, and, though he could not feel it with his fingers, he could hear its crisp rustling as he fumbled for it. Try as he would, he could not clutch hold of it. And all the time, in his consciousness, was the knowledge that each instant his feet were freezing. This thought tended to put him in a panic, but ❷ he fought against it and kept calm. He pulled on his mittens with his teeth, and threshed his arms back and forth, beating his hands with all his might against his sides. He did this sitting down, and he stood up to do it; and all the while the dog sat in the snow, its wolf brush of a tail curled around warmly over its forefeet, its sharp wolf ears pricked forward intently as it watched the man. And the man, as he beat and threshed with his arms and hands, felt a great surge of envy as he regarded the creature that was warm and secure in its natural covering.

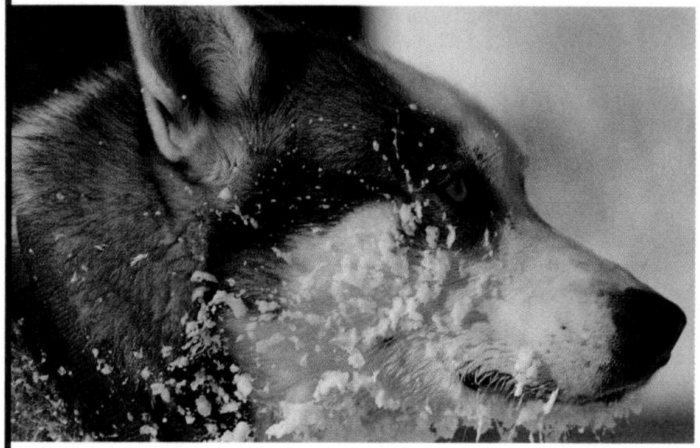

❸ ▲ **Critical Viewing** Study the eyes of this husky. What human characteristics would you attribute to its eyes? Which, if any, of those characteristics apply to the dog in the story? **[Infer; Relate]**

After a time he was aware of the first faraway signals of sensation in his beaten fingers. The faint tingling grew stronger till it evolved into a stinging ache that was excruciating, but which the man hailed with satisfaction. He stripped the mitten from his right hand and fetched forth the birch bark. The exposed fingers were quickly going numb again. Next he brought out his bunch of sulphur matches. But the tremendous cold had already driven the life out of his fingers. In his effort to separate one match from the others, the whole bunch fell in the snow. He tried to pick it out of the snow, but failed. The dead fingers could neither touch nor clutch. He was very careful. He drove the thought of his freezing feet, and nose, and cheeks, out of his mind, devoting his whole soul to the matches. He watched, using the sense of vision in place of that of touch, and when he saw his fingers on each side the bunch, he closed them—that is, he willed to close them, for the wires were down, and the fingers did not obey. He pulled the mitten on the right hand, and beat it fiercely against his knee. Then, with both mittened hands, he scooped the bunch of matches, along with much snow, into his lap. Yet he was no better off.

After some manipulation he managed to get the bunch between the heels of his mittened hands. In this fashion he carried it to his mouth. The ice crackled and snapped when by a violent effort he opened his mouth. He drew the lower jaw in, curled the upper lip out of the way, and scraped the bunch with his upper teeth in order to separate a match. He succeeded in getting one, which he dropped on his ❹
lap. He was no better off. He could not pick it up. Then he devised a way. He picked it up in his teeth and scratched it on his leg. Twenty times he scratched before he succeeded in lighting it. As it flamed he held it with his teeth to the birch bark. But the burning brimstone went up his nostrils and into his lungs, causing him to cough spasmodically. The match fell into the snow and went out.

The old-timer on Sulphur Creek was right, he thought in the moment of controlled despair that ensued: after fifty below, a man should travel with a partner. He beat his hands, but failed in exciting any sensation. Suddenly he

Beyond the Classroom

Career Connection

Eco-Tourism There are few people who would want venture into the Arctic wilderness by themselves like the man in this story. However, there is a growing tourist industry that fulfills people's desire to travel into areas of unspoiled wilderness in all parts of the world, from Alaska to the Antarctic and from the rainforests of Central America to the African savannah. This industry is called eco-tourism. Explain to students that there are many career opportunities in eco-tourism. Cooks, naturalists, pilots, and booking agents are just a few of the types of people employed by eco-tourism companies. Encourage students to conduct research to learn about this growing industry and the opportunities it provides, and to share their findings with their classmates.

bared both hands, removing the mittens with his teeth. He caught the whole bunch between the heels of his hands. His arm muscles not being frozen enabled him to press the hand heels tightly against the matches. Then he scratched the bunch along his leg. It flared into flame, seventy sulphur matches at once! There was no wind to blow them out. He kept his head to one side to escape the strangling fumes, and held the blazing bunch to the birch bark. As he so
5 held it, he became aware of sensation in his hand. His flesh was burning. He could smell it. Deep down below the surface he could feel it. The sensation developed into pain that grew acute. And still he endured it, holding the flame of the matches clumsily to the bark that would not light readily because his own burning hands were in the way, absorbing most of the flame.

At last, when he could endure no more, he jerked his hands apart. The blazing matches fell sizzling into the snow, but the birch bark was alight. He began laying dry grasses and the tiniest twigs on the flame. He could not pick and choose, for he had to lift the fuel between the heels of his hands. Small pieces of rotten wood and green moss clung to the twigs, and he bit them off as well as he could with his teeth. He cherished the flame carefully and awkwardly. It meant life, and it must not perish. The withdrawal of blood from the surface of his body now made him begin to shiver, and he grew more awkward. A large piece of green moss fell squarely on the little fire. He tried to poke it out with his fingers, but his shivering frame made him poke too far, and he disrupted the nucleus of the little fire, the burning grasses and tiny twigs separating and scattering. He tried to poke them together again, but in spite of the tenseness of the effort, his shivering got away with him, and the twigs were hopelessly scattered. Each twig gushed a puff of smoke and went out. The fire provider had failed. As he looked apathetically about him, his eyes chanced on the dog, sitting across the ruins of the fire from him, in the snow, making restless, hunching movements, slightly lifting one forefoot and then the other, shifting its weight back and forth on them with wistful eagerness.

The sight of the dog put a wild idea into his head. He remembered the tale of the man, caught in a blizzard, who killed a steer and crawled inside the carcass, and so was saved. He would kill the dog and bury his hands in the warm body until the numbness went out of them. Then he could build another fire. He spoke to the dog, calling it to him; but in his voice was a strange note of fear that frightened the animal, who had never known the man to speak in such way before. Something was the matter, and its suspicious nature sensed danger—it knew not what danger, but somewhere,
somehow, in its brain arose an apprehension of 6
the man. It flattened its ears down at the sound of the man's voice, and its restless, hunching movements and the liftings and shiftings of its forefeet became more pronounced; but it would not come to the man. He got on his hands and knees and crawled toward the dog. This unusual posture again excited suspicion, and the animal sidled mincingly away.

The man sat up in the snow for a moment and struggled for calmness. Then he pulled on his mittens, by means of his teeth, and got upon his feet. He glanced down at first in order to assure himself that he was really standing up, for the absence of sensation in his feet left him unrelated to the earth. His erect position in itself started to drive the webs of suspicion from the dog's mind; and when he spoke peremptorily, with the sound of whiplashes in his voice, the dog rendered its customary allegiance and came to him. As it came within reaching distance, the man lost his control. His arms flashed out to the dog, and he experienced genuine surprise when he discovered that his hands could not clutch, that there was neither bend nor feeling in the fingers. He had
forgotten for the moment that they were frozen 7
and that they were freezing more and more. All this happened quickly, and before the animal could get away, he encircled its body with his arms. He sat down in the snow, and in this fashion held the dog, while it snarled and whined and struggled.

◆ Build Vocabulary

peremptorily (pər empʹ tər ə lē) *adj.*: Decisively; commandingly

Comprehension Check ☑

5 How does the man learn that the sensation in his hand is the result of his hand being burned by the flame? *He can smell the burning flesh.*

Customize for *Less Proficient Readers*

6 Have students summarize what is happening here between the man and the dog. Guide them to understand that the man is making an awkward, desperate attempt to capture the dog, kill it, and use its body warmth to undo his numbness, and that his movements and sounds make the dog apprehensive.

◆ Reading Strategy

7 **Predict** Ask students to predict whether the man will survive and whether the dog will. Students should support both predictions with details from the story. *Based on the fact that the man has no means by which to start a fire, it is unlikely that he will survive. The dog, on the other hand, is likely to survive because of its protective coat and strong survival skills.*

Analyze Literary Criticism

Arthur Calder-Marshall, in his Introduction to a collection of Jack London's works, commented: "Jack London's stories still compel the reader to read on. He learned to tell a tale, he says, when he was bumming across the United States . . . . He tells his stories like a tramp. At the end you are left with no distillation of truth, no new vision of life. But you have experienced something vicariously . . . ." After students have finished reading the story, share Calder-Marshall's remarks with them. Make sure they understand the meaning of the words *distillation* and *vicariously.* Invite students to discuss what Calder-Marshall might have meant by saying that Jack London "tells his stories like a tramp." How do they feel about this remark? Do they think he means this as a compliment or a criticism? Then have them answer the following questions in their journals:

1. On the basis of your experience, do you agree with Calder-Marshall that a Jack London story "compel[s] the reader to read on"? Do you agree that "To Build a Fire" leaves the reader "with no distillation of truth, no new vision of life"? Explain. *Students' responses will vary, but should be supported by examples from the text.*
2. Do you agree that after reading a London story you have "experienced something vicariously"? If so, describe what you have experienced and how it felt. If you disagree with the critic's observation, explain why. *Students may say that they vicariously experienced the main character's anxiety, fear, solitude, increasing cold, despair, and even his gradual drifting off into death.*

❶ **Clarification** Point out that the man's disorientation is a result of severe hypothermia. (Refer to the bottom note on page 558.)

◆ Reading Strategy

❷ **Predict** Students might say that the man will die because his hypothermia is too severe and the camp is too far away. Others might suggest that there's a hope that someone will catch up to him on the trail and save him.

◆ Literary Focus

❸ **Conflict** Ask students to describe what they know of the man's will to live. *Students may say that the man has a very strong will to live as evidenced by his frantic efforts to stop from freezing and his attempts to think of things other than death.*

❹ **Clarification** Point out to students that the man is no longer shivering even though he is faced with extreme cold. This behavior is another symptom of severe hypothermia; the man's condition is worsening.

Customize for
Less Proficient Readers

❺ Guide students to recognize the change the man undergoes here; for the first time he accepts the inevitability of his death.

Customize for
AP Students

❻ Ask students to ponder Jack London's attitude toward animal instinct. Ask them to explain what the dog represents in this story. *Students may say that London places high value on natural instinct as a survival mechanism. They may suggest that the dog symbolizes that despite man's follies (like prospecting in inhospitable lands), life goes on, instinctually.*

But it was all he could do, hold its body encircled in his arms and sit there. He realized that he could not kill the dog. There was no way to do it. With his helpless hands he could neither draw nor hold his sheath-knife nor throttle the animal. He released it, and it plunged wildly away, with tail between its legs, and still snarling. It halted forty feet away and surveyed him curiously, with ears sharply pricked forward. ❶ The man looked down at his hands in order to locate them, and found them hanging on the ends of his arms. It struck him as curious that one should have to use his eyes in order to find out where his hands were. He began threshing his arms back and forth, beating the mittened hands against his sides. He did this for five minutes, violently, and his heart pumped enough blood up to the surface to put a stop to his shivering. But no sensation was aroused in the hands. He had an impression that they hung like weights on the ends of his arms, but when he tried to run the impression down, he could not find it.

A certain fear of death, dull and oppressive, came to him. This fear quickly became poignant as he realized that it was no longer a mere matter of freezing his fingers and toes, or of losing his hands and feet, but that it was a matter of life and death with the chances against him. This threw him into a panic, and he turned and ran up the creek-bed along the old, dim trail. The dog joined in behind and kept up with him. He ran blindly, without intention, in fear such as he had never known in his life. Slowly, as he plowed and floundered through the snow, he began to see things again—the banks of the creek, the old timber jams, the leafless aspens, and the sky. The running made him feel better. He did not shiver. Maybe, if he ran on, his feet would thaw out; and, anyway, if he ran far enough, he would reach camp and the boys. Without doubt he would lose some fingers and toes and some of his face; but the boys would take care of him, and save the rest of him when he got there. ❸ And at the same time there was another thought in his mind that said he would never get to the camp and the boys; that it was too many miles away, that the freezing had too great a start on him, and that he would soon be stiff and dead. This thought he kept in the background and refused to consider. Sometimes it pushed itself forward and demanded to be heard, but he thrust it back and strove to think of other things.

❷ **◆ Reading Strategy** Does the man still have a chance for survival? Explain why or why not.

It struck him as curious that he could run at all on feet so frozen that he could not feel them when they struck the earth and took the weight of his body. He seemed to himself to skim along above the surface, and to have no connection with the earth. Somewhere he had once seen a winged Mercury,[6] and he wondered if Mercury felt as he felt when skimming over the earth.

His theory of running until he reached camp and the boys had one flaw in it: he lacked the endurance. Several times he stumbled, and finally he tottered, crumpled up, and fell. When he tried to rise, he failed. He must sit and rest, he decided, and next time he would merely walk and keep on going. As he sat and regained his breath, he noted that he was feeling quite warm and comfortable. ❹ He was not shivering, and it even seemed that a warm glow had come to his chest and trunk. And yet, when he touched his nose or cheeks, there was no sensation. Running would not thaw them out. Nor would it thaw out his hands and feet. Then the thought came to him that the frozen portions of his body must be extending. He tried to keep this thought down, to forget it, to think of something else; he was aware of the panicky feeling that it caused, and he was afraid of the panic. But the thought asserted itself, and persisted, until it produced a vision of his body totally frozen. This was too much, and he made another wild run along the trail. Once he slowed down to a walk, but the thought of the freezing extending itself made him run again.

And all the time the dog ran with him, at his heels. When he fell down a second time, it curled its tail over its forefeet and sat in front of him, facing him, curiously eager and intent. The warmth and security of the animal angered him, and he cursed it till it flattened down its

6. **Mercury:** From Roman mythology, the wing-footed messenger of the gods.

Reteach

If some students need help understanding the concept of conflict in this story, they may benefit from the use of a graphic organizer. Remind them that conflict is a common ingredient in fictional plots, and that it follows a pattern: the struggles, mistakes, or problems of the main character accumulate, becoming more and more complicated or serious, until a crisis or particular event causes a crisis, or turning point (called the climax), in the sequence of events. The events following this turning point resolve the conflict, by gradually or suddenly guiding the action to an end. Show students the graphic organizer below and suggest that they copy it. On the left side, have them list the events leading up to the event which is the turning point, or climax, of the main character's conflict in "To Build a Fire." On the right side, have them list the events that follow this turning point.

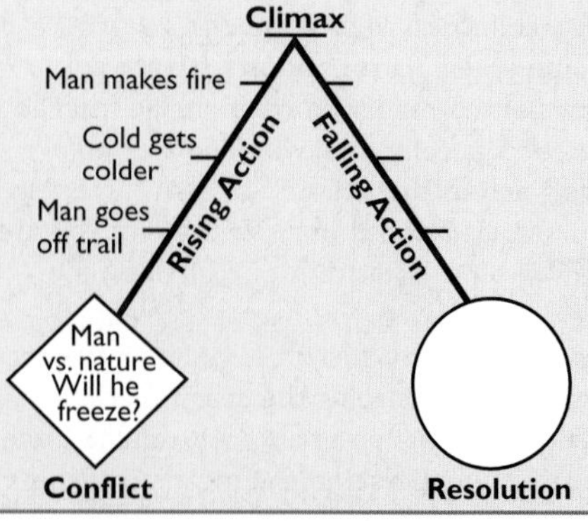

ears appeasingly. This time the shivering came more quickly upon the man. He was losing in his battle with the frost. It was creeping into his body from all sides. The thought of it drove him on, but he ran no more than a hundred feet, when he staggered and pitched headlong. It was his last panic. When he had recovered his breath and control, he sat up and entertained in his mind the conception of meeting death with dignity. However, the conception did not come to him in such terms. His idea of it was that he had been making a fool of himself, running around like a chicken with its head cut
5 off—such was the simile that occurred to him. Well, he was bound to freeze anyway, and he might as well take it decently. With this newfound peace of mind came the first glimmerings of drowsiness. A good idea, he thought, to sleep off to death. It was like taking an anaesthetic. Freezing was not so bad as people thought. There were lots worse ways to die.

He pictured the boys finding his body next day. Suddenly he found himself with them, coming along the trail and looking for himself. And, still with them, he came around a turn in the trail and found himself lying in the snow. He did not belong with himself any more, for even then he was out of himself; standing with the boys and looking at himself in the snow. It certainly was cold, was his thought. When he got back to the States he could tell the folks what real cold was. He drifted on from this to a vision of the old-timer on Sulphur Creek. He could see him quite clearly, warm and comfortable, and smoking a pipe.

"You were right, old hoss; you were right," the man mumbled to the old-timer of Sulphur Creek.

Then the man drowsed off into what seemed to him the most comfortable and satisfying sleep he had ever known. The dog sat facing him and waiting. The brief day drew to a close in a long, slow twilight. There were no signs of a fire to be made, and, besides, never in the dog's experience had it known a man to sit like that in the snow and make no fire. As the twilight drew on, its eager yearning for the fire mastered it, and with a great lifting and shifting of forefeet, it whined softly, then flattened 6
its ears down in anticipation of being chidden[7] by the man. But the man remained silent. Later, the dog whined loudly. And still later it crept close to the man and caught the scent of death. This made the animal bristle and back away. A little longer it delayed, howling under the stars that leaped and danced and shone brightly in the cold sky. Then it turned and trotted up the trail in the direction of the camp it knew, where were the other food providers and fire providers.

7. **chidden:** Scolded.

Guide for Responding

◆ *Literature and Your Life*

Reader's Response Could you imagine yourself falling into the same circumstances as the man? How could you avoid them?

Thematic Focus Adventurers seek different things when they challenge themselves. Are the risks worth the possible consequences?

Group Discussion With a group, discuss your attitudes toward the positives and negatives of high-risk sports and adventures.

☑ Check Your Comprehension

1. What advice from an old-timer does the man choose to ignore?
2. (a) What traps does the man try to avoid? (b) What happens despite his precautions?
3. What careless mistake does the man make when he tries to build a fire to thaw out his feet?
4. Why is the man unable to build another fire?
5. What happens to the man and the dog at the end of the story?

Beyond the Selection

FURTHER READING

Other Works by Jack London

The Call of the Wild
The Sea Wolf
White Fang
Martin Eden

Other Works With the Theme of Battling the Elements

The Perfect Storm, Sebastian Junger
"The Open Boat," Stephen Crane

INTERNET

You and your students can find additional information about Jack London on the Internet. We suggest the following site. Please be aware, however, that sites may have changed from the time we published this information. For biographical information, images of Jack London, documents, some of his writings, a bibliography, and research aids, go to **http://sunsite.berkeley.edu/London/**

We *strongly recommend* that you preview the site before you send students to it.

Reinforce and Extend

Customize for
Less Proficient Readers
Ask students to summarize, chronologically, the man's fatal errors. *Students may say that he chose to travel alone, that he misgauged the temperature, that he stepped through the ice, and that he built his fire under a tree.*

Enrichment To extend students' knowledge of the powerful elements, use the Media Connections: Films about Survival page in ***Beyond Literature*** (p. 35).

Answers

◆ *Literature and Your Life*

Reader's Response Students may respond that they would never have set out alone or would have chosen not to travel in such harsh weather.

Thematic Focus Students may reply that much depends on what is to be gained by taking the risk, and how dangerous the consequences. For some, the thrill of forging new frontiers may outweigh the risks.

☑ Check Your Comprehension

1. No one should travel alone in the Klondike if the temperature is colder than fifty below zero.
2. (a) The man carefully avoids the hidden pools under the thin skins of ice that are covered by snow. (b) He falls though the ice that covers the stream he is following and wets his legs.
3. He builds the fire under a tree that has snow on its boughs, and the snow falls down, putting out the fire.
4. His hands are too numb to rebuild the fire.
5. The man freezes to death, and the dog makes his way to the camp.

Guide for Responding (continued)

◆ Critical Thinking

INTERPRET

1. Why does the extreme cold "make no impression" on the man? **[Deduce]**

2. Compare the dog's relationship with nature to the man's relationship with nature. Which is better equipped to survive? **[Compare]**

3. Why might London have chosen not to give the man in the story a name? **[Speculate]**

4. What does the story suggest about humanity's place in the natural world? **[Draw Conclusions]**

EVALUATE

5. At one point, the man gets angry and curses his fate. Is the outcome of the story due to fate or something within the man? Explain. **[Evaluate]**

EXTEND

6. How might the outcome of the story be different if it were set in today's world? Why? **[Connect]**

◆ Reading Strategy

PREDICT

Jack London includes a variety of clues that can help you **predict**, or make educated guesses about, the outcome of the story.

1. How do the man's recollections of his conversation with the old man from Sulphur Creek help you predict the end of the story?

2. (a) At what point did you first predict that the man would not survive his journey? (b) On what clues did you base your prediction?

◆ Literary Focus

CONFLICT

Conflict—a struggle between two opposing forces—may be **internal,** occurring in the mind of a character, or **external,** occurring between a character and society, a character and nature, or between a character and fate.

1. What external conflict is central to the plot of "To Build a Fire"?

2. How does the conflict intensify as the plot unfolds and how is it resolved?

3. Describe the internal conflict that develops as the story progresses.

◆ Build Vocabulary

USING THE LATIN ROOT *-ject-*

Each word below contains the Latin root *-ject-*, meaning "to throw." Use the clues to match each word with the situation to which it applies.

1. reject (*re* = again; back)

2. object (*ob* = toward; over; against)

3. conjecture (*con* = with; *ure* = noun of action)

4. abject (*ab* = away from)

a. you throw your thoughts in with others
b. you throw back fish that are too small
c. you speak out against something
d. you feel this way when your friends shun you

USING THE WORD BANK: Sentence Completions

Copy this passage. Then fill in the blanks with the appropriate vocabulary words from the Word Bank.

A lightning storm in the parched woodland sparked a ___?___. The mild-mannered fire chief acted with ___?___ speed and authority, ___?___ ordering all firefighters to work round the clock, though his estimates of how long it would take to overcome the fire were ___?___, at best.

◆ Grammar and Style

ADVERB CLAUSES

Adverb clauses modify verbs, adjectives, or other adverbs, explaining *how, where, when, why, to what extent,* or *under what circumstances.*

Practice Identify the adverb clause in each item and indicate whether it tells *where, when, why, how, to what extent,* or *under what circumstances.*

1. North and south, as far as the eye could see, it was unbroken white . . .

2. A foot of snow had fallen since the last sled had passed over.

3. He made a new foundation for a fire, this time in the open, where no treacherous tree could blot it out.

4. If he kept it up, he would certainly be with the boys by six.

Writing Application Write a brief description of extreme weather. Use at least four adverb clauses.

Answers

◆ Critical Thinking

1. The man does not have the imagination to understand the significance of the cold or to imagine the possible consequences of traveling in such weather.
2. The dog instinctively understands how to respond to nature. The man sees nature as a problem his mind can solve as long as he "keeps his head."
3. Suggested response: London did not name his character because the man serves as a symbol for the human desire to control or disregard the power of nature.
4. Students may respond that the man's own character flaws—lack of imagination, overconfidence, unwillingness to listen to others—contribute to his downfall. Had he heeded the advice he was given, he would probably have survived the elements.
5. Suggested response: It suggests that humanity cannot control nature and must respect it. Nature is a much more powerful force than humanity.
6. Students may suggest that search teams might be able to rescue the man.

◆ Reading Strategy

1. Because the old-timer's warnings are based on years of experience, readers know that the man is running a terrible risk by ignoring them. Each time he recalls the old-timer's advice and laughs, it is a reminder of the fatal danger he faces.
2. Some students may respond that they knew the man was doomed when his fire was blotted out by the snow and the narrator says: *It was as though he had just heard his own sentence of death.* Others, alerted by the descriptions of the dog's apprehensions, may have felt from the beginning that the man would not make it to the camp.

◆ Literary Focus

1. The conflict is between man and nature.
2. The forces of nature have more and more of an effect on the man as the story progresses.
3. The man's lack of judgment and overconfidence conflict with his genuine fear for his own safety as he battles to stay calm in the face of rising panic.

◆ Build Vocabulary

Using the Word Root *-ject-*
1. b 2. c 3. a 4. d

Using the Word Bank: Sentence Completions
conflagration; unwonted; peremptorily; conjectural

◆ Grammar and Style

1. as far as the eye could see; *to what extent*
2. since the last sled had passed over; *when*
3. where no treacherous tree could blot it out; *where*
4. If he kept it up; *under what circumstances*

Grammar Reinforcement

For additional instruction and practice, use the practice page on adverb clauses in the *Writer's Solution Grammar Practice Book* (p. 36). For practice using clauses to vary sentence length and structure, use the Varying Sentence Structure Lesson in the Writing Style unit of the **Language Lab CD-ROM.**

Build Your Portfolio

Idea Bank

Writing

1. Diary Entry Imagine that you are the man in the story, keeping a diary of your journey. Write the last entry that you'd be capable of creating.

2. Sequel Add another episode to the story in which you describe the dog's journey to the camp and the reactions of the campers on seeing him.

3. Character Analysis London tells us little about the main character of his story, but the man's decisions and actions are revealing. Write an analysis of the man's character, citing examples from the story to support your conclusions.

Speaking, Listening, and Viewing

4. Enactment If the dog could voice its thoughts about the man's behavior, what would it say? Write and present your version of what the dog might be thinking as a particular scene from the story unfolds. **[Performing Arts Link]**

5. Oral Storytelling Given his warnings, how might the old-timer from Sulphur Creek have reacted to the news of the man's death? Tell the tale of the man's fate as the old-timer would have told it by the campfire. **[Performing Arts Link]**

Researching and Representing

6. Graphic Display Long-term survival in the cold is very different from staying warm on short trips or camping. Research a cold-climate culture to learn more about living in extreme conditions. Create a poster highlighting issues of warmth, food, and resources.

7. Pamphlet The man in the story died from hypothermia, or subnormal body temperature. Research this condition, then create a booklet of tips and guidelines for avoiding hypothermia and detecting its warning signs. **[Health Link]**

Online Activity www.phlit.phschool.com

Guided Writing Lesson

Literary Analysis

Although "To Build a Fire" remains a classic story, many of London's works are no longer as highly regarded. Public opinion of fiction is often swayed by critiques and literary analyses. A **literary analysis** explores how the different elements of a piece of literature—such as plot, setting, characters, point of view, and theme—work together to convey a message or create an overall effect. Write a literary analysis in which you explain the message that London conveys in "To Build a Fire" and discuss how the various story elements contribute to this message.

Writing Skills Focus: Elaborate to Support an Argument

Unlike a book report that simply restates what happened in a literary work, a literary analysis digs beneath the surface to present an individual interpretation of the work or an aspect of the work. This interpretation forms the thesis, or main point, of the analysis. To write an effective literary analysis effective, you have to present an argument to back up the thesis. **Elaborate on each point in your argument** by providing details and passages from the literature that back up what you are saying.

Prewriting First review the story to identify its message. What is London saying about the relationship between humanity and nature? Gather details and passages that support your interpretation.

Drafting Start with an introduction in which you state your thesis in a single sentence and outline each of your main points. Focus each body paragraph on one main point. Cite supporting passages and details from the story.

Revising Read your draft as though seeing it for the first time. Is your thesis clear? Is your support convincing? Look for opportunities to elaborate on your key points.

Idea Bank

Customizing for
Performance Levels
Following are suggestions for matching Idea Bank topics with your students' performance levels:
Less Advanced Students: 1, 5,
Average Students: 2, 4, 6
More Advanced Students: 3, 7

Customizing for
Learning Modalities
Following are suggestions for matching Idea Bank topics with your students' learning modalities:
Verbal/Linguistic: 4, 5
Body/Kinesthetic: 6
Logical/Mathematical: 6, 7

Guided Writing Lesson

For more instruction on prewriting, elaboration, and revision, see *Prentice Hall Writing and Grammar*.

Writers at Work Videodisc
Have students view the videodisc segment (Ch. 7) featuring literary agent Theresa Park to see how she responds to literature. Have students discuss how she reviews and evaluates the literature she receives for consideration.

Play frames 22513 to 31258

Writing Lab CD-ROM
Have students work in the tutorial on Response to Literature to complete their literary analyses. Follow these steps:

1. Have students use the Sunburst Diagram to gather details.
2. To help students organize the elements they will cover in an analysis, encourage students to use the Topic Web in the Focusing Your Response section.
3. Have students draft on computer and use the Interactive Self-Evaluation Checklist to aid revision.

ASSESSMENT OPTIONS

Formal Assessment, Selection Test, pp. 167–169, and Assessment Resources Software. The selection test is designed so that it can be easily customized to the performance levels of your students.

Alternative Assessment, p. 35, includes options for less advanced students, more advanced students, verbal/linguistic learners, bodily/kinesthetic learners, and visual/spatial learners.

PORTFOLIO ASSESSMENT
Use the following rubrics in the ***Alternative Assessment*** booklet to assess student writing:
Diary Entry: Narrative Based on Personal Experience Rubric, p. 111
Sequel: Fictional Narrative Rubric, p. 110
Character Analysis: Literary Analysis/Interpretation Rubric, p. 127
Guided Writing Lesson: Literary Analysis/Interpretation Rubric, p. 127

Prepare and Engage

LESSON OBJECTIVES

1. **To develop vocabulary and word identification skills**
   - Latin Suffixes: *-ance* and *-ence*
   - Using the Word Bank: Sentence Completions
2. **To use a variety of reading strategies to comprehend folk literature**
   - Reading Strategy: Recognize Cultural Details
3. **To express and support responses to the text**
   - Critical Thinking
   - Idea Bank: Dialogue
   - Idea Bank: Prosecution Argument
   - Idea Bank: Fantasy Creature
   - Idea Bank: Analytic Essay
4. **To analyze literary elements**
   - Literary Focus: Folk Literature
   - Compare Literary Works
5. **To read in order to research self-selected and assigned topics**
   - Idea Bank: Oral Report
   - Idea Bank: Western Ballads
   - Idea Bank: Graphic Display
6. **To use recursive writing processes to write a legend about a heroic figure**
   - Guided Writing Lesson
7. **To increase knowledge of the rules of grammar and usage**
   - Grammar and Style: Compound Predicates

Test Preparation

Reading Comprehension: Context (ATE, p. 569)

The teaching tips and sample test item in this workshop support the instruction and practice in the unit workshop:

Reading Comprehension: Using Context (ATE, p. 631)

Guide for Interpreting

Oral Tradition: Tales of the Old West

Tall tales with larger-than-life-heroes, folk tales, and ballads are all part of the oral tradition—tales that have been passed down from generation to generation. In America, this oral tradition has preserved myths of Native Americans, folk tales, spirituals, legends, and ballads. All were originally spoken and memorized rather than written down. Most oral works have changed over time as their tellers elaborate, exaggerate, and add and subtract details.The folk literature that follows includes a folk tale, a legend, and a ballad that will give you a glimpse into life in the Old West.

Folk Tales Folk tales are traditional stories, often based on fanciful heroes with mythical qualities. Pecos Bill, whom you'll read about here, Paul Bunyan, and Febold Feboldson are a few well-known subjects of folk tales. Folk tale heroes are frequently common people who display extraordinary strength and perform great acts of courage.

Courtesy of the Museum of Texas Tech University

Legends Legends are traditional stories that often deal with a particular person, such as King Arthur or Gregorio Cortez (gre gōr´ ē ō kôr tez´), the Mexican hero you'll soon read about. Legends typically reflect the cultural values of the people who originally told them. For example, "The Legend of Gregorio Cortez," told in the form of a ballad, gives you a taste of what life was like for Mexicans living in Texas at the beginning of the 1900's. By emphasizing the heroic qualities of their subjects, legends have immortalized many figures who were famous in their own time, such as Daniel Boone, Davy Crockett, Calamity Jane, and Gregorio Cortez.

Ballads Ballads are song-like poems that tell a story, often dealing with adventure and romance. Folk ballads, such as "The Streets of Laredo," which features an unnamed gunman, originated in the oral tradition and were passed down over time. Ballads usually feature simple language, four- or six-line stanzas, rhyme, and regular meter—all characteristics of "The Streets of Laredo."

◆ Background for Understanding

HISTORY: GREGORIO CORTEZ

"The Legend of Gregorio Cortez" centers on a Mexican man who became a famous fugitive in Texas at the turn of the century, a time when tensions around the United States–Texas border ran high, fueled by the lynching of Mexicans. On June 12, 1901, Cortez shot and killed Sheriff Brack Morris in retribution for Morris's having killed Cotez's brother while trying to arrest him for a crime he didn't commit. In his flight to the Mexican border, Cortez walked more than 100 miles and rode another 400 miles—killing another sheriff along the way. Three hundred men searched for Cortez with no luck. Finally, he was captured, exhausted and out of ammunition. He was acquitted for killing the first sheriff, but sentenced to life for killing the second. After serving twelve years for his crime, Cortez was pardoned by the governor of Texas in 1913.

Prentice Hall Literature Program Resources

REINFORCE / RETEACH / EXTEND

Selection Support Pages
Build Vocabulary: Suffixes: *-ance* and *-ence*, p. 167
Grammar and Style: Compound Predicates, p. 168
Reading Strategy: Recognize Cultural Details, p. 169
Literary Focus: Folk Literature, p. 170

Strategies for Diverse Student Needs, p. 36

Beyond Literature
Humanities Connection: Art, p. 36

Formal Assessment Selection Test, pp. 170–172; Assessment Resources Software

Alternative Assessment, p. 36

Writing and Language Transparencies
Cubing Organizer, p. 75

Resource Pro CD-ROM

Listening to Literature Audiocassettes

◆ Pecos Bill Becomes a Coyote ◆ The Legend of Gregorio Cortez ◆ The Streets of Laredo

◆ Literature and Your Life

CONNECT YOUR EXPERIENCE

Think about your favorite cultural heroes. Do they stand for your idea of America today? Frequently faced with danger, the folk heroes of the American West exhibited courage and strength. As you read, compare their behavior with that of the people you think of as heroes. Ask yourself whether the people you admire are likely to become tomorrow's legendary heroes.

Journal Writing List characteristics that you think would make someone a hero of legendary proportions today.

THEMATIC FOCUS: FORGING NEW FRONTIERS

The many dangers awaiting frontier settlers often required the bold and heroic actions that inspired much of our culture's folk literature.

◆ Build Vocabulary

LATIN SUFFIXES: *-ance* AND *-ence*

The Latin suffixes *-ance* and *-ence,* which indicate a quality or state of being, change adjectives into nouns. For words ending in *-ent* or *-ant,* drop the *t* and add only *ce*. For example, the adjective *defiant,* meaning "refusing to submit," becomes the noun *defiance*—a quality Bull Rattlesnake displays in this tale about Pecos Bill.

WORD BANK

Preview these words from the selections.

defiance
pall

◆ Grammar and Style

COMPOUND PREDICATES

Picture a storyteller spinning a long, drawn-out tale. The sentences might well include some **compound predicates**—two or more verbs that share the same subject. Using compound predicates avoids the necessity of having to repeat the subject. The following examples of compound predicates come from "Pecos Bill Becomes a Coyote."

- He *became* a member of a pack of wild coyotes, and . . . *believed* that his name was Cropear . . .
- Later he *discovered* that he was a human being and very shortly thereafter *became* the greatest cowboy . . .

◆ Literary Focus

FOLK LITERATURE

Folk literature—stories and ballads handed down orally—originated in a time before electronic media or the printing press. This literature was often passed along by people who did not read or write. Most folk literature is not attributed to any one person because the first teller of the tale has long been forgotten. However, people have written down particular versions of many tales, making them permanent. They do not tell the tale for the first time, but *retell* it. James Bowman, for example, retells "Pecos Bill," stamping his own special mark on this famous folk tale.

◆ Reading Strategy

RECOGNIZE CULTURAL DETAILS

Just by looking up from this page, you'll notice **cultural details** that root you to your time and place. Perhaps you see a computer. The mention of a computer in writing is a cultural detail because it reveals something about modern society—just as mention of a fife in "The Streets of Laredo" reveals something about the culture of Laredo at the time the ballad was written. Notice other cultural details that show what life was like during the late nineteenth century.

Interest Grabber A film version of *The Legend of Gregorio Cortez* was produced in 1982 for public television. The film, which stars Edward James Olmos as Cortez, presents an authentic retelling of the story. Show students a piece of it, such as the scene where Cortez escapes his pursuers by leaping over a corral. Discuss the scene with students. Ask them to identify the characteristics that make Cortez larger than life. Tell students the folk literature they are about to read presents characters whose abilities make them legendary.

Customize for
Less Proficient Readers
To help readers make visual connections to the western setting, show them photos or pictures of things associated with the West that are mentioned in the pieces. For example, show them what sagebrush, corrals, covered wagons, mesquite, and pronghorn antelope look like.

Customize for
AP Students
Guide students to compare and contrast these pieces with legends and myths they know that originate in other times or from other places. Have them look for common threads and identify any unique features of the selections in this grouping.

Customize for
English Language Learners
These students may have little familiarity with the genre of "cowboy tales" and with the history of the American West. Provide background information—in the form of pictures as well as explanation—and help them recognize revealing cultural details.

Customize for
Interpersonal Learners
Students may enjoy reading these tales aloud in groups. Encourage readers to read dramatically in an attempt to re-create the flavor of the Old West.

Test Preparation Workshop

Reading Comprehension: Context The reading sections of standardized reading tests require students to use context clues to determine the meaning of unfamiliar words. Students can practice this skill with the following sample test item.

He led Cropear to the berries that were good to eat, and dug up roots that were sweet and spicy. He showed the boy how to break open the small nuts from the <u>piñon.</u>

In this passage, a <u>piñon</u> is most likely a —

A tree
B root
C berry
D dirt

The fact that a piñon has nuts is a context clue that it is a tree or a shrub. Students should be able to determine that *A* is the correct answer.

Develop Understanding

One-Minute Insight This folk tale, one of the many that feature the adventures of Pecos Bill, describes how the young Bill was saved by coyotes and then raised as one.

◆ Background for Understanding

Geography Tell students that the Pecos River flows south from the mountains east of Santa Fe, New Mexico, through Carlsbad, New Mexico, and then into West Texas. There, it flows in a southeasterly direction until it empties into the Rio Grande on the Texas-Mexico border.

◆ Literary Focus

❶ Folk Literature Guide students to notice this typical exaggerated beginning of a tall tale. Point out how the last line indicates the oral roots of the tale.

◆ Literary Focus

❷ Folk Literature Students can notice the exaggeration here as another clue that what follows is a folk tale. Although pioneer families were large as a rule, eighteen children is an exaggeration, as is the volume of their *medley of noises* that drowned out the sound of thunder.

◆ Reading Strategy

❸ Recognize Cultural Details Guide students to understand that in the course of a dangerous and rigorous journey west, sickness and accidents were common, and that families had to absorb tragedy and move on with the other wagons.

◆ Grammar and Style

❹ Compound Predicates Ask students to identify the subject *He,* and all parts of the compound predicate *sniffed, yelped, ran* in this sentence.

Customize for
Gifted/Talented Students
Ask students to consider how they would change this folk tale if they were retelling it. What details and events would they delete, add, or exaggerate?

Pecos Bill Becomes a Coyote

RETOLD BY JAMES CLOYD BOWMAN

Pecos Bill had the strangest and most exciting experience any boy ever had. He became a member of a pack of wild Coyotes, and until he was a grown man, believed that his name was Cropear, and that he was a full-blooded Coyote. Later he discovered that he was a human being and very shortly thereafter became the greatest cowboy of all time. This is how it all came about.

Pecos Bill's family was migrating westward through Texas in the early days, in an old covered wagon with wheels made from cross sections of a sycamore log. His father and mother were riding in the front seat, and his father was driving a wall-eyed, spavined[1] roan horse and a red and white spotted milch cow hitched side by side. The eighteen children in the back of the wagon were making such a medley of noises that their mother said it wasn't possible even to hear thunder.

Just as the wagon was rattling down to the ford across the Pecos River, the rear left wheel bounced over a great piece of rock, and Bill, his red hair bristling like porcupine quills, rolled out of the rear of the wagon, and landed, up to his neck, in a pile of loose sand. He was only four years old at the time, and he lay dazed until the wagon had crossed the river and disappeared into the sage brush. It wasn't until his mother rounded up the family for the noonday meal that Bill was missed. The last anyone remembered seeing him was just before they had forded the river.

The mother and eight or ten of the older children hurried back to the river and hunted everywhere, but they could find no trace of the lost boy. When evening came, they were forced to go back to the covered wagon, and later, to continue their journey without him. Ever after, when they thought of Bill, they remembered the river, and so they naturally came to speak of him as Pecos Bill.

What had happened to Bill was this. He had strayed off into the mesquite,[2] and a few hours later was found by a wise old Coyote, who was the undisputed leader of the Loyal and Approved Packs of the Pecos and Rio Grande Valleys. He was, in fact, the Granddaddy of the entire race of Coyotes, and so his followers, out of affection to him, called him Grandy.

When he accidentally met Bill, Grandy was curious, but shy. He sniffed and he yelped, and he ran this way and that, the better to get the scent, and to make sure there was no danger. After a while he came quite near, sat up on his haunches, and waited to see what the boy would do. Bill trotted up to Grandy and began running his hands through the long shaggy hair.

1. **spavined** (spav´ ind) *adj.*: Afflicted with spavin, a horse disease that can cause lameness.

2. **mesquite** (mes kēt´) *n.*: Thorny trees or shrubs commonly found in the southwestern United States and Mexico.

▶ **Critical Viewing** How does this story's description of Pecos Bill as a child hint at the extraordinary adult he was to become? **[Connect]**

Block Scheduling Strategies

Consider these suggestions to take advantage of extended class time:

- Introduce folk tales, legends, and ballads by discussing the section titled Oral Tradition: Tales of the Old West (p. 568). Ask students to name additional folk tales, legends, or ballads.
- Suggest that students research western folk literature on the Internet before or after they read.
- Play one of more of the audiocassettes of the selections. Have students discuss how listening to the selections increases their appreciation of cultural details and of the characteristics of folk literature.
- Set up peer discussion groups in which students can answer and talk about the Critical Thinking questions (pp. 573, 576).
- Focus attention on the Guided Writing Lesson (p. 577). Before students begin, discuss how using vivid details and exaggeration makes writing more entertaining. Guide students to look for specific examples of this kind of elaboration in the selections.

▶Critical Viewing◀

5 Connect The story's description of Pecos Bill as a child hints at the extraordinary adult he was to become by showing that Pecos Bill was not only raised by the coyotes, but was also able to do learn to live as a coyote lives in the wilderness. Pecos Bill learned, among other things, to hunt for food, to twirl his body, and to stand in the "silent, rigid pose of invisibility."

Customize for *Visual/Spatial Learners*

To build background about the American West, you might show your students pictures of paintings and sculptures done by artists who captured the images of the Old West.

Ask students what images come to mind when they think of the Old West. The best known artist among those who focused on the Old West is Frederic Remington (1861–1909). His illustration titled "In a Stampede" is shown on this page. Both a painter and a sculptor, Remington painted and molded images of the romanticized West of the cowboy, the Native American, the bronco buster, the soldier, and the gunfighter. Americans in Remington's time thirsted for the West, a place where life was unique. For this reason, Remington's art works were immensely popular. By 1888, he was one of the nation's most popular magazine illustrators. Visiting the West on an annual basis for inspiration, Remington noticed as time went by that the Old West was fast disappearing, that townspeople in derby hats had replaced the western individualist. For Remington, the loss of the Old West was a sad one. While time marched on, Remington's art crystallized a way of life that had vanished forever.

Humanities: Art

In a Stampede (illustration), 1888, by Frederic Remington.

Through his paintings and sculptures, Remington preserved a unique era of American history. For more on Remington's life and work, see the Customize for Visual/Spatial Learners note on this page.

This action-packed piece of art shows a cowboy of the Old West on horseback in the midst of a stampeding herd of livestock. The picture illustrates the rugged and at times dangerous life of the cowboy, having to stay in the saddle for long periods of time herding cattle and coping with potentially dangerous situations, such as stampedes.

Use these questions for discussion:

1. What dangers does the cowboy in this painting face? *Dangers include a riding accident and the possible stampeding of the cattle.*
2. What character traits of the real cowboy are the same as that of Pecos Bill? *Like Pecos Bill, a real cowboy is brave, physically fit, and dedicated to his rugged work.*

▶Critical Viewing◀

❶ Analyze The coyote shows confidence, dignity, and poise—traits that are also human attributes.

❷ Clarification Explain that coyotes, who are members of the dog family, have large ears, and that "Cropear" (Crop-ear) is a humorous way to describe humans, who have smaller ears.

◆Reading Strategy

❸ Recognize Cultural Details Guide students to appreciate that animals and humans alike make use of what their environment provides in the way of food, medicine, and shelter; their survival demands it.

◆Reading Strategy

❹ Recognize Cultural Details Students may say that survival on the frontier demanded cooperation, knowledge of how to live off the land, and the preparedness and care needed to face its many dangers.

Enrichment The coyote is a member of a dog family that is noted for its distinctive nocturnal howl. Coyotes live in the United States, Canada, and Mexico. The fur of the coyote ranges from light yellow to brownish yellow. Standing about two feet high and weighing about twenty-five pounds, coyotes live alone, in pairs, or sometimes in larger groups. Coyotes eat rabbits, rodents—such as mice, gophers, squirrels, and prairie dogs—the remains of large dead animals—such as cattle and deer—and juniper berries, watermelons, and other fruits.

▲ **Critical Viewing** What human personality traits are reflected in this coyote's face? **[Analyze]** ❶

❷ "What a nice doggy you are," he repeated again and again.

"Yes, and what a nice Cropear you are," yelped Grandy joyously.

And so, ever after, the Coyotes called the child Cropear.

Grandy was much pleased with his find and so, by running ahead and stopping and barking softly, he led the boy to the jagged side of Cabezon, or the Big Head, as it was called. This was a towering mass of mountain that rose abruptly, as if by magic, from the prairie. Around the base of this mountain the various families of the Loyal and Approved Packs had burrowed out their dens.

❸ Here, far away from the nearest human dwelling, Grandy made a home for Cropear, and taught him all the knowledge of the wild out-of-doors. He led Cropear to the berries that were good to eat, and dug up roots that were sweet and spicy. He showed the boy how to break open the small nuts from the piñon;[3] and when Cropear wanted a drink, he led him to a vigorous young mother coyote who gave him of her milk. Cropear thus drank the very life blood of a thousand generations of wild life and became a native beast of the prairie, without at all knowing that he was a man-child.

Grandy became his teacher and schooled him in the knowledge that had been handed down through thousands of generations of the Pack's life. He taught Cropear the many signal calls, and the code of right and wrong, and the gentle art of loyalty to the leader. He also trained him to leap long distances and to dance; and to flip-flop and to twirl his body so fast that the eye could not follow his movements. And most important of all, he instructed him in the silent, rigid pose of invisibility, so that he could see all that was going on around him without being seen.

And Cropear grew tall and strong, he became the pet of the Pack. The Coyotes were always bringing him what they thought he would like to eat, and were ever showing him the many secrets of the fine art of hunting. They taught him where the Field-mouse nested, where the Song Thrush hid her eggs, where the Squirrel stored his nuts; and where the Mountain Sheep concealed their young among the towering rocks.

◆ **Reading Strategy** What do these details reveal about the culture of the western frontier? ❹

When the Jack-rabbit was to be hunted, they gave Cropear his station and taught him to do his turn in the relay race. And when the prong-horn Antelope was to be captured, Cropear took his place among the encircling pack and helped bring the fleeting animal to bay and pull him down, in spite of his darting, charging antlers.

Grandy took pains to introduce Cropear to each of the animals and made every one of them promise he would not harm the growing man-child. "Au-g-gh!" growled the Mountain Lion, "I will be as careful as I can. But be sure to tell your child to be careful, too!"

"Gr-r-rr!" growled the fierce Grizzly Bear, "I have crunched many a marrow bone, but I will not harm your boy. Gr-r-rr!"

"Yes, we'll keep our perfumery and our quills in our inside vest pockets," mumbled

3. **piñon** (pēn´ yän´) *n.*: Small pine trees with large, edible seeds or nuts.

Cultural Connection

Tricksters Stories about tricks and pranks, especially when played by the small and weak against the great and powerful, have delighted audiences for as long as there has been storytelling. To Native Americans, that trickster is Coyote, a clever mischief-maker whose exploits are recounted by groups across the continent.

To Native American groups in the Great Plains and plateau regions of the West, Coyote is a prominent figure who is clever, clowning, lecherous, thieving, and untrustworthy. He can transform himself into other forms when necessary. In stories from these regions, as in all others, Coyote periodically gets his comeuppance. Invite students to read a few Coyote legends, and then choose one to read aloud to the class. Have students compare the characteristics of Coyote in each tale and discuss what the stories have in common.

the silly Skunk and Porcupine, as if suffering from adenoids.[4]

But when Grandy talked things over with the Bull Rattlesnake, he was met with the <u>defiance</u> of hissing rattles. "Nobody will ever make me promise to protect anybody or anything! S-s-s-s-ss! I'll do just as I please!"

"Be careful of your wicked tongue," warned Grandy, "or you'll be very sorry."

But when Grandy met the Wouser, things were even worse. The Wouser was a cross between the Mountain Lion and the Grizzly Bear, and was ten times larger than either. Besides that, he was the nastiest creature in the world. 5 "I can only give you fair warning," yowled the Wouser, "and if you prize your man-child, as you say you do, you will have to keep him out of harm's way!" And as the Wouser continued, he stalked back and forth, lashing his tail and gnashing his jaws, and acting as if he were ready to snap somebody's head off. "What's more, you know that nobody treats me as a friend. Everybody runs around behind my back spreading lies about me. Everybody says I carry hydrophobia[5]—the deadly poison—about on my person, and because of all these lies, I am shunned like a leper. Now you come sneaking around asking me to help you. Get out of my sight before I do something I shall be sorry for!"

"I'm not sneaking," barked Grandy in defiance, "and besides, you're the one who will be sorry in the end."

So it happened that all the animals, save only the Bull Rattlesnake and the Wouser, promised to help Cropear bear a charmed life so that no harm should come near him. And by good fortune, the boy was never sick. The vigorous exercise and the fresh air and the constant sunlight helped him to become the healthiest, strongest, most active boy in the world.

When Pecos Bill, the Coyotes' *Cropear,* met Chuck, a cowpuncher, and discovered that he was human, he learned to speak and joined Chuck's company of cowpunchers at the I. X. L. Ranch.

4. **adenoids** (ad′ ən oidz′) *n.*: Growth of lymph tissue in the upper part of the throat that, when swollen, can obstruct breathing and result in nasal-sounding speech.

5. **hydrophobia** (hī′ drō fō′ bē ə) *n.*: Rabies.

◆ Build Vocabulary

defiance (dē fī′ əns) *n.*: Act of defying authority or opposition; open, bold resistance

Guide for Responding

◆ Literature and Your Life

Reader's Response What are your impressions of Grandy as a caretaker? Explain why you would or would not want him to care for you as a young child.

Thematic Focus Do you think the animals in this tale were the kinds that populated the western frontier? Explain.

Group Discussion What unique lessons does the animal world teach? With a group, discuss how each of these lessons would be useful to Pecos Bill.

☑ Check Your Comprehension

1. How did Pecos Bill get his name?
2. Who raised the boy?
3. How did Pecos Bill discover that he was a human?

◆ Critical Thinking

INTERPRET

1. What evidence in this tale suggests Pecos Bill may have problems in the future? **[Support]**
2. Why do most of the animals agree not to harm Cropear? **[Infer]**
3. What are one or two underlying reasons for Wouser's behavior? **[Analyze]**

EVALUATE

4. Do you think Pecos Bill is a good example of a folk hero? Support your answer. **[Evaluate]**

EXTEND

5. Where in the United States would you be likely to find wildlife like that which appears in this tale? Explain. **[Science Link]**

◆ Literary Focus

5 Folk Literature Guide students to recognize another characteristic of a tall tale: a made-up animal with a funny name and certain exaggerated attributes, in this instance the Wouser demonstrates a bad case of nastiness.

Reinforce and Extend

Answers

◆ Literature and Your Life

Reader's Response Students may say that Grandy is a good caretaker, citing that Grandy taught Cropear all about the wild.

Thematic Focus While some animals, such as the coyote and mountain sheep, are authentic animals, the Wouser is an imaginary one.

☑ Check Your Comprehension

1. He fell out of a wagon as his family was crossing the Pecos River.
2. He was found and reared by Grandy, the Granddaddy of the race of Coyotes.
3. He finally encountered Chuck, a cowpuncher, and found he was not a coyote.

◆ Critical Thinking

1. The rattlesnake and the Wouser refuse to agree not to harm him.
2. They respect Grandy as an important figure and heed his request.
3. He is unsociable because others have treated him poorly in the past.
4. Possible response: He survives an extraordinary event; he has supernatural powers such as invisibility and an ability to communicate with animals; he is a common man.
5. Students should cite details from both works in their response.

Speaking, Listening, and Viewing Mini-Lesson

Oral Report

This mini-lesson supports the Speaking, Listening, and Viewing activity in the Idea Bank on p. 577.

Introduce the Concept Tell students they are going to choose a legendary figure from the American West, find out about that figure, then give an oral presentation to the class.

Develop Background Have groups of students brainstorm for a list of candidates for research. To help them come up with ideas, suggest that they break down their research into categories, such as "Cowboys," "Outlaws," "Prospectors," "Law Officers," "Scouts and Trailblazers," "Mountain Men," "Frontier Women," and "Native American Leaders."

Students can work alone, in pairs, or in small groups to find what they can about their figure. Guide them to look for information in songs and in videos as well as in print materials. Point out that magazines such as *Smithsonian* or *National Geographic* might have articles on some of these people.

Apply the Information Have students organize their information logically in writing and then present their oral reports to the class.

Assess the Outcome Use the following criteria to evaluate students' reports: Is there evidence of sufficient research? Is the report organized logically? Does the report capture the essence of its subject? Is any especially illuminating or entertaining episode recounted in the report?

Develop Understanding

One-Minute Insight This poem retells the legend of Gregorio Cortez who, in 1901, killed a sheriff for revenge and then fled from a posse intent on his capture. Cortez's reputation as a folk hero grew out of respect for his dramatic escapes from the clutches of his numerous pursuers.

◆ Reading Strategy

❶ **Recognize Cultural Details** Guide students to recognize one feature of frontier justice: the posse. Point out that Cortez's pursuers were mercenaries who banded together to capture him, not so much for ethical or moral reasons, but for the reward they hoped to collect.

◆ Literary Focus

❷ **Folk Literature** Point out the exaggeration here that identifies this piece as a legend. Although the real Cortez had hundreds on his trail and undoubtably slipped out of some traps and made some improbable get-aways, it is unlikely that he was able to escape the grip of three hundred men who had him penned in.

◆ Reading Strategy

❸ **Recognize Cultural Details** Students may recognize another theme in western cultural lore, that of the the lone man, hopelessly pitted against many opponents, fighting bravely on despite slim prospects for survival. The lasting appeal of the story of Davy Crockett and the small band of Americans who desperately but heroically fought a huge Mexican army at the Alamo is a vivid example of this. For a literary example, students can read the sections of Larry McMurtry's *Lonesome Dove* in which Augustus single-handedly fights off large, hostile groups of attackers.

▶Critical Viewing◀

❹ **Analyze** Students may point to the agitated, racing horse, to the fiery yellow colors and the waving red blanket, to the rifle butt, and to the serious look on the face of the man riding tall in the saddle.

The Legend Of Gregorio Cortez

Translated by Américo Paredes

Headin' Up the Range, Edward Borein, Gerald Peters Gallery, Sante Fe, New Mexico

▲ Critical Viewing: How does this painting convey the fiery spirit of Cortez? **[Analyze]**

In the county of El Carmen
A great misfortune befell;
The Major Sheriff is dead;
Who killed him no one can tell.

At two in the afternoon
In half an hour or less,
They knew that the man who killed him
Had been Gregorio Cortez.

They let loose the bloodhound dogs;
They followed him from afar.
But trying to catch Cortez
Was like following a star.

❶ All the rangers of the county
Were flying, they rode so hard;
What they wanted was to get
The thousand-dollar reward.

❷ And in the county of Kiansis
They cornered him after all;
Though they were more than three hundred
He leaped out of their corral.

Then the Major Sheriff said,
As if he was going to cry,
"Cortez, hand over your weapons;
We want to take you alive."

Then said Gregorio Cortez,
And his voice was like a bell,
"You will never get my weapons
Till you put me in a cell."

Then said Gregorio Cortez,
❸ With his pistol in his hand,
"Ah, so many mounted Rangers
Just to take one Mexican!"

Humanities: Art

Headin' Up the Range by Edward Borein.

This painting evokes the Old West by depicting perhaps the most defining image of that place and time, the man on his horse in wide open country.

Use this question for discussion: Does this painting accurately represent Gregorio Cortez as you imagine him? Explain. *Students may suggest that it does and support their answer by pointing to his Mexican cowboy attire, including chaps, rifle, lasso, hat, belt, and beaded reins. They may point to the intent look on his face.*

Follow up instruction with the Humanities Connection: Art page in ***Beyond Literature*** (p. 36).

The Streets of Laredo

Anonymous

As I walked out in the streets of Laredo,
As I walked out in Laredo one day,
I spied a poor cowboy all wrapped in white linen,
All wrapped in white linen as cold as the clay.

"I see by your outfit that you are a cowboy,"
These words he did say as I calmly went by.
"Come sit down beside me and hear my sad
  story,
I'm shot in the breast and I know I must die."

"It was once in the saddle I used to go dashing,
❺ With no one as quick on the trigger as I.
I sat in a card-game in back of the bar-room,
Got shot in the back and today I must die."

"Get six of my buddies to carry my coffin,
And six pretty maidens to sing a sad song,
Take me to the valley and lay the sod o'er me,
For I'm a young cowboy who played the game
  wrong."

"Oh, beat the drum slowly and play the fife lowly,
❻ And play the dead march as they carry my pall.
Put bunches of roses all over my coffin,
The roses will deaden the clods as they fall."

"Go gather around you a crowd of young
  cowboys,
And tell them the story of this my sad fate.
Tell one and the other before they go further,
To stop their wild roving before it's too late."

"Go fetch me a cup, just a cup of cold water,
To cool my parched lips," the cowboy then said.
Before I returned, his brave spirit had left him,
And gone to his Master, the cowboy was dead.

◆ Build Vocabulary

pall (pôl) *n.*: Cloth used to cover a coffin; used here to represent a draped coffin

Guide for Responding

◆ Literature and Your Life

Reader's Response Not everyone would agree that Gregorio Cortez is a hero. What's your opinion on Cortez's status as a hero? Explain your answer.

Thematic Focus Judging by this legend and ballad, violence seems to have been rampant on the western frontier. Why do you think this was so?

☑ Check Your Comprehension

1. Why did the rangers chase after Gregorio Cortez?
2. What did Cortez do to escape three hundred men?
3. Under what circumstances did the Laredo cowboy get shot?

◆ Critical Thinking

INTERPRET

1. What evidence suggests that Cortez was unwilling to give himself up? **[Support]**
2. What does the last line of "The Legend of Gregorio Cortez" suggest about Cortez's attitude toward his nationality? **[Infer]**
3. What is the central message of "The Streets of Laredo?" **[Interpret]**

EVALUATE

4. Did Cortez or the Laredo cowboy deserve their fates? Explain. **[Make a Judgment]**

COMPARE LITERARY WORKS

5. Read another piece of literature in which the hero is one who resists authority. Compare its themes with the story of Gregorio Cortez. What are the similarities? **[Compare and Contrast]**

Develop Understanding

One-Minute Insight This song is a cautionary tale, a "cowboy's lament." A dying young cowboy, who has lived a wild, carefree, fast life, asks his listener to warn others of the pitfalls of such a life.

◆ Reading Strategy

❺ Recognize Cultural Details Guide students to recognize the commonly held perception of frontier towns as lawless, dangerous places frequented by gamblers.

◆ Grammar and Style

❻ Compound Predicates Ask students to identify the subject *understood, you*, and all parts of the compound predicate *beat, play, play* of this sentence.

Reinforce and Extend

Customize for
Musical/Rhythmic Learners
Students may appreciate the sadness of this song even more by listening to a recording of it or by singing it themselves. Invite an interested student to obtain the music, grab a guitar, don a bandana and cowboy hat and perform for classmates.

Answers

◆ Literature and Your Life

Reader's Response Students should support their opinions with evidence from the selection.

Thematic Focus Students may say that violence was rampant because of the lack of many law enforcement officials in a vast expanse of relatively unsettled land.

☑ Check Your Comprehension

1. He had killed a sheriff.
2. He leaped out of their corral.
3. He was playing cards in the back of a barroom.

(Answers continue on p. 576)

Beyond the Selection

FURTHER READING

Other Works About Western Folk Literature

Narrative, Davy Crockett
Paul Bunyan, Esther Shephard
"The Day the Cisco Kid Shot John Wayne," Nash Candelaria
Pecos Bill stories, by Edward O'Reilly, in *Century* magazine

We suggest that you preview these works before recommending them to students.

INTERNET

Laredo is a real place. It is located in south Texas, on the Rio Grande along the border with Mexico, about 150 miles south of San Antonio. You and your students may find additional information about Laredo on the Internet. Please be aware, however, that the following site may have changed from the time we published this information.

For information on the history of Laredo, go to **http://www.border.net/cvb/facts/history/index.htm**

We *strongly recommend* that you preview the site before you send students to it.

Answers *(continued from p. 575)*

◆ Critical Thinking

1. He says "You will never get my weapons till you put me in a cell," suggesting that he will not surrender.
2. The last line suggests that Cortez is proud of his nationality.
3. "The Streets of Laredo" warns others not to live a wild life, that it might lead to death.
4. Students should support their opinions with evidence from the selections.
5. Students should name appropriate pieces of literature and give logical explanations.

◆ Reading Strategy

1. Every member in the society takes part in activities that are for the good of all.
2. Sample response: Two cultural details are the cowboy dashing around quick on the trigger, and the cowboy playing a card game in the back of a barroom.

◆ Literary Focus

1. Pecos Bill's ability to talk to and hunt with coyotes is exaggerated, as is Gregorio Cortez's ability to escape from three hundred rangers.
2. Sample response: The ballad format gives the sad story even more poignant.
3. Suggested response: While folk literature provides a general picture of what life was like in a given period, it also contains exaggerations or distortions of truths.
4. Student responses should include logical explanations based upon the selections.

◆ Build Vocabulary

Using the Suffixes *-ance* and *-ence*

1. significance; 2. diligence; 3. defiance; 4. munificence; 5. independence

Using the Word Bank: Sentence Completion

defiance; pall

◆ Grammar and Style

1. The Coyotes were always bringing him what they thought he would like to eat and ever showing him the many secrets of the fine art of hunting.
2. After a while he came quite near, sat up on his haunches, and waited to see what the boy would do.
3. Grandy made a home for Cropear and taught him all about the out-of-doors.

Guide for Responding *(continued)*

◆ Reading Strategy

RECOGNIZE CULTURAL DETAILS

Literature set in a different time or place from your own can reveal much through cultural details. Think of **cultural details**—such as mention of a clothing or furniture style, kind of music or food, or slang expression—as clues that show the way people lived and what they regarded as important in their lives.

1. What does mention of the relay race in "Pecos Bill Becomes a Coyote" tell you about the culture of the time and place?
2. Find two cultural details in "The Streets of Laredo" that indicate cowboys led reckless lives.

◆ Literary Focus

FOLK LITERATURE

Each of these selections represents a different form of folk literature. "Pecos Bill Becomes a Coyote" is a **folk tale** because it focuses upon a fanciful hero who possesses mythical qualities. It can be further characterized as a **tall tale** because it exaggerates the attributes of the hero. "The Legend of Gregorio Cortez" has typical features of a **legend:** It's about a person who really existed, and it emphasizes that person's heroic qualities. "The Streets of Laredo" is a **ballad**—a rhymed, songlike poem that tells a story.

Having been passed down from generation to generation, these pieces preserve aspects of an important period in American history—the settling of the West.

1. What characteristics of Pecos Bill and Gregorio Cortez are exaggerated or fanciful?
2. How does the ballad format of "The Streets of Laredo" enhance your appreciation of the story?
3. What are some pros and cons of reading folk literature to gain information about a period in history?
4. Based on the examples you read in this group, which form of folk literature do you prefer? Explain your choice.

◆ Build Vocabulary

USING THE LATIN SUFFIXES *-ance* AND *-ence*

Using the Latin suffix *-ance* or *-ence*, rewrite the following adjectives so that they become nouns indicating a state of being. Use each new noun in a sentence in your notebook.

1. significant (full of meaning)
2. diligent (hard-working)
3. defiant (refusing to submit)
4. munificent (very generous)
5. independent (free from the rule of another)

USING THE WORD BANK: Sentence Completions

Copy the following passage in your notebook, filling the blanks with appropriate words from the Word Bank.

In __?__ of the sheriff's orders, the townsfolk filled the streets as the outlaw's __?__-draped coffin was carried to the graveyard.

◆ Grammar and Style

COMPOUND PREDICATES

Using **compound predicates** helps you to avoid repeating subjects in your sentences.

> **Compound predicates** combine two or more verbs with the same subject into one sentence.

Practice In your notebook, rewrite each group of sentences as one sentence with a compound predicate.

1. The Coyotes were always bringing him what they thought he would like to eat. The Coyotes were ever showing him the many secrets of the fine art of hunting.
2. After a while he came quite near. He sat up on his haunches. He waited to see what the boy would do.
3. Grandy made a home for Cropear. Grandy taught him all about the out-of-doors.

Grammar Reinforcement

For additional instruction and practice, use lesson in the **Language Lab CD-ROM** on Writing With Nouns and Verbs, and the practice pages on Subjects and Verbs, pp. 16–18, in the *Writer's Solution Grammar Practice Book.*

Reteach

To reteach this selection, use ***Strategies for Diverse Student Needs,*** p. 35.

Build Your Portfolio

Idea Bank

Writing

1. **Fantasy Creature** A cross between two animals, Wouser is the only fantasy creature in the folk tale about Pecos Bill. Write a paragraph describing another fantasy creature. Decide which animals this creature combines and describe the new animal's personality and characteristics.
2. **Dialogue** Several heroes in these pieces brag or exaggerate. Choose two characters from among the tales, and write a dialogue in which they boast to each other about their feats.
3. **Analytic Essay** Based on these selections, what was society like in the early American West? Considering issues such as violence, roles of women, and attitudes about work, write a brief social analysis of the times.

Speaking, Listening, and Viewing

4. **Oral Report** Research another legendary figure of the western frontier, such as Davy Crockett, Kit Carson, or Paul Bunyan and report to the class on your findings. **[Social Studies Link]**
5. **Prosecution Argument** As a prosecuting attorney, deliver a closing argument to convince a jury to convict Gregorio Cortez for murder. **[Social Studies Link]**

Researching and Representing

6. **Western Ballads** Find a collection of folk songs that includes western ballads. Sing or play one or more of the songs for your classmates; then lead a discussion on the cultural details revealed in the ballads. **[Music Link]**
7. **Graphic Display** Research events that occurred in Texas around the time Cortez murdered the sheriffs. Create an illustrated timeline of important events, including Cortez's crime. **[History Link]**

Online Activity www.phlit.phschool.com

Guided Writing Lesson

Legend About a Heroic Figure

Now is your chance to create a legend about your favorite heroic figure. Choose someone known for a particular act of courage or greatness. Then write a legend about that person, filling in for your audience all the details about why your hero is heroic.

Writing Skills Focus: Elaboration to Entertain

One technique for making writing entertaining is **elaborating**—adding vivid details or exaggerating. Notice how James Cloyd Bowman elaborates in his retelling of the Pecos Bill tale:

Model From the Selection

Just as the wagon was rattling down to the ford across the Pecos River, the rear left wheel bounced over a great piece of rock, and Bill, his red hair bristling like porcupine quills, rolled out of the rear of the wagon, and landed, up to his neck, in a pile of loose sand.

Prewriting Before you begin to write, brainstorm for a list of physical traits, qualities, and actions that make your hero legendary in your eyes. Then list several specific details that reinforce each trait, quality, or action.

Drafting Develop your ideas into a written legend. Begin with an exciting event or an engaging bit of dialogue to hook your readers. Then refer to your prewriting notes to help you find interesting ways to elaborate on the main accomplishments of your hero.

Revising Read your legend aloud as if you were telling it to someone, and listen to the way the words work together. Be sure your characterization reveals the heroic qualities of your hero. Look for ways to clarify the action, heighten the suspense, and make the dialogue sound more natural or realistic.

✓ ASSESSMENT OPTIONS

Formal Assessment, Selection Test, pp. 170–172, and Assessment Resources Software. The selection test is designed so that it can be easily customized to the performance levels of your students.

Alternative Assessment, p. 36, includes options for less advanced students, more advanced students, visual/spatial learners and verbal/linguistic learners.

PORTFOLIO ASSESSMENT

Use the following rubrics in the ***Alternative Assessment*** booklet to assess student writing:
Fantasy Creature: Description Rubric, p. 112
Dialogue: Drama Rubric, p. 124
Analytic Essay: Definition/Classification Rubric, p. 114
Guided Writing Lesson: Fictional Narrative Rubric, p. 110

Idea Bank

Customizing for
Performance Levels

Following are suggestions for matching Idea Bank topics with your students' performance levels:
Less Advanced Students: 1
Average Students: 2, 4, 6
More Advanced Students: 3, 5, 7

Customizing for
Learning Modalities

Following are suggestions for matching Idea Bank topics with your students' learning modalities:
Verbal/Linguistic: 4
Logical/Mathematical: 5
Musical/Rhythmic: 6
Visual/Spatial: 7

Guided Writing Lesson

For more instruction on prewriting, elaboration, and revision, see *Prentice Hall Writing and Grammar.*

Writing and Language Transparencies Have students use the Cubing Organizer, p. 75, to organize their prewriting lists of physical traits, qualities, and actions.

Writers at Work Videodisc
Have students view the videodisc segment (Ch. 2) featuring novelist, poet, and essayist N. Scott Momaday speaking about choosing a topic. Ask students how discussing something or listening to music can trigger a writing idea.

Play frames 11644 to 20980

Writing Lab CD-ROM
Have students complete the tutorial on Narration. Follow these steps:

1. Have students use the Character Trait Word Bin to help develop the legendary character.
2. Have students draft on the computer.
3. Have students use the Language Variety Checker to replace overused words.

Prepare and Engage

LESSON OBJECTIVES

1. To analyze literary elements
- Thematic Connection
- Idea Bank: Literary Critique

2. To express and support responses to the text
- Idea Bank: Audition
- Idea Bank: Western Scenario

3. To read in order to research self-selected and assigned topics
- Idea Bank: Report
- Idea Bank: Annotated Movie List

Connections to Today's World

Tales of the American West remain popular to this day. This excerpt from contemporary novelist Larry McMurtry's Pulitzer Prize-winning *Lonesome Dove* has all the elements of the classic tale of the American West: cowboys, horses, cattle, and the challenge of forging new frontiers in the untamed wilderness. As students read, prompt them to look for connections to the plots and themes of the selections in Part 3, particularly the folk literature and the works of Bret Harte, Miriam Davis Colt, and Jack London.

CONNECTIONS TO TODAY'S WORLD

from Lonesome Dove

Larry McMurtry

Thematic Connection

FORGING NEW FRONTIERS

Americans have been heading west ever since the first immigrants crossed the Atlantic to reach this country. In the 1700's, adventurers left the settled East for the wilds of Kentucky and Ohio. Gradually, Americans pushed on toward the Mississippi, and by the mid-1800's, they were thronging the 2,000-mile trail that led from the Missouri River to Oregon.

COWBOYS AND THE LONG TRAIL

Among the greatest legends of the American West were the cowboys, who drove longhorn cattle from the open ranges of Texas up to the railroad yards in Kansas. As they made the two- or three-month journey, cowboys faced loneliness, and danger—yet they seemed glamourous to those who lived more settled lives. As more of the wilderness was tamed, the cowboy came to symbolize a side of the American dream that was being lost.

Toward the end of the nineteenth century, the spread of the railroads and the fencing of the range spelled the end for most working cowboys. However, the national obsession with the cowboy myth refused to die.

THE WESTERN

For most of the twentieth century, fictional cowboys pursued their lonely quests in thousands of books and movies. Beginning in 1912, an Ohio dentist named Zane Grey published over eighty westerns, many of which are still popular today. The first western movie, *The Great Train Robbery,* was made in 1903, and hundreds of low-budget, hugely popular westerns were filmed in the decades that followed. In all of them, the cowboy was a mythical American figure: a solitary hero forced to prove himself in the wilderness.

Contemporary writers like Larry McMurtry and Cormac McCarthy have tapped into a uniquely American interest. Their novels set in the West have captured the public's imagination and enjoyed both popular and critical success.

LARRY McMURTRY
(1936–)

Larry McMurtry, a descendant of Texas cattle ranchers, published his first western when he was only twenty-six. In his many novels, McMurtry has trained a humorous, critical eye on the culture of the American West, which, he believes, tries to create a tradition out of rootlessness.

Labeled by some critics as the creator of the "urban western," McMurtry first attracted attention as a new kind of writer of western novels, who mixed the traditional elements of the genre with sharp social observation and a strong dose of dark humor.

When it was published in 1985, *Lonesome Dove* and its portrayal of the frontier heritage of the West were seen as a dramatic departure from McMurtry's earlier works—such as *The Last Picture Show* (1966), *Moving On* (1970), and *Terms of Endearment* (1975)—which focus on the ever-changing character of contemporary life.

Prentice Hall Literature Program Resources

REINFORCE / RETEACH / EXTEND

Selection Support Pages
Build Vocabulary p. 171
Thematic Connection: Forging New Frontiers, p. 172

Formal Assessment Selection Test, pp. 173–174

Resource Pro CD-ROM

Listening to Literature Audiocassettes

from

Lonesome Dove

Larry McMurtry

❶ *Captain Woodrow Call and Augustus McCrae are two former Texas Rangers who helped bring peace to the Texas frontier. Call now feels a yearning for adventure. With his friend Augustus, he gathers together a ragtag bunch of cowboys and embarks on a cattle drive from Lonesome Dove, Texas, on the Rio Grande, to the wilderness of Montana.*

In the late afternoon they strung a rope corral around the remuda,[1] so each hand could pick himself a set of mounts, each being allowed four picks. It was slow work, for Jasper Fant and Needle Nelson could not make up their minds. The Irishmen and the boys had to take what was left after the more experienced hands had chosen.

❷ Augustus did not deign to make a choice at all. "I intend to ride old Malaria all the way," he said, "or if not I'll ride Greasy."

Once the horses were assigned, the positions had to be assigned as well.

"Dish, you take the right point," Call said. "Soupy can take the left and Bert and Needle will back you up."

Dish had assumed that, as a top hand, he would have a point, and no one disputed his right, but both Bert and Needle were unhappy that Soupy had the other point. They had been with the outfit longer, and felt aggrieved.

The Spettle boys were told to help Lippy with the horse herd, and Newt, the Raineys and the Irishmen were left with the drags. Call saw that each of them had bandanas, for the dust at the rear of the herd would be bad.

They spent an hour patching on the wagon, a vehicle Augustus regarded with scorn. "That dern wagon won't get us to the Brazos,"[2] he said.

"Well, it's the only wagon we got," Call said.

"You didn't assign me no duties, nor yourself either," Augustus pointed out.

1. **remuda** (rə mo͞o′ də) *n.:* Group of extra saddle horses kept as a supply of remounts.

2. **the Brazos** (brä′ zəs): River in central and southeastern Texas.

◆ **Build Vocabulary**

aggrieved (ə grēvd′) *adj.:* Offended; wronged

Develop Understanding

One-Minute Insight

Middle-aged old friends Woodrow Call and Augustus McCrae begin a 2,500-mile cattle drive from their small Texas ranch to the unfamiliar wilds of Montana. Call, a hard, silent man, initiates the plan and runs the crew; easygoing Augustus, who has gotten used to a lazy life of drinking and stargazing, regrets leaving Lonesome Dove. This excerpt recounts the first day of the long journey toward Montana.

Customize for
Less Proficient Readers

This selection contains many "cowboy" terms and colorful Western verbs that may be unfamiliar to students. Examples include *hand, point, drags, spooked,* and *reckon.* Help students use context clues to determine the meanings of these words, or substitute more familiar words as needed.

Customize for
ESL Students

These students may lack familiarity with the concept of a cattle drive. Explain that the point was to raise beef cattle on a ranch and then, when the animals were ready to be sold for slaughter, the cowboys would travel with the herd to a major railroad junction, such as Omaha or Kansas City, where the cattle could be sold and transported to other parts of the country.

◆ Background for Understanding

❶ **Literature** This excerpt is from Chapter 25, which ends the first of the three parts of McMurtry's sprawling novel. Call and McCrae are not cattlemen and they know nothing of Montana. They are middle-aged men who are not quite sure that they are ready to settle down. They argue about how to keep up an interest in life, but finally agree to one last big adventure; on the strength of advice from an old acquaintance, they set out together on a dangerous cattle drive.

◆ Critical Thinking

❷ **Infer** Ask students to infer what kind of man Augustus is, based on the names of his horses. *Students may say that he has a dry sense of humor.*

Beyond the Classroom

Media Connection

Several of Larry McMurtry's novels have been adapted for film, including *The Last Picture Show, Terms of Endearment, Streets of Laredo,* and *Lonesome Dove.* Discuss with students the difficulties involved in adapting a novel for film. Guide them to consider how screenwriters must make a decision about issues like these:

- whether to cut back the plot by deleting certain characters or story lines
- how to convey information provided by the narrator in the novel
- how to develop characterization, conflict, and drama

Students may be interested in reading *Lonesome Dove* and then in seeing the video adaptation to compare and contrast the two versions. You might also encourage them to read other western novels and then view their film adaptations. Suggest westerns such as *Shane, The Big Sky,* and *The Ox-Bow Incident.* We *strongly suggest* that you preview these works before recommending them to your students.

▶Critical Viewing◀

❶ Distinguish Students may say that McMurtry's descriptions of the drive emphasize the thick dust, hard work, and fatigue. By contrast, this work idealizes the cowboys. They are clean and tall in their saddles; bright, sunny colors illuminate the background. The forms may be realistic, but the sense is entirely romantic.

Thematic Connection

❷ Forging New Frontiers Point out to students that because the men are about to leave Lonesome Dove and the Rio Grande, where they have spent so many years, Augustus feels a need to acknowledge the step they are about to take. He is forging a new frontier, but with reluctance.

Humanities: Art

Open Range, 1942, by Maynard Dixon.

Dixon (1875–1946), who was born in Fresno, California, was essentially a self-taught artist. Most of his works portray the West, through which he traveled extensively as a young man. He even worked as a cowboy to support himself before launching a career as an illustrator at the age of twenty. His works appeared in top magazines, including *Harper's* and *Collier's*. After seventeen successful years, Dixon gave up illustration to devote himself to painting in the West.

This painting, which displays Dixon's characteristically bold approach to composition, attempts to capture a scene synonymous with the Old West: a cattle drive across the wide-open western landscape.

Use these questions for discussion:

1. What does this painting suggest about the role or importance of the cowboy? *The fact that the figures of the cowboys are relatively small and faceless suggests that they are of small importance in the greater landscape. Yet, in keeping with the romantic myth of the American cowboy, the artist shows them tall in the saddle, nearly alone.*
2. Like parts of the Southwest, Montana is called "Big Sky Country." How does Dixon evoke this image of the West? *The sky fills more than half the painting; despite the dramatic land forms, the eye goes first to the big sky.*

CONNECTIONS TO TODAY'S WORLD

Open Range, 1942, Maynard Dixon, Museum of Western Art, Denver, Colorado

❶ **Critical Viewing** Based on the descriptions in the selection, would you characterize this depiction of a cattle drive as realistic or romanticized? Explain. **[Distinguish]**

"That simple," Call said. "I'll scare off bandits and you can talk to Indian chiefs."

"You boys let these cattle string out," he said to the men. "We ain't in no big hurry."

Augustus had ridden through the cattle and had come back with a count of slightly over twenty-six hundred.

"Make it twenty-six hundred cattle and two pigs," he said. "I guess we've seen the last of the dern Rio Grande. One of us ought to make a speech, Call. Think of how long we've rode this river." ❷

Call was not willing to indulge him in any dramatics. He mounted the mare and went over to help the boys get the cattle started. It was not a hard task. Most of the cattle were still wild as antelope and instinctively moved away from the horsemen. In a few minutes they were on the trail, strung out for more than a mile. The point riders soon disappeared in the low brush.

Lippy and the Spettle boys were with the wagon. With the dust so bad, they intended to keep the horses a fair distance behind.

Bolivar sat on the wagon seat, his ten-gauge across his lap. In his experience trouble usually came quick, when it came, and he meant to keep the ten-gauge handy to discourage it.

Newt had heard much talk of dust, but had paid little attention to it until they actually started the cattle. Then he couldn't help noticing it, for there was nothing else to notice. The grass was sparse, and every hoof sent up its little spurt of dust. Before they had gone a mile he himself was white with it, and for moments actually felt lost, it was so thick. He had to tie the bandana around his nose to get a good breath. He understood why Dish and the other ❸ boys were so anxious to draw assignments ❹ near the front of the herd. If the dust was going to be that bad all the way, he might as well be riding to Montana with his eyes shut. He would see nothing but his own horse and the few cattle that happened to be within ten yards of him. A grizzly bear could walk in and eat him and his horse both, and they wouldn't be missed until breakfast the next day.

But he had no intention of complaining. They were on their way, and he was part of the outfit. After waiting for the moment so long, what was a little dust?

◆ Critical Thinking

❸ **Connect** The language of western story telling and writing has often used humor and caricature. Guide students to notice how Larry McMurtry infuses his modern writing with the tall-tale elements of understatement, exaggeration, and dry wit. Examples include statements like "might as well be riding to Montana with his eyes shut" and "wouldn't be missed until breakfast the next day." Ask students which selections in Part 3 make use of similar techniques. *Suggested responses include "The Notorious Jumping Frog of Calaveras County" and "Pecos Bill Becomes a Coyote."*

◆ *Literature and Your Life*

❹ Newt, a young apprentice, has the lowest rank among the hands on the cattle drive. He accepts his menial role for the sheer excitement of being part of the adventure. Ask students whether they have ever been in a similar situation. Were they, like Newt, able to swallow their pride in exchange for a chance at gaining experience? Or, as another possibility, did they voice their complaints and try to take on extra responsibilities? Groups might discuss the value of being an apprentice, even if it means doing lowly tasks.

Analyze an Author's Comment

About *Lonesome Dove,* the reviewer Walter Clemons wrote in *Newsweek* that "McMurtry has laconic Texas talk and leathery, slim-hipped machismo down pat, and he's able to refresh heroic clichés with exact observations about cowboy prudery, ignorance and fear of losing face. . . . The whole book moves with joyous energy." Share these comments with students, and invite them to discuss various points. Have students answer the following questions in their journals:

1. From the excerpt you've just read, what examples could you cite to support the reviewer's comment that McMurtry manages to "refresh heroic clichés with exact observations about cowboy prudery, ignorance and fear of losing face"? *Students may mention, for example, Newt's lack of experience, the fact that "for moments he actually felt lost, [the dust] was so thick," and yet the fact that he "had no intention of complaining."*
2. Clemons has commented that "The whole book moves with joyous energy." Do you agree or disagree that this observation accurately describes the excerpt you've just read? Support your answer with evidence from the text. *Students may disagree, arguing that the "energy" of the excerpt is matter-of-fact and somewhat subdued, and moves slowly, like the cattle drive.*

Thematic Connection

❶ **Forging New Frontiers** Have students contrast the glory and romance of forging new frontiers with the gritty realities of the cattle drive. Students may point out that the young hands are glad to be along, but because they have the worst rank, they have the most uncomfortable position in the drive. They must learn how to manage the dust, heat, and almost overwhelming responsibility of trying to keep valuable cattle from straying from the herd.

❷ **Clarification** The men discuss Jake Spoon in this passage. Jake is also a former Texas Ranger. Augustus and Call know that Jake is a scoundrel and a man who rarely keeps his word. It is Jake's enthusiastic description of the rich opportunities in Montana, however, that prompt Call to plan the drive.

◆ Critical Thinking

❸ **Compare and Contrast** Ask students to compare and contrast the characters of Augustus McCrae and Woodrow Call. Why would they still be friends if they seem to have so little in common any more? *Students may see that Augustus and Call seem like an old married couple who have shared so much that they can't imagine not staying together. Their different personalities balance one another. Call is strict, orderly, and works too hard; Augustus is easy-going, funny, even lazy. Call is tough on the young cowhands, while Augustus is more lenient. Call is driven, but Augustus tries to be conciliatory.*

◆ Critical Thinking

❹ **Speculate** Invite students to speculate what thoughts are in Augustus's mind. *Students may say that he is torn about leaving Lonesome Dove, does not relish the rigors of the drive, and wonders if he will ever return.*

Once in a while, though, he dropped back a little. His bandana got sweaty, and the dust caked on it so that he felt he was inhaling mud. He had to take it off and beat it against his leg once in a while. He was riding Mouse, who looked like he could use a bandana of his own. The dust seemed to make the heat worse, or else the heat made the dust worse.

The second time he stopped to beat his bandana, he happened to notice Sean leaning off his horse as if he were trying to vomit. The horse and Sean were both white, as if they had been rolled in powder, though the horse Sean rode was a dark bay.

"Are you hurt?" he asked anxiously.

"No, I was trying to spit," Sean said. "I've got some mud in my mouth. I didn't know it would be like this."

"I didn't either," Newt said.

"Well, we better keep up," he added nervously—he didn't want to neglect his responsibilities. Then to his dismay, he looked back and ❶ saw twenty or thirty cattle standing behind them. He had ridden right past them in the dust. He immediately loped back to get them, hoping the Captain hadn't noticed. When he turned back, two of the wild heifers spooked. Mouse, a good cow horse, twisted and jumped a medium-sized chaparral[3] bush in an effort to gain a step on the cows. Newt had not expected the jump and lost both stirrups, but fortunately diverted the heifers so that they turned back into the main herd. He found his heart was beating fast, partly because he had almost been thrown and partly because he had nearly left thirty cattle behind. With such a start, it seemed to him he would be lucky to get to Montana without disgracing himself.

Call and Augustus rode along together, some distance from the herd. They were moving through fairly open country, flats of chaparral with only here and there a strand of mesquite.[4] That would soon change: the first challenge would be the brush country, an almost impenetrable band of thick mesquite between them and San Antonio. Only a few of the hands were experienced in the brush, and a bad run of some kind might cost them hundreds of cattle.

"What do you think, Gus?" Call asked. "Think we can get through the brush, or had we better go around?"

Augustus looked amused. "Why, these cattle are like deer, only faster." he said. "They'll get through the brush fine. The problem will be with the hands. Half of them will probably get their eyes poked out."

"I still don't know what you think," Call said.

"The problem is, I ain't used to being consulted," Augustus said. "I'm usually sitting on the porch drinking whiskey at this hour. As for the brush, my choice would be to go through. It's that or go down to the coast and get et by the mosquitoes."

"Where do you reckon Jake will end up?" Call asked.

"In a hole in the ground, like you and me," Augustus said.

"I don't know why I ever ask you a question," ❷ Call said.

"Well, last time I seen Jake he had a thorn in his hand," Augustus said. "He was wishing he'd stayed in Arkansas and taken to his hanging."

They rode up on a little knobby hill and stopped for a moment to watch the cattle. The late sun shone through the dust cloud, making the white dust rosy. The riders to each side of the herd were spread wide, giving the cattle lots of room. Most of them were horned stock, thin and light, their hides a mixture of colors. The riders at the rear were all but hidden in the rosy dust.

"Them boys on the drags won't even be able to get down from their horses unless we take a spade and spade 'em off a little," Augustus said.

"It won't hurt 'em," Call said. "They're young."

In the clear late afternoon light they could see all the way back to Lonesome Dove and the river and Mexico. Augustus regretted not tying a jug to his saddle—he would have liked to sit ❸ on the little hill and drink for an hour. Although Lonesome Dove had not been much of a town, he felt sure that a little whiskey would have made him feel sentimental about it. Call merely sat on the hill, studying the cattle. It was clear to Augustus that he was not troubled in any way by leaving the border or the town.

"It's odd I partnered with a man like you, Call," Augustus said. "If we was to meet now

3. **chaparral** (chap′ ə ral′) *n.*: Thicket of shrubs or thorny bushes.
4. **mesquite** (mes kēt′) *n.*: Type of small, thorny tree.

Cultural Connection

The Diversity of the American West The American West was a magnet that drew settlers from all backgrounds. Each culture lent things of its own to establish a rich multicultural tradition that continues to this day. Freed blacks came from the southeast after the Civil War to set up new lives in western territories; Mexicans arrived from south of the border; and immigrants from all parts of Europe sought their fortunes. Different languages left their marks on the region. Travel west and you will see and hear many English words borrowed from Spanish, such as *chaparral, mesa,* and *arroyo*. Place names, such as Wichita, Muskogee, and Ogallala, reflect Native American languages. Invite students to examine aspects of Western culture to find more evidence of its multicultural roots.

CONNECTIONS TO TODAY'S WORLD

instead of when we did, I doubt we'd have two words to say to one another."

"I wish it could happen, then, if it would hold you to two words," Call said. Though everything seemed peaceful, he had an odd, confused feeling at the thought of what they had undertaken. He had quickly convinced himself it was necessary, this drive. Fighting the Indians had been necessary, if Texas was to be settled. Protecting the border was necessary, else the Mex-
3 icans would have taken south Texas back.

A cattle drive, for all its difficulty, wasn't so imperative. He didn't feel the old sense of adventure, though perhaps it would come once they got beyond the settled country.

Augustus, who could almost read his mind, almost read it as they were stopped on the little knob of a hill.

"I hope this is hard enough for you, Call," he said. "I hope it makes you happy. If it don't, I give up. Driving all these skinny cattle all that way is a funny way to maintain an interest in life, if you ask me."

"Well, I didn't," Call said.

"No, but then you seldom ask," Augustus said. "You should have died in the line of duty, Woodrow. You'd know how to do that fine. The problem is you don't know how to live."

"Whereas you do?" Call asked.

"Most certainly," Augustus said. "I've lived about a hundred to your one. I'll be a little riled if I end up being the one to die in the line of duty, because this ain't my duty and it ain't yours, either. This is just fortune hunting."

"Well, we wasn't finding one in Lonesome
Dove," Call said. He saw Deets returning from 4
the northwest, ready to lead them to the bedground. Call was glad to see him—he was tired of Gus and his talk. He spurred the mare on off the hill. It was only when he met Deets that he realized Augustus hadn't followed. He was still sitting on old Malaria, back on the little hill, watching the sunset and the cattle herd.

Guide for Responding

◆ *Literature and Your Life*

Reader's Response If you had been invited to go along on a cattle drive, would you have accepted? Why or why not?

Thematic Focus Augustus implies that the cattle drive has a purpose beyond making money. What is its symbolic meaning for Call and himself, and how does it relate to the romance of the West?

Journal Entry With which character do you identify more—Augustus or Call? List the qualities you share with this character.

☑ Check Your Comprehension

1. Why is riding point a more desirable position than riding at the back of the herd?
2. Why is Call concerned about the stretch of the trail that the cowboys are about to reach?
3. At the end, at what is Augustus staring?

◆ Critical Thinking

INTERPRET

1. Who seems to be more in charge of the cattle drive—Call or Augustus? How can you tell? **[Analyze]**
2. How do you know that the cowboys face danger as well as discomfort? Cite two clues from the story. **[Draw Conclusions]**
3. Give two examples of humor from this selection. **[Analyze]**

EVALUATE

4. How effective is McMurtry in painting a picture of the cattle drive? **[Make a Judgment]**

APPLY

5. List examples of famous people or people whom you know who seem to need a major challenge in order to enjoy life. **[Synthesize]**

Beyond the Selection

FURTHER READING

Other Works by Larry McMurtry

Texasville
Cadillac Jack
The Desert Rose

Other Works About the West

All the Pretty Horses, Cormac McCarthy
The Riders of the Purple Sage, Zane Grey

We suggest that you preview these works before recommending them to students.

4. Students may point out that McMurtry effectively describes the cowboys' actions, the dust, and the scenery.
5. Students should be prepared to explain their answers.

Reinforce and Extend

Customize for
Less Proficient Readers and Visual/Spatial Learners
Students may benefit from seeing portions of the video adaptation of *Lonesome Dove* to get a better understanding of the relationship between Augustus and Call, and of the rigors of the cattle drive. The video will also provide a panoramic sense of the landscape. After viewing the video, students should compare the mental images they had formed in their own minds with the images they saw on screen.

Answers

◆ *Literature and Your Life*

Reader's Response Students should be prepared to explain their responses.

Thematic Focus Call hopes that the cattle drive will give him the sense of purpose that fighting had given him in the past. Call's quest fits the romantic vision of a man proving himself in the wilderness.

☑ Check Your Comprehension

1. The point riders in front are less affected by all the dust kicked up by the cattle.
2. It is so full of thick, thorny mesquite that it may be difficult to drive the cattle through.
3. Augustus is staring back at Lonesome Dove, the Rio Grande, and Mexico.

◆ Critical Thinking

1. Call is more in charge. He assigns riders their positions, and the drive seems to have been his idea.
2. Call jokes that he will scare off the bandits, Bolivar sits in a wagon seat, holding a gun and watching for trouble, and Augustus talks about the possibility of dying "in the line of duty."
3. Examples might include Augustus answering Call's question about where Jake will end up with, "In a hole in the ground, like you and me," or Augustus's observation, "Them boys on the drags won't even be able to get down from their horses unless we take a spade and spade 'em off a little."

Thematic Connection

1. The cattle drive feels less "imperative" than war did.
2. Students may note that this story reflects a very popular interpretation of the "wild West," complete with cowboys, cattle, wide open plains, and the potential for danger. Colt's account, on the other hand, is probably more historically accurate, even though students may find its descriptions of travel by train and covered wagon to be less exciting or "Western."
3. Students may cite the elements of danger, excitement, and wide-open spaces that characterize most stories about the American West.

Idea Bank

Customizing for
Performance Levels

Following are suggestions for matching Idea Bank topics with your students' performance levels:
Less Advanced Students: 3, 4
Average Students: 1, 5
More Advanced Students: 2, 5

Customizing for
Learning Modalities

Following are suggestions for matching Idea Bank topics with your students' learning modalities:
Verbal/Linguistic: 3
Logical/Mathematical: 4, 5

Thematic Connection

Forging New Frontiers

Lonesome Dove, Larry McMurtry's Pulitzer Prize-winning novel, was written in the 1980's. However, it was set over a century earlier and describes an 1870 cattle drive from the Rio Grande River to Northern Montana.

The reality of the West often differed dramatically from the romanticized vision of the West held by so many people.

1. How does the cattle drive on which Woodrow Call has embarked fail to live up to his romantic expectations?
2. How does this fictional story compare with Miriam Davis Colt's account "Heading West"? Explain.
3. Not all historical periods capture the modern imagination. Why do you think stories about the American West are still popular today?

Idea Bank

Writing

1. **Western Scenario** Write a scenario that could serve as the basis for a classic western movie. Identify basic elements, such as a lonely and heroic protagonist, a wild and desolate setting, and some kind of conflict that the protagonist must win alone using his bravery and skill. Explain your premise. Then briefly outline the hero's situation and how the story would unfold.
2. **Literary Critique** *Lonesome Dove* won the Pulitzer Prize—a major literary award. Such awards are given on the basis of many criteria, including literary style. Evaluate McMurtry's style, and explain whether or not you think it deserves to win an award.

Speaking, Listening, and Viewing

3. **Audition** *Lonesome Dove* is full of dialogue that is both entertaining and revealing of character. "Audition" for the role of either Call or Augustus. Read a few lines of dialogue for your classmates. When everyone is finished, discuss which readings best seem to convey each character. **[Performing Arts Link]**

Researching and Representing

4. **Report** Though there are far fewer today than a century ago, professional cowboys still exist. What functions do they perform? What skills must they have? Where and how do they live? Research the answers to these questions, and present your findings in a written report. You may find it helpful to visit cowboy-related Internet Web sites, such as the Home Page of the professional Rodeo Cowboys Association at http://www. ProRodeo. com. **[Career Link]**
5. **Annotated Movie List** To study a unique genre of film, watch several westerns. Develop a set of criteria to use as you evaluate each film. Then rate each film and create an annotated list for classmates. In each entry, identify the name of the film, the year it was made, and any comments. You might devise a rating system—four lassos—to help organize your list. **[Media Link]**

Online Activity www.phlit.phschool.com

ASSESSMENT OPTIONS

Formal Assessment, Selection Test, pp. 173–174, and Assessment Resources Software. The selection test is designed so that it can be easily customized to the performance levels of your students.

PORTFOLIO ASSESSMENT
Use the following rubrics in the ***Alternative Assessment*** booklet to assess student writing:
Western Scenario: Fictional Narrative Rubric, p. 110
Literary Critique: Evaluation/Review Rubric, p. 119
Report: Research Report/Paper Rubric, p. 121

Writing Process Workshop

Comparison-and-Contrast Essay

In *Life on the Mississippi*, Mark Twain captures the glamour and excitement of life aboard a steamboat by contrasting it with the humdrum life in Hannibal, Missouri. As Twain's writing illustrates, comparisons are one of the most effective ways to give readers a clear sense of one or more subjects. Develop your ability to create comparisons by writing a comparison-and-contrast essay—an essay that examines the similarities and differences between two or more persons, places, things, or ideas. The following skills, introduced in this section's Guided Writing Lessons, will help you.

Writing Skills Focus

- **Use precise details** to make your comparisons clear to readers. (See p. 543.)
- **Elaborate for vividness.** Provide enough details so readers will get a complete picture. (See p. 531.)
- **Write coherently.** Use a logical organization and provide transitions to connect your details. (See p. 553.)

Look at Twain's use of comparisons in his description of a boy who had left home to work on a steamboat.

Model From Literature

from *Life on the Mississippi*
by Mark Twain

By and by one of our boys went away. He was not heard of for a long time. At last he turned up as apprentice engineer or striker on a steamboat. This thing shook the bottom out of all my Sunday-school teachings. ① That boy had been notoriously worldly, and I just the reverse: yet he was exalted to this eminence, and I left in obscurity and misery. ② He would always manage to have a rusty bolt to scrub while his boat tarried at our town, and he would sit on the inside guard and scrub it, where we could all see him and envy him and loathe him. . . . ③

① Twain captures the intensity of his reaction to the reappearance of the boy.

② Here, Twain creates a clear contrast by alternating descriptions of "that boy" and himself.

③ The precise details "rusty bolt to scrub" and "sit on the inside guard" sharpen the picture of the striker.

Prepare and Engage

LESSON OBJECTIVES

- To use recursive writing processes to write a comparison-and-contrast essay
- To recognize and avoid faulty logic
- To identify and correct errors in subject-verb agreement in inverted sentences

Distribute the scoring rubric for Comparison/ Contrast (p. 118) in ***Alternative Assessment*** to make students aware of the criteria on which their work will be evaluated. For suggestions on customizing the rubric to this workshop see p. 587.

Refer students to the Writing Handbook, p. 1192, for instruction in the writing process, and p. 1194 for further information on expository writing. You may also use the Comparison-and-Contrast Organizer in the ***Writing and Language Transparencies*** (pp. 87–89).

Writers at Work Videodisc
To introduce the elements of expository writing, play the videodisc segment featuring museum curator Thom Harrington (Ch. 3).

Play frames 23159 to 33243

Writing Lab CD-ROM
If your students have access to computers, you may want to have them work in the tutorial on Exposition. Have students follow these steps:

1. Use the Comparison-and-Contrast Subject Generator to choose a topic for their comparison-and-contrast essay.
2. Draft their comparison-and-contrast essays on the computer.
3. Review the interactive Self-Evaluation Checklist to help them revise.

Cross-Curricular Connection: Physical Education

Choosing a Sports-Related Topic Many students may be familiar with the elements of a comparison-and-contrast organization from print and broadcast coverage of sporting events. Commentators frequently provide information or analysis by presenting easy-to-understand comparisons for the audience. In addition, sports buffs often compare players from different eras, or the skills required by one sport to those of another. If students choose to write their essays on a sports-related topic, here are possible topics:

- An athlete's performance in the playoffs versus the regular season, or that of an athlete before and after being injured and recovering.
- A comparison of the ways a sport has changed due to a change in rules, or the way the same sport is played in different countries or venues (e.g., indoors vs. outdoors).
- A veteran athlete's skills now versus early in his or her career.

Finally, students may want to write from their own athletic experience, contrasting seasonal demands, coed versus unisex sports, or varsity versus junior varsity and intramural teams.

Prewriting Strategy

The Venn Diagram approach can be applied to each of the topic ideas provided by the student edition. You may want to work with students to narrow the topics first in order to focus the activity.

Customize for *Less Advanced Students*

To help these students organize their details, offer them the following alternative to using a Venn diagram. Ask them to list details in two columns, one for each of their subjects. After brainstorming items for each list individually, students can draw lines between the two lists to make connections—both similarities and differences—that they want to explore in their essays. Students may find this process easier than using the Venn diagram method, which entails their making decisions about details before placing them in the circles.

Customize for *Logical/Mathematical Learners*

These students may enjoy writing about topics for which they can gather statistics to support their analyses. Remind logical/mathematical learners to treat statistics as evidence that must be organized like any other.

Writing Lab CD-ROM

The Organizing Details section of the tutorial includes audio-annotated models for comparison-and-contrast organization. Students can learn why writers chose to use either a point-by-point or a subject-by-subject format.

Elaboration Strategy

After students have identified points of comparison and contrast, have them use a trifold for each point to explore examples, facts, and other forms of elaboration they can use to illustrate each point.

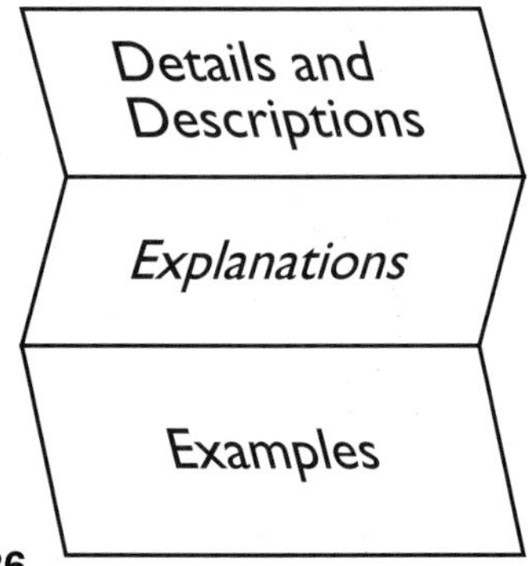

APPLYING LANGUAGE SKILLS: Avoiding Faulty Logic

Be careful to avoid making incomplete comparisons, such as these:

Incomplete Comparisons:

Dent-o toothpaste is better for tartar control. (Better than what?)

Dent-o toothpaste is the best. (The best compared to what, and in what way?)

Revised Comparisons:

Dent-o toothpaste is better than Smilex for tartar control.

Dent-o toothpaste is the best of all the leading brands for tartar control.

Practice Correct any flaws you see in the following comparisons.

1. Vote for Tino for class president. He's better than Melissa.
2. Senator Woolf's budget proposal is far superior.
3. Health care is not as big an issue in the campaign.

Writing Application As you draft and revise your essay, be sure that your comparisons are complete.

Writer's Solution Connection
Writing Lab

For help gathering your details, use the Venn diagram in the Exposition tutorial.

Prewriting

Choose a Topic To select a topic for a comparison-and-contrast essay, note interesting places, things, and people that are in some ways similar. Review your notes, and focus on the topic that you think will most appeal to others. You may also choose one of the topic ideas listed here.

Topic Ideas

- Earth and Mars
- Movies and stage plays
- Two rock stars
- Two sports

Gather Details Use a Venn diagram to help you identify the similarities and differences between your subjects. Draw two circles that overlap each other. Label each with one of your two subjects. In each nonoverlapping portion, list the characteristics unique to each subject. In the overlapping portion, list the shared characteristics. Refer to your Venn diagram as you develop and draft your paper.

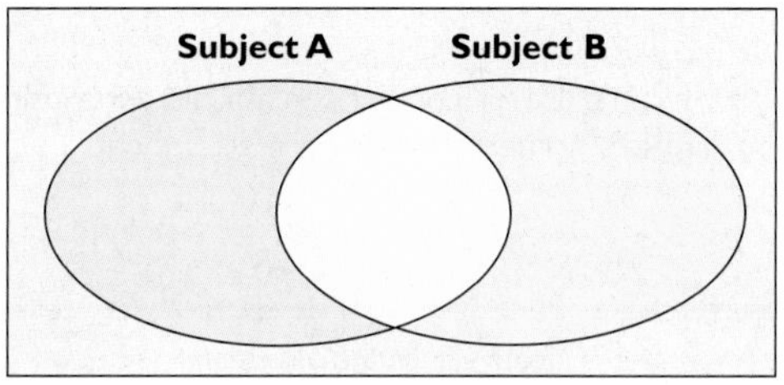

Drafting

Introduce Your Main Points Begin your essay with an introduction in which you present your overall conclusions about the similarities and differences between your subjects.

Organize Your Details Clearly As you develop your body paragraphs, use a clear organization to avoid getting details jumbled and confused. You might discuss all the aspects of one subject fully before going on to the next subject, or you might move back and forth between your two subjects, explaining each point of similarity or difference.

Mark Places to Add Precise Details If you can't come up with the right word to describe an aspect of one of your subjects, simply mark the spot and move on.

Applying Language Skills

Avoiding Faulty Logic

Introduce this skill by explaining to students that an incomplete comparison—the core problem this language skill addresses—goes against the main purpose of their essay, which is to provide clear and complete comparisons.

Suggested Answers

1. Vote for Tino for class president. He's better than Melissa in terms of athletic and academic accomplishments.
2. Because it addresses emergency aid issues, Senator Woolf's budget is far superior to the President's plan.
3. Health care is not as big an issue in the campaign as foreign policy is.

Grammar Reinforcement

For additional instruction and practice, refer to the *Sourcebook* lesson on Avoiding Faulty Logic (p. 119), and p. 75 in the *Writer's Solution Grammar Practice Book*.

Revising

Use a Checklist Use these questions to help you revise your essay:

- Where can you add details or replace vague words with more precise language to make your comparisons more clear? Remember to fill in details or replace words in passages that you marked while drafting.
- How can you improve the organization of your essay to make it easier for readers to follow?
- Where can you add transitions, such as *in contrast, as opposed to,* and *similarly,* to make your comparisons more obvious to readers?

Revision Model

① You can put out the litter box and a big bowl of food and take off for the weekend.

Cats are easy to care for. Dogs require more attention.

② —regular walking and scheduled feeding are a must—

but they repay your efforts many times over because they

③ : while your cat checks in for an occasional nuzzle on his schedule, your dog is always there for you, with a sloppy, consoling lick at the ready.

are more affectionate.

①②The addition of these precise details makes the comparison clear for the reader.

③ The vivid images in this sentence develop the comparison in an amusing and entertaining way.

Use a Peer Reviewer Once you've finished revising your essay on your own, have a classmate read your paper. Ask your peer to suggest where you might add details to make your comparisons more complete and to suggest how you can improve your organization. Encourage your classmate to be as specific as possible in making suggestions.

Publishing

Read Your Essay Aloud to the Class A great way to share your ideas with others is to read your essay aloud. Before delivering your reading, practice on your own or with a friend or family member. Work on varying the volume and tone of your voice and on using hand gestures to emphasize key points. In addition, practice looking up from your paper to meet the eyes of the members of your audience. After you present your essay, hold a question-and-answer session.

Applying Language Skills: Inverted Sentences

In most sentences, the subject comes before the verb. In inverted sentences, the subject comes after the verb, but the subject and verb must still agree in number. Many inverted sentences start with *here, there,* or *where.*

Incorrect:

Here comes (V) the happy winners (S).

Correct:

Here come (V) the happy winners (S).

Practice On your paper, correct any errors in subject-verb agreement in the following inverted sentences.

1. Here in this magazine is two great articles.
2. Down the hillside rumbles the huge boulders.
3. There has to be three cookies left.

Writing Application Review your essay to be sure that all sentences with inverted word order have correct subject-verb agreement.

Writer's Solution Connection
Language Lab

For more practice, complete the Language Lab lesson on Correct and Effective Use of Verbs.

Revision Strategy

Ask peer reviewers to draw their own Venn Diagrams based on their reading, and then contrast them with the one the writer developed in the prewriting stage.

Writing Lab CD-ROM

The Revising and Editing section includes Revision Checkers for transition words and language variety.

Publishing

If students elect to read their essays aloud, encourage them to supplement their text with props and other visual aids to engage the audience.

Applying Language Skills

Inverted Sentences

To improve sentence variety and structure, encourage students to use inverted order in their comparison-and-contrast essays.

Answers

1. Here in this magazine are two great articles.
2. Down the hillside rumble the huge boulders.
3. There have to be three cookies left.

Grammar Reinforcement

For additional practice, refer to the **Language Lab CD-ROM** lesson on Special Problems in Agreement, and the section on Agreement in the *Writer's Solution Grammar Practice Book* (pp. 66–72).

Reinforce and Extend

Prentice Hall Writing and Grammar For more prewriting, elaboration, and revision strategies, see *Prentice Hall Writing and Grammar.*

ASSESSMENT

		4	3	2	1
PORTFOLIO ASSESSMENT Use the rubric on Comparison/Contrast in ***Alternative Assessment*** (p. 118) to assess students' writing. Add these criteria to customize the rubric to this assignment.	**Balance Between Two Subjects**	The writer shows a thorough knowledge of both subjects and presents a balanced selection of details about each.	The writer clearly focuses on one of the subjects, but overall the two subjects are thoughtfully compared and contrasted.	The purpose of the essay suffers because the writer heavily favors one of his subjects over the other.	The writer dwells on one of his subjects to the virtual exclusion of the other.
	Complete Comparisons	The writer consistently makes comparisons that are clear and complete.	The writer makes some comparisons that are elliptical or slightly unclear.	The writer rarely makes complete comparisons; the result is many instances of faulty logic.	The writer consistently makes incomplete comparisons, or avoids making comparisons altogether.

Prepare and Engage

LESSON OBJECTIVES

- To use print resources for research
- To use research questions to guide selection of resources
- To evaluate information sources

Customize for
AP Students
Students may expand their appreciation of three standard reference sources—dictionaries, multivolume encyclopedias, and atlases—by examining the supplemental material in each. For example, students can list what they discover in the front and back matter of an unabridged dictionary. They may explain why an encyclopedia index is the first volume to consult.

Apply the Strategies

Answers

1. Additional print resources include articles in periodicals located through a computer database. Periodicals about science, nature, and plants seem most likely to have information.
2. Possible questions and print sources that might lead to answers: What are the different kinds of tropisms? (encyclopedia, dictionary) How did scientists learn about tropisms? (bibliography in encyclopedia article, periodicals database) What current research is there on plant hormones related to tropisms? (database of academic journals)
3. Students should name a research topic and use standard bibliographic style to list three print sources containing information.

Student Success Workshop

Research Skills — Using Print Resources for Research

Strategies for Success

If you want to research the meaning of a technical term, the demographics of a city, the reproduction cycle of a cactus, or the history of jazz, there are many print resources available. You can research using an encyclopedia, atlas, newspaper, dictionary, or academic journal. Use a variety of resources:

Encyclopedias and Atlases If you need a starting point or are looking for reliable general information, consult an encyclopedia. Encyclopedias contain information about a variety of topics; however, they are not exhaustive, and you should use other resources also. Atlases—books of maps—are good resources for finding political, geographic, agricultural, and economic information about a particular region or place.

Academic Journals, Magazines, and Newspapers Periodicals are also useful resources. Academic journals contain the published research of scholars, covering almost every subject. They are excellent resources for research, and their bibliographies list even more resources related to their topics. Newspapers and magazines can also be powerful research tools for finding time-specific information. For example, if you want to research Topeka, Kansas, in 1929, these resources may reveal perspectives not found in history books. Whichever source you choose, learning to find the information is an important step.

Computer Databases These can help direct your research. They contain lists of print resources and can be searched by key word. Entries often give abstracts, or summaries, of information in the source.

Microfilm and Microfiche Since libraries don't have room to store every periodical, they use microfilm and microfiche. *Microfilm* is a roll of film and *microfiche* is a sheet of film, each containing reduced pages from a periodical. Use the library's magnifying machines to read them.

Apply the Strategies

Read this encyclopedia entry about plant tropisms, and answer the questions that follow.

> Plants grow in response to cues from their environment. These responses are known as *tropisms.* The term tropism is derived from a Greek word that means "to turn." There are several common tropisms, each of which demonstrates the ability of plants to respond to changes in their environment. Geotropism allows seedlings to grow up out of the soil while their roots spread downward. Phototropism is the name of a plant's responsive growth toward light. Thigmotropism describes the response some plants, such as ivy, have to touch. Tropisms, in general, are caused by plant hormones.

1. What print resource could you use to learn more about plant hormones?
2. How would you research tropisms in depth? Write questions to help you research in three of the print resources.
3. Choose a topic for research, and find one example from each of the resources that contains information you can use.

✔ *Print materials for research can be useful when you want to:*

- ▶ *Trace a historical event*
- ▶ *Learn more about the lifestyles in a different country*
- ▶ *Figure out how to fix your bike*

Test-Taking Tip

Evaluating Sources of Information

Many standardized tests require students to evaluate information and the reliability of a source. Use the following sample test item to demonstrate.

> Plants grow in response to cues from their environment. These responses are known as tropism. The term *tropism* is derived from a Greek word that means "to turn." There are several common tropisms, each of which demonstrates the ability of plants to respond to change in the environment.

The information in this source would be most useful when writing a—

A poem about plants
B poem about the environment
C persuasive essay on the environment
D research paper on plants

By evaluating the type of information presented in the source, students should be able to recognize that the information is most useful and appropriate for a research paper on plants. The correct answer is D.

PART 4

Living in a Changing World

Channel to the Mills, 1913,
Edwin M. Dawes, Minneapolis Institute of Arts

One-Minute Planning Guide

These works examine the effects of the societal changes taking place at the turn of the twentieth century. Students will be interested to learn that Kate Chopin's dark tale, "The Story of an Hour," was considered scandalous because it suggested that a woman might be happier without her husband. African Americans' struggle for acceptance and equality is reflected in the poems of Paul Laurence Dunbar. Edwin Arlington Robinson and Edgar Lee Masters paint memorable verbal portraits of four uniquely American characters who reflect the changing values of their day. Willa Cather contrasts the rigors of American frontier life with the cultural centers of the East in "A Wagner Matinée." The recurring theme of social alienation takes on a contemporary setting in Anna Quindlen's "Cats."

Customize for *Varying Student Needs*

When assigning the selections in this part, keep the following factors in mind:

"The Story of an Hour"
- Short story set in span of one hour
- Darkly ironic surprise ending should capture student interest

"Douglass" and "We Wear the Mask"
- Brief, emotionally-charged poems
- Formal, antiquated language of "Douglass" may challenge less proficient readers

"Luke Havergal," "Richard Cory," "Lucinda Matlock" and "Richard Bone"
- Four portraits in verse
- Vivid character profiles

"A Wagner Matinée"
- Accessible short story
- Concert setting will intrigue musical/rhythmic learners

"Cats"
- Accessible contemporary account

Humanities: Art

Channel to the Mills, 1913 by Edwin M. Dawes.

Encourage students to contrast this artwork with pieces like ***Early Morning at Cold Spring*** (which introduces Unit 3, Part 3). Help them see that the natural landscape had dominated earlier paintings, In contrast, Dawes chooses a group of mills to dominate the landscape of this painting.

Have your students link the painting to the focus of this part (Living in a Changing World) by answering the following questions:

1. What changes in the American environment does this artwork suggest? *The artwork focuses on the change from a rural to an industrial society.*
2. What attitude toward these changes does the artist communicate, and how? *Students who see a positive attitude may focus on the soft, shimmering colors of the artwork. Students who see a negative attitude may focus on the title, which draws attention to the water that the mills are polluting and the way the buildings loom so large and blot out the horizon.*

LESSON OBJECTIVES

1. To develop vocabulary and word identification skills
- Anglo-Saxon Prefixes: *fore-*
- Using the Word Bank: Word Choice

2. To use a variety of reading strategies to comprehend a short story
- Connect Your Experience
- Reading Strategy: Recognize Ironic Details
- Background for Understanding

3. To increase knowledge of other cultures and to connect common elements across cultures
- Connecting Themes Across Cultures (ATE)

4. To express and support responses to the text
- Critical Thinking
- Idea Bank: Diary Entry
- Idea Bank: Commentary
- Idea Bank: Pantomime

5. To analyze literary elements
- Literary Focus: Irony
- Read to Appreciate an Author's Craft (ATE)

6. To read in order to research self-selected and assigned topics
- Idea Bank: Culture Comparison

7. To plan, prepare, organize, and present literary interpretations
- Idea Bank: Soliloquy
- Idea Bank: Visual Interpretation
- Idea Bank: New Version

8. To use recursive writing processes to write a reflective essay
- Guided Writing Lesson

9. To increase knowledge of the rules of grammar and usage
- Grammar and Style: Appositives and Appositive Phrases

Test Preparation

Reading Comprehension: Context (ATE, p. 591)

The teaching tips and sample test item in this workshop support the instruction and practice in the unit workshop:

Reading Comprehension: Using Context (SE, p. 631)

Guide for Interpreting

Kate Chopin *(1851–1904)*

Despite her conservative, aristocratic upbringing, Kate Chopin (shō′ pan) became one of the most powerful and controversial writers of her time. In her stories, sketches, and novels, she not only captured the local color of Louisiana, but also boldly explored the role of women in society.

Family Life Kate O'Flaherty, who was born in St. Louis, Missouri, married Oscar Chopin, a Louisiana cotton trader, when she was only nineteen. She moved with her husband to New Orleans, where they lived for ten years before settling on a plantation in rural Louisiana. In 1883, Chopin's husband died, leaving her to raise their six children alone. She managed the plantation on her own for a year, developing her financial and business skills. Eventually, however, she gave in to her mother's urging to sell her home and return with her children to St. Louis.

Her mother's sudden death in 1885 left Chopin in deep sorrow. It was at the suggestion of a family doctor, who was concerned about her emotional health, that she began to write fiction. Chopin kept St. Louis as her home and devoted much of her energy to writing.

Chopin the Writer and Rebel Chopin's writing is noted for its ability to present the essence of Louisiana life. Like most of her works, Chopin's first novel, *At Fault* (1890), was set in a Louisiana town inhabited by Creoles, descendants of the original French and Spanish settlers, and Cajuns, descendants of French Canadian settlers who arrived later. Through vivid descriptions and dialect, Chopin captured the local color of the region. Her stories, published in *Bayou Folk* (1894) and *Acadie* (1897), exhibited a deep understanding of the different attitudes of the Louisiana natives.

Kate Chopin's charming portraits of Louisiana life often obscured their underlying radical themes.

She examined the nature of marriage, racial prejudice, and women's desire for social, economic and political equality. "The Story of an Hour" explores several of these issues.

Chopin's finest novel, *The Awakening* (1899), is an account of a woman's search for independence and fulfillment. The novel aroused a storm of protest and was eventually banned. Her reputation was so badly damaged that her work was ignored for decades after her death. Today, however, she is widely respected for her portrayal of the psychology of women and her ability to capture local color.

◆ Background for Understanding

CULTURE: CHOPIN'S WORKS STIR THE SOCIAL CONSCIENCE OF A NATION

"The Story of an Hour" was considered daring in the nineteenth century. At least two magazines refused the story because they thought it was unethical. They wanted Chopin to soften her female characters, to make them less independent and assertive. Undaunted, she continued to deal with issues of women's growth and emancipation in her writing, advancing ideas that are widely accepted today.

In Chopin's time, however, activists were just beginning to stir the national conscience. Women and minorities were seeking to expand their civil rights. In addition, psychologists such as William James were debating free will, the ability of individuals to control their own destiny. These developments began a social revolution whose effects are still being felt today.

Prentice Hall Literature Program Resources

REINFORCE / RETEACH / EXTEND

Selection Support Pages
Build Vocabulary: Using the Prefix: *fore-*, p. 173
Grammar and Style: Appositives and Appositive Phrases, p. 174
Reading Strategy: Recognizing Ironic Details, p. 175
Literary Focus: Irony, p. 176

Strategies for Diverse Student Needs, p. 37

Beyond Literature
Cross-Curricular Connection: Social Studies, p. 37

Formal Assessment Selection Test, pp. 179–181

Alternative Assessment, p. 37

Writing and Language Transparencies
Writing Process Model 1: Reflective Essay, pp. 5–8

Resource Pro CD-ROM

Listening to Literature Audiocassettes

The Story of an Hour

◆ *Literature and Your Life*

Connect Your Experience

Often, life-changing events sneak up on us unexpectedly—a chance encounter with someone who becomes important in our lives, the loss of a loved one, a change in a parent's employment situation, a sudden move to a new place. The story you're about to read focuses on a woman's surprising reaction to a shocking piece of news.

Thematic Focus: Living in a Changing World

As you read this story, remember that it was very controversial in its time. However, the inner transformation of the main character foreshadows great social changes that would soon transform the nation.

Journal Writing In a journal entry, explore one facet of life in our culture that has changed significantly since the late nineteenth century.

◆ Literary Focus

Irony

Irony is a contrast between what is stated and what is intended or between what is expected and what actually happens. There are a number of different types of irony to be found in literature. **Verbal irony** is the use of words to suggest the opposite of their usual meaning. **Dramatic irony** occurs when readers are aware of something that a character in a literary work does not know. **Situational irony** occurs when the outcome of an action or situation is quite different from what one expects. As you read, decide which type of irony best describes the events in this story.

◆ Reading Strategy

Recognize Ironic Details

A story's details often lead readers to have certain expectations. When events don't turn out as details lead us to expect, it creates irony. As you read "The Story of an Hour," use a chart like this one to note how specific details imply certain feelings, circumstances, or events that may not, in fact, be what they appear. After reading the story, note whether your expectations were or were not met.

Detail	Expected Outcome	Actual Outcome
Care is taken to reveal bad news to Mrs. Mallard.	She would be upset.	

◆ Build Vocabulary

Using the Anglo-Saxon Prefix *fore-*

If you have *foreknowledge* of an event, you can take steps to prepare for it or even to *forestall* it. The Anglo-Saxon prefix *fore-* means "before," either in time, place, or condition. Words with this prefix include *foreshadow, forethought* (time); *forearm, forehead, forecourt* (place); *foremost, forefront* (condition). In which category does *forestall* fit?

Word Bank

Preview this list of words from "The Story of an Hour."

forestall
repression
elusive
tumultuously
importunities

◆ Grammar and Style

Appositives and Appositive Phrases

An **appositive** is a noun or pronoun placed near another noun or pronoun to provide more information about it. When an appositive is accompanied by its own modifiers, it forms an **appositive phrase.** Look at this example from "The Story of an Hour."

What could love, the unsolved mystery, count for in the face of this possession . . . (appositive phrase renaming *love*)

Test Preparation Workshop

Reading Comprehension: Context The reading sections of many standardized tests specify that students use the context of a targeted word or phrase to determine its meaning. Because figurative expressions are not literally true, students must try to infer the meaning of the expression from the surrounding context. Use the following sample test item to demonstrate.

Her fancy was running riot along those days ahead of her. Spring days, and summer days, and all sorts of days that would be her own.

In this passage, the words running riot most nearly mean—

A quietly contemplating
B causing a public disturbance
C becoming overactive
D going numb

The excitement communicated in the second sentence should lead students to recognize that *C* is the correct answer based on the context.

Interest Grabber To get started, have students generate a list of "news flashes" that would change their lives. For example, you might suggest winning the lottery, the death of a loved one, or early admission to college.

Then tell students that in the story they are about to read, a character has unexpected reactions to unanticipated news. Discuss that in life, things are not always as they appear, that there's often more than one way to look at them.

Connecting Themes Across Cultures

"The Story of an Hour" is a story of personal change. Lead students to consider the effects of cultural change on personal change as the world continues to become "smaller." Many cultures normally untouched by changes around them now face encroachment from the outside. In east Africa, for example, the Masai and Datoga continually struggle to maintain their cultures as nomadic pastoralists. The surrounding population growth, however, forces the respective governments to take much needed land away from these tribes.

Customize for
Less Proficient Readers

To help students get the most from this piece, have them read it through twice, once to follow the plot and once more to notice the ironic details.

Customize for
AP Students

Guide students to look for examples of ideas in this story that were ahead of their time. Examples include the connection Chopin makes between the psychological and the physical.

Customize for
English Language Learners

Students may come from cultures in which gender roles are very strictly defined. Discuss the role of women and the conventions of marriage in the late nineteenth century in America, making clear the contrast between life then and now in America. Guide students to recognize the radical ideas Chopin presents.

Develop Understanding

One-Minute Insight Chopin's story presents its heroine with one unexpected shock and its readers with another.

Mrs. Mallard gets the unexpected news that her husband has been killed in an accident. She quickly recovers from the shock to discover that what she really feels is relief. Though she mourns his passing, she delights in the freedom that is now hers. She shuts herself in her room and relishes the opportunities ahead of her. When Mr. Mallard returns as unexpectedly as he died, Mrs. Mallard suffers a fatal heart attacks caused by the shock of the sudden loss of independence. The doctors, mistakenly assuming that she had been grieving, attribute the death to "joy that kills."

◆ Background for Understanding

Culture Chopin's story addresses issues of women's liberation in a time when these issues were not frequently raised. In this selection, Mrs. Mallard reveals thoughts about her life and her marriage. Ask students: What benefits does marriage offer? How do the demands of marriage conflict with each spouse's needs as an individual?

Art Transparency After students have read "The Story of an Hour," redisplay Art Transparency 6 and have students apply that description to the woman in Cassatt's painting. Review the contrast between seeming normalcy of Mallard's domestic life and the deep unhappiness and desire for escape that she actually felt.

The Story of an Hour

Kate Chopin

Knowing that Mrs. Mallard was afflicted with a heart trouble, great care was taken to break to her as gently as possible the news of her husband's death.

It was her sister Josephine who told her, in broken sentences; veiled hints that revealed in half concealing.

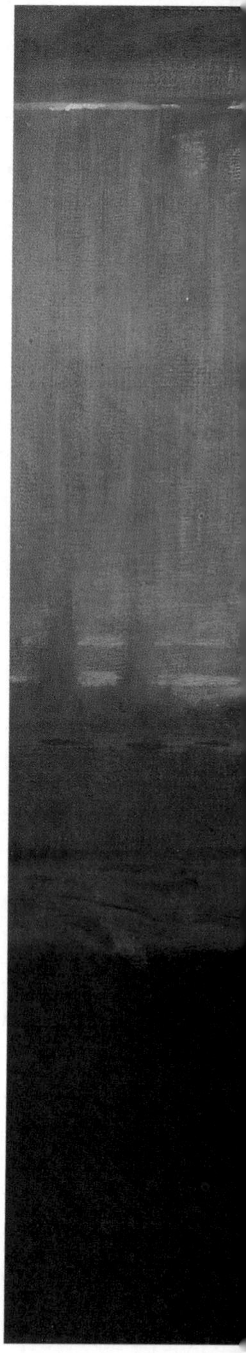

❶ ▶ Critical Viewing How does the light shining through the uncovered portion of the window reflect the "subtle and elusive" revelation that will come to Mrs. Mallard? **[Connect]**

Block Scheduling Strategies

Consider these suggestions to take advantage of extended class time:

- Introduce the selection with the Interest Grabber provided in the ATE. Ask students to choose one event from their list and then create a cause-and-effect chart to the possible results of the dramatic event they chose.
- Have students read the Background for Understanding section (p. 590) to help them complete the journal activity in Literature and Your Life (p. 591). Encourage students to discuss their entries in small groups. Ask them to choose a "top ten" list of those facets that have undergone the greatest change.
- Introduce the reading strategy and ask students to create a chart like the one on p. 591. Students can use their completed charts to help them answer the Reading Strategy question on p. 596.
- Assign the Guided Writing Lesson (p. 597). Before students begin, use the Reflective Essay model on pp. 5–8 in the ***Writing and Language Transparencies.*** Have students identify specific examples of how Kate Chopin conveys her personal attitudes in the story.

Afternoon in Piedmont, Xavier Martinez, Courtesy of the Oakland Museum

Humanities: Art

Afternoon in Piedmont by Xavier Martinez.

Xavier Martinez was born in Guadalajara, Mexico, in 1869. He eventually moved to San Francisco, where he later taught at the California School of Fine Arts. Martinez's work has been described as poetic. His *Afternoon at Piedmont* used as its inspiration James Whistler's famous painting of his mother. In his work, Martinez moved the scene to his house and used his wife as the model.

After students have read the selection, return to this painting and use these questions for discussion:

1. How would you describe the mood of this painting? *Students may see the yellow light entering the dark interior as the coming of dawn, bringing with it a comforting awakening.*
2. What scene in the story does the painting best represent? *Students may say that it describes the scene in which Mrs. Mallard is looking out at the signs of early spring and is herself awakening to her true feelings and a new approach to life.*

◆ Background for Understanding

Literature Chopin wrote "The Story of an Hour" on April 19, 1894, a day on which she herself was feeling as triumphant as the heroine of the story. Chopin's collection of regional stories *Bayou Folk* (1894) had just been favorably reviewed; she knew that her own dreams of literary and financial success were to be fulfilled. In its emphatic theme of female self-assertion, this story is different from Chopin's previous writing, and it sets the tone for much of her subsequent work.

▶Critical Viewing◀

❶ **Connect** Students may say that the light shows her calm contentment upon recognizing the first stages of her newly found freedom. They may suggest that the light is the yellow light of dawn and is symbolic of the new beginning of her life.

Read to Appreciate Author's Craft

Kate Chopin speaks loudly about women's issues in "The Story of an Hour," (a defined issue in her time,) yet she initially leads the reader into thinking she holds traditional beliefs. Help students recognize how she places emphasis on women's issues by building the first half of the story on the sadness and concern which accompanies the death—the expected response in Mrs. Mallard and those around her—and then turns the story upside down with an unexpected ending. This technique of Chopin's emphasizes the focus on women's rights by catching the reader unaware.

◆ Grammar and Style

❶ Appositives and Appositive Phrases Guide students to note the appositive in this sentence. Point out that *Richards* is not preceded by a comma because it is so closely related to the pronoun it modifies. Tell students that this kind of appositive is called a restrictive appositive because it is essential to the meaning of the sentence.

❷ Clarification Tell students that telegrams were the main form of long-distance communication at that time.

◆ Literary Focus

❸ Irony Guide students to appreciate the situational irony in this passage. It is ironic that Mrs. Mallard, newly widowed, should look out her window and see signs of the new life of spring, breaks in the clouds, and hear the sounds and songs of life.

◆ Reading Strategy

❹ Recognize Ironic Details Ask students whether they think that Mrs. Mallard is about to be possessed by some horrible "thing," as these details suggest, or whether they think the author is setting the stage for an ironic twist. *Students may say that an ironic twist is in store, basing their predictions on her seeing and hearing the signs of spring and spotting patches of blue sky. They may also refer to the hints that she feels something she didn't understand, thinking that she would understand and recognize grief.*

Thematic Focus

❺ Living in a Changing World Discuss that Mrs. Mallard recognizes that she is free for the first time. Out from under her husband's thumb, she is eager to pursue what she wants for herself and not what has been imposed upon her. Discuss that the idea of an emancipated woman was a radical notion in the 1890's.

❶ Her husband's friend Richards was there, too, near her. It was he who had been in the newspaper office when intelligence of the railroad disaster was received, with Brently Mallard's name leading the list of "killed." He had only taken the time to assure himself of ❷ its truth by a second telegram, and had hastened to forestall any less careful, less tender friend in bearing the sad message.

She did not hear the story as many women have heard the same, with a paralyzed inability to accept its significance. She wept at once, with sudden, wild abandonment, in her sister's arms. When the storm of grief had spent itself she went away to her room alone. She would have no one follow her.

There stood, facing the open window, a comfortable, roomy armchair. Into this she sank, pressed down by a physical exhaustion that haunted her body and seemed to reach into her soul.

She could see in the open square before her house the tops of trees that were all aquiver with the new spring life. The delicious breath of rain was in the air. ❸ In the street below a peddler was crying his wares. The notes of a distant song which someone was singing reached her faintly, and countless sparrows were twittering in the eaves.

There were patches of blue sky showing here and there through the clouds that had met and piled one above the other in the west facing her window.

She sat with her head thrown back upon the cushion of the chair, quite motionless, except when a sob came up into her throat and shook her, as a child who has cried itself to sleep continues to sob in its dreams.

She was young, with a fair, calm face, whose lines bespoke repression and even a certain strength. But now there was a dull stare in her eyes, whose gaze was fixed away off yonder on one of those patches of blue sky. It was not a glance of reflection, but rather indicated a suspension of intelligent thought.

There was something coming to her and she was waiting for it, fearfully. What was ❹ it? She did not know; it was too subtle and elusive to name. But she felt it, creeping out of the sky, reaching toward her through the sounds, the scents, the color that filled ❹ the air.

Now her bosom rose and fell tumultuously. She was beginning to recognize this thing that was approaching to possess her, and she was striving to beat it back with her will—as powerless as her two white slender hands would have been.

When she abandoned herself, a little whispered word escaped her slightly parted lips. She said it over and over under her breath: "free, free, free!" The vacant stare and the look of terror that had followed it went from her eyes. They stayed keen and bright. Her pulses beat fast, and the coursing blood warmed and relaxed every inch of her body.

She did not stop to ask if it were or were not a monstrous joy that held her. A clear and exalted perception enabled her to dismiss the suggestion as trivial.

She knew that she would weep again when she saw the kind, tender hands folded in death; the face that had never looked save with love upon her, fixed and gray and dead. But she saw beyond that bitter moment a long procession of years to come that would belong to her absolutely. And she opened and spread her arms out to them in welcome.

There would be no one to live for her during those coming years; she would live for herself. There would be no powerful will bending hers in that blind persistence with which men and women believe they have a right to impose a private will upon a fellow ❺ creature. A kind intention or a cruel intention made the act seem no less a crime as she looked upon it in that brief moment of illumination.

◆ Build Vocabulary

forestall (fôr stôl′) *v.*: Prevent by acting ahead of time

repression (ri presh′ ən) *n.*: Restraint

elusive (ē lo͞o′ siv) *adj.*: Hard to grasp

tumultuously (to͞o mul′ cho͞o wəs lē) *adv.*: In an agitated way

importunities (im′ pôr to͞on′ ə tēz) *n.*: Persistent requests or demands

Beyond the Classroom

Workplace Skills Connection

Communications Technology Point out that the failure of long-distance communication in this story leads to a fatal misunderstanding. While the telegram was a major method of long-distance communication in Chopin's time, newer faster modes have since made the telegram obsolete.

By 1887, the telephone was becoming widely available and U. S. telephone companies served more than 150,000 customers. One hundred years later, fax machines became a popular mode of communication, allowing people to send reproductions of documents through telephone lines. In the early 1990's, the Internet was introduced to the general public with the highly designed World Wide Web. Personal Internet access services allowed people to send and receive e-mail from the comfort of their homes.

Use this information to spark a discussion about the advantages and disadvantages of our highly technological age.

And yet she had loved him—sometimes. Often she had not. What did it matter! What could love, the unsolved mystery, count for in face of this possession of self-assertion which she suddenly recognized as the strongest impulse of her being!

> ◆ **Literary Focus**
> 6 Why is Josephine's reaction an example of dramatic irony?

"Free! Body and soul free!" she kept whispering.

Josephine was kneeling before the closed door with her lips to the keyhole, imploring for admission. "Louise, open the door! I beg; open the door—you will make yourself ill. What are you doing, Louise? For heaven's sake open the door."

"Go away. I am not making myself ill." No; she was drinking in a very elixir of life[1] through that open window.

Her fancy was running riot along those days ahead of her. Spring days, and summer days, and all sorts of days that would be her own. She breathed a quick prayer that life might be long. It was only yesterday she had thought with a shudder that life might be long. 7

She arose at length and opened the door to her sister's importunities. There was a feverish triumph in her eyes, and she carried herself unwittingly like a goddess of Victory. She clasped her sister's waist, and together they descended the stairs. Richards stood waiting for them at the bottom.

Someone was opening the front door with a latchkey. It was Brently Mallard who entered, a little travel-stained, composedly carrying his gripsack[2] and umbrella. He had been far from the scene of accident, and did not know there had been one. He stood amazed at Josephine's piercing cry; at Richards's quick motion to screen him from the view of his wife.

But Richards was too late.

When the doctors came they said she had died of heart disease—of joy that kills. 8

1. **elixir of life** (i lik´ sər): Imaginary substance believed in medieval times to prolong life indefinitely.

2. **gripsack** (grip´ sak) *n.*: Small bag for holding clothes.

Guide for Responding

◆ Literature and Your Life

Reader's Response Were you surprised by the end of the story? Explain why or why not.

Thematic Focus Kate Chopin lived and wrote in a time in which great social changes were brewing. How might Mrs. Mallard's life been different if the story were set in the late twentieth century?

Journal Writing What did you feel as you read about Mrs. Mallard's joy at her husband's death? Why? Describe your response in a journal entry.

☑ Check Your Comprehension

1. How does Mrs. Mallard react at first?
2. How does Mrs. Mallard's reaction change?
3. (a) What happens to Mrs. Mallard at the end of the story? (b) What prompts this occurrence?

◆ Critical Thinking

INTERPRET

1. At the beginning of the story, the author writes that Mrs. Mallard was afflicted with "a heart trouble." What, in addition to a medical condition, might she mean by this statement? **[Interpret]**
2. How does the scene outside Mrs. Mallard's window foreshadow the feelings that sweep over her as she sits in her chair? **[Connect]**
3. What has Mrs. Mallard apparently resented about her marriage? **[Infer]**
4. What do you believe is the actual reason for Mrs. Mallard's death? **[Draw a Conclusion]**

EVALUATE

5. Would "The Story of an Hour" seem believable as a modern tale? Explain. **[Evaluate]**

Beyond the Selection

FURTHER READING

Other Works by Kate Chopin

The Awakening

Bayou Folk

Other Works With the Theme of Women Living in a Changing World

The Kitchen God's Wife, Amy Tan

The Color Purple, Alice Walker

We suggest that you preview these works before recommending them to students.

INTERNET

You and your students may find additional information about Kate Chopin on the Internet. We suggest the following site. Please be aware, however, that sites may have changed since this information was published.

To learn about Kate Chopin, to see a list of her works, and to learn about the authors that influenced her, go to

http://www.dsu.edu/~freierm/chopin.htm

We *strongly recommend* that you preview the site before you send students to it.

◆ Literary Focus

6 Irony Students may say that the irony is that Josephine is worried that her sister is suffering but is unaware of Louise's sense of relief.

◆ Reading Strategy

7 Recognize Ironic Details Students can recognize the irony in this passage: whereas on the previous day Mrs. Mallard dreaded that her life might be a long one, today, now that she is a free woman, she is thrilled about it. Students can look back to this passage when they've finished reading to notice that, ironically, her life turned out to be quite short after all.

◆ Literary Focus

8 Irony Ask students to explain the irony in the doctors' diagnosis. *Students may say that Mrs. Mallard died of the shock of disappointment, not joy, as the doctors thought.*

Reinforce and Extend

Answers

◆ Literature and Your Life

Reader's Response Students should support their opinions with details from the story. Invite students who disagree to defend their positions.

Thematic Focus Mrs. Mallard might have found fulfillment in a career. She also may not have chosen to be married.

☑ Check Your Comprehension

1. She weeps with wild abandon.
2. Her reaction changes to joy as she develops a sense of freedom.
3. (a) She has a fatal heart attack. (b) Her husband—whom she believed was dead—returned home.

◆ Critical Thinking

1. It might refer to her lack of love for her husband and her unenthusiastic outlook on life.
2. The spring scene conveys a sense of rebirth.
3. Possible response: Mrs. Mallard resented the limits placed upon her freedom.
4. Possible response: Her death is caused by the feelings of shock and disappointment that result from the return of her husband.
5. Students should support their responses.

Answers

◆ Literary Focus

1. Neither the reader nor Mrs. Mallard knows that Mr. Mallard is actually alive.
2. Mrs. Mallard's has just begun to look forward to leading a long life.
3. Readers know that the doctors diagnosis is wrong.

◆ Build Vocabulary

Using the Anglo-Saxon Prefix *fore-*

1. forestall
2. foretell
3. foreman
4. forefathers

Using the Word Bank

1. importunities
2. forestall
3. repression
4. tumultuously
5. elusive

◆ Reading Strategy

1. Her family is careful to share the news gently.
2. Two sources confirmed Mallard's death.
3. Possible response: She has been "drinking in the very elixir of life" and she had "breathed a quick prayer that life might be long."

◆ Grammar and Style

Writing Application

2. She sank gratefully into the chair, *a comfortable, roomy, armchair.*
3. She felt like a new woman, *the goddess of Victory,* as she left her room.
4. Her husband's friend *Richards* tried to shield the visitor from Mrs. Mallard's sight.

Grammar Reinforcement

For additional instruction and practice, use the Recognizing and Using Phrases lesson in the **Language Lab CD-ROM**, and the pages on Prepositional Phrases and Appositives pp. 30–31 in the *Writer's Solution Grammar Practice Book.*

Guide for Responding (continued)

◆ Literary Focus

IRONY

Irony is the contrast between what is stated and what is meant or between what is expected and what actually happens. "The Story of an Hour" contains both **dramatic irony,** which occurs when the reader knows something a character does not, and **situational irony,** which occurs when a reader is surprised by an unexpected turn of events.

1. How is Mrs. Mallard's reaction to her husband's death an example of situational irony?
2. Why is Mrs. Mallard's sudden death also an example of situational irony?
3. Where is the dramatic irony in the diagnosis of Mrs. Mallard's cause of death?

◆ Build Vocabulary

USING THE ANGLO-SAXON PREFIX *fore-*

Knowing that the Anglo-Saxon prefix *fore-* means "before," select the word from the box below that you could expect to find in each of these book titles.

foretell	foreman	forestall	forefathers

1. *Why Pay Taxes Now When You Can Pay Them Later?*
2. *Amazing Predictions for the Twenty-first Century*
3. *Twenty Years on an Assembly Line*
4. *How to Trace Your Family History*

USING THE WORD BANK: Word Choice

Write the following sentences in your notebook, replacing the italicized word or phrase in each with the appropriate word from the Word Bank.

1. After her husband's death, Kate Chopin gave in to her mother's *insistent pleas* and returned to live in St. Louis.
2. Following her mother's death, a doctor suggested Chopin take up writing in the hope that it would *head off* a slide into depression.
3. Kate Chopin strove in her writing to expose the social conventions that kept women in a state of near constant *restraint.*
4. Her characters often lived *in a state of agitation,* their lives fraught with upheaval and change.
5. Though she initially enjoyed success as a writer, outrage over her finest novel taught Chopin that lasting acclaim is *difficult to hold on to.*

◆ Reading Strategy

RECOGNIZE IRONIC DETAILS

"The Story of an Hour" is filled with **details** that lead the reader to have certain expectations. When readers draw conclusions or make predictions based on the details, the actual turn of events is often surprising.

1. What detail leads you to believe that Mrs. Mallard will be truly grieved by her husband's death?
2. Which detail in the second paragraph makes Mr. Mallard's arrival at the end all the more ironic?
3. Identify two details that help create the surprise of Mrs. Mallard's death.

◆ Grammar and Style

APPOSITIVES AND APPOSITIVE PHRASES

If an **appositive** can be omitted from a sentence without altering the sentence's basic meaning, it must be set off by commas. If, however, the appositive is essential to the meaning of the sentence, commas are not used. **Appositive phrases** are always set off by commas or dashes.

An **appositive** is a noun or pronoun placed near another noun or pronoun to provide more information about it. When an appositive is accompanied by its own modifiers, it forms an **appositive phrase.**

Writing Application Combine the information in each pair of sentences into a single sentence containing an appositive. The first one has been done for you.

1. Mrs. Mallard was not grieved by her husband's death. She was an unconventional woman.
   Mrs. Mallard, *an unconventional woman,* was not grieved by her husband's death.
2. She sank gratefully into the chair. The chair was a comfortable, roomy armchair.
3. She felt like a new woman as she left her room. She felt like the goddess of Victory.
4. Her husband's friend tried to shield the visitor from Mrs. Mallard's sight. The friend's name was Richards.

Reteach

"The Story of an Hour" is filled with irony. Points of verbal, dramatic, and situational irony can each be found. Students may, however, have difficulty recognizing irony as it occurs in this story. To help them better understand the different types of irony, create a chart similar to the one in the Reading Strategy on p. 591. While students follow along, read the story aloud, pausing to explain the different ironies as they occur. (Use the teaching notes to help you.) After completing several examples, ask students to point out irony as you continue reading.

Detail	Expected Outcome	Actual Outcome	Type of Irony
"There was something coming to her and she was waiting for it, fearfully."	grief, even death	signs of spring coming through the window (rebirth)	situational

Build Your Portfolio

Idea Bank

Writing

1. Diary Entry Imagine that Louise Mallard survives the shock of her husband's return. Writing as Mrs. Mallard, create a diary entry describing the day's emotional ordeal.

2. New Version Write a new version of the story, setting it in modern times. Consider how the details and Mrs. Mallard's options might be different.

3. Commentary Shortly after completing this story, Chopin wrote that if she could get her husband back, she would be willing to give up "... the past ten years of [her] growth—[her] real growth." In a brief essay, explain how her comment affects your interpretation of "The Story of an Hour."

Speaking, Listening, and Viewing

4. Soliloquy What might Mrs. Mallard have made of her life if her husband had not returned? Present a soliloquy in which she reflects on her life and thoughts ten years later. Have the years fulfilled their promise? **[Performing Arts Link]**

5. Culture Comparison Give an oral presentation comparing the roles of women in the United States today with those of women in another culture that interests you. Lead your class in a discussion. **[Social Studies Link]**

Researching and Representing

6. Visual Interpretation Create a work of art that expresses the joy of freedom experienced by Mrs. Mallard. Be prepared to explain your piece, in particular any symbolism that reflects details or events from the story. **[Art Link]**

7. Pantomime With a small group, act out "The Story of an Hour" using facial expressions and gestures but no dialogue. **[Performing Arts Link]**

Online Activity www.phlit.phschool.com

Guided Writing Lesson

Reflective Essay

In a reflective essay, a writer describes personal experiences or pivotal events and conveys his or her feelings about them. In addition, the writer often reflects on the significance of his or her subject. Draw upon your memory and your observations to come up with a topic for a reflective essay. Recall interesting people, places, and events; think about issues of importance to you. In writing your essay, use a personal tone.

Writing Skills Focus: Personal Tone

Just as your tone of voice can convey your attitude about an event or a situation, the tone of your writing can convey how you feel about your topic. You can achieve a **personal tone** in your reflective essay by incorporating these strategies:

- Write in the first person.
- Use an informal conversational style.
- Include your personal opinions and feelings about your topic.

Prewriting To gather details for your reflective essay, use a sunburst diagram like this one. Write your topic in the center circle; then write your observations and feelings about the topic on spokes radiating from the circle.

Drafting Organize your details in a way that fits your topic; consider chronological order or order of importance. As you write, use a personal tone that reflects your attitude toward your subject. To keep the tone of your essay informal, avoid high-level vocabulary.

Revising Read over your essay, focusing on parts that could be made clearer. Add or eliminate details as necessary to strengthen the impression you wish to convey to your readers.

Idea Bank

Customizing for
Performance Levels
Following are suggestions for matching Idea Bank topics with your students' performance levels:
Less Advanced Students: 1, 7
Average Students: 2, 4, 6
More Advanced Students: 3, 5

Customizing for
Learning Modalities
Following are suggestions for matching Idea Bank topics with your students' learning modalities:
Verbal/Linguistic: 5
Logical/Mathematical: 5
Bodily/Kinesthetic: 7
Visual/Spatial: 6
Intrapersonal: 4

Guided Writing Lesson

For more instruction on prewriting, elaboration, and revision, see *Prentice Hall Writing and Grammar.*

Writing and Language Transparencies
Use Writing Process Model 1: Reflective Essay on pages 5–8 to introduce students to the features of a reflective essay.

Writing Lab CD-ROM
Have students complete the tutorial on Description. Follow these steps:

1. Have students use the sensory word bins to choose modifiers, nouns and verbs to enhance their reflective essay.
2. After using the interactive models of different tones, have students draft on the computer
3. Refer students to the audio-annotated student model to help them see how and why another student revised.

✓ ASSESSMENT OPTIONS

Formal Assessment, Selection Test, pp. 179–181, and Assessment Resources Software. The selection test is designed so that it can be easily customized to the performance levels of your students.

Alternative Assessment, p. 37, includes options for less advanced students, more advanced students, verbal/linguistic learners and interpersonal learners.

PORTFOLIO ASSESSMENT
Use the following rubrics in the ***Alternative Assessment*** booklet to assess student writing:
Diary Entry: Response to Literature Rubric, p. 125
New Version: Response to Literature Rubric, p. 125
Commentary: Critical Review Rubric, p. 126
Guided Writing Lesson: Description Rubric, p. 112

Prepare and Engage

LESSON OBJECTIVES

1. **To develop vocabulary and word identification skills**
   - Word Origins: Forms of *Guile*
   - Using the Word Bank: Antonyms
2. **To use a variety of reading strategies to comprehend a poem**
   - Connect Your Experience
   - Reading Strategy: Interpret
3. **To increase knowledge of other cultures and to connect common elements across cultures**
   - Background for Understanding
   - Idea Bank: Other Cultures
4. **To express and support responses to the text**
   - Critical Thinking
   - Idea Bank: Diary Entry
5. **To analyze literary elements**
   - Literary Focus: Rhyme
   - Idea Bank: Literary Analysis
6. **To read in order to research self-selected and assigned topics**
   - Idea Bank: Report
   - Idea Bank: Timeline
7. **To plan, prepare, organize, and present literary interpretations**
   - Idea Bank: Oral Interpretation
8. **To use recursive writing processes to write a poem to honor a hero**
   - Guided Writing Lesson
9. **To increase knowledge of the rules of grammar and usage**
   - Grammar and Style: Punctuation of Interjections

Test Preparation

Reading Comprehension: Context (ATE, p. 599)

The teaching tips and sample test item in this workshop support the instruction and practice in the unit workshop:

Reading Comprehension: Using Context (SE, p. 631)

Guide for Interpreting

Paul Laurence Dunbar

(1872–1906)

The first African American to support himself entirely by writing, Paul Laurence Dunbar displayed great versatility as a writer throughout his short career.

Dunbar was born in Dayton, Ohio, the son of former slaves. Encouraged by his mother, he began writing poetry at an early age. During high school, Dunbar, who was the only African America student in his class, frequently recited his poetry before school assemblies. He also served as the president of the literary society, as class poet, and as editor of the school newspaper. Following his graduation, he supported himself by working as an elevator operator while continuing to write. He first earned recognition when he gave a poetry reading during a meeting of the Western Association of Writers.

Characters, Themes, and Forms In his lifetime, he published seven volumes of poetry, four novels, and four volumes of short stories. Dunbar's writing cast a nostalgic light on the lost world of the southern plantation. Dunbar also focused on social problems facing African Americans at the turn of the century. His characters included farmers, politicians, preachers, traders, entertainers, and professional people.

By his late twenties, Dunbar was a nationally prominent poet. His reputation resulted largely from the readings he gave throughout the United States and Europe.

Popularity at a Price Dunbar composed poems in two styles—one formal, elegant, and serious; the other, a rural dialect. This split was echoed in people's reactions to his work. Called the "Poet Laureate of the Negro Race" by Booker T. Washington, Dunbar was criticized by some blacks who believed that his dialect poems pandered to white readers' desire for sentimental stereotypes of prewar African Americans.

Despite his success as a poet, Dunbar was disillusioned by the critics' tendency to focus on the poetry he wrote in black dialect, while virtually ignoring the poetry he wrote in more formal verse.

By the end of his life, his poetry was so popular that he was able to write from Florida, "Down here one finds my poems recited everywhere."

In poems such as"Douglass" and "We Wear the Mask," Dunbar demonstrates a command of the English language that was often overlooked, capturing the despair of African Americans in a dignified, graceful manner.

◆ Background for Understanding

CULTURE: DUNBAR AND INDEPENDENCE DAY

Dunbar wrote during a period of racial injustice. In a July 1903 letter, he uses bitter irony to express his feelings about observing Independence Day as a black American. Parts of the letter follow.

> [W]e have celebrated the Nation's birthday. Yes, and we black folks have celebrated. . . . Like a dark cloud, pregnant with terror and destruction, disenfranchisement has spread its wings over our brethren of the South. Like the same dark cloud, industrial prejudice glooms about us in the North . . . And yet we celebrate. . . .
>
> With bleeding hands uplifted, still sore and smarting from long beating at the door of opportunity, we raise our voices and sing, "My Country, Tis of Thee"; . . . while from the four points of the compass comes our brothers' unavailing cry, and so we celebrate.

Prentice Hall Literature Program Resources

REINFORCE / RETEACH / EXTEND

Selection Support Pages
Build Vocabulary: Forms of *guile*, p. 177
Grammar and Style: Punctuation of Interjections, p. 178
Reading Strategy: Interpret, p. 179
Literary Focus: Rhyme, p. 180

Strategies for Diverse Student Needs, p. 38

Beyond Literature
Humanities Connection: Art, p. 38

Formal Assessment Selection Test, pp. 182–184; Assessment Resources Software

Alternative Assessment, p. 38

Writing and Language Transparencies
Branching Organizer, pp. 67–69

Resource Pro CD-ROM

Listening to Literature Audiocassettes

◆ Literature and Your Life

CONNECT YOUR EXPERIENCE

At the end of most sporting events, the competitors shake hands. Despite anger or frustration, the loser usually smiles and congratulates the winner. The rules of courtesy often dictate that people smile even when they really feel sad or disappointed. Paul Laurence Dunbar describes such a reaction in his poems as he explores conflicts arising from the struggle for identity and truth.

Journal Writing Write about a time when your appearance or behavior was contrary to the way you felt inside.

THEMATIC FOCUS: LIVING IN A CHANGING WORLD

Dunbar was among the first generation of African Americans born into a nation that no longer tolerated slavery. However, change came slowly for African Americans and brought with it struggle and self-doubt. In these poems, Dunbar confronts directly some of the difficulties and anxieties of living in a changing world.

◆ Build Vocabulary

RELATED WORDS: FORMS OF *GUILE*

The word *guile* is a noun meaning "craftiness." By adding one or more prefixes or suffixes to *guile,* you can form related words, such as the adjective *guileless,* meaning "innocent or naive," and the verb *beguile,* meaning "to mislead or trick."

WORD BANK

Preview this list of words from the poems.

salient
tempest
stark
guile
myriad

◆ Grammar and Style

PUNCTUATION OF INTERJECTIONS

Dunbar writes, "Ah, Douglass, we have fall'n on evil days . . ." In this line, *Ah* is an **interjection**—a word or phrase used to express emotion. An interjection has no grammatical relation to other words in a sentence. Depending on the degree of emotion being expressed, you can use either an exclamation point or a comma after an interjection. For example:

No! Don't touch that doorknob!

Yes, she agrees with me.

◆ Literary Focus

RHYME

Rhyme—which gives poetry a musical quality—is the repetition of sounds in the accented syllables of two or more words appearing close to each other. In a **true rhyme,** the vowel sounds and any consonants that appear after them must be the same, as in *flag* and *stag.* A **slant rhyme** links two similar (but not exact) vowel sounds, as in *prove* and *love.*

Poets use rhyme in different ways. **End rhymes** occur at the ends of two or more poetic lines; an **internal rhyme** appears within a single line.

◆ Reading Strategy

INTERPRET

Poets often mean much more than their lines say literally. To **interpret** the poet's words, you have to read between and beyond the lines to discover what the poet really means.

For example, in order to interpret "We Wear the Mask," you must consider who "we" refers to. It also helps to know the time and historical context in which the poem was written. Then you need to consider what a mask suggests and what it might cover.

Thinking about these issues as you read the poem will help you to interpret it.

Interest Grabber Prepare students for reading and interpreting these poems by asking them to wear a mask to class. It can be a simple eye mask, surgical face mask, or, if they have no mask, they can make one of paper or fabric. Have groups discuss what it is like to try to communicate when they all have masks on. Guide them to notice that masks can fool, hide, frighten, or amuse, but rarely do they encourage honesty or frankness. Then, have students remove the physical masks but assume mask-like facial expressions: joy, fear, boredom, or any emotion of their choice. How convincing can they be in maintaining the mask of an emotion when talking with friends? With strangers?

Customize for
Less Proficient Readers
To help students with these works, have them follow along in their text as they listen to the recording of the poems.

Listening to Literature Audiocassettes

Customize for
AP Students
Post-Civil War African Americans faced new kinds of struggles for dignity and equality, despite what the law said. Many found that they had to forge new identities in the emancipated world. Have students research more about the post-Civil War period for African Americans. Have them relate what they have learned to their understanding of what Dunbar asks for in these poems, and why he implores Frederick Douglass to help.

Customize for
English Language Learners
Like other poets, Dunbar often uses poetic license in his works. He adjusts inflections ("heard thee with amaze"), reverses typical word order ("to thee from tortured souls arise"), and uses unfamiliar word forms ("dispraise"). Help students identify and understand cases like these in the poems.

Test Preparation Workshop

Reading Comprehension:
Context Some standardized tests require students to use context to determine the meanings of unfamiliar words. Write the following passage from p. 600 on the chalkboard, then have students answer the question that follows.

We ride amid a tempest of dispraise,/Now, when the waves of swift dissension swarm,/And Honor, the strong pilot lieth stark,/Oh, for thy voice high-sounding o'er the storm

In this passage, tempest means—

A storm
B sinking boat
C discussion
D voice

The first part of the passage says the speaker rides amid a tempest. *Amid,* in combination with the references to waves and a storm, should provide the context that helps students choose *A* as the correct answer.

Develop Understanding

One-Minute Insight In both poems, the writer addresses the struggles of African Americans. In the first poem, the speaker cries out to a hero of an earlier generation.

In the second poem, the speaker suggests that African Americans hide their despair from the eyes of white America.

▶Critical Viewing◀

❶ **Speculate** *Douglass was an abolitionist who helped to bring about great change.*

◆ Reading Strategy

❷ **Interpret** Ask students what the poet means by "evil days." *Slavery is over, but the progress of African Americans is still in check.*

◆ Critical Thinking

❸ **Assess** Why does Dunbar use the formal address of *thee* and *thou*? *Dunbar honors Douglass. This language creates a formal tone.*

◆ Literary Focus

❹ **Rhyme** Guide students to identify examples of true and slant rhyme. *Examples include know/ago/flow for true rhyme and swarm/storm for slant rhyme.* Point out that "Douglass" is a Petrarchan sonnet—a fourteen line poem with an ABBA ABBA CDCDCD rhyme scheme.

◆ Reading Strategy

❺ **Interpret** Show students that the tempest metaphor casts Douglass as a captain who can guide the ship. The storm metaphor implies that trouble will end, but that guidance is needed to get through it safely.

Humanities: Art

Frederick Douglass, artist unknown.

This portrait of the abolitionist Frederick Douglass (1817–1895) appeared in the November 24, 1883, issue of *Harper's Weekly.*

Use this question for discussion: What qualities of Douglass's does the artist capture in this portrait? *Students might cite the strong face, intense stare, and determination.*

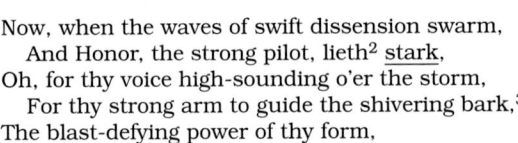

▲ ❶ Critical Viewing: Why is a civil rights activist like Frederick Douglass an appropriate inspiration for Dunbar? **[Speculate]**

DOUGLASS

Paul Laurence Dunbar

Ah, Douglass,[1] we have fall'n on evil days,
  Such days as thou, not even thou didst know,
  When thee, the eyes of that harsh long ago ❷
Saw, <u>salient</u>, at the cross of devious ways,
And all the country heard thee with amaze. ❸
  Not ended then, the passionate ebb and flow, ❹
  The awful tide that battled to and fro;
We ride amid a <u>tempest</u> of dispraise.

Now, when the waves of swift dissension swarm,
  And Honor, the strong pilot, lieth[2] <u>stark</u>, ❺
Oh, for thy voice high-sounding o'er the storm,
  For thy strong arm to guide the shivering bark,[3]
The blast-defying power of thy form,
  To give us comfort through the lonely dark.

---

1. **Douglass:** Frederick Douglass, an American abolitionist (1817?–1895).
2. **lieth** (lī′ eth) *v.*: Lies.
3. **bark:** Boat.

◆ Build Vocabulary

salient (sāl′ yənt) *adj.*: Standing out from the rest
tempest (tem′ pist) *n.*: Violent storm
stark (stärk) *adj.*: Stiff or rigid, as a corpse

Block Scheduling Strategies

Consider these suggestions to take advantage of extended class time.

- Introduce the selection with the interest grabber in the ATE. Follow up with the Literature and Your Life feature on p. 599.
- Provide students with an appropriate framework for interpreting Dunbar's poetry. Refer to the author biography and the Background for Understanding on p. 598, and the Thematic Focus on p. 599.
- Using their answers to Critical Thinking questions and the Reading Strategy questions on p. 602 as a guide, invite students to explain their own interpretations of each poem.
- Provide class time to allow students to prepare for the Panel Discussion activity on p. 603. Once students are ready, stage the discussion.
- Have students complete one of the writing assignments in the Idea Bank (p. 603) as a homework assignment. Then, using a Scoring Rubric, found in ***Alternative Assessment,*** have pairs assess each other's work.

We Wear the Mask

Paul Laurence Dunbar

We wear the mask that grins and lies,
It hides our cheeks and shades our eyes—
This debt we pay to human guile;
With torn and bleeding hearts we smile,
And mouth with myriad subtleties.

Why should the world be overwise,
❻ In counting all our tears and sighs?
❼ Nay, let them only see us, while
We wear the mask.

We smile, but, O great Christ, our cries
To thee from tortured souls arise.
We sing, but oh the clay is vile
Beneath our feet, and long the mile;
But let the world dream otherwise,
We wear the mask!

◆ Build Vocabulary

guile (gīl) *n.*: Craftiness

myriad (mir′ ē əd) *adj.*: Countless

Guide for Responding

◆ Literature and Your Life

Reader's Response How do you feel when you must appear or behave as others want you to?

Thematic Focus How might Paul Laurence Dunbar like to see the world change?

Questions for Research In these two poems by Dunbar, look for common themes about social issues faced by post-war African Americans. Ask questions that will guide your research about this subject.

☑ Check Your Comprehension

1. According to the speaker of "Douglass," when was Frederick Douglass's voice heard by the whole nation?
2. Why does the speaker wish that Douglass were alive to "guide the shivering bark"?
3. According to the speaker of "We Wear the Mask," what emotions does the mask hide?

◆ Literary Focus

❻ **Rhyme** Have students identify the rhyme scheme in this poem, in which most lines are either true rhymes or slant rhymes. Ask about the impact of the lack of rhyme in lines 9 and 15, where the poet repeats the title. Students may sense that these lines stand out; perhaps Dunbar feels as isolated.

◆ Grammar and Style

❼ **Punctuation of Interjections** Point out the interjection in line 10, "O great Christ," which is separated from the rest of the line by commas.

Reinforce and Extend

Customize for
AP Students
Maya Angelou's 1970 autobiography *I Know Why the Caged Bird Sings* gets its title from Dunbar's poem, "Sympathy." Share the poem with students and explore the meaning of its title. Have students analyze Dunbar's sense of being a caged bird who sang to avoid crying. Hold a group discussion on how his sympathy for the caged bird grew from his experience as a black writer forced by circumstances to write for largely white audiences. Ask students to draw a conclusion about the question that Dunbar didn't ask but that was most important to him. (Caged by market-place expectations, Dunbar avoided writing about the crucially important question of how to end racial discrimination.)

Answers

◆ Literature and Your Life

Reader's Response Students may say that they feel awkward or angry.

Thematic Focus Possible response: Dunbar would like to see greater honesty and equality.

☑ Check Your Comprehension

1. Douglass's voice was heard "long ago" in a harsher time.
2. He believes that Douglass would guide the ship and offer comfort.
3. The mask hides pain and torment.

Beyond the Selection

FURTHER READING

Other Works by Paul Laurence Dunbar

Oak and Ivy
Majors and Minors
Lyrics of Lowly Life

Other Works with the Theme of Equal Rights

"I, Too," Langston Hughes
"Tableau," Countee Cullen

We suggest that you preview these works before recommending them to students.

INTERNET

You can find additional information about Dunbar on the Internet. We suggest the following site. Please be aware, however, that sites may have changed since this information was published. For a database that covers the work of fifty-four African American poets who wrote between 1760 and 1900, go to **http://www.hti.umich.edu/english/daap/index.html**

We *strongly recommend* that you preview the site before you send students to it.

Answers

◆ Critical Thinking

1. (a) The speaker is the African Americans. (b) They are distressed by their condition.
2. It symbolized their attempt to hide their feelings.
3. He compares their struggles to the ocean, an awful tide that ebbs and flows and now is a rough, stormy sea.
4. The speaker calls for a leader like Douglass to guide African Americans through troubled times.
5. Possible response: He would see great improvements but also see the need for true equality.

◆ Literary Focus

1. The words are *eyes, overwise, sighs, cries, arise,* and *otherwise.*
2. The slant rhyme is *lies/subtleties.*
3. The rhyme scheme is CDCDCD.

◆ Reading Strategy

1. Possible response: The speaker may be describing a situation where friends, family, co-workers, or community expected him to act in a certain way.
2. Possible response: The speaker may be referring to the effects of segregation.
3. Even though the violent fight to end slavery eventually succeeded, racism continues to cause problems.

◆ Build Vocabulary

Using Forms of *Guile*

guileful, *(adj.);* guilefully, *(adv.);* guilefullness, *(n.);* guileless, *(adj.);* guilelessly, *(adv.);* guilelessness, *(n.)*

Using the Word Bank

1. e 2. a 3. d 4. c 5. b

◆ Grammar and Style

1. Hey! Don't leave without me!
2. Ah, this warm bath feels soothing.
3. No, I'm afraid I wont' be able to attend your party.
4. (a) Oh! Is that what you think? (b) Well, you should know you're wrong.
5. Yes! You've got to hurry!

Guide for Responding *(continued)*

◆ Critical Thinking

Interpret

1. (a) Who is the speaker of "We Wear the Mask"? (b) How would you describe the speaker's emotional condition? **[Analyze]**

2. (a) What does the mask symbolize? (b) Whom does it deceive? **[Interpret]**

3. To what does the speaker of "Douglass" compare the plight of African Americans?

4. Summarize the main idea of "Douglass." **[Draw Conclusions]**

Extend

5. How do you think Dunbar might have characterized the situation of African Americans in the 1990's? **[Social Studies Link]**

◆ Literary Focus

Rhyme

Rhyme occurs in two or more words that have similar or identical vowel and final consonant sounds in their accented syllables. For example, in the first two lines of "We Wear the Mask," Paul Laurence Dunbar rhymes the words *lies* and *eyes.*

1. List all the words in "We Wear the Mask" that are true rhymes with the word *lies.*

2. What slant rhyme does Dunbar use in this poem?

3. The **rhyme scheme** or pattern of rhyme in the first stanza of "Douglass" can be expressed as ABBAABBA (A stands for words rhyming with *days* and B stands for words rhyming with *know.*) What is the rhyme scheme for the second stanza?

◆ Reading Strategy

Interpret

As you **interpret** a work of literature, you explain its meaning and significance. Interpreting a work of literature can reveal several layers of meaning.

1. How might you interpret "We Wear the Mask" on the level of Dunbar's personal experience?

2. What situation might he be describing for African Americans in general?

3. In "Douglass," how would you interpret the situation described in lines 6–10?

◆ Build Vocabulary

Using Forms of *Guile*

Several English words are related to the noun *guile.* Combine *guile,* meaning "craftiness," with the suffixes *-ful, -fully, -fullness, -less, -lessly,* and *-lessness* to create six words. Label each word's part of speech.

Using the Word Bank: Antonyms

On your paper, match each word in the left column with its antonym in the right column.

1. guile	**a.** tranquility; stillness
2. tempest	**b.** not many
3. salient	**c.** elastic; flexible
4. stark	**d.** unimportant
5. myriad	**e.** honesty

◆ Grammar and Style

Punctuation of Interjections

Interjections are grammatically unrelated to the other words in a sentence. Use a comma to punctuate an interjection that expresses mild emotion. Use an exclamation point to punctuate an interjection that expresses strong emotion. Note that any words following the exclamation point constitute a new sentence, which must begin with a capital letter.

An **interjection** is a word or phrase that expresses emotion in a sentence.

Practice Add a comma or an exclamation point to correct the punctuation of the interjections in each of the following sentences. Capitalize the sentences as necessary.

1. Hey don't leave without me!

2. Ah this warm bath feels soothing.

3. No I'm afraid I won't be able to attend your party.

4. (a) Oh is that what you think? (b) Well you should know you're wrong.

5. Yes you've got to hurry!

Reteach

Give students who are having difficulty interpreting the poem some strategies for reading between the lines to determine what the poet really means. Point out the words *We* and *Mask* in the title of the poem.

Tell them to ask themselves three questions as they read the poem: What's the purpose of the mask? What is the mask hiding? Who does *we* represent? Draw the following visual on the chalkboard to get students started.

Tell student to fill in more information as they read the poem.

We Represents	Purpose of a Mask	What Mask Hides
(African Americans) torn and bleeding hearts	lies hides	our cheeks and eyes

Build Your Portfolio

Idea Bank

Writing

1. Diary Entry Imagine that you are the speaker of "We Wear the Mask." Write a diary entry describing a day in your life. Focus on encounters in which you are required to "wear the mask."

2. Report Research one aspect of racial discrimination in the United States during Dunbar's lifetime. Present your findings in a written report. **[Social Studies Link]**

3. Literary Analysis Choose one Dunbar poem, and write a literary analysis in which you examine the imagery, word choice, rhyme, and rhythm and show how, together, these elements convey Dunbar's thoughts and feelings.

Speaking, Listening, and Viewing

4. Panel Discussion With several of your classmates, stage a panel discussion on how important figures in history can affect the generations that follow them. **[Social Studies Link]**

5. Oral Interpretation Prepare an oral interpretation of one of the two Dunbar poems. Begin by analyzing the meaning and form of each line. Then read the poem aloud many times, trying different tones of voice and cadences. Present your interpretation to the class. **[Drama Link]**

Researching and Representing

6. Other Cultures Since the Stone Age, human beings have constructed and worn masks. Explore types of masks used around the world. Then create a replica of one. Explain to your class the mask's cultural significance. **[Art Link]**

7. Timeline Research the life of activist Frederick Douglass; then create a timeline showing the important events and achievements of his career. **[Social Studies Link]**

Online Activity www.phlit.phschool.com

Guided Writing Lesson

Poem to Honor a Hero

In "Douglass," Paul Laurence Dunbar expresses the wish that his hero were still alive to help comfort and guide African Americans through continuing difficult times. Think of another historical figure who, if alive today, might help solve some of society's problems. Compose a poem in which you address this hero as Dunbar addresses Douglass.

Writing Skills Focus: Main Impression

The ideas and details in your poem should combine to create a single, dominant impression of your subject. Use language and images that contribute to the impression you're striving for, and avoid details that do not. Notice how the images in "Douglass" work together to convey the sense of the subject as a powerful figure.

Model From the Poem

Oh, for thy voice high-sounding o'er the storm, / For thy strong arm to guide the shivering bark . . .

Prewriting First, list the accomplishments and character traits that contributed to your subject's heroism. Then brainstorm for sensory words and images that relate this person to aspects of today's world that your hero might affect.

Drafting Choose a form for your poem—a regular rhythm and rhyme scheme or free verse, for example. Use images and sound devices that convey a vivid main impression of your subject.

Revising Reread your poem. What details should you add or eliminate to sharpen the impression of your subject? How can you improve your sound devices, such as rhyme or alliteration? How can you use images and figurative language—similes and metaphors—to convey your ideas more effectively?

ASSESSMENT OPTIONS

Formal Assessment, Selection Test, pp. 182–184, and Assessment Resources Software. The selection test is designed so that it can be easily customized to the performance levels of your students.

Alternative Assessment, p. 38, includes options for less advanced students, more advanced students, visual/spatial learners, verbal/linguistic learners, and bodily/kinesthetic learners.

PORTFOLIO ASSESSMENT

Use the following rubrics in the ***Alternative Assessment*** booklet to assess student writing:
Diary Entry: Response to Literature Rubric, p. 125
Report: Research Report/Paper Rubric, p. 121
Literary Analysis: Literary Analysis/Interpretation Rubric, p. 127
Guided Writing Lesson: Poetry Rubric, p. 123

Idea Bank

Customizing for
Performance Levels
Following are suggestions for matching Idea Bank topics with your students' performance levels:
Less Advanced Students: 1, 6
Average Students: 2, 4, 5
More Advanced Students: 3, 7

Customizing for
Learning Modalities
Following are suggestions for matching Idea Bank topics with your students' learning modalities:
Logical/Mathematical: 7
Musical/Rhythmic: 5
Visual/Spatial: 6
Interpersonal: 4

Guided Writing Lesson

For more instruction on prewriting, elaboration, and revision, see *Prentice Hall Writing and Grammar.*

Writing and Language Transparencies
Use the Branching organizer on pages 67–69 in ***Writing and Language Transparencies*** to help students gather images for their poems.

Writers at Work Videodisc
Have students view the videodisc segment on Creative Writing (Ch. 6) featuring Martín Espada to learn how Martín Espada feels about sound devices. Have students discuss how they can apply his advice to their own poetry.

Play frames 20514 to 20978

Writing Lab CD-ROM
Have students complete the tutorial on Creative Writing. Follow these steps:

1. Have students use the sensory word bins to gather vivid language.
2. As students draft on the computer, encourage them to use the audio-annotated models that demonstrate the use of sound devices.
3. Have students use the Revision Checker for vague adjectives.

Prepare and Engage

LESSON OBJECTIVES

1. **To develop vocabulary and word identification skills**
   - Latin Word Roots: *-pose-*
   - Using the Word Bank: Synonyms
2. **To use a variety of reading strategies to comprehend poetry**
   - Connect Your Experience
   - Reading Strategy: Recognize Attitudes
3. **To increase knowledge of other cultures and to connect common elements across cultures**
   - Connecting Themes Across Cultures (ATE)
5. **To express and support responses to the text**
   - Critical Thinking
   - Idea Bank: Comparison/Contrast
   - Idea Bank: Persuasive Letter
6. **To analyze literary elements**
   - Literary Focus: Speaker
7. **To read in order to research self-selected and assigned topics**
   - Idea Bank: Illustration
   - Idea Bank: Map
8. **To plan, prepare, organize, and present literary interpretations**
   - Idea Bank: Biographical Sketch
   - Idea Bank: Music Appreciation
   - Idea Bank: Dramatic Reading
9. **To use recursive writing processes to write a firsthand biography**
   - Guided Writing Lesson
10. **To increase knowledge of the rules of grammar and usage**
    - Grammar and Style: Noun Clauses

Test Preparation

Reading Comprehension: Context (ATE, p. 605)

The teaching tips and sample test item in this workshop support the instruction and practice in the unit workshop:

Reading Comprehension: Using Context (SE, p. 631)

Guide for Interpreting

Edwin Arlington Robinson *(1869–1935)*

As a New York City subway inspector in his mid-thirties, Edwin Arlington Robinson earned twenty cents an hour. Yet friends helped him arrange the private printing of three books of poetry during these lean times, helping Robinson establish himself as the most successful American poet of the 1920's.

Robinson grew up in Gardiner, Maine, a small town that was the model for Tilbury Town, the fictional setting of many of his poems. He attended college for two years, but he was forced to return to Gardiner after his father's death. Upon his return, Robinson began writing poetry; by the time he moved to New York four years later, he had established his poetic voice. Most of Robinson's best poems focus on people's inner struggles. They paint portraits of desperate characters who view their lives as trivial and meaningless or who long to live in another place or time.

Robinson lived and worked in New York for many years before achieving success with *The Town Down the River* in 1910. He went on to publish many acclaimed books, including *The Man Against the Sky* (1915) and *Avon's Harvest* (1922), and received three Pulitzer Prizes.

Edgar Lee Masters *(1868–1950)*

For years, Edgar Lee Masters practiced criminal law by day in a successful Chicago firm and wrote poems, plays, and essays by night. In 1915, he published *Spoon River Anthology,* a series of poems about the lives of people in rural southern Illinois. The volume was so successful that Masters decided to quit his law career and move to New York City to earn a living as a writer.

Masters went on to produce many other volumes of poetry, in addition to novels, biographies, and his autobiography, *Across Spoon River*. However, he is still remembered almost exclusively for *Spoon River Anthology*, and the collection is widely regarded as his masterpiece.

The *Anthology* consists of 244 epitaphs for characters buried in the mythical Spoon River cemetery. The dead themselves serve as the speakers of the poems, often revealing secrets they kept hidden during their lifetimes. Many types of people are represented, including storekeepers, housewives, and murderers. Some of the characters lived happy lives, but many more lived lives filled with frustration and despair. Presented together, the epitaphs paint a vivid portrait of what life was like in small midwestern towns around the turn of the century.

◆ Background for Understanding

Literature: The Roots of Masters's Spoon River

In his essay "The Genesis of Spoon River," Edgar Lee Masters describes experiences from his youth that contributed to his writing of the *Spoon River Anthology.* He points out that the characters are based on a variety of interesting and unusual people he observed as a boy. He also explains that no one single town inspired his famous fictional village. Instead, he refers to the general area lining the Spoon River, which flows through west-central Illinois:

> People ask me over and over where the town of Spoon River is located. As there is no such town, I have to answer that there is only a river. And what a river! . . . It goes by little towns as ugly and lonely as the tin-roofed hamlets of Kansas. Yet this is the town, or one of the towns, and this is the river and the country from which I extracted whatever beauty there is in that part of *Spoon River Anthology* which relates to a village depiction. . . .

Prentice Hall Literature Program Resources

REINFORCE / RETEACH / EXTEND

Selection Support Pages
Build Vocabulary: Latin Word Roots: *-pose-*, p. 181
Grammar and Style: Noun Clauses, p. 182
Reading Strategy: Recognize Attitudes, p. 183
Literary Focus: Speaker, p. 184

Strategies for Diverse Student Needs, p. 39

Beyond Literature
Humanities Connection: Dance, p. 39

Formal Assessment Selection Test, pp. 185–187; Assessment Resources Software

Alternative Assessment, p. 39

Writing and Language Transparencies
Descriptive and Observational Report, pp. 9–12

Resource Pro CD-ROM

Listening to Literature Audiocassettes

Luke Havergal ◆ Richard Cory
Lucinda Matlock ◆ Richard Bone

◆ Literature and Your Life

CONNECT YOUR EXPERIENCE

Have you ever wondered how you'll be remembered a century from now? Perhaps you'd like to be remembered for professional achievements or for your personal characteristics. The following poems create a memorable impression of four characters from small-town America one hundred years ago. How do your impressions of them compare with the impression you'd like to leave behind?

Journal Writing Jot down your thoughts about how you'd like to be remembered one hundred years from now.

THEMATIC FOCUS: LIVING IN A CHANGING WORLD

The characters in these poems lived in a time when our nation was changing from an agricultural to an industrial society. How do the poems capture both a sense of change and a sense of tradition?

◆ Literary Focus

SPEAKER

The **speaker** is the voice of a poem. Although the speaker is often the poet, it can also be a fictional character or some non-human entity. For example, the speakers of the poems in Masters's *Spoon River Anthology* are characters buried in a cemetery in fictional Spoon River. Instead of using a neutral speaker, Masters lets characters speak candidly for themselves. In this way, the poet can delve deeply into the minds and hearts of Spoon River's former citizens.

◆ Build Vocabulary

LATIN WORD ROOTS: *-pose-*

Edgar Lee Masters uses the word *repose* to describe Lucinda Matlock's death. This word combines the Latin root *-pose-* ("place" or "rest") with the prefix *re-* ("back"); the word *repose* can be defined as "the state of being at rest."

WORD BANK

Preview this list of words before you read.

imperially
repose
degenerate
epitaph

◆ Reading Strategy

RECOGNIZE ATTITUDES

The attitudes and beliefs of a poem's speaker—whether the speaker is the poet or a fictional character—are likely to color the depiction of the characters, settings, and events in the poem. As you read a poem, determine who the speaker is and look for clues to the speaker's outlook on life and **attitudes** toward the poem's subject. For example, "Lucinda Matlock" includes the lines, "Degenerate sons and daughters,/Life is too strong for you—" These lines suggest that the speaker, Lucinda Matlock, believes that the younger generation isn't as tough and hard-working as she was.

◆ Grammar and Style

NOUN CLAUSES

These poems contain **noun clauses**—subordinate clauses (word groups with subjects and verbs that cannot stand alone as sentences) used as nouns in sentences. Noun clauses can act as a subject, direct or indirect object, predicate nominative, or object of a preposition.

Direct Object: In fine, we thought *that he was everything*

Object of a Preposition: . . . wait for *what will come.*

Noun clauses are commonly introduced by: *that, which, whomever, how, where, what, who, whose, whether, whatever, whoever, when,* and *why.*

Test Preparation Workshop

Reading Comprehension: Context The reading sections of many standardized tests require students to use context clues to identify the appropriate meaning of a multiple-meaning word in a given passage. Use the following sample test item to demonstrate.

Whenever Richard Corey went to town,
We people on the pavement looked at him:
He was a gentleman from sole to crown.
Clean favored and imperially slim.

In this passage, the word crown most nearly means—

A symbol of royalty
B hit on the head
C top of head
D royal government

The juxtaposition of *sole* and *crown*, and the general context of describing a gentleman's appearance should lead students to recognize that *C* is the most appropriate choice.

Interest Grabber Bring in several obituary notices from newspapers or news magazines. Duplicate them for students or read them aloud. Or have students visit a local cemetery to see the kinds of messages inscribed on gravestones there. Then challenge students to write their own obituary notice or gravestone epitaph in the style of the ones they have seen. Allow about ten minutes for this task, then invite volunteers to share the obituaries or epitaphs. Then tell students that all the poems in this grouping are about people who died, but are neither typical obituaries nor epitaphs.

Connecting Themes Across Cultures

Point out that just as songs relate a singer's emotions, dreams, and ambitions, poetry expresses the poet's emotions and observations about life. Have students reflect on their own lives in the changing world. What do they think people their own age would write about in a poem? What would people their age in other cultures want to express about the changes that have occurred as a result of the technological age?

Customize for
Less Proficient Readers

Help these students recognize and interpret symbolism in these poems. For instance, in "Luke Havergal," "the western gate" can represent not just an actual cemetery gate, but death itself.

Customize for
AP Students

Review the meaning of situational irony and dramatic irony. (See the *Literary Terms Handbook,* p. 1184, or the instruction accompanying "The Story of an Hour," p. 591). Have students look for examples of both kinds of irony in the poems in this grouping. Have them determine which examples deliver comic effect and which carry great emotional impact.

Connecting to World Literature

To connect "Luke Havergal" to a world literature selection, see p. 1191.

Develop Understanding

One-Minute Insight Each of these poems addresses the pain of loss. Luke Havergal grieves for his beloved and questions whether he can go on living. The speaker urges him to, suggesting that he can commune with her spirit until it is his rightful time to die and they can meet again in the next life.

In contrast, "Richard Cory" reveals a whole town in shock and grief. The ordinary townsfolk so idealized the life that they believed the wealthy, elegant Richard Cory led that they were unprepared for his sudden suicide.

Customize for
Less Proficient Readers
It may help students to paraphrase lines to get at the meaning of the poem. For instance, students might paraphrase lines 9 and 10 as "This is not just a bad dream that you can awake from."

Customize for
Verbal/Linguistic Learners
❶ Students may notice repetition in the last two lines of each stanza as well as the western gate image that is introduced in the first stanza and echoed in the last. Discuss the effects of repetition in this poem. *Students may find the repetition to be both soothing and hypnotic.*

◆ Critical Thinking

❷ **Infer** What details in this stanza suggest death? *The western gate, the twilight, the autumn seem to point to the approach of death.*

◆ Literary Focus

❸ **Speaker** Discuss with students who the speaker is in this poem. *Students might suggest that the speaker is a supreme being, the spirit of Havergal's lost love, or part of Havergal's inner self.*

▶Critical Viewing◀

❹ **Analyze** Students may say that the gate creates an imposing mood that separates Luke from his beloved; they might say that the autumn leaves suggest dying.

Luke Havergal

Edwin Arlington Robinson

Connections to World Literature, *page 1189*

Go to the western gate, Luke Havergal,
There where the vines cling crimson on the wall,
❶ And in the twilight wait for what will come.
❷ The leaves will whisper there of her, and some,
Like flying words, will strike you as they fall;
But go, and if you listen she will call.
Go to the western gate, Luke Havergal—
Luke Havergal.

No, there is not a dawn in eastern skies
To rift the fiery night that's in your eyes;
But there, where western glooms are gathering,
The dark will end the dark, if anything:
God slays Himself with every leaf that flies,
And hell is more than half of paradise.
No, there is not a dawn in eastern skies—
In eastern skies.

Out of a grave I come to tell you this,
Out of a grave I come to quench the kiss
That flames upon your forehead with a glow
That blinds you to the way that you must go.
❸ Yes, there is yet one way to where she is,
Bitter, but one that faith may never miss.
Out of a grave I come to tell you this—
To tell you this.

There is the western gate, Luke Havergal,
There are the crimson leaves upon the wall.
Go, for the winds are tearing them away,—
Nor think to riddle the dead words they say,
Nor any more to feel them as they fall;
But go, and if you trust her she will call.
There is the western gate, Luke Havergal—
Luke Havergal.

▲ Critical Viewing
Picture this gate as Luke Havergal will see it: at twilight with the winds whipping the dead leaves from the trees. Describe the mood evoked by that image. **[Analyze]** ❹

Block Scheduling Strategies

Consider these suggestions to take advantage of extended class time:

- Use the Interest Grabber activity or the journal writing activity in Literature and Your Life (p. 605) and discuss students' responses in groups.
- To enrich students' knowledge of the authors, use the features on Robinson and Masters in the **Literature CD-ROM.**
- Introduce the Literary Focus before students read the poems. Guide students' awareness of each poem's speaker using the notes provided in the Annotated Teacher's edition.
- Have students work in discussion groups to answer the Critical Thinking questions (pp. 607 and 609).
- After students have read and interpreted "Richard Cory" use the Music Appreciation activity in the Idea Bank. Ask students to identify the effect of Simon and Garfunkel's interpretation of the poem.

The Thinker (Portrait of Louis N. Kenton, 1900), Thomas Eakins, The Metropolitan Museum of Art

Richard Cory

Edwin Arlington Robinson

Whenever Richard Cory went down town,
We people on the pavement looked at him:
He was a gentleman from sole to crown,
Clean favored, and imperially slim.

And he was always quietly arrayed,
And he was always human when he talked;
But still he fluttered pulses when he said,
"Good-morning," and he glittered when he walked.

And he was rich—yes, richer than a king—
And admirably schooled in every grace:
In fine, we thought that he was everything
To make us wish that we were in his place. ❻ ❼

So on we worked, and waited for the light,
And went without the meat, and cursed the bread;
And Richard Cory, one calm summer night,
Went home and put a bullet through his head.

❺ ▲ **Critical Viewing** Is this painting an appropriate illustration for "Richard Cory"? Explain. **[Evaluate]**

◆ **Build Vocabulary**

imperially (im pir′ ē əl ē) *adv.*: Majestically

Guide for Responding

◆ Literature and Your Life

Reader's Response Would you like to read more poems about the residents of Tilbury Town? Why or why not?

Thematic Focus What characteristics does a person need in order to thrive in a changing world?

☑ Check Your Comprehension

1. According to the speaker, why should Luke Havergal go to the western gate?
2. In "Luke Havergal," from where has the speaker come to deliver a message?
3. Why was Richard Cory envied?
4. What does he do "one calm summer night"?

◆ Critical Thinking

INTERPRET

1. What do you think was Luke Havergal's relationship to the woman? Why? **[Speculate]**
2. (a) What might the western gate symbolize? (b) What might the "dawn in eastern skies" symbolize? **[Interpret]**
3. Would the townspeople have expected Richard Cory to take his life? Why or why not? **[Support]**

APPLY

4. (a) Why do you think a person like Richard Cory might be miserable? (b) What do you think are the keys to a person's happiness? **[Relate]**

Humanities: Art

The Thinker (Portrait of Louis N. Kenton, 1900), by Thomas Eakins.

Thomas Eakins (1844–1916) was an American portrait and genre painter from Philadelphia. He studied art in Paris and at the Pennsylvania Academy of Fine Arts, where he later became the director. He also studied anatomy. Eakins grew interested in using photography to record human and animal locomotion. Some of his photographic studies served as a basis for paintings that show a penetrating knowledge of the structure and motion of the human body. His later work reveals deep psychological insights, especially in representing contemplative moods. *The Thinker* is a fine example of Eakins's presentation of a state of mind. The intense and haunting image of a man embodies sadness, frustration, and resignation. Ask:

1. What might the man in the portrait be thinking? *Responses should reflect the serious and somber expression on the man's face.*
2. How does the artist's use of color affect the message of the portrait? *Students may say that the black suit and the brown walls suggest depression, dark thoughts, and a lack of hope.*

▶Critical Viewing◀

❺ **Evaluate** Student may feel that the demeanor of the man, his fine clothes, and the expression make this image appropriate.

◆ Reading Strategy

❻ **Recognize Attitudes** Ask students to identify the speaker's attitude toward Richard Cory in lines 9–12. *The speaker reveals the envy that he and the others felt about him, and how much they wished they could be in his place.*

◆ Critical Thinking

❼ **Assess** How does line 12 set up the irony of the last stanza? *The townspeople idolized Cory and had no idea that he was suicidal.*

Answers

◆ Literature and Your Life

Reader's Response Encourage students to select other Robinson poems to share with the class.

Thematic Response Possible responses include courage, compassion, and self-esteem.

☑ Check Your Comprehension

1. The speaker says that Luke Havergal will hear "her" speak to him at the western gate.
2. The speaker has come "Out of a grave."
3. Richard Cory was envied for his wealth, grace, and social position.
4. He killed himself.

◆ Critical Thinking

1. Possible response: He loved her.
2. Possible response: (a) The western gate may symbolize death. (b) It may symbolize rebirth, renewal, or hope.
3. Possible response: Since they imagined Cory had everything, they wouldn't expect him to take his life.
4. (a) Possible response: Cory may not have had close relationships; he may have achieved success and still felt empty. (b) Students should support their answers.

One-Minute Insight These two selections from *Spoon River Anthology* demonstrate two characters' abilities to face life in a changing world. From the detached distance of the grave, Lucinda Matlock and Richard Bone speak frankly about their lives. Matlock died when she was ninety-six, after a hard but full life. She dismisses the complaints she hears from the younger generation, whom she feels never developed the power to embrace life and survive its many troubles. As a carver of tombstones, Richard Bone came to know the people in Spoon River and learn how closeness and affection caused relatives to ask him to carve "false chronicles" into the stone.

▶Critical Viewing◀

1 Connect Students may say that the painting of a barn dance depicts some of Lucinda's memories and seems to illustrate the small-town life she so enjoyed.

◆Literary Focus

2 Speaker Have students identify the time of Lucinda Matlock's life she describes in lines 1–5. *She talks about events in her life prior to the time she met the man she would marry.*

◆Reading Strategy

3 Recognize Attitudes Call attention to the speaker's matter-of-fact tone, even when she describes the loss of eight children. Ask students what they can gather about Lucinda Matlock's attitude toward life. *She was a tough woman who just kept going, no matter what blows life dealt her.*

◆Literary Focus

4 Speaker After listing activities that shaped her life, Lucinda Matlock, at the age of ninety-six, is ready to die. Discuss why she may have felt this way. *Students may say that she felt she'd lived long enough and was tired and ready to rest; she felt she didn't have enough energy left in her body to appreciate life as she had before.*

Barn Dance, Grandma Moses, © 1989, Grandma Moses Properties Co., New York

◀ **Critical Viewing** In what ways does this painting reflect the life of Lucinda Matlock? **[Connect]** 1

Lucinda Matlock

Edgar Lee Masters

I went to the dances at Chandlerville,
And played snap-out[1] at Winchester.
(2) One time we changed partners,
Driving home in the moonlight of middle June,
And then I found Davis.
We were married and lived together for seventy years,
(3) Enjoying, working, raising the twelve children,
Eight of whom we lost
Ere I had reached the age of sixty.
I spun, I wove, I kept the house, I nursed the sick,
I made the garden, and for holiday
Rambled over the fields where sang the larks,
And by Spoon River gathering many a shell,
And many a flower and medicinal weed—
Shouting to the wooded hills, singing to the green valleys.
(4) At ninety-six I had lived enough, that is all,
And passed to a sweet repose.
What is this I hear of sorrow and weariness,
Anger, discontent and drooping hopes?
Degenerate sons and daughters,
Life is too strong for you—
It takes life to love Life.

◆ Build Vocabulary

repose (ri pōz′) *n.*: State of being at rest

degenerate (dē jen′ ər it) *adj.*: Morally corrupt

1. **Snap-out:** Game often referred to as Crack-the-Whip, in which a long line of players who are holding hands spin around in a circle, causing the players on the ends to be flung off by centrifugal force.

Humanities: Art

Barn Dance, 1950, by Grandma Moses.

Anna Mary Robertson Moses (1860–1961) did not begin to paint seriously until she was in her seventies. She had no formal art training. Her unaffected scenes of happy rural life, with simple forms, lively colors, and immense detail made her name a household word. Her work blazed a trail for later folk artists by increasing public awareness and by appealing to a wide audience.

Barn Dance is a typical Grandma Moses painting that portrays personal memories in a primitive style. Almost ninety when she painted this work, she includes meticulous detail in the landscape and in the people. The composition is reminiscent of the Currier and Ives prints that were popular during her lifetime.

Use this question for discussion:

1. Describe what might be called the "charming appeal" of this painting. *Students might cite the colorful gathering of neighbors at a dance; the lively touches of carriages arriving, of live musicians playing, and the resplendent hillside in the background.*

Richard Bone

Edgar Lee Masters

When I first came to Spoon River
I did not know whether what they told me
Was true or false.
They would bring me the epitaph
And stand around the shop while I worked
and say "He was so kind," "He was wonderful,"
"She was the sweetest woman," "He was a consistent Christian."
And I chiseled for them whatever they wished,
All in ignorance of its truth.
But later, as I lived among the people here,
I knew how near to the life
Were the epitaphs that were ordered for them as they died.

But still I chiseled whatever they paid me to chisel
and made myself party to the false chronicles ❺
Of the stones,
Even as the historian does who writes
Without knowing the truth,
Or because he is influenced to hide it.

◆ **Build Vocabulary**

epitaph (ep′ ə taf′) *n.*: Inscription on a tombstone or grave marker

Guide for Responding

◆ Literature and Your Life

Reader's Response (a) What is your opinion of Lucinda Matlock? (b) Is she someone you would strive to emulate? Why or why not?

Thematic Focus How do Lucinda Matlock and Richard Bone deal with change in a similar manner?

☑ Check Your Comprehension

1. (a) Who is the speaker of "Lucinda Matlock"? (b) How old was Matlock when she died? (c) Use the poem to write a summary of Matlock's life.

2. (a) What is Richard Bone's occupation? (b) What change occurs in Bone after years of living in Spoon River?

◆ Critical Thinking

INTERPRET

1. (a) Characterize Lucinda Matlock's life. (b) What is her attitude about her life? **[Analyze]**

2. (a) Who are the "sons and daughters" Matlock addresses? (b) What is the meaning of her message to them? **[Interpret]**

3. Why do you think the townspeople in "Richard Bone" composed false epitaphs for their loved ones? **[Analyze]**

APPLY

4. How might Lucinda Matlock respond to the complaint that life today is too complex? **[Relate]**

5. Why do you think two generations' attitudes toward life are often so different? **[Speculate]**

Beyond the Selection

FURTHER READING

Other Works by Edwin Arlington Robinson

The Man Against the Sky
Collected Poems
The Man Who Died Twice

Other Works by Edgar Lee Masters

Vachel Lindsay: A Poet in America
Across Spoon River
Mitch Miller

We suggest that you preview these works before recommending them to students.

INTERNET

You can find additional information about Robinson and Masters on the Internet. To learn more about Edgar Lee Masters, go to **http:// www.outfitters.com/illinois/fulton/ masters.html**

For information on Pulitzer-Prize-winning poets, including Edwin Arlington Robinson, go to **http:// www.ccc.govt.nz/Library/Lit_Prizes/ Pulitzer_Poetry.html**

We *strongly suggest* that you preview the sites before you send students to them.

◆ Reading Strategy

❺ Recognize Attitudes Discuss the speaker's attitude toward the epitaphs he was asked to carve. *He seems to have disdain for what he calls "false chronicles."* Ask whether students agree that epitaphs are "false chronicles" or whether they could be explained or characterized in other ways. *They may be seen as acts of forgiveness or love.*

Reinforce and Extend

Answers

◆ Literature and Your Life

Reader's Response Whether students like or dislike Matlock, they should support their opinions with evidence from the poem.

Thematic Focus Both Matlock and Bone seem to have their own values that are separate and distinct from those of their community.

☑ Check Your Comprehension

1. (a) The speaker is Lucinda Matlock. (b) She died at 96. (c) Matlock led a full life: a happy childhood, a marriage which produced twelve children although eight died before Matlock was 60. Matlock was charitable and hardworking. At 96, she died.
2. (a) Bone is a tombstone carver. (b) After years of living in Spoon River, Bone could determine whether the epitaphs he carved were in fact true.

◆ Critical Thinking

1. (a) Possible response: Matlock led a busy, difficult life, filled with small pleasures. (b) She seems to think she lived well.
2. (a) They are the members of the following generation. (b) They must live and experience the joys and stand up to the sorrows.
3. Possible responses: They believed them; they wanted to show their love.
4. Matlock would probably disagree. She might say her life was equally complex.
5. Possible response: Each generation is raised in a unique world. The Depression or the rise of technology, for example, leaves a lasting imprint on the values of each generation.

Answers

◆ Literary Focus

1. The speaker uses the term "we."
2. The speaker creates Cory as a sympathetic character and readers may find themselves also revering Cory. Cory's death is a shock not only to the speaker but to the reader as well.
3. Because Matlock speaks for herself. The use of another speaker would have created a biased view.
4. Speakers who are "dead" are detached from the world and therefore have nothing to gain or lose from their honesty.

◆ Grammar and Style

1. *where she is:* object of a preposition.
2. *whatever they wished:* direct object.
3. *whether what they told me was true or false:* direct object
4. *the epitaphs that were ordered:* predication noun.
5. *whatever they paid me to chisel:* direct object.

Grammar Reinforcement

For additional instruction and practice, use the page on Noun Clauses, p. 37, in the *Writer's Solution Grammar Practice Book.*

◆ Reading Strategy

1. Richard Cory does not believe that he has everything to live for; the speaker thinks Cory does.
2. Possible response: He had difficulty relating to them and felt isolated.
3. The speaker of Richard Bone seems disdainful of the people he serves.
4. Matlock believes that people must face life's challenges directly.
5. Line 21 reveals that Matlock thinks they are weak.

◆ Build Vocabulary

Using the Latin Word Root *-pose-*

1. b 2. c 3. a

Using the Word Bank

1. a 2. b 3. a 4. a

Guide for Responding *(continued)*

◆ Literary Focus

Speaker

The **speaker** is the the voice of a poem. A poem's speaker may be the poet or a fictional character, an animal, or even an inanimate object. The speaker in "Lucinda Matlock" is Lucinda Matlock herself.

1. How can you tell that the speaker of "Richard Cory" is speaking for the entire town?
2. How does the fact that the speaker admires Richard Cory add to the impact of the poem?
3. How would "Lucinda Matlock" be different if Masters had used a different speaker?
4. Lucinda Matlock, Richard Bone, and the other speakers in *Spoon River Anthology* are dead. Why might this allow them to discuss their lives more openly than if they were alive?

◆ Grammar and Style

Noun Clauses

A **noun clause** is a subordinate clause used as a noun. A noun clause can be used as a subject, predicate noun, direct object, indirect object, or object of a preposition.

Practice On your paper, write the following sentences and underline the noun clause in each. Explain the function of each noun clause.

1. There is yet one way to where she is.
2. I chiseled for them whatever they wished.
3. I did not know whether what they told me was true or false.
4. I knew how near to the life were the epitaphs that were ordered.
5. I chiseled whatever they paid me to chisel.

Writing Application Combine the following pairs of sentences by turning one of the sentences into a noun clause.

1. The speaker knew what was right. Luke Havergal must go to the western gate.
2. Lucinda Matlock gave advice. She would give it to anyone who would listen.

◆ Reading Strategy

Recognize Attitudes

To fully understand a person, you have to be aware of his or her outlook on life. The same is true of a poem's speaker. When you read a poem, look closely at the choice of words and the presentation of details, and think about what they reveal about the speaker's attitudes and beliefs. **Recognizing the speaker's attitudes** will help you unlock the meaning of the poem.

1. In "Richard Cory," how does the speaker's attitude toward Richard Cory differ from Cory's attitude toward himself? Support your answer.
2. What do you think might have been Richard Cory's attitude toward the townspeople?
3. How would you describe the attitude of the speaker in "Richard Bone"? Support your answer.
4. How would you describe Lucinda Matlock's outlook on life?
5. What seems to be Lucinda Matlock's attitude toward the people who have survived her? Support your answer.

◆ Build Vocabulary

Using the Latin Root *-pose-*

Use each of these words containing the Latin root *-pose-*, meaning "place" or "rest," to complete one of the sentences.

a. depose **b.** impose **c.** interpose

1. He hated to __?__ on his friends, but he was unable to find a hotel room.
2. Each time audience members __?__ comments, the speaker loses his train of thought.
3. When we __?__ the prime minister, we will set this nation on a course toward true freedom.

Using the Word Bank: Synonyms

Write the letter of the best synonym for the first word.

1. imperially: (a) grandly, (b) scornfully, (c) strongly
2. repose: (a) model, (b) silence, (c) ease
3. degenerate: (a) evil, (b) degraded, (c) slow
4. epitaph: (a) inscription, (b) homily, (c) graph

Reteach

To reteach speaker, have students fill out a graphic organizer like the one here to analyze the personality of the speaker in "Lucinda Matlock" and "Richard Bone." Then, lead a group discussion in which students compare and contrast the speakers. Lead students to recognize that even though both poems are written in the first person, the distinct voices in these poems cannot both belong to one person. They are individual voices that the poet has "put on" in much the same way that an actor puts on a costume and acts a certain way to portray a character.

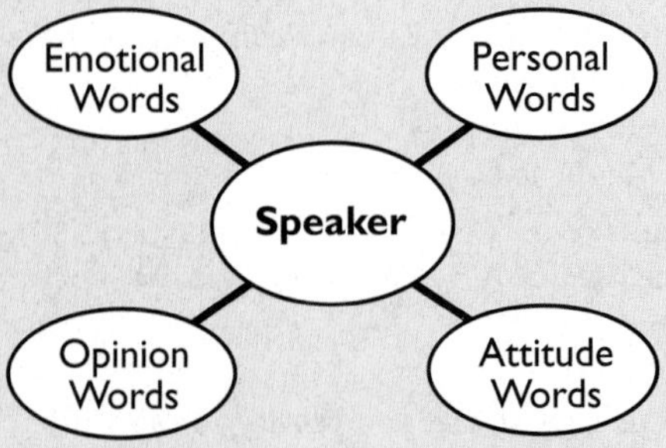

Build Your Portfolio

Idea Bank

Writing

1. **Biographical Sketch** Using details from the poems, along with additional details that you concoct in your imagination, write a biographical sketch of one of the characters in these poems.
2. **Comparison/Contrast** Write an essay comparing and contrasting the poems of Robinson and Masters. Explore similarities and differences in the settings, characters, moods, and themes.
3. **Persuasive Letter** How would you convince Lucinda Matlock that her assessment of the younger generation is wrong? Look closely at the last few lines of the poem. Then write a persuasive letter to Matlock convincing her that life is not "too strong" for today's younger generation.

Speaking, Listening, and Viewing

4. **Music Appreciation** Find a copy of folk duo Simon and Garfunkel's adaptation of "Richard Cory," and play it for the class. Lead a discussion of the song's effectiveness. **[Music Link]**
5. **Dramatic Reading** Read one of the poems aloud to the class in a way that you think fits the poem's speaker and subject matter. For example, if you read "Lucinda Matlock," try to capture how you imagine the poem's speaker would sound. **[Performing Arts Link]**

Researching and Representing

6. **Illustration** Create or find an illustration that could accompany one of the four poems in a poetry collection. **[Art Link]**
7. **Map** Like Robinson and Masters, many American writers have focused their works on one specific location. Conduct research to learn about places associated with various writers. Then create a literary map identifying these locations.

Online Activity www.phlit.phschool.com

Guided Writing Lesson

Firsthand Biography

Poems like Robinson's and Masters's are one way to create vivid portraits of people. Another way to present a portrait of a person is through a firsthand biography—a story about events in the life of a person with whom the writer has a personal relationship. Think of an interesting, special, or unusual person who stands out in your memory. Then write a firsthand biography in which you share your impressions of the person and describe one or more events that capture his or her personality.

Writing Skills Focus: Transitions to Show Order of Importance

In your firsthand biography, you'll want to give readers a strong impression of the personality traits and details of the person's life that stand out most in your own mind. One way to make it clear to readers which details are most important is to use **transitional words that show order of importance.** These words include: *first, second, more importantly, least importantly, mainly, last, finally, good, better, best, primarily, secondarily, above all, worst of all, few, most effective,* and *unnecessary.*

Prewriting After you've decided on your subject, list key personality traits and events in the person's life that illustrate the personality traits. Then arrange these details in their order of importance.

Drafting Focus your firsthand biography on a single event or a series of events that illustrate the person's most important personality traits. As you describe the event or events, include your own impressions of the person. Use transitional words to indicate which impressions are most important.

Revising Have you included details that reveal your subject's personality? Review your biography to make sure that it conveys the impression of your subject that you intended.

ASSESSMENT OPTIONS

Formal Assessment, Selection Test, pp. 185–187, and Assessment Resources Software. The selection test is designed so that it can be easily customized to the performance levels of your students.

Alternative Assessment, p. 39, includes options for less advanced students, more advanced students, interpersonal learners, musical/rhythmic learners and verbal/linguistic learners.

PORTFOLIO ASSESSMENT

Use the following rubrics in the ***Alternative Assessment*** booklet to assess student writing:
Biographical Sketch: Description Rubric, p. 112
Comparison/Contrast: Comparison/Contrast Rubric, p. 118
Persuasive Letter: Persuasion Rubric, p. 120
Guided Writing Lesson: Narrative Based on Personal Experience Rubric, p. 111

Idea Bank

Customizing for ***Performance Levels***

Following are suggestions for matching Idea Bank topics with your students' performance levels:
Less Advanced Students: 1, 6
Average Students: 2, 4, 5
More Advanced Students: 3, 7

Customizing for ***Learning Modalities***

Following are suggestions for matching Idea Bank topics with your students' learning modalities:
Musical/Rhythmic: 4
Visual/Spatial: 5, 6, 7
Logical/Mathematical: 7

Guided Writing Lesson

For more instruction on prewriting, elaboration, and revision, see *Prentice Hall Writing and Grammar.*

Writing and Language Transparencies
Use the Descriptive and Observational Report on pages 9–12 to introduce students to the characteristics of narrative writing.

Writers at Work Videodisc
Have students view the videodisc segment on Narration (Ch. 2) featuring N. Scott Momaday to see how to develop narrative elements. Have students discuss what Momaday thinks are important features of narrative writing.

Play frames 18612 to 19873

Writing Lab CD-ROM
Have students complete the tutorial on Narration. Follow these steps:

1. Have students look at the interactive model of a firsthand biography in the "About Narration" section.
2. Have students use the character trait word bin to help them gather details.
3. Have students draft on the computer.
4. Have students use the self-evaluation checklist to help students revise their work.

LESSON OBJECTIVES

1. To develop vocabulary and word identification skills
- Words from Music
- Using the Word Bank: Connotations
- Extending Word Study: Word Origins (ATE)

2. To use a variety of reading strategies to comprehend a short story
- Connect Your Experience
- Reading Strategy: Clarifying

3. To increase knowledge of other cultures and to connect common elements across cultures
- Cultural Connection (ATE)

4. To express and support responses to the text
- Critical Thinking
- Idea Bank: Diary Entry
- Idea Bank: Editorial
- Idea Bank: Debate
- Idea Bank: School Brochure

5. To analyze literary elements
- Literary Focus: Characterization

6. To read in order to research self-selected and assigned topics
- Idea Bank: Research Project

7. To plan, prepare, organize, and present literary interpretations
- Idea Bank: Oral Storytelling
- Idea Bank: A Wagner Matinée

8. To use recursive writing processes to write a travel brochure
- Guided Writing Lesson

9. To increase knowledge of the rules of grammar and usage
- Grammar and Style: Reflexive and Intensive Pronouns

Test Preparation

Reading Comprehension: Context (ATE, p. 613)

The teaching tips and sample test item in this workshop support the instruction and practice in the unit workshop:

Reading Comprehension: Using Context (SE, p. 631)

Guide for Interpreting

Featured in AUTHORS IN DEPTH Series

Willa Cather *(1873–1947)*

Although Willa Cather lived more than half her life in New York City, she turned again and again to the Nebraska prairie of her youth—at the time, a recently settled area of the American frontier—for inspiration and material for her writing.

Cather captured with unflinching honesty the difficulties of life on the expanding frontier.

A Prairie Childhood Born in a small town in western Virginia, Cather moved to the Nebraska frontier when she was ten. Many of her new neighbors were immigrants struggling to build new lives while preserving their native cultures. Commenting on the diversity that surrounded her during her childhood, Cather once wrote: "On Sundays we could drive to a Norwegian church and listen to a sermon in that language, or to a Danish or Swedish church. We could go to a French Catholic settlement or into a Bohemian township and hear one in Czech, or we could go to the church with the German Lutherans." In addition to all that she learned from observing the diverse group of people who surrounded her, Cather received a rich formal education, studying foreign languages, history, classical music, and opera.

The Making of a Literary Giant After graduating from the University of Nebraska in 1895, Cather worked as an editor at a Pittsburgh newspaper, while writing poems and short stories in her spare time. In 1904, she moved to New York, where she joined the editorial staff of *McClure's Magazine.* Her first collection of stories, *The Troll Garden,* was published in 1905. After her first novel, *Alexander's Bridge,* was published in 1911, Cather left *McClure's* to devote herself to writing.

Over the next 35 years, Cather produced some ten novels, two short-story collections, and two collections of essays. Among her outstanding works are *O Pioneers!* (1913), *My Antonia* (1918), and *One of Ours* (1922), which capture the flavor of life on the midwestern prairie. *One of Ours* won Cather the Pulitzer Prize in 1923.

Portraits of Prairie Life Although Cather's fiction was by no means limited to "prairie stories"—her fictional settings ranged from contemporary New York City to the American Southwest to seventeenth-century Quebec—it was her stories about Nebraska immigrants that most appealed to readers and critics. In these stories, she displayed her admiration for the courage and spirit of the immigrants and other settlers of the frontier. At the same time, she conveyed an intense awareness of the loss felt by the pioneers and the loneliness and isolation from which they suffered. In "A Wagner Matinée," Cather captures this sense of loneliness and isolation by contrasting the stark realities of frontier life with the possibilities of life in a more cultured world.

◆ Background for Understanding

Music: The Operas of Richard Wagner

When "A Wagner Matinée" first appeared in 1904, Cather's readers would have been as familiar with Richard Wagner (Väg nər) as people are today with the Beatles. Wagner, who was German, was one of the nineteenth century's greatest composers. His operas are characterized by their adventurous harmonic language and their innovative intermarriage of music and drama. Although many critics judged Wagner's music unfavorably during his lifetime, his operas became enormously popular after his death in 1883.

Prentice Hall Literature Program Resources

REINFORCE / RETEACH / EXTEND

Selection Support Pages
Build Vocabulary: Words From Music: *prelude*, p. 185
Grammar and Style: Reflexive and Intensive Pronouns, p. 186
Reading Strategy: Clarifying, p. 187
Literary Focus: Characterization, p. 188

Strategies for Diverse Student Needs, p. 40

Beyond Literature
Cross-Curricular Connection: Music, p. 40

Formal Assessment Selection Test, pp. 188–190; Assessment Resources Software

Alternative Assessment, p. 40

Writing and Language Transparencies
Branching Organizer (pp. 67–69)

Resource Pro CD-ROM

Literature CD-ROM

Listening to Literature Audiocassettes

A Wagner Matinée

◆ Literature and Your Life

CONNECT YOUR EXPERIENCE

Have you ever heard a song that grabbed at your emotions, pulling you out of the moment and into another time or place? Music can exert a powerful pull on our feelings, memories, and fantasies. In this story, a woman experiences a flood of long-buried emotions when she attends a special concert.

Journal Writing Briefly describe a time when a song or piece of music stirred up your emotions.

THEMATIC FOCUS: LIVING IN A CHANGING WORLD

The music that this story's central character hears stirs up memories of the world she left behind when she and her husband headed to the frontier. Why do you think people often feel isolated or disillusioned when they undergo major changes in their lives?

◆ Build Vocabulary

WORDS FROM MUSIC: *PRELUDE*

Vocabulary from the field of music can often have two meanings—one specific musical meaning and one for use in a nonmusical context. A *prelude,* for example, is a musical introduction. However, *prelude* also refers to any preparation for an important matter.

WORD BANK

Before you read, preview this list of words from the selection.

- reverential
- tremulously
- semi-somnambulant
- inert
- prelude
- jocularity

◆ Grammar and Style

REFLEXIVE AND INTENSIVE PRONOUNS

Reflexive pronouns end in *-self* or *-selves,* refer to the subject, and are necessary to complete the meaning of a sentence. **Intensive pronouns,** which also end in *-self* or *-selves,* simply add emphasis to a noun or pronoun in the same sentence and can be omitted without changing the meaning of the sentence.

Reflexive Pronoun: . . . she had surrendered *herself* unquestioningly into the hands of a country dressmaker.

Intensive Pronoun: *Myself,* I saw my aunt's misshapen figure with that feeling of awe and respect . . .

◆ Literary Focus

CHARACTERIZATION

Characterization is the means by which a writer reveals a character's personality. Writers generally develop characters through one of the following methods: direct statements about the character, physical descriptions of the character, actions of the character, thoughts and comments of the character, or comments about the character made by other characters. As you read, look for the ways in which this story's main character is developed.

◆ Reading Strategy

CLARIFYING

Cather's story is packed with details about its main character. To fully understand the character's actions, it is important to **clarify**—check your understanding of—the details that are provided. This may simply involve reading a footnote or looking up a word in the dictionary. In other instances, you may need to reread a passage to refresh your memory about previous details. In still other cases, when you come across a passage you don't fully understand, you may want to read ahead to find details that clarify its meaning.

Test Preparation Workshop

Reading Comprehension: Context Many standardized tests require students to use context clues to choose the appropriate definition of multiple-meaning words. Use the following sample test item to demonstrate.

> When the train arrived I had some difficulty in finding my aunt. She was the last of the passengers to alight, and when I got her into the carriage she looked not unlike one of those charred, smoked bodies that firemen lift from the débris of a burned building. She had come all the way in a day coach . . .

In this passage, the word alight means—

A light a fire on the platform
B descend from the train
C turn on the light
D enter her compartment

Although *alight* can mean *illuminated,* that definition does not fit the sentence in the passage. The narrator is waiting for his aunt and has trouble finding her because she is the last passenger to get off the train. B is the correct answer.

Interest Grabber Before class, write "Wagner Matinée" on the chalkboard, as if to announce a concert, and give the composer's full name and dates (1813–1883). Prepare a list of the pieces mentioned in the story: Overture from *Tannhäuser,* Prelude to *Tristan and Isolde,* selections from *The Flying Dutchman, The Ring (The Rheingold, The Valkyrie, Siegfried,* and *Dusk of the Gods),* Forest Music from *Siegfried,* and Siegfried's funeral march. As students enter, pass out the "program" and dim the lights, as if in a concert hall. Play one or more excerpts from these pieces, all of which are readily available. Invite them to respond to the emotion of the music. Then tell them that an afternoon concert with this program is a key event in the story they are about to read.

Literature CD-ROM
To introduce students to Willa Cather, use *The History of American Literature:* Part 2, Disk 1, Feature 2, which discusses Cather's famous portrayal of prairie life in *My Ántonia.*

Customize for
Less Proficient Readers
Cather's story includes long sentences that may prove challenging for these students. To help meet this challenge, show them how they can get to the core of a sentence by finding its subject and predicate, then looking to see how the other sentence parts relate to the subject and predicate.

Customize for
AP Students
In Aunt Georgiana, Cather has created a character who literally has layers of meaning. Invite students to analyze her and peel back those layers. Create a chart that shows the type of person she is on the outside. As students read the story, have them fill in the chart, showing the layers of character until they have reached her inner being.

Customize for
English Language Learners
The story has many musical terms, such as *scale, score, strain, motif, melody, chorus,* and *tenor,* as well as the names of instruments. Review these terms, using sheet music, recordings, and photographs to illustrate them.

Develop Understanding

One-Minute Insight This story delves into the contrast between cultured city life and the rugged life that nineteenth-century settlers led after moving to the frontier. The narrator's Aunt Georgiana returns to Boston for a visit years after moving to Nebraska with her husband. A former music teacher, Georgiana has been hardened by frontier life. When her nephew takes her to the opera, she has a deep emotional response. She cries with joy at the music and with grief at the culture she has forfeited to live with her husband in Nebraska. Through his aunt's pain, the narrator learns that the soul never really dies, but "withers to the outward eye only" as it waits to be reawakened.

◆ Background for Understanding

Literature "A Wagner Matinée" was included in Willa Cather's first short story collection, *The Troll Garden.* Those stories dealt with art or artists. One of Cather's long-held, deeply felt concerns was conflict between the artist and the workaday world. This story explores the conflict between a woman's love for music and the withering effects of the rude farming life in the pioneer West that leaves neither time nor energy for the pursuit of fine arts.

◆ Literary Focus

1 Characterization Discuss Clark's reaction to thinking about his aunt: he is shocked at how her name so quickly transports him to his own modest past as "the gangling farmer boy" his aunt had once known, yet recalls with affection the influences she had upon him when he was young.

▶Critical Viewing◀

2 Connect; Interpret Students may say that both women look misshapen, weary, and worn from suffering and hard work.

Connections to Real-World Literature To connect this selection to a real-world text, see "Old-Time Cowboys in the Modern World," p. 1215.

A Wagner Matinée

Willa Cather

I received one morning a letter written in pale ink, on glassy, blue-lined notepaper, and bearing the postmark of a little Nebraska village. This communication, worn and rubbed, looking as though it had been carried for some days in a coat pocket that was none too clean, was from my Uncle Howard. It informed me that his wife had been left a small legacy by a bachelor relative who had recently died, and that it had become necessary for her to come to Boston to attend to the settling of the estate. He requested me to meet her at the station, and render her whatever services might prove necessary. On examining the date indicated as that of her arrival, I found it no later than tomorrow. He had characteristically delayed writing until, had I been away from home for a day, I must have missed the good woman altogether.

1 The name of my Aunt Georgiana called up not alone her own figure, at once pathetic and grotesque, but opened before my feet a gulf of recollections so wide and deep that, as the letter dropped from my hand, I felt suddenly a stranger to all the present conditions of my existence, wholly ill at ease and out of place amid the surroundings of my study. I became, in short, the gangling farmer boy my aunt had known, scourged with chilblains and bashfulness, my hands cracked and raw from the corn husking. I felt the knuckles of my thumb tentatively, as though they were raw again. I sat again before her parlor organ, thumbing the scales with my stiff, red hands, while she beside me made canvas mittens for the huskers.

The next morning, after preparing my landlady somewhat, I set out for the station. When the train arrived I had some difficulty in finding my aunt. She was the last of the passengers to alight, and when I got her into the carriage she looked not unlike one of those charred, smoked bodies that firemen lift from the *débris* of a burned building. She had come all the way in a day coach; her linen duster[1] had become black with soot and her black bonnet gray with dust during the journey. When we arrived at my

From Arkansas, George Schreiber, Sheldon Swope Art Museum, Terre Haute, Indiana

▲ **Critical Viewing** In what ways does the woman in the painting seem like Aunt Georgiana? **[Connect; Interpret]** 2

1. **duster** *n.*: Short, loose smock worn to protect clothing from dust.

Humanities: Art

From Arkansas, 1939, by George Schreiber (1904–1977).

Belgian-born George Schreiber came to the United States in the 1920's. Like many artists during the Depression, Schreiber turned his focus to the great midwestern farmlands. Although Schreiber was not a major figure in the Regionalist art movement, this painting demonstrated his talent and interest in recording the spirit of rural America during one of its most trying times. He portrays this woman with stark realism. Her face, her ragged apron, and her stance reflect the hardships she has endured and the strength with which she has met them.

Use these questions for discussion:

1. What can you infer about the woman's feeling from the way she holds her arms? *Students may say that she is weary, resigned to a difficult life, or frustrated.*
2. What details of the setting reflect the description of Aunt Georgiana's homestead? *The flat, barren land, bare tree branches, and dilapidated building are similar to those described in the story.*

boardinghouse the landlady put her to bed at once, and I did not see her again until the next morning.

Whatever shock Mrs. Springer experienced at my aunt's appearance she considerately concealed. Myself, I saw my aunt's misshapen figure with that feeling of awe and respect with which we behold explorers who have left their ears and fingers north of Franz Josef Land,[2] or their health somewhere along the upper Congo.[3] My Aunt Georgiana had been a music teacher at the Boston Conservatory, somewhere back in the latter sixties. One summer, which she had spent in the little village in the Green Mountains[4] where her ancestors had dwelt for generations, she had kindled the callow[5] fancy of the most idle and shiftless of all the village lads, and had conceived for this Howard Carpenter one of those absurd and extravagant passions which a handsome country boy of twenty-one sometimes inspires in a plain, angular, spectacled woman of thirty. When she returned to her duties in Boston, Howard followed her; and the upshot of this inexplicable infatuation was that she eloped with him, eluding the reproaches of her family and the criticism of her friends by going with him to the Nebraska frontier. Carpenter, who of course had no money, took a homestead in Red Willow County,[6] fifty miles from the railroad. There ❸ they measured off their eighty acres by driving across the prairie in a wagon, to the wheel of which they had tied a red cotton handkerchief, and counting its revolutions. They built a dugout in the red hillside, one of those cave dwellings whose inmates usually reverted to the conditions of primitive savagery. Their water they got from the lagoons where the buffalo drank, and their slender stock of provisions was always at the mercy of bands of roving Indians. For thirty years my aunt had not been farther than fifty miles from the homestead. ❸

◆ Literary Focus
❹ What do the contrasting details of Aunt Georgiana's life in Boston and Nebraska reveal about her character?

But Mrs. Springer knew nothing of all this, and must have been considerably shocked at what was left of my kinswoman. Beneath the soiled linen duster, which on her arrival was the most conspicuous feature of her costume, she wore a black stuff dress whose ornamentation showed that she had surrendered herself unquestioningly into the hands of a country dressmaker. My poor aunt's figure, however, would have presented astonishing difficulties to any dressmaker. ❺ Her skin was yellow from constant exposure to a pitiless wind, and to the alkaline water which transforms the most transparent cuticle into a sort of flexible leather. She wore ill-fitting false teeth. The most striking thing about her physiognomy, however, was an incessant twitching of the mouth and eyebrows, a form of nervous disorder resulting from isolation and monotony, and from frequent physical suffering.

In my boyhood this affliction had possessed a sort of horrible fascination for me, of which I was secretly very much ashamed, for in those days I owed to this woman most of the good that ever came my way, and had a reverential affection for her. During the three winters when I was riding herd for my uncle, my aunt, after cooking three meals for half a dozen farmhands, and putting the six children to bed, would often stand until midnight at her ironing board, hearing me at the kitchen table beside her recite Latin declensions and conjugations, and gently shaking me when my drowsy head sank down over a page of irregular verbs. It was to her, at her ironing or mending, that I read my first Shakespeare; and her old textbook of mythology was the first that ever came into my empty hands. She taught me my scales and exercises, too, on the little parlor organ which her husband had bought her after fifteen years, during which she had not so much as seen any instrument except an accordion, that belonged to one of the

2. **Franz Josef Land:** Group of islands in the Arctic Ocean.
3. **Congo:** River in central Africa.
4. **Green Mountains:** Mountains in Vermont.
5. **callow** (kal´ ō) *adj.*: Immature; inexperienced
6. **Red Willow County:** County in southwestern Nebraska that borders on Kansas.

◆ Build Vocabulary

reverential (rev´ ə ren´ shəl) *adj.*: Showing or caused by a feeling of deep respect, love, and awe

Block Scheduling Strategies

Consider these suggestions to take advantage of extended class time:

- Use the Interest Grabber to prepare students for "A Wagner Matinée." Review the Literature and Your Life section (p. 613), then have students complete the journal activity.
- To provide more background on Willa Cather, use the **Literature CD-ROM.**
- Introduce the Literary Focus and Reading Strategy. After students have read the selection, they can answer the corresponding Guide for Responding questions on page 620. Assign the pages in ***Selection Support*** (pp. 187 and 188) for additional practice or as homework.
- As a class, discuss the Critical Thinking questions (p. 620).
- If you have access to technology, have students work in the **Writer's Solution Writing Lab CD-ROM** to complete the Guided Writing Lesson (p. 621). Then have peers evaluate one another's work, using a Scoring Rubric in ***Alternative Assessment.***

◆ Background for Understanding

Literature When this story appeared, it created a hue and cry among some of Willa Cather's fellow Nebraskans, who claimed it was unfair to the state in which she had been raised. The story also offended Cather's family, because her uncle, George Cather, and his wife, Aunt Franc, were obviously the models for the fictional Uncle Howard and Aunt Georgiana. (Cather's aunt, who had attended Smith and Mount Holyoke, had married George Cather and gone to live in a sod house in Nebraska.) Cather defended her story, saying that it paid tribute to the brave women who endured the desolation and loneliness of life on the frontier.

Customize for
Musical/Rhythmic Learners
Have these students listen to the pieces mentioned in the story and comment on their emotional power. Also have them identify terms, used here and elsewhere, that have broad as well as specific musical meanings. Examples include *motif, crescendo, development,* and *counterpoint.*

❸ Clarification In 1862, Congress passed the Homestead Act to advance settlement of the prairie lands of the West. The Act offered 160 acres of free land to anyone over twenty-one years of age who was a citizen or who had declared intention to become one. Permanent ownership of the land came after five years of residence or after six months and payment of $1.50 an acre.

◆ Literary Focus

❹ Characterization They reveal that she was once a refined and cultured woman who, for the sake of romantic passion, exchanged life in Boston for a life that transformed her into a figure "at once pathetic and grotesque."

◆ Literary Focus

❺ Characterization Guide students to notice that this passage presents physical descriptions of Georgiana that provide further insight into her character and express Clark's attitude toward her.

◆ Critical Thinking

1 Connect; Analyze In *Euryanthe,* the opera by Carl Maria von Weber (1786–1826), Euryanthe is falsely accused and led by the man she loves to the desert to die. Notice how Euryanthe's story echoes the theme of martyrdom to which Cather alludes in this passage. Prompt students to discuss Aunt Georgiana's martyrdom, how the music aroused such a strong reaction in her, and how this fact informs her admonition to Clark. *Students may say that Aunt Georgiana was a martyr because she left something she deeply loved to be with her husband; recognizing the pain of her decision, she advises Clark to moderate his love for music lest he lose it, as she did.*

◆ Reading Strategy

2 Clarify Encourage students to use footnotes 7–9 to clarify the meaning of three terms mentioned here.

◆ Literary Focus

3 Characterization Ask students what they learn of Aunt Georgiana's character by her comments and concerns. *Students may say that she seems to have become a prairie wife whose main concerns are the well-being of her livestock and the necessity to use her precious food supply wisely. She seems to have little interest in music or the city that was once her home.*

Extending Word Study

Word Origins Have students look up the origins of the word *conservatory* as a strategy to understanding its meaning. Ask them to trace the changes in the word's usage. Then, have some students explain to the class how the origins of *conservatory* relate to its use in the story.

Norwegian farmhands. She would sit beside me by the hour, darning and counting, while I struggled with the "Harmonious Blacksmith"; but she seldom talked to me about music, and I understood why. She was a pious woman; she had the consolation of religion; and to 1 her at least her martyrdom was not wholly sordid. Once when I had been doggedly beating out some passages from an old score of "Euryanthe" I had found among her music books, she came up to me and, putting her hands over my eyes, gently drew my head back upon her shoulder, saying tremulously, "Don't love it so well, Clark, or it may be taken from you. Oh! dear boy, pray that whatever your sacrifice be it is not that."

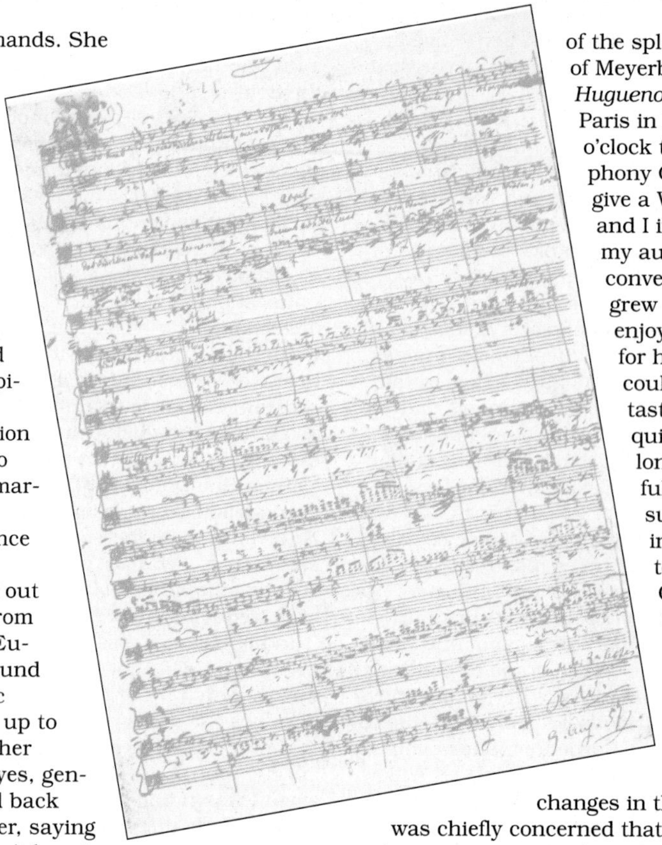

When my aunt appeared on the morning after her arrival, she was still in a semi-somnambulant state. She seemed not to realize that she was in the city where she had spent her youth, the place longed for hungrily for half a lifetime. She had been so wretchedly trainsick throughout the journey that she had no recollection of anything but her discomfort, and, to all intents and purposes, there were but a few hours of nightmare between the farm in Red Willow County and my study on Newbury Street. I had planned a little pleasure for her that afternoon, to repay her for some of the glorious moments she had given me when we used to milk together in the straw-thatched cowshed, and she, because I was more than usually tired, or because her husband had spoken sharply to me, would tell me of the splendid performance of Meyerbeer's *Les Huguenots*[7] she had seen in Paris in her youth. At two o'clock the Boston Symphony Orchestra was to give a Wagner[8] program, and I intended to take my aunt, though as I conversed with her I grew doubtful about her enjoyment of it. Indeed, for her own sake, I could only wish her 2 taste for such things quite dead, and the long struggle mercifully ended at last. I suggested our visiting the Conservatory and the Common[9] before lunch, but she seemed altogether too timid to wish to venture out. She questioned me absently about various changes in the city, but she was chiefly concerned that she had forgotten to leave instructions about feeding half-skimmed milk to a certain weakling calf, "Old Maggie's calf, you know, Clark," she explained, evidently 3 having forgotten how long I had been away. She was further troubled because she had neglected to tell her daughter about the freshly opened kit of mackerel in the cellar, that would spoil if it were not used directly.

7. ***Les Huguenots*** (lāz hyōō´ gə nät´): Opera written in 1836 by Giacomo Meyerbeer (1791–1864).
8. **Wagner** (väg´ nər): Richard Wagner (1813–1883), a great German composer who is responsible for the development of the musical drama.
9. **Common:** Boston Common, a small park in Boston.

◆ Build Vocabulary

tremulously (trem´ yōō ləs lē) *adv.*: Fearfully; timidly

semi-somnambulant (sem´ i säm nam´ byōō lənt) *adj.*: Half-sleepwalking

Speaking, Listening, and Viewing Mini-Lesson

Debate

This mini-lesson supports the Speaking, Listening, and Viewing activity in the Idea Bank (p. 621).

Introduce the Concept Divide participating students into two debate teams to argue the question: "Which was a healthier environment, the Nebraska frontier or Boston at the same period of time?" Review the general rules of debate—how to present statements, rebuttals, and summaries in logical and well-reasoned ways.

Develop Background Help teams determine how to prepare and present objective information, not just personal opinions. Have them review the story for key details that support their position. They might also read first-hand journals of the times, or archival newspaper accounts of life in those places. Have students consider the advantages and drawbacks of each lifestyle.

Apply the Information Announce formal rules so that both teams operate under equal and fair conditions. Then stage the debate. Students who are not members of the debate teams should participate as audience members who will vote on the presentations.

Assess the Outcome After audience members have selected a winner, discuss what elements made that team more persuasive. For example: which arguments were most compelling? Which team seemed better prepared? Which team supported its points or rebuttals more effectively?

I asked her whether she had ever heard any of the Wagnerian operas, and found that she had not, though she was perfectly familiar with their respective situations and had once pos-
4 sessed the piano score of *The Flying Dutchman.* I began to think it would have been best to get her back to Red Willow County without waking her, and regretted having suggested the concert.

From the time we entered the concert hall, however, she was a trifle less passive and inert, and seemed to begin to perceive her surroundings. I had felt some trepidation[10] lest one might become aware of the absurdities of her attire, or might experience some painful embarrassment at stepping suddenly into the world to which she had been dead for a quarter of a century. But again I found how superficially I had judged her. She sat looking about her with eyes as impersonal, almost as stony, as those with which
5 the granite Ramses[11] in a museum watches the froth and fret that ebbs and flows about his pedestal, separated from it by the lonely stretch of centuries. I have seen this same aloofness in old miners who drift into the Brown Hotel at Denver, their pockets full of bullion, their linen soiled, their haggard faces unshorn, and who stand in the thronged corridors as solitary as though they were still in a frozen camp on the Yukon, or in the yellow blaze of the Arizona desert, conscious that certain experiences have isolated them from their fellows by a gulf no haberdasher could conceal.

The audience was made up chiefly of women. One lost the contour of faces and figures, indeed any effect of line whatever, and there was only the color contrast of bodices past counting, the shimmer and shading of fabrics soft and firm, silky and sheer, resisting and yielding: red, mauve, pink, blue, lilac, purple, ecru, rose, yellow, cream, and white, all the colors that an impressionist finds in a sunlit landscape, with here and there the dead black shadow of a frock coat. My Aunt Georgiana regarded them as though they had been so many daubs of tube paint on a palette.

When the musicians came out and took their places, she gave a little stir of anticipation, and looked with quickening interest down over the rail at that invariable grouping; perhaps the first wholly familiar thing that had greeted her eye since she had left old Maggie and her weakling calf. I could feel how all those details sank into her soul, for I had not forgotten how they had sunk into mine when I came fresh from plowing forever and forever between green aisles of corn, where, as in a treadmill, one might walk from daybreak to dusk without perceiving a shadow of change in one's environment. I reminded myself of the impression made on me by the clean profiles of the musicians, the 7
gloss of their linen; the dull black of their coats, the beloved shapes of the instruments, the patches of yellow light thrown by the green-shaded stand-lamps on the smooth, varnished bellies of the cellos and the bass viols in the rear, the restless, wind-tossed forest of fiddle necks and bows; I recalled how, in the first orchestra I had ever heard, those long bow strokes seemed to draw the soul out of me, as a conjuror's stick reels out paper ribbon from a hat.

> **◆ Literary Focus**
> What does Aunt Georgiana's excitement about the upcoming performance reveal about her? 6

The first number was the Tannhäuser overture. When the violins drew out the first strain of the Pilgrims' chorus, my Aunt Georgiana clutched my coat sleeve. Then it was that I first realized that for her this singing of basses and stinging frenzy of lighter strings broke a silence 8
of thirty years, the inconceivable silence of the plains. With the battle between the two motifs, with the bitter frenzy of the Venusberg[12] theme and its ripping of strings, came to me an overwhelming sense of the waste and wear we are so powerless to combat. I saw again the tall, naked house on the prairie, black and grim as a wooden fortress; the black pond where I had learned to swim, the rain-gullied clay about the naked house; the four dwarf ash seedlings on

10. **trepidation** (trep´ ə dā´ shən) *n.*: Fearful anxiety; apprehension.
11. **Ramses** (ram´ sēz): One of the eleven Egyptian kings by that name who ruled from c. 1315 to c. 1090 B.C.
12. **Venusberg** (vē´ nəs burg´): Legendary mountain in Germany where Venus, the Roman goddess of love, held court.

◆ Build Vocabulary
inert (in urt´) *adj.*: Motionless

Cultural Connection

Opera Opera is as rich culturally as it is musically. Richard Wagner's opera brought German mythology to life with stirring music and drama. Earlier opera composers, such as Claudio Monteverdi and Christoph Gluck, relied on classical stories of ancient Greece and Rome for their subjects. Nationalism burst onto the musical scene in Czechoslovakia and Russia in the operas of Anton Dvorák and Modest Mussorgsky, who incorporated their cultures' rich folk music into their operas. English composer Gustav Holst's opera *Savitri* is based on an episode from the Hindu epic *Mahabharata,* and George Gershwin dramatized African American life in *Porgy and Bess.* Today, opera is truly an international art form; singers perform in many languages in opera houses around the world.

Have students listen to some or all of an opera or watch a video of an operatic performance. Ask them to analyze how the music conveys the characters' feelings and thoughts, and reaches audiences in ways that differ from nonmusical theatrical productions.

◆ Reading Strategy

4 Clarify Explain to students that they can dig deeper into Cather's meaning by understanding more about her references to Wagner and his operas. For example, *The Flying Dutchman,* a milestone in Wagner's career, is about a Dutch sea captain who is doomed forever to roam the seas until a curse he rashly uttered can be broken by the love of a faithful woman. Discuss how Aunt Georgiana's rash decision doomed her to a similar fate.

◆ Reading Strategy

5 Clarify Discuss Clark's growing understanding of his aunt. Encourage students to reread this passage to appreciate it. Help them notice that Clark was at first embarrassed by being seen with Aunt Georgiana because she looked so out of place, yet it was his idea to bring her to the concert in the first place. Clark still thinks of her as a haggard pioneer, a confused stranger in her own land. His appreciation for her must change as he realizes how much she must overcome to return to the cultural world that has become so foreign to her.

◆ Literary Focus

6 Characterization Her excitement reveals that her love for music is reawakening; her suffering has not completely numbed or withered her soul.

◆ Grammar and Style

7 Reflexive and Intensive Pronouns Point out the reflexive pronoun *myself* in this sentence. It is used to clarify *who* was reminded.

◆ Build Vocabulary

8 Words From Music This passage contains many words from music, including *overture, violins, strain, chorus, basses,* and *motifs,* as well as descriptions of the way the violin passages sound: *singing, lighter strings, ripping of strings.* Direct students to use a musical dictionary or other resource to explore the meaning of any terms they may not understand.

◆ Reading Strategy

❶ **Clarify** Students should realize that, in this context, films are probably thin layers of grime or thin membranes that grow over aging eyes, separating Aunt Georgiana from the music and the world she once knew. When this story was written, film did not have the connotation of *movie* that it has today.

◆ Background for Understanding

❷ **Music** Richard Wagner's tragic opera *Tristan and Isolde* is another example of a tragic ending brought on by love. Isolde has been promised to the King, and Tristan must deliver her to him. As Tristan and Isolde declare their love for one another, one of the King's knights surprises them in the King's garden. Tristan is mortally wounded and Isolde breathes her last breath over his body.

◆ Build Vocabulary

❸ **Words From Music** The term *motif* (also *motive* or *motiv*) is a brief rhythmic or melodic figure too short to be a theme. A motif can be associated with a character, idea, or object. In Wagner, such a musical idea is often called a *leitmotiv*. Help students understand that the "warfare of motifs" literally describes a compositional technique Wagner used to build symbolism into his music. It is also, however, symbolic of the conflicting needs and desires that clash within Aunt Georgiana.

◆ Critical Thinking

❹ **Interpret** Ask students what Clark's "quivering eyelids" signify. What emotions is he feeling?

Students should realize that Clark is himself close to tears as he remembers all that his aunt has done for him.

which the dishcloths were always hung to dry before the kitchen door. The world there is the flat world of the ancients; to the east, a cornfield that stretched to daybreak; to the west, a corral that stretched to sunset; between, the sordid conquests of peace, more merciless than those of war.

The overture closed. My aunt released my coat sleeve, but she said nothing. She sat staring at the orchestra through a dullness of thirty years, through the films made, little by little, by each of the three hundred and sixty-five days in every one of them. What, I wondered, did she get from it? She had been a good pianist in her day, I knew, and her musical education had been broader than that of most music teachers of a quarter of a century ago. She had often told me of Mozart's operas and Meyerbeer's, and I could remember hearing her sing, years ago, certain melodies of Verdi. When I had fallen ill with a fever she used to sit by my cot in the evening, while the cool night wind blew in through the faded mosquito netting tacked over the window, and I lay watching a bright star that burned red above the cornfield, and sing "Home to our mountains, oh, let us return!" in a way fit to break the heart of a Vermont boy near dead of homesickness already.

> **◆ Reading Strategy** ❶
> What does the author mean by "films"? To help clarify, consider when the story was written.

I watched her closely through the prelude to *Tristan and Isolde*, trying vainly to conjecture what that warfare of motifs, that seething turmoil of strings and winds, might mean to her. ❷ Had this music any message for her? Did or did ❸ not a new planet swim into her ken? Wagner had been a sealed book to Americans before the sixties. Had she anything left with which to comprehend this glory that had flashed around the world since she had gone from it? I was in a fever of curiosity, but Aunt Georgiana sat silent upon her peak in Darien.[13] She preserved this utter immobility throughout the numbers from the *Flying Dutchman*, though her fingers worked mechanically upon her black dress, as though of themselves they were recalling the piano score they had once played. Poor old hands! They were stretched and pulled and twisted into mere tentacles to hold, and lift, and knead with; the palms unduly swollen, the fingers bent and knotted, on one of them a thin worn band that had once been a wedding ring. As I pressed and gently quieted one of those groping hands, I remembered, with quivering eyelids, their services for me in other days. ❹

Soon after the tenor began the "Prize Song," I heard a quick-drawn breath, and turned to my aunt. Her eyes were closed, but the tears were glistening on her cheeks, and I think in a moment more they were in my eyes as well. It never really dies, then, the soul? It withers to the outward eye only, like that strange moss which can lie on a dusty shelf half a century and yet, if placed in water, grows green again. My aunt wept gently throughout the development and elaboration of the melody.

During the intermission before the second half of the concert, I questioned my aunt and found that the "Prize Song" was not new to her. Some years before there had drifted to the farm in Red Willow County a young German, a tramp cow puncher who had sung in the chorus at Bayreuth,[14] when he was a boy, along with the other peasant boys and girls. Of a Sunday morning he used to sit on his blue gingham-sheeted bed in the hands' bedroom, which opened off the kitchen, cleaning the leather of his boots and saddle, and singing the "Prize Song," while my aunt went about her work in the kitchen. She had hovered about him until she had prevailed upon him to join the country church, though his sole fitness for this step, so far as I could gather, lay in his boyish face and his possession of this divine melody. Shortly afterward he had gone to town on the Fourth of July, lost his money at a faro[15] table, ridden a saddled Texas steer on a

13. **peak in Darien** (derʹ ē ən): Mountain on the Isthmus of Panama; from "On First Looking at Chapman's Homer" by English poet John Keats (1795–1821).

14. **Bayreuth** (bī roitʹ): City in Germany known for its annual Wagnerian music festivals.

15. **faro** (ferʹ ō): Gambling game in which players bet on the cards to be turned up from the top of the dealer's deck.

◆ Build Vocabulary

prelude (prelʹ yo͞od) *n.*: Introductory section or movement of a suite, fugue, or work of music

Reteach

Students may not immediately recognize examples of characterization as they appear in the story. Create a chart like the one here and distribute it to the class. Read the first two pages of the story aloud to students, pausing to fill in the chart when characterization takes place. Then, have students read the rest of the story silently, filling out the chart when they encounter characterization.

Detail from Text	Characterization of Georgiana	Characterization of Clark
yellow skin; ill-fitting false teeth; twitching of mouth and eyebrows	physical description (direct)	He feels life in Nebraska is a poor choice Georgiana's physical traits are a result of this life (indirect)

bet, and disappeared with a fractured collarbone.

"Well, we have come to better things than the old *Trovatore* at any rate, Aunt Georgie?" I queried, with well-meant jocularity.

Her lip quivered and she hastily put her handkerchief up to her mouth. From behind it she murmured, "And you've been hearing this
5 ever since you left me, Clark?" Her question was the gentlest and saddest of reproaches.

"But do you get it, Aunt Georgiana, the astonishing structure of it all?" I persisted.

"Who could?" she said, absently; "why should one?"

6 The second half of the program consisted of four numbers from the *Ring*. This was followed by the forest music from *Siegfried*[16] and the program closed with Siegfried's funeral march. My aunt wept quietly, but almost continuously. I was perplexed as to what measure of musical comprehension was left to her, to her who had heard nothing for so many years but the singing of gospel hymns in Methodist services at the square frame schoolhouse on Section Thirteen. I was unable to gauge how much of it had been dissolved in soapsuds, or worked into bread, or milked into the bottom of a pail.

The deluge of sound poured on and on; I never knew what she found in the shining current of it; I never knew how far it bore her, or past what happy islands, or under what skies. From the trembling of her face I could well believe that the *Siegfried* march, at least, carried her out where the myriad graves are, out into the gray, burying grounds of the sea; or into some world of death vaster yet, where, from the beginning of the world, hope has lain down with hope, and dream with dream and, renouncing, slept.

The concert was over; the people filed out of the hall chattering and laughing, glad to 7
relax and find the living level again, but my kinswoman made no effort to rise. I spoke gently to her. She burst into tears and sobbed pleadingly, "I don't want to go, Clark, I don't want to go!"

I understood. For her, just outside the door of the concert hall, lay the black pond with the cattle-tracked bluffs, the tall, unpainted house, naked as a tower, with weather-curled boards; the crook-backed ash seedlings where the dishcloths hung to dry, the gaunt, moulting turkeys picking up refuse about the kitchen door.

16. ***Siegfried*** (sēg´ frēd): Opera based on the adventures of Siegfried, a legendary hero in medieval German literature.

◆ **Build Vocabulary**

jocularity (jäk´ yə lar´ ə tē) *n.*: Joking good humor

Guide for Responding

◆ *Literature and Your Life*

Reader's Response Did you feel sorry for Aunt Georgiana? Why or why not?

Thematic Focus At one point, the narrator suggests that it would have been better to have sent Aunt Georgiana back to Red Willow "without waking her." Do you agree? Why or why not?

Group Discussion Aunt Georgiana gave up her greatest joy—music—for the chance to marry the man she loved. Did she make the right choice? Discuss the question in a small group.

☑ Check Your Comprehension

1. Summarize the sequence of events leading up to the matinée.
2. Describe Aunt Georgiana in your own words.
3. When and under what circumstances did the narrator live with Aunt Georgiana?
4. What happens to make the narrator realize that "it never really dies, then, the soul"?
5. How does Aunt Georgiana react when the concert ends?

Beyond the Selection

FURTHER READING

Other Works by Willa Cather

O Pioneers!
My Antonia
Death Comes to the Archbishop

Other Works About Prairie Life

The Great Plains, Ian Frazier
Little Big Man, Thomas Berger

We suggest that you preview these works before recommending them to students.

INTERNET

You and your students may find additional information about Willa Cather on the Internet. We suggest the following site. Please be aware, however, that sites may have changed since this information was published.

For a comprehensive look at the life and work of Willa Cather, go to the home page for her at **http://icg.harvard.edu/~cather/**

We *strongly recommend* that you preview the site before you send students to it.

◆ Literary Focus

5 Characterization Discuss how this conversation reveals the characters of Clark and Aunt Georgiana. Ask students to contrast the way nephew and aunt respond to the music. *Students should realize that Clark is being intellectual, even patronizing, in his response, while Aunt Georgiana reacts on a purely emotional level.*

◆ Background for Understanding

6 Music *The Ring* refers to a set of four operas based on the Nibelung sagas of German mythology. The operas are *The Rheingold, The Valkyrie, Siegfried,* and *Dusk of the Gods.*

Customize for
Less Proficient Readers

7 Help students understand the meaning of the end of this story. "Just outside the door" is not to be taken literally. Rather, the concert hall symbolizes an oasis in Aunt Georgiana's life; once she leaves its spell, she must return to prairie life.

Reinforce and Extend

Answers

◆ ***Literature and Your Life***

Reader's Response Students should be prepared to explain their answers.

Thematic Focus Students may agree that it would have been better never to remind Aunt Georgiana of all that she left behind when she moved to Nebraska.

☑ **Check Your Comprehension**

1. Clark receives a letter informing him that his Aunt Georgiana is coming to Boston to settle some legal affairs. He meets her at the station, and takes her to his rooming house where she spends the night. The next day they attend an afternoon performance of the music of Wagner.
2. Descriptions will vary but should convey Aunt Georgiana's desiccated and passive quality.
3. He lived with her for three winters of his childhood while he helped his uncle work the farm.
4. Aunt Georgiana begins to cry at the beauty of the music.
5. She doesn't get up, and cries out that she doesn't want to leave.

Guide for Responding (continued)

◆ Critical Thinking

INTERPRET

1. Contrast the impression the story conveys of life in Red Willow County with life in Boston. **[Compare and Contrast]**
2. What does Aunt Georgiana mean when she says "Don't love it so well, Clark, or it may be taken from you"? **[Interpret]**
3. (a) Why does the opera have such a powerful effect on Aunt Georgiana? **[Analyze]** (b) How does her reaction, in turn, awaken Clark? **[Connect]**

EVALUATE

4. Would it have been better for Aunt Georgiana if she had not come to Boston? Explain. **[Speculate]**

APPLY

5. How are people's personalities shaped by the environment in which they live? **[Apply]**

◆ Reading Strategy

CLARIFYING

To understand Aunt Georgiana's actions in this story, it is important to **clarify**—check your understanding of—the details that Cather provides about her background.

Review the details that Cather provides about Aunt Georgiana's life on the frontier. How do these details help explain how she behaves in Boston?

◆ Literary Focus

CHARACTERIZATION

Characterization is the means by which an author reveals a character's personality. Because of Cather's use of a first-person narrator, much of what we learn about Aunt Georgiana comes from Clark's thoughts and feelings about her.

1. What is revealed about Aunt Georgiana through descriptions of her appearance?
2. What does Aunt Georgiana's reaction to the opera reveal about her personality?
3. What is revealed about Clark's personality through his thoughts and feelings about his aunt?
4. How does the fact that much of what we learn about Aunt Georgiana is revealed through Clark's thoughts help us shape our impressions of her?

◆ Build Vocabulary

USING WORDS FROM MUSIC

Look at the following definitions. Then choose the response to each item that better fits the situation.

overture: (a) an introductory movement to an extended musical work, (b) any first move

concert: (a) a public performance of several short compositions, (b) the act of working together

1. **concerted** effort: (a) competitive, (b) united
2. **overture** at a car sale: (a) "Would you like to take a test drive?" (b) "Step away from the car."

USING THE WORD BANK: Connotions

Answer the following questions in your notebook.

1. If students are *reverential* toward a teacher, do they ignore her, worship her, or avoid her?
2. Who is most likely to speak *tremulously*—a musician, a truck driver, or a child?
3. Does *semi-somnambulant* describe someone who is angry, dazed, or busy?
4. Is an *inert* substance motionless or weightless?
5. Is *jocularity* the trademark of a funeral director, a talk-show host, or a surgeon?
6. As a *prelude* to bad news, would you expect humor or seriousness?

◆ Grammar and Style

REFLEXIVE AND INTENSIVE PRONOUNS

Reflexive and **intensive pronouns** end in *-self* or *-selves* but function differently. Reflexive pronouns refer to the subject and are necessary to the meaning of the sentence. Intensive pronouns emphasize a word mentioned earlier. They can be omitted without changing the meaning of the sentence.

Practice Identify the reflexive or intensive pronouns in these sentences.

1. Cather quit her job to devote herself to writing.
2. If you're a writer, you have to ask yourself whether you would have the courage to do the same.
3. For Cather, writing was itself a full-time job.
4. Writing is hard—books don't write themselves.

Writing Application Write four sentences describing some of your interests. Use two reflexive and two intensive pronouns.

Answers

◆ Critical Thinking

1. Life in Red Willow County is physically and psychologically brutal: the climate is harsh; the work never-ending and backbreaking; there are few people with whom to socialize; there is no music or culture. Life in Boston, by contrast, where there is an abundance of culture, people, and society, seems stimulating and enjoyable.
2. She's referring to her own profound love of music, which was taken from her.
3. (a) She hasn't heard such music in decades and it awakens her long dormant passion for music. (b) It makes him see that Aunt Georgiana is not just a pathetic symbol of isolation, toil, and self-sacrifice; that she is still, after all these years, a deeply feeling person.
4. Some may agree that it would be better if she had not come because her visit is just a cruel reminder of all that she lost when she moved to Nebraska.
5. Students' responses should reflect their understanding of how Aunt Georgiana was changed by her years on the farm.

◆ Reading Strategy

Students should note the details that portray the harshness of life in Nebraska, such as the dugout likened to a "cave dwelling," and "the conditions of primitive savagery." After decades of isolation from the elegance and culture of Boston, Aunt Georgiana feels and acts as though she is walking through a dream world that contrasts sharply with her desolate home.

◆ Literary Focus

1. We learn that she has been roughened and aged by her years in Nebraska. Her nervous twitching hints at the isolation and suffering she has endured.
2. Her reaction reveals that her passionate love for music is still very much alive; her harsh life has not deadened her inner spirit.
3. Suggested response: Clark is grateful and affectionate toward his aunt for all she has done for him, yet, as a cultured Bostonian, he is a bit embarrassed by his aunt's appearance.
4. Clark provides the background that makes Aunt Georgiana into something more than just a pathetic and slightly ridiculous figure. He describes her life before Nebraska—her great love of music and her prestigious position at the Boston Conservatory. He also relates her kindness to him as a boy. Because we learn about the type of person she once was and all that she has done for Clark, we come to view Aunt Georgiana with respect and sympathy.

◆ Build Vocabulary

Using Words From Music

1. b 2. a

Using the Word Bank

1. They worship her.
2. a child 3. dazed
4. motionless 5. a talk-show host 6. seriousness

◆ Grammar and Style

Practice

1. herself; reflexive
2. yourself; reflexive
3. itself; intensive
4. themselves; reflexive

Writing Application

Students should identify which pronouns they use are reflexive and which are intensive.

Build Your Portfolio

Idea Bank

Writing

1. **Diary Entry** For the most part, Clark cannot gauge the effect of the music on his aunt. Let Aunt Georgiana speak for herself. Write a diary entry recording her reactions to the matinée.

2. **School Brochure** Aunt Georgiana has decided to open a music school in Red Willow County. Create an informational brochure aimed at convincing Nebraskans to send their children to the school. **[Media Link]**

3. **Editorial** "A Wagner Matinée" provoked an outcry among Nebraskans who felt Cather had portrayed the state unfairly. Cather said the story was a tribute to pioneer strength and endurance. As the editor of a Nebraska newspaper, write an editorial stating and defending your view.

Speaking, Listening, and Viewing

4. **Debate** Create two teams to debate the question: Which is a healthier environment, the Nebraska frontier or Boston?

5. **Oral Storytelling** Tell the story of Aunt Georgiana's visit as you imagine Clark would have described it to friends after his aunt left.

Researching and Representing

6. **A Wagner Matinée** Locate a recording of one of Wagner's operas. Do research to learn its story. Play one of the songs for the class, explaining to them the piece's significance in the opera. **[Music Link]**

7. **Research Project** Find out how the Homestead Act of 1862 opened the frontier for settlement. Does Cather present an accurate portrait of life on a homestead? Use your findings to create an oral report. **[Social Studies Link]**

Online Activity www.phlit.phschool.com

Guided Writing Lesson

Travel Brochure

Cather's rendering of Aunt Georgiana's Nebraska homestead is strikingly vivid, but it doesn't exactly make you want to visit. Think of a place that captures your imagination—a place you've visited, seen on television, or read about—and create a travel brochure that does make people want to visit.

Writing Skills Focus: Sensory Details

Travel brochures use description to make vacation destinations seem appealing. Make your descriptions rich and vivid by including **sensory details**—details that appeal to one or more of the five senses—as Cather does in this description of the matinée audience.

Model From the Selection

. . . there was only the color contrast of bodices past counting, the shimmer and shadowing of fabrics soft and firm, silky and sheer, resisting and yielding: red mauve, pink, blue, lilac, purple, ecru, rose, yellow, cream, and white.

Prewriting Once you've chosen a place, think about the features you might describe, such as culture, architecture, music, foods, museums, or scenic locales. Gather and list sensory details you could use to describe them. Then find photographs and other visuals you can include in your brochure.

Drafting Arrange the visuals you've gathered into an order that makes sense. Then write a paragraph to accompany each visual. In each paragraph, focus on presenting vivid descriptions that will make your readers want to visit the destination.

Revising Review your draft, looking for places where you can add or change sensory details to make the descriptions more vivid and appealing.

Idea Bank

Customizing for
Performance Levels

Following are suggestions for matching Idea Bank topics with your students' performance levels:

Less Advanced Students: 1, 5
Average Students: 2, 4, 6
More Advanced Students: 3, 7

Customizing for
Learning Modalities

Following are suggestions for matching Idea Bank topics with your students' learning modalities:

Logical/Mathematical: 4, 7
Verbal/Linguistic: 5
Interpersonal: 5
Musical/Rhythmic: 6

Guided Writing Lesson

For more instruction on prewriting, elaboration, and revision, see *Prentice Hall Writing and Grammar.*

Writing and Language Transparencies To aid students with Prewriting, use the Branching Transparency (p. 67) to help students organize key points and sensory details.

Writing Lab CD-ROM

Have students complete the Tutorial on Description. Follow these steps:

1. Have students review the annotated model of a travel brochure in the About Description section.
2. Have students use the Sensory Word Bins in the Gathering Details section to aid them as they draft on the computer.
3. Use the revision checker for vague or overused adjectives to aid revision.

✓ ASSESSMENT OPTIONS

Formal Assessment, Selection Test, pp. 188–190, and Assessment Resources Software. The selection test is designed so that it can be easily customized to the performance levels of your students.

Alternative Assessment, p. 40, includes options for less advanced students, more advanced students, visual/spatial learners, musical/rhythmic learners, and verbal/linguistic learners.

PORTFOLIO ASSESSMENT

Use the following rubrics in the ***Alternative Assessment*** booklet to assess student writing:
Diary Entry: Expression Rubric, p. 109
School Brochure: Persuasion Rubric, p. 120
Editorial: Persuasion Rubric, p. 120
Guided Writing Lesson: Description Rubric, p. 112

LESSON OBJECTIVES

1. To express and support responses to the text
- Critical Thinking
- Idea Bank: Letter to the Editor

2. To analyze literary elements
- Thematic Connection

3. To read in order to research self-selected and assigned topics
- Idea Bank: Report

4. To plan, prepare, organize, and present literary interpretations
- Idea Bank: Epitaph
- Idea Bank: Song
- Idea Bank: Dramatic Monologue

5. To write a character sketch
- Idea Bank: Character Sketch

Interest Grabber Invite students to listen as you play the Beatles song "Eleanor Rigby" (from the *Revolver* album). Invite their responses to the song ("All the lonely people / Where do they all come from? / All the lonely people / Where do they all belong?") in light of today's technological age. Ask them how they think people can make meaningful connections in a fast-moving world.

Connections to Today's World

Alienation, isolation, loneliness—though universal, these themes began to emerge more strongly at the dawning of the twentieth century. The authors featured in Part 4 lived and wrote in a time of tremendous change. As they read this contemporary essay about an elderly woman's alienation from society, students should recognize emotions and themes that echo the works of Chopin, Dunbar, Robinson, Masters, and Cather.

CONNECTIONS TO TODAY'S WORLD

Cats

Anna Quindlen

Thematic Connection

LIVING IN A CHANGING WORLD

Writer Joyce Carol Oates once described Willa Cather as "a passionate chronicler of her time and place." The same can be said of novelist and former *New York Times* columnist Anna Quindlen. Although separated by nearly a century, both writers explore similar emotional terrain, charting the inner struggles and conflicts of the individual in a changing society.

A NEW LITERARY SENSIBILITY

The America of Willa Cather's youth was a nation in the midst of rapid and massive change. Industry and technology were booming. Immigrants swelled urban populations and fanned out westward across the plains. Cities burgeoned, and the pace of life quickened.

Confronted by these changes in society and its values, many writers struggled to find meaning in lives that were isolated from others. Out of this struggle, a new literary movement, known as Realism, emerged. Realism emphasized the honest rendering of life, and the works of the Realists were often colored by loneliness and alienation.

A LOSS OF COMMUNITY

With the Information Age dawning, America is again undergoing a transformation, and many find the changes exciting. However, for some, the loneliness and alienation of a century ago are still a reality.

The symptoms aren't hard to spot. People log anonymously onto chat rooms or spend hours watching television instead of chatting with flesh-and-blood neighbors. They pursue high-powered careers that leave little time for an emotional life. They move every few years in pursuit of better jobs, but at the expense of family and community ties.

The emotional isolation that results is the subtext of many of Anna Quindlen's columns. In her column "Life in the '30s," Quindlen took the school, the neighborhood, and the office as her territory. These are the places where human bonds should be strongest. Yet, as Quindlen reveals, there is a profound underside of loneliness and isolation.

ANNA QUINDLEN
(1953–)

Anna Quindlen was a *New York Times* reporter and editor and an aspiring novelist when the *Times* asked her to write a weekly column. She accepted the offer, never dreaming of where it might lead. "I thought of the column as a way to make a little bit of money while writing my novel," she said. "I was just trying hard not to disgrace myself."

Far from it. Quindlen's column, "Life in the '30s," was a well-loved *Times* feature for five years, beginning in 1990. Quindlen's approach to the column—honest, personal, empathetic, astute—helps explain its immense popularity. She also had a knack for pinpointing the concerns of her readers. "I think of a column as having a conversation with a person that it just so happens I can't see," Quindlen said after winning a Pulitzer Prize for commentary in 1992. "It's nice to know that my end of the conversation was heard."

Prentice Hall Literature Program Resources

REINFORCE / RETEACH / EXTEND

Selection Support Pages
Build Vocabulary, p. 189
Thematic Connection: Living in a Changing World, p. 190

Formal Assessment Selection Test, pp. 191–192; Assessment Resources Software

Resource Pro CD-ROM

Listening to Literature Audiocassettes

Cats

Anna Quindlen

The cats came with the house. They lived in the backyards, tiger gray, orange marmalade, calico, black. They slithered through the evergreens at the back perimeter, and during mating season their screams were terrible. Sometimes I shook black pepper along the property line, and for a night or two all was still. Then the rain came and they were back.

❶ The cats came because of the woman next door. She and her husband, said to be bedridden, had lived on the third floor for many years. Every evening after dinner she went into the alley with a foil pie plate heaped with cat food and scraps: cabbage, rice, the noodles from chicken noodle soup, whatever they had had for dinner. Before she would even get to the bottom of the stairs the cats would begin to assemble, narrowing their eyes. She would talk to them roughly in a voice like sandpaper, coarse from years of cigarette smoke. ". . . Cats," she grumbled as she bent to put the food down.

She had only two interests besides the cats: my son and her own. She and her husband had one grown child. I never heard her say a bad word about him. He had reportedly walked and talked early, been as beautiful as a child star, never given a bit of trouble. He always sent a large card on Mother's Day, and each Christmas a poinsettia came, wrapped in green foil with a red bow. He was in the military, stationed here and there. During the time we lived next door to her, he came home once. She said it broke his heart not to see his father more. She said they had always been close when he lived at home, that he played baseball for the high school team and that his father never missed a game. He was a crack shortstop, she said, and a superior hitter. ❷

She called my son "Bop Bop" because of the way he bounced in my arms. It was one of the first things he learned to say, and when he was in the backyard on summer evenings he would call "Bop Bop" plaintively until she came to her apartment window. As she raised the screen the cats would begin to mass in a great Pavlovian[1] gesture at the head of the alley. "Are you being a good boy?" she would call down. Bop Bop would smile up, his eyes shining. "Cat," he said, pointing, and the cats looked, too. Some summer nights she and my little boy would sit together companionably on the front stoop, watching the cars go by. She did not talk to him very much, and she wasn't tender, but when he was very good and not terribly dirty she sometimes said he looked just like her own little boy, only his hair wasn't quite as thick. ❸

Last year she fell on the street and broke her hip, but while she was in the hospital, they found that she had fallen because she had had a stroke, and she had had a stroke because

1. **Pavlovian** (pav lō´ vē ən) *adj.*: Referring to Russian physiologist Ivan Pavlov (1849–1936), who showed that acquired habits depend on chains of conditioned reflexes.

Develop Understanding

One-Minute Insight

Anna Quindlen writes of an elderly neighbor woman who felt a certain connection to Quindlen's small son because of his resemblance to her own estranged son. Quindlen muses about what her boy may remember of the woman, who has since died, and describes the inexorable end of her modest influence on the animals of the neighborhood. By extension, she examines the impact of life and death in any family or community far less close-knit than communities once were.

Customize for
Less Proficient Readers
Help students read this story on several levels. Most simply, it is a narrative observation with facts and details. On a deeper level, it is a personal essay that explores how an interaction between the author and a lonely neighbor made her examine the value of connections in the world.

◆ Critical Thinking

❶ **Analyze** Discuss students' first impressions of the woman next door. Encourage them to support their opinions. Students may find her eccentric, lovable, strange, or sad.

◆ Critical Thinking

❷ **Infer** Ask students to explain whether they think the young man is really as devoted to his parents as his mother says he is. On what do they base their responses? *Students should realize that the son is actually estranged from his parents; he visits only rarely, preferring to send hollow gestures of filial devotion.*

Thematic Connection

❸ **Living in a Changing World**
Talk with students about how the woman's life reflects her alienation from others. Students may note that she has little or no relationship with her own son, and although she is neighborly to Bop-Bop, she isn't really affectionate or friendly to him. Even the cats she cares for cause her to grumble and complain.

Thematic Connection

❶ Living in a Changing World
Guide students to notice that, according to Quindlen's description in this passage, the death of even an alienated, lonely, disconnected person leaves a gap.

Reinforce and Extend

Answers

◆ Literature and Your Life

Reader's Response Some students will pity her inability to build meaningful relationships.

Thematic Focus "Cats" is really about the loneliness of a woman who isn't close to anyone. When she dies, her bird dies, the cats in the neighborhood lose a provider, and Quindlen's son loses a companion.

☑ Check Your Comprehension

1. The neighbor is interested in her cats, her son, and Quindlen's son.
2. She sits with him, gives him an affectionate nickname, and, significantly, compares him favorably to her own son.
3. She becomes ill and goes into the hospital. When she returns she has changed. She dies not long afterward.

◆ Critical Thinking

1. The cats make the woman feel needed and connected to other living creatures.
2. He reminds the woman of her own son; he is a link to a time when her own little boy still needed and loved her.
3. Though she speaks glowingly of her son and their relationship, they are not close and he expends no thought or effort on his mother. He sends her routine, impersonal gifts twice a year; he visits only once.
4. Suggested response: He is not really a good son because he does not appear to care about his parents.
5. Students may say that Quindlen has learned the dangers of allowing community and family ties to weaken and, ultimately, to break.

of brain cancer. I went to see her in the hospital, and brought a picture of my son. She propped it against the water pitcher. She asked me to take care of her parakeet until she came home, to look in on her husband and to feed the cats. At night, when I came back from work, they would be prowling the yards, crying pitifully. My dogs lunged at the back windows.

When the ambulance brought her home, she looked like a scarecrow, her arms broomsticks in the armholes of her housecoat, her white hair wild. A home health-care aide came and cared for her and her husband. The woman across the street told me she was not well enough to take the bird back. The cats climbed the fire escape and banged against the screens with their bullet heads, but the aide shooed them away. My son would stand in the backyard and call "Bop Bop" at the window. One evening she threw it open and leaned out, a death's head, and shouted at him, and he cried. "Bop Bop is very sick," I said, and gave him a Popsicle.

She died this winter, a month after her husband. Her son came home for the funerals with his wife, and together they cleaned out the apartment. We sent roses to the funeral home, and the son's wife sent a nice thank-you note. The bird died the next month. Slowly the cats began to disperse. The two biggest, a tom and a female, seem to have stayed. I don't really feed them, but sometimes my son will eat lunch out back; if he doesn't finish his food, I will leave it on the table. When I look out again it is gone, and the dogs are a little wild.

My son likes to look through photo albums. In one there is a picture of her leaning out the window, and a picture of him looking up with a self-conscious smile. He calls them both "Bop Bop." I wonder for how long he will remember, and what it will mean to him, years from now, when he looks at the picture and sees her at her window, what reverberations will begin, what lasting lessons will she have subliminally taught him, what lasting lessons will she not so subliminally have taught me.

Guide for Responding

◆ Literature and Your Life

Reader's Response Did you feel sorry for the woman next door? Why or why not?

Thematic Focus Is "Cats" really about cats? What changes result from the neighbor's illness and eventual death?

Journal Entry Think about someone to whom you are emotionally close. Briefly describe your relationship, and tell what makes you so close to the other person.

☑ Check Your Comprehension

1. What are the main interests of the neighbor?
2. How does the woman express her affection for Quindlen's son?
3. What happens to the woman to end her relationship with Quindlen and her son?

◆ Critical Thinking

INTERPRET

1. What role do the cats play in the life of the woman next door? **[Interpret]**
2. Why is the woman so interested in Quindlen's son? **[Infer]**
3. Does the woman's perception of her own son equate with his actions? Support your answer with examples from the text. **[Analyze; Support]**

EVALUATE

4. Is the neighbor's son really a "good son"? Explain. **[Criticize]**

APPLY

5. What "lasting lessons" do you think Quindlen might have learned from her neighbor? **[Generalize]**

Beyond the Selection

FURTHER READING

Other Works by Anna Quindlen

Living Out Loud
Thinking Out Loud
Object Lessons
One True Thing

We suggest that you preview these works before recommending them to students.

INTERNET

You and your students may find additional information about Anna Quindlen on the Internet. We suggest the following site. Please be aware, however, that sites may have changed from the time we published this information.

For the transcript of an interview with Anna Quindlen, go to **http://www.booknotes.org/transcripts/50148. htm**

We *strongly recommend* that you preview the site before you send students to it.

Thematic Connection

LIVING IN A CHANGING WORLD

An old woman sickens and dies, estranged from her only son. Another woman, after years of physical and mental isolation, weeps inconsolably when that isolation is broken. A rich and successful man stuns his community by taking his own life.

What do these scenarios—taken from the selections in this section—have in common? They all show people in emotional pain, people who are disconnected from other people. Although all but one are drawn from the fiction and poetry of the past, it's not hard to imagine them taking place today, just about anywhere in the United States.

People in every age have suffered from loneliness; our need for other people is part of what makes us human. However, alienation—withdrawal or disconnection from society—is a modern condition, peculiar to highly developed, fast-paced, industrial and post-industrial societies. The authors in this section, all writing at the dawn of this century, searched for meaning in the emotional detachment and suffering of ordinary people. As the century comes to a close, the search goes on.

1. How does Quindlen's neighbor try to give meaning to her lonely life?
2. With which character from the selections in this section does Quindlen's neighbor have the most in common? Explain.
3. Could "Cats" have been written a hundred years ago? Why or why not?

Idea Bank

Writing

1. **Epitaph** In *Spoon River Anthology*, Edgar Lee Masters lets the dead speak for themselves in their own revealing epitaphs. Using them as a model, write an epitaph for Quindlen's neighbor.
2. **Letter to the Editor** "Cats" originally appeared as a "Life in the 30's" column in the *New York Times*. Write a letter to the editor of the *New York Times* expressing your reaction to "Cats." **[Media Link]**
3. **Song** Drawing on any of the situations and characters in this section, write a song about loneliness. **[Music Link]**
4. **Character Sketch** Write a character sketch of a lonely or isolated person—either real or imaginary. In the sketch, suggest the reasons for the person's situation.

Speaking, Listening, and Viewing

5. **Dramatic Monologue** Write and deliver a monologue in which you, as Quindlen's neighbor, reveal your inner feelings about your son and his behavior toward you. Alternatively, take the role of the son, and write and perform a dramatic monologue in which you reveal your feelings and the history of your relationship with your mother.

Researching and Representing

6. **Report** The writers in this section have drawn on experience and creative imagination for their portrayals of the effects of social and emotional isolation, but have the effects of isolation been scientifically documented? Do research to find out what kinds of effects isolation can have on people. Present your findings in the form of an oral or written report. **[Science Link]**

Online Activity www.phlit.phschool.com

Answers
Thematic Connection

1. She "adopts" cats and her neighbor's small son.
2. Students should be prepared to explain the connection between the neighbor and the character they cite. Some may suggest that Quindlen's neighbor is similar to Aunt Georgiana in that both have been wounded by life.
3. Students may say that stripped of contemporary details, the basic premise of an emotionally isolated old woman who loses any real ties to her adored son could have been adapted by any of the writers in Part 4; its themes and emotions are timeless and universally human. Others may disagree, saying that part of the author's argument centers on today's increasingly impersonal world, one that is devoid of strong communal ties.

Idea Bank

Customizing for
Performance Levels

Following are suggestions for matching Idea Bank topics with your students' performance levels:
Less Advanced Students: 2
Average Students: 1, 3, 6
More Advanced Students: 4, 5

Customizing for
Learning Modalities

Following are suggestions for matching Idea Bank topics with your students' learning modalities:
Intrapersonal: 2, 3
Musical/Rhythmic: 3
Bodily/Kinesthetic: 5
Logical/Mathematical: 6

ASSESSMENT OPTIONS

Formal Assessment, Selection Test, pp. 191–192, and Assessment Resources Software. The selection test is designed so that it can be easily customized to the performance levels of your students.

PORTFOLIO ASSESSMENT

Use the following rubrics in the ***Alternative Assessment*** booklet to assess student writing:
Epitaph: Expression Rubric, p. 109
Letter to the Editor: Response to Literature Rubric, p. 125
Song: Expression Rubric, p. 109
Character Sketch: Description Rubric, p. 112

Prepare and Engage

LESSON OBJECTIVES

- To use recursive writing processes to write a character profile
- To recognize and use correct punctuation of quotations
- To recognize and use appropriate sentence combining as a revision strategy

Distribute the scoring rubric for Description in ***Alternative Assessment*** (p. 112) to make students aware of the criteria on which their work will be evaluated. See the suggestions on page 628 for customizing the rubric to this workshop.

Refer students to the Writing Handbook, page 1192, for instruction in the writing process, and page 1194 for further information on descriptive writing. You may also want to present Writing Process Model 2: Descriptive and Observational Writing in ***Writing and Language Transparencies*** (pp. 9–12).

Connect to Literature Point out that any effective work of fiction contains elements of a character profile.

Writers at Work Videodisc
To introduce the elements of descriptive writing, play the videodisc segment featuring Pulitzer Prize-winning poet and novelist Rita Dove (Ch. 1).

Play frames 335 to 10985

Writing Lab CD-ROM
If your students have access to computers, you may want to have them use the tutorial on Description. Have students follow these steps:

1. Use the Word Bins to choose sensory details and character traits.
2. Draft on the computer.
3. Use the Self-Evaluation Checklist to help them revise their character profile.

Character Profile — Writing Process Workshop

A character sketch describes the physical appearance and personality of a real person or a fictional character and often provides insights into the subject's behavior and motivations. The sketch might also include other people's or characters' responses to the subject. Although character studies are usually prose pieces, a poem can be an equally effective vehicle for this purpose: Witness Edward Arlington Robinson's arresting poetic portraits of Miniver Cheevy and Richard Cory, and Edgar Lee Master's study of Lucinda Matlock.

The following skills, introduced in this section's Guided Writing Lessons, will help you write a character sketch:

Writing Skills Focus

- ▶ **Create a main impression** of your subject. Focus on presenting details that support this impression. (See p. 603.)
- ▶ **Use sensory details** to make your subject's appearance and personality come alive for your readers. (See p. 621.)
- ▶ **Use a personal tone** that conveys your attitude toward your subject. (See p. 597.)
- ▶ **Use transitions** to make clear connections among the details you include. (See p. 597.)

Edward Arlington Robinson uses all these skills in his poetic character sketch of the fictional Richard Cory.

① Robinson establishes a main impression of Cory in the opening line.

② Transitions such as "and" and "but" make clear connections among the details.

③ Sensory details such as "imperially slim," and "glittered" help to create a portrait of Cory's physical appearance.

Model From Literature

He was a gentleman from sole to crown, ①
Clean favored, and imperially slim,
And he was always quietly arrayed,
And he was always human when he talked;
But ② still he fluttered pulses when he said,
"Good-morning," and he glittered ③ when he
  walked.

Beyond the Classroom

Career Connection

Psychology Students may not be aware that psychologists work in a variety of settings and capacities—clinical, research, industrial, consultative, forensic, and so on. A common element across many of these applications is detailed note-taking used later to assess and sometimes "inventory" individuals, developing personality summaries that are similar to character profiles. Whether appraising a prospective worker or evaluating a suspect, a psychologist must make close observations of behavior, speech, and appearance to form opinions that are supported by specific examples. Encourage interested students to speak to guidance counselors or other individuals with a background in psychology to learn more about this field. Ask students how formal psychological profiles might differ from the ones they will write. *Students may respond that psychologists may express themselves in more formal language and use specialized jargon. Also, psychological profiles might be required to follow a uniform format dictated by a professional organization, or by legal or scientific convention.*

Prewriting

Choose a Topic Search your memory to identify the most interesting or unusual people you've encountered at some time in your life. Choose one of these individuals as the subject for your character profile, or consider one of the following topic ideas:

Topic Ideas

- An inspiring coach or teacher
- A character in a mystery
- A family member or close friend

Gather Sensory Details Use a cluster diagram like the one below to gather details that vividly capture your subject's physical appearance and personality:

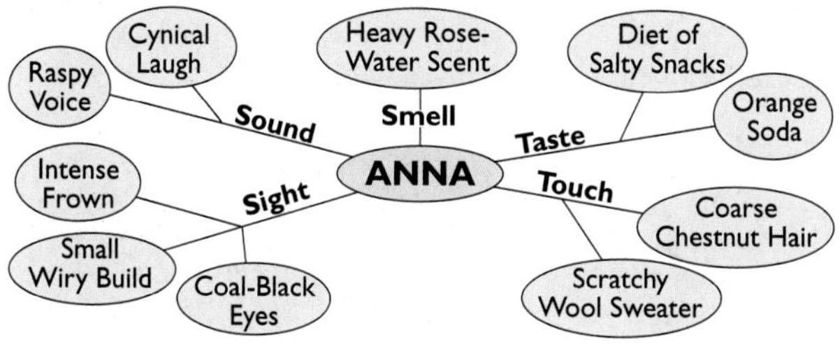

Drafting

Create a Main Impression All of the details in your profile should work together to create a single impression of the subject. Focus on capturing physical characteristics and personality traits that contribrute to the impression you're striving to convey to readers.

Organize by Order of Importance When you organize by order of importance, you place details from the least to most important, or vice versa. Decide which order will help you portray your subject most effectively. Then use appropriate transition words to clarify the order you've chosen and guide your readers from point to point. These transition words show order of importance:

and, but, first, second, more importantly, most importantly, less importantly, least importantly, mainly, last, finally, even better, not as good, primarily, secondarily, above all, worst of all.

Applying Language Skills: Using Quotations

Including appropriate quotations from or about your subject is a great way to capture his or her personality.

Description: Mrs. Drake was a kindly woman who cared for stray cats. She seemed to love the animals and worry about their welfare.

Enhanced With a Quotation: Mrs. Drake was a kindly woman who cared for stray cats. She once lamented, "I worry so about all the poor, homeless kitties. If I can give a few of them some food and a place to stay, I feel I've done some good."

Practice Enhance each of the following descriptions by adding a quotation or two or three lines of dialogue.

1. When Zoltron got angry, he roared at his crew, and they tried to calm him.
2. Coach Jones revved us up with his weekly pep talks.

Writing Application As you draft your character sketch, look for places where you can include dialogue or quotations.

Writer's Solution Connection
Writing Lab

To help you gather details, use the Character Trait Word Bin in the Description tutorial.

Prewriting Strategy

To help students apply the cluster diagram technique provided in the student edition, consider drawing the "skeleton" (the topic surrounded by the branches corresponding to each sense) for the topic ideas listed. Invite students to come to the chalkboard to complete the diagram with appropriate details.

Customize for *Intrapersonal Learners*

These students may benefit from choosing a person to profile who has been an inspiration to them in some way. In this manner students can use their feelings and reflections as a springboard for writing.

Writing Lab CD-ROM

The Gathering Details section of the tutorial includes interactive examples of figurative language that may help add color to their profiles. Students can explore examples and definitions of simile, metaphor, personification, and hyperbole.

Elaboration Strategy

Advise students that their profiles may be more intriguing if they deliberately note exceptions or details that contradict their initial impressions, as if closer inspection or reflection caused them to question surface appearances. Such an approach may add depth and complexity to their profiles. However, warn students that this advanced approach needs to be handled delicately to avoid confusing readers.

Applying Language Skills

Using Quotation Marks

To introduce this language skill, point out that including quotations in a character profile will help students *show* rather than *tell.*

Suggested Answers

1. When Zoltron got angry, he roared at his crew: "I must the biggest fool of all! Why do I keep paying good money for substandard work?" "Please calm down, sir," and "We'll work late if we need to" came the usual sheepish replies.
2. It was game day, which meant that Coach Jones was thundering at us. "You think the crowd out there came here to watch a bunch of *quitters* play ball? They came here to watch *warriors* in action!"

Grammar Reinforcement

For additional instruction on using quotations, refer to the *Sourcebook* lesson on page 226; for more information on correctly punctuating quotations, use the **Language Lab CD-ROM** lesson Quotation Marks, Colons, and Semicolons and practice page 90 in the *Writer's Solution Grammar Practice Book.*

Revision Strategy

Encourage students to discuss the checklist in the studnet edition and the questions below in their writing groups and peer conferencing.

- Have you used quotations to convey personality aspects directly?
- Do the details describe not only appearance, but also physical gestures and speech patterns?

Writing Lab CD-ROM
The Revising and Editing section of the tutorial includes interactive instruction on point of view to help students avoid shifts in perspective.

Applying Language Skills

Combining Sentences
Introduce this skill by explaining that effective sentence combining is a key stylistic element in all writing.

Answers

1. Zoe's blue eyes twinkle while her brown hair glistens.
2. Grandpa reads the morning paper, and then goes for a stroll.

Grammar Reinforcement

For instruction and practice, refer to the **Language Lab CD-ROM** lesson Varying Sentence Structure, and pages 16–27 in the *Writer's Solution Grammar Practice Book.*

Publishing

Students may want to invite the subjects of their profiles to act as the audience for their finished writing.

Reinforce and Extend

Prentice Hall Writing and Grammar For more prewriting, elaboration, and revision strategies, see *Prentice Hall Writing and Grammar.*

APPLYING LANGUAGE SKILLS: Combining Sentences

To avoid choppy writing, look for places to combine two or more short sentences into one longer one by using a coordinating conjunction (*and, but, or*) or a subordinating conjunction (*if, after, because,* and so on).

Short Sentences:

Tom lifts weights every day. He also runs three miles.

Revised Sentences:

Tom is dedicated to keeping fit. He eats nutritious meals.

Tom lifts weights <u>and</u> runs three miles every day.

<u>Because</u> Tom is dedicated to keeping fit, he eats nutritious meals.

Practice Combine each of the following pairs of short sentences into a longer sentence.

1. Zoe's blue eyes twinkle. Her brown hair glistens.
2. Grandpa reads the morning paper. Then he goes for a stroll.

Writing Application As you revise your character sketch, smooth your writing by combining short, choppy sentences into longer ones.

Writer's Solution Connection Writing Lab

For help revising your profile, use the Vague Adjective Checker in the Description tutorial.

Revising

Use a Checklist Use the following checklist to help you revise your character sketch:

- ▶ How can you strengthen the main impression of your subject?
- ▶ Where can you add sensory details to sharpen the picture of your subject's appearance and personality?
- ▶ What details might you delete?
- ▶ What transitions can you add to connect your paragraphs more smoothly and clarify the relationships among your ideas?

REVISION MODEL

① one of the kindest, most considerate people I know
Kathy is ~~a nice person~~. She's always trying to do things to
② For example, ③ to Hawaii she'd been planning for years
help other people. ^She ^canceled a ~~planned~~ vacation ^to take
recently
care of a close friend who was sick.

① Notice how the writer clarifies her main impression of her subject.
② The writer adds this transition to introduce an example.
③ This precise detail helps the reader to understand the sacrifice that was made.

Consult a Peer Reviewer Have a classmate read your profile and jot down his or her key impressions of your subject based on your paper. Check to see that the main impressions your peer reviewer has noted match the impressions you were trying to convey. If not, consult with your classmate to find ways that you can strengthen your writing to better achieve your purpose.

Publishing

Prepare a Documentary If your subject is nearby, consider creating a documentary-style character portrait on video, adapting your written text for use as a voice-over narration. You might even include an on-camera interview. Show the video in class.

Create a Bulletin Board Display Assemble the character sketches from your classmates and display them on a wall or bulletin board, together with photographs and drawings of the subjects.

✓ ASSESSMENT

PORTFOLIO ASSESSMENT
Use the rubric on Description in ***Alternative Assessment*** (p. 112) to assess students' writing. Add these criteria to customize the rubric to this assignment.

	4	3	2	1
Main Impression	The writer effectively creates a memorable main impression through the presentation of select details.	The writer creates several impressions of the subject, with some more vivid than others.	The writer's attempts to create an impression are unclear or seriously flawed.	A random organization of details hampers the formation of any impression.
Uses Quotations	The writer consistently chooses strong and revealing quotations to enhance the profile.	The writer uses quotations in the profile, some of which support the main impression of the subject.	The writer chooses quotations that reveal little about the subject.	The writer avoids using quotations, or does so in a way that adds nothing to the description.

Student Success Workshop

Real-World Reading Skills

Reading an Application Form

Strategies for Success

Summer job applications, standardized test forms, warranty registrations, club memberships—all these require you to fill out application forms. While some forms are more complex than others, correctly reading any application helps you complete it accurately and completely.

Know What You're Being Asked Determine the purpose of the application. Is it intended to gather information about your personal life, your medical history, or your employment experience? Will you gain access to services or privileges by completing the form, or does it merely identify you and your work for reviewers? Recognizing what information an application is seeking will help you focus your answers.

Verify the Form Confirm that you are completing the correct form. Check its title, and briefly scan labeled boxes or lines. Quickly skim any directions before writing.

Read the Application Once you're sure you have the correct form, read the directions thoroughly. Check the information requested against the purpose of the form. If you're applying for a job in another city, for example, you'll want to include an address in that city along with your home address. Work slowly and carefully.

Apply the Strategies

In order to work at the next national political convention, you must complete the application form for an internship position.

1. What is this form entitled?

Internship Application Form

Name ____________________________

Address ____________________________

____

SS# ____-___-____ Date of birth __/__/__

Phone ____________________

Health restrictions ____________________

Will you need housing in Convention City?

Yes ___ No ___ (If *no*, please list your Convention City address.) ____________________________

How many hours per day are you available to work? ____

Check all the communications operations with which you are familiar.
___ word processing ___ e-mail
___ live broadcast ___ still photography
___ video recording ___ cell phones

Write a brief paragraph explaining why you want to work as an intern and listing some experiences you think qualify you for the job.

2. Complete the application, using a separate piece of paper.
3. After completing the application, what else would you have to do if you were actually submitting it?

Here are other situations in which reading an application form can be important:
- Armed services entry
- Sports or activity tryouts
- Automobile or home loan qualification

Answers

1. The title is "Internship Application Form."
2. Review the completed applications for both accuracy and completeness. You may want to make sure the following items are included as needed: apartment number and zip code in the address section; an explanatory note and attached immigration documentation if the student does not have a social security number; health information only as it is relevant to the demands of working the long, fast-paced hours of a political convention; a specific address if students are handling their own local housing.
3. Possible responses include: proofreading what they wrote and adding neat and legible corrections as needed; photocopying the completed form so that they have their own record; following up with a thank-you note or a phone call soon afterwards.

Prepare and Engage

LESSON OBJECTIVE
- To read an application form

Customize for
English Language Learners
The text of the application form may contain terms that are unfamiliar to these students—an everyday obstacle faced by many nonnative speakers who seek employment. Pair English language learners with native speakers as necessary to define words and phrases such as *cell telephones* and *communications operations*.

Customize for
Intrapersonal Learners
Draw these students' attention to the paragraph they are requested to write at the close of the application form. Explain that this is their opportunity to convey thoughtful reflection about themselves and the internship, and reply in a considered, careful way—without the anxiety that might accompany a live interview. Allow students to substitute a real-world goal of theirs for the political convention premise if this will motivate student writing.

Apply the Strategies

Before answering the questions in the student edition, you may want to discuss the following points to help orient readers:

- Point out that the form asks for experience, but not job experience *per se*. Experience gained from extracurricular pursuits and hobbies is probably acceptable.
- Point out that the proper noun *Convention City* is clearly an abstraction and not a real place.
- Remind students that it is acceptable to write the final paragraph on a separate page if it will make the text more legible.

Introduce the Strategy

LESSON OBJECTIVES

- To interpret texts for performance
- To use verbal and nonverbal performance techniques

Customize for
Interpersonal Learners
These students may enjoy role-modeling the strategies with you in front of the class. You may want at first to place yourself in the role of "mediator" to ensure that students see the strategies. Gradually allow students to interact directly, without your direct intervention.

Apply the Strategy

1. Before breaking the class into work groups, you may want to brainstorm and role-play as a class first—in effect modeling the process of role-playing itself.
2. If students choose to participate in a formal conflict-resolution program, encourage them to paraphrase or expand upon the tips in the student edition in a handout that they can distribute to participants. Alternatively, they can share their experiences with the class.
3. Take care here not to bring up student conflicts that may have roots and causes deeper than this workshop's strategies can address. However, if students choose to recount only petty conflicts, they may not benefit from practicing the strategies in the type of emotional context that in the real world necessitates conflict resolution in the first place.

Speaking, Listening, and Viewing Workshop

Verbal and Nonverbal Performance Techniques

Performers use a variety of techniques—both verbal and nonverbal—to express the meaning of a text. The power of Dr. Martin Luther King's "I Have a Dream" speech comes partly from the fervor in his voice as he speaks. Similarly, such nonverbal techniques as gestures and posture add meaning to words.

Analyze and Interpret When you read or recite literature orally, you can use these techniques to interpret the work. First, analyze the text. For example, an analysis and interpretation of the Gettysburg Address should focus on Abraham Lincoln's compassion and sense of honor. If you are presenting an oral interpretation of a poem, you need to understand the components of the poem—its speaker and message, as well as its technical aspects, such as meter and rhyme. To analyze a text for a literary interpretation, ask yourself these questions:

- ▶ Whose words am I speaking?
- ▶ Who is my audience?
- ▶ What message do I want to convey?

Use Verbal and Nonverbal Techniques
Experiment with different interpretations of the text. While there is no one right way to "say" something, always keep in mind the mood and tone of the work. Change your intonation, pitch, and emphasis to find the most effective ways to deliver the lines. Nonverbal techniques are just as important as your voice. Facial expressions, gestures, posture, and eye contact are all nonverbal ways to "say" something. Another important nonverbal technique is timing, since pauses can be just as meaningful as words.

Apply the Strategies

Use verbal and nonverbal techniques to interpret one of these literary texts:

1. In a small group, interpret Sojourner Truth's "An Account of an Experience With Discrimination." Justify your performance techniques by explaining your text analysis.
2. Interpret Chief Joseph's speech, "I Will Fight No More Forever." Focus on the use of pauses.
3. Analyze Lincoln's "The Gettysburg Address," and write a guide for literary interpretation. Include verbal and nonverbal techniques.

Tips for Applying Verbal and Nonverbal Techniques

✔ *When you analyze a text for a literary interpretation, follow these strategies:*

- ▶ Be certain that you have a clear understanding of the text.
- ▶ Determine the mood and tone of the text.
- ▶ Make sure your verbal and nonverbal techniques convey the author's intent.

Beyond the Classroom

Workplace Skills Connection

Building Consensus Explain to students that even if they choose to pursue career paths that can be described as "low-stress," conflicts between workers can still develop and affect them. Frequently, customer conflicts arise in retail and telemarketing. Just as often, trouble develops between co-workers or clients and vendors.

Point out that in many ways conflicts are inevitable—for example, an unexpected crisis or a demanding schedule may put pressure on everyone in the workplace environment. However, it is the way that people handle conflicts that shapes their professional reputation and, perhaps, the future course of their careers. Discuss the concept of "building consensus" with students, sharing any examples from your own career that you feel are appropriate.

Test Preparation Workshop

Reading Comprehension — Using Context

Strategies for Success

The reading sections of standardized tests often require you to use context to determine the meaning of unfamiliar and uncommon words and figurative expressions. The following strategies will help you answer such test questions:

Be Aware of Context Context is defined as the words and phrases that surround a word or figurative expression, which provide clues to its meaning. In a test, you might be asked to determine the meaning of certain words and figurative expressions, such as those contained in the following passage:

> The practice of celebrating Thanksgiving in the United States dates back to the year 1621, when the Pilgrims of Plymouth, Massachusetts, joined with local Wampanoag Indians to give thanks for the bountiful harvest. The feast included ducks, geese, corn, potatoes, lobsters, bass, clams, and dried fruit. In the eyes of the deeply religious Pilgrims, the food was like manna to the Israelites.

1 Judging from the context of the passage, what might you determine the meaning of the word *bountiful* to be?

A lacking
B spoiled
C abundant
D tasty

Answers **A** and **B** describe a harvest that would not be worth celebrating. **D** could be correct, but no information in the text supports the idea that the food tasted good. The context of *bountiful* includes a lengthy list of food and "giving thanks." The correct answer is **C.**

2 From the context of the passage, what might be the meaning of the figurative expression "the food was like manna to the Israelites"?

A The food is what people in Israel eat.
B The food seemed like a gift from God.
C The food seemed foreign and strange.
D The food was tasteless and poorly prepared.

There is no contextual information leading to **A, C,** or **D.** The Pilgrims are "deeply religious" and are "giving thanks" for the harvest. It is likely that they might view the harvest as "a gift from God." The context clues support **B.**

Apply the Strategies

Read the following passage, and answer the questions:

> Amy and Jane listened closely to the weather forecast as they packed their bags. For nearly a year, they had eagerly anticipated taking a ski trip to Colorado. As they listened to the ominous predictions of freezing rain, sleet, and snow, their hearts sank like lead. Such dangerous weather conditions would surely ground their plane and force them to cancel their plans.

1 Judging from the context of the passage in which it is used, which of these words best defines the word *ominous?*

A optimistic
B troubling
C incorrect
D long range

2 Taken in context, what could the figurative expression "their hearts sank like lead" mean?

A They experienced a rapid heartbeat.
B They were overwhelmed with fear.
C They were greatly disappointed.
D They felt confidence in their hearts.

Correlations to Standardized Tests

The reading comprehension skills reviewed in this Workshop correspond to the following standardized test sections:

SAT Critical Reading
ACT Reading

Test Preparation

Each ATE workshop in Unit 4 supports the instruction here by providing teaching suggestions and a sample test item:

Reading Comprehension: Context: (ATE, pp. 441, 451, 457, 467, 479, 486, 495, 520, 533, 545, 555, 569, 591, 599, 605, 613)

LESSON OBJECTIVES

- To acquire an extensive vocabulary through reading and systematic word study; to rely on context to determine meanings of words and phrases such as figurative language, connotation and denotation of words, analogies, idioms, and technical vocabulary

Answers

1. (B) troubling
2. (C) They were greatly disappointed.

Test-Taking Tip

Process of Elimination

Students may find that when they are looking for the correct meaning of a word, they do not know the definitions of all the choices. Tell students that in these cases they should use the process of elimination. Use the following example to demonstrate.

> Her eyes burned with hatred and she glared with malevolence at the stranger.

By using the context clues of *hatred* and *glared,* students can arrive at the conclusion that *malevolence* is an antagonistic feeling. Offer students the following choices:

A kindness
B anxiety
C invidiousness
D exhaustion

Even if students do not know the meaning of *invidiousness,* they should be able to recognize it as the correct choice because none of the others fit the definition they formed through context. Point out to students that even if two of the choices are unfamiliar to them, by using the process of elimination they will have increased their chances of guessing correctly,

Planning Instruction and Assessment

Unit Objectives

1. To read American literature selections written between 1914–1946
2. To apply strategies for reading poetry, appropriate for reading these selections
3. To analyze literary elements
4. To use a variety of strategies to read unfamiliar words and to build vocabulary
5. To learn elements of grammar, usage, and style
6. To use recursive writing processes to write in a variety of forms
7. To express and support responses to various types of texts
8. To prepare, organize, and present literary interpretations

Meeting the Objectives

With each selection, you will find instructional material and portfolio opportunities through which students can meet these objectives. You will find practice pages for reading strategies, literary elements, vocabulary, and grammar in the ***Selection Support*** booklet in ***Teaching Resources.***

Test Preparation

The unit workshop, **Reading Comprehension: Sentence-Completion Questions** (SE, p. 863), is supported by teaching tips and a sample test item in the ATE workshop with each selection grouping.

- **Anticipate Missing Words** (ATE, pp. 645, 655, 759, 785, 817, 829, 847)
- **Analyze Sentence Meaning** (ATE, pp. 669, 687, 729, 769, 775)
- **Try Words in the Sentence** (ATE, pp. 693, 701, 803, 839)

The following additional workshops in the ATE give teaching tips and a sample test item for applying the skill taught in the Student Success Workshops:

- **Using Study Strategies to Understand Text** (ATE, p. 726)
- **Reading Silently for an Extended Period** (ATE, p. 756)
- **Analyzing Text Structure** (ATE, p. 861)

Nighthawks, 1942, Edward Hopper, The Art Institute of Chicago

Humanities: Art

Nighthawks, 1942, by Edward Hopper.

Born in Nyack, New York, Edward Hopper (1882–1967) worked for 20 years as a commercial illustrator; only after he was forty was he able to begin to focus entirely on art. Hopper specialized in two types of subject matter: New England rural life and New York City urban scenes. Both subjects allowed him to express a deep sense of loneliness.

1. What mood does the painting create, and how? *Most students will respond that the painting creates a mood of loneliness. They may indicate that the nighttime setting and apparent isolation of the people contribute to this mood.*
2. Make up a story about one of the people in the coffee shop. *Students should indicate why the person is there and how he or she feels in the moment.*

UNIT 5

Disillusion, Defiance, and Discontent (1914–1946)

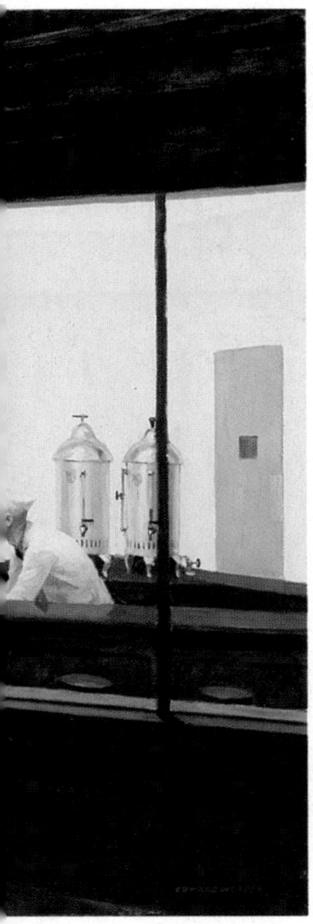

"We asked the cyclone
to go around our barn but
it didn't hear us."

—Carl Sandburg
from The People, Yes

Assessing Student Progress

The following tools are available to measure the degree to which students meet the unit objectives:

Informal Assessment

The questions on the Guide for Responding sections are a first level of response to the concepts and skills presented with the selection. Students' responses are a brief informal measure of their grasp of the material. Their responses on this level can indicate where further instruction and practice are needed. You may then follow up with the practice pages in the ***Selection Support*** booklet.

You will find literature and reading guides in the ***Alternative Assessment*** booklet, which you may give students on an individual basis for informal assessment of their performance.

Formal Assessment

In the ***Formal Assessment*** booklet, you will find selection tests and part tests.

Selection Tests The selection tests measure comprehension and skills acquisition for each selection or group of selections.

Part Tests Each part test, which calls on students to read a passage of literature they have not previously seen, applies the part skills on a broader level. The Critical Reading section measures Unit Objectives 1, 2, and 3. The Vocabulary and Grammar section measures Objectives 4 and 5. The Essay section measures Objectives 1 and 6. Both the Critical Reading and Vocabulary and Grammar sections use formats similar to those found on many standardized tests, including the SAT.

Alternative Assessment

Portfolios As you review individual pieces or the collected work in students' portfolios, you will find assessment sheets available in the portfolio section of the ***Alternative Assessment*** booklet.

Scoring Rubrics You will find scoring rubrics for writing modes in the ***Alternative Assessment*** booklet. You can apply these to Guided Writing Lessons and to Writing Process Workshop lessons.

Speaking, Listening, and Viewing The ***Alternative Assessment*** booklet contains assessment sheets for speaking, listening, and viewing activities.

Learning Modalities The ***Alternative Assessment*** booklet contains activities that appeal to different learning styles. You may use these too as an alternative measurement of students' growth.

Using the Timeline

The Timeline can serve a number of instructional purposes, as follows:

Getting an Overview Use the Timeline to help students get a quick overview of themes and events of the period. This approach will benefit all students but may be especially helpful for visually oriented students, English language learners, and those less proficient in reading. (For strategies in using the Timeline as an overview, see the bottom of this page.)

Thinking Critically Questions are provided on the facing page. Use these questions to have students review the events, discuss their significance, and examine the *so what* behind the *what happened*.

Connecting to Selections Have students refer back to the Timeline when beginning to read individual selections. By consulting the Timeline regularly, they will gain a better sense of the period's chronology. In addition, they will appreciate what was occurring in the world that gave rise to these works of literature.

Projects Students can use the Timeline as a launching pad for projects like these:

- **Focused Timelines** Have students research the events leading up to an item on the Timeline and create a smaller, more focused timeline to record them. For example, students can use the biography of T. S. Eliot on page 644, as well as other surces, to show the events leading up to the publication of *The Waste Land* in 1922.
- **News Presentations** Have students scan a section of the Timeline, assimilate the information on it, and summarize the important events of this period in a brief oral presentation for their classmates. They can model their presentation on a television or radio news report.

Timeline

1915–1945

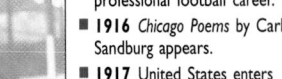

1915 | 1920 | 1925

American Events

- **1915** Olympic track and field champion Jim Thorpe begins his professional football career. ◀

- **1916** *Chicago Poems* by Carl Sandburg appears.
- **1917** United States enters World War I.
- **1918** President Wilson announces his 14 Points in peace plan. ▼
- **1919** Prohibition becomes law; repealed in 1933.
- **1919** Sherwood Anderson publishes *Winesburg, Ohio.*

- **1920** Nineteenth Amendment to Constitution gives U.S. women the right to vote. ▼

- **1922** T. S. Eliot publishes *The Waste Land.*
- **1923** Wallace Stevens publishes *Harmonium.*

- **1925** F. Scott Fitzgerald publishes *The Great Gatsby.*
- **1926** Langston Hughes publishes *The Weary Blues.*
- **1926** Ernest Hemingway publishes *The Sun Also Rises.*
- **1927** Charles Lindbergh flies solo and nonstop from New York to Paris.
- **1929** Stock market crashes in October, followed by Great Depression of the 1930's. ▶

World Events

- **1914** Panama: Built by the United States, the Panama Canal is opened. ▲
- **1915** England: Because of the war in Europe, travelers are cautioned against transatlantic voyages. *The Lusitania* would be sunk despite these warnings. ◀

- **1917** Russia: Bolsheviks seize control of Russia in October Revolution.
- **1918** Worldwide influenza epidemic kills as many as 20 million people.
- **1919** France: Treaty of Versailles ends World War I. ▶

- **1921** England: D. H. Lawrence publishes *Women in Love.*

- **1922** Ireland: James Joyce publishes *Ulysses.* ▲
- **1924** Germany: Thomas Mann publishes *The Magic Mountain.*

- **1925** England: Virginia Woolf publishes *Mrs. Dalloway.*
- **1928** China: Chiang Kai-shek becomes head of Nationalist government. ▼
- **1928** Germany: Kurt Weill and Bertolt Brecht write and produce *The Threepenny Opera.*

Getting an Overview of the Period

Introduction To give students an overview of the period, indicate the span of dates in the title of the Timeline. *A period of 30 years is covered.* Into what units is this period divided? *It is divided into five-year units, with one ten-year unit, 1930–1940.* Next, point out that the Timeline is divided into American Events (on top) and World Events (on bottom). Have them scan the Timeline, looking at the American Events and the World Events. Point out that these events often represent beginnings, turning points, and endings (for example, the start of WW II in 1939).

Key Events Have students identify key events related to disillusion, defiance, and discontent. *Reasonable answers include: events related to World War I, the stock market crash of 1929, and the start of World War II in 1939.* Judging from the events going on in the United States and the world during this period, what adjectives would you use to describe this period of history? *Reasonable answers include adjectives like* violent, turbulent, destructive*—in response to the two world wars. Some students may call the artistic developments* creative *and* exciting*.*

1930 1940 1945

American Events

- **1930** Katherine Anne Porter publishes *Flowering Judas.*
- **1933** President Roosevelt closes banks; Congress passes New Deal laws. ▲
- **1938** Thornton Wilder's play *Our Town* opens.
- **1939** John Steinbeck publishes *The Grapes of Wrath.*
- **1939** *The Wizard of Oz* and *Gone With the Wind* appear in movie theaters. ▼
- **1939** United States declares neutrality as World War II breaks out in Europe.

- **1940** Richard Wright publishes *Native Son.*
- **1940** Civil Aeronautics Board is created to regulate U.S. commercial air traffic.
- **1941** Federal Communications Commission grants first commercial television station licenses to NBC and CBS in New York.
- **1941** *A Curtain of Green* by Eudora Welty appears.
- **1941** Japanese bomb American naval base at Pearl Harbor, bringing U.S. into World War II. ▼
- **1944** Roosevelt is reelected president for an unprecedented fourth term.

- **1945** First atomic bomb is successfully exploded by U.S. in secret test, July 16.
- **1945** Truman declares September 2 V-J Day, or Victory Over Japan Day. World War II ends. ▼

- **1945** Karl Shapiro's collection *V-Letter and Other Poems* wins Pulitzer Prize for poetry.

World Events

- **1930** India: Mahatma Gandhi leads famous march to the sea to protest British tax on salt. ◀
- **1931** Spain: Salvador Dali paints *Persistence of Memory.* ▶
- **1933** Germany: Adolf Hitler becomes German chancellor.
- **1936** USSR: Stalin starts Great Purge to rid government and armed forces of opposition.
- **1936** Spain: Spanish Civil War begins.
- **1939** Poland: German blitzkrieg invasion of Poland sets off World War II.

- **1940** France: French government signs armistice with Germany.
- **1942** France: Albert Camus completes *The Stranger.*

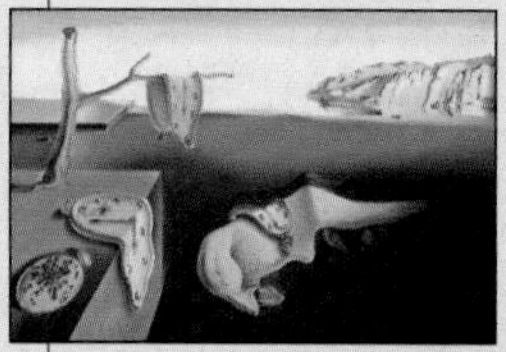

- **1944** Poland: Warsaw uprising. Polish underground unsuccessfully attempts to capture Warsaw from Germans before Soviets can take city.

- **1945** Germany: Dresden is hit by Allied firebombing raid. Firestorm virtually destroys city.
- **1945** Germany: First attempt at manned rocket flight. Pilot is killed.
- **1945** United Nations Charter signed at end of World War II. ▼

▶Critical Viewing◀

1. What does the poster supporting the Nineteenth Amendment (1920) indicate about the mood of those seeking the vote for women? **[Infer]** *The word demand on the poster suggests that supporters were not in a mood to wait.*
2. What does the photograph of President Roosevelt (1933) suggest about him? **[Analyze]** *The photograph, showing Roosevelt posed with a small girl, suggests he is kind and comforting.*
3. Compare and contrast the photograph of Roosevelt and the young girl (1933) with that of Dorothy, the straw man and the tin man (1939). **[Compare and Contrast]** *Roosevelt seems to comfort the young girl, while Dorothy seems to comfort the tin man.*
4. What mood does Salvador Dali's painting (1931) convey? **[Analyze]** *With its limp watches, apparently dead horse, and stretch of open ground, the painting conveys a mood of fear and uncertainty.*

◆Critical Thinking

1. When did the United States enter World War I? *The United States entered World War I in 1917.* What does this date of entry suggest about feelings in the United States toward the war? *The lateness of this date—the war had been going on for several years—suggests that the United States was reluctant to become involved in a European conflict.* **[Speculate]**
2. Name an important engineering event that occurred in the period before 1920 and a feat of flying that occurred in the period 1925–1930. *In 1914, the United States opened the Panama Canal. In 1927, Charles Lindbergh flew solo and nonstop from New York to Paris.* What do these events indicate about the development of technology? *Better methods of transportation were shrinking the globe.* **[Infer]**
3. What is the time span between the end of World War I and the beginning of World War II? *The time span is a period of 20 years, from 1919 to 1939.* Judging by this Timeline, how would you characterize the ten years leading up to World War II? *In 1929, the stock market crashed, leading to the Great Depression of the 1930's. This item suggests that the 1930's were a time of economic hardship.* **[Analyze]**
4. When World War II broke out in Europe, what was the response of the United States? *In 1939, the United States declared neutrality as war broke out in Europe.* What connection can you make between this response and the behavior of the United States in World War I? *In World War I, the United States also seemed to have been reluctant to join in the fighting.* **[Connect]**
5. For how many terms was President Roosevelt elected? *In 1944, he won an unprecedented fourth term.* Judging by the events on this Timeline, what might account for this success? *Judging by a 1933 entry, he seems to have dealt decisively with the Depression. Also, people in the United States may have wanted to keep a trusted leader during a time of crisis like World War II.* **[Speculate]**

Develop Understanding

Customize for
Less Proficient Readers
Help less proficient readers understand The Story of the Times by having them set a purpose for reading. For example, you might have them focus on the two world wars and their effects on life and literature. To motivate them, build background about the issues or events on which they will focus.

Customize for
English Language Learners
Use A Graphic Look at the Period to engage these students. Have them look at the photographs and posters, and have them speculate about them. Ask them which of these they would choose to represent the period and why.

Customize for
Visual Learners
Have visual learners use information from The Story of the Times and A Graphic Look at the Period to sketch a symbol that expresses a key theme of this era.

Customize for
AP Students
Ask more advanced students to search The Story of the Times for events and developments that still have influence today.

Answers to

A GRAPHIC LOOK

Evaluate an Advertisement
Some students may respond that the poster is corny. Others may feel that its inspirational, patriotic message—with a heroic-looking sailor beckoning toward the flag and liberty hovering at the top—would have been effective.

Hypothesize The experience of responsible work may have prompted women to demand the right to vote. It may also have demonstrated to many people that women were as capable as men and therefore deserved the right to vote.

A Graphic Look at the Period

▲ **Evaluate an Advertisement** Recruiting posters like this one urged Americans to help the war effort during World War I by joining the armed forces. Why do you think this poster would or would not have been effective in persuading people to enlist?

▲ **Hypothesize** As World War I took men away from home industries, women took over their jobs. These shipyard workers are holding the tools they used to work with red-hot steel rivets. How do you think their wartime work helped women win the right to vote after the war?

The Story of the Times

1914–1946

The America that entered the twentieth century was a nation achieving world dominance, but at the same time losing some of its youthful innocence and brash confidence. Two world wars, a dizzying decade of prosperity, and a devastating worldwide depression marked this era. With these events came a new age in American literature. The upheavals of the early twentieth century ushered in a period of artistic experimentation and lasting literary achievement.

Historical Background

The years immediately preceding World War I were characterized by an overwhelming sense of optimism. Numerous technological advances occurred, dramatically affecting people's lives and creating a sense of promise for the future. While a number of serious social problems still existed, reforms aimed at solving these problems began to be instituted. When World War I broke out in 1914, however, President Woodrow Wilson was forced to turn his attention away from the troubles at home and focus on the events in Europe.

War in Europe World War I was one of the bloodiest and most tragic conflicts ever to occur. The introduction of the machine gun changed the methods of battle, and the war dragged on for several years, claiming almost an entire generation of European men.

President Wilson wanted the United States to remain neutral in the war, but that proved impossible. In 1915, a German submarine sank the *Lusitania*, pride of the British merchant fleet. More than 1,200 people on board lost their lives, including 128 Americans. After the sinking, American public opinion favored the Allies—England, France, Italy, and Russia. When Germany resumed unrestricted submarine warfare two years later, the United States joined the Allied cause.

Cross-Curricular Connection: Social Studies

Ethnic Groups in the U.S. Army
People from every ethnic group enlisted to fight in WW I. About 20,000 Puerto Ricans served in the armed forces. Many Filipinos also served. Scores of soldiers were immigrants who had recently arrived in the United States.

Because Native Americans could not be citizens, they also could not be drafted. Large numbers of Native Americans enlisted anyway. From one family of Winnebago Indians came 35 volunteers. They served together in the same unit.

At first, the armed forces did not allow African Americans in combat. When the government changed the rules, more than two million African Americans registered for the draft. Nearly 400,000 were accepted for duty. They were forced into segregated "black-only" units commanded mostly by white officers.

Ask students what the willingness to serve in the army, despite barriers, indicates about the loyalty of ethnic groups. *It suggests that ethnic Americans felt a strong commitment to the country and its cause.*

Americans were confident and carefree as the troops set off overseas. That cheerful mood soon passed. A number of famous American writers saw the war firsthand and learned of its horror. E. E. Cummings, Ernest Hemingway, and John Dos Passos served as ambulance drivers. Hemingway later served in the Italian infantry and was seriously wounded.

Prosperity and Depression The end of the Great War in November 1918 brought little peace to the big cities of America. In 1919, Prohibition made the sale of liquor illegal, leading to bootlegging, speak-easies, widespread law breaking, and sporadic warfare among competing gangs.

Throughout the 1920's, the nation seemed on a binge. After a brief recession in 1920 and 1921, the economy boomed. New buildings rose everywhere, creating new downtown sections in many cities—Omaha, Des Moines, and Minneapolis among them. Radio arrived, and so did jazz. Movies became big business, and spectacular movie palaces sprang up across the country. Fads abounded: raccoon coats, flagpole sitting, a dance called the Charleston. The great literary interpreter of the Roaring Twenties was F. Scott Fitzgerald. In *This Side of Paradise* and *The Great Gatsby,* Fitzgerald vividly captured the essence of life during this frenzied decade.

In late October 1929, the stock market crashed, marking the beginning of the Great Depression. By mid-1932, about 12 million people—one quarter of the work force—were out of work. Even as bread lines formed and the numbers of unemployed grew, most business leaders remained optimistic. However, the situation continued to worsen. In the presidential election of 1932, New York's governor Franklin D. Roosevelt defeated incumbent president Herbert Hoover. Roosevelt initiated a package of major economic reforms, the New Deal, to turn the economic tide. Roosevelt's policies helped bring an end to the Depression and earned him reelection in 1936 and again in 1940.

World War II Only twenty years after the Treaty of Versailles had ended World War I, the German invasion of Poland touched off World War II. As in the earlier war, most Americans wanted to remain neutral. When the Japanese

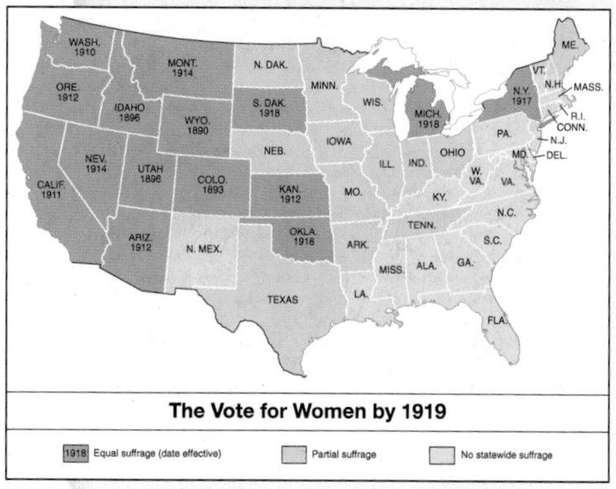

▲ **Read a Map** By 1919, women in most states had won the right to vote in state and local elections. (a) Which state was the first to grant women full suffrage? (b) Using the information on this map, make a generalization about the relationship between women's suffrage and regions of the country.

▲ **Make an Inference** In the 1920's, Americans were eager to buy new devices that made life easier. What does the clothing the model is wearing suggest about lifestyles at that time?

Connection to the Literature

- Amid the optimism of pre-World War I America, T. S. Eliot was hearing a more melancholy strain and helping to create a new kind of verse. Students can appreciate his achievement by reading "The Love Song of J. Alfred Prufrock," p. 647.
- In Ernest Hemingway's short story "In Another Country," p. 731, students will experience the sense of loss and disillusionment that resulted from World War I.
- As they read F. Scott Fitzgerald's story "Winter Dreams," p. 670, students will come to understand the dreams that tantalized Americans during the 1920's.

More About the 1920's

During the 1920's, artists and writers flocked to Greenwich Village in New York City. Older buildings in the area, including barns, stables, and houses, were converted to studios, nightclubs, theaters, and shops. In 1923, playwright Eugene O'Neill founded the Greenwich Village Theatre, where experimental dramas were performed.

Answers to

A GRAPHIC LOOK

Read a Map (a) Wyoming (1890) was the first state to grant women the right to vote. (b) It seems that western states were the first to grant women the right to vote. Most states that did not grant suffrage were in the East, especially the Southeast.

Make an Inference Reasonable answers include: The model is wearing a stylish apron that suggests a woman's role is to be a graceful homemaker, taking advantage of the latest devices and gadgets.

Cross-Curricular Connection: Science

Growth of the Auto Industry The auto industry was the engine of the American economy in the 1920's. Car sales grew rapidly during the decade. The auto boom spurred growth in related fields such as steel and rubber.

One reason for the auto boom was a drop in prices. By 1924, the cost of a Model T had decreased from $850 to $290. As a result, ordinary Americans—not just the rich—could afford to buy a car.

Car prices fell because factories became more efficient. Henry Ford had introduced the assembly line in his factory in 1913. The goal, he said, was to make the cars identical. Before the assembly line, it took 14 hours to put together a Model T. In Ford's new factory, workers could assemble a Model T in 93 minutes!

Other companies copied Ford's methods. In 1927, General Motors passed Ford as the top auto maker. General Motors sold cars in a variety of models and colors.

Ask students why the assembly line was such a key idea. *It could apply to many industries, ensuring rapid manufacture of less expensive goods.*

Historical Background

Comprehension Check ☑

1. What was the prevailing mood in the years preceding World War I? *There was a mood of optimism.*
2. What tragic event during World War I turned opinion in America toward the Allies? *This event was the sinking of the* Lusitania, *which resulted in 128 American deaths.*
3. After World War I, what law caused an outbreak of criminal activity in American cities? *In 1919, Prohibition made the sale of liquor illegal, a measure that caused widespread crime as liquor was smuggled into America and sold illegally.*
4. How healthy was the economy during most of the 1920's? *During most of the 1920's, the economy boomed.*
5. Name the event that, in 1929, started the economic downturn known as the Depression. *That event was the stock market crash.*
6. What caused the United States to enter World War II? *The Japanese attack on Pearl Harbor on December 7, 1941, caused the United States to enter the war.*

◆ Critical Thinking

1. In what way could you support the assertion that, between 1914 and 1939, the mood of Americans alternated between optimism and pessimism? **[Support]** *Before World War I, Americans were optimistic. The war brought Americans face to face with bitter realities. However, the 1920's produced a new optimism as the economy boomed. Then spirits declined as the Depression set in.*
2. Judging by what you know about the 1920's, what do you think F. Scott Fitzgerald's stories and novels are like? **[Infer]** *Reasonable answers include: they capture the dazzle, dreams—and perhaps the disillusion—of a fast-moving, showy era.*
3. Do the historical events suggest that 1914–1946 would be a time of experimentation in literature? Why or why not? **[Draw Conclusions]** *The rapid changes, dramatic world events, and fluctuations in mood might inspire writers to experiment with new forms and new approaches to language.*

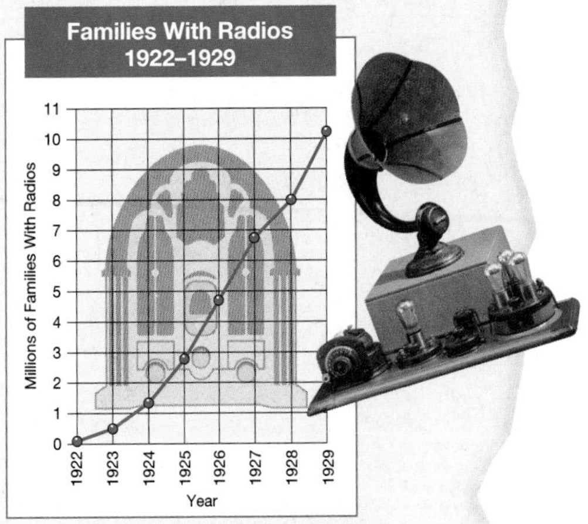

▲ **Read a Graph** The 1920's could be called the age of radio. Millions of American families bought radios and listened to popular programming. About how many families had radios in 1924? In 1928? What later trends in home entertainment did the growth in popularity of the radio foreshadow?

▲ **Make an Inference** The Charleston was a popular dance during the Roaring Twenties. Why do nightclubs featuring music and dance flourish during periods of prosperity?

attacked Pearl Harbor in Hawaii on December 7, 1941, however, America could stay neutral no longer. The United States declared war on the Axis powers—Japan, Germany, and Italy.

After years of bitter fighting on two fronts, the Allies—including the United States, Great Britain, the Soviet Union, and France—defeated Nazi Germany. Japan surrendered three months later, after the United States had dropped atomic bombs on two Japanese cities. Peace, and the atomic age, had arrived.

Literature of the Period

The Birth of Modernism The devastation of World War I left many people with a feeling of uncertainty and disillusionment. No longer trusting the ideas and values of the world out of which the war had developed, people sought to find new ideas that better suited twentieth-century life. A major literary movement known as Modernism was born. Modernists experimented with a wide variety of new approaches and techniques, producing a remarkably diverse body of literature. Yet, the Modernists shared a common purpose. They sought to capture the essence of modern life in both the form and content of their work. To reflect the fragmentation of the modern world, the Modernists constructed their works out of fragments, omitting the expositions, transitions, resolutions, and explanations used in traditional literature. The themes of their works were usually implied, rather than directly stated, creating a sense of uncertainty and forcing readers to draw their own conclusions.

Imagism The Modernist movement was ushered in by a poetic movement known as Imagism. This movement, which lasted from 1909 to 1917, attracted followers in both the United States and England. The Imagists rebelled against the sentimentality of nineteenth-century poetry. They demanded instead hard, clear expression, concrete images, and the language of everyday speech. Their models came from Greek and Roman classics, Chinese and Japanese poetry, and the free verse of the French poets of their day. The early leader of the Imagist movement was Ezra Pound. When Pound abandoned Imagism, other Imagists assumed leadership, among them the poet H. D. (Hilda Doolittle).

Humanities: Film

The Movies Leisure gained a new meaning in the 1920's. Rising wages and labor-saving appliances gave families more money, and they looked for new ways to have fun.

In the 1920's, the movie industry came of age and provided Americans with the fun they were seeking. Southern California's warm sunny climate allowed filming all year round. Soon, Hollywood became the movie capital of the world.

In the 1920's, millions of Americans went to the movies. They thrilled to westerns, romances, adventures, and comedies. In small towns, theaters were bare rooms with hard chairs. In cities, they were huge palaces with red velvet seats.

The first movies had no sound. Audiences followed the plot by reading "title cards" that appeared on the screen. A pianist in the theater played music that went with the action. What recent development may be hurting movie attendance? *The use of VCRs for home viewing might be having such an effect.*

The Expatriates Postwar disenchantment led a number of American writers to become expatriates, or exiles. Many of these writers settled in Paris, where they were influenced by Gertrude Stein, the writer who coined the phrase "lost generation" to describe those who were disillusioned by World War I. Stein lived in Paris from 1902 until her death in 1946, and her home attracted many major authors, including Sherwood Anderson, F. Scott Fitzgerald, and Ernest Hemingway.

Fitzgerald and Hemingway are the best known of the expatriates, but they are by no means the only ones. Ezra Pound spent most of his adult life in England, France, and Italy. T. S. Eliot, born in St. Louis, went to Europe in 1914 and died in London in 1965. Some critics have called Eliot's long, despairing poem *The Waste Land* the most important poem of the century.

New Approaches During the years between the two world wars, writers in both the United States and Europe explored new literary territories. Influenced by developments in modern psychology, writers began using the stream-of-consciousness technique, attempting to re-create the natural flow of a character's thoughts. Named by psychologist William James, the stream-of-consciousness technique involves the presentation of a series of thoughts, memories, and insights, connected only by a character's natural associations. The landmark stream-of-consciousness novel is *Ulysses*, published in 1922 by the Irish writer James Joyce. A number of American novelists soon adopted the technique, most notably William Faulkner in *The Sound and the Fury*. Katherine Anne Porter's short stories also employ stream of consciousness.

Poets also sought to stretch the old boundaries. E. E. Cummings's poems attracted special attention because of their wordplay, unique typography, and special punctuation. These devices are more than mere oddities in Cummings's poetry. They are vital to its intent and its meaning. William Carlos Williams, a

▲ **Analyze Art** Aaron Douglas, an African American artist who lived and painted during the Harlem Renaissance, became one of the nation's leading muralists. How does "From Slavery Through Reconstruction," the painting shown here, communicate the experience of African Americans?

▲ **Make an Inference** The government
▼ struggled to stop the illegal flow of liquor during Prohibition. In the photograph below, federal agents destroy cases of beer found during a raid in Philadelphia. The two men in disguise in the picture above were among the most effective Prohibition agents. Working undercover, the partners made more than 4,000 arrests. Given the many advances during this period of history, why do you think many Americans supported Prohibition?

More About the "Lost Generation" Most of the lost generation saw very little in their civilization to praise or even accept. Archibald MacLeish, an expatriate from 1923 to 1928, wrote several volumes of verse expressing the chaos and hopelessness of those years. MacLeish eventually broke with the expatriates, however. He returned to the United States in the 1930's and became increasingly concerned about the rise of dictatorships. A supporter of President Roosevelt's New Deal, he served as Librarian of Congress during the Second World War.

Answers to

A GRAPHIC LOOK

(from page 638)

Read a Graph In 1924, about one million families had radios. In 1928, about eight million families had radios. The growth in popularity of the radio foreshadowed the later popularity of television.

Make an Inference They probably flourish because people have money to spend and more leisure time in which to enjoy themselves.

(from page 639)

Analyze Art In a single panorama, it dramatizes a sequence of events in the history of African Americans. Figures are shown in silhouette, gesturing dramatically, while a rising sun symbolizes hope for the future.

Make an Inference Some Americans may have felt that it was immoral to drink. Others, who did not believe this, may have felt bound to support any law established by the government.

Humanities: Music

Jazz The early part of the twentieth century was an era of experimentation and innovation in music and art, as well as literature. Drawing upon the complex rhythms of traditional West African music and the harmonies of the black folk music of the nineteenth century, African Americans created a vibrant new type of music known as jazz. By the 1920's listening and dancing to jazz had become a national craze. Due to the success of performers like Duke Ellington (1899–1974) and Fats Waller (1904–1943), Harlem became the nation's jazz center.

Often regarded as the greatest single figure in jazz history, Ellington made his first professional appearance as a jazz pianist at the age of seventeen. He went on to form his own orchestra and write and record hundreds of compositions.

Play for students Ellington's "Take the A Train" from the ***Listening to Music: The American Experience CD.*** Ask these questions:

1. Describe this piece of music for someone who has never heard it. *Students may say that the music is free-flowing but also seems to know where it's going.*
2. How does the music reflect the spirit of the modern age? *It is quick and innovative, and it has a nervous energy.*

More About the Harlem Renaissance The Harlem Renaissance was publicly recognized in March 1924 when young African American writers met the literary editors of the city. Carl Van Doren, editor of the *Century,* noted that black writers, long "oppressed and handicapped . . . have gathered stores of emotion and are ready to burst forth with a new eloquence."

Literature CD-ROMS To build background, use the CD-ROM *The History of American Literature*, Part 2, Disk 1, Feature 4, which contains information on African American writers Claude McKay, W. E. B. DuBois, James Weldon Johnson, and Langston Hughes.

Answers to

A GRAPHIC LOOK

(from page 640)

Interpret a Pattern According to this graph, the percentage of unemployed workers was highest in 1933. The percentage of unemployed workers fell from 1936 to 1937 (from about 17% to 14%), rose again from 1937 to 1938 from 14% to about 19%), and then declined from 1938 to 1941 (from about 19% to 10%).

Draw a Conclusion Photographs provide visual documentation of details and emotions; images are sometimes so powerful and "say" so much that they become symbolic of an era.

(from page 641)

Draw a Conclusion The attack was an act of war that could only be met with a declaration of war.

Draw a Conclusion It would provide needed hospitals, schools, parks, airports, and public art. At the same time, it would give unemployed people a chance to earn money.

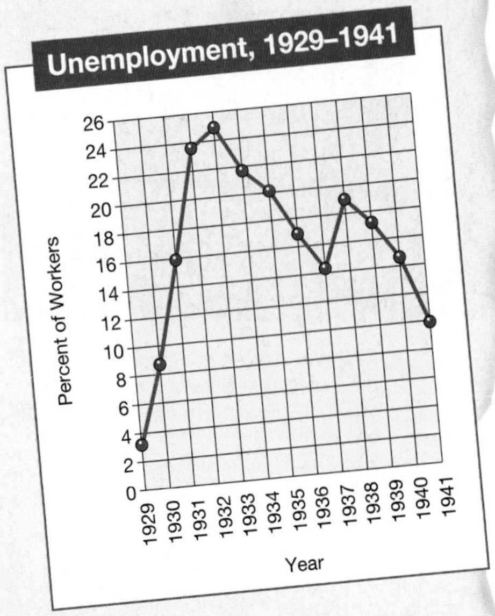

▲ **Interpret a Pattern** During the Depression, millions of Americans were out of work. According to the graph, in which year was unemployment the highest? What happened to unemployment between 1936 and 1941?

▲ **Draw a Conclusion** During the Depression, photographers captured the suffering of the rural poor in powerful pictures. Dorothea Lange took this photograph, which has become a symbol of the Great Depression. Why do you think photographs are such valuable records of the times?

New Jersey physician and poet, wrote poetry so spare and cryptic that one cannot say for sure what the poems "mean." This obscurity of meaning did not bother Williams. Likewise, it did not concern other poets who shared Archibald MacLeish's belief that "a poem should not mean but be."

Writers of International Renown The Modernists dramatically altered the complexion of American literature. At the same time, many of these writers earned international acclaim that equaled that of their European literary contemporaries.

The Nobel Prize for Literature is an international award. It was established in 1901 with funds bequeathed by Alfred Nobel, the Swedish inventor of dynamite. The first American to win the Nobel Prize for Literature was Sinclair Lewis. A native of Minnesota, Lewis fictionalized his hometown in his first important novel, *Main Street.*

Lewis's Nobel Prize in 1930 was the first of many for American writers. In 1936, the prize went to Eugene O'Neill, ranked by most critics as America's greatest playwright. Among his best-known plays are *Desire Under the Elms, The Iceman Cometh,* and *Long Day's Journey Into Night.* O'Neill's plays are sometimes autobiographical, generally tragic, and often experimental.

In 1938, the Nobel Prize for Literature went to Pearl S. Buck, an American who spent her early years in China. Buck wrote about that country with understanding and compassion. *The Good Earth* is considered her finest work.

T. S. Eliot, who had become a British subject in 1927, won the award in 1948. William Faulkner won it the following year. In addition to *The Sound and the Fury,* Faulkner wrote such enduring works as *Light in August* and *The Hamlet.*

In later years, Ernest Hemingway and John Steinbeck also won Nobel Prizes for Literature. Hemingway's simple, direct, journalistic style of writing, evident in such novels as *The Sun Also Rises* and *A Farewell to Arms,* influenced a generation of young writers. Much of his best writing captures aspects of World War I and its after-

Humanities: Art

Flashes of Wit and Humor So much of the outstanding writing between the wars echoed disenchantment and despair that the bright, cheery voices of the period tend to be forgotten. The best-known humorist of the time was Will Rogers, the "Cowboy Philosopher" from Oklahoma. He earned that nickname with his homespun humor and wry comments on politics and current events. Rogers died in a 1935 plane crash along with noted American aviator Wiley Post.

The drama critic and popular humorist Robert Benchley wrote clever works with amusing titles. James Thurber was one of a number of humorous writers associated with *The New Yorker* magazine. Thurber, who was also a cartoonist, showed real psychological insight into the odd characters in his works. One of these characters, Walter Mitty, dreams of spectacular achievements while in real life, he is a meek and timid man. Another *New Yorker* writer was E. B. White, a subtle humorist and brilliant stylist. White later wrote *Charlotte's Web, Stuart Little,* and several other classic stories for children.

Ask students to name some of the writers they think are funny and to give examples of their work.

math. Many of Steinbeck's works depict the Depression, especially as it affected migrant workers and dust-bowl farmers. Two of Steinbeck's most memorable novels are *Of Mice and Men* and *The Grapes of Wrath.*

The Harlem Renaissance A new literary age was dawning—not only in Greenwich Village and among expatriates in Paris, but also in northern Manhattan, in Harlem. African American writers, mostly newcomers from the South, were creating their own renaissance there. It began in 1921 with the publication of Countee Cullen's "I Have a Rendezvous With Life (with apologies to Alan Seeger)." Another poem by a promising young African American writer—"The Negro Speaks of Rivers," by Langston Hughes—followed six months later.

What occurred thereafter would come to be known as the Harlem Renaissance. It was a burst of creative activity by black writers and artists, few of whom, other than Cullen, had been born in New York City. Most of those involved in the movement moved to Harlem during the renaissance. Claude McKay, for example, was from Jamaica. His most famous book was *Harlem Shadows*, a collection of poems published in 1922. A year later came Jean Toomer's *Cane*, a collection of stories, verses, and a play.

The Harlem phenomenon continued throughout the 1920's and into the 1930's, producing a body of exceptional works. In addition, Harlem Renaissance artists opened the door for later generations of African American writers who would follow them.

A Continuing Tradition World War II did not end the literary revival that had begun after World War I. Many of the older writers continued to produce novels, short stories, plays, and poems. Meanwhile, a new generation of writers arose after World War II to keep American literature at the leading edge of the world's artistic achievement.

▲ **Draw a Conclusion** This photograph was taken soon after the surprise bombing of Pearl Harbor, December 7, 1941. Within hours, newspaper "extras" were on the street with the story of the Japanese sneak attack. Why would such an attack make the United States entry into WWII inevitable?

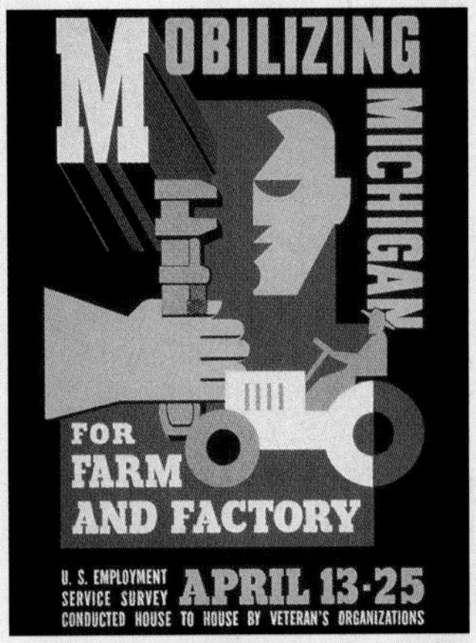

▲ **Draw a Conclusion** The Works Progress Administration (WPA) employed men and women to build hospitals, schools, parks, and airports. The WPA also employed artists, writers, and musicians. How would this program benefit both the government and the unemployed?

Literature of the Period

Comprehension Check ☑

1. What purpose was shared by Modernist writers? *They sought to capture the essence of modern life in the form and content of their work.*
2. Name three qualities favored by Imagist poets. *They wanted clear expression, concrete images, and the language of everyday speech.*
3. What prompted writers to leave the United States and become expatriates in Europe? *Disenchantment stemming from World War I prompted writers to move to Europe.* Which two writers are the best known of the expatriates? *Hemingway and Fitzgerald are the best-known expatriate writers.*
4. What is the stream-of-consciousness technique pioneered by writers during this era? *It involves the presentation of a series of thoughts, memories, and insights, linked only by a character's natural associations.*
5. Name at least two American writers who won the Nobel Prize for Literature during this era. *Sinclair Lewis (1930), Eugene O'Neill (1936), and Pearl Buck (1938) all won the Nobel Prize for Literature. In later years, Eliot, Faulkner, Hemingway, and Steinbeck won the prize.*
6. What was the Harlem Renaissance? *It was a flowering of creative activity by black writers and artists associated with the New York City community of Harlem. It occurred in the 1920's and 1930's.*

◆ Critical Thinking

1. What qualities of the modern world are reflected in the literary movement known as Modernism? **[Connect]** *Modernism reflects the nervous energy, quick and baffling transitions, and fragmentary qualities of the modern world.*
2. What do you think the expatriates were looking for in Europe that they couldn't find in America? **[Speculate]** *Reasonable answers include: They may have been looking for a chance to cut free from traditional ties and develop their own viewpoint. They may have seen Europe as a place where moral standards were not so rigid.*
3. What factors might have brought about the Harlem Renaissance? **[Analyze Causes and Effects]** *Young African Americans from more rural areas may have been inspired by the freedom of the big city and by the loose-flowing free rhythms of jazz, a form of music newly invented by African Americans.*

Activities

1. **Graph of National Mood** Have students create a line graph for the period. One axis should measure the country's optimism or pessimism, and the other should indicate key events affecting the country's mood.
2. **Planning a Historical Exhibition** Have groups of students plan a museum exhibition that would make The Story of the Times come alive for other teenagers. Encourage them to be creative in using a variety of media and exhibit designs.
3. **Sketch for a Mural** Have students sketch scenes for a mural—in the spirit of Aaron Douglass's, p. 639—that summarizes the key events of the era 1914–1946.
4. **Connect to the Literature** Challenge students to find passages from the literature in this section that illustrate the literary experiments discussed in The Story of the Times. Then ask them to read these passages aloud to the class and explain how they are experimental.

◆ Critical Thinking

1. Why do you think people use slang? **[Speculate]** *Reasonable answers include: Certain types of slang qualify the user as part of an "in" crowd. Slang may also have an appeal because it is fresh and new.*
2. How much slang do you use? **[Relate]** *Give students some methods by which they can evaluate the slang quotient of their own speech, to see whether slang makes up more than or less than a fifth of the words they use. For example, they could tape record a brief phone conversation with a friend and then analyze its slang content.*

Activity

Encourage students to develop a consistent format for their glossary. They may want to include pronunciations as well as definitions.

More on Outdated Slang Ask students if they have ever heard any of these older slang terms, all of which express the same idea:

Skedaddle
Vamoose
Twenty-three skiddoo
Beat it
Scram
Buzz off

Literature CD-ROM To build background, use the CD-ROM *The History of American Literature*, Part 2, Disc 1, Feature 3, which contains information about H. L. Mencken's *The American Language*.

The Development of American English

Slang as It Is Slung

by Richard Lederer

Slang is hot and slang is cool. Slang is nifty and slang is wicked. Slang is the bee's knees and the cat's whiskers. Slang is far out, groovy, and outa sight. Slang is fresh, fly, and phat. Slang is bodacious and fantabulous. Slang is ace, awesome, copacetic, the max, and totally tubular.

Those are many ways of saying that, if variety is the spice of life, slang is the spice of language. Slang adds gusto to the feast of words, as long as speakers and writers remember that too much spice can kill the feast of any dish.

Slang has added spice to the feast of American literature as American writers have increasingly written in an American voice, with the words and rhythms of everyday American discourse. Listen to the Harlem Renaissance poet Langston Hughes:

> Good morning, daddy!
> Ain't you heard
> The boogie-woogie rumble
> Of a dream deferred?

Defining the "Lingo" What is slang? In the preface to their *Dictionary of American Slang*, Harold Wentworth and Stuart Berg Flexner define slang as "the body of words and expressions frequently used by or intelligible to a rather large portion of the general American public, but not accepted as good, formal usage by the majority." Slang, then, is seen as a kind of vagabond language that prowls the outskirts of respectable speech, yet few of us can get along without it. Even our statespersons have a hard time getting by without such colloquial or slang expressions as "hit the nail on the head," "team effort," or "pass the buck."

What's in This Name? Nobody is quite sure where the word *slang* comes from. According to H. L. Mencken, the word *slang* developed in the eighteenth century (it was first recorded in 1756) either from an erroneous past tense of *sling* (*sling-slang-slung*) or from *language* itself, as in *(thieve)s'lang(uage)* and *(beggar)s'lang(uage)*. The second theory makes the point that jargon and slang originate and are used by a particular trade or class group, but slang words come to be slung around to some extent by a whole population.

Slang is a prominent part of our American wordscape. In fact, *The Dictionary of American Slang* estimates that slang makes up perhaps a fifth of the words we use. Many of our most valuable and pungent words have begun their lives keeping company with thieves, vagrants, and hipsters. As Mr. Dooley, a fictional Irish saloon keeper, once observed, "When we Americans get through with the English language, it will look as if it has been run over by a musical comedy."

Activity

Student slang is a rich vein of metaphor and word formation. With your classmates, compile a glossary of the slang used in your school.

More on Slang

Point out to students that slang can contribute to the growth of the language. Often words that we take for granted today were once regarded as outrageous and unacceptable examples of slang.

Following are several slang terms that have gradually become acceptable to most speakers:

joke	row [meaning a fight]
boom	slump
crank	fad

Ask students if it surprises them that any of these words were once regarded as slang. *Most students will probably be surprised that the word joke was originally a slang term.*

Have students list slang terms that they use. Ask them to keep the chart in mind and predict which of their slang terms will have staying power and which will fall away. If possible, have them express the criteria they are using to make this judgment. *One factor predictive of a word's lasting value may be its ability to describe something better than a more standard word does or its ability to describe something for which there is no standard word.*

Part 1 Facing Troubled Times

No Place to Go, 1935, Maynard Dixon, The Herald Clark Memorial Collection, Courtesy of Brigham Young University Museum of Fine Arts

The devastation of World War I and the calamity of the Great Depression left many Americans disillusioned with the world. However, as in other chapters of our nation's history, Americans showed the ability to endure these troubled times and to build something positive out of them. One of the positive effects was a new brand of experimental literature that carried the American literary tradition to new heights.

One-Minute Planning Guide

The selections in this section reflect the pain and disillusionment Americans felt during the years between the two world wars—a time when many Americans questioned an increasingly complex and impersonal society. "The Love Song of J. Alfred Prufrock" provides students with a glimpse of a troubled individual trapped in conventions. Pound's "In a Station of the Metro," reflects the transient nature of relationships and of society. Similarly, Fitzgerald's short story "Winter Dreams" shows the tentative nature of love in a status-conscious world. "The Unknown Citizen" raises questions about the nature of conformity. This section ends with the Billy Joel song "Allentown," a 1980's lament over a dying steel town.

Customize for *Varying Student Needs*

When assigning the selections in this part, keep in mind these factors:

"The Love Song of J. Alfred Prufrock"
- Lengthy poem may present difficulty for some students.

"This Is Just to Say"
- An Imagist poem with appealing sensory imagery

"old age sticks"; "any one lived . . ."
- Cummings's poetry may delight some students while presenting challenges to others; you may need to clarify unconventional punctuation.

"The Unknown Citizen"
- An accessible poem about the dangers of uniformity in society.

"Of Modern Poetry"; "Ars Poetica"; "Poetry"
- Three poems demonstrate their subject—the techniques and subject matter of poetry.

"Allentown"
- A contemporary song about a serious economic problem in society.

Humanities: Art

No Place to Go, 1935, by Maynard Dixon.

Point out that this painting dates from the Great Depression; elicit students' knowledge about that time in American history. Encourage students to contrast this painting with the painting on page 215 that shows a man taking in the wonders of Niagara Falls. Both paintings show a traveler in a natural setting. However, elicit the many differences in content and mood, and ask students to relate these differences to historical and social developments.

Have your students link the painting to the focus of this part (Facing Troubled Times) by answering the following questions:

1. Considering the painting's title, who might the man in this painting be, and what reasons might he have for traveling on foot in the American West? *Sample response: He may be a factory worker who has lost his job and is looking for another one. He may be a farmer whose farm has been repossessed and whose quest for an agricultural job has been fruitless.*
2. How is this man similar to and different from the men helping to build the fort at Jamestown in the opener for Unit 1, Part 2 (p. 63)? *All are facing difficulties and potential dangers; all are on their own in the American landscape. He is alone; they are working together. He seems to have come to the end of his road; they are starting a new future.*

Prepare and Engage

LESSON OBJECTIVES

1. **To develop vocabulary and word identification skills**
   - Greek Prefixes: *-di-*
   - Using the Word Bank: Synonyms
   - Extending Word Study: Thesaurus (ATE)
   - Extending Word Study: Connotations (ATE)
2. **To use a variety of reading strategies to comprehend a poem**
   - Connect Your Experience
   - Reading for Success: Strategies for Reading Poetry
3. **To increase knowledge of other cultures and to connect common elements across cultures**
   - Connecting Themes Across Cultures (ATE)
   - Cultural Connection
4. **To express and support responses to the text**
   - Critical Thinking
   - Idea Bank: Letter
   - Idea Bank: Character Analysis
5. **To analyze literary elements**
   - Literary Focus: Dramatic Monologue
   - Idea Bank: Allusions Essay
6. **To read in order to research self-selected and assigned topics**
   - Idea Bank: Report
   - Idea Bank: Art Exhibit
7. **To plan, prepare, organize, and present literary interpretations**
   - Idea Bank: Oral Interpretation
   - Idea Bank: Role Play
   - Speaking, Listening, and Viewing Mini-Lesson
8. **To use recursive writing processes to write a monologue**
   - Guided Writing Lesson
9. **To increase knowledge of the rules of grammar and usage**
   - Grammar and Style: Adjectival Modifiers

Test Preparation

Reading Comprehension: Anticipate Missing Words
(ATE, p. 645)
The teaching tips and sample test item in this workshop support the instruction and practice in the unit workshop:
Reading Comprehension: Sentence-Completion Questions
(SE, p. 863)

Guide for Interpreting

T. S. Eliot *(1888–1965)*

Always somberly attired and well-spoken, Thomas Stearns Eliot was outwardly the model of convention. His work, in contrast, was revolutionary in both form and content.

Beginnings Born into a wealthy family in St. Louis, Missouri, Eliot grew up in an environment that promoted his intellectual development. He attended Harvard University, and in 1910, the year he received his master's degree in philosophy, he completed "The Love Song of J. Alfred Prufrock."

A Literary Sensation When World War I broke out, Eliot moved to England. There he became acquainted with Ezra Pound, another young American poet. Pound helped influence a magazine editor to publish "Prufrock," making Eliot's work available to the public for the first time. A short time later, Eliot published a collection, *Prufrock and Other Observations* (1917), that contained "Prufrock" and a variety of other poems. The book caused a sensation, earning Eliot a lasting place among the finest writers of this century.

Eliot's exploration of the uncertainty of modern life struck a chord among readers, who were stunned by his revolutionary poetic imagery.

In 1922, Eliot published *The Waste Land*, his most celebrated work. Although Eliot himself once dismissed *The Waste Land* as "a piece of rhythmical grumbling," most readers saw it as a profound critique of the spiritual barrenness of the modern world. The poem, which had an enormous impact on writers and critics, was a crowning achievement of the Modernist literary movement and is still considered one of the finest works ever written.

A Return to Tradition In his search for something beyond the "waste land" of modern society, Eliot became a member of the Church of England in 1927. He began to explore religious themes in poems such as "Ash Wednesday" (1930) and *Four Quartets* (1943)—works which suggest that he believed religion could heal the wounds inflicted by society. In later years, he wrote several plays, including *Murder in the Cathedral* (1935) and *The Cocktail Party* (1950).

◆ Background for Understanding

LITERATURE: ELIOT AND THE MODERNIST MOVEMENT

Telephones, radios, automobiles—all were transforming life at an unprecedented pace in the early decades of the twentieth century. Long-held traditions seemingly had no place in this new and modern way of life. Uncertain and disillusioned with the values and ideologies that produced the devastation of World War I, many people were searching for new ideas, values, and ways of looking at life.

Within the literary world, the quest for all things new gave rise to Modernism, a movement that represented a break with literary traditions. In an effort to reflect a world that no longer held simple answers or permanent truths, Modernist leaders T. S. Eliot and Ezra Pound began creating literature that was often fragmented in structure and avoided providing directly stated themes. Rather than providing answers, the Modernists most often left it up to readers to draw their own conclusions about the meaning of a work. In some works, including "Prufrock," Eliot and other Modernists used a technique known as stream of consciousness, in which they tried to reproduce the natural tendency of the human mind to jump from association to association.

Prentice Hall Literature Program Resources

REINFORCE / RETEACH / EXTEND

Selection Support Pages
Build Vocabulary: Prefixes: *di-*, p. 191
Grammar and Style: Adjectival Modifiers, p. 192
Reading for Success: Reading Poetry, pp. 193–194
Literary Focus: Dramatic Monologue, p. 195
Strategies for Diverse Students Needs, p. 41

Beyond Literature
Cross-Curricular Connection: Art, p. 41
Formal Assessment Selection Test, pp. 197–199; Assessment Resources Software
Alternative Assessment, p. 41
Writing and Language Transparencies
Outline Organizer, p. 47

Resource Pro CD-R🅾M
Listening to Literature Audiocassettes
Literature CD-R🅾M
Daily Language Practice
Week 26

MODEL SELECTION

The Love Song of J. Alfred Prufrock

◆ Literature and Your Life

CONNECT YOUR EXPERIENCE

Think of the times you have wished you had a different personality. Maybe you would have preferred to be more outgoing or more assertive, the type of person who "makes things happen." The character J. Alfred Prufrock speaks to this feeling in all of us.

Journal Writing Recall an occasion in which you wish you had behaved more boldly. What actually happened? Describe the scenario you wish you had acted out.

THEMATIC FOCUS: FACING TROUBLED TIMES

J. Alfred Prufrock's public face is that of a proper gentleman, a member of society. Inwardly, however, he is lonely and suffering, paralyzed by his inability to act in ways that might bring meaning to his empty life. He is discontented by his timidity, his physical imperfections, and his insignificance; he is also disillusioned with other people. Prufrock symbolizes all of the characteristics that the Modernists associated with life in the early 1900's.

◆ Build Vocabulary

GREEK PREFIXES: *di-*

The Greek prefix *di-* (or *dis-*) means "apart" or "away." You'll notice that this prefix appears in the word *digress*, meaning "to turn aside from," in Eliot's poem. How does the prefix contribute to the overall meaning of the word? What other words include this prefix?

WORD BANK

Before you read, preview this list of words from "The Love Song of J. Alfred Prufrock."

insidious
digress
malingers
meticulous
obtuse

◆ Grammar and Style

ADJECTIVAL MODIFIERS

There are many different grammatical structures that can function as adjectives to modify nouns or pronouns. For example, Eliot uses a variety of phrases and clauses to modify nouns:

Prepositional Phrases: sawdust restaurants *with oyster-shells*
Participial Phrases: a patient *etherized upon a table*
Adjective Clauses: Streets *that follow like a tedious argument*
Infinitive Phrases: prepare a face *to meet the faces that you meet*

◆ Literary Focus

DRAMATIC MONOLOGUE

A troubled J. Alfred Prufrock invites an unidentified companion—perhaps a part of his own personality—to walk with him as he reflects aloud about his inhibitions and the bitter realization that life and love are passing him by. Prufrock's so-called love song is actually a **dramatic monologue**—a poem or speech in which a character addresses a silent listener, in this case, at a critical point in the speaker's life.

As you read Eliot's dramatic monologue, use a chart like the one below to record Prufrock's observations about life, along with details about his personality and the situation that he faces.

Prufrock's Situation	Personality Traits	Observations About Life

Interest Grabber This dramatic monologue about a critical turning point in the speaker's life surrounds a theme students will find universal—the challenge of seizing an opportunity for emotional connection and the anguish when that opportunity goes unrealized. To get students involved in the theme, ask students to imagine you have invited a much-admired celebrity to visit the class. Ask students to record their feelings about such a visit in a journal. How would they express their admiration? What apprehensions might they have about the visitor's reactions? How might their feelings for the visitor affect their ability to communicate during the visit? Invite willing students to share their entries.

Connecting Themes Across Cultures

Lead students to notice that Prufrock's actions and attitudes in troubled times make him an antihero. His qualities are the opposite of the qualities of most heroes. Have students brainstorm for a list of qualities they expect from a hero in American culture and in several other cultures. Then have students contrast Prufrock's qualities with the heroic qualities they have identified.

Customize for
Less Proficient Readers

Urge less proficient readers to study the Reading for Success strategies carefully before beginning this difficult poem. Direct them to use the embedded examples of the strategies as a springboard to understanding.

Customize for
AP Students

Point out that Eliot's language is full of cultural references and historical allusions. Have more advanced students select a list of these references to share with the class.

Customize for
Gifted/Talented Students

Have students look for clues in the poem that will help them create a cartoon character based on the speaker.

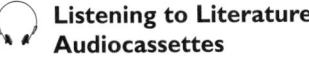

Listening to Literature Audiocassettes

Test Preparation Workshop

Reading Comprehension:
Anticipate Missing Words Many standardized tests ask students to correctly answer sentence-completion questions. Use the following example to show students how to use context and their own knowledge to choose the word that would best complete the following passage.

Always somberly attired and well-spoken, Thomas Stearns Eliot was outwardly the model of ____. His work, in contrast, was revolutionary in both form and content.

A rebellion
B convention
C illiteracy
D fashion

The context clues "somberly attired" and "well-spoken" provide the key to completing the sentence. In addition, "in contrast" indicates that the word must be the opposite of *revolutionary*. B is the most logical choice.

Reading for Success

The Reading for Success page in each unit presents a set of problem-solving procedures to help readers understand authors' words and ideas on multiple levels. Good readers develop a bank of strategies from which they can draw as needed.

Unit 5 introduces strategies for reading poetry. Because the meaning of a poem is often not readily apparent, it is important for students to learn these strategies to improve their comprehension. Both the unfamiliar form of some poems and the often circuitous route to meaning within a poem demand strategies to help guide students on the road to understanding poetry.

These strategies for reading poetry are modeled with "The Love Song of J. Alfred Prufrock." Each green box shows an example of the thinking process involved in applying one of the strategies.

How to Use the Reading for Success Page

- Introduce the strategies for reading poetry, presenting each as a problem-solving procedure. Be sure students understand what each strategy involves and under what circumstances to apply it.
- Before students read the poem, have them preview it, looking at the annotations in the green boxes that model the strategies.

To reinforce these strategies after students have read "The Love Song of J. Alfred Prufrock," have students do the Reading for Success pages in ***Selection Support,*** pp. 193–194. These pages give students an opportunity to read a selection and practice strategies for reading poetry by writing their own annotations.

Reading for Success

Strategies for Reading Poetry

Poetry is one of the richest and most mysterious forms of literature. Because a poem generally comes at the truth sideways rather than head on, you must use a number of strategies to help you unravel the meaning the poet has hidden within the lines. Here are several:

Identify the poem's speaker.
Identifying its speaker is an important first step in gaining insight into a poem. The speaker may be the poet or a fictional character created by the poet. What is the speaker's outlook on life? How is it reflected in the poem?

Engage your senses.
Poems, especially the Imagist poems you will study in this unit, use images—words or phrases that appeal to the five senses—to convey meaning. As you read, picture the visual images in all their detail. Hear the sounds described, and imagine the textures and scents. When you engage your senses, you will find greater enjoyment and meaning in the poem.

Relate structure to meaning.
A poem's structure—the length of its lines, the way it is broken into lines and stanzas—is often closely tied to its meaning. Avoid the temptation to read a poem rigidly, pausing or stopping at the end of each line. Notice where sentences begin and end and how ideas are grouped into stanzas; the start of a new stanza can signal the introduction of a new thought or idea.

Paraphrase.
Pause every so often and try restating passages in your own words. How might you describe the speaker's experiences and feelings?

Respond.
Think about what the poem is saying. How does it make you feel? What thoughts does it set off in your mind?

Connect to a historical context.
Understanding the social, political, economic, and literary environment in which a poem was written will help you grasp its meaning. To help you better understand each poem, review the background in the unit introduction.

Listen.
To fully appreciate a poem, you must listen to it. Try reading the poem aloud. Analyze the melodies of literary language, paying attention to rhythms and to the repetition of certain sounds. Consider how they contribute to the mood and meaning of the work.

As you read "The Love Song of J. Alfred Prufrock," look at the notes along the side of each page. They demonstrate how to apply these strategies.

Reading Strategies: Support and Reinforcement

Appropriate Reading Strategies Students are given a reading strategy to apply in reading each selection in this unit. In those selections in which understanding a poet's meaning may be challenging, students are given one of these strategies for understanding poetry. In other cases, a strategy is suggested that is appropriate to the selection.

Reading Prompts To encourage application of the given reading strategy, there are occasional prompts, within green boxes, at appropriate and significant points. In addition, there are red boxes prompting application of the Literary Focus concept and maroon boxes prompting students to connect with their lives.

Using the Boxed Annotations and Prompts
The material in the green, red, and maroon boxes along the sides of selections is intended to help students apply the literary element and the reading strategy and to make a connection with their lives.

You may use the boxed material in several ways:

- Have students pause when they come to a box and respond to its prompt before they continue reading.
- Urge students to read through the selection ignoring the boxes. After they have read the selection completely, they may go back and review the selection, responding to the prompts.

The Love Song of J. Alfred Prufrock

MODEL

T. S. Eliot

Connections to World Literature, *page 1190*

S'io credessi che mia risposta fosse
a persona che mai tornasse al mondo,
questa fiamma staria senza più scosse.
Ma per ciò che giammai di questo fondo
non tornò vivo alcun, s'i'odo il vero,
senza tema d'infamia ti rispondo.[1]

Let us go then, you and I,
When the evening is spread out against the sky
Like a patient etherized[2] upon a table;
Let us go, through certain half-deserted streets,
The muttering retreats
Of restless nights in one-night cheap hotels
❶ And sawdust restaurants with oyster-shells:
Streets that follow like a tedious argument
Of insidious intent
To lead you to an overwhelming question . . .
Oh, do not ask, "What is it?"
Let us go and make our visit.

In the room the women come and go
Talking of Michelangelo.[3]

Who is the "I" referred to in this line? Is it the poet, T. S. Eliot, or a character in the poem? The poem's title provides a clue to **identifying the poem's speaker,** J. Alfred Prufrock.

1. ***S'io credessi . . . ti rispondo:*** The epigraph is a passage from Dante's *Inferno,* in which one of the damned, upon being requested to tell his story, says: "If I believed my answer were being given to someone who could ever return to the world, this flame (his voice) would shake no more. But since no one has ever returned alive from this depth, if what I hear is true, I will answer you without fear of disgrace."
2. **etherized** (ē´ thə rīzd) *v.*: Anesthetized with ether.
3. **Michelangelo** (mī´ kəl an´ jə lō): A famous Italian artist and sculptor (1475–1564).

◆ Build Vocabulary

insidious (in sid´ ē əs) *adj.*: Secretly treacherous

Develop Understanding

One-Minute Insight

This poem invites readers into the dramatic monologue of its speaker, J. Alfred Prufrock, as he agonizes over whether and how to declare his love to a woman. Prufrock reviews the superficial tea parties of his days, and recognizes his sense of disconnection and failure, all the while visualizing the scene of declaration that may take place if he summons the courage. By accompanying Prufrock on his internal journey, the poem demonstrates how a person can vacillate over which path to take at a fork in life's road, and how that decision-making process can reveal important facets of the person's character.

◆ Critical Thinking

❶ **Infer** What can you infer about the characters of the speaker and his "companion" from these lines? *Students should note that the speaker is timid; for example, he is hesitant to name the question he wants to ask, while his companion appears more outspoken, directly asking what the pertinent issue is.* If this dialogue is occurring between Prufrock and himself, what does this suggest about him? *If these two voices represent parts of Prufrock, he is a divided and ambivalent character.*

Extending Word Study

Thesaurus Have students use a thesaurus to find three synonyms for *insidious.* After listing several together, ask students to explain the shades of meaning that make each synonym distinct.

Block Scheduling Strategies

Consider these suggestions to take advantage of extended class time.

- Use the Daily Language Practice page for Week 26. You may dictate the passages to students, or you may use the transparency and have students correct the passages in groups.
- To build background for the selection, discuss with students the Background for Understanding on T. S. Eliot and the Modernist Movement (p. 644) and the Literary Focus on Dramatic Monologue (p. 645).
- Have students listen to the poem on audiocassette. Discuss how the characterizations portrayed enhance comprehension of the poem.
- To build comprehension, have student pairs read the poem aloud, pausing to analyze any unclear passages. Pairs can use the Check Comprehension questions (p. 651) as a guide.
- To build understanding of the poem, have students apply the Reading for Success strategies (p. 646), responding as a class to the embedded prompts.
- Before students begin the Role Play assignment in the Idea Bank (p. 653), present the Speaking, Listening, and Viewing Mini-Lesson (teacher edition, p. 649).
- If you have access to technology, have groups of students learn more by reviewing the feature about Eliot on *The History of American Literature CD-ROM.*

▶Critical Viewing◀

❶ **Analyze** The painting's light and fog reflect the poem's mood and Prufrock's loneliness.

◆Reading for Success

❷ **Relate Structure to Meaning** Students should note how repetition of "yellow" and "that rubs its . . ." in the first two lines clearly establishes the subject sentence; pronoun references throughout refer back to that subject, and the stanza/sentence ends with a period.

◆Reading for Success

❸ **Engage Your Senses** Ask students to visualize and experience the yellow fog as it moves around the building. Have students think about fog or smoke as it "slipped" and "curled." What would fog look like as it "lingers" or "rubs"?

◆Reading for Success

❹ **Connect to a Historical Context** To help students understand Eliot's reference to a line from a poem written by ancient Greek poet Hesiod, note that the Modernists often used other works of literature, from Greek and Roman classics to Chinese and Japanese poetry. They saw these as models for clear and straightforward expression.

Customize for *Less Proficient Readers*

To help these students employ a strategy for understanding the meaning of this poem, use the Paraphrase page in ***Strategies for Diverse Student Needs***, p. 41.

Customize for *Bodily/Kinesthetic Learners*

These students may find it easier to understand Eliot's description of the fog if they experience it physically. Encourage students to recreate the movements of the fog around an imaginary building.

Moonlight, Dovehouse Street, Chelsea, Algernon Newton, Fine Art Society, London

❶ ▶ Critical Viewing In what ways does this painting reflect aspects of the poem? **[Analyze]**

The yellow fog that rubs its back upon the window-panes,
The yellow smoke that rubs its muzzle on the window-panes,
Licked its tongue into the corners of the evening,
❸ Lingered upon the pools that stand in drains,
Let fall upon its back the soot that falls from chimneys,
Slipped by the terrace, made a sudden leap,
And seeing that it was a soft October night,
Curled once about the house, and fell asleep.

Relate the structure of the poem to its meaning by recognizing that these eight lines are part of a single sentence describing the actions of the fog. ❷

And indeed there will be time[4]
For the yellow smoke that slides along the street
Rubbing its back upon the window-panes;
There will be time, there will be time
To prepare a face to meet the faces that you meet;
❹ There will be time to murder and create,
And time for all the works and days[5] of hands
That lift and drop a question on your plate;
Time for you and time for me,
And time yet for a hundred indecisions,
And for a hundred visions and revisions,
Before the taking of a toast and tea.

In the room the women come and go
Talking of Michelangelo.

---

4. **there will be time:** Echoes the narrator's plea in English poet Andrew Marvell's "To His Coy Mistress": "Had we but world enough and time . . ."
5. **works and days:** Ancient Greek poet Hesiod wrote a poem about farming called "Works and Days."

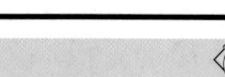

Humanities: Art

Moonlight, Dovehouse Street, Chelsea by Algernon Newton.

This watercolor painting illustrates a half-darkened city street similar to the one on Prufrock's journey.

Algernon Newton (1880–1968) was a British artist of the late nineteenth and early twentieth centuries. Newton was known for his watercolors, of which *Moonlight, Dovehouse Street, Chelsea* is an example. Its delicate colors and realistic style create a dramatic atmosphere of twilight and mystery. The painting's composition—with a strong perspective line—draws viewers into the scene.

Use these questions for discussion.

1. With what elements does this painting reflect the mood of the poem? *The lack of human figures, the twilight street, and darkened buildings all suggest Prufrock's isolation during his walk.*
2. How might walking down a street like this affect Prufrock's decision about asking the "overwhelming question"? *The street is dreary and would likely influence Prufrock toward returning home.*

And indeed there will be time
To wonder, "Do I dare?" and, "Do I dare?"
Time to turn back and descend the stair,
With a bald spot in the middle of my hair—
❻ (They will say: "How his hair is growing thin!")
My morning coat, my collar mounting firmly to the chin,
My necktie rich and modest, but asserted by a simple pin—
(They will say: "But how his arms and legs are thin!")
Do I dare
❼ Disturb the universe?
In a minute there is time
For decisions and revisions which a minute will reverse.

For I have known them all already, known them all—
Have known the evenings, mornings, afternoons,
❽ I have measured out my life with coffee spoons;
I know the voices dying with a dying fall
Beneath the music from a farther room.
So how should I presume?

And I have known the eyes already, known them all—
The eyes that fix you in a formulated phrase,
And when I am formulated, sprawling on a pin,
When I am pinned and wriggling on the wall,
Then how should I begin
To spit out all the butt-ends of my days and ways?
And how should I presume?

❾ And I have known the arms already, known them all—
Arms that are braceleted and white and bare
(But in the lamplight, downed with light brown hair!)
Is it perfume from a dress
That makes me so digress?
Arms that lie along a table, or wrap about a shawl.
And should I then presume?
And how should I begin?

. . . . . .

Shall I say, I have gone at dusk through narrow streets
And watched the smoke that rises from the pipes
Of lonely men in shirt-sleeves, leaning out of windows? . . .

I should have been a pair of ragged claws
Scuttling across the floors of silent seas.[6]

. . . . . .

6. **I should . . . seas:** In Shakespeare's *Hamlet*, the hero, Hamlet, mocks the aging Lord Chamberlain, Polonius, saying, "You yourself, sir, should be old as I am, if like a crab you could go backward" (II.ii. 205–206).

◆ Build Vocabulary

digress (dī gres´) *v.*: Depart temporarily from the main subject

❺ **Respond** emotionally to the speaker's indecisiveness and self-consciousness. Do you empathize with him or not?

Engage your senses by imagining the sounds of "voices dying" and music coming "from a farther room." They suggest that Prufrock feels removed from other people.

To help you understand the speaker's feelings, you might **paraphrase** lines 55–61 in these words: "I know what it feels like to have people inspect and discuss me like an insect on display in a collection. I feel exposed, helpless, and unable to explain myself."

◆ Reading for Success

❺ **Respond** Students may say that they empathize with Prufrock's feelings, having had similar experiences. Others may say they feel impatient with Prufrock's extreme timidity and insecurity.

◆ Literary Focus

❻ **Dramatic Monologue** How do the party guests' imaginary comments contribute to the character portrait this dramatic monologue paints? *They are the comments Prufrock thinks others will make. They show that Prufrock views himself as neatly dressed but more noticeable for being unattractively thin and balding.*

◆ Build Vocabulary

❼ **The Greek Prefix *di-*** Ask students to identify the word in this line containing the prefix *di-*. With their knowledge of the prefix, what meaning can students construe for this word? *The word "disturb" builds on the prefix "di," meaning "away" or "apart," to mean "to put order apart" or "interfere with."*

◆ Critical Thinking

❽ **Interpret** What does Prufrock's description of his life "measured out . . . with coffee spoons" indicate about his feelings toward the many tea parties he has attended? *Students should note that Prufrock feels the time has been wasted and that opportunity is passing him by.*

◆ Grammar and Style

❾ **Adjectival Modifiers** Have students identify the adjectival modifier in this sentence, explain its grammatical structure, and label the noun which it modifies. *The phrase "downed with light brown hair" is a participial phrase modifying "the arms."*

Speaking, Listening, and Viewing Mini-Lesson

Role Play

This mini-lesson supports the Speaking, Listening, and Viewing activity in the Idea bank on p. 653.

Introduce the Concept Invite students to share recent examples of radio or television talk-show conversations. Compare the various styles and focuses, ranging from highly intellectual analyses to intensely personal grilling sessions. You might have students identify talk-show hosts whose styles they admire. Whose approach might be appropriate to engage a character like Prufrock?

Develop Background Before students begin their role-playing, review some basic guidelines for effective interviewing.

- Interviewers should be respectful of their subject's privacy and emotions, while still seeking relevant and interesting information.
- Carefully developed questions help interviewers keep the discussion focused.
- When interviewed, subjects should respond as frankly and completely as is comfortable.

Apply the Information With this background, students should be able to portray a realistic dialogue and gain new insights into Prufrock's character.

Assess the Outcome Use the following criteria to evaluate each pair's role play: Was the interview interesting? Was it well planned? Did it reveal insight into Prufrock's low self-esteem?

◆ Reading for Success

❶ **Engage Your Senses** Students may say that a "smoothed evening" seems quiet and uneventful, and also recalls the earlier image of an etherized patient.

◆ Critical Thinking

❷ **Interpret** What has Prufrock decided about his declaration of love? *He has decided not to express his feelings to the woman he loves.*

◆ Reading for Success

❸ **Relate Structure to Meaning** Note that these two lines are additionally indented to set them off from the previous text. Why might Eliot have done this? *Students may say to emphasize the importance of the lines or to suggest that they are the woman's words instead of Prufrock's.*

Customize for
AP Students
Ask students what advice they would give to the speaker of this poem. Some students may offer advice that encourages Prufrock to speak up. *Others may say that if he is concerned about the opinions of others, than is safer saying nothing.*

Customize for
English Language Learners
These students will be challenged by Eliot's stanza-long sentences. Encourage students to break the sentences into meaningful chunks, perhaps omitting repeated words or phrases, and rewrite the sentences in prose form.

Extending Word Study

Context Clues Have students use the context of the poem to identify the connotations of *malingers*, *meticulous*, and *obtuse* as positive, negative, or neutral. Allow time for students to share the reasons for their responses.

And the afternoon, the evening, sleeps so peacefully!
Smoothed by long fingers,
Asleep . . . tired . . . or it malingers,
Stretched on the floor, here beside you and me.
Should I, after tea and cakes and ices,
Have the strength to force the moment to its crisis?
But though I have wept and fasted, wept and prayed,
Though I have seen my head (grown slightly bald) brought in
upon a platter,[7]
I am no prophet—and here's no great matter;
I have seen the moment of my greatness flicker,
And I have seen the eternal Footman[8] hold my coat, and
❷ snicker.
And in short, I was afraid.

Engage your senses to imagine the soothing touch of "long fingers." Think about how a "smoothed" evening would look and feel. ❶

And would it have been worth it, after all,
After the cups, the marmalade, the tea,
Among the porcelain, among some talk of you and me,
Would it have been worth while,
To have bitten off the matter with a smile,
To have squeezed the universe into a ball
To roll it towards some overwhelming question,
To say: "I am Lazarus,[9] come from the dead,
Come back to tell you all, I shall tell you all"—
If one, settling a pillow by her head,
❸ Should say: "That is not what I meant at all.
That is not it, at all."

And would it have been worth it, after all,
Would it have been worth while,
After the sunsets and the dooryards and the sprinkled streets,
After the novels, after the teacups, after the skirts that trail
along the floor—
And this, and so much more?—
It is impossible to say just what I mean!
But as if a magic lantern[10] threw the nerves in patterns on a
screen:
Would it have been worth while
If one, settling a pillow or throwing off a shawl,
And turning toward the window, should say:

---

7. **head . . . platter:** A reference to the prophet John the Baptist, whose head was delivered on a platter to Salome as a reward for her dancing (Matthew 14:1–11).
8. **eternal Footman:** Death.
9. **Lazarus** (laz′ ə rəs): Lazarus is resurrected from the dead by Jesus in John 11:1–44.
10. **magic lantern:** An early device used to project images on a screen.

◆ Build Vocabulary

malingers (mə liŋ′ gərz) *v.*: Pretends to be ill
meticulous (mə tik′ yo͞o ləs) *adj.*: Extremely careful about details
obtuse (äb to͞os′) *adj.*: Slow to understand or perceive

Cultural Connection

The Importance of Tea Eliot's poem revolves around the anticipation of an afternoon tea party. In the late eighteenth and early twentieth centuries, afternoon tea parties were social events; people dressed up for the occasion and tables were elegantly set. Small sandwiches and pastries were served in addition to tea. The tea party provided an opportunity for well-born people to "see and be seen." Tea parties were quiet, well-mannered affairs.

Have students compare and contrast tea parties with their own social gatherings. Points of comparison might include:
- reasons for the gathering,
- accepted social behavior at the gathering,
- appropriate dress,
- refreshments served.

Tell students to represent the similarities and differences that they find on a chart or a Venn diagram.

"That is not it at all,
That is not what I meant, at all."

. . . . . .

No! I am not Prince Hamlet, nor was meant to be;
Am an attendant lord, one that will do
To swell a progress,[11] start a scene or two,
Advise the prince; no doubt, an easy tool,
Deferential, glad to be of use, ❹
Politic, cautious, and meticulous;
Full of high sentence,[12] but a bit obtuse;
At times, indeed, almost ridiculous—
Almost, at times, the Fool.

I grow old . . . I grow old . . .
I shall wear the bottoms of my trousers rolled.

Shall I part my hair behind? Do I dare to eat a peach? ❺
I shall wear white flannel trousers, and walk upon the beach.
I have heard the mermaids singing, each to each.

I do not think that they will sing to me.

I have seen them riding seaward on the waves
Combing the white hair of the waves blown back
When the wind blows the water white and black.

We have lingered in the chambers of the sea
By sea-girls wreathed with seaweed red and brown
Till human voices wake us, and we drown.

Listen to the musical quality of line 130. Notice how the soft "s" sounds mimic the rhythmic sound of ocean waves.

---

11. **To swell a progress:** To add to the number of people in a parade or scene from a play.
12. **Full of high sentence:** Speaking in a very ornate manner, often offering advice.

Guide for Responding

◆ Literature and Your Life

Reader's Response What do you mostly feel for Prufrock: pity or irritation? Why? What advice would you give him if he were your friend?

Thematic Focus In what way does Prufrock represent many modern people?

Journal Writing How do the particular disillusionments and discontents of our present age affect you as an individual? Explore your answer in a journal entry.

☑ Check Your Comprehension

1. What time of day is it when the poem begins?
2. What is the weather like?
3. In roughly what stage of life is Prufrock?
4. To which character from Shakespeare does Prufrock unfavorably compare himself?
5. At the end of the poem, whom does Prufrock hear singing?

◆ Reading for Success

❹ **Listen** Read this stanza aloud to the students. Have students listen to the rhythm and rhyme. Note how the stanza reinforces, with its almost-happy cadence, the silly character Prufrock sees as himself.

◆ Reading for Success

❺ **Paraphrase** Have students paraphrase Prufrock's description of his older self. *Sample paraphrase: As I continue to grow old, I'll wear my trousers with the pant legs rolled up. How shall I part my hair or eat a peach? I shall wear white flannel trousers and walk on the beach, where I've heard girls singing to each other.* What kind of person will the older Prufrock be? *Suggested response: The aging Prufrock will be awkward and timid, ineffectual and unnoticed.*

Reinforce and Extend

◆ Literature and Your Life

Reader's Response Students' responses should indicate clear understanding of the poem.

Thematic Focus Prufrock represents the large number of modern people who feel confused and uncertain.

☑ Check Your Comprehension

1. When poem begins, it is night.
2. The weather is foggy.
3. Prufrock is probably in middle age.
4. He unfavorably compares himself to Polonius.
5. He hears mermaids singing.

Reteach

Remind students that a dramatic monologue consists of the things a single person says, either to another person or while alone. Ask students what the purpose of a dramatic monologue might be. Guide them to see that it allows the speaker to give voice freely to his or her inner state. This is what Prufrock does, saying things that he wouldn't dare speak aloud to others.

Beyond the Selection

FURTHER READING

Other Works by T. S. Eliot

The Waste Land
Four Quartets
The Confidential Clerk

Other Works About Self-Realization

The Heart of Darkness, Joseph Conrad
"One day I asked the mirror facing me," Tialuga Sunia Seloti

We suggest that you preview these works before recommending them to students.

INTERNET

You may find additional information about Eliot on the Internet. Please be aware, that sites may have changed since this information was published.

For discussion of Eliot and links to other Eliot sites, visit **http://killdevilhill.com/tseliotchat/wwwboard.html**

To read on-line analysis of Eliot's works, visit **http://www.missouri.edu/~enggf/tsebase.html**

We *strongly recommend* that you preview sites before you send students to them.

Answers

◆ Critical Thinking

1. The quotation from Dante's *Inferno* suggests that the content of the poem will be depressing.
2. His constant references to time reveal that he is procrastinating. He also questions his personal appearance and repeatedly asks the question "Do I dare?"; he says that he has seen his "greatness flicker"; and he says, "I grow old."
3. (a) He feels they are superficial. (b) He expects them to be painfully aware of his shortcomings.
4. (a) He expresses his fear of death. (b) He begins speaking about his intentions of declaring his love in the past tense.
5. (a) The vision at the end of the poem suggest dreams and imagination of the beautiful; the images in the first stanza capture the bleakness of city life. (b) The references to human voices and drowning suggest an abrupt return to reality.
6. Some students might say that in light of Prufrock's behavior, the self-assessment is accurate. Others may say he is being too hard on himself.
7. He might be suggesting that his generation takes life much too seriously.

◆ Literary Focus

1. The gloomy images, such as that of an etherized patient and of cheap hotels, infer a pessimistic outlook on life.
2. In the first line, Prufrock refers to himself as "you and I."
3. Suggested responses: (a) Prufrock has probably never been in a successful relationship. (b) His lack of confidence to say what he feels indicates inexperience in relationships.

◆ Reading for Success

Reading Strategy

1. The yellow fog suggests gloominess and an inability to express feelings. It may also represent a way of hiding the true self from others.
2. The structural space between stanzas indicates a jump to a new thought.
3. Sample paraphrase: I have seen Death, with a mocking smile, getting ready to take me.

Guide for Responding *(continued)*

◆ Critical Thinking

Interpret

1. What does the opening quotation from Dante's *Inferno* suggest about the content of the poem that follows? **[Interpret]**
2. Prufrock, who is on his way to a tea party, is trying to raise the courage to tell a woman of his love for her. How does he convey his apprehension and uncertainty in lines 23–48? **[Analyze]**
3. (a) What feelings about the other guests he expects to find at the party does Prufrock express in lines 49–69? (b) How does he expect to be treated by the other guests? **[Interpret]**
4. (a) In lines 87–109, how does Prufrock convey the fact that he has decided not to express his love? (b) How does he justify his decision? **[Analyze]**
5. (a) Contrast the vision at the end of the poem with the images at the beginning. (b) How does the final line suggest that reality has intruded on Prufrock's thoughts? **[Compare and Contrast; Interpret]**

Evaluate

6. Toward the end of the poem, Prufrock labels himself "almost ridiculous." Explain whether you believe his self-assessment is accurate. **[Assess]**

Apply

7. When Eliot writes that the mermaids, who represent beauty and happiness, will not sing for Prufrock, what might he be suggesting about his entire generation? **[Generalize]**

◆ Literary Focus

Dramatic Monologue

Although Prufrock's thoughts are presented in a sometimes disjointed and confusing stream and he says little about the actual circumstances and events of his life, Eliot's **dramatic monologue** does build a detailed portrait of the speaker's personality.

1. What can you infer about Prufrock's outlook on life from the images he uses in lines 1–12?
2. How does the monologue reveal that Prufrock sees himself as a man divided in two parts?
3. (a) Do you think Prufrock has ever been in a successful relationship? (b) How do you know?

◆ Reading Strategy

Strategies for Reading Poetry

Review the strategies outlined for reading poetry.

1. What is suggested by the image of the "yellow fog" described in lines 15–22?
2. How does the structure of the poem signal that Prufrock is jumping to a new thought in the lines "In the room the women come and go / Talking of Michelangelo."
3. Paraphrase the line, "And I have seen the eternal Footman hold my coat, and snicker."

◆ Build Vocabulary

Using the Greek Prefix *di-*

Each of the following sentences includes a word that contains the Greek prefix *di-*, meaning "away" or "apart." Decide whether each is true or false.

1. A path *diverges* if it branches off.
2. When you *divide* something, you join its parts.
3. When you are *diverted,* your attention is focused.
4. A *diverse* menu features many similar foods.

Using the Word Bank: Synonyms

On your paper, write the letter of the word that is the best synonym of the first word.

1. insidious: (a) innocent, (b) wealthy, (c) dangerous
2. digress: (a) wander, (b) contain, (c) hesitate
3. malingers: (a) fakes, (b) studies, (c) boasts
4. meticulous: (a) messy, (b) absurd, (c) careful
5. obtuse: (a) wide, (b) stupid, (c) friendly

◆ Grammar and Style

Adjectival Modifiers

Eliot creates vivid images in his poems by using a variety of phrases and clauses to modify nouns.

Practice Copy each sentence below. Underline the adjectival modifier, and circle the noun it modifies.

1. The cups full of tea sat on the tray.
2. The guests talking in the next room were gossiping about J. Alfred Prufrock.
3. People who secretly disliked each other chatted politely.
4. The hostess announced it was time to serve tea.

◆ Build Vocabulary

Using the Greek Prefix *di-*

1. true 2. false 3. false 4. false

Using the Word Bank

1. c 2. a 3. a 4. c 5. b

◆ Grammar and Style

Adjectival Modifiers

1. modifier: full of tea; modifies: cups
2. modifier: talking in the next room; modifies: guests
3. modifier: who secretly disliked each other; modifies: People
4. modifier: to serve tea; modifies: time

Grammar Reinforcement

For additional instruction and practice, use the lesson in the **Language Lab CD-ROM** on Misplaced Modifiers, and the pages on Misplaced and Dangling Modifiers, pp. 47–48, in the *Writer's Solution Grammar Practice Book.*

Build Your Portfolio

Idea Bank

Writing

1. Letter Imagine that an aged J. Alfred Prufrock finally summons the courage to tell the woman he loves of his feelings. Write a letter to her in which he explains why he hid his feelings for so long.

2. Character Analysis Write an analysis of Prufrock's character in which you describe his personal and physical qualities. How does he appear to others? How does he perceive himself?

3. Allusions Essay The poem contains several allusions—references to other literary, historic, religious, or mythological people or events. Identify two allusions and research their origins. Use your findings to write an essay in which you interpret what each means within the context of the poem.

Speaking, Listening, and Viewing

4. Oral Interpretation Read the poem aloud for the class as Prufrock might have spoken it. Lead a class discussion about your interpretation. Did anyone notice anything new about the poem as a result of hearing it? **[Performing Arts Link]**

5. Role Play With a fellow student, role-play a talk-show host's interview with Prufrock. Explore the reasons for Prufrock's poor self-esteem, and try to build his self-image. **[Media Link]**

Researching and Representing

6. Report Modernism has had a lasting effect on art, literature, and popular culture. Research the movement and its impact, and present your findings in a report. **[Social Studies Link]**

7. Art Exhibit Locate reproductions of artworks produced around the same time as "Prufrock." Create a classroom exhibit of works that share the poem's themes, images, or moods. **[Art Link]**

Online Activity www.phlit.phschool.com

Guided Writing Lesson

A Day-in-the-Life Monologue

Through J. Alfred Prufrock's dramatic monologue, we learn much about the character's daily life—how he passed his days taking tea with people he disliked and who cared little for him. Create your own dramatic monologue describing a typical day in the life of a character—either one from another literary work or one of your own creation. Focus on conveying the character's personality and capturing his or her observations about life. Remember that it is your character, not you, who is speaking.

Writing Skills Focus: Consistent Point of View

To make your dialogue believable, you must maintain a **consistent point of view** by conveying all of your information from the point of view of the individual who is supposed to be talking. Be careful not to slip into your own voice; relate all of the events as the character would perceive them. Any information you include should fit within the context of

- what the character would see and know
- how he or she would feel about the events
- how she or he would use language

Prewriting Jot down notes on your character's age, personality, occupation, place of origin, and so on. Then imagine what that character would do on a typical day. Think about how you might reveal his or her personality through the description of those events.

Drafting Describe the character's day in her or his own words. Portray events as the character would perceive them, and avoid using language or statements inconsistent with his or her point of view.

Revising Does the monologue consistently reflect only your character's point of view? Does it reveal anything about your character's personality? Refer to your prewriting notes to guide your revisions.

Idea Bank

Customizing for
Performance Levels

Following are suggestions for matching Idea Bank topics with your students' performance levels:
Less Advanced Students: 1
Average Students: 2, 4, 7
More Advanced Students: 3, 5, 6

Customizing for
Learning Modalities

Following are suggestions for matching Idea Bank topics with your students' learning modalities:
Interpersonal: 4
Bodily/Kinesthetic: 5
Logical/Mathematical: 6
Visual/Spatial: 7

Guided Writing Lesson

Refer students to the Writing Process Handbook, page 1192, for instruction on the writing process, and p. 1195 for further information on creative writing.

For more prewriting, elaboration, and revision strategies, see *Prentice Hall Writing and Grammar.*

Writing and Language Transparencies Have students use the Outline Organizer, p. 47, to help organize the daily events they will include.

Writing Lab CD-ROM
Have students complete the tutorial on Creative Writing. Follow these steps:

1. Have students use the Word Bins for Poetry and Drama to sample words for such elements as sensory details and character traits.
2. Have students draft on the computer.
3. Encourage students to use the Interactive Self-Evaluation Checklists to aid revision.

✓ ASSESSMENT OPTIONS

Formal Assessment, Selection Test, pp. 197–199, and Assessment Resources Software. The selection test is designed so that it can be easily customized to the performance levels of your students.

Alternative Assessment, p. 41, includes options for less advanced students, more advanced students, verbal/linguistic learners, visual/spatial learners, bodily/kinesthetic learners, and interpersonal learners.

PORTFOLIO ASSESSMENT
Use the following rubrics in the ***Alternative Assessment*** booklet to assess student writing:
Letter: Cause-Effect Rubric, p. 117
Character Analysis: Definition/Classification Rubric, p. 114
Allusions Essay: Literary Analysis/Interpretation Rubric, p. 127
Guided Writing Lesson: Fictional Narrative Rubric, p. 110

LESSON OBJECTIVES

1. **To develop vocabulary and word identification skills**
   - Forms of *Appear*
   - Using the Word Bank: Synonyms
2. **To use a variety of reading strategies to comprehend a poem**
   - Connect Your Experience
   - Reading Strategy: Engage Your Senses
3. **To increase knowledge of other cultures and to connect common elements across cultures**
   - Background for Understanding
4. **To express and support responses to the text**
   - Critical Thinking
   - Idea Bank: Description
   - Idea Bank: Critical Essay
5. **To analyze literary elements**
   - Literary Focus: Imagist Poetry
6. **To read in order to research self-selected and assigned topics**
   - Idea Bank: Poetry Collection
   - Idea Bank: Art
   - Questions for Research
7. **To plan, prepare, organize, and present literary interpretations**
   - Idea Bank: Oral Interpretation
   - Idea Bank: Informal Debate
   - Idea Bank: Poem
8. **To use recursive writing processes to write an editor's review**
   - Guided Writing Lesson
9. **To increase knowledge of the rules of grammar and usage**
   - Grammar and Style: Concrete and Abstract Nouns

Test Preparation

Reading Comprehension: Anticipate Missing Words (ATE, p. 655)
The teaching tips and sample test item in this workshop support the instruction and practice in the unit workshop:
Reading Comprehension: Sentence-Completion Questions (SE, p. 863)

Guide for Interpreting

Ezra Pound *(1885–1972)*

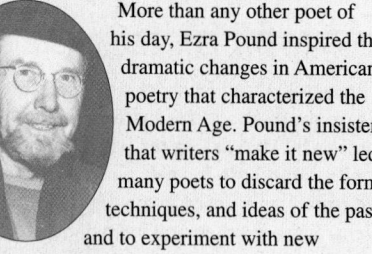

More than any other poet of his day, Ezra Pound inspired the dramatic changes in American poetry that characterized the Modern Age. Pound's insistence that writers "make it new" led many poets to discard the forms, techniques, and ideas of the past and to experiment with new approaches to poetry.

Pound influenced the work of the noted Irish poet William Butler Yeats and that of many American writers, including T. S. Eliot, William Carlos Williams, H. D., Marianne Moore, and Ernest Hemingway—a "who's who" of the literary voices of the age. Pound spent most of his life in Europe, where he became a vital part of the Modernist movement. He is perhaps best remembered, however, for his role in the development of Imagism, a literary movement that included H. D., Williams, and Moore.

Despite his preoccupation with originality and inventiveness, Pound's work often drew upon the poetry of ancient cultures. Many of his poems are filled with literary and historical allusions, which can make the poems difficult to interpret without having the appropriate background information.

After 1920, Pound focused his efforts on writing *The Cantos,* a long poetic sequence in which he expresses his beliefs, reflects upon history and politics, and alludes to a variety of foreign languages and literatures. In all, he produced 116 cantos of varying quality.

Fall From Grace In 1925, Pound settled in Italy. Motivated by the mistaken belief that a country governed by a powerful dictator was the most conducive environment for the creation of art, Pound became an outspoken supporter of Italian dictator Benito Mussolini during World War II. In 1943, the American government indicted Pound for treason; in 1945, he was arrested by American troops and imprisoned. After being flown back to the United States in 1945, he was judged psychologically unfit to stand trial and was confined to a hospital for the criminally insane. There he remained until 1958, when he was released due largely to the efforts of the literary community. He returned to Italy, where he lived until his death.

William Carlos Williams *(1883–1963)*

Unlike his fellow Imagists, William Carlos Williams spent most of his life in the United States, where he pursued a double career as a poet and a pediatrician in New Jersey. He felt that his experiences as a doctor helped provide him with inspiration as a poet, crediting medicine for his ability to "gain entrance to . . . the secret gardens of the self."

Although his father was English and his mother Puerto Rican, Williams was enamored of American language and life. He rejected the views of his college friend, Ezra Pound, who believed in using allusions to history, religion, and ancient literature. Williams focused instead on capturing the essence of modern American life by depicting a variety of ordinary people, objects, and experiences using current, everyday language.

The Poetry of Daily Life In volumes such as *Spring and All* (1923) and *In the American Grain* (1925), Williams captured the essence of American life by using commonplace objects and experiences in writing his poetry. He avoided presenting explanations, remarking that a poet should deal in "No ideas but in things"—concrete images that speak for themselves, evoking emotions and ideas.

Williams continued to write even after his failing health forced him to give up his medical practice. In 1963, he received a Pulitzer Prize for *Pictures from Breughel and Other Poems*, his final volume of poetry.

Prentice Hall Literature Program Resources

REINFORCE / RETEACH / EXTEND

Selection Support Pages
Build Vocabulary: Forms of *Appear,* p. 196
Grammar: Concrete and Abstract Nouns, p. 197
Reading Strategy: Engage Your Senses, p. 198
Literary Focus: Imagist Poetry, p. 199

Strategies for Diverse Students Needs
Identify Sensory Imagery, p. 42

Beyond Literature
Cross-Curricular Connection: Music, p. 42

Formal Assessment Selection Test, pp. 200–202; Assessment Resources Software

Alternative Assessment, p. 42

Writing and Language Transparencies

Resource Pro CD-ROM

Listening to Literature Audiocassettes

Literature CD-ROM

The Imagist Poets

H. D. (Hilda Doolittle) *(1886–1961)*

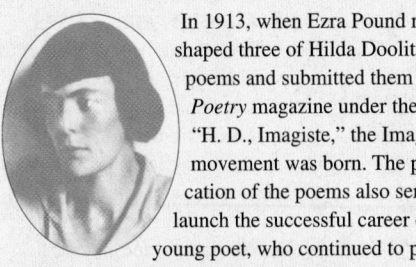

In 1913, when Ezra Pound reshaped three of Hilda Doolittle's poems and submitted them to *Poetry* magazine under the name "H. D., Imagiste," the Imagist movement was born. The publication of the poems also served to launch the successful career of the young poet, who continued to publish under the name H. D. throughout her life.

Born in Pennsylvania, Doolittle was only fifteen when she first met Ezra Pound, who was studying at the University of Pennsylvania. In 1911, Doolittle moved to London and renewed her acquaintance with Pound. She married a close friend of his, English poet Richard Aldington, but the marriage failed during World War I when Aldington left to fight in France. Doolittle remained a short while in London, where she became a leader of the Imagist group. She returned to the United States and settled in California, where she remained for a year before going back to England. In 1921, she moved to Switzerland, where she lived until her death.

Classically Inspired Like the Greek lyrics that she so greatly admired, H. D.'s early poems were brief, precise, and direct. Often emphasizing light, color, and physical textures, she created vivid, emotive images. She also abandoned traditional rhythmical patterns, instead creating innovative musical rhythms in her poetry.

In 1925, almost all of H. D.'s early poems were gathered in *Collected Poems,* a volume that also contained her translations from the *Odyssey* and from the Greek poet Sappho. She also wrote a play, *Hippolytus Temporizes,* which appeared in 1927, and two prose works: *Palimpsest* (1926) and *Hedylus* (1928). During the later stages of her career, she focused on writing longer works, including an epic poem. H. D. is best remembered, however, for her early Imagist poetry.

◆ Background for Understanding

LITERATURE: THE IMAGIST MOVEMENT

Imagism was a literary movement established in the early 1900's by Ezra Pound and other poets. As the name suggests, the Imagists concentrated on the direct presentation of images, or word pictures. An Imagist poem expressed the essence of an object, person, or incident, without providing explanations. Through the spare, clean presentation of an image, the Imagists hoped to evoke an emotional response—they hoped to freeze a single moment in time and to capture the emotions of that moment. To accomplish this purpose, the Imagists used the language of everyday speech, carefully choosing each word and avoiding unnecessary words. In addition, they also shied away from traditional poetic patterns, focusing instead on creating new, musical rhythms in their poetry.

The Imagists were strongly influenced by traditional Chinese and Japanese poetry. Many Imagist poems bear a close resemblance to the Japanese verse forms of haiku and tanka. The haiku consists of three lines of five, seven, and five syllables. The tanka consists of five lines of five, seven, five, seven, and five syllables. Like Imagist poems, haiku and tanka generally evoke an emotional response through the presentation of a single image or a pair of contrasting images.

The Imagist movement was short-lived, lasting only until about 1918. However, for many years that followed, the poems of Pound, Williams, H. D., and other Imagists continued to influence the works of other poets, including Wallace Stevens, T. S. Eliot, and Hart Crane.

Test Preparation Workshop

Reading Comprehension: Anticipate Missing Words Many standardized tests ask students to correctly answer sentence-completion questions. Use the following example to show students how to use context and their own knowledge to choose the word that best completes the following passage.

The Imagist poets strove for a spare, clean presentation of an image. To accomplish this purpose, the Imagists carefully avoided using ____ words.

A easy
B everyday
C simple
D unnecessary

The context clues *spare* and *clean* provide the key to completing the sentence. The correct answer will describe words that would prevent something from being spare and clean. D is the most logical choice.

Interest Grabber When students read Pound's essay and these vivid poems, their senses will stand at attention. To jump-start students' interest in the selections, arrange a variety of sensory stimuli in the classroom: several dramatic photographs; a strongly scented item of food or greenery; textural examples such as carpet or a bowl of dried beans; musical objects or audiotaped sounds. Invite students to tour and interact with the stimuli. Then urge them to free write for a few moments about the images generated by the stimuli. What do they expect to encounter in poetry created under the banner: "It is better to present one Image in a lifetime than to produce voluminous work"?

Customize for
Less Proficient Readers
Direct students to read Pound's essay before reading the poetry. Discuss and explain the footnoted material beneath the essay. Urge students to then read the poetry for a sensory and emotional response rather than for literal meaning.

Customize for
AP Students
To draw these students' attention to the sparse and precise language of Imagist poetry, have them write brief descriptive paragraphs about the scenes each poem describes. Ask students to respond analytically to the following question: How do the Imagists convey so much with so few words?

Customize for
English Language Learners
The free verse of Imagist poetry may be confusing to English language learners. To navigate the poems more easily, urge these students to read the poems aloud to find the natural pauses.

Customize for
Visual/Spatial Learners
Point out that Imagist poetry is highly visual. Have students preview the illustrations that accompany the poems. What images and moods do these illustrations evoke?

Guide for Interpreting *(continued)*

◆ Literature and Your Life

Connect Your Experience

You may know what it's like to have a song stick in your mind for hours, but have you ever had an *image* lodge there? The poems you're about to read capture in words some of the striking images that lodged in the minds and emotions of the Imagists.

Journal Writing Think of an image that you find striking—a skyscraper, a shiny new car, sunset, a pizza hot from the oven. List sensory details that vividly convey this image. What emotions do you associate with the image?

Thematic Focus: Facing Troubled Times

The first decades of the twentieth century were times of great change in the social and literary worlds. How do these works reflect a new and unique way of seeing both poetry and everyday life?

◆ Literary Focus

Imagist Poetry

Imagist poems focus on evoking emotion and sparking the reader's imagination through the vivid presentation of a limited number of images. "In a Station of the Metro," for example, presents just two images, and consists of only two lines and fourteen words. The words were chosen with extreme precision, however. They paint a vivid picture of each image and prompt the reader to consider the meaning of each word and to think about the connection between the two images.

◆ Grammar and Style

Concrete and Abstract Nouns

A **concrete noun** names something that can be perceived with one or more of the five senses. An **abstract noun** names something that cannot be seen, heard, smelled, tasted, or touched. By their very nature, Imagist poems tend to include more concrete than abstract nouns. For instance, there are thirteen nouns in the first stanza of "The River-Merchant's Wife." Two of these—*dislike* and *suspicion*—are abstract, whereas the remainder—words such as *hair, forehead,* and *gate*—are concrete nouns.

◆ Reading Strategy

Engage Your Senses

These poems are filled with vivid imagery—words or phrases that appeal to one or more of the five senses. As you encounter each image, **engage your senses**—experience in your mind the sights, sounds, smells, tastes, and physical sensations associated with the image. Recreating these sensations will enrich your enjoyment and understanding of the work.

While you might think of images as being primarily visual, many appeal to more than one sense. For example, you can almost see and feel the thickness of the air as H. D. calls on the wind in "Heat": "Cut the heat— / plow through it, / turning it on either side / of your path."

◆ Build Vocabulary

Forms of *Appear*

Ezra Pound uses the word *apparition* in his description of people standing in a train station. This noun is based on the verb *appear,* meaning "to come into sight or into being" or "to become understood." What do you think *apparition* means?

Word Bank

Before you read, preview this list of words from the poems.

voluminous
dogma
apparition

Block Scheduling Strategies

Consider these suggestions to take advantage of extended class time:

- If you have access to technology, build background by playing the **Literature CD-ROM,** *The History of American Literature:* Part 2, Disc 1, Feature 5, for H. D. (Hilda Doolittle); and Part 2, Disc 1, Feature 10, for William Carlos Williams.
- Have students listen—with closed eyes—to the audiocassette recording of the poetry. Then have students record the mental pictures generated by the poetic images.
- Before students read the poetry, have them brainstorm for lists of concrete and abstract nouns. Then ask students to complete the Grammar and Style activity, p. 666.
- After students read the poetry, ask them to work in groups to respond to the Critical Thinking questions (pp. 659, 661, and 663).
- Before students begin the Guided Writing Lesson, discuss—with examples from the poetry selections—the merits of brevity and clarity, the Writing Skills Focus of the Guided Writing Lesson.

❶ # A Few Don'ts by an IMAGISTE[1]

Ezra Pound

An "Image" is that which presents an intellectual and emotional complex in an instant of time. I use the term "complex" rather in the technical sense employed by the newer psychologists, such as Hart, though we might not agree absolutely in our application.

❷ It is the presentation of such a "complex" instantaneously which gives that sense of sudden liberation; that sense of freedom from time limits and space limits; that sense of sudden growth, which we experience in the presence of the greatest works of art.

It is better to present one Image in a lifetime than to produce voluminous works.

All this, however, some may consider open to debate. The immediate necessity is to tabulate A LIST OF DON'TS for those beginning to write verses. But I can not put all of them into Mosaic negative.[2]

To begin with, consider the three rules recorded by Mr. Flint,[3] . . . not as dogma—never consider anything as dogma—but as

◆ Build Vocabulary

voluminous (və lo͞om´ ə nəs) *adj*.: Of enough material to fill volumes

dogma (dôg´ mə) *n*.: Formalized and authoritative doctrines or beliefs

1. **Imagiste:** French for *Imagist*.
2. **Mosaic negative:** Refers to the ten commandments presented by Moses to the Israelites in the Old Testament of the Bible. Many of the commandments are in the negative and begin with the words "Thou shalt not . . ."
3. **the three rules recorded by Mr. Flint:** English Imagist poet Frank Stuart Flint noted that Imagist poets adhered to the following three rules or guidelines.
   1. Direct treatment of the "thing," whether subjective or objective.
   2. To use absolutely no word that did not contribute to the presentation.
   3. As regarding rhythm: to compose in sequence of the musical phrase, not in sequence of a metronome.

Develop Understanding

One-Minute Insight

As one of the founders of Imagism, Ezra Pound helped define its parameters. In his essay warning Imagist poets against writing pitfalls, Pound quickly establishes his essential idea: less is more. His poems then exemplify this credo—"In a Station of the Metro" evokes the complex imagery of a train station in just fourteen words. In "The River-Merchant's Wife: A Letter," the speaker, who was married as a young girl by the arrangement of her parents, comes gradually to love her husband. By vividly describing her emotions and experiences during his absence, she demonstrates the power of human emotion.

◆ Literature and Your Life

❶ Highlight Pound's choice to list *Don'ts* rather than *Do's* of writing. Ask students to recall times they have learned a new task or skill. Which do they prefer for guidance? *Many students will prefer* do's *as positive direction rather than* don'ts, *which stress the negative. Others will prefer* don'ts *as insurance against mistakes.*

◆ Grammar and Style

❷ Concrete and Abstract Nouns

Ask students to identify which type of noun is most appropriate in Pound's prose. *Students should note that abstract nouns are more appropriate than concrete nouns in Pound's prose because he is discussing ideas rather than objects.* Which type of noun is most consistent with Pound's criteria for good poetry? *Concrete nouns would be most consistent with Pound's criteria for poetry because they reflect specific, real objects.*

Speaking, Listening, and Viewing Mini-Lesson

Formulating Questions

Introduce the Concept Tell students that when they conduct research for an assignment such as exploring the nature of Imagist poetry, the project can be seen in terms of asking and answering the right questions.

Develop Background Remind students of the way schools of poetry grow by touching on Wordsworth's career and the development of Romanticism. Note that schools like Romanticism develop in reaction to previous literary or intellectual trends, and that movements like Romanticism are often guided by common themes. In Romanticism, the fundamental theme was of Nature and the encounter of humans with its forces.

Apply the Information With this in mind, have students prepare to research the Imagist movement by formulating questions that explore any parallels that might exist between it and Romanticism. For example, what intellectual or poetic movements, if any, did the Imagists react against? Students should actually prepare a list of such questions, along with basic resources for answering each question.

Assess the Outcome Evaluate students on the value of their questions for exploring the basic themes of the Imagist movement and its place in the broader scope of intellectual and poetic life.

▶Critical Viewing◀

❶ **Synthesize** Responses might include the following: *Sleeping man and papers; meditative writer at rest; a quiet moment.*

◆Critical Thinking

❷ **Infer** What does Pound's comparison between poetry and prose suggest about the standards he applied to each? *Students should note that Pound applied extremely high standards to all writing but felt that writers often set lower standards for writing poetry than prose.*

Customize for *AP Students*

Provide, or have students locate, the complete text of Pound's essay. Challenge them to summarize this essay which is also known as "The Imagist Manifesto." How, if at all, does the full text impact their understanding of Pound's ideas?

Customize for *Less Proficient Readers*

Less proficient readers may struggle with Pound's sometimes elaborate sentences. To help students glean the essence of the writer's position, have them paraphrase each "Don't."

Literature CD-ROM To build background on Ezra Pound, use the CD-ROM *The History of American Literature:* Part 2, Disk 1, Feature 5, which focuses in part on Ezra Pound.

Read to Be Informed

Remind students about Ezra Pound's extraordinary influence during this century, and that this brief essay on Imagism was one of Pound's best efforts to convey to a broader audience some of what he had imparted to fellow poets. One strategy for developing an understanding of this selection is to find or create examples of all the "negatives" he warns against. For example, when students read Pound's caution against using superfluous words in a poem, they should find superfluous words in another source or make up an example of poetic superfluity.

❶ ▲ Critical Viewing How might an Imagist describe the scene depicted in this portrait of Ezra Pound? **[Synthesize]**

the result of long contemplation, which, even if it is some one else's contemplation, may be worth consideration. . . .

LANGUAGE

Use no superfluous word, no adjective, which does not reveal something.

Don't use such an expression as "dim lands *of peace*." It dulls the image. It mixes an abstraction with the concrete. It comes from the writer's not realizing that the natural object is always the *adequate* symbol.

Go in fear of abstractions. Don't retell in mediocre verse what has already been done in good prose. Don't think any intelligent person is going to be deceived when you try to shirk all the difficulties of the unspeakably difficult art of good prose by chopping your composition into line lengths. . . . ❷

Don't imagine that the art of poetry is any simpler than the art of music, or that you can please the expert before you have spent at least as much effort on the art of verse as the average piano teacher spends on the art of music. . . .

Humanities: Art

Ezra Pound by Wyndham Lewis.

This painting is a portrait of the poet, Ezra Pound, perhaps resting or silently contemplating his work.

Use these questions for discussion:

1. How does the painting's style mirror Pound's preference for the "concrete"? *The sharp edges render each depicted form highly concretely, almost tangibly.*
2. According to Pound, a painter can best describe a landscape. What elements does Lewis incorporate to capture the landscape of his subject? *These elements include: black clothing, a contemplative and somewhat serious expression—even at rest; the newspaper; the importance of the figure in the composition. Like a landscape, the portrait includes a wide area around the subject rather than focusing on a face.*

RHYTHM AND RHYME

. . . Don't imagine that a thing will "go" in verse just because it's too dull to go in prose.

Don't be "viewy"—leave that to the writers of pretty little philosophic essays. Don't be descriptive; remember that the painter can describe a landscape much better than you can, and that he has to know a deal more about it.

When Shakespeare talks of the "Dawn in russet mantle clad" he presents something which the painter does not present. There is in this line of his nothing that one can call description; he presents. . . .

3 Don't chop your stuff into separate *iambs.*[4] Don't make each line stop dead at the end, and then begin every next line with a heave. Let the beginning of the next line catch the rise of the rhythm wave, unless you want a definite longish pause.

In short, behave as a musician, a good musician, when dealing with that phase of your art which has exact parallels in music. The same laws govern, and you are bound by no others. . . .

A rhyme must have in it some slight element of surprise if it is to give pleasure; it need not be bizarre or curious, but it must be well used if used at all. . . .

Don't mess up the perception of one sense by trying to define it in terms of another. This is usually only the result of being too lazy to find the exact word. To this clause there are possibly exceptions. 4

The first three simple proscriptions[5] will throw out nine-tenths of all the bad poetry now accepted as standard and classic; and will prevent you from many a crime of production. . . .

4. **iambs** (ī´ amz´) *n.:* Metrical feet consisting of two syllables, the first unaccented, the other accented.

5. **The first three simple proscriptions:** Reference to Flint's three rules outlined in footnote #3.

Guide for Responding

◆ Literature and Your Life

Reader's Response What is your reaction to Ezra Pound's ideas about great poetry?

Thematic Focus Why might you expect that new literary movements develop during periods of societal change?

☑ Check Your Comprehension

1. How did the Imagists measure the success of a poetic career?
2. What do the Imagists consider preferable to abstractions?
3. Summarize Pound's attitude toward adjectives.
4. With which other art does Pound compare the art of poetry?

◆ Critical Thinking

INTERPRET

1. Why do you think Pound preferred a list of "don'ts" to a list of "do's"? **[Speculate]**
2. Name at least two stated or implied differences between prose and poetry, according to Pound. **[Interpret]**
3. (a) Does Pound consider Shakespeare's image of "Dawn in russet mantle clad" as an example of description or presentation? (b) According to Pound, how are the two different? **[Distinguish]**

EVALUATE

4. Do you think following Pound's rules would make it easier or more difficult to write poetry? Explain. **[Evaluate]**

Beyond the Selection

FURTHER READING

Other Works by Ezra Pound

The Cantos, A Lume Spento, Ripostes, Cathay

Other Works About Creativity

"Inspiration," Henry David Thoreau
"Lamento," Tomas Transtömer
"Freedom," Wimal Dissanayake

We suggest that you preview these works before recommending them to students.

INTERNET

You and your students may find additional information about Ezra Pound and Imagist poetry on the Internet. We suggest the following sites. Please be aware, however, that sites may have changed since this information was published. Visit the Ezra Pound Home Page at
http://wings.buffalo.edu/epc/authors/pound/
For links to commentary, excerpts, and chronology, visit
http://www.lit.kobeu.ac.jp/~hishika/pound.htm

We *strongly recommend* that you preview the sites before you send students to them.

◆ Reading Strategy

3 Engage Your Senses Challenge students to use their senses to apply Pound's idea to his poem "The River-Merchant's Wife: A Letter." Students can find the rising wave of rhythm he describes. What physical sensations does it evoke? *Students may note a lifting feeling or a swelling feeling that propels them forward.*

◆ Literary Focus

4 Imagist Poetry Ask students to explain how discussing one sense in the terms of another conflicts with the basic tenets of Imagism. *Imagism seeks to express the essence of an object, person, or event. Language that describes in removed terms is diluting and fails to present the subject as it is.*

Reinforce and Extend

Answers

◆ Literature and Your Life

Reader's Response Students' opinions should be supported by citations from the text.

Thematic Focus Dramatic social change may alter the ways in which people, including writers, perceive their world.

☑ Check Your Comprehension

1. The Imagists believed that "it is better to present one Image in a lifetime than to produce voluminous works."
2. Imagists consider the concrete better than the abstract.
3. Adjectives are to be avoided unless they reveal something.
4. Pound compares poetry to music.

◆ Critical Thinking

1. A list of "do's" might be infinitely long, while a list of key "don'ts" is manageable.
2. Prose can express abstractions while poetry can express images. Unlike prose, poetry has a rhythm similar to music.
3. (a) Pound considers it presentation. (b) Presentation puts forth only the concrete object. Description explains the nuances of the concrete object in detail.
4. Students may say that Pound's rules place restrictions on content.

Develop Understanding

◆ Critical Thinking

❶ Infer As the poem begins, how old is the speaker as a character in the story? How can you tell? *Students should note that the speaker is a child; the haircut and playful activities serve as clues.*

❷ Clarification Pound's poem was adapted from a Chinese poem by Li T'ai Po. At the time that Li T'ai Po was writing, marriages in China were commonly arranged by family leaders rather than by the bride and groom. Love was expected to grow after the marriage. As they read, ask students to consider whether that system worked for the speaker and her husband. *Students should note that the system worked, recognizing as proof the growing love between the young speaker and her husband.*

◆ *Literature and Your Life*

❸ Point out the changing emotions experienced by the speaker. Ask students to recall times in their lives when their feelings about a person changed dramatically over time. Invite them to share their memories or record them in a journal for privacy. *Students may mention new family members, close friends, or even romantic relationships.*

◆ Reading Strategy

❹ Engage Your Senses Challenge students to experience the falling leaves, wind, and colorful butterflies. What senses are they able to engage? *Students should engage sight to see the falling leaves and colorful butterflies, touch to feel the wind, and sound to hear the falling leaves.*

▶Critical Viewing◀

❺ Analyze Students should note the somewhat desolate mood, created by bare trees, an isolated house, and a stark landscape.

Customize for
Less Proficient Readers
To help these students understand the concept of imagery, use the Identify Sensory Imagery page in ***Strategies for Diverse Student Needs,*** p. 42.

The River-Merchant's Wife: A Letter

Ezra Pound

❶
While my hair was still cut straight across my forehead
I played about the front gate, pulling flowers.
You came by on bamboo stilts, playing horse,
You walked about my seat, playing with blue plums.
And we went on living in the village of Chokan:[1]
Two small people, without dislike or suspicion.

❷
At fourteen I married My Lord you.
I never laughed, being bashful.
Lowering my head, I looked at the wall.
Called to, a thousand times, I never looked back.

❸
At fifteen I stopped scowling,
I desired my dust to be mingled with yours
Forever and forever and forever.
Why should I climb the lookout?

At sixteen you departed,
You went into far Ku-to-yen,[2] by the river of swirling eddies,
And you have been gone five months.
The monkeys make sorrowful noise overhead.

You dragged your feet when you went out.
By the gate now, the moss is grown, the different mosses,
Too deep to clear them away!
❹
The leaves fall early this autumn, in wind.
The paired butterflies are already yellow with August
Over the grass in the West garden;
They hurt me. I grow older.
If you are coming down through the narrows of the river Kiang,

Please let me know beforehand,
And I will come out to meet you
As far as Cho-fu-Sa.[3]

By Rihaku

---

1. **Chokan** (chō´ kän´): A suburb of Nanking, a city in the People's Republic of China.
2. **Ku-to-yen** (ko͞o´ tō´ yen´): An island in the Yangtze (yäng´ tsē) River.
3. **Cho-fu-Sa** (chō´ fo͞o´ sä´): A beach along the Yangtze River, several hundred miles from Nanking.

Beyond the Classroom

Community Connection
Customs Acknowledge with students that arranged marriages, while common in Li T'ai Po's time, are more unusual now. Customs such as this one are often unique to a time and culture. Invite students to brainstorm for customs of your community—annual festivals, young people's gathering places, decorated doorways on special holidays. Then urge students to interview long-time residents of the community to learn how these customs originated and changed over time.

Workplace Skills Connection
Communication In this poem, the speaker shares her feelings in the form of a letter. Explain that letters are also an important communication vehicle for people working in business. Refer students to the proper form for business letters. Then have students gather examples of business letters—such as those accompanying advertisements and offers mailed to homes—for analysis. Which letters are most and least effective

❺ ▼ **Critical Viewing** How does the mood of this drawing mirror the mood of "The River-Merchant's Wife: A Letter"? **[Analyze]**

Landscape Album in Various Styles, Ch'a Shih-piao, The Cleveland Museum of Art

In a Station of the Metro[1]

Ezra Pound

The apparition of these faces in the crowd; ❻
Petals on a wet, black bough. ❼

1. **Metro:** The Paris subway.

◆ **Build Vocabulary**

apparition (ap´ ə rish´ ən) *n.*: The act of appearing or becoming visible

Guide for Responding

◆ *Literature and Your Life*

Reader's Response Of all the images contained in these two poems, which did you find the most striking? Why?

Thematic Focus What troubled times does the river-merchant's wife face?

☑ Check Your Comprehension

1. Summarize the events in the life of the river-merchant's wife.
2. Describe in your own words the setting of "In a Station of the Metro."

◆ Critical Thinking

1. (a) How did the river-merchant's wife feel at the time of her marriage? (b) How have her feelings for her husband changed since then? **[Analyze]**
2. (a) How does she feel about her husband's absence? (b) How do the descriptions of the animals and insects reflect her feelings? **[Analyze]**
3. What does the comparison Pound makes in "In a Station of the Metro" suggest about how society affects individuality? **[Interpret]**

EXTEND

4. Many cultures have practiced the custom of arranged marriages. What are its potential benefits and drawbacks? **[Social Studies Link]**

◆ Critical Thinking

❻ **Interpret** How does the speaker see the faces in the crowd? *The faces appear and disappear as if from nowhere.*

◆ Grammar and Style

❼ **Concrete and Abstract Nouns** Ask students to label the poem's nouns as either concrete or abstract. *Abstract: apparition; Concrete: faces, crowd, petals, bough.*

Customize for ***Less Proficient Readers***
Explain to these students that Pound's poem presents a single comparison linking two images: faces in a crowd and individual flower petals against a wet, black tree branch. Urge students to use their senses to visualize each image. Then have them work in pairs to discuss how the images are similar.

Reinforce and Extend

Answers

◆ ***Literature and Your Life***

Reader's Response Encourage students to share their responses.

Thematic Focus She is troubled because her husband has been away.

☑ **Check Your Comprehension**

1. She married the river-merchant at fourteen. She began to love at fifteen. Her husband left when she was sixteen.
2. The station is damp and dark with countless anonymous people crowded together.

◆ **Critical Thinking**

1. (a) At the time of her marriage she was unhappy because she did not love her husband. (b) She now loves her husband.
2. (a) She is unhappy. (b) The unhappiness is reflected in the monkeys' "sorrowful noise" and in her hurt as she watches the butterflies pairing.
3. Individuality is obscured by society.
4. Advantages may be no need to search for the right marriage partner and a guarantee of companionship. Disadvantages might include not being able to marry for love and not having the right to remain single.

Humanities: Art

Landscape Album in Various Styles, Seventeenth-century, by Ch'a Shih-piao, ink and color on paper, 9 7/16" x 12 3/4".

This piece of art depicts a landscape similar to the one described by the river-merchant's wife. The artist, Ch'a Shih-piao, was born in 1615 to a wealthy family in China's Anhui Province. He first encountered art through his family's extensive private collection. The many styles in the collection influenced Ch'a Shih-piao and led to a tremendous diversity in his work. *Landscape Album in Various Styles* is an example of his most enduring and well-known style, the somber and melancholy landscape modeled after the fourteenth-century great, Ni Tsan.

Use these questions for discussion:

1. How would the setting depicted in this painting make it difficult for the speaker to learn of her husband's progress home? *The setting is isolated, making long-distance communication difficult.*
2. What contrasts can you identify between the painting and your image of the poem's setting? *Students may note the lack of a village, animals, lookout, and the small home.*

Develop Understanding

One-Minute Insight These poems by William Carlos Williams illustrate the power of strong sensory images to evoke emotions and responses from readers. Whether capturing an everyday farm scene of animals and equipment, interpreting a letter of apology for eating the last plums, or freezing in time the tension of a speeding fire engine, the poems use straightforward language to create images that demand attention.

Customize for *ESL Students*
Guide these students to realize that the language of these poems is quite simple. To avoid the possibility of students stumbling over the free-verse format, suggest that they write the poems out in prose format.

Literature CD-ROM To build background on William Carlos Williams, use the CD-ROM *The History of American Literature:* Part 2, Disc 1, Feature 10, which focuses in part on William Carlos Williams.

◆ Reading Strategy

❶ **Engage Your Senses** Have students identify descriptive language in "The Red Wheelbarrow." *Students should note these words and phrases: "red," "glazed with rain water," and "white."* Ask: How does this language help you engage your senses? *Descriptive language creates mental pictures that add detail and stimulate readers' senses.*

◆ Critical Thinking

❷ **Infer** How do you think the speaker in "The Great Figure" might feel in the moment described? *Students may say the speaker feels frightened, excited, or alarmed. He may also admire the fire engine's speed and technology.*

▶ Critical Viewing ◀

❸ **Connect** Students should note the expanding and repeated "5" which seems to shout at viewers, the fragmented bands of lights that explode from the center of the image, and the bright colors against a dark background. All of these create a mood of urgency and clamor.

The Red Wheelbarrow

William Carlos Williams

so much depends
upon

a red wheel
barrow

❶ glazed with rain
water

beside the white
chickens.

The Great Figure

William Carlos Williams

Among the rain
and lights
I saw the figure 5
in gold
on a red
fire truck
moving
❷ tense
unheeded
to gong clangs
siren howls
and wheels rumbling
through the dark city.

The Figure 5 in Gold, Charles Demuth, Metropolitan Museum of Art

❸ ▲ **Critical Viewing** Artist Charles Demuth created this work of art to accompany his friend Williams's poem. How does his illustration convey the energy and clamor of "gong clangs / siren howls / and wheels rumbling / through the dark city"? **[Connect]**

Humanities: Art

The Figure 5 in Gold, 1928, by Charles Demuth, oil on composition board, 36" X 29 ¾".

This painting evokes many of the images in "The Great Figure" as well the character of the poet Williams. Point out the artist's inclusion of the nickname Bill at the top of the image, referencing William Carlos Williams even more deliberately.

After studying at the Pennsylvania Academy of Fine Arts and in Paris, Demuth worked in many media and styles, from still-lifes to watercolor illustrations. *The Figure 5 in Gold* is considered an outstanding example of the poster-portrait format Demuth himself invented. The painting also captures the modern world's growing awareness of machines and technology. Use these questions for discussion:

1. How do the painting and the poem contribute to a "portrait" of William Carlos Williams? *The poem shows Williams's ambivalence about modern technology. The painting, which suggests Williams's spare poetry, mirrors that tug-of-war.*
2. How does the painting respond to the poem? *It distills the poem's essence to its raw visual core.*

This Is Just to Say

I have eaten
the plums
that were in
the icebox
and which
you were probably
saving
for breakfast

Forgive me
they were delicious
❹ so sweet
and so cold

William Carlos Williams

Guide for Responding

◆ Literature and Your Life

Reader's Response Which of these three poems evokes the strongest emotional response in you? Why?

Thematic Focus How is everyday life transformed in Williams's poetry?

Journal Writing Choose another food to take the place of "the plums" in line two of "This Is Just to Say" and revise the poem accordingly. Is your new poem more or less effective than the original?

☑ Check Your Comprehension

1. To what sense do the images in "The Red Wheelbarrow" directly appeal?
2. What detail is the focus of the speaker's experience of the fire truck?
3. What is the intention of the speaker in "This Is Just to Say"?

◆ Critical Thinking

INTERPRET

1. In your view, *what* depends on the red wheelbarrow? **[Speculate]**
2. In "The Great Figure," what might Williams be saying about (a) beauty? (b) modern life? **[Interpret]**
3. (a) Why is the incident in "This Is Just to Say" important to the speaker? (b) How do lines 10–12 reveal its importance? **[Infer, Analyze]**

APPLY

4. How would you describe the philosophy of life suggested by "This Is Just to Say"? **[Synthesize]**

COMPARE LITERARY WORKS

5. Williams accentuates his imagery with short, concise wording. Examine the topics of these three poems. Is this style more effective in one of the poems? Explain. **[Evaluate]**

Analyze Literary Criticism

William Carlos Williams occupies a special place among modern poets. He has been admired for his directness, especially in comparison to poets like Eliot, whose poetry features obscure literary references and quotations in foreign languages. According to critic R. P. Blackmur, Williams's poetry grew from everyday life, "the commonplace made unique because violently felt." Elsewhere Blackmur writes of Williams's basic approach: "He isolates and calls attention to what we are already presently in possession of."

Have students respond to these observations in a discussion. Pose the following questions:

1. How are Blackmur's observations illustrated in the poetry on these pages? *The imagery in the poems is commonplace, though rendered with intensity.*
2. Do students find anything reflective or spiritual behind Williams's images "isolated" from the commonplace? *Students may say that the poems could have come only after a kind of reflection that increases the intensity of the image.*

◆ Reading Strategy

❹ **Engage Your Senses** Ask students: What senses are stimulated by these lines? Cite specific words to explain your answer. *Students' answers should include: the senses of taste and touch; taste in delicious and sweet; touch in cold.*

Reinforce and Extend

Customize for *AP Students*
Highlight the varied emotions Williams has packed into his sparsely worded poem. To illustrate the poem's impact, challenge these students to write a similar response from the poem's recipient.

Answers

◆ Literature and Your Life

Reader's Response Students' responses should include citations from the poems.

Thematic Focus Williams transforms everyday life in his poetry by distilling events into poetry.

☑ Check Your Comprehension

1. They appeal to the sense of sight.
2. The detail is the figure 5.
3. The speaker intends to apologize.

◆ Critical Thinking

1. Students may say that the wheelbarrow is used for daily chores.
2. (a) He may be saying that beauty can be found in unlikely places. (b) Sample response: Modern life is so hectic and impersonal that people don't notice what's going on around them.
3. (a) It is important because of the sensations the speaker experiences. (b) They reveal the importance by describing the enjoyment the speaker experienced.
4. Students may debate whether the poem expresses selfishness, humility, or a "live in the moment" attitude.
5. William's short, concise phrases work well with all the poems, but students may give voice to their own preferences. For instance, the images in "This Is Just to Say" are especially immediate and apt for the subject.

Develop Understanding

One-Minute Insight These Imagist poems illustrate nature with words so evocative they hardly need accompanying illustrations. In both poems, the poet describes and responds to nature. "Pear Tree" presents H. D.'s glorious emotional response to the wonder of a pear tree in bloom while "Heat" brings the physical experience of a sweltering day into sharp focus for readers. One poem adores nature while the other complains to it, but together they demonstrate the emotional and sensory impact of carefully chosen words.

Customize for *Visual/Spatial Learners*
Though the language in this poem is simple, it is almost entirely figurative. Urge these learners to use the photo of a pear tree on p. 664 to help them visualize the poem's central image. Then, for greater understanding, have them reread the poem, listing all the visually descriptive words.

Customize for *Less Proficient Readers*
These students may benefit from the page on identifying sensory images in ***Strategies for Diverse Student Needs,*** p. 42.

Literature CD-ROM
To build background on H. D. (Hilda Doolittle), use the CD-ROM *The History of American Literature:* Part 2, Disc 1, Feature 5, which focuses in part on H. D.

◆ Critical Thinking

❶ **Infer** Ask students: What is the effect of the repetition of the phrase "higher than my arms reach"? *Students may say the repetition emphasizes the great height of the tree.*

◆ Reading Strategy

❷ **Engage Your Senses** Ask students to name the frequently repeated sensory image in the poem. *The repeated image is "silver." It engages the visual sense.* What senses does it engage? How does repeating it effect readers? *Repeating it stresses its importance in the poet's description.*

Pear Tree H. D.

Silver dust
lifted from the earth,
higher than my arms reach,
you have mounted,
O silver,
❶ higher than my arms reach
you front us with great mass;

no flower ever opened
so staunch a white leaf,
❷ no flower ever parted silver
from such rare silver;

O white pear,
your flower-tufts
thick on the branch
bring summer and ripe fruits
in their purple hearts.

Humanities: Art

Landscape Painting Describing nature in words and pictures is a long-standing artistic tradition. Although Native Americans had been painting the landscape for centuries, many art historians assert that landscape painting in America reached its peak during the nineteenth century when artists of the Hudson River School were active. Characterized by contrast between primarily untouched land and a smaller human element, these landscapes highlighted the magnificence of the wild American landscape and the relative transience of human occupancy.

Later important painting movements include the Rocky Mountain School—immortalizing the dramatic impact of the West on settlers—and the Luminists, who focused on the effect of light in the landscape.

Have students view examples of American landscape painting in books or museums. Discuss how these images capture the same sense of responsive wonder as does the poem "Pear Tree."

***Overhanging Cloud in July,* (1947/1959),** Charles Burchfield, Watercolor on paper, 39 1/2" x 35 1/2", Collection of Whitney Museum of American Art, Purchase, with funds from the Friends of the Whitney Museum of American Art

Heat

H. D.

O wind, rend open the heat,
cut apart the heat,
rend it to tatters.

Fruit cannot drop
through this thick air— ❸
fruit cannot fall into heat
that presses up and blunts
the points of pears
and rounds the grapes.

Cut the heat—
plow through it,
turning it on either side
of your path.

◀ **Critical Viewing** Does this painting capture the oppressive heat of a humid summer day as effectively as the poem does? Explain. **[Evaluate]** ❹

Guide for Responding

◆ *Literature and Your Life*

Reader's Response How do these two poems by H. D. make you feel?

Thematic Focus In the world presented in "Heat," are troubles natural or man-made?

Questions for Research Develop questions that would guide you in beginning to research common themes in Imagist poetry.

☑ Check Your Comprehension

1. What is the "silver dust" in "Pear Tree"?
2. According to the speaker of "Heat," how is wind potentially stronger than heat?

◆ Critical Thinking

INTERPRET

1. In "Pear Tree," in what sense is the silver dust "lifted from the earth"? **[Interpret]**
2. (a) What time of year is the speaker describing in "Pear Tree"? (b) How is this information conveyed? **[Infer, Analyze]**
3. What specific type of heat is the speaker in "Heat" describing? **[Interpret]**
4. How does H. D. create the impression that heat is almost a solid substance? **[Analyze]**

APPLY

5. H. D. uses the color silver several times. What associations do you have with this color? **[Relate]**

◆ Reading Strategy

❸ **Engage Your Senses** To what senses do these lines appeal? *The description of fruit hanging or dropping appeals to sight. The image of air so thick it is nearly impenetrable appeals to the sense of touch.*

▶Critical Viewing◀

❹ **Evaluate** Some students will say the image is effective for its depiction of the thick and hanging air, bright light, and bowed vegetation. Others will say it is not, citing the painting's scene as less oppressive than the feelings of the poem.

Reinforce and Extend

Customize for
Bodily/Kinesthetic Learners
To help these students relate to the tactile sensations suggested by the poem, suggest experiences that evoke the density and closeness of the poem's images. For example, ask students to describe pushing through a crowded room or swimming upstream in a current.

Answers

◆ *Literature and Your Life*

Reader's Response Encourage students to share their responses. Have them support their answers with specific images and phrases from the poems.

Thematic Focus The troubles are natural.

☑ Check Your Comprehension

1. The silver dust refers to the leaves and flowers of the pear tree.
2. The wind can cut through the heat.

◆ Critical Thinking

1. The pear tree grows upward.
2. (a) It is spring. (b) The pear tree's blossom anticipates the arrival of summer and its fruits.
3. The speaker seems to describe the heat of the sun on a torrid summer day.
4. H. D. creates the impression by speaking of heat being rent, cut, and plowed through.
5. Relate student responses to reactions to the poem.

Beyond the Selection

FURTHER READING

Other Works by William Carlos Williams and H. D.
Spring and All; In the American Grain, Williams
Sea Garden; Helen in Egypt, H. D.

Other Works About Nature and Machines
Walden, Henry David Thoreau
"The Pear Tree," Edna St. Vincent Millay
"Mending Wall," Robert Frost

We suggest that you preview these works before recommending them to students.

INTERNET

You may find additional information on the Internet. We suggest these sites. Please be aware that sites may have changed since this information was published.

For a discussion of H. D.'s work, visit **http://www.poets.org/lit/poet/hdoolitt.htm**
For information on modernism, go to **http://www. poets.org/lit/EXH/exoolfst.htm**

We *strongly recommend* that you preview the sites before you send students to them.

Answers

◆ Reading Strategy

1. The sense of touch can be engaged to feel the petals and the wet bough. The sense of smell can be engaged to smell the wet bough and the petals.
2. Passages include "I played about the front gate, pulling flowers," and "The paired butterflies are already yellow with August / Over the grass in the West garden."
3. Image: "Among the rain / and lights," Senses: touch, sight; Image: "the figure 5 / in gold," Sense: sight; Image: "a red / fire truck / moving /tense," Sense: sight; Image: "gong clangs / siren howls / and wheels rumbling," Sense: hearing; Image: "the dark city," Sense: sight.

◆ Literary Focus

1. The poem is not a purely Imagist poem. It includes descriptive lines and abstract words.
2. The word *apparition* enhances the feeling of isolation and anonymity within the crowd.
3. H.D.'s images of extreme heat evoke feelings of lethargy and fatigue.
4. Students may agree with the comment because H.D.'s poetry is not overly descriptive. "Heat," for example, provides the effects of heat more than it provides a description of heat.

◆ Build Vocabulary

Using Forms of *Appear*

1. appearance
2. apparent
3. apparition

Using the Word Bank

1. a 2. c 3. b

◆ Grammar and Style

Concrete and Abstract Nouns

1. abstract
2. concrete, concrete
3. concrete, concrete, concrete
4. concrete, concrete

Grammar Reinforcement

For additional instruction and practice, use the lesson in the **Language Lab CD-ROM** on Types of Nouns and the pages on Nouns, pp. 5–6, in the *Writer's Solution Grammar Practice Book*.

Guide for Responding (continued)

◆ Reading Strategy

ENGAGE YOUR SENSES

By **engaging your senses** to fully experience the images created by a writer, you can deepen your involvement in a literary work. For instance, experiencing the range of sensations brought to life in "The Red Wheelbarrow" may trigger a range of associations from experiences with rainstorms to memories of a childhood.

1. What other senses, besides sight, can you engage to recreate the image of "Petals on a wet, black bough"? Explain.
2. Give examples of two passages in "The River-Merchant's Wife" where you were able to engage the sense of smell.
3. List each of the images in "The Great Figure" and identify the sense or senses to which each appeals.

◆ Literary Focus

IMAGIST POETRY

Imagism was a literary movement that focused on presenting unadorned images in poetry. The Imagists used common language, which emphasized the creation of new poetic rhythms. They chose words with great precision in the belief that a single, well-crafted image could spark readers' associations and evoke powerful emotions.

1. Based on what you've learned of Imagism, does "The River-Merchant's Wife: A Letter" qualify as a purely Imagist poem? Why or why not?
2. How does Pound's choice of the word *apparition*—which is commonly used to describe a ghostly figure—to mean *appearance* contribute to the emotional impact of the image of "In a Station of the Metro"?
3. What types of feelings do H.D.'s images evoke in "Heat"?
4. Use your understanding of "A Few Don'ts by an Imagiste" to explain whether you agree or disagree with this comment about H. D. made by poet and critic Louis Untermeyer: "She was the only one who steadfastly held to the letter as well as the spirit of [the Imagist] *credo*."

◆ Build Vocabulary

USING FORMS OF *APPEAR*

Several common English words are forms of the word *appear*. Complete each of the following sentences with the correct word from the box below.

apparent	appearance	apparition

1. He made a brief __?__ at the awards dinner—just long enough to pick up his trophy and say a few words.
2. When midnight found the toddlers still running around the house, it became __?__ that the babysitter was no longer in control.
3. The __?__ of a face at the window nearly stopped her heart with fear.

USING THE WORD BANK: Synonyms

On your paper, write the letter of the best synonym for the first word.

1. dogma: (a) doctrine, (b) legality, (c) statement
2. voluminous: (a) loud, (b) arrogant, (c) comprehensive
3. apparition: (a) suspicion, (b) vision, (c) face

◆ Grammar and Style

CONCRETE AND ABSTRACT NOUNS

A **concrete noun** names a physical thing that can be perceived with one of the five senses. An **abstract noun** names something that cannot be seen, heard, felt, tasted, or touched.

Practice On your paper, label the italicized noun(s) in each passage as *concrete* or *abstract*.

1. Don't use such an expression as "dim lands of *peace*."
2. The *leaves* fall early this autumn, in *wind*.
3. Among the *rain* and lights I saw the figure 5 in gold on a red firetruck moving tense unheeded to gong *clangs* siren howls and wheels rumbling through the dark *city*.
4. Cut the *heat*—plow through it, turning it on either side of your *path*.

Looking at Style Explain why you'd expect to find mainly concrete nouns in an Imagist poem.

Reteach

To help students engage poetry on a sensory level, you may want to use the graphic organizer at right. Have students add words or images from a given poem in the appropriate area of the graphic.

Imagist poetry is especially appropriate for learning how to engage the senses. Remind students of the admonition that Ezra Pound includes in his essay on Imagist poetry: "Go in fear of abstractions." The opposite of an abstraction is the concrete image, which impresses itself on the senses upon reading.

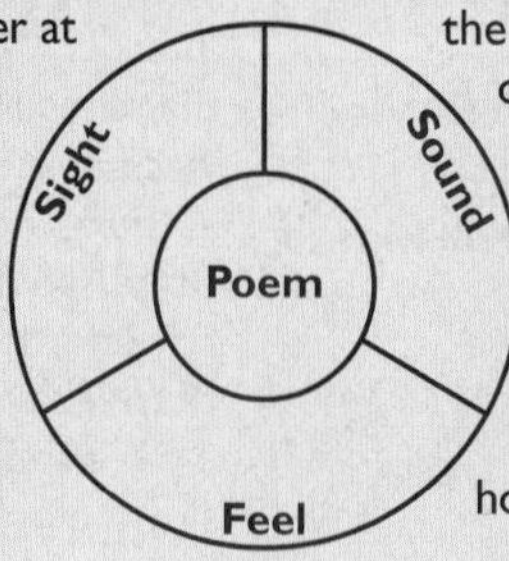

All the poems included in this section should have this effect. Use the poem "The Great Figure" as an example, and ask students for sensory impressions from it. Ask, what sense is affected by the words "gong clangs/siren howls/ and wheels rumbling"?

Build Your Portfolio

Idea Bank

Writing

1. **Description** Critic Louis Untermeyer claims that in "Heat," H. D. goes beyond describing heat; rather, she presents "the effect of it." Write a description that captures the effect of heat, cold, or some other weather condition. **[Science Link]**
2. **Poem** Capture the essence of an object, person, or incident in a brief Imagist poem of your own. Use language that is precise and suggestive.
3. **Critical Essay** Select one of the poems you have just read, and write a critical essay explaining how it meets—or fails to meet—each of the key guidelines for Imagist poetry set forth in Pound's "A Few Don'ts."

Speaking, Listening, and Viewing

4. **Informal Debate** Discussing "The Red Wheelbarrow," critic Roy Harvey Pearce comments: "At its worst this is togetherness in a chickenyard. At its best it is an exercise in the creation of the poetic out of the anti-poetic." To which view do you subscribe? Defend your assessment of Williams's poem in an informal debate with classmates.
5. **Oral Interpretation** What type of music elicits the feel of a hot summer day? Select a piece of music that suggests the effect of heat and play it as you read "Heat" aloud. **[Music Link]**

Researching and Representing

6. **Art** Draw or paint the way *you* envision the image of "In a Station of the Metro." **[Art Link]**
7. **Poetry Collection** Explore the poetry of Pound, Williams, H. D., and other Imagists. Create a collection of your favorite Imagist poems. Accompany each poem with a brief explanation of why you chose it. Share copies with the class.

Online Activity www.phlit.phschool.com

Guided Writing Lesson

An Editor's Review of Manuscript

Magazine editors (such as Ezra Pound was) receive manuscripts from writers. An editor reviews each manuscript, makes a decision about publishing it, and sends a letter of acceptance or rejection to the writer. Often these letters contain constructive criticism about the work's merits and weaknesses. Imagine that you are a literary magazine editor who has just received a manuscript from an Imagist poet. Critique the poems of Pound, Williams, or H. D., in a letter explaining why you will or will not publish this work. Make your points clearly and concisely in a professional manner.

Writing Skills Focus: Brevity and Clarity

A business letter—like most examples of good prose—should present ideas with **brevity and clarity**. Here are a few tips to keep your letter precise and to the point:

- Avoid general, vague nouns. Instead, use specific, concrete words that express ideas exactly.
- Eliminate unnecessary words or sentences.
- Present your ideas in a logical sequence—don't jump from point to point.

Prewriting Decide to which of the three poets you will address your review, then reread his or her poems. As you read, take notes on the strengths and weaknesses of each poem, noting relevant passages.

Drafting Draft a letter that briefly and clearly explains why you will or will not publish the poems. Discuss what you particularly liked or disliked about each poem, citing examples from the work. Be simple, honest, and kind in your analysis.

Revising Trim any excess words, sharpen your word choices, and then read your letter aloud as if you were the recipient. Do you understand exactly what the editor thought of your writing?

✓ ASSESSMENT OPTIONS

ASSESSMENT OPTIONS

Formal Assessment, Selection Test, pp. 200–202, and Assessment Resources Software. The selection test is designed so that it can be easily customized to the performance levels of your students.

Alternative Assessment, p. 42, includes options for less advanced students, more advanced students, verbal/linguistic learners, visual/spatial learners, musical/rhythmic learners, and interpersonal learners.

PORTFOLIO ASSESSMENT

Use the following rubrics in the ***Alternative Assessment*** booklet to assess student writing:
Description: Description Rubric, p. 112
Poem: Poetry Rubric, p. 123
Critical Essay: Literary Analysis/Interpretation Rubric, p. 127
Guided Writing Lesson: Response to Literature Rubric, p. 125

Idea Bank

Customizing for *Performance Levels*

Following are suggestions for matching Idea Bank topics with your students' performance levels:
Less Advanced Students: 1, 5
Average Students: 2, 6, 7
More Advanced Students: 3, 4

Customizing for *Learning Modalities*

Following are suggestions for matching Idea Bank topics with your students' learning modalities:
Interpersonal: 4
Musical/Rhythmic: 5
Visual/Spatial: 6
Logical/Mathematical: 7

Guided Writing Lesson

Refer students to p. 1192, for instruction on the writing process, and p. 1196 for further information on response to literature.

For more prewriting, elaboration, and revision strategies, see *Prentice Hall Writing and Grammar.*

Writing and Language Transparencies Use the Cubing Organizer (p. 71), to help students organize the strengths and weaknesses of their selected poems.

Writers at Work Videodisc

Have students view the videodisc segment on response to literature (Ch. 7) featuring literary agent Theresa Park speaking about her job. Ask students: In what ways does Park typically respond to the literature she reads?

Play frames 22513 to 31258

Writing Lab CD-ROM

Have students complete the tutorial on Response to Literature. Follow these steps:

1. To help students capture their reactions to literature exactly, have them use the Evaluation Word Bins.
2. Have students draft on computer.
3. Have students use the Interactive Self-Evaluation Checklist to aid revision.

LESSON OBJECTIVES

1. **To develop vocabulary and word identification skills**
   - Latin Word Roots: *-somn-*
   - Using the Word Bank: Antonyms
   - Extending Word Study (ATE)
2. **To use a variety of reading strategies to comprehend a short story**
   - Connect Your Experience
   - Reading Strategy: Draw Conclusions About Characters
3. **To increase knowledge of other cultures and to connect common elements across cultures**
   - Cultural Connection (ATE)
4. **To express and support responses to the text**
   - Critical Thinking
   - Idea Bank: Diary Entry
   - Idea Bank: Dialogue
5. **To analyze literary elements**
   - Literary Focus: Characterization
   - Idea Bank: Montage
6. **To read in order to research self-selected and assigned topics**
   - Idea Bank: Report
   - Questions for Research
7. **To plan, prepare, organize, and present literary interpretations**
   - Idea Bank: Résumé
   - Idea Bank: Essay
   - Idea Bank: Musical Interpretation
8. **To use recursive writing processes to write a character analysis**
   - Guided Writing Lesson
9. **To increase knowledge of the rules of grammar and usage**
   - Grammar and Style: Dashes

Test Preparation

Reading Comprehension: Analyze Sentence Meaning (ATE, p. 669) The teaching tips and sample test item in this workshop support the instruction and practice in the unit workshop:
Reading Comprehension: Sentence-Completion Questions (SE, p. 863)

Guide for Interpreting

F. Scott Fitzgerald *(1896–1940)*

When you open the pages of F. Scott Fitgerald's books, you're transported back in time to the Roaring 20's, a frantic decade unlike any other in American history. Fitzgerald was able to successfully capture the glittering, materialistic, and often self-destructive lifestyle of the time because he actually lived it. Like many of his characters, he led a fast-paced life and longed to attain the wealth and social status of the upper class.

A Quick Rise to Fame Francis Scott Key Fitzgerald was born in St. Paul, Minnesota, into a family with high social aspirations but little money. He entered Princeton University in 1913, where he began leading the type of high profile social life for which he'd become famous in the 1920's.

His first novel, *This Side of Paradise* (1920), published shortly after his discharge from army service, was an instant success. With the fame and wealth the novel brought him, Fitzgerald was able to persuade Zelda Sayre, a lovely southern belle with whom he had fallen in love while in the army, to be his wife. Together, they blazed an extravagant trail across the societies of both New York and Europe, mingling with rich and famous artists and aristocrats and spending money recklessly. Despite the couple's pleasure-seeking lifestyle, Fitzgerald remained a productive writer, publishing dozens of short stories. In 1925 he published his most successful novel, *The Great Gatsby*, the story of a self-made man whose dreams of love and social acceptance lead to scandal and corruption and ultimately end in tragedy. The novel displayed Fitzgerald's fascination with and growing distrust of the wealthy society he had embraced.

Fortunes Turn After the 1929 stock-market crash, Fitzgerald's world began to crumble. His wife suffered a series of nervous breakdowns, his reputation as a writer declined, and financial setbacks forced him to seek work as a Hollywood screenwriter. Despite these setbacks, however, he managed to produce many more short stories and a fine second novel, *Tender Is the Night (1934).* Focusing on the decline of a young American psychiatrist following his marriage to a wealthy patient, the novel reflects Fitzgerald's growing awareness of the tragedy that can result from an obsession with wealth and social status.

Fitzgerald was in the midst of writing a novel about a Hollywood film mogul, *The Last Tycoon,* when he died of a heart attack in 1940.

◆ Background for Understanding

CULTURE: FITZGERALD AS THE VOICE OF THE JAZZ AGE

After World War I—a war that politicians had once promised would end war forever but turned out to be the bloodiest war in history—it seemed to many that modern advances had created more problems rather than solving those that already existed. Frustrated and disappointed, Americans were desperate for a good time. They roared into the 1920's at breakneck pace, overthrowing rules about clothing and personal style. Shorter dresses, sporty automobiles, and dancing until dawn were just a few of the hallmarks of the age.

Another feature of the time was the quest for personal fulfillment through material wealth. The restricted world of America's established wealthy families had begun to open its doors. Making money—rather than inheriting it—became honorable and admired. Yet there was something frantic and despairing about the urgent quest for pleasure and money. F. Scott Fitzgerald's work and life reflected both the gaiety and the emptiness of this time—named "The Jazz Age" after the free-flowing music that dominated the time.

Prentice Hall Literature Program Resources

REINFORCE / RETEACH / EXTEND

Selection Support Pages
Build Vocabulary: Word Roots *-somn-*, p. 200
Grammar and Style: Dashes, p. 201
Reading Strategy: Drawing Conclusion About Characters, p. 202
Literary Focus: Characterization, p. 203

Strategies for Diverse Student Needs, p. 43

Beyond Literature
Media Connection: Film, p. 43

Formal Assessment Selection Test, pp. 203–205; Assessment Resources Software

Alternative Assessment, p. 43

Resource Pro CD-ROM

Literature CD-ROM

Listening to Literature Audiocassettes

Winter Dreams

◆ Literature and Your Life

Connect Your Experience

What you long for isn't always what's good for you. The little voice inside your head tells you that someone or something—as much as you want it—isn't right for you, but you still go on wanting.

Journal Writing Think of an episode in your own life when your desire for something left you caught in a struggle between reason and emotion. Write a dialogue that tells what the two voices in your head were saying to you.

Thematic Focus: Facing Troubled Times

The battle between the voice of reason and the voice of desire sometimes leaves scars. In this story of destructive love, a young man, Dexter Green, defies convention and sensibility to pursue his romantic ideal—a woman who embodies the wealth and social standing for which he yearns. Consider how Green's devotion to that ideal comes at the cost of his own happiness.

◆ Literary Focus

Characterization

As Dexter and Judy's story unfolds, you'll feel you have known them a long time. Fitzgerald creates this feeling of intimacy through **characterization**—the revelation of characters' personalities. In **direct characterization,** the writer directly states the traits of the characters. In **indirect characterization,** characters' traits are revealed through their own words, thoughts, and actions and by what other characters say to or about them. Notice how Fitzgerald brings the personalities of Dexter and Judy into sharp focus through both methods of characterization.

◆ Grammar and Style

Dashes

Dashes (—), which create a longer, more emphatic pause than commas, signal information that interrupts the flow of text. As you'll discover in this story, dashes tend to draw readers' attention to the information they set off. Look at this example:

When he was twenty-three, Mr. Hart—*one of the gray-haired men who liked to say "Now there's a boy"*—gave him a guest card to the Sherry Island Golf Club for a weekend.

◆ Reading Strategy

Draw Conclusions About Characters

F. Scott Fitzgerald paints a vivid picture of Dexter's and Judy's personalities but sometimes leaves it up to you to draw conclusions about their motivations and emotions. To **draw conclusions,** combine information from the story with your own knowledge of human behavior. Look at the example:

Dexter stood perfectly still . . . if he moved forward a step his stare would be in her line of vision—if he moved backward he would lose his full view of her face.

If you've ever wanted to hide your own interest in someone but couldn't stop looking, you can conclude from his behavior that Dexter is enthralled by Judy's beauty.

◆ Build Vocabulary

Latin Roots: *-somn-*

The word *somnolent* in this story is built on the Latin root *-somn-,* which means "sleep." Knowing its meaning is related to sleep can help you define *somnolent*—which means "sleepy or likely to induce sleep"—and other words that contain *-somn-*.

Word Bank

Before you read, preview this list of words.

fallowness
preposterous
fortuitous
sinuous
mundane
poignant
pugilistic
somnolent

Interest Grabber Students may discover that this sad story of obsessive love is reminiscent of many films, books, and real-life experiences. The power of any love story evolves from its characters. Introduce students to Fitzgerald's vividly drawn and alluring centerpiece character—Judy Jones—by reading aloud the following passage:

"She drew down the corners of her mouth, smiled, glanced furtively around, her eyes in transit falling for an instant on Dexter. . . . The smile again—radiant, blatantly artificial—convincing."

Have students discuss what this description reveals about the character on which it focuses. Then have them predict what might happen when another character falls desperately in love with her. Record students' predictions on the chalkboard. Then, after students have completed the story, check to see which prediction was closest.

Customize for
Less Proficient Readers
Less proficient readers may find the abrupt time shifts in this long story quite confusing. Suggest that they use a timeline to chart the story events in the sequence in which they occur.

Customize for
AP Students
Drawing conclusions about character can help more advanced students appreciate Fitzgerald's power-packed portrayal of even minor characters. Have students locate details from the text to support conclusions about one or more minor characters.

Test Preparation Workshop

Reading Comprehension:
Analyze Sentence Meaning Many standardized tests ask students to correctly answer sentence-completion questions. Use the following example to show students how to use the meaning of a sentence to choose the word that best completes the following passage.

F. Scott Fitzgerald was able to successfully capture the glittering and ____ lifestyle of the Roaring 20's. Like many of his characters, he longed to attain the wealth and social status of the upper class.

A repressed
B materialistic
C simplistic
D frugal

The meaning of the second sentence supports answer B, *materialistic,* as the most logical answer. Answer choices C and D contradict the second sentence, and choice A, *repressed,* does not fit with the meaning of *glittering.*

Develop Understanding

One-Minute Insight This story illustrates the powerful magnetism of love and suggests the extremes to which a person might pursue it. Dexter Green, an up and coming young man, becomes passionately obsessed with capturing Judy Jones and an entrée into her wealthy society. No matter how badly she behaves, Dexter finds her and the glittering life around her both captivating and desirable. As Dexter repeatedly returns to Judy's side to hungrily grasp at her erratic goodwill, he demonstrates with poignant force the glory and despair of loving a fantasy—a romantic ideal for which sacrificing all seems worthwhile.

◆ Literary Focus

1 Characterization What do Dexter's fantasies suggest about his character? *Students should note that Dexter is an idealist who romanticizes himself and his future.*

◆ Grammar and Style

2 Dashes Have students explain Fitzgerald's use of dashes in this paragraph. *The first and last sets of dashes function as commas would to set off an aside; the middle two uses of dashes stand for words Fitzgerald omitted because they were considered improper.*

Customize for
English Language Learners
Fitzgerald's creative sentence structure, especially his use of dashes, will likely challenge these students. Grouped with a more advanced reader, urge these students to read the story in manageable chunks, rephrasing difficult sentences for clarity. You may want to break the story into the numbered sections the author has already created.

Customize for
Gifted/Talented Students
Point out to students that Dexter Green's family comes from a place called Black Bear, while the area's wealthier families come from Sherry Island. Have students discuss what meanings these names are meant to convey, and challenge them to invent similar names that fit your region.

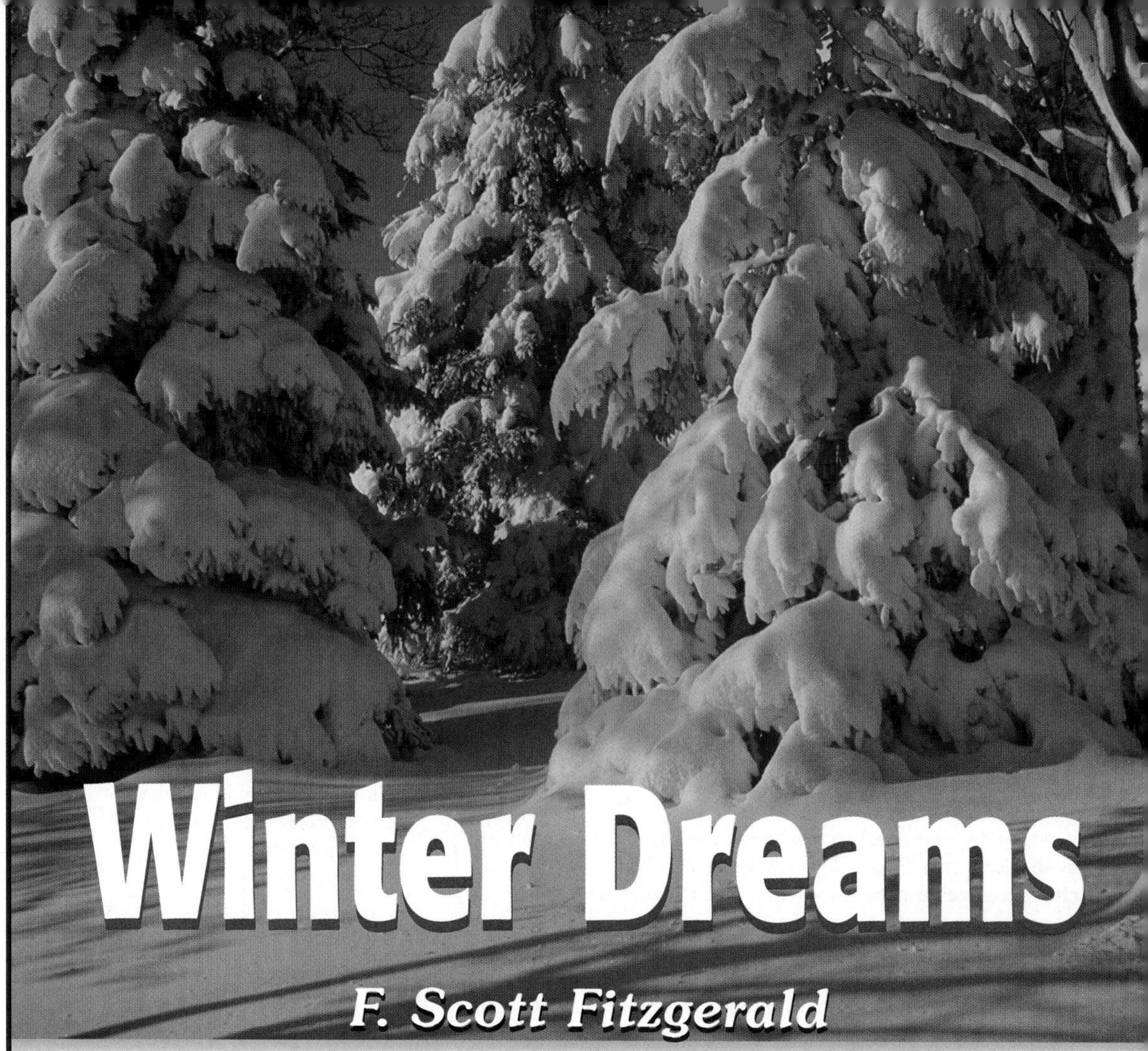

Winter Dreams

F. Scott Fitzgerald

I

Some of the caddies were poor as sin and lived in one-room houses with a neurasthenic[1] cow in the front yard, but Dexter Green's father owned the second best grocery store in Black Bear—the best one was "The Hub," patronized by the wealthy people from Sherry Island—and Dexter caddied only for pocket money.

In the fall when the days became crisp and gray, and the long Minnesota winter shut down like the white lid of a box, Dexter's skis moved over the snow that hid the fairways of the golf course. At these times the country gave him a feeling of profound melancholy—it offended him that the links should lie in enforced fallowness,

1. **neurasthenic** (no͞or´ əs then´ ik) *adj.*: Here, weak, tired.

◆ Build Vocabulary
fallowness (fal´ ō nis) *n.*: Inactivity

Block Scheduling Strategies

Consider these suggestions to take advantage of extended class time:

- After students complete the journal activity in Literature and Your Life (p. 669), engage the class in a debate between proponents for the voice of reason and the voice of passion.
- Have students listen to one or more sections of the story on audiotape. Have them discuss how listening to the story differs from reading it.
- Have student groups work together to answer the Critical Thinking questions (p. 683). Then have the groups share their responses with the class.
- If you have access to computers, have students work in the **Writer's Solution Writing Lab CD-ROM** to complete the Guided Writing Lesson (p. 685) or one of the Idea Bank activities (p. 685).
- Have student pairs exchange drafts from an Idea Bank (p. 685) writing activity or the Guided Writing Lesson (p. 685) for peer editing and/or peer assessment.

haunted by ragged sparrows for the long season. It was dreary, too, that on the tees where the gay colors fluttered in summer there were now only the desolate sandboxes knee deep in crusted ice. When he crossed the hills the wind blew cold as misery, and if the sun was out he tramped with his eyes squinted up against the hard dimensionless glare.

In April the winter ceased abruptly. The snow ran down into Black Bear Lake scarcely tarrying for the early golfers to brave the season with red and black balls. Without elation, without an interval of moist glory, the cold was gone. Dexter knew that there was something dismal about this Northern spring, just as he knew there was something gorgeous about the fall. Fall made him clinch his hands and tremble and repeat idiotic sentences to himself, and make brisk abrupt gestures of command to imaginary audiences and armies. October filled him with hope which November raised to a sort of ecstatic triumph, and in this mood the fleeting brilliant impressions of the summer at Sherry Island were ready grist to his mill. ❶ He became a golf champion and defeated Mr. T. A. Hedrick in a marvelous match played a hundred times over the fairways of his imagination, a match each detail of which he changed about untiringly—sometimes he won with almost laughable ease, sometimes he came up magnificently from behind. Again, stepping from a Pierce-Arrow automobile, like Mr. Mortimer Jones, he strolled frigidly into the lounge of the Sherry Island Golf Club—or perhaps, surrounded by an admiring crowd, he gave an exhibition of fancy diving from the springboard of the club raft. . . . Among those who watched him in open-mouthed wonder was Mr. Mortimer Jones.

❷ And one day it came to pass that Mr. Jones—himself and not his ghost—came up to Dexter with tears in his eyes and said that Dexter was the——best caddy in the club, and wouldn't he decide not to quit if Mr. Jones made it worth his while, because every other——caddy in the club lost one ball a hole for him—regularly——

"No, sir," said Dexter decisively, "I don't want to caddy any more." Then, after a pause: "I'm too old."

"You're not more than fourteen. Why the devil did you decide just this morning that you wanted to quit? You promised that next week you'd go over to the state tournament with me."

"I decided I was too old."

Dexter handed in his "A Class" badge, collected what money was due him from the caddy master, and walked home to Black Bear Village.

"The best——caddy I ever saw," shouted Mr. Mortimer Jones over a drink that afternoon. "Never lost a ball! Willing! Intelligent! Quiet! Honest! Grateful!"

❸ The little girl who had done this was eleven—beautifully ugly as little girls are apt to be who are destined after a few years to be inexpressibly lovely and bring no end of misery to a great number of men. The spark, however, was perceptible. There was a general ungodliness in the way her lips twisted down at the corners when she smiled, and in the—Heaven help us!—in the almost passionate quality of her eyes. Vitality is born early in such women. It was utterly in evidence now, shining through her thin frame in a sort of glow.

She had come eagerly out on to the course at nine o'clock with a white linen nurse and five small new golf clubs in a white canvas bag which the nurse was carrying. When Dexter first saw her she was standing by the caddy house, rather ill at ease and trying to conceal the fact by engaging her nurse in an obviously unnatural conversation graced by startling and irrelevant grimaces from herself.

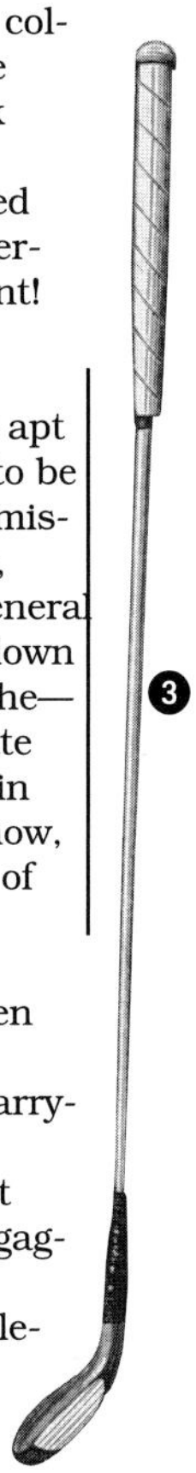

Customize for
Less Proficient Readers
Point out the link between Dexter's "winter dreams" and his covetous perception of Judy, noting the adjectives such as "brilliant" and "glow" Fitzgerald uses to describe both. Encourage students to look for additional examples of this connection as they read.

Humanities: Photography

Invite students to respond to the photograph on pp. 670–671.
Use these questions for discussion:

1. What impression does the photograph convey of winter? *Students may respond that the photograph presents an impression of winter as being both cold and beautiful.*
2. How might the long, snowy Minnesota winters shape Dexter's vision of his life? *The winter landscape provides a blank slate for Dexter's fantasies. Also, the landscape is so cold Dexter must escape from it to a warmer, more pleasurable vision.*
3. What might a person dream of or long for during winter? *Students may suggest that during the winter people are likely to dream of warmth, longer days, and the freedom and happiness often associated with summer.*

Enrichment Tell students that Fitzgerald once said "Winter Dreams" was a first version of his novel *The Great Gatsby*. Read, or have students read, the section of the novel in which the two main characters meet. Discuss how the opening scene of "Winter Dreams" might give rise to the novel text.

◆ Reading Strategy

❸ Drawing Conclusions About Character Ask students: What can you conclude about Judy from Fitzgerald's description? *Students may say she is beautiful and passionate, but not to be trusted.*

Beyond the Classroom

Workplace Skills Connection
Job Search Review with students the characteristics associated with Judy—vital, beautiful, athletic, superficial, flirtatious, charming, greedy, self-centered. Encourage students to brainstorm for ways that these skills and physical traits could serve Judy in the workplace. What jobs might she be suited for and why? Have students examine the employment ads in a local newspaper or online source to see if they can find a match.

Customize for
English Language Learners
To help these students keep track of the rapid dialogue between Dexter, Judy, and Hilda, encourage them to identify the speaker of each line of dialogue.

Customize for
AP Students
Challenge these students to draw on their knowledge of F. Scott Fitzgerald's life to link his hopes and dreams with those of Dexter Green. Fitzgerald too came from a modest background but aspired to wealth and glamour. Given this link, how might Fitzgerald want readers to feel about his character? *He wants readers to care about Dexter, to understand, and to sympathize with his longings.*

◆ Literature and Your Life

❶ Direct students to consider Dexter's involuntary laughter. In what situations have they laughed without any humorous stimuli? *Students may recall moments of embarrassment, nervousness, or disgust.*

◆ Literary Focus

❷ **Characterization** Fitzgerald uses indirect characterization, showing Judy's nasty actions toward her nurse and Hilda's impatience with what is clearly common behavior for Judy.

◆ Critical Thinking

❸ **Interpret** Why has Dexter decided to quit his caddy job? *He is overwhelmed by his attraction for Judy. He doesn't want to work as her servant; instead, he wants to show himself as uncaring and unaffected by her.*

"Well, it's certainly a nice day, Hilda," Dexter heard her say. She drew down the corners of her mouth, smiled, and glanced furtively around, her eyes in transit falling for an instant on Dexter.

Then to the nurse:

"Well, I guess there aren't very many people out here this morning, are there?"

The smile again—radiant, blatantly artificial—convincing.

"I don't know what we're supposed to do now," said the nurse looking nowhere in particular.

"Oh, that's all right. I'll fix it up."

Dexter stood perfectly still, his mouth slightly ajar. He knew that if he moved forward a step his stare would be in her line of vision—if he moved backward he would lose his full view of her face. For a moment he had not realized how young she was. Now he remembered having seen her several times the year before—in bloomers.

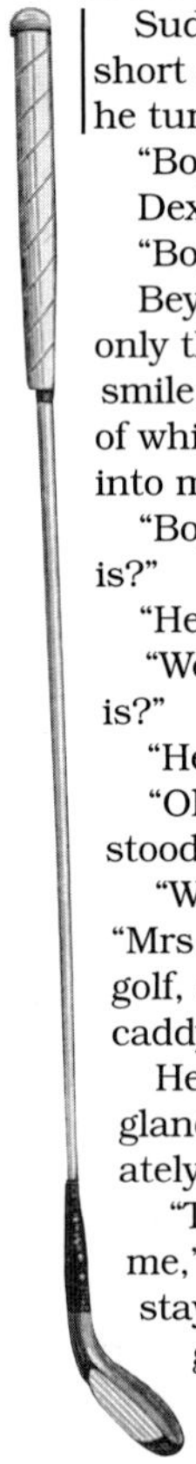

❶ Suddenly, involuntarily, he laughed, a short abrupt laugh—then, startled by himself, he turned and began to walk quickly away.

"Boy!"

Dexter stopped.

"Boy——"

Beyond question he was addressed. Not only that, but he was treated to that absurd smile, that preposterous smile—the memory of which at least a dozen men were to carry into middle age.

"Boy, do you know where the golf teacher is?"

"He's giving a lesson."

"Well, do you know where the caddy master is?"

"He isn't here yet this morning."

"Oh." For a moment this baffled her. She stood alternately on her right and left foot.

"We'd like to get a caddy," said the nurse. "Mrs. Mortimer Jones sent us out to play golf, and we don't know how without we get a caddy."

Here she was stopped by an ominous glance from Miss Jones, followed immediately by the smile.

"There aren't any caddies here except me," said Dexter to the nurse, "and I got to stay here in charge until the caddy master gets here."

"Oh."

Miss Jones and her retinue now withdrew, and at a proper distance from Dexter became involved in a heated conversation, which was concluded by Miss Jones taking one of the clubs and hitting it on the ground with violence. For further emphasis she raised it again and was about to bring it down smartly upon the nurse's bosom, when the nurse seized the club and twisted it from her hands.

> **◆ Literary Focus**
> What methods of characterization does Fitzgerald use to introduce the character of Judy Jones? ❷

"You little mean old *thing!*" cried Miss Jones wildly.

Another argument ensued. Realizing that the elements of the comedy were implied in the scene, Dexter several times began to laugh, but each time restrained the laugh before it reached audibility. He could not resist the monstrous conviction that the little girl was justified in beating the nurse.

The situation was resolved by the fortuitous appearance of the caddy master, who was appealed to immediately by the nurse.

"Miss Jones is to have a little caddy, and this one says he can't go."

"Mr. McKenna said I was to wait here till you came," said Dexter quickly.

"Well, he's here now." Miss Jones smiled cheerfully at the caddy master. Then she dropped her bag and set off at a haughty mince toward the first tee.

"Well?" The caddy master turned to Dexter. "What you standing there like a dummy for? Go pick up the young lady's clubs." ❸

"I don't think I'll go out today," said Dexter.

"You don't——"

"I think I'll quit."

The enormity of his decision frightened him. He was a favorite caddy, and the thirty dollars a month he earned through the summer were not to be made elsewhere around the lake. But he had received a strong emotional shock,

> **◆ Build Vocabulary**
> **preposterous** (pri päs′ tər əs) *adj.*: Ridiculous
> **fortuitous** (fôr to͞o′ ə təs) *adj.*: Fortunate

Speaking, Listening, and Viewing Mini-Lesson

Enactment
This mini-lesson supports the Speaking, Listening, and Viewing activity in the Idea Bank on p. 685.

Introduce the Concept Point out to students that well-drawn story characters, like real people, usually behave consistently with their personality, beliefs, and experience. Have students explain, for example, why either Judy's or Dexter's behavior in a given story situation was predictable.

Develop Background Before students begin writing their dialogue, have them consider and discuss these points:

- To be believable, dialogue must be consistent with the characters' experiences and beliefs.
- Incorporating individual diction, speech patterns, and gestures creates more vivid dialogue.

Apply the Information With this background, students should be able to draft realistic conversations between Judy and Dexter. As students perform their dialogues, remind the class to observe respectfully.

Assess the Outcome Ask students to rate the enactments for plausibility and character consistency. Then initiate a discussion about how, if at all, Judy or Dexter has changed since the story's close.

and his perturbation required a violent and immediate outlet.

It is not so simple as that, either. As so frequently would be the case in the future, Dexter was unconsciously dictated to by his winter dreams.

II

Now, of course, the quality and the seasonability of these winter dreams varied, but the stuff of them remained. They persuaded Dexter several years later to pass up a business course at the State university—his father, prospering now, would have paid his way—for the precarious advantage of attending an older and more famous university in the East, where he was bothered by his scanty funds. But do not get the impression, because his winter dreams happened to be concerned at first with musings on the rich, that there was anything merely snobbish in the boy. He wanted not association with glittering things and glittering people—he wanted the glittering things themselves. Often he reached out for the best without knowing why he wanted it—and sometimes he ran up against the mysterious denials and prohibitions in which life indulges. It is with one of those denials and not with his career as a whole that this story deals.

He made money. It was rather amazing. After college he went to the city from which Black Bear Lake draws its wealthy patrons. When he was only twenty-three and had been there not quite two years, there were already people who liked to say: "Now *there's* a boy—" All about him rich men's sons were peddling bonds precariously, or investing patrimonies precariously, or plodding through the two dozen volumes of the "George Washington Commercial Course," but Dexter borrowed a thousand dollars on his college degree and his confident mouth, and bought a partnership in a laundry.

It was a small laundry when he went into it, but Dexter made a specialty of learning how the English washed fine woolen golf stockings without shrinking them, and within a year he was catering to the trade that wore knickerbockers. Men were insisting that their Shetland hose and sweaters go to his laundry, just as they had insisted on a caddy who could find golf balls. A little later he was doing their wives' lingerie as well—and running five branches in different parts of the city. Before he was twenty-seven he owned the largest string of laundries in his section of the country. It was then that he sold out and went to New York. But the part of his story that concerns us goes back to the days when he was making his first big success.

> ❹ **◆ Reading Strategy**
> What conclusion can you draw about Dexter from his high standards for his laundry business?

When he was twenty-three Mr. Hart—one of the gray-haired men who like to say "Now there's a boy"—gave him a guest card to the Sherry Island Golf Club for a weekend. So he signed his name one day on the register, and that afternoon played golf in a foursome with Mr. Hart and Mr. Sandwood and Mr. T. A. Hedrick. He did not consider it necessary to remark that he had once carried Mr. Hart's bag over this same links, and that he knew every trap and gully with his eyes shut—but he found himself glancing at the four caddies who trailed them, trying to catch a gleam or gesture that would remind him of himself, that would lessen the gap which lay between his present and his past.

It was a curious day, slashed abruptly with fleeting, familiar impressions. One minute he had the sense of being a trespasser—in the next he was impressed by the tremendous superiority he felt toward Mr. T. A. Hedrick, who was a bore and not even a good golfer any more.

Then, because of a ball Mr. Hart lost near the fifteenth green, an enormous thing happened. While they were searching the stiff grasses of the rough there was a clear call of "Fore!" from behind a hill in their rear. And as they all turned abruptly from their search a bright new ball sliced abruptly over the hill and caught Mr. T. A. Hedrick in the abdomen. ❺

"By Gad!" cried Mr. T. A. Hedrick, "they ought to put some of these crazy women off the course. It's getting to be outrageous."

A head and a voice came up together over the hill:

"Do you mind if we go through?"

"You hit me in the stomach!" declared Mr. Hedrick wildly.

"Did I?" The girl approached the group of men. "I'm sorry. I yelled 'Fore!' "

Her glance fell casually on each of the men—then scanned the fairway for her ball. ❻

Customize for
Less Proficient Readers

Draw these students' attention to the time shift that has occurred in Part II. Point out that the events described here take place many years after Dexter's caddying job. Have students note the time shift on a sequential record, if they are keeping one.

◆ Reading Strategy

❹ **Draw Conclusions About Characters** Students should note that Dexter wants to succeed very badly and believes that giving others what they want is the way to achieve that success.

❺ **Clarification** Explain that the word "fore" is a golf term of caution meant to announce a swing to people in the foreground (or ahead of a golfer).

◆ Grammar and Style

❻ **Dashes** Ask students why they think Fitzgerald used a dash in this sentence. Urge them to incorporate knowledge of Judy's character in their answer. *This dash creates a dramatic pause to indicate Judy's perusal of each man as a possible audience for her charms. When she finds each lacking, she moves on.*

Tips to Guide Reading

Sustained Reading A story of this length may challenge the capacity of students to sustain interest over its course. One way to help students with this challenge is to have them note the import of the section breaks inserted by the author. Tell students that each of these provide a place to pause and reflect on what has passed so far in the story, and prepare for surprises to come.

Cultural Connection

The Rising Popularity of Golf Though golf was once a game played mostly in closed clubs reserved for the wealthy and often mostly by whites, in recent years it has become more widely accessible and popular in America. As a result, top golfers can now be found among many American cultures and ethnic groups. In 1997, for example, Tiger Woods—whose mother is Southeast Asian and whose father is African American, Native American, and Chinese—won golf's most prestigious prize, the Masters Tournament. At just 21 years old, Tiger was the youngest Masters champion in history.

▶Critical Viewing◀

❶ **Analyze** Students may note that in this private and privileged setting, Dexter would see Judy as somewhat unattainable and more attractive.

◆Literary Focus

❷ **Characterization** Ask students to identify the method of characterization Fitzgerald uses here to develop Judy Jones's character. *Fitzgerald uses indirect characterization, revealing Judy's character through the comments of other characters.*

Customize for *Musical/Rhythmic Learners*

Give these students the opportunity to share Dexter's sensory experience. Play a recording of the noted songs—available on Jazz Age song collections. Have students identify other sounds in the scene. As they listen to the recording, urge them to imagine the other sounds Dexter hears. Lead students to appreciate how these various sounds might affect Dexter's mood.

Customize for *AP Students*

Point out to these students the carefully crafted mood Fitzgerald weaves as Dexter bathes and rests. To help these students appreciate Fitzgerald's style, urge them to focus on the techniques Fitzgerald uses to create a mood. Fitzgerald both directly states Dexter's mood and also uses sensory language to envelop readers in that mood. Challenge students to find examples of this strategy in this scene and elsewhere throughout the story.

***Golf Course—California*, 1917,** George Wesley Bellows, Cincinnati Art Museum

❶ ▲ **Critical Viewing** Golf was once a game reserved for the wealthy. It is on a golf course like the one in this painting that Dexter meets Judy for the first time, then again nine years later. How might this setting have affected Dexter's perception of Judy? **[Analyze]**

"Did I bounce into the rough?"

It was impossible to determine whether this question was ingenuous or malicious. In a moment, however, she left no doubt, for as her partner came up over the hill she called cheerfully:

"Here I am! I'd have gone on the green except that I hit something."

As she took her stance for a short mashie shot, Dexter looked at her closely. She wore a blue gingham dress, rimmed at throat and shoulders with a white edging that accentuated her tan. The quality of exaggeration, of thinness, which had made her passionate eyes and down-turning mouth absurd at eleven, was gone now. She was arrestingly beautiful. The color in her cheeks was centered like the color in a picture—it was not a "high" color, but a sort of fluctuating and feverish warmth, so shaded that it seemed at any moment it would recede and disappear. This color and the mobility of her mouth gave a continual impression of flux, of intense life, of passionate vitality—balanced only partially by the sad luxury of her eyes.

She swung her mashie impatiently and without interest, pitching the ball into a sand pit on the other side of the green. With a quick, insincere smile and a careless "Thank you!" she went on after it.

"That Judy Jones!" remarked Mr. Hedrick on the next tee, as they waited—some moments—for her to play on ahead. "All she needs is to be turned up and spanked for six months and then to be married off to an old-fashioned cavalry captain." ❷

"My God, she's good looking!" said Mr. Sandwood, who was just over thirty.

"Good looking!" cried Mr. Hedrick contemptuously, "she always looks as if she wanted to be kissed! Turning those big coweyes on every calf in town!"

It was doubtful if Mr. Hedrick intended a reference to the maternal instinct.

"She'd play pretty good golf if she'd try," said Mr. Sandwood.

"She has no form," said Mr. Hedrick solemnly.

"She has a nice figure," said Mr. Sandwood.

"Better thank the Lord she doesn't drive a swifter ball," said Mr. Hart, winking at Dexter.

Later in the afternoon the sun went down with a riotous swirl of gold and varying blues and scarlets, and left the dry, rustling night of Western summer. Dexter watched from the veranda of the golf club, watched the even overlap of the waters in the little wind, silver molasses under the harvest moon. Then the moon held a finger to her lips and the lake became a clear pool, pale and quiet. Dexter put on his bathing suit and swam out to the farthest raft, where he stretched dripping on the wet canvas of the springboard.

There was a fish jumping and a star shining and the lights around the lake were gleaming. Over on a dark peninsula a piano was playing the songs of last summer and of summers be-

Humanities: Art

Golf Course–California, 1917, by George Wesley Bellows.

This picture is a lithograph—a picture printed from an inked stone or metal plate. It depicts a golf course much like the one where Dexter and Judy meet in the story.

George Wesley Bellows (also known as George Bellows) was well known for both lithography and painting, especially of sports and action scenes. These were activities he knew personally as a serious amateur athlete. *Golf Course–California,* like Bellows' other work, captures the motion and energy in sports almost like a photograph. Though some viewers were unused to the realistic quality of his pictures, this immediacy makes the pictures effective.

Use these questions for discussion:

1. What do the people depicted here suggest about the manners and expectations of Fitzgerald's characters? *They are dressed in almost uniform like clothing, suggesting a "club" which only some can enter. They appear to be moving slowly and gently, as if they have few cares.*
2. How does the golf club and its members depicted here compare to your image of Dexter and Judy at their golf club? *Students may say that they envisioned the course more densely covered in trees, and the people, therefore, less exposed to one another.*

fore that—songs from *Chin-Chin* and *The Count of Luxemburg* and *The Chocolate Soldier*[2]—and because the sound of a piano over a stretch of water had always seemed beautiful to Dexter he lay perfectly quiet and listened.

The tune the piano was playing at that moment had been gay and new five years before when Dexter was a sophomore at college. They had played it at a prom once when he could not afford the luxury of proms, and he had stood outside the gymnasium and listened. The sound of the tune precipitated in him a sort of ecstasy and it was with that ecstasy he viewed what happened to him now. It was a mood of intense appreciation, a sense that, for once, he was magnificently attuned to life and that everything about him was radiating a brightness and a glamor he might never know again.

A low, pale oblong detached itself suddenly from the darkness of the Island, spitting forth the reverberate sound of a racing motorboat. Two white streamers of cleft water rolled themselves out behind it and almost immediately the boat was beside him, drowning out the hot tinkle of the piano in the drone of its spray. Dexter raising himself on his arms was aware of a figure standing at the wheel, of two dark eyes regarding him over the lengthening space of water—then the boat had gone by and was sweeping in an immense and purposeless circle of spray round and round in the middle of the lake. With equal eccentricity one of the circles flattened out and headed back toward the raft.

"Who's that?" she called, shutting off her motor. She was so near now that Dexter could see her bathing suit, which consisted apparently of pink rompers.

The nose of the boat bumped the raft, and as the latter tilted rakishly he was precipitated toward her. With different degrees of interest they recognized each other.

"Aren't you one of those men we played through this afternoon?" she demanded.

He was.

❸ "Well, do you know how to drive a motorboat? Because if you do I wish you'd drive this one so I can ride on the surfboard behind. My name is Judy Jones"—she favored him with an absurd smirk—rather, what tried to be a smirk, for, twist her mouth as she might, it was not grotesque, it was merely beautiful—❹ "and I live in a house over there on the Island, and in that house there is a man waiting for me. When he drove up at the door I drove out of the dock because he says I'm his ideal."

There was a fish jumping and a star shining and the lights around the lake were gleaming. Dexter sat beside Judy Jones and she explained how her boat was driven. Then she was in the water, swimming to the floating surfboard with a sinuous crawl. Watching her was without effort to the eye, watching a branch waving or a sea gull flying. Her arms, burned to butternut, moved sinuously among the dull platinum ripples, elbow appearing first, casting the forearm back with a cadence of falling water, then reaching out and down, stabbing a path ahead.

They moved out into the lake; turning, Dexter saw that she was kneeling on the low rear of the now uptilted surfboard.

"Go faster," she called, "fast as it'll go."

Obediently he jammed the lever forward and the white spray mounted at the bow. When he looked around again the girl was standing up on the rushing board, her arms spread wide, her eyes lifted toward the moon.

"It's awful cold," she shouted. "What's your name?"

He told her.

"Well, why don't you come to dinner tomorrow night?"

His heart turned over like the flywheel of the boat, and, for the second time, her casual whim gave a new direction to his life. ❺

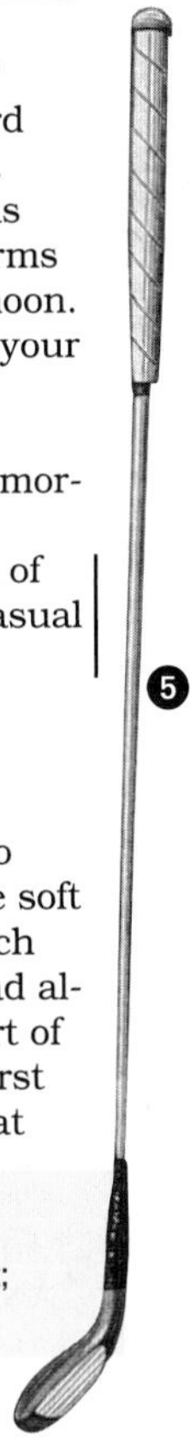

III

Next evening while he waited for her to come downstairs, Dexter peopled the soft deep summer room and the sun porch that opened from it with the men who had already loved Judy Jones. He knew the sort of men they were—the men who when he first went to college had entered from the great

2. ***Chin-Chin . . . The Chocolate Soldier***: Popular operettas of the time.

◆ Build Vocabulary

sinuous (sin′ yo͞o wəs) *adj.*: Moving in and out; wavy

Customize for
Less Proficient Readers

❸ Review the Grammar and Style lesson (p. 669) on Dashes with these students. Then work with them to break down the complicated sentence in which Judy introduces herself to Dexter as the narrator inserts comments.

◆ Reading Strategy

❹ **Drawing Conclusions About Characters** Ask students: What can you conclude about Judy Jones's character from this remark? *She wants to be admired but is uncomfortable if too obviously idealized. She prefers the tension of the chase.*

◆ Critical Thinking

❺ **Interpret** Why might Judy's invitation have such an effect on Dexter's feelings and on his life? *Dexter is strongly attracted to Judy. More importantly, his attraction for her is so strong that he will change the direction of his life to follow it. Fitzgerald is hinting that something important will happen to Dexter as a result of his feelings for Judy.*

Beyond the Classroom

Career Connection

Costume Design Dexter believes that part of his ticket to enter the wealthy world of golf clubs and Judy Jones is the right clothing. By donning the costume of the privileged class, Dexter hopes to become of it.

Film and theatrical costume designers develop clothing that enables actors to enter the life and cultural setting of a character. Have interested students read about costume design. Then invite students to apply costume design methods to create costumes appropriate to several subgroups in contemporary American culture.

Community Connection

Sports Venues Point out to students that the golf course featured in Dexter's story is a significant physical element in the community. A typical golf course has 18 holes that require walking 7,000 yards (70 football fields) to complete. Most are carefully landscaped and may even incorporate natural features such as ponds. Ask students to identify some sports venues, whether indoor or outdoor, in your community. How do these affect the community? Urge students to consider the business activity, traffic flow, visitor density, and visual impact of the venues.

◆ Background for Understanding

❶ **Culture** Explain that the wealthy society Dexter admires is comprised mostly of families whose ancestors have been in America a long time. These early settlers came largely from England, Scotland, and other parts of Northern Europe where names like Jones are more common. Dexter's reference to his mother's name acknowledges his family's origins in Eastern Europe where emigration to America is more recent—his mother speaks broken English because it is not her first language.

◆ Critical Thinking

❷ **Draw Conclusions** Draw students' attention to Fitzgerald's repeated description of Judy Jones' smile. Lead students to identify the casual but manipulative way Judy smiles. What does it suggest about how she views herself? *She sees herself as the focus of attention, ready to deliver the dramatic action necessary to captivate her audience.* Challenge students to consider the motivations and emotions they associate with smiling.

◆ Literary Focus

❸ **Characterization** Students should note that Dexter is basically honest, sympathetic, and eager to be accepted. Judy is superficial, petty, and coy.

Extending Word Study

Connotation The author F. Scott Fitzgerald has Judy Jones tell Dexter that a boyfriend had upset her by admitting that he was poor. She asked Dexter, "Does this sound horribly mundane?" Have students look up the word *mundane* to help them understand its connotations. Then ask students to speculate about what effect Fitzgerald was trying to achieve by having Judy use this word. Was she appealing to, or manipulating, something high-minded in Dexter? *Students may say that she was being coy and somewhat manipulative.*

---

prep schools with graceful clothes and the deep tan of healthy summers. He had seen that, in one sense, he was better than these men. He was newer and stronger. Yet in acknowledging to himself that he wished his children to be like them he was admitting that he was but the rough, strong stuff from which they eternally sprang.

❶ When the time had come for him to wear good clothes, he had known who were the best tailors in America, and the best tailors in America had made him the suit he wore this evening. He had acquired that particular reserve peculiar to his university, that set it off from other universities. He recognized the value to him of such a mannerism and he had adopted it; he knew that to be careless in dress and manner required more confidence than to be careful. But carelessness was for his children. His mother's name had been Krimelich. She was a Bohemian of the peasant class and she had talked broken English to the end of her days. Her son must keep to the set patterns.

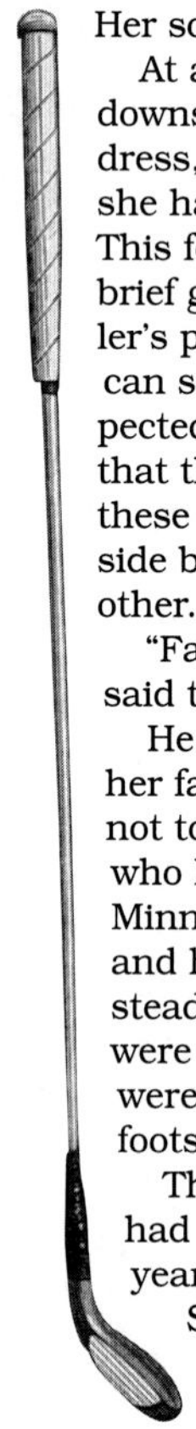

At a little after seven Judy Jones came downstairs. She wore a blue silk afternoon dress, and he was disappointed at first that she had not put on something more elaborate. This feeling was accentuated when, after a brief greeting, she went to the door of a butler's pantry and pushing it open called: "You can serve dinner, Martha." He had rather expected that a butler would announce dinner, that there would be a cocktail. Then he put these thoughts behind him as they sat down side by side on a lounge and looked at each other.

"Father and mother won't be here," she said thoughtfully.

He remembered the last time he had seen her father, and he was glad the parents were not to be here tonight—they might wonder who he was. He had been born in Keeble, a Minnesota village fifty miles farther north, and he always gave Keeble as his home instead of Black Bear Village. Country towns were well enough to come from if they weren't inconveniently in sight and used as footstools by fashionable lakes.

They talked of his university, which she had visited frequently during the past two years, and of the nearby city which supplied Sherry Island with its patrons, and whither Dexter would return next day to his prospering laundries.

During dinner she slipped into a moody depression which gave Dexter a feeling of uneasiness. Whatever petulance she uttered in her throaty voice worried him. Whatever she smiled at—at him, at a chicken liver, at nothing—it disturbed him that her smile could have no root in mirth, or even in amusement. When the scarlet corners of her lips curved down, it was less a smile than an invitation to a kiss. ❷

Then, after dinner, she led him out on the dark sun porch and deliberately changed the atmosphere.

"Do you mind if I weep a little?" she said.

"I'm afraid I'm boring you," he responded quickly.

"You're not. I like you. But I've just had a terrible afternoon. There was a man I cared about, and this afternoon he told me out of a clear sky that he was poor as a church mouse. He'd never even hinted it before. Does this sound horribly mundane?"

> **◆ Literary Focus**
> What does this conversation reveal to you about the personalities of Dexter and Judy? ❸

"Perhaps he was afraid to tell you."

"Suppose he was," she answered. "He didn't start right. You see, if I'd thought of him as poor—well, I've been mad about loads of poor men, and fully intended to marry them all. But in this case, I hadn't thought of him that way, and my interest in him wasn't strong enough to survive the shock. As if a girl calmly informed her fiancé that she was a widow. He might not object to widows, but——

"Let's start right," she interrupted herself suddenly. "Who are you, anyhow?"

For a moment Dexter hesitated. Then:

"I'm nobody," he announced. "My career is largely a matter of futures."

"Are you poor?"

"No," he said frankly, "I'm probably making more money than any man my age in the Northwest. I know that's an obnoxious remark, but you advised me to start right."

There was a pause. Then she smiled and the corners of her mouth drooped and an al-

> **◆ Build Vocabulary**
> **mundane** (mun dān′) *adj.*: Commonplace; ordinary

Beyond the Classroom

Community Connection

The Grape Vine Because Judy's suitors are obsessed by her, they continually "report" her actions to each other. Even if the information is true, remind students that this method of communication may be considered gossip and could have potentially dangerous results.

Ask students to consider how news and information travel through communities large or small. Beyond the formal channels of television, radio, and print journalism, community leaders such as school prinicipals, police personnel, and the clergy can also distribute news. Point out that students get only a percentage of their information through these official sources. Students may get their news in the halls between classes, or in the other free time they spend with friends.

Link the discussion to the story by asking how Dexter feels about hearing that Judy dates several men. Would he have felt differently if he'd *seen* newspaper photos of Judy with the many other men in her life?

4 ▶ **Critical Viewing** The mood of this painting is serene. How might this portrait be different if the artist were striving to communicate Judy Jones's energy and magnetic beauty? **[Modify]**

The Morning Sun, © 1920, Pauline Palmer, Rockford Art Museum

most imperceptible sway brought her closer to him, looking up into his eyes. A lump rose in Dexter's throat, and he waited breathless for the experiment, facing the unpredictable compound that would form mysteriously from the elements of their lips. Then he saw—she communicated her excitement to him, lavishly, deeply, with kisses that were not a promise but a fulfillment. They aroused in him not hunger demanding renewal but surfeit that would demand more surfeit . . . kisses that were like charity, creating want by holding back nothing at all.

It did not take him many hours to decide that he had wanted Judy Jones ever since he was a proud, desirous little boy.

IV

5 It began like that—and continued, with varying shades of intensity, on such a note right up to the denouement. Dexter surrendered a part of himself to the most direct and unprincipled personality with which he had ever come in contact. Whatever Judy wanted, she went after with the full pressure of her charm. There was no divergence of method, no jockeying for position or premeditation of ef-
6 fects—there was a very little mental side to any of her affairs. She simply made men conscious to the highest degree of her physical loveliness. Dexter had no desire to change her. Her deficiencies were knit up with a passionate energy that transcended and justified them.

When, as Judy's head lay against his shoulder that first night, she whispered, "I don't know what's the matter with me. Last night I thought I was in love with a man and tonight I think I'm in love with you——" it seemed to him a beautiful and romantic thing to say. It was the exquisite excitability that for the moment he controlled and owned. But a week later he was compelled to view this same quality in a different light. She took him in her roadster to a picnic supper, and after supper she disappeared, likewise in her roadster, with another man. Dexter became enormously upset and was scarcely able to be decently civil to the other people present. When she assured him that she had not kissed the other man, he knew she was lying—yet he was glad that she had taken the trouble to lie to him.

He was, as he found before the summer ended, one of a varying dozen who circulated about her. Each of them had at one time been favored above all others—about half of them still basked in the solace of occasional sentimental revivals. Whenever one showed signs of dropping out through long neglect, she granted him a brief honeyed hour, which encouraged him to tag along for a year or so longer. Judy

▶Critical Viewing◀

❹ **Modify** The painting would show the woman's full face and more movement. It might also depict the young woman interacting with others.

❺ **Clarification** Explain that the word *denouement* is a French word literally meaning "untying" but used to refer to the final outcome or resolution of a complex situation. The word has been absorbed into English with its original French spelling intact.

◆ Literary Focus

❻ **Characterization** What method of characterization does Fitzgerald use here to develop Judy's character? *Students should note that Fitzgerald uses direct characterization, telling readers outright that Judy is simple, not terribly bright, and beautiful.*

Humanities: Art

The Morning Sun, 1920, by Pauline Palmer, oil on canvas, 50 ¼" X 40".

This painting shows a young woman much like Judy Jones contemplating herself in the mirror.

The artist, Pauline Palmer, was a first generation American born to German and French parents. She studied in Chicago and Paris, where she became interested in the soft brushwork of Impressionism.

The Morning Sun is typical of Palmer's work, capturing its atmosphere through the use of light and color. Though Palmer is relatively unknown today, in her time she was hugely popular both with critics and art collectors, especially for her portraits of high Chicago society. This popularity was challenged briefly by painters who focused more on social content than portraiture.

Use these questions for discussion:

1. If this portrait were of Judy Jones, what might the young woman be thinking at this moment? *Judy would likely be thinking about what dress to wear or which man she would see that day—her thoughts would not be analytical or introspective.*
2. How does this painting reflect the privileged world in which Judy Jones lives? *The room is furnished with delicate fabrics and decorative objects such as flowers and a painted lamp. Even the mirror is decorative. The young woman is dressed in very impractical clothing as if for a day of leisure.*

◆ Reading Strategy

❶ Drawing Conclusion About Character Ask students to explain this passage. What conclusions can they draw about Judy's behavior and appearance from the reactions of her suitors? *Students should conclude that Judy is very beautiful but also that she is a skillful manipulator.*

◆ Critical Thinking

❷ Support The Jazz Age was a time of parties and the pursuit of a good time. Young men and women were increasingly breaking long-held rules about relationships, engaging in casual love affairs without serious commitment. Identify details from Dexter and Judy's interaction to support this statement. *Students should note that the relationship seems almost entirely physical, despite Dexter's acknowledgment that they are not engaged.*

◆ Grammar and Style

❸ Dashes Point out the set of dashes in this sentence. Ask students: What meaning does Fitzgerald add to the sentence by using these dashes? *Inserted around "she said" at the end of a list of Judy's prevarications, the dashes emphasize the final word "nothing."*

◆ Reading Strategy

❹ Draw Conclusions About Characters Students should be able to conclude that Dexter is so smitten by Judy and the world she symbolizes that despite his better judgment about her character, he can't turn away.

Customize for
Less Proficient Readers

Have students review the chronology of Dexter's and Judy's relationship, including the entrance of Irene Scheerer into Dexter's life. *Chronologies should show the following sequence: Dexter and Judy meet while he is a caddy (ages 14 and 11); Dexter and Judy meet again on the golf course with Mr. Hedrick and Mr. Hart (ages 23 and 20); for 18 months Dexter and Judy date; Dexter becomes engaged to Irene Scheerer (age 25).*

made these forays upon the helpless and defeated without malice, indeed half unconscious that there was anything mischievous in what she did.

When a new man came to town everyone dropped out—dates were automatically canceled.

The helpless part of trying to do anything about it was that she did it all herself. She was not a girl who could be "won" in the kinetic sense—she was proof against cleverness, she
❶ was proof against charm; if any of these assailed her too strongly she would immediately resolve the affair to a physical basis, and under the magic of her physical splendor the strong as well as the brilliant played her game and not their own. She was entertained only by the gratification of her desires and by the direct exercise of her own charm. Perhaps from so much youthful love, so many youthful lovers, she had come, in self-defense, to nourish herself wholly from within.

Succeeding Dexter's first exhilaration came restlessness and dissatisfaction. The helpless ecstasy of losing himself in her was opiate rather than tonic. It was fortunate for his work during the winter that those moments of ecstasy came infrequently. Early in their acquaintance it had seemed for a while that there was a deep and spontaneous mutual attraction—that first August, for example—three days of long evenings on her dusky veranda, of strange wan kisses through the late afternoon, in shadowy alcoves or behind the protecting trellises of the garden arbors, of mornings when she was fresh as a dream and almost shy at meeting him in the clarity of the rising day. There was all the ecstasy of an engagement about it,
❷ sharpened by his realization that there was no engagement. It was during those three days that, for the first time, he had asked her to marry him. She said "maybe some day," she
❸ said "kiss me," she said, "I'd like to marry you," she said "I love you"—she said—nothing.

The three days were interrupted by the arrival of a New York man who visited at her house for half September. To Dexter's agony, rumor engaged them. The man was the son of the president of a great trust company. But at the end of a month it was reported that Judy was yawning. At a dance one night she sat all evening in a motorboat with a local beau, while the New Yorker searched the club for her frantically. She told the local beau that she was bored with her visitor, and two days later he left. She was seen with him at the station, and it was reported that he looked very mournful indeed.

On this note the summer ended. Dexter was twenty-four, and he found himself increasingly in a position to do as he wished. He joined two clubs in the city and lived at one of them. Though he was by no means an integral part of the stag lines at these clubs, he managed to be on hand at dances where Judy Jones was likely to appear. He could have gone out socially as much as he liked—he was an eligible young man, now, and popular with downtown fathers. His confessed devotion to Judy Jones had rather solidified his position. But he had no social aspirations and rather despised the dancing men who were always on tap for the Thursday or Saturday parties and who filled in at dinners with the younger married set. Already he was playing with the idea of going East to New York. He wanted to take Judy Jones with him. No disillusion as to the world in which she had grown up could cure his illusion as to her desirability. ❹

> **◆ Reading Strategy** What does this observation reveal about the way in which Dexter regards Judy?

Remember that—for only in the light of it can what he did for her be understood.

Eighteen months after he first met Judy Jones he became engaged to another girl. Her name was Irene Scheerer, and her father was one of the men who had always believed in Dexter. Irene was light-haired and sweet and honorable, and a little stout, and she had two suitors whom she pleasantly relinquished when Dexter formally asked her to marry him.

Summer, fall, winter, spring, another summer, another fall—so much he had given of his active life to the incorrigible lips of Judy Jones. She had treated him with interest, with encouragement, with malice, with indifference, with contempt. She had inflicted on him the innumerable little slights and indignities possible in such a case—as if in revenge for having ever cared for him at all. She had beckoned him and yawned at him and beckoned him again and he had responded often with bitterness and

Cross-Curricular Connection: Science

Anatomy of Emotion As Dexter struggles to forsake Judy Jones, his reason battles with his emotions. Reason and decision-making are governed by the cerebrum, the largest part of the human brain. The cerebrum has two parts known as the left brain and the right brain, each of which controls the opposite side of the body. Scientists now believe there are important contrasts between the right and left brains of men and women which contribute to differences in behavior.

Emotions, while they arise from the brain, are associated with the heart. In fact, the heart and other physical elements change in response to emotion. Feelings of love, for example, may result in a faster heart rate, sweaty palms, weak knees, and loss of concentration.

Have students use this information to analyze Dexter's reactions to and decisions about Judy.

narrowed eyes. She had brought him ecstatic happiness and intolerable agony of spirit. She had caused him untold inconvenience and not a little trouble. She had insulted him, and she had ridden over him, and she had played his interest in her against his interest in his work—for fun. She had done everything to him except to criticize him—this she had not done—it seemed to him only because it might have sullied the utter indifference she manifested and sincerely felt toward him.

When autumn had come and gone again it occurred to him that he could not have Judy Jones. He had to beat this into his mind but he convinced himself at last. He lay awake at night for a while and argued it over. He told himself the trouble and the pain she had caused him, he enumerated her glaring deficiencies as a wife. Then he said to himself that he loved her, and after a while he fell asleep. For a week, lest he imagined her husky voice over the telephone or her eyes opposite him at lunch, he worked hard and late, and at night he went to his office and plotted out his years.

5 At the end of a week he went to a dance and cut in on her once. For almost the first time since they had met he did not ask her to sit out with him or tell her that she was lovely. It hurt him that she did not miss these things—that was all. He was not jealous when he saw that there was a new man tonight. He had been hardened against jealousy long before.

He stayed late at the dance. He sat for an hour with Irene Scheerer and talked about books and about music. He knew very little about either. But he was beginning to be master of his own time now, and he had a rather priggish[3] notion that he—the young and already fabulously successful Dexter Green—should know more about such things.

That was in October, when he was twenty-five. In January, Dexter and Irene became engaged. It was to be announced in June, and they were to be married three months later.

The Minnesota winter prolonged itself interminably, and it was almost May when the winds came soft and the snow ran down into Black Bear Lake at last. For the first time in over a year Dexter was enjoying a certain tranquility of spirit. Judy Jones had been in Florida, and afterward in Hot Springs, and somewhere she had been engaged, and somewhere she had broken it off. At first, when Dexter had definitely given her up, it had made him sad that people still linked them together and asked for news of her, but when he began to be placed at dinner next to Irene Scheerer people didn't ask him about her any more—they told him about her. He ceased to be an authority on her.

May at last. Dexter walked the streets at night when the darkness was damp as rain, wondering that so soon, with so little done, so much of ecstasy had gone from him. May one year back had been marked by Judy's poignant, unforgivable, yet forgiven turbulence—it had been one of those rare times when he fancied she had grown to care for him. That old penny's worth of happiness he had spent for this bushel of content. He knew that Irene would be no more than a curtain spread behind him, a hand moving among gleaming teacups, a voice calling to children . . . fire and loveliness were gone, the magic of nights and the wonder of the varying hours and seasons . . . slender lips, down-turning, dropping to his lips and bearing him up into a heaven of eyes . . . The thing was deep in him. He was too strong and alive for it to die lightly.

In the middle of May when the weather balanced for a few days on the thin bridge that led to deep summer he turned in one night at Irene's house. Their engagement was to be announced in a week now—no one would be surprised at it. And tonight they would sit together on the lounge at the University Club and look on for an hour at the dancers. It gave him a sense of solidity to go with her—she was so sturdily popular, so intensely "great." 6

He mounted the steps of the brownstone house and stepped inside.

"Irene," he called.

Mrs. Scheerer came out of the living room to meet him.

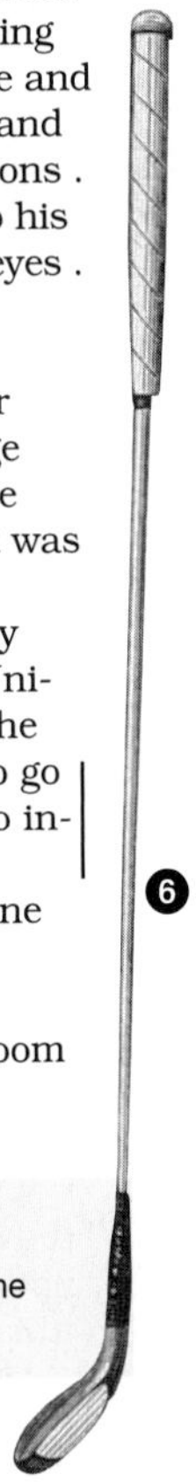

◆ Build Vocabulary

poignant (poin′ yənt) *adj.*: Sharply painful to the feelings

3. **priggish** (prig′ ish) *adj.*: Excessively proper and smug.

Customize for *Verbal/Linguistic Learners*

To help these students cull a word picture of Judy Jones, ask them to pare Dexter's recounting of Judy's behavior down to its essential words. Looking only at these lists, have student pairs brainstorm a description of the person revealed. *Descriptions might include qualities such as troublemaker, inconsistent, indifferent, and insensitive.*

Customize for *AP Students*

Help these students to appreciate the depth of Dexter's tumult. Six months after renouncing Judy in favor of sturdy Irene Scheerer, Dexter remains painfully saddened by his memories. Challenge students to look back to find other examples of Dexter's doomed struggle to stop wanting Judy Jones. *They might mention his distraught decision-making night or his willingness to find comfort in deceit.*

◆ Critical Thinking

5 Compare and Contrast How does Dexter's behavior toward Judy change after his decision to stop pursuing her? *He deliberately keeps his physical and emotional distance.*

◆ Literary Focus

6 Characterization Ask students: What method of characterization does Fitzgerald use to portray Irene? *He tells readers about Dexter's reaction to Irene–indirectly characterizing Irene in the process.*

Humanities: Music

Jazz The music Dexter hears as Judy Jones sweeps by is surely jazz. Jazz traces its roots to African music brought to America by the Africans forced into slavery. Unique African rhythms later blended with gospel music and other influences to create jazz—a music characterized by improvisational rhythms woven from trumpet, trombone, clarinet, and later saxophone, as well as piano and vocals.

By the early 1900's, jazz was flourishing in the African American community in cities such as New Orleans. With riverboat traffic bringing Northerners up and down the Mississippi, this exciting music began to spread to the North and into white communities. Important jazz musicians like Joe "King" Oliver and Louis Armstrong migrated north to Chicago where they spearheaded the explosion of jazz onto the international scene.

Have students discuss their responses to jazz music and describe the mood it would generate for Judy and Dexter.

◆ Grammar and Style

1 Dashes Highlight the use of a single dash in Dexter's comment. Ask students to explain its function here. *Students should note that the dash replaces the unspoken remainder of Dexter's sentence, which Fitzgerald here implies is too mundane to mention.* What words might replace the dash? *Words might include "hope" or "trust."*

◆ *Literature and Your Life*

2 Draw students' attention to Dexter's reaction to Judy. Prompt them to recall a situation in which they re-met someone who was once very important. How did they react and what were their emotions? *Students may recall discovering with surprise that their emotions and reactions were still quite strong.*

◆ Reading Strategy

3 Draw Conclusions About Characters What do Dexter's thoughts suggest about his feelings for Judy? *He is still strongly affected by her, despite his efforts to control his reactions.*

◆ Critical Thinking

4 Compare and Contrast How is Judy different from the previous times she and Dexter have met? *She no longer smiles, she seems sad, she's lost some of her originality and charm.* In what ways is she the same? *She is still beautiful and still seeks attention.*

◆ *Literature and Your Life*

5 Students may mention times when they knew a sibling or friend had done something wrong or times when they should have acknowledged their own culpability but didn't.

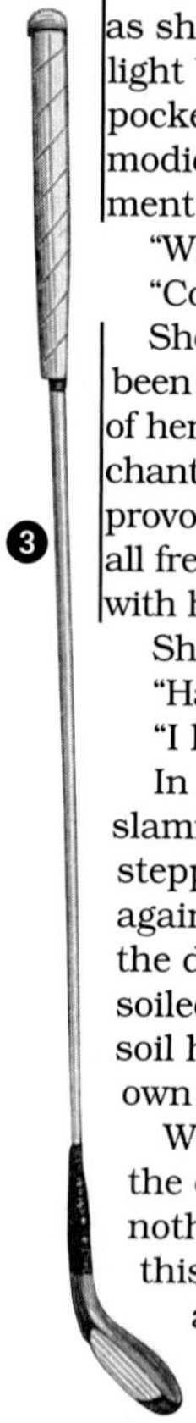

"Dexter," she said, "Irene's gone upstairs with a splitting headache. She wanted to go with you but I made her go to bed."

1 "Nothing serious, I——"

"Oh, no. She's going to play golf with you in the morning. You can spare her for just one night, can't you, Dexter?"

Her smile was kind. She and Dexter liked each other. In the living room he talked for a moment before he said good night.

Returning to the University Club, where he had rooms, he stood in the doorway for a moment and watched the dancers. He leaned against the doorpost, nodded at a man or two—yawned.

"Hello, darling."

The familiar voice at his elbow startled him. Judy Jones had left a man and crossed the room to him—Judy Jones, a slender enameled doll in cloth of gold: gold in a band at her head, gold in two slipper points at her dress's hem. The fragile glow of her face seemed to blossom as she smiled at him. A breeze of warmth and light blew through the room. His hands in the pockets of his dinner jacket tightened spasmodically. He was filled with a sudden excitement.

"When did you get back?" he asked casually.

"Come here and I'll tell you about it."

3 She turned and he followed her. She had been away—he could have wept at the wonder of her return. She had passed through enchanted streets, doing things that were like provocative music. All mysterious happenings, all fresh and quickening hopes, had gone away with her, come back with her now.

She turned in the doorway.

"Have you a car here? If you haven't, I have."

"I have a coupé."

In then, with a rustle of golden cloth. He slammed the door. Into so many cars she had stepped—like this—like that—her back against the leather, so—her elbow resting on the door—waiting. She would have been soiled long since had there been anything to soil her—except herself—but this was her own self outpouring.

With an effort he forced himself to start the car and back into the street. This was nothing, he must remember. She had done this before, and he had put her behind him, as he would have crossed a bad account from his books.

He drove slowly downtown and, affecting abstraction, traversed the deserted streets of the business section, peopled here and there where a movie was giving out its crowd or where consumptive or pugilistic youth lounged in front of pool halls. The clink of glasses and the slap of hands on the bars issued from saloons, cloisters of glazed glass and dirty yellow light.

She was watching him closely and the silence was embarrassing, yet in this crisis he could find no casual word with which to profane the hour. At a convenient turning he began to zigzag back toward the University Club.

"Have you missed me?" she asked suddenly.

"Everybody missed you."

He wondered if she knew of Irene Scheerer. She had been back only a day—her absence had been almost contemporaneous with his engagement.

"What a remark!" Judy laughed sadly—without sadness. She looked at him searchingly. He became absorbed in the dashboard. 4

"You're handsomer than you used to be," she said thoughtfully. "Dexter, you have the most rememberable eyes."

He could have laughed at this, but he did not laugh. It was the sort of thing that was said to sophomores. Yet it stabbed at him.

"I'm awfully tired of everything, darling." She called everyone darling, endowing the endearment with careless, individual camaraderie.[4] "I wish you'd marry me."

The directness of this confused him. He should have told her now that he was going to marry another girl, but he could not tell her. He could as easily have sworn that he had never loved her.

> ◆ ***Literature and Your Life***
>
> Like Dexter, have you ever kept quiet when you knew that telling the truth was the right thing to do? 5

"I think we'd get along," she continued, on the same note, "unless probably you've forgotten me and fallen in love with another girl."

Her confidence was obviously enormous. She had said, in effect, that she found such a thing

4. **camaraderie** (käm´ ə räd´ ər ē) *n.*: Warm, friendly feelings.

Cultural Connection

Marriage Customs In other times and cultures Dexter and Judy might have had little to say about whether they married. The choice of marriage partner is sometimes severely restricted by cultural and religious beliefs. For example, in cultures such as apartheid South Africa with very distinct ethnic and social groups, intermarriage amongst groups was strongly discouraged. In other cultures—Islam or Orthodox Judaism, for example—marriages might be arranged by parents of the couple. Couples are restricted from marrying before a certain age in many cultures. Even in the largely open culture of America, the idea of marrying for love without parental guidance is a fairly recent trend. Marriages have often been influenced by economic reasons, as families seek to expand holdings or shore up finances.

Ask students to contribute information about marriage customs in cultures with which they are familiar. Research as a class if necessary. Then discuss which methods students feel are most likely to produce successful marriages.

impossible to believe, that if it were true he had merely committed a childish indiscretion—and probably to show off. She would forgive him, because it was not a matter of any moment but rather something to be brushed aside lightly.

"Of course you could never love anybody but me," she continued, "I like the way you love me. Oh, Dexter, have you forgotten last year?"

"No, I haven't forgotten."

"Neither have I!"

Was she sincerely moved—or was she carried along by the wave of her own acting?

"I wish we could be like that again," she said, and he forced himself to answer:

"I don't think we can."

"I suppose not. . . . I hear you're giving Irene Scheerer a violent rush."

There was not the faintest emphasis on the name, yet Dexter was suddenly ashamed.

"Oh, take me home," cried Judy suddenly; "I don't want to go back to that idiotic dance—with those children."

Then, as he turned up the street that led to the residence district, Judy began to cry quietly to herself. He had never seen her cry before.

The dark street lightened, the dwellings of the rich loomed up around them, he stopped his coupé in front of the great white bulk of the
6 Mortimer Joneses' house, somnolent, gorgeous, drenched with the splendor of the damp moonlight. Its solidity startled him. The strong walls, the steel of the girders, the breadth and beam and pomp of it were there only to bring out the contrast with the young beauty beside him. It was sturdy to accentuate her slightness—as if to show what a breeze could be generated by a butterfly's wing.

He sat perfectly quiet, his nerves in wild clamor, afraid that if he moved he would find her irresistibly in his arms. Two tears had rolled down her wet face and trembled on her upper lip.

"I'm more beautiful than anybody else," she said brokenly, "why can't I be happy?" Her moist eyes tore at his stability—her mouth turned slowly downward with an exquisite sadness: "I'd like to marry you if you'll have me, Dexter. I suppose you think I'm not worth having, but I'll be so beautiful for you, Dexter."

> **◆ Literary Focus**
> 7 How does this wistful remark add to Fitzgerald's portrait of Judy's character? Do you think Judy has changed?

A million phrases of anger, pride, passion, hatred, tenderness fought on his lips. Then a perfect wave of emotion washed over him, carrying off with it a sediment of wisdom, of convention, of doubt, of honor. This was his girl who was speaking, his own, his beautiful, his pride.

"Won't you come in?" He heard her draw in her breath sharply.

Waiting.

"All right," his voice was trembling, "I'll come in." 8

V

It was strange that neither when it was over nor a long time afterward did he regret that night. Looking at it from the perspective of ten years, the fact that Judy's flare for him endured just one month seemed of little importance. Nor did it matter that by his yielding he subjected himself to a deeper agony in the end and gave serious hurt to Irene Scheerer and to Irene's parents, who had befriended him. There was nothing sufficiently pictorial about Irene's grief to stamp itself on his mind.

Dexter was at bottom hard-minded. The attitude of the city on his action was of no importance to him, not because he was going to leave the city, but because any outside attitude on the situation seemed superficial. He was completely indifferent to popular opinion. Nor, when he had seen that it was no use, that he did not possess in himself the power to move fundamentally or to hold Judy Jones, did he bear any malice toward her. He loved her, and he would love her until the day he was too old for loving—but he could not have her. So he tasted the deep pain that is reserved only for the strong, just as he had tasted for a little while the deep happiness. 9

Even the ultimate falsity of the grounds upon which Judy terminated the engagement that she did not want to "take him away" from Irene—Judy who had wanted nothing else—did

> **◆ Build Vocabulary**
> **pugilistic** (pyo͞o´ jə lis´ tik) *adj.*: Looking for a fight
> **somnolent** (säm´ nə lənt) *adj.*: Sleepy; drowsy

◆ Build Vocabulary

6 The Latin Root *-somn-* Point out the word *somnolent* and have students define it using the word root *-somn-*. *The word means "to induce sleep."* Then ask them to describe Mortimer Jones' house. Ask: How does understanding the word root enhance your image of the house? *Descriptions should recognize the house's size and sense of immobility and should reflect students' understanding of "somnolent."*

◆ Literary Focus

7 Characterization The comment shows that Judy is capable of some self-awareness. Still, with all the previous information about her character, most students should feel that Judy is not capable of true growth or lasting change.

◆ Critical Thinking

8 Make a Judgment Ask students: Do you think Dexter is making a wise choice here? Why or why not? *Students should sense that no good will come of Dexter and Judy meeting again. Each earlier meeting has led to pain as Judy abandons Dexter as soon as her ego was sufficiently stroked.*

◆ Literary Focus

9 Characterization Ask students to summarize what this passage reveals about Dexter. *Dexter is not concerned for convention or the views of others. He follows his emotions. He is an idealist.*

Beyond the Classroom

Community Connection

Men at War Some 16 million American men and women served in World War II. Many were overseas for several years. Encourage the class to discuss the possible effects their absence had on the communities left behind. For example, students may mention families left with only one parent, an insufficient labor force, a call for more women in the labor force, and an increase in financial struggles. Urge students to study town records, speak with older residents, and visit historical societies to learn how your community was affected by World War II.

Career Connection

Service Jobs In this story, Dexter makes his initial fortune with a chain of laundries. He maintains high standards to ensure that his customers' clothing is never damaged. These standards and attention to customers' specific requests establish his laundries' reputation.

Today, service businesses are among the fastest growing sectors of the American economy, expected to double by the year 2005. Have students survey local service businesses. What standards must be met to achieve success? How do businesses strive to meet these standards?

◆ *Literature and Your Life*

1 Discuss Dexter's relief over going to war. Ask students if they have ever wished so strongly to get away from an emotional situation that they would welcome an unpleasant or even horrible alternative with relief. *Students may mention unhappy romantic relationships, difficulties with parents, or family changes such as death or divorce. Students should be given the option of keeping their response private.*

◆ Reading Strategy

2 Drawing Conclusions About Character Ask students: What do you think has happened to Judy to bring about this change? *Suggested responses: Students should grasp that while Judy was once unhappy but beautiful and desirable, she is now unhappy and neglected. They should be able to conclude that Judy is a person who will wilt without admiration.*

◆ Critical Thinking

3 Interpret Why does Dexter become angry with Devlin? *Dexter views Devlin as the bearer of bad news, the person who has shattered his belief that Judy's beauty still exists somewhere in the world.*

◆ Literary Focus

4 Characterization Ask students how Fitzgerald paints his final picture of Judy's character. *Fitzgerald uses the comments of another character, Devlin, along with Dexter's reactions, to complete his portrait of Judy.*

not revolt him. He was beyond any revulsion or any amusement.

He went East in February with the intention of selling out his laundries and settling in New York—but the war came to America in March and changed his plans. He returned to the West, handed over the management of the business to his partner, and went into the first officers' training camp in late April. He was one
1 of those young thousands who greeted the war with a certain amount of relief, welcoming the liberation from webs of tangled emotion.

VI

This story is not his biography, remember, although things creep into it which have nothing to do with those dreams he had when he was young. We are almost done with them and with him now. There is only one more incident to be related here, and it happens seven years farther on.

It took place in New York, where he had done well—so well that there were no barriers too high for him. He was thirty-two years old, and, except for one flying trip immediately after the war, he had not been West in seven years. A man named Devlin from Detroit came into his office to see him in a business way, and then and there this incident occurred, and closed out, so to speak, this particular side of his life.

"So you're from the Middle West," said the man Devlin with careless curiosity. "That's funny—I thought men like you were probably born and raised on Wall Street. You know—wife of one of my best friends in Detroit came from your city. I was an usher at the wedding."

Dexter waited with no apprehension of what was coming.

"Judy Simms," said Devlin with no particular interest; "Judy Jones she was once."

"Yes, I knew her." A dull impatience spread over him. He had heard, of course, that she was married—perhaps deliberately he had heard no more.

"Awfully nice girl," brooded Devlin meaninglessly, "I'm sort of sorry for her."

"Why?" Something in Dexter was alert, re-
2 ceptive, at once.

"Oh, Lud Simms has gone to pieces in a way. I don't mean he ill-uses her, but he drinks and runs around——"

"Doesn't she run around?"

"No. Stays at home with her kids."

"Oh."

"She's a little too old for him," said Devlin. 2

"Too old!" cried Dexter. "Why, man, she's only twenty-seven."

He was possessed with a wild notion of rushing out into the streets and taking a train to Detroit. He rose to his feet spasmodically.

"I guess you're busy," Devlin apologized quickly. "I didn't realize——"

"No, I'm not busy," said Dexter, steadying his voice. "I'm not busy at all. Not busy at all. Did you say she was—twenty-seven? No, I said she was twenty-seven."

"Yes, you did," agreed Devlin dryly.

"Go on, then. Go on."

"What do you mean?"

"About Judy Jones."

Devlin looked at him helplessly.

"Well, that's—I told you all there is to it. He treats her like the devil. Oh, they're not going to get divorced or anything. When he's particularly outrageous she forgives him. In fact, I'm inclined to think she loves him. She was a pretty girl when she first came to Detroit. "

A pretty girl! The phrase struck Dexter as ludicrous.

"Isn't she—a pretty girl, anymore?"

"Oh, she's all right."

"Look here," said Dexter, sitting down suddenly. "I don't understand. You say she was a 'pretty girl' and now you say she's 'all right.' I
don't understand what you mean—Judy Jones 3
wasn't a pretty girl, at all. She was a great beauty. Why, I knew her. I knew her. She was ——"

Devlin laughed pleasantly.

"I'm not trying to start a row," he said. "I think Judy's a nice girl and I like her. I can't understand how a man like Lud Simms could fall madly in love with her, but he did." Then he added: "Most of the women like her."

Dexter looked closely at Devlin, thinking wildly that there must be a reason for this, some insensitivity in the man or some private malice.

"Lots of women fade just like *that*," Devlin snapped his fingers. "You must have seen it
happen. Perhaps I've forgotten how pretty she 4
was at her wedding. I've seen her so much since then, you see. She has nice eyes."

A sort of dullness settled down upon Dexter.

Reteach

Tell students that one of the qualities that made Fitzgerald a great writer was his capacity to develop characters with psychological depth and realism. His characters can surprise readers, just as real people may do.

Draw a graphic organizer like the one shown to help students draw conclusions about Judy Jones's character: Was she a selfish person in the end? Upon what actions do students base their conclusions? Have students suggest actions to fill out both sides of the organizer. If students have trouble finding unselfish actions, remind them about the final scene of the story.

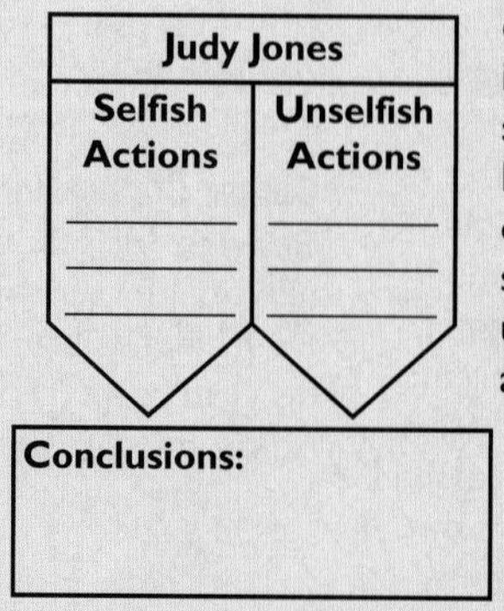

For the first time in his life he felt like getting very drunk. He knew that he was laughing loudly at something Devlin had said, but he did not know what it was or why it was funny. When, in a few minutes, Devlin went he lay down on his lounge and looked out the window at the New York skyline into which the sun was sinking in dull lovely shades of pink and gold.

5 He had thought that having nothing else to lose he was invulnerable at last—but he knew that he had just lost something more, as surely as if he had married Judy Jones and seen her fade away before his eyes.

The dream was gone. Something had been taken from him. In a sort of panic he pushed the palms of his hands into his eyes and tried to bring up a picture of the waters lapping on Sherry Island and the moonlit veranda, and gingham on the golf links and the dry sun and the gold color of her neck's soft down. And her mouth damp to his kisses and her eyes plaintive with melancholy and her freshness like new fine linen in the morning. Why, these things were no longer in the world! They had existed and they existed no longer.

For the first time in years the tears were streaming down his face. But they were for himself now. He did not care about mouth and eyes and moving hands. He wanted to care, and he could not care. For he had gone away and he could never go back any more. The gates were closed, the sun was gone down, and there was no beauty but the gray beauty of steel that withstands all time. Even the grief he could have borne was left behind in the country of illusion, of youth, of the richness of life, where his winter dreams had flourished.

"Long ago," he said, "long ago, there was something in me, but now that thing is gone. Now that thing is gone, that thing is gone. I cannot cry. I cannot care. That thing will come back no more."

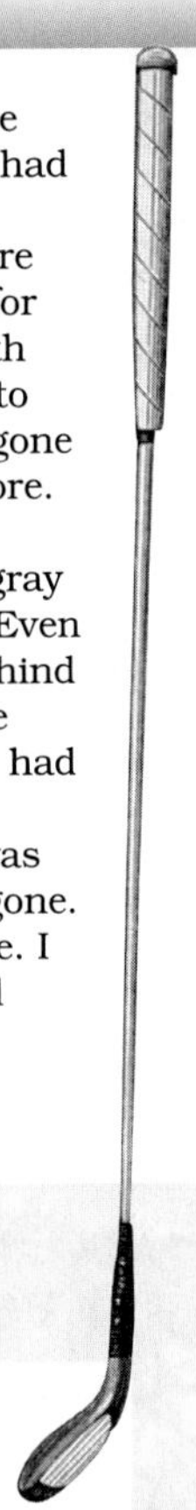

Guide for Responding

◆ Literature and Your Life

Reader's Response Do you feel sorry for Judy? For Dexter? Why or why not?

Thematic Response How do Dexter's feelings for Judy dictate the course of his life?

Questions for Research Generate questions that would help you research themes in Fitzgerald's stories. Consider settings, character similarities, and tones. What sources could you use to begin your research?

☑ Check Your Comprehension

1. (a) What action does Dexter take as a result of his first meeting with Judy Jones? (b) What happens the second time they meet?
2. How does Judy behave during her romance with Dexter?
3. Why does Dexter become engaged to another woman but later break the engagement?
4. What happens to Dexter and Judy's relationship after he breaks his engagement with Irene?
5. How does Devlin shatter Dexter's image of Judy?

◆ Critical Thinking

INTERPRETING

1. What are Dexter's "winter dreams," and how does Judy fit into those dreams? **[Interpret]**
2. Find two examples in the story that demonstrate how Judy's casual decisions or behavior changes Dexter's life in important ways. **[Connect]**
3. What does the decision to become engaged to Irene symbolize for Dexter? **[Infer]**
4. (a) What does Judy represent to Dexter? (b) Why does Dexter keep loving Judy even after he has lost her? **[Analyze]**

EVALUATE

5. Are Dexter's values and ideals influenced by the times in which he lived, or would his feelings for Judy Jones have been the same in any era? Explain. **[Assess]**

APPLY

6. How might the story have been different if Dexter had married Judy? **[Modify]**

Beyond the Selection

FURTHER READING

Other Works by F. Scott Fitzgerald

This Side of Paradise, The Great Gatsby, Tender Is the Night, The Last Tycoon

Other Works With the Theme of Coming of Age

Invisible Man, Ralph Ellison
Lord of the Flies, William Golding
"Everyday Use," Alice Walker

We suggest that you preview these works before recommending them to students.

INTERNET

You and your students may find additional information about F. Scott Fitzgerald on the Internet. We suggest the following site. Please be aware, however, that sites may have changed since this information was published.

For a comprehensive site devoted to the works of Fitzgerald, visit **http://www.sc.edu/fitzgerald**

We *strongly recommend* that you preview sites before you send students to them.

◆ Reading Strategy

5 Draw Conclusions About Characters Ask students to explain what Dexter's reaction to news of Judy suggests about his character? *Students may say that Dexter has remained an idealist, holding onto the idea of Judy's desirability even through his own loss.*

Reinforce and Extend

Customize for
Less Proficient Readers
Less proficient readers will benefit greatly from reviewing story events. Urge students to identify passages they found confusing and try to place these in the overall story sequence.

Answers

Reader's Response Students should support their answers with clear reasons.

Thematic Focus Dexter's love for Judy leads him to break off his engagement with another woman.

☑ Check Your Comprehension

1. (a) He quits his job as a caddy. (b) He falls in love with her.
2. She sees other men and has little regard for his feelings.
3. Irene is sweet, dependable, and devoted, the opposite of Judy. He breaks the engagement because Judy shows interest in him.
4. She loses interest in him.
5. He reveals that Judy has lost her good looks and is unhappily married.

◆ Critical Thinking

1. His "winter dreams" are dreams of acquiring "glittering things."
2. She causes him to quit his caddying job, and later leads him to break off an engagement.
3. It represents a more stable life.
4. (a) She represents the ultimate "glittering thing" to Dexter. (b) He is obsessed with her and the ideal that she represents to him.
5. Students may answer that many people in today's world are also obsessed with money and status.
6. Possible response: Dexter might have discovered that his feelings toward Judy would change as a result of spending every day with her.

Guide for Responding *(continued)*

◆ Literary Focus

Characterization

Fitzgerald uses **characterization**—a variety of techniques that reveal characters' personalities—to paint multi-dimensional portraits of Judy and Dexter. We learn about Judy and Dexter through **direct characterization**—the narrator's comments about their personalities—as well as through **indirect characterization**—their own actions and words and other characters' reactions to them.

1. Cite at least two examples from the story of Fitzgerald's use of direct characterization to characterize Judy and Dexter.

2. Cite two examples of indirect characterization of Judy and Dexter, and explain what you learn from each example.

3. (a) In what ways are Dexter and Judy alike? (b) In what ways are they different? (c) Explain which details of characterization lead you to draw your conclusions.

◆ Build Vocabulary

Using the Latin Root *-somn-*

The Latin root *-somn-* means "sleep." Using each of the words defined below, write a brief paragraph about a student who keeps nodding off in class because he or she can't sleep at night.

insomnia *n.*: Prolonged inability to sleep
somnolent *adj.*: Sleepy; drowsy
somniloquist *n.*: One who talks in his or her sleep
somnambulation *n.*: The action of walking while sleeping

Using the Word Bank: Antonyms

On a separate sheet of paper, write the letter of the word that is the best antonym of the first word.

1. fallowness	**a.** activity	**b.** emptiness
2. preposterous	**a.** serious	**b.** sarcastic
3. fortuitous	**a.** wealthy	**b.** cursed
4. sinuous	**a.** straight	**b.** slippery
5. mundane	**a.** legal	**b.** amazing
6. poignant	**a.** dull	**b.** moving
7. pugilistic	**a.** tough	**b.** peace-loving
8. somnolent	**a.** alert	**b.** hard

◆ Reading Strategy

Draw Conclusions About Character

As you read, you **drew conclusions** about Judy and Dexter. You gathered details about their actions and words and, using your own knowledge of human behavior, read between the lines to infer emotions and motivations not directly stated. Now demonstrate what you have learned by writing an account of Dexter and Judy's last meeting. What did they say and how did they act as she broke off their engagement? Use the conclusions you have drawn to help you develop your descriptions of their behavior. Include dialogue in your account.

◆ Grammar and Style

Dashes

Fitzgerald makes abundant use of dashes to introduce asides that seem to compete for the reader's attention. These dashes reflect the frenetic competition for the spotlight that characterized the writer's life and times. In your writing, use dashes only occasionally for dramatic effect, to surprise, or to emphasize.

Dashes are punctuation marks that set off information that interrupts the flow of a sentence. Dashes are stronger and more emphatic than commas.

Practice In your notebook, write the following sentences. Insert dashes where necessary to set off dramatic ideas or abrupt changes in thought.

1. Mr. Hart one of those golfers who like to yell *Fore!* at the top of their lungs gave him a guest card to a prestigious local golf club.

2. He was glad her parents were not there they might wonder who he was.

3. Whatever she smiled at at him, at a chicken liver, at nothing it disturbed him that her smile could have no root in mirth.

4. He had the notion that she and this was the really strange part actually had feelings for him.

Writing Application Write a brief description of someone you admire. Use dashes to set off a few pieces of information you want readers to notice.

◆ Literary Focus

Answers

1. Possible answers include: The narrator comments, "do not get the impression . . . that there was anything merely snobbish in the boy." The narrator also points out that Dexter wanted the "glittering things themselves." The narrator observes that Judy Jones was "not a girl who could be 'won' in the kinetic sense . . ." The narrator later observes that perhaps Judy had come "to nourish herself totally from within."
2. Possible answer: Judy Jones's treatment of Dexter at the beginning of the story is an example of indirect characterization, as is Mr. Hedrick's remark that Judy "always looks as if she wanted to be kissed . . ." Dexter's reaction to Judy Jones's treatment of him at the beginning of the story reveals his pride. Dexter's decision to break off his engagement when Judy shows renewed interest in him illustrates the degree to which he can be manipulated.
3. (a) Students may point out that they are both materialistic. (b) Students may note that Judy comes from a wealthy background, while Dexter does not. (c) Students should use evidence from the text to support their responses.

◆ Build Vocabulary

Using the Latin Root *-somn-*
Check to see that students have used each word correctly.

Using the Word Bank
1. a 2. a 3. b 4. a 5. b
6. a 7. b 8. a

◆ Reading Strategy

You may want to have students exchange papers to evaluate one another's work. Students should base their assessments on each writer's ability to create likely scenarios.

◆ Grammar and Style

1. Mr. Hart—one of those golfers who like to yell *Fore!* at the top of their lungs—gave him a guest card to a prestigious local golf club.
2. He was glad her parents were not there—they might wonder who he was.
3. Whatever she smiled at—at him, at a chicken liver, at nothing—it disturbed him that her smile could have no root in mirth.
4. He had the notion that she—and this was the really strange part—actually had feelings for him.

Writing Application
Check to see that students do not overuse dashes in their descriptions.

Grammar Reinforcement

For additional instruction and practice, use the page on dashes, p. 93, in the *Writer's Solution Grammar Practice Book.*

Build Your Portfolio

Idea Bank

Writing

1. **Diary Entry** Fitzgerald never tells us what Judy thinks of or feels for Dexter. Write the diary entry she might have written to describe their meeting on the lake. What are her impressions?

2. **Résumé** Consider the skills and character traits Dexter demonstrates in the story. Then write a résumé that he might use to be considered for a management job. **[Career Link]**

3. **Essay** According to one critic, Fitzgerald's best work "caught not only the irresponsibility of the years following [World War I] but pointed also to the sources of personal and moral corruption implicit in a society based upon the social and moral prerogatives of wealth." Write an essay in which you demonstrate how this observation applies to "Winter Dreams."

Speaking, Listening, and Viewing

4. **Enactment** Imagine that Dexter and Judy meet a month after the story's close. With a partner, write and perform the conversation they might have. **[Performing Arts Link]**

5. **Musical Interpretation** Select a song that might remind Dexter of his relationship with Judy. Play the song for the class, and discuss why it is appropriate. **[Music Link]**

Researching and Representing

6. **Montage** Create a montage of words and images that reflect the values, fads, and fashions of the "Roaring Twenties." **[Social Studies Link]**

7. **Report** Research the lives of F. Scott and Zelda Fitzgerald. Then write a report on the couple's relationship and lifestyle and how they may have influenced Fitzgerald's works.

Online Activity www.phlit.phschool.com

Guided Writing Lesson

Character Analysis

Dexter Green comes vividly to life because F. Scott Fitzgerald portrays him as a fully-rounded character with believable thoughts and feelings, strengths and weaknesses. Explore Dexter's behavior, motivations, and weak and strong traits in a character analysis. Support your ideas with specific examples from the story.

Writing Skills Focus: Elaboration to Give Information

Elaborate by providing information that supports your analysis of Dexter's personality:

- After making general statements about the character's personality, elaborate with precise details from the story.
- Describe Dexter's behavior with specific examples.
- Paraphrase or quote exactly from the text to support your judgments of the character.
- Identify Dexter's strengths and weaknesses, using the reactions of other characters to him.

Prewriting Scan the story for examples of Dexter's appearance, words, actions, and motivations. Note how he changes during the story and whether his actions seem heroic or simply foolish.

Drafting In your opening statement, name the author and title of the work, identify the character to be discussed, then grab readers' attention by stating your most important idea about the character. You might organize the rest of your analysis around strengths and weaknesses, addressing first one and then the other.

Revising Read your essay. Have you conveyed your opinion? Have you supported your view with elaboration? Where needed, add specific quotations or other details to support your points.

Idea Bank

Customizing for
Performance Levels

Following are suggestions for matching Idea Bank topics with your students' performance levels:
Less Advanced Students: 1, 5, 6
Average Students: 2, 4, 6, 7
More Advanced Students: 3, 4, 7

Customizing for
Learning Modalities

Following are suggestions for matching Idea Bank topics with your students' learning modalities:
Interpersonal: 4
Musical/Rhythmic: 5
Visual/Spatial: 6

Guided Writing Lesson

Writers at Work Videodisc

Have students view the videodisc segment on Response to Literature (Ch. 7) featuring literary agent Theresa Park to learn how she analyzes a piece of literature. Have students discuss what they can learn from Park that they can apply to writing a character analysis.

Play frames 22513 to 31258

For more prewriting, elaboration, and revision strategies, see *Prentice Hall Writing and Grammar.*

Writing Lab CD-ROM

Have students complete the tutorial on Response to Literature. Follow these steps:

1. Have students look at the interactive model of a literary analysis.
2. Have students use the Character Personality Profile activity to help them gather details.
3. Have students draft on computer.
4. Have students use the Self-Evaluation Checklist to aid in revision.

✓ ASSESSMENT OPTIONS

Formal Assessment, Selection Test, pp. 203–205, and Assessment Resources Software. The selection test is designed so that it can be easily customized to the performance levels of your students.

Alternative Assessment, p. 43, includes options for less advanced students, more advanced students, intrapersonal learners, interpersonal learners, and visual/spatial learners.

PORTFOLIO ASSESSMENT

Use the following rubrics in the ***Alternative Assessment*** booklet to assess student writing:
Diary Entry: Expression Rubric, p. 109
Resume: Resume and Cover Letter Rubric, p. 129
Essay: Literary Analysis/Interpretation Rubric, p. 127
Guided Writing Lesson: Literary Analysis/Interpretation Rubric, p. 127

Prepare and Engage

LESSON OBJECTIVES

1. **To develop vocabulary and word identification skills**
   - Latin Prefixes: *pro-*
   - Using the Word Bank: True or False?
2. **To use a variety of reading strategies to comprehend a poem**
   - Connect Your Experience
   - Reading Strategy: Find Clues to Theme
3. **To express and support responses to the text**
   - Critical Thinking Questions
   - Idea Bank: Description
4. **To analyze literary elements**
   - Literary Focus: Theme
   - Idea Bank: Literary Analysis
5. **To read to do research on a self-selected or an assigned topic**
   - Idea Bank: Essay
   - Idea Bank: Interview
   - Idea Bank: Environmental Report
6. **To plan, prepare, organize, and present literary interpretations**
   - Idea Bank: Monologue
   - Idea Bank: Cartoon
7. **To use recursive writing processes to write an observation**
   - Guided Writing Lesson
8. **To increase knowledge of the rules of grammar and usage**
   - Grammar and Style: Parallel Structure

Test Preparation

Reading Comprehension: Analyze Sentence Meaning (ATE, p. 687)
The teaching tips and sample test item in this workshop support the instruction and practice in the unit workshop:
Reading Comprehension: Sentence-Completion Questions (SE, p. 863)

Guide for Interpreting

John Steinbeck *(1902–1968)*

No writer more vividly captures what it was like to live through the Great Depression of the 1930's than John Steinbeck.

His stories and novels, many of which are set in the agricultural region of Northern California where he grew up, capture the poverty, desperation, and social injustice experienced by many working class Americans during this bleak period in our nation's history. As in the works of Naturalist writers like Stephen Crane and Jack London, Steinbeck's characters struggle desperately against forces beyond their understanding or control. Many of his characters suffer tragic fates, yet they almost always manage to exhibit bravery and retain a sense of dignity throughout their struggles.

Modest Beginnings Steinbeck was born in Salinas, California, the son of a county official and a schoolteacher. By his late teens, he was already supporting himself by working as a laborer. After graduating from high school, he enrolled at Stanford University. He left before graduating, however, and spent the next five years drifting across the country, working as a fish hatcher, fruit picker, and apprentice painter. Through these experiences, Steinbeck discovered firsthand what it means to survive by manual labor.

Steinbeck also gathered material that he would later be able to use in his literary works to create authentic portraits of working-class life.

Even before he was paid for his words, Steinbeck always found time to write. However, he had little success as a writer until 1935 when he published *Tortilla Flat*, his third novel. Two years later, he earned widespread recognition and critical acclaim with *Of Mice and Men* (1937). This novel, which portrays two migrant workers whose dream of owning a farm ends in tragedy, became a best seller and was made into a Broadway play and a movie.

The Great American Novel Steinbeck went on to write what is generally regarded as his finest novel. *The Grapes of Wrath* (1939) is the accurate and emotional story of the Joad family, Oklahoma farmers dispossessed of their land and forced to become migrant farmers in California. "The Turtle" is an excerpt from the opening pages of this novel which won the National Book Award and the Pulitzer Prize. The book established Steinbeck as one of the most highly regarded writers of his day.

Steinbeck produced several more successful works during his later years, including *Cannery Row* (1945), *The Pearl* (1947), *East of Eden* (1951), and *The Winter of Our Discontent* (1961). Steinbeck received the Nobel Prize for Literature in 1962.

◆ Background for Understanding

HISTORY: THE GREAT DEPRESSION

The Great Depression of the 1930's was a time of unparalleled financial hardship. In 1932 a quarter of Americans—at least 12 million—were out of work. One of many factors contributing to the Depression was a massive drought in Oklahoma. The drought was so bad that farmlands literally blew away in massive dust storms that sometimes lasted several days. Many farmers fled the land for the city, hoping to find relief away from nature's failure. This is the situation faced by the Joad family who, like the turtle in this piece, are repelled by a commercial world that cares nothing for them.

Prentice Hall Literature Program Resources

REINFORCE / RETEACH / EXTEND

Selection Support Pages
Build Vocabulary: Prefixes: *pro-*, p. 204
Grammar and Style: Parallel Structure, p. 205
Reading Strategy: Find Clues to Theme, p. 206
Literary Focus: Theme, p. 207

Strategies for Diverse Student Needs Outline Main Idea and Supporting Details, p. 44

Beyond Literature
Workplace Skills: Survival, p. 44

Formal Assessment Selection Test, pp. 206–208; Assessment Resources Software

Alternative Assessment, p. 44

Writing and Language Transparencies
Research Report (pp. 41–50)

Resource Pro CD-ROM

Literature CD-ROM

Listening to Literature Audiocassettes

The Turtle

◆ Literature and Your Life

CONNECT YOUR EXPERIENCE

Sometimes a single event can seem to mirror all of life. For example, one long and complicated journey with many detours and wrong turns might be seen as representing the experience of growing up. As you read, think about how the small events in this story could reflect something much bigger about the times in which the story takes place.

Journal Writing Describe a past experience that seemed to reflect the way your life was going at the time. What qualities made the experience seem so loaded with meaning?

THEMATIC FOCUS: FACING TROUBLED TIMES

In this tale, a turtle perseveres in the face of many obstacles. As you move through the story, remember what you've read about the Joads and other Oklahoma farmers. How might the turtle's plight relate to their struggle in the Great Depression?

◆ Build Vocabulary

LATIN PREFIXES: *pro-*

In this story, Steinbeck uses the word *protruded*, which begins with the Latin prefix *pro-*, meaning "forward." Knowing this meaning helps you to define the whole word *protruded*—"thrust forward"—and other words beginning with the prefix *pro-*.

WORD BANK

Preview this list of words from the story.

embankment
protruded

◆ Grammar and Style

PARALLEL STRUCTURE

Parallel structure—the expression of similar ideas in similar grammatical form—helps to emphasize key ideas and link similar concepts. In this story, Steinbeck uses parallel structure to draw attention to the details in his descriptions and to give equal weighting to these details. In this example he uses parallel infinitive phrases:

> . . . the grass heads were heavy with oat beards *to catch on a dog's coat*, and foxtails *to tangle in a horse's fetlocks*, and clover burrs *to fasten in sheep's wool* . . .

◆ Literary Focus

THEME

John Steinbeck's story about a brief episode in a turtle's life conveys an important **theme,** or insight into life. An author's theme is rarely directly stated. Instead, it is revealed indirectly through the characters' comments and actions, the events in the plot, and the author's use of literary devices, such as symbols. Sometimes, even small details can serve an important role in conveying a theme.

◆ Reading Strategy

FIND CLUES TO THEME

The process of interpreting the theme of a story is almost like being a detective—you have to look carefully for **clues to the theme** in the writer's choice of details, in the comments that characters make, in the ways they react to one another, and so on. In a brief story like this one, each detail is especially important. For example, Steinbeck includes only slight descriptions of how two motorists react when they encounter the turtle. However, these brief descriptions are important clues to the theme. When you encounter such clues, ask yourself: What broader or underlying meaning do the clues suggest?

Interest Grabber Students can appreciate this "Little Engine That Could" story on two levels: as a highly detailed and literal account of a turtle's efforts to cross the road and as a thematic statement about the human struggles of the Great Depression. You might engage students' interest in the story by focusing on the first level. Read aloud the following passages:

> "As the embankment grew steeper and steeper, the more frantic were the efforts of the land turtle."

> "Pushing hind legs strained and slipped, . . ."

> "Little by little the shell slid up the embankment . . ."

Ask students whether they think the turtle will succeed in climbing the embankment. Invite students to empathize with the turtle as they read the story.

Customize for
Less Proficient Students
Urge less proficient readers to read the story through once without pause, then reread slowly to break down the exact sequence of the turtle's movements. They might number the turtle's efforts in sequence for clarity.

Customize for
AP Students
Direct more advanced students to study Steinbeck's descriptive vocabulary. Have students list some words Steinbeck uses to describe the turtle's progress. Challenge them to brainstorm for additional descriptive language.

Customize for
English Language Learners
Steinbeck's sometimes complex syntax may challenge English language learners. To help these students, have them paraphrase difficult passages. Direct them as well to pay special attention to the Reading Strategy suggestions.

Customize for
Verbal/Linguistic Learners
This story is highly visual. To help these students grasp the movement in the story, pair them with visual/spatial learners to create a map of the turtle's progress.

Test Preparation Workshop

Reading Comprehension: Analyze Sentence Meaning Many standardized tests require students to correctly answer sentence-completion questions. Often, more than one choice can complete a sentence. Use the following sample item to show students how to analyze sentence meaning, decide whether it is positive or negative, and eliminate choices that have the opposite sense.

John Steinbeck captured the poverty and desperation experienced by many Americans during the Great Depression, a _____ period in our nation's history.

A comfortable
B inconvenient
C bleak
D prosperous

The context of the sentence indicates that the correct answer will have a negative connotation, so *A* and *D* are eliminated. Answer choice *B* is too mild to compare to the words *poverty* and *desperation*. *C* is the best choice.

Develop Understanding

One-Minute Insight This story proclaims the virtues of persistence and commitment, illustrating how a character can achieve a difficult goal through steady effort and flexibility. Readers may initially doubt the turtle's ability to achieve its goal—climbing the embankment of a highway—but will increasingly admire its dogged efforts. When the turtle is rebuffed, first by the landscape and then by speeding cars, its response—taking another path—symbolizes the underlying ability of both nature and people to adapt to the environment.

◆ Reading Strategy

❶ **Find Clues to Theme** Guide students to see that while Steinbeck might have chosen to describe other types of plant life, Steinbeck focuses on the variety of seeds on the side of the road. Ask what the word "seed" conveys and have students speculate about why Steinbeck identifies the "appliances of dispersal." *Seeds are potential life; however, in this environment, they need assistance to survive.*

▶Critical Viewing◀

❷ **Connect** Student may respond that it has short legs well suited to steady progress and a tough shell to protect it from any bumps along the way.

◆ Critical Thinking

❸ **Make Inferences** Ask students: What can you infer about the turtle's character from this description? *Responses can include: the turtle is persistent; the turtle is inspired by adversity; the turtle is determined to climb that embankment, no matter what.*

The Turtle

John Steinbeck

▲ **Critical Viewing** What elements of this turtle's anatomy make it especially suited for the landscape Steinbeck describes? **[Connect]** ❷

❶ The concrete highway was edged with a mat of tangled, broken, dry grass, and the grass heads were heavy with oat beards to catch on a dog's coat, and foxtails to tangle in a horse's fetlocks, and clover burrs to fasten in sheep's wool; sleeping life waiting to be spread and dispersed, every seed armed with an appliance of dispersal, twisting darts and parachutes for the wind, little spears and balls of tiny thorns, and all waiting for animals or the hem of a woman's skirt, all passive but armed with appliances of activity, still, but each possessed of the anlage[1] of movement.

The sun lay on the grass and warmed it, and in the shade under the grass the insects moved, ants and ant lions to set traps for them, grasshoppers to jump into the air and flick their yellow wings for a second, sow bugs like little armadillos, plodding restlessly on many tender feet. And over the grass at the roadside a land turtle crawled, turning aside for nothing, dragging his high-domed shell over the grass: His hard legs and yellow-nailed feet threshed slowly through the grass, not really walking, but boosting and dragging his shell along. The barley beards slid off his shell, and the clover burrs fell on him and rolled to the ground. His horny beak was partly opened, and his fierce, humorous eyes, under brows like fingernails, stared straight ahead. He came over the grass leaving a beaten trail behind him, and the hill, which was the highway embankment, reared up ahead of him. For a moment he stopped, his head held high. He blinked and looked up and down. At last he started to climb the embankment. Front clawed feet reached forward but did ❸

1. **anlage** (än′ lä′gə) *n.*: Foundation; basis; the initial cell structure from which an embryonic part develops.

Block Scheduling Strategies

Consider these suggestions to take advantage of extended class time:

- To build knowledge of the Great Depression and the *Grapes of Wrath,* have students read the Background for Understanding. Follow up with the CD-ROM *The History of American Literature:* Part 2, Disk 1, Feature 9. Invite students who have read *The Grapes of Wrath* to share their understanding of the story and its Depression events.
- After groups complete the Journal activity on p. 687, have them exchange experiences and ideas with other groups to identify common features of their "meaningful" experiences. They may use these discussions as prewriting material for the Guided Writing Lesson.
- Have students work in pairs or small groups to answer the Critical Thinking and Literary Focus questions (p. 690).
- Invite students to present the results of their Interview or Environmental Report (p. 691).

not touch. The hind feet kicked his shell along, and it scraped on the grass, and on the gravel. As the embankment grew steeper and steeper, the more frantic were the efforts of the land turtle. Pushing hind legs strained and slipped, boosting the shell along, and the horny head protruded as far as the neck could stretch. Little by little the shell slid up the embankment
3 until at last a parapet[2] cut straight across its line of march, the shoulder of the road, a concrete wall four inches high. As though they worked independently the hind legs pushed the shell against the wall. The head upraised and peered over the wall to the broad smooth plain of cement. Now the hands, braced on top of the wall, strained and lifted, and the shell came slowly up and rested its front end on the wall. For a moment the turtle rested. A red ant ran into the shell, into the soft skin inside the shell, and suddenly head and legs snapped in, and the armored tail clamped in sideways. The red ant was crushed between body and legs. And one head of wild oats was clamped into the shell by a front leg. For a long moment the turtle lay still, and then the neck crept out and the old humorous frowning eyes looked about and the legs and tail came out. The back legs went to work, straining like elephant legs, and the shell tipped to an angle so that the front legs could not reach the level cement plain. But higher and higher the hind legs boosted it, until at last the center of balance was reached,
4 the front tipped down, the front legs scratched at the pavement, and it was up. But the head of wild oats was held by its stem around the front legs.

Now the going was easy, and all the legs worked, and the shell boosted along, waggling from side to side. A sedan driven by a forty-year-old woman approached. She saw the turtle and swung to the right, off the highway, the wheels screamed and a cloud of dust boiled up. Two wheels lifted for a moment and then settled. The car skidded back onto the road, and went on, but more slowly. The turtle had jerked into its shell, but now it hurried on, for the highway was burning hot.

And now a light truck approached, and as it came near, the driver saw the turtle and swerved to hit it. His front wheel struck the edge of the shell, flipped the turtle like a tiddly-wink, spun it like a coin, and rolled it off the highway. The truck went back to its course along the right side. Lying on its back, the turtle was tight in its shell for a long time. But at last its legs waved in the air, reaching for something to pull it over. Its front foot caught a piece of quartz and little by little the shell pulled over and flopped upright. The wild oat head fell out and three of the spearhead seeds stuck in the ground. And as the turtle crawled on down the embankment, its shell dragged
dirt over the seeds. The turtle entered a dust 5
road and jerked itself along, drawing a wavy 6
shallow trench in the dust with its shell. The old humorous eyes looked ahead, and the horny beak opened a little. His yellow toe nails slipped a fraction in the dust.

2. **parapet** (par´ ə pet´) *n.*: A low, protective wall or edge of a roof, balcony, or similar structure.

◆ Build Vocabulary

embankment (em bangk´ mənt) *n.*: A mound of earth or stone built to hold back water or support a roadway

protruded (prō tro͞od´ id) *v.*: Pushed or thrusted outward

Guide for Responding

◆ *Literature and Your Life*

Reader's Response Describe how you felt as you watched the turtle slowly proceed.

Thematic Response Identify two challenges the turtle faces that might symbolize the plight of ordinary Americans facing the uncaring modern world.

☑ Check Your Comprehension

1. What is the turtle's goal?
2. What obstacles does the turtle encounter?
3. How does the turtle react to the final obstacles?
4. What happens to the wild oat head at the end of the story?

◆ Literary Focus

4 Theme Discuss with students how the turtle's persistence and ultimate successes can be linked with Steinbeck's theme of people struggling and persevering amid the challenges of the Great Depression.

◆ Reading Strategy

5 Find Clues to Theme Be sure students notice that the seed mentioned at the start of the narrative has crossed the road and been planted.

◆ *Literature and Your Life*

6 Ask students to recall situations in which after facing insurmountable obstacles to reaching a goal, they developed an alternative strategy for achieving the goal.

Reinforce and Extend

Writing and Language Transparencies Use the Writing Process Model of a Research Report (pp. 41–50) to enrich students' knowledge of the Great Depression.

Answers

◆ *Literature and Your Life*

Reader's Response Students may report they felt nervous for the turtle's success.

Thematic Response The parapet and the cars present obstacles.

☑ Check Your Comprehension

1. To cross the road to safety.
2. The turtle encounters the highway embankment, the parapet, the hot surface of the road, and traffic.
3. It rights itself after being flipped on its back. It proceeds.
4. The seed is planted.

Beyond the Selection

FURTHER READING

Other Works by John Steinbeck

The Pearl
The Red Pony

Other Works With the Theme of Quests

The Old Man and the Sea, Ernest Hemingway
Moby-Dick, Herman Melville
"A Worn Path," Eudora Welty

We suggest that you preview these works before recommending them to students.

INTERNET

You and your students may find additional information about John Steinbeck and "The Turtle" on the Internet. We suggest the following sites. Please be aware, however, that sites may have changed since this information was published.

Visit the John Steinbeck page at **http://ocean.st.usm.edu/~wsimkins/steinb.html**

To view a photo essay about *The Grapes of Wrath* and the Great Depression, visit **http://www2.uncwil.edu/english/newlin/224/grapes/grapes2.htm**

We *strongly recommend* that you preview sites before you send students to them.

Answers

◆ Critical Thinking

1. He seems to know no other way.
2. The first driver altruistically swerves to avoid the turtle and the second driver does not.
3. His experiences in crossing the road demonstrate the dangers of the modern world. He is wise to return to a more natural setting.
4. Possible Response: The turtle makes a good symbol because he encounters many obstacles yet perseveres and finally succeeds.
5. They would be advantageous because they would allow a person to weather hard times. They would be disadvantageous because they might prevent a person from dropping an idea that was misguided.

◆ Reading Strategy

1. (a) Three obstacles are: the embankment, the parapet, and the traffic. (b) The turtle overcomes the embankment and the parapet through sheer physical determination. It overcomes the traffic through luck. (c) The obstacles and the turtle's responses can represent the determination people summon when facing "uphill" battles.
2. (a) These words personify the turtle and make readers perceive it as a fighter. (b) He wants them to be sympathetic of it.
3. (a) The turtle and the woman who swerves to avoid it can be seen as representing nature and the simple life. The truck driver may represent the modern world. (b) Steinbeck probably feels nature is more important.

◆ Literary Focus

1. Life presents many challenges, and still people persevere.
2. The wild oat seed represents potential life; without help it cannot succeed. The turtle's struggle allows it to be planted and therefore succeed. This may symbolize the larger theme of success through struggle and the help of others.
3. Possible responses: Life is difficult, but obstacles—including those presented by the modern world—can be overcome.

Guide for Responding (continued)

◆ Critical Thinking

Interpret

1. Why is the turtle so persistent in working toward his goal? **[Analyze]**

2. Compare and contrast the actions of the two vehicle drivers in this story. **[Compare and Contrast]**

Evaluate

3. Do you think the turtle made the right decision in retreating from the embankment? Why or why not? **[Make a Judgment]**

4. Do you think the turtle would make an effective symbol of the experiences of ordinary people during the Great Depression of the 1930's? Explain. **[Evaluate]**

Extend

5. How would the personal qualities of the turtle be advantageous or disadvantageous in today's business world? **[Career Link]**

◆ Reading Strategy

Find Clues to Theme

To arrive at an understanding of a story's theme, or central insight into life, it is important to analyze the writing carefully. Look for **clues to the theme** by considering each detail the writer provides and thinking about whether it might have a broader or underlying meaning.

1. (a) List three obstacles the turtle faces. (b) How does the turtle respond to each obstacle? (c) What underlying meaning can you find in these obstacles and the turtle's responses to them?

2. Steinbeck uses the words *dragging, turning aside for nothing,* and *thrashed slowly* to describe the turtle. (a) What effect do these words have on how the reader perceives the turtle? (b) How do you think Steinbeck wants readers to respond to the turtle?

3. (a) Which story characters can be seen as representing nature—or the simple life—and which represent the modern commercial world? Give reasons for your choices. (b) What do you think Steinbeck feels is more important? Explain.

◆ Literary Focus

Theme

Although it is an extremely brief piece, "The Turtle" conveys an important **theme,** or central message about life. This message is closely tied to the overall theme of Steinbeck's novel *The Grapes of Wrath,* for which "The Turtle" serves as an introduction.

1. How can the experiences of the turtle be connected to human experiences?

2. Explain the significance of the wild oat seed. How might it relate to the story's theme?

3. Using your answers to the previous questions, state the theme of the story.

◆ Build Vocabulary

Using the Latin Prefix *pro-*

Add the prefix *pro-* meaning "forward" to these word roots. Then use each word in a sentence.

1. -ject **2.** -ceed **3.** -gress **4.** -hibit

Using the Word Bank: True or False?

Using your knowledge of the word bank words, decide if these statements are true or false.

1. An **embankment** is at the bottom of a lake.

2. When the cat's paw **protruded** from the cat carrier, it stuck out.

◆ Grammar and Style

Using Parallel Structure

Writers use **parallel structure**—the expression of similar ideas in similar grammatical form—to emphasize key ideas and link similar concepts.

Practice On your paper, write these passages. Underline the parallel grammatical elements.

1. . . . all waiting for animals and for the wind, for a man's trouser cuff. . .

2. . . . a land turtle crawled, turning aside for nothing, dragging his high-domed shell over the grass.

3. His front wheel struck the edge of the shell, flipped the turtle like a tiddly-wink, spun it like a coin, and rolled it off the highway.

Writing Application Write a short description of an event in nature. Use parallel structure to call attention to the key details in your description.

◆ Build Vocabulary

Using the Latin Prefix *pro-*

1. We *project* high sales next quarter.
2. *Proceed* to the next corner and turn left.
3. The turtle's steady *progress* is amazing.
4. Because of the danger they present, we *prohibit* trucks on this road.

Using the Word Bank

1. False 2. True

◆ Grammar and Style

1. . . .all waiting for animals and for the wind, for a man's trouser cuff . . .
2. . . . a land turtle crawled, turning aside for nothing, dragging his high domed shell over the grass.
3. His front wheel struck the edge of the shell, flipped the turtle like a tiddly-wink, spun it like a coin, and rolled it off the highway.

Writing Application

Encourage students to share their responses with the class. For additional practice, use the Strengthening Sentences lesson on the **Language Lab CD-ROM.**

Reteach

To reteach the selection, refer to the booklet ***Strategies for Diverse Student Needs,*** p. 44.

Build Your Portfolio

Idea Bank

Writing

1. Description Write a description of the events in the story from the point of view of one of the two motorists.

2. Literary Analysis Write a brief essay in which you analyze the theme of "The Turtle." Cite passages and details from the story to support your interpretation.

3. Essay About Historical Context Research the Great Depression. Then write an essay in which you connect the events described in "The Turtle" to the experiences of ordinary people during the 1930's. **[Social Studies Link]**

Speaking, Listening, and Viewing

4. Interview After preparing a list of questions, interview someone who lived through the Great Depression. Ask open-ended questions and encourage detailed answers. Share your findings with the class. **[Social Studies Link]**

5. Monologue Imagine you're the turtle in the story, and you're talking to yourself as you proceed on your journey. Present a monologue of your interior speech. **[Performing Arts Link]**

Researching and Representing

6. Environmental Report Research the impact of human settlement on a particular turtle population. Gather data about species type, anatomy, movement, and feeding habits. Present your findings in an oral report with visuals. **[Science Link]**

7. Cartoon With a partner, pare "The Turtle" down to its essential thematic message. Write and illustrate a cartoon conveying that message. **[Art Link]**

Online Activity www.phlit.phschool.com

Guided Writing Lesson

Scientific Observation

John Steinbeck describes the turtle's progress up the embankment with specific language that accounts for everything the reptile does. Observe an animal of your choice as it completes a specific task. Then create a piece of writing in which you present your observations.

Writing Skills Focus: Clear Sequence of Events

Arrange your details in chronological order to make it easy for readers to follow the sequence of events in your observation. Use signal words such as *first, next, now,* and *at last* to clearly place each step in sequence. Notice how Steinbeck uses time order words to trace the turtle's progress across the grass:

Model From the Story

For a moment he stopped, his head held high . . . *At last* he started to climb the embankment. . . . *Now* the hands . . . lifted

Prewriting Find an animal to describe. For example, you might describe a dog exploring its surroundings during a walk or a fish reacting to feeding time. Then carefully observe the animal you've chosen, recording as many details as you can.

Drafting Begin your observation with a detailed description of the animal's physical appearance. Then follow with a detailed, step-by-step description of its actions. Use precise nouns and verbs; avoid using an excessive number of adjectives and adverbs.

Revising As you revise, look for any details you might have left out. Also make sure that the sequence of events is clear. Where possible, add transitions to clarify the connection among details.

Idea Bank

Customizing for *Performance Levels*

Following are suggestions for matching Idea Bank topics with your students' performance levels:
Less Advanced Students: 1, 4
Average Students: 2, 5, 7
More Advanced Students: 3, 6

Customizing for *Learning Modalities*

Following are suggestions for matching Idea Bank topics with your students' learning modalities:
Verbal/Linguistic: 4, 5
Logical/Mathematical: 6
Visual/Spatial: 6, 7
Intrapersonal: 5
Gifted/Talented: 5, 7

Guided Writing Lesson

Refer students to the Writing Process Handbook, p. 1192, for instruction on the writing process, and p. 1194 for further information on description.

Writing and Language Transparencies Use the Writing Process Model of a Descriptive and Observational Report (pp. 9–12) to introduce students to the elements of observational writing.

For more prewriting, elaboration, and revision strategies, see *Prentice Hall Writing and Grammar.*

Writing Lab CD-ROM

Have students complete the tutorial on Description. Follow these steps:

1. Have students use the Transition Word Bin activity to help them come up with words to link their ideas.
2. Have students draft on the computer.
3. Have students use the Transitions Checker to help them revise.

✓ ASSESSMENT OPTIONS

Formal Assessment, Selection Test, pp. 206–208, and Assessment Resources Software. The selection test is designed so that it can be easily customized to the performance levels of your students.

Alternative Assessment, p. 44, includes options for less advanced students, more advanced students, visual/spatial learners, verbal/linguistic learners, and intrapersonal learners.

PORTFOLIO ASSESSMENT

Use the following rubrics in the ***Alternative Assessment*** booklet to assess student writing:
Description: Description Rubric, p. 112
Literary Analysis: Literary Analysis/Interpretation Rubric, p. 127
Essay About Historical Context: Literary Analysis/Interpretation Rubric, p. 127
Guided Writing Lesson: Technical Description/Explanation Rubric, p. 130

Prepare and Engage

LESSON OBJECTIVES

1. **To develop vocabulary and word identification skills**
   - Greek Roots: *-psych-*
   - Using the Word Bank: Context
2. **To use a variety of reading strategies to comprehend poetry**
   - Connect Your Experience
   - Idea Bank: Summary
3. **To increase knowledge of other cultures and to connect common elements across cultures**
   - Cultural Connection: African Art
4. **To express and support responses to the text**
   - Critical Thinking Questions
   - Idea Bank: Critical Essay
   - Idea Bank: Group Discussion
   - Idea Bank: Art
   - Idea Bank: Double Diary Entry
5. **To analyze literary elements**
   - Literary Focus: Satire
   - Reading Strategy: Relate Structure to Meaning
6. **To read to do research on a self-selected or an assigned topic**
   - Idea Bank: Internet Research
7. **To plan, prepare, organize, and present literary interpretations**
   - Idea Bank: Poetry Reading
   - Speaking, Listen, and Viewing Mini-Lesson: Poetry Reading (ATE)
8. **To use recursive writing processes to write an introduction to a poetry reading**
   - Guided Writing Lesson
9. **To increase knowledge of the rules of grammar and usage**
   - Grammar and Style: Parentheses

Test Preparation

Reading Comprehension: Try Words in the Sentence
(ATE, p. 693)
The teaching tips and sample test item in this workshop support the instruction and practice in the unit workshop:
Reading Comprehension: Sentence-Completion Questions
(SE, p. 863)

Guide for Interpreting

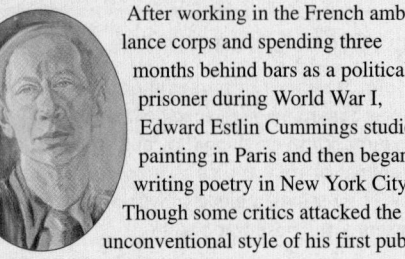

E. E. Cummings *(1894–1962)*

After working in the French ambulance corps and spending three months behind bars as a political prisoner during World War I, Edward Estlin Cummings studied painting in Paris and then began writing poetry in New York City. Though some critics attacked the unconventional style of his first published poems, Cummings's work was popular with general readers. People admired his playful use of language, his distinctive approach to using grammar and punctuation, and his interest in a poem's appearance—an interest that might have stemmed from his gifts as a painter.

Although Cummings's poems tend to be unconventional in form and style, they generally embody traditional thought. In his finest poems, Cummings explores love and nature while innovatively using grammar and punctuation to reinforce meaning. Many of his poems also contain a touch of humor, as Cummings addresses the confusing aspects of modern life.

Cummings received a number of awards for his work, including the Boston Fine Arts Poetry Festival Award and the Bollingen Prize in Poetry. In 1968, six years after his death, a complete volume of his poetry, *The Complete Poems, 1913–1968,* was published.

W. H. Auden *(1907–1973)*

Although he was influenced by the Modernist poets, Wystan Hugh Auden adopted only those aspects of Modernism with which he felt comfortable. At the same time, he maintained many elements of traditional poetry. Throughout his career, he wrote with insight about people struggling to preserve their individuality in an increasingly conformist society.

Auden was born in England, and attended Oxford University. At age twenty-three, W. H. Auden published his first volume of poems and developed a passionate interest in politics. He spoke out against poverty in England and the rise of Nazism in German.

Just before World War II, in 1939, Auden moved from England to the United States, and around that same time he rediscovered his Christian beliefs. He expressed his beliefs in *Double Man* (1941) and *For the Times Being* (1944), depicting religion as a way of coping with the disjointedness of modern society.

Auden earned the Pulitzer Prize in 1948 for his long narrative poem *The Age of Anxiety* (1947) which explores the confusion associated with post-World War II life. He went on to produce several more volumes of poetry and a large body of literary criticism.

◆ Background for Understanding

LITERATURE: E. E. CUMMINGS'S STYLE

Cummings's style is among the most distinctive of any American poet. He molded his poems into unconventional shapes by varying line lengths and inserting unusual spaces between letters and lines. He also wrote **concrete poetry**—poetry in which the shape of the poem reinforces its meaning. For example, his poem about a grasshopper, "r-p-o-p-h-e-s-s-a-g-r" forms the shape of a grasshopper hopping and reforming itself.

Many of E. E. Cummings's poems contain little punctuation; the few marks that do appear often highlight important ideas. In addition, Cummings rarely used capital letters, except for emphasis. Another distinguishing mark of his style was his use of a lower-case *i* when his speakers refer to themselves. This small *i* was meant to convey the idea of the self as a small part of mass society and Cummings's belief in the need for modesty.

Prentice Hall Literature Program Resources

REINFORCE / RETEACH / EXTEND

Selection Support Pages
Build Vocabulary: Word Roots: *-psych-*, p. 208
Grammar and Style: Parentheses, p. 209
Reading Strategy: Relate Structure to Meaning, p. 210
Literary Focus: Satire, p. 211

Strategies for Diverse Student Needs, p. 45

Beyond Literature
Humanities Connection: Art, p. 45

Formal Assessment Selection Test, pp. 209–211; Assessment Resources Software

Alternative Assessment, p. 45

Writing and Language Transparencies
Comparison-and-Contrast Organizer, pp. 87–89

Resource Pro CD-ROM

Listening to Literature Audiocassettes

◆ Literature and Your Life

Connect Your Experience

In this country, you are both an individual and a member of a vast society. Have you ever felt a conflict between asserting your individuality and maintaining your responsibility toward society? Do you wonder how you can distinguish yourself from the rest of humanity—or even from a group of your friends? The following poems address these issues.

Journal Writing Jot down examples of television, radio, and print advertising that encourage people to conform to certain ways of thought, appearance, and behavior.

Thematic Focus: Facing Troubled Times

As you read, think about what these poems suggest about some of the negative aspects of today's world. Does modern society sometimes lose track of the needs of certain individuals?

◆ Build Vocabulary

Greek Roots: *-psych-*

The name Psyche—a heroine in a Greek myth—comes from a Greek word meaning "breath" or "soul." The Greek root *-psych-* means "soul" or "mind," and it forms the basis for a number of English words, including *psychology,* which appears in Auden's poem.

Word Bank

Preview this list before you read.

statistics
psychology

◆ Literary Focus

Satire

Satire is writing in which an author uses humor to ridicule or criticize certain individuals, institutions, types of behavior, or even humanity. Satire ranges in tone; it might be tolerant, humorous, or bitter. The purpose of satire is to promote changes in society or humanity. Satirists write about what they perceive to be problems in the world. By poking fun at these problems, they use the force of laughter to persuade readers to accept their point of view.

◆ Grammar and Style

Parentheses

Generally, **parentheses, ( ),** are used to enclose extra information. They set off material that does not merit special attention but is relevant enough to be included in a sentence.

Although E. E. Cummings uses parentheses conventionally, he also uses them for his own stylistic purposes. In "old age sticks," for example, he uses parentheses to highlight the contrast in attitudes between the old and young.

◆ Reading Strategy

Relate Structure to Meaning

You can often relate a poem's **structure**—the way it is put together in words, lines, and stanzas—to its **meaning**—the central ideas the poet wants you to take away. For example, you'll see that Cummings's poems play typographical games and break rules of grammar and syntax. "Look at me," the structure of the poems seems to say, "I'm an individual." It is no coincidence that the meaning of many of Cummings's poems *also* centers on the individual challenging conventional boundaries.

Interest Grabber Read an excerpt from Jerry Seinfeld's book *Seinlanguage,* a column by Dave Barry, or share a video of the stand-up comedy of Paula Poundstone, Jay Leno, or David Letterman to show that no subject is off limits to columnists and comedians who challenge and satirize society and its rituals. Ask students whether they enjoyed the contemporary satire and how they view the role of writers and artists in analyzing society. Tell them that they're about to encounter a group of poems that comment on society.

Customize for
Less Proficient Readers
These readers will be extremely challenged by the unusual syntax in Cummings's poems and the long sentences in Auden's poem. Point out that Cummings often plays with word order, and urge students to organize words as necessary to gain understanding. Suggest that they use the line breaks in Auden's poem to break down his long sentences into manageable phrases.

Customize for
AP Students
Challenge more advanced students to analyze Cummings's syntax by punctuating a stanza or two from either poem. What do the punctuated versions highlight about Cummings's syntax?

Customize for
English Language Learners
Warn these students that E. E. Cummings breaks many punctuation rules. To help these students negotiate Cummings's work, pair them with more advanced students to read aloud and analyze the poems.

Test Preparation Workshop

Reading Comprehension:
Try Words in the Sentence Many standardized tests require students to correctly answer sentence-completion questions. Use the following sample item to show students that they can often eliminate choices because they are illogical, the wrong part of speech, or inconsistent with the sentence meaning.

Thomas Wolfe's first novel, *Look Homeward, Angel,* was a critical and ____ success and earned Wolfe widespread ____.

A moral; abuse
B financial; recognition
C personal; apathy
D profit; applause

D uses the wrong part of speech. The context of the sentence indicates that the second word will have a positive meaning, eliminating choices *A* and *C.* Answer *B* is the best choice.

One-Minute Insight Cummings challenges the way people live in both of these poems. "anyone lived in a pretty how town" paints a picture for readers of an anonymous town in which people live routine and unremarkable lives. The seasons pass with regular predictability as the main characters, "anyone" and his wife "noone," do nothing special and are basically unnoticed by the town's other occupants. In "old age sticks," Cummings illustrates the cyclical nature of human experience. Youth's liveliness is contrasted with old age's conservatism but gradually youth becomes old age. With the unusual syntax and satirical view, these poems explore the relationship between the individual and society's structure.

◆ Critical Thinking

❶ **Interpret** Who is "anyone"? What is "anyone's" relationship to "noone," introduced in line 12? *"Anyone" and "noone" are two characters, married to one another. Some students may say that "noone" is not a person but rather the statement that nobody loves "anyone."*

◆ Literary Focus

❷ **Satire** What does Cummings think happens to children as they grow up? *Their perceptiveness and honesty diminishes, they lose their individuality and blend into society's sameness.*

◆ Reading Strategy

❸ **Relate Structure to Meaning** Which lines in the poem convey the passage of time? *Lines 3, 8, 11, 21, 34, and 36 show the passage of time.* Why might Cummings vary the order of the words in these lines? *It reinforces the idea of time passing.*

◆ Grammar and Style

❹ **Parentheses** Have students explain the use of parentheses in this stanza. How does the text within the parentheses relate to the surrounding text? *The parentheses set aside the text about noone's behavior. This renders it less important, but still relevant.*

anyone lived in a pretty how town

E. E. Cummings

anyone lived in a pretty how town
(with up so floating many bells down)
spring summer autumn winter
he sang his didn't he danced his did.

Women and men(both little and small)
cared for anyone not at all
❶ they sowed their isn't they reaped their same
sun moon stars rain

children guessed(but only a few
and down they forgot as up they grew
autumn winter spring summer)
that noone loved him more by more

when by now and tree by leaf
she laughed his joy she cried his grief
bird by snow and stir by still
anyone's any was all to he

someones married their everyones
laughed their cryings and did their dance
(sleep wake hope and then)they
said their nevers they slept their dream

stars rain sun moon
❷ (and only the snow can begin to explain
how children are apt to forget to remember
with up so floating many bells down)

one day anyone died i guess
(and noone stooped to kiss his face)
busy folk buried them side by side
little by little and was by was

all by all and deep by deep
and more by more they dream their sleep
❸ noone and anyone earth by april
❹ wish by spirit and if by yes.

Women and men(both dong and ding)
summer autumn winter spring
reaped their sowing and went their came
sun moon stars rain

Block Scheduling Strategies

Consider these suggestions to take advantage of extended class time.

- Have student groups analyze the poems, line by line, constructing literal and symbolic meaning. Then have groups discuss and answer the Critical Thinking questions (pp. 695, 697).
- Have students listen to the three poems on audiotape. Initiate a class discussion about the rhythm of the spoken poetry. Ask students how hearing the poems spoken enhances their comprehension or appreciation.
- As a class, visit and interact with the Internet sites linked to Cummings and Auden.
- Have students stage a Cummings and Auden Poetry Reading (p. 699). Assign groups to complete the Guided Writing Lesson as part of the project, using group discussion to develop a comparison of the two poets.
- Have students complete the Beyond Literature Activity in ***Selection Support,*** p. 45. Then urge them to complement their analysis by completing the Art Project (p. 697).

old age sticks

E. E. Cummings

old age sticks
up Keep
Off
signs)&

youth yanks them
down(old
age
❺ cries No

❻ Tres)&(pas)
youth laughs
(sing
old age

scolds Forbid
den Stop
Must
n't Don't

&)youth goes
right on
gr
owing old

Remember Now the Days of Thy Youth, 1950, Paul Starrett Sample, Hood Museum of Art, Dartmouth College, Hanover, NH

▲ **Critical Viewing** Do you think that the elderly men in this painting belong to the group that Cummings describes or are they a different sort? On what details did you base your conclusion? **[Speculate]** ❼

Guide for Responding

◆ *Literature and Your Life*

Reader's Response Did you enjoy the language play in these poems? Why, or why not?

Thematic Focus In what sense does Cummings address the issue of personal or national identity?

☑ Check Your Comprehension

1. In "anyone lived in a pretty how town," what does "anyone" sing and dance?
2. (a) In "old age sticks," what actions does old age take? (b) What are youth's three responses to old age's actions?

◆ Critical Thinking

INTERPRET

1. (a) In "anyone lived in a pretty how town," why might Cummings have chosen the names "anyone" for the man and "noone" for his wife? **[Speculate]**
2. What is the meaning of "laughed their cryings" and "slept their dream"? **[Interpret]**
3. In "old age sticks," explain the difference Cummings is pointing out between youth and old age. **[Compare and Contrast]**
4. Explain the irony in the final stanza of "old age sticks." **[Interpret]**

Humanities: Art

Remember Now the Days of Thy Youth, 1950, by Paul Starrett Sample; 34" x 48"; oil on canvas.

American painter Paul Starrett Sample discovered art while convalescing from tuberculosis. While living in Los Angeles and later New England, Sample painted scenes of American life that made him immensely popular. His work was included in exhibitions such as the 1939 New York World's Fair. Many critics today consider Sample one of America's most important but underrecognized painters. *Remember Now the Days of Thy Youth,* much like Sample's famous *Maple Sugaring in Vermont,* captures an everyday moment in the lives of ordinary people. Ask:

1. How do the figures in the painting represent the contrasting groups in the poem? *The old men on the porch represent "old age." The mother and baby and the two lovers represent "youth."*
2. In the world of the poem, how would you expect the young lovers depicted here to behave toward "old age" on the porch? *They would either ignore or overrule "old age," perhaps blocking their view.*

◆ Critical Thinking

❺ **Synthesize** What would youth say if asked to explain its views about old age? *Old age is unimportant to me; old age will never happen to me.*

◆ Reading Strategy

❻ **Relate Structure to Meaning** Ask students how Cummings's continual interruption of words and sentences, especially those of old age by those of youth, highlights the meaning of his poem. *Cummings depicts youth as unconcerned about old age. Interrupting the comments about old age suggests that its views aren't even worth hearing.*

►Critical Viewing◄

❼ **Speculate** Students may say the men are of the "sticks up Keep Off signs" group. Reasons include: They are old, they are watching instead of participating. Others may say the men are not interfering with youth as it heads on its way.

Reinforce and Extend

Answers

◆ *Literature and Your Life*

Reader's Response Some students may be intrigued by the language play; others may find it too challenging.

Thematic Focus Possible response: In "anyone lived . . ." Cummings examines the way individuals can be swallowed by society.

☑ Check Your Comprehension

1. He sings his didn't. He dances his did.
2. (a) It puts up signs; it scolds. (b) It yanks down signs, laughs, and grows old anyway.

◆ Critical Thinking

1. These names are anonymous. He wanted to suggest these people could be anyone.
2. "Laughed their cryings" implies that they hid their feelings. "Slept their dream" means they lived unimaginative, unfulfilled lives.
3. Youth is carefree and lively; old age is conservative and authoritarian.
4. Youth shows no concern for old age, yet youth is growing old.

Develop Understanding

One-Minute Insight This poem highlights how society can become so concerned with recording data that it obliterates individuals and their emotions or beliefs. The poem's central character, the unknown citizen, is documented, analyzed, and studied yet no one knows anything about his true personal experience of the world. Organizations that imagine themselves immensely important ask every question except the most important ones: Was he free? Was he happy? By blotting out what is unique in the individual, modern society appears hostile to human nature.

◆ Reading Strategy

❶ Relate Structure to Meaning Have students identify the terms Auden has capitalized. What is Auden suggesting about these groups and the society by capitalizing so many names? *Auden implies that these groups are falsely elevating their own status.*

▶Critical Viewing◀

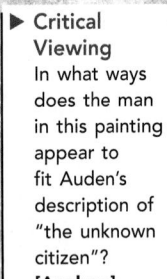

❷ Analyze *Students may respond that he looks like an ordinary man who wouldn't challenge or surprise anyone. He works in a factory where as long as his machine keeps going, no one will notice him.*

Humanities: Art

The Turret Lathe Operator, 1925, by Grant Wood; 18 3/4" x 24"; oil on composition board.

This painting depicts an everyday, average man much like the unknown citizen in the poem.

Grant Wood was born and lived much of his life in or near Anamosa, Iowa. There he painted, taught art, and promoted regional art, especially that capturing the unique midwestern experience. *The Turret Lathe Operator* is part of a series commissioned by a dairy equipment manufacturer to show quality craftsmanship in their factory. Ask:

Why might the unknown citizen in the painting or poem not communicate his unhappiness to the world? *He might assume the world is not interested in his opinions.*

The Unknown Citizen

W. H. Auden

(To JS/07/M/378 This Marble Monument Is Erected by the State)

He was found by the Bureau of Statistics to be
One against whom there was no official complaint,
And all the reports on his conduct agree
That, in the modern sense of an old-fashioned word, he was a saint,
For in everything he did he served the Greater Community.
Except for the War till the day he retired
He worked in a factory and never got fired,
But satisfied his employers, Fudge Motors Inc.
❶ Yet he wasn't a scab[1] or odd in his views,
For his Union reports that he paid his dues,
(Our report on his Union shows it was sound)
And our Social Psychology workers found
That he was popular with his mates and liked a drink.
The Press are convinced that he bought a paper every day
And that his reactions to advertisements were normal in every way.
Policies taken out in his name prove that he was fully insured,
And his Health-card shows he was once in hospital but left it cured.
Both Producers Research and High-Grade Living declare
He was fully sensible to the advantages of the Installment Plan
And had everything necessary to the Modern Man,
A phonograph, a radio, a car and a frigidaire.
Our researchers into Public Opinion are content
That he held the proper opinions for the time of year;
When there was peace, he was for peace; when there was war, he went.

1. **scab** *n.*: A worker who refuses to strike or takes the place of a striking worker.

❷ ▶ **Critical Viewing** In what ways does the man in this painting appear to fit Auden's description of "the unknown citizen"? **[Analyze]**

Turret Lathe Operator, Grant Wood, Cedar Rapids Museum of Art, Cedar Rapids, Iowa. Courtesy Associated American Artists, © Estate of Grant Wood/Licensed by VAGA, New York, NY

Speaking, Listening, and Viewing Mini-Lesson

Poetry Reading
This mini-lesson supports the Speaking, Listening, and Viewing activity in the Idea Bank on p. 699.

Introduce the Concept Have students recall discussions in which peers have read aloud their work for comment. Point out that these sessions are similar in structure to poetry readings.

Develop Background To facilitate students' efforts, have them consider and discuss necessary features of poetry readings. Share these tips:

- Choose poems you truly like—you will read with greater enthusiasm and emotion.
- Gather accurate information on the poet and poem to create an authentic presentation.
- Listen respectfully and support comments with specific examples from the text.

Apply the Information With this background, students should be able to enact their poetry reading effectively.

Assess the Outcome Invite students from the "audience" to assess the readers, evaluating their performances based on the Peer Assessments for Speaker/Speech and Oral Interpretation on pp. 133–134 in the ***Alternative Assessment*** booklet.

He was married and added five children to the population.
Which our Eugenist[2] says was the right number for a parent of his generation,
And our teachers report that he never interfered with their education.
Was he free? Was he happy? The question is absurd:
Had anything been wrong, we should certainly have heard.

2. **Eugenist** (yo͞o jen´ ist) *n.*: A specialist in eugenics, the movement devoted to improving the human species through genetic control.

◆ Build Vocabulary

statistics (sta tis´ tiks) *n.*: The science of collecting and arranging facts about a particular subject in the form of numbers

psychology (sī käl´ ə jē) *n.*: The science dealing with the mind and with mental and emotional processes

Beyond Literature

Math Connection

The Census In "The Unknown Citizen," W.H. Auden pokes fun at the amount of data collected on people in the United States. One of the most basic means of collecting such data is through the census. In the United States, a population census—a count of the number of people—is taken every ten years. The census was provided for by the United States Constitution. The first United States Census was a population count that began in 1790. At that time, the data collection lasted about eighteen months and revealed that fewer than four million people lived in the country. Since then, the country's population—and the way it is counted—has grown.

The census is now conducted by the Bureau of the Census, which is an agency of the Department of Commerce. In 1990, the U.S. population was more than 280 million. Data collected in that census included information such as population, age, sex, ethnicity, marital status, and more.

Why is the information collected by the census useful to the government and the American people?

Guide for Responding

◆ Literature and Your Life

Reader's Response Have you ever felt reduced to a number? Explain your answer.

Thematic Focus How have large bureaucracies, such as government offices and some corporations, affected our sense of American identity?

☑ Check Your Comprehension

Name four groups that report on the unknown citizen's activities.

◆ Critical Thinking

INTERPRET

1. (a) What is suggested by the numbers and letters referring to the citizen? (b) How is the citizen "unknown" to the state? **[Interpret]**
2. (a) Describe the nature of the the state's interest in the citizen in this poem. (b) What do the concerns of the state and the group reveal about society as a whole? **[Infer; Interpret]**
3. Why might the state have heard nothing about the citizen's freedom and happiness? **[Deduce]**

APPLY

4. What aspects of the society portrayed in the poem are like contemporary American society? What aspects are different? **[Relate]**

Customize for *English Language Learners*

Stress that Auden's poem is not meant to be read literally. Help them locate examples of exaggeration (lines 14, 15, 19, 24, and 26) in the poem and discuss the tone these examples convey.

Reinforce and Extend

Answers

◆ Literature and Your Life

Reader's Response Students who have interaction with bureaucracies—from government offices to answer sheets for standardized tests—may have experienced this feeling.

Thematic Focus Bureaucracies and large corporations depersonalize American citizens. The emergence of "superstores," for example, has obliterated many neighborhood businesses and made main streets more conformist.

☑ Check Your Comprehension

1. Responses include: his Union, High-Grade Living, Public Opinion researchers, and the Eugenist.

◆ Critical Thinking

1. (a) It suggests the impersonal, mechanical nature of the society; it suggests he has no true identity. (b) The state knows nothing about his feelings or concerns.
2. (a) The state is concerned that citizens conform and avoid creating disturbances. (b) It is a society in which people have no freedom and are controlled by the state.
3. These are not data that can be monitored.
4. Possible responses: While there is a bureaucratic system in place today, the society portrayed in the poem is different from our society because freedom is protected in our society.

Reteach

To further help students understand the relationships of structure and meaning in poetry, refer to ***Strategies for Diverse Student Needs,*** Interpret Poetic Images, p. 45.

Beyond the Selection

FURTHER READING

Other Works by E. E. Cummings & W. H. Auden

The Enormous Room, Cummings
Tulips and Chimneys, Cummings
Poems, Auden
The Shield of Achilles, Auden

We suggest that you preview these works before recommending them to students.

INTERNET

You and your students may find information about E.E. Cummings and W. H. Auden on the Internet. We suggest the following sites. Please be aware, however, that sites may have changed from the time we published this information.

For a Cummings page, go to **http://www.poets.org/lit/poet/eecummin.htm**

For more poetry by Auden, go to **http://www.pmb.net/poetry/auden.html**

We *strongly recommend* that you preview sites before you send students to them.

Answers

◆ Literary Focus

1. Cummings tone is disdainful of the way in which most people lead lives that lack imagination, creativity, or a sense of meaning. Lines such as "they sowed their isn't they reaped their same" express the poet's belief that people are caught up in their own negativity and rigid routine.
2. He has a tremendous amount of contempt for it.
3. They reveal that he believes that society itself is absurd and he is angered by its indifference to people's freedom and happiness.
4. He probably supports a society that places greater emphasis on individuality and freedom. His satirical references to a large number of experts and institutions, such as "the Bureau of Statistics," "his Union," "Social Psychology workers," "the Press," "Producers Research and High-Grade Living,"etc., suggest that he feels that society is too controlling and regulated.

◆ Build Vocabulary

Suggested responses:

1. psychiatry: the branch of medicine concerned with the study, treatment, and prevention of disorders of the mind. Possible response: He specialized in psychiatry in medical school.
2. psychosomatic: a physical disorder of the body originating in or aggravated by the psychic or emotional process. Possible response: The doctor labeled his patients symptoms as psychosomatic when he could find no physical cause for them.
3. psychotic: of, or having the nature of, a psychosis. Possible response: The serial killer was a confirmed psychotic.
4. psychiatrist: a doctor of medicine specializing in psychiatry after postgraduate training. Possible response: The psychiatrist diagnosed the patient with schizophrenia.
5. psychodrama: a form of cathartic therapy in which a patient acts out by improvisation situations related to his or her problem. Possible response: The therapist used psychodrama to help her patients work through their problems.

Guide for Responding *(continued)*

◆ Literary Focus

Satire

In **satire,** a writer ridicules specific individuals or institutions or human behavior or society in general in a humorous manner. In "The Unknown Citizen," for example, W. H. Auden criticizes the impersonal and bureaucratic nature of modern society by presenting an exaggerated vision of a state in which people are stripped of their individuality.

1. Describe the tone in Cummings's satiric poem "anyone lived in a pretty how town." Give reasons or examples to support your answer.
2. What is Auden's attitude toward the type of society portrayed in his poem?
3. How do the final two lines clarify his attitude?
4. Considering Auden's attitude toward the society he portrays, what type of society do you think he supports? Provide details from the poem to support your answer.

◆ Build Vocabulary

Using the Greek Root *-psych-*

The root *-psych-* derives from the mythological Greek heroine Psyche and means "mind" or "soul." Using a dictionary, write definitions in your notebook for the following *-psych-* words. Then write a sentence using each word.

1. psychiatry
2. psychosomatic
3. psychotic
4. psychiatrist
5. psychodrama

Using the Word Bank: Context

The word *psychology* refers to the science dealing with mental and emotional processes. The word *statistics* refers to the science of tabulation or counting. In a small group, discuss whether each of the following descriptions relates more closely to psychology or statistics.

1. Teacher assigns class lesson on grieving process.
2. Teacher keeps records of completed assignments.
3. You explain your dream to a friend.
4. Scientist publishes paper on blood diseases in New York State.
5. A star athlete's endorsement boosts product sales.

◆ Reading Strategy

Relate Structure to Meaning

You can often relate a poem's **structure**—the way it is put together in words, lines, and stanzas—to its **meaning**—the central ideas the poet wants you to take away. For example, E. E. Cummings uses regular stanzas, rhythms, and rhymes in "anyone lived in a pretty how town," yet he also uses little punctuation and only two capital letters. This blend of formal and informal structural elements echoes Cummings's central ideas about the lives being led in "a pretty how town."

1. How does the structure of "old age sticks" relate to the idea of rules and rule-breaking as it is presented in the poem? Use examples to support your answer.
2. Discuss how Auden's style of capitalization affects the meaning and tone of his poems.

◆ Grammar and Style

Parentheses

Parentheses are used for slightly different purposes than commas and dashes. Use commas to set off material that is especially closely connected to the rest of a sentence. Dashes are appropriate if you want to call attention to the extra information. You should use parentheses when the material is interruptive (but not deserving of special attention) or loosely related to the rest of the sentence.

> **Parentheses** enclose extra material that does not deserve special attention but is relevant enough to be included in a sentence.

Practice Rewrite each of the following sentences, adding parentheses to improve the clarity.

1. No person at least no sensible person could accuse Cummings of being a conformist.
2. Cummings's poetry except for the love poems can be silly and serious at the same time.
3. Auden's poetry especially when read by an actor always affects listeners.
4. Auden's political viewpoints I'd guess were formed over time.

Using the Word Bank

1. psychology; 2. statistics; 3. psychology; 4. statistics; 5. psychology

◆ Reading Strategy

1. The lines within the five stanzas are (with the exception of line 20) regular in the number of syllables they contain; this corresponds to old age's tendency toward rules. Yet all other structural elements are nontraditional and more in keeping with rule-breaking youth. Also, references to old age and its rules are presented in parentheses, suggesting that they are less important than the actions of youthful rule breakers.
2. Auden capitalizes state and societal institutions, reinforcing their formality and officiality.

◆ Grammar and Style

1. (at least no sensible person); 2. (except for the love poems); 3. (especially when read by an actor); 4. (I'd guess)

Grammar Reinforcement

For additional practice, use the page on Parentheses, p. 94, in the *Writer's Solution Grammar Practice Book.*

Build Your Portfolio

Idea Bank

Writing

1. Summary Write a paragraph summarizing the events described in "anyone lived in a pretty how town." Follow with a paragraph explaining how the impact of reading your summary compares to the impact of reading the poem.

2. Double Diary Entry Write a diary entry describing a recent experience. Then write a second account of the same experience as if you knew someone were monitoring your diary.

3. Critical Essay Write an essay in which you explain how Cummings's style reinforces the meaning in his poems. Use at least one passage from each poem to support your argument.

Speaking, Listening, and Viewing

4. Poetry Reading You are at a poetry reading in a New York coffee house in the 1920's. Choose your favorite poems from the early twentieth century. Then, read them aloud to your audience of fellow artists and intellectuals.

5. Group Discussion How might "anyone lived in a pretty how town" be different if it were set in a city? Discuss this question with a group of classmates. To start, suggest points of revision.

Researching and Representing

6. Internet Research Auden speaks out against totalitarianism, or a system in which the government takes complete control. Use the Internet to investigate totalitarian governments in Europe after World War I. Share your findings in an informal oral report. **[Social Studies Link]**

7. Art Choose one of the three poems, and capture and create a piece of art that could accompany it in a poetry collection. **[Art Link]**

Online Activity www.phlit.phschool.com

Guided Writing Lesson

Introduction to a Poetry Reading

Poetry readings—oral readings of poetry often held in bookstores, libraries, coffee houses, and community centers—often feature the work of more than one writer. Imagine that you've been asked to organize a reading of several poems by E. E. Cummings and W. H. Auden. Write an introduction that welcomes your audience and provides brief background information on the poets and a comparison of their work.

Writing Skills Focus: Types of Support—Details

To support or illustrate general statements about literary works, provide quotations and other specific details from the works. Consider using examples that show the poets' themes, as well as their use of rhythm, sound devices, imagery, structure, and figurative language. For instance, you'll probably want to share several examples of E. E. Cummings's unique writing style.

Prewriting Reread the poems. Develop a central idea about how the works of Cummings and Auden are related. Then jot down details or examples from the poems that support this main idea.

Drafting Keep your audience in mind as you draft your introduction. Make your remarks about the poems brief but informative. Remember that you'll be reading your introduction aloud, so use a conversational writing style and keep in mind the sound of the language you choose.

Revising Ask a classmate to read your introduction aloud. As you're listening, ask yourself if your ideas can be clearly understood. Do you prepare your audience adequately for the poetry they're about to hear? Are the details that support your main points relevant and important?

Idea Bank

Customizing for Performance Levels

Following are suggestions for matching Idea Bank topics with your students' performance levels:
Less Advanced Students: 1, 7
Average Students: 2, 4, 6
More Advanced Students: 3, 5

Customizing for Learning Modalities

Following are suggestions for matching Idea Bank topics with your students' learning modalities:
Musical/Rhythmic: 4
Interpersonal: 5
Logical/Mathematical: 6
Visual/Spatial: 7

Guided Writing Lesson

Writing and Language Transparencies Display the Comparison and Contrast Transparency, p. 87, to help students organize the ideas and details they will include in their introductions.

For more prewriting, elaboration, and revision strategies, see *Prentice Hall Writing and Grammar.*

Writing Lab CD-ROM

Have students complete the tutorial on Response to Literature. Follow these steps:

1. Students can use the Venn Diagram in the Gathering Details section to organize their comparison of the two poets.
2. Have students draft their introductions on the computer.
3. Have students use the Evaluation Word Bins to aid revision.

✓ ASSESSMENT OPTIONS

Formal Assessment, Selection Test, pp. 209–211, and Assessment Resources Software. The selection test is designed so that it can be easily customized to the performance levels of your students.

Alternative Assessment, p. 45, includes options for less advanced students, more advanced students, bodily/kinesthetic learners, interpersonal learners, visual/spatial learners, and verbal/linguistic learners.

PORTFOLIO ASSESSMENT

Use the following rubrics in the ***Alternative Assessment*** booklet to assess student writing:
Summary: Summary Rubric, p. 113
Double Diary Entry: Expression Rubric, p. 109
Critical Essay: Critical Review Rubric, p. 126
Guided Writing Lesson: Comparison/Contrast Rubric, p. 118

Prepare and Engage

LESSON OBJECTIVES

1. **To develop vocabulary and word identification skills**
   - Latin Roots: *-temp-*
   - Using the Word Bank: Context
2. **To use a variety of reading strategies to comprehend a short story**
   - Connect Your Experience
   - Reading Strategy: Predict
   - Read to Interpret (ATE)
3. **To express and support responses to the text**
   - Critical Thinking Questions
   - Idea Bank: Description
   - Idea Bank: First-Person Account
   - Idea Bank: Comparison-and-Contrast Essay
   - Idea Bank: Interview
   - Idea Bank: Map
4. **To analyze literary elements**
   - Literary Focus: Climax and Anticlimax
   - Reteach: Predict (ATE)
5. **To read to do research on a self-selected or assigned topics**
   - Idea Bank: Railroad Report
6. **To plan, prepare, organize, and present literary interpretations**
   - Idea Bank: Music Critique
7. **To use recursive writing processes to write a brochure**
   - Guided Writing Lesson
8. **To increase knowledge of the rules of grammar and usage**
   - Grammar and Style: Restrictive and Nonrestrictive Participial Phrases

Test Preparation

Reading Comprehension: Try Words in the Sentence
(ATE, p. 701)
The teaching tips and sample test item in this workshop support the instruction and practice in the unit workshop:
Reading Comprehension: Sentence-Completion Questions
(SE, p. 863)

Guide for Interpreting

Thomas Wolfe *(1900–1938)*

A man of tremendous energy, appetites, and size, Thomas Wolfe poured out thousands of pages of fiction during his brief career.

Wolfe was driven by the desire to experience all life had to offer.

He sought a range of experiences throughout his life: living in the city and in the country, in America and in Europe, in the North and in the South. He reflected them in his work: in its sheer volume, in the expanses of time and territory it covers, in his characters who were symbols of greater humanity.

An Instant Success Born in Asheville, North Carolina, Wolfe grew up in a large, eccentric family whose members later served as models for his fiction. He attended the University of North Carolina. There he became interested in playwriting, a focus he pursued during and after his postgraduate studies at Harvard. Wolfe eventually moved to New York City where he taught composition at New York University and wrote plays in his spare time. Unable to find success as a playwright, Wolfe turned to writing fiction. With the assistance of Maxwell Perkins, the leading editor of the time, Wolfe published his first novel, the loosely autobiographical *Look Homeward, Angel,* in 1929. The novel was a critical and financial success and earned Wolfe widespread recognition.

A New Direction Inspired by the success of his first novel, Wolfe began working on a sequel. Once again Perkins helped him to shorten and shape the novel, which was published as *Of Time and the River* in 1935. The novel sold well, yet Wolfe was criticized for basing his work too closely on his own life and for his reliance on Perkins. Stung by the criticism, Wolfe switched publishers and struck out on a new course, obsessed with the idea that his duty as a writer was to act as a social historian, to interpret his time and place. Unfortunately, he died of a brain infection before he could finish another novel. He did, however leave several thousand pages of manuscript in the hands of another editor, Edward Aswell, who shaped them into two more books, *The Web and the Rock* (1939) and *You Can't Go Home Again* (1940).

◆ Background for Understanding

HISTORY: AMERICA'S ROMANCE WITH THE RAILROAD

With the driving of the "golden spike"on May 10, 1869, at Promontory, Utah, the first transcontinental rail link was completed. Finishing the western half had taken more than six years, the work of thousands, and the lives of many. With its completion, America's love affair with the railways had officially begun. Now people could travel the young nation in relative comfort; they could strike out for the inexpensive land available to homesteaders; they could return East to visit relatives. The railroad also gave western farmers and ranchers access to the markets of the East.

Songs and literature about the emerging railroad abounded, including folksongs like "I've Been Working on the Railroad." The railroad influenced more than popular culture, however; it also affected the development of the United States. The nation grew smaller and in some ways more united. Cities grew at railroad hubs such as Chicago and St. Louis. As the railroad crisscrossed the nation, untamed land and lifestyles, like those of cowboys, disappeared. America was becoming a nation of towns like the one the engineer in "The Far and the Near" observes from his perch in the train engine.

Prentice Hall Literature Program Resources

REINFORCE / RETEACH / EXTEND

Selection Support Pages
Build Vocabulary: Latin Roots *-temp-*, p. 212
Grammar and Style: Restrictive and Nonrestrictive Participial Phrases, p. 213
Reading Strategy: Predict, p. 214
Literary Focus: Climax and Anticlimax, p. 215

Strategies for Diverse Student Needs Identify Key Ideas, p. 46

Beyond Literature
Humanities Connection: Art p. 46

Formal Assessment Selection Test, pp. 212–214; Assessment Resources Software

Alternative Assessment, p. 46

Resource Pro CD-ROM

Listening to Literature Audiocassettes

Literature CD-ROM
The History of Am. Lit., Part 2, Disk 1, Feature 8

The Far and the Near

◆ Literature and Your Life

Connect Your Experience

At some time in your life, you've probably looked forward to an experience for days, weeks, even months, only to find that it wasn't all you had hoped it would be. In this story a character actually spends years eagerly anticipating an event and building it up in his mind. Do you think it will live up to his expectations?

Journal Writing Describe a time in your life when an anticipated experience proved disappointing.

Thematic Focus: Facing Troubled Times

In this story of one man's very personal experience, you can find a nation's disillusionment with a future it thought endlessly bright.

◆ Literary Focus

Climax and Anticlimax

The **climax** is the high point of interest or suspense in a story, the moment at which the conflict is resolved. When that resolution is unexpectedly disappointing, ridiculous, or trivial, it is called an **anticlimax.** Like a climax, an anticlimax is the biggest moment of the story, but it is more a low point than a high point in the action. The reader, who has been led to expect that something important or serious is about to occur, is suddenly confronted with the letdown of a seemingly inappropriate resolution. When used intentionally and effectively, anticlimax can create a variety of effects, from pathos—sorrow or sympathy—to humor.

◆ Grammar and Style

Restrictive and Nonrestrictive Participial Phrases

A **participle** is a form of a verb that acts as an adjective. A **participial phrase** consists of a participle and its modifiers or complements. The entire phrase acts as an adjective. If the phrase is essential to the meaning of the sentence, it is **restrictive** and not set off by commas. If the phrase is not essential to the sentence, it is **nonrestrictive** and should be set off by commas.

Restrictive: a light spring wagon *filled with children.*

Nonrestrictive: And finally, *stammering a crude farewell,* he departed.

◆ Reading Strategy

Predict

This story about a train engineer's life is a bit like a real train ride—signposts guide the way to the final destination. These clues enable you to **predict,** or make educated guesses about, upcoming events and outcomes. Watch for signals in statements about characters, in the author's use of language, and in events you can connect to your own experiences. You'll find that they can help you predict where the story is headed. For example:

Detail Every day, a few minutes after two o'clock in the afternoon, the limited express . . . passed this spot.

Prediction The story will involve "this spot" in a way different from "every day."

◆ Build Vocabulary

Latin Roots: *-temp-*

Wolfe uses the word *tempo* to describe the timing of the train's noises. Built on the Latin root *-temp-*, meaning "time," *tempo* means "pace" or "the rate of activity of a sound or motion." What other *-temp-* words can you think of?

Word Bank

Preview these words before you read.

tempo
sallow
sullen
timorous
visage

Interest Grabber Thomas Wolfe's story juxtaposes two perspectives on life—the far and the near views. As students read, they will discover the sharp contrast between these two perspectives. Engage students' interest in the story by involving them in the following demonstration. Have students describe a distant part of the school, such as the gymnasium or library. Then visit the identified location as a class. Again, invite students to describe it. How do the two descriptions differ? Challenge students to explain the contrast.

Customize for
Less Proficient Readers
Although Wolfe's story is very brief, it covers a time period of twenty years. To ensure that less proficient readers have a clear understanding of when events are taking place, urge them to note words and phrases related to time.

Customize for
AP Students
This story depicts experiences that don't live up to a character's expectations. Encourage students to extend their exploration of the story by comparing and contrasting it with other pieces of literature or movies that deal with a similar theme.

Art Transparency

Before students read "The Far and the Near," display Art Transparency 10. Discuss Hopper's painting, directing students' attention to the railroad tracks. Have students describe what it might be like to live in the house and have at least one train pass by each day. Explain that such a situation is key to Wolfe's story. After students have read the story, display the transparency again. Use these questions for discussion:

1. How did the engineer feel about the house while he was on the job and then after he visited it personally?
2. How did the women feel about the train before and after they met the engineer?

Test Preparation Workshop

Reading Comprehension:
Try Words in the Sentence Many standardized tests require students to correctly answer sentence-completion questions. Use the following sample item to show students that they can often eliminate choices because they are illogical, the wrong part of speech, or inconsistent with the sentence meaning.

Have you ever felt a conflict between asserting your ____ and maintaining your ____ toward society?

A duty; obligation
B uniqueness; separateness
C independence; indifference
D individuality; responsibility

Because the sentence uses the word *conflict,* the correct pair of words will have somewhat opposite meanings, eliminating *A* and *B*. *C* is illogical. Answer *D* is the best choice.

Develop Understanding

One-Minute Insight This story conveys the human desire to latch onto something enduring in the face of change. The story's central character, a train engineer, passes by a house every day for twenty years. Each time he passes the house, a woman and her daughter appear on the back porch and wave at him. Through all of the difficulties and changes he endures during his career, the image of the woman and her daughter is the one thing that remains constant. The anonymous family takes on a larger meaning for him, representing warmth, love, and stability. When he retires, he goes to visit the woman and her daughter, only to make the shocking discovery that the woman is unattractive and unfriendly—nothing like what he had expected. His experience underscores people's ability to build up an event in their minds to such an extent that it is unlikely that the event will ever live up to their expectations.

Literature CD-ROM To build background, use the CD-ROM *The History of American Literature:* Part 2, Disk 1, Feature 8.

◆ Critical Thinking

❶ **Interpret** Ask students to choose an adjective to describe this house. *Students may suggest "unreal" or "picture-perfect" or "idyllic."* Prompt them to discuss how the details indicate that the engineer's impressions of the house are not completely accurate. *Signal details might include the description of the oak trees' shade as "clean" and the overall impression that it is "too good to be true."*

◆ Literature and Your Life

❷ Point out that, like this house, people often seem perfect when viewed from afar. Ask students if they have ever met a much-admired athlete, local personage, or other celebrity. Did he or she live up to students' imaginings? How did students feel after confronting this person up close? *Students probably recognized more ordinary qualities in the celebrity upon closer inspection and felt some disappointment.*

The Far and the Near

Thomas Wolfe

On the outskirts of a little town upon a rise of land that swept back from the railway there was a tidy little cottage of white boards, trimmed vividly with green blinds. To one side of the house there was a garden neatly pat-
❶ terned with plots of growing vegetables, and an
❷ arbor for the grapes which ripened late in August. Before the house there were three mighty oaks which sheltered it in their clean and massive shade in summer, and to the other side there was a border of gay flowers. The whole place had an air of tidiness, thrift, and modest comfort.

Block Scheduling Strategies

Consider these suggestions to take advantage of extended class time:

- After reading Background for Understanding (p. 700), invite students to discuss their own knowledge of the American railroad.
- Have students complete the journal activity in Connect Your Experience (p. 701).
- If you have access to technology, have students learn more by reviewing *The History of American Literature* CD-ROM feature about the author.
- Have students complete the Humanities Connection: Art page in ***Beyond Literature,*** p. 46.
- Work as a class to complete the Grammar and Style activity (p. 701).
- Have students complete the Interview activity (p. 707), contacting interviewees through Internet usergroups if possible.
- Before students complete the Guided Writing Lesson (p. 707) invite them to analyze the accuracy and effectiveness of sample promotional brochures you provide.

Stone City, Iowa, Grant Wood, Joslyn Art Museum, Omaha, Nebraska, © Estate of Grant Wood/Licensed by VAGA, New York, NY

3 ▲ **Critical Viewing** How does this painting reflect the engineer's perspective on the farms and villages he sees along his train route? **[Analyze]**

Every day, a few minutes after two o'clock in the afternoon, the limited express between two cities passed this spot. At that moment the great train, having halted for a breathing space at the town nearby, was beginning to lengthen evenly into its stroke, but it had not yet reached the full drive of its terrific speed. It swung into view deliberately, swept past with a powerful swaying motion of the engine, a low smooth rumble of its heavy cars upon pressed steel, and then it vanished in the cut. For a moment the progress of the engine could be marked by heavy bellowing puffs of smoke that burst at spaced intervals above the edges of the meadow grass, and finally nothing could be heard but
4 the solid clacking tempo of the wheels receding into the drowsy stillness of the afternoon.

Every day for more than twenty years, as the train had approached this house, the engineer had blown on the whistle, and every day, as soon as she heard this signal, a woman had appeared on the back porch of the little house and waved to him. 5 At first she had a small child clinging to her skirts, and now this child had grown to full womanhood, and every day she, too, came with her mother to the porch and waved.

The engineer had grown old and gray in service. He had driven his great train, loaded with its weight of lives, across the land ten thousand times. His own children had grown up and married, and four times he had seen before him on the tracks the ghastly dot of

◆ **Build Vocabulary**

tempo (tem´ pō) *n.*: Rate of activity of a sound or motion; pace

Customize for
ESL Students

Some of Wolfe's sophisticated sentences may challenge these students. Suggest that they rephrase difficult sentences using a simple subject-verb-object construction. These students may also benefit from using the Identify Key Ideas page in ***Strategies for Diverse Student Needs,*** p. 46.

▶Critical Viewing◀

3 Analyze Students may note that the painting depicts the town from afar and above, as a train engineer would view it.

◆ Build Vocabulary

4 The Word Root *-temp-*
Remind students of *tempo's* root: *-temp-*. How does understanding the word's root and meaning help students visualize and hear the train's movement? *Linking tempo to -temp- and "time" may help students hear and experience the rhythmic motion of the train.*

◆ Critical Thinking

5 Interpret The narrator uses the phrase "every day" three times in the same paragraph. Have students discuss possible reasons for this repetition. What might the narrator be telling readers about the life of the engineer? *The narrator uses the repetition of the phrase "every day" to emphasize the monotony of the engineer's life.*

Read to
Interpret

Before students begin reading this story, tell them it has meaning which reaches deeper than just the plot and that they should read with a purpose to interpret. A good strategy is to ask questions. Encourage them to ask "Why?" as they read: "What is the author saying by describing this detail or action?" "Why did he or she include it?

Humanities: Art

Stone City, Iowa, 1930, by Grant Wood.

This painting illustrates what some might call a typical midwestern American small town, similar to that viewed by the engineer in "The Far and the Near."

Grant Wood, an American painter, was a lifelong resident of Iowa, a state where rural small towns abound. He studied painting in Europe before returning to Iowa to embrace the inspiration he found in its familiar people and places.

Stone City, Iowa, is a perfect example of Wood's move toward painting everyday objects and scenes. Although the painting depicts realistic elements, the almost geometric forms give the picture a surrealistic air. Use these questions for discussion:

1. What elements in this painting underscore the importance of perspective addressed in Wolfe's story? *The picture's rising foreground and diminishing background frame the town, making it seem more important. Similarly, the engineer's distant perspective on the woman diminishes the details around her.*
2. How does the painting capture the unreal quality of the engineer's view of the town and the woman? *The composition and smooth-edged outline of individual elements make these seem artificial, like toys modeled on the real thing.*

Follow up with the Humanities Connection: Art page in Beyond Literature, p. 46.

Customize for
Bodily/Kinesthetic Learners
These students will better appreciate the engineer's changing perspective by experiencing it physically. Have them choose a distant classroom object to observe as they approach nearer and nearer to it. Discuss how the changing perspective affects their responses to the object.

◆ Grammar and Style

❶ Participial Phrases Have students identify the participial phrase in this passage and label it restrictive or nonrestrictive. Then have them explain their answer. *The participial phrase "schooled by the qualities of faith and courage and humbleness that attended his labor," modifies "he." It is nonrestrictive because it is not essential to the sentence.*

◆ Critical Thinking

❷ Infer The narrator uses the word *sorcery,* meaning "witchcraft" in an unusual context. Ask students: What does this word suggest to you about the engineer's view of the two women? *Responses can include: He has imbued them with special, almost magical powers.*

◆ Reading Strategy

❸ Predict Students should be able to predict that the engineer will be surprised somehow when he carries out his resolution.

◆ Literary Focus

❹ Climax and Anticlimax Responses may include: The engineer initially expects the woman to be "beautiful and enduring." Now he sees that she appears ordinary and unattractive. This contrast creates an anticlimactic feeling.

tragedy converging like a cannon ball to its eclipse of horror at the boiler head[1]—a light spring wagon filled with children, with its clustered row of small stunned faces; a cheap automobile stalled upon the tracks, set with the wooden figures of people paralyzed with fear; a battered hobo walking by the rail, too deaf and old to hear the whistle's warning; and a form flung past his window with a scream—all this the man had seen and known. He had known all the grief, the joy, the peril and the labor such a man could know; he had grown seamed and weathered in his loyal service, and now, ❶ schooled by the qualities of faith and courage and humbleness that attended his labor, he had grown old, and had the grandeur and the wisdom these men have.

But no matter what peril or tragedy he had known, the vision of the little house and the women waving to him with a brave free motion of the arm had become fixed in the mind of the engineer as something beautiful and enduring, something beyond all change and ruin, and something that would always be the same, no matter what mishap, grief or error might break the iron schedule of his days.

The sight of the little house and of these two women gave him the most extraordinary happiness he had ever known. He had seen them in a thousand lights, a hundred weathers. He had seen them through the harsh bare light of wintry gray across the ❷ brown and frosted stubble of the earth, and he had seen them again in the green luring sorcery of April.

He felt for them and for the little house in which they lived such tenderness as a man might feel for his own children, and at length the picture of their lives was carved so sharply in his heart that he felt that he knew their lives completely, to every hour and moment of the day, and he resolved that one day, when his years of service should be ended, he would go and find these people and speak at last with them whose lives had been so wrought into his own.

> ❸ **◆ Reading Strategy**
> Can you predict what will happen when the engineer carries out his resolution?

That day came. At last the engineer stepped from a train onto the station platform of the town where these two women lived. His years upon the rail had ended. He was a pensioned servant of his company, with no more work to do. The engineer walked slowly through the station and out into the streets of the town. Everything was as strange to him as if he had never seen this town before. As he walked on, his sense of bewilderment and confusion grew. Could this be the town he had passed ten thousand times? Were these the same houses he had seen so often from the high windows of his cab? It was all as unfamiliar, as disquieting as a city in a dream, and the perplexity of his spirit increased as he went on.

Presently the houses thinned into the straggling outposts of the town, and the street faded into a country road—the one on which the women lived. And the man plodded on slowly in the heat and dust. At length he stood before the house he sought. He knew at once that he had found the proper place. He saw the lordly oaks before the house, the flower beds, the garden and the arbor, and farther off, the glint of rails.

Yes, this was the house he sought, the place he had passed so many times, the destination he had longed for with such happiness. But now that he had found it, now that he was here, why did his hand falter on the gate; why had the town, the road, the earth, the very entrance to this place he loved turned unfamiliar as the landscape of some ugly dream? Why did he now feel this sense of confusion, doubt and hopelessness?

At length he entered by the gate, walked slowly up the path and in a moment more had mounted three short steps that led up to the porch, and was knocking at the door. Presently he heard steps in the hall, the door was opened, and a woman stood facing him.

And instantly, with a sense of bitter loss and grief, he was sorry he had come. He knew at once that the woman who stood there looking at him with a mistrustful eye was the same woman who had waved to

1. **boiler head:** The front section of a steam locomotive.

Speaking, Listening, and Viewing Mini-Lesson

Music Critique

This mini-lesson supports the Speaking, Listening, and Viewing activity in the Idea Bank on p. 707.

Introduce the Concept Tell students that songs can capture an experience or subject by describing it or evoking its mood. A critique enables listeners to analyze how a particular song address its topic.

Develop Background The following suggestions will help students prepare for their critique.

- Present criticism objectively and respectfully.
- Cite specific examples or reasons from the song lyrics or melody to support your critique.
- Use adjectives to describe the mood evoked by a song: How does it make you feel about railroad travel?

Apply the Information With this background, students should be able to conduct a constructive discussion about the music they have heard. Remind them there is no "right" answer in a critique, only poorly or well supported opinions.

Assess the Outcome Poll the class on students' success as music critics. Were they able to support their ideas with details from the songs?

him so many thousand times. But her face was harsh and pinched and meager; the flesh sagged wearily in sallow folds, and the small eyes peered at him with timid suspicion and uneasy doubt. All the brave freedom, the warmth and the affection that he had read into her gesture, vanished in the moment that he saw her and heard her unfriendly tongue.

> ◆ **Literary Focus**
> 4 How is the woman's appearance anticlimactic?

5 And now his own voice sounded unreal and ghastly to him as he tried to explain his presence, to tell her who he was and the reason he had come. But he faltered on, fighting stubbornly against the horror of regret, confusion, disbelief that surged up in his spirit, drowning all his former joy and making his act of hope and tenderness seem shameful to him.

At length the woman invited him almost unwillingly into the house, and called her daughter in a harsh shrill voice. Then, for a brief agony of time, the man sat in an ugly little parlor, and he tried to talk while the two women stared at him with a dull, bewildered hostility, a sullen, timorous restraint.

And finally, stammering a crude farewell, he departed. He walked away down the path and then along the road toward town, and suddenly he knew that he was an old man. His heart, which had been brave and confident when it looked along the familiar vista of the rails, was now sick with doubt and horror as it saw the strange and unsuspected visage of an earth which had always been within a stone's throw of him, and which he had never seen or known. And he knew that all the magic of that bright lost way, the vista of that shining line, the imagined corner of that small good universe of hope's desire, was gone forever, could never be got back again.

◆ Build Vocabulary

sallow (sal´ ō) *adj.*: Sickly; pale yellow

sullen (sul´ ən) *adj.*: Sulky; glum

timorous (tim´ ər əs) *adj.*: Full of fear

visage (viz´ ij) *n.*: Appearance

Guide for Responding

◆ Literature and Your Life

Reader's Response As you read about the engineer's approaching visit to the little town, what did you hope he would find?

Thematic Focus The engineer is crushed when he discovers that his optimism was falsely based. Is it possible to confront reality and remain hopeful about life? Explain.

☑ Check Your Comprehension

1. Describe the engineer's daily experience for the last twenty years.
2. How does the engineer feel about the little house and the two women?
3. How does the engineer's life change during the story?
4. What realization does the engineer come to at the end of the story?

◆ Critical Thinking

INTERPRET

1. The narrator uses the phrase "every day" several times in the opening paragraphs. What does this tell you about the engineer's life? **[Interpret]**
2. What does the house represent to the engineer? **[Infer]**
3. When does the engineer first sense that his experience is unlikely to match his expectations? **[Connect]**
4. How do the engineer's observations in the final scene contrast with his expectations? **[Contrast]**
5. How does the title of the story relate to its content? **[Interpret]**

APPLY

6. What is Wolfe saying about life through this story? **[Generalize]**

Beyond the Selection

FURTHER READING

Other Works By Thomas Wolfe

Look Homeward Angel
Of Time and the River
You Can't Go Home Again

Other Works With the Theme of Changing Perspective

To Kill a Mockingbird, Harper Lee
Catcher in the Rye, J. D. Salinger

Preview these works before recommending them to students.

INTERNET

You and your students may find additional information about Thomas Wolfe and "The Far and the Near" on the Internet. We suggest the following sites. Please be aware, however, that sites may have changed since this information was published.

For selected quotations from Wolfe's life and writings, go to **http://www.cms.uncwil.edu/~connelly/quote2.htm**

For a chronology of Wolfe's life, go to **http:// www.cms.uncwil.edu/~connelly/calendar.htm**

We *strongly recommend* that you preview sites before you send students to them.

◆ Literature and Your Life

5 Ask students to recall times when they felt strongly about a particular course of action only to discover later that it was a mistake. How did they feel about their earlier hopes and aspirations? *Students may recall feeling regret for a poor decision or sadness for setting sights on a foolish goal.*

Customize for AP Students

Help these students to appreciate how Wolfe crafts the changing mood as the story progresses. Challenge them to contrast connotations in the story's early and later language.

Reinforce and Extend

Answers

◆ Literature and Your Life

Reader's Response Students should offer reasons for their answers.

Thematic Focus Encourage students to discuss their opinions.

☑ Check Your Comprehension

1. He travels the same route, passes a house outside a little town, and sees a woman and her daughter who wave to him.
2. He idealizes them.
3. He finishes his career and retires.
4. He realizes that his magical vision is gone forever.

◆ Critical Thinking

1. It suggests that his life is monotonous.
2. It represents enduring values and a simple way of life.
3. He realizes it as soon as he steps off the train.
4. Suggested response: The woman had come to represent warmth and beauty. As it turns out, she is unfriendly and unattractive.
5. Both the title and the story focus on contrasting views of something from two different vantage points.
6. Suggested response: He suggests that reality rarely lives up to people's idealized views.

Answers

◆ Reading Strategy

1. Students will most likely respond that they anticipated that the engineer's experience of actually meeting the two woman would not live up to his expectations. As support, students may suggest that these women were too wonderful or that the engineer had given them too much power.
2. Students may respond that they expected that the engineer's experiences of actually interacting with people would be dramatically different from viewing them from a distance.
3. Students should support their answers with solid reasons.

◆ Build Vocabulary

Using the Latin Root *-temp-*

1. tempo; 2. extemporaneous; 3. contemporary; 4. temporary

Using the Word Bank

Sentences should contain the following words:

1. sallow; 2. timorous; 3. visage; 4. sullen; 5. tempo

◆ Literary Focus

1. The rising action is built around the engineer's anticipation of meeting the woman and her daughter. The fact that the engineer's actual experience of meeting them sharply contrasts with his expectations makes the ending an anticlimax.
2. Suggested response: The anticlimax is a letdown for both the engineer and the reader. This leads to an examination of the underlying significance of the event.

◆ Grammar and Style

Practice

1. . . . and now, schooled by the qualities of faith and courage and humbleness that attended his labor, he had grown old . . .
2. . . . tragedy converging like a cannon ball to its eclipse of horror at the boiler head . . .
3. He had driven his great train, loaded with its weight of lives, across the land ten thousand times.
4. . . . nothing could be heard but the solid clacking tempo of wheels receding into the drowsy stillness of the afternoon.

Guide for Responding *(continued)*

◆ Reading Strategy

PREDICT

"The Far and the Near" offered several clues to help you **predict** upcoming events or emotions. Use those clues to answer these questions.

1. When you read about the engineer's resolution to visit the two women after retiring, what did you think would happen? Identify the details from the story that support the prediction you made.
2. Based on your own experience, how did you predict the engineer's view of the world would change when he stepped down from the "high windows of his cab"?
3. (a) What prediction did you make about the woman's likely reception of the engineer?
(b) How, if at all, did you revise your prediction as you read the story's ending?

◆ Build Vocabulary

USING THE LATIN ROOT *-temp-*

The Latin root *-temp-* means "time." Use your knowledge of this root to replace the italicized word or phrase in each of the following sentences with the appropriate word from this list:

temporary	extemporaneous
tempo	contemporary

1. The band slowed the *pace* of the music.
2. His *spur of the moment* wedding proposal caught his girlfriend off guard.
3. Judging from the age of the paper, these two documents appear to be *of the same time period*.
4. I have to walk to school until the car is fixed, but I'm hoping that it will be just *for a short time*.

USING THE WORD BANK: Context

For each item, follow the directions by writing a sentence using a word from the word bank.

1. Describe a man who has been ill for many weeks.
2. Describe how a child might feel before visiting the dentist.
3. Describe a student giving an outrageous reason for not having completed her research paper.
4. Write the first sentence of a story about a girl who is unhappy and angry about her life.
5. Describe activity in a busy office.

◆ Literary Focus

CLIMAX AND ANTICLIMAX

Although you might have predicted that all would not turn out exactly as the engineer hoped, the reception he receives at the "tidy little cottage" is a devastating **anticlimax**.

1. Explain how the rising action of the story makes the story's resolution an anticlimax rather than a climax.
2. What effect does the anticlimax have on the engineer and on the reader?

◆ Grammar and Style

RESTRICTIVE AND NONRESTRICTIVE PARTICIPIAL PHRASES

Participial phrases can help writers insert action into a description. A **participle** is a form of a verb that acts as an adjective. A **participial phrase** consists of a participle and its modifiers or complements. The entire phrase acts as an adjective.

If a participial phrase is essential to the meaning of the sentence, it is **restrictive** and not set off by commas. If the phrase is not essential to the sentence, it is **nonrestrictive** and should be set off by commas.

Practice Write the following passages on your paper. Underline the participial phrases and add commas as necessary.

1. . . . and now schooled by the qualities of faith and courage and humbleness that attended his labor he had grown old . . .
2. . . . four times he had seen before him on the tracks the ghastly dot of tragedy converging like a cannon ball to its eclipse of horror at the boiler head . . .
3. . . . He had driven his great train loaded with its weight of lives across the land ten thousand times.
4. . . . nothing could be heard but the solid clacking tempo of the wheels receding into the drowsy stillness of the afternoon.

Looking at Style Explain how each of the participial phrases in the Practice enables Wolfe to insert action into a description.

Looking at Style

Suggested response: In the first example, the participial phrase captures the effect of the engineer's experiences on his personality. The other three examples capture actions associated with the train.

Grammar Reinforcement

For additional instruction and practice, use the page on Participial Phrases, p. 32, in the *Writer's Solution Grammar Practice Book.*

Reteach

To help students make predictions, read the story to them and have them follow along. At appropriate points, stop and have students write down their predictions. When you finish reading, retrace the story, asking students to explain why they made the predictions they did, and upon what textual evidence they based their predictions.

Build Your Portfolio

Idea Bank

Writing

1. Description Using details from the story and your imagination, write a description of the countryside and sights the engineer sees as he travels his daily train route.

2. First-Person Account What did the woman who lives in the green and white cottage think of the engineer's visit? Write an account of the visit as she might have described it to a neighbor.

3. Comparison-and-Contrast Essay Write an essay in which you compare the two viewpoints suggested by the title "The Far and the Near." How does the engineer's view of his world depend on his proximity to it? What does the story suggest about the dreams we dream from afar?

Speaking, Listening, and Viewing

4. Interview Is there really something special about train travel? Interview someone who has traveled great distances by train about their experiences. Share your findings with the class.

5. Music Critique Locate recordings of several songs about trains. Play them for the class, then lead a discussion on how rail travel is portrayed. Are the songs realistic? Romantic? **[Music Link]**

Researching and Representing

6. Railroad Report Research the evolution of the railroad and the nation's love affair with it. In a written report, explain one aspect of the history of the railroad and the changes that have taken place in recent decades. **[Social Studies Link]**

7. Map Create a map or three-dimensional diagram of a train route, and embellish it with real or imagined details. The route may be short—between two towns—or long. **[Geography Link]**

Online Activity www.phlit.phschool.com

Guided Writing Lesson

Brochure on Train Travel

"The Far and the Near" is built on the simple premise that the world can appear better than it really is when viewed from a train. Think like a salesperson and use this insight to promote rail travel. Write a brochure to encourage people to travel by train rather than by car, bus, or plane. Describe the benefits of seeing America by rail. Be careful, however, to keep your brochure believable by insuring that all your information is accurate.

Writing Skills Focus: Accuracy

Accuracy in your brochure is essential. Tell the truth so that the readers you convince to travel by train won't be disappointed. Keep these tips in mind:

- Don't exaggerate benefits or make unrealistic promises about services that train travel could never realistically deliver.
- Gather facts from reliable sources, and verify information obtained from unofficial sources.
- Include quotations from real people, recorded accurately word for word.

Prewriting Research information about train travel, focusing if you like on a particular area of the country. Note facts about routes, schedules, prices, seating and sleeping accommodations, and meals. Then jot down sensory details you might use to flesh out your descriptions.

Drafting Open with an anecdote, a quotation about train travel, or a vivid description of a place viewed from a train. Use your notes to highlight each of the features you identified, adding descriptive and sensory words to entice passengers.

Revising Read your brochure aloud, checking for promises that sound "too good to be true." Can you verify the accuracy of your statements?

Idea Bank

Customizing for ***Performance Levels***

Following are suggestions for matching Idea Bank topics with your students' performance levels:
Less Advanced Students: 1, 4
Average Students: 2, 5, 6, 7
More Advanced Students: 3, 6

Customizing for ***Learning Modalities***

Following are suggestions for matching Idea Bank topics with your students' learning modalities:
Interpersonal: 4
Musical/Rhythmic: 4, 5
Visual/Spatial: 6
Logical/Mathematical: 7

Guided Writing Lesson

For more prewriting, elaboration, and revision strategies, see *Prentice Hall Writing and Grammar.*

Writing Lab CD-ROM

Have students complete the tutorial on Description. Follow these steps:

1. Have students view the interactive model of a travel brochure.
2. Have students use the Sensory Word Bins to help them gather details.
3. Have students draft on computer.
4. Have students use the revision checkers to help them revise.

ASSESSMENT OPTIONS

Formal Assessment, Selection Test, pp. 212–214, and Assessment Resources Software. The selection test is designed so that it can be easily customized to the performance levels of your students.

Alternative Assessment, p. 46, includes options for less advanced students, more advanced students, musical/rhythmic learners, interpersonal learners, and visual/spatial learners.

PORTFOLIO ASSESSMENT

Use the following rubrics in the ***Alternative Assessment*** booklet to assess student writing:
Description: Description Rubric, p. 112
First-Person Account: Fictional Narrative Rubric, p. 110
Comparison and Contrast: Comparison and Contrast Rubric, p. 118
Guided Writing Lesson: Description Rubric, p. 112

Prepare and Engage

LESSON OBJECTIVES

1. **To develop vocabulary and word identification skills**
   - Latin Word Roots: *-satis-*
   - Using the Word Bank: Context
2. **To use a variety of reading strategies to comprehend poetry**
   - Connect Your Experience
   - Reading Strategy: Paraphrase
   - Background for Understanding
3. **To increase knowledge of other cultures and to connect common elements across cultures**
   - Connecting Themes Across Cultures (ATE)
4. **To express and support responses to the text**
   - Critical Thinking Questions
   - Viewing and Representing Mini-Lesson (ATE)
   - Idea Bank: Ars Poetica
   - Idea Bank: Comparison and Contrast
   - Idea Bank: Response to Criticism
   - Idea Bank: Round Table Discussion
5. **To analyze literary elements**
   - Literary Focus
6. **To plan, prepare, organize, and present literary interpretations**
   - Idea Bank: Introduction
   - Idea Bank: Illustration
   - Idea Bank: Poetry Collection
7. **To use recursive writing processes to write a definition**
   - Guided Writing Lesson
8. **To increase knowledge of the rules of grammar and usage**
   - Grammar and Style: Subject Complements

Test Preparation

Reading Comprehension: Analyze Sentence Meaning (ATE, p. 709)
The teaching tips and sample test item in this workshop support the instruction and practice in the unit workshop:
Reading Comprehension: Sentence-Completion Questions (SE, p. 863)

Guide for Interpreting

Wallace Stevens *(1879–1955)*

Wallace Stevens believed that the goal of poetry was to capture the interaction of fantasy and reality. He spent his career writing poems that delve into the ways in which the imagination can shape the way in which we perceive the physical world.

Stevens was born and raised in Reading, Pennsylvania. After completing his education, he took a job at an insurance company in Hartford, Connecticut, and eventually became the company's vice president. He didn't publish his first collection of poetry, *Harmonium* (1923), until he was over forty. In this book, Stevens uses dazzling imagery to capture the beauty of the physical world, while expressing the dependence of that beauty on the perceptions of the observer. Although the book received little public attention, it was praised by critics and launched Stevens into a successful literary career.

Stevens went on to publish many volumes of poetry, including *Ideas of Order* (1935), *Parts of a World* (1942), *Transport to Summer* (1947), and *The Auroras of Autumn* (1950). His *Collected Poems* earned him the Pulitzer Prize in 1955. Despite his success as a poet, however, Stevens continued his career in insurance. He rarely appeared in public and only began giving readings toward the end of his life.

Archibald MacLeish *(1892–1982)*

Archibald MacLeish was trained as a lawyer, but unlike Stevens, he turned his back on his first career to devote himself completely to poetry. MacLeish's early poems, such as "Ars Poetica," are experimental in form, reflecting the influence of the Modernists. However, in an effort to help his readers more easily understand his work, he later tried to make his poems more traditional. As unrest spread through the world in the 1930's, MacLeish used poetry to explore political and social issues.

Marianne Moore *(1887–1972)*

Born in Kirkwood, Missouri, Marianne Moore first became an influential literary figure when she became the editor of *The Dial*, a highly regarded literary journal. In that role, she encouraged many new writers by publishing their work. However, she was hesitant to publish her own work, despite the fact that it had been read and admired by many noted poets. In fact, her first book, *Poems* (1921), was published without her knowledge.

◆ Background for Understanding

LITERATURE: STEVENS'S VIEWS OF POETRY

Stevens believed that the Modern Age was a time of uncertainty and that it was the duty of the poet to provide new ways of understanding the world. His views of poetry reflect the influence of Symbolism, a literary movement that originated in France in the last half of the nineteenth century. Because people perceive the physical world in different ways, the Symbolist poets believed that the ideas and emotions that people experience are personal and difficult to communicate. As a result, these poets avoided directly stating their ideas in their poetry. Instead, they tried to convey meaning through clusters of symbols—people, places, and objects that have meanings in themselves and also represent something larger than themselves. Because of this reliance on symbols, Symbolist poems—and the works of Stevens—can often be interpreted in a number of different ways.

Prentice Hall Literature Program Resources

REINFORCE / RETEACH / EXTEND

Selection Support Pages
Build Vocabulary: Word Roots: *-satis-*, p. 216
Grammar and Style: Subject Complements, p. 217
Reading Strategy: Paraphrase, p. 218
Literary Focus: Simile, p. 219

Strategies for Diverse Student Needs, p. 47

Beyond Literature
Humanities Connection: Photography, p. 47

Formal Assessment Selection Test, pp. 215–217; Assessment Resources Software

Alternative Assessment, p. 47

Resource Pro CD-ROM

Listening to Literature Audiocassettes

Literature CD-ROM *The History of American Literature:* Part 2, Disk 1, Feature 10, and Part 2, Disk 2, Feature 5.

Of Modern Poetry ◆ Anecdote of the Jar Ars Poetica ◆ Poetry

◆ Literature and Your Life

Connect Your Experience

You probably have your own special ways of looking at the activities you care about most deeply. Maybe you have strong views of what makes good music or a unique way of looking at your favorite sport. In the selections you're about to read, the writers present their views on a subject that they are passionate about: poetry.

Journal Writing Although people have debated the rules of the genre for ages, poetry defies definition. What is your definition of poetry?

Thematic Focus: Facing Troubled Times

During the time in which these poets lived, technological advances and wars with an unparalleled scale of destruction changed how people viewed the world. At the same time, the arts, including literature, underwent major changes. With these changes, writers had to develop new ways of defining literary forms and techniques. These selections present new ways of looking at poetry.

◆ Literary Focus

Simile

A **simile** is a comparison between two seemingly dissimilar things. A signal word such as "like" or "as" indicates the comparison. For example, the word *like* signals the comparison in the following simile:

The sound of the explosion echoed through the air *like thunder*.

Like poetry itself, similes enable us to see the world in startling new ways.

◆ Grammar and Style

Subject Complements

A **subject complement** follows a linking verb and identifies or describes the subject. It may be a noun, a pronoun, or an adjective. Sentences containing subject complements are especially effective when a writer's purpose is to define something. For example, in several of the selections that follow, the poets use subject complements in defining poetry. Look at this example:

A poem should be <u>wordless</u> . . .

◆ Reading Strategy

Paraphrase

Because poetry is written in verse and is likely to contain unexpected words and images, it can be difficult to understand. One way to make sure that you grasp what you are reading is to **paraphrase**—to identify key ideas and restate them. For example, you might restate the opening lines of Moore's "Poetry" *("I, too, dislike it: there are things that are important beyond/all this fiddle.")* as "I also dislike poetry. It's nonsense, and a lot of other things are more important." Paraphrasing can remove barriers that make some poems seem too difficult to understand.

◆ Build Vocabulary

Latin Roots: *-satis-*

In "Of Modern Poetry," Wallace Stevens uses the word *insatiable*. This word contains the Latin root *-satis-*, which means "enough." How does the root contribute to the meaning of *insatiable*—"constantly wanting more"? What other words can you think of that contain this root?

Word Bank

Preview this list of words.

suffice
insatiable
slovenly
dominion
palpable
derivative
literalists

Test Preparation Workshop

Reading Comprehension: Analyze Sentence Meaning Many standardized tests require students to correctly answer sentence-completion questions. Often, more than one choice can complete a sentence. Use the following sample item to show students how to analyze sentence meaning to eliminate incorrect choices.

The Symbolist poets believed that the Modern Age was a time of uncertainty, and that people's ideas and emotions were _____ to communicate.

A easy
B fair
C difficult
D enjoyable

The context of the sentence indicates that the correct answer will have a negative connotation, so *A* and *D* are eliminated. Answer choice *B* does not make sense in the sentence. *C* is the best choice.

Interest Grabber Use students' interest in music as a hook to motivate them to read these poems. Start with a class activity in which students share the ways in which their favorite music affects them. Write the responses on the chalkboard. Then have students discuss the role that song lyrics play in eliciting the types of responses they've noted. Using the ideas that have been gathered, work as a class to come up with a short definition of what song lyrics are and how they affect people. Then point out that poetry shares many of the same qualities as song lyrics, and explain to students that they are about to read three poets' definitions of poetry and its impact. Focus their reading by having them compare the poets' definitions of poetry with their own definition of song lyrics.

Connecting Themes Across Cultures

The poets in this section lived in the United States during some very tumultuous times, including both world wars. This unrest affected the themes and styles of writers and the thoughts of leaders, and it also can be seen reflected in the thoughts and writings of prominent figures from other countries. In Russia, for example, the Bolshevik Revolution took place during this time, turning the whole of Russian society upside-down.

Customize for
Less Proficient Readers

The difficult vocabulary and abstract nature of these poems will challenge these students. Preview the vocabulary words in the Word Bank, then use the page on explaining and responding to poetry, p. 47 in ***Strategies for Diverse Student Needs,*** to prepare these students to read. Have students pause to paraphrase after every few lines to aid comprehension.

Customize for
AP Students

More advanced readers can analyze the symbolism in the poems through critical reading and paraphrasing. Have student teams or groups identify and explain symbolic elements in their own words.

Develop Understanding

One-Minute Insight These two poems explore the creative process as defined by Wallace Stevens. They break down that process into the intimate moments of imagination, inspiration, and painstaking perfectionism that together work to create poetry. Stevens presents as symbols of creativity a dialogue between actor and audience—mind and ear, and a jar, perhaps holding the human imagination. In exploring Stevens' symbols, readers can bring their own instincts to understanding the core of human creativity.

Literature CD-ROM To introduce students to the poetry of Wallace Stevens, use *The History of American Literature:* Part 2, Disk 1, Feature 10.

◆ Literary Focus

❶ **Simile** Have students identify the simile in this line. Ask students how the comparison adds to the definition of poetry. *The simile is "like an insatiable actor" with the first element, "poetry," implied from earlier lines. Students may note that comparing poetry to a human being makes it easier for readers to visualize.*

◆ Reading Strategy

❷ **Paraphrase** Ask students to restate in their own words the content of these lines. *Students' paraphrases should include: The poet must listen carefully to inspiration, experimenting with different forms and testing each word and approach against an inner and trusted instant until satisfied.*

Customize for
Gifted/Talented Students
"Of Modern Poetry" is about creativity, reflecting a writer's thoughts during times of change. Ask students to choose an idea in the poem and use it as the starting point for a collage. Challenge them to express some of Stevens's ideas in this visual format.

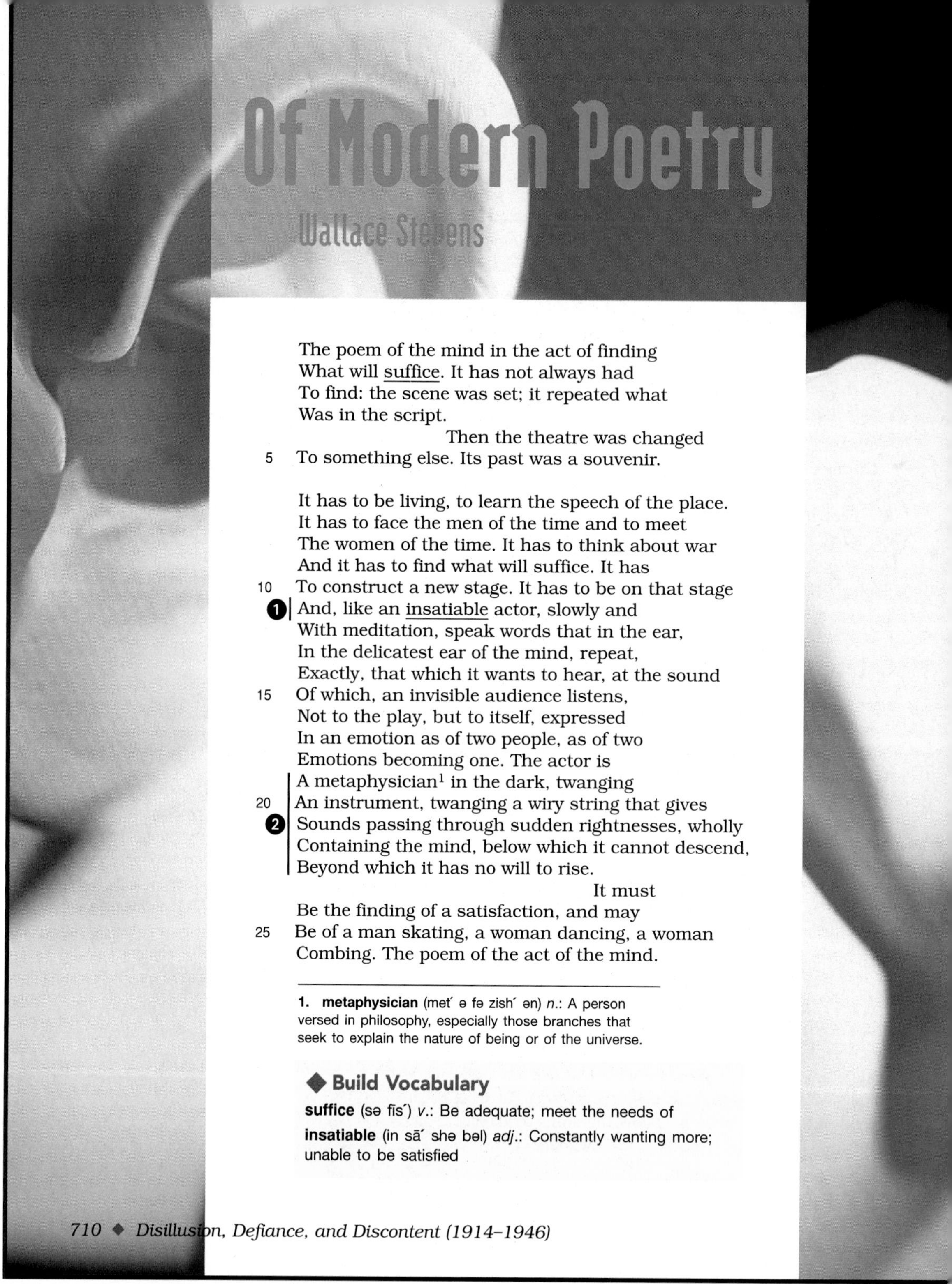

Of Modern Poetry

Wallace Stevens

The poem of the mind in the act of finding
What will <u>suffice</u>. It has not always had
To find: the scene was set; it repeated what
Was in the script.
                    Then the theatre was changed
To something else. Its past was a souvenir.

It has to be living, to learn the speech of the place.
It has to face the men of the time and to meet
The women of the time. It has to think about war
And it has to find what will suffice. It has
To construct a new stage. It has to be on that stage
❶ And, like an <u>insatiable</u> actor, slowly and
With meditation, speak words that in the ear,
In the delicatest ear of the mind, repeat,
Exactly, that which it wants to hear, at the sound
Of which, an invisible audience listens,
Not to the play, but to itself, expressed
In an emotion as of two people, as of two
Emotions becoming one. The actor is
A metaphysician[1] in the dark, twanging
An instrument, twanging a wiry string that gives
❷ Sounds passing through sudden rightnesses, wholly
Containing the mind, below which it cannot descend,
Beyond which it has no will to rise.
                    It must
Be the finding of a satisfaction, and may
Be of a man skating, a woman dancing, a woman
Combing. The poem of the act of the mind.

---

1. **metaphysician** (met´ ə fə zish´ ən) *n.*: A person versed in philosophy, especially those branches that seek to explain the nature of being or of the universe.

◆ Build Vocabulary

suffice (sə fīs´) *v.*: Be adequate; meet the needs of

insatiable (in sā´ shə bəl) *adj.*: Constantly wanting more; unable to be satisfied

Block Scheduling Strategies

Consider these suggestions to take advantage of extended class time:

- Have students complete the journal activity in Literature and Your Life (p. 709) and exchange their poetry definitions for discussion.
- Prior to reading, have students read criticism and analysis of the poets on the Internet.
- Have students complete the Illustration Project (p. 717) and discuss together how interpreting poetry visually adds to readers' appreciation.
- Have student pairs quiz each other with the Check Your Comprehension questions (pp. 711 and 715). Discuss any remaining confusions.
- Have students complete the Reading Strategy activity (p. 716), continuing through the full selection text if time allows.
- Have students complete one of the Writing assignments in the Idea Bank (p. 717). Before students write, prompt student groups to brainstorm definitions, comparisons, or arguments.

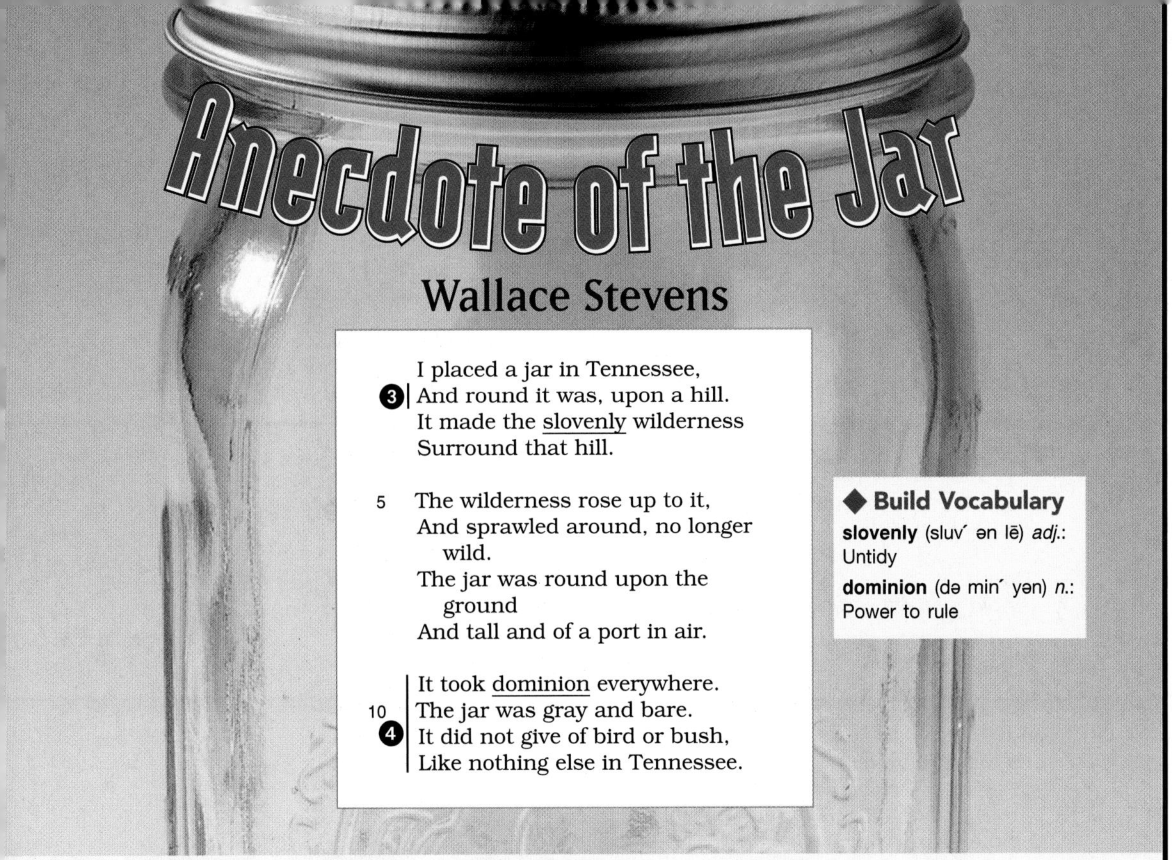

Anecdote of the Jar

Wallace Stevens

I placed a jar in Tennessee,
❸ And round it was, upon a hill.
It made the slovenly wilderness
Surround that hill.

The wilderness rose up to it,
And sprawled around, no longer
wild.
The jar was round upon the
ground
And tall and of a port in air.

It took dominion everywhere.
The jar was gray and bare.
❹ It did not give of bird or bush,
Like nothing else in Tennessee.

◆ Build Vocabulary

slovenly (sluv´ ən lē) *adj.*: Untidy

dominion (də min´ yən) *n.*: Power to rule

Guide for Responding

◆ Literature and Your Life

Reader's Response What is your reaction to the ideas Stevens presents in "Of Modern Poetry"? Why?

Thematic Focus In "Of Modern Poetry," what does Stevens mean by the line, "Then the theater was changed"?

☑ Check Your Comprehension

1. What does "Of Modern Poetry" suggest about the relationship modern poetry needs to have with the people of its time?
2. Where does the speaker in "Anecdote of the Jar" place the jar?

◆ Critical Thinking

INTERPRET

1. Describe the jar's effect on the wilderness in "Anecdote of the Jar." **[Analyze]**
2. How is the impression of the jar that the speaker conveys in the third stanza different from that conveyed in the first two stanzas? **[Compare and Contrast]**
3. Find evidence in "Anecdote of the Jar" to support this interpretation: The jar symbolizes the human imagination, and the poem says nature is shaped by our perceptions. **[Support]**
4. Find two lines from "Of Modern Poetry" that suggest that writing poetry requires effort and precision. **[Support]**

Viewing and Representing Mini-Lesson

Illustration This mini-lesson supports activity 6 in the Idea Bank, p. 717.

Introduce the Concept Remind students that each word in a poem is carefully and deliberately chosen for its sound, appearance, and meaning. Poets craft their work until it says exactly what they want it to say.

Develop Background Have students work in groups to think of possible ideas for their illustrations. Tell students that they can paint, draw, or create a collage. What is important, however, is to capture the essence of the poem in an illustration.

Apply the Information Have students display their illustrations for the class and explain their motivation for representing the scene as they did.

Assess the Outcome Assess students' work on their ability to depict and explain the essence of the scene in the poem.

Customize for
Less Proficient Readers
Encourage these students to first read instinctively for an overall impression of the poem, rather than trying to break down its literal meaning. Then have them reread the poem, focusing on Stevens' use of symbolism to generate meaning.

◆ Grammar and Style

❸ Subject Complements
Challenge students to identify the subject complement in this line. Have them explain its function in this inverted sentence. *The subject complement is "round." It describes "it" or the jar but is placed before it in the sentence for poetic purposes.*

◆ Critical Thinking

❹ Interpret Assuming the jar is the human imagination, what effect does imagination have on our perception of the natural surroundings? *Students may say that the imagination dictates, "takes dominion" over how we perceive our natural surroundings. Imagination is empty without nature as a stimulus.*

Reinforce and Extend

Answers

◆ Literature and Your Life

Reader's Response Students should provide a clear explanation of their reactions.

Thematic Focus Suggested response: The world went through major changes as the modern age began.

☑ Check Your Comprehension

1. It has to "face the men of the time" and "meet the women of the time."
2. He places it in Tennessee.

◆ Critical Thinking

1. Suggested response: The jar gives form to the wilderness.
2. The first two stanzas almost suggest that the jar is attractive; the third tells us that it is not.
3. Suggested response: The jar's effect on the wilderness supports this interpretation.
4. Possible answer: "It has to be living, to learn the speech of the place, . . ." "It has / to construct a new stage. . . ."

Develop Understanding

One-Minute Insight This poem catalogs—by describing what poetry should be—the myriad ways poetry can touch the human spirit. MacLeish uses vivid sensory and figurative language to portray poetry as a living force, rendering it as the outlet for human emotion expressed through concrete and accessible images.

More About the Author
In addition to poetry, Archibald MacLeish wrote criticism and drama—his play *J.B.* was a success on Broadway and won both a Pulitzer Prize and a Tony Award.

◆ Literary Focus

❶ **Simile** After eliciting an identification of the stanza's simile and signal word, ask students to explain the comparison. *The entire stanza is a simile surrounding the signal word "as." MacLeish is comparing poetry with a smooth and mossy stone. The comparison stresses that poetry should communicate through its sensory experiences, not through rhetoric.*

◆ Critical Thinking

❷ **Analyze** How is the statement that poetry should be "wordless" a paradox? *Students should recognize that poetry, which is composed of words, cannot be literally wordless but rather MacLeish is suggesting poetry should rest on its images instead of its words.*

▶Critical Viewing◀

❸ **Interpret** Students should should identify the images in lines 9–14: the moon climbing, bare trees against a moonlit night, and the moon behind the winter leaves.

Ars Poetica[1]

Archibald MacLeish

A poem should be palpable and mute
As a globed fruit.

Dumb
As old medallions to the thumb,

❶ Silent as the sleeve-worn stone
Of casement ledges where the moss has grown—

❷ A poem should be wordless
As the flight of birds.

A poem should be motionless in time
As the moon climbs,

Leaving, as the moon releases
Twig by twig the night-entangled trees,

1. **Ars Poetica:** The title is an allusion to Horace's "Ars Poetica," or "The Art of Poetry," which was composed about 20 B.C.

❸ ▶ Critical Viewing
Which of the poem's images can be found in this photograph? **[Interpret]**

Cross-Curricular Connection: Science

The Moon's Orbit The moon's climb is not really motionless, of course, just slow enough that the movement is difficult to see. It takes 27 days, 7 hours, and 43 minutes for the moon to complete an orbit around the Earth. Each night the moon appears to rise in the sky, both because of its orbiting motion and because the Earth itself is turning. The moon's light—a reflection of the Sun's light—takes different shapes, or phases, as the lit portion of moon surface rotates through our path of vision.

Have students work in groups to calculate the moon's rate of movement through the night sky and create an accurate movable model of the moon and Earth.

Leaving, as the moon behind the winter leaves,
Memory by memory the mind—

A poem should be motionless in time
As the moon climbs. ❹

A poem should be equal to:
Not true.

For all the history of grief
An empty doorway and a maple leaf.

For love
The leaning grasses and two lights above the sea—

A poem should not mean
But be. ❺

◆ Build Vocabulary

palpable (pal′ pə bəl) *adj.*: Able to be touched, felt, or handled

◆ Grammar and Style

❹ Subject Complements Have students name the subject complement in this stanza. Ask them to explain how it modifies the sentence subject. *The subject complement is "motionless." It describes the subject "the poem."*

◆ Literature and Your Life

❺ Ask students what the poem's final stanza means to them. Urge them to consider the role poetry has played in their lives and to recall specific examples of its impact. *Students may mention times of grief or love when poetry moved them, moments when poetry vividly captured a physical experience or setting.*

Customize for *AP Students*

Provide students with the following passage from Horace's "Ars Poetica," to which MacLeish alludes in his title: "It is not enough that poems have beauty of form; they must have charm. . . ."

Ask students to explain the passage and tell whether they think MacLeish would agree with it or not.

Customize for *Verbal/Linguistic Learners*

Pair these students with visual/spatial learners to expand their experience of the poem's imagery. Have students read the poem aloud as their visual/spatial partners illustrate its images with original or located visuals.

Speaking, Listening, and Viewing Mini-Lesson

Round Table Discussion

This mini-lesson supports the Speaking, Listening, and Viewing activity in the Idea Bank on p. 717.

Introduce the Concept Have students review some of the poetry definitions they created in Literature and Your Life (p. 709). Highlight the similarities and differences in the various definitions, pointing out that the poets featured in this selection also had common and divergent views about "What is Poetry?"

Develop Background Before students begin their discussion, have them consider ways to analyze poetry and conduct productive interchanges of ideas. Stress the following points:

- Poetry analysis can be highly subjective. Develop ideas which can be supported, rather than looking for one "right" meaning.
- Remain consistent to the poet's ideas, avoiding the influence of your own personal concept of poetry.

Apply the Information Divide the class into two groups. They should begin by analyzing each poet's views before moving on to the round table discussion. Remind them to adopt appropriate discussion behavior, listening and speaking respectfully.

Assess the Outcome Evaluate group discussions for structure and content. Were the poets' positions accurately and believable presented? Was the discussion productively handled?

Develop Understanding

One-Minute Insight This poem explains why poetry must be accessible to be effective. The speaker acknowledges, with a self-effacing tone, that poetry is unimportant next to world affairs, but insists nonetheless on its place in people's lives. Poetry can command strong emotional reaction. It can be found in nature and in people. Though imperfect when obscure and unfinished, when inexpertly rendered, genuine poetry is worthy of interest.

Literature CD-ROM To introduce students to the poetry of Marianne Moore, use *The History of American Literature:* Part 2, Disk 2, Feature 5.

▶Critical Viewing◀

1 Draw Conclusions Students will likely note a strong contrast, as the painting requires interpretation. It does not present its message in a simple or accessible manner.

◆ Critical Thinking

2 Connect What does this sentence suggest about how poetry can effect readers? What contrast is suggested with the speaker's opening statement? *These lines describe how poetry can evoke such vivid images and emotions that readers clench their fists, open wide their eyes, and feel their hairs rise. Though poetry may be "unimportant" in the larger scheme of things, it remains a powerful communicator.*

◆ Literary Focus

3 Simile Ask: What comparison is made by the simile in this line? How does the simile enhance Moore's description of poetry? *The simile compares a nervous critic to an irritated horse. Students should note that the simile enables Moore to link both people and animals to poetry.*

◆ Reading Strategy

4 Paraphrase Ask students to restate these lines in their own words. *Poetry is not more important as a communication form than business papers, schoolbooks, or other types of writing.*

Poetry

Marianne Moore

Untitled, 1984, Alexander Calder, Solomon R. Guggenheim Museum, New York

▶ **Critical Viewing** 1 How does this modern image compare or contrast with the ideas in Moore's poem? **[Draw Conclusions]**

I, too, dislike it: there are things that are important beyond
  all this fiddle.
 Reading it, however, with a perfect contempt for it, one
   discovers in
 it after all, a place for the genuine.
   Hands that can grasp, eyes
   that can dilate, hair that can rise
   if it must, these things are important not because a

2 high-sounding interpretation can be put upon them but
   because they are
   useful. When they become so <u>derivative</u> as to become
     unintelligible,
 the same thing may be said for all of us, that we do not
   admire what
     we cannot understand: the bat
       holding on upside down or in quest of something to

 eat, elephants pushing, a wild horse taking a roll, a
   tireless wolf under
3 a tree, the immovable critic twitching his skin like a
     horse that feels a flea, the base-
   ball fan, the statistician—
     nor is it valid
4   to discriminate against "business documents and

 schoolbooks"; all these phenomena are important. One
   must make a distinction
   however: when dragged into prominence by half poets,
     the result is not poetry,
 nor till the poets among us can be

Humanities: Art

Untitled, 1984, by Alexander Calder.

This painting is of the modern school, much like Marianne Moore's poetry.

The painter, Alexander Calder, was born in Philadelphia into a family of artists. He studied at the Art Students League and later in Paris. Best known for his innovative mobiles in which—as in this painting—geometric shapes play off one another.

Use the following questions for discussion:

1. How do you think Moore would have felt about this painting? *She might have felt it was too abstract to be useful.*
2. What elements of the painting's style reflect the structure of Moore's poem? *Its whimsical shapes remind readers of Moore's creative punctuation and sentence structure.*

"literalists of
the imagination"—above
insolence and triviality and can present

for inspection, "imaginary gardens with real toads in
them," shall we have
it. In the meantime, if you demand on the one hand,
the raw material of poetry in
all its rawness and
that which is on the other hand
genuine, you are interested in poetry.

◆ Build Vocabulary

derivative (də riv′ ə tiv) *adj.*: Not original; based on something else

literalists (lit′ ər əl ists) *n.*: People who insist on taking words at their exact meaning

Guide for Responding

◆ Literature and Your Life

Reader's Response (a) Are you interested in poetry? Explain. (b) In your opinion, which word or phrase best describes Moore's poem—"fiddle," "derivative," or "genuine"? Explain.

Thematic Focus According to Marianne Moore, what characteristics make poetry useful to its readers?

Group Discussion Some have suggested that the lyrics of popular music are the poetry of today's generation. With classmates, discuss this assertion.

☑ Check Your Comprehension

1. (a) To what does the speaker of "Ars Poetica" compare a poem? (b) How should a poem show the history of grief? (c) How should it show love?
2. (a) What does the speaker of "Poetry" say a person discovers when reading poetry "with a perfect contempt for it"? (b) What happens when poetry is "dragged into prominence by half poets"?

◆ Critical Thinking

INTERPRET

1. What do you think the speaker of "Ars Poetica" means by saying that a poem should be (a) "palpable and mute" (line 1); (b) "wordless" (line 7); and (c) "motionless in time" (line 9)? **[Analyze]**
2. Why do you think MacLeish chose to focus on the emotions of love and grief? **[Infer]**
3. How does the final line of "Ars Poetica" sum up the ideas expressed in the poem? **[Analyze]**
4. What type of poetry does the speaker of "Poetry" dislike? **[Interpret]**
5. (a) What does the speaker mean by saying that poets should be "literalists of the imagination"? (b) What is meant by "imaginary gardens with real toads in them"? **[Interpret]**
6. What qualities does the speaker believe good poetry should possess? **[Interpret]**

COMPARE LITERARY WORKS

7. Explain the similarities and the differences between Moore's views of poetry and MacLeish's label. **[Compare and Contrast]**

Beyond the Selection

FURTHER READING

Other Works by the Poets

Harmonium, Wallace Stevens
The Man with the Blue Guitar, Wallace Stevens
Parts of a World, Wallace Stevens
J. B.: A Play in Verse, Archibald MacLeish
Poetry and Experience, Archibald MacLeish
Complete Poems of Marianne Moore

We suggest that you preview these works before recommending them to students.

INTERNET

You can find additional information about the lives and works of Wallace Stevens, Archibald MacLeish, and Marianne Moore on the Internet. We suggest the following site. Please be aware that sites may have changed since the publication of this information.

For information on the Modernists, with links to Stevens and Moore, go to **http://www.poets.org/lit/EXH/ex001fst.html**

We *strongly recommend* that you preview the sites before you send students to them.

Customize for *Less Proficient Readers*

Less proficient readers may benefit from reading the Check Your Comprehension and Critical Thinking questions prior to rereading the poem(s). Facilitate exploration and discussion of the questions by pairing these students with more advanced readers.

Reinforce and Extend

Answers

◆ Literature and Your Life

Reader's Response Students should offer clear explanations for their answers.

Thematic Focus Suggested response: It can lead people to new discoveries.

☑ Check Your Comprehension

1. (a) The speaker compares a poem to a "globed fruit," "old medallions," "sleeve-worn stone of casement ledges," and "the flight of birds." (b) A poem shows the history of grief in "an empty doorway and a maple leaf." (c) It shows love in "leaning grasses and two lights above the sea."
2. (a) There is a place for the genuine, a physical contact. (b) The result is not real poetry.

◆ Critical Thinking

1. Suggested responses: (a) Poetry appeals to the sense of touch. (b) Poetry expresses through concrete visual images. (c) Poetry is timeless.
2. They are two of the strongest emotions.
3. It reinforces the idea that poetry should be concrete.
4. The speaker dislikes poetry that needs high-sounding interpretations.
5. (a) They should be able to create imaginary but concrete images. (b) She is referring to imaginary but concrete images grounded in reality.
6. Suggested response: She believes that poems should be accessible and concrete.
7. The two poets both emphasize the fact that poetry must be concrete. Moore also states her belief that poetry should not be inaccessible.

Answers

◆ Literary Focus

1. It should approach some ideal, rounded form.
2. Suggested response: It can appeal to many senses and have many textures.
3. Possible answers include the following: "Dumb/As old medallions to the thumb" suggests that poetry should convey a sense of touch. The simile "wordless as the flight of the birds" suggests that poetry should convey movement rather than the words that describe movement. The comparison to being motionless "as the moon climbs" suggests that poetry should be timeless.
4. The combination of similes demonstrates that poetry is concrete and sparks associations by appealing to the senses.

◆ Reading Strategy

Suggested responses:

1. The wilderness enveloped the jar, and both the landscape and jar were improved.
2. A poem should be timeless.
3. A poem should be a living thing to its readers.
4. These things are important because they are practical, not lofty or intellectual.
5. If you want poetry in its roughest and truest form, you are interested in poetry.

◆ Build Vocabulary

Using the Word Root *-satis-*

Sample responses:

1. A sweet apple can *satisfy* my craving for dessert.
2. That report was too short to be *satisfactory.*
3. The elaborate meal *satiated* the guests.
4. After devouring its meal, the cat wore an expression of *satiety.*

Using the Word Bank

Sample responses:

1. Someone who has no imagination is a *literalist.*
2. The territory governed by a king is his *dominion.*
3. In a beautiful painting, a peach looks *palpable* and ripe.
4. My friend has *slovenly* habits.
5. The musician is very *derivative.*
6. That amount of food will not *suffice* to maintain your health.
7. My sibling has an *insatiable* appetite for possessions.

Guide for Responding *(continued)*

◆ Literary Focus

Simile

A **simile** is an explicit comparison between two seemingly dissimilar things, clearly indicated by a connecting word such as *like* or *as*. For example, MacLeish presents a simile in lines 1 and 2 in which he compares a poem to a globed fruit.

1. What does "globed" suggest about a poem?
2. In what ways can a poem be like a fruit?
3. Find three other similes in "Ars Poetica" and interpret their meaning.
4. How do all of the similes work together to create a vision of poetry as something that "should not mean/But be"?

◆ Reading Strategy

Paraphrasing

When you **paraphrase**, you identify key ideas in a passage and restate them in your own words. Paraphrase the following passages from the poems. Try to make your paraphrased version as straightforward, direct, and comprehensible as possible.

1. The wilderness rose up to it,
And sprawled around, no longer wild.
The jar was round upon the ground
And tall and of a port in air.

2. A poem should be motionless in time
As the moon climbs.

As poem should be equal to:
Not true.

3. A poem should not mean
But be.

4. . . . these things are important not because a
high sounding interpretation can be put upon
them but
because they are
useful. . .

5. . . . In the meantime, if you demand on the one
hand,
the raw material of poetry in
all its rawness and
that which is on the other hand
genuine, you are interested in poetry.

◆ Build Vocabulary

Using the Latin Root *-satis-*

Each of the following words contains the Latin root *-satis-*, meaning "enough." Use your knowledge of the root to guess their meanings—and use a dictionary to confirm the precise definition. Then use each of the words correctly in a sentence.

1. satisfy
2. satisfactory
3. satiate
4. satiety

Using the Word Bank: Context

Follow the instructions below by writing a sentence for each item that uses one word from the Word Bank. Use each word once.

1. Describe someone who has no imagination.
2. Define the territory governed by a king.
3. Describe the quality of a peach in a beautiful painting.
4. Explain why a friend's room is such a mess.
5. Criticize a musician who lacks originality.
6. Explain why a certain amount of food is not enough to maintain one's health.
7. Criticize a sibling who always wants more possessions.

◆ Grammar and Style

Subject Complements

Subject complements are nouns, pronouns, or adjectives that follow linking verbs (often forms of the verb "to be") and identify or describe the subject of a sentence. Sentences containing subject complements are especially effective when a writer's purpose is to define something.

Practice Copy each of the following sentences. Underline the subject complement and label it as a noun, pronoun, or adjective.

1. The winner of this year's poetry prize is you!
2. The subject of the poem was a waterfall.
3. Good poetry should be thrilling.
4. Poets are deep thinkers.
5. The oldest book in the library is a volume of poems.

Writing Application Write a brief descriptive poem about a familiar person or object. Begin each line with the name of the person or object. Follow it with a linking verb and a noun, pronoun, or adjective that renames or describes the person or object.

◆ Grammar and Style

Practice

1. you; pronoun
2. waterfall; noun
3. thrilling; adjective
4. dreamy; adjective
5. volume; noun

Writing Application

Check to see that each line of students' poems contains a subject complement.

Grammar Reinforcement

For additional instruction and practice, use the page on Subject Complements, p. 24 in the *Writer's Solution Grammar Practice Book.*

Reteach

In order to paraphrase a poem, students must first understand what the poet it saying. To guide students, use ***Strategies for Diverse Student Needs,*** Explain and Respond to Poetry, p. 47.

Build Your Portfolio

Idea Bank

Writing

1. **Ars Poetica** MacLeish's poem is a listing of the different characteristics a poem should have. Using his similes as a model, write five new couplets (two-line verses) that express your ideas about the characteristics of a good poem.

2. **Comparison and Contrast** Write an essay in which you compare and contrast two of the definitions of poetry presented in this group. Cite passages from the poems to support your points.

3. **Response to Criticism** Wallace Stevens felt that the goal of a poet is "to help people live their lives." Choose one of Stevens's poems. Then write an essay in which you discuss how effectively that poem achieves this goal. Support your argument with passages from the poem.

Speaking, Listening, and Viewing

4. **Round-Table Discussion** With a small group, analyze the views of poetry held by the different poets. Then stage a round-table discussion on the issue "What Is Poetry?" Each group member should take the position of one of the poets.

5. **Introduction** When poets read their work, they often introduce each poem with a brief explanation of it. Plan and present remarks to introduce one of these poems.

Researching and Representing

6. **Illustration** Create an illustration that captures the scene in "Anecdote of the Jar." **[Art Link]**

7. **Poetry Collection** These poems focus on a specific topic: What is poetry? Create a collection of poems on another topic—such as sports or nature. Include an introduction that explains how the poems relate to one another.

Online Activity www.phlit.phschool.com

Guided Writing Lesson

Definition

In these selections, Stevens, MacLeish, and Moore define something about which they care very deeply: poetry. Choose something that you care deeply about—for example, your favorite type of music, your favorite ice cream, or your favorite season—and write a definition of it in which you use one or more striking comparisons to capture how you feel about the subject. Keep this tip in mind as you develop your definition.

Writing Skills Focus: Necessary Background

When you write a definition, it's essential that you provide readers with any necessary background information about your subject. Think about what someone who is not an expert on your topic would and wouldn't know about it. You'll need to provide any details that your audience wouldn't already know. In addition, you'll need to define any specialized terms with which your audience is likely to be unfamiliar.

Prewriting Freewrite about what your topic means to you. What aspects of it interest you most? Review what you've written and underline details that you can use in your definition. Then create comparisons that you can use to capture what your topic means to you.

Drafting You can either develop your definition around a single comparison, or present a series of comparisons. Whichever approach you choose, make sure to include enough details to give your readers a clear understanding of your topic.

Revising Give your definition to a classmate who is not familiar with your topic. Ask your reader to suggest places where you can add details to make it more clear.

Idea Bank

Customizing for *Performance Levels*
Following are suggestions for matching Idea Bank topics with your students' performance levels:
Less Advanced Students: 1, 6
Average Students: 2, 5, 7
More Advanced Students: 3, 4, 7

Customizing for *Learning Modalities*
Following are suggestions for matching Idea Bank topics with your students' learning modalities:
Interpersonal: 4
Visual/Spatial: 6
Verbal/Linguistic: 5, 7

Guided Writing Lesson

For more prewriting, elaboration, and revision strategies, see *Prentice Hall Writing and Grammar.*

Writing and Language Transparencies Display the Analysis Transparency, p. 83, to help students organize the information they will present in their definitions.

Writers at Work Videodisc
Have students view the videodisc segment on Exposition (Ch. 3) featuring writer Thom Harrington to see how he explains artifacts found in the museum of the New York City Subway. Have students discuss how they can apply what they learn to their writing.

Play frames 23159 to 33243

Writing Lab CD-ROM
Have students complete the tutorial on Exposition. Follow these steps:
1. Have students use the Cluster Diagram to help them gather details.
2. Have them draft on computer.
3. Have them use the Self-Evaluation Checklist to aid in revision.

✓ ASSESSMENT OPTIONS

Formal Assessment, Selection Test, pp. 215–217, and Assessment Resources Software. The selection test is designed so that it can be easily customized to the performance levels of your students.

Alternative Assessment, p. 47, includes options for less advanced students, more advanced students, musical/rhythmic learners, visual/spatial learners and interpersonal learners.

PORTFOLIO ASSESSMENT
Use the following rubrics in the ***Alternative Assessment*** booklet to assess student writing:
Ars Poetica: Poetry Rubric, p. 123
Comparison and Contrast: Comparison/Contrast Rubric, p. 118
Response to Criticism: Literary Analysis Rubric, p. 127
Guided Writing Lesson: Definition Rubric, p. 114

LESSON OBJECTIVES

1. **To use a variety of reading strategies to comprehend song lyrics**
   - Thematic Connection
2. **To express and support responses to the text**
   - Critical Thinking Questions
   - Idea Bank: Letter to Congress
   - Idea Bank: Newspaper Interview
   - Idea Bank: Interview
3. **To read in order to research self-selected and assigned topics**
   - Idea Bank: Diagram
   - Idea Bank: City Profile
4. **To plan, prepare, organize, and present literary interpretations**
   - Idea Bank: Role Play

CONNECTIONS TO TODAY'S WORLD

Allentown
Billy Joel

Thematic Connection

TROUBLED TIMES

Through their novels and stories, Fitzgerald, Steinbeck, and other writers spoke for many Americans who felt confused and alienated in the period between the two world wars. The brutality and carnage of World War I had shocked our still young nation. The war highlighted the most destructive capabilities of modern technology and made many people begin to question whether traditional values could still be applied to the modern world.

More recent American writers have also addressed social problems and their effects. The Vietnam War and the unrest it caused, the issues relating to civil rights and inequality, concern for the environment—these are all themes that contemporary American writers have dealt with in recent years. Every age has its troubles, and writers often give voice to these concerns, moving readers to deeper reflection and sometimes to action.

Singers also frequently address social concerns. One such artist is Billy Joel, who addressed some of the dominant issues of the 1980's. For many Americans, this period was one of economic prosperity, with average incomes rising and the financial markets booming. Yet for others, the 1980's was the decade when the American dream died. Factories, which had long been a reliable source of employment, began to streamline their work forces, move overseas to take advantage of cheap labor, or close down altogether. Many skilled laborers were forced to take lower-paying service jobs. A sense of betrayal and confusion permeated towns that had long been dominated by huge steel mills, automobile manufacturing plants, and other large industries.

The lyrics of many of Billy Joel's songs written during this period show the plight of legions of abandoned workers. Through words and music, Joel drew attention to situations that some would prefer to overlook. Like many writers before him, Joel had the courage and compassion to write movingly of those who were left behind.

BILLY JOEL (1949–)

The son of Jewish immigrants, Billy Joel grew up in Hicksville, New York. When Joel was a child, his engineer father left the family, forcing his mother to raise her two children on a secretary's salary. Although the family was poor, Joel had a rich cultural life learning to play the piano and going to classical concerts with his grandfather. He also boxed and spent time with friends.

At age sixteen, Joel became the pianist for a local band called the Hassles. He worked a lot of late nights, earning money that helped his mother pay the mortgage.

His first album was a failure, but his second album, released in 1973, was the hugely successful *Piano Man.* Hit song after hit song has followed. Yet Joel warns people against assessing him as a "pop meister who just churns out these hit singles." Unlike many pop artists, Joel has tackled a range of social issues from unemployment to the legacy of the Vietnam War.

In the late 1980's, Joel toured Russia, playing songs that emphasized similarities between people despite political divisions. More recently, he has lectured at colleges to help young musicians learn from his experiences.

Prentice Hall Literature Program Resources

REINFORCE / RETEACH / EXTEND

Selection Support Pages
Thematic Connection: Troubled Times, p. 220

Formal Assessment Selection Test, p. 218–219; Assessment Resources Software

Resource Pro CD-ROM
"Allentown"—includes all resource material and customizable lesson plan

Allentown

Words and Music by Billy Joel

Well we're living here in Allentown[1]
And they're closing all the factories down
Out in Bethlehem[2] they're killing time
Filling out forms
Standing in line

Well our fathers fought the Second World War
Spent their weekends on the Jersey shore

---

1. **Allentown:** A city on the Lehigh River in eastern Pennsylvania, once home to a thriving steel industry that began to collapse during the 1970's, leaving thousands of workers unemployed.
2. **Bethlehem:** A neighboring city located within the Allentown, Pennsylvania, metropolitan area.

Connections to Today's World

Many of the literary works in Part I deal with the disillusionment felt by many people between the two world wars. The carnage caused by the new weapons of World War I underscored a growing distrust of the promise of modern technology. In addition, the economic hardships of the Great Depression and the increasingly impersonal nature of society fanned the flames of insecurity. Reflecting those troubled times in their works were writers like Eliot, Fitzgerald, and Steinbeck. But troubles were not the exclusive province of the decades between the World Wars; contemporary society has also had its share of uncertainty. In his song "Allentown," Billy Joel explores one painful aspect of modern life.

Develop Understanding

One-Minute Insight This contemporary song acknowledges the dilemma facing young people in difficult economic times. The song's speaker describes life in the Pennsylvania steel belt during the 1970's, when unemployment grew as a result of the steel industry's collapse. He recounts the sacrifices his parents made for America, the promises of a better life he feels the country has made to young people, and the despair of seeing those promises unfulfilled. By questioning whether to stay in Allentown or go, the speaker struggles with the common American quandary: whether to embrace continuity with its restriction and problems or strike out for new opportunity despite its risks.

Customize for
English Language Learners
English language learners may find the song's loosely structured punctuation difficult to follow. Encourage these students to read entire stanzas for meaning before rereading slowly for syntax and flow.

Speaking, Listening, and Viewing Mini-Lesson

Interview
This mini-lesson supports the Speaking, Listening, and Viewing activity in the Idea Bank on p. 722.

Introduce the Concept Have students define financial hard times. Ask students to imagine the difficulties such a situation would pose. Point out that "Allentown" presents a specific and vivid view of hard times in a particular time and place.

Develop Background Before students begin, suggest that they consider the following strategies:

- Learn about the economic circumstances of the chosen time period prior to the interview.
- Ask questions designed to elicit open-ended responses rather than yes or no.
- Record all direct quotations word for word.

Apply the Information Suggest that students locate interview subjects through family, friends, or community organizations. Remind students that they should respect their subject's privacy and emotions, especially when discussing difficult times.

Assess the Outcome Evaluate interview results according to the following criteria: interest level, logical organization, and relevance of content to the assignment parameters.

▶Critical Viewing◀

❶ **Connect** Lines 3–5 describe such a scene: "Out in Bethlehem they're killing time / Filling out forms / Standing in line"

◆Critical Thinking

❷ **Assess** Point out to students the speaker's uncertainty about whether to stay in Allentown or leave the troubles behind. Ask students: What are the advantages of staying or going in such a situation? *Students should note that staying may offer the continuing support of community and family, while going may offer the hope of greater economic opportunity.*

Thematic Focus

❸ **Troubled Times** Remind students of the disillusionment evident in Thomas Wolfe's "The Far and the Near." Discuss how that story's central character feels when promises he has believed prove unfulfilled. Point out that here the speaker rails at the broken promises of his time.

Customize for *Less Proficient Readers*

"Allentown" appears on Billy Joel's album *The Nylon Curtain.* To help these readers find the cadence and pauses in the song, have them follow along in their texts as they listen to the selection. Urge students to note where the singer pauses, using the song's structure to identify related ideas.

Customize for *Musical/Rhythmic Learners*

Help these students enjoy Joel's song by playing the musical version for them. Ask them to listen to the interplay between words and music. How does the music support the themes of the lyrics?

Customize for *Visual/Spatial Learners*

Encourage these students to use both Joel's lyrics and the photographs on these pages to engage their senses in the song. What images can students envision? What sounds can they hear? Discuss how these sensory images enhance students' appreciation of the song.

▲ **Critical Viewing** Lines of unemployed workers were a common sight in "steel towns" like Allentown during the 1970's and early 1980's. Which lines of the song describe a scene like this one? **[Connect]** ❶

Met our mothers in the USO[3]
Asked them to dance
Danced with them slow

And we're living here in Allentown
❷ But the restlessness was handed down
and it's getting very hard to stay

Well we're waiting here in Allentown
For the Pennsylvania we never found
For the promises our teachers gave
If we worked hard
❸ If we behaved
So the graduations hang on the wall
But they never really helped us at all
No they never told us what was real
Iron and coke[4]
And chromium steel

And we're waiting here in Allentown
But they've taken all the coal from the ground
And the union people crawled away

---

3. **USO:** Refers to a social club sponsored by the United Service Organizations, a group that provides entertainment and many other services to U.S. military personnel and their families worldwide.
4. **coke:** A form of coal used as industrial fuel.

Cross-Curricular Connection: Social Studies

The Rise and Fall of Unemployment In 1982, the unemployment rate in the United States was 10.8 percent of the working population. This rate was the highest since the Great Depression, when nearly a third of workers had no jobs. During the prosperous postwar decades of the 1950's and 1960's, United States unemployment was only about 4 percent. In recent decades, unemployment has worsened dramatically amongst certain segments of the population. For example, in 1982, nearly 50 percent of African American urban teenage workers were unemployed.

Have students gather additional statistics on the rise and fall of unemployment in the United States since 1914. After graphing the change in the unemployment rate through time, ask students to link their findings to the information learned in the selections in Part 1 of this unit.

CONNECTIONS TO TODAY'S WORLD

Every child had a pretty good shot
To get at least as far as their old man got
But something happened on the way to that place
They threw an American flag in our face **4**

Well I'm waiting here in Allentown
And it's hard to keep a good man down
But I won't be getting up today
And it's getting very hard to stay
And we're living here in Allentown **5**

Guide for Responding

◆ Literature and Your Life

Reader's Response If you were the speaker in this song, would you stay in Allentown? Explain.

Thematic Focus Which has a greater influence on a person's fate—his or her character or the surrounding environment? Support your opinion.

☑ Check Your Comprehension

1. For what is Allentown famous?
2. According to the speaker, what is "real" in Allentown?
3. What happened to the union in Allentown?
4. What did the speaker expect to do for a living?

◆ Critical Thinking

INTERPRET

1. According to the speaker, how did his education fail him? **[Interpret]**
2. Why does the speaker mention his father's war experience? **[Connect]**
3. What is the speaker's attitude toward America? **[Draw Conclusions]**

EVALUATE

4. Is the speaker's attitude justified? Explain. **[Assess]**

EXTEND

5. What might Stevens, MacLeish, or Moore think of "Allentown"? Explain. **[Literature Link]**

◆ Literature and Your Life

4 American children no longer have a chance to live at least as well as their parents. Ask students whether they think children ever had this chance and whether their knowledge and experience support or refute Joel's statement. *Students may say that their parents or grandparents have succeeded and that economic conditions such as the rising cost of health care and housing make it difficult for them to match their parents' experiences.*

Thematic Connection

5 Troubled Times Ask students to compare the speaker in "Allentown" with the central character in Steinbeck's "The Turtle." How does each character respond to obstacles? *Both characters are persistent; they don't give up easily when challenged. Both consider taking other paths.*

Reinforce and Extend

Answers

◆ Literature and Your Life

Reader's Response Students should support their responses with citations from the song.

Thematic Focus Students should present logical arguments in support of their opinions.

☑ Check Your Comprehension

1. Allentown is famous for its steel industry.
2. Iron, coke, and chromium steel are real.
3. The union was disbanded.
4. He expected to work in the steel industry.

◆ Critical Thinking

1. His education misled him with hollow promises.
2. The speaker believes his father deserved better for the sacrifice of fighting for his country.
3. He is disillusioned about America.
4. Most students will believe that the speaker's attitude is justified because without a job, life becomes a desperate struggle for survival.
5. The writers would probably like "Allentown" because the song, while dealing with the real world, also incorporates symbols.

Beyond the Selection

FURTHER READING

Other Works by Billy Joel

"The River of Dreams"
"The Storm Front"
"The Bridge"

Other Works About Troubled Times

"Brother, Can You Spare a Dime"
The Road from Coorain, Jill Ker Conway
Growing Up, Russell Baker

We suggest that you preview these works before recommending them to students.

INTERNET

You and your students may find additional information about the Billy Joel on the Internet. We suggest the following site. Please be aware, however, that sites may have changed from the time we published this information.

For information about Joel's music, visit **http://www. music.sony.com/Music/ArtistInfo/ BillyJoel.html**

We *strongly recommend* that you preview the sites before you send students to them.

Answers
Thematic Connection

1. Sample response: Some students may say the mood of "Allentown" is sad, as exemplified by such lines as "And they're closing all the factories down / Out in Bethlehem they're killing time / Filling out forms / Standing in line." Others may find anger in the speaker's voice.
2. Students' opinions should be supported by lines from the song.
3. Sample response: The future seems bleak for both the speaker and the town. Excerpts such as the following attest to this: "Well I'm waiting here in Allentown / And it's hard to keep a good man down / But I won't be getting up today" and "But they've taken all the coal from the ground / And the union people crawled away."

Idea Bank

Customizing for *Performance Levels*

Following are suggestions for matching Idea Bank topics with your students' performance levels:
Less Advanced Students: 1, 4
Average Students: 3, 5, 6
More Advanced Students: 2, 7

Customizing for *Learning Modalities*

Following are suggestions for matching Idea Bank topics with your students' learning modalities:
Bodily/Kinesthetic: 4
Interpersonal: 5
Visual/Spatial: 6
Logical/Mathematical: 7

Thematic Connection

TROUBLED TIMES

Economic and social changes can happen quickly. Sometimes individuals have to struggle to keep up. Sometimes whole cities find themselves without the resources to keep up. This was the case for Allentown, Pennsylvania, which lost its most important industry—the steel industry—which had once been vital to our nation's prosperity.

Joel's song expresses the inner turmoil of a man living in troubled times. In addition to suffering from financial problems, the speaker suffers spiritually—his most deeply rooted beliefs are being held up to question. He has lost the security of a world where "Every child had a pretty good shot / To get at least as far as their old man got." Many people feel the same even today.

Billy Joel's song might leave you with the question: Will the speaker remake himself, or will he surrender?

1. What is the mood of "Allentown"? Give examples to support your answer.
2. Do you think the speaker could have changed his destiny? Why or why not?
3. What does the future seem to hold for the speaker and the town? Support your answer with evidence from the song.

Idea Bank

Writing

1. **Application Essay** You are the speaker in the song "Allentown," and you've decided to seek training for another career. Write an application essay for a technical school or training program. Stress the experience and personal qualities that would make you a good student. **[Career Link]**
2. **Letter to Congress** As the speaker in "Allentown," write a letter to your congressional representative. Summarize the state of the local economy and its effect upon the population. Make suggestions about what the government might do to help. **[Social Studies Link]**
3. **Newspaper Interview** You are a journalist assigned the task of profiling an individual personally affected by economic changes. With this goal in mind, write up an interview with the speaker of "Allentown." **[Media Link]**

Speaking, Listening, and Viewing

4. **Enactment** With a partner, role-play two retired steelworkers reminiscing about their working days. They might recall working conditions, union strikes, or financial matters. **[Social Studies Link]**
5. **Interview** Interview an adult who lived through—or knew someone who lived through—financial hard times resulting from an economic change or a job layoff. Relate what you learn. **[Social Studies Link]**

Researching and Representing

6. **Diagram** Research the process of manufacturing steel. Create a diagram illustrating the basic steps in the process. **[Science Link]**
7. **City Profile** Research Allentown before and after the collapse of the steel industry. If possible, find pictures. Share your findings with the class. **[Social Studies Link]**

Online Activity www.phlit.phschool.com

✓ ASSESSMENT OPTIONS

Formal Assessment, Selection Test, pp. 218–219, and Assessment Resources Software. The selection test is designed so that it can be easily customized to the performance levels of your students.

PORTFOLIO ASSESSMENT
Use the following rubrics in the ***Alternative Assessment*** booklet to assess student writing:
Application Essay: Persuasion Rubric, p. 120
Letter to Congress: Problem-Solution Rubric, p. 116
Newspaper Interview: Comparison/Contrast Rubric, p. 118

Writing Process Workshop

Essay for a Test

During the Modern Age, many fiction writers and poets abandoned traditional structures and began experimenting with new forms and techniques. You can also experiment with forms and techniques when you write creatively. When you write an essay for a test, however, it is essential that your writing fit into the format that the test dictates. In addition, you must work quickly and efficiently, outlining your ideas, crafting your essay, and making revisions within a matter of minutes.

The following skills, introduced in this section's Guided Writing Lessons, will help you write a concise, complete test essay.

Writing Skills Focus

- **Elaborate on your key points.** Provide enough facts and details to thoroughly answer the question. (See p. 685.)
- **Maintain brevity and clarity.** Make sure your essay is clear and direct. Avoid including unnecessary details, and check to see that each word conveys your intended meaning. (See p. 667.)
- **Pay attention to accuracy.** Make sure that any facts, names, and dates you cite are correct. (See p. 707.)
- **Provide necessary background information.** Present definitions and historical details that give a framework for your answer. (See p. 717.)

Consider how the following essay demonstrates these skills:

Writing Model

Excerpt from a test essay on the importance of voting

I believe that all eligible citizens should vote in every election. ① The right to vote is a freedom that we should not take for granted. . . . Even in this country, people could not always vote. For example, African American men could not vote until after the Civil War. Women could not vote until early in this century. ② History tells of several presidential elections that were determined by no more than a hundred thousand votes . . . a very small margin. ③

① The writer begins with a clear statement of his thesis, or main point.

② The writer accurately cites historical details that support his thesis.

③ This fact further elaborates on the essay's main point.

Prepare and Engage

LESSON OBJECTIVES

- To use recursive writing processes to write an essay for a test
- To recognize appropriate sentence construction, including the avoidance of both sentence fragments and repetition of words and phrases

Establish Writing Guidelines

Distribute the scoring rubric for Technical Description/Explanation in ***Alternative Assessment*** (p. 130) to make students aware of the criteria on which their work will be evaluated. For suggestions on customizing these rubrics to this workshop, see p. 725.

You may also want to present the Outline Graphic Organizer in ***Writing and Language Transparencies,*** p. 47.

Writers at Work Videodisc To introduce the elements of practical writing, play the videodisc segment featuring NASA's David Herring (Ch. 8).

Play frames 33063 to 43439

Writing Lab CD-ROM

If your students have access to computers, you may want to have them use the tutorial on Practical and Technical Writing. Have students follow these steps:

1. Explore the interactive tips designed to help them gather details for a timed-test essay.
2. Practice drafting a timed-test essay on the computer.
3. Use the Self-Evaluation Checklist to help them revise their essays.

Beyond the Classroom

Workplace Skills Connection

Examinations Tests in schools or for college admissions are not the only times in life when people are required to respond in writing to examination questions. Explain to students that all over the world entrance exams are used to screen applicants for civil service jobs in areas like law enforcement, health care, education, and government administration.

Some questions may be designed to gauge how an employee would handle new responsibilities and situations that are beyond his or her present experience. Other questions may help determine whether individuals are aware of trends and developments in their fields. Discuss jobs that require such exams, drawing examples from your own experience or that of other adults whom students may know.

Develop Student Writing

Prewriting Strategy
One problem students encounter when writing essays for tests is covering a topic too broadly; the result is often that their work is full of generalizations, or that they find themselves "running out of time." Because the topic ideas provided in the student edition are still fairly broad, you may want to brainstorm as a class for ways these ideas might be narrowed. For example, for the first topic ask students how they might limit the writers or events under consideration.

Customize for
Intrapersonal Learners
Generally, the details students use must come from memory or experience. Guide intrapersonal learners to enhance the process of recall by practicing "free associating" techniques, or by helping them develop mnemonic devices to remember specific information.

Customize for
Less Advanced Students
These students may find it difficult to go straight from a brainstormed list of details to a neat, formal outline such as the one shown in the student edition. Explain that in the margin of their lists of details they can use numbers, letters, or brief one- or two-word prompts to mark items that belong together. Explain that these "like items" should become the "logical categories" of ideas that are grouped together in an outline.

Writing Lab CD-ROM The Organizing Details section of the tutorial includes several graphic organizers, including an Outliner, that students can use to choose a type of order for the information they have gathered.

Elaboration Strategy
When drafting their essays, students may become flustered by test anxiety. To help students master the skills of this workshop, consider conducting a "mock test" with flexible time constraints.

Applying Language Skills: Sentence Fragments
A **sentence fragment** is a group of words incorrectly punctuated as a sentence. Most often, fragments are missing a subject, a verb, or both.

Missing Subject and Verb:
Responsible for changes in American poetry.

Missing Subject:
Writes about a pear tree in spring.

Missing Verb:
W. H. Auden, known for his use of satire to comment on modern society.

To correct a fragment, supply the missing element or combine the fragment with a nearby sentence.

Practice Rewrite the examples as complete sentences.

Writing Application In a timed situation, use complete sentences when you are outlining your essay to give you a head start on your draft.

Writer's Solution Connection
Language Lab
For additional practice correcting sentence fragments, complete the Fragments and Run-on Sentences lesson in the Sentence Errors unit.

Prewriting
Choose a Topic Some tests provide a highly structured topic; others offer a general question that requires you to narrow the topic. It is a good idea to be prepared for all types of questions by practicing ahead of time. Practice writing a test essay either by responding to a question you think you're likely to be asked on an upcoming test or by using the suggestion given below.

Topic Idea
Some states offer money for bottle deposits. Do you feel your state should encourage recycling in this way? Write a letter to the local newspaper stating and strongly supporting your position.

Organize Your Ideas About the Topic Allow yourself five minutes to outline your essay. Begin by quickly brainstorming for all the details that you can remember about your topic. Jot them down, and organize them in logical categories. Determine and state your thesis—the statement that summarizes your main idea. Use the following outline format to organize the main ideas and supporting details for your essay, or adapt it to fit your topic:

I. Introduction/Thesis Statement
II. Background
  A. Detail
  B. Detail
III. Supporting Information
  A. Detail
  B. Detail
IV. Conclusion/Restatement of Thesis

Drafting
Consider the Audience For most essay tests, the audience will be your teacher. For standardized writing tests, your audience will be an impartial, but interested, reader. Some tests may ask you to write for a specific audience. Let your audience govern your word choice, level of formality, and content.

Write With a Persuasive Purpose Some test essay questions will ask you for information and analysis. Others may ask you to take a position on a given subject. Your answer may have narrative, descriptive, and expository elements, but it should be focused on your main purpose. Effective organization and choice of language will help you achieve your purpose.

Applying Language Skills
Sentence Fragments Introduce this skill by pointing out that the pressure of a timed-test may force students to rush their thoughts. However, as writers they should not allow the expression of those thoughts to be sacrificed, with the result being missing words and sometimes sentence fragments.

Answers
1. Many factors were responsible for changes in American poetry.
2. My favorite poet writes about a pear tree in spring.
3. W. H. Auden, known for his use of satire to comment on modern society, wrote poems that are still highly relevant to today's world.

Grammar Reinforcement
In addition to the **Language Lab CD-ROM** lesson cited in the student edition, refer students to practice p. 45 in the *Writer's Solution Grammar Practice Book.*

Revising

Do a Quick Check While you won't have time to do a full-scale revision, take a few minutes at the end of the test to do a quick scan of your essay. Whenever you revise a test essay, use questions like these to guide your editing:

- Have you left out any important facts or details? *Add any information that will improve your argument.*
- Are all of your facts accurate? *Eliminate or replace any facts about which you are unsure.*
- Is the writing legible? *If there are any words that can't be read, take the time to make them more clear.*
- Are all your ideas expressed in full sentences? *Revise any sentence fragments or run-ons.*
- Is the order of extra pages clear? *Take a minute to number the pages so your reader reads the information in the way that you intend.*

Revision Model

① during the time between the two world wars,

Influenced by developments in modern psychology ^ writers began using the stream-of-consciousness technique. ~~The term originated with American psychologist William James.~~ ② The technique, unlike traditional literary forms, attempts to present thoughts, memories, and insights connected by a character's natural associations. ~~James Joyce~~ ③ and William Faulkner, ^an American novelists, used stream of consciousness successfully. ^

④ Other prose authors who employed this technique include Katherine Anne Porter and John Dos Passos.

① The author adds a historical detail to clarify the time frame of the events.

② By deleting a detail that is not necessary or true, the author maintains a clear, brief presentation.

③ The author deletes a factually incorrect detail: James Joyce was Irish.

④ Additional details help support the thesis.

Publishing

- **Share Your Essay** Ask family members to read your essay and give their reactions. Did they learn something new?

Applying Language Skills: Language Variety

Avoid repeating the same words and phrases. Think of synonyms or alternative ways to structure your sentences. Notice how the example is improved:

Example:

Many of the expatriates settled in Paris. The expatriates were named the "lost generation" by Gertrude Stein, who influenced the writing of many of the expatriates.

Revision:

The expatriate writers were named "the lost generation" by Gertrude Stein. Much of their writing was influenced by Stein, who entertained them at her Paris home.

Practice Revise the following to improve language variety.

Thomas Wolfe is a native of Asheville, N.C. He is best known for his first novel, *Look Homeward Angel.* Thomas Wolfe's novel is about his experiences in Asheville, N.C.

Writer's Solution Connection
Writing Lab

For more help on test essays, use the instruction and activities in the tutorial on Practical and Technical Writing in the Writing Lab CD-ROM.

Revision Strategy

Errors, legibility, misspellings, and sentence fragments are a top priority for revising in a test environment. Adding modifiers or details should be considered priority.

Writing Lab CD-ROM The Revising and Editing section of the tutorial on Practical Writing includes helpful tips for revising a timed-test essay.

Publishing

If students share their essays with family members, they may want to recopy their work more legibly. They will be less likely to trip over their own words—and readers can later read the essay more easily.

Applying Language Skills

Language Variety Under the pressure of a test, students may use familiar vocabulary or unknowingly repeat phrases they have already used.

Suggested Answer

Thomas Wolfe is best known for his first novel *Look Homeward Angel,* which is about his experience in his native Asheville, N.C.

Grammar Reinforcement

For additional practice, refer students to the section on Vocabulary Building (pp. 148–153) in the *Writer's Solution Grammar Practice Book.*

Reinforce and Extend

Prentice Hall Writing and Grammar For more prewriting, elaboration, and revision strategies, see *Prentice Hall Writing and Grammar.*

✓ ASSESSMENT		4	3	2	1
PORTFOLIO ASSESSMENT To assess student writing use a rubric in the ***Alternative Assessment*** booklet that corresponds to the writing purpose and the thesis, such as Cause-Effect, p. 117, or Comparison/Contrast, p. 119. Add these criteria to customize the rubrics to this assignment.	**Language Variety**	The writer consistently avoids repetition, skillfully using a knowledge of synonyms and sentence structure.	The writer rarely repeats words or phrases unnecessarily.	The writer often repeats words or phrases in cases where there are alternatives.	The writer consistently repeats the same words and phrases, hampering the essay's effectiveness.
	Readability	The writer consistently produces highly readable pages—they are legible, and the order of the passages is clear.	The writer includes some passages that are difficult to read because the order is unclear or the text is illegible.	The writer includes several passages that are difficult to read because the order is unclear or the text is illegible.	The writer consistently produces unreadable pages.

Prepare and Engage

LESSON OBJECTIVES

- To comprehend selections using a variety of strategies, including study strategies such as note taking, outlining, and using study-guide questions to better understand texts

Customize for
Musical/Rhythmic Learners
Have students present rhythmical mnemonic devices they know, such as rhymes and raps, that have helped them recall facts and sequences. Encourage them to create rhythmical mnemonics whenever memorization of names, terms, or events is required.

Apply the Strategies

Answers

1. Possible notes:
   Archaeologists learning about ancient, largest Mesoamerican city of Teotihuacán
   —first discoveries in 1960's
   —tomb uncovered in 1998
   —hieroglyphic writing yet to be deciphered
   —about 15,000 people in about A.D. 500
2. Possible formal outline:
   Ancient Mesoamerican City of Teotihuacán
   I. What Archaeologists Know
   A. Largest Mesoamerican city
   1. about A.D. 500
   2. one of world's largest
3. peak population approx. 15,000
   B. Discovered in 1960's
   C. Tomb uncovered in 1998
   D. Hieroglyphs on artifacts
   II. What Is Still Unknown
   A. Who were the people?
   B. What do the hieroglyphs mean?
3. a. The city of Teotihuacán has significance because its large size means that it probably had great influence in the ancient Mesoamerican world.
   b. Archaeologists are continuing to explore the city to uncover still-buried tombs and artifacts and to learn about the people's written language and way of life.

Student Success Workshop

Study Skills — Using Study Strategies

Strategies for Success

Sometimes, understanding a piece of writing requires more than reading words on a page. Study strategies—such as taking notes, creating an outline, and using study-guide questions—can help you understand more of what you read. Here are some pointers for choosing and using study strategies:

Take Notes If you take notes as you read, you'll understand more in a text. Taking notes helps you comprehend a complicated text because it keeps you focused on the main ideas. Take notes, for example, when reading a medical article, a detailed newspaper report, or a history book. For each paragraph, briefly summarize the main idea, and, if necessary, include important details, such as names and dates.

Outline It Outlines are useful for sorting out main ideas and details in a long, detailed text. Using an outline, you can sift through the information and visually arrange the important ideas. You can make a traditional text outline by writing down the main ideas, numbering each with a Roman numeral. Then, below each main idea, write down the supporting ideas, labeling these with capital letters. Alternatively, you can make a cluster outline: Put the main ideas in larger circles and supporting details in smaller circles. Draw lines to connect the main ideas and details.

Let Study Questions Be Your Guide Study-guide questions in a textbook focus on the most important concepts in a text. They are designed to lead you through the facts and help reinforce the information in your mind. When using study-guide questions as a strategy for understanding, it is helpful to write out the answers or discuss the questions with a friend.

Apply the Strategies

Read this article, and apply study strategies:

> In 1998, archaeologists uncovered a tomb at the site of the ancient Mesoamerican city, Teotihuacán. Although evidence of Teotihuacán was first discovered in the 1960's, we know little about the people who lived there. It is estimated that as many as 15,000 people lived there when the city was at its largest, in about A.D. 500. It was the largest city in Mesoamerica, and one of the largest in the world. Archaeologists still cannot read the hieroglyphic language inscribed on artifacts they discovered in Teotihuacán. They are working to uncover other information about the city's residents.

1. Take notes on the article. Keep them brief, and focus on the main ideas.
2. Create a formal or informal outline of the piece, showing main ideas and details.
3. Answer these study questions:
   a. What makes the city of Teotihuacán significant?
   b. Why are archaeologists continuing to explore the city?

✔ *Study strategies can be useful in situations like these:*
- ▶ Studying for a test
- ▶ Understanding a complicated plot in a book
- ▶ Researching a topic in several sources

Test Preparation Workshop

Using Study Strategies
Offer this test item about the study strategies presented in this workshop:

I. Basic Study Strategies
  A. Notetaking
  B. Outlines
    1. Traditional
    2. ?
  C. Study-guide Questions

Choose the best answer for item 2.

A Main ideas and important supporting details
B Focus on main ideas
C Roman numerals and capital letters
D Cluster

Students should recognize that the correct answer is a detail about "Outlines," parallel to "Traditional"; D is the only answer choice that fits. The workshop describes a cluster outline as an alternative to a traditional, formal outline.

PART 2

Focus on Literary Forms: The Short Story

Do It Yourself Landscape,
Andy Warhol, Museum Ludwig, Cologne,
photo courtesy of Rheinisches Bildarchiv Köln

The short story has been a part of American literature since Edgar Allan Poe defined the genre in the 1800's. Every generation of writers brings a new energy to the form, revitalizing it by reflecting the changing values, attitudes and issues of the times. The Modern Age was a critical period in the growth of the American short story, as writers such as Hemingway and Fitzgerald carried the form to new heights.

One-Minute Planning Guide

The selections in this section deal with the anxiety and fear felt by many during the modern era, that is, from the period of World War I to the present. "In Another Country" is told though the eyes of a wounded American World-War-I volunteer recuperating in a hospital in Italy. A soldier's fear of death, the fragility of life, the disillusionment with modern technology, and the futility of careful planning are poignantly brought out in this Hemingway story. In "The Corn Planting," an American farm couple, isolated from fast-paced society, cope with the unexpected death of their son by communing with nature through the planting of corn. "A Worn Path" presents an elderly woman with a mission. In spite of her anxiety over making an arduous journey, and over becoming confused at times, a grandmother walks many miles into town to pick up medicine for her injured grandson. She has made this ritualistic journey many times since the young boy swallowed lye long ago. Part 2 ends with a story appropriately titled "Anxiety." This short story examines a particular fear of contemporary society, that of annihilation from nuclear war.

Customize for *Varying Student Needs*

When assigning the selections in this part, keep in mind these factors:

"In Another Country"
- An accessible short story dealing with poignant human emotions
- Background information on World War I will aid understanding

"The Corn Planting"
- A deceptively simple story that reveals much about life's trials
- Less proficient readers may need to read the story in sections

"A Worn Path"
- Less proficient readers may need help distinguishing between actual events and the main character's lapses into reverie
- English language learners may need help with story dialect

"Anxiety"
- Students may need help following dialogue written without quotation marks
- Accessible message about fear of nuclear annihilation

Humanities: Art

Do It Yourself Landscape, 1962, by Andy Warhol.

Andy Warhol (1930–1987) led the Pop Art movement during the 1960's, making artworks out of commonplace elements of popular culture. In this artwork, Warhol cleverly imitates the look of a partially finished paint-by-number painting, popular during the 1950's and early 1960's. Explain that such a painting would start out like the outlined white spaces on this work, the numbers indicating which color to use within each space. The idea was to make ordinary people feel like artists. Ask:

1. Imagine a fantasy story in which the setting looks like this artwork. What kinds of characters would live in such a world, and what idea about life could such a story convey? *Sample response: Such a story could contain characters whose faces look like the partly-filled-in setting, or who long for a more full-bodied world.*
2. What seems peculiarly American and twentieth-century about the idea of do-it-yourself art? *Such art is democratic—no one needs to be specially skilled or inspired. It also reflects the techniques of modern mass-production.*

Prepare and Engage

LESSON OBJECTIVES

1. **To develop vocabulary and word identification skills**
   - Latin Word Roots: *-val-*
   - Using the Word Bank: Denotations
2. **To use a variety of reading strategies to comprehend a story**
   - Connect Your Experience
   - Reading Strategy: Identify With Characters
   - Tips to Guide Reading
   - Read to Appreciate Author's Craft (ATE)
3. **To increase knowledge of other cultures and to connect common elements across cultures**
   - Cultural Connection (ATE)
4. **To express and support responses to the text**
   - Critical Thinking
   - Idea Bank: Memorial Speech
   - Idea Bank: Magazine Article
   - Idea Bank: Grant Proposal
   - Idea Bank: Enactment
   - Analyze an Author's Comment (ATE)
5. **To analyze literary elements**
   - Literary Focus: Point of View
6. **To read in order to research self-selected or assigned topics**
   - Idea Bank: Report on Rehabilitation
   - Idea Bank: Military Report
   - Research Skills Mini-Lesson (ATE)
7. **To plan, prepare, organize, and present literary interpretations**
   - Idea Bank: Oral Story
8. **To use recursive writing processes to write a personal narrative**
   - Guided Writing Lesson: Personal Narrative
9. **To increase knowledge of the rules of grammar and usage**
   - Grammar and Style: Punctuating Dialogue

Test Preparation

Reading Comprehension: Sentence Completion (ATE, p. 729) The teaching tips and sample test item in this workshop support the instruction and practice in the unit workshop:
Reading Comprehension: Sentence-Completion Questions (SE, p. 863)

Guide for Interpreting

Ernest Hemingway *(1899–1961)*

In his short stories, Ernest Hemingway vividly and forcefully expressed the sentiments of many members of the post-World War I generation. Using a concise, direct style, he wrote about people's struggles to maintain a sense of dignity while living in a seemingly hostile and confusing world.

After graduating from high school, Hemingway got a job as a reporter for the *Kansas City Star.* Eager to serve in World War I, however, he joined the Red Cross ambulance corps in 1918 and was sent to the Italian front. Shortly after his arrival, he was severely wounded and he spent several months recovering in a Milan hospital. His experiences during the war shaped his views and provided material for his writing.

After the war, Hemingway had an especially hard time readjusting to life in the United States. Hoping to find personal contentment and establish himself as a writer, he went to Paris where he became friends with Ezra Pound, Gertrude Stein, and other expatriate writers and artists. His new friends provided him with valuable advice and helped him to develop his writing style.

In 1925, Hemingway published his first major work, *In Our Time*, a series of loosely connected short stories. A year later he published *The Sun Also Rises*, a novel about a group of British and American expatriates trying to overcome the pain and disillusionment of life in the modern world. The novel earned him international acclaim and he remained famous for the rest of his life.

Hemingway was as well known for his lifestyle as he was for his writing.

Constantly pursuing adventure, he hunted in Africa, fished in the Caribbean, and skied in Europe.

The full body of Hemingway's work—including *A Farewell to Arms* (1929), *For Whom the Bell Tolls* (1940) and *The Old Man and the Sea* (1952)—earned him the Nobel Prize for Literature in 1954.

Sherwood Anderson *(1876–1941)*

Sherwood Anderson was one of the most influential writers of the modern age. Born and raised in a small town in Ohio, Anderson used his boyhood observations and experiences as material for his best-known work: *Winesburg, Ohio* (1919), a unified collection of short stories. In this work, Anderson presents a portrait of small-town life that is strikingly different from the portraits presented in most earlier works of literature. He captures the sense of isolation hidden beneath the surface of the characters' seemingly uneventful lives. He also uses everyday language to capture the true flavor of his characters—a technique that influenced such other twentieth-century writers as Ernest Hemingway.

Success in the City In his own life, Anderson eventually left small-town life behind, moving to Chicago, to pursue a writing career. There, he met Carl Sandburg, Theodore Dreiser, Edgar Lee Masters, and other writers.When he saw the success of Masters's *Spoon River Anthology*, he began to write about life in rural America.

Psychology and Literature While he was concerned with the troubles of modern life, Anderson was one of the first American writers to incorporate the ideas of contemporary psychology in his works. Inspired by the insights of Austrian psychologist Sigmund Freud, Anderson developed a type of character known as *grotesque* that had a singular focus on one truth, value, or assumption.

Although Anderson's reputation rests mainly on the success of *Winesburg, Ohio*, he published several other books, including *Windy McPherson's Son* (1916), *The Triumph of the Egg* (1921), *Horses and Men* (1923), and *Death in the Woods and Other Stories* (1933).

Prentice Hall Literature Program Resources

REINFORCE / RETEACH / EXTEND

Selection Support Pages
Build Vocabulary: Latin Roots: *-val-*, p. 221
Grammar and Style: Punctuating Dialogue, p. 222
Reading Strategy: Identify With Characters, p. 223
Literary Focus: Point of View, p. 224

Strategies for Diverse Student Needs, p. 48

Beyond Literature Cross-Curricular Connection: Health, p. 48

Formal Assessment Selection Test, pp. 224–226; Assessment Resources Software

Alternative Assessment, p. 48

Resource Pro CD-ROM

Listening to Literature Audiocassettes

Literature CD-ROM

In Another Country ◆ The Corn Planting ◆ A Worn Path ◆

Eudora Welty *(1909–)*

In her short stories and novels. Eudora Welty vividly captures life in the deep South, creating powerful images of the landscape and conveying the shared attitudes and values of the people. She often confronts the hardships and sorrows of life in poor rural areas.

Despite her awareness of people's suffering, her outlook remains positive and optimistic.

Welty was born in Jackson, Mississippi, where she has spent most of her life. She attended Mississippi State College for Women before transferring to the University of Wisconsin, from which she graduated in 1929. Hoping to pursue a career in advertising, she moved to New York and enrolled at Columbia University School of Business. However, because of the worsening Depression, she was unable to find a steady job and returned to Jackson in 1931.

After accepting a job as a publicist for a government agency, she spent several years traveling throughout Mississippi, taking photographs and interviewing people. Her experiences and observations inspired her to write fiction, and in 1936, her first short story, "Death of a Travelling Salesman," was published in a small magazine.

Throughout her work, Welty displays an acute sense of detail and a deep sense of compassion toward her characters. In "A Worn Path," for example, she paints a sympathetic portrait of an old woman whose feelings of love and sense of duty motivate her to make a long, painful journey through the woods.

Welty is one of the leading American writers of the twentieth century. Over the years, she has published numerous collections of short stories and novels. In 1973, her novel *The Optimist's Daughter* won the Pulitzer Prize.

◆ Background for Understanding

History: World War I

World War I was the first truly global war, involving nations on every continent but Antarctica. The Great War, as it was also called, began in Europe in 1914, sparked by nationalistic pride and systems of alliances among nations. The Central Powers (Germany, Austria, Turkey) fought the Allies (England, France, Russia) with other nations joining one side or the other. Italy, where Hemingway's "In Another Country" takes place, was not strategically important but helped the Allies by drawing Central Power troops away from other battle areas.

The war lasted four brutal years and took the lives of nine million soldiers. Throughout most of the conflict, a stalemate existed. Both sides were dug into trenches and took turns rushing one another. Each rush was greeted by a barrage of machine fire, with thousands falling dead. Other soldiers fell to new weapons of killing—inventions such as airplanes, long-range artillery, and poison gas, which many people had hoped would deter aggressors and prevent war. Many of the wounded were saved, however, by advances in medical treatment, such as surgically disinfected wounds, plastic surgery, and rehabilitation to strengthen injured limbs. Ironically, despite the war's devastation, modern medicine leapt forward during World War I.

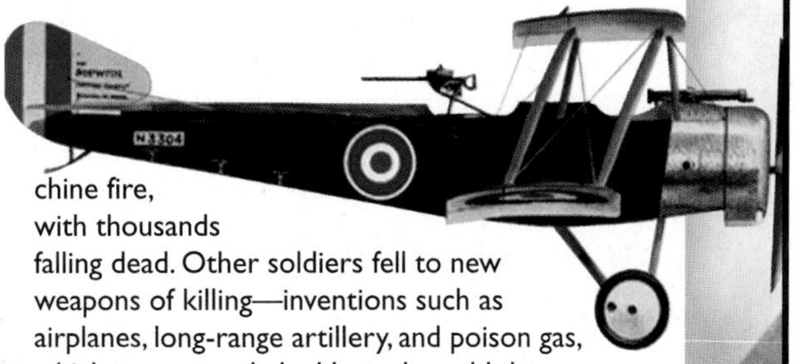

Customize for
Less Proficient Readers
Some of the situations and ideas presented in these stories may be confusing. You may find it useful to stop and clarify things periodically, asking *Who? Where? Why? What? How?* and *When?* questions to make sure students are on track.

Customize for
AP Students
Each of the stories includes references that add levels of meaning and degrees of complexity. Have students analyze examples in the poem of irony, symbolism, imagery, and foreshadowing.

Customize for
English Language Learners
Guide students to use context clues or a dictionary to discover the meanings of words not highlighted and defined on the page. *Pavilions, lurched,* and *jostle* are examples from the first story. *Gnarled, loitered,* and *harrowing* are examples from the second. In the last story, students may not know the meanings of *meditative, ravine,* and *lolling.*

Test Preparation Workshop

Reading Comprehension:
Analyze Sentence Meaning Many standardized tests require students to correctly answer sentence-completion questions. Often, more than one choice can complete a sentence. Use the following sample item to show students how to analyze sentence meaning, decide whether it is positive or negative, and eliminate choices that have the opposite sense.

Ironically, despite the devastation of World War I, modern medicine ____during the period.

A advanced
B declined
C regressed
D changed

The signal words *Ironically* and *despite* indicate the correct answer will have a positive connotation. *B* and *C* can be eliminated. *D* is too mild an answer. *A* is the best choice.

Interest Grabber Tell students that it is likely that at some time in their lives they will find themselves in the unenviable position of being the bearer of bad news. Then divide students into groups. Hand each group an index card with news of an injury, accident, incarceration, dire financial reversal, etc. Tell them that it is their job to pass on that news to someone who will probably find it very upsetting. Give a different piece of bad news to each group.

Groups can discuss and role-play ways to break the news to the person(s) most affected by it. Should they be direct? Should they try to soften the blow? Should they be comforting? Should they speak and then disappear? Have students talk or write about how they think it would feel to give bad news. Students who actually have had that responsibility can volunteer to describe their approach and their feelings at the time. Explain to students that each of the stories they're about to read focuses on how people handle difficult situations such as the ones they dealt with in the activity.

Guide for Interpreting *(continued)*

◆ Literature and Your Life

CONNECT YOUR EXPERIENCE

During the course of your life, you'll journey to countless places. Through these journeys you'll learn about yourself and the world around you. In each of these stories, you'll encounter characters who make journeys that dramatically impact their lives. How do their journeys compare to ones you've made?

Journal Writing Jot down some thoughts you might have during a journey. Your journey may be real or imagined.

THEMATIC FOCUS: FACING TROUBLED TIMES

War, poverty, illness—such hardships affect people's personal journeys. How are these story characters affected by hardships?

◆ Literary Focus

POINT OF VIEW

Each of these stories is told from a different **point of view,** or perspective. "In Another Country" features a narrator who is the central character in the story. He uses the **first-person point of view** referring to himself as "I" and telling the story in his own words. "The Corn Planting" also uses the first-person point of view but the narrator is a minor character. In both these stories, readers learn only what is in the narrator's range of experience. "A Worn Path" is told from the **limited third-person point of view,** in which a narrator who doesn't participate in the action tells the story and conveys the thoughts of one of the characters.

◆ Grammar and Style

PUNCTUATING DIALOGUE

Like most short stories, these pieces include dialogue. Notice that the dialogue follows these rules.

Quotation marks appear immediately before and after a character's words. When a quotation is inserted into a longer sentence, place a comma before each set of marks. (*"Dance old scarecrow," she said, "while I dance with you."*) **Periods** are placed inside the quotation marks. **Question** and **exclamation marks** appear inside the quotation marks if they are part of the quoted material. (*"How could we?" he said.*) Place them outside the marks if they belong to the overall sentence. (*Did he really mean, "I loved that story"?*)

◆ Reading Strategy

IDENTIFY WITH CHARACTERS

Even if your journeys have differed greatly from the ones taken by these characters, you might feel as if you know them. When you **identify with characters,** you try to relate to their thoughts and feelings, connecting them with your own experience. For example, when the doctor consoles the injured soldier in this story, you might find yourself remembering an injury *you* recovered from, or you may just feel you know how the soldier feels. In either case, you're identifying with the character—taking him into your personal world.

◆ Build Vocabulary

LATIN ROOTS: *-val-*

The word *invalided* means "removed from active duty by illness or injury." You can construct this meaning—and the meaning of other *-val-* words—with the help of the Latin root *-val-*, which means "strength or value."

WORD BANK

Preview this list of words from the stories.

invalided
grave
limber
obstinate

Research Skills Mini-Lesson

Using Visuals in a Report

This mini-lesson supports the Report on Rehabilitation activity on p. 747.

Introduce the Concept Tell students that in writing a research report on current practices of rehabilitation medicine, they will look for appropriate photographs, diagrams, and illustrations as well as written information. Remind them to research in a variety of print and nonprint sources, including medical journals, hospital and clinic publications, periodicals, texts, databases, and the Internet.

Develop Background Explain that rehabilitation is the process by which an incapacitated person is restored to health or put back into good condition. For example, a person recovering from a broken leg might go to a rehabilitation facility to get physical therapy. Suggest that students collect photos of people using various kinds of exercise machines.

Apply the Information After collecting information, have students evaluate the materials they have gathered to determine if they need more visuals to support their report. They should also check that their visual displays are interesting and relevant.

Assess the Outcome Assess students' work on their ability to collect interesting, relevant visuals to support their report. You might have students use the Peer Assessment form for Research Report/Paper, p. 121 in ***Alternative Assessment.***

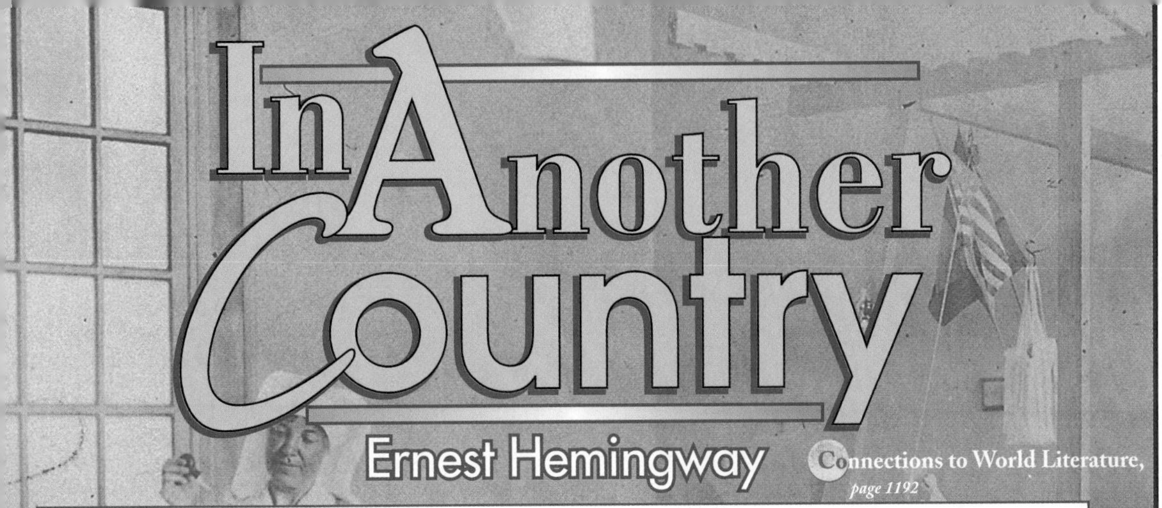

In Another Country

Ernest Hemingway

Connections to World Literature, page 1192

❶ In the fall the war[1] was always there, but we did not go to it any more. It was cold in the fall in Milan[2] and the dark came very early. Then the electric lights came on, and it was pleasant along the streets looking in the windows. There was much game hanging outside the shops, and the snow powdered in the fur of the foxes and the wind blew their tails. The deer hung stiff and heavy and empty, and small birds blew in the wind and the wind turned their feathers. It was a cold fall and the wind came down from the mountains.

We were all at the hospital every afternoon, and there were different ways of walking across the town through the dusk to the hospital. Two of the ways were alongside canals, but they were long. Always, though, you crossed a bridge across a canal to enter the hospital. There was a choice of three bridges. On one of them a woman sold roasted chestnuts. It was warm, standing in front of her charcoal fire, and the chestnuts were warm afterward in your pocket. The hospital was very old and very beautiful, and you entered through a gate and walked across a courtyard and out a gate on the other side. There were usually funerals starting from the courtyard. Beyond the old hospital were the new brick pavilions, and there we met every afternoon and were all very polite and interested in what was the matter, and sat in the machines that were to make so much difference.

The doctor came up to the machine where I was sitting and said: "What did you like best to do before the war? Did you practice a sport?"

I said: "Yes, football."

"Good," he said. "You will be able to play football again better than ever." ❷

My knee did not bend and the leg dropped straight from the knee to the ankle without a calf, and the machine was to bend the knee and make it move as in riding a tricycle. But it did not bend yet, and instead the machine lurched when it came to the bending part. The doctor said: "That will all pass. You are a fortunate young man. You will play football again like a champion."

In the next machine was a major who had a little hand like a baby's. He winked at me when the doctor examined his hand, which was between two leather straps that bounced up and down and flapped the stiff fingers, and said: "And will I too play football, captain-doctor?" He had been a very great fencer, and before the war the greatest fencer in Italy.

The doctor went to his office in a back room and brought a photograph which showed a hand that had been withered almost as small as the major's, before it had taken a machine course, and after was a little larger. The major held the photograph with his good hand and

1. **the war:** World War I (1914–1918).
2. **Milan** (mi lan´): A city in northern Italy.

Develop Understanding

One-Minute Insight

True to Hemingway's style, this story of a soldier in a World War I military hospital describes a time, but does not create and then resolve a single conflict. The narrator, an American serving as an officer in the Italian army during World War I, convalesces in Milan after a serious injury to his leg. He befriends other wounded soldiers, but once they decide his medals are because he is an American while their medals were much more hard-won, he feels isolated from even the men with whom he has so much in common. The narrator is "in another country," one where he feels no connection to anyone else. Hemingway's story deals with the meaningless of war and the false hope that such hospitals create.

Customize for *Gifted/Talented Students*

Invite students to develop an exercise program for someone like the major or the narrator in the story. Their goal is to strengthen or increase the use of a particular injured limb. Students should assume that the complex, scientific equipment that exists today is not available.

◆ Literary Focus

❶ **Point of View** Ask students how they can tell, right from the start, that the story is told from a first-person point of view. *Students can identify the word we in the first sentence.*

◆ Grammar and Style

❷ **Punctuating Dialogue** Point out the convention of starting a new paragraph for a change in speakers, as well as the unconventional use of the colon preceding the first sentence of dialogue. For the second piece of dialogue, guide students to notice the period after *he said,* and the capital *Y* in the "You" that follows, indicating that the character says not one long sentence but two shorter ones.

Connecting to World Literature

To connect "In Another Country" to the world literature selection, "War," see p. 1192.

Block Scheduling Strategies

Consider these suggestions to take advantage of extended class time:

- Build background about World War I by having students view Chapter 9 of the **Looking at Literature Videodisc.** Follow with a class discussion.
- Introduce Point of View by discussing with students the Literary Focus on p. 730. Make sure students understand the points of view represented in the three selections.
- Play all or some of the stories on audiocassette. Have students discuss how hearing the stories adds to their ability to identify with the characters or appreciate the authors' choice of point of view.
- Provide time for students to review and respond to the Critical Viewing questions accompanying the art and photos.
- Ask students to work in discussion groups to answer the Critical Thinking questions that follow each story.

◆ Critical Thinking

❶ Speculate Ask students to tell how old they think the narrator and the other "boys" are. *Students may say that the young soldiers are perhaps 18–20 years old. Remind them that wars, for the most part, are fought by soldiers who are their age and just a little older.*

▶Critical Viewing◀

❷ Compare and Contrast Students may say that the place Hemingway has described seems to be an out-patient clinic housed in an impressive building. It appears to be full of machines, not crowded with beds filled with badly wounded men.

◆ Background for Understanding

❸ History World War I was a nineteenth-century war fought with twentieth-century weapons: the military tactics lagged behind the capability of the weaponry. As a result, casualties were staggering and the wounds extraordinary and appalling. Although some soldiers came home with psychological wounds and others with illnesses, some were simply ripped apart. It has been estimated that more than 12 percent of all injured soldiers suffered from facial wounds. Perhaps a third of these unfortunate men were permanently disfigured. Polite society sometimes shunned them. Much of the support the hundreds of thousands of mutilated veterans received was from their fellow victims. Attempting to dignify their experience, they bonded together to form mutual-aid societies.

❹ Clarification Point out that here the narrator rephrases the opening sentence of the story.

◆ Literature and Your Life

❺ Have students discuss what it means to feel detached. Ask them to explain why all these men are "a little detached," and offer reasons why other people come to feel aloof and indifferent. Then have students discuss the nature of the relationship these young soldiers share. Ask them to think of relationships they have with people that are based solely on shared experiences, such as taking the bus together each day, or being in the same math class.

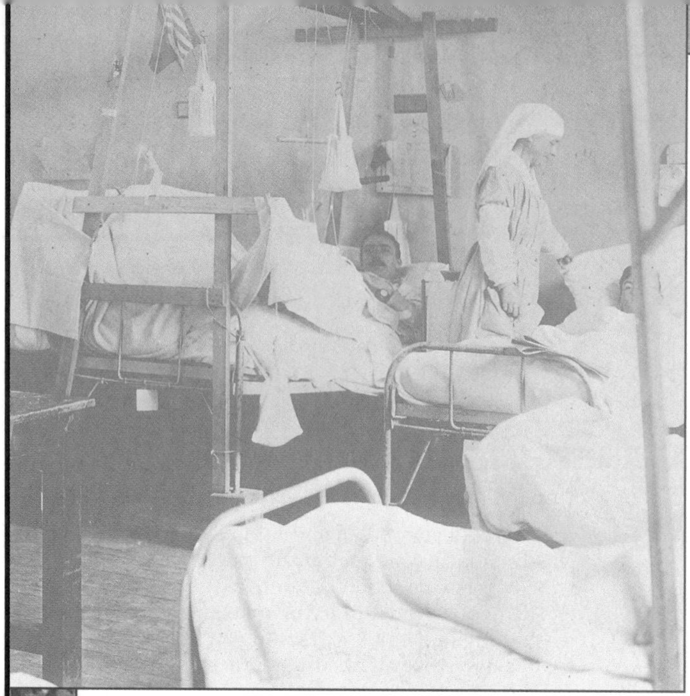

◀ **Critical Viewing** How does the World War I military hospital in this photo compare with the hospital Hemingway describes? **[Compare and Contrast]** ❷

looked at it very carefully. "A wound?" he asked.

"An industrial accident," the doctor said.

"Very interesting, very interesting," the major said, and handed it back to the doctor.

"You have confidence?"

"No," said the major.

❶ There were three boys who came each day who were about the same age I was. They were all three from Milan, and one of them was to be a lawyer, and one was to be a painter, and one had intended to be a soldier, and after we were finished with the machines, sometimes we walked back together to the Café Cova, which was next door to the Scala.[3] We walked the short way through the communist quarter because we were four together. The people hated us because we were officers, and from a wine-shop someone called out, "A basso gli ufficiali!"[4] as we passed. Another boy who walked with us sometimes and made us five wore a black silk handkerchief across his face because he had no nose then and his face was to be rebuilt. He had gone out to the front from the military academy and been wounded within an hour after he had gone into the front line for the first time. They rebuilt his face, but he came from a very old family and they could never get the nose exactly right. He went to South America and worked in a bank. But this was a long time ago, and then we did not any of us know how it was going to be afterward. We only knew then that there was always the war, but that we were not going to it any more. ❸ ❹

> **◆ Literary Focus**
> Who is telling this story? How is the narrator identified?

We all had the same medals, except the boy with the black silk bandage across his face, and he had not been at the front long enough to get any medals. The tall boy with a very pale face who was to be a lawyer had been a lieutenant of Arditi[5] and had three medals of the sort we each had only one of. He had lived a very long time with death and was a little detached. We were all a little detached, and there was nothing that held us together except that we met every afternoon at the hospital. ❺ Although, as we walked to the Cova through the tough part of town, walking in the dark, with light and singing coming out of the wine-shops, and sometimes having to walk into the street when the men and women would crowd together on the sidewalk so that we would have had to jostle them to get by, we felt held together by there being something that had happened that they, the people who disliked us, did not understand.

3. **the Scala** (skä´ lä): An opera house in Milan.
4. **"A basso gli ufficiali!"** (ä bä´ sō lye ōō fē chä´ lē): "Down with officers!" (Italian).
5. **Arditi** (är dē´ tē): A select group of soldiers chosen specifically for dangerous campaigns.

Beyond the Classroom

Career Connection

Physical Therapist Physical therapy is the treatment of injury or disease by physical means. Physical therapists work with a wide range of patients, from those who have severe injuries and are in need of intensive therapy, to athletes or dancers with knee or ankle problems, to the throngs of Americans suffering from lower back pain. The tools of the physical therapist are exercise, massage, infrared or ultraviolet light, electrotherapy, hydrotherapy, and heat.

Invite students to visit a physical therapy clinic to find out more about the daily activities of physical therapists. Students can interview therapists to learn about how their approach to healing physical injuries differs from that of chiropractors, physiatrists, orthopedists, acupuncturists, and other practitioners. Interested students can research the nature of the education and training physical therapists undergo, as well as the necessary licensing requirements.

We ourselves all understood the Cova, where it was rich and warm and not too brightly lighted, and noisy and smoky at certain hours, and there were always girls at the tables and the illustrated papers on a rack on the wall. The girls at the Cova were very patriotic, and I found that the most patriotic people in Italy were the café girls—and I believe they are still patriotic.

The boys at first were very polite about my medals and asked me what I had done to get them. I showed them the papers, which were written in very beautiful language and full of *fratellanza* and *abnegazione*,[6] but which really said, with the adjectives removed, that I had been given the medals because I was an American. After that their manner changed a little toward me, although I was their friend against outsiders. I was a friend, but I was never really one of them after they had read the citations, because it had been different with them 6 and they had done very different things to get their medals. I had been wounded, it was true; but we all knew that being wounded, after all, was really an accident. I was never ashamed of the ribbons, though, and sometimes, after the cocktail hour, I would imagine myself having done all the things they had done to get their medals; but walking home at night through the empty streets with the cold wind and all the shops closed, trying to keep near the street lights, I knew that I would never have done such things, and I was very much afraid to die, and often lay in bed at night by myself, afraid to die and wondering how I would be when I went back to the front again.

The three with the medals were like hunting-hawks; and I was not a hawk, although I might seem a hawk to those who had never hunted; they, the three, knew better and so we drifted apart. But I stayed good friends with the boy who had been wounded his first day at the front, because he would never know now how he would have turned out; so he could never be accepted either, and I liked him because I thought perhaps he would not have turned out to be a hawk either.

The major, who had been the great fencer, did not believe in bravery, and spent much time while we sat in the machines correcting my grammar. He had complimented me on how I spoke Italian, and we talked together very easily. One day I had said that Italian seemed such an easy language to me that I 7 could not take a great interest in it; everything was so easy to say. "Ah yes," the major said. "Why, then, do you not take up the use of grammar?" So we took up the use of grammar, and soon Italian was such a difficult language that I was afraid to talk to him until I had the grammar straight in my mind.

The major came very regularly to the hospital. I do not think he ever missed a day, although I am sure he did not believe in the machines. There was a time when none of us believed in the machines, and one day the major said it was all nonsense. The machines were new then and it was we who were to prove them. It was an idiotic idea, he said, "a theory, like another." I had not learned my grammar, and he said I was a stupid impossible disgrace, and he was a fool to have bothered with me. He was a small man and he sat straight up in his chair with his right hand thrust into the machine and looked straight ahead at the wall while the straps thumped up and down with his fingers in them.

"What will you do when the war is over if it is over?" he asked me. "Speak grammatically!"

"I will go to the States."

"Are you married?"

"No, but I hope to be."

"The more of a fool you are," he said. He seemed very angry. "A man must not marry."

"Why, Signor Maggiore?"[7]

"Don't call me 'Signor Maggiore.'"

"Why must not a man marry?"

"He cannot marry. He cannot marry," he 8 said angrily. "If he is to lose everything, he should not place himself in a position to lose that. He should not place himself in a position to lose. He should find things he cannot lose."

He spoke very angrily and bitterly, and looked straight ahead while he talked.

---

6. ***fratellanza*** (frä tāl än´ tsä) **and *abnegazione*** (äb´ nā gä tzyō´ nā): "Brotherhood" and "self-denial" (Italian).

7. **Signor Maggiore** (sēn yōr´ mäj jō´ rā): "Mr. Major" (Italian); a respectful way of addressing an officer.

Literature CD-ROM To build background on Ernest Hemingway, use the CD-ROM *The History of American Literature:* Part 2, Disc 1, Feature 7. Part of this segment focuses upon Ernest Hemingway.

◆ Background for Understanding

❻ History This paragraph describes an experience much like Hemingway's own as a Red Cross volunteer during World War I. He didn't take part in the fighting; his job was to deliver food to troops in the trenches. During one run he was wounded, hit by several fragments from a mortar shell. For this he received medals and glowing citations.

Customize for *English Language Learners*

❼ You may wish to use this paragraph for class discussion. Students can understand that speaking Italian was easy for the narrator when he was unaware of correct grammar. Then, as soon as he tried to speak correctly, Italian became difficult. Ask students learning English if they face the same problem. Discuss whether there is an everyday English that is easy to speak and a "classroom" grammar that is difficult to learn.

◆ Reading Strategy

❽ Identify With Characters Ask students to try to explain why the major has such a negative attitude toward marriage. Ask them to keep their explanations in mind as they read the remainder of the story.

Cross-Curricular Connection: Science

Medical Advances Advances in medicine and in the treatment of wounds are often the by-products of war. During the Civil War, for example, in which medical care was abysmal by twentieth-century standards, nursing care was transformed from a menial service to a genuine profession. That war also introduced the idea of a special ambulance corps to give first aid to the wounded and then transport them from the battlefield. Following World War I, the problem of dealing with the hundreds of thousands of disfigured and mutilated soldiers led to advancements in plastic surgery and the prosthetic arts. Many men, whom the French called "the men with the broken faces," endured a series of painful operations meant to correct or minimize the disfigurement.

Interested students can do research to learn more about war-related advancements in medical care. For a unique look at several "before-and-after" photos of some of the first reconstructive surgery patients, students can view the PBS series *The Great War* (1996). As an alternative, they can read the companion book to the series, written by Jay Winter and Blaine Baggett.

◆ Critical Thinking

❶ Connect Ask students why the major responded to learning of his loss by being angry? *Some students might say that anger is a common reaction to tragedy. Others might say that the major has not yet accepted the tragedy.*

Customize for *AP Students*

❷ Point out that this story ends without a resolution, reflecting the Modernist perception of life as being uncertain and confusing. Also, guide students to recognize that this story, like some of those in the previous unit, contains dramatic irony; the major postponed marriage until he was finished with the war and could assure his young bride of his well-being, only to have her die unexpectedly.

"But why should he necessarily lose it?"

"He'll lose it," the major said. He was looking at the wall. Then he looked down at the machine and jerked his little hand out from between the straps and slapped it hard against his thigh. "He'll lose it," he almost shouted. "Don't argue with me!" Then he called to the attendant who ran the machines. "Come and turn this damned thing off."

He went back into the other room for the light treatment and the massage. Then I heard him ask the doctor if he might use his telephone and he shut the door. When he came back into the room, I was sitting in another machine. He was wearing his cape and had his cap on, and he came directly toward my machine and put his arm on my shoulder.

❶ "I am so sorry," he said, and patted me on the shoulder with his good hand. "I would not be rude. My wife has just died. You must forgive me."

"Oh—" I said, feeling sick for him. "I am so sorry."

He stood there biting his lower lip. "It is very difficult," he said. "I cannot resign myself."

He looked straight past me and out through the window. Then he began to cry. "I am utterly unable to resign myself," he said and choked. And then crying, his head up looking at nothing, carrying himself straight and soldierly, with tears on both his cheeks and biting his lips, he walked past the machines and out the door.

The doctor told me that the major's wife, who was very young and whom he had not married until he was definitely invalided out of the war, had died of pneumonia. She had been sick only a few days. No one expected her to die. The major did not come to the hospital for three days. Then he came at the usual hour, wearing a black band on the sleeve of his uniform. When he came back, there were large framed photographs around the wall of all sorts of wounds before and after they had been cured by the machines. In front of the machine the major used were three photographs of hands like his that were completely restored. I do not know where the doctor got them. I always understood we were the first to use the machines. The photographs did not make much difference to the major because he only looked out of the window. ❷

◆ Build Vocabulary

invalided (in´ və lid´ id) *v.*: Released because of illness or disability

Guide for Responding

◆ *Literature and Your Life*

Reader's Response What emotion did this story arouse most strongly in you? Explain.

Thematic Focus What qualities allow the characters in this story to deal with hardship? Explain.

Journal Writing Describe what you learned about World War I from the story.

☑ Check Your Comprehension

1. Why does the narrator go to the hospital every afternoon?
2. How do the people in the communist quarter react to the officers as they walked by?
3. (a) What happens to the major's wife? (b) How does he react?

◆ Critical Thinking

INTERPRET

1. How would you describe the story's mood? **[Deduce]**
2. How do the three boys' attitude about the war relate to their nationalities? **[Connect]**
3. What might be the significance of the major's interest in grammar? **[Interpret]**
4. Find examples to support this statement: In this story, the machines symbolize the false hopes and promises of the Modern Age. **[Support]**
5. What is ironic, or surprising, about the major's wife's death? **[Analyze]**

APPLY

6. How does the story reflect the sense of disillusionment that arose during World War I? **[Apply]**

Reinforce and Extend

Answers

◆ *Literature and Your Life*

Reader's Response Students may say that the story aroused pity for all the injured men and especially for the major. They may also note anger at a world which so cruelly and seemingly randomly punishes people who have already suffered.

Thematic Focus Sample response: The characters display courage and adaptability as well as the ability to not constantly think about their hardships.

☑ Check Your Comprehension

1. The narrator was wounded in the leg and is receiving physical therapy treatments to help restore muscle activity.
2. The people in the communist quarter hate the officers just because they are officers.
3. (a) The major's wife dies. (b) He reacts with anger.

◆ Critical Thinking

1. The story's mood is melancholic.
2. The Italian boys are proud of their accomplishments during the war because they are fighting for their country. The narrator dislikes war in part because he is fighting a foreign war.
3. Grammar is understandable because it follows set rules while the war is difficult to understand and seemingly has no rules.
4. Suggested response: The examples include the photographs that supposedly demonstrate the machines' effectiveness; the narrator's comment that the machines "were to make so much difference"; and his comment that they were the first to use the machines.
5. The major escaped death in the war but his wife, away from the dangers of war, died after a short illness.
6. Suggested response: The men are disillusioned about the machines; the major is disillusioned about his young wife's sudden death; some townspeople are disillusioned with the officers fighting for them.

The Corn Planting

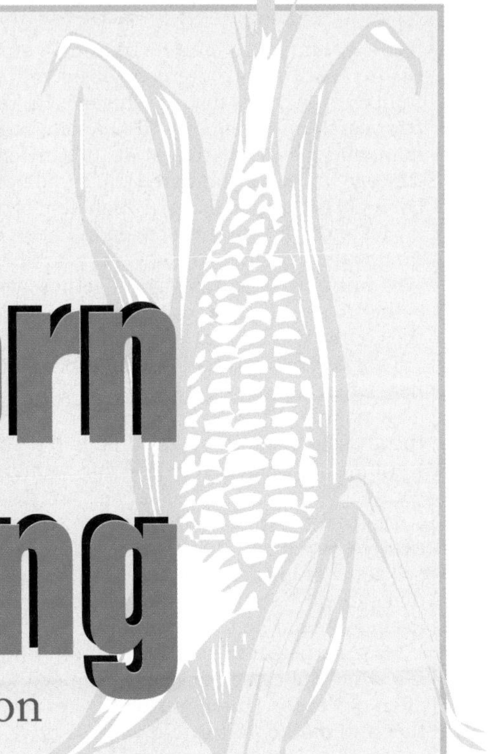

Sherwood Anderson

The farmers who come to our town to trade are a part of the town life. Saturday is the big day. Often the children come to the high school in town.

It is so with Hatch Hutchenson. Although his farm, some three miles from town, is small, it is known to be one of the best-kept and best-worked places in all our section. Hatch is a little gnarled old figure of a man. His place is on
3 the Scratch Gravel Road and there are plenty of poorly kept places out that way.

Hatch's place stands out. The little frame house is always kept painted, the trees in his orchard are whitened with lime halfway up the trunks, and the barn and sheds are in repair, and his fields are always clean-looking.

Hatch is nearly seventy. He got a rather late start in life. His father, who owned the same farm, was a Civil War man and came home badly wounded, so that, although he lived a long time after the war, he couldn't work much. Hatch was the only son and stayed at home, working the place until his father died. Then, when he was nearing fifty, he married a schoolteacher of forty, and they had a son. The schoolteacher was a small one like Hatch. After they married, they both stuck close to the land. They seemed to fit into their farm life as certain people fit into the clothes they wear. I have noticed something about people who make a go of marriage. They grow more and more alike. Then even grow to look alike.

Their one son, Will Hutchenson, was a small 4
but remarkably strong boy. He came to our high school in town and pitched on our town baseball team. He was a fellow always cheerful, bright and alert, and a great favorite with all of us.

For one thing, he began as a young boy to make amusing little drawings. It was a talent. He made drawings of fish and pigs and cows, and they looked like people you knew. I never did know, before, that people could look so much like cows and horses and pigs and fish.

When he had finished in the town high school, Will went to Chicago, where his mother

Develop Understanding

One-Minute Insight Told from the point of view of a friend of the family, this story describes the alienation of a son from his parents. The narrator describes the Hutchensons as people who "fit into their farm life." When their son, Will, leaves to study art in Chicago, his parents live for news of his life; he frequently sends letters that they treasure. The Hutchensons claim that they can never visit Will in Chicago because of the demands of the farm. When a friend of the narrator gets a telegraph about Will's death, he and the narrator both go out to the farm to inform his parents. In an eerily silent reaction to the news, the Hutchensons grieve in the only way they know how: they go out into the night to plant corn.

◆ Critical Thinking

3 Form a Mental Picture Have students consider the name *Scratch Gravel Road.* Invite them to visualize what a place with that name might look like. *Students are likely to envision unproductive, dry, lifeless, land with some shacks and other evidence of hard times.*

◆ Literary Focus

4 Point of View Guide students to notice that here and in the first two paragraphs are indications that the story is being told in the first-person point of view by someone who lives in the place he is describing and who knows its inhabitants.

Tips to Guide Reading

Shared Reading To help students get started, read aloud the first few paragraphs of "The Corn Planting" while they follow along in their texts. Afterward, discuss what you've read and answer any questions that students might have. Then tell students to continue reading silently.

Viewing and Representing Mini-Lesson

This mini-lesson supports the Military Report activity in the Idea Bank on p. 747.

Introduce the Concept Remind students to collect information for creating maps, graphs, charts, and other visuals. Tell students to use a variety of print and nonprint resources in gathering information, such as text books, encyclopedias, atlases, databases, and the Internet.

Develop Background If students have difficulty finding information on the Italian Arditi, tell them to search under: "Italian Front in World War I" and "Hemingway." Suggest that they look at maps of Europe during the war, investigate military maneuvers, and gather data on the numbers of volunteers, and so on.

Apply the Information After they gather their research materials, have students determine if they have appropriate information to use as maps, charts, and diagrams.

Assess the Outcome Assess students' work on their ability to use maps, charts, and other visuals and to present a well-organized report.

◆ Background for Understanding

❶ History Chicago was a major city in the Midwest when Will Hutchenson went there to study at the Art Institute. In 1830, when it was incorporated, Chicago had a population of about 300. By the time of its Great Fire in 1871, the population had soared to 300,000. By 1893, the city had sufficiently recovered to host the World Columbian Exposition commemorating the 400th anniversary of the European discovery of America. With unlimited opportunities to rebuild after the Great Fire, Chicago provided America's finest architects with an unprecedented boost; the city filled up with decorative and monumental buildings. The Art Institute is one such structure which today houses an impressive collection of artwork. Tell students that Ernest Hemingway grew up in Chicago.

◆ Critical Thinking

❷ Compare and Contrast Have students contrast the life Will was living in Chicago with the farm life his parents knew. Point out that Hal bridged the two generations; he served as the link between Will and his parents.

◆ Grammar and Style

❸ Punctuating Dialogue Point out that it is unconventional to present in one paragraph what two different speakers say. Tell students that here this style makes sense because the narrator is relating the information and because the Hutchensons are essentially saying the same thing.

❶ had a cousin living, and he became a student in the Art Institute out there. Another young fellow from our town was also in Chicago. He really went two years before Will did. His name was Hal Weyman, and he was a student at the University of Chicago. After he graduated, he came home and got a job as principal of our high school.

Hal and Will Hutchenson hadn't been close friends before, Hal being several years older than Will, but in Chicago they got together, went together to see plays, and, as Hal later told me, they had a good many long talks.

I got it from Hal that, in Chicago, as at home here when he was a young boy, Will was immediately popular. He was good-looking, so the girls in the art school liked him, and he had a straightforwardness that made him popular with all the young fellows.

Hal told me that Will was out to some party nearly every night, and right away he began to sell some of his amusing little drawings and to make money. The drawings were used in advertisements, and he was well paid.

He even began to send some money home. You ❷ see, after Hal came back here, he used to go quite often out to the Hutchenson place to see Will's father and mother. He would walk or drive out there in the afternoon or on summer evenings and sit with them. The talk was always of Will.

Hal said it was touching how much the father and mother depended on their one son, how much they talked about him and dreamed of his future. They had never been people who went about much with the town folks or even with their neighbors. They were of the sort who work all the time, from early morning till late in the evenings, and on moonlight nights, Hal said, and after the little old wife had got the supper, they often went out into the fields and worked again.

You see, by this time old Hatch was nearing seventy and his wife would have been ten years younger. Hal said that whenever he went out to the farm they quit work and came to sit with him. They might be in one of the fields, working together, but when they saw him in the road, they came running. They had got a letter from Will. He wrote every week.

The little old mother would come running following the father. "We got another letter, Mr. ❸ Weyman," Hatch would cry, and then his wife, quite breathless, would say the same thing, "Mr. Weyman, we got a letter."

Cultural Connection

Corn Corn, a member of the grass family, was first cultivated in Central America. In the domestication of plants, corn is actually a latecomer, trailing by a thousand years the cultivation of beans and squash. The original tiny wild corn is small. The much larger size and shape of the modern corncob is a result of centuries of selective breeding.

Corn has long been a staple of Native American societies throughout North America, and different groups have celebrated its cultivation in one way or another. For example, the Pueblo people have traditionally honored their Corn Mothers by providing all new born children with corn fetishes. Mississippian groups like the Muskogee, Chickasaw, Choctaw, and Cherokee have held Green Corn Dances after each summer's harvest. Invite students to learn more about the specifics of the Green Corn Dance or other Native American ceremonies that honor this key crop. They can share their findings with the class.

The letter would be brought out at once and read aloud. Hal said the letters were always delicious. Will larded them with little sketches. There were humorous drawings of people he had seen or been with, rivers of automobiles on Michigan Avenue in Chicago, a policeman at a street crossing, young stenographers hurrying into office buildings. Neither of the old people had ever been to the city and they were curious and eager. They wanted the drawings explained, and Hal said they were like two children wanting to know every little detail Hal could remember about their son's life in the big city. He was always at them to come there on a visit and they would spend hours talking of that.

◆ **Literary Focus** How does the narrator interact with other characters? 4

"Of course," Hatch said, "we couldn't go."

"How could we?" he said. He had been on that one little farm since he was a boy. When he was a young fellow, his father was an invalid and so Hatch had to run things. A farm, if you run it right, is very exacting. You have to fight weeds all the time. There are the farm animals to take care of. "Who would milk our cows?" Hatch said. The idea of anyone but him or his wife touching one of the Hutchenson cows seemed to hurt him. While he was alive, he didn't want anyone else plowing one of his fields, tending his corn, looking after things about the barn. He felt that way about his farm. It was a thing you couldn't explain, Hal said. He seemed to understand the two old people. 5 6

It was a spring night, past midnight, when Hal came to my house and told me the news. In our town we have a night telegraph operator at the railroad station and Hal got a wire. It was really addressed to Hatch Hutchenson, but the operator brought it to Hal. Will Hutchenson was dead, had been killed. It turned out later that he was at a party with some other young fellows and there might have been some drinking. Anyway, the car was wrecked, and Will Hutchenson was killed. The operator wanted Hal to go out and take the message to Hatch and his wife, and Hal wanted me to go along. 7

I offered to take my car, but Hal said no, "Let's

◀ **Critical Viewing** What does a harvest usually symbolize? How does corn play an important part of this story? **[Connect]** 8

◆ Literary Focus

4 Point of View Students may say that the narrator appears to be in regular communication with Hal, who informs him of what the Hutchensons are saying and doing.

◆ Build Vocabulary

5 Word Roots: *-val-* Students can use their understanding of the word root *-val-* along with their knowledge of the root *-in-,* which means "not," to construct the definition of *invalid,* in this case a noun that means "a disabled person." Hatch's father did *not* have the physical capacity to work the farm.

◆ Critical Thinking

6 Speculate Students may wonder why, if they love their son so much and are so curious about his life in Chicago, the Hutchensons do not visit him there. Invite them to discuss possible interpretations of the Hutchensons' choice. *Students may suggest that their reluctance stems from both a powerful sense of responsibility and connection to their land and a fear of and disconnection from modern life.*

◆ Critical Thinking

7 Analyze Ask students to explain why the night operator gave the Hutchensons' telegram to Hal. *Students may say that in the small town, people knew one another and looked after one another protectively.*

▶Critical Viewing◀

8 Connect A corn harvest usually symbolizes something good, such as nature's reward for hard work. Corn plays an important part in this story because the Hutchensons grow corn on their farm.

Research Skills Mini-Lesson

Presenting Reports in Different Forms

This mini-lesson supports the Cultural Connection on p. 736.

Introduce the Concept Tell students that they will research Native American ceremonies that celebrate corn, and then present their findings to the class. Explain that they can use an oral, written, or artistic form for their presentations. Remind students that as they gather information, they should periodically evaluate whether or not their material is complete and relevant.

Develop Background Give students some suggestions about different forms for their report. For example, they could create a poster, make a comparison chart, draw a map, compose a song about corn, invent a dance, write a dialogue, and so on. Tell students that as they research, they should think about how best to present their information.

Apply the Information Guide students in choosing a form for their presentation. In choosing, they should consider what they do best and are most confident in, as well as what form is best suited to the subject matter.

Assess the Outcome Assess students' work on their ability to choose a form of presentation that is appropriate, interesting, and entertaining.

◆ Critical Thinking

❶ Analyze Guide students to notice the situational irony in this paragraph: although the characters are on their way to bear news of death, they do so on an early spring night, a time of rebirth, with little leaves just coming on the trees and with streams seemingly alive in the moonlight.

◆ Reading Strategy

❷ Identify with Characters Ask students to put themselves in Hal's place as he approaches Hatch Hutchenson's house with the news of Will's death.

▶Critical Viewing◀

❸ Compare and Contrast Students may say that this surreal sunny image of a fertile well-tended farm is in no way evocative of the hardscrabble Hutchenson farm, either in mood or appearance. They may think of the Hutchenson farm as one on poor, ungiving land from which each crop is harvested only through the tireless work of the Hutchensons. By the time in the story students see this painting, their view of the Hutchenson place is likely to be that of a sad, lonely, isolated spot.

◆ Critical Thinking

❹ Speculate Ask students to predict what the Hutchensons are going to do once they emerge from the house. *Students' predictions will vary but may include ideas such as: they will kill themselves; they will begin digging a grave; they will sit somewhere in the field and pray or meditate; they will bury his letters, and so on.*

Farm Landscape, Grant Wood, Coe College, Cedar Rapids, Iowa, © Estate of Grant Wood/Licensed by VAGA, New York, NY

walk out," he said. He wanted to put off the moment, I could see that. So we did walk. It was early spring, and I remember every moment of the silent walk we took, the little leaves
❶ just coming on the trees, the little streams we crossed, how the moonlight made the water seem alive. We loitered and loitered, not talking, hating to go on.

Then we got out there, and Hal went to the front door of the farmhouse while I stayed in the road. I heard a dog bark, away off somewhere. I heard a child crying in some distant house. I think that Hal, after he got to the front door of the house, must have stood there for ten minutes, hating to knock.

Then he did knock, and the sound his fist made on the door seemed terrible. It seemed
❷ like guns going off. Old Hatch came to the door, and I heard Hal tell him. I know what happened. Hal had been trying, all the way out from town, to think up words to tell the old couple in some gentle way, but when it came to the scratch, he couldn't. He blurted everything right out, right into old Hatch's face.

That was all. Old Hatch didn't say a word. The door was opened, he stood there in the moonlight, wearing a funny long white nightgown, Hal told him, and the door went shut again with a bang, and Hal was left standing there.

He stood for a time, and then came back out into the road to me. "Well," he said, and "Well," I said. We stood in the road looking and listening. There wasn't a sound from the house.

And then—it might have been ten minutes or it might have been a half-hour—we stood silently, listening and watching, not knowing what to do—we couldn't go away——"I guess they are trying to get so they can believe it," Hal whispered to me. I got his notion all right. The two old people must have thought of their son Will always only in terms of life, never of death.

We stood watching and listening, and then, suddenly, after a long time, Hal touched me on the arm. "Look," he whispered. There were two white-clad figures going from the house to the ❹
barn. It turned out, you see, that old Hatch had been plowing that day. He had finished plowing and harrowing a field near the barn.

The two figures went into the barn and presently came out. They went into the field, and Hal and I crept across the farmyard to the barn and got to where we could see what was going on without being seen.

It was an incredible thing. The old man had got a hand corn-planter out of the barn and his wife had got a bag of seed corn, and there, in

▲ **Critical Viewing** How does the mood of this idealized image of a farm compare with the mood conveyed in the story? Explain. **[Compare and Contrast]** ❸

Humanities: Art

Farm Landscape by Grant Wood.

Grant Wood (1891–1942) was a lifelong resident of Iowa. In the 1920's, he traveled to Europe. His painting, especially his landscapes, showed the influence of impressionism and of the work of the German and Flemish primitives. Once back in the United States, Wood found inspiration in the people and places of Iowa. He became one of the exponents of Regionalism, an artistic movement in America during the 1930's, which strove to elevate everyday local experiences.

Use these questions for discussion:

1. Does this painting look like the vision of the Hutchenson farm that you have from reading the story? *Student responses should be supported by examples from the selection.*
2. How does Wood's unusual use of perspective and composition give this painting a surreal, or bizarre, quality? *Students may notice that Wood has included no people or animals; that the flat land seems to roll; that stacks of grain look like chess pawns; and that there are shadows but no apparent sunlight.*
3. What can you say about the forms of the various buildings, crops, trees, and other features of the landscape? *Students may say that these elements are stiffly geometric and unnaturally regular; the clumps of trees look more like rock formations than plants; there is an overall lack of vitality and life.*

the moonlight, that night, after they got that news, they were planting corn.

It was a thing to curl your hair—it was so ghostly. They were both in their nightgowns. They would do a row across the field, coming quite close to us as we stood in the shadow of the barn, and then, at the end of each row, they would kneel side by side by the fence and stay silent for a time. The whole thing went on in silence. It was the first time in my life I ever understood something, and I am far from sure now that I can put down what I understood and felt that night—I mean something about the connection between certain people and the earth—a kind of silent cry, down into the earth, of these two old people, putting corn down into the earth. It was as though they were putting death down into the ground that life might grow again—something like that.

They must have been asking something of the earth, too. But what's the use? What they were up to in connection with the life in their field and the lost life in their son is something you can't very well make clear in words. All I know is that Hal and I stood the sight as long as we could, and then we crept away and went back to town, but Hatch Hutchenson and his wife must have got what they were after that night, because Hal told me that when he went out in the morning to see them and to make the arrangements for bringing their dead son home, they were both curiously quiet and Hal thought in command of themselves. Hal said he thought they had got something. "They have their farm and they have still got Will's letters to read," Hal said.

◆ *Literature and Your Life*
Use empathy and your own experience to explain why Hal and the narrator find it difficult to watch the Hutchensons plant corn. 5

Guide for Responding

◆ *Literature and Your Life*

Reader's Response Which character did you identify the most with in this story? Why?

Thematic Focus If you were Mr. or Mrs. Hutchenson, how would you have faced the terrible news of Will's death?

Journal Writing Each person has his or her own way of dealing with grief. In a journal entry, discuss coping methods you have used or observed.

☑ Check Your Comprehension

1. Why didn't Hatch Hutchenson go off to make his own way in the world?
2. What did the Hutchensons always do when Hal came to visit?
3. Why is Hal given the task of bringing the bad news to the Hutchensons?

◆ Critical Thinking

INTERPRET

1. Why do the Hutchensons spend so much time working in their fields? **[Infer]**
2. Why do the Hutchensons react as they do to the news Hal Weyman brings? **[Interpret]**
3. Compare the Hutchensons at the story's beginning and at its end. **[Compare and Contrast]**
4. What message about life does this story convey? Support your answer. **[Draw Conclusions]**

EVALUATE

5. Do you think Hal did a good job of telling the Hutchensons about Will's death? Why or why not? **[Make a Judgment]**

COMPARE LITERARY WORKS

6. Compare and contrast this story with others you've read that deal with grief. List the similarities and differences. **[Compare and Contrast]**

Speaking, Listening, and Viewing Mini-Lesson

Enactment

This mini-lesson supports the Speaking, Listening, and Viewing activity in the Idea Bank on p. 747.

Introduce the Concept Tell students that their task in this activity is to plan and act out a conversation that the Hutchensons might have had after learning of Will's death.

Develop Background Have students discuss what they know or can infer about the Hutchensons from the story.

Apply the Information Direct students to write out the Hutchensons' conversation. Encourage them to practice. Have pairs present their role plays in front of the class.

Assess the Outcome Use these criteria for assessment: Does the role play capture the personality and perspective of the Hutchensons? Does the role play re-create what the couple might have said to one another? Does the content of the conversation logically lead to the planting of corn? Is the role play presented clearly with appropriate use of voice and gesture?

◆ *Literature and Your Life*

5 Students may respond that it is difficult to watch anybody grieve, and that the narrator and Hal, at least initially, had trouble understanding the unusual way the Hutchensons expressed their grief. They may also say that grieving is a very personal experience and that watching someone grieve is an invasion of privacy, almost a form of spying.

Reinforce and Extend

Answers

◆ *Literature and Your Life*

Reader's Response Student explanations should include citations from the story

Thematic Focus Accept reasonable responses that are consistent with the Hutchensons' character traits.

☑ **Check Your Comprehension**

1. Hatch has to care for an injured father before he can marry.
2. The Hutchensons talked with Hal about their son.
3. Hal is quite close to the Hutchensons and has always acted as a conduit for information about Will.

◆ **Critical Thinking**

1. They love the farm and the land more than anything except their son. They feel more comfortable working the land than doing anything else.
2. They turn to the other love in their lives, the land—to gain control in an unpredictable world, to create new life, and to find comfort.
3. At the story's outset and ending, they are closely tied to the land. In a way they haven't changed at all.
4. The story conveys the message that life is unpredictable and that tragedy can strike anyone at any time.
5. Suggested response: Some students will say Hal did a poor job because he blurted the news out without any preamble. Others will say it is a difficult enough task and that his willingness to do it at all makes it a good job.
6. Student responses should include details from the other stories.

Develop Understanding

One-Minute Insight This story is a prose portrait of Phoenix Jackson, an elderly southern black woman who selflessly makes an arduous journey into town to obtain medicine for her ailing grandson. In this errand of "love carried out," she overcomes one real or imagined obstacle after another. Her interactions with the people she meets reveal more of her character—she is at once determined, confused, and tired. When she reaches her destination—where the reader first learns the nature of her mission—she rises to the occasion. She leaves the doctor's office with the medicine, proudly determined to purchase a simple Christmas gift for her grandson despite the nurse's deliberate references to the "charity" status of her nephew's treatment.

Literature CD-ROM To build background, use the CD-ROM *The History of American Literature,* Part 2, Disc 2, Feature 10.

◆ Critical Thinking

❶ **Connect** Birds play a key symbolic role in the story. Point out, for example, that the name *Phoenix* refers to the Egyptian bird that rose from the ashes of its own funeral pyre. Suggest that students lookout for other references to birds as they read.

Customize for
Visual/Spatial Learners

❷ Ask students to visualize what Phoenix looks like and how she moves along the path. Ask them to tell what they can infer about her situation based on the description of what she wears. *Students may say that she leads a simple rural life, that she makes her own clothes, that she is used to and can withstand discomfort, and that she is poor. Some may infer that she might have been a slave.*

▶Critical Viewing◀

❸ **Evaluate** Some students may say that the surrealistic nature of the painting is representative of the dreamlike state in which Phoenix seems to exist. Others may say that Phoenix was walking a path through dense pine woods, not a road passing farmhouses and a few hardwood trees, as depicted in the painting.

A Worn Path

Eudora Welty

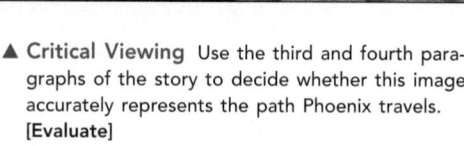

▲ **Critical Viewing** Use the third and fourth paragraphs of the story to decide whether this image accurately represents the path Phoenix travels. **[Evaluate]** ❸

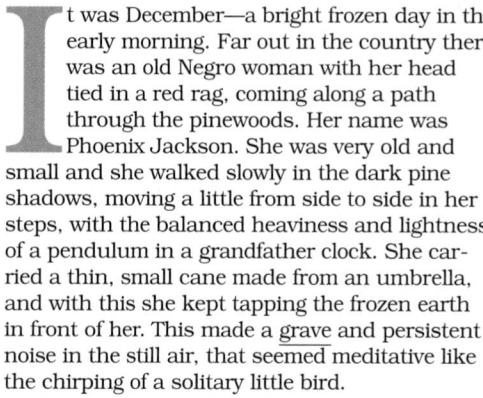

It was December—a bright frozen day in the early morning. Far out in the country there was an old Negro woman with her head tied in a red rag, coming along a path through the pinewoods. Her name was Phoenix Jackson. She was very old and small and she walked slowly in the dark pine shadows, moving a little from side to side in her steps, with the balanced heaviness and lightness of a pendulum in a grandfather clock. She carried a thin, small cane made from an umbrella, and with this she kept tapping the frozen earth
❶ in front of her. This made a grave and persistent noise in the still air, that seemed meditative like the chirping of a solitary little bird.

❷ She wore a dark striped dress reaching down to her shoe tops, and an equally long apron of bleached sugar sacks, with a full pocket all neat and tidy, but every time she took a step she might have fallen over her shoelaces, which dragged from her unlaced shoes. She looked straight ahead. Her eyes were blue with age. Her skin had a pattern all its own of numberless branching wrinkles and as though a whole little tree stood in the middle of her forehead, but a golden color ran underneath, and the two knobs of her cheeks were illumined by a yellow burning under the dark. Under the red rag her hair came down on her neck in the frailest of ringlets, still black, and with an odor like copper.

Now and then there was a quivering in the thicket. Old Phoenix said, "Out of my way, all you foxes, owls, beetles, jack rabbits, coons ❹

Humanities: Art

Georgia Red Clay, 1946, by Nell Choate Jones.

This oil painting offers a surreal representation of a dirt road winding through the Georgia countryside.

Use these questions for discussion:

1. How would you describe the mood of this painting? *Students may describe it as dark, foreboding, eerie, dreamlike.*
2. This painting depicts a rural scene in Georgia. What about this work fits the story, which is set in Mississippi? *Students may say that this scene depicts a hilly, winding country path, such as the one described in the story. The gnarled trees are foreboding, suggesting Phoenix's frame of mind during parts of her walk. The odd light suggests the haze through which she viewed events.*

Georgia Red Clay, 1946, Nell Choate Jones, Morris Museum of Art, Augusta, Georgia

and wild animals! . . . Keep out from under these feet, little bobwhites[1]. . . . 4 Keep the big wild hogs out of my path. Don't let none of those come running my direction. I got a long way." Under her small black-freckled hand her cane, limber as a buggy whip, would switch at the brush as if to rouse up any hiding things. On she went. The woods were deep and still. The sun made the pine needles almost too bright to look at, up where the wind rocked. The cones dropped as light as feathers. Down in the hollow was the mourning dove—it was not too late for him.

The path ran up a hill. "Seem like there is chains about my feet, time I get this far," she said, in the voice of argument old people keep to use with themselves. "Something always take a
5 hold of me on this hill—pleads I should stay."

After she got to the top she turned and gave a full, severe look behind her where she had come. "Up through pines," she said at length. "Now down through oaks."

Her eyes opened their widest, and she started down gently. But before she got to the bottom of the hill a bush caught her dress.

Her fingers were busy and intent, but her skirts were full and long, so that before she could pull them free in one place they were caught in another. It was not possible to allow the dress to tear. "I in the thorny bush," she said. "Thorns, you doing your appointed work. Never want to let folks pass, no sir. Old eyes thought you was a pretty little *green* bush."

Finally, trembling all over, she stood free, and 6
after a moment dared to stoop for her cane.

"Sun so high!" she cried, leaning back and looking, while the thick tears went over her eyes. "The time getting all gone here."

At the foot of this hill was a place where a log was laid across the creek.

"Now comes the trial," said Phoenix.

Putting her right foot out, she mounted the log and shut her eyes. Lifting her skirt, leveling her cane fiercely before her, like a festival figure in some parade, she began to march across. Then she opened her eyes and she was safe on the other side.

"I wasn't as old as I thought," she said.

But she sat down to rest. She spread her skirts on the bank around her and folded her hands over her knees. Up above her was a tree in a pearly cloud of mistletoe. She did not dare to close her eyes, and when a little boy brought her a plate with a slice of marble cake on it she spoke to him. "That would be acceptable," she said. But when she went to take it there was just her own hand in the air. 7

So she left that tree, and had to go through a barbed-wire fence. There she had to creep and crawl, spreading her knees and stretching her fingers like a baby trying to climb the steps. But she talked loudly to herself: she could not let her dress be torn now, so late in the day, and she could not pay for having her arm or her leg sawed off if she got caught fast where she was.

At last she was safe through the fence and risen up out in the clearing. Big dead trees, like black men with one arm, were standing in the purple stalks of the withered cotton field. There sat a buzzard.

"Who you watching?"

In the furrow she made her way along.

"Glad this not the season for bulls," she said, looking sideways, "and the good Lord made his

◆ Build Vocabulary

grave (grāv) *adj.*: Serious; solemn

limber (lim´ bər) *adj.*: Flexible

1. **bobwhites** *n.*: Partridges.

Analyze an Author's Comment

Eudora Welty has this to say regarding the purpose of fiction:

"I don't think literature—I'm talking about fiction now—I don't think it can exhort, or it loses every bit of its reality and value. I think it speaks to what is more deeply within, that is, the personal, and conveys its meaning that way. And then one hopes that a person made alert or aroused to be more sensitive to other human beings would go on to look at things on a larger scale by himself. I wouldn't want to read a work of fiction that I thought had an ulterior motive, to persuade me politically. I automatically react the other way. . . . I think things should be in a column or an editorial or a speech. But perfectly on the up and up. That's because I understand as a person, not as a motto."

Have students answers these questions in their journals:

1. Do you agree that fiction should not be written to give advice or to persuade? Why or why not?
2. Do you think "A Worn Path" is a good example of fiction—as Welty defines it— that affects people personally and encourages them to be more sensitive to other people? Support your answer.

Customize for *Less Proficient Readers*

To help these students understand the character traits of Phoenix Jackson, use ***Strategies for Diverse Student Needs,*** p. 48, "Make a Character Chart." Have students complete the chart as they read.

◆ Critical Thinking

4 Analyze Ask students to explain what Phoenix's warning to the animals reveals about Phoenix herself. *Students may say that she has not actually seen any animals; they may infer that for Phoenix, the real and the imagined are intertwined.*

◆ Reading Strategy

5 Identify With Characters
Guide students to recognize Phoenix's familiarity with the path she is walking, and to notice that she uses figurative language to describe its difficult parts. Point out Jackson's running commentary and ask students why she may be talking her way through the woods. *Students may note that the sound of her voice may soothe her. By identifying the obstacles, she may eliminate her fear that the woods present an unknown challenge.*

Customize for *English Language Learners*

6 You can help students who are learning English to understand the meaning of the dialectical grammar Phoenix uses by supplying missing verbs and helping verbs, pronouns, and inflected endings.

◆ Literary Focus

7 Point of View The third-person narration includes Phoenix's rambling fantasies. Help students not to be distracted by the things she imagines, and to separate what is real about her journey from what is fantasy.

Read to Appreciate Author's Craft

Welty uses descriptive adjectives and strong images to develop the character of Phoenix. For example, she describes "a whole little tree that stood in the middle of her forehead." Tell students that these details help readers connect the woman with their own experience. As students read, have them look for other examples of Welty's use of adjectives and images to build character.

❶ **Enrichment** Tell students that the bull and the two-headed snake are two of the many Egyptian mythical creatures who guard the underworld. For more information, see the Cultural Connection note on the bottom of this page.

Customize for
Verbal/Linguistic Learners
❷ Guide students to note the double meaning of *maze* here—labyrinth and corn (maize).

Customize for
AP Students
❸ Ghosts are one of the many images of death in the story. Ask students to identify other words and images the author has used so far to create a grim atmosphere. *Students may mention, in addition to the bull and two-headed snake, "dark pine shadows," "frozen earth," "mourning dove," "something [that] always take a hold on me," "big dead trees," "dancing with the [scarecrow]," and "buzzard."*

◆ Literary Focus

❹ **Point of View** The story is told through a limited third-person point of view, in which events are viewed from the perspective of Phoenix Jackson. Students should note that the story includes both real and imagined events that could only be known by the main character.

Customize for
Less Proficient Readers
Guide these students to distinguish the story's concrete details that describe Jackson's journey from the imagined details that reveal the daydreams her mind creates.

❶ snakes to curl up and sleep in the winter. A pleasure I don't see no two-headed snake coming around that tree, where it come once. It took a while to get by him, back in the summer."

❷ She passed through the old cotton and went into a field of dead corn. It whispered and shook and was taller than her head. "Through the maze now," she said, for there was no path.

Then there was something tall, black, and skinny there, moving before her.

❸ At first she took it for a man. It could have been a man dancing in the field. But she stood still and listened, and it did not make a sound. It was as silent as a ghost.

"Ghost," she said sharply, "who be you the ghost of? For I have heard of nary death close by."

But there was no answer—only the ragged dancing in the wind.

She shut her eyes, reached out her hand, and touched a sleeve. She found a coat and inside that an emptiness, cold as ice.

"You scarecrow," she said. Her face lighted. "I ought to be shut up for good," she said with laughter. "My senses is gone. I too old. I the oldest people I ever know. Dance, old scarecrow," she said, "while I dancing with you."

❹ **◆ Literary Focus**
From what point of view is the story being told? How do you know?

She kicked her foot over the furrow, and with mouth drawn down, shook her head once or twice in a little strutting way. Some husks blew down and whirled in streamers about her skirts.

Then she went on, parting her way from side to side with the cane, through the whispering field. At last she came to the end, to a wagon track where the silver grass blew between the red ruts. The quail were walking around like pullets, seeming all dainty and unseen.

"Walk pretty," she said. "This the easy place. This the easy going."

She followed the track, swaying through the quiet bare fields, through the little strings of trees silver in their dead leaves, past cabins silver from weather, with the doors and windows boarded shut, all like old women under a spell sitting there. "I walking in their sleep," she said, nodding her head vigorously.

In a ravine she went where a spring was silently flowing through a hollow log. Old Phoenix bent and drank. "Sweet gum[2] makes the water sweet," she said, and drank more. "Nobody know who made this well, for it was here when I was born."

The track crossed a swampy part where the moss hung as white as lace from every limb. "Sleep on, alligators, and blow your bubbles." Then the track went into the road.

Deep, deep the road went down between the high green-colored banks. Overhead the live-oaks met, and it was as dark as a cave.

A black dog with a lolling tongue came up out of the weeds by the ditch. She was meditating, and not ready, and when he came at her she only hit him a little with her cane. Over she went in the ditch, like a little puff of milkweed.[3]

Down there, her senses drifted away. A dream visited her, and she reached her hand up, but nothing reached down and gave her a pull. So she lay there and presently went to talking. "Old woman," she said to herself, "that black dog come up out of the weeds to stall you off, and now there he sitting on his fine tail, smiling at you."

A white man finally came along and found her—a hunter, a young man, with his dog on a chain.

"Well, Granny!" he laughed. "What are you doing there?"

"Lying on my back like a June bug waiting to be turned over, mister," she said, reaching up her hand.

He lifted her up, gave her a swing in the air, and set her down. "Anything broken, Granny?"

"No sir, them old dead weeds is springy enough," said Phoenix, when she had got her breath. "I thank you for your trouble."

"Where do you live, Granny?" he asked, while the two dogs were growling at each other.

"Away back yonder, sir, behind the ridge. You can't even see it from here."

"On your way home?"

"No sir, I going to town."

"Why, that's too far! That's as far as I walk when I come out myself, and I get something for my trouble." He patted the stuffed bag he carried, and there hung down a little closed claw. It was one of the bobwhites, with its beak

2. **sweet gum** *n.*: A tree that produces a fragrant juice.
3. **milkweed** *n.*: A plant with pods that, when ripe, release feathery seeds.

Cultural Connection

Egyptian Myths The journey, with its obstacles and travails, has been a common element in literature for thousands of years. Phoenix Jackson's story parallels Egyptian myths relating the journey of the dead through the twelve gates of Osiris's underworld. That journey ended when the travelers faced the god, who pronounced judgment on them. The dead person's heart was weighed on a balancing scale overseen by Truth. If the person failed the test, he or she was destroyed by a ferocious beast called the Devourer of Souls. If the person passed and was judged worthy of the afterlife, he or she entered eternity, free to pursue the same pleasures enjoyed on earth.

Invite interested students to investigate journey or quest myths of other cultures. For example, they might look into the Buddhist story of Siddhartha, or the Nibelung saga of ancient Teutonic mythology.

hooked bitterly to show it was dead. "Now you go on home, Granny!"

"I bound to go to town, mister," said Phoenix. "The time come around."

He gave another laugh, filling the whole landscape.
5 "I know you old colored people! Wouldn't miss going to town to see Santa Claus!"

But something held old Phoenix very still. The deep lines in her face went into a fierce and different radiation. Without warning, she had seen with her own eyes a flashing nickel fall out of the man's pocket onto the ground.

6 ◆ **Literary Focus** What might you learn about the young man's thoughts if the story were told from his point of view?

"How old are you, Granny?" he was saying.

"There is no telling, mister," she said, "no telling."

Then she gave a little cry and clapped her hands and said, "Git on away from here, dog!
7 Look! Look at that dog!" She laughed as if in admiration. "He ain't scared of nobody. He a big black dog." She whispered, "Sic him!"

"Watch me get rid of that cur," said the man. "Sic him, Pete! Sic him!"

Phoenix heard the dogs fighting, and heard the man running and throwing sticks. She even heard a gunshot. But she was slowly bending forward by that time, further and further forward, the lids stretched down over her eyes, as if she were doing this in her sleep. Her chin was lowered almost to her knees. The yellow palm of her hand came out from the fold of her apron. Her fingers slid down and along the ground under the piece of money with the grace and care they would have in lifting an egg from under a setting hen. Then she slowly straightened up,
8 she stood erect, and the nickel was in her apron pocket. A bird flew by. Her lips moved. "God watching me the whole time. I come to stealing."

The man came back, and his own dog panted about them. "Well, I scared him off that time," he said, and then he laughed and lifted his gun and pointed it at Phoenix.

She stood straight and faced him.

"Doesn't the gun scare you?" he said, still pointing it.

"No, sir, I seen plenty go off closer by, in my day, and for less than what I done," she said, holding utterly still.

Miz Emily, Joseph Holston, Holston Reproductions

▲ **Critical Viewing** What details in this image suggest the woman's strong character? What details in the story suggest Phoenix's strong character? **[Connect]** 9

He smiled, and shouldered the gun. "Well, Granny," he said, "you must be a hundred years old, and scared of nothing. I'd give you a dime if I had any money with me. But you take my advice and stay home, and nothing will happen to you."

"I bound to go on my way, mister," said Phoenix. She inclined her head in the red rag. Then they went in different directions, but she could hear the gun shooting again and again over the hill.

She walked on. The shadows hung from the oak trees to the road like curtains. Then she smelled woodsmoke, and smelled the river, and she saw a steeple and the cabins on their steep steps. Dozens of little black children whirled

Humanities: Art

Miz Emily by Joseph Holston.

This piece of art shows an African American woman pausing to look out into the distance. The dramatic juxtaposition of light and shadow as well as the facial expression and posture of the woman help to bring out her character.

Use these questions for discussion:

1. What can you infer about this woman and her life based on her facial expression, her stance, and her clothing? *Students may say that the woman looks like she is used to hard work; she wears an apron and a head wrap, which indicate that she is some kind of laborer; her loose sweater indicates a cool climate. She grasps a walking stick, suggesting that she is taking a walk. She may be pausing for a rest or to take stock of her work for the day.*
2. Notice how the light streams in on the woman's face. What might the artist mean by this? *Students may say that the light represents a higher calling, a gleam of hope in the distance to contrast with the hard life she seems to lead. The light could signify sunrise or sunset, suggesting a change: either a new dawn or an ending.*

5 **Clarification** Tell students that when this story was first published in 1949, the term *colored people* was commonly used to refer to African Americans. The term is no longer considered acceptable.

◆ Literary Focus

6 **Point of View** Students might say that if the story were told from the hunter's viewpoint, they would learn that he was being condescending and patronizing toward Phoenix, whom he probably regarded as dull, odd, and inferior to himself.

◆ Grammar and Style

7 **Punctuating Dialogue** Guide students to contrast the punctuation in cases where a sentence is broken up with cases in which two separate sentences are interrupted by a reference to the speaker. In the first instance, students can notice that commas set off the speaker and that the continuation of the dialogue is not capitalized. In the other case, the continuation of the dialogue begins with a capital letter because it is a new sentence.

◆ Reading Strategy

8 **Identify With Characters** Point out that Phoenix's act of taking a nickel that fell and her awareness that she is stealing show both how poor she is and that she has a sense of honor. Ask students what it says about her that she is used to having a gun pointed at her or near to her. *Students may say that it indicates that she was once a slave and had experienced the bullying of armed overseers or perhaps that she was a poor sharecropper accustomed to harsh treatment by callous landowners.*

▶Critical Viewing◀

9 **Connect** Students may say that the determined look on her face of the woman in the picture suggests her strong character. They may point to the steadfastness with which Phoenix undertakes her journey and the fearlessness with which she deals with both the dog and the man with the gun as evidence of her strength of character.

◆ Critical Thinking

❶ Speculate Ask students to explain why Welty does not identify the building with the gold seal. *Students may suggest that the narrator is describing the building as Phoenix herself sees it.*

Customize for
Less Proficient Readers
❷ Guide students to recognize that the place to which Phoenix has come is probably a hospital or a clinic. Evidence includes the presence of a nurse and the fact that Phoenix has been asked about her history.

❸ Clarification Tell students that the Old Natchez Trace is a road that runs from the city of Natchez diagonally through the entire state of Mississippi. Point out that the name probably derives from the Natchez, an Indian nation of the Southeast, and identifies a hunting or trading route.

❹ Clarification Inform students that lye is a strongly alkaline substance, usually sodium hydroxide or potassium hydroxide, that is used in cleaning or making soap.

◆ Reading Strategy

❺ Identify with Characters Students are likely to be empathetic toward Phoenix, who has just made a formidable journey on her grandson's behalf. They may infer that Phoenix has had a hard life, and reason that she asks little of the attendants at the clinic.

◆ Literary Focus

❻ Point of View Ask students to explain how the narrator lets the reader know how Phoenix feels about her grandson. *Students can appreciate that not only does Phoenix make such an arduous journey just to get his medicine, but she finds a way to bring him a holiday treat as well.*

around her. There ahead was Natchez[4] shining. Bells were ringing. She walked on.

In the paved city it was Christmas time. There were red and green electric lights strung and criss-crossed everywhere, and all turned on in the daytime. Old Phoenix would have been lost if she had not distrusted her eyesight and depended on her feet to know where to take her.

She paused quietly on the sidewalk where people were passing by. A lady came along in the crowd, carrying an armful of red-, green- and silver-wrapped presents; she gave off perfume like the red roses in hot summer, and Phoenix stopped her.

"Please, missy, will you lace up my shoe?" She held up her foot.

"What do you want, Grandma?"

"See my shoe," said Phoenix. "Do all right for out in the country, but wouldn't look right to go in a big building."

"Stand still then, Grandma," said the lady. She put her packages down on the sidewalk beside her and laced and tied both shoes tightly.

"Can't lace em with a cane," said Phoenix. "Thank you, missy. I doesn't mind asking a nice lady to tie up my shoe, when I gets out on the street."

❶ Moving slowly and from side to side, she went into the big building, and into a tower of steps, where she walked up and around and around until her feet knew to stop.

She entered a door, and there she saw nailed up on the wall the document that had been stamped with the gold seal and framed in the gold frame, which matched the dream that was hung up in her head.

"Here I be," she said. There was a fixed and ceremonial stiffness over her body.

"A charity case, I suppose," said an attendant who sat at the desk before her.

But Phoenix only looked above her head. There was sweat on her face, the wrinkles in her skin shone like a bright net.

❷ "Speak up, Grandma," the woman said. "What's your name? We must have your history, you know. Have you been here before? What seems to be the trouble with you?"

Old Phoenix only gave a twitch to her face as if a fly were bothering her.

"Are you deaf?" cried the attendant. But then the nurse came in. ❷

"Oh, that's just old Aunt Phoenix," she said. "She doesn't come for herself—she has a little grandson. She makes these trips just as regular as clockwork. She lives away back off the Old Natchez Trace." She bent down. "Well, Aunt Phoenix, why don't you just take a seat? We won't keep you standing after your long trip." ❸ She pointed.

The old woman sat down, bolt upright in the chair.

"Now, how is the boy?" asked the nurse.

Old Phoenix did not speak.

"I said, how is the boy?"

But Phoenix only waited and stared straight ahead, her face very solemn and withdrawn into rigidity.

"Is his throat any better?" asked the nurse. "Aunt Phoenix, don't you hear me? Is your grandson's throat any better since the last time you came for the medicine?"

With her hands on her knees, the old woman waited, silent, erect and motionless, just as if she were in armor.

"You mustn't take up our time this way, Aunt Phoenix," the nurse said. "Tell us quickly about your grandson, and get it over. He isn't dead, is he?"

At last there came a flicker and then a flame of comprehension across her face, and she spoke.

"My grandson. It was my memory had left me. There I sat and forgot why I made my long trip."

"Forgot?" The nurse frowned. "After you came so far?"

Then Phoenix was like an old woman begging a dignified forgiveness for waking up frightened in the night. "I never did go to school. I was too old at the Surrender,"[5] she said in a soft voice. "I'm an old woman without an education. It was my memory fail me. My little grandson, he is just the same, and I forgot it in the coming."

"Throat never heals, does it?" said the nurse, speaking in a loud, sure voice to old Phoenix. By now she had a card with something written on it, a little list. "Yes. Swallowed lye. When was it?—January—two-three years ago—" ❹

Phoenix spoke unasked now. "No, missy, he not dead, he just the same. Every little while his

4. **Natchez** (nach´ iz): A town in southern Mississippi.

5. **the Surrender:** The surrender of the Confederate army, which ended the Civil War.

Reteach

Use this strategy with students who are having difficulty understanding point of view. Have students cut out three large circles. In the center of each, have them draw a smaller circle and write the name of one of the three stories—"In Another Country," "The Corn Planting," and "A Worn Path." Around the outside, students should fill in the narrator and his or her part in the story.
Guide students in filling in the rest of the circles.

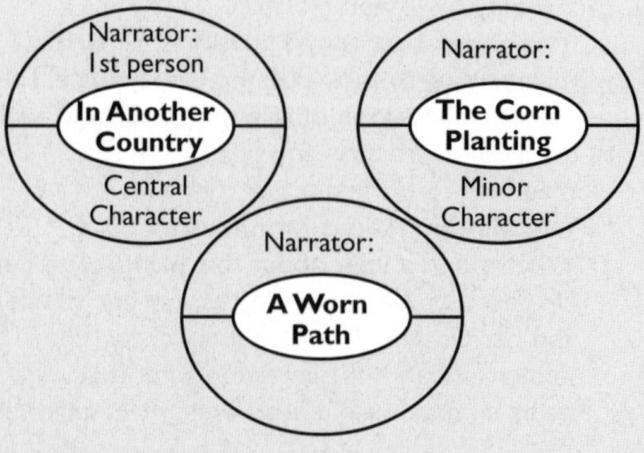

throat begin to close up again, and he not able to swallow. He not get his breath. He not able to help himself. So the time come around, and I go on another trip for the soothing medicine."

"All right. The doctor said as long as you came to get it, you could have it," said the nurse. "But it's an obstinate case."

"My little grandson, he sit up there in the house all wrapped up, waiting by himself," Phoenix went on. "We is the only two left in the world. He suffer and it don't seem to put him back at all. He got a sweet look. He going to last. He wear a little patch quilt and peep out holding his mouth open like a little bird. I remembers so plain now. I not going to forget him again, no, the whole enduring time. I could tell him from all the others in creation."

5 ◆ **Reading Strategy** Can you identify with Phoenix Jackson's feelings in this situation?

"All right." The nurse was trying to hush her now. She brought her a bottle of medicine. "Charity," she said, making a check mark in a book.

Old Phoenix held the bottle close to her eyes, and then carefully put it into her pocket.

"I thank you," she said.

"It's Christmas time, Grandma," said the attendant. "Could I give you a few pennies out of my purse?"

"Five pennies is a nickel," said Phoenix stiffly.

"Here's a nickel," said the attendant.

Phoenix rose carefully and held out her hand. She received the nickel and then fished the other nickel out of her pocket and laid it beside the new one. She stared at her palm closely, with her head on one side.

Then she gave a tap with her cane on the floor.

"This is what come to me to do," she said. "I going to the store and buy my child a little windmill they sells, made out of paper. He going to find it hard to believe there such a thing in the world. I'll march myself back where he is waiting, holding it straight up in this hand." 6

She lifted her free hand, gave a little nod, turned around, and walked out of the doctor's office. Then her slow step began on the stairs, going down.

◆ Build Vocabulary

obstinate (äb′ stə nit) *adj.*: Stubborn

Guide for Responding

◆ *Literature and Your Life*

Reader's Response Do you think Welty's use of language suits her story, or would you have used language differently? Explain.

Thematic Focus In what specific ways has a life of troubled times shaped Phoenix Jackson's character?

Compare Cultures Read about the elderly in another culture. Compare your findings to Welty's portrayal of Phoenix Jackson's life.

☑ Check Your Comprehension

1. Why does Phoenix make her journey?
2. What obstacles does Phoenix Jackson encounter on her journey?
3. (a) What does the nurse ask Phoenix? (b) How does Phoenix explain her inability to answer?

◆ Critical Thinking

INTERPRET

1. Compare and contrast the attitudes of the hunter, the attendant, and the nurse toward Phoenix. **[Compare and Contrast]**
2. Why do you think Phoenix does not immediately respond to the questions of the nurse and the attendant? **[Infer]**
3. What is the significance of the story's taking place at Christmas time? **[Interpret]**
4. What does Phoenix's journey symbolize, or represent? **[Draw Conclusions]**

EVALUATE

5. Do you think Phoenix sees herself as others see her? Explain. **[Assess]**

EXTEND

6. How might this story change if the setting were changed? **[Social Studies Link]**

Reinforce and Extend

◆ Critical Thinking

Speculate Readers cannot be sure that Phoenix's grandson is still alive or, for that matter, whether he exists at all. Challenge students to find two details from the story that support the interpretation that the boy is alive and two that support the possibility that he is dead. *In support of the theory that he is alive, students may say that Phoenix talks about him as if he is alive and that she buys him a gift. To support the possibility that he is dead, they may refer to the fact that she was slow in answering questions about him and that she describes him sitting and waiting "all wrapped up" (as if dead).*

Answers

◆ *Literature and Your Life*

Reader's Response Students may say that Welty's use of language suits her story because the language lets readers know what Phoenix is thinking and feeling.

Thematic Focus Phoenix shows perseverance during her long journey as well as optimism when difficulties occur, as when she falls into the ditch. Life in troubled times has made Phoenix a strong person.

☑ Check Your Comprehension

1. Phoenix goes to Natchez to pick up her grandson's medicine from a state agency.
2. Suggested response: Examples include the distance Phoenix must travel on foot, a thorny bush, a log bridge across a creek, barbed-wire fencing, a pathless field, a scarecrow, a dog, a hunter, and a desk attendant.
3. (a) The nurse asks about Phoenix's sick grandson. (b) She says that she momentarily forgot why she had come.

(Answers continue on p. 746)

Beyond the Selection

FURTHER READING

Other Works by Hemingway
The Sun Also Rises, A Farewell to Arms, For Whom the Bell Tolls, The Old Man and the Sea

Other Works by Anderson
Winesburg, Ohio; Windy McPherson's Sons; Triumph of the Egg; Horses and Men

Other Works by Welty
The Optimist's Daughter, Delta Wedding, The Ponder Heart, Losing Battles

We suggest that you preview these works.

INTERNET

You can find additional information about Hemingway, Anderson, and Welty on the Internet. We suggest the following sites. Please be aware that sites may have changed since this information was published.

For the Hemingway Home Page, go to **http://www.atlantic.net/~gagne/hem/**

For the Anderson Home Page, visit **http://urich.edu/~jounalm/sahome.html**

For information on Welty, go to **http://www.cssc.olemiss.edu/welty/homepage.html**

We *strongly recommend* that you preview the sites.

Guide for Responding *(continued)*

◆ Literary Focus

Point of View

Point of view refers to the perspective from which a narrative is told. Each of these stories is told from a different point of view. "In Another Country" is told by a main character from a **first-person point of view**. "The Corn Planting" is told from a first-person point of view by a minor character who primarily observes. "A Worn Path" is told from a **limited third-person point of view** by an outside narrator who reveals the thoughts of one character. In each case, the story's point of view determines the level of information you receive about the characters and events.

1. (a) List three details that you learn about the thoughts, feelings, or emotions of the narrator of "In Another Country." (b) How would the story be different if Hemingway had used a third-person point of view?

2. In what ways is the narrator of "The Corn Planting" the best character to tell the story?

3. How would "A Worn Path" be different if Welty had told the story from Phoenix Jackson's point of view?

4. Choose one of the stories in this grouping. Using a different point of view from the original, rewrite one of the paragraphs. Then compare the two versions. (a) What is gained in your version? (b) What is lost?

◆ Reading Strategy

Identify With Characters

When you **identify with characters** such as Phoenix Jackson, the Hutchensons, or the disillusioned soldiers, you place yourself in their shoes and try to see life as they do. You can imagine yourself behaving or feeling as they do, and consider how you'd react in their situation.

1. Among the three stories, choose the characters with whom you identify the most *and* the least. Give reasons in both cases.

2. For a reader to identify with a character, that character needs to be sympathetic—able to arouse feelings in others. Discuss why Phoenix Jackson is—or isn't—a sympathetic character.

◆ Build Vocabulary

Using the Latin Root *-val-*

The Latin root *-val-* means "strength" or "value." Use a dictionary to define each of the words below. Then write a sentence explaining how each word's definition might relate to the meaning of *-val-*.

1. valid
2. equivalent
3. valor
4. prevail

Using the Word Bank: Denotations

On your paper, answer yes or no to each question. Explain each of your answers.

1. If a soldier is **invalided**, has he or she been transferred to combat duty?

2. Would someone bringing **grave** news be smiling?

3. Would a gymnast need to be **limber** before performing?

4. Would you want to pair up for a project with someone described as **obstinate**?

◆ Grammar and Style

Punctuating Dialogue

In these stories, dialogue brings the characters to life by letting readers "hear" the characters' own words. Because each writer carefully punctuated the **dialogue**, you could easily tell who was speaking each line.

Practice The punctuation marks in the following pieces of dialogue have been misplaced. Rewrite each item, correctly placing punctuation marks.

1. "No", said the major.

2. "Well," he said, and "Well", I said.

3. "Don't argue with me"!

4. I offered to take my car, but Hal said no ",Let's walk out," he said.

5. "How old are you, Granny"? he was saying.

6. "Very interesting, very interesting", the major said, and handed it back to the doctor.

Looking at Style When you compare the amount of dialogue in these three stories, you'll notice that "The Corn Planting" has the least dialogue. How does this difference affect the way you relate to the characters? Explain.

Answers *(continued from p. 745)*

◆ Critical Thinking

1. The hunter, the attendant, and the nurse regard Phoenix with a mixture of helpfulness, irritation, and wondrous disbelief.
2. Students may say that Phoenix's grandson is dead but she refuses to accept or admit this fact. Others may say she is intimidated or simply elderly and forgetful.
3. Suggested response: The behavior of the other characters toward Phoenix contrasts with the Christmas spirit.
4. Suggested response: Phoenix's journey symbolizes one of the habits of love.
5. Students may say that Phoenix sees herself as more physically fit and mentally sharp than others see her.
6. Suggested response: The story might change very little because it deals with a situation that is universal.

◆ Literary Focus

1. (a) Details include the narrator's dislike of war, fear of death, and feeling of not being accepted by the soldiers who were wounded while taking part in combat. (b) If Hemingway had used a third-person point of view, the thoughts and feelings of all the characters might have been given.
2. The narrator is best because his relationship with Hal enables him to learn pertinent information, sort it out, and retell that information in an objective manner.
3. It might have focused in greater detail on Phoenix's emotions.
4. Paragraphs must demonstrate an understanding of point of view.

◆ Reading Strategy

1. Students' responses should show familiarity with the characters.
2. Student's may say that Phoenix is a sympathetic character because she undertakes an arduous journey in order to help her grandson.

◆ Build Vocabulary

Using the Latin Word Root *-val-*

1. Having legal force or power, correct. Something that is *valid* has the strength of accuracy behind it.
2. Equal in value, amount, or force. things which are *equivalent* are of equal value or strength.
3. Strength of mind or spirit, especially in the face of danger. It takes great strength to have *valor.*
4. To gain the advantage; to be victorious or triumphant. One must be strong to *prevail.*

Using the Word Bank

1. No. Someone who is invalided has been removed from service to recover from an injury.
2. No. Grave news is serious or solemn; therefore, the bearer of the news would be in a similar mood.
3. Yes. Athletes, especially gymnasts, need to make their limbs limber before attempting difficult movements.
4. No. An obstinate person would be unlikely to compromise as is needed in a successful collaborative effort.

◆ Grammar and Style

Punctuating Dialogue

1. "No," said the major.
2. "Well," he said, and "Well," I said.
3. "Don't argue with me!"
4. I offered to take my car, but Hal said no. "Let's walk out," he said.
5. "How old are you, Granny?" he was saying.
6. "Very interesting, very interesting," the major said, and handed it back to the doctor.

Build Your Portfolio

Idea Bank

Writing

1. Memorial Speech As Hal Weyman in "The Corn Planting," write a speech you might give at Will's memorial service. In your remarks, acknowledge both Will's family and his dreams.

2. Magazine Article Write a feature article about the hospital machines in the story "In Another Country." Explain why World War I doctors were hopeful about this new medical technology.

3. Grant Proposal Assume the role of a fundraiser for a social service agency, and use Phoenix Jackson's story to generate support. Write a proposal for a program to help grandparents who raise grandchildren alone.

Speaking, Listening, and Viewing

4. Oral Story What happens to Phoenix Jackson when she gets home? Use your imagination to come up with a plot for the events that might occur. Present your story orally to classmates.

5. Enactment With a partner, role-play the conversations that may have occurred between Hatch Hutchenson and his wife—in the house or the cornfield—after they learn of Will's death.

Researching and Representing

6. Report on Rehabilitation Gather information about current practices in rehabilitation medicine. Present your findings in a brief written report with visuals. **[Science Link; Health Link]**

7. Military Report Hemingway's story drew upon his service in the Italian Arditi (volunteer infantry). Report on the role of the Italian Arditi in World War I, as well as Hemingway's participation in it. Use maps and charts in presenting your findings. **[Social Studies Link]**

Online Activity www.phlit.phschool.com

Guided Writing Lesson

Personal Narrative

Each of the three stories you've just read recounts a memorable event or time in one character's personal experience. Write a personal narrative highlighting a memorable event in your life. Help readers appreciate what the experience meant to you by using elaboration to add emotional depth.

Writing Skills Focus: Elaboration to Add Emotional Depth

Use these tips to **elaborate** upon the event:

1. Create sensory descriptions to help put your reader at the scene of your experience.
2. Carefully describe your true feelings. Your readers might have had similar feelings, and they'll identify with you.
3. Let other people speak in their own words. Honest dialogue often moves readers.

Prewriting Off the top of your head, write the names of four or five events that have made major impressions on you. Under each, write two or three reasons why the events might interest others. Then decide which event you'll describe.

Drafting Writing in the first-person, you may want to begin your narrative with a remembered detail or an observation. To create a mood suited to the event you describe, use carefully chosen language and details.

Revising Ask a partner to read your narrative, and summarize what its topic means to you. Check your partner's response against your own perception. Does he or she understand the importance of the experience? If not, ask what changes you can make to help your reader identify with your experience.

ASSESSMENT OPTIONS

Formal Assessment, Selection Test, pp. 224–226, and Assessment Resources Software. The selection test is designed so that it can be easily customized to the performance levels of your students.

Alternative Assessment, p. 48, includes options for less advanced students and more advanced students as well as options for students with various learning modalities.

PORTFOLIO ASSESSMENT

Use the following rubrics in the ***Alternative Assessment*** booklet to assess student writing:
Memorial Speech: Summary Rubric, p. 113
Magazine Article: Technical Description/ Explanation Rubric, p. 130
Grant Proposal: Persuasion Rubric, p. 120
Guided Writing Lesson: Narrative Based on Personal Experience Rubric, p. 111

Idea Bank

Customizing for *Performance Levels*

Following are suggestions for matching Idea Bank topics with your students' performance levels:
Less Advanced Students: 1, 4
Average Students: 2, 5
More Advanced Students: 3, 6, 7

Customizing for *Learning Modalities*

Following are suggestions for matching Idea Bank topics with your students' learning modalities:
Verbal/Linguistic: 4, 5
Bodily/Kinesthetic: 5
Logical/Mathematical: 6
Visual/Spatial: 7

Guided Writing Lesson

Writing and Language Transparencies Use the Writing Process Model 3: Personal Narrative in ***Writing and Language Transparencies,*** pp. 13–16, to guide students in writing their narratives.

For more prewriting, elaboration, and revision strategies, see *Prentice Hall Writing and Grammar.*

Writers at Work Videodisc

Have students view the videodisc segment (Ch. 2) featuring novelist, poet, and essayist N. Scott Momaday speaking about developing narrative elements. Ask students what they think Momaday means when he says that you should place plot events in a "... meaningful or symmetrical or beautiful relationship ..."?

Play frames 15695 to 18560

Writing Lab CD-ROM

Have students complete the tutorial on Narration. Follow these steps:

1. Have students use the Plot Diagram to develop their narratives.
2. Have students draft on computer.
3. Have students use the Self-Evaluation Checklist to help them revise.

Prepare and Engage

LESSON OBJECTIVES

1. **To express and support responses to the text**
   - Critical Thinking Questions
2. **To analyze literary elements**
   - Literary Connections
   - Thematic Connections
   - Idea Bank: Critical Analysis
   - Idea Bank: Future Projection
3. **To read in order to research self-selected and assigned topics**
   - Idea Bank: Historical Newspaper
4. **To use recursive writing processes to write an expository essay**
   - Idea Bank: Expository Essay

CONNECTIONS TO TODAY'S WORLD

Anxiety
Grace Paley

Thematic Connection

FACING TROUBLED TIMES

The Modernists writing after World War I had a deep sense of uncertainty about their time. The war that had cost the world dearly seemed to have accomplished little. Technology such as airplanes and long-range artillery expected to help prevent war instead caused terrible suffering within war. Searching for values suited to a new era, Modernists focused on themes of confusion and the apparent meaninglessness of life. Their themes were often implied, not directly stated, and readers were expected to draw their own conclusions. Modernist stories had fragmented structures, seeming to begin arbitrarily and to end without resolution.

For contemporary Americans, the world is even more fragmented, with rapid technological advances, shifting national boundaries, and terrorist threats. Grace Paley's story "Anxiety," with its implied theme of world doom, reflects the uncertainty brought about by these changes.

Literary Connection

CONTEMPORARY SHORT STORIES

Ernest Hemingway, Sherwood Anderson, Eudora Welty, and Grace Paley all wrote **short stories**—brief fictional narratives with a limited number of characters and settings. The short story genre remains popular in current times—suited to the fast-paced lives of readers who sometimes have limited time to satisfy their literary appetites.

As twentieth-century stories, the four examples in this section share common themes of uncertainty, ambiguity, and some disillusionment. However, you'll notice some differences, too. Welty and Anderson's stories unfold in small-town America, and their characters reflect its values. In contrast, Paley's contemporary short story is set in a city, and its straight-to-the-point style reflects the pace of our increasingly urban culture. Additionally, Paley's story raises new issues of concern—nuclear warfare, for example—and, consisting almost entirely of unpunctuated dialogue, blurs structural form further than the other stories.

GRACE PALEY (1922–)

Grace Paley is a New Yorker through and through. Born, raised, and often living in the boisterous city, Paley has a strong concern for urban community life. This concern, along with her interest in social issues, is reflected in her highly praised short story collections, such as *Enormous Changes at the Last Minute* (1974) and *Later the Same Day* (1985).

Sometimes referred to as a writer's writer, Paley is often studied in writing workshops. Her style is crisp and deceptively simple. Nonetheless, "Anxiety" embodies an implicit theme of moral concern worth consideration in our age.

Prentice Hall Literature Program Resources

REINFORCE / RETEACH / EXTEND

Selection Support Worksheets
Build Vocabulary, p. 225
Thematic Connection: Facing Troubled Times, p. 226

Formal Assessment Selection Test, pp. 227–228; Assessment Resources Software

Listening to Literature Audiocassettes

ANXIETY

Grace Paley

CONNECTIONS TO TODAY'S WORLD

Woman in a Window, Richard Diebenkorn, Albright-Knox Art Gallery, Buffalo, New York

▶ Critical Viewing ❶ How do the colors in this image create a sense of anxiety? **[Support]**

❷ The young fathers are waiting outside the school. What curly heads! Such graceful brown mustaches. They're sitting on their haunches eating pizza and exchanging information. They're waiting for the 3 P.M. bell. It's springtime, the season of first looking out the window. I have a window box of greenhouse marigolds. The young fathers can be seen through the ferny leaves.

Humanities: Art

Woman in a Window by Richard Diebenkorn.

American painter Richard Diebenkorn was born in 1922. His extensive study of art included work at Stanford University, the University of California, the California School of Fine Art, and the University of New Mexico.

Use the following questions for discussion.

1. In what ways does the woman in this painting reflect the character of the narrator? In what ways does it contradict your impression of her? *Students may say that the woman in the painting seems overwhelmed as she holds her head in her hands and leans on the table as if she can barely manage. However, the woman in the story seems more animated and attentive to what's outside her window than this figure does.*
2. Diebenkorn often uses geometric figures in his work. What geometric figures appear in this piece and how do they influence your perception of the woman? *Students may notice rectangles, triangles—the table, the angle of the woman's right arm—and part of a curve—the chair. Most of the shapes have sharp angles, which could signify rigidity or lack of warmth.*

Develop Understanding

One-Minute Insight A solitary woman watches the world from her window. One day, as fathers pick up their young children from school, she criticizes one of them for being too self-involved and removed from the world of his own youth to treat his young daughter with the kindness she deserves. In her scolding, she reveals her fears about the present condition of the world. She is afraid that "madmen" will destroy the planet Earth, thus wiping out the entire human race. The woman's worries are representative of the anxiety experienced by many people living under the constant threat of nuclear war during the Cold War era.

Customize for
Less Proficient Readers
Students may be confused by the lack of standard quotation punctuation in this work. Suggest that they read in groups, round-robin style, to "hear" the dialogue and to determine who is speaking to whom.

▶Critical Viewing◀

❶ **Support** Suggested response: The colors in this painting are bold and bright, with green, orange, blue, and black predominant. The boldness of the colors, the use of the colors in specific geometric areas, and the sharp contrasts between the juxtaposed colors create an unsettling anxious mood.

Customize for
Less Proficient Readers
❷ Help students understand both the literary and physical points of view of the narrator. The story is told in the first person, which allows readers to glimpse the narrator's views and feelings through the words she says and the inner thoughts she reveals. Because the narrator's is the only point of view given, her participation influences how readers perceive others. Furthermore, the narrator observes from her window, perched above the street. She looks down at a vibrant world below, while her own life is limited by her isolation and distance.

◆ Critical Thinking

❶ **Interpret** Have students summarize the events of this passage. Discuss whether or not the father has overreacted to his daughter. *Students may say that the girl is simply being playful, and for some reason the father seems to lack reasonable patience.*

◆ Literary Connection

❷ **Contemporary Short Stories** Focus on the element of characterization in this story. Ask students to describe the narrator, telling who she is and what link she has to the fathers and children. *Students may say that she is a lonely old woman who intrudes in the lives of others because she feels that her age and experience justify her to admonish anyone younger, even those who are themselves adults.*

Customize for
Less Proficient Readers

❸ Be sure students understand that the woman begins by offering the father a compliment: she notices his involvement in his daughter's life as being greater than she saw among fathers of previous generations. Ask students why they think she does this. *They may say that this is her way to grab the father's attention so she can subsequently scold him.*

Thematic Connection

❹ **Facing Troubled Times** Have students restate the narrator's concern. *Students may say that she worries that the planet will be destroyed soon, so the father should control himself and ignore a small child's minor transgressions in light of a far greater doom that is imminent.*

❺ **Clarification** During the Vietnam War, public protest demonstrations were common. At the Democratic National Convention held in Chicago in 1968, city police overreacted to the protesters and earned the derogatory nickname of "pigs." After that event, protesters would taunt the police by making oinking sounds.

The bell rings. The children fall out of school, tumbling through the open door. One of the fathers sees his child. A small child. Is she Chinese? A little. Up u-u-p, he says and hoists her to his shoulders. U-u-p, says the second father, and hoists his little boy. The little boy sits on top of his father's head for a couple of seconds before sliding to his shoulders. Very funny, says the father.

❶ They start off down the street, right under and past my window. The two children are still laughing. They try to whisper a secret. The fathers haven't finished their conversation. The frailer father is uncomfortable; his little girl wiggles too much.

Stop it this minute, he says.

Oink oink, says the little girl.

What'd you say?

Oink oink, she says.

The young father says What! three times. Then he seizes the child, raises her high above his head, and sets her hard on her feet.

What'd I do so bad, she says, rubbing her ankle. Just hold my hand, screams the frail and angry father.

❷ I lean far out the window. Stop! Stop! I cry.

The young father turns, shading his eyes, but sees. What? he says. His friend says, Hey? Who's that? He probably thinks I'm a family friend, a teacher maybe.

Who're you? he says.

I move the pots of marigold aside. Then I'm able to lean my elbow way out into unshadowed visibility. Once, not too long ago, the tenements were speckled with women like me in every third window up to the fifth story, calling the children from play to receive orders and instruction. This memory enables me to say strictly, Young man, I am an older person who feels free because of that to ask questions and give advice.

Oh? he says, laughs with a little embarrassment, says to his friend, Shoot if you will that old gray head.[1] But he's joking, I know, because he has established himself, legs apart, hands behind his back, his neck arched to see and hear me out.

How old are you? I call. About thirty or so?

Thirty-three.

First I want to say you're about a generation ahead of your father in your attitude and behavior toward your child. ❸

Really? Well? Anything else, ma'am.

Son, I said, leaning another two, three dangerous inches toward him. Son, I must tell you that madmen intend to destroy this beautifully made planet. That the murder of our children by these men has got to become a terror and a sorrow to you, and starting now, it had better interfere with any daily pleasure.

Speech, speech, he called.

I waited a minute, but he continued to look up. So, I said, I can tell by your general appearance and loping walk that you agree with me. ❹

I do, he said, winking at his friend; but turning a serious face to mine, he said again, Yes, yes, I do.

Well then, why do you become so angry at that little girl whose future is like a film which suddenly cuts to white. Why did you nearly slam this little doomed person to the ground in your uncontrollable anger.

Let's not go too far, said the young father. She *was* jumping around on my poor back and hollering oink oink.

When were you angriest—when she wiggled and jumped or when she said oink?

He scratched his wonderful head of dark well-cut hair. I guess when she said oink.

Have you ever said oink oink? Think carefully. Years ago, perhaps? ❺

No. Well maybe. Maybe.

Whom did you refer to in this way?

He laughed. He called to his friend, Hey Ken, this old person's got something. The cops. In a demonstration. Oink oink, he said, remembering, laughing.

The little girl smiled and said, Oink oink.

Shut up, he said.

What do you deduce from this?

That I was angry at Rosie because she was

1. **Shoot . . . head:** A reference to John Greenleaf Whittier's 1864 Civil War poem, "Barbara Frietchie," which contains the line, "'Shoot, if you must, this old gray head,/But spare your country's flag,' she said."

Humanities: Music

Symphony No. 2: The Age of Anxiety, 1949, Leonard Bernstein.

American composer, conductor, teacher, and pianist Leonard Bernstein (1918–1990) created a broadly diverse body of work. Some of his best-known pieces include the beloved Broadway musical "West Side Story," ballet music ("Fancy Free"), film scores ("On the Waterfront"), operas ("Trouble in Tahiti"), liturgical music ("Chichester Psalms"), and three symphonies. His second symphony, written during the early years of the Cold War, is known as "The Age of Anxiety." Written for piano and orchestra, it was based on the W. H. Auden poem of the same name. Play some or all of this work for the class. Encourage students to listen for tonal, rhythmic, or harmonic passages that suggest feelings of anxiety. You might have interested students research the composition of this piece to learn more about why Bernstein gave it this name and what inspired him to create this work.

dealing with me as though I was a figure of authority, and it's not my thing, never has been, never will be.

I could see his happiness, his nice grin, as he remembered this.

So, I continued, since those children are such lovely examples of what may well be the last generation of humankind, why don't you start all over again, right from the school door, as though none of this had ever happened.

Thank you, said the young father. Thank you. It would be nice to be a horse, he said, grabbing little Rosie's hand. Come on Rosie, let's go. I don't have all day.

U-up, says the first father. U-up, says the second.

Giddap, shout the children, and the fathers yell neigh neigh, as horses do. The children kick their fathers' horsechests, screaming giddap giddap, and they gallop wildly westward.

I lean way out to cry once more, Be careful! Stop! But they've gone too far. Oh, anyone would love to be a fierce fast horse carrying a beloved beautiful rider, but they are galloping toward one of the most dangerous street corners in the world. And they live beyond that trisection across other dangerous avenues.

So I must shut the window after patting the April-cooled marigolds with their rusty smell of summer. Then I sit in the nice light and wonder how to make sure that they gallop safely home through the airy scary dreams of scientists and the bulky dreams of automakers. I wish I could see just how they sit down at their kitchen tables for a healthy snack (orange juice or milk and cookies) before going out into the new spring afternoon to play. ❻

CONNECTIONS TO TODAY'S WORLD

Guide for Responding

◆ Literature and Your Life

Reader's Response What was your first response to the old woman in the story? Explain.

Thematic Focus Which time period do you find more uncertain and troubling—post-World War I or Grace Paley's nuclear age? Why?

☑ Check Your Comprehension

1. What do the young fathers do while they are waiting outside the school?
2. Explain the circumstances in which the young father said "oink oink" when he was a young man.
3. The young father eventually says he was angry at his daughter. What does he discover was the underlying reason for his anger?

◆ Critical Thinking

INTERPRET

1. What does the father's response to the narrator's remarks reveal about his character? **[Interpret]**
2. What makes the narrator anxious? **[Draw Conclusions]**

APPLY

3. What does this story suggest to you about the emotional climate of the late twentieth century? **[Generalize]**

COMPARE LITERARY WORKS

4. What social and political circumstances suggested in Hemingway's story would most concern the narrator of "Anxiety"? Why? **[Connect]**

Beyond the Selection

FURTHER READING

Other Works About an Uncertain Future

"The Age of Anxiety," W. H. Auden

"The Slump," John Updike

"Player Piano," Kurt Vonnegut

We suggest that you preview these works before recommending them to students.

INTERNET

You and your students may find additional information about Grace Paley on the Internet. We suggest the following site. Please be aware, however, that the site may have changed since this information was published.

For a literary chat with Grace Paley, including questions and answers about her work, visit **http://www.salon1999. com/11/departments/litchat1.html**

We *strongly recommend* that you preview the site before you send students to it.

◆ Literary Connection

❻ Contemporary Short Stories
Focus again on the element of characterization and how the woman reveals more of herself at the end of the story. The father has deferred to her criticism, which was unsolicited but seemingly well-intentioned. Yet this passage reveals new details about the woman that influence readers' impressions of her. Discuss this with the class. *Students may say that now they realize that anxieties completely overwhelm the woman, and that whatever concern she may address, there will always be another one to worry about next.*

Reinforce and Extend

Answers

◆ Literature and Your Life

Reader's Response Students may say that at first they regarded the old woman as a nosy person who meddles in other people's business.

Thematic Focus Some students may say that the nuclear age is more troubling because a nuclear war could destroy the planet. Others might say that the post-World War I period is more troubling because they find living in the contemporary world not particularly unsettling.

☑ Check Your Comprehension

1. They chat and eat pizza.
2. He said "oink oink" at police officers while he was taking part in a demonstration.
3. He was angry because he felt his daughter was dealing with him as though he were a figure of authority.

◆ Critical Thinking

1. The father's response shows that he loves his daughter very much and is willing to admit when he makes a mistake.
2. The narrator is anxious about the angry manner in which the father treats his daughter.
3. The story suggests that the emotional climate is one of anxiety and tension over world affairs.
4. The social and political circumstances arising from war would most concern the narrator of "Anxiety." The narrator's fear of the destructiveness of war would draw the narrator toward those issues.

Answers
Thematic Connection

1. Sample response: Paley's narrator reaches out personally to others. Hemingway's soldiers distrust the claims made about technology's benefits to people. Anderson's Hutchensons go back to nature.
2. Following World War I, people were concerned with national economies, the availability of jobs, and anxiety over the rapid development of new technologies. In the post World War II period, they were concerned with civil rights and the possibility of nuclear war.
3. Sample response: The soldiers are anxious about physical recovery and death. The Hutchensons are anxious about the world complexity and the meaning of their son's death. Welty's Phoenix Jackson is anxious about not being able to complete her long journey.

◆ Literary Connection

1. The central characters of Hemingway's story view their world with skepticism and disillusionment. Those of Anderson view their world with fear of its complexity. Welty's central character views her world with fear and suspicion. The narrator of Paley's story views her world with anxiety about future events.
2. Words that evoke the mood of each story are as follows: "In Another Country": cold, dark, cried; "The Corn Planting": silent, exacting, night; "A Worn Path": mourning, senses, withdrawn; "Anxiety": laughing, terror, careful.

Idea Bank

Customizing for
Performance Levels
Following are suggestions for matching Idea Bank topics with your students' performance levels:
Less Advanced Students: 1
Average Students: 2, 4, 6
More Advanced Students: 3, 5

Customizing for
Learning Modalities
Following are suggestions for matching Idea Bank topics with your students' learning modalities:
Interpersonal: 4
Visual/Spatial: 5
Logical/Mathematical: 6

Thematic Connection

Facing Troubled Times: An Uncertain Future

The short stories written just after World War I and those written today share a sense of disillusionment and anxiety about the future.

1. Compare and contrast how Paley's narrator, Hemingway's soldiers, and Anderson's Hutchensons respond to the advancing technology of their eras. Give examples.
2. How are the concerns of the post-World War II era—when Paley wrote—different from those of the period following World War I?
3. Explain how the title "Anxiety" might fit the stories by Hemingway, Anderson, and Welty. What issues concern key characters in each of these stories?

Literary Connection

Contemporary Short Stories

The world created within a short story is defined by limitations of plot complexity and numbers of characters and settings. In contrast to longer works, elements of character, setting, and mood become key parts of the story. As you reflect on Grace Paley's portrait of modern anxiety, think about how each of these key elements contributes to the overall effect of the story. Compare and contrast the characters, setting, and moods with those created by Hemingway, Anderson, and Welty in their stories.

1. Explain how you think the central characters in each story view their world.
2. Cite three descriptive words in each story that help evoke the story's mood.

Idea Bank

Writing

1. **Dialogue** Write a dialogue between the Hutchensons in Sherwood Anderson's story and the old woman in "Anxiety." The Hutchensons should argue for coping with modern uncertainty by burying oneself in work. The old woman should advocate combating uncertainty by taking action to change society.
2. **Expository Essay** A common generalization calls the period following World War II an age of anxiety. Identify the world, national, social, and personal factors that might lead to this growing sense of anxiety. In an essay, explain how these factors might affect the people living at this time.
3. **Critical Analysis** Grace Paley has said, "There isn't a story written that isn't about blood and money. People and their relationships to each other is the blood, the family. And how they live, the money of it." Write a brief essay in which you connect this idea to specific issues and examples in Paley's story "Anxiety."

Speaking, Listening, and Viewing

4. **Interview** Interview two or three adults—family members or others—about the threat of nuclear war. How do they feel about it? Ask what has been done—and what can yet be done—to minimize the threat. **[Social Studies Link; Science Link]**

Researching and Representing

5. **Historical Newspaper** With a group, research the times and settings of the stories you've read in this section. Create the front page of a historical newspaper; then devote one page to the time period of each story. Fill each page with news, pictures, and advertisements that would be typical of the times. **[Social Studies Link]**
6. **Future Projection** Think about the rate at which technology advanced from the time of Hemingway's story to Grace Paley's. Create a presentation explaining and showing (with drawings and graphs) where technology is expected to be in twenty-five years. **[Science Link]**

Online Activity www.phlit.phschool.com

✓ ASSESSMENT OPTIONS

Formal Assessment, Selection Test, pp. 227–228, and Assessment Resources Software. The selection test is designed so that it can be easily customized to the performance levels of your students.

PORTFOLIO ASSESSMENT
Use the following rubrics in the ***Alternative Assessment*** booklet to assess student writing:
Dialogue: Persuasion Rubric, p. 120
Expository Essay: Definition/Classification Rubric, p. 114
Critical Analysis: Literary Analysis/Interpretation Rubric, p. 127

Writing Process Workshop

Literary Analysis

Any one of the short stories in this section would make an excellent topic for a literary analysis—a formal piece of writing that examines the underlying meaning or significance of one or more elements of a literary work or of the work as a whole. By writing a literary analysis, you can demonstrate your ability to think critically about what you read and to dig beneath the surface to unlock meaning. The skills below and the instructions on the following pages will help you develop an effective literary analysis of any work you choose.

The skills below will help you write a literary analysis.

Writing Skills Focus

- **Use an appropriate level of formality.** Use formal language and a serious, thoughtful tone.
- **Present a clear thesis statement** in which you offer your interpretation of the literary work or an element of that work.
- **Use precise details** from the literary work to support your thesis—the main idea of your analysis. Wherever possible, use direct quotations from the work.
- **Elaborate** by discussing how the elements in a work of literature elicit an emotional response. (See p. 747.)

This excerpt from an introduction to a literary analysis of "Winter Dreams" includes some of the features of a strong analysis:

Writing Model

F. Scott Fitzgerald's "Winter Dreams" suggests that a single-minded pursuit of wealth and social status is unlikely to lead to personal fulfillment. ① The story's main character, Dexter Green, accumulates great wealth, yet is unable to find happiness because of his obsession with Judy Jones, a beautiful woman who symbolizes for Dexter all that is exciting and glamourous about upper-class life. ② ③

① The writer opens with her thesis statement.

② The writer then develops her thesis statement with details from the story.

③ A formal vocabulary and presentation lend an authoritative tone to the essay.

Prepare and Engage

LESSON OBJECTIVES

- To use recursive writing processes to write a literary analysis
- To understand and use parallel structure
- To understand and use infinitives and infinitive phrases

Establish Writing Guidelines
Distribute the scoring rubric for Literary Analysis/Interpretation (p. 127) in ***Alternative Assessment*** to make students aware of the criteria on which their work will be evaluated. See the suggestions on p. 755 for customizing the rubric to this workshop.

You may also want to present the Writing Process Model for Interpreting a Work of Literature in ***Writing and Language Transparencies,*** pp. 37–40.

Connect to Literature William Faulkner's Nobel Prize Acceptance Speech (p. 798), points out the many responsibilities of the writer in today's world. Encourage students to keep these larger issues in mind while writing their own analyses.

Writers at Work Videodisc To show how agent Theresa Park analyzes literary work, play the videodisc segment on Response to Literature (Ch. 7).

Play frames 22513 to 31258

Writing Lab CD-ROM
If your students have access to computers, you may want to have them use the tutorial on Responding to Literature. Have students follow these steps:

1. Explore the Response Wheels to see combinations of literary elements and response methods.
2. Draft on the computer.
3. Use the Evaluation Word Bin to select precise modifiers.
4. Review the Self-Evaluation Checklist to help them revise.

Beyond the Classroom

Career Connection

Book Reviewing Students who enjoy writing about literature should consider the many opportunities that exist to do so professionally. Established critics who write for newspapers and magazines are often well-paid to do something that they claim they would do anyway—read voraciously. However, landing such a position at a major publication may require several years of "apprenticeship" as reviewers try to amass impressive "clippings" in a writing portfolio. Many reviewers begin by writing for high school and college literary magazines. Local newspapers and company newsletters may accept reviews by new critics though they may not pay very much, if they pay anything at all. Eventually a writer can graduate to producing brief "capsule" reviews in magazines or Sunday newspapers. If editors like the work, the writer is offered more substantial assignments.

Develop Student Writing

Prewriting Strategy
In the student edition, students are asked to consider choosing a topic from the selections in this section. If students opt for such a topic, suggest that they review notes from class discussions on the work to suggest elements for analysis. However, remind students that they will be expected to go beyond classroom observations by thoroughly referencing specific passages of text.

Customize for
English Language Learners
Encourage students to choose a work whose reading level matches their own and to focus on elements with which they feel most comfortable. For example, if writing about poetry, some English language learners may find it easier to discuss rhyme scheme than the nuances in meaning of certain word choices.

Elaboration Strategy
As students begin drafting, remind them of their purpose: to analyze, not to evaluate.

Writing Lab CD-ROM Students may benefit from reviewing audio-annotated literary models of poetic and dramatic elements in the Gathering Details section of the tutorial on Response to Literature.

Revision Strategy
Consider supplementing the peer review checklist in the student edition with the following:

- Does the writer seem to have a thorough or superficial grasp of the literary elements under consideration?
- Does the analysis include insights that strike the reader as original and eye-opening?
- Does the writing exhibit variety in terms of its language, or are certain words repeated too frequently?

Applying Language Skills: Parallel Structure

Parallel structure is the placement of equal ideas in words, phrases, or clauses of similar types. Notice that all of the elements must be parallel.

First Draft: Fads of the Roaring Twenties included the Charleston, raccoon coats, and they sat on flagpoles.

Revision: Fads of the Roaring Twenties included the Charleston, raccoon coats, and flagpole sitting.

Practice Correct the faulty parallelism in each sentence:

1. The writer Eudora Welty is also a photographer and paints pictures.
2. Many American writers were affected by experiencing the horrors of WWI firsthand or they heard about them from friends who served in the military.
3. After the end of WWII, President Truman ordered full restoration of civilian consumer production and to return to free markets.

Writer's Solution Connection
Language Lab
For help on parallel structure, see the Strengthening Sentences lesson in the Writing Style unit.

Prewriting

Choose a Topic If you found one of the stories in this section especially thought-provoking, you may want to use that story as the focus of your literary analysis. As an alternative, choose another literary work that you've recently read that had a strong impact on you.

Review the Literature Carefully review the literary work you've selected. Jot down answers to the following questions:

- ▶ Which of the characters stand out? Why? What motivates the characters actions?
- ▶ How does the setting shape the characters and the plot?
- ▶ Which images are most striking? Why? What associations do these images call to mind? Which images seem to have an underlying meaning?
- ▶ What, if any, symbolic meaning can be found in the characters, setting, or events?
- ▶ What lessons can be learned from the characters and events that can be applied to real life?

Review your answers to these questions. Then decide whether to focus your analysis on one or more elements of the work or to concentrate on analyzing the work as a whole.

Gather Precise Details Once you've decided on the focus of your analysis, write a sentence or two stating the main point that you'll make in your paper. Then gather details and passages from the work that you can use to support this thesis.

Drafting

Begin With a Strong Introduction Your introduction should have an attention-grabbing beginning, a statement of the title and author of the work to be discussed, and a clearly stated thesis. Notice how the following example meets all three criteria:

> Will Phoenix rise again? In her story "A Worn Path," Eudora Welty's use of the name Phoenix for her main character is an allusion to the phoenix that rises from the ashes in ancient Egyptian mythology. Like the mythological phoenix, the character Phoenix Jackson is able to endure and rise above the hardships that her life presents to her.

Maintain a Serious Tone A literary analysis calls for formal sentence structure and a serious tone. Avoid slang and familiar, informal language and use a more scholarly tone.

Applying Language Skills

Parallel Structure
Explain that analytical writing may require more complex sentence structures than students might regularly use. That is why it is important that they keep such structures internally coherent and consistent—to ensure elements are parallel.

Answers

1. The writer Eudora Welty is also a photographer and a painter.
2. Many American writers were affected by experiencing the horrors of WWI firsthand or hearing about them from friends who served in the military.
3. After the end of WWII, President Truman ordered the full restoration of civilian consumer production and the return to free markets.

Grammar Reinforcement

In addition to the instruction in the **Language Lab CD-ROM** cited in the student edition, you can refer to the *Sourcebook* lesson titled Developing Your Style 2, Using Parallel Structures (p. 262) and practice p. 49 in the *Writer's Solution Grammar Practice Book.*

Revising

Check Your Language Variety Reread your essay to determine whether you overuse any words. For example, if you use the word "writer" too frequently, revise by inserting synonyms or the author's name. You may want to rewrite some sentences to improve language variety.

Consult a Peer Reviewer Ask a classmate who is familiar with your topic to read your literary analysis. Provide your peer reviewer with a checklist based on the following points:

- ▶ How can you more clearly express the thesis in the introduction of the analysis?
- ▶ What quotations or other details could you add in the body of the analysis to strengthen support for your ideas?
- ▶ Have you restated the thesis in your conclusion?
- ▶ What personal reactions should you include?
- ▶ Have you been consistently and appropriately formal?

Revision Model

Welty leaves unanswered the question of whether Phoenix Jackson's grandson is still alive. ~~On one hand,~~ ① a nurse at the clinic to which Phoenix walks says, "She doesn't come in for herself—she has a little grandson." ② However, Later in the story, the same nurse asks ~~if Phoenix's granson is dead~~ ③ , "Tell us about your grandson. . . . He's dead, isn't he?" In an essay on this topic, Welty herself answers the question by stating, "*Phoenix* is alive."

① The writer deletes this awkward transition.

② Here, a transition is added to make a smoother connection between sentences.

③ A quotation from the work replaces a vague reference.

Publishing

▶ **Literary Magazine** Create a class literary magazine featuring the literary analysis of several members of the class. Organize the analysis by time period, author, or genre; include a table of contents; and consider adding illustrations.

Applying Language Skills: Infinitives and Infinitive Phrases

An **infinitive** is the base form of a verb—usually preceded by the word *to* as in *to sing*. An **infinitive phrase** consists of an infinitive plus complements and/or modifiers (*to sing a song merrily*). Both an infinitive and an infinitive phrase can function as a noun, an adjective, or an adverb.

Examples:

To write (n) was her dream. She had the will to succeed (adj). Still, she found it hard to complete her first novel (adv).

Practice Identify the infinitive phrases in the following sentences, and label their function (noun, adjective, or adverb).

1. I like to read literature about the South.
2. My career goal is to be a published writer.

Writing Application Use infinitive phrases to avoid dull, repetitious writing.

Writer's Solution Connection Writing Lab

For help revising your analysis, view the video tip from writer Ralph Ellison in the Revising and Editing section of the tutorial on Response to Literature.

Writing Lab CD-ROM The Revising and Editing section of the tutorial includes a Revision Checker for language variety to help students avoid excess repetition.

Publishing

If students choose to produce a literary magazine, encourage them to incorporate illustrations and intriguing magazine style display quotes in their design to attract the interest of readers who may not be familiar with the works being analyzed.

Applying Language Skills

Infinitives and Infinitive Phrases

Explain to students that the effective use of infinitives can help lend writing a sophisticated, serious tone and can help express complex ideas efficiently.

Answers

1. I like to read literature about the South. *noun, direct object*
2. My career goal is to be a published writer. *noun, predicate nominative*

Grammar Reinforcement

For additional instruction and practice, refer students to the **Language Lab CD-ROM** lesson on Recognizing and Using Phrases.

Reinforce and Extend

Prentice Hall Writing and Grammar For more prewriting, elaboration, and revision strategies, see *Prentice Hall Writing and Grammar.*

Reflect on Writing Connect the assignment back to the reading curriculum by asking students which literary elements they will now look for in future reading.

✓ ASSESSMENT		4	3	2	1
PORTFOLIO ASSESSMENT Use the rubric on Literary Analysis/Interpretation in the ***Alternative Assessment*** booklet (p. 127) to assess students' writing. Add the following criteria to further customize the rubric to this assignment.	**Appropriate Formality**	The writer consistently uses language and a tone that are appropriate to the formality of the topic.	For the most part the writer uses language and a tone that are appropriate to the formality of the topic.	The writer rarely uses language and a tone that are appropriate to the formality of the topic.	The writer avoids using appropriately formal language and tone.
	Parallel Structure	The writer consistently employs a parallel structure of elements within a sentence.	The writer sometimes fails to use a parallel structure for elements within a sentence.	The writer rarely uses a parallel structure correctly.	The writer consistently makes errors in parallel structure.

Prepare and Engage

LESSON OBJECTIVES

- To comprehend selections using a variety of strategies; to read silently with comprehension for a sustained period of time

Customize for
Less Proficient Readers
Guide students in setting two kinds of goals: to increase time spent every day in focused, sustained silent reading; and to increase the number of pages read with comprehension at each sitting. Students can determine reasonable goals by assessing their own reading behaviors. Answering questions such as these can help them with self-assessment: "What is a 'long' book you have read?" "How often do you become so absorbed in a book that time passes quickly?" "How long do you think it should take you to read ten pages with comprehension?"

Apply the Strategies

Answers

1. Three main sections take the reader to three locations important in the author's narrative: Sconset, Boise, and New Orleans. The reader could set goals to read a chapter a day, for example, or a four-chapter section a week.
2. The story seems to be a nonfiction personal narrative. The author is telling about his childhood, so the reader will meet family members and share the boy's experiences in three places.
3. Students should keep track of the number of pages they were able to read at a sitting and assess their own comprehension. Among the difficulties students may note in their self-assessments (along with ideas for solutions) are concentration lapses, lack of a quiet place, and loss of interest in the work.

Student Success Workshop

Real-World Reading Skills

Reading Silently for Extended Periods

Strategies for Success

This book is filled with brief literary works, most of which can be read in a single sitting. Novels, biographies, and full-length plays, on the other hand, require extended reading periods. Follow these strategies to help you read silently with comprehension for an extended period:

Define Your Interest Before you begin a lengthy reading project, read the book jacket, author's notes and foreword, and reviewers' comments, to assess your interest in the text.

Get an Overview Survey the structure. Are there parts or sections? Look at the table of contents, prologue or foreword, and other explanatory notes. Identify the organization of events and ideas to guide your reading.

Create an Atmosphere Reading for an extended period requires concentration. Create an atmosphere that allows you to read. Most important, eliminate distractions. Avoid sitting in the busiest place in the house or blasting your stereo while you read.

Be Determined Set goals for yourself. Start by reading for thirty minutes each day. Then see if you can increase that time to an hour. Take a break if you need one. Get up, stretch, get some water, and return to your book. If you have the initial determination to read, the book's content will carry you once you get into it.

✔ *Here are situations in which you can apply strategies for reading silently for extended periods:*

- ▶ Reading a novel for pleasure
- ▶ Reading a book for a book report
- ▶ Reading nonfiction for a research report

Apply the Strategies

Read the contents and review. Use the strategies in this workshop to answer the questions.

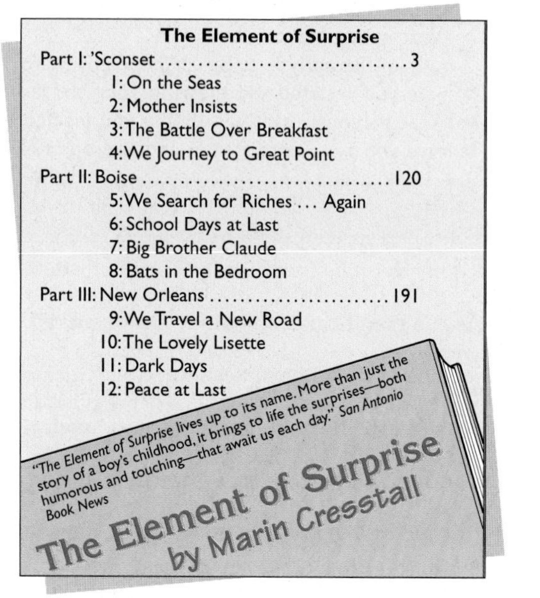

1. Examine the table of contents above. How is the book organized? How can the organization guide you through the book?
2. What does the structure suggest to you about the story?
3. Choose a book or play to read for an extended period. Set aside one-hour increments for reading. After each session, assess your success. What did you accomplish? List any difficulties, and plan how you can improve the next time.

Test Preparation Workshop

Reading Silently for Extended Periods Point out that the strategies students develop to read long written works will also help them with the shorter passages that are common on standardized tests. Present this test item about information in the workshop:

What question can you answer by reading the foreword to a book?

A Is this book likely to hold my interest?
B What do reviewers say about this book?
C Will I need to concentrate to read this book?
D How many chapters are in this book?

Students should be able to tell why *A* is the correct answer by describing categories of information usually contained in a foreword. They may also note that *B* and *D* are incorrect because they refer to information not found in the forward. Choice *C* is incorrect because all reading requires concentration.

PART 3 *From Every Corner of the Land*

The Tower, Charles Demuth, Columbus Museum of Art, Ohio

Humanities: Art

The Tower, 1920 by Charles Demuth.

Sir Christopher Wren (1632–1723), to whom this painting pays tribute, was England's most famous architect. After the Great Fire of London in 1666, he redesigned at least portions of more than half of the churches that had been burnt. His church spires, in particular, are admired for their grace and variety. Ask students why this painting is called *The Tower.* Most will see the connection with the old-fashioned spire in the center of the painting, but point out the other towers in the painting, including the faceted, blue, futuristic structure in the background.

Have your students link the painting to the theme of Part 3 ("From Every Corner of the Land") by answering the following question:

What various facets of America do you see reflected in this painting? *This painting reflects America's New England roots, its combination of past and future, its social variety.*

One-Minute Planning Guide

The works in this section reflect the breadth of American literature in the early-to-mid-twentieth century. This literary look at the regional diversity of the United States takes students from Carl Sandburg's rough and ready "Chicago" and E. B. White's dynamic urban portrait in *Here is New York,* to the Southern bayous of Faulkner's Mississippi in "Race at Morning." Katherine Anne Porter uses a stream-of-consciousness style to tell the tale of a rural woman's life in "The Jilting of Granny Weatherall," a story that is likely to both challenge and intrigue students. Frost's poetry, set against a vividly-painted New England backdrop, has a depth and power that belie its simple language. The engaging excerpt from Zora Neale Hurston's *Dust Tracks on a Road* introduces a sampling of poetry by the leading writers of the Harlem Renaissance. These easy-to-read poems are rich with images and metaphors that express what it meant to be an African American at a time when memories of both slavery and the Civil War were still fresh in the American consciousness.

Customize for *Varying Student Needs*

When assigning these particular selections from this part, keep in mind these factors:

"April Showers"
- Accessible short story

"The Jilting of Granny Weatherall"
- Short story written in stream-of-consciousness style
- Less proficient readers may need help clarifying the sequence of events

"Race at Morning"
- Short story filled with regional dialect will challenge English Language Learners and less proficient readers

Frost Poetry
- Musical/rhythmic learners and visual/spatial learners will enjoy the rhythm and imagery of these poems

Poetry of the Harlem Renaissance
- Challenge intrapersonal learners and more advanced students to interpret the many layers of meaning in these brief, easy-to-read poems

Prepare and Engage

LESSON OBJECTIVES

1. **To develop vocabulary and word identification skills**
   - Latin Word Roots: *-man-*, *-manu-*
   - Using the Word Bank: Synonyms
   - Extending Word Study: Prefixes (ATE)
2. **To use a variety of reading strategies to comprehend a story**
   - Connect Your Experience
   - Reading Strategy: Anticipate Events
   - Idea Bank: Critical Response
3. **To express and support responses to the text**
   - Critical Thinking
   - Idea Bank: Flier Copy
   - Idea Bank: Movie Scene
   - Idea Bank: Contest Announcement
4. **To analyze literary elements**
   - Literary Focus: Elements of Plot
5. **To read in order to research self-selected and assigned topics**
   - Idea Bank: Interior Design Project
6. **To plan, prepare, organize, and present literary interpretations**
   - Idea Bank: Casting Discussion
   - Idea Bank: Dramatic Monologue
   - Speaking Listening, and Viewing Mini-Lesson (ATE)
7. **To use recursive writing processes to write a short story**
   - Guided Writing Lesson: Short Story
8. **To increase knowledge of the rules of grammar and usage**
   - Grammar and Styles: Gerund Phrases

Test Preparation

Reading Comprehension: Anticipate Missing Words (ATE, p. 759)
The teaching tips and sample test item in this workshop support the instruction and practice in the unit workshop:
Reading Comprehension: Sentence-Completion Questions (SE, p. 863)

Guide for Interpreting

Edith Wharton *(1862–1937)*

Colorful Old New York, the high society of London and Paris, The French Riviera—these settings from the late nineteenth century through the 1930's were all part of Edith Wharton's world. They also played an important role in the making of her books—more than fifty published volumes—and her remarkable literary career.

Wharton was a master at re-creating the staid, rule-bound atmosphere of the upper-class society of her time.

A Daughter of Privilege Born Edith Newbold Jones, Wharton was the daughter of a socially prominent New York City family. Educated privately in New York and Europe, she married Edward Wharton, a Boston banker, in 1885. The couple spent the next few years immersing themselves in the social life of the high society in Newport, Rhode Island; in Lenox, Massachusetts; and in Europe.

Interestingly, it was on the advice of a doctor that Wharton began to write fiction. Wharton was caring for her husband, known as Teddy, who had become chronically ill, and the doctor advised Wharton to take up writing as a way to relieve stress. Her first stories appeared in *Scribner's* magazine, and several volumes of her fiction were published around the turn of the century. However, it was her best-selling novel *The House of Mirth* (1905)—a devastating portrait of a young woman who tries and fails to survive in New York high society—that established her as an important writer.

An Expatriate Writer In 1913, Wharton moved to Paris. She began a friendship with the novelist Henry James and other writers who helped her refine her work. As World War I loomed, she produced some of her finest novels: *Ethan Frome* (1911), *The Reef* (1912), and *The Custom of the Country* (1913). During the war, Wharton remained in France, organizing aid for Belgian refugees. In 1920, her novel *The Age of Innocence*—which was recently made into a popular movie—won the Pulitzer Prize. Wharton also published *Old New York* (1924), *The Mothers Recompense* (1925), and 85 short stories. In addition, she published an autobiography, *A Backward Glance*, in 1934.

In her fiction, which continues to attract readers and earn critical acclaim, Wharton explores the conflict between money and morality and exposes the cruelty of the social "game," with its rivalries, rules, and punishments.

◆ Background for Understanding

History: Publishing at the Turn of the Century

The publishing world of the late nineteenth and early twentieth centuries was far different from today's book world. If Wharton's novels were published today, they would stand on bookstore shelves crowded with many other novels. Wharton's publisher would probably send her on a whirlwind book tour; perhaps she'd appear on Oprah Winfrey's show. You could even hear her books read on audiotape by a famous actor.

Around the turn of century, however, things were different. Novels were customarily serialized in magazines and newspapers. *The House of Mirth*, one of Wharton's most famous novels, appeared in *Scribner's* magazine before it was published as a book in 1905. Readers of the time would eagerly await the next monthly installment of the latest novel by their favorite author. Some great writers, including England's Charles Dickens earlier in the century, established their reputations this way.

Prentice Hall Literature Program Resources

REINFORCE / RETEACH / EXTEND

Selection Support Pages
Build Vocabulary: Latin Word Roots: *-man-*, *-manu-*, p. 227
Grammar and Style: Gerund Phrases, p. 228
Reading Strategy: Anticipate Events, p. 229
Literary Focus: Elements of Plot, p. 230

Strategies for Diverse Student Needs, p. 49

Beyond Literature
Career Connection: Publishing, p. 49

Formal Assessment Selection Test, pp. 232–234; Assessment Resources Software

Alternative Assessment, p. 49

Writing and Language Transparencies
Story Map Organizer, pp. 99–101

Resource Pro CD-ROM

Listening to Literature Audiocassettes

April Showers

◆ Literature and Your Life

CONNECT YOUR EXPERIENCE

You submit a poem to a literary magazine or audition for the lead in the play. Suddenly, you seem to be waiting for a world of strangers to pass judgment. It takes courage to risk having your work criticized or rejected. In this story, a young writer braves the world of publishing—and gets not one surprise, but two.

Journal Writing Do you ever dream of being "discovered" and shooting to fame? Describe your dream.

THEMATIC FOCUS: FROM EVERY CORNER OF THE LAND

Most of this story is set in a small Massachusetts town where neighbors know one another. As you read, think how the story would be different if all the action had taken place in the city of Boston.

◆ Literary Focus

ELEMENTS OF PLOT

Like most short story writers, Wharton brings together the **elements of plot** to lead readers through the events of a story. The **exposition** introduces the story's characters, setting, and situation. This is followed by an event that sets out the **conflict**, or struggle, whether internal or external. The conflict increases until it reaches a **climax,** or high point of suspense. The events leading up to the climax comprise the **rising action.** The climax is followed by the end, or **resolution,** of the central conflict. Anything that occurs after the resolution is the **denouement,** or **falling action.** Use a chart like this one to describe the development of the plot.

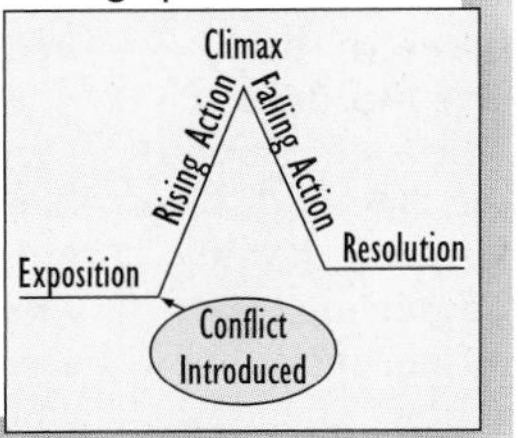

◆ Build Vocabulary

LATIN ROOTS: *-man-, -manu-*

The word *manuscript* is formed from the Latin word *manus,* meaning "hand," and the Latin root *-script-,* meaning "write." Using this information and the surrounding context, you might guess that *manuscript* means "a handwritten document."

WORD BANK

Preview this list of words from the story.

- admonitory
- retrospective
- antagonism
- contrition
- manuscript
- commiseration

◆ Reading Strategy

ANTICIPATE EVENTS

As you read "April Showers," you will probably find yourself **anticipating events**—eagerly looking forward to what is going to happen. Anticipating events differs from predicting in that it's less a conscious, mental process and more an emotional one. When you anticipate events, you forge a connection to characters who, like you, are watching their lives unfold.

As you read this story, join the central character, Theodora, in anticipating what will happen.

◆ Grammar and Style

GERUND PHRASES

A **gerund** is a verb form that ends in *-ing* and is used as a noun. A **gerund phrase,** which also serves as a noun, includes a gerund and any modifiers or complements. Like nouns, gerund phrases function as subjects, direct objects, subject complements, and objects of prepositions. This gerund phrase functions as an object of the preposition *in.*

> I don't believe in *feeding* youngsters on sentimental trash; . . .

As you read, notice the author's frequent use of gerund phrases.

Interest Grabber Hold up four envelopes. Tell students to imagine that you have in your hand awards for *Student Most Likely to Become President, Student Most Likely to Become a Writer, Student Most Likely to Win a Nobel Prize,* and *Student Most Likely to Be a Celebrity.* Ask students to jot down their feelings and ideas about their chances to win one or more of those awards, and to describe how they would feel if their expectations are or are not met. Tell students that in the story they are about to read, expectations play a key part; a young woman eagerly awaits the fate of a novel she wrote and submitted for publication.

Customize for
Less Proficient Readers
Help students to use context clues and a dictionary to determine the meanings of unfamiliar words, such as *prosperous, obscure, complement, abject, derision, consumptive,* and *sacrilege.* Invite students to work in pairs to formulate definitions.

Customize for
AP Students
Theodora is a young woman who is about the same age as your students. Ask them to identify the ways that her actions and reactions are typical of someone her age. After students have finished reading the piece, ask them to speculate about how the story might have turned out differently if Theodora had been an older, more experienced person.

Customize for
English Language Learners
Edith Wharton's story contains several phrases and expressions that either are not used today or no longer appear in the same construction. Help students to decipher the meanings and to rephrase these groups of words, using simpler language or substitute words.

Test Preparation Workshop

Reading Comprehension: Anticipate Missing Words Many standardized tests ask students to correctly answer sentence-completion questions. Use the following example to show students how to use context and their own knowledge to guess a word that completes the following passage.

> On the advice of a doctor, Edith Wharton began to write fiction to relieve the ____ of caring for her chronically ill husband.

A relaxation
B stress
C amusement
D annoyance

After reading the passage, students might think the word *pressure* completes the sentence. Looking at the choices, they would find that *B, stress,* comes closest to the meaning of their guess.

One-Minute Insight A romantic, suggestible young woman distracts herself from the responsibilities of running the family household by writing a florid novel and submitting it to a magazine. After much anxious anticipation, she is surprised and thrilled to learn that her work has been accepted for publication. To her dismay, she soon learns that it was another story with the same name that the publisher really wanted. Though she fears her father's derision, she is surprised and comforted when he exhibits uncharacteristic compassion for her disappointment; he, too, once harbored dreams of becoming a writer.

◆ Background for Understanding

❶ History Point out to students that many writers have historically chosen to publish under a pseudonym. For example, remind students that Mark Twain was Samuel Clemens's pen name, and tell them that best-selling author Stephen King wrote five novels using the name Richard Bachman. Ask students to speculate why writers choose to use pen names.

◆ Reading Strategy

❷ Anticipate Events Ask students to say what they think Theodora expects to happen. Then have them tell what they themselves anticipate for her novel.

❸ Clarification Inform students that Uncle James was excited about a new upgrade in home construction: indoor plumbing. At the turn of the century few homes, the White House among them, had this modern luxury.

◆ Critical Thinking

❹ Infer Ask students to infer what Uncle James meant by his distinction between a "pleasant, sociable kind of woman" and one that is a writer. *Students should realize that Uncle James does not think very highly of writers; he makes it clear that he does not usually consider writers to be pleasant or sociable people.*

April Showers

Edith Wharton

"But Guy's heart slept under the violets on Muriel's grave."

❶ It was a beautiful ending; Theodora had seen girls cry over last chapters that weren't half as pathetic. She laid her pen aside and read the words over, letting her voice linger on the fall of the sentence; then, drawing a deep breath, she wrote across the foot of the page the name by which she had decided to become known in literature—Gladys Glyn.

Downstairs the library clock struck two. Its muffled thump sounded like an admonitory knock against her bedroom floor. Two o'clock! and she had promised her mother to be up early enough to see that the buttons were sewn on Johnny's reefer, and that Kate had her cod-liver oil before starting for school!

❷ Lingeringly, tenderly she gathered up the pages of her novel—there were five hundred of them—and tied them with the blue satin ribbon that her Aunt Julia had given her. She had meant to wear the ribbon with her new dotted muslin on Sundays, but this was putting it to a nobler use. She bound it round her manuscript, tying the ends in a pretty bow. Theodora was clever at making bows, and could have trimmed hats beautifully, had not all her spare moments been given to literature. Then, with a last look at the precious pages, she sealed and addressed the package. She meant to send it off next morning to the *Home Circle*. She knew it would be hard to obtain access to a paper which numbered so many popular authors among its contributors, but she had been encouraged to make the venture by something her Uncle James had said the last time he had come down from Boston.

He had been telling his brother, Doctor Dace, about his new house out at Brookline. Uncle James was prosperous, and was always moving into new houses with more "modern improvements." Hygiene was his passion, and he migrated in the wake of sanitary plumbing. ❸

"The bathrooms alone are worth the money," he was saying, cheerfully, "although it *is* a big rent. But then, when a man's got no children to save up for—" he glanced compassionately round Doctor Dace's crowded table "—and it is something to be in a neighborhood where the drainage is A-one. That's what I was telling our neighbor. Who do you suppose she is, by the way?" He smiled at Theodora. "I rather think that young lady knows all about her. Ever heard of Kathleen Kyd?"

Kathleen Kyd! The famous "society novelist," the creator of more "favorite heroines" than all her predecessors put together had ever turned out, the author of *Fashion and Passion, An American Duchess, Rhona's Revolt*. Was there any intelligent girl from Maine to California whose heart would not have beat faster at the mention of that name?

"Why, yes," Uncle James was saying, "Kathleen Kyd lives next door. Frances G. Wollop is her real name, and her husband's a dentist. She's a very pleasant, sociable kind of woman; ❹ you'd never think she was a writer. Ever hear how she began to write? She told me the whole story. It seems she was a saleswoman in a store, working on starvation wages, with a mother and a consumptive sister to support. Well, she wrote a story one day, just for fun,

Block Scheduling Strategies

Consider these suggestions to take advantage of extended class time:

- Introduce the selection with the Interest Grabber. Ask students to think about awards ceremonies they have seen, such as those for the Academy Awards and MTV Music Awards. Invite students to discuss what it must be like to be nominated for an award and then await the outcome.
- Explain the elements of plot outlined in the Literary Focus. Using the Story Map transparency or the diagram on p. 759, guide students to record the elements of the story as they read. At what points in the story does one element end and another begin? Use the Literary Focus questions on p. 766 to direct discussion.
- Using the Speaking, Listening, and Viewing Mini-Lesson (p. 762), divide students into groups to hold casting discussions. Invite groups to share their casting decisions.
- Assign the Guided Writing Lesson (p. 767). Before students begin, introduce the Writing Skills Focus: creating a mood.

and sent it to the *Home Circle*. They'd never heard of her, of course, and she never expected to hear from them. She did, though. They took the story and passed their plate for more. She became a regular contributor and eventually was known all over the country. Now she tells me her books bring her in about ten thousand a year. Rather more than you and I can boast of, eh, John? Well, I hope *this* household doesn't contribute to her support." He glanced sharply at Theodora. "I don't believe in feeding youngsters on sentimental trash; it's like sewer gas—doesn't smell bad, and infects the system without your knowing it."

Memories, 1885–86, William Merritt Chase, Munson-Williams-Proctor Institute Museum of Art, Utica, New York

7 ▲ **Critical Viewing** What emotions are evoked by this portrait? How do they relate to Theodora's literary hopes and dreams? **[Connect]**

Theodora listened breathlessly. Kathleen Kyd's first story had been accepted by the *Home Circle*, and they had asked
5 for more! Why should Gladys Glyn be less fortunate? Theodora had done a great deal of novel reading—far more than her parents were aware of—and felt herself competent to pronounce upon the quality of her own work. She was almost sure that "April Showers" was a remarkable book. If it lacked Kathleen Kyd's lightness of touch, it had an emotional intensity never achieved by that brilliant writer. Theodora did not care to amuse her readers; she left that to more frivolous talents. Her aim was to stir the depths of human nature, and she felt she had succeeded. It was a great thing for a girl to be able to feel that about her first novel. Theodora was only seventeen; and she remembered, with a touch of retrospective compassion, that George Eliot[1] had not become famous till she was nearly forty.

6 No, there was no doubt about the merit of "April Showers." But would not an inferior work have had a better chance of success? Theodora recalled the early struggles of famous authors, the notorious antagonism of publishers and editors to any new writer of exceptional promise. Would it not be wiser to write the book down to the average reader's level, reserving for some later work the great "effects" into which she had thrown all the fever of her imagination? The thought was sacrilege! Never would she lay hands on the sacred structure she had reared; never would she resort to the inartistic expedient of modifying her work to suit the popular taste. Better obscure failure than a vulgar triumph. The great authors never stooped to such concessions, and Theodora felt herself included in their ranks by the firmness with which she rejected all thought of conciliating an unappreciative public. The manuscript should be sent as it was. 6

She woke with a start and a heavy sense of apprehension. The *Home Circle* had refused "April Showers!" No, that couldn't be it; there lay the precious manuscript, waiting to be posted. What was it, then? Ah, that ominous thump below stairs—nine o'clock striking! It was Johnny's buttons!

◆ **Literary Focus** Where does the exposition end and the rising action begin? 8

She sprang out of bed in dismay. She had been so determined not to disappoint her mother about Johnny's buttons! Mrs. Dace, helpless from chronic rheumatism, had to entrust the care of the household to her

1. **George Eliot:** Pseudonym of Mary Ann Evans (1819–1880), a celebrated English novelist.

◆ Build Vocabulary

admonitory (ad män′ i tôr′ ē) *adj.*: Warning

retrospective (re trə spek′ tiv) *adj.*: Looking back on or directed to the past

antagonism (an tag′ ə niz′ əm) *n.*: Hostility

◆ Critical Thinking

5 **Speculate** In this passage, readers learn how one famous writer got her start, and more about how Theodora had been preparing for her own fame. Ask students to suggest reasons she might have had for keeping the quantity of her reading from her parents. *Students may suggest that although things would be different today, at that time it might have been considered inappropriate for a young women to forsake household chores in order to read popular or romantic novels. Even more unconventional was the idea of a woman pursuing a career as a writer, a career that many viewed as both undesirable and improbable.*

◆ Literature and Your Life

6 Ask students if they agree with Theodora's opinion of the idea of writers "dumbing down" their early work in order to get the opportunity to put their best feet forward in subsequent books. Invite them to argue for or against her notions about what a writer should do to achieve success and recognition.

▶Critical Viewing◀

7 **Connect** Students may say that this portrait presents a dreamy, romanticized look at the writing process, one that accurately captures how Theodora sees herself. (See the Humanities Note at the bottom of this page.)

◆ Literary Focus

8 **Elements of Plot** Students may say that the exposition of the story ends and the rising actions begins when Theodora awakens after working late to complete her book and realizes she has failed to take care of her household responsibilities.

Extending Word Study

Prefixes Direct students to the word *retrospective* at the bottom of the first column on p. 761. Tell students that the word contains the Latin prefix *retro-*, which means "backward," "back," or "behind." Students who know that the Latin root *-spect-* means "look" will know that *retrospective* means "looking back on things in the past." Invite students to find the meaning of other words that use the prefix *-retro*, such as *retroactive*, *retrogression*, and others.

Humanities: Art

Memories, 1885–1886, by William Merritt Chase.

After a brief stint with the U.S. Navy, William Merritt Chase (1849–1916) studied in New York with artist Joseph O. Eaton and then took classes at the National Academy of Design. After his painting *Keying Up—The Court Jester* established his credibility, he enjoyed a successful career as an artist and teacher for the rest of his life.

Use these questions for discussion:

1. In what ways does this painting capture Theodora's attitude toward her writing? *Students may say that her dreamy faraway expression portrays her romantic view of the craft and that the manuscript lights up the table, her heart, and her face, that it alone glows, while all else is in darkness.*
2. The painting is entitled *Memories*; it is not specifically about Theodora and her book. What other interpretations can you suggest? *Students may suggest that the young woman is looking over old photos, wistfully recalling events, people, and feelings from her past.*

◆ Literary Focus

1 Elements of Plot Guide students to recognize the conflict between Theodora's desire to be a novelist and the practical demands of her domestic obligations, between her romantic fantasies and the realities of her mundane responsibilities.

◆ Grammar and Style

2 Gerund Phrases Point out that the gerund phrase "*sewing on his buttons*" serves as a noun. You might substitute a noun such as *science* or *Latin* to demonstrate.

◆ Reading Strategy

3 Anticipate Events Theodora assumes that if her book is published, her parents will be enamored with her success and she, in turn, will forgive *them* for misunderstanding her during the time she fell behind in her chores. Ask students if they think she is being realistic in her expectations. Ask them what they anticipate the parents' response will be.

◆ Grammar and Style

4 Gerund Phrases Ask students to identify the gerund in this sentence and to tell how it is used. *The gerund is mending, and it serves as a noun in the form of an object of a preposition.*

5 Clarification Paraphrase the sentence that includes the expression ". . . but had the benefit of her personal supervision" to help students understand its meaning: that every house in town has experienced Miss Brill's "supervision" of affairs. Also explain that houses with "a crepe bow on the bell" were homes whose residents were in mourning.

eldest daughter; and Theodora honestly meant to see that Johnny had his full complement of buttons, and that Kate and Bertha went to school tidy. Unfortunately, the writing of a great novel leaves little time or memory for the lesser obligations of life, and Theodore usually found that her good intentions matured too late for
1 practical results.

Her contrition was softened by the thought that literary success would enable her to make up for all the little negligences of which she was guilty. She meant to spend all her money on her family; and already she had visions of a wheeled chair for her mother, a fresh wallpaper for the doctor's shabby office, bicycles for the girls, and
2 Johnny's establishment at a boarding school where sewing on his buttons would be included in the curriculum. If her parents could have guessed her intentions, they would not have found fault with her as they did; and Doctor Dace, on this particular morning, would not have looked up to say, with his fagged, ironical air:

> *She turned aside to hide the dismay that flushed her face.*

"I suppose you didn't get home from the ball till morning?"

Theodora's sense of being in the right enabled her to take the thrust with a dignity that would have awed the unfeeling parent of fiction.

"I'm sorry to be late, father," she said.

Doctor Dace, who could never be counted on to behave like a father in a book, shrugged his shoulders impatiently.

"Your sentiments do you credit, but they haven't kept your mother's breakfast warm."

"Hasn't mother's tray gone up yet?"

"Who was to take it, I should like to know? The girls came down so late that I had to hustle them off before they'd finished breakfast, and Johnny's hands were so dirty that I sent him back to his room to make himself decent. It's a pretty thing for the doctor's children to be the dirtiest little savages in Norton!"

Theodora had hastily prepared her mother's tray, leaving her own breakfast untouched. As she entered the room upstairs, Mrs. Dace's patient face turned to her with a smile much harder to bear than her father's reproaches.

"Mother, I'm *so* sorry—"

"No matter, dear. I suppose Johnny's buttons kept you. I can't think what they boy does to his clothes!"

Theodora sat the tray down without speaking. It was impossible to own to having forgotten Johnny's buttons without revealing the cause of her forgetfulness. For a few weeks longer she must bear to be misunderstood; then—ah, then if her novel were accepted, how gladly would she 3
forget and forgive! But what if it were refused? She turned aside to hide the dismay that flushed her face. Well, then she would admit the truth—she would ask her parents' pardon, and settle down without a murmur to an obscure existence of mending and combing.

She had said to herself that after the manuscript had been sent, she would have time to look after the children and catch up with the mending; but 4
she had reckoned without the postman. He came three times a day; for an hour before each ring she was too excited to do anything but wonder if he would bring an answer this time, and for an hour afterward she moved about in a leaden stupor of disappointment. The children had never been so trying. They seemed to be always coming to pieces, like cheap furniture; one would have supposed they had been put together with bad glue. Mrs. Dace worried herself ill over Johnny's tatters, Bertha's bad marks at school, and Kate's open abstention from cod-liver oil; and Doctor Dace, coming back late from a long round of visits to a fireless office with a smoky lamp, called out furiously to know if Theodora would kindly come down and remove the "East, West, home's best" that hung above the empty grate.

In the midst of it all, Miss Sophy Brill called. It was very kind of her to come, for she was the busiest woman in Norton. She made it her duty to look after other people's affairs, and there was not a house in town but had the benefit of 5
her personal supervision. She generally came when things were going wrong, and the sight of her bonnet on the doorstep was a surer sign of calamity than a crepe bow on the bell. After she left, Mrs. Dace looked very sad, and the doctor punished Johnny for warbling down the entry:

"Miss Sophy Brill
Is a bitter pill!"

Speaking, Listening, and Viewing Mini-Lesson

Casting Discussion
This mini-lesson supports the Speaking, Listening, and Viewing activity in the Idea Bank on p. 767.

Introduce the Concept Explain that students will use their understanding of the characters in "April Showers," along with what they know about the acting talents and physical appearance of today's film actors, to cast a movie version of the story.

Develop Background Have students work in groups to list the story's characters and write a capsule description of each. Descriptions should include the character's approximate age and anything students can infer about physical appearance. Groups can brainstorm for a list of potential actors for each role, and then pare down each list to a few candidates before making a final decision. Students can refer to a movie video guide or the movie section of a newspaper for inspiration.

Apply the Information Have groups present their casts in an entertaining way. They can, for example, make a movie poster that lists the characters and actors, or perhaps write a press release announcing the cast.

Assess the Outcome Informally assess students by questioning groups about their choices. Your questions should relate specifically to the students' understanding of the characters in the story and why they chose one actor over another for the roles.

while Theodora, locking herself in her room, resolved with tears that she would never write another novel.

The week was a long nightmare. Theodora could neither eat nor sleep. She was up early enough, but instead of looking after the children and seeing that breakfast was ready, she wandered down the road to meet the postman, and came back wan and empty-handed, oblivious of her morning duties. She had no idea how long the suspense would last; but she didn't see how authors could live if they were kept waiting more than a week.

Then, suddenly, one afternoon—she never quite knew how or when it happened—she found herself with a *Home Circle* envelope in her hands, and her dazzled eyes flashing over a wild dance of words that wouldn't settle down and make sense.

6 "Dear Madam:" [They called her *Madam!* And then; yes, the words were beginning to fall into line now.] "Your novel, 'April Showers,' has been received, and we are glad to accept it on the usual terms. A serial on which we were counting for immediate publication has been delayed by the author's illness, and the first chapters of 'April Showers' will therefore appear in our midsummer number. Thanking you for favoring us with your manuscript, we remain," and so forth.

> 7 ◆ **Reading Strategy**
> Here, Theodora begins to anticipate the publication of her story. What do you feel?

Theodora found herself in the wood beyond the schoolhouse. She was kneeling on the ground, brushing aside the dead leaves and pressing her lips to the little bursting green things that pushed up eager tips through last year's decay. It was spring—spring! Everything was crowding toward the light and in her own heart hundreds 8 of germinating hopes had burst into sudden leaf. She wondered if the thrust of those little green fingers hurt the surface of the earth as her springing raptures hurt—yes, actually hurt!—her hot, constricted breast! She looked up through interlacing boughs at a tender, opaque blue sky full of the coming of a milky moon. She seemed enveloped in an atmosphere of loving comprehension. The brown earth throbbed with her joy, the treetops trembled with it, and a sudden star broke through the branches with an audible "I know!"

Theodora, on the whole, behaved very well. Her mother cried, her father whistled and said he supposed he must put up with grounds in his coffee now, and be thankful if he ever got a hot meal again; while the children took the most deafening and harassing advantage of what seemed a sudden suspension of the laws of nature.

Within a week everybody in Norton knew that Theodora had written a novel, and that it was coming out in the *Home Circle*. On Sundays, when she walked up the aisle, her friends dropped their prayer books and the soprano sang false in her excitement. Girls with more pin money than Theodora had ever dreamed of copied her hats and imitated her way of speaking. The local paper asked her for a poem; her old school teachers stopped to shake hands and grew shy over their congratulations; and Miss Sophy Brill came to call. She had put on her Sunday bonnet and her manner was almost abject. She ventured, very timidly, to ask her young friend how she wrote, whether it "just came to her," and if she had found that the kind of pen she used made any difference; and wound up by begging Theodora to write a sentiment in her album. 9

Even Uncle James came down from Boston to talk the wonder over. He called Theodora a "sly baggage," and proposed that she should give him her earnings to invest in a new patent grease-trap company. From what Kathleen Kyd had told him, he thought Theodora would probably get a thousand dollars for her story. He concluded by suggesting that she should base her next romance on the subject of sanitation, making the heroine nearly die of sewer gas poisoning because her parents won't listen to the handsome young doctor next door, when he warns them that their plumbing is out of order. That was a subject that would interest everybody, and do a lot more good than the sentimental trash most women wrote.

◆ **Build Vocabulary**

contrition (kən trish´ ən) *n.*: Remorse for having done wrong

manuscript (man´ yo͞o skript´) *n.*: Written or typed document, especially one submitted to a publisher or printer

Customize for *Less Proficient Readers*

❻ Help students understand that the author uses brackets here to show that these are Theodora's thoughts as she reads the letter. Guide them to see that, as a 17-year-old, she is excited to be called "Madam," which she interprets as an address of maturity and respect.

◆ Reading Strategy

❼ **Anticipate Events** Students are likely to be completely unaware of the surprise twist to come and therefore may anticipate for Theodora the same success she herself anticipates. Others may sense that she may be in for an unhappy surprise.

Customize for *AP Students*

❽ Have students read this passage aloud to appreciate how Edith Wharton is herself using the florid style of the sentimental romance potboiler to express Theodora's own sentimental feelings and romantic fantasies. Guide them to examine other examples of this technique.

◆ Literary Focus

❾ **Elements of Plot** Guide students to recognize the rising action in the plot of the story. Help them notice how Edith Wharton picks up the pace here in the build-up to the publication of Theodora's novel. This pace continues right up to the climax—the point at which Theodora barges into the magazine's offices and learns of the mistake.

Beyond the Classroom

Workplace Skill

Attention to Detail Theodora sees the editors at *Home Circle* as zoo specimens. However, editors perform a vital function in the publishing process. Guide students to appreciate that the success and quality of the final version of any kind of book is often due in large part to the efforts of the book's editor. Essential to the many technical, managerial, financial, and interpersonal skills required of a successful editor is an ability to focus on details.

Guide students to think about and discuss the variety of details they themselves need to consider when they edit classmates' essays and stories. Then tell students that editing is one kind of job in which the ability to pay attention to details is critical to success. Ask students to brainstorm for a list of other jobs that require this kind of thinking. Invite them to defend their choices.

◆ Critical Thinking

❶ **Analyze** Why is it so ironic that Kathleen Kyd's name appear beneath the title of the story? *It is ironic that Theodora is "cheated" of her chance to see her name in print by the very person whose story inspired her to dream of being published in the first place.*

◆ Critical Thinking

❷ **Speculate** Ask students to speculate about what might have happened here. Has there been a typographer's error? Has her story been changed by someone whose name now appears beneath it? Was the title to her story placed above another by mistake? Is the actuality immediately clear—that another writer wrote a story with the same title and that the other writer's story, not Theodora's, was accepted? If so, why did Theodora get the acceptance letter? Have students discuss the possibilities.

Customize for *AP Students*

❸ Have students discuss the zoological images Wharton uses here. Students can interpret the irony in Theodora's perceptions of the editors as specimens: it is she who is the outsider in those offices, the one who is not part of the publishing process, the one who is the curiosity.

◆ Literary Focus

❹ **Elements of Plot** Theodora must relinquish her dreams of being published when she learns that she and the established writer Kathleen Kyd coincidentally wrote and submitted a story with the same title. Although Ms. Kyd's story was the one accepted, Theodora was the one to whom the acceptance letter was mistakenly sent.

At last the great day came. Theodora had left an order with the bookseller for the midsummer number of the *Home Circle* and before the shop was open she was waiting on the sidewalk. She clutched the precious paper and ran home without opening it. Her excitement was almost more than she could bear. Not heeding her father's call to breakfast, she rushed upstairs and locked herself in her room. Her hands trembled so that she could hardly turn the pages. At last—yes, there it was: "April Showers."

❶ The paper dropped from her hands. What name had she read beneath the title? Had her emotion blinded her?

"April Showers, by *Kathleen Kyd*."

❷ Kathleen Kyd! Oh, cruel misprint! Oh, dastardly typographer! Through tears of rage and disappointment Theodora looked again; yes, there was no mistaking the hateful name. Her glance ran on. She found herself reading a first paragraph that she had never seen before. She read farther. All was strange. The horrible truth burst upon her: *It was not her story!*

She never knew how she got back to the station. She struggled through the crowd on the platform, and a gold-banded arm pushed her into the train just starting for Norton. It would be dark when she reached home; but that didn't matter—nothing mattered now. She sank into her seat, closing her eyes in the vain attempt to shut out the vision of the last few hours; but minute by minute memory forced her to relive it; she felt like a rebellious school child dragged forth to repeat the same detested "piece."

Although she did not know Boston well, she had made her way easily enough to the *Home Circle* building; at least, she supposed she had, since she remembered nothing till she found herself ascending the editorial stairs as easily as one does incredible things in dreams. ❸ She must have walked very fast, for her heart was beating furiously, and she had barely breath to whisper the editor's name to a young man who looked out at her from a glass case, like a zoological specimen. The young man led her past other glass cases containing similar specimens to an inner enclosure which seemed filled by an enormous presence. Theodora felt herself enveloped in the presence, submerged by it, gasping for air as she sank under its rising surges.

Gradually fragments of speech floated to the surface. "'April Showers?' Mrs. Kyd's new serial? *Your* manuscript, you say? You have a letter from me? The name, please? Evidently some unfortunate misunderstanding. One moment." And then a bell ringing, a zoological specimen ordered to unlock a safe, her name asked for again, the manuscript, her own precious manuscript, tied with Aunt Julia's ribbon, laid on the table before her, and her outcries, her protests, her interrogations, drowned in a flood of bland apology: "An unfortunate accident—Mrs. Kyd's manuscript received the same day—extraordinary coincidence in the choice of a title—duplicate answers sent by mistake—Miss Dace's novel hardly suited to their purpose—should of course have been returned—regrettable oversight—accidents would happen—sure she understood."

> **◆ Literary Focus**
> What is the resolution of the central conflict? ❹

The voice went on, like the steady pressure of a surgeon's hand on a shrieking nerve. When it stopped she was in the street. A cab nearly ran her down, and a car bell jangled furiously in her ears. She clutched her manuscript, carrying it tenderly through the crowd, like a live thing that had been hurt. She could not bear to look at its soiled edges and the ink stain on Aunt Julia's ribbon.

The train stopped with a jerk and she opened her eyes. It was dark, and by the windy flare of gas on the platform she saw the Norton passengers getting out. She stood up stiffly and followed them. A warm wind blew into her face the fragrance of the summer woods, and she remembered how, two months earlier, she had knelt among the dead leaves, pressing her lips to the first shoots of green. Then for the first time she thought of home. She had fled away in the morning without a word, and her heart sank at the thought of her mother's fears. And her father—how angry he would be! She bent her head under the coming storm of his derision.

The night was cloudy, and as she stepped into the darkness beyond the station a hand was slipped in hers. She stood still, too weary to feel frightened, and a voice said, quietly:

"Don't walk so fast, child. You look tired."

"Father!" Her hand dropped from his, but he recaptured it and drew it through his arm. When she found voice, it was to whisper, "You

Reteach

To help students understand plot, review with them its different elements:

- **exposition** introduces the story
- **conflict** sets up the struggle
- **rising action** consists of events that lead up to the climax
- **climax** is the height of the struggle
- **falling action** consists of events that follow the climax
- **resolution** is the end of the central conflict

Have students fill in the following visual with information from the story.

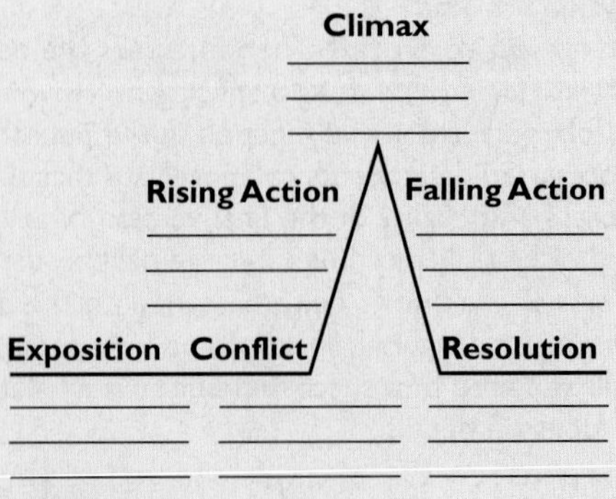

◆ **Reading Strategy**
5 Theodora is anticipating a negative reaction from her father. What are you anticipating?

were at the station?"

"It's such a good night I thought I'd stroll down and meet you."

Her arm trembled against his. She could not see his face in the dimness, but the light of his cigar looked down on her like a friendly eye, and she took courage to falter out: "Then you knew—"

"That you'd gone to Boston? Well, I rather thought you had."

They walked on slowly, and presently he added, "You see, you left the *Home Circle* lying in your room."

How she blessed the darkness and the muffled sky! She could not have borne the scrutiny of the tiniest star.

"Then mother wasn't very much frightened?"

"Why, no, she didn't appear to be. She's been busy all day over some toggery of Bertha's."

Theodora choked. "Father, I'll—" She groped for words, but they eluded her. "I'll do things—differently; I haven't meant—" Suddenly she heard herself bursting out: "It was all a mistake, you know—about my story. They didn't want it; they won't have it!" and she shrank back involuntarily from his impending mirth.

She felt the pressure of his arm, but he didn't speak, and she figured his mute hilarity. They moved on in silence. Presently he said:

"It hurts a bit just at first, doesn't it?"

"O father!"

He stood still, and the gleam of his cigar showed a face of unexpected participation.

"You see I've been through it myself."

"You, father? You?"

"Why, yes. Didn't I ever tell you? I wrote a novel once. I was just out of college, and didn't want to be a doctor. No; I wanted to be a genius, so I wrote a novel." 6

The doctor paused, and Theodora clung to him in a mute passion of commiseration. It was as if a drowning creature caught a live hand through the murderous fury of the waves.

"Father—O father!"

"It took me a year—a whole year's hard work; and when I'd finished it the public wouldn't have it, either; not at any price and that's why I came down to meet you, because I remembered my walk home."

◆ **Build Vocabulary**

commiseration (kə miz´ ər ā´ shən) *n.*: Sympathy; condolence

Guide for Responding

◆ *Literature and Your Life*

Reader's Response Did this story surprise you? Explain.

Thematic Focus How might "April Showers" have been different if it had been set in a different region of the country?

☑ Check Your Comprehension

1. What is Theodora's job in the family?
2. What is Theodora planning to do when the story begins?
3. How does the acceptance of Theodora's story change the way others behave toward her?
4. What does Theodora do when she sees that the story in the magazine is not her story?
5. What is her father's reaction to the mistake?

◆ Critical Thinking

INTERPRET

1. (a) What is the author's tone in "April Showers"? (b) How does the author's tone influence your view of Theodora? **[Analyze]**
2. How does Theodora change during the story? **[Compare and Contrast]**
3. Does this story support the saying: "If it seems too good to be true, it probably is"? Explain. **[Support]**

EVALUATE

4. What is the importance of Doctor Dace as a character in the story? **[Assess]**

APPLY

5. What lesson(s) from this story might apply to your own life? **[Generalize]**

Beyond the Selection

FURTHER READING

Other Works by Edith Wharton

Ethan Frome, The House of Mirth,
The Age of Innocence, The Buccaneers
A Backward Glance

Other Works About Upper Class Society

Washington Square, Henry James
The Great Gatsby, F. Scott Fitzgerald

We suggest that you preview these works before recommending them to students.

INTERNET

You can visit these sites for information about Edith Wharton. Please be aware that sites may have changed since this information was published.

To post your reactions to "April Showers," go to Daphne's Dream, a bookstore of reviews at **http://www.mindspring.com/~driordan/authors/wharton.htm** To learn about the Wharton Restoration in Lenox, MA, go to **http://www. berkshireweb.com/themount/**

We *strongly recommend* that you preview sites.

◆ Reading Strategy

5 Anticipate Events Few students are likely to expect the father's reaction. Some may have noticed, however, that he was amused and supportive in his own way when she got the good news.

◆ Literary Focus

6 Elements of Plot Remind students that Theodora had said that she couldn't count on her father to act like a father in a book. Point out that here, in the denouement, she comes to see him differently. Ask them to characterize their new relationship. *They are closer because of their shared disappointment.*

Reinforce and Extend

◆ *Literature and Your Life*

Theodora found a silver lining in her unfortunate publishing experience. Invite students to talk or write about a misfortune or disappointment they have experienced that led to something good unanticipated.

Answers

◆ *Literature and Your Life*

Reader's Response Students may express surprise at Dr. Dace's compassion.

Thematic Focus Students may note that, while some of the details might have varied, the essence of the story does not depend on its setting and would not change.

☑ Check Your Comprehension

1. She is responsible for running the house.
2. She's planning to submit her manuscript to *Home Circle* magazine for consideration.
3. Her family becomes more tolerant and the townspeople view her with awe.
4. She takes the train into Boston to visit the publisher and find out what happened.
5. He is sympathetic and consoling.

(Answers continue on p. 766)

Answers *(continued from p. 765)*

◆ Critical Thinking

Interpret

1. (a) The tone is ironic and satirical until the end, when it becomes compassionate. (b) It makes her seem naive.
2. At first, she is naive and self-absorbed; at the end, she is miserable, but she has a clearer sense of reality and a stronger tie to her father.
3. Yes; A prestigious magazine might not publish an unknown writer's first effort.
4. Though Dr. Dace is a secondary character, his experience enables Theodora to put her failure into perspective.
5. Students may see the silver lining in their own disappointments.

◆ Reading Strategy

1. (a) Students may have been excited for Theodora, but the ironic tone at the beginning was a clue that things were not going to turn out well. (b) Students should be prepared to support their answers.
2. Students' sense of anticipation was probably heightened by the discovery; they may have wondered what caused the mistake, what Theodora would do next, and how her family would react.

◆ Literary Focus

1. (a) The central conflict is Theodora's inner struggle between fulfilling her dream of becoming a novelist and fulfilling her real-life obligations to her family. (b) The conflict is introduced when Theodora fails to awaken in time to complete her household duties because she stayed up late completing her novel.
2. The climax is Theodora's horrified discovery that the "April Showers" in the magazine is not her "April Showers."
3. Suggested response: Everything that happens after Theodora learns from the magazine editor that her work will not be published can be considered the denouement.

◆ Build Vocabulary

Using the Latin Roots *-man-* *-manu-*

1. manual; 2. emancipate; 3. manipulated; 4. manufactures

Guide for Responding *(continued)*

◆ Reading Strategy

ANTICIPATE EVENTS

As you read, you—along with Theodora—**anticipated events**, or looked forward to what was going to happen. Anticipating can take a variety of forms: eagerness, excitement, uncertainty, dread, or foreboding are a few examples.

1. (a) What was your emotional response to the letter Theodora got from *Home Circle*? Why? (b) What did you think would happen next?
2. How did the news that *Home Circle* had published the wrong story affect your sense of anticipation?

◆ Literary Focus

DEVELOPMENT OF PLOT

The anticipation you felt when reading "April Showers" was partly a result of the twists and turns of the plot. The author skillfully handles the **development of plot**—exposition, conflict, rising action, climax, resolution, denouement—to evoke curiosity, surprise, and empathy in the reader.

1. (a) Describe the central conflict of the story. (b) What incident introduces this conflict?
2. What is the climax of the story? Explain.
3. Does this story have a denouement? Explain.

Beyond Literature

Cultural Connection

Freedom of Speech The decision not to publish Theodora's novel was a matter of taste and economics. In other parts of the world, some writers have to deal with censorship, too. In Nigeria, for example, the government banned the writings of contemporary poet and playwright Wole Soyinka. The first black African to receive the Nobel Prize for Literature, Soyinka spoke out against the dictatorship in Nigeria and called for human rights. In 1998, after several years of exile, Soyinka was allowed to return to Nigeria, where he continues to write. Should speech ever be limited? If so, where do you draw the line?

◆ Build Vocabulary

USING THE LATIN ROOTS *-man-, -manu-*

Replace the italicized word or phrase in each sentence with a word from the box that contains the Latin prefix *man-* (also spelled *manu-*).

manufactures	manual	manipulated	emancipate

1. A hammer is a *hand-operated* tool.
2. He decided to *free* his caged birds *from restraint*.
3. The potter *kneaded* the clay *with his hands* until it was soft.
4. That company *makes* motorcycles *into finished products*.

USING THE WORD BANK: Synonyms

Write the letter of the word closest in meaning to each of the following words from the word bank.

1. admonitory: (a) sorry, (b) warning, (c) financial
2. retrospective: (a) futuristic, (b) under, (c) back
3. antagonism: (a) hostility, (b) fright, (c) arrogance
4. contrition: (a) regret, (b) jocularity, (c) passivity
5. manuscript: (a) draft, (b) map, (c) autograph
6. commiseration: (a) wrath, (b) sympathy, (c) angst

◆ Grammar and Style

GERUND PHRASES

"April Showers" includes **gerund phrases**, which perform as subjects, direct objects, subject complements, and objects of prepositions.

A **gerund phrase** is a group of words serving as a noun and consisting of a gerund (*-ing* verb form that is used as a noun) and any modifiers or complements.

Practice Copy these examples into your notebook. For each one, underline at least one gerund phrase and identify how it is used in the sentence.

1. Unfortunately, the writing of a great novel leaves little time or memory for the lesser obligations of life . . .
2. . . . instead of looking after the children and seeing that breakfast was ready . . .
3. Theodora's sense of being in the right enabled her . . .
4. . . . there was no mistaking the hateful name.

Beyond Literature

Career Connection

Students may suggest that Theodora might have enjoyed working as an editor or a writer of romance novels, or as the fiction editor of a women's magazine.

Using the Word Bank

1. b 2. c 3. a 4. a 5. a 6. b

◆ Grammar and Style

1. writing of a great novel; subject
2. looking after the children and seeing that breakfast was ready; objects of preposition
3. being in the right; object of preposition
4. mistaking the hateful name; subject

Grammar Reinforcement

For additional instruction and practice, use the Recognizing and Using Phrases lesson on **Language Lab CD-ROM** and the page on Gerunds and Gerund Phrases, p. 33, in the *Writer's Solution Grammar Practice Book.*

Build Your Portfolio

Idea Bank

Writing

1. **Flier Copy** Theodora could have been in a writer's group—a group where writers read and appraise one another's work. Create a flier to advertise such a group and explain its benefits.
2. **Movie Scene** Choose one scene from the story to adapt for the big screen. Write a script based on the scene. Include set descriptions, camera directions, and dialogue. **[Career Link]**
3. **Critical Response** Wharton's publishers wrote that she had a "magnificent gift of story telling, pure and simple." Based on your reading of "April Showers," write an essay in which you critically respond to this appraisal.

Speaking, Listening, and Viewing

4. **Casting Discussion** In a small group, list the roles necessary for a movie version of "April Showers." Then discuss which actors would be right for each role, and why. **[Media Link]**
5. **Dramatic Monologue** Imagine that Theodora's neighbors throw a surprise party to celebrate her story. As Theodora, deliver a brief speech explaining to your neighbors what happened in Boston. **[Performing Arts Link]**

Researching and Representing

6. **Interior Design Project** Wharton had a special interest in interior decoration. Research principles of interior decor of the time the story was set, and create an oral and visual presentation showing what Theodora's house might have looked like. **[Art Link; Social Studies Link]**
7. **Contest Announcement** For *Home Circle*'s new story contest, write and design an eye-catching ad detailing submission guidelines and announcing awards for winning stories. **[Media Link]**

Online Activity www.phlit.phschool.com

Guided Writing Lesson

Short Story

Theodora might have done better to launch her writing career with a short story—a brief fictional narrative. Using a single setting, a simple plot, and just a few characters, write a short story that will succeed as well as "April Showers" does in holding audience attention.

Writing Skills Focus: Creating a Mood

Your single setting should include details that convey a particular **mood**, or atmosphere, as well as a sense of time and place.

Model From the Story

Downstairs the library clock struck two. Its muffled thump sounded like an admonitory knock against her bedroom floor. Two o'clock! and she had promised her mother to be up early . . .

In this passage, the author creates a hushed atmosphere with the words *muffled* and *admonitory*. The exclamation *Two o'clock!* throws a bit of fright into the mood. Choose vivid details to create a mood for your story.

Prewriting Ask yourself: What central idea do I want to convey? Who is my audience? Then decide on the narrative elements of your story: plot, characters, setting, theme, narrator, and point of view.

Drafting Begin your draft by describing your setting and creating a mood. Use vivid language to make your setting and mood enticing. Then introduce the characters and the conflict. Be sure to bring the conflict to a climax and resolution.

Revising Think about ways to strengthen your story. For example, can the plot and conflict be made clearer? You may go through several rounds of revision before you are satisfied with your story.

✓ ASSESSMENT OPTIONS

Formal Assessment, Selection Test, pp. 232–234, and Assessment Resources Software. The selection test is designed so that it can be easily customized to the performance levels of your students.

Alternative Assessment, p. 49, includes options for less advanced students, more advanced students, verbal/linguistic learners, bodily/kinesthetic learners, and visual/spatial learners.

PORTFOLIO ASSESSMENT
Use the following rubrics in the ***Alternative Assessment*** booklet to assess student writing:
Flier Copy: Persuasion Rubric, p. 120
Movie Scene: Drama Rubric, p. 124
Critical Response: Critical Review Rubric, p. 126
Guided Writing Lesson: Fictional Narrative Rubric, p. 110

Idea Bank

Customizing for
Performance Levels
Following are suggestions for matching Idea Bank topics with your students' performance levels:
Less Advanced Students: 1, 4
Average Students: 2, 5, 7
More Advanced Students: 3, 6

Customizing for
Learning Modalities
Following are suggestions for matching Idea Bank topics with your students' learning modalities:
Interpersonal: 4
Verbal/Linguistic: 4, 5
Visual/Spatial: 6, 7

Guided Writing Lesson

Refer students to the Writing Process Handbook, p. 1192, for instruction on the writing process, and p. 1194 for further information on Narration.

For more prewriting, elaboration, and revision strategies, see *Prentice Hall Writing and Grammar.*

Writing and Language Transparencies Display the Story Map Transparency, p. 99, to help students organize the elements of their short stories.

Writers at Work Videodisc
Have students view the videodisc segment on Narration (Ch. 2) featuring N. Scott Momaday to learn his approach to narrative writing. Have students discuss their response to Momaday's rules for writing.

Play frames 18612 to 19873

Writing Lab CD-ROM
Have students complete the tutorial on Narration. Follow these steps:

1. Use the Inspirations for Narration section to help students come up with an idea for their short stories.
2. To develop their settings, students can complete the Setting Profile Activity.
3. After drafting on the computer, students can use the Self-Evaluation Checklist to aid revision.

Prepare and Engage

LESSON OBJECTIVES

1. **To develop vocabulary and word identification skills**
   - Related Words: *Brutal*
   - Using the Word Bank: Synonyms
2. **To use a variety of reading strategies to comprehend a poem**
   - Connect Your Experience
   - Reading Strategy: Respond
3. **To express and support responses to the text**
   - Critical Thinking
   - Idea Bank: Postcard
4. **To analyze literary elements**
   - Literary Focus: Apostrophe
   - Idea Bank: Analysis of Repetition
5. **To read in order to research self-selected and assigned topics**
   - Idea Bank: Research Project
   - Idea Bank: Population Breakdown
6. **To plan, prepare, organize, and present literary interpretations**
   - Idea Bank: Stand-Up Routine
   - Idea Bank: Disagreement
   - Speaking, Listening, and Viewing Mini-Lesson (ATE)
7. **To use recursive writing processes to write a description for a travel guide**
   - Guided Writing Lesson
8. **To increase knowledge of the rules of grammar and usage**
   - Grammar and Style: Four Types of Sentences

Test Preparation

Reading Comprehension: Analyze Sentence Meaning (ATE, p. 769)
The teaching tips and sample test item in this workshop support the instruction and practice in the unit workshop:
Reading Comprehension: Sentence-Completion Questions (SE, p. 863)

Guide for Interpreting

Carl Sandburg *(1878–1967)*

You may know the work of a contemporary poet or songwriter who seems to speak right to you. The poetry of Carl Sandburg seemed to speak directly to many of the people of his time. It celebrated the lives and the spirit of ordinary Americans of that era.

Modest Beginnings The son of Swedish immigrants, Sandburg was born and raised in Galesburg, Illinois. Forced to go to work at an early age, Sandburg attended school on an irregular basis. As an adolescent, he knew firsthand the life of a laborer.

By writing about mills and factories, Sandburg paid tribute to the struggles and hopes of the poor.

After spending six years working at a variety of jobs, Sandburg enlisted in the army in 1898, at the time of the Spanish-American War. After the war, he attended college, but dropped out before graduating. He then spent several years traveling around the country, again working at a variety of jobs.

The Bard of Chicago In 1912, Sandburg settled in Chicago, one of the nation's great industrial cities. He worked as a newspaper reporter and began to publish poetry. His first book, *Chicago Poems*, published in 1916, met with success. Sandburg soon earned widespread recognition, and helped establish Chicago as a leading literary center. During the next ten years, Sandburg published three more successful collections of poetry: *Cornhuskers* (1918), *Smoke and Steel* (1920), and *Slabs of the Sunburst West* (1922). While continuing to write poetry, Sandburg then began touring the country delivering lectures on Walt Whitman and Abraham Lincoln—two men whom he greatly admired—and started a career as a folk singer. He also spent a great deal of time collecting material for a biography of Lincoln and he prepared an anthology of American folk songs, *The American Songbook* (1927). In 1940, Carl Sandburg received a Pulitzer Prize for his multi-volume biography of Lincoln, and in 1951 he received a second Pulitzer Prize for his *Complete Poems*.

Power of Positive Thinking Sandburg was an optimist who believed in the power of ordinary Americans to fulfill their dreams. Throughout his career, Sandburg reached out to his readers with poems that were concrete and direct. He was not interested in experimenting with complicated syntax or images, as were some other poets of his generation.

Sandburg offered a variety of definitions of poetry, among them these two: "Poetry is a search for syllables to shoot at the barriers of the unknown and the unknowable" and "Poetry is the opening and closing of a door, leaving those who look through to guess about what is seen during a moment."

◆ Background for Understanding

SOCIAL STUDIES: SANDBURG AND 1920'S AMERICA

The 1920's, the decade when Sandburg wrote many of his greatest poems, was a time of activity and excitement in America. The economy was booming, jazz filled the airwaves, the Charleston was the rage at dance halls, and Hollywood started producing talking films. Called the Roaring Twenties, this decade was celebrated in the literature of F. Scott Fitzgerald, among other writers.

Sandburg's poems, too, reflected what many Americans believed in the 1920's: There was no limit to what they could achieve. However, Sandburg also focused attention on the lives of those who weren't getting rich: workers in meatpacking houses, mills, and factories. The result was a simple and straightforward verse that captured the energy of industrial America.

Prentice Hall Literature Program Resources

REINFORCE / RETEACH / EXTEND

Selection Support Pages
Build Vocabulary: Using Related Words: *Brutal*, p. 231
Grammar and Style: Types of Sentences, p. 232
Reading Strategy: Respond, p. 233
Literary Focus: Apostrophe, p. 234

Strategies for Diverse Student Needs Reword Poet's Ideas, p. 50

Beyond Literature
Career Connection: Marketing, p. 50

Formal Assessment Selection Test, pp. 235–237; Assessment Resources Software

Alternative Assessment, p. 50

Resource Pro CD-ROM

Literature CD-ROM
The History of American Literature: Part 2, Disc 1, Feature 5

Listening to Literature Audiocassettes

Chicago ◆ Grass

◆ Literature and Your Life

Connect Your Experience

If you've ever celebrated the comeback of someone who seemed to have been defeated—a team scoring four runs in the bottom of the ninth, for example—then you understand the spirit in which Carl Sandburg wrote. In reading these poems, you'll see that Sandburg recognized people's (and cities') failures—but he cheered the invincibility of their souls.

Journal Writing Do you think that most of the residents of your town or city have a strong spirit? Write about one or two events that illustrate their general outlook on life.

Thematic Focus: From Every Corner of the Land

Carl Sandburg paid special attention to the voices of industrial workers in the nation's heartland. Think about the ways in which these voices differ from those in other regions of the country.

◆ Build Vocabulary

Related Words: *Brutal*

Sandburg uses the word *brutal* to refer to Chicago. Knowing the meaning of *brutal*—cruel or harsh—can help you determine the meanings of related words such as *brute*, *brutality*, and *brutish*.

Word Bank

Preview this list of words from the poems.

brutal
wanton
cunning

◆ Grammar and Style

Four Types of Sentences

In these poems, Sandburg uses all four types of sentences:

I am the grass. This sentence is **declarative** because it makes a statement and ends with a period.

What place is this? This sentence is **interrogative** because it asks a question and ends with a question mark.

Pile the bodies high at Austerlitz and Waterloo. This sentence is **imperative** because it is a statement that gives a command or makes a request.

. . . under his wrist is the pulse, and under his ribs the heart of the people, Laughing! This sentence is **exclamatory** because it expresses a strong emotion and ends with an exclamation point.

◆ Literary Focus

Apostrophe

Apostrophe is a literary device in which the speaker or narrator directly addresses a person or thing. For example, in "Chicago," Sandburg addresses the city as if it were a person:

> They tell me you are wicked
> and I believe them . . .
>
> And they tell me you are
> crooked and I answer:
> Yes . . .

As you read "Chicago," think about the effect this technique creates. Why do you think Sandburg chose to speak directly to the city of Chicago?

◆ Reading Strategy

Respond

When you **respond** to a poem, you think about the message that the poet has conveyed and reflect on how you personally feel about the topic. Consider how the poet's message relates to your own life and to the world in which you live, and think about how you can use or apply what you learned from the poem.

As you read these poems, connect your own experiences to the images and ideas presented, and react to the message Sandburg conveys.

Interest Grabber Obtain the video of the John Hughes 1986 film *Ferris Bueller's Day Off,* which offers viewers a whirlwind tour of the "City of the Big Shoulders" as it looks today. Play portions of the movie to show scenes in which the teen and his high school friends are in the Loop, at the Board of Trade, at a Cubs game at Wrigley Field, at a parade down Michigan Avenue, and at a posh French restaurant. Ask students to give their impressions of the city. Then tell students that they are going to read a famous poem about Chicago, written nearly a century ago. Have them keep modern Chicago in mind as they read. Invite them to compare the images from the film with images Sandburg presents.

Customize for
Less Proficient Readers
Guide students to understand that with the rough, robust, and coarse images at the beginning of the poem, Sandburg is celebrating the essence of Chicago, not complaining about the city. Help them to appreciate that to him these images are rich and heroic. Read the poem aloud or play audiocassette to convey the poem's gusto.

Listening to Literature Audiocassettes

Customize for
AP Students
Have students contrast the general feelings and emotions behind the two poems as they read them. Also ask them to compare the techniques Sandburg applies in both, such as his use of parallelism and the way he varies the lengths of the lines for effect.

Customize for
Visual/Spatial Learners
Provide photos of the Chicago Sandburg portrays as well as "before and after" photos of Gettysburg and the World War I battlefields. Ask students to think about whether the tone of the poems matches the visual images in these pictures.

Test Preparation Workshop

Reading Comprehension:
Analyze Sentence Meaning Many standardized tests require students to correctly answer sentence-completion questions. Often, more than one choice can complete a sentence. Use the following sample item to show students how to analyze sentence meaning, decide whether it is positive or negative, and eliminate choices that have the opposite sense.

Carl Sandburg's poems focus on the lives of the working classes. By writing about mills and factories, he honored the _____ and hopes of the poor.

A cowardice
B avarice
C struggles
D idleness

The context indicates that the missing word will have a positive connotation. *A, B,* and *D* are all negative. *C* is the best choice.

Develop Understanding

One-Minute Insight Using spirited but simple words and phrases, Sandburg expresses his love and admiration for what he sees as a vital, brawny, hearty, sweating giant of a city.

Literature CD-ROM To introduce the poem, use *The History of American Literature:* Part 2, Disc 1, Feature 5, which features Sandburg's "Chicago."

◆ Background for Understanding

❶ History When Sandburg wrote his poem, Chicago was the center of the nation's meat packing industry, thanks to the city's ideal geographical location and to new developments in the shipping of beef. As a way to reduce the freight charges of transporting live cattle, the animals were slaughtered in Chicago and the cuts of beef shipped at great savings.

◆ Critical Thinking

❷ Analyze Point out the changes in imagery, and the speaker's pride in the city's accomplishments and resiliency. Ask student to analyze the effect of following lengthy lines with very short ones. *It draws attention to the characteristics presented in the brief lines.*

◆ Reading Strategy

❸ Respond Ask students to respond to Sandburg's use of personification here. *The poet's Chicago is tough, resilient, young, enduring, and full of heart.*

◆ Critical Thinking

❹ Connect Point out that the last line is a more positive version of the poem's opening lines. This technique, known as parallelism, helps to emphasize important ideas and to contribute to the natural rhythm of a poem.

Connecting to World Literature

To connect "Chicago" to a world literature selection, see "Discoverers of Chile," p. 1196.

CHICAGO

CARL SANDBURG

Connections to World Literature, *page 1196*

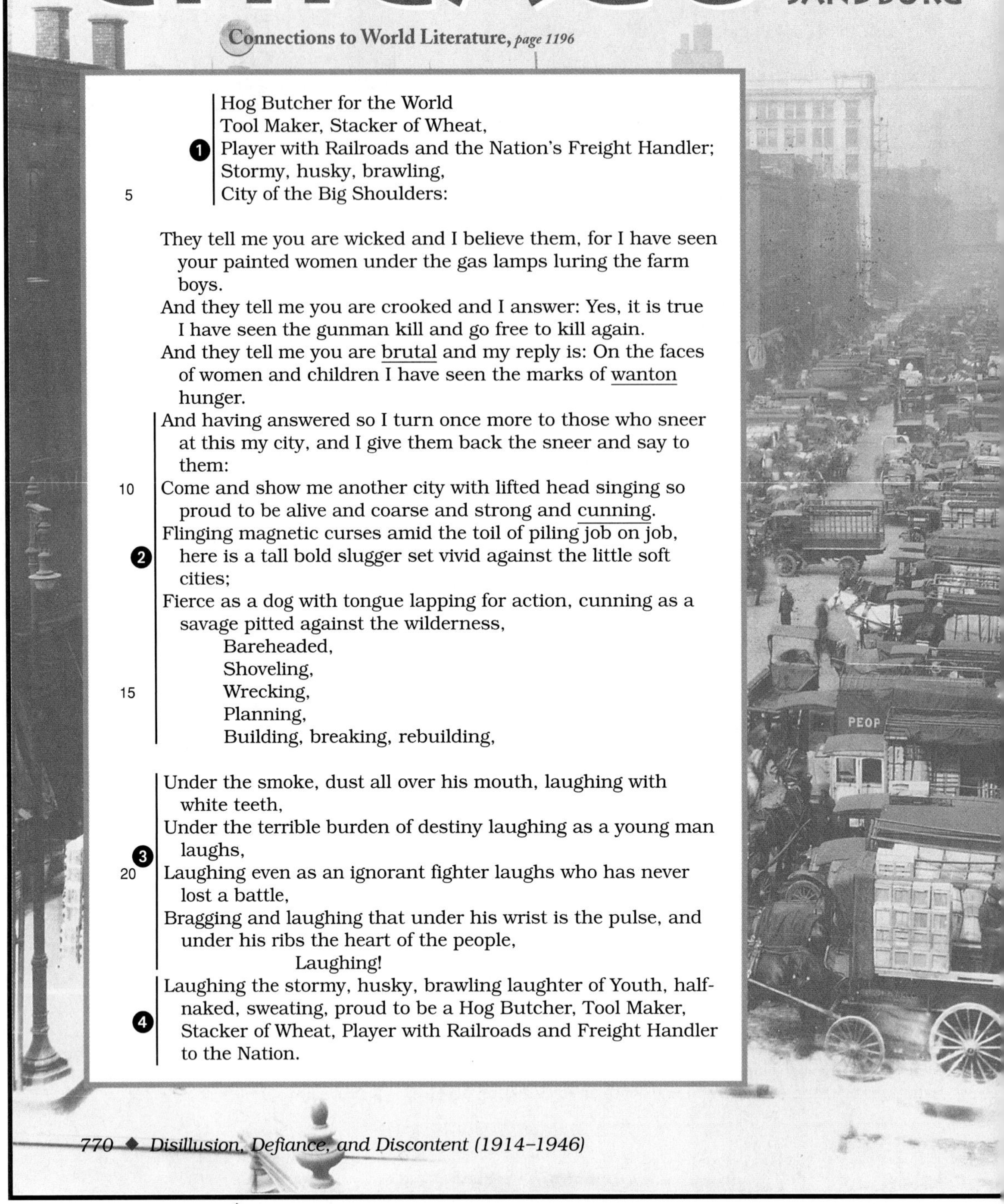

❶
Hog Butcher for the World
Tool Maker, Stacker of Wheat,
Player with Railroads and the Nation's Freight Handler;
Stormy, husky, brawling,
City of the Big Shoulders:

They tell me you are wicked and I believe them, for I have seen your painted women under the gas lamps luring the farm boys.
And they tell me you are crooked and I answer: Yes, it is true I have seen the gunman kill and go free to kill again.
And they tell me you are brutal and my reply is: On the faces of women and children I have seen the marks of wanton hunger.
❷
And having answered so I turn once more to those who sneer at this my city, and I give them back the sneer and say to them:
Come and show me another city with lifted head singing so proud to be alive and coarse and strong and cunning.
Flinging magnetic curses amid the toil of piling job on job, here is a tall bold slugger set vivid against the little soft cities;
Fierce as a dog with tongue lapping for action, cunning as a savage pitted against the wilderness,
　　Bareheaded,
　　Shoveling,
　　Wrecking,
　　Planning,
　　Building, breaking, rebuilding,

❸
Under the smoke, dust all over his mouth, laughing with white teeth,
Under the terrible burden of destiny laughing as a young man laughs,
Laughing even as an ignorant fighter laughs who has never lost a battle,
Bragging and laughing that under his wrist is the pulse, and under his ribs the heart of the people,
　　　　Laughing!
❹
Laughing the stormy, husky, brawling laughter of Youth, half-naked, sweating, proud to be a Hog Butcher, Tool Maker, Stacker of Wheat, Player with Railroads and Freight Handler to the Nation.

Speaking, Listening, and Viewing Mini-Lesson

Disagreement
This mini-lesson supports the Speaking, Listening, and Viewing activity in the Idea Bank (p. 773).

Introduce the Concept Review the description of the activity. Inform students that participants will be judged on the persuasiveness and pertinence of their arguments. Suggest that they consider using appropriate humor to enhance their points.

Develop Background Have students review the poem, listing opinions for and against the city. They can brainstorm for additional items that reflect the spirit of the poet's views.

Apply the Information Emphasize that students should attempt to act like proud, brawling Chicagoans, but they should also listen to each other's points with respect. Audience members can monitor the interactions to make sure that they stay at the level of healthy disagreement.

Assess the Outcome Assess students' performances on how thoughtfully and persuasively they have made their arguments, and how accurately they have captured or disputed Sandburg's views.

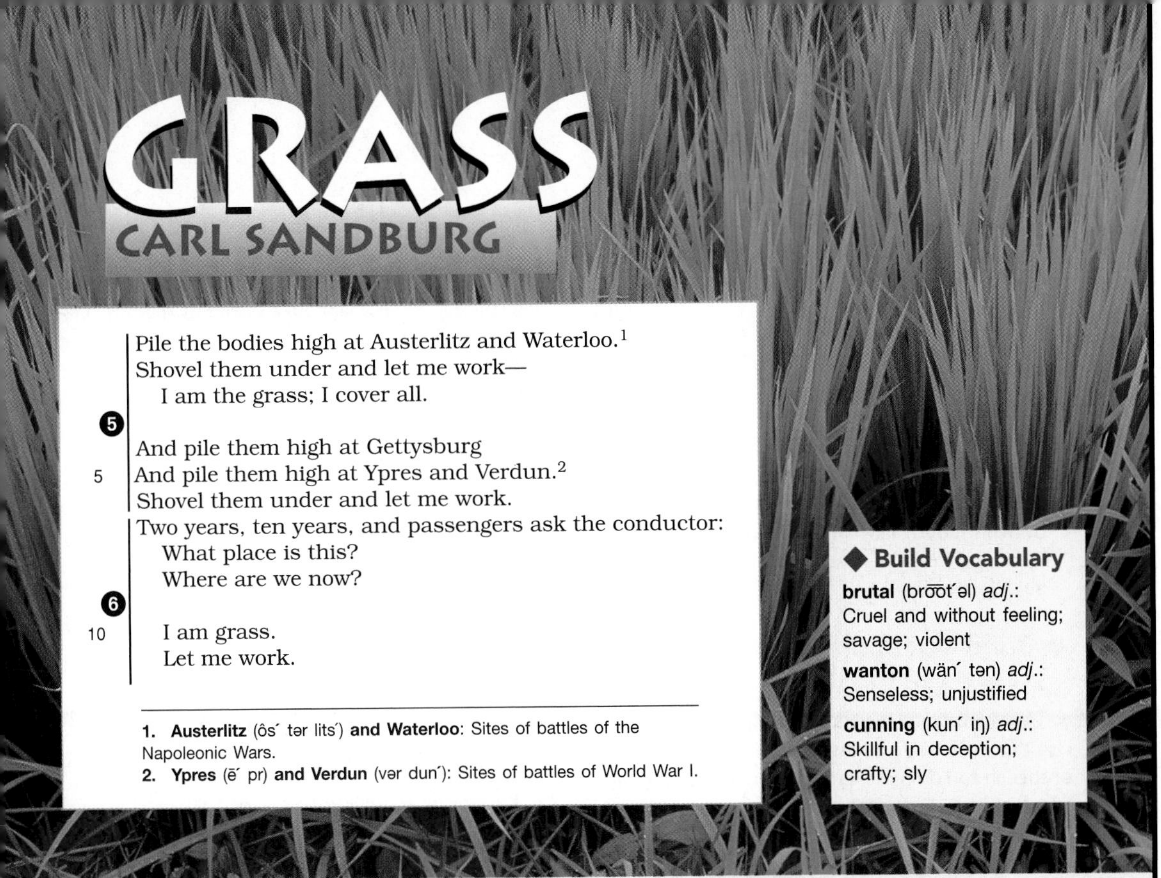

GRASS

CARL SANDBURG

Pile the bodies high at Austerlitz and Waterloo.[1]
Shovel them under and let me work—
  I am the grass; I cover all.

❺

And pile them high at Gettysburg
And pile them high at Ypres and Verdun.[2]
Shovel them under and let me work.
Two years, ten years, and passengers ask the conductor:
  What place is this?
  Where are we now?

❻

  I am grass.
  Let me work.

1. **Austerlitz** (ôs´ tər lits´) **and Waterloo**: Sites of battles of the Napoleonic Wars.
2. **Ypres** (ē´ pr) **and Verdun** (vər dun´): Sites of battles of World War I.

◆ Build Vocabulary

brutal (bro͞ot´əl) *adj.*: Cruel and without feeling; savage; violent

wanton (wän´ tən) *adj.*: Senseless; unjustified

cunning (kun´ iŋ) *adj.*: Skillful in deception; crafty; sly

Guide for Responding

◆ Literature and Your Life

Reader's Response Unlike some poets, Sandburg tells you what to feel and what to think. How do you react to this directness? Do you enjoy, admire, or resent it? Why?

Thematic Focus How does Chicago differ from your town? (Or, if you live in Chicago, how does Sandburg's Chicago differ from the city you know?)

☑ Check Your Comprehension

1. What do the different places mentioned in "Grass" have in common?
2. Name two of the industries for which Chicago was famous.

◆ Critical Thinking

INTERPRET

1. According to the speaker, how do other people see Chicago? Support your answer. **[Interpret]**
2. Why does the speaker appreciate Chicago? **[Interpret]**
3. What does "Grass" say about the end result of war? **[Draw Conclusions]**
4. What does "Grass" say about the relationship between people and nature? **[Draw Conclusions]**

EVALUATE

5. In "Grass," Sandburg uses only 11 lines to get his message across. Does he achieve his goal? Explain. **[Make a Judgment]**

Develop Understanding

One-Minute Insight

In this brief poem, Carl Sandburg observes that today there is only grass where once monumental battles between great armies took place; where there was once the deafening booms of cannons and the gruesome cries of the dying, there is now only grass. The serenity of nature obscures the horror and futility of war.

◆ Critical Thinking

❺ **Interpret** Ask students to tell who is speaking and who is being addressed. *The grass is speaking to humanity.*

◆ Critical Thinking

❻ **Analyze** Ask students to explain how the questions asked by the passengers reflect the pointlessness of war. *The fact that no one recognizes or remembers the battle sites suggests that many have forgotten the reasons for the wars in which so many lost their lives.*

Reinforce and Extend

Answers

◆ Literature and Your Life

Reader's Response Students should be prepared to explain their responses.

Thematic Response Responses should show an awareness of regional variations.

☑ Check Your Comprehension

1. All the places are battlefields.
2. Answers include meatpacking, toolmaking, grain supplying, and transportation.

(Answers continue on p. 772)

Beyond the Selection

FURTHER READING

Other Works by Carl Sandburg

Rootabaga Stories; Complete Poems; Abraham Lincoln: The Prairie Years; Abraham Lincoln: The War Years; Steichen the Photographer

Other Works About Chicago

The Jungle, Upton Sinclair
Eight Men Out, Eliot Asinof
Hard Times, Studs Turkel

We suggest that you preview these works before recommending them to students.

INTERNET

To enhance students' knowledge of Chicago, encourage them to visit the following site. Be aware, however, that the site may have changed since this information was published.

To find out more about the city of Chicago, go to **http://www.chicago.thelinks.com/**

We *strongly recommend* that you preview the site before you send students to them.

Answers *(continued from p. 771)*

◆ Critical Thinking

1. Other people see Chicago in mostly negative terms, as wicked, crooked, and brutal.
2. The speaker appreciates Chicago because, despite its brutality, it is vigorous, powerful, brave, and representative of the strength of ordinary people.
3. "Grass" suggests that the end result of war is death and futility.
4. It suggests that nature is more powerful than human beings.
5. Students may respond that Sandburg does, in just a few lines, convey the idea that throughout the world and throughout history, the forces of nature have blotted out the results of human wars and human history.

◆ Reading Strategy

1. (a) Sandburg is emphasizing the pointlessness of war. (b) Most students will probably say that the simple imagery of the poem helped bring home the futility of losing lives in wars that are so soon forgotten.
2. (a) Students may say that they used the senses of smell (smoke), vision, and hearing (laughing) to respond. (b) Sample response: I pictured someone strong, reckless, and powerful who thrives on the filth and chaos of the city.

◆ Build Vocabulary

Using Related Words: *Brutal*

1. brute; 2. brutality; 3. brutish; 4. brutalize

Using the Word Bank

1. b 2. c 3. c

◆ Literary Focus

1. Sandburg uses apostrophe in lines 6–8.
2. (a) The section addressed to the city's critics contains more positive images of Chicago's vitality and pride. (b) The section that uses apostrophe contains many negative images of the city, such as murder and hunger, while the speaker uses more positive images to address the city's critics. It is as if the speaker is willing to acknowledge the city's flaws to the city itself, but not to critics or outsiders.

Guide for Responding *(continued)*

◆ Reading Strategy

RESPOND

To **respond** to a poem, think about what the writing says. Consider how the poem makes you feel, and notice what thoughts the poem sets off in your mind.

Combine your knowledge with your emotional reactions to "Grass" and "Chicago" to answer these questions.

1. (a) What is Sandburg's message in "Grass"? (b) How do you react to that message? Why?
2. (a) What senses did you draw upon to respond to the description "Under the smoke, dust all over his mouth, laughing with white teeth" from "Chicago"? (b) What was your response to the description? Explain.

◆ Build Vocabulary

USING RELATED WORDS: *BRUTAL*

The word *brutal* means "cruel; crude; harsh." Use this knowledge and what you know about parts of speech to complete each sentence with *brutish, brutalize, brute,* or *brutality.*

1. Sam was so rough with my brother that I told him he was behaving like a __?__ and asked him to leave.
2. Many who participated in World War I were stunned by the __?__ on the front lines.
3. Use your knife and fork, and stop that __?__ behavior at once!
4. Those who __?__ innocent animals should receive the harshest punishment.

USING THE WORD BANK: Synonyms

Write the letter of the word closest in meaning to each of the following words from the word bank:

1. brutal: (a) unwise, (b) violent, (c) heavy
2. cunning: (a) suspicious, (b) diligent, (c) crafty
3. wanton: (a) rapid, (b) kind, (c) rash

◆ Literary Focus

APOSTROPHE

Carl Sandburg uses **apostrophe**—the literary technique of directly addressing a person or thing—to make the city of Chicago come alive. By addressing Chicago as *you,* Sandburg shows us that his relationship with the city resembles a close relationship with a person.

1. Identify the lines in which Sandburg uses apostrophe.
2. Compare the lines that directly address the city with those that are addressed to the people who criticize Chicago. (a) Which section contains more positive images? (b) Analyze the difference between the two sections.
3. Identify at least one feeling Sandburg has for Chicago that he might feel toward a close friend. Support your answer with examples from the poem.

◆ Grammar and Style

SENTENCE TYPES

By varying sentence types, writers can add interest to their creative works.

> The four types of sentences are **declarative, imperative, interrogative,** and **exclamatory**.

Practice On your paper, write each sentence, add the correct end punctuation, and label the sentence type.

1. Shovel me under and let me work
2. I am the grass
3. Where are we now
4. Come and show me another city
5. What place is this

Writing Application Write an essay in which you praise and/or criticize your city or town. Use all four types of sentences in your essay.

3. Possible answer: Sandburg has warm feelings toward the city.

◆ Grammar and Style

Practice

1. Shovel me under and let me work. (Imperative)
2. I am the grass. (Declarative)
3. Where are we now? (Interrogative)
4. Come and show me another city. (Imperative)
5. What place is this? (Interrogative)

Writing Application

Check to see that students have included and properly punctuated all four types of sentences.

Grammar Reinforcement

For more instruction and practice, use the page on the four functions of sentences (p. 19) in the *Grammar Practice Book.*

Reteach

To reteach this selection, use ***Strategies for Diverse Student Needs,*** p. 50.

Build Your Portfolio

Idea Bank

Writing

1. **Postcard** Imagine that you've traveled to Chicago, and write a postcard to a friend back home, describing your impressions of the city.
2. **Apostrophe** Write a poem to the place that means the most to you, making sure to address the place as *you*. In your poem, reflect upon the positive and negative aspects of the place.
3. **Analysis of Repetition** Sandburg is famous for repetition. Using either of his poems, write an analysis that explains the effect that the repeated elements (words, phrases, sentence structure, grammatical elements, and so on) have on the overall effect of the poem.

Speaking, Listening, and Viewing

4. **Disagreement** With a partner, role-play a disagreement between two Chicago residents. One defends the city, and one attacks it. Use the opinions expressed in "Chicago" as a guide.
5. **Stand-up Routine** Acting as the city of Chicago, deliver a comedy routine. You can either brag about how tough you are or whine about how everyone criticizes you. **[Performing Arts Link]**

Researching and Representing

6. **Research Project** "Grass" mentions two battles from the Napoleonic Wars. Conduct research to learn more about these wars. Present your findings in a report along with illustrations or other graphic aids. **[Social Studies Link]**
7. **Population Breakdown** Using the Internet or the library, find the total population of Chicago. Collect statistics related to that population (male/female totals, totals by ethnic group, and so on). Calculate percentages of the total represented by each category. **[Math Link]**

Online Activity www.phlit.phschool.com

Guided Writing Lesson

Description for a Travel Guide

In "Chicago," Carl Sandburg conveys that city's energy through descriptive details of the activities that go on there. As a writer assigned to produce a travel guide, write a vivid, exciting description of a place you want to sell to an audience of travelers.

Writing Skills Focus: Precise Details

Use specific examples to create a vivid and precise picture of a place. Don't just say a city has great ethnic restaurants; tell your readers they can find Mexican, Thai, and Ethiopian food there. *Describe* that food.

Take "Chicago" as your example. Sandburg doesn't just say the city resembles a powerful young laborer; he uses verbs that show the power:

Model From the Poem

Bareheaded,/Shoveling,/Wrecking,/Planning,/Building, breaking, rebuilding, . . .

Prewriting Think of a place you know well. On a chart like this one, jot down its most positive features—interesting architecture, great museums, crystal-clear freshwater lakes. Then list specific examples of each.

Features	Examples

Drafting You might want to chose your subject's strongest feature first. Describe exactly why visitors must see this feature, and why it reflects the place as a whole.

Revising Review your draft. Did you bring a place alive with description? Check to see where you can replace vague or general language with precise nouns and vivid verbs.

✓ ASSESSMENT OPTIONS

Formal Assessment, Selection Test, pp. 235–237, and Assessment Resources Software. The selection test is designed so that it can be easily customized to the performance levels of your students.

Alternative Assessment, p. 50, includes options for less advanced students, more advanced students, intrapersonal learners, visual/spatial learners, and verbal/linguistic learners.

PORTFOLIO ASSESSMENT
Use the following rubrics in the ***Alternative Assessment*** booklet to assess student writing:
Postcard: Expression Rubric, p. 109
Apostrophe: Poetry Rubric, p. 123
Analysis of Repetition: Literary Analysis/Interpretation Rubric, p. 127
Guided Writing Lesson: Description Rubric, p. 112

Idea Bank

Customizing for
Performance Levels
Following are suggestions for matching Idea Bank topics with your students' performance levels:
Less Advanced Students: 1, 5
Average Students: 2, 4, 6
More Advanced Students: 3, 7

Customizing for
Learning Modalities
Following are suggestions for matching Idea Bank topics with your students' learning modalities:
Interpersonal: 4
Verbal/Linguistic: 4, 5, 6
Visual/Spatial: 6
Logical/Mathematical: 7

Customize for
Less Proficient Readers and English Language Learners
As an alternate means of assessing these students, you may wish to use the ***Strategies for Diverse Students Needs*** page titled Reword Poet's Ideas, p. 50, in ***Teaching Resources.***

Guided Writing Lesson

Refer students to the Writing Process Handbook, p. 1192, for instruction on the writing process, and p. 1194 for further information on Description.

For more prewriting, elaboration, and revision strategies, see *Prentice Hall Writing and Grammar.*

Writer's Solution

Writing Lab CD-ROM
Have students complete the tutorial on Description. Follow these steps:

1. Refer students to the annotated model of a travel brochure in the About Description section.
2. Use the Word Bins for Places and Sensory Words in the Drafting section to help Students create precise details as they draft on the computer.
3. To aid revision, students can use the revision checker to identify vague or overused adjectives.

Prepare and Engage

LESSON OBJECTIVES

1. **To develop vocabulary and word identification skills**
   - Greek Prefixes: *dys*
   - Using the Word Bank: Sentence Completions
2. **To use a variety of reading strategies to comprehend a short story**
   - Connect Your Experience
   - Reading Strategy: Clarify Sequence of Events
3. **To increase knowledge of other cultures and to connect common elements across cultures**
   - Connecting Themes Across Cultures (ATE)
4. **To express and support responses to the text**
   - Critical Thinking
   - Idea Bank: Doctor's Report
   - Idea Bank: Letter to George
   - Idea Bank: Course Description
5. **To analyze literary elements**
   - Literary Focus: Stream of Consciousness
   - Background for Understanding: Culture
   - Viewing and Representing Mini-Lesson (ATE)
   - Idea Bank: Free Painting
6. **To read in order to research self-selected or assigned topics**
   - Questions for Research
   - Idea Bank: Report on Hospice Care
7. **To plan, prepare, organize, and present literary interpretations**
   - Idea Bank: Conversation
   - Idea Bank: Lecture
8. **To use recursive writing processes to write a dramatic monologue**
   - Guided Writing Lesson
9. **To increase knowledge of the rules of grammar and usage**
   - Grammar and Style: Imperative Sentences

Test Preparation

Reading Comprehension: Analyze Sentence Meaning (ATE, p. 775)
The teaching tips and sample test item in this workshop support the instruction and practice in the unit workshop:
Reading Comprehension: Sentence-Completion Questions (SE, p. 863)

Guide for Interpreting

Katherine Anne Porter
(1890–1980)

The exceptionally well-crafted fiction of Katherine Anne Porter focuses primarily on human relationships and on people's varied responses to a rapidly changing world.

In her writing, Porter sought to understand people's motivations and emotions.

Porter's dual interests in people's religious attitudes and the rural South—pursued in much of her work—may have originated in her childhood. Born in Indian Creek, Texas, she was raised in poverty and haphazardly educated in convent schools.

Beginnings as a Writer Porter began writing at an early age; as a young adult, she worked as a journalist. Her work took her to many places, including Mexico City, where she lived for eight years. There she developed an interest in writing fiction and in 1922 she published her first story, "María Concepción," in *Century*, a highly regarded literary magazine. Eight years later, she published her first book, *Flowering Judas* (1930). The book, a collection of six short stories, was praised by critics and earned Porter widespread recognition. *Flowering Judas and Other Stories*, an expanded edition of the book containing ten stories, was published in 1935.

Literary Achievements Katherine Anne Porter went on to produce several other major works, including *Noon Wine* (1937), *Pale Horse, Pale Rider* (1939), *No Safe Harbor* (1941), *The Leaning Tower and Other Stories* (1944), and *Ship of Fools* (1962)—Porter's only novel. Although her body of work was relatively small in comparison to some of the other major writers of her time, her works consistently received high praise from critics and earned her a place among the finest writers of this century. Her *Collected Stories* (1965), was awarded the Pulitzer Prize and the National Book Award. In addition, her novel, *Ship of Fools*, was made into a popular film.

In his review of *The Leaning Tower and Other Stories,* critic Edmund Wilson tried to account for the "elusive" quality that made Porter an "absolutely first-rate artist." He said, "These stories are not illustrations of anything that is reducible to a moral law or a political or social analysis or even a principle of human behavior. What they show us are human relationships in their constantly shifting phases and in the moments of which their existence is made. There is not place for general reflections; you are to live through the experiences as the characters do." You'll discover that Wilson's observations can be applied to "The Jilting of Granny Weatherall," which takes readers on a journey through the various phases of an old woman's life in the moments leading up to her death.

◆ Background for Understanding

CULTURE: POST-WAR DESPAIR

Katherine Anne Porter's life view was shaped by the universal sense of disillusionment resulting from World War I, the despair of the Great Depression, and the World War II horrors of Nazism and nuclear warfare. In her words, she lived life "under the heavy threat of world catastrophe." In response, Porter poured all her energies into "the effort to grasp the meaning of those threats. . . ." Sometimes, as in the novel *Ship of Fools,* this exploration focused on large-scale social and political issues such as Nazism. In contrast, works like "The Jilting of Granny Weatherall" pinpointed the drifting and dissolving families and communities of the modern age.

Prentice Hall Literature Program Resources

REINFORCE / RETEACH / EXTEND

Selection Support Pages
Build Vocabulary: Greek Prefixes: *dys-*, p. 235
Grammar and Style: Imperative Sentences, p. 236
Reading Strategy: Clarify Chronological Order, p. 237
Literary Focus: Stream of Consciousness, p. 238

Strategies for Diverse Student Needs
Make a Timeline, p. 51

Beyond Literature
Media Connection: Film Biography, p. 51

Formal Assessment Selection Test, pp. 238–240; Assessment Resources Software

Alternative Assessment, p. 51

Writing and Language Transparencies
Branching Organizer, pp. 67–69

Resource Pro CD-ROM

The Jilting of Granny Weatherall

◆ Literature and Your Life

CONNECT YOUR EXPERIENCE

Think about the memories and images your mind offers up just as you're falling asleep. They are probably strange, disjointed, and a little fuzzy. If you can remember these semi-conscious thoughts of yours, you may be able to understand Granny Weatherall a little better. The old woman in this story is being visited by a host of images from her past. As you read, try to piece together the meaning of those memories.

Journal Writing Choose an event from the recent past. Without trying to write perfectly formed sentences, write down some associations that flow through your mind.

THEMATIC FOCUS: FROM EVERY CORNER OF THE LAND

This story is set in the rural South where families often lived far from town. In what specific ways does the setting capture a sense of isolation?

◆ Reading Strategy

CLARIFY SEQUENCE OF EVENTS

This story evokes many different time periods as Granny Weatherall drifts in and out of the present. To stay oriented, you should **clarify the sequence of events.** Watch for jumps in Granny Weatherall's thinking, often signaled by a shift from present-moment dialogue to Granny's inner thoughts. Notice flashbacks, in which Granny's thoughts return to an earlier time in her life. List key moments in a chart under the headings Past and Present. Number them in order as you unravel the sequence of Granny's life.

Past	Present

◆ Build Vocabulary

GREEK PREFIXES: *dys-*

You'll find the word *dyspepsia,* which means "indigestion," in this story. The word contains the Greek prefix *dys-*, meaning "difficult" or "bad." How does the prefix contribute to the overall meaning of the word?

WORD BANK

Preview this list of words from the story.

piety
frippery
dyspepsia

◆ Literary Focus

STREAM OF CONSCIOUSNESS

People's thoughts don't usually flow in a neat, organized manner. Instead, they proceed in an unorganized flow of insights, memories, and reflections. During the early 1900's some writers began using a literary device called **stream of consciousness,** in which they tried to capture the natural flow of people's thoughts. When writers use this technique, they present a sequence of thoughts as if they were coming directly from a character's mind. Transitions found in ordinary prose are omitted, and details are connected only by a character's associations.

◆ Grammar and Style

IMPERATIVE SENTENCES

To portray Granny Weatherall's attempt to regain control of her life—and death—Katherine Anne Porter uses imperative sentences. An **imperative sentence** states a request, or, in Granny Weatherall's case, gives an order. The subject, *you*, is understood, not stated. Look at the example from the story:

The word *you*, or a character's name, is implied here.

"Get along now, take your schoolbooks and go."

Interest Grabber Write the word "granny" on the chalkboard. Ask students to begin with that word and then freewrite their thoughts and associations as they occur. Encourage them to write quickly whatever comes to mind for about five minutes, without stopping to organize or order their impressions. Have small groups of students share what they wrote and discuss the associations that led them from one thought to the next. Are there any common threads? Tell students that they have just created a piece of stream-of-consciousness writing—the same style used in the short story they are about to read.

Connecting Themes Across Cultures

Have students identify some of the effects of living in a geographically isolated area: in an isolated environment, things are taken care of within the immediate community and people's survival depends on their self-reliance. Have students consider what people in other cultures experience when living in an isolated area, for example, in the mountains of Asia.

Customize for
Less Proficient Readers

Suggest that students read this difficult story at least twice in order to better grasp the meaning of Granny Weatherall's stream-of-consciousness thoughts. As they read, encourage students to jot down the events Granny relates; they can then label them "Past" or "Present" to help clarify their understanding of the sequence of events.

Customize for
AP Students

Have students compare and contrast the stream-of-consciousness technique in "The Jilting of Granny Weatherall" with that in "The Love Song of J. Alfred Prufrock."

Customize for
English Language Learners

Help students to use context clues and a dictionary to figure out the meanings of unfamiliar words in the story that are not otherwise addressed, such as *rummaging, plague, jilted, nimbus,* and *swindled.*

Test Preparation Workshop

Reading Comprehension: Analyze Sentence Meaning Many standardized tests require students to correctly answer sentence-completion questions. Often, more than one choice can complete a sentence. Use the following sample item to show students how to analyze sentence meaning, decide whether it is positive or negative, and eliminate choices that have the opposite sense.

Katherine Anne Porter's work reflects the disillusionment of the postwar era. Many of her works examine the drifting and ____ families and communities of the modern age.

A growing
B uniting
C reflective
D dissolving

The context clues *disillusionment* and *drifting* indicate the correct answer will have a negative connotation. *D* is the best choice.

Develop Understanding

One-Minute Insight On her deathbed, between visits from her daughter, her doctor, and her priest, old Granny Weatherall thinks back on her life as she slips in and out of consciousness. She recalls George, who left her standing at the altar on their wedding day, and John, who became her husband but died when their five children were still young. She reflects with pleasure and pride on her raising of the children, but remains deeply troubled by the recollection of having been jilted sixty years earlier. Granny, unable to come to terms with the pain of that experience and haunted by the death of her daughter, Hapsy, suddenly realizes that death has come to claim her. As Granny is about to die, she suffers one last jilting—her loss of faith—when God fails to provide a sign that would indicate that He is waiting for her with open arms.

❶ **Clarification** You may wish to review the title with students, discussing the meaning of *jilting* and the implications of the name *Weatherall.* Students may suggest that the name identifies someone who can weather, or endure, all situations.

◆ Literary Focus

❷ **Stream of Consciousness** To prepare students for the ways in which Granny's thoughts wander, go over these and the following paragraphs together. Help students make the distinction between what is memory or hallucination, and what is real (the doctor examining her and speaking with Cornelia; Cornelia caring for her).

◆ Critical Thinking

❸ **Analyze** Ask students to explain what is ironic about the fact that Granny wants to spank Cornelia for being dutiful. *Granny wants to punish her for being so good and thoughtful, rather than for bad behavior.*

❶

The Jilting of Granny Weatherall

Katherine Anne Porter

She flicked her wrist neatly out of Doctor Harry's pudgy careful fingers and pulled the sheet up to her chin. The brat ought to be in knee breeches. Doctoring around the country with spectacles on his nose! "Get along now, take your schoolbooks and go. There's nothing wrong with me."

Doctor Harry spread a warm paw like a cushion on her forehead where the forked green vein danced and made her eyelids twitch. "Now, now, be a good girl, and we'll have you up in no time."

"That's no way to speak to a woman nearly eighty years old just because she's down. I'd have you respect your elders, young man."

"Well, Missy, excuse me," Doctor Harry patted her cheek. "But I've got to warn you, haven't I? You're a marvel, but you must be careful or you're going to be good and sorry."

"Don't tell me what I'm going to be. I'm on my feet now, morally speaking. It's Cornelia. I had to go to bed to get rid of her."

Her bones felt loose, and floated around in her skin, and Doctor Harry floated like a balloon around the foot of the bed. He floated and pulled down his waistcoat and swung his glasses on a cord. "Well, stay where you are, it certainly can't hurt you."

❷ "Get along and doctor your sick," said Granny Weatherall. "Leave a well woman alone. I'll call for you when I want you. . . . Where were you forty years ago when I pulled through milk leg[1] and double pneumonia? You weren't even born. Don't let Cornelia lead you on," she shouted, because Doctor Harry appeared to float up to the ceiling and out. "I pay my own bills, and I don't throw my money away on nonsense!"

She meant to wave good-bye, but it was too much trouble. Her eyes closed of themselves, it was like a dark curtain drawn around the bed. The pillow rose and floated under her, pleasant as a hammock in a light wind. She listened to the leaves rustling outside the window. No, somebody was swishing newspapers: no, Cornelia and Doctor Harry were whispering together. She leaped broad awake, thinking they whispered in her ear. ❷

"She was never like this, never like this!" "Well, what can we expect?" "Yes, eighty years old. . . ."

Well, and what if she was? She still had ears. It was like Cornelia to whisper around doors. She always kept things secret in such a public way. She was always being tactful and kind. Cornelia was dutiful; that was the trouble with her. Dutiful and good: "So good and dutiful," said Granny, "that I'd like to spank her." She saw herself spanking Cornelia and making a fine job of it. ❸

"What'd you say, Mother?"

Granny felt her face tying up in hard knots.

"Can't a body think, I'd like to know?"

"I thought you might want something."

"I do. I want a lot of things. First off, go away and don't whisper."

She lay and drowsed, hoping in her sleep that the children would keep out and let her rest a minute. It had been a long day. Not that she was tired. It was always pleasant to snatch a minute now and then. There was always so much to be done, let me see: tomorrow.

1. **milk leg:** Painful swelling of the leg.

Block Scheduling Strategies

Consider these suggestions to take advantage of extended class time:

- Introduce the selection and the Literary Focus with the Interest Grabber (p. 775).
- Discuss the Literary Focus and the Reading Strategy. Alert students to watch for shifts in time frame as Granny's mind jumps from the present to the past and back again.
- Organize discussion groups in which students can answer the Critical Thinking questions and complete the Reading Strategy exercise (p. 782).
- Have students complete a Writing or Speaking, Listening, and Viewing activity from the Idea Bank (p. 783). Use the Speaking, Listening, and Viewing Mini-Lesson (p. 780) to help those students who are assigned the Conversation activity.
- To encourage students to consider the way they would tell the story of someone's life in film, organize students into small groups. Distribute the Media Connection: Film Biography page in ***Beyond Literature*** (p. 51).

Tomorrow was far away and there was nothing to trouble about. Things were finished somehow when the time came; thank God there was always a little margin over for peace: then a person could spread out the plan of life and tuck in the edges orderly. It was good to have everything clean and folded away, with the hair brushes and tonic bottles sitting straight on the white embroidered linen: the day started without fuss and the pantry shelves laid out with rows of jelly glasses and brown jugs and white
4 stone-china jars with blue whirligigs
5 and words painted on them: coffee, tea, sugar, ginger, cinnamon, allspice: and the bronze clock with the lion on top nicely dusted off. The dust that lion could collect in twenty-four hours! The box in the attic with all those letters tied up, well, she'd have to go through that tomorrow. All those letters—George's letters and John's letters and her letters to them both—lying around for the children to find afterwards made her uneasy. Yes, that would be tomorrow's business. No use to let them know how silly she had been once.

While she was rummaging around she found death in her mind and it felt clammy and unfamiliar. She had spent so much time preparing for death there was no need for bringing it up again. Let it take care of itself now. When she was sixty she had felt very old, finished, and went around making farewell trips to see her children and grandchildren, with a secret in her mind: This is the very last of your mother,
6 children! Then she made her will and came down with a long fever. That was all just a notion like a lot of other things, but it was lucky too, for she had once for all got over the idea of dying for a long time. Now she couldn't be worried. She hoped she had better sense now. Her father had lived to be one hundred and two years old and had drunk a noggin of strong hot toddy on his last birthday. He told the reporters it was his daily habit, and he owed his long life to that. He had made quite a scandal and was very pleased about it. She believed she'd just plague Cornelia a little.

"Cornelia! Cornelia!" No footsteps, but a sudden hand on her cheek. "Bless you, where have you been?"

"Here, mother."

"Well, Cornelia, I want a noggin of hot toddy."

"Are you cold, darling?"

"I'm chilly, Cornelia. Lying in bed stops the circulation. I must have told you that a thousand times."

Well, she could just hear Cornelia telling her husband that Mother was getting a little childish and they'd have to humor her. The thing that most annoyed her was that Cornelia thought she was deaf, dumb, and blind. Little hasty glances and tiny gestures tossed around 8
her and over her head saying, "Don't cross her, let her have her way, she's eighty years old," and she sitting there as if she lived in a thin glass cage. Sometimes Granny almost made up her mind to pack up and move back to her own

Garden of Memories, Charles Burchfield, The Museum of Modern Art

▲ **Critical Viewing** How might the figure in this surreal illustration of an old woman in her "garden of memories" represent Granny Weatherall? **[Connect]** 7

◆ Critical Thinking

4 Infer Ask student what Granny's thoughts reveal about her character. *She likes her home—and her life—to be neat, orderly, and well-planned.*

◆ Critical Thinking

5 Speculate Have students speculate about why Granny might be concerned about the possibility that her children will find her letters. *Students should realize that Granny may be keeping some kind of secret from her children about her involvement with one or both men; she may also consider the letters too personal for anyone else's eyes.*

Customize for *Less Proficient Readers*

6 Help students understand Granny's attitude toward death. Guide them to see that she is resigned to it now, unafraid, having had the experience twenty years earlier of thinking that she was dying and preparing for the inevitability by getting her things in order and visiting her children.

▶Critical Viewing◀

7 Connect Students may respond that, like the old woman in the painting, who is sunk in a chair and seeing apparitions all around her, Granny is immobile in bed, floating in and out of consciousness, imagining all kinds of surreal things.

Customize for *Interpersonal Learners*

8 Discuss with students that Granny goes in and out of lucidity, but when she is lucid, she feels proud and doesn't want her daughter humoring or babying her. Help students recognize that Granny is in Cornelia's home, under her care, and that Cornelia believes that her mother is not thinking clearly and can no longer care for herself.

Humanities: Art

Garden of Memories, 1917, by Charles Burchfield.

Charles Burchfield (1893–1967) learned his craft at the Cleveland Institute of Art, where he developed his individualistic style. Burchfield's early work, of which this surrealistic crayon and water color is an example, evoke his childhood memories and emotions and produce a haunting sense of imagination.

Use these questions for discussion:

1. How would you describe the mood of this piece of art? *Students may say that the painting is sinister and filled with strange apparitions and melancholy.*
2. How does the artist create its melancholy, sinister quality? *Students may point to the gloomy palette of colors; the sadness of the old woman with her head on her chin, dressed all in black; the phantom-like trees and drooping flowers; the uninviting home with its dark doorway and bat-like designs; the rough land; and the gray trees encroaching on the house.*

Customize for
Less Proficient Readers

❶ To help students through Granny's stream-of-consciousness thoughts here, ask them to tell which of her accomplishments she is most proud. *She is most proud of her homemaking skills and her common sense.*

Comprehension Check ☑

❷ Ask students to explain why Granny envisions her husband as a young man. *Students should understand that when John died, he was younger than the children are now.*

◆ Literary Focus

❸ **Stream of Consciousness** Students may say that Granny's thoughts run back to the past when she was responsible for raising a family and running a farm. She revels in the successes of that time.

❹ **Clarification** Rural women, living far from hospitals and medical doctors, often depended on the services of neighbors and midwives in delivering their babies. Students may be surprised at Granny's elation in recalling that she "hardly ever lost one" of the sick children or animals she nursed. Inform them that at that time, infant mortality rates were far higher than they are today; it was not uncommon for children to die of illnesses or diseases that are easily treated with modern medicine.

◆ Grammar and Style

❺ **Imperative Sentences** Ask students to explain why the author has Granny speaking in a flurry of imperative sentences here. *Students may suggest that Granny is giving a set of orders, an indication that at a time when she is becoming more and more helpless and out of control, she is trying to take charge and get a handle on her life.*

house where nobody could remind her every minute that she was old. Wait, wait, Cornelia, till your own children whisper behind your back!

❶ In her day she had kept a better house and had got more work done. She wasn't too old yet for Lydia to be driving eighty miles for advice when one of the children jumped the track, and Jimmy still dropped in and talked things over: "Now, Mammy, you've a good business head, I want to know what you think of this?. . . " Old. Cornelia couldn't change the furniture around without asking. Little things, little things! They had been so sweet when they were little. Granny wished the old days were back again with the children young and everything to be done over. It had been a hard pull, but not too much for her. When she thought of all the food she had cooked, and all the clothes she had cut and sewed, and all the gardens she had made—well, the children showed it. There they were, made out of her, and they couldn't get away from that. ❷ Sometimes she wanted to see John again and point to them and say, Well, I didn't do so badly, did I? But that would have to wait. That was for tomorrow. She used to think of him as a man, but now all the children were older than their father, and he would be a child beside her if she saw him now. It seemed strange and there was something wrong in the idea. Why, he couldn't possibly recognize her. She had fenced in a hundred acres once, digging the post holes herself and clamping the wires with just a negro boy to help. That changed a woman. John would be looking for a young woman with the peaked Spanish comb in her hair and the painted fan. Digging post holes changed a woman. ❹ Riding country roads in the winter when women had their babies was another thing: sitting up nights with sick horses and sick children and hardly ever losing one. John, I hardly ever lost one of them! John would see that in a minute, that would be something he could understand, she wouldn't have to explain anything!

> ❸ **◆ Literary Focus**
> Notice the random path of Granny's thoughts. What are some topics she touches on, and how are they linked in her mind?

Granny wished the old days were back again with the children young and everything to be done over.

It made her feel like rolling up her sleeves and putting the whole place to rights again. No matter if Cornelia was determined to be everywhere at once, there were a great many things left undone on this place. She would start tomorrow and do them. It was good to be strong enough for everything, even if all you made melted and changed and slipped under your hands, so that by the time you finished you almost forgot what you were working for. What was it I set out to do? she asked herself intently, but she could not remember. A fog rose over the valley, she saw it marching across the creek swallowing the trees and moving up the hill like an army of ghosts. Soon it would be at the near edge of the orchard, and then it was time to go in and light the lamps. Come in, children, don't stay out in the night air.

Lighting the lamps had been beautiful. The children huddled up to her and breathed like little calves waiting at the bars in the twilight. Their eyes followed the match and watched the flame rise and settle in a blue curve, then they moved away from her. The lamp was lit, they didn't have to be scared and hang on to mother any more. Never, never, never more. God, for all my life I thank Thee. Without Thee, my God, I could never have done it. Hail Mary, full of grace.

I want you to pick all the fruit this year and see that nothing is wasted. There's always someone who can use it. Don't let good things rot for want of using. You waste life when you waste good food. Don't let things get lost. It's bitter to lose things. Now, don't let me get to thinking, not when I am tired and taking a little nap before supper. . . . ❺

The pillow rose about her shoulders and pressed against her heart and the memory was being squeezed out of it: oh, push down the pillow, somebody: it would smother her if she tried to hold it. Such a fresh breeze blowing and such a green day with no threats in it. But

Viewing and Representing Mini-Lesson

Free Painting

This mini-lesson supports the Researching and Representing Activity in the Idea Bank on p. 783.

Introduce the Concept Explain that a painting that represents the stream-of-consciousness writing technique should reflect the characteristics of this writing style.

Develop the Background Have students brainstorm for words or phrases that describe the stream-of-consciousness style of writing, and record their ideas in a word map. *Possible answers may include: wandering, random thoughts, free associations, no boundaries, broad thoughts and fine details, personal and intimate thoughts, emotions, reflections, joys, pain, and so on.* Suggest that students discuss how these words could be interpreted in a painting. Explain that in a free painting, the strokes of the brush are not planned; the free association of thoughts directs the paintbrush just as thoughts direct the writing in the stream-of-consciousness technique.

Apply the Information Have students choose whatever medium is appropriate to create the free painting. Some students may have difficulty expressing their thoughts. Playing music may enhance their creativity.

Assess the Outcome Evaluate students' ability to create a painting that reflects the characteristics of the stream-of-consciousness writing style.

he had not come, just the same. What does a woman do when she has put on the white veil and set out the white cake for a man and he doesn't come? She tried to remember. No, I swear he never harmed me but in that. He never harmed me but in that . . . and what if he did? There was the day, the day, but a whirl of dark smoke rose and covered it, crept up and over into the bright field where everything was planted so carefully in orderly rows. That was hell, she knew hell when she saw it. For sixty years she had prayed against remembering him and against losing her soul in the deep pit of hell, and now the two things were
6 mingled in one and the thought of him was a smoky cloud from hell that moved and crept
7 in her head when she had just got rid of Doctor Harry and was trying to rest a minute. Wounded vanity, Ellen, said a sharp voice in the top of her mind. Don't let your wounded vanity get the upper hand of you. Plenty of girls get jilted. You were jilted, weren't you? Then stand up to it. Her eyelids wavered and let in streamers of blue-gray light like tissue paper over her eyes. She must get up and pull the shades down or she'd never sleep. She was in bed again and the shades were not down. How could that happen? Better turn over, hide from the light, sleeping in the light gave you nightmares. "Mother, how do you feel now?" and a stinging wetness on her forehead. But I don't like having my face washed in cold water!

Hapsy? George? Lydia? Jimmy? No, Cornelia, and her features were swollen and full of little puddles. "They're coming, darling, they'll all be here soon." Go wash your face, child, you look funny.

Instead of obeying, Cornelia knelt down and put her head on the pillow. She seemed to be talking but there was no sound. "Well, are you tongue-tied? Whose birthday is it? Are you
8 going to give a party?"

Cornelia's mouth moved urgently in strange shapes. "Don't do that, you bother me, daughter."

"Oh, no, Mother. Oh, no. . . ."

Nonsense. It was strange about children. They disputed your every word. "No what, Cornelia?"

"Here's Doctor Harry."

"I won't see that boy again. He just left five minutes ago."

"That was this morning, Mother. It's night now. Here's the nurse."

"This is Doctor Harry, Mrs. Weatherall. I never saw you look so young and happy!"

"Ah, I'll never be young again—but I'd be happy if they'd let me lie in peace and get rested."

She thought she spoke up loudly, but no one answered. A warm weight on her forehead, a warm bracelet on her wrist, and a breeze went on whispering, trying to tell her something. A shuffle of leaves in the everlasting hand of God, He blew on them and they danced and rattled. "Mother, don't mind, we're going to give you a little hypodermic." "Look here, daughter, how do ants get in this bed? I saw sugar ants
yesterday." Did you send for Hapsy too? 8

It was Hapsy she really wanted. She had to go a long way back through a great many rooms to find Hapsy standing with a baby on her arm. She seemed to herself to be Hapsy also, and the baby on Hapsy's arm was Hapsy and himself and herself, all at once, and there was no surprise in the meeting. Then Hapsy melted from within and turned flimsy as gray gauze and the baby was a gauzy shadow, and Hapsy came up close and said, "I thought you'd never come," and looked at her very searchingly and said, "You haven't changed a bit!" They leaned forward to kiss, when Cornelia began whispering from a long way off, "Oh, is there anything you want to tell me? Is there anything I can do for you?"

Yes, she had changed her mind after sixty years and she would like to see George. I want you to find George. Find him and be sure to tell him I forgot him. I want him to know I had my husband just the same and my children and my house like any other woman. A good house too and a good husband that I loved and fine children out of him. Better than I hoped for even. Tell him I was given back everything he took away and more. Oh, no, oh, God, no, there was something else besides the house and the man and the children. Oh, surely they were not all? What was it? Something not given back. . . . Her breath crowded down under her ribs and grew into a monstrous frightening shape with cutting

◆ **Reading Strategy** 9
Who are George and John, and in what sequence did they appear in Granny's life?

Customize for
English Language Learners

❻ Explain to students that when Granny recalls the time she "put on the white veil and set out the white cake" and the man didn't come, she is remembering a time when she was jilted, left standing at the altar by the prospective groom.

◆ Critical Thinking

❼ **Infer; Support** Ask students whether they believe Granny has fully recovered from her jilting. Ask them to support their response with evidence from this passage. *Students are likely to say that Granny has not fully recovered from what she refers to as a hellish experience. As evidence, they should cite the fact that she has prayed for sixty years against remembering it, and that she says the memory of George is like "a smoky cloud from hell."*

Comprehension Check ☑

❽ Review with students what is happening in the present. Make sure they recognize that Granny is drifting in and out of consciousness and that her daughter and the doctor are at her bedside caring for her, giving her medication and washing her face. Elicit from students that Granny, at the moment, is thinking way back into her past and her memories ("a long way back through a great many rooms") and imagining that Hapsy, her deceased daughter, is there with her now. She barely hears or recognizes Cornelia, who *is* right there offering comfort.

◆ Reading Strategy

❾ **Clarify Chronological Order**
George is the man who jilted Granny; she then married John, who is the father of her children.

Beyond the Classroom

Career Connection

Gerontology As people today live longer and longer, the care and treatment of older people and issues involving the elderly have grown in prominence. Those interested in the problems facing America's elderly population will find many career opportunities. From jobs in geriatric medicine, dentistry, psychology, social work, and physical and occupational therapy, to work in estate planning and elder law, there are many jobs geared to planning for old age and improving the circumstances of the elderly.

Invite interested students to explore career opportunities in one or more of the aforementioned fields. Ask them to do research to track the changes the field has undergone in recent years and to predict the direction in which it is going. Students can gather their information from the library, by contacting associations like the AARP, and by interviewing people working in the field.

❶ **Clarification** Point out that Granny is close to death and that Father Connolly has arrived to administer the last rites of the Catholic Church.

◆ Critical Thinking

❷ **Speculate** Ask students to speculate about who the man Granny refers to might have been. *Students might speculate that "he" is John, threatening to kill George for the hurt he has caused her.*

◆ Literary Focus

❸ **Stream of Consciousness** Guide students to notice how the image of Cornelia's voice faltering "like a cart in a bad road" leads Granny to picture herself on a cart ride, seated next to an unidentified man—John? George? Death?—who is no stranger to her.

◆ Critical Thinking

❹ **Connect** Students may recall a similar carriage ride with Death in the Emily Dickinson poem "Because I could not stop for death." Students may wish to reread that poem.

Reteach

To reteach sequence of events, have students create timelines. Instruct them to write the events of the story on note cards or paper cut into strips. Each event should be written in a few words. When all the events are written, they are put in order and numbered. Then the numbered events are put into a timeline as shown here.

Story Events Timeline

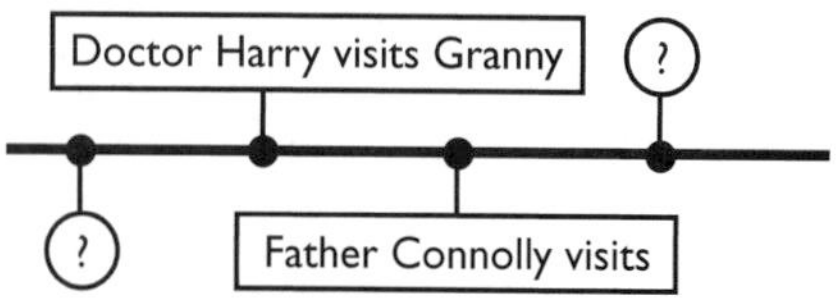

edges; it bored up into her head, and the agony was unbelievable: Yes, John, get the Doctor now, no more talk, my time has come.

When this one was born it should be the last. The last. It should have been born first, for it was the one she had truly wanted. Everything came in good time. Nothing left out, left over. She was strong, in three days she would be as well as ever. Better. A woman needed milk in her to have her full health.

"Mother, do you hear me?"

"I've been telling you—"

❶ "Mother, Father Connolly's here."

"I went to Holy Communion only last week. Tell him I'm not so sinful as all that."

"Father just wants to speak to you."

He could speak as much as he pleased. It was like him to drop in and inquire about her soul as if it were a teething baby, and then stay on for a cup of tea and a round of cards and gossip. He always had a funny story of some sort, usually about an Irishman who made his little mistakes and confessed them, and the point lay in some absurd thing he would blurt out in the confessional showing his struggles between native piety and original sin. Granny felt easy about her soul. Cornelia, where are your manners? Give Father Connolly a chair. She had her secret comfortable understanding with a few favorite saints who cleared a straight road to God for her. All as surely signed and sealed as the papers for the new Forty Acres. Forever . . . heirs and assigns[2] forever. Since the day the wedding cake was not cut, but thrown out and wasted. The whole bottom dropped out of the world, and there she was blind and sweating with nothing under her feet and the walls falling away. His hand had caught her under the breast, she had not fallen, there was the freshly polished floor with the green rug on it, just as
❷ before. He had cursed like a sailor's parrot and said, "I'll kill him for you." Don't lay a hand on him, for my sake leave something to God. "Now, Ellen, you must believe what I tell you. . . ."

So there was nothing, nothing to worry about any more, except sometimes in the night one of the children screamed in a nightmare, and they both hustled out shaking and hunting for the matches and calling, "There, wait a minute, here we are!" John, get the doctor now, Hapsy's time has come. But there was Hapsy standing by the bed in a white cap. "Cornelia, tell Hapsy to take off her cap. I can't see her plain."

Her eyes opened very wide and the room stood out like a picture she had seen somewhere. Dark colors with the shadows rising towards the ceiling in long angles. The tall black dresser gleamed with nothing on it but John's picture, enlarged from a little one, with John's eyes very black when they should have been blue. You never saw him, so how do you know how he looked? But the man insisted the copy was perfect, it was very rich and handsome. For a picture, yes, but it's not my husband. The table by the bed had a linen cover and a candle and a crucifix. The light was blue from Cornelia's silk lampshades. No sort of light at all, just frippery. You had to live forty years with kerosene lamps to appreciate honest electricity. She felt very strong and she saw Doctor Harry with a rosy nimbus around him.

"You look like a saint, Doctor Harry, and I vow that's as near as you'll ever come to it."

"She's saying something."

"I heard you, Cornelia. What's all this carrying on?"

"Father Connolly's saying—"

Cornelia's voice staggered and bumped like a cart in a bad road. It rounded corners and turned back again and arrived nowhere. Granny stepped up in the cart very lightly and ❸ reached for the reins, but a man sat beside her and she knew him by his hands, driving the cart. She did not look in his face, for she knew without seeing, but looked instead down the road where the trees leaned over and bowed to each other and a thousand birds were singing a Mass. She felt like singing too, but she put her ❹ hand in the bosom of her dress and pulled out a rosary, and Father Connolly murmured Latin in a very solemn voice and tickled her feet.[3] My God, will you stop that nonsense? I'm a married woman. What if he did run away and leave me to face the priest by myself? I found another a whole world better. I wouldn't have exchanged my husband for anybody except St. Michael[4] himself, and you may tell him that

2. **assigns:** Persons to whom property is transferred.

3. **murmured . . . feet:** Administered the last rites of the Catholic Church.

4. **St. Michael:** One of the archangels.

Speaking, Listening, and Viewing Mini-Lesson

Conversation

This mini-lesson supports the Speaking, Listening, and Viewing activity in the Idea Bank (p. 783).

Introduce the Concept Review the activity. Tell students that their efforts will be judged based on the following criteria:

- how well their dialogue conveys the likely feelings of the two people
- the creativity and credibility of George's explanation for his behavior

Develop Background Students can begin by asking themselves questions such as:

- Why did George do it?
- How would he explain himself to Granny ten years later and what would he be feeling then?
- What would Granny be feeling?
- How would she treat George?

Students should examine what they know of Granny and her feelings about the jilting. They should also come up with a reason for George's fateful choice.

Apply the Information Have students use their notes to develop a rough script. Encourage pairs to practice their role-playing to refine it before they perform for the class.

Assess the Outcome Focus on how imaginatively, yet plausibly, students have captured the jilting scenario as well as the feelings and reactions that Granny and George might have experienced.

for me with a thank you in the bargain.

Light flashed on her closed eyelids, and a deep roaring shook her. Cornelia, is that lightning? I hear thunder. There's going to be a storm. Close all the windows. Call the children in. . . . "Mother, here we are, all of us." "Is that you, Hapsy?" "Oh, no, I'm Lydia. We drove as fast as we could." Their faces drifted above her, drifted away. The rosary fell out of her hands and Lydia put it back. Jimmy tried to help, their hands fumbled together, and Granny closed two fingers around Jimmy's thumb. Beads wouldn't do, it must be something alive. She was so amazed her thoughts ran round and round. So, my dear Lord, this is my death and I wasn't even thinking about it. My children have come to see me die. But I can't, it's not time. Oh, I always hated surprises. I wanted to give Cornelia the amethyst set—Cornelia, you're to have the amethyst set, but Hapsy's to wear it when she wants, and, Doctor Harry, do shut up. Nobody sent for you. Oh, my dear Lord, do wait a minute. I meant to do something about the Forty Acres, Jimmy doesn't need it and Lydia will later on, with that worthless husband of hers. I meant to finish the altar cloth and send six bottles of wine to Sister Borgia for her dyspepsia. I want to send six bottles of wine to Sister Borgia, Father Connolly, now don't let me forget.

5 **◆ Literary Focus**
What is the connecting link between Granny's seemingly random thoughts?

Cornelia's voice made short turns and tilted over and crashed. "Oh, Mother, oh, Mother, oh Mother. . . ."

"I'm not going, Cornelia. I'm taken by surprise. I can't go." 6

You'll see Hapsy again. What about her? "I thought you'd never come." Granny made a long journey outward, looking for Hapsy. What if I don't find her? What then? Her heart sank down and down, there was no bottom to death, she couldn't come to the end of it. The blue light from Cornelia's lampshade drew into a tiny point in the center of her brain, it flickered and winked like an eye, quietly it fluttered and dwindled. Granny lay curled down within herself, amazed and watchful, staring at the point of light that was herself; her body was now only a deeper mass of shadow in an endless darkness and this darkness would curl around the light and swallow it up. God, give a sign!

For the second time there was no sign. Again no bridegroom and the priest in the house. She could not remember any other sorrow because this grief wiped them all away. Oh, no, there's nothing more cruel than this—I'll never forgive it. She stretched herself with a deep breath and blew out the light. 7

◆ Build Vocabulary

piety (pī´ ə tē) *n.*: Devotion to religious duties

frippery (frip´ ər ē) *n.*: Showy display of elegance

dyspepsia (dis pep´ shə) *n.*: Indigestion

Guide for Responding

◆ *Literature and Your Life*

Reader's Response If you were at Granny Weatherall's deathbed, what would you say to help comfort her?

Thematic Focus Identify three clues from the story that indicate it is set in a rural area.

Questions for Research List questions to begin researching the psychological effects of anger turned inward. What key words could you use to locate information in computer databases?

☑ Check Your Comprehension

1. (a) Which memory is most painful to Granny as she reviews her life? (b) With what thought does this memory become mingled?
2. How does Granny respond to her children's arrival?
3. What happens at the end of the story just before Granny "[blows] out the light"?

Beyond the Selection

FURTHER READING

Other Works by Katherine Anne Porter

Flowering Judas; Pale Horse, Pale Rider; The Leaning Tower; Collected Short Stories; Ship of Fools

Other Works With the Theme of Death and Dying

One True Thing, Anna Quindlen

Spoon River Anthology, Edgar Lee Masters

We suggest that you preview these works before recommending them to students.

INTERNET

You can find additional information about Porter on the Internet. We suggest the following site. Please be aware that sites may have changed since this information was published.

For information about the author and about the Katherine Anne Porter Room at the University of Maryland, go to

http://www.lib.umd.edu/UMCP/ARCV/kporter

We *strongly recommend* that you preview sites before you send students to them.

◆ Literary Focus

5 Stream of Consciousness She is thinking of all the things she intended to accomplish before her death.

◆ Critical Thinking

6 Analyze Why does Granny tell Cornelia that she has been "taken by surprise"? *Suggested response: She can't believe God would let her die without first sending her a sign that her time has come.*

◆ Critical Thinking

7 Connect Discuss with students that Granny believes that she is being jilted again; Guide them to see that rejection is even worse this time because she thinks that God is jilting her by not giving her a sign or accompanying her along the road to death.

Reinforce and Extend

Answers

◆ *Literature and Your Life*

Reader's Response Student might tell Granny that her life has been a success: she married a good man and had children whose lives have pleased her.

Thematic Response Clues include Granny's recollections of fencing the land, caring for sick horses, picking fruit, and driving country roads to deliver babies. The fact that Granny is being cared for at home rather than a hospital, her attitude about surviving serious illnesses without a doctor, and various details about the care of the house and land also indicate a rural setting.

☑ Check Your Comprehension

1. (a) The memory of being jilted on her wedding day is the most painful. (b) It had become mingled with the thought of losing her soul in hell.
2. She realizes she is truly dying, she thinks of all the things that she wanted to do before she died.
3. She asks God to give her a sign that it is time to die. The sign never comes and instead she relives the memory of her long-ago jilting, blowing out the light of her life to end its pain.

Answers

◆ Critical Thinking

1. It is appropriate because she has weathered many difficult situations in the course of her life.
2. Suggested response: The events of Granny's life are classified in relation to the experience of being jilted by George on their wedding day.
3. The fact that she wants to find George indicates that she hasn't forgotten him at all.
4. The "something not gotten back" might be her self-esteem and pride.
5. Suggested response: Granny cannot forgive the fact that, just as with her jilting by George, she has been left alone without a comforting, vindicating sign from God to face the greatest emotional pain she has ever known. When she perceives no sign, she feels that her achievements in life have been overshadowed by the pain and humiliation of the first jilting.
6. It represent Granny's life.
7. Students should offer explanations for their answers.

◆ Literary Focus

Sample responses: Granny thinks of tasks to be done, and her thoughts drift to her possessions and her fears that her children will discover her letters from John and George. Thoughts of how she organized her possessions leads her to think about the letters and her fears concerning their discovery. When the priest arrives, Granny's thoughts drift from the peculiarities of his personality, to the need to provide him a chair, to her conviction that a direct relationship with the saints ensures her soul's safety. Granny's thoughts about the priest are linked to her thoughts about saints and salvation by their association with God.

◆ Reading Strategy

Suggested responses: As a young woman, Granny is jilted by George. She later marries John and has five children, one of whom dies. After John dies, Granny continues to raise her children and run the household alone. At age sixty, she prepares for death and visits her children. She eventually moves into Cornelia's home, and, at age eighty, Granny dies.

Guide for Responding *(continued)*

◆ Critical Thinking

INTERPRET

1. Why is "Weatherall" an appropriate surname for Granny? **[Interpret]**
2. How might Granny summarize the important turning point of her life? **[Synthesize]**
3. What is ironic or surprising about Granny's desire to find George to tell him she has forgotten him? **[Interpret]**
4. What has George taken from Granny that she hopes to regain as the story ends? **[Analyze]**
5. At the end of the story, Granny says "I'll never forgive it." What is *it*, and what does her comment reveal about her? **[Draw Conclusions]**
6. What does the light referred to in the last two paragraphs symbolize? **[Draw Conclusions]**

APPLY

7. How might this story have been different if Granny had confronted George after he jilted her? **[Hypothesize]**

◆ Literary Focus

STREAM OF CONSCIOUSNESS

Porter's **stream-of-consciousness** technique captures the natural flow of Granny Weatherall's thoughts. She deliberately avoids using transition phrases such as *when she was younger* or *looking back at it now*. Rather, Porter lets Granny's associations bridge the gap between thoughts.

Cite two examples in which Granny's thoughts drift from one subject to a seemingly unrelated subject. For each example, explain the natural associations that connect Granny's thoughts.

◆ Reading Strategy

CLARIFY SEQUENCE OF EVENTS

When the stream-of-consciousness technique is used in a story, events are organized according to a character's associations, rather than in chronological order. This means that the narrative jumps around in time. As a result, to understand the order, you must be able to reorganize the events in the sequence in which they occurred.

Rearrange the events presented in "The Jilting of Granny Weatherall" in chronological order.

◆ Build Vocabulary

USING THE GREEK PREFIX *dys-*

The Greek prefix *dys-* means "difficult" or "bad." Add this meaning to each of the clues in parentheses to define the numbered words. Check your definitions in the dictionary. Revise if necessary.

1. dysentery (*entery* = intestine)
2. dysfunctional (*functional* = working properly)
3. dyslexia (*lexis* = word or speech)

USING THE WORD BANK: Sentence Completions

On your paper, write the word from the word bank that fits best in each sentence.

1. Kelly showed her __?__ by attending religious services daily.
2. "Pizza aggravates my __?__," said Mr. Otis.
3. The skaters strutted by, displaying their __?__ for all to admire.

◆ Grammar and Style

USING IMPERATIVE SENTENCES

Each time Granny Weatherall gives a command in this story, she is using an **imperative sentence**—a sentence that gives an order or states a request.

Practice On your paper, write the letter of the imperative sentence.

1. a. Will you get along and doctor your sick?
   b. Your sick need doctoring.
   c. Get along and doctor your sick.
2. a. Could you stay where you are?
   b. I want you to stay where you are.
   c. Stay where you are.
3. a. They shouldn't be whispering.
   b. Go away and don't whisper.
   c. I wish they wouldn't whisper.

Looking at Style Explain what Granny's use of imperative sentences reveals about her character.

Writing Application Rewrite these sentences to make them imperative sentences.

1. Won't you please leave a well woman alone?
2. You shouldn't let Cornelia lead you on.
3. Can't a body think?

◆ Build Vocabulary

Using the Greek Prefix dys-

Suggested responses:

1. dysentery: a disturbance or disease of the intestines
2. dysfunctional: not working properly
3. dyslexia: a difficulty with words and reading

Using the Word Bank

1. piety; 2. dyspepsia;
3. frippery

◆ Grammar and Style

Practice 1. c 2. c 3. b

Looking at Style It reveals that Granny is accustomed to giving orders and being in charge of situations.

Writing Application

Suggested responses:

1. Leave a well woman alone.
2. Don't let Cornelia lead you on.
3. Let a body think.

Build Your Portfolio

Idea Bank

Writing

1. **Doctor's Report** Imagine you're Doctor Harry. Write a report describing the physical and mental changes you've observed in Granny over the course of the day. **[Career Link]**

2. **Letter to George** As Cornelia, write a letter to George informing him of Granny's death. In whatever tone you choose, discuss the impact he had on Granny's life.

3. **Course Description** For a college catalog, write a page-long description of a course on stream-of-consciousness writing. Use examples from Porter's story to support your points. **[Career Link]**

Speaking, Listening, and Viewing

4. **Conversation** Suppose that Granny and George happened to meet ten years after the jilting. With a partner, role-play a conversation between them. **[Performing Arts Link]**

5. **Lecture** You are Doctor Harry fifteen years after Granny's death. More experience has taught you better ways of interacting with the elderly and infirm. In a lecture to a group of colleagues, share what you've learned. **[Health Link]**

Researching and Representing

6. **Free Painting** In a painting, illustrate the stream-of-consciousness writing technique. Using the medium of your choice, make a painting of free-associated images. Listening to music might help you to paint from your subconscious. **[Art Link; Music Link]**

7. **Report on Hospice Care** Hospice care—benevolent care of terminally ill people—is a growing area of medical specialization. Prepare a report detailing how Granny might have been cared for in a modern hospice. **[Health Link]**

Online Activity www.phlit.phschool.com

Guided Writing Lesson

Dramatic Monologue

A **dramatic monologue** is a speech in which an imaginary character speaks to a silent listener. It might be said that Granny Weatherall's silent listener is herself, or her younger self.

Create a character who interests you; it may or may not be an elderly person. Write a dramatic monologue incorporating that character's stream-of-consciousness thoughts and memories. As you write, focus on effective characterizations that reveal what the character is like as a person.

Writing Skills Focus: Characterization

Choose memories, thoughts, language, and details that contribute to your characterization. For example, notice that Porter returns again and again to the incident of the jilting to show its impact on Granny's character and attitudes. Knowing what has hurt Granny helps readers know her better.

If your character is dominated by a particular emotion, show a memory that clearly and consistently explains the reason for that emotion.

Prewriting List descriptive words you associate with your character. Group these under "Actions," "Feelings," "Comments," and "Attitudes."

Drafting Select one or two key memories, events, or details around which to organize your monologue. Introduce one of these early in your draft. Experiment with the stream-of-consciousness technique by writing without transitions.

Revising Read your dramatic monologue aloud to yourself. Does it sound like the voice in someone's head? If you have been successful in making the sequence of events sound as though it were entirely random, you may want to add clues to help your audience follow the thought stream and clarify the purpose of the character's monologue.

Idea Bank

Customizing for
Performance Levels
Following are suggestions for matching Idea Bank topics with your students' performance levels:
Less Advanced Students: 1, 6
Average Students: 2, 4, 7
More Advanced Students: 3, 5

Customizing for
Learning Modalities
Following are suggestions for matching Idea Bank topics with your students' learning modalities:
Interpersonal: 4
Verbal/Linguistic: 4, 5
Intrapersonal: 5, 6
Visual/Spatial: 6
Logical/Mathematical: 6

Guided Writing Lesson

Writing and Language Transparencies Display the Branching Transparency, p. 67, to help students organize key personality traits and descriptive words and phrases for their monologues.

For more prewriting, elaboration, and revision strategies, see *Prentice Hall Writing and Grammar.*

Writing Lab CD-ROM
Have students complete the tutorial on Creative Writing. Follow these steps:

1. Students can use the Situation Word Bins in the Choosing a Topic section to help spark ideas for their monologues.
2. Direct students to use their choice of activities in the Gathering Details section to help them organize the details or events around which they will organize their monologue.
3. After they have drafted on the computer, students can use the tips for peer revision before soliciting input from a partner.

ASSESSMENT OPTIONS

Formal Assessment, Selection Test, pp. 238–240, and Assessment Resources Software. The selection test is designed so that it can be easily customized to the performance levels of your students.

Alternative Assessment, p. 51, includes options for less advanced students, more advanced students, verbal/linguistic learners, visual/spatial learners, bodily/kinesthetic learners, and interpersonal learners.

PORTFOLIO ASSESSMENT
Use the following rubrics in the ***Alternative Assessment*** booklet to assess student writing:
Doctor's Report: Description Rubric, p. 112
Letter to George: Expression Rubric, p. 109
Course Description: Definition/Classification Rubric, p. 114
Guided Writing Lesson: Drama Rubric, p. 124

Prepare and Engage

LESSON OBJECTIVES

1. **To develop vocabulary and word identification skills**
   - Build Vocabulary: Latin Suffixes
   - Using the Word Bank: Definitions
2. **To use a variety of reading strategies to comprehend a short story**
   - Connect Your Experience
   - Reading Strategy: Break Down Long Sentences
   - Tips to Guide Reading
3. **To increase knowledge of other cultures and to connect common elements across cultures**
   - Connecting Themes Across Cultures (ATE)
   - Background for Understanding
4. **To express and support responses to the text**
   - Critical Thinking
   - Idea Bank: Letter of Support
   - Idea Bank: Acceptance Speech
   - Analyze Literary Criticism (ATE)
5. **To analyze literary elements**
   - Literary Focus: Dialect
   - Idea Bank: Analysis of Dialect
6. **To read to do research on self-selected and assigned topics**
   - Questions for Research
   - Research Skills Mini-Lesson (ATE)
7. **To plan, prepare, organize, and present literary interpretations**
   - Idea Bank: Debate
   - Idea Bank: Broadcast
   - Idea Bank: Pantomime
   - Idea Bank: Musical Research
8. **To use recursive writing processes to write a critical review**
   - Guided Writing Lesson
9. **To increase knowledge of the rules of grammar and usage**
   - Grammar and Style: Irregular Verb Forms

Test Preparation

Reading Comprehension: Anticipate Missing Words
(ATE, p. 785)
The teaching tips and sample test item in this workshop support the instruction and practice in the unit workshop:
Reading Comprehension: Sentence-Completion Questions
(SE, p. 863)

Guide for Interpreting

William Faulkner *(1897–1962)*

For some writers, the place of their roots is a wellspring of story material. Oxford, Mississippi, was such a place for William Faulkner. It became the basis for the imaginary world of Yoknapatawpha County—the setting of many of his novels.

A Writer's Roots Although Faulkner never finished high school, he read a great deal and developed an interest in writing from an early age. In 1918, he enlisted in the British Royal Flying Corps and was sent to Canada for training. However, World War I ended before he had a chance to see combat, and he returned to Mississippi. A few years later, longing for a change of scene, Faulkner moved to New Orleans. There he became friends with Sherwood Anderson, who offered encouragement and helped get Faulkner's first novel, *A Soldier's Pay,* published. In 1926, he returned home to Oxford, Mississippi, to devote himself to his writing.

A Gold Mine of Inspiration In what he called his "own little postage stamp of native soil," Faulkner uncovered a "gold mine" of inspiration. From there, he wrote a series of novels about the decay of traditional values as small communities became swept up in the changes of the modern age. Faulkner saw immense dramas acted out in his small, rural environment, and he used jumbled time sequences, stream-of-consciousness narration, dialect, and other difficult techniques to show what he called "the human heart in conflict with itself."

A Slow Spread of Recognition For many years, Faulkner was dismissed as an eccentric—an unimportant regional writer. Gradually, however, critics began to take him seriously.

Today, Faulkner is generally considered the most innovative writer of his time.

The novel that first earned him critical acclaim was *The Sound and the Fury* (1929), a complex novel exploring the downfall of an old southern family. A year later, he published *As I Lay Dying,* the story of a poor family's six-day journey to bury their mother. Told from fifteen different points of view and exploring people's varying perspectives of death, the novel was a masterpiece in narrative experimentation. Other innovative works followed, including *Absalom, Absalom!* (1936), which is told by four speakers with different interpretations of events.

Despite the critical success of his works, Faulkner did not earn widespread public recognition until 1946, when *The Portable Faulkner*—an anthology in which many of his writings about Yoknapatawpha County were presented in chronological order—was published. Four years later, he was awarded the Nobel Prize following the publication of *Intruder in the Dust* (1948), a novel in which he confronted the issue of racism.

◆ Background for Understanding

LITERATURE: THE NOBEL PRIZE

Alfred Nobel, a Swedish chemist, first earned fame as the inventor of dynamite, and at one time many people associated him with death. Nobel had intended dynamite to be used safely in mining and construction, but disasters often occurred. Nobel was determined to make dynamite safer, and he eventually succeeded in his goal. Later, he sought to use his success to help bring about good in the world by establishing a multimillion-dollar foundation to encourage achievement and diplomacy by awarding annual prizes in the fields of physics, chemistry, medicine, literature, and world peace.

Prentice Hall Literature Program Resources

REINFORCE / RETEACH / EXTEND

Selection Support Pages
Build Vocabulary: Latin Suffixes: *-ery*, p. 239
Grammar and Style: Irregular Verb Forms, p. 240
Reading Strategy: Break Down Sentences, p. 241
Literary Focus: Dialect, p. 242

Strategies for Diverse Student Needs, p. 52

Beyond Literature
Workplace Skills: Taking Recess, p. 52

Formal Assessment Selection Test, pp. 241–243; Assessment Resources Software

Alternative Assessment, p. 52

Writing and Language Transparencies
Argument Transparency, p. 75

Resource Pro CD-ROM

◆ Race at Morning ◆
Nobel Prize Acceptance Speech

◆ Literature and Your Life

CONNECT YOUR EXPERIENCE

People's interests are often determined largely by where they live. For example, if you live in the city, your idea of fun might be a pick-up basketball game. In contrast, if you live in the country, you might choose to spend a free afternoon fishing in a local stream. "Race at Morning" captures one of the favorite activities of a group of characters from rural Mississippi—an annual hunting expedition.

Journal Writing Think of an activity you have enjoyed that was somehow linked to a particular place. Describe the place and the activity.

THEMATIC FOCUS: FROM EVERY CORNER OF THE LAND

In this story, Faulkner creates a vivid portrait of life in rural Mississippi. As you read, take note of how the characteristics of the setting and the characters contribute to the flavor of the story.

◆ Build Vocabulary

LATIN SUFFIXES: *-ery*

"Race at Morning" includes the word *distillery,* which contains the Latin suffix *-ery* (sometimes spelled *-ry).* The suffix, meaning "state or quality of" or "place of," is used to form nouns from verbs or other nouns. The verb *distill* means "to refine" or "to extract." The noun *distillery* means a place where something is distilled.

WORD BANK

Preview this list of words.

bayou
distillery
buck
moiling
switch
scrabbling
swag
glade

◆ Grammar and Style

CORRECT USE OF IRREGULAR VERB FORMS

The narrator of "Race at Morning" is an uneducated boy who often mistakenly conjugates **irregular verbs**—verbs whose past tenses and past participles are *not* formed by adding *-ed* or *-d* to the present form—as regular verbs. Notice how examples such as this one help capture the narrator's dialect.

Incorrect: I *knowed* it was him.

Correct: I *knew* it was he.

◆ Literary Focus

DIALECT

One way in which Faulkner captures the flavor of life in rural Mississippi is by using **dialect,** a manner of speaking that is common to a particular region or group. Dialect affects pronunciation, word choice, and grammatical structure. Look at this example:

> It was *jest dust-dark;* I had *jest* fed the horses and *clumb* back down the bank. . .

Jest is the way the speaker pronounces *just. Dust-dark* is his word for *dusk,* and *clumb* is the way he forms the past participle of *climb.*

◆ Reading Strategy

BREAK DOWN LONG SENTENCES

Faulkner is famous for his use of long sentences, which can make his works difficult to read. To avoid letting the length of his sentences cause confusion or disrupt your enjoyment of his stories, **break each long sentence down** into smaller units of meaning. Using the punctuation as a guide, divide the sentence into sections. Determine the meaning of each section. Then look for transitions that show how the sections fit together. With an extremely long sentence, you may find it helpful to divide the sentence into a series of shorter ones.

Test Preparation Workshop

Reading Comprehension: Anticipate Missing Words Many standardized tests ask students to correctly answer sentence-completion questions. Use the following example to show students how to use context and their own knowledge to guess a word that would complete the following passage.

Because he wrote about his home in Oxford, Mississippi, William Faulkner was for many years dismissed as an unimportant ____ writer.

A experimental
B regional
C eccentric
D untalented

After reading the passage, students might think that the word *local* completes the sentence. B, *regional,* is the best choice.

Interest Grabber On one side of the classroom, post a sign that says, "Hunting is a worthwhile activity that serves a purpose." On the other side, post a sign that says, "Hunting is wrong. Place more restrictions on it." Invite students to take one side or the other and, with their group, develop a list of points that make their case. Record their points on the chalkboard. Then tell students that the story they are about to read centers around a hunting trip through the bayous of Mississippi. Explain, however, that hunting is not the true focus of the story; prompt them to respond to the symbolic significance of the story as they read.

Customize for
Less Proficient Readers

To help readers keep track of who's who in the story, help them make a list of key characters that they can refer to as needed. Guide students to understand, for example, that Dan is a horse and that Eagle is a dog. Prompt students to apply the reading strategy by breaking down lengthy sentences to aid comprehension. To help them digest this dense story, encourage them to reread passages as needed.

Customize for
AP Students

Tell students that according to critic Cleanth Brooks, Faulkner writes "up to the hilt." His works burst at the seams with life; they have what the Elizabethans called *copia*—an abundance and fullness of life. Encourage students to look for evidence of *copia* when they read this story.

Customize for
English Language Learners

Students learning English will probably not be the only ones who find Faulkner's long sentences full of regional dialect difficult to follow. Encourage students to read in small groups so that they can work together to use context clues to figure out the meanings of expressions heavy in Mississippi dialect. They may also find it helpful to read difficult passages aloud; the pronunciation of certain dialect words can provide clues to their meaning.

Develop Understanding

One-Minute Insight This story is narrated by a twelve-year-old boy, whose parents have abandoned him to the care of the Mississippi farmer the boy refers to as Mister Ernest. Every year, Mister Ernest and his men—along with dozens of other hunters—spend the two-week hunting season in the bayou on a quest for one large, elusive buck. In his distinctive Southern dialect, the boy relates the events of the final day of hunting season, when he and Mister Ernest embark on a battle of wits and instincts with the legendary buck. When given the opportunity, Mister Ernest intentionally fails to shoot the deer, teaching the boy in the process about the importance of respecting nature and valuing the possibilities of life. The hunt becomes a rite of passage or turning point in the boy's life; it prompts Mister Ernest's decision to formally educate the boy so that he can learn the reasons for choosing right over wrong.

Literature CD-ROM To introduce students to the works of William Faulkner, use *The History of American Literature:* Part 2, Disc 1, Feature 8

Customize for
Visual/Spatial Learners
The story takes place in the bayou, a sluggish swampy region with which few students will be familiar. Obtain and show a geography video or sets of photos of bayou country to acquaint them with this unique environment and its inhabitants.

▶Critical Viewing◀

❶ **Compare** Students may say that both the painting and Faulkner's description convey the uneasiness and excitement that would precede a hunt.

◆Grammar and Style

❷ **Irregular Verb Forms** Point out that in the very first line, the word *seen* is a dialectical variation of the past tense of "see," used instead of the correct form: *saw*. Tell students to notice other examples of this kind of irregular usage.

RACE AT MORNING

William Faulkner

Buck and Doe Alerted, Arthur Fitzwilliam Tait, Superstock

❶ ▲ **Critical Viewing** Compare the mood of this painting with the feeling you get from the narrator's description of the bayou on page 788. **[Compare]**

I was in the boat when I seen him. It was ❷ jest dust-dark; I had jest fed the horses and clumb back down the bank to the boat and shoved off to cross back to camp when I seen him, about half a quarter up the river, swimming; just his head above the water, and it no more than a dot in that light. But I could see that rocking chair he toted on it and ❸ I knowed it was him, going right back to that ❹ canebrake[1] in the fork of the bayou where he

1. **canebrake** *n.*: Area overgrown with the tall, woody reeds of cane plants.

Humanities: Art

Buck and Doe Alerted by Arthur Fitzwilliam Tait (1819–1905).

This realistic landscape painting depicts a scene common to anyone who has ever viewed a video about North American wildlife or examined a diorama at a natural history museum. A pair of deer have stopped in their tracks, alerted perhaps by the sound of hunters in the distance. The sense of danger is also suggested by the receding line of geese in flight; they seem to be escaping.

Use these questions for discussion:

1. How does the artist express his attitude toward nature in this picture? *His respect for nature is evident from the way he positions the deer in the center of the canvas and depicts them—particularly the buck—as beautiful, powerful, majestic, and vulnerable to danger.*
2. How does this attitude compare with Faulkner's attitude in the story? *Students should realize that the author and artist share a great respect for nature.*

lived all year until the day before the season opened, like the game wardens had give him a calendar, when he would clear out and disappear, nobody knowed where, until the day after the season closed. But here he was, coming
❸ back a day ahead of time, like maybe he had
❹ got mixed up and was using last year's calendar by mistake. Which was jest too bad for him, because me and Mister Ernest would be setting on the horse right over him when the sun rose tomorrow morning.

So I told Mister Ernest and we et supper and fed the dogs, and then I holp Mister Ernest in the poker game, standing behind his chair until about ten o'clock, when Roth Edmonds said, "Why don't you go to bed, boy?"

"Or if you're going to set up," Willy Legate said, "why don't you take a spelling book to set up over? He knows every cuss word in the dic-
❺ tionary, every poker hand in the deck and every whisky label in the distillery, but he can't even write his name. Can you?" he says to me.

"I don't need to write my name down," I said. "I can remember in my mind who I am."

"You're twelve years old," Walter Ewell said. "Man to man now, how many days in your life did you ever spend in school?"

"He ain't got time to go to school," Willy Legate said. "What's the use in going to school from September to middle of November, when he'll have to quit then to come in here and do Ernest's hearing for him? And what's the use in going back to school in January, when in jest eleven months it will be November fifteenth again and he'll have to start all over telling
❻ Ernest which way the dogs went?"

"Well, stop looking into my hand, anyway," Roth Edmonds said.

"What's that? What's that?" Mister Ernest said. He wore his listening button in his ear all the time, but he never brought the battery to camp with him because the cord would bound to get snagged ever time we run through a thicket.

"Willy says for me to go to bed!" I hollered.

"Don't you never call nobody 'mister'?" Willy said.

"I call Mister Ernest 'mister.'" I said.

"All right," Mister Ernest said. "Go to bed then. I don't need you."

"That ain't no lie," Willy said. "Deaf or no deaf, he can hear a fifty-dollar raise if you don't even move your lips." ❻

So I went to bed, and after a while Mister Ernest come in and I wanted to tell him again how big them horns looked even half a quarter away in the river. Only I would 'a' had to holler, ❼ and the only time Mister Ernest agreed he couldn't hear was when we would be setting on Dan, waiting for me to point which way the dogs was going. So we jest laid down, and it wasn't no time Simon was beating the bottom of the dishpan with the spoon, hollering, "Raise up and get your four-o'clock coffee!" and I crossed the river in the dark this time, with the lantern, and fed Dan and Roth Edmondziz horse. It was going to be a fine day, cold and bright; even in the dark I could see the white frost on the leaves and bushes—jest exactly the kind of day that big old son of a gun laying up there in that brake would like to run.

Then we et, and set the stand-holder across for Uncle Ike McCaslin to put them on the stands where he thought they ought to be, because he was the oldest one in camp. He had been hunting deer in these woods for about a hundred years, I reckon, and if anybody would know where a buck would pass, it would be ❽ him. Maybe with a big old buck like this one, that had been running the woods for what would amount to a hundred years in a deer's life, too, him and Uncle Ike would sholy manage to be at the same place at the same time this morning—provided, of course, he managed to git away from me and Mister Ernest on the jump. Because me and Mister Ernest was going to git him.

Then me and Mister Ernest and Roth Edmonds sent the dogs over, with Simon holding Eagle and the other old dogs on leash because the young ones, the puppies, wasn't going nowhere until Eagle let him, nohow. Then me and Mister Ernest and Roth saddled up, and Mr. Ernest got up and I handed him up his

◆ Build Vocabulary

bayou (bī´ o͞o) *n.*: Sluggish, marshy inlet

distillery (dis til´ ə rē) *n.*: Place where alcoholic liquors are distilled

buck (bək) *n.*: Male animal, especially a male deer

Block Scheduling Strategies

Consider these suggestions to take advantage of extended class time:

- If you have access to technology, build background on Faulkner using the *History of American Literature* CD-ROM.
- Introduce the reading strategy and any other skills you wish to emphasize. Point out that the story students are about to read contains many uncommonly lengthy sentences. You may wish to use the Reading Strategy practice page in ***Selection Support,*** p. 241, at this point.
- After students have read the selections, use the questions in the Critical Viewing and Humanities Notes to prompt discussion of the illustrations that accompany the story.
- Put students into small groups to have them brainstorm for a list of "the responsibilities of writers, and screenwriters." Compare and contrast these lists with the points Faulkner makes in his acceptance speech.

❸ **Enrichment** A recurring theme in Faulkner's writing is humanity's destruction of nature. Faulkner's description of the deer's behavior reveals the animal's uncanny instinct for survival in the presence of hunters.

Customize for
Less Proficient Readers

❹ Guide students to see that the *him* the boy refers to here is the buck the hunters are after. What the boy refers to as "the rocking chair he toted" is the buck's impressive rack of antlers.

◆ Literary Focus

❺ **Dialect** Point out that by *set up,* Willy Legate means "stay awake," and that by *cuss,* he means "curse." Guide students to appreciate that without being formally educated, these bayou folk know what they need to know for the lives they lead. As they read, prompt students to consider what the narrator's language reveals about him, his background, and the area in which he lives.

Comprehension Check ☑

❻ Before students read on, ask them to identify the men in this group and infer how they are related. *Students should realize that Mister Ernest is the leader of the group, which has just begun an annual deer hunt, and that the boy is his charge. They may infer that the others—Willy, Walter, and Roth (Simon and others are introduced later) are men who know or may work for Mister Ernest.*

Customize for
Logical/Mathematical Learners

❼ Explain that the boy is using an expression for distance, *half a quarter,* that translates to a distance of half of a quarter-mile, or an eighth of a mile. This is a distance of 220 yards, a little longer than two football fields.

◆ Critical Thinking

❽ **Speculate** Based on the self-confidence the speaker expresses, prompt students to predict the outcome of the hunt. *Students may say that anyone so overly-confident is sure to fail.*

◆ Reading Strategy

❶ **Break Down Long Sentences** Encourage students to break this sentence down into smaller units of meaning to help them understand the sensations and emotions the speaker is describing.

Thematic Focus

❷ **From Every Corner of the Land** Guide students to note that this passage is filled with references that reflect the Mississippi bayou setting: the mud, the canebreak island in the center of the bayou, the deer's escape route from the bayou to the river. As students read, have them consider how the "race" might have been different had it taken place in another part of the country.

❸ **Clarification** Inform students that *standers* are the members of a hunting party who do not participate in the chase but, rather, who wait in readiness for game to be driven within shooting range.

◆ Literary Focus

❹ **Dialect** The word *souple* is dialect; students may infer that the expression means "to get excited" or "revved up."

Customize for *Visual/Spatial Learners*

❺ Students can picture this scene to see the humor in it—as the horse is galloping along, the boy, who sits behind Mister Ernest, is hanging on to the man's belt for dear life; he is horizontal to the ground, practically lifted off the horse's back. Students may enjoy sketching their interpretation of this image.

pump gun and let Dan's bridle[2] go for him to git rid of the spell of bucking he had to git shut of ever morning until Mister Ernest hit him between the ears with a gun barrel. Then Mister Ernest loaded the gun and give me the stirrup,[3] and I got up behind him and we taken the fire road up toward the bayou, the four big dogs dragging Simon along in front with his single-barrel britch-loader slung on a piece of plow line across his back, and the puppies moiling along in ever'body's way. It was light now and it was going to be jest fine; the east already yellow for the sun and our breaths smoking in the cold still bright air until the sun would come up and warm it, and a little skim of ice in the ruts, and ever leaf and twig and switch and even the frozen clods frosted over, waiting to sparkle like a rainbow when the sun finally come up and hit them. Until all my insides felt light and strong as a balloon, full of that light cold strong air, so that it seemed to me like I couldn't even feel the horse's back I was straddle of—jest the hot strong muscles moving under the hot strong skin, setting up there without no wait atall, so that when old Eagle struck and jumped, me and Dan and Mister Ernest would go jest like a bird, not even touching the ground. It was jest fine. When that big old buck got killed today, I knowed that even if he had put it off another ten years, he couldn't 'a' picked a better one. ❶

And sho enough, as soon as we come to the bayou we seen his foot in the mud where he had come up out of the river last night, spread in the soft mud like a cow's foot, big as a cow's, big as a mule's, with Eagle and the other dogs laying into the leash rope now until Mister Ernest told me to jump down and help Simon hold them. Because me and Mister Ernest knowed exactly where he would be—a little canebrake island in the middle of the bayou, where he could lay up until whatever doe or little deer the dogs had happened to jump could go up or down the bayou in either direction and take the dogs on away, so he could steal out and creep back down the bayou to the river and swim it, and leave the country like he always done the day the season opened. ❷

Which is jest what we never aimed for him to do this time. So we left Roth on his horse to cut him off and turn him over Uncle Ike's standers if he tried to slip back down the bayou, and me and Simon, with the leashed dogs, walked on up the bayou until Mister Ernest on the horse said it was fur enough; then turned up into the woods about half a quarter above the brake because the wind was going to be south this morning when it riz, and turned down toward the brake, and Mister Ernest give the word to cast them,[4] and we slipped the leash and Mr. Ernest give me the stirrup again and I got up. ❸

Old Eagle had done already took off because he knowed where that old son of a gun would be laying as good as we did, not making no racket atall yet, but jest boring on through the buck vines with the other dogs trailing along behind him, and even Dan seemed to know about that buck, too, beginning to souple up and jump a little through the vines, so that I taken my holt in Mister Ernest's belt already before the time had come for Mister Ernest to touch him. ❹ Because when we got strung out, going fast behind a deer, I wasn't on Dan's back much of the time nohow, but mostly jest strung out from my holt on Mister Ernest's belt, so that Willy Legate said that when we was going through the woods fast, it looked like Mister Ernest had a boy-size pair of empty overalls blowing out of his hind pocket. ❺

> ◆ **Literary Focus**
> Which word here shows the speaker is using dialect, and what does the word mean in standard English?

So it wasn't even a strike, it was a jump. Eagle must 'a' walked right up behind him or maybe even stepped on him while he was laying there still thinking it was day after tomorrow. Eagle jest throwed his head back and up and said, "There he goes," and we even heard the buck crashing through the first of the cane. Then all the other dogs was hollering behind him, and Dan give a squat to jump, but it was against the curb[5] this time, not jest the snaffle,[6] and Mister Ernest let him down into

2. **bridle** *n.*: Headgear with which a horse is guided.
3. **stirrup** *n.*: Rings or other devices attached to the saddle of a horse and used to support the rider's feet.
4. **cast them:** Send them ranging overland in search of a trail.
5. **curb** *n.*: Chain or strap used to restrain a horse.
6. **snaffle** *n.*: The part of a bridle that is inserted into the mouth of a horse.

Cultural Connection

Deer as Symbols Many Native American peoples use the deer as symbolic figures in their dance rituals and ceremonies. To gain power over the deer before a hunt, the Yaqui perform a deer dance at fiestas. The footwork, postures, and gestures of the dance are meant to represent the deer's behavior during the hunt. While this ceremony is performed as a solo dance, the deer dance in San Juan, Puerto Rico, is performed by eighteen men, fourteen of whom run away at the end of the dance, leaving four to be symbolically hunted and killed. For many nations, such as the Hopi, the deer dance is performed to help bring rain and to promote abundant harvests.

Among the Zuñi, the deer dance is performed to help cure sickness. During the performance, dancers use actual parts or symbolic representations of parts of a deer, such as antlers, hoofs, and hide.

Rattles made with deer hoofs are particularly prevalent among the Native American nations of North America. They are used in mourning rites by the Diegueno Indians of California and in the rituals of many men's societies of the Great Plains. Among the Flatheads of Montana, deer-hoof rattles were used by shamans, or medicine people, to conduct dances for cures. In California and South America, these rattles, as well as hoof-tipped poles, are associated with girls' rites of initiation into adulthood.

the bayou and swung him around the brake and up the other bank. Only he never had to say, "Which way?" because I was already pointing past his shoulder, freshening my holt on the belt jest as Mister Ernest touched Dan with that big old rusty spur on his nigh heel, because when Dan felt it he would go off jest like a stick of dynamite, straight through whatever he could bust and over and under what he couldn't, over it like a bird or under it crawling on his knees like a mole or a big coon, with Mister Ernest still on him because he had the saddle to hold on to, and me still there because I had Mister Ernest to hold on to; me and Mister Ernest not riding him, but jest going along with him, provided we held on. Because when the jump come, Dan never cared who else was there neither; I believe to my soul he could 'a' cast and run them dogs by hisself, without me or Mister Ernest or Simon or nobody.

That's what he done. He had to; the dogs was already almost out of hearing. Eagle must 'a' been looking right up that big son of a gun's tail until he finally decided he better git on out of there. And now they must 'a' been getting pretty close to Uncle Ike's standers, and Mister Ernest reined Dan back and held him, squatting and bouncing and trembling like a mule having his tail roached,[7] while we listened for the shots. But never none come, and I hollered to Mister Ernest we better go on while I could still hear the dogs, and he let Dan off, but still there wasn't no shots, and now we knowed the
6 race had done already passed the standers, like that old son of a gun actually was a hant,[8] like Simon and the other field hands said he was, and we busted out of a thicket, and sho enough there was Uncle Ike and Willy standing beside his foot in a soft patch.

"He got through us all," Uncle Ike said. "I don't know how he done it. I just had a glimpse of him. He looked big as a elephant, with a rack on his head you could cradle a yellin' calf in. He went right on down the ridge. You better get on, too; that Hog Bayou camp might not miss him."

So I freshened my holt and Mister Ernest touched Dan again. The ridge run due south; it was clear of vines and bushes so we could go fast, into the wind, too, because it had riz now, and now the sun was up, too; though I hadn't had time to notice it, bright and strong and level through the woods, shining and sparkling like a rainbow on the frosted leaves. So we would hear the dogs again any time now as the wind got up; we could make time now, but still holding Dan back to a canter,[9] because it was either going to be quick, when he got down to the standers from that Hog Bayou camp eight miles below ourn, or a long time, in case he got by them, too. And sho enough, after a while we heard the dogs; we was walking Dan now to let him blow a while, and we heard them, the sound coming faint up the wind, not running now, but trailing because the big son of a gun had decided a good piece back, probably, to put a end to this foolishness, and picked hisself up and soupled out and put about a mile between hisself and the dogs—until he run up on them other standers from that camp below. I could almost see him stopped behind a bush, peeping out and saying, "What's this? What's this? Is this whole durn country full of folks this morning?" 7 Then looking back over his shoulder at where old Eagle and others was hollering along after him while he decided how much time he had to decide what to do next.

Except he almost shaved it too fine. We heard the shots; it sounded like a war. Old Eagle must 'a' been looking right up his tail again and he had to bust on through the best way he could. "Pow, pow, pow, pow" and then "Pow, pow, pow, pow," like it must 'a' been three or 8 four ganged right up on him before he had time 9 even to swerve, and me hollering, "No! No! No! No!" because he was ourn. It was our beans and oats he et and our brake he laid in; we had been watching him every year, and it was like we had raised him, to be killed at last on our jump, in front of our dogs, by some strangers that would probably try to beat the dogs off

7. **roached** *v.*: Cut so that the remainder stands upright, as with an animal's tail.
8. **hant** *n.*: Ghost.

9. **canter** *n.*: Three-beat gait resembling, but smoother and slower than, a gallop.

◆ Build Vocabulary

moiling (moi′ liŋ) *v.*: Churning; swirling
switch (swich) *n.*: Slender, flexible twig or whip

◆ Reading Strategy

6 Break Down Long Sentences Guide students to break down this lengthy sentence, as needed, to understand what is happening here: the buck, like the ghost he is thought to be, has eluded the dogs and the standers, too.

◆ Literary Focus

7 Dialect Point out that here the boy humorously imbues the buck with human characteristics; the animal thinks and even speaks like one of the hunters in the bayou.

Customize for *Less Proficient Readers*

8 Guide students to understand that another group of hunters has spotted the buck and is firing at it. The boy is outraged because he believes that the prize belongs to his group alone.

◆ Critical Thinking

9 Interpret; Evaluate Ask students to explain why the speaker believes that the deer belongs to him and Mister Ernest. *They have been chasing the deer so long that they feel that they alone have the right to shoot him.* Have students explain whether they feel that the boy is justified in his belief.

Tips to Guide Reading

Summarizing Suggest that students work in pairs as they read to summarize and discuss any questions. Explain that discussing their summaries will help students clarify information, answer questions, and focus on the main ideas.

Analyze Literary Criticism

The critic Irving Howe commented on William Faulkner's work: "...At a time when men in mass society often believe that their possibilities for significant experience are shrinking, Faulkner insists upon the largeness of human possibility. He returned to traditional dramatic gestures; he reasserted the claims of uncompromising tragedy, extreme melodrama, wild comedy. The force of human desire breaks through in his novels with a grandeur and terror that are almost unequaled in our time. Indeed, it is this readiness for confronting the largest ranges of experience which helps explain the hold Faulkner has won upon modern readers ..."

Read aloud Howe's critique and work with students to paraphrase it. Then have students discuss these questions:

1. How does Faulkner express the force of human desire in *Race at Morning?*
2. Do you agree that the experience described in this story will hold interest for modern readers? Why or why not?

Listening to Literature Audiocassettes At any time, feel free to stop and play the audiocassette version of the story or parts of it to enhance comprehension or to help students appreciate the vitality, richness, and the humor of the prose.

Customize for
AP Students
In this story, Faulkner makes references to Yoknapatawpha County, a fictional place that he used as the setting for several of his novels, including *The Hamlet.* Have more advanced students learn more about Faulkner's imaginary setting. Ask them to find and present a map showing Lafayette County, Mississippi, the actual location on which Yoknapatawpha was based. Certain editions of Faulkner's works include maps of the author's fictional setting.

▶Critical Viewing◀
❶ **Connect** Students may respond that the bayou is more dense, watery, and impenetrable than they had imagined. The painting can also help students appreciate the eerie beauty of such a setting.

Winter in Southern Louisiana, Ellsworth Woodward, Mississippi Museum of Art

❶ ▲ **Critical Viewing** How does this painting add to your appreciation of the story's bayou setting? **[Connect]**

Humanities: Art

Winter in Southern Louisiana by Ellsworth Woodward.

This colorful landscape depicts a serene, still bayou scene. The long shadows and silhouetted trees in the background suggest that it is either early morning or late afternoon. The painting shows the bayou to consist of water, low-lying land, and towering trees that provide little shade. It is early winter, judging by the shades of red, yellow, brown, and orange in the foliage.

Use these questions for discussion:

1. Although this painting does not make specific reference to hunting, how does it illustrate some of the difficulties deer hunters would face? *Students may cite the dense, high brush, mucky, watery areas, straggling branches, and limited visibility.*
2. How would you describes the mood created by such as setting. Explain. *Students may respond that the bayou has an eerie or mystical feel to it. Others may simply see it as forbidding.*

and drag him away before we could even git a piece of the meat.

"Shut up and listen," Mister Ernest said. So I done it and we could hear the dogs; not just the others, but Eagle, too, not trailing no scent now and not baying[10] no downed meat neither, but running hot on sight long after the shooting was over. I jest had time to freshen my holt. Yes, sir, they was running on sight. Like Willy Legate would say, if Eagle jest had a drink of whisky he would ketch that deer; going on, done already gone when we broke out of the thicket and seen the fellers that had done the shooting, five or six of them, squatting and crawling around, looking at the ground and the bushes, like maybe if they looked hard enough, spots of blood would bloom out on the stalks
2 and leaves like frogstools or hawberries, with old Eagle still in hearing and still telling them that what blood they found wasn't coming out of nothing in front of him.

"Have any luck, boys?" Mister Ernest said.

"I think I hit him," one of them said. "I know I did. We're hunting blood now."

"Well, when you find him, blow your horn and I'll come back and tote him in to camp for you," Mister Ernest said.

So we went on, going fast now because the race was almost out of hearing again, going fast, too, like not jest the buck, but the dogs, too, had took a new leash on life from all the
3 excitement and shooting.

We was in strange country now because we never had to run this fur before, we had always killed before now; now we had come to Hog Bayou that runs into the river a good fifteen miles below our camp. It had water in it, not to mention a mess of down trees and logs and such, and Mister Ernest checked Dan again, saying, "Which way?" I could just barely hear them, off to the east a little, like the old son of a gun had give up the idea of Vicksburg or New Orleans, like he first seemed to have, and had decided to have a look at Alabama, maybe, since he was already up and moving; so I pointed and we turned up the bayou hunting for a crossing, and maybe we could 'a' found one, except that I reckon Mister Ernest decided we never had time to wait.

10. **baying** *v.*: Barking with long, deep tones.

We come to a place where the bayou had narrowed down to about twelve or fifteen feet, and Mister Ernest said, "Look out, I'm going to touch him," and done it; I didn't even have time to freshen my holt when we was already in the air, and then I seen the vine—it was a loop of grapevine nigh as big as my wrist, looping down right across the middle of the bayou—and I thought he seen it, too, and was jest waiting to grab it and fling it over our heads to go under it, and I know Dan seen it because he even ducked his head to jump under it. But Mister Ernest never seen it atall until it skun back along Dan's neck and hooked under the head of the saddle horn,[11] us flying on through the air, the loop of the vine gitting tighter and tighter until something somewhere was going to have to give. It was the saddle girth. It broke, and Dan going on and scrabbling up the other bank bare nekkid except for the bridle, and me and Mister Ernest and the saddle, Mister Ernest still setting in the saddle holding the gun, and me still holding onto Mister Ernest's belt, hanging in the air over the bayou in the tightened loop of that vine like in the drawed-back loop of a big rubber-banded slingshot, until it snapped back and shot across the
4 bayou and flang us clear, me still holding onto Mister Ernest's belt and on the bottom now, so that when we lit I would 'a' had Mister Ernest and the saddle both on top of me if I hadn't clumb fast around the saddle and up Mister Ernest's side, so that when we landed, it was the saddle first, then Mister Ernest, and
5 me on top, until I jumped up, and Mister Ernest still laying there with jest the white rim of his eyes showing.

◆ Reading Strategy
How can you break down this sentence into a series of shorter sentences?

"Mister Ernest!" I hollered, and then clumb down to the bayou and scooped my cap full of water and clumb back and throwed it in his face, and he opened his eyes and laid there on the saddle cussing me.

11. **saddle horn** *n.*: Knob at the front and top of a saddle.

◆ Build Vocabulary
scrabbling (skrab′ liŋ) *v.*: Scrambling

Customize for
English Language Learners

2 Discuss with students that when the man says that they are *hunting blood,* he means that they think the buck has been hit and that they are looking for the trail of blood stains that will lead them to their prey.

Customize for
Verbal/Linguistic Learners

3 Students may notice the play on words in the expression *new leash* (lease) *on life.* In a hunting dog's world, having a new lease on life would mean having renewed eagerness to hunt.

◆ Reading Strategy

4 Break Down Long Sentences Students first need to understand that the riders have been hooked by a vine. One way to break down the sentence, including paraphrasing, is as follows: *The saddle girth broke and Dan scrabbled up the other bank. He wore only the bridle. Mister Ernest was still in the saddle, holding the gun. I was still holding on to Mister Ernest's belt. We both were hanging in the air over the bayou, hooked in the tightened loop of the vine. This ever-tightening vine was like a slingshot. Then the vine snapped back and flung us across the bayou. I was still holding on to Mister Ernest's belt. It appeared to me that when we landed, I would have Mister Ernest and the saddle on top of me. But I quickly climbed around the saddle and up Mister Ernest's side. So, when we landed, it was the saddle first, then Mister Ernest, and then me, on top. When I jumped up, Mister Ernest was still laying there with just the white rim of his eyes showing.*

Customize for
Body/Kinesthetic Learners

5 Have students picture this very humorous and improbable scene.

Research Skills Mini-Lesson

Finding Up-to-Date Information

This mini-lesson supports activity 4, p. 801.

Introduce the Concept Explain that the success of a debate depends on both sides having the most up-to-date information.

Develop the Background Have students brainstorm for the kinds of information they need, and for where to find that information. A chart such as the one here can be used to organize the information. Students can research this information on the Internet or at the library in print form.

Apply the Information Have students form teams and practice their debates. Several teams may represent the various positions on the hunting issue. Ask the listeners to determine the winning side of the debate and to give reasons why.

Pro Hunting	Information/Sources
Hunters	

Con Hunting	Information/Sources
Animals Advocates	Articles, Bills passed

Assess the Outcome Evaluate students' ability to find up-to-date information using a variety of sources and to organize and use the information in the debate. You may want to use Peer Assessment: Speaking /Speech on p. 133 in ***Alternative Assessment.***

◆ Critical Thinking

1 Infer Ask students what they can infer about the relationship between Mister Ernest and the boy from this exchange. Is Mister Ernest really angry at his ward? Is the boy frightened of his guardian's wrath? *Students should realize that the boy has no qualms about speaking his mind to Mister Ernest, and knows that he has nothing to fear from him. There is not real anger between them—the two are obviously fond of each other.*

◆ Critical Thinking

2 Analyze What does this passage express about human beings' experience of time while in the domain of nature? How does it relate to other passages in the story that refer to time? *In this passage and others in the story, the author suggests that people lose track of time when they are in a natural setting, away from the schedules and clocks that normally regulate our days.*

Customize for *Less Proficient Readers*

3 Clarify for students that when the boy yells, *"Don't touch him!"* he means "Don't spur him!" He knows that making the horse run fast will cause the makeshift cinch to let go and make them fall off again.

◆ Critical Thinking

4 Evaluate Ask students: How effective would you say the other hunters are? What evidence do you have to support your answer? *Students may respond that they are not very effective because they are still looking for blood when it is obvious from Eagle the dog's response that there is none to be found.*

"God dawg it," he said, "why didn't you stay behind where you started out?"

"You was the biggest!" I said. "You would 'a' mashed me flat!"

"What do you think you done to me?" Mister Ernest said. "Next time, if you can't stay where you start out, jump clear. Don't climb on top of me no more. You hear?"

"Yes, sir," I said.

So he got up then, still cussing and holding his back, and clumb down to the water and dipped some in his hand onto his face and neck and dipped some more up and drunk it, and I drunk some, too, and clumb back and got (1) the saddle and the gun, and we crossed the bayou on the down logs. If we could jest ketch Dan; not that he would have went them fifteen miles back to camp, because, if anything, he would have went on by hisself to try to help Eagle ketch that buck. But he was about fifty yards away, eating buck vines, so I brought him back, and we taken Mister Ernest's galluses[12] and my belt and tied the saddle back on Dan. It didn't look like much, but maybe it would hold.

"Provided you don't let me jump him through no more grapevines without hollering first," Mister Ernest said.

"Yes, sir," I said. "I'll holler first next time—provided you'll holler a little quicker when you touch him next time, too." But it was all right; we jest had to be a little easy getting up. "Now which-a-way?" I said. Because we couldn't hear nothing now, after wasting all this time. And this was new country, sho enough. It had been cut over and growed up in thickets we couldn't 'a' seen over even standing up on Dan.

But Mister Ernest never even answered. He jest turned Dan along the bank of the bayou where it was a little more open and we could move faster again, soon as Dan and us got used to that homemade cinch strop[13] and got a little confidence in it. Which jest happened to be east, or so I thought then, because I never paid no particular attention to east then be- (2) cause the sun—I don't know where the morning had went, but it was gone, the morning and the frost, too—was up high now, even if my insides had told me it was past dinnertime. (2)

And then we heard him. No, that's wrong; what we heard was shots. And that was when we realized how fur he had come, because the only camp we knowed about in that direction was the Hollyknowe camp, and Hollyknowe was exactly twenty-eight miles from Van Dorn, where me and Mister Ernest lived—jest the shots, no dogs nor nothing. If old Eagle was still behind him and the buck was still alive, he was too wore out now to even say, "Here he comes."

"Don't touch him!" I hollered. But Mister Ernest remembered that cinch strop, too, and (3) he jest let Dan off the snaffle. And Dan heard them shots, too; picking his way through the thickets, hopping the vines and logs when he could and going under them when he couldn't. And sho enough, it was jest like before—two or three men squatting and creeping among the (4) bushes, looking for blood that Eagle had done already told them wasn't there. But we never stopped this time, jest trotting on by with Dan hopping and dodging among the brush and vines dainty as a dancer. Then Mister Ernest swung Dan until we was going due north.

"Wait!" I hollered. "Not this way."

But Mister Ernest jest turned his face back over his shoulder. It looked tired, too, and there was a smear of mud on it where that ere grapevine had snatched him off the horse.

"Don't you know where he's heading?" he said. "He's done done his part, give everybody a fair open shot at him, and now he's going home, back to that brake in our bayou. He ought to make it exactly at dark."

And that's what he was doing. We went on. It didn't matter to hurry now. There wasn't no sound nowhere; it was that time in the early afternoon in November when don't nothing move or cry, not even birds, the peckerwoods and yellowhammers and jays, and it seemed to me like I could see all three of us—me and Mister Ernest and Dan—and Eagle, and the other dogs, and that big old buck, moving through the quiet woods in the same direction, headed for the same place, not running now but walking, that had all run the fine race the best we knowed how, and all three of us now turned like on a agreement to walk back home, not together in a bunch because we didn't want to worry or tempt one another, because what we had all three spent this morning doing was no

12. **galluses** *n.*: Suspenders.
13. **cinch strop** *n.*: Strap that encircles the body of an animal and is used to fasten something on its back.

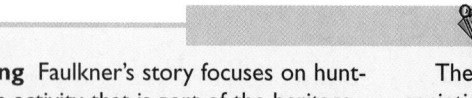

Cultural Connection

Hunting Faulkner's story focuses on hunting—an activity that is part of the heritage of all cultures. While farming has been practiced for about one percent of human history, hunting was humankind's occupation for more than half a million years. Anthropologists think hunting may have encouraged many traits common to human beings in modern societies, including cooperation, organization, and aggression.

There are few hunting and gathering societies left in the world. The only people who still exist solely by hunting are the Mbuti Pygmies of the Central African rain forest and the disappearing Bushmen of the Kalahari in Southern Africa. Societies that combine hunting with other means of sustenance include the Eskimos, the Pacific Northwest Indians, some Plains Indians, the Siriono Indians of Bolivia, and the Aborigines of Australia.

These hunting societies are equally egalitarian: Cooperation is paramount for successful hunting, and individualism and authoritarianism are discouraged. Identification with the environment is very strong, as reflected in such religious ceremonies as the Mbuti songs to the forest god, Eskimo poetry celebrating the sea goddess, and the giraffe dance of the Kalahari Bushmen.

playacting jest for fun, but was serious, and all three of us was still what we was—that old buck that had to run, not because he was skeered, but because running was what he done the best and was proudest at; and Eagle and the dogs that chased him, not because they hated or feared him, but because that was the thing they done the best and was proudest at; and me and Mister Ernest and Dan, that run him not because we wanted his meat, which would be too tough to eat anyhow, or his head to hang on a wall, but because now we could go back and work hard for eleven months making a crop, so we would have the right to come back here next November—all three of us going back home now, peaceful and separate, but still side by side, until next year, next time.

> **◆ Reading Strategy**
> 5 Why do you think Faulkner chose to combine all of this information into one sentence?

6 Then we seen him for the first time. We was out of the cut-over now; we could even 'a' cantered, except that all three of us was long past that, and now you could tell where west was because the sun was already half-way down it. So we was walking, too, when we come on the dogs—the puppies and one of the old ones—played out, laying in a little wet swag, panting, jest looking up at us when we passed, but not moving when we went on. Then we come to a long open glade, you could see about half a quarter, and we seen the three other old dogs and about a hundred yards ahead of them Eagle, all walking, not making no sound; and then suddenly, at the fur end of the glade, the buck hisself getting up from where he had been resting for the dogs to come up, getting up without no hurry, big, big as a mule, tall as a mule, and turned without no hurry still, and the white underside of his tail for a second or two more before the thicket taken him.

It might 'a' been a signal, a good-bye, a farewell. Still walking, we passed the other three old dogs in the middle of the glade, laying down, too, now jest where they was when the buck vanished, and not trying to get up neither when we passed; and still that hundred yards ahead of them, Eagle, too, not laying down, because he was still on his feet, but his legs was spraddled and his head was down; maybe jest waiting until we was out of sight of his shame, his eyes saying plain as talk when we passed, "I'm sorry, boys, but this here is all." 7

Mister Ernest stopped Dan. "Jump down and look at his feet," he said.

"Ain't nothing wrong with his feet," I said. "It's his wind has done give out."

"Jump down and look at his feet," Mister Ernest said.

So I done it, and while I was stooping over Eagle I could hear the pump gun go, "Snick-cluck, Snick-cluck. Snick-cluck" three times, except that I never thought nothing then. Maybe he was jest running the shells through to be sho it would work when we seen him again or maybe to make sho they was all buckshot.[14] 8 Then I got up again, and we went on, still walking; a little west of north now, because when we seen his white flag that second or two before the thicket hid it, it was on a beeline for that notch in the bayou. And it was evening, too, now. The wind had done dropped and there was a edge to the air and the sun jest touched the tops of the trees now, except jest now and then, when it found a hole to come almost level through onto the ground. And he was taking the easiest way, too, now, going straight as he could. When we seen his foot in the soft places he was running for a while at first after his rest. But soon he was walking, too, like he knowed, too, where Eagle and the dogs was.

And then we seen him again. It was the last time—a thicket, with the sun coming through a hole onto it like a searchlight. He crashed jest once; then he was standing there broadside to us, not twenty yards away, big as a statue and red as gold in the sun, and the sun sparking on the tips of his horns—they was twelve of them—so that he looked like he had twelve lighted candles branched around his head, standing there looking at us while Mister Ernest raised the gun and aimed at his neck, and the gun went, "Click. Snick-cluck. Click, 9

◆ Build Vocabulary

swag (swag) *n.*: Suspended cluster of branches

glade (glād) *n.*: Open space surrounded by woods

14. buckshot *n.*: Large lead shot used for shooting deer and other big game.

◆ Reading Strategy

5 Break Down Long Sentences Students may suggest that Faulkner uses just one sentence here because he is describing a cycle of life as these men live it, and summarizing the essence of his story.

Customize for *AP Students*

6 Students may notice the change in tone in this passage. Even though the men spot the buck, the frenetic chase is essentially over. Everyone, including the dogs, is spent, weary. Readers can catch their breath, too.

7 Enrichment Point out to students that here and in other places throughout the story, animals communicate messages to people in a variety of ways. Ask students to identify examples as they read or reread the story.

◆ Critical Thinking

8 Analyze Ask students to explain what is going on here. Why does Mister Ernest insist that the boy dismount to check a nonexistent problem with the horse? *Students should realize that Mister Ernest is trying to divert the boy's attention from his actions with the gun. They will find out later that Mister Ernest is actually unloading the gun; he plans not to kill the buck if the opportunity arises.*

◆ Critical Thinking

9 Analyze What kind of imagery does the speaker use to describe the deer? Why do you think he chooses the kind of imagery he does? *The speaker uses imagery that conveys the majesty of the animal because he respects the buck's size, intelligence, and brazenness. He views the buck with awe—even a type of reverence.*

Customize for *Gifted/Talented Students*

Students may be challenged to write what happened the last day from the buck's point of view. Suggest that they write about what he saw, what he would say to Mister Ernest and the boy, and how he feels about not being killed.

Beyond the Classroom

Community Connection

Hunting Season The characters in the story wait all year for the opening day of deer-hunting season. Explain to students that states carefully regulate when, where, and for how long particular animals can be hunted or fish caught. Have them imagine what it would be like for casual hikers and campers if hunters were let loose year round! Point out that regulations also require most people to obtain licenses before they may hunt or fish. Have students discuss the reasons for allowing the shooting of certain animals, and also for limiting hunting and fishing seasons. Invite interested students to contact your state's fish and game office to learn about hunting regulations in your area, including what precautionary measures hunters need to take. Have them find out about the procedures and requirements for obtaining a license.

▶Critical Viewing◀

❶ **Evaluate** Students may say that the painting is effective because it pictures an older man and a young boy with a dog who appear to be roughly the same ages as Mister Ernest and his ward. They may also point out, however, that neither figures carries a gun like those in Faulkner's story, that the hunters in the story are on horseback, and that the environment shown in the painting does not closely resemble that of the bayou.

◆Critical Thinking

❷ **Compare** Students can compare the sounds the gun makes now with those it made while the boy was checking the horse's feet (p. 793) to recognize that they are the same sounds. The gun is empty; Mister Ernest had unloaded it.

◆Grammar and Style

❸ **Irregular Verb Forms** Have students take note of the way the boy, using regional dialect, incorrectly conjugates the verbs *throw* and *take* to express them in the past tense.

◆Critical Thinking

❹ **Analyze** Have students discuss whether Mister Ernest really forget to load his gun. Does the boy really believe that he did? *Students should realize that Mister Ernest emptied his gun because he never intended to kill the buck. Some students may recognize that the boy understands exactly what happened, even though he doesn't know why Mister Ernest would have purposely unloaded the gun.*

Old Man and the Boy, John Head, Russell A. Fink Gallery

❶ ▲ Critical Viewing Do you think this painting effectively illustrates the story? Explain. **[Evaluate]**

❷ Snick-cluck. Click. Snick-cluck" three times, and Mister Ernest still holding the gun aimed while the buck turned and give one long bound, the white underside of his tail like a blaze of fire, too, until the thicket and the shadows put it out; and Mister Ernest laid the gun slow and gentle back across the saddle in front of him, saying quiet and peaceful, and not much louder than jest breathing, "God dawg. God dawg."

Then he jogged me with his elbow and we got down, easy and careful because of that ere cinch strop and he reached into his vest and taken out one of the cigars. It was busted where I had fell on it, I reckon, when we hit the ground. ❸ He throwed it away and taken out the other one. It was busted, too, so he bit off a hunk of it to chew and throwed the rest away. And now the sun was gone even from the tops of the trees and there wasn't nothing left but a big red glare in the west.

"Don't worry," I said. "I ain't going to tell them you forgot to load your gun. For that matter, they don't need to know we ever seed him." ❹

"Much oblige," Mister Ernest said. There wasn't going to be no moon tonight neither, so he taken the compass off the whang leather loop in his buttonhole and handed me the gun and set the compass on a stump and stepped back and looked at it. "Just about the way we're headed now," he said, and taken the gun from me and opened it and put one shell in the britch and taken up the compass, and I taken Dan's reins and we started, with him in front with the compass in his hand.

And after a while it was full dark; Mister Ernest would have to strike a match ever now and then to read the compass, until the stars come out good and we could pick out one to follow, because I said, "How fur do you reckon it is?" A little more than one box of matches." So we used a star when we could, only we couldn't see it all the time because the woods was too dense and we would git a little off until he would have to spend another match. And

Humanities: Art

Old Man and the Boy by John Head.

This painting shows an old man and a young boy and his dog, presumably out for a walk by a secluded lake or stream. Our eyes are drawn to the boy in his red hat, the only splash of bold color in the landscape. He and the dog have spotted or heard something in the distance, perhaps a deer, a turkey, or a waterfowl.

Use this question for discussion: How can you tell that the man and boy are on a casual walk rather than a hunting trip? *Students may suggest that they are not dressed like hunters and that neither carries a gun, bow, or other hunting gear.*

now it was good and late, and he stopped and said, "Get on the horse."

"I ain't tired," I said.

"Get on the horse," he said. "We don't want to spoil him."

5 Because he had been a good feller ever since I had knowed him, which was even before that day two years ago when maw went off with the Vicksburg roadhouse feller and the next day pap didn't come home neither, and on the third one Mister Ernest rid Dan up to the door of the cabin on the river he let us live in, so pap could work his piece of land and run his fish line, too, and said, "Put that gun down and come on here and climb up behind."

6 So I got in the saddle even if I couldn't reach the stirrups, and Mister Ernest taken the reins and I must 'a' went to sleep, because the next thing I knowed a button hole of my lumberjack was tied to the saddle horn with that ere whang cord off the compass, and it was good and late now and we wasn't fur, because Dan was already smelling water, the river. Or maybe it was the feed lot itself he smelled, because we struck the fire road not a quarter below it, and soon I could see the river, too, with the white mist laying on it soft and still as cotton. Then the lot, home; and up yonder in the dark, not no piece akchully, close enough to hear us unsaddling and shucking corn prob'ly, and sholy close enough to hear Mister Ernest blowing his horn at the dark camp for Simon to come in the boat and git us, that old buck in his brake in the bayou; home, too, resting, too, after the hard run, waking hisself now and then, dreaming of dogs behind him or maybe it was the racket we was making would wake him, but not neither of them for more than jest a little while before sleeping again.

7 ◆ **Literary Focus**
How would you restate this passage in standard English?

Then Mister Ernest stood on the bank blowing until Simon's lantern went bobbing down into the mist; then we clumb down to the landing and Mister Ernest blowed again now and then to guide Simon, until we seen the lantern in the mist, and then Simon and the boat; only it looked like ever time I set down and got still, I went back to sleep, because Mister Ernest was shaking me again to git out and climb the bank into the dark camp, until I felt a bed against my knees and tumbled into it.

Then it was morning, tomorrow; it was all over now until next November, next year, and we could come back. Uncle Ike and Willy and Walter and Roth and the rest of them had come in yestiddy, soon as Eagle taken the buck out of hearing and they knowed that deer was gone, to pack up and be ready to leave this morning for Yoknapatawpha, where they lived, until it would be November again and they could come back again. 8

So, as soon as we et breakfast, Simon run them back up the river in the big boat to where they left their cars and pickups, and now it wasn't nobody but jest me and Mister Ernest setting on the back against the kitchen wall in the sun; Mister Ernest smoking a cigar—a whole one this time that Dan hadn't had no chance to jump through a grapevine and bust. He hadn't washed his face neither where that vine had throwed him into the mud.

◆ Critical Thinking

5 Interpret What does this passage reveal about Mister Ernest's character? *He is a good-hearted man who took it upon himself to take care of the son his tenants had abandoned.* How does it help you understand the speaker's attitude toward Mister Ernest? *When you realize all that Mister Ernest has done for the speaker, you understand why the boy is inseparable from his guardian and why he addresses him alone with the respectful title of "Mister."*

◆ Critical Thinking

6 Analyze Ask students to explain how Faulkner plays with time in this passage. *He seamlessly blends the boy's first horse ride with Mister Ernest two years earlier into the present; the boy falls asleep as Mister Ernest is taking him to his new home, but wakes to find himself returning from the hunt.*

◆ Literary Focus

7 Dialect Students' restatements will vary, but should express the ideas that night has fallen, that the boy and Mister Ernest have left the hunt and have arrived at a point across the river from home, that Simon has come to ferry them back home, and that the buck, too, is resting after the chase.

◆ Critical Thinking

8 Assess; Speculate Are Uncle Ike and the others smarter hunters than Mister Ernest and the speaker? *Students may note that they don't possess the same sense of perseverance and purpose that drove the older man and the boy. Others may respond that they were smart enough to realize that they would never be able to catch the buck on their own, so they were smarter not to waste time pursuing him.* How do you think they might view the pair's efforts during the hunt? *They would probably think that the two were a bit crazy for giving the chase as much effort as they did, particularly if they knew that they had forfeited their chance at slaying the buck.*

Speaking, Listening, and Viewing Mini-Lesson

Broadcast

This mini-lesson supports the Speaking, Listening, and Viewing activity in the Idea Bank, p. 801.

Introduce the Concept Guide students to understand that their broadcasts will be judged according to how clearly and accurately they describe the experience and how well they capture its drama, excitement, and humor.

Develop Background Have students work in small groups to gather their information.

Apply the Information Have groups write and edit their broadcast scripts. One member of the group can present the broadcast, or students can divide up the "air time."

Assess the Outcome Have listeners comment on the accuracy and effectiveness of the broadcasts. Guide them to evaluate how clearly information is presented and how well the reporters have captured the excitement, tension, and humor of the hunt. You may wish to have students tape record the broadcasts so you can listen to them more than once for further evaluation.

Thematic Focus

❶ **From Every Corner of the Land** Discuss with students how people look after one another in rural communities, particularly in earlier times. Although Mister Ernest probably feels no real connection to or affection for the boy at this point in time, he knows he cannot just leave him alone in the cabin. He does the right thing by taking the boy into his care, with no questions asked, no legalities considered.

◆ Critical Thinking

❷ **Analyze** The speaker uses the word *home* several times in this passage. What might make the idea of home especially meaningful to him? *The home he shares with Mister Ernest is probably the first real home he's ever known. It is his place of refuge and the only place where anyone has ever truly cared for him.*

◆ Reading Strategy

❸ **Break Down Long Sentences** Students can break down this paragraph into smaller units to get at its essential meaning: the hunting ritual is about affirming the lives of the participants; it is about taking pride in what they do during the rest of the year so that, once a year, every year, they can celebrate by going on the quest. It is also about how the buck's pride in avoiding these men for two weeks each year is rewarded with fifty weeks free of bother.

◆ Critical Thinking

❹ **Interpret** What does Mister Ernest mean when he says the boy must "belong to the business of mankind"? *He is expressing his belief in the moral or ethical obligation to concern oneself with the welfare of others.*

❺ **Evaluate** Ask students to explain why Mister Ernest is so insistent that the boy go to school. *Students may say that success in changing times requires a change in attitude and skills. They should realize, however, that Mister Ernest wants to develop the boy's character and give him the education he needs to make his own moral judgments. He may also be looking forward to the day when the boy will take his place as the owner of the farm; he will then have to look out for his tenants as Mister Ernest did.*

But that was all right, too; his face usually did have a smudge of mud or tractor grease or beard stubble on it, because he wasn't jest a planter; he was a farmer, he worked as hard as ara one of his hands and tenants—which is why I knowed from the very first that we would git along, that I wouldn't have no trouble with him and he wouldn't have no trouble with me, from that very first day when I woke up and maw had done gone off with that Vicksburg roadhouse feller without even waiting to cook breakfast, and the next morning pap was gone, too, and it was almost night the next day when I heard a horse coming up and I taken the gun that I had already throwed a shell into the britch when pap never came home last night, and stood in the door while Mister Ernest rid up and said, "Come on. Your paw ain't coming back neither." ❶

"You mean he give me to you?" I said.

"Who cares?" He said. "Come on. I brought a lock for the door. We'll send the pickup back tomorrow for whatever you want."

So I come home with him and it was all right, it was jest fine—his wife had died about three years ago—without no women to worry us or take off in the middle of the night with a durn Vicksburg roadhouse jake without even wanting to cook breakfast. And we would go home this afternoon, too, but not jest yet; we always stayed one more day after the others left because Uncle Ike always left what grub they hadn't et, and the rest of the homemade corn whisky he drunk and that town whisky of Roth Edmondziz he called Scotch that smelled like it come out of a old bucket of roof paint; setting in the sun for one more day before we went back home to get ready to put in next year's crop of cotton and oats and beans and hay; and across the river yonder, behind the wall of trees where the big woods started, that old buck laying up today in the sun, too—resting today, too, without nobody to bother him until next November. ❷

So at least one of us was glad it would be eleven months and two weeks before he would have to run that fur that fast again. So he was glad of the very same thing we was sorry of, and so all of a sudden I thought about how maybe planting and working and then harvesting oats and cotton and beans and hay wasn't jest something me and Mister Ernest done three hundred and fifty-one days to fill in the time until we could come back hunting again, but it was something we had to do, and do honest and good during the three hundred and fifty-one days, to have the right to come back into the big woods and hunt for the other fourteen; and the fourteen days that old buck run in front of dogs wasn't jest something to fill his time until the three hundred and fifty-one when he didn't have to, but the running and the risking in front of guns and dogs was something he had to do for fourteen days to have the right not to be bothered for the other three hundred and fifty-one. And so the hunting and the farming wasn't two different things atall—they was jest the other side of each other. ❸

"Yes," I said. "All we got to do now is put in that next year's crop. Then November won't be no time away atall."

"You ain't going to put in the crop next year," Mister Ernest said. "You're going to school."

So at first I didn't even believe I had heard him. "What?" I said. "Me? Go to school?"

"Yes," Mister Ernest said. "You must make something out of yourself."

"I am," I said. "I'm doing it now. I'm going to be a hunter and a farmer like you."

"No," Mister Ernest said. "That ain't enough any more. Time was when all a man had to do was just farm eleven and a half months, and hunt the other half. But not now. Now just to belong to the farming business and the hunting business ain't enough. You got to belong to the business of mankind." ❹

"Mankind?" I said.

"Yes," Mister Ernest said. "So you're going to school. Because you got to know why. You can belong to the farming and hunting business and you can learn the difference between what's right and what's wrong, and do right. And that used to be enough—just to do right. But not now. You got to know why it's right and why it's wrong, and be able to tell the folks that never had no chance to learn it; teach them how to do what's right, not just because they know it's right, but because they know now why it's right because you just showed them, told them, taught them why. So you're going to school." ❺

"It's because you been listening to that durn

Reteach

Suggest that students break a long sentence into shorter segments using punctuation as a guide. Have students write a sentence from this page on the left side of the chart. Then have them put a box around each thought within the longer sentence. Finally, have students restate the text in their own words on the right side. An example is shown.

Text	In My Own Words
"And that was when we realized how fur he had come, because the only camp we knowed about in that direction was the Hollyknowe camp, and Hollyknowe was exactly twenty-eight miles from Van Dorn, where me and Mister Ernest lived—jest the shots, no dogs or nothing."	We realized how far he had come. The only camp we knew about in that direction was the Hollyknowe. Hollyknowe was twenty-eight miles from Van Dorn. We heard shots and no dogs.

Will Legate and Walter Ewell!" I said.

"No," Mister Ernest said.

"Yes!" I said. "No wonder you missed that buck yestiddy, taking ideas from the very fellers that let him get away, after me and you had run Dan and the dogs durn nigh clean to
6 death! Because you never even missed him! You never forgot to load that gun! You had done already unloaded it a purpose! I heard you!"

"All right, all right," Mister Ernest said. "Which would you rather have? His bloody head and hide on the kitchen floor yonder and half his meat in a pickup truck on the way to Yoknapatawpha County, or him with his head and hide and meat still together over yonder in that brake, waiting for next November for us to run him again?"

"And git him, too," I said. "We won't even fool with no Willy Legate and Walter Ewell next time."

"Maybe," Mister Ernest said.

"Yes," I said.

"Maybe," Mister Ernest said. "The best word in our language, the best of all. That's what mankind keeps going on: Maybe. The best days 7
of his life ain't the ones when he said 'Yes' beforehand: they're the ones when all he knew to say was 'Maybe.' He can't say 'Yes' until afterward because he not only don't know it until then, he don't want to know 'Yes' until then . . . Step in the kitchen and make me a toddy. Then we'll see about dinner." 8

> ◆ *Literature and Your Life*
> Mister Ernest is the speaker's role model. Who is yours? Why?

"All right," I said. I got up. "You want some of Uncle Ike's corn or that town whisky of Roth Edmondziz?"

"Can't you say Mister Roth or Mister Edmonds?" Mister Ernest said.

"Yes, sir," I said. "Well, which do you want? 9
Uncle Ike's corn or that ere stuff of Roth Edmondziz?"

Guide for Responding

◆ *Literature and Your Life*

Reader's Response If you had the opportunity, would you join Mister Ernest and the narrator on the yearly trip to the bayou? Explain.

Thematic Focus Does Faulkner's description make you want to visit this region of the country?

Journal Entry Think of a place that you will remember all your life the way that the boy in this story will remember the hunting camp and the bayou. In a brief journal entry, describe the setting and the effect it had on you.

☑ Check Your Comprehension

1. When does this story take place?
2. What is the relationship of the speaker to Mister Ernest?
3. When Mister Ernest fires at the deer at the end of the day, why doesn't the deer die?
4. Why won't the boy be planting next year's crop?

◆ Critical Thinking

INTERPRET

1. At the beginning of the story, why does Faulkner include a discussion about school? **[Connect]**
2. Find two examples from the story that support the conclusion that the boy trusts and feels relaxed with Mister Ernest. **[Support]**
3. According to the boy, what is the true function of work on the farm for him and Mister Ernest? **[Analyze]**
4. According to Mister Ernest, why is it better to have the deer still alive than to have killed it? **[Analyze]**

EVALUATE

5. Evaluate Faulkner's success in connecting the significance of the hunt to the significance of Mister Ernest's plans for the boy's future. **[Evaluate]**

EXTEND

6. Why are wetlands such as bayous ecologically important? **[Science Link]**

◆ Critical Thinking

6 Analyze Ask students what they think might have motivated the boy to suddenly accuse Mister Ernest of deception when he had been willing to pretend it was all a mistake. *Students may say that the boy is feeling betrayed or deceived by Mister Ernest, and is lashing out at him in anger.*

◆ Critical Thinking

7 Evaluate Ask students to explain Mister Ernest's philosophy of life, as he describes it to the boy. Do they agree with his points? *Students may say that Mister Ernest feels that one must be open to the possibilities of life. To say "yes" to one thing closes the door to other things that might have been if only one had been more open to the potential of life.*

◆ *Literature and Your Life*

8 Invite students to talk about their role models and to share the reasons for their choice.

Customize for
Intrapersonal Learners
9 Guide students to appreciate that the boy saves this address of respect for the only man he truly does respect: Mister Ernest.

Reinforce and Extend

Answers

◆ *Literature and Your Life*

Reader's Response Students should be prepared to explain their responses.

Thematic Response Students should be prepared to explain their responses.

☑ Check Your Comprehension

1. The story takes place in November on the last day of hunting season.
2. The speaker is Mister Ernest's ward, the abandoned child of a former tenant.
3. Mister Ernest has secretly unloaded the gun.
4. The boy will be sent to school.

◆ Critical Thinking

1. The discussion foreshadows the end of the story, when the boy learns he will be attending school.
2. Examples might include the trust with which the boy holds onto Mister Ernest atop a galloping horse, and the way he speaks his mind to Mister Ernest.
3. The boy realizes that the function of farming is to afford them the pleasure of hunting.
4. According to Mister Ernest, there is more pleasure in possibility (in "maybe") than in certainty.
5. Suggested response: Faulkner successfully connects the two events by making the point that the boy needs an education in order to understand why Mister Ernest's decision not to shoot the buck was the right decision.
6. Students should discuss some of the features of the wetlands: that they support endangered wildlife, that they often act as buffer zones between areas prone to flooding and areas of human habitation, that they are important to migrating birds, and so on.

Develop Understanding

One-Minute Insight In his gracious acceptance speech, Faulkner expresses his concern that the question of physical survival has diverted young writers from writing about what truly matters in life and literature: love, honor, compassion, and sacrifice. He states his belief that humanity will not only endure, but prevail, because man alone has an immortal soul and compassionate spirit. The writer is both obliged and privileged to remind humanity of its nobler capabilities and, thus, can help ensure the success of the human race.

Enrichment Inform students that the main point of Faulkner's speech is echoed in the theme of his short story "The Bear."

Customize for *Visual/Spatial Learners* Ask students to look closely at the photograph of Faulkner receiving his Nobel Prize. Based on the clothing of those pictured, what can they conclude about the ceremony itself? *Students should note that the white tie and tails on the men and full length gowns on the women suggest that the event is quite formal and prestigious.*

◆ Background for Understanding

❶ Literature: The Nobel Prize The fund for the Nobel Prize awards was established in the will of Alfred Nobel (1833–1896). Nobel specified that the annual awards should go to those persons who, during the preceding year, conferred the greatest benefit on humankind. William Faulkner received his award in 1950 for his contributions in 1949.

❷ Clarification Inform students that the financial benefits of the Nobel Prize are significant; the prize now brings a reward of about $1 million.

❶ Nobel Prize Acceptance Speech

William Faulkner

Stockholm, Sweden December 10, 1950

I feel that this award was not made to me as a man, but to my work—a life's work in the agony and sweat of the human spirit, not for glory and least of all for profit, but to create out of the materials of the human spirit something which did not exist before. So this award is only mine in trust. ❷ It will not be difficult to find a dedication for the money part of it commensurate with the purpose

Cultural Connection

The Nobel Prize The Nobel Prize for Literature, awarded each year by the Swedish Academy of Literature in Stockholm, is awarded without regard to national origin. It is usually based on an author's entire body of work, rather than on any single book. Tell students that recent award winners in literature include Seamus Heaney (Ireland), Kenzaburō Oe (Japan), Toni Morrison (United States), Derek Walcott (West Indies), Nadine Gordimer (South Africa), and Octavio Paz (Mexico).

Encourage interested students to explore the works of Nobel Prize winners from countries other than the United States. Students can read with the purpose of learning how the literature reflects the values and culture of its country of origin. You may wish to have each student select a different Nobel Prize–winning author to research. Students can then share their findings in a series of oral reports. As a class, discuss which themes or concerns the authors share in common, despite their different cultural backgrounds. Do their works meet Faulkner's criteria for good literature?

❷ and significance of its origin. But I would like to do the same with the acclaim too, by using this moment as a pinnacle from which I might be listened to by the young men and women already dedicated to the same anguish and travail, among whom is already that one who will some day stand here where I am standing.

Our tragedy today is a general and universal physical fear so long sustained by now that we
❸ can even bear it. There are no longer problems of the spirit. There is only the question: When will I be blown up? Because of this, the young man or woman writing today has forgotten the problems of the human heart in conflict with itself which alone can make good writing because only that is worth writing about, worth the agony and the sweat.

He must learn them again. He must teach himself that the basest of all things is to be afraid; and, teaching himself that, forget it forever, leaving no room in his workshop for anything but the old verities and truths of the heart, the old universal truths lacking which any story is ephemeral and doomed—love and honor and pity and pride and compassion and sacrifice. Until he does so, he labors under a curse. He writes not of love but of lust, of defeats in which nobody loses anything of value, of victories without hope and, worst of all, without pity or compassion. His griefs grieve on no universal bones, leaving no scars. He writes not of the heart but of the glands.

Until he relearns these things, he will write as though he stood among and watched the end of man. I decline to accept the end of man. It is easy enough to say that man is immortal simply because he will endure: that when the last ding-dong of doom has clanged and faded from the last worthless rock hanging tideless in the last red and dying evening, that even then there will still be one more sound: that of his puny inexhaustible voice, still talking. I refuse to accept this. I believe that man will not merely endure: he will prevail. He is immortal, not because he alone among creatures has an inexhaustible voice, but because he has a soul, a spirit capable of compassion and sacrifice and endurance. The poet's, the writer's, duty is to write about these things. It is his privilege to help man endure by lifting his heart, by reminding him of the courage and honor and hope and pride and compassion and pity and sacrifice which have been the glory of his past. The poet's voice need not merely be the record of man, it can be one of the props, the pillars to help him endure and prevail.

Guide for Responding

◆ Literature and Your Life

Reader's Response Do you agree with Faulkner's definition of good literature? If not, how would you revise it?

Thematic Focus How does Faulkner's criticism of contemporary literature reflect his experience as a writer living in a specific place and time?

☑ Check Your Comprehension

1. Of what specific physical fear does Faulkner speak?
2. According to Faulkner, what is the basest of all things?
3. According to Faulkner's Nobel acceptance speech, what is "Our tragedy today"?
4. What must young writers teach themselves?

◆ Critical Thinking

INTERPRET

1. Why does Faulkner see the Nobel Prize as something he holds in trust? **[Analyze]**
2. Why does Faulkner see modern literature as ephemeral? **[Interpret]**
3. Why does he think that people will prevail over the threats that face them? **[Draw Conclusions]**
4. How can the writer help people endure? **[Draw Conclusions]**

APPLY

5. Describe a time when a piece of literature helped you overcome some obstacle. **[Relate]**

EXTEND

6. What events not long before 1950 gave rise to the fear of which Faulkner speaks? **[Social Studies Link]**

❸ **Clarification** In 1950 the United States was involved in the Cold War with the Soviet Union. The relationship between the two nations was strained, and the buildup of nuclear weapons in both countries produced a tremendous amount of distrust and fear.

Reinforce and Extend

Answers

◆ Literature and Your Life

Reader's Response Students' responses should reflect an understanding of Faulkner's criteria for good literature.

Thematic Response Faulkner's criticisms arise from his having grown up in the traditional South and from his experience of living during the Cold War era.

☑ Check Your Comprehension

1. He speaks of the fear of being blown up.
2. Faulkner considers fear to be the basest of all things.
3. The tragedy is the fact that so many live with an unbearable burden of fear.
4. They must first teach themselves that fear is base, and then forget fear entirely.

◆ Critical Thinking

1. He considers the prize not as a personal award, but as a recognition of his work, which is drawn "from the material of the human spirit."
2. He sees modern literature as concerned with trivial or passing emotions and problems rather than with "old universal truths."
3. The human soul's capacity for compassion, nobility, and selflessness will enable humans to prevail.
4. They can remind them of the noble qualities of which they are capable.
5. Students may respond that a character's response to a tragedy or disability showed them a way to respond to a similar challenge.
6. The use of atom bombs in World War II and Russia's testing of an atom bomb soon afterward led to widespread fear that nuclear war was about to destroy the human race.

Beyond the Selection

FURTHER READING

Other Works by William Faulkner

"The Bear"; *A Soldier's Pay; The Sound and the Fury; As I Lay Dying*

Other Works With the Theme of Life in the Rural South

The Collected Stories of Eudora Welty, Eudora Welty
The Member of the Wedding, Carson McCullers
The Complete Stories, Flannery O'Connor

We suggest that you preview these works before recommending them to students.

INTERNET

To learn more about Faulkner, we suggest the following Internet site. Please note that sites may have changed since this information was published.

To explore fictional Yoknapatawpha County and for a Faulkner biography, trivia, links to other Web sites, and information on specific works, film, and stage adaptations, go to **http://www.mcsr.olemiss.edu/~egjbp/faulkner/**

We *strongly recommend* that you preview sites before you send students to them.

Answers

◆ Literary Focus

1. Students should note use of informal, anecdotal language, the parenthetical comments, the unusual grammatical structure and length of the sentence, and regional pronunciations such as "sholy" and "git."
2. Possible response: If the big old buck, which had been running the woods for the equivalent of a hundred years in a deer's life, managed to get away from me and Mister Ernest at the start, then Uncle Ike would surely manage to be at the same place at the same time as the deer.
3. Sample response: (a) " . . . let Dan's bridle go for him to git rid of the spell of bucking he had to git shut of ever morning . . ." (b) "let Dan's bridle go so that he could go through the period of bucking he had to get over every morning"

◆ Reading Strategy

1. Then Mister Ernest loaded the gun and give me the stirrup, / and I got up behind him and we taken the fire road up toward the bayou, / the four big dogs dragging Simon along in front with his single-barrel britch-loader slung on a piece of plow line across his back, / and the puppies moiling along in ever'body's way.
2. Two sections have subjects: the first section contains the subject *Mister Ernest;* the second contains the subjects *I* and *we*.
3. Suggested response: Then Mister Ernest loaded the gun and give me the stirrup. So I got up behind him and we taken the fire road up toward the bayou. Meanwhile, the four big dogs were dragging Simon along in front with his single-barrel britch-loader slung on a piece of plow line across his back. At the same time, the puppies were moiling along in ever'body's way.

Guide for Responding (continued)

◆ Literary Focus

Dialect

Every **dialect**—a manner of speaking that is common to a particular region or group—has a unique set of characteristics that affect word choice, grammar, and pronunciation. Faulkner's use of southern rural dialect goes a long way in helping "Race at Morning" to achieve its authentic ring. Consider the effects of the use of dialect in this sentence:

> Maybe with a big old buck like this one, that had been running the woods for what would amount to a hundred years in a deer's life, too, him and Uncle Ike would sholy manage to be at the same place at the same time this morning—provided, of course, he managed to git away from me and Mister Ernest on the jump.

1. Explain what makes this passage an example of dialect. Analyze it in terms of word choice, nonstandard grammatical constructions, pronunciations, and word order.
2. Rewrite the passage in standard English.
3. (a) Find two or three other examples of dialect in "Race at Morning." (b) Translate each example into standard English.

◆ Reading Strategy

Break Down Long Sentences

Breaking down long sentences into smaller units of meaning will help you to understand them. Read this sentence from the story:

> Then Mister Ernest loaded the gun and give me the stirrup, and I got up behind him and we taken the fire road up toward the bayou, the four big dogs dragging Simon along in front with his single-barrel britch-loader slung on a piece of plow line across his back, and the puppies moiling along in ever'body's way.

1. Divide the sentence into sections, using the punctuation as a guide.
2. Identify the section of the sentence that contains its subject.
3. Rewrite these sections as separate sentences, connected by transitions.

◆ Build Vocabulary

Using the Latin Suffix *-ery*

The Latin suffix *-ery (-ry)* means "state or quality of" or "place of." It can also mean a "kind of behavior." Use this information and the meaning of base words or roots to define each of the following words. Then write each word in a sentence.

1. creamery	**3.** hatchery	**5.** slavery
2. finery	**4.** snobbery	**6.** bravery

Using the Word Bank: Definitions

Basing your answer on the meaning of the italicized words in the following questions, answer *yes* or *no* to each question.

1. Can you plow a *bayou?*
2. Are the typical products of a *distillery* suitable for children to consume?
3. Is a *buck* a male animal?
4. Would a *moiling* puppy be standing still?
5. Might you find a *switch* in the woods?
6. Is *scrabbling* a quick movement?
7. Is a *swag* something you'd find in the forest?
8. If you wanted to get some sun, would you head for a *glade?*

◆ Grammar and Style

Correct Use of Irregular Verb Forms

The English language contains many **irregular verbs**. If you're unsure whether a verb in your writing has an irregular past tense or past participle, check a dictionary or grammar book. In writing, it's acceptable to use incorrect verb forms only when constructing dialogue in dialect.

Practice Rewrite each incorrect verb that follows in its correct irregular form. Then write a context sentence for each verb.

1. eated	**4.** gived	**7.** taked
2. rised	**5.** throwed	**8.** getted
3. goed	**6.** heared	**9.** weared

Writing Application Using dialect, write a conversation between two characters in "Race at Morning." Underline at least three irregular verbs you've used *incorrectly*.

◆ Build Vocabulary

Using the Latin Suffix -ery

1. A *creamery* is a place where products made from cream are produced; We get our butter from the creamery.
2. *Finery* is showy or elaborate decoration, clothing, or jewels; The women at the ball were dressed in their finery.
3. A hatchery is a place where creatures are hatched; The baby chicks stayed at the hatchery for two weeks.
4. *Snobbery* is snobbish behavior; Her snobbery and scorn of those with less money than she made her unpopular with her neighbors.
5. *Slavery* is the state of being enslaved; The Emancipation Proclamation decreed the abolition of slavery.
6. *Bravery* is the quality or state of being brave; The battle was won thanks to the bravery of the men on the front lines.

Using the Word Bank

1. No; 2. No; 3. Yes; 4. No; 5. Yes; 6. Yes; 7. Yes; 8. Yes

◆ Grammar and Style

Practice

1. *ate;* We ate by the campfire. 2. *rose;* I rose with the sun. 3. *went;* We went east when we heard the dogs barking. 4. *gave;* We gave the chase all our effort. 5. *threw;* The tension of the vine threw the saddle through the air. 6. *heard;* I heard the dogs barking in the forest. 7. *took;* We took the path along the bayou. 8. *got;* Mister Ernest got just one chance at the buck. 9. *wore;* The long chase wore out the dogs.

Writing Application

Student dialogues should be properly punctuated and should reflect the speech patterns of the characters in the short story.

Build Your Portfolio

Idea Bank

Writing

1. Letter of Support A judge is considering whether to make Mister Ernest the narrator's legal guardian. Write a letter to the judge explaining why Mister Ernest is suited for this role.

2. Acceptance Speech Write a brief speech accepting an honor. As Faulkner did when he received the Nobel Prize, use your speech to express your deepest beliefs and convictions.

3. Analysis of Dialect Write a short essay in which you explain how Faulkner's use of dialect contributes to the effectiveness of his story.

Speaking, Listening, and Viewing

4. Debate With a classmate, debate the pros and cons of hunting. Discuss the subject from the point of view of farmers, animal rights supporters, hunters, and others. **[Social Studies Link]**

5. Broadcast As a radio announcer, broadcast the hunt in "Race at Morning" as it occurs in real time. Report on the progress of all participants. **[Performing Arts Link]**

Researching and Representing

6. Pantomime Convert your classroom into a model of the landscape of "Race at Morning" by identifying parts of the room as the canebrake, the place where the grapevines hang over the bayou, and so on. Assign classmates different roles. Then act out the day without words. **[Performing Arts Link]**

7. Musical Research Find a piece of music that could serve as a score (music composed for film) for the hunt. Play it for the class, and then explain why you chose it. **[Music Link]**

Online Activity www.phlit.phschool.com

Guided Writing Lesson

Critical Review

In his Nobel Prize acceptance speech, Faulkner says that the writer's duty is to help people "endure by lifting their hearts, by reminding them of the courage and honor and hope and pride and compassion and pity and sacrifice which have been the glory of their past."

Choose a story and evaluate it in terms of how well its author fulfilled Faulkner's idea of the writer's duty. Explain why the author succeeded or failed. Use the following tip to help you.

Writing Skills Focus: Elaboration to Support an Argument

Your main argument should be that the selected story either does or does not live up to Faulkner's standard for good writing. Once you have made this statement, you need to **elaborate** on your argument by providing precise details and examples that back up your points. Look at how Faulkner develops and supports one of his key points.

Model From the Selection

Argument: Our tragedy today is a general and universal physical fear . . .

Elaboration: There is only the question: When will I be blown up?

Prewriting Choose your story. Review Faulkner's ideals and then decide whether the author succeeds or fails according to Faulkner's standards. Jot down some reasons why the author meets or doesn't meet the criteria.

Drafting Begin your review with a clear statement of your position. Then use details and passages from the story to create a convincing argument.

Revising Did you state Faulkner's standard clearly? Do all of the details in your review show how the story does or doesn't live up to this standard? Make any necessary revisions.

Idea Bank

Customizing for
Performance Levels
Following are suggestions for matching Idea Bank activities with student performance levels:
Less Advanced Students: 1, 6, 7
Average Students: 2, 4, 5
More Advanced Students: 3, 4

Customizing for
Learning Modalities
Following are suggestions for matching Idea Bank activities with learning modalities:
Logical/Mathematical: 4
Verbal/Linguistic: 4, 5
Bodily/Kinesthetic: 6
Musical/Rhythmic: 7

Guided Writing Lesson

Writing and Language Transparencies Use the Argument Transparency, p. 75, to help students organize details they can use to elaborate on their arguments.

Writing Lab CD-ROM
Have students complete the tutorial on Response to Literature. Follow these steps:

1. Refer students to the annotated model of a Critical Review in the Response to Literature section.
2. Students can refer to the Evaluation Word Bins as they draft on the computer.
3. Use the Proofreading Checklist to help students revise and edit their drafts.

✓ ASSESSMENT OPTIONS

Formal Assessment, Selection Test, pp. 241–243, and Assessment Resources Software. The Selection Test is designed so that it can be easily customized to the performance levels of your students.

Alternative Assessment, p. 52, includes options for less advanced students, more advanced students, interpersonal learners, verbal/linguistic learners, and visual/spatial learners.

PORTFOLIO ASSESSMENT
Use the following rubrics in the ***Alternative Assessment*** booklet to assess student writing:
Letter of Support: Persuasion Rubric, p. 120
Acceptance Speech: Expression Rubric, p. 109
Analysis of Dialect: Literary Analysis/Interpretation Rubric, p. 127
Guided Writing Lesson: Critical Review Rubric, p. 126

LESSON OBJECTIVES

1. **To develop vocabulary and word identification skills**
   - Latin Word Roots: *-lum-*
   - Using the Word Bank: Analogies
2. **To use a variety of reading strategies to comprehend a short story**
   - Connect Your Experience
   - Reading Strategy: Reading Blank Verse
3. **To increase knowledge of other cultures and to connect common elements across cultures**
   - Connecting Themes Across Cultures (ATE)
4. **To express and support responses to the text**
   - Critical Thinking
   - Idea Bank: Character Sketch
   - Idea Bank: News Story
   - Idea Bank: Essay
   - Idea Bank: Graphic Display
5. **To analyze literary elements**
   - Literary Focus: Blank Verse
   - Background for Understanding
6. **To read in order to research self-selected and assigned topics**
   - Idea Bank: Travel Brochure
7. **To plan, prepare, organize, and present literary interpretations**
   - Idea Bank: Eulogy
   - Idea Bank: Poetry Reading
8. **To use recursive writing processes to write an introduction**
   - Guided Writing Lesson
9. **To increase knowledge of the rules of grammar and usage**
   - Grammar and Style: Infinitives

Test Preparation

Reading Comprehension: Try Words in the Sentence (ATE, p. 803)
The teaching tips and sample test item in this workshop support the instruction and practice in the unit workshop:
Reading Comprehension: Sentence-Completion Questions (SE, p. 863)

Guide for Interpreting

Featured in AUTHORS IN DEPTH Series

Robert Frost *(1874–1963)*

In becoming one of America's most loved and respected poets, Robert Frost displayed the same rugged persistence and determination exhibited by the rural New Englanders he depicted in his poems. Although he eventually received four Pulitzer Prizes and read at a presidential inauguration, Frost's success as a poet didn't come easily. Only after years of rejection by book and magazine publishers did he finally achieve the acceptance for which he worked so hard.

Early Struggles Frost was born in San Francisco, California, but at the age of eleven moved with his family to the gritty textile city of Lawrence, Massachusetts. After briefly attending Dartmouth College, he left school and spent time working as a farmer, mill hand, newspaper writer, and schoolteacher. During his spare time, he wrote poetry and dreamed of someday being able to support himself solely by writing.

The English Years Frost married and spent ten years farming in New Hampshire. Unable to get his poems published, he sold his farm and moved his family to England in 1912, hoping to establish himself there as a poet. He became a friend of a number of other poets, including Ezra Pound, and he succeeded in publishing two collections of poetry, *A Boy's Will* (1913) and *North of Boston* (1914).

When Frost returned to the United States in 1915, he discovered that his success in England had spread and he was on the road to fame.

Acclaim Frost went on to publish several more volumes of poetry, for which he received many awards. He also taught at Amherst, the University of Michigan, Harvard, and Dartmouth; lectured and read at dozens of other schools; and farmed in Vermont and New Hampshire. In 1960, at John F. Kennedy's invitation, he became the first poet to read his work at a presidential inauguration.

Frost's poetry was popular not only with critics and intellectuals, but also among the general public. He used traditional verse forms and conversational language to paint vivid verbal portraits of the New England landscape and lifestyle. Despite their apparent simplicity, however, his poems are filled with hidden meanings, compelling readers to delve beneath the surface to fully appreciate his work.

Like his poetry, Frost's personality also had multiple levels. In his public appearances, Frost liked to present himself as a jovial, folksy farmer who just happened to write poetry. In reality, however, Frost was a deep thinker who was described as a complicated personality by those who knew him well.

◆ Background for Understanding

CULTURE: FROST THE NEW ENGLANDER

In the minds of many, Robert Frost is inseparable from the New England countryside he so loved. Much of his poetry reflects not only the landscape, but the characteristic personalities of the region. Proud, hard-working, and occasionally stubborn, the New Englanders who populate Frost's poetry are drawn from his experience. Frost spent most of his life in New Hampshire, Vermont, and Massachusetts, often living in rural communities. Despite his city roots, he was able to gain the acceptance of his country neighbors and to enter their world—a world that was usually closed to outsiders. In doing so, he gathered a wealth of material for his poetry.

Prentice Hall Literature Program Resources

REINFORCE /RETEACH / EXTEND

Selection Support Pages
Build Vocabulary: Latin Word Roots: *-lum-*, p. 243
Grammar and Style: Uses of Infinitives, p. 244
Reading Strategy: Reading Blank Verse, p. 245
Literary Focus: Blank Verse, p. 246

Strategies for Diverse Student Needs, p. 53

Beyond Literature Humanities Connection, p. 53

Formal Assessment Selection Test, pp. 244–246; Assessment Resources Software

Alternative Assessment, p. 53

Writing and Language Transparencies
Analysis Map, pp. 83–85

Resource Pro CD-ROM

Listening to Literature Audiocassettes

The Poetry of Robert Frost

◆ Literature and Your Life

Connect Your Experience

Think for a moment about how your surroundings affect you. Popular psychology holds that we are products of our environments. Do you feel and act differently when you're on a busy city street from the way you do when you're in a natural setting? How might your personality and style be different if you lived in another part of the country?

Journal Writing Write a paragraph about your favorite type of landscape—the seaside, mountains, the city, or prairie, for instance. How do you feel when you're in that environment?

Thematic Focus: From Every Corner of the Land

Had Robert Frost remained in San Francisco, his life and his poetry might well have been very different. Frost's works are shaped by, and reflective of, New England values, people, and landscapes.

◆ Build Vocabulary

Latin Roots: *-lum-*

In "Acquainted With the Night," Frost uses the word *luminary* to describe the moon. Along with several related English words, including *luminous* and *illuminate,* the word *luminary*, which means "giving off light," is based on the Latin root *-lum-*, meaning "light."

Word Bank

Preview these words from the poems.

poise
rueful
luminary

◆ Literary Focus

Blank Verse

Many of Frost's poems do not contain rhyme, but their lines have a regular meter, or pattern of stressed and unstressed syllables. The basic unit of meter is a foot, which usually consists of one stressed syllable and one or more unstressed syllables. The most common foot in American and English poetry is the iamb, which consists of one unstressed syllable followed by a stressed syllable. A line containing five iambs is written in **iambic pentameter.** Verse consisting of unrhymed lines of iambic pentameter is called **blank verse.** Look at this example :

> When I see birches bend to left and right
> Across the lines of straighter darker trees,

Notice how blank verse re-creates the natural flow of speech.

◆ Grammar and Style

Uses of Infinitives

"He will not see me stopping here / To watch his woods fill up with snow." In these lines from "Stopping by Woods on a Snowy Evening," the infinitive *to watch* modifies *stopping*. Both **infinitives**—the base form of a verb preceded by *to*—and **infinitive phrases**—which consist of the infinitive plus any complements or modifiers—can act as nouns, adjectives, or adverbs. In "Birches," for example, Frost writes, "But swinging doesn't bend them down *to stay*." Here the infinitive *to stay* acts as an adverb modifying the verb *bend*.

◆ Reading Strategy

Reading Blank Verse

One way to appreciate **blank verse** is to read it aloud in sentences rather than in poetic lines. Don't pause at the end of each line. Instead, follow the punctuation as if you were reading prose: Pause briefly after commas, and pause longer after periods.

Test Preparation Workshop

Reading Comprehension:
Try Words in the Sentence Many standardized tests require students to correctly answer sentence completion questions. Use the following sample item to show students that they can often eliminate choices because they are illogical, the wrong part of speech, or inconsistent with sentence meaning.

Robert Frost moved to England in 1912 hoping to have his poetry accepted, and his strategy worked. When he returned, he found that his ____ abroad had spread and that he was on the road to ____.

A failure; ruin
B success; fame
C reputation; despair
D defeat; glory

From the context, students can tell that the correct words should be positive and should have similar meanings. B is the best choice.

Interest Grabber Before class, set up a low wall down the center of the room out of boxes, desks, chairs, or masking tape. On either side of the "wall" post a sign that says, "Good fences make good neighbors." As students enter, have them sit on either side of the wall so that about half the class is on each side. Ask students to tell how it feels to be separated from each other. Draw attention to the quotation and ask them to respond to it. Then tell students that they will be reading poems by Robert Frost, one of which explores a response to the line they have discussed.

Connecting Themes Across Cultures

Discuss the idea that each region has its own customs, values, attitudes, dialect, and idioms, among other things. People may feel more comfortable in their own environment because they know the ways of people like themselves. Discuss students' observations about people they have met from other regions. Why would they expect to find cultural differences from region to region?

Customize for *Less Proficient Readers*

Poetry should be read many times to allow the reader to grasp the meaning and dig for deeper symbolism or significance. Tell students that it is useful, if not essential, to reread lines, parts, or whole poems. It can also help to hear the poems several times. Play the audiotaped versions both before and after students read.

Listening to Literature Audiocassettes

Customize for *AP Students*

Robert Frost's poetry, which is full of symbolism, can usually be interpreted on more than one level. Review the meaning of a literary symbol as a person, place, or thing that has meaning in itself and also represents something larger. Encourage students to identify symbols and suggest larger meanings.

Develop Understanding

One-Minute Insight The speaker, an older man, remembers the childhood pleasure of swinging from birches. He muses about how exploring his environment prepared him for life's greater challenges. Yet, despite preparation, adulthood sometimes feels so burdensome that it helps to recall carefree times as a boy swinging birches, when his whole life was still ahead of him.

◆ Reading Strategy

❶ Reading Blank Verse Help students to read these lines as sentences rather than stopping at line breaks. Ask students to paraphrase the passage to elicit its broader meaning. *Students might say that human interaction is fleeting and has little impact, unlike the forces of nature, which destroy.*

◆ Critical Thinking

❷ Interpret Help students interpret the metaphor Frost creates here. *Students may say that birches represent people under the pressures of age or of life's burdens that weigh them down and take away their resiliency.*

Customize for
AP Students

❸ Guide students to understand that the speaker longs to see traces of human experience to know that life has been lived to the fullest, and that others have taken pleasure in interacting with their environment.

◆ Critical Thinking

❹ Analyze Discuss with students why swinging birches replaces playing baseball in the life of "some boy" and how what he learns can be applied to living his life. *Students may say that because a country boy lives far from others, he cannot learn rules by playing a team sport. Instead, he learns his life lessons, such as developing an ability to determine limits, from his own experiments and explorations.*

Birches

Robert Frost

When I see birches bend to left and right
Across the lines of straighter darker trees,
❶ I like to think some boy's been swinging them.
But swinging doesn't bend them down to stay
As ice storms do. Often you must have seen them
Loaded with ice a sunny winter morning
After a rain. They click upon themselves
As the breeze rises, and turn many-colored
As the stir cracks and crazes their enamel.
Soon the sun's warmth makes them shed crystal shells
Shattering and avalanching on the snow crust—
Such heaps of broken glass to sweep away
You'd think the inner dome of heaven had fallen.
They are dragged to the withered bracken by the load,
And they seem not to break; though once they are bowed
❷ So low for long, they never right themselves:
You may see their trunks arching in the woods
Years afterwards, trailing their leaves on the ground
Like girls on hands and knees that throw their hair
Before them over their heads to dry in the sun.
But I was going to say when Truth broke in
❸ With all her matter of fact about the ice storm,
I should prefer to have some boy bend them
As he went out and in to fetch the cows—
Some boy too far from town to learn baseball,
Whose only play was what he found himself,
Summer or winter, and could play alone.
❹ One by one he subdued his father's trees
❺ By riding them down over and over again
Until he took the stiffness out of them,
And not one but hung limp, not one was left
For him to conquer. He learned all there was
To learn about not launching out too soon
And not carrying the tree away

Block Scheduling Strategies

Consider these suggestions to take advantage of extended class time:

- Have students read and discuss the Background for Understanding (p. 802). Combine this with a display of pictures of New England scenes to provide literary and visual background.
- Introduce the Reading Strategy and Literary Focus (p. 803). You may wish to use the Reading Strategy practice page found in ***Selection Support*** at this point, if appropriate.
- Divide the class into groups to read and respond to the poems. Guide class discussion using the questions and notes given in the ATE.
- Assign the Guided Writing Lesson (p. 815). Before students begin, display a collection of poetry anthologies so students can scan the introductions for ideas and examples. To help students plan their introductions, distribute copies of the Analysis Map Organizer in ***Writing and Language Transparencies*** (pp. 83–85).
- Use the multiple-choice portion of the Selection Test, pp. 244–246 in ***Formal Assessment.***

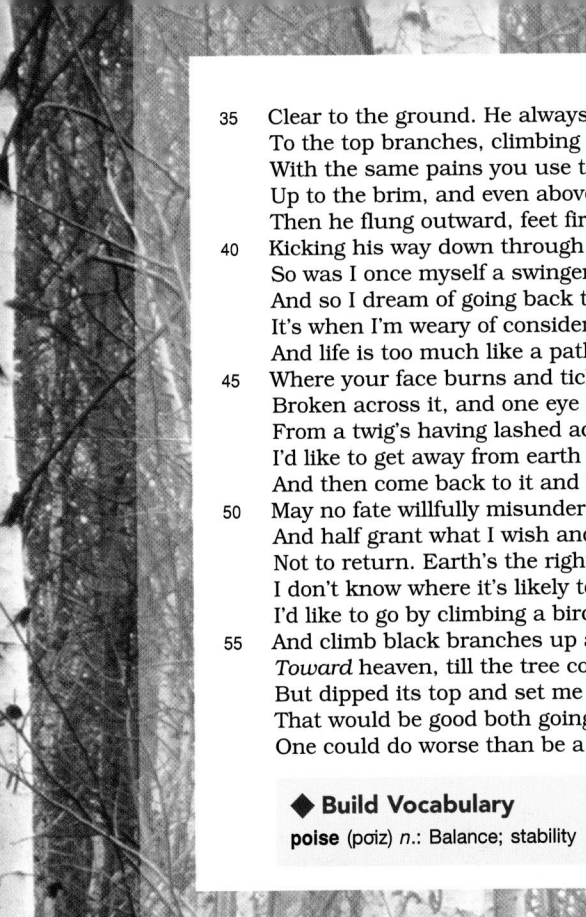

Clear to the ground. He always kept his <u>poise</u>
To the top branches, climbing carefully
With the same pains you use to fill a cup
Up to the brim, and even above the brim.
Then he flung outward, feet first, with a swish,
Kicking his way down through the air to the ground. ❺
So was I once myself a swinger of birches.
And so I dream of going back to be.
It's when I'm weary of considerations,
And life is too much like a pathless wood
Where your face burns and tickles with the cobwebs ❻
Broken across it, and one eye is weeping
From a twig's having lashed across it open.
I'd like to get away from earth awhile
And then come back to it and begin over.
May no fate willfully misunderstand me
And half grant what I wish and snatch me away
Not to return. Earth's the right place for love:
I don't know where it's likely to go better.
I'd like to go by climbing a birch tree,
And climb black branches up a snow-white trunk
Toward heaven, till the tree could bear no more,
But dipped its top and set me down again.
That would be good both going and coming back.
One could do worse than be a swinger of birches.

◆ Build Vocabulary

poise (poiz) *n.*: Balance; stability

Guide for Responding

◆ *Literature and Your Life*

Reader's Response Do you ever yearn to escape from reality for a while? Why or why not?

Thematic Response What do the speaker's activities reveal about the place where he lives?

☑ Check Your Comprehension

1. What does the speaker of "Birches" prefer to think when he sees birches "bend to left and right"?
2. When does he "dream of going back" to swing again on birches?

◆ Critical Thinking

INTERPRET

1. What is the connection between the boy in "Birches" and the poem's speaker? **[Infer]**
2. What does the activity of swinging on birches symbolize for the speaker? **[Interpret]**
3. What message does this poem convey that applies to people of all ages? **[Draw Conclusion]**

APPLY

4. What kinds of events, experiences, and feelings in his life might have caused the speaker to make the admission contained in lines 48–49? **[Speculate]**

Cultural Connection

Trees as Symbols Certain trees have come to symbolize a culture or nation. The cedars of Lebanon are included in the nation's flag and have been associated with that Middle East country since Biblical times. Unfortunately, few giant cedars remain in Lebanon today; most were cut down in previous centuries to provide wood for building ships and temples. The graceful weeping willow tree, native to China, appears frequently in Chinese art. The American elm has long been part of our nation's heritage. Elms lined many streets in early American villages; to this day most towns and cities still have an Elm Street.

Have students discuss what characteristics might make trees meaningful and enduring symbols. *While trees are a visual reference to the cycles of the seasons and therefore life and death, they withstand harsh weather and storms and live for many years.*

◆ Critical Thinking

❺ **Apply** Invite students to paraphrase the message Frost gives in lines 28–40 as it can apply to the process of growing up. *Students may say that young people should learn all they can in the safety of home, move step-by-step beyond the circle their parents created, and leap into life, taking calculated chances.*

◆ Critical Thinking

❻ **Analyze** Discuss with students how the woods in lines 43–47 become a metaphor for life and its assaults. Clarify that when the speaker longs "to get away from earth awhile," he means he'd like to leave behind the pressures life puts in his path. Swinging birches represents the chance to feel free and bold, yet still be part of the earth.

Reinforce and Extend

Answers

◆ *Literature and Your Life*

Reader's Response Many students will admit to the occasional need to escape. They may point to stress, aggravation, and others' expectations as factors contributing to this need.

Thematic Response The speaker grew up in a rural setting.

☑ Check Your Comprehension

1. He hopes they are bent because a boy has been playing on them, not because of violent storms.
2. He dreams of swinging on birches when the troubles of the world make him weary.

◆ Critical Thinking

1. The boy is the speaker as a youth.
2. It symbolizes freedom and the experience of learning.
3. Possible response: Playfully exploring the environment can prepare young people for life's challenges. It can also provide memories that make adults long for the freedom of childhood.
4. Possible responses: The adult may be troubled by relationships, responsibilities, or frustrations.

Develop Understanding

One-Minute Insight The speaker and his neighbor make an annual walk along the fieldstone wall that separates their property to repair the breaks they find. The speaker see this as a futile act, but the neighbor holds that "Good fences make good neighbors." The speaker feels that because walls create unnatural separations, natural forces will always work to break them down.

Customize for
Less Proficient Readers
❶ Brainstorm with the class for reasons not to love a wall, as well as for valid reasons to support putting up walls. You may use the Interest Grabber Activity on page 803 to help students visualize the concept. Encourage students to think metaphorically as well as concretely.

◆ Grammar and Style

❷ **Uses of Infinitives** Ask students to identify the infinitives and infinitive phrases in these lines and determine how each is used. *Students should identify "To please the yelping dogs" as an adverbial phrase that explains why; "to walk the line" also acts as an adverbial phrase that modifies the verb meet.*

▶Critical Viewing◀

❸ **Analyze** Students may respond that weeds grow right up through the rock wall as if it offers no resistance. Also, some rocks have fallen, due perhaps to frost heaves or animals or people climbing on them.

Mending Wall

Robert Frost

❶ Something there is that doesn't love a wall,
That sends the frozen-ground-swell under it
And spills the upper boulders in the sun,
And makes gaps even two can pass abreast.
The work of hunters is another thing:
I have come after them and made repair
Where they have left not one stone on a stone,
But they would have the rabbit out of hiding,
To please the yelping dogs. The gaps I mean,
No one has seen them made or heard them made,
❷ But at spring mending-time we find them there.
I let my neighbor know beyond the hill;
And on a day we meet to walk the line
And set the wall between us once again.

▼ **Critical Viewing** How does this picture suggest that walls don't belong in the natural world? **[Analyze]** ❸

Beyond the Classroom

Career Connection

Surveyor Anyone who has ever flown over a rural area has seen the patchwork quilt of land parcels of different farms or properties. Boundaries are usually not arbitrary. They have been determined by technical measurements, called surveys, which become part of the legal documentation of land ownership.

Federal surveying of public lands for private purchase began in 1785. Surveyors walked the land, took measurements, recorded their findings, and created fairly accurate maps of most of the privately owned land in America.

Invite interested students to find out more about the process of surveying. For example, what skills or talents are required, which tools are used, and what training and education are needed. Students can investigate what working conditions can be expected and what kinds of job opportunities are available. Students might interview a working surveyor, or contact a public agency to learn more about the role of surveying to determine or validate property boundaries.

We keep the wall between us as we go.
To each the boulders that have fallen to each.
And some are loaves and some so nearly balls
We have to use a spell to make them balance:
"Stay where you are until our backs are turned!"
We wear our fingers rough with handling them.
Oh, just another kind of outdoor game, ❹
One on a side. It comes to little more:
There where it is we do not need the wall:
He is all pine and I am apple orchard.
My apple trees will never get across
And eat the cones under his pines, I tell him.
He only says, "Good fences make good neighbors."
Spring is the mischief in me, and I wonder
If I could put a notion in his head:
"*Why* do they make good neighbors? Isn't it
Where there are cows? But here there are no cows. ❺
Before I built a wall I'd ask to know
What I was walling in or walling out,
And to whom I was like to give offense.
Something there is that doesn't love a wall,
That wants it down." I could say "Elves" to him,
But it's not elves exactly, and I'd rather
He said it for himself. I see him there,
Bringing a stone grasped firmly by the top
In each hand, like an old-stone savage armed. ❻
He moves in darkness as it seems to me,
Not of woods only and the shade of trees.
He will not go behind his father's saying,
And he likes having thought of it so well
He says again, "Good fences make good neighbors."

Guide for Responding

◆ Literature and Your Life

Reader's Response With which character do you more closely identify—the speaker or his neighbor? Why?

Thematic Focus Is the central conflict in "Mending Wall" specifically a rural problem? Why or why not?

☑ Check Your Comprehension

1. What two causes of gaps in walls does the speaker identify?
2. Why does the speaker feel that the wall is unnecessary?
3. What is his neighbor's attitude about it?

◆ Critical Thinking

INTERPRET

1. What is the "something" that "doesn't love a wall" and why doesn't it love the wall? **[Interpret]**
2. Compare and contrast the speaker and his neighbor. **[Compare and Contrast]**
3. (a) What does the wall symbolize? (b) What is the significance of the fact that the wall breaks apart each winter? **[Interpret]**

EVALUATE

4. How valid are the neighbor's (and the speaker's) ideas about the value of walls? Explain. **[Criticize]**

◆ Reading Strategy

❹ Reading Blank Verse
Encourage students to read this passage aloud in sentences to better grasp the speaker's relationship with his neighbor. This may help isolate the speaker's views about walls and about the annual process of mending them.

Customize for
AP Students
❺ Challenge students to restate the logic the speaker puts forth in lines 28–34 to argue against his neighbor's viewpoint about walls. *The speaker questions whether any fence is needed since there are no animals who can migrate from one yard to another. He thinks stubbornness is not reason enough to maintain the wall.*

◆ Critical Thinking

❻ Infer Ask students to make inferences about how the speaker feels about his neighbor. *Students may say that Frost's descriptions make the neighbor seem rigid, unenlightened, and unimaginative.*

Reinforce and Extend

Enrichment Challenge students to make the case that good fences do make good neighbors. *They provide these benefits: clearly defining boundaries or limitations to help people learn how far they can go, or how not to intrude upon others.*

Looking at Literature Videodisc Play Chapter 10 of the videodisc for a presentation of "Mending Wall" followed by one student's response to the poem. Ask students to compare and contrast their responses with the response of the student.

Chapter 10

☑ Check Your Comprehension

1. The speaker names the freezing and thawing of the earth and the work of hunters as culprits.
2. Nothing needs to be kept out where he has a wall.
3. The neighbor believes "Good fences make good neighbors."

◆ Critical Thinking

1. Possible response: The forces of nature do not love a wall because it marks territories and claims a false ownership.
2. Possible responses: The speaker does not believe in the wall; the neighbor does. The speaker is open to change; the neighbor is not.
3. (a) The wall symbolizes human interference with nature. (b) Nature, more powerful than humans, makes a statement each winter.
4. Possible responses: Each view is valid. While walls may be unnecessary in certain circumstances, they may keep the peace between enemies.

Answers

◆ Literature and Your Life

Reader's Response Students should support their responses.

Thematic Focus It is not specific to rural areas; people create artificial boundaries in all types of living environments.

Develop Understanding

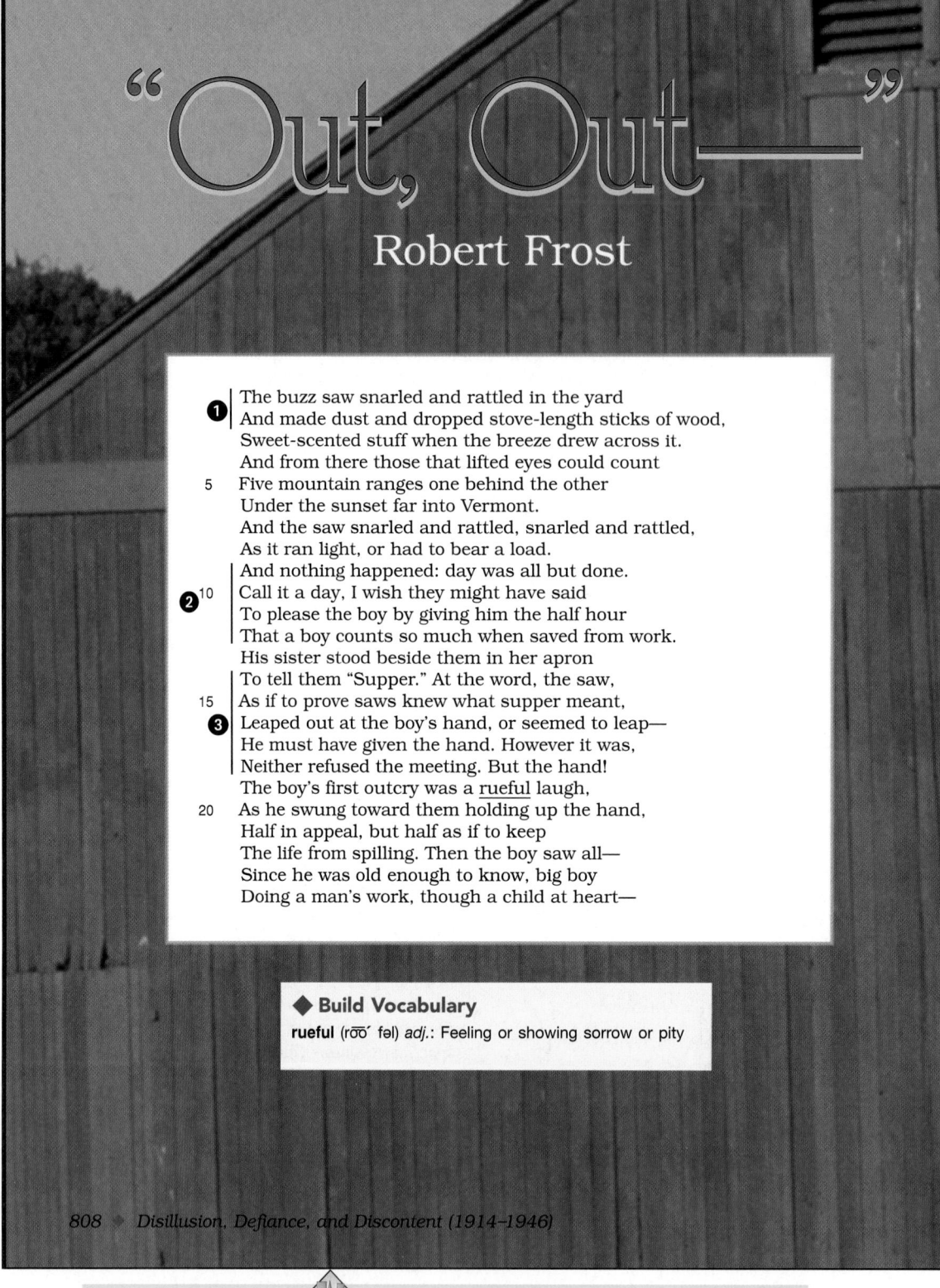

One-Minute Insight This shocking, understated poem presents a horrific story of death. Late one ordinary day, a young boy using a power saw to cut wood momentarily loses his concentration and severely cuts his hand. Unfortunately, not only does the boy lose his hand, he loses his life. However, the harsh reality of rural life demands that family members go about their chores because farm life must go on even after a senseless death.

Customize for
AP Students
Remind students of the Sherwood Anderson short story, "The Corn Planting" (pp. 735–739). After students have read this poem, encourage them to compare the two families' responses to death.

Customize for
ESL Students
To help students visualize the tool that plays such a key role in this poem, display pictures of buzz saws or bring in a buzz saw blade for students to carefully examine. Students who have used a buzz saw or have heard one in operation can describe its loud whining sound.

Customize for
Verbal/Linguistic Learners
❶ Ask students to identify the words in the opening lines that create an uneasy sense of foreboding. *Students may cite vivid verbs that personify the saw (snarled and rattled), and the idea of making dust as an allusion to death.*

◆ Critical Thinking

❷ **Analyze** Ask a volunteer to read lines 9–12 aloud to emphasize the sense of "calm before a storm" that Frost creates here. Discuss what Frost means by time "That a boy counts so much when saved from work." *Students may say that the time the boy would count so much may be like "found money"—an unexpected delight that is all the more wonderful because it is unanticipated.*

"Out, Out—"

Robert Frost

❶ The buzz saw snarled and rattled in the yard
And made dust and dropped stove-length sticks of wood,
Sweet-scented stuff when the breeze drew across it.
And from there those that lifted eyes could count
Five mountain ranges one behind the other
Under the sunset far into Vermont.
And the saw snarled and rattled, snarled and rattled,
As it ran light, or had to bear a load.
❷ And nothing happened: day was all but done.
Call it a day, I wish they might have said
To please the boy by giving him the half hour
That a boy counts so much when saved from work.
His sister stood beside them in her apron
❸ To tell them "Supper." At the word, the saw,
As if to prove saws knew what supper meant,
Leaped out at the boy's hand, or seemed to leap—
He must have given the hand. However it was,
Neither refused the meeting. But the hand!
The boy's first outcry was a rueful laugh,
As he swung toward them holding up the hand,
Half in appeal, but half as if to keep
The life from spilling. Then the boy saw all—
Since he was old enough to know, big boy
Doing a man's work, though a child at heart—

◆ Build Vocabulary
rueful (ro͞o′ fəl) *adj.*: Feeling or showing sorrow or pity

Beyond the Classroom

Workplace Skills Connection
On the Job Safety Statistics for fatalities from plane crashes, natural disasters, or epidemic illnesses are widely publicized. However, we rarely hear about the significant number of casualties that occur each year on farms. Nearly one-third of all reported farm accidents involve contact with equipment or machinery.

Brainstorm with the class for different types of farm equipment or machinery that could cause injury, and then for measures workers could take to protect themselves. Have interested students contact the U.S. Labor Department to gather recent statistics on farm-related injuries. Students can present their findings in a chart or graph, and provide a list of safety measures.

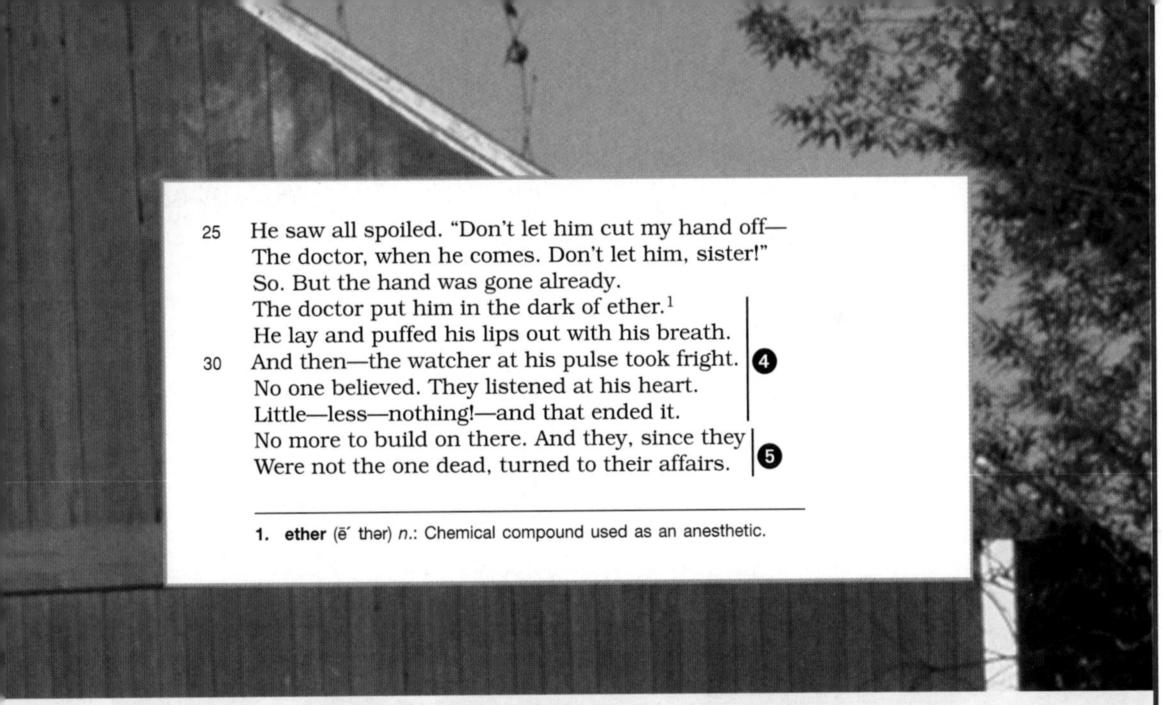

He saw all spoiled. "Don't let him cut my hand off—
The doctor, when he comes. Don't let him, sister!"
So. But the hand was gone already.
The doctor put him in the dark of ether.[1]
He lay and puffed his lips out with his breath.
And then—the watcher at his pulse took fright. ❹
No one believed. They listened at his heart.
Little—less—nothing!—and that ended it.
No more to build on there. And they, since they
Were not the one dead, turned to their affairs. ❺

1. **ether** (ē´ thər) *n.*: Chemical compound used as an anesthetic.

Guide for Responding

◆ Literature and Your Life

Reader's Response What do you find more disturbing—the boy's death or the onlookers' reaction to it? Explain.

Thematic Focus What does this poem suggest about rural life?

Other Cultures Choose a culture of another country and read about the views of death held by its people. What connections can you make between these beliefs and the culture's lifestyle? Compare your findings with the society in which you live.

☑ Check Your Comprehension

1. (a) When does the accident occur? (b) How does it happen?
2. (a) What is the boy's very first response? (b) What is his second response?
3. What happens to the boy after the doctor arrives?
4. What is the family's reaction?

◆ Critical Thinking

INTERPRET

1. How does the setting contrast with the events of the poem? **[Compare and Contrast]**
2. What is ironic about the fact that the boy is cut just as his sister says the word *supper*? **[Support]**
3. What does the speaker mean by the expression "the boy saw all" in line 22? **[Interpret]**
4. The poem's title comes from a scene in Shakespeare's *Macbeth* in which Macbeth laments the premature death of his wife with these words:

   Out, out, brief candle!
   Life's but a walking shadow, a poor player,
   That struts and frets his hour upon the
   stage,
   And then is heard no more.

   What does this quotation reveal about the poem's theme? **[Connect]**

APPLY

5. How do you explain the family's response to the incident and to the boy's death? **[Speculate]**

Customize for *Less Proficient Readers*

❸ Guide students to recognize the impact Frost creates in lines 14–18 by personifying the saw. Help them understand that Frost describes the saw as if it had a mind and could understand that it was time to be fed, as if the saw "eats" the boy's hand for its cruel nourishment.

◆ Critical Thinking

❹ **Analyze** Discuss with students how the speaker achieves a dramatic effect as he describes the boy's death. *Students may notice that Frost describes the decreasing pulse:* Little-less-nothing! *Also, they may say that the understatement leading up to this scene makes the impact of the death more powerful.*

Thematic Focus

❺ **From Every Corner of the Land** Discuss what the final two lines of the poem say about farm life in general, whether in New England or elsewhere. *Students may say that the relentless demands of farm life allow little time to pause, even in the face of tragedy.*

Reinforce and Extend

◆ Critical Thinking

Interpret Challenge students to interpret the meaning of the buzz saw as a symbol, and support their answer with evidence from the poem. *Students may say that the buzz saw represents a technological invention that humans have created but cannot completely control.*

Answers

◆ Literature and Your Life

Reader's Response Students should support their responses.

Thematic Focus Rural life is not as simple and idyllic as some postcard images suggest.

☑ Check Your Comprehension

1. (a) The accident occurs just before supper. (b) The saw leaped out of the boy's hand as he was called to supper.
2. (a) He laughs ruefully. (b) He asks his sister not to let them cut off his hand.
3. He is given ether and dies.
4. They go on with their affairs.

◆ Critical Thinking

1. The setting seems serene but the events are violent and fatal.
2. The boy was finished with work for the day and—theoretically—out of danger.
3. Possible response: The boy understood the severity of his injury.
4. It conveys the fact that life is short and fragile in nature.
5. Possible response: They were in shock and unable to process the reality of the death.

One-Minute Insight Drawing on the darkness as a time of isolation and loneliness, these poems can be seen as the city and country versions of a similar theme. The speaker of the first poem, on a nighttime journey through a wintry forest, stops to observe the beauty of the scene and to temporarily escape the demands of his life. Although he would like to rest and take in the beauty of the scene, he realizes the many tasks he must complete. This decision suggests he forestalls death to keep the promises of his life. An accessible poem on the surface, "Stopping by Woods on a Snowy Evening" mines the meaning of life and the things people value most. In the second poem, the speaker views his life as having had times of isolation, loneliness, and despair, but he accepts this as his lot.

◆ Literary Focus

❶ Blank Verse Point out that this poem is *not* an example of blank verse. Challenge students to explain why. *It has a regular rhyme scheme.*

❷ Clarification "The darkest evening of the year" refers to the winter solstice, the time of the year (about December 21 in the Northern Hemisphere) when the sun is at its greatest distance from the equator. The winter solstice has the least amount of daytime and greatest amount of nighttime of any day of the year.

◆ Critical Thinking

❸ Analyze Ask students to comment on the effect of repeating the last line. *The repetition suggests resignation or determination.*

▶Critical Viewing◀

❹ Compare and Contrast Students should note that the wooded area in the photo is brightly moonlit, open, and still, rather than dark, windy, and filled with falling snow. Both scenes are peaceful nighttime depcitions of snow-covered woods.

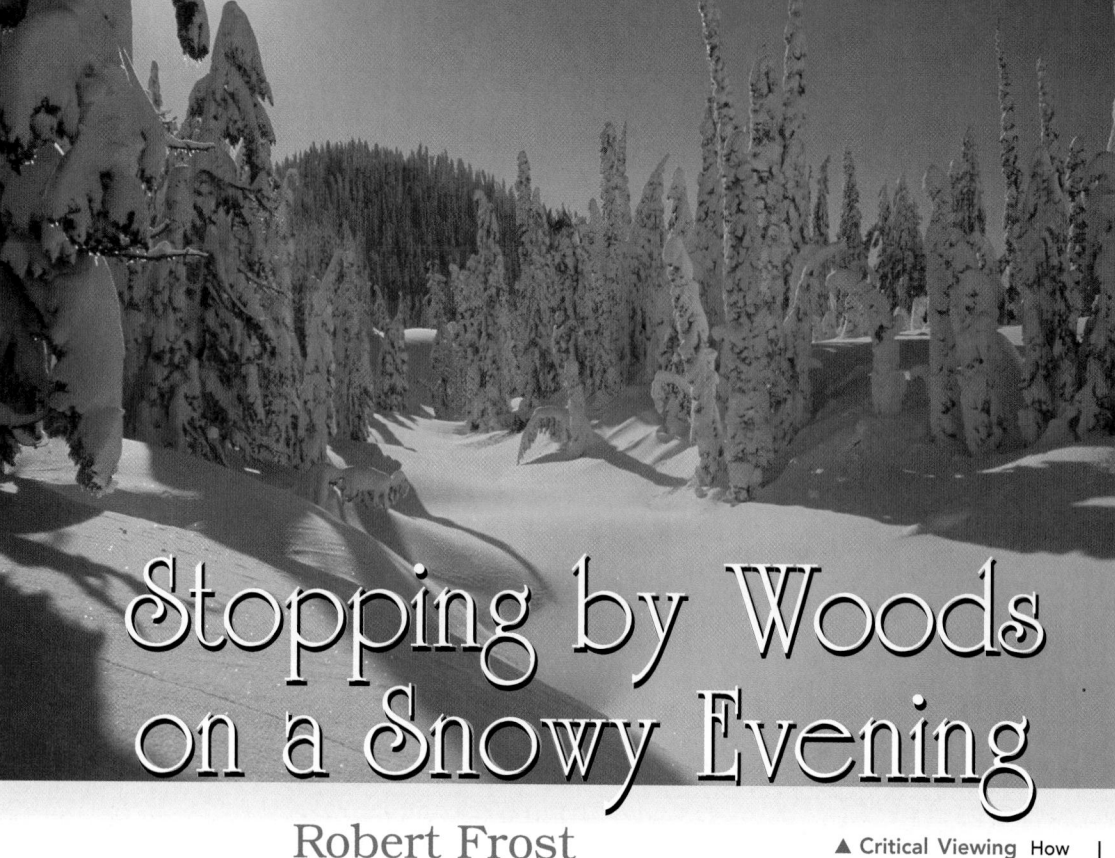

Stopping by Woods on a Snowy Evening

Robert Frost

Whose woods these are I think I know.
His house is in the village though;
He will not see me stopping here
To watch his woods fill up with snow.

My little horse must think it queer
To stop without a farmhouse near
Between the woods and frozen lake
The darkest evening of the year.

He gives his harness bells a shake
To ask if there is some mistake.
The only other sound's the sweep
Of easy wind and downy flake.

The woods are lovely, dark and deep,
But I have promises to keep,
And miles to go before I sleep,
And miles to go before I sleep.

▲ Critical Viewing How does the scene of moonlit trees differ from the one the speaker describes? What do they have in common? **[Compare and Contrast]**

▶ Critical Viewing How does the mood of this image reflect the mood of "Acquainted With the Night"? **[Connect]**

Cultural Connection

The Winter Solstice Light is a universal symbol of life, hope, and spiritual connection. Many cultures hold feasts of light during the darkest times of the year, often near the winter solstice. Celebrations may involve candles, lanterns, star tales, and wish-making rituals meant to encourage light to return. At the Thai festival of Loy Krathong, people use lotus flowers, banana leaves, or paper to make small boats. They place a lighted candle or piece of burning incense into the boats, which they set sail on a river as they make a wish. If the candle or incense stays lit until the boat sails out of view, the wish is said to come true.

Have students find out more about solstice rituals in any culture or tradition of their choice. They can prepare a report for inclusion in a class anthology of solstice stories.

Acquainted With the Night

5

Robert Frost

I have been one acquainted with the night.
I have walked out in rain—and back in rain.
I have outwalked the furthest city light.

I have looked down the saddest city lane.
6 I have passed by the watchman on his beat
And dropped my eyes, unwilling to explain.

I have stood still and stopped the sound of feet
When far away an interrupted cry
Came over houses from another street,

But not to call me back or say good-by;
And further still at an unearthly height
7 One <u>luminary</u> clock against the sky
8
Proclaimed the time was neither wrong nor right.
I have been one acquainted with the night.

◆ Build Vocabulary

luminary (lōō′ mə ner′ ē) *adj.*: Giving off light

Humanities: Art

Rural landscapes and farm scenes are a popular subject for artists. American artists such as Martin Johnson Heade, Winslow Homer, and George Inness have experimented with many techniques while concentrating on rural subjects. Invite visual/artistic learners to work together to study the work of these artists and choose images that illustrate Frost's settings. Students can collect photos or copies of them from public sources. Encourage students to put together a display that includes captions that are lines from Robert Frost's poetry, such as "As he went out and in to fetch the cows" ("Birches") to accompany a photograph of a farmer rounding up cows for milking.

Customize for
Intrapersonal Learners

5 Guide students to examine the possible metaphorical meanings of the word "night." Have students explore the possible meanings of the poem's title.

◆ Critical Thinking

6 **Analyze** Invite a volunteer to read lines 1–9 aloud as other students listen for the mood the lines convey. Discuss what the images bring to mind and how the repetition of "I have . . ." influences their understanding of the speaker. *Students may respond that the lines convey loneliness, isolation, despair, and weariness. The repetition of "I have . . ." can reinforce the speaker's experience or convey a sense of resignation.*

◆ Critical Thinking

7 **Infer** Using the last five lines as a guide, ask students to summarize the speaker's attitude toward city life. *Students may say that the speaker characterizes city life as having a sense of loneliness and isolation, that its inhuman proportions dwarf people and make them feel unwanted or insignificant.*

Comprehension Check ☑

8 What is the "luminary clock" suspended at "an unearthly height" in the night sky? *The speaker is describing the moon.*

Customize for
Visual/Spatial Learners

Encourage students to compare the mood of the photograph accompanying the poem with the poem. Ask them to identify the details of the photography that convey a mood. *Students may say that a snowy winter night and a lone figure on a city street create a mood of tranquillity. Others may notice the umbrella and say that the figure does not see the calming power of the snow.*

Customize for
Intrapersonal Learners

Although Frost's poetry invokes natural outdoor settings, it also mines the inner landscape of human values and beliefs. Encourage students to compare their own reactions to Frost's ideas. For example, ask students to consider their own views on walls or to respond to "Stopping by Woods on a Snowy Evening."

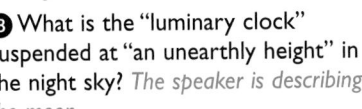

One-Minute Insight This poem celebrates the birth of a nation and reminds readers of the human connection to the hope and potential of the landscape. The speaker examines the American colonists' struggle to understand their future on the strange continent. He suggests that—spurred on by a love of the land and high hopes for a future that was as yet unformed—colonists broke free from English rule to form an independent nation.

Customize for
Less Proficient Readers
Provide or discuss prior knowledge about United States colonial history and independence from England to help students understand the meaning of this poem. Encourage these students to read or listen to the poem several times to try to grasp the problems inherent in the idea of trading dependence for independence.

❶ **Clarification** If necessary, remind students that these lines refer to the Plymouth and Massachusetts Bay colonies and Jamestown.

◆ Reading Strategy

❷ **Reading Blank Verse** Help students grasp the meaning of these lines. Suggest that they read them aloud as sentences to find a logical interpretation. *Students might say that the colonists were possessed by a love of the land that was not yet theirs because they still belonged to England. Colonists withheld the strength they would need to break away from England and had not yet discovered the courage and will to demand freedom.*

◆ Critical Thinking

❸ **Interpret** Ask students to explain what they think Frost is saying about the American people who gave themselves the "gift outright." *Students may say that these early Americans gave us all the gift of freedom by accepting that they had to shed blood to achieve it; they paid a dear price for a country they believed had great promise but was at that time still unrealized.*

The Gift Outright

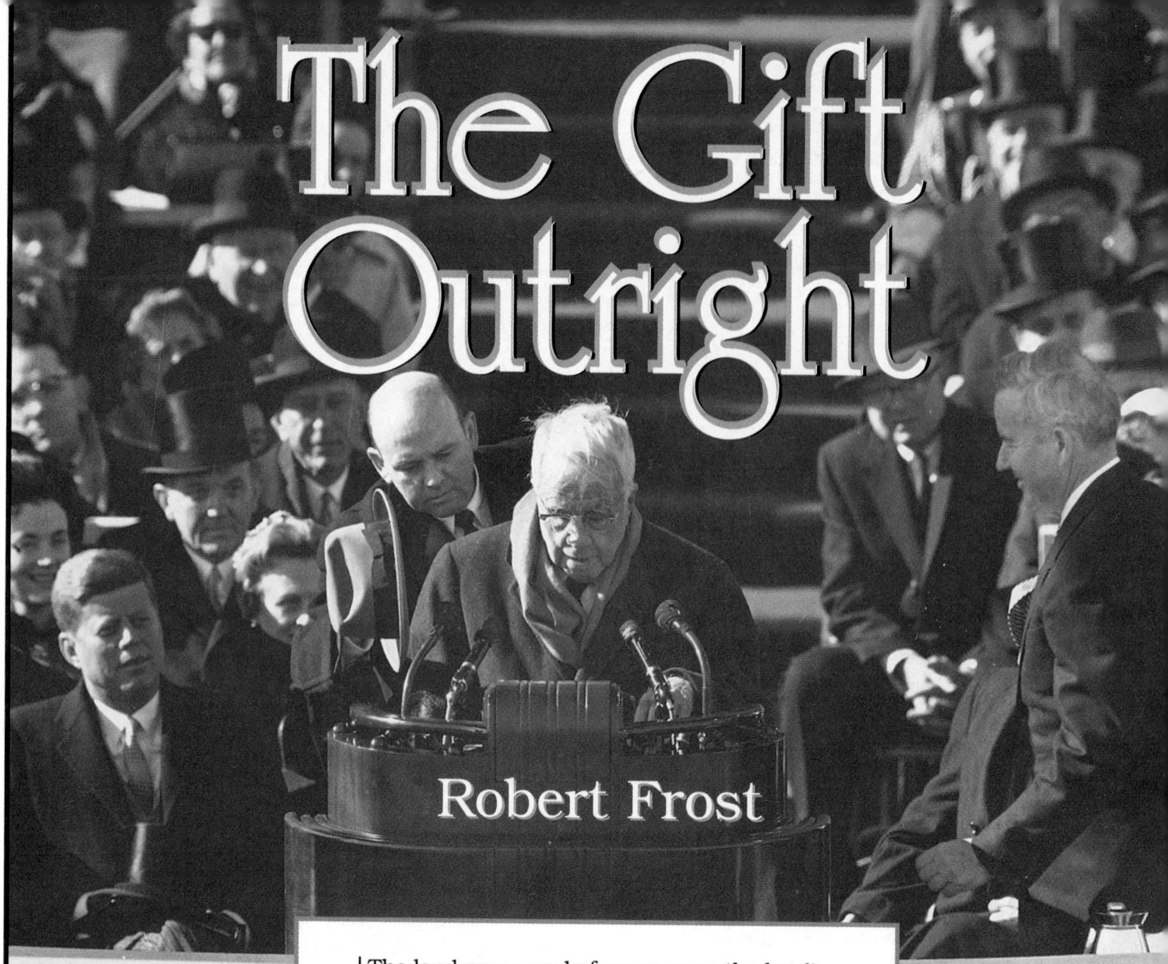

Robert Frost

The land was ours before we were the land's.
She was our land more than a hundred years
❶ Before we were her people. She was ours
In Massachusetts, in Virginia,
But we were England's, still colonials,
Possessing what we still were unpossessed by,
Possessed by what we now no more possessed.
❷ Something we were withholding made us weak
Until we found out that it was ourselves
We were withholding from our land of living,
And forthwith found salvation in surrender.
Such as we were we gave ourselves outright
(The deed of gift was many deeds of war)
❸ To the land vaguely realizing westward,
But still unstoried, artless, unenhanced,
Such as she was, such as she would become.

Speaking, Listening, and Viewing Mini-Lesson

Eulogy
This mini-lesson supports the Speaking, Listening, and Viewing activity in the Idea Bank on p. 815.

Introduce the Concept Review the activity and explain that eulogies will be judged on the basis of eloquence, ability to move listeners, and faithfulness to the event as described in the poem.

Develop Background Obtain a variety of written eulogies students can browse through for inspiration. Students who have attended a memorial service can share their ideas on what makes an effective eulogy. Discuss the importance of a respectful and sincere tone.

Apply the Information Have students write, edit, revise, practice, and then deliver their eulogies, first to a small group, then finally as part of the class memorial service.

Assess the Outcome Provide checklists students can use to evaluate each other's eulogies in terms of appropriateness of language, depth of feeling, sincerity of tone, method of delivery, and coherence of thought.

Beyond Literature

History Connection

Frost and the Inauguration of John F. Kennedy During the planning stages of John F. Kennedy's presidential inauguration, his staff approached Robert Frost with a request: Would the poet write and recite a poem for the inauguration? Frost declined to write something new for the occasion but agreed to recite "The Gift Outright." President Kennedy had a second request: Would Frost change the word "would" to "will" in the last line of the poem? The poet agreed.

Shortly before the inauguration date, Frost was struck by inspiration and, despite his earlier refusal, drafted a forty-two-line poem, "Dedication," especially for the ceremonies. The weather on January 21, 1961, Inauguration Day, was windy, clear, and sunny. As Frost stood at the presidential podium reading his new poem, the glare of the sun and the whipping wind made it almost impossible for him to see the words on the page. After struggling through the first half of "Dedication," he gave up the effort and began instead to recite "The Gift Outright" from memory. He even remembered President Kennedy's request to change the last line.

Why do you think President Kennedy might have invited Robert Frost, rather than another poet of the time, to speak at his inauguration?

Activity Use a *Readers' Guide to Periodical Literature* or the Internet to locate news articles dating from the last two presidential inaugurations. Which literary figures were invited to appear at the ceremonies? Distribute to your classmates copies of the works they recited.

Guide for Responding

◆ Literature and Your Life

Reader's Response Which of the poems on pages 810–812 made the strongest impression on you? Explain why, citing examples from the poem.

Thematic Focus In what way does land or landscape play a role in each of these poems?

Group Discussion What words would you use to describe Robert Frost's view of the natural world? What words would you use to describe his view of human society?

☑ Check Your Comprehension

1. In your own words, summarize what occurs in "Stopping by Woods on a Snowy Evening."
2. What actions does the speaker of "Acquainted With the Night" perform?
3. According to the speaker of "The Gift Outright," what did Americans do to cease being English colonials?

◆ Critical Thinking

INTERPRET

1. (a) What internal conflict does the speaker of "Stopping by Woods . . ." experience? (b) What choice does he make? **[Interpret; Infer]**
2. How does the repetition in the last two lines reinforce the meaning of "Stopping by Woods . . ."? **[Analyze]**
3. (a) In line 6 of "Acquainted With the Night," what is the speaker "unwilling to explain"? (b) What can you infer from line 10 about the speaker's hopes about the "interrupted cry"? **[Interpret; Infer]**
4. In lines 6 and 7 of "The Gift Outright," to what is the speaker referring? **[Interpret]**
5. In "The Gift Outright," to what does the speaker suggest the people surrender in order to become true Americans? **[Infer]**

COMPARE LITERARY WORKS

6. Many people enjoy Frost's poems for their sentimentality. Yet, these same poems also have a dark side with deeper levels of meaning. Examine Frost's poems, looking for these other themes. Are there similarities? **[Distinguish]**

Beyond Literature

History Connection Maya Angelou read "On the Pulse of Morning" at President Clinton's inauguration in 1993. Miller Williams read "Of History and Hope" at Clinton's inauguration in 1997.

Reinforce and Extend

Answers

◆ Literature and Your Life

Reader's Response Invite students to defend their responses.

Thematic Focus "Birches" is set in a forest. "Mending Wall" and "Out, Out—" are set in farm towns. "Stopping by Woods on a Snowy Evening" and "Acquainted With the Night" are set in outdoor landscapes. The subject of "The Gift Outright" is the American land.

Group Discussion Words that describe Frost's view of the natural world include *enduring, powerful,* and *inspirational.* Words that describe Frost's view of human society include *controlling, overpowering,* and *isolating.*

☑ Check Your Comprehension

1. A man stops to enjoy a snowfall and then continues on his journey.
2. The speaker has walked in the city at night and experienced the quiet and the activity.
3. They surrendered to the need to fight for freedom.

◆ Critical Thinking

1. (a) He is torn between the desire to enjoy nature's beauty and the awareness that he has commitments to fulfill. (b) He decides to move on.
2. The repetition creates a finality in the poem and reinforces the conflict between life's commitments and the sleep of death.
3. Possible responses: (a) He is unwilling to explain his own presence. (b) He wishes someone would interact with him.
4. He is referring to the relationship of the colonists to the land and to England.
5. They surrender to the need to fight and sacrifice for freedom.
6. Themes might include death, conflict, loneliness, isolation, and the struggle for freedom.

Beyond the Selection

FURTHER READING

Other Works by Robert Frost

"The Road Not Taken"; "The Death of the Hired Man"; *A Boy's Will*

Other Works About New England Life

Cape Cod, Henry David Thoreau
"Cousin Nancy," T. S. Eliot
"A Village Singer," Mary Wilkins Freeman

We suggest that you preview these works before recommending them to students.

INTERNET

For additional information about Robert Frost, we suggest these sites. Be aware that sites may have changed.

For a comprehensive list of Frost's works and a selected bibliography, go to **http://www.pro net.co.uk/home/catalyst/rf/bib1.html**

For more on Frost, visit **www.columbia.edu/acis/bartleby/frost**

We *strongly recommend* that you preview sites before you send students to them.

Answers

◆ Literary Focus

1. The land was ours before we were the land's/She was our land more than a hundred years/Before we were her people. She was ours/In Massachusetts, in Virginia/
2. While blank verse is frequently not exact, Frost makes clear breaks in lines 27 and 32.
3. The breaks in lines 27 and 32 emphasize the severity of the injury.

◆ Grammar and Style

Practice

1. to fetch the cows: adv.
2. to walk the line: adv.
3. to keep, to go: adj.
4. to know: noun (dir. obj.)
5. to sweep: adj.

Writing Application Students' paragraphs should be free of mechanical errors and make proper use of at least three infinitives or infinitive phrases.

For additional instruction and practice, use the Recognizing and Using Phrases lesson in the Writing Style unit of the **Language Lab CD-ROM.**

◆ Reading Strategy

Students may find that reading the poem and pausing at line breaks produces a choppy effect that interferes with comprehension. Reading blank verse as a series of sentences is a more effective method for retaining meaning.

Customize for
English Language Learners
Students who need additional help with reading blank verse may benefit from completing the page on restating poetry as prose, p. 53, in ***Stategies for Diverse Student Needs.***

◆ Build Vocabulary

Using the Latin Root *-lum-*
1. b 2. a 3. c

Using the Word Bank
1. b 2. a 3. a

Guide for Responding (continued)

◆ Literary Focus

BLANK VERSE

Blank verse is composed of unrhymed lines of iambic pentameter. In iambic pentameter, there are five feet per line, with each foot consisting of one unstressed syllable followed by a stressed syllable. Robert Frost uses blank verse in "The Gift Outright," "Out, Out—," and "Birches."

1. Copy the first four lines of "The Gift Outright"; then mark the stressed and unstressed syllables.
2. Find two examples in "Out, Out—" where Frost deviates from blank verse.
3. Explain how Frost uses each metrical variation to emphasize an idea or an image.

◆ Grammar and Style

USES OF INFINITIVES

An **infinitive** is a verb form consisting of the base form of a verb, usually with the word *to.* It can function as a noun, adjective, or adverb. An **infinitive phrase** consists of an infinitive plus any modifiers or complements. Infinitives and infinitive phrases can be used as adjectives, adverbs, or nouns.

Practice On your paper, copy the following lines from Frost's poems. For each item, underline the infinitive or infinitive phrase and identify whether it functions as a noun, adjective, or adverb.

1. As he went out and in to fetch the cows— . . .
2. And on a day we meet to walk the line . . .
3. But I have promises to keep,/ And miles to go before I sleep, . . .
4. Before I built a wall I'd ask to know/What I was walling in or walling out, . . .
5. Such heaps of broken glass to sweep away . . .

Writing Application Write a few lines of verse describing an outdoor activity you recently participated in or witnessed. Use at least three infinitives or infinitive phrases.

◆ Reading Strategy

READING BLANK VERSE

Reading blank verse in sentences, rather than pausing at the end of each line, helps you to appreciate how this type of verse captures the rhythms of everyday speech. For example, reading the sixteen-line poem "The Gift Outright" as five sentences underscores Frost's use of direct and common language.

"Out, Out—" is also written largely in blank verse. Read the poem twice—first pausing at the end of each of the thirty-four poetic lines, then again, reading the poem as a series of twenty-three sentences. Describe the differences between the two readings. Which approach to reading is more effective? Why?

◆ Build Vocabulary

USING THE LATIN ROOT *-lum-*

Many English words are based on the Latin root *-lum-*, meaning "light." In your notebook, complete these sentences using the appropriate *-lum-* word.

a. luminous **b.** illuminate **c.** illumination

1. Is that single bulb enough to __?__ the entire room?
2. The leaves of the linden tree were bathed in __?__ sunlight.
3. The students found __?__ in the wise words of the philosopher.

USING THE WORD BANK: Analogies

On your paper, complete the following analogies using the words from the Word Bank.

1. *Scorching* is to *fire* as __?__ is to *moon.*
2. *Swiftness* is to *runner* as __?__ is to *dancer.*
3. *Joyful* is to *celebrant* as __?__ is to *mourner.*

Reteach

Reading Blank Verse To help students get meaning from reading blank verse, suggest that they read the sentences and not stop or pause at the end of a line unless there is punctuation. Explain that stopping at the end of every line will produce a choppy effect and will distract from the meaning.

Have students work in groups of two or three to read one of Frost's poems aloud. Ask one person to read aloud, stopping at the end of each complete thought, which usually ends in punctuation. Instruct the others to listen. Then the listeners should briefly state the idea in the lines that were read aloud. Students may exchange roles of reader and listener.

To help students get the rhythm when reading the lines aloud, they can highlight the stressed syllable in each word as shown here.

"But they would have the rabbit out of hiding,
To please the yelping dogs. The gaps I mean. . ."

Build Your Portfolio

Idea Bank

Writing

1. **Character Sketch** Using your imagination to fill in missing details, write a character sketch about the speaker in "Stopping by Woods." Who is he? Where is he coming from, and where is he headed? What are the promises he must keep?
2. **News Story** Building on the facts presented in the poem, reshape "Out, Out—" into a newspaper article. **[Media Link]**
3. **Essay** Critic Robert DiYanni commented that Frost's poetry often "'begins in delight and ends in wisdom,' offering along the way what [Frost] called 'a momentary stay against confusion.'" Write an essay in which you explain how that statement relates to "Birches."

Speaking, Listening, and Viewing

4. **Eulogy** Prepare a eulogy for the young boy in "Out, Out—" in which you lament his early death and pay tribute to a boy who did "a man's work." Deliver the eulogy at a "memorial service" in the classroom. **[Performing Arts Link]**
5. **Poetry Reading** Ask a librarian to help you locate recordings of Frost reciting his own poems. Select two or three poems that appeal to you, and play them for the class. Lead a discussion of the impressions created by Frost's delivery.

Researching and Representing

6. **Graphic Display** Which line from "Mending Wall" best captures your own ideas about walls? Design a poster to illustrate this line. **[Art Link]**
7. **Travel Brochure** Create a travel brochure promoting New England tourism. Refer to travel guides or Internet sites to learn what draws visitors to the region. Include text, photos, and passages from Frost's poetry. **[Social Studies Link]**

Online Activity www.phlit.phschool.com

Guided Writing Lesson

Introduction to an Anthology

An **anthology** is a collection of literary works often focused on a specific theme (poems about nature, for example) or on a specific time period (for instance, twentieth-century short stories). Usually anthologies include an introduction that provides an overview of the content, as well as commentary on the works. Write an introduction to an anthology featuring poems by Robert Frost. Identify the key characteristics of his work, providing examples to support each of your points.

Writing Skills Focus: Transitions to Show Examples

Each time you cite a supporting example, introduce the example with a transition, such as the ones in this list.

for example	such as
along with	for instance
in other words	like

Prewriting Review the Frost poems in this group. As you read, jot down ideas about the topics, style, and themes of the works. Note the elements they have in common. Decide which characteristics you will address in your introduction; then identify supporting poems or specific lines. Finally, sketch out a table of contents that indicates which selections you will include.

Drafting Begin your introduction with a general statement about the poems, and follow by touching on a few key points related to this statement. Focus each body paragraph on one key point. Support each point with passages from the poems.

Revising Read your work for clarity and correctness. Does it reveal insights into the works and the relationships among them? Does it provide enough information to encourage readers to read the anthology? Add transitions to introduce examples where necessary.

Idea Bank

Customizing for
Performance Levels

Following are suggestions for matching Idea Bank topics with your students' performance levels:
Less Advanced Students: 1, 4
Average Students: 2, 6, 7
More Advanced Students: 3, 5

Customizing for
Learning Modalities

Following are suggestions for matching Idea Bank topics with your students' learning modalities:
Verbal/Linguistic: 4
Interpersonal: 4
Musical/Rhythmic: 5
Visual/Spatial: 6, 7

Guided Writing Lesson

Writing and Language Transparencies Use the Analysis Map (pp. 83–85) or the Outline Organizer (pp. 95–97) to help students plan their introductions.

For more prewriting, elaboration, and revision strategies, see *Prentice Hall Writing and Grammar.*

Writers at Work Videodisc
Have students view the videodisc segment on Exposition (Ch. 3), featuring Thom Harrington, to see how to use an outline to help organize ideas. Have students discuss the type of information they might include in their outlines.

Play frames 26184 to 27200

Writing Lab CD-ROM
Have students complete the tutorial on Exposition. Follow these steps:

1. Direct students to use the Outliner activity in the Organizing Details section to plan their introductions.
2. Have students draft on computer.
3. Have students use the revision checker for transition words.

ASSESSMENT OPTIONS

Formal Assessment, Selection Test, pp. 244–246, and Assessment Resources Software. The selection test is designed so that it can be easily customized to the performance levels of your students.

Alternative Assessment, p. 53, includes options for less advanced students, more advanced students, musical/rhythmic learners, interpersonal learners, visual/spatial learners, and bodily/kinesthetic learners.

PORTFOLIO ASSESSMENT
Use the following rubrics in the ***Alternative Assessment*** booklet to assess student writing:
Character Sketch: Description Rubric, p. 112
News Story : Summary Rubric, p. 113
Essay: Critical Review Rubric, p.126
Guided Writing Lesson: Literary Analysis/Interpretation Rubric, p.127

Prepare and Engage

LESSON OBJECTIVES

1. **To develop vocabulary and word identification skills**
   - Latin Roots: *-terr-*
   - Using the Word Bank: Context
2. **To use a variety of reading strategies to comprehend informal essays**
   - Reading Strategy: Recognize Hyperbole
3. **To express and support responses to the text**
   - Critical Thinking
   - Idea Bank: Humorous Tourist Guide
   - Idea Bank: Police Report
   - Idea Bank: Critical Response
   - Idea Bank: Set Design
   - Idea Bank: Audition
4. **To analyze literary elements**
   - Literary Focus: Informal Essay
   - Idea Bank: Essay Critique
5. **To read in order to research self-selected and assigned topics**
   - Idea Bank: Historical Re-creation
6. **To use recursive writing processes to write a toast**
   - Guided Writing Lesson
7. **To increase knowledge of the rules of grammar and usage**
   - Build Grammar Skills: Commas in Series

Test Preparation

Reading Comprehension: Anticipate Missing Words (ATE, p. 817)
The teaching tips and sample test item in this workshop support the instruction and practice in the unit workshop:
Reading Comprehension: Sentence-Completion Questions (ATE, p. 863)

Guide for Interpreting

James Thurber *(1894–1961)*

James Thurber's essays and other writings—plays, sketches, and short stories such as the well-known "The Secret Life of Walter Mitty"—generally evolved from his own experiences. In his humorous autobiographical sketches, Thurber embellishes the facts and describes events in an amusing manner. In his short stories, Thurber's characters struggle against the unpleasant realities of modern life—often with humorous consequences.

Thurber was born in Columbus, Ohio. After attending Ohio State University, he joined *The New Yorker* magazine staff in 1927. Thurber enjoyed a relationship with the magazine that lasted for years.

Thurber published many collections of his writing. For example, *The Owl in the Attic and Other Perplexities* (1931) and *The Seal in the Bedroom and Other Predicaments* (1932) contain a mixture of short stories, parodies, and cartoons. Thurber was also an able cartoonist—often creating cartoons to illustrate his writing and sometimes writing stories or essays to explain his cartoons. Thurber's humor shows a glint of unhappiness, especially in the later years when his failing vision made him increasingly bitter.

E. B. White *(1899–1985)*

Creating writings that capture the interest of adults as well as pieces that entertained children, E(lwyn) B(rooks) White established himself as one of the best-loved twentieth-century writers. His direct and precisely worded essays set a standard against which today's essays can be judged. White strongly believed in individualism and simplicity, values that come through in his writing.

The relatively simple youth White has recalled with yearning took place in Mount Vernon, New York. From there, he went to study literature at Cornell University. As an undergraduate, White served as the editor of the Cornell *Daily Sun*. Later, he began a long association with *The New Yorker* magazine. His humorous, topical essays helped to establish *The New Yorker* as one of the nation's most successful general-interest magazines.

White wrote two of the most beloved children's books of all time, *Stuart Little* (1945) and *Charlotte's Web* (1952), along with many adult essays, columns, poems, and stories. In addition, his revision of William Strunk, Jr.'s classic style manual, *The Elements of Style,* has become a classic in its own right.

◆ Background for Understanding

CULTURE: HUMOR IN AMERICA

America has a strong tradition of humorous writing. Much of that humor builds on self-ridicule, with people poking fun at their own missteps and failures. Americans seem especially willing to laugh at themselves when they don't achieve everything they attempt.

Magazines have played a key role in nurturing American humor. For years, *The Saturday Evening Post* and *The New Yorker* magazine have showcased the work of cartoonists and humorous writers. Founded in 1925 as a magazine of satire, *The New Yorker* published the work of humorists Robert Benchley, S. J. Perelman, Dorothy Parker, and Frank Sullivan, in addition to James Thurber and E. B. White.

Many of today's best writers of humor reach out into other media. Garrison Keillor, for example, writes humorous essays but is most popularly known as the host of "Prairie Home Companion," a radio program that spoofs the people of the imaginary Lake Wobegon, Minnesota, much as White satirized New Yorkers.

Prentice Hall Literature Program Resources

REINFORCE /RETEACH / EXTEND
Selection Support Pages
Build Vocabulary: Word Roots: *-terr-*, p. 247
Grammar and Style: Commas in Series, p. 248
Reading Strategy: Recognize Hyperbole, p. 249
Literary Focus: Informal Essay, p. 250

Strategies for Diverse Student Needs,
Identify Paragraph Topics, p. 54
Beyond Literature
Community Connection: The Police, p. 54
Formal Assessment Selection Test, pp. 247–249; Assessment Resources Software
Alternative Assessment, p. 54

Writing and Language Transparencies
Cubing Organizer, pp. 71–73
Resource Pro CD-ROM
Listening to Literature Audiocassettes

◆ Literature and Your Life

Connect Your Experience

What makes you laugh? Different people are amused by different things—movie characters slipping on banana peels, the irreverent jokes of a stand-up comedian, or the subtle wit of the humorous essay. Notice as you read these essays which parts make you laugh—or smile. How does your laughter relate to your own experiences?

Group Discussion In a small group, discuss the kind of humor you most enjoy, and why.

Thematic Focus: From Every Corner of the Land

As you read E. B. White's essay about New York City, think about what gives any place its unique character.

◆ Build Vocabulary

Latin Word Roots: *-terr-*

The word *subterranean* appears in "Here Is New York." Knowing that the prefix *sub-* means "under" and the Latin root *-terr-* means "earth" will help you guess that *subterranean* means "occurring under the earth's surface."

Word Bank

Before you read, preview this list of words from the essays.

intuitively
blaspheming
aspiration
subterranean
claustrophobia
cosmopolitan

◆ Grammar and Style

Commas in Series

Both Thurber and White use **commas in series**—three or more parallel items linked by commas with a conjunction usually preceding the final item—to string together humorous details. Look at these examples:

White: . . . it has been hit by an airplane in a fog, struck countless times by lightning, and been jumped off of by so many unhappy people that . . .

Thurber: Bodwell was at the window in a minute, shouting, frothing a little, shaking his fist.

◆ Literary Focus

Informal Essay

"The Night the Ghost Got In" and "Here Is New York" are both **informal essays**, brief nonfiction pieces characterized by a relaxed, conversational style and structure. Informal essays are intended to entertain. Using informal language, they address a narrow subject, and they tend to be loosely organized. They often include digressions in which the author expresses an opinion or discusses related matters.

When you read informal essays, you'll get to glimpse the writer's personality. What do these essays suggest about James Thurber and E. B. White?

◆ Reading Strategy

Recognize Hyperbole

These essays draw humor from **hyperbole**—lavish exaggerations of fact and outrageous overstatements. The series of bizarre events in Thurber's essays and White's litany of probable New York City disasters are good examples of how writers use hyperbole to amuse their audiences.

Watch for details that seem too absurd to be true. When Thurber describes an army of police and reporters arriving at his house, you'd be right to suspect hyperbole. Jot down a hyperbole that you find especially amusing.

Test Preparation Workshop

Reading Comprehension: Anticipate Missing Words Many standardized tests ask students to correctly answer sentence-completion questions. Use the following example to show students how to use context and their own knowledge to guess a word that would complete the following passage.

Magazines have been important in nurturing American humor. For years *The New Yorker* has ____ the work of cartoonists and humor writers.

A concealed
B reserved
C showcased
D hidden

After reading the question, students may guess that the word *shown* completes the sentence. Answer C is closest in meaning to that guess.

Interest Grabber For the Thurber essay, you might play a videotape of an especially memorable and quirky character in a television sitcom. Consider featuring Ted from "The Mary Tyler Moore Show," Lucy from "I Love Lucy," or Louie or Latka from "Taxi." Point out that character traits are often exaggerated for effect. The humorous essay they are about to read has characters that might make interesting members of a sitcom family.

Before students read E. B. White's appealing essay about New York City, show the opening sequence from Woody Allen's film *Manhattan*, which provides striking black and white footage of New York while George Gershwin's romantic *Rhapsody in Blue* plays in the background. Next, show the opening credits from the TV show "NYPD Blue," which offers an entirely different, grittier view of the city. Then ask students to give their own views on what images of New York City come immediately to their minds.

Customize for
Less Proficient Readers
Have these students read aloud in small groups, stopping periodically to check comprehension. When students read the E. B. White piece, help them ascertain the meanings of difficult vocabulary not otherwise highlighted, such as *ferments, succumbed,* and *patronized.*

Customize for
English Language Learners
Help students interpret any unfamiliar figures of speech the writers use. For example, in the Thurber piece, the boys' mother tells them that they "haven't a stitch on" and that they'll "catch [their] death." You can point out that she means the boys are undressed and they'll freeze. If possible, suggest more current expressions that mean the same thing as the unfamiliar ones.

Customize for
Verbal/Linguistic Learners
Both essayists use sensory images in their pieces. Guide students to look for examples and to discuss how they add liveliness to the descriptions.

Develop Understanding

One-Minute Insight This humorous informal essay has the following ingredients: a strange noise in the night, a quirky mother, an unpredictable grandfather, a frothing neighbor, a fumbling army of police officers, and the deadpan narration of a witty teen amused by it all. It features a comical situation described with overstatement, understatement, and, on occasion, accuracy.

Customize for
Visual/Spatial Learners
Have students preview the story by flipping through the pages and examining the three cartoons by the writer. Ask them to predict the plot and tone of the story, based on the title and illustrations. Have them describe the clues that tell them more about the nature of the piece. *Students should not predict a scary ghost story, but instead anticipate a humorous tale.*

Customize for
AP Students
Guide students to look for examples of understatement and hyperbole as they read. You may find it helpful to relate understatement to the comic technique students may know as "deadpan"—the style of many comedians, such as Bob Newhart.

◆ Reading Strategy

❶ **Recognize Hyperbole** Students can appreciate how Thurber immediately captures the reader's interest with this list of absurd, but related details in the first paragraph. The active reader wants to know how they all fit together.

❷ **Clarification** Point out that this sentence is a reference to another story by James Thurber, called "The Night the Bed Fell In."

▶Critical Viewing◀

❸ **Analyze** Students may suggest that the humor in the sketch stems from the depiction of the ghost; it seems more comical than frightening, the kind that might say, "Boo!" and scare itself with the remark! Students may also find the faces of both figures comical.

The Night the Ghost Got In

James Thurber

The Night the Ghost Got In, Copyright 1933, 1961, James Thurber, From *My Life and Hard Times,* published by Harper & Row.

▲ **Critical Viewing** The humor in Thurber's drawing echoes the humor in his story. What makes this sketch humorous? **[Analyze]** ❸

❶ The ghost that got into our house on the night of November 17, 1915, raised such a hullabaloo of misunderstandings that I am sorry I didn't just let it keep on walking, and go to bed. Its advent caused my mother to throw a shoe through a window of the house next door and ended up with my grandfather shooting a patrolman. I am sorry, therefore, as I have said, that I ever paid any attention to the footsteps.

❷ They began about a quarter past one o'clock in the morning, a rhythmic, quick-cadenced walking around the dining-room table. My mother was asleep in one room upstairs, my brother Herman in another; grandfather was in the attic, in the old walnut bed which, as you will remember, once fell on my father. I had just stepped out of the bathtub and was busily rubbing myself with a towel when I heard the steps. They were the steps of a man walking rapidly around the dining-room table downstairs. The light from the bathroom shone down the back steps, which dropped directly into the dining-room; I could see the faint shine of plates on the plate-rail; I couldn't see the table. The steps kept going round and round the table; at regular intervals a board creaked, when it was trod upon. I supposed at first that it was my father or my brother Roy, who had gone to Indianapolis but were expected home at any time. I suspected next that it was a burglar. It did not enter my mind until later that it was a ghost.

After the walking had gone on for perhaps three minutes, I tiptoed to Herman's room. "Psst!" I hissed, in the dark, shaking him. "Awp," he said, in the low, hopeless tone of a despondent beagle—he always half suspected that something would "get him" in the night. I told him who I was. "There's something

Block Scheduling Strategies

Consider these suggestions to take advantage of extended class time:

- Have students complete the Group Discussion activity in Literature and Your Life (p. 817). Each group can present its findings about what students think is funny.
- Use the Interest Grabber activity to spark interest in Thurber's essay and to elicit student reaction to the way New York is presented in film and television.
- Introduce the Reading Strategy and any other skills you wish to emphasize.
- Have students read the selections and respond to the Critical Viewing questions.
- Assign the Humorous Tourist Guide writing activity from the Idea Bank (p. 827). Invite students to write about a city with which they are familiar. Before students begin, discuss the elements of an informal essay and how to use hyperbole to make points or create humor.
- Use a scoring rubric, found in ***Alternative Assessment,*** to quickly assess students' writing.

downstairs!" I said. He got up and followed me to the head of the back staircase. We listened together. There was no sound. The steps had ceased. Herman looked at me in some alarm: I had only the bath towel around my waist. He wanted to go back to bed, but I gripped his arm. "There's something down there!" I said. Instantly the steps began again, circled the dining-room table like a man running, and started up the stairs toward us, heavily, two at a time. The light still shone palely down the stairs; we saw nothing coming; we only heard the steps. Herman rushed to his room and slammed the door. I slammed shut the door at the stairs top and held my knee against it. After a long minute, I slowly opened it again. There was nothing there. There was no sound. None of us ever heard the ghost again.

The slamming of the doors had aroused mother: she peered out of her room. "What on earth are you boys doing?" she demanded. Herman ventured out of his room. "Nothing," he said, gruffly, but he was, in color, a light green. "What was all that running around downstairs?" said mother. So she had heard the steps, too! We just looked at her. "Burglars!" she shouted intuitively. I tried to quiet her by starting lightly downstairs.

"Come on, Herman," I said.

4 "I'll stay with Mother," he said. "She's all excited."

I stepped back onto the landing.

"Don't either of you go a step," said mother. "We'll call the police." Since the phone was downstairs, I didn't see how we were going to call the police—nor did I want the police—but mother made one of her quick, incomparable decisions. She flung up a window of her bedroom which faced the bedroom windows of the
5 house of a neighbor, picked up a shoe, and whammed it through a pane of glass across the narrow space that separated the two houses. Glass tinkled into the bedroom occupied by a retired engraver named Bodwell and his wife. Bodwell had been for some years in rather a bad way and was subject to mild "attacks." Most everybody we knew or lived near had *some* kind of attacks.

It was now about two o'clock of a moonless night; clouds hung black and low. Bodwell was at the window in a minute, shouting, frothing a little, shaking his fist. "We'll sell the house and go back to Peoria," we could hear Mrs. Bodwell saying. It was some time before mother "got through" to Bodwell. "Burglars!" she shouted. "Burglars in the house!" Herman and I hadn't dared to tell her that it was not burglars but ghosts, for she was even more afraid of ghosts than of burglars. Bodwell at first thought that she meant there were burglars in his house, but finally he quieted down and called the police for us over an extension phone by his bed. After he had disappeared from the window, mother suddenly made as if to throw another shoe, not because there was further need of it, but, as she later explained, because the thrill of heaving a shoe through a window glass had enormously taken her fancy. I prevented her.

The police were on hand in a commendably short time: a Ford sedan full of them, two on motorcycles, and a patrol wagon with about eight in it and a few reporters. They began banging at our front door. Flashlights shot streaks of gleam up and down the walls, across the yard, down the walk between our house and Bodwell's. "Open up!" cried a hoarse voice. "We're men from Headquarters!" I wanted to go down and let them in, since there they were, but mother wouldn't hear of it. "You haven't a stitch on," she pointed out. "You'd catch your death." I wound the towel around me again. Finally the cops put their shoulders to our big heavy front door with its thick beveled glass and broke it in: I could hear a rending of wood and a splash of glass on the floor of the hall. Their lights played all over the living-room and crisscrossed nervously in the dining-room, stabbed into hallways, shot up the front stairs and finally up the back. They caught me standing in my towel at the top. A heavy policeman bounded up the steps. "Who are you?" he demanded. "I live here," I said. "Well, whattsa matta, ya hot?" he asked. I was, as a matter of fact, cold; I went to my room and pulled on some trousers. On my way out, a cop stuck a gun into my ribs. "Whatta you doin' here?" he demanded. "I live here," I said.

> **◆ Reading Strategy**
> Why is this clearly an example of exaggeration? 6

◆ Build Vocabulary

intuitively (in to͞o´ i tiv lē) *adv.*: Instinctively

Customize for
Interpersonal Learners

4 Guide students to see the humor in this exchange. It is Herman who is "all excited," not the mother; he is frightened and just looking for a way to avoid going downstairs.

◆ *Literature and Your Life*

5 Help students analyze the comedy of this passage. Although the mother does a very dramatic and comical thing here, the narrator takes it in stride, describing the act with almost no effect at all. In fact, in the middle of describing what she does, he digresses to include what he knows about the neighbor and other neighbors. Discuss with students that the humor stems as much from the way he describes the act as from the act itself.

◆ Reading Strategy

6 **Recognize Hyperbole** Students may say that the overreaction of the police is a clear example of hyperbole. They can point out that in response to a report of a possible break-in, it is highly improbable that the police would appear in such force and act in such a frantic, absurd manner.

Read to
Be Entertained

Thurber's essay provides ample amusement, so most students will probably realize that their purpose for reading is to be entertained. Invite students to identify or analyze aspects of the text that amuse, such as: suspense, eccentric characters (including the narrator), humorously realistic dialogue, and unpredictable events. They may also mention Thurber's use of detailed descriptions, which—together with his cartoons—invites readers to visualize the humorous situation, the characters, and the events.

Humanities: Art

Cartoons by James Thurber for "The Night the Ghost Got In," 1933.

James Thurber was a cartoonist and illustrator as well as a writer. Many of his essays, like this one, are illustrated with his own cartoons. These drawings could be called gesture drawings, simple in the use of line and space, yet involving a wild, dark humor.

In his mid-50's, Thurber went blind. Many of his drawings were made with the aid of special visual equipment such as a microscope and an illuminated board. He used a mechanized pencil that produced a glowing neon line. This may explain the lack of detail that has become part of Thurber's trademark artistic style.

Use these questions to guide students' interpretation of the cartoons in this story:

1. What part of the story does the cartoon on page 818 reflect? *Students may say that since at no time in the story is a character visited by a ghost while in bed, this picture serves to illustrate the opening paragraph and to create the impression that the story about to be told is a humorous one.*
2. Thurber is able to convey a variety of expressions with simple line drawings. What expressions are shown on the faces of the police officers in the cartoon on page 821? *The officers in action are puzzled. The one who is in charge appears to be equally perplexed despite his stiff-upper-lip stance.*

▶Critical Viewing◀

❶ **Assess** Students may say that the cartoon presents the mother as a comic, mischievous figure.

◆ Grammar and Style

❷ **Commas in Series** Guide students to examine Thurber's use of commas here. He strings together the effects of the police behavior on household objects. Students can note the stylistic effect created by the writer's decision to omit a coordinating conjunction to link the last police action to the others.

❸ **Clarification** Point out Thurber's use of malapropism here to poke fun at the police officer. Elicit from students that the word he meant to use was "hysterical." Inform students that the humorous misuse of words has a long-standing comic tradition.

❹ **Clarification** This story is set in 1915; it would not have been too uncommon at that time for men of Grandfather's age to use the Civil War as the source of their military fantasies. Point out that Grandfather's "phase" might be analogous to someone of his age today being infatuated with events in World War II.

◆ Literary Focus

❺ **Informal Essay** Students may point to the relaxed, understated, conversational style the boy uses to describe the odd events in the attic, or to the informality of placing dialogue from several people within one paragraph. They might say that the passage reflects the author's keen wit.

Extending Word Study

Context Students can use context to determine the meaning of *report* ("a loud, resounding noise, especially one made by an explosion") near the bottom of the second column on p. 820. Guide students to notice that the preceding sentence mentions a gun; "let fly" implies that a bullet was shot; and the effect of the report is that it "seemed to crack the rafters," not with the bullet's impact, but presumably with loudness.

The Night the Ghost Got In, Copyright 1933, 1961, James Thurber, From *My Life and Hard Times,* published by Harper & Row.

▲ ❶ **Critical Viewing** Thurber created this cartoon to accompany "The Night the Ghost Got In." How does the illustration add to the humorous effect of the essay? **[Assess]**

The officer in charge reported to mother. "No sign of nobody, lady," he said. "Musta got away—whatt'd he look like?" "There were two or three of them," mother said, "whooping and carrying on and slamming doors." "Funny," said the cop. "All ya windows and doors was locked on the inside tight as a tick."

Downstairs, we could hear the tromping of ❷ the other police. Police were all over the place; doors were yanked open, drawers were yanked open, windows were shot up and pulled down, furniture fell with dull thumps. A half-dozen policemen emerged out of the darkness of the front hallway upstairs. They began to ransack the floor: pulled beds away from walls, tore clothes off hooks in the closets, pulled suitcases and boxes off shelves. One of them found an old zither[1] that Roy had won in a pool tournament. "Looky here, Joe," he said, strumming it with a big paw. The cop named Joe took it and turned it over. "What is it?" he asked me. "It's an old zither our guinea pig used to sleep on," I said. It was true that a pet guinea pig we once had would never sleep anywhere except on the zither, but I should never have said so. Joe and the other cop looked at me a long time. They put the zither back on a shelf.

"No sign o' nuthin'," said the cop who had first spoken to mother. "This guy," he explained to the others, jerking a thumb at me, "was nekked. The lady seems historical." They all nodded, but said nothing; just looked at me. In the small silence we all heard a creaking in the attic. ❸ Grandfather was turning over in bed. "What's 'at?" snapped Joe. Five or six cops sprang for the attic door before I could intervene or explain. I realized that it would be bad if they burst in on grandfather unannounced, or even announced. He was going through a phase in which he believed that General Meade's men, under steady hammering by Stonewall Jackson, were beginning to retreat and even desert. ❹

When I got to the attic, things were pretty confused. Grandfather had evidently jumped to the conclusion that the police were deserters from Meade's army, trying to hide away in his attic. He bounded out of bed wearing a long flannel nightgown over long woolen underwear, a nightcap, and a leather jacket around his chest. The cops must have realized at once that the indignant white-haired old man belonged in the house, but they had no chance to say so. "Back, ye cowardly dogs!" roared grandfather. "Back t' the lines, ye yellow, lily-livered cattle!" With that, he fetched the officer who found the zither a flat-handed smack alongside his head that sent him sprawling. The others beat a retreat, but not fast enough; grandfather grabbed Zither's gun from its holster and let fly. The report seemed to crack the rafters; smoke filled the attic. ❺ A cop cursed and shot his hand to his shoulder. Somehow, we all finally got downstairs again and locked the door against the old gentleman. He fired once or twice more in the darkness and then went back to bed. "That was grandfather," I explained to Joe, out of breath. "He thinks you're deserters." "I'll say he does," said Joe.

> **◆ Literary Focus**
> What features of this passage are typical of an informal essay?

The cops were reluctant to leave without getting their hands on somebody besides

1. **zither** (zith´ ər) *n.*: Musical instrument with thirty to forty strings stretched across a flat soundboard and played with the fingers.

◆ Build Vocabulary

blaspheming (blas fēm´ iŋ) *v.*: Cursing

Humanities: Music

Thurber's Dogs Inspired by James Thurber's canine drawings, Peter Schickele, the creative composer of P.D.Q. Bach fame, has written a musical composition called "Thurber's Dogs." Assign students the task of locating a selection of these drawings and either describing them for classmates or photocopying them for display. Have a volunteer locate and bring in a recording of the Schickele piece. Invite students to listen to the music and respond to its representation of the drawings.

grandfather; the night had been distinctly a defeat for them. Furthermore, they obviously didn't like the "layout"; something looked—and I can see their viewpoint—phony. They began to poke into things again. A reporter, a thin-faced, wispy man, came up to me. I had put on one of mother's blouses, not being able to find anything else. The reporter looked at me with mingled suspicion and interest. "Just what the heck is the real lowdown here, Bud?" he asked. I decided to be frank with him. "We had ghosts," I said. He gazed at me a long time as if I were a slot machine into which he had, without results, dropped a nickel. Then he walked away. The cops followed him, the one grandfather shot holding his now-bandaged arm, cursing and blaspheming. "I'm gonna get my gun back from that old bird," said the zither-cop. "Yeh," said Joe. "You—and who else?" I told them I would bring it to the station house the next day.

6 "What was the matter with that one policeman?" mother asked, after they had gone. "Grandfather shot him," I said. "What for?" she demanded. I told her he was a deserter. "Of all things!" said mother. "He was such a nice-looking young man." 6

Grandfather was fresh as a daisy and full of jokes at breakfast next morning. We thought at first he had forgotten all about what had happened, but he hadn't. Over his third cup of coffee, he glared at Herman and me. "What was the idee of all them cops tarry-hootin' round the house last night?" he demanded. He had us there.

The Night the Ghost Got In, Copyright 1933, 1961, James Thurber, From *My Life and Hard Times*, published by Harper & Row.

▲ Critical Viewing Compare this illustration with Thurber's description of the police investigation. What makes each funny? **[Evaluate]** 7

Guide for Responding

◆ *Literature and Your Life*

Reader's Response What did you find the most humorous point in the essay? Why?

Thematic Response Could this humorous essay have take place in a distant land—for example, Argentina or Nigeria? Explain.

☑ Check Your Comprehension

1. What event sets off the family's reactions?
2. Describe what each character in the narrator's family does on the night "the ghost" got into the house.

◆ Critical Thinking

INTERPRET

1. How does Thurber's portrayal of himself differ from his portrayal of the other characters? **[Compare and Contrast]**
2. How does lack of communication contribute to the humor of this essay? **[Support]**
3. What does the grandfather's question at breakfast reveal about him? **[Interpret]**

EXTEND

4. Explain why these characters would probably not succeed in business. **[Career Link]**

◆ Reading Strategy

6 Recognize Hyperbole Guide students to appreciate the humor in the calm way the boy describes the shooting of a police officer.

▶Critical Viewing◀

7 Evaluate It shows that it takes four men to look in a drawer. The cartoon matches the fumbling attempts of the police officers.

◆ Critical Thinking

Assess Ask students to decide whether the story's characters are likable.

Reinforce and Extend

Enrichment Have students contrast contemporary police procedures with those practiced by Thurber's team of police officers using p. 54 in ***Beyond Literature***, entitled Community Connection: The Police.

Answers

◆ *Literature and Your Life*

Reader's Response Students should support their choices with explanations.

Thematic Focus While the story's conflict—confusion over noises in the night—could take place anywhere, Thurber's telling is strongly anchored in the United States in 1915.

☑ Check Your Comprehension

1. Late at night, the narrator hears noises on the first floor.
2. The narrator wraps himself in a towel and wakes his brother. The two slam doors against the "ghost" running up the stairs. Mother throws a shoe through her neighbor's window. Grandfather fights off the police then goes back to bed.

◆ Critical Thinking

1. He depicts himself as the only person acting rationally.
2. A lack of communication sets off the entire sequence of events.
3. His question reveals that he is more aware than people think.
4. Possible response: These characters act on impulse rather than following a deliberate, rational plan.

Beyond the Selection

FURTHER READING

Other Works by James Thurber

Thurber: A Collection of Critical Essays
"The Secret Life of Walter Mitty"
The Owl in the Attic and Other Perplexities
The Seal in the Bedroom and Other Predicaments

We suggest that you preview these works before recommending them to students.

INTERNET

You and your students may find additional information about the work of James Thurber on the Internet. We suggest the following sites. Please be aware, however, that sites may have changed since this information was published.

To visit the James Thurber Web page, go to **http://home.earthlink.net/~ritter/thurber/index.html**

We *strongly recommend* that you preview sites before you send students to them.

Develop Understanding

One-Minute Insight In this informal essay, E. B. White affectionately describes the city he loves, paying tribute to its unique features and characteristics, and explaining how these more than make up for the deficiencies visitors are bound to notice.

Clarification Tell students that this essay first appeared in *Holiday Magazine* in 1948, and that it came out in book form in the following year.

Customize for
AP Students
Guide students to look for examples of the author's precisely-worded style, a style that many see as the standard against which today's essayists are judged. For example, in the first paragraph, in describing the Empire State Building, White writes that it ". . . managed to reach the highest point in the sky at the lowest moment of . . ." Have students find other examples of White's craft.

◆ Literary Focus

❶ **Informal Essay** Here, White presents some entertaining information about the Empire State Building. This digression suits the relaxed, conversational style of an informal essay.

▶Critical Viewing◀

❷ **Connect** Students may say that the photograph shows the skyward expanse of Manhattan and the energetic urban details that set it apart from other cities as "the loftiest of cities." They may also notice the American flags and conclude that the city dwellers take pride in their city and their nation.

◆ *Literature and Your Life*

Ask students to share their experiences visiting cosmopolitan places. You may even have students briefly discuss the difference between visiting a place and living there. Encourage students to list the positive and negative aspects of living in a busy city like New York, Los Angeles, or Chicago.

from Here Is New York

E. B. White

New York is nothing like Paris; it is nothing like London; and it is not Spokane multiplied by sixty, or Detroit multiplied by four. It is by all odds the loftiest of cities. It even managed to reach the highest point in the sky at the lowest moment of the Depression. The Empire State Building shot 1250 feet into the air when it was madness to put out as much as six inches of new growth. (The building has a mooring mast that no dirigible[1] has ever tied to; it employs a man to flush toilets in slack times; it has been hit by an airplane in a fog, struck ❶

1. **dirigible** (dir′ə jə bəl) *n.*: Large, long airship.

◀ **Critical Viewing** What objects in this photograph confirm White's attitude about New York? Explain. **[Connect]** ❷

Analyze an Author's Comment

E.B. White once said, "The only way to dwell in cities these days, whether it be wise or foolish, is in the conviction that the city itself is a monument of one's own making, to which each shall be faithful in his own fashion."

Share this comment with students and invite them to discuss what White might mean by calling the city "a monument of one's own making." *Students might paraphrase this remark, for example, saying that according to White, the city is what each person makes of it in his or her own experience.*

Then have students answer the following questions in their journals:

1. Relate White's comment to his essay on New York. In your opinion, does White's attitude seem similar or different in these two pieces of writing?
2. Do you agree or disagree with White's remark about "the only way to dwell in cities these days"? Explain your answer.

3 ▲ Critical Viewing How does this scene compare with the New York White describes? **[Compare and Contrast]**

1 countless times by lightning, and been jumped off of by so many unhappy people that pedestrians instinctively quicken step when passing Fifth Avenue and Thirty-fourth Street.)

Manhattan has been compelled to expand skyward because of the absence of any other direction in which to grow. This, more than any other thing, is responsible for its physical majesty. It is to the nation what the white church spire is to the village—the visible symbol of aspiration and faith, the white plume saying that the way is up. The summer traveler swings in over Hell Gate Bridge and from the window of his sleeping car as it glides above the pigeon lofts and back yards of Queens looks southwest to where the morning light first strikes the steel peaks of midtown, and he
4 sees its upward thrust unmistakable: the great walls and towers rising, the smoke rising, the heat not yet rising, the hopes and ferments of so many awakening millions rising—this vigorous spear that presses heaven hard.

It is a miracle that New York works at all. The whole thing is implausible. Every time the residents brush their teeth, millions of gallons of water must be drawn from the Catskills and the hills of Westchester. When a young man in Manhattan writes a letter to his girl in Brooklyn, the love message gets blown to her through a pneumatic[2] tube—*pfft*—just like that. The subterranean system of telephone cables, power lines, steam pipes, gas mains, and sewer pipes is reason enough to abandon the island to the gods and the weevils. Every time an incision is made in the 6

◆ **Literary Focus** In what specific ways is White's tone typical of an informal essay? 5

2. **pneumatic** (no͞o mat′ik) *adj.*: Filled with compressed air.

◆ Build Vocabulary

aspiration (as′pə rā′shən) *n.*: Strong ambition
subterranean (sub′tə rā′nē ən) *adj.*: Underground

▶Critical Viewing◀

3 Compare and Contrast Students may respond that although the photograph doesn't show the neighborhoods White describes, it does present his view of a crowded, claustrophobic, congested, bustling urban scene.

◆ Grammar and Style

4 Commas in Series Guide students to notice how White uses commas in series to string together a traveler's views of and reactions to the upward thrust of the Manhattan skyline.

◆ Literary Focus

5 Informal Essay Students may say that the engaging, conversational, and light-hearted tone of this passage is typical of the tone of an informal essay.

6 Clarification For the benefit of those students who might not be aware of the fact, explain that Manhattan is a literal island, surrounded by water and reachable only by bridge or tunnel.

Customize for
Gifted/Talented Students
As students read, encourage them to notice the abundance of details, comparisons, and metaphors White uses to describe New York. Ask them to envision an elaborate cartoon or illustration they could draw, sketch, or paint to communicate the urban complexity White describes.

Cultural Connection

On the Town The 1949 movie musical *On the Town* provides a look at the 1940's New York City that E. B. White describes. Based on the exuberant Betty Comden/Adolph Green/Leonard Bernstein stage production of the same name, the film is about three sailors who have twenty-four hours to spend taking in the sights and sounds of the city. Invite students to view the film, which is available in video, and compare its portrayal of New York with that which White presents.

Have students suppose that, like the sailors in *On the Town,* they have a short time to spend in New York City. Challenge groups of students to put together a realistic itinerary of artistic and cultural events that would give them a sense of the multicultural make-up of the city. Encourage students to not only plan visits to museums and cultural societies, but to music, dance, and sporting events; poetry readings; theaters; events in parks and at community centers; and neighborhood restaurants. Guide students' research by providing New York newspapers and magazines and by sending away for brochures put out by tourist offices, automobile associations, and museums, or by calling the toll-free travel information number at 1-800-CALLNYS. Have groups present and post their reports.

pavement, the noisy surgeons expose ganglia[3] that are tangled beyond belief. By rights New York should have destroyed itself long ago, from panic or fire or rioting or failure of some vital supply line in its circulatory system or from some deep labyrinthine short circuit. Long ago the city should have experienced an insoluble traffic snarl at some impossible bottleneck. It should have perished of hunger when food lines filed for a few days. It should have been
❶ wiped out by a plague starting in its slums or carried in by ships' rats. It should have been overwhelmed by the sea that licks at it on every side. The workers in its myriad cells should have succumbed to nerves, from the fearful pall of smoke-fog that drifts over every few days from Jersey, blotting out all light at noon and leaving the high offices suspended, men groping and depressed, and the sense of world's end. It should have been touched in the head by the August heat and gone off its rocker.

Mass hysteria is a terrible force, yet New Yorkers seem always to escape it by some tiny margin: they sit in stalled subways without claustrophobia, they extricate themselves from panic situations by some lucky wisecrack, they meet confusion and congestion with patience and grit—a sort of perpetual muddling through. Every facility is inadequate—the hospitals and
❷ schools and the playgrounds are overcrowded, the express highways are feverish, the unimproved highways and bridges are bottlenecks, there is not enough air and not enough light, and there is usually either too much heat or too little. But the city makes up for its hazards and its deficiencies by supplying its citizens with massive doses of a supplementary vitamin: the sense of belonging to something unique, cosmopolitan, mighty, and unparalleled.

To an outlander a stay in New York can be and often is a series of small embarrassments and discomforts and disappointments: not understanding the waiter, not being able to distinguish between a sucker joint and a friendly saloon, riding the wrong subway, being slapped down by a bus driver for asking an innocent question, enduring sleepless nights when the street noises fill the bedroom. Tourists make for New York, particularly in summertime—they swarm all over the Statue of Liberty (where many a resident of the town has never set foot), they invade the Automat,[4] visit radio studios, St. Patrick's Cathedral, and they window shop. Mostly they have a pretty good time. But sometimes in New York you run across the disillusioned—a young couple who are obviously visitors, newlyweds perhaps, for whom the bright dream has vanished. The place has been too much for them; they sit languishing in a cheap restaurant over a speechless meal.

The oft-quoted thumbnail sketch of New York is, of course: "It's a wonderful place, but I'd hate to live there." I have an idea that people from villages and small towns, people accustomed to the convenience and the friendliness of neighborhood over-the-fence living, are unaware that life in New York follows the neighborhood pattern. The city is literally a ❸
composite of tens of thousands of tiny neighborhood units. There are, of course, the big districts and big units: Chelsea and Murray Hill and Gramercy (which are residential units), . . . Greenwich Village (a unit dedicated to the arts and other matters), and there is Radio City (a commercial development), Peter Cooper Village (a housing unit), the Medical Center (a sickness unit) and many other sections each of which has some distinguishing characteristic. But the curious thing about New York is that each large geographical unit is composed of countless small neighborhoods. Each neighborhood is virtually self-sufficient. Usually it is no more than two or three blocks long and a couple of blocks wide. Each area is a city within a city within a city. Thus, no matter where you live in New ❹
York, you will find within a block or two a grocery store, a barbershop, a newsstand and shoeshine shack, an ice-coal-and-wood cellar (where you write your order on a pad outside as you walk by), a dry cleaner, a laundry, a

3. **ganglia** (gaŋ′glē ə) *n.*: Mass of nerve cells serving as center of force, energy, activity.

4. **Automat** *n.*: Restaurant in which patrons get food from small compartments with doors opened by putting coins into slots.

◆ Build Vocabulary

claustrophobia (klôs′trə fō′bē ə) *n.*: Fear of being in a confined space

cosmopolitan (käz′mə päl′ə tən) *adj.*: Common to or representative of all or many parts of the world

◆ Reading Strategy

❶ Recognize Hyperbole In this paragraph White humorously restates the views of naysayers. Ask students to identify the examples of exaggeration he uses here to state the reasons for suggesting that New York City should have self-destructed long ago. *Students may note the suggestion of a potential short-circuit or a traffic jam that would destroy the whole city. White also names death by hunger, plague, heat and smoke.*

Thematic Focus

❷ From Every Corner of the Land Ask students what White means when he writes that the city supplies "massive doses of a supplementary vitamin." *New York City, with its excitement, glamour, and opportunities, has the ability to energize people. This "vitamin" helps people overcome the city's challenges.*

◆ Literary Focus

❸ Informal Essay Point out that in this personal commentary, White presents his views on New York City: it is an aggregate of neighborhoods. Discuss that here he means both to enlighten and entertain, and to correct some negative notions about life in the city.

❹ Enrichment New Yorkers have always relied on their neighborhoods to provide the services they need when they need them. While this attitude has changed little since 1948, there have been many changes in the kinds of services available. Have students replace the list of stores and activities White presents with more modern examples. *Students may suggest video stores, coffee bars, multiplex movie theaters, a variety of take-out ethnic restaurants, ATMs, health food stores, and chain stores of many kinds.*

Speaking, Listening, and Viewing Mini-Lesson

Audition

This mini-lesson supports the Speaking, Listening, and Viewing activity in the Idea Bank (p. 827).

Introduce the Concept Tell students that this activity consists of an audition for the role of narrator in either "The Night the Ghost Got In" or "Here is New York." Inform them that their performance will be evaluated according to the extent to which they capture the tone and personality of the writer's work. Emphasize the importance of selecting a representative portion of the essay to read.

Develop Background Have students list words that characterize the style of each of these informal essays. Students should refer to this list when planning the tone of their performance. They can also use gestures to convey that tone.

Apply the Information Students should select an excerpt, practice reading it aloud, and then stage their auditions. To increase the speaking and listening opportunities, you might have students audition within groups. When each group selects a winner for each essay, those students can audition for the whole class. Classmates can vote for the student whose performance best captures the tone of each writer.

Assess the Outcome Judge students' performances by how well they capture the writer's personality and his efforts at amusing the audience.

delicatessen (beer and sandwiches delivered at any hour to your door), a flower shop, an undertaker's parlor, a movie house, a radio-repair shop, a stationer, a haberdasher,[5] a tailor, a drugstore, a garage, a tearoom, a saloon, a hardware store, a liquor store, a shoe-repair shop. Every block or two, in most residential sections of New York, is a little main street. A man starts for work in the morning and before he has gone two hundred yards he has com-
4 pleted half a dozen missions: bought a paper, left a pair of shoes to be soled, picked up a pack of cigarettes, . . . written a message to the unseen forces of the wood cellar, and notified the dry cleaner that a pair of trousers awaits call. Homeward-bound eight hours later, he buys a bunch of pussy willows, a Mazda bulb, a drink, a shine—all between the corner where he steps off the bus and his apartment. So complete is each neighborhood, and so strong the sense of neighborhood, that many a New Yorker spends a lifetime within the confines of an area smaller than a country village. Let him walk two blocks from his corner and he is in a strange land and will feel uneasy till he gets back.

Storekeepers are particularly conscious of neighborhood boundary lines. A woman friend of mine moved recently from one apartment to another, a distance of three blocks. When she turned up, the day after the move, at the same grocer's that she had patronized for years, the proprietor was in ecstasy—almost in tears— at seeing her. "I was afraid," he said, "now that you've moved away I wouldn't be seeing you anymore." To him, *away* was three blocks, or about 750 feet. 5

> ◆ **Reading Strategy** Is this description an example of hyperbole? Why, or why not?

I am, at the moment of writing this, living not as a neighborhood man in New York but as a transient, or vagrant, in from the country for a few days. Summertime is a good time to reexamine New York and to receive again the gift of privacy, the jewel of loneliness. In summer the city contains (except for tourists) only die- 6 hards and authentic characters. No casual, spotty dwellers are around, only the real article. And the town has a somewhat relaxed air, and one can lie in a loincloth, gasping and remembering things.

5. **haberdasher** *n.*: Person whose work is selling men's clothing, such as hats, shirts, neckties, and gloves.

Guide for Responding

◆ Literature and Your Life

Reader's Response Would you like to visit the New York City of E. B. White's description? Why or why not?

Thematic Response What are some memorable characteristics of New York City as E. B. White describes it?

Thumbnail Sketch E. B. White says a thumbnail sketch of New York is "It's a wonderful place, but I'd hate to live there." Write a "thumbnail sketch" of your town or city.

☑ Check Your Comprehension

1. List three ways in which New Yorkers escape mass hysteria, according to the essay.
2. According to E. B. White, what is New York City like in summertime?

◆ Critical Thinking

INTERPRET

1. How do New York City's neighborhoods compare to those of small towns? **[Compare and Contrast]**
2. What qualities about New York City enable it to function against all odds? **[Draw Conclusions]**
3. What general conclusion does White's essay reach about the city? **[Summarize]**

EVALUATE

4. E. B. White takes a bemused tone in this essay. Do you think he uses that tone effectively? Explain. **[Assess]**

EXTEND

5. How might someone working in the tourist industry in New York City respond to E. B. White's representation of the city? **[Career Link]**

Beyond the Selection

FURTHER READING

Other Works by E. B. White

The Wild Flag

The Elements of Style

"Walden," from *One Man's Meat*

We suggest that you preview these works before recommending them to students.

INTERNET

You and your students may find additional information about the work of E. B. White on the Internet. We suggest the following site. Please be aware, however, that sites may have changed since this information was published.

To visit the E. B. White home page, go to **http://www.tiac.net/users/winlib/ebwhite.htm**

We *strongly recommend* that you preview sites before you send students to them.

◆ Reading Strategy

5 Recognize Hyperbole Some students may argue that this is an example of hyperbole. Others may defend the New York notion that three blocks can seem like a great distance, particularly if the move means living in a new neighborhood.

◆ Critical Thinking

6 Compare and Contrast Guide students to think about how White's views on New York compare with Carl Sandburg's views on Chicago, another giant of a city. *Both men applaud the energy, defiance, resilience, and endurance of a city.*

Reinforce and Extend

Answers

◆ Literature and Your Life

Reader's Response Some students may suggest that White makes New York sound enticing. Others may disagree.

Thematic Response The city is spirited, energetic, and diversified.

☑ Check Your Comprehension

1. New Yorkers escape mass hysteria through patience, luck, and grit.
2. The city is less crowded in summer because only tourists and "diehards and authentic characters" spend time there.

◆ Critical Thinking

1. Neighborhoods are similar to small towns because they are self-sufficient. However, neighborhoods within the city are more compressed and contain the full spectrum of New York in close range.
2. Possible response: The energy of people of all backgrounds and interests keeps the city moving.
3. New York is a city like no other.
4. Possible response: Since the writing conveys a feeling of disbelief, readers may connect with the narrator. It is therefore effective.
5. A travel agent may put an even more positive spin on his ideas.

Answers

◆ Literary Focus

1. Possible response: The last clause of the first sentence, "I am sorry I didn't just let it keep on walking." reflects an unusual and casual grammatical structure, and gives the reader a sense of the writer's personality.
2. White is in love with the energy of New York, although the last paragraph suggests that everyone needs a rest from it for reflection.

◆ Reading Strategy

1. Possible responses: Thurber's description of the action of the policemen's lights (p. 819) is funny for its language and the long and winding path of the light. White's description of pedestrians walking faster when they pass the Empire State Building is amusing because it is a broad generalization.
2. Making Grandfather appear more quirky than the others creates a comic effect by contrast.
3. Hyperbole emphasizes the fact that New York is a city of extremes.

◆ Build Vocabulary

Using the Word Root *-terr-*

1. b 2. c 3. a

Using the Word Bank: Context

1. No; she has an ambition.
2. Yes; they are underground.
3. Yes; cursing is disrespectful.
4. No; he would be afraid of the enclosed space of the cockpit.
5. Yes; the city is a mix of many cultures.
6. Yes; the wince would be automatic.

◆ Grammar and Style

1. The subterranean system of telephone cables, power lines, steam pipes, gas mains, and sewer pipes is the reason to . . .
2. Instantly the steps began again, circled the dining-room table like a man running, and started up the stairs toward us . . .
3. Their lights . . . crisscrossed nervously in the dining-room, stabbed into hallways, shot up the front stairs, and finally up the back.

Grammar Reinforcement

See the page on Commas, p. 86, in the *Writer's Solution Grammar Practice Book.*

Guide for Responding (continued)

◆ Literary Focus

INFORMAL ESSAY

As **informal essays**, both "The Night the Ghost Got In" and "Here Is New York" aim to entertain. They use a conversational style, relaxed language, and narrowly defined subjects. Notice in each example how the writer's personality and opinion of the world emerge.

> **Thurber**: I decided to be frank with him. "We had ghosts," I said. He gazed at me a long time as if I were a slot machine into which he had, without results, dropped a nickel.
>
> **White**: Summertime is a good time to reexamine New York and to receive again the gift of privacy, the jewel of loneliness.

1. Cite an especially strong example of language that reflects the conversational style of Thurber's essay. Explain your choice.
2. What does "Here Is New York" suggest about White's attitude toward New York and the modern world it symbolizes? Support your answer.

◆ Reading Strategy

RECOGNIZE HYPERBOLE

White and Thurber use **hyperbole**—bold overstatements and extreme exaggerations—to create humor or make a point in their essays. Note this example from "Here Is New York." It tells you twice what you need to know to envision the Empire State Building—and makes you smile in the process:

> The building has a mooring mast no dirigible has ever tied to; it employs a man to flush toilets in slack times; it has been hit by an airplane in a fog, struck countless times by lightning, and been jumped off of by so many unhappy people that pedestrians instinctively quicken step when passing Fifth Avenue and Thirty-fourth Street.

1. Cite an example of hyperbole from each essay and explain why you find each amusing.
2. For what purpose do you think Thurber exaggerates the behavior of his grandfather in the essay?
3. Why is White's use of hyperbole appropriate for his subject?

◆ Build Vocabulary

USING THE LATIN ROOT *-terr-*

Using the meaning of *-terr-* ("earth" or "land") and context clues, choose the best word for each sentence.

a. terrain **b.** extraterrestrial **c.** terrarium

1. The __?__ was our first visitor from another planet.
2. Put some earth in a glass jar and plant some seeds to make a __?__.
3. Westward pioneers settled new __?__ .

USING THE WORD BANK: Context

Answer *yes* or *no* to each question. Then, explain your response.

1. If Sheila has an *aspiration* to sail around the world, does she have a vague notion?
2. Must you dig a hole to reach *subterranean* pipes?
3. Could you get in trouble for *blaspheming* in class?
4. Would *claustrophobia* help an airplane pilot?
5. Would a *cosmopolitan* person enjoy Paris?
6. If you heard a very loud bang, would you *intuitively* wince?

◆ Grammar and Style

COMMAS IN SERIES

Thurber and White frequently use commas in series to string together several humorous details in a single sentence.

Commas in series are placed between three or more parallel items to link them. A conjunction usually precedes the final item.

Practice Rewrite these sentences, inserting commas in their appropriate places.

1. The subterranean system of telephone cables power lines steam pipe gas mains and sewer pipes is the reason to . . .
2. Instantly the steps began again circled the dining-room table like a man running and started up the stairs toward us . . .
3. Their lights . . . crisscrossed nervously in the dining-room stabbed into hallways shot up the front stairs and finally up the back.

Reteach

If some students have trouble recognizing hyperbole, they may benefit from the following exercise. Pass out photocopies of the first paragraph of "Here Is New York." Suggest that students reread the passage carefully and use a marker to highlight each part of a sentence that states an exaggeration. For example, in the last sentence, have students highlight "been jumped off of by so many unhappy people that pedestrians instinctively quicken step when passing Fifth Avenue and Thirty-fourth Street." Point out the difference between this comment and the statement that New York has nothing in common with Paris or London, which is a simple exaggeration. The last sentence in the paragraph contains hyperbole.

Students may benefit from writing some hyperbole of their own. Suggest that they make a list of statements that are deliberate exaggerations. Then tell them to try turning these exaggerations into hyperbole by making them outrageous. If students need more examples to get them started, you might offer the sample exaggeration, "He was as wide as a barn door" turned into the sample hyperbole, "He was as wide as the barn."

Build Your Portfolio

Idea Bank

Writing

1. **Humorous Tourist Guide** Using "Here Is New York" as a model, write a humorous guide to New York. Give your guide a witty title.

2. **Police Report** Suppose you're one of the police officers called to Thurber's home. Write a report describing the scene and the actions of each family member. To contrast Thurber's account, use a completely objective tone.

3. **Critical Response** E. B. White once said, "The most widely appreciated humorists are those who create characters and tell tales . . ." Write an essay responding to this statement. Cite passages from one or both essays for support.

Speaking, Listening, and Viewing

4. **Audition** Try out for a one-actor show about either E. B. White or James Thurber. Audition for the starring (and only) role by reading aloud excerpts from the writer's essay. Try to capture its tone in your reading. **[Performing Arts Link]**

5. **Essay Critique** With a partner, role-play Thurber and White discussing their essays in the offices of *The New Yorker*. Constructively criticize each other's essays. **[Career Link]**

Researching and Representing

6. **Historical Re-creation** Research "The Roundtable," a group of very funny people associated with *The New Yorker* who gathered together on a regular basis. With classmates, take roles and stage a mock Roundtable. **[Performing Arts Link]**

7. **Set Design** Draw a graph or plan for a dramatic enactment of either essay. In your proposed set design, show movement with arrows or other graphic devices. **[Art Link]**

Online Activity www.phlit.phschool.com

Guided Writing Lesson

Toast at a Party

The essays of E. B. White and James Thurber tell humorous stories but also have subtle messages. Use the tone of their essays as a model to write a toast for a party—you might even toast White or Thurber! Grab listeners' attention quickly to engage their interest. Then use anecdotes or humor to make a point while you have "the floor."

Writing Skills Focus: Grabbing Listeners' Attention

When speaking to an audience, it's important to **grab listeners' attention**. Opening with a funny anecdote or outrageous statement can entice your audience to keep listening. See how skillfully Thurber hooks his audience and makes them eager to know what is to come:

Model From the Story

The ghost that got into our house . . . raised such a hullabaloo of misunderstanding that I am sorry I didn't just let it keep on walking. . . . Its advent caused my mother to throw a shoe through a window . . . and ended up with my grandfather shooting a patrolman.

Prewriting What are the stand-out characteristics of the person you will honor with a toast? Sort your responses by category, such as *physical appearance, world view*, or *special abilities*. Then list the person's accomplishments and the noteworthy events in his or her life.

Drafting Begin with a funny anecdote or startling comment. Review your catalogued responses to find something that will grab listeners' attention. In the body of your toast, convey the general message you want your listeners to understand.

Revising Read your toast to a friend. Notice how it flows and invite comment about its interest level. Add transitions where appropriate to make it flow more smoothly.

Idea Bank

Customizing for
Performance Levels
Following are suggestions for matching Idea Bank topics with your students' performance levels:
Less Advanced Students: 1, 7
Average Students: 2, 4, 6
More Advanced Students: 3, 5

Customizing for
Learning Modalities
Following are suggestions for matching Idea Bank topics with your students' learning modalities:
Bodily/Kinesthetic: 4
Interpersonal: 4, 5
Verbal/Linguistic: 6
Logical/Mathematical: 7
Visual/Spatial: 7

Guided Writing Lesson

Writing and Language Transparencies Use the Cubing Organizer in the Writing and Language Transparencies to help students in the prewriting stage (pp. 71–73).

For more prewriting, elaboration, and revision strategies, see *Prentice Hall Writing and Grammar.*

Writing Lab CD-ROM
Have students complete the tutorial on Description. Follow these steps:

1. Have students use the Checklist for narrowing a topic in the Narrowing Your Topic section.
2. Students can use the Character Traits Word Bin in the Gathering Details section to help them select the right adjectives to describe the subject of their toast.
3. After students have drafted on the computer, have them use the Revision Checker for vague or overused adjectives to aid revision.

✓ ASSESSMENT OPTIONS

Formal Assessment, Selection Test, pp. 247–249, and Assessment Resources Software. The selection test is designed so that it can be easily customized to the performance levels of your students.

Alternative Assessment, p. 54, includes options for less advanced students, more advanced students, visual/spatial learners and verbal/linguistic learners.

PORTFOLIO ASSESSMENT
Use the following rubrics in the ***Alternative Assessment*** booklet to assess student writing:
Humorous Tourist Guide: Description Rubric, p. 112
Police Report: Technical Description/Explanation Rubric, p. 130
Critical Response: Response to Literature Rubric, p. 125
Guided Writing Lesson: Expression Rubric, p. 109

LESSON OBJECTIVES

1. **To develop vocabulary and word identification skills**
   - Greek Word Roots: *-graph-*
   - Using the Word Bank: Synonyms
2. **To use a variety of reading strategies to comprehend autobiography**
   - Reading Strategy: Analyze How a Writer Achieves Purpose
3. **To increase knowledge of other cultures and to connect common elements across cultures**
   - Connecting Themes Across Cultures (ATE)
4. **To express and support responses to the text**
   - Critical Thinking
   - Idea Bank: Eulogy
   - Idea Bank: Opinion Essay
5. **To analyze literary elements**
   - Literary Focus: Purpose in Autobiography
6. **To read in order to research self-selected and assigned topics**
   - Idea Bank: Reading List
   - Idea Bank: Folk-Tale Collection
7. **To plan, prepare, organize, and present literary interpretations**
   - Idea Bank: Campaign Speech
   - Idea Bank: Interview
8. **To use recursive writing processes to write about a moment of inspiration**
   - Guided Writing Lesson
9. **To increase knowledge of the rules of grammar and usage**
   - Grammar and Style: Parallelism in Coordinate Elements

Test Preparation

Reading Comprehension: Anticipate Missing Words
(ATE, p. 829)
The teaching tips and sample test item in this workshop support the instruction and practice in the unit workshop:

Reading Comprehension: Sentence-Completion Questions
(ATE, p. 863)

Guide for Interpreting

Zora Neale Hurston
(1891–1960)

When Zora Neale Hurston died in January 1960, she was buried in an unmarked grave in a segregated cemetery in Fort Pierce, Florida. There she lay, forgotten until 1973, when writer Alice Walker located and marked Hurston's grave, recording the experience in a 1975 *Ms.* magazine article. Walker's efforts restored Hurston to her rightful place in American literature, as "the dominant black woman writer" of her time and a pioneering force in the celebration of African American culture.

Hurston was the first writer of her day to recognize that cultural heritage was valuable in its own right.

Her unshakable self-confidence and strong sense of personal and racial worth were fostered by a childhood in Eatonville, Florida, America's first fully incorporated African American township. One of eight children, Hurston was, by her own account, a spirited, curious child who "always wanted to go." Her mother explained this urge to wander by claiming that travel dust had been sprinkled at the door the day Zora was born.

Hurston's childhood abruptly ended, however, when her mother died. Hurston went to live with a series of friends and relatives, attending school whenever she could. By age fourteen, she was supporting herself.

Two Careers Hurston developed an interest in writing while studying at Howard University. In 1925, she moved to New York City. She soon published a story and a play, firmly establishing herself as one of the bright new talents of the Harlem Renaissance. She began attending Barnard College, where her work came to the attention of prominent anthropologist Franz Boas, who convinced Hurston to begin graduate studies in anthropology at Columbia University. With an academic grant, she began a second career as a folklorist, returning to the South to collect African American folk tales and to research customs, especially those of people from her native Florida. She published two folklore collections, *Mules and Men* (1935) and *Tell My Horse* (1938).

The Road to Obscurity Hurston achieved strong critical and popular success during the 1930's and 1940's, publishing the novels *Jonah's Gourd Vine* (1934), *Their Eyes Were Watching God* (1937), and *Moses, Man of the Mountain* (1939), along with numerous short stories, plays, and her prize-winning autobiography, *Dust Tracks on a Road* (1942). Personal scandal, however, led Hurston's career into obscurity. The 1970's saw a resurgence of interest in Hurston's work that continues to gain momentum.

◆ Background for Understanding

CULTURE: HURSTON AND THE FOLKLORE TRADITION

Folklore refers to traditional stories passed down from generation to generation by word of mouth within a particular culture or region. Most cultures, from the ancient Greeks and Romans to peoples from Eastern Europe and Latin America, have their own folk traditions. One of the world's richest and most vibrant collections of folklore is that of African Americans. The roots of African American folklore stretch back to the tales, myths, and songs that had been passed down among generations of Africans long before the first Africans were brought to America and forced into slavery. For enslaved Africans and their ancestors, folklore has served as an important means of preserving their cultural heritage, and the folk tradition has continued to grow and expand. Thanks to Zora Neale Hurston and others, this rich folk traditional is now permanently preserved in writing.

Prentice Hall Literature Program Resources

REINFORCE / RETEACH / EXTEND

Selection Support Pages
Build Vocabulary: Word Roots: *-graph-*, p. 251
Grammar and Style: Parallelism, p. 252
Reading Strategy: Analyze How a Writer Achieves Purpose, p. 253
Literary Focus: Purpose in Autobiography, p. 254

Strategies for Diverse Student Needs, Analyze Characters, p. 55

Beyond Literature
Community Connection: Community and Personal Identity, p. 55

Formal Assessment Selection Test, pp. 250–252; Assessment Resources Software

Alternative Assessment, p. 55

Writing and Language Transparencies
Writing Process Model 3: Personal Narrative (pp. 13–16) and Cause-and-Effect Transparency (p. 91)

Resource Pro CD-ROM

Listening to Literature Audiocassettes

from Dust Tracks on a Road

◆ Literature and Your Life

CONNECT YOUR EXPERIENCE

Even as a child, Zora Neale Hurston was passionate about literature. What excites your interest? As you read, think about how an interest can shape your character and change your life.

Journal Writing Jot down some of your own interests—sports, hobbies, movies, travel—and trace their origins.

THEMATIC FOCUS: FROM EVERY CORNER OF THE LAND

In this excerpt from the life of an African American girl growing up in a small Florida town, character and community play important roles. What does the story reveal about the girl and her town?

◆ Literary Focus

PURPOSE IN AUTOBIOGRAPHY

All writers draw on their own experiences in their work. Autobiography, however, makes the author's life its central concern. An **autobiography** is an account of a person's life written by that person, generally in the first person. In an autobiography, the writer presents a continuous narrative of signficant events from his or her perspective. The reader sees events through the writer's eyes and comes to understand the writer's point of view.

An author's **purpose in writing an autobiography** varies. Some writers strive to justify their beliefs or sort out conflicts. Others wish to present their lives as an example for readers to follow. In her autobiography, Zora Neale Hurston strives to show that while she and other African Americans of her day suffered from racial injustice, they lived rich lives filled with laughter and had promising hopes and dreams for the future.

◆ Grammar and Style

PARALLELISM IN COORDINATE ELEMENTS

By using coordinating conjunctions—such as *and, but, or,* and *nor*—Zora Neale Hurston packs a lot of information into her sentences and creates a rhythm in her writing. Notice that she is careful to maintain **parallelism in coordinate structures** by using the same form of each grammatically equivalent element linked by coordinating conjunctions within a sentence. Look at this example:

They also *came* and *went, came* and *went.*

◆ Reading Strategy

ANALYZE HOW A WRITER ACHIEVES PURPOSE

Hurston's purpose—to share her personal experience and show the vitality of the African American community of her childhood—determines her choice of words, details, characters, and events. By linking her choices to her goals, you can analyze how she achieves her purpose. For example:

Writer's Choice

Hurston describes herself as befriending white passersby despite her family's disapproval.

Analysis

This scene shows her self-assurance and ability to feel comfortable with people of every kind. It helps the reader sense her spunk and see her outlook on life.

◆ Build Vocabulary

GREEK ROOTS: *-graph-*

You have known the word *geography* since grade school, but do you know how the Greek root *-graph-*, meaning "write," contributes to its definition? In fact, *geography* means "the study of—or writing about—the Earth."

WORD BANK

Before you read, preview this list of words from *Dust Tracks on a Road.*

foreknowledge
brazenness
caper
exalted
geography
avarice

Interest Grabber Ask students to think about the books that they most enjoyed when they were in the fifth or sixth grade. Have them bring one such book—or the titles of several—to class. Ask volunteers to share their selections and explain how their reading influenced them. Tell students that they are about to read an autobiographical sketch about a child whose love of reading was to shape her entire adult life.

Connecting Themes Across Cultures

Ask students to name autobiographical accounts they have read or heard of, by people whose cultural community has played important roles in determining who they are or were. For example, they might mention Jill Kerr Conway's *The Road From Coorain* (about the author's experience of growing up in a rural part of Australia); or Maya Angelou's *I Know Why the Caged Bird Sings.*

Customize for
Less Proficient Readers

Tell students that writers of autobiographies believe that their life is interesting or important and can in some way serve as an example to others. When they read the excerpt, guide students to think about why Hurston has chosen to include this episode from her childhood, and what the episode reveals about her character.

Customize for
AP Students

All the adults the young Hurston mentions in this excerpt have some motive for wanting her to behave in a particular way. For instance, Mr. Calhoun wants to show off his prized pupil. As they read, students should identify and analyze the reasons behind what each adult does or says.

Customize for
English Language Learners

Hurston uses several words, idiomatic phrases, and figures of speech that might be unfamiliar to students. Have students work in pairs to try to figure out the meanings using context clues or a dictionary.

Test Preparation Workshop

Reading Comprehension:
Anticipate Missing Words Many standardized tests ask students to correctly answer sentence-completion questions. Use the following example to show students how to use context and their own knowledge to guess a word that would complete the following passage.

For African Americans, folklore and oral history served as an important means of preserving their cultural heritage. Thanks to anthropologists and writers such as Zora Neale Hurston, this folk tradition is now ____ preserved in writing.

A permanently
B temporarily
C emphatically
D tentatively

After reading the passage, students may guess that the word *always* completes the sentence. Answer *A, permanently,* is closest in meaning to that guess.

Develop Understanding

One-Minute Insight Hurston provides a glimpse of life in a small African American community in Florida as well as a vivid portrait of herself as a child. Self-assured, spunky, and filled with curiosity, she defied her parents and grandmother, often stopping white travelers and asking to accompany them for a short distance. Hurston devotes much of the excerpt to her first real interaction with white people and the role this played in developing her literary tastes and direction in life. During a school visit by two white women from Minnesota, Zora is singled out for her impressive reading skills. The ladies treat her to gifts of money, clothing and—most importantly—books. She develops a deep love for a broad range of literature, particularly enjoying biblical and mythological tales of adventurous heroes.

◆ Reading Strategy

Analyze How a Writer Achieves Purpose Guide students to understand that in writing her autobiography, Hurston does not merely document her past. She chooses memorable or significant events from her life and interprets them to clarify the experiences and to present insights she gained from them. Discuss the idea that although facts in an autobiography may be somewhat distorted, the significance of the retelling is in what readers make of it.

◆ Background for Understanding

Culture Zora Neale Hurston was born in a small hamlet near Tuskegee, Alabama. When she was a child, her family resettled in Eatonville, Florida, the first incorporated African American community in America. Her father served three terms as mayor there. Her Eatonville experience was an empowering one. There, Hurston did not experience the sting of racism. Instead, pride in African culture was openly shared and celebrated. This environment led the future folklorist to develop a deep appreciation of the riches to be found in folklore and literature.

from Dust Tracks on a Road

Zora Neale Hurston

I used to take a seat on top of the gatepost and watch the world go by. One way to Orlando[1] ran past my house, so the carriages and cars would pass before me. The movement made me glad to see it. Often the white travelers would hail me, but more often I hailed
1 them, and asked, "Don't you want me to go a piece of the way with you?"

They always did. I know now that I must have caused a great deal of amusement among them, but my self-assurance must have carried the point, for I was always invited to come along. I'd ride up the road for perhaps a half-mile, then walk back. I did not do this with the permission of my parents, nor with their foreknowledge. When they found out about it later, I usually got a whipping. My grandmother worried about my forward ways a great deal. She had known slavery and to her my brazenness was unthinkable.

"Git down offa dat gate-post! You li'l sow, you! Git down! Setting up dere looking dem white folks right in de face! They's gowine[2] to lynch you, yet. And don't stand in dat doorway gazing out at 'em neither. Youse too brazen to live long."[3]

Nevertheless, I kept right on gazing at them, and "going a piece of the way" whenever I could make it. The village seemed dull to me most of the time. If the village was singing a chorus, I must have missed the tune.

Perhaps a year before the old man[4] died, I came to know two other white people for myself. They were women.

It came about this way. The whites who came down from the North were often brought by their friends to visit the village school. A Negro school was something strange to them, and while they were always sympathetic and kind, curiosity must have been present, also. They came and went, came and went. Always, the room was hurriedly put in order, and we were threatened with a prompt and bloody death if 2
we cut one caper while the visitors were present. We always sang a spiritual, led by Mr. Calhoun himself. Mrs. Calhoun always stood in the back, with a palmetto switch[5] in her hand as a squelcher. We were all little angels for the duration, because we'd better be. She would cut her eyes and give us a glare that meant trouble, then turn her face towards the visitors and beam as much as to say it was a great privilege and pleasure to teach lovely children like us. They couldn't see that palmetto hickory

---

1. **Orlando** (ôr lan´ dō): City in central Florida, about five miles from Eatonville, Hurston's hometown.
2. **gowine:** "Going."
3. **"Git down . . . live long":** Hurston's grandmother's fears reflect the belief of many people at the time that it was inappropriate for African Americans to be assertive toward whites.
4. **the old man:** White farmer who had developed a friendship with Hurston.
5. **palmetto** (pal met´ ō) **switch:** Whip made from the fan-shaped leaves of the palmetto, a type of palm tree.

Block Scheduling Strategies

Consider these suggestions to take advantage of extended class time:

- After reading Hurston's biography, have students complete the journal activity in Literature and Your Life (p. 829).
- Introduce the Reading Strategy and Literary Focus. You may wish to follow up with the corresponding pages in ***Selection Support.***
- To develop context and background for the Campaign Speech activity in the Idea Bank (p. 837), use the Speaking and Listening Mini-Lesson on page 834 of the teachers edition. Allow time for students to rehearse their speeches in small groups before presenting their finished work to the entire class.
- Assign the Guided Writing Lesson (p. 837) or the Autobiographical Episode from the Idea Bank. Before students begin, discuss the technique of *showing* rather than *telling* how characters feel, look, and act.

The Mather School, Jonathan Green

▲ **Critical Viewing** Do you think the students in this painting enjoy going to school? On what elements of the painting do you base your decision? **[Evaluate]** ❸

in her hand behind all those benches, but we knew where our angelic behavior was coming from.

❹ Usually, the visitors gave warning a day ahead and we would be cautioned to put on shoes, comb our heads, and see to ears and fingernails. There was a close inspection of every one of us before we marched in that morning. Knotty heads, dirty ears and fingernails got hauled out of line, strapped and sent home to lick the calf over again.

This particular afternoon, the two young ladies just popped in. Mr. Calhoun was flustered,

◆ Build Vocabulary

foreknowledge (fôr′ näl′ ij) *n.*: Awareness of something before it happens or exists

brazenness (brā′ zən nis) *n.*: Shamelessness; boldness; impudence

caper (kā′ pər) *n.*: Prank

Customize for
Less Proficient Readers and ESL Students

To help these students get more from their reading, use the page on analyzing characters in ***Strategies for Diverse Student Needs*** (p. 55).

◆ Reading Strategy

❶ **Analyze How a Writer Achieves Purpose** Ask students to explain why Hurston may have recounted the fact she phrased her question in this way. *Students should note that she wants to show that she was a clever and assertive girl who knew how to get what she wanted—it's much harder to say no to a question phrased in such a way.*

◆ Grammar and Style

❷ **Parallelism in Coordinate Elements** Point out this example of how Hurston maintains the parallelism of her grammatical structure by using the past tense (*was hurriedly put in order . . . were threatened*) on both sides of the coordinating conjunction, *and*.

▶Critical Viewing◀

❸ **Evaluate** Students may note the bright colors of the children's dress. Some might suggest that these children from a rural area might enjoy leaving their farm chores, putting on their good clothes, grabbing their books, and joining their friends at school.

◆ *Literature and Your Life*

❹ Invite students to imagine that an important community leader will be visiting your classroom as an observer. Ask them to think about how they might act differently than usual. What might they do, if anything, to prepare for the visit? What would they want to demonstrate for the visitor? Have them explain what they would want that person to think of them when the visit was over.

Humanities: Art

The Mather School, 1988, by Jonathan Green.

Jonathan Green is a contemporary African American artist whose bold paintings with their musical rhythms celebrate the rich heritage of his people. In this painting, he uses repetition of powerful colors and shapes to create a musical rhythm. Green's distinctive style was heavily influenced by the work of two great African American painters, Romare Bearden and Jacob Lawrence.

Use these questions for discussion:

1. At first glance, what part of the picture gets your attention? *Students may cite the boldness of the colors and shapes of the large figures in the foreground.*
2. What details of this painting make it an appropriate illustration for this excerpt from Hurston's autobiography? *Students should note the fact that, as in Hurston's school, all of the students pictured are African American. Like students expecting a visitor to Mr. Calhoun's classroom, they are neatly dressed and wearing bright, tropical colors that seem to echo the Florida landscape in which Hurston's excerpt is set.*

Customize for
Less Proficient Readers

❶ Help students recognize that this paragraph is an example of how an autobiographer reveals something about herself by describing what she was like as a child. Here readers learn that Hurston was always a voracious reader who devoured whatever book she had, even a school textbook.

◆ Critical Thinking

❷ **Speculate** Ask students to suggest why the writer was so transfixed by the visitors' hands. *Students should realize that Hurston had never closely observed the hands of a white woman, which were unlike those hands she had observed all her life.*

◆ Build Vocabulary

❸ **Word Roots: *-graph-*** Inform students of the etymology of the word *paragraph,* which comes from the Greek term *paragraphos,* which combines *graph,* meaning "write," with *para,* meaning "beside." The word originally meant a sign or symbol that separated writing into parts or sections.

❹ **Clarification** Summarize for students what has happened here: Pluto, the god who rules over the lower world, has captured Persephone and has taken her to his underground realm, as Jupiter looks on.

◆ Reading Strategy

❺ **Analyze How a Writer Achieves Purpose** This passage reveals the fact that Zora was not always well loved by her classmates, who were pleased at the prospect of seeing her punished. The reader realizes that Zora's intelligence and self-confidence sometimes alienated her from her classmates. From a young age, she was already "different."

◆ Critical Thinking

❻ **Analyze** Ask students to explain why the writer finds it necessary to lie to the visitors. *Zora was intelligent and realized that it was in her own best interest—both to avoid a whipping from her teacher and to please the ladies—to bend the truth.*

but he put on the best show he could. He dismissed the class that he was teaching up at the front of the room, then called the fifth grade in reading. That was my class.

So we took our readers and went up front. We stood up in the usual line, and opened to the lesson. It was the story of Pluto and Persephone. It was new and hard to the class in general, and Mr. Calhoun was very uncomfortable as the readers stumbled along, spelling out words with their lips, and in mumbling undertones before they exposed them experimentally to the teacher's ears.

❶ Then it came to me. I was fifth or sixth down the line. The story was not new to me, because I had read my reader through from lid to lid, the first week that Papa had bought it for me.

That is how it was that my eyes were not in the book, working out the paragraph which I knew would be mine by counting the children ahead of me. I was observing our visitors, who held a book between them, following the lesson. They had shiny hair, mostly brownish. One had a looping gold chain around her neck. The other one was dressed all over in black and ❷ white with a pretty finger ring on her left hand. But the thing that held my eyes were their fingers. They were long and thin, and very white, except up near the tips. There they were baby pink. I had never seen such hands. It was a fascinating discovery for me. I wondered how they felt. I would have given those hands more attention, but the child before me was almost through. My turn next, so I got on my mark, bringing my eyes back to the book and made sure of my place. Some of the stories I had reread several times, and this Greco-Roman ❸ myth was one of my favorites. I was exalted by it, and that is the way I read my paragraph.

❹ "Yes, Jupiter had seen her (Persephone). He had seen the maiden picking flowers in the field. He had seen the chariot of the dark monarch pause by the maiden's side. He had seen him when he seized Persephone. He had seen the black horses leap down Mount Aetna's fiery throat. Persephone was now in Pluto's dark realm and he had made her his wife."

The two women looked at each other and then back to me. Mr. Calhoun broke out with a proud smile beneath his bristly moustache, and instead of the next child taking up where I had ended, he nodded to me to go on. So I read the story to the end, where flying Mercury, the messenger of the Gods, brought Persephone back to the sunlit earth and restored her to the arms of Dame Ceres, her mother, that the world might have springtime and summer flowers, autumn and harvest. But because she had bitten the pomegranate[6] while in Pluto's kingdom, she must return to him for three months of each year, and be his queen. Then the world had winter, until she returned to earth.

The class was dismissed, and the visitors smiled us away and went into a low-voiced conversation with Mr. Calhoun for a few minutes. They glanced my way once or twice and I began to worry. Not only was I barefooted, but my feet and legs were dusty. My hair was more uncombed than usual, and my nails were not shiny clean. Oh, I'm going to catch it now. Those ladies saw me, too. Mr. Calhoun is promising to 'tend to me. So I thought.

Then Mr. Calhoun called me. I went up thinking how awful it was to get a whipping before company. Furthermore, I heard a snicker run over the room. Hennie Clark and Stell Brazzle did it out loud, so I would be sure to hear them. The smart-aleck was going to get it. I slipped one hand behind me and switched my dress tail at them, indicating scorn.

> **◆ Reading Strategy**
> Analyze why Hurston includes this incident. How does it help you to step into young Zora's experience? ❺

"Come here, Zora Neale," Mr. Calhoun cooed as I reached the desk. He put his hand on my shoulder and gave me little pats. The ladies smiled and held out those flower-looking fingers towards me. I seized the opportunity for a good look.

"Shake hands with the ladies, Zora Neale," Mr. Calhoun prompted and they took my hand one after the other and smiled. They asked if I loved school, and I lied that I did. There was *some* truth in it, because I liked geography and ❻ reading, and I liked to play at recess time. Whoever it was invented writing and arithmetic got no thanks from me. Neither did I like the arrangement where the teacher could sit up there with a palmetto stem and lick me

6. **pomegranate** (päm′ gran′ it) *n.*: Round, red-skinned fruit with many seeds.

Cultural Connection

Keeping Cultures Alive Through Folklore
In 1927, Zora Neale Hurston left New York City and returned to Eatonville to collect folktales, spirituals, sermons, work songs, blues, and children's games. At a time of the Great Migration to northern cities, Hurston went south, against the tide; she spent the next six years documenting the forms of African American cultural expression that she believed had made the greatest contribution to American culture. She worked in lumber camps to learn work songs and joined in initiation rituals in order to research voodoo curses in New Orleans.

Thanks to folklorists like Hurston, the rich contributions of many cultures have been preserved. From recording Native American chants to trying to keep the Yiddish language alive, folklorists document and protect our national bounty of diverse cultures. Invite students to choose a culture with which they are familiar and then find out about what is being done and by whom to preserve its art, music, stories, crafts, and practices for future generations.

School Bell Time, *1978 From the Profile/Part 1: The Twenties series (Mecklenburg County),* Romare Bearden, Collection: Kingsborough Community College, The City University of New York; © Romare Bearden Foundation/ Licensed by VAGA, New York, NY

7 ▲ Critical Viewing How does the mood of this image compare or contrast with the mood of Hurston's writing? Explain. **[Compare and Contrast]**

whenever he saw fit. I hated things I couldn't do
6 anything about. But I knew better than to bring that up right there, so I said yes, I *loved* school.

8 "I can tell you do," Brown Taffeta gleamed. She patted my head, and was lucky enough not to get sandspurs in her hand. Children who roll and tumble in the grass in Florida are apt to get sandspurs in their hair. They shook hands with me again and I went back to my seat.

When school let out at three o'clock, Mr. Calhoun told me to wait. When everybody had gone, he told me I was to go to the Park House,
9 that was the hotel in Maitland,[7] the next after-
10 noon to call upon Mrs. Johnstone and Miss Hurd. I must tell Mama to see that I was clean and brushed from head to feet, and I must wear shoes and stockings. The ladies liked me, he said, and I must be on my best behavior. 10

The next day I was let out of school an hour early, and went home to be stood up in a tub full of suds and be scrubbed and have my ears dug into. My sandy hair sported a red ribbon to match my red and white checked gingham dress, starched until it could stand alone. Mama saw to it that my shoes were on the right feet, since I was careless about left and right. Last thing, I was given a handkerchief to carry, warned again about my behavior, and sent off, with my big brother John to go as far as the hotel gate with me.

7. **Maitland** (mat´ lənd): City in Florida, close to Eatonville.

◆ Build Vocabulary

exalted (eg zôlt´ id) *adj.*: Filled with joy or pride; elated

geography (jē ôg´ rə fē) *n.*: The study of the surface of the earth

▶Critical Viewing◀

7 Compare and Contrast Some students may respond that figures in the painting and its composition convey a sense of gloom and darkness, in contrast to the upbeat tone of Hurston's writing.

8 Enrichment Point out the writer's technique of referring to the woman as "Brown Taffeta." To describe her simply in terms of her clothing implies a dismissiveness on the part of young Hurston.

◆Critical Thinking

9 Speculate Ask students why Mr. Calhoun thinks it is so important that the ladies take a liking to Zora. Why is everyone so eager to please them? *Students should realize that these ladies are patrons of some sort, who are in a position to offer educational or monetary support to promising students like Zora.*

10 Clarification You may wish to explain that the ladies are representatives of a progressive northern church engaged in a form of social work that sought to recognize and support the efforts of poor southern African Americans to get an education. Point out that parents and teachers like those in Zora's community took these visits very seriously because they wanted to show how well their students were doing.

Customize for
Intrapersonal Learners
To help these students consider the elements that contribute to a sense of self, use the Community Connection: Community and Personal Identity page in ***Beyond Literature*** (p. 55).

Humanities: Art

School Bell Time, 1978, by Romare Bearden.

Romare Bearden (1914–1988) grew up in Harlem. During the Depression years, he became a member of the Harlem Artists' Guild, along with other established African American artists such as Jacob Lawrence and Aaron Douglas. After World War II, he studied at the Sorbonne in Paris.

Bearden was greatly influenced by the Cubist painters, especially Picasso. *School Bell Time* demonstrates this Cubist influence. He eventually achieved a very personal style, a collage technique full of vitality and energy.

Use these questions for discussion:

1. How would you describe the composition of this painting? *Students may say that it is an abstract painting with a collage-like design and geometrical patterns.*
2. Which figures in the painting are suggestive of characters in the story? *The woman ringing the school bell (lower right corner) may remind students of Mrs. Calhoun, while they may identify the man in the schoolyard as Mr. Calhoun.*

◆ Critical Thinking

1 Draw Conclusions Ask students: What is the purpose of Zora's visit? *Students should realize that the ladies want to get to know Zora and to gain a better idea of her potential.*

◆ Literary Focus

2 Purpose in Autobiography Hurston wants readers to appreciate that she and her family believed in saving wisely and valued the experience of doing and achieving more than they valued money itself. Students may suggest that Hurston wants to convey the message that recognition comes to those who strive for it and earn it.

◆ Critical Thinking

3 Connect How does young Zora's appreciation for the hymns relate to her career choices as an adult? *Her appreciation of the hymns reflects her love of the rhythms of language—a love that influenced her careers has both a writer and a folklorist.*

4 Enrichment According to Norse mythology, Odin is the supreme god as well as the god of wisdom, poetry, war, and agriculture. He became the All-Wise by drinking from the fountain of Mimir, a water demon and giant who was previously the god of wisdom; however, Odin purchased his distinction at the cost of one eye. Thor, his son, is the god of thunder and the benevolent protector of humankind. His most precious possessions are his magic hammer, a belt of strength, and a pair of iron gloves.

---

1 First thing, the ladies gave me strange things, like stuffed dates and preserved ginger, and encouraged me to eat all that I wanted. Then they showed me their Japanese dolls and just talked. I was then handed a copy of *Scribner's Magazine*,[8] and asked to read a place that was pointed out to me. After a paragraph or two, I was told with smiles, that that would do.

I was led out on the grounds and they took my picture under a palm tree. They handed me what was to me then a heavy cylinder done up in fancy paper, tied with a ribbon, and they told me goodbye, asking me not to open it until I got home.

My brother was waiting for me down by the lake, and we hurried home, eager to see what was in the thing. It was too heavy to be candy or anything like that. John insisted on toting it for me.

My mother made John give it back to me and let me open it. Perhaps, I shall never experience such joy again. The nearest thing to that moment was the telegram accepting my first book.

> **◆ Literary Focus**
> 2 What does Hurston want you to know about her family's values and her own?

One hundred goldy-new pennies rolled out of the cylinder. Their gleam lit up the world. It was not avarice that moved me. It was the beauty of the thing. I stood on the mountain. Mama let me play with my pennies for a while, then put them away for me to keep.

That was only the beginning. The next day I received an Episcopal hymn-book bound in white leather with a golden cross stamped into the front cover, a copy of *The Swiss Family Robinson*, and a book of fairy tales.

3 I set about to commit the song words to memory. There was no music written there, just the words. But there was to my consciousness music in between them just the same. "When I Survey the Wondrous Cross" seemed the most beautiful to me, so I committed that to memory first of all. Some of them seemed dull and without life, and I pretended they were not there. If white people liked trashy singing like that, there must be something funny about them that I had not noticed before. I stuck to the pretty ones where the words marched to a throb I could feel. 3

A month or so after the young ladies returned to Minnesota, they sent me a huge box packed with clothes and books. The red coat with a wide circular collar and the red tam[9] pleased me more than any of the other things. My chums pretended not to like anything that I had, but even then I knew that they were jealous. Old Smarty had gotten by them again. The clothes were not new, but they were very good. I shone like the morning sun.

But the books gave me more pleasure than the clothes. I had never been too keen on dressing up. It called for hard scrubbings with Octagon soap suds getting in my eyes, and none too gentle fingers scrubbing my neck and gouging in my ears.

4 In that box were *Gulliver's Travels*, *Grimm's Fairy Tales*, *Dick Whittington*, *Greek and Roman Myths*, and best of all, *Norse Tales*. Why did the Norse tales strike so deeply into my soul? I do not know, but they did. I seemed to remember seeing Thor swing his mighty short-handled hammer as he sped across the sky in rumbling thunder, lightning flashing from the tread of his steeds and the wheels of his chariot. The great and good Odin, who went down to the well of knowledge to drink, and was told that the price of a drink from that fountain was an eye. Odin drank deeply, then plucked out one eye without a murmur and handed it to the grizzly keeper, and walked away. That held majesty for me.

Of the Greeks, Hercules moved me most. I followed him eagerly on his tasks. The story of the choice of Hercules as a boy when he met Pleasure and Duty, and put his hand in that of Duty and followed her steep way to the blue hills of fame and glory, which she pointed out at the end, moved me profoundly. I resolved to be like him. The tricks and turns of the other Gods and Goddesses left me cold. There were other thin books about this and that sweet and

8. ***Scribner's Magazine***: Literary magazine no longer published.

9. **tam** (tam) *n.*: Cap with a wide, round, flat top and sometimes a center pompom.

> **◆ Build Vocabulary**
> **avarice** (av´ ər is) *n.*: Extreme desire for wealth; greed

Speaking, Listening, and Viewing Mini-Lesson

Campaign Speech

This mini-lesson supports the Speaking, Listening, and Viewing activity in the Idea Bank (p. 837).

Introduce the Concept Ask students to share the knowledge of campaign speeches. Point out that these speeches generally tout the strengths of candidates, explain the benefits of their leadership to their audience, and urge listeners to vote.

Develop Background Briefly review how a persuasive speech should state a narrowly focused opinion, offer emotional or logical reasons to back the speaker's position, present facts and supporting details whenever possible, and call upon listeners to take a specific action.

Apply the Information Have students gather evidence in favor of Zora's candidacy, organize their information, and then write their speeches. Prompt them to keep in mind the fact that they are writing for an audience of Zora's young schoolmates. Allow time for students to practice their speeches.

Assess the Outcome To assess each speech, rate students on their ability to state opinions clearly and persuasively, use evidence from the selection to support the opinions, and organize their speech coherently. Ask students to vote on which speech they feel was most effective.

gentle little girl who gave up her heart to Christ and good works. Almost always they died from it, preaching as they passed. I was utterly indifferent to their deaths. In the first place I could not conceive of death, and in the next place they never had any funerals that amounted to a hill of beans, so I didn't care how soon they rolled up their big, soulful, blue eyes and kicked the bucket. They had no meat on their bones.

5 But I also met Hans Andersen and Robert Louis Stevenson. They seemed to know what I wanted to hear and said it in a way that tingled me. Just a little below these friends was Rudyard Kipling in his *Jungle Books*. I loved his talking snakes as much as I did the hero.

I came to start reading the Bible through my mother. She gave me a licking one afternoon for repeating something I had overheard a neighbor telling her. She locked me in her room after the whipping, and the Bible was the only thing in there for me to read. I happened to open to the place where David[10] was doing some mighty smiting, and I got interested. David went here and he went there, and no matter where he went, he smote 'em hip and thigh. Then he sung songs to his harp awhile, and went out and smote some more. Not one time did David stop and preach about sins and other things. All David wanted to know from God was who to kill and when. He took care of the other details himself. Never a quiet moment. I liked him a lot. So I read a great deal more in the Bible, hunting for some more active people like David. Except for the beautiful language of Luke and Paul,[11] the New Testament still plays a poor second to the Old Testament for me. The Jews had a God who laid about Him when they needed Him. I could see no use waiting until Judgment Day to see a man who was just crying for a good killing, to be told to go and roast. My idea was to give him a good killing first, and then if he got roasted later on, so much the better.

10. **David:** In the Bible, the second king of Israel, the land of the Hebrews.

11. **Luke and Paul:** Two Christian Apostles, who wrote parts of the New Testament.

Guide for Responding

◆ Literature and Your Life

Reader's Response What do you think about young Zora's taste in reading? Which, if any, of the stories she read would you like to read?

Thematic Focus How does the town of Zora Neale's youth compare with the community in which you live?

☑ Check Your Comprehension

1. Why does Zora ask for rides from travelers passing by her home?
2. Who are the two white women Zora meets, and why are they at her school?
3. How does Zora command special attention from the women?
4. How does Zora respond to the gifts and attention she receives?

◆ Critical Thinking

INTERPRET

1. What do you learn from Hurston's statement "if the village was singing a chorus, I must have missed the tune"? **[Infer]**
2. (a) Why does Zora find the visitor's hands so fascinating? (b) What does her fascination suggest about her life experiences so far? **[Interpret]**
3. How can you tell that the two visitors from Minnesota made a great impression on Hurston? **[Support]**
4. What do Hurston's taste in reading reveal about her? **[Infer]**

EXTEND

5. How do you think the interests of young Zora Neale helped her succeed at the adult careers of fiction writer and folklorist? **[Career Link]**

Beyond the Selection

FURTHER READING

Other Works by Zora Neale Hurston

Their Eyes Were Watching God, Jonah's Gourd Vine, Mules and Men

Other Works With Autobiographical Origins

I Know Why the Caged Bird Sings, Maya Angelou
Bearing Witness, Henry Louis Gates, Jr.
A Long Way From Home, Claude McKay

We suggest that you preview these works before recommending them to students.

INTERNET

You and your students may find additional information about Zora Neale Hurston on the Internet. We suggest the following site. Please be aware, however, that sites may have changed since this information was published.

For general information on Hurston, including her stories and photos, go to **http://pages.prodigy.com/zora/**

We *strongly recommend* that you preview sites before you send students to them.

5 Clarification Inform students that Hans Christian Andersen ("The Ugly Duckling," "The Emperor's New Clothes") was a nineteenth-century Danish writer known for giving folk tales and legends a rare combination of whimsy, irony, and wisdom. Robert Louis Stevenson (1850–1894) was a Scottish novelist best known for his novels *Treasure Island, Kidnapped,* and *The Strange Case of Dr. Jekyll and Mr. Hyde.* Rudyard Kipling (1865–1936) was an English writer who was adept at using precise, vivid imagery. He is known for his novels *Captains Courageous* and *Kim,* and his *Just So* stories.

Reinforce and Extend

Answers

◆ Literature and Your Life

Reader's Response Some students will prefer different reading but recognize that Zora's taste reflects her quest for knowledge and adventure.

Thematic Focus Students should recognize the rural character of Zora's town, the strong sense of community, and the homogeneity of the entirely African American population.

☑ Check Your Comprehension

1. She is bored by life on her street.
2. The two women are potential patrons from Minnesota.
3. She reads aloud with assurance and enthusiasm.
4. She enjoys and appreciates the beauty of the objects and is enthralled by the many books.

◆ Critical Thinking

1. She found her village uninspiring.
2. (a) She has never seen a white person's hands up close before. (b) Her fascination draws attention to the fact that she has had limited experience with white people.
3. She remembers them in great detail long after the incident.
4. She likes action and adventure.
5. Suggested responses: Hurston exhibits an early appreciation for the sound of words and for a well-told tale.

Answers

◆ Reading Strategy

1. Suggested response: She wished to portray an authentic characterization of a Southern African American woman. Hurston wanted readers to envision her grandmother as she herself experienced her.
2. She *shows* her behavior and allows readers to make inferences about the kind of child she was.
3. It demonstrates her early intelligence, her eagerness for learning, and her self-confidence. The two women also introduced her to literature that inspired her.

◆ Build Vocabulary

Using the Word Root *-graph-*
1. c 2. b 3. a 4. d

Using the Word Bank: Synonyms
1. b 2. a 3. c 4. b 5. c 6. a

◆ Literary Focus

1. Suggested responses: (a) Hurston wants to show her childhood community as endearing and admirable. (b) The reader learns that the community was tightly knit and that it valued courtesy, integrity, and education.
2. Hurston seems to regard her young self with affection, and her writing reflects a certain respect for the spunkiness, intelligence, and self-confidence of her youthful character. She is not intimidated by her peers' negative reactions to her intelligence and appearance.
3. She has the courage to ask strangers if she can join them, and she seems to enjoy the attention of the ladies from Minnesota.

◆ Grammar and Style

Practice

1. gazing at them, (and) "going a piece of the way"
2. with the permission of my parents, (nor) with their foreknowledge
3. sung songs . . . (and) went out (and) smote some more

Guide for Responding *(continued)*

◆ Reading Strategy

Analyze How a Writer Achieves Purpose

With the goal of drawing readers into her particular childhood experiences and showing the vitality of her community, Zora Neale Hurston carefully chooses words, details, characters, and events to craft her autobiography. To **analyze how the writer has achieved her purpose**, there are several issues to consider: how her details reflect her self-assurance, how the main events of the excerpt focus on her abilities, and how she uses words that capture the rural Florida setting.

1. Why does Hurston include the actual words of her grandmother in dialect?
2. How does she use small incidents and details to reveal her reputation as a school smart-aleck?
3. Why might Hurston have included her meeting with the Minnesotans in her autobiography?

◆ Build Vocabulary

Using the Greek Root *-graph-*

The Greek root *-graph-* means "write." On your paper, complete the following sentences using one of these common *-graph-* words:

a. autograph **b.** telegraph **c.** biography **d.** graphic

1. She researched Zora Neale Hurston's life and wrote a __?__ of the artist.
2. The __?__ enabled people to transmit messages quickly over long distances.
3. The actor was bombarded by fans seeking his __?__.
4. A __?__ organizer helps you visually plan your writing.

Using the Word Bank: Analogies

On your paper,complete the following analogies using the words from the Word Bank.

1. *Hindsight* is to *past* as __?__ is to *future.*
2. *Trick* is to *magician* as __?__ is to *prankster.*
3. *Indifference* is to *concern* as __?__ is to *shyness.*
4. *Dejected* is to *loser* as __?__ is to *winner.*
5. *Zoology* is to *animals* as __?__ is to *the earth's surface.*
6. *Cruelty* is to *kindness* as __?__ is to *selflessness.*

◆ Literary Focus

Purpose in Autobiography

Zora Neal Hurston had a very specific **purpose in writing her autobiography**: to share her personal experiences and to portray the African American culture of her childhood.

1. (a) What impression of her childhood community does Hurston create? (b) What do you learn about the values that were important to her and to her community?
2. What does this excerpt suggest about Hurston's self-image? Explain.
3. How does Hurston convey the fact that she was comfortable in the presence of people who were not part of her African American community?

◆ Grammar and Style

Parallelism in Coordinate Elements

Parallel coordinate elements—those linked by coordinating conjunctions—may be nouns, adjectives, adverbs, clauses, or phrases. When you link grammatical elements of equal rank with a coordinate conjunction, the elements must have parallel grammatical structure.

Practice On your paper, write the following sentences. Circle the coordinate conjunction(s) and underline the parallel coordinate elements.

1. Nevertheless, I kept right on gazing at them, and "going a piece of the way" . . .
2. I did not do this with the permission of my parents, nor with their foreknowledge.
3. Then [David] sung songs to his harp awhile, and went out and smote some more.

Writing Application Rewrite the following sentences, correcting any flaws in parallelism.

1. Zora likes to watch the passing cars and reading mythology.
2. According to her grandmother, Zora shows signs of intelligence, spunk, and being brazen.
3. Zora finds something memorable or to enjoy in every book she reads.

Writing Application

1. Zora likes to watch the passing cars and to read mythology.
2. According to her grandmother, Zora shows signs of intelligence, spunk, and brazenness.
3. Zora find something memorable or enjoyable in every book she reads.

Grammar Reinforcement

For additional instruction and practice, use the Strengthening Sentences lesson in the Writing Style unit of the **Language Lab CD-ROM,** and the pages on Faulty Parallelism, pp. 49–50, in the *Writer's Solution Grammar Practice Book.*

Reteach

To reteach this selection, use ***Strategies for Diverse Student Needs,*** p. 55.

Build Your Portfolio

Idea Bank

Writing

1. **Autobiographical Episode** Write an autobiographical episode describing how you first developed one of your major interests. Like Hurston, turn the experience into a story.

2. **Eulogy** Suppose you had been at Hurston's funeral. What would you have said about her life? Write a eulogy, drawing on details from the excerpt and the background information.

3. **Opinion Essay** Critics felt Hurston's autobiography ignored issues of racism and inequality. Did she have a responsibility to address these topics? Can *Dust Tracks*... be considered effective without them? Take a stand on this issue in an essay.

Speaking, Listening, and Viewing

4. **Campaign Speech** Develop and deliver a speech in which young Zora persuades her classmates to elect her class president. Include details that show Zora's self-image and portray her character. **[Performing Arts Link]**

5. **Interview** Work with a partner to re-create a talk-show interview with Hurston. Prepare questions about her childhood based on the excerpt. Rehearse your questions and answers; then stage the interview for the class. **[Media Link]**

Researching and Representing

6. **Reading List** Imagine you are a librarian in young Zora's town. Investigate and recommend literature she might enjoy. Explain your choices.

7. **Folk-Tale Collection** Select three folk tales from Hurston's *Mules and Men* or from another book of folk tales. Compile them in a booklet and include a brief review of each.

Online Activity www.phlit.phschool.com

Guided Writing Lesson

Moment of Inspiration

Hurston's encounter with the Minnesotans was a turning point in her life, leading to a greater love of reading and learning. Write a personal narrative about a moment in your life that inspired you to act or think differently. Emphasize its power by showing, rather than telling about, its impact on you.

Writing Skills Focus: Show, Don't Tell

When you **show instead of tell** how characters feel, look, and behave, readers can easily step into written experiences. For example, if you were inspired by a great athlete, you could *show* yourself planning a new fitness program rather than just recounting your feelings.

Prewriting Complete the journal activity on page 829. Which incidents that you recalled might qualify as "moments of inspiration"? Select one such incident as the focus of your narrative, and explore its impact on your life in a cause-and-effect diagram like this one:

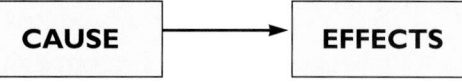

CAUSE → **EFFECTS**

Drafting You might start your essay by showing the effects of your moment of inspiration, then flashing back to reconstruct the moment itself. Use the details in your cause-and-effect diagram to help you.

Revising Reread your narrative to make sure the connection between inspiration and reaction is clear. Have you demonstrated, rather than explained, its impact on your life?

ASSESSMENT OPTIONS

Formal Assessment, Selection Test, pp. 250–252, and Assessment Resources Software. The selection test is designed so that it can be easily customized to the performance levels of your students.

Alternative Assessment, p. 55, includes options for less advanced students, more advanced students, verbal/linguistic learners, visual/spatial learners, musical/rhythmic learners, and bodily/kinesthetic learners.

PORTFOLIO ASSESSMENT

Use the following rubrics in the ***Alternative Assessment*** booklet to assess student writing:
Autobiographical Episode: Narrative Based on Personal Experience Rubric, p. 111
Eulogy: Expression Rubric, p. 109
Opinion Essay: Persuasion Rubric, p. 120
Guided Writing Lesson: Narrative Based on Personal Experience Rubric, p. 111

Idea Bank

Customizing for *Performance Levels*

Use these suggestions to match Idea Bank activities with student performance levels:
Less Advanced Students: 1, 5, 7
Average Students: 2, 4, 6
More Advanced Students: 3, 5

Customizing for *Learning Modalities*

Use these suggestions to match Idea Bank activities with student learning modalities:
Intrapersonal: 1, 6
Verbal/Linguistic: 4, 5, 7
Interpersonal: 5

Guided Writing Lesson

Refer students to p. 1194 for further information on Narration.

For more prewriting, elaboration, and revision strategies, *see Prentice Hall Writing and Grammar.*

Writing and Language Transparencies Display the Writing Process Model of a Personal Narrative (pp. 13–16), then use the Cause-and-Effect Transparency (p. 91) to help students organize details for their narratives.

Writers at Work Videodisc

Have students view the videodisc segment on Narration (Ch. 2) featuring Native American author M. Scott Momaday to see how he approaches narrative writing. Have students discuss how Momaday's sources of inspiration can help them choose topics for their narratives.

Play frames 335 to 10985

Writing Lab CD-ROM

Have students complete the tutorial on Narration. Follow these steps:

1. After reviewing the model of a Personal Narrative, students can use the Personal Experience Wheel to decide on a topic.
2. Have students use the models of different ways to organize and develop a narrative as they draft on the computer.
3. Students can use the revision tools to edit and revise their drafts.

Prepare and Engage

LESSON OBJECTIVES

1. To develop vocabulary and word identification skills
- Latin Word Roots: *-lib-*
- Using the Word Bank: Sentence Completions

2. To use a variety of reading strategies to comprehend poetry
- Reading Strategy: Draw Inferences About the Speaker

3. To express and support responses to the text
- Critical Thinking
- Idea Bank: Description
- Idea Bank: Journal Entry
- Idea Bank: Poem

4. To analyze literary elements
- Literary Focus: Speaker

5. To read in order to research self-selected and assigned topics
- Idea Bank: Viewing
- Idea Bank: Posters
- Idea Bank: Travel Brochure

6. To plan, prepare, organize, and present literary interpretations
- Idea Bank: Speech

7. To use recursive writing processes to write a profile of an immigrant group
- Guided Writing Lesson

8. To increase knowledge of the rules of grammar and usage
- Grammar and Style: Verb Tenses: Past and Present Perfect

Test Preparation

Reading Comprehension: Try Words in the Sentence (ATE, p. 839)

The teaching tips and sample test item in this workshop support the instruction and practice in the unit workshop:

Reading Comprehension: Sentence-Completion Questions (ATE, p. 863)

Guide for Interpreting

Featured in AUTHORS IN DEPTH Series

Langston Hughes (1902–1967)

Langston Hughes emerged from the Harlem Renaissance—a cultural movement in the 1920's—as the most prolific and successful African American writer. In his poetry, he expressed pride in his heritage and voiced displeasure with the oppression he saw. Although Hughes is best known for his powerful poetry, he also wrote plays, fiction, autobiographical sketches, and movie screenplays.

Born in Missouri and raised in Kansas, Illinois, and Ohio, Hughes attended high school in Cleveland, where he contributed poetry to the school literary magazine. In 1921, he moved to New York City to attend Columbia University, but a year later he left school to work as a merchant seaman.

On his return to New York, he published his first volume of poetry, *The Weary Blues* (1926). The book attracted attention and earned him wide recognition. Hughes went on to publish several other volumes of poetry, including *The Dream Keeper* (1932), *Fields of Wonder* (1947), and *Montage of a Dream Deferred* (1951). In his poetry, he experimented with a variety of forms and techniques and often tried to re-create the rhythms of contemporary jazz.

Claude McKay (1890–1948)

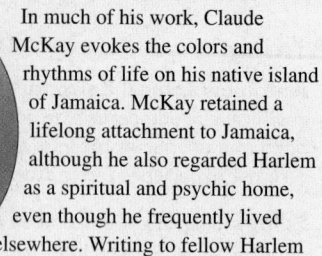

In much of his work, Claude McKay evokes the colors and rhythms of life on his native island of Jamaica. McKay retained a lifelong attachment to Jamaica, although he also regarded Harlem as a spiritual and psychic home, even though he frequently lived elsewhere. Writing to fellow Harlem Renaissance poet Langston Hughes from abroad in 1930, McKay said, "I write of America as home [although] I am really a poet without a country."

Jamaican Roots The son of farm workers, McKay moved to Kingston, the capital of the Caribbean island, when he was fourteen. While living in Kingston, he began writing poetry. When his collection *Songs of Jamaica* (1912) won an award from the Institute of Arts and Letters, he was able to emigrate to the United States.

When McKay moved to Harlem in 1914, he opened a restaurant with a friend. The business failed, but McKay's writing continued to improve. McKay's poem "The Tropics in New York" is marked by a nostalgia for his homeland—a feeling echoed in the title of his autobiography, *A Long Way From Home* (1937).

◆ Background for Understanding

LITERATURE: THE HARLEM RENAISSANCE

During the late 1800's and early 1900's, many southern African Americans moved north, hoping to find opportunities in the northern industrial centers. With this shift in population, the New York City community of Harlem developed into the cultural center for African Americans. There, in the 1920's, a cultural movement known as the Harlem Renaissance was established. The movement encompassed music, art, and literature and included such writers as Countee Cullen, Claude McKay, Langston Hughes, Jean Toomer, Zora Neale Hurston, and Arna Bontemps. The Harlem Renaissance produced such musicians as Duke Ellington, Fats Waller, Ethel Waters, and Bessie Smith. Visual artists active at the same time include James Van Der Zee and Aaron Douglas.

Although Hughes and McKay, like many of the Harlem Renaissance writers, were not born in Harlem and lived a large part of their life somewhere else, they identified Harlem as a source of inspiration and life for African American artists. Harlem was where they felt nourished, where they felt a sense of community.

Prentice Hall Literature Program Resources

REINFORCE / RETEACH / EXTEND

Selection Support Pages
Build Vocabulary: Word Roots: *-lib-*, p. 255
Grammar and Style: Past and Present Perfect, p. 256
Reading Strategy: Make Inferences, p. 257
Literary Focus: Speaker, p. 258

Strategies for Diverse Student Needs, p. 56

Beyond Literature
Cross-Curricular Connection: Science, p. 56

Formal Assessment Selection Test, pp. 253–255; Assessment Resources Software

Alternative Assessment, p. 56

Writing and Language Transparencies
Daily Language Practice, Week 28, p. 135

Resource Pro CD-ROM

Literature CD-ROM

Listening to Literature Audiocassettes

Refugee in America ◆ Ardella
The Negro Speaks of Rivers ◆ Dream Variations
◆ The Tropics in New York ◆

◆ *Literature and Your Life*

CONNECT YOUR EXPERIENCE

There are many factors that go into shaping each of our identities—the place we come from, the people who surround us, experiences that have touched our lives and those of our ancestors. Think about the things that make you who you are. Then compare them to what you learn about the places and experiences that have shaped these poets' identities.

Journal Writing Describe one place or experience that has had a great impact on you.

THEMATIC FOCUS: FROM EVERY CORNER OF THE LAND

What do these poems reveal about the shared experiences of African Americans with different backgrounds or from different regions of the country?

◆ Literary Focus

SPEAKER

The **speaker** is the voice of a poem. Often the speaker is the poet. However, a speaker may also be an imaginary person, a group of people, an animal, an inanimate thing, or another type of nonhuman entity. In the poem "The Tropics in New York," for example, Claude McKay's speaker is a homesick adult who is probably the poet himself.

◆ Build Vocabulary

LATIN WORD ROOTS: *-lib-*

In "Refugee in America," Langston Hughes uses the word *liberty* with an uppercase *L*. The root *-lib-* derives from *liber,* the Latin word for "free." Other English words that contain this root include *liberal, liberate, libertarian,* and *ad-lib*.

WORD BANK

Before you read, preview this list of words from the poems.

liberty
lulled
dusky

◆ Reading Strategy

DRAW INFERENCES ABOUT THE SPEAKER

Most often, a poem's speaker isn't revealed directly. Instead, it's left up to the reader to **draw inferences,** or come to conclusions, about the speaker's identity based on the speaker's choice of words and the details included in the poem. For instance, details in the third stanza of "The Negro Speaks of Rivers" help you infer that "I" is not an individual—since a person could not have lived long enough to experience both "the Euphrates when dawns were young" and "the Mississippi when Abe Lincoln went down to New Orleans." Once you've determined the speaker's identity, you can draw inferences about the speaker's attitudes, feelings, and experiences.

◆ Grammar and Style

VERB TENSES: PAST AND PRESENT PERFECT

The **past tense** shows an action or condition that occurred at a given time in the past; it is formed without helping verbs. In contrast, the **present perfect tense** shows an action or condition that occurred at an unnamed time in the past—or one that began in the past and continues in the present. This tense is formed with the helping verb *have* or *has* placed before the past participle of the main verb. Langston Hughes uses both tenses in his poem "The Negro Speaks of Rivers":

Past: I *built* my hut near the Congo and it *lulled* me to sleep.
Present Perfect: I've *known* rivers . . .

Interest Grabber Harlem during the 1920's was, for anyone interested in African American culture, the center of the world. Play for the class the **Listening to Music: Audio CD** recording of Duke Ellington's jazz classic "Take the A Train." Invite students to respond to the music, which was popular in the 1920's as well as afterward. Tell students that the music scene was not the only hotbed of creativity during this vibrant period; the Harlem Renaissance enabled many African American writers, dancers, and visual artists to express their longings and dreams to broad audiences, often for the first time. Tell them that in this selection, they will be reading poems by two of the movement's greatest voices.

Listening to Music: The American Experience Audio CD

Literature CD-ROM To introduce the works of McKay and Hughes, use *The History of American Literature:* Part 2, Disk 1, Feature 4.

Customize for
Less Proficient Readers
These students may benefit from the React to Poetry page in ***Strategies for Diverse Students Needs*** (p. 56).

Customize for
AP Students
All the poems in this grouping use a first-person point of view. As students read, they should consider the impact of each poet's decision and consider whether or how the poems might have evoked different responses had they been written in the third person.

Customize for
English Language Learners
Despite the complex feelings and ideas evoked, the language in the Langston Hughes poems here is fairly direct. These poems also have a rhythmic foundation that makes them suitable for oral or choral reading. Encourage students with emerging English abilities to select one or more of the poems to present aloud, individually or in groups.

Test Preparation Workshop

Reading Comprehension:
Try Words in the Sentence Many standardized tests require students to correctly answer sentence-completion questions. Use the following sample item to show students that they can often eliminate choices because they are illogical, the wrong part of speech, or inconsistent with sentence meaning.

Many writers in the 1920s identified Harlem as a source of ____ for African American artists, a supportive place where they felt a sense of ____.

A embarrassment; loss
B inspiration; community
C comfort; bewilderment
D pride; abandonment

From the context, students can tell that both the correct words should be positive. B is the best choice.

Develop Understanding

One-Minute Insight In "Refugee in America," a speaker who has escaped some, but not all, oppression in his life poignantly describes his responses to the precious words *freedom* and *liberty*.

The speaker of "Ardella" cannot find comparisons that aptly describe his beloved, who moves him beyond words.

"The Negro Speaks of Rivers" conveys the musings of a universal speaker who recalls ancient rivers and the people who lived along their shores to evoke the long history of black people and how their heritage has been shaped by generations of hardship.

Customize for
Less Proficient Readers

❶ Be sure students know that a "refugee" is someone who has fled danger or persecution, usually from another country.

◆ Critical Thinking

❷ **Distinguish** Discuss with students the distinctions between *freedom* and *liberty*, and how the poet differentiates the two in his poem. *Freedom suggests a broad absence of limitation, curbs, or frustrations, while liberty implies release from former restraint. They may say that the poet rejoices at the notion of freedom, but thinking about liberty reminds him that he hasn't always enjoyed true freedom.*

◆ Reading Strategy

❸ **Make Inferences About the Speaker** Ask students to speculate on the relationship between Ardella and the speaker. *Ardella is someone the speaker loves and takes inspiration from: his mother, a beloved, perhaps even a daughter or friend.*

▶Critical Viewing◀

❹ **Compare and Contrast** Students may say that the woman in the image has striking eyes, just as Ardella does. The woman in the painting, like Ardella, has dark skin that can be likened to a "night without stars."

❶

Refugee in America

Langston Hughes

There are words like *Freedom*
Sweet and wonderful to say.
On my heart-strings freedom sings
All day everyday.

❷

There are words like <u>*Liberty*</u>
That almost make me cry.
If you had known what I knew
You would know why.

Ardella

Langston Hughes

I would liken you
To a night without stars
❸ Were it not for your eyes.
I would liken you
To a sleep without dreams
Were it not for your songs.

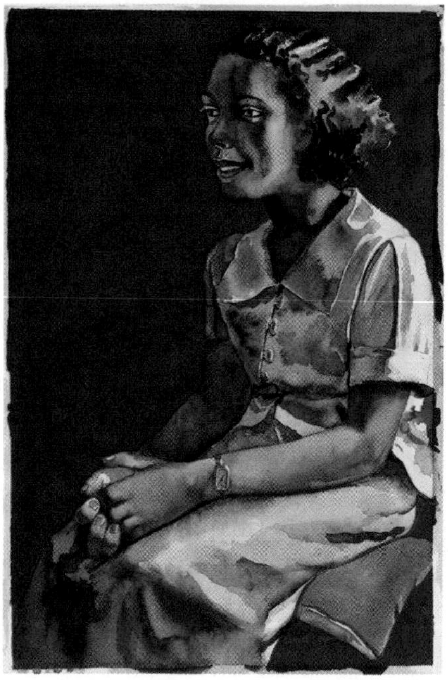

Girl in Blue Dress, 1936, Samuel Joseph Brown, Jr., Metropolitan Museum of Art

❹ ▶ **Critical Viewing** Compare the woman in this image with the subject of the poem. **[Compare and Contrast]**

Block Scheduling Strategies

Consider these suggestions to take advantage of extended class time:

- To spark interest in the period, play "Take the A Train" in **Listening to Music: The American Experience Audio CD.**
- Split the class into groups and assign each group one of the poems. As "experts," these students can lead class discussion of the poem they study.
- Use the Daily Language Practice sentences for Week 28 in the Teaching Resources and in the ***Writing and Language Transparencies.*** Display the transparency and have students correct the sentences, or dictate the sentences to students.
- Tell students to select and complete an activity from the Idea Bank (p. 845). Students can work independently, in pairs, or in small groups, depending on the chosen activity.

The Negro Speaks of Rivers

Langston Hughes

I've known rivers:
I've known rivers ancient as the world and older than
  the flow of human blood in human veins.

My soul has grown deep like the rivers.

I bathed in the Euphrates when dawns were young.
I built my hut near the Congo and it lulled me to sleep.
❺ I looked upon the Nile and raised the pyramids
  above it.
❻ I heard the singing of the Mississippi when Abe
  Lincoln went down to New Orleans, and I've seen
  its muddy bosom turn all golden in the sunset.

I've known rivers:
Ancient, dusky rivers.

My soul has grown deep like the rivers.

◆ Build Vocabulary

liberty (lib´ ər tē) *n.*: The condition of being free from control by others

lulled (luld) *v.*: Calmed or soothed by a gentle sound or motion

dusky (dus´ kē) *adj.*: Dim; shadowy

Guide for Responding

◆ Literature and Your Life

Reader's Response What associations do you have with the places Hughes describes in "The Negro Speaks of Rivers"? What places do you associate with your culture or your ancestry?

Thematic Focus In what sense is place important to the speaker in each of these poems?

List Write a list of words that describe ideas, places, people and things you associate with the word "refugee."

☑ Check Your Comprehension

1. In "Refugee in America," what is the speaker's reaction to words like "freedom"?
2. Identify four rivers the speaker names in "The Negro Speaks of Rivers."

◆ Critical Thinking

INTERPRET

1. (a) How does the title "Refugee in America" relate to the poem itself? (b)How would you describe the contrast between this poem's first and second stanzas? **[Interpret; Contrast]**
2. (a) Why does the subject of "Ardella" defy comparison? (b) What is the speaker's feeling toward her? **[Infer]**
3. (a) In "The Negro Speaks of River," what does the age of rivers imply about people of African ancestry? (b) How do lines 3 and 10 reflect the poem's theme? **[Interpret]**

APPLY

4. In what respects can the human race as a whole be compared with rivers? **[Support]**

Humanities: Art

Girl in Blue Dress, 1936, by Samuel Joseph Brown, Jr.

Brown (1907–1994) received international attention in 1939 as the only African American artist to be included in a contemporary art exhibit organized by the Metropolitan Museum of Art in New York.

Just as you can make inferences about the speaker in the poem, you can make inferences about the painter of this portrait. Ask students: How do you think he regarded his subject? *Based upon the way the artist portrays her eager face and the way he uses light to illuminate her, students should infer that the artist wants others to see her in the same way he does: young, happy, and full of life.*

◆ Literary Focus

Speaker Guide students to recognize that the speaker of "The Negro Speaks . . ." is a universal black voice that speaks for all blacks, condensing their long and diverse heritage.

◆ Critical Thinking

❺ **Interpret** Ask students what the references to specific rivers in lines 4–7 convey about the black experience. *Reference to the four rivers suggests the depth of the black experience by tracing the path of African Americans from the beginnings of civilization in Mesopotamia (the Euphrates) to black cultures on the African continent (Congo and Nile) to slavery in the American South (Mississippi).*

❻ **Clarification** When he was about nineteen, Lincoln worked on a Mississippi flatboat, where he first encountered slaves in great numbers. This experience left a lasting impression upon him.

Answers

◆ Literature and Your Life

Reader's Response Answers will vary.

Thematic Focus The title of the first poem suggests that the speaker feels out of place in his surroundings. The third speaker uses places to mark his self-identity.

☑ Check Your Comprehension

1. They bring him joy.
2. The speaker identifies the Euphrates, Congo, Nile, and Mississippi rivers.

◆ Critical Thinking

1. (a)The word *refugee* suggests that the speaker does not feel like a full citizen. (b) The first stanza describes the speaker's positive response to the word *freedom*; the second stanza focuses on a bitter or sad response to the word *liberty*.
2. Suggested responses: (a) Her eyes and her songs cannot be defined in words. (b) Students should infer that the speaker is captivated by the subject of the poem.
3. (a) It implies that people with African ancestry have existed for ages. (b) The lines convey the idea that black people have grown strong from their experiences.
4. Suggested response: Like rivers, the human race has survived for ages.

Develop Understanding

One-Minute Insight The speaker of "Dream Variations" dreams of the exhilaration he would feel if he could freely express himself in the light of day anywhere or anytime, and know that he would have the calm and peace to rest and renew himself each evening without fear.

In "The Tropics in New York," a window display of tropical fruits evokes vivid memories of the bountiful, distant countryside where the fruits might have grown. Overcome by a longing for his homeland, the speaker weeps.

◆ Reading Strategy

Make Inferences About the Speaker Ask students to determine who the speaker is as they read this poem, and to characterize him. *Students may say that the speaker is an African American who is full of enthusiasm for a life he has imagined but has not yet been able to lead.*

▶Critical Viewing◀

❶ **Connect** Students may say that the bright, swirling figures reflect the same vigorous, life-affirming energy the speaker longs to express.

◆ Critical Thinking

❷ **Interpret** Discuss with students what they think the poet means by describing a day as "white." *Students may say that it simply implies light, as opposed to the dark of night; others may think that it implies that the speaker's days are dominated by white people. You might point out that other meanings of white include upright; meaning to cause no harm, as in a "white lie"; or passionate, as in "white with rage."*

◆ Reading Strategy

❸ **Make Inferences About the Speaker** Guide students to notice how the poet describes the approach of night in lines 7 and 16: " . . . comes on gently" and " . . . coming tenderly." Discuss what the speaker wishes to express by comparing himself to the night in these terms. *Students may say that the speaker wants people not to fear the black man: like the night, he, too, is gentle and tender.*

Dream Variations

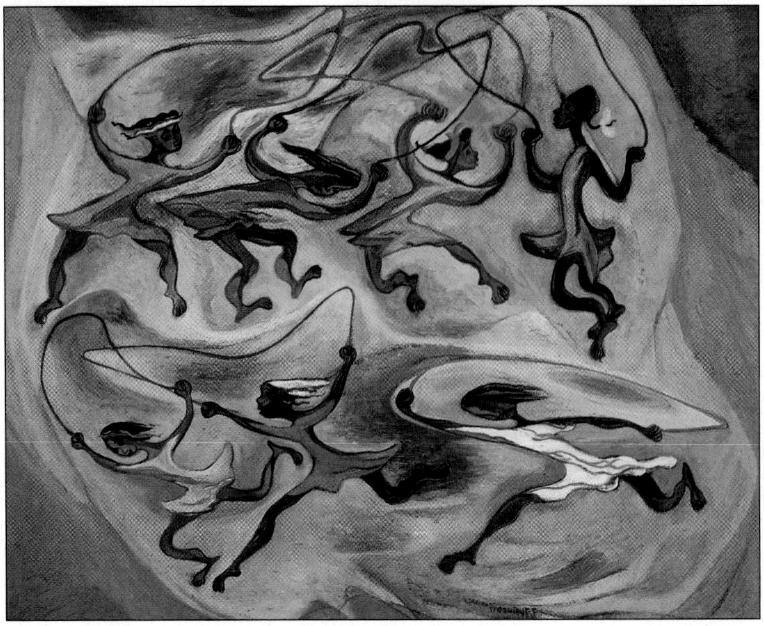

Girls Skipping, 1949, Hale Woodruff, Michael Rosenfeld Gallery

❶ ▲ **Critical Viewing** How does the motion of the figures in this drawing reflect the mood of the poem? **[Connect]**

Langston Hughes

To fling my arms wide
In some place of the sun,
To whirl and to dance
❷ Till the white day is done.
Then rest at cool evening
Beneath a tall tree
While night comes on gently,
  Dark like me —
That is my dream!
❸

To fling my arms wide
In the face of the sun,
Dance! Whirl! Whirl!
Till the quick day is done.
Rest at pale evening . . .
A tall, slim tree . . .
Night coming tenderly
  Black like me.

Humanities: Art

Girls Skipping, 1949, by Hale Woodruff.

African American artist Hale Woodruff (1900–1980) was a painter, printmaker, muralist, and educator. Born in Cairo, Illinois, he studied at the John Herron Art Institute in Indianapolis and at the Fogg Art Museum at Harvard University, and worked with Diego Rivera in Mexico. Woodruff's murals are on display at the University of Atlanta in Georgia, where he once taught. In "Girls Skipping," the artist uses whirling ropes to divide the canvas into segments and create a dizzying sense of motion. Use these questions for discussion:

1. How does the artist use color, shape, and line to give stationary figures the illusion of motion and energy? *The bright colors lend a sense of energy, the swirling shapes suggest change and motion, and the lines of the jump ropes intertwine and connect the colors, segments, and figures into a whirling whole.*
2. What other real-life activities might the artist have chosen to convey the sense of motion and energy of the poem? *Possible answers include dancing, skating, or playing basketball.*

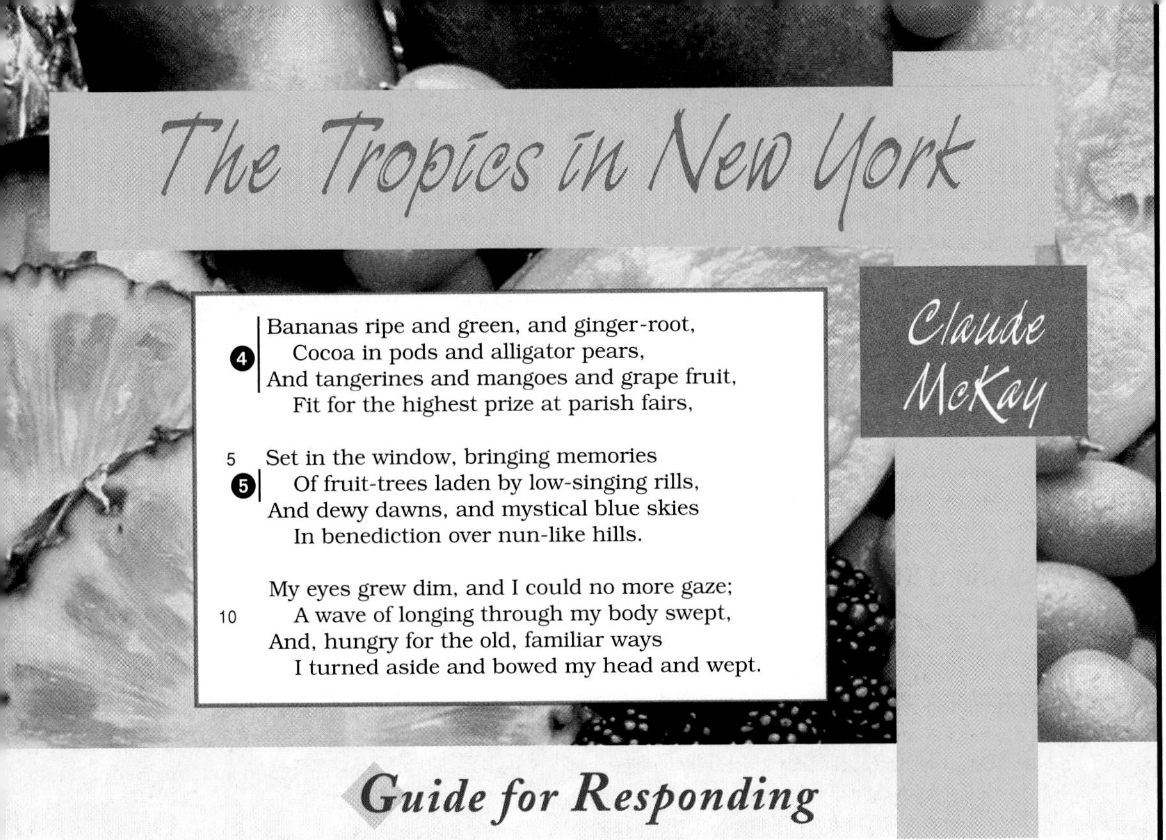

The Tropics in New York

Claude McKay

❹ Bananas ripe and green, and ginger-root,
Cocoa in pods and alligator pears,
And tangerines and mangoes and grape fruit,
Fit for the highest prize at parish fairs,

Set in the window, bringing memories
❺ Of fruit-trees laden by low-singing rills,
And dewy dawns, and mystical blue skies
In benediction over nun-like hills.

My eyes grew dim, and I could no more gaze;
A wave of longing through my body swept,
And, hungry for the old, familiar ways
I turned aside and bowed my head and wept.

Guide for Responding

◆ Literature and Your Life

Reader's Response In "The Tropics in New York," the fruit in the window evokes memories of the poet's birthplace. What objects could evoke memories of your own past in you?

Thematic Focus Is the idea of home always associated with the past?

Questions for Research Compare the themes of a contemporary African American poet with those of Hughes. List questions you would ask to begin researching your project. Then narrow your list.

☑ Check Your Comprehension

1. In "Dream Variations," what is the speaker's ideal experience?
2. (a) In "The Tropics in New York," what fruits are "set in the window"? (b) What memories do they stir in the speaker? (c) Why does the speaker weep?

◆ Critical Thinking

INTERPRET

1. (a) In "Dream Variations," how would you describe the speaker's daily life? (b) How do you think the speaker feels about his ethnicity? Explain. **[Infer]**
2. How does the title of "The Tropics in New York" contribute to the poem's meaning? **[Interpret]**
3. (a) In "The Tropics in New York," what impression of his homeland does the speaker convey? (b) Which words create especially vivid images? **[Infer; Analyze]**

EVALUATE

4. Do you think the speakers of these poems have a realistic impression of life? Explain. **[Assess]**

COMPARE LITERARY WORKS

5. Notice how Langston Hughes uses images of darkness in these poems. List the different ideas he explores through these images. **[Evaluate]**

Beyond the Selection

FURTHER READING

Other Works by Langston Hughes

The Weary Blues
Not Without Laughter
Mulebone (with Zora Neale Hurston)

Other Works by Claude McKay

Home to Harlem
Spring in New Hampshire
Banana Bottom

We suggest that you preview these works before recommending them to students.

INTERNET

We suggest you visit the following Internet sites to learn more.

For information on Hughes and links to other artists of the Harlem Renaissance, visit "It's a Hughes Thang!!!!" at **http://www.cwrl.utexas.edu/~mmaynard/Hughes/hughes/.htm**

Visit the Harlem Renaissance page at **http://www.geocities.com/athens/forum/4722/big.html**

We *strongly recommend* that you preview sites before you send students to them.

◆ Critical Thinking

❹ **Analyze** Ask students to reread lines 1–3. Which senses do the images engage? *They appeal to the sense of sight, smell, taste, and touch.*

❺ **Clarification** "Rills" are small streams.

◆ Critical Thinking

Connect Ask students to suggest a relationship among the poem's three stanzas. *The first stanza describes the sight which, in the second stanza, triggers a memory that transports the speaker; in the third stanza, he returns to the present, overcome by homesickness.*

Reinforce and Extend

Answers

◆ Literature and Your Life

Reader's Response Encourage volunteers to share their responses.

Thematic Focus Suggested response: For people who live in the place of their birth, home is related to the past and the present; for others, the relationship between "home" and "past" is a strong one.

☑ Check Your Comprehension

1. He wishes to dance in the sun, then rest as evening sets in.
2. (a) Tropical fruit are set in the window. (b) They stir memories of his homeland. (c) He is homesick.

◆ Critical Thinking

Interpret

1. (a) The speaker's daily life is probably filled with hard work, affording him little time to play or rest. (b) He seems to long to celebrate or embrace his ethnicity.
2. It provides the setting of the poem and reveals its conflict.
3. (a) He conveys an impression of a tropical paradise. (b) Students may mention words such as *ripe, green, dewy,* and *mystical.*
4. The speaker of "Dream Variations" is not realistic; he wishes to do nothing but play and rest. The speaker of the second poem idealizes his homeland by omitting negative details.
5. Possible response: People often associate places from the past with times when they felt happier or more secure.

Answers

◆ Literary Focus

1. The speaker resides in America but does not feel free.
2. The speaker is most likely a man with strong feelings for the woman of whom he writes.
3. (a) The speaker is the Negro people. (b) It states that it is "The Negro" who is speaking of rivers.
4. The intense personal emotion of longing might be diluted if the poem were spoken by someone who had not actually experienced life in the speaker's faraway homeland.

◆ Reading Strategy

1. The speaker may be an "ordinary" African American.
2. The speaker must be many black people, for it took hundreds or thousands of people to erect a pyramid.

◆ Build Vocabulary

Using the Word Root *-lib-*

1 c 2. a 3. d 4. b

Using the Word Bank: Sentence Completions

dusky, lulled, liberty

◆ Grammar and Style

1. *has grown;* present perfect
2. *turned, bowed, wept;* past
3. *(have) known;* present perfect

Grammar Reinforcement

For additional instruction and practice, use the Correct and Effective Use of Verbs lesson in the Using Verbs unit of the **Language Lab CD-ROM.**

Beyond Literature

To increase awareness of the artist's style, direct students to his work on p. 639 and p. 848 of this book. Students who do further research should discover that Douglas's murals helped build awareness of the richness of the African cultural heritage.

Guide for Responding (continued)

◆ Literary Focus

Speaker

Each poem has a **speaker,** or voice. The speaker can be the poet, a character, a group of people, or an inanimate or nonhuman entity.

1. How would you describe the speaker of "Refugee in America"?
2. What can you tell about the speaker of "Ardella"?
3. (a) Who is the speaker of "The Negro Speaks of Rivers"? (b) How does the title help to reveal the speaker's identity?
4. How would the effect of "Tropics in New York" be different if it were delivered by an adolescent son or daughter of the speaker?

◆ Reading Strategy

Draw Inferences About the Speaker

By looking closely at the details in a poem, you can **draw inferences** about the speaker's attitudes, feelings, and background. For instance, you can infer from the vivid descriptions of fruits in "The Tropics in New York" that the speaker is intimately familiar with a tropical landscape like Jamaica.

1. What can you infer about the speaker of "Refugee in America" from the plain, straightforward language in the poem?
2. What can you infer about the speaker of "The Negro Speaks of Rivers" from line 6?

◆ Build Vocabulary

Using the Latin Root *-lib-*

Several English words contain the Latin root *-lib-*. Match the following words with their definitions.

1. liberty	**a.** improvise
2. ad-lib	**b.** generous
3. liberate	**c.** freedom
4. liberal	**d.** release from slavery

Using the Word Bank: Sentence Completions

On your paper, use the words from the word bank to complete the following sentence.

The light, ___?___ and soft, ___?___ the prisoner to sleep, and soon he was dreaming once again of his ___?___.

◆ Grammar and Style

Verb Tenses: Past and Present Perfect

The **present perfect tense** is formed with the helping verb *have* or *has* placed before the past participle of the main verb. The **past tense** requires no helping verbs.

The **past tense** names or describes an action or condition that began and ended at a given time in the past. The **present perfect tense** names or describes an action or condition that occurred at an indefinite past time—or one that began in the past and continues into the present.

Practice Circle the verbs in the following sentences from Hughes's and McKay's poems. Label each verb as past tense or present perfect tense.

1. My soul has grown deep like the rivers.
2. I turned aside and bowed my head and wept.
3. I've known rivers ancient as the world and older than the flow of human blood in human veins.

Beyond Literature

Cultural Connection

African Art Through the Harlem Renaissance, many writers and artists explored their African heritage. A common form in African art is the carved figure. African artists, however, do not always aim for accuracy in portraying figures. Instead, they use human and animal images to express ideas about spiritual or human reality. For example, a smooth, polished surface on a carving represents healthy skin on a living person.

Activity Although there are common themes in African art, it is important to remember that Africa is a diverse continent composed of fifty-five countries, each with a variety of cultural and tribal ideas. Choose two regions of Africa, and compare their art forms. How are the themes similar? How are they different?

Reteach

Explain to students that drawing inferences about the identity of a poem's speaker helps a reader clarify the poet's intent. By contrast, assuming that a poem's speaker is the poet may lead a reader to an invalid interpretation of the poem itself.

To determine who or what the speaker is in Langston Hughes's poem "The Negro Speaks of Rivers," use a graphic organizer like the one shown.

As students complete the organizer, help them see that that the final lines of the poem underscore the collective, or nonindividual, nature of the speaker: "My soul has grown deep like the rivers." Tie the clues together by returning to the title.

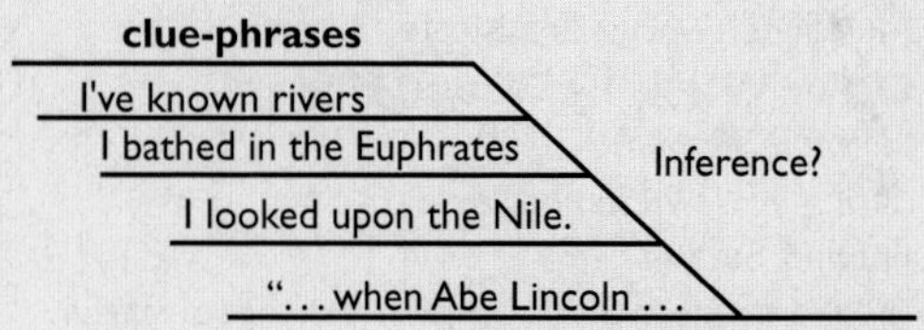
clue-phrases
I've known rivers
I bathed in the Euphrates
I looked upon the Nile.
"... when Abe Lincoln ...
Inference?

Build Your Portfolio

Idea Bank

Writing

1. **Journal Entry** Langston Hughes's poems are full of rhythmic language. For several days, pay special attention to the rhythms of the speech you hear around you. For example, compare the speech of news reporters with the sound of every day talk. Write your observations in a journal.

2. **Description** Imagine that the speaker of "The Tropics in New York" returns home after twenty years. Tell the story of this visit. Would his former home live up to his memories of it?

3. **Poem** Write a poem in which vivid, memorable images lead your speaker to recall a place that evokes powerful feelings.

Speaking, Listening, and Viewing

4. **Speech** Deliver a political stump speech on the topic of "liberty and freedom." Refer to the themes of Hughes's poem at some point in your speech. **[Performing Arts Link; Social Studies Link]**

5. **Viewing** Examine pictures of Jamaican life, and list those characteristics you find most intriguing. What aspects of Jamaican culture can you discover from photos? Make a chart in which you compare and contrast aspects of Jamaican culture with those of the United States. **[Social Studies Link]**

Researching and Representing

6. **Posters** Design a series of subway or bus posters to create public awareness of the cultural contributions of African Americans during the 1920's. **[Art Link; Social Studies Link]**

7. **Travel Brochure** Imagine that you are a travel agent booking vacations to Jamaica. Create a travel brochure to attract visitors to the island. **[Art Link; Social Studies Link]**

Online Activity www.phlit.phschool.com

Guided Writing Lesson

Profile of an Immigrant Group

Create a profile of an immigrant group providing factual historical information about a group's experience of immigration. Your profile can contain material on immigrants' reasons for moving from one place to another, as well as facts about their activities, interests, lifestyles, challenges, and triumphs in their new home.

Writing Skills Focus: Objective Tone

In order to write a balanced and informative profile, you will need to establish and maintain an **objective tone**—a neutral attitude toward your subject. Consider these suggestions as you write your profile:

- Avoid words that have strong positive or negative connotations.
- Use long, straightforward sentences. They often lend a more serious, objective tone than short sentences do.
- Stick to the facts and steer clear of opinions.

Prewriting Do research on an immigrant group that interests you. Take notes on the conditions in their country of origin, their reasons for leaving, the years of their emigration, and their experiences in their adopted country. Review this material, and decide on an organizational plan for your profile.

Drafting Tell the story of the group's emigration patterns and history, using facts expressed in straightforward, neutral language. When possible, include charts, maps or graphs to help readers see the patterns you are describing.

Revising Carefully review your work with an eye for any biased or unsupported ideas. Also look for places where you can add or delete details to make your paragraphs clearer and more informative.

✓ ASSESSMENT OPTIONS

Formal Assessment, Selection Test, pp. 253–255, and Assessment Resources Software. The selection test is designed so that it can be easily customized to the performance levels of your students.

Alternative Assessment, p. 56, includes options for less advanced students, more advanced students, intrapersonal learners, musical/rhythmic learners, and interpersonal learners.

PORTFOLIO ASSESSMENT

Use the following rubrics in the ***Alternative Assessment*** booklet to assess student writing:
Journal Entry: Description Rubric, p. 112
Description: Fictional Narrative Rubric, p. 110
Poem: Poetry Rubric, p. 123
Guided Writing Lesson: Research Report/Paper Rubric, p. 121

Idea Bank

Customizing for *Performance Levels*

Following are suggestions for matching Idea Bank topics with your students' performance levels:
Less Advanced Students: 1, 5
Average Students: 2, 6, 7
More Advanced Students: 3, 4

Customizing for *Learning Modalities*

Following are suggestions for matching Idea Bank topics with your students' learning modalities:
Verbal/Linguistic: 4, 5, 7
Bodily/Kinesthetic: 5
Visual/Spatial: 6

Guided Writing Lesson

Refer students to the Writing Process Handbook, p. 1192, for instruction on the writing process, and p. 1195 for further information on Research Writing.

Writers at Work Videodisc

Have students view the videodisc segment on Research Writing (Ch. 5) featuring journalist Gillian Gaar to see how she approaches research writing. Have students discuss how they can use Gaar's insights to help them create more lively, informative profiles.

Play frames 3 to 9643

Writing Lab CD-ROM

Have students complete the tutorial on Research Writing. Follow these steps:

1. To facilitate their research efforts, students can use the audio-annotated instruction on using library resources and on-line services.
2. Have students draft on computer.
3. Direct students to the interactive instruction on improving content to aid revision.

Prepare and Engage

LESSON OBJECTIVES

1. **To develop vocabulary and word identification skills**
   - Latin Word Roots: *-cre-*
   - Using the Word Bank: Synonyms
2. **To use a variety of reading strategies to comprehend poetry**
   - Reading Strategy: Connect to Historical Context
3. **To increase knowledge of other cultures and to connect common elements across cultures**
   - Connecting Themes Across Cultures (ATE)
4. **To express and support responses to the text**
   - Critical Thinking
   - Idea Bank: List
   - Idea Bank: Painting
   - Idea Bank: Essay
5. **To analyze literary elements**
   - Literary Focus: Metaphor
   - Idea Bank: Poem
6. **To read in order to research self-selected and assigned topics**
   - Idea Bank: Research Report
7. **To plan, prepare, organize, and present literary interpretations**
   - Idea Bank: Weather Report
8. **To use recursive writing processes to write a description**
   - Guided Writing Lesson
9. **To increase knowledge of the rules of grammar and usage**
   - Grammar and Style: Placement of Adjectives

Test Preparation

Reading Comprehension: Anticipate Missing Words
(ATE, p. 847)
The teaching tips and sample test item in this workshop support the instruction and practice in the unit workshop:

Reading Comprehension: Sentence-Completion Questions
(ATE, p. 863)

Guide for Interpreting

Countee Cullen *(1903–1946)*

Unlike most other poets of his time, Countee Cullen used traditional forms and methods. However, no poet expressed the general sentiments of African Americans during the early 1900's more eloquently than Cullen.

Cullen was born in Louisville, Kentucky. He graduated from New York University and later earned a master's degree from Harvard. His first collection of poetry, *Color*, was published in 1925. This was followed by *Copper Sun* (1927), *The Ballad of the Brown Girl* (1927) and *The Black Christ* (1929). In 1932, he published *One Way to Heaven*, a satirical novel about life in Harlem. During his later years, he published two children's books, *The Lost Zoo* (1940) and *My Lives and How I Lost Them* (1942).

Arna Bontemps *(1902–1973)*

Arna Bontemps was one of the most scholarly figures of the Harlem Renaissance. After working as a postal worker and a teacher in several religious academies, Bontemps wrote a highly acclaimed novel, *Black Thunder* (1936), about a Virginia slave revolt. In the years that followed, he published poetry, dramas, anthologies, and children's books. He also ran the library at Fisk University in Nashville and transformed it into an important center for African American studies.

Jean Toomer *(1894–1967)*

Following the appearance of *Cane* (1923)—an unusual book of prose sketches, poems, stories, and a one-act play—Jean Toomer was widely considered among the most talented writers of the Harlem Renaissance. For a few years he published in leading black journals and in the Imagist journal, *The Little Review.* However, Toomer's publishing output dwindled and *Cane* fell into obscurity. As a result, Toomer was virtually forgotten as a writer. In recent years, however, *Cane* has come to be recognized as one of the greatest works of the Harlem Renaissance.

◆ Background for Understanding

LITERATURE: THE HARLEM RENAISSANCE

When Southern African Americans made the move north in the late 1800's and the early 1900's, the population shift made the New York community of Harlem a thriving cultural center. While many southerners moved north in search of industrial jobs, African American culture—art, music, and literature—experienced a huge growth.

The 1920's movement known as the Harlem Renaissance produced literature of many styles. Although the forms and techniques used by Harlem Renaissance writers varied widely, the poets, essayists, novelists, and playwrights shared a common purpose: to create art and literature that reflected the African American experience. At the same time, the Harlem Renaissance writers focused on capturing the general sentiments of the time. In doing so, they expressed their displeasure concerning their overall condition and articulated their cultural heritage.

The Harlem Renaissance helped make the general public aware of African American life. By eloquently chronicling the heritage of African Americans and expressing their pride and determination, Harlem Renaissance writers provided African Americans with a link to their cultural roots and a promise for a better future.

Prentice Hall Literature Program Resources

REINFORCE / RETEACH / EXTEND

Selection Support Pages
Build Vocabulary: Word Roots: *-cre-*, p. 259
Grammar and Style: Placement of Adjectives, p. 260
Reading Strategy: Apply Historical Context, p. 261
Literary Focus: Metaphor, p. 262

Strategies for Diverse Student Needs, p. 57

Beyond Literature
Cross-Curricular Connection: Social Studies, p. 57

Formal Assessment Selection Test, pp. 256–258; Assessment Resources Software

Alternative Assessment, p. 57

Resource Pro CD-ROM

Listening to Literature Audiocassettes

◆ From the Dark Tower ◆
A Black Man Talks of Reaping ◆ Storm Ending

◆ Literature and Your Life

CONNECT YOUR EXPERIENCE

When you tell someone how you're feeling at a particular time, you probably make comparisons to familiar activities or events in nature. For example, if you see trouble ahead, you might say that a storm is brewing. In the same way, these poems capture the experiences of the African American people through striking images of activities and events.

Journal Writing In "Storm Ending," Jean Toomer describes a thunderstorm. Write about the types of images you associate with thunderstorms.

THEMATIC FOCUS: FROM EVERY CORNER OF THE LAND

Each of these poems emerged from a specific time and place: Harlem in the 1920's. However, the poems capture experiences shared by African Americans throughout the land.

◆ Build Vocabulary

LATIN WORD ROOTS: *-cre-*

Countee Cullen describes a bountiful harvest as a "golden increment." Like *increase, crescendo,* and *create,* the word *increment* contains the Latin root *-cre-*, which means "to grow." *Increment* means an "increase or gain." How does the Latin root *-cre-* contribute to its meaning?

increment
countenance
beguile
stark
reaping
glean

WORD BANK

Before you read, preview this list of words from the poems.

◆ Grammar and Style

PLACEMENT OF ADJECTIVES

Ordinarily, **adjectives** precede the noun or pronoun they modify. However, for reasons of style, emphasis, or variety, writers sometimes choose to place adjectives after the words they modify. Look at these examples from "A Black Man Talks of Reaping":

Before Noun: this *stark, lean* year

After Noun: I've scattered seed *enough* to plant the land

Even in poetry, writers take care to place adjectives so that readers do not misunderstand what each word modifies.

◆ Literary Focus

METAPHOR

A **metaphor** is an implied comparison between two seemingly dissimilar things. For example, Countee Cullen compares African American life to the toil of planting.

Although metaphors are often brief, they may also be elaborate, lengthy comparisons. An **extended metaphor** is a comparison that is developed throughout the course of a poem. As you read "Storm Ending," look for the extended metaphor Toomer employs.

◆ Reading Strategy

CONNECT TO HISTORICAL CONTEXT

Many works of literature bear a direct relation to the time and place in which they were written. For this reason, a reader must connect such works to their **historical contexts** in order to understand and appreciate them thoroughly. For example, to fully appreciate the following poems, it is important to recognize that the writers were part of the cultural movement known as the Harlem Renaissance in the 1920's.

Read the Background for Understanding on pp. 838 and 846. Then apply this information to your reading of these poems.

Test Preparation Workshop

Reading Comprehension: Anticipate Missing Words Many standardized tests ask students to correctly answer sentence-completion questions. Use the following example to show students how to use context and their own knowledge to guess a word that would complete the following passage.

Although the forms and techniques used by Harlem Renaissance writers varied widely, the poets and novelists had ____ purposes for creating their art.

A complex
B unusual
C similar
D different

From the context clue *although,* students may guess that the correct word is the opposite of "varied widely." Answer *C, similar,* is correct.

Interest Grabber Obtain and display some works by Harlem Renaissance artists, such as Aaron Douglas, Hale Woodruff, Palmer Hayden, William H. Johnson, Laura Wheeler Waring, or Romare Bearden. Encourage volunteers to share their responses to the art. Tell students that both the art they have seen and the poems they are about to read are the product of some of the leading lights of the Harlem Renaissance. As they read, have students look for images or ideas in the poems that reflect what they saw in the art.

Connecting Themes Across Cultures

Invite students to identify other literature which expresses the shared experiences of other cultural groups, such as the reflective essays of Native American authors N. Scott Momaday *(The Way to Rainy Mountain)* and Leslie Marmon Silko *(Yellow Woman and a Beauty of the Spirit)*.

Customize for *Less Proficient Readers*

Help students to paraphrase or restate in simpler terms lines or phrases of these poems to get at the poet's meaning. For example, "We shall not always plant while others reap" might be restated as "We won't always do the work while others get the benefits."

Customize for *AP Students*

Tell students that the poets may have had grandparents who had firsthand knowledge of slavery, or who passed down family stories about such experiences. In addition, many recalled life in the Jim Crow South, and experienced discrimination in every aspect of life. Such recollections profoundly influenced their writings.

Customize for *Interpersonal Learners*

Encourage students to remember that the poets experienced the struggle through a difficult time in American history. Encourage them to list questions they would like to ask the poets. These lists can help students solidify their understanding of the poems, the period, and the role of art among African Americans.

Develop Understanding

One-Minute Insight The speaker recalls the endless indignities of slavery and oppression. He knows he must hide his true feelings in order to survive in a hostile world, but he longs for a day when racism will finally end.

◆ Literary Focus

Metaphor Ask students, as they read, to identify metaphors Countee Cullen uses in this poem, and to notice the details he uses to extend them. *Students may cite the metaphors of planting and reaping; the temptation of bursting fruit that the speaker cannot enjoy; or the dark night that represents the black person.*

◆ Reading Strategy

❶ Apply Historical Context Students may wonder about the person to whom the poet dedicated this work. Point out that knowing who this person was may clarify the intent of the poem, or shed light on the relationship between the poet and the dedicatee. You might have students research Charles S. Johnson. Or you can tell them that he was a brilliant sociologist, editor of many National Urban League publications, and a major promoter of the Harlem Renaissance.

▶Critical Viewing◀

❷ Assess Students may say that the image suggests the chance to move from the shadows into the light of opportunity. They may say that Aaron Douglas presents a more hopeful view of aspiration, while Cullen's view is more bitter, tinged by repression and despair.

◆ Critical Thinking

❸ Analyze Ask students to analyze the tone of this section of the poem. *Students may say that its tone reflects anger, impatience, injustice, and frustration.*

Connecting to Real-World Texts

To connect this selection to a real-world text, see "Harlem: A Paradise of My Own People," pp. 1217–1219.

From the Dark Tower

❶ **Countee Cullen** *(To Charles S. Johnson)*

Aspiration, Aaron Douglas

❷ ▶ **Critical Viewing** What do you think is the message of this image? Do you think Countee Cullen would agree with the artist's interpretation of "aspiration"? **[Assess]**

We shall not always plant while others reap
The golden increment of bursting fruit,
❸ Not always countenance, abject and mute,
That lesser men should hold their brothers cheap;
Not everlastingly while others sleep

Block Scheduling Strategies

Consider these suggestions to take advantage of extended class time:

- After students have read the Background for Understanding (p. 846), invite them to share any prior knowledge.
- Introduce the Literary Focus. Review the use of metaphor in other literary works students have recently read, or use the Literary Focus page in ***Selection Support*** for additional instruction and practice.
- Extend your students' knowledge of the Harlem Renaissance by sharing the Humanities notes that accompany the paintings on pp. 849 and 850.
- Use the viewing and representing Mini-Lesson to help groups of students complete the Painting activity in the Idea Bank (p. 853).
- Students can use any remaining class time to begin their homework assignment: the Guided Writing Lesson (p. 853). Before they begin, have students identify some vivid verbs in these or other poems. Encourage them to use a thesaurus.

Shall we beguile their limbs with mellow flute, ❸
Not always bend to some more subtle brute; ❹
We were not made eternally to weep.

The night whose sable breast relieves the stark, ❺
White stars is no less lovely being dark,
And there are buds that cannot bloom at all ❻
In light, but crumple, piteous, and fall;
So in the dark we hide the heart that bleeds,
And wait, and tend our agonizing seeds.

◆ Build Vocabulary

increment (in´ krə mənt) *n.*: Increase, as in a series
countenance (koun´ tə nəns) *v.*: Approve; tolerate
beguile (bē gīl´) *v.*: Charm or delight

Guide for Responding

◆ Literature and Your Life

Reader's Response Can you identify or empathize with the speaker of this poem? Why or why not?

Thematic Focus To which groups of people in today's America can this poem's message be applied? Explain.

Journal Writing In your journal, write a few sentences in which you explore the possible meanings of the title "From the Dark Tower."

☑ Check Your Comprehension

1. (a) According to the speaker, who is "abject and mute"? (b) Who is being tended in lines 5–6?
2. What contrast or opposition does the speaker set up in lines 9–10?

◆ Critical Thinking

INTERPRET

1. (a) Who is the "we" of the poem? (b) What distinction does the speaker draw between the circumstances of "we" and those of "others"? **[Infer; Interpret]**
2. What is the effect of Cullen's repetition of phrases using the word *not* in the first stanza? **[Analyze; Interpret]**
3. How do the ideas in the first and second stanzas differ? **[Compare and Contrast]**
4. What is the poem's theme, or central message? Support your answer. **[Draw Conclusions]**

EVALUATE

5. Do you think the waiting mentioned in the final line is an appropriate response to the conflicts described in the poem? Explain. **[Criticize]**

Humanities: Art

Aspiration by Aaron Douglas.

In 1924, Aaron Douglas (1898–1979) left his high school teaching job in Kansas City and came to Harlem to become the official painter of the Harlem Renaissance movement. He did so at the invitation of Charles S. Johnson, editor of *Opportunity,* the voice of the Harlem Renaissance literary movement. Douglas became a central figure among intellectuals, and writers, artists, musicians, and scholars gathered at his home. He pioneered the "synthetic cubist" style of painting, which incorporates flat, shadowy figures silhouetted against blocks of color. Some of Douglas's finest murals can been seen at the Harlem branch of the New York Public Library and at Fisk University's library.

Ask students: In what ways does this image fit the poem? *The golden skyscrapers in the distance symbolize the goal for which the speaker and his people long: they represent a new time or place where African Americans would be able to fulfill their dreams of equality and justice.*

◆ Critical Thinking

❹ **Interpret** Help students understand what the speaker means by "more subtle brute." Unlike a bully, those who discriminate are "subtle brutes" because they appear civilized, yet they inflict an insidious form of cruelty.

Customize for
Verbal/Linguistic Learners
❺ Ask students to comment on the connotations of the word *sable* in this context. *Sable mean blackness, but it also connotes the richness and softness of fur—a velvet night sky.*

◆ Literary Focus

❻ **Metaphor** Show how Cullen's reference to "seeds" extends the metaphor of a flowering plant. Discuss how these seeds symbolize African Americans' precious but fragile hopes for the future.

Answers

◆ Literature and Your Life

Reader's Response Answers will vary.

Thematic Focus Students may suggest groups that still experience discrimination.

☑ Check Your Comprehension

1. (a) "We" are "abject and mute." (b) "Others" are being tended by the "we" of the poem.
2. He presents the contrast between the black night sky and white stars.

◆ Critical Thinking

1. (a) The "we" are African Americans. (b) They are oppressed by the "others" who exploit them.
2. Possible response: The repetition signals that the speaker is not content.
3. Suggested response: The first stanza presents the speaker's idea of current race relations; the second stanza conveys the beauty of his people, and describes their long wait for social change.
4. Suggested response: The poem explores both the conflict between the oppressor and the oppressed, and the internal conflict of the oppressed.
5. Some students may feel that rebellion or positive action is the more appropriate response; others may favor patience.

Develop Understanding

One-Minute Insight The speaker of "A Black Man . . ." recalls with bitterness the injustices of slavery—how hard he has worked to benefit others and to protect himself from an uncertain future. Neither his "brothers" nor the world itself has been fair to him or to his children.

On a literal level, "Storm Ending" describes the awesome power of a thunderstorm. Metaphorically, the poet may allude to the storm of racial injustice, or the thunder of the Civil War.

◆ Reading Strategy

❶ Apply Historical Context Ask students to discuss how a black man's view of reaping might differ from a white man's view of the same task. *Students may say that reaping time was historically a time for enslaved Africans to do the harvesting work, but the profits would go to the white owners. Thus, reaping was a frustrating act that gave little satisfaction to the worker.*

▶Critical Viewing◀

❷ Compare and Contrast The posture of the figures and the barren landscape suggest weariness and despair that echo the general mood of the poem.

◆ Literary Focus

❸ Metaphor Ask students to explain what the speaker means by "my brother's sons" and the "bitter fruit" his children must feed on. *"My brother's sons" are the white man's sons, his brothers perhaps in age but not in status; the "bitter fruit" is the injustice and pain of slavery.*

Humanities

Hoeing by Robert Gwathmey.

This large-scale painting (it measures more than three feet by four feet in size) is particularly unsettling in its depiction of workers toiling with little to show for their work.

Ask students: Which elements of the painting make it an appropriate illustration for the poem? *The central figure of an exhausted African American, the depressing barrenness of the landscape, and the muddy, gloomy colors echo the speaker's pain.*

❶

A Black Man Talks of Reaping

Arna Bontemps

Hoeing, Robert Gwathmey, Carnegie Institute Museum of Art, Pittsburgh, Pennsylvania, © Estate of Robert Gwathmey/Licensed by VAGA, New York, NY

❷ ▲ **Critical Viewing** What emotion does the image convey? How does it compare with the mood of the poem? **[Compare and Contrast]**

I have sown beside all waters in my day.
I planted deep, within my heart the fear
that wind or fowl would take the grain away.
I planted safe against this stark, lean year.

I scattered seed enough to plant the land
in rows from Canada to Mexico
but for my reaping only what the hand
can hold at once is all that I can show.

Yet what I sowed and what the orchard yields
my brother's sons are gathering stalk and root;
small wonder then my children glean in fields
they have not sown, and feed on bitter fruit. ❸

◆ Build Vocabulary

stark (stärk) *adj.*: Severe

reaping (rēp′ iŋ) *v.*: Cutting or harvesting grain from a field

glean (glēn) *v.*: Collect the remaining grain after reaping

Viewing and Representing Mini-Lesson

This mini-lesson supports activity 7, p. 853.

Introduce Point out that this activity will allow students to use visual art in ways that support the vivid and evocative imagery of a poem.

Develop Have students select a poem, then choose one image from that poem that powerfully conveys the poem's message. Emphasize that in choosing an image to paint, students should not worry about their artistic "talent" or training.

Apply Provide students with supplies, or let them furnish their own. Suggest that before students begin painting, they close their eyes and picture their image in as much detail as possible. They may want to do some preliminary sketches to evaluate different visual concepts. When students are ready to paint, encourage them to use colors and lines any way they like, to convey the mood of the poem.

Assess Assess students' paintings on the basis of how clearly or effectively they illustrate an image from one of the poems. You may want to exhibit the paintings in the classroom.

Storm Ending ❹

Jean Toomer

Thunder blossoms gorgeously above our heads,
Great, hollow, bell-like flowers,
Rumbling in the wind,
Stretching clappers to strike our ears . . .
Full-lipped flowers ❺
Bitten by the sun
Bleeding rain
Dripping rain like golden honey—
And the sweet earth flying from the thunder.

Guide for Responding

◆ Literature and Your Life

Reader's Response What did you see as you read these poems? What did you hear?

Thematic Focus What statement do you think Bontemps is making about the experience of African Americans in the United States?

☑ Check Your Comprehension

1. In "A Black Man Talks of Reaping," why does the speaker plant "deep"?
2. (a) In "A Black Man Talks of Reaping," how much seed does the speaker scatter? (b) How much grain is he allowed to harvest? (c) Who reaps what the speaker has sown?
3. In "Storm Ending," what natural event does the poem describe?

◆ Critical Thinking

INTERPRET

1. (a) How would you describe the tone of Bontemps's poem? (b) What images or lines illustrate this tone especially vividly? **[Infer, Analyze]**
2. What does Bontemps's poem suggest about what African Americans have received in exchange for their hard work? **[Draw Conclusions]**
3. (a) In "Storm Ending," what is the speaker's attitude toward the event described? (b) How is the attitude conveyed? **[Analyze; Support]**

APPLY

4. A well-known aphorism states, "Whatsoever a man soweth, that shall he also reap." How does Bontemps's poem comment on this idea? **[Apply]**

Beyond the Selection

FURTHER READING

Other Works by Countee Cullen
Color, Copper Sun, The Ballad of the Brown Girl

Other Works by Arna Bontemps
God Sends Sunday, Black Thunder, Drums at Dusk

Other Works by Jean Toomer
Cane, Essentials, The Blue Meridian

We suggest that you preview these works before recommending them to students.

INTERNET

We suggest the following sites for additional information about the Harlem Renaissance and its well-known poets.

For information on the poets and on the Harlem Renaissance, go to **http://www.geocities.com/ athens/forum/4722/big.html** The Black Poetry Page is a good source for poetry by African Americans. Go to **http://www.sas.upenn.edu/~vbead**

We *strongly recommend* that you preview sites before you send students to them.

◆ Reading Strategy

❹ Apply Historical Context Discuss with students the layers of meaning in this poem. Aside from the literal weather event, they may be able to imagine events in the American past that could be seen as a powerful storm that broke and ended. *Students might suggest the end of slavery, brought on by the catastrophic Civil War.*

◆ Literary Focus

❺ Metaphor Challenge students to link the bell imagery to messages of freedom. *Students may connect the "bell-like flowers" and "clappers" (strikers that hang inside the bell) to the Liberty Bell, an American symbol of freedom.*

Reinforce and Extend

Answers

◆ Literature and Your Life

Reader's Response Responses should reflect the imagery in the two poems.

Thematic Focus Bontemps is conveying the injustice of seeing others reap what you have sown.

☑ Check Your Comprehension

1. He plants seeds deep to protect them from wind or birds.
2. (a) He scatters enough seeds to plant the area from Canada to Mexico. (b) He ends up with just a handful. (c) His "brother's sons" reap what the speaker has sown.
3. It describes a thunderstorm.

◆ Critical Thinking

1. (a) The tone might be described as bitterly ironic. (b) Answers include lines 7–8 and 11–12.
2. The poem suggests that African Americans have been treated extremely unfairly and that their hard work was rewarded with the bitter fruits of slavery.
3. (a) The speaker considers it both beautiful and majestic. (b) Images of flowers and honey, as well as word choices such as *gorgeously* and *sweet* indicate the speaker's appreciation.
4. The poem suggests that because injustice has been sown, injustice will be reaped.

Answers

◆ Reading Strategy

1. Students should realize that African Americans left the South with the hope of leaving oppression behind and finding a new life and new opportunities in the north.
2. By considering when it was written, students can appreciate how the poem reflects the bitter experience of slavery—a not-so-distant memory for African Americans in the first decades of the twentieth century.
3. Some students may feel that the poem is purely descriptive and exists apart from any historical context. Others may interpret the title as symbolizing an end to the storms of oppression or injustice and the start of a new era in African American life. Still others may see the poem's imagery as a reflection of rural life in the South.

◆ Build Vocabulary

Word Roots: *-cre-*
1. c 2. a 3. b

Using the Word Bank: Synonyms
1. a 2. b 3. a 4. c 5. c 6. a

◆ Literary Focus

1. (a) Cullen uses a metaphor of planting seeds and reaping fruit. (b) He uses the images of "bursting fruit," "buds," "bloom," and "seeds."
2. Bontemps uses the metaphor of sowing and reaping grain.
3. (a) Thunder is compared to a lush flowering plant. (b) He describes the plant's bell-like flowers. (c) He describes the flowers in more specific detail, likening them to bitten flowers that bleed or drip rain like nectar or honey.

◆ Grammar and Style

Possible responses include
1. The wind, cold and merciless, swept through the shack and chilled the woman.
2. Vast and cobalt, the ocean was visible through the porthole.
3. Many refugees arrived in this country penniless but determined to start anew.

Guide for Responding *(continued)*

◆ Reading Strategy

Connect to Historical Context

You can enrich your understanding of many literary works by connecting them to their historical contexts as you read. For example, reflecting on the fact that nearly a million blacks migrated to industrial northern cities from rural areas in the South in the late 1800's and early 1900's can help you appreciate Countee Cullen's and Arna Bontemps's use of agricultural metaphors in their work.

1. How can you deepen your appreciation of "From the Dark Tower" by reflecting on the northern migration of nearly a million African Americans in the late 1800's and early 1900's?
2. How can you enrich your reading of "A Black Man Talks of Reaping" by applying historical context?
3. Does your interpretation of "Storm Ending" change when you apply historical context? Explain.

◆ Build Vocabulary

Using the Latin Root *-cre-*

Many familiar words include the Latin root *-cre-*, meaning "to grow." Use the words that follow to complete the sentences.

a. crescendo **b.** creation **c.** increment

1. The salary schedule indicates the __?__ employees receive after each year's service.
2. The symphony begins quietly, but soon a __?__ introduces the central celebratory theme.
3. The __?__ of a new sports pavilion will bring thousands of dollars to the city.

Using the Word Bank: Synonyms

On your paper write the letter of the best synonym for each given word.

1. reap: (a) harvest, (b) sow, (c) plow
2. countenance: (a) cheer, (b) tolerate, (c) disregard
3. increment: (a) increase, (b) stability, (c) decrease
4. stark: (a) gentle, (b) steep, (c) severe
5. glean: (a) spread, (b) weigh, (c) collect
6. beguile: (a) delight, (b) annoy, (c) correspond

◆ Literary Focus

Metaphor

A **metaphor** is an implied comparison between two dissimilar things. An **extended metaphor** develops such a comparison throughout a literary work.

1. (a) What metaphor does Countee Cullen use to evoke the struggle between African Americans and other Americans? (b) What images does he use to extend this metaphor?
2. What metaphor appears in Bontemps's poem?
3. (a) What two things are compared in the extended metaphor presented in "Storm Ending"? (b) How does Toomer establish this comparison in the first four lines? (c) How does he develop it in the lines that follow?

◆ Grammar and Style

Placement of Adjectives

Although adjectives usually precede the words they modify, adjectives can sometimes be more effective if they are placed after the modified word.

In "From the Dark Tower," for example, Cullen places the adjectives *object* and *mute* at the end of the sentence—far from the pronoun *we* they modify.

We shall . . . /
Not always countenance, *object* and *mute*

In this position, adjectives sometimes need to be set off with commas.

An **adjective** can be **placed** before or after the noun or pronoun it modifies.

Practice On your paper, rewrite the following sentences, altering the position of the italicized adjectives. Be sure that the adjectives modify the same noun in your sentence. Make any necessary changes in wording and punctuation.

1. The *cold, merciless* wind swept through the shack and chilled the woman.
2. The ocean, *vast and cobalt,* was visible through the porthole.
3. Many *penniless but determined* refugees arrived in this country to start anew.

Reteach

Reteach extended metaphor with a written exercise. Suggest that students imitate the poetic method of Arna Bontemps in "A Black Man Talks of Reaping." Tell them that they will write their own extended metaphor, creating either a poem or a passage of prose. Call students' attention to Bontemps's first line, and discuss the fact that "I have sown" is a simple metaphor. Guide students to see that Bontemps adds detail upon detail, extending this metaphor throughout the poem. Suggest that students make up a simple metaphor of their own that expresses something important to them. Tell them to write this as a short, clear sentence. Then have them add more sentences and more details, sustaining and extending the metaphor.

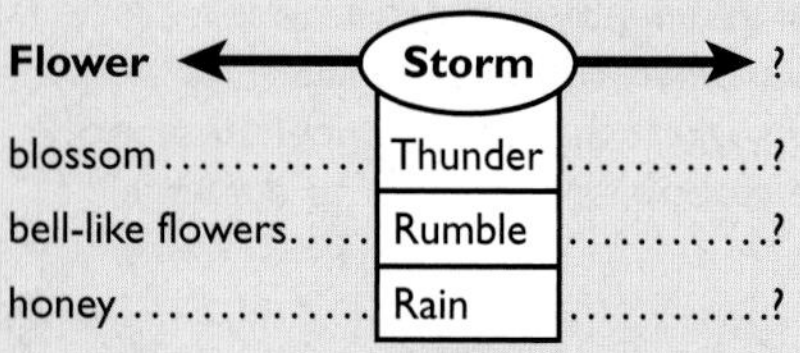

Build Your Portfolio

Idea Bank

Writing

1. List What was it like to live in Harlem during the 1920's among a community of artists? Ask the poets. Generate a list of questions you would ask if you had the opportunity. Then trade lists and try to answer the questions of a classmate.

2. Poem Write a poem in which you present an extended metaphor. Establish the comparison you are making early in the poem, and develop it using a variety of words and images.

3. Essay Although Cullen and Toomer were associated with the same literary movement, each had a distinct style. In an essay, compare and contrast the qualities of Cullen's sonnet and Toomer's lyric.

Speaking, Listening, and Viewing

4. Weather Report Take the part of a meteorologist and create a report providing a scientific explanation of a thunderstorm. In your report, use some of the words and images from Toomer's poem. **[Science Link]**

5. Visual Display Design a visual display that reflects some themes of the Harlem Renaissance. Include both prints and poetry. Remember the importance of layout when creating a visual display.

Researching and Representing

6. Research Report Choose an artist or musician from the Harlem Renaissance period and research his or her life and accomplishments. Present your findings in a report. **[History Link; Art Link; Music Link]**

7. Painting Use watercolors to create a painting that captures a striking image from one of these poems. **[Art Link]**

Online Activity www.phlit.phschool.com

Guided Writing Lesson

Description of Weather Conditions

Jean Toomer used poetry to describe a storm. You can use the same language—strong images and precise words—to describe a storm in prose. Think about the most memorable storm you've encountered and then write a few paragraphs that convey the experience.

Writing Skills Focus: Vivid Verbs

Poetry's conciseness demands careful attention to word choice. Use vivid verbs to describe action and evoke strong, clear images and ideas. Use action verbs instead of linking verbs to make your writing more lively. For example, look at the first line of Jean Toomer's "Storm Ending":

Model From the Poem

Thunder blossoms gorgeously above our heads . . .

The line could have read, "Thunder sounds gorgeous above our heads." However, since Toomer chose the vivid "blossoms" instead, the image of the storm is richer.

Prewriting Take a minute to imagine the storm you will describe. Consider the mood your essay will convey. It may help to personify the storm in your mind. It may be violent and dangerous, or it may be calm and reserved. Make a list of words to bring this mood across to your readers.

Drafting As you write your essay, choose precise words that communicate exactly what is happening. Include sensory details—sounds, smells, sights, textures, or tastes—that make your writing more vivid.

Revising Look for vague words to replace with more precise ones. Make sure your essay provides enough detail to bring the storm to life.

Idea Bank

Customizing for
Performance Levels

Following are suggestions for matching Idea Bank topics with your students' performance levels:
Less Advanced Students: 1, 7
Average Students: 2, 4, 6
More Advanced Students: 3, 5

Customizing for
Learning Modalities

Following are suggestions for matching Idea Bank topics with your students' learning modalities:
Logical/Mathematical: 4
Verbal/Linguistic: 6
Visual/Spatial: 5, 7

Guided Writing Lesson

Refer students to the Writing Process Handbook, p. 1192, for instruction on the writing process, and p. 1194 for further information on Description.

For more prewriting, elaboration, and revision strategies, see *Prentice Hall Writing and Grammar.*

Writers at Work Videodisc

Play the videodisc segment on Description (Ch. 1) featuring poet and author Rita Dove to see how she paints verbal pictures for her readers. Have students discuss how Dove gathers details for her descriptive writing.

Play frames 335 to 10985

Writing Lab CD-ROM

Have students complete the tutorial on Description. Follow these steps:

1. Students can use the Note Card Activity and Word Bins in the Gathering Details section to help them collect details.
2. Have students draft on computer.
3. Use the checker for vague or overused adjectives to aid revision.

ASSESSMENT OPTIONS

Formal Assessment, Selection Test, pp. 256–258, and Assessment Resources Software. The selection test is designed so that it can be easily customized to the performance levels of your students.

Alternative Assessment, p. 57, includes options for less advanced students, more advanced students, intrapersonal learners, verbal/linguistic learners, and interpersonal learners.

PORTFOLIO ASSESSMENT

Use the following rubrics in the ***Alternative Assessment*** booklet to assess student writing:
Poem: Poetry Rubric, p. 123
Essay: Comparison/Contrast Rubric, p. 118
Guided Writing Lesson: Description Rubric, p. 112

Prepare and Engage

LESSON OBJECTIVES

1. **To express and support responses to the text**
   - Critical Thinking Questions
   - Idea Bank: Dear Ricardo
   - Idea Bank: You Yearn
2. **To analyze literary elements**
   - Idea Bank: Literary Analysis
3. **To read in order to research self-selected and assigned topics**
   - Idea Bank: Graph
   - Idea Bank: Interview

Interest Grabber Ask students to imagine that they have been away from home for about a year, living somewhere quite different from their usual home. Have students brainstorm in groups for a list of things they imagine they would miss the most. Invite volunteers to share items from their lists; look for common threads. Then tell students that they are about to read a poem called "i yearn," which expresses one man's longings.

CONNECTIONS TO TODAY'S WORLD

i yearn

Ricardo Sánchez

Thematic Connection

FROM EVERY CORNER OF THE LAND

American writers in the first half of the twentieth century celebrated the nation's diversity by focusing on the environments from which they came. A writer's world may be defined by a geographic area, such as Robert Frost's New England, or by ethnic or racial connections, such as the African American identity celebrated in the Harlem Renaissance.

Historians used to describe the United States as a "melting pot" to suggest that people of different ethnic backgrounds came to the United States and blended into a single American culture. Today, many Americans argue that the "melting pot" metaphor is not accurate. They say that the United States is a multicultural society in which many distinct cultures exist side by side, retaining their individual identities. New phrases that describe the country's diversity call the United States a quilt, a rainbow, a salad bowl, or a mosaic.

In today's United States, ethnic communities nurture their own cultures and traditions while at the same time holding many distinctly American beliefs, such as freedom and equality. Just a few examples of such communities are the Chinatowns in New York and San Francisco, Arab communities in Michigan, and Scandinavian communities in the Midwest.

WRITERS CELEBRATE DIFFERENCES

Today's writers continue to explore the many ways of being an American. Hispanic Americans are growing in numbers and becoming increasingly vocal. Between 1980 and 1990, there was a 44 percent increase in the number of Hispanics living in the United States, and experts predict that by the middle of the twenty-first century, 21 percent of the U.S. population will be people of Spanish-speaking origin. Hispanic novelists, playwrights, and poets such as Ricardo Sánchez reflect on the ways in which their Hispanic roots intersect with U.S. culture to create new influences and identities.

RICARDO SÁNCHEZ (1941–1995)

Born in El Paso, Texas, and raised in a *barrio,* or Hispanic neighborhood, Ricardo Sánchez believed that his mission was to bring Mexican culture and traditions into the lives of his fellow Mexican Americans. He often wrote about the challenge faced by those who try to create a coherent identity from a mix of two cultures: Mexican and American.

Sánchez was an activist as well as a writer and an academic: He directed a health project for migrant workers, sat on the board of an El Paso health clinic, and founded a number of organizations for Mexican Americans. As a lecturer, consultant, and developer of television programs as well as a poet, Sánchez worked to educate all Americans about Mexican American culture.

Prentice Hall Literature Program Resources

REINFORCE / RETEACH / EXTEND

Selection Support Pages
Build Vocabulary, p. 263
Thematic Connection: From Every Corner of the Land, p. 264

Formal Assessment Selection Test, pp. 259–260; Assessment Resources Software

Resource Pro CD-ROM

Listening to Literature Audiocassettes

i yearn

Ricardo Sánchez

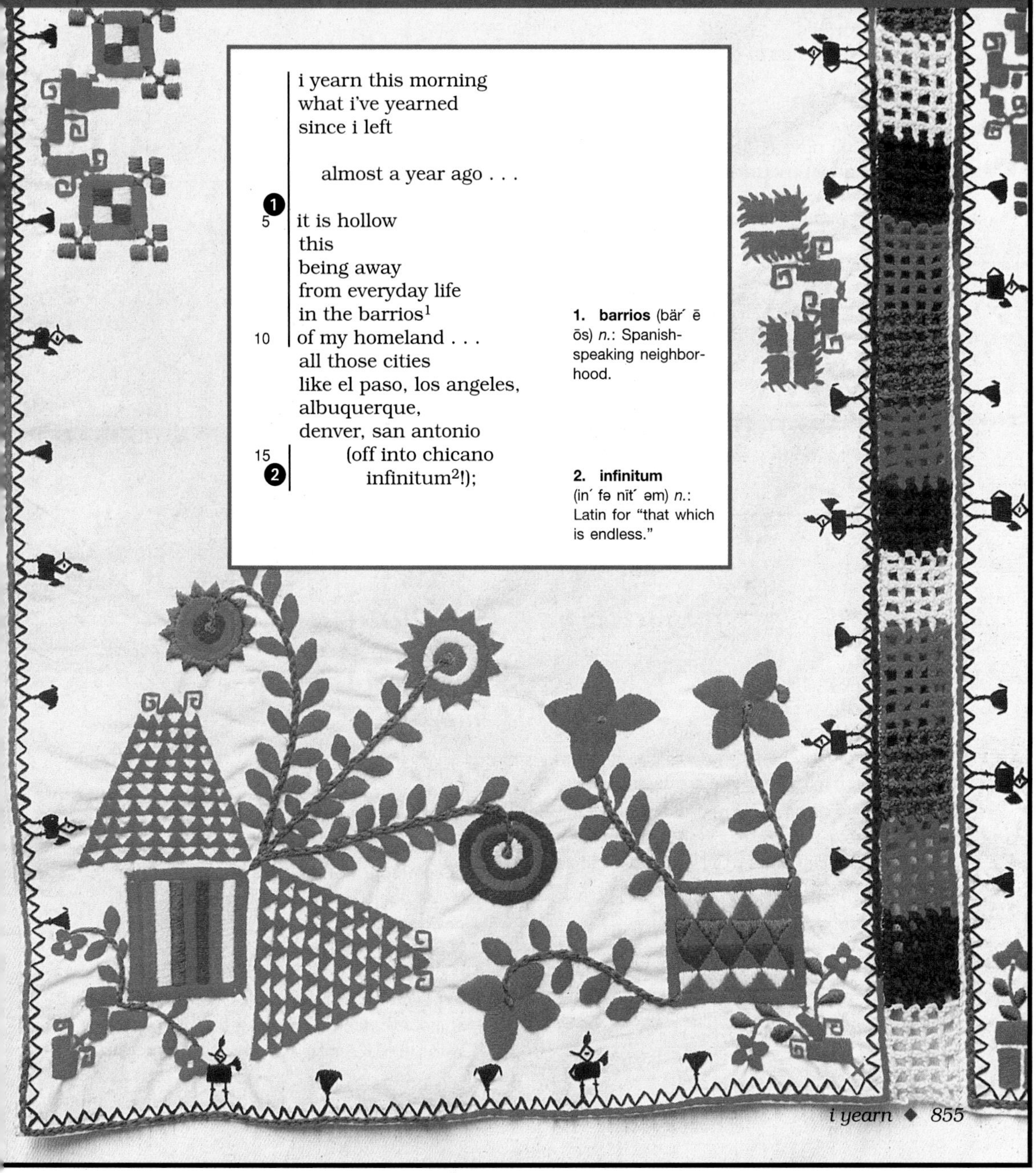

i yearn this morning
what i've yearned
since i left

almost a year ago . . .

❶ it is hollow
this
being away
from everyday life
in the barrios[1]
of my homeland . . .
all those cities
like el paso, los angeles,
albuquerque,
denver, san antonio
(off into chicano
❷ infinitum[2]!);

1. **barrios** (bär′ ē ōs) *n.*: Spanish-speaking neighborhood.

2. **infinitum** (in′ fə nīt′ əm) *n.*: Latin for "that which is endless."

Humanities: Art

Folk Art Identify the embroidered object that forms the background for the poem as a huipil (blouse) from the Tarascan people of Michoacan. Michoacan is a state in Mexico that borders on the Pacific Ocean, about two-thirds of the way to Guatemala; the Tarascans are Native Americans who live there.

Invite students to find out more about the folk arts associated with a culture of their choice. For example, they might investigate and describe the characteristic pottery of the Acoma people of New Mexico, the beautiful hand-woven *dhurrie* rugs of India, the dramatic batik work of Indonesia, or the delicate lacework of the people of Saba, in the Caribbean. Students can find representative examples of the folk art, and research how particular techniques or styles developed and how they are preserved and continued today.

Develop Understanding

One-Minute Insight The speaker reveals how much he misses being with fellow Chicanos: to hear the slang they speak, to eat the zesty foods they enjoy, and, most of all, to be relaxed and easy with people who share common bonds.

Connections to Today's World

Authors of diverse ethnic backgrounds have been gaining wide audiences today by writing about how their own culture both meshes and conflicts with mainstream American attitudes and values. These works tap the universality of the struggle to belong to two worlds, and a behind-the-mask look into at once familiar and foreign emotions and ways of life.

Customize for *Less Proficient Readers*

Ricardo Sánchez chooses to eschew standard punctuation and capitalization in his poem, and to include the Spanish style of punctuation around a question. This may be confusing to some students. Help them read the poem and discuss why Sánchez may have made this artistic choice. *Students may suggest that his use of the lower case with the pronoun I suggests a lack of self-esteem of the Chicano speaker in American culture, or suggests that everyone is equal; that no one should stand out more than others.*

Thematic Connection

❶ **From Every Corner of the Land** Help students recognize that although the poet writes specifically about what *he* yearns for, his plaintive cry has a universal appeal. Guide students to substitute something else for the word *barrios* to understand this. *Students may suggest words like the village, the city, the town, the suburb, the 'hood, the kibbutz, the encampment.*

❷ **Clarification** *Ad infinitum* is a Latin phrase that means without limit or end. Help students to apply this meaning to line 15 to better understand what the poet is saying. *"... off into chicano infinitum! ..." means that the cities he named are just some of many American cities with large Chicano populations.*

Thematic Connection

❶ **From Every Corner of the Land** Discuss with students how the speaker reflects a longing similar to that felt by many immigrants, and by Americans who come from parts of the country where regional dialects, accents, or figures of speech are spoken.

❷ **Enrichment** Point out to students that many cultures in warm or hot climates tend to have spicy foods in their traditional cuisine. This may be due in part to the fact that spiciness induces perspiration, which has a cooling effect on the body.

Reinforce and Extend

Answers

◆ *Literature and Your Life*

Reader's Response Encourage students to explain their responses.

Thematic Focus Students may point to the problems of intolerance, language barriers, and conflicting cultural values. They should recognize the benefits of diversity, including the opportunity to appreciate the heritage of many cultures.

☑ **Check Your Comprehension**

1. He misses the sound of Spanish being spoken by Chicanos, foods with "character" and the warmth of his fellow Chicanos.
2. He misses the warmth of his fellow Chicanos and their shared love for their culture.

◆ Critical Thinking

1. The poem begins with sadness, but becomes a celebration of the speaker's ethnicity.
2. The speaker feels no longer part of the everyday life of the barrios.
3. All the cities mentioned have Chicano populations.
4. He suggests that few or no Chicanos live in this environment.
5. People need to share a common heritage to feel a sense of belonging and to reaffirm their own ethnicity.

i yearn
to hear spanish
spoken in caló[3]—
that special way
❶ chicanos[4] roll their
tongues
to form
words
which dart or glide;

i yearn
for foods
that have character
❷ and strength—the kind
that assail yet caress
you with the zest of life;

more than anything,
i yearn, my people,
for the warmth of you
greeting me with "¿qué tal,
hermano?"[5]
and the knowing that you
mean it
when you tell me that you love
the fact that we exist . . .

3. **caló** (kä lō´) *n.*: Slang.
4. **chicanos** (chē kä´ nōs) *n.*: Mexican Americans, usually capitalized.
5. **¿qué tal, hermano?** (kā täl´ er mä´ nō): Spanish for "How are things, brother?"

Guide for Responding

◆ *Literature and Your Life*

Reader's Response The speaker describes a feeling of homesickness. What objects or experiences do you miss when you are away from home?

Thematic Focus Language and culture can bring people together or create a wall between them. What are the difficulties of a multicultural society? What are the benefits?

☑ **Check Your Comprehension**

1. List three things the speaker misses about his home.
2. What does the speaker miss most of all?

◆ Critical Thinking

INTERPRET

1. What is the poem's tone, or attitude? **[Interpret]**
2. What experiences make the speaker feel as he does? **[Infer]**
3. What do the cities mentioned in the poem have in common? **[Connect]**
4. What does the speaker suggest about the environment where he is currently living? **[Compare and Contrast]**

APPLY

5. What does this poem suggest about why people sometimes feel the need to be among others who share a similar background? **[Generalize]**

Beyond the Selection

FURTHER READING

Other Works by Ricardo Sánchez

The Loves, Ricardo Sánchez

Other Works by Chicano Writers

The House on Mango Street, Sandra Cisneros
"Barrio Boy," Ernesto Galarza
Bless Me, Ultima, Rudolfo A. Anaya

We suggest that you preview these works before recommending them to students.

INTERNET

To learn more, we suggest the following Internet site. Please be aware, however, that sites may have changed since this information was published.

The Sánchez family maintains a Web site that provides biographical information about Ricardo Sánchez, go to
http://www.dr-ricardo-sanchez.com/link.html

We *strongly recommend* that you preview sites before you send students to them.

Thematic Connection

From Every Corner of the Land

Successive waves of immigrants have made the United States a nation of enormous diversity. Although the immigration wave of the early 1900's mostly brought new citizens from both Eastern and Western Europe, many of today's immigrants arrive from Asia and Central and South America.

Spanish-speaking immigrants live in many states; notably large numbers inhabit California, New York, New Mexico, and Florida. As of 1990, nearly four-and-a-half million Americans were born in Mexico, the country from which Ricardo Sánchez's ancestors came.

For nearly all immigrant groups, the process of becoming an American may be difficult. During this period of transition, immigrants may savor the opportunities that America offers while they simultaneously miss their country of birth and feel that their identity is threatened.

1. What does Ricardo Sánchez mean when he refers to his "homeland"?
2. What aspects of life does Sánchez particularly associate with his Mexican roots?
3. To whom is Sánchez referring when he says, "my people"?

Idea Bank

Writing

1. **Dear Ricardo** Write a letter to Ricardo Sánchez, offering him moral support and urging him to concentrate on the positive aspects of being away from home.
2. **You Yearn** Write your own poem about the things you would yearn for if you were away from home for a year. Concentrate on the distinctive features of your community that you most enjoy. **[Social Studies Link]**
3. **Literary Analysis** Analyze the way in which "i yearn" begins as a poem with a negative mood and ends in a mood of celebration. Support your points with details and passages from the poem.

Speaking, Listening, and Viewing

4. **Interview** Interview friends, relatives, or others in the community to learn about the ethnic or regional foods they most enjoy. Ask questions to discover what images or associations people have with these foods. Record your interviews, and share highlights with the class. **[Community Link]**

Researching and Representing

5. **Graph** Using the census or other government documents, locate statistics about the immigration of a particular group to the United States. Graph the rise and fall over a set number of years. **[Math Link; Social Studies Link]**

Online Activity www.phlit.phschool.com

✓ ASSESSMENT OPTIONS

Formal Assessment, Selection Test, pp. 259–260, and Assessment Resources Software. The selection test is designed so that it can be easily customized to the performance levels of your students.

PORTFOLIO ASSESSMENT

Use the following rubrics in the ***Alternative Assessment*** booklet to assess student writing:
Dear Ricardo (letter): Expression Rubric, p. 109
You Yearn (poem): Poetry Rubric, p. 123
Literary Analysis: Literary Analysis/Interpretation Rubric, p. 127

Answers

Thematic Connection

1. The word "homeland" seems to refer to U.S. cities with large Chicano populations.
2. Sánchez associates a certain way of speaking, certain foods, and a certain kind of welcoming attitude with his culture.
3. Sánchez is referring to other Mexican-Americans.

Customize for
AP Students

Sánchez is generally regarded as one of the founding fathers of the Chicano literary movement. As an alternate Idea Bank activity, suggest that interested students research and report on Sánchez's remarkable life as a poet, activist, and teacher. The Internet site listed in the Beyond the Selection feature on the bottom of page 856 is a good source of information. They can also obtain a copy of *The Loves of Ricardo Sánchez,* a posthumous collection of his poetry, to learn more about how Sánchez's Chicano roots influenced his poetry.

Enrichment Challenge students to debate these questions: Is it possible to preserve one's own cultural identity and also have an identity as an American? What does it mean to be an American now? What will it mean in thirty years? A hundred years?

Idea Bank

Customizing for
Performance Levels

Following are suggestions for matching Idea Bank topics with your students' performance levels:
Less Advanced Students: 1
Average Students: 2, 4
More Advanced Students: 3, 5

Customizing for
Learning Modalities

Following are suggestions for matching Idea Bank topics with your students' learning modalities:
Intrapersonal: 2
Interpersonal: 4
Logical/Mathematical: 5

Prepare and Engage

LESSON OBJECTIVES

- To use recursive writing processes to write a statistical report
- To show correct use of the conventions of punctuation, including the correct use of semicolons

Establish Writing Guidelines

Distribute the scoring rubric for Research Report/Paper (p. 121 in ***Alternative Assessment***) to make students aware of the criteria on which their work will be evaluated. To customize the rubric to this workshop, see page 860.

You may also want to present the Writing Process Model of a Research Report from the ***Writing and Language Transparencies,*** pp.41–50.

Writers at Work Videodisc To introduce students to the elements of research writing, play the videodisc segment on Research Writing (Ch. 5) featuring music writer Gillian Gaar.

Play frames 3 to 9643

Writing Lab CD-ROM

If your students have access to computers, you may want to have them work in the tutorial on Research. Have students follow these steps:

1. Complete a Brainstormer activity designed to spark ideas for statistical reports.
2. Draft on the computer.
3. Use the tools in the proofreading section to ensure that their reports are accurate.
4. Review the Self-Evaluation Checklist to help them revise.

Statistical Report — Writing Process Workshop

The writers of the modern era often intentionally obscured the meaning or outcome of their literary works, leaving readers to draw their own conclusions. In a statistical report, however, the writer presents numerical data, interprets them, then draws conclusions for the reader. Although the subjects of statistical reports are diverse, they share a common characteristic: They use numbers to support a thesis, or main idea. These reports often include tables, charts, and graphs, as well as written text.

The following skills, introduced in this section's Guided Writing Lessons, will help you write a statistical report.

Writing Skills Focus

- ▶ **Use precise details,** including numerical data, to thoroughly support your thesis. (See p. 773.)
- ▶ **Define a clear and consistent purpose.** Decide on what you want your audience to learn, and focus your writing to achieve that purpose.
- ▶ **Maintain an objective tone.** Avoid argumentative, judgmental, or overly emotional language. (See p. 845.)
- ▶ **Elaborate on your main points** using a variety of methods, including charts and graphs. (See p. 801.)

MODEL FROM LITERATURE

Excerpt from "Most Immigrants Find the Dream"
by Brad Edmondson

In 1996, 9.3 percent of the U.S. population was foreign-born, according to the Census Bureau's Current Population Survey. Urban neighborhoods are crowded with Mexican, Chinese, Russian, and Filipino immigrants. ① Native-born Americans are revisiting concerns of the early 20th century. ② But there is strong evidence that today's immigrants will join the middle class just as the children of 1910 immigrants did. ③ The 1995 median income of foreign-born Americans who entered the U.S. in the 1970's ($17,400) is nearly equal to the national median for all persons with income ($17,500). Among naturalized citizens, median personal income is even higher than average ($18,500). ④

① The author names specific examples of nationalities of immigrants.

② Notice the writer's objective tone.

③ Here, the writer presents his thesis.

④ Statistics support the author's thesis.

Cross-Curricular Connection: Physical Education

Statistics and Sports Most students will be familiar with the use of statistics in televised sporting events. The information constantly provided by commentators is often supplemented by on-screen charts or tables to clarify its meaning for the viewing audience. To stimulate student interest in this writing workshop, you may want to have a class discussion on how an appreciation of statistics has enhanced students' understanding of their favorite sports. The following are possible topic ideas for students who choose to write their reports on a sports-related topic:

- An analysis of an athlete's performance over an entire career.
- A statistical comparison of stars from different eras in a sport's history.
- A prediction for the upcoming season of one of your school's varsity teams based on a statistical evaluation of returning players.

Prewriting

Choose a Topic Begin by considering statistics associated with areas of interest to you, such as sports, politics, or music. You might also scan newspaper articles to find other possible topics. Another option is to base your report on one of the following:

Topic Ideas

- World War I
- The World Series
- Population trends
- A career that interests you

Determine Your Purpose Use a K-W-L chart like the following example to define your purpose:

KNOW:	WANT to COVER:	LEARN:
a little about local charities	the giving habits of the citizens of this community	who gives money to charities in our community, and how much they give

Gather Data There are many sources for statistical data, including reference books on specific topics, such as *The Baseball Encyclopedia.* Almanacs, vertical files, and journals or magazines may also contain statistics. Search the Internet to find the most recent data.

Write a Thesis Statement Once you've gathered your data, look for one idea or conclusion that can be supported by the majority of the statistics you have found. Summarize this idea in a sentence in your opening paragraph.

Drafting

Cite Relevant Data Use only examples or statistics that directly relate to your thesis. Don't hesitate to return to the library for additional supporting data. Where appropriate, include charts or graphs. Introduce and explain each one you present.

Avoid Argumentative Language Don't inject your personal viewpoint; your thesis should be backed by facts and statistics. Note the differences between these examples:

- **Argumentative:** Only a fool could ignore the warnings about the cancer-causing effects of the sun.
- **Research-based:** People who want to stay healthy should protect themselves from the sun. An estimated 90 percent of skin cancers are caused by exposure to sunlight.

Applying Language Skills: Semicolons

Use **semicolons** to join clauses that are not already joined by a conjunction or to avoid confusion when independent clauses or items in a series already contain commas.

Examples:

Cornelia was dutiful; that was the trouble with her.

Zora learned much from her mother, who taught her to save; her teachers, who taught her to read; and the young ladies, who fostered her love for reading.

Practice Rewrite the following sentences, correcting or clarifying each with semicolons:

1. Countee Cullen graduated from New York University, he later earned a master's degree from Harvard.
2. It was a challenging assignment; I had to do research, which took hours, interview the county council members, and create my own charts.

Writer's Solution Connection
Language Lab

For more practice with semicolons, see the Quotation Marks, Colons, and Semicolons lesson in the Capitalization and Punctuation unit of the Language Lab CD-ROM.

Prewriting Strategy

To help students use a K-W-L chart in planning their own reports, have the class discuss what a chart might look like for each of the topic ideas provided in the student edition.

Customize for *Logical/Mathematical Students*

Challenge these students to use statistics that they gather and evaluate themselves according to professional standards of statistical analysis. Suggest that they conduct surveys with simple binary ("yes" or "no") responses in order to limit the number of variables in their results.

Writing Lab CD-ROM

The Organizing Details section of the tutorial on Research Writing includes many features to help students organize their reports: audio-annotated examples of thesis statements and organizational strategies; interactive instruction on grouping information; and video tips on organizing information.

Elaboration Strategy

Guide students to avoid writing reports that become bogged down in too many statistics. Though students may understand the theory of citing only relevant data, they may find it difficult in practice to omit many of the statistics that they worked so hard to gather. Point out that an asterisk or explanatory note can refer readers to more extensive tables or lists of statistics in an appendix that students can include with their reports.

Applying Language Skills

Semicolons Introduce this skill by explaining to students that writing a statistical report may necessitate that they present related items in a series. The proper use of semicolons is crucial to the clear presentation of such information.

Answers

1. Countee Cullen graduated from New York University; he later earned a master's degree from Harvard.
2. It was a challenging assignment: I had to do research, which took hours; interview the county council members; and create my own charts.

Grammar Reinforcement

In addition to the **Language Lab CD-ROM** lesson cited in the student edition, you can refer students to practice p. 89 in the *Writer's Solution Grammar Practice Book.*

Revision Strategy

One of the hazards of using statistics is the potential misinterpretation of data to draw spurious conclusions. A classic case of this practice often occurs in political campaigns, when a rival might claim that the incumbent candidate "cut spending" on a vital program when in actuality it was the annual *increase* in spending that was cut from previous years. Remind students to be critical of similar misstatements or errors in logic, such as claiming that a correlation implies a causal relationship.

Writing Lab CD-ROM

Refer students to the Revising and Editing section, which includes Revision Checkers for unity and coherence, transitions, and sentence length.

Publishing

If students choose to present their reports to family members or friends, remind them to add clarifying material to suit the audience.

Applying Language Skills

Accuracy of Charts and Graphs

Introduce the skill by explaining that using charts and graphs enables writers to connect with a wider audience.

Reinforce and Extend

Prentice Hall Writing and Grammar For more prewriting, elaboration, and revision strategies, see *Prentice Hall Writing and Grammar.*

Applying Language Skills: Accuracy of Charts and Graphs

Use these tips to ensure that the data in your charts and graphs are clear and accurate:

- Write labels and provide a legend for a chart or graph and its data.
- Be sure that percentages add up to 100; explain any discrepancies.
- Be consistent in labeling information (hours, minutes, seconds, and so on).
- Carefully copy the data when transferring them from one type of graph to another.

Writing Application Wherever possible, use charts and graphs to report numerical data in your statistical report. A chart conveys information that might take paragraphs to present in writing. A graph can highlight changes over a period of time. These visual aids will lend impact and clarity to your report.

Writer's Solution Connection Writing Lab

For help gathering statistical data, use the instruction in the Gathering Information section of the tutorial on Research Writing.

Revising

Review the Numbers It is easy to make typographical errors. To be sure the numbers in your report are accurate, check your statistics against your original source.

Use a Revision Checklist Use your answers to these questions, which are based on this lesson's focus points, to help you improve your statistical analysis:

- ▶ Does my introduction clearly state my purpose and present the thesis developed in the body of my report?
- ▶ Have I included enough specific examples, numerical data, and charts and graphs to support my thesis?
- ▶ Do I need to delete any examples or data that don't relate directly to my argument or thesis?
- ▶ Have I avoided argumentative, threatening, or judgmental language?

Revision Model

~~Through the insensitivity of cigarette smokers, many Americans face serious health risks.~~ ① Environmental tobacco smoke (ETS) represents a serious threat to public health in the United States. ② Conditions such as aggravated asthma, impaired blood circulation, bronchitis, and pneumonia can be linked to ETS. The American Cancer Society reports that ~~thousands of~~ ③ 3,000 people will die each year as a result of breathing the smoke of other people's cigarettes. ~~In the 1980's there were over 4.5 million cancer deaths.~~ ④

① The author deletes an argumentative and unnecessary sentence.
② Specific examples are added.
③ Numerical data is added to replace a vague reference.
④ The author deletes an irrelevant statement.

Publishing

▶ **Presentation** Share your report with an interested audience—your classmates or family members and friends. Add visual aids, and allow time for questions.

✓ ASSESSMENT		4	3	2	1
PORTFOLIO ASSESSMENT Use the rubric on Research Report/Paper in the ***Alternative Assessment*** booklet (p. 121) to assess students' writing. Add these criteria to customize the rubric to this assignment.	**Charts and Graphs**	The writer presents clear and appealing charts and graphs to heighten the impact of the report.	The writer presents charts and graphs with accurate information.	The writer rarely uses charts and graphs effectively.	The writer either avoids using charts and graphs altogether, or does so in an incoherent or inaccurate manner.
	Semicolons	The writer consistently uses semicolons to separate ideas or items in a series.	The writer makes at least one error in using semicolons.	The writer rarely uses semicolons or makes several errors when attempting to.	The writer avoids using semicolons altogether, or does so in an incorrect manner.

Student Success Workshop

Real-World Reading Skills — Analyzing Text Structure

Strategies for Success

Writers present their ideas using different text structures. Examples of organizing structures are comparison and contrast, cause and effect, and chronological order. Recognizing and analyzing these text structures can help you sort through the information in a text and give you the background to better understand what you read.

Comparison and Contrast A text that is trying to point out similarities and differences between two things or ideas will often have a structure that allows you to compare and contrast information. A good example of this is a newspaper article in which two solutions to a local problem are discussed. After you analyze the organizing structure, construct a comparison-and-contrast chart to show what the writer is saying.

Cause and Effect Writing often shows cause-and-effect relationships among pieces of information. A magazine article on changing weather patterns, for instance, may include a paragraph explaining that some scientists believe that global warming causes oceans to rise, thus affecting the number of hurricanes and floods in some areas. Here, the writer uses a cause-and-effect text structure to explain a point. As you recognize cause-and-effect relationships in a text, write them down to aid your understanding.

Chronological Order Text that is structured in chronological order shows the time in which events occurred. You might see a chronological structure when you are reading about a historical event or a scientific process. As you analyze a text that is structured chronologically, creating a timeline with dates, events, or procedures listed can help you comprehend the text more fully.

Apply the Strategies

Read the sample article. Then answer the questions.

> A 1998 study shows that children and teenagers who spend long hours in Internet chat rooms do not get enough exercise. In the 1970's, the study says, outdoor activities were extremely popular with teens. But as home video game systems and personal computers became popular in the 1980's, more and more kids spent their time sitting indoors. Today, many young people are experiencing health problems normally experienced by people in their thirties and forties. The study explains this phenomena by showing a link between the lack of exercise and the increase in the size and popularity of the Internet. The study suggests that teenagers should balance "chat time" with physical activity.

1. What does the writer compare and contrast? Explain how this organizing structure is effective for conveying the writer's message.
2. Create a cause-and-effect chart based on the information you've read.
3. Analyze the chronological structure by creating a timeline. Point out how the comparison-and-contrast and cause-and-effect relationships are correlated to the chronological structure.

✔ *Here are some situations in which to analyze text structures:*

- ▶ *Reading a memoir*
- ▶ *Comparing features and costs when planning to buy a new stereo system*
- ▶ *Reading a magazine article about political events*

Test Preparation Workshop

Analyzing Text Structure

Tell students that informational passages on standardized tests often contain one or more of the text structures named in this workshop. Present this sample test item:

The article above continues with information about four kinds of health problems that are seen in young Web surfers today. How might the paragraph be organized?

A The health problems are contrasted with health problems of teenagers in times past.

B The health problems are described to show what they have in common.

C The writer introduces ideas about the causes of the health problems.

D The writer traces the development of the health problems over time.

Discuss why a paragraph about "four kinds of health problems" is likely to have a comparison-contrast organization—making B the correct answer.

Prepare and Engage

LESSON OBJECTIVES

- To comprehend selections using a variety of strategies, including analyzing text structures such as compare/contrast, cause/effect, and chronological order for how they influence understanding

Customize for
Visual/Spatial Learners

Combine discussion of common text structures with examples of graphic organizers. Tables with labeled rows and columns, frames connected with arrows, and other concept drawings can help learners see the organization of ideas.

Apply the Strategies

Answers

1. The writer contrasts the activities of children and teenagers in the 1970's with activities since the growth of home video games and computers in the 1980's. The contrast is linked to the writer's message that young people today do not get enough exercise.
2. Possible chart:

Causes	Effects
increased popularity of video games, computers, and Internet	increased time spent sitting indoors
increased time spent sitting indoors	not enough exercise
not enough exercise	health problems

3. One possible timeline could show three decades and popular activities in each: the 1970's, outdoor activities; the 1980's, video game systems and personal computers; the 1990's, Internet chat rooms. The timeline compares and contrasts activities and shows possible causes of today's health problems among young people.

Prepare and Engage

LESSON OBJECTIVES

- To understand and interpret visual representations
- To analyze and critique the significance of visual representations

Customize for
Gifted/Talented Students
Groups may evaluate television news reporting for such standards as thoroughness, objectivity, and professional polish. One way to evaluate is to devise a rating scale to show how each program meets the standards. Students may publish their results, including supporting evidence for their ratings.

1. The main purpose of a television news story is usually to inform, but students should recognize that stories may also be chosen to entertain, to shock, to stir emotion, and so on. Sources of information include unbiased witnesses and people who want news reporters to draw attention to an issue.
2. After viewing local and national news reports on different network and cable channels, students may contrast features such as these: the number of stories covered, the depth of coverage, the kinds of feature stories chosen, the quantity of pictures, the quantity of talk, the selection of interviewees, the informational value of interviewees' remarks, number and kinds of commercials, and editorializing that is presented as objective reporting.
3. Partners' written evaluations of the content and effectiveness of a documentary should discuss these elements: viewpoints, depth of treatment, and sources of information.

Speaking, Listening, and Viewing Workshop

Viewing Media Critically

Every day, you have the opportunity to view the media in a variety of formats, including television news programs, documentaries, and the Internet. Before taking action or developing views about information presented by the media, it is important to evaluate it. Learning strategies to view the media critically will help you become a critical viewer.

Identify the Purpose What is the purpose of the program you are viewing? Straightforward news reports recount information objectively. Feature stories offer in-depth exploration and description of a topic. Editorials present persuasive views. Knowing what you are viewing and its purpose will help you evaluate the information.

Think Critically To establish criteria for viewing the media critically, think about the source of the information. Some news sources are better than others. Evaluate the journalist's experience, especially with the topic. Think about the reputation and objectivity of the news program. Remember that you are hearing and seeing only what the producer has chosen to include in the program. You are also getting the reporter's opinions. Ask yourself, "Is this an unbiased or a slanted viewpoint?" "How do the reporter's opinions affect my understanding?" "Am I getting the whole story?"

Apply the Strategies

Use the strategies for viewing the media critically to do these activities:

1. As a class, view a daytime news program. Identify the purpose of each story, and evaluate the source of the information.
2. View local and national news reports from several different news sources. Compare them, and explain your findings in an oral report.
3. With a partner, view a documentary. Write an evaluation of the program's content and effectiveness using the criteria for viewing.

Tips for Viewing the Media Critically

- Listen carefully to the information reported.
- Check surprising or questionable news in other sources.
- Note the "experts" interviewed or quoted and consider their qualifications to comment authoritatively.
- Be aware that not every news report is objective; determine if the journalist is sensationalizing the news or focusing on only one side of a story or issue.
- Develop your own views about the issues, people, and information reported in the news.
- View the complete report before taking any action or reaching a conclusion.

Beyond the Classroom

Career Connection
The Careers shelves of the library may have books about careers in broadcast journalism; students can also use the library catalog to find books under the Subject "Broadcasting—Vocational guidance." They may work together to create and fill out a fact sheet for each career: reporters, writers, editors, producers, directors, computer graphics and animation artists, technicians and engineers in digital media, sales and marketing specialists, and more. Possible fact sheet sections: job title, job description, salary range, employment prospects, advancement prospects, and prerequisites.

Test Preparation Workshop

Reading Comprehension — Sentence-Completion Questions

Strategies for Success

The reading sections of some standardized tests require you to correctly answer sentence completion questions. Use the following strategies to help you understand and answer these types of questions.

Anticipate Missing Words Read the question, using the context and your own knowledge to guess what word would best complete it. Then look among the answers. If your anticipated word isn't among the choices, look for synonyms or related words. For example:

1 When Julie skipped three classes and two band practices after months of perfect attendance, her friends wondered at her ___?___ behavior.

A erratic **C** slow
B reasonable **D** arrogant

After reading the question, you might think that the word "unusual" completes the sentence. Looking at the choices, you find that **A,** "erratic," is closest in meaning to your guess.

Analyze Sentence Meaning Often, more than one choice can complete the sentence. Analyze the sentence meaning, deciding if it is positive or negative, and eliminate choices that have the opposite sense. Look for context clues. Is another part of the sentence compared to or contrasted with the missing word? For example:

2 Those who believe it is barbaric and cruel to keep large animals in captivity think that to visit a zoo is ___?___.

A unfortunate **C** immoral
B advisable **D** courageous

It's clear from the context of the sentence that the correct answer will have a negative connotation, so **B** and **D** can be eliminated. The comparison to the words "barbaric" and "cruel" in the first part of the sentence makes **A** too mild an answer. **C** is the best choice.

Try Words in the Sentence You can often eliminate choices because they are illogical, the wrong part of speech, or inconsistent with the sentence meaning. If you are left with more than one possible response, use each remaining choice in the sentence. Choose the response that best fits. For example, look at the following question:

3 Although my good friend had ___?___ the movie, I was ___?___ by the weak plot.

A recommended; disappointed
B enjoyed; impressed
C criticized; convinced
D proposed; upset

C is illogical. Because the sentence begins with "although," the correct pair of words will have somewhat opposite meanings, eliminating **B.** Both **A** and **D** are possible, but using them in the sentence reveals that **A** is the best choice.

Apply the Strategies

Choose the answer that best completes each sentence.

1 In a court case, an impartial ruling, made without prejudice, is described as ___?___.

A fairly **C** unbiased
B absurd **D** unjust

2 After her book received scathing reviews, the embittered writer ___?___ the literary critics and their ___?___ followers.

A applauded; brilliant **C** revered; devoted
B resented; petty **D** forgave; deluded

Correlations to Standardized Tests

The reading comprehension skills reviewed in this workshop correspond to the following standardized test section:

SAT Sentence Completions

Test Preparation

Each ATE workshop in Unit 5 supports the instruction here by providing teaching suggestions and a sample test item:

- **Anticipate Missing Words** (ATE, pp. 645, 655, 759, 785, 817, 829, 847)
- **Analyze Sentence Meaning** (ATE, pp. 669, 687, 729, 769, 775)
- **Try Words in the Sentence** (ATE, pp. 693, 701, 803, 839)

LESSON OBJECTIVES

- To acquire an extensive vocabulary through reading and systematic word study; to rely on context to determine meanings of words and phrases such as figurative language, connotation and denotation of words, analogies, idioms, and technical vocabulary

Answers

1. (C) unbiased
2. (B) resented; petty

Test-Taking Tip

Anticipate

The workshop advises students to anticipate missing words in order to choose the most likely sentence-completion responses. Anticipating is a useful strategy for answering all kinds of multiple-choice questions. The test taker (1) reads the question or the stem (partial sentence) carefully; (2) thinks of a reasonable response; and (3) looks among the answer choices for a similar response.

Have students tell how they anticipated answers to the two questions at the end of this workshop. For item 1, the words *impartial ruling* and *without prejudice*, should have suggested synonyms such as *just, fair,* and *neutral,* which lead to the correct answer choice, *unbiased.* For item 2, the phrases *scathing reviews* and *embittered writer* should have suggested verb/adjective pairs such as *hated/foolish* and *despised/mindless.* The correct answer, *resented/petty,* comes closest to the anticipated one.

Planning Instruction and Assessment

Unit Objectives

1. To read selections from American literature written during the period 1946 to Present
2. To apply a variety of reading strategies, particularly strategies for reading fiction, appropriate for reading these selections
3. To analyze literary elements
4. To use a variety of strategies to read unfamiliar words and to build vocabulary
5. To learn elements of grammar, usage, and style
6. To use recursive writing processes to write in a variety of forms
7. To prepare, organize, and present literary interpretations

Meeting the Objectives

With each selection, you will find instructional material and portfolio opportunities through which students can meet these objectives. Further, you will find additional practice pages for reading strategies, literary elements, vocabulary, and grammar in the ***Selection Support*** booklet in the ***Teaching Resources*** box.

Test Preparation

The unit workshop, **Writing Skills: Punctuation, Usage, and Sentence Structure** (SE, p. 1143) is supported by teaching tips and a sample test item in the ATE workshop with each selection grouping.

- **Punctuation** (ATE, pp. 877, 891, 956, 992, 1025)
- **Grammar and Usage** (ATE, pp. 913, 925, 947, 1067)
- **Sentence Structure** (ATE, pp. 903, 935, 977, 1047, 1078)
- **Identifying Errors** (ATE, pp. 1005, 1059)

The following additional workshops in the ATE give teaching tips and a sample test item for applying the skill taught in the Student Success Workshop:

- **Written Composition** (ATE, p. 990)
- **Locating Facts and Details** (ATE, p. 1022)

Telephones (detail), 1954, Colleen Browning, Butler Institute of American Art

Humanities: Art

Telephones (detail), 1954 by Colleen Browning.

In this painting, the artist has painted on plywood, which gives the image a rough, grainy quality

Have your students link the painting to the focus of Unit 6, Prosperity and Protest, by answering the following questions:

1. Does the painting emphasize a sense of community or a sense of isolation? Explain. *The painting emphasizes people's isolation by showing them in separate phone booths, with no person relating to the others.*
2. In what ways does the painting relate to the unit's theme, prosperity and protest? *Some students may say that, by showing people in separate telephone conversations, the painting demonstrates that prosperity and technology isolate people rather than bringing them together.*

UNIT 6

Prosperity and Protest (1946–Present)

"Sometimes I can see the future stretched out in front of me—just as plain as day. The future hanging over there at the edge of my days. Just waiting for me."

—Lorraine Hansberry

Assessing Student Progress

The following tools are available to measure the degree to which students meet the unit objectives:

Informal Assessment

The questions on the Guide for Responding sections are a first level of response to the concepts and skills presented with the selection. Students' responses are a brief informal measure of their grasp of the material. Their responses on this level can indicate where further instruction and practice are needed. You may then follow up with the practice pages in the ***Selection Support*** booklet.

You will find literature and reading guides in the ***Alternative Assessment*** booklet, which you may give students on an individual basis for informal assessment of their performance.

Formal Assessment

In the ***Formal Assessment*** booklet, you will find selection tests and part tests.

Selection Tests The selection tests measure comprehension and skills acquisition for each selection or group of selections.

Part Tests Each part test, which calls on students to read a passage of literature they have not previously seen, applies the unit skills on a broader level. The Critical Reading section measures Unit Objectives 1, 2, and 3. The Vocabulary and Grammar section measures Objectives 4 and 5. The Essay section measures Objectives 1 and 6. Both the Critical Reading and Vocabulary and Grammar sections use formats similar to those found on many standardized tests, including the SAT.

Alternative Assessment

Portfolios As you review individual pieces or the collected work in students' portfolios, you will find assessment sheets available in the portfolio section of the ***Alternative Assessment*** booklet.

Scoring Rubrics You will find scoring rubrics for writing modes in the ***Alternative Assessment*** booklet. You can apply these to Guided Writing Lessons and to Writing Process Workshop lessons.

Speaking, Listening, and Viewing The ***Alternative Assessment*** booklet contains assessment sheets for speaking, listening, and viewing activities.

Learning Modalities The ***Alternative Assessment*** booklet contains activities that appeal to different learning styles. You may use these as an alternative measurement of students' growth.

Using the Timeline

The Timeline can serve a number of instructional purposes, as follows:

Getting an Overview Use the Timeline to help students get a quick overview of themes and events of the period. This approach will benefit all students but may be especially helpful for visually oriented students, English language learners, and those less proficient in reading. (For strategies in using the Timeline as an overview, see the bottom of this page.)

Thinking Critically Questions are provided on the facing page. Use these questions to have students review the events, discuss their significance, and examine the *so what* behind the *what happened.*

Connecting to Selections Have students refer back to the Timeline when beginning to read individual selections. By consulting the Timeline regularly, they will gain a better sense of the period's chronology. In addition, they will appreciate what was occurring in the world that gave rise to these works of literature.

Projects Students can use the Timeline as a launching pad for projects like these:

- **Timeline Follow-up** Have students bring the Timeline up to date by drawing an additional column in their notebooks and entering significant new American and world events. These can include new works of literature, scientific achievements, and political events.
- **Oral Reports** Have students choose an item on the Timeline and report to the class on some of its effects. For example, students might report on public reaction to the Vietnam Veterans Memorial, which was dedicated in 1982.

Timeline

1945 – Present

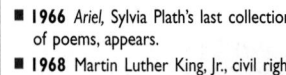

1945 | 1955 | 1965

American Events

- **1945** United States grants independence to the Philippines.
- **1946** Carson McCullers publishes *The Member of the Wedding.*
- **1949** *Death of a Salesman* by Arthur Miller is first produced.
- **1950** President Harry S. Truman sends troops to South Korea after North Korean invasion.
- **1952** Ralph Ellison publishes *Invisible Man.* ▼
- **1954** Supreme Court rules public school segregation to be unconstitutional.

- **1955** Flannery O'Connor publishes *A Good Man Is Hard to Find.* ◀
- **1959** Alaska and Hawaii admitted to the Union as the 49th and 50th states.
- **1959** Robert Lowell's *Life Studies* appears.
- **1960** John Updike publishes *Rabbit Run.*
- **1961** Joseph Heller publishes *Catch-22.*
- **1962** Environmental protection movement spurred by Rachel Carson's book *Silent Spring.*
- **1963** President John F. Kennedy assassinated in Dallas.

- **1966** *Ariel,* Sylvia Plath's last collection of poems, appears.
- **1968** Martin Luther King, Jr., civil rights leader, murdered in Memphis.
- **1969** Astronaut Neil Armstrong becomes the first person to set foot on the moon. ▲
- **1969** Joyce Carol Oates publishes *Them.*
- **1972** Last U.S. combat troops leave Vietnam; peace pact signed in 1973. ▲
- **1974** President Richard M. Nixon resigns. ▼

World Events

- **1947** India-Pakistan: India and Pakistan granted independence from Great Britain.
- **1948** Israel: United Nations establishes state of Israel.
- **1948** Germany: Soviet Union blockades Allied sectors of Berlin.
- **1950** England: Doris Lessing publishes *The Grass Is Singing.*
- **1954** England: *Lord of the Flies* by William Golding appears.

- **1955** Argentina: Jorge Luis Borges publishes *Extraordinary Tales.*
- **1957** Ghana: Ghana emerges as independent nation.
- **1957** USSR: *Doctor Zhivago* by Boris Pasternak appears.
- **1959** Cuba: Fidel Castro comes to power. ▲
- **1959** Germany: East Germany builds Berlin Wall.
- **1962** USSR: *One Day in the Life of Ivan Denisovich* by Alexander Solzhenitsyn appears.

- **1967** Israel: Israel gains territory from Arab states in Six-Day War.
- **1967** South Africa: Dr. Christiaan Barnard performs first human heart transplant.
- **1969** Northern Ireland: Long period of violence begins between Catholics and Protestants.

- **1972** China: Nixon makes historic visit to China. ◀
- **1972** Mexico: Octavio Paz publishes *The Other Mexico.*
- **1973** Middle East: Embargo on Middle East oil produces world shortages.

Getting an Overview of the Period

Introduction To give students an overview of the period, indicate the span of dates covered in the Timeline. *Subtract 1945 from 1997 to get 42 years.* Into what units is this period divided? *It's divided into ten-year units.* Next, point out that the Timeline is divided into American Events (on top) and World Events (on bottom). Have them scan the Timeline, looking both at the American Events and the World Events. Point out that the events in the Timeline often represent beginnings, turning points, and endings (for example, astronauts first landed on the moon in 1969).

Key Events Have students identify key events related to protest, one of the unit's themes. *Such events might include the Supreme Court ruling against segregation (1954), the beginning of the environmental movement (1962), the assassination of Martin Luther King, Jr. (1968), and the end of the Vietnam War (1972).* What events indicate progress or setbacks in space travel and exploration? *These include the first landing of humans on the moon (1969); Sally Ride's experience as the first American woman in space (1983); the explosion of the space shuttle* Challenger *(1986); and the mission to Mars (1997).*

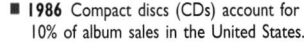

1975 | 1985 | 1995

American Events

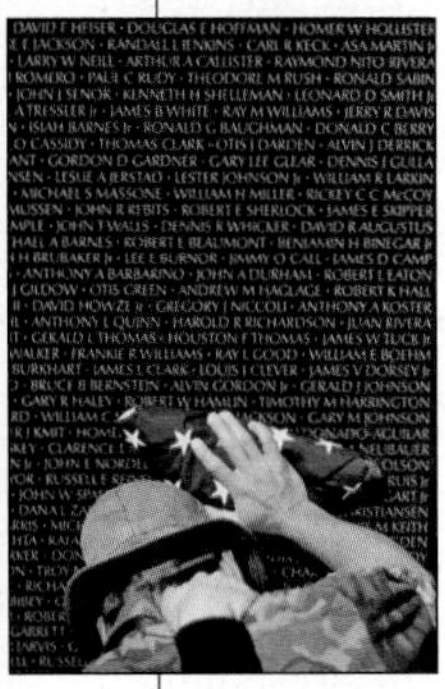

- **1979** Militant Iranian students take more than 50 Americans hostage in Teheran.
- **1980** Ronald Reagan elected president.
- **1982** Vietnam Veterans Memorial dedicated in Washington, D.C. ◀
- **1982** Alice Walker publishes *The Color Purple*.
- **1983** Sally Ride becomes the first American woman to travel in space.

- **1986** Compact discs (CDs) account for 10% of album sales in the United States.
- **1986** Space shuttle *Challenger* explodes after launch from Cape Canaveral.
- **1987** President Reagan and Soviet leader Mikhail Gorbachev sign the INF treaty, agreeing to ban short-range and medium-range nuclear missiles. ▲
- **1988** George Bush elected president.
- **1990** Carol Moseley Braun becomes the first African American woman elected to the Senate.
- **1990** Congress passes the Americans With Disabilities Act, prohibiting discrimination against people with disabilities. ▶
- **1992** Bill Clinton elected president.
- **1993** Toni Morrison wins Nobel Prize for Literature.
- **1993** Congress passes the North American Free Trade Agreement.

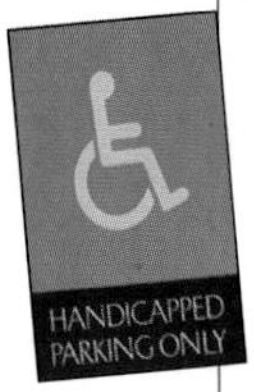

- **1995** Amy Tan publishes her third novel, *The Kitchen God's Wife*.
- **1996** Summer Olympic Games held in Atlanta, Georgia.
- **1997** Frank McCourt's autobiography *Angela's Ashes* wins Pulitzer Prize.
- **1997** Pathfinder mission and lander/rover Sojourner reach Mars; photographs of planet's landscape sent back to Earth.
- **1997** Congress passes a law allowing the line item veto. President Clinton is the first president to exercise the power.

World Events

- **1979** India: Mother Teresa wins Nobel Prize for Peace.
- **1979** Vietnam: Hundreds of thousands of "boat people" flee Vietnam.
- **1979** Trinidad: V. S. Naipaul publishes *A Bend in the River*.
- **1979** England: Margaret Thatcher becomes British prime minister.
- **1981** Poland: Polish trade union movement, Solidarity, suppressed.

- **1986** USSR: Chernobyl nuclear disaster spreads radioactive cloud across Eastern Europe.
- **1989** Eastern Europe: Berlin Wall comes down.
- **1989** China: Pro-democracy demonstrations violently suppressed at Tiananmen Square.
- **1991** Middle East: Unified forces led by U.S. defeat Iraq in Persian Gulf War.
- **1992** Russia: Boris Yeltsin is elected president.
- **1993** Middle East: Israel and the PLO sign an unprecedented peace agreement.
- **1994** South Africa: Nelson Mandela becomes the first democratically elected president. ▲

- **1997** China: Hong Kong returns to Chinese rule, ending 155 years of British rule. ▼

▶Critical Viewing◀

1. What is the mood of the image of the Vietnam Veterans Memorial (1982)? **[Interpret]** *Students may say the names of the dead overpower the image of the soldier and that the image has a somber, sad mood.*
2. What is unusual about the flags in the 1987 photo featuring U. S. President Reagan and Soviet leader Gorbachev? **[Make Connections]** *Each leader is sitting in front of the flag of the other's country.* How does this add to the moment as the men sign a treaty to ban certain nuclear missiles? **[Assess]** *It suggests they are not enemies.*
3. What are the benefits of using a symbol like the one on the "Handicapped Parking Only" sign (1990)? **[Evaluate]** *Such a symbol can be understood in areas where a number of languages are spoken.* What are the disadvantages of such a symbol? **[Evaluate]** *It suggests that all people with disabilities travel in wheelchairs.*

◆Critical Thinking

1. (a)When did the Supreme Court rule that public school segregation is unconstitutional? *The Supreme Court's ruling was in 1954.* (b) What is the relationship between that ruling and the civil rights movement of the 1950's and 1960's? *Many students will realize that the Brown decision prompted further efforts to integrate schools.* **[Analyze Cause and Effect]**
2. (a) Name two important public figures that were assassinated during this period. *John F. Kennedy was assassinated in 1963 and Martin Luther King, Jr. in 1968.* (b) What do these events suggest about the decade in which they occurred? *They suggest that the decade of the 1960's was turbulent.* **[Infer]**
3. (a) Identify two important political events occurring in Eastern Europe in the 1980s. *In 1981 the Polish trade union movement, Solidarity, was suppressed. In 1989, the Berlin Wall came down.* (b) Taken together, what story do these events tell about Soviet control of Eastern Europe? *The first event suggests that the Soviet Union was having trouble with protest movements. The second suggests that the Soviet Union was coming apart.* **[Connect]**
4. (a) How long after the end of the Vietnam War was the Vietnam Veterans Memorial dedicated? *The memorial was dedicated in 1982, 9 years after the peace pact was signed in 1973.* (b) Do you think the dedication of the memorial meant that arguments over the war were finally coming to an end? *Some students may speculate that the dedication of a monument meant that some sense of conciliation had been reached. Others may point out that to this day, people disagree about the Vietnam War.* **[Speculate]**
5. What recent events after 1997 could be possible entries in a timeline like this one? **[Relate]** *The events that students choose should be important turning points, firsts, or milestones in the fields of politics, literature, science, music, or art.*

Customize for
Less Proficient Readers
Have students brainstorm to list issues and trends of contemporary life. After they have developed this framework of prior knowledge, have them look for evidence of these issues and trends in The Story of the Times.

Customize for
English Language Learners
Give these students the opportunity to supplement The Story of the Times with background information from their own culture.

Customize for
Musical/Rhythmic Learners
Have these students identify and present to the class examples of contemporary styles in music. These presentations can include the playing of recordings. Then students can discuss how, or if, the music relates to issues and trends mentioned in The Story of the Times.

Customize for
AP Students
Ask more advanced students to create a time capsule for later generations that gives background on the era 1946 to Present. Have them refer to The Story of the Times and A Graphic Look at the Period in devising a collection of artifacts, manuscripts, timelines, recordings, and any other items they choose.

Answers to
A GRAPHIC LOOK

Analyze Cause and Effect By demonstrating that African Americans could compete in professional baseball, Robinson prompted people to think that African Americans could succeed in other professional sports and in all professions and trades.

Contrast Highways enable commuters to move more quickly between work and home than high-access local roads would allow.

A GRAPHIC LOOK AT THE PERIOD

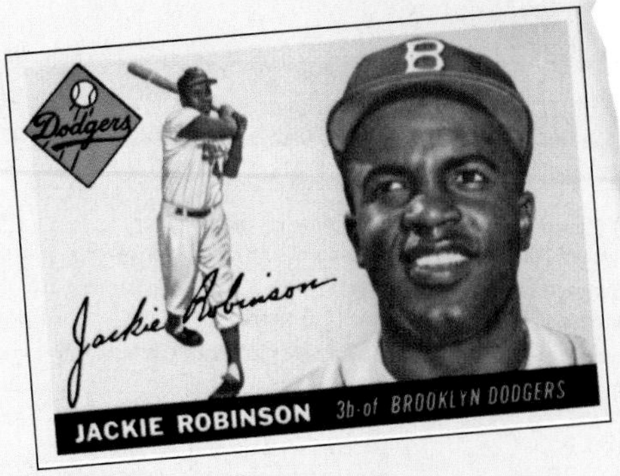

▲ **Analyze Cause and Effect** Astonishing as it may seem today, African Americans could not play baseball in the major leagues until Jackie Robinson broke the color barrier in 1947. How might Robinson have paved the way for African Americans in other sports and other occupations?

▲ **Contrast** Automobiles like this 1958 Oldsmobile would change a great deal about the United States. The Interstate Highway Act of 1956, for example, set plans in motion for a 41,000-mile national network of roadways. What benefits do highways provide commuters that local roads do not?

The Story of the Times

1946 – Present

Looking to the future is a natural part of the human experience. Much of the technology that has become widespread since 1945—television and computers in particular—shows us a brighter future. The new technology does make life easier and more pleasant. Paradoxically, it also introduces complexities that were unknown in earlier days.

The years from the end of World War II to the present day have been a time of change. Great strides have been made in civil rights and women's rights. Popular entertainment has changed dramatically, not just in presentation (from radio to television, from phonographs to CDs) but also in style (from big bands to rock music). These changes and others have had an effect on American literature. Their effect seems somehow less dramatic than the changes themselves, however.

Historical Background

The United States emerged from World War II as the most powerful nation on Earth. Proud of their role in the Allied victory, Americans now wanted life to return to normal. Soldiers came home, the rationing of scarce goods ended, and the nation prospered. Despite postwar jubilation, however, the dawn of the nuclear age and the ominous actions of the Soviet Union, including the establishment of dominance throughout Eastern Europe, meant that nothing would be the same again.

In 1945, the United Nations was created amid high hopes that it would prevent future wars. Nonetheless, a Cold War between the Soviet Union and the West began as soon as World War II ended. It was in Asia, however, that the first armed conflict came. In 1950, President Harry S. Truman sent American troops to help anti-Communist South Korean forces turn back a North Korean invasion.

Cross-Curricular Connection: Social Studies

Brown v. Board of Education In 1951, Oliver Brown sued the Topeka, Kansas, Board of Education to allow his eight-year-old daughter Linda to attend a school that only white children were allowed to attend. She had been going to a school farther away that was intended for African Americans only. When the case was argued before the Supreme Court, the African American lawyer Thurgood Marshall argued for Brown and against segregation in any of America's schools.

The court's ruling on May 17, 1954 was a historic one. It declared that "separate facilities are inherently unequal." President Eisenhower, who privately disagreed with the ruling, did not speak out for it publicly but said he would support "constitutional processes." Soon after, the court ruled that local school boards should move to desegregate "with all deliberate speed."

Ask students why this ruling was so important. *Many will see that it challenged the decades-old doctrine of segregation.*

From Quiet Pride to Activism Americans of the 1950's are sometimes referred to as "the Silent Generation." Many of them had lived through both the Great Depression and World War II. When peace finally arrived, they were glad to adopt a quiet, somewhat complacent attitude. They greatly admired President Dwight D. Eisenhower, one of America's wartime heroes.

Near the end of the 1950's, the Soviet Union launched *Sputnik*, the first artificial satellite to orbit the Earth. This Soviet space triumph spurred many people to call for changes in American science and education. President John F. Kennedy, elected in 1960, promised to "get the nation moving again." He had little time to do so, however, before his tragic assassination in 1963.

Kennedy's assassination was followed by an escalating and increasingly unpopular war in Vietnam. A wave of protest followed. Gone were the calm of the Eisenhower years and the high hopes of Kennedy's brief administration. In their place came idealistic but strident demands for rapid change: greater "relevance" in education, more progress on civil rights, an immediate end to the Vietnam War. It was a time of crisis and confrontations.

Real and lasting gains were made in civil rights after World War II. Segregation in the public schools was outlawed by the Supreme Court in 1954. Tragedy struck in 1968, however, when civil rights leader Martin Luther King, Jr., was assassinated in Memphis, Tennessee. Riots broke out in many cities across the nation.

A Quest for Stability The upheavals of the 1960's brought a conservative reaction. Many Americans longed for a return to "the good old days." President Richard M. Nixon, elected in 1968, promised to end the Vietnam War and to restore order in the nation. Nixon's achievements were soon overshadowed by the Watergate affair. This scandal forced his resignation from the presidency in 1974.

Civil rights activism continued during the 1970's, and another movement attracted growing

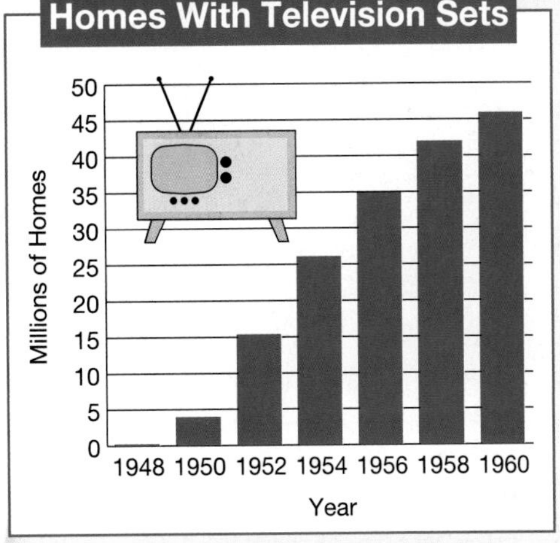

▲ **Draw a Conclusion** Before 1950, television was a novelty. By the end of the decade, however, television sets were a common feature in American homes. What factors might have influenced the steady rise in television ownership?

▲ **Make a Connection** The Beatles—an enormously successful British rock band—took over the American music scene in 1964. They created a sensation wherever they appeared. What role does television play in creating celebrities?

Connection to the Literature

- In reading Flannery O'Connor's "The Life You Save May Be Your Own," p. 879, students will experience a work that runs counter to the complacency of the 1950's. (The story first appeared in a full-length collection in 1955.)
- As students will read in The Story of the Times, this era is one in which diverse groups have asserted their rights. Students have a chance to appreciate the diversity of contemporary literature by reading selections like the excerpt from *The Names* by N. Scott Momaday, p. 936; "Mint Snowball" by Naomi Shihab Nye, p. 940; "Suspended," by Joy Harjo, p. 942; "Everyday Use," by Alice Walker, p. 948; "Freeway 280," by Lorna Dee Cervantes, p. 978; "Who Burns for the Perfection of Paper," by Martín Espada, p. 979, and others.

Answers to

A Graphic Look

Draw a Conclusion The steady rise in television ownership might have resulted from falling prices, improving technology, increased advertising and appealing programs.

Make a Connection Television allows audiences of thousands or millions to see a performer or a group. This kind of publicity can make people into instant celebrities, household names across the country.

Cross-Curricular Connection: Social Studies

The Civil Rights Movement After scoring major legal victories through the 1950's, including the famous decision in the Brown v. Board of Education case (see the note on page 868), the civil rights movement gained support in the 1960's. African Americans and others attempted to end segregation and secure voting rights in the South. This battle was hard fought and sometimes violent, but it began to produce results by the mid-1960's. With desegregation progressing, the movement began to focus on economic injustice in cities.

Martin Luther King, Jr., was perhaps the most important leader in the civil rights movement. Both his father and grandfather were ministers, and he followed in their footsteps. He was also influenced by the teachings of the Indian leader Mohandas Gandhi, who believed that strong foes could be vanquished through nonviolence.

Ask students why King chose a nonviolent approach. *Reasonable answers include: It is morally preferable to avoid violence. Also, when you are in the minority, it makes strategic sense to appeal to people's better instincts.*

Historical Background

Comprehension Check ☑

1. What international organization was created in 1945? Briefly describe this organization's chief goal. *The United Nations was founded in 1945. Its goal was to prevent future wars.*
2. Why are Americans of the 1950's sometimes referred to as "the Silent Generation"? *Having lived through the Great Depression and World War II, they were glad to live quietly.*
3. In what way did the 1960's differ from the 1950's? *The 1960's—which saw the assassinations of Kennedy and King and protests against the Vietnam War—were years of crisis and confrontation. The 1950's were characterized by a greater acceptance of things as they are.*
4. In the years after World War II, what new medium changed the leisure habits of Americans? *Television changed the leisure habits of Americans.*
5. What type of regions grew most rapidly as a result of the automobile? *The automobile made possible an explosive suburban growth.*

▶Critical Viewing◀

1. In what ways would America be different without cars and televisions? **[Speculate]** *Students may say that more people might travel by public transportation and that there might be more extensive rail lines connecting cities. Also, people might provide more of their own entertainment.*
2. Is it accurate to describe this era as one of protest? **[Evaluate]** *Students agreeing with the premise will point out the civil rights movement, the women's movement, and Vietnam War protests. Other students may distinguish among decades, pointing to the 1960's as a time of protest, with various movements continuing past that decade.*
3. What is the one most important development of this era? Explain. **[Support]** *Students should justify the importance of whatever issue or trend they choose to emphasize. For example, students might point to the civil rights movement as an attempt to fulfill the founders' promise of equality for all.*

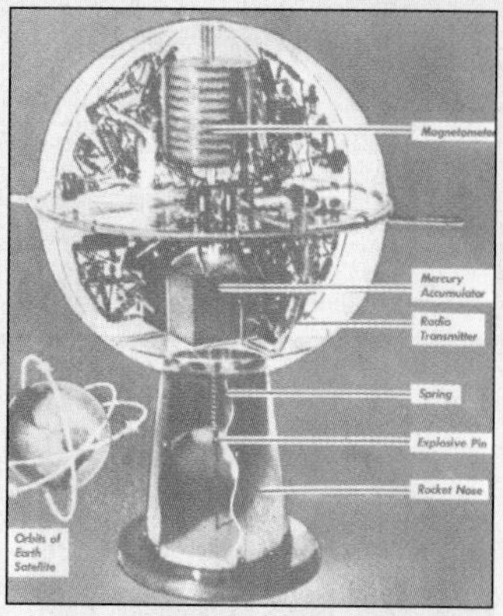

▲ **Analyze Cause and Effect** On October 5, 1957, the Soviet Union launched the world's first artificial satellite. The satellite, called *Sputnik I*, orbited the Earth once every hour and 35 minutes. The following year, the Congress National Defense Education Act of 1958 was passed, endorsing reforms in education. Why would the Soviet Union's success lead to changes in science and math education in American schools?

▲ **Make an Inference** The American Indian Movement (AIM) was formed in 1968 to address Native American rights. One goal of Native American activists has been to force the federal government to honor treaties made in the 1800's. In this photograph, AIM leader Dennis Banks leads a protest at Mount Rushmore, South Dakota. Why were so many treaties made and then broken?

attention—the women's liberation movement. Although women had earned the right to vote in 1920, discrimination still existed. Women received lower pay than men did for the same jobs, and promotion was more difficult. Betty Friedan's *The Feminine Mystique,* published in 1963, called for change. The women's movement grew steadily through the 1970's.

After Jimmy Carter's one-term presidency, the nation sent Ronald Reagan to the White House. A former film star and governor of California, Reagan proved to be a popular and persuasive president. His reelection in 1984 was one of the biggest landslide victories in American history. In 1988, George Bush, Reagan's vice president, was elected to the presidency. Seeking reelection in 1992, Bush faced a tough fight against high unemployment, a recession, growing dissatisfaction with government, and his youthful opponent. Democrats Bill Clinton and Al Gore, the youngest ticket in American history, won the election. Despite the 1994 elections that voted many Democratic Congress members out of office, Clinton won reelection in 1996.

The Changing Scene Commercial television was still in its infancy at the end of World War II, but it was on the verge of spectacular growth. Over the next few years, television changed the leisure habits of Americans.

The postwar period was a time of explosive suburban growth, made possible by the automobile. At first, most suburban homeowners worked in the nearby city and commuted to their jobs by train, bus, or car. Then, major corporations began establishing suburban headquarters, and workers could live nearby or commute short distances from one suburb to another. Even more recently, advanced technology allows people to "telecommute"—working in home offices and staying connected by Internet, phone, and fax.

The world has changed dramatically since 1945, and it is still changing. These changes have had an impact on the literature of the time, although this impact has not always been obvious.

Literature of the Period

Variety and Promise The turbulence of contemporary times has not fostered a literary revolu-

Humanities: Music

The Music of Aaron Copland Play for students the excerpt from Copland's *Appalachian Spring* on the **Listening to Music: The American Experience Audio CD.** Tell them that Copland (1900–1990) is widely regarded as America's greatest composer. His works range from jazz- and blues-influenced compositions to orchestral pieces to ballets reflecting the influence of folk music.

Appalachian Spring, a ballet composed in 1944, is one of Copland's most popular works. It tells the story of a "pioneer celebration of Spring in a newly built farmhouse in Pennsylvania in the early 1800's." The movement students will hear celebrates a young couple's new life together. Based on the Shaker hymn "Simple Gifts," the movement is a theme with variations, the theme being introduced by a solo clarinet and each variation becoming more elaborate.

Ask students what is specifically American about this work. *Even if students do not know, or have not been told about, "Simple Gifts," they will probably recognize that the melody comes from an old American song or hymn.*

tion of the kind that occurred in the 1920's, yet it has contributed to the development of a variety of literary movements that are often collectively referred to as Postmodernism. While many writers have been content to build on the experiments of the Modernists, others have sought to create works that stand apart from the past. Some writers have explored new literary forms and techniques, composing works from dialogue alone, creating works that blend fiction and nonfiction, and/or experimenting with the physical appearance of their work. Other writers have focused on capturing the essence of contemporary life in the content of their works, often expressing themes concerning the impersonal and commercial nature of today's world.

Authors for a New Era Although contemporary writers have produced a wide variety of impressive works, it is all but impossible to predict which writers will achieve lasting fame and which will not. Time is needed to certify greatness. Modern readers and critics have their favorites, of course. Some of them will undoubtedly become part of America's enduring literary legacy.

Every writer owes a debt to those writers who have gone before. In that sense, literature is cumulative. The earliest American literature, except for that of the Native Americans, was based on European models. Writers in the United States today can look to a rich heritage of their own. Contemporary novelists are well aware of Nathaniel Hawthorne, Mark Twain, Ernest Hemingway, and William Faulkner. Short-story writers know Edgar Allan Poe, Willa Cather, and Eudora Welty. Poets study Emily Dickinson, Walt Whitman, and Langston Hughes. Playwrights are familiar with Eugene O'Neill and Thornton Wilder.

Contemporary novelists of stature include Carson McCullers, Norman Mailer, Bernard Malamud, John Updike, Flannery O'Connor, Joyce Carol Oates, Anne Tyler, and Alice Walker. Many of these novelists have written short stories as well. Flannery O'Connor and John Updike are modern masters of the short-story form. Other writers, such as Donald Barthelme and Ann Beattie, have written novels but are better known for their short stories. Isaac Bashevis Singer, a Polish-born New Yorker who

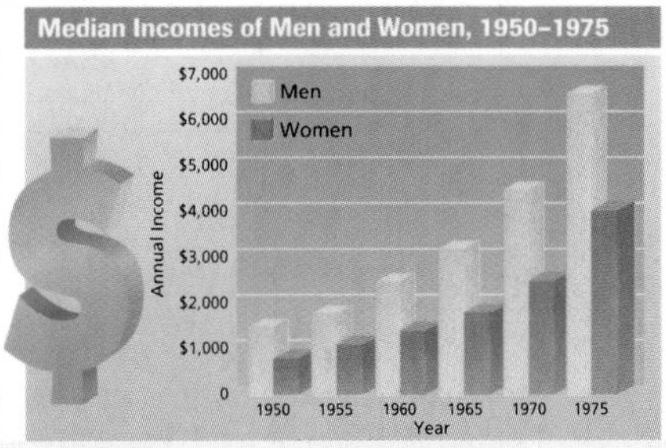

▲ **Interpret a Graph** Between 1950 and 1975, women's incomes continued to lag behind men's earnings, partly because many low-paying fields such as nursing and teaching were traditionally considered "women's work." Did the gap increase or decrease between 1950 and 1975?

▲ **Make an Inference** In May 1973, Senate committee hearings nearly a year after a break-in at Democratic party headquarters revealed that Nixon and several close advisors had been involved in trying to cover up the truth about the burglary. How would such an incident shake the public's faith in government?

Art Transparency Use Art Transparency 11, Asian Women United Commemorative Quilt, to help students appreciate that diversity and the assertion of ethnic identity have been issues in the visual arts as well as in literature.

Answers to

A Graphic Look

(from page 870)

Analyze Cause and Effect The Soviet success probably caused Americans to think about the education of scientists, and led them to think schools should place more emphasis on curriculum that would help the country compete with the Soviet Union.

Make an Inference Students may speculate that the United States government never intended to keep the treaties or that it intended to keep them but was overtaken by events as increasing numbers of settlers moved into areas promised to Native Americans exclusively.

(from page 871)

Interpret a Graph In 1950, the ratio of women's incomes to men's was about $800 to $1200 or 2/3. In 1975, the ratio was $4000 to $6500, which is less than 2/3. Although the ratios seem to remain relatively constant, the difference between men's and women's income in 1950 was $400, while the difference grew to $2,500 in 1975.

Make an Inference Most people believe or want to believe that their elected officials, especially at the highest levels, are honest and trustworthy. A coverup by the nation's highest elected official might suggest to some that crime and corruption exist at every level of government.

Humanities: Music

Rock and Roll Play for students "Rock Around the Clock" from the **Listening to Music Audio CD:** *The American Experience.*

Tell them that after World War II, the United States entered a period of economic prosperity and rapid change. The population expanded dramatically, altering the age balance of the American people. Making up an increasingly large percentage of the population, American teenagers became a major social and economic force. The emerging importance of young Americans prompted major changes in popular entertainment. Among these was the development of rock and roll, a rebellious new type of music. This song, released in 1955, was one of the earliest rock and roll hits.

Ask students how "Rock Around the Clock" expresses the rebelliousness of early rock and roll. *Its quick, insistent rhythms and lyrics advocating all-night dancing are rebellious.*

Literature CD-ROM To build background, use the CD-ROM *The History of American Literature,* Part 2, Disk 2, Features 2–11, which contain information on many of the authors mentioned in this section. However, it is advisable to preview these features before referring students to them. Note, for instance, that in Feature 5, Alan Ginsberg denounces what he sees as a culturally sterile society and advocates drugs and social permissiveness.

Answers to

A GRAPHIC LOOK

(from page 872)

Interpret a Graph The deficit was just below $90 billion in 1980. The deficit decreased during the two-year period 1986–1988.

Draw a Conclusion The United States is interested in safeguarding the supplies of oil and maintaining access to them. Also, it is clear that a conflict in the Middle East could spread rapidly to other parts of the world.

(from page 873)

Make a Judgment Some students may say that people find the Internet a cause for concern because children can use it to access material that their parents might not want them to see. Others may point to issues such as problems in retaining control of intellectual property.

Evaluate Technology Students may point to such advantages as the ability to use the computer while traveling and the potential to have students carry it to classes or study sessions. Some students may point to examples of on-the-job use—for example, an architect may find use for a computer at a building site.

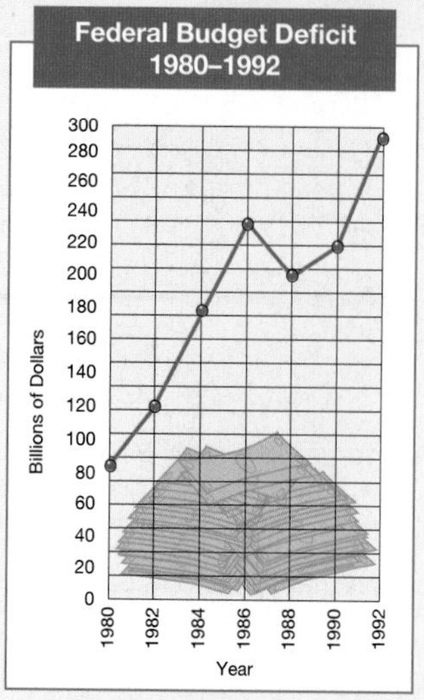

▲ **Interpret a Graph** The rapidly growing federal budget deficit worried many Americans in the 1980's and early 1990's. (a) What was the budget deficit in 1980? (b) During which two-year period did the deficit decrease?

▲ **Draw a Conclusion** The creation of Israel in 1948 led to tension between Israel and surrounding Arab states. In 1993, Israel and the PLO stunned the world by signing a peace agreement. Here, President Clinton watches as Israeli prime minister Yitzhak Rabin shakes hands with PLO leader Yasir Arafat. Considering the Middle East's large supplies of oil as well as other factors, why do you think the United States maintains an interest in peace in the region?

wrote in Yiddish, was renowned for both his novels and his short stories. He won the Nobel Prize for Literature in 1978. John Cheever, a respected novelist, won the Pulitzer Prize for Fiction in 1979 for his collected short stories, many of which concern suburban life.

Just as realism and romanticism have tended to merge in recent literature, so, curiously, have fiction and nonfiction. Truman Capote's *In Cold Blood,* published in 1966, was billed as a "nonfiction novel." Capote, primarily a novelist and short-story writer, used fictional techniques to analyze a real and seemingly senseless crime. Later authors, such as E. L. Doctorow in his novel *Ragtime,* combined historical figures with purely fictional characters. This technique has aroused considerable controversy.

Increasing attention has been paid recently to the place of nonfiction in the literary hierarchy. The essay has always been considered an important literary form, and some outstanding essays are published every year. James Baldwin and John McPhee are accomplished essayists. Among the many notable longer works of nonfiction are Paul Theroux's *The Great Railway Bazaar,* N. Scott Momaday's *The Names,* and Barry Lopez's *Arctic Dreams.*

Poetry Within the Tradition A number of the famous prewar poets continued to publish extensively after the war. Robert Frost, Marianne Moore, Wallace Stevens, E. E. Cummings, William Carlos Williams, and Ezra Pound all produced major collections of their works. Younger poets, starting out in the shadow of these great names, were mostly content to work within the advances made in the 1920's and 1930's. One critic observed that to a beginning poet "the reassurance of sounding like something already acclaimed" was hard to resist.

The tumultuous 1960's brought great changes in social behavior, which affected the subject matter of all literature. In poetry, as in

Humanities: Literature

A Poetry Renaissance in the 1990's Tell students that poetry experienced a renaissance in the 1990's, with many Americans becoming more aware of this art form. Signs of this renaissance include the broadcast of Bill Moyers's television show about poets and poetry, *The Language of Life;* the increasing popularity of poetry readings, including contests known as poetry slams; the activism of poetry organizations like Poets House in New York, with its archive of literary magazines, its schedule of readings, and its outreach program for libraries and high schools.

Tell students that poetry often appears in small literary magazines before it is collected and published in books. Explain to students that thousands of these magazines are published throughout the country—Beloit Poetry Journal (Maine), Atlanta Review (Georgia), Threepenny Review (California), and Descant (Texas), to name just a few. There is even a poetry magazine on the Internet, Poetry Daily that features a new poem each day. It can be accessed at **http://www.poems.com/home.htm.** We *strongly urge* you to preview the site before referring students to it.

fiction, the resulting changes were often more personal and thematic than innovative. It seems ironic that out of the turmoil of the 1960's, the finest poetry to emerge follows older patterns.

One of the most respected contemporary poets is Robert Lowell. Lowell, a great-nephew of the poet James Russell Lowell, writes poetry that is traditional in form. However, his range in theme, method, and tone is breathtaking.

Theodore Roethke, a master of poetic rhythm, was deeply influenced by his father, a strong-willed greenhouse owner in Saginaw, Michigan. The best of Roethke's poems are often referred to as his "greenhouse poems."

Two other poets of note are Elizabeth Bishop and Gwendolyn Brooks. Bishop's poems are beautifully crafted, with precise and memorable descriptions. Two of Brooks's collections, *A Street in Bronzeville* (1945) and *Annie Allen* (1949), assured her reputation.

Many fine poets are at work today. Nowhere perhaps is America's pluralism displayed more vividly than in its poets. Although it is too early to assess these poets' achievements, it seems likely that some of their works will become the classics of tomorrow.

▲ **Make a Judgment** Introduced to the American public in the 1990's, the Internet has radically changed the way we live, study, and work. Why are some people finding the Internet a cause for concern?

Beyond the Horizon

One of the features of literary history is its unpredictability. No one knows what will happen next. Of this, however, we can be reasonably sure: The novel is not dead, as some were proclaiming in the 1950's and 1960's. Poetry is not dead, nor is the short story. Literature has great resilience. While it may be profoundly influenced by other media—radio, television, film—it has not been replaced by them. Indeed, for sheer technical virtuosity, there has probably never been a more impressive group of American writers at work than at the present time.

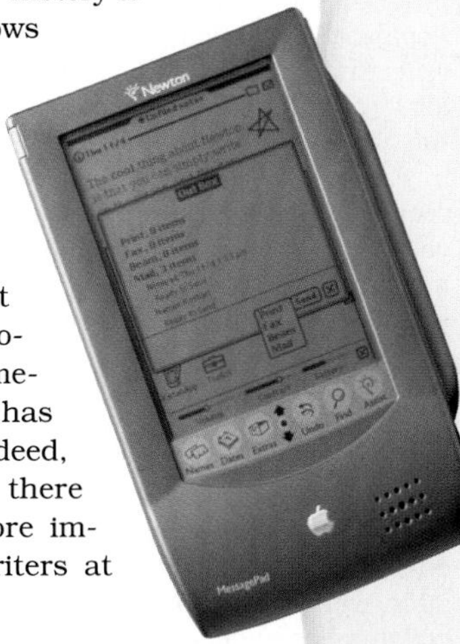

◀ **Evaluate Technology** The ability of a single silicon chip to store and process information has dramatically reduced the size of computers. A person can carry this hand-held computer anywhere and operate it at any time with a small stylus. What are the advantages of a portable computer?

Literature of the Period

Comprehension Check ☑

1. In what way does the literature of this era differ from that written in the early part of the century? *Our time has not seen a literary revolution of the kind that occurred in the 1920's.*
2. What new type of book did Truman Capote create? *He created the nonfiction novel, which blends fiction and truth.*
3. Name three important fiction writers from this era. *Important fiction writers include Carson McCullers, Norman Mailer, Bernard Malamud, John Updike, Flannery O'Connor, Joyce Carol Oates, and Alice Walker, among others.*
4. What important contemporary poet was a descendant of a well-known nineteenth-century poet? *Robert Lowell was a great-nephew of James Russell Lowell.*
5. What type of prose has received increased attention in recent years? *Nonfiction and the essay have received increased attention.*

▶Critical Viewing◀

1. What trends in the history of this era explain the greater diversity among authors? **[Analyze Cause and Effect]** *Students may point out that this was an era of protest, in which various groups asserted their identities and claimed their rights. The increased diversity among authors represents a literary reflection of these themes.*
2. Why do you think that the turbulence of this era did not foster a literary revolution of the kind that occurred in the 1920's? **[Speculate]** *Students may argue that issues of identity and self-assertion took precedence over literary experimentation.*
3. Do you think that advances in computer technology will eventually lead to the disappearance of books? In other words, will literature be written for the screen? **[Analyze Cause and Effect]** *Some students may feel that the book is a resilient medium that will co-exist with computers. Other, more technologically oriented students may believe that the computer is bringing about an information revolution comparable to that created by the invention of printed books in 1450. However, students should support their answers with facts and examples.*

Activities

1. **Predictions** Have students use specific events and trends discussed in the Story of the Times to make predictions about future literary developments. They should be able to explain the thinking behind their predictions.
2. **Graphic Organizer** Have students use the Outline Organizer, p. 95, in ***Writing and Language Transparencies*** to summarize the key ideas and supporting details in The Story of the Times and A Graphic Look at the Period.
3. **Role-Play a Modern Rip Van Winkle** Have students role-play a person who went to sleep in 1946 and woke up in the late 1990's. Ask them to improvise a monologue in which they discuss what surprises them.
4. **News Story of the Half Century** Have students scan The Story of the Times in order to choose the single most important news story of this time period. Then, have them summarize the story for the class and explain why it is so important.

◆ Critical Thinking

1. What do you think accounts for the success of English as a worldwide language? **[Speculate]** *Students may point to English's large vocabulary and rich supply of synonyms or to the success of America as a superpower that can "export" its language and culture through popular music and feature films.*
2. Why do you think Russians are especially interested in business English? **[Infer]** *Russia is in the process of changing from a communist to a capitalist society. American capitalism is seen as a role model for this process. Therefore, American capitalist terms are especially popular.*

▸Critical Viewing◂

In what way does the picture accompanying Lederer's article support his argument that English is a worldwide language? **[Connect]** *The picture seems to show a newsstand with international publications—an English language magazine is featured prominently.*

Answers to Activity

(a) beefsteak; (b) bull dog; (c) baseball; (d) pullover

Additional Activities

1. Many people have argued that if everyone in the world could speak the same language, understanding would be greater and war less likely. Discuss whether or not you agree with this statement—and why. *You might want to structure this activity as a debate. Be sure that students support their statements.*
2. There have been attempts to construct an international language. Prepare a report on Esperanto, the best known of these languages, or Volapuk, Novial, or Interlingua.

More About English in Space

When the spacecraft *Voyager* embarked on its late 1970's journey to Jupiter and beyond, it carried a recorded message addressed to extraterrestrial beings, beginning with a statement from the Secretary General of the United Nations—in English.

The Development of American English

THE GLOBALIZATION OF ENGLISH

by Richard Lederer

English—the linguistic wonder of the modern world—has been transported around the globe and has become the most widely spoken language in the history of humankind.

A Worldwide Language The majority of the world's books, newspapers, and magazines are written in English. Most international telephone calls are made in English. Sixty percent of the world's radio programs are beamed in English, and more than seventy percent of international mail and seventy-five percent of cable messages and telexes are written and addressed in English. It is the language in which more than eighty percent of all stored computer texts and Web sites are written.

Reverse English Planet Earth is spinning with "reverse English." The very English that through the centuries has imported so many words from so many other languages is today one of the world's most popular exports. Through its contributions to other tongues, English is beginning to repay its historical debts and establish a linguistic balance of trade.

By reverse English, we mean, for the most part, American English. If you were to read German newspapers, for example, you would recognize English words such as *scoop, holiday, paperbacks, teenagers, blue jeans, toasters,* and *mixers,* as well as the sports terms *ref, goalkeeper, puck, body check, punch,* and *boxing.*

American words have entered Russian stores with products like *miksers, tosters, komputers,* and *antifriz,* reflecting the fact that half of all foreign language classes in the Soviet Union are courses in English. By popular Soviet request, the British Broadcasting Corporation is supplying Moscow Radio with a series of programs emphasizing the essential English vocabulary of a capitalist society. To help Soviet listeners tell a stock from a bond and a bull from a bear, the BBC-Moscow Radio broadcasts encourage familiarity with such words and phrases as *collateral, management buy-outs, export guarantees, Let's talk about that over lunch,* and *Do we have a deal?*

English Is Alive and Well The English language continues to be one of the world's great growth industries, adding more than a thousand new words a year to its word store and, since World War II, garnering new speakers at an annual rate of about two percent. Over the course of a millennium and a half, it has evolved from the rude tongue of a few isolated Germanic tribes into an international medium of exchange in science, commerce, politics, diplomacy, tourism, literature, and pop culture—the closest thing we have ever had to a global language.

Activity

Identify each English word as it has been adapted by another language:

(a) *bifuteki* (Japanese)
(b) *bouledogue* (French)
(c) *beisbol* (Spanish)
(d) *pulova* (Italian)

More on the Globalization of English

English is the first or official language of forty-five countries covering one-fifth of the earth's land surface. More than ten percent of the populations of other countries, such as India, Pakistan, Malaysia, Switzerland, Holland, Denmark, and Sweden, are able to converse in English. One out of every seven people in the world understands and speaks the English language in some form.

Explain that pilots and air controllers in all international airports use English to communicate. Also, English lyrics pervade rock music the world over. India, with almost two hundred different languages, relies on English to unify itself. From Athens to Baghdad, from Finland to Kabul, people stand in long lines to sign up for English classes that are vastly oversubscribed.

Students may be amused to hear that many a Japanese businessman has a *kakuteiru* ("cocktail") with his *fantazikku garufurendo* ("fantastic girl friend"). For a snack later in the evening the couple might choose to have *aisukurimu* or *yoguruto*. If you're not sure what *aisukurimu* and *yoguruto* are, consider that they come in a variety of flavors, among them *chokoreto, banira,* and *sutoroberi*. *The words are, respectively, ice cream and yogurt, chocolate, vanilla, and strawberry.*

PART 1 *Literature Confronts the Everyday*

Television Moon, 1978–79, Alfred Leslie, Wichita Art Museum, Wichita, Kansas

One-Minute Planning Guide

The writers whose work appears in this section reveal the variety of angles from which one can view everyday events. Both O'Connor's "The Life You Save May Be Your Own," and Malamud's "The First Seven Years" ask readers to consider the level of honesty between strangers, acquaintances, and co-workers. Updike's "The Brown Chest" presents the objects a family treasures and Walker's "Everyday Use" challenges students to decide the value of such family heirlooms. Essays by Nye and Harjo reveal that ordinary happenings can be momentous. Finally, poetry by Cervantes, Espada, Ortiz, Chang, and Hongo suggests the filter that ethnicity, and personal experience bring to the daily tasks of living.

Customize for
Varying Student Needs

When assigning the selections in this part, keep in mind these factors:

"The Life You Save May Be Your Own"
- Accessible story will appeal to almost all students.

"The First Seven Years"
- Charming period piece will spark discussions about independence.

"Hawthorne," "Gold Glade," "The Light Comes Brighter," "The Adamant"
- Abstract concepts may make these poems difficult for less-proficient students.

from *The Names*, "Mint Snowball," "Suspended"
- Three brief selections will appeal to students of all levels.
- Musical/rhythmic learners may especially relate to "Suspended."

"Everyday Use"
- Interpersonal learners will find sympathetic characters that bring the conflict of this story to life.

Humanities: Art

Television Moon, 1978–1979, by Alfred Leslie.

Like the writers of this period, Alfred Leslie has chosen an ordinary subject for this still life, adding significance to an otherwise mundane piece of furniture. Leslie converts the broad landscapes of earlier American artists into a limited, dim rendering shown on a television screen. Instead of facing the frontier through rugged exploration, technology now allows citizens to passively examine the landscape without leaving their armchairs.

Link the art to the theme of Part 1, "Literature Confronts the Everyday," with the following questions:

1. What might the artist be saying about American society by focusing on the mundane items shown in this painting? *Possible response: Americans are caught up in daily trivial and material goods, rather than focusing on more important issues.*
2. Would this painting be a good one to include in a time capsule to show future generations? *Students who say "yes" might point to the way the painting accurately records the small items and especially the television at the center of so many American lives; students who say "no" might argue that the painting overemphasizes the trivial, that other things not shown here are more important to Americans.*

Prepare and Engage

LESSON OBJECTIVES

1. **To develop vocabulary and word identification skills**
   - Latin Word Roots: *-sol-*
   - Using the Word Bank: Context
2. **To use a variety of reading strategies to comprehend fiction**
   - Connect Your Experience
   - Reading for Success: Strategies for Reading Fiction
3. **To increase knowledge of other cultures and to connect common elements across cultures**
   - Connecting Themes Across Cultures (ATE)
4. **To express and support responses to the text**
   - Critical Thinking
   - Idea Bank: Missing Person Report
5. **To analyze literary elements**
   - Literary Focus: Grotesque Characters
   - Idea Bank: Moral Analysis
6. **To read in order to research self-selected and assigned topics**
   - Idea Bank: Body Language Presentation
   - Idea Bank: Special Education Research
7. **To plan, prepare, organize, and present literary interpretations**
   - Idea Bank: Staged Reading
   - Idea Bank: Magazine Illustration
   - Speaking, Listening, and Viewing Mini-Lesson
8. **To use recursive writing processes to write a deposition**
   - Guided Writing Lesson
9. **To increase knowledge of the rules of grammar and usage**
   - Grammar and Style: Subjunctive Mood

Test Preparation

Writing Skills: Punctuation (ATE, p. 877)
The teaching tips and sample test item in this workshop support the instruction and practice in the unit workshop:

Writing Skills: Punctuation, Usage, and Sentence Structure (SE, p. 1143)

Guide for Interpreting

Flannery O'Connor

(1925–1964)

Flannery O'Connor's work reflects her intense commitment to her personal beliefs. In her exaggerated, tragic, and at times shockingly violent tales, she forces readers to confront such human faults as hypocrisy, insensitivity, self-centeredness, and prejudice.

O'Connor once said, "People are always complaining that the modern novelist has no hope and that the picture he paints of the world is unbearable. The only answer to this is that people without hope do not write novels."

"The Habit of Art" Born in Savannah, Georgia, Flannery O'Connor was raised in the small town of Milledgeville. She earned her undergraduate degree from Georgia State College for Women and then left her home state to attend the celebrated University of Iowa Writers' Workshop. In 1950, O'Connor became ill with lupus, a serious disease which restricted her independence. O'Connor moved back to the family farm outside Milledgeville, where she lived with her mother. There, she committed herself not only to her writing but to "the habit of art," an enlivened way of thinking and seeing. In 1952, she published her first novel, *Wise Blood,* the story of a violent rivalry among members of a fictional religious sect in the South. In 1955, she published a collection of stories, *A Good Man Is Hard to Find.* It was followed by a second novel, *The Violent Bear It Away* (1960), and *Everything That Rises Must Converge* (1965), a collection of short stories.

A Triumphant Spirit O'Connor lived with physical suffering and the awareness that she would probably die young. Despite her condition, she often seemed joyous, entertaining many friends at home and painting watercolors of the peacocks that she and her mother raised on the farm. In her fiction, however, she clearly feels a strong kinship with those who are outcast or suffering. Many of her characters are social outcasts or people who are physically or mentally challenged. Although she portrays these characters in an unsentimental way, there is an underlying sense of sympathy concerning their pain and suffering, which reflects both her own physical problems and her strong Catholic faith.

Background on this Story "The Life You Save May Be Your Own" is a typical O'Connor story. In its grim depiction of a group of outcasts with sharply exaggerated physical characteristics and personality traits, the story conveys a powerful moral message and captures many of the tragic realities of life in the modern world.

◆ Background for Understanding

LITERATURE: O'CONNOR AND GOTHIC LITERATURE

In England in the late 1700's, a literary style known as Gothic flourished. Gothic novels featured horror and violence, and the settings were often weird and exaggerated. In **Gothic literature,** evil is acknowledged as a real force in the world, and characters are assumed to have a dark side that lures them into violent or wicked acts.

In the twentieth century, a number of southern American writers such as Truman Capote, Carson McCullers, Tennessee Williams, William Faulkner, and Flannery O'Connor borrowed devices from Gothic literature. Their works often contain a foreboding atmosphere and doomed or grotesque characters.

Flannery O'Connor used Gothic elements to help expose the gap she saw between some people's professed religious beliefs and their morally irresponsible behavior.

Prentice Hall Literature Program Resources

REINFORCE / RETEACH / EXTEND

Selection Support Pages
Build Vocabulary: Latin Word Roots: *-sol-*, p. 265
Grammar and Style: Subjunctive Mood, p. 266
Reading for Success: Reading Fiction, pp. 267–268
Literary Focus: Grotesque Characters, p. 269

Strategies for Diverse Student Needs, p. 58

Beyond Literature Career Connection: Human Resources Interview, p. 58

Formal Assessment Selection Test, pp. 265–267; Assessment Resources Software

Alternative Assessment, p. 58

Writing and Language Transparencies
Cause-and-Effect Transparency, p. 91
Daily Language Practice, Week 29

Resource Pro CD-ROM
Includes all resource materials and a customizable lesson plan.

Literature CD-ROM

Listening to Literature Audiocassettes

The Life You Save May Be Your Own

MODEL SELECTION

◆ Literature and Your Life

CONNECT YOUR EXPERIENCE

In this story, a stranger appears at a remote farm where an elderly widow lives alone with her daughter. The woman must decide whether to trust him and whether to allow him into her home. What would you do if you were in her place? Why?

Journal Writing Discuss how you think people should react to strangers.

THEMATIC FOCUS: LITERATURE CONFRONTS THE EVERYDAY

Like many modern stories, "The Life You Save May Be Your Own" captures the everyday lives of less fortunate people. What lessons can be learned from the lives of such people?

◆ Build Vocabulary

LATIN WORD ROOTS: *-sol-*

O'Connor uses the word *desolate,* which has several meanings, including "forlorn." The word contains the Latin root *-sol-,* meaning "alone." Knowing the meaning of this root and drawing from your prior knowledge, what are some other definitions for *desolate*?

WORD BANK

Preview this list of words from the story.

desolate
listed
ominous
ravenous
morose
guffawing

◆ Grammar and Style

SUBJUNCTIVE MOOD

The **subjunctive mood** is any verb form indicating possibility, supposition, or desire. The verb form has two functions. One is to express a condition that is contrary to fact:

Mr. Shiftlet talked *as if he were an ethical person.*

This sentence suggests that Mr. Shiftlet may not be an ethical person. In this function, the verb form is always *were* rather than *was.*

The subjunctive mood is also used to indirectly express a demand, recommendation, suggestion, or statement of necessity:

Mrs. Crater suggested *that Shiftlet marry her daughter.*

Here, the third-person singular verb form does not have the usual *-s, -es,* or *-ies* ending.

◆ Literary Focus

GROTESQUE CHARACTERS

A key element in gothic literature, the **grotesque character** is one who has become bizarre, usually through some kind of obsession. A grotesque character may be obsessed with an idea, a value, or an assumption. Typically, grotesque characters are one-dimensional and possess one or more exaggerated personality traits.

Many of Flannery O'Connor's characters, including those in this story, can be considered grotesque. Notice how O'Connor uses these bizarre characters to communicate a universal message.

Interest Grabber The title of this story is a slogan that once commonly appeared on American highways. Such slogans—like this story—challenge readers' consciences and try to raise their moral standards. To spark students' interest in the story, post the title along with other common slogans, such as anti-drug or safety belt warnings. Discuss the motives to which these warnings appeal. Invite them to predict what this story may reveal about human nature.

Connecting Themes Across Cultures

Among Flannery O'Connor's strongest influences were writers associated with a movement sometimes called "Nashville Agrarianism," who wrote in defense of the humanism embodied in traditional, agrarian cultures, and against the dehumanizing effects of industrial economies. Interestingly, the Nashville Agrarians found allies in movements far beyond the American South where they were centered. They felt a strong affinity for many regional cultures, including Russian, Irish, and Native American traditions that were threatened by new economic trends.

Customize for
Less Proficient Readers

This complex story may be difficult for less proficient readers. To help these readers, review the Strategies for Reading Fiction, perhaps modeling each strategy with examples from previous selections.

Customize for
AP Students

Remind these students of O'Connor's deep religious convictions and of her concern for the world's moral bankruptcy. Careful analysis can enable these students to link these issues to the story content.

Customize for
English Language Learners

The regional manners and dialect in this story may be obstacles for language learners. To help these students, provide them with a dictionary of American slang or dialect. Working with you or native speakers, have students "translate" the dialect into standard English.

Test Preparation Workshop

Writing Skills: Punctuation

The writing sections of some standardized tests, such as the ACT, require students to proofread for errors in spelling, capitalization, and punctuation within the context of a written passage. Use the following sample item to give students practice in this skill

"The Life You Save May Be Your Own" is a story of a drifter who meets a woman and her daughter. In the course of the story; the daughter is treated as if she were a piece of property.

Which type of error, if any, appears in the underlined section of the passage?

A Spelling error
B Capitalization error
C Punctuation error
D No error

The semicolon after *story* separates a prepositional phrase from an independent clause; it should be replaced by a comma. Therefore, C is the correct answer.

Reading for Success

The Reading for Success page in each unit presents a set of problem-solving procedures to help readers understand authors' words and ideas on multiple levels. Good readers develop a bank of strategies from which they can draw as needed.

Unit 6 introduces strategies for reading fiction. These strategies will give students the tools they need to analyze and appreciate the nuances of meaning contained in a literary work of fiction.

These strategies for reading fiction are modeled with "The Life You Save May Be Your Own." Each green box shows an example of the thinking process involved in applying one of these strategies.

How to Use the Reading for Success Page

- Introduce the strategies for reading fiction, presenting each as a problem-solving procedure. Be sure students understand what each strategy involves and under what circumstances to apply it.
- Before students read the story, have them preview it, looking at the annotations in the green boxes that model the strategies.
- To reinforce these strategies after students have read "The Life You Save May Be Your Own," have students do the Reading for Success pages in ***Selection Support,*** pp. 267–268. These pages give students an opportunity to read a selection and practice strategies for reading fiction by writing their own annotations.

Reading for Success

Strategies for Reading Fiction

In a great work of fiction, every word has been chosen carefully to express a precise meaning. A plot has been structured, characters delineated, hints dropped, and themes deliberately implied to create a unique and yet believable world. By applying the following strategies, you can more fully appreciate the fictional world a writer has so carefully created.

Envision the action in your mind.
A skilled writer describes action clearly and vividly to help you picture the scenes of a story in your mind. Allow yourself to be carried away by the pictures painted by the author's words.

Connect the literature to your own experiences.
If you empathize, or feel as another does, you'll be able to put yourself in a character's shoes. Imagine yourself in the story's setting and in the character's situations.

Question.
In life, you ask yourself questions about people's actions and motivations. What was he *really* doing? Why did she say that? Relate to a work of literature in the same way. Ask yourself why the characters behave as they do.

Predict.
When you find yourself wondering how a series of events will unfold, pause and predict what will happen. When you are trying to predict outcomes, look back, recall, and carefully weigh what you've experienced so far.

Draw inferences.
Fictional characters and situations don't come neatly labeled "Villain" or "Disaster"—you have to infer information from the clues you're given. Use a character's attitudes and actions to read "between the lines."

Draw conclusions.
When you've finished reading a piece of fiction, reflect on its overall meaning. What general ideas does the writer want you to carry away?

Respond.
As you read a story, respond mentally and emotionally. A story may evoke positive responses—like laughter or recognition—or negative responses—such as disappointment or disgust with a character.

As you read "The Life You Save May Be Your Own," look at the notes along the sides. They demonstrate how to apply these strategies to your reading.

Reading Strategies: Support and Reinforcement

Appropriate Reading Strategies Students are given a reading strategy to apply in reading each selection in this unit. When the selection is a short story or novel excerpt, students are given one of these strategies for reading fiction. In other selections a strategy is suggested that is appropriate to the selection.

Reading Prompts To encourage application of the given reading strategy, there are occasional prompts, within green boxes, at appropriate and significant points.

In addition, there are red boxes prompting application of the Literary Focus concept and maroon boxes prompting students to connect with their lives.

Using the Boxed Annotations and Prompts
The material in the green, red, and maroon boxes along the sides of selections is intended to help students apply the literary element and the reading strategy and to make a connection with their lives.

You may use the boxed material in several ways:

- Have students pause when they come to a box and respond to its prompt before they continue reading.
- Urge students to read through the selection ignoring the boxes. After they have read the selection completely, they may go back and review the selection, responding to the prompts.

MODEL

The Life You Save May Be Your Own

Flannery O'Connor

The old woman and her daughter were sitting on their porch when Mr. Shiftlet came up their road for the first time. The old woman slid to the edge of her chair and leaned forward, shading her eyes from the piercing sunset with her hand. The daughter could not see far in front of her and continued to play with her fingers. Although the old woman lived in this desolate spot with only her daughter and she had never seen Mr. Shiftlet before, she could tell, even from a distance, that he was a tramp and no one to be afraid of. His left coat sleeve was folded up to show there was only half an arm in it and his gaunt figure listed slightly to the side as if the breeze were pushing him. He had on a black town suit and a brown felt hat that was turned up in the front and down in the back and he carried a tin tool box by a handle. He came on, at an amble, up her road, his face turned toward the sun which appeared to be balancing itself on the peak of a small mountain.

❶ The old woman didn't change her position until he was almost into her yard; then she rose with one hand fisted on her hip. ❷ The daughter, a large girl in a short blue organdy dress, saw him all at once and jumped up and began to stamp and point and make excited speechless sounds.

Mr. Shiftlet stopped just inside the yard and set his box on the ground and tipped his hat at her as if she were not in the least afflicted; then he turned toward the old woman and swung the hat all the way off. He had long black slick hair that hung flat from a part in the middle to beyond the tips of his ears on either side. His face descended in forehead for more than half its length and ended suddenly with his features just balanced over a jutting steel-trap jaw. He seemed to be a young man but he had a look of composed dissatisfaction as if he understood life thoroughly. ❸

> This description allows you to establish a **picture in your mind**. Its effect is like that of a camera pausing on a scene before the action begins.

"Good evening," the old woman said. She was about the size of a cedar fence post and she had a man's gray hat pulled down low over her head.

The tramp stood looking at her and didn't answer. He turned his back and faced the sunset. He swung both his whole and his short arm up slowly so that they indicated an expanse of sky and his figure formed a crooked cross. The old woman watched him with her arms folded across her chest as if she were the owner of the sun, and the daughter watched, her head thrust forward and her fat helpless hands hanging at the wrists. She had long pink-gold hair and eyes as blue as a peacock's neck.

He held the pose for almost fifty seconds and then he picked up his box and came on to the porch and dropped down on the bottom step. "Lady," he said in a firm nasal voice, "I'd give a

◆ Build Vocabulary

desolate (des´ə lit) *adj.*: Forlorn; wretched

listed (list´ id) *v.*: Tilted; inclined

Develop Understanding

One-Minute Insight This story of grotesque characters obsessed with outmaneuvering each other becomes a morality tale about the spiritual desert facing those who behave immorally. Mr. Shiftlet and Mrs. Lucynell Crater appear as good people, who denounce the moral deterioration of the world. They are motivated by goals that are not outwardly evil: Shiftlet wants a car and Mrs. Crater wants a husband for her daughter, who is mentally retarded, deaf, and mute. As they plot to achieve their cherished goals, however, they show themselves willing to sacrifice both human decency and the younger Lucynell's future. Their hypocrisy comes at a high price.

◆ Critical Thinking

❶ **Interpret** What does the old wo-man's body language tell you about how she plans to deal with the stranger? *She seems to be prepared for a fight.*

◆ Critical Thinking

❷ **Infer** What do the young girl's actions in the first two paragraphs suggest about her? *Students should recognize that she is mentally or possibly physically challenged in some way, citing her jumping, finger play and excited speechless sounds as clues.*

◆ Grammar and Style

❸ **Subjunctive Mood** Explain that the verb "understand" is in the subjunctive mood because the phrase "as if he" indicates that this sentence expresses a condition that is contrary to fact. Point out that most of the time, a verb in the subjunctive mood does not appear any different than it would in the indicative mood. If the sentence involved the verb "to be," however (as in "as if he *were* enlightened"), the subjunctive verb (*were*) would be noticeably different from the indicative form (*was*).

Block Scheduling Strategies

Consider these suggestions to take advantage of extended class time:

- After students have read the biography and Background for Understanding on p. 876, introduce the Literary Focus. Ask students to discuss why they think O'Connor may have been drawn to grotesque characters.
- Introduce and discuss the Strategies for Reading Fiction (p. 878).
- If you have access to technology, have groups of students build background on O'Connor with the **Literature CD-ROM:** *The History of Am. Lit.*
- Present the Speaking, Listening, and Viewing Mini-Lesson (ATE, p. 886) before assigning the parts of the narrator, Mr. Shiftlet, Mrs. Crater, the diner worker, and the hitchhiker. Have volunteers read the selection aloud for the class.
- Use the Daily Language Practice sentences for Week 29. You can display the transparency (p. 136 in ***Writing and Language Transparencies***) and have students write the sentences correctly, or dictate the sentences.

◆ Critical Thinking

1 Compare and Contrast Ask students: How are Mr. Shiftlet's and the woman's views of the sunset different? *He seems to appreciate its beauty, while she takes it completely for granted.*

◆ Reading for Success

2 Question Point out to students that Mr. Shiftlet does not answer the old woman's question. Invite students to formulate a reading question in response to this bit of dialogue. *Students may wish to discover where Mr. Shiflet is from.* Encourage them to read on for an answer to their question.

◆ Reading for Success

3 Infer Ask students what they can infer about Mr. Shiftlet's interest in the car from his initial conversation with the old woman. What evidence from the text can students cite to support their inference? *Students should notice Mr. Shiftlet's strong focus on the car, evidenced by his glance stopping when he reaches the car, his question about the car, his examination of the tires, and his assessment of the car's age.*

▶Critical Viewing◀

4 Connect Students should cite the rural setting and general air of dilapidation, the large tree, the shed, and the old car.

Read to Appreciate Author's Craft

Flannery O'Connor liked to employ her biting sense of irony in playing off of Southern manners. For instance, on this page, the author has Tom Shiftlet mouthing the platitudes of what she called elsewhere "good country people." We see this when he says to Lucynell Crater that "Nothing is like it used to be, lady, . . . The world is almost rotten." The humor of his words come from his timing—he offers this morally charged declaration after being told that the Craters' car stopped running some years back. Encourage students to be aware of similar ironies in stereotypes and mannerisms.

1 fortune to live where I could see me a sun do that every evening."

"Does it every evening," the old woman said and sat back down. The daughter sat down too and watched him with a cautious sly look as if he were a bird that had come up very close. He leaned to one side, rooting in his pants pocket, and in a second he brought out a package of chewing gum and offered her a piece. She took it and unpeeled it and began to chew without taking her eyes off him. He offered the old woman a piece but she only raised her upper lip to indicate she had no teeth.

Mr. Shiftlet's pale sharp glance had already passed over everything in the yard—the pump near the corner of the house and the big fig tree that three or four chickens were preparing to roost in—and had moved to a shed where he saw the square rusted back of an automobile. "You ladies drive?" he asked.

"That car ain't run in fifteen year," the old woman said. "The day my husband died, it quit running."

"Nothing is like it used to be, lady," he said. "The world is almost rotten."

2 "That's right," the old woman said. "You from around here?"

"Name Tom T. Shiftlet," he murmured, looking at the tires.

"I'm pleased to meet you," the old woman said. "Name Lucynell Crater and daughter Lucynell Crater. What you doing around here, Mr. Shiftlet?"

3 He judged the car to be about a 1928 or '29 Ford. "Lady," he said, and turned and gave her his full attention, "lemme tell you something. There's one of these doctors in Atlanta that's taken a knife and cut the human heart—the human heart," he repeated, leaning forward, "out of a man's chest and held it in his hand," and he held his hand out, palm up, as if it were slightly weighted with the human heart, "and studied it like it was a day-old chicken, and lady," he said, allowing a long significant pause in which his head slid forward and his clay-colored eyes brightened, "he don't know no more about it than you or me."

"That's right," the old woman said.

"Why, if he was to take that knife and cut into every corner of it, he still wouldn't know no more than you or me. What you want to bet?"

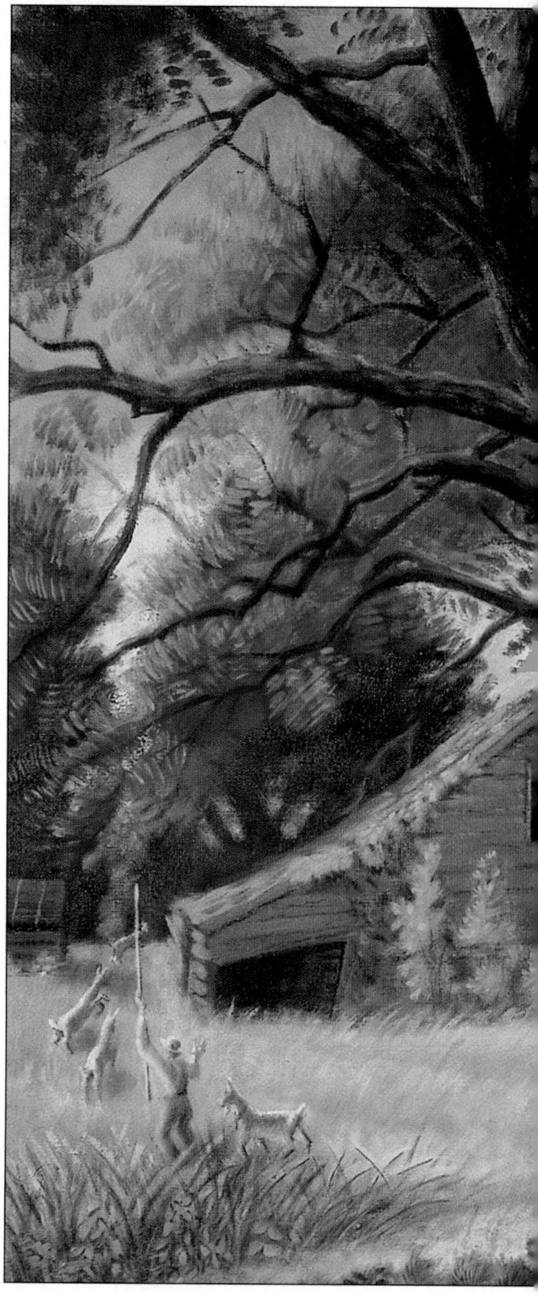

▲ Critical Viewing What aspects of the story are reflected in this painting? **[Connect]** 4

Cultural Connection

The "Southern" Accent Though accents vary throughout the American South, the region as a whole is known for its distinctive cadences and patterns of speech. These unique qualities were influenced by a number of circumstances. In the small towns of this agricultural region, people entertained themselves with storytelling and long chatting sessions. They also heard only each other's voices—often seeing few outsiders. The strong religious current in the southern states, sometimes referred to as "the Bible Belt," helped infuse the cadences of the King James Bible into Southern speech. In the years following the Civil War, Southerners struggled to retain a semblance of their pre-war lives. People preserved their speech patterns, which varied with social position, as a way of associating themselves with a particular social group.

Have students discuss how varying speech patterns could help story characters make inferences about each other.

Black Walnuts, 1945, Joseph Pollet, Oil on canvas, 30" x 40", Collection of Whitney Museum of American Art, Purchase, Gift of Gertrude Vanderbilt Whitney, by exchange

Humanities: Art

Black Walnuts, 1945, by Joseph Pollet.

This painting illustrates an everyday scene amidst a rural setting much like that of the story: an old and dilapidated homestead in an isolated rural area.

The painter was Swiss-American Joseph Pollet. He studied at the Art Students' League in New York City with American realist painter, John Sloan. *Black Walnuts* shows both Sloan's influence—a highly realistic stop-action quality that still conveys much more emotion than a photograph would—and the general focus of painting during the depression—capturing everyday American images for American viewers.

Use these questions for discussion:

1. How does the mood this painting conveys compare to that of the story? *The painting has a happier, brighter mood than the story.*
2. Do you think the story characters would fit in the painting's setting? Why or why not? *They would fit into the setting itself because it is rural; however, they would not belong in the sense that the scene is one of purity and goodness and they—as students will see—are morally bankrupt.*

◆ *Literature and Your Life*

Draw students' attention to the contradictions between characters' actions and words, for example, Mr. Shiftlet complains about the world's rotten state while himself coveting the Craters' car. What experiences have students had with people whose actions contradict their professed beliefs? Invite students to respond in their journals for privacy.

Customize for *AP Students*

To help these students appreciate O'Connor's skill in portraying her characters' moral duplicity, ask them to cite examples of descriptive language with negative connotations. For example, they might note that Mr. Shiftlet's glance is described as "pale" and "sharp." What do these words suggest about his character? *They suggest that it is ultimately transparent and without substance, and that he is possibly dangerous.*

Customize for *Visual/Spatial Learners*

Encourage these students to pay close attention to the details of the setting. Discuss how the details of the setting reflect the events in the story, for example, suggesting the decay in the characters' morality.

Customize for *Gifted/Talented Students*

The names Tom T. Shiftlet and Lucynell Crater are unusual and evocative, but what do they suggest to students? Have them free-associate phrases, adjectives, and images that come to mind upon hearing or reading these names early in the story.

Literature CD-ROM Use *The History of American Literature:* Part 2, Disk 2, Feature 4, to introduce students to Flannery O'Connor and her distinctive literary style.

◆ Critical Thinking

❶ Analyze Point out that this is the second time Mr. Shiftlet has failed to answer the woman's question about his place of origin. Ask students to analyze his behavior. *Students should realize that Mr. Shiftlet is being intentionally evasive, perhaps because he wishes to hide something unsavory in his past.*

◆ Grammar and Style

❷ Subjunctive Mood Ask students to identify the verb in the subjunctive mood and explain its function in the sentence. *The verb were is in the subjunctive mood. It serves to express a condition contrary to fact.*

◆ Reading for Success

❸ Predict Challenge students to predict how the interaction between Mr. Shiftlet and Mrs. Crater will unfold. Do students think Mr. Shiftlet will be honest with Lucynell? *Students may be able to predict that he will not, as a function of his duplicity thus far and the way he almost dares Lucynell to disbelieve him.*

◆ Critical Thinking

❹ Evaluate Mr. Shiftlet's patter is like that of a seductive con man. He boasts loudly and constantly of his own virtues, favorably comparing his own personal values with those of "most people." Ask students whether they believe Mr. Shiftlet truly is the type of person he would like others to think he is. Students should recognize the irony of these statements once they are aware of Shiftlet's actions later in the story.

◆ Reading for Success

❺ Question Some students should begin to have an instinctive answer to their question: Mr. Shiftlet was probably not raised the way he claims because he's shown himself to be a hypocrite.

◆ Literary Focus

❻ Grotesque Characters Ask students: In what specific way does this description fit into the definition of a grotesque character? *Students should note that young Lucynell's behavior is bizarre, that she expresses her fascination with Mr. Shiftlet by sneaking looks at him through her hair, and that she is unable to communicate.*

"Nothing," the old woman said wisely.
❶ "Where you come from, Mr. Shiftlet?"

He didn't answer. He reached into his pocket and brought out a sack of tobacco and a package of cigarette papers and rolled himself a cigarette, expertly with one hand, and attached it in a hanging position to his upper lip. Then he took a box of wooden matches from his pocket and struck one on his shoe. He held the burning match as if he were studying the mystery of
❷ flame while it traveled dangerously toward his skin. The daughter began to make loud noises and to point to his hand and shake her finger at him, but when the flame was just before touching him, he leaned down with his hand cupped over it as if he were going to set fire to his nose and lit the cigarette.

He flipped away the dead match and blew a stream of gray into the evening. A sly look came over his face. "Lady," he said, "nowadays, people'll do anything anyways. I can tell you my name is Tom T. Shiftlet and I come from
❸ Tarwater, Tennessee, but you never have seen me before: how you know I ain't lying? How you know my name ain't Aaron Sparks, lady, and I come from Singleberry, Georgia, or how you know it's not George Speeds and I come from Lucy, Alabama, or how you know I ain't Thompson Bright from Toolafalls, Mississippi?"

"I don't know nothing about you," the old woman muttered, irked.

"Lady," he said, "people don't care how they lie. Maybe the best I can tell you is, I'm a man; but listen lady," he said and paused and made his tone more <u>ominous</u> still, "what is a man?"

The old woman began to gum a seed. "What you carry in that tin box, Mr. Shiftlet?" she asked.

"Tools," he said, put back. "I'm a carpenter."

"Well, if you come out here to work, I'll be able to feed you and give you a place to sleep but I can't pay. I'll tell you that before you begin," she said.

There was no answer at once and no particular expression on his face. He leaned back against the two-by-four that helped support the porch roof. "Lady," he said slowly, "there's
❹ some men that some things mean more to them than money." The old woman rocked without comment and the daughter watched the trigger that moved up and down in his neck. He told the old woman then that all most people were interested in was money, but he asked what a man was made for. He asked her if a man was made for money, or what. He asked her what she thought she was made for but she didn't answer, she only sat rocking and wondered if a one-armed man could put a new roof on her garden house. He asked a lot of questions that she didn't answer. He told her that he was twenty-eight years old and had lived a varied life. He had been a gospel singer, a foreman on the railroad, an assistant in an undertaking parlor, and he come over the radio for three months with Uncle Roy and his Red Creek Wranglers. He said he had fought and bled in the Arm Service of his country and visited every foreign land and that everywhere he had seen people that didn't care if they did a thing one way or another. He said he hadn't been raised thataway.

> **Connect the literature to your own experience** by reflecting on a time when a person was talking to you about one thing, but you were reflecting on your own concerns. ❹

> **Ask yourself:** *How was Shiftlet raised?* ❺

A fat yellow moon appeared in the branches of the fig tree as if it were going to roost there with the chickens. He said that a man had to escape to the country to see the world whole and that he wished he lived in a desolate place like this where he could see the sun go down every evening like God made it to do.

"Are you married or are you single?" the old woman asked.

There was a long silence. "Lady," he asked finally, "where would you find you an innocent woman today? I wouldn't have any of this trash I could just pick up."

The daughter was leaning very far down, hanging her head almost between her knees watching him through a triangular door she had made in her overturned hair; and she suddenly fell in a heap on the floor and began ❻
to whimper. Mr. Shiftlet straightened her out and helped her get back in the chair.

"Is she your baby girl?" he asked.

"My only," the old woman said "and she's the sweetest girl in the world. I would give her up for nothing on earth. She's smart too. She can sweep the floor, cook, wash, feed the chickens, and hoe. I wouldn't give her up for a casket of jewels."

Cross-Curricular Connection: Physical Education

The Special Olympics

Explain to students that many mentally challenged people lead full and productive lives, sometimes holding jobs or pursuing athletic excellence. Events such as the Special Olympics provide an opportunity for mentally challenged athletes to build self-confidence by competing in a supportive and appropriate setting. Nearly 7,000 mentally challenged athletes from 140 countries participated in the 1995 Special Olympics World Summer Games, competing in sporting events ranging from swimming and tennis to basketball and weight lifting.

You might discuss with students programs in your school or community that enable mentally challenged people to become and remain physically fit.

"No," he said kindly, "don't ever let any man take her away from you."

"Any man come after her," the old woman said, "'ll have to stay around the place."

Mr. Shiftlet's eye in the darkness was focused on a part of the automobile bumper that glittered in the distance. "Lady," he said, jerking his short arm up as if he could point with it to her house and yard and pump, "there ain't a broken thing on this plantation that I couldn't fix for you, one-arm jackleg or not. I'm a man," he said with a sullen dignity, "even if I ain't a whole one. I got," he said, tapping his knuckles on the floor to emphasize the immensity of what he was going to say, "a moral intelligence!" and his face pierced out of the darkness into a shaft of doorlight and he stared at her as if he were astonished himself at this impossible truth.

The old woman was not impressed with the phrase. "I told you you could hang around and work for food," she said, "if you don't mind sleeping in that car yonder."

"Why listen, lady, " he said with a grin of delight, "the monks of old slept in their coffins!"

"They wasn't as advanced as we are," the old woman said.

The next morning he began on the roof of the garden house while Lucynell, the daughter, sat on a rock and watched him work. He had not been around a week before the change he had made in the place was apparent. He had patched the front and back steps, built a new hog pen, restored a fence, and taught Lucynell, who was completely deaf and had never said a word in her life, to say the word "bird." The big rosy-faced girl followed him everywhere, saying "Burrttddt ddbirrrttdt," and clapping her hands. The old woman watched from a distance, secretly pleased. She was ravenous for a son-in-law. ❼

> Shiftlet's capable performance in his new job gives you a good basis upon which to **predict** what might happen next.

Mr. Shiftlet slept on the hard narrow back seat of the car with his feet out the side window. He had his razor and a can of water on a crate that served him as a bedside table and he put up a piece of mirror against the back glass and kept his coat neatly on a hanger that he hung over one of the windows.

In the evenings he sat on the steps and talked while the old woman and Lucynell rocked violently in their chairs on either side of him. The old woman's three mountains were black against the dark blue sky and were visited off and on by various planets and by the moon after it had left the chickens. Mr. Shiftlet pointed out that the reason he had improved this plantation was because he had taken a personal interest in it. He said he was even going to make the automobile run. ❽

He had raised the hood and studied the mechanism and he said he could tell that the car had been built in the days when cars were really built. You take now, he said, one man puts in one bolt and another man puts in another bolt and another man puts in another bolt so that it's a man for a bolt. That's why you have to pay so much for a car: you're paying all those men. Now if you didn't have to pay but one man, you could get you a cheaper car and one that had had a personal interest taken in it, and it would be a better car. The old woman agreed with him that this was so. ❾

Mr. Shiftlet said that the trouble with the world was that nobody cared, or stopped and took any trouble. He said he never would have been able to teach Lucynell to say a word if he hadn't cared and stopped long enough. ❿

"Teach her to say something else," the old woman said.

"What you want her to say next?" Mr. Shiftlet asked.

The old woman's smile was broad and toothless and suggestive. "Teach her to say 'sugarpie,'" she said.

Mr. Shiftlet already knew what was on her mind. ⓫

The next day he began to tinker with the automobile and that evening he told her that if she would buy a fan belt, he would be able to make the car run.

The old woman said she would give him the money. "You see that girl yonder?" she asked, pointing to Lucynell who was sitting on the floor a foot away, watching him, her eyes blue even in the dark. "If it was ever a man wanted to take her away, I would say, 'No man on

◆ Build Vocabulary

ominous (äm´ ə nəs) *adj.*: Threatening; sinister

ravenous (rav´ ə nəs) *adj.*: Extremely eager

◆ Background for Understanding

Literature: O'Connor and Gothic Literature Point out that the author's treatment of both physically and mentally challenged characters is not meant to make fun of them. Emphasize that Flannery O'Connor's fiction is filled with black humor and that many of her characters are depicted as grotesque in order to make a serious point.

◆ Critical Thinking

❼ **Make a Judgment** Ask students: Do you think a husband would be good for Lucynell? Do you think Lucynell's mother has her daughter's best interests in mind in seeking a husband for her? Explain. *Students will probably judge Lucynell harshly for wanting a son-in-law. You might help them see that a husband would care for young Lucynell after her elderly mother's death.*

◆ Reading for Success

❽ **Envision the Action** Point out to students the descriptive language in this sentence and encourage them to use it to paint a mental picture of the scene.

❾ **Clarification:** Shiflet complains about the quality of cars built on assembly lines. See the note at the bottom of this page for more information on the 1913 introduction of a modernized way to build cars.

Customize for *AP Students*

❿ Point out how Mr. Shiftlet often passes judgment on the world around him. Ask students to explain why he does this. *He wishes to show his own moral superiority.* Then discuss whether students think his observations are accurate.

◆ Literary Focus

⓫ **Grotesque Characters** Ask students how this exchange hints at the old woman's obsession and thereby emphasizes her as a grotesque character. *Students should note that the old woman's smile and suggestive request hints at her obsession for a son-in-law. This desire is so distorted from reality as to render her a grotesque character.*

Beyond the Classroom

Workplace Skills Connection

The Assembly Line The assembly line was introduced by Henry Ford in 1913. Although it greatly increased the efficiency of production, many people feared that the quality of the product might suffer. Others have questioned how the repetitive efforts assembly lines require of workers cause both physical and emotional strains. Have interested students learn about workplace problems that have arisen because of assembly line work and identify some of the efforts being made to address the issues.

Community Connection

Access for All Point out to students that Mr. Shiftlet is a very effective worker, despite his physical challenges. Explain that today there are laws to prevent discrimination against the physically challenged, both in and outside the workplace. One of these laws, the Americans with Disabilities Act, re-quires that public buildings be accessible to both the visually impaired and those in wheelchairs. Have student groups survey buildings in your community, beginning with your school, to identify which comply with ADA requirements.

Customize for
Less Proficient Readers

To insure that these students have grasped the essential interaction occurring between Mr. Shiftlet and the old woman, have them summarize the story up to this point. *Summaries should include: Mr. Shiftlet, a tramp, remains at the Crater home in the hopes of acquiring a car spotted there. The senior Lucynell Crater welcomes him as a potential son-in-law for her mentally challenged daughter, offering the car as bait. Each claims moral motives while scheming against the other.*

◆ Critical Thinking

❶ **Analyze** Why might the old woman have lied about Lucynell's age? *She probably didn't want Mr. Shiftlet to know that Lucynell was older than he was. She wanted him to think that he would be marrying a docile, young girl.*

◆ Reading for Success

❷ **Predict** Ask students to predict whether Mr. Shiftlet will be interested in marrying young Lucynell. *Students should be able to predict that Mr. Shiftlet will want to marry young Lucynell because he will do anything to fulfill his desire for the car.*

▶Critical Viewing◀

❸ **Draw Conclusions** Students should conclude that travel in a rural area would be next to impossible without a car—there would be little or no public transportation. An automobile would provide the ability to reach services, entertainment, and other destinations.

earth is going to take that sweet girl of mine away from me!' but if he was to say, 'Lady, I don't want to take her away, I want her right here,' I would say, 'Mister, I don't blame you none. I wouldn't pass up a chance to live in a permanent place and get the sweetest girl in the world myself. You ain't no fool,' I would say."

❶ "How old is she?" Mr. Shiftlet asked casually.

"Fifteen, sixteen," the old woman said. The girl was nearly thirty but because of her innocence it was impossible to guess.

"It would be a good idea to paint it too," Mr. Shiftlet remarked. "You don't want it to rust out."

"We'll see about that later," the old woman said.

The next day he walked into town and returned with the parts he needed and a can of gasoline. Late in the afternoon, terrible noises issued from the shed and the old woman rushed out of the house, thinking Lucynell was somewhere having a fit. Lucynell was sitting on a chicken crate, stamping her feet and screaming, "Burrddtt! bddurrddttt!" but her fuss was drowned out by the car. With a volley of blasts it emerged from the shed, moving in a fierce and stately way. Mr. Shiftlet was in the driver's seat, sitting very erect. He had an expression of serious modesty on his face as if he had just raised the dead.

❷ That night, rocking on the porch, the old woman began her business, at once. "You want you an innocent woman, don't you?" she asked sympathetically. "You don't want none of this trash."

"No'm, I don't," Mr. Shiftlet said.

"One that can't talk," she continued, "can't sass you back or use foul language. That's the

Deep Fork Overlook, Joan Marron-LaRue

▲ **Critical Viewing** Why might an automobile be so valuable in a rural area like the one in this story? **[Draw Conclusions]** ❸

Humanities: Art

Deep Fork Overlook, c. 1989, by Joan Marron-LaRue.

This oil-on-canvas painting depicts a rural gas station in an area much like the story's setting. The artist, Joan Marron-LaRue, grew up in rural Oklahoma. Though interested in painting since early childhood, she nonetheless worked in fashion design for a time, painting only in her spare time. She later re-turned to formal study with various master painters. *Deep Fork Overlook,* painted gratis to adorn the cover of a Central State University anthology of student poetry, holds a special place in the artist's heart—she once lived just down the road from the real gas station and barn it depicts.

Use these questions for discussion:

1. What element of this scene would probably hold the most interest for Mr. Shiftlet? *He would be very interested in the truck.*
2. What elements in the painting suggest the time period of the story? *The older truck, the historic barn, the antiquated gas pumps, and the presence of chickens wandering suggest both the Depression time period and the rural setting.*

kind for you to have. Right there," and she pointed to Lucynell sitting crosslegged in her chair, holding both feet in her hands.

"That's right," he admitted. "She wouldn't give me any trouble."

"Saturday," the old woman said, "you and her and me can drive into town and get married."

Mr. Shiftlet eased his position on the steps.

"I can't get married right now," he said. "Everything you want to do takes money and I ain't got any."

"What you need with money?" she asked.

4 "It takes money," he said. "Some people'll do anything anyhow these days, but the way I think, I wouldn't marry no woman that I couldn't take on a trip like she was somebody. I mean take her to a hotel and treat her. I wouldn't marry the Duchesser Windsor," he said firmly, "unless I could take her to a hotel and giver something good to eat.

"I was raised thataway and there ain't a thing I can do about it. My old mother taught me how to do."

"Lucynell don't even know what a hotel is," the old woman muttered. "Listen here, Mr. Shiftlet," she said, sliding forward in her chair, "you'd be getting a permanent house and a deep well and the most innocent girl in the world. You don't need no money. Lemme tell you something: there ain't any place in the world for a poor disabled friendless drifting man."

The ugly words settled in Mr. Shiftlet's head like a group of buzzards in the top of a tree. He didn't answer at once. He rolled himself a cigarette and lit it and then he said in an even voice, "Lady, a man is divided into two parts, body and spirit."

The old woman clamped her gums together.

"A body and a spirit," he repeated. "The body, lady, is like a house: it don't go anywhere; but the spirit, lady, is like a automobile: always on the move, always . . ."

5 "Listen, Mr. Shiftlet," she said, "my well never goes dry and my house is always warm in the winter and there's no mortgage on a thing about this place. You can go to the courthouse and see for yourself. And yonder under that shed is a fine automobile." She laid the bait carefully. "You can have it painted by Saturday. I'll pay for the paint."

6 In the darkness, Mr. Shiftlet's smile stretched like a weary snake waking up by a fire. After a second he recalled himself and said, "I'm only saying a man's spirit means more to him than anything else. I would have to take my wife off for the weekend without no regards at all for cost. I got to follow where my spirit says to go."

> Here Shiftlet begins to change his tone with the old woman. You might **infer** that he has some scheme in mind.

"I'll give you fifteen dollars for a weekend trip," the old woman said in a crabbed voice. "That's the best I can do."

"That wouldn't hardly pay for more than the gas and the hotel," he said. "It wouldn't feed her."

"Seventeen-fifty," the old woman said. "That's all I got so it isn't any use you trying to milk me. You can take a lunch."

Mr. Shiftlet was deeply hurt by the word "milk." He didn't doubt that she had more money sewed up in her mattress but he had already told her he was not interested in her money. "I'll make that do," he said and rose and walked off without treating with her further.

7 On Saturday the three of them drove into town in the car that the paint had barely dried on and Mr. Shiftlet and Lucynell were married in the Ordinary's office while the old woman witnessed. As they came out of the courthouse, Mr. Shiftlet began twisting his neck in his collar. He looked morose and bitter as if he had been insulted while someone held him. "That didn't satisfy me none," he said. "That was just something a woman in an office did, nothing but paper work and blood tests. What do they know about my blood? If they was to take my heart and cut it out," he said, "they wouldn't know a thing about me. It didn't satisfy me at all."

"It satisfied the law," the old woman said sharply.

"The law," Mr. Shiftlet said and spit. "It's the law that don't satisfy me."

He had painted the car dark green with a yellow band around it just under the windows. The three of them climbed in the front seat and

◆ Build Vocabulary

morose (mə rōs´) *adj.*: Gloomy; sullen

◆ Reading for Success

4 Draw Conclusions Ask students: Do you think Mr. Shiftlet really wants the money to provide Lucynell with a proper honeymoon? *Students should be able to conclude from Mr. Shiftlet's hypocrisy to date that he will not use the money honestly, that behind his high-flown talk is a self-serving goal.*

Customize for *AP Students*

Draw students' attention to the old woman's repeated description of young Lucynell as "innocent." Ask students to explain what that innocence symbolizes for Flannery O'Connor. *These students should recognize that young Lucynell is innocent because she is mentally childlike, but that O'Connor is also suggesting that only the childlike are the only moral innocents in the modern world.*

◆ Literary Focus

5 Grotesque Characters Point out that in this interchange, both Mr. Shiftlet and the old woman are closing in on the object of their obsessions. Meanwhile, any real concern for young Lucynell's future has been abandoned.

◆ Critical Thinking

6 Interpret What does the description of Mr. Shiftlet's smile suggest? *It implies a sense of hidden evil and treachery.* Guide students to look for other instances in which the narrator reveals the characters' personalities through physical descriptions.

◆ Reading for Success

7 Respond Invite students to describe their response to this scene in a journal or to a classmate. How does the scene make them feel? What questions or issues does it raise?

Cross-Curricular Connection: Science

Marriage Blood Tests The blood tests Mr. Shiftlet and young Lucynell must take prior to marrying are part of an effort to control the passage of hereditary illnesses. Some hereditary abnormalities are carried by recessive genes, or genes that do not manifest themselves unless a person receives one from each parent. Therefore, without a blood test, two such potential parents might marry and produce a child bearing both recessive genes and the related abnormality. This is just one reason why marriage between first cousins is discouraged and even illegal in most societies. It is possible, however, in small communities such as the story setting, that such an intermarriage contributed to young Lucynell's condition.

Have students discuss whether society has the moral obligation to impose restrictions on who can marry whom.

◆ Build Vocabulary

❶ **Latin Word Roots: *-sol-*** Point out the word *isolated* to students. Challenge them to use their knowledge of the root *-sol-* to define the word. *Isolated means "set apart from others" and can be linked to the root -sol- meaning "alone" as well as to the root insula meaning "island."*

Comprehension Check ☑

❷ Why does Mr. Shiftlet leave Lucynell in the diner? *He married her only in order to get the car and the honeymoon money; now that he has both, he no longer needs her.*

◆ Critical Thinking

❸ **Make a Judgment** Ask students: How do you feel about Mr. Shiftlet's actions? *Most students will say they dislike Mr. Shiftlet's actions and find them immoral and unkind.*

◆ Reading for Success

❹ **Identify With the Characters and the Situation** Ask students to put themselves in Mr. Shiftlet's position—they've just done something they're not especially proud of. Why might they offer a ride to this young boy? *Students should note that Mr. Shiftlet may want to make amends for abandoning young Lucynell. Also, he may want a chance to show off his car and flaunt his claimed moral superiority.*

Customize for *AP Students*

To encourage these students to respond thoughtfully to the story, initiate an analysis of Mr. Shiftlet's motivations throughout the story. Discuss whether he had always planned to abandon young Lucynell or was in fact willing to live with the Craters if only to gain access to the car.

the old woman said, "Don't Lucynell look pretty? Looks like a baby doll." Lucynell was dressed up in a white dress that her mother had uprooted from a trunk and there was a Panama hat on her head with a bunch of red wooden cherries on the brim. Every now and then her placid ❶ expression was changed by a sly isolated little thought like a shoot of green in the desert. "You got a prize!" the old woman said.

Mr. Shiftlet didn't even look at her. They drove back to the house to let the old woman off and pick up the lunch. When they were ready to leave, she stood staring in the window of the car, with her fingers clenched around the glass. Tears began to seep sideways out of her eyes and run along the dirty creases in her face. "I ain't ever been parted with her for two days before," she said.

Mr. Shiftlet started the motor.

"And I wouldn't let no man have her but you because I seen you would do right. Goodbye, Sugarbaby," she said, clutching at the sleeve of the white dress. Lucynell looked straight at her and didn't seem to see her there at all. Mr. Shiftlet eased the car forward so that she had to move her hands.

The early afternoon was clear and open and surrounded by pale blue sky. Although the car would go only thirty miles an hour, Mr. Shiftlet imagined a terrific climb and dip and swerve that went entirely to his head so that he forgot his morning bitterness. He had always wanted an automobile but he had never been able to afford one before. He drove very fast because he wanted to make Mobile by nightfall.

Occasionally he stopped his thoughts long enough to look at Lucynell in the seat beside him. She had eaten the lunch as soon as they were out of the yard and now she was pulling the cherries off the hat one by one and throwing them out the window. He became depressed in spite of the car. He had driven about a hundred miles when he decided that she must be hungry again and at the next small town they came to, he stopped in front of an aluminum-painted eating place called The Hot Spot and took her in and ordered her a plate of ham and grits. The ride had made her sleepy and as soon as she got up on the stool, she rested her head on the counter and shut her eyes. There was no one in The Hot Spot but Mr. Shiftlet and the boy behind the counter, a pale youth with a greasy rag hung over his shoulder. Before he could dish up the food, she was snoring gently.

"Give it to her when she wakes up," Mr. Shiftlet said. "I'll pay for it now."

The boy bent over her and stared at the long pink-gold hair and the half-shut sleeping ❷ eyes. Then he looked up and stared at Mr. Shiftlet. "She looks like an angel of Gawd," ❸ he murmured.

"Hitchhiker," Mr. Shiftlet explained. "I can't wait. I got to make Tuscaloosa."

The boy bent over again and very carefully touched his finger to a strand of the golden hair and Mr. Shiftlet left.

He was more depressed than ever as he drove on by himself. The late afternoon had grown hot and sultry and the country had flattened out. Deep in the sky a storm was preparing very slowly and without thunder as if it meant to drain every drop of air from the earth before it broke. There were times when Mr. Shiftlet preferred not to be alone. He felt too that a man with a car had a responsibility to others and he kept his eye out for a hitchhiker. Occasionally he saw a sign that warned: "Drive carefully. The life you save may be your own."

The narrow road dropped off on either side into dry fields and here and there a shack or a filling station stood in a clearing. The sun began to set directly in front of the automobile. It was a reddening ball that through his windshield was slightly flat on the bottom and top. He saw a boy in overalls and a gray hat standing on the edge of the road and he slowed the car down and stopped in front of him. The boy didn't have his hand raised to thumb the ride, he was only standing there, but he had a small cardboard suitcase and his hat was set on his ❹ head in a way to indicate that he had left somewhere for good. "Son," Mr. Shiftlet said, "I see you want a ride."

The boy didn't say he did or he didn't but he opened the door of the car and got in, and Mr. Shiftlet started driving again. The child held the suitcase on his lap and folded his arms on top of it. He turned his head and looked out the window away from Shiftlet. Mr. Shiftlet felt

◆ Build Vocabulary

guffawing (gə fô´ iŋ) *adj.*: Laughing in a loud, coarse manner

Speaking, Listening, and Viewing Mini-Lesson

Staged Reading

This mini-lesson supports the Speaking, Listening, and Viewing activity in the Idea Bank on p. 889.

Introduce the Concept Review the activity description on p. 889. Have students discuss dramatic presentations they have seen. If students have seen performances adapted from books, did these add to their appreciation of the original work?

Develop Background Before students begin their readings, have them review and discuss these strategies:

- Once parts are assigned, players should reread the story, noting any description that may shed light on how they should deliver their character's lines.
- Gesture, tone of voice, and body language can greatly enhance each player's reading.
- Players should time their responses to flow as a real conversation would.

Apply the Information Have groups present their readings to the class. If students wish to work without scripts, station a prompter near the "stage." Remind students to treat each other's dramatic efforts with respect.

Assess the Outcome Have students evaluate each group in writing using the following criteria: fidelity to the text, plausibility of characters, and overall effectiveness. Ask the class to identify any insights about the story generated by the readings.

oppressed. "Son," he said after a minute, "I got the best old mother in the world so I reckon you only got the second best."

The boy gave him a quick dark glance and then turned his face back out the window.

"It's nothing so sweet," Mr. Shiftlet continued, "as a boy's mother. She taught him his first prayers at her knee, she give him love when no other would, she told him what was right and what wasn't, and she seen that he done the right thing. Son," he said, "I never rued a day in my life like the one I rued when I left that old mother of mine."

The boy shifted in his seat but he didn't look at Mr. Shiftlet. He unfolded his arms and put one hand on the door handle.

"My mother was a angel of Gawd," Mr. Shiftlet said in a very strained voice. "He took her
5 from heaven and giver to me and I left her." His eyes were instantly clouded over with a mist of tears. The car was barely moving.

The boy turned angrily in the seat. "You go to the devil!" he cried. "My old woman is a flea bag and yours is a stinking pole cat!" and with that he flung the door open and jumped out with his suitcase into the ditch.

Mr. Shiftlet was so shocked that for about a hundred feet he drove along slowly with the door still open. A cloud, the exact color of the boy's hat and shaped like a turnip, had descended over the sun, and another, worse looking, crouched behind the car. Mr. Shiftlet felt that the rottenness of the world was about to engulf him. He raised his arm and let it fall again to his breast. "Oh Lord!" he prayed. "Break forth and wash the slime from this earth!"

The turnip continued slowly to descend. After a few minutes there was a guffawing peal of thunder from behind and fantastic raindrops, like tin-can tops, crashed over the rear of Mr. Shiftlet's car. Very quickly he stepped on the gas and with his stump sticking out the window he raced the galloping shower into Mobile.

Guide for Responding

◆ Literature and Your Life

Reader's Response How did you react to Shiftlet's final protest, his prayer that God "Break forth and wash the slime from this earth!"?

Thematic Focus Who do you think has the most difficult time coping with the demands of everyday living: Shiftlet, the mother, or the daughter?

Journal Writing In your journal, discuss your reactions to the characters in this story and their behavior. In what ways, if any, do they remind you of people you've met?

☑ Check Your Comprehension

1. What is Mr. Shiftlet's physical disability?
2. Which of the Craters' possessions does he want?
3. (a) What arguments does the old woman use to persuade Shiftlet to marry Lucynell? (b) Why does Shiftlet say he cannot marry her? (c) What causes him to change his mind?
4. What is the outcome of the story?

◆ Critical Thinking

INTERPRET

1. Explain how Shiftlet's comment that the spirit is "always on the move" foreshadows or hints at the story's outcome. **[Analyze]**
2. Why is it ironic that at the end of the story "Mr. Shiftlet felt that the rottenness of the world was about to engulf him"? **[Analyze]**
3. Shiftlet observes that "the world is almost rotten." What does the story suggest about the cause of this condition? **[Draw Conclusions]**
4. (a) What is ironic about how Shiftlet's prayer is answered at the end? (b) What does the event suggest about those whose behavior contradicts their professed beliefs? **[Draw Conclusions]**

EVALUATE

5. Mrs. Crater decides to marry Lucynell to Shiftlet; the girl seems to have no control over her fate. Does Mrs. Crater's action have any moral justification? Explain. **[Make a Judgment]**

Beyond the Selection

FURTHER READING

Other Works by Flannery O'Connor
The Complete Stories, The Violent Bear It Away, Wise Blood

Other Works With Themes Related to the Mentally Challenged
Choices: Within Reach, ed. Donald R. Gallo
Flowers for Algernon, Daniel Keyes

We suggest that you preview these works before recommending them to students.

INTERNET

To learn more about Flannery O'Connor, we suggest the following Internet sites:

For an on-line Flannery O'Connor bulletin board, go to **http://peacock.gac.peachnet.edu/~sc/focbull.html**

To read frequently asked questions and answers about her works, visit **http://peacock.gac.peachnet.edu/~sc/focfaq.html**

We *strongly recommend* that you preview sites before you send students to them.

◆ Critical Thinking

5 Connect Ask students: What is the significance of Mr. Shiftlet's use of the phrase "angel of Gawd" in referring to his mother? *Students should note that the restaurant worker described young Lucynell as an "angel of Gawd." Mr. Shiftlet is incorporating evidence of his own immoral behavior into his newest posture of high morality.*

Reinforce and Extend

Answers

Reader's Response Students may react with amusement or anger at Shiftlet's hypocrisy, or with sympathy for his complete lack of self-awareness.

Thematic Focus Students should support their responses with details from the story.

☑ Check Your Comprehension

1. He is missing part of an arm.
2. He wants their old car.
3. (a) She boasts of Lucynell's innocence and youth. (b) He says marriage is contrary to his wandering spirit; he says that he needs money to treat his wife to a honeymoon. (c) The woman offers him the car, as well as $17.50 for the honeymoon.
4. Shiftlet abandons Lucynell in a diner far from her home, and heads to Mobile in the Craters' car.

◆ Critical Thinking

1. Shiftlet himself is always on the move, as evidenced by the way he abandons Lucynell so that he can go on to Mobile.
2. Shiftlet's actions contribute to the rottenness that he senses.
3. The story suggests that the deterioration is caused by people's hypocrisy and self-centeredness.
4. (a) When he asks God to "wash the slime from the earth," a storm breaks out that threatens to wash him from the earth. (b) It suggests that people will ultimately pay for their hypocrisy.
5. Students may say that, given the mother's poverty, ignorance, and isolated, rural existence, she has few ways of providing for her daughter's future security. They may feel that she is therefore justified in her actions, since the daughter seems so unaware of her circumstances and since her limited reactions to Shiftlet are positive.

◆ Literary Focus

1. Suggested responses include the following: Shiftlet has lost part of one arm and his figure is described as forming "a crooked cross"; the old woman is described as resembling "a cedar fence post;" and Lucynell is described as having "fat helpless hands hanging at the wrists."
2. Mrs. Crater is obsessed with finding a son-in-law.
3. Suggested responses include his complaint about the lack of innocent women in the world and his criticism of automobile assembly lines.
4. Suggested responses: (a) Rather than appear as kind, polished, and false, O'Connor's characters have problems and have been hurt by the world. (b) It may be hard for readers to believe that people as mean-spirited as these exist.

◆ Reading Strategy

1. Students should select passages with strong descriptive qualities and should cite specific, vivid phrases or images.
2. Students may identify with or pity Shiftlet because of his disability and the impression that his life has never been an easy one.
3. Students may have questioned Mr. Shiftlet's motives for staying on at the Crater homestead and Mrs. Crater's motives for hiring the stranger.
4. Responses will vary with each student's predictions.
5. Her reply suggests that she would like Lucynell to talk romantically with Mr. Shiftlet, whom she is considering as a potential husband for the girl.
6. He is a hollow hypocrite who is as morally rotten as the state of the world he decries.
7. Students may suggest that it gave them a new angle on moral hypocrisy.

Guide for Responding *(continued)*

◆ Literary Focus

Grotesque Characters

All three of the main characters in O'Connor's short story are **grotesque** in some way. They exhibit exaggerated characteristics in both appearance and behavior. Both Shiftlet and old Mrs. Crater are driven by obsessions.

1. Find one physical description for each character that creates a grotesque effect.
2. What is Mrs. Crater's obsession?
3. Give an example of Mr. Shiftlet's obsession with the dire state of the world.
4. In what ways are the characters realistic? In what ways are they exaggerated?

◆ Reading Strategy

Strategies for Reading Fiction

By applying certain strategies, you can get more information and gain a greater understanding of a work of fiction. Review the strategies for reading fiction, and use them to answer these questions:

1. Find a description that helps you to envision the action. What images and descriptive phrases create a picture in your mind?
2. To be believable, even villainous characters exhibit some qualities—or find themselves in situations—that are sympathetic. Discuss one or two aspects of Shiftlet's character or situation that allow you occasionally to identify with him.
3. As you read this story, what questions did you ask yourself about the motivations of Shiftlet or Mrs. Crater? Did you find the answers as you read on? Explain.
4. Did your predictions about events in this story match the outcome? Explain.
5. When Shiftlet asks Mrs. Crater what word she wants him to teach Lucynell next, she says, "Teach her to say 'sugarpie.'" What inference can you draw from this reply?
6. Consider the full range of Shiftlet's behavior and actions in this story. What conclusions can you draw about him at the story's end?
7. Describe your personal response to this story. Did the story give you a new idea or a new angle on an old idea? Explain.

◆ Build Vocabulary

Using the Latin Root *-sol-*

Using your knowledge of the Latin root *-sol-* (alone), answer the following questions.

1. Is *solitaire* a game played by a single person or a group of players?
2. In a *soliloquy*, do two actors have an exchange or does one character address the audience?
3. Would a pilot have a co-pilot on a *solo* flight?
4. Would a person who loves to take walks alone enjoy the state of *solitude*?

Using the Word Bank: Context

For each sentence, indicate whether the word in italics is used correctly. If the word is used incorrectly, write a new sentence that uses the word properly.

1. The cottage with lace curtains, flower boxes, and a fresh paint job had a *desolate* appearance.
2. The rickety fence *listed* in the strong winds.
3. With an *ominous* expression, the jury foreman pronounced the guilty sentence.
4. After the huge dinner, the guest was *ravenous*.
5. Your *morose* reaction tells me you love the gift.
6. He was *guffawing* at the comedian's antics.

◆ Grammar and Style

Subjunctive Mood

The use of the **subjunctive mood** in contrary-to-fact statements always requires the past-tense form *were* (If she *were* nicer, she would have more friends). In statements that recommend, demand, or suggest, *be* is used instead of *am, is,* or *are* (I recommend that you *be* well prepared for the exam).

Practice Determine whether the subjunctive mood is necessary in each example. Choose the correct form of the verb in parentheses to complete each sentence.

1. I wouldn't trust that salesman, if I (be) you.
2. He requires that everyone (pay) in cash.
3. He comes every summer and (rent) a storefront.
4. He requests that each passerby (try) a sample.
5. The sample usually (taste) better than the items he delivers later.

◆ Build Vocabulary

Using the Latin Root *-sol-*

1. Solitaire is played by one player.
2. In a soliloquy, one character talks to the audience.
3. A pilot would not have a co-pilot on a solo flight.
4. A person who likes to walk alone enjoys solitude.

Using the Word Bank

1. The unpainted, windowless cottage had a *desolate* appearance.
2. Correct
3. Correct
4. Before the huge dinner, the guest felt ravenous.
5. From your morose expression, I see you loathe the gift.
6. Correct

◆ Grammar and Style

1. were; 2. pay; 3. rents; 4. try; 5. tastes

Grammar Reinforcement

For additional instruction and practice, use the page titled The Subjunctive Mood, p. 59, in the *Writer's Solution Grammar Practice Book*.

Reteach

To reteach grotesque characters, show students caricatures of famous people. Point out that the artist exaggerates a physical feature, making the portrait unrealistic but recognizable. Then, lead students to connect the exaggeration of qualities that writers sometimes use. Have students identify the quality they would exaggerate for Tom T. Shiftlet if they could "sketch" his personality.

Build Your Portfolio

Idea Bank

Writing

1. Missing Person Report As a police officer, write a detailed description of Lucynell Crater to circulate in the community following her disappearance. **[Career Link]**

2. Moral Analysis Shiftlet boasts that he has "a moral intelligence." Write an analysis in which you comment on this statement in light of his behavior.

3. Short Story Write a short story featuring a deceitful character or a character who commits a deceitful act. Provide action and dialogue that let your readers draw their own conclusions.

Speaking, Listening, and Viewing

4. Staged Reading In a small group, conduct a staged reading of the story. Speaking parts should include a narrator, Shiftlet, and Mrs. Crater. A fourth student can act out the part of Lucynell as the narrator describes her. **[Performing Arts Link]**

5. Body Language Presentation People's postures or gestures can often "speak" louder than their words. Do some research on body language and share your findings with the class.

Researching and Representing

6. Magazine Illustration It is 1953, and you are assigned to illustrate O'Connor's story for a popular magazine. Research illustration styles of the period, and apply what you've learned to illustrate a scene from the story. **[Art Link; Career Link]**

7. Special Education Research In the modern world, a mentally challenged young woman such as Lucynell would have educational opportunities. Research and report on the legislation that has led to these opportunities. **[Social Studies Link]**

Online Activity www.phlit.phschool.com

Guided Writing Lesson

Deposition

A deposition is a witness's formal, written testimony—a legal first-person recounting of events. Imagine that Shiflet has been formally accused of stealing Mrs. Crater's car and of abandoning and endangering Lucynell. As a witness to the events, write a deposition that may be used against Shiftlet. Use transitions to show the causes and effects of the man's actions.

Writing Skills Focus: Transitions to Show Cause and Effect

If you were testifying about an individual's alleged criminal actions, you would use transition words carefully to show how the individual caused certain things to happen and to demonstrate how those events had harmful effects. **Transition words that show cause and effect** include *because, as a result, consequently, if, then, as an effect, so,* and *therefore.*

Prewriting List Shiflet's statements and actions and the effects you know or imagine they had. Carefully copy quotations from the story to support your position.

Drafting Begin by explaining what Shiftlet did. Establish clear transitions that show cause and effect. Include relevant quotations to back up your statements. Finally, suggest why you believe his actions were criminal or harmful.

Revising Reread your deposition to be sure that you have described Shiflet's actions in a clear and logical way. What details can you add to sharpen the picture of his criminal behavior? What transition words can you add to clarify the causes and effects of the events? Knowing that the audience for your deposition will be lawyers or law-enforcement personnel, be sure that all your information is accurate, that you have used formal language, and that your spelling and punctuation are correct.

Idea Bank

Customizing for
Performance Levels

Following are suggestions for matching Idea Bank topics with your students' performance levels:
Less Advanced Students: 1, 4
Average Students: 2, 5, 7
More Advanced Students: 3, 6

Customizing for
Learning Modalities

Following are suggestions for matching Idea Bank topics with your students' learning modalities:
Verbal/Linguistic: 4
Bodily/Kinesthetic: 5
Visual/Spatial: 6
Logical/Mathematical: 7

Guided Writing Lesson

For more instruction on prewriting, elaboration, and revision, see *Prentice Hall Writing and Grammar.*

Writing and Language Transparencies Display the Cause-and-Effect Transparency, p. 95, to help students organize their ideas about Mr. Shiftlet's motivations and actions, and their consequences.

Writing Lab CD-ROM
Have students complete the tutorial on Exposition. Follow these steps:

1. Students can review the model of a cause-and-effect essay in the About Exposition section.
2. Have students use the Chain of Events or Timeline activity to help gather details for the deposition.
3. After students have drafted on the computer, they can use the Transition Word Bin to aid revision.

✓ ASSESSMENT OPTIONS

Formal Assessment, Selection Test, pp. 265–267, and Assessment Resources Software. The selection test is designed so that it can be easily customized to the performance levels of your students.

Alternative Assessment, p. 58, includes options for less advanced students, more advanced students, intrapersonal learners, verbal/linguistic learners, and visual/spatial learners.

PORTFOLIO ASSESSMENT
Use the following rubrics in the ***Alternative Assessment*** booklet to assess student writing:
Missing Person Report: Description Rubric, p. 112
Moral Analysis: Literary Analysis/Interpretation Rubric, p. 127
Short Story: Fictional Narrative Rubric, p. 110
Guided Writing Lesson: Cause/Effect Rubric, p. 117

LESSON OBJECTIVES

1. **To develop vocabulary and word identification skills**
   - Latin Word Roots: *-liter-*
   - Using the Word Bank: Context
2. **To use a variety of reading strategies to comprehend fiction**
   - Connect Your Experience
   - Reading Strategy: Identify with Characters
3. **To increase knowledge of other cultures and to connect common elements across cultures**
   - Background for Understanding
   - Cross-Curricular Connection (ATE)
4. **To express and support responses to the text**
   - Critical Thinking
   - Idea Bank: Diary Entry
   - Idea Bank: Matchmaker's Letter
   - Idea Bank: Group Discussion
   - Analyze Literary Criticism (ATE)
5. **To analyze literary elements**
   - Literary Focus: Epiphany
6. **To read in order to research self-selected and assigned topics**
   - Idea Bank: Accounting Curriculum
   - Idea Bank: Cultural Research
7. **To plan, prepare, organize, and present literary interpretations**
   - Idea Bank: Literary Analysis
   - Idea Bank: Role Play
   - Speaking, Listening, and Viewing Mini-Lesson
8. **To use recursive writing processes to write a personality profile**
   - Guided Writing Lesson
9. **To increase knowledge of the rules of grammar and usage**
   - Grammar and Style: Correct Use of *Who* and *Whom*

Test Preparation

Writing Skills: Punctuation (ATE, p. 891)

The teaching tips and sample test item in this workshop support the instruction and practice in the unit workshop:

Writing Skills: Punctuation, Usage, and Sentence Structure (SE, p. 1143)

Guide for Interpreting

Bernard Malamud *(1914–1986)*

"I write . . . to explain life to myself and to keep me related to men," Bernard Malamud once commented when explaining his life's work.

Childhood of Two Cultures Malamud was born in Brooklyn, New York, the son of Russian immigrants. According to his own account, Malamud's boyhood was "comparatively happy." He grew up hearing the constant mingling of Yiddish and English—an experience that contributed to his fine ear for the rhythms of spoken dialogue. A favored boyhood pastime was listening to his father recount tales of Jewish life in czarist Russia. Young Bernard soon took up this family pastime, recording stories he'd made up to tell his friends.

A Literary Range Malamud attended City College of New York and Columbia University and began publishing stories in a number of well-known magazines. Despite Malamud's strong connection to Yiddish folk tales—many stories are drawn from this oral tradition—his work depicts a broad range of settings and characters. From the gifted baseball player in *The Natural* (1952) to the handyman living in czarist Russia in the Pulitzer Prize-winning *The Fixer* (1966), all of his characters come across to readers as real and accessible, with universal hopes and concerns.

Malamud's other novels include *The Assistant* (1957), *A New Life* (1961), *The Tenants* (1971), and *Dubin's Lives* (1979). He also wrote numerous short stories, many of which were published in *The Magic Barrel* (1958), which won the National Book Award.

Capturing Life's Lessons In much of his work, Malamud uses people who share his Jewish heritage to represent all of humanity, capturing their attempts to maintain a link to their cultural heritage while trying to cope with modern realities. While some of his characters achieve success, others experience failure. By portraying failures as well as triumphs, he captures the essence of the human experience and creates a delicate balance between tragedy and comedy. Some of his stories amuse readers as the characters try to negotiate between fulfilling their ideals and meeting the practical demands of their lives. Other Malamud stories move readers to sadness as characters struggle courageously within tragic circumstances. "The First Seven Years" depicts a Polish immigrant's desire to see his daughter achieve a better life. His notion of that life, however, is not the same as hers.

◆ Background for Understanding

CULTURE: A GENERATION'S VALUES

Bernard Malamud's father was a grocer who, like many immigrants, worked diligently to forge a better life for his family. Similarly, the Polish immigrant father in "The First Seven Years" works hard to make his business succeed and dreams that his daughter will achieve a better life. The character's desire to see his daughter go to college or marry an educated man is typical of the hopes of parents of his generation and experience.

The 1950's, when this story takes place, were a prosperous decade in the United States. Many people were upwardly mobile; they worked hard and were virtually assured that their status in society would improve. Parents labored hard for material wealth so that their children would struggle less than they had; children took material comfort for granted and became more interested in matters of the spirit. Malamud's story explores the gap in values that sometimes occurred between children of the 1950's and their parents.

Prentice Hall Literature Program Resources

REINFORCE / RETEACH / EXTEND

Selection Support Pages
Build Vocabulary: Latin Word Roots: *-liter-*, p. 270
Grammar and Style: Correct Use of *Who* and *Whom*, p. 271
Reading Strategy: Identify With Characters, p. 272
Literary Focus: Epiphany, p. 273

Strategies for Diverse Student Needs, p. 59

Beyond Literature
Career Connection: Workplace Skills, p. 59

Formal Assessment Selection Test, pp. 268–270; Assessment Resources Software

Alternative Assessment, p. 59

Writing and Language Transparencies
Branching Organizer, pp. 67–69

Resource Pro CD-ROM
Includes all resource material and customizable lesson plan.

Literature CD-ROM

Listening to Literature Audiocassettes

The First Seven Years

◆ Literature and Your Life

Connect Your Experience

When parents or teachers push you to take college entrance exams, learn a skill, or take up an instrument, they hope to help you achieve a better life. Similarly, the father in this story pushes his daughter in a certain direction in the hope that she'll achieve happiness. However, her idea of happiness doesn't match his.

Journal Writing Describe the goals you have for your future, and discuss any goals that adult relatives have for you.

Thematic Focus: Literature Confronts the Everyday

In this story, everyday choices prove important. As you read, consider which choices young people should make on their own and which ones adult relatives might expect to make for them.

◆ Literary Focus

Epiphany

In a traditional short story, the plot moves toward a resolution, a point at which the conflict is resolved and the outcome of the action becomes clear. However, in an effort to capture the uncertainty of life in the modern world, many twentieth-century fiction writers have turned away from the traditional plot structure by ending their stories without a resolution. Instead, writers often construct plots that move toward an **epiphany**, a moment when a character has a flash of insight about himself or herself, another character, or life in general. In this story, the main character has an epiphany in which he suddenly sees into another character's emotions and, as a result, reexamines some long-held assumptions.

◆ Grammar and Style

Correct Use of *Who* and *Whom*

In this story, you'll find may examples of the **use of *who* and *whom***. Notice that *who*—like *he* or *she*—is used as a subject or subject complement. *Whom*—like *him* or *her*—is used as a direct object or as an object of the preposition. Look at these examples:

direct object of *respected*

. . . could turn his thoughts from Max, the college boy . . . *whom* he so much respected . . .

subject

Yet he could not help but contrast the diligence of the college boy, *who* was a peddler's son, with Miriam's unconcern . . .

◆ Reading Strategy

Identify With Characters

When you **identify with characters** in literature, you connect their thoughts, actions, and situations to your own experience. Look at this example:

Story Situation

He had begged her to go, pointing out how many fathers could not afford to send their children to college, but she said she wanted to be independent.

Identifying With the Character

I can identify with the daughter in this situation. Last summer my mother wanted me to be a camp counselor, but I wanted to have a summer of freedom.

Identifying with characters will help you to understand their problems better and relate to the decisions they make.

◆ Build Vocabulary

Latin Roots: *-liter-*

Malamud uses the word *illiterate,* which contains the Latin root *-liter-,* meaning "letter." Notice how the root contributes to the overall meaning of the word: "unable to read written letters."

Word Bank

Preview this list of words from the story.

- diligence
- connivance
- illiterate
- unscrupulous
- repugnant
- discern

Interest Grabber Write the following statements on the chalkboard before students enter the classroom:

I want you to have all the things I never had.

I want you to make something of yourself.

I only want what's best for you.

Ask students to respond to these statements. Do they sound familiar? Who might be the speaker? Who is the "you" being addressed? Students should recognize that these are expressions of parental aspirations—their hopes and dreams for their children's lives. Encourage students to add to the list by contributing other such expressions they have heard their own parents or grandparents say. Explain to students that they are about to read the story of a father who has ambitious dreams for his daughter's future that, unfortunately for him, she does not share.

Customize for
Less Proficient Readers
These students may have difficulty understanding the concept of an epiphany. It may be helpful to relate it to a conventional conflict and resolution. Explain that many contemporary writers do not wish to entirely resolve the conflict of a story. Instead, an epiphany is used to focus attention on a particular insight or understanding.

Customize for
AP Students
Prompt students to analyze how Malamud crafts a complex character portrait with relatively simple, almost spare, language. Ask students to find examples of particularly vivid passages portraying Feld and explain why these are so effective.

Customize for
English Language Learners
These students may be challenged by the way the objective narrator suddenly begins revealing Feld's thoughts and opinions, then shifts back into objective narration. Urge students to watch for signal words such as "thought" to locate the shifts.

Test Preparation Workshop

Writing Skills: Punctuation
Many standardized tests, including the ACT, require students to identify the best way to correct an error in punctuation. Use the following sample test item to demonstrate for students.

Feld is a shoemaker. Who immigrated to America from Poland.

Which is the best way to correct the underlined section of the passage?

A shoemaker who immigrated
B shoemaker—who immigrated
C shoemaker; who immigrated
D Correct as is

Answers *B* and *C* replace the incorrect punctuation with other incorrect punctuation. A period is incorrect punctuation, so *D* is not correct. No punctuation is needed between *shoemaker* and *who,* so the correct answer is *A*.

Develop Understanding

One-Minute Insight This poignant story portrays the potentially tragic results that can occur as parents struggle to let go of their maturing children. The main character, the shoemaker Feld, loves his only child, Miriam, with a fierce and ambitious love. Wanting an easier life for her than the immigrant trials of his own young adulthood, Feld plots what he believes will be an advantageous relationship with a young accounting student, Max. When Sobel, Feld's assistant, hears Feld and Max talking about Miriam, he flees the store. After her second date with Max, Miriam reports that the aspiring CPA is a soulless bore. Circumstance forces Feld to swallow his pride and visit Sobel, who reveals that he has worked for the shoemaker for five years solely out of love for Miriam. Feld, devastated, relinquishes his plans for his daughter's brilliant future as he agrees to let the apprentice ask for Miriam's hand in marriage in two years. Feld discovers the hard way that emotions cannot be dictated and that children must choose their own path in life.

◆ Literary Focus

Epiphany The term "epiphany" is derived from Greek mythology where it was used to describe the occasion when a god or goddess, wearing a disguise or concealed in a cloud, would suddenly reveal his or her true identity to a mortal. In many Christian churches, Epiphany (spelled with a capital letter) refers to an annual festival held on January 6 (the twelfth day of Christmas), commemorating the revelation of the baby Jesus to the three wise men. Influenced by his religious upbringing, the Irish novelist James Joyce (1882–1941) was the first writer to use the word as a literary term, defining it as a profound mental or spiritual revelation experienced by a character in a literary work. Although the term is still most often associated with the works of Joyce, epiphanies also occur in works by many other twentieth-century writers.

Customize for
Interpersonal Readers
Have students keep a response log as they read, considering the question "How would I feel and behave in this character's place?"

Cross-Curricular Connection: Social Studies

America's Immigrants This story is about Polish immigrants in America. The Poles are just one of many groups whose members have left their homes to seek a better life in America. For example, a huge immigration surge occurred in the mid-1800s as Irish, Chinese, and Germans—along with many others—fled economic or political difficulties. Additional immigration waves have swelled America's population since that time, whether comprised of Russian Jews escaping mob attacks in the late 1870's or Vietnamese in boats seeking freedom from a changing government in the 1980's.

Immigrants often settle first in coastal cities, straining the urban infrastructure. During the nineteenth and early twentieth centuries, large numbers of newcomers were forced to live in dark and dreary tenement house apartments, which often lacked windows, indoor plumbing, and fire escapes. Many new Americans arrived with limited financial resources, and even more limited English.

Invite students, especially those born elsewhere or with immigrant relatives, to discuss the challenges facing new arrivals. How might these affect parents' hopes for their "American" children?

The First Seven Years

Bernard Malamud

Connections to World Literature, *page 1193*

Feld, the shoemaker, was annoyed that his helper, Sobel, was so insensitive to his reverie that he wouldn't for a minute cease his fanatic pounding at the other bench. He gave him a look, but Sobel's bald head was bent over the last[1] as he worked and he didn't notice. The shoemaker shrugged and continued to peer through the partly frosted window at the nearsighted haze of falling February snow. Neither the shifting white blur outside, nor the sudden deep remembrance of the snowy Polish village where he had wasted his youth could turn his thoughts from Max the college boy, (a constant visitor in the mind since early that morning when Feld saw him trudging through the snowdrifts on his way to school) whom he so much respected because of the sacrifices he had made throughout the years—in winter or direst heat—to further his education. An old wish returned to haunt the shoemaker: that he had had a son instead of a daughter, but this blew away in ❶

1. **last** *n.*: Block shaped like a person's foot, on which shoes are made or repaired.

◀ Critical Viewing What does this image reveal about the setting of the story? **[Predict]** ❷

Block Scheduling Strategies

Consider these suggestions to take advantage of extended class time:

- Begin the class with the Interest Grabber activity on p. 891 of the teacher edition.
- Have students read the Literature and Your Life section (p. 891) and complete the Journal Writing activity. Students can discuss their responses in pairs.
- Review the Reading Strategy and discuss the concept of an epiphany. Distribute the Literary Focus page in ***Selection Support,*** p. 273.
- Use the Speaking and Listening Mini-Lesson (p. 895) to help students complete the Role Play activity (p. 901).
- Use the Career Connection: Workplace Skills in ***Beyond Literature*** to generate a discussion of the character traits necessary for resolving conflict in a workplace environment.
- Group students into writing teams to complete the Guided Writing Lesson (p. 901). Challenge them to review the story together in search of character details.

Customize for
Less Proficient Readers and English Language Learners
These students may benefit from completing page 59 in ***Strategies for Diverse Student Needs.*** The page provides a summary of "The First Seven Years" in English and Spanish, and asks students to complete a timeline of events.

Customize for
English Language Learners
Point out that the main character in this story, Feld, speaks English as his second language. His sentences are sometimes awkward. Urge students to reread these sentences slowly for comprehension.

Customize for
Musical/Rhythmic Learners
Explain that Feld's manner of speaking indicates a Yiddish accent characterized by a musical quality and an uprising tone at the end of each sentence. To help musical/rhythmic learners appreciate Feld's speech patterns, have them listen to the audiocassette recording of the selection.

Listening to Literature Audiocassettes

◆ Critical Thinking

❶ **Infer** Ask students: What do you learn about the characters of Feld, Sobel, and Max from the opening lines? *Students should infer that Feld is an immigrant who values education and feels his life has been somewhat wasted; Sobel is either insensitive or angry, and his bald head suggests he may be old. Max is a college boy who also values education.*

▶Critical Viewing◀

❷ **Predict** Students should realize that the setting is a commercial section of a fairly large city. The automobiles in the photograph reveal that the story is probably set in the first half of the twentieth century. The prominent shoe repair sign suggests that the story involves a shoemaker.

Connecting to World Literature

To connect this selection to world literature, see "The Pig," p. 1198.

the snow for Feld, if anything, was a practical man. Yet he could not help but contrast the diligence of the boy, who was a peddler's son, with Miriam's unconcern for an education. True, she was always with a book in her hand, yet when the opportunity arose for a college education, she had said no she would rather (1) find a job. He had begged her to go, pointing out how many fathers could not afford to send their children to college, but she said she wanted to be independent. As for education, what was it, she asked, but books, which Sobel, who diligently read the classics, would as usual advise her on. Her answer greatly grieved her father.

A figure emerged from the snow and the door opened. At the counter the man withdrew from a wet paper bag a pair of battered shoes for repair. Who he was the shoemaker for a moment had no idea, then his heart trembled as he realized, before he had thoroughly discerned the face, that Max himself was standing there, embarrassedly explaining what he wanted done to his old shoes. Though Feld listened eagerly, he (2) couldn't hear a word, for the opportunity that had burst upon him was deafening.

He couldn't exactly recall when the thought had occurred to him, because it was clear he had more than once considered suggesting to the boy that he go out with Miriam. But he had not dared speak, for if Max said no, how would he face him again? Or suppose Miriam, who harped so often on independence, blew up in anger and shouted at him for his meddling? Still, the chance was too good to let by: all it meant was an introduction. They might long ago have become friends had they happened to meet somewhere, therefore was it not his duty—an obligation—to bring them together, nothing more, a harmless connivance to replace an accidental encounter in the subway, let's say, or a mutual friend's introduction in the street? Just let him once see and talk to her and he would for sure be interested. As for Miriam, what possible harm for a working girl in an office, who met only loud-mouthed salesmen and illiterate shipping clerks, to make the acquaintance of a fine scholarly boy? Maybe he (3) would awaken in her a desire to go to college; if not—the shoemaker's mind at last came to grips with the truth—let her marry an educated man and live a better life.

When Max finished describing what he wanted done to his shoes, Feld marked them, both with enormous holes in the soles which he pretended not to notice, with large white-chalk x's, and the rubber heels, thinned to the nails, he marked with o's, though it troubled him he might have mixed up the letters. Max inquired the price, and the shoemaker cleared his throat and asked the boy, above Sobel's insistent hammering, would he please step through the side door there into the hall. Though surprised, Max did as the shoemaker requested, and Feld went in after him. For a minute they were both silent, because Sobel had stopped banging, and it seemed they (4) understood neither was to say anything until the noise began again. When it did, loudly, the shoemaker quickly told Max why he had asked to talk to him.

"Ever since you went to high school," he said, in the dimly-lit hallway, "I watched you in the morning go to the subway to school, and I (5) said always to myself, this is a fine boy that he wants so much an education."

"Thanks," Max said, nervously alert. He was tall and grotesquely thin, with sharply cut features, particularly a beak-like nose. He was wearing a loose, long slushy overcoat that hung down to his ankles, looking like a rug draped over his bony shoulders, and a soggy, old brown hat, as battered as the shoes he had brought in.

"I am a business man," the shoemaker abruptly said to conceal his embarrassment, "so I will explain you right away why I talk to you. I have a girl, my daughter Miriam—she is nineteen—a very nice girl and also so pretty that everybody looks on her when she passes by in the street. She is smart, always with a book, and I thought to myself that a boy like you, an educated boy—I thought maybe you will be interested sometime to meet a girl like

◆ Build Vocabulary

diligence (dil′ ə jəns) *n.*: Constant, careful effort; perseverance

connivance (kə nī′ vəns) *n.*: Secret cooperation

illiterate (i lit′ ər it) *adj.*: Unable to read or write

unscrupulous (un skro͞op′ yə ləs) *adj.*: Not restrained by ideas of right and wrong

◆ Reading Strategy

❶ Identify With Characters Ask: If you were in Feld's place, would you want your daughter to attend college? Why or why not? *Students should support their answers with specific reasons, for example saying that they too would want to make life easier for their child or that they believe life experience is more valuable than college.*

◆ Literary Focus

❷ Epiphany Point out the mini-epiphany Feld experiences in this sentence. What is the opportunity that presented itself so urgently to Feld? *This is his chance to introduce Max and Miriam.* Urge students to watch for other moments of insight that may presage the story's final and central epiphany.

◆ Build Vocabulary

❸ Latin Roots: *-liter-* Point out the word *illiterate* in this sentence. Ask students to recall the word's meaning and explain its basis in the root *-liter-*. *Illiterate means "unable to read written letters" and derives from -liter- meaning "letter."*

◆ Critical Thinking

❹ Interpret; Infer Ask students: Why does Feld wait for Sobel to resume his work before talking to Max? *He wants to be sure that Sobel cannot hear him.* What does this reveal about Feld's attitude toward Sobel? *He considers him merely as an employee, rather than as a trusted friend.*

◆ Critical Thinking

❺ Connect Why does Feld value Max's education so highly? *Harsh childhood conditions limited his own education. In addition, he believes that education holds the key to a higher status than his own as tradesman.*

Beyond the Classroom

Career Connection

Apprenticeships Sobel's period of training in shoe repair is a form of apprenticeship. An apprentice receives training in an art, trade, or craft from an experienced practitioner.

Apprenticeships once made it possible for unskilled workers to enter a trade, perhaps that of an older relative, and learn that trade while working. Today, on-the-job training more often occurs through formal courses and printed material. Have interested students survey parents or other workers to learn about job training they have person-ally undertaken.

Community Connection

Ethnic Neighborhoods Point out to students that many cities have ethnic neighborhoods such as Chinatown, Little Italy or Little Poland. Have students identify examples of such neighborhoods in your community or in a nearby city. Challenge students to outline features of such neighborhoods. For example, students may mention shops selling ethnic foods and street or shop signs in languages other than English. Have students discuss the reasons why these neighborhoods exist. How do these neighborhoods make it easier for immigrants to adjust to life in America? What are the possible drawbacks of such communities?

this." He laughed a bit when he had finished and was tempted to say more but had the good sense not to.

Max stared down like a hawk. For an uncomfortable second he was silent, then he asked, "Did you say nineteen?"

6 "Yes."

"Would it be all right to inquire if you have a picture of her?"

> **◆ Reading Strategy**
> 7 Put yourself in Feld's place. How do you think he feels during this exchange?

"Just a minute." The shoemaker went into the store and hastily returned with a snapshot that Max held up to the light.

"She's all right," he said.

Feld waited.

"And is she sensible—not the flighty kind?"

"She is very sensible."

After another short pause, Max said it was okay with him if he met her.

"Here is my telephone," said the shoemaker, hurriedly handing him a slip of paper. "Call her up. She comes home from work six o'clock."

Max folded the paper and tucked it away into his worn leather wallet.

"About the shoes," he said. "How much did you say they will cost me?"

"Don't worry about the price."

"I just like to have an idea."

"A dollar—dollar fifty. A dollar fifty," the shoemaker said.

At once he felt bad, for he usually charged two twenty-five for this kind of job. Either he should have asked the regular price or done the work for nothing.

Later, as he entered the store, he was startled by a violent clanging and looked up to see Sobel pounding with all his might upon the
8 naked last. It broke, the iron striking the floor and jumping with a thump against the wall, but before the enraged shoemaker could cry out, the assistant had torn his hat and coat from the hook and rushed out into the snow.

So Feld, who had looked forward to anticipating how it would go with his daughter and Max, instead had a great worry on his mind. Without his temperamental helper he was a lost man, especially since it was years now that he had carried the store alone. The shoemaker had for an age suffered from a heart condition that threatened collapse if he dared exert himself. Five years ago, after an attack, it had appeared as though he would have either to sacrifice his business upon the auction block and live on a pittance thereafter, or put himself at the mercy of some unscrupulous employee who would in the end probably ruin him. But just at the moment of his darkest despair, this Polish refugee, Sobel, appeared one night from the street and begged for work. He was a stocky man, poorly dressed, with a bald head that had once been blond, a severely plain face and soft blue eyes prone to tears over the sad books he read, a young man but old—no one would have guessed thirty. Though he confessed he knew nothing of shoemaking, he said he was apt and would work for a very little if Feld taught him the trade. Thinking that with, after all, a landsman,[2] he would have less to fear than from a complete stranger, Feld took him on and within six weeks the refugee rebuilt as good a shoe as he, and not long thereafter expertly ran the business for the thoroughly relieved shoemaker. 9

Feld could trust him with anything and did, frequently going home after an hour or two at the store, leaving all the money in the till, knowing Sobel would guard every cent of it. The amazing thing was that he demanded so little. His wants were few; in money he wasn't interested—in nothing but books, it seemed—which he one by one lent to Miriam, together with his profuse, queer written comments, manufactured during his lonely rooming house evenings, thick pads of commentary which the shoemaker peered at and twitched his shoulders over as his daughter, from her fourteenth year, read page by sanctified page, as if the word of God were inscribed on them. To protect Sobel, Feld himself had to see that he received more than he asked for. Yet his conscience bothered him for not insisting that the assistant accept a better wage than he was getting, though Feld had honestly told him he could earn a handsome salary if he worked elsewhere, or maybe opened a place of his own. But the assistant answered, somewhat ungraciously, that he was not interested in going elsewhere, and though Feld frequently asked himself what keeps him here? why does he stay? he finally answered it that the man, no

2. **landsman** *n.*: Fellow countryman.

◆ Critical Thinking

6 Infer Ask students: What can you infer about Max's character based on this passage? *Students should recognize that the narrator's use of the word* hawk *suggests that Max is sharp and calculating, a suggestion further supported by his request to see a picture of Miriam. He wants to make sure that her appearance is acceptable to him—despite the fact that readers have already learned that Max himself is quite unattractive.*

◆ Reading Strategy

7 Identify With Characters Students should recognize Feld's embarrassment about the conversation, his pride in his daughter's qualities, and his almost reverential respect for Max's educated status.

◆ Critical Thinking

8 Speculate Ask students to speculate about the reasons behind Sobel's outburst.

◆ Reading Strategy

9 Identify With Characters Ask: If you were Sobel, why might you be willing to work for so little to learn a trade in your new home? *Students should identify with Sobel's vulnerability as an immigrant and his desire to build a new life for himself.*

◆ Critical Thinking

10 Draw Conclusions What do books represent for Sobel? *Students should note that Sobel clearly reads books both for their inherent value and for the bridge they create with Miriam.*

Speaking, Listening, and Viewing Mini-Lesson

Role Play

This mini-lesson supports the Speaking, Listening, and Viewing activity in the Idea Bank on p. 901.

Introduce the Concept Review the description of the activity in the Idea Bank. Prompt students to keep these guidelines in mind as they develop their role play:

- Characters in a role play should behave consistently with earlier words and actions.
- Characters, like living people, can and do grow or change; however, there should be recognizable causes for the growth and change.

Develop Background Have students recall situations in which they finally engaged in a long-awaited conversation or activity. Did others who were involved behave as students predicted? You might point out that Sobel has already demonstrated tremendous persistence where Miriam is concerned, while Feld has shown his commitment to a particular future for his daughter.

Apply the Information Suggest that student pairs brainstorm possible outcomes of the conversation, sketching out dialogue together. Then encourage students to enter the character's thinking, adding new dialogue, gestures, and behavior as the role play proceeds.

Assess the Outcome Use the bulleted guidelines above to help you evaluate the credibility, originality, and audience appeal of each performance.

◆ Reading Strategy

❶ **Identify With Characters** Considering your own past experience, why do you think Sobel continues working for the shoemaker? *Students should conclude that Sobel must have a personal motive for remaining. Some may note that he may have felt comfortable in such a familiar environment and may have been hesitant to take the risk of changing his daily routine. More advanced students may suspect it is his attachment to Miriam.*

◆ Literary Focus

❷ **Epiphany** Ask students why they think Feld finds it repugnant to send Miriam to Sobel's house. Point out that his feelings may anticipate his later insight and challenge students to make predictions about that insight. *Students should note that Feld likely senses the bond between Miriam and Sobel though he clearly hasn't yet acknowledged this awareness. They should speculate that Feld's ultimate epiphany will concern the strength of that bond.*

▶Critical Viewing◀

❸ **Connect** Students should use prior knowledge or context clues from the story to identify the last pictured in this photograph.

◆ Literature and Your Life

❹ Discuss with students the hopes Feld has for the date between Miriam and Max. Ask: What experiences have you had with dates arranged by others? How do you think Max and Miriam's date will turn out? *Students may mention disastrous arranged dates or their surprise at successful arrangements. They will likely speculate that the date between Max and Miriam will not go well.*

◀ Critical Viewing Which item mentioned in the story is shown in this photograph? **[Connect]** ❸

❶ doubt because of his terrible experiences as a refugee, was afraid of the world.

After the incident with the broken last, angered by Sobel's behavior, the shoemaker decided to let him stew for a week in the rooming house, although his own strength was taxed dangerously and the business suffered. However, after several sharp nagging warnings from both his wife and daughter, he went finally in search of Sobel, as he had once before, quite recently, when over some fancied slight—Feld had merely asked him not to give Miriam so many books to read because her eyes were strained and red—the assistant had left the place in a huff, an incident which, as usual, came to nothing for he had returned after the shoemaker had talked to him, and taken his seat at the bench. But this time, after Feld had plodded through the snow to Sobel's house—he had thought of sending Miriam but the idea became ❷ repugnant to him—the burly landlady at the door informed him in a nasal voice that Sobel was not at home, and though Feld knew this was a nasty lie, for where had the refugee to go? still for some reason he was not completely sure of—it may have been the cold and his fatigue—he decided not to insist on seeing him. Instead he went home and hired a new helper.

Having settled the matter, though not entirely to his satisfaction, for he had much more to do than before, and so, for example, could no longer lie late in bed mornings because he had to get up to open the store for the new assistant, a speechless, dark man with an irritating rasp as he worked, whom he would not trust with the key as he had Sobel. Furthermore, this one, though able to do a fair repair job, knew nothing of grades of leather or prices, so Feld had to make his own purchases: and every night at closing time it was necessary to count the money in the till and lock up. However, he was not dissatisfied, for he lived much in his thoughts of Max and Miriam. The college boy had called her, and they had arranged a meeting for this coming Friday night. The shoemaker would personally have preferred Saturday, which he felt would make it a date of the first magnitude, but ❹ he learned Friday was Miriam's choice, so he said nothing. The day of the week did not matter. What mattered was the aftermath. Would they like each other and want to be friends? He sighed at all the time that would have to go by before he knew for sure. Often he was tempted to talk to Miriam about the boy, to ask whether she thought she would like his type—he had told her only that he considered Max a nice boy and had suggested he call her—but the one time he tried she snapped at him—justly—how should she know?

At last Friday came. Feld was not feeling particularly well so he stayed in bed, and Mrs. Feld thought it better to remain in the bedroom with him when Max called. Miriam received the boy, and her parents could hear their voices, his throaty one, as they talked. Just before leaving, Miriam brought Max to the bedroom door and he stood there a minute, a tall, slightly hunched figure wearing a thick, droopy ❺ suit, and apparently at ease as he greeted the shoemaker and his wife, which was surely a good sign. And Miriam, although she had

Analyze an Author's Comment

Bernard Malamud began publishing fiction in the 1950's, one of a generation of gifted Jewish writers that included Saul Bellow, Norman Mailer, and Isaac Bashevis Singer. Among these, Malamud has been praised for the accessibility of his style and themes. The author himself in speaking of the value of ordinary narrative forms said, "The human race needs the novel . . . . Those who say the novel is dead can't write them."

Malamud's place among writers of his generation is further defined by his moral vision. The characters in his fiction often seem to struggle against base instincts in an attempt to lead better, more virtuous lives. Moreover, the virtues Malamud treats in his fiction are not inverted, revolutionary, or abstract. As one critic said, "Our image of Bernard Malamud is so bound up with certain familiar sentiments concerning conscience and moral accountability that scarcely anyone writes about him without paying tribute to them." The critic sums up this aspect of Malamud's writing as being a "mission of moral improvement."

Read these statements to students and have them discuss the following questions as a group.

1. In "The First Seven Years," does Malamud display a strong "mission of moral improvement?" *Student answers should reflect an awareness that the author's moral view is quite plain in the story.*
2. What virtues, if any, does the author seem to favor, and which characters bear those virtues? *The author seems to especially admire Sobel's intelligence, patience, and capacity for faithful, enduring love.*

5 worked all day, looked fresh and pretty. She was a large-framed girl with a well-shaped body, and she had a fine open face and soft hair. They made, Feld thought, a first-class couple.

Miriam returned after 11:30. Her mother was already asleep, but the shoemaker got out of bed and after locating his bathrobe went into the kitchen, where Miriam, to his surprise, sat at the table, reading.

"So where did you go?" Feld asked pleasantly.

"For a walk," she said, not looking up.

"I advised him," Feld said, clearing his throat, "he shouldn't spend so much money."

"I didn't care."

The shoemaker boiled up some water for tea and sat down at the table with a cupful and a thick slice of lemon.

"So how," he sighed after a sip, "did you enjoy?"

"It was all right."

He was silent. She must have sensed his disappointment, for she added, "You can't really tell much the first time."

"You will see him again?"

Turning a page, she said that Max had asked for another date.

"For when?"

"Saturday."

"So what did you say?"

"What did I say?" she asked, delaying for a moment—"I said yes."

7 Afterwards she inquired about Sobel, and Feld, without exactly knowing why, said the assistant had got another job. Miriam said nothing more and began to read. The shoemaker's conscience did not trouble him; he was satisfied with the Saturday date.

During the week, by placing here and there a deft question, he managed to get from Miriam some information about Max. It surprised him to learn that the boy was not studying to be either a doctor or lawyer but was taking a business course leading to a degree in accountancy. Feld was a little disappointed because he thought of accountants as bookkeepers and would have preferred "a higher profession." However, it was not long before he had investigated the subject and discovered that Certified Public Accountants were highly respected people, so he was thoroughly content as Saturday approached. But because Saturday was a busy day, he was much in the store and therefore did not see Max when he came to call for Miriam. From his wife he learned there had been nothing especially revealing about their meeting. Max had rung the bell and Miriam had got her coat and left with him—nothing more. Feld did not probe, for his wife was not particularly observant. Instead, he waited up for Miriam with a newspaper on his lap, which he scarcely looked at so lost was he in thinking of the future. He awoke to find her in the room with him, tiredly removing her hat. Greeting her, he was suddenly inexplicably afraid to ask anything about the evening. But since she volunteered nothing he was at last forced to inquire how she had enjoyed herself. Miriam began something noncommittal but apparently changed her mind, for she said after a minute, "I was bored."

When Feld had sufficiently recovered from his anguished disappointment to ask why, she answered without hesitation, "Because he's nothing more than a materialist." 8

"What means this word?"

"He has no soul. He's only interested in things."

He considered her statement for a long time but then asked, "Will you see him again?"

"He didn't ask."

"Suppose he will ask you?"

"I won't see him."

He did not argue: however, as the days went by he hoped increasingly she would change her mind. He wished the boy would telephone, because he was sure there was more to him than Miriam, with her inexperienced eye, could discern. But Max didn't call. As a matter of fact he took a different route to school, no longer passing the shoemaker's store, and Feld was deeply hurt.

Then one afternoon Max came in and asked for his shoes. The shoemaker took them down

6 **◆ Reading Strategy**
Looking into your own experience, why do you think Feld ends up asking Miriam about her date?

◆ Build Vocabulary

repugnant (ri pug´ nənt) *adj.*: Offensive; disagreeable

discern (di sʉrn´) *v.*: To perceive or recognize; make out clearly

Beyond the Classroom

Community Connection

Local Business The main drama of this story takes place in a shoe repair shop, where people like Feld and Max have become acquainted while transacting routine business. Have students analyze the kinds of interactions they have with businesses in your community. Have they worked in local businesses?Are they acquainted with any proprietors or workers? Then discuss how local business owners participate in the community. Do they live locally? What, if any, role do they play in community decisions?

Customize for AP Students

Help these students to appreciate the character Malamud has portrayed in Max, despite the fact that readers only briefly encounter Max directly. Challenge students to look back through the text for characteristics of Max's appearance and behavior.

Customize for Visual/Spatial Learners

5 Read aloud the descriptions of Max and Miriam. Ask students to compare and contrast the two characters' appearances. What impression of each character is suggested by the comparison? Why is Feld's description of the couple ironic? *Max appears physically unattractive—"droopy"—while Miriam is "fresh and pretty." Ironically, though Feld describes the two as a "first-class couple," readers can see that they are obviously ill suited to each other.*

◆ Reading Strategy

6 Identify With Characters Students should recognize that Feld's curiosity simply gets the better of him. He is so invested in his dream of their marriage that his anxiety over its outcome is stronger than his respect for Miriam's privacy. Students should re-call from their own lives situations in which their curiosity about something overpowered politeness and better judgment.

◆ Critical Thinking

7 Infer Ask: What can you infer about Miriam's feelings for Sobel from her inquiry? What does Feld's concealment of Sobel's real situation suggest about his feelings? *Students should recognize that Miriam cares for Sobel. Feld's concealment shows that he senses her feelings and wants to discourage them.*

8 Clarification Draw students' at-tention to the word *materialist*, used by Miriam to describe Max. Explain that it is commonly used with a negative connotation. It is a difficult word, and the Polish-born Feld is unlikely to know its meaning. Discuss what it means for Miriam to know the meaning of a word that Feld does not. *Miriam probably feels a certain sense of superiority.*

◆ Literary Focus

❶ Epiphany The story of Max and Miriam's relationship "ends" here. However, Malamud continues the story past its resolution of the two dates in order to tell of Feld's epiphany. Ask students to predict what that upcoming insight may be. *Students may say Feld will realize he should not have meddled in Miriam's love life or that he will recognize the affection between Miriam and Sobel.*

Customize for *English Language Learners*

❷ Acknowledge with these students the difficulty in reading the unpunctuated dialogue presented here. Encourage students to rewrite the paragraph, adding quotation marks to indicate dialogue.

◆ Reading Strategy

❸ Identify With Characters Ask: If you were in Miriam's position, would you be aware of Sobel's feelings? Explain why or why not. *Students should identify with Miriam's situation as the admired party, saying that they usually sense it when someone admires them. Some students may comment that people, especially those who are insecure or preoccupied, may not notice admiration.*

◆ Literary Focus

❹ Epiphany Malamud announces Feld's epiphany with the text: "Feld had a sudden insight."

Customize for *Less Proficient Readers*

Have students summarize the plot up to this point. *Summaries should include the following: Feld, a Polish-born shoemaker, arranges a date between his daughter Miriam and a young college student Max in the hopes of securing for Miriam an educated husband and "better life." Feld's employee, Sobel, who loves Miriam, quits his job in response, leaving Feld overworked. Max and Miriam have two dates but do not respond to one another. Feld, who is in ill health, has a heart attack under the strain of matchmaking and running his business without Sobel.*

from the shelf where he had placed them, apart from the other pairs. He had done the work himself and the soles and heels were well built and firm. The shoes had been highly polished and somehow looked better than new. Max's Adam's apple went up once when he saw them, and his eyes had little lights in them.

"How much?" he asked, without directly looking at the shoemaker.

"Like I told you before," Feld answered sadly. "One dollar fifty cents."

Max handed him two crumpled bills and received in return a newly-minted silver half dollar.

❶ He left. Miriam had not been mentioned. That night the shoemaker discovered that his new assistant had been all the while stealing from him, and he suffered a heart attack.

Though the attack was very mild, he lay in bed for three weeks. Miriam spoke of going for Sobel, but sick as he was Feld rose in wrath against the idea. Yet in his heart he knew there was no other way, and the first weary day back in the shop thoroughly convinced him, so that night after supper he dragged himself to Sobel's rooming house.

He toiled up the stairs, though he knew it was bad for him, and at the top knocked at the door. Sobel opened it and the shoemaker entered. The room was a small, poor one, with a single window facing the street. It contained a narrow cot, a low table and several stacks of books piled haphazardly around on the floor along the wall, which made him think how queer Sobel was, to be uneducated and read so much. He had once asked him, Sobel, why you read so much? and the assistant could not answer him. Did you ever study in a college someplace? he had asked but Sobel shook his head.
❷ He read, he said, to know. But to know what, the shoemaker demanded, and to know, why? Sobel never explained, which proved he read much because he was queer.

Feld sat down to recover his breath. The assistant was resting on his bed with his heavy back to the wall. His shirt and trousers were clean, and his stubby fingers, away from the shoemaker's bench, were strangely pallid. His face was thin and pale, as if he had been shut in this room since the day he had bolted from the store.

"So when you will come back to work?" Feld asked him.

To his surprise, Sobel burst out, "Never."

Jumping up, he strode over to the window that looked out upon the miserable street. "Why should I come back?" he cried.

"I will raise your wages."

"Who cares for your wages!"

The shoemaker, knowing he didn't care, was at a loss what else to say.

"What do you want from me, Sobel?"

"Nothing."

"I always treated you like you was my son."

Sobel vehemently denied it. "So why you look for strange boys in the street they should go out with Miriam? Why you don't think of me?"

The shoemaker's hands and feet turned freezing cold. His voice became so hoarse he couldn't speak. At last he cleared his throat and croaked, "So what has my daughter got to do with a shoemaker thirty-five years old who works for me?"

"Why do you think I worked so long for you?" Sobel cried out. "For the stingy wages I sacrificed five years of my life so you could have to eat and drink and where to sleep?"

"Then for what?" shouted the shoemaker.

"For Miriam," he blurted—"for her."

The shoemaker, after a time, managed to say, "I pay wages in cash, Sobel," and lapsed into silence. Though he was seething with excitement, his mind was coldly clear, and he had to admit to himself he had sensed all along that Sobel felt this way. He had never so much as thought it consciously, but he had felt it and was afraid.

"Miriam knows?" he muttered hoarsely.

"She knows."

"You told her?"

"No."

"Then how does she know?" ❸

"How does she know?" Sobel said, "because she knows. She knows who I am and what is in my heart."

> **◆ Literary Focus**
> How can you tell Feld is having an epiphany?

Feld had a sudden insight. In some devious way, with his books and commentary, Sobel had given Miriam to understand that he loved her. ❹ The shoemaker felt a terrible anger at him for his deceit.

Reteach

To reteach epiphany, use a graphic organizer like the one at right. As students identify how Feld's view changes, they will find their way to the moment at which his view changes. When students have identified the moment of change, ask them who or what changes, Sobel, Feld, or something else? *Students should recognize that an epiphany is a change in the character. While it may be initiated by an external event, the change is internal.*

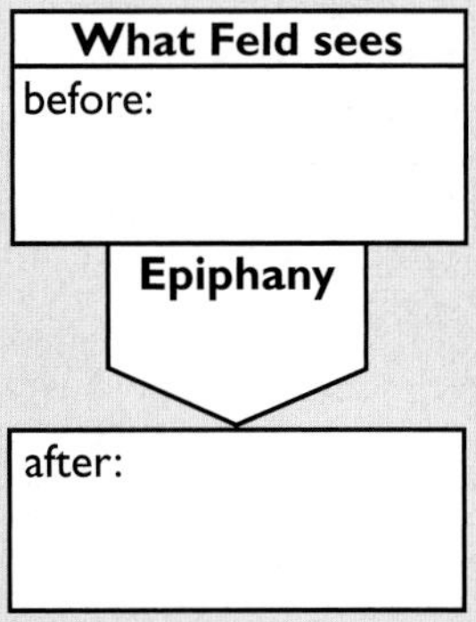

"Sobel, you are crazy," he said bitterly. "She will never marry a man so old and ugly like you."

Sobel turned black with rage. He cursed the shoemaker, but then, though he trembled to hold it in, his eyes filled with tears and he broke into deep sobs. With his back to Feld, he stood at the window, fists clenched, and his shoulders shook with his choked sobbing.

Watching him, the shoemaker's anger diminished. His teeth were on edge with pity for the man, and his eyes grew moist. How strange and sad that a refugee, a grown man, bald and old with his miseries, who had by the skin of his teeth escaped Hitler's incinerators,[3] should fall in love, when he had got to America, with a girl less than half his age. Day after day, for five years he had sat at his bench, cutting and hammering away, waiting for the girl to become a woman, unable to ease his heart with speech, knowing no protest but desperation.

"Ugly I didn't mean," he said half aloud.

Then he realized that what he had called ugly was not Sobel but Miriam's life if she married him. He felt for his daughter a strange and gripping sorrow, as if she were already Sobel's bride, the wife, after all, of a shoemaker, and had in her life no more than her mother had had. And all his dreams for her—why he had slaved and destroyed his heart with anxiety and labor—all these dreams of a better life were dead.

The room was quiet. Sobel was standing by the window reading, and it was curious that when he read he looked young.

"She is only nineteen," Feld said brokenly. "This is too young yet to get married. Don't ask her for two years more, till she is twenty-one, then you can talk to her."

Sobel didn't answer. Feld rose and left. He went slowly down the stairs but once outside, though it was an icy night and the crisp falling snow whitened the street, he walked with a stronger stride.

But the next morning, when the shoemaker arrived, heavy-hearted, to open the store, he saw he needn't have come, for his assistant was already seated at the last, pounding leather for his love.

3. **Hitler's incinerators:** During World War II, millions of Jews were murdered by the Nazis under the direction of German dictator Adolf Hitler (1889–1945).

Guide for Responding

◆ Literature and Your Life

Reader's Response Which ambitions for Miriam's future seem more worthy to you, Feld's or Miriam's? Explain.

Thematic Focus Explain how the everyday event of having shoes repaired becomes more than an ordinary errand in this story.

☑ Check Your Comprehension

1. (a) Why does Feld want to introduce Max to his daughter? (b) What about Max appeals to Feld?
2. How does the introduction take place?
3. How does Miriam react to her second date with Max?
4. What causes Sobel to quit his job with Feld?
5. How does Feld respond to Sobel's revelation about his feelings for Miriam?

◆ Critical Thinking

INTERPRET

1. How does Feld's belief that he wasted his youth shape his actions? **[Analyze]**
2. (a) What does education represent to Feld? (b) What does it represent to Sobel? **[Interpret]**
3. How might Feld's meddling in Miriam's life change her future? **[Speculate]**
4. In what ways are Feld and Sobel similar, despite their different goals for Miriam? **[Compare and Contrast]**

EVALUATE

5. Do you think Feld was right to interfere in Miriam's life? Explain. **[Make a Judgment]**

EXTEND

6. Discuss some pros and cons of having particular career aspirations for someone you love. **[Career Link]**

Beyond the Selection

FURTHER READING

Other Works by Bernard Malamud

The Natural, The Fixer, The Magic Barrel, The Tenants

Other Works With the Theme of Accepting Change

Davita's Harp, Chaim Potok

A Gathering of Days, Joan W. Blos

Tevye the Dairyman, Sholom Aleichem

We suggest that you preview these works before recommending them to students.

INTERNET

You and your students may find additional information about Bernard Malamud on the Internet.

We suggest the following sites. Please be aware, however, that sites may have changed since this information was published.

Go to **http://www.emanuelnyc.org/bulletin/archive/35.html**

We *strongly recommend* that you preview sites before you send students to them.

Reinforce and Extend

Customize for
AP Students

Challenge these students to speculate about whether Feld will tell Miriam about his discussion with Sobel. *Students may say that Feld won't tell Miriam as he wants to discourage the relationship. On the other hand, he might tell her in the hope that she will respond negatively and end Sobel's hopes herself.*

Answers

◆ Literature and Your Life

Reader's Response Students may admire Feld for seeking a better life for his daughter. Others may sympathize with Miriam, who wants a man with soul rather than a materialist.

Thematic Focus Max's visit to the shoe repair shop becomes the key, in Feld's mind, that opens the door to a great future for Miriam.

☑ Check Your Comprehension

1. (a) He hopes they will date and possibly marry. (b) Feld admires Max's college education and the comfortable future he thinks it will achieve.
2. Feld suggests a date to Max, showing him Miriam's picture and providing her phone number.
3. She is disappointed and shows no interest in future dates.
4. He realizes that Feld is trying to arrange a match between Max and Miriam, whom Sobel loves.
5. He is shocked, but recognizes that the choice is Miriam's. He asks Sobel to wait two years before proposing to Miriam.

◆ Critical Thinking

1. He wants Miriam to have the advantages he lacked.
2. (a) Feld views education as a means of gaining respect and achieving financial success. (b) Sobel views education as an opportunity to expand his knowledge and understanding of the world.
3. Possible responses: She may become resentful of her father's meddling and may even become estranged from him. She may, on the other hand, come to see things his way, and decide not to marry Sobel.

(Answers continue on p. 900)

Answers *(continued from p. 899)*

4. They both love Miriam and are willing to make sacrifices for her, both value education, and both are immigrants who have struggled to improve themselves.
5. Some students will say Feld had the right as Miriam's parent, others will say he should have stayed out of her love life.
6. Possible responses: Aspirations can inspire a loved one to achieve those goals. On the other hand, aspirations which conflict with someone else's reality or plans can lead to problems.

◆ Reading Strategy

Students should draw plausible links from the story character to their own experience, explaining their imagined actions and emotions with reference to the links.

◆ Literary Focus

1. Feld suddenly understands that Sobel's love for Miriam is the center of meaning in Sobel's life.
2. Feld has to give up his long-cherished dream of a "better life" for Miriam.
3. Suggested responses: (a) He may become more sensitive to the wishes and feelings of others.
   (b) Feld may feel saddened and even a bit resentful toward his daughter for not sharing or fulfilling his dreams for her future.
   (c) Feld's epiphany will probably result in his allowing Miriam to marry Sobel when he asks her.

◆ Build Vocabulary

Using the Latin Root: *-liter-*
Suggested responses:

1. literary: related to letters
2. literal: exactly as the letters say
3. alliteration: the repetition of sounds from a letter or letters, used to create a particular effect in writing
4. literacy: the ability to read

Using the Word Bank
1. illiterate; 2. repugnant; 3. diligence; 4. unscrupulous; 5. discern; 6. connivance

Guide for Responding *(continued)*

◆ Reading Strategy

IDENTIFY WITH CHARACTERS

When you **identify with characters,** you connect to their experiences, emotions, and actions by drawing links to your own life. This strategy of connecting with the story allows you to get more emotionally involved in your reading.

Choose a character from "The First Seven Years" and find as many links as possible to your own experience. Then imagine yourself in the character's situation. How would you feel? What actions might you take? Answer these questions in a short paragraph that explains the connections you discovered to your own life. You may want to use an outline like this one to organize your thoughts:

I. How the Character Is Like Me
  a.
  b.
II. How I Might React in the Character's Situation
  a.
  b.
III. Actions I Might Take If I Were the Character
  a.
  b.

◆ Literary Focus

EPIPHANY

In "The First Seven Years," as in many modern stories, the action moves toward an **epiphany,** or sudden flash of insight, rather than a traditional resolution.

1. What is the epiphany that Feld experiences at the end of the story?
2. What long-held assumptions does Feld reevaluate as a result of his epiphany?
3. Speculate how this epiphany might
   (a) change Feld's way of thinking in the future.
   (b) affect Feld's attitude toward Miriam.
   (c) affect a future course of events.

◆ Build Vocabulary

USING THE LATIN ROOT *-liter-*

Use your knowledge of the Latin root *-liter-*, meaning "letter," to expand your vocabulary. Suggest a definition for each of the following words. Then check your definitions against those in a dictionary.

1. literary **2.** literal **3.** alliteration **4.** literacy

USING THE WORD BANK: Context

On your paper, write the Word Bank word you might find in each of these newspaper articles:

1. *Reading Rate Declines Among American Adults*
2. *Residents Complain of Dump's Disagreeable Smell*
3. *Hard-Working Teenagers Turn Vacant Lot Into Garden*
4. *Dishonorable Band of Thieves Gets Nabbed*
5. *Girl of Ten Recognizes Error in Mayor's Speech*
6. *Five Executives Caught Plotting a Takeover*

◆ Grammar and Style

CORRECT USE OF *WHO* AND *WHOM*

Using *who* and *whom* correctly helps Malamud clarify which character he's describing.

Correct use of *who* and *whom* is determined by the word's function in the sentence. *Who* is used as a subject; *whom* is used as an object.

Practice On your paper, write each sentence, replacing the blank with the correct word—*who* or *whom*. Then identify the word's function in the sentence.

1. __?__ he was the shoemaker for a moment had no idea . . .
2. So Feld, __?__ had looked forward to anticipating how it would go with his daughter and Max . . .
3. . . . what possible harm for a working girl in an office, __?__ met only loud-mouthed salesmen . . .
4. . . . he had to get up to open the store for the new assistant . . . __?__ he would not trust with the key . . .
5. He called Sobel __?__ he expected would be immediately available.

◆ Grammar and Style

1. who; subject complement
2. who; subject
3. who; subject
4. whom; direct object
5. who; subject

Grammar Reinforcement

For additional instruction and practice, use the page on Using *Who* and *Whom* Correctly, p. 65, in the *Writer's Solution Grammar Practice Book.*

Build Your Portfolio

Idea Bank

Writing

1. Diary Entry Consider Sobel's anger and disappointment after hearing Feld's conversation with Max. Write a diary entry in which he responds to what he's heard.

2. Matchmaker's Letter In many times and cultures, marriages have been arranged by matchmakers. As a matchmaker, write a letter introducing Miriam to a prospective match.

3. Literary Analysis Considering Miriam's great interest in books, why would she turn down the opportunity to go to college? Using details from the story, write an essay answering this question.

Speaking, Listening, and Viewing

4. Group Discussion In a group, review what you know about Sobel's past. Discuss ways in which his past might have affected his personality, values, and decisions. **[Social Studies Link]**

5. Role Play Imagine two years have passed since the story's end. With a classmate, role-play a conversation in which Sobel reminds Feld of his earlier promise. **[Performing Arts Link]**

Researching and Representing

6. Cultural Research Learn about a present-day culture in which marriages are commonly arranged. In a report, describe the system and its acceptance by those within the culture.

7. Accounting Curriculum If Max were studying accounting today, what courses would he be taking? First, research the requirements for becoming a certified public accountant. Then describe four courses in detail. Like a true curriculum, each course should teach a different aspect of accounting. **[Career Link; Math Link]**

Online Activity www.phlit.phschool.com

Guided Writing Lesson

Personality Profile

Malamud creates a believable and engaging character in Feld, the shoemaker. Suppose you are going to develop a television show based on "The First Seven Years." Write a personality profile of Feld to be used by your producers. Use this tip to help you provide a clear picture to the producer:

Writing Skills Focus: Elaboration to Give Information

When you provide information about a character or anything else, **elaborate** on each of your main ideas through the presentation of details and examples. Notice how the details in this paragraph help Malamud develop Sobel's character:

Model From the Story

Sobel opened [the door] and the shoemaker entered. The room was a small, poor one, with a single window facing the street. It contained a narrow cot, a low table and several stacks of books piled haphazardly around on the floor along the wall, which made [Max] think how queer Sobel was, to be uneducated and read so much.

Prewriting Before Feld's television character can be fully crafted, actors and producers need to know what he looks like and how he behaves. In a cluster diagram, jot down physical characteristics and personal qualities you observe in Feld.

Drafting Begin with a particularly informative detail or image of Feld. Expand your profile in layers, adding information about the shoemaker and referring to your cluster diagram as needed. Keep in mind the main impression you want to create.

Revising Have a classmate create a new cluster diagram from your profile. Compare it to your prewriting diagram to discover key information you may have omitted.

Idea Bank

Customizing for Performance Levels

Following are suggestions for matching Idea Bank topics with your students' performance levels:
Less Advanced Students: 1, 5
Average Students: 2, 6, 7
More Advanced Students: 3, 4

Customizing for Learning Modalities

Following are suggestions for matching Idea Bank topics with your students' learning modalities:
Interpersonal: 4, 5
Verbal/Linguistic: 4, 5
Logical/Mathematical: 6, 7

Guided Writing Lesson

For more instruction on prewriting, elaboration, and revision, see *Prentice Hall Writing and Grammar.*

Writing and Language Transparencies Display the Branching Transparency (p. 67) to help students organize the supporting details they will present in their profiles.

Writing Lab CD-ROM

Have students complete the tutorial on Description. Follow these steps:

1. Refer students to the annotated model of a character profile in the About Description section.
2. Have students use the Cluster Diagram in the Organizing Details section to record characteristics and qualities they will include in their profiles.
3. After they have drafted on the computer, have students use the Word Bins in the Revising and Editing section to enhance their profiles.

✓ ASSESSMENT OPTIONS

Formal Assessment, Selection Test, pp. 268–270, and Assessment Resources Software. The selection test is designed so that it can be easily customized to the performance levels of your students.

Alternative Assessment, p. 59, includes options for less advanced students, more advanced students, logical/mathematical learners, verbal/linguistic learners, and visual/spatial learners.

PORTFOLIO ASSESSMENT

Use the following rubrics in the ***Alternative Assessment*** booklet to assess student writing:
Diary Entry: Expression Rubric, p. 109
Matchmaker's Letter: Description Rubric, p. 112
Literary Analysis: Literary Analysis/Interpretation Rubric, p. 127
Guided Writing Lesson: Description Rubric, p. 112

Prepare and Engage

LESSON OBJECTIVES

1. **To develop vocabulary and word identification skills**
   - Latin Word Roots: *-sim-*
   - Using the Word Bank: Word Choice
2. **To use a variety of reading strategies to comprehend fiction**
   - Connect Your Experience
   - Reading Strategy: Break Down Long Sentences
3. **To increase knowledge of other cultures and to connect common elements across cultures**
   - Background for Understanding
   - Connecting Themes Across Cultures (ATE)
4. **To express and support responses to the text**
   - Critical Thinking
   - Idea Bank: Bequest
   - Idea Bank: Conversation
   - Speaking, Listening, and Viewing Mini-Lesson (ATE)
5. **To analyze literary elements**
   - Literary Focus: Atmosphere
   - Idea Bank: Analysis of a Symbol
6. **To read in order to research self-selected and assigned topics**
   - Idea Bank: Fashion Report
   - Idea Bank: Music
7. **To plan, prepare, organize, and present literary interpretations**
   - Idea Bank: Inventory
   - Idea Bank: Poem
8. **To use recursive writing processes to write a guide for collectors**
   - Guided Writing Lesson
9. **To increase knowledge of the rules of grammar and usage**
   - Grammar and Style: Beginning Sentences with Adverb Clauses

Test Preparation

Writing Skills: Sentence Structure (ATE, p. 903)

The teaching tips in and sample test item in this workshop support the instruction and practice in the unit workshop:

Writing Skills: Punctuation, Usage, and Sentence Structure (SE, p. 1143)

Guide for Interpreting

John Updike *(1932–)*

John Updike's fiction spins the gold of insight from the straw of everyday experience. Through his depictions of ordinary situations and events, Updike explores some of the most important issues of our time and offers glimpses of the underlying significance of everyday life in contemporary America.

Updike transfigures outwardly ordinary people, places, objects, and events with flashes of insight, grief, and love.

His short stories, novels, plays and poems have given shape to the lives of many Americans—children and adults, rich and poor, ordinary and gifted.

Small Town to Big City John Updike was born in Reading, Pennsylvania, and raised in the nearby town of Shillington. His father was a high-school teacher and his mother a writer. Updike thinks his experience as an only child helped to nurture his artistic temperament: "I'm sure that my capacities to fantasize and to make coherent fantasies, to have patience to sit down day after day and to whittle a fantasy out of paper, all that relates to being an only child."

Updike excelled in drawing as well as writing. In early years, he focused his hopes on a career as a cartoonist, following in the path of James Thurber. As he matured, his interest shifted toward writing, and by age eighteen, he had decided to pursue a career in writing. This aspiration may have been fostered by his mother, who had literary ambitions of her own. After graduating from Harvard, Updike studied for a year in England. When he returned to the United States, he became a staff writer for the *New Yorker* magazine, where James Thurber and E. B. White had made names for themselves earlier.

The Personal and the Global Updike has received wide acclaim for his many novels, as well as for volumes of poetry, criticism, and short stories. His thematic concerns are broad: Four novels featuring a character called Rabbit magnify the meaning of everyday moments. Novels such as *The Coup* (1978), *Brazil* (1994), and *In the Beauty of the Lilies* (1997) use a wider lens to examine how historical and political issues have affected people across the globe. Updike is also a master of the short story form, which is ideal for capturing flashes of insight into ordinary existence. In the story "The Brown Chest," a man sifts through his deceased mother's belongings, focusing again and again on a chest filled with odds and ends that call up significant memories.

◆ Background for Understanding

CULTURE: THE BROWN CHEST AS A TIME CAPSULE

The brown chest in Updike's story is a kind of time capsule of early-twentieth century popular culture. For example, it contains auburn curls from a haircut in 1919, recalling the "bobbed" haircuts that were popular just after World War I. The 1925 wedding dress was probably not the full-length style that brides wear today. Most likely, it was a short dress or had a short hem in the front and a long one in the back. Another item in the chest is a photograph of the main character's father as a college football player in the early 1920's. At that time, players wore little padding, and skull-hugging leather helmets provided much less protection than the large synthetic padded helmets of today.

During the period profiled by the items in the chest, there was no videotape to help future generations grasp what life was like. As a result, the items provide one of the few means of gaining insight into the times.

Prentice Hall Literature Program Resources

REINFORCE / RETEACH / EXTEND

Selection Support Pages
Build Vocabulary: Latin Root: *-sim-*, p. 274
Grammar and Style: Beginning Sentences With Adverb Clauses, p. 275
Reading Strategy: Break Down Long Sentences, p. 276
Literary Focus: Atmosphere, p. 277

Strategies for Diverse Student Needs, p. 60

Beyond Literature
Cross-Curricular Connection: Social Studies, p. 60

Formal Assessment Selection Test, pp. 271–273; Assessment Resources Software

Alternative Assessment, p. 60

Resource Pro CD-ROM
Includes all resource material and customizable lesson plan.

Literature CD-ROM

Listening to Literature Audiocassettes

The Brown Chest

◆ Literature and Your Life

Connect Your Experience

Whether it is a drawer stuffed with old Scout badges or valentines from the third grade, most of us have a place for keeping those things we no longer need but cannot bear to throw away. The character in this story looks through a chest that has been in his family for many years, a chest that holds a lifetime of family memories.

Thematic Focus: Literature Confronts the Everyday

The man in Updike's story makes many personal associations with the everyday objects in the chest. As you read, look for these associations—the unique meanings the objects have for the man.

Journal Writing Make a list of five items that you've kept from years ago. For each item, jot down your reasons for keeping it.

◆ Literary Focus

Atmosphere

Atmosphere refers to the feeling or mood evoked in the reader by a piece of writing. In works of fiction, atmosphere arises from events and from descriptions of the setting—especially the effect the setting has on particular characters.

A storage chest full of family mementos is a key element in the setting of Updike's story. As you read, notice how this brown chest and its contents affect the atmosphere of the story over time.

◆ Build Vocabulary

Latin Word Roots: *-sim-*

You'll come across the word *assimilate* in this story. It is based on the Latin root *-sim-*, which means "the same." To *assimilate* means to blend into or "to become the same."

Word Bank

Before you read, preview this list of words from the selection.

mottled
assimilate
unfathomable
egregious
proprietorial
evanescent

◆ Reading Strategy

Break Down Long Sentences

Updike tends to use long sentences filled with details. Follow these tips to **break down** these long sentences:

1. Use punctuation marks—dashes, commas, parentheses, colons, and semicolons—to help you break up the sentence into manageable sections.
2. Identify the core of the sentence—the subject and the verb that accompanies it.
3. Identify how other phrases and clauses in the sentence relate to the subject.
4. Check your understanding by paraphrasing the entire sentence or portions of the sentence.

◆ Grammar and Style

Beginning Sentences With Adverb Clauses

You'll discover that Updike's sentences flow smoothly from one to another and that the ideas in the sentences are clearly connected. One of the ways in which Updike makes clear connections among sentences is by beginning many of his sentences with **adverb clauses**—subordinate clauses that modify verbs, adjectives, or adverbs. Adverb clauses begin with conjunctions like *when, where, as if, if, because, in,* and *so.* Look at this example:

If she had never done this, the room would have become haunted. . .

Interest Grabber This sweetly moving story of family attachments and history is in turns poignant and eerie. To engage students' interest in the story, ask them to bring to class at least one item that holds special memories for them or their families. Encourage volunteers to explain why their families have held onto these items, despite the fact that they have outgrown their usefulness. Explain that the story they are about to read reveals how visual tokens of shared memories take on more and more value as time goes on.

Connecting Themes Across Cultures

Updike's concern with family mementos, like those in the brown chest, is not uniquely American. As the poet Virgil relates, when Aeneas left Troy to found the Roman nation, he brought practically nothing with him. He did carry his *lares* and *penates*, however. These were the gods of the household and subjects of family devotions. Have students discuss the objects that might represent home or family in different cultures.

Customize for
Less Proficient Readers
Point out the breaks in the text, which indicate shifts in the story. To help less proficient readers, suggest that students stop at each break to summarize the story to that point.

Customize for
AP Students
Draw these students' attention to the carefully crafted descriptive language Updike uses. Challenge students to find examples of such language and to explain how it generates a vivid picture of the story setting and characters.

Customize for
English Language Learners
Review the reading strategy—break down long sentences—with these students. As they implement the strategy, urge them to paraphrase each section of a given sentence to insure comprehension.

Listening to Literature Audiocassettes

Test Preparation Workshop

Writing Skills: Punctuation, Usage, and Sentence Structure: Choose the Best Change Many standardized tests, including the ACT, require students to choose the best change to make to a sentence in order to improve its punctuation, usage, or structure. Use the following sample item to show students how to choose the best way to change a sentence.

Looking through the chest, old and unused things repulse the boy.

Which of the following is needed in the passage?

A Change the comma to a semicolon.
B Change "Looking through the chest" to "As he looks through the chest."
C Change "repulse the boy" to "are repulsed by the boy."
D Delete the comma.

Answer B is correct because it is the only choice that corrects the dangling modifier, "Looking through the chest."

Develop Understanding

One-Minute Insight Like members of the secret clubs many students created as youngsters, the family in this story has imbued certain objects with special importance. Stored in a brown trunk which makes its way from home to home over the years, these objects trace the family's history. As the narrator ages from childhood to middle-age, his feelings about the trunk and its cherished memories change from an almost fearful fascination to deep affection. At the story's end, he is about to share the contents of the now precious chest with his son and the young man's fiancée—a new generation of family that will continue the story told by the mementos contained within the brown chest.

Literature CD-ROM To introduce students to author John Updike, use *The History of American Literature:* Part 2, Disk 2, Feature 10.

◆ Literary Focus

❶ Atmosphere Ask students to picture this room in their mind's eye. Is it a bright, cheerful place, or does it seem less welcoming? Have students back their responses with details from the story. *Students should see the room as a vaguely forbidding place. The narrator's description of only two pieces of furniture create an image of a barren, unused room, and his use of words such as "haunted," "frightening shadows" and "sad spirits" suggest a menacing air.*

The Brown Chest

John Updike

In the first house he lived in, it sat up on the second floor, a big wooden chest, out of the way and yet not. For in this house, the house that he inhabited as if he would never live in any other, there were popular cheerful places, where the radio played and the legs of grown-ups went back and forth, and there were haunted bad places, like the coal bin behind the furnace, and the attic with its spiders and smell of old carpet, where he would never go without a grown-up close with him, and there were places in between, that were out of the main current but were not menacing, either, just neutral, and neglected. The entire front of the house had this neglected quality, with its guest bedroom where guests hardly ever stayed; it held a gray-painted bed with silver moons on the headboard and corner posts shaped at the top like mushrooms, and a little desk by the window where his mother sometimes, but not often, wrote letters and confided
❶ sentences to her diary in her tiny backslanting hand. If she had never done this, the room would have become haunted, even though it looked out on the busy street with its telephone wires and daytime swish of cars; but the occasional scratch of her pen exerted just enough pressure to keep away the frightening shadows, the sad spirits from long ago, locked into events that couldn't change.

Outside the guest-bedroom door, the upstairs hall, having narrowly sneaked past his grandparents' bedroom's door, broadened to be almost a room, with a window all its own, and a geranium on the sill shedding brown leaves when the women of the house forgot to water it,
and curtains of dotted swiss[1] he could see the ❷
telephone wires through, and a rug of braided rags shaped like the oval tracks his Lionel train[2] went around and around the Christmas tree on, and, to one side, its front feet planted on the rag rug, with just enough space left for the attic door to swing open, the chest.

It was big enough for him to lie in, but he had never dared try. It was painted brown, but in such a way that the wood grain showed through, as if paint very thinned with turpentine had been used. On the side, wavy stripes of paint had been allowed to run, making dribbles like the teeth of a big wobbly comb. The lid on its brown had patches of yellow freckles. The hinges were small and black, and there was a keyhole that had no key. All this made the chest, simple in shape as it was, strange, and ancient, and almost frightening. And when

1. **dotted swiss:** Sheer fabric covered in woven dots.
2. **Lionel train:** The Lionel Company is a famous manufacturer of model trains, which were a very popular hobby during Updike's youth.

Block Scheduling Strategies

Consider these suggestions to take advantage of extended class time:

- Have students complete the Cross-Curricular Connection: Social Studies page in ***Beyond Literature***, (p. 60).
- Review the Literature and Your Life section (p. 903), then introduce the Literary Focus and any other skills you wish to emphasize. You may wish to follow up by assigning the corresponding ***Selection Support*** pages as homework.
- Prompt students to look for changes in atmosphere as they read. Ask volunteers to respond to the Literary Focus prompts on pp. 906 and 908.
- Organize student pairs to complete the Partner Discussion activity (p. 909).
- Discuss and answer the Critical Thinking questions (p. 909) as a class.
- Have students complete the multiple choice section of the Selection Test found in the ***Formal Assessment,*** pp. 271–273.
- Use any remaining class time to introduce the Guided Writing Lesson (p. 911). Have students discuss the organizing priorities in the story's brown chest. Students can begin work in class and complete the assignment for homework.

he, or the grown-up with him, lifted the lid of the chest, an amazing smell rushed out—deeply sweet and musty, of mothballs and cedar, but that wasn't all of it. The smell seemed also to belong to the contents—lace tablecloths and wool blankets on top, but much more underneath. The full contents of the chest never came quite clear, perhaps because he didn't want to know. His parents' college diplomas seemed to be under the blankets, and other documents going back still farther, having to do with his grandparents, their marriage, or the marriage of someone beyond even them. There was a folded old piece of paper with drawn-on hearts and designs and words in German. His mother had once tried to explain the paper to him, but he hadn't wanted to listen. A thing so old disgusted him. And there were giant Bibles, and squat books with plush covers and a little square mottled mirror buried in the plush of one. These books had fat pages edged in gold, thick enough to hold, on both sides, stiff brown pictures, often oval, of dead people. He didn't like looking into these albums, even when his mother was explaining them to him. The chest went down and down, into the past, and he hated the feeling of that well of time, with its sweet deep smell of things
❸ unstirring, waiting, taking on the moldy flavor of time, not moving unless somebody touched them.

Then everything moved: the moving men came one day and everything in the house that had always been in a certain place was swiftly and casually uplifted and carried out the door. In the general upheaval the week before, he had been shocked to discover, glancing in, that at some point the chest had come to contain drawings he had done as a child, and his elementary-school report cards, and photographs—studio photographs lovingly mounted in folders of dove-gray cardboard with deckle edges[3]—of him when he was five. He was now thirteen.

The new house was smaller, with more outdoors around it. He liked it less on both accounts. Country space frightened him, much as the coal bin and the dark triangles under the attic eaves had—spaces that didn't have enough to do with people. Fields that were plowed one day in the spring and harvested one day in the fall, woods where dead trees were allowed to topple and slowly rot without anyone noticing, brambled-around spaces where he felt nobody had ever been before he himself came upon them. Heaps and rows of overgrown stones and dumps of rusty cans and tinted bottles indicated that other people
in fact had been here, people like those who ❹
had posed in their Sunday clothes in the gilded albums, but the traces they left weren't usable, the way city sidewalks and trolley-car tracks were usable. His instinct was to stay in the little thick-walled country house, and read, and eat sandwiches he made for himself of raisins and peanut butter, and wait for this phase of his life to pass. Moving from the first house, leaving it behind, had taught him that a life had phases.

The chest, on that day of moving, had been set in the new attic, which was smaller than the other, and less frightening, perhaps because gaps in the cedar-shingled roof let dabs of daylight in. When the roof was being repaired, the whole space was thrown open
to the weather, and it rained in, on all the ❺
furniture there was no longer room for, except up here or in the barn. The chest was too important for the barn; it perched on the edge of the attic steps, so an unpainted back he had never seen before, of two very wide pale boards, became visible. At the ends of each board were careless splashes of the thin brown paint—stain, really—left by the chestmaker when he had covered the sides.

The chest's contents, unseen, darkened in his mind. Once in a great while his mother had to search in there for something, or to confide a treasure to its depths, and in those moments, peeking in, he was surprised at how full the

3. **deckle edges:** Rough edges of paper, often regarded as decorative.

◆ Build Vocabulary

mottled (mät' ld) *adj.*: Blotched or streaked

Customize for
Verbal/Linguistic Learners

Challenge these students to identify sensory language in Updike's story, listing words under the headings: sight, smell, touch, sound, and taste. Discuss how these words evoke the narrator's emotional responses and ask students to describe their own responses to these words.

◆ Reading Strategy

❷ Break Down Long Sentences Point out this paragraph-long sentence to students. Ask them to identify logical places to break down the sentences and to explain their choices. *Students may break the sentence at "all its own," "the Christmas tree on," and "the chest" because each of these sections focuses on a particular aspect of the physical description.*

◆ *Literature and Your Life*

❸ Invite a student to read this sentence aloud. Point out the boy's negative reaction to the chest and the emotions it evokes. How do students feel about objects or stories from their family's history, about spending time with older relatives or acquaintances, about collecting or interacting with elements of their community's past? Students may respond privately in journals. *Students may express emotions ranging from strong interest and affiliation with both family and community history to feelings of revulsion and discomfort similar to those expressed by the narrator.*

◆ Literary Focus

❹ Atmosphere By describing decay in both the natural and human surroundings, the narrator creates an atmosphere of gloom and a sense of time's relentless attempt to blot out the past. Readers can then understand why the narrator wants to hide in his room and escape into books.

◆ Grammar and Style

❺ Beginning Sentences With Adverb Clauses Have students identify the adverb clause beginning this sentence. *It is "When the roof was being repaired."* How does it set the stage for the main sentence clause? *It answers the question "when?"*

Cross-Curricular Connection: Social Studies

American Portraiture For generations, families have recorded their history through portraits—both formal and informal—of family members. Whether paintings or, as is more common today, photographs, portraits can effectively capture both the personality of the subject and the atmosphere of their surroundings.

American colonists and their simmering revolution were recorded through the work of portrait painter John Singleton Copley. Later, as westward expansion threatened the Native American way of life, artist George Catlin captured that passing civilization. The "poster" portraits of Charles Demuth incorporate many symbolic objects to evoke the subject's personality.

Whether famous or ordinary, Americans and their portraits offer a close-up glimpse of earlier times and places. Have students locate an American portrait, from a book or from their own family collection. Discuss how the portraits capture the time and setting depicted.

▶Critical Viewing◀

❶ Distinguish The gloomy colors and dismal, deserted air give the room in this painting a definite feeling of neglect and disuse.

Customize for
Less Proficient Readers

❷ Clarify the story sequence and passage of time by asking students: How much time has passed since the story began? What details indicate the passage of time? Help students understand that at least forty years have passed, dated from the boy's first move to the smaller country house. Point out details and language that suggest the passage of time. For example, details include a description of the narrator as once a boy, as a man with grown children, with a grandmother who has "at last died," and as "the only survivor."

◆Reading Strategy

❸ Break Down Long Sentences Prompt students to break this long sentence into more manageable sections to facilitate their comprehension.

◆Literary Focus

❹ Atmosphere The atmosphere is one of aging and decay, with details such as "damp," "heavy," and "rust stains" contributing.

Customize for
English Language Learners

These students may benefit from the Form a Mental Picture page in ***Strategies for Diverse Student Needs*** (p. 60).

Winter Bouquet, Charles Burchfield, Museum of Fine Arts, Boston

❶ ▲ **Critical Viewing** In what part of the narrator's boyhood home might this room be found—in the "popular cheerful places" or the parts of the house that he describes as "neutral and neglected"? Explain. **[Distinguish]**

chest seemed, fuller than he remembered, of dotted-swiss curtains and crocheted lap rugs and photographs in folders of soft cardboard, all smelling of camphor and cedar. There the chest perched, an inch from the attic stairwell, and there it stayed, for over forty years.

Then it moved again. His children, adults all, came from afar and joined him in the house, where their grandmother had at last died, and divided up the furniture—some for them ❷ to carry away, some for the local auctioneer ❸ to sell, and some for him, the only survivor of that first house, with its long halls and haunted places, to keep and to assimilate to his own house, hundreds of miles away.

Two of the three children, the two that were married, had many responsibilities and soon left; he and his younger son, without a wife and without a job, remained to empty the house and pack the U-Haul van they rented. For days they lived together, eating takeout food, poisoning mice and trapping cats, moving from crowded cellar to jammed attic like sick men changing position in bed, overwhelmed by decisions, by accumulated possessions, now and then fleeing the house to escape the oppression of the past. He found the iron scales, quite rusted by the cellar damp, whereon his grandmother used to weigh out bundles of asparagus against a set of cylindrical weights. The weights were still heavy in his hand, and left rust stains on his palm. He studied a tin basin, painted in a white-on-gray spatter-pattern that had puzzled him as a child with its apparent sloppiness, and he could see again his grandfather's paper-white feet soaking in suds that rustled as the bubbles popped one by one.

> **◆ Literary Focus** How would you describe the atmosphere in this paragraph? What details contribute to that atmosphere? ❹

The chest, up there in the attic along with old rolled carpets and rocking chairs with broken cane seats, stacked hatboxes from the Thirties and paperback mysteries from the Forties, was too heavy to lift, loaded as it was. He and his younger son took out layers of blankets and plush-covered albums, lace tablecloths and linen napkins; they uncovered a long cardboard box labelled in his mother's handwriting "Wedding Dress 1925," and, underneath that, rumpled silk dresses that a small girl might have worn when the century was young, and patent-leather baby shoes, and a gold-plated horseshoe, and faithful notations of the last century's weather kept by his grandfather's father in limp dairies bound in red leather, and a buggy-whip. A little box labelled in his mother's handwriting "Haircut July 1919" held, wrapped in tissue paper, coils of auburn hair startlingly silky to the touch. There were stiff brown photographs of his father's college football team, his father crouching at right tackle in an unpadded helmet, and of a stageful of posing

Humanities: Art

Winter Bouquet, 1933, by Charles Burchfield (1893–1967).

Charles Burchfield, an Ohio-born American artist, began recording observations of his surroundings at the age of fifteen. Despite a financially difficult childhood, Burchfield studied at the Cleveland School of Art; he also studied briefly at the National Academy of Design.

Winter Bouquet—a watercolor over graphite and charcoal—depicts Burchfield's own studio in Gardenville, New York. Similar to the richly detailed rooms of the story narrator's boyhood home, the painting depicts a bouquet of dried flowers set before a studio window filled with the fading November light. Though a departure for Burchfield, who rarely painted still-lifes or interior scenes, the painting was an immediate sensation.

Use these questions for discussion.

1. What element in this painting conveys the sometimes sinister atmosphere of the narrator's boyhood home? *The stuffed raven, the dead flowers, and the half-light give the scene an air of gloomy neglect.*
2. How might the story narrator feel about spending time in this room? How do you know? *Given his dislike for the neglected rooms of his childhood and the way he avoided, as an adult, the barn filled with old furniture, he would probably prefer to be hesitant to spend time here.*

young people among whom he finally found his mother, wearing a flimsy fairy dress and looking as if she had been crying. And so on and on, until he couldn't bear it and asked his son to help him carry the chest, half unemptied, down the narrow attic stairs whose bare ⑤ wooden treads had been troughed[4] by generations of use, and then down the slightly broader stairs carpeted decades ago, and out the back door to the van. It didn't fit; they had to go back to the city ten miles away to rent a bigger van. Even so, packing everything in was a struggle. At one point, exasperated and anxious to be gone, his broad-backed son, hunched in the body of the U-Haul van, picked up the chest single-handed, and inverted it, lid open, over some smaller items to save space. The old thin-painted wood gave off a sharp *crack*, a piercing quick cry of injury.

The chest came to rest in his barn. He now owned a barn, not a Pennsylvania barn with stone sides and pegged oak beams but a skimpier, New England barn, with a flat tarred roof and a long-abandoned horse stall. He found the place in the chest lid, near one of the little dark hinges, where a split had occurred, and with a few carefully driven nails repaired the damage well enough. He could not blame the boy, who was named Gordon, after his paternal grandfather, the one-time football player crouching for his picture in some sunny autumn when Harding[5] was President. On the drive north in a downpour, Gordon had driven the truck, and his father tried to read the map, and in the dim light of the cab failed, and headed him the wrong way out of Westchester County, so they wound up across ⑥ the Hudson River, amid blinding headlights, ⑦ on an unfathomable, exitless highway. After that egregious piece of guidance, he could not blame the boy for anything, even for failing to get a job while concentrating instead on perfecting his dart game in the fake pubs of Boston. In a way not then immediately realized, the map-reading blunder righted the balance between them, himself and his son, as when under his grandmother's gnarled hands another stalk of asparagus would cause the tray holding the rusty cylindrical weights to rise with a soft *clunk*.

> **◆ Reading Strategy** ⑧
> Notice that this long sentence has two focuses: the man and his son, and the man's grandmother using a scale.

They arrived an hour late, after midnight. The unloading, including the reloading of the righted chest, all took place by flashlight, hurriedly, under the drumming sound of rain on the flat roof.

Now his barn felt haunted. He could scarcely bear to examine his inherited treasure, the chairs and cabinets and chinaware and faded best-sellers and old-fashioned bridge lamps clustered in a corner beyond the leaf-mulcher and the snow-blower and the rack of motorcycle tires left by the youngest son of the previous owner of the barn. He was the present owner. He had never imagined, as a child, owning so much. His wife saw no place in their ⑨ house for even the curly-maple[6] kitchen table and the walnut corner cupboard, his mother's pride. This section of the barn became, if not as frightening as the old coal bin, a place he avoided. These pieces that his infant eyes had grazed, and that had framed his parents' lives, seemed sadly shabby now, cheap in their time, most of them, and yet devoid of antique value: useless used furniture he had lacked the courage to discard.

So he was pleased, one winter day, two years after their wayward drive north, to have Gordon call and ask if he could come look at

4. **troughed** (trôf'd) *v.*: Worn into troughs or grooves.
5. **Harding:** Warren G. Harding (1865–1923), twenty-ninth president of the United States, from 1921 to 1923.

6. **curly-maple:** Maple wood with a pronounced wavy grain.

◆ Build Vocabulary

assimilate (ə sim´ ə lāt´) *v.*: To absorb or incorporate

unfathomable (un fath´ əm ə bəl) *adj.*: Unable to be understood

egregious (ē grē´ jəs) *adj.*: Outstanding for undesirable qualities; remarkably bad

◆ Reading Strategy

⑤ Break Down Long Sentences Point out to students that this sentence contains many clauses, joined by the conjunction *and*, which are organized around the chest's physical progression out of the house.

Customize for *Bodily/Kinesthetic Learners*
Draw these students' attention to the physical efforts undertaken by the narrator and his adult son. Ask them to describe how *they* would move a chest of "treasured" belongings, given strongly ambivalent feelings about those belongings.

◆ Grammar and Style

⑥ Beginning Sentences With Adverb Clauses Ask: What questions does the opening adverb clause answer in this first sentence? *Where and when: on the drive north, in a downpour.*

◆ Critical Thinking

⑦ Analyze Why does the narrator's simple mistake have the power to release Gordon from blame of any kind? *The narrator somehow failed in his fundamental duty as a father—to lead his son in the right direction, both literally and figuratively.*

◆ Reading Strategy

⑧ Break Down Long Sentences Guide students to break this sentence into two distinct sections at "as when."

◆ Literary Focus

⑨ Atmosphere Ask students: How does the atmosphere in this paragraph recall the mood of the narrator's boyhood home? *Students should note the narrator's references to his childhood, his infant eyes, his move from child occupant to owner of a house, and the frightening coal bin of his childhood.*

Speaking, Listening, and Viewing Mini-Lesson

Bequest
This mini-lesson supports the Speaking, Listening, and Viewing activity in the Idea Bank on p. 911.

Introduce the Concept After you have reviewed the description of the activity given on p. 911, discuss these points:

- Items for bequest needn't be valuable financially, only important to the giver.
- To communicate an item's significance, offer details about its role in the giver's life.
- The giver's hopes for an item's future will help the recipient appreciate it.

Develop Background Have students discuss whether they have received or given an item that was laden with meaning. What information did they wish to communicate or receive about the item? How were they able to convey or understand the item's significance? Point out that the story narrator's family never discusses the importance of the chest and its contents. Students will have to draw—and express—their own conclusions about just how meaningful the chest has become to the narrator by the story's end.

Apply the Information Remind students to speak as the story narrator, incorporating his feelings about the chest. Ask audience members to listen carefully to each speaker.

Assess the Outcome Ask students to contribute their evaluations as you assess each bequest performance for character, consistency, and effectiveness.

Customize for
ESL Students

❶ Point out the repeated pronoun *he* in these sentences. Explain to students that in the first sentence, he is the narrator while in the second sentence, *he* refers to Gordon.

▶Critical Viewing◀

❷ **Analyze** They capture both trivial important moments in family members' lives, thus creating a picture of daily life—for example, the weather diary—and of rites of passage, such as cutting hair always worn long.

Customize for
AP Students

❸ Challenge students to explain the significance of describing Morna as a Celtic and elfin name. What associations do students have with Celtic culture and traditions? How do these fit with the other atmosphere details in the paragraph? *Students may associate Celtic culture with magical stories, a reverence for the past, and the ever-intertwined emotions of hope and doom. Details such as "ogre" and "ancestral . . . figure" support the Celtic reference.*

◆ Literary Focus

❹ **Atmosphere** Morna's presence is slightly other-worldly and charged with delicate energy. Details such as the puffs of visible breath, Morna's quick movements, narrow white hands, and shyness, along with the description of the narrator as "a kind of ogre" contribute to the atmosphere.

Customize for
Visual/Spatial Learners

Ask these students to study the objects in the montage. Which items or photographs are similar to those cherished by their family?

◆ Critical Thinking

❺ **Connect** What feature of Morna's appearance recalls the narrator's mother? *They both have auburn hair.*

◆ Literary Focus

❻ **Atmosphere** Point out the sensory details with which Updike describes the atmosphere as an almost physical thing. Readers experience an upsurge of hope and possibility, mingled with a new, more positive perspective on the past, created by Morna's refreshing approach to the chest.

❶ the furniture in the barn. He had a job, he said, or almost, and was moving into a bigger place, out from the city. He would be bringing a friend, he vaguely added. A male friend, presumably, to help him lift and load what he chose to take away.

But the friend was a female, small and exquisite, with fascinating large eyes, the whites white as china, and a way of darting back and forth like a hummingbird, her wings invisible. "Oh," she exclaimed, over this and that, explaining to Gordon in a breathy small voice how this would be useful, and that would fit right in. "Lamps!" she said. "I love lamps."

"You see, Dad," the boy explained, the words pronounced softly yet in a manner so momentous that it seemed to take all the air in the barn to give them utterance, "Morna and I are planning to get married."

"Morna"—a Celtic name, fittingly elfin. The ❸ girl was magical, there in the cold barn, emitting puffs of visible breath, moving through the clutter with quick twists of her denim-clad hips and graceful stabs of her narrow white hands. She spoke only to Gordon, as if a pane of shyness protected her from his hoary[7] father—at this late phase of his life a kind of ogre, an ancestral, proprietorial figure full of potency and ugliness. "Gordon, what's this?" she asked.

> **◆ Literary Focus** In what specific ways does this description of Morna change the story's atmosphere? ❹

The boy was embarrassed, perhaps by her innocent avidity.[8] "Tell her, Dad."

"Our old guest bed." Which he used to lie diagonally across, listening to his mother's pen

❷ ▼ **Critical Viewing** How do the items in the chest tell the story of the family that owns it? **[Analyze]**

7. **hoary** (hôr´ē) *adj.*: Ancient; old.
8. **avidity** (ə vid´ ə tē) *n.*: Eagerness.

Beyond the Classroom

Community Connection

Artifacts This story revolves around the potency of objects imbued with historical significance. Such objects, or artifacts, can tell the stories of recent or ancient people, families, and civilizations. Historians, especially archaeologists, weave together an understanding of how people lived, using everyday objects and carefully preserved mementos as clues.

In this tale, the narrator's family has collected artifacts of its history. Challenge students to search your community for artifacts of its history, for example, books written by local authors, samples of products created in the community, newspaper clippings about key local events. When students have gathered and exchanged these many artifacts (or descriptions of them), discuss the portrait these paint of your community.

scratch as her diary tried to hold fast her days. Even then he knew it couldn't be done.

"We could strip off the ghastly gray, I guess," the boy conceded, frowning in the attempt to envision it and the work involved. "We *have* a bed," he reminded her.

5 "And this?" she went on, leaving the bed hanging in a realm of future possibility. Her headscarf had slipped back, exposing auburn hair glinting above the vapor of her breath, in evanescent present time.

She had paused at the chest. Her glance darted at Gordon, and then, receiving no response, at the present owner, looking him in the eyes for the first time. The ogre smiled. "Open it."

"What's in it?" she asked.

He said, "I forget, actually."

Delicately but fearlessly, she lifted the lid, and out swooped, with the same vividness that had astonished and alarmed his nostrils as a child, the sweetish deep cedary smell, undiminished, cedar and camphor and paper and cloth, the smell of family, family without end. 6

◆ Build Vocabulary

proprietorial (prō prī´ ə tôr´ ē əl) *adj.*: Like someone who owns something

evanescent (ev´ ə nes´ ənt) *adj.*: Tendency to fade or disappear

Guide for Responding

◆ Literature and Your Life

Reader's Response The brown chest clearly has had a profound effect upon the man in the story. What object or objects in your life seem to have emotional power over you, and why?

Thematic Focus Find three pieces of evidence in the story to support this statement: Everyday experiences can end up making the most powerful memories.

Partner Discussion Are you a "purger"—someone who is always throwing things away—or a "pack rat"—someone who saves every little thing? Pair up with a partner of the opposite inclination, and persuade him or her that your way is best.

☑ Check Your Comprehension

1. Describe the boy's earliest impressions of the chest and its contents.
2. What does he notice has been added to the chest when he is older?
3. (a) How much time passes in the story? (b) How do you know?
4. For whom does the man open the chest at the end of the story?

◆ Critical Thinking

INTERPRET

1. (a) What event "righted the balance" between the man and his son? (b) Why does that event cause the man to reevaluate his feelings toward his son? **[Analyze]**
2. How does the main character seem to feel toward Morna, and how can you tell? **[Infer]**
3. (a) Which detail about Morna connects her to the chest: her narrow white hands? her auburn hair? her large eyes? (b) Why is this detail significant? **[Support; Infer]**
4. Explain how the main character's attitude toward the chest changes from the beginning to the end of the story. **[Synthesize]**

EVALUATE

5. How well do you think Updike succeeds in showing the passing of many decades within the confines of the short-story form? Explain. **[Criticize]**

COMPARE LITERARY WORKS

6. Reread the final paragraphs of "The Brown Chest" and "The Life You Save May Be Your Own." Characterize the differences in tone and the ways each author creates the tone. **[Distinguish]**

Beyond the Selection

FURTHER READING

Other Works by John Updike

Hugging the Shore, Problems and Other Stories, Rabbit, Run (and the other *Rabbit* novels), *Trust Me*

Other Works With the Theme of Family History/Special Memories

"The Memento," O. Henry

"The Christmas Box," Richard Evans

The Notebook, Nicholas Sparks

We strongly suggest that you preview these works before recommending them to students.

INTERNET

To learn more about John Updike, we suggest the following Internet site. Please be aware, however, that sites may have changed since this information was published.

For a site that offers several links to other pages of Updike information, go to **http://www.mala.bc.ca/~mcneil/updike.htm**

We *strongly recommend* that you preview sites before you send students to them.

Reinforce and Extend

Answers

◆ Literature and Your Life

Reader's Response Responses should reflect students' understanding of the chest's effect upon the narrator.

Thematic Focus Responses may include the following "everyday" memories: the narrator's mother writing at the guest room desk, the toy train tracks under the Christmas tree, and the opening of the brown chest.

☑ Check You Comprehension

1. He recalls the chest as "strange, ancient, and almost frightening," and filled with a smell of mothballs and cedar. He hated the idea that the chest was full of mementos that stretched so far back in time.
2. He notices that souvenirs of his own youth have been added.
3. (a) Approximately fifty years. (b) It begins when the narrator is young; after ten years, the family moves to a house where the chest remains for forty years, until the narrator brings it to his barn, where it sits for two years.
4. He opens it for his son's fiancée, Morna.

◆ Critical Thinking

1. (a) The man misreads a map and sends his son miles off course. (b) After his own mistake, he feels he can no longer blame his son for the mistakes he makes in life.
2. He seems to find her captivating and refreshing. He likens her to a delicate hummingbird, and describes her as "elfin" and "magical."
3. (a) Her auburn hair connects her to the chest. (b) It is a link to his mother's auburn curls, which lie in the trunk; it bridges past and present generations of his family.
4. As a young boy, he is repelled by the trunk and its contents; by the end of the story, he has come to appreciate their value as family history.
5. Students should support their opinions using specific examples from the story.
6. O'Connor's final paragraphs are full of shattered illusions about family attachments and much else. They are full of foreboding. Updike's ending, by contrast, offer a scene of reconciliation and deepening family ties. It is sweetly optimistic.

Answers

◆ Literary Focus

1. Suggested responses: (a) neglect: "guests hardly ever stayed"; (b) tenderness: "lovingly"; (c) nostalgia: "faithful" and "grandfather's father"
2. Suggested responses: (a) The atmos-phere is gloomy or oppressive. (b) The skimpy barn with its "long-abandoned" horse stall, the dim light of the truck cab, the "unfathomable, exitless" highway, and the rusty weights suggest a depressed atmosphere.
3. (a) The atmosphere becomes filled with life again. (b) She arrives like a delicate breath of fresh air, as suggested by the comparison to a hummingbird, her love of lamps (light), her "puffs of visible" breath, the "quick twists" and "graceful stabs" of her body, the glint of her hair, and her enthusiasm for all she sees. (c) The change occurs because Morna is young and filled with life, and represents a fresh new generation of the narrator's family.

◆ Reading Strategy

1. The commas divide the sentence into sections: the first two relate to the narrator's mother's actions; the third is a transition to the narrator's actions; the fourth through sixth sections describe his actions; and the remaining sections describe the contents of the trunk.
2. His mother opens the chest to search for or add something. The narrator is surprised by how full the chest has become.
3. Possible response: He fills it with words, just as the chest is filled with objects.

◆ Build Vocabulary

Using the Latin Root *-sim-*

1. simultaneous; 2. similar; 3. simulation

Using the Word Bank

1. unfathomable; 2. mottled; 3. proprietorial; 4. evanescent; 5. assimilate; 6. egregious

Guide for Responding *(continued)*

◆ Literary Focus

ATMOSPHERE

Through his vivid descriptions of the items in the chest and the main character's feelings about them, Updike creates a powerful **atmosphere,** or mood, in "The Brown Chest."

1. Reread each detail that follows and tell what emotion it suggests the narrator might be feeling. Identify the word or words that led you to your answer.
   (a) *. . . its guest bedroom where guests hardly ever stayed*
   (b) *studio photographs lovingly mounted in folders of dove-gray cardboard*
   (c) *faithful notations of the last century's weather kept by his grandfather's father . . .*

2. Reread the paragraph on p. 907 that begins "The chest came to rest in his barn." (a) How would you describe the atmosphere in this paragraph? (b) What details contribute to that atmosphere?

3. (a) Describe how the atmosphere changes when Morna enters the story. (b) What words signal the change? (c) Why do you think the atmos-phere changes?

◆ Reading Strategy

BREAK DOWN LONG SENTENCES

To create sentence variety, writers use sentences with different lengths and structures. "The Brown Chest" includes a number of long sentences. Use the strategies presented on p. 903 to **break down** the following long sentence:

> Once in a great while his mother had to search in there for something, or to confide a treasure to its depths, and in those moments, peeking in, he was surprised at how full the chest seemed, fuller than he remembered, of dotted-swiss curtains and crocheted lap rugs and photographs in folders of soft cardboard, all smelling of camphor and cedar.

1. How does punctuation help break this sentence into meaningful sections?

2. What action or actions are being performed in this sentence?

3. Why do you think Updike used a long sentence to convey this information?

◆ Build Vocabulary

USING THE LATIN ROOT *-sim-*

Knowing that the Latin root *-sim-* means "the same," complete each sentence with one of the words from the box.

similar	simultaneous	simulation

1. My arrival at the party and his departure from it were almost ___?___; I ran into him at the door.

2. Her hair style is ___?___ to mine, except hers is longer in the front.

3. The spaceflight ___?___ was so realistic that I felt weightless!

USING THE WORD BANK: Word Choice

Write the following sentences in your notebook, replacing the italicized word or phrase in each with the appropriate word from the Word Bank.

1. The small boy found the adults' attachment to the chest *impossible to figure out.*

2. The covers of the old books were *spotted.*

3. The man had *an ownerlike* interest in the chest.

4. His joy in the smell of the chest was *likely to disappear soon,* yet it was powerful.

5. Try as he might, he couldn't make the chest *fit* into his everyday life two hundred miles away.

6. If the man's parents had made any *outstandingly bad* errors, there was no evidence in the chest.

◆ Grammar and Style

BEGINNING SENTENCES WITH ADVERB CLAUSES

Beginning sentences with **adverb clauses** helps to make sentences flow smoothly from one to another and to connect ideas clearly.

Practice Write a sentence that might have preceded each of the following.

1. *Because Updike is so beloved by his readers,* he receives much fan mail.

2. *Before Updike became a writer,* he dreamed of becoming a cartoonist.

3. *Although many years have passed since Updike lived in rural Pennsylvania,* he still has vivid memories.

Writing Application Write a paragraph describing a vivid memory. Use at least three sentences containing adverb clauses.

◆ Grammar and Style

Practice

Sample responses:

1. John Updike has a loyal following of devoted readers.
2. John Updike did not always aspire to a career as an author.
3. In his story, Updike unfavorably compares New England barns with those found in the Pennsylvania countryside.

Writing Application

Look for at least three examples of sentences that begin with properly constructed adverb clauses. Paragraphs should be free of major mechanical errors.

Writer's Solution

For additional instruction and practice, use the Varying Sentence Structure lesson in the Writing Style unit of the **Language Lab CD-ROM.**

Reteach

To reteach this selection, use ***Strategies for Diverse Student Needs***, *page 60.*

Build Your Portfolio

Idea Bank

Writing

1. Inventory At several points, Updike lists items in the chest. Write an inventory list of important mementos you or family members keep in your house. Arrange the list by category.

2. Poem What object have you had the most feelings about over time? Write a poem in which each stanza describes your attitude toward that object at a different point in your life.

3. Analysis of a Symbol The significance of the chest for the main character in this story changes over time. Write an essay analyzing what the chest symbolizes at different points in his life.

Speaking, Listening, and Viewing

4. Bequest As the main character in the story, create and deliver a future bequest of the chest to your youngest son. In a brief oral explanation, share the reasons the chest is important to you, and tell why he should have it.

5. Conversation With another student, role-play a conversation between Gordon and Morna on their way home from visiting the barn. Each character should exchange impressions of the visit. **[Performing Arts Link]**

Researching and Representing

6. Fashion Report Create a feature article on women's fashions of the 1920's. Illustrate it with examples, and draw connections between fashions and the social atmosphere of the time. **[Social Studies Link; Art Link]**

7. Music Present background music for a film based on this story. Find recordings of music from each period mentioned in the story—the 1920's to the 1980's—and put them together on an audiotape for your presentation. **[Music Link]**

Online Activity www.phlit.phschool.com

Guided Writing Lesson

Guide for Collectors

Behind every great collection—whether it consists of action heroes or family mementos—is a great organizing scheme. Choose a type of item you are particularly interested in—for example, baseball cards, stamps, or coins—and create a guide for collectors. Provide clear directions on methods for assembling and organizing a superb collection.

Writing Skills Focus: Using Clear and Logical Organization

To help your readers assemble an impressive collection, give them detailed, step-by-step instructions. Use a **clear and logical organization.** Since you'll be presenting information in a series of steps, use **chronological order,** starting by detailing the first step and continuing to the last.

Prewriting Decide what your readers most need to know. Create a priority list. For a foreign stamp collection, for example, it's important to provide tips for gathering the stamps, for storing and preserving them, and for presenting them. It's less important to provide a history of stamp collecting.

Drafting Begin by providing a clear explanation of collection techniques. Organization and preservation methods should come next. Write about the organization method that best fits the type of collection. (For example, organize foreign stamps by country, and then by value within each country.)

Revising Review your guide. Does it tell your readers everything they need to know to collect, organize, and preserve the items in their collection? Is the organization method the best, and is it clearly explained? If necessary, you might want to number each step or use bullets to clarify your organization for collectors. You may also want to include graphics and illustrations to make your guide more helpful.

Idea Bank

Customizing for
Performance Levels
Following are suggestions for matching Idea Bank topics with your students' performance levels:
Less Advanced Students: 1, 4
Average Students: 2, 5, 6
More Advanced Students: 3, 7

Customizing for
Learning Modalities
Following are suggestions for matching Idea Bank topics with your students' learning modalities:
Verbal/Linguistic: 4, 5
Interpersonal: 5
Visual/Spatial: 6
Musical/Rhythmic: 7

Guided Writing Lesson

For more instruction on prewriting, elaboration, and revision, see *Prentice Hall Writing and Grammar.*

Writing Lab CD-ROM
Have students complete the tutorial on Practical and Technical Writing. Follow these steps:

1. Have students complete the Audience and Purpose Profiles in the Considering Audience and Purpose section to help them decide what to include and how to present it.
2. Have students use the Chain of Events activity in Gathering Details to help students organize their ideas in chronological order.
3. After they have drafted on the computer, pairs of students can use the Peer Evaluation Checklist for technical writing to evaluate one another's work.

✓ ASSESSMENT OPTIONS

Formal Assessment, Selection Test, pp. 271–273, and Assessment Resources Software. The selection test is designed so that it can be easily customized to the performance levels of your students.

Alternative Assessment, p. 60, includes options for less advanced students, more advanced students, intrapersonal learners, visual/spatial learners, and interpersonal learners.

PORTFOLIO ASSESSMENT
Use the following rubrics in the ***Alternative Assessment*** booklet to assess student writing:
Inventory: Description Rubric, p. 112
Poem: Poetry Rubric, p. 123
Analysis of a Symbol: Literary Analysis/Interpretation Rubric, p. 127
Guided Writing Lesson: How-to/Process Explanation Rubric, p. 115

Prepare and Engage

LESSON OBJECTIVES

1. To develop vocabulary and word identification skills
- Related Words: *Exhaust*
- Using the Word Bank: Synonyms

2. To use a variety of reading strategies to comprehend poetry
- Connect Your Experience
- Reading Strategy: Paraphrase
- Background for Understanding
- Read to Interpret (ATE)

3. To increase knowledge of other cultures and to connect common elements across cultures
- Cultural Connection (ATE)

4. To express and support responses to the text
- Critical Thinking
- Idea Bank: Poem
- Idea Bank: Critical Response
- Idea Bank: Dictionary

5. To analyze literary elements
- Literary Focus: Diction and Style

6. To read in order to research self-selected and assigned topics
- Idea Bank: Oral Presentation
- Speaking, Listening, and Viewing Mini-Lesson (ATE)

7. To plan, prepare, organize, and present literary interpretations
- Idea Bank: Movie Summary
- Idea Bank: Mural
- Viewing and Representing Mini-Lesson

8. To use recursive writing processes to write a a review
- Guided Writing Lesson
- Idea Bank: Explanation

9. To increase knowledge of the rules of grammar and usage
- Grammar and Style: Subject and Verb Agreement

Test Preparation

Reading Comprehension: Grammar and Usage (ATE, p. 913) The teaching tips and sample test item in this workshop support the instruction and practice in the unit workshop:

Writing Skills: Punctuation, Usage, and Sentence Structure (SE, p. 1143)

Guide for Interpreting

Robert Lowell *(1917–1977)*

Robert Lowell was born into one of America's oldest, most prominent families. Early in his career, he used traditional poetic forms and techniques. In the late 1950's, however, Lowell began writing freer, more direct poems in what came to be called the "confessional" mode. His volume *Life Studies* (1959) launched a school of confessional poets that included Sylvia Plath, John Berryman, and Anne Sexton.

Robert Penn Warren *(1905–1989)*

Among the most versatile, prolific, and distinguished writers of our time, Robert Penn Warren won the first of his three Pulitzer Prizes for *All the King's Men* (1946), a fictional study of a Southern politician (based on Louisiana Governor Huey Long). Warren's poetry collections include *Promises* (1957), and *Now and Then: Poems* (1978). Though Warren consistently used Southern settings and characters in his writing, he treated universal themes, such as the love of the land that fills the poem "Gold Glade."

Theodore Roethke *(1908–1963)*

As a child Theodore Roethke (ret′ kē) was a passionate observer of the plants that grew in his family's acres of commercial greenhouses. Through adolescence and well into adulthood, he found it difficult to relate to other people. Following the ideas of his heroes, Emerson and Thoreau, he took refuge in nature. At age thirty-three he published the first of several volumes of poetry; he grew eventually into one of the most acclaimed poets of his day. He received the Pulitzer Prize for his collection *The Waking* (1954) and the National Book Award for *The Far Field* (1964).

William Stafford *(1914–1993)*

Focusing on such subjects as the threat of nuclear war and the beauty of untamed nature, William Stafford wrote about his fear that modern technology would someday destroy the wilderness. He did not publish his first volume of verse, *West of Your City* (1960), until age forty-six, after years of working in the United States Forest Service.

◆ Background for Understanding

CULTURE: ROBERT PENN WARREN NAMED FIRST POET LAUREATE OF THE UNITED STATES

Following an English tradition that dates back to 1619, the Library of Congress named Robert Penn Warren Poet Laureate of the United States in 1985. Warren was the first poet to be elevated to this honorary position. Before 1986, the year in which Warren actually served his term, the Library of Congress had appointed only consultants in poetry (William Stafford among them).

Since then, some of America's best and brightest literary talents—including Richard Wilbur and Rita Dove—have held the title of Poet Laureate. Unlike their British counterparts, American poets laureate are under no obligation to compose poems to commemorate special occasions. Though they receive a sizable stipend and an office in the Library of Congress for the duration of the one-year term, poets laureate are free to continue writing (or not writing) as they choose.

Prentice Hall Literature Program Resources

REINFORCE / RETEACH / EXTEND

Selection Support Pages
Build Vocabulary: Related Words: *exhaust,* p. 278
Grammar and Style: Agreement, p. 279
Reading Strategy: Paraphrase, p. 280
Literary Focus: Diction and Style, p. 281

Strategies for Diverse Student Needs, p. 61

Beyond Literature
Community Connection: Community Identity, p. 61

Formal Assessment Selection Test, pp. 274–276; Assessment Resources Software

Alternative Assessment, p. 61

Resource Pro CD-ROM
Includes all resource materials and a customizable lesson plan

Literature CD-ROM

Listening to Literature Audiocassettes

Hawthorne ◆ Gold Glade ◆ The Light Comes Brighter The Adamant ◆ Traveling Through the Dark

◆ Literature and Your Life

Connect Your Experience

Sometimes, when you least expect it, you make the most surprising and important discoveries about yourself, other people, and the world around you. In the following works, you will see how four poets make discoveries and find inspiration in diverse places.

Journal Writing In your journal, write about an important and unexpected discovery you've made in the past year or so. How has your new understanding affected your life?

Thematic Focus: Literature Confronts the Everyday

These poems address ideas drawn from the poets' everyday observations and interests—from the effect of machines on people and animals to the vitality of an artistic ancestor. How do your everyday observations compare to theirs?

◆ Build Vocabulary

Related Words: *Exhaust*

William Stafford uses the word *exhaust* as a noun meaning "the discharge of used steam or gas from an engine." This word may also function as a verb meaning "to empty completely" or "to tire out." Other words related to *exhaust* include *exhausted, exhaustive, exhaustible, exhaustibility,* and *exhaustion.*

Word Bank

Before you read, preview this list of words from the poems.

brooding
furtive
meditation
declivity
vestiges
exhaust

◆ Grammar and Style

Subject and Verb Agreement

A **subject** and **verb** must **agree** in number, even if the verb is separated from its subject by several intervening words. Look, for example, at this passage from "The Light Comes Brighter":

. . . the caw (s) / Of restive crows is (v) sharper on the ear

The singular verb *is* agrees with the singular subject *caw.* Notice that the verb does not agree with the plural noun *crows,* which is part of an intervening prepositional phrase—not the subject of the clause.

◆ Literary Focus

Diction and Style

A writer's **style** is the manner in which he or she puts ideas into words; style generally concerns *form* rather than *content.* In poetry, style is determined by a poet's use of tone, rhythm, sound devices, figurative language, symbolism, punctuation, and capitalization, as well as the length and arrangement of lines.

An important aspect of style is a poet's **diction**, or word choice. The way a poet chooses and arranges words not only reflects varying degrees of formality and abstraction, but also helps establish a unique voice.

◆ Reading Strategy

Paraphrase

Some poems contain passages that are especially difficult to understand because of sophisticated or unusual vocabulary, complicated sentence structure, or the ambiguities of poetic language. To improve your understanding, take a moment to **paraphrase**, or restate in your own words, any difficult passages you encounter. For example:

Roethke's Version:

Soon field and wood will
wear an April look. . .

Paraphrased Version:

Soon spring will come.

Test Preparation Workshop

Writing Skills:
Grammar and Usage The writing sections of standardized tests often require students to choose the correct pronoun or form of a verb to complete a sentence. Use the following sample item to give students practice in this skill.

Robert Penn Warren published *All the King's Men* in 1946 and ____ the Pulitzer Prize for it that year.

Choose the word or group of words that belongs in the blank.

A wins
B had won
C won
D has won

A and *D* put the event in the present and near-present, and *B* puts it in the past prior to the publication of the book. *C* puts the Pulitzer Prize in the simple past along with the book's publication.

Interest Grabber Anyone who has ever swelled with emotion in response to an inspirational figure or a scene of nature's power will discover a friend in these poems. Introduce students to the poetry by asking students what inspires awe or strong emotions in them. You might show students some photographs of natural and human-made wonders as a stimulus. Then list together the emotions students experience. How might these feelings take root in poetic form? Urge students to read on for the answer four poets gave.

Customize for
Less Proficient Readers
Poetic diction is often challenging to less proficient readers. Encourage these students to paraphrase any text they find confusing. Pair them with classmates to test the clarity of the restatements.

Customize for
AP Students
Encourage AP students to analyze the poets' diction and style, using paraphrasing to highlight figurative language, alliteration, and unusual word choice.

Customize for
English Language Learners
The diction in these poems may pose a particular problem for these students. Encourage them to break down compound or hyphenated words, such as *wharf-piles, dial-clock, firelight, leaf-fall, and winter-sealed*, into individual parts to help them develop definitions.

Customize for
Musical/Rhythmic Learners
Have these students listen to the recording of the selection as they follow along in their texts. What effects do the sounds of the words have on their meaning?

Listening to Literature Audiocassettes

Literature CD-ROM To build background on Robert Lowell and Theodore Roethke, use *The History of American Literature:* Part 2, Disc 2, Feature 5. Information on Robert Penn Warren is included in Feature 11 on the same disc.

Hawthorne

Robert Lowell

Crowninshield's Wharf, George Ropes, Peabody Museum of Salem

▲ Critical Viewing ❶ What does this scene suggest about the port of Salem? How does the painting compare to Lowell's description of the town? **[Contrast]**

Follow its lazy main street lounging
from the alms house to Gallows Hill[1]
along a flat, unvaried surface
covered with wooden houses
aged by yellow drain
like the unhealthy hair of an old dog.
You'll walk to no purpose
in Hawthorne's Salem.

I cannot resilver the smudged plate.[2]

I drop to Hawthorne, the customs officer,[3]
measuring coal and mostly trying to keep warm—
to the stunted black schooner,
the dismal South-end dock,
the wharf-piles with their fungus of ice.
On State Street[4]
a steeple with a glowing dial-clock
measures the weary hours,
❷ the merciless march of professional feet.

❸ Even this shy distrustful ego
sometimes walked on top of the blazing roof,

1. **Gallows Hill:** Hill in Salem, Massachusetts, where nineteen people who were accused of practicing witchcraft were hanged.
2. **resilver . . . plate:** Early photographs were taken on a metal plate coated with silver.
3. **customs officer:** Nathaniel Hawthorne worked as a customs officer in Salem.
4. **State Street:** Street in the business district of Boston.

Develop Understanding

One-Minute Insight This poem demonstrates the myriad sources of artistic inspiration. Its speaker, presumably the poet, pays homage to American writer Nathaniel Hawthorne with a walk through Hawthorne's home town of Salem, Massachusetts. As the speaker passes the apparently peaceful main street, he senses its stagnant present and troubled history. He raises the memory of Hawthorne, whose work also had a dark side, as an inspirational beacon for his own creative process.

Enrichment This poem describes the Salem of Nathaniel Hawthorne (1804–1864), the renowned American novelist and short story writer. Salem was a world-famous port city from its earliest colonial days. Its infamous history includes the witchcraft scare of the seventeenth century.

▶Critical Viewing◀

❶ **Contrast** The scene suggests that Salem's port is thriving. The brightly waving flags, tall ships, and air of bustle suggest a proud, vibrant seaside town, while Lowell's poem focuses on Salem's decay.

◆Critical Thinking

❷ **Infer** What is the speaker's opinion of "professional" life? *He views it as a life of drudgery, dictated by the clock.*

◆Critical Thinking

❸ **Connect** Who is the "shy distrustful ego" in these lines? *The poet is speaking of Hawthorne, but also perhaps of himself.*

Humanities

Crowninshield's Wharf, 1805, by George Ropes.

This oil painting depicts Salem during its most active years as a port town, slightly before Hawthorne's tenure as customs officer.

Have students discuss which of the elements mentioned in the poem might be found in this painting. *The schooner, South-end dock, and wharf-piles could all be in the painting's scene.*

Block Scheduling Strategies

Consider these suggestions to take advantage of extended class time:

- Introduce the Literary Focus and any other skills you wish to emphasize.
- Together, read and discuss the author biographies and Background for Understanding (p. 912). Allow time for students to research the poets on the Internet and share their findings.
- Break the class into five groups and assign each a single poem from this grouping. Students should read the poems, answer the critical thinking questions to aid their study, and then, as "experts," lead the class discussion of the work they've been assigned.
- Have students listen to the poems on audiocassette as they follow along in their texts. Discuss how listening to the poems affects their awareness of the poets' diction and style.
- To extend learning, share your choice of the Beyond the Classroom, Humanities, or Cross-Curricular notes in the ATE.

and felt those flashes
that char the discharged cells of the brain. ❸

Look at the faces—
Longfellow, Lowell, Holmes and Whittier!
Study the grizzled silver of their beards.
Hawthorne's picture,
however, has a blond mustache
and golden General Custer[5] scalp.
He looks like a Civil War officer.
He shines in the firelight. His hard
survivor's smile is touched with fire.

Leave him alone for a moment or two,
and you'll see him with his head
bent down, brooding, brooding,
eyes fixed on some chip,
some stone, some common plant,
the commonest thing,
as if it were the clue. ❹
The disturbed eyes rise,
furtive, foiled, dissatisfied
from meditation on the true
and insignificant.

◆ Build Vocabulary

brooding (bro͞od′ iŋ) *v.*: Pondering in a troubled or mournful way

furtive (fʉr′ tiv) *adj.*: Sneaky; stealthy

meditation (med′ ə tā′ shən) *n.*: Deep thought or solemn reflection

5. **General Custer:** George Armstrong Custer (1839–1876), a general who served in the Civil War and was killed along with his troops by the Sioux at the Battle of Little Big Horn, had long blond hair.

Guide for Responding

◆ Literature and Your Life

Reader's Response Based on the way he is portrayed in this poem, what is your opinion of Nathaniel Hawthorne?

Thematic Focus How does the poet's focus on the "true and insignificant" aspects of daily life in Salem and Boston contribute to his portrait of Hawthorne?

Questions for Research Generate research questions to explore the differences between Hawthorne and the contemporaries in the poem.

☑ Check Your Comprehension

1. What action is detailed in the first stanza?
2. To whom does the speaker compare Hawthorne in the fifth stanza?
3. What is described in the final stanza?

◆ Critical Thinking

INTERPRET

1. List at least three words or images from the first stanza that contribute to the impression of Salem as a stagnant, decaying town. **[Support]**
2. What impression of professional people is created by the images in lines 15–18? **[Interpret]**
3. (a) What is the significance of the image of Hawthorne walking "on top of the blazing roof"? (b) Based on lines 23–31, how would you contrast Hawthorne with his literary contemporaries? **[Analyze; Compare and Contrast]**

APPLY

4. (a) Why do you think Lowell wrote this poem? (b) What does it reveal about the poet? **[Speculate; Apply]**

Beyond the Selection

FURTHER READING

Other Works by Robert Lowell

Lord Weary's Castle, The Mills of the Kavanaughs

Life Studies, "For the Union Dead," "Concord,"

Other Works With the Theme of History/Inspiration

"Inspiration," Henry David Thoreau

"Help From History," William Stafford

"What Happened Here Before," Gary Snyder

We suggest that you preview these works before recommending them to students.

INTERNET

You and your students may find additional information about Robert Lowell on the Internet. We suggest the following site. Please be aware, however, that sites may have changed since this information was published.

For essays providing a chronological review of Lowell's work and life, visit **http://www.lit.kobe-u.ac.jp/~hishika/lowell.htm**

We *strongly recommend* that you preview sites before you send students to them.

◆ Literary Focus

❹ **Diction and Style** Have students identify repetition and alliteration in these lines. Ask students how these stylistic devices enhance the poem's emotional impact. *Students should note the repetition of "brooding," "some," and "common," and alliteration in "furtive, foiled." These create a haunting effect which emphasizes the content in the lines.*

Reinforce and Extend

Answers

◆ Literature and Your Life

Reader's Response Encourage students to support their opinion of Hawthorne with details from the poem.

Thematic Focus Suggested response: Salem is a dreary, tired place, and Boston's commerce is dull and unimaginative, whereas Hawthorne's creations are vital and profound.

☑ Check Your Comprehension

1. The speaker walks through Salem.
2. He compares him with the Fireside Poets of the nineteenth century: Longfellow, Lowell, Holmes, and Whittier.
3. The speaker describes Hawthorne "brooding" on some seemingly unimportant thing.

◆ Critical Thinking

1. Suggested responses include "lazy main street," "lounging," "Gallows Hill," "flat, unvaried surfaces," "aged by yellow drain like the unhealthy hair of an old dog," and "no purpose."
2. Lowell's images imply that professional people are blindly absorbed in daily routines and have lost interest in everything else.
3. (a) The image suggests that Hawthorne took risks and was passionate, brilliant, and insightful. (b) Lowell's descriptions imply that the four poets are bland and lack originality, whereas Hawthorne is strong, energetic, and unique.
4. (a) Lowell may have wished to distinguish Hawthorne from other New England poets and to identify himself with Hawthorne. (b) Lowell obviously respects—even idolizes—Hawthorne.

Develop Understanding

One-Minute Insight This intensely visual, auditory, and tactile poem explodes with the natural imagery of Warren's childhood memory. The speaker wends his way through woods, over rocks, past a stream to a hidden glade of golden trees. Capturing the cherished glory of that childhood place as it shimmers with autumn light, "Gold Glade" spotlights an important poetic inspiration: nature.

Customize for
Visual/Spatial Learners and Verbal/Linguistic Learners
Have these students work together to map out the speaker's route. Where is the speaker in each stanza? What does he see? What time of day is it? Encourage students to illustrate their analyses with maps and drawings.

◆ Literary Focus

❶ **Diction and Style** Ask students to supply the missing words in these lines. How does the omission of these words affect the rhythm of the poem? *"To" and "the" are missing in line 4; "the" is missing in line 5; "my" is missing in line 7. Students should note that omitting these words reduces the number of syllables per line and enables the poet to maintain the rhythm he has established. This pattern of speech also recalls early childhood speech when words are commonly dropped.*

◆ Critical Thinking

❷ **Interpret** What is it that the speaker is admiring? *Students should use their own understanding along with the footnote to realize that he is admiring a large, golden hickory tree.*

Gold Glade

Robert Penn Warren

Wandering, in autumn, the woods of boyhood,
Where cedar, black, thick, rode the ridge,
Heart aimless as rifle, boy-blankness of mood,
I came where ridge broke, and the great ledge,
Limestone, set the toe high as treetop by dark edge

Of a gorge, and water hid, grudging and grumbling,
And I saw, in mind's eye, foam white on
Wet stone, stone wet-black, white water tumbling,
And so went down, and with some fright on
Slick boulders, crossed over. The gorge-depth drew night on,

But high over high rock and leaf-lacing, sky
Showed yet bright, and declivity wooed
My foot by the quietening stream, and so I
Went on, in quiet, through the beech wood:
There, in gold light, where the glade gave, it stood.

The glade was geometric, circular, gold,
No brush or weed breaking that bright gold of leaf-fall.
In the center it stood, absolute and bold
Beyond any heart-hurt, or eye's grief-fall.
Gold-massy in air, it stood in gold light-fall,

No breathing of air, no leaf now gold-falling,
No tooth-stitch of squirrel, or any far fox bark,
No woodpecker coding, or late jay calling.
Silence: gray-shagged, the great shagbark[1]
Gave forth gold light. There could be no dark.

1. **shagbark:** Hickory tree.

◆ Build Vocabulary
declivity (di kliv′ ə tē) *n.*: Downward slope

Viewing and Representing Mini-Lesson

Mural

This mini-lesson supports the Viewing and Representing activity on p. 923.

Introduce the Concept Show students several panels from the mural *The Chronicle of Salem,* or call their attention to the panel pictured on p. 914. Tell students that they will create a panel based on the descriptions in Lowell's poem.

Develop Background Form students into groups to search the poems for details they can represent visually. Draw students' attention to figurative descriptions such as *lazy, lounging streets,* and literal descriptions such as *flat, unvaried surface.*

Apply the Information Have students work independently to create a continuous image or a montage of images. Allow time for students to explain the connections between their images and the poem.

Assess the Outcome Assess students on their ability to identify descriptive details, to represent them, and to explain them.

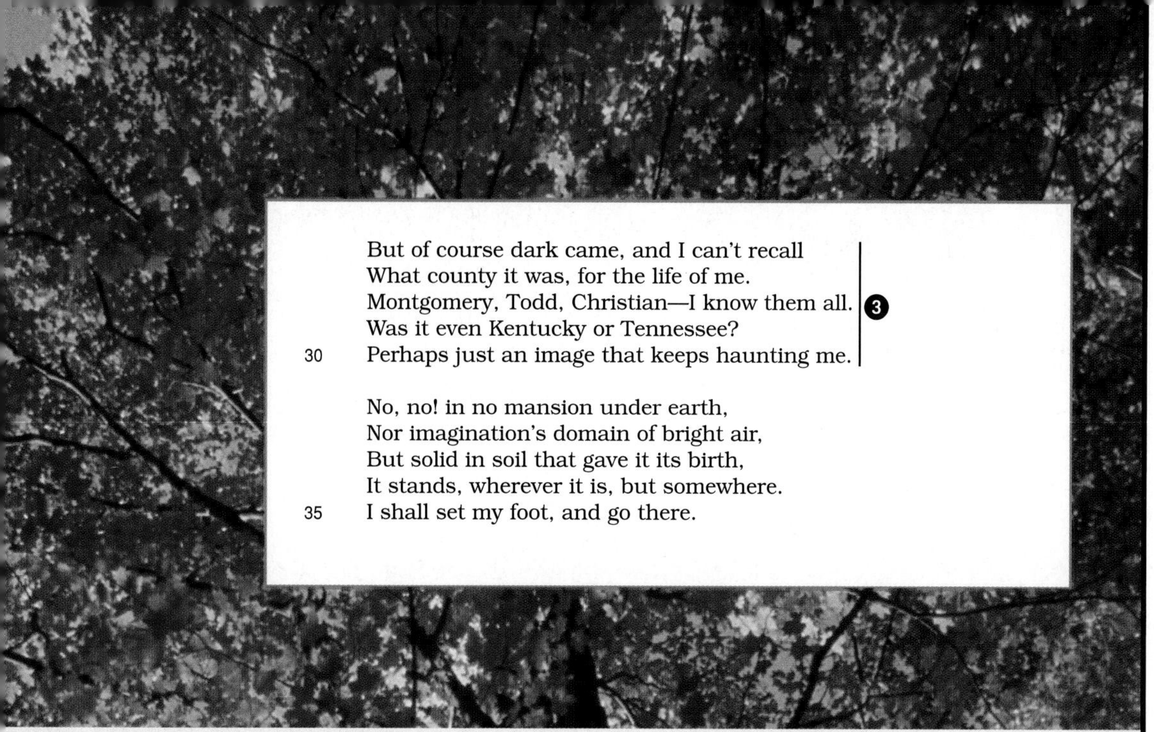

But of course dark came, and I can't recall
What county it was, for the life of me.
Montgomery, Todd, Christian—I know them all. ❸
Was it even Kentucky or Tennessee?
Perhaps just an image that keeps haunting me.

No, no! in no mansion under earth,
Nor imagination's domain of bright air,
But solid in soil that gave it its birth,
It stands, wherever it is, but somewhere.
I shall set my foot, and go there.

Guide for Responding

◆ Literature and Your Life

Reader's Response What are some of your memories of autumn? How do they compare with the speaker's memories?

Thematic Focus How does the speaker compare experiences in the glade with experiences of everyday life?

Cluster Diagrams Robert Penn Warren uses the colors black, white, gold, and gray in "Gold Glade." Make four cluster diagrams containing words and images you associate with each of these colors.

☑ Check Your Comprehension

1. How does the speaker describe the glade?
2. What majestic thing does the speaker find in the center of the glade?
3. What is the speaker unable to recall about the glade?
4. What does the speaker vow to do?

◆ Critical Thinking

INTERPRET

1. At what point does the action of the poem shift from the past to the present? **[Analyze]**
2. What is the significance of the speaker's descriptions of the ledge, the gorge, and the "slick boulders" he encounters before reaching the glade? **[Interpret]**
3. (a) What does the speaker mean by the comment that the glade is "beyond any heart-hurt, or eye's grief-fall"? (b) What does he mean by the saying, "There could be no dark"? **[Interpret]**
4. (a) What does the gold glade represent to the speaker? (b) Why is he so anxious to return to the glade? **[Interpret; Infer]**

COMPARE LITERARY WORKS

5. What does this poem have in common with Robert Frost's "Birches"? **[Connect]**

◆ Critical Thinking

❸ **Interpret** What does "dark" refer to in this line? *Help students to understand that "dark" is both the darkness of evening and maturity—the forgetting that occurs as the speaker grows older and leaves behind the clarity of his childhood vision and innocence.*

Reinforce and Extend

Customize for
Less Proficient Readers
Pair these students with experienced poetry readers to analyze the poem line by line. As they work to construct meaning by breaking down long sentences into meaningful chunks, and interpreting Warren's figurative language, encourage less proficient readers to enjoy the musical rhythm of the lines.

Answers

◆ Literature and Your Life

Reader's Response Students' responses will be personal.

Thematic Focus His experience in the glade was unique, even magical, and unlike his everyday experiences.

☑ Check Your Comprehension

1. He describes it as "geometric, circular, gold."
2. He finds a hickory tree.
3. He cannot recall the glade's location.
4. He vows to find and stand in the glade someday.

◆ Critical Thinking

1. This shift occurs in the first line of the sixth stanza.
2. Suggested response: These descriptions draw attention to the difficulty and exhilaration of the journey to the glade.
3. Suggested responses: (a) The awe inspired by the sight of the glade is beyond any human emotion; it cannot be touched or affected by human cares and griefs. (b) The glade was majestic and eternally beautiful.
4. (a) The glade represents the speaker's youth and innocence. (b) He is anxious to return to confirm his remembered impressions of the glade.
5. Warren's poem concerns a moment of peace he experienced as a young man in a "Gold Glade." That moment haunts him, and he determines to find the place again and regain that moment beyond grief or hurt. The poem tends to be romantic and nostalgic. Frost remembers heightened moments—not a single moment, as in "Gold Glade"—he achieved as a swinger of "Birches." Like Warren, he is haunted by the memory of going beyond earthly hurt. However, Frost's poem is shrewder and more accepting of life's bittersweet realities. He wants to reexperience the heightened moment at the top of the tree, but he also wants to return to earth.

Read to Interpret

Help students interpret "Gold Glade" or "Hawthorne" by having them identify a main idea or image in each stanza. Encourage students to write one sentence to capture this idea or image. Then, discuss with students the cumulative effect of the images and ideas. Finally, have students state the theme of the poem.

Develop Understanding

One-Minute Insight These poems celebrate the power of endurance despite challenge and even violence. "The Light Comes Brighter" recognizes nature's endurance amidst dramatic changes wrought by the seasonal cycle. "The Adamant" describes the innate and inviolate strength of truth. With his vivid imagery, the poet captures the glorious determination of both nature and truth to survive.

◆ Reading Strategy

❶ **Paraphrase** What natural activity does this line describe? Have students restate the line in their own words to answer this question. *Warming temperatures are causing cracks to form in the ice along the river's edge.*

◆ Literary Focus

❷ **Diction and Style** Point out Roethke's use of words that suggest action, even violence, such as "cuts," "buckled,"

◆ Critical Thinking

Analyze Ask students to examine the poem's images. To which senses do they appeal? *The images appeal to the senses of sight, touch, and hearing.*

The Light Comes Brighter

Theodore Roethke

The light comes brighter from the east; the caw
Of restive crows is sharper on the ear.
A walker at the river's edge may hear
❶ A cannon crack announce an early thaw.

The sun cuts deep into the heavy drift,
❷ Though still the guarded snow is winter-sealed,
At bridgeheads buckled ice begins to shift,
The river overflows the level field.

Once more the trees assume familiar shapes,
As branches loose last vestiges of snow.
The water stored in narrow pools escapes
In rivulets; the cold roots stir below.

Soon field and wood will wear an April look,
The frost be gone, for green is breaking now;
The ovenbird[1] will match the vocal brook,
The young fruit swell upon the pear-tree bough.

And soon a branch, part of a hidden scene,
The leafy mind, that long was tightly furled,
Will turn its private substance into green,
And young shoots spread upon our inner world.

---

1. **ovenbird:** Common name for any of the many birds that build a domelike nest on the ground.

◆ Build Vocabulary
vestiges (ves´ tij iz) *n.*: Traces

Beyond the Classroom

Community Connection

Seasonal Cycles Point out to students that the seasonal changes Roethke describes are particular to certain climate and geographic regions. Challenge students to analyze—through research if necessary—and then record the seasonal changes evident in your community. Tell students to consider noting changing foliage, temperature, animal and plant life, human and natural activities. Interested students may wish to track seasonal economic cycles as well.

Career Connection

Environmental Science The speaker in this poem observes natural environmental changes that occur with the change of seasons. Environmentalists work to insure that nature's cycles can survive the earth's ever-expanding human presence. Have interested students learn more about the ways in which environmentalists evaluate and attempt to minimize threats to the environment. Encourage them to research both government and grass-roots programs related to deforestation, air pollution, global warming, or another issue. What types of job opportunities are available to environmentalists? What kind of training is required? Have students share their findings.

The Adamant

Theodore Roethke

Thought does not crush to stone.
The great sledge drops in vain.
Truth never is undone;
Its shafts remain.

The teeth of knitted gears
Turn slowly through the night,
But the true substance bears
The hammer's weight.

Compression cannot break
A center so congealed;
The tool can chip no flake:
The core lies sealed.

❸

Guide for Responding

◆ Literature and Your Life

Reader's Response Which of these poems made a stronger impression on you? Why?

Thematic Focus These poems use imagery and comparison to turn ordinary experiences into moments of discovery. How does "The Light Comes Brighter" make sense of the passage of time?

☑ Check Your Comprehension

1. What is the subject of "The Light Comes Brighter"?

2. (a) In line 4 of "The Light . . . ," what does the speaker indicate a walker might hear near a river? (b) What event does the speaker describe in the final stanza?

3. In "The Adamant," what is "the true substance"?

◆ Critical Thinking

INTERPRET

1. Identify two images or words in "The Light . . ." that suggest that the change in seasons involves action and even some violence. **[Support]**

2. What does the phrase "the leafy mind" tell you about Roethke's world view? **[Infer]**

3. An *adamant* is an extremely hard surface, such as that of a diamond. In "The Adamant," what is described as an adamant? **[Interpret]**

4. How does this imagery in "The Adamant" emphasize the indestructibility of truth? **[Analyze]**

EVALUATE

5. Does Roethke demonstrate an optimistic or a pessimistic outlook in "The Adamant"? Explain. **[Make a Judgment]**

◆ Literature and Your Life

❸ Discuss with students the qualities Roethke ascribes to truth. How have students' own experiences with truth confirmed or denied these qualities? *Students may note that in today's world, truth is sometimes treated as if it were open to interpretation, rather than an unshakable absolute.*

Reinforce and Extend

Answers

◆ Literature and Your Life

Reader's Response Students should be prepared to explain their responses.

Thematic Focus Suggested response: It reveals how one season unfolds into the next in a never-ending progression.

☑ Check Your Comprehension

1. The change in seasons from winter to spring is the subject of the poem.
2. (a) A walker might hear ice cracking. (b) The speaker describes the emergence of leaves on the branches of trees.
3. The "true substance" is truth or thought.

◆ Critical Thinking

1. Suggested responses include "cannon crack," "sun cuts deep," "guarded snow," "escapes," and "breaking."
2. Suggested response: The poet believes in the power and "intelligence" of nature.
3. "Thought" or "truth" is an adamant.
4. Roethke uses imagery that has to do with manual tools and industrial machinery. Since truth and thought are abstractions, they cannot be broken down by machinery—no matter how technologically advanced.
5. Suggested response: Despite his sober, clenched tone and his blunt imagery, Roethke ultimately maintains the optimistic idea that thought ("the true substance") is unbreakable.

Speaking, Listening, and Viewing Mini-Lesson

Oral Presentation

This mini-lesson supports the Speaking, Listening, and Viewing activity in the Idea Bank on p. 923.

Introduce the Concept Review the assignment. Point out the need to include poetic recitations in each presentation.

Develop Background Explain that presentations will be graded based on adherence to these key strategies:

- Orally presented information must be thoroughly documented—just as a written report would be.
- Students should speak slowly and clearly, but with feeling; presentations should engage the audience.
- Successful oral reports are carefully structured around an outline.

Apply the Information As students begin their research, assist them with source ideas as needed. Focus students' efforts to minimize overlap in the reports.

Assess the Outcome Evaluate the presentations for clarity, thoroughness, and creativity.

One-Minute Insight By juxtaposing nature and technology, this poem reminds readers of the dangers created by expanding civilization. On one level, the poem traces the speaker's experience removing a dead—and pregnant—deer from the road as his almost-living car looks on. At a more symbolic level, this poem follows the speaker into the dark recesses of life where the death and destruction of nature at the hands of modern technology seem inevitable.

Customize for
Visual/Spatial Learners
Have these students study the photograph on pages 920–921. What does it suggest about the poem's setting? *It is an isolated rural setting.*

◆ Literary Focus

❶ **Diction and Style** Ask: How would you describe William Stafford's diction in this poem? What stylistic techniques does he employ to craft poetry here? *Stafford's diction is much like ordinary conversational speech. He creates poetry through line arrangement, punctuation, and capitalization.*

◆ Critical Thinking

❷ **Analyze** How is the mood of the poem affected by the time of day in which it is set? *Nighttime creates a mood of loneliness, isolation, and danger.*

◆ Critical Thinking

❸ **Connect** Have students note the image of the warm doe within the belly of the stiffened deer. Ask them to look for a parallel image in the poem. *Students should link the image with that of the warm engine purring beneath the metal hood of the car.*

Traveling Through

William Stafford

❶
Traveling through the dark I found a deer
dead on the edge of the Wilson River road.
It is usually best to roll them into the canyon:
that road is narrow; to swerve might make more dead.

❷
By glow of the tail-light I stumbled back of the car
and stood by the heap, a doe, a recent killing;
she had stiffened already, almost cold.
I dragged her off; she was large in the belly.

❸
My fingers touching her side brought me the reason—
her side was warm; her fawn lay there waiting,
alive, still, never to be born.
Beside that mountain road I hesitated.

Cultural Connection

Deer and Algonquian Life Like many Native American groups, the Algonquian relied on deer for food and clothing. Living in what is now America's northeast, the Algonquian hunted deer with weapons, traps, and disguises. They particularly favored the white-tailed deer for its hide. Skins were cured into a soft leather, then crafted into shirts, leggings, skirts, dresses, and moccasins. The skins were often embellished with decorative painting or fringed edges. After white settlers introduced glass beads, buckskin clothing sometimes featured beaded fringed.

White settlers also brought horses to North America, enabling the Algonquian to hunt deer on horseback. As a result of extensive hunting by both Native Americans and European settlers, the white-tailed deer population was nearly obliterated. It has since been restored in the eastern United States, where many communities consider an abundance of these deer to be a nuisance.

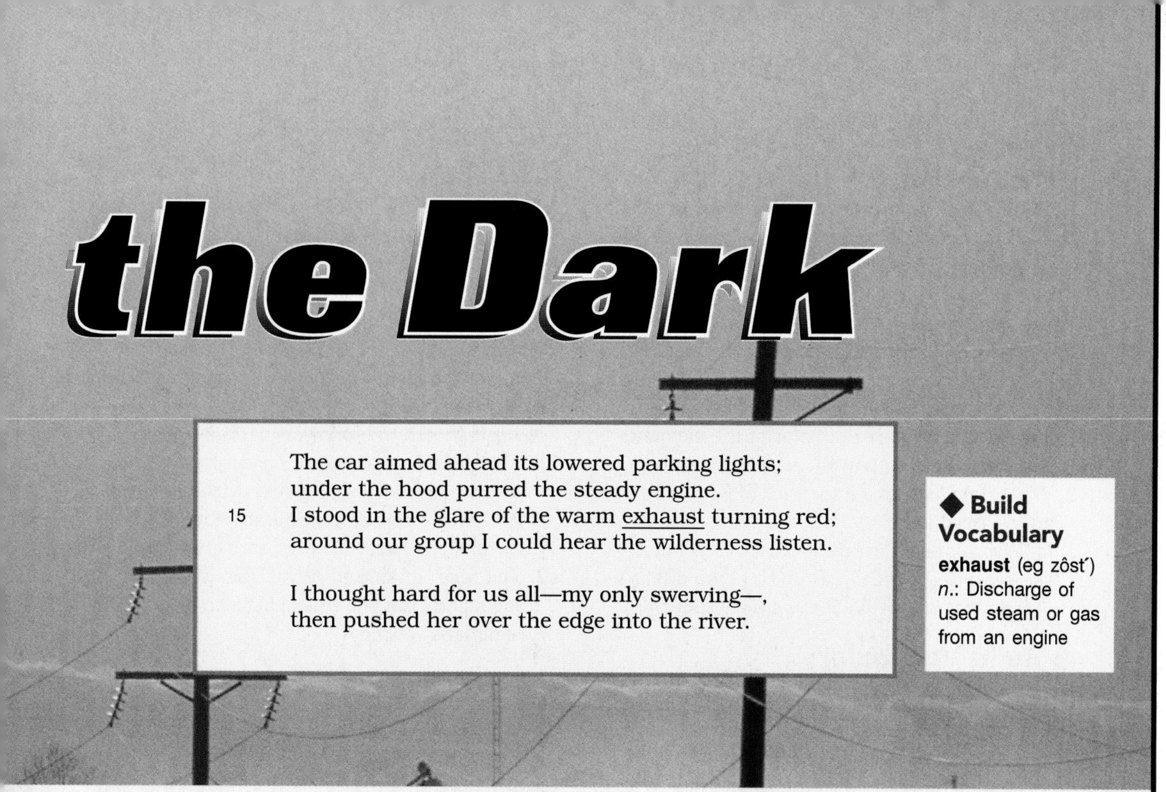

the Dark

The car aimed ahead its lowered parking lights;
under the hood purred the steady engine.
I stood in the glare of the warm exhaust turning red;
around our group I could hear the wilderness listen.

I thought hard for us all—my only swerving—,
then pushed her over the edge into the river.

◆ Build Vocabulary

exhaust (eg zôst′) *n.*: Discharge of used steam or gas from an engine

Guide for Responding

◆ *Literature and Your Life*

Reader's Response How did you feel as you read this poem? What would you say to the poet if you could meet him?

Thematic Focus In an otherwise ordinary day, the speaker stumbles into a difficult dilemma. What factors does the speaker weigh in the decision?

☑ Check Your Comprehension

1. Where does the speaker find the deer?
2. What does he observe about the deer "By glow of the tail-light . . ."?
3. What does he discover when he touches the deer?
4. What does the speaker do at the end of the poem?

◆ Critical Thinking

INTERPRET

1. (a) With what details does the speaker personify his car in the fourth stanza? (b) How does the speaker's description of the car echo his discovery about the deer? **[Support; Connect]**
2. What does the speaker mean when he says, "I thought hard for all of us"? **[Interpret]**
3. What does this poem reveal about the relationship between humanity and nature in the modern world? **[Draw Conclusions]**
4. In literature, a journey is often used to symbolize life. Assuming that this applies to Stafford's poem, how might you interpret its title? **[Interpret]**

APPLY

5. If you had been traveling with the speaker, what would you have suggested that he do? **[Relate]**

Beyond the Selection

FURTHER READING

Other Works by the Poets
All the King's Men, Promises, Warren
The Waking, The Far Field, Roethke
West of Your City, Down in My Heart, Stafford

Other Works With the Theme of the Natural World
"Creative Force," Maude Miner Hadden
Silent Spring, Rachel Carson

We suggest that you preview these works before recommending them to students.

INTERNET

We suggest the following Internet sites. Please be aware, however, that sites may have changed since this information was published.

For information about Warren, go to **http:// www.system.missouri.edu/upress/ spring1998grimshaw.htm**

The Roethke Home Page is at **http://www. thebrothers.com/eraaz/index.html**

We *strongly recommend* that you preview sites before you send students to them.

Reinforce and Extend

Customize for
AP Students
Point out to students the moral and medical dilemmas facing the speaker when he realizes the fawn is still alive. Challenge students to develop alternative courses of action the speaker might take to save the fawn. How practical and successful might these be?

Answers

◆ *Literature and Your Life*

Reader's Response Student responses will vary.

Thematic Focus He considers what is best for himself, the people traveling the road, and the unborn fawn.

☑ Check Your Comprehension

1. He finds the deer on the edge of the Wilson River road.
2. He observes that she is dead, has stiffened, and is almost cold.
3. He discovers that the deer is pregnant and that the fawn inside the doe is alive.
4. He pushes the deer over the edge of the road into the river.

◆ Critical Thinking

1. (a) The car seems to control its own headlights, as if holding a flashlight. Its engine purrs as if it is an animal. It has a warm exhaust, like warm breath. (b) The car is a cold, stiff object on the outside, but inside its engine is warm and "purring." Inside the body of the cold, stiff doe is a living fawn.
2. Suggested response: He tried to consider what course of action would be best for the people traveling the road, his own conscience, and the unborn fawn.
3. Suggested response: Nature is threatened by the development of human civilization.
4. Suggested response: The title suggests that there are many depressing, sad, or unpleasant aspects of life.
5. Encourage students to brainstorm for a list of options available to the speaker. Have them evaluate the consequences of the different options they have listed.

◆ Literary Focus

1. Suggested response: In this poem, Lowell's style is evident in his precise and yet informal diction *(you'll walk, mostly trying to keep warm)*, figurative language *(the blazing roof, touched with fire)*, and loosely arranged lines and stanzas.
2. Suggested response: These poems demonstrate the use of rhyme, formal meter, vivid imagery, precise diction, figurative language, and symbolism that characterize Roethke's style.
3. (a) Most students will cite "Traveling Through the Dark" as having the most ordinary diction. (b) Warren's "Gold Glade" uses language that is least like everyday language.

◆ Build Vocabulary

Using Related Words: *Exhaust*

1. exhaustion, noun
2. exhausted, adj.
3. exhaust, noun
4. exhaustive, adj.

Using the Word Bank: Synonyms

1. d 2. f 3. e 4. a 5. c 6. b

◆ Reading Strategy

Suggested responses:

1. The glade was shaped like a circle and dominated by golden leaves. In the center of the glade stood something very important that seemed more monumental than anything human—such as emotional pain or tears.
2. Although powerful machines run continuously, truth and human thought are strong enough to resist their control.

◆ Grammar and Style

1. water/escapes
2. Walkers/hear
3. teeth/turn
4. fingers/reveal
5. mind/turns

Grammar Reinforcement

For additional instruction and practice, use the Agreement in Number and Special Problems in Agreement lessons in the Subject-Verb Agreement unit of the **Language Lab CD-ROM,** and the pages on Subject and Verb Agreement, pp. 66–67, in the *Writer's Solution Grammar Practice Book.*

Guide for Responding *(continued)*

◆ Literary Focus

Diction and Style

Style refers to the way in which a writer puts ideas into words. Although many writers may address the same topic, each writer's style produces a unique literary expression. Poetic style is established through the writer's use of tone, rhythm, sound devices, figurative language, symbols, punctuation and capitalization, line length and arrangement, stanza format, and **diction**—or word choice.

1. Identify and provide examples of the elements that contribute to Lowell's style in "Hawthorne."
2. What dominant characteristics of Roethke's style are revealed in his two poems?
3. (a) Which poem displays diction that is most like everyday speech? (b) Which poem displays diction that is most unlike everyday speech?

◆ Build Vocabulary

Using Related Words: *Exhaust*

Several English words are related to the word *exhaust.* Write the following sentences on your paper, completing each with the appropriate word from the box below. Then label the part of speech of each of the four related words.

exhaust	exhaustive	exhausted	exhaustion

1. The ___?___ I felt was due to lack of sleep.
2. The runner had become completely ___?___ by the time she neared the finish line.
3. The truck's thick, black ___?___ obscured my vision.
4. The congressman spoke for more than twenty-three hours in an ___?___ attempt to block a vote on the proposed new legislation.

Using the Word Bank: Synonyms

On your paper, write the letter of the word in the right column that is the best synonym for the word in the left column.

1. brooding	**a.** slope
2. furtive	**b.** fumes
3. meditation	**c.** traces
4. declivity	**d.** worrying
5. vestiges	**e.** pensiveness
6. exhaust	**f.** sneaky

◆ Reading Strategy

Paraphrase

You can clarify difficult phrases, lines, or passages by **paraphrasing**—or restating them in your own words. In fact, you may find it useful to paraphrase every sentence of especially challenging poems. For example, you might paraphrase lines 19–22 of "Hawthorne" as *Though he was a shy and distrustful man, Hawthorne was capable of passionate feelings and extraordinary mental and artistic insights.* How would you paraphrase the following passages?

1. The glade was geometric, circular, gold, / No brush or weed breaking that bright gold of leaf-fall. / In the center it stood, absolute and bold / Beyond any heart-hurt, or eye's grief-fall.
2. The teeth of knitted gears / Turn slowly through the night, / But the true substance bears / The hammer's weight.

◆ Grammar and Style

Subject and Verb Agreement

Remember in your own writing that the subject is not always the noun or pronoun that immediately precedes the verb. Sometimes you have to look closely to identify the subject—who or what is actually performing the action of the verb.

Subjects and **verbs** must **agree** in number, even when they are separated by intervening words.

Practice Write the following sentences on a sheet of paper. For each sentence, underline the subject, and then choose the correct form of the verb in parentheses.

1. The water stored in narrow pools (escapes, escape) in rivulets.
2. Walkers at the river's edge (hears, hear) a cannon crack.
3. The teeth of knitted gears (turns, turn) slowly through the night.
4. My fingers touching her side (reveals, reveal) the reason.
5. The leafy mind, that long was tightly furled, (turn, turns) its private substance into green.

Reteach

Students may have difficulty identifying the differences among poets' writing. To help them understand and recognize varying poetic style and diction, use a chart like the one shown here. Guide students to examine each poet's work for very specific aspects of style and diction. (You may wish to add other details to this chart.) Work as a group to help students complete the chart, then explain how these details contribute to the diction and overall style of the work.

	formal language	informal language	strong regular rhythm	no regular rhythm	short lines	long lines	standard punctuation and capitalization	nonstandard punctuation and capitalization
Lowell								
Penn Warren	X							
Roethke								
Stafford		X						

Build Your Portfolio

Idea Bank

Writing

1. **Explanation** If you were going to write a poem about one of your favorite writers, whom would you choose? Explain your choice in a paragraph.

2. **Poem** Using Warren's "Gold Glade" for inspiration, write a poem in which you use vivid imagery to re-create an important childhood experience.

3. **Critical Response** Critic Robert Boyers has commented that Roethke's best poems "permit us to embrace the principle of change as the root of stability." Write an essay in which you discuss this comment in relation to "The Light Comes Brighter" or "The Adamant."

Speaking, Listening, and Viewing

4. **Oral Presentation** Conduct research to learn more about Lowell and confessional poetry. In an oral report, share your findings on the confessional poets and their works. Include recitations of two or three poems.

5. **Movie Summary** Robert Penn Warren was one of the outstanding figures in twentieth-century southern literature. Watch the film based on his novel "All the King's Men," and prepare a summary for your classmates.

Researching and Representing

6. **Mural** The Peabody Museum in Salem houses a fifty-panel mural, *The Chronicle of Salem.* Create another panel (based on Lowell's description of Hawthorne's Salem) for this mural. **[Art Link]**

7. **Dictionary** In "Gold Glade," Warren invents a number of compound words: boy-blankness, grief-fall, and so on. Create a "Warren dictionary" in which you define each word as it is used in the context of the poem.

Online Activity www.phlit.phschool.com

Guided Writing Lesson

One Writer Reviews Another

In the book review section of many newspapers, magazines, and literary journals, you can read a writer's review of another writer's work. Often writers review works within their own genre—for instance, poets review the work of other poets and novelists review works of fiction. Choose two poets from this section. Using one poet's work as a guide, decide what that poet might consider to be the criteria for good poetry. Then review the other poet's work using those criteria.

Writing Skills Focus: Suitable Criteria

A critical review evaluates a work of literature by discussing its positive and negative aspects. Responsible reviewers use **suitable criteria** to judge literary works. Although many of these criteria are universally accepted, some criteria reflect the reviewer's unique perspective. William Stafford's idea of what makes a good poem, for example, might be very different from Robert Lowell's. Some suitable criteria for evaluating poems include:

- skillful or inspired use of language
- effective use of poetic devices
- appropriate relationship between form and content
- compelling subject matter

Prewriting Decide on the poet from whose point of view you will speak. Review his or her poetry to determine and list the elements of writing that he values. Using these criteria, read and make notes about the poems you will review.

Drafting Establish and maintain a tone that is appropriate for a poet reviewing the work of a peer.

Revising Read the review aloud. Is your tone respectful? How thoroughly did you review the second poet's work? Did you use criteria that the first poet would have deemed especially important?

✓ ASSESSMENT OPTIONS

Formal Assessment, Selection Test, pp. 274–276, and Assessment Resources Software. The selection test is designed so that it can be easily customized to the performance levels of your students.

Alternative Assessment, p. 61, includes options for less advanced students, more advanced students, visual/spatial learners, musical/rhythmic learners, verbal/linguistic learners, and bodily/kinesthetic learners.

PORTFOLIO ASSESSMENT

Use the following rubrics in the ***Alternative Assessment*** booklet to assess student writing:
Explanation: Expression Rubric, p. 109
Poem: Poetry Rubric, p. 123
Critical Response: Critical Review Rubric, p. 126
Guided Writing Lesson: Evaluation/Review Rubric, p. 119

Idea Bank

Customizing for
Performance Levels

Following are suggestions for matching Idea Bank topics with your students' performance levels:
Less Advanced Students: 1, 6
Average Students: 2, 4, 5
More Advanced Students: 3, 7

Customizing for
Learning Modalities

Following are suggestions for matching Idea Bank topics with your students' learning modalities:
Verbal/Linguistic: 4, 5, 7
Interpersonal: 5
Visual/Spatial: 6

Guided Writing Lesson

For more instruction on prewriting, elaboration, and revision, see *Prentice Hall Writing and Grammar.*

Writers at Work Videodisc

Have students view the videodisc segment on Response to Literature (Ch. 7) featuring Theresa Park to see how this professional literary agent approaches the process of reviewing the manuscripts she receives. Have students discuss how her ideas can help them shape their writer reviews.

Play frames 22513 to 31258

Writing Lab CD-ROM

Have students complete the tutorial on Response to Literature. Follow these steps:

1. Refer students to the audio-annotated Literary Models of poetic elements in the Gathering Details section to help them focus their reviews.
2. Have students draft on the computer.
3. Students can use the Evaluation Word Bins to help strengthen their reviews.

Prepare and Engage

LESSON OBJECTIVES

1. To develop vocabulary and word identification skills
- Latin Prefixes: *trans-*
- Using the Word Bank: Sentence Completions
- Extending Word Study: Greek Roots (ATE)

2. To use a variety of reading strategies to comprehend a short story
- Connect Your Experience
- Reading Strategy: Order Events

3. To increase knowledge of other cultures and to connect common elements across cultures
- Connecting Themes Across Cultures (ATE)

4. To express and support responses to the text
- Critical Thinking
- Idea Bank: Letter
- Idea Bank: Critical Response
- Idea Bank: Conversation

5. To analyze literary elements
- Literary Focus: Foreshadowing

6. To read in order to research self-selected and assigned topics
- Idea Bank: Fact-Finding Report
- Research Skills Mini-Lesson (ATE)
- Idea Bank: Medical Brochure

7. To plan, prepare, organize, and present literary interpretations
- Idea Bank: New Version
- Idea Bank: Political Speech

8. To use recursive writing processes to write a social worker's report
- Guided Writing Lesson

9. To increase knowledge of the rules of grammar and usage
- Grammar and Style: Correct Use of Adjectives and Adverbs

Test Preparation

Writing Skills: Grammar and Usage (ATE, p. 925)

The teaching tips and sample test item in this workshop support the instruction and practice in the unit workshop:

Writing Skills: Punctuation, Usage, and Sentence Structure (SE, p. 1143)

Guide for Interpreting

Anne Tyler *(1941–)*

As the wife of a child psychiatrist and the mother of two daughters, Anne Tyler has for years successfully juggled the demands of family life while maintaining her commitment to writing. Mondays through Thursdays she writes; Fridays she reserves for errands; weekends she devotes entirely to family matters. She works on a daybed in a starkly plain study, penning her fiction in longhand so that, as she explains it, she can hear her characters speak. During occasional bouts of insomnia, she often records her ideas in boxes of index cards.

Young Talent Born in Minneapolis, Tyler spent most of her childhood in Quaker communes in the Midwest and South. After attending high school in Raleigh, North Carolina, she went on to study Russian at Duke University when she was only sixteen. She published her first novel, *If Morning Ever Comes* (1964), at age twenty-four and since then has produced a string of novels to ever-increasing acclaim. Among them are *Dinner at the Homesick Restaurant* (1982), *The Accidental Tourist* (1985), and *Ladder of Years* (1995). Tyler has also published numerous short stories in prestigious literary magazines such as *The New Yorker*.

Serious Fiction Tyler's characters are not fictionalized versions of people from her own quiet life; they are products of a fertile imagination, drawn with her gift for fine, realistic detail. When Tyler works on a novel, she follows a pattern that entails writing out a first draft in longhand. She then reads the draft to "find out what it means." She revises the draft to enhance "the subconscious intentions" she has discovered in the work. Tyler keeps the goal of writing "serious fiction" firmly in sight.

"A serious book," Tyler explains, "is one that removes me to another life as I am reading it. It has to have layers and layers, like life does. It has to be an extremely believable lie."

"Average Waves in Unprotected Waters" displays Tyler's ability to create well-developed, realistic characters and evoke an emotional response through an unsentimental portrayal of the characters' tragic lives.

Tyler, who has remained a private person despite her fame, now lives in Baltimore, Maryland. Preferring this to living in a larger city, she has been called "the nearest thing we have to an urban southern writer."

◆ Background for Understanding

SOCIAL STUDIES: CARING FOR MENTALLY OR PHYSICALLY CHALLENGED CHILDREN

In "Average Waves in Unprotected Waters," Anne Tyler explores a mother's attempts to cope with a severely challenged child. The decision to institutionalize a child is an extremely difficult one. When this story was written in the mid-1970's, however, a single parent like the mother in "Average Waves" may have felt that she had few other options available to her. That knowledge probably offered little comfort to the parents facing such decisions. Then, as now, the cost of private care was so high that many patients wound up in state-run or charitable hospitals that were often severely underfunded. Lack of funds sometimes resulted in grim conditions, outdated equipment, and an inadequate staff.

Fortunately, today's ever-increasing array of educational, medical, and counseling programs for children with special needs makes it possible for many children who might once have been institutionalized to remain at home.

Journal Writing Explore the difficulties and emotions that parents might face in dealing with a severely challenged child.

Prentice Hall Literature Program Resources

REINFORCE / RETEACH / EXTEND

Selection Support Pages
Build Vocabulary: Prefixes: *trans-*, p. 282
Grammar and Style: Correct Use of Adjectives and Adverbs, p. 283
Reading Strategy: Order Events, p. 284
Literary Focus: Foreshadowing, p. 285

Strategies for Diverse Student Needs, p. 62

Beyond Literature
Humanities Connection: Art, p. 62

Formal Assessment Selection Test, pp. 277–279; Assessment Resources Software

Alternative Assessment, p. 62

Writing and Language Transparencies
Cause-and-Effect Transparency, p. 91

Resource Pro CD-ROM
Includes all resource material and customizable lesson plan

Listening to Literature Audiocassettes

Average Waves in Unprotected Waters

◆ Literature and Your Life

Connect Your Experience

A family move, a new school, the change of seasons—these situations can present either a terrible problem to overcome or an exciting challenge to greet. Some changes present difficulties and others offer great rewards. In this story, the main character, Bet, faces a tremendous change in her life. Are you willing to make difficult changes if they are for the better?

Thematic Focus: Literature Confronts the Everyday

Tyler depicts the unchanging nature of Bet's character through her use of details that are ordinary as well as extraordinary. How do the everyday details enhance the emotions underlying both Bet's experiences and her resistance to change?

◆ Literary Focus

Foreshadowing

Foreshadowing is the use of details or clues that hint at what will occur later in a plot or suggest a certain outcome. In the opening paragraphs of this story, for example, readers learn that Bet is wearing the dress "she usually saved for Sundays." This detail suggests that this day will be special or important in some way.

Foreshadowing builds suspense, because it makes the reader wonder what will happen next and what will happen at the end of the story. As you read, notice how Tyler's use of foreshadowing keeps you guessing about how the story will turn out.

◆ Grammar and Style

Correct Use of Adjectives and Adverbs

Adjectives modify nouns or pronouns; **adverbs** modify verbs, adjectives, and other adverbs. You could not, for example, use the adjective *slow* in the following sentence; the adverb *slowly* is required to modify the verb *went.*

They went down the stairs *slowly.* [not *slow*]

However, use an adjective, rather than an adverb, after a linking verb, such as a form of *be.* You must use an adjective because you are modifying the subject of the sentence, not the verb.

The collar was *askew.* She always felt *bad.* [not *badly*]

◆ Reading Strategy

Order Events

Most stories are written in chronological order, the order in which events happened. Sometimes, however, the writer interrupts the sequence to present a **flashback,** a scene or an event from an earlier time. As you read Tyler's story, **order events** by noting the sequence, or order, in which events actually occurred. Using an expanded version of a chain-of-events diagram like the one below, record the earliest event at the top and the latest at the bottom.

Event:

↓

Event:

↓

Event:

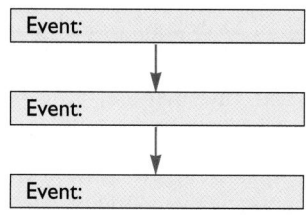

◆ Build Vocabulary

Latin Prefixes: *trans-*

Bet describes her son Arnold's skin as so *transparent* that "she imagined she could see the blood traveling in his veins." The Latin prefix *trans-* means "across," "over," or "through." Something *transparent* is "clear or thin enough to be seen through."

Word Bank

Before you read, preview this list of words from the selection.

orthopedic
transparent
stocky
staunch
viper

Test Preparation Workshop

Writing Skills: Grammar and Usage The writing sections of standardized tests such as the ACT often require students to choose the correct word or group of words to complete a sentence. Use the following sample item to show students how to recognize correct and incorrect grammar and choose the correct word to complete a sentence.

A writer who wishes to create serious fiction should be willing to revise ____ work as many times as is necessary.

Choose the word or group of words that belongs in the blank.

A their
B they're
C him or her
D his or her

A is plural, whereas the antecedent is singular. *B* is not a possessive pronoun, but a contraction meaning "they are." *C* is not possessive. *D* is both singular and possessive, and is therefore the correct answer.

Interest Grabber Students may find this story of ambivalence in the face of seemingly unavoidable change both uplifting and depressing. Engage them in considering the range of human reactions to change by presenting the following dramatization. Ask the school principal to announce to your class only an impending major change—relocating the school, retirement of a much-loved teacher, or closing of the athletic program. Challenge students to identify both positive and negative reactions to the proposed changes. Explain that in this story, the main character experiences emotional extremes in facing an important life change.

Connecting Themes Across Cultures

Tell students that in ancient cultures, a weak, infirm, or mentally disabled member of the community would often be cast out or abandoned. In most modern societies, accomodations are made for the care and maintenance of those unable to care for themselves. Ask students for possible reasons that attitudes have changed. Students may recognize that in ancient cultures, caring for an individual who did not produce for the group would have endangered the group by depleting a food supply that varied from hunt to hunt. Some students may also point out that we know more today about disabilities, eliminating the fear that uninformed cultures may have felt.

Customize for *Less Proficient Readers*

At the start of the story, Tyler gives only clues about the challenge Bet faces. Encourage these students to read on, despite any early confusion, as the situation will ultimately become clear.

Customize for *AP Students*

Draw students' attention to the challenge Tyler faces in truthfully and respectfully portraying a mentally challenged boy. Have students identify Tyler's characterization techniques, for example distinguishing between direct and indirect characterization.

Develop Understanding

One-Minute Insight In this story, students meet Bet, a woman emotionally torn apart by the difficult decision she has made about the care of her mentally challenged son. As Bet accompanies Arnold to his new home, guiding him and negotiating the obstacles of travel with him, she recalls the events which have brought her to this point in life. Readers learn of the gritty sense of perseverance that has enabled her to endure, rather than truly overcome, the catastrophic events of her life which have washed over her like "average waves in unprotected waters." As she leaves her son behind in a mental hospital, Bet is torn with ambivalent feelings of guilt and relief as she realizes that she will no longer have to participate in the daily agonies of her former life.

◆ Literary Focus

❶ **Foreshadowing** Point out this very early signal from Tyler that something unusual, and possibly, unpleasant, may be ahead.

◆ Grammar and Style

❷ **Correct Use of Adjectives and Adverbs** Ask students to identify the modifier "slight" as an adjective or an adverb. Then have them explain why their identification is correct. *It is an adjective, used here instead of an adverb because it follows a linking verb and modifies the subject "she."*

◆ Literary Focus

❸ **Foreshadowing** Bet's last look around, the suitcase, and her tone of voice all foreshadow the importance and finality of an upcoming journey.

Average Waves in Unprotected Waters

Anne Tyler

As soon as it got light, Bet woke him and dressed him, and then she walked him over to the table and tried to make him ❶ eat a little cereal. He wouldn't, though. He could tell something was up. She pressed the edge of the spoon against his lips till she heard it click on his teeth, but he just looked off at a corner of the ceiling—a knobby child with great glassy eyes and her own fair hair. Like any other nine-year-old, he wore a striped shirt and jeans, but the shirt was too neat and the jeans too blue, unpatched and unfaded, and would stay that way till he outgrew them. And his face was elderly—pinched, strained, tired—though it should have looked as unused as his jeans. He hardly ever changed his expression.

She left him in his chair and went to make the beds. Then she raised the yellowed shade, rinsed a few spoons in the bathroom sink, picked up some bits of magazines he'd torn the night before. This was a rented room in an ancient, crumbling house, and nothing you could do to it would lighten its cluttered look. There was always that feeling of too many lives layered over other lives, like the layers of brownish wallpaper her child had peeled away in the corner by his bed.

She slipped her feet into flat-heeled loafers and absently patted the front of her dress, a worn beige knit she usually saved for Sundays. Maybe she should take it in a little; it ❷ hung from her shoulders like a sack. She felt too slight and frail, too wispy for all she had to do today. ❷ But she reached for her coat anyhow, and put it on and tied a blue kerchief under her chin. Then she went over to the table and slowly spun, modeling the coat. "See, Arnold?" she said. "We're going out."

Arnold went on looking at the ceiling, but his gaze turned wild and she knew he'd heard.

She fetched his jacket from the closet—brown corduroy, with a hood. It had set her back half a week's salary. But Arnold didn't like it; he always wanted his old one, a little red duffel coat he'd long ago outgrown. When she came toward him, he started moaning and rocking and shaking his head. She had to struggle to stuff his arms in the sleeves. Small though he was, he was strong, wiry; he was getting to be too much for her. He shook free of her hands and ran over to his bed. The jacket was on, though. It wasn't buttoned, the collar was askew, but never mind; that just made him look more real. She always felt bad at how he stood inside his clothes, separate from them, passive, unaware of all the buttons and snaps she'd fastened as carefully as she would a doll's.

She gave a last look around the room, checked to make sure the hot plate was off, and then picked up her purse and Arnold's suitcase. "Come along, Arnold," she said. ❸

He came, dragging out every step. He looked at the suitcase suspiciously, but only

Block Scheduling Strategies

Consider these suggestions to take advantage of extended class time:

- After reading the Background for Understanding, have students complete and discuss the journal activity (p. 924).
- Introduce the Literary Focus and Reading Strategy, as well as any other skills you wish to emphasize.
- Have students create foreshadowing logs so that they can record appropriate story details as they read.
- Use the Critical Viewing question (p. 929) and Group Discussion activity in the Guide for Responding (p. 931) to guide discussion of the story.
- Work as a class to order story events in a chain-of-events diagram (p. 925).
- Assist students in identifying appropriate research paths for the Fact-Finding Report or Medical Brochure (p. 933). Allow class time for students to conduct Internet research.

because it was new. It didn't have any meaning for him. "See?" she said. "It's yours. It's Arnold's. It's going on the train with us."

But her voice was all wrong. He would pick it up, for sure. She paused in the middle of locking the door and glanced over at him fearfully. Anything could set him off nowadays. He hadn't noticed, though. He was too busy staring around the hallway, goggling at a freckled, walnut-framed mirror as if he'd never seen it before. She touched his shoulder. "Come, Arnold," she said.

They went down the stairs slowly, both of them clinging to the sticky mahogany railing. The suitcase banged against her shins. In the entrance hall, old Mrs. Puckett stood waiting outside her door—a huge, soft lady in a black crepe dress and orthopedic shoes. She was holding a plastic bag of peanutbutter cookies, Arnold's favorites. There were tears in her eyes. "Here, Arnold," she said, quavering. Maybe she felt to blame that he was going.

> **◆ Literary Focus**
> 4 What does Mrs. Puckett's behavior hint about subsequent events?

But she'd done the best she could: babysat
5 him all these years and only given up when
he'd grown too strong and wild to manage. Bet wished Arnold would give the old lady some sign—hug her, make his little crowing noise, just take the cookies, even. But he was too excited. He raced on out the front door, and it was Bet who had to take them. "Well, thank you, Mrs. Puckett," she said. "I know he'll enjoy them later."

"Oh, no . . ." said Mrs. Puckett, and she flapped her large hands and gave up, sobbing.

They were lucky and caught a bus first thing. Arnold sat by the window. He must have thought he was going to work with her; when they passed the red-and-gold Kresge's sign, he jabbered and tried to stand up. "No, honey," she said, and took hold of his arm. He settled down then and let his hand stay curled in hers awhile. He had very small, cool fingers, and nails as smooth as thumbtack heads.

At the train station, she bought the tickets
6 and then a pack of Wrigley's spearmint gum.
Arnold stood gaping at the vaulted ceiling, with his head flopped back and his arms hanging limp at his sides. People stared at him. She would have liked to push their faces in. "Over here, honey," she said, and she nudged him toward the gate, straightening his collar as they walked. 7

He hadn't been on a train before and acted a little nervous, bouncing up and down in his seat and flipping the lid of his ashtray and craning forward to see the man ahead of them. When the train started moving, he crowed and pulled at her sleeve. "That's right, Arnold. Train. We're taking a trip," Bet said. She unwrapped a stick of chewing gum and gave it to him. He loved gum. If she didn't watch him closely, he sometimes swallowed it—which worried her a little because she'd heard it clogged your kidneys; but at least it would keep him busy. She looked down at the top of his head. Through the blond prickles of his hair, cut short for practical reasons, she could see his skull bones moving as he chewed. He was so thin-skinned, almost transparent; sometimes she imagined she could see the blood traveling in his veins.

When the train reached a steady speed, he grew calmer, and after a while he nodded over against her and let his hands sag on his knees. She watched his eyelashes slowly drooping—two colorless, fringed crescents, heavier and heavier, every now and then flying up as he tried to fight off sleep. He had
never slept well, not ever, not even as a baby. 8
Even before they'd noticed anything wrong, they'd wondered at his jittery, jerky catnaps, his tiny hands clutching tight and springing open, his strange single wail sailing out while he went right on sleeping. Avery said it gave him the chills. And after the doctor talked to them Avery wouldn't have anything to do

> **◆ Build Vocabulary**
> **orthopedic** (ôr´ thō pē´ dik) *adj.*: Correcting posture or other disorders of the skeletal system and related muscles and joints
>
> **transparent** (trans per´ ənt) *adj.*: Capable of being seen through

Customize for *Musical/Rhythmic Learners*

Point out the care with which Bet modulates her tone of voice, sure that it will reveal too much of her feelings to Arnold. As Bet, have students read portions of the text aloud, listening for the intonations that might signal to Arnold that something was amiss.

Customize for *Less Proficient Readers*

Help these students improve comprehension with the Identify Chain of Events page in ***Strategies for Diverse Student Needs,*** p. 62

◆ Literary Focus

4 Foreshadowing Her distress suggests that she expects something unpleasant will happen to Arnold.

◆ Reading Strategy

5 Order Events Ask: When, in the chronology of the story, do the events in this line occur? How does inserting this information about past events help clarify the current situation? *Mrs. Puckett had cared for Arnold from early childhood to the present. The reference to the change in Arnold's behavior explains why his mother must make new arrangements for his care.*

◆ Critical Thinking

6 Predict Have students predict where Bet and Arnold may be going.

Customize for *Less Proficient Readers*

7 Have students pause at each text break to consider its purpose. Lead students to understand that the story setting changes at each break. Here, Arnold and Bet's train journey has begun.

◆ Reading Strategy

8 Order Events Ask students: Which sentence in this paragraph begins a flashback? *"He had never slept well, not ever, not even as a baby."*

Extending Word Study

Greek Roots: *-ortho-* Arrange students into groups and have them look up the root *-ortho-* and write its meaning. Then, have students make posters illustrating several words with the root, showing the commonality among the words.

Beyond the Classroom

Community Connection

Institutions and Services for the Mentally Challenged In this story, a single mother faces difficulty in caring for her mentally challenged son. Invite interested students to learn about the help such a parent might locate in your community. Direct students to libraries, social service agencies, and hospitals for resources. As a class, evaluate your community's services and suggest ways to fill any gaps. You may wish to have students complete the Fact-Finding Report in the Idea Bank (p. 933).

Workplace Skills Connection

Specialized Training Several characters in the story—the narrator, Mrs. Puckett, and the nurse—must care for a young mentally challenged boy. Challenge students to brainstorm the skills a care-giver would need to properly and kindly care for the mentally challenged. Discuss how these skills might be useful in other workplace or family situations.

❶ Enrichment Some forms of mental retardation are hereditarily linked. For example, Down's syndrome results from an extra chromosome or genetic message, which prevents normal development. There is no direct indication that Arnold's condition results from a hereditary link. In fact, when Bet moves from blaming it on a gene to the marriage in general, the narrator seems to indicate that there is no hereditary link. At the very least, the narrator shows the insignificance of assigning blame in the situation.

◆ Critical Thinking

❷ Synthesize Ask students to consider what Bet might say if she were able to explain why she stands staunchly against the waves. *Students may suggest that Bet would say she feels as though there's something noble about the ability to withstand the force of the waves, rather than using that force to carry her to shore.*

◆ Reading Strategy

❸ Order Events Draw students' attention to the fact that the flashback begins with Arnold's childhood, then moves to Bet's childhood, and finally explores her marriage to Avery. Ask students to explain why Bet recalls events out of chronological order. *Students may point out that thinking of Arnold's childhood naturally leads Bet to contrast it with her own childhood. The memory of her father then leads to memories of Avery, Arnold's father.*

◆ Critical Thinking

❹ Connect Ask students how this sentence reflects events from Bet's childhood. *Students should recognize that this attitude is the same one that led Bet to stand staunchly in the face of crashing waves.*

◆ Literature and Your Life

❺ Discuss with students Bet's concern that Arnold will behave inappropriately on the train. What experiences have students had in which they felt anxious that a friend or family member would behave inappropriately and perhaps embarrass them? *Students may mention their parents at school athletic events, the introduction between a friend and new romantic attachment, or the behavior of a younger sibling.*

with Arnold anymore—just walked in wide circles around the crib, looking stunned and sick. A few weeks later, he left. She wasn't surprised. She even knew how he felt, more or less. Halfway, he blamed her; halfway, he blamed himself. You can't believe a thing like this will just fall on you out of nowhere.

She'd had moments herself of picturing some kind of evil gene in her husband's ordinary, stocky body—a dark little egg like a black jelly bean, she imagined it. All his fault. ❶ But other times she was sure the gene was hers. It seemed so natural; she never could do anything as well as most people. And then other times she blamed their marriage. They'd married too young, against her parents' wishes. All she'd wanted was to get away from home. Now she couldn't remember why. What was wrong with home? She thought of her parents' humped green trailer, perched on cinder blocks near a forest of masts in Salt Spray, Maryland. At this distance (parents dead, trailer rusted to bits, even Salt Spray changed past recognition), it seemed to her that her old life had been beautifully free and spacious. She closed her eyes and saw wide gray skies. Everything had been ruled by the sea. Her father (who'd run a fishing boat for tourists) couldn't arrange his day till he'd heard the marine forecast—the wind, the tides, the small-craft warnings, the height of average waves in unprotected waters. He loved to fish, offshore and on, and he swam every chance he could get. He'd tried to teach her to bodysurf, but it hadn't worked out. There was something about the breakers: she just gritted her teeth ❷ and stood staunch and let them slam into her. As if standing staunch were a virtue, really. She couldn't explain it. Her father thought she was scared, but it wasn't that at all.

She'd married Avery against their wishes and been sorry ever since—sorry to move so far from home, sorrier when her parents died within a year of each other, sorriest of all when ❸ the marriage turned grim and cranky. But she never would have thought of leaving him. It was Avery who left; she would have stayed forever. In fact, she did stay on in their apartment for months after he'd gone, though the rent was far too high. It wasn't that she expected him back. She just took some comfort from enduring. ❹

Arnold's head snapped up. He looked around him and made a gurgling sound. His chewing gum fell onto the front of his jacket. "Here, honey," she told him. She put the gum in her ashtray. "Look out the window. See the cows?"

He wouldn't look. He began bouncing in his seat, rubbing his hands together rapidly.

"Arnold? Want a cookie?"

If only she'd brought a picture book. She'd meant to and then forgot. She wondered if the train people sold magazines. If she let him get too bored, he'd go into one of his tantrums, and then she wouldn't be able to handle him. ❺ The doctor had given her pills just in case, but she was always afraid that while he was screaming he would choke on them. She looked around the car. "Arnold," she said, "see the . . . see the hat with feathers on? Isn't it pretty? See the red suitcase? See the, um . . ."

The car door opened with a rush of clattering wheels and the conductor burst in, singing "Girl of my dreams, I love you." He lurched down the aisle, plucking pink tickets from the back of each seat. Just across from Bet and Arnold, he stopped. He was looking down at a tiny black lady in a purple coat, with a fox fur piece biting its own tail around her neck. "You!" he said.

The lady stared straight ahead.

"You, I saw you. You're the one in the washroom."

A little muscle twitched in her cheek.

"You got on this train in Beulah, didn't you. Snuck in the washroom. Darted back like you thought you could put something over on me. I saw that bit of purple! Where's your ticket gone to?"

She started fumbling in a blue cloth purse. The fumbling went on and on. The conductor shifted his weight.

"Why!" she said finally. "I must've left it back in my other seat."

"What other seat?"

"Oh, the one back . . ." She waved a spidery hand.

The conductor sighed. "Lady," he said, "you owe me money."

Research Skills Mini-Lesson

Fact-Finding Report

This mini-lesson supports the Researching and Representing project on p. 933.

Introduce Discuss with students that the goal of research is usually not just to report facts, but to draw meaning from a group of related facts.

Develop Have students share some of the facts they have found. Discuss individual facts and what they might indicate. For example, if an institution spends a great deal of money per client, it might mean that the quality of care is very good, or that the adminstration of finances is very careless. Guide students to recognize that in order to draw a conclusion, they will need to look at combinations of related facts.

Apply Have students complete their reports and present their conclusions.

Assess Assess students on how well they use facts to support their conclusions. You may also assess the completed report using the Scoring Rubric for a Research Report/Paper on p. 121 of ***Alternative Assessment*** .

"I do no such thing!" she said. "Viper! Monger! Hitler!"[1] Her voice screeched up all at once; she sounded like a parrot. Bet winced and felt herself flushing, as if *she* were the one. But then at her shoulder she heard a sudden, rusty clang, and she turned and saw that Arnold was laughing. He had his mouth wide open and his tongue curled, the way he did when he watched "Sesame Street." Even after the scene had worn itself out, and the lady had paid and the conductor had moved on, Arnold went on chortling and la-la-ing, and Bet looked gratefully at the little black lady, who was settling 6 her fur piece fussily and muttering under her breath.

Girl Looking at Landscape, 1957, Richard Diebenkorn, oil on canvas, 59 x 60 3/8 inches, (149.9 x 153.4 cm), Gift of Mr. and Mrs. Alan H. Temple, 61.49, Collection of Whitney Museum of American Art, photograph by Geoffrey Clements, N.Y., Photograph copyright © 1997: Whitney Museum of American Art

▲ **Critical Viewing** Bet probably experienced a range of emotions after leaving the hospital. Which of her possible emotions are reflected in this painting? **[Interpret]** 9

From the Parkinsville Railroad Station, which they seemed to be tearing down or else remodeling—she couldn't tell which—they took a taxicab to Parkins State Hospital. "Oh, I been out there many and many a time," said the driver. "Went out there just the other—"

But she couldn't stop herself; she had to tell him before she forgot. "Listen," she said, "I want you to wait for me right in the driveway. I don't want you to go on away."

7 "Well, fine," he said.

"Can you do that? I want you to be sitting right by the porch or the steps or whatever, right where I come out of, ready to take me back to the station. Don't just go off, and—"

"I *got* you, I got you," he said.

She sank back. She hoped he understood.

Arnold wanted a peanut-butter cookie. He was reaching and whimpering. She didn't know what to do. She wanted to give him anything he asked for, anything; but he'd get 8 it all over his face and arrive not looking his best. She couldn't stand it if they thought he was just ordinary and unattractive. She wanted them to see how small and neat he was, how somebody cherished him. But it 8 would be awful if he went into one of his rages. She broke off a little piece of cookie from the bag. "Here," she told him. "Don't mess, now."

He flung himself back in the corner and ate it, keeping one hand flattened across his mouth while he chewed.

The hospital looked like someone's great, pillared mansion, with square brick buildings all around it. "Here we are," the driver said.

"Thank you," she said. "Now you wait here, please. Just wait till I get—" 10

"*Lady,*" he said. "I'll wait."

◆ Build Vocabulary

stocky (stäk′ ē) *adj.*: Solidly built; sturdy

staunch (stônch) *adj.*: Strong; unyielding

viper (vī′pər) *n.*: Type of snake; here, a malicious person

1. **Hitler:** German dictator Adolf Hitler (1889–1945).

◆ Grammar and Style

6 Correct Use of Adjectives and Adverbs Ask students to explain why the word "gratefully" is used rather than "grateful" in this sentence. Have them label "gratefully" as an adjective or an adverb and name the word it modifies. *"Gratefully" is an adverb modifying the verb "looked," which serves as an action verb, rather than a linking verb, in this sentence.*

◆ Critical Thinking

7 Infer What do Bet's interactions with the cab driver reveal about her state of mind? *She is clearly anxious about leaving promptly, perhaps afraid that if she hesitates it will be impossible to leave.*

◆ Critical Thinking

8 Interpret What do Bet's thoughts reveal about her feelings for her son? *She loves him and wants others to see that he is special in the hope that they will cherish him as she does.* Who is the "they" to which she refers? *They are Arnold's new caretakers.*

▶Critical Viewing◀

9 Interpret Students may suggest that this painting portrays Bet's sadness about leaving her son. This emotion is conveyed in the posture of the slumped, still figure of the woman.

◆ Literary Focus

10 Foreshadowing Help students see that the sense of urgency Bet conveys in her conversation with the taxi driver heightens the story's suspense. Readers want to know, "Why does she expect to be in such a hurry to leave?"

Reteach

Reteach foreshadowing by playing a suspenseful scene from a thriller in which music, lighting, or mysterious noises hint at an upcoming danger. Discuss with students how these elements raise expectations about upcoming events. Then, guide students to recognize that while literary foreshadowing is not usually as obvious or dramatic, an alert reader can notice words and actions that hint at future events in the story.

Humanities: Art

Girl Looking at Landscape, 1957, by Richard Diebenkorn.

This painting illustrates a young woman similar to Bet looking at a landscape viewed through a large window.

Richard Diebenkorn was born and raised on America's west coast, later studying at Stanford University under Victor Arnautoff and Daniel Mendelowitz. The G.I. Bill facilitated additional study at the University of New Mexico, Albuquerque. On an airplane trip home to boyhood San Francisco, Diebenkorn delighted in the landscape and began a long artistic interest in its forms. *Girl Looking at Landscape* was painted during a period of focus on figurative and representational painting.

Use the following question to guide discussion: In what ways does the painting symbolize Bet's relationship to the world around her? *The girl in the painting is separated from the landscape by a window. Like Bet, she is an observer of, rather than a participant in, the events of the world that surround her.*

She opened the door and nudged Arnold out ahead of her. Lugging the suitcase, she started toward the steps. "Come on, Arnold," she said.

He hung back.

❶ "Arnold?"

Maybe he wouldn't allow it, and they would go on home and never think of this again.

But he came, finally, climbing the steps in his little hobbled way. His face was clean, but there were a few cookie crumbs on his jacket. She set down the suitcase to brush them off. Then she buttoned all his buttons and smoothed his shirt collar over his jacket collar before she pushed open the door.

In the admitting office, a lady behind a wooden counter showed her what papers to sign. Secretaries were clacketing typewriters all around. Bet thought Arnold might like that, but instead he got lost in the lights—chilly, hanging ice-cube-tray lights with a little flicker to them. He gazed upward, looking astonished. Finally a flat-fronted nurse came in and touched his elbow. "Come along, ❷ Arnold. Come, Mommy. We'll show you where Arnold is staying," she said.

They walked back across the entrance hall, then up wide marble steps with hollows worn in them. Arnold clung to the banister. There was a smell Bet hated, pine-oil disinfectant, but Arnold didn't seem to notice. You never knew; sometimes smells could just put him in a state.

The nurse unlocked a double door that had chicken-wired windows. They walked through a corridor, passing several fat, ugly women in shapeless gray dresses and ankle socks. "Ha!" one of the women said, and fell giggling into the arms of a friend. The nurse said, "*Here* we are." She led them into an enormous hallway lined with little white cots. Nobody else was in it; there wasn't a sign that children lived here except for a tiny cardboard clown picture hanging on one vacant wall. "This one is your bed, Arnold," said the nurse. Bet laid the ❸ suitcase on it. It was made up so neatly, the sheets might have been painted on. A steely-gray blanket was folded across the foot. She looked over at Arnold, but he was pivoting back and forth to hear how his new sneakers squeaked on the linoleum.

❹ "Usually," said the nurse, "we like to give new residents six months before the family visits. That way they settle in quicker, don't you see." She turned away and adjusted the clown picture, though as far as Bet could tell ❹ it was fine the way it was. Over her shoulder, the nurse said, "You can tell him goodbye now, if you like."

"Oh," Bet said. "All right." She set her hands on Arnold's shoulders. Then she laid her face against his hair, which felt warm and fuzzy. "Honey," she said. But he went on pivoting. She straightened and told the nurse, "I brought his special blanket."

"Oh, fine," said the nurse, turning toward her again. "We'll see that he gets it."

"He always likes to sleep with it; he has ever since he was little."

"All right." ❺

"Don't wash it. He hates if you wash it."

"Yes. Say goodbye to Mommy now, Arnold."

"A lot of times he'll surprise you. I mean there's a whole lot to him. He's not just—"

"We'll take very good care of him, Mrs. Blevins, don't worry."

"Well," she said. " 'Bye, Arnold."

She left the ward with the nurse and went down the corridor. As the nurse was unlocking the doors for her, she heard a single, terrible scream, but the nurse only patted her shoulder and pushed her gently on through.

In the taxi, Bet said, "Now, I've just got fifteen minutes to get to the station. I wonder if you could hurry?"

"Sure thing," the driver said.

She folded her hands and looked straight ahead. Tears seemed to be coming down her face in sheets.

Once she'd reached the station, she went to the ticket window. "Am I in time for the twelve-thirty-two?" she asked.

"Easily," said the man. "It's twenty minutes late."

"What?"

"Got held up in Norton somehow." ❻

"But you can't!" she said. The man looked startled. She must be a sight, all swollen-eyed and wet-cheeked. "Look," she said, in a lower voice. "I figured this on purpose. I chose the one train from Beulah that would let me catch another one back without waiting. I do not

◆ Critical Thinking

❶ **Draw Conclusions** Ask: To what degree does Bet feel she has control over her life? Explain, using this example and others from the story. *Students should recognize a pattern of passive endurance in Bet, dating from the ocean waves incident and including her response to Avery's departure. Here, she hopes Arnold, who is not objectively capable of making a decision, will take the matter out of her hands.*

◆ Critical Thinking

❷ **Evaluate** The nurse calls Bet "Mommy." Ask students whether they feel this is appropriate. *Students may say that she is being condescending or overly-familiar; she has dealt with thousands of "mommies" and Arnolds—and they are all the same to her.*

Thematic Focus

❸ **Literature Confronts the Everyday** What effect is created by the everyday details in this passage? *Details such as the vacant wall, painted-on sheets, steely-gray blanket, and linoleum floors convey the starkness and sterility of the setting. The clown picture seems forlorn and strikingly out of place.*

◆ Critical Thinking

❹ **Make a Judgment** Ask students: Why might the hospital prefer that new patients wait six months before seeing relatives? Do you agree or disagree with this policy? *Students may say that it's easier for patients to accept their new environment if they are not reminded of their former lives. Other students may feel that such a tremendous adjustment can be made only with the support of family members.*

◆ Critical Thinking

❺ **Analyze** What is the nurse's attitude toward the situation? *She is indifferent; she has seen and heard it all before.*

◆ *Literature and Your Life*

❻ Discuss whether Bet's response to the news that her train has been delayed is an appropriate one. Then ask students to recall times when their emotional state caused them to overreact to seemingly minor matters.

Speaking, Listening, and Viewing Mini-Lesson

Political Speech

This mini-lesson supports the Speaking, Listening, and Viewing activity in the Idea Bank on p. 933.

Introduce the Concept Have students discuss issues about which they have strong feelings. Recall together recent efforts to support these or other goals. Ask students what they think makes such political or fund-raising appeals effective.

Develop Background Before students begin, review basic persuasive techniques.

- A persuasive speech convinces an audience to act or think a certain way.
- A successful speech includes supporting evidence such as facts, reasons, and examples.
- Emotionally-charged language, repetition, and rhetorical questions make a speech effective.

Apply the Information As they deliver their speeches, encourage students to use gesture and expression to emphasize their points.

Assess the Outcome Have students use the Self-Assessment for Speech, in **Alternative Assessment**, p. 132.

6 want to sit and wait in this station."

"Twenty *minutes*, lady. That's all it is."

"What am I going to do?" she asked him.

He turned back to his ledgers.

She went over to a bench and sat down. Ladders and scaffolding towered above her, and only ten or twelve passengers were dotted through the rest of the station. The place looked bombed out—nothing but a shell. "Twenty minutes!" she said aloud. "What am I going to do?"

Through the double glass doors at the far end of the station, a procession of gray-suited men arrived with briefcases. More men came behind them, dressed in work clothes, carrying folding chairs, black trunklike boxes with silver hinges, microphones, a wooden lectern, and an armload of bunting. They set the lectern down in the center of the floor, not six feet from Bet. They draped the bunting across it—an arc of red, white, and blue. Wires were connected, floodlights were lit. A microphone screeched. One of the workmen said, "Try her, Mayor." He held the microphone out to a fat man in a suit, who cleared his throat and said, "Ladies and gentlemen, on the occasion of the expansion of this fine old railway station—"

"Sure do get an echo here," the workman said. "Keep on going."

The Mayor cleared his throat again. "If I may," he said, "I'd like to take about twenty minutes of your time, friends."

He straightened his tie. Bet blew her nose, and then she wiped her eyes and smiled. They had come just for her sake, you might think. They were putting on a sort of private play. From now on, all the world was going to be like that—just something on a stage, for her to sit back and watch.

Guide for Responding

◆ Literature and Your Life

Reader's Response What do you think of Bet's new outlook on life? Explain.

Thematic Focus Which details of everyday life enhance or underscore the emotions at work beneath the story's surface?

Group Discussion Do you think that Bet will be able to cope with the consequences of her choice? In a group, discuss the evidence in the story that supports your predictions.

☑ Check Your Comprehension

1. Where is Bet taking Arnold?
2. Why is she caring for Arnold without the support of her husband or family?
3. Summarize what you learned of Bet's childhood and marriage.
4. What does Bet hear just as she leaves Arnold?
5. What happens while Bet is waiting for the train home?

◆ Critical Thinking

INTERPRET

1. How does Bet's behavior when her father tried teaching her to bodysurf relate to her behavior later in life? **[Connect]**
2. Why does Bet insist that the cab driver wait for her outside the hospital? **[Infer]**
3. (a) What impression does Tyler convey in her description of the hospital? (b) What seems to be the nurse's attitude concerning Arnold's situation? **[Draw Conclusions]**
4. Explain the single, terrible scream that Mrs. Blevins hears as the nurse unlocks the doors for her. **[Interpret]**
5. What is ironic, or surprising, about the mayor's plans to speak in the train station for twenty minutes? **[Support]**
6. (a) What is the meaning of the story's final sentence? (b) How does the story's title relate to its meaning? **[Analyze]**

APPLY

7. Do you think that most people would act as Bet did if they were in her place? Why or why not? **[Generalize]**

Beyond the Selection

FURTHER READING

Other Works by Anne Tyler

Ladder of Years; The Accidental Tourist; Dinner at the Homesick Restaurant

Other Works With the Theme of Decisions/Coping With Mental Challenge

Choices: Within Reach, (ed.) Donald R. Gallo

Flowers for Algernon, Daniel Keyes

The Keeper, Phyllis Reynolds Naylor

We suggest that you preview these works before recommending them to students.

INTERNET

You and your students may find additional information about Anne Tyler on the Internet. We suggest the following site. Please be aware, however, that the site may have changed since this information was published.

For information on Tyler, go to **http://lime.weeg.uiowa.edu/~uipress/newbooks/salwak-anne.html**

We *strongly recommend* that you preview sites before you send students to them.

Reinforce and Extend

Customize for
Interpersonal Readers
Invite these students to role play the scene between Bet and the nurse. Ask students playing Bet how the nurse's behavior makes them feel. Discuss with those playing the nurse the conflicting emotions they may feel about taking on the care of another child.

Answers

◆ Literature and Your Life

Reader's Response Have students discuss whether Bet's new outlook is temporary or permanent.

Thematic Focus Students may note details such as the chicken-wired windows and smell of pine-oil disinfectant that underscore the sterility of the mental hospital.

☑ Check Your Comprehension

1. She is taking him to a state hospital.
2. Her parents are dead and her husband has left her.
3. She grew up in a trailer and married at a young age to get away from home. She and her husband moved away. He left her when Arnold was still an infant.
4. She hears "a single, terrible scream."
5. The mayor of the town delivers a speech at the train station.

◆ Critical Thinking

1. Bet takes pride in enduring. She does little to change the flow of events.
2. She wants to escape from the hospital as soon as possible because she feels guilty about leaving Arnold there.
3. (a) The hospital is an unsympathetic, institutional place. (b) She seems indifferent to Arnold's situation.
4. The scream is probably Arnold's response to the realization that his mother has left him behind.
5. Twenty minutes is the amount of time that Bet's train has been delayed.

(Answers continue on p. 932)

Answers *(continued from p. 931)*

6. (a) Bet feels that she will no longer have to participate in the daily chores that made up her life to this point. (b) The title refers to those events in life that can catch a person off guard, such as Bet's son's condition and her husband's decision to leave her.
7. Most students will probably feel that Bet did the only thing she could under the circumstances. Students should realize that there were not as many options for quality care available at that time, particularly for those who, like Bet, lacked financial resources.

◆ Literary Focus

1. Examples include the descriptions of Arnold in the opening paragraph, Arnold's eyeing the suitcase suspiciously, Mrs. Puckett giving Arnold a going-away present, Arnold never having been on a train before, and Bet's nervousness.
2. The foreshadowing helps to increase the reader's interest in discovering the purpose of Bet's trip.
3. The foreshadowing gives the reader a sense of suspenseful anticipation; without it, the flashbacks would have less significance and the story itself would probably have less appeal.

◆ Build Vocabulary

Using the Latin Prefix *trans-*

1. To *translate* is to convey, or put across, the same meaning in a different language.
2. A *transatlantic* journey takes the traveler across the Atlantic Ocean.
3. To *transfer* an object is to move it from one place over to another.
4. *Transportation* is a means or system for conveying people or goods from one place to another.

Using the Word Bank

1. a 2. c 3. b 4. b 5. a

◆ Reading Strategy

1. When Bet was young, her father tried to teach her to bodysurf. She married Avery against her parents' wishes. Her parents died. She and Avery had Arnold, and soon learned about his condition. A few weeks later, Avery left. Nine years later, Bet left her rented room with Arnold. She took him by train to a state hospital where he would be institutionalized. When she returned to the train station, she found the train delayed. The mayor came to deliver a speech at the station, and she sat back to watch.
2. (a) She flashes back to Arnold's behavior as a baby, her husband's desertion, and the history of her childhood and marriage. (b) It is prompted by remembering, as Arnold drifts off to sleep, that he never slept well; it ends when Arnold's head snaps up. (c) It sheds new light on Bet's personality and the circumstances that led to her and Arnold's current situation.

◆ Grammar and Style

1. suspiciously; modifies *stared*
2. pathetic; modifies *Arnold*
3. well; modifies *behaved*
4. carefully; modifies *chew*
5. awful; modifies *hospital*
6. bad; modifies *she*

Grammar Reinforcement

For additional instruction and practice, use the Problems With Modifiers lesson in the Using Modifiers unit of the **Language Lab CD-ROM.**

Guide for Responding (continued)

◆ Literary Focus

FORESHADOWING

Foreshadowing is the use of hints or clues in a narrative to suggest later events. For example, in the first paragraph of the story, Tyler hints at later events when she writes that Arnold "could tell something was up."

1. Find three more examples of foreshadowing in the story. Explain each example.
2. How does Tyler's use of foreshadowing help to build suspense?
3. Why would the story be less effective if Tyler had not used foreshadowing?

◆ Build Vocabulary

USING THE LATIN PREFIX *trans-*

The Latin prefix *trans-* means "across," "over," or "through." For each of the following words, write a sentence on your paper, explaining how the meaning of the prefix relates to the meaning of the given word.

1. translate **3.** transfer
2. transatlantic **4.** transportation

USING THE WORD BANK: Sentence Completions

On a separate sheet of paper, write the letter of the choice that best completes each of the following statements.

1. Something *transparent* is often made of (a) glass, (b) wool, (c) polished brass.
2. A *stocky* person looks (a) sloppy, (b) rich, (c) sturdy.
3. A *staunch* ally (a) betrays you, (b) stands by you through thick and thin, (c) abandons you at the first sign of trouble.
4. *Orthopedic* shoes are designed to (a) make you look thinner, (b) correct your posture, (c) cost less than most shoes.
5. A *viper* might (a) bite you, (b) sing to you, (c) walk up and shake your hand.

◆ Reading Strategy

ORDER EVENTS

Because Tyler's story includes a flashback that interrupts the chronological sequence of events to present an event from an earlier time, you have to pay careful attention to the **order of events** in the story.

1. State the main events and details of the story in chronological order.
2. (a) What flashback does Bet have? (b) What prompts this flashback, and what causes it to end? (c) What does it add to your understanding of the story?

◆ Grammar and Style

CORRECT USE OF ADJECTIVES AND ADVERBS

Use an **adjective** to modify a noun or a pronoun. Use an **adverb** to modify a verb, an adjective, or another adverb.

Be careful to use an adverb, never an adjective, to modify an action verb. Look at this passage from the story.

She never could do anything as *well* as most people.

Notice how Tyler uses the adverb *well,* rather than the adjective *good*, to modify the verb *do*. Remember, however, to use an adjective, not an adverb, after a linking verb such as *be*, *am*, *is*, or *seem* if the modifier describes the subject.

Practice For each item, choose the correct modifier and write the complete sentence in your notebook. Circle the word being modified.

1. Arnold stared (suspicious, suspiciously) at the suitcase.
2. Sometimes Arnold looked (pathetic, pathetically) in his neatly buttoned clothes.
3. Arnold behaved (good, well) when he had something to entertain him.
4. His mother told him to chew his gum (careful, carefully).
5. The hospital smelled (awful, awfully).
6. After she left Arnold there, she felt very (bad, badly).

Build Your Portfolio

Idea Bank

Writing

1. New Version Write an account of the story's events as Arnold might have perceived them.

2. Letter Writing as Bet, draft a letter to the director of the hospital, in which you make a case for the need to institutionalize Arnold.

3. Critical Response Write an essay in which you use examples from the story to explore one critic's observation that Tyler "does not trivialize motives with rationalizations. She launches her imagined lives and describes their trajectories with an unpretentious sense of fate."

Speaking, Listening, and Viewing

4. Conversation With another student, role-play the conversation that might take place between Bet and Mrs. Puckett when Bet returns to her rented room after bringing Arnold to the institution. **[Performing Arts Link]**

5. Political Speech Imagine that the subject of the mayor's speech was the need for more funding and improved care at state-run institutions like the one in which Arnold was placed. Present the speech he might have given, using Arnold's case to support your points. **[Social Studies Link]**

Researching and Representing

6. Fact-Finding Report Work with a classmate to find out more about a state-run institution in your area. Would you conclude that it is well run and/or well funded? Present your facts and conclusions in a written report. **[Social Studies Link]**

7. Medical Brochure Find out more about autism, childhood schizophrenia, Downs syndrome, or another childhood illness or condition that can result in severe mental or emotional challenges. Present your findings in a medical brochure like the kind often found in a doctor's office. **[Health Link]**

Online Activity www.phlit.phschool.com

Guided Writing Lesson

Social Worker's Report

Imagine that you are the social worker assigned to Bet and Arnold's case. Write a report explaining Arnold's condition and the events and situations that led to the decision to have him institutionalized.

Writing Skills Focus: Transitions to Show Cause and Effect

In writing about Arnold's illness and the decision to institutionalize him, you will be tracing **cause-and-effect** relationships. Words and phrases like these can help make those relationships clear:

Transitions to Show Cause and Effect

• because	• as a result	• thus
• since	• as a consequence	• if . . . then
• as	• consequently	• arising from
• owing to	• therefore	• stemming from

Prewriting Scan the story for details that indicate that Bet can no longer care for Arnold. Use a diagram like this one to categorize this information and show how it contributes to the decision to institutionalize him.

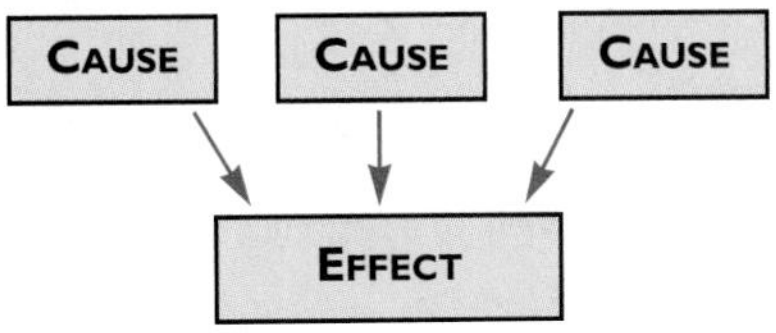

Drafting Build your report on the information you outlined in your graphic organizer. Use clear transitions like those listed above to show cause-and-effect and other relationships. Try to maintain the objective tone of an effective social worker.

Revising Read your report as though you were a supervisor reviewing the case for the first time. Are there sufficient details to support the report's general conclusions? Check that your facts are accurate, your word choice precise, and your transitions adequate to make the cause-and-effect relationships clear.

Idea Bank

Customizing for *Performance Levels*
Following are suggestions for matching Idea Bank topics with your students' performance levels:
Less Advanced Students: 1, 4
Average Students: 2, 7
More Advanced Students: 3, 5, 6

Customizing for *Learning Modalities*
Following are suggestions for matching Idea Bank topics with your students' learning modalities:
Interpersonal: 4
Verbal/Linguistic: 4, 5, 7
Logical/Mathematical: 5, 6, 7

Guided Writing Lesson

For more instruction on prewriting, elaboration, and revision see *Prentice Hall Writing and Grammar.*

Writing and Language Transparencies Display the Cause-and-Effect Transparency, p. 91, to help students with the Prewriting phase of their report.

Writing Lab CD-ROM
Have students complete the tutorial on Exposition. Follow these steps:

1. Students can complete the Note Cards Activities in the Gathering Details section to help them organize details they will use in their reports.
2. Have students refer to the Transition Word Bins as they draft on the computer.
3. Students can use the Interactive Self-Evaluation Checklist for cause-and-effect essays to help them revise their reports.

✓ ASSESSMENT OPTIONS

Formal Assessment, Selection Test, pp. 277–279, and Assessment Resources Software. The selection test is designed so that it can be easily customized to the performance levels of your students.

Alternative Assessment, p. 62, includes options for less advanced students, more advanced students, interpersonal learners, verbal/linguistic learners, bodily/kinesthetic learners, logical/mathematical learners, and visual/spatial learners.

PORTFOLIO ASSESSMENT
Use the following rubrics in the ***Alternative Assessment*** booklet to assess student writing:
New Version: Fictional Narrative Rubric, p. 110
Letter: Persuasion Rubric, p. 120
Critical Response: Literary Analysis/Interpretation Rubric, p. 127
Guided Writing Lesson: Cause/Effect Rubric, p. 117

Prepare and Engage

LESSON OBJECTIVES

1. **To develop vocabulary and word identification skills**
   - Latin Prefixes: *con-*
   - Using the Word Bank: Analogies
2. **To use a variety of reading strategies to comprehend a personal essay**
   - Connect Your Experience
   - Reading Strategy: Relate to Your Own Experiences
   - Read to Discover Models for Writing (ATE)
3. **To express and support responses to the text**
   - Critical Thinking
   - Idea Bank: Photographs and Memories
   - Idea Bank: Illustration
4. **To analyze literary elements**
   - Literary Focus: Anecdotes
   - Idea Bank: Analytical Essay
   - Background for Understanding
5. **To plan, prepare, organize, and present literary interpretations**
   - Idea Bank: Evocative Music
   - Idea Bank: Movie Review
6. **To use recursive writing processes**
   - Guided Writing Lesson
   - Idea Bank: Recipe
   - Idea Bank: Description
7. **To increase knowledge of the rules of grammar and usage**
   - Grammar and Style: Elliptical Clauses

Test Preparation

Writing Skills: Sentence Structure (ATE, p. 935)
The teaching tips and sample test item in this workshop support the instruction and practice in the unit workshop:
Writing Skills: Punctuation, Usage, and Sentence Structure (SE, p. 1143)

Guide for Interpreting

N. Scott Momaday

(1934–)

A member of the Kiowa nation, N. Scott Momaday has devoted his life to preserving Native American culture. As a young boy, he often visited his grandparents, whose home was a meeting place for elderly Kiowas, whom Momaday describes as people made of "lean leather." Inspired by his boyhood experiences, Momaday devoted himself to preserving his Kiowa heritage. After receiving his doctorate from Stanford University, he wrote his first book, a novel about a young Native American torn between his roots and white society. Momaday has since published poetry, essays, anecdotes, and retellings of Kiowa legends. His works provide the reader with a deeper understanding of Native American culture, both past and present.

Naomi Shihab Nye

(1952–)

Arab-American poet Naomi Shihab Nye spent her teenage years in Jerusalem—far from the American cities of St. Louis, Missouri, and San Antonio, Texas, where she grew up. In addition to publishing award-winning volumes of poetry, this versatile writer has also created picture books for children. Nye, whose works are built on the sturdy foundation of everyday experiences, believes that "the primary source of poetry has always been local life, random characters met on the streets, our own ancestry sifting down to us through small essential daily tasks."

Joy Harjo ***(1951–)***

The influence of Joy Harjo's Native American Creek (or Muscogee) and Cherokee heritage is evident in many aspects of her life, including her writing. As a teenager, she became interested in dance and joined a troupe of Native American dancers. She attended the Institute of American Indian Arts, the University of New Mexico, and the Writers' Workshop of the University of Iowa. In addition to publishing books of poetry and prose, Harjo has also written film scripts and taught at the state universities of California, New Mexico, and Montana.

◆ Background for Understanding

LITERATURE: PERSONAL AND CULTURAL EXPRESSION IN ESSAYS

If you were asked to name a literary form that you associate with personal, creative expression, what would you say—poetry? short stories? novels? The essay might not be your immediate response; however, its flexible form may provide the best arena for personal expression.

You're probably not accustomed to thinking of essays as personal or expressive. Though they are a form of nonfiction, essays can be as moving, entertaining, and enriching as your favorite piece of fiction. Because they can explore any topic the writer chooses, there are as many types of personal essays as there are people who write them.

In personal essays (like those you are about to read), the writers approach their subjects in a rather casual and intimate way, often providing a personal insight into a general subject. In each of the three essays that follow, the writer uses a vivid memory of a particular experience or object—a journey on a horse, a special dessert, the dawning of a childhood awareness—as the springboard to an analysis of her or his identity. The essay then explores how that identity is related to the writer's ancestors, place of birth, and culture. When taken together, these essays provide new insight into the rich and varied cultures that make up our nation.

Prentice Hall Literature Program Resources

REINFORCE / RETEACH / EXTEND

Selection Support Pages
Build Vocabulary: Latin Prefixes: *con-* p. 286
Grammar and Style: Elliptical Clauses, p. 287
Reading Strategy: Relate to Your Own Experiences, p. 288
Literary Focus: Anecdotes, p. 289

Strategies for Diverse Student Needs, p.63

Beyond Literature, Science Connection, p. 63

Formal Assessment Selection Test, pp. 280–282; Assessment Resources Software

Alternative Assessment, p. 63

Writing and Language Transparencies
Context Chart Organizer, pp. 103–105

Resource Pro CD-ROM

Listening to Literature Audiocassettes

Art Transparencies
Transparency 1

from The Names ◆ Mint Snowball ◆ Suspended ◆

◆ Literature and Your Life

Connect Your Experience

Watching home videos or flipping through a family photo album may bring back some very special memories of your childhood. You may recognize the comfort of a treasured toy, react to the smile of a long-forgotten friend, or remember the warmth of special occasions. Think about childhood experiences that you remember most vividly. Do you think they have helped form your identity? Why did they have such a strong effect on you?

Journal Writing Describe a childhood memory. The act of writing about it may help you remember more details.

Thematic Focus: Literature Confronts the Everyday

Two of these essays deal with details and everyday experiences: the taste of a favorite dessert, the sound of music on a car radio. How do the essays lend greater meaning to seemingly ordinary experiences?

◆ Reading Strategy

Relate to Your Own Experiences

As you start to read these essays, you may think at first you have little in common with a Kiowa youth seeking adventure on horseback, or the great-granddaughter of a Midwestern pharmacist, or a little Creek girl riding in her father's Cadillac. However, if you have ever taken a journey, yearned for the past, or experienced a mysterious inner awakening, you can find a connection between your experiences and theirs. Making such a connection will increase your understanding and enjoyment of the essay.

◆ Grammar and Style

Elliptical Clauses

An **elliptical clause** is one in which certain words are omitted because they are understood. In the following sentences from the essays by Momaday and Nye, the elliptical clauses are in italics. Notice that the elliptical clauses make the writing flow smoothly.

> . . . the Kiowas owned more horses . . . *than any other tribe on the Great Plains [owned]*." (The verb *owned* is understood rather than stated.)
>
> My grandfather thought *[that] he should have inherited it*. . . . " (The relative pronoun *that* is understood.)

◆ Literary Focus

Anecdotes

An **anecdote** is a short account of an amusing or interesting event. People tell anecdotes all the time—mostly for entertainment. Some anecdotes can be used to make a point. For example, you might share an anecdote about a favorite gift to demonstrate the giver's thoughtfulness. A reporter writing an article might grab the reader's attention with an anecdote about an individual who suffers from an illness before providing medical data about it.

An essayist often recounts an anecdote and then draws a conclusion or makes a generalization based on the anecdote. As you read, identify the anecdotes in these essays.

◆ Build Vocabulary

Latin Prefixes: *con-*

The Latin prefix *con-* (or *com-*) means "with" or "together." In "Suspended," Joy Harjo uses the word *confluence*, which means "a flowing together."

Word Bank

Preview these words from the essays.

supple
concocted
flamboyant
elixir
permeated
replicate
revelatory
confluence

Test Preparation Workshop

Writing Skills:
Sentence Structure Standardized tests often require students to choose the best way to correct the structure of a sentence. Use the sample test item below to demonstrate.

> If you don't know much about horses, riding one can be quite dangerous. <u>A horse can easily throw an inexperienced rider, this can cause serious injury</u>.

Choose the best way to write the underlined section of the passage.

A A horse can easily throw an inexperienced rider, can cause serious injury.
B A horse can easily throw an inexperienced rider, causing serious injury.
C A horse, easily throwing an inexperienced rider, causing serious injury.
D Correct as is.

B is the best answer; it is the only complete sentence that is correctly structured and punctuated.

Interest Grabber In preparation for these essays, ask students to find a piece of music that is especially meaningful to them. Invite students to bring recordings to class and, in small groups, share the feelings or memories that the music evokes. Alternatively, you might play segments of music and ask the class to respond. Consider using music that will evoke childhood memories: the sound of the ice-cream truck, music from "A Charlie Brown Christmas," or a lullaby.

Customize for
Less Proficient Readers
Less proficient readers may need help with the sentence fragments contained in these essays. Encourage students to paraphrase to complete fragments, using information from the context, before reading on.

Customize for
AP Students
Ask students to explain the connections between the essays in this section and the authors' cultural backgrounds. Urge these students to supply and exchange information about the cultures and settings of each essay.

Customize for
English Language Learners
Point out the first-person voice to these students, explaining how this voice impacts verb forms. Pair these students with native speakers to work through the text one paragraph at a time.

Customize for
Visual/Spatial Learners
Refer to ***Art Transparencies*** to build background for the selections. For Momaday's essay in which he discusses his Kiowa heritage, use Art Transparency 1: *Kiowa Apache,* by Native American artist John Nieto (p. 7). For Harjo's essay celebrating the power of music, use Art Transparency 9: *Battle of the Big Horns,* (p. 39). Refer to the Humanities Notes and Learning Options pages that accompany each work in the ***Art Transparencies*** booklet.

Develop Understanding

One-Minute Insight In reading this essay, students will travel with a young Kiowa boy on a journey of discovery and personal growth. The speaker, presumably young Momaday, recounts his travels on the horse he receives as a thirteenth birthday gift. As he journeys across his southwestern homelands, the boy recognizes how his physical journey is intertwined with a spiritual journey toward connection with his Kiowa heritage.

Writers at Work Videodisc
To build background about Momaday's literary style, use the videodisc segment for Chapter 2, Narration. Ask students to listen to Momaday's ideas about what is important in a narrative. Students can use his criteria to judge this essay.

Play frames 18612 to 19873

◆ Critical Thinking

1 Analyze What details of the Kiowa culture are revealed in this opening paragraph? *Kiowas lived on the Great Plains; horses were an important element of Kiowa life and folklore.*

◆ Build Vocabulary

2 The Latin Prefix *con-* Point out that the word *concentrated* contains the Latin prefix *con-*. Ask students to use their knowledge of the prefix to define the word. *Added to the root meaning "center," concentrated means "together at the center."*

Customize for
Less Proficient Readers
3 Point out the text breaks in the opening, explaining that each moves the reader closer to the beginning of the speaker's journey.

◆ Literary Focus

4 Anecdotes What prediction can students make about the essayist's goal for this anecdote, based on his opening remarks? *Momaday has acknowledged his cultural attachment to horses, thus he may want to show his close connection with Pecos.*

from THE NAMES

N. Scott Momaday

1 I sometimes think of what it means that in their heyday—in 1830, say—the Kiowas owned more horses *per capita* than any other tribe on the Great Plains, that the Plains Indian culture, the last culture to evolve in North America, is also known as "the horse culture" and "the centaur[1] culture," that the Kiowas tell the story of a horse that died of shame after its owner committed an act of cowardice, that I am a Kiowa, that therefore there is in me, as there is in the Tartars,[2] an old, sacred notion of the horse. I believe that at some point in my racial life, this notion must needs be expressed in order that I may be true to my nature.

It happened so: I was thirteen years old, and my parents gave me a horse. It was a small nine-year-old gelding of that rare, soft color that is called strawberry roan. This my horse and I came to be, in the course of our life together, in good understanding, of one mind, a true story and history of that large landscape in which we made the one entity of whole motion, one and the same center of an intricate, pastoral composition, evanescent,[3] ever changing. And to this my horse I gave the name Pecos.

On the back of my horse I had a different view of the world. I could see more of it, how it reached away beyond all the horizons I had ever seen; and yet it was more concentrated in its appearance, too, and more accessible to my mind, my imagination. My mind loomed upon the farthest edges of the earth, where I could feel the full force of the planet whirling into space. There was nothing of the air and light that was not pure exhilaration, and nothing of time and eternity. Oh, Pecos, *un poquito mas*! Oh, my hunting horse! Bear me away, bear me away! 2

It was appropriate that I should make a long journey. Accordingly I set out one early morning, traveling light. Such a journey must begin in the nick of time, on the spur of the moment, and one must say to himself at the outset: Let there be wonderful things along the way; let me hold to the way and be thoughtful in my going; let this journey be made in beauty and belief. 3

I sang in the sunshine and heard the birds call out on either side. Bits of down from the cottonwoods drifted across the air, and butterflies fluttered in the sage. I could feel my horse under me, rocking at my legs, the bobbing of the reins to my hand; I could feel the sun on my face and the stirring of a little wind at my hair. And through the hard hooves, the slender limbs, the supple shoulders, the fluent back of my horse I felt the earth under me. Everything was under me, buoying me up; I rode across the top of the world. My mind soared; time and again I saw the fleeting shadow of my mind moving about me as it went winding upon the sun. 4

When the song, which was a song of riding, was finished, I had Pecos pick up the pace. Far down on the road to San Ysidro I overtook my

1. **centaur** (sen´ tôr) *adj.*: Pertaining to a mythical creature with the head and upper body of a man and the lower body of a horse.
2. **Tartars** (tär´ tərz) *n.*: Nomadic Turkish peoples that took part in the invasions of Eastern Europe during the Middle Ages.
3. **evanescent** (ev´ ə nes´ ənt) *adj.*: Transient; tending to fade from sight.

Block Scheduling Strategies

Consider these suggestions to take advantage of extended class time:

- To introduce students to Kiowa culture, use the ***Writers at Work*** videodisc segment featuring N. Scott Momaday (Ch. 2) or Art Transparency 1, *Kiowa Apache,* (p. 7 in ***Art Transparencies***).
- To introduce students to the power of music that Harjo describes, use the interest grabber activity or Art Transparency 9, *The Battle of the Big Horns.* (p. 39 in ***Art Transparencies***).
- Have students discuss the Literary Focus in small groups, exchanging anecdotes from their own personal experience.
- Have students work in groups to answer the Critical Thinking questions (pp. 939, 941, 943).
- To introduce the Guided Writing Lesson (p. 945) give students the opportunity to listen to a recorded or live oral history. Then have students find examples of necessary context in the selection essays.
- Guide students to complete the Science Connection: Sensory Experiences activity, p. 63 in ***Beyond Literature.***

Passion of Paints, Bob Peters

friend Pasqual Fragua. He was riding a rangy, stiff-legged black and white stallion, half wild, which horse he was breaking for the rancher Cass Goodner. The horse skittered and blew as I drew up beside him. Pecos began to prance, as he did always in the company of another horse. "Where are you going?" I asked in the Jemez language. And he replied, "I am going down the road." The stallion was hard to manage, and Pasqual had to keep his mind upon it; I saw that I had taken him by surprise. "You know," he said after a moment, "when you rode up just now I did not know who you were." We rode on for a time in silence, and our horses got used to each other, but still they wanted their heads.[4] The longer I looked at the stallion the more I admired it, and I suppose that Pasqual knew this, for he began to say good things about it: that it was a thing of good blood, that it was very strong and fast, that it felt very good to ride it. The thing was this: that the stallion was half wild, and I came to wonder about the wild half of it; I wanted to know what its wildness was worth in the riding. "Let us trade horses for a while," I said, and, well, all right, he agreed. At first it was exciting to ride the stallion, for every once in a while it pitched and bucked and wanted to run. But it was heavy and raw-boned and full of resistance, and every step was a jolt that I could feel deep down in my bones. I saw soon enough that I had made a bad bargain, and I wanted my horse back, but I was ashamed to admit it. There came a time in the late afternoon, in the vast plain far south of San Ysidro, after thirty miles, perhaps, when I no longer knew whether it was I who was riding the stallion or the stallion who was riding me. "Well, let us go back now," said Pasqual at last. "No. I am going on; and I will have my horse back, please," I said, and he was surprised and sorry to hear it, and we said goodbye. "If you are going south or east," he said, "look out for the sun, and keep

5 6 7 8

▲ **Critical Viewing** Using the third paragraph of the essay as a guide, how do you think Momaday would describe this painting? **[Hypothesize]**

4. **. . . they wanted their heads:** The horses wanted to be free of the control of the reins.

◆ **Build Vocabulary**

supple (sup´ əl) *adj.*: Able to bend and move easily and nimbly; flexible

Humanities: Art

Passion of Paints by Bob Peters.

This painting illustrates a stampede of horses, much like those the Kiowa once so proudly harnessed and perhaps like the story narrator's own horse, Pecos.

Bob Peters, a contemporary American artist, began his career in the competitive world of freelance illustration. Peters made a shift from commercial art to fine art, and began working in oils instead of acrylics. He uses his love of horses and the inspiration of the Arizona and Colorado landscape to capture the beauty of the American West.

Use these questions for discussion:

1. How does the painting reflect the narrator's emotions about his horse? *The sense of movement and speed in the painting convey the narrator's feelings of excitement and adventure.*
2. How might a small boy respond to seeing these horses approach? *He might be frightened or fascinated.*

◆ Critical Thinking

5 Infer Ask: What does Pasqual hope to gain by praising his horse so highly? *Students should infer that Pasqual wants to trade horses, possibly to show up his friend as unable to ride the stallion.*

▶Critical Viewing◀

6 Hypothesize Sample description: The horizon loomed invitingly in the distance and the glorious power of the horses filled the air.

◆ Reading Strategy

7 Relate to Your Own Experiences Highlight for students the emotions felt by the speaker in this moment. Have students ever made a decision or accepted a dare only to regret their choice? Challenge students to recount their own experience and explain how it relates to the speaker's.

Customize for *Less Proficient Readers*

8 Less proficient readers may find this passage of recounted dialogue confusing. To help them navigate it, point out that when Pasqual speaks, "I" refers to Pasqual, not to the story narrator. Students may wish to rewrite the paragraph in formal dialogue form.

Read to Discover Models for Writing

Have students read this essay as a model for autobiographical writing. Help them to see that autobiographical narratives may be individual vignettes from the author's life or may focus on one aspect of his or her life, rather than be comprehensive accounts.

Art Transparency After students have read Momaday's account, display Art Transparency 1, *Kiowa Apache*. Discuss the painting, emphasizing the very modern presentation of a very traditional subject. Have students discuss how young Momaday's experience with Pecos suggests the power of tradition in the midst of modern life. Interested students might want to explore the mix of tradition and modernity in their own lives, using a form such as a reflective essay to capture their thoughts.

Humanities: Art

Indian on Galloping Horse after Remington, No. 2, 1976, by Fritz Scholder.

Fritz Scholder uses his art to challenge Native American stereotypes. This lithograph of single horse and rider is a contemporary version of a familiar image.

Use this question for discussion: What is the effect of the artist's decision to present the image without a landscape? *It creates a sense of motion or flight.*

Customize for
Visual/Spatial Learners

To help these students follow the speaker's journey, have them work with Verbal/Linguistic Learners to create a journey log. As the verbal learners read aloud for clues to movement and time passage, visual learners can draw a map of the journey. Together, have pairs add a visual time line to the map.

▶Critical Viewing◀

❶ **Connect** They are similar; both are exhilarating and filled with motion.

◆ Literary Focus

❷ **Anecdotes** Here students can enjoy an anecdote within an anecdote as the speaker describes a very brief moment on his journey. How does this anecdote contribute to the overall essay? *Students may say it shows the boy's resilience and his openness to the journey.*

Customize for
Bodily/Kinesthetic Learners

❸ Discuss with these students the riding races and tricks the narrator engages in. Then challenge students to pantomime—at home if they wish—the speaker's movements as a means of understanding the complexity of the actions.

◆ Reading Strategy

❹ **Relate to Your Own Experiences** Challenge students to link the narrator's repeated efforts to master a trick to their own experiences. What lessons have they learned from these experiences? *Students may mention attempts to master driving, an athletic skill, or a new game, and should note the development of confidence that results from working successfully toward a goal.*

Indian on Galloping Horse after Remington, No. 2, 1976, Fritz Scholder, Courtesy Museum of Fine Arts, Museum of New Mexico

❶ ▲ **Critical Viewing** How do Momaday's feelings about riding his horse compare with the mood of this image? **[Connect]**

your face in the shadow of your hat. *Vaya con Dios.*"[5] And I went on my way alone then, wiser and better mounted, and thereafter I held on to my horse. I saw no one for a long time, but I saw four falling stars and any number of jackrabbits, roadrunners, and coyotes, and once, across a distance, I saw a bear, small and black, lumbering in the ravine. The mountains drew close and withdrew and drew close again, and after several days I swung east.

❷ Now and then I came upon settlements. For the most part they were dry, burnt places with Spanish names: Arroyo Seco, Las Piedras, Tres Casas. In one of these I found myself in a narrow street between high adobe walls. Just ahead, on my left, was a door in the wall. As I approached the door was flung open, and a small boy came running out, rolling a hoop. This happened so suddenly that Pecos shied very sharply, and I fell to the ground, jamming the thumb of my left hand. The little boy looked very worried and said that he was sorry to have caused such an accident. I ❷ waved the matter off, as if it were nothing; but as a matter of fact my hand hurt so much that tears welled up in my eyes. And the pain lasted for many days. I have fallen many times from a horse, both before and after that, and a few times I fell from a running horse on dangerous ground, but that was the most painful of them all.

In another settlement there were some boys who were interested in racing. They had good horses, some of them, but their horses were not so good as mine, and I won easily. After that, I began to think of ways in which I might even the odds a little, might give some advantage to my competitors. Once or twice I gave them a head start, a reasonable head start of, say, five or ten yards to the hundred, but that was too simple, and I won anyway. Then it came to me that I might try this: we should all line up in the usual way, side by side, but my competitors should be mounted and I should not. When the signal was given I should then have to get up on my horse while the others were breaking away; I should have to mount my horse during the race. This idea appealed to me greatly, for it was both imaginative and difficult, not to mention dangerous; Pecos and I should have to work very closely together. The first few times we tried this I had little success, and over a course of a hundred yards I lost four races out ❸ of five. The principal problem was that Pecos ❹ simply could not hold still among the other horses. Even before they broke away he was hard to manage, and when they were set running nothing could hold him back, even for an instant. I could not get my foot in the stirrup, but I had to throw myself up across the saddle on my stomach, hold on as best I could, and twist myself into position, and all this while racing at full speed. I could ride well enough to accomplish this feat, but it was a very awkward and inefficient business. I had to find some way to use the whole energy of my horse, to get it all

5. ***Vaya con Dios*** (vī yə kən dē´ ōs): "Go with God" (Spanish).

Analyze a Book Review

P. L. Adams, in a review of N. Scott Momaday's book *The Names*, says about Momaday: "Behind his parents are the interwoven strands of his ancestry, the reckless, tough, successful white men on his mother's side, and the proud, austere Kiowans of his father's line. In Momaday these divergent lines comes (sic) together, and the primary narrative of the book describes his development as an individual, and the ways in which each strand uniquely influenced him. . . . This brief, eloquent memoir is a celebration of individual life, of one's people, and of the 'human spirit, which endures.' " Read this review to students and have them write a journal entry in which they respond to the following questions:

1. Using the text, describe how Adams' description of Momaday is evident in this excerpt from *The Names*.
2. What makes *The Names* a celebration of the " 'human spirit, which endures' "?

Students can use their journal entries as a starting point for the Analytical Essay in Idea Bank on p. 945.

into the race. Thus far I had managed only to break his motion, to divert him from his purpose and mine. To correct this I took Pecos away and worked with him through the better part of a long afternoon on a broad reach of level ground beside an irrigation ditch. And it was hot, hard work. I began by teaching him to run straight away while I ran beside him a few steps, holding on to the saddle horn, with no pressure on the reins. Then, when we had mastered this trick, we proceeded to the next one, which was this: I placed my weight on my arms, hanging from the saddle horn, threw my
❸ feet out in front of me, struck them to the
❹ ground, and sprang up against the saddle.
This I did again and again, until Pecos came
❺ to expect it and did not flinch or lose his stride.
I sprang a little higher each time. It was in all a slow process of trial and error, and after two or three hours both Pecos and I were covered with bruises and soaked through with perspiration. But we had much to show for our efforts, and at last the moment came when we must put the whole performance together. I had not yet leaped into the saddle, but I was quite confident that I could now do so; only I must be sure to get high enough. We began this dress rehearsal then from a standing position. At my signal Pecos lurched and was running at once, straight away and smoothly. And at the same time I sprinted forward two steps and gathered myself up, placing my weight
precisely at my wrists, throwing my feet out ❸
and together, perfectly. I brought my feet down sharply to the ground and sprang up hard, as hard as I could, bringing my legs astraddle of my horse—and everything was just right, except that I sprang too high. I vaulted all the way over my horse, clearing the saddle by a considerable margin, and came down into the irrigation ditch. It was a good trick, but it was not the one I had in mind, and I wonder what Pecos thought of it after all. Anyway, after a while I could mount my horse in this way and so well that there was no challenge in it, and I went on winning race after race.

> **◆ Literary Focus** ❻
> What is the point of this anecdote?

I went on, farther and farther into the wide world. Many things happened. And in all this I knew one thing: I knew where the journey was begun, that it was itself a learning of the beginning, that the beginning was infinitely worth the learning. The journey was well undertaken, and somewhere in it I sold my horse to an old Spanish man of Vallecitos. I do not know how long Pecos lived. I had used him hard and well, and it may be that in his last days an image of me like thought shimmered in his brain.

Guide for Responding

◆ Literature and Your Life

Reader's Response What kind of animal seems "sacred" or special in some way to you? Why?

Journal Writing Describe an especially positive or negative relationship or encounter with an animal.

☑ Check Your Comprehension

1. What inspires Momaday's decision to take a journey?
2. List the highlights of the journey. What did young Momaday see and do in his travels?
3. In the end, how did Momaday get rid of his horse?

◆ Critical Thinking

INTERPRET

1. What motivated Momaday to temporarily trade Pecos for the horse his friend Pasqual was riding? **[Analyze]**
2. Provide one detail that supports the statement that Pecos was an extremely good horse. **[Support]**
3. Why is it significant that Momaday's first long journey was on horseback? **[Draw Conclusions]**

APPLY

4. What life lesson have you learned that was "infinitely worth the learning"? **[Connect]**

Beyond the Selection

FURTHER READING

Other Works by N. Scott Momaday

House Made of Dawn
The Way to Rainy Mountain
The Gourd Dancer

Other Works With the Themes of Adventure/Coming of Age

Crazy Horse: Great Warrior of the Sioux, Dorothy Shannon Garst
Don Quixote, Miguel de Cervantes Saavedra

We suggest that you preview these works before recommending them to students.

INTERNET

You may find additional information about N. Scott Momaday and Native American culture on the Internet. We suggest the following site. Please be aware, however, that the site may have changed since this information was published.

For biographical, literary, and cultural information, visit **http://users.mwci.net/~apoz/N.Scott.Momaday.html**

We *strongly recommend* that you preview sites before you send students to them.

Customize for
AP Students

❺ Ask these students to explain the self-image the speaker seeks to create. For example, here he shows himself mastering a trick to become the unbeatable race champion. Have students look for other examples that show the boy's self-character portrait.

◆ Literary Focus

❻ **Anecdotes** Possible response: The anecdote shows that the narrator is resourceful, quick-witted, persistent, and athletic.

Reinforce and Extend

Customize for
Interpersonal Readers

These students will benefit from dramatic reading or role-play of the story anecdotes. Encourage small groups to participate, using voice, gesture, and pantomime to create realistic effects.

Answers

◆ Literature and Your Life

Reader's Response Students should support their answers.

☑ Check Your Comprehension

1. He was given a horse when he was thirteen; the feeling of being on a horse was so exhilarating, he felt that it was appropriate for him to take a journey.
2. He met a friend and traded horses; he accidentally hurt his hand; he traveled through many settlements and experienced the beauty of nights and nature; he came to a settlement where he became involved in horse racing.
3. He sold his horse to an old Spanish man of Vallecitos.

◆ Critical Thinking

1. He was intrigued by the stallion's wildness.
2. Possible response: Pecos allows himself to be trained.
3. Since horses are an important element of Kiowa culture, this journey connects him with his heritage.
4. Possible responses include learning about responsibility, courage, or friendship.

Develop Understanding

One-Minute Insight This brief essay vividly captures a flash of memory that illuminates the present with the power of the past. The speaker recalls the atmosphere of her great-grandfather's soda shop as *her* mother had described it. In this magical place, Nye's great-grandfather had concocted a wondrous dessert called a Mint Snowball. Since it was lost to the family. Naomi and her mother feel a palpable loss, a break in the chain of memories leading to heritage and identity.

◆ Reading Strategy

❶ Relate to Your Own Experiences Discuss what is universal about the activities of the opening paragraph. *Students may note that the slow time of summer, the magical perspective of childhood, and perhaps the childish love of sweets are fairly universal. Students may link this scene to other special memories they have of time spent in a well-known place with a loved one.*

◆ Build Vocabulary

❷ The Latin Prefix *con-* Invite a student to read aloud the definition of *concocted.* Then ask students to link their knowledge of the Latin prefix *con-* to the definition. *Concocted means "made by combining various ingredients." The prefix con- is combined with the root "coquere," meaning "to cook."*

◆ Reading Strategy

❸ Relate to Your Own Experiences Most students will have at least one example, perhaps foods they always eat when studying or a special treat served only on certain holidays.

Mint Snowball

Naomi Shihab Nye

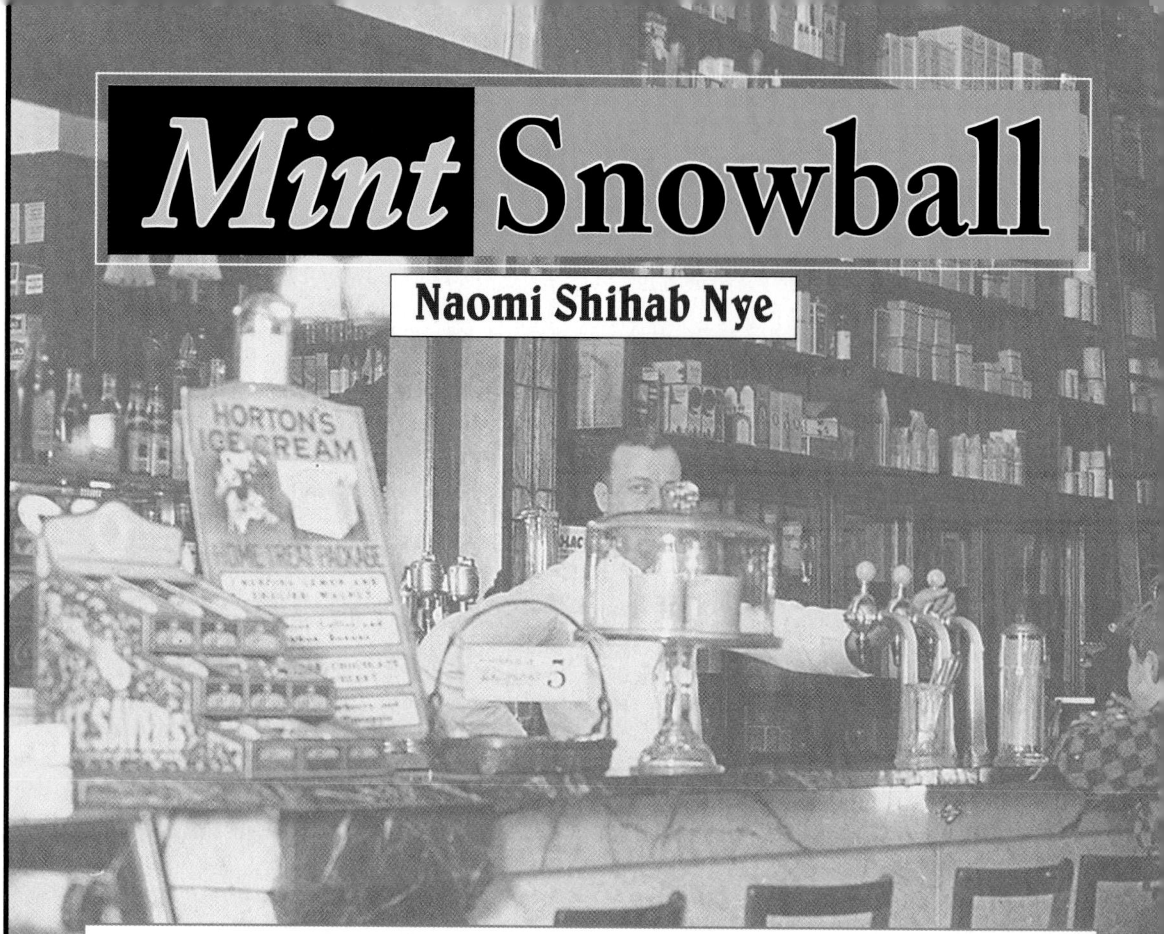

❶ My great-grandfather on my mother's side ran a drugstore in a small town in central Illinois. He sold pills and rubbing alcohol from behind the big cash register and creamy ice cream from the soda fountain. My mother remembers the counter's long polished sweep, its shining face. She twirled on the stools. Dreamy fans. Wide summer afternoons. Clink of nickels in anybody's hand. He sold milkshakes, cherry cokes, old fashioned sandwiches. What did an old fashioned sandwich look like? Dark wooden shelves. Silver spigots on chocolate dispensers.

My great-grandfather had one specialty: a Mint Snowball which he invented. Some people drove all the way in from Decatur just to taste it. First he stirred fresh mint leaves with sugar and secret ingredients in a small pot on the stove for a very long time. He concocted a flamboyant elixir of mint. ❷ Its scent clung to his fingers even after he washed his hands. Then he shaved ice into tiny particles and served it mounted in a glass dish. Permeated with mint syrup. Scoops of rich vanilla ice cream to each side. My mother took a bite of minty ice and ice cream mixed together. The Mint Snowball tasted like winter. She closed her eyes to see the Swiss village my great-grandfather's parents came from.

◆ Reading Strategy Are there certain foods that you associate with a particular time, place, or emotion? ❸

Beyond the Classroom

Community Connection

The Corner Drugstore The drugstore that Naomi Shihab Nye describes in *Mint Snowball* is reflective of a time past. In the first half of the twentieth century, the drugstore served as coffee shop, luncheonette, ice-cream parlor, card store, and pharmacy on American's main streets. While some of these old-fashioned stores still exist, they have lost much of their business to a fragmented market: chain drug stores, 90's style coffeehouses, and specialty restaurants.

To help students imagine the hey-day of stores like the one Nye describes, locate the artwork of Norman Rockwell. Share "After the Prom" or "The Runaway," two of his well-known drugstore images, with students.

Guide students in a discussion of their community. What are the social gathering areas in their community today?

Snow frosting the roofs. Glistening, dangling spokes of ice.

Before my great-grandfather died, he sold the recipe for the mint syrup to someone in town for one hundred dollars. This hurt my grandfather's feelings. My grandfather thought he should have inherited it to carry on the tradition. As far as the family knew, the person who bought the recipe never used it. At least not in public. My mother had watched my grandfather make the syrup so often she thought she could replicate it. But
4 what did he have in those little unmarked bottles? She experimented. Once she came close. She wrote down what she did. Now she has lost the paper.

5 ❖

Perhaps the clue to my entire personality connects to the lost Mint Snowball. I have always felt out-of-step with my environment, disjointed in the modern world. The crisp flush of cities makes me weep. Strip centers, Poodle grooming and Take-out Thai. I am angry over lost department stores, wistful for something I have never tasted or seen.

Although I know how to do everything one needs to know—change airplanes, find my exit off the interstate, charge gas, send a fax—there is something missing. Perhaps the stoop of my great-grandfather over the pan, the slow patient swish of his spoon. The spin of my mother on the high stool with her whole life in front of her, something fine and fragrant still to happen. When I breathe a handful of mint, even pathetic sprigs from my sunbaked Texas earth, I close my eyes. Little chips of ice on the tongue, their cool slide down. Can we follow the long river of the word "refreshment" back to its spring? Is there another land for me? Can I find any lasting solace in the color green?

◆ Build Vocabulary

concocted (kən käkt´ əd) *v.*: Made by combining various ingredients

flamboyant (flam boi´ ənt) *adj.*: Too extravagant

elixir (ē liks´ ir) *n.*: Supposed remedy for all ailments

permeated (pur´ mē āt id) *adj.*: Penetrated and spread through

replicate (rep´ li kāt) *v.*: Duplicate

Guide for Responding

◆ Literature and Your Life

Reader's Response Do you feel out of step with the modern world or in tune with it? Explain your feelings.

Thematic Focus Naomi Shihab Nye is primarily a poet. What are some of the ways in which her essay transforms the everyday into a type of poetry?

Journal Writing Jot down images that come to mind when you think of your parents' or grandparents' generation.

☑ Check Your Comprehension

1. What happened to the original Mint Snowball recipe?
2. Which family member came close to duplicating the recipe?

◆ Critical Thinking

INTERPRET

1. How did the Mint Snowball remind Nye's mother of the country from which her ancestors came? **[Connect]**
2. Contrast Nye's images of the past and present. **[Compare and Contrast]**
3. (a) What is the mood of the final paragraph of this essay? (b) Which details create it? **[Analyze]**

EVALUATE

4. Does the image of the Mint Snowball successfully capture a past time? Explain. **[Evaluate]**

EXTEND

5. Relate "Mint Snowball" to another literary work that expresses the theme of yearning for a way of life that is long gone. **[Literature Link]**

Beyond the Selection

FURTHER READING

Other Works by Naomi Shahib Nye

Different Ways to Pray; Hugging the Jukebox; Yellow Glove

Other Works With the Theme of Special Memories

"The Memento," O'Henry

The Endless Steppe, Esther Hautzig

The Road from Coorain, Jill Ker Conway

We suggest that you preview these works before recommending them to students.

INTERNET

You and your students may find additional information about Naomi Shahib Nye on the Internet. We suggest the following site. Please be aware, however, that sites may have changed since this information was published.

To read an interview with the poet about her views on poetry for young readers, visit **http://207.222.194.222.naomi.htm**

We *strongly recommend* that you preview sites before you send students to them.

◆ Grammar and Style

4 Elliptical Clauses Ask students to identify the elliptical clauses here and to suggest possible missing words. *Both "She experimented." and "Once she came close." are elliptical, with words such as "with it" or "to succeeding" missing.*

Customize for *Less Proficient Readers*

5 Explain that the text break here indicates a shift in focus. Prior to the break, the essay describes an earlier time. After the break, Nye jumps forward in time to focus on her own personal experiences.

Reinforce and Extend

Answers

◆ Literature and Your Life

Reader's Response Students should support their feelings with their own experience.

Thematic Focus By using sentence fragments and descriptive sensory language to describe the Mint Snowball, she brings her experiences into the realm of magic or poetry.

Journal Writing Invite students to compare their lists.

☑ Check Your Comprehension

1. It was sold by Nye's great-grandfather.
2. Nye's mother created a version of her own.

◆ Critical Thinking

1. She thought it tasted like winter in the Swiss village of her ancestors.
2. Nye describes the past as a small town where people cherish the taste of unique drinks. She describes modern society as big cities with anonymous strip malls.
3. (a) The mood is one of despair and loss. (b) Images of her grandfather and mother with their whole lives before them create this mood.
4. Students should support their responses.
5. Possible responses from this text include "Winter Dreams," "Big Yellow Taxi," and "A Wagner Matinée."

Develop Understanding

One-Minute Insight This essay illustrates how a single sensory experience can radically change a person's life. The speaker recalls a critical moment in which the glory of music—jazz, for her—reached her pre-verbal childhood mind. Blended with the heat of the day and the scent of her father's aftershave, the music became a catalyst, a medium through which the author could suddenly connect her creative dream world to the everyday world.

Customize for
Musical/Rhythmic Learners
Encourage students who are involved with school jazz bands, choirs, or orchestras to share their talent with the class. If students perform for their peers invite both the musicians and the student audience to talk about their emotional responses to the music.

▶Critical Viewing◀

❶ **Evaluate** Students may say that the emotions conveyed by the painting—excitement, moodiness, pleasure—show how music can communicate without words.

Art Transparency Introduce "Suspended" by displaying Art Transparency 9, *Battle of the Big Horns*. Invite students to comment upon Beasley's vibrant depiction of jazz musicians and to share what they already may know about jazz. Leave the transparency on the overhead as students read Harjo's essay. Afterward, discuss how she uses both literal and figurative interpretations of *jazz* to express her ideas. Students may enjoy writing or talking about what a particular style of music means to them, as well.

SUSPENDED

Joy Harjo

Getting Down, Joseph Holston

❶ ▲ **Critical Viewing** Does this illustration of a jazz musician effectively convey Harjo's belief that jazz is "a way to speak beyond the confines of ordinary language"? Explain. **[Evaluate]**

Once I was so small that I could barely peer over the top of the backseat of the black Cadillac my father polished and tuned daily; I wanted to see everything. It was around the time I acquired language, or even before that time, when something happened that changed my relationship to the spin of the world. My concept of

Humanities: Art

Getting Down 1990, by Joseph Holston, gouache on paper.

This painting illustrates an African American jazz musician, like Miles Davis, whom the speaker hears on the radio.

Joseph Holston was born in Washington D. C. Self-taught during a career in advertising art, he also studied with Marcos Blahove and Richard Goetz. Encouraged by Harlem Renaissance artists Lois Mailou Jones and James Wells, Holston developed a cubist abstractionist style in both his paintings and prints. *Getting Down*, with its fragmented forms and emphasis on lines, tone, and shading, demonstrates that style.

Use these questions for discussion.

1. How does this painting convey the unique perspective of the speaker's childhood? *The abstract lines and distortion are reminiscent of a child's limited, and therefore distorted, view of the adult world.*
2. How might the speaker respond to this painting? *She would likely enjoy it as a bridge between reality—the musical and his instrument—and art—the play of shadow and form.*

language, of what was possible with music was changed by this revelatory moment. It changed even the way I looked at the sun. This suspended integer of time probably escaped ordinary notice in my parents' universe, which informed most of my vision in the ordinary world. They were still omnipresent gods. We were driving somewhere in Tulsa, the northern border of the Creek Nation.[1] I don't know where we were going or where we had been, but I know the sun was boiling the asphalt, the car windows open for any breeze as I stood on tiptoes on the floorboard behind my father, a handsome god who smelled of Old Spice, whose slick black hair was always impeccably groomed, his clothes perfectly creased and ironed. The radio was on. I loved the radio, jukeboxes or any magic thing containing music even then.

◆ *Literature and Your Life*

2 What everyday objects were fascinating or magical to you as a small child?

I wonder now what signaled this moment, a loop of time that on first glance could be any place in time. I became acutely aware of the line the jazz trumpeter was playing (a sound I later associated with Miles Davis). I didn't know the word jazz or trumpet, or the concepts. I don't know how to say it, with what sounds or words, but in that confluence of hot southern afternoon, in the breeze of aftershave and humidity, I followed that sound to the beginning, to the place of the birth of sound. I was suspended in whirling stars, a moon to which I'd traveled often by then. I grieved my parents' failings, my own life which I saw stretched the length of that rhapsody.

My rite of passage into the world of humanity occurred then, via jazz. The music made a startling bridge between familiar and strange lands, an appropriate vehicle, for though the music is predominantly west African in concept, with European associations, jazz was influenced by the Creek (or Muscogee) people, for we were there when jazz was born. I recognized it, that humid afternoon in my formative years, as a way to speak beyond the confines of ordinary language. I still hear it. 3

1. **Creek Nation:** Nation of Native American peoples, mainly Muscogean, formerly of Georgia and Alabama. Most now live in Oklahoma and Florida.

◆ **Build Vocabulary**

revelatory (rev´ ə lə tôr´ ē) *adj.*: Revealing; disclosing

confluence (kän´ flo͞o əns) *n.*: A flowing together

Guide for Responding

◆ *Literature and Your Life*

Reader's Response Can you recall a personal experience that was important in your life, but which is difficult for you to analyze or describe?

Thematic Focus How does Harjo's essay lend a sense of wonder and mystery to the ordinary experiences of childhood?

Questions for Research Who besides the Creek were present when jazz was born? Generate research questions on the social context of the birth of jazz.

☑ **Check Your Comprehension**

1. During what season did Harjo's experience take place?
2. What kind of music was playing on the radio?

◆ Critical Thinking

INTERPRET

1. Roughly, what age was Harjo at the time she describes? **[Infer]**
2. How did she feel about her father? **[Analyze]**
3. What did the music teach Harjo about communication? **[Draw Conclusions]**
4. How does Harjo suggest that growing up involves sadness and disillusion? **[Deduce]**

APPLY

5. What does this essay suggest about the mysterious workings of each individual's inner world? **[Generalize]**

Beyond the Selection

FURTHER READING

Other Works by Joy Harjo

Secrets from the Center of the World; In Mad Love and War; The Last Song

Other Works With the Theme of Special Memories

The Notebook, Nicholas Sparks

Memories of My Life in a Polish Village, Toby Knobel Flvek

We suggest that you preview these works before recommending them to students.

INTERNET

For additional information about Joy Harjo, we suggest the following sites.

For a comprehensive look at her life and literature, visit **http://hanksville.phast.umass.edu/poems/poets/joy**

To learn about Harjo's musical efforts, visit **http://www.silverwave.com/music/native.html**

We *strongly recommend* that you preview sites before you send students to them.

Customize for *English Language Learners*

These students may have difficulty with the essay's occasionally lengthy sentences. Remind them to use commas as signposts for breaking down long sentences into manageable sections.

◆ *Literature and Your Life*

2 Students may mention everyday objects belonging to a parent, such as watches or keychains, appliances, or particular toys.

◆ **Critical Thinking**

3 **Synthesize** In this concluding paragraph, Harjo connects the experience with a larger meaning. What message does the anecdote convey? *This moment of discovery opens the doors to art and creativity, connecting everyday experiences with the rest of the world.*

Reinforce and Extend

Enrichment Joy Harjo's experience reveals that she may be a musical/rhythmic learner. Introduce the theory of multiple intelligences, which identifies seven ways of knowing, perceiving, and understanding the world around us. Refer to "Addressing Diverse Learning Styles," in ***Professional Development*** (p. 28).

Answers

◆ *Literature and Your Life*

Reader's Response Encourage students to think about why words cannot always communicate completely.

Thematic Focus Harjo talks about the power of a specific, ordinary moment to change her life forever.

☑ **Check Your Comprehension**

1. It probably took place in summer.
2. Jazz was playing on the radio.

◆ **Critical Thinking**

1. Since it was "around the time [she] acquired language," she was probably between one and three years old.
2. She thought her father was a god.
3. She realized that communication was not limited to the verbal.
4. Childhood has an innocence that is soon lost.
5. It suggests that each person has his or her own thinking and learning style.

Answers

◆ Reading Strategy

Sample response:
Writer's Experience: Momaday's solitary journey
My Experience: The flight I took by myself last year
How They Relate: We both took risks and learned we could take care of ourselves; we learned independence.

◆ Literary Focus

1. Momaday talks about the importance of horses to his Kiowa ancestors. The anecdote reveal the importance of a horse to his own development.
2. Nye feels that the lost recipe has somehow separated her from her family history.
3. (a) At that moment, she made a connection that had not been there before; she thought clearly about the meaning of her surroundings for the first time. (b) She sees this revelation as a rite of passage.

◆ Build Vocabulary

Using the Latin Prefix *con-*
Possible response: The group *congregated* in the first floor room to discuss the company's latest policy. Rather than accept the news lightly, many of the employees adopted a *combative* stance. They met to *concoct* a response which would explain their decision to resist *conforming* to the new policy.

Using the Word Bank
1. permeated
2. confluence
3. flamboyant
4. revelatory
5. concocted
6. replicate
7. elixir
8. supple

◆ Grammar and Style

1. Pecos ran faster than the other horses [ran].
2. Momaday thought the stallion was better than his own horse [was].
3. Nye's grandfather sold the recipe [that] he invented.
4. Harjo recalls hearing the music in the car more vividly than she does [remember] any other early experience.

Guide for Responding (continued)

◆ Reading Strategy

Relate to Your Own Experiences

For most people, it is quite natural to **relate reading to personal experiences**. By identifying similar situations, emotions, attitudes, and behaviors, readers can connect and compare a writer's ideas and experiences with their own. Completing a chart like the one below will help you to analyze the ways in which your experiences connect to those of Momaday, Nye, and Harjo.

In the first column, use short phrases to refer to elements from each essay. List at least one image or experience from each essay. In the second column, describe an experience or emotion of your own that parallels the item in the first column. In the third column, briefly analyze the relationship between the two experiences.

Writer's Experience	My Experience	How They Relate

◆ Literary Focus

Anecdotes

Each of the three essays you have just read contains one or more **anecdotes**—brief accounts of entertaining or interesting events and experiences. N. Scott Momaday tells several stories about a horse. Naomi Shihab Nye relates how her great-grandfather sold a secret recipe. Joy Harjo recalls a very early memory of hearing jazz on the radio. Think about each writer's reasons for recounting his or her anecdote as you answer these questions.

1. How do Momaday's anecdotes relate to the theme sounded in his opening paragraph?
2. What is the significance of the lost recipe to Nye's life and personality?
3. (a) How did Harjo's experience of hearing jazz affect her at the moment? (b) How did that experience change her life?

◆ Build Vocabulary

Using the Latin Prefix *con-*

Each of the words in the following list contains the Latin prefix *con-* (or *com-*), meaning "with" or "together." Using at least four of the words, write a paragraph about a group of workers who have gathered to protest a new company policy. You may change the form of a word if necessary.

conference	congregated	conform
communication	concocted	combative

Using the Word Bank: Analogies

Write the word that best completes the analogy.

1. comfortable : chair :: supple :
   (a) table (b) enemy (c) dancer (d) flexible
2. stitched : clothing :: concocted :
   (a) potion (b) scientist (c) created
   (d) contradiction
3. shy : timid :: flamboyant :
   (a) flaming (b) showy (c) watchful (d) nervous
4. treatment : disease :: elixir :
   (a) harm (b) ailment (c) mixture (d) doctor
5. spread : rumor :: permeated :
   (a) filled (b) odor (c) solid (d) permanence
6. design : create :: replicate :
   (a) represent (b) destroy (c) count (d) copy
7. illuminating : lamp :: revelatory :
   (a) concealment (b) celebration (c) news
   (d) reversal
8. join : split :: confluence :
   (a) divergence (b) port (c) river (d) fluency

◆ Grammar and Style

Elliptical Clauses

Practice Copy each sentence on your paper, underline the elliptical clause, and write the understood word(s).

In an **elliptical clause,** one or more words are omitted because they are understood.

1. Pecos ran faster than the other horses.
2. Momaday thought the stallion was better than his own horse.
3. Nye's grandfather sold the recipe he invented.
4. Harjo recalls hearing the music in the car more vividly than she does any other early experience.

Reteach

To reteach these selections, have students practice retelling the anecdotes aloud. Discuss with students which details in each anecdote contribute to the entertaining quality of the story. Guide students to use these details in their retellings and think about ways they can use voice, gestures, and body language to emphasize the details.

To aid students' recall, you may want to have them use the summarizing activity in ***Strategies for Diverse Student Needs,*** p. 63.

Build Your Portfolio

Idea Bank

Writing

1. Recipe Write a recipe in your own words. List the precise ingredients and each step involved in preparation. Make sure that your instructions are clear, concise, and complete, and that each step is presented in the correct order.

2. Description In his essay, Momaday describes in great physical detail his attempts to vault his horse while it was running. Write one or two paragraphs in which you describe, in similar detail, a series of physical maneuvers that you have executed. **[Physical Education Link]**

3. Analytical Essay Momaday's journey on his horse, Nye's family's Mint Snowball, and Harjo's jazz song all have both a literal and a symbolic meaning. Choose one and analyze its symbolic meaning.

Speaking, Listening, and Viewing

4. Evocative Music A line of jazz gave Joy Harjo a new vision of the world. Perform or play a recording of a piece of music that does the same for you. Explain how it affected you. **[Music Link]**

5. Movie Review The film "When the Legends Die" tells the story of a young Native American who struggles to find a balance between his culture and the demands of the modern world. Watch the film, and review it for your class. **[Media Link]**

Researching and Representing

6. Photographs and Memories With a group of classmates, put together a class anthology consisting of personal photographs and accompanying anecdotes.

7. Illustration Create a two-paneled illustration for "Mint Snowball." The first panel should portray Nye's image of the past, and the other, her impressions of contemporary life. **[Art Link]**

Online Activity www.phlit.phschool.com

Guided Writing Lesson

Oral History

Have you ever heard family friends or relatives recall how their ancestors immigrated to the United States or describe what it was like to watch live coverage of the first moon walk? Stories like these are a form of *oral history*—a spoken record of personally or historically significant events. Collect a bit of oral history, and record it in writing. To make the history understandable to your readers, you will need to supply relevant background information.

Writing Skills Focus: Necessary Context

An oral history flows from the speaker's personality, experiences, and cultural background. To create a successful oral history, you must decide what **context**, or background information, is necessary in order for your readers to understand the full meaning of the experiences you present. In *The Names*, for example, Momaday explains his special connection to horses by informing his readers that the animals are sacred to his Kiowa heritage.

Model From the Selection

. . . I am a Kiowa . . .therefore there is in me, as there is in the Tartars, an old sacred notion of the horse.

Prewriting Interview an interesting person about significant events in his or her life. Take careful notes or tape record the interview. Then review your notes and select one experience which you will present. Determine what background information you will need to provide.

Drafting Draft the oral history, using the exact words of the teller. Incorporate necessary background information to provide a context for it.

Revising Ask a friend to read your draft. Does the history have a clear beginning, middle, and end? Is it written in the "voice" of the teller? Does your friend have any questions about it that are not answered by the background information?

ASSESSMENT OPTIONS

ASSESSMENT OPTIONS

Formal Assessment, Selection Test, pp. 280–282, and Assessment Resources Software. The selection test is designed so that it can be easily customized to the performance levels of your students.

Alternative Assessment, p. 63, includes options for less advanced students, more advanced students, bodily/kinesthetic learners, logical/mathematical learners, and visual/spatial learners.

PORTFOLIO ASSESSMENT

Use the following rubrics in the ***Alternative Assessment*** booklet to assess student writing:
Recipe: How-to/Process Explanation Rubric, p. 115
Description: Description Rubric, p. 112
Analytic Essay: Literary Analysis/Interpretation Rubric, p. 127
Guided Writing Lesson: Technical Description/Explanation Rubric, p. 130

Idea Bank

Customizing for
Performance Levels
Following are suggestions for matching Idea Bank topics with your students' performance levels:
Less Advanced Students: 1, 5
Average Students: 2, 6, 7
More Advanced Students: 3, 4

Customizing for
Learning Modalities
Following are suggestions for matching Idea Bank topics with your students' learning modalities:
Musical/Rhythmic: 4
Verbal/Linguistic: 4
Interpersonal: 6
Visual/Spatial: 6, 7

Guided Writing Lesson

For more instruction on prewriting, elaboration, and revision, see *Prentice Hall Writing and Grammar.*

Writing and Language Transparencies Use the Context Chart Organizer to help students gather details about the context of their subject's oral histories (pp. 103–105).

Writers at Work Videodisc
Have students view the videodisc segment on Exposition (Ch. 3) featuring Thom Harrington to learn how Harrington keeps his audience and purpose in mind when writing about museum exhibits.

Play frames 29740 to 30502

Play frames 30616 to 31352

Writing Lab CD-ROM
Have students complete the tutorial on Exposition. Follow these steps:
1. Have students use the Timeline Activity in the Gathering Details section to organize key events in their oral history.
2. Have students draft on computer.
3. Encourage students to use the interactive Self-Evaluation Checklists to aid their revision.

Prepare and Engage

LESSON OBJECTIVES

1. To develop vocabulary and word identification skills
- Build Vocabulary: Latin Word Roots
- Using the Word Bank: Analogies

2. To use a variety of reading strategies to comprehend a short story
- Connect Your Experience
- Reading Strategy: Contrasting Characters

3. To increase knowledge of other cultures and to connect common elements across cultures
- Connecting Themes Across Cultures (ATE)
- Background for Understanding: Culture

4. To express and support responses to the text
- Critical Thinking
- Idea Bank: Journal Entry
- Idea Bank: Debate

5. To analyze literary elements
- Literary Focus: Character's Motivation
- Idea Bank: Character Analysis

6 To read in order to research self-selected and assigned topics
- Idea Bank: African Languages Project
- Idea Bank: Heritage Exhibit
- Research Skills Mini-Lesson (ATE)

7. To plan, prepare, organize, and present literary interpretations
- Idea Bank: Speech
- Idea Bank: Television Talk Show

8. To use recursive writing processes to write a review of a short story
- Guided Writing Lesson

9. To increase knowledge of the rules of grammar and usage
- Grammar and Style: Sentence Fragments

Test Preparation

Writing Skills: Grammar and Usage (ATE, p. 947)

The teaching tips and sample test item in this workshop support the instruction and practice in the unit workshop:

Writing Skills: Punctuation, Usage, and Sentence Structure (SE, p. 1143)

Guide for Interpreting

Alice Walker *(1944–)*

Born in Eatonton, Georgia, Alice Walker was the youngest child in a family of sharecroppers.

Of her childhood, Walker writes, "It was great fun being cute. But then, one day, it ended."

Her childhood self-confidence was challenged by an accident with a BB-gun that scarred and nearly blinded her. Walker reports that she did not lift her head for six years.

When the scar tissue on her eye was removed, her self-confidence returned. Walker left high school as the valedictorian and the most popular student. She attended Spelman College in Atlanta, an elite college for African American women, and after two years she transferred to Sarah Lawrence College in Bronxville, New York. *Once* (1968), Walker's first book of poetry, was written when she was a student there.

The Movement After graduating from Sarah Lawrence, Walker moved to Mississippi to work in the civil rights movement, demonstrating with African Americans and whites alike who were fighting for equality on all fronts. During this period, Walker also taught African American studies at Jackson State University, where she was writer-in-residence.

Cultural Pride Much of Alice Walker's fiction—novels including *The Third Life of Grange Copeland* (1970), story collections including *You Can't Keep a Good Woman Down* (1981), and *In Love and Trouble* (1973)—delves into the lives of African American women. Her fiction and essays reflect a pride in her personal heritage and the heritage of her people. The title essay from *In Search of Our Mothers' Gardens* (1983), often described as the nonfiction relative of "Everyday Use," explores Walker's maternal heritage, describing the creative legacy of "ordinary" black southern women. The 1982 publication of her third novel, *The Color Purple*, transformed "an intense reputation into a national one." This novel about an indomitable woman named Celie was both a critical and a popular success. Awarded both a Pulitzer Prize and an American Book Award, it was later made into a successful motion picture.

◆ Background for Understanding

CULTURE: PRESERVING TRADITIONS THROUGH FOLK ART

In this story, the character Dee is interested in the artifacts that reveal her family's history. Today, folk art is much celebrated for its beauty, originality, and connection to a culture's history. Most "folk art," however, was originally created for utilitarian purposes. In America, European settlers, Native Americans, and enslaved Africans took pride in creating items that were attractive as well as useful.

When families moved, they brought a few treasured items with them. In each new home, objects would again be created from locally available materials and tools. Families thus accumulated a cherished collection of heirlooms.

Quilts—an important symbol in this story—are an example of American folk art; they have been made in America since colonial times. Like most folk art, they served a number of purposes—keeping people warm; recycling pieces of cloth from worn-out clothing; providing a focal point for creative, recreational, and social gatherings of women; and, perhaps most important, recording bits of family history.

Prentice Hall Literature Program Resources

REINFORCE / RETEACH / EXTEND

Selection Support Pages
Build Vocabulary: Latin Roots: *-doc-/-doct-*, p. 290
Grammar and Style: Sentence Fragments, p. 291
Reading Strategy: Contrasting Characters, p. 292
Literary Focus: Character's Motivation, p. 293

Strategies for Diverse Student Needs, p. 64

Beyond Literature
Art Connection: Quilting

Formal Assessment Selection Test, pp. 283–285; Assessment Resources Software

Alternative Assessment, p. 64

Writing and Language Transparencies
Outline Transparency, p. 95

Resource Pro CD-ROM
Includes all resource material and customizable lesson plan

Literature CD-ROM

Listening to Literature Audiocassettes

Everyday Use

◆ Literature and Your Life

CONNECT YOUR EXPERIENCE

A cousin now living far away comes to visit your family, and you think, "She sure lives in a different world than I do!" Time and new experiences can create gaps between people—even relatives. In this story, you'll see how distance and the passage of time have caused a mother and her daughter to have very different views of the world.

Journal Writing Brainstorm for a list of reasons why people leave home. Note some reasons why they return home.

THEMATIC FOCUS: LITERATURE CONFRONTS THE EVERYDAY

In this story of a reunion between a rural southern family and an urban daughter, Walker explores how everyday experiences change people. As you read, ask yourself how family members can remain close despite experiences that might divide them.

◆ Build Vocabulary

LATIN ROOTS: *-doc-,-doct-*

The word *doctrines* includes the Latin root *-doc-* or *-doct-*, meaning "teach." Notice how the root contributes to the meaning of *doctrines*: "ideas, beliefs, or rules that are taught."

WORD BANK

Preview this list of words from the story.

furtive
lye
oppress
doctrines

◆ Literary Focus

CHARACTER'S MOTIVATION

To know a character truly, you need to understand that **character's motivation**—the reasons for his or her thoughts, feelings, actions, or speech. Sometimes a character's motivation results from his or her values or experiences. At other times, characters are motivated by their needs or dreams.

The characters in "Everyday Use" reveal their motivations through their actions and speech. As you read, ask: Why is this character doing or saying this? What need is she trying to satisfy? What goal does she have in mind? The answers will help you piece together each character's motivation.

◆ Grammar and Style

SENTENCE FRAGMENTS

A **sentence fragment** is a group of words that is punctuated as a sentence but fails to express a complete thought because it lacks a subject, a verb, or both. Look at this example from "Everyday Use." Notice that it lacks a subject.

Never could carry a tune.

While fragments are not generally acceptable in formal writing, writers do use them to re-create the way people speak. In this story, Walker uses fragments to make it seem as if the story's first-person narrator is speaking informally to the reader.

◆ Reading Strategy

CONTRASTING CHARACTERS

As this story opens, one sister awaits the arrival of another. You learn almost immediately that the two sisters and their experiences are quite different. By **contrasting characters,** or identifying the ways in which they differ, you can begin to uncover the major conflict in the story. As you read, use a graphic organizer like this one to note the personality characteristics and details of behavior that distinguish Dee from Maggie. Think about how their individual experiences have shaped their differences.

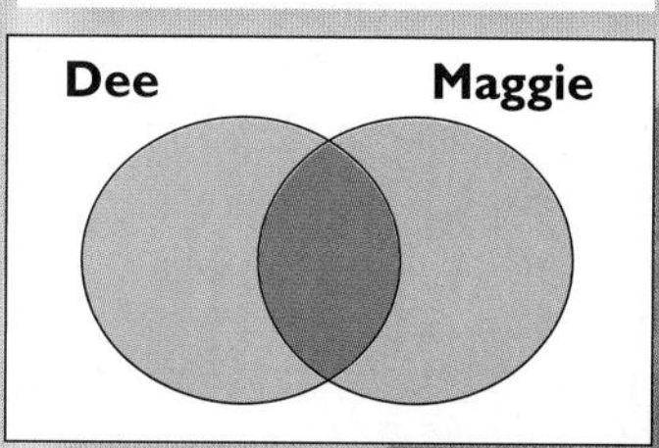

Interest Grabber Ask students to bring to class—or be prepared to discuss—a memento that represents their heritage. These items might be anything from a treasured photograph or great-grandfather's watch to an china teapot that has been in the family for generations. Ask students how their families use or display these items: Are they tucked away in storage or display cabinets, or do their families make use of them on a regular basis? Is the risk of damaging the objects outweighed by the pleasure of seeing and using them regularly? Tell students that the story they are about to read poses the question of whether such family mementos belong in "everyday use."

Connecting Themes Across Cultures

Portrayal of the human experience is a major theme in literature. Explain that literature "confronts the everyday" by showing how people face challenges, growth, and change through life experiences. Initiate a discussion about the ways literature has portrayed human growth and change in different cultures. For example, compare and contrast literature about life in the rural South today with life in the South prior to the Civil War.

Customize for
Less Proficient Readers

Clarify the story's first-person point of view with less proficient readers, explaining that it is the voice of a mother but is not the author's voice. To help them access the narrator's experiences, encourage them to read the story aloud in her voice.

Customize for
AP Students

Suggest that students explore Walker's style by highlighting examples of dialect and sentence fragments, explaining in each case how the writing adds to Walker's portrait of the story's characters.

Literature CD-ROM To introduce students to Alice Walker and her unique brand of literature, use *The History of American Literature:* Part 2, Disk 2, Feature 6.

Test Preparation Workshop

Writing Skills:
Grammar and Usage The writing sections of standardized tests often require students to choose the correct word or group of words to complete a sentence. Use the following sample item to demonstrate.

The pieces of the unfinished quilt ____ scattered on the floor.

Choose the word that belongs in the blank.

A lay
B lied
C laid
D lain

B is the past tense of the wrong *lie,* meaning "to tell an untruth"; *C* is the past tense of the transitive verb *lay; D* is the past participle of *lie; A* is the simple past tense of *lie,* meaning "to rest or recline," and is therefore the correct answer.

Develop Understanding

One-Minute Insight In this story, a mother and daughter struggle to make themselves known to each other across the considerable chasm that time and change have created between them. Educated and self-assured, Dee, who now uses the African name Wangero, visits her rural Georgia home. She has returned after a long absence, ostensibly to reintroduce herself to her cultural heritage but also to display her spiritual growth to the mother and sister she left behind. As Dee tries to extract the material trappings of her African American heritage from the house, her mother and sister discover their own personal brand of cultural pride.

❶ **Enrichment** The Piedmont region of Georgia, a gently rolling wide belt running east and west through the central part of the state, is covered by clay loams with red clay subsoils. The clay often gives the hillsides a red color. The soil hardens, almost like natural brick, in hot weather. Augusta, the town mentioned later, is located in this region, and so is Eatonton, the town in which Alice Walker grew up.

❷ **Clarification** This is a reference to the popular television show "This is Your Life," which aired during the 1950's. The program reunited celebrities with surprise visitors from the past.

◆ Reading Strategy

❸ **Contrasting Characters** Urge students to contrast the narrator's "real life" appearance and behavior with that in the dream—"the way [her] daughter would want [her] to be." *Students should note that in real life the narrator is a sturdy, hard-working, taciturn, practical woman with little interest in her appearance. In the dream, she is thin with lighter skin, carefully arranged hair, and a witty tongue.*

Everyday Use

Alice Walker

I will wait for her in the yard that Maggie and I made so clean and wavy yesterday afternoon. A yard like this is more comfortable than most people know. It is not just a yard. It is like an extended living room. When the hard clay is swept clean as a floor and the fine sand around the edges lined with tiny, irregular grooves, anyone can come and sit and look up into the elm tree and wait for the breezes that never come inside the house. ❶

Maggie will be nervous until after her sister goes: she will stand hopelessly in corners, homely and ashamed of the burn scars down her arms and legs, eyeing her sister with a mixture of envy and awe. She thinks her sister has held life always in the palm of one hand, that "no" is a word the world never learned to say to her.

You've no doubt seen those TV shows where the child who has "made it" is confronted, as a surprise, by her own mother and father, tottering in weakly from backstage. (A pleasant surprise, of course: What would they do if parent and child came on the show only to curse out and insult each other?) ❷ On TV mother and child embrace and smile into each other's faces. Sometimes the mother and father weep, the child wraps them in her arms and leans across the table to tell how she would not have made it without their help. I have seen these programs.

Sometimes I dream a dream in which Dee and I are suddenly brought together on a TV program of this sort. Out of a dark and soft-seated limousine I am ushered into a bright room filled with many people. There I meet a smiling, gray, sporty man like Johnny Carson who shakes my hand and tells me what a fine girl I have. Then we are on the stage and Dee is embracing me with tears in her eyes. She pins on my dress a large orchid, even though she has told me once that she thinks orchids are tacky flowers. ❸

In real life I am a large, big-boned woman with rough, man-working hands. In the winter I wear flannel nightgowns to bed and overalls during the day. I can kill and clean a hog as mercilessly as a man. My fat keeps me hot in zero weather. I can work outside all day, breaking ice to get water for washing; I can eat pork liver cooked over the open fire minutes after it comes steaming from the hog. One winter I knocked a bull calf straight in the brain between the eyes with

Humanities: Media

TV Talk Shows The story's narrator alludes to several popular television shows that were a well established part of American pop culture in the mid-to-late-twentieth century. The popular television talk show "This Is Your Life" ran from 1952 to 1961. Hosted by Ralph Edwards, the show staged reunions between celebrities and influential people from various phases of their lives. The narrator also mentions popular comedian Johnny Carson, who hosted late-night television's "Tonight Show" from 1962 until 1992, when Jay Leno took over. With wry humor, Carson interviewed people who had "made it."

Today, TV talk show hosts such as Oprah Winfrey often invite audience members to participate by joining them in questioning and commenting on controversial and sometimes quite intimate aspects of guests' lives.

Have students discuss how meeting in a public and televised situation would affect the behavior of a parent and child.

a sledge hammer and had the meat hung up to chill before nightfall. But of course all of this does not show on television. I am the way my daughter would want me to be: a
3 hundred pounds lighter, my skin like an uncooked barley pancake. My hair glistens in the hot bright lights. Johnny Carson has much to do to keep up with my quick and witty tongue.

But that is a mistake. I know even before I wake up. Who ever knew a Johnson with a quick tongue? Who can even imagine me looking a strange white man in the eye? It
4 seems to me I have talked to them always with one foot raised in flight, with my head turned in whichever way is farthest from them. Dee, though. She would always look anyone in the eye. Hesitation was no part of her nature.

"How do I look, Mama?" Maggie says, showing just enough of her thin body enveloped in pink skirt and red blouse for me to know she's there, almost hidden by the door.

"Come out into the yard," I say.

Have you ever seen a lame animal, perhaps a dog run over by some careless person rich enough to own a car, sidle up to someone who is ignorant enough to be kind to him? That is the way my Maggie walks. She has been like this, chin on chest, eyes on ground, feet in shuffle, ever since the fire that burned the other house to the ground.

Dee is lighter than Maggie, with nicer hair and a fuller figure. She's a woman now, though sometimes I forget. How long ago was it that the other house burned? Ten, twelve years? Sometimes I can still hear the flames and feel Maggie's arms sticking to me, her hair smoking and her dress falling off her in little black papery flakes. Her eyes seemed stretched open, blazed open by the flames reflected in them. And Dee. I see her standing off under the sweet gum tree she used to dig gum out of; a look of concentration on her face as she watched the last dingy gray board of the house fall in toward the red-hot brick chimney. Why don't you do a dance around the ashes? I'd want to ask her. She had hated the house that much.

I used to think she hated Maggie, too. But that was before we raised the money, the church and me, to send her to Augusta to school. She used to read to us without pity; forcing words, lies, other folks' habits, whole lives upon us two, sitting trapped and ignorant underneath her voice. 5 She washed us in a river of make-believe, burned us with a lot of knowledge we didn't necessarily need to know. Pressed us to her with the serious way she read, to shove us away at just the moment, like dimwits, we seemed about to understand.

Dee wanted nice things. A yellow organdy dress to wear to her graduation from high school; black pumps to match a green suit she'd made from an old suit somebody gave me. She was determined to stare 6 down any disaster in her efforts. Her eyelids would not flicker for minutes at a time. Often I fought off the temptation to shake her. At sixteen she had a style of her own, and knew what style was.

> ◆ **Reading Strategy**
> Explain why Maggie might not care about "nice things" in the same way Dee does.

I never had an education myself. After second grade the school was closed down. Don't ask me why: in 1927 colored asked fewer questions than they do now. 7 Sometimes Maggie reads to me. She stumbles along good-naturedly but can't see well. She knows she is not bright. Like good looks and money, quickness passed her by. She will marry John Thomas (who has mossy teeth in an earnest face) and then I'll be free to sit here and I guess just sing church songs to myself. 8 Although I never was a good singer. Never could carry a tune. I was always better at a man's job. I used to love to milk till I was hooved in the side in '49. Cows are soothing and slow and don't bother you, unless you try to milk them the wrong way.

I have deliberately turned my back on the house. It is three rooms, just like the one that burned, except the roof is tin; they

◆ Reading Strategy

4 Contrasting Characters Point out the contrast between the way the narrator responds to a strange white man and the way she believes her daughter would respond. What do we learn about both women? *The narrator seems to fear white strangers, while Dee seems confident and unafraid of anyone.*

◆ Literary Focus

5 Character's Motivations Ask: What do you think motivated the narrator to head up a fund-raising drive to send Dee away to school? *Besides recognizing her academic abilities, the narrator may have wanted to send Dee away from home so that she and Maggie could be free of her condescension.*

◆ Reading Strategy

6 Contrasting Characters
Students should recognize that Maggie might be self-conscious about her appearance, wishing to "hide" in unremarkable clothing.

◆ Reading Strategy

7 Contrasting Characters Ask: How does Dee's formal education contrast with her mother and sister's educational experiences? *The narrator had little or no education and Maggie has had only rudimentary schooling. Dee, on the other hand, was educated at a presumably superior school.*

◆ Literature and Your Life

8 Draw students' attention to the self-awareness of both the narrator and her daughter Maggie about their individual strengths and weaknesses. What do students identify as their own strengths and weaknesses?

Block Scheduling Strategies

Consider these suggestions to take advantage of extended class time:

- Open the class with the Interest Grabber (ATE, p. 947).
- Have students read and discuss the Background for Understanding (p. 946).
- After they have completed the journal activity in Literature and Your Life (p. 947), encourage willing students to exchange and compare lists.
- Introduce the Reading Strategy. Have students create a graphic organizer like the one on page 947 in which they can record details as they read. Follow up with the Reading Strategy questions (p. 954).
- Have students complete the ***Beyond Literature*** activity, p. 64, in ***Selection Support.*** Before beginning, urge students to discuss the importance of the quilts in the story.
- Use the Speaking, Listening, and Viewing Lesson (p. 952) to help students stage the Debate activity in the Idea Bank.
- Begin the Guided Writing Lesson by reviewing the Writing Skills Focus tips. Students can use the remaining class time to organize and draft their reviews. Have them finish the assignment for homework.

◆ Critical Thinking

1 Infer What do Dee's friends show us about Dee? *She likes to be surrounded by those who admire her superiority.*

◆ Critical Thinking

2 Interpret What does Maggie's reaction to Dee's companion suggest about him? *It suggests that she finds his appearance somehow shocking or repugnant—like that of a snake in her path.*

◆ Grammar and Style

3 Sentence Fragments After students identify the sentence fragments and the missing parts of speech in each, ask them how the fragments reflect the narrator's frame of mind in this moment. *"Dee next." "A dress down to the ground, in this hot weather." "A dress so loud it hurts my eyes" are all fragments. The first is missing a verb, the second a subject and verb, the third a subject and verb. Fragments here suggest the narrator's emotionally jumbled reaction to seeing her daughter much changed.*

4 Clarification Dee and her companion are wearing their hair in the style known as an Afro.

◆ Reading Strategy

5 Contrasting Characters How do Dee and Maggie appear different in this scene? *Maggie is hesitant, shy, and inarticulate while Dee appears graceful, well-dressed, and outgoing.*

◆ Literary Focus

6 Character's Motivation Dee wants to document the house as a quaint reminder of her "heritage," thereby diminishing her family by portraying their home as a curiosity. She wants to elevate her interest to what she views as a more acceptable intellectual level.

Customize for *English Language Learners*

The dialect and sentence fragments in this story may confuse these students. To help these students, remind them how fragmented and personal their own internal monologue is. Urge them to complete fragmented sentences and restate dialect to ensure comprehension.

don't make shingle roofs any more. There are no real windows, just some holes cut in the sides, like the portholes in a ship, but not round and not square, with rawhide holding the shutters up on the outside. This house is in a pasture, too, like the other one. No doubt when Dee sees it she will want to tear it down. She wrote me once that no matter where we "choose" to live, she will manage to come see us. But she will never bring her friends. Maggie and I thought about this and Maggie asked me, "Mama, when did Dee ever *have* any friends?"

1 She had a few. Furtive boys in pink shirts hanging about on washday after school. Nervous girls who never laughed. Impressed with her they worshiped the well-turned phrase, the cute shape, the scalding humor that erupted like bubbles in lye. She read to them.

When she was courting Jimmy T she didn't have much time to pay to us, but turned all her faultfinding power on him. He *flew* to marry a cheap city girl from a family of ignorant flashy people. She hardly had time to recompose herself.

When she comes I will meet—but there they are!

Maggie attempts to make a dash for the house, in her shuffling way, but I stay her with my hand. "Come back here," I say. And she stops and tries to dig a well in the sand with her toe.

It is hard to see them clearly through the strong sun. But even the first glimpse of leg out of the car tells me it is Dee. Her feet were always neat-looking, as if God himself had shaped them with a certain style. From the other side of the car comes a short, stocky man. Hair is all over his head a foot long and hanging from his chin like a kinky mule tail. 2 I hear Maggie suck in her breath. "Uhnnnh," is what it sounds like. Like when you see the wriggling end of a snake just in front of your foot on the road. "Uhnnnh."

3 Dee next. A dress down to the ground, in this hot weather. A dress so loud it hurts my eyes. There are yellows and oranges enough to throw back the light of the sun. I feel my whole face warming from the heat waves it throws out. Earrings gold, too, and hanging down to her shoulders. Bracelets dangling and making noises when she moves her arm up to shake the folds of the dress out of her armpits. The dress is loose and flows, and as she walks closer, I like it. I hear Maggie go "Uhnnnh" again. It is her sister's hair. It stands straight up like the wool on a sheep. 4
It is black as night and around the edges are two long pigtails that rope about like small lizards disappearing behind her ears.

"Wa-su-zo-Tean-o!"[1] she says, coming on in that gliding way the dress makes her move. The short stocky fellow with the hair to his navel is all grinning and he follows up with "Asalamalakim,[2] my mother and sister!" 5
He moves to hug Maggie but she falls back, right up against the back of my chair. I feel her trembling there and when I look up I see the perspiration falling off her chin.

"Don't get up," says Dee. Since I am stout it takes something of a push. You can see me trying to move a second or two before I make it. She turns, showing white heels through her sandals, and goes back to the car. Out she peeks next with a Polaroid. She stoops down quickly and lines up picture after picture of me sitting there in front of the house with Maggie cowering behind me. She never takes a shot without making 6 sure the house is included. When a cow comes nibbling around the edge of the yard she snaps it and me and Maggie and the house. Then she puts the Polaroid in the back seat of the car, and comes up and kisses me on the forehead.

> **◆ Literary Focus**
> Considering that Dee is not proud of the house, what is her motivation for taking these pictures?

Meanwhile Asalamalakim is going through motions with Maggie's hand. Maggie's hand is as limp as a fish, and probably as cold, despite the sweat, and she keeps trying to pull it back. It looks like Asalamalakim wants to shake hands but wants to do it fancy. Or maybe he don't know how people

1. **Wa-su-zo-Tean-o** (wä sōō zō tēn´ ō): African greeting.
2. **Asalamalakim:** *Salaam aleikhim* (sə läm´ ä lī´ kēm´): Islamic greeting meaning "Peace be with you."

Cultural Connection

Islam As part of their quest for an African American identity, many African Americans during the 1960's and early 1970's emphasized their links to their African ancestry and worked toward gaining universal recognition of the African American identity. Members celebrated their cultural heritage, dressed in African style, and wore their hair in the natural "Afro" style. Many took African or Arabic names, rejecting the names given to them through their American slave ancestry.

As followers of the Islamic faith established by Mohammed in the seventh century, some African Americans followed the teachings of the Koran, the Muslim holy book. The book denounces usury, games of chance, and the consumption of pork and alcohol.

shake hands. Anyhow, he soon gives up on Maggie.

"Well," I say. "Dee."

"No, Mama," she says. "Not 'Dee,' Wangero Leewanika Kemanjo!"

"What happened to 'Dee'?" I wanted to know.

"She's dead," Wangero said. "I couldn't bear it any longer, being named after the people who oppress me."

"You know as well as me you was named after your aunt Dicie," I said. Dicie is my sister. She named Dee. We called her "Big Dee" after Dee was born.

"But who was *she* named after?" asked Wangero.

"I guess after Grandma Dee," I said.

"And who was she named after?" asked Wangero.

"Her mother," I said, and saw Wangero was getting tired. "That's about as far back as I can trace it," I said. Though, in fact, I probably could have carried it back beyond the Civil War through the branches.

"Well," said Asalamalakim, "there you are."

"Uhnnnh," I heard Maggie say.

"There I was not," I said, "before 'Dicie' cropped up in our family, so why should I try to trace it that far back?"

7 He just stood there grinning, looking down on me like somebody inspecting a Model A car. Every once in a while he and Wangero sent eye signals over my head.

8 "How do you pronounce this name?" I asked.

"You don't have to call me by it if you don't want to," said Wangero.

"Why shouldn't I?" I asked. "If that's what you want us to call you, we'll call you."

"I know it might sound awkward at first," said Wangero.

"I'll get used to it," I said. "Ream it out again."

Well, soon we got the name out of the way. Asalamalakim had a name twice as long and three times as hard. After I tripped over it two or three times he told me to just call him Hakim-a-barber. I wanted to ask him was he a barber, but I didn't really think he was, so I didn't ask.

"You must belong to those beef-cattle people down the road," I said. They said "Asalamalakim" when they met you, too, but they didn't shake hands. Always too busy: feeding the cattle, fixing the fences, putting up salt-lick shelters, throwing down hay. When the white folks poisoned some of the herd the men stayed up all night with rifles in their hands. I walked a mile and a half just to see the sight.

Hakim-a-barber said, "I accept some of their doctrines, but farming and raising cattle is not my style." (They didn't tell me, and I didn't ask, whether Wangero (Dee) had really gone and married him.)

We sat down to eat and right away he said he didn't eat collards[3] and pork was unclean. Wangero, though, went on through the chitlins[4] and corn bread, the greens and everything else. She talked a blue streak over the sweet potatoes. Everything delighted her. Even the fact that we still used the benches her daddy made for the table when we couldn't afford to buy chairs. 9

"Oh, Mama!" she cried. Then turned to Hakim-a-barber. "I never knew how lovely these benches are. You can feel the rump prints," she said, running her hands underneath her and along the bench. Then she gave a sigh and her hand closed over Grandma Dee's butter dish. "That's it!" she said. "I knew there was something I wanted to ask you if I could have." She jumped up from the table and went over in the corner

◆ Build Vocabulary

furtive (fur´ tiv) *adj.*: Sneaky

lye (lī) *n.*: Strong alkaline solution used in cleaning and making soap

oppress (ə pres´) *v.*: Keep down by cruel or unjust use of power or authority

doctrines (däk´ trinz) *n.*: Religious beliefs or principles

---

3. **collards** (käl´ ərdz) *n.*: Leaves of the collard plant, often referred to as "collard greens."

4. **chitlins** (chit´ lənz) *n.*: Chitterlings, a pork dish popular among southern African Americans.

Customize for *Less Proficient Readers*

Help less proficient readers keep track of the story characters by clarifying that Dee has changed her name to Wangero. If they find it helpful, students may mentally replace "Wangero" with "Dee" as they read.

Customize for *AP Students*

After presenting the Cultural Connection note (ATE, p. 950), challenge more advanced students to research other African-American identity movements throughout American history. Urge them to share their findings with each other and the class, working to develop a timeline tracing African Americans' continuous efforts to establish a cultural identity in an often-hostile environment.

Customize for *Bodily/Kinesthetic Learners*

7 Ask these students to enact their interpretation of the "eye signals" exchanged by Dee and her companion.

◆ *Literature and Your Life*

8 Discuss with students the fact that Dee has changed her name. Ask students if they have ever wanted to change their name. How did changing their names relate to changes in their characters? *Students may mention abandoning a childhood or family nickname for a more "grown-up" formal version of their name or taking on a new nickname designed to present a desired image.*

9 **Clarification** Hakim-a-barber is a follower of Islam, a religion which proscribes the consumption of pork. See Cultural Connection (ATE, p. 950) for more information.

Research Skills Mini-Lesson

Using Non-Print Resources

This mini-lesson supports both Researching and Representing projects in Build Your Portfolio, p. 955.

Introduce the Concept Discuss with students that in addition to print resources, they can find information in audio and video archives, through interviews, and in museum exhibits.

Develop Background Talk with students about the two projects and the kinds of resources they might need. Suggest that students make phone calls or write letters to museum curators or individuals in charge of audio and video archives.

Apply the Information Have students locate three non-print sources they could use for the heritage exhibit or the African languages project.

Assess the Outcome Assess students on their ability to identify and access non-print resources.

Customize for
Visual/Spatial Learners
To help these learners visualize the objects over which Dee, her mother, and Maggie confront one another, show students a book of American artifacts from colonial times through the present. Discuss the careful and loving labor required to create these objects, usually with limited tools. Then challenge students to locate illustrations of items similar to those in the story, for example, the quilts.

◆ Literary Focus

1 Character's Motivation Ask students: What is Dee's motivation in asking for the churn top? What personal need is she fulfilling? *She wants to gain status with her new friends by displaying her cultural heritage. Students may suggest that she is fulfilling the personal need to get attention.*

◆ Reading Strategy

2 Contrasting Characters Ask students to contrast the behavior of the two sisters in this passage. What does it reveal about the differences in their personalities? *Dee does not help clean up, but begins looking for more treasure she can take. Maggie humbly retreats to the kitchen to wash dishes.*

◆ Literary Focus

3 Character's Motivation Why does Dee become immediately possessive of the quilts? *Students should note that Dee already believes the quilts are hers, simply because she wants them.*

◆ Reading Strategy

4 Contrasting Characters Ask students: What specific differences between the sisters does this statement reflect? *Dee has been more formally educated than Maggie. She is also more selfish and less respectful of others' values.*

where the churn stood, the milk in it clabber by now. She looked at the churn and looked at it.

1 "This churn top is what I need," she said. "Didn't Uncle Buddy whittle it out of a tree you all used to have?"

"Yes," I said.

"Uh huh," she said happily. "And I want the dasher, too."

"Uncle Buddy whittle that, too?" asked the barber.

Dee (Wangero) looked up at me.

"Aunt Dee's first husband whittled the dash, " said Maggie so low you almost couldn't hear her. "His name was Henry, but they called him Stash."

"Maggie's brain is like an elephant's," Wangero said, laughing. "I can use the churn top as a centerpiece for the alcove table," she said, sliding a plate over the churn, "and I'll think of something artistic to do with the dasher."

When she finished wrapping the dasher the handle stuck out. I took it for a moment in my hands. You didn't even have to look close to see where hands pushing the dasher up and down to make butter had left a kind of sink in the wood. In fact, there were a lot of small sinks; you could see where thumbs and fingers had sunk into the wood. It was beautiful light yellow wood, from a tree that grew in the yard where Big Dee and Stash had lived.

2 After dinner Dee (Wangero) went to the trunk at the foot of my bed and started rifling through it. Maggie hung back in the kitchen over the dishpan. Out came Wangero with two quilts. They had been pieced by Grandma Dee and then Big Dee and me had hung them on the quilt frames on the front porch and quilted them. One was in the Lone Star pattern. The other was Walk Around the Mountain. In both of them were scraps of dresses Grandma Dee had worn fifty and more years ago. Bits and pieces of Grandpa Jarrell's Paisley shirts. And one teeny faded blue piece, about the size of a penny matchbox, that was from Great Grandpa Ezra's uniform that he wore in the Civil War.

"Mama," Wangero said sweet as a bird. "Can I have these old quilts?"

I heard something fall in the kitchen, and a minute later the kitchen door slammed.

"Why don't you take one or two of the others?" I asked. "These old things was just done by me and Big Dee from some tops your grandma pieced before she died."

"No," said Wangero. "I don't want those. They are stitched around the borders by machine."

"That'll make them last better," I said.

"That's not the point," said Wangero. "These are all pieces of dresses Grandma used to wear. She did all this stitching by hand. Imagine!" She held the quilts securely in her arms, stroking them.

"Some of the pieces, like those lavender ones, come from old clothes her mother handed down to her," I said, moving up to touch the quilts. Dee (Wangero) moved back just enough so that I couldn't reach the quilts. They already belonged to her. 3

"Imagine!" she breathed again, clutching them closely to her bosom.

"The truth is," I said, "I promised to give them quilts to Maggie, for when she marries John Thomas."

She gasped like a bee had stung her.

"Maggie can't appreciate these quilts!" she said. "She'd probably be backward enough to put them to everyday use." 4

"I reckon she would," I said. "God knows I been saving 'em for long enough with nobody using 'em. I hope she will!" I didn't want to bring up how I had offered Dee (Wangero) a quilt when she went away to college. Then she had told me they were old-fashioned, out of style.

"But they're *priceless*!" she was saying now, furiously; for she has a temper. "Maggie would put them on the bed and in five years they'd be in rags. Less than that!"

"She can always make some more," I said. "Maggie knows how to quilt."

Dee (Wangero) looked at me with hatred. "You just will not understand. The point is these quilts, *these quilts*!"

"Well," I said, stumped. "What would *you* do with them?"

Speaking, Listening, and Viewing Mini-Lesson

Debate
This mini-lesson supports the Speaking, Listening, and Viewing activity in the Idea Bank on p. 955.

Introduce the Concept Review and discuss effective strategies for debate. Consider the following points:

- Arguments should be developed thoroughly, with logical as well as emotional support.
- Individuals involved in debate must listen and respond respectfully to the views of others.

Develop Background Point out that Maggie and Dee represent two very divergent views of how best to recognize and integrate one's heritage. Ask students to generate arguments for both points of view.

Apply the Information Organize participating students into two teams representing opposing points of view. You may want to assign a mediator to oversee the debate process. After each side presents a statement, allow time for the opposition to present its rebuttal.

Assess the Outcome Ask students to vote on which team they feel won the debate. Then challenge them to explain why the winning team's argument was more convincing than that of the opposing team. You might also discuss which viewpoint—or character—students found most convincing in the story.

"Hang them," she said. As if that was the only thing you *could* do with quilts.

Maggie by now was standing in the door. I could almost hear the sound her feet made as they scraped over each other.

"She can have them, Mama," she said, like somebody used to never winning anything, or having anything reserved for her. "I can 'member Grandma Dee without the quilts."

I looked at her hard. She had filled her bottom lip with checkerberry snuff and it gave her face a kind of dopey, hangdog look. It was Grandma Dee and Big Dee who taught her how to quilt herself. She stood there with her scarred hands hidden in the folds of her skirt. She looked at her sister with something like fear but she wasn't mad at her. This was Maggie's portion. This was the way she knew God to work.

When I looked at her like that something hit me in the top of my head and ran down to the soles of my feet. Just like when I'm in church and the spirit of God touches me and I get happy and shout. I did something I never had done before: hugged Maggie to me, then dragged her on into the room, snatched the quilts out of Miss Wangero's hands and dumped them into Maggie's lap. Maggie just sat there on my bed with her mouth open.

"Take one or two of the others," I said to Dee.

But she turned without a word and went out to Hakim-a-barber.

"You just don't understand," she said, as Maggie and I came out to the car.

"What don't I understand?" I wanted to know.

"Your heritage," she said. And then she turned to Maggie, kissed her, and said, "You ought to try to make something of yourself, too, Maggie. It's really a new day for us. But from the way you and Mama still live you'd never know it."

She put on some sunglasses that hid everything above the tip of her nose and her chin.

Maggie smiled; maybe at the sunglasses. But a real smile, not scared. After we watched the car dust settle I asked Maggie to bring me a dip of snuff. And then the two of us sat there just enjoying, until it was time to go in the house and go to bed.

Guide for Responding

◆ Literature and Your Life

Reader's Response How did you feel about Dee's behavior on her visit home? Explain.

Thematic Focus Do you think Dee has effectively blended an awareness of her African heritage with her everyday life? Explain.

☑ Check Your Comprehension

1. (a) How was Maggie injured? (b) How did she and her sister react to that experience?
2. (a) What objects does Dee ask to have? (b) What does she intend to do with each one?
3. What is Dee's response when the narrator says that she has promised to give the quilts to Maggie?

◆ Critical Thinking

INTERPRET

1. (a) What is revealed about the narrator's relationships with her daughters early in the story? (b) How does the mother's relationship with each daughter change? **[Infer]**
2. What is ironic about Dee's professed interest in her heritage? **[Interpret]**
3. (a) What do the quilts mean to Dee? (b) What do they mean to Maggie? **[Interpret]**
4. What message does this story convey about family relationships and the meaning of a family's heritage? **[Draw Conclusions]**

APPLY

5. What does your heritage mean to you? **[Define]**

Beyond the Selection

FURTHER READING

Other Works by Alice Walker

The Color Purple; In Search of Our Mothers' Gardens; You Can't Keep a Good Woman Down

Other Works With the Theme of Family Relationships/Mothers and Daughters

The Birds of Summer, Zilpha Keatley Snyder

Little Women, Louisa May Alcott

We suggest that you preview these works before recommending them to students.

INTERNET

To learn more about the works of Alice Walker, we suggest the following Internet sites. Be aware that sites may have changed since this information was published.

For articles by Alice Walker, go to **http://wwwvms.utexas.edu/~melindaj/journals.html**

For an annotated bibliography, go to **http://www.edtech.vt.edu/idi/fdi/Paradigms.html**

We *strongly recommend* that you preview sites before you send students to them.

Reinforce and Extend

Reteach

To reteach this selection, use ***Strategies for Diverse Student Needs,*** page 64.

Answers

◆ Literature and Your Life

Reader's Response Students may express outrage at Dee's attitudes and actions.

Thematic Focus Suggested response: Dee has not effectively blended her awareness of her African heritage into her life; she has, instead, allowed it to dominate her life.

☑ Check Your Comprehension

1. (a) She was badly burned when the family home caught fire. (b) Maggie appears horrified, while Dee seems glad to see the house burn down.
2. (a) Dee asks for the butter churn top, the dasher, and two handmade quilts. (b) She intends to use the churn top as a centerpiece, do "something artistic" with the dasher, and display the quilts.
3. Dee becomes outraged; she says that Maggie can't appreciate the quilts, that she'll put them to everyday use.

◆ Critical Thinking

1. Suggested responses: (a) Her comments reveal that she feels compassion and kinship toward Maggie, but feels some resentment toward Dee, with whom she has little in common. (b) These feelings become even more pronounced as the story unfolds.
2. Although she claims to care deeply about her heritage, she treats her mother, her sister, and their possessions with selfish disrespect.
3. (a) To Dee, they are pieces of the past to be artistically displayed. (b) To Maggie, they are memories of family, to be used every day.
4. Possible response: Family relationships and heritage mean different things to different people.
5. Students' responses will be personal.

Answers

◆ Reading Strategy

1. (a) Maggie is younger, darker-skinned, and thinner. She is badly scarred, while Dee is attractive. (b) Maggie is not bright or well-educated; Dee is clever and well-educated. (c) Maggie is shy and nervous; Dee is arrogant, determined, and self-absorbed.
2. (a) Maggie knows little or nothing; Dee seems to know much more. (b) Maggie has embraced it; Dee seems to have rejected it.
3. Maggie trusts and obeys her mother; they seem to get along quite well because they are, in fact, alike in many ways. Dee, on the other hand, seems to be contemptuous of her mother's lack of education and "understanding"; she has no real relationship with or respect for her mother.

◆ Build Vocabulary

Using the Latin Word Roots: *-doc-/-doct-*

1. documentary 2. docile
3. indoctrinate 4. documents

Using the Word Bank

1. b 2. a 3. c 4. a

◆ Literary Focus

1. Suggested response: The people she has met, such as Hakim-a-barber, and the trends of the time in which she is living—many African Americans explored their African heritage in the 1960's and 1970's—seem to have motivated her interest.
2. Dee is used to getting her own way and taking whatever she wants. She seems arrogant and filled with ideas of her own self-worth and self-importance.
3. Suggested response: She is not willing to stand by and watch one daughter rob another of what is rightfully hers; she is willing to stand up for what she believes is right.

◆ Grammar and Style

Practice

1.–4. Students may say that these fragments are missing a verb or both a subject and a verb. Either answer is acceptable, depending on whether the fragments are viewed objectively or within the context of the story.

Guide for Responding *(continued)*

◆ Reading Strategy

Contrasting Characters

Although Dee and Maggie are sisters, they have very little in common, aside from their mother and their interest in the two quilts. By **contrasting characters**—analyzing the differences between them—you can better understand each character and gain insight into the story's conflict and theme.

1. How do Maggie and Dee differ (a) physically, (b) intellectually, and (c) emotionally?

2. (a) What does each sister know about her African heritage and her American heritage?
(b) To what extent does each sister think it is important to incorporate knowledge of her African heritage into her daily life? Support your answers with examples from the story.

3. Contrast the relationship each daughter has with her mother.

◆ Build Vocabulary

Using the Latin Roots *-doc-,-doct-*

Using the meaning of *-doc-,-doct-* ("teach") and context clues, choose the best word in the box to complete each sentence.

documents	docile
indoctrinate	documentary

1. We watched a film __?__ that traced the history of quilt-making in the United States.

2. A __?__ learner is one who accepts without question anything he or she is taught.

3. The political leader tried to __?__ his followers by repeating his ideology every day.

4. Immigrants were asked to show __?__ to prove their citizenship in other countries.

Using the Word Bank: Analogies

On your paper, complete the following analogies using the words from the Word Bank.

1. *Flour* is to *pie crust* as __?__ is to *soap*.

2. *Encourage* is to *coach* as __?__ is to *dictator*.

3. *Competitive* is to *athlete* as __?__ is to *prowler*.

4. *Moral* is to *lesson* as __?__ is to *belief*.

◆ Literary Focus

Characters' Motivations

It is particularly important to understand the **characters' motivations**—reasons for behavior—in "Everyday Use," a story about how people change over time. For example, Walker shows you that Maggie's hesitancy results, in part, from the childhood accident that has left more than a physical scar. Analyze the characters' motivations to answer these questions:

1. What appears to motivate Dee's interest in her heritage?

2. Discuss the personality characteristics that enable Dee to return home after a long absence and immediately assume she can get the churn top, the dasher, and the quilts.

3. What does the narrator's act of snatching up the quilts from Dee reveal about her personal values?

◆ Grammar and Style

Sentence Fragments

In this story, Walker uses **sentence fragments** to make it seem as if the first-person narrator is speaking informally to readers.

Sentence fragments are parts of sentences incorrectly punctuated as complete.

Practice On your paper, explain why each example is a sentence fragment, and identify the missing part or parts of speech. Rewrite each fragment as a complete sentence.

1. Furtive boys in pink shirts hanging about on washday after school.

2. Nervous girls who never laughed.

3. Earrings gold, too, and hanging down to her shoulder.

4. Always too busy: feeding the cattle, fixing the fences, putting up salt-lick shelters, throwing down hay.

Writing Application Write a short dialogue featuring characters from "Everyday Use." Incorporate sentence fragments to capture speech and thought patterns.

Possible responses for 1–4 include the following:

1. Her friends were furtive boys in pink shirts, hanging about on wash day; *or* Furtive boys in pink shirts hung about on wash day.
2. Her friends were nervous girls who never laughed; *or* Nervous girls who never laughed befriended Dee.
3. Her earrings were gold, too, and hanging down to her shoulder; *or* She wore gold earrings, too, hanging down to her shoulder.
4. There is no subject or verb. Possible response: They were always too busy: . . .

Writing Application

Dialogues should be properly punctuated and should incorporate sentence fragments that reflect the speech patterns of the characters from the story.

Grammar Reinforcement

For additional instruction and practice, use the Fragments and Run-on Sentences lesson in the Sentence Errors unit of the **Language Lab CD-ROM** and the page on Fragments, p. 45, in the *Writer's Solution Grammar Practice Book.*

Build Your Portfolio

Idea Bank

Writing

1. **Journal Entry** Write a journal entry describing the events in this story from either Maggie's or Dee's point of view.
2. **Speech** In the character of either Maggie or Dee, write a speech to a local women's group about the value of cultural heritage. **[Social Studies Link]**
3. **Character Analysis** Write a character analysis of Maggie. In your analysis, respond to one critic's suggestion that Maggie is a "silent, suffering" character. Using evidence from the story, argue for or against the critic's analysis of Maggie.

Speaking, Listening, and Viewing

4. **Television Talk Show** With a partner, dramatize the narrator's dream of a television reunion between herself and Dee. Add dialogue of your own to extend and elaborate on the dream in the story. **[Performing Arts Link]**
5. **Debate** In two teams, take pro and con positions to argue this statement: Handicrafts that reflect a culture's heritage should be taken out of general use and displayed in museums. **[Social Studies Link]**

Researching and Representing

6. **Heritage Exhibit** As a class, gather examples or pictures of folk art from cultures represented in the class. Create an exhibit with explanatory captions. **[Social Studies Link; Art Link]**
7. **African Languages Project** The names *Wangero* and *Hakim-a-barber* come from one of the 800–1,000 languages spoken in Africa today. Gather information on one of the four major language families, and present your findings to the class, along with audiotaped examples, if possible. **[Social Studies Link]**

Online Activity www.phlit.phschool.com

Guided Writing Lesson

Review of a Short Story

What are your reactions to Walker's story? Were the characters interesting and believable? Did the story convey a message that you feel is important? Write a critical review of the story in which you respond to these and other questions that come to mind. Explain the ways in which you think the story is and is not effective. Keep the following tip in mind as you develop your review:

Writing Skills Focus: Accuracy

Focus on **accuracy** when gathering examples or evidence to support your opinions:

- Double-check any quotations to make sure they reflect the source word for word.
- Test and prove any cause-and-effect links you discuss.
- To avoid confusion, organize evidence about individual characters on separate pieces of paper.
- Clearly distinguish your opinions, and those of any critics you quote, from facts about the story and its characters.

Prewriting Create a two-column chart in which you list some positive and negative aspects of the story. Next to each item, note relevant page numbers of appropriate examples. Review the information on your chart and try to sum up your overall opinion in a sentence or two.

Drafting Begin by stating your overall opinion of the story. Then present a series of paragraphs in which you back up your opinion by accurately citing details from the story.

Revising Replace weak modifiers (such as *poor, good, nicely*) with precise adjectives and adverbs that capture your reactions (such as *cleverly, gripping, bold, challenging*). Be sure that your facts are accurate and that you've copied all quotations word for word.

✓ ASSESSMENT OPTIONS

Formal Assessment, Selection Test, pp. 283–285, and Assessment Resources Software. The selection test is designed so that it can be easily customized to the performance levels of your students.

Alternative Assessment, p. 64, includes options for less advanced students, more advanced students, verbal/linguistic learners, logical/mathematical learners, visual/spatial learners, and interpersonal learners.

PORTFOLIO ASSESSMENT

Use the following rubrics in the ***Alternative Assessment*** booklet to assess student writing:
Journal Entry: Description Rubric, p. 112
Speech: Persuasion Rubric, p. 120
Character Analysis: Literary Analysis/Interpretation Rubric, p. 127
Guided Writing Lesson: Critical Review Rubric, p. 126

Idea Bank

Customizing for *Performance Levels*

Following are suggestions for matching Idea Bank topics with your students' performance levels:
Less Advanced Students: 1, 6
Average Students: 2, 4, 5
More Advanced Students: 3, 7

Customizing for *Learning Modalities*

Following are suggestions for matching Idea Bank topics with your students' learning modalities:
Bodily/Kinesthetic: 4
Verbal/Linguistics: 4, 5, 7
Logical/Mathematical: 5
Visual/Spatial: 6

Guided Writing Lesson

For more instruction on prewriting, elaboration, and revision, see *Prentice Hall Writing and Grammar.*

Writing and Language Transparencies Display the Outline Transparency, p. 95, to help students organize the main points and supporting details they will include in their review.

Writers at Work Videodisc
Have students view the videodisc segment on Response to Literature (Ch. 7) featuring Theresa Park to see how a literary agent critiques the works she reads. Have students discuss how they can use insights from the interview with Park to help them evaluate "Everyday Use."

Play frames 22513 to 31258

Writing Lab CD-ROM
Have students complete the tutorial on Response to Literature. Follow these steps:

1. Refer students to the annotated model of a Critical Review.
2. Direct students to the interactive tips for using quotations before they begin drafting on the computer.
3. Use the Evaluation Word Bins to help students strengthen their reviews.

Prepare and Engage

LESSON OBJECTIVES

1. To develop vocabulary and word identification skills
- Build Vocabulary: Latin Word Roots: *-aud-*
- Using the Word Bank: Sentence Completions

2. To use a variety of reading strategies to comprehend a short story
- Connect Your Experience
- Reading Strategy: Apply Background Information

3. To increase knowledge of other cultures and to connect common elements across cultures
- Connecting Themes Across Cultures (ATE)
- Background for Understanding: Culture

4. To express and support responses to the text
- Critical Thinking
- Idea Bank: Diary Entry
- Analyze a Book Review

5. To analyze literary elements
- Literary Focus: Memoirs
- Idea Bank: Prequel
- Idea Bank: Character Analysis

6. To read to do research on self-selected and assigned topics
- Idea Bank: Written Report
- Idea Bank: Historical Travelogue

7. To plan, prepare, organize, and present literary interpretations
- Idea Bank: Talk Story
- Idea Bank: Panel Discussion

8. To use recursive writing processes to write a guide for planning a family reunion
- Guided Writing Lesson

9. To increase knowledge of the rules of grammar and usage
- Grammar and Style: Punctuating a Quotation Within a Quotation

Test Preparation

Writing Skills: Punctuation (ATE, p. 957)
The teaching tips and sample test item in this workshop support the instruction and practice in the unit workshop:
Writing Skills: Punctuation, Usage, and Sentence Structure (SE, p. 1143)

Guide for Interpreting

Maxine Hong Kingston
(1940–)

"I was born to be a writer," Maxine Hong Kingston once told an interviewer. "In the midst of any adventure, a born writer has a desire to hurry home and put it into words."

Crossing Cultures Kingston did not begin describing her adventures in English until she was nearly ten, because at home her first language was a form of Cantonese—a Chinese dialect spoken around Canton, now Guangzhou, China. Both her parents came from a village near Canton: Her father left first for "the Golden Mountain" of America, settling in New York City. Her mother used the money he sent home to run a clinic in their native village until 1939, when she escaped war-torn China and joined her husband. Not long afterward the couple resettled in Stockton, California, where Maxine Hong was born.

Young Maxine was a shy girl who earned straight A's in school. She won a scholarship to the University of California at Berkeley, which she attended in its heyday as a center of intellectual activity and political activism in the 1960's. Kingston recalls those years fondly: "Peace on earth. Friendship. We in Berkeley thought we were going to change the world."

At Berkeley, Maxine Hong met Earll Kingston, whom she married in 1962. After graduation the couple supported themselves as teachers while pursuing success in their chosen fields—Earll in acting, Maxine in writing.

Maxine Hong Kingston shot to success with her first book, The Woman Warrior.

The Woman Warrior, a unique blend of folklore, myth, feminism and autobiography, won the National Book Critics' Circle Award in 1976. The major focus of the book is on Brave Orchid (Kingston's mother) and the "talk stories" she tells her daughter about China and the female members of their family.

Kingston also earned the National Book Critics' Circle Award for *China Men* in 1980. In 1989, she published the novel *Tripmaster Monkey*. After living in Hawaii for many years, Kingston and her husband and son returned to the mainland, settling in Oakland, California.

◆ Background for Understanding

CULTURE: *THE WOMAN WARRIOR* AND THE CHINESE AMERICAN EXPERIENCE

The Woman Warrior is an innovative autobiography that attempts to capture both the outer and inner experience of growing up in a bicultural world—part Chinese, part American—and feeling torn between the two. To accomplish her purpose, Kingston often presents the "talk stories" that she heard as a girl growing up among native Chinese speakers. The book's subtitle, *Memoirs of a Girlhood Among Ghosts,* refers to the pale ghosts of white America as well as the ghosts of the narrator's ancestors back in China.

The woman warrior of the title is one of the latter ghosts, the brave heroine of a "talk story" from China's past, with whom the narrator identifies so strongly that at one point she practically becomes her. However, the title *Woman Warrior* may have a double meaning; it may also refer to the other Chinese and Chinese American women portrayed in the book, including the narrator's mother, Brave Orchid, on whom this selection focuses. This selection comes from a section of the book called "At the Western Palace."

Prentice Hall Literature Program Resources

REINFORCE / RETEACH / EXTEND

Selection Support Pages
Build Vocabulary: Latin Roots: *-aud-*, p. 294
Grammar and Style: Punctuating a Quotation Within a Quotation, p. 295
Reading Strategy: Apply Background Information, p. 296
Literary Focus: Memoirs, p. 297

Strategies for Diverse Student Needs, p. 65

Beyond Literature
Career Connection: Memoir Writing, p. 65

Formal Assessment Selection Test, pp. 286–288; Assessment Resources Software

Alternative Assessment, p. 65

Resource Pro CD-ROM

from The Woman Warrior

◆ Literature and Your Life

Connect Your Experience

If you've ever felt a gap between the way you and older relatives view the world, you'll appreciate this selection. In families whose adults and children were born in different countries, this gap can be particularly pronounced. As you read, think about the many ways in which the culture you grow up in influences your general outlook.

Journal Writing Jot down a "talk story," or oral tale or anecdote, that you recall. It might be a family tale or something you heard from a neighbor.

Thematic Focus: Literature Confronts the Everyday

This selection captures the details of everyday American life through the eyes of a woman who is something of an outsider.

◆ Build Vocabulary

Latin Roots: *-aud-*

From the Latin word *audire,* which means "to hear," comes the root *-aud-,* which also conveys the idea of sound or hearing. The adverb *inaudibly* means "in a tone too low to be heard."

Word Bank

Preview this list of words.

- hysterically
- encampment
- inaudibly
- gravity
- oblivious

◆ Literary Focus

Memoirs

Most **memoirs** are first-person nonfiction narratives. Most recount historically or personally significant events in which the writer was a participant or an eyewitness. While *The Woman Warrior* is not a traditional memoir, Kingston subtitled her writing *Memoirs of a Girlhood Among Ghosts.* As you read this selection from *The Woman Warrior,* consider how it does and does not conform to the standard definition of a memoir.

◆ Grammar and Style

Punctuating a Quotation Within a Quotation

Use single quotation marks to enclose a **quotation within a quotation.** As with double quotation marks, place commas and periods inside the closing single quotation marks. Place colons and semicolons outside, and place question and exclamation marks inside or outside, depending on who is speaking. Look at these examples:

"He will say, 'Abandon ship,' but my son won't hear."

"The captain will say, 'Abandon ship'; or he might say, 'Watch out for bombs.' "

"Did the captain say, 'I believe we are under attack'?" Brave Orchid asked.

◆ Reading Strategy

Apply Background Information

Background information can often help you fully appreciate a piece of literature. Information found in book-jacket copy, a foreword or introduction, footnotes, or your own knowledge from prior experience can help you understand a work's central message and subtleties.

In this textbook, you can gain background information from reading the author biography and Background for Understanding sections in the Guide for Interpreting. For example, by reading the background information for this selection from *The Woman Warrior,* you'll gain a frame of reference for details in the selection that are not otherwise explained.

Interest Grabber In reading this memoir, students will experience the excitement, impatience, and surprise of a long-awaited family reunion. Engage students' interest with the following activity. Provide childhood pictures of yourself and other teachers or ask students to contribute their own baby photos. Challenge the class to match up the photos with the correct people. How difficult might it be to recognize someone who has changed this much? What feelings might such a reunion produce in both parties?

Customize for
Less Proficient Readers
Brave Orchid's description of American culture includes contextual references some readers may find confusing. Encourage less proficient readers to pause as necessary and carefully read the explanatory footnotes.

Customize for
AP Students
Comparison and contrast can enable these students to appreciate the cultural dualities presented in Maxine Hong Kingston's memoir. Have students identify and record elements of description about both Chinese and American cultures, as seen through Brave Orchid's eyes. What does the comparison reveal about Brave Orchid's character?

Customize for
English Language Learners
Explain that the memoir focuses on the experiences of a Chinese American woman for whom English is also a second language. Her thoughts are sometimes awkwardly stated and she uses unfamiliar figurative language. Urge students to study context as they decipher any confusing passages.

Literature CD-ROM To build background on the author and the selection, use *The History of American Literature:* Part 2, Disk 2, Feature 7, which profiles Kingston's *The Woman Warrior.*

Test Preparation Workshop

Writing Skills:
Punctuation Many standardized tests require students to identify the type of error. Use the following sample test item to demonstrate.

> Immigrants who arrived at Ellis Island had often spent months at sea; and were thin and weak by the time they landed.

Read the passage and decide which type of error, if any, appears in the underlined section.

A Spelling error
B Capitalization error
C Punctuation error
D No error

C is the correct answer. The underlined section contains a semicolon separating two parts of a compound predicate. Remind students that semicolons are used to separate independent clauses.

Develop Understanding

One-Minute Insight This memoir captures perfectly the strange distortions passing time can create. When the main character, Brave Orchid, arrives at the airport to meet the sister she has not seen in thirty years, she brings the unique perspective of her memories along—sure that she and Moon Orchid remain unchanged by time. Determined as well to resist the effects of the alien American culture in which she now lives, Brave Orchid evokes the universal struggle between tradition and change.

◆ Literature and Your Life

❶ Recap Brave Orchid's situation in the opening paragraphs. What emotions have students experienced when waiting eagerly for someone special to arrive? *Students may describe excitement, anxiety, annoyance over delays, or restlessness.*

◆ Reading Strategy

❷ **Apply Background Information** Ask: What does the footnoted information suggest about Moon Orchid's life since she and Brave Orchid last saw each other? How have the two women's lives differed and overlapped? *Students should infer that Moon Orchid fled mainland China and may have lived for some time in Hong Kong. Both women have lived in countries other than China, but have likely faced very different challenges in their new homes.*

◆ Literary Focus

❸ **Memoirs** Students should note that the paragraph provides Brave Orchid's impressions of her children and their America.

◆ Critical Thinking

❹ **Infer** Based on the niece's solicitous question and her aunt's reply, what can you infer about Brave Orchid's age or physical condition? *She is probably relatively elderly and frail.*

from The Woman Warrior

Maxine Hong Kingston

❶ When she was about sixty-eight years old, Brave Orchid took a day off to wait at San Francisco International Airport for the plane that was bringing her sister to the United States. She had not seen Moon Orchid for thirty years. ❷ She had begun this waiting at home, getting up a half-hour before Moon Orchid's plane took off in Hong Kong.[1] Brave Orchid would add her will power to the forces that keep an airplane up. Her head hurt with the concentration. The plane had to be light, so no matter how tired she felt, she dared not rest her spirit on a wing but continuously and gently pushed up on the plane's belly. She had already been waiting at the airport for nine hours. She was wakeful.

❸ Next to Brave Orchid sat Moon Orchid's only daughter, who was helping her aunt wait. Brave Orchid had made two of her own children come too because they could drive, but they had been lured away by the magazine racks and the gift shops and coffee shops. Her American children could not sit for very long. They did not understand sitting; they had wandering feet. She hoped they would get back from the pay TV's or the pay toilets or wherever they were spending their money before the plane arrived. If they did not come back soon, she would go look for them. If her son thought he could hide in the men's room, he was wrong.

> **◆ Literary Focus** Whose impressions are provided in this paragraph?

❹ "Are you all right, Aunt?" asked her niece.

"No, this chair hurts me. Help me pull some chairs together so I can put my feet up."

She unbundled a blanket and spread it out to make a bed for herself. On the floor she had two shopping bags full of canned peaches, real peaches, beans wrapped in taro leaves,[2] cookies, Thermos bottles,[3] enough food for everybody, though only her niece would eat with her. Her bad boy and bad girl were probably sneaking hamburgers, wasting their money. She would scold them.

Many soldiers and sailors sat about, oddly calm, like little boys in cowboy uniforms. (She thought "cowboy" was what you would call a Boy Scout.) They should have been crying hysterically on their way to Vietnam.[4] "If I see one that looks Chinese," she thought, "I'll go over and give him some advice." She sat up suddenly; she had forgotten about her own son, who was even now in Vietnam. Carefully she split her attention, beaming half of it to the ocean, into the water to keep him afloat. He was on a ship. He was in Vietnamese waters. She was sure of it. He and the other children were lying to her. They had said he was in Japan, and then they said he was in the Philippines. But when she sent him her help, she could feel that he was on a ship in Da Nang.[5] Also she had seen the children hide the envelopes that his letters came in.

"Do you think my son is in Vietnam?" she asked her niece, who was dutifully eating.

---

1. **took off in Hong Kong:** After mainland China fell to the Communists in the late 1940's, many native Chinese fled first to Hong Kong (a British colony until 1997) before emigrating to the United States.

2. **taro** (te´ rō) **leaves:** Leaves of an edible tuberous plant widely eaten in Asia.
3. **Thermos** (thur´ məs) **bottles:** Insulated containers for holding liquids and keeping them warm or cold.
4. **Vietnam:** Southeast Asian nation where, in the late 1960's when this selection takes place, the U.S. had joined the fighting known as the Vietnam War (1954–1975).
5. **Da Nang** (da naŋ): City in central Vietnam that was the site of an important U.S. military base during the Vietnam War; also spelled Danang.

Analyze Literary Criticism

The critic Sharon Wong reviewed Kingston's work: "In this beautifully written collection of interrelated reminiscences, Kingston tells the story of a Chinese-American woman searching for her past to explain her present. . . . Kingston grows painfully aware that she cannot accept the old values, yet she is somehow saddened by her loss."

Discuss this review with students and then explore the answers to these questions:

1. In her story, how does Kingston use the characters to reveal the conflict within her? *The two sisters have changed and seem to disapprove of each other; they might be compared as the products of two cultures.*
2. In what ways is "The Warrior Woman" a story of many women growing up in bicultural worlds? *They could possess the same conflicts and struggles of trying to live in two cultures.*

"No. Didn't your children say he was in the Philippines?"

"Have you ever seen any of his letters with Philippine stamps on them?"

"Oh, yes. Your children showed me one."

"I wouldn't put it past them to send the letters to some Filipino they know. He puts Manila[6] postmarks on them to fool me."

"Yes, I can imagine them doing that. But don't worry. Your son can take care of himself. All your children can take care of themselves."

5 "Not him. He's not like other people. Not normal at all. He sticks erasers in his ears, and the erasers are still attached to the pencil stubs. The captain will say, 'Abandon ship,' or 'Watch out for bombs,' and he won't hear. He doesn't listen to orders. I told him to flee to Canada,[7] but he wouldn't go."

She closed her eyes. After a short while, plane and ship under control, she looked again at the children in uniforms. Some of the blond ones looked like baby chicks, their crew cuts like the downy yellow on baby chicks. You had to feel sorry for them even though they were Army and Navy Ghosts.

Suddenly her son and daughter came running. "Come, Mother. The plane's landed early. She's here already." They hurried, folding up their mother's encampment. She was glad her children were not useless. They must have known what this trip to San Francisco was about then. "It's a good thing I made you come early," she said.

Brave Orchid pushed to the front of the crowd. She had to be in front. The passengers were separated from the people waiting for them by glass doors and walls. Immigration Ghosts were stamping papers. The travellers crowded along some conveyor belts to have their luggage searched. Brave Orchid did not see her sister anywhere. She stood watching for four hours. Her children left and came back. "Why don't you sit down?" they asked.

"The chairs are too far away," she said.

"Why don't you sit on the floor then?"

No, she would stand, as her sister was probably standing in a line she could not see from here. Her American children had no feelings and no memory.

To while away time, she and her niece talked about the Chinese passengers. These new immigrants had it easy. On Ellis Island[8] the people were thin after forty days at sea and had no fancy luggage. 6

"That one looks like her," Brave Orchid would say.

"No, that's not her."

Ellis Island had been made out of wood and iron. Here everything was new plastic, a ghost trick to lure immigrants into feeling safe and spilling their secrets. Then the Alien Office could send them right back. Otherwise, why did they lock her out, not letting her help her sister answer questions and spell her name? At Ellis Island when the ghost asked Brave Orchid what year her husband had cut off his pigtail, a Chinese who was crouching on the floor motioned her not to talk. "I don't know," she had said. If it weren't for that Chinese man, she might not be here today, or her husband either. She hoped some Chinese, a janitor or a clerk, would look out for Moon Orchid. Luggage conveyors fooled immigrants into thinking the Gold Mountain was going to be easy. 7

> ◆ **Reading Strategy** What does the background information in the Guide for Interpreting indicate that "the Gold Mountain" is? 8

Brave Orchid felt her heart jump—Moon Orchid. "There she is," she shouted. But her niece saw it was not her mother at all. And it shocked her to discover the woman her aunt was pointing out. This was a young woman, younger than herself, no older than Moon Orchid the day the sisters parted. "Moon Orchid will have changed a little, of course," Brave Orchid was saying. "She will have learned to wear western clothes." The woman wore a navy blue suit with a bunch of dark cherries at the shoulder.

6. **Manila** (mə nil′ ə): Capital of the Philippines.

7. **flee to Canada:** During the Vietnam War era, thousands of Americans fled to Canada to escape the military draft, even though such draft dodgers were subject to prosecution upon returning to the U.S.

8. **Ellis Island:** Island in the harbor off New York City that was the chief U.S. immigration station from 1892 to 1943.

◆ Build Vocabulary

hysterically (hi ster′ ik lē) *adv.*: In a highly emotional or uncontrolled manner

encampment (en kamp′ mənt) *n.*: Place where a person has set up camp

◆ Grammar and Style

5 Punctuating a Quotation Within a Quotation After students point out the interior and exterior quotation marks in Brave Orchid's words, ask them what purpose the interior quotation marks serve in the sentence. Whose words do they surround? *Students should identify interior quotation marks around 'Abandon ship' and 'Watch out for bombs.' These marks serve to distinguish the words of the captain from those of Brave Orchid herself.*

◆ Reading Strategy

6 Apply Background Information Ask students to apply background information in explaining why Brave Orchid, who lives in California, would be familiar with Ellis Island. *Students should recall from the Guide for Interpreting that the author's mother, upon whom Brave Orchid's character is based, was an immigrant to America who arrived in New York City and would therefore have passed through Ellis Island.*

◆ Literary Focus

7 Memoirs Would students expect to find a memory such as this one in traditional memoirs? Why or why not? *Students should say yes, such a memory would be an expected element in a traditional memoir because memoirs often includes significant events in the writer's personal history—such as this life-altering moment.*

◆ Reading Strategy

8 Apply Background Information The Gold Mountain is America.

Block Scheduling Strategies

Consider these suggestions to take advantage of extended class time:

- Introduce the Reading Strategy, then discuss the Background for Understanding and author biography (p. 956).
- After students have read the Literature and Your Life section (p. 957) and completed the Journal Writing activity, invite volunteers to share their journal entries. You may wish to use the Speaking, Listening, and Viewing Mini-Lesson (ATE, p. 960) to expand this reading into the Talk Story activity in the Idea Bank.
- Define and discuss memoirs. Have students evaluate other memoirs they have read against the criteria presented in Literary Focus (p. 957).
- As students read, have them pause to read the footnoted references throughout the selection.
- Have partners exchange and evaluate each other's responses to the Critical Thinking (p. 961) and Reading Strategy (p. 962) questions.
- Stage the Panel Discussion (p. 963). Before students begin, explore and specify a definition of nonfiction.
- To assess student learning, use one of the activities on p. 65 in ***Alternative Assessment,*** or administer the multiple-choice section of the Selection Test, pp. 286–288, in ***Formal Assessment.***

Customize for *English Language Learners*

Point out that the three main characters in the memoir are all women. In describing the actions and feelings of these three women (Brave Orchid, her niece, Moon Orchid), Hong Kingston uses the pronouns *her* and *she* frequently. To help language learners avoid confusions, suggest that they replace pronouns with proper nouns to clarify which character is concerned.

Customize for *Visual/Spatial Learners*

❶ To help these students visualize the story setting, suggest the examples of grocery store automatic doors, through which two people can see but probably cannot hear each another. When these doors open, the two can briefly interact until the channel slowly narrows as the door closes.

Comprehension Check ☑

❷ Why is Brave Orchid so shocked by her sister's age? *She still pictures her as the young woman she left behind in China.*

◆ Critical Thinking

❸ **Infer** How do you think Brave Orchid feels about her children's American manners? *She feels dissatisfied by them and judges them inferior to Chinese behavior.*

◆ Critical Thinking

❹ **Interpret** To whom is Brave Orchid speaking? *Students should recognize that Brave Orchid is literally speaking to her sister but metaphorically speaking to herself as well.*

"No, Aunt," said the niece. "That's not my mother."

"Perhaps not. It's been so many years. Yes, it is your mother. It must be. Let her come closer, and we can tell. Do you think she's too far away for me to tell, or is it my eyes getting bad?"

"It's too many years gone by," said the niece.

Brave Orchid turned suddenly—another Moon Orchid, this one a neat little woman with a bun. She was laughing at something the person ahead of her in line said. Moon Orchid was just like that, laughing at nothing. "I would be able to tell the difference if one of them would only come closer," Brave Orchid said with tears, which she did not wipe. Two children met the woman with the cherries, and she shook their hands. The other woman was met by a young man. They looked at each other gladly, then walked away side by side.

Up close neither one of those women looked like Moon Orchid at all. "Don't worry, Aunt," said the niece. "I'll know her."

"I'll know her too. I knew her before you did."

The niece said nothing, although she had seen her mother only five years ago. Her aunt liked having the last word.

Finally Brave Orchid's children quit wandering and drooped on a railing. Who knew what they were thinking? At last the niece called out, "I see her! I see her! Mother! Mother!" Whenever the doors parted, she shouted, probably embarrassing the American cousins, but she didn't care. She called ❶ out, "Mama! Mama!" until the crack in the sliding doors became too small to let in her voice. "Mama!" What a strange word in an adult voice. Many people turned to see what adult was calling, "Mama!" like a child. Brave Orchid saw an old, old woman jerk her head up, her little eyes blinking confusedly, a woman whose nerves leapt toward the sound anytime she heard "Mama!" Then she relaxed to her own business again. She was a tiny, tiny lady, very thin, with little fluttering hands, and her hair was in a gray knot. She was dressed in a gray wool suit; she wore pearls around her neck and in her earlobes. Moon Orchid *would* travel with her jewels showing. Brave Orchid momentarily saw, like a larger, younger outline around this old woman, the sister she had been waiting ❷ for. The familiar dim halo faded, leaving the woman so old, so gray. So old. Brave Orchid pressed against the glass. *That* old lady? Yes, that old lady facing the ghost who stamped her papers without questioning her was her sister. Then, without noticing her family, Moon Orchid walked smiling over to the Suitcase Inspector Ghost, who took her boxes apart, pulling out puffs of tissue. From where she was, Brave Orchid could not see what her sister had chosen to carry across the ocean. She wished her sister would look her way. Brave Orchid thought that if *she* were entering a new country, she would be at the windows. Instead Moon Orchid hovered over the unwrapping, surprised at each reappearance as if she were opening presents after a birthday party.

"Mama!" Moon Orchid's daughter kept calling. Brave Orchid said to her children, "Why don't you call your aunt too? Maybe she'll hear us if all of you call out together." ❸ But her children slunk away. Maybe that shame-face they so often wore was American politeness.

"Mama!" Moon Orchid's daughter called again, and this time her mother looked right at her. She left her bundles in a heap and came running. "Hey!" the Customs Ghost yelled at her. She went back to clear up her mess, talking inaudibly to her daughter all the while. Her daughter pointed toward Brave Orchid. And at last Moon Orchid looked at her—two old women with faces like mirrors.

Their hands reached out as if to touch the other's face, then returned to their own, the fingers checking the grooves in the forehead

◆ Build Vocabulary

inaudibly (in ôd′ ə blē) *adv.*: In a manner that cannot be heard; in a low tone

gravity (grav′ i tē) *n.*: Seriousness

oblivious (ə bliv′ ē əs) *adj.*: Lacking all awareness; having totally forgotten

Speaking, Listening, and Viewing Mini-Lesson

Talk Story

This mini-lesson supports the Speaking, Listening, and Viewing activity in the Idea Bank on p. 963.

Introduce the Concept To help students understand the assignment, review the following points:

- Events need be dramatic only in the teller's experience and reactions; the situations themselves may be quite ordinary.
- Effective stories use descriptive language to create vivid mental pictures and portray believable characters and actions.
- When recounting an experience from childhood, choose carefully whether to present the child's view or your more mature current perspective.

Develop Background Have students recall dramatic moments from their childhood—transitions such as births or deaths, emergencies such as injury or natural calamity, or emotional peaks of anger or joy.

Apply the Information Some students may wish to write down their story, record it on audiotape, or practice before a mirror before telling it aloud to the class. Remind students to be respectful of one another's significant memories.

Assess the Outcome Have students rank the stories and storytelling according to headings such as "Funniest," "Most Poignant," or "Most Revealing." Discuss how the stories, like those of Brave Orchid, add to the portrait of their tellers.

and along the sides of the mouth. Moon Orchid, who never understood the gravity of things, started smiling and laughing, pointing at Brave Orchid. Finally Moon Orchid gathered up her stuff, strings hanging and papers loose, and met her sister at the door, where they shook hands, oblivious to blocking the way.

"You're an old woman," said Brave Orchid.

"Aiaa. *You're* an old woman."

"But you are really old. Surely, you can't say that about me. I'm not old the way you're old."

"But *you* really are old. You're one year older than I am."

"Your hair is white and your face all wrinkled."

"You're so skinny."

"You're so fat."

"Fat women are more beautiful than skinny women."

The children pulled them out of the doorway. One of Brave Orchid's children brought the car from the parking lot, and the other heaved the luggage into the trunk. They put the two old ladies and the niece in the back seat. All the way home—across the Bay Bridge,[9] over the Diablo hills,[10] across the San Joaquin River[11] to the valley, the valley moon so white at dusk—all the way home, the two sisters exclaimed every time they turned to look at each other, "Aiaa! How old!"

Brave Orchid forgot that she got sick in cars, that all vehicles but palanquins[12] made her dizzy. "You're so old," she kept saying. "How did you get so old?" 4

Brave Orchid had tears in her eyes. But Moon Orchid said, "You look older than I. You *are* older than I," and again she'd laugh. "You're wearing an old mask to tease me." It surprised Brave Orchid that after thirty years she could still get annoyed at her sister's silliness.

---

9. **Bay Bridge:** One of the bridges across San Francisco Bay.
10. **Diablo** (dē äb´ lō) **hills:** Hills outside San Francisco.
11. **San Joaquin** (wô kēn´) **River:** River of central California; its valley is one of the state's richest agricultural areas.
12. **palanquins** (pal´ ən kēnz´): Hand-carried covered litters once widely used to transport people in China and elsewhere in eastern Asia.

Guide for Responding

◆ Literature and Your Life

Reader's Response With which character did you identify the most? Why?

Thematic Focus The mother and children in this selection might have contrasting definitions of "everyday events." Cite an example of such an event and explain the generational difference it reveals.

☑ Check Your Comprehension

1. Identify the family members waiting for Moon Orchid at the airport, and briefly describe each one's behavior.
2. What two things does Brave Orchid try to keep safe by applying her will power?
3. What is Brave Orchid's main impression when she finally sees her sister?

◆ Critical Thinking

INTERPRET

1. What sort of person is Brave Orchid? **[Connect]**
2. What seems to be her attitude toward America and American culture? **[Infer]**
3. When the two sisters finally meet, why do they speak to each other as they do? **[Interpret]**

EVALUATE

4. Did Kingston succeed in evoking the lives of people from very different cultures? Explain. **[Assess]**

APPLY

5. What does this selection suggest about the conflicts that face immigrants and the children of immigrants in America? **[Generalize]**

Beyond the Selection

FURTHER READING

Other Works by Maxine Hong Kingston

China Men

Tripmaster Monkey

Other Works With the Theme of Immigrant Experiences

Ethnic Islands, Ronald T. Takaki

Chinese American Family Album, Dorothy Hoobler

Join In, ed. Donald R. Gallo

We suggest that you preview these works before recommending them to students.

INTERNET

You may find additional information about Maxine Hong Kingston on the Internet. We suggest the following site. Be aware that sites may have changed since this information was published.

For critical responses to Maxine Hong Kingston's work, visit **http://www.tufts.edu/as/stu-org/tuftsdaily/archives/fall96/features/F1011bo~.html**

We *strongly recommend* that you preview sites before you send students to them.

Reinforce and Extend

Customize for
AP Readers

Challenge students to create, from their own knowledge or research, additional footnotes to explain Brave Orchid's references to American culture and to the events of the memoir's historical setting (late 1960's).

Answers

◆ Literature and Your Life

Reader's Response Students should be prepared to explain their responses.

Thematic Focus The trip to the airport is an everyday experience for Brave Orchid's children, but it is a major excursion for her, requiring bags of bedding and food.

☑ Check Your Comprehension

1. Brave Orchid is nervous and full of anticipation; Moon Orchid's daughter remains dutifully with her aunt; and Brave Orchid's son and daughter restlessly roam the airport.
2. She tries to keep her sister's plane in the air and her son's ship afloat.
3. She cannot believe how old her sister has grown.

◆ Critical Thinking

1. She seems to be a reserved, dignified woman who clings to traditional Chinese values and customs.
2. She seems to feel that they are inferior to China and its culture.
3. Suggested response: They fall back into old habits, bickering with one another as they did in their youth.
4. Students may suggest that Kingston succeeds in showing how Brave Orchid is still staunchly Chinese in her attitudes and behavior, despite her many years in the United States. They may cite Brave Orchid's supply of Chinese foods, her insistence on standing for hours as her sister goes through customs, and the way she formally shakes her sister's hand when they finally meet.
5. It suggests that immigrants struggle simultaneously to hold on to their cultural heritage while making their way in a new culture. Their children are often caught between the old and new cultures, and may feel that they do not fully belong in either.

Guide for Responding (continued)

◆ Literary Focus

MEMOIRS

If you were comparing the features of this selection with those of traditional **memoirs**—nonfiction narratives similar to autobiographies—you would notice both similarities and differences.

1. Upon whose impressions does this selection focus? Cite examples to support your answer.

2. (a) From what narrative point of view is this selection told? (b) Explain the difference between the point of view of this selection and that of traditional memoirs.

3. (a) Cite two memories Brave Orchid has while waiting in the airport. (b) Explain why these memories are—or are not—features typical of the memoir form.

4. Based on this selection, would you classify *The Woman Warrior* as a standard memoir? Why or why not?

◆ Reading Strategy

APPLY BACKGROUND INFORMATION

The **background information** provided for a piece of literature can help you to understand the details and cultural and historical references in that work. Knowing a bit about a country's history, for example, enables you to understand named historic events.

The background information from the Guide for Interpreting, footnotes, or your own knowledge can help you better understand the selection. Using this background knowledge, answer these questions.

1. (a) From what province in China might Moon Orchid be coming? (b) What evidence did you use to draw your conclusion?

2. What does the narrator mean by (a) Army and Navy Ghosts? (b) Customs Ghost?

3. (a) Where might the family be headed in the last paragraphs? (b) How do you know?

4. Brave Orchid has packed beans wrapped in taro leaves. How does knowing what taro leaves are increase your understanding of her character?

◆ Build Vocabulary

USING THE LATIN ROOT *-aud-*

The Latin root *-aud-* indicates "hearing" or "sound." Explain how its meaning is connected to each of these words:

1. audiocassette **3.** auditorium
2. auditory **4.** audition

USING THE WORD BANK: Sentence Completions

In your notebook, write each sentence, replacing the blank with the appropriate word from the Word Bank.

1. We left our homey ___?___ and hiked up the mountain.

2. ___?___ to the time, she worked on into the night.

3. When she answered ___?___, I asked her to speak up.

4. The boy yelled ___?___ when he thought he was lost.

5. The ___?___ of the situation silenced us all.

◆ Grammar and Style

PUNCTUATING A QUOTATION WITHIN A QUOTATION

Remember to place commas and periods inside closing quotation marks, colons and semicolons outside, and question marks and exclamation points inside or outside, depending on the words to which they apply.

Use single quotation marks to enclose a **quotation within a quotation**.

Practice Copy this paragraph about the characters in *The Woman Warrior* into your notebook, adding all the missing single quotation marks.

"My sister wrote, I am coming to America," Brave Orchid told her family. "She asked, Will you be able to pick me up? I told her, Yes, I will leave my house before your plane takes off from Hong Kong. Do you think she knows I am excited?"

Writing Application Write a second paragraph in which Brave Orchid quotes her sister. Use single quotation marks to indicate quotations within quotations. Punctuate according to the rules that apply.

Answers

◆ Literary Focus

1. It focuses on the impressions of Brave Orchid. The narrator reveals her impressions of her children's behavior in the airport, and her impressions of the soldiers waiting to fly to Vietnam.
2. (a) It is told from a limited third-person point of view. (b) Most traditional memoirs are first-person narratives.
3. (a) She remembers how her children have been hiding information about where her son is stationed and she recalls her immigration interview when she entered the United States. (b) The memories are not typical in that they recall events in which the writer was not directly involved. The memories are, on the other hand, personally significant to the subject of the memoir, Brave Orchid—a typical feature of the events recounted in memoirs.
4. Suggested response: It is not a standard memoir because it is not written in the first person, nor did the writer experience all of the events recounted.

◆ Reading Strategy

1. (a) She is probably coming from Canton. (b) The author's biography reveals that her family came from this region.
2. (a) Army and Navy Ghosts are white soldiers. (b) The Customs Ghost is the white customs officer.
3. (a) They are probably headed for Stockton, California. (b) The author's biography reveals that her family relocated to this area.
4. The fact that they are the leaves of an Asian plant tells us that Brave Orchid still eats traditional Chinese foods; she has preserved her Chinese cultural heritage.

Reteach

To reteach this selection, use ***Strategies for Diverse Student Needs,*** page 65.

◆ Build Vocabulary

Using the Latin Word Root *-aud-*

Suggested responses:

1. Sound is recorded and played back on audiocassettes.
2. Auditory describes something that has to do with hearing.
3. An auditorium is where one goes to hear a speaker.
4. An audition is a chance to be heard.

Using the Word Bank Sentence Completions

1. encampment; 2. Oblivious; 3. inaudibly; 4. hysterically; 5. gravity

◆ Grammar and Style

Practice "My sister wrote, 'I am coming to America,'" Brave Orchid told her family. "She asked, 'Will you be able to pick me up?' I told her, 'Yes, I will leave my house before your plane takes off from Hong Kong.' Do you think she knows I am excited?"

Writing Application

Paragraphs should be consistent with the content of the selection and should include at least two examples of properly punctuated quotations within quotations.

Grammar Reinforcement

For additional instruction and practice, use the Quotation Marks, Colons, and Semicolons lesson in the Capitalization and Punctuation unit of the **Language Lab CD-ROM,** and the page on Quotation Marks, p. 91, in the *Writer's Solution Grammar Practice Book.*

Build Your Portfolio

Idea Bank

Writing

1. Diary Entry Write the diary entry that Moon Orchid might have written on the night of her arrival in California.

2. Prequel Write a scene that explains why Moon Orchid and her daughter were separated. In your prequel to the story, reveal why Moon Orchid is coming to America now or why Moon Orchid's daughter came to America earlier.

3. Character Analysis In an essay, analyze Brave Orchid's character. Identify three or four of her character traits, and connect these traits to her background and her behavior. Cite appropriate supporting examples from the selection.

Speaking, Listening, and Viewing

4. Talk Story As an adult, tell your grown children a "talk story"—an oral account of a dramatic event that took place when you were a child.

5. Panel Discussion When *The Woman Warrior* won a 1976 national award for nonfiction, many debated its qualifications. Based on what you've read, hold a panel discussion to decide whether this work fits the definition of nonfiction.

Researching and Representing

6. Written Report Research and report on the history of Chinese immigration to the United States. Study the arrivals of immigrants and their patterns of settlement. Create a supplementary chart of statistical information. **[Math Link]**

7. Historical Travelogue Suppose you were traveling to Guangzhou (Canton), China, during the 1930's when Brave Orchid still lived there. Present an audiotaped travelogue describing what you saw. Show pictures if possible. **[Social Studies Link]**

Online Activity www.phlit.phschool.com

Guided Writing Lesson

Guide for Planning a Family Reunion

Many families hold organized reunions to bring family members living in distant places together for a visit. Such a reunion takes a lot of planning. Relatives in far-flung places must be contacted; travel routes must be suggested; a meeting place has to be chosen; menus must be planned. Create a guide in which you cover these essentials as well as any details that you think go into making a successful family reunion.

Writing Skills Focus: Explain a Procedure

In writing your guide, it's important to explain a procedure clearly.

- Use headings or spacing to make the main parts of the procedure clear. One main part might be "Compiling a Guest List," another might be "Arranging the Picnic," and so on.
- Divide each main part of the procedure into numbered or lettered steps.
- Include diagrams or graphic aids to clarify your information. For example, you might include a checklist to help readers chart their progress.

Prewriting List the main parts of the plan in an outline or on index cards organized in separate piles.

Drafting Include an introduction that states the purpose of reunions and your reunion plan; a body that uses subheadings, numerals, and other graphic aids; and a conclusion that sums up the key points of your plan.

Revising Make sure you have included all necessary steps and details, including appropriate information on organizing *who, what, where, when, why,* and *how.* Check that all steps are presented in logical order with headings, spacing, and numerals used to make the reading easy.

Idea Bank

Customizing for *Performance Levels*

Following are suggestions for matching Idea Bank topics with your students' performance levels:
Less Advanced Students: 1, 4
Average Students: 2, 6
More Advanced Students: 3, 5, 7

Customizing for *Learning Modalities*

Following are suggestions for matching Idea Bank topics with your students' learning modalities:
Verbal/Linguistic: 4, 5, 7
Logical/Mathematical: 5, 6
Visual/Spatial: 7

Guided Writing Lesson

For more instruction on prewriting, elaboration, and revision, see *Prentice Hall Writing and Grammar.*

Writing Lab CD-ROM

Have students complete the tutorial on Practical and Technical Writing. Follow these steps:

1. Refer students to the annotated models of a user's manual and a process explanation found in the About Practical and Technical Writing section.
2. Have students use the Chain of Events for technical writing activity to help them organize details about steps or instructions.
3. After they have drafted on the computer, students can use the Self-Evaluation Checklist for technical writing to guide revision.

✓ ASSESSMENT OPTIONS

Formal Assessment, Selection Test, pp. 286–288, and Assessment Resources Software. The selection test is designed so that it can be easily customized to the performance levels of your students.

Alternative Assessment, p. 65, includes options for less advanced students, more advanced students, verbal/linguistic learners, visual/spatial learners, and interpersonal learners.

PORTFOLIO ASSESSMENT

Use the following rubrics in the ***Alternative Assessment*** booklet to assess student writing:
Diary Entry: Expression Rubric, p. 109
Prequel: Fictional Narrative Rubric, p. 110
Character Analysis: Literary Analysis/Interpretation Rubric, p. 127
Guided Writing Lesson: How-to/Process Explanation Rubric, p. 115

Prepare and Engage

LESSON OBJECTIVES

1. **To develop vocabulary and word identification skills**
   - Build Vocabulary: Words From Spanish
   - Using the Word Bank: Synonyms or Antonyms?
   - Extending Word Study: Using Context (ATE)
2. **To use a variety of reading strategies to comprehend a short story**
   - Connect Your Experience
   - Reading Strategy: Identify With a Character
   - Idea Bank: Postcard Message
3. **To increase knowledge of other cultures and to connect common elements across cultures**
   - Connecting Themes Across Cultures (ATE)
   - Background for Understanding
4. **To express and support responses to the text**
   - Critical Thinking
   - Idea Bank: Personal Essay
   - Idea Bank: Set Design
5. **To analyze literary elements**
   - Literary Focus: Flashback
6. **To read to do research on self-selected and assigned topics**
   - Viewing and Representing Mini-Lesson (ATE)
   - Idea Bank: Multimedia Report
   - Idea Bank: Flowchart
7. **To plan, prepare, organize, and present literary interpretations**
   - Idea Bank: New Version
   - Idea Bank: Dialogue
8. **To use recursive writing processes to write pointers for travel safety**
   - Guided Writing Lesson
9. **To increase knowledge of the rules of grammar and usage**
   - Grammar and Style: Absolute Phrases

Test Preparation

Writing Skills: Grammar and Usage (ATE, p. 965)
The teaching tips and sample test item in this workshop support the instruction and practice in the unit workshop:
Writing Skills: Punctuation, Usage, and Sentence Structure (SE, p. 1143)

Guide for Interpreting

Featured in AUTHORS IN DEPTH Series

Julia Alvarez *(1950–)*

"I came into English as a ten-year-old from the Dominican Republic, and I consider this radical uprooting from my culture, my native language, my country, the reason I began writing," Julia Alvarez once explained.

Writing to Ease the Pain While moving to a new country changed her world forever, Alvarez quickly found her voice as a writer.

As a young adult, Alvarez found that writing helped her deal with the pain of trying to adjust to a new culture and language.

"In high school, I fell in love with how words can make you feel complete in a way that I hadn't felt complete since leaving the island," she said.

After graduating from college, where she was awarded several poetry prizes, Alvarez earned a masters degree in creative writing at Syracuse University. She went on to join the Kentucky Arts Commission's poetry-in-the-schools program. For two years, she traveled around Kentucky teaching poetry. She then held a variety of teaching jobs before settling in Vermont as a Professor of English at Middlebury College.

New Directions Alvarez's poetry often focuses on details of daily life as well as her Caribbean heritage. She has published two volumes of poetry, *Homecomings* (1984) and *The Other Side* (1995). After *Homecomings* was published, Alvarez began to focus on a new area of writing: fiction.

"My own island background was steeped in a tradition of storytelling that I wanted to explore in prose," Alvarez explained. The move to prose proved fruitful, for Alvarez has won fame for three semi-autobiographical novels rooted in Hispanic American tradition: *How the García Girls Lost Their Accents* (1991), *In the Time of the Butterflies* (1994), and *¡Yo!* (1997).

As the story "Antojos" illustrates, Alvarez has also shown that she is a talented short-story writer. Like her novels, "Antojos" tells the story of a Dominican woman who has settled in the United States. The story captures what happens when she revisits her homeland.

◆ Background for Understanding

SOCIAL STUDIES: JULIA ALVAREZ AND DOMINICAN POLITICS

Alvarez's homeland, the Dominican Republic, takes up the eastern two thirds of Hispaniola, an island that is part of the West Indies. The western third of the island is the country of Haiti.

The Dominican Republic won independence in 1844, after a successful rebellion against Haitian rule. Since then, however, the country has suffered through several dictatorships and frequent foreign domination. One of the most ruthless dictators was Rafael Trujillo, who ruled the country from 1930 until he was assassinated in 1961.

Julia Alvarez's father was part of the underground movement against Trujillo, and it was this involvement that forced the family to flee the country. Three months after they left, three of her father's co-conspirators were killed. Alvarez's emigration experience and the political turmoil of the time have influenced much of her writing.

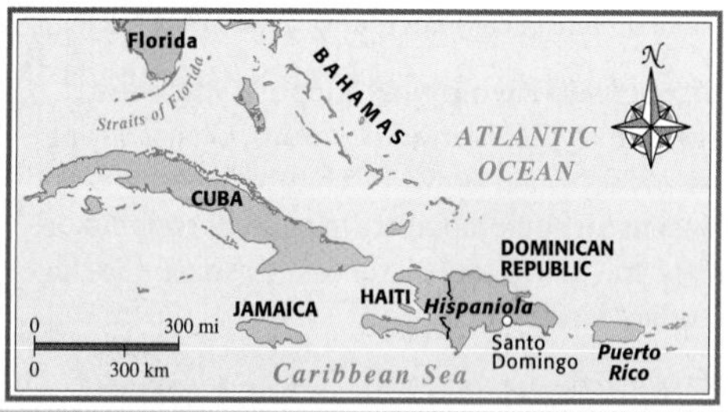

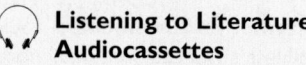

Prentice Hall Literature Program Resources

REINFORCE / RETEACH / EXTEND

Selection Support Pages
Build Vocabulary: Words From Spanish, p. 298
Grammar and Style: Absolute Phrases, p. 299
Reading Strategy: Identify With a Character, p. 300
Literary Focus: Flashback, p. 301

Strategies for Diverse Student Needs, Sequence Events, p. 66

Beyond Literature
Cross-Curricular Connection: World Languages, p. 66

Formal Assessment Selection Test, pp. 289–291; Assessment Resources Software

Alternative Assessment, p. 66

Writing and Language Transparencies
Outline Organizer, pp. 95–97

Listening to Literature Audiocassettes

Antojos

◆ Literature and Your Life

Connect Your Experience

In this story, the main character becomes fearful because she is unsure of the motives of two strangers. Have you ever been in a similar situation? Why are we more comfortable dealing with familiar people?

Journal Writing Think back to your first impression of someone whom you now know well. How much has your initial impression of that person changed? In what way is it the same?

Thematic Focus: Literature Confronts the Everyday

People are constantly confronted with conflict; we disagree with others or struggle to make decisions daily. Sometimes, an unforeseen event can put the resolution of even a small problem in doubt. The main character in "Antojos" faces such a situation.

◆ Literary Focus

Flashback

A **flashback** is an interruption in the chronological presentation of events in a story to present a scene or event from an earlier time. Flashbacks often provide valuable information about characters' backgrounds, personalities, and motives. When you come to a flashback in "Antojos," consider what it reveals about the main character.

◆ Build Vocabulary

Words From Spanish

This story contains many words that come to English from Spanish. For example, a *machete* (mə shet´ ē) is a large, heavy knife used to cut down vegetation. The word is taken directly from Spanish (pronounced mä che´ tā). It is a form of the Spanish word *macho*, meaning "sledge hammer."

Word Bank

Preview this list of words from the story.

dissuade
loath
appease
machetes
collusion
docile
enunciated

◆ Reading Strategy

Identify With a Character

You can often understand a literary work better if you **identify with a character** who appears in the work. Think about what you and the character have in common in terms of background, personality, attitudes, motives, or behavior. For example, as you read "Antojos," think about ways in which you are like the main character, Yolanda. List similarities in a chart like this one.

	Yolanda	Me
Background		
Personality		
Attitudes		
Motives		
Behavior		

◆ Grammar and Style

Absolute Phrases

An **absolute phrase** usually consists of a noun or noun phrase modified by a participle or participial phrase. It has no direct grammatical connection with any single word in the sentence; instead, it stands absolutely by itself and modifies the entire clause to which it is attached. Absolute phrases can open, interrupt, or conclude sentences and are always set off with commas, as in these sentences:

A bus came lurching around the curve, *the driver saluting.*

His friend bracing him, he pumped the jack vigorously.

Sometimes the participle is omitted as understood:

His friend (being) weary, they exchanged places.

Test Preparation Workshop

Writing Skills: Grammar and Usage The writing sections of many standardized tests require students to recognize and correct errors in grammar. Use the following sample test item to give students practice in this skill.

The latest sales reports indicate that the popularity of guavas are growing in the United States.

Choose the best way to rewrite the underlined section of the passage. If the underlined section needs no change, choose "Correct as is."

A of guavas were growing
B of guavas is growing
C of guavas was growing
D Correct as is

A does not agree with the subject. *C* is in the past tense, while the passage refers to the present. The verb *are* does not agree with the subject *popularity*, so *D* is incorrect. The correct choice is *B*.

Interest Grabber Like a travel diary, this story of a young woman's journey to her homeland is immediate and engaging. To entice travelers to visit particular places, tourism agents often show photographs and excerpt travel diaries. Invite your students into the world of the Dominican Republic by displaying some photos of the region and travel advertisements. Write these passages on the chalkboard:

"She hadn't had her favorite *antojo, guavas,* since her last trip seven years ago."

"She ate right on the spot, relishing the slightly bumpy feel of the skin in her hand, devouring the crunchy, sweet, white meat."

Ask students to describe journeys they have taken and identify moments they found enjoyable.

Connecting Themes Across Cultures

The main character in this story fears strangers because of the violence she witnessed during a revolution. Most students, however, will acknowledge that most cultures teach their children to be cautious of strangers for a variety of reasons. Point out to students that most cultures have cautionary fairy tales such as "Little Red Riding Hood" that reinforce the message of caution. Discuss with students folk literature for various cultures that communicates similar messages.

Customize for ***Less Proficient Readers***

Before students begin reading, review and explain the footnoted Spanish words.

Customize for ***AP Students***

Help these students to appreciate the subtle changes of mood Alvarez creates through her choice of words. Encourage students to keep a log of words that enhance story mood.

Customize for ***English Language Learners***

Students who are native Spanish speakers can enjoy the opportunity to help others—through pairing with both language learners and native English speakers—understand the Spanish words and Hispanic context of the story.

Develop Understanding

One-Minute Insight If students have ever taken a journey alone—near or far—they will recognize the inextricable mix of confidence, anticipation, and fear that permeates this story. The main character, Yolanda, has returned to her Caribbean island homeland intent on demonstrating her adult independence to the family. As she travels through the countryside, aware of the region's unpredictable political climate, Yolanda must decide whom to trust and whom to fear. By facing some risks and making choices, she begins to consider how high a price she is willing to pay for her independence.

▶Critical Viewing◀

❶ **Compare** The painting shows the fruit as colorful, ripe, and inviting. Yolanda also thinks of guavas as inviting, craving them as a much-enjoyed treat and sensual experience.

◆ Literature and Your Life

❷ Ask students to recall times when they have returned home, even from an evening out with friends. What emotions do they associate with home? *While students may mention warmth, familiarity, security, they may also focus on concern over family problems, sadness over changes they see, or anger over an aspect of the family's living situation.*

Customize for *Gifted/Talented Students*

Have students role-play the visit between Yolanda and her aunts. Encourage students to find prompts for their role play in Yolanda's reflections as she drives.

Antojos[1]

Julia Alvarez

Fruit Vendor, 1951, Olga Costa, Museo de Arte Moderno, Mexico

❶ ▲ **Critical Viewing** How is the artist's portrayal of fruit similar to Yolanda's feelings about guavas? **[Compare]**

For the first time since Yolanda had reached the hills, there was a shoulder on the left side of the narrow road. She pulled the car over out of a sense of homecoming: every other visit she had stayed with her family in the capital. ❷

1. **Antojos** (än tō´ hōs)

Humanities: Art

Fruit Vendor, 1951, Olga Costa, oil on canvas.

This painting vividly illustrates a fruit stand similar to those Yolanda passes in the story.

The artist, Olga Costa, was born in Leipzig, Germany, but had been a resident of Mexico since 1945. Largely self-taught, Costa's realistic style has been exhibited countless times during her years in Mexico and was ultimately honored by Mexico's National Art Prize in 1990. The artist died in 1993. *Fruit Vendor*, as it is titled here in English, bears a subtitle *Frutas Mexicanas (Mexican Fruits),* its original Spanish title.

Use these questions for discussion.

1. What elements of the painting capture the sensory images of the story setting? *The bright colors, bountiful quantities, and tropical nature of the fruits all reflect the vivid sensory images of the story setting.*
2. How would Yolanda likely feel about approaching this fruit vendor? *She would probably feel excited about finding her guavas and friendly toward the vendor.*

Once her own engine was off, she heard the sound of another motor, approaching, a pained roar as if the engine were falling apart. She
3 made out an undertow of men's voices. Quickly, she got back into the car, locked the door, and pulled off the shoulder, hugging her right side of the road.

—Just in time too. A bus came lurching around the curve, obscuring her view with a belching of exhaust, the driver saluting or warning with a series of blasts on his horn. It was an old army bus, the official name brushed over with paint that didn't quite match the regulation gray. The passengers saw her only at the last moment, and all up and down her side of the bus, men poked out of the windows, hooting and yelling, waving purple party flags, holding out bottles and beckoning to her. She speeded up and left them behind, the small compact climbing easily up the snakey highway, its well-oiled hum a gratifying sound after the hullabaloo of the bus.

She tried the radio again, but all she could tune to was static even here on the summit hills. She would have to wait until she got to the coast to hear news of the hunger march in the capital. Her family had been worried that trouble would break out, for the march had been scheduled on the anniversary of the failed revolution nineteen years ago today. A huge turnout was expected. She bet that bus she had just passed had been delayed by breakdowns on its way to the capital. In fact, earlier on the road when she had first set out, Yolanda had passed buses and truckloads of men, drinking and shouting slogans. It crossed her mind that her family had finally agreed to loan
4 her a car because they knew she'd be far safer on the north coast than in the capital city where revolutions always broke out.

The hills began to plane out into a high plateau, the road widening. Left and right, roadside stands began appearing. Yolanda slowed down and kept an eye out for guavas, supposedly in season this far north. Piled high on wooden stands were fruits she hadn't seen in so many years: pinkish-yellow mangoes, and tamarind pods oozing their rich sap, and small cashew fruits strung on a rope to keep them from bruising each other. There were little brown packets of roasted cashews and bars of milk fudge wrapped in waxed paper and tied with a string, the color of which told what filling was inside the bar. Strips of meat, buzzing with flies, hung from the windows of butcher stalls. An occasional display of straw hats and baskets and hammocks told that tourists 5
sometimes did pass by here. Looking at the stores spread before her, it was hard to believe the poverty the organizers of the march kept discussing on the radio. There seemed to be plenty here to eat—except for guavas.

In the capital, her aunts had plied her with what she most craved after so many years 6
away. "Any little *antojo*, you must tell us!" They wanted to spoil her, so she'd stay on in her nativeland before she forgot where she had come from. "What exactly does it mean, *antojo*?" Yolanda asked. Her aunts were proven right: After so many years away, their niece was losing her Spanish.

"An *antojo*—" The aunts exchanged quizzical looks. "How to put it? An *antojo* is like a crav- 7
ing for something you have to eat."

A cousin blew out her cheeks. "Calories."

An *antojo*, one of the older aunts continued, was a very old Spanish word from before "your United States was thought of," she added tartly. In the countryside some *campesinos*[2] still used the word to mean possession by an island spirit demanding its due.

Her island spirit certainly was a patient soul, Yolanda joked. She hadn't had her favorite *antojo*, guavas, since her last trip seven years ago. Well, on this trip, her aunts promised, Yoyo could eat guavas to her heart's content. But when the gardener was summoned, he

---

2. ***campesinos*** (käm´ pe sē´ nōs): "Poor farmers; simple rural dwellers" (Spanish).

◆ Reading Strategy

3 Identify With a Character While she got out of the car for sentimental reasons, she was quickly forced back in by the dangers she perceived. Ask students to imagine Yolanda's feelings at this moment. *She may have been scared or bewildered.*

◆ Critical Thinking

4 Compare and Contrast How are Yolanda's feelings about taking risks different than those of her family in the capital? *Students should note that Yolanda's family is concerned about her safety, both in the capital and on the journey. Yolanda, on the surface, seems unconcerned about her journey. She does however, respond quickly to protect herself from the oncoming bus.*

◆ Build Vocabulary

5 Words From Spanish Ask students to find the word in this sentence that comes from the Spanish *hamaca,* meaning a swinging couch or bed, often woven of netting or fabric. The word is *hammock*.

◆ Literary Focus

6 Flashback Point out the opening modifier "In the capital" and explain that it signals readers of the coming flashback by indicating a change in location. If the events described didn't happen where Yolanda is now, they must have occurred earlier. Urge students to pay particular attention to the flashback—questioning why Yolanda recalls the conversation with her aunts.

◆ Reading Strategy

7 Identify With a Character Prompt students to think of times when they've craved something, especially something linked to a special place in their lives. Can they identify with Yolanda's desire for guavas? Invite students to name their own *antojos,* or cravings, and use these to explain their answer. *Students should be able to identify easily with Yolanda's craving, naming a range of food cravings as examples.*

Block Scheduling Strategies

Consider these suggestions to take advantage of extended class time:

- Have students complete the journal activity in Literature and Your Life (p. 964). As a class, discuss students responses.
- Introduce the Build Vocabulary lesson (p. 965), then have students complete the Build Vocabulary page (p. 298), in ***Selection Support.*** Invite any native Spanish speakers to share additional words from Spanish.
- Use the author biography and the Background For Understanding (p. 964) to give students insight into Alvarez and her writing.
- Have groups brainstorm ideas for the New Version or Multimedia Idea Bank activities (p. 975).
- Begin the Guided Writing Lesson (p. 975) with a discussion of safety measures Yolanda might have employed.
- Invite students to learn more about the Dominican Republic and Julia Alvarez on the Internet.

Customize for
Less Proficient Readers

❶ Explain to these students that one way to remain focused when reading a story is to make predictions about story outcomes. Urge students to use information from the text and their own experiences to predict whether Yolanda will face difficulties up north by herself. *Students may predict that Yolanda will prove her independence and confidence well-placed by traveling with no problems. Alternatively, they may guess that her aunts' concern is a signal that Yolanda's confidence is misplaced.*

◆ Literary Focus

❷ **Flashback** It reveals that Yolanda and her aunts come from very different worlds and have contrasting views and expectations.

◆ Critical Thinking

❸ **Infer** Ask students: What can you infer about Yolanda's family from this description of an estate similar to theirs? How might her family's social standing affect Yolanda's expectations of the people she will meet in the countryside? *Students should infer that Yolanda's family is wealthy, that the wealthy feel unsafe in the capital and even in the countryside. They may also infer that Yolanda is likely to be somewhat mistrustful of the common people, despite her claims to the contrary.*

Customize for
AP Readers

❹ In this passage, Alvarez alludes to "troubles in the capital." Offer these students the opportunity to learn more about the real-life political history of the Dominican Republic. Have them research one or more key figures in the nation's struggle for independence.

Extending Word Study

Context Have students read the text on this page with the word *cantina*. Although students may know the meaning of this word, discuss the context clues that reveal the word's meaning. As students identify words such as *menu, poster, thatched roof, thirstier,* write the words in a concept map on the board. Then have students write a definition of a *cantina* using the context clues. Finally, have students illustrate the *cantina* described in the story using the context clues.

wasn't so sure. Guavas were no longer in season, at least not in the hotter lowlands of the south. Maybe up north, the chauffeur could pick her up some on his way back from some errand. Yolanda took this opportunity to inform her aunts of her plans: she could pick the guavas herself when she went up north in a few days.

❶ —She was going up north? By herself? A woman alone on the road! "This is not the States." Her old aunts had tried to dissuade her. "Anything can happen." When Yolanda challenged them, "What?" they came up with boogeymen stories that made her feel as if she were talking to china dolls.[3] Haitian hougans[4] and Communist kidnappers. "And Martians?" Yolanda wanted to tease them. They had led such sheltered lives, riding from one safe place to another in their air-conditioned cars.

> ❷ **◆ Literary Focus**
> What does this flashback reveal about Yolanda and her aunts?

❸ ❹ She had left the fruit stands behind her and was approaching a compound very much like her family's in the capital. The underbrush stopped abruptly at a high concrete wall, topped with broken bottle glass. Parked at the door was a chocolate brown Mercedes. Perhaps the owners had come up to their country home for the weekend to avoid the troubles in the capital?

Just beyond the estate, Yolanda came upon a small village—ALTAMIRA in rippling letters on the corrugated tin roof of the first little house. It was a little cluster of houses on either side of the road, a good place to stretch her legs before what she'd heard was a steep and slightly (her aunts had warned "very") dangerous descent to the coast. Yolanda pulled up at a cantina, the thatched roof held up by several posts. Instead of a menu, there was a yellowing, grimy poster for Palmolive soap tacked on one of the posts with a picture of a blonde woman under a spraying shower, her head thrown back in seeming ecstasy, her mouth opened in a wordless cry. ("Palmolive"? Yolanda wondered.) She felt even thirstier and grimier looking at this lathered beauty after her hot day on the road.

An old woman emerged at last from a shack behind the cabana, buttoning up a torn housedress, and followed closely by a little boy, who kept ducking behind her whenever Yolanda smiled at him. Asking him his name just drove him further into the folds of the old woman's skirt.

"You must excuse him, Doña,"[5] she apologized. "He's not used to being among people." But Yolanda knew the old woman meant, not the people in the village, but the people with money who drove through Altamira to the beaches on the coast. "Your name," the old woman repeated, as if Yolanda hadn't asked him in Spanish. The little boy mumbled at the ground. "Speak up!" the old woman scolded, but her voice betrayed pride when she spoke up for him. "This little know-nothing is Jose Duarte Sanchez y Mella Garcia."

Yolanda laughed. Not only were those a lot of names for such a little boy, but they certainly were momentous: the surnames of the three liberators of the country!

"Can I serve the Doña in any way?" the woman asked. Yolanda gave the tree line beyond the woman's shack a glance. "You think you might have some guavas around?"

The old woman's face scrunched up. "Guavas?" she murmured and thought to herself a second. "Why, they're all around, Doña. But I can't say as I've seen any."

"With your permission—" Jose Duarte had joined a group of little boys who had come out

3. **china dolls:** Old-fashioned, delicate dolls made of fragile high-quality porcelain or ceramic ware.
4. **Haitian hougans** (o͞o gänz′): Voodoo priests or cult leaders.
5. **Doña** (dō′ nyä): "Madam" (Spanish).

Cross-Curricular Connection: Geography

The Terrain of the Dominican Republic
The capital of the Dominican Republic, Santo Domingo, sits on the southern coast. To reach the north from this city, Yolanda would have to drive across the Cordillera Central, a highland area containing the West Indies' highest mountain (the Pico Duarte at 10,417 ft./3,175 m). While the transportation system in the Dominican Republic is generally considered adequate, this mountainous center is challenging to motorists. A route through the mountains would be slow though quite scenic. In fact, the name of village at which Yolanda stops—Altamira—can be translated as "View from Above."

Discuss with students how the experience of driving through the mountains on a questionable road might affect Yolanda's sense of security.

of nowhere and were milling around the car, boasting how many automobiles they had ridden in. At Yolanda's mention of guavas, he sprung forward, pointing across the road towards the summit of the western hills. "I know where there's a whole grove of them." Behind him, his little companions nodded.

"Go on, then!" His grandmother stamped her foot as if she were scatting a little animal. "Get the Doña some."

A few boys dashed across the road and disappeared up a steep path on the hillside, but before Jose could follow, Yolanda called him back. She wanted to go along too. The little boy looked towards his grandmother, unsure of what to think. The old woman shook her head. The Doña would get hot, her nice clothes would get all dirty. Jose would get the Doña as many guavas as she was wanting.

"But they taste so much better when you've picked them yourself," Yolanda's voice had an edge, for suddenly, it was as if the woman had turned into the long arm of her family, keeping her away from seeing her country on her own.

5 **◆ Reading Strategy** Can you identify with Yolanda's feelings at this point in the story? Why or why not?

6 The few boys who had stayed behind with Jose had congregated around the car. Each one claimed to be guarding it for the Doña. It occurred to Yolanda that there was a way to make this a treat all the way around. "What do you say we take the car?"

"*Sí, Sí, Sí,*"[6] the boys screamed in a riot of excitement.

The old woman hushed them but agreed that was not a bad idea if the Doña insisted on going. There was a dirt road up ahead she could follow a ways and then cross over onto the road that was paved all the way to the coffee barns. The woman pointed south in the direction of the big house. Many workers took that short cut to work.

They piled into the car, half a dozen boys in the back, and Jose as co-pilot in the passenger seat beside Yolanda. They turned onto a bumpy road off the highway, which got bumpier and bumpier, and climbed up into wilder, more desolate country. Branches scraped the sides and pebbles pelted the underside of the car. Yolanda wanted to turn back, but there was no room to maneuver the car around. Finally, with a great 7
snapping of twigs and thrashing of branches across the windshield, as if the countryside were loath to release them, the car burst forth onto smooth pavement and the light of day. On either side of the road were groves of guava trees. Among them, the boys who had gone ahead on foot were already pulling down branches and shaking loose a rain of guavas. The fruit was definitely in season.

For the next hour or so, Yolanda and her crew scavenged the grove, the best of the pick going into the beach basket Yolanda had gotten out of the trunk, with the exception of the ones she ate right on the spot, relishing the slightly 8
bumpy feel of the skin in her hand, devouring the crunchy, sweet, white meat. The boys watched her, surprised by her odd hunger.

Yolanda and Jose, partners, wandered far from the path that cut through the grove. Soon they were bent double to avoid getting entangled in the thick canopy of branches overhead. Each addition to the basket caused a spill from the stash already piled high above the brim. Finally, it was a case of abandoning the treasure in order to cart some of it home. With Jose hugging the basket to himself and Yolanda parting the wayward branches in front of them, they headed back toward the car.

When they finally cleared the thicket of guava branches, the sun was low on the

6. ***Sí, Sí, Sí*** (sē): "Yes, Yes, Yes" (Spanish).

◆ Build Vocabulary

dissuade (di swād′) *v.*: Convince someone not to do something; discourage

loath (lōth) *adj.*: Reluctant

◆ Reading Strategy

5 Identify With a Character Students will likely say that they can identify with Yolanda, citing times when parents or other authority figures have restricted their independence, even from a distance.

◆ Critical Thinking

6 Analyze Ask students: Why do you think the boys are so concerned about the car? What does this suggest about their experience with cars? *Students should recognize that the boys want desperately to ride in the car. This suggests that cars are not common in their lives. The boys may also be concerned for the car's safety in an unstable surrounding.*

Customize for *Bodily/Kinesthetic Learners*

7 Have these students use classroom materials to generate a life-size representation of the story setting, focusing especially on the crowded car traveling through a restricted roadway. Invite students to take turns experiencing the physical sensations of constraint. Discuss how such a situation might affect Yolanda's sense of independence and security.

◆ Critical Thinking

8 Connect Invite students to put themselves in Yolanda's position. What might her "odd hunger" symbolize? *Students may suggest that Yolanda's hunger symbolizes her desire for independence or her hunger for a connection to her homeland.*

Beyond the Classroom

Community Connection

Estates Point out to students that in the story setting, the big house provides a focal point for the community. Such agricultural estates often date back centuries to a time when the landed and wealthy offered protection and patronage to workers in exchange for their loyalty and poorly-paid efforts. Have interested students learn about similar relationships in your community, or state. For example ask students to consider relationships between workers/citizens and wealthy families or important businesses. Have these businesses or families funded community services? What is expected in return for such contributions? Encourage students to consider the advantages and disadvantages to both patrons and workers/citizens in such a relationship. *Advantages may include funding for arts or charities that improves the quality of life. Disadvantages may include a sense of elitism or dependence that inspires jealousy, anger, or political obligation.*

◆ *Literature and Your Life*

❶ Point out Yolanda's feelings of regret. Ask students to recall times when they pursued a desire only to later regret their course of action. How did they resolve the situation? *Students may mention skipped homework or practices, money spent unwisely, or friendship choices they later regretted. They should be able to describe new choices made or corrective actions taken.*

◆ Critical Thinking

❷ **Evaluate** Ask students to evaluate Yolanda's success at being independent. *Students should note that at the first sign of trouble, Yolanda needs help. On the other hand, she doesn't panic but quickly implements a plan.*

Customize for
Musical/Rhythmic Learners

❸ To help these students understand Yolanda's moment of connection to her homeland, invite them to listen as you or a student reads this passage aloud. Urge students to engage all their senses to see, hear, and feel Yolanda's surroundings and to experience her emotions.

◆ Reading Strategy

❹ **Identify With a Character** Challenge students, both male and female, to consider how they would react in Yolanda's situation. As a class, compare the reactions of male and female students. *All students should appreciate Yolanda's feelings of vulnerability at this moment. Female students may identify more strongly with her, while male students may feel less physically vulnerable.*

western horizon. There was no sign of the other boys. "They must have gone to round up the goats," Jose observed.

Yolanda glanced at her watch: it was past six o'clock. She'd never make the north coast by nightfall, but at least she could get off the dangerous mountain roads while it was still light. She hurried Jose back to the car, where they found a heap of guavas the other boys had left behind on the shoulder of the road. Enough guavas to appease even the greediest island spirit for life!

They packed the guavas in the trunk quickly and climbed in, but the car had not gone a foot before it lurched forward with a horrible hobble. Yolanda closed her eyes and laid her head down on the wheel, then glanced over at Jose. The way his eyes were searching the inside of the car for a clue as to what could have happened, she could tell he didn't know how to change a flat tire either.

❶ It was no use regretting having brought the car up that bad stretch of road. The thing to do now was to act quickly. Soon the sun would set and night would fall swiftly, no lingering dusk as in the States. She explained to Jose that they had a flat tire and had to hike back to town and send for help down the road to the big house. Whoever tended to the brown Mercedes would know how to change the tire on her car.

"With your permission," Jose offered meekly. He pointed down the paved road. "This goes directly to the big house." The Doña could just wait in the car and he would be back in no time with someone from the Miranda place.

❷ She did not like the idea of staying behind in the car, but Jose could probably go and come back much quicker without her. "All right," she said to the boy. "I'll tell you what." She pointed to her watch. It was almost six thirty. "If you're back by the time this hand is over here, I'll give you"—she held up one finger "a dollar." The boy's mouth fell open. In no time, he had shot out of his side of the car and was headed at a run toward the Miranda place. Yolanda climbed out as well and walked down a pace, until the boy had disappeared in one of the turnings of the road. ❷

❸ Suddenly, the countryside was so very quiet. She looked up at the purple sky. A breeze was blowing through the grove, rustling the leaves, so they whispered like voices, something indistinct. Here and there a light flickered on the hills, a *campesino* living out his solitary life. This was what she had been missing without really knowing that she was missing it all these years. She had never felt at home in the States, never, though she knew she was lucky to have a job, so she could afford her own life and not be run by her family. But independence didn't have to be exile. She could come home, home to places like these very hills, and live here on her own terms.

❹ Heading back to the car, Yolanda stopped. She had heard footsteps in the grove. Could Jose be back already? Branches were being thrust aside, twigs snapped. Suddenly, a short, dark man, and then a slender, light-skin man emerged from a footpath on the opposite side of the grove from the one she and Jose had scavenged. They wore ragged work clothes stained with patches of sweat; their faces were drawn and tired. Yolanda's glance fell on the machetes that hung from their belts.

The men's faces snapped awake from their stupor at the sight of her. They looked beyond her at the car. "Yours?" the darker man spoke first. It struck her, even then, as an absurd question. Who else's would it be here in the middle of nowhere?

"Is there some problem?" the darker man spoke up again. The taller one was looking her up and down with interest. They were now both in front of her on the road, blocking her escape. Both—she had looked them up and down as well—were strong and quite capable of catching her if she made a run for the Miranda's. Not that she could have moved, for her legs seemed suddenly to have been hammered into the ground beneath her. She thought of explaining

Cross-Curricular Connection: Science

Raising Mangoes The warm, tropical climate of the Dominican Republic is well suited to growing fruits such as guavas, mangoes, tamarind pods, and cashew nuts. In fact, mangoes are one of the nation's major agricultural products. Like many tropical fruits, mangoes are evergreen while also extremely sensitive to cold temperatures. Grown widely in India and other parts of Asia, as well as tropical parts of Central and South America, mangoes range from plum-size to almost five pounds. A reddish-yellow to green skin covers orangy-yellow flesh and a single large stone. Mangoes contain vitamins A, C, and D. Unfortunately, they are highly perishable and therefore difficult and expensive to transport.

If possible, offer students the opportunity to taste a mango. Otherwise, display pictures of the fruit and some foods prepared with it. Discuss how its succulence suggests the tropical setting of the story.

> ◆ *Literature and Your Life*
>
> How do you react to situations in which you feel a threat? Do you think you would react in a different manner than Yolanda? Explain.

5 that she was just out for a drive before dinner at the big house, so that these men would think someone knew where she was, someone would come looking for her if they tried to carry her off. But she found she could not speak. Her tongue felt as if it'd been stuffed in her mouth like a rag to keep her quiet.

The men exchanged a look—it seemed to Yolanda of collusion. Then the shorter, darker one spoke up again, "Señorita,[7] are you all right?" He peered at her. The darkness of his complexion in the growing darkness of the evening made it difficult to distinguish an expression. He was no taller than Yolanda, but he gave the impression of being quite large, for he was broad and solid, like something not yet completely carved out of a piece of wood. His companion was tall and of a rich honey-brown color that matched his honey-brown eyes. Anywhere else, Yolanda would have found him extremely attractive, but here on a lonely road, with the sky growing darker by seconds, his good looks seemed dangerous, a lure to catch her off her guard.

"Can we help you?" the shorter man repeated.

The handsome one smiled knowingly. Two long, deep dimples appeared like gashes on either side of his mouth. "*Americana*," he said to
6 the other in Spanish, pointing to the car. "She doesn't understand."

The darker man narrowed his eyes and studied Yolanda a moment. "*Americana*?" he asked her as if not quite sure what to make of her.

She had been too frightened to carry out any strategy, but now a road was opening before her. She laid her hand on her chest—she could feel her pounding heart—and nodded. Then, as if the admission itself loosened her tongue, she explained in English how it came that she was on a back road by herself, her craving for guavas, her never having learned to change a flat. The two men stared at her, uncomprehendingly, rendered docile by her gibberish. Strangely enough, it soothed her to hear herself speaking something they could not understand. She thought of something her teacher used to say to her when as a young immigrant girl she 7 was learning English, "Language is power." It was her only defense now.

Yolanda made the motions of pumping. The darker man looked at the other, who had shown better luck at understanding the foreign lady. But his companion shrugged, baffled as well. "I'll show you," Yolanda waved for them to follow her. And suddenly, as if after pulling and pulling at roots, she had finally managed to yank them free of the soil they had clung to, she found she could move her own feet forward to the car. 8

The small group stood staring at the sagging tire a moment, the two men kicking at it as if punishing it for having failed the Señorita. They squatted by the passenger's side, conversing in low tones. Yolanda led them to the rear of the car, where the men lifted the spare out of its sunken nest—then set to work, fitting the interlocking pieces of the jack, unpacking the tools from the deeper hollows of the trunk. They laid their machetes down on the side of the road,

> ### ◆ Build Vocabulary
>
> **appease** (ə pēz′) *v.*: Satisfy
>
> **machetes** (mə shet′ ēz) *n.*: Large heavy knives with broad blades, used to clear overgrown paths or cut down vegetation
>
> **collusion** (kə lo͞o′ zhən) *n.*: Secret agreement; conspiracy
>
> **docile** (däs′ əl) *adj.*: Easy to direct or manage; obedient

---

7. **Señorita** (se′ nyō rē′ tä): "Miss" (Spanish).

◆ *Literature and Your Life*

5 Students may say they become aggressive, creative, withdrawn, clumsy, or panicky. Some will identify with Yolanda's responses, while others will find her fears unnecessary.

◆ Critical Thinking

6 **Interpret** Ask students to question why Yolanda doesn't answer the men. *Students should recognize that Yolanda is so frightened she cannot speak.*

Customize for *English Language Learners*

7 Read aloud this passage containing the statement "Language is power." Ask students to use their own experiences to confirm or refute this statement. Discuss how their growing knowledge of English might help them navigate situations such as Yolanda's, and explore whether there are ever times it may seem useful to minimize their developing expertise.

◆ Critical Thinking

8 **Evaluate** Ask students to determine whether Yolanda should have feared these men. *Students may say that the men prove to be helpful and not dangerous. However, Yolanda did not know that they would help her and had every reason to be frightened.*

Cultural Connection

Language Most people living in the Dominican Republic speak Spanish, though there are a noticeable number of immigrants from neighboring Haiti who speak a form of French. As people move about the world easily, many nations lack this cohesion of languages. In the United States, for example, though the principal language is English, at least 12.5 percent of the population speaks another language. Over half of these non-native English speakers speak Spanish.

When entering a U.S. school, a young immigrant girl like Yolanda likely had to learn English quickly in order to keep up. Today, many school systems offer instruction in students' primary languages until they are proficient in English.

Ask students to develop proposals for improving communication among people of all cultures. Would an international language, which all children must learn, be appropriate or might this limit children's sense of cultural identity? Encourage students to debate this issue.

◆ Critical Thinking

❶ Compare and Contrast Challenge students to describe the first impression Yolanda had about the men and their motivations. Ask them to distinguish that idea from the reality of the two men's behavior. *She originally thought they would harm her; instead, one of them is hurt in the process of helping Yolanda.*

◆ Reading Strategy

❷ Identify With a Character Ask students how they react when thanked for a favor. Urge them to identify with the two men and consider whether they would respond as the men have to Yolanda's offer. *Students may say they find receiving thanks, especially with money, uncomfortable. Others may say the men were justified in accepting thanks and that they would personally feel comfortable accepting the money.*

Customize for *Interpersonal Learners*

❸ Draw these students' attention to the conversation Jose reports having with the Mirandas. Challenge students to role-play that dialogue with a partner, brainstorming first about the likely behaviors and comments of the interaction.

out of the way. Yolanda turned on the headlights to help them see in the growing darkness. Above the small group, the sky was purple with twilight.

There was a problem with the jack. It squeaked and labored, but the car would not rise. The shorter man squirmed his way underneath and placed the mechanism deeper under the bowels of the car. There, he pumped vigorously, his friend bracing him by holding him down by the ankles. Slowly, the car rose until the wheel hung suspended. When the man came out from under the car, his hand was bloody where his knuckles had scraped against the pavement.

❶ Yolanda pointed to the man's hand. She had been sure that if any blood were going to be spilled tonight, it would be hers. She offered him the towel she kept draped on her car seat to absorb her perspiration. But he waved it away and sucked his knuckles to make the bleeding stop.

Once the flat had been replaced with the spare, the two men lifted the deflated tire into the trunk and put away the tools. They handed Yolanda her keys. There was still no sign of Jose and the Miranda's. Yolanda was relieved. As she had waited, watching the two men hard at work, she had begun to dread the boy's return with help. The two men would realize she spoke Spanish. It was too late to admit that she had tricked them, to explain she had done so only because she thought her survival was on the line. The least she could do now was to try and repay them, handsomely, for their trouble.

"I'd like to give you something," she began reaching for the purse she'd retrieved from the trunk. The English words sounded hollow on her tongue. She rolled up a couple of American bills and offered them to the men. The shorter man held up his hand. Yolanda could see where the blood had dried dark streaks on his palm. "No, no, Señorita. *Nuestro placer.*"[8] Our pleasure.

❷ Yolanda turned to the other man, who had struck her as more pliant than his sterner companion. "Please," she urged the bills on him. But he too looked down at the ground with the bashfulness she had observed in Jose of country people not wanting to offend. She felt the poverty of her response and stuffed the bills quickly into his pocket.

The two men picked up their machetes and raised them to their shoulders like soldiers their guns. The tall man motioned towards the big house. "*Directo, directo,*"[9] he <u>enunciated</u> the words carefully. Yolanda looked in the direction of his hand. In the faint light of what was left of day, she could barely make out the road ahead. It was as if the guava grove had overgrown into the road and woven its mat of branches so securely and tightly in all directions, she would not be able to escape.

But finally, she was off! While the two men waited a moment on the shoulder to see if the tire would hold, Yolanda drove a few yards, poking her head out the window before speeding up. "*Gracias!*"[10] she called, and they waved, appreciatively, at the foreign lady making an effort in their native tongue. When she looked for them in her rear-view mirror, they had disappeared into the darkness of the guava grove.

Just ahead, her lights described the figure of a small boy: Jose was walking alone, listlessly, as if he did not particularly want to get to where he was going.

Yolanda leaned over and opened the door for him. The small overhead light came on; she saw that the boy's face was streaked with tears.

"Why, what's wrong, Jose?"

❸ The boy swallowed hard. "They would not come. They didn't believe me." He took little breaths between words to keep his tears at bay. He had lost his chance at a whole dollar. "And the guard, he said if I didn't stop telling stories, he was going to whip me."

"What did you tell him, Jose?"

8. ***Nuestro placer*** (no͞o es´ trō plä ser´): "Our pleasure" (Spanish).

9. ***Directo, directo*** (dē rek´ tō): "Straight, straight" (Spanish).

10. ***Gracias*** (grä´ sē äs): "Thank you" (Spanish).

Viewing and Representing Mini-Lesson

Set Design

This mini-lesson supports the Researching and Representing activity in the Idea Bank on p. 975.

Introduce the Concept Discuss with students that a set design is more than just a drawing, it is a floor plan that shows the spatial relationships between parts of the set.

Develop the Background Give students graph paper and show them how the squares can be used to designate a scale for the set design. Show students how to create an aerial view by using the classroom as an example. Use symbols and shapes to indicate placement of desks, shelves, etc. Then, have students work in groups to discuss how elements from the story can be represented.

Apply the Information Have students work in groups or independently to create their set designs.

Assess the Outcome Evaluate students on how effectively they use details from the story in their set designs. Assess also that students have used an appropriate scale for the parts of the set. Allow time for students to share their set designs and offer one another suggestions.

(3) "I told him you had broken your car and you needed help fixing it."

She should have gone along with Jose to the Miranda's. Given all the trouble in the country, they would be suspicious of a boy coming to their door at nightfall with some story about a lady on a back road with a broken car. "Don't you worry, Jose," Yolanda patted the boy. She could feel the bony shoulder through the thin fabric of his worn shirt. "You can still have your dollar. You did your part."

But the shame of being suspected of lying seemed to have obscured any immediate pleasure he might feel in her offer. Yolanda tried to distract him by asking what he would buy with his money, what he most craved, thinking that on a subsequent trip, she might bring him his little *antojo*. But Jose Duarte Sanchez y Mella (4) said nothing, except a bashful thank you when she left him off at the cantina with his promised dollar. In the glow of the headlights, Yolanda made out the figure of the old woman in the black square of her doorway, waving good-bye. Above the picnic table on a near post, the Palmolive woman's skin shone; her head was thrown back, her mouth opened as if she were calling someone over a great distance.

◆ Build Vocabulary

enunciated (ē nun´ sē āt´əd) *v.*: Pronounced; stated precisely

Guide for Responding

◆ Literature and Your Life

Reader's Response Did this story surprise you in any way? Explain.

Thematic Focus How does a commonplace annoyance like a flat tire become an opportunity for highlighting the kindness of strangers?

Journal Entry Put yourself in Yolanda's place and write the journal entry she might have written about her adventure.

☑ Check Your Comprehension

1. What warnings do family members give Yolanda?
2. What are *antojos*?
3. (a) What deal with Yolanda prompts Jose to go with her? (b) What happens to that deal?
4. Summarize what happens after the car gets a flat tire.

◆ Critical Thinking

INTERPRET

1. (a) How is Yolanda different from her aunts? (b) How is she different from the men who change her flat tire? **[Compare and Contrast]**
2. (a) Why does Yolanda pretend she has no island background? (b) Why is she suspicious of the two men? **[Analyze]**
3. What theme do you think the story title stresses? **[Connect]**
4. What might the Palmolive poster on p. 968 and p. 973 symbolize? **[Interpret]**

EVALUATE

5. Are Yolanda's suspicions of the men warranted? Cite details to support your evaluation. **[Evaluate]**
6. Does Yolanda learn or grow in the story? Explain. **[Assess]**

Beyond the Selection

FURTHER READING

Other Works by Julia Alvarez

The Other Side
In the Time of the Butterflies
How the Garcia Girls Lost Their Accents

Other Works With the Themes of Independence/Homecoming

"Initiation," C. Mattingly
"The Homecoming," Laurence Yep

We suggest that you preview these works before recommending them to students.

INTERNET

You may find additional information about Alvarez or the Dominican Republic on the Internet. We suggest the following site. Please be aware, however, that sites may have changed since this information was published.

For an autobiography and bibliography of Julia Alvarez, visit **http://www.middlebury.edu/~english/facpub/Alv-autobio.html**

We *strongly recommend* that you preview sites before you send students to them.

Customize for *Less Proficient Readers*

(4) Verify that these students understand *antojos* as it was defined earlier in the story. Explain that here Jose's *antojo* wouldn't be guavas but something of *his* choosing.

Reinforce and Extend

Answers

◆ Literature and Your Life

Reader's Response Encourage students to analyze their reactions.

Thematic Focus We normally interact with only those people we know. For some, a flat tire seems to break down the invisible walls between strangers.

☑ Check Your Comprehension

1. They tell her not to go north by herself.
2. *Antojos* are cravings.
3. (a) She offers him a ride in her car. (b) With several other boys, they pick guavas and return to a car with a flat tire.
4. Jose goes to get help and Yolanda waits in the car. A group of men approach Yolanda. Although she feels threatened by them, they fix her tire.

◆ Critical Thinking

1. (a) She lives in America, she is young, and she is more adventurous than her aunts. (b) She imagines strangers to be dangerous; they do not. They know how to fix a flat; she does not.
2. (a) Yolanda plays "tourist" to elicit sympathy and, perhaps, save her life. (b) She thinks they want to hurt her.
3. *Antojos,* while technically referring to food cravings, can also refer to the emotional need to belong, to succeed, or to be independent.
4. The poster represents a lifestyle that many in the Dominican countryside do not have.
5. Possible response: While they appear strong and appear to Yolanda as frightening, their actions prove her first impressions wrong.
6. Possible response: Yolanda grows because she learns not to make snap judgments about people. She may also have learned to consider the advice of others.

Answers

◆ Reading Strategy

1. (a) and (b) Students should support their answers but may focus on Yolanda's main character traits: stubbornness, ability to focus on a goal, and fearful reaction to threatening situations.
2. Students should explain their answers.

◆ Build Vocabulary

Using Words From Spanish

1. guava
2. canteen
3. It is probably a small store since the context shows it has an advertisement but no menu.

Using the Word Bank

1. synonym
2. antonym
3. antonym
4. synonym
5. synonym
6. antonym
7. antonym

◆ Literary Focus

1. The flashback shows that Yolanda's family employs a gardener and a chauffeur, suggesting a high social and economic status.
2. It suggests that she takes the trip in part to prove her aunts wrong.

◆ Grammar and Style

1. the official name brushed over with paint that didn't quite match the regulation gray
2. the small compact climbing easily up the snakey highway
3. the thatched roof held up by several posts
4. the best of the pick going into the beach basket
5. the two men kicking it as if punishing it

Writing Application

Sample response: When I was three, my parents introduced me to ice skating. I screamed when they walked me toward the ice, *my ankles wiggling beneath me*. My parents seemed astonished, *my mother staring in quiet surprise*. Instead of skating, I watched as others glided around the satin ring, *their faces glowing with the cold.*

Guide for Responding *(continued)*

◆ Reading Strategy

Identify With a Character

When you **identify with the story's main character**, you imagine yourself in the situation the story presents. At the same time, you consider any similarities in your backgrounds, personalities, attitudes, motives, and behavior.

1. (a) What would you identify as the chief similarities between yourself and Yolanda? (b) What are the chief differences?

2. Do you think you would have reacted as she did to the two men who came by when she had the flat tire? Explain.

◆ Build Vocabulary

Using Words From Spanish

Machete comes to English directly from Spanish, a language in which it has the same meaning. Many other English words also come from Spanish. Use the story context to help you answer these questions about three more such words.

1. What English word used in the story probably comes from *guayaba,* the Spanish name for the same tropical fruit?

2. *Cantina,* from the Spanish for "bar" or "tavern," is related to an Italian word for "wine cellar." What other English word probably has a similar origin?

3. In English, a *cabana* or *cabaña* is usually a small building used as a beach house at a swimming pool or beach. Is that the word's meaning on p. 968 in the story? Explain.

Using the Word Bank: Synonyms or Antonyms?

On a separate sheet of paper, indicate whether the following pairs of words are synonyms or antonyms.

1. dissuade, discourage
2. loath, eager
3. appease, arouse
4. machetes, knives
5. collusion, plotting
6. docile, cantankerous
7. enunciated, slurred

◆ Literary Focus

Flashback

You can often obtain valuable information about characters' backgrounds, personalities, and motives from a **flashback**—a section of a literary work that interrupts the chronological presentation of events to relate an event from an earlier time. Alvarez's story contains a revealing flashback to Yolanda's time with her aunts in the capital.

1. What does the flashback reveal about the social and economic situation of Yolanda's family?

2. What does the flashback reveal about Yolanda's reasons for making the car trip up north?

◆ Grammar and Style

Absolute Phrases

An **absolute phrase** is made up of a subject and a participle or participial phrase. It stands absolutely by itself and is not considered part of the subject or predicate. It is set off from the rest of the sentence by a comma or commas.

Practice Copy these sentences into your notebook, and underline all the absolute phrases. If a sentence contains no absolute phrase, write *none.*

1. It was an old army bus, the official name brushed over with paint that didn't quite match the regulation gray.

2. She speeded up and left them behind, the small compact climbing easily up the snakey highway.

3. Yolanda pulled up at a cantina, the thatched roof held up by several posts.

4. Yolanda and her crew scavenged the grove, the best of the pick going into the beach basket.

5. The small group stood staring at the sagging tire a moment, the two men kicking it as if punishing it.

Writing Application Write a description of an important childhood memory. Include at least three absolute phrases.

Reteach

Reteach flashback by using a modified plot diagram like the one shown here. Point out that the author interrupts the telling of the story in the present to give the reader information about the past. By viewing this diagram, students should be able to recognize that the event in the flashback influences the character's perception of and reaction to events in the present. Seeing a visual representation like this should help students understand that the flashback is a significant part of the plot, not just a departure from it.

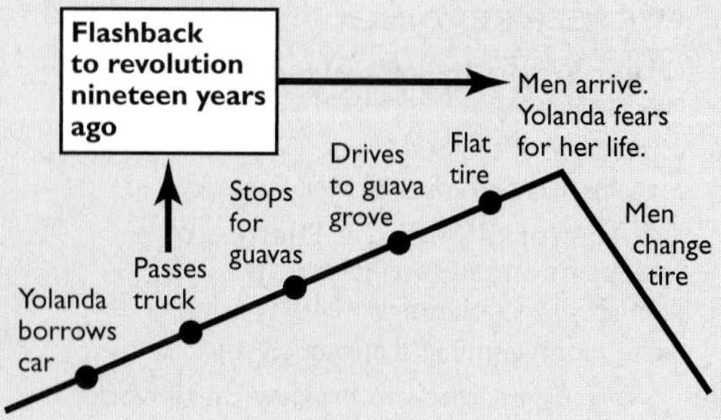

Build Your Portfolio

Idea Bank

Writing

1. **Postcard Message** Write the postcard message that Yolanda might have sent to a close friend back in the States. Briefly describe her adventure.
2. **New Version** Write a new version of this story from the point of view of one of the men who changed the flat tire for Yolanda.
3. **Personal Essay** Like Yolanda, have you ever encountered goodness or kindness where you expected only trouble? How was your response like—or unlike—Yolanda's? Describe your experience and what you learned from it in an essay.

Speaking, Listening, and Viewing

4. **Multimedia Report** Working with several classmates, contribute to a multimedia group report about the Dominican Republic. Choose one area to research—geography, for example, or economics. Add music and images and report your findings in a presentation to the class. **[Social Studies Link]**
5. **Dialogue** Role-play the conversation the two men might have held after watching Yolanda drive away, or the conversation Jose might have had with the old woman. **[Performing Arts Link]**

Researching and Representing

6. **Flowchart** Create a cause-and-effect flowchart illustrating how the decisions made by Yolanda and the story's other characters affect the plot. Diagram the characters' choices in each situation, and show how the action of the story stems from their decisions. **[Math Link]**
7. **Set Design** Use the details of the story to design sets and scenery for a dramatic version of "Antojos." Provide a detailed sketch for two different scenes. **[Art Link]**

Online Activity www.phlit.phschool.com

Guided Writing Lesson

Pointers for Travel Safety

Write a brief essay or magazine article giving pointers for travel safety. If you prefer, you can give safety tips on a particular method of travel—flying, for example, or traveling by car across unknown terrain.

Writing Skills Focus: Transitions to Show Importance

In offering your pointers for travel safety, it's probably a good idea to organize them in order of importance. You can put the most important tip first or last. No matter which order you choose, use **transitions** like these to clarify the importance of the information:

- first and foremost
- of primary importance
- more/more importantly
- more/most crucial
- less importantly
- above all
- primarily
- secondarily
- even better
- best of all
- finally
- last but not least

Prewriting Choose the area or mode of transportation you will discuss, and list your safety pointers. You may want to use note cards and devote one card to each tip. Then organize the cards in order of importance, placing the most important tip first or last.

Drafting Incorporate all your travel tips in a logical order, using transitions to make the order of importance clear. Include a catchy introduction and a brief conclusion. Avoid using a tone that might frighten your readers.

Revising Ask a friend to read your pointers and identify the most important tip. Did you succeed in conveying the order of importance to your reader? If not, revise your pointers by adding clear transitions to indicate which ideas are more, or less, important. Make sure that your word choice is precise and clear and that your sentences flow smoothly.

Idea Bank

Customizing for *Performance Levels*

Following are suggestions for matching Idea Bank topics with your students' performance levels:
Less Advanced Students: 1, 5
Average Students: 2, 6, 7
More Advanced Students: 3, 4

Customizing for *Learning Modalities*

Following are suggestions for matching Idea Bank topics with your students' learning modalities:
Musical/Rhythmic: 4
Visual/Spatial: 4, 7
Verbal/Linguistic: 5
Interpersonal: 5
Logical/Mathematical: 6
Bodily/Kinesthetic: 7

Guided Writing Lesson

For more instruction on prewriting, elaboration, and revision, see *Prentice Hall Writing and Grammar.*

Writing and Language Transparencies Use the Outline Organizer (pp. 95–97) to help students plan their essays.

Writing Lab CD-ROM
Have students complete the tutorial on Exposition. Follow these steps:

1. Refer students to the note card activity to help them organize their ideas.
2. Encourage students to use the transitions word bins. Have students draft on the computer.
3. Have students check their drafts with the revision checker for transition words.

ASSESSMENT OPTIONS

Formal Assessment, Selection Test, pp. 289–291, and Assessment Resources Software. The selection test is designed so that it can be easily customized to the performance levels of your students.

Alternative Assessment, p. 66, includes options for less advanced students, more advanced students, interpersonal learners, bodily/kinesthetic learners, and visual/spatial learners.

PORTFOLIO ASSESSMENT
Use the following rubrics in the ***Alternative Assessment*** booklet to assess student writing:
Postcard Message: Summary Rubric, p. 113
New Version: Response to Literature Rubric, p. 125
Personal Essay: Narrative Based on Personal Experience Rubric, p. 111
Guided Writing Lesson: How-to/Process Explanation Rubric, p. 115

Prepare and Engage

LESSON OBJECTIVES

1. **To develop vocabulary and word identification skills**
   - Word Origins: Greek Prefixes *auto-*
   - Using the Word Bank: Sentence Completions
2. **To use a variety of reading strategies to comprehend poetry**
   - Connect Your Experience
   - Reading Strategy: Summarize
   - Idea Bank: Anthology
3. **To increase knowledge of other cultures and to connect common elements across cultures**
   - Connect Your Experience
   - Background for Understanding
4. **To express and support responses to the text**
   - Critical Thinking
   - Idea Bank: Letter
   - Idea Bank: Editorial
5. **To analyze literary elements**
   - Literary Focus: Voice
   - Idea Bank: Compare-and-Contrast
6. **To read to do research on self-selected and assigned topics**
   - Idea Bank: Cultural Report
   - Research Skills Mini-Lesson (ATE)
7. **To plan, prepare, organize, and present literary interpretations**
   - Idea Bank: Interview
   - Idea Bank: Oral Interpretation
   - Speaking, Listening, and Viewing Mini-Lesson (ATE)
8. **To use recursive writing processes to write an observation of a storm**
   - Guided Writing Lesson
9. **To increase knowledge of the rules of grammar and usage**
   - Grammar and Style: Participial Phrases

Test Preparation

Writing Skills: Sentence Structure (ATE, p. 977)
The teaching tips and sample test item in this workshop support the instruction and practice in the unit workshop:

Writing Skills: Punctuation, Usage, and Sentence Structure (SE, p. 1143)

Guide for Interpreting

Lorna Dee Cervantes *(1954–)*

California native Lorna Dee Cervantes has been writing poetry since she was eight years old. A committed feminist and Hispanic rights activist, she founded her own small press in 1976 "in order to broaden not only the horizons but also the definitions of what was Chicana literature." Cervantes published her own first book of poetry, *Emplumada,* in 1981. She also established the literary magazine *Mango* to help nurture other Hispanic American writers.

Martín Espada *(1957–)*

Not many lawyers pursue simultaneous careers as poets, but Martín Espada was—until 1993—an exception. Born in Brooklyn, New York, Espada was inspired to creativity by his father, a talented photographer with whom he helped produce a 1981 photo documentary called *The Puerto Rican Diaspora Documentary Project.* A year later came Espada's own first volume of poetry, *The Immigrant Iceboy's Bolero.* He now teaches poetry at the University of Massachusetts at Amherst.

Simon Ortiz *(1941–)*

A native of the Acoma Pueblo in New Mexico, Simon Ortiz grew up steeped in the oral tradition of his people. Writing came naturally to him, and in 1980 he was honored at a White House "Salute to Poetry and American Poets." Ortiz has published more than a dozen books of poetry and prose. A creative-writing teacher, he also edits the literary magazine *Wanbli Ho.*

Diana Chang *(1934–)*

Born in New York City, Diana Chang spent most of her childhood in China. She returned to the United States following World War II and attended Barnard College in New York. In addition to writing poetry, she has written several novels, including *The Frontiers of Love* (1993). Chang's spare, introspective poetry, collected in volumes such as *What Matisse Is After* (1984), shows the influence of traditional Asian verse forms. She has also translated Asian writings into English.

Garrett Hongo *(1951–)*

One of the shining stars among recent Asian American poets, Garrett Hongo is a fourth-generation Japanese American who spent most of his early boyhood in Hawaii. His father, an electrical technician, figures prominently in Hongo's poems and is profiled in his book *Volcano: A Memoir of Hawaii* (1995). Hongo has won numerous awards including fellowships from the Thomas Watson and Guggenheim foundations. Among Hongo's other works are *Yellow Light* (1982) and *The River of Heaven* (1988).

◆ Background for Understanding

CULTURE: REFLECTING MULTICULTURAL ROOTS

The poems you are about to read reflect the cultural roots of their authors. Cervantes writes of her Chicana heritage in a familiar California setting, a barrio beside a freeway. Ortiz describes how life in New York City prompts a hunger for his southwestern Native American home. Chinese American writer Chang offers a poem whose subject (nature) and style are reminiscent of Asian verse. Garrett Hongo's poem draws on his heritage as one of many Japanese Americans in Hawaii, some of whom practice the Buddhist faith of their Japanese ancestors.

Prentice Hall Literature Program Resources

REINFORCE / RETEACH / EXTEND

Selection Support Pages
Build Vocabulary: Greek Prefixes: *auto-*, p. 302
Grammar and Style: Participial Phrases, p. 303
Reading Strategy: Summarize, p. 304
Literary Focus: Voice, p. 305

Strategies for Diverse Student Needs, p. 67

Beyond Literature
Cross-Curricular Connection: Social Studies, p. 67

Formal Assessment Selection Test, pp. 292–294; Assessment Resources Software

Alternative Assessment, p. 67

Writing and Language Transparencies
Writing Process Model 2: Descriptive and Observational Writing, pp. 9–12

Resource Pro CD-ROM
Includes all resource materials and a customizable lesson plan

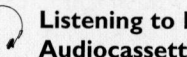

Listening to Literature Audiocassettes

Looking at Literature Videodisc, Ch. 11

Freeway 280 ◆ Who Burns for the Perfection of Paper
Hunger in New York City ◆ Most Satisfied by Snow ◆ What For

◆ *Literature and Your Life*

Connect Your Experience

Although the citizens of the United States share national traditions, people also bring their own unique backgrounds and heritages to their community. What role does family heritage play in your life? What are the benefits of strong cultural ties? Share your experiences in a group discussion.

Journal Writing Describe an activity or tradition associated with your cultural background or heritage.

Thematic Focus: Literature Confronts the Everyday

As you read each of these poems, think about the role that family background or heritage plays in each speaker's everyday life.

◆ Build Vocabulary

Greek Prefixes: *auto-*

From the Greek word *autos* comes the prefix *auto-*, which means "self." For example, the word *automation* refers to manufacturing conducted using self-operating machinery.

Word Bank

Preview this list of words from the poems.

crevices
automation
pervade
liturgy
conjure
calligraphy
trough

◆ Grammar and Style

Participial Phrases

A **participial phrase** consists of a participle—a verb acting as an adjective—and the words that modify or complete it. The entire phrase works as an adjective to modify a noun or a pronoun. A participial phrase must be placed so that it is clear what word it modifies. Usually this means placing it as close as possible to the modified noun or pronoun, as in these examples:

We made legal pads from yellow paper *stacked seven feet high.*

My hands, *smoothing the exact rectangle,* would slide along the paper.

Occupied by snow, I see that matter matters.

◆ Literary Focus

Voice

Every person has a distinctive way of speaking. Similarly, every poet has an individual **voice.** A poet's distinctive sound is based on word choice and combinations, rhyme (or lack of it), pace, attitude, and even the pattern of vowels and consonants.

◆ Reading Strategy

Summarize

Sometimes you can understand a poem better if you briefly restate the main points in a **summary.** Consider these passages from Espada's poem and the summary that follows.

At sixteen, I worked after high school hours / at a printing plant / that manufactured legal pads: /. . . I slipped cardboard / between the pages, / then brushed red glue / up and down the stack. . . ./ Sluggish by 9 PM, the hands / would slide along suddenly sharp paper, / and gather slits thinner than the crevices / of the skin, hidden.

Summary

At sixteen, the speaker had a routine but often painful evening job at a plant that manufactured legal pads.

Interest Grabber As students question and define their own identities within a context of cultural heritage, they will find these poems—statements of cultural pride and definition—intensely personal and relevant. Begin a discussion by displaying a collection of magazine advertisements featuring a variety of ethnicities and cultures. Ask students to draw conclusions about the advertisers' decisions to use the models they chose. *They know their market; they want to reflect the variety of people in the country.* Ask students whether seeing this diversity in commercials and advertisements would prompt them to make a purchase. To further mine students' thoughts about the poems, challenge willing student pairs to interview each other about their cultural heritage and sense of affiliation. Discuss as a class the growing role of cultural identity in America's multicultural society.

Customize for
Less Proficient Readers
Poetic syntax is often challenging to less proficient readers. To help these readers understand the poems, encourage them to punctuate or rewrite text in sentence form. Use Reword Poets' Ideas in ***Strategies for Diverse Student Needs,*** p. 67.

Customize for
AP Students
Analyzing figurative language can help more advanced students appreciate the literary style of these poems. Urge students to pay particular attention to this figurative language, noting examples they find especially effective.

Customize for
English Language Learners
The specific cultural references in these poems may be difficult for language learners. Encourage these students to read footnotes carefully, working with native speakers to apply the footnote content to each poem.

Customize for
Visual/Spatial Readers
Invite these students to respond to the illustrations throughout the selection. Challenge them to make predictions about the poems based on these visual images.

Test Preparation Workshop

Writing Skills: Sentence Structure Many standardized tests require students to identify correctly written sentences that should be combined. Use the following sample item to demonstrate.

<u>Poets often do other work. They work to support themselves.</u> Among the members of most professions, you can find a poet or two.

Choose the best way to write the underlined section. If the underlined section needs no change, choose "Correct as is."

A Poets often do other work to support themselves.
B Poets often do other work, or they work to support themselves.
C Among the members of most professions, poets work to support themselves
D Correct as is.

Students should recognize that choice *A* combines two choppy sentences, but maintains the sense of both.

Develop Understanding

One-Minute Insight These poems illustrate how the bond of cultural heritage and childhood experience help to shape people's adult identities. In "Freeway 280," the poet traces the path of her own rediscovered cultural identity by blending Spanish and English, and focusing on the endurance of nature despite human interference. The speaker of "Who Burns for the Perfection of Paper," presumably the poet, recalls the harsh physical labor of a childhood job to remind readers that behind his outward accomplishments are the painful memories of hard work and sacrifice.

◆ Critical Thinking

❶ **Connect** Ask students: What does the speaker seek to escape in lines 14–19 and then hopes to rediscover in the final stanza? *She hopes to rediscover her Hispanic identity, her connection to a part of her past and self.*

◆ Grammar and Style

❷ **Participial Phrases** Help students find the participial phrase in this sentence and identify the noun or pronoun that it modifies. *The participial phrase is "burning on swing shift in the greasy summer air." It modifies "the smell of tomatoes."*

Customize for *English Language Learners*

❸ Use the footnotes to review the meaning of the Spanish phrases to aid comprehension of the poem.

▶ Critical Viewing ◀

❹ **Interpret** Students may say it represents a road to the future.

Humanities: Fine Art

Untitled, 1986, by Peter Malone.

Both painter Peter Malone and the poet create a relatively accurate physical representation of a real place. They make these places their own by presenting them through the colors and images of personal perspective.

Ask students: How might the poem's speaker characterize the place depicted in the painting? *First as a means of escape from her Chicano community and heritage, but later as a symbol of outside interference with her community.*

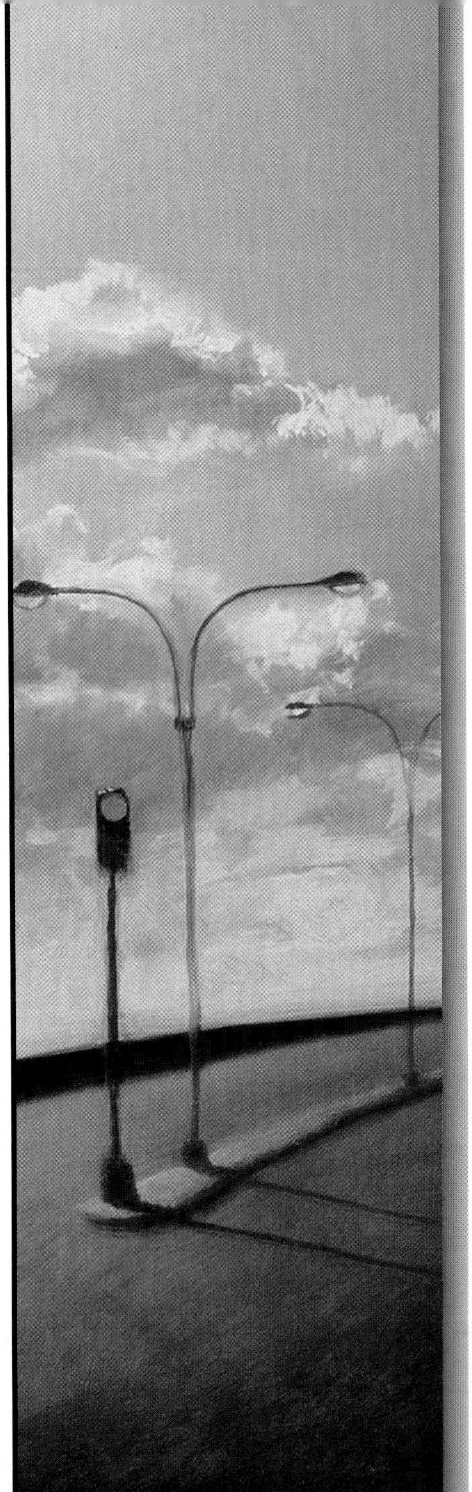

Untitled (detail), Peter Malone

Freeway 280[1]

Lorna Dee Cervantes

Las casitas[2] near the gray cannery,
nestled amid wild abrazos[3] of climbing roses
and man-high red geraniums
are gone now. The freeway conceals it
all beneath a raised scar.

But under the fake windsounds of the open lanes,
in the abandoned lots below, new grasses sprout,
wild mustard remembers, old gardens
come back stronger than they were,
trees have been left standing in their yards.
Albaricoqueros, cerezos, nogales . . .[4]
Viejitas[5] come here with paper bags to gather greens.
Espinaca, verdolagas, yerbabuena . . .[6]

I scramble over the wire fence
that would have kept me out.
Once, I wanted out, wanted the rigid lanes ❶
to take me to a place without sun,
without the smell of tomatoes burning ❷
on swing shift in the greasy summer air.

Maybe it's here
en los campos extraños de esta ciudad[7]
where I'll find it, that part of me
mown under
like a corpse
or a loose seed.

1. **Freeway 280:** Freeway in California.
2. **Las casitas** (läs kä sē´ täs): "The little houses" (Spanish).
3. **abrazos** (ä brä´ sōs): "Hugs" (Spanish).
4. **Albaricoqueros, cerezos, nogales** (äl bär´ rē kō ker´ ōs, se rē´ sōs, nō gä´ les): "Apricot trees, cherry trees, walnut trees" (Spanish).
5. **Viejitas** (bye hē´ täs): "Old women" (Spanish).
6. **Espinaca, verdolagas, yerbabuena** (es pē nä´ kä, ber thō lä´ gäs, yer´ bä bwe´ nä): "Spinach, purslane, peppermint" (Spanish).
7. **en los campos estraños de esta ciudad** (en lōs käm´ pōs es trä´ nyōs de es´ tä syōō thath): "In the strange fields of this city" (Spanish). ❸

◀ **Critical Viewing** What do you think this freeway scene represents for the artist? **[Interpret]** ❹

Block Scheduling Strategies

Consider these suggestions to take advantage of extended class time:

- Have students work together to organize a volume containing their journal entries from Literature and Your Life (p. 977).
- Challenge students to brainstorm additional words containing the prefix *auto-*.
- Stage the Oral Interpretation activity (p. 986), comparing students' interpretations of the poems.
- As a class, read some of the additional works by these poets listed on pp. 979, 981, and 984.
- Have students work in pairs to answer the Critical Thinking questions (pp. 979, 981, 984).
- Have students begin the Guided Writing Lesson (p. 986) by identifying and analyzing figurative language in the poems.
- Have students complete the Cultural Report (p. 986) and share their findings with the class.

Who Burns for the Perfection of Paper

Martín Espada

At sixteen, I worked after high school hours
at a printing plant
that manufactured legal pads:
Yellow paper
stacked seven feet high
and leaning
as I slipped cardboard
between the pages,
❺ then brushed red glue
up and down the stack.
No gloves: fingertips required
for the perfection of paper,
smoothing the exact rectangle.
Sluggish by 9 PM, the hands
would slide along suddenly sharp paper,
and gather slits thinner than the <u>crevices</u>
of the skin, hidden.
Then the glue would sting,
hands oozing
till both palms burned
at the punchclock.

❻

Ten years later, in law school,
I knew that every legal pad
was glued with the sting of hidden cuts,
that every open lawbook
was a pair of hands
upturned and burning.

◆ **Build Vocabulary**

crevices (krev′ is iz) *n.*: Narrow cracks or splits

Guide for Responding

◆ *Literature and Your Life*

Reader's Response Each of these poems reflects back on the speaker's childhood. With which one could you relate more strongly? Explain.

Thematic Focus Did these poems change the way you look at everyday objects such as legal pads and highways? How?

☑ Check Your Comprehension

1. What sort of neighborhood once stood on the site of "Freeway 280"?
2. In "Who Burns . . . ," cite the two ways the speaker has come to know legal pads.

◆ Critical Thinking

INTERPRET

1. (a) How is "Freeway 280" like a scar? (b) What might it represent? **[Interpret]**
2. (a) In "Freeway 280," why does the speaker liken a part of herself to a "corpse" and a "loose seed"? (b) How do lines 7–10 imply that the "loose seed" will take root? **[Infer; Connect]**
3. (a) In "Who Burns . . . ," how would you describe the printing plant job? (b) What did the speaker learn from his experience making legal pads? **[Classify; Connect]**
4. What aspects of the law student's background might the hidden cuts represent? **[Interpret]**

Beyond the Selection

FURTHER READING

Other Works by Lorna Dee Cervantes and Martín Espada

Emplumada (Cervantes)
From the Cables of Genocide (Cervantes)
The Immigrant Iceboy's Bolero (Espada)
Trumpets from the Islands of Their Eviction (Espada)

We suggest that you preview these works before recommending them to students.

INTERNET

To learn more about Lorna Dee Cervantes and Martín Espada we suggest the following sites. Sites may have changed since this information was published.

For Cervantes, visit **http://www.en.utexas.edu/~sheilac/cervantes.html**

For an article on Espada visit **http:www.pacificnews.org/jinn/stories/3.11/970520censor.html**

We *strongly recommend* that you preview sites before you send students to them.

Customize for
Bodily/Kinesthetic Learners

❺ Draw students' attention to the highly tactile imagery of the poem. Ask them what these images reveal about the speaker's experiences.

◆ Critical Thinking

❻ **Analyze** Ask students why Espada may have written this poem in two stanzas. *He did so in order to contrast his two experiences with legal pads.*

Answers

Reader's Response Responses will reflect students' personal experiences.

Thematic Focus Students may say that they no longer take these things for granted; they now think about how such items come into being.

☑ Check Your Comprehension

1. It was a poor Hispanic neighborhood of small houses.
2. He knows them through his work at the plant and in law school.

Reinforce and Extend

◆ Critical Thinking

1. (a) It has healed over the decaying barrio. (b) The freeway may represent the way prosperous America passes the barrio by, or it may symbolize changes or modern ways that disrupt ethnic traditions.
2. (a) Without her heritage she has felt dead as a corpse or adrift like a loose seed. (b) The regeneration of abandoned gardens suggests it is also possible for the speaker to experience new growth.
3. (a) The job is physically demanding, sometimes painful, and always routine. (b) He learns to appreciate the hard work and sacrifices that are required to create the items we take for granted.
4. They represent the hard work and sacrifices that enabled him to attend law school.

Develop Understanding

One-Minute Insight These poems explore the relationship between humans and nature. Both demonstrate the knowledge people can gain from interacting with nature. The speaker in "Hunger in New York City" acknowledges a longing for his home, where nature is more accessible, and draws on memories of a closer connection to the earth to satisfy his longing. In "Most Satisfied by Snow," the speaker contrasts the empty spaces of fog with the substance of snow, characterizing nature as a teacher urging awareness of both physical and spiritual components.

▶Critical Viewing◀

❶ **Interpret** Students may suggest words such as *stark, sad,* and *isolated.*

◆ Literary Focus

❷ **Voice** Ask: Based on these lines, how would you describe the speaker's personality? *Students should note that the speaker is honest, thoughtful, and dedicated—he is attempting to connect with his urban home, but honest about his inability to do so.*

◆ Reading Strategy

❸ **Summarize** Have students summarize the poem. *The speaker, who is living in the harsh urban setting of New York City, misses the connection with nature found in his childhood home.*

◆ Critical Thinking

❹ **Generalize** Ask students: In what way might this be typical of Native American beliefs? *Students may note that Native American philosophy demands a respect for the earth.*

Hunger in New York City

Simon Ortiz

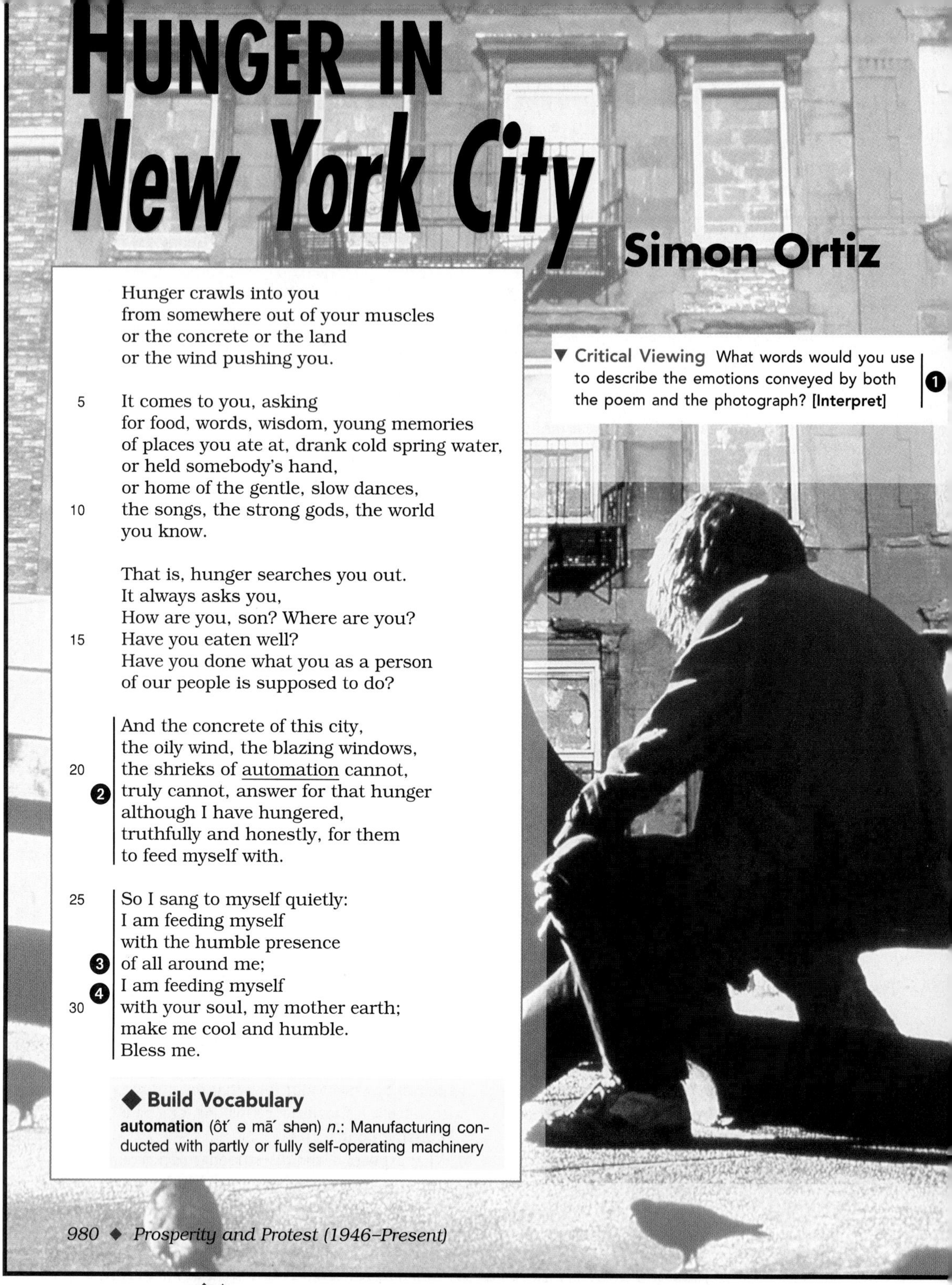

▼ **Critical Viewing** What words would you use to describe the emotions conveyed by both the poem and the photograph? **[Interpret]** ❶

Hunger crawls into you
from somewhere out of your muscles
or the concrete or the land
or the wind pushing you.

It comes to you, asking
for food, words, wisdom, young memories
of places you ate at, drank cold spring water,
or held somebody's hand,
or home of the gentle, slow dances,
the songs, the strong gods, the world
you know.

That is, hunger searches you out.
It always asks you,
How are you, son? Where are you?
Have you eaten well?
Have you done what you as a person
of our people is supposed to do?

And the concrete of this city,
the oily wind, the blazing windows,
the shrieks of <u>automation</u> cannot,
❷ truly cannot, answer for that hunger
although I have hungered,
truthfully and honestly, for them
to feed myself with.

So I sang to myself quietly:
I am feeding myself
with the humble presence
❸ of all around me;
❹ I am feeding myself
with your soul, my mother earth;
make me cool and humble.
Bless me.

◆ Build Vocabulary

automation (ôt´ ə mā´ shən) *n.*: Manufacturing conducted with partly or fully self-operating machinery

Cross-Curricular Connection: Social Studies

The Acoma Pueblo People Although Ortiz writes about New York City, he is an Acoma Pueblo of the Southwest. His background is almost exactly the opposite of the area he describes in "Hunger in New York City."

The Acomas live some seventy miles west of Albuquerque. A small mesa rises roughly three hundred feet in a vast landscape of low brown mountains and cliffs, and a shallow valley rests green with centuries of nurturing and carefully guarded fertility. On top of this mesa sit the irregular adobe houses of Acoma Pueblo, the Sky City, of the same color as the cliffs below and invisible from a distance. This is the matrix of the Acoma people, first built, they say, sometime before history when Masaweh, one of the Divine Twins, created by the earth herself, led the people up the cliffs. Share this information with students and then ask: What might be the emotional perspective of a Native American from this southwestern environment who is suffering from hunger in the urban Northwest? *He or she might be feeling cut off from the earth and nature; overwhelmed by people and machinery; or lonely for home.*

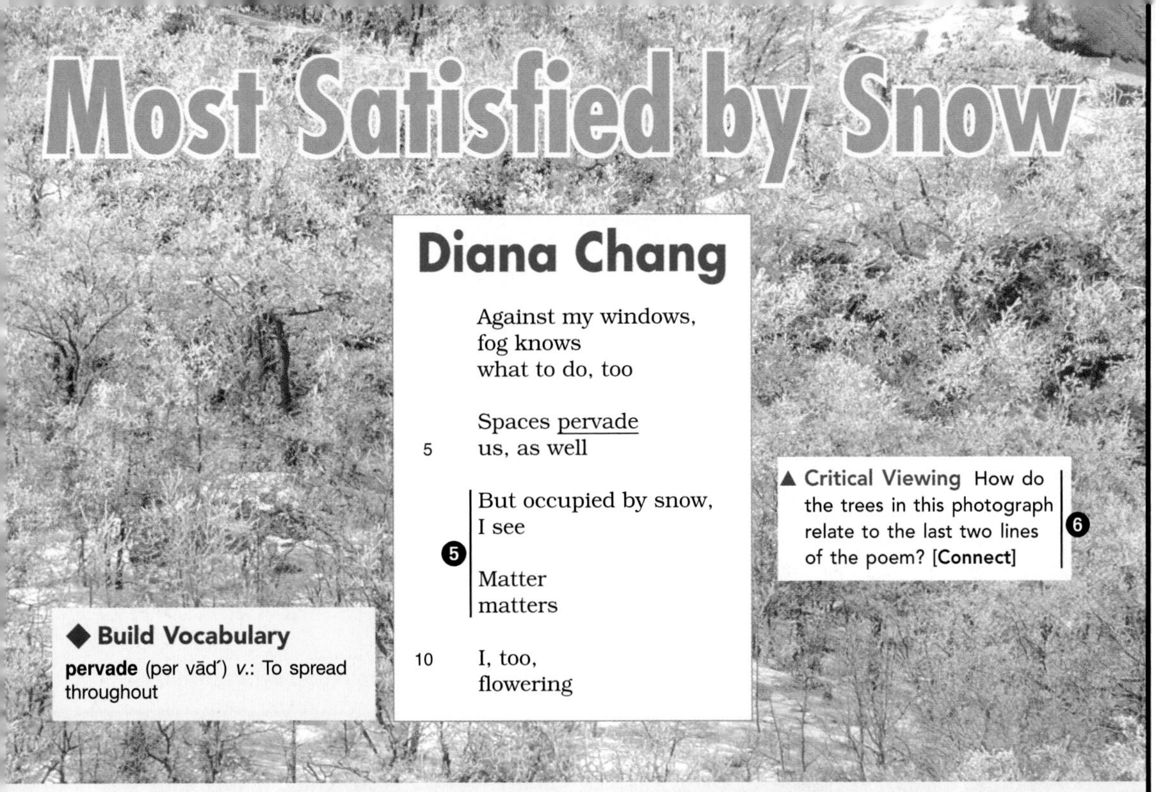

Most Satisfied by Snow

Diana Chang

Against my windows,
fog knows
what to do, too

Spaces pervade
us, as well

❺ But occupied by snow,
I see

Matter
matters

I, too,
flowering

▲ **Critical Viewing** How do the trees in this photograph relate to the last two lines of the poem? **[Connect]** ❻

◆ **Build Vocabulary**

pervade (pər vād′) *v.*: To spread throughout

Guide for Responding

◆ *Literature and Your Life*

Reader's Response Did the contents of either poem surprise you, given the titles? Explain.

Thematic Focus How can your everyday surroundings either emotionally nourish or starve you?

Journal Writing Chang makes an observation about herself after watching a natural event. What feelings do storms evoke in you?

☑ Check Your Comprehension

1. (a) In "Hunger in New York City," what four questions does the hunger ask? (b) What four things cannot answer for that hunger? (c) With what does the speaker feed himself in the end?

2. (a) In "Most Satisfied by Snow," what two aspects of nature does the speaker observe? (b) What does she conclude?

◆ Critical Thinking

INTERPRET

1. What kind of hunger does "Hunger in New York City" describe? **[Interpret]**

2. (a) What impressions does the speaker give of New York City and of his home? (b) Compare the two sets of impressions. **[Compare and Contrast]**

3. In "Most Satisfied by Snow," what might the speaker mean when she comments that "spaces pervade us"? **[Interpret]**

4. (a) What differences between fog and snow does this poem highlight? (b) How is this contrast embodied in humans? **[Analyze]**

APPLY

5. Chang's poem suggests that we can learn about ourselves by observing nature. Do you agree? Why or why not? **[Apply]**

Beyond the Selection

FURTHER READING

Other Works by Simon Ortiz and Diana Chang

A Good Journey (Ortiz)
From Sand Creek (Ortiz)
The Frontiers of Love (Chang)
The Horizon Is Definitely Speaking (Chang)

We suggest that you preview these works before recommending them to students.

INTERNET

You and your students may find additional information about Simon Ortiz and Diana Chang on the Internet. We suggest the following site. Please be aware, however, that sites may have changed since this information was published.

For a biography and links to on-line resources on Simon Ortiz, visit **http://www.ipl.org/cgi/ref/native/browse.pl/A93**

We *strongly recommend* that you preview sites before you send students to them.

◆ *Literature and Your Life*

❺ Point out how nature helps the speaker "see." What insights has nature revealed or inspired in students? *Students may mention strong emotions inspired by nature or lessons about renewal and conservation.*

▶Critical Viewing◀

❻ **Connect** Students may say that the trees in the photograph appear to be flowering (like the poem's speaker) though in fact they are covered (or, like the speaker, occupied by) with snow.

Reinforce and Extend

Answers

◆ *Literature and Your Life*

Reader's Response Students may have expected "Hunger" to be about the social problem of physical hunger.

Thematic Focus Our surroundings influence us emotionally and psychologically, as well as physically.

☑ Check Your Comprehension

1. (a) It asks how he is, where he is, whether he has eaten well, and whether he has done what he should as a member of his people. (b) The concrete of this city, the oily wind, the blazing windows, and the shrieks of automation cannot answer for it. (c) He feeds himself with the humble presence of all around him, mother earth.
2. (a) She observes the fog and the snow. (b) She concludes that "matter matters."

◆ Critical Thinking

1. It describes the hunger for home, his cultural roots, and family.
2. (a) New York City is a modern, windy, mechanized environment. His home is filled with beloved places, people, music, and dance. (b) New York City is a cold, heartless, foreign place, while his home is full of warm, familiar, soul-satisfying people and experiences.
3. She means that we have a nonphysical, spiritual component.
4. (a) The fog represents space; the snow represents substance. (b) We possess both spiritual and physical components.
5. Sample response: Yes, because many aspects of human existence are reflected in nature.

Develop Understanding

One-Minute Insight Any student who has felt concern for a hard-working parent or friend will appreciate the central sentiment of this poem—the desire to lighten a loved one's load. The speaker recalls childhood moments of waiting patiently for his father to come home from a physically demanding job and the fervent wish to use the power of his Japanese and Hawaiian heritage—richly detailed in the early stanzas—to ease his father's pain.

Customize for
AP Students
Encourage students to work in teams to explain more about the various cultural references footnoted beneath the poem.

◆ Literary Focus

❶ **Voice** Ask students to describe the speaker's voice as the poem opens. *Students should note that though the speaker is now an adult, the voice being presented is that of a child.*

◆ Grammar and Style

❷ **Participial Phrases** Have students identify the participial phrases in this stanza. Ask them to explain each one's role in the sentence. *The participial phrases are "stirring curry into a thick stew," and "weaving a calligraphy of Kannon's love into grass mats and straw sandals." They both modify "my grandmother."*

◆ Critical Thinking

❸ **Infer** Ask: As a child, how did the speaker feel about his grandmother? *Students should recognize the child's love for his grandmother and his reliance on her for guidance.*

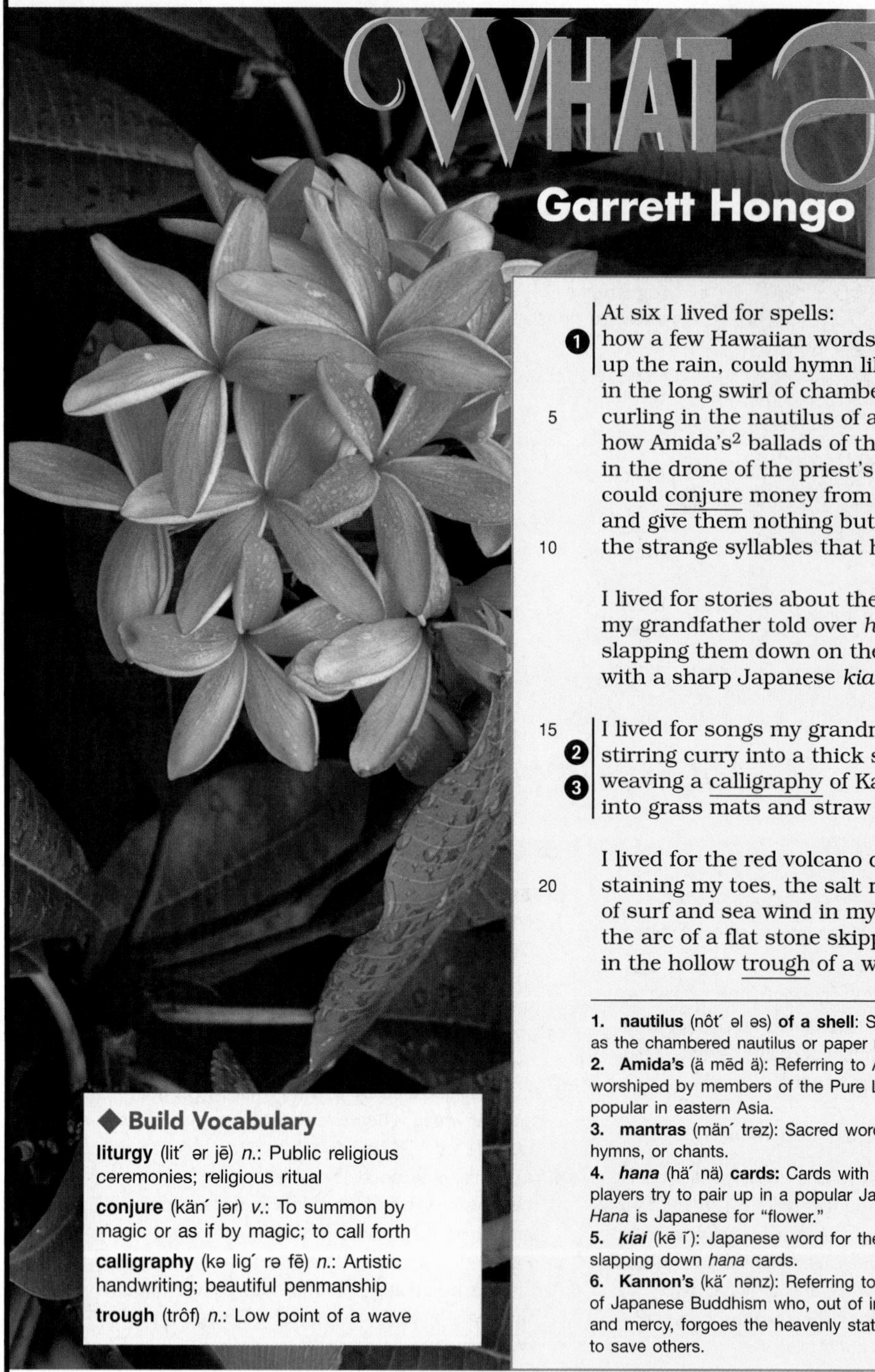

WHAT FOR

Garrett Hongo

At six I lived for spells:
❶ how a few Hawaiian words could call
up the rain, could hymn like the sea
in the long swirl of chambers
curling in the nautilus of a shell,[1]
how Amida's[2] ballads of the Buddhaland
in the drone of the priest's liturgy
could conjure money from the poor
and give them nothing but mantras,[3]
the strange syllables that healed desire.

I lived for stories about the war
my grandfather told over *hana* cards,[4]
slapping them down on the mats
with a sharp Japanese *kiai.*[5]

I lived for songs my grandmother sang
❷ stirring curry into a thick stew,
❸ weaving a calligraphy of Kannon's[6] love
into grass mats and straw sandals.

I lived for the red volcano dirt
staining my toes, the salt residue
of surf and sea wind in my hair,
the arc of a flat stone skipping
in the hollow trough of a wave.

◆ Build Vocabulary

liturgy (lit´ ər jē) *n.*: Public religious ceremonies; religious ritual

conjure (kän´ jər) *v.*: To summon by magic or as if by magic; to call forth

calligraphy (kə lig´ rə fē) *n.*: Artistic handwriting; beautiful penmanship

trough (trôf) *n.*: Low point of a wave

---

1. **nautilus** (nôt´ əl əs) **of a shell**: Spiral of a seashell such as the chambered nautilus or paper nautilus.
2. **Amida's** (ä mēd ä): Referring to Amida, the great savior worshiped by members of the Pure Land sect of Buddhism popular in eastern Asia.
3. **mantras** (män´ trəz): Sacred words repeated in prayers, hymns, or chants.
4. ***hana*** (hä´ nä) **cards:** Cards with flower patterns that players try to pair up in a popular Japanese card game. *Hana* is Japanese for "flower."
5. ***kiai*** (kē ī´): Japanese word for the sound made by slapping down *hana* cards.
6. **Kannon's** (kä´ nənz): Referring to an enlightened savior of Japanese Buddhism who, out of infinite compassion and mercy, forgoes the heavenly state of nirvana in order to save others.

Research Skills Mini-Lesson

Evaluating Sources

This mini-lesson supports the Cultural Report in the Idea Bank on p. 986.

Introduce the Concept Tell students that they will write a research report on an aspect of the culture background reflected in one of the poems. Stress the importance of using reliable, unbiased sources of information.

Develop Background Suggest that students review the poems to choose a culture to research, such as Puerto Rico, Acoma Pueblo of New Mexico, Confucianism in China, or Japanese Buddhism. Remind students to evaluate their sources for the bias of the writer as well as for the validity of the source. For example, an encyclopedia or reputable newspaper like *The Wall Street Journal* would be more reliable then information from a political speech.

Apply the Information After collecting information, have students evaluate the credibility of their sources. Encourage students to verify the accuracy of their facts by researching in more than one source, by evaluating the author for bias and accuracy, and by checking that the text is logical and balanced.

Assess the Outcome Assess students' work on the accuracy, validity, and reliability of their sources. You might have students use the Peer Assessment form for Research Report/Paper, p. 121 in ***Alternative Assessment.***

I lived a child's world, waited
for my father to drag himself home,
dusted with blasts of sand, powdered rock,
and the strange ash of raw cement,
his deafness made worse by the clang
of pneumatic drills,[7] sore in his bones
from the buckings of a jackhammer.
He'd hand me a scarred lunchpail,
let me unlace the hightop G.I. boots,[8]
call him the new name I'd invented
❹ that day in school, write it for him
on his newspaper. He'd rub my face
❺ with hands that felt like gravel roads,
tell me to move, go play, and then he'd
walk to the laundry sink to scrub,
rinse the dirt of his long day
from a face brown and grained as koa wood.[9]

I wanted to take away the pain
in his legs, the swelling in his joints,
give him back his hearing,
❻ clear and rare as crystal chimes,
the fins of glass that wrinkled
and sparked the air with their sound.

I wanted to heal the sores that work
and war had sent to him,
let him play catch in the backyard
with me, tossing a tennis ball
past papaya trees without the shoulders
of pain shrugging back his arms.

▲ **Critical Viewing**
❼ How does the poet use the image of the fragrant plumeria flower to communicate his desire to heal his father's pain? **[Analyze]**

7. **pneumatic** (nōō mat´ ik) **drills:** Air drills used in construction.
8. **hightop G.I. boots:** Army boots.
9. **koa** (kō´ ə) **wood:** Grainy wood of the Hawaiian acacia tree.

◆ Reading Strategy

❹ **Summarize** Have students briefly restate the main point of this stanza. *Possible summary: Every day the speaker's father came home from work, greeted his son with affection, and cleaned up.*

◆ Critical Thinking

❺ **Connect** Ask: What is one way you can tell that the speaker's father has been a soldier? *Students should recall the reference in line 32 to the father's G.I. boots.*

Customize for
Less Proficient Readers
❻ Point out the change in opening lines beginning with the sixth stanza. Explain that this change signals readers to take notice. Urge students to read the stanzas that follow especially carefully to discover what the speaker wanted for his father.

▶Critical Viewing◀

❼ **Analyze** In line 56, the poet links the pleasant fragrance of the plumeria to his words, thereby helping readers imagine the sweetness of the words by offering them a positive sensory prompt of a fragrant flower.

Customize for
Bodily/Kinesthetic Learners
Invite students to pantomime the father's actions, defining how he would move according to the descriptive language of the poem.

Reteach

To reteach summarizing, have students recall details aloud. Write the details on the board, and work with students to group related details and arrive at a concise and accurate summary.

Speaking, Listening, and Viewing Mini-Lesson

Interview

This mini-lesson supports the Speaking, Listening, and Viewing activity in the Idea Bank on p. 986.

Introduce the Concept Have students read or view recent interviews from print or electronic media. Discuss what makes an interview effective and interesting, listing suggestions on the chalkboard.

Develop Background Before students undertake their interview, review and discuss the following guidelines:

- Interview questions are most effective when they are open-ended, requiring in-depth, rather than yes or no responses.
- Interviewers should always consider their subject's privacy, respecting potential limitations of discussion topics.
- Brief research about the subject's background will enable interviewers to ask interesting and effective questions.

Apply the Information Assist students as necessary in arranging the interviews.

Remind students to be polite, thorough, and accurate. Before their official meetings, encourage students to exchange questions with a peer for comment.

Assess the Outcome Using the ideas about effective interviewing reviewed earlier, have students develop rating criteria. With these, invite the class to evaluate all the interviews for interest level and effectiveness.

◆ Critical Thinking

❶ Modify The speaker's hopes for helping his father reflect his Hawaiian background. Encourage students to revise this stanza, capturing the speaker's sentiment in figurative language that describes their background or geography.

Reinforce and Extend

Answers

◆ *Literature and Your Life*

Reader's Response Suggested response: Yes, he enjoyed life by the sea and the company of his family.

Thematic Focus It very effectively captures his childhood through descriptions of the spells, ballads, and stories that captivated him; sensory images of his seaside experiences; and specific details about the family members who were at the center of his childhood world.

☑ Check Your Comprehension

1. He lived for spells, ballads of the Buddhaland, war stories, and his grandmother's songs.
2. He lived near the ocean. He refers to the surf, sea wind, and waves.
3. (a) He is dusted with blasting residue, deafened by the drills, and is sore in his bones. (b) He wants to take away his pain, restore his hearing, and heal his sores.

◆ Critical Thinking

1. He suggests that his grandmother follows the example of selfless Kannon by weaving to supplement the family income. He describes the suffering his father endured in order to support his family.
2. (a) He is a work-battered, deafened war veteran. (b) He loves him so much that he wishes he could become a "doctor of pure magic" and erase his father's suffering.
3. He values self-sacrifice and family.
4. The title asks a question which the poem answers by listing the things for which he lived as a boy.
5. Both focus on the physical suffering and sacrifices that the speakers knew in their youth from personal experience or observation.

Beyond Literature

American media and pop culture reflect the influence of many cultures.

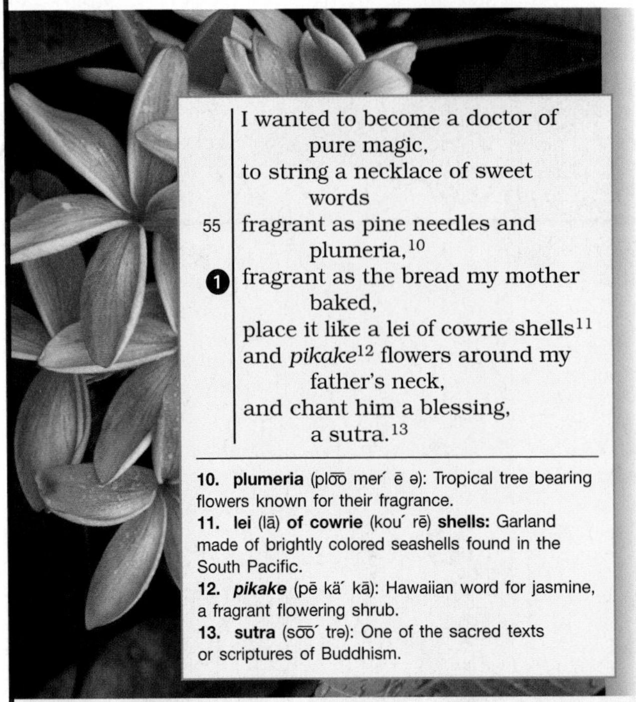

I wanted to become a doctor of
  pure magic,
to string a necklace of sweet
  words
fragrant as pine needles and
  plumeria,[10]
❶ fragrant as the bread my mother
  baked,
place it like a lei of cowrie shells[11]
and *pikake*[12] flowers around my
  father's neck,
and chant him a blessing,
  a sutra.[13]

---

10. plumeria (plo͞o mer´ ē ə): Tropical tree bearing flowers known for their fragrance.
11. lei (lā) **of cowrie** (kou´ rē) **shells:** Garland made of brightly colored seashells found in the South Pacific.
12. *pikake* (pē kä´ kā): Hawaiian word for jasmine, a fragrant flowering shrub.
13. sutra (so͞o´ trə): One of the sacred texts or scriptures of Buddhism.

Beyond Literature

Culture Connection

American Diversity As it has for centuries, the United States continues to attract immigrants seeking a new life in the "land of opportunity." For hundreds of years, those immigrants came mainly from European countries. Today, however, newcomers are just as likely to come from Asia, Mexico, Latin America, or the Caribbean. This new influx of immigration, paired with dramatic growth in the existing immigrant populations, has made the United States a nation of true ethnic and cultural diversity. More than ever before, our country reflects the motto adopted by our founding fathers: *E pluribus unum*—"Out of many, one."

How is America's growing diversity mirrored in popular culture and fashions, including music, television, and films?

Guide for Responding

◆ *Literature and Your Life*

Reader's Response Do you think the speaker had a happy childhood? Why or why not?

Thematic Focus How effectively does the poem capture the details of the speaker's childhood days? Cite details to support your opinion.

Journal Writing What do you remember of the people who formed your world as a six-year-old child? Record your memories in a journal entry.

☑ Check Your Comprehension

1. What kinds of songs or other forms of communication does the speaker say he lived for?
2. Did the speaker live near the desert, the ocean, or the mountains? How do you know?
3. (a) Cite three details in "What For" that describe the father's condition when he returns from work. (b) What does the speaker want to do for his father?

◆ Critical Thinking

INTERPRET

1. Cite examples from the text that suggest that the speaker considers at least two members of his family as models of compassion and self-sacrifice. **[Support]**
2. (a) What sort of person is the speaker's father? (b) How does the speaker feel about him? Support your answer. **[Infer]**
3. Based on this poem, what values do you think are important to the poet? **[Draw Conclusions]**

EVALUATE

4. Evaluate the title's relationship to the content of the poem. Is the title an effective one? Explain. **[Evaluate]**

COMPARE LITERARY WORKS

5. What parallels can you draw between "What For" and Espada's "Who Burns for the Perfection of Paper"? **[Connect]**

Beyond the Selection

FURTHER READING

Other Works by Garrett Hongo
Yellow Light
The River of Heaven
Volcano

Other Works With the Theme of Fathers
"And This Is My Father," Marcus J. Grapes
"Lines to My Father," Leslie Daiken
"Remember My Father," Jonathan Holden

We suggest that you preview these works before recommending them to students.

INTERNET

You and your students may find additional information about Garrett Hongo on the Internet. We suggest the following Web sites. Please be aware, however, that sites may have changed since this information was published.

To read an interview with Hongo about his memoir *Volcano*, go to **http://dcn.davis.ca.us/~gizmo/ongo.html**

We *strongly recommend* that you preview sites before you send students to them.

Guide for Responding (continued)

◆ Literary Focus

Voice

Each one of these poets has a distinctive **voice**, or sound, which results from word choice, tone, pace, and use of sound devices.

1. What adjectives would you use to describe each poet's voice? Why?
2. Which of the five voices do you find most appealing? Why?

◆ Build Vocabulary

Using the Greek Prefix *auto-*

Automation, "manufacturing conducted with self-operating machinery," contains the Greek prefix *auto-*, which means "self." Explain how the meaning of *auto-* is conveyed in each of these words.

1. automobile
2. autopilot
3. autograph (The root *-graph-* means "writing.")

Using the Word Bank: Sentence Completions

Choose the letter of the word or phrase that best completes each statement. Write your answers on your paper.

1. A wave's *trough* is its (a) high point, (b) low point, (c) surf.
2. Someone trying to *conjure* a rabbit is most likely (a) a magician, (b) an animal-rights activist, (c) a French chef.
3. You'd most likely use *calligraphy* on (a) a merry-go-round, (b) a woman's hairdo, (c) a wedding invitation.
4. For information on Jewish *liturgy*, it would be best to consult (a) a prayer book, (b) an atlas, (c) a cookbook.
5. After *automation*, the plant probably had (a) more workers, (b) fewer workers, (c) the same number of workers.
6. *Crevices* in rock are likely to (a) be brightly colored, (b) be used in jewelry, (c) fill up with rainwater.
7. If bad odors *pervade*, people are likely to (a) hold their noses, (b) not notice them, (c) breathe a sigh of relief.

◆ Reading Strategy

Summarize

As you read these poems, you may have created mental **summaries** of the main points. This strategy can often help you better understand the poems you read.

1. "Freeway 280" is divided into four stanzas, or groups of lines. Write a four-sentence summary in which each sentence sums up a different stanza of the poem.
2. Write a summary of each of the following two poems: (a) "Hunger in New York City," (b) "What For."

◆ Grammar and Style

Participial Phrases

In choosing where to place a participial phrase, make sure that it is clear what word it modifies.

A **participial phrase** is a participle—a verb form that can be used as an adjective—and the words that modify or complete it.

Practice Copy the following sentences into your notebook and underline each participial phrase. Draw an arrow to the noun or pronoun it modifies.

1. Seeking an after-school job, I found one at a printing plant.
2. I worked hard, slipping cardboard between the papers.
3. Cut by the sharp edges, my hands were often stinging.
4. The glue, oozing over them, made the stinging worse.
5. I can still visualize my hands, upturned in pain.

Writing Application For each numbered item, write a sentence that uses the participial phrase provided. Be sure to place the participial phrase so that it is clear what word it modifies. If you like, you can base your sentences on "Freeway 280."

1. nestled among climbing roses
2. sitting beside the freeway
3. abandoned in the open lots
4. scrambling over a wire fence
5. burning in the greasy summer air

◆ Literary Focus

1. Possible responses: *Cervantes'* voice may be described as sensory or Hispanic. She uses descriptive language and many Spanish words in her poem. *Espada's* voice may be described as straightforward and direct since his poem is written without flowery or complex language. *Ortiz's* voice may be described as repetitive or rhythmic since the poet repeats key words and phrases in his poem. *Chang's* voice might be described as spare and thoughtful since she addresses an abstract concept in very few words. *Hongo's* voice might be described as rhythmic, descriptive and anecdotal since his poetry incorporates long sentences that create images by telling stories of the people and places he describes.
2. Students should support their choice with examples from the poems.

◆ Build Vocabulary

Using the Greek Prefix *auto-*

1. An *automobile* moves under its own power.
2. The *autopilot* setting allows a plane to fly and navigate itself.
3. An *autograph* is a signature, written with one's own hand.

Using the Word Bank: Sentence Completions

1. b 2. a 3. c 4. a
5. b 6. c 7. a

◆ Reading Strategy

1. Possible response: The freeway has paved over a Spanish community of houses. In the abandoned lots it created, nature is rebuilding. I have come back to look at the place I was once so eager to leave. Maybe this place holds a part of me that I have lost.
2. Possible responses: (a) *Hunger in New York City:* Hunger can seek you out, reviving memories of food, people, and experiences. It makes you long for those things again. It makes you question your achievements and your goals. The city cannot soothe the pain of this hunger, so one needs to turn inward. (b) *What For:* At six, the speaker loved his family and the warmth they created. He knew each person—especially his father—had sacrificed and he wanted to soothe their pain.

◆ Grammar and Style

1. *Seeking an after-school job* modifies *I*.
2. *Slipping cardboard between the papers* modifies *I*.
3. *Cut by the sharp edges* modifies *hands*.
4. *Oozing over them* modifies *glue*.
5. *Upturned in pain* modifies *hands*.

Writing Application

Possible responses:

1. The house, *nestled among climbing roses*, was abandoned. (house)
2. *Sitting beside the freeway,* Cervantes wrote a poem. (Cervantes)
3. She was amazed to see the buildings *abandoned in the open lots*. (buildings)
4. The writer, *scrambling over a wire fence*, lost all sense of time and place. (writer)
5. The smell of tar *burning in the greasy summer air* emphasized the heat. (tar)

Grammar Reinforcement

For additional instruction and practice, use the Recognizing and Using Phrases lesson in the Writing Style unit of the **Language Lab CD-ROM,** and the page on Participles and Participial Phrases, p. 32, in the *Writer's Solution Grammar Practice Book*.

Idea Bank

Customizing for
Performance Levels
Following are suggestions for matching Idea Bank topics with your students' performance levels:
Less Advanced Students: 1, 5
Average Students: 2, 4, 6
More Advanced Students: 3, 7

Customizing for
Learning Modalities
Following are suggestions for matching Idea Bank topics with your students' learning modalities:
Interpersonal: 4
Musical/Rhythmic: 5
Logical/Mathematical: 6, 7

Guided Writing Lesson

For more intruction on prewriting, elaboration, and revision, see *Prentice Hall Writing and Grammar.*

Writing and Language Transparencies Use Writing Process Model 2, Descriptive and Observational Writing, (pp. 9–12) to demonstrate the elements of observational writing.

Writers at Work Videodisc
Have students view the videodisc segment on Description (Ch. 1) featuring Rita Dove to see how language choice can play a key part in description. Have students discuss Dove's ideas about using "compelling" language.

Play frames 1481 to 2687

Writing Lab CD-ROM
Have students complete the tutorial on Description. Follow these steps:
1. Encourage students to use Word Bins to help them gather sensory details.
2. Have students draft on computer.
3. Refer students to interactive tips for revising figurative language.

Build Your Portfolio

Idea Bank

Writing

1. **Letter** Choose one of the poems and turn it into a letter the speaker might write to a friend.
2. **Editorial** Write a newspaper editorial inspired by the details in one of these poems. You might focus, for example, on how to redevelop the area around Freeway 280 or how to improve the quality of life in the New York City of Ortiz's poem.
3. **Comparison-and-Contrast Essay** Write an essay in which you compare and contrast two of these poems. Focus on the poems' messages and the poets' use of language.

Speaking, Listening, and Viewing

4. **Interview** Do you know someone whose personal or professional life reflects his or her cultural heritage? Prepare a list of questions; then interview that person about the influences in his or her life. Videotape or record the interview to share with the class. **[Social Studies Link]**
5. **Oral Interpretation** Using background music or other sound effects, give an oral reading of one of the poems. **[Performing Arts Link]**

Researching and Representing

6. **Cultural Report** Find out more about the cultural background reflected in one of the poems. For example, you might research and report on Japanese Buddhism or customs of New Mexico's Acoma Pueblo. **[Social Studies Link]**
7. **Anthology** Locate and gather Asian poetry in English translations. Create an anthology of these poems. In a brief introduction to your anthology, explain how Diana Chang's "Most Satisfied by Snow" shows the influence of Asian verse. **[Literature Link]**

Online Activity www.phlit.phschool.com

Guided Writing Lesson

Observation of a Storm

Carefully observe a rainstorm, snowstorm, or windstorm. Then write a description of it. Your description may take the form of a poem or a prose passage. Use language creatively to convey the physical and emotional effects of the storm.

Writing Skills Focus: Figurative Language

To help you capture the storm and the feelings it inspires, you will probably want to use **figurative language**—language not meant to be taken literally. Most types of figurative language compare something vague or abstract to an image that can readily be perceived by the senses.

- A **simile** compares two unlike things using *like* or *as* to show that a comparison is being made: *His hearing was as clear as crystal chimes.*
- A **metaphor** equates two unlike things without using *like* or *as: The freeway is a raised scar.*
- **Personification** describes something nonhuman as if it were human: *Hunger crawls into you, asking for food, words, wisdom.*

Prewriting Jot down details that describe the storm—perhaps using a cluster diagram to help you recall and organize them. Review your notes, writing down any comparisons they inspire.

Drafting Decide what comparison you'd like to develop in your observation. Get your ideas down on paper; you can polish your language later.

Revising Make sure that your language is vivid and your word choice is clear and precise. Did you use figurative language to bring the sights and sounds of the storm to life for the reader? If you are writing prose, check that you have used transitions to make your sentences flow logically and smoothly. Correct any grammar, spelling, and mechanical errors.

ASSESSMENT OPTIONS

Formal Assessment, Selection Test, pp. 292–294, and Assessment Resources Software. The selection test is designed so that it can be easily customized to the performance levels of your students.

Alternative Assessment, p. 67, includes options for less advanced students, more advanced students, verbal/linguistic learners, and visual/spatial learners.

PORTFOLIO ASSESSMENT
Use the following rubrics in ***Alternative Assessment*** to assess student writing:
Letter: Expression Rubric, p. 109
Editorial: Persuasion Rubric, p. 120
Comparison-and-Contrast Essay: Comparison/Contrast Rubric, p. 118
Guided Writing Lesson: Technical Description/Explanation Rubric, p. 130

Writing Process Workshop

Research Paper

The process of writing a piece of nonfiction doesn't begin with setting words down on paper. Writers often spend days, weeks, or even months researching and gathering information on their topics before ever writing a word. Scholars and students use these same skills when writing a research paper—a formal paper that presents and supports a thesis statement, or main idea, with research gathered from a variety of reliable sources.

Use the following writing skills, introduced in this section's Guided Writing Lessons, to help you write a strong, coherent research paper.

Writing Skills Focus

- **Use a clear organization.** Begin with an introduction that states the thesis, and develop and support the thesis in the body of the paper. Conclude with a restatement of the main points. (See p. 911.)
- **Elaborate** by including direct quotations from a variety of credible sources. (See p. 901.)
- To clearly link your ideas and details, **use transitions that show cause and effect**. (See p. 889.)

This passage from a research paper on Amy Tan demonstrates these skills.

Writing Model

Though Amy Tan did not begin writing fiction until age thirty-three, she quickly established herself as a unique and powerful literary voice. ① She had wanted to write fiction from the time she won an essay contest at age eight, but was told "if you liked doing something, it wasn't worth doing." (Clark, 36) ② It was 1985 before she entered a creative writing workshop because ③ she realized that she was not satisfied with her hectic career as a business writer. Though Tan claims her first few short stories were barely understandable, she found her literary voice when she began to envision her Chinese mother as her reader. (Grieg, 89)

① *The writer opens with a thesis statement that clearly establishes the paper's topic.*

② *Parenthetical notes indicate the source of the information.*

③ *The transition word "because" clearly shows the cause-and-effect relationship between Tan's dissatisfaction with her career and the decision to join the workshop.*

Prepare and Engage

LESSON OBJECTIVES

- To use recursive writing processes to write a research paper
- To write paragraphs with topic sentences and supporting sentences
- To use proper bibliographic style

Distribute the scoring rubric for Research Report/Paper (p. 121 in ***Alternative Assessment***) to make students aware of evaluation criteria. To customize the rubric to this workshop, see page 989.

You may also want to present to the class the Writing Process Model of a Research Report from the ***Writing and Language Transparencies.***

Writers at Work Videodisc

To introduce students to elements of research writing, play the videodisc segment on Research (Ch. 5) featuring music writer Gillian Gaar.

Play frames 3 to 9643

Writing Lab CD-ROM

If your students have access to computers, you may want to have them work in the tutorial on Research to complete all or part of their research papers. Have students follow these steps:

1. Review the interactive model of a research paper.
2. Complete a Research Profile, a questionnaire they can refer to to save time conducting research.
3 Draft their research papers on the computer.
4. Revise using Revision Checkers for unity and coherence, transitions, and sentence lengths.
5. Review the Self-Evaluation Checklist to help them revise.

Beyond the Classroom

Career Connection

Fact Checking There are many opportunities to use research skills in the job market. Most major magazines, newspapers and book publishers employ fact checkers to verify information before it is published. A fact checker is given a manuscript and then confirms facts through research. When information in an manuscript can not be confirmed independently, an editor must decide whether it should be printed. Ask students to identify some reasons why a manuscript might contain incorrect information. *Possible replies include: reference material that is no longer up-to-date; the sources used were not correct; the writer misinterpreted or misapplied information.* Ask students what they can do to prevent these types of situations in their writing. *Possible replies include: using primary sources; double checking reference material against other references; noting the date of a publication, and clarifying the currency of its information for readers as in, "Crime rates have been falling drastically according to a 1996 FBI report."*

Develop Student Writing

Prewriting Strategy

Before students begin writing, emphasize that research writing is a recursive process. Display and discuss a research loop like the one shown here. Call students' attention to the discussion and interviewing that follows reading and the conferencing that precedes students' reentering their writing.

Customize for *AP Students*

These students may enjoy supplementing conventional information resources—libraries or on/line sources—by conducting original research. Have them consider taking an interdisciplinary approach, and enlisting another teacher to serve as a subject area consultant.

Customize for *English Language Learners*

Review the sources of information that these students use in order to check for special jargon or advanced vocabulary—many reference books contain glossaries of key terms. Guide students to locate such tools, or to narrow their topics to match their level of comprehension.

Writing Lab CD-ROM

The Gathering Information section of the tutorial contains audio-annotated instruction in using library resources including a computer catalog screen, conventional card catalog systems, almanacs, atlases, encyclopedias, and bibliographic references.

Elaboration Strategy

Caution students about including information that does not directly support their thesis statements. Explain that extraneous facts, no matter how interesting, will detract from the effectiveness of their papers.

Applying Language Skills: Topic and Supporting Sentences

A **topic sentence**—which most often appears at the beginning of a paragraph—states the main idea of the paragraph. The rest of the sentences in the paragraph should support the main idea; these are called **supporting sentences.** The topic sentence in this example is underlined:

Julia Alvarez uses her Dominican heritage as inspiration for her fiction. Books like *¡Yo!* detail the life of fictional characters and include details of the Hispanic American tradition.

Practice In a brief paragraph, describe one of the selections you read in this section. Include a topic sentence and a series of supporting sentences.

Writing Application Keep your paper clear and focused by building each paragraph around a topic sentence.

> **Writer's Solution Connection Writing Lab**
>
> For additional support on gathering information, see the instruction and activities in the tutorial on Research Writing.

Prewriting

Choose a Topic Choose a subject that you would like to study. You might browse through a newspaper or skim a history text for inspiration. Keep in mind that your topic must be narrow enough to research and present in a single paper, yet broad enough to enable you to find information in a variety of sources. If you can't come up with a topic on your own, consider one of these:

> **Topic Ideas**
>
> - The life and literature of N. Scott Momaday
> - A local historical event
> - The effects of the end of the Cold War
> - The planet Mars

Gather Information To create an effective research paper, you will need a variety of quality sources. Locate at least three sources on your topic by consulting reference resources such as the *Readers' Guide to Periodical Literature*; a library card or computer catalog; vertical files; or Internet search engines that can help you locate Web sites related to your topic.

Take Notes As you research, record each item of information on an individual note card. Record all direct quotations accurately and note the source of the information. Group note cards by subtopic.

Write a Thesis Statement The thesis statement is a concise presentation of your main point. To develop yours, organize and review your notes. Draw a conclusion that synthesizes the information in your notes, and then summarize it in a single sentence. Use your thesis to develop an outline for your paper.

Drafting

Create an Introduction, Body, and Conclusion An organized paper begins with an effective introduction that includes the thesis statement. Consider opening with a dramatic quote or startling fact for greater impact. Develop your thesis in the body of the paper. Be sure the topic sentence and details of each paragraph support the thesis statement, and use transition words to clarify relationships among details and ideas. Finish with a conclusion that summarizes the main idea or findings presented in your paper.

Applying Language Skills

Topic and Supporting Sentences

Introduce this skill by explaining that adhering to a topic-and-supporting/ sentence structure will make writing—and reading—their papers much easier. Sentences that do not support the topic sentence should be eliminated

Answer

When reviewing students' practice paragraphs, you may want to label the topic sentence and place a check mark next to each supporting sentence to provide graphic feedback to students. Before having students write these paragraphs you may lead the class in composing a paragraph on the chalkboard to illustrate the process; for some students, the example in the book may be too brief.

Grammar Reinforcement

For additional instruction and practice, refer students to the **Language Lab CD-ROM** lesson on Topic Sentence and Support, and the Developing Your Style 2 lesson in the *Sourcebook* (p. 163).

Credit Sources Each time you use another person's exact words, present an original idea that is not your own, or report a fact available only in one source, you must credit the original source in a footnote, endnote, or parenthetical citation. Include a complete bibliography listing each of your research sources.

Revising

Review the Essay's Coherence Confirm that your introduction and conclusion agree. Then check the first and last sentence of every paragraph to be sure that each idea follows in a logical sequence. If necessary, add transitional sentences to make connections in your essay more clear.

Use a Checklist Set aside some time to step back and evaluate your work using a checklist like the following:

- Have I clearly stated my thesis in the introduction? Is the thesis supported with enough information?
- Is the paper organized, with a clear introduction, body, and conclusion? Does every paragraph have a topic sentence?
- Have I used transitions to show how the ideas in successive sentences and paragraphs are related?
- Have I used—and cited—a variety of credible sources?

Revision Model

When a bill is introduced in Congress, it has already passed a number of hurdles. ^① House members introduce bills by dropping them in the hopper at the clerk's desk in the House chamber. Then, Subcommittees made up of members of both parties review each bill. ^② When the bill has been thoroughly researched and reviewed, ~~Next,~~ the subcommittee reports to the full Congress with a recommendation.

① The author adds an interesting, little known detail to maintain the reader's interest.

② A cause-and-effect transition and explanatory phrase help the reader link the work of the subcommittee to the process.

Publishing

- **Multimedia Presentation** Enhance your research paper with pictures, videotape, or other appropriate media. Invite classmates or family members to see your presentation.

Applying Language Skills: Proper Bibliographic Form

When you use **proper bibliographic form**, you present sources in a standardized format based on the type of resource. This enables readers to check the accuracy of information or learn more about the topic.

For a Book With One Author:

Welty, Eudora. *One Writer's Beginnings.* New York: Warner Books, Inc., 1984.

For a Reference Book:

"Hockey." *The World Book Encyclopedia.* 1998 ed.

For a Magazine Article:

Corliss, Richard. "The Deal That Wasn't." *Time,* June 19, 1995: 51.

Writing Application During the research phase of your work, keep a list of the sources you consult. Following the style your teacher requires, create a bibliography of your sources.

Writer's Solution Connection
Writing Lab

For additional information on citing sources, consult the instruction in the Drafting section of the tutorial on Research Writing.

Revision Strategy

Make sure that peer reviewers are familiar with the method of source citation used by the writer.

Writing Lab CD-ROM

The Revising and Editing section of the tutorial includes tips on checking for accuracy.

Publishing

If students create a multimedia presentation, refer them to helpful instruction found in the workshop on multimedia presentations (p. 208) and on giving an oral presentation (p. 114).

Applying Language Skills

Proper Bibliographic Form Point out that an accurate bibliography is not a mere formality or afterthought in a research paper. Indeed, in their later academic careers, teachers, critics, and colleagues will actively investigate any items they cite.

Writing Application Decide on a class standard for bibliographic form, and make sure that a reference guide such as the *Chicago Manual of Style* is available for students to consult.

Grammar Reinforcement

Refer to the pages on Library and Reference Materials in the *Writer's Solution Grammar Practice Book* (pp. 169–171).

Reinforce and Extend

Prentice Hall Writing and Grammar For more prewriting, elaboration, and revision strategies, see *Prentice Hall Writing and Grammar.*

✓ ASSESSMENT		4	3	2	1
PORTFOLIO ASSESSMENT Use the rubric on Research Report/Paper in the ***Alternative Assessment*** booklet (p. 121) to assess students' writing. Add these criteria to customize the rubric to this assignment.	**Topic Sentences**	The writer makes sure that every paragraph has a topic sentence that is supported by other sentences.	The writer includes topic and supporting sentences in most paragraphs.	The writer's paragraphs rarely have topic sentences, or these sentences are not well supported by others	The paper does not reflect the use of topic and supporting sentences.
	Proper Bibliographic Form	The writer consistently follows proper bibliographic form.	The writer makes some errors in proper bibliographic form.	The writer rarely uses proper bibliographic form.	The writer demonstrates no ability to use proper bibliographic form.

Prepare and Engage

LESSON OBJECTIVES

- To adapt reports and research projects for different audiences
- To respond appropriately in a written composition to the purpose/audience in a given topic

Customize for
Less Advanced Students
Prepare two sets of cards, one naming research topics and one naming different audiences. Each card should show only one topic or audience. Invite students to select a card from each stack. Have him or her write the research topic and audience on the board as column heads. With the help of the entire class or a small group, discuss characteristics or qualities associated with each topic and audience. List them on the board under the correct headings. Repeat the procedure several times, pointing out to students that the more they know about their topic and audience the better they can focus their research and ensure that their message will be received well.

Apply the Strategies

Answers

1. Teachers or students doing research on Mark Twain.
2. Student revisions should focus on the topic of Mark Twain's humorous characterizations, reflect more grade-appropriate word choices, and provide simpler sentence constructions.
3. Students should be able to identify three different audiences, and then give advice about the audience for each. For example, students might write this for third graders, "Be sure to use words that people who read or hear your report will understand."

Student Success Workshop

Research Skills — Adapt Research Presentations to Your Audience

Strategies for Success

When writing a research paper, the way you present the information is often determined by your audience. For instance, a research paper on rain forests presented to elementary-school students would look different from one presented to college biology students. Use the strategies to tailor research papers for specific audiences:

Identify Your Audience The purpose of a research report is to present your findings on a particular subject with an organized collection of information from different sources that supports your findings. Ask yourself some questions as you prepare and write to help you direct the topic to your audience: Who will be reading this paper? Why are they interested in this topic? What information will they find most important? How much do they already know about the topic?

Choose a Format Not all research reports have the same appearance. A report that contains technical information may include charts and graphs. Biographical research papers may contain pictures from that person's life. Carefully assess the information you need to present, and choose the form of presentation that suits it best.

Write for Your Audience Your intended audience determines the tone and style of your research paper. If your audience is a business group, you would minimize informal language and humor. A research report presented to teenagers might include flashy graphics and have a more conversational tone. Papers written for your teacher should discuss the material thoroughly. As you write your research paper, always keep your audience in mind.

Apply the Strategies

Read this excerpt from a research paper, and do the activities that following.

> In addition to his use of cynicism and ironic endings, Mark Twain's ability to create and define quirky characters—their words, clothes, and mannerisms—also contributes to his humor. Few other authors have so successfully depicted the idiosyncratic nature of individuals. In "The Notorious Jumping Frog of Calaveras County," Twain exemplifies this in the character of Jim Smiley, the subject of the story. However, not content with one singularly noticeable individual, Twain adds flavor to the story by telling it through the voice of Simon Wheeler, an equally unique person. . . .

1. Describe the audience who would most likely read this research paper.
2. Imagine your audience to be a middle-school language arts class. Rewrite this excerpt accordingly.
3. Choose three possible audiences. Write a section of a writer's manual telling how to tailor writing toward each audience.

Here are other situations in which you might tailor research findings for different audiences:

- *A report on a new vaccine delivered to parents of young children*
- *A research paper on school testing methods delivered to educators*
- *A presentation to children about environmental responsibility*

Test Preparation Workshop

Written Communication: Composition for a Specific Audience and Purpose Many standardized tests have students respond to writing prompts with a specific purpose or audience. Most prompts will require students to respond to a formal audience of objective and impartial adults. Students are assessed on their ability to vary word choice, to incorporate information from sources other than personal experience, to use persuasive discourse, and to use formal and informal language appropriately. Have students respond to the following prompt. Then, assist students in evaluating their own writing based on the given criteria.

> In an effort to decrease the number of automobile fatalities, many states have established a speed limit of 55 mph on highways that formerly had a 65 mph speed limit. What is your position on this change? Write a letter to your state senator explaining your position and supporting it with convincing reasons.

PART 2 # *Focus on Literary Forms: Essay*

My Mother's Book of Life, Lee Lawson

Analytic, expository, satiric, or personal, the essay has been used for centuries to express ideas that range from personal reflection to national revolution. In the busy modern world, readers have embraced the essay form, which presents ideas in a limited space. From comedy to personal triumph, the essays in this section demonstrate the flexibility of the form.

Humanities: Art

My Mother's Book of Life, 1987, by Lee Lawson.

Encourage students to contrast this painting with Television Moon (p. 875), which introduced Part 1. Help them to see not only the difference in subject matter—a real, as opposed to televised, moon, along with a human being reading—but also the difference in style. This painting has visible texture, which softens the edges of the images, as opposed to the hard, almost photographic quality of Television Moon.

Have your students link the painting to the focus of this part (The Essay) by answering the following questions:

1. What mood would you say this painting creates, and how? *The painting creates a quiet, reflective, tender mood, through the use of soft colors and interesting textures and through its title.*
2. An essay is a highly personal form of literature, directly expressing the author's thoughts, feelings, and opinions. What do you feel this painting reveals about its creator? *The artist expresses love for a mother who loved books and natural beauty.*

One-Minute Planning Guide

The selections in this section offer students a sampling of a wide range of styles and subjects. Carson McCuller's analytical essay from "The Mortgaged Heart" addresses the issue of loneliness. Safire's expository essay "Onomatopoeia" presents an interesting segment of language. Frazier's satirical "Coyote v. Acme" takes a humorous look at the court system. Reflective essays by Cisneros, Dove, and Tan address each author's contemplations on life experiences.

Customize for
Varying Student Needs

When assigning selections in this part, keep these factors in mind:

from "The Mortgaged Heart"
- Contains high-level analysis of an abstract concept
- Intrapersonal learners may be especially interested in McCuller's analysis.

"Onomatopoeia"
- An accessible essay about the unusual words which bring lively sounds to everyday speech

"Coyote v. Acme"
- High-interest, comical "opening argument" pitting Wile E. Coyote against the explosive company from which he frequently makes purchases
- Logical/Mathematic learners may enjoy the essay's legal wranglings.

"Straw Into Gold"
- An inspirational essay about success despite obstacles

"For the Love of Books"
- In an accessible, short essay, a poet-laureate describes her childhood passion for reading.

"Mother Tongue"
- Tan describes stereotypes sparked by her mother's trouble with English.
- English Language learners may relate and respond favorably to Tan's message.

Prepare and Engage

LESSON OBJECTIVES

1. To develop vocabulary and word identification skills
- Word Origins: Latin Root *-ten-*
- Using the Word Bank: Word Choice
- Idea Bank: Analytical Essay

2. To use a variety of reading strategies to comprehend an essay
- Connect Your Experience
- Read to Form an Opinion (ATE)

3. To increase knowledge of other cultures and to connect common elements across cultures
- Connecting Themes Across Cultures (ATE)

4. To express and support responses to the text
- Critical Thinking
- Idea Bank: Letter
- Idea Bank: News Article
- Idea Bank: Cartoon Strip

5. To read critically and analyze literary elements
- Literary Focus: Essays
- Reading Strategy: Identify Line of Reasoning
- Idea Bank: Invented Words
- Idea Bank: Essay Collection

6. To plan, prepare, organize, and present literary interpretations
- Idea Bank: Opening Statement for the Defense
- Speaking Listening, and Viewing Mini-Lesson (ATE)

7. To use recursive writing processes to write a résumé
- Guided Writing Lesson

8. To increase knowledge of the rules of grammar and usage
- Grammar and Style: Pronouns With Appositives
- Extending Word Study: Mnemonic Spelling(ATE)

Test Preparation

Writing Skills: Punctuation (ATE, p. 993)

The teaching tips and sample test item in this workshop support the instruction and practice in the unit workshop:

Writing Skills: Punctuation, Usage, and Sentence Structure (SE, p. 1143)

Guide for Interpreting

Carson McCullers *(1917–1967)*

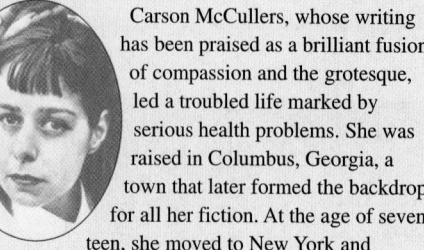

Carson McCullers, whose writing has been praised as a brilliant fusion of compassion and the grotesque, led a troubled life marked by serious health problems. She was raised in Columbus, Georgia, a town that later formed the backdrop for all her fiction. At the age of seventeen, she moved to New York and married Reeves McCullers three years later. While still in her twenties, she suffered a series of strokes, which incapacitated her for long periods. In later years, partial paralysis confined her to a wheelchair, yet she still managed to type new manuscripts. Her loneliness and suffering are reflected in her novels, which include *The Heart Is a Lonely Hunter* (1940), *The Member of the Wedding* (1946), and *Clock Without Hands* (1961).

William Safire *(1929–)*

When it comes to questions about the use—and misuse—of the English language, few people have more answers or observations than William Safire. A political commentator and the author of the "On Language" column of *The New York Times,* Safire is one of the world's most widely read writers on language in America today. The 1978 Pulitzer Prize winner for distinguished commentary, Safire was once a political speech writer for the White House. His books include *On Language* (1980), *What's the Good Word?* (1982), *I Stand Corrected* (1984), *Take My Word for It* (1986), *You Could Look It Up* (1988), and *Coming to Terms* (1991). He has also written two novels, *Full Disclosure* (1977) and *Freedom* (1987).

Ian Frazier *(1951–)*

Known for humorous essays and for affectionate descriptions of rural America, Ian Frazier brings "an antic sense of fun" to whatever he writes. He was born in Cleveland, Ohio, and now lives in New York City, where he works as a staff writer for *The New Yorker* magazine.

Frazier's humorous and often ironic essays are collected in a series of nonfiction books, including *Dating Your Mom* (1986), *Nobody Better, Better Than Nobody* (1987), *Great Plains* (1989), and *Family* (1994). "Coyote v. Acme" is typical of his work: a ludicrous premise packaged in serious style. As you read the essay, ask yourself what Frazier is really satirizing—the cartoon character who is his subject or the legal profession.

◆ Background for Understanding

POPULAR CULTURE: HALF A CENTURY OF CARTOONS

Ian Frazier's essay "Coyote v. Acme" is the fictional opening statement of a lawsuit by Mr. Wile E. Coyote, charging the Acme Company with the sale of defective merchandise. Do those names sound familiar? You may have a childhood memory of watching Wile E. Coyote chase the Road Runner through the desert. The Warner Brothers cartoon "Road Runner and Coyote" made its debut in 1948; half a century later, both the coyote and the elusive bird are still going strong. Perhaps fifty years from now your grandchildren will be watching Coyote's ill-fated attempts—many involving Acme products—to capture the fleet-footed bird.

Prentice Hall Literature Program Resources

REINFORCE / RETEACH / EXTEND

Selection Support Pages
Build Vocabulary: Word Roots *-ten-*, p. 306
Grammar and Style: Pronouns w/ Appositives, p. 307
Reading Strategy: Identify Line of Reasoning, p. 308
Literary Focus: Essays, p. 309

Strategies for Diverse Student Needs, p. 68

Beyond Literature
Cross-Curricular Connection: Social Studies, p. 68

Formal Assessment Selection Test, pp. 299–301; Assessment Resources Software

Alternative Assessment, p. 68

Writing and Language Transparencies
Writing Process Model: Résumé (pp. 53–56)

Resource Pro CD-ROM
Includes all resources and customizable lesson plan.

Listening to Literature Audiocassettes

Art Transparency 3

from The Mortgaged Heart ◆ Onomatopoeia ◆ Coyote v. Acme

◆ Literature and Your Life

Connect Your Experience

Think about what is important to you. It might be enjoying friendship, overcoming loneliness, or finding your own personal identity. You may explore the ideas that mean the most to you in your journal or in letters or e-mails to close friends. Some writers use a more public form of writing—the essay—to express themes or to make a point about something that they consider important.

Thematic Focus: Literature Confronts the Everyday

In these essays, writers confront common elements of American culture: loneliness, language, and our legal system. As you read, consider whether you share the writers' views on their subjects.

Journal Writing Safire's essay is about words that sound like what they name, such as *buzz* and *hum*. How many of these words can you list?

◆ Reading Strategy

Identify Line of Reasoning

When presenting an argument in an essay, a writer offers a **line of reasoning** in an attempt to convince readers of the essay's key points. As you read these essays, identify the writers' main points and note the reasons, facts, and examples each writer offers to back up the points. Also look carefully at the relationships among the pieces of evidence cited. Are the cause-and-effect relationships valid?

◆ Grammar and Style

Pronouns With Appositives

McCullers observes that "... we Americans are always seeking." Notice that the pronoun *we* is followed by the noun *Americans* and acts as the subject of the clause. When a pronoun is followed by an **appositive**—a noun that renames the pronoun—choose the correct pronoun by mentally dropping the appositive.

Subject:	**Object:**
[Us/We] players had to win.	It was up to [us/we] players.
[Us/We] ~~players~~ had to win.	It was up to *us* ~~players~~.
We players had to win.	It was up to *us* players.

When a pronoun renames a sentence's subject, use *I, he, she, we,* or *they*. To rename an object, use *me, him, her, us,* or *them*.

◆ Literary Focus

Essays

An **essay** is a short piece of nonfiction in which a writer expresses a personal view or a topic. Among the many types of essays are the analytical essay, the satirical essay, and the expository essay.

- An **analytical essay** attempts to analyze—or break down and explain the parts of—a topic.
- A **satirical essay** uses irony, ridicule, or sarcasm to comment on a topic.
- An **expository essay** provides information about or explains a topic. As you read, look for details that help you decide how you might classify each of these essays.

◆ Build Vocabulary

Latin Roots: *-ten-*

In "Coyote v. Acme," Frazier describes the *tensile* strength of Acme springs. The word *tensile* contains the Latin root *-ten-*, meaning "to stretch tightly." Tensile springs would be "stretchable."

Word Bank

Preview this list of words from the essays.

pristine
corollary
aesthetic
maverick
contiguous
precipitate
caveat
tensile

Interest Grabber As you play a Roadrunner cartoon for the class, ask students to count the times Coyote meets with disaster. Ask students to draw a few conclusions about Coyote as a predator. Students may call him incompetent. Then ask for student reaction to the cartoon. Point out that essays—like cartoons, movies, or advertisements—generate a variety of responses. Invite students to be open to the range of expression this genre—and this grouping—offers.

Connecting Themes Across Cultures

The essays in this grouping address specific aspects of American culture: cartoons, television commercials, and social norms. Encourage students to consider how they can move from the specific to the universal. Discuss how these reflections on American life can draw students' attention to the similarities and differences from other cultures.

Customize for ***Less Proficient Readers***

All three essays contain specialized or difficult vocabulary. To help less proficient readers, encourage them to read with a dictionary at hand. By pausing to define unfamiliar words, they can insure comprehension.

Customize for ***AP Students***

Comparative analysis can enable these students to appreciate the stylistic differences among the three essays. Have students describe the diction, tone, and syntax of each writer, then link these to each essay's message.

Customize for ***English Language Learners***

The complex ideas, difficult language, and sometimes satirical tone of these essays will likely prove difficult for language learners. It may be helpful to introduce more vocabulary than the student edition features or to focus on only one of the three essays presented here.

Test Preparation Workshop

Writing Skills:
Punctuation The writing sections of standardized tests often require students to identify and correct punctuation errors. Use the following sample test item to give students practice in this skill.

A coyote could not possibly use the following items! a rocket sled, rocket skates, a bomb, and spring-powered shoes.

What is the BEST way to rewrite the underlined section of the passage?

A NO CHANGE
B items: a rocket
C items a rocket
D items. A rocket

An exclamation mark is not appropriate preceding a list, so *A* is incorrect. *C* requires punctuation between the clause and the list. *D* creates a sentence fragment. *B* includes a colon before the list. *B* is the correct answer.

Develop Understanding

One-Minute Insight As young adults working to define their own place in the world, students will find "The Mortgaged Heart," both poignant and highly pertinent. McCullers begins with the challenge of understanding American loneliness. She follows the path of human growth to track the development of Americans' sense of isolation and offers examples of real-life responses to loneliness. By analyzing this apparently ingrained element of the human experience and urging self-examination as method for relief, McCullers offers hope to any reader who has ever felt like an outsider.

Customize for
Musical/Rhythmic Learners
Remind students that loneliness is a prime topic for songwriters. Many, many songs, whether popular, jazz, or country-western, focus on the speaker's isolation. Invite students to share favorite songs, prompting them with classics such as The Beatles' "Eleanor Rigby," or more recent titles such as Sarah McLachlan's "Out of the Shadows."

Literature CD-ROM Invite students to learn more about *The Member of the Wedding*, using the CD-ROM *The History of American Literature:* Part 2, Disk 2, Feature 3. How can the novel's characters and themes be linked to those of this essay?

◆ Literature and Your Life

❶ Point out McCullers' initial definition of loneliness as a quest for identity. Invite students to use examples from their own lives to verify or refute the definition. Offer the option of responding privately in a journal. *Some students may argue that loneliness stems from not feeling part of any group.*

◆ Reading Strategy

❷ Identify Line of Reasoning
Draw students' attention to this paragraph in which McCullers introduces an element in her argument. Invite students to paraphrase the text and restate the position. *Paraphrases may include: Love helps people reduce their loneliness by offering a bridge to others, by creating a positive lens through which to view the world, and by casting out fear.*

from The Mortgaged Heart

Carson McCullers

Connections to World Literature, *page 1204*

This city, New York—consider the people in it, the eight million of us. An English friend of mine, when asked why he lived in New York City, said that he liked it here because he could be so alone. While it was my friend's desire to be alone, the aloneness of many Americans who live in cities is an involuntary and fearful thing. It has been said that loneliness is the great American malady. What ❶ is the nature of this loneliness? It would seem essentially to be a quest for identity.

To the spectator, the amateur philosopher, no motive among the complex ricochets of our desires and rejections seems stronger or more enduring than the will of the individual to claim his identity and belong. From infancy to death, the human being is obsessed by these dual motives. During our first weeks of life, the question of identity shares urgency with the need for milk. The baby reaches for his toes, then explores the bars of his crib; again and again he compares the difference between his own body and the objects around him, and in the wavering, infant eyes there comes a pristine wonder.

Consciousness of self is the first abstract problem that the human being solves. Indeed, it is this self-consciousness that removes us from lower animals. This primitive grasp of identity develops with constantly shifting emphasis through all our years. Perhaps maturity is simply the history of those mutations that reveal to the individual the relation between himself and the world in which he finds himself.

After the first establishment of identity there comes the imperative need to lose this newfound sense of separateness and to belong to something larger and more powerful than the weak, lonely self. The sense of moral isolation is intolerable to us.

In *The Member of the Wedding*[1] the lonely twelve-year-old girl, Frankie Addams, articulates this universal need: "The trouble with me is that for a long time I have just been an *I* person. All people belong to a *We* except me. Not to belong to a *We* makes you too lonesome."

Love is the bridge that leads from the *I* sense to the *We*, and there is a paradox about personal love. Love of another individual opens a new relation between the personality and the world. The lover responds in a new way to nature and may even write poetry. Love is affirmation; it motivates the *yes* responses and the ❷ sense of wider communication. Love casts out fear, and in the security of this togetherness we find contentment, courage. We no longer fear the age-old haunting questions: "Who am I?" "Why am I?" "Where am I going?"—and having cast out fear, we can be honest and charitable.

◆ Build Vocabulary

pristine (pris´ tēn) *adj.*: Pure; uncorrupted

corollary (kôr´ ə ler´ ē) *n.*: Easily drawn conclusion

aesthetic (es *thet*´ ik) *adj.*: Pertaining to the study or theory of beauty and of the psychological response to it

maverick (mav´ ər ik) *n.*: Nonconformist

1. ***The Member of the Wedding:*** Novel and play by Carson McCullers.

Block Scheduling Strategies

Consider these strategies to take advantage of extended class time:

- Refer to the Literature and Your Life and Literary Focus features to introduce students to the idea that essays address a wide range of subjects.
- Use Art Transparency 3 to elicit a discussion of the legal system. The transparency features a painting of a courtroom scene and is best suited for use with Ian Frazier's essay.
- Have students work in groups to answer the selection page Guide for Responding questions (pp. 995, 997, 1001).
- Use the Speaking, Listening and Viewing Lesson (ATE, p. 998) to help students with the Opening Statement for the Defense activity (p. 1003).
- Use the rubrics suggested on page 1003 to assess one another's writing, after completing either an Idea Bank activity or the Guided Writing Lesson.
- Have students exchange and enjoy each other's work from the Cartoon Strip and Essay Collection activities (p. 1003).

For fear is a primary source of evil. And when the question "Who am I?" recurs and is unanswered, then fear and frustration project a negative attitude. The bewildered soul can answer only: "Since I do not understand 'Who I am,' I only know what I am *not*." The corollary of this emotional incertitude is snobbism, intolerance and racial hate. The xenophobic[2] individual can only reject and destroy, as the xenophobic nation inevitably makes war.

The loneliness of Americans does not have its source in xenophobia; as a nation we are an outgoing people, reaching always for immediate contacts, further experience. But we tend to seek out things as individuals, alone. The European, secure in his family ties and rigid
❸ class loyalties, knows little of the moral loneliness that is native to us Americans. While the European artists tend to form groups or aesthetic schools, the American artist is the eternal maverick—not only from society in the way of all creative minds, but within the orbit of his own art.

Thoreau took to the woods to seek the ultimate meaning of his life. His creed was simplicity and his *modus vivendi*[3] the deliberate stripping of external life to the Spartan[4] necessities in order that his inward life could freely flourish. His objective, as he put it, was to back the world into a corner. And in that way did he discover "What a man thinks of himself, that it is which determines, or rather indicates, his fate." ❹

On the other hand, Thomas Wolfe turned to the city, and in his wanderings around New York he continued his frenetic and lifelong search for the lost brother, the magic door. He too backed the world into a corner, and as he passed among the city's millions, returning their stares, he experienced "That silent meeting [that] is the summary of all the meetings of men's lives."

Whether in the pastoral joys of country life or in the labyrinthine city, we Americans are always seeking. We wander, question. But the answer waits in each separate heart—the answer of our own identity and the way by which we can master loneliness and feel that at last we belong.

2. **xenophobic** (zen´ ə fō´ bik) *adj.*: Afraid of strangers or foreigners.

3. ***modus vivendi*** (mō´ dəs vi ven´ dī): "Manner of living" (Latin).

4. **Spartan** (spär´ tən) *adj.*: Characteristic of the people of ancient Sparta: hardy, stoical, severe, frugal.

Guide for Responding

◆ Literature and Your Life

Reader's Response If you could meet Carson McCullers, which of the observations in this essay would you most like to discuss with her? Explain your reasons for choosing this observation.

Thematic Focus McCullers says that love "is the bridge that leads from the *I* sense to the *We*." How do the situations you encounter in everyday life support her observation?

Check Your Comprehension

1. Why does McCullers's English friend like living in New York City?
2. What does McCullers believe is the biggest problem for most Americans?
3. How does she say we can find contentment and courage and get rid of our fears?

◆ Critical Thinking

INTERPRET

1. What is McCullers's opinion about the cause of loneliness in America? **[Analyze]**
2. Find evidence in the essay that McCullers thinks love helps a person find true happiness. **[Support]**
3. (a) What does McCullers mean by the terms "moral isolation" and "moral loneliness"? (b) What does she mean when she comments that love "motivates the *yes* response"? **[Interpret]**

EXTEND

4. Do you think Americans today are likely to be more or less lonely than the early settlers? Explain the societal changes that prompted your answer. **[Social Studies Link]**

Beyond the Selection

FURTHER READING

Other Works by Carson McCullers

Reflections in a Golden Eye
Seven
The Square Root of Wonderful

Other Works With the Theme of Isolation

Walden, Henry David Thoreau
Are You In the House Alone?, Richard Peck
Invisible Man, Ralph Ellison

We suggest that you preview these works before recommending them to students.

INTERNET

You can find additional information about McCullers on the Internet. We suggest the following sites. Please be aware that sites may have changed since this information was published.

For information about McCullers and the study of her work, visit **http://educeth.ethz.ch/english/reading list/mccullers,carson.html**
To find out about the McCullers Society, go to **http://www.uwf. edu/~english/McCullers/main.htm**

We *strongly recommend* that you preview each site.

◆ Literary Focus

❸ **Essays** Ask students: How does this paragraph signal that this is an analytic essay? *A comparison of Europeans and Americans suggests the writer is trying to explain the sense of loneliness experienced by Americans.*

❹ **Clarification** Remind students that Henry David Thoreau wrote about his experiences living alone in a natural environment in his book *Walden* and that New York City was an important source of inspiration for Thomas Wolfe's work.

Reinforce and Extend

Answers

◆ **Literature and Your Life**

Reader's Response Possible response: Some students may want to question McCullers's assertion that "fear is a primary source of evil."

Thematic Focus Possible response: People who feel loved may find they have a stronger self-confidence.

Check Your Comprehension

1. He liked it because it allowed him to be alone.
2. The American quality of independence and individuality is the biggest problem.
3. She says that love will help us break free from fear.

◆ **Critical Thinking**

1. She believes that loneliness is caused by both a need for individuality and a quest for identity.
2. The sixth paragraph provides evidence to support the statement.
3. (a) She uses "moral" to imply conformity to accepted ideas of right and wrong. A child loses its "moral isolation" by learning the standards of family and society. Without the strict class structure of Europeans, Americans experience the "moral loneliness" of deciding correct behavior for themselves. (b) She means that people don't like to deny anything to someone they love.
4. Make sure that students thoroughly support their answers.

Develop Understanding

One-Minute Insight This expository essay explains the origin and meaning of *onomatopoeia.* As a linguistic tool, onomatopoeia—"words that are made by people making sounds like the action to be described"—have proved appealing to writers, both serious and commercial, as well as to readers and consumers, for centuries. In recounting some history and applications of onomatopoeia, Safire humorously confirms the extraordinary power of words and sounds to engage the human mind.

Customize for
Less Proficient Readers

❶ Review the pronunciation of *onomatopoeia* and its variations within the essay. Provide some common examples, such as *hum* and verify students' grasp of the linguistic definition.

▶Critical Viewing◀

❷ **Connect** Students should recognize that the illustration depicts cartoon action with an onomatopoetic word BLAM such as Safire describes in his text.

◆Literary Focus

❸ **Essays** Ask students: What is the author's purpose in the first paragraph? *Students should recognize that Safire defines, or explains, what onomatopoeia is.*

Extending Word Study

Mnemonic Spelling Help students remember the spelling of *onomotopoeia* by pointing out that they can remember the silent *oe* by thinking of onomotopoeia as a poetic device. Connecting *poetry* and onomo*topoeia* may help students remember to include the silent letters. Allow time for students to meet in groups, make lists of troublesome words, and find mnemonic devices for remembering the correct spelling or usage. You might suggest that students concentrate especially on frequently confused words, such as *their* and *there, affect* and *effect,* or *insure* and *ensure.* Encourage students to use reference materials to identify

❶ Onomatopoeia

William Safire

Blam, 1962, Roy Lichtenstein

▲ **Critical Viewing** What is the connection between this illustration and the subject of the essay? **[Connect]** ❷

The word *onomatopoeia* was used above, and it had better be spelled right or one usage dictator and six copy editors will get zapped. That word is based on the Greek for "word making"—the *poe* is the same as in *poetry,* "something made"—and is synonymous with *imitative* and *echoic,* denoting words that are made by people making sounds like the action to be described. (The *poe* in *onomatopoeia* has its own rule for pronunciation. Whenever a vowel follows *poe,* the *oe* combination is pronounced as a long *e*: *onomato-PEE-ia.* Whenever a consonant follows, as in *poetry* and *onomatopoetic,* pronounce the long *o* of Edgar Allan's name.) ❸

Henry Peacham, in his 1577 book on grammar and rhetoric called *The Garden of Eloquence,* first used *onomatopoeia* and defined it as "when we invent, devise, fayne, and make a

Humanities: Art

Blam, 1962, by Roy Lichtenstein.

This illustration depicts a cartoon character ejecting from an exploding airplane and features an onomatopoetic word—BLAM.

The artist, Roy Lichtenstein, was born and raised in New York City, where in his boyhood he was a fan of science and science fiction. He studied at the Art Students League and later with Hoyt Sherman at Ohio State University.

Use these questions for discussion:

1. How is the word BLAM an example of the onomatopoetic effects explained in the essay? *It imitates the sound of the explosion as it is heard in the viewer's ear.*
2. According to the essay, why are words and images like those in the painting so enduring? *They engage the human imagination through multiple senses.*

name intimating the sound of that it signifieth, as *hurlyburly*, for an uprore and tumultuous stirre." He also gave *flibergib* to "a gossip," from which we derive *flibbertigibbet*, and the long-lost *clapperclaw* and *kickle-kackle*.

Since Willard Espy borrowed the title of Peacham's work for his rhetorical bestiary in 1983, the author went beyond the usual examples of *buzz, hiss, bobwhite* and *babble*. He pointed out that one speculation about the origin of language was the *bow-wow theory*, holding that words originated in imitation of natural sounds of animals and thunder. (Proponents of the *pooh-pooh theory* argued that interjections like *ow!* and *oof!* started us all yakking toward language. Other theories—arrgh!—abound.)

Reaching for an alliterative onomatope, the poet Milton chose "melodious *murmurs*;" Edgar Allan Poe one-upped him with "the *tintinnabulation* of the bells." When carried too far, an obsession with words is called *onomatomania*; in the crunch (a word imitating the sound of an icebreaker breaking through ice) Gertrude Stein turned into an *onomatomaniac*.

What makes a word like *zap* of particular interest is that it imitates an imaginary noise—the sound of a paralyzing ray gun. Thus we can see another way that the human mind creates new words: imitating what can be heard only in the mind's ear. The coinage filled a need for an unheard sound and—*pow!*—slammed the vocabulary right in the kisser. Steadily, surely, under the watchful eye of great lexicographers and with the encouragement of columnists and writers who ache for color in verbs, the creation of Buck Rogers's creator has blasted its way into the dictionaries. The verb will live long after superpowers agree to ban ray guns; no sound thunders or crackles like an imaginary sound turned into a new word. ❹

Took me a while to get to the point today, but that is because I did not know what the point was when I started.

"I now zap all the commercials," says the merry Ellen Goodman. "I zap to the memory of white tornadoes past. I zap headaches, arthritis, bad breath and laundry detergent. I zap diet-drink maidens and hand-lotion mavens . . . Wiping out commercials could entirely and joyfully upend the TV industry. Take the word of The Boston Zapper."

Guide for Responding

◆ Literature and Your Life

Reader's Response Had you ever noticed the connection between the onomatopoetic words Safire discusses and the sounds they describe?

Thematic Focus How might the origins of many onomatopoetic words be tied to everyday situations and events?

☑ Check Your Comprehension

1. What is onomatopoeia?
2. What is the *bow-wow theory* concerning the origin of language?
3. What does Safire find so interesting about the word *zap*?

◆ Critical Thinking

INTERPRET

1. What is the origin of the word *onomatopoeia*? **[Classify]**
2. Compare and contrast the *bow-wow* and the *pooh-pooh theories* of language. **[Compare and Contrast]**
3. Why does Safire believe that the word *zap* will "live long after superpowers agree to ban ray guns"? **[Analyze]**

EVALUATE

4. Do you think Safire's humorous style is more or less effective than a factual explanation as a way of speaking about language? Explain. **[Assess]**

Beyond the Selection

FURTHER READING

Other Works by William Safire

Coming to Terms
Full Disclosure

Other Works With the Theme of Language and Its Power

"Words of Power," Jane Yolen
Crazy English, Richard Lederer

We suggest that you preview these works.

INTERNET

You and your students may find additional information about William Safire on the Internet. We suggest the following sites. Please be aware, however, that sites may have changed since this information was published.

For a profile of Safire posted by the high school which he attended, and other links, visit **http://voyager.bxscience.edu/alum/safire.html**

We *strongly recommend* that you preview sites before you send students to them.

Customize for
English Language Learners
Onomatopoetic words are invented and therefore reflect the sounds of the inventor's language. For example, a turkey says "gobble gobble" in English, but "glou-glou" in French. Invite students to share onomatopoetic words from their own language.

◆ Reading Strategy

❹ Identify Line of Reasoning
Challenge students to restate Safire's main point. *Invented words are enduring and powerful because they stimulate and engage the human imagination.*

Reinforce and Extend

Customize for
AP Students
Encourage students to read some writings by Edgar Allan Poe or Gertrude Stein and share a selection of onomatopoeia from these works. Discuss which examples students find most effective.

Answers

◆ Literature and Your Life

Reader's Response Most students should have some knowledge of these types of words.

Thematic Focus People find themselves describing sounds for which there are no words.

☑ Check Your Comprehension

1. Onomatopoeia is a word which makes the sound of the action it describes.
2. The *bow-wow* theory holds that words were derived as imitations of natural sounds.
3. *Zap* is an onomatopoeia to describe an imaginary sound no one has ever heard.

◆ Critical Thinking

1. The word is based on the Greek word for word making. It was first used by Henry Peacham in 1577.
2. The *bow-wow theory* says that language formed from an effort to imitate sound; the *pooh-pooh theory* says that language was formed from the grunts that humans already emitted.
3. *Zap* will live longer than ray guns, because it is a created product of imagination.
4. Make sure that students support their answers.

Develop Understanding

One-Minute Insight Students will find this satirical take on a legal brief amusing and enjoyable. The fictional defendant, Wile E. Coyote of cartoon fame, becomes an outraged victim whose terrible injuries are listed in great detail. This "brief's" lambaste of the Acme Company for its supposed negligence presents a scathing—but hilarious—commentary on the overly litigious relationship that currently exists between consumers and business.

Art Transparencies To build background for this selection, use Art Transparency 3: *Trial by Jury* by Thomas Hart Benton in ***Art Transparencies,*** (p. 15–17).

◆ Critical Thinking

❶ **Assess** Ask students to determine the effect of this opening heading. *The legal heading sets up the tone and purpose of the "essay."*

◆ Reading Strategy

❷ **Identify Line of Reasoning** The speaker will claim that defective products cause Coyote's injury.

◆ Critical Thinking

❸ **Make Inferences** Ask students: What can you infer about Coyote from the movements his body is able to make? *Students should recognize that Wile E. Coyote is a cartoon figure, with limbs able to stretch to fifty feet.*

◆ Reading Strategy

❹ **Identify Line of Reasoning** Point out to students how this evidence supports the speaker's argument that Acme's products are not well made.

COYOTE V. ACME

IAN FRAZIER

❶ In the United States District Court,
Southwestern District,
Tempe, Arizona
Case No. B19294,
JUDGE JOAN KUJAVA, PRESIDING

WILE E. COYOTE, Plaintiff
—v.—
ACME COMPANY, Defendant

Opening Statement of Mr. Harold Schoff, attorney for Mr. Coyote: My client, Mr. Wile E. Coyote, a resident of Arizona and contiguous states, does hereby bring suit for damages against the Acme Company, manufacturer and retail distributor of assorted merchandise, incorporated in Delaware and doing business in every state, district and territory. Mr. Coyote seeks compensation for personal injuries, loss of business income, and mental suffering caused as a direct result of the actions and/or gross negligence of said company, under Title 15 of the United States Code, Chapter 47, section 2072, subsection (a), relating to product liability.

Mr. Coyote states that on eighty-five separate occasions he has purchased of the Acme Company (hereinafter, "Defendant"), through that company's mail-order department, certain products which did cause him bodily injury due to defects in manufacture or improper cautionary labeling. Sales slips made out to Mr. Coyote as proof of purchase are at present in the possession of the Court, marked Exhibit A. Such injuries sustained by Mr. Coyote have temporarily restricted his ability to make a living in his profession of predator. Mr. Coyote is self-employed and thus not eligible for Workmen's Compensation.[1]

❷ **◆ Reading Strategy** What line of reasoning will the speaker use to make his case for an award of damages to his client, Wile E. Coyote?

Mr. Coyote states that on December 13th he received of Defendant via parcel post one Acme Rocket Sled. The intention of Mr. Coyote was to use the Rocket Sled to aid him in pursuit of his prey. Upon receipt of the Rocket Sled Mr. Coyote removed it from its wooden shipping crate and, sighting his prey in the distance, activated the ignition. As Mr. Coyote gripped the handlebars, the Rocket Sled accelerated with such sudden and precipitate force as to stretch Mr. Coyote's forelimbs to a length of fifty feet. ❸ Subsequently, the rest of Mr. Coyote's body shot forward with a violent jolt, causing severe strain to his back and neck and placing him unexpectedly astride the Rocket Sled. Disappearing over the horizon at such speed as to leave a diminishing jet trail along its path, the Rocket Sled soon brought Mr. Coyote abreast of his prey. At that moment the animal he was pursuing veered sharply to the right. Mr. Coyote vigorously attempted to follow this maneuver but was unable to, due to poorly designed steering on the Rocket Sled and a faulty or nonexistent braking system. ❹ Shortly thereafter, the unchecked progress of the Rocket Sled brought it and Mr. Coyote into collision with the side of a mesa.[2]

Paragraph One of the Report of Attending Physician (Exhibit B), prepared by Dr. Ernest Grosscup, M.D., D.O., details the multiple fractures, contusions, and tissue damage suffered by Mr. Coyote as a result of this collision. Repair of the injuries required a full bandage around the head (excluding the ears), a neck brace, and full or partial casts on all four legs.

Hampered by these injuries, Mr. Coyote was nevertheless obliged to support himself. With

1. **Workmen's Compensation:** Form of disability insurance that provides income to workers who are unable to work due to injuries sustained on the job.
2. **mesa** (mā´ sə) *n.*: Small, high plateau with steep sides.

Speaking, Listening, and Viewing Mini-Lesson

Opening Statement for the Defense
This mini-lesson supports the Speaking, Listening, and Viewing activity in the Idea Bank on p. 1003.

Introduce the Concept Have students discuss the goals and context of a legal defense. They might use cases recently in the news to clarify the role of a defending attorney's opening statement. Point out that the legal brief presented in the essay is written from the plaintiff's view.

Develop Background Before students present their arguments, urge them to consider the following defense strategies:

- Develop an overall responding argument. State arguments clearly in the opening and again in closing.
- Answer each point made in the plaintiff's argument, constructing it from the defense's view.
- Use vocal tone and body language to emphasize important points.

Apply the Information Place the class as "jury." Then have a student narrator read Frazier's essay aloud in a mock courtroom style, inviting each defense attorney to respond. Remind students to be respectful of the court and its participants.

Assess the Outcome Invite the "jury" to evaluate the defense arguments they have heard. Which were most convincing? Why?

5 ▶ Critical Viewing Based on this illustration, how might you describe Coyote's occupational goals as a professional predator? **[Analyze]**

this in mind, he purchased of Defendant as an aid to mobility one pair of Acme Rocket Skates. When he attempted to use this product, however, he became involved in an accident remarkably similar to that which occurred with the Rocket Sled. Again, Defendant sold over the counter, without <u>caveat</u>, a product which attached powerful jet engines (in this case, two) to inadequate vehicles, with little or no provision for passenger safety. Encumbered by his heavy casts, Mr. Coyote lost control of the Rocket
6 Skates soon after strapping them on, and collided with a roadside billboard so violently as to leave a hole in the shape of his full silhouette.

Mr. Coyote states that on occasions too numerous to list in this document he has suffered mishaps with explosives purchased of Defendant: the Acme "Little Giant" Firecracker, the Acme Self-Guided Aerial Bomb, etc. (For a full listing, see the Acme Mail Order Explosives Catalogue and attached deposition,[3] entered in
7 evidence as Exhibit C.) Indeed, it is safe to say
8 that not once has an explosive purchased of Defendant by Mr. Coyote performed in an expected manner. To cite just one example: At the expense of much time and personal effort, Mr. Coyote constructed around the outer rim of a butte[4] a wooden trough beginning at the top of the butte and spiraling downward around it to some few feet above a black X painted on the desert floor. The trough was designed in such a way that a spherical explosive of the type sold by Defendant would roll easily and swiftly down to the point of detonation indicated by the X. Mr. Coyote placed a generous pile of birdseed directly on the X, and then, carrying the spherical Acme Bomb (Catalogue #78-832), climbed to the top of the butte. Mr. Coyote's prey, seeing the birdseed, approached, and Mr. Coyote proceeded to light the fuse. In an instant, the fuse burned down to the stem, causing the bomb to detonate.

In addition to reducing all Mr. Coyote's careful preparations to naught, the premature detonation of Defendant's product resulted in the following disfigurements to Mr. Coyote:

1. Severe singeing of the hair on the head, neck, and muzzle.
2. Sooty discoloration.
3. Fracture of the left ear at the stem, causing the ear to dangle in the aftershock with a cracking noise.
4. Radical widening of the eyes, due to brow and lid charring.

◆ Build Vocabulary

contiguous (kən tig´ yo͞o əs) *adj.*: Bordering; adjacent

precipitate (prē sip´ ə tit) *adj.*: Very sudden; unexpected or abrupt

caveat (kā´ vē at´) *n.*: Formal notice; warning

3. **deposition** (dep´ ə zish´ ən) *n.*: Legal term for the written testimony of a witness.
4. **butte** (byo͞ot) *n.*: Steep hill standing alone in a plain.

Humanities: Art

Road Runner and Wile E. Coyote by Chuck Jones, still-photo from animated film.

This illustration shows the cartoon figure of Wile E. Coyote chasing his prey, the Road Runner, in a situation similar to those described in the essay.

Chuck Jones, an animator and producer, studied at Los Angeles's Chouinard Art Institute before joining the animation team at Warner Bros. With colleagues, he has designed such cartoon favorites as Bugs Bunny, Tweetie Pie, and Daffy Duck. In the 1960's, Jones founded his own company, creating animation for TV.

Use these questions for discussion:

1. What elements in the illustration convey Wile E. Coyote's personality as it is characterized in the essay? *His flight through air and crazed expression reflect the obsessive recklessness described in the essay.*
2. What effect might such an illustration have on the jury? *A character poised for the kill with such relish would probably not elicit much sympathy.*

Customize for
Visual/Spatial Learners
These learners may miss some of the essay's humorous tone because of its subtlety. Urge these learners to view the illustrations on page 999 and 1000 as a way to access the essay's humorous tone.

▶Critical Viewing◀

5 **Analyze** Students may comment that Coyote is a hunter—a very poor one—obsessed with catching his prey.

◆ Critical Thinking

6 **Interpret** Ask students to explain, verbally or with illustration, what has actually happened to Mr. Coyote. *Students explanation should include the fact that Mr. Coyote has been exploded completely <u>through</u> the billboard, leaving a cut-out silhouette behind.*

◆ Literary Focus

7 **Essays** Discuss with students how this text supports the comment Ian Frazier is making about the legal system. Guide students to see that this overabundance of evidence meant to blame Acme actually shows Mr. Coyote's obsessiveness and gullibility. Frazier undercuts the literal text with his satirical view: Why should consumers be allowed to hold companies responsible for their own stupidity or obsessiveness?

◆ *Literature and Your Life*

8 Point out to students Mr. Coyote's willingness, even determination, to keep buying Acme products despite the problems he has had with them. Have students ever been so focused on a goal that they perhaps lost perspective about the best methods for achieving it? *Students may mention efforts to achieve an athletic or academic goal in which they persisted on an unproductive path or times they were determined to befriend someone despite negative impacts on other parts of their lives.*

▶Critical Viewing◀

❶ **Connect** *Tensile*, meaning stretchable, could be used to describe "Mr. Coyote's body and the bow."

◆ *Literature and Your Life*

❷ Students might recall times when they very carefully planned a situation's logistics only to have these explode, figuratively or literally, in their faces.

Humanities: Art

Chariots of Fur by Chuck Jones, still photo from animated film.

This illustration, like the one on page 999, depicts the essay's plaintiff, Wile E. Coyote, engaged in a scheme to capture his prey, the Road Runner.

Among Chuck Jones' many accomplishments are much-loved animated TV specials based on Dr. Seuss stories, Rudyard Kipling tales, and the full-length novel *The Phantom Tollbooth*. Jones has won four Academy Awards for his work. Even in still-photo form, *Chariots of Fur* captures Wile E. Coyote's crazed personality.

Use these questions for discussion:

1. How does this illustration support the essay's comment about the legal system? *It shows Mr. Coyote clearly misusing the product for his own purposes.*
2. Based on the essay, what might the frame of film following this image show? *Wile E. Coyote slamming into something, while the Road Runner dashes away.*

Read to Form an Opinion

Tell students that in this humorous satire, Wile E. Coyote, the plaintiff, states his case against Acme Company, the defendant. In a true trial, the court would listen to both sides and render an opinion.

Explain to students that when they read to form an opinion, they must consider and evaluate all sides of an issue. Before they form an opinion, tell them to ask themselves these questions: Is the information on all sides is complete? Is the supporting evidence accurate and relevant? Is the speaker credible?

◀ Critical Viewing Which word from the Word Bank might be used to describe Coyote's bow? Explain. **[Connect]** ❶

We come now to the Acme Spring-Powered Shoes. The remains of a pair of these purchased by Mr. Coyote on June 23rd are Plaintiff's Exhibit D. Selected fragments have been shipped to the metallurgical laboratories of the University of California at Santa Barbara for analysis, but to date no explanation has been found for this product's sudden and extreme malfunction. As advertised by Defendant, this product is simplicity itself: two wood-and-metal sandals, each attached to milled-steel springs of high <u>tensile</u> strength and compressed in a tightly coiled position by a cocking device with a lanyard release. Mr. Coyote believed that this product would enable him to pounce upon his prey in the initial moments of the chase, when swift reflexes are at a premium.

To increase the shoes' thrusting still further, Mr. Coyote affixed them by their bottoms to the side of a large boulder. Adjacent to the boulder was a path which Mr. Coyote's prey was known to frequent. Mr. Coyote put his hind feet in the wood-and-metal sandals and crouched in readiness, his right forepaw holding firmly to the lanyard release. Within a short time Mr. Coyote's prey did indeed appear on the path coming toward him. Unsuspecting, the prey stopped near Mr. Coyote, well within range of the springs at full extension. Mr. Coyote gauged the distance with care and proceeded to pull the lanyard release.

At this point, Defendant's product should have thrust Mr. Coyote forward and away from the boulder. Instead, for reasons yet unknown, the Acme Spring-Powered Shoes thrust the boulder away from Mr. Coyote. ❷ As the intended prey looked on unharmed, Mr. Coyote hung suspended in air. Then the twin springs recoiled, bringing Mr. Coyote to a violent feet-first collision with the boulder, the full weight of his head and forequarters falling upon his lower extremities.

The force of this impact then caused the springs to rebound, whereupon Mr. Coyote was thrust skyward. A second recoil and collision followed. The boulder, meanwhile, which was roughly ovoid in shape, had begun to bounce down a hillside, the coiling and recoiling of the springs adding to its velocity. At each bounce, Mr. Coyote came into contact with the boulder, or the boulder came into contact with Mr. Coyote, or both came into contact with the ground. As the grade was a long one, this process continued for some time.

The sequence of collisions resulted in systemic physical damage to Mr. Coyote, viz., flattening of the cranium, sideways displacement of the tongue, reduction of length of legs and upper body, and compression of vertebrae from base of tail to head. Repetition of blows along a vertical axis produced a series of

Humanities: Art

Animation The animation techniques used to create cartoon figures such as Wile E. Coyote date back to 1908 when Frenchman Émile Cohl drew white matchstick figures on a black ground. Later methods, such as those used by Walt Disney, were based on drawings either inked or painted onto clear plastic sheets. Repeated or unmoving elements could be reproduced on many sheets, while moving elements had to be redrawn in their new position for each image. When the many images were photographed and linked together, the elements appeared animated or moving. Today's animation is often computer generated, saving a great deal of time and enhancing the range of possible effects.

Have students discuss why an animated character is so suited for the satirical essay Ian Frazier chose to write. How does the animated process lend itself to portraying exaggeration and irony?

regular horizontal folds in Mr. Coyote's body tissues—a rare and painful condition which caused Mr. Coyote to expand upward and contract downward alternately as he walked, and to emit an off-key accordion-like wheezing with every step. The distracting and embarrassing nature of this symptom has been a major impediment to Mr. Coyote's pursuit of a normal social life. ❸

As the Court is no doubt aware, Defendant has a virtual monopoly of manufacture and sale of goods required by Mr. Coyote's work. It is our contention that Defendant has used its market advantage to the detriment of the consumer of such specialized products as itching powder, giant kites, Burmese tiger traps, anvils, and two-hundred-foot-long rubber bands. Much as he has come to mistrust Defendant's products, Mr. Coyote has no other domestic source of supply to which to turn. One can only wonder what our trading partners in Western Europe and Japan would make of such a situation, where a giant company is allowed to victimize the consumer in the most reckless and wrongful manner over and over again.

Mr. Coyote respectfully requests that the Court regard these larger economic implications and assess punitive damages in the amount of seventeen million dollars. In addition, Mr. Coyote seeks actual damages (missed meals, medical expenses, days lost from professional occupation) of one million dollars; general damages (mental suffering, injury to reputation) of twenty million dollars; and attorney's fees of seven hundred and fifty thousand dollars. Total damages: thirty-eight million seven hundred and fifty thousand dollars. By awarding Mr. Coyote the full amount, this Court will censure Defendant, its directors, officers, shareholders, successors, and assigns, in the only language they understand, and reaffirm the right of the individual predator to equal protection under the law. ❹

◆ Build Vocabulary

tensile (ten′ sil) *adj.*: Stretchable

Guide for Responding

◆ Literature and Your Life

Reader's Response As you read the attorney's statement, did you sympathize with Wile E. Coyote? Why or why not?

Thematic Focus How does this essay suggest that product liability lawsuits have become an all-too-common occurrence?

☑ Check Your Comprehension

1. Why is Coyote suing the Acme Company?
2. What pieces of evidence does the attorney submit to the court?
3. (a) Describe the way in which the Rocket Sled malfunctioned. (b) How was Wile E. Coyote injured while using the Rocket Skates?
4. (a) Where did the lawyer for Wile E. Coyote send fragments of the Spring-Powered Shoes? (b) Why?
5. What action is Wile E. Coyote seeking from the court?

◆ Critical Thinking

INTERPRET

1. What is the relationship between Wile E. Coyote and (a) Harold Schoff? (b) the Acme Company? (c) Dr. Ernest Grosscup? **[Classify]**
2. What details in this essay suggest that Wile E. Coyote is a cartoon character? **[Support]**
3. Find evidence to explain why Wile E. Coyote kept buying from Acme, even though eighty-five products did not work properly. **[Support]**

EVALUATE

4. What do you believe was Frazier's purpose in writing this essay—was he simply trying to be funny or was he making a point? Explain your answer. **[Evaluate]**

COMPARE LITERARY WORKS

5. Both "Onomatopoeia" and "Coyote v. Acme" rely on humor, but of different kinds. Choose two words to describe each. **[Distinguish]**

Beyond the Selection

FURTHER READING

Other Works by Ian Frazier

Dating Your Mom
Nobody Better, Better Than Nobody
Great Plains

Other Works Providing Social Commentary

Animal Farm, George Orwell
Gulliver's Travels, Jonathan Swift

We suggest that you preview these works before recommending them to students.

INTERNET

You and your students may find additional information about Ian Frazier on the Internet. We suggest the following site. Please be aware, however, that sites may have changed since this information was published.

For a preview and review of *Coyote vs. Acme,* visit **http://www.salon1999.com/sneaks/sneakpeeks960513.html**

We *strongly recommend* that you preview sites before you send students to them.

◆ Literary Focus

❸ **Essays** How does this sentence contribute to the essay's satirical tone? *The exaggeration in the text shows the absurdity of Coyote's claim.*

◆ Critical Thinking

❹ **Assess** What is the effect of the tone of this paragraph? *It uses the language of a legal brief and maintains the tone of the opening heading.*

Reinforce and Extend

Answers

◆ Literature and Your Life

Reader's Response Some students may find Coyote so pathetic that he elicits sympathy.

Thematic Focus The humor of the Roadrunner cartoons is based on Coyote's ineptitude. With this character as a plaintiff, Frazier lets us question other liability cases.

☑ Check Your Comprehension

1. Coyote sues because Acme products have caused him injury.
2. He presents receipts, a doctor's report, fragments of spring-powered shoes, and the Acme catalog.
3. (a) The Rocket Sled could not be steered and Coyote crashed into a mesa. (b) The Rocket Skates thrust Coyote through a billboard.
4. (a) They have been sent to a university lab. (b)They are being analyzed.
5. He asks the court to assess punitive damages, actual damages, general damages, and attorney's fees.

◆ Critical Thinking

1. (a) Harold Schoff is Coyote's attorney. (b) Coyote is a frequent customer of Acme. (c) Dr. Grosscup wrote the medical report confirming Coyote's injuries.
2. Possible responses include the physical injuries Coyote survives and Coyote's instant recovery from injuries.
3. The brief suggests that Coyote continued to buy from Acme because there were no other companies from which to purchase.
4. By following the legal formats and using a familiar character, Frazier was satirizing the court system.
5. "Onomotopeia," silly, exaggerated; "acme" sophisticated, dry.

◆ Literary Focus

1. (a) "The Mortgaged Heart" is an analytical essay. (b) McCullers explores the development of a social consciousness from birth and American tendencies toward loneliness.
2. (a) "Onomatopoeia" is an expository essay. (b) Possible responses: Safire explains the etymology of the word and two different theories of language development.
3. The idea that even Coyote would be the plaintiff in a lawsuit is comical, but suggests that the legal system has heard from everyone.

◆ Build Vocabulary

Using the Word Root *-ten-*

Possible Response: We went camping to ease the *tension* of finals week. Little did we know the *extent* of trouble that awaited us at the campsite. As we put the *tent* up, I ripped a *tendon* in my heel and hit my brother with the stake. I was screaming, he was yelling, and everything was more *tense* than when we left.

Using the Word Bank

1. contiguous
2. corollary
3. precipitate
4. caveat
5. maverick
6. tensile
7. aesthetic
8. pristine

◆ Reading Strategy

1. (a) McCullers explains that human development ensures that babies understand their separate identities. This separateness has the power to create a universal loneliness. (b) When "I" becomes "We" loneliness disappears because love elicits the yes response and banishes fear.
2. (a) The attorney argues that Coyote was victim to products that were designed without safety features. (b) Exhibit A proves Coyote bought the products; B proves he suffered injury; C proves the catalog offers a variety of products, each of which caused harm; D proves the damage that one product sustained.

Guide for Responding *(continued)*

◆ Literary Focus

Essays

You have just read three very different types of essays: an **analytical essay,** in which the writer considers many aspects of a topic in an attempt to define, understand, or clarify it; a **satirical essay,** which uses irony, ridicule, or sarcasm to comment on a topic; and an **expository essay,** which explains or provides information about a topic.

1. (a) What type of essay is "The Mortgaged Heart"? (b) What aspects of loneliness does McCullers explore?
2. (a) What type of essay is "Onomatopoeia"? (b) Give an example of something that is explained in the essay.
3. How does "Coyote v. Acme" use humor to make a point about the increasing number of product liability suits?

◆ Build Vocabulary

Using the Latin Root *-ten-*

The Latin root *-ten-* means "to stretch tightly." The words in the box each take their meaning from the root *-ten-*. Use at least four of the words to write a paragraph about a disastrous camping trip in which everything seems to go wrong. If you are unsure about a word, look it up in a dictionary.

tension	tense	tent	extent	tendon	intensify

Using the Word Bank: Word Choice

For each sentence, choose the word from the Word Bank that is suggested by the italicized word or phrase. Write the answers on your paper.

1. California and Oregon *share a common border.*
2. Redheads sunburn easily; *therefore, they must use sunscreen.*
3. Since he was usually gracious, we were all surprised by his *sudden, abrupt* exit.
4. The sign gave this *formal notice: Danger! Beware!*
5. The film director was a *nonconformist* in every way.
6. The *stretchable quality* of the rubber band was amazing.
7. The garish colors and loud music of the theater offended my *sense of appropriate decor.*
8. The newly fallen snow was *completely untouched.*

◆ Reading Strategy

Identify Line of Reasoning

As you read these essays you **identified the line of reasoning** by asking yourself how the writer made a case for the main ideas he or she presented.

1. In "The Mortgaged Heart," how does McCullers convince the reader that (a) loneliness stems from the quest for identity and (b) love is the means of overcoming loneliness?
2. (a) Summarize the attorney's case for Mr. Coyote's compensation in "Coyote v. Acme." (b) What is the connection between Exhibits A–D and the main points of the attorney's argument?

◆ Grammar and Style

Pronouns With Appositives

When you use a pronoun preceding an appositive—a noun that renames the pronoun—you may be confused about which pronoun form to use. To choose the proper pronoun form, drop the noun or noun phrase the pronoun replaces as you say the sentence aloud.

When a pronoun acts as a subject, use *I, he, she, we,* or *they.* When a pronoun acts as an object, use *me, him, her, us,* or *them.*

Practice For each item, choose the correct form of the pronoun in parentheses. Then write the completed sentence in your notebook.

1. Loneliness is common among (we, us) Americans.
2. Love can help us, you and (I, me), feel less lonely.
3. Two students, (she, her) and Carlos, were tied for the longest list of examples of onomatopoeia.
4. (We, Us) cartoon lovers all know Wile E. Coyote.

Writing Application Rewrite this paragraph using the correct form of the pronouns in parentheses.

The whole family, Mom, Dad, Grandma, Caroline, and (I, me), settled in front of the TV. The young people—Caroline and (I, me), that is—wanted to watch Road Runner cartoons. "That's not very entertaining for (we, us) adults," said Mom. I told Caroline that I hoped we, meaning (she, her) and (I, me), would never outgrow our love of cartoons.

◆ Grammar and Style

1. us
2. me
3. she
4. We

Writing Application

I, I, us, she, I

Grammar Reinforcement

For additional instruction and practice, use the Pronoun Case lesson on the **Language Lab CD-ROM.**

Reteach

To help students who are having difficulty identifying the line of reasoning in the text, have them set up a question-and-answer chart to answer these questions: What are the main statements that the writer makes? What supporting reasons, evidence, facts does the writer give? What cause-and-effect relationships do you find?

Build Your Portfolio

Idea Bank

Writing

1. **Letter** Write a letter to Carson McCullers in which you respond to one of the ideas in her essay. Do you agree or disagree with her analysis?

2. **News Article** Write a newspaper article based on "Coyote v. Acme." You may wish to include details about the plaintiff's appearance in court and his reaction to the verdict. **[Media Link]**

3. **Analytical Essay** McCullers describes the American artist as "the eternal maverick." Use a dictionary to trace the origin of *maverick.* In an essay, explore the connection between the American origin and current usage of the word. Is being a *maverick* an "American" quality? Explain.

Speaking, Listening, and Viewing

4. **Opening Statement for the Defense** As the attorney defending the Acme Company, how would you respond to the arguments presented in "Coyote v. Acme"? Present your statement to the class. **[Social Studies Link]**

5. **Invented Words** Working with a partner, take turns inventing onomatopoetic words for everyday sounds. Present eight to ten new words to the class, and see whether your classmates can identify the sound each word describes.

Researching and Representing

6. **Essay Collection** Look through a book of Safire's "On Language" columns. Select five or six that you find most appealing, and collect them in a booklet for display in the classroom. Include an introduction explaining your choices.

7. **Cartoon Strip** Create a cartoon strip showing one of Coyote's experiences with an Acme product as described in "Coyote v. Acme." **[Art Link]**

Online Activity www.phlit.phschool.com

Guided Writing Lesson

Résumé for Wile E. Coyote

Wile E. Coyote's attorney frequently refers to his client's profession of predator. He mentions the tools his clients uses (or tries to use), and he implies that his client is quite well experienced in his field. Write a résumé that Wile E. Coyote might use to search for a job. Follow Ian Frazier's example, and use your sense of humor as you compose a satirical version of a standard résumé.

Writing Skills Focus: Keeping to a Format

Successful résumés generally follow a standard format. After a name, address, and phone number, the writer divides information into clearly labeled sections. For example, you might establish these categories for Coyote's résumé:

- Objective or Goal
- Qualifications
- Work Experience
- Education
- Awards
- References

Prewriting Jot down some notes concerning the kinds of experience and training Coyote might include in his résumé. How did he prepare himself for his career? What jobs might he have had before becoming a full-fledged predator? Refer to Frazier's essay for ideas about Coyote's experience.

Drafting Begin your draft with the résumé heading described in the above format. Then use your notes to complete the résumé by organizing the appropriate qualifications under each heading.

Revising Ask a classmate to read the résumé and tell you which sections need more detail. Replace any vague verbs with more powerful, active ones. For example, change "kept inventory" to "organized and maintained inventory."

ASSESSMENT OPTIONS

Formal Assessment, Selection Test, pp. 299–301, and Assessment Resources Software. The selection test is designed so that it can be easily customized to the performance levels of your students.

Alternative Assessment, p. 68, includes options for less advanced students, more advanced students, musical/rhythmic learners, verbal/linguistic learners, logical/mathematic learners, intrapersonal learners, and visual/spatial learners.

PORTFOLIO ASSESSMENT

Use the following rubrics in the ***Alternative Assessment*** booklet to assess student writing:
Letter: Evaluation/Review Rubric, p. 119
News Article: Response to Literature Rubric, p. 125
Analytical Essay: Definition/Classification Rubric, p. 114
Guided Writing Lesson: Résumé and Cover Letter Rubric, p. 129

Idea Bank

Customizing for *Performance Levels*

Following are suggestions for matching Idea Bank topics with your students' performance levels:
Less Advanced Students: 1, 7
Average Students: 2, 4, 5
More Advanced Students: 3, 6

Customizing for *Learning Modalities*

Following are suggestions for matching Idea Bank topics with your students' learning modalities:
Logical/Mathematical: 4
Verbal/Linguistic: 4, 5, 6
Musical/Rhythmic: 5
Visual/Spatial: 7

Guided Writing Lesson

For more prewriting, elaboration, and revision strategies, see *Prentice Hall Writing and Grammar.*

Writing and Language Transparencies Use the Writing Process Model of a Résumé, pp. 53–56, to introduce students to the résumé format.

Writing Lab CD-ROM

Have students complete the tutorial on Practical and Technical Writing. Follow these steps:

1. Refer to the annotated model of a resume in the About Practical and Technical Writing Section.
2. Have students draft on the computer.
3. Use the revision checkers to help students revise their résumés.

Prepare and Engage

LESSON OBJECTIVES

1. To develop vocabulary and word identification skills
- Word Origins: Latin Roots *-scrib-*, *-script-*
- Using the Word Bank: Sentence Completions

2. To use a variety of reading strategies to comprehend reflective essays
- Connect Your Experience
- Reading Strategy: Evaluate a Writer's Message
- Idea Bank: Readers' Club

3. To express and support responses to the text
- Critical Thinking
- Letter to the Author
- Idea Bank: Science Fiction Story
- Idea Bank: Television Pilot
- Idea Bank: Monologue
- Idea Bank: Icons

4. To analyze literary elements
- Literary Focus: Reflective Essay

5. To plan, prepare, organize, and present literary interpretations
- Idea Bank: Speech
- Speaking, Listening, and Viewing Mini-Lesson (ATE)

6. To use recursive writing processes to write about a treasured memory
- Guided Writing Lesson

7. To increase knowledge of the rules of grammar and usage
- Grammar and Style: Varying Sentence Structure

Test Preparation

Writing Skills: Identifying Errors (ATE, p. 1005)
The teaching tips and sample test item in this workshop support the instruction and practice in the unit workshop:
Writing Skills: Punctuation, Usage, and Sentence Structure (SE, p. 1143)

Guide for Interpreting

Sandra Cisneros *(1954–)*

Sandra Cisneros was born in Chicago into a large Mexican American family. Because her family was poor, Cisneros moved frequently and lived for the most part in small, cramped apartments. To cope with these conditions, she retreated into herself, spending much of her time reading fairy tales and classic literature. Cisneros attended Loyola University in Chicago and the Writer's Workshop at the University of Iowa. Her book *The House on Mango Street* (1984) was a modest success. However, her later book, *Woman Hollering Creek* (1991), won critical acclaim and earned Cisneros widespread recognition.

Rita Dove *(1953–)*

Now a famous poet, Rita Dove's first writing efforts—at the age of nine or ten—were comic books with female superheroines. Born in Akron, Ohio, she attended Miami University in Oxford, Ohio, and later the University of Iowa. Dove has published several volumes of poetry, including the Pulitzer Prize-winning *Thomas and Beulah* (1986). In 1993, Dove was appointed Poet Laureate of the United States. She was the first African American and the youngest person ever to hold that position. Dove has also written a play, a novel, and a collection of short stories.

Featured in AUTHORS IN DEPTH Series

Amy Tan *(1952–)*

When Amy Tan was thirty-five, she visited China with her mother. Until then, Tan, who was born in Oakland, California, to Chinese immigrants, had rejected her Chinese heritage. On that trip, however, she made peace with her Chinese roots. At the time, she was leaving a successful career as a business writer to become a fiction writer. When she returned to the United States, she began *The Joy Luck Club* (1989), a novel about four Chinese American women and their mothers. The book made Tan an overnight celebrity. *The Kitchen God's Wife* (1991) was even more enthusiastically received. Her third novel, *The Hundred Secret Senses,* was published in 1995.

◆ Background for Understanding

LITERATURE: THE DEVELOPMENT OF THE ESSAY

Although writers were using the form earlier, the word *essai* was not coined until 1580, when the French philosopher Montaigne published a book called *Essais*. Translated, the French word *essai* means "try," which describes the essay's original sense: an exploratory piece of writing that lacked finish. In 1597, the English philosopher Francis Bacon said that his own *Essays* were "grains of salt which will rather give an appetite than offend with satiety." Montaigne and Bacon share fame for the development of the genre.

Eventually, the essay lost its original "unfinished" sense and writers began to think of it as an elegant, well-thought-out, polished piece of writing. Today, the essay has become one of the most popular literary forms—both among writers and readers.

Essays are one of the most flexible of all literary forms. They can be as short as a few hundred words or as long as a few hundred pages. They can be formal or informal, and they can discuss a wide variety of subjects, ranging from philosophy, literature, history, and current events to personal reflections on just about anything.

Prentice Hall Literature Program Resources

REINFORCE / RETEACH / EXTEND

Selection Support Pages
Build Vocabulary: *-scrib-* and *-script-*, p. 310
Grammar and Style: Sentence Variety, p. 311
Reading Strategy: Evaluate Writer's Message, p. 312
Literary Focus: Reflective Essay, p. 313

Strategies for Diverse Student Needs, Summarize Main Idea, p. 69

Beyond Literature Career Connection: Writing, p. 69

Formal Assessment Selection Test, pp. 302–304; Assessment Resources Software

Alternative Assessment, p. 69

Writing and Language Transparencies Reflective Essay Writing Process Model (p. 5–8)

Resource Pro CD-ROM Includes all resource materials and a customizable lesson plan.

Listening to Literature Audiocassettes

Art Transparencies Art Transparency 8, *The Tortilla Maker,* p. 35; Transparency 11, *Asian Women United Commemorative Quilt,* p. 47

Straw Into Gold ◆ For the Love of Books ◆ Mother Tongue ◆

◆ Literature and Your Life

Connect Your Experience

Are you confident around other people, or are you often a little insecure? The writers of these essays say they were shy or insecure as girls. They retreated to the world of books, and their love of reading led them to write—and in writing, each found her voice.

Journal Writing Imagine that ten years from now you have become a writer. Consider the kind of writer you might be. Then draft a short biographical sketch highlighting your background and interests for the jacket of your first book.

Thematic Focus: Literature Confronts the Everyday

Each of these essays focuses on an ordinary aspect of the writer's past, turning everyday events into material for reflective thought.

◆ Literary Focus

Reflective Essay

An essay is a short piece of nonfiction in which a writer expresses a personal view of a topic. In a **reflective essay,** the writer uses an informal tone to describe personal experiences or pivotal events. The essay conveys the writer's feelings about these events or experiences. The writer often considers the significance of the experience being described and arrives at a deeper understanding through this reflection.

◆ Reading Strategy

Evaluate a Writer's Message

Most writers write essays to communicate an idea. As the reader, your job is not only to get the point, but also to decide what you think about it. When you **evaluate a writer's message,** you think about whether the writer's idea is valid and whether you agree or disagree with it. As you read each essay that follows, identify and then evaluate the writer's message.

◆ Build Vocabulary

Latin Roots: *-scrib-*, *-script-*

In "Mother Tongue," Amy Tan transcribes a taped conversation. The word *transcribe* is formed from the Latin root *-scrib-*, which means "write." *Transcribe* means "write out or type out in full." Other familiar words containing *-scrib-* or *-script-* include *scribble, scripture,* and *inscribe.*

Word Bank

Before you read, preview this list of words from the essays.

nomadic
transcribed
empirical
benign
semantic
quandary
nascent

◆ Grammar and Style

Varying Sentence Structure

The right mix of sentence structures helps keep writing lively and interesting. **Simple sentences**—those consisting of one independent clause—can convey ideas concisely and directly. **Compound sentences,** which contain two or more independent clauses, and **complex sentences,** which contain an independent clause and one or more subordinate clauses, can enhance the flow of ideas. In this example from "Straw Into Gold," Cisneros follows a complex sentence with a simple one:

> To make matters worse, I had left before any of my six brothers had ventured away from home. I had broken a terrible taboo.

As you read these essays, notice how each author varies her sentences to create interesting, readable prose.

Interest Grabber These essays offer a convincing mosaic of the many reasons people write and the myriad experiences that fan writers' imaginations. To interest students in the essays, ask students to bring or suggest a favorite title for a classroom library from each student's most recently enjoyed reading material. Urge students to be candid—all reading is worthwhile. Discuss what inspired these many writers to share their experiences, topics, and issues; what makes an idea worth writing about?

Customize for
Less Proficient Readers
Writing that contains specific contextual references, in this case to the writers' cultures, can challenge less proficient readers. Urge students to use footnotes, background information, and peer exchange to explain any confusing references.

Customize for
AP Students
Outlining can help draw more advanced students' analyze the structure of each essay. Have students compare and contrast the three outlines with one another. What do the outlines suggest about each writer's method of communicating a message?

Customize for
Visual/Spatial Learners
Refer to ***Art Transparencies*** to build background for the selections. For Cisneros's essay, use Art Transparency 8, *The Tortilla Maker,* by Diego Rivera (p. 35). To build background for Tan's essay, use Art Transparency 11, *Asian Women United Quilt* by Debbie Lee (p. 47). For information and activities, use the Humanities Notes and Learning Options pages that accompany the art.

To link the art to the selections in each case, ask students to reflect on the images and discuss whether they create or challenge stereotypes.

Test Preparation Workshop

Writing Skills:
Identifying Errors The writing sections of many standardized tests require students to identify the type of error, if any, present in a sentence or phrase. Use the following sample item to show students how to determine the type of error a passage contains.

> <u>Many people have too different selves: the one they show to the outside world</u> and the one they keep hidden.

Which type of error, if any, appears in the underlined section of the passage?

A Spelling error
B Capitalization error
C Punctuation error
D No error

There are no capitalization errors or punctuation errors, but *too* should be spelled "two." The correct answer is A.

Develop Understanding

One-Minute Insight This essay draws a carefully woven connection between life experiences and a writer's imaginative powers. The essayist, Sandra Cisneros, shares anecdotes about her childhood in a Mexican American family and her travels through Europe as a fledgling writer. In recounting some unexpected turns in her life, Cisneros highlights the contrast between her inner experience and the world's view looking at her, and emphasizes strengths she has been surprised to discover in herself.

◆ Literature and Your Life

❶ Point out the assumptions being made about Cisneros in this paragraph. What experiences have students had in which they were expected to know something simply because of their background? How did they react in these situations? *Students may mention situations linked to culturally-related holidays or customs.*

❷ **Clarification** Explain that this is a reference to the miller's daughter in the fairy tale *Rumpelstilskin.* For those unfamiliar with the tale, it centers on a miller's daughter who is married off to a prince on the promise that she can spin straw into gold. When she fails, the magical Rumpelstilskin appears to help her.

◆ Critical Thinking

❸ **Connect** For Cisneros, how are making tortillas and taking the MFA exam like spinning straw into gold? *She feels she does not know the strict rules for completing either task.*

Customize for
English Language Learners
Offer Spanish speakers the opportunity to share their expertise with the class by pronouncing Spanish words from the essay.

Straw Into Gold: *The Metamorphosis of the Everyday*

Sandra Cisneros

When I was living in an artists' colony in the south of France, some fellow Latin-Americans who taught at the university in Aix-en-Provence[1] invited me to share a home-cooked meal with them. I had been living abroad almost a year then on an NEA[2] grant, subsisting mainly on French bread and lentils while in France so that my money could last longer. So when the invitation to dinner arrived, I accepted without hesitation. Especially since they had promised Mexican food.

❶ What I didn't realize when they made this invitation was that I was supposed to be involved in preparing this meal. I guess they assumed I knew how to cook Mexican food because I was Mexican. They wanted specifically tortillas, though I'd never made a tortilla in my life.

It's true I had witnessed my mother rolling the little armies of dough into perfect circles, but my mother's family is from Guanajuato,[3] *provinciales*,[4] country folk. They only know how to make flour tortillas. My father's family, on the other hand, is *chilango*,[5] from Mexico City. We ate corn tortillas but we didn't make them. Someone was sent to the corner tortilleria to buy some. I'd never seen anybody make corn tortillas. Ever.

Well, somehow my Latino hosts had gotten a hold of a packet of corn flour, and this is what they tossed my way with orders to produce tortillas. *Asi como sea.* Any ol' way, they said and went back to their cooking.

Why did I feel like the woman in the fairy tale who was locked in a room and ordered to spin straw into gold? I had the same sick feeling when I was required to write my critical essay for my MFA[6] exam—the only piece of noncreative writing necessary in order to get my graduate degree. ❷ How was I to start? There were rules involved here, unlike writing a poem ❸ or story, which I did intuitively. There was a step-by-step process needed and I had better know it. I felt as if making tortillas, or writing a critical paper for that matter, were tasks so impossible I wanted to break down into tears.

Somehow though, I managed to make those tortillas—crooked and burnt, but edible nonetheless. My hosts were absolutely ignorant when it came to Mexican food; they thought my tortillas were delicious. (I'm glad my mama wasn't there.) Thinking back and looking at that photograph documenting the three of us consuming those lopsided circles I am amazed. Just as I am amazed I could finish my MFA exam (lopsided and crooked, but finished all the same). Didn't think I could do it. But I did.

I've managed to do a lot of things in my life I didn't think I was capable of and which many others didn't think me capable of either.

1. **Aix-en-Provence** (eks än prō väns´): City in southeastern France.
2. **NEA:** National Endowment for the Arts.
3. **Guanajuato** (gwä´ nä hwä´ tō): State in central Mexico.
4. ***provinciales*** (prō bēn sē ä´ läs): "Country folk" (Spanish).
5. ***chilango*** (chē län´ gō): "City folk" (Spanish).
6. **MFA:** Master of Fine Arts.

1006 ◆ Prosperity and Protest (1946–Present)

Block Scheduling Strategies

Consider these strategies to take advantage of extended class time:

- Use the Journal Writing activity (p. 1005) to spark a discussion of the variety of subjects for writing. Follow up with the Beyond Literature activity in ***Selection Support*** (p. 69).
- As a class, answer the Reading Strategy questions (p. 1017).
- After students complete the Literary Focus page in ***Selection Support*** (p. 313), lead a comparison-contrast of the three essays and their respective authors.
- Have students gather and exchange information from the Internet about the three essayists.
- Have students complete the Icons project (p. 1018) individually or in teams. Challenge them to organize an exhibit of the art for display in a central school location.
- Invite students to begin the Guided Writing Lesson (p. 1018) with a discussion of the main impressions created by each essay. Then have student pairs brainstorm topics for their own essays.

Biography, 1988, Marina Gutierrez, Courtesy of the artist

4 ▲ **Critical Viewing** This painting, titled *Biography*, challenges the viewer to piece together the experiences of a lifetime from a variety of small objects. What parallels can you draw between the picture and the essay? **[Connect]**

5 ◆ **Literary Focus** How does this paragraph signal the fact that this is a reflective essay?

Especially because I am a woman, a Latina, an only daughter in a family of six men. My father would've liked to have seen me married long ago. In our culture, men and women
6 don't leave their father's house except by way of marriage. I crossed my father's threshold with nothing carrying me but my own two feet. A woman whom no one came for and no one chased away.

To make matters worse, I had left before any of my six brothers had ventured away from home. I had broken a terrible taboo. Somehow, looking back at photos of myself as a child, I wonder if I was aware of having begun already my own quiet war.

I like to think that somehow my family, my Mexicanness, my poverty all had something to 7 do with shaping me into a writer. I like to think my parents were preparing me all along for my life as an artist even though they didn't know it. From my father I inherited a love of wandering. He was born in Mexico City but as a young man he traveled into the U.S. vagabonding. He eventually was drafted and thus became a citizen. Some of the stories he has told about his

Customize for
Bodily/Kinesthetic Learners
Invite these students to demonstrate for the class a physical skill—analogous to tortilla making—they have recently mastered. As all students attempt the task, urge them to share their feelings about facing and managing challenges.

▶Critical Viewing◀

4 Connect Students should note that Cisneros also pieces together a picture of her life experiences from a collection of anecdotes and moments.

◆ Literary Focus

5 Reflective Essay Cisneros reconsiders the meaning of an action she took years earlier by linking her heritage to her decision to leave the house. She also points out the bravery of this decision.

◆ *Literature and Your Life*

6 Ask students to consider the ways their culture defines the roles of men and women. Guide students to see that despite expanding roles since the 1950's, there are still clear expectations for men and women.

◆ Reading Strategy

7 Evaluate Writer's Message Point out that Cisneros here recognizes how her family, her Mexican heritage, and her poverty have influenced her and her writing.

Customize for
Gifted/Talented Students
Sandra Cisneros says, "I've managed to do a lot of things in my life I didn't think I was capable of and which many others didn't think me capable of either." Develop a personality profile for someone who succeeds in spite of difficult obstacles.

Humanities: Art

Biography, 1988, by Marina Gutierrez.

This painting illustrates a young Hispanic woman similar to Sandra Cisneros, the writer and speaker of the essay.

The creator of the painting is Marina Gutierrez, a contemporary Latin American artist (1954–). In titling this painting *Biography,* Gutierrez offers viewers a guiding hand through the painting's complexity, just as Sandra Cisneros points the way for readers of her "biography," each recognizing that a life and a personality is often more complex than it initially appears to be.

Use these questions for discussion.

1. Which objects in the painting suggest experiences mentioned in the essay? *The apartment building, red house, table with food, and open book all suggest aspects of Cisneros's life experiences.*
2. How might each of the young women depicted in the painting represent aspects of Sandra Cisneros? *One might be her eleven-year-old self, one her intellectual/ writer self, and one her proud Mexican American self.*

◆ Grammar and Style

❶ Varying Sentence Structures Point out the different sentence structures in this paragraph, including the final two fragments punctuated as sentences. Discuss how the varying structures contribute to the flow of the paragraph. *In order, the sentences are complex, simple, fragment, fragment. In terms of length, they are long, long, short, short. The effect is to decorate the first two foundation sentences with lighter dollops of detail and to reduce the last two sentences to the bare facts.*

Customize for *AP Students*

❷ You might encourage students to read Cisneros's short stories, "Tepeyac," in which she describes her grandparents' house in detail, and "Eleven," in which she recounts a painful, but significant eleventh birthday. Have students evaluate the stories and make a report to the class.

◆ Critical Thinking

❸ Connect; Infer Ask students: Where else in the essay does Cisneros mention rules? How do you think she feels about rules? Why might Cisneros include this anecdote in her essay about sources of imaginative thought? *Students should connect this text to Cisneros' earlier comment about making the tortilla, writing the MFA essay, and breaking a taboo in leaving home. They should infer that she dislikes rules and is willing to break them. However, students should also infer that the anecdote is included to support Cisneros's message that all experiences are possible story fodder.*

◆ Reading Strategy

❹ Evaluate Writer's Message Invite students to compare the young girl described here with the proud young woman who found her own way in an unfamiliar culture. What does the comparison reveal about Cisneros's personality? *Students may say that Cisneros is a complex person for whom writing has been the cement between a shy, insecure self and a proud, outspoken self.*

first months in the U.S. with little or no English surface in my stories in *The House on Mango Street* as well as others I have in mind to write in the future. From him I inherited a sappy heart. (He still cries when he watches the Mexican soaps—especially if they deal with children who have forsaken their parents.)

❶ My mother was born like me—in Chicago but of Mexican descent. It would be her tough, streetwise voice that would haunt all my stories and poems. An amazing woman who loves to draw and read books and can sing an opera. A smart cookie.

❷ When I was a little girl we traveled to Mexico City so much I thought my grandparents' house on La Fortuna, Number 12, was home. It was the only constant in our nomadic ramblings from one Chicago flat to another. The house on Destiny Street, Number 12, in the colonia Tepeyac,[7] would be perhaps the only home I knew, and that nostalgia for a home would be a theme that would obsess me.

My brothers also figured greatly in my art. Especially the oldest two; I grew up in their shadows. Henry, the second oldest and my favorite, appears often in poems I have written and in stories which at times only borrow his nickname, Kiki. He played a major role in my childhood. We were bunkbed mates. We were co-conspirators. We were pals. Until my oldest brother came back from studying in Mexico and left me odd-woman-out for always.

What would my teachers say if they knew I was a writer? Who would've guessed it? I wasn't a very bright student. I didn't much like school because we moved so much and I was always new and funny-looking. In my fifth-grade report card, I have nothing but an avalanche of C's and D's, but I don't remember being that stupid. I was good at art and I read plenty of library books and Kiki laughed at all my jokes. At home I was fine, but at school I never opened my mouth except when the teacher called on me, the first time I'd speak all day.

When I think how I see myself, it would have to be at age eleven. I know I'm thirty-two on the outside, but inside I'm eleven. I'm the girl in the picture with skinny arms and a crumpled shirt and crooked hair. I didn't like school because all they saw was the outside me. School was lots of rules and sitting with your hands folded and being very afraid all the time. I liked looking out the window and thinking. I liked staring at the girl across the way writing her name over and over again in red ink. I wondered why the boy with the dirty collar in front of me didn't have a mama who took better care of him. ❸

I think my mama and papa did the best they could to keep us warm and clean and never hungry. We had birthday and graduation parties and things like that, but there was another hunger that had to be fed. There was a hunger I didn't even have a name for. Was this when I began writing?

In 1966 we moved into a house, a real one, our first real home. This meant we didn't have to change schools and be the new kids on the block every couple of years. We could make friends and not be afraid we'd have to say goodbye to them and start all over. My brothers and the flock of boys they brought home would become important characters eventually for my stories—Louie and his cousins, Meme Ortiz and his dog with two names, one in English and one in Spanish.

My mother flourished in her own home. She took books out of the library and taught herself to garden, producing flowers so envied we had to put a lock on the gate to keep out the midnight flower thieves. My mother is still gardening to this day.

This was the period in my life, that slippery age when you are both child and woman and neither, I was to record in *The House on Mango Street.* I was still shy. I was a girl who couldn't come out of her shell. ❹

How was I to know I would be recording and documenting the women who sat their sadness on an elbow and stared out a window? It would be the city streets of Chicago I would later record, but from a child's eyes.

I've done all kinds of things I didn't think I could do since then. I've gone to a prestigious university, studied with famous writers, and taken away an MFA degree. I've taught poetry in the schools in Illinois and Texas. I've gotten

7. **colonia Tepeyac** (cô lō´ nēä tā pā´ yäc): District of Mexico City.

◆ Build Vocabulary

nomadic (nō mad´ ik) *adj.*: Wandering; leading the life of a nomad

Beyond the Classroom

Community Connection

Housing In this essay, Cisneros describes some of the places she has lived and the importance to her of moving into a house and of having a permanent home. Encourage students to explore your community. What kinds of dwellings do most people occupy? Students might also use local census information to determine how many community residents own and rent their homes and to estimate the proportions of transient or permanent residents. Discuss how these factors affect residents' roles in the community.

Workplace Skills

Interpersonal Relations Point out Cisneros' comments about the challenges of meeting and making friends each time she moved. Challenge students to brainstorm how these experiences might help and hinder someone in the workplace. For example, students might note that the ability to get along with changing staff and people of many backgrounds would be very useful in a company situation. Invite interested students to interview parents or other adults about the importance of interpersonal relations in the workplace.

5 **◆ Reading Strategy** Why do you think Cisneros emphasizes the fact that her life has unfolded in ways she never expected?

an NEA grant and run away with it as far as my courage would take me. I've seen the bleached and bitter mountains of the Peloponnesus.[8] I've lived on a Greek island. I've been to Venice[9] twice. In Rapallo, I met Ilona once and forever and took her sad heart with me across the south of France and into Spain.

I've lived in Yugoslavia. I've been to the famous Nice[10] flower market behind the opera house. I've lived in a village in the pre-Alps[11] and witnessed the daily parade of promenaders.

I've moved since Europe to the strange and wonderful country of Texas, land of polaroid-blue skies and big bugs. I met a mayor with my last name. I met famous Chicana/o artists and writers and *politicos*.[12]

Texas is another chapter in my life. It brought with it the Dobie-Paisano Fellowship, a six-month residency on a 265-acre ranch. But most important Texas brought Mexico back to me.

Sitting at my favorite people-watching spot, the snaky Woolworth's counter across the street from the Alamo,[13] I can't think of anything else I'd rather be than a writer. I've traveled and lectured from Cape Cod to San Francisco, to Spain, Yugoslavia, Greece, Mexico, France, Italy, and finally today to Seguin, Texas. Along the way there is straw for the taking. With a little imagination, it can be spun into gold.

---

8. **Peloponnesus** (pel´ ə pə nē´ səs): Peninsula forming the southeastern part of the Greek mainland.
9. **Venice** (ven´ is): Seaport in northern Italy.
10. **Nice** (nēs): Seaport and resort in southeastern France.
11. **pre-Alps:** Foothills of the Alps, a mountain range in south-central Europe.
12. ***politicos*** (pō lē´ tē cōs): "Politicians" (Spanish).
13. **the Alamo** (al´ ə mō´): Mission in San Antonio, Texas, that was the scene of a famous battle between Texans and Mexican troops in 1836.

Guide for Responding

◆ Literature and Your Life

Reader's Response Does Cisneros seem to be someone you would like to meet? Why or why not?

Thematic Focus What phase of Cisneros's life seems to have been the most important in shaping her writing? Support your answer.

Questions for Research Sandra Cisneros mentions receiving grants and fellowships, but what are such things? Generate research questions about grants and fellowships and how they relate to careers.

☑ Check Your Comprehension

1. What experience reminded Cisneros of the woman who had to spin straw into gold?
2. What obstacles stood in the way of Cisneros's goal of becoming a writer?
3. What does Cisneros believe contributed to shaping her as a writer?

◆ Critical Thinking

INTERPRET

1. (a) What point is Cisneros trying to make through her anecdote about making tortillas? (b) How is this anecdote connected to the rest of her essay? **[Interpret; Connect]**
2. What does the essay suggest about Cisneros's imagination and eye for detail? **[Infer]**
3. What is the main point of the essay? Support your answer. **[Draw Conclusions]**

EVALUATE

4. Do you agree with Cisneros that "with a little imagination, [straw] can be spun into gold"? Explain. **[Evaluate]**

APPLY

5. How could you apply Cisneros's message to your own life? Explain. **[Apply]**

Beyond the Selection

FURTHER READING

Other Works by Sandra Cisneros

The House on Mango Street

Woman Hollering Creek and Other Stories

Other Works With the Theme of Inspirations/Influences

Inspirations, Leslie Sills

To Kill a Mockingbird, Harper Lee

"Journey," Joyce Carol Oates

We suggest that you preview these works before recommending them to students.

INTERNET

You and your students may find additional information about Sandra Cisneros on the Internet. We suggest the following sites. Please be aware, however, that sites may have changed since this information was published.

For a profile of Cisneros, visit **http://www.engl.cla. umn.edu/LKD/VFG/Authors/SandraCisneros**

To read an interview with Cisneros, visit **http://latino.sscnet.ucla.edu/women/interviews.html**

We *strongly recommend* that you preview sites before you send students to them.

◆ Reading Strategy

5 Evaluate Writer's Message She wants to stress that following life's unexpected turns has been an important source of inspiration.

Reinforce and Extend

Answers

◆ Literature and Your Life

Reader's Response Students should support their impressions of the writer with evidence from the text.

Thematic Focus Cisneros suggests that childhood experiences turned her toward writing.

☑ Check Your Comprehension

1. Cisneros was once asked to make tortillas at a party.
2. Possible responses include poverty, frequent moves, and poor grades.
3. Cisneros cites her family, her heritage, and her experiences as contributing factors.

◆ Critical Thinking

1. (a) The tortilla anecdote explains the need to face challenges. (b) Facing challenges allows her to spin straw into gold.
2. Cisneros uses her imagination to see ordinary things in new ways. Students may note the image of Cisneros's mother making tortillas by "rolling the little armies of dough," and her reference to the teenage years as "that slippery age."
3. If you are a writer, don't deny any of your experiences. Everything can be a springboard for a story.
4. Some students may agree while others may argue that some obstacles cannot be overcome.
5. Possible response: You should not be afraid to accept challenges; by accepting them you learn and grow.

For the Love of Books

Rita Dove

When I am asked: "What made you want to be a writer?" my answer has always been: "Books." First and foremost, now, then, and always, I have been passionate about books. From the time I began to read, as a child, I loved to feel their heft in my hand and the warm spot caused by their intimate weight in my lap; I loved the crisp whisper of a page turning, the musky odor of old paper and the sharp inky whiff of new pages. Leather bindings sent me into ecstasy. I even loved to gaze at a closed book and daydream about the possibilities inside—it was like contemplating a genie's lamp. Of course, my favorite fairy tale was *A Thousand and One Nights*—imagine buying your life with stories!—and my favorite cartoons were those where animated characters popped out of books and partied while the unsuspecting humans slept. In books, I could travel anywhere, be anybody, understand worlds long past and imaginary colonies in the future. My idea of a bargain was to go to the public library, wander along the bookshelves, and emerge with a chin-high stack of books that were mine, all mine, for two weeks—free of charge!

What I remember most about long summer days is browsing the bookshelves in our solarium to see if there were any new additions. I grew up with those rows of books; I knew where each one was shelved and immediately spotted newcomers. And after months had gone by and there'd be no new books, I would think: Okay, I guess I'll try this one—and then discover that the very book I had been avoiding because of a drab cover or small print was actually a wonderful read. Louis Untermeyer's *Treasury of Best Loved Poems* had a sickeningly sweet lilac and gold cover and was forbiddingly thick, but I finally pulled it off the shelf and discovered a cornucopia of emotional and linguistic delights, from "The Ballad of Barbara Fritchie," which I adored for its sheer length and rather numbing rhymes, to Langston Hughes's dazzlingly syncopated "Dream Boogie." Then there was Shakespeare—daunting for many years because it was his entire oeuvre,[1] in matching wine-red volumes that were so thick they looked more like over-sized bouillon cubes than books, and yet it ❷ was that ponderous title—*The Complete Works of William Shakespeare*—that enticed me, because here was a lifetime's work—a lifetime!—in two compact, dense packages. I began with the long poem "The Rape of Lucrece" . . . I sampled a few sonnets, which I found beautiful but rather adult; and finally wandered into the plays—first *Romeo and Juliet*, then *Macbeth, Julius Caesar, A Midsummer Night's Dream, Twelfth Night*—enthralled by the language, by the fact that poetry was spinning the story. Of course I did not understand every single word, but I was too young to know that this was supposed to be difficult; ❸ besides, no one was waiting to test me on anything, so, free from pressure, I dove in.

At the same time, my brother, two years my senior, had become a science fiction buff, so I'd read his *Analog* and *Fantasy and Science Fiction* magazines after he was finished with them. One story particularly fascinated me: A retarded boy in a small town begins building a sculpture in his backyard, using old and discarded

◆ Reading Strategy
What point is Dove making when she talks about a "wonderful read" being concealed behind a drab cover? Explain whether you agree with her point. ❶

1. **oeuvre** (ë´ vrə) *n.*: All the works, usually of a lifetime, of a particular writer, artist, or composer.

Develop Understanding

One-Minute Insight

In this essay, Rita Dove vividly communicates her love of books and the critical influence that passion had on her decision to become a writer. As a young child, Rita adored books, not just reading them but holding them, smelling them, turning their pages. As she matured to discover the magic of language and the places it could take her, Rita encountered many literary voices. When she met a real writer (poet John Ciardi), the possibility of living her adult life among these literary voices—and perhaps adding her own to theirs—became startlingly and wonderfully tangible.

Customize for *AP Students*

Urge these students to divide up and read the literary works Rita Dove mentions. Then challenge students to compare Dove's responses to the works with their own. Discuss also how these early literary experiences contributed to Dove's later goals as Poet Laureate of the United States.

◆ Reading Strategy

❶ Evaluate Writer's Message Students should recognize Dove's point that a fruitful experience may sometimes seem very ordinary, that writers can draw inspiration from everyday events. Students should be able to support their reactions to this idea.

◆ Grammar and Style

❷ Varying Sentence Structures Have students define this sentence as complex, compound, or simple. Ask them to describe the rhythm created by this sentence. *The sentence is compound. Its three main clauses, interrupted by dashes and commas, flow a bit like a burbling stream—first rapidly, then slowly.*

◆ Literary Focus

❸ Reflective Essay Ask students: What insight does Dove suggest about the value of reading to her development and that of other young people? *She suggests that reading works somewhat beyond understanding, was worthwhile for her, and can broaden readers' horizons.*

Beyond the Classroom

Career Connection

Publishing The art of bookbinding, which so enchants young Rita Dove, began with decorated books used in churches. These magnificently adorned bookbindings sometimes included ivory carvings, jewels, gold leaf, or embroidery. Later, decorated leather bindings became the norm. These books were hand-bound with carefully tooled leather.

Today's books are usually machine-bound, though they can still be quite beautiful. Some contain lettering or illustrations impressed into the fabric covering. Paper jackets, often designed to include paintings, illustrations, or stylized text, remain as a modern grandchild of the bookbinder's art.

Ask students to comment on objects they enjoy for both beauty and function. Invite students to share examples of their enthusiasm with the class.

materials—coke bottles, scrap iron, string, and bottle caps. Everyone laughs at him, but he continues building. Then one day he disappears. And when the neighbors investigate, they discover that the sculpture has been dragged onto the back porch and that the screen door is open. Somehow the narrator of the story figures out how to switch on the sculpture: The back door frame begins to glow, and when he steps through it, he's in an alternate universe, a town the mirror image of his own—even down to the colors, with green roses and an orange sky. And he walks through this town until he comes to the main square, where there is a statue erected to—who else?—the village idiot.

I loved this story, the idea that the dreamy, mild, scatter-brained boy of one world could be the hero of another. And in a way, I identified with that village idiot because in real life I was painfully shy and awkward; the place where I felt most alive was between the pages of a book.

Although I loved books, for a long time I had no aspirations to be a writer. The possibility was beyond my imagination. I liked to write, however—and on long summer days when I ran out of reading material or my legs had fallen asleep because I had been curled up on the couch for hours on end, I made up my own stories. Most were abandoned midway. Those that I did bring to a conclusion I neither showed to others nor considered saving.

My first piece of writing I thought enough of to keep was a novel called *Chaos*, which was about robots taking over the earth. I had just entered third or fourth grade; the novel had forty-three chapters, and each chapter was twenty lines or less because I used each week's spelling list as the basis for each chapter, and there were twenty words per list. In the course of the year I wrote one installment per week, and I never knew what was going to happen next—the words led me, not the other way around.

At that time I didn't think of writing as an activity people admited doing. I had no living role models—a "real" writer was a long-dead white male, usually with a white beard to match. (4) Much later, when I was in eleventh grade, my English teacher, Miss Oechsner, took me to a book-signing in a downtown hotel. She didn't ask me if I'd like to go—she asked my parents instead, signed me and a classmate (who is now a professor of literature) out of school one day, and took us to meet a writer. The writer was John Ciardi, a poet who also had translated Dante's *Divine Comedy*, which I had heard of, vaguely. At that moment I realized that writers were real people and how it was possible to write down a poem or story in the intimate sphere of one's own room and then share it with the world.

Guide for Responding

◆ Literature and Your Life

Reader's Response Might you have been friends with Rita Dove if you had known her as a child? Why or why not?

Thematic Focus Why do you think reading and writing are often the favorite pastime of shy people?

Journal Writing List your five favorite activities. Is reading one of them? Explore your answer.

☑ Check Your Comprehension

1. How does Rita Dove feel about books?
2. What was the first piece of writing Dove liked well enough to keep?
3. What made Dove realize that she could be a "real" writer?

◆ Critical Thinking

INTERPRET

1. What does Dove mean when she says that gazing at a closed book was "like contemplating a genie's lamp"? **[Interpret]**
2. What influences contributed to Dove's goal of becoming a writer? **[Deduce]**
3. Do you think Dove would have gone on to become a writer if she had not attended the book signing? **[Speculate]**

EVALUATE

4. In an interview, Dove has said, "My first and really only piece of advice [to young writers] is to read, read, read." After reading this essay, do you think this is good advice? Explain. **[Criticize]**

Beyond the Selection

FURTHER READING

Other Works by Rita Dove

Under the Ivory Gate
Thomas and Beulah
Fifth Sunday
The Yellow House on the Corner

Other Works With the Theme of Influences

Dust Tracks on a Road, Zora Neale Hurston
"The Observer," Adrienne Rich

We suggest that you preview these works before recommending them to students.

INTERNET

You can find additional information about Rita Dove on the Internet. We suggest the following sites. Please be aware, however, that sites may have changed since this information was published.

For a biography and bibliography, visit **http://members.aol.com/vonvibre/rdove.html** The Rita Dove Home Page can be visited at **http://www.wilmington.net/arts/poets/dove.html**

We *strongly recommend* that you preview sites before you send students to them.

◆ Reading Strategy

(4) Evaluate Writer's Message Discuss with students Dove's point about the value of accessible role models. Challenge them to take a stand for or against the importance of familiar role models; For example, does an Asian American child need an Asian American role model?

Reinforce and Extend

Writers at Work Videodisc To show students what has become of the young girl in this essay, use the videodisc segment on description (Ch. 1) featuring Rita Dove. Ask students whether "For the Love of Books" meets the criteria Dove lists in this interview.

Play frames 335 to 10985

Answers

◆ Literature and Your Life

Reader's Response Students should support their responses.

Thematic Focus Books allow people to live vicariously, letting shy people experience things they might feel too awkward to actually do.

☑ Check Your Comprehension

1. She loves them for their content and their weight, smell, and texture.
2. A science-fiction novel called *Chaos*.
3. She realized she could be a writer when she met a living author.

◆ Critical Thinking

1. The comparison suggests that books contain as much wonder and potential power as genie's lamps.
2. Dove was shy, she loved to read, she loved to write, and she met a professional writer.
3. Possible response: Dove's interests may have led her to this field even if she hadn't met Ciardi.
4. Possible response: As you read, you learn more about writing, so this is good advice.

Develop Understanding

One-Minute Insight This essay demonstrates how much people miss when they reach snap judgments or apply stereotypes. Amy Tan paints a portrait of her mother as an intelligent and perceptive woman who encounters difficulties because English is her second language. Tan contrasts the valuable lessons she has learned from her mother with the English world's view of her mother. This essay celebrates the many ways people can communicate and identifies Tan's central goal as a writer: to be readable.

◆ Grammar and Style

❶ **Varying Sentence Structure** Work with students to identify and label each sentence of this text as simple, compound, or complex. Then ask students how Tan's variation in sentence structure helps emphasize her text message. *Starting with "The talk was going . . .," the sentences are complex, simple, complex. A short, simple sentence after a long, complex one draws attention and emphasizes its main idea.*

▶Critical Viewing◀

❷ **Infer** Students should be able to infer that Tan and her mother have a close relationship today. The picture shows them working together or sharing the pleasure of reading together.

◆ *Literature and Your Life*

❸ Call attention to Tan's idea of different Englishes. How are the languages they speak at home similar to or different from those they speak at school? *Most students will acknowledge a difference between private, family language and public, school, or formal language. These languages may be entirely different or simply subtle variations of English.*

◆ Critical Thinking

❹ **Infer** Ask students why Tan may have recorded her mother's speech. *She was doing research for her writing.*

Mother Tongue

Amy Tan

▲ **Critical Viewing** Based on this photograph of Amy Tan and her mother, what kind of a relationship do you think they now share? Explain. **[Infer]** ❷

I am not a scholar of English or literature. I cannot give you much more than personal opinions on the English language and its variations in this country or others.

I am a writer. And by that definition, I am someone who has always loved language. I am fascinated by language in daily life. I spend a great deal of my time thinking about the power of language—the way it can evoke an emotion, a visual image, a complex idea, or a simple truth. Language is the tool of my trade. And I use them all—all the Englishes I grew up with.

Recently, I was made keenly aware of the different Englishes I do use. I was giving a talk to a large group of people, the same talk I had already given to half a dozen other groups. The nature of the talk was about my writing, my life, and my book, *The Joy Luck Club*. The talk was going along well enough, until I remembered one major difference that made the whole ❶ talk sound wrong. My mother was in the room. And it was perhaps the first time she had heard me give a lengthy speech, using the kind of English I have never used with her. I was saying things like, "The intersection of memory upon imagination" and "There is an aspect of my fiction that relates to thus-and-thus"—a speech filled with carefully wrought grammatical phrases, burdened, it suddenly seemed to me, with nominalized forms, past perfect tenses, conditional phrases, all the forms of standard English that I had learned in school and through books, the forms of English I did not use at home with my mother.

Just last week, I was walking down the street with my mother, and I again found myself conscious of the English I was using, the English I do use with her. We were talking about the price of new and used furniture and I heard myself saying this: "Not waste money that way." My husband was with us as well, and he didn't notice any switch in my English. And then I realized why. It's because over the twenty years we've been together I've often used the same kind of English with him, and sometimes he even uses it with me. It has become our language of intimacy, a different sort of English that relates to family talk, the language ❸ I grew up with.

So you'll have some idea of what this family talk I heard sounds like, I'll quote what my mother said during a recent conversation ❹ which I videotaped and then transcribed. During this conversation, my mother was

Cultural Connection

Chinese or American The issue of maintaining a cultural identity and being part of mainstream society requires a delicate balancing act. The dual status of the Chinese American and the confusion this entails is one of Amy Tan's main themes in both her interviews and her writing. "They [her parents] wanted us to have American circumstances and Chinese character," Tan said in an interview with Elaine Woo for the *Los Angeles Times* (March 12, 1989) "We should always think like a Chinese person but we should always speak perfect English so we can take advantage of circumstances." Assimilation carried a price, as she told Dorothy Wang of *Newsweek* (April 17, 1989). "There is a myth that America is a melting pot, but what happens in assimilation is that we end up deliberately choosing the American things—hot dogs and apple pie—and ignoring the Chinese offerings."

talking about a political gangster in Shanghai[1] who had the same last name as her family's, Du, and how the gangster in his early years wanted to be adopted by her family, which was rich by comparison. Later, the gangster became more powerful, far richer than my mother's family, and one day showed up at my mother's wedding to pay his respects. Here's what she said in part:

"Du Yusong having business like fruit stand. Like off the street kind. He is Du like Du Zong—but not Tsung-ming Island people. The local people call putong, the river east side, he belong to that side local people. That man want to ask Du Zong father take him in like become own family. Du Zong father wasn't look down on him, but didn't take seriously, until that
5 man big like become a mafia. Now important person, very hard to inviting him. Chinese way, come only to show respect, don't stay for dinner. Respect for making big celebration, he shows up. Mean gives lots of respect. Chinese custom. Chinese social life that way. If too important won't have to stay too long. He come to my wedding. I didn't see, I heard it. I gone to boy's side, they have YMCA[2] dinner. Chinese age I was nineteen."

You should know that my mother's expressive command of English belies how much she actually understands. She reads the *Forbes*[3] report, listens to *Wall Street Week*,[4] converses daily with her stockbroker, reads all of Shirley MacLaine's[5] books with ease—all kinds of things I can't begin to understand. Yet some of my friends tell me they understand 50 percent of what my mother says. Some say they understand 80 to 90 percent. Some say they understand none of it, as if she were speaking pure Chinese. But to me, my mother's English is perfectly clear, perfectly natural. It's my mother tongue. Her language, as I hear it, is vivid, direct, full of observation and imagery. That was the language that helped shape the way I saw things, expressed things, made sense of the world.

Lately, I've been giving more thought to the kind of English my mother speaks. Like others, I have described it to people as "broken," or
"fractured" English. But I wince when I say 6
that. It has always bothered me that I can think of no way to describe it other than "broken," as if it were damaged and needed to be fixed, as if it lacked a certain wholeness and soundness. I've heard other terms used, "limited English," for example. But they seem just as bad, as if everything is limited, including people's perceptions of the limited English speaker.

I know this for a fact, because when I was growing up, my mother's "limited" English limited *my* perception of her. I was ashamed of her English. I believed that her English reflected the quality of what she had to say. That is, because she expressed them imperfectly her thoughts were imperfect. And I had plenty of empirical evidence to support me: the fact that people in department stores, at banks, and at restaurants did not take her seriously, did not give her good service, pretended not to understand her, or even acted as if they did not hear her.

> ◆ **Literary Focus**
> What significance does Tan attach to this personal experience? 7

My mother has long realized the limitations of her English as well. When I was fifteen, she used to have me call people on the phone to pretend I was she. In this guise, I was forced to ask for information or even to complain and yell at people who had been rude to her. One time it was a call to her stockbroker in New York. She had cashed out her small portfolio and it just so happened we were going to go to New York the next week, our very first trip outside California. I had to get on the phone and say in an adolescent voice that was not very convincing, "This is Mrs. Tan."

And my mother was standing in the back whispering loudly, "Why he don't send me check, already two weeks late. So mad he lie to me, losing me money."

And then I said in perfect English, "Yes, I'm getting rather concerned. You had agreed to

1. **Shanghai** (shaŋ´ hī´): Seaport in eastern China.
2. **YMCA:** Young Men's Christian Association.
3. ***Forbes*:** Magazine of business and finance.
4. ***Wall Street Week*:** Weekly television program that reports business and investment news.
5. **Shirley MacLaine's** (mək lānz´): Shirley MacLaine is an American actress who has written several books.

◆ Build Vocabulary

transcribed (tran skrībd´) *v.*: Wrote or typed a copy of

empirical (em pir´ i kəl) *adj.*: Derived from observation or experiment

Customize for *English Language Learners*

Explain that English has different levels of usage, ranging from formal to informal. Each level is appropriate to a given set of situations. Formal English, which follows certain rules of word choice and grammar, is used in most writing and in speaking unless the conversation is a casual one. Informal English, including colloquial expressions and slang, is used appropriately in everyday conversations or when writing dialogue or informal communications. Urge students to adjust their reading rate to fit each type of English used in the essay.

Customize for *Musical/Rhythmic Learners*

5 Have one student in a pair read aloud Amy Tan's mother's paragraph as the other "translates" the text into standard English. Pairs can then agree on a translation to present to the class. Discuss what the passages gained and/or lost in the translation.

◆ Build Vocabulary

6 **Word Roots: *-scrib-* and *-script-*** Prompt students to identify and define the word in this sentence based on the root *-scrib-*. Discuss how knowing the word root enhances students' understanding of the complete word. *Described means "to represent or give an account of in words." Knowing that -scrib- means "write" helps students see that describe is linked to writing down words, though it now commonly refers also to words delivered orally.*

◆ Literary Focus

7 **Reflective Essay** Students should recognize that even Tan misjudged her own mother by drawing inaccurate conclusions on the basis of stereotypes.

Speaking, Listening, and Viewing Mini-Lesson

Speech

This mini-lesson supports the Speaking, Listening, and Viewing activity in the Idea Bank on p. 1018.

Introduce the Concept Have students read, view, or listen to recent or historical speeches, especially some of renown.

Develop Background Before students create their speeches, offer the following suggestions for their consideration and review:

- When taking on another person's voice, be consistent to that person's views and experiences.
- Effective speeches blend concepts with specifics, rhetoric with anecdote.
- Consider the audience in choosing the style of English for the speech.

Apply the Information Encourage students to begin with an outline of their writer's basic ideas, searching the essay for clues to these. Stress the value of private practice prior to formal speech delivery. Urge speakers to use gesture and tone of voice for emphasis and remind listeners to be respectful.

Assess the Outcome Refer students to the self-assessment rubric for a speech (p.132) and the peer assessment rubric for speaker/speech (p. 133) in ***Alternative Assessment.***

◆ Literature and Your Life

❶ Point out the difficult position young Amy was in with her mother. Have students ever been in similar situations with an adult? How did they feel? *Students may mention language barrier situations or times when differences in education or cultural familiarity forced them to "interpret" for a parent. Some students will say they were embarrassed by the attention or strained by playing two roles at once. Others will say they felt proud to be able to help their parents.*

◆ Reading Strategy

❷ **Evaluate Writer's Message** Ask students to restate Amy Tan's point here and to cite the supporting evidence in the surrounding text. Then poll the class on their agreement or disagreement with Tan's point. *Tan's point is that people are responded to unfairly, according to the status assigned them as a function of their grasp of English. The doctor's courteous response to Tan contrasted with a disinterested response to Tan's mother supports the point. Most students will agree with Tan.*

◆ Literary Focus

❸ **Reflective Essay** Ask students to explain the link Tan makes between her personal experience and an insight about the general culture. *Students should link Tan's experience of language skills limiting her possibilities with her statement that the language and life possibilities of children, especially immigrant children, are dramatically shaped by the language of the home.*

Customize for *Less Proficient Readers*

❹ These readers may have difficulty with the insertion of test item examples into Tan's essay. To help these students, encourage them to pull out the example text. Then point out and clarify the general statements Tan makes about her difficulties with English tests. Finally, show students sample standardized tests if they are not already familiar with these. Then, have students reinsert the example text before rereading.

send the check two weeks ago, but it hasn't arrived."

Then she began to talk more loudly. "What he want, I come to New York tell him front of ❶ his boss, you cheating me?" And I was trying to calm her down, make her be quiet, while telling the stockbroker, "I can't tolerate any more excuses. If I don't receive the check immediately, I am going to have to speak to your manager when I'm in New York next week." And sure enough, the following week there we were in front of this astonished stockbroker, and I was sitting there red-faced and quiet, and my mother, the real Mrs. Tan, was shouting at his boss in her impeccable broken English.

We used a similar routine just five days ago, for a situation that was far less humorous. My mother had gone to the hospital for an appointment, to find out about a benign brain tumor a CAT scan[6] had revealed a month ago. She said she had spoken very good English, her best English, no mistakes. Still, she said, the hospital did not apologize when they said they had lost the CAT scan and she had come for nothing. She said they did not seem to have any sympathy when she told them she was anxious to know the exact diagnosis, since her husband and son had both died of brain tumors. She said they would not give her any more information until the next time and she would have to make another appointment for that. So she said she would not leave until the doctor called her daughter. She wouldn't ❷ budge. And when the doctor finally called her daughter, me, who spoke in perfect English—lo and behold—we had assurances the CAT scan would be found, promises that a conference call on Monday would be held, and apologies for any suffering my mother had gone through for a most regrettable mistake.

❸ I think my mother's English almost had an effect on limiting my possibilities in life as well. Sociologists and linguists probably will tell you that a person's developing language skills are more influenced by peers. But I do think that the language spoken in the family, especially in immigrant families which are more insular, plays a large role in shaping the language of the child. And I believe that it affected my results on achievement tests, IQ tests, and the SAT.[7] While my English skills were never judged as poor, compared to math, English could not be considered my strong suit. In ❸ grade school I did moderately well, getting perhaps B's, sometimes B-pluses, in English and scoring perhaps in the sixtieth or seventieth percentile on achievement tests. But those scores were not good enough to override the opinion that my true abilities lay in math and science, because in those areas I achieved A's and scored in the ninetieth percentile or higher.

This was understandable. Math is precise; there is only one correct answer. Whereas, for me at least, the answers on English tests were always a judgment call, a matter of opinion and personal experience. Those tests were constructed around items like fill-in-the-blank sentence completion, such as, "Even though Tom was _____, Mary thought he was _____." And the correct answer always seemed to be the most bland combinations of thoughts, for ❹ example, "Even though Tom was shy, Mary thought he was charming," with the grammatical structure "even though" limiting the correct answer to some sort of semantic opposites, so you wouldn't get answers like, "Even though Tom was foolish, Mary thought he was ridiculous." Well, according to my mother, there were very few limitations as to what Tom could have been and what Mary might have thought of him. So I never did well on tests like that.

The same was true with word analogies, pairs of words in which you were supposed to find some sort of logical, semantic relationship—for example, "*Sunset* is to *nightfall* as _____ is to _____." And here you would be presented with a list of four possible pairs, one of which showed the same kind of relationship: *red* is to *stoplight, bus* is to *arrival, chills* is to *fever, yawn* is to *boring.* Well, I could never think that way. I knew what the tests were asking, but I could not block out of my mind the images already created by the first pair, "*sunset* is to *nightfall*"—and I would see a burst of colors against a darkening sky, the moon rising, the lowering of a curtain of stars. And all the other pairs of words—red, bus, stoplight,

6. **CAT scan:** Method used by doctors to diagnose brain disorders.

7. **SAT:** Scholastic Aptitude Test; national college entrance exam.

Beyond the Classroom

Community Connection

Languages Explain to students that Amy Tan's essay comments on the ways people's life experiences are impacted by their speech. Encourage students to survey your community for speech types commonly presented, for example, immigrants speaking English as a second language, newcomers speaking an unfamiliar regional dialect, long-time residents speaking a local jargon. Challenge students to consider how these different styles of English play a role in the community.

Workplace Skills Connection

Communication Amy Tan's mother has difficulty achieving her goals because her English is viewed as inferior. In a workplace situation, a competent grasp of formal English is extremely important.

Have students brainstorm for some ways workers and employers rely on the existence of a common language to communicate. Point out that many businesses rely on formal letters, presentations, and customer interaction. These activities make language essential.

5 ▶ **Critical Viewing** Is the language on these signs in San Francisco's Chinatown district the "mother tongue" to which Tan refers? Explain. **[Distinguish]**

boring—just threw up a mass of confusing images, making it impossible for me to sort out something as logical as saying: "A sunset precedes nightfall" is the same as "a chill
6 precedes a fever." The only way I would have gotten that answer right would have been to imagine an associative situation, for example, my being disobedient and staying out past sunset, catching a chill at night, which turns into feverish pneumonia as punishment, which indeed did happen to me.

I have been thinking about all this lately, about my mother's English, about achievement tests. Because lately I've been asked, as a writer, why there are not more Asian Ameri-
7 cans represented in American literature. Why are there few Asian Americans enrolled in creative writing programs? Why do so many Chinese students go into engineering? Well, these are broad sociological questions I can't begin to answer. But I have noticed in surveys—in fact, just last week—that Asian students, as a whole, always do significantly better on math achievement tests than in English. And this makes me think that there are other Asian-
8 American students whose English spoken in the home might also be described as "broken" or "limited." And perhaps they also have teachers who are steering them away from writing and into math and science, which is what happened to me.

Fortunately, I happen to be rebellious in nature and enjoy the challenge of disproving assumptions made about me. I became an English major my first year in college, after being enrolled as pre-med. I started writing nonfiction as a freelancer the week after I was told by my former boss that writing was my worst skill and I should hone my talents toward account management.

◆ Build Vocabulary

benign (bi nīn′) *adj.*: Not injurious or malignant; not cancerous

semantic (sə man′ tik) *adj.*: Pertaining to meaning in language

▶Critical Viewing◀

5 Distinguish Students should recall that Tan describes her mother's "broken English," not Chinese, as her mother tongue.

Customize for *Visual/Spatial Learners*

6 Ask students whether they experience the problem Tan describes with images obstructing their thinking process. Suggest to students that recording what the images evokes, either visually or in writing, will free their minds to focus on the content and required response.

Customize for *AP Students*

7 Challenge these students to disprove the statement that "there are not more Asian Americans represented in American literature." Urge them to cite specific examples. *This textbook contains writing by Tan and Maxine Hong Kingston. Students may also be familiar with work of Toshio Mori, Bette Bao Lord, Belle Yang, Li-Young Lee, and Marie G. Lee. Prentice Hall also offers a mini-anthology of Asian American literature.*

◆ Critical Thinking

8 Interpret Ask students: How does Tan explain the failure of Asian Americans with language arts relative to their success with math and science? *She believes Asian American students may have received mixed messages from educators about their capacity for language arts, partly as a result of language differences arising from "limited" English spoken in these students' homes.*

Reteach

To help students who are having difficulty evaluating a writer's message, suggest that they use the following visual.

What's the writer's message? → **Is the message valid, logical, and complete?** → **Do I agree or disagree with the writer's message? Why or why not?**

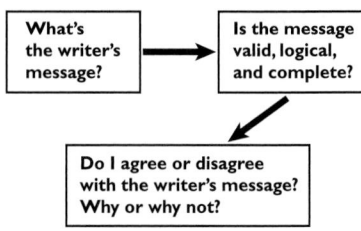

Have students identify the writer's message, analyze its validity, and evaluate whether or not they agree or disagree with the message.

Cross-Curricular Connection: Math

Data Analysis Tan makes several assertions about the cultural groups and their achievements on standardized tests. Provide, or have students locate through libraries, educational organizations, and governmental institutions, educational surveys about the standardized test performances of various cultural subgroups. Encourage students to review data from several different points in time. Then have students create a multiple-line graph comparing the performances of different subgroups over time. Urge students to draw conclusions from the graph. Challenge them as well to discuss the factors contributing to varying results, for example, cultural familiarity with test situations.

Reinforce and Extend

Answers

◆ Literature and Your Life

Reader's Response Among other responses, students may feel that the women have a strong relationship.

Thematic Focus Tan's use of different languages helps her characterization.

☑ Check Your Comprehension

1. Amy Tan realized that she has developed the ability to speak an English that her mother may not understand.
2. Tan has had to speak with doctors and brokers on her mother's behalf. Both situations were awkward; Tan was able to speak more clearly than her mother.
3. Tan believes that math is more precise than English; there is only one correct answer.
4. She uses what she calls simple English, broken English, and formal English.

◆ Critical Thinking

1. Possible response: Because Tan's mother has a language that is vivid and full of observation, she helped shape the way her daughter saw and expressed things.
2. While Tan understands perfectly, others still have difficulty understanding Tan's mother.
3. (a) Tan is thoughtful, sincere, and honest. (b) Tan's mother is depicted as stubborn, intelligent, and unintimidated by others.
4. Possible response: While other criteria —such as an ability to inform, describe, or persuade—can be applied to evaluate writing, readability is most critical.
5. Possible responses: (a) It would be frustrating to try to make myself understood or trying to understand others. (b) I would try to learn the language as soon as possible.
6. Possible responses include providing information in many languages and offering language classes.

But it wasn't until 1985 that I finally began to write fiction. And at first I wrote using what I thought to be wittily crafted sentences, sentences that would finally prove I had mastery over the English language. Here's an example from the first draft of a story that later made its way into *The Joy Luck Club*, but without this line: "That was my mental quandary in its nascent state." A terrible line, which I can barely pronounce.

Fortunately, for reasons I won't get into today, I later decided I should envision a reader for the stories I would write. And the reader I decided upon was my mother, because these were stories about mothers. So with this reader in mind—and in fact she did read my early drafts—I began to write stories using all the Englishes I grew up with: the English I spoke to my mother, which for lack of a better term might be described as "simple"; the English she used with me, which for lack of a better term might be described as "broken"; my translation of her Chinese, which could certainly be described as "watered down"; and what I imagined to be her translation of her Chinese if she could speak in perfect English, her internal language, and for that I sought to preserve the essence, but neither an English nor a Chinese structure. I wanted to capture what language ability tests can never reveal: her intent, her passion, her imagery, the rhythms of her speech and the nature of her thoughts.

Apart from what any critic had to say about my writing, I knew I had succeeded where it counted when my mother finished reading my book and gave me her verdict: "So easy to read."

◆ Build Vocabulary

quandary (kwän´ dä rē) *n.*: State of uncertainty; dilemma

nascent (nas´ ənt, nā´ sənt) *adj.*: Coming into existence; emerging

Guide for Responding

◆ Literature and Your Life

Reader's Response Having read this essay, what are your feelings about Tan and her mother? Explain.

Thematic Focus What effect do you think using different "Englishes" might have on Tan's fiction?

Journal Writing Consider the obstacles that might be faced by a person who has a limited understanding of the English language. Then write about the obstacle you think would be most difficult for you.

☑ Check Your Comprehension

1. When her mother was present at a speech she was giving, Amy Tan had a realization about the way each of them spoke English. What was it?
2. Summarize one experience Tan has had involving her mother's difficulty with English.
3. Why does Tan believe Asian students, including herself, generally score higher on math achievement tests than on English tests?
4. What different kinds of English does Tan use when she writes fiction?

◆ Critical Thinking

INTERPRET

1. How has her mother shaped Tan's writing? Support your answer. **[Analyze]**
2. How does the way Tan views her mother's English differ from how others view it? **[Compare and Contrast]**
3. (a) What can you infer from this essay about Amy Tan's character? (b) What can you infer about her mother's character? **[Infer]**

EVALUATE

4. Assess Tan's conclusion that successful writing is "easy to read." **[Assess]**

APPLY

5. (a) What would it be like to live in a place where a language barrier made it difficult for you to communicate with others? (b) How would you try to overcome the barrier? **[Speculate]**

EXTEND

6. What services can a government or community provide to people with a limited understanding of English? **[Community Link]**

Beyond the Selection

FURTHER READING

Other Works by Amy Tan

The Joy Luck Club
The Kitchen God's Wife

Other Works With the Theme of Mother/Daughter Relationships

Roll of Thunder Hear My Cry, Mildred D. Taylor
Pride and Prejudice, Jane Austen

We suggest that you preview these works.

INTERNET

You and your students may find additional information about Amy Tan on the Internet. We suggest the following sites. Please be aware, however, that sites may have changed since this information was published.

The Amy Tan Home Page can be viewed at **http://www.lumiarium.org/contemporary/amytan/**

For the text of an interview with Amy Tan, visit **http://www.salon1999.com/12nov1995/feature/tan.html**

We *strongly recommend* that you preview sites before you send students to them.

Guide for Responding *(continued)*

◆ Reading Strategy

Evaluate a Writer's Message

All of these writers use their own experiences to convey messages that readers may be able to apply to their own lives. As a reader, it's your job to **evaluate each writer's message**—to judge it critically and to decide whether you do or do not agree with it.

1. (a) What does Rita Dove believe about the power of books? (b) What evidence does she provide to support her opinion? (c) How might someone disagree with this opinion? (d) Considering your answers to the previous questions, explain whether you do or do not agree with the author's message. Support your answer.
2. (a) What does Amy Tan's essay reveal about how language differences can lead to misconceptions or stereotypes? (b) What evidence does she provide to support her opinion? (c) How might someone disagree with this opinion? (d) Considering your answers to the previous questions, explain whether you do or do not agree with the author's message. Support your answer.

◆ Literary Focus

Reflective Essay

A **reflective essay** explores the meaning of a writer's personal experiences or observations. Because of their informal and autobiographical nature, reflective essays generally reveal something about the writer's personality and values.

1. (a) What does Cisneros's list of accomplishments suggest about her values? (b) Does the last paragraph confirm or contradict that idea? Explain.
2. (a) What kind of child does Dove say she was? (b) How do you think Dove feels about her childhood?
3. How has Tan's attitude toward her mother changed as she has grown older? Support your answer with evidence from her essay.

◆ Build Vocabulary

Using the Latin Roots *-scrib-, -script-*

The Latin roots *-scrib-* and *-script-* mean "write." Using each pair of words below, write a sentence that demonstrates the meaning of this root.

1. scribble, child
2. prescription, doctor
3. inscription, trophy
4. author, manuscript

Using the Word Bank: Sentence Completions

Write the following sentences in your notebook. Fill in each blank with a word from the Word Bank.

1. The wandering tribe led a __?__ life in the desert.
2. A person who loves language and words might pursue __?__ studies.
3. The kindly old neighbor had a __?__ influence on the children.
4. Her __?__ social extroversion began to reveal itself even before she could talk.
5. The archaeologist __?__ the message that was carved on the wall of the tomb.
6. Having accepted two invitations for the same date, he found himself in a social __?__.
7. Scientists use __?__ evidence to prove or disprove a hypothesis.

◆ Grammar and Style

Varying Sentence Structure

Writers use a variety of sentence structures to lend a rhythmic flow to their work and avoid choppiness and dull predictability. As you read these essays, you may have noticed that the writers used a variety of simple, compound, and complex sentences.

Looking at Style Compare Tan's first two paragraphs with the rest of her essay. (a) What do you notice? (b) How does choice of sentence structure affect the rhythm of her writing? (c) How does this style relate to Tan's message?

Writing Application Using a variety of sentence structures, write a paragraph in which you discuss the essay you enjoyed most. Explain the reasons.

◆ Grammar and Style

Looking at Style

(a) The first two paragraphs are written in short, simple sentences. The following paragraphs make more use of a variety of sentence styles. (b) The first two paragraphs present information forcefully. The following paragraphs are more fluent. (c) The first two paragraphs may represent the simpler writing of a mother tongue. The next paragraphs are more fluent. Tan's message is about fluency and ability to communicate with ease.

Grammar Reinforcement

For additional instruction and practice, use the Varying Sentence Structure on the **Language Lab CD-ROM,** and the page on Sentences Classified by Structure, p. 38, in the *Writer's Solution Grammar Practice Book.*

◆ Reading Strategy

1. (a) Dove believes that books have power to transport and educate. (b) She talks about her own childhood and the ways that books were magical to her. (c) Possible response: Like watching television, reading books is a passive experience; those who read may not actually "do" anything. (d) Students should offer reasons to support their opinion.
2. (a) Tan says that people judge others based on their ability to speak a language fluently. (b) She provides the personal experiences of her mother and herself. (c) Possible response: People should not allow themselves to be judged this way; they ought to learn the language. (d) Students should offer reasons to support their opinion.

◆ Literary Focus

1. (a) She thinks that education, travel, and writing about a variety of experiences are important. (b) The final paragraph confirms these values.
2. (a) She says she was "painfully shy and awkward." (b) Dove seems to treasure the experiences of childhood.
3. Responses should confirm that as a child, Tan was embarrassed by her mother's language difficulties. As an adult, she has grown to understand and respect her mother.

◆ Build Vocabulary

Using the Latin Roots *-scrib-* and *-script-*

1. The child used the crayon to *scribble* on the wall.
2. The doctor wrote a *prescription* for the medication.
3. What will you write as the *inscription* on the trophy?
4. The author spent months on the revision of his *manuscript.*

Using the Word Bank: Sentence Completions

1. nomadic
2. semantic
3. benign
4. nascent
5. transcribed
6. quandary
7. empirical

Idea Bank

Customizing for
Performance Levels
Following are suggestions for matching Idea Bank topics with your students' performance levels:
Less Advanced Students: 1, 5
Average Students: 2, 4, 6
More Advanced Students: 3, 7

Customizing for
Learning Modalities
Following are suggestions for matching Idea Bank topics with your students' learning modalities:
Interpersonal: 4
Verbal/Linguistic: 4, 5, 7
Logical/Mathematical: 6
Visual/Spatial: 6

Guided Writing Lesson

For more instruction on prewriting, elaboration, and revision, see *Prentice Hall Writing and Grammar.*

Writing and Language Transparencies Use the Reflective Essay Writing Process Model (pp. 5–8) to reinforce the elements of descriptive writing.

Writers at Work Videodisc
Have students view the videodisc segment on description (Ch. 1) in which Rita Dove discusses the importance of language choice. Have students discuss how they can apply Dove's advice to their work.

Play frames 1481 to 2687

Writing Lab CD-ROM
Have students complete the tutorial on Description. Follow these steps:
1. Use the Word Bins to gather sensory details.
2. Refer to the interactive examples of tone. Have students draft on the computer.
3. Encourage students to consult the audio-annotated student revision model.

Build Your Portfolio

Idea Bank

Writing

1. **Letter to the Author** Respond to one of these essays by writing a letter to the author. Explain what you liked, what you didn't like, and ask any questions you might have.
2. **Science-Fiction Story** In "For the Love of Books," Rita Dove summarizes a science-fiction story she read as a child that made a big impression on her. Write your own science-fiction story in which you are the central character.
3. **Television Pilot** Imagine Sandra (Cisneros), Rita (Dove), and Amy (Tan) spending the summer of 1967 together at a creative-writing camp. Using this as a premise, write a script for a television sit-com pilot. Use your imagination as well as what you know from the essays you have read. **[Media Link]**

Speaking, Listening, and Viewing

4. **Speech** What message would Cisneros, Dove, or Tan convey in a speech to aspiring young writers? Develop and deliver the speech that one of these writers might present.
5. **Monologue** As Tan argues, do you use more than one kind of English in your daily life? Write and deliver a monologue that utilizes all the "Englishes" in your life. **[Performing Arts Link]**

Researching and Representing

6. **Icons** To overcome language barriers, icons or symbols are often used in place of words in public places. Create a series of icons to represent places and people in your school. **[Art Link]**
7. **Readers' Club** In a group, choose another work by Cisneros, Dove, or Tan. After reading the work, discuss it—taking into account what you know about the author.

Online Activity www.phlit.phschool.com

Guided Writing Lesson

A Treasured Memory

In each of the essays you read, the author vividly describes memories from childhood. Such remembrances are an integral part of personal and reflective essays. Think of an event or moment from your past that meant a great deal to you. Write a remembrance of it. In describing your experience, concentrate on creating a single impression that will stand out in your reader's mind.

Writing Skills Focus: Main Impression

To create a **main impression,** use language and sensory details that contribute to the impression you're developing, and avoid details that don't fit in.

Model From the Essay

From the time I began to read, as a child, I loved to feel [books's] heft in my hand and the warm spot caused by their intimate weight in my lap; I loved the crisp whisper of a page turning, the musky odor of old paper and the sharp inky whiff of new pages. . . .

Notice how Rita Dove uses precise sensory details, like "warm spot," "crisp whisper," and "sharp inky whiff." Together these details add up to a single impression: her passion for books.

Prewriting Once you have decided on the topic for your remembrance, gather descriptive details. Make lists of sensory words and images that relate to the moment or event you are going to describe.

Drafting Refer to your list of sensory details as you draft your remembrance. Include only those details that will help build the impression you're creating. Be aware that the tone of your writing also conveys your attitude toward your subject.

Revising Think about whether you've created a single strong impression. To focus your impression, consider adding or eliminating details. Check that your organization is clear and that the tone of your writing accurately reflects your feelings.

ASSESSMENT OPTIONS

Formal Assessment, Selection Test, pp. 302–304, and Assessment Resources Software. The selection test is designed so that it can be easily customized to the performance levels of your students.

Alternative Assessment, p. 69, includes options for less advanced students, more advanced students, intrapersonal learners, verbal/linguistic learners, and visual/spatial learners.

PORTFOLIO ASSESSMENT
Use the following rubrics in ***Alternative Assessment*** to assess student writing:
Letter to the Author: Expression Rubric, p. 109
Science-Fiction Story: Fictional Narrative Rubric, p. 110
Television Pilot: Drama Rubric, p. 124
Guided Writing Lesson: Description Rubric, p. 112

Writing Process Workshop

Job Portfolio

Essays like the ones in this section serve as a written record of where our culture has been—and perhaps as an indication of where it is going. A résumé serves a similar purpose for the individual; it is a written summary of education, qualifications, and work experience that a prospective employer can use to evaluate your suitability for a new position. A job portfolio that includes a résumé, a cover letter, and, where appropriate, job samples or references gives an employer a quick summary of what you have to offer. The portfolio often determines whether you will progress to the next step in the job-seeking process: the interview.

Use these skills, introduced in this section's Guided Writing Lessons, to help you develop a professional job portfolio.

Writing Skills Focus

- **Keep to a format** by following the conventions of business letters and résumés. (See p. 1003.)
- **Convey a main impression.** Highlight information that is relevant to the prospective job and downplay irrelevant details. (See p. 1018.)
- **Maintain accuracy** by truthfully representing job descriptions, achievements, and other details.

Look at this sample résumé.

WRITING MODEL

Excerpt from a résumé

QUALIFICATIONS
Experienced musician. Own two guitars; familiar with all major brands. ①

WORK EXPERIENCE ②
Sept. 1997–Present: Cashier
Carlyle Clothing, Riverview Mall.
- Ring up sales and returns.
- Keep inventory up to date.

Summer 1995–1996 ③: Library Clerk
Holmstead Branch Library.
- Helped patrons locate resources.
- Shelved and repaired books. ④

① The author includes information that is relevant to the music store job she is seeking.
② Each section of the résumé is clearly labeled.
③ The résumé accurately reflects the dates of employment.
④ Beyond job titles, the résumé provides details about responsibilities.

Prepare and Engage

LESSON OBJECTIVES

- To use recursive writing processes to write a job portfolio
- To recognize and correct errors in capitalization
- To recognize and use action verbs

Distribute the scoring rubric for Résumé and Cover Letter (p. 129) in ***Alternative Assessment*** to make students aware of the evaluation criteria. See the note on page 1021 to customize the rubric to this workshop.

Refer students to the Writing Handbook, page 1192, for instruction in the writing process, and page 1196 for more information on practical and technical writing. You may also want to present the Outline Graphic Organizer in ***Writing and Language Transparencies,*** p. 47.

Writers at Work Videodisc
To introduce practical writing, play the videodisc segment featuring NASA's David Herring (Ch. 8).

Play frames 33063 to 43439

Writing Lab CD-ROM
If your students have access to computers, you may want to have them use the tutorial on Practical and Technical Writing. Have students follow these steps:

1. Complete a questionnaire to learn how to tailor their work to a specific audience or purpose.
2. Draft on the computer.
3. Compare the draft of a business letter with a revised version to get ideas for revising their cover letters.
4. Use the Self-Evaluation Checklist to evaluate their portfolios.

Beyond the Classroom

Workplace Skills Connection

Job Hunting Students may already be familiar with the components of a job portfolio from their experience applying for summer or after-school positions. Encourage these students to share these documents with the class, as writing models or as pieces to be revised or updated to fit a current job prospect. Alternately, students can ask adults they know for copies of their résumés to refer to in the course of this workshop. Explain to students that many adults constantly update their résumés and keep copies handy even if they are not actively job hunting—just in case an opportunity should present itself. In addition, a current employer should receive an updated version of a résumé if it includes an advance in education level or the acquisition of new skills.

Prewriting Strategy
Have students use a web to explore the skills associated with their extracurricular activities and their hobbies.

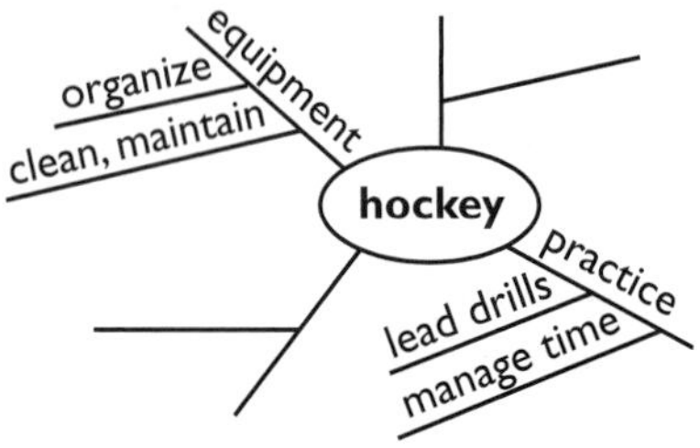

Customize for
Interpersonal Learners
Encourage these students to speak to past employers, coaches, or teachers as they develop their résumés. These adults may be able to provide written references, positive opinions on students' aptitude and past performance, or offer ideas that students can incorporate into their résumés or cover letters.

Writing Lab CD-ROM
The Gathering Details section of the tutorial on Practical writing includes a Cluster Diagram and a Details Checklist. Students can use these tools to help plan their résumés.

Elaboration Strategy
When students recall previous experience on note cards or elsewhere, encourage them to elaborate by quantifying their achievements in a way that presents them in an impressive light. For instance, the sample note card in the student edition might be modified to read "Assisted in the page layout of six trade books in the space of three months" or "Copyedited over 400 pages of manuscript of technical writing." Urge students to be specific, but warn them to present details that are completely factual.

Revision Strategy
As students revise their résumés, have them consider saving slightly different versions to fit different audiences and purposes, a common technique used by veteran job hunters. For example, one résumé may be geared to finding an internship in a new field, whereas another may be written to land a high-paying job in an area in which the student is quite experienced.

Applying Language Skills: Capitalization

Capitalize all proper nouns and adjectives; months and days of the week; and geographical names, such as the name of a street, city, state, country, or body of water.

Examples:

WORK EXPERIENCE:
May 1998–August 1998
Computer Corner
660 King's Highway, Grenville
EDUCATION:
June 1998–July 1998
Oxford University, England
Young Scholars of America study program

Practice Revise the following, correcting any errors in capitalization.

As my Résumé indicates, I was a student at Kennedy high school in dallas until last may, when I moved to Austin.

Writing Application Check that you have capitalized businesses, organizations, or schools in your job portfolio.

Writer's Solution Connection
Writing Lab

For tips on formatting business letters and résumés, review the Interactive Workplace Writing Models in the Organizing Details section of the tutorial on Practical and Technical Writing.

Prewriting

Choose a Topic Look through the help wanted ads in a newspaper. Find a job that interests you, and create either your own job portfolio or that of an "ideal candidate" for that job. You may find it helpful to learn more about the backgrounds of people who have held similar positions. You may also use any of the career openings suggested below:

Topic Ideas
- Intern at a law office
- Tour guide in Mexico
- Poet Laureate of your town or community
- President of the United States

Make Note Cards For each skill or experience you wish to include on your résumé, create an individual note card on which you record the *who*, *what*, *where*, and *when* of the experience. Here's how a note card might look:

1997–1998	**Production assistant**
	Mayer's Printing Co.
	Detroit, MI
Assisted with page layout and copyediting.	

Include All Relevant Abilities Don't forget to record additional qualifications or skills, such as fluency in a foreign language, computer skills, and so on.

Drafting

Follow a Clear Organization Organize your note cards to help you decide which section headings—Objective, Qualifications, Work Experience, Related Experience, Education, Awards, References, and so on—to use. Record the headings, then fill in the information from the appropriate note cards.

Use a Template Use a consistent format; for example, if you write the first section heading in bold capital letters, use the same type style for subsequent headings. Follow a standard business letter format for your cover letter. Most word-processing programs include templates for résumés and business letters. Adapt them to fit your needs.

Be Accurate Do not exaggerate your duties, skills, or other details when describing your personal job experiences. Make sure all employment dates and job titles are correct.

Applying Language Skills

Capitalization To introduce this language skill, point out that prospective employers often have difficulty comparing the many résumés and letters of applicants who have similar qualifications. In this case, they may look for small "negative details" to eliminate candidates who are otherwise promising. Advise students not to make the decision-making process easier for employers: misspellings, poor punctuation, and incorrect capitalization can quickly eliminate them from the consideration.

Answer
As my résumé indicates, I was a student at Kennedy High School in Dallas until last May, when I moved to Austin.

Grammar Reinforcement

For additional instruction and practice, refer students to the **Language Lab CD-ROM** unit on Capitalization and Punctuation, and practice page 81 in the *Writer's Solution Grammar Practice Book.*

Revising

Use a Peer Reviewer Ask a classmate to take on the role of a potential employer. Have him or her review and critique your portfolio, paying particular attention to the following:

- Is the portfolio well organized and professional?
- Is the résumé consistent in format? Has the writer used formal business letter format for the cover letter?
- Does the portfolio emphasize experiences and qualifications that are relevant to the prospective job?
- Is information truthful and accurate?

Proofread Reread your portfolio, checking for errors in spelling, capitalization, punctuation, and formatting. Finally, review each component to be sure that any personal information is accurate and factually correct.

Revision Model

Dear ~~Anne,~~ ① Ms. Singer:

I am currently a junior at J.L. Mann High School and the president of the ② National Championship Debate team. ~~I have extensive experience in radio.~~ ③ I have enjoyed spending the last two semesters as a disc jockey for my school's dances. I am interested in a summer internship at your radio station so that I can learn more about the field of communications and media.

① In keeping with the format of a business letter, an informal greeting is replaced with a formal salutation.

② Inserting this detail reinforces the writer's qualifications as a skilled communicator.

③ By deleting a misleading statement and adding a more accurate one, the writer avoids exaggerating her experience.

Publishing

- **Send Your Portfolio Out** Submit your portfolio to several prospective employers. If your work is fictitious, ask employers in appropriate professions to review your writing.
- **Personal Portfolio** Keep copies of all your cover letters and résumés in a binder for future reference. Date each copy, noting any responses it may have received. Use your samples as models the next time you need to prepare a job portfolio.

Applying Language Skills: Action Verbs

An **action verb** expresses physical or mental action and tells what the subject is doing or thinking. Wherever possible, replace the linking verbs *am, is, are, was,* and *were* with action verbs to make your résumé stronger and more effective:

Linking Verb:

I was the manager.

Action Verb:

I managed four clerks and organized the schedule.

Practice Replace each italicized phrase with an action verb, revising the sentences as necessary.

1. He *was a* stock clerk.
2. She *is* a camp counselor.
3. I *am* the director.

Writing Application Use a variety of action verbs to describe work-related responsibilities and experiences.

Writer's Solution Connection
Language Lab

For more help with action verbs, see the Writing With Nouns and Verbs lesson in the Writing Style Unit of the Language Lab CD-ROM.

Writing Lab CD-ROM
The Practical Writing tutorial includes audio-annotated models of business letters that show changes made in the revision process.

Publishing

If students choose to send part or all of their portfolios to prospective employers, encourage students to keep track of the exact dates on which they send material so that they can follow up intelligently with phone calls.

Applying Language Skills

Action Verbs Introduce this skill by explaining that action verbs not only enhance the description of past experiences, but also convey a sense of energy about the writer's personality.

Answers

1. He mastered all duties associated with the position of stock clerk.
2. She teaches and motivates young children as a camp counselor.
3. I plan, coordinate, and lead in my role as the director.

Reinforce and Extend

Reflect on Writing To extend the assignment, encourage students to share potential employers' responses to their portfolio.

Prentice Hall Writing and Grammar For more prewriting, elaboration, and revision strategies, see *Prentice Hall Writing and Grammar.*

✓ ASSESSMENT		4	3	2	1
PORTFOLIO ASSESSMENT Use the rubric on Résumé and Cover Letter in the ***Alternative Assessment*** booklet (p. 129) to assess students' writing. Add these criteria to customize the rubric to this assignment.	**Action Verbs**	The writer consistently uses action verbs to lend greater impact to the résumé.	The writer uses action verbs in several cases.	The writer rarely uses action verbs.	The writer avoids using action verbs altogether, giving the portfolio a lackluster tone.
	Capitalization	The writer consistently capitalizes words correctly.	The writer uses correct capitalization in most cases.	The writer rarely capitalizes words correctly, making the portfolio appear somewhat thoughtless and sloppy.	The writer either avoids capitalizing altogether, or applies capitalization to words that do not require it.

Prepare and Engage

LESSON OBJECTIVES

- To use text organizers such as overviews, headings, and graphic features to locate and categorize information
- To locate facts and details

Customize for
Gifted/Talented Students
Invite students to select an article from a newspaper or magazine that has no headings or graphic features. Challenge them to provide text organizers that will help a reader locate information in the article quickly. Have them create a table of contents, headings, a graphic feature such as a chart or timeline, and an index for the article. Students can cut the article into sections and mount them on paper, allowing space for inserting headings and graphic features.

Apply the Strategies

Answers

1. Possible research topics are: bike helmet laws, bike injuries of children, head injuries, and bike accidents.
2. Section 3
3. Students' graphics should focus on specific information from the article that can be visually presented such as a diagram of a bike helmet showing its protective features.

Student Success Workshop

Research Skills — Using Text Organizers as a Research Tool

Strategies for Success

When you search for information about a particular topic, are you surprised by the amount of information available? You can find the information most relevant to your topic by using text organizers, such as tables of contents, chapter headings and subheadings, indexes, and graphics, which highlight the important points in the material.

Tables of Contents and Indexes A table of contents is found at the beginning of a book and provides a chronological outline of the book's contents. Use the table of contents to determine whether the book discusses your topic. Indexes, located at the back of a book, contain alphabetical listings of the contents. Here you can search for more specific information.

Overviews, Headings, and Graphic Features These features can help you research:

- **Overviews,** such as introductions or prefaces, preview the material you are about to read. Found at the beginning of a text or of a section of text, they may contain information about main ideas and the author's purpose.
- **Headings** organize a text into manageable pieces. They often state the main point of the following section and can be quick guides for scanning a book's material.
- **Graphic features,** such as maps, charts, graphs, timelines, and illustrations, often review or summarize the information in a text. Sometimes, they explain ideas better than words alone and are useful research tools.

Apply the Strategies

Read the sample article, and do the activities.

It's Time for Helmets
Every year, thousands of children receive serious head injuries in bike accidents, many of which could be prevented by the use of bike helmets. Laws requiring their use can help.

Helmets Provide Protection
Many children fall from their bicycles with little effect, but 2 percent of bike accidents cause serious injuries that are permanent, even life-threatening. A helmet absorbs the impact of falls, often preventing serious injuries. Studies show that bike helmets reduce the risk of head injury by 85 percent!

Bike Helmet Laws Work
In 1998, the state of Florida began requiring cyclists under the age of 16 to wear a helmet. The police issue a fine of $15 to violators. Kids, however, can avoid the fine by purchasing a bike helmet within 30 days. In this way, authorities hope more kids will use helmets. States with similar laws have experienced a 20 to 40 percent drop in head injuries sustained by children while biking.

1. List three research topics for which this article might be a useful source.
2. Based on the headings, which section would be a useful source if you wanted to convince your community to pass helmet laws?
3. Create a sketch, diagram, or other graphic to represent information in the article.

Here are other situations in which you can use text organizers for research:

- *Sorting through multiple sources for a research paper*
- *Looking at the help-wanted ads*
- *Using a bus or train schedule*

Test-Taking Tip

Locating Facts and Details

Knowing how to locate information efficiently in a reading passage can help students perform well on any standardized test. The ACT and SAT tests contain sections that require students to locate facts and details. Have students use the passage about bike helmets in the student edition to locate the detail asked for in the following sample test item.

By what percent have injuries to children been reduced in states that enforce bike helmet laws?

A 2–5 percent
B 15–16 percent
C 20–40 percent
D 85–90 percent

By using the headings, students can quickly locate which part of the passage has information about the results of the laws. The correct answer is C, but more important, students should notice that by using heads, they found the correct information quickly.

PART 3 Social Protest

Choke, 1964, Robert Rauschenberg, Oil and screenprint on canvas, 60" x 48", Washington University Gallery of Art, St. Louis, © Robert Rauschenberg/Licensed by VAGA, New York, NY

The freedom to speak out against policies we disagree with and to fight against injustices we see has always been one of the rights that Americans most cherish. During the 1950's, 1960's, and early 1970's, Americans passionately exercised this right, fighting for civil rights, opposing an unpopular war, and pointing out the dangers of nuclear proliferation. The literature in this section illustrates the important contributions made by writers in addressing such issues.

One-Minute Planning Guide

From Hersey's account of the bombing of Hiroshima to the dark themes of *The Glass Menagerie,* the selections in this section capture the mood of the second half of the twentieth century. Social protest threads through poems such as "Mirror," which questions society's emphasis on youth, and "Frederick Douglass," which assesses the progress African Americans have made toward equality. Writings by Komunyakaa and O'Brien bring home the lessons of the Vietnam War.

Customize for *Varying Student Needs*

When assigning the selections in this part, keep these factors in mind:

"The Rockpile"
- Engaging short story about family relationships
- Dialect may prove challenging to English Language Learners.

from *Hiroshima*
- A compelling story of four survivors of the atomic bomb
- Less proficient readers may need help keeping narratives separate.

"Death of the Ball Turret Gunner," "Losses"
- In simple language, these poems ask what becomes of human values in war.

"Runagate Runagate," "Frederick Douglass"
- Accessible poems will appeal to most students.

"Ambush"
- Brief, accessible, high-interest story of a veteran's memories of war

The Glass Menagerie
- Full-length play which can be read on many levels

Humanities: Art

Choke, 1964, by Robert Rauschenberg.

Born in Texas in 1925, Robert Rauschenberg has been one of the leading experimental American artists of the late twentieth century. Rauschenberg studied art at Black Mountain College in North Carolina. After creating a series of all-white and all-black paintings, Rauschenberg invented what he called the "combine"—a collage incorporating actual objects into paintings. The work shown here uses another technique he developed in the early 1960's: combining images from media and other artifacts of everyday life in silk-screen prints.

Encourage students to identify as many images in this work as they can. For example, guide students to see the upside-down Public Shelter sign, the One Way sign, the grainy Army helicopter, and the Statue of Liberty.

Have your students link the painting to the theme of Social Protest by answering the following questions:

1. There are references to the military and bomb shelters in this work. Given that Rauschenberg created this work a few years after the Cuban Missile Crisis, what aspect of American life might he be protesting? *He might be protesting the possibility of nuclear war or the power of the military.*
2. The term *choke* means to clog something to the point of constriction or even suffocation. What aspects of American life might create such a feeling? *This feeling might be created by the way people are bombarded by media images and information or the fear of nuclear war.*

Prepare and Engage

LESSON OBJECTIVES

1. **To develop vocabulary and word identification skills**
   - Latin Prefixes: *mal-*
   - Using the Word Bank: Synonyms or Antonyms
2. **To use a variety of reading strategies to comprehend fiction**
   - Reading Strategy: Analyze Cause and Effect
3. **To increase knowledge of other cultures and to connect common elements across cultures**
   - Connecting Themes Across Cultures (ATE)
4. **To express and support responses to the text**
   - Critical Thinking
   - Idea Bank: Flyer
   - Idea Bank: Book Jacket
   - Idea Bank: Movie Proposal
   - Idea Bank: Public Service Announcement
5. **To analyze literary elements**
   - Literary Focus: Setting
6. **To read in order to research self-selected and assigned topics**
   - Idea Bank: Illustrated Report
7. **To plan, prepare, organize, and present literary interpretations**
   - Idea Bank: Radio Play
   - Idea Bank: Psychological Profile
8. **To use recursive writing processes to write a fictional journal**
   - Guided Writing Lesson
9. **To increase knowledge of the rules of grammar and usage**
   - Grammar and Style: Restrictive and Nonrestrictive Adjective Clauses

Test Preparation

Writing Skills: Punctuation (ATE, p. 1025)
The teaching tips and sample test item in this workshop support the instruction and practice in the unit workshop:

Writing Skills: Punctuation, Usage, and Sentence Structure (ATE, p. 1143)

Guide for Interpreting

James Baldwin *(1924–1987)*

James Baldwin once told an interviewer that he "never had a childhood." Because his stepfather worked long hours as both a preacher and a factory hand, Baldwin had much of the responsibility for raising his eight siblings. The only leisure activity he was able to pursue was reading, and Baldwin read *Uncle Tom's Cabin* and *A Tale of Two Cities* "over and over again." This early passion for reading fueled his imagination, planting the seeds of inspiration for his later success as a writer.

A Harlem Childhood Baldwin was born in Harlem, New York. Even as a boy, it was clear that he had a gift for words, but his deeply religious parents disapproved of his interest in literature. They wanted him to become a preacher like his stepfather. At age fourteen, he did. He didn't give up his literary pursuits, however.

Baldwin was encouraged by African American poet Countee Cullen, who taught at his junior high school.

With Cullen's support, he wrote poetry and worked on his school's literary magazine. Inspired by the success of Richard Wright's novel *Native Son,* which proved to him that an African American could have success as a writer, Baldwin eventually decided to abandon preaching and devote his life to writing.

The Road to "Writer" For several years, Baldwin worked at odd jobs while writing and reading in his spare time. At age twenty-four, he won a fellowship that enabled him to travel to Europe and write. In 1953, he published his first novel, *Go Tell It on the Mountain*, a semi-autobiographical story about a boy preacher. The novel marked the beginning of a distinguished literary career that included the novels *Giovanni's Room* (1956), *Another Country* (1962), and *Tell Me How Long the Train's Been Gone* (1968); a play set in the American South called *Blues for Mr. Charlie* (1964); and several notable essay collections.

A Powerful Witness Baldwin once said, "One writes out of one thing only—one's own experience. Everything depends on how relentlessly one forces from this experience the last drop, sweet or bitter, it can possibly give." Baldwin's work bears powerful witness to his own experience as an African American. In his writing, he expresses the need for social justice, while delving into such universal concerns as the desire for love and the need for acceptance. His books, which dig deeply into contemporary life, are sometimes painful to read, but the pain is always tempered by hope.

Baldwin often repeated one phrase—"People can be better than they are." This simple idea is woven into everything he wrote.

◆ Background for Understanding

Art: Harlem as a Cultural Center

Harlem, the New York City neighborhood where James Baldwin grew up, has been a vital center of African American life and culture since southern blacks began migrating there in the 1910's. In the 1920's, it was the hub of the Harlem Renaissance, an African American literary and artistic movement. One of the leading writers of that movement was James Baldwin's teacher, Countee Cullen.

When the Depression hit in the 1930's, the largely poor population of Harlem plunged even deeper into poverty. Despite economic hardships, however, Harlem's culture—its churches, theaters, music, and dance centers—remained strong.

Prentice Hall Literature Program Resources

REINFORCE / RETEACH / EXTEND

Selection Support Pages
Build Vocabulary: Prefixes: *mal-*, p. 314
Grammar and Style: Restrictive and Nonrestrictive Adjective Clauses, p. 315
Reading Strategy: Identify Cause and Effect, p. 316
Literary Focus: Setting, p. 317

Strategies for Diverse Student Needs, p. 70

Beyond Literature
Community Connection: Emergency Services, p. 70

Formal Assessment Selection Test, pp. 308–310; Assessment Resources Software

Alternative Assessment, p. 70

Writing and Language Transparencies
Cause-and-Effect Organizer, pp. 91–93

Resource Pro CD-ROM
Includes all resource materials and a customizable lesson plan.

Literature CD-ROM

Listening to Literature Audiocassettes

The Rockpile

◆ Literature and Your Life

Connect Your Experience

As you'll see, "The Rockpile" takes place in a poor urban community where people faced difficult obstacles. However, from the penthouse apartments on the wealthiest city block to the sprawling acres of land in isolated farm communities, every neighborhood has distinct advantages and unique problems.

Journal Writing How do you think communities can shape people's actions, attitudes, or values? Jot down your response.

Thematic Focus: Social Protest

Although Baldwin may have written this story to explore the way people interact when under pressure, he also reveals how poverty's problems can extend beyond simple finances.

◆ Build Vocabulary

Latin Prefixes: *mal-*

In this story, you'll find the word *malevolence,* which begins with *mal-*, a Latin prefix meaning "bad" or "wrong." *Mal-* is a clue that *malevolence* refers to something bad. In fact, it means "ill will" or "the state of wishing evil toward others."

Word Bank

Before you read, preview this list of words from the story.

intriguing
benevolent
decorously
latent
engrossed
jubilant
arrested
malevolence
perdition

◆ Grammar and Style

Restrictive and Nonrestrictive Adjective Clauses

"The Rockpile" contains examples of **adjective clauses** — subordinate clauses used as adjectives to modify nouns or pronouns. **Restrictive adjective clauses** are necessary to complete the meaning of the noun or pronoun they modify. **Nonrestrictive adjective clauses** provide additional but not necessary information. They are set off from the rest of the sentence with commas. Here are two examples from the story:

. . . he was afraid of the rockpile and of the boys *who played there.*
[restrictive clause explains essential information—which *boys* he fears]

Once a boy, *whose name was Richard*, drowned in the river.
[nonrestrictive clause provides more information about the *boy*]

◆ Literary Focus

Setting

Just as real people are shaped to some extent by the environments in which they live, the characters in a work of fiction are often shaped by the **setting**—the specific time and place in which the action of the story occurs. Drawn from Baldwin's childhood experiences, "The Rockpile" is set in Harlem during the 1930's. Life in that place and time was influenced by the difficult economic and social realities that people faced. In addition, Harlem's physical features at times had a direct impact on people's lives. As you read, think about how the setting affects the characters' personalities and actions.

◆ Reading Strategy

Analyze Cause and Effect

In "The Rockpile," a child's disobedience sparks a painful family confrontation. You will understand the characters better if you **analyze cause-and-effect** relationships in the text. This means determining what causes the characters' behavior and noting what effects each character's words or actions have on other characters or on the situation. Identifying causes and effects can give you insight into the complicated family dynamics exposed in "The Rockpile."

Interest Grabber Write the following statement on the board: "I am not my brother's keeper." Discuss its meaning with students. You might use some of the following questions to shape the discussion:

- To whom does the word *brother* refer?
- What does the word *keeper* mean in this context?
- When would someone be apt to make such a statement?
- Do you agree with the sentiments of the statement? Why or why not?

Encourage students to keep this statement in mind as they read "The Rockpile" and to note which characters might agree with the statement.

Connecting Themes Across Cultures

Ask students to compare and contrast types of social protest that have occurred in various communities and cultures. For example, they might compare and contrast other literary, visual, or performance art works, created as expressions of social protest, with mass protests such as the 1989 student demonstrations in Beijing, China's Tiananmen Square.

Customize for ***Less Proficient Readers***
To help students better understand the story, point out that the first two pages convey setting and background information and that the main incident is recounted immediately afterward. Encourage students to make a timeline of the incident.

Customize for ***AP Students***
Setting plays a major role in this story. Suggest that students consider: What is the greatest danger that the characters face? Is it a danger from the setting or from other characters? Have students take notes to support their answers.

Customize for ***English Language Learners***
The dialogue in this story is in dialect. Have students paraphrase portions of dialect that they find difficult. Use the page titled Rephrase Characters' Speech, p. 70, in ***Strategies for Diverse Student Needs.***

Test Preparation Workshop

Writing Skills: Punctuation
Some standardized tests require students to identify the best way to correct an error in punctuation. Use the following sample test item to demonstrate.

Because he had much of the responsibility of raising his eight siblings—James Baldwin claimed that he "never had a childhood."

Which is the best way to correct the underlined section of this passage?

A Because he had much of the responsibility of raising his eight siblings; James Baldwin claimed that he "never had a childhood."
B Because he had much of the responsibility of raising his eight siblings: James Baldwin claimed that he "never had a childhood."
C Because he had much of the responsibility of raising his eight siblings, James Baldwin claimed that he "never had a childhood."
D Correct as is

C correctly places a comma after an adverb clause preceding an independent clause.

Develop Understanding

One-Minute Insight Family relationships are complicated matters, and family conflicts, like all conflicts, are studies in cause and effect. As students read this story about one family's response to a child's seemingly simple and commonplace act of disobedience, they will see that the characters' actions have both apparent and underlying causes and both immediate and far-reaching effects. Tracing these strands will help students understand the forces of love, need, resentment, and fear that bind and divide Baldwin's fictional family.

▶Critical Viewing◀

❶ **Connect** Sample response: Both the painting and the story depict urban neighborhoods that seem to be settings for both ordinary, everyday life and for danger and drama. The painting suggests the crowded and confusing nature of life on city streets.

◆ Literary Focus

❷ **Setting** Ask students to identify the details that let the reader know the story is set in a city. *Reference to a subway immediately places the narrative in a city.*

Customize for
Gifted/Talented Students
Aunt Florence offers one explanation of why the rockpile cannot be removed. Challenge students to invent an alternative explanation, and to account for the rockpile's mysterious origin.

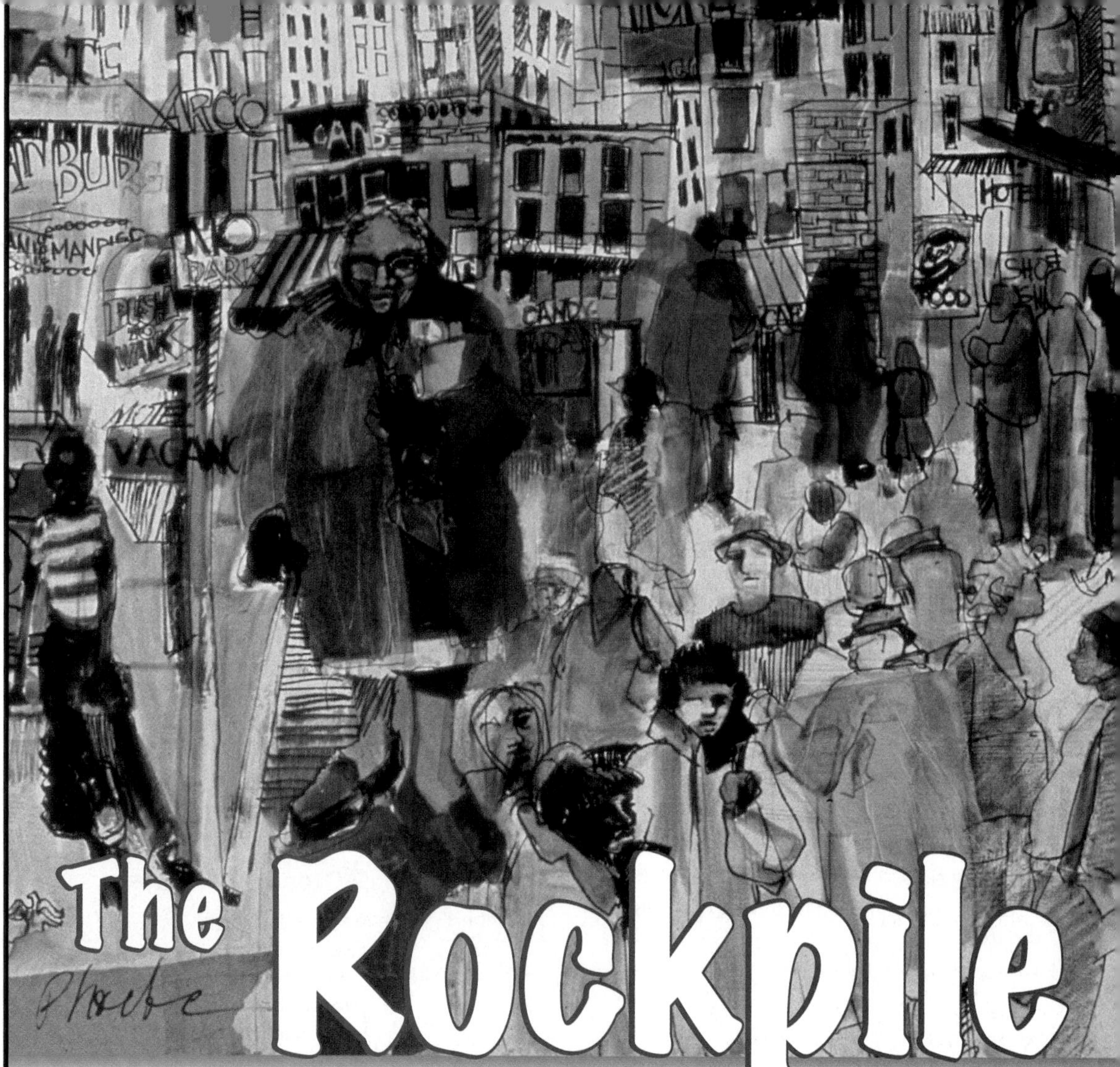

The Rockpile

James Baldwin

Push to Walk, (collage 48" x 48"), Phoebe Be

❶ ▲ Critical Viewing How does the setting depicted in this painting connect to Baldwin's story? **[Connect]**

❷ Across the street from their house, in an empty lot between two houses, stood the rockpile. It was a strange place to find a mass of natural rock jutting out of the ground; and someone, probably Aunt Florence, had once told them that the rock was there and could not be taken away because without it the subway cars underground would fly apart, killing all the people. ❷ This, touching on some natural mystery concerning the surface and the center of the earth, was far too intriguing an explanation to be challenged, and it invested the rockpile, moreover, with such mysterious importance

Block Scheduling Strategies

Consider these suggestions to take advantage of extended class time:

- Before students read, have them complete and discuss responses to the journal activity in Literature and Your Life (p. 1025).
- Have students review the biographical information about James Baldwin on p. 1024. You might also share the **Literature CD-ROM,** *The History of American Literature*: Part 2, Disk 2, Feature 4 to build background on Baldwin's career.
- Introduce the Reading Strategy, Identify Cause and Effect (p. 1025). Distribute copies of Cause-and-Effect Organizer in ***Writing and Language Transparencies***, (pp. 91–93) and encourage students to fill them out with details from the story.
- As a strategy to help students get into the mind of a character, have them write a journal entry for Roy, as outlined in the Guided Writing Lesson (p. 1033). Before students get started, discuss the appropriate personal tone for the entry.

that Roy felt it to be his right, not to say his duty, to play there.

Other boys were to be seen there each afternoon after school and all day Saturday and Sunday. They fought on the rockpile. Sure footed, dangerous, and reckless, they rushed each other and grappled on the heights, sometimes disappearing down the other side in a confusion of dust and screams and upended, flying feet. "It's a wonder they don't kill themselves," their mother said, watching sometimes from the fire escape. "You children stay away from there, you hear me?" Though she said "children" she was looking at Roy, where he sat beside John on the fire escape. "The good Lord knows," she continued, "I don't want you to come home bleeding like a hog every day the Lord sends." Roy shifted impatiently, and continued to stare at the street, as though in this gazing he might somehow acquire wings. John said nothing. He had not really been spoken to: he was afraid of the rockpile and of the boys who played there.

3 ◆ **Literary Focus** Note that the story begins with the setting. What is the significance of this?

4

Each Saturday morning John and Roy sat on the fire escape and watched the forbidden street below. Sometimes their mother sat in the room behind them, sewing, or dressing their younger sister, or nursing the baby, Paul. The sun fell across them and across the fire escape with a high, benevolent indifference; below them, men and women, and boys and girls, sinners all, loitered; sometimes one of the church-members passed and saw them and waved. Then, for the moment that they waved decorously back, they were intimidated. They watched the saint, man or woman, until he or she had disappeared from sight. The passage of one of the redeemed made them consider, however vacantly, the wickedness of the street, their own latent wickedness in sitting where they sat; and made them think of their father, who came home early on Saturdays and who would soon be turning this corner and entering the dark hall below them. 5

But until he came to end their freedom, they sat, watching and longing above the street. At the end of the street nearest their house was the bridge which spanned the Harlem River[1] and led to a city called the Bronx; which was where Aunt Florence lived. Nevertheless, when they saw her coming, she did not come from the bridge, but from the opposite end of the street. This, weakly, to their minds, she explained by saying that she had taken the subway, not wishing to walk, and that, besides, she did not live in *that* section of the Bronx. Knowing that the Bronx was across the river, they did not believe this story ever, but, adopting toward her their father's attitude, assumed that she had just left some sinful place which she dared not name, as, for example, a movie palace. 6

In the summertime boys swam in the river, diving off the wooden dock, or wading in from the garbage-heavy bank. Once a boy, whose name was Richard, drowned in the river. His mother had not known where he was; she had even come to their house, to ask if he was there. Then, in the evening, at six o'clock, they had heard from the street a woman screaming and wailing; and they ran to the windows and looked out. Down the street came the woman, Richard's mother, screaming, her face raised to the sky and tears running down her face. A woman walked beside her, trying to make her quiet and trying to hold her up. Behind them walked a man, Richard's father, with Richard's body in his arms. There were two white policemen walking in the gutter, who did not seem to know what should be done. Richard's father and Richard were wet, and Richard's body lay across his father's arms like a cotton baby. The woman's screaming filled all the street; cars slowed down and the people in the cars stared; people opened their windows and looked out and came rushing out of doors to stand in the gutter, watching. Then the small procession disappeared within the house which stood beside the rockpile. Then, *"Lord, Lord, Lord!"* 7

◆ **Build Vocabulary**

intriguing (in trēg´ iŋ) *adj.*: Interesting or curious

benevolent (bə nev´ ə lənt) *adj.*: Kindly; charitable

decorously (dek´ ər əs lē) *adv.*: Characterized by or showing decorum and good taste

latent (lāt´ ənt) *adj.*: Present but invisible or inactive

1. **Harlem River:** River that separates Manhattan Island from the Bronx in New York City.

◆ Literary Focus

3 Setting Possible responses: The setting must be of great importance to the story; the rockpile will probably play a major role in the plot—perhaps someone will be hurt there. The author may be suggesting that this setting is the only place where the events of this story could happen.

◆ Critical Thinking

4 Analyze Point out that brothers Roy and John are introduced into the setting. Ask students what they can tell about the two boys from this description. *Students should point out that Roy "tunes out" their mother's scolding—this suggests that he is rebellious or disobedient. John appears to be the opposite—he has no intention of misbehaving.*

◆ Critical Thinking

5 Draw Conclusions What does the boys' perception of the contrast between the "redeemed" and the "wickedness of the street" suggest about their upbringing? *They belong to a strictly religious family that makes a great distinction between those who do and those who do not belong to their church.*

◆ Grammar and Style

6 Restrictive and Nonrestrictive Adjective Clauses Point out the adjective clause *which she dared not name*. Ask: What noun does the clause describe? Is the clause restrictive or nonrestrictive? Why? *The clause describes the noun place. It is restrictive because it is necessary to the meaning of the sentence.*

◆ Literary Focus

7 Setting Ask students what this description of the river and the boy who drowned adds to their understanding of the setting. *Responses may include: There are many dangers in the setting; people who live in the neighborhood face danger not only from the streets but also from the river; the reaction to accidents is swift and dramatic.*

Humanities: Art

Push to Walk by Phoebe Beasley.

This urban image captures the busy setting that Baldwin's story describes.

An African American born in Ohio, Phoebe Beasley studied at the Cleveland Art Institute and received her BFA from Ohio University. She became a high school art teacher and eventually moved to Los Angeles to pursue her art full-time. Beasley has created work to celebrate the inaugurations of Presidents Bush and Clinton and the official artwork for the 1987 Los Angeles Marathon. She has won many awards, including the Presidential Seal.

Use these questions for discussion:

1. Draw students' attention to the artist's vibrant use of color. What is the effect of this feature? *Students may say that it makes the scene seem vividly real and alive.*
2. In "The Rockpile," Baldwin offers a glimpse into the lives and relationships of one family living in Harlem in the 1930's. How does Beasley suggest that there are many "stories" waiting to be told on the block that he depicts? *Students may point out numerous figures on the street.*

◆ Grammar and Style

1 Restrictive and Nonrestrictive Adjective Clauses Have students identify the adjective clause in this sentence and explain whether it is restrictive or nonrestrictive. *Students should identify the clause* which featured a new electric locomotive; *it is restrictive because it is necessary to the meaning of the sentence.*

◆ Critical Thinking

2 Infer Encourage students to make inferences about John's character, based on this argument that he has with his brother Roy. *Inferences may include: John is older, and he believes he needs to watch out for Roy. He is fearful that something bad will happen.*

◆ Reading Strategy

3 Identify Cause and Effect
Roy goes to the rockpile because his friends are there and are calling him. He goes because he has a defiant streak in him.

◆ Literary Focus

4 Setting Draw students' attention to this striking description of the setting. Encourage them to comment on its effect. *Students should note that the "arrested" quality of the sun reinforces the arrested quality of the motionless boys. The effect is suspenseful and ominous.*

◆ Reading Strategy

5 Identify Cause and Effect
Students may point to the following effects: The fight stops and the adults rush over to help Roy. His mother is filled with fear and worry.

---

cried Elizabeth, their mother, and slammed the window down.

One Saturday, an hour before his father would be coming home, Roy was wounded on the rockpile and brought screaming upstairs. He and John had been sitting on the fire escape and their mother had gone into the kitchen to sip tea with Sister McCandless. By and by Roy became bored and sat beside John
1 in restless silence; and John began drawing into his schoolbook a newspaper advertisement which featured a new electric locomotive. Some friends of Roy passed beneath the fire escape and called him. Roy began to fidget, yelling down to them through the bars. Then a silence fell. John looked up. Roy stood looking at him.

"I'm going downstairs," he said.

"You better stay where you is, boy. You know Mama don't want you going downstairs."

"I be right *back*. She won't even know I'm
2 gone, less you run and tell her."

"I ain't *got* to tell her. What's going to stop her from coming in here and looking out the window?"

"She's talking," Roy said. He started into the house.

> **◆ Reading Strategy**
> 3 What causes Roy to go to the rockpile?

"But Daddy's going to be home soon!"

"I be back before *that*. What you all the time got to be so *scared* for?" He was already in the house and he now turned, leaning on the windowsill, to swear impatiently, "I be back in *five* minutes."

John watched him sourly as he carefully unlocked the door and disappeared. In a moment he saw him on the sidewalk with his friends. He did not dare to go and tell his mother that Roy had left the fire escape because he had practically promised not to. He started to shout, *Remember, you said five minutes*! but one of Roy's friends was looking up at the fire escape. John looked down at his schoolbook: he became engrossed again in the problem of the locomotive.

When he looked up again he did not know how much time had passed, but now there was a gang fight on the rockpile. Dozens of boys fought each other in the harsh sun: clambering up the rocks and battling hand to hand, scuffed shoes sliding on the slippery rock; filling the bright air with curses and jubilant cries. They filled the air, too, with flying weapons: stones, sticks, tin cans, garbage, whatever could be picked up and thrown. John watched in a kind of absent amazement—until he remembered that Roy was still downstairs, and that he was one of the boys on the rockpile. Then he was afraid; he could not see his brother among the figures in the sun; and he stood up, leaning over the fire-escape railing. Then Roy appeared from the other side of the rocks; John saw that his shirt was torn; he was laughing. He moved until he stood at the very top of the rockpile. Then, something, an empty tin can, flew out of the air and hit him on the forehead, just above the eye. Immediately, one side of Roy's face ran with blood, he fell and rolled on his face down the rocks. Then for a moment there was no movement at all, no
sound, the sun, arrested, lay on the street 4
and the sidewalk and the arrested boys. Then someone screamed or shouted; boys began to run away, down the street, toward the bridge. The figure on the ground, having caught its breath and felt its own blood, began to shout. John cried, "Mama! Mama!" and ran inside.

"Don't fret, don't fret," panted Sister McCandless as they rushed down the dark, narrow, swaying stairs, "don't fret. Ain't a boy been born don't get his knocks every now and again. *Lord*!" they hurried into the sun. A man had picked Roy up and now walked slowly toward them. One or two boys sat silent on their stoops; at either end of the street there was a group of boys watching. "He ain't hurt bad," the man said, "wouldn't be making this kind of noise if he was hurt real bad."

Elizabeth, trembling, reached out to take Roy, but Sister McCandless, bigger, calmer, took him from the man and threw him over her shoulder as she once might have handled a sack of cotton. "God bless you," she said to the man, "God bless you, son." Roy was still screaming.

> **◆ Reading Strategy**
> What is the immediate effect of Roy's accident? 5

◆ Build Vocabulary

engrossed (in grōst′) *adj.*: Occupied wholly; absorbed

jubilant (jo͞o′ bəl ənt) *adj.*: Joyful and triumphant

arrested (ə rest′ id) *adj.*: Stopped

Humanities: Literature

Countee Cullen
Countee Cullen, who taught and encouraged James Baldwin, was a leading writer of the Harlem Renaissance. You might share the following information about Cullen with students. Follow up by encouraging students to read some of Cullen's work on their own.

Countee Cullen grew up in Kentucky and moved to Harlem when he was fifteen. He received several important poetry awards while he was a college student at New York University and published *Color*, his first book of poetry, shortly after his graduation.

Cullen went on to earn a Masters degree at Harvard; to teach French and English in New York City's public schools; and to publish several more volumes of poetry, a novel, two collections of children's stories, and several plays. He is best known for his poems, which he often wrote in sonnet form, and in which he explored such themes as race, creativity, and spirituality. Refer students to Cullen's poem, "From the Dark Tower," p. 848.

Ask students how Countee Cullen and other Harlem Renaissance writers and artists might have influenced the writing of James Baldwin.

Elizabeth stood behind Sister McCandless to stare at his bloody face.

"It's just a flesh wound," the man kept saying, "just broke the skin, that's all." They were moving across the sidewalk, toward the house. John, not now afraid of the staring boys, looked toward the corner to see if his father was yet in sight.

Upstairs, they hushed Roy's crying. They bathed the blood away, to find, just above the left eyebrow, the jagged, superficial scar. "Lord, have mercy," murmured Elizabeth, "another inch and it would've been his eye." And she looked with apprehension toward the clock. "Ain't it the truth," said Sister McCandless, busy with bandages and iodine.

"When did he go downstairs?" his mother asked at last.

Sister McCandless now sat fanning herself in the easy chair, at the head of the sofa where Roy lay, bound and silent. She paused for a moment to look sharply at John. John stood near the window, holding the newspaper advertisement and the drawing he had done.

"We was sitting on the fire escape," he said. "Some boys he knew called him."

"When?"

"He said he'd be back in five minutes."

"Why didn't you tell me he was downstairs?"

He looked at his hands, clasping his note-
6 book, and did not answer.

"Boy," said Sister McCandless, "you hear your mother a-talking to you?"

He looked at his mother. He repeated:

"He said he'd be back in five minutes."

"He said he'd be back in five minutes," said Sister McCandless with scorn, "don't look to me like that's no right answer. You's the man of the house, you supposed to look after your baby
7 brothers and sisters—you ain't supposed to let them run off and get half-killed. But I expect," she added, rising from the chair, dropping the cardboard fan, "your Daddy'll make you tell the truth. Your Ma's way too soft with you."

He did not look at her, but at the fan where it lay in the dark red, depressed seat where she had been. The fan advertised a pomade[2] for the hair and showed a brown woman and her baby, both with glistening hair, smiling happily at each other.

"Honey," said Sister McCandless, "I got to be moving along. Maybe I drop in later tonight. I don't reckon you going to be at Tarry Service tonight?"

Tarry Service was the prayer meeting held every Saturday night at church to strengthen believers and prepare the church for the coming of the Holy Ghost on Sunday.

"I don't reckon," said Elizabeth. She stood up; she and Sister McCandless kissed each other on the cheek. "But you be sure to remember me in your prayers."

"I surely will do that." She paused, with her hand on the door knob, and looked down at Roy and laughed. "Poor little man," she said, "reckon he'll be content to sit on the fire escape *now*."

Elizabeth laughed with her. "It sure ought to be a lesson to him. You don't reckon," she asked nervously, still smiling, "he going to keep that scar, do you?"

"Lord, no," said Sister McCandless, "ain't nothing but a scratch. I declare, Sister Grimes, you worse than a child. Another couple of weeks and you won't be able to *see* no scar. No, you go on about your housework, honey, and thank the Lord it weren't no worse." She opened the door; they heard the sound of feet on the stairs. "I expect that's the Reverend," said Sister McCand- 8
less, placidly, "I *bet* he going to raise cain."[3]

"Maybe it's Florence," Elizabeth said. "Sometimes she get here about this time." They stood in the doorway, staring, while the steps reached the landing below and began again climbing to their floor. "No," said Elizabeth then, "that ain't her walk. That's Gabriel."

"Well, I'll just go on," said Sister McCandless, "and kind of prepare his mind." She pressed Elizabeth's hand as she spoke and started into the hall, leaving the door behind her slightly ajar. Elizabeth turned slowly back
into the room. Roy did not open his eyes, or 9
move; but she knew that he was not sleeping; he wished to delay until the last possible moment any contact with his father. John put his newspaper and his notebook on the table and stood, leaning on the table, staring at her.

"It wasn't my fault," he said. "I couldn't stop him from going downstairs."

"No," she said, "you ain't got nothing to worry about. You just tell your Daddy the truth."

2. **pomade** (päm ād′) *n.*: Perfumed ointment.

3. **raise cain:** Slang for "cause trouble."

◆ Critical Thinking

6 Modify If John had chosen to give his mother a real answer, what might he have told her? *Students may suggest the following: He might have said that his brother wouldn't listen to him, that he told him not to go. He also might have said more disparaging things about Roy.*

◆ Critical Thinking

7 Make a Judgment Ask students whether they think that Sister McCandless's scolding of John is justified or not. *Some students may say that it is not justified, pointing out that John tried to stop his brother from going downstairs. Others may say that the scolding is justified—John could and should have been firmer with his brother.*

Comprehension Check ☑

8 What is the father's occupation? *He is a preacher or minister—he is referred to as "the Reverend."*

◆ Critical Thinking

9 Analyze Point out that Sister McCandless says she feels that it is necessary to "prepare" Gabriel before he enters the apartment. Then ask: How does John seem to feel about his father's homecoming? *Suggested response: John is afraid that his father will blame him for Roy's behavior and subsequent accident.*

Reteach

Students who have difficulty recognizing or analyzing cause-and-effect relationships in literature may benefit from a visual demonstration. Use a graphic organizer like the one shown to help students chart the sequence of causes and effects in the story. By the time the chart is complete, students should realize that the causes and effects in this story become increasingly complex.

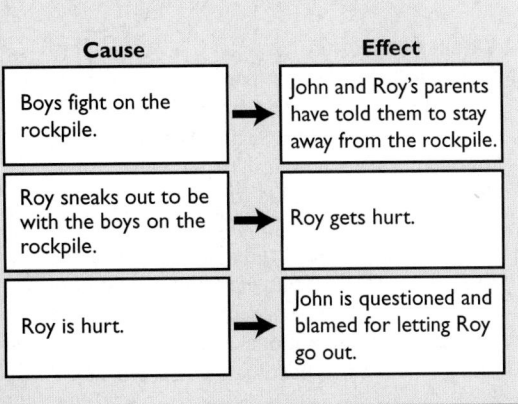

Cause		Effect
Boys fight on the rockpile.	→	John and Roy's parents have told them to stay away from the rockpile.
Roy sneaks out to be with the boys on the rockpile.	→	Roy gets hurt.
Roy is hurt.	→	John is questioned and blamed for letting Roy go out.

◆ Critical Thinking

❶ Infer Ask: Does Elizabeth feel confident that everything is going to be all right when her husband comes home? How do you know? *Elizabeth does not feel confident; her thoughts and actions indicate that she is anxious. She wonders what Sister McCandless is telling Gabriel, she becomes upset over the baby's crying, and she notices that Gabriel slams the door when he comes in.*

◆ Critical Thinking

❷ Analyze Call students' attention to this description of the children. Ask students whose point of view it expresses. Then have them identify the important fact about John that it reveals. *Students should note that the description conveys Elizabeth's and—probably to an even greater extent—her husband Gabriel's point of view. Through the description we learn that John is Gabriel's stepson.*

◆ Reading Strategy

❸ Identify Cause and Effect Roy appears to be Gabriel's favorite child; Gabriel is very protective—perhaps overly protective—where Roy is concerned.

◆ Critical Thinking

❹ Interpret Draw attention to Gabriel's words to Elizabeth. Ask students what these remarks reveal about the way that Gabriel views himself. *Gabriel apparently views himself as the head of the household; he thinks of himself as an authority figure and speaks to his wife as if she were a naughty child.*

Listening to Literature Audiocassettes The family discussion that begins on this page with Gabriel's entrance would be a good point to play the audiocassette recording. Students can listen to the dialogue and draw their own conclusions about the relationships within the family.

❶ He looked directly at her, and she turned to the window, staring into the street. What was Sister McCandless saying? Then from her bedroom she heard Delilah's thin wail and she turned, frowning, looking toward the bedroom and toward the still open door. She knew that John was watching her. Delilah continued to wail, she thought, angrily, *Now that girl's getting too big for that*, but she feared that Delilah would awaken Paul and she hurried into the bedroom. She tried to soothe Delilah back to sleep. Then she heard the front door open and close—too loud, Delilah raised her voice, with an exasperated sigh Elizabeth picked the child up. ❷ Her child and Gabriel's, her children and Gabriel's: Roy, Delilah, Paul. Only John was nameless and a stranger, living, unalterable testimony to his mother's days in sin.

"What happened?" Gabriel demanded. He stood, enormous, in the center of the room, his black lunchbox dangling from his hand, staring at the sofa where Roy lay. John stood just before him, it seemed to her astonished vision just below him, beneath his fist, his heavy shoe. The child stared at the man in fascination and terror—when a girl down home she had seen rabbits stand so paralyzed before the barking dog. She hurried past Gabriel to the sofa, feeling the weight of Delilah in her arms like the weight of a shield, and stood over Roy, saying:

"Now, ain't a thing to get upset about, Gabriel. This boy sneaked downstairs while I had my back turned and got hisself hurt a little. He's alright now."

Roy, as though in confirmation, now opened his eyes and looked gravely at his father. Gabriel dropped his lunchbox with a clatter and knelt by the sofa.

"How you feel, son? Tell your Daddy what happened?"

Roy opened his mouth to speak and then, relapsing into panic, began to cry. His father held him by the shoulder.

"You don't want to cry. You's Daddy's little man. Tell your Daddy what happened."

"He went downstairs," said Elizabeth, "where he didn't have no business to be, and got to fighting with them bad boys playing on the rockpile. That's what happened and it's a mercy it weren't nothing worse."

He looked up at her. "Can't you let this boy answer me for hisself?"

Ignoring this, she went on, more gently: "He got cut on the forehead, but it ain't nothing to worry about."

"You call a doctor? How you know it ain't nothing to worry about?"

> **◆ Reading Strategy** ❸
> Why is Gabriel so upset by Roy's injury?

"Is you got money to be throwing away on doctors? No, I ain't called no doctor. Ain't nothing wrong with my eyes that I can't tell whether he's hurt bad or not. He got a fright more'n anything else, and you ought to pray God it teaches him a lesson."

❹ "You got a lot to say *now*," he said, "but I'll have *me* something to say in a minute. I'll be wanting to know when all this happened, what you was doing with your eyes *then*." He turned back to Roy, who had lain quietly sobbing eyes wide open and body held rigid: and who now, at his father's touch, remembered the height, the sharp, sliding rock beneath his feet, the sun, the explosion of the sun, his plunge into darkness and his salty blood; and recoiled, beginning to scream, as his father touched his forehead. "Hold still, hold still," crooned his father, shaking, "hold still. Don't cry. Daddy ain't going to hurt you, he just wants to see this bandage, see what they've done to his little man." But Roy continued to scream and would not be still and Gabriel dared not lift the bandage for fear of hurting him more. And he looked at Elizabeth in fury: "Can't you put that child down and help me with this boy? John, take your baby sister from your mother—don't look like neither of you got good sense."

John took Delilah and sat down with her in the easy chair. His mother bent over Roy, and held him still, while his father, carefully—but still Roy screamed—lifted the bandage and stared at the wound. Roy's sobs began to lessen. Gabriel readjusted the bandage. "You see," said Elizabeth, finally, "he ain't nowhere near dead."

"It sure ain't your fault that he ain't dead." He and Elizabeth considered each other for a moment in silence. "He came mightly close to losing an eye. Course, his eyes ain't as big as your'n, so I reckon you don't think it matters so much." At this her face hardened; he smiled. "Lord, have mercy," he said, "you think you ever going to learn to do right? Where was you when all this happened? Who let him go downstairs?"

Beyond the Classroom

Career Connection

Social Work Writers like James Baldwin delve into family problems and family dynamics as part of their creative work. Social workers deal with these areas on a practical, real-life level; these professionals are trained to provide support and counseling to individuals and families who need help. Have interested students gather information about the various types of services social workers provide. In addition, encourage students to investigate the educational requirements and training needed to become a social worker.

Community Connection

Programs for Kids One of the problems that contribute to the conflict in this story is that John and Roy did not have a place where they could safely play. What kinds of programs and facilities does your community provide for kids—both children and teenagers? Have students brainstorm for a list. Students can check resources such as local newspapers and community bulletins to add more places and programs to their list. Interested students can make a resource booklet and offer it to the school or local library.

"Ain't nobody let him go downstairs, he just went. He got a head just like his father, it got to be broken before it'll bow. I was in the kitchen."

"Where was Johnnie?"

"He was in here."

"Where?"

"He was on the fire escape."

"Didn't he know Roy was downstairs?"

"I reckon."

5 "What you mean, you reckon? He ain't got your big eyes for nothing, does he?" He looked over at John. "Boy, you see your brother go downstairs?"

"Gabriel, ain't no sense in trying to blame Johnnie. You know right well if you have trouble making Roy behave, he ain't going to listen to his brother. He don't hardly listen to me."

"How come you didn't tell your mother Roy was downstairs?"

John said nothing, staring at the blanket which covered Delilah.

"Boy, you hear me? You want me to take a strap to you?"

"No, you ain't," she said. "You ain't going to taken no strap to this boy, not today you ain't. Ain't a soul to blame for Roy's lying up there now but you—you because you done spoiled him so that he thinks he can do just anything and get away with it. I'm here to tell you that ain't no way to raise no child. You don't pray to the Lord to help you do better than you been doing, you going to live to shed bitter tears that the Lord didn't take his soul today." And she was trembling. She moved, unseeing, toward John and took Delilah from his arms. She looked back at Gabriel, who had risen, who stood near the sofa, staring at her. And she found in his face not fury alone, which would not have surprised her; but hatred so deep as to become insupportable in its lack of personality. His eyes were struck alive, unmoving, blind with malevolence—she felt, like the pull of the earth at her feet, his longing to witness her perdition. Again, as though it might be propitiation, she moved the child in her arms. And at this his eyes changed, he looked at Elizabeth, the mother of his children, the helpmeet given by the Lord. Then her eyes clouded; she moved to leave the room; her foot struck the lunchbox lying on the floor. 7

> ◆ **Reading Strategy** What is the effect of John's silence on Gabriel? On Elizabeth? 6

"John," she said, "pick up your father's lunchbox like a good boy."

She heard, behind her, his scrambling movement as he left the easy chair, the scrape and jangle of the lunchbox as he picked it up, bending his dark head near the toe of his father's heavy shoe.

◆ Build Vocabulary

malevolence (mə lev′ ə ləns) *n.*: Malice; spitefulness

perdition (pər dish′ ən) *n.*: Complete and irreparable loss; ruin

Guide for Responding

◆ *Literature and Your Life*

Reader's Response Does this story call to mind any of your own childhood experiences? Explain.

Thematic Focus Do you think the author is making a statement about families, about society, or about both in this story? Explain.

Role Play With a partner, act out a conversation between Roy and John after their father and mother have left them alone.

☑ Check Your Comprehension

1. Where are the various characters when the action of the story begins?
2. What draws Roy to the rockpile?
3. What happens at the rockpile?
4. (a) Whom does Gabriel blame for Roy's injury? (b) Whom does Elizabeth blame?

◆ Critical Thinking

5 Infer Ask students what they can tell about the relationship between John and Gabriel, based on this conversation. *The relationship is tense. Gabriel blames John for events that are beyond his control and expects nothing less than perfect behavior.*

◆ Reading Strategy

6 Identify Cause and Effect John's silence infuriates Gabriel; he perceives it as blatant disrespect. Elizabeth recognizes that John is afraid, so she speaks in his defense.

◆ Critical Thinking

7 Evaluate Ask: Is Gabriel a completely bad person? Explain your answer. *Sample response: Gabriel is not a completely bad person. He is domineering and quick-tempered, but he also feels tenderness for his family.*

Reinforce and Extend

Answers

◆ *Literature and Your Life*

Reader's Response Students may recall times when they disobeyed a parent's request.

Thematic Focus While some students may argue that the author is making a statement about both society and the family, a stronger case can be made for Baldwin's family-related theme.

☑ Check Your Comprehension

1. Gabriel is at work; Elizabeth is in the kitchen with Sister McCandless; Roy and John are sitting on the fire escape.
2. He is bored and friends encourage him to come and play.
3. There was a fight on the rockpile and Roy got cut just above his eye.
4. (a) Gabriel blames John and Elizabeth. (b) Elizabeth blames Gabriel.

Beyond the Selection

FURTHER READING

Other Works by James Baldwin

Go Tell It on the Mountain
Giovanni's Room
Another Country
Tell Me How Long the Train's Been Gone
Nobody Knows My Name
The Fire Next Time
Blues for Mr. Charlie

We suggest that you preview these works before recommending them to students.

INTERNET

You and your students may find additional information about James Baldwin on the Internet. We suggest the following site. Please be aware, however, that sites may have changed since this information was published.

For a biographical sketch of this author, direct students to **http://www.bridgesweb.com/baldwin.html**

We *strongly recommend* that you preview sites before you send students to them.

Answers

◆ Critical Thinking

1. Possible responses: John is thought of as the "man of the house" while his father is away.
2. Students should mention the fact that John is the only child who is not Gabriel's son.
3. Possible responses: (a) They have a somewhat strained relationship in which Gabriel plays the dominant role. (b) He remembers that she is his partner and the mother of his children.
4. Many students may wish to blame Roy himself for his injury. Students should support their opinions.
5. Answers should reflect an understanding of the insights of the story, especially with regard to parents' treatment of children.

◆ Reading Strategy

1. (a) John was afraid to tell his mother immediately because he had "practically promised not to." (b) When Roy is hurt, people look to John for an explanation.
2. (a) Elizabeth is protective of John because she is his mother; she may be trying to compensate for the fact that Gabriel doesn't treat John the same way he treats his own children. (b) It makes Gabriel angry.

◆ Literary Focus

1. Possible response: Because they feel the neighborhood is not a safe place to play, the parents need to impose strict rules on their children. The 1930's setting also affects the clear gender roles in the story.
2. Possible responses: (a) There is the danger of succumbing to violence, of killing or being killed in the fight for survival. (b) The rockpile is a gathering place where boys act out their frustrations in gang fights.

Guide for Responding (continued)

◆ Critical Thinking

Interpret

1. What role does John serve in the family? Support your answer. **[Analyze]**
2. What evidence is there that John's relationship with Gabriel is different from that of the other children? **[Support]**
3. (a) What conclusions can you draw about Gabriel's relationship with Elizabeth? Explain. (b) Why do his feelings toward Elizabeth soften at the end of the story? **[Draw Conclusions]**

Evaluate

4. Whom do you blame for Roy's injury? Explain. **[Make a Judgment]**

Apply

5. What lessons can you learn from this story that you could apply to your own life? Explain. **[Apply]**

◆ Reading Strategy

Analyze Cause and Effect

When you **analyze cause-and-effect** relationships in the text, you think about what causes the characters' behavior and what effects their behavior has on others.

1. (a) Why doesn't John immediately tell his mother that Roy went to the rockpile? (b) What is the effect of this decision?
2. (a) What are the causes of Elizabeth's protectiveness toward John? (b) What is the effect on Gabriel of this protectiveness?

◆ Literary Focus

Setting

The setting of "The Rockpile"—Harlem during the 1930's—clearly plays a dominant role in the characters' lives, shaping both their attitudes and their behavior.

1. What can you infer, or conclude, about how the setting affects the way Gabriel and Elizabeth raise their children?
2. (a) What are some of the potential dangers that the setting presents? (b) What evidence is there that the rockpile symbolizes these dangers?

◆ Build Vocabulary

Using the Latin Prefix *mal-*

Knowing that the Latin prefix *mal-* means "bad," "wrong," or "ill," write a definition in your notebook for these words:

1. maladjusted
2. malfunction
3. malnutrition
4. malodorous

Using the Word Bank: Synonyms or Antonyms?

Decide whether the words in each of the following pairs are synonyms or antonyms. On your paper, write *S* for *Synonyms* or *A* for *Antonyms*.

1. intriguing, boring
2. benevolent, charitable
3. decorously, tastefully
4. latent, obvious
5. engrossed, detached
6. jubilant, despondent
7. arrested, halted
8. malevolence, kindness
9. perdition, salvation

◆ Grammar and Style

Restrictive and Nonrestrictive Adjective Clauses

A **restrictive adjective clause** is necessary to complete the meaning of the noun or pronoun it modifies. A **nonrestrictive adjective clause**, set off by commas, provides additional but not essential information.

Practice Copy the sentences into your notebook. Underline the adjective clause(s) in each one. For each clause, identify whether it is restrictive or nonrestrictive.

1. There were two white policemen, who did not seem to know what should be done, walking in the gutter.
2. At the end of the street nearest their house was the bridge which spanned the Harlem River . . .
3. . . . made them think of their father, who came home early on Saturdays and who . . .
4. Then the small procession disappeared within the house which stood beside the rockpile.
5. He did not look at her, but at the fan where it lay in the dark red, depressed seat where she had been.

◆ Build Vocabulary

Using the Latin Prefix *mal-*

1. poorly adjusted to the conditions of life
2. to work improperly
3. a disease resulting from a poor diet
4. producing an unpleasant scent

Using the Word Bank: Synonyms

1. *A* 2. *S* 3. *S* 4. *A* 5. *A* 6. *A* 7. *S* 8. *A* 9. *A*

◆ Grammar and Style

Note: These sentences were selected from the story. Stress to students that Baldwin has used *that* and *which* interchangeably, and therefore incorrectly.

1. who did not seem to know what should be done: *nonrestrictive*
2. which spanned the Harlem River: *restrictive*
3. who came home early on Saturdays: *nonrestrictive*
4. which stood beside the rockpile: *restrictive*
5. where it lay: *restrictive;* where she had been: *restrictive*

Build Your Portfolio

Idea Bank

Writing

1. Flyer Create a flyer announcing the start-up meeting of a block association for Roy's block. Your first goal will be to find ways to keep children from playing on the rockpile.

2. Movie Proposal Write a proposal for a film based on the characters in Baldwin's story. Explain the issues and events that will be explored in the film. **[Media Link]**

3. Psychological Profile Imagine that you are a therapist and that Roy's family has come to you for family counseling. Write a profile of each family member and summarize the issues they face as a family. Include your recommendations for resolving these issues. **[Career Link]**

Speaking, Listening, and Viewing

4. Radio Play Turn "The Rockpile" into a radio play. Divide the story into scenes and develop a script. Include a narrator and sound effects. Record your play and share it with the class.

5. Public-Service Announcement Many communities have recreation or after-school programs to keep kids off the streets. Write and record a public-service announcement for a program in Roy's neighborhood. **[Community Link]**

Researching and Representing

6. Book Jacket Create a cover design for a short-story collection featuring "The Rockpile." Include a photograph, fine art, or an original drawing. Explain your concept and design. **[Art Link]**

7. Illustrated Report Prepare an illustrated report, based on research, comparing Harlem today with Harlem in the 1930's. Share your report with the class. **[Social Studies Link]**

Online Activity www.phlit.phschool.com

Guided Writing Lesson

Roy's Journal

In "The Rockpile," Roy's actions spark a family crisis in which much is revealed about Elizabeth, Gabriel, and John. But we never really get to look inside Roy. What is his side of the story? Write a journal entry for Roy in which he reveals his inner thoughts and conflicts. Make it convincing by using the kind of thoughts and feelings that Roy might express.

Writing Skills Focus: Personal Tone

Any time you put words in a character's mouth, it's important to make the ideas sound realistic. To make Roy's journal true to Roy's character, use a **personal tone.** To do so, consider the following suggestions:

- Use informal language—the language of everyday speech. Since journals are not meant for a wide audience, they can include sentence fragments, contractions, and slang.
- Choose words that Roy would use.
- Instead of simply recording events, include Roy's reactions, thoughts, and emotions. This may mean including details that only Roy would know.

Prewriting Consider what you already know about Roy and his relationships with his family members. Reread the story to create a timeline of events. Then, for each point on the line, jot down ideas about what Roy may be thinking and feeling.

Drafting Your primary goal is to make sure that the feelings and conflicts you present make sense for this particular character. As you draft Roy's journal, refer to your notes and keep the language personal and informal.

Revising As you revise, look for opportunities to make the tone of the journal more personal. Change words that may be too formal. Then ask yourself whether your writing shows Roy's side of the story. Does it provide insight into his behavior?

Idea Bank

Customizing for
Performance Levels
Following are suggestions for matching Idea Bank topics with your students' performance levels:
Less Advanced Students: 1, 4, 6
Average Students: 2, 5
More Advanced Students: 3, 7

Customizing for
Learning Modalities
Following are suggestions for matching Idea Bank topics with your students' learning modalities:
Verbal/Linguistic: 4
Musical/Rhythmic: 4
Interpersonal: 5
Visual/Spatial: 6, 7
Logical/Mathematical: 7

Guided Writing Lesson

For more instruction on prewriting, elaboration, and revision, see *Prentice Hall Writing and Grammar.*

Writing Lab CD-ROM
Have students complete the tutorial on Response to Literature. Follow these steps:

1. Students can use the Character Personality Profile in Prewriting to gather details about Roy.
2. Have students draft on the computer.
3. Encourage students to use revision checkers to ensure language variety.

ASSESSMENT OPTIONS

Formal Assessment, Selection Test, pp. 308–310, and Assessment Resources Software. The selection test is designed so that it can be easily customized to the performance levels of your students.

Alternative Assessment, p. 70, includes options for less advanced students, more advanced students, bodily/kinesthetic learners, visual/spatial learners, and logical/mathematical learners.

PORTFOLIO ASSESSMENT
Use the following rubrics in ***Alternative Assessment*** to assess student writing:
Flyer: Problem-Solution Rubric, p. 116
Movie Proposal: Summary Rubric, p. 113
Psychological Profile: Definition/Classification Rubric, p. 114
Guided Writing Lesson: Response to Literature Rubric, p. 125

LESSON OBJECTIVES

1. **To develop vocabulary and word identification skills**
   - Latin Roots: *-vol-*
   - Using the Word Bank: Sentence Completions
2. **To use a variety of reading strategies to comprehend literature**
   - Reading Strategy: Draw Inferences About Theme
   - Tips to Guide Reading (ATE)
3. **To express and support responses to the text**
   - Critical Thinking
   - Idea Bank: Journal
   - Idea Bank: Dramatic Reading
   - Speaking, Listening, and Viewing Mini-Lesson (ATE)
   - Idea Bank: Debate
   - Analyze Literary Criticism
4. **To analyze literary elements**
   - Literary Focus: Implied Theme
   - Idea Bank: Poem
5. **To read in order to research self-selected and assigned topics**
   - Idea Bank: Map
   - Viewing and Representing Mini-Lesson (ATE)
   - Idea Bank: Research Report
6. **To plan, prepare, organize, and present literary interpretations**
   - Idea Bank: Essay
7. **To use recursive writing processes to write an introduction to a documentary**
   - Guided Writing Lesson
8. **To increase knowledge of the rules of grammar and usage**
   - Grammar and Style: Transitions and Transitional Phrases

Test Preparation

Writing Skills: Grammar and Usage (ATE, p. 1035)
The teaching tips and sample test item in this workshop support the instruction and practice in the unit workshop:
Writing Skills: Punctuation, Usage, and Sentence Structure (SE, p. 1143)

Guide for Interpreting

John Hersey *(1914–1993)*

Born in China and raised there until age ten, John Hersey returned repeatedly to East Asia during his long career as a war correspondent, novelist, and essayist.

Hersey's novels and essays examined the moral implications of the major political and historical events of his day. In 1945, he won a Pulitzer Prize for his novel *A Bell for Adano,* in which an American major discovers the human dignity of the villagers who were his enemies in World War II.

During the next two years, Hersey traveled to China and Japan for *New Yorker* and *Life* magazines, gathering material for his most famous and acclaimed book, *Hiroshima* (1946), a shocking, graphic depiction of the devastation caused by the atomic bomb that was dropped on the Japanese city of Hiroshima at the end of World War II.

Randall Jarrell *(1914–1965)*

Randall Jarrell was a talented poet, literary critic, and teacher whose poetry was praised by both writers and critics. His literary essays, many of which appear in his book *Poetry and the Age* (1953), have been credited with changing the critical tastes and trends of his time.

Born in Tennessee, Jarrell graduated from Vanderbilt University and served in the U.S. Air Force during World War II. His war experiences provided him with the material for the poems in his book *Losses* (1948). Jarrell's collections *The Seven-League Crutches* (1951) and *The Lost World* (1965) focus on childhood and innocence. *The Woman at the Washington Zoo* (1960) deals with aging and loneliness.

"The Death of the Ball Turret Gunner"—a brief poem told in the first person of a soldier experiencing his last moments in a World War II bomber plane—is one of Jarrell's most famous poems.

◆ Background for Understanding

History: World War II

World War II began in August 1939, when German forces, following the orders of the dictator Adolf Hitler, invaded Poland. In response to this unprovoked invasion, France and Great Britain declared war on Germany. Just over two years later, the United States entered the war when Japan, a German ally, launched a surprise attack on an American naval base at Pearl Harbor in Hawaii. The war continued to escalate during the early 1940's. More than two dozen nations were eventually drawn into the conflict, and tens of millions of soldiers and civilians were killed. By 1945, the tide had turned strongly in favor of the United States and its allies. In early May 1945, the German forces surrendered. Fighting continued in the Pacific, however, as the Japanese refused to surrender.

In August 1945, American President Harry Truman faced a difficult choice. The United States had just finished developing an atomic bomb capable of mass destruction. President Truman pondered whether to use this new technology in the hope of bringing a swift end to the war, knowing that it would cause thousands of deaths. The president ultimately decided that the potential losses from a prolonged war outweighed the damage that using the bomb would cause. On August 6, an atomic bomb was dropped on Hiroshima. Three days later, one was dropped on Nagasaki. These two bombs killed more than 200,000 people, and forced the Japanese to surrender. The dropping of the bombs also marked the start of a nuclear arms race that dominated the next several decades.

Prentice Hall Literature Program Resources

REINFORCE / RETEACH / EXTEND

Selection Support Pages
Build Vocabulary: Word Roots: *-vol-*, p. 318
Grammar and Style: Transitions, p. 319
Reading Strategy: Inferences About Theme, p. 320
Literary Focus: Implied Theme, p. 321

Strategies for Diverse Student Needs, "Question Author's Purpose," p. 71

Beyond Literature Cultural Connection: Ethics of Warfare, p. 71

Formal Assessment Selection Test, pp. 311–313; Assessment Resources Software

Alternative Assessment, p. 71

Resource Pro CD-ROM
Includes all resources and a customizable lesson plan.

Literature CD-ROM

Listening to Literature Audiocassettes

from Hiroshima ◆ Losses
The Death of the Ball Turret Gunner

◆ Literature and Your Life

Connect Your Experience

You may have seen movies that captured heroic deeds and bloody battles from World War II. You may even have a relative who has described firsthand experiences during the war. Yet it's probably still difficult for you to imagine what it was truly like to live through the war. These pieces will give you a better sense of what it was like to be involved in the war and help provide a picture of the events that ended the war and changed the world forever.

Journal Writing Jot down what you know about World War II. Then share this information with your classmates.

Thematic Focus: Social Protest

These selections all express concerns relating to the cruelties of war. Why do you think war is a frequent subject of social protest?

◆ Build Vocabulary

Latin Roots: *-vol-*

In *Hiroshima*, John Hersey uses the word *volition*, meaning "the act of using the will." The meaning of the word is derived largely from the Latin root *-vol-*, meaning "to will" or "to wish." How does this root contribute to the meaning of *volunteer* and *voluntary*?

Word Bank

Preview these words from the story before you read.

evacuated
volition
rendezvous
philanthropies
incessant
convivial

◆ Grammar and Style

Transitions and Transitional Phrases

Hiroshima begins: "At exactly fifteen minutes past eight in the morning, on August 6, 1945, . . ." With these words, John Hersey pins down the precise moment at which the atomic bomb exploded over Hiroshima. Hersey's opening words are an excellent example of a **transitional phrase**, a group of words that shows the relationship among ideas and details in a piece of writing. A single word that functions in the same way is a **transition**. Often, as in the example from Hersey's book, transitions and transitional phrases show time relationships, but they can also show comparisons, degrees of importance, and spatial relationships.

◆ Literary Focus

Implied Theme

The **theme** is the central idea that a writer hopes to convey in a work of literature. Most often a theme is **implied**, or revealed indirectly, through the writer's choice of details, portrayal of characters and events, and use of literary devices. All three of these pieces have implied themes about war.

◆ Reading Strategy

Draw Inferences About Theme

When the theme of a literary work is conveyed indirectly, it's left up to the reader to **draw inferences,** or conclusions, about the theme by looking closely at the writer's choice of details, events, characters, and literary devices. Look at this line from "Losses":

> . . . we burned,/The cities we had learned about in school—

From this ironic, or surprising, contrast between education and destruction, you can infer that one of the themes of the poem is the apparent senselessness of war.

As you read, jot down details that strike you as particularly important. They will probably point to an implied theme.

Interest Grabber What do today's young people fear most? Have a brief discussion in which students offer their responses to this question. Follow the discussion by explaining that about a half century ago, young people lived with the very real fear of atomic war and its massive destructive force. In elementary schools of the post-World War II age, students were taught to duck beneath their desks and cover their heads to protect themselves from bombs (a response that, from John Hersey's description, we know would have been futile in a real atomic bomb attack). Tell students that the selections they are about to read will give them a glimpse of the horrors of modern warfare and help them understand people's anxieties and fears in the aftermath of World War II.

Customize for
Less Proficient Readers
Help students keep track of the characters in *Hiroshima* by making a chart with the following headings and filling it in as they read:
Character:
Description:
Before the Bomb:
After the Bomb:

Customize for
AP Students
Ask students to watch for and discuss details and literary devices in *Hiroshima* that move the work beyond a typical news article and into the realm of literature.

Customize for
English Language Learners
Movement back and forth in time in *Hiroshima* may confuse some English language learners. As students read, ask them to determine whether each paragraph deals with a time well before the bomb drops, early on the day when the bomb drops, or immediately after the bomb drops.

Customize for
Intrapersonal Learners
Before they read, ask students to think about and record in writing their personal feelings about war. As they read, have them note particular phrases or descriptions that they find especially moving or disturbing. After they read, discuss how the three works affected their original feelings.

Test Preparation Workshop

Writing Skills:
Grammar and Usage The writing sections of many standardized tests require students to choose the correct word to complete a sentence. Use the following sample item to show students how to recognize correct and incorrect grammar and choose the correct word to complete a sentence.

If you ever see photographs of the devastation of Hiroshima, ____ senses will be overwhelmed.

Choose the word or group of words that belongs in the blank.

A yourself
B your
C you're
D you

A, C, and *D* are not possessive forms. *B* is the correct possessive form.

Develop Understanding

One-Minute Insight World War II was a so-called "popular" war, one in which issues were clearly defined. With the future of many of the nations of the world in grave danger, the majority of Americans believed that fighting the enemy was both just and necessary for survival. Nevertheless, technological advances in air, land, and sea weaponry; the sheer magnitude of the global conflict; and the ability to report on the progress of the war from virtually any location around the world via the print, radio, and film media, brought the horrors of war home to many people in a way that previous wars had not. Although the antiwar movement did not become a political force until the 1960's, these works by Hersey and Jarrell take their place in the ranks of early antiwar literature.

Tips to Guide Reading

Sustained Reading This long selection provides a good opportunity for students to develop their ability to read independently for a sustained period of time. Suggest to students that, while reading independently, they use sticky notes to mark any passages that have confusing ideas or vocabulary and continue reading. Reading further may clarify points. If not, students can use the sticky notes to return to these pages and ask questions during a class discussion that follows a sustained reading period. For suggestions for more sustained reading opportunities, see pp. 1234–1236.

Connections to World Literature, *page 1206*

from Hiroshima

John Hersey

▲ Critical Viewing How effectively do these remains of the sacred tree of a Hiroshima temple convey the physical and emotional devastation of the blast? Explain. **[Evaluate]**

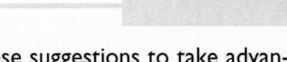

Block Scheduling Strategies

Consider these suggestions to take advantage of extended class time:

- Help build background on World War II by discussing with students the Background for Understanding (p. 1034).
- Provide students with background on the dropping of the atomic bomb on Hiroshima by showing the **Literature CD-ROM** *The History of American Literature,* Part 2, Disc 2, Feature 2 on John Hersey and *Hiroshima.*
- Introduce the Reading Strategy, Make Inferences About Theme by having students read the Reading Strategy section (p. 1035). After students read the selections, have them complete the Reading Strategy activities (p. 1046).
- Students can meet in small groups to discuss their answers to the Critical Thinking questions (pp. 1043 and 1045).
- Have students complete the Practice and Writing Application activities on Transitions and Transitional Phrases in Grammar and Style (p. 1046). Follow up by asking students to analyze the use of transitions and transitional phrases in their own writing.
- If possible, share a World War II documentary with students before they work on the Guided Writing Lesson (p. 1047). Your local library or video store can help.

At exactly fifteen minutes past eight in the morning, on August 6, 1945, Japanese time, at the moment when the atomic bomb flashed above Hiroshima, Miss Toshiko Sasaki, a clerk in the personnel department of the East Asia Tin Works, had just sat down at her place in the plant office and was turning her head to speak to the girl at the next desk. At that same moment, Dr. Masakazu Fujii was settling down cross-legged to read the Osaka *Asahi* on the porch of his private hospital, overhanging one of the seven deltaic rivers which divide Hiroshima; Mrs. Hatsuyo Nakamura, a tailor's widow, stood by the window of her kitchen, watching a neighbor tearing down his house because it lay in the path of an air-raid-defense fire lane . . . and the Reverend Mr. Kiyoshi Tanimoto, pastor of the Hiroshima Methodist Church, paused at the door of a rich man's house in Koi, the city's western suburb, and prepared to unload a handcart full of things he had <u>evacuated</u> from town in fear of the massive B-29 raid which everyone expected Hiroshima to suffer. ❷ A hundred thousand people were killed by the atomic bomb, and these [four] were among the survivors. They still wonder why they lived when so many others died. Each of them counts many small items of chance or <u>volition</u>—a step taken in time, a decision to go indoors, catching one streetcar instead of the next—that spared him. And now each knows that in the act of survival he lived a dozen lives and saw more death than he ever thought he would see. At the time, none of them knew anything.

❸

> **◆ Reading Strategy**
> What underlying meaning can you draw from these details about the survivors?

The Reverend Mr. Tanimoto got up at five o'clock that morning. He was alone in the parsonage, because for some time his wife had been commuting with their year-old baby to spend nights with a friend in Ushida, a suburb to the north. Of all the important cities of Japan, only two, Kyoto and Hiroshima, had not been visited in strength by *B-san*, or Mr. B, as the Japanese, with a mixture of respect and unhappy familiarity, called the B-29; and Mr. Tanimoto, like all his neighbors and friends, was almost sick with anxiety. He had heard uncomfortably detailed accounts of mass raids on Kure, Iwakuni, Tokuyama, and other nearby towns; he was sure Hiroshima's turn would come soon. He had slept badly the night before, because there had been several air-raid warnings. Hiroshima had been getting such warnings almost every night for weeks, for at that time the B-29s were using Lake Biwa, northeast of Hiroshima, as a <u>rendezvous</u> point, and no matter what city the Americans planned to hit, the Superfortresses streamed in over the coast near Hiroshima. The frequency of the warning and the continued abstinence of Mr. B with respect to Hiroshima had made its citizens jittery; a rumor was going around that the Americans were saving something special for the city.

Mr. Tanimoto was a small man, quick to talk, laugh, and cry. He wore his black hair parted in the middle and rather long; the prominence of the frontal bones just above his eyebrows and the smallness of his mustache, mouth, and chin gave him a strange old-young look, boyish and yet wise, weak and yet fiery. He moved nervously and fast, but with a restraint which suggested that he is a cautious, thoughtful man. He showed, indeed, just those qualities in the uneasy days before the bomb fell. Mr. Tanimoto had been carrying all the portable things from his church, in the close-packed residential district called Nagaragawa, to a house that belonged to a rayon manufacturer in Koi, two miles from the center of town.

◆ Build Vocabulary

evacuated (ē vak′ yo͞o āt′ əd) *v.*: To have made empty; withdrawn

volition (vō lish′ ən) *n.*: Act of using the will

rendezvous (rän′dā vo͞o′) *n.*: Meeting place

▶Critical Viewing◀

❶ **Evaluate** Sample response: The remains of the sacred tree convey the physical and emotional devastation of the blast quite effectively. First of all, the gnarled remnants of the tree and the bricks and debris scattered about the tree illustrate the physical damage in the area. Perhaps more importantly, the magnitude of the physical destruction, as well as the fact that the decimated tree is a sacred one, helps to underscore the emotional pain that the people of Hiroshima must have felt.

◆ Critical Thinking

❷ **Speculate** Point out that Hersey chooses to tell the story of the dropping of the bomb through the lives of six survivors. Ask students why they think he chose these six survivors as his focus. *Responses may include: The survivors may have been chosen for their very ordinariness; by describing typical, ordinary people living in Hiroshima at the time of the bombing, Hersey makes the point that helpless civilians were victims of the bomb.*

◆ Reading Strategy

❸ **Draw Inferences About Theme** Hersey notes that small acts and decisions spelled the difference between life and death for the survivors. Students may infer that this and related details suggest the arbitrariness and senselessness of war.

Cross-Curricular Connection: Social Studies

Hiroshima and Nagasaki Share with the class the following information about Japan and the cities of Hiroshima and Nagasaki. Have one or more volunteers point out the places you cite on a wall map.

Japan is a chain of islands—which means that it can be attacked only by air or by sea. Its western neighbors are North and South Korea, Russia, and China. The four main islands of Japan are Hokkaido, Honshu, Shikoku, and Kyushu.

Hiroshima is a port city on the southwest coast of Honshu. Nagasaki is a port city on the west coast of Kyushu. Both had a certain amount of industry and military installations in 1945, but neither was as major a target as the capital, Tokyo, was. The cities were in large part destroyed by the bombs but were reconstructed throughout the 1950's. Today both house important tourist sites and monuments that attract antiwar and antinuclear supporters from around the world.

You might follow up by explaining that bombing raids on Japan generally started from bases in China or from islands in the central Pacific. Have volunteers estimate in miles the distance of a typical bombing run from an air base on the island of Tinian in the Marianas to the Japanese home islands.

◆ **Background for Understanding**

History Explain that the Second World War saw major advances in the technology of mechanized warfare—warfare that relied heavily on machines. The B-29 Superfortress was an aircraft capable of long-range, heavy bombing runs and was used frequently against Japan during 1944 and 1945. Firebomb B-29 raids against industrial cities in Japan totaled nearly 7,000 flights, which dropped 41,600 tons of bombs. Ask students: What makes mechanized warfare different from the hand-to-hand or face-to-face combat of the past? *Mechanized warfare is both more effective and more impersonal.*

▶Critical Viewing◀

❶ **Relate** Students may say that they relate the devastation more to real people's lives now that they have read about some real people affected by bombing.

◆ **Background for Understanding**

❷ **World War II** The Japanese were not the only people who had "a fear of being spied upon." The United States government rounded up Japanese American families living in the West and locked them up in detention camps for the duration of the war. Have students speculate on why times of war can bring out irrational fears. *Sample response: Thinking in terms of enemies versus allies can lead to mistrust of anyone who seems different or anyone who, like Mr. Tanimoto, has connections to a foreign country.*

Literature CD-ROM To build background about the selection, use the CD-ROM *The History of American Literature,* Part 2, Disc 2, Feature 2, which focuses in part on John Hersey and *Hiroshima.*

Customize for *Less Proficient Readers*
To help these students to grasp the author's implied themes, use ***Strategies for Diverse Student Needs,*** p. 71, "Question Author's Purpose."

The rayon man, a Mr. Matsui, had opened his then unoccupied estate to a large number of his friends and acquaintances, so that they might evacuate whatever they wished to a safe distance from the probable target area. Mr. Tanimoto had had no difficulty in moving chairs, hymnals, Bibles, altar gear, and church records by pushcart himself, but the organ console and an upright piano required some aid. A friend of his named Matsuo had, the day before, helped him get the piano out to Koi; in return, he had promised this day to assist Mr. Matsuo in hauling out a daughter's belongings. That is why he had risen so early.

Mr. Tanimoto cooked his own breakfast. He felt awfully tired. The effort of moving the piano the day before, a sleepless night, weeks of worry and unbalanced diet, the cares of his parish—all combined to make him feel hardly adequate to the new day's work. There was another thing, too: Mr. Tanimoto had studied theology at Emory College, in Atlanta, Georgia; he had graduated in 1940; he spoke excellent English; he dressed in American clothes; he had corresponded with many American friends right up to the time the war began; and among a people obsessed with a fear of being spied upon—perhaps almost obsessed himself—he found himself growing increasingly uneasy. ❷ The police had questioned him several times, and just a few days before, he had heard that an influential acquaintance, a Mr. Tanaka, a retired officer of the Toyo Kisen Kaisha

▲ **Critical Viewing** You may have seen photographs like this one of the aftermath of the Hiroshima bombing. How does Hersey's account change the way you view such pictures? **[Relate]** ❶

Analyze Literary Criticism

Commenting on John Hersey's "Hiroshima," one reviewer wrote: "This is not a treatise. It is a factual account, in straightforward reportorial style, of what happened in Hiroshima on the morning of August 6, 1945, and in the sad days that followed. It is John Hersey at his best." Share this comment with students. Then have students respond to the following question in their journals:

Do you agree that Hersey's book is "a factual account," written "in straightforward reportorial style"? Explain, using details from the text to support your answer. *Students may feel that the attention to details of time and activity make the narrative factual. Some may say that the focus on individuals makes the narrative less than objective.*

steamship line, an anti-Christian, a man famous in Hiroshima for his showy philanthropies and notorious for his personal tyrannies, had been telling people that Tanimoto should not be trusted. In compensation, to show himself publicly a good Japanese, Mr. Tanimoto had taken on the chairmanship of his local *tonarigumi*, or Neighborhood Association, and to his other duties and concerns this position had added the business of organizing air-raid defense for about twenty families. ❸

Before six o'clock that morning, Mr. Tanimoto started for Mr. Matsuo's house. There he found that their burden was to be a *tansu*, a large Japanese cabinet, full of clothing and household goods. The two men set out. The morning was perfectly clear and so warm that the day promised to be uncomfortable. A few minutes after they started, the air-raid siren went off—a minute-long blast that warned of approaching planes but indicated to the people of Hiroshima only a slight degree of danger, since it sounded every morning at this time, when an American weather plane came over. ❹ The two men pulled and pushed the handcart through the city streets. Hiroshima was a fan-shaped city, lying mostly on the six islands formed by the seven estuarial rivers that branch out from the Ota River; its main commercial and residential districts, covering about four square miles in the center of the city, contained three-quarters of its population, which had been reduced by several evacuation programs from a wartime peak of 380,000 to about 245,000. Factories and other residential districts, or suburbs, lay compactly around the edges of the city. To the south were the docks, an airport, and the island-studded Inland Sea. A rim of mountains runs around the other three sides of the delta. Mr. Tanimoto and Mr. Matsuo took their way through the shopping center, already full of people, and across two of the rivers to the sloping streets of Koi, and up them to the outskirts and foothills. As they started up a valley away from the tight-ranked houses, the all-clear sounded. (The Japanese radar operators, detecting only three planes, supposed that they comprised a reconnaissance.) Pushing the handcart up to the rayon man's house was tiring, and the men, after they had maneuvered their load into the driveway and to the front steps, paused to rest awhile. They stood with a wing of the house between them and the city. Like most homes in this part of Japan, the house consisted of a wooden frame and wooden walls supporting a heavy tile roof. Its front hall, packed with rolls of bedding and clothing, looked like a cool cave full of fat cushions. Opposite the house, to the right of the front door, there was a large, finicky rock garden. There was no sound of planes. The morning was still; the place was cool and pleasant.

Then a tremendous flash of light cut across the sky. ❺ Mr. Tanimoto has a distinct recollection that it travelled from east to west, from the city toward the hills. It seemed a sheet of sun. Both he and Mr. Matsuo reacted in terror—and both had time to react (for they were 3,500 yards, or two miles, from the center of the explosion). Mr. Matsuo dashed up the front steps into the house and dived among the bedrolls and buried himself there. Mr. Tanimoto took four or five steps and threw himself between two big rocks in the garden. He bellied up very hard against one of them. As his face was against the stone, he did not see what happened. He felt a sudden pressure, and then splinters and pieces of board and fragments of tile fell on him. He heard no roar. (Almost no one in Hiroshima recalls hearing any noise of the bomb. But a fisherman in his sampan on the Inland Sea near Tsuzu, the man with whom Mr. Tanimoto's mother-in-law and sister-in-law were living, saw the flash and heard a tremendous explosion; he was nearly twenty miles from Hiroshima, but the thunder was greater than when the B-29s hit Iwakuni, only five miles away.) ❻

When he dared, Mr. Tanimoto raised his head and saw that the rayon man's house had collapsed. He thought a bomb had fallen directly on it. Such clouds of dust had risen that there was a sort of twilight around. In panic, not thinking for the moment of Mr. Matsuo under the ruins, he dashed out into the street. He noticed as he ran that the concrete wall of the estate had fallen over—toward the house rather than away from it. In the street, the first thing

◆ Build Vocabulary

philanthropies (fə lan´ thrə pēz) *n.*: Charitable acts or gifts

◆ Literary Focus

❸ Implied Theme Hersey often uses irony to underscore one of his themes: the irrationality and unpredictability of war. Ask: In light of what happens to his neighborhood, what is ironic about Mr. Tanimoto's *tonarigumi* job? *Although he organizes air raid defense for twenty families, when such defense is needed, there is nothing anyone can do.*

◆ Grammar and Style

❹ Transitions and Transitional Phrases Have students identify the transitional phrase in this sentence. Then have them explain its function. *Students should identify the phrase* a few minutes after they started; *the phrase shows the time relationship between actions.*

◆ Grammar and Style

❺ Transitions and Transitional Phrases Here Hersey uses the simplest of transitions to mark the shift from life before the bomb to life after the bomb. Have students identify the transition and explain why it may be more powerful than a more complex transitional phrase. *The transition is "Then"; its power lies in its simplicity, because it echoes the terrifying suddenness of the shift.*

◆ Reading Strategy

❻ Draw Inferences About Theme Ask students to explain what these parenthetical details suggest about nuclear warfare. *Students should note that although the bomb was clearly far greater in strength than the usual B-29 bombs, those who were directly affected could not even hear it. This information suggests the terrifying and unnatural qualities of nuclear war.*

Viewing and Representing Mini-Lesson

Map

This mini-lesson supports the Researching and Representing activity on p. 1047 of the Idea Bank.

Introduce Point out that libraries and the Internet offer a variety of reference materials that students will find helpful both for creating an accurate world map and for gathering information about major events of World War II. Library sources of world maps include atlases; the Internet has graphic and photographic maps (taken by satellite); information about events of World War II is available in books, periodicals, and via the Internet.

Develop Suggest that students take notes on the name, date, and exact location of each event. To make the map most readable and informative, they may want to simplify it, showing only the borders and names of countries, icons or labels marking the World War II sites, and a map key. Encourage students to give some thought to types of icons they can design to impart information, such as the year or the nature of an event.

Apply Some students may wish to create their maps entirely on computers. Others may prefer to print out an Internet map, then enlarge and/or trace it. Some may decide to photocopy an oversized map from an atlas in several steps, paste together the pages, then trace the map onto the butcher paper, using colored markers.

Assess Evaluate students' maps on the basis of their informational content, attention to detail, and accuracy.

◆ Reading Strategy

❶ Draw Inferences About Theme Ask: What does the detail about the soldiers imply about the catastrophe that has just taken place? What does it imply about Hersey's theme? *Responses may include: Whatever has happened was worse than anything the soldiers had prepared for; it was unpredictable and impossible to defend against. The atomic bomb is a weapon of tremendous and almost unthinkable power.*

◆ Grammar and Style

❷ Transitions and Transitional Phrases Have students identify the transitional phrase in this sentence. What is the function of this phrase? *Students should identify the phrase* At nearly midnight, the night before the bomb was dropped *and note that it shows a time relationship.*

❸ Clarification Honshu is the large Japanese island on which the city of Hiroshima is located.

◆ Literary Focus

❹ Implied Theme Here Hersey again uses an ironic detail to point to the idea that one cannot prepare for nuclear warfare. Ask students to look at the picture on page 1041 and explain what makes this passage ironic. *Mrs. Nakamura's neighbor is knocking down his house to make way for a fire lane; however, the house will soon be hit by a bomb more devastating than any incendiary device ever seen.*

◆ Literary Focus

❺ Implied Theme Sample response: Mrs. Nakamura has been through so much that it seems impossible she will have to face more, but the reader knows that she will. In this way, she embodies the resilience and strength of the human spirit.

❶ he saw was a squad of soldiers who had been burrowing into the hillside opposite, making one of the thousands of dugouts in which the Japanese apparently intended to resist invasion, hill by hill, life for life; the soldiers were coming out of the hole, where they should have been safe, and blood was running from their heads, chests, and backs. They were silent and dazed.

Under what seemed to be a local dust cloud, the day grew darker and darker.

❷ ❸ At nearly midnight, the night before the bomb was dropped, an announcer on the city's radio station said that about two hundred B-29s were approaching southern Honshu and advised the population of Hiroshima to evacuate to their designated "safe areas." Mrs. Hatsuyo Nakamura, the tailor's widow, who lived in the section called Nobori-cho and who had long had a habit of doing as she was told, got her three children—a ten-year-old boy, Toshio, an eight-year-old girl, Yaeko, and a five-year-old girl, Myeko—out of bed and dressed them and walked with them to the military area known as the East Parade Ground, on the northeast edge of the city. There she unrolled some mats and the children lay down on them. They slept until about two, when they were awakened by the roar of the planes going over Hiroshima.

As soon as the planes had passed, Mrs. Nakamura started back with her children. They reached home a little after two-thirty and she immediately turned on the radio, which, to her distress, was just then broadcasting a fresh warning. When she looked at the children and saw how tired they were, and when she thought of the number of trips they had made in past weeks, all to no purpose, to the East Parade Ground, she decided that in spite of the instructions on the radio, she simply could not face starting out all over again. She put the children in their bedrolls on the floor, lay down herself at three o'clock, and fell asleep at once, so soundly that when planes passed over later, she did not waken to their sound.

The siren jarred her awake at about seven. She arose, dressed quickly, and hurried to the house of Mr. Nakamoto, the head of her Neighborhood Association, and asked him what she should do. He said that she should remain at home unless an urgent warning—a series of intermittent blasts of the siren—was sounded. She returned home, lit the stove in the kitchen, set some rice to cook, and sat down to read that mornings Hiroshima *Chugoku*. To her relief, the all-clear sounded at eight o'clock. She heard the children stirring, so she went and gave each of them a handful of peanuts and told them to stay in their bedrolls, because they were tired from the night's walk. She had hoped that they would go back to sleep, but the man in the house directly to the south began to make a terrible hullabaloo of hammering, wedging, ripping, and splitting. The prefectural government,[1] convinced, as everyone in Hiroshima was, that the city would be attacked soon, had begun to press with threats and warnings for the completion of wide fire lanes, which, it was hoped, might act in conjunction with the rivers to localize any fires started by an incendiary[2] raid; and the neighbor was reluctantly sacrificing his home to the city's safety. Just the day before, the prefecture had ordered all able-bodied girls from the secondary schools to spend a few days helping to clear these lanes, and they started work soon after the all-clear sounded. ❹

Mrs. Nakamura went back to the kitchen, looked at the rice, and began watching the man next door. At first, she was annoyed with him for making so much noise, but then she was moved almost to tears by pity. Her emotion was specifically directed toward her neighbor, tearing down his home, board by board, at a time when there was so much unavoidable destruction, but undoubtedly she also felt a generalized, community pity, to say nothing of self-pity. She had not had an easy time. Her husband, Isawa, had gone into the Army just after Myeko was born, and she had heard nothing from or of him for a long time, until, on March 5, 1942, she received a seven-word telegram: "Isawa died an honorable death at Singapore." She learned later that he

> **◆ Literary Focus**
> How does Hersey's characterization of Mrs. Nakamura hint at an implied theme related to the strength of the human spirit? ❺

1. **prefectural government:** Regional districts of Japan which are administered by a governor.
2. **incendiary** (in sen´ dē er´ ē) *adj.*: Designed to cause fires.

Beyond the Classroom

Career Connection

Radio Broadcasting The Second World War occurred at a time when there was as yet only limited television broadcasting. Therefore, the most important source of up-to-the-minute-news about the war was radio. Radio broadcasting is still a vital link to the news of the day for thousands of people, many of whom keep the radio on as they go about their business at work.

Just as in the golden age of radio (from about 1925 until the early 1950's), today's on-air news reporters must have a good grasp of standard English, a good speaking voice, and the ability to interview, paraphrase, and distill key ideas from masses of information.

Encourage students to tell how they get information about what is happening in your area, in the country, and in the world. To what extent do they rely on radio? What other sources do they rely on, and to what extent? Invite students interested in a career in radio to research the various kinds of jobs in the radio field as well as the requirements for those jobs.

6 ▲ Critical Viewing There are no people shown in this photograph—nor in many others—depicting the devastation wrought by the Hiroshima bomb. Does the lack of humanity lessen or intensify the impact of the image? Explain. **[Assess]**

had died on February 15th, the day Singapore fell, and that he had been a corporal. Isawa had been a not particularly prosperous tailor, and his only capital was a Sankoku sewing machine. After his death, when his allotments stopped coming, Mrs. Nakamura got out the machine and began to take in piecework herself, and since then had supported the children, but poorly, by sewing.

7 As Mrs. Nakamura stood watching her neighbor, everything flashed whiter than any white she had ever seen. She did not notice what happened to the man next door; the reflex of a mother set her in motion toward her children. She had taken a single step (the house was 1,350 yards, or three-quarters of a mile, from the center of the explosion) when something picked her up and she seemed to fly into the next room over the raised sleeping platform, pursued by parts of her house.

Timbers fell around her as she landed, and a shower of tiles pommelled her; everything became dark, for she was buried. The debris did not cover her deeply. She rose up and freed herself. She heard a child cry, "Mother, help me!" and saw her youngest—Myeko, the five-year-old—buried up to her breast and unable to move. As Mrs. Nakamura started frantically to claw her way toward the baby, she could see or hear nothing of her other children.

In the days right before the bombing, Dr. Masakazu Fujii, being prosperous, hedonistic,[3] and at the time not too busy, had been allowing himself the luxury of sleeping until nine or nine-thirty, but fortunately he had to get up early the morning the bomb was dropped to see a house guest off on a train. He rose at six, and half an hour later walked with his friend to the station, not far away, across two of the rivers. He was back home by seven, just as the siren sounded its sustained warning. He ate breakfast and then, because the morning was already hot, undressed down to his underwear and went out on the porch to read the paper. This porch—in fact, the whole building—was curiously constructed. Dr. Fujii was the proprietor of a peculiarly Japanese institution; a private, single-doctor hospital. This building, perched beside and over the water of the Kyo River, and next to the bridge of the same name, contained thirty rooms for thirty patients and their kinfolk—for, according to Japanese custom, when a person falls sick and goes to a hospital, one or more members 8

3. **hedonistic** (he de nis´ tik) *adj.*: Indulgently seeking out pleasure.

▶Critical Viewing◀

6 Assess Students may say that the impact of the image is greater without people because the bomb appears to have erased all signs of life.

◆ Critical Thinking

7 Analyze Ask students to explain why using a mother of three as one of his six subjects would be an effective way for Hersey to make his points about war. *Responses may include: A mother's desire to protect her children is something every reader understands; the fate of a mother and her children will touch readers in a way that other subjects might not.*

◆ Grammar and Style

8 Transitions and Transitional Phrases Ask students what difficulty a reader might have if Hersey did not include the transitional phrase that begins this section. *The reader might have difficulty following the story, becoming confused by the sudden movement back in time.*

Beyond the Classroom

Career Connection

Medicine In this country, it is almost unheard of for a doctor to operate a private hospital, as Dr. Fuji does. It is typical here for physicians to have private practices and be affiliated with large privately, or publicly, operated hospitals.

Have students share what they know about the training of a physician in the United States. What kind of schooling is required? How difficult is it to become a doctor? What does it mean to specialize?

Community Connection

Community Hospitals The role of a community hospital in times of emergency is absolutely vital. Although local hospitals in the United States have not been immediately involved in treating battle injuries since the Civil War, they still serve as the primary emergency facilities in cases of major accidents and natural disasters. Have students identify the hospitals in your area. Do all of the hospitals have emergency facilities? What other services and facilities do the hospitals provide?

◆ Reading Strategy

❶ Draw Inferences About Theme Ask: Considering what is about to happen, what is Hersey saying about nuclear warfare when he uses this image of a house standing fast against a flood? *Elicit the following: He compares the devastation of which nature is capable to the devastation caused by war and finds the latter more powerful.*

◆ Reading Strategy

❷ Draw Inferences About Theme Students may say that decisions made during wartime have little to do with day-to-day existence during other times. Dr. Fuji is no longer concerned with making a good living or healing but only with staying relatively safe and keeping his patients safe.

❸ Clarification Explain that the word *affected* here means "showed a liking for" with a connotation of trying to make an impression by putting on airs.

◆ Reading Strategy

❹ Draw Inferences About Theme Ask students what theme this ironic statement might be expressing. *Sample response: The statement might be expressing the theme that the devastation wrought by nuclear weapons is swift.*

◆ Critical Thinking

❺ Analyze Hersey includes a number of mundane details about Miss Sasaki's morning. Ask: Knowing that the bomb is about to fall, how do these details affect your response to the article? *Responses may include: The details help you relate to Miss Sasaki as a fellow human being; the details make the coming disaster seem more tragic and painful.*

of his family go and live there with him, to cook for him, bathe, massage, and read to him, and to offer incessant familial sympathy, without which a Japanese patient would be miserable indeed. Dr. Fujii had no beds—only straw mats—for his patients. He did, however, have all sorts of modern equipment: an X-ray machine, diathermy[4] apparatus, and a fine tiled laboratory. The structure rested two-thirds on the land, one-third on piles over the tidal waters of the Kyo. This overhang, the part of the building where Dr. Fujii lived, was queer-looking, but it was cool in summer and from the porch, which faced away from the center of the city, the prospect of the river, with pleasure boats drifting up and down it, was always refreshing. ❶ Dr. Fujii had occasionally had anxious moments when the Ota and its mouth branches rose to flood, but the piling was apparently firm enough and the house had always held.

Dr. Fujii had been relatively idle for about a month because in July, as the number of untouched cities in Japan dwindled and as Hiroshima seemed more and more inevitably a target, he began turning patients away, on the ground that in case of a fire raid he would not be able to evacuate them. Now he had only two patients left—a woman from Yano, injured in the shoulder, and a young man of twenty-five recovering from burns he had suffered when the steel factory near Hiroshima in which he worked had been hit. Dr. Fujii had six nurses to tend his patients. His wife and children were safe; his wife and one son were living outside Osaka, and another son and two daughters were in the country on Kyushu. A niece was living with him, and a maid and a manservant. He had little to do and did not mind, for he had saved some money. At fifty, he was healthy, convivial, and calm, and he was pleased to pass the evenings drinking whiskey with friends, always sensibly and for the sake of conversation. ❸ Before the war, he had affected brands imported from Scotland and America; now he was perfectly satisfied with the best Japanese brand, Suntory.

> ❷ **◆ Reading Strategy**
> What does this detail about Dr. Fujii suggest about the effects of war on people's decisions?

4. **diathermy** (dī´ ə thʉr´ mē) *n*: Medical treatment in which heat is produced beneath the skin to warm or destroy tissue.

Dr. Fujii sat down cross-legged in his underwear on the spotless matting of the porch, put on his glasses, and started reading the Osaka *Asahi*. He liked to read the Osaka news because his wife was there. He saw the flash. To him—faced away from the center and looking at his paper—it seemed a brilliant yellow. Startled, he began to rise to his feet. In that moment (he was 1,550 yards from the center), the hospital leaned behind his rising and, with a terrible ripping noise, toppled into the river. The Doctor, still in the act of getting to his feet, was thrown forward and around and over; he was buffeted and gripped; he lost track of everything, because things were so speeded up; he felt the water.

Dr. Fujii hardly had time to think that he was dying before he realized that he was alive, ❹ squeezed tightly by two long timbers in a V across his chest, like a morsel suspended between two huge chopsticks—held upright, so that he could not move, with his head miraculously above water and his torso and legs in it. The remains of his hospital were all around him in a mad assortment of splintered lumber and materials for the relief of pain. His left shoulder hurt terribly. His glasses were gone. . . .

Miss Toshiko Sasaki, the East Asia Tin Works clerk, . . . got up at three o'clock in the morning on the day the bomb fell. There was extra housework to do. Her eleven-month-old brother, Akio, had come down the day before with a serious stomach upset; her mother had taken him to the Tamura Pediatric Hospital and was staying there with him. Miss Sasaki, who was about twenty, had to cook breakfast for her father, ❺ a brother, a sister, and herself, and—since the hospital, because of the war, was unable to provide food—to prepare a whole day's meals for her mother and the baby, in time for her father, who worked in a factory making rubber earplugs for artillery crews, to take the food by on his way to the plant. When she had finished

◆ Build Vocabulary

incessant (in ses´ənt) *adj.*: Constant; continuing or repeating in a way that seems endless

convivial (kən viv´ ē əl) *adj.*: Fond of eating, drinking, and good company; sociable

Reteach

Students who experience difficulty when asked to draw inferences about theme may benefit from a visual demonstration. Use the following graphic organizer to present a list of simple details, such as those shown, together with an inference that may be drawn from them. Then suggest that during or after reading students use the same type of graphic organizer to draw inferences about theme, based on key lines or passages.

Details
- a white light flashed
- buildings collapsed
- a hospital fell into the river
- a woman flew through a house

↓

Inference
An atomic bomb had exploded.

and had cleaned and put away the cooking things, it was nearly seven. The family lived in Koi, and she had a forty-five-minute trip to the tin works, in the section of town called Kannonmachi. She was in charge of the personnel records in the factory. She left Koi at seven, and as soon as she reached the plant, she went with some of the other girls from the personnel department to the factory auditorium. A prominent local Navy man, a former employee, had committed suicide the day before by throwing himself under a train—a death considered honorable enough to warrant a memorial service, which was to be held at the tin works at ten o'clock that morning. In the large hall, Miss Sasaki and the others made suitable preparations for the meeting. This work took about twenty minutes.

Miss Sasaki went back to her office and sat down at her desk. She was quite far from the windows, which were off to her left, and behind her were a couple of tall bookcases containing all the books of the factory library, which the personnel department had organized. She settled herself at her desk, put some things in a drawer, and shifted papers. She thought that before she began to make entries in her lists of new employees, discharges, and departures for the Army, she would chat for a moment with the girl at her right. Just as she turned her head away from the windows, the room was filled with a blinding light. She was paralyzed by fear, fixed still in her chair for a long moment (the plant was 1,600 yards from the center).

Everything fell, and Miss Sasaki lost consciousness. The ceiling dropped suddenly and the wooden floor above collapsed in splinters and the people up there came down and the roof above them gave way; but principally and first of all, the bookcases right behind her swooped forward and the contents threw her down, with her left leg horribly twisted and breaking underneath her. There, in the tin factory, in the first moment of the atomic age, a human being was crushed by books. ❻

Guide for Responding

◆ Literature and Your Life

Reader's Response What thoughts remain with you after reading this account of the bombing of Hiroshima?

Thematic Focus What details imply that the author does not condone, or agree with, the bombing of Japanese cities?

Questions for Research Generate questions to find out how Hersey learned about the explosion's impact on specific individuals.

☑ Check Your Comprehension

1. Describe the city of Hiroshima in the hours and days preceding the explosion of the atomic bomb.
2. What factors determined whether certain individuals in Hiroshima survived or perished when the bomb exploded?
3. Describe the roles of the following people in this story: Miss Toshiko Sasaki, Dr. Masakazu Fujii, and Mrs. Hatsuyo Nakamura.

◆ Critical Thinking

INTERPRET

1. Why does Hersey spend so much time describing details of the hours preceding the bomb? **[Draw Conclusions]**
2. What is the effect of Hersey's returning to the moment of the actual explosion in his account of each individual's experience? **[Interpret]**
3. Explain the effect Hersey probably intended for the ending—Miss Sasaki's being "crushed by books"—to have on the reader. **[Infer]**
4. Why do you think Hersey told this story through the experiences and perceptions of these individuals? **[Draw Conclusions]**

APPLY

5. What does this selection reveal to you about nuclear war in general? **[Generalize]**

EXTEND

6. Compare this account of war with fictional accounts of war you have read or seen in films. **[Literature Link]**

◆ Critical Thinking

❻ Analyze Draw students' attention to the transitional phrase *principally* and *first of all.* Why does Hersey use these particular words in describing the fall of the bookcases? What might the bookcases and the books they hold represent? *Suggested response: Hersey is calling attention to a great irony—in the atomic age the knowledge embodied in books can be used not only to help and enlighten people but also to destroy them.*

Reinforce and Extend

Customize for Logical/Mathematical Learners

An interesting exercise might be to draw a time line of the various citizens' days immediately preceding and immediately following the explosion. Seeing, for example, Miss Sasaki's morning laid out in time sequence can help students understand the enormous tragedy and disruption that the bomb brings to Hiroshima.

Answers

◆ Literature and Your Life

Reader's Response Responses will probably focus upon the terrible destructive power of an atomic bomb.

Thematic Focus The close detail with which Hersey observes and reports each and every scene (from each individual's point of view) implies his protest.

☑ Check Your Comprehension

1. The residents of Hiroshima were making preparations for possible attacks by American B-29 bombers.
2. A person's nearness to the center of the bomb's explosion and the solidity of his or her immediate surroundings were two key factors that determined whether a Hiroshima resident lived or died.
3. When the bomb exploded, Miss Sasaki was seated at her desk in the factory in which she worked, Dr. Fuji—a physician—was reading a newspaper at his nearly empty hospital, and Mrs. Nakamura was at home with her children. All three survived the atomic explosion.

◆ Critical Thinking

1. These small, everyday details personalize and humanize the awesome effect of the bomb far beyond what statistics could do.
2. Suggested response: By returning to the moments surrounding the explosion, the author forces the reader to witness the bomb's destructive power again and again.
3. Suggested response: The effect is sadly ironic. Miss Sasaki is crushed by the weight of "knowledge" and "learning"; the explosion that caused the books to fall, of course, was the fruit of many expert scientists' labors.
4. Suggested response: These six people represent a cross-section of the city's citizenry. By telling the story through their eyes, Hersey is able to show that the atomic bomb devastated everyone similarly—regardless of background, class, or vocation.
5. Sample response: Nuclear war causes unparalleled death and destruction in but a moment's time.
6. Students' comparisons should be supported by citations from the selection text.

Develop Understanding

One-Minute Insight The indifference with which the powers that be sacrifice the lives of others during wartime is the implied theme of this poem. According to the speaker, this indifference extends to both the young World War II fliers like himself—men whose deaths were regarded as either "accidents" or "mistakes"—and to the enemy they fired at—"the people we had killed and never seen.'

◆ Critical Thinking

❶ **Analyze** Have students describe the two reasons the speaker ironically gives to explain why "it was not dying." What attitudes toward the deaths of pilots like himself do these explanations reveal? *The pilots' deaths are regarded as either normal occurances ("everybody died") or routine events ("we had died before").*

Customize for
Less Proficient Readers

❷ Check students' understanding by having them explain what the poet means by this parenthetical sentence. *He means that we were so young and untouched by death that we had no frame of reference other than "aunts," "pets," or "foreigners" to which we might compare our deaths.*

◆ Reading Strategy

❸ **Draw Inferences About Theme** Ask students: What is the poet saying about death in war by citing the difference between death during training and death during air combat with the words, ". . . but if we died / It was not an accident but a mistake"? *The only difference is merely semantics; death during training is called "an accident," while death during combat is called "a mistake." An individual's death in war is impersonal and glossed over.*

◆ Literary Focus

❹ **Implied Theme** Have students explain what the poet is saying about the impersonal quality of modern warfare. *Sample response: Bombers and other modern weapons make it possible to kill people from a distance; therefore those who fight do not have a good sense of whom they are killing.*

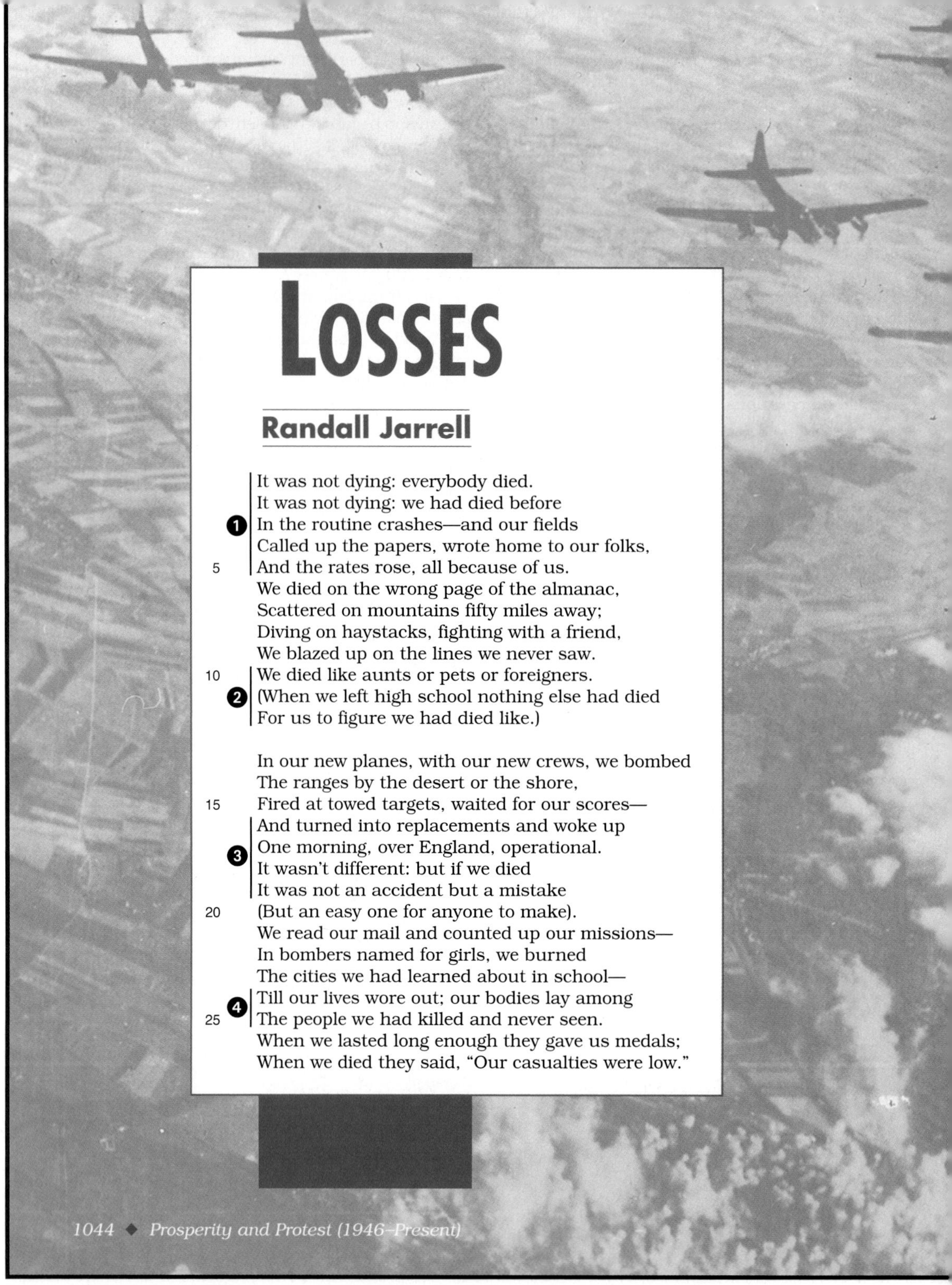

LOSSES

Randall Jarrell

It was not dying: everybody died.
It was not dying: we had died before
❶ In the routine crashes—and our fields
Called up the papers, wrote home to our folks,
And the rates rose, all because of us.
We died on the wrong page of the almanac,
Scattered on mountains fifty miles away;
Diving on haystacks, fighting with a friend,
We blazed up on the lines we never saw.
We died like aunts or pets or foreigners.
❷ (When we left high school nothing else had died
For us to figure we had died like.)

In our new planes, with our new crews, we bombed
The ranges by the desert or the shore,
Fired at towed targets, waited for our scores—
And turned into replacements and woke up
❸ One morning, over England, operational.
It wasn't different: but if we died
It was not an accident but a mistake
(But an easy one for anyone to make).
We read our mail and counted up our missions—
In bombers named for girls, we burned
The cities we had learned about in school—
❹ Till our lives wore out; our bodies lay among
The people we had killed and never seen.
When we lasted long enough they gave us medals;
When we died they said, "Our casualties were low."

Speaking, Listening, and Viewing Mini-Lesson

Dramatic Reading

This mini-lesson supports the Speaking, Listening, and Viewing activity in the Idea Bank on p. 1047.

Introduce the Concept Explain that a dramatic reading is similar to a reading of a play. The reader uses vocal expression to show emotion and may incorporate movement as well.

Develop Background Have each participant choose one of the two Jarrell poems. Provide time for students to locate music if they wish to use it to supplement their readings. Students with a special interest in music might record their own musical interpretations.

Apply the Information Have students take turns performing for the class. Provide cassette players if necessary.

Assess the Outcome Have each student complete Self-Assessment: Dramatic Performance in ***Alternative Assessment,*** p. 71. Discuss students' performances in terms of the emotional quality and clarity of their voices.

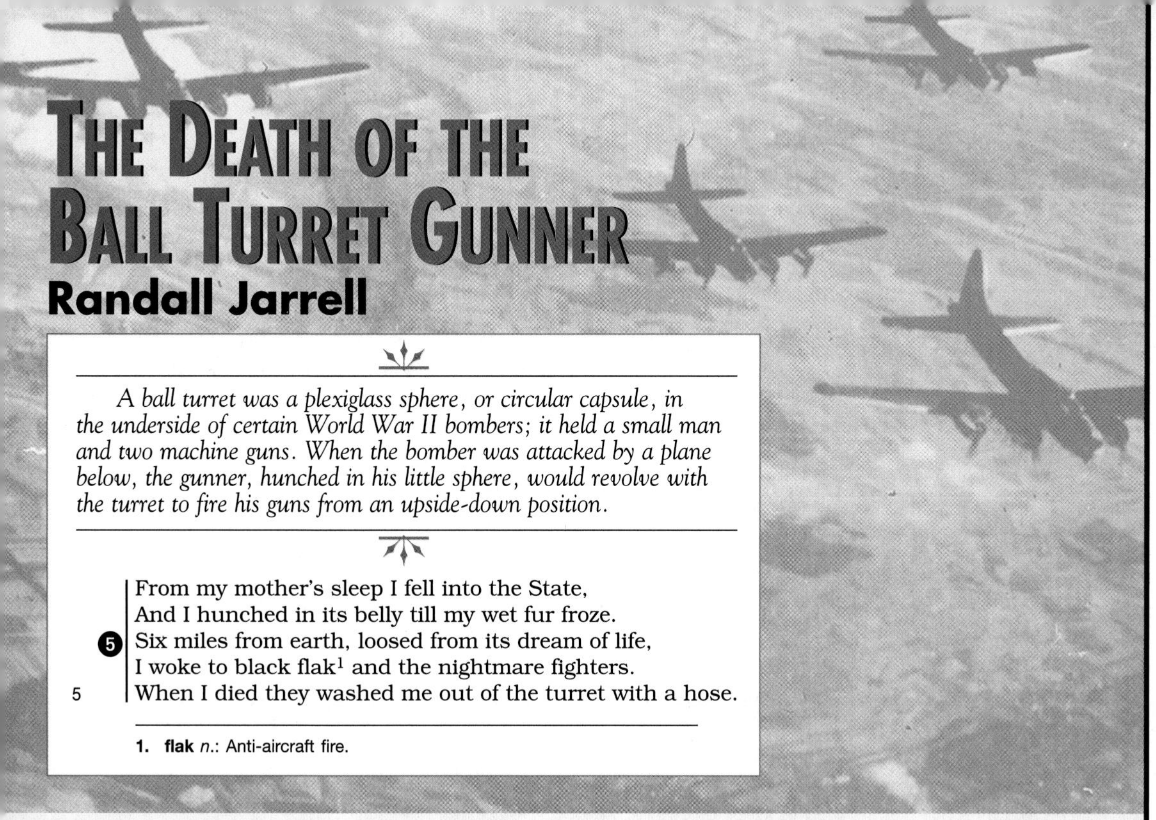

The Death of the Ball Turret Gunner

Randall Jarrell

A ball turret was a plexiglass sphere, or circular capsule, in the underside of certain World War II bombers; it held a small man and two machine guns. When the bomber was attacked by a plane below, the gunner, hunched in his little sphere, would revolve with the turret to fire his guns from an upside-down position.

From my mother's sleep I fell into the State,
And I hunched in its belly till my wet fur froze.
❺ Six miles from earth, loosed from its dream of life,
I woke to black flak[1] and the nightmare fighters.
When I died they washed me out of the turret with a hose.

1. **flak** *n.*: Anti-aircraft fire.

Guide for Responding

◆ Literature and Your Life

Reader's Response Do you share the poet's attitude toward war as he expresses it in "Losses"? Why or why not?

Thematic Focus How would you describe Randall Jarrell's view of war?

☑ Check Your Comprehension

1. In "Losses," to whom do the words *we, our,* and *us* refer?
2. For what reason did the soldiers get medals in "Losses"?
3. In "The Death of the Ball Turret Gunner," what woke the speaker when he was six miles from Earth?

◆ Critical Thinking

Interpret

1. In "Losses," what is the impact of the various ways in which the pilots' deaths are described in the opening stanza? **[Interpret]**
2. What is the significance of the fact that the pilots never see the people they kill? **[Analyze]**
3. (a) Who is the "they" referred to in the final line? (b) What does their comment reveal about their attitude toward the pilots? **[Infer]**
4. In "The Death . . . ," why might the gunner view life on Earth as a "dream"? **[Speculate]**
5. What does the final line reveal about the realities of war? **[Interpret]**

Compare Literary Works

6. Compare the treatment of the bombing victims in "Hiroshima" and in "Losses," and speculate on each author's intent. **[Connect]**

Beyond the Selection

FURTHER READING

Other Works by John Hersey

A Bell for Adano
The Wall

Other Works by Randall Jarrell

Little Friend, Little Friend
The Woman at the Washington Zoo

We suggest that you preview these works before recommending them to students.

INTERNET

You and your students may find additional information about John Hersey and Randall Jarrell on the Internet. We suggest the following sites. Please be aware, however, that the sites may have changed from the time we published this information.

For an essay on the original publication of "Hiroshima" in *The New Yorker* and the impact made by the work, go to **http://www.geocities.com/Heartland/Hills/6556/**

Information on Randall Jarrell's life and work can be found at **http://www.uncg.edn/lib/speccoll/Jarrell**

We *strongly recommend* that you preview sites.

Develop Understanding

One-Minute Insight In this poem, Jarrell juxtaposes images of sleeping, waking, birth, and death to expose the deadly and all-powerful nature of war.

◆ Reading Strategy

❺ Draw Inferences About Theme Have students discuss how this glimpse of war differs from the heroic view often portrayed in the movies. Then have them discuss what this contrast suggests about the implied theme. *Suggested response: The hero of the poem lacks any conventionally heroic qualities, and his death seems to have no meaning. The contrast implies that, in Jarrell's view, war is often meaningless to those who must fight and die.*

Reinforce and Extend

Answers

◆ Literature and Your Life

Reader's Response Student responses should be supported by citations from the poem.

Thematic Focus Suggested response: Jarrell seems to have abhorred war.

☑ Check Your Comprehension

1. The words refer to fighter pilots.
2. They get medals for surviving battle.
3. Black flak and enemy fighters woke the speaker.

◆ Critical Thinking

1. The impact is one of a casual and inevitable attitude toward death.
2. It demonstrates the impersonal nature of war.
3. (a) "They" refers to the military establishment. (b) They place little value on individual lives.
4. He might view life on earth as a dream because he is completely removed from it while in the plane.
5. The line reveals the cruel, impersonal, and unfeeling nature of war.
6. "Hiroshima" makes the deaths personal; "Losses" stresses the impersonal.

Answers

◆ Reading Strategy

1. These words mean that the survivors witnessed more death and destruction and felt more physical and emotional pain than can be imagined in countless lives.
2. These lines present the underlying meaning that there were no "safe areas" from a nuclear explosion.
3. These words show that the military pilots died so young that aunts, pets, and foreigners comprised their only frame of reference for death.
4. This statement indicates that to the military leaders, the individuals who died meant little; only death statistics were important.

◆ Literary Focus

Suggested response: By juxtaposing the monumental damage of the atomic explosion with the humbler manual activities of the Japanese soldiers, Hersey uses irony to underscore the theme of the great destructive power of war.

The theme of both poems is that war is violent, cruel, and impersonal. Relevant details in "Losses" include the speaker's comment that they never saw the people they killed and the officers' comment that the casualties were low; relevant details in "The Death of the Ball Turret Gunner" include images such as *State, wet fur froze, nightmare fighters,* and *the final line.*

◆ Build Vocabulary

Using the Latin Root *-vol-*

1. *volunteer:* A person who wishes to do something.
2. *benevolence:* An inclination or wish to do good; kindliness.
3. *malevolence:* The quality or state of wishing evil or harm to others.

Using the Word Bank; Sentence Completions

1. evacuated; 4. philanthropies
2. volition; 5. incessant
3. rendezvous; 6. convivial

◆ Grammar and Style

Transitions and Transitional Phrases

Practice

A sample paragraph follows:

After Mr. Tanimoto cooked his own breakfast, he started for Mr. Matsuo's house. Later, as the two men set out, an air-raid siren went off. Then, the all-clear sounded. Suddenly, although there was no sound of planes, a tremendous flash of light cut across the sky. Both Mr. Tanimoto and Mr. Matsuo reacted in terror.

Writing Application

Details within paragraphs should be logically linked by transitions.

Grammar Reinforcement

For additional instruction and practice, use the lesson in the **Language Lab CD-ROM** on transitional Words and the page on Connecting Ideas Clearly, p. 114, in the *Writer's Solution Grammar Practice Book.*

Guide for Responding (continued)

◆ Reading Strategy

Draw Inferences About Theme

All three pieces convey important messages about war. To grasp these messages, however, you have to **draw inferences,** or conclusions, from key lines or passages. Explain what underlying meaning you can grasp from each of these lines.

1. ". . . each knows that in the act of survival he lived a dozen lives . . ." (*Hiroshima*)
2. ". . . the night before the bomb was dropped, an announcer . . . advised the population . . . to evacuate to their designated 'safe areas.' " (*Hiroshima*)
3. "We died like aunts or pets or foreigners." ("Losses")
4. "When we died, they said, 'Our casualties were low.' " ("Losses")

◆ Literary Focus

Implied Theme

In each of these selections, the **theme** is **implied**, rather than directly stated. State the theme of each selection, using lines like those above to support your answer. Why would the selections be less effective if their themes were directly stated?

Beyond Literature

History Connection

The Manhattan Project The Manhattan Project was the American effort to create the atomic bomb. It was a top-secret undertaking that took seven years, employed over 120,000 people, and cost more than $2 billion. On July 16, 1945, the first atomic device was set off in the desert at Alamogordo, New Mexico. It left a huge crater and shattered windows 125 miles away. As he watched the blast, physicist J. Robert Oppenheimer, who had spearheaded the entire project, remembered the words of the *Bhagavad Gita*, the Hindu holy book: "Now I am become Death, the destroyer of worlds." Do you think this quote is an appropriate description of nuclear weapons? Explain.

◆ Build Vocabulary

Using the Latin Root *-vol-*

Several English words come from the Latin root *-vol-*, meaning "to will" or "to wish." Use a dictionary to find and write the definitions of the following words in your notebook.

1. volunteer **2.** benevolence **3.** malevolence

Using the Word Bank: Sentence Completions

On your paper, write the word that best completes each sentence.

a. incessant **c.** rendezvous **e.** evacuated
b. convivial **d.** volition **f.** philanthropies

1. The birds ___?___ their nest and never returned to it.
2. She did extra homework of her own ___?___, not because it was expected of her.
3. Let's establish a ___?___, so we don't miss each other.
4. Among the financier's ___?___ was a fund to send talented young musicians to music camp.
5. The child's ___?___ whining bothered fellow train passengers.
6. The ___?___ friends attend parties together regularly.

◆ Grammar and Style

Transitions and Transitional Phrases

John Hersey makes it easy for the reader to place events in time order through his frequent use of **transitional phrases**—groups of words that show relationships among ideas—and **transitions**—single words that function in the same way.

Practice Add transitions to this paragraph summarizing some of the events in Hersey's account.

Mr. Tanimoto cooked his own breakfast. He started for Mr. Matsuo's house. The two men set out. An air-raid siren went off. The all-clear sounded. There was no sound of planes. A tremendous flash of light cut across the sky. Both Mr. Tanimoto and Mr. Matsuo reacted in terror.

Writing Application Write a series of paragraphs summarizing your activities one day during the past week. Use transitions to link your details.

Build Your Portfolio

Idea Bank

Writing

1. **Journal** Suppose you were aboard the airplane that dropped the atomic bomb on Hiroshima. Write a journal entry that you might have written before going to sleep that night.

2. **Poem** Write a poem of three stanzas or more in which you state your feelings about war. Imply your theme through the details you choose.

3. **Essay** Write an essay in which you explain what you can infer about either Jarrell's or Hersey's attitude toward war based on what you've just read. Cite details from the literature for support.

Speaking, Listening, and Viewing

4. **Debate** These selections concern events and observations of World War II, once known as "the good war." Is a "good war" possible? With classmates, divide into teams to debate this question. **[Social Studies Link]**

5. **Dramatic Reading** Rehearse and present a dramatic reading of one of Jarrell's poems. If you wish, you can supplement the reading with music. **[Performing Arts Link]**

Researching and Representing

6. **Map** Prepare a world map that shows the locations of major events of World War II, including the bombings of Hiroshima and Nagasaki. **[Social Studies Link; Art Link]**

7. **Research Report** Use library or Internet resources to learn more about Hiroshima before and after August 1945. Report on your findings in a written report. If possible, include eyewitness accounts of Japanese people near the bombing sites. **[Social Studies Link]**

Online Activity www.phlit.phschool.com

Guided Writing Lesson

Introduction to a Documentary on World War II

In a film documentary on World War II, still photographs, film clips, and the recollections of eyewitnesses might be tied together with commentary provided by a narrator. Write an introduction to be read by a narrator at the beginning of such a documentary. Capture the interest of viewers and help prepare them for the events to come.

Writing Skills Focus: Knowledge Level of Readers

To write an effective introduction to a documentary, consider how much your audience already knows about the topic. Reflect on the type of audience likely to watch your documentary, and think about the following points as you decide what information to include:

- An audience familiar with World War II requires fewer basic details than one not familiar with it.
- A general audience may be bored by the small details that are apt to fascinate real World War II buffs.
- For a less-knowledgeable audience, it is important to define specialized terms and provide adequate background information.

Prewriting Conduct research in the library or on the Internet to gather information for the documentary. Choose an event of special interest or relevance on which to focus. Then decide which events you will highlight in your introduction.

Drafting Begin with a vivid introductory sentence that grabs viewers' attention. Then describe the documentary they are about to see, using a conversational style that lends itself to oral presentation.

Revising Read your introduction aloud to make sure it is interesting and informative. Ask yourself whether you have appropriately targeted the knowledge level of your expected audience.

Idea Bank

Customizing for *Performance Levels*

Following are suggestions for matching Idea Bank topics with your students' performance levels:
Less Advanced Students: 1, 5
Average Students: 2, 4, 6
More Advanced Students: 3, 7

Customizing for *Learning Modalities*

Following are suggestions for matching Idea Bank topics with your students' learning modalities:
Interpersonal: 4
Musical/Rhythmic: 5
Visual/Spatial: 6
Logical/Mathematical: 7

Guided Writing Lesson

For more instruction on prewriting, elaboration, and revision, see *Prentice Hall Writing and Grammar.*

Writers at Work Videodisc

Have students view the videodisc segment (Ch. 5) featuring music writer and editor Gillian Gaar speaking about research writing. Discuss with students what Gaar says about the place of research in the writing process.

Play frames 3 to 9643

Writing Lab CD-ROM

Have students complete the tutorial on Research Writing. Follow these steps:

1. To help students conduct research, have them use the Audio-Annotated Instruction on Using Library Resources.
2. While students draft, have them use the Transition Word Bin to help connect their events.
3. Use the Interactive Self-Evaluation Checklist to aid revision.

ASSESSMENT OPTIONS

Formal Assessment, Selection Test, pp. 311–313, and Assessment Resources Software. The selection test is designed so that it can be easily customized to the performance levels of your students.

Alternative Assessment, p. 71, includes options for less advanced students, more advanced students, verbal/linguistic learners, logical/mathematical learners, and visual/spatial learners.

PORTFOLIO ASSESSMENT

Use the following rubrics in the ***Alternative Assessment*** booklet to assess student writing:
Journal: Fictional Narrative Rubric, p. 110
Poem: Poetry Rubric, p. 123
Essay: Literary Analysis/Interpretation Rubric, p. 127
Guided Writing Lesson: Summary Rubric, p. 113

Prepare and Engage

LESSON OBJECTIVES

1. **To develop vocabulary and word identification skills**
   - Latin Word Roots: *-cep-*, *-cept-*
   - Using the Word Bank: Sentence Completions
2. **To use a variety of reading strategies to comprehend poetry**
   - Reading Strategy: Interpret
3. **To increase knowledge of other cultures and to connect common elements across cultures**
   - Connecting Themes Across Cultures (ATE)
4. **To express and support responses to the text**
   - Critical Thinking
   - Idea Bank: Poem or Paragraph
   - Idea Bank: Debate
   - Idea Bank: Letter
5. **To analyze literary elements**
   - Literary Focus: Implied Theme and Context
6. **To read in order to research self-selected and assigned topics**
   - Idea Bank: Multimedia Presentation
   - Idea Bank: Collage
7. **To plan, prepare, organize, and present literary interpretations**
   - Idea Bank: Comparison-and-Contrast Essay
   - Idea Bank: Oral Interpretation
8. **To use recursive writing processes to write a literary analysis**
   - Guided Writing Lesson
9. **To increase knowledge of the rules of grammar and usage**
   - Grammar and Style: Parallel Structure

Test Preparation

Writing Skills: Sentence Structure (ATE, p. 1049)
The teaching tips and sample test item in this workshop support the instruction and practice in the unit workshop:
Reading Comprehension: Context Clues and Prefixes/Suffixes (SE, p. 1143)

Guide for Interpreting

Sylvia Plath *(1932–1963)*

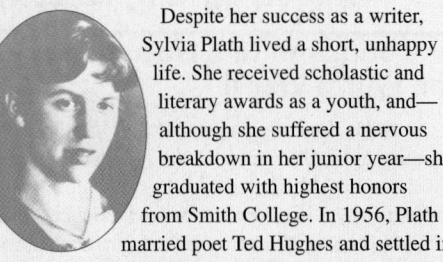

Despite her success as a writer, Sylvia Plath lived a short, unhappy life. She received scholastic and literary awards as a youth, and—although she suffered a nervous breakdown in her junior year—she graduated with highest honors from Smith College. In 1956, Plath married poet Ted Hughes and settled in England. Her first book of verse, *The Colossus* (1960), was the only one published during her lifetime. Four more books of poetry and a novel, *The Bell Jar* (1963), were published posthumously.

Adrienne Rich *(1929–)*

Adrienne Rich's career can be divided into two distinct stages. During the early part of her career, she wrote neatly crafted traditional verse. In contrast, her later poems are written in free verse and often explore her deepest personal feelings.

Her first volume of poetry, *A Change of World* (1951), was published just after she graduated from Radcliffe College. Since abandoning traditional poetic forms for free verse in the early 1960's, she has produced several other collections of poetry. Her later books include *An Atlas of the Difficult World* (1991) and *Dark Fields of the Republic* (1995).

Gwendolyn Brooks *(1917–)*

Gwendolyn Brooks was raised in a Chicago neighborhood known as "Bronzeville"—the setting for her first book, *A Street in Bronzeville* (1945). Though her early poems focus on suffering urban blacks who feel uprooted and are unable to make a living, Brooks's own youth was quite different—her home was warm, and her family loving and supportive. Of her childhood, she recalls, "I began to put rhymes together at about seven, at which time my parents expressed most earnest confidence that I would one day be a writer." In 1950, Brooks became the first African American writer to win a Pulitzer Prize.

Robert Hayden *(1913–1980)*

As a young, politically active writer in the 1930's, Robert Hayden protested not only the condition of African Americans, but also what he saw as the nation's inadequate care of the poor. In the 1940's, he became a poet, and he began to focus his writing on a wide range of topics; he wrote about mythology, folklore, and spiritual matters, as well as historical and current events. His volumes include *Heart-Shape in the Dust* (1940) and *A Ballad of Remembrance* (1966).

◆ Background for Understanding

LITERATURE: ROBERT HAYDEN AS POET-HISTORIOGRAPHER

Though Robert Hayden's poetry spans the range of human experience, much of it reflects his passionate, lifelong interest in African American history. His first job after graduating from Detroit City College was as a researcher of local African American history with Detroit's Federal Writer's Project. Throughout his career as a professor of literature, Hayden continued to research and write about his heritage. Several of his most significant poems deal with figures from African and African American history. In "Frederick Douglass," he pays tribute to the famous African American abolitionist; "Runagate Runagate" brings the experiences of the Underground Railroad vividly to life.

Prentice Hall Literature Program Resources

REINFORCE / RETEACH / EXTEND

Selection Support Pages
Build Vocabulary: Word Roots: *-cep-* and *-cept-*, p. 322
Grammar and Style: Parallel Structure, p. 323
Reading Strategy: Interpret, p. 324
Literary Focus: Theme and Context, p. 325

Strategies for Diverse Student Needs, Interpret and Explain Poetry, p. 72

Beyond Literature
Humanities Connection: Poetry of Protest, p. 72

Formal Assessment Selection Test, pp. 314–316; Assessment Resources Software

Alternative Assessment, p. 72

Resource Pro CD-ROM
Includes all resources and a customizable lesson plan.

Listening to Literature Audiocassettes

Literature CD-ROM

Mirror ◆ In a Classroom ◆ The Explorer
Frederick Douglass ◆ Runagate Runagate

◆ Literature and Your Life

CONNECT YOUR EXPERIENCE

It's human nature to find fault with the situations, policies, and attitudes reflected in everyday life. Maybe you think we should recycle more, or you dislike society's emphasis on appearance. While you may discuss your social concerns with your family and friends or volunteer for causes you believe in, poets often use their writing as a means of expressing their views.

Journal Writing What social issues or attitudes bother you? How do you express your concern about them?

THEMATIC FOCUS: SOCIAL PROTEST

Several of these poems reflect dissatisfaction with societal values and attitudes. What aspect of society is each poet critiquing?

◆ Reading Strategy

INTERPRET

In most poems, the central message isn't directly stated. Instead, it's left up to you to **interpret** the poem's message by looking for an underlying meaning in the words and images. Because poems tend to be brief, every word is important. Consider the connotations of words and the associations that each calls to mind. What common thread ties together these impressions? The answer to this question will lead you to the poem's message.

◆ Grammar and Style

PARALLEL STRUCTURE

Parallel structure is the expression of similar ideas in similar grammatical forms. Poets often use parallel structure for emphasis. For example, in "The Explorer," Brooks repeats the phrase *there were* twice, to emphasize her subject's failure to find peace. While parallel structure is an effective literary device, it's important to be careful to avoid faulty parallelism—the incorrect use of dissimilar grammatical structures to express similar ideas.

Faulty: We hiked, we biked, and *camping was another activity.*

Parallel: We hiked, we biked, *and we camped.*

◆ Literary Focus

THEME AND CONTEXT

Poems often contain references, images, symbols, or ideas closely connected to historical events, mythology, or the poet's own life. To understand the **theme**, or central message, of such poems it is essential to place the details in an appropriate **context**. For example, the historical context of "Runagate Runagate" is the Underground Railroad—the method by which many slaves escaped to freedom during the 1800's. Knowing this context can help a reader determine that the theme of the poem is that people are willing to take risks and make great sacrifices to gain their freedom.

◆ Build Vocabulary

LATIN ROOTS: *-cep-, -cept-*

The speaker of "Mirror" asserts that it has no *preconceptions,* or "ideas formed beforehand." This word is built around the Latin root *-cep-* or *-cept-,* meaning "to take, hold, or seize."

WORD BANK

Preview these words from the poems.

preconceptions
meditate
din
wily

Interest Grabber

As we look back on the twentieth century, it's fascinating to see how close we are to a time when women rarely worked outside the home, African Americans and whites attended separate schools, and the word *opportunity* had little meaning for many Americans. How far have we come? How far do we yet have to go?

Ask students to suggest ways that they themselves might cope with injustice and lack of opportunity. Would they give up? Protest actively? Express their anger in writing? Why or why not? Remind them that the writers of these poems protest through poetry.

Connecting Themes Across Cultures

Through literature, the poets in this group protest attitudes and circumstances, Ask students to identify and describe values or attitudes in various parts of the world which they might find difficult to accept. If they were a poet living in each place, what might they feel compelled to challenge through their art?

Customize for
Less Proficient Readers
Suggest that students use these questions to focus their reading: Who is speaking? What does the title refer to? If I expressed the poet's main idea in a sentence, what would it be? Have them jot down notes to answer the questions as they read.

Customize for
AP Students
Have students consider these questions and discuss them after they read: To admire and enjoy a poem, is it necessary to identify with the poet or the speaker? For example, must you be African American to respond to "Frederick Douglass"? Must you be female to respond to "Mirror"?

Art Transparency After students have read "The Explorer," display Art Transparency 20. Call on volunteers to describe its overall impression and to speculate about the sights and sounds that would be part of that scene if they were to see it for themselves.

Test Preparation Workshop

Writing Skills:
Sentence Structure Many standardized tests require students to choose the best way to correct the structure of a sentence. Use the sample item below to demonstrate.

Robert Hayden wrote about folklore, mythology, spiritual matters, and he also wrote about historical and current events.

Choose the best way to write the passage.

A Robert Hayden wrote about folklore, mythology, and spiritual matters, he also wrote about historical and current events.

B Robert Hayden wrote about folklore, mythology, spiritual matters, historical and current events.

C Robert Hayden wrote about folklore, mythology, and spiritual matters, about historical and current events.

D Robert Hayden wrote about folklore, mythology, spiritual matters, and historical and current events.

D is correct. It is a complete sentence with parallel structure.

Develop Understanding

One-Minute Insight The speaker of this poem, a mirror, describes a woman's reaction to viewing her image day after day. The woman, aware that she is growing older, responds "with tears and agitation of hands."

▶Critical Viewing◀

❶ Connect; Synthesize Students may note that both painting and poem contain the images of a young woman, a mirror, and the old woman who waits just beyond the mirror. Both suggest that aging is an inevitable, though not necessarily welcome, part of the human condition.

◆ Reading Strategy

❷ Interpret Point out that these opening lines establish the identity of the speaker. Have students identify this speaker as well as its qualities or traits. *The speaker is a mirror. It is accurate, truthful, and objective.*

❸ Clarification This line alludes to Narcissus, the beautiful youth in ancient Greek mythology who fell in love with his own image in a pool, whereupon he turned into a flower. What is meant when we say someone is narcissistic? *A narcissistic person is excessively interested in his or her appearance and importance.* In what way is Narcissus similar to the woman in the poem? *Narcissus, like the woman in the poem, is obsessed with his appearance.*

◆ Literary Focus

❹ Theme and Context Point out that Sylvia Plath wrote at a time before women were expected to have much of a role outside the home. Ask: How does the woman's agitation make sense in the context of the times? *Responses might include: She is preoccupied with her appearance because she doesn't have much of an outside life; she is preoccupied with her appearance because society expects her to be.*

MIRROR

Sylvia Plath

Mirror II, George Tooker, © Addison Gallery of American Art, Phillips Academy, Andover, Massachusetts

❶ ▶ **Critical Viewing** The artist titled this painting *Mirror II.* What ideas are common to both the painting and poem? What do both names say about the human condition? **[Connect; Synthesize]**

I am silver and exact. I have no preconceptions.
❷ Whatever I see I swallow immediately
Just as it is, unmisted by love or dislike.
I am not cruel, only truthful—
The eye of a little god, four-cornered.
Most of the time I meditate on the opposite wall.
It is pink, with speckles. I have looked at it so long
I think it is a part of my heart. But it flickers.
Faces and darkness separate us over and over.
❸ Now I am a lake. A woman bends over me,
Searching my reaches for what she really is.
Then she turns to those liars, the candles or the moon.
❹ I see her back, and reflect it faithfully.
She rewards me with tears and an agitation of hands.
I am important to her. She comes and goes.
Each morning it is her face that replaces the darkness.
In me she has drowned a young girl, and in me an old woman
Rises toward her day after day, like a terrible fish.

◆ Build Vocabulary

preconceptions (prē´ kən sep´ shənz) *n.*: Ideas formed beforehand

meditate (med´ ə tāt´) *v.*: Think deeply; ponder

Block Scheduling Strategies

Consider these suggestions to take advantage of extended class time:

- To build background on the poets Sylvia Plath and Adrienne Rich, use Part 2, Feature 7 of *The History of American Literature,* on the **Literature CD-ROM.** For background on Gwendolyn Brooks, use Part 2, Feature 6 of *The History of American Literature,* on the **Literature CD-ROM.**
- As you review the information in Background for Understanding (p. 1048), ask students to share any facts they know about Frederick Douglass, Harriet Tubman, and other heroes of the antislavery movement.
- Students can meet in small groups to discuss their answers to the Critical Thinking questions (pp. 1051, 1052, 1053, and 1055).
- For practice on the relationship between theme and context, have students complete Literary Focus: Theme and Context in ***Selection Support,*** p. 325.

In a CLASSROOM

Adrienne Rich

Talking of poetry, hauling the books
arm-full to the table where the heads
bend or gaze upward, listening, reading aloud,
talking of consonants, elision,[1]
caught in the how, oblivious of why:
I look in your face, Jude,
neither frowning nor nodding,
opaque in the slant of dust-motes over the table:
a presence like a stone, if a stone were thinking
What I cannot say, is me. For that I came.

1. **elision** (ē lizh′ ən) *n.*: Omission or slurring over of a vowel or syllable; often used in poetry to preserve meter.

Guide for Responding

◆ Literature and Your Life

Reader's Response The speaker of "Mirror" maintains: "I am not cruel, only truthful—." If the truth hurts, do you think that being truthful is cruel? Explain.

Thematic Focus What is Plath saying about the way society conditions people—particularly women—to regard the natural process of aging?

Journal Writing How would life be different if there were no mirrors? Explore this idea in a journal entry.

☑ Check Your Comprehension

1. In "Mirror," what two reflecting surfaces does the speaker name?
2. Why does the woman react to the mirror "with tears and an agitation of hands"?

◆ Critical Thinking

INTERPRET

1. (a) Who is the speaker in "Mirror"? (b) How is the speaker personified? (c) How is the speaker *unlike* a person? **[Analyze; Distinguish]**
2. In what way are the candle and the moon "liars"? **[Interpret]**
3. (a) Who is the "young girl" who has drowned? (b) Who is the "old woman"? **[Infer]**
4. (a) How does the woman feel about aging? (b) How is her attitude revealed? **[Analyze; Support]**

EVALUATE

5. Would it be possible for the woman in "Mirror" to change her attitude toward aging? Why or why not? **[Assess]**

APPLY

6. Do you think that most people share the woman's attitude toward aging? Why or why not? **[Synthesize]**

Customize for
Less Proficient Readers
To help these students to understand these poems, use ***Strategies for Diverse Student Needs,*** p. 72, Interpret and Explain Poetry.

Reinforce and Extend

Answers

◆ Literature and Your Life

Reader's Response Accept reasonable responses.

Thematic Focus Sample response: Society conditions people to regard the natural aging process as something tragic.

☑ Check Your Comprehension

1. The speaker mentions a "four-cornered" mirror and a lake.
2. She reacts that way because she is upset by seeing herself age.

◆ Critical Thinking

1. (a) The mirror is the speaker in the poem. (b) Plath uses words such as "swallow," "meditate," "I think," and "my heart" to personify the mirror. (c) Unlike human beings, the speaker is "silver and exact," and has "no preconceptions."
2. Suggested response: The candle and the moon produce dim and pleasant light in which the woman appears younger or more attractive than she really is.
3. (a) The girl is the woman's younger self. (b) The old woman is the person the woman is becoming.
4. (a) She is unhappy about aging and has difficulty accepting it. (b) Her attitude is revealed through her actions—crying and wringing her hands, turning her back on the mirror, and searching desperately for signs of youth.
5. Some students may point out that—despite the fact that she is experiencing feelings typical in society—some people are able to have a more accepting view of the natural process of aging.
6. Sample response: Many older people do share the woman's attitude toward aging because of society's preoccupation with linking youth with good looks and usefulness.

Humanities: Art

Mirror II by George Tooker.

Born in 1920, George Tooker is an American painter whose style is known as "Magic Realism." Magic Realism is realistic art that uses everyday images symbolically, as Tooker uses the mirror in this painting. As in most of Tooker's paintings, the setting, lighting, and mood of *Mirror II* are clean, cold, and barren.

Use these questions for discussion:

1. In what way does the woman in the painting resemble the woman in the poem? *Like the woman in the poem, she "searches . . . for what she really is" as she looks at her reflection; also, she senses an older woman "rising toward her."*
2. Do you think that the mood of the painting matches the mood of the poem? Why or why not? *Students may say that it does match—the mood of both is serious and slightly fantastic.*

Develop Understanding

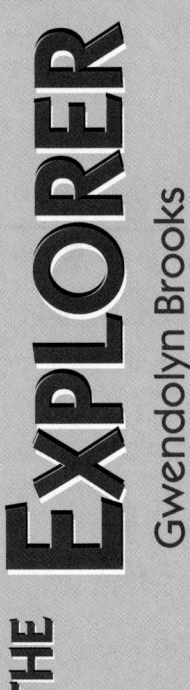

One-Minute Insight A person, identified only as "he," explores an apartment building, searching for "a still spot in the noise." His search for peace—for inner peace—is unsuccessful, however, as all he finds are noises connected with human activity and the frightening prospect of "choices, that cried to be taken."

◆ Literary Focus

❶ Theme and Context
Gwendolyn Brooks uses the imagery of a bustling apartment building to stand for something greater. Ask: What is the poet saying about life in the twentieth century? *Responses may include: It is impossible to avoid choices or find complete peace in the fast-paced, crowded world of today.*

Reinforce and Extend

Answers

◆ *Literature and Your Life*

Reader's Response Students should support their responses.

Thematic Focus Students should support their responses.

☑ Check Your Comprehension

1. The "inner want" is peace of mind.
2. He is searching the halls to find a quiet room.

◆ Critical Thinking

1. (a) They appeal to the sense of hearing. (b) It is fitting because the poem is about a person seeking quiet and solace in a crowded and chaotic apartment building.
2. Suggested responses: (a) The apartment building may represent the explorer's life, and the rooms represent his choices in life. (b) His actions and feelings might symbolize his inability to find solace and the limitations of the choices with which he is presented.
3. Suggested responses: He realizes that he will never be able to find solace in this home.
4. Suggested response: He's afraid of the risk involved in making choices.
5. Suggested response: People are afraid they will not be happy with the results of their decision.

THE EXPLORER

Gwendolyn Brooks

Somehow to find a still spot in the noise
Was the frayed inner want, the winding, the frayed hope
Whose tatters he kept hunting through the din.
A satin peace somewhere.
A room of wily hush somewhere within.

So tipping down the scrambled halls he set
Vague hands on throbbing knobs. There were behind
Only spiraling, high human voices,
The scream of nervous affairs,
Wee griefs,
Grand griefs. And choices.

He feared most of all the choices, that cried to be taken.

❶ There were no bourns.[1]
There were no quiet rooms.

1. **bourns** (bōrnz) *n.*: Limits; boundaries

◆ Build Vocabulary

din (din) *n.*: Loud continuous noise or clamor
wily (wī′ lē) *adj.*: Sly; cunning

Guide for Responding

◆ *Literature and Your Life*

Reader's Response What did you see and hear as you read this poem?

Thematic Focus Are those who live in apartment buildings deprived by their environment of the opportunity to enjoy inner—and outer—peace?

Group Discussion With a small group of classmates, share your thoughts about living in a large apartment building. What do you think are the benefits of living in such an environment? What are the drawbacks?

☑ Check Your Comprehension

1. What is the "inner want" of the poem's speaker?
2. What is he doing to find it?

◆ Critical Thinking

INTERPRET

1. (a) To which sense do Brooks's images most often appeal? Give three examples to support your answer. (b) Why is it fitting for this poem to be filled with images like these? **[Analyze]**
2. The poem's title casts a symbolic light on the lines that follow. (a) What might the explorer's apartment building symbolize? (b) What might his actions and feelings symbolize? **[Interpret]**
3. What conclusion does the explorer reach in the final two lines? **[Interpret]**
4. Why might the explorer fear choices "most of all"? **[Speculate]**

APPLY

5. Why do you think people often fear having to make choices? **[Speculate]**

Humanities: Art

Part II, The Free Man, No. 30, The Frederick Douglass Series by Jacob Lawrence.

Black American artist Jacob Lawrence was born in Atlantic City, New Jersey, in 1917. His work utilizes bold geometric shapes and bright colors to depict the daily lives of ordinary black Americans as well as the lives of distinguished blacks. The painting shown here is of the later variety, part of a series of paintings completed during 1938 and 1939 on the life of Frederick Douglass. Use these questions for discussion:

1. Does the painting correspond with the image of Frederick Douglass presented in the poem? *Sample response: Yes, because the poem alludes to a highly intelligent man "superb in love and logic," who would therefore probably be fond of reading.*
2. Keeping in mind what is said in the poem about Frederick Douglass, what might he be reading in the painting? *He might be reading the United States Constitution.*
3. What does the style and context of Lawrence's depiction of his subject say about Douglass as a person? *It shows Douglass to be a bold, resolute, and scholarly person.*

Frederick Douglass[1]

Robert Hayden

When it is finally ours, this freedom, this liberty, this
    beautiful
and terrible thing, needful to man as air,
❷ usable as earth; when it belongs at last to all,
when it is truly instinct, brain matter, diastole, systole,[2]
reflex action; when it is finally won; when it is more
than the gaudy mumbo jumbo of politicians:
this man, this Douglass, this former slave, this Negro
beaten to his knees, exiled, visioning a world
where none is lonely, none hunted, alien,
this man, superb in love and logic, this man
shall be remembered. Oh, not with statues' rhetoric,
not with legends and poems and wreaths of bronze alone,
but with the lives grown out of his life, the lives
❸ fleshing his dream of the beautiful, needful thing.

1. **Frederick Douglass:** American abolitionist (1817?–1895).
2. **diastole** (dī as´ tə lē´), **systole** (sis´ tə lē´): Diastole is the normal rhythmic dilation, or opening, of the heart. Systole is the normal rhythmic closing of the heart.

Part II, The Free Man, No. 30, The Frederick Douglass Series, Jacob Lawrence, Hampton University Museum, Hampton, Virginia

▲ Critical Viewing What impression of Douglass does this painting convey? **[Analyze]** ❹

Guide for Responding

◆ Literature and Your Life

Reader's Response What impression do you have of Frederick Douglass after reading this poem? What kind of a person was he?

Thematic Focus What is the poet saying about the condition of African Americans in the United States at the time the poem was written?

☑ Check Your Comprehension

1. According to the speaker of "Frederick Douglass," what does not yet belong to African Americans?
2. What does the speaker say will happen when African Americans finally possess this prize?
3. In what way does the speaker say Douglass will truly be memorialized?

◆ Critical Thinking

INTERPRET

1. (a) What is paradoxical about Hayden's notion that freedom is both a beautiful and terrible thing? (b) How would you explain this characterization of freedom? **[Analyze; Interpret]**
2. What does the speaker think of the value of statues and memorials as a way of remembering a person's achievements? **[Infer]**
3. What does the speaker mean when he says that Douglass will be remembered "with the lives grown out of his life"? **[Interpret]**

APPLY

4. How do you think Frederick Douglass would respond to this poem? Explain. **[Speculate]**

Develop Understanding

One-Minute Insight In this poem, the speaker describes the way Frederick Douglass will be remembered when freedom "is finally ours": not through statues, legends, poems, or wreaths, but through the lives that will realize the visionary's dream.

◆ Grammar and Style

❷ **Parallel Structure** Have students find the repeated phrase in these lines and explain the effect of the parallel structure. *The poet repeats "when it is" to emphasize that the time of freedom is not yet here.*

◆ Reading Strategy

❸ **Interpret** Ask students to explain in their own words this final line, based on their understanding of the rest of the poem. *In this line, the poet refers to people giving life to Douglass's dream by living in freedom.*

▶Critical Viewing◀

❹ **Analyze** The impression is one of a thoughtful, scholarly Douglass.

Reinforce and Extend

Answers

◆ Literature and Your Life

Reader's Response Sample response: Frederick Douglas was a man who had a difficult life, but kept alive the dream of freedom for all.

Thematic Focus At the time the poem was written, African Americans did not as yet achieve the dream freedom and equality.

☑ Check Your Comprehension

1. Freedom does not yet belong to them.
2. Frederick Douglass will be remembered.
3. Douglas will be memorialized by the lives of people living in freedom.

◆ Critical Thinking

1. (a) Most things that are beautiful are not also terrible and vice versa. (b) Suggested response: Freedom is beautiful because it is dignifying and precious, especially if it is won after a long, hard struggle; it can also be terrible if it comes as the result of a huge price.
2. Suggested response: The speaker thinks that statues and memorials aren't the best ways of remembering a person's achievements.
3. Suggested response: The lives of people who have achieved the dream of freedom—for which Douglass fought—will be the best memorial to him.
4. Sample response: Frederick Douglass would be proud to think that the work that he began is still ongoing.

Develop Understanding

One-Minute Insight A chorus of voices conveys the risks, the rewards, and the emotions that accompany a journey on the Underground Railroad.

Literature CD-ROM To build background on Sylvia Plath and Adriene Rich, use the CD-ROM *The History of American Literature:* Part 2, Disc 2, Feature 7. To build background on Gwendolyn Brooks, use Part 2, Disc 2, Feature 6 of the same CD-ROM.

◆ Grammar and Style

❶ **Parallel Structure** Point out that here Hayden uses parallel structure to help create a mood. Ask: How does the repetition of the word and affect your understanding of the action? *Responses may include: It suggests constant movement and an unending assortment of obstacles. It suggests someone who is running and out of breath.*

◆ Critical Thinking

❷ **Contrast** Encourage students to contrast these lines with lines 1–7. How would they describe the overall effect of each passage? What might be the purpose of the change in mood and tone? *Students may say that the first passage seems to convey the agitated thoughts of a person running away from pursuers, while the second passage represents a more formal style of poetry and, in fact, resembles a song. They may conclude that Hayden is expressing multiple voices, experiences, and points of view in this poem.*

◆ Literary Focus

❸ **Theme and Context** Robert Hayden fills this poem with allusions to African American spirituals and folk songs. Ask: How does this line from a spiritual illuminate the poem's theme? *The theme has to do with the risks people take to be free, and this line expresses the sentiment that death is better than slavery.*

Runagate Runagate[1]

Robert Hayden

I

Runs falls rises stumbles on from darkness into darkness
and the darkness thicketed with shapes of terror
and the hunters pursuing and the hounds pursuing
❶ and the night cold and the night long and the river
to cross and the jack-muh-lanterns beckoning beckoning
and blackness ahead and when shall I reach that somewhere
morning and keep on going and never turn back and keep on going

Runagate
Runagate
Runagate

Many thousands rise and go
many thousands crossing over

O mythic North
O star-shaped yonder Bible city[2]

❷ Some go weeping and some rejoicing
some in coffins and some in carriages
some in silks and some in shackles

Rise and go or fare you well

No more auction block for me
no more driver's lash for me

If you see my Pompey, 30 yrs of age,
new breeches, plain stockings, negro shoes;
if you see my Anna, likely young mulatto
branded E on the right cheek, R on the left
catch them if you can and notify subscriber.[3]
Catch them if you can, but it won't be easy.
They'll dart underground when you try to catch them,
plunge into quicksand, whirlpools, mazes,
turn into scorpions when you try to catch them.

❸ And before I'll be a slave
I'll be buried in my grave

North star and bonanza gold
I'm bound for the freedom, freedom-bound
and oh Susyanna don't you cry for me.

---

1. **Runagate** (run´ ə gāt): Runaway; fugitive.
2. **star-shaped yonder Bible city:** Bethlehem, a town in the free state of Pennsylvania.
3. **subscriber:** Slave holder from whom the slaves are fleeing.

Reteach

Students who experience difficulty when asked to interpret the underlying message of a poem may benefit from the use of a graphic organizer. Remind them that the process of interpretation requires thinking carefully about individual words and images in order to discover their underlying meaning. Suggest that students visualize a thread of meaning linking a poem's words and images together, and point out that their interpretive challenge is to state what that thread of meaning may be. On the board, draw the following graphic organizer, depicting a thread linking images from "The Explorer." Have students reproduce the graphic, adding more images from the poem. Finally, ask them to write one sentence on the line labeled "Interpretation," stating the underlying idea that links the images together.

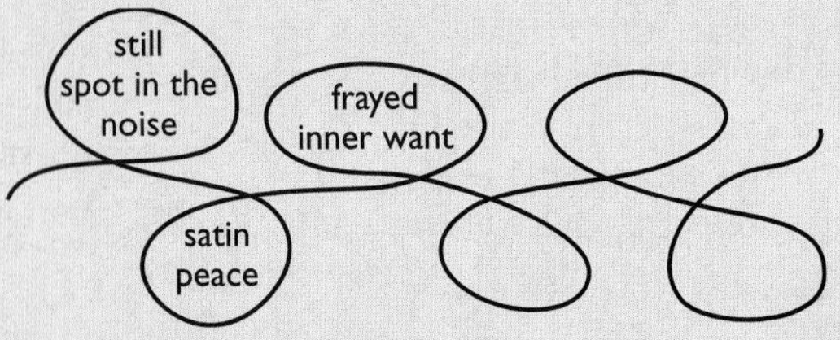

Runagate

Runagate

II

Rises from their anguish and their power,

Harriet Tubman,[4]

woman of earth, whip-scarred,
a summoning, a shining

Mean to be free

(4) And this was the way of it, brethren
brethren,
way we journeyed from Can't to Can.

Moon so bright and no place to hide,
the cry up and the patterollers[5] riding,
hound dogs belling in bladed air.
And fear starts a-murbling, Never make it,
we'll never make it. *Hush that now,*
and she's turned upon us, leveled pistol
glinting in the moonlight:
Dead folks can't jaybird-talk, she says;
You keep on going now or die, she says.

Wanted Harriet Tubman alias The
General
alias Moses Stealer of Slaves

In league with Garrison Alcott
Emerson
Garrett Douglass Thoreau
John Brown[6]

Armed and known to be Dangerous

Wanted Reward Dead or Alive

Tell me, Ezekiel, oh tell me do you see
mailed Jehovah[7] coming to deliver me? (5)
Hoot-owl calling in the ghosted air,
five times calling to the hants[8] in the air.
Shadow of a face in the scary leaves,
shadow of a voice in the talking leaves:

Come ride-a my train

Oh that train, ghost-story train
through swamp and savanna
movering movering,
over trestles of dew, through caves of
the wish
Midnight Special on a sabre track
movering movering,
first stop Mercy and the last
Hallelujah.

Come ride-a my train

Mean mean mean to be free.

---

4. **Harriet Tubman:** (c. 1820–1913) Escaped enslaved African American who led other slaves to safety in the North.
5. **patterollers:** Patrollers, hunting the escaped slaves.
6. **Garrison . . . John Brown:** Prominent abolitionists.
7. **Ezekiel . . . mailed Jehovah** (ē zē´ kē əl, ji hō´ və): Ezekiel was a sixth-century B.C. Hebrew prophet; Jehovah is an Old Testament name for the Judeo-Christian God.
8. **hants:** Haunts; ghosts.

Guide for Responding

◆ Literature and Your Life

Reader's Response How did your response to this poem change from stanza to stanza?

Thematic Focus What are the risks involved in the struggle for freedom?

☑ Check Your Comprehension

1. What is being described in this poem?
2. How does Harriet Tubman prevent frightened fugitives from giving themselves up?

◆ Critical Thinking

INTERPRET

1. How do lines 1–7 convey the feeling of running? **[Analyze]**
2. (a) Do you think that this poem reflects the experiences of a single speaker, or does it reflect a chorus of voices? (b) If there is more than one voice, whose voices are they? Explain your answers and support them with examples from the poem. **[Interpret; Support]**

Beyond the Selection

FURTHER READING

Other Works by Sylvia Plath
Ariel

Other Works by Adrienne Rich
Dark Fields of the Republic: Poems 1991–1995

Other Works by Gwendolyn Brooks
Bronzeville Boys and Girls

Other Works by Robert Hayden
Angle of Ascent: New and Selected Poems

We suggest that you preview these works.

INTERNET

You and your students may find additional information about the poets featured in these selections on the Internet. We suggest the following sites. Please be aware, however, that sites may have changed since this information was published.

For more about Plath, go to **http://www.humboldt.edu/~tegl/syllabus/406/students/2/1783.html**

For more about Richard Hayden, go to **http://ie.windsor.ca/jazz/soledad.html**

We *strongly recommend* that you preview the sites.

◆ Reading Strategy

(4) Interpret Based on their understanding of the poem, have students explain what "Can't" and "Can" represent. *Sample response: Can't represents places where there are no possibilities—places where slavery exists; "Can" represents places where there are possibilities—places where people are free.*

(5) Clarification In this context, *mailed* means "armored" rather than "sent by mail."

Reinforce and Extend

Answers

◆ Literature and Your Life

Reader's Response Accept reasonable responses grounded in the poem.

Thematic Focus The risks involve being captured or killed.

☑ Check Your Comprehension

1. A trip on the Underground Railroad is being described.
2. She threatens to kill them if they try to give themselves up.

◆ Critical Thinking

1. The poet's repetition of the word and with the nonstop litany of actions and imagery create the feeling of running.
2. (a) Sample response: This poem's shifts in viewpoint from stanza to stanza reflects a chorus of voices. (b) The first seven lines voice the words of a slave on the run; the references to obstacles and the determination to "keep on going" are supporting examples. Lines 19–27 give the voice of a slave owner asking people to catch runaway slaves. Evidence of this are the descriptions of the slaves and the pleas to "catch them if you can." Lines 30–32 again represent the voice of a runaway slave. Lines 34–49 give the voice of a runaway slave describing Harriet Tubman. Lines 50–55 present the voice of a slave owner wanting Harriet Tubman captured or killed. The remaining lines of the poem present the voice of a runaway slave's impressions of the underground railroad.

Answers

◆ Reading Strategy

1. (a) The word *swallow* personifies the mirror and also indicates that the mirror takes in anything it sees without question. (b) The word contributes to the message that the mirror reflects the stark reality it takes in.
2. The medical terms describe involuntary phenomena that occur naturally without thinking, the way Hayden hopes freedom will occur for everyone.
3. The runaway slave will do anything to be free, even die.

◆ Grammar and Style

Parallel Structure

1. The woman rewards the mirror's faithful accuracy with tears, tantrums, and depression.
2. High human voices are heard in one room, and the scream of nervous affairs is heard from another room.
3. There is no quiet or peace for the explorer.
4. The runagates escaped from slavery, some in coffins, some in carriages, some in silks, and some in shackles.
5. They saw the shadow of a face in the scary leaves and heard the shadow of a voice in the talking leaves.

Looking at Style

Examples include the repeated use of *when it is* and *not with*. The parallel structures emphasize key ideas.

Grammar Reinforcement

For additional instruction and practice, use the lesson in the **Language Lab CD-ROM** on Strengthening Sentences and the pages on Faulty Parallelism, pp. 49–50, in the *Writer's Solution Grammar Practice Book*.

◆ Literary Focus

1. Suggested response: Knowing the biographical context allows a reader to appreciate the poet's insistence that freedom and liberty have not yet been secured by African Americans.
2. Suggested response: This knowledge helps a reader determine that the poem's setting is not a single-family house, but rather a tenement apartment building filled with various tenants in different rooms. This discovery can lead to a deeper appreciation of the sameness of the lives being led in the building—and of the seriousness of the explorer's conflict.

◆ Build Vocabulary

Using the Latin Roots *-cep-* and *-cept-*

Students' paragraphs should reflect knowledge of the precise meanings of the given words.

Using the Word Bank: Sentence Completions

1. meditate
2. preconceptions
3. din
4. wily

Guide for Responding (continued)

◆ Reading Strategy

INTERPRET

To **interpret** the underlying message of most poems, it's necessary to look closely at individual words and images to find their underlying meaning. Then look for a common thread that ties together the meanings of the individual words and images.

1. (a) In "Mirror," what is the significance of the word *swallow* in line 2? (b) How does this word contribute to the message of the poem?
2. What is the significance of the medical terms Hayden uses in describing a time when freedom is "brain matter, diastole, systole, reflex action"?
3. Based on the subject of the poem, how do you interpret the meaning of lines 26–29 of "Runagate Runagate"?

◆ Grammar and Style

PARALLEL STRUCTURE

Parallel structure is the expression of similar ideas in similar grammatical forms. Be careful to avoid faulty parallelism—the incorrect use of dissimilar grammatical structures to express similar ideas.

Practice On your paper, rewrite the following sentences using correct parallel structure.

1. The woman rewards the mirror's faithful accuracy with tears, tantrums, and getting depressed.
2. High human voices are heard in one room, and from another room comes the scream of nervous affairs.
3. There is no quiet for the explorer and he's not finding any peace.
4. The runagates escaped from slavery, some in coffins, some in carriages, some in silks, and some were wearing shackles.
5. They saw the shadow of a face in the scary leaves and heard the shadow of a voice in the leaves that were talking.

Looking at Style Give at least two examples of parallel structure in the poem "Frederick Douglass." Explain how Hayden's use of parallel structure in each example reinforces key ideas.

◆ Literary Focus

THEME AND CONTEXT

Putting a poem in its historical or biographical **context** can help you reach a deeper understanding of the **theme,** or central message, of the work. For instance, in reading "Runagate Runagate," an understanding of the Underground Railroad can help you appreciate how the images in lines 37–54 contribute to the theme—the willingness of people to make sacrifices and take risks for freedom.

1. How is your understanding of "Frederick Douglass" deepened by knowing that Robert Hayden was an African American whose birth occurred a century after that of the African American abolitionist Frederick Douglass?
2. How is your understanding of the setting and theme of "The Explorer" enhanced by knowing that Gwendolyn Brooks grew up in a poor urban neighborhood?

◆ Build Vocabulary

USING THE LATIN ROOTS *-cep-, -cept-*

The word *preconception*—like other English words such as *deception, inception, conception, concept, reception,* and *intercept*—derives from the Latin root *-cep-* or *-cept-*, meaning "to take, hold, or seize."

Write a paragraph about a football game using the words *concept, deceptive, reception,* and *intercept.* Refer to a dictionary if you are unsure of the meaning of a word.

USING THE WORD BANK: Sentence Completions

Write each sentence on your paper, filling in the blank with the appropriate word from the Word Bank.

1. The guru said she needed to ___?___ on the question I had posed.
2. All the jurors were required to state under oath that they had no ___?___ about the honesty of journalists.
3. The factory workers wore earplugs to protect them from the ___?___ of the machines.
4. The clever raccoon is one of the most ___?___ of animals.

Build Your Portfolio

Idea Bank

Writing

1. Letter Imagine that you are the person described in "The Explorer." In a letter to an advice columnist, outline your dilemma and ask for help in resolving it.

2. Poem or Paragraph Review "Mirror" and then rewrite it from the woman's point of view.

3. Comparison-and-Contrast Essay Write an essay in which you compare and contrast Hayden's poem about Frederick Douglass with the one written by Paul Laurence Dunbar (p. 600).

Speaking, Listening, and Viewing

4. Oral Interpretation "Runagate Runagate" contains vivid imagery, sound devices, and a compelling theme. Deliver a reading of the poem in which you use your voice to reinforce these elements. **[Performing Arts Link]**

5. Debate What does freedom mean to you? Do you believe that everyone in present-day America is free? With a group of classmates, stage a debate on these questions. **[Social Studies Link]**

Researching and Representing

6. Multimedia Presentation Using a mix of media—such as magazine ads, song tracks, and oral commentary—create a presentation showing our culture's emphasis on youth. **[Social Studies Link]**

7. Collage Create an illustrated profile of someone who, like Frederick Douglass, has affected the lives of many people. Use photographs, drawings, and words to capture the nature of the person's influence. **[Art Link]**

Online Activity www.phlit.phschool.com

Guided Writing Lesson

Literary Analysis

The purpose of a literary analysis is to show how various elements of a work of literature combine to convey an overall meaning or effect. Write a literary analysis of one of the poems you have just read.

Writing Skills Focus: Use of Specific Examples

A successful literary analysis contains examples and details from the work that illustrate or support the ideas presented. Review all the elements of the poetry—from form and sound devices, to figurative language, mood, and theme. Consider the following tips as you analyze a poem:

- Jot down examples of any sound devices, such as repetition, rhyme, alliteration, or onomatopoeia.
- Find examples of figurative language—language not meant to be interpreted literally—and other imagery that contribute to the poem's meaning.
- Provide several examples of how the poet's diction—or word choice—affects the tone—or the poet's or speaker's attitude toward the subject.

Prewriting Review the five poems, and decide which will be the subject of your literary analysis. Read the poem you select several times, and take notes on how you would describe its overall effect or meaning. Then gather examples of the poet's use of various elements to achieve this effect.

Drafting Begin your analysis with a general statement about the poem, including the points you plan to cover. Then, in the body, discuss each point in a separate paragraph, supporting each point with examples and direct quotations from the poem.

Revising Strengthen your analysis by adding support for your interpretation and replacing vague language with precise words. Double-check the accuracy of quotations and examples from the poem.

Idea Bank

Customizing for
Performance Levels
Following are suggestions for matching Idea Bank topics with your students' performance levels:
Less Advanced Students: 1, 4
Average Students: 2, 6, 7
More Advanced Students: 3, 5

Customizing for
Learning Modalities
Following are suggestions for matching Idea Bank topics with your students' learning modalities:
Verbal/Linguistic: 4, 5
Musical/Rhythmic: 4
Interpersonal: 5
Logical/Mathematical: 6
Visual/Spatial: 7

Guided Writing Lesson

For more prewriting, elaboration, and revision strategies, see *Prentice Hall Writing and Grammar.*

Writers at Work Videodisc Have students view the videodisc segment of Chapter 7 featuring literary agent Theresa Park speaking about starting a draft. Ask students whether a literary response, like a literary work, should "start with a bang."

Play frames 31772 to 32535

Writing Lab CD-ROM
Have students complete the tutorial on Response to Literature. Follow these steps:

1. To help students gather poetic elements, have them use the Audio-annotated Literary Models of Poetic Elements.
2. Have students use the Evaluation Word Bin while they draft.
3. To focus peer evaluation, students can use the Peer Evaluation Checklist.

✓ ASSESSMENT OPTIONS

Formal Assessment, Selection Test, pp. 314–316, and Assessment Resources Software. The selection test is designed so that it can be easily customized to the performance levels of your students.

Alternative Assessment, p. 72, includes options for less advanced students, more advanced students, and students of various learning modalities.

PORTFOLIO ASSESSMENT
Use the following rubrics in the ***Alternative Assessment*** booklet to assess student writing:
Letter: Summary Rubric, p. 113
Poem or Paragraph: Response to Literature Rubric, p. 125
Comparison-and-Contrast Essay: Comparison/Contrast Rubric, p. 118
Guided Writing Lesson: Literary Analysis/Interpretation Rubric, p. 127

Prepare and Engage

LESSON OBJECTIVES

1. To develop vocabulary and word identification skills
   - Related Words: *Heritage*
2. To use a variety of reading strategies to comprehend poetry
   - Connect Your Experience
   - Reading Strategy: Read in Sentences
3. To increase knowledge of other cultures and to connect common elements across cultures
   - Idea Bank: Oral Report
4. To express and support responses to the text
   - Critical Thinking
   - Idea Bank: Letter
   - Idea Bank: Song Lyrics
   - Idea Bank: Drawing or Painting
5. To analyze literary elements
   - Literary Focus: Lyric Poetry
   - Idea Bank: Comparison and Contrast Essay
6. To read to do research on a self-selected and assigned topics
   - Idea Bank: Illustrated Report
7. To plan, prepare, organize, and present literary interpretations
   - Idea Bank: Legend
8. To use recursive writing processes to write a ghost story
   - Guided Writing Lesson
9. To increase knowledge of the rules of grammar and usage
   - Grammar and Style: Sequence of Tenses

Test Preparation

Writing Skills: Identify Errors (ATE, p. 1059)
The teaching tips and sample test item in this workshop support the instruction and practice in the unit workshop:
Writing Skills: Punctuation, Usage, and Sentence Structure (SE, p. 1143)

Guide for Interpreting

Colleen McElroy *(1935–)*

Like a modern-day explorer, Colleen McElroy enjoys experiencing new places and has traveled widely throughout the United States and abroad. This wandering spirit is reflected in many of her poems, which are inspired by people and scenes she has discovered during her travels. McElroy's love of travel has led her to embark on ancestral searches. In her poetry, she often delves into her rich African American heritage to find connections between experiences of the past, realities of the present, and hope for the future.

After growing up in St. Louis, Missouri, McElroy graduated from Kansas State University and earned a doctorate from the University of Washington, where she is now a professor of English. A prolific writer, she has published several collections of poetry, including *The Mules Done Long Since Gone* (1973), *Music from Home: Selected Poems* (1976), and *Bone Flames* (1987). She has also published numerous short stories, as well as educational books, articles, and film scripts.

Louise Erdrich *(1954–)*

Louise Erdrich, whose Chippewa ancestry has shaped her identity, was born in Little Falls, Minnesota. After receiving degrees from Dartmouth College and Johns Hopkins University, she settled in central New Hampshire and published her first volume of poems, *Jacklight* (1984). Her debut novel, *Love Medicine* (1984), is the story of three Chippewa families living on a North Dakota reservation in the early part of the twentieth century. The novel, planned and written as part of a four-novel series, enjoyed great critical and commercial success. Erdrich's reputation grew with the publication of two sequels to this book, *The Beet Queen* (1986) and *Tracks* (1988). The following year she released a second volume of poetry, *Baptism of Fire*, and in 1991 she co-wrote *The Crown of Columbus*, which offers a Native American perspective of American historical events.

Although she is principally known to the public through her fiction, Erdrich has also been praised for her poetry.

◆ Background for Understanding

SOCIAL STUDIES: ORAL HISTORY

In recent years, many Americans have grown fascinated by history gathered through interviews with individuals—especially older people—who can recall events and people of years past. Oral histories of families (containing stories, jokes, legends, and facts) are especially popular, and oral histories of communities have blossomed as well.

Oral history is as old as the study of history itself. As early as the fifth century B.C., the Greek historians Herodotus and Thucydides were relying upon the oral accounts of survivors of wars to provide a basis for their written histories. In other societies without a written language, oral information passed down from one generation to the next took the place of written historical accounts.

Oral history has been advanced by a growing interest in the lives of ordinary people from all cultures and by the commitment of anthropologists, sociologists, historians, and artists who regard oral history as a serious and vital part of all cultures.

The speaker of "For My Children" is a collector of the oral history of her people; in telling this poem, she sifts through many facts and images of the past and hands down to you those she finds most striking.

Prentice Hall Literature Program Resources

REINFORCE / RETEACH / EXTEND

Selection Support Pages
Build Vocabulary: Related Words: *Heritage*, p. 326
Grammar and Style: Sequence of Tenses, p. 327
Reading Strategy: Read in Sentences, p. 328
Literary Focus: Lyric Poetry, p. 329

Strategies for Diverse Student Needs, Identify Sensory Words, p. 73

Beyond Literature
Cross-Curricular Connection: Geography, p. 73

Formal Assessment Selection Test, p. 317–319; Assessment Resources Software

Alternative Assessment, p. 73

Writing and Language Transparencies
Story Map Organizer, pp. 99–101

Resource Pro CD-ROM
Includes all resource material and customizable lesson plan

Listening to Literature Audiocassettes

◆ Literature and Your Life

Connect Your Experience

The stories we hear from relatives, family friends, and neighbors help shape our awareness of our heritage. "For My Children" vividly captures how a sense of identity is passed on from one generation to the next.

Journal Writing Make a list of images you associate with your ethnic or cultural heritage. Your list could be any combination of names of people, places, kinds of clothing, customs, or rituals.

Thematic Focus: Social Protest

These poems focus on Native American and African cultures. As you read, think about whether each poet is writing to celebrate, to educate, to protest—or to achieve some other purpose.

◆ Build Vocabulary

Related Words: *Heritage*

In "For My Children," McElroy uses the word *heritage,* which means "something handed down from ancestors." It derives from the Latin word *heres,* meaning "heir." This root also forms the basis for words such as *inherit* and *hereditary.*

Word Bank

Before you read, preview this list of words from the selections.

shackles
heritage
effigies

◆ Grammar and Style

Sequence of Tenses

By using the correct **sequence of tenses,** writers make the relationship of events in time clear. Look at these examples from "Bidwell Ghost":

Line 1: Each night she *waits* (present) by the road

Lines 4–5: It *has been* (present perfect) twenty years/since her house *surged* and *burst* (past) in the dark trees

The **present tense** in line 1 indicates habitual action. In lines 4–5, the **present perfect** indicates something that began in the past and continues to the present; the **past-tense** verbs indicate the point in the past at which the present-perfect action began.

◆ Literary Focus

Lyric Poetry

One of the oldest and most popular verse forms, **lyric poetry** is melodic poetry that expresses the observations and feelings of a single speaker. Lyric poems were originally sung to the accompaniment of a stringed instrument called a lyre. Though no longer set to music, lyric poems still tend to be brief and melodic.

Unlike a narrative poem, which focuses on relating a story, a lyric poem focuses on producing a single, unified effect. "Bidwell Ghost," for example, focuses on the speaker's vivid impressions of a fiery tragedy that occurred twenty years before.

◆ Reading Strategy

Read in Sentences

Like prose, many poems are written in sentences. They are also written in lines. However, poets don't always complete a sentence at the end of a line. A sentence may extend for several lines and then end in the middle of a line so that the poet can keep to the chosen rhythm and rhyme scheme. To understand the meaning of a poem, **read in sentences.** Notice the punctuation. Don't make a full stop at the end of a line unless there is a period, comma, colon, semicolon, or dash.

Test Preparation Workshop

Writing Skills:
Identify Errors Many standardized tests require students to identify the type of error in a written passage. Use the following sample test item to give students practice in this skill.

Poets often use details of culture to add depth to their poems. The poem's details communicate its theme.

Read the passage and decide which type of error, if any, appears in the underlined section.

A Spelling error
B Capitalization error
C Punctuation error
D No error

Some students may choose *A*, thinking that *its* should have an apostrophe. Have a volunteer explain why this is not an error. Use this example to show students that some test items will contain no errors. D is the correct choice here.

Interest Grabber

Is one generation's history and experience important to share with the children of future generations? How can one generation help educate another when the world changes so drastically over the years? Ask students to consider these questions and the ideas they would stress if they were to write a letter to the children of the future. What important lessons about life, or what lessons from history would they want to convey? You might pair students to encourage them to write the letters and then have the class compare their ideas with those expressed in McElroy's poem.

Customize for
Less Proficient Readers
Less proficient readers may find the figurative language of the poems confusing, particularly the metaphors in "For My Children." Encourage students to identify difficult images as they read and guide them in questioning and determining the meaning of each one. Use ***Strategies for Diverse Student Needs,*** Identify Sensory Words, page 73, to facilitate comprehension.

Customize for
AP Students
Advanced readers can be challenged to help analyze some of the more difficult images in the poems. Encourage them to explain the meaning of phrases such as "yearly rituals for alabaster beauty," "the wrought-iron rail of first stairs," and "her house surged and burst."

Customize for
English Language Learners
To help students understand the cultural references in "For My Children," encourage them to make a chart listing the references to the speaker's culture. Then have them jot down a brief explanation of each reference, using information from the numbered side notes.

Customize for
Intrapersonal Learners
Encourage students to respond to the poems by writing journal entries. Suggest that the entries might take the form of poems based on their thoughts about their own cultural heritages or on stories that have been passed down to them.

Develop Understanding

One-Minute Insight

The speaker of "For My Children" searches for a heritage to share with her children, an African American heritage that extends "beyond St. Louis" all the way back "to Ashanti mysteries and rituals." As she delves into her store of tales, thoughts, and memories, she invokes many rich possibilities. She also discovers that the present and past are not as separate and discontinuous as they may seem–they mingle joyously in the children she sees.

▶Critical Viewing◀

1 Analyze Possible response: In the painting, a mother dressed in traditional African clothing and surrounded by a stylized African landscape holds and nurtures her child.

◆ Literary Focus

2 Lyric Poetry Have students paraphrase the thoughts that the speaker expresses in this opening stanza. *Possible paraphrase: My children, I will tell you of our history in this land, but I must begin with tales of Africa, because that is where our history began.*

◆ Critical Thinking

3 Assess Ask students to explain why a calabash is an effective metaphor. *Possible response: It is a reference to an African object.*

◆ Reading Strategy

4 Read in Sentences Have three volunteers read this stanza aloud, pausing at the ends of sentences. Guide students to see that a brief third sentence—in reality, a sentence fragment—follows two longer ones. Ask students to assess the effect of this short sentence. *Suggested response: The brevity reinforces the speaker's feeling that her knowledge of her heritage is incomplete.*

Art Transparency Before students read "For My Children," display Art Transparency 11. Discuss the way in which Debbie Lee has linked a diverse group of women and which details communicate a sense of heritage.

For My Children

Colleen McElroy

The Madonna and Child 1990, Momodou Ceesay

◀ Critical Viewing How does this painting reflect the heritage that the speaker seeks to hand on to her children? **[Analyze]** (1)

(2)
I have stored up tales for you, my children
    My favorite children, my only children;
Of shackles and slaves and a bill of rights.
But skin of honey and beauty of ebony begins
    In the land called Bilad as-Sudan,[1]
So I search for a heritage beyond St. Louis.

(3)
My memory floats down a long narrow hall,
    A calabash[2] of history.
Grandpa stood high in Watusi[3] shadows
    In this land of yearly rituals for alabaster beauty;
Where effigies of my ancestors are captured
    In Beatle tunes,
And crowns never touch Bantu[4] heads.

(4)
My past is a slender dancer reflected briefly
    Like a leopard in fingers of fire.
The future of Dahomey[5] is a house of 16 doors,
The totem of the Burundi[6] counts 17 warriors—
    In reverse generations.
While I cling to one stray Seminole.[7]

1. **Bilad as-Sudan** (bē läd′ äs so͞o dan′): "Land of the blacks," an Arabic expression by which Arab geographers referred to the settled African countries north of the southern edge of the Sahara.
2. **calabash** (kal′ ə bash′) *n.*: Dried, hollow shell of a gourd, used as a bowl or a cup.
3. **Watusi** (wä to͞o′ sē): People of east-central Africa.
4. **Bantu** (ban′ to͞o): Bantu-speaking peoples of southern Africa.
5. **Dahomey** (də hō′ mē): Old name for Benin, in west-central Africa.
6. **Burundi** (bo͝o ro͞on′ dē): Country in east-central Africa.
7. **Seminole** (sem′ ə nōl′): Native American people from Florida.

Block Scheduling Strategies

Consider these suggestions to take advantage of extended class time:

- Before students read, have them list images that they associate with their cultural heritages, as outlined in the Journal Writing activity in Literature and Your Life (p. 1059). Let students meet in small groups to discuss their lists.
- Have students listen to the poems on audiocassette. Suggest that students read along with the tape, noting how the readers' intonations correspond to the sentence punctuation within the poems.
- Assign students to work in discussion groups to answer the Critical Thinking questions (pp. 1061 and 1063).
- To help students learn more about the places in Africa that Colleen McElroy refers to in "For My Children," have them complete the ***Beyond Literature*** page on Cross-Curricular Connection: Geography, p. 73. Students may also choose to complete the Oral Report activity described on page 1065.
- Have students complete Literary Focus: Lyric Poetry page in ***Selection Support***, p. 329.

My thoughts grow thin in the urge to travel
  Beyond Grandma's tale
Of why cat fur is for kitten britches;
(5) Past the wrought-iron rail of first stairs
  In baby white shoes,
To Ashanti[8] mysteries and rituals.

Back in the narrow hallway of my childhood.
  I cradled my knees
In limbs as smooth and long as the neck of a bud vase,
I began this ancestral search that you children yield now
  In profile and bust
By common invention, in being and belonging.
(6)
The line of your cheeks recalls Ibo[9] melodies
  As surely as oboe and flute.
The sun dances a honey and cocoa duet on your faces.
I see smiles that mirror schoolboy smiles
  In the land called Bilad as-Sudan;
I see the link between the Mississippi and the Congo.

8. **Ashanti** (ə shän´ tə): People of western Africa.

9. **Ibo** (ē´ bō´): African people of southeastern Nigeria.

◆ Build Vocabulary

shackles (shak´ əlz) *n.*: Any things that restrain a freedom or expression or action

heritage (her´ i tij´) *n.*: Something handed down from one's ancestors or the past

effigies (ef´ i jēz) *n.*: Likenesses

Guide for Responding

◆ Literature and Your Life

Reader's Response What is your reaction to this poem? Does it stir up thoughts about your own ancestors and cultural traditions? Why or why not?

Thematic Focus Could the poet's "ancestral search" be understood as a form of social protest? If so, how?

☑ Check Your Comprehension

1. Identify the cultures in which the speaker searches for evidence of her heritage.
2. Which culture mentioned in this poem is not associated with Africa?
3. To whom does the speaker address this poem?

◆ Critical Thinking

INTERPRET

1. What is the meaning of the word *travel* as the speaker uses it in line 20? **[Interpret]**
2. (a) What impressions of her ancestors does the speaker convey in the second and third stanzas? (b) Which images shape these impressions? **[Analyze]**
3. Describe this poem's theme. **[Interpret]**

APPLY

4. In what specific ways might educating one's children about their heritage affect the way they live today? **[Generalize]**

EXTEND

5. Identify three facts related to the heritage of a culture that is not your own—such as a friend's or neighbor's. **[Social Studies Link]**

Humanities: Art

The Madonna and Child, 1990, by Momodou Ceesay.

In this watercolor, contemporary artist Momodou Ceesay combines traditional elements of African art and European art. The effect is both tender and vibrant.

Ceesay follows in the footsteps of the famous African American artists of an earlier generation. In fact, the influence of Jacob Lawrence's work is evident in this painting. As Lawrence's work does, Ceesay's painting pulses with life and contrast. In addition, it is filled with strong angles, vivid colors, and intense repetition of patterns.

Use these questions to promote discussion:

1. How does the subject of the painting reflect the theme of the poem? *The mother in the painting looks closely at the child, just as the speaker in the poem looks closely at her children to find links between the past and the present.*
2. How does the artist's use of color correspond to the images in the poem? *The painting's vibrant colors appeal to the sense of sight; sensory images in the poem appeal to the sense of sight as well as hearing and touch.*

◆ Critical Thinking

(5) Interpret Have students explain where the speaker's thoughts are "traveling" in this stanza. *Her thoughts are moving backward in time, past her grandmother's stories and her own childhood to an ancestral past rooted in Africa.*

◆ Critical Thinking

(6) Draw Conclusions Ask students what the speaker discovers in her search. Elicit the following: *She discovers her children are the link between the present and the past, between the Mississippi River, which represents the land where they now live, and the Congo River, which represents the land of their heritage.*

Reinforce and Extend

Answers

◆ Literature and Your Life

Reader's Response Encourage students to generalize beyond the specific cultures mentioned in the poem.

Thematic Focus Possible response: If the speaker doesn't feel that the country she lives in acknowledges her heritage, this poem could be considered a form of social protest.

☑ Check Your Comprehension

1. She names the Watusi, Bantu, Seminole, Ashanti, and Ibo cultures.
2. The Seminole are Native Americans based in Florida.
3. She addresses her children.

◆ Critical Thinking

1. In this context, to travel means to know or to connect.
2. (a) Her impressions are of vast and grand families. (b) Images include a house of 16 doors and a 17-warrior totem.
3. Possible response: Sometimes it's easier to see our ancestral heritage in our children than in our parents.
4. Possible responses: Children who are aware of their heritage can appreciate not only their own ancestral culture, but may also be more respectful of or open to cultural diversity in general; they may be able to share their heritage with others; and they may develop more self-confidence.
5. Ask students to share their knowledge.

Develop Understanding

One-Minute Insight Like "For My Children," "Bidwell Ghost" is a multi-layered lyric poem that explores the effect of the past on the present. On one level, the poem presents a legend passed on to the poet and storyteller, who in turn passes it on to the reader. On another, it probes the fate of a figure who is haunted and tormented by a tragic past.

Customize for
Verbal/Linguistic Learners
The word *bidwell* is not in a dictionary. Perhaps it is a surname or the name of a place, or perhaps the poet invented the word by combining the verb *bid* and the adverb *well*. Ask verbal/linguistic learners to read the poem and decide whether the imagery of the poem "bids well."

▶Critical Viewing◀

❶ **Connect** Responses may include: The woman in the painting appears to have a "blackened nest of hair," and the images of cold in the poem are reflected in her posture. Like the ghost, the woman in the painting is alone dressed in a white garment edged in flame-like color that suggests that it has been "embroidered with fire."

◆ Literary Focus

❷ **Lyric Poetry** Invite a volunteer to read these opening lines aloud. Then have students describe the mood that the poet creates. *Students may describe the mood as mysterious, eerie, or chilling.*

◆ Critical Thinking

❸ **Compare** Have students carefully read these lines, along with lines 7–9. Then ask: In what way are the apple trees and the ghost alike? *Just as nothing can kill the trees, which keep coming back each spring, nothing can*

BIDWELL GHOST

Louise Erdrich

Winter, Ozz Franca

◀ **Critical Viewing** What features of this painting are reminiscent of phrases from the poem? Explain. **[Connect]** ❶

Each night she waits by the road
in a thin white dress
embroidered with fire.
❷
It has been twenty years
since her house surged and burst in the dark trees.
Still nobody goes there.

Humanities: Art

Winter, by Ozz Franca.

Like the Bidwell ghost, the figure in *Winter* emanates mystery and seems immersed in her own thoughts.

Ozz Franca is a contemporary painter whose works are exhibited widely throughout the American Southwest. In this painting, Franca uses the form of a woman as the embodiment of a season. The shadowy features give the figure an air of mystery. The red area on the left adds a warmth that could symbolize fire or blood but remains enigmatic.

1. In what ways is the mood of this illustration similar to the mood of the poem? *Students may describe the mood of both works as mysterious, dramatic, or somber.*
2. Does the illustration reflect the mental image you have of the Bidwell ghost? Explain. *Students may say that, for the most part, the illustration matches the image they formed while reading. They may point out however, that the ghost in the poem wears a "thin white dress," while the figure in the illustration appears to be wrapped in a warm blanket.*

The heat charred the branches
of the apple trees,
but nothing can kill that wood.

She will climb into your car
but not say where she is going
and you shouldn't ask.

Nor should you try to comb the blackened nest of hair
or press the agates of tears
back into her eyes.

First the orchard bowed low and complained
of the unpicked fruit,
then the branches cracked apart and fell. 3

The windfalls sweetened to wine
beneath the ruined arms and snow.
Each spring now, in the grass, buds form on the tattered wood.

The child, the child, why is she so persistent
in her need? Is it so terrible 4
to be alone when the cold white blossoms 5
come to life and burn?

Guide for Responding

◆ Literature and Your Life

Reader's Response What question or questions arose in your mind as you read this poem? Were they answered? Explain.

Thematic Focus In your view, how does the speaker feel about the predicament and behavior of the Bidwell ghost?

Cluster Diagram Explore your own associations by creating a cluster diagram with the word *ghost* at the center. Use the diagram as a basis for writing a ghost story.

☑ Check Your Comprehension

1. What occurred twenty years ago?
2. How does the Bidwell ghost respond to people driving along the road?
3. What happens each spring at the site in the orchard where the branches once cracked apart?

◆ Critical Thinking

INTERPRET

1. (a) How would you describe the Bidwell ghost's attitude or behavior? (b) Why might the ghost feel or behave this way? **[Interpret; Speculate]**
2. How does Erdrich suggest nature's resilience? **[Analyze]**
3. (a) Who is "the child" in the final stanza? (b) Why do you think the speaker uses this term? **[Interpret; Speculate]**

APPLY

4. Why do you think people from so many cultures are fascinated with ghosts? **[Speculate]**

COMPARE LITERARY WORKS

5. Both of these poems are retrospective. Does one seem to be more optimistic about the future? Explain. **[Distinguish]**

Beyond the Selection

FURTHER READING

Other Works by Colleen McElroy

Queen of the Ebony Islands
What Madness Brought Me Here: New and Selected Poems, 1968–1988
Driving Under the Cardboard Pines

Other Works by Louise Erdrich

Love Medicine; The Crown of Columbus; The Bingo Palace

We suggest that you preview these works before recommending them to students.

INTERNET

You can find additional information about Colleen McElroy and Louise Erdrich on the Internet. We suggest the following sites. Please be aware, that sites may have changed since this information was published.

To hear a reading of another McElroy poem, go to **http://www.sonarchy.org/archives/florence.html**

For more about Louise Erdrich, go to: **http://www.nativeauthors.com/search/bio/bioerdrich.html**

We *strongly recommend* that you preview sites before you send students to them.

◆ Reading Strategy

4 Read in Sentences Invite a volunteer to read the last stanza aloud, pausing at the ends of sentences. Have students discuss why the poet chose to break the lines where she did. *The line breaks emphasize the words "persistent," "need," "terrible," and "burn," words that are important to the meaning of the poem.*

◆ Critical Thinking

5 Connect Ask students if they think that the last stanza answers the question alluded to in lines 10–12. In what way? *Students may say that this stanza indirectly explains where the ghost is going and why—apparently she is fleeing the loneliness of death and the scene of the tragic fire.*

Reinforce and Extend

Answers

◆ Literature and Your Life

Reader's Response Students may have questions about the identity or history of the woman the poem describes.

Thematic Focus Students may suggest that, although the speaker finds the ghost's behavior odd, she seems to pity her and wants to comfort her.

☑ Check Your Comprehension

1. A house burned down.
2. She watches them silently; in some cases, she climbs into their cars.
3. New life emerges.

◆ Critical Thinking

1. (a) Her behavior is strange, antisocial, and pained. (b) She might behave this way because she has been hurt by the loss of her house.
2. She describes the growth of buds in the charred remains of the house.
3. (a) The child is the ghost. (b) Erdrich uses this word to suggest that the ghost is vulnerable to pain and dependent on others.
4. Possible response: Ghosts are one way in which people deal with the mystery of death.
5. Students will probably suggest that "For My Children" is more optimistic because it looks to future generations.

Answers

◆ Literary Focus

Possible responses:

1. The feelings reflect sadness, mystery, and helplessness.
2. Generations and cultures are connected across time and geography.

◆ Reading Strategy

1. (a) Most stanzas are complete sentences. (b) Possible response: The punctuation clarifies the separate images the writer conveys.
2. By breaking this stanza into sentences, most students will see that first sentence compares a face with music and the second sentence personifies the sun.

◆ Build Vocabulary

Using Related Words: *Heritage*

1. hereditary
2. inheritance
3. heritage
4. inherit

Using the Word Bank

1. a 2. c 3. b

◆ Grammar and Style

1. *stood:* past. The house existed in the past, whereas the waiting takes place in the present.
2. *charred:* past. The *charring* was completed in the past; the rest of the sentence's action is in the present.
3. *come, burn:* present. All the action of the sentence is in the present tense.
4. *has wondered:* present-perfect. The action of this sentence started in the past and continues to the present.

Grammar Reinforcement

For additional instruction and practice, use the pages on Verb Tenses (pp. 54–58), or the page on the correct use of tenses, (p. 58) in the *Writer's Solution Grammar Practice Book.*

Guide for Responding *(continued)*

◆ Literary Focus

Lyric Poetry

Lyric poetry is melodic verse that conveys the personal observations and feelings of a single speaker and produces a single, unified effect. "For My Children" is an example of a lyric poem—a half-dozen highly musical stanzas expressing a woman's thoughts and emotions.

1. How would you describe the "observations and feelings" the speaker expresses in "Bidwell Ghost"?
2. What philosophy of life does "For My Children" convey?

◆ Reading Strategy

Read in Sentences

Part of the nature of poetry is its unique form. Poets write in lines and stanzas, often breaking sentences in the process. However, sentences express complete thoughts and are critical to the poet's ability to communicate.

Reading a poem in sentences rather than in poetic lines can help you understand and appreciate the writer's ideas. For example, reading the first stanza of "For My Children" in sentences allows you to focus on the contrast between the tales of America ("shackles and slaves and a bill of rights") and those of Africa ("Skin of honey and beauty of ebony begins/In the land called Bilad as-Sudan"). Once you've become familiar with the ideas in "For My Children," you may want to read it again, pausing at line breaks to appreciate the poem's rhythms.

1. (a) By focusing on Louise Erdrich's use of punctuation, what do you notice about every stanza in "Bidwell Ghost"? (b) Why do you think Erdrich chose to punctuate this poem as she did?
2. Identify the figurative language in the last stanza of "For My Children," and explain how reading the stanza in sentences helped you to understand and appreciate this figurative language.

◆ Build Vocabulary

Using Related Words: *Heritage*

Several English words—such as *hereditary, inherit,* and *inheritance*—are related to the word *heritage* ("something handed down from one's ancestors or the past"). Use these four related words to complete the four sentences below.

1. His slender physique has nothing to do with lack of exercise; it's ___?___.
2. The siblings' ___?___ included their uncle's prized collection of hand tools.
3. My twin cousins are very proud of their Scandinavian ___?___.
4. Most children ___?___ some physical and emotional characteristics from both parents.

Using the Word Bank: Synonyms

On your paper, write the letter of the best synonym for each of the first words.

1. effigies: (a) representations, (b) toys, (c) machines
2. shackles: (a) imprisoned, (b) worries, (c) chains
3. heritage: (a) folk art, (b) traditions, (c) society

◆ Grammar and Style

Sequence of Tenses

Using the correct **sequence of verb tenses** allows you to show the relationship of events in time.

The **present tense** shows action that exists at the present time.

The **present-perfect tense** indicates something that began in the past and continues to the present.

The **past tense** shows action that began and ended at a given time in the past.

Practice For each of the following sentences, identify the tense of the italicized verb. Then, for each sentence, explain the relationship of events in time that the verbs express.

1. Each night she *waits* by the road where her house once stood.
2. The heat *charred* the branches of the apple trees, but nothing can kill that wood.
3. Is it so terrible to be alone when the cold white blossoms *come* to life and *burn?*
4. She *has wondered* about this all her life.

Reteach

For students who have difficulty grasping the definition of lyric poetry, provide a graphic demonstration. Draw this visual on the board. Challenge students to fill in the circles around the edge with images and observations from the poem "For My Children." Then help them synthesize those images into a statement that reflects the single effect of the poem.

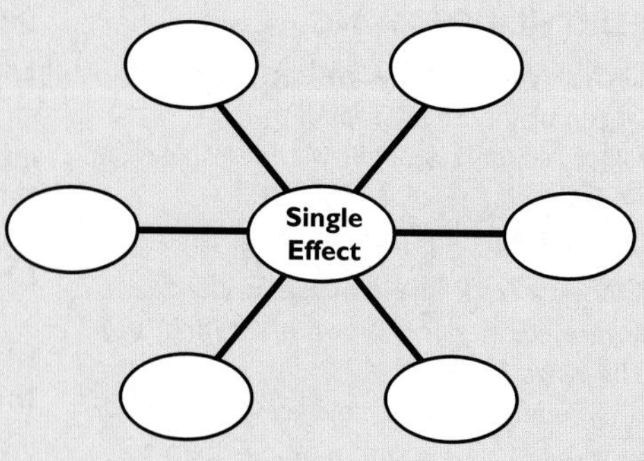

Build Your Portfolio

Idea Bank

Writing

1. Letter As yourself or as a fictional character, write a letter to the children of the future in which you convey something important you have learned about your heritage.

2. Song Lyrics Rewrite one of these poems in the form of popular song lyrics. If you like, use details of your own cultural heritage.

3. Comparison-and-Contrast Essay Write a short essay comparing and contrasting the two lyric poems in this section. Consider such literary elements as figurative language, rhythm, and imagery.

Speaking, Listening, and Viewing

4. Legend Share a tale or legend—one you remember from childhood or one you create—with your classmates. Use pacing and gestures to heighten the story's suspense or interest level. **[Performing Arts Link]**

5. Oral Report Research and deliver a short oral presentation about the visual arts of the African cultures noted in "For My Children"—Watusi, Bantu, Dahomey, Burundi, Ashanti, or Ibo. **[Social Studies Link]**

Researching and Representing

6. Drawing or Painting Choose a single stanza from "Bidwell Ghost" to use as the subject of a drawing or painting. **[Art Link]**

7. Illustrated Report Erdrich uses an image featuring embroidery, an ancient art involving stitching patterns or designs on cloth. Prepare an illustrated research report on distinctive embroideries of various Native American tribes. **[Social Studies Link; Art Link]**

Online Activity www.phlit.phschool.com

Guided Writing Lesson

Ghost Story

Stories involving ghosts are common in Gothic fiction, folk literature, legends, and oral histories. Almost all ghost stories contain an element of mystery and eeriness; some also feature a noticeable air of humor or melancholy. Write an original ghost story based on a story you heard as a child or a new idea you develop in your imagination.

Writing Skills Focus: Sensory Details

In works of imaginative writing, it is important to create a vivid impression using **sensory details**—those that tell how something looks, smells, feels, sounds, and tastes. In a single stanza of "Bidwell Ghost," for example, Louise Erdrich uses details involving touch, smell, sight, and taste:

Model From the Selection

The heat charred the branches / of the apple trees, / but nothing can kill that wood.

Prewriting Consider the story line you will develop. Once you know the *who, what, where, when,* and *how,* begin to plan the eerie quality of the story. Use a chart like this one to categorize the sensory details.

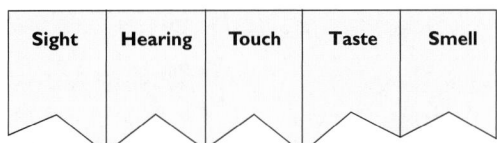

Sight	Hearing	Touch	Taste	Smell

Drafting Try to grab your audience's interest from the start. You can do this with a vivid description of the setting or by starting off with a description of an eerie event. As you develop your story, focus on building suspense.

Revising Read your story several times—both silently and aloud. How can you make it more suspenseful? What, if any, details should you add or delete? How can you sharpen your language?

Idea Bank

Customizing for ***Performance Levels***

Following are suggestions for matching Idea Bank topics with your students' performance levels:
Less Advanced Students: 1, 4
Average Students: 2, 6, 7
More Advanced Students: 3, 5

Customizing for ***Learning Modalities***

Following are suggestions for matching Idea Bank topics with your students' learning modalities:
Bodily/Kinesthetic: 4
Verbal/Linguistic: 4, 5
Logical/Mathematical: 5, 7
Visual/Spatial: 6, 7

Guided Writing Lesson

For more instruction on prewriting, elaboration, and revision, see *Prentice Hall Writing and Grammar.*

Writing and Language Transparencies Use the Story Map Organizer (pp. 99–101) to help students plan their ghost stories.

Writers at Work Videodisc
Have students view the videodisc segment on Narration (Ch. 2) featuring N. Scott Momaday to see how Momaday selects descriptive words. Have students discuss why he tells writers to use simple language.

Play frames 11291 to 21755

Writing Lab CD-ROM
Have students complete the tutorial on Narration. Follow these steps:

1. Students can use the Story Line Diagram and Sensory Word Bins to help them organize their plots and create vivid sensory details.
2. Have students draft on the computer.
3. Suggest that students use the Vague Adjectives Checker to sharpen sensory images as they revise.

ASSESSMENT OPTIONS

Formal Assessment, Selection Test, pp. 317–319, and Assessment Resources Software. The selection test is designed so that it can be easily customized to the performance levels of your students.

Alternative Assessment, p. 73, includes options for less advanced students, more advanced students, musical/rhythmic learners, verbal/linguistic learners, and visual/spatial learners.

PORTFOLIO ASSESSMENT
Use the following rubrics in ***Alternative Assessment*** to assess student writing:
Letter: Expression Rubric, p. 109
Song Lyrics: Response to Literature Rubric, p. 125
Comparison-and-Contrast Essay: Comparison/Contrast Rubric, p. 118
Guided Writing Lesson: Fictional Narrative Rubric, p. 110

LESSON OBJECTIVES

1. **To develop vocabulary and word identification skills**
   - Greek Suffixes: *-itis*
   - Using the Word Bank: Sentence Completions
   - Extending Word Study: Connotations
2. **To use a variety of reading strategies to comprehend a short story**
   - Connect Your Experience
   - Reading Strategy: Judge the Characters' Actions
3. **To increase knowledge of other cultures and to connect common elements across cultures**
   - Connecting Themes Across Cultures (ATE)
4. **To express and support responses to the text**
   - Critical Thinking
   - Idea Bank: Final Letter
   - Idea Bank: Eulogy
   - Idea Bank: Critical Essay
   - Idea Bank: Debate
   - Idea Bank: Costume Proposal
5. **To analyze literary elements**
   - Literary Focus: Static and Dynamic Characters
6. **To read to do research on self-selected and assigned topics**
   - Idea Bank: Grief Hotline
7. **To plan, prepare, organize, and present literary interpretations**
   - Idea Bank: Family Conference
   - Speaking, Listening, and Viewing Mini-Lesson (ATE)
8. **To use recursive writing processes to write an advice column**
   - Guided Writing Lesson
9. **To increase knowledge of the rules of grammar and usage**
   - Grammar and Style: Commonly Confused Words: *Affect* and *Effect*

Test Preparation

Writing Skills: Grammar and Usage (ATE, p. 1067)
The teaching tips and sample test item in this workshop support the instruction and practice in the unit workshop:

Writing Skills: Punctuation, Usage, and Sentence Structure (SE, p. 1143)

Guide for Interpreting

E. L. Doctorow *(1931–)*

The literary work of E(dgar) L(awrence) Doctorow defies strict categorization. It is distinguished by a unique and authoritative blend of fact and fiction—sometimes called "faction," a term first coined around Doctorow's work.

Doctorow's work is known for pushing the limits of style, form, and content.

Doctorow has always been aware of the political unrest, social rootlessness, and constant motion of his time; his literary experimentation seems both to respond to and reflect an era brimming with contradiction and irony.

Rising to a Challenge As a reader for Columbia Pictures, Doctorow was dismayed at the inferior scripts he read. Certain he could make up better stories, Doctorow started writing himself. In his first novel, *Welcome to Hard Times* (1960), he focused on stretching the boundaries of western fiction by addressing serious themes not usually treated in this type of literature. He continued writing, producing novels, short stories, essays, plays, and screen adaptations that exhibit the same type of inventiveness that he showed in his first novel.

Mixing Fact and Fiction Doctorow frequently incorporates fact and fiction in his writing to create powerful dramatic effects. *The Book of Daniel* (1971) weaves factual details about Ethel and Julius Rosenberg—Communists found guilty of treason and sentenced to die—into a story centering on the lives of fictional children parted from their parents amidst political scandal. Doctorow's 1975 novel, *Ragtime,* also blends fictional characters with the invented and real experiences of historical figures such as Harry Houdini and J. P. Morgan. Doctorow has won two National Book Critic Circle Awards, one for *Ragtime* and another for the 1990 novel, *Billy Bathgate*. Four of his novels have been made into major motion pictures. "The Writer in the Family" is a traditionally structured short story written from the point of view of a young writer who finds himself in a strange dilemma.

◆ Background for Understanding

CULTURE: SHI'VA

Most cultures have unique mourning rituals. For Jews, that ritual is called shi'va, meaning "seven" in Hebrew. When a parent, child, sibling, or spouse dies, the family observes shi'va for seven days.

During shi'va, mourners follow certain traditional rules. They remain at home and conduct no ordinary business. Comfortable furniture is exchanged for seating on low stools or the floor. Men and women neither shave nor cut their hair. Mourners do not wear leather footwear or don new clothes. Traditionally, friends and fellow mourners join the family in their home to express sympathy and recite prayers.

Many Jews in contemporary society observe these traditions in modified ways—perhaps shortening the length of the traditional shi'va or choosing only a few rituals to follow.

In "The Writer in the Family," the shi'va's ritual acknowledgment of death contrasts sharply with the pretense at the story's center.

Prentice Hall Literature Program Resources

REINFORCE / RETEACH / EXTEND

Selection Support Pages
Build Vocabulary: Greek Suffixes: *-itis,* p. 330
Grammar and Style: Commonly Confused Words: *Affect* and *Effect,* p. 331
Reading Strategy: Judge the Characters' Actions, p. 332
Literary Focus: Static and Dynamic Characters, p. 333

Strategies for Diverse Student Needs, p. 74

Beyond Literature
Cultural Connection: Rituals of Mourning, p. 74

Formal Assessment Selection Test, pp. 320–322; Assessment Resources Software

Alternative Assessment, p. 74

Writing and Language Transparencies
Problem/Solution Organizer, pp. 79–81

Resource Pro CD-ROM

Listening to Literature Audiocassettes

Literature CD-ROM *The History of American Literature:* Part 2, Disk 2, Feature 9

The Writer in the Family

◆ *Literature and Your Life*

CONNECT YOUR EXPERIENCE

One of the most difficult aspects of life is coping with the loss of loved ones. People cope with such a loss in a variety of ways. In this story, the characters deal with the death of a loved one in a complicated way that will probably surprise you.

Journal Writing Jot down your thoughts about how people should deal with the loss of a loved one. What types of behavior might you consider unacceptable in such a situation?

THEMATIC FOCUS: SOCIAL PROTEST

Social protest in the twentieth century has involved the questioning of a wide range of rules and codes of conduct. As you read, ask yourself whether there are some rules that should never be bent or questioned.

◆ Build Vocabulary

GREEK SUFFIXES: *-itis*

A character in this story is said to have *bronchitis*. You can piece together a meaning for this word by learning that the Greek suffix *-itis* means "disease" or "inflammation." *Bronchitis* means "inflammation of the bronchial tubes."

WORD BANK

Before you read, preview this list of words from the story.

bronchitis
cronies
barometer
anthology

◆ Grammar and Style

COMMONLY CONFUSED WORDS: *AFFECT* AND *EFFECT*

Commonly confused words are those that look or sound alike but have different meanings. In this story, for example, Doctorow uses the word *effect* in its most frequently used form—as a noun to describe the result of an action. **Affect**, which is often confused with **effect**, is a verb meaning "to influence."

My aunt called some days later and told me it was when she read this letter aloud to the old lady that the full *effect* of Jack's death came over her.

◆ Literary Focus

STATIC AND DYNAMIC CHARACTERS

Doctorow uses static and dynamic characters to create a heightened sense of contrast in his story. A **static character** is one whose attitudes and behavior remain essentially stable throughout a literary work. **Dynamic characters**, on the other hand, experience a shift or change in attitude and behavior during the course of the work. As you read "The Writer in the Family," identify each of the main characters as either static or dynamic. Consider how the contrasts between these character types add to the story's impact.

◆ Reading Strategy

JUDGE THE CHARACTERS' ACTIONS

The characters in this story bend the rules relating to a pivotal event in their lives—the death of a family member. Would you behave the same way faced with similar circumstances? When you **judge the characters' actions**, you evaluate their behavior against moral or other criteria. As you read, consider the actions of each character in light of the circumstances Doctorow describes. Are their actions morally defensible? Against what standards are you judging?

Test Preparation Workshop

Writing Skills:
Grammar and Usage Many standardized tests require students to recognize and correct errors in grammar and usage. Use the following sample item to give students practice in this skill.

E. L. Doctorow has written numerous novels. Four of them are made into major motion pictures.

Choose the best way to rewrite the underlined section of the passage. If the underlined section needs no change, choose "Correct as is."

A have been made
B had been made
C could be made
D Correct as is.

The best way to rewrite the underlined section is to rewrite it for consistent verb tense. The correct answer is *A*.

Interest Grabber Ask students to picture this situation: A young man whose father has recently died is asked by a family member to write a letter in his father's name, making it seem as if the father is still alive. Then ask: What might the purpose of such a letter be? Will the young man refuse or comply? You might take an informal classroom poll to ask students what they would do in a similar situation. After students have made their guesses and predictions, invite them to begin reading to learn the answers to these questions.

Connecting Themes Across Cultures

Remind students that rules and codes of conduct vary from culture to culture. For example, while individual liberties are highly valued in the United States, other cultures place a greater priority on group survival and solidarity. Ask students to discuss the implications of conflicting codes of social behavior in today's "global village."

Customize for
Less Proficient Readers
To help students better understand the story's characters, have them list the following family members and take notes on what they learn about each character: Jonathan, mother, Aunt Frances, Harold, and father.

Customize for
AP Students
Explain that there are a number of conflicts, both internal and external, in the story. Have students make a list of the conflicts and consider how these conflicts affect the development (or lack of development) of the characters.

Customize for
Intrapersonal Learners
Have students reflect on the narrator's perceptions, motives, and actions. Encourage them to write a journal entry in which they both speculate about why Jonathan acts as he does and assess the ethics of his actions.

Develop Understanding

One-Minute Insight This story raises the thorny question: Which is more important, loyalty or integrity? The relatives of a young man named Jonathan come up with an unusual scheme for maintaining the status quo within the family: They ask Jonathan to write a series of letters in the voice of his recently deceased father. The letters relieve the relatives of the difficult task of telling Jonathan's grandmother that her son has died. Jonathan goes along with the scheme until he realizes that the high value that his family places on the status quo is a burden on him—just as it was a burden on his late father. By choosing integrity over loyalty and refusing to remain "the writer in the family," Jonathan makes a declaration of independence, both on his own and on his father's behalf.

◆ Reading Strategy

❶ Judge the Characters' Actions Doctorow sets up the conflict immediately. Ask: Do you approve of the aunts' motives in not informing their mother about the death? Why or why not? *Some students may say that they approve because the aunts' motive—to spare their mother a shock—is a good one; others will likely say that they disapprove, because one dishonest act often sets a whole chain of dishonest acts in motion.*

◆ Critical Thinking

❷ Support Ask students if they think that the narrator's mother is justified in her claim. What evidence from the text can they offer in support of their answers? *Possible response: The mother's claim is justified; the fact that the aunts made up the story about Arizona without consulting her shows that they treat her as an outsider.*

◆ Critical Thinking

❸ Analyze Ask: What type of person would go to such lengths to conceal a death? *Based on her words and actions, students may describe Aunt Frances as domineering, deceitful, or manipulative.*

The Writer in the Family

E. L. Doctorow

❶ In 1955 my father died with his ancient mother still alive in a nursing home. The old lady was ninety and hadn't even known he was ill. Thinking the shock might kill her, my aunts told her that he had moved to Arizona for his <u>bronchitis</u>. To the immigrant generation of my grandmother, Arizona was the American equivalent of the Alps, it was where you went for your health. More accurately, it was where you went if you had the money. Since my father had failed in all the business enterprises of his life, this was the aspect of the news my grandmother dwelled on, that he had finally had some success. And so it came about that as we mourned him at home in our stocking feet,[1] my grandmother was bragging to her <u>cronies</u> about her son's new life in the dry air of the desert.

My aunts had decided on their course of action without consulting us. It meant neither my mother nor my brother nor I could visit Grandma because we were supposed to have moved west too, a family, after all. My brother Harold and I didn't mind—it was always a nightmare at the old people's home, where they all sat around staring at us while we tried to make conversation with Grandma. She looked terrible, had numbers of ailments, and her mind wandered. Not seeing her was no disappointment either for my mother, who had never gotten along with the old woman and did not visit when she could have. But what was disturbing was that my aunts had acted in the manner of that side of the family of making government on everyone's behalf, the true citizens by blood and the lesser citizens by marriage. It was exactly this attitude that had tormented my mother all her married life. She claimed Jack's family had never accepted her. She had battled them for twenty-five years as an outsider. ❷

A few weeks after the end of our ritual mourning my Aunt Frances phoned us from her home in Larchmont. Aunt Frances was the wealthier of my father's sisters. Her husband was a lawyer, and both her sons were at Amherst.[2] She had called to say that Grandma was asking why she didn't hear from Jack. I had answered the phone. "You're the writer in the family," my aunt said. "Your father had so much faith in you. Would you mind making up something? Send it to me and I'll read it to her. She won't know the difference." ❸

That evening, at the kitchen table, I pushed my homework aside and composed a letter. I tried to imagine my father's response to his new life. He had never been west. He had never traveled anywhere. In his generation the great journey was from the working class to the professional class. He hadn't managed that either. But he loved New York, where he had been born and lived all his life, and he was always discovering new things about it. He especially loved the old parts of the city below Canal Street, where he would find ships' chandlers or firms that wholesaled in spices and teas. He was a salesman for an appliance jobber[3] with accounts all over the city. He liked to bring home rare cheeses or exotic foreign vegetables that were sold only in certain neighborhoods. Once he brought home a <u>barometer</u>, another

---

1. **as we mourned . . . in our stocking feet:** Refers to the Jewish custom of not wearing leather footwear during the traditional mourning period known as shi'va.

2. **Amherst:** Amherst College in Amherst, Massachusetts.
3. **jobber:** Industry jargon for a person who buys goods in quantity from manufacturers and sells them to dealers; a wholesaler or middleman.

Block Scheduling Strategies

Consider these suggestions to take advantage of extended class time:

- Have students complete the Journal Writing activity in Literature and Your Life. (p. 1067).
- Review the Grammar and Style lesson (p. 1067) on the commonly confused words *affect* and *effect*. After students have completed the follow-up exercise on page 1076, have partners create and exchange quizzes to test one another on the correct use of *affect* and *effect*.
- Use the Interest Grabber (p. 1067) to introduce the story's central issue. After students have read the story, invite partners to engage in the Debate activity in the Idea Bank (p. 1077).
- Have students work in pairs to complete the Guided Writing Lesson (p. 1077). One student can take the role of Jonathan and write a letter explaining his dilemma. Acting as the advice columnist, the partner can answer the letter.
- Have students complete Reading Strategy: Judge the Characters' Actions in ***Selection Support***, page 332.

4 ▶ **Critical Viewing** How might the boy in this picture use the familiar surroundings to help him concoct a believable letter? **[Connect]**

Laurence Typing, 1952, Fairfield Porter, Oil on canvas 40" × 30 1/8", The Parrish Art Museum, Southampton, New York, Gift of the Estate of Fairfield Porter

time an antique ship's telescope in a wooden case with a brass snap.

"Dear Mama," I wrote. "Arizona is beautiful. The sun shines all day and the air is warm and I feel better then I have in years. The desert is not as barren as you would expect, but filled with wildflowers and cactus plants and peculiar crooked trees that look like men holding their arms out. You can see great distances in whatever direction you turn and to the west is a range of mountains maybe fifty miles from here, but in the morning with the sun on them you can see the snow on their crests."

My aunt called some days later and told me it was when she read this letter aloud to the old lady that the full
5 effect of Jack's death came over her. She had to excuse herself and went out in the parking lot to cry. "I wept so," she said. "I felt such terrible longing for him. You're so right, he loved to go places, he loved life, he loved everything."

We began trying to organize our lives. My father had borrowed money against his
6 insurance and there was very little left. Some commissions were still due but it didn't look as if his firm would honor them. There was

◆ Build Vocabulary

bronchitis (bräŋ kīt´ is) *n.*: Inflammation of the lining of the major air passageways of the lungs

cronies (krō´ nēz) *n.*: Close companions

barometer (bə räm´ ət ər) *n.*: Instrument for measuring atmospheric pressure; used in forecasting weather or finding height above sea level

▶Critical Viewing◀

❹ **Connect** Students should note that in his letter, the narrator did an excellent job of imagining how his father would respond to and describe Arizona. They may therefore conclude that he would use the familiar surroundings in the room as the basis for comparisons in his letter.

◆ Literary Focus

❺ **Static and Dynamic Characters** Have students summarize the narrator's role so far in the letter-writing scheme. Also have them comment on what his action up to this point reveals about his personality traits. *Students should note that the narrator went along with his aunt's rather unusual request. They may say that he is imaginative but also timid and obedient.*

◆ Literature and Your Life

❻ In the wake of his father's death, Jonathan says, "We began trying to organize our lives." Ask students to identify the moments in life when people might feel the need to restore organization. *Possible response: When people have a great deal of upheaval in their lives, such as a divorce, a move, the loss of a job, or a death, they will often respond by organizing everything around them; doing so helps them to feel that they have some measure of control over their lives.*

Extending Word Study

Connotations The narrator refers to his grandmother's friends as her "cronies." Have students look up the word in a thesaurus to find synonyms for it. Then, have students work in groups to create charts of synonyms for "companions", dividing the synonyms into words that have positive, negative, and neutral connotations. Allow time for students to share and discuss their charts.

Humanities: Art

Laurence Typing, 1952, by Fairfield Porter.

This piece of art shows a young man typing in a homey setting. Both his surroundings and the typewriter suggest the 1950's—the time in which the story is set.

American artist Fairfield Porter (1907–1975) was born in Winnetka, Illinois. The subjects of his paintings are those he knows best—himself, his family, his friends, and the landscapes that surrounded him. The young man in the picture is the artist's son Laurence, who was born in 1936.

Use these questions for discussion:

1. What do the details in the picture tell you about the young man? *He looks as if he is thinking hard about what he is typing. The books on the desk suggest that he is interested in intellectual pursuits.*
2. What traits do you think the young man in the painting might have in common with the story's narrator? *Responses may include: seriousness, introspection, a good imagination, a gift for writing.*

1 Clarification The Grand Concourse is a wide, residential boulevard in the Bronx, a borough of New York City. Many middle-class Jewish families lived on the Grand Concourse in the 1950's.

◆ Reading Strategy

2 Judge the Characters' Actions Point out that the mother wants the boys to have their father's clothes. Ask: Are the boys wrong to refuse? What standards did you use in arriving at your answer? *Students may say that the boys are not wrong to refuse, because wearing their father's clothes would remind them of him and therefore upset them. In evaluating the boys' behavior, students may say that they used their knowledge of human emotions and behavior.*

◆ Critical Thinking

3 Analyze In this conversation, Aunt Frances tells Jonathan's mother that it's not so terrible to make things easier for the grandmother. Ask: Why does Jonathan's mother disagree? *Jonathan's mother disagrees because Aunt Frances's story is causing Jonathan and his family to live a lie. They are unable to put the past behind them, accept the death, and move on with their lives as long as they are a part of Aunt Frances's scheme.*

◆ Critical Thinking

4 Infer Why is the second letter harder for Jonathan to write than the first? *Possible responses: He knows it upsets his mother; he begins to see that it is deceitful.*

a couple of thousand dollars in a savings bank that had to be maintained there until the estate was settled. The lawyer involved was Aunt Frances' husband and he was very proper. "The estate!" my mother muttered, gesturing as if to pull out her hair. "The estate!" She applied for a job part-time in the admissions office of the hospital where my father's terminal illness had been diagnosed, and where he had spent some months until they had sent him home to die. She knew a lot of the doctors and staff and she had learned "from bitter experience," as she told them, about the hospital routine. She was hired.

I hated that hospital, it was dark and grim and full of tortured people. I thought it was masochistic[4] of my mother to seek out a job there, but did not tell her so.

We lived in an apartment on the corner of
1 175th Street and the Grand Concourse, one flight up. Three rooms. I shared the bedroom with my brother. It was jammed with furniture because when my father had required a hospital bed in the last weeks of his illness we had moved some of the living-room pieces into the bedroom and made over the living room for him. We had to navigate bookcases, beds, a gateleg table, bureaus, a record player and radio console, stacks of 78 albums, my brother's trombone and music stand, and so on. My mother continued to sleep on the convertible sofa in the living room that had been their bed before his illness. The two rooms were connected by a narrow hall made even narrower by bookcases along the wall. Off the hall were a small kitchen and dinette and a bathroom. There were lots of appliances in the kitchen—broiler, toaster, pressure cooker, counter-top dishwasher, blender—that my father had gotten through his job, at cost. A treasured phrase in our house: *at cost.* But most of these fixtures went unused because my mother did not care for them. Chromium devices with timers or gauges that required the reading of elaborate instructions were not for her. They were in part responsible for the awful clutter of our lives and now she wanted to get rid of them. "We're being buried," she said. "Who needs them!"

So we agreed to throw out or sell anything inessential. While I found boxes for the appliances and my brother tied the boxes with twine, my mother opened my father's closet and took out his clothes. He had several suits because as a salesman he needed to look his best. My mother wanted us to try on his suits to see which of them could be altered and used. My brother refused to try them on. I tried on one jacket which was too large for me. The lining inside the sleeves chilled my arms and the vaguest scent of my father's being came to me.

"This is way too big," I said.

"Don't worry," my mother said. "I had it cleaned. Would I let you wear it if I hadn't?" 2

It was the evening, the end of winter, and snow was coming down on the windowsill and melting as it settled. The ceiling bulb glared on a pile of my father's suits and trousers on hangers flung across the bed in the shape of a dead man. We refused to try on anything more, and my mother began to cry.

"What are you crying for?" my brother shouted. "You wanted to get rid of things, didn't you?"

A few weeks later my aunt phoned again and said she thought it would be necessary to have another letter from Jack. Grandma had fallen out of her chair and bruised herself and was very depressed.

"How long does this go on?" my mother said.

"It's not so terrible," my aunt said, "for the little time left to make things easier for her."

My mother slammed down the phone. "He can't even die when he wants to!" she cried. 3 "Even death comes second to Mama! What are they afraid of, the shock will kill her? Nothing can kill her. She's indestructible! A stake through the heart couldn't kill her!"

When I sat down in the kitchen to write the letter I found it more difficult than the first one. "Don't watch me," I said to my brother. "It's 4 hard enough."

"You don't have to do something just because someone wants you to," Harold said. He was two years older than me and had started at City College; but when my father became ill he had switched to night school and gotten a job in a record store.

"Dear Mama," I wrote. "I hope you're feeling well. We're all fit as a fiddle. The life here is 5

4. **masochistic** (mas´ ə kis´ tik) *adj.*: Deriving pleasure from physical or psychological pain.

Speaking, Listening, and Viewing Mini-Lesson

Family Conference

This mini-lesson supports the Speaking, Listening, and Viewing activity in the Idea Bank on p. 1077.

Introduce the Concept Explain that a family conference is a meeting in which members of a family get together to plan, discuss, and decide upon a course of action that will affect one or more family members.

Develop Background Before students begin their role playing, discuss the issues involved. Lead students to consider these points:

- Those students playing the aunts need to come up with reasons for the deception—for example, it is in the grandmother's best interest.
- Those students playing Ruth, Harold, and Jonathan have to come up with reasons for not supporting the deception—for example, it is disrespectful to Jack's memory.
- By speaking and behaving the way the family members would, students on both sides of the discussion should remain "in character."

Apply the Information Have students plan and perform their conferences. Remind them that Aunt Frances is a controlling personality and that Ruth feels hostility toward her.

Assess the Outcome Ask students to evaluate the conferences based on how persuasive the reasons were and how well each student stayed in character.

good and the people are very friendly and informal. Nobody wears suits and ties here. Just a pair of slacks and a short-sleeved shirt. Perhaps a sweater in the evening. I have bought
5 into a very successful radio and record business and I'm doing very well. You remember Jack's Electric, my old place on Forty-third Street? Well, now it's Jack's Arizona Electric and we have a line of television sets as well."

I sent that letter off to my Aunt Frances, and as we all knew she would, she phoned soon after. My brother held his hand over the mouthpiece. "It's Frances with her latest review," he said.

"Jonathan? You're a very talented young
6 man. I just wanted to tell you what a blessing your letter was. Her whole face lit up when I read the part about Jack's store. That would be an excellent way to continue."

> **◆ Reading Strategy**
> 7 Do you agree with the narrator's statement that the letter writing is dishonest? Why or why not?

"Well, I hope I don't have to do this anymore, Aunt Frances. It's not very honest."

Her tone changed. "Is your mother there? Let me talk to her."

"She's not here," I said.

"Tell her not to worry," my aunt said. "A poor old lady who has never wished anything but the best for her will soon die."

I did not repeat this to my mother, for whom it would have been one more in the family anthology of unforgivable remarks. But then I had to suffer it myself for the possible truth it might embody. Each side defended its position with rhetoric, but I, who wanted peace, rationalized the snubs and rebuffs each inflicted on the other, taking no stands, like my father himself.

Years ago his life had fallen into a pattern of business failures and missed opportunities. The great debate between his family on one side, and my mother Ruth on the other, was this: who was responsible for the fact that he had not lived up to anyone's expectations?

As to the prophecies, when spring came my mother's prevailed. Grandma was still alive.

One balmy Sunday my mother and brother and I took the bus to the Beth El cemetery in New Jersey to visit my father's grave. It was situated on a slight rise. We stood looking over rolling fields embedded with monuments. Here and there processions of black cars wound their way through the lanes, or clusters of people stood at open graves. My father's grave was planted with tiny shoots of evergreen but it lacked a headstone. We had chosen one and paid for it and then the stonecutters had gone on strike. Without a headstone my father did not seem to be honorably dead. He didn't seem to me properly buried.

My mother gazed at the plot beside his, reserved for her coffin. "They were always too fine for other people," she said. "Even in the old days on Stanton Street. They put on airs. Nobody was ever good enough for them. Finally Jack himself was not good enough for them. Except to get them things wholesale. Then he was good enough for them."

"Mom, please," my brother said.

"If I had known. Before I ever met him he was tied to his mama's apron strings. And Essie's apron strings were like chains, let me tell you. We had to live where we could be near them for the Sunday visits. Every Sunday, that was my life, a visit to mamaleh. Whatever she knew I wanted, a better apartment, a stick of furniture, a summer camp for the boys, she spoke against it. You know your father, every decision had to be considered and reconsidered. And nothing changed. Nothing ever changed."

She began to cry. We sat her down on a nearby bench. My brother walked off and read 8
the names on stones. I looked at my mother, who was crying, and I went off after my brother.

"Mom's still crying," I said. "Shouldn't we do something?"

"It's all right," he said. "It's what she came here for."

"Yes," I said, and then a sob escaped from my throat. "But I feel like crying too."

My brother Harold put his arm around me. "Look at this old black stone here," he said. "The way it's carved. You can see the changing fashion in monuments—just like everything else."

> **◆ Build Vocabulary**
> **anthology** (an thäl´ ə jē) *n.*: Collection of poems, stories, songs, excerpts, etc.

Customize for
AP Students

5 Ask these students to carefully reread Jonathan's letter. Encourage them to point out how Jonathan uses the letter to "remake" his father. *Students should note the following: His father always wore suits and ties, and now Jonathan has him wearing slacks and short-sleeved shirts. Also, his businesses were unsuccessful, but Jack's Arizona Electric is very successful.*

◆ Critical Thinking

6 Ask: How do you think Aunt Frances views her actions? Do you think she is being honest with herself? *Suggested responses: Aunt Frances probably thinks she is doing the merciful thing by protecting her mother from bad news. However, Aunt Frances is also protecting herself because the course of action she has chosen ensures that she doesn't have to deal with either the old woman's grief or her own. In this sense, she is not being honest with herself.*

◆ Reading Strategy

7 **Judge the Characters' Actions** Some students may agree that the letter writing is both dishonest and wrong. Others may say that it is dishonest but not really wrong because it would be a terrible and painful blow for the old woman to find out that her son had died.

◆ Critical Thinking

8 **Analyze** Point out that both Ruth and Harold talk about change. Have these students compare their attitudes and explain what the attitude tells about each character. *Ruth felt that nothing ever changed when her husband was alive; she seems to feel disappointed and defeated by life. Harold, on the other hand, recognizes that change is always occurring; he uses the different monument styles to point out to Jonathan that everything changes—even objects made from stone. He seems to be more philosophical and optimistic than his mother.*

Cross-Curricular Connection: Math

Trip Planner In the story that Aunt Frances told her mother, Jack, Ruth, Harold, and Jonathan relocate to Arizona. Although today people can fly from New York to Arizona in several hours, in the 1950's, the car trip would have taken at least a week. Have students compare the trip with one taken today. Would the same amount of time be needed? How much would such a trip cost? Have students map out a road trip for a family of four between New York and Phoenix. Ask them to work out an itinerary that takes into consideration where the family will eat, where they will stop for the night, and where they will get gasoline. Then have students figure out the mileage and cost of such a trip. Students can also find out the mileage and cost of airplane tickets for four people from New York to Phoenix. Is it more economical for a family of four to drive or to fly to Phoenix today? Ask students to share their findings with the class.

◆ Critical Thinking

❶ Connect Jonathan says that in his dream, there was always "something we had to fix." Remind students that writers are deliberate in the details they include. Then ask them to connect these dreams to Jonathan's real-life situation. *Possible response: Aunt Frances and Jonathan have been trying to "fix" Jack's death by keeping him alive through the letters.*

▶Critical Viewing◀

❷ Infer Sample response: A person who save letters probably thinks of the contents as part of a personal history. Such a person would disapprove of the narrator because he is attempting to rewrite history.

◆ Critical Thinking

❸ Analyze Point out that Jonathan becomes fearful of dreaming about his father and that the dream makes him feel guilty. Then ask students to identify the real source of his guilt. *Suggested response: He believes that his letters are not allowing his father to rest in peace.*

◆ *Literature and Your Life*

Ask volunteers to share dreams they have had in times of great stress. Then discuss whether students place any value on dream interpretation.

Customize for *Gifted/Talented Students*

Have students use found objects and mementoes to make a bulletin board such as the one pictured on this page. Tell students to create a board that communicates something about their interests and personality.

Somewhere in this time I began dreaming of my father. Not the robust father of my childhood, the handsome man with healthy pink skin and brown eyes and a mustache and the thinning hair parted in the middle. My dead father. We were taking him home from the hospital. It was understood that he had come back from death. This was amazing and joyous. On the other hand, he was terribly mysteriously damaged, or, more accurately, spoiled and unclean. He was very yellowed and debilitated by his death, and there were no guarantees that he wouldn't soon die again. He seemed aware of this and his entire personality was changed. He was angry and impatient with all of us. We were trying to help him in some way, struggling to get him home, but something prevented us, something we had to fix, ❶ a tattered suitcase that had sprung open, some mechanical thing: he had a car but it wouldn't start; or the car was made of wood; or his clothes, which had become too large for him, had caught in the door. In one version he was all bandaged and as we tried to lift him from his wheelchair into a taxi the bandage began to unroll and catch in the spokes of the wheelchair. This seemed to be some unreasonableness on his part. My mother looked on sadly and tried to get him to cooperate.

That was the dream. I shared it with no one. Once when I woke, crying out, my brother turned on the light. He wanted to know what I'd been dreaming but I pretended I didn't remember. The dream made me feel guilty. I felt guilty *in* the dream too because my enraged father knew we didn't want to live with him. The dream represented us taking him home, or trying to, but it was nevertheless understood by all of us that he was to live alone. He was this derelict back from death, but what we were doing was taking him to some place where he would live by himself without help from anyone until he died again.

At one point I became so fearful of this dream that I tried not to go to sleep. ❸ I tried to think of good things about my father and to remember him before his illness. He used to call me "matey." "Hello, matey," he would say when he came home from work. He always wanted us to go someplace—to the store, to the park, to a ball game. He loved to walk. When I went walking with him he would say: "Hold your shoulders back, don't slump. Hold your head up and look at the world. Walk as if you meant it!" As he strode down the street his shoulders moved from side to side, as if he was hearing some kind of cakewalk. He moved with a bounce. He was always eager to see what was around the corner.

Letters and Postcards, Reid Christman

▲ ❷ **Critical Viewing** How would a person who might save letters and mementos like these feel about the narrator of this story? **[Infer]**

The next request for a letter coincided with a special occasion in the house. My brother Harold had met a girl he liked and had gone out with her several times. Now she was coming to our house for dinner.

We had prepared for this for days, cleaning everything in sight, giving the house a going-

Humanities: Art

Letters and Postcards, by Reid Christman.

In this piece of art, letters and everyday objects add up to suggest a life story.

Use these questions for discussion:

1. What do you notice about the letters in this collage? What inferences can you make about the letters? *The letters are addressed to Reid Christman, the artist who created the piece. The letters may be from important people in his life and/or mark important events.*
2. Why do people save mementos like letters, ticket stubs, and photographs? *Possible responses: We like to stay in touch with people; we like to remember good times; we like to read and reread special notes from friends to remind us of ourselves at earlier points in life.*

over, washing the dust of disuse from the glasses and good dishes. My mother came home early from work to get the dinner going. We opened the gateleg table in the living room and brought in the kitchen chairs. My mother spread the table with a laundered white cloth and put out her silver. It was the first family occasion since my father's illness.

I liked my brother's girlfriend a lot. She was a thin girl with very straight hair and she had a terrific smile. Her presence seemed to excite the air. It was amazing to have a living breathing girl in our house. She looked around and what she said was: "Oh, I've never seen so many books!" While she and my brother sat at the table my mother was in the kitchen putting the food into serving bowls and I was going from the kitchen to the living room, kidding around like a waiter, with a white cloth over my arm and a high style of service, placing the serving dish of green beans on the table with a flourish. In the kitchen my mother's eyes were sparkling. She looked at me and nodded and mimed the words: "She's adorable!"

My brother suffered himself to be waited on. He was wary of what we might say. He kept glancing at the girl—her name was Susan—to see if we met with her approval. She worked in an insurance office and was taking courses in accounting at City College. Harold was under a terrible strain but he was excited and happy too. He had bought a bottle of Concord-grape wine to go with the roast chicken. He held up his glass and proposed a toast. My mother said: "To good health and happiness," and we all drank, even I. At that moment the phone rang and I went into the bedroom to get it.

"Jonathan? This is your Aunt Frances. How is everyone?"

"Fine, thank you."

"I want to ask one last favor of you. I need a letter from Jack. Your grandma's very ill. Do you think you can?"

> **◆ Reading Strategy**
> 4 Do you think the narrator is making the right choice here? Why or why not?

"Who is it?" my mother called from the living room.

"OK, Aunt Frances," I said quickly. "I have to go now, we're eating dinner." And I hung up the phone.

5 "It was my friend Louie," I said, sitting back down. "He didn't know the math pages to review."

The dinner was very fine. Harold and Susan washed the dishes and by the time they were done my mother and I had folded up the gateleg table and put it back against the wall and I had swept the crumbs up with the carpet sweeper. We all sat and talked and listened to records for a while and then my brother took Susan home. The evening had gone very well.

Once when my mother wasn't home my brother had pointed out something: the letters from Jack weren't really necessary. "What is this ritual?" he said, holding his palms up. "Grandma is almost totally blind, she's half deaf and crippled. Does the situation really call for a literary composition? Does it need verisimilitude? Would the old lady know the difference if she was read the phone book?"

"Then why did Aunt Frances ask me?"

"That is the question, Jonathan. Why did she? After all, she could write the letter herself—what difference would it make? And if not Frances, why not Frances' sons, the Amherst students? They should have learned by now to write."

"But they're not Jack's sons," I said.

"That's exactly the point," my brother said. 6 "The idea is *service*. Dad used to break his back getting them things wholesale, getting them deals on things. Frances of Westchester really needed things at cost. And Aunt Molly. And Aunt Molly's husband, and Aunt Molly's ex-husband. Grandma, if she needed an errand done. He was always on the hook for something. They never thought his time was important. They never thought every favor he got was one he had to pay back. Appliances, records, watches, china, opera tickets, . . . anything. Call Jack."

"It was a matter of pride to him to be able to do things for them," I said. "To have connections."

"Yeah, I wonder why," my brother said. He looked out the window.

Then suddenly it dawned on me that I was being implicated.

"You should use your head more," my brother said.

Yet I had agreed once again to write a letter from the desert and so I did. I mailed it off to Aunt Frances. A few days later, when I came home from school, I thought

◆ Reading Strategy

4 Judge the Characters' Actions Students may suggest that Jonathan is making the wrong choice, because he is postponing the inevitable. He cannot continue writing the letters because the lie is weighing heavily on him; on the other hand, he made the right decision because this moment would not be the right time for an extended discussion with Frances.

◆ Reading Strategy

5 Judge the Characters' Actions Point out that Jonathan tells his mother a lie immediately. Ask students whether it is wrong in this instance for Jonathan to lie to his mother. *Some students are likely to say that it is wrong to lie under any circumstances; others will recognize that if Jonathan told his mother the truth about who was on the telephone, it would ruin the evening for everyone.*

◆ Literary Focus

6 Static and Dynamic Characters This conversation between Harold and Jonathan is an important one. Ask: What does the conversation reveal about Jonathan's development as a character? *Students should note that Harold causes Jonathan to think about what he is doing. He helps Jonathan recognize that if he continues writing letters, he's going to step into the role in the family that his father had occupied—the person everyone depends on but takes for granted. This conversation represents a step toward change for Jonathan.*

Humanities: Literature

Great Sea Novels Jonathan refers to his father's collection of Great Sea Novels (p. 1075). He states that the collection contains books by "Melville, Conrad, Victor Hugo and Captain Marryat." Discuss what students know about each author. Share the following information:

- Herman Melville (1819–1891): an American author who worked on merchant ships and whalers; best known for novels of the sea such as *Moby-Dick* and *Billy Budd*.
- Joseph Conrad (1857–1924): a writer who was born in Poland but wrote in English and who spent much of his life on the sea; two of his most famous novels are *Heart of Darkness* and *Lord Jim*.
- Victor Hugo (1802–1885): a French writer, who is not known for his connection to the sea; two of his most famous novels are *The Hunchback of Notre Dame* and *Les Miserables*.
- Frederick Marryat (1792–1848): an English novelist and naval officer who used his experiences at sea in his books; two of his novels are *Peter Simple* and *Mr. Midshipman Easy*.

Ask students: What does this reading material suggests about the character? *This book list suggests that Jonathan's late father liked adventure. Ironically, the story suggests he didn't have a great deal of adventure in his life.* Ask students to locate other details in the story which suggest the character's love of adventure.

Customize for
AP Students

There is a great deal of irony in the conversation that Aunt Frances has with Jonathan. Have students identify some examples of this irony. *Students may note the following: (1) Aunt Frances says that Jonathan's mother is strong-willed and selfish. However, Aunt Frances has also shown herself to be strong-willed and selfish. (2) Aunt Frances lists all the demands that Jonathan's mother made on Jack. It has been revealed, however, that Aunt Frances and her mother made many demands on Jack. (3) Aunt Frances refers to the "marvelous" letter, but the reader knows that she means the letter is anything but marvelous. (4) Aunt Frances says that she would invite the narrator's family for Passover if she thought that his mother would accept the invitation. However, it is likely that Aunt Frances does not extend the invitation because she does not accept them as part of the family and is making her point by not inviting them.*

◆ Literary Focus

❶ Static and Dynamic Characters Sample response: The fact that Aunt Frances never questions her beliefs shows that she is a static character. She still believes that Grandma should not be told about Jack's death, and she still blames the narrator's mother for preventing Jack from achieving success.

❷ Clarification Explain that sepia is a shade of brown. Many old photographs have a sepia tone.

Reteach

Students who have trouble seeing the difference between static and dynamic characters may be helped by a visual demonstration. Draw the visual below on the board. Ask students which character each pair of figures represents.

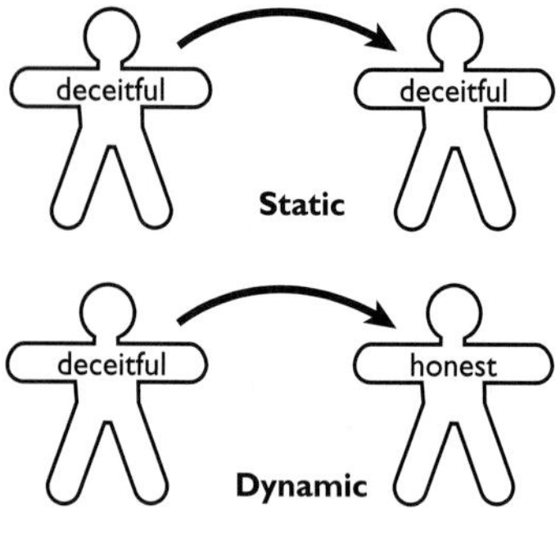

I saw her sitting in her car in front of our house. She drove a black Buick Roadmaster, a very large clean car with whitewall tires. It was Aunt Frances all right. She blew the horn when she saw me. I went over and leaned in at the window.

"Hello, Jonathan," she said. "I haven't long. Can you get in the car?"

"Mom's not home," I said. "She's working."

"I know that. I came to talk to you."

"Would you like to come upstairs?"

"I can't, I have to get back to Larchmont. Can you get in for a moment, please?"

I got in the car. My Aunt Frances was a very pretty white-haired woman, very elegant, and she wore tasteful clothes. I had always liked her and from the time I was a child she had enjoyed pointing out to everyone that I looked more like her son than Jack's. She wore white gloves and held the steering wheel and looked straight ahead as she talked, as if the car was in traffic and not sitting at the curb.

"Jonathan," she said, "there is your letter on the seat. Needless to say I didn't read it to Grandma. I'm giving it back to you and I won't ever say a word to anyone. This is just between us. I never expected cruelty from you. I never thought you were capable of doing something so deliberately cruel and perverse."

I said nothing.

> **◆ Literary Focus**
> ❶ In what ways do her comments show that Aunt Frances is a static character?

"Your mother has very bitter feelings and now I see she has poisoned you with them. She has always resented the family. She is a very strong-willed, selfish person."

"No she isn't," I said.

"I wouldn't expect you to agree. She drove poor Jack crazy with her demands. She always had the highest aspirations and he could never fulfill them to her satisfaction. When he still had his store he kept your mother's brother . . . on salary. After the war when he began to make a little money he had to buy Ruth a mink jacket because she was so desperate to have one. He had debts to pay but she wanted a mink. He was a very special person, my brother, he should have accomplished something special, but he loved your mother and devoted his life to her. And all she ever thought about was keeping up with the Joneses."

I watched the traffic going up the Grand Concourse. A bunch of kids were waiting at the bus stop at the corner. They had put their books on the ground and were horsing around.

"I'm sorry I have to descend to this," Aunt Frances said. "I don't like talking about people this way. If I have nothing good to say about someone, I'd rather not say anything. How is Harold?"

"Fine."

"Did he help you write this marvelous letter?"

"No."

After a moment she said more softly: "How are you all getting along?"

"Fine."

"I would invite you up for Passover if I thought your mother would accept."

I didn't answer.

She turned on the engine. "I'll say good-bye now, Jonathan. Take your letter. I hope you give some time to thinking about what you've done."

That evening when my mother came home from work I saw that she wasn't as pretty as my Aunt Frances. I usually thought my mother was a good-looking woman, but I saw now that she was too heavy and that her hair was undistinguished.

"Why are you looking at me?" she said.

"I'm not."

"I learned something interesting today," my mother said. "We may be eligible for a V.A. pension because of the time your father spent in the Navy."

That took me by surprise. Nobody had ever told me my father was in the Navy.

"In World War I," she said, "he went to Webb's Naval Academy on the Harlem River. He was training to be an ensign. But the war ended and he never got his commission."

After dinner the three of us went through the closets looking for my father's papers, hoping to find some proof that could be filed with the Veterans Administration. We came up with two things, a Victory medal, which my brother said everyone got for being in the service during the Great War, and an astounding sepia photograph of my father and his shipmates on the deck of a ship. They were dressed ❷

Humanities: Religion

Passover Aunt Frances tells Jonathan that she would invite him and his family for Passover if she thought his mother would accept the invitation (p. 1074). An eight-day festival, Passover is a Jewish celebration of freedom. It commemorates the angel of death's "passing over" the homes of Israelites during a plague and the subsequent flight of the Israelites from slavery in Egypt. The date of Passover varies, but it is in March or April; it begins on the fifteenth day of the Hebrew month of Nisan.

Invite students with a Jewish background to explain more about Passover and the *Seder*—the ceremonial feast that families hold during this holiday period.

in bell-bottoms and T-shirts and armed with mops and pails, brooms and brushes.

"I never knew this," I found myself saying. "I never knew this."

"You just don't remember," my brother said.

I was able to pick out my father. He stood at the end of the row, a thin, handsome boy with a full head of hair, a mustache, and an intelligent smiling countenance. . . .

Neither the picture nor the medal was proof of anything, but my brother thought a duplicate of my father's service record had to be in Washington somewhere and that it was just a matter of learning how to go about finding it.

"The pension wouldn't amount to much," my mother said. "Twenty or thirty dollars. But it would certainly help."

I took the picture of my father and his shipmates and propped it against the lamp at my bedside. I looked into his youthful face and tried to relate it to the Father I knew. I looked at the picture a long time. Only gradually did my eye connect it to the set of Great Sea Novels in the bottom shelf of the bookcase a few feet away. My father had given that set to me: it was uniformly bound in green with gilt lettering and it included works by Melville, Conrad, Victor Hugo and Captain Marryat. And lying across the top of the books, jammed in under the sagging shelf above, was his old ship's telescope in its wooden case with the brass snap.

I thought how stupid, and imperceptive, and self-centered I had been never to have understood while he was alive what my father's dream for his life had been.

> ◆ **Literary Focus**
> In what ways has Jonathan changed since the story's opening scene? **3**

On the other hand, I had written in my last letter from Arizona—the one that had so angered Aunt Frances—something that might allow me, the writer in the family, to soften my judgment of myself. I will conclude by giving the letter here in its entirety.

Dear Mama,

This will be my final letter to you since I have been told by the doctors that I am dying.

I have sold my store at a very fine profit and am sending Frances a check for five thousand dollars to be deposited in your account. My present to you, Mamaleh. Let Frances show you the passbook.

As for the nature of my ailment, the doctors haven't told me what it is, but I know that I am simply dying of the wrong life. I should never have come to the desert. It wasn't the place for me.

I have asked Ruth and the boys to have my body cremated and the ashes scattered in the ocean. **4**

Your loving son,
Jack

Guide for Responding

◆ Literature and Your Life

Reader's Response What did you find admirable or disappointing about the narrator?

Thematic Response: As you read this story, did you want Jonathan to keep writing the letters? Why or why not?

Group Activity As a class, develop a "yes" or "no" question to address the central dilemma of this story. Then poll friends, family, and schoolmates for their responses. Submit and total the responses as a class.

☑ Check Your Comprehension

1. What has happened to the narrator's father?
2. What is the narrator's grandmother told about her son's whereabouts and situation?
3. (a) What key decision is made about communicating with the grandmother? (b) Who makes this decision?
4. What does the narrator do to help his Aunt Frances with her plan?
5. What point of view does the narrator express in the final paragraphs of the story?

◆ Literary Focus

3 Static and Dynamic Characters Possible response: At the beginning of the story, Jonathan had a tendency to try to please others, particularly his Aunt Frances. By the end of the story, he realizes that some things are more important, namely, being true to oneself and acting on one's beliefs. Also, Jonathan has learned a great deal about who his father really was.

Customize for
Less Proficient Readers
4 Help students see the significance of the final paragraph of the letter. Point out that in it, Jonathan pays tribute to his father's love of the sea.

Reinforce and Extend

Answers

◆ Literature and Your Life

Reader's Response Students should support their responses with details from the story.

Thematic Focus Encourage students to share their responses with the class.

☑ Check Your Comprehension

1. He has died.
2. She is told that he has moved to Arizona for health reasons.
3. (a) The family decides that Jonathan's grandmother should not be told of her son's death. Instead, Jonathan will write letters in his voice. (b) Jonathan's aunts make this decision.
4. He agrees to write the letters.
5. He says that although the letters may have been deceitful, the experience of writing them has helped him better understand his father.

Beyond the Selection

FURTHER READING

Other Works by E.L. Doctorow

Welcome to Hard Times
The Book of Daniel
Ragtime
World's Fair
The Waterworks
Billy Bathgate

We suggest that you preview these works before recommending them to students

INTERNET

Encourage students to use the Internet to find out more about E. L. Doctorow. Please be aware, however, that sites may have changed since this information was published.

For biographical information and a critical essay, students can visit the following site: **http://hsl.hst.msu.edu/~cal/celeb/doctorow.html**

We *strongly recommend* that you preview the site before you send students to it.

Answers

◆ Critical Thinking

1. Possible response: They reverted to the immediate family; the aunts were the dead man's sisters and they may have thought that their blood relation to him was more valid than that of his wife and children.
2. She is willing to be deceitful to protect her mother's feelings.
3. (a) She feels the letters are dishonest; she feels they are an extension of the control under which she and her husband had lived. (b) She values honesty and independence.
4. Possible responses: It symbolizes the notion that the dead man cannot rest until his relatives accept his death.
5. His brother helps him to see that Frances is forcing him to do something he may not want to do; he sees that his father was frequently in the same situation.
6. Students should support their responses with reference to film, literature, or life experience.

◆ Grammar and Style

Practice

1. *Affect,* a verb, is correct.
2. *Effect,* a noun, is correct.
3. *Effected* is wrong. The verb *affected* is correct.
4. *Affect* is wrong. The noun *effect* is correct.

Writing Application

Essays should be consistent with the characters and events of the story. Check to see that students have used both *affect* and *effect* correctly at least once.

◆ Literary Focus

1. Jonathan is a dynamic character for the following reasons: He decides to stand up to his aunt and not write the letters; he goes through the grieving process; and he sees his father in a new light.
2. Aunt Frances is a static character. Throughout the story, she wants to keep things as they were.

◆ Reading Strategy

1. Ruth wants to grieve a death and move on. Frances wants to deny a death ever occurred. Students should support their own decisions about which approach is more productive.
2. Using their own moral code, students should explain their response.

◆ Build Vocabulary

Using the Greek Suffix *-itis*

1. Inflammation of the sinuses.
2. Inflammation of the appendix.
3. Inflammation of a tendon.
4. Inflammation of the tonsils.

Using the Word Bank

1. barometer
2. cronies
3. bronchitis
4. anthology

Guide for Responding (continued)

◆ Critical Thinking

INTERPRET

1. Why do the aunts make such a key family decision without consulting the narrator and his mother? **[Interpret]**

2. What does Aunt Frances's desire to conceal Jack's death from their mother reveal about her character? **[Analyze]**

3. (a) How does Jonathan's mother feel about deceiving Grandma? (b) What do these feelings suggest about her values? **[Infer]**

4. What do you think the narrator's dream symbolizes? **[Interpret]**

5. Why does Jonathan ultimately change his mind about writing the letters? **[Connect]**

EVALUATE

6. Do you think Doctorow's portrayal of a family in mourning is realistic? Explain. **[Criticize]**

◆ Grammar and Style

COMMONLY CONFUSED WORDS: *AFFECT* AND *EFFECT*

Affect and *effect* are commonly confused words that look or sound alike but have different meanings. If you're confused about when to use a particular word, check the meanings in a dictionary or grammar book.

> ***Effect*** is usually used as a noun, meaning "the result of some action." ***Affect*** is a verb, meaning "to influence."

Practice On your paper, name the part of speech for each italicized word, and indicate whether the word is used correctly, explaining why or why not.

1. How did her husband's death *affect* Ruth?

2. Jack's illness had a serious *effect* on his business.

3. How was Jonathan *effected* by his family?

4. What *affect* might Arizona's climate have on bronchitis?

Writing Application Write a brief essay explaining the impact you think Jack's death had on Jonathan. Use the commonly confused words *affect* and *effect* at least once.

◆ Literary Focus

STATIC AND DYNAMIC CHARACTERS

In this story, the characters' approaches to life, decision making, and death contrast sharply. Doctorow's use of both **static characters**—who remain basically unchanged during the story—and **dynamic characters**—who undergo a shift during the story—adds to these contrasts.

1. Is Jonathan a dynamic character? Give three reasons or examples to support your answer.

2. Identify Aunt Frances as either a static or dynamic character. Support your answer.

◆ Reading Strategy

JUDGE THE CHARACTERS' ACTIONS

When you **judge the characters' actions,** you evaluate each character's behaviors and actions by weighing them according to your own standards of right and wrong.

1. Contrast Aunt Frances's and Ruth's approach to death. Which do you think is more productive?

2. Who do you think was "right" at the end of the story—Aunt Frances or Jonathan? Why?

◆ Build Vocabulary

USING THE GREEK SUFFIX *-ITIS*

The Greek suffix *-itis* means "disease or inflammation." With that knowledge, define each of these words on your paper. If necessary, use a dictionary to define the root or base word indicated.

1. sinusitis (*sinus*)
2. appendicitis (*appendix*)
3. tendonitis (*tendon*)
4. tonsilitis (*tonsil*)

USING THE WORD BANK: Sentence Completions

On your paper, write the word from the Word Bank that fits best in each sentence.

1. According to the __?__, it will probably rain in a day or two.

2. Grandpa and his __?__ play golf every week.

3. My bout with __?__ left me coughing for days.

4. We developed an __?__ of short stories to share with the children.

Build Your Portfolio

Idea Bank

Writing

1. **Final Letter** If you were in Jonathan's situation, what would you have written in Jack's final letter to Grandma? Write a final letter in your own voice.

2. **Eulogy** As Jonathan, write a speech you might deliver at your father's memorial service. Write about the unique value of your father's life.

3. **Critical Essay** E. L. Doctorow once said, "A novelist is someone who lives in other people's skins." In a critical essay, link this statement to "The Writer in the Family."

Speaking, Listening, and Viewing

4. **Family Conference** With a group, role-play the family conference at which the aunts decide to deceive their mother. Introduce Jonathan, Ruth, and Harold into the discussion to argue against this approach. **[Performing Arts Link]**

5. **Debate** In pairs, take turns debating the morality of Jonathan's deceptive letters. Invite questions from the audience to further the discussion. **[Social Studies Link]**

Researching and Representing

6. **Costume Proposal** This story takes place in the 1950's. How would the characters dress and wear their hair? Discuss, plan, and illustrate the costumes and makeup you would propose for a dramatic presentation of the story. **[Art Link]**

7. **Grief Hotline** Research a crisis center in your area. Collect brochures and information on how the center helps people in need. If possible, interview a counselor. Share your findings with classmates. **[Community Link]**

Online Activity www.phlit.phschool.com

Guided Writing Lesson

Advice Column

Doctorow's story explores a difficult dilemma. How should Jonathan handle the situation with his Aunt Frances? Write an advice column that includes a brief letter from Jonathan describing his problem and a response from the columnist proposing certain actions. As the columnist, use elaboration to support your argument.

Writing Skills Focus: Elaboration to Support an Argument

When you write persuasively, use **elaboration to support your argument.** Use the following techniques to help you create a convincing case for your position:

- Give coherent, logical reasons for each of your points.
- Support your reasons with facts and statistics.
- If appropriate, include statements from experts.

Prewriting First, list the elements of the dilemma that Jonathan's letter will include; then decide on the advice you will give him in response. Next, identify several reasons you might use to persuade Jonathan to follow your advice. To back up your reasons, do some research to collect facts about how older people cope with news of the death of a loved one.

Drafting After drafting Jonathan's letter, begin your response with a sympathetic line about his problem and a summary statement of the action you believe he should take. Follow up with a clear and logical argument to convince him to take your advice, elaborating each point with reasons and facts.

Revising Reread your column to be sure that Jonathan's problem and the response are clearly stated. Ask yourself whether you have made a strong case that will persuade Jonathan to follow the advice. How can you strengthen your argument? What additional reasons and support can you add?

ASSESSMENT OPTIONS

Formal Assessment, Selection Test, pp. 320–322, and Assessment Resources Software. The selection test is designed so that it can be easily customized to the performance levels of your students.

Alternative Assessment, p. 74, includes options for less advanced students, more advanced students, interpersonal learners, verbal/linguistic learners, and visual/spatial learners.

PORTFOLIO ASSESSMENT

Use the following rubrics in the ***Alternative Assessment*** booklet to assess student writing:
Final Letter: Expression Rubric, p. 109
Eulogy: Description Rubric, p. 112
Critical Essay: Critical Review Rubric, p. 126
Guided Writing Lesson: Problem-Solution Rubric, p. 116

Idea Bank

Customizing for *Performance Levels*

Following are suggestions for matching Idea Bank topics with your students' performance levels:
Less Advanced Students: 1
Average Students: 2, 4, 6, 7
More Advanced Students: 3, 5

Customizing for *Learning Modalities*

Following are suggestions for matching Idea Bank topics with your students' learning modalities:
Interpersonal: 4, 7
Logical/Mathematical: 5
Visual/Spatial: 6

Guided Writing Lesson

For more prewriting, elaboration, and revision strategies, see *Prentice Hall Writing and Grammar.*

Writing and Language Transparencies Use the Problem/Solution Organizer to help students prepare ideas for their advice columns (pp. 79–81).

Writers at Work Videodisc

Have students view the videodisc segment on Persuasion (Ch. 4), featuring Gasby Greely to see how Greely considers the needs of her audience. Have students discuss how a sensitivity to a reader's concerns can make an advice column more persuasive.

Play frames 41841 to 42690

Writing Lab CD-ROM

Have students complete the tutorial on Persuasion. Follow these steps:

1. Review the elements of persuasive writing using the models of an editorial and a persuasive essay.
2. Have students draft on the computer.
3. Encourage students to use the Persuasive Word Bin to strengthen their arguments.

LESSON OBJECTIVES

1. **To develop vocabulary and word identification skills**
   - Words From War
   - Using the Word Bank: Context
2. **To use a variety of reading strategies to comprehend a short story**
   - Connect Your Experience
   - Reading Strategy: Envision the Action
3. **To increase knowledge of other cultures and to connect common elements across cultures**
   - Background for Understanding
4. **To express and support responses to the text**
   - Critical Thinking
   - Idea Bank: Letter to an Author
   - Idea Bank: Newspaper Article
   - Idea Bank: Dance
5. **To analyze literary elements**
   - Literary Focus: First-Person Narrator
   - Idea Bank: Literary Analysis
6. **To read to do research on self-selected and assigned topics**
   - Idea Bank: Multimedia Presentation
   - Idea Bank: Interview
   - Speaking, Listening, and Viewing Mini-Lesson
7. **To plan, prepare, organize, and present literary interpretations**
   - Idea Bank: Choral Reading
8. **To use recursive writing processes to write a suspenseful personal account**
   - Guided Writing Lesson
9. **To increase knowledge of the rules of grammar and usage**
   - Grammar and Style: Noun Clauses

Test Preparation

Writing Skills: Sentence Structure (ATE, p. 1079)
The teaching tips and sample test item in this workshop support the instruction and practice in the unit workshop:

Writing Skills: Punctuation, Usage, and Sentence Structure (SE, p. 1143)

Guide for Interpreting

Yusef Komunyakaa *(1947–)*

"It took me fourteen years to write poems about Vietnam," said Yusef Komunyakaa (yo͞o′ sef kō mun yä′ kä) in 1994, shortly after winning the Pulitzer Prize for *Neon Vernacular,* the collection from which "Camouflaging the Chimera" is taken. "I had never thought about writing about it, and in a way I had been systematically writing around it."

Komunyakaa joined the army and went to Vietnam in 1965. Serving as an "information specialist," he reported from the front lines, edited a military newspaper, and earned a Bronze Star. After the war, he pursued his education, earning a B.A. and an M.A. at the University of Colorado and an M.F.A. at the University of California, Irvine. He then took a variety of teaching jobs, and in 1977 published his first collection of poetry. In 1983, he returned to his native Louisiana, working as a poet-in-the-schools in New Orleans. During this time, he let Vietnam reenter his consciousness. "And it was as if I had uncapped some hidden place in me," Komunyakaa said. "Poem after poem came spilling out."

Tim O'Brien *(1946–)*

No writer has more effectively captured the Vietnam War than Tim O'Brien. O'Brien has written five books that focus on the war, providing readers with vivid pictures of the fighting in the dense Vietnamese jungles and allowing them to share the fear and homesickness experienced by American soldiers during this bitter conflict.

Born in Austin, Minnesota, O'Brien was drafted a month after graduating from college and was sent to Vietnam. After coming home in 1970, he began writing essays about his experiences. His first published work, *If I Die in a Combat Zone, Box Me Up and Ship Me Home* (1973), is a memoir. Several subsequent novels include a National Book Award winner, *Going After Cacciato* (1978), and the widely praised *The Things They Carried* (1990), from which "Ambush" is taken. In this fictional memoir of Vietnam—narrated by a character named Tim O'Brien—the author artfully straddles the line between fact and fiction. O'Brien has said that he writes fiction ". . . to get at the essence of things, not merely the surface."

◆ Background for Understanding

History: The Vietnam War

In 1961, President John F. Kennedy sent 400 military advisors to aid the South Vietnamese government in its fight against communist rebels supported by North Vietnam. As the war escalated, the United States poured massive military resources into defeating the rebels, known as Vietcong, or—as you'll read in "Camouflaging the Chimera"—the VC. However, traditional military strategies were useless in dense jungle, against a guerrilla army that could blend in at will with the civilian population. American soldiers grew increasingly frustrated, fighting a tenacious but elusive enemy.

At home, the war sparked mass protests. College students and other citizens demonstrated against what they saw as a pointless war and a useless sacrifice of lives on both sides. The United States became deeply divided between those who supported the war and those who opposed it. In 1968, the United States began peace talks, even as the war continued. The talks failed. By 1973, when the United States finally pulled out of Vietnam, more than 58,000 Americans had died and thousands more had been wounded.

Many American writers continue to produce memoirs, analyses, novels, short stories, and poems reflecting on the Vietnam War and its aftermath.

Prentice Hall Literature Program Resources

REINFORCE / RETEACH / EXTEND

Selection Support Pages
Build Vocabulary: Words From War, p. 334
Grammar and Style: Noun Clauses, p. 335
Reading Strategy: Envision the Action, p. 336
Literary Focus: First-Person Narrator, p. 337

Strategies for Diverse Student Needs, Form a Mental Picture, p. 75

Beyond Literature
Cross-Curricular Connection: Social Studies, p. 75

Formal Assessment Selection Test, pp. 323–325; Assessment Resources Software

Alternative Assessment, p. 75

Writing and Language Transparencies Writing Process Model 3: Personal Narrative, pp. 13–16.

Resource Pro CD-ROM
Includes all resource material and customizable lesson plan

Listening to Literature Audiocassettes

◆ Camouflaging the Chimera ◆
Ambush *from* The Things They Carried

◆ Literature and Your Life

Connect Your Experience

Most soldiers who went to Vietnam were only a few years older than you are now. Can you imagine finding yourself in a jungle, far from home, where you must kill or be killed? This is the reality that faces the narrators of "Camouflaging the Chimera" and "Ambush."

Thematic Focus: Social Protest

Tim O'Brien was a war protester who went to Vietnam, he says, in order "not to be thought of as a coward. . . ." Reading "Ambush" might leave you wondering: Which takes more courage—to fight a war or to refuse to fight?

Journal Writing Describe one or two examples of courageous behavior that you have admired in another person.

◆ Literary Focus

First-Person Narrator

Sometimes the most compelling stories are those told in the **first person**; that is, by a narrator who—using the pronouns *I* and *we*—takes part in the action and reveals his or her thoughts and feelings about the events being described. Both selections you are about to read are narrated in the first person. As you read, think about how this point of view pulls you inside the narrator's head, making you feel as though you are actually living through the events.

◆ Grammar and Style

Noun Clauses

A **noun clause** is a subordinate clause (a group of words with a subject and a verb that cannot stand by itself as a sentence) that functions as a noun. Here is an example from "Ambush":

. . . my daughter Kathleen asked *if I had ever killed anyone.*

In this sentence, "if I had ever killed anyone" is a noun clause functioning as the direct object of *asked.* Several common words that introduce noun clauses are *that, which, what, if, how, when, where, why, whatever, whoever,* and *whether.* Sometimes, the introductory word *that* is understood, not stated. In this example, *that* is understood before "I'd been a soldier":

. . . She knew *I'd been a soldier.*

◆ Reading Strategy

Envision the Action

As you read these suspenseful pieces set during wartime in remote jungles of Southeast Asia, utilize the details the writers provide to **envision the action**—form a mental picture of what you are reading. Both pieces describe soldiers lying in wait for the enemy—a particularly suspenseful action. When Komunyakaa writes, "We painted our faces & rifles/with mud from a riverbank," picture doing what he says. Like a movie in your head, these mental images will help the works come alive.

◆ Build Vocabulary

Words From War

Throughout history, soldiers have spoken their own language, the language of warfare. Each war produces unique terms. World War I, for example, gave us *doughboy, over the top,* and *no man's land.* Many words of war, such as *ambush* and *ammunition,* have long since entered our everyday language. As you read these selections, notice which words are specifically military in origin.

Word Bank

Before you read, preview this list of words from the selections.

refuge
ambush
ammunition
muzzle
gape

Test Preparation Workshop

Writing Skills: Sentence Structure Many standardized tests require students to combine sentences. Demonstrate with this example.

Many people who have experienced war have horrifying memories. These memories often stay with them for a lifetime.

Which of the following is the BEST way to combine the two sentences in the passage?

A Many people who have experienced war have horrifying memories, these memories stay with them for a lifetime.

B Many people who have experienced war have horrifying memories, stay with them for a lifetime.

C Many people who have experienced war have horrifying memories that stay with them for a lifetime.

D Staying with them for a lifetime, many people who have experienced war have horrifying memories.

A is a comma splice. *B* is a run-on. *D* has a misplaced modifier. *C* is the correct answer.

Interest Grabber Before reading the selections, have students read the Beyond Literature feature (p. 1081) about the Vietnam Veterans Memorial. Tell students that decades have passed since the war ended, yet crowds continue to visit this memorial, leaving mementos and notes. If possible, share photos and notes from Michael Katakis' book *The Vietnam Veterans Memorial,* or ask students who have seen the memorial to describe it and their response to it for the class. Lead students to reflect on how the war continues to haunt many people who lived through that period, as these selections demonstrate.

Customize for *Less Proficient Readers*

To help these students envision the action of the selections, have them describe movies they have seen about the Vietnam War. Encourage them to focus their descriptions on the jungle terrain of the country, the protective camouflage worn by American soldiers, and the difficulties of fighting a guerrilla war.

Customize for *AP Students*

Encourage these students to compare the two works. What similar ideas and images, if any, do they convey about the Vietnam War? Which piece did they prefer, and why?

Customize for *English Language Learners*

Your class may include Vietnamese or Hmong immigrants whose older relatives fought alongside American troops in the Vietnam War, or whose families were forced into refugee camps and then relocated to the United States as a result of the war. Speak to these students privately before beginning these selections and ask if there are any family stories about the war they would be willing to share with the class.

Customize for *Visual/Spatial Learners*

Have these students preview the illustrations accompanying the selection before reading. Ask them to try to imagine themselves in the American soldiers' situation in Vietnam.

Develop Understanding

One-Minute Insight "Camouflaging the Chimera" is a suspenseful, first-person description of how it feels to lie in ambush for hours, waiting for the approach of enemy soldiers.

◆ Literary Focus

❶ **First-Person Narrator** Guide students to see that the poem's first-person narrator is not a single soldier, but a group.

◆ Build Vocabulary

❷ **Words From War** Ask students why the soldiers might refer to their camouflage uniforms as "tiger suits." *Just as tigers have black stripes and golden coats that help camouflage them in the jungle, the soldiers have uniforms with splotches of jungle colors to camouflage them.*

❸ **Clarification** Explain that Saigon was the capital of South Vietnam, while Bangkok is the capital of Thailand, another Southeast Asian country.

◆ Critical Thinking

❹ **Analyze** Ask students what details the narrator provides to help readers understand what it felt like for the soldiers to lie in ambush for hours. *Details include the chameleons crawling on their spines, watching the sunset, the eventual appearance of the moonlight shining on the metal of their guns, and the feeling of something breaking inside them.*

Customize for
Visual/Spatial Learners
Have these students study the camouflage fabric on the soldier's helmet in the photo on this page. Ask how the appearance of the helmet relates to the changes in the chameleons described in lines 17–20. *Possible response: Chameleons change color to match their surroundings. Because the camouflage fabric worn by the soldiers is made up of splotches of green, gold, and black, these are the colors the chameleons turn as they crawl up the soldiers' backs.*

Camouflaging the Chimera[1]

Yusef Komunyakaa

❶ We tied branches to our helmets.
We painted our faces & rifles
with mud from a riverbank,

❷ blades of grass hung from the pockets
of our tiger suits. We wove
ourselves into the terrain,
content to be a hummingbird's target.

We hugged bamboo & leaned
against a breeze off the river,
slow-dragging with ghosts

❸ from Saigon to Bangkok,
with women left in doorways
reaching in from America.
We aimed at dark-hearted songbirds.

In our way station of shadows
rock apes tried to blow our cover,
throwing stones at the sunset. Chameleons

❹ crawled our spines, changing from day
to night: green to gold,
gold to black. But we waited
till the moon touched metal,

1. **Chimera** (kī´ mir´ ə): From Greek mythology, a firebreathing monster with a lion's head, a goat's body, and a serpent's tail.

Block Scheduling Strategies

Consider these suggestions to take advantage of extended class time:

- Your students can find a wealth of information about the Vietnam War experience at the Vietnam Veterans' home page on the Internet: **http://www.vietvet.org** Before students read the selection, have them research images, facts, and maps of Vietnam, as well as a history of the Vietnam War at the site. After they read the selections, have them search the site for stories, poems, and pictures submitted by veterans in the Remembrances section.
- Have pairs or small groups of students discuss how they envisioned the action in both Komunyakaa's and O'Brien's work by responding to the Reading Strategy questions on page 1084.
- Have students complete Literary Focus: First-Person Narrator in ***Selection Support***, p. 337.

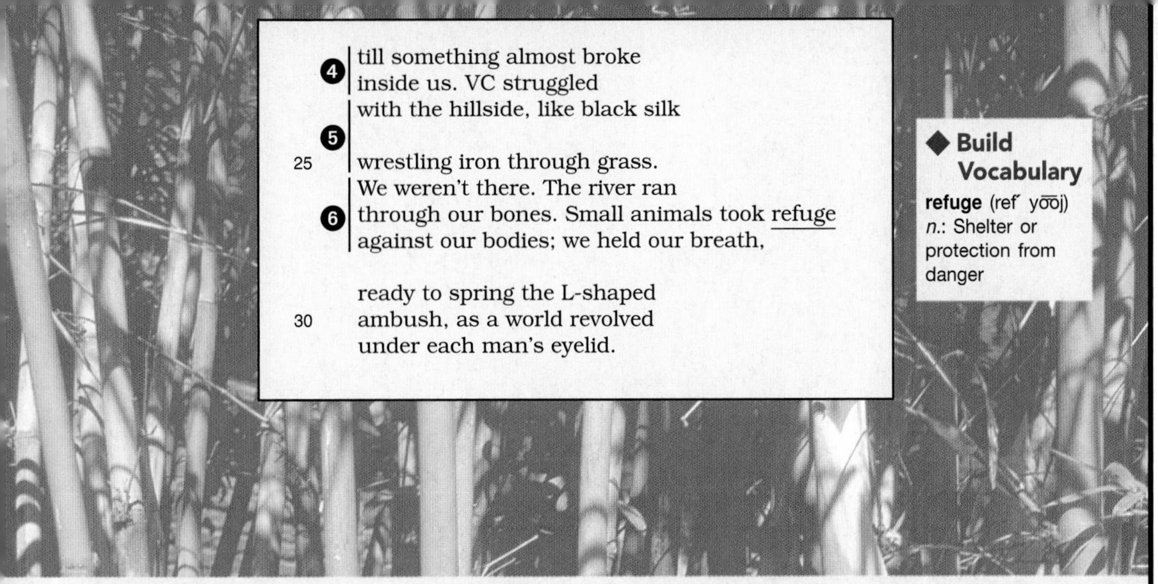

❹ till something almost broke
inside us. VC struggled
with the hillside, like black silk
❺
wrestling iron through grass.
We weren't there. The river ran
❻ through our bones. Small animals took refuge
against our bodies; we held our breath,

ready to spring the L-shaped
ambush, as a world revolved
under each man's eyelid.

◆ Build Vocabulary

refuge (ref′ yo͞oj) *n.:* Shelter or protection from danger

Beyond Literature

Architecture Connection

The Vietnam Veterans Memorial Since its completion in 1982, millions of people have visited the Vietnam Veterans Memorial in Washington, D.C. Designed by architect Maya Ying Lin, the memorial honoring those who died in the Vietnam War consists of two black granite walls which slope down into the ground and meet to form a V. Etched into the wall are the names of more than 58,000 Americans who died in Vietnam.

Lin has said of her design, "It does not glorify the war or make an antiwar statement. It is a place for private reckoning." Visitors from across the nation leave notes and small mementos at the wall. The National Park Service collects these items and plans to exhibit them.

Locate a photograph of the memorial. How does its design support Lin's description of its purpose?

Guide for Responding

◆ Literature and Your Life

Reader's Response With what emotion were you left as you finished the poem? Explain.

Thematic Focus Do the images in this poem suggest that the speaker is opposed to the war he is fighting? Explain.

☑ Check Your Comprehension

1. Where does this poem take place?
2. What happens in this poem?
3. Who are the VC in the seventh stanza?

◆ Critical Thinking

INTERPRET

1. What obstacles and burdens does the speaker face in this poem? **[Interpret]**
2. What images suggest that the speaker is merging with his surroundings? **[Support]**
3. What is the meaning of the title? Support your answer. **[Interpret]**

EVALUATE

4. Komunyakaa has said: "I like connecting the abstract to the concrete." Has he succeeded in this poem? Explain. **[Assess]**

Cross-Curricular Connection: Music

Protest Songs Much of the antiwar protest of the 1960's and 1970's was expressed in popular music of the time.

Encourage students to listen to and analyze the feelings expressed in such songs as "Masters of War," "Blowin' in the Wind," and "With God on Our Side," by Bob Dylan; "I Feel Like I'm Fixin' to Die Rag," by Country Joe McDonald; and "For What It's Worth," by Stephen Stills (p. 487).

Bruce Springsteen's "Born in the U.S.A." and Billy Joel's "Goodnight Saigon" also address the Vietnam veterans' experience.

Ask students to describe popular music of today that expresses messages of social protest. We suggest you preview these songs before sharing them with your students.

◆ Reading Strategy

❺ Envisioning the Action Tell students that the Viet Cong often dressed in black. Ask how the imagery of these lines helps them envision the Viet Cong climbing up the hill. *Dressed in black and carrying their guns, the Viet Cong look like "black silk wrestling iron" as they crawl through the grass clutching their guns.*

◆ Critical Thinking

❻ Interpret What idea does the narrator convey when he says, "The river ran through our bones"? *The soldiers have merged with their surroundings.*

Reinforce and Extend

Customize for
Visualize/Spatial Learners
Encourage students to research images of the Vietnam War using magazines and newspapers from the 1960's and 1970's. Have them interpret the images for the class.

Answers

◆ Literature and Your Life

Reader's Response Possible responses include fear, anticipation, anxiety, and excitement.

Thematic Focus The poem is descriptive but does not indicate any anger toward the war. Instead, the images suggest nature's interaction with the soldiers.

☑ Check Your Comprehension

1. It is set in the jungles of Vietnam.
2. Soldiers spend an evening and night waiting to ambush their enemies.
3. They are the enemy.

◆ Critical Thinking

1. The speaker faces the danger of being seen and the burden of remaining silent and motionless despite the growing tension.
2. Possible responses include the chameleon, the river running through their bones, and the animals snuggling up against them.
3. The soldiers are a terrible monster ready to ambush; they are trying to keep themselves camouflaged or covered.
4. Possible response: The poet successfully uses many concrete details of the jungle to convey the abstract feelings of anticipation.

Develop Understanding

One-Minute Insight Tim O'Brien's memory of the Viet Cong soldier he killed in the Vietnam War is a haunting portrait of the fear and ambivalence experienced by many soldiers as they balance their struggle to survive with their personal values and respect for human life.

Customize for
Intrapersonal Learners
Before these students read the selection, ask them to consider their own ideas about military combat. Explain that wars frequently require soldiers to "kill or be killed." Ask students whether killing in the name of country is more acceptable than killing for other reasons.

◆ Grammar and Style

❶ **Noun Clauses** Have students find all the noun clauses in this passage. Then ask whether each clause functions as a direct object, as the object of a preposition, or as a predicate noun. *The noun clauses are "what seemed right," "she's a grown-up," "exactly what happened," and "what I remember happening." All four clauses function as direct objects.*

◆ Literary Focus

❷ **First-Person Narrator** Ask students what effect the use of first person has on their perception of the narrator in the opening paragraph. *The use of the first-person helps readers identify with the narrator. He reveals his conflicted feelings about having killed someone. He is a loving father who is uncertain about what to tell his young daughter. Readers see both his concern for his daughter and his desire to tell the truth.*

◆ Critical Thinking

❸ **Analyze** Ask students which of the narrator's remembered thoughts and sensations capture and convey the feeling of attack. *Thoughts and sensations include the narrator's automatic responses, the sour taste in his mouth, the way his feeling of fear drowns out all other motivations and reasoning.*

AMBUSH

from The Things They Carried

Tim O'Brien

When she was nine, my daughter Kathleen asked if I had ever killed anyone. She knew about the war; she knew I'd been a soldier. "You keep writing these war stories," she said, "so I guess you must've killed somebody." It was a difficult moment, but I did what seemed right, which was to say, "Of course not," and then to take her onto my lap and hold
❶ her for a while. Someday, I hope, she'll ask again. But here I want to pretend she's a grown-up. I want to tell her exactly what happened, or what I remember happening, and then I want to say to
❷ her that as a little girl she was absolutely right. This is why I keep writing war stories:

He was a short, slender young man of about twenty. I was afraid of him—afraid of something—and as he passed me on the trail I threw a grenade that exploded at his feet and killed him.

Or to go back:

Shortly after midnight we moved into the ambush site outside My Khe. The whole platoon was there, spread out in the dense brush along the trail, and for five hours nothing at all happened. We were working in two-man teams—one man on guard while the other slept, switching off every two hours—and I remember it was still dark when Kiowa shook me awake for the final watch. The night was foggy and hot. For the first few moments I felt lost, not sure about directions, groping for my helmet and weapon. I reached out and found three grenades and lined them up in front of me; the pins had already been straightened for quick throwing. And then for maybe half an hour I kneeled there and waited. Very gradually, in tiny slivers, dawn began to break through the fog, and from my position in the brush I could see ten or fifteen meters up the trail. The mosquitoes were fierce. I remember slapping at them, wondering if I should wake up Kiowa and ask for some repellent, then thinking it was a bad idea, then looking up and seeing the young man come out of the fog. He wore black clothing and rubber sandals and a gray ammunition belt. His shoulders were slightly stooped, his head cocked to the side as if listening for something. He seemed at ease. He carried his weapon in one hand, muzzle down, moving without any hurry up the center of the trail. There was no sound at all—none that I can remember. In a way, it seemed, he was part of the morning fog, or my own imagination, but there was also the reality of what was happening in my stomach. I had already pulled the pin on a grenade. I had come up to a crouch. It was entirely automatic. I did not hate the young man; I did not see him as the enemy; I did not ponder issues of morality or politics or military duty. I crouched and kept my head low. I tried to swallow whatever was rising from my stomach, which tasted like lemonade, something fruity and sour. ❸
I was terrified. There were no thoughts about killing. The grenade was to make him go away—just evaporate—and I leaned back and felt my mind go empty and then felt it fill up again. I had already thrown the grenade before telling myself to throw it. The brush was thick and I had to lob

Speaking, Listening, and Viewing Mini-Lesson

Interview
This mini-lesson supports the Speaking, Listening, and Viewing activity in the Idea Bank on p. 1085.

Introduce the Concept Through an interview, students gather information on a subject by questioning a knowledgeable person.

Develop Background Tell students that effective interviewers prepare by writing a list of questions in advance and by anticipating follow-up questions. Lead students to develop questions based on the 5W's and an H:

- Where exactly did you serve?
- When did you arrive? When did you leave?
- Why did you serve? Were you drafted?
- How did you cope with fear?
- What did you learn from your experiences?

Apply the Information Remind students to tape-record their interviews and to be prepared to ask follow-up questions.

Assess the Outcome Have students evaluate one another's interviews based on how well each achieved its purpose of getting the subject to describe memorable events and lessons learned.

it high, not aiming, and I remember the grenade seeming to freeze above me for an instant, as if a camera had clicked, and I remember ducking down and holding my breath and seeing little wisps of fog rise from the earth. The grenade bounced once and rolled across the trail. I did not hear it, but there must've been a sound, because the young man dropped his weapon and began to run, just two or three quick steps, then he hesitated, swiveling to his right, and he
4 glanced down at the grenade and tried to cover his head but never did. It occurred to me then that he was about to die. I wanted to warn him. The grenade made a popping noise—not soft but not loud either—not what I'd expected—and there was a puff of dust and smoke—a small white puff—and the young man seemed to jerk upward as if pulled by invisible wires. He fell on his back. His rubber sandals had been blown off. There was no wind. He lay at the center of the trail, his right leg bent beneath him, his one eye shut, his other eye a huge star-shaped hole.

It was not a matter of live or die. There was no real peril. Almost certainly the young man would have passed by. And it will always be that way.

Later, I remember, Kiowa tried to tell me that the man would've died anyway. He told me that it was a good kill, that I was a soldier and this was a war, that I should shape up and stop staring and ask myself what the dead man would've done if things were reversed.

None of it mattered. The words seemed far too complicated. All I could do was gape at the fact of the young man's body.

Even now I haven't finished sorting it out. Sometimes I forgive myself, other times I don't. In the ordinary hours of life I try not to dwell on it, but now and then, when I'm reading a newspaper or just sitting alone in a room, I'll look up and see the young man coming out of the morn- 5
ing fog. I'll watch him walk toward me, his shoulders slightly stooped, his head cocked to the side, and he'll pass within a few yards of me and suddenly smile at some secret thought and then continue up the trail to where it bends back into the fog.

◆ Build Vocabulary

ambush (am´ boosh´) *n.*: Lying in wait to attack by surprise

ammunition (am´ yoo nish´ ən) *n.*: Anything hurled by a weapon or exploded as a weapon; for example, bullets, shot, shells, etc.

muzzle (muz´ əl) *n.*: Front end of a barrel of a gun; the snout of an animal

gape (gāp) *v.*: Stare, open-mouthed

Guide for Responding

◆ Literature and Your Life

Reader's Response If you had been the narrator, would you have told your nine-year-old this story? Explain.

Thematic Focus Is this a war story or an anti-war story? Explain.

☑ Check Your Comprehension

1. Why does the narrator throw the grenade?
2. What is the narrator's reaction to what he has done?
3. How did Kiowa respond to the narrator's reaction to the killing?

◆ Critical Thinking

INTERPRET

1. What does the narrator mean when he says "And it will always be that way"? **[Interpret]**
2. (a) Why does the narrator have the fantasy he describes at the end of the story? (b)What effect does this fantasy have on the story? **[Infer]**

EVALUATE

3. Kiowa uses the expression "a good kill." Is there such a thing? Explain. **[Make a Judgment]**

EXTEND

4. Both of these selections look at Vietnam through a soldier's eyes. Compare and contrast the thoughts, feelings, and perceptions of the narrators of the two selections. **[Literature Link]**

Beyond the Selection

FURTHER READING

Other Works by Tim O'Brien
Going After Cacciato, In the Lake of the Woods

Other Works by Yusef Komunyakaa
Dien Cai Dan

Other Works About the Vietnam War
American Daughter Gone to War: On the Front Lines with an Army Nurse in Vietnam, Winnie Smith
Born on the Fourth of July, Ron Kovic

We suggest that you preview these works before recommending them to students.

INTERNET

In addition to the Vietnam Veterans' home page described in Block Scheduling Strategies (p. 1080), students can visit a site about Tim O'Brien at **http://www.illyria.com/tobsites.html** and read poems by Yusef Komunyakaa at the Poems from the Planet Earth site: **http://redfrog.nor-connect. no/~poems/mb/18.html**
Sites may have changed since this information was published.

We *strongly recommend* that you preview sites before you send students to them.

◆ Reading Strategy

4 Envision the Action Ask students which images from this passage helped them visualize the scene in their minds. *Images may include the grenade freezing as if a camera had clicked; wisps of fog; the motion of the victim; and the star-shaped hole.*

◆ Critical Thinking

5 Support Ask students how they know the narrator wishes he had not killed the young man. *He still finds it hard to forgive himself. He fantasizes a different ending to the story.*

Reinforce and Extend

Customize for
AP Students
To help these students learn more about soldiers' experiences in Vietnam, use the Internet search idea described in Block Scheduling Strategies (teacher edition, p. 1080).

Answers

◆ Literature and Your Life

Reader's Response Some students will argue that a father should be truthful; others will respect his decision to protect his daughter.

Thematic Focus Because it describes a war experience, it is a war story. Because the veteran regrets the killing, it is an anti-war story.

☑ Check Your Comprehension

1. He throws the grenade to protect himself from an enemy soldier.
2. He is stunned.
3. Kiowa tells him to accept the realities of war.

◆ Critical Thinking

1. He means he will never be able to accept that he killed without being in real danger.
2. (a) He wishes the memory could be different; he regrets the killing. (b) The fantasy emphasizes the narrator's ambiguity.
3. Some students will argue that a killing in wartime is justified. Others will argue that no killing is ever good.
4. Possible response: In "Camouflaging the Chimera," the soldier accepts his job as a killer; in "Ambush," he does not.

Answers

◆ Literary Focus

1. Komunyakaa uses sensory details which allow readers to imagine that they are part of the "we" who are in hiding. Words like "hugged bamboo," "crawled our spines," and "held our breath," bring reader into the action of the poem.
2. Possible responses: (a) The poet suggests a group of soldiers instead of just one. (b) "We" brings the reader into the poem more than "I" or "they."
3. Possible response: O'Brien's use of the first person allows readers to feel closer to, and therefore more sympathetic toward, the main character. It allows the reader to enter more fully into the narrator's internal conflict over the killing.

◆ Reading Strategy

1. Students may suggest the first, sixth, and seventh stanzas of the poem and the description of the killing in the short story. All of these segments use vivid language to bring the action to life.
2. Possible responses: These images from the poem may be especially vivid: "moon touched metal," and "river ran through our bones." From the short story, students may mention the soldier's jerking "upward as if pulled by invisible wires," and "star-shaped hole."
3. These images create a sensory experience that readers might otherwise be unable to imagine.
4. Readers are drawn into the story by imagining the fog and seeing the dawn break slowly, as the narrator sees it.

◆ Build Vocabulary

Using Words From War

Possible response: To help them imagine an *ambush* attack, the recruits were sent to the underbrush to wait. Each soldier was given rounds of *ammunition* and a *grenade* and assigned to a *platoon* of twenty others.

Using the Word Bank: Context

Possible responses:

1. I would seek *refuge*.
2. "Hold it by the *muzzle*."
3. I could only *gape* in amazement.
4. We might *ambush* her at lunch.
5. Guns and *ammunition* must be locked away separately.

Guide for Responding *(continued)*

◆ Literary Focus

First-Person Narrator

Both "Ambush" and "Camouflaging the Chimera" are told by a first-person narrator who participates in the action and reveals inner thoughts, feelings, and perceptions. Writers often use the first person when they want to show the narrator's personal responses or to focus on the narrator's personality or viewpoint.

1. Komunyakaa has said, "I believe the reader or listener should be able to enter the poem as a participant." In what specific ways does his use of the first person in "Camouflaging the Chimera" help make that happen?

2. (a) Why do you think that Komunyakaa uses "we" instead of "I" in "Camouflaging the Chimera"? (b) What is the impact of this choice?

3. Do you think O'Brien's use of the first person makes you more sympathetic to his protagonist? Why or why not?

◆ Reading Strategy

Envision the Action

When you use your imagination and your experience, along with the details that a writer provides, to **envision the action** of a literary work, you can picture the events in your mind—almost as if you're watching a movie.

1. Which action segments from these selections were easiest for you to picture in your mind as you read? Why?

2. What specific images especially helped you to envision the action? Why?

3. How does envisioning images such as "We hugged bamboo & leaned/against a breeze off the river" help you understand and appreciate "Camouflaging the Chimera"?

4. Explain how your ability to envision the action in the following passage from "Ambush" draws you into Tim O'Brien's world.

> Very gradually, in tiny slivers, dawn began to break through the fog, and from my position in the brush I could see ten or fifteen meters up the trail.

◆ Build Vocabulary

Using Words From War

In these selections, you encountered terms of warfare and words drawn from military jargon. Write a paragraph about a military practice maneuver using these words: ammunition, ambush, platoon, grenade.

Using the Word Bank: Context

In your notebook, write a sentence responding to each of the following specific instructions. Include one word from the Word Bank in each sentence.

a. refuge **b.** gape **c.** ambush **d.** ammunition **e.** muzzle

1. Tell what you would do if you were caught outside in a thunderstorm.

2. Tell how a sergeant might instruct recruits to hold a gun when standing at ease.

3. Describe your reaction when your best friend reveals that she's really from Mars.

4. Explain your strategy for capturing the leader of a rival team at camp.

5. Make a rule that would prevent children from injuring themselves with guns in the home.

◆ Grammar and Style

Noun Clauses

When identifying a **noun clause,** remember that the word *that* is often implied and not stated.

A **noun clause** is a subordinate clause that functions as a noun.

Practice Write each sentence in your notebook, and underline the noun clause.

1. This is why I keep writing war stories.

2. . . . but there was also the reality of what was happening in my stomach.

3. I tried to swallow whatever was rising from my stomach . . .

4. Later, I remember, Kiowa tried to tell me that the man would've died anyway.

5. . . . she said, "so I guess you must've killed somebody."

◆ Grammar and Style

1. Why I keep writing war stories.
2. what was happening in my stomach.
3. whatever was rising from my stomach
4. that the man would've died anyway
5. [that] you must've killed somebody.

Grammar Reinforcement

For additional instruction and practice, use the page on Noun Clauses, p. 37, in the *Writer's Solution Grammar Practice Book.*

Reteach

Students who have difficulty envisioning the action of the story or poem may benefit from your modeling the skill for them. Read aloud the first part of the long paragraph that begins in the middle of the first column on page 1082, stopping at intervals to tell students what you are "seeing." For example: "I see a dirt path with dense vegetation on either side. Soldiers, grouped in pairs, are waiting in the brush alongside the path." After you have done this a few times, ask volunteers to describe the action that they envision.

Build Your Portfolio

Idea Bank

Writing

1. **Letter to an Author** Writer a letter to either O'Brien or Komunyakaa, sharing your reactions to his work and asking any questions you have about his experiences during the war.
2. **Newspaper Article** Retell the events from "Ambush" in the form of a brief news article. Make sure to answer the questions *who, what, when, where, why,* and *how.* **[Social Studies Link]**
3. **Literary Analysis** Write an essay in which you analyze the message about war that one of the two selections conveys. Support your points with details and passages from the work.

Speaking, Listening, and Viewing

4. **Interview** Interview a Vietnam War veteran about his or her wartime experiences. Ask questions about the events that stand out in his or her memory and about the lessons that he or she feels can be learned from the war. Tape-record the interview, and share highlights with the class. **[Social Studies Link]**
5. **Choral Reading** With a group of classmates, perform a choral reading of Komunyakaa's poem. Practice reading the poem in unison before performing for the class. **[Performing Arts Link]**

Researching and Representing

6. **Dance** "Camouflaging the Chimera" is filled with images of body movement. Create a dance, with or without music, that captures the events of the poem. **[Performing Arts Link]**
7. **Multimedia Presentation** Create a multimedia presentation about the Vietnam War and the controversy surrounding it during the 1960's. Use newspaper and magazine articles, photographs, political cartoons, television news reports, and protest songs. **[Media Link]**

Online Activity www.phlit.phschool.com

Guided Writing Lesson

Suspenseful Personal Account

Both Tim O'Brien and Yusef Komunyakaa turned suspenseful personal experiences into gripping and moving pieces of literature. Follow their examples by writing a personal account about a suspenseful experience that you've had. For example, you might focus on a time when you were caught in a natural disaster, such as an earthquake or a hurricane.

Writing Skills Focus: Suspense

As you develop your account, create suspense by providing details that create a mood of uncertainty and make readers want to find out what's going to happen next. Notice the details that Tim O'Brien uses to create suspense in this passage:

Model From the Selection

. . . I remember it was still dark when Kiowa shook me awake for the final watch. The night was foggy and hot. For the first few moments I felt lost, not sure about directions, groping for my helmet and weapons. I reached out and found three grenades and lined them up in front of me; the pins had already been straightened for quick throwing. And then for maybe half an hour I kneeled there and waited.

The details of the setting create an ominous atmosphere, and the narrator's descriptions of his preparations make you feel that something dramatic is going to happen.

Prewriting After you decide on your topic, jot down the key details of the event. Then arrange them in the order in which they happened.

Drafting Begin by grabbing the reader's interest—for example, by jumping right into the action or describing the tremendous impact that the experience had on you. As you continue writing, create suspense by including details that create a mood of uncertainty and by withholding key details.

Revising As you revise, look for ways in which you can make your account more suspenseful.

Idea Bank

Customizing for
Performance Levels
Following are suggestions for matching Idea Bank topics with your students' performance levels:
Less Advanced Students: 1, 6
Average Students: 2, 4, 5
More Advanced Students: 3, 7

Customizing for
Learning Modalities
Following are suggestions for matching Idea Bank topics with your students' learning modalities:
Interpersonal: 4
Verbal/Linguistic: 4, 5, 7
Bodily/Kinesthetic: 6
Musical/Rhythmic: 6
Visual/Spatial: 7

Guided Writing Lesson

For more prewriting, elaboration, and revision strategies, see *Prentice Hall Writing and Grammar.*

Writing and Language Transparencies Use Writing Process Model 3: Personal Narrative, (pp. 13–16) to review the elements of a narrative account.

Writers at Work Videodisc
Have students view the videodisc segment on Narration (Ch. 2), featuring N. Scott Momaday, to see how the writer chooses a topic for narration.

Play frames 11644 to 20980

Writing Lab CD-ROM
Have students complete the tutorial on Narration. Follow these steps:

1. Use the Story Line Diagram to help students organize their narratives.
2. Have students view the Slide Show on beginning a draft. Have students draft on computer.
3. Encourage students to use the Language Variety Checker to aid their revision.

ASSESSMENT OPTIONS

Formal Assessment, Selection Test, pp. 323–325, and Assessment Resources Software. The selection test is designed so that it can be easily customized to the performance levels of your students.

Alternative Assessment, p. 75, includes options for less advanced students, more advanced students, verbal/linguistic learners, and visual/spatial learners.

PORTFOLIO ASSESSMENT
Use the following rubrics in ***Alternative Assessment*** to assess student writing:
Letter to an Author: Expression Rubric, p. 109
Newspaper Article: Summary Rubric, p. 113
Literary Analysis: Literary Analysis/Interpretation Rubric, p. 127
Guided Writing Lesson: Narrative Based on Personal Experience Rubric, p. 111

LESSON OBJECTIVES

1. **To develop vocabulary and word identification skills**
   - Latin Roots: *-grat-*
   - Using the Word Bank: Sentence Completion
2. **To use a variety of reading strategies to comprehend a drama**
   - Connect Your Experience
   - Reading Strategy: Question the Characters' Motives
3. **To increase knowledge of other cultures and to connect common elements across cultures**
   - Background for Understanding
   - Cross-Curricular Connection: Social Studies (ATE)
4. **To express and support responses to the text**
   - Critical Thinking
   - Idea Bank: Medical Chart
5. **To analyze literary elements**
   - Literary Focus: Dialogue and Stage Directions
6. **To plan, prepare, organize, and present literary interpretations**
   - Idea Bank: Dramatization
   - Speaking, Listening, and Viewing Mini-Lesson (ATE)
7. **To research self-selected and assigned topics and to produce reports in a variety of forms**
   - Idea Bank: Oral Presentation
   - Idea Bank: News Account
8. **To increase knowledge of the rules of grammar and usage**
   - Grammar and Style: Pronoun Case in Incomplete Constructions

Guide for Interpreting

Arthur Miller *(1915–)*

On October 20, 1995, the stars were out at a theater called Town Hall in New York City. The occasion was the eightieth birthday of playwright Arthur Miller, and dozens of celebrities from the world of literature and the theater had come together to honor one of their own.

A living legend of the American theater, Miller has chronicled the dilemma of common people pitted against powerful and unyielding social forces.

A native New Yorker, Miller has known bad times as well as good. During the Depression, his family lost its money and was forced to move from Manhattan to more modest living quarters in Brooklyn. Miller had to drop out of high school to take a job as a shipping clerk in a warehouse—an experience that he later dramatized in *A Memory of Two Mondays* (1955). Despite his inability to finish high school, he persuaded the University of Michigan to accept him as a student and used his savings from the warehouse job to finance his first year of studies.

Promising Playwright Miller first began writing drama while still in college. Though he held a variety of jobs after graduation, he continued to write. In 1947, his play *All My Sons* opened on Broadway to immediate acclaim, establishing Miller as a bright new talent. Two years later, he won international fame and a Pulitzer Prize for *Death of a Salesman* (1949), which critics hailed as a modern American tragedy.

His next play, *The Crucible* (1953), was less warmly received, for it used the Salem witchcraft trials of 1692 as a means of attacking the anti-communist "witch hunts" in Congress. Miller believed that the hysteria surrounding the witchcraft trials paralleled the contemporary political climate of McCarthyism—Senator Joseph McCarthy's obsessive quest to uncover Communist party infiltration of American institutions.

In the introduction to his *Collected Plays* (1957), Miller described his perceptions of the atmosphere during the McCarthy era and the way in which those perceptions influenced the writing of *The Crucible*: "It was as though the whole country had been born anew, without a memory even of certain elemental decencies which a year or two earlier no one would have imagined could be altered, let alone forgotten. Astounded, I watched men pass me by without a nod whom I had known rather well for years; and again, the astonishment was produced by my knowledge, which I could not give up, that the terror in these people was being knowingly planned and consciously engineered, and yet that all they knew was terror. That so interior and subjective an emotion could have been so manifestly created from without was a marvel to me. It underlies every word in *The Crucible*."

In the Shadows of McCarthyism During the two years following the publication and production of *The Crucible*, Miller was investigated for possible associations with the Communist party. In 1956, he was called to testify before the House Committee on Un-American Activities. Although he never became a member of the Communist party, Miller, like so many of his contemporaries, had advocated principles of social justice and equality among the classes. He had become disillusioned, however, by the reality of communism as practiced in the Soviet Union. At the hearings, he testified about his own experiences, but he refused to discuss his colleagues and associates. He was found guilty of contempt (a sentence later overturned) for his refusal.

In 1956, the spotlight was focused on Miller's personal life when he married glamorous film star Marilyn Monroe. Though he did little writing during their five-year marriage, he did pen a screenplay of a film, *The Misfits* (1961), in which Monroe starred. After their divorce, Miller went on to write other noteworthy plays, including *The Price* (1968) and *The Last Yankee* (1991).

Prentice Hall Literature Program Resources

REINFORCE / RETEACH / EXTEND

Selection Support Pages
Build Vocabulary: Latin Roots: *-grat-*, p. 338
Grammar and Style: Pronoun Case in Incomplete Constructions, p. 339
Reading Strategy: Question the Characters' Motives, p. 340
Literary Focus: Drama: Dialogue and Stage Directions, p. 341

Strategies for Diverse Student Needs, Make a Character Chart, p. 76

Beyond Literature
Cross-Curricular Connection: Social Studies, p. 76

Formal Assessment Selection Test, pp. 326–328; Assessment Resources Software

Alternative Assessment, p. 76

Resource Pro CD-ROM
The Crucible, Act I

Literature CD-ROM
The History of Am. Lit.: Part 2, Disc 2, Feature 4
How to Read and Understand Drama: Feature 12

The Crucible

◆ Background for Understanding

History: The Salem Witchcraft Trials

In 1692, the British colony of Massachusetts was swept by a witchcraft hysteria that resulted in the execution of twenty people and the jailing of at least 150 others. The incident was not isolated: It is estimated that between one million and nine million Europeans were executed as witches in the sixteenth and seventeenth centuries. Many of these individuals were merely practicing folk customs that had survived in Europe since pre-Christian times. In addition, in an era when religion and politics were closely allied, witch hunts were often politically motivated. England's James I, for example, wrote a treatise on witchcraft and sometimes accused his enemies of practicing the black arts. It was a cry that resonated well in a superstitious populace.

The Trial of "Two Witches" at Salem, Massachusetts, in 1662, Howard Pyle

For the New England colonies, however, the witchcraft episode was unusual, though perhaps inevitable. The colonists endured harsh conditions and punishing hardship in their lives. Finding themselves at the mercy of forces beyond their control—bitter weather, sickness and death, devastating fires, drought, and insect infestations that killed their crops—many colonists attributed their misfortunes to the Devil. They were fearful (some would say paranoid) people, and their Puritan faith stressed the biblical teaching that witches were real and dangerous.

In the small parish of Salem Village, many were quick to blame witchcraft when the minister's daughter and several other girls were afflicted by seizures and lapses into unconsciousness, especially after it was learned that the girls had been dabbling in fortune-telling with the minister's slave Tituba. (They were not dancing in the woods, as they were in the play.) At first, only Tituba and two elderly women were named as witches, but then the hunt spread, until some of the colony's most prominent citizens stood accused. Many historians have seen a pattern of social and economic animosity behind the accusations, but most feel that mass hysteria was also a strong contributing factor.

When *The Crucible* was first published, Arthur Miller added a note about the play's historical accuracy: "This play is not history in the sense in which the word is used by the academic historian. Dramatic purposes have sometimes required many characters to be fused into one; the number of girls involved in the 'crying-out' has been reduced; Abigail's age has been raised; while there were several judges of almost equal authority, I have symbolized them in Hathorne and Danforth. However, I believe that the reader will discover here the essential nature of one of the strangest and most awful chapters in human history. The fate of each character is exactly that of his historical model, and there is no one in the drama who did not play a similar—and in some cases exactly the same—role in history."

◆ Background for Understanding

Literature *The Crucible* opened on Broadway on January 22, 1953, and ran for only 197 performances. It received lukewarm but polite reviews—what Miller himself called "respectable notices, the kind that bury you decently." Audiences and critics alike were uncomfortable with the theme of witch-hunting in the McCarthy era. Although the play ran for only a short time in America, it was very popular in Europe, and Miller was planning to attend the Brussels opening in 1954 when he was denied a passport by the State Department. The denial of the passport was just the beginning of Miller's troubles with the government over his alleged leftist sympathies.

The opening of *The Crucible,* however, did establish Arthur Miller as a playwright who brought a new seriousness to the American theater. Drama critic Eric Bentley commented on Miller's commitment to weighty moral issues shortly after *The Crucible* opened:

> Few events on Broadway have any importance whatsoever except to that small section of the community . . . that sees Broadway plays. A play by Arthur Miller is an exception. Such a play is not only better than the majority; it belongs in the mainstream of our culture. Such an author has something to say about America that is worth discussing. In *The Crucible,* Mr. Miller says something that has to be discussed.

Interest Grabber Write the phrase *courtroom drama* on the chalkboard and invite students to name dramatic legal cases they know of, from both fiction and real life. Then invite students to offer their opinions on why specific cases as well as courtroom situations in general capture people's attention. Follow by letting students know that the play they are about to read explores the legal, political, and moral issues surrounding two notorious sets of trials from American history.

Customize for
Less Proficient Readers
Portions of the commentaries within Miller's stage directions may pose difficulties for less proficient readers. Suggest that students read through the play twice, focusing more on the plot during the first reading and more on the commentaries during the second.

Customize for
AP Students
Many ironies present themselves in Act I. Encourage more advanced students to notice and discuss this aspect of Miller's writing as they read.

Customize for
English Language Learners
To lend authenticity to his characters' speech, Miller uses certain archaic phrases and forms. Help students anticipate and adapt to this style by previewing examples such as "he *have been* searchin'" and "it *were* sport."

Customize for
Gifted/Talented Students
The play's stage directions include gestures and movements that help to reveal the characters' feelings and motives. Have students give performances that capture these important nonverbal details.

Guide for Interpreting, Act I

◆ Literature and Your Life

CONNECT YOUR EXPERIENCE

If you have ever observed a rumor spread through your school or helped to spread one yourself, you know how easy it is to be swept along with a crowd, believing blindly rather than using your judgment.

Journal Writing Briefly describe an incident from a film or your own life in which a false rumor was accepted by many as the truth. What were the consequences?

THEMATIC FOCUS: SOCIAL PROTEST

As you read Act I of *The Crucible*, think about what Miller is saying about the weaknesses and faults of people past and present.

◆ Reading Strategy

QUESTION THE CHARACTERS' MOTIVES

"A man can smile and smile and be a villain," William Shakespeare once observed. And indeed, like people in real life, characters in plays are not always what they seem. Often we must **question their motives**, or reasons, for behaving in a certain way. Ambition, fear, greed, guilt, jealousy, love, loyalty, revenge—these are just some of the driving forces behind human behavior. As you read Act I of *The Crucible*, ask yourself the following questions about each character:

- What motivates the character to speak or act in this way?
- Does the character hide his or her true motives? If so, how?
- Might the character be unaware of his or her true motives?

◆ Grammar and Style

PRONOUN CASE IN INCOMPLETE CONSTRUCTIONS

In written and, especially, in spoken English, some sentences use **incomplete constructions,** omitting words that are understood. In such cases, it may be hard to determine whether to use a subject or an object pronoun. The best way to decide is to mentally complete the incomplete construction. You can then tell whether the pronoun should be a subject such as *I*, *he*, *she*, *we*, or *they* or an object such as *me*, *him*, *her*, *us*, or *them*. In the following examples, the words that mentally complete each sentence are in brackets.

They want slaves, not such as *I* [am]. (subject)

They want slaves more than [they want] *me*. (object)

◆ Literary Focus

DRAMA: DIALOGUE AND STAGE DIRECTIONS

Drama consists of **dialogue,** or the words characters speak, and **stage directions,** or the instructions the playwright gives actors, the director, and technicians involved in putting on the play. Dialogue not only moves the plot along, but also reveals the characters' personalities and backgrounds to the audience. Stage directions usually indicate where a scene takes place, what it should look like, and how the characters should move and speak. Stage directions may also convey valuable background information. As you read Act I of *The Crucible*, look for information in both the stage directions and dialogue.

◆ Build Vocabulary

LATIN WORD ROOTS: *-grat-*

From *gratus*, Latin for "pleasing," comes the root *-grat-*, which means "pleasing" or "agreeable." An *ingratiating* act, for example, is one done to please others.

WORD BANK

Before you read, preview this list of words from Act I.

predilection
ingratiating
dissembling
calumny
inculcation
propitiation
licentious

Test Preparation Workshop

Writing Skills: Grammar and Usage
Many standardized tests require students to choose the best word or group of words to complete a sentence. Use the following sample item to give students practice in this skill.

Among the many plays written by Arthur Miller ______ *The Crucible*, *Death of a Salesman*, and *A View From the Bridge*.

Choose the best word to fill in the blank.

A is
B are
C was
D remains

A, *C*, and *D* are singular. *B* is plural, matching the plural subject. Therefore, *B* is the best answer.

The Crucible[1]

Arthur Miller

CHARACTERS

Reverend Parris	**Mercy Lewis**	**Francis Nurse**
Betty Parris	**Mary Warren**	**Ezekiel Cheever**
Tituba	**John Proctor**	**Marshal Herrick**
Abigail Williams	**Rebecca Nurse**	**Judge Hathorne**
Susanna Walcott	**Giles Corey**	**Deputy Governor Danforth**
Mrs. Ann Putnam	**Reverend John Hale**	**Sarah Good**
Thomas Putnam	**Elizabeth Proctor**	**Hopkins**

ACT I

(An Overture)

1 *A small upper bedroom in the home of* REVEREND SAMUEL PARRIS, *Salem, Massachusetts, in the spring of the year 1692.*

There is a narrow window at the left. Through its leaded panes the morning sunlight streams. A candle still burns near the bed, which is at the right. A chest, a chair, and a small table are the other furnishings. At the back a door opens on the landing of the stairway to the ground floor. The room gives off an air of clean spareness. The roof rafters are exposed, and the wood colors are raw and unmellowed.

As the curtain rises, REVEREND PARRIS *is discovered kneeling beside the bed, evidently in prayer. His daughter,* BETTY PARRIS, *aged ten, is lying on the bed, inert.*

At the time of these events Parris was in his middle forties. In history he cut a villainous path, and there is very little good to be said for him. He believed he was being persecuted wherever he went, despite his best efforts to win people and God to his side. In meeting, he felt insulted if someone rose to shut the door without first asking his permission. He was a widower with no interest in children, or talent with them. He regarded them as young adults, and until this strange crisis he, like the rest of Salem, never conceived that the children were anything but thankful for being permitted to walk straight, eyes slightly lowered, arms at the sides, and mouths shut until bidden to speak. 2

1. **crucible** (kro͞o′ sə bəl) *n.*: Heat-resistant container in which metals are melted or fused at very high temperatures; thus, a severe trial or test.

Develop Understanding

One-Minute Insight Conflicts, resentments, and motives for accusing others all surface in this act, which begins with intimations of witchcraft and ends with a chilling "crying out" of names of those who supposedly kept company with the Devil. Through the characters' words and actions, as well as Miller's revealing stage directions, we learn that some act out of fear and self-preservation, that others act on not-so-deeply buried feelings of spite and malice, and that still others seem to represent the voice of reason. In other words, we begin to understand who will stand as an accuser, who will stand accused, and why, as the tragedy of Salem is set in motion.

◆ Literary Focus

1 Drama: Dialogue and Stage Directions Ask students what important information is revealed in this opening paragraph of the stage directions. *Students should note that the time and place in which the act is set is revealed here.*

◆ Literary Focus

2 Drama: Dialogue and Stage Directions Explain that Miller's stage directions for *The Crucible* are unusual in that they include a lengthy commentary in addition to information about settings, props, gestures, and movements. Then have students identify the kind of information that Miller provides here. *Sample responses: He provides background information about one of the characters, Reverend Parris, and about the Puritans; he provides information about Parris's personality traits and motives.*

Block Scheduling Strategies

Consider these suggestions to take advantage of extended class time:

- To build background on playwright Arthur Miller, use the **Literature CD-ROM,** *The History of American Literature:* Part 2, Disk 2, Feature 4, which focuses on Miller and his play *Death of a Salesman.*
- Before students read, have a brief discussion on rumors and how easily they can be spread. Then have students complete the journal activity in Literature and Your Life (p. 1088). Students might then meet in small groups to discuss their entries.
- To help students understand the conventions of drama, discuss with them, before they read the play, the Literary Focus, (p. 1088). After students read the play, have them complete the Literary Focus questions on p. 1112. For reinforcement, use the Literary Focus page in ***Selection Support***, p. 341.
- Ask groups of students to choose, practice, and perform scenes from Act I. Afterwards, let students critique their own performances.
- Students can work in small groups to answer the Critical Thinking questions (p. 1111).
- Have students complete one of the writing assignments in the Idea Bank (p. 1112).

❶ **Enrichment** Explain to students that one of the reasons the Puritans felt the Church of England needed to be purified was their belief that there were too many rituals and sacraments. One of the rituals to which they objected was the celebration of Christmas.

◆ Critical Thinking

❷ **Draw Conclusions** Encourage students to draw conclusions about Salem and its inhabitants, based on this passage. *Responses may include: Salem is an extremely close-knit community—too close-knit for some people; it is a place where individual freedom is not highly valued.*

◆ Literary Focus

❸ **Drama: Dialogue and Stage Directions** Sample response: The information that Miller provides about the experiences, temperaments, and beliefs of the Puritans of Salem will help to explain their actions as the play unfolds.

Customize for *AP Students*

Encourage students to analyze and describe Miller's attitude toward the Puritans. Have them cite specific passages and phrases to support their responses. *Some students may describe Miller's attitude as critical, disapproving, or wary; in support, they might cite such passages and phrases as "To the European, . . . sect of fanatics"; "strict and somber way of life"; and "the coming madness." Other students may point out that Miller shows a sense of irony; this sentiment is revealed in his description of the Puritans' attitude toward the Indians and in the passage "The fathers had of course been persecuted . . . deny any other sect its freedom."*

His house stood in the "town"—but we today would hardly call it a village. The meeting house was nearby, and from this point outward—toward the bay or inland—there were a few small-windowed, dark houses snuggling against the raw Massachusetts winter. Salem had been established hardly forty years before. To the European world the whole province was a barbaric frontier inhabited by a sect of fanatics who, nevertheless, were shipping out products of slowly increasing quantity and value.

No one can really know what their lives were like. They had no novelists—and would not have permitted anyone to read a novel if one were handy. Their creed forbade anything resembling a theater or "vain enjoyment." They
❶ did not celebrate Christmas, and a holiday from work meant only that they must concentrate even more upon prayer.

Which is not to say that nothing broke into this strict and somber way of life. When a new farmhouse was built, friends assembled to "raise the roof," and there would be special foods cooked and probably some potent cider passed around. There was a good supply of ne'er-do-wells in Salem, who dallied at the shovelboard[2] in Bridget Bishop's tavern. Probably more than the creed, hard work kept the morals of the place from spoiling, for the people were forced to fight the land like heroes for every grain of corn, and no man had very much time for fooling around.

That there were some jokers, however, is indicated by the practice of appointing a two-man patrol whose duty was to "walk forth in the time of God's worship to take notice of such as either lie about the meeting house, without attending to the word and ordinances, or that lie at home or in the fields without giving good account thereof, and to take the names of such persons, and to present them to the magistrates, whereby they may be accordingly proceeded against." This predilection for minding other people's business was time-honored
❷ among the people of Salem, and it undoubtedly created many of the suspicions which were to feed the coming madness. It was also, in my opinion, one of the things that a John Proctor would rebel against, for the time of the armed camp had almost passed, and since the country was reasonably—although not wholly—safe, the old disciplines were beginning to rankle. ❷
But, as in all such matters, the issue was not clear-cut, for danger was still a possibility, and in unity still lay the best promise of safety.

The edge of the wilderness was close by. The American continent stretched endlessly west, and it was full of mystery for them. It stood, dark and threatening, over their shoulders night and day, for out of it Indian tribes marauded from time to time, and Reverend Parris had parishioners who had lost relatives to these heathen.

The parochial snobbery of these people was partly responsible for their failure to convert the Indians. Probably they also preferred to take land from heathens rather than from fellow Christians. At any rate, very few Indians were converted, and the Salem folk believed that the virgin forest was the Devil's last preserve, his home base and the citadel of his final stand. To the best of their knowledge the American forest was the last place on earth that was not paying homage to God.

For these reasons, among others, they carried about an air of innate resistance, even of persecution. Their fathers had, of course, been persecuted in England. So now they and their church found it necessary to deny any other sect its freedom, lest their New Jerusalem[3] be defiled and corrupted by wrong ways and deceitful ideas.

They believed, in short, that they held in their steady hands the candle that would light the world. We have inherited this belief, and it has helped and hurt us. It helped them with the discipline it gave them. They were a dedicated folk, by and large, and they had to be to survive the life they had chosen or been born into in this country.

> **◆ Literary Focus** Why is this background information about the situation in Salem important to your understanding of the play? ❸

The proof of their belief's value to them may be taken from the opposite character of the

2. **shovelboard:** Game in which a coin or other disk is driven with the hand along a highly polished board, floor, or table marked with transverse lines.

3. **New Jerusalem:** In the Bible, the holy city of heaven.

Cross-Curricular Connection: Social Studies

Puritanism As students read Miller's description of Salem's Puritan settlers and their "strict and somber way of life," they may become curious about the historical roots of Puritanism.

During the late 1500's, a party within the Church of England—that country's national church—began to gain strength as it campaigned for reforms. The object of these reforms was to "purify" the church, for example, by granting more authority to individual congregations and less to high-ranking church officials and by simplifying the sacraments. The solemn and devout people who pressed for such reforms came to call themselves *Puritans.*

The Puritans came into increasing conflict not only with the Church of England but also with the English monarchy during the 1600's. The conflict escalated to the point that from 1642–1649 Puritan forces and royalist forces fought a civil war. The Puritans were victorious and gained control of the government. The monarchy was restored, however, in 1660.

Ask students what other highly significant event took place during this period of Puritan history. *Some Puritans journeyed to New England to establish settlements such as Salem.*

first Jamestown settlement, farther south, in Virginia. The Englishmen who landed there were motivated mainly by a hunt for profit. They had thought to pick off the wealth of the new country and then return rich to England. They were a band of individualists, and a much more ingratiating group than the Massachusetts men. But Virginia destroyed them. Massachusetts tried to kill off the Puritans, but they combined; they set up a communal society which, in the beginning, was little more than an armed camp with an autocratic and very devoted leadership. It was, however, an autocracy by consent, for they were united from top to bottom by a commonly held ideology whose perpetuation was the reason and justification for all their sufferings. So their self-denial, their purposefulness, their suspicion of all vain pursuits, their hard-handed justice, were altogether perfect instruments for the conquest of this space so antagonistic to man.

But the people of Salem in 1692 were not quite the dedicated folk that arrived on the *Mayflower*. A vast differentiation had taken place, and in their own time a revolution had unseated the royal government and substituted a junta[4] which was at this moment in power. The times, to their eyes, must have been out of joint, and to the common folk must have seemed as insoluble and complicated as do ours today. It is not hard to see how easily many could have been led to believe that the time of confusion had been brought upon them by deep and darkling forces. No hint of such speculation appears on the court record, but social disorder in any age breeds such mystical suspicions, and when, as in Salem, wonders are brought forth from below the social surface, it is too much to expect people to hold back very long from laying on the victims with all the force of their frustrations.

EXECUTION OF REV. STEPHEN BURROUGHS.

The Execution of the Reverend Stephen Burroughs for Witchcraft at Salem, Massachusetts, in 1692, 19th-Century Engraving

▲ **Critical Viewing** This nineteenth-century engraving shows the hanging of the Reverend Stephen Burroughs during the Salem witchcraft trials. What does it suggest about the condemned man's state of mind? **[Infer]**

The Salem tragedy, which is about to begin in these pages, developed from a paradox. It is a paradox in whose grip we still live, and there is no prospect yet that we will discover its resolution. Simply, it was this: for good purposes, even high purposes, the people of Salem developed a theocracy, a combine of state and religious power whose function was to keep the community together, and to prevent any kind of disunity that might open it to destruction by material or ideological enemies. It was forged for a necessary purpose and accomplished that purpose. But all organization is and must be grounded on the idea of exclusion and prohibition, just as two objects cannot occupy the same space. Evidently the

◆ Build Vocabulary

predilection (pred´ əl ek´ shən) *n.*: Preexisting liking; preference

ingratiating (in grā´ shē āt iŋ) *adj.*: Having a quality that brings oneself into favor; charming or flattering

4. **junta** (hoon´ tə) *n.*: Assembly or council.

Literature CD-ROM
To build background, use *The History of American Literature:* Part 2, Disc 2, Feature 4, which focuses in part on Arthur Miller and his play, *Death of a Salesman.*

Customize for
Less Proficient Readers
To help these students understand the actions and dialogue of the various characters, use ***Strategies for Diverse Student Needs,*** p. 76, "Make a Character Chart."

▶Critical Viewing◀

❹ **Infer** Students may infer that the condemned man faced his death with courage and that he spent his final moments in prayer.

❺ **Clarification** The revolution in England to which Miller refers took place in 1688 and is known as the Glorious Revolution. In this rebellion, members of England's Parliament forced King James II to abandon his throne and flee to France.

◆ Critical Thinking

❻ **Contrast** Have students explain in their own words the contrast that Miller points up between the people of Salem in 1692 and their predecessors who arrived on the *Mayflower.* *According to Miller, the people who arrived on the Mayflower were united by hardship and suffering. The Puritans of 1692, on the other hand, lived in a period of social and political turmoil; they experienced disorder and confusion rather than a sense of common purpose.*

❼ **Clarification** If students are not familiar with the term *paradox,* explain that a paradox is a statement that seems contradictory but that actually presents a truth.

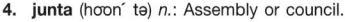

Humanities: Art

The Execution of the Reverend Stephen Burroughs at Salem, Massachusetts, in 1692.

This nineteenth-century engraving captures the execution of one of the people accused of witchcraft during the hysteria in Salem. Like many nineteenth-century engravers who focused on historical subjects, the artist has attempted to be historically accurate. Yet, probably because the artist had access to little factual material about the witchcraft trials, a number of the details in the picture seem out of place. Although the executioner, the minister on horseback, and the accused are all dressed in Puritan attire, the guards are dressed in costumes that seem to be taken from medieval Europe rather than colonial America. The weapons the guards are holding also seem to be taken from the distant past. Ask:

1. What does the engraving suggest about Burroughs's state of mind in the moments preceding his execution? *Students should note that he looks pensive. He seems to be looking skyward, perhaps religiously.*
2. What role does the minister on horseback seem to be playing in the proceedings? *He may be keeping the crowd back.*
3. What emotions does this engraving evoke in you? Why? *Students may be saddened by the image since the "criminal" may not fit their expectations.*

◆ Reading Strategy

❶ Question the Characters' Motives Point out that in these paragraphs Miller discusses two different motives that people in Salem might have had for accusing their neighbors of witchcraft. Have students identify the motives. *Psychologically repressed people could project their own sins and guilt onto others through the accusations. Envious and economically frustrated people could take revenge on others by accusing them.*

◆ Reading Strategy

❷ Question the Characters' Motives Students should note that the stage directions reveal conflicting motives on Tituba's part. She genuinely cares about Betty, but she also has a justifiable fear of being blamed for anything that goes wrong in Reverend Parris's household.

◆ Literary Focus

❸ Drama: Dialogue and Stage Directions Have a volunteer interpret both the dialogue and stage directions by acting out this passage. Afterward, review the print conventions behind both types of text. Point out that dialogue is printed in Roman, or "normal," type, while stage directions appear in italics.

◆ Reading Strategy

❹ Question the Characters' Motives Based on what Miller reveals about Abigail's personality, what can students conclude about her being "all worry and apprehension and propriety" as she enters the scene? *Students may say that she is putting on an act; she is hiding her true feelings and motives.*

---

time came in New England when the repressions of order were heavier than seemed warranted by the dangers against which the order was organized. The witch-hunt was a perverse manifestation of the panic which set in among all classes when the balance began to turn toward greater individual freedom.

When one rises above the individual villainy displayed, one can only pity them all, just as we shall be pitied someday. It is still impossible for man to organize his social life without repressions, and the balance has yet to be struck between order and freedom.

The witch-hunt was not, however, a mere repression. It was also, and as importantly, a long overdue opportunity for everyone so inclined to express publicly his guilt and sins, under the cover of accusations against the victims. It suddenly became possible—and patriotic and holy—for a man to say that Martha Corey had come into his bedroom at night, and that, while his wife was sleeping at his side, Martha laid herself down on his chest and "nearly suffocated him." Of course it was her
❶ spirit only, but his satisfaction at confessing himself was no lighter than if it had been Martha herself. One could not ordinarily speak such things in public.

Long-held hatreds of neighbors could now be openly expressed, and vengeance taken, despite the Bible's charitable injunctions. Landlust which had been expressed before by constant bickering over boundaries and deeds, could now be elevated to the arena of morality; one could cry witch against one's neighbor and feel perfectly justified in the bargain. Old scores could be settled on a plane of heavenly combat between Lucifer[5] and the Lord; suspicions and the envy of the miserable toward the happy could and did burst out in the general revenge.

REVEREND PARRIS *is praying now, and, though we cannot hear his words, a sense of his confusion hangs about him. He mumbles, then seems about to weep; then he weeps, then prays again; but his daughter does not stir on the bed.*

The door opens, and his Negro slave enters. TITUBA *is in her forties.* PARRIS *brought her with him from Barbados, where he spent some years as a merchant before entering the ministry. She enters as one does who can no longer bear to be barred from the sight of her beloved, but she is also very frightened because her slave sense has warned her that, as always, trouble in this house eventually lands on her back.*

> **◆ Reading Strategy** What do you learn here about Tituba's motives? ❷

TITUBA, *already taking a step backward:* My Betty be hearty soon?

PARRIS: Out of here!

TITUBA, *backing to the door:* My Betty not goin' die . . .

PARRIS, *scrambling to his feet in a fury:* Out of my sight! *She is gone.* Out of my— *He is overcome with sobs. He clamps his teeth against them and closes the door and leans against it, exhausted.* Oh, my God! God help me! *Quaking with fear, mumbling to himself through his sobs, he goes to the bed and gently takes* BETTY'*s hand.* Betty. Child. Dear child. Will you wake, will you open up your eyes! Betty, little one . . . ❸

He is bending to kneel again when his niece, ABIGAIL WILLIAMS, *seventeen, enters—a strikingly beautiful girl, an orphan, with an endless capacity for* dissembling. *Now she is all worry and apprehension and propriety.* ❹

ABIGAIL: Uncle? *He looks to her.* Susanna Walcott's here from Doctor Griggs.

PARRIS: Oh? Let her come, let her come.

ABIGAIL, *leaning out the door to call to Susanna, who is down the hall a few steps:* Come in, Susanna.

SUSANNA WALCOTT, *a little younger than* ABIGAIL, *a nervous, hurried girl, enters.*

PARRIS, *eagerly:* What does the doctor say, child?

SUSANNA, *craning around* PARRIS *to get a look at* BETTY: He bid me come and tell you, reverend sir, that he cannot discover no medicine for it in his books.

PARRIS: Then he must search on.

SUSANNA: Aye, sir, he have been searchin' his

---

5. **Lucifer** (lo͞o sə fər): The Devil.

Cross-Curricular Connection: Social Studies

Early Settlers In his commentary, Miller contrasts the Puritans of Salem with two other groups: the Jamestown settlers and the settlers who arrived on the *Mayflower*. You might share the following information to help students better understand each of these communities.

- **Jamestown, Virginia,** was the first English settlement in America. It was founded in 1607. As Miller notes, the people who settled Jamestown were not religious dissidents but rather were largely motivated by profit. These settlers generally belonged to the Church of England and supported the English monarchy.
- The people who journeyed from England to Plymouth, Massachusetts, on the ***Mayflower*** in 1620 established the second permanent English settlement in America. Some, but not all, of those aboard the ship belonged to a Puritan group known as the Separatists. These settlers are also commonly known as the Pilgrims.
- The people who lived in **Salem** in 1692 were not descendants of the Pilgrims. Rather, they were the descendants of a group of Puritans who arrived in Massachusetts in 1630.

Have groups of students do research to learn more about each of these communities and the role each played in the growth of Colonial America.

books since he left you, sir. But he bid me tell you, that you might look to unnatural things for the cause of it.

PARRIS, *his eyes going wide:* No—no. There be no unnatural cause here. Tell him I have sent for Reverend Hale of Beverly, and Mr. Hale will surely confirm that. Let him look to medicine and put out all thought of unnatural causes here. There be none.

5 **SUSANNA:** Aye, sir. He bid me tell you. *She turns*
6 *to go.*

ABIGAIL: Speak nothin' of it in the village, Susanna.

PARRIS: Go directly home and speak nothing of unnatural causes.

SUSANNA: Aye, sir. I pray for her. *She goes out.*

ABIGAIL: Uncle, the rumor of witchcraft is all about; I think you'd best go down and deny it yourself. The parlor's packed with people, sir. I'll sit with her.

PARRIS, *pressed, turns on her:* And what shall I say to them? That my daughter and my niece I discovered dancing like heathen in the forest?

ABIGAIL: Uncle, we did dance; let you tell them I confessed it—and I'll be whipped if I must be. But they're speakin' of witchcraft. Betty's not witched.

PARRIS: Abigail, I cannot go before the congregation when I know you have not opened with me. What did you do with her in the forest?

ABIGAIL: We did dance, uncle, and when you leaped out of the bush so suddenly, Betty was frightened and then she fainted. And there's the whole of it.

PARRIS: Child. Sit you down.

ABIGAIL, *quavering, as she sits:* I would never hurt Betty. I love her dearly.

PARRIS: Now look you, child, your punishment will come in its time. But if you trafficked with spirits in the forest I must know it now, for surely my enemies will, and they will ruin me with it.

ABIGAIL: But we never conjured spirits.

PARRIS: Then why can she not move herself since midnight? This child is desperate! *Abigail lowers her eyes.* It must come out—my enemies will bring it out. Let me know what you done there. Abigail, do you understand that I have many enemies?

ABIGAIL: I have heard of it, uncle. 7

PARRIS: There is a faction that is sworn to drive me from my pulpit. Do you understand that?

ABIGAIL: I think so, sir.

PARRIS: Now then, in the midst of such disruption, my own household is discovered to be the very center of some obscene practice. Abominations are done in the forest—

ABIGAIL: It were sport, uncle!

PARRIS, *pointing at* BETTY: You call this sport? *She lowers her eyes. He pleads:* Abigail, if you know something that may help the doctor, for God's sake tell it to me. *She is silent.* I saw Tituba waving her arms over the fire when I came on you. Why was she doing that? And I heard a screeching and gibberish coming from her mouth. She were swaying like a dumb beast over that fire!

ABIGAIL: She always sings her Barbados songs, and we dance.

PARRIS: I cannot blink what I saw, Abigail, for my enemies will not blink it. I saw a dress lying 8
on the grass.

ABIGAIL, *innocently:* A dress?

PARRIS—*it is very hard to say:* Aye, a dress. And I thought I saw—someone naked running through the trees!

ABIGAIL, *in terror:* No one was naked! You mistake yourself, uncle!

PARRIS, *with anger:* I saw it! *He moves from her. Then, resolved:* Now tell me true, Abigail. And I pray you feel the weight of truth upon you, for now my ministry's at stake, my ministry and

◆ Build Vocabulary

dissembling (di sem´ bliŋ) *n.*: Disguising one's real nature or motives; pretense

5 Clarification Like Salem, Beverly was a town in the Massachusetts Bay Colony, the large New England settlement established by Puritans in 1628.

◆ Reading Strategy

6 Question the Characters' Motives Have students speculate about why Parris is so quick to dismiss the possibility that Betty's ailment is the result of "unnatural causes." Why does he instruct her to "Go directly home and speak nothing of unnatural causes"? *Students may say that Parris does not want a witch hunt to begin over the matter.*

◆ Reading Strategy

7 Question the Characters' Motives Ask students what this dialogue reveals about Reverend Parris. What seems to be the main motive behind his decisions and actions at this point? *Students should note that he is primarily concerned with his reputation and his position in the community. He is determined to keep his enemies from using the strange circumstances surrounding Betty's illness against him.*

Comprehension Check ☑

8 Have students use context clues to determine the meaning of the word *blink* in this sentence. *Responses may include: ignore, disregard, overlook.*

Tips to Guide Reading

Sustained Reading Encourage students to keep a character map as they read, creating links between characters and making annotations on the relationships between characters. Tell students that creating the map will help them identify the major characters and how they relate to one another. Having the map as a reference will help students confirm relationships between characters as the play progresses.

◆ Critical Thinking

❶ **Support** Ask students if they think that Abigail is telling the truth as she responds to her uncle's questions. Have them give reasons in support of their answers. *Students should note that Abigail is probably not being truthful. In support, they should recall that earlier in this act, she was described as having "an endless capacity for dissembling"—in other words, she is an accomplished liar.*

◆ Literary Focus

❷ **Drama: Dialogue and Stage Directions** Have two volunteers read this exchange aloud. Then have students explain how the stage directions help to reveal Mrs. Putnam's thoughts and motives. *Students should note that Mrs. Putnam is described as being "full of breath, shiny-eyed" and "very pleased" as she repeats the specifics of the rumors of witchcraft. She is apparently excited—almost ecstatic—at the prospect of scandalous goings-on.*

◆ Literary Focus

❸ **Drama: Dialogue and Stage Directions** Encourage students to comment on the significance of the stage directions that accompany this remark. *Students should note that Mrs. Putnam speaks of the presence of the Devil with a "vicious certainty." From this, they may conclude that she will be one of the main sources of rumors about witchcraft or that she will be one of the main accusers once people start pointing fingers.*

perhaps your cousin's life. Whatever abomination you have done, give me all of it now, for I dare not be taken unaware when I go before them down there.

ABIGAIL: There is nothin' more. I swear it, uncle.

PARRIS, *studies her, then nods, half convinced:* Abigail, I have fought here three long years to bend these stiff-necked people to me, and now, just now when some good respect is rising for me in the parish, you compromise my very character. I have given you a home, child, I have put clothes upon your back—now give me upright answer. Your name in the town—it is entirely white, is it not?

ABIGAIL, *with an edge of resentment:* Why, I am sure it is, sir. There be no blush about my name.

PARRIS, *to the point:* Abigail, is there any other cause than you have told me, for your being discharged from Goody[6] Proctor's service? I have heard it said, and I tell you as I heard it,
❶ that she comes so rarely to the church this year for she will not sit so close to something soiled. What signified that remark?

ABIGAIL: She hates me, uncle, she must, for I would not be her slave. It's a bitter woman, a lying, cold, sniveling woman, and I will not work for such a woman!

PARRIS: She may be. And yet it has troubled me that you are now seven month out of their house, and in all this time no other family has ever called for your service.

ABIGAIL: They want slaves, not such as I. Let them send to Barbados for that. I will not black my face for any of them! *With ill-concealed resentment at him:* Do you begrudge my bed, uncle?

PARRIS: No—no.

ABIGAIL, *in a temper:* My name is good in the village! I will not have it said my name is soiled! Goody Proctor is a gossiping liar!

Enter MRS. ANN PUTNAM. *She is a twisted soul of forty-five, a death-ridden woman, haunted by dreams.*

PARRIS, *as soon as the door begins to open:* No—no, I cannot have anyone. *He sees her, and a certain deference springs into him, although his worry remains.* Why, Goody Putnam, come in.

MRS. PUTNAM, *full of breath, shiny-eyed:* It is a marvel. It is surely a stroke of hell upon you.

PARRIS: No, Goody Putnam, it is—

MRS. PUTNAM, *glancing at* BETTY: How high did she fly, how high?

PARRIS: No, no, she never flew—

MRS. PUTNAM, *very pleased with it*: Why, it's sure she did. Mr. Collins saw her goin' over Ingersoll's barn, and come down light as bird, he says!

PARRIS: Now, look you, Goody Putnam, she never—*Enter* THOMAS PUTNAM, *a well-to-do, hard-handed landowner, near fifty.* Oh, good morning, Mr. Putnam.

PUTNAM: It is a providence the thing is out now! It is a providence. *He goes directly to the bed.*

PARRIS: What's out, sir, what's—?

MRS. PUTNAM *goes to the bed.*

PUTNAM, *looking down at* BETTY: Why, *her* eyes is closed! Look you, Ann.

MRS. PUTNAM: Why, that's strange. *To* PARRIS: Ours is open.

PARRIS, *shocked*: Your Ruth is sick?

MRS. PUTNAM, *with vicious certainty:* I'd not call it sick; the Devil's touch is heavier than sick. It's death, y'know, it's death drivin' into them, ❸
forked and hoofed.

PARRIS: Oh, pray not! Why, how does Ruth ail?

MRS. PUTNAM: She ails as she must—she never waked this morning, but her eyes open and she walks, and hears naught, sees naught, and cannot eat. Her soul is taken, surely.

PARRIS *is struck.*

PUTNAM, *as though for further details:* They say you've sent for Reverend Hale of Beverly?

PARRIS *with dwindling conviction now:* A precaution only. He has much experience in all demonic arts, and I—

---

6. **Goody:** Title used for a married woman; short for *Goodwife.*

Cross-Curricular Connection: Science

Metal Manufacturing The primary meaning of *crucible*—a heat-resistant container in which metals are melted or fused at very high temperatures—comes from the field of metallurgy. You might extend this science and technology connection by sharing the following facts with students:

- *Metallurgy* is the science of separating metals from their ores and preparing them for use. It is one of the world's oldest sciences.
- In the process used to make such metals as iron and steel, the temperature inside a furnace housing a crucible may reach 3000°F.
- Modern crucibles are most commonly made from graphite, porcelain, and platinum, all highly heat-resistant materials. Graphite, for example, melts at more than 7000°F.
- Iron making was a thriving trade in the Europe of the 1600's, and English colonists brought the iron-making technology of their day with them to America. The crucibles they used were made of highly heat-resistant clay.

You might follow up by having groups of students develop questions about iron and steel manufacturing of the past and present. Students can then research the answers to their questions and share their findings with the class.

MRS. PUTNAM: He has indeed; and found a witch in Beverly last year, and let you remember that.

PARRIS: Now, Goody Ann, they only thought that were a witch, and I am certain there be no element of witchcraft here.

PUTNAM: No witchcraft! Now look you, Mr. Parris—

PARRIS: Thomas, Thomas, I pray you, leap not to witchcraft. I know that you—you least of all, Thomas, would ever wish so disastrous a charge laid upon me. We cannot leap to witchcraft. They will howl me out of Salem for such corruption in my house.

A word about Thomas Putnam. He was a man with many grievances, at least one of which appears justified. Some time before, his wife's brother-in-law, James Bayley, had been turned down as minister at Salem. Bayley had all the qualifications, and a two-thirds vote into the bargain, but a faction stopped his acceptance, for reasons that are not clear.

4 Thomas Putnam was the eldest son of the richest man in the village. He had fought the Indians at Narragansett, and was deeply interested in parish affairs. He undoubtedly felt it poor payment that the village should so blatantly disregard his candidate for one of its more important offices, especially since he regarded himself as the intellectual superior of most of the people around him.

> 5 ◆ **Reading Strategy**
> What does Miller tell you about Putnam's motives?

His vindictive nature was demonstrated long before the witchcraft began. Another former Salem minister, George Burroughs, had had to borrow money to pay for his wife's funeral, and, since the parish was remiss in his salary, he was soon bankrupt. Thomas and his brother John had Burroughs jailed for debts the man did not owe. The incident is important only in that Burroughs succeeded in becoming minister where Bayley, Thomas Putnam's brother-in-law, had been rejected; the motif of resentment is clear here. Thomas Putnam felt that his own name and the honor of his family had been smirched by the village, and he meant to right matters however he could.

Another reason to believe him a deeply embittered man was his attempt to break his father's will, which left a disproportionate amount to a stepbrother. As with every other public cause in which he tried to force his way, he failed in this.

So it is not surprising to find that so many accusations against people are in the handwriting of Thomas Putnam, or that his name is so often found as a witness corroborating the supernatural testimony, or that his daughter led the crying-out at the most opportune junctures of the trials, especially when—But we'll speak of that when we come to it.

PUTNAM—*at the moment he is intent upon getting* PARRIS, *for whom he has only contempt, to move toward the abyss:*[7] Mr. Parris, I have taken your part in all contention here, and I would continue; but I cannot if you hold back in this. There are hurtful, vengeful spirits layin' hands on these children. 6

PARRIS: But, Thomas, you cannot—

PUTNAM: Ann! Tell Mr. Parris what you have done.

MRS. PUTNAM: Reverend Parris, I have laid seven babies unbaptized in the earth. Believe me, sir, you never saw more hearty babies born. And yet, each would wither in my arms the very night of their birth. I have spoke nothin', but my heart has clamored intimations. And now, this year, my Ruth, my only—I see her turning strange. A secret child she has become this year, and shrivels like a sucking mouth were pullin' on her life too. And so I thought to send her to your Tituba—

PARRIS: To Tituba! What may Tituba—?

MRS. PUTNAM: Tituba knows how to speak to the dead, Mr. Parris.

PARRIS: Goody Ann, it is a formidable sin to conjure up the dead!

MRS. PUTNAM: I take it on my soul, but who else may surely tell us what person murdered my babies?

PARRIS, *horrified:* Woman!

---

7. **abyss** (ə bis′) *n.*: Deep crack in the Earth.

4 Enrichment In 1676 and 1677, a group of Native American tribes led by Chief Philip, the leader of the Wampanoags, launched an assault against the settlers, prompted by the settlers' encroachments of tribal hunting lands. The settlers retaliated by attacking the stronghold of the Narragansetts near what is now Kingston, Rhode Island. The settlers inflicted heavy losses on the Native Americans, and in a later skirmish they killed Chief Philip. This series of battles came to be known as King Philip's War.

◆ Reading Strategy

5 Question the Characters' Motives Miller says that Putnam is out for revenge. The following words from the passage support this motive: "He was a man of many grievances . . ."; "His vindictive nature was demonstrated . . ."; "Another reason to believe him a deeply embittered man. . . ."

◆ Reading Strategy

6 Question the Characters' Motives Have students identify Putnam's immediate objective and his motive, both of which are clearly revealed in the stage directions. *Objective: He is determined to get Parris to "move toward the abyss"—in other words, to acknowledge the presence of witchcraft. Motive: He feels contempt for Parris.* Then ask students if Putnam is successful at hiding his true motive. How do they know? *Students should note that he is successful; Parris's previous speech reveals that Parris is unaware of Putnam's ill feelings toward him.*

◆ Background for Understanding

❶ Ask students what characteristic of seventeenth-century Puritans Mrs. Putnam embodies. If necessary, have them review the information about the Salem witchcraft trials on page 1087. *Students should note that Mrs. Putnam exemplifies the tendency that many Puritans showed to blame the devil for terrible events beyond their control.*

◆ Grammar and Style

❷ **Pronoun Case in Incomplete Constructions** Ask students whether the subjective pronoun *I* is correct in this incomplete construction. Have them mentally complete the sentence to determine the answer. *I is the correct pronoun. Completed sentence: It was not I, sir—it was Tituba and Ruth.*

◆ Reading Strategy

❸ **Question the Characters' Motives** Have two volunteers read these lines aloud. Then have students discuss the motive or motives behind each character's words. *Responses may include: Parris is motivated by fear and anxiety over his reputation. Putnam is motivated by envy and contempt—he would in fact like to see Parris "toppled."*

Customize for *AP Students*

❹ Call students' attention to the stage directions that introduce Mercy Lewis. Have them explain what is ironic about this character. *Her name is Mercy, but she is a merciless person.*

◆ Literary Focus

❺ **Drama: Dialogue and Stage Directions** Point out that Reverend Parris and the Putnams have left the room, and Abigail and Mercy are now alone with Betty. Ask students what this conversation reveals about the two young women. *Students should note that with the others gone, Abigail and Mercy drop their proper façades and reveal their true selves. They show callous attitudes toward Betty, and they talk in a conspiratorial manner about what really happened in the woods.*

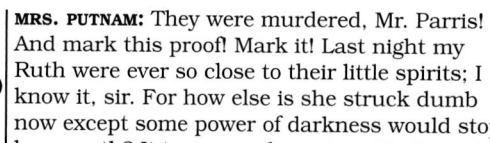

❶ **MRS. PUTNAM:** They were murdered, Mr. Parris! And mark this proof! Mark it! Last night my Ruth were ever so close to their little spirits; I know it, sir. For how else is she struck dumb now except some power of darkness would stop her mouth? It is a marvelous sign, Mr. Parris!

PUTNAM: Don't you understand it, sir? There is a murdering witch among us, bound to keep herself in the dark. PARRIS *turns to* BETTY, *a frantic terror rising in him.* Let your names make of it what they will, you cannot blink it more.

PARRIS, *to* ABIGAIL: Then you were conjuring spirits last night.

❷ **ABIGAIL,** *whispering:* Not I, sir—Tituba and Ruth.

PARRIS *turns now, with new fear, and goes to* BETTY, *looks down at her, and then, gazing off:* Oh, Abigail, what proper payment for my charity! Now I am undone.

❸ **PUTNAM:** You are not undone! Let you take hold here. Wait for no one to charge you—declare it yourself. You have discovered witchcraft—

PARRIS: In my house? In my house, Thomas? They will topple me with this! They will make of it a—

❹ *Enter* MERCY LEWIS, *the Putnams' servant, a fat, sly, merciless girl of eighteen.*

MERCY: Your pardons. I only thought to see how Betty is.

PUTNAM: Why aren't you home? Who's with Ruth?

MERCY: Her grandma come. She's improved a little, I think—she give a powerful sneeze before.

MRS. PUTNAM: Ah, there's a sign of life!

MERCY: I'd fear no more, Goody Putnam. It were a grand sneeze; another like it will shake her wits together, I'm sure. *She goes to the bed to look.*

PARRIS: Will you leave me now, Thomas? I would pray a while alone.

ABIGAIL: Uncle, you've prayed since midnight. Why do you not go down and—

PARRIS: No—no. *To* PUTNAM: I have no answer for that crowd. I'll wait till Mr. Hale arrives. *To get* MRS. PUTNAM *to leave:* If you will, Goody Ann . . .

PUTNAM: Now look you, sir. Let you strike out against the Devil, and the village will bless you for it! Come down, speak to them—pray with them. They're thirsting for your word, Mister! Surely you'll pray with them.

PARRIS, *swayed:* I'll lead them in a psalm, but let you say nothing of witchcraft yet. I will not discuss it. The cause is yet unknown. I have had enough contention since I came; I want no more.

MRS. PUTNAM: Mercy, you go home to Ruth, d'y'hear?

MERCY: Aye, mum.

MRS. PUTNAM *goes out.*

PARRIS, *to* ABIGAIL: If she starts for the window, cry for me at once.

ABIGAIL: I will, uncle.

PARRIS, *to* PUTNAM: There is a terrible power in her arms today. *He goes out with* PUTNAM.

ABIGAIL, *with hushed trepidation:* How is Ruth sick?

MERCY: It's weirdish, I know not—she seems to walk like a dead one since last night.

ABIGAIL, *turns at once and goes to* BETTY, *and now, with fear in her voice:* Betty? BETTY *doesn't move. She shakes her.* Now stop this! Betty! Sit up now!

BETTY *doesn't stir.* MERCY *comes over.* ❺

MERCY: Have you tried beatin' her? I gave Ruth a good one and it waked her for a minute. Here, let me have her.

ABIGAIL, *holding* MERCY *back:* No, he'll be comin' up. Listen, now; if they be questioning us, tell them we danced—I told him as much already.

MERCY: Aye. And what more?

ABIGAIL: He knows Tituba conjured Ruth's sisters to come out of the grave.

MERCY: And what more?

ABIGAIL: He saw you naked.

MERCY: *clapping her hands together with a frightened laugh:* Oh, Jesus!

Beyond the Classroom

Community Connection

Local History Salem, Miller notes, had been established about forty years before the fateful spring of 1692. Do your students know when their city, town, or community was established? In a class discussion, encourage them to share their prior knowledge as well as identify sources from which they can learn more about their community's origins. Then have groups of students investigate such questions as: When was the city, town, or community first formed? When was it officially chartered or incorporated? What is the meaning or significance of its name?

Native American History Native Americans were the first people to live in America. As part of their research into their community's history, have one or more groups find out about the history and way of life of the area's original inhabitants. Have the groups share their findings with the class.

6 *Enter* MARY WARREN, *breathless. She is seventeen, a subservient, naive, lonely girl.*

MARY WARREN: What'll we do? The village is out! I just come from the farm; the whole country's talkin' witchcraft! They'll be callin' us witches, Abby!

MERCY, *pointing and looking at* MARY WARREN: She means to tell, I know it.

MARY WARREN: Abby, we've got to tell. Witchery's a hangin' error, a hangin' like they done in Boston two year ago! We must tell the truth, Abby! You'll only be whipped for dancin', and the other things!

ABIGAIL: Oh, *we'll* be whipped!

MARY WARREN: I never done none of it, Abby. I only looked!

MERCY, *moving menacingly toward* MARY: Oh, you're a great one for lookin', aren't you, Mary Warren? What a grand peeping courage you have!

BETTY, *on the bed, whimpers.* ABIGAIL *turns to her at once.*

ABIGAIL: Betty? *She goes to* BETTY. Now, Betty, dear, wake up now. It's Abigail. *She sits* BETTY *up and furiously shakes her.* I'll beat you, Betty! BETTY *whimpers.* My, you seem improving. I talked to your papa and I told him everything. So there's nothing to—

7 **BETTY,** *darts off the bed, frightened of* ABIGAIL, *and flattens herself against the wall:* I want my mama!

ABIGAIL, *with alarm, as she cautiously approaches* BETTY: What ails you, Betty? Your mama's dead and buried.

BETTY: I'll fly to Mama. Let me fly! *She raises her arms as though to fly, and streaks for the window, gets one leg out.*

ABIGAIL, *pulling her away from the window:* I told him everything; he knows now, he knows everything we—

8 **BETTY:** You drank blood, Abby! You didn't tell him that!

ABIGAIL: Betty, you never say that again! You will never—

▲ Critical Viewing You'll find movie stills from the 1996 film version of *The Crucible* throughout the text. As you come across each photograph, identify the character(s) or scene it portrays. 9

BETTY: You did, you did! You drank a charm to kill John Proctor's wife! You drank a charm to kill Goody Proctor! 8

ABIGAIL, *smashes her across the face:* Shut it! Now shut it!

BETTY: *collapsing on the bed:* Mama, Mama! *She dissolves into sobs.*

ABIGAIL: Now look you. All of you. We danced. And Tituba conjured Ruth Putnam's dead sisters. And that is all. And mark this. Let either of you breathe a word, or the edge of a word, about the other things, and I will come to you in the black of some terrible night and I will bring a pointy reckoning that will shudder you. And you know I can do it; I saw Indians smash my dear parents' heads on the pillow next to mine, and I have seen some reddish work done at night, and I can make you wish you had never seen the sun go down! *She goes to* BETTY *and roughly sits her up.* Now, you—sit up and stop this!

But BETTY *collapses in her hands and lies inert on the bed.*

◆ Literary Focus

6 Drama: Dialogue and Stage Directions Encourage students to note the contrast between Mary Warren's character traits and Mercy Lewis's character traits, which were revealed on the previous page. *Students should note that Mary is described as "subservient," "naive," and "lonely," while Mercy was described as being "sly" and "merciless."* You might also have students use this information to make predictions about how Mary, Mercy, and Abigail will interact. *Predictions may include: Mary will be manipulated by Mercy and Abigail; Mercy and Abigail will scapegoat Mary in order to protect themselves.*

◆ Literary Focus

7 Drama: Dialogue and Stage Directions How might the detail that Betty is frightened of Abigail be important to students' understanding of the play? *Students should note that this detail helps the audience see Abigail as a cruel and intimidating person. They may speculate that Abigail might have done something to harm Betty or someone else the night before in the woods or that Betty will do as Abigail tells her to as the action unfolds.*

◆ Critical Thinking

8 Interpret Ask students what these revelations suggest about Abigail's role in the activities that took place in the woods. Also, what do the revelations suggest about what really happened while Abigail was working for Goody Proctor? *Responses may include: Betty's exclamations prove that Abigail actually was involved in witchcraft; the fact that Abigail drank a charm to kill Goody Proctor suggests that she did in fact do something shameful and scandalous while working for Goody Proctor.*

▶Critical Viewing◀

9 Students should point out that this photo depicts Betty as she darts from her bed to the window and tries to "fly."

◆ Literary Focus

❶ Drama: Dialogue and Stage Directions Ask students to imagine that they are actors playing the role of John Proctor. How would this information help them with their portrayals? *Students may say that they would try to portray Proctor as a strong yet complicated person—according to this description, he carries with him both a commanding presence and a sense of private disappointment in himself.*

❷ Clarification Make sure students are aware that a *pilgrimage* is a journey to a holy place undertaken as a religious act. Ask students: What is ironic about John Proctor's use of this word? *Proctor himself is a hypocrite in religious matters.*

◆ Literary Focus

❸ Drama: Dialogue and Stage Directions The stage directions call attention to the fact that Proctor and Abigail are attracted to each other and know each other well, explaining Abigail's behavior.

❹ Clarification Make sure students realize that stocks were a device used for the punishment of minor offenses. The stocks were generally located in a place that was highly visible to the general public.

MARY WARREN, *with hysterical fright:* What's got her? ABIGAIL *stares in fright at* BETTY. Abby, she's going to die! It's a sin to conjure, and we—

ABIGAIL, *starting for* MARY: I say shut it, Mary Warren!

Enter JOHN PROCTOR. *On seeing him,* MARY WARREN *leaps in fright.*

Proctor was a farmer in his middle thirties. He need not have been a partisan of any faction in the town, but there is evidence to suggest that he had a sharp and biting way with hypocrites. He was the kind of man—powerful of body, even-tempered, and not easily led—who cannot refuse support to partisans without drawing their deepest resentment. In Proctor's presence a fool felt his foolishness instantly—and a Proctor is always marked for calumny therefore.

But as we shall see, the steady manner he displays does not spring from an untroubled soul. He is a sinner, a sinner not only against the moral fashion of the time, but against his own vision of decent conduct. These people had no ritual for the washing away of sins. It is another trait we inherited from them, and it has helped to discipline us as well as to breed hypocrisy among us. Proctor, respected and even feared in Salem, has come to regard himself as a kind of fraud. But no hint of this has yet appeared on the surface, and as he enters from the crowded parlor below it is a man in his prime we see, with a quiet confidence and an unexpressed, hidden force. Mary Warren, his servant, can barely speak for embarrassment and fear. ❶

MARY WARREN: Oh! I'm just going home, Mr. Proctor.

PROCTOR: Be you foolish, Mary Warren? Be you deaf? I forbid you leave the house, did I not? Why shall I pay you? I am looking for you more often than my cows!

MARY WARREN: I only come to see the great doings in the world.

PROCTOR: I'll show you a great doin' on your arse one of these days. Now get you home; my wife is waitin' with your work! *Trying to retain a shred of dignity, she goes slowly out.*

MERCY LEWIS, *both afraid of him and strangely titillated:* I'd best be off. I have my Ruth to watch. Good morning, Mr. Proctor.

MERCY *sidles out. Since* PROCTOR'S *entrance,* ABIGAIL *has stood as though on tiptoe, absorbing his presence, wide-eyed. He glances at her then goes to* BETTY *on the bed.*

ABIGAIL: Gad. I'd almost forgot how strong you are, John Proctor!

PROCTOR, *looking at* ABIGAIL *now, the faintest suggestion of a knowing smile on his face:* What's this mischief here?

ABIGAIL, *with a nervous laugh:* Oh, she's only gone silly somehow.

PROCTOR: The road past my house is a pilgrimage to Salem all morning. The town's mumbling witchcraft. ❷

ABIGAIL: Oh, posh! *Winningly she comes a little closer, with a confidential, wicked air.* We were dancin' in the woods last night, and my uncle leaped in on us. She took fright, is all.

PROCTOR, *his smile widening:* Ah, you're wicked yet, aren't y'! *A trill of expectant laughter escapes her, and she dares come closer, feverishly looking into his eyes.* You'll be clapped in the stocks before you're twenty. ❸ ❹

> **◆ Literary Focus**
> How do the stage directions help you interpret Abigail's behavior?

He takes a step to go, and she springs into his path.

ABIGAIL: Give me a word, John. A soft word. *Her concentrated desire destroys his smile.*

PROCTOR: No, no, Abby. That's done with.

ABIGAIL, *tauntingly:* You come five mile to see a silly girl fly? I know you better.

PROCTOR, *setting her firmly out of his path:* I come to see what mischief your uncle's brewin' now. *With final emphasis:* Put it out of mind, Abby.

◆ Build Vocabulary

calumny (kal′ əm nē) *n.*: False accusation; slander

Speaking, Listening, and Viewing Mini-Lesson

Dramatization

This mini-lesson supports the Speaking, Listening, and Viewing activity in the Idea Bank on page 1112.

Introduce the Concept Point out that Act I contains suspenseful scenes, shocking scenes, and scenes that introduce some of the play's main characters. Let students know that they will now perform their own scenes.

Develop Background Help students identify approaches that will help them better understand their roles. Lead them to consider the following:

- Study the stage directions. Look for information about the characters' personality traits and background as well as instructions about gestures, movements, actions, and reactions.
- Examine the character's motives. What drives his or her behavior? Is the character hiding or unaware of his or her true motives?
- Review the rest of the act. The character's earlier or later actions will help reveal who he or she is.

Apply the Information Let students practice and perform their scenes.

Assess the Outcome Have each student complete a Peer Assessment: Dramatic Performance page in ***Alternative Assessment***, p. 76.

ABIGAIL, *grasping his hand before he can release her:* John—I am waitin' for you every night.

PROCTOR: Abby, I never give you hope to wait for me.

ABIGAIL, *now beginning to anger—she can't believe it:* I have something better than hope, I think!

PROCTOR: Abby, you'll put it out of mind. I'll not be comin' for you more.

ABIGAIL: You're surely sportin' with me.

PROCTOR: You know me better.

ABIGAIL: I know how you clutched my back behind your house and sweated like a stallion whenever I come near! Or did I dream that? It's she put me out, you cannot pretend it were you. I saw your face when she put me out, and ❺ you loved me then and you do now!

PROCTOR: Abby, that's a wild thing to say—

ABIGAIL: A wild thing may say wild things. But not so wild, I think. I have seen you since she put me out; I have seen you nights.

PROCTOR: I have hardly stepped off my farm this seven-month.

ABIGAIL: I have a sense for heat, John, and yours has drawn me to my window, and I have seen you looking up, burning in your loneliness. Do you tell me you've never looked up at my window?

PROCTOR: I may have looked up.

ABIGAIL, *now softening:* And you must. You are no wintry man. I know you, John. I *know* you. *She is weeping.* I cannot sleep for dreamin'; I cannot dream but I wake and walk about the house as though I'd find you comin' through some door. *She clutches him desperately.*

PROCTOR, *gently pressing her from him, with great sympathy but firmly:* Child—

ABIGAIL, *with a flash of anger:* How do you call me child!

PROCTOR: Abby, I may think of you softly from time to time. But I will cut off my hand before ❻ I'll ever reach for you again. Wipe it out of mind. We never touched, Abby.

ABIGAIL: Aye, but we did.

PROCTOR: Aye, but we did not.

ABIGAIL, *with a bitter anger:* Oh, I marvel how such a strong man may let such a sickly wife be—

PROCTOR, *angered—at himself as well:* You'll speak nothin' of Elizabeth!

ABIGAIL: She is blackening my name in the village! She is telling lies about me! She is a cold, sniveling woman, and you bend to her! Let her turn you like a—

PROCTOR, *shaking her:* Do you look for whippin'?

A psalm is heard being sung below.

ABIGAIL, *in tears:* I look for John Proctor that took me from my sleep and put knowledge in my heart! I never knew what pretense Salem was, I never knew the lying lessons I was taught by all these Christian women and their ❼ covenanted men! And now you bid me tear the light out of my eyes? I will not, I cannot! You loved me, John Proctor, and whatever sin it is, you love me yet! *He turns abruptly to go out. She rushes to him.* John, pity me, pity me!

The words "going up to Jesus" are heard in the psalm, and BETTY *claps her ears suddenly and whines loudly.*

ABIGAIL: Betty? *She hurries to* BETTY, who is now *sitting up and screaming.* PROCTOR *goes to* BETTY *as* ABIGAIL *is trying to pull her hands down, calling "Betty!"*

PROCTOR, *growing unnerved:* What's she doing? Girl, what ails you? Stop that wailing!

The singing has stopped in the midst of this, and now PARRIS *rushes in.*

PARRIS: What happened? What are you doing to her? Betty! *He rushes to the bed, crying,* "Betty, Betty!" MRS. PUTNAM *enters, feverish with curiosity, and with her* PUTNAM *and* MERCY LEWIS. PARRIS, *at the bed, keeps lightly slapping* BETTY's *face, while she moans and tries to get up.*

ABIGAIL: She heard you singin' and suddenly she's up and screamin'.

MRS. PUTNAM: The psalm! The psalm! She cannot bear to hear the Lord's name!

PARRIS: No, God forbid. Mercy, run to the

◆ Critical Thinking

❺ **Connect** Have students identify the "she" to whom Abigail refers. *Goody Proctor* Then ask: How does this speech explain why Abigail would drink a charm to kill Goody Proctor? *Elicit the following: Abigail reveals her love for John Proctor as well as her bitter resentment of his wife, who apparently suspected the adulterous relationship and sent Abigail away.*

Comprehension Check ☑

❻ What are Proctor's feelings toward Abigail? *He still has some fondness for her, but he is adamant that the affair they had is over.*

◆ Literary Focus

❼ **Drama: Dialogue and Stage Directions** Point out the stage directions that accompany Abigail's speech. Then ask students what effect they think the sound of a psalm being sung below would have on this scene. *Responses may include: It would reinforce the tension between the strict and proper atmosphere of Salem and the shocking realities that Abigail brings up in her speech; it would heighten the drama of the scene.*

◆ Literary Focus

❶ Drama: Dialogue and Stage Directions Invite three volunteers to read Mrs. Putnam's, Parris's, and Mr. Putnam's lines aloud. Then have students discuss what these lines reveal about each character. *Students may say that Mrs. Putnam and her husband continue to promote the idea that witchcraft is at work, while Parris continues to be confused and frightened.*

◆ Reading Strategy

❷ Question the Characters' Motives Remind students that earlier in this act, Miller had discussed both economic and psychological forces that may have driven people to denounce their neighbors as witches. Then ask: To which category do the theories that Miller brings up here belong? *Both of the theories have to do with social and economic reasons that people might have for resenting and accusing the Nurses.*

Customize for *AP Students*

❸ Encourage students to explain the irony in the last sentence of Miller's commentary. *On one hand, Mrs. Putnam made a false accusation when she claimed that Rebecca's spirit tempted her to "iniquity," or wickedness. On the other hand, there is truth to this statement, since falsely accusing Rebecca was indeed a wicked act.*

doctor! Tell him what's happened here! MERCY LEWIS *rushes out.*

MRS. PUTNAM: Mark it for a sign, mark it!

REBECCA NURSE, *seventy-two, enters. She is white-haired, leaning upon her walking-stick.*

❶ **PUTNAM,** *pointing at the whimpering* BETTY: That is a notorious sign of witchcraft afoot, Goody Nurse, a prodigious sign!

MRS. PUTNAM: My mother told me that! When they cannot bear to hear the name of—

PARRIS, *trembling*: Rebecca, Rebecca, go to her, we're lost. She suddenly cannot bear to hear the Lord's—

GILES COREY, *eighty-three, enters. He is knotted with muscle, canny, inquisitive, and still powerful.*

REBECCA: There is hard sickness here, Giles Corey, so please to keep the quiet.

GILES: I've not said a word. No one here can testify I've said a word. Is she going to fly again? I hear she flies.

PUTNAM: Man, be quiet now!

Everything is quiet. REBECCA *walks across the room to the bed. Gentleness exudes from her.* BETTY *is quietly whimpering, eyes shut.* REBECCA *simply stands over the child, who gradually quiets.*

And while they are so absorbed, we may put a word in for Rebecca. Rebecca was the wife of Francis Nurse, who, from all accounts, was one of those men for whom both sides of the argument had to have respect. He was called upon to arbitrate disputes as though he were an unofficial judge, and Rebecca also enjoyed the high opinion most people had for him. By the time of the delusion, they had three hundred acres, and their children were settled in separate homesteads within the same estate. However, Francis had originally rented the land, and one theory has it that, as he gradually paid for it and raised his social status, ❷ there were those who resented his rise.

Another suggestion to explain the systematic campaign against Rebecca, and inferentially against Francis, is the land war he fought with his neighbors, one of whom was a Putnam. This squabble grew to the proportions of a battle in the woods between partisans of both sides, and it ❷ is said to have lasted for two days. As for Rebecca herself, the general opinion of her character was so high that to explain how anyone dared cry her out for a witch—and more, how adults could bring themselves to lay hands on her—we must look to the fields and boundaries of that time.

As we have seen, Thomas Putnam's man for the Salem ministry was Bayley. The Nurse clan had been in the faction that prevented Bayley's taking office. In addition, certain families allied to the Nurses by blood or friendship, and whose farms were contiguous with the Nurse farm or close to it, combined to break away from the Salem town authority and set up Topsfield, a new and independent entity whose existence was resented by old Salemites.

That the guiding hand behind the outcry was Putnam's is indicated by the fact that, as soon as it began, this Topsfield-Nurse faction absented themselves from church in protest and disbelief. It was Edward and Jonathan Putnam who signed the first complaint against Rebecca; and Thomas Putnam's little daughter was the one who fell into a fit at the hearing and pointed to Rebecca as her attacker. To top it all, Mrs. Putnam—who is now staring at the bewitched child on the bed—soon accused Rebecca's spirit ❸ of "tempting her to iniquity," a charge that had more truth in it than Mrs. Putnam could know.

MRS. PUTNAM, *astonished*: What have you done?

REBECCA, *in thought, now leaves the bedside and sits.*

PARRIS, *wondrous and relieved:* What do you make of it, Rebecca?

PUTNAM, *eagerly:* Goody Nurse, will you go to my Ruth and see if you can wake her?

REBECCA, *sitting:* I think she'll wake in time. Pray calm yourselves. I have eleven children, and I am twenty-six times a grandma, and I have seen them all through their silly seasons, and when it come on them they will run the Devil bowlegged keeping up with their mischief. I think she'll wake when she tires of it. A child's spirit is like a child, you can never catch it by running after it; you must stand still, and, for

Beyond the Classroom

Career Connection

Court Reporter While many documents pertaining to the Salem witchcraft trials have survived, there is no complete word-for-word account of the proceedings. Such accounts do exist in the case of modern trials, however, thanks to the work of court reporters.

Court reporters, sometimes called court stenographers, record every word that is spoken at a trial. The only exceptions are remarks that a judge rules to be "off the record" and testimony that the judge declares to be inadmissible. Using a shorthand machine—a specially designed machine with a 21-character keyboard—a trained court reporter can record 200 words or even more per minute.

Have interested students gather more information about court reporting and stenography. For example, some students might work together to develop a brief explanation of why it is essential that court proceedings be accurately recorded and saved. Others might do research to find out how operating a shorthand machine differs from conventional typing. Students can share their findings with the class.

love, it will soon itself come back.

PROCTOR: Aye, that's the truth of it, Rebecca.

4 **MRS. PUTNAM:** This is no silly season, Rebecca. My Ruth is bewildered, Rebecca; she cannot eat.

REBECCA: Perhaps she is not hungered yet. *To* PARRIS: I hope you are not decided to go in search of loose spirits, Mr. Parris. I've heard promise of that outside.

PARRIS: A wide opinion's running in the parish that the Devil may be among us, and I would satisfy them that they are wrong.

PROCTOR: Then let you come out and call them wrong. Did you consult the wardens before you called this minister to look for devils?

PARRIS: He is not coming to look for devils!

PROCTOR: Then what's he coming for?

PUTNAM: There be children dyin' in the village, Mister!

PROCTOR: I seen none dyin'. This society will not be a bag to swing around your head, Mr. Putnam. *To* PARRIS: Did you call a meeting before you—? 5

PUTNAM: I am sick of meetings; cannot the man turn his head without he have a meeting?

PROCTOR: He may turn his head, but not to Hell!

REBECCA: Pray, John, be calm. *Pause. He defers to her.* Mr. Parris, I think you'd best send Reverend Hale back as soon as he come. This will set us all to arguin' again in the society, and we thought to have peace this year. I think we ought rely on the doctor now, and good prayer. 6

MRS. PUTNAM: Rebecca, the doctor's baffled!

REBECCA: If so he is, then let us go to God for the cause of it. There is prodigious danger in the seeking of loose spirits. I fear it, I fear it. Let us rather blame ourselves and—

PUTNAM: How may we blame ourselves? I am one of nine sons; the Putnam seed have peopled this province. And yet I have but one child left of eight—and now she shrivels!

REBECCA: I cannot fathom that. 7

MRS. PUTNAM, *with a growing edge of sarcasm:* But I must! You think it God's work you should never lose a child, nor grandchild either, and I bury all but one? There are wheels within wheels in this village, and fires within fires!

PUTNAM, *to* PARRIS: When Reverend Hale comes, you will proceed to look for signs of witchcraft here.

PROCTOR, *to* PUTNAM: You cannot command Mr. Parris. We vote by name in this society, not by acreage.

PUTNAM: I never heard you worried so on this society, Mr. Proctor. I do not think I saw you at Sabbath meeting since snow flew.

PROCTOR: I have trouble enough without I come five mile to hear him preach only hellfire and bloody damnation. Take it to heart, Mr. Parris. There are many others who stay away from

4 Clarification Explain to students that Goody Putnam is using the word *bewilder* in its original sense, meaning that Ruth has "gone wild."

Comprehension Check ☑

5 What does Proctor mean when he tells Putnam that "this society will not be a bag to swing around your head"? *You are not in charge of this community; you cannot tell people what to do.*

◆ Critical Thinking

6 Compare and Contrast Encourage students to compare and contrast Rebecca Nurse's behavior and motives with those of Mr. and Mrs. Putnam. *Students may point out that Rebecca behaves with dignity, reason, and patience, while the Putnams behave in an irrational and alarmist manner. Rebecca is motivated by a desire to maintain peace, while the Putnams are motivated by a desire to stir up trouble.*

◆ Reading Strategy

7 Question the Characters' Motives Have students restate the point that the Putnams make here. Then have them identify the motive or motives suggested by the Putnams remarks. *The Putnams point out that they have lost several children, while Rebecca has many children and grandchildren. Students may identify the motive that surfaces here as jealousy, envy, or resentment.*

▶Critical Viewing◀

Students should identify the character in the photograph as John Proctor, "a farmer in his middle thirties."

❶ **Clarification** Explain that a minister's yearly salary usually included a number of cords of wood.

❷ **Enrichment** Founded in 1636, Harvard College was the first college in the Western Hemisphere. One of its most illustrious early graduates was Cotton Mather, who wrote about the Salem witchcraft trials in *Wonders of the Invisible World.*

❸ **Enrichment** As succeeding generations drifted away from the goals and standards of the first Puritan settlers, many ministers began angrily denouncing this trend and threatening their congregations with the prospect of eternal suffering in Hell.

◆ Critical Thinking

❹ **Draw Conclusions** Have students identify the specific issues that Parris, Putnam, Proctor, and Giles have been arguing about—that is, the issues that led up to this angry exchange. *They have argued over Reverend Parris's style of preaching, firewood and money matters, and church politics.* Then encourage students to draw general conclusions about Salem based on these details. *Responses may include: The town is full of conflict and contention; people are harboring all sorts of resentments.*

church these days because you hardly ever mention God any more.

PARRIS, *now aroused:* Why, that's a drastic charge!

REBECCA: It's somewhat true; there are many that quail to bring their children—

PARRIS: I do not preach for children, Rebecca. It is not the children who are unmindful of their obligations toward this ministry.

REBECCA: Are there really those unmindful?

PARRIS: I should say the better half of Salem village—

PUTNAM: And more than that!

PARRIS: Where is my wood? My contract provides I be supplied with all my firewood. I am waiting since November for a stick, and even in November I had to show my frostbitten hands like some London beggar!

❶ **GILES:** You are allowed six pound a year to buy your wood, Mr. Parris.

PARRIS: I regard that six pound as part of my salary. I am paid little enough without I spend six pound on firewood.

PROCTOR: Sixty, plus six for firewood—

❷ **PARRIS:** The salary is sixty-six pound, Mr. Proctor! I am not some preaching farmer with a book under my arm; I am a graduate of Harvard College.

GILES: Aye, and well instructed in arithmetic!

PARRIS: Mr. Corey, you will look far for a man of my kind at sixty pound a year! I am not used to this poverty; I left a thrifty business in the Barbados to serve the Lord. I do not fathom it, why am I persecuted here? I cannot offer one proposition but there be a howling riot of argument. I have often wondered if the Devil be in it somewhere; I cannot understand you people otherwise.

PROCTOR: Mr. Parris, you are the first minister ever did demand the deed to this house—

PARRIS: Man! Don't a minister deserve a house to live in?

PROCTOR: To live in, yes. But to ask ownership is like you shall own the meeting house itself; the last meeting I were at you spoke so long on deeds and mortgages I thought it were an auction.

PARRIS: I want a mark of confidence, is all! I am your third preacher in seven years. I do not wish to be put out like the cat whenever some majority feels the whim. You people seem not to comprehend that a minister is the Lord's man in the parish; a minister is not to be so lightly crossed and contradicted—

PUTNAM: Aye!

PARRIS: There is either obedience or the church will burn like Hell is burning!

PROCTOR: Can you speak one minute without we land in Hell again? I am sick of Hell! ❸

PARRIS: It is not for you to say what is good for you to hear!

PROCTOR: I may speak my heart, I think!

PARRIS, *in a fury:* What, are we Quakers?[8] We are not Quakers here yet, Mr. Proctor. And you may tell that to your followers! ❹

PROCTOR: My followers!

PARRIS—*now he's out with it:* There is a party in this church. I am not blind; there is a faction and a party.

PROCTOR: Against you?

PUTNAM: Against him and all authority!

PROCTOR: Why, then I must find it and join it.

There is shock among the others.

REBECCA: He does not mean that.

PUTNAM: He confessed it now!

PROCTOR: I mean it solemnly, Rebecca; I like not the smell of this "authority."

REBECCA: No, you cannot break charity with your minister. You are another kind, John. Clasp his hand, make your peace.

8. **Quakers:** Members of the Society of Friends, a Christian religious sect that was founded in the mid-17th century and has no formal creed, rites, or priesthood. Unlike the Quakers, the Puritans had a rigid code of conduct and were expected to heed the words of their ministers.

Cross-Curricular Connection: Social Studies

Harvard University The Harvard College that Parris attended has since become a world-famous institution of higher learning. The undergraduate division is still known as Harvard College, and the entire institution, which comprises both graduate and undergraduate programs, is known as Harvard University. The College was founded by Puritans in 1636 and was named after John Harvard, a Puritan minister. Harvard University is the oldest institution of higher learning in the United States.

Have students work in groups to learn more about the history of Harvard University and about the Puritans' approach to education in colonial America. Groups can share their findings with the class.

PROCTOR: I have a crop to sow and lumber to drag home. *He goes angrily to the door and turns to* COREY *with a smile.* What say you, GILES, let's find the party. He says there's a party.

GILES: I've changed my opinion of this man, John. Mr. Parris, I beg your pardon. I never thought you had so much iron in you.

PARRIS, *surprised:* Why, thank you, Giles!

GILES: It suggests to the mind what the trouble be among us all these years. *To all:* Think on it. Wherefore is everybody suing everybody else? Think on it now, it's a deep thing, and dark as a pit. I have been six time in court this year—

❺ **PROCTOR,** *familiarly, with warmth, although he knows he is approaching the edge of Giles' tolerance with this:* Is it the Devil's fault that a man cannot say you good morning without you clap him for defamation? You're old, Giles, and you're not hearin' so well as you did.

GILES—*he cannot be crossed:* John Proctor, I have only last month collected four pound damages for you publicly sayin' I burned the roof off your house, and I—

PROCTOR, *laughing:* I never said no such thing, but I've paid you for it, so I hope I can call you deaf without charge. Now come along, Giles, and help me drag my lumber home.

PUTNAM: A moment, Mr. Proctor. What lumber is that you're draggin', if I may ask you?

PROCTOR: My lumber. From out my forest by the riverside.

PUTNAM: Why, we are surely gone wild this year. What anarchy is this? That tract is in my bounds, it's in my bounds, Mr. Proctor.

❻ **PROCTOR:** In your bounds! *Indicating* REBECCA: I bought that tract from Goody Nurse's husband five months ago.

PUTNAM: He had no right to sell it. It stands clear in my grandfather's will that all the land between the river and—

PROCTOR: Your grandfather had a habit of willing land that never belonged to him, if I may say it plain.

GILES: That's God's truth; he nearly willed away my north pasture but he knew I'd break his fingers before he'd set his name to it. Let's get your lumber home, John. I feel a sudden will to work coming on.

PUTNAM: You load one oak of mine and you'll fight to drag it home!

GILES: Aye, and we'll win too, Putnam—this fool and I. Come on! *He turns to* PROCTOR *and starts out.*

PUTNAM: I'll have my men on you, Corey! I'll clap a writ on you!

Enter REVEREND JOHN HALE *of Beverly.*

Mr. Hale is nearing forty, a tight-skinned, eager-eyed intellectual. This is a beloved errand for him; on being called here to ascertain witchcraft he felt the pride of the specialist whose unique knowledge has at last been publicly called for. Like almost all men of learning, he spent a good deal of time pondering the invisible world, especially since he had himself encountered a witch in his parish not long before. That woman, however, turned into a mere pest under his searching scrutiny, and the child she had allegedly been afflicting recovered her normal behavior after Hale had given her his kindness and a few days of rest in his own house. However, that experience never raised a doubt in his mind as to the reality of the underworld or the existence of Lucifer's many-faced lieutenants. And his belief is not to his discredit. Better minds than Hale's were—and still are—convinced that there is a society of spirits beyond our ken. One cannot help noting that one of his lines has never yet raised a laugh in any audience that has seen this play; it is his assurance that "We cannot look to superstition in this. The Devil is precise." Evidently we are not quite certain even now whether diabolism is holy and not to be scoffed at. And it is no accident that we should be so bemused. ❼

Like Reverend Hale and the others on this stage, we conceive the Devil as a necessary part of a respectable view of cosmology. Ours is a divided empire in which certain ideas and emotions and actions are of God, and their

◆ Literary Focus

❺ Drama: Dialogue and Stage Directions Ask two volunteers to read this exchange aloud. Then have students comment on what it reveals about the mood and atmosphere in Salem. *Elicit the following: Giles's suggestion that there are "deep" and "dark" forces behind the fact that everyone is suing everyone else shows that people are quick to blame the Devil for their problems—just as John Proctor points out.*

Customize for *Less Proficient Readers*

❻ Check students' understanding by having them summarize the dispute that takes places here. *Proctor and Putnam argue over the ownership of a piece of land. Putnam claims that the land belongs to his family, as stated in his grandfather's will; Proctor states that he bought it from its rightful owner—Rebecca Nurse.*

◆ Literary Focus

❼ Drama: Dialogue and Stage Directions Remind students that in earlier portions of his stage directions, Miller provided background information about Salem and its inhabitants. Point out that in this portion, after discussing Reverend Hale and his view of the Devil, Miller goes on to discuss later views and interpretations of the Devil.

Comprehension Check ☑

❶ Why does Miller call the change that has taken place since 1692 "great but superficial"? *The image of the Devil has changed, but people still believe in the concept of absolute good versus absolute evil with which the Devil is associated.*

Comprehension Check ☑

❷ According to Miller, in what way has the Devil been used as a "weapon" in every age? *In every age, the Devil has been used to coerce people into submission to a particular church or theocracy.*

◆ Critical Thinking

❸ **Analyze; Support** Point out that in his commentary, Miller makes a direct reference to the political climates of both America and Communist countries in the 1950's. Have students explain in their own words Miller's notion of "contemporary diabolism." *Responses may include: In Communist countries, any type of political opposition is blamed on capitalist "devils," while in America, anyone who does not agree with certain reactionary views is labeled a Communist.* You might then have students look back over this paragraph to identify the general phenomenon that these examples illustrate. *The examples illustrate the tendency of religious and political groups to demonize—or make devils of—those who oppose them.*

opposites are of Lucifer. It is as impossible for most men to conceive of a morality without sin as of an earth without "sky." ❶ Since 1692 a great but superficial change has wiped out God's beard and the Devil's horns, but the world is still gripped between two diametrically opposed absolutes. The concept of unity, in which positive and negative are attributes of the same force, in which good and evil are relative, ever-changing, and always joined to the same phenomenon—such a concept is still reserved to the physical sciences and to the few who have grasped the history of ideas. ❷ When it is recalled that until the Christian era the underworld was never regarded as a hostile area, that all gods were useful and essentially friendly to man despite occasional lapses; when we see the steady and methodical <u>inculcation</u> into humanity of the idea of man's worthlessness—until redeemed—the necessity of the Devil may become evident as a weapon, a weapon designed and used time and time again in every age to whip men into a surrender to a particular church or church-state.

Our difficulty in believing the—for want of a better word—political inspiration of the Devil is due in great part to the fact that he is called up and damned not only by our social antagonists but by our own side, whatever it may be. The Catholic Church, through its Inquisition,[9] is famous for cultivating Lucifer as the arch-fiend, but the Church's enemies relied no less upon the Old Boy to keep the human mind enthralled. Luther[10] was himself accused of alliance with Hell, and he in turn accused his enemies. To complicate matters further, he believed that he had had contact with the Devil and had argued theology with him. I am not surprised at this, for at my own university a professor of history—a Lutheran,[11] by the way—used to assemble his graduate students, draw the shades, and commune in the classroom with Erasmus.[12] He was never, to my knowledge, officially scoffed at for this, the reason being that the university officials, like most of us, are the children of a history which still sucks at the Devil's teats. ❸ At this writing, only England has held back before the temptations of contemporary diabolism. In the countries of the Communist ideology, all resistance of any import is linked to the totally malign capitalist succubi,[13] and in America any man who is not reactionary in his views is open to the charge of alliance with the Red hell. Political opposition, thereby, is given an inhumane overlay which then justifies the abrogation[14] of all normally applied customs of civilized intercourse. A political policy is equated with moral right, and opposition to it with diabolical malevolence. Once such an equation is effectively made, society becomes a congerie[15] of plots and counterplots, and the main role of government changes from that of the arbiter to that of the scourge of God.

The results of this process are no different now from what they ever were, except sometimes in the degree of cruelty inflicted, and not always even in that department. Normally, the actions and deeds of a man were all that society felt comfortable in judging. The secret intent of an action was left to the ministers, priests, and rabbis to deal with. When diabolism rises, however, actions are the least important manifests of the true nature of a man. The Devil, as Reverend Hale said, is a wily one, and until an hour before he fell, even God thought him beautiful in Heaven.

❹ The analogy, however, seems to falter when one considers that, while there were no witches then, there are Communists and capitalists now, and in each camp there is certain proof that spies of each side are at work undermining the other. But this is a snobbish objection and not at all warranted by the facts. I have no doubt that people *were* communing with, and even worshiping, the Devil in Salem, and if the

9. **Inquisition:** General tribunal established in the 13th century for the discovery and suppression of beliefs and opinions opposed to the orthodox doctrines of the Church.
10. **Luther:** Martin Luther (1483–1546), German theologian who led the Protestant Reformation.
11. **Lutheran:** Member of the Protestant denomination founded by Martin Luther.
12. **Erasmus:** Desiderius Erasmus (1466?–1536), Dutch humanist, scholar, and theologian.
13. **succubi** (suk´ yoo bī): Female demons thought to lie on sleeping men.
14. **abrogation** (ab´ rō gā´ shən): Abolishment.
15. **congerie** (kän´ jə rē´): Heap; pile.

Humanities: Art

The Decorative Arts in Puritan America Although Puritans generally preferred a plain style and were suspicious of ornamentation, they did produce works of beautiful craftsmanship for their homes.

Salem was noted for its fine furniture makers. The furniture was often painted in light colors and then stenciled with designs of fruits, flowers, vines, and leaves. Floors were also often stenciled.

Women in colonial New England were known for their fine needlework and quilting. "Crazy quilts" were an innovation colonial women developed as a practical necessity. When blankets became worn, women would patch them with whatever fabric scraps they had on hand. Over time, the surface of the blanket became completely covered with a wild assortment of overlapping patches. Girls were taught embroidery at an early age and spent long winter months working on samplers that demonstrated their repertoire of stitches and also taught them to read as they stitched the alphabet and sayings from the Bible.

Have students do library research to find photos of the decorative art forms mentioned here.

whole truth could be known in this case, as it is in others, we should discover a regular and conventionalized propitiation of the dark spirit. 4 One certain evidence of this is the confession of Tituba, the slave of Reverend Parris, and another is the behavior of the children who were known to have indulged in sorceries with her.

There are accounts of similar *klatches*[16] in Europe, where the daughters of the towns would assemble at night and, sometimes with fetishes,[17] sometimes with a selected young man, give themselves to love, with some bastardly results. The Church, sharp-eyed as it must be when gods long dead are brought to life, condemned these orgies as witchcraft and interpreted them, rightly, as a resurgence of the Dionysiac[18] forces it had crushed long before. Sex, sin, and the Devil were early linked, and so they continued to be in Salem, and are today. From all accounts there are no more puritanical mores in the world than those enforced by the Communists in Russia, where women's fashions, for instance, are as prudent and all-covering as any American Baptist would desire. The divorce laws lay a tremendous responsibility on the father for the care of his children. Even the laxity of divorce regulations in the early years of the revolution was undoubtedly a revulsion from the nineteenth-century Victorian[19] immobility of marriage and the consequent hypocrisy that developed from it. If for no other reasons, a state so powerful, so jealous of the uniformity of its citizens, cannot long tolerate the atomization of the family. And yet, in American eyes at least, there remains the conviction that the Russian attitude toward women is lascivious. It is the Devil working again, just as he is working within the Slav who is shocked at the very idea of a woman's disrobing herself in a burlesque show. Our opposites are always robed in sexual sin, and it is from this unconscious conviction that demonology gains both its attractive sensuality and its capacity to infuriate and frighten.

Coming into Salem now, Reverend Hale conceives of himself much as a young doctor on his first call. His painfully acquired armory of symptoms, catchwords, and diagnostic procedures are now to be put to use at last. The road from Beverly is unusually busy this morning, and he has passed a hundred rumors that make him smile at the ignorance of the yeomanry in this most precise science. He feels himself allied with the best minds of Europe—kings, philosophers, scientists, and ecclesiasts of all churches. His goal is light, goodness and its preservation, and he knows the exaltation of the blessed whose intelligence, sharpened by minute examinations of enormous tracts, is finally called upon to face what may be a bloody fight with the Fiend himself. 5 6

He appears loaded down with half a dozen heavy books.

HALE: Pray you, someone take these!

PARRIS, *delighted:* Mr. Hale! Oh! it's good to see you again! *Taking some books:* My, they're heavy!

HALE, *setting down his books:* They must be; they are weighted with authority.

PARRIS, *a little scared:* Well, you do come prepared!

HALE: We shall need hard study if it comes to tracking down the Old Boy. *Noticing* REBECCA: You cannot be Rebecca Nurse?

REBECCA: I am, sir. Do you know me?

HALE: It's strange how I knew you, but I suppose you look as such a good soul should. We have all heard of your great charities in Beverly.

---

16. ***klatches*** (klächz): Informal gatherings.
17. **fetishes** (fet′ ish iz): Objects believed to have magical power.
18. **Dionysiac** (dī′ ə nish′ ē ak): Characteristic of Dionysus, Greek god of wine and revelry; thus, wild, frenzied, sensuous.
19. **Victorian:** Characteristic of the time when Victoria was queen of England (1837–1901), an era associated with respectability, prudery, and hypocrisy.

◆ Build Vocabulary

inculcation (in′ kul kā′ shən) *n.*: Teaching by repetition and insistent urging

propitiation (prə pish′ ē ā′ shən) *n.*: Action designed to soothe or satisfy a person, a cause, etc.; conciliation

◆ Critical Thinking

4 Identify; Summarize Have students identify the analogy to which Miller refers here. *It is the analogy between the Salem witchcraft trials and the 1950's political "witch hunts."* Then have them summarize the argument that he makes in this paragraph. *He argues that the analogy is valid; some people in Salem really did practice witchcraft, just as some people in Communist and capitalist countries really do try to undermine the system in power.*

◆ Reading Strategy

5 Question the Characters' Motives According to this passage, what motivates Reverend Hale to work in the field of ascertaining witchcraft? To what extent do students think that he is aware of his motive or motives? *Students may identify the following motives: He is dedicated to fighting the Devil; this type of work makes him feel important and somewhat superior. They may note that he is fully aware of the first motive but not of the second.*

Customize for
AP Students

6 Have students explain the irony behind this sentence found in the last paragraph of Miller's commentary: ". . . he [Reverend Hale] has passed a hundred rumors that make him smile at the ignorance of the yeomanry in this most precise science." *Reverend Hale regards the diagnosis of witchcraft as "this most precise science." To Miller, and presumably to the modern reader, it is anything but a science.*

Customize for
Interpersonal Learners

1 Have four volunteers read this section aloud. Then ask students what they can tell about Reverend Hale from his words. *Responses may include: He is extremely courteous; he is a flatterer; he is a smooth talker.*

◆ Literary Focus

2 **Drama: Dialogue and Stage Directions** Encourage students to comment on what this speech reveals about Hale. *Some students may say that he takes his job seriously and has a sincere belief in his methods. Others may suggest that he is responding to Proctor's parting words and is making an effort to act "sensibly."*

Customize for
Body/Kinesthetic Learners

3 Have a group of six students, representing the Putnams, Parris, Hale, Giles, and Rebecca Nurse, act out the stage directions that follow Mrs. Putnam's broken-voiced "Aye." Afterwards, encourage students to discuss the effect of their silent actions. *Students may point out that the actions create suspense; they heighten the drama.*

PARRIS: Do you know this gentleman? Mr. Thomas Putnam. And his good wife Ann.

HALE: Putnam! I had not expected such distinguished company, sir. 1

PUTNAM, *pleased:* It does seem to help us today, Mr. Hale. We look to you to come to our house and save our child.

HALE: Your child ails too?

MRS. PUTNAM: Her soul, her soul seems flown away. She sleeps and yet she walks . . .

PUTNAM: She cannot eat.

HALE: Cannot eat! *Thinks on it. Then, to* PROCTOR *and* GILES COREY: Do you men have afflicted children?

PARRIS: No, no, these are farmers. John Proctor—

GILES COREY: He don't believe in witches.

PROCTOR, *to* HALE: I never spoke on witches one way or the other. Will you come, Giles?

GILES: No—no, John, I think not. I have some few queer questions of my own to ask this fellow.

PROCTOR: I've heard you to be a sensible man, Mr. Hale. I hope you'll leave some of it in Salem.

PROCTOR *goes.* HALE *stands embarrassed for an instant.*

PARRIS, *quickly:* Will you look at my daughter, sir? *Leads* HALE *to the bed.* She has tried to leap out the window; we discovered her this morning on the highroad, waving her arms as though she'd fly.

HALE, *narrowing his eyes:* Tries to fly.

PUTNAM: She cannot bear to hear the Lord's name, Mr. Hale; that's a sure sign of witchcraft afloat.

HALE, *holding up his hands:* No, no. Now let me instruct you. We cannot look to superstition in this. The Devil is precise; the marks of his presence are definite as stone, and I must tell you all that I shall not proceed unless you are prepared to believe me if I should find no bruise of hell upon her. 2

PARRIS: It is agreed, sir—it is agreed—we will abide by your judgment.

HALE: Good then. *He goes to the bed, looks down at* BETTY. *To* PARRIS: Now, sir, what were your first warning of this strangeness?

PARRIS: Why, sir—I discovered her—*indicating* ABIGAIL—and my niece and ten or twelve of the other girls, dancing in the forest last night.

HALE, *surprised:* You permit dancing?

PARRIS: No, no, it were secret—

MRS. PUTNAM, *unable to wait:* Mr. Parris's slave has knowledge of conjurin', sir.

PARRIS, *to* MRS. PUTNAM: We cannot be sure of that, Goody Ann—

MRS. PUTNAM, *frightened, very softly:* I know it, sir. I sent my child—she should learn from Tituba who murdered her sisters.

REBECCA, *horrified:* Goody Ann! You sent a child to conjure up the dead?

MRS. PUTNAM: Let God blame me, not you, not you, Rebecca! I'll not have you judging me any more! *To* HALE: Is it a natural work to lose seven children before they live a day?

PARRIS: Sssh!

REBECCA, *with great pain, turns her face away. There is a pause.*

HALE: Seven dead in childbirth.

MRS. PUTNAM, *softly:* Aye. *Her voice breaks; she looks up at him. Silence.* HALE *is impressed.* PARRIS *looks to him. He goes to his books, opens one, turns pages, then reads. All wait, avidly.* 3

PARRIS, *hushed:* What book is that?

MRS. PUTNAM: What's there, sir?

HALE, *with a tasty love of intellectual pursuit:* Here is all the invisible world, caught, defined, and calculated. In these books the Devil stands stripped of all his brute disguises. Here are all your familiar spirits—your incubi[20] and succubi, your witches that go by land, by air, and by sea;

20. **incubi** (in´ kyoo bī): Spirits or demons thought to lie on sleeping women.

Beyond the Classroom

Community Connection

Houses of Worship Most of the inhabitants of Salem in the late 1600's would have been members of the Puritan church, and all would have been required to attend services. Have students discuss the various houses of worship in your community. How many are there? What denominations do they serve? When was each house of worship established? Encourage students to contrast current notions of religious freedom with the Puritans' notion of religious freedom.

your wizards of the night and of the day. Have no fear now—we shall find him out if he has come among us, and I mean to crush him utterly if he has shown his face! *He starts for the bed.*

REBECCA: Will it hurt the child, sir?

HALE: I cannot tell, If she is truly in the Devil's grip we may have to rip and tear to get her free.

REBECCA: I think I'll go, then. I am too old for this. *She rises.*

PARRIS, *striving for conviction:* Why, Rebecca, we may open up the boil of all our troubles today! ❹

REBECCA: Let us hope for that. I go to God for you, sir.

PARRIS, *with trepidation—and resentment:* I hope you do not mean to go to Satan here! *Slight pause.*

REBECCA: I wish I knew. *She goes out; they feel resentful of her note of moral superiority.*

PUTNAM, *abruptly:* Come, Mr. Hale, let's get on. Sit you here.

GILES: Mr. Hale, I have always wanted to ask a learned man—what signifies the readin' of strange books?

HALE: What books?

GILES: I cannot tell; she hides them.

HALE: Who does this?

GILES: Martha, my wife. I have waked at night many a time and found her in a corner, readin' of a book. Now what do you make of that?

HALE: Why, that's not necessarily—

GILES: It discomfits me! Last night—mark this—I tried and tried and could not say my prayers. And then she close her book and walks out of the house, and suddenly—mark this—I could pray again!

Old Giles must be spoken for, if only because his fate was to be so remarkable and so different from that of all the others. He was in his early eighties at this time, and was the most comical hero in the history. No man has ever been blamed for so much. If a cow was missed, the first thought was to look for her around Corey's house; a fire blazing up at night brought suspicion of arson to his door. He didn't give a hoot for public opinion, and only in his last years—after he had married Martha—did he bother much with the church. That she stopped his prayer is very probable, but he forgot to say that he'd only recently learned any prayers and it didn't take much to make him stumble over them. He was a crank and a nuisance, but withal a deeply innocent and brave man. In court, once, he was asked if it were true that he had been frightened by the strange behavior of a hog and had then said he knew it to be the Devil in an animal's shape. "What frighted you?" he was asked. He forgot everything but the word "frighted," and instantly replied, "I do not know that I ever spoke that word in my life." ❺

HALE: Ah! The stoppage of prayer—that is strange. I'll speak further on that with you.

GILES: I'm not sayin' she's touched the Devil, now, but I'd admire to know what books she reads and why she hides them. She'll not answer me, y' see. ❻

HALE: Aye, we'll discuss it. *To all:* Now mark me, if the Devil is in her you will witness some frightful wonders in this room, so please to keep your wits about you. Mr. Putnam, stand close in case she flies. Now, Betty, dear, will you sit up? PUTNAM *comes in closer, ready-handed.* HALE *sits* BETTY *up, but she hangs limp in his hands.* Hmmm. *He observes her carefully. The others watch breathlessly.* Can you hear me? I am John Hale, minister of Beverly. I have come to help you, dear. Do you remember my two little girls in Beverly? *She does not stir in his hands.*

PARRIS, *in fright:* How can it be the Devil? Why would he choose my house to strike? We have all manner of licentious people in the village!

HALE: What victory would the Devil have to win a soul already bad? It is the best the Devil

◆ Build Vocabulary

licentious (lī sen′ shəs) *adj.*: Lacking moral restraint; disregarding accepted rules, especially in moral conduct

◆ Critical Thinking

❹ Compare and Contrast Have students contrast Rebecca's attitude in this scene with that of Hale and Parris. *Rebecca is genuinely concerned about Betty, while Hale and Parris seem more concerned with the pursuit of witchcraft; Rebecca seems skeptical about the possibility of witchcraft in Salem, while Hale and Parris seem eager to uncover it.*

◆ Literary Focus

❺ Drama: Dialogue and Stage Directions How does this background information about Giles Corey help us to understand his remarks about his wife Martha and her behavior? *Students should note that Miller describes Giles as a "deeply innocent" man. Therefore, we can conclude that he did not mean to implicate Martha by describing her "strange" behavior; rather, he brought the subject up out of naive curiosity.*

◆ Critical Thinking

❻ Analyze Encourage students to discuss why Miller includes the short scene in which Giles seeks Hale's opinion of Martha's actions. *Sample response: The scene is meant to show how easily—and inadvertently—innocent people can be implicated in witchcraft.*

▶Critical Viewing◀

Students should note that the photo on this page portrays the scene in which Tituba, Abigail, Betty, Mercy Lewis, Mary Warren, and several others dance and "conjure" in the woods. Students may also note that this scene is apparently depicted in the movie, from which the stills are taken, while it is only referred to in the stage version of the play.

◆Literary Focus

❶ Drama: Dialogue and Stage Directions Have a volunteer read this speech aloud. Then ask students what they notice about the questions that Hale puts to Betty. *Responses may include: He asks leading questions; his questions are likely to plant ideas in her head.*

◆Literary Focus

❷ Drama: Dialogue and Stage Directions Point out that Hale again asks leading questions as he interrogates Abigail.

wants, and who is better than the minister?

GILES: That's deep, Mr. Parris, deep, deep!

PARRIS, *with resolution now:* Betty! Answer Mr. Hale! Betty!

HALE: Does someone afflict you, child? It need not be a woman, mind you, or a man. Perhaps some bird invisible to others comes to you—perhaps a pig, a mouse, or any beast at all. Is there some figure bids you fly? *The child remains limp in his hands. In silence he lays her*
❶ *back on the pillow. Now, holding out his hands toward her, he intones:* In nomine Domini Sabaoth sui filiique ite ad infernos.[21] *She does not stir. He turns to* ABIGAIL, *his eyes narrowing.* Abigail, what sort of dancing were you doing with her in the forest?

ABIGAIL: Why—common dancing is all.

PARRIS: I think I ought to say that I—I saw a kettle in the grass where they were dancing.

ABIGAIL: That were only soup.

HALE: What sort of soup were in this kettle, Abigail?

ABIGAIL: Why, it were beans—and lentils, I think, and—

HALE: Mr. Parris, you did not notice, did you, any living thing in the kettle? A mouse, perhaps, a spider, a frog—?

PARRIS, *fearfully:* I—do believe there were some movement—in the soup.

ABIGAIL: That jumped in, we never put it in!

HALE, *quickly:* What jumped in?

ABIGAIL: Why, a very little frog jumped—

PARRIS: A frog, Abby!

HALE, *grasping* ABIGAIL: Abigail, it may be your cousin is dying. Did you call the Devil last night?

ABIGAIL: I never called him! Tituba, Tituba . . .

PARRIS, *blanched:* She called the Devil?

HALE: I should like to speak with Tituba.

PARRIS: Goody Ann, will you bring her up? MRS. PUTNAM *exits.*

HALE: How did she call him?

ABIGAIL: I know not—she spoke Barbados.

HALE: Did you feel any strangeness when she called him? A sudden cold wind, perhaps? A ❷
trembling below the ground?

ABIGAIL: I didn't see no Devil! *Shaking* BETTY: Betty, wake up. Betty! Betty!

HALE: You cannot evade me, Abigail. Did your cousin drink any of the brew in that kettle?

---

21. **In nomine Domini Sabaoth sui filiique ite ad infernos** (in nō´mē nā dō´ mē nē sab´ ā äth so͞o´ ē fē´ lēē kwā ē´ tā äd in fur´ nōs): "In the name of the lord of hosts and his son, get thee to the lower world" (Latin).

Humanities: Art

The Salem Memorial Explain to students that in 1986, in preparation for the tercentenary, or three-hundred year, remembrance of the Salem witchcraft trials, the official Tercentenary Committee held a design competition for a memorial to the victims. The winning design, by architect Jim Cutler and artist Maggie Smith, was in part inspired by Cutler's childhood reactions both to learning about the McCarthy hearings and to viewing a performance of *The Crucible.* The memorial is a granite wall, built adjacent to the cemetery where Hathorne is buried. On its threshold are engraved words from the trial itself, and farther along the wall are horizontal slabs, each of which features the name of a victim, along with the date and method of death. The memorial stands beside a grove of locust trees, thought to be the type of tree from which the victims were hanged. When the memorial was unveiled, in November of 1991, the honored guest at the ceremony was Arthur Miller, author of *The Crucible.*

ABIGAIL: She never drank it!

HALE: Did you drink it?

ABIGAIL: No, sir!

HALE: Did Tituba ask you to drink it?

ABIGAIL: She tried, but I refused.

HALE: Why are you concealing? Have you sold yourself to Lucifer?

ABIGAIL: I never sold myself! I'm a good girl! I'm a proper girl!

MRS. PUTNAM *enters with* TITUBA, *and instantly* ABIGAIL *points at* TITUBA.

3 **ABIGAIL:** She made me do it! She made Betty do it!

TITUBA, *shocked and angry:* Abby!

ABIGAIL: She makes me drink blood!

PARRIS: Blood!!

MRS. PUTNAM: My baby's blood?

TITUBA: No, no, chicken blood. I give she chicken blood!

HALE: Woman, have you enlisted these children for the Devil?

TITUBA: No, no, sir, I don't truck with no Devil!

HALE: Why can she not wake? Are you silencing this child?

TITUBA: I love me Betty!

HALE: You have sent your spirit out upon this child, have you not? Are you gathering souls for the Devil?

ABIGAIL: She sends her spirit on me in church; she makes me laugh at prayer!

PARRIS: She have often laughed at prayer!

ABIGAIL: She comes to me every night to go and drink blood!

TITUBA: You beg *me* to conjure! She beg *me* make charm—

ABIGAIL: Don't lie! *To* HALE: She comes to me while I sleep; she's always making me dream corruptions!

TITUBA: Why you say that, Abby?

ABIGAIL: Sometimes I wake and find myself standing in the open doorway and not a stitch on my body! I always hear her laughing in my sleep. I hear her singing her Barbados songs and tempting me with—

TITUBA: Mister Reverend, I never—

HALE, *resolved now:* Tituba, I want you to wake this child.

TITUBA: I have no power on this child, sir.

HALE: You most certainly do, and you will free her from it now! When did you compact with the Devil?

TITUBA: I don't compact with no Devil!

PARRIS: You will confess yourself or I will take you out and whip you to your death, Tituba!

PUTNAM: This woman must be hanged! She must be taken and hanged!

TITUBA, *terrified, falls to her knees:* No, no, don't hang Tituba! I tell him I don't desire to work for him, sir. 4

PARRIS: The Devil?

HALE: Then you saw him! TITUBA *weeps.* Now Tituba, I know that when we bind ourselves to Hell it is very hard to break with it. We are going to help you tear yourself free— 5

> **◆ Reading Strategy**
> What does this dialogue reveal about Tituba's motives for suddenly admitting that she has trafficked with the Devil?

TITUBA, *frightened by the coming process:* Mister Reverend, I do believe somebody else be witchin' these children.

HALE: Who? 6

TITUBA: I don't know, sir, but the Devil got him numerous witches.

HALE: Does he! *It is a clue.* Tituba, look into my eyes. Come, look into me. *She raises her eyes to his fearfully.* You would be a good Christian woman, would you not, Tituba?

TITUBA: Aye, sir, a good Christian woman.

HALE: And you love these little children? 7

TITUBA: Oh, yes, sir, I don't desire to hurt little children.

◆ Reading Strategy

3 Question the Characters' Motives Encourage students to comment on Abigail's motives for accusing Tituba. *Responses may include the following: She wants to deflect attention and blame away from herself; she hopes to win the questioners' approval by providing them with a culprit.*

4 Enrichment Explain to students that it was believed that witches had transferred their allegiance from God to the Devil and had signed their names in the Devil's book.

◆ Reading Strategy

5 Question the Characters' Motives Students should note that Parris has threatened Tituba with being "whipped to death," while Putnam has threatened hanging. Tituba is intimidated and frightened into her sudden admission.

◆ Critical Thinking

6 Identify Cause and Effect Point out that, like Abigail, Tituba points the finger at others. How do students explain her reasons for doing so? *Responses may include the following: Like Abigail, Tituba means to clear herself by naming others; she is making an effort to appease Hale by telling him what he wants to hear.*

◆ Critical Thinking

7 Analyze Ask students what they notice about the way in which Tituba responds to Hale's questions. What does this reveal about her state of mind? *At this point, Tituba is closely attuned to Hale's questions—her answers tend to repeat or elaborate on words and ideas within them. Tituba's responses reveal that she is clearly following Hale's lead.*

◆ Reading Strategy

❶ **Question the Characters' Motives** Encourage students to speculate about Putnam's motives for asking whether Tituba saw these two people in particular in the company of the Devil. *Some students may say that Putnam actually suspects these two of witchcraft. Others may say that he has personal grudges against them and is hoping to see them ruined.*

❷ **Enrichment** Tell students that although the term *witch* was used to refer to both men and women, ninety percent of the people accused of witchcraft over the centuries were women. Also point out that the terms *wizard* and *warlock* were sometimes used to refer to male witches.

◆ Critical Thinking

❸ **Infer** Based on this speech, what inferences can students make about Tituba's actions and her personality traits? *Students may point out that she has a fertile and vivid imagination. Others may say that consciously or unconsciously, she is trying to please and impress her interrogators; in the spirit of going along with what is expected of her, she names Goody Good and Goody Osburn—the two people whom Putnam had specifically asked about.*

HALE: And you love God, Tituba?

TITUBA: I love God with all my bein'.

HALE: Now, in God's holy name—

TITUBA: Bless Him. Bless Him. *She is rocking on her knees, sobbing in terror.*

HALE: And to His glory—

TITUBA: Eternal glory. Bless Him—bless God . . .

HALE: Open yourself, Tituba—open yourself and let God's holy light shine on you.

TITUBA: Oh, bless the Lord.

HALE: When the Devil come to you does he ever come—with another person? *She stares up into his face.* Perhaps another person in the village? Someone you know.

PARRIS: Who came with him?

❶ **PUTNAM:** Sarah Good? Did you ever see Sarah Good with him? Or Osburn?

PARRIS: Was it man or woman came with him?

TITUBA: Man or woman. Was—was woman.

❷ **PARRIS:** What woman? A woman, you said. What woman?

TITUBA: It was black dark, and I—

PARRIS: You could see him, why could you not see her?

TITUBA: Well, they was always talking; they was always runnin' round and carryin' on—

PARRIS: You mean out of Salem? Salem witches?

TITUBA: I believe so, yes, sir.

Now HALE *takes her hand. She is surprised.*

HALE: Tituba. You must have no fear to tell us who they are, do you understand? We will protect you. The Devil can never overcome a minister. You know that, do you not?

TITUBA, *kisses* HALE*'s hand:* Aye, sir, oh, I do.

HALE: You have confessed yourself to witchcraft, and that speaks a wish to come to Heaven's side. And we will bless you, Tituba.

TITUBA, *deeply relieved:* Oh, God bless you, Mr. Hale!

HALE, *with rising exaltation:* You are God's instrument put in our hands to discover the Devil's agent among us. You are selected, Tituba, you are chosen to help us cleanse our village. So speak utterly, Tituba, turn your back on him and face God—face God, Tituba, and God will protect you.

TITUBA, *joining with him:* Oh, God, protect Tituba!

HALE, *kindly:* Who came to you with the Devil? Two? Three? Four? How many?

Tituba pants, and begins rocking back and forth again, staring ahead.

TITUBA: There was four. There was four.

PARRIS, *pressing in on her:* Who? Who? Their names, their names!

TITUBA, *suddenly bursting out:* Oh, how many times he bid me kill you, Mr. Parris!

PARRIS: Kill me!

TITUBA, *in a fury:* He say Mr. Parris must be kill! Mr. Parris no goodly man, Mr. Parris mean man and no gentle man, and he bid me rise out of my bed and cut your throat! *They gasp.* But I tell him "No! I don't hate that man. I don't want kill that man." But he say, "You work for me, Tituba, and I make you free! I give you pretty dress to wear, and put you way high up in the air, and you gone fly back to Barbados!" And I ❸ say, "You lie, Devil, you lie!" And then he come one stormy night to me, and he say, "Look! I have *white* people belong to me." And I look—and there was Goody Good.

PARRIS: Sarah Good!

TITUBA, *rocking and weeping:* Aye, sir, and Goody Osburn.

MRS. PUTNAM: I knew it! Goody Osburn were midwife to me three times. I begged you, Thomas, did I not? I begged him not to call Osburn because I feared her. My babies always shriveled in her hands!

HALE: Take courage, you must give us all their names. How can you bear to see this child suffering? Look at her, Tituba. *He is indicating* BETTY *on the bed.* Look at her God-given innocence; her soul is so tender; we must protect her, Tituba; the Devil is out and preying on her like a beast upon the flesh of the pure lamb. God will bless you for your help.

ABIGAIL *rises, staring as though inspired, and cries out.*

ABIGAIL: I want to open myself! *They turn to her, startled. She is enraptured, as though in a pearly light.* I want the light of God, I want the sweet love of Jesus! I danced for the Devil; I saw him; I wrote in his book; I go back to Jesus; I kiss His hand. I saw Sarah Good with the Devil! I saw Goody Osburn with the Devil! I saw Bridget Bishop with the Devil! ❹

As she is speaking, BETTY *is rising from the bed, a fever in her eyes, and picks up the chant.*

BETTY, *staring too:* I saw George Jacobs with the Devil! I saw Goody Howe with the Devil!

PARRIS: She speaks! *He rushes to embrace* BETTY. She speaks!

HALE: Glory to God! It is broken, they are free!

BETTY, *calling out hysterically and with great relief:* I saw Martha Bellows with the Devil!

ABIGAIL: I saw Goody Sibber with the Devil! *It is rising to a great glee.*

PUTNAM: The marshal, I'll call the marshal!

PARRIS *is shouting a prayer of thanksgiving.*

BETTY: I saw Alice Barrow with the Devil! ❹

The curtain begins to fall.

HALE, *as* PUTNAM *goes out:* Let the marshal bring irons!

ABIGAIL: I saw Goody Hawkins with the Devil!

BETTY: I saw Goody Bibber with the Devil!

ABIGAIL: I saw Goody Booth with the Devil!

On their ecstatic cries—

THE CURTAIN FALLS

Guide for Responding

◆ Literature and Your Life

Reader's Response Were you surprised when the accusations multiplied? Explain.

Thematic Focus: What aspects of society does Miller seem to be criticizing through the characters of Reverend Parris and the Putnams?

Group Discussion Discuss the types of situations that could cause a contemporary American town to become afflicted by a general hysteria.

☑ Check Your Comprehension

1. (a) What is Betty's condition as the play opens? (b) What were she and her cousin Abigail doing the night before?
2. Summarize Abigail's prior relationship with the Proctors.
3. (a) Who is Reverend Hale? (b) Why is he contacted?

◆ Critical Thinking

INTERPRET

1. What seems to be the main motivation for Reverend Parris's concern about Abigail and Betty's behavior in the forest? **[Infer]**
2. (a) When Reverend Parris leaves the room, Abigail, Mercy, Mary, and Betty talk in private. What does their discussion reveal? (b) How does this scene hint at events that will occur later in the play? **[Interpret; Speculate]**
3. (a) How does Betty's reaction to the psalm support the assertion that there is "witchcraft afoot"? (b) What other incidents do the various characters use to support this assertion? **[Infer]**
4. What evidence is there that sharp divisions exist among the people of Salem Village? **[Support]**

APPLY

5. (a) Name two others you think will be accused. (b) Who will accuse them? Why? **[Speculate]**

◆ Literary Focus

❹ Drama: Dialogue and Stage Directions Have six volunteers read these lines aloud. Then have students comment on the effect of this closing scene. *Students may describe it as chilling or ominous. The ecstatic and contagious nature of the accusations suggests that superstition and hysteria have won out and that many innocent people will be victimized.*

Reinforce and Extend

Answers

◆ Literature and Your Life

Reader's Response Accept all reasonable responses.

Thematic Focus Miller seems to be criticizing hypocrisy and vindictiveness.

☑ Check Your Comprehension

1. (a) She is seemingly unconscious or in an inexplicable swoon. (b) They were cavorting with other girls and the slave woman, Tituba.
2. She worked as a servant in the Proctor home, had an affair with John Proctor, and was dismissed.
3. (a) He is a neighboring minister with expertise in witchcraft. (b) The doctor does not know what is wrong with Betty; given her activities in the woods the night before, witchcraft is suspected.

◆ Critical Thinking

1. Suggested response: He seems most concerned about how it will affect his own status in the village.
2. (a) Suggested response: It reveals that they have not divulged the truth about their behavior and that they are afraid they will be accused of being witches. (b) Suggested response: It shows the girls plotting to save themselves and hints at the fact that they will ultimately do almost anything to avoid punishment.
3. (a) It suggests that she cannot bear to hear God's name. (b) Students should note Mrs. Putnam's frequent references to the deaths of her babies and her descriptions of her daughter's strange behavior.
4. Suggested response: The people are involved in frequent lawsuits. There is talk about "factions" within the village. Several of the characters become involved in arguments during the course of the act.
5. (a) Some students may name Rebecca Nurse and John or Elizabeth Proctor. (b) Students who name either of the Proctors should recognize that Abby will probably want to implicate Elizabeth out of jealousy and/or John out of revenge for his scorn. Students who name Rebecca Nurse should recognize that the Putnams will probably want to implicate their rivals.

Answers

◆ Literary Focus

1. (a) She is an immoral, manipulative person motivated by lust for John Proctor, jealousy for his wife, and a desire to be the center of attention. (b) She has an endless gift for dissembling.
2. (a) He includes it to show he has researched events carefully and to tie the events to the Communist "witch hunts" of the 1950's. (b) Possible answer: It is addressed toward those involved in the McCarthy hearings.

◆ Reading Strategy

1. Reverend Parris is motivated by self-importance to keep his reputation intact.
2. Mary Warren seems to be motivated by fear of being labeled a witch.
3. Abigail Williams is motivated by lust for John Proctor.
4. Tituba seems to be motivated by fear of being executed.

◆ Grammar and Style

Pronoun Case in Incomplete Constructions

1. he; 2. her; 3. she; 4. me

◆ Build Vocabulary

Using the Latin Root *-grat-*

1. gratify: to please
2. ingrate: someone who isn't pleased
3. congratulate: to express pleasure in the achievement or good fortune of another

Using the Word Bank

1. calumny; 2. inculcation; 3. dissembling; 4. licentious; 5. propitiation; 6. ingratiating; 7. predilection

Idea Bank

Customizing for *Performance Levels*

Following are suggestions for matching Idea Bank topics with your students' performance levels:
Average Students: 1, 4
More Advanced Students: 2, 3

Customizing for *Learning Modalities*

Following are suggestions for matching Idea Bank topics with your students' learning modalities:
Interpersonal: 3
Bodily/Kinesthetic: 4

Guide for Responding, Act I (continued)

◆ Literary Focus

Drama: Dialogue and Stage Directions

Drama consists of **dialogue** that the characters speak and **stage directions** that the playwright gives to the actors, director, and others reading or staging the play. Though the extent of stage directions varies from playwright to playwright, Miller's inclusion of such lengthy background information is unusual.

1. (a) What does the dialogue reveal about Abby's personality and motives? (b) In the stage directions, what does Miller state directly about her personality?

2. (a) Why do you think Miller includes such extensive background information about Salem and its inhabitants? (b) To whom do you think this information is addressed?

◆ Reading Strategy

Question the Characters' Motives

To improve your ability to interpret and analyze the characters in a drama, you should **question the characters' motives**, or consider the reasons they behave as they do. Identify what each of the following character's comments and actions reveal about his or her motivations.

1. Reverend Parris
2. Mary Warren
3. Abigail Williams
4. Tituba

◆ Grammar and Style

Pronoun Case in Incomplete Constructions

In an **incomplete construction**—a sentence where understood words are omitted—you may be uncertain about which form of a pronoun to use. Mentally complete the construction by inserting the missing words to help you decide

Practice Indicate which pronoun would best complete each sentence.

1. Proctor is a sinner, but others are more sinful than (he, him).
2. Proctor has some lingering affection for Abigail but cares more for his wife than (she, her).
3. Betty lies, but Abigail is craftier than (she, her).
4. "Blame others more than (I, me)," Tituba says.

◆ Build Vocabulary

Using the Latin Word Root *-grat-*

The root *-grat-* means "pleasing" or "agreeable." Explain how *-grat-* relates to the meaning of each of these words. Use a dictionary, if necessary.

1. gratify **2.** ingrate **3.** congratulate

Using the Word Bank: Sentence Completion

Write these sentences in your notebook, completing each with the appropriate word bank word.

1. Gossip and ___?___ can destroy a person's reputation.
2. Months of ___?___ helped me master Latin.
3. A born actor, he hid his true nature by ___?___.
4. His ___?___ behavior was the town scandal.
5. To soothe their gods, they made sacrifices as an act of ___?___.
6. Her ___?___ manner pleased the most demanding customers.
7. With my ___?___ for historical settings, it was predictable that I would enjoy *The Crucible*.

Idea Bank

Writing

1. Medical Chart Imagine that you are Betty's doctor. Write her medical chart for the day she takes ill. Describe her condition and its possible cause. **[Science Link]**

2. News Account Write an account of the events in Salem as they might be described in a Boston newspaper of the day. **[Media Link]**

Speaking, Listening, and Viewing

3. Oral Presentation Working in a small group, research and report on the belief in witches in seventeenth-century Europe. Present your findings to the class in an oral report. **[Social Studies Link]**

4. Dramatization Working in a small group, choose a scene from Act I to rehearse and perform for classmates. **[Performing Arts Link]**

✓ ASSESSMENT OPTIONS

Formal Assessment, Selection Test, pp. 326–328, and Assessment Resources Software. The selection test is designed so that it can be easily customized to the performance levels of your students. ***Alternative Assessment,*** p. 76, includes options for less advanced students, more advanced students, visual/spatial learners, verbal/linguistic learners, and interpersonal learners.

PORTFOLIO ASSESSMENT

Use the following rubrics in the ***Alternative Assessment*** booklet to assess student writing:
Medical Chart: Cause-Effect Rubric, p. 117
News Article: Fictional Narrative Rubric, p. 110

Guide for Interpreting, Act II

◆ Review and Anticipate

As Act I draws to a close, Salem is in the grip of mounting hysteria. What had begun as concern over the strange behavior of Betty, the minister's daughter—a reaction that may have stemmed from guilty feelings about her activities in the woods the night before—had by the act's end swelled to a mass hysteria in which accusations of witchcraft were being made and accepted against a growing number of Salem's citizens.

Which characters do you think will most readily believe the accusations of witchcraft? Who do you think will be accused next? Record your predictions about the characters from Act I in a chart like the one below. Then read Act II to see whether your predictions are correct.

Character	Prediction	Is Prediction Correct?

◆ Build Vocabulary

GREEK SUFFIXES: *-logy*

The suffix *-logy* means "the science, theory, or study of." Combining it with the Greek root *-theo-*, which means "god," you get *theology*, "the study of religion or a particular religious philosophy."

WORD BANK

Preview this list of words from Act II.

pallor
ameliorate
avidly
base
deference
theology
quail
gingerly
abomination
blasphemy

◆ Grammar and Style

COMMAS AFTER INTRODUCTORY WORDS

Use a comma to set off a mild interjection or another interrupter that introduces a sentence. Look at these examples from Act II:

Oh, you're not done then.
Aye, the farm is seeded.
No, she walked into the house this afternoon.
Why, she's weepin'!

◆ Literary Focus

ALLUSION

An **allusion** is a brief reference within a work to something outside the work, such as another literary work, a well-known person, a place, or a historical event. *The Crucible*, not surprisingly, makes many allusions to the Bible. For example, Act I mentions the New Jerusalem, a term for the holy city of heaven. Look for other biblical allusions as you read Act II.

◆ Reading Strategy

READ DRAMA

When you view a play, action and staging elements such as sets, lighting, and costumes work with the dialogue to advance the play's plot and develop the characters. When you **read a play**, instead of watching the action and staging, you read stage directions. Because stage directions often interrupt the dialogue, the experience of reading a play is usually not as smooth as that of reading a novel or story. The stage directions, however, can provide crucial information. In this passage from Act II of *The Crucible*, for example, you might think Elizabeth's words are cheerful and happy if you did not read the two words of stage directions in italics.

ELIZABETH—*it is hard to say:* I know it, John.

LESSON OBJECTIVES

1. **To develop vocabulary and word identification skills**
   - Greek Suffixes: *-logy*
   - Using the Word Bank: True or False?
2. **To use a variety of reading strategies to comprehend a drama**
   - Review and Anticipate
   - Reading Strategy: Read Drama
3. **To increase knowledge of other cultures and to connect common elements across cultures**
   - Background for Understanding (ATE)
   - Cross-Curricular Connection: Social Studies (ATE)
4. **To express and support responses to the text**
   - Critical Thinking
5. **To analyze literary elements**
   - Literary Focus: Allusion
6. **To research self-selected and assigned topics and produce reports in a variety of forms**
   - Idea Bank: Wanted Poster
   - Career Connection: Law Enforcement (ATE)
7. **To plan, prepare, organize, and present literary interpretations**
   - Idea Bank: Additional Scene
   - Idea Bank: Pantomime
   - Speaking, Listening, and Viewing Mini-Lesson (ATE)
8. **To increase knowledge of the rules of grammar and usage**
   - Grammar and Style: Commas After Introductory Words

Interest Grabber Tell students that in this act John Proctor must decide whether he is willing to risk his own life to save his wife from the consequences of unjust accusations. Have students write in their journals about times they had to decide how far to go to help a friend or loved one. What conflicts did they experience at that time? How did they resolve the conflicts and decide what to do in this difficult circumstance?

Prentice Hall Literature Program Resources

REINFORCE / RETEACH / EXTEND

Selection Support Pages
Build Vocabulary: Greek Suffixes: *-logy*, p. 342
Grammar and Style: Commas After Introductory Words, p. 343
Reading Strategy: Read Drama, p. 344
Literary Focus: Allusion, p. 345

Strategies for Diverse Student Needs, Paraphrase Dialogue, p. 77

Beyond Literature
Media Connection: Film Adaptations, p. 77

Formal Assessment Selection Test, pp. 329–331; Assessment Resources Software

Alternative Assessment, p. 77

Resource Pro CD-ROM
The Crucible, Act II—includes all resource material and customizable lesson plan

Literature CD-ROM
The History of American Literature: Part 2, Disc 2, Feature 4; *How to Read and Understand Drama:* Feature 12

One-Minute Insight Salem's troubles invade the Proctor family's home in Act II, as we learn that Abigail has accused Elizabeth Proctor of witchcraft. Haunted by the knowledge that Abigail's accusation is a consequence of his affair with her, John Proctor must decide whether he has the courage to publicly admit his affair in order to save his wife.

Customize for
Interpersonal Learners
Invite these students to act out the opening scene between John and Elizabeth Proctor. Suggest that they keep in mind how John has hurt Elizabeth in the past and that they pay close attention to the stage directions in order to express the tension and conflict between the couple at this point in the play.

Customize for
AP Students
Encourage these students to research the source of the biblical allusions in Act II and report back to the class on the full story behind each one.

◆ Reading Strategy

1 Read Drama The opening stage directions state that Act II opens eight days after the events of Act I.

Literature CD-ROM To build background, use *How to Read and Understand Drama,* Feature 12, which discusses Miller's work.

ACT II

The common room of PROCTOR*'s house, eight days later.*

> **◆ Reading Strategy**
> What important information do you learn here about when Act II takes place in relation to Act I?

1

At the right is a door opening on the fields outside. A fireplace is at the left, and behind it a stairway leading upstairs. It is the low, dark, and rather long living room of the time. As the curtain rises, the room is empty. From above, ELIZABETH *is heard softly singing to the children. Presently the door opens and* JOHN PROCTOR *enters, carrying his gun. He glances about the room as he comes toward the fireplace, then halts for an instant as he hears her singing. He continues on to the fireplace, leans the gun against the wall as he swings a pot out of the fire and smells it. Then he lifts out the ladle and tastes. He is not quite pleased. He reaches to a cupboard, takes a pinch of salt, and drops it into the pot. As he is tasting again, her footsteps are heard on the stair. He swings the pot into the fireplace and goes to a basin and washes his hands and face.* ELIZABETH *enters.*

ELIZABETH: What keeps you so late? It's almost dark.

PROCTOR: I were planting far out to the forest edge.

ELIZABETH: Oh, you're done then.

PROCTOR: Aye, the farm is seeded. The boys asleep?

ELIZABETH: They will be soon. *And she goes to the fireplace, proceeds to ladle up stew in a dish.*

PROCTOR: Pray now for a fair summer.

ELIZABETH: Aye.

PROCTOR: Are you well today?

ELIZABETH: I am. *She brings the plate to the table, and, indicating the food:* It is a rabbit.

PROCTOR, *going to the table:* Oh, is it! In Jonathan's trap?

ELIZABETH: No, she walked into the house this afternoon; I found her sittin' in the corner like she come to visit.

PROCTOR: Oh, that's a good sign walkin' in.

ELIZABETH: Pray God. It hurt my heart to strip her, poor rabbit. *She sits and watches him taste it.*

PROCTOR: It's well seasoned.

ELIZABETH, *blushing with pleasure:* I took great care. She's tender?

PROCTOR: Aye. *He eats. She watches him.* I think we'll see green fields soon. It's warm as blood beneath the clods.

ELIZABETH: That's well.

PROCTOR *eats, then looks up.*

PROCTOR: If the crop is good I'll buy George Jacob's heifer. How would that please you?

ELIZABETH: Aye, it would.

PROCTOR, *with a grin:* I mean to please you, Elizabeth.

ELIZABETH—*it is hard to say:* I know it, John.

He gets up, goes to her, kisses her. She receives it. With a certain disappointment, he returns to the table.

PROCTOR, *as gently as he can:* Cider?

ELIZABETH, *with a sense of reprimanding herself for having forgot:* Aye! *She gets up and goes and pours a glass for him. He now arches his back.*

PROCTOR: This farm's a continent when you go foot by foot droppin' seeds in it.

ELIZABETH, *coming with the cider:* It must be.

PROCTOR, *drinks a long draught, then, putting the glass down:* You ought to bring some flowers in the house.

ELIZABETH: Oh! I forgot! I will tomorrow.

PROCTOR: It's winter in here yet. On Sunday let you come with me, and we'll walk the farm together; I never see such a load of flowers on the earth. *With good feeling he goes and looks up at*

Test Preparation Workshop

Writing Skills: Grammar and Usage
Many standardized tests require students to identify errors in a sentence and choose how they should be corrected. Use the following sample test item to give students practice in this skill. Choose the best way to rewrite the underlined portion of the sentence. If the sentence does not need to be rewritten, choose "Correct as is."

> I wish you were able to help her and me, but I understand why you can't.

A I wish you are able to help her and me
B I wish you were able to help she and I
C I wish you were able to help her and I
D Correct as is.

Students may be tempted to choose *B* or *C* because changing *me* to *I* is often a needed correction. Guide students to check their choice carefully to be sure there is an error. With a second look, students should recognize that the objective case (*her* and *me)* is used correctly to receive the action of *help*. The sentence is *D:* Correct as is.

the sky through the open doorway. Lilacs have a purple smell. Lilac is the smell of nightfall, I think. Massachusetts is a beauty in the spring!

ELIZABETH: Aye, it is.

❷ *There is a pause. She is watching him from the table as he stands there absorbing the night. It is as though she would speak but cannot. Instead, now, she takes up his plate and glass and fork and goes with them to the basin. Her back is turned to him. He turns to her and watches her. A sense of their separation rises.*

PROCTOR: I think you're sad again. Are you?

ELIZABETH—*she doesn't want friction, and yet she must:* You come so late I thought you'd gone to Salem this afternoon.

PROCTOR: Why? I have no business in Salem.

ELIZABETH: You did speak of going, earlier this week.

PROCTOR—*he knows what she means:* I thought better of it since.

ELIZABETH: Mary Warren's there today.

PROCTOR: Why'd you let her? You heard me forbid her go to Salem any more!

ELIZABETH: I couldn't stop her.

PROCTOR, *holding back a full condemnation of her:* It is a fault, it is a fault, Elizabeth—you're the mistress here, not Mary Warren.

ELIZABETH: She frightened all my strength away.

PROCTOR: How may that mouse frighten you, Elizabeth? You—

ELIZABETH: It is a mouse no more. I forbid her go, and she raises up her chin like the daughter of a prince and says to me, "I must go to Salem, Goody Proctor; I am an official of the court!"

PROCTOR: Court! What court?

❸ **ELIZABETH:** Aye, it is a proper court they have now. They've sent four judges out of Boston, she says, weighty magistrates of the General Court, and at the head sits the Deputy Governor of the Province.

PROCTOR, *astonished:* Why, she's mad.

ELIZABETH: I would to God she were. There be fourteen people in the jail now, she says. PROCTOR *simply looks at her, unable to grasp it.* And they'll be tried, and the court have power to hang them too, she says.

PROCTOR, *scoffing but without conviction:* Ah, they'd never hang—

ELIZABETH: The Deputy Governor promise hangin' if they'll not confess, John. The town's gone wild, I think. She speak of Abigail, and I thought she were a saint, to hear her. Abigail brings the other girls into the court, and where she walks the crowd will part like the sea for Israel.[1] And folks are brought before them, and if they scream and howl and fall to the floor—the person's clapped in the jail for bewitchin' them.

> ◆ **Literary Focus** ❹
> What does the allusion to Moses parting the Red Sea suggest about Abby?

PROCTOR, *wide-eyed:* Oh, it is a black mischief.

❺ **ELIZABETH:** I think you must go to Salem, John. *He turns to her.* I think so. You must tell them it is a fraud.

PROCTOR, *thinking beyond this:* Aye, it is, it is surely.

ELIZABETH: Let you go to Ezekiel Cheever—he knows you well. And tell him what she said to you last week in her uncle's house. She said it had naught to do with witchcraft, did she not?

PROCTOR, *in thought:* Aye, she did, she did. *Now, a pause.*

ELIZABETH, *quietly, fearing to anger him by prodding:* God forbid you keep that from the court, John. I think they must be told.

PROCTOR, *quietly, struggling with his thought:* Aye, they must, they must. It is a wonder they do believe her.

ELIZABETH: I would go to Salem now, John—let you go tonight.

PROCTOR: I'll think on it.

---

1. **part like . . . Israel:** In the Bible, God commanded Moses, the leader of the Jews, to part the Red Sea to enable the Jews to escape from the Egyptians into Canaan.

◆ Reading Strategy

❷ **Read Drama** Ask students how the stage directions help prepare them for Proctor's remark that Elizabeth seems sad. *The stage directions convey Elizabeth's tentative movements, her conflict and ambivalence about saying what she feels, and the fact that John is watching her.*

◆ Grammar and Style

❸ **Commas After Introductory Words** Ask students why a comma appears after the word *Aye* and after the word *Why*. *Both are interrupters that introduce a sentence and need to be set off from the rest of the sentence.*

◆ Literary Focus

❹ **Allusion** Suggested response: The allusion suggests that Abby is a powerful, charismatic leader whom people consider a righteous messenger from God. She has the power to influence people and make things happen.

Customize for *Less Proficient Readers*

❺ Remind these students of the scene in Act I in which Abby confessed to John that the charges of witchcraft were a fraud (see page 1098).

Block Scheduling Strategies

Consider these suggestions to take advantage of extended class time:

- To help students better understand the play, discuss the Reading Strategy. Stress the importance of reading stage directions. Reinforce learning with the Reading Strategy page of ***Selection Support,*** p. 344.
- Either before or after students read Act II, they can participate in on-line discussions of the Puritan era and the Salem Witch Trials in the Town Crier section of the Archiving Early America Web site: **http://early america.com** They can also see a timeline of the witch trials at a Web site established by the city of Salem, Massachusetts: **www.salemweb.com/memorial/default.html** Please be aware, however, that sites may have changed since this information was published. We *strongly recommend* that you preview sites before you send students to them.
- Rent the videotape of the recent film version of the play starring Daniel Day Lewis and have students view the scenes corresponding to Act II. Suggest that students pay attention to how the actors convey the actions cited in the stage directions.
- Have students complete either one of the Writing ideas or the Speaking, Listening, and Viewing idea in the Idea Bank (p. 1130).

◆ Reading Strategy

❶ **Read Drama** Have students use the stage directions to describe Elizabeth's changing emotions and level of confidence as she challenges John to publicly reveal what Abby has told him. *Sample response: She begins her challenge quietly and fearfully. However, as John continues to resist her challenge and also reveals that he saw Abby alone, Elizabeth becomes colder and more hurt. She becomes less confident of John's ability to do the right thing and more sure of her own suspicions about him.*

◆ Critical Thinking

❷ **Analyze** Ask students what John Proctor's reaction to Elizabeth's suspicion reveals about his character. *Students may say that his highly argumentative reaction reveals that he is a volatile person who gives in to his feelings. His reaction may also reveal that he does not have enough courage to reveal the truth about himself to others.*

▶Critical Viewing◀

Evaluate Ask students to describe how the actor visually expresses John Proctor's mood in the illustration on this page. *Suggested response: The actor's bared teeth, tight jaw, and flashing eyes express Proctor's growing anger.*

Customize for
Less Proficient Readers
To help these students better understand the main ideas of the dialogue of the play, use ***Strategies for Diverse Student Needs,*** p. 77, "Paraphrase Dialogue."

ELIZABETH, *with her courage now:* You cannot keep it, John.

PROCTOR, *angering:* I know I cannot keep it. I say I will think on it!

ELIZABETH, *hurt, and very coldly:* Good, then, let you think on it. *She stands and starts to walk out of the room.*

❶ **PROCTOR:** I am only wondering how I may prove what she told me, Elizabeth. If the girl's a saint now, I think it is not easy to prove she's fraud, and the town gone so silly. She told it to me in a room alone—I have no proof for it.

ELIZABETH: You were alone with her?

PROCTOR, *stubbornly:* For a moment alone, aye.

ELIZABETH: Why, then, it is not as you told me.

PROCTOR, *his anger rising:* For a moment, I say. The others come in soon after.

ELIZABETH, *quietly—she has suddenly lost all faith in him:* Do as you wish, then. *She starts to turn.*

PROCTOR: Woman. *She turns to him.* I'll not have your suspicion any more.

ELIZABETH, *a little loftily:* I have no—

PROCTOR: I'll not have it!

ELIZABETH: Then let you not earn it.

PROCTOR, *with a violent undertone:* You doubt me yet?

ELIZABETH, *with a smile, to keep her dignity:* John, if it were not Abigail that you must go to hurt, would you falter now? I think not.

PROCTOR: Now look you—

ELIZABETH: I see what I see, John.

PROCTOR, *with solemn warning:* You will not judge me more, Elizabeth. I have good reason to think before I charge fraud on Abigail, and I will think on it. Let you look to your own ❷

improvement before you go to judge your husband any more. I have forgot Abigail, and—

ELIZABETH: And I.

PROCTOR: Spare me! You forget nothin' and forgive nothin'. Learn charity, woman. I have gone tiptoe in this house all seven month since she is gone. I have not moved from there to there without I think to please you, and still an everlasting funeral marches round your heart. I cannot speak but I am doubted, every moment judged for lies, as though I come into a court when I come into this house! ❷

ELIZABETH: John, you are not open with me. You saw her with a crowd, you said. Now you—

Cross-Curricular Connection: Social Studies

Women's Roles in Puritan Society In Puritan New England, a woman's role was limited to housekeeping, and domesticity was considered a major virtue. Husbands and fathers ruled their households with an iron hand. Women were encouraged to read the Bible and make their own covenants with God, but they were warned not to read too much and not to neglect their household chores. Women had no political rights, and when a woman married, her husband acquired all rights to her property, income, and any debts owed her.

Ask students if they see any connection between the status of women in Puritan society and the fact that it was usually women who were accused of witchcraft.

PROCTOR: I'll plead my honesty no more, Elizabeth.

ELIZABETH—*now she would justify herself:* John, I am only—

PROCTOR: No more! I should have roared you down when first you told me your suspicion. But I wilted, and, like a Christian, I confessed. Confessed! Some dream I had must have mistaken you for God that day. But you're not,
❸ you're not, and let you remember it! Let you look sometimes for the goodness in me, and judge me not.

ELIZABETH: I do not judge you. The magistrate sits in your heart that judges you. I never thought you but a good man, John—*with a smile*—only somewhat bewildered.

PROCTOR, *laughing bitterly:* Oh, Elizabeth, your justice would freeze beer! *He turns suddenly toward a sound outside. He starts for the door as* MARY WARREN *enters. As soon as he sees her, he goes directly to her and grabs her by the cloak, furious.* How do you go to Salem when I forbid it? Do you mock me? *Shaking her.* I'll whip you if you dare leave this house again!

Strangely, she doesn't resist him, but hangs limply by his grip.

MARY WARREN: I am sick, I am sick, Mr. Proctor. Pray, pray, hurt me not. *Her strangeness throws him off, and her evident* pallor *and weakness. He frees her.* My insides are all shuddery; I am in the proceedings all day, sir.

❹ **◆ Reading Strategy**
What do the stage directions here clarify?

PROCTOR, *with draining anger—his curiosity is draining it:* And what of these proceedings here? When will you proceed to keep this house, as you are paid nine pound a year to do—and my wife not wholly well?

As though to compensate, MARY WARREN *goes to* ELIZABETH *with a small rag doll.*

MARY WARREN: I made a gift for you today, Goody Proctor. I had to sit long hours in a chair, and passed the time with sewing.

❺ **ELIZABETH,** *perplexed, looking at the doll:* Why, thank you, it's a fair poppet.[2]

MARY WARREN, *with a trembling, decayed voice:* We must all love each other now, Goody Proctor. ❺

ELIZABETH, *amazed at her strangeness:* Aye, indeed we must.

MARY WARREN, *glancing at the room:* I'll get up early in the morning and clean the house. I must sleep now. *She turns and starts off.*

PROCTOR: Mary. *She halts.* Is it true? There be fourteen women arrested?

MARY WARREN: No, sir. There be thirty-nine now— *She suddenly breaks off and sobs and sits down, exhausted.*

ELIZABETH: Why, she's weepin'! What ails you, child?

MARY WARREN: Goody Osburn—will hang!

There is a shocked pause, while she sobs.

PROCTOR: Hang! *He calls into her face.* Hang, y'say?

MARY WARREN, *through her weeping:* Aye.

PROCTOR: The Deputy Governor will permit it?

MARY WARREN: He sentenced her. He must. *To* ameliorate *it:* But not Sarah Good. For Sarah Good confessed, y'see.

PROCTOR: Confessed! To what?

MARY WARREN: That she—*in horror at the memory*—she sometimes made a compact with Lucifer, and wrote her name in his black
book—with her blood—and bound herself to ❻
torment Christians till God's thrown down—and we all must worship Hell forevermore.

Pause.

PROCTOR: But—surely you know what a jabberer she is. Did you tell them that?

---

2. **poppet:** Doll.

◆ Build Vocabulary

pallor (pal′ ər) *n.:* Paleness

ameliorate (ə mēl′ yə rāt) *v.:* Make better

❸ **Clarification** Public confession and repentance were important aspects of Puritan life. Offenders were expected to read a written confession to the congregation. Those who refused might first receive a warning, but if they continued to refuse to confess, they could be subject to excommunication from the church.

◆ Reading Strategy

❹ **Read Drama** Suggested response: *The stage directions clarify Proctor's reaction to Mary's strange behavior.*

◆ Grammar and Style

❺ **Commas After Introductory Words** Have students identify the two introductory words set off by commas in this passage. *Students should identify the words* Why *and* Aye.

◆ Literary Focus

❻ **Allusion** Tell students that Lucifer is another name for Satan, or the devil. The original Hebrew word for Lucifer means "the morning star." It was first applied in the Bible by Isaiah to describe Nebuchadnezzar, the sinfully proud king of Babylon. Later, the word was applied to the devil, who was said to have originally been an angel who was driven out of heaven for his pride. The name Lucifer was used for the devil in Christopher Marlowe's *Dr. Faustus,* Dante's *Inferno,* and John Milton's *Paradise Lost.* In *Paradise Lost,* Lucifer's name is changed to Satan after his fall from heaven.

◆ Critical Thinking

❶ Analyze Ask students how they can tell that Mary Warren really believes what she is saying about Goody Osburn. *The stage directions indicate that she speaks "like one awakened to a marvelous secret insight."*

Comprehension Check ☑

❷ What evidence does Mary Warren use as proof that Goody Osburn is a witch? *When Mary refused to give Goody Osburn bread and cider, the beggar woman walked away mumbling. For two days after that, Mary Warren was sick to her stomach. Mary therefore concludes that Goody Osburn is a witch and that Osburn put a curse on her.*

◆ Critical Thinking

❸ Compare and Contrast Ask students why Mary Warren's story about Goody Osburn would not be accepted as evidence in a trial today. *Suggested response: Mary Warren's "evidence" would not be accepted because people no longer believe in witchcraft. Even if they did, the evidence would still be considered circumstantial. The fact that one event follows another does not prove that the first event caused the second.*

◆ Reading Strategy

❹ Read Drama Ask students what change Mary's participation in the court proceedings seems to have brought about in her attitude toward the Proctors and her obligations to them. Remind students to read both the dialogue and the stage directions before they answer. *Sample response: Mary is now more proud of herself. She stands up for herself and says she will not stand whipping any more.*

MARY WARREN: Mr. Proctor, in open court she near to choked us all to death.

PROCTOR: How, choked you?

MARY WARREN: She sent her spirit out.

ELIZABETH: Oh, Mary, Mary, surely you—

MARY WARREN, *with an indignant edge:* She tried to kill me many times, Goody Proctor!

ELIZABETH: Why, I never heard you mention that before.

MARY WARREN: I never knew it before. I never knew anything before. When she come into the court I say to myself, I must not accuse this woman, for she sleep in ditches, and so very old and poor. But then—then she sit there, denying and denying, and I feel a misty coldness climbin' up my back, and the skin on my skull begin to creep, and I feel a clamp around my neck and I cannot breathe air; and then—*entranced*—I hear a voice, a screamin' voice, and it were my voice—and all at once I remembered everything she done to me!

PROCTOR: Why? What did she do to you?

❶ **MARY WARREN,** *like one awakened to a marvelous secret insight:* So many time, Mr. Proctor, she come to this very door, beggin' bread and a cup of cider—and mark this: whenever I turned her away empty, she *mumbled.*

ELIZABETH: Mumbled! She may mumble if she's hungry.

MARY WARREN: But *what* does she mumble? You must remember, Goody Proctor. Last month—a Monday, I think—she walked away, and I thought my guts would burst for two days after. Do you remember it?

ELIZABETH: Why—I do, I think, but—

❷ **MARY WARREN:** And so I told that to Judge Hathorne, and he asks her so. "Goody Osburn," says he, "what curse do you mumble that this girl must fall sick after turning you away?" And then she replies—*mimicking an old crone*—"Why, your excellence, no curse at all. I only say my commandments; I hope I may say my commandments," says she!

ELIZABETH: And that's an upright answer.

MARY WARREN: Aye, but then Judge Hathorne say, "Recite for us your commandments!"—*leaning avidly toward them*—and of all the ten she could not say a single one. She never knew no commandments, and they had her in a flat lie!

PROCTOR: And so condemned her?

MARY WARREN, *now a little strained, seeing his stubborn doubt:* Why, they must when she condemned herself.

PROCTOR: But the proof, the proof!

MARY WARREN, *with greater impatience with him:* ❸ I told you the proof. It's hard proof, hard as rock, the judges said.

PROCTOR, *pauses an instant, then:* You will not go to court again, Mary Warren.

MARY WARREN: I must tell you, sir, I will be gone every day now. I am amazed you do not see what weighty work we do.

PROCTOR: What work you do! It's strange work for a Christian girl to hang old women!

MARY WARREN: But, Mr. Proctor, they will not hang them if they confess. Sarah Good will only sit in jail some time—*recalling*—and here's a wonder for you; think on this. Goody Good is pregnant!

ELIZABETH: Pregnant! Are they mad? The woman's near to sixty!

MARY WARREN: They had Doctor Griggs examine her, and she's full to the brim. And smokin' a pipe all these years, and no husband either! But she's safe, thank God, for they'll not hurt the innocent child. But be that not a marvel? You must see it, sir, it's God's work we do. So I'll be gone every day for some time. I'm—I am ❹ an official of the court, they say, and I—*She has been edging toward offstage.*

PROCTOR: I'll official you! *He strides to the mantel, takes down the whip hanging there.*

MARY WARREN, *terrified, but coming erect, striving for her authority:* I'll not stand whipping any more!

ELIZABETH, *hurriedly, as* PROCTOR *approaches:* Mary, promise you'll stay at home—

Cross-Curricular Connection: Social Studies

Witchcraft in Europe There was a widespread belief in witches throughout Europe well into modern times. In medieval Europe, witchcraft became associated with an alliance with the devil, and so it became a concern not only to civil authorities but to religious leaders as well. From the Middle Ages until the eighteenth century, millions of women were put on trial for witchcraft in Europe, and hundreds of thousands of them were hanged or burned at the stake. Today, some women still claim to practice witchcraft as a form of nature worship that emphasizes healing through herbs and ceremonies associated with, among other things, the phases of the moon.

MARY WARREN, *backing from him, but keeping her erect posture, striving, striving for her way:* The Devil's loose in Salem, Mr. Proctor; we must discover where he's hiding!

PROCTOR: I'll whip the Devil out of you! *With whip raised he reaches out for her, and she streaks away and yells.*

MARY WARREN, *pointing at* ELIZABETH: I saved her life today!

Silence. His whip comes down.

ELIZABETH, *softly:* I am accused?

5 **MARY WARREN,** *quaking:* Somewhat mentioned. But I said I never see no sign you ever sent your spirit out to hurt no one, and seeing I do live so closely with you, they dismissed it.

ELIZABETH: Who accused me?

MARY WARREN: I am bound by law, I cannot tell it. *To* PROCTOR: I only hope you'll not be so sarcastical no more. Four judges and the King's deputy sat to dinner with us but an hour ago. I—I would have you speak civilly to me, from this out.

PROCTOR, *in horror, muttering in disgust at her:* Go to bed.

MARY WARREN, *with a stamp of her foot:* I'll not be ordered to bed no more, Mr. Proctor! I am eighteen and a woman, however single!

PROCTOR: Do you wish to sit up? Then sit up.

MARY WARREN: I wish to go to bed!

PROCTOR, *in anger:* Good night, then!

MARY WARREN: Good night. *Dissatisfied, uncertain of herself, she goes out. Wide-eyed, both* PROCTOR *and* ELIZABETH *stand staring.*

ELIZABETH, *quietly:* Oh, the noose, the noose is up!

PROCTOR: There'll be no noose.

◆ Build Vocabulary

avidly (av′ id lē) *adv.:* Eagerly; intently

ELIZABETH: She wants me dead. I knew all week it would come to this! 6

PROCTOR, *without conviction:* They dismissed it. You heard her say— 7

> ◆ **Reading Strategy**
> How do the stage directions affect your understanding of Proctor's line?

ELIZABETH: And what of tomorrow? She will cry me out until they take me!

PROCTOR: Sit you down.

ELIZABETH: She wants me dead, John, you know it!

PROCTOR: I say sit down! *She sits, trembling. He speaks quickly, trying to keep his wits.* Now we must be wise, Elizabeth.

ELIZABETH, *with sarcasm, and a sense of being lost:* Oh, indeed, indeed!

PROCTOR: Fear nothing. I'll find Ezekiel Cheever. I'll tell him she said it were all sport.

ELIZABETH: John, with so many in the jail, more than Cheever's help is needed now, I think. Would you favor me with this? Go to Abigail.

PROCTOR, *his soul hardening as he senses . . .:* What have I to say to Abigail?

ELIZABETH, *delicately:* John—grant me this. You have a faulty understanding of young girls. There is a promise made in any bed—

PROCTOR, *striving against his anger:* What promise! 8

ELIZABETH: Spoke or silent, a promise is surely made. And she may dote on it now—I am sure she does—and thinks to kill me, then to take my place.

PROCTOR'S *anger is rising; he cannot speak.*

ELIZABETH: It is her dearest hope, John, I know it. There be a thousand names; why does she call mine? There be a certain danger in calling such a name—I am no Goody Good that sleeps in ditches, nor Osburn, drunk and half-witted. She'd dare not call out such a farmer's wife but there be monstrous profit in it. She thinks to take my place, John.

PROCTOR: She cannot think it! *He knows it is true.*

◆ Critical Thinking

5 Analyze Ask students how they can tell that Mary Warren is acquiring a new sense of strength and power from her participation in the witchcraft trials. *Suggested response: Although she is physically afraid of John Proctor, Mary keeps standing up to him and demanding her rights. She boasts about her association with the judges and the King's deputy and mentions that she saved Elizabeth's life that day. The stage directions describe her as "keeping her erect posture, striving, striving for her way" and stamping her foot at Proctor.*

Customize for *Less Proficient Readers*

6 Make sure students understand that the "she" who wants Elizabeth dead is Abby, not Mary Warren.

◆ Reading Strategy

7 Read Drama The words "without conviction" in the stage directions let the reader know that Proctor doesn't really believe that Elizabeth's name won't come up in court again, and he transmits that disbelief to his wife by the irresolute way in which he says "They dismissed it. You heard her say–."

Comprehension Check ☑

8 What "promise" does Elizabeth think that John has implicitly made to Abby by having an affair with her? *Elicit the following: From Abby's point of view, by having an affair with her, John has implicitly promised that he will marry her someday.*

◆ Critical Thinking

❶ Analyze Causes and Effects Ask students the reason John Proctor blushes when Abigail passes by him in church. Have them support their reason with facts from the text. *Some students may say that John Proctor blushes because he is still in love with Abigail. His protestations are an attempt to hide how he truly feels. Other students may say that John Proctor blushes because he is ashamed of his sin and that although Proctor is argumentative, he usually is truthful in what he says.*

Comprehension Check ☑

❷ What does Elizabeth's outburst reveal about her feelings? *She is jealous of Abigail.*

◆ Critical Thinking

❸ Speculate Ask students why they think Mr. Hale is visiting the Proctors. *Some students may say that Mr. Hale is going to discuss the fact that Elizabeth's name came up in court. Other students may say that Mr. Hale is going to charge Elizabeth with witchcraft.*

◆ Reading Strategy

❹ Read Drama Ask students why the silent pause indicated by the stage directions is important here. *Suggested response: It builds suspense as to the purpose of Hale's visit. It suggests that the Proctors are nervous that Elizabeth will be accused and that Hale may be reluctant to question them.*

ELIZABETH, *"reasonably":* John, have you ever shown her somewhat of contempt? She cannot pass you in the church but you will blush—

PROCTOR: I may blush for my sin.

ELIZABETH: I think she sees another meaning in that blush.

❶ PROCTOR: And what see you? What see you, Elizabeth?

ELIZABETH, *"conceding":* I think you be somewhat ashamed, for I am there, and she so close.

PROCTOR: When will you know me, woman? Were I stone I would have cracked for shame this seven month!

ELIZABETH: Then go and tell her she's a whore. Whatever promise she may sense—break it, John, break it.

PROCTOR, *between his teeth:* Good, then. I'll go. *He starts for his rifle.*

ELIZABETH, *trembling, fearfully:* Oh, how unwillingly!

PROCTOR, *turning on her, rifle in hand:* I will curse her hotter than the oldest cinder in hell. But pray, begrudge me not my anger!

ELIZABETH: Your anger! I only ask you—

PROCTOR: Woman, am I so base? Do you truly think me base?

ELIZABETH: I never called you base.

PROCTOR: Then how do you charge me with such a promise? The promise that a stallion gives a mare I gave that girl!

ELIZABETH: Then why do you anger with me when I bid you break it?

PROCTOR: Because it speaks deceit, and I am honest! But I'll plead no more! I see now your spirit twists around the single error of my life, and I will never tear it free!

ELIZABETH, *crying out:* You'll tear it free—when ❷ you come to know that I will be your only wife, or no wife at all! She has an arrow in you yet, John Proctor, and you know it well!

❸ *Quite suddenly, as though from the air, a figure appears in the doorway. They start slightly. It is* MR. HALE. *He is different now—drawn a little, and there is a quality of deference, even of guilt, about his manner now.* ❸

HALE: Good evening.

PROCTOR, *still in his shock:* Why, Mr. Hale! Good evening to you, sir. Come in, come in.

HALE, *to Elizabeth:* I hope I do not startle you.

ELIZABETH: No, no, it's only that I heard no horse—

HALE: You are Goodwife Proctor.

PROCTOR: Aye; Elizabeth.

HALE, *nods, then:* I hope you're not off to bed yet.

PROCTOR, *setting down his gun:* No, no. HALE *comes further into the room. And* PROCTOR, *to explain his nervousness:* We are not used to visitors after dark, but you're welcome here. Will you sit you down, sir?

HALE: I will. *He sits.* Let you sit, Goodwife Proctor.

She does, never letting him out of her sight. There is a pause as HALE *looks about the room.* ❹

PROCTOR, *to break the silence:* Will you drink cider, Mr. Hale?

HALE: No, it rebels my stomach; I have some further traveling yet tonight. Sit you down, sir. PROCTOR *sits.* I will not keep you long, but I have some business with you.

PROCTOR: Business of the court?

HALE: No—no, I come of my own, without the court's authority. Hear me. *He wets his lips.* I know not if you are aware, but your wife's name is—mentioned in the court.

PROCTOR: We know it, sir. Our Mary Warren told us. We are entirely amazed.

HALE: I am a stranger here, as you know. And in my ignorance I find it hard to draw a clear opinion of them that come accused before the court. And so this afternoon, and now tonight, I go from house to house—I come now from Rebecca Nurse's house and—

ELIZABETH, *shocked:* Rebecca's charged!

Cross-Curricular Connection: Science

Impact of Medical Advances on Beliefs Belief in witchcraft flourished in the centuries before the rise of the scientific method and scientific discoveries about the causes of disease and death. Until such discoveries were made, disease was often seen as the result of either punishment from a supernatural source or vengeance dispensed by human witches.

It wasn't until the seventeenth century—the century of the Salem witchcraft trials—that Anton van Leeuwenhoek invented the microscope and discovered the existence of blood cells and bacteria in the human body. In the eighteenth century, Edward Jenner demonstrated that smallpox could be prevented by vaccination. It was only in the nineteenth century, however, that the germ theory of disease and the practice of widespread immunization began to take hold, thanks to the experiments of Louis Pasteur and Robert Koch. The British surgeon Joseph Lister applied Pasteur's work to preventing infection in the operating room through sterilization.

Have students research in more detail the work of one of the scientists mentioned here and report to the class on the scientist's discoveries.

HALE: God forbid such a one be charged. She is, however—mentioned somewhat.

ELIZABETH, *with an attempt at a laugh:* You will never believe, I hope, that Rebecca trafficked with the Devil.

HALE: Woman, it is possible.

PROCTOR, *taken aback:* Surely you cannot think so.

5 **HALE:** This is a strange time, Mister. No man may longer doubt the powers of the dark are gathered in monstrous attack upon this village. There is too much evidence now to deny it. You will agree, sir?

PROCTOR, *evading:* I—have no knowledge in that line. But it's hard to think so pious a woman be secretly a Devil's bitch after seventy year of such good prayer.

HALE: Aye. But the Devil is a wily one, you cannot deny it. However, she is far from accused, and I know she will not be. *Pause.* I thought, sir, to put some questions as to the Christian character of this house, if you'll permit me.

PROCTOR, *coldly, resentful:* Why, we—have no fear of questions, sir.

HALE: Good, then. *He makes himself more comfortable.* In the book of record that Mr. Parris keeps, I note that you are rarely in the church on Sabbath Day.

PROCTOR: No, sir, you are mistaken.

HALE: Twenty-six time in seventeen month, sir. I must call that rare. Will you tell me why you are so absent?

PROCTOR: Mr. Hale, I never knew I must account to that man for I come to church or stay at home. My wife were sick this winter.

HALE: So I am told. But you, Mister, why could you not come alone?

PROCTOR: I surely did come when I could, and when I could not I prayed in this house.

HALE: Mr. Proctor, your house is not a church; your theology must tell you that.

PROCTOR: It does, sir, it does; and it tells me that a minister may pray to God without he have golden candlesticks upon the altar.

HALE: What golden candlesticks?

PROCTOR: Since we built the church there were pewter candlesticks upon the altar; Francis Nurse made them y'know, and a sweeter hand never touched the metal. But Parris came, and for twenty week he preach nothin' but golden candlesticks until he had them. I labor the earth from dawn of day to blink of night, and I tell you true when I look to heaven and see my money glaring at his elbows—it hurt my prayer, sir, it hurt my prayer. I think, sometimes, the man dreams cathedrals, not clapboard meetin' houses. 6

HALE, *thinks, then:* And yet, Mister, a Christian on Sabbath Day must be in church. *Pause.* Tell me—you have three children?

PROCTOR: Aye. Boys.

HALE: How comes it that only two are baptized? 7

PROCTOR, *starts to speak, then stops, then, as though unable to restrain this:* I like it not that Mr. Parris should lay his hand upon my baby. I see no light of God in that man. I'll not conceal it.

HALE: I must say it, Mr. Proctor; that is not for you to decide. The man's ordained, therefore the light of God is in him.

PROCTOR, *flushed with resentment but trying to smile:* What's your suspicion, Mr. Hale?

HALE: No, no, I have no—

PROCTOR: I nailed the roof upon the church, I hung the door—

HALE: Oh, did you! That's a good sign, then.

PROCTOR: It may be I have been too quick to bring the man to book, but you cannot think we ever desired the destruction of religion. I think that's in your mind, is it not?

◆ Build Vocabulary

base (bās) *adj.*: Low; contemptible

deference (def′ ər əns) *n.*: Courteous regard or respect

theology (thē äl′ ə jē) *n.*: Religious philosophy or teachings; the study of religion

◆ Critical Thinking

5 Analyze Causes and Effects Ask students why Rebecca Nurse is a highly unlikely suspect for the witch hunt. *She is an unlikely suspect because she has always been a pious, prayerful Puritan and an upstanding, well-respected member of the community.*

◆ Background for Understanding

6 History The Puritans sought to "purify" the practice of Christianity in accordance with their reading of the Bible (hence the name of this religious group). In these lines, Proctor expresses the general Puritan disapproval of the opulence displayed by the Catholic Church and the Church of England.

◆ Background for Understanding

7 History To help students understand the seriousness of Hale's admonitions, explain that attendance at church services and the general observance of the Sabbath as a day of rest and prayer were strictly enforced in the Puritan colonies. Likewise, church members who criticized their church or their minister could be severely punished.

◆ Critical Thinking

❶ **Infer** Ask students how they can tell that the Proctors' ability to name the Commandments will play an important part in the play. *The stage directions indicate that Hale asks the question "with the voice of one administering a secret test."*

❷ **Clarification** The authority of the Puritan churches was based on the idea of a covenant, or contract, between church members and God and among the members of the church. A person who wanted to become a member of the church had to make a public confession of faith and then sign his name to the covenant the church members agreed to abide by.

Customize for *English Language Learners*

❸ Some of your English language learners may come from religious backgrounds outside the Judeo-Christian tradition. Explain that, according to the Bible, the Ten Commandments were given to Moses after the Hebrews were set free from bondage in Egypt. For Christians and Jews, the Commandments represent the rules of proper behavior expected by God. Any violations of the commandments is considered a sin. In Puritan Massachusetts, even the civil laws were based on the Ten Commandments.

◆ Critical Thinking

❹ **Interpret** Ask students to explain the reason behind Proctor's pain and embarrassment. *Suggested response: By having an affair with Abby, John has committed the sin of adultery. His omission of the commandment points to his guilt.*

◆ Reading Strategy

❺ **Read Drama** Ask students how they can tell that Hale is beginning to think that the Proctors are guilty of witchcraft. *The stage directions indicate that he tries to smile at them, but "his misgivings are clear." They also indicate that he is "obviously disturbed" by their replies to his question, and he is "evasive" in responding to Elizabeth's question about whether he now suspects her.*

HALE, *not altogether giving way:* I—have—there is a softness in your record, sir, a softness.

ELIZABETH: I think, maybe, we have been too hard with Mr. Parris. I think so. But sure we never loved the Devil here.

❶ **HALE,** *nods, deliberating this. Then, with the voice of one administering a secret test:* Do you know your Commandments, Elizabeth?

❷ **ELIZABETH,** *without hesitation, even eagerly:* I surely do. There be no mark of blame upon my life, Mr. Hale. I am a covenanted Christian woman.

HALE: And you, Mister?

PROCTOR, *a trifle unsteadily:* I—am sure I do, sir.

HALE, *glances at her open face, then at* JOHN, *then:* Let you repeat them, if you will.

PROCTOR: The Commandments.

HALE: Aye.

PROCTOR, *looking off, beginning to sweat:* Thou shalt not kill.

HALE: Aye.

❸ **PROCTOR,** *counting on his fingers:* Thou shalt not steal. Thou shalt not covet thy neighbor's goods, nor make unto thee any graven image. Thou shalt not take the name of the Lord in vain; thou shalt have no other gods before me. *With some hesitation:* Thou shalt remember the Sabbath Day and keep it holy. *Pause. Then:* Thou shalt honor thy father and mother. Thou shalt not bear false witness. *He is stuck. He counts back on his fingers, knowing one is missing.* Thou shalt not make unto thee any graven image.

HALE: You have said that twice, sir.

PROCTOR, *lost:* Aye. *He is flailing for it.*

ELIZABETH, *delicately:* Adultery, John.

❹ **PROCTOR,** *as though a secret arrow had pained his heart:* Aye. *Trying to grin it away—to* HALE: You see, sir, between the two of us we do know them all. HALE *only looks at* PROCTOR, *deep in his attempt to define this man.* PROCTOR *grows more uneasy.* I think it be a small fault.

HALE: Theology, sir, is a fortress; no crack in a fortress may be accounted small. *He rises; he seems worried now. He paces a little, in deep thought.*

PROCTOR: There be no love for Satan in this house, Mister.

HALE: I pray it, I pray it dearly. *He looks to both of them, an attempt at a smile on his face, but his misgivings are clear.* Well, then—I'll bid you good night.

ELIZABETH, *unable to restrain herself:* Mr. Hale. *He turns.* I do think you are suspecting me somewhat? Are you not? ❺

HALE, *obviously disturbed—and evasive:* Goody Proctor, I do not judge you. My duty is to add what I may to the godly wisdom of the court. I pray you both good health and good fortune. *To* JOHN: Good night, sir. *He starts out.*

ELIZABETH, *with a note of desperation:* I think you must tell him, John.

HALE: What's that?

ELIZABETH, *restraining a call:* Will you tell him?

Slight pause. HALE *looks questioningly at* JOHN.

PROCTOR, *with difficulty:* I—I have no witness and cannot prove it, except my word be taken. But I know the children's sickness had naught to do with witchcraft.

HALE, *stopped, struck:* Naught to do—?

PROCTOR: Mr. Parris discovered them sportin' in the woods. They were startled and took sick.

Pause.

HALE: Who told you this?

PROCTOR, *hesitates, then:* Abigail Williams.

HALE: Abigail.

PROCTOR: Aye.

HALE, *his eyes wide:* Abigail Williams told you it had naught to do with witchcraft!

PROCTOR: She told me the day you came, sir.

HALE, *suspiciously:* Why—why did you keep this?

PROCTOR: I never knew until tonight that the world is gone daft with this nonsense.

HALE: Nonsense! Mister, I have myself examined Tituba, Sarah Good, and numerous others that have confessed to dealing with the Devil. They have *confessed* it.

PROCTOR: And why not, if they must hang for denyin' it? There are them that will swear to anything before they'll hang; have you never thought of that?

HALE: I have. I—I have indeed. *It is his own suspicion, but he resists it. He glances at* ELIZABETH, *then at* JOHN. And you—would you testify to this in court?

PROCTOR: I—had not reckoned with goin' into court. But if I must I will.

6 **HALE:** Do you falter here?

PROCTOR: I falter nothing, but I may wonder if my story will be credited in such a court. I do wonder on it, when such a steady-minded minister as you will suspicion such a woman that never lied, and cannot, and the world knows she cannot! I may falter somewhat, Mister; I am no fool.

HALE, *quietly—it has impressed him:* Proctor, let you open with me now, for I have a rumor that troubles me. It's said you hold no belief that there may even be witches in the world. Is that true, sir?

PROCTOR—*he knows this is critical, and is striving against his disgust with* HALE *and with himself for even answering:* I know not what I have said, I may have said it. I have wondered if there be witches in the world—although I cannot believe they come among us now.

HALE: Then you do not believe—

7 **PROCTOR:** I have no knowledge of it; the Bible speaks of witches, and I will not deny them.

HALE: And you, woman?

ELIZABETH: I—I cannot believe it.

HALE, *shocked:* You cannot!

PROCTOR: Elizabeth, you bewilder him!

ELIZABETH, *to* HALE: I cannot think the Devil may own a woman's soul, Mr. Hale, when she keeps an upright way, as I have. I am a good woman, I know it; and if you believe I may do only good work in the world, and yet be secretly bound to Satan, then I must tell you, sir, I do not believe it.

HALE: But, woman, you do believe there are witches in—

ELIZABETH: If you think that I am one, then I say there are none.

HALE: You surely do not fly against the Gospel, the Gospel—

PROCTOR: She believe in the Gospel, every word! 8

ELIZABETH: Question Abigail Williams about the Gospel, not myself!

HALE *stares at her.*

PROCTOR: She do not mean to doubt the Gospel, sir, you cannot think it. This be a Christian house, sir, a Christian house.

HALE: God keep you both; let the third child be quickly baptized, and go you without fail each Sunday to Sabbath prayer; and keep a solemn, quiet way among you. I think—

GILES COREY *appears in doorway.*

GILES: John!

PROCTOR: Giles! What's the matter?

GILES: They take my wife.

FRANCIS NURSE *enters.*

GILES: And his Rebecca!

PROCTOR, *to* FRANCIS: Rebecca's in the *jail!*

FRANCIS: Aye, Cheever come and take her in his wagon. We've only now come from the jail, and they'll not even let us in to see them.

ELIZABETH: They've surely gone wild now, Mr. Hale!

FRANCIS, *going to* HALE: Reverend Hale! Can you not speak to the Deputy Governor? I'm sure he mistakes these people—

HALE: Pray calm yourself, Mr. Nurse.

FRANCIS: My wife is the very brick and mortar of the church, Mr. Hale—*indicating* GILES—and Martha Corey, there cannot be a woman closer yet to God than Martha.

◆ Reading Strategy

6 Read Drama Ask students how the stage directions help them understand that Hale is vacillating and that he wants to believe the Proctors are good people. *According to the stage directions, Hale suspects, as Proctor does, that women are confessing to witchcraft out of fear—that is, to avoid hanging. The stage directions also indicate that Proctor's explanation of his fear of being treated unfairly by the court makes an impression on Hale.*

◆ Background for Understanding

7 Culture The Bible includes several references to witchcraft. Among them is the warning given to Moses by God: "Thou shalt not suffer a witch to live." (Exodus 22:18)

◆ Background for Understanding

8 Culture The Gospels of Matthew, Mark, Luke, and John chronicle slightly different versions of the life of Jesus and form the foundation of the Christian New Testament. They include the purported words of Jesus himself about the essence of a good Christian life.

▶Critical Viewing◀

Analyze Tell students that this still photo from the movie version of *The Crucible* represents the moment when Elizabeth Proctor is taken off to jail. Have students analyze the facial expressions of the actors portraying Elizabeth, Hale, and the two deputies. Have them analyze what each character seems to be feeling at this moment in the play. *Sample responses: Elizabeth looks cold and angry but resigned to her fate. Hale looks sad and reflective. One of the deputies appears stern, while the other may have a hint of a self-satisfied smile on his face.*

◆ Background for Understanding

Literature After the first performance of the play, Miller reacted to critics' reviews by writing an additional scene that took place between Act II and Act III. In this scene, which is set in the woods, Abigail voices her determination to get rid of Elizabeth and to reestablish her relationship with John. However, John vows to thwart her plan. The scene was felt by many to be unnecessary and to disturb the rhythm of the play. Miller came to agree with this assessment and decided not to include the scene in the version of the play that he published in his *Collected Plays*.

Cross-Curricular Connection: Social Studies

Puritan Clothing Share the following information with students. You might follow up by having interested students do research to learn more about colonial textiles and clothing.

Flax was an important crop on colonial farms, and most Puritan women spun the flax fibers into linen thread on their own spinning wheels. This thread was then woven into cloth by the women themselves or by professional weavers. Later, sheep were imported into the colonies, and warm woolen clothing became more available. Because wool was scarce, however, colonists invented a new kind of cloth called "linsey-woolsey," which was woven with a warp of strong linen threads and a weft of wool. Most clothing was made in solid colors; printed cloth was not widely available until the eighteenth century, when the British and Dutch East India Companies began importing flowered calico and patterned chintz into the colonies.

HALE: How is Rebecca charged, Mr. Nurse?

FRANCIS, *with a mocking, half-hearted laugh:* For murder, she's charged! *Mockingly quoting the warrant:* "For the marvelous and supernatural murder of Goody Putnam's babies." What am I to do, Mr. Hale?

HALE, *turns from* FRANCIS, *deeply troubled, then:* Believe me, Mr. Nurse, if Rebecca Nurse be tainted, then nothing's left to stop the whole green world from burning. Let you rest upon the justice of the court; the court will send her home. I know it.

FRANCIS: You cannot mean she will be tried in court!

HALE, *pleading:* Nurse, though our hearts break, we cannot flinch; these are new times, sir. There is a misty plot afoot so subtle we
1 should be criminal to cling to old respects and ancient friendships. I have seen too many frightful proofs in court—the Devil is alive in Salem, and we dare not quail to follow wherever the accusing finger points!

PROCTOR, *angered:* How may such a woman murder children?

HALE, *in great pain:* Man, remember, until an
2 hour before the Devil fell, God thought him beautiful in Heaven.

GILES: I never said my wife were a witch, Mr. Hale; I only said she were reading books!

HALE: Mr. Corey, exactly what complaint were made on your wife?

GILES: That bloody mongrel Walcott charge her. Y'see, he buy a pig of my wife four or five years ago, and the pig died soon after. So he come dancin' in for his money back. So my Martha, she says to him, "Walcott, if you haven't the
3 wit to feed a pig properly, you'll not live to own many," she says. Now he goes to court and claims that from that day to this he cannot keep a pig alive for more than four weeks because my Martha bewitch them with her books!

Enter EZEKIEL CHEEVER. *A shocked silence.*

CHEEVER: Good evening to you, Proctor.

PROCTOR: Why, Mr. Cheever. Good evening.

CHEEVER: Good evening, all. Good evening, Mr. Hale.

PROCTOR: I hope you come not on business of the court.

CHEEVER: I do, Proctor, aye. I am clerk of the court now, y'know.

Enter MARSHAL HERRICK, *a man in his early thirties, who is somewhat shamefaced at the moment.*

GILES: It's a pity, Ezekiel, that an honest tailor might have gone to Heaven must burn in Hell. 4
You'll burn for this, do you know it?

CHEEVER: You know yourself I must do as I'm told. You surely know that, Giles. And I'd as lief[3] you'd not be sending me to Hell. I like not the sound of it, I tell you; I like not the sound of it. *He fears* PROCTOR, *but starts to reach inside his coat.* Now believe me, Proctor, how heavy be the law, all its tonnage I do carry on my back tonight. *He takes out a warrant.* I have a warrant for your wife.

PROCTOR, *to* HALE: You said she were not charged!

HALE: I know nothin' of it. *To* CHEEVER: When were she charged?

CHEEVER: I am given sixteen warrant tonight, sir, and she is one.

PROCTOR: Who charged her?

CHEEVER: Why, Abigail Williams charge her.

PROCTOR: On what proof, what proof?

CHEEVER, *looking about the room:* Mr. Proctor, I have little time. The court bid me search your house, but I like not to search a house. So will you hand me any poppets that your wife may keep here?

PROCTOR: Poppets?

◆ Build Vocabulary

quail (kwāl) *v.*: Cringe from; pull back in fear

3. **as lief** (as lēf) *adv.*: Rather.

Comprehension Check ☑

1 Encourage students to restate Hale's remark in their own words. *Possible paraphrase: Something very strange is going on, and we can no longer trust our friends or the people we used to respect.*

◆ Literary Focus

2 Allusion The reference here is once again to the story of Lucifer, or Satan. This story is alluded to in the New Testament: "For . . . God did not spare the angels when they sinned, but cast them into hell and committed them to chains of deepest darkness until the judgment." (2 Peter 2:4)

◆ Critical Thinking

3 Compare and Contrast Have students compare the evidence offered against Martha Corey with that offered against Goody Osburn. *Suggested response: Like the evidence offered against Goody Osburn, this claim is a circumstantial one. It is based on superstitious belief, rather than proof of a logical connection between two events.*

◆ Critical Thinking

4 Connect Have students discuss the irony of Giles Corey's suggestion that Ezekiel Cheever will "burn in Hell" for his role in the witchcraft proceedings. *It is ironic that Giles Corey is being told that his actions of bringing innocent people to court—to be judged as witches and condemned to be hanged and to spend the afterlife in hell—will merit him an everlasting place in hell.*

Beyond the Classroom

Career Connection

Law Enforcement Point out to students that rules of search and seizure and arrest are much more strict in the United States today than they were in the Puritan New England colonies. Police must obtain a search warrant based on "probable cause" before they can search a suspect's home, and people who are arrested must be read their "Miranda Rights," which include the right to speak to a defense attorney before being questioned by police. Have students research the constitutional bases of these rights and the legal cases that have reinforced them.

Arrange for students to visit a local police station and interview officers about their experiences with search warrants, informing suspects of their Miranda Rights, and holding suspects until trial.

◆ Reading Strategy

❶ **Read Drama** Ask students how they can tell that Cheever does not at first believe the charges against Elizabeth and is reluctant to arrest her. *The stage directions describe him as "embarrassed" and "shy" as he asks about the poppet.*

◆ Grammar and Style

❷ **Commas After Introductory Words** Have students identify the interrupter that Cheever uses twice in these lines. How is it punctuated and why? *The interrupter is* Why. *It is set off by a comma; it introduces the sentence.*

Comprehension Check ☑

❸ What connection do Elizabeth's accusers see between the poppet and Abigail's injury? *They believe that Elizabeth used the poppet to cast an evil spell on Abigail; by plunging a needle into the doll's stomach, Elizabeth made an evil spirit plunge a needle into Abigail's stomach.*

ELIZABETH: I never kept no poppets, not since I were a girl.

❶ **CHEEVER,** *embarrassed, glancing toward the mantel where sits* MARY WARREN*'s poppet:* I spy a poppet, Goody Proctor.

ELIZABETH: Oh! *Going for it:* Why, this is Mary's.

CHEEVER, *shyly:* Would you please to give it to me?

ELIZABETH, *handing it to him, asks* HALE: Has the court discovered a text in poppets now?

CHEEVER, *carefully holding the poppet:* Do you keep any others in this house?

PROCTOR: No, nor this one either till tonight. What signifies a poppet?

CHEEVER: Why, a poppet—*he gingerly turns the poppet over*—a poppet may signify—Now, woman, will you please to come with me?

PROCTOR: She will not! *To* ELIZABETH: Fetch Mary here.

CHEEVER, *ineptly reaching toward* ELIZABETH: No, no, I am forbid to leave her from my sight.

PROCTOR, *pushing his arm away:* You'll leave her out of sight and out of mind, Mister. Fetch Mary, Elizabeth. ELIZABETH *goes upstairs.*

HALE: What signifies a poppet, Mr. Cheever?

❷ **CHEEVER,** *turning the poppet over in his hands:* Why, they say it may signify that she—*he has lifted the poppet's skirt, and his eyes widen in astonished fear.* Why, this, this—

> **◆ Reading Strategy**
> What is the tone of this scene?

PROCTOR, *reaching for the poppet:* What's there?

CHEEVER: Why—*He draws out a long needle from the poppet*—it is a needle! Herrick, Herrick, it is a needle!

HERRICK *comes toward him.*

PROCTOR, *angrily, bewildered:* And what signifies a needle!

CHEEVER, *his hands shaking:* Why, this go hard with her, Proctor, this—I had my doubts, Proctor, I had my doubts, but here's calamity. *To* HALE, *showing the needle:* You see it, sir, it is a needle!

HALE: Why? What meanin' has it?

CHEEVER, *wide-eyed, trembling:* The girl, the Williams girl, Abigail Williams, sir. She sat to dinner in Reverend Parris's house tonight, and without word nor warnin' she falls to the floor. Like a struck beast, he says, and screamed a scream that a bull would weep to hear. And he goes to save her, and, stuck two inches in the flesh of her belly, he draw a needle out. And demandin' of her how she come to be so stabbed, she—*to* PROCTOR *now*—testify it were your wife's ❸
familiar spirit pushed it in.

PROCTOR: Why, she done it herself! *To* HALE: I hope you're not takin' this for proof, Mister!

HALE, *struck by the proof, is silent.*

CHEEVER: 'Tis hard proof! *To* HALE: I find here a poppet Goody Proctor keeps. I have found it, sir. And in the belly of the poppet a needle's stuck. I tell you true, Proctor, I never warranted to see such proof of Hell, and I bid you obstruct me not, for I—

Enter ELIZABETH *with* MARY WARREN. PROCTOR, *seeing* MARY WARREN, *draws her by the arm to* HALE.

PROCTOR: Here now! Mary, how did this poppet come into my house?

MARY WARREN, *frightened for herself, her voice very small:* What poppet's that, sir?

PROCTOR, *impatiently, points at the doll in* CHEEVER'S *hand:* This poppet, this poppet.

MARY WARREN, *evasively, looking at it:* Why, I—I think it is mine.

PROCTOR: It is your poppet, is it not?

MARY WARREN, *not understanding the direction of this:* It—is, sir.

PROCTOR: And how did it come into this house?

MARY WARREN, *glancing about at the avid faces:* Why—I made it in the court, sir, and—give it to Goody Proctor tonight.

PROCTOR, *to* HALE: Now, sir—do you have it?

> **◆ Build Vocabulary**
> **gingerly** (jin′ jər lē) *adv.*: With delicate care; cautiously

Speaking, Listening, and Viewing Mini-Lesson

Preparing a Pantomime

This mini-lesson supports the Speaking, Listening, and Viewing Mini-Lesson in the Idea Bank on page 1130.

Introduce the Concept Tell students that a pantomime is a silent enactment of a scene. It requires nonverbal communication—the communication of messages by unspoken cues such as gestures and facial expressions rather than words.

Develop Background Ask students if they have ever seen a silent movie. Point out the features of pantomime, or silent acting:

- Facial expressions and gestures are exaggerated in order to vividly express emotion.
- Actors need to find gestures to convey a question being asked or an explanation being given.

Apply the Information Have groups of students reread Cheever's description of Abigail's finding the needle on this page. Who, besides Abigail and Parris, might have been present? Have students assign roles and figure out what gestures and expressions to use to convey the scene's actions, emotions, questions, and explanations.

Assess the Outcome Evaluate each pantomime according to the following criteria: Were students' expressions and gestures appropriate for the emotions expressed? Did the pantomime flow logically? Was the action easy to follow?

HALE: Mary Warren, a needle have been found inside this poppet.

MARY WARREN, *bewildered:* Why, I meant no harm by it, sir.

PROCTOR, *quickly:* You stuck that needle in yourself?

MARY WARREN: I—I believe I did, sir, I—

4 **PROCTOR,** *to* HALE: What say you now?

HALE, *watching* MARY WARREN *closely:* Child, you are certain this be your natural memory? May it be, perhaps that someone conjures you even now to say this?

MARY WARREN: Conjures me? Why, no, sir, I am entirely myself, I think. Let you ask Susanna Walcott—she saw me sewin' it in court. *Or better still:* Ask Abby, Abby sat beside me when I made it.

PROCTOR, *to* HALE, *of* CHEEVER: Bid him begone. Your mind is surely settled now. Bid him out, Mr. Hale.

ELIZABETH: What signifies a needle?

HALE: Mary—you charge a cold and cruel murder on Abigail.

MARY WARREN: Murder! I charge no—

HALE: Abigail were stabbed tonight; a needle were found stuck into her belly—

ELIZABETH: And she charges me?

HALE: Aye.

ELIZABETH, *her breath knocked out:* Why—! The girl is murder! She must be ripped out of the world!

CHEEVER, *pointing at* ELIZABETH: You've heard that, sir! Ripped out of the world! Herrick, you heard it!

PROCTOR, *suddenly snatching the warrant out of* CHEEVER'S *hands:* Out with you.

CHEEVER: Proctor, you dare not touch the warrant.

PROCTOR, *ripping the warrant:* Out with you!

CHEEVER: You've ripped the Deputy Governor's warrant, man!

PROCTOR: Damn the Deputy Governor! Out of my house!

HALE: Now, Proctor, Proctor!

PROCTOR: Get y'gone with them! You are a broken minister.

HALE: Proctor, if she is innocent, the court—

PROCTOR: If *she* is innocent! Why do you never wonder if Parris be innocent, or Abigail? Is the accuser always holy now? Were they born this morning as clean as God's fingers? I'll tell you what's walking Salem—vengeance is walking Salem. We are what we always were in Salem, but now the little crazy children are jangling the keys of the kingdom, and common vengeance writes the law! This warrant's vengeance! I'll not give my wife to vengeance! 5

ELIZABETH: I'll go, John—

PROCTOR: You will not go!

HERRICK: I have nine men outside. You cannot keep her. The law binds me, John, I cannot budge.

PROCTOR, *to* HALE, *ready to break him:* Will you see her taken?

HALE: Proctor, the court is just—

PROCTOR: Pontius Pilate![4] God will not let you wash your hands of this! 6

ELIZABETH: John—I think I must go with them. *He cannot bear to look at her.* Mary, there is bread enough for the morning; you will bake, in the afternoon. Help Mr. Proctor as you were his daughter—you owe me that, and much more. *She is fighting her weeping. To* PROCTOR: When the children wake, speak nothing of witchcraft—it will frighten them. *She cannot go on.*

PROCTOR: I will bring you home. I will bring you soon.

ELIZABETH: Oh, John, bring me soon!

PROCTOR: I will fall like an ocean on that court! Fear nothing, Elizabeth.

4. **Pontius** (pän´ shəs) **Pilate** (pī´lət): Roman leader who condemned Jesus to be crucified.

◆ Critical Thinking

4 Make Inferences Ask students to explain how Abigail has used Mary Warren, without Mary's knowledge, to achieve her own ends. *Elicit the following: When Abigail saw Mary Warren sewing a doll and leaving her needle in the doll's stomach, Abigail knew that Mary would take the doll home. That evening, Abigail put a needle into her own stomach, claiming that Elizabeth had cast a spell on her. She knew the officers of the court would find the doll with the needle in it in the Proctors' home and that they would consider the doll proof of Abby's charges against Elizabeth.*

◆ Critical Thinking

5 Interpret Ask students what Proctor means when he says that "vengeance is walking Salem." *Suggested response: People are using the charge of witchcraft to get even with anyone who has ever hurt or offended them. Specifically, Abby is accusing Elizabeth to get revenge on Proctor because he ended their affair.*

◆ Literary Focus

6 Allusion In the Gospel of Matthew, when Jesus is turned over to the Roman governor Pontius Pilate, Pilate's wife warns him not to condemn Jesus, because she has had a dream that he is innocent. Pilate tells the crowd at Jesus' trial that he will set one prisoner free that day and asks whether he should set free Jesus or the thief Barabbas. The crowd yells to set Barabbas free and crucify Jesus. Pilate then turns Jesus over to the crowd and publicly washes his hands, saying "I am innocent of this man's blood; see to it yourselves." Ask students what similarity Proctor sees between Hale and Pontius Pilate. *Hale is not convinced that Elizabeth is guilty, but he "washes his hands" of responsibility of interceding and preventing her arrest.*

◆ Reading Strategy

❶ **Read Drama** What conclusions can students draw from Elizabeth's words and actions? *Responses may include: She is putting up a brave front; she is afraid that she may never come back home.*

◆ Reading Strategy

❷ **Read Drama** Ask students what important information they learn from the stage directions in this passage. *They learn that Elizabeth is being chained, that the deputies are resisting Proctor's efforts to have the chains removed, that Hale is feeling guilty and confused, and that Mary Warren is shocked and upset over Elizabeth's arrest.*

Comprehension Check ☑

❸ Have students explain in their own words the advice that Hale gives to Proctor in this speech. *Sample response: He says that the citizens of Salem must have committed some terrible crime in the past for which God is now punishing them in the form of the witchcraft trials. He advises the men to think hard about what they might have done to deserve such punishment from God.*

◆ Critical Thinking

Classify Ask students their opinions, at this point in the play, of John Proctor, Elizabeth Proctor, Reverend Hale, and Abigail Williams. *Students may say that John Proctor now understands how wrong it was to have an affair and is trying to do what is right. Elizabeth Proctor is a good and selfless person. Reverend Hale is beginning to see what is right but is not courageous enough to act. Abigail Williams is selfish, and she is willing to do anything—including letting Elizabeth hang—for revenge.*

◆ Literary Focus

❹ **Allusion** Tell students that at this time in history, Christians thought of hell as a fiery pit. Miller's use of the phrase "slide together into our pit" echoes language from Puritan author Michael Wigglesworth's widely read poem "Day of Doom" (1662), which describes the punishment of sinners on Judgment Day, as well as a famous sermon by Puritan preacher Jonathan Edwards, who actually lived several decades after the Salem Witch Trials.

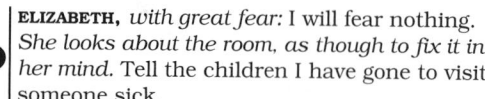

❶ **ELIZABETH,** *with great fear:* I will fear nothing. *She looks about the room, as though to fix it in her mind.* Tell the children I have gone to visit someone sick.

She walks out the door, HERRICK *and* CHEEVER *behind her. For a moment,* PROCTOR *watches from the doorway. The clank of chain is heard.*

❷ **PROCTOR:** Herrick! Herrick, don't chain her! *He rushes out the door. From outside:* Damn you, man, you will not chain her! Off with them! I'll not have it! I will not have her chained!

There are other men's voices against his. HALE, *in a fever of guilt and uncertainty, turns from the door to avoid the sight:* MARY WARREN *bursts into tears and sits weeping.* GILES COREY *calls to* HALE.

GILES: And yet silent, minister? It is fraud, you know it is fraud! What keeps you, man?

PROCTOR *is half braced, half pushed into the room by two deputies and* HERRICK.

PROCTOR: I'll pay you, Herrick, I will surely pay you!

HERRICK, *panting:* In God's name, John, I cannot help myself. I must chain them all. Now let you keep inside this house till I am gone! *He goes out with his deputies.*

PROCTOR *stands there, gulping air. Horses and a wagon creaking are heard.*

HALE, *in great uncertainty:* Mr. Proctor—

PROCTOR: Out of my sight!

HALE: Charity, Proctor, charity. What I have heard in her favor, I will not fear to testify in court. God help me, I cannot judge her guilty or innocent—I know not. Only this consider: the world goes mad, and it profit nothing you should lay the cause to the vengeance of a little girl.

PROCTOR: You are a coward! Though you be ordained in God's own tears, you are a coward now!

HALE: Proctor, I cannot think God be provoked so grandly by such a petty cause. The jails are packed—our greatest judges sit in Salem now—and hangin's promised. Man, we must look to cause proportionate. Were there murder done, perhaps, and never brought to light? Abomination? Some secret blasphemy that stinks to Heaven? Think on cause, man, and let you help me to discover it. For there's your way, believe it, there is your only way, when such confusion strikes upon the world. *He goes to* GILES *and* FRANCIS. Let you counsel among yourselves; think on your village and what may have drawn from heaven such thundering wrath upon you all. I shall pray God open up our eyes. ❸

HALE *goes out.*

FRANCIS, *struck by* HALE'S *mood:* I never heard no murder done in Salem.

PROCTOR—*he has been reached by* HALE'S *words:* Leave me, Francis, leave me.

GILES, *shaken:* John—tell me, are we lost?

PROCTOR: Go home now, Giles. We'll speak on it tomorrow.

GILES: Let you think on it. We'll come early, eh?

PROCTOR: Aye. Go now, Giles.

GILES: Good night, then.

GILES COREY *goes out. After a moment:*

MARY WARREN, *in a fearful squeak of a voice:* Mr. Proctor, very likely they'll let her come home once they're given proper evidence.

PROCTOR: You're coming to the court with me, Mary. You will tell it in the court.

MARY WARREN: I cannot charge murder on Abigail.

◆ Build Vocabulary

abomination (ə bäm′ ə nā′ shən) *n.*: Something that causes great horror or disgust

blasphemy (blas′ fə mē) *n.*: Sinful act or remark

PROCTOR, *moving menacingly toward her:* You will tell the court how that poppet come here and who stuck the needle in.

MARY WARREN: She'll kill me for sayin' that! PROCTOR *continues toward her.* Abby'll charge lechery[5] on you, Mr. Proctor!

PROCTOR, *halting:* She's told you!

MARY WARREN: I have known it, sir. She'll ruin you with it, I know she will.

4 **PROCTOR,** *hesitating, and with deep hatred of himself:* Good. Then her saintliness is done with. MARY *backs from him.* We will slide together into our pit; you will tell the court what you know.

MARY WARREN, *in terror:* I cannot, they'll turn on me—

PROCTOR *strides and catches her, and she is repeating, "I cannot, I cannot!"*

PROCTOR: My wife will never die for me! I will bring your guts into your mouth but that goodness will not die for me!

MARY WARREN, *struggling to escape him:* I cannot do it. I cannot!

PROCTOR, *grasping her by the throat as though he would strangle her:* Make your peace with it! Now Hell and Heaven grapple on our backs, and all our pretense is ripped away—make your peace! *He throws her to the floor, where she sobs, "I cannot, I cannot . . ." And now, half to himself, staring, and turning to the open door:* Peace. It is a providence, and no great change; we are only what we always were, but naked now. *He walks as though toward a great horror, facing the open sky.* Aye, naked! And the wind, God's icy wind, will blow!

And she is over and over again sobbing, "I cannot, I cannot, I cannot."

5. **lechery** (lech´ ər ē) *n.:* Lust; adultery—a charge almost as serious as witchcraft in this Puritan community.

Guide for Responding

◆ Literature and Your Life

Reader's Response Which character do you find the most intriguing? Why?

Thematic Response What criticisms of society does this act make?

Journal Activity Write the report that Reverend Hale might have written following his visit to the Proctors.

☑ Check Your Comprehension

1. What evidence is used to support Abigail Williams's assertion that Elizabeth Proctor is guilty of witchcraft?
2. What does Sarah Good do to save herself from hanging?

◆ Critical Thinking

INTERPRET

1. At one point, John Proctor identifies revenge as the true evil that is afflicting Salem Village. What evidence is there to support Proctor's assertion? **[Interpret]**
2. (a) What is ironic about John Proctor's comment that the witchcraft trials are "a black mischief"? (b) Why is it ironic that Rebecca Nurse is charged with witchcraft? (c) What is ironic about the fact that Ezekiel Cheever is the one who arrests Elizabeth Proctor? **[Analyze]**

EXTEND

3. How are legal principles and evidence-gathering procedures different in America today? **[Social Studies Link]**

Reinforce and Extend

Customize for
Less Proficient Readers
Before continuing on to Act III, help students summarize the important events of Act II: Elizabeth urges Proctor to give the court evidence that Abby is a fraud; Mary Warren returns from the trials, gives Elizabeth a doll, and reveals that Elizabeth has been accused by Abby; Hale appears and tests the Proctors on their knowledge of the Ten Commandments; Proctor tells Hale about his evidence against Abby, and Hale urges him to give the evidence in court; Cheever finds the doll with the needle in it and explains its significance; Elizabeth is arrested and taken away.

Answers

◆ Literature and Your Life

Reader's Response Students should support their opinions with examples from the play.

Thematic Focus Among the criticisms are the following: Petty jealousies can lead to great disharmony; public opinion tries and convicts people on flimsy evidence; self-important or self-righteous people can do much damage; supposedly religious people often ignore the basic teachings of their religion and instead use their faith to better their own social and economic positions and/or to persecute others.

☑ Check Your Comprehension

1. In the Proctor house, a poppet is found with a needle in its stomach, providing "evidence" that the Proctor household has been involved in the witchcraft against Abigail, who finds a needle in her stomach.
2. She confesses to being a witch.

◆ Critical Thinking

1. Among the evidence is the following: Abigail's earlier comments to John reveal that she is still deeply attached to him and support the notion that she has accused Elizabeth as a means of seeking revenge on her; Walcott accuses Giles Corey's wife of witchcraft because she had refused to refund his money after a pig she had sold him died; Goody Putnam is seeking someone to blame for the loss of her children.
2. (a) Suggested response: Although the trials are supposed to rid the community of evil, Proctor recognizes that in reality it is the trials themselves that are evil. (b) Suggested response: It is ironic because she has always been the most respected and admired member of the community and her actions have always demonstrated her deep moral commitment. (c) Suggested response: Several times John and Elizabeth had spoken of going to him for help in combating the girls' accusations.
3. Accept all reasonable responses that students support with facts or examples. Among the things they may mention are recent advances in evidence gathering, such as DNA testing and the guiding principle that in an American court of law today, a person is innocent until proven guilty.

Answers

◆ Literary Focus

1. The crowd views Abigail as a dangerous person who might accuse anyone of wrongdoing.
2. (a) Proctor implies that Reverend Hale does not have the courage to back his convictions. (b) This implies that the witchcraft proceedings are a cruel and spiteful sham.

◆ Build Vocabulary

Using the Greek Suffix *-logy*

1. *astrology:* the ancient study of the stars to see what they can predict about people's personalities and futures
2. *biology:* the science that studies living things
3. *geology:* the study of the surface and interior of the Earth
4. *phonology:* the study of speech sounds in a language

Using the Word Bank

1. true; 2. false; 3. false; 4. true; 5. true; 6. true; 7. false; 8. false; 9. false; 10. true

◆ Reading Strategy

Read Drama

1. Students should explain each example.
2. The stage directions also reveal characters' movements, to whom they address their remarks, and information about the setting.

◆ Grammar and Style

Commas After Introductory Words

Practice

1. Hey, did you ever see *The Crucible?*
2. Yes, I saw a local theater group's production.
3. Well, which characters did you find the most sympathetic?
4. correct
5. Perhaps, but the problem could have been with the performances you saw.

Idea Bank

Customizing for

Performance Levels

Following are suggestions for matching Idea Bank topics with your students' performance levels:

Less Advanced Students: 3

Average Students: 1

More Advanced Students: 2

Guide for Responding, Act II (continued)

◆ Literary Focus

ALLUSION

An **allusion** is a brief reference within a work, to something outside the work, such as another literary work, a well-known person, a place, or a historical event. *The Crucible* contains many allusions to the Bible and to Christianity.

1. Early in Act II, Elizabeth Proctor comments that when Abigail walks into the court, the crowd parts "like the sea for Israel." What does this biblical allusion to Moses and the parting of the Red Sea suggest about how the crowd views Abigail?
2. (a) With the allusion to Pontius Pilate on p. 1127, what does John Proctor imply about Reverend Hale? (b) What does he imply about the witchcraft proceedings in Salem?

◆ Build Vocabulary

USING THE GREEK SUFFIX *-logy*

The suffix *-logy* means "the science, theory, or study of." For each item below, write a word that combines the root with the suffix *-logy*, and then explain the new word's meaning.

1. *astro-*, "star"
2. *bio-*, "life"
3. *geo-*, "earth"
4. *phono-*, "sound"

USING THE WORD BANK: True or False?

Indicate whether each statement is *true* or *false*.

1. Lying and stealing are examples of *base* behaviors.
2. Someone who steps *gingerly* really pounds the pavement.
3. Someone who watches sports *avidly* probably knows very little about them.
4. Well-behaved youngsters show *deference* to their elders.
5. For the Puritans, witchcraft was an *abomination*.
6. A fearful animal may *quail* at the sight of a whip.
7. A minister is always pleased to hear *blasphemy*.
8. A *pallor* usually comes over the face of a blushing person.
9. The Puritans encouraged community members to question their *theology*.
10. People who *ameliorate* a situation are likely to win praise.

◆ Reading Strategy

READ DRAMA

As you read Act II, you paid attention to the stage directions as well as to the dialogue in order to understand the play's plot, characters, and themes.

1. Cite two examples of dialogue in which a character's attitudes would have been unclear to you if you had not read the stage directions. Explain.
2. In addition to characters' attitudes, what other significant information did the stage directions in Act II reveal to you?

◆ Grammar and Style

COMMAS AFTER INTRODUCTORY WORDS

Use a comma to set off an introductory word from the rest of the sentence in which it appears.

Practice Copy the following sentences into your notebook, and add commas to set off introductory words. If a sentence is correct as is, write *correct*.

1. Hey did you ever see *The Crucible?*
2. Yes I saw a local theater group's production.
3. Well which characters did you find the most sympathetic?
4. Perhaps it is a fine play but I found all the characters unpleasant.
5. Perhaps but the problem could have been with the performance you saw.

Idea Bank

Writing

1. **Wanted Poster** Imagine that one of the accused witches has disappeared. Describe her and her crimes in a wanted poster. **[Art Link]**
2. **Additional Scene** Write a scene showing Rebecca Nurse's arrest. Make the style of your scene consistent with that of the rest of the play.

Speaking, Listening, and Viewing

3. **Pantomime** Working in a small group, use gestures—not words—to act out the incident in which Abigail finds the needle in her stomach. **[Performing Arts Link]**

ASSESSMENT OPTIONS

Formal Assessment, Selection Test, pp. 329–331, and Assessment Resources Software. The selection test is designed so that it can be easily customized to the performance levels of your students. ***Alternative Assessment***, p. 77, includes options for less advanced students, more advanced students, interpersonal learners, bodily/kinesthetic learners, musical/rhythmic learners, and visual/spatial learners.

PORTFOLIO ASSESSMENT

Use the following rubrics in the ***Alternative Assessment*** booklet to assess student writing:

Wanted Poster: Description Rubric, p. 112

Additional Scene: Drama Rubric, p. 124

Guide for Interpreting, Act III

◆ Review and Anticipate

Act II ends as Elizabeth Proctor is accused of witchcraft and carted off to jail at the connivance of Abigail Williams. John Proctor demands that Mary Warren tell the court the truth; Mary, though aware of Abigail's ploys, is terrified of exposing her. Do you think John will convince Mary to overcome her fears and testify against Abby? If she does, how will the judges receive her testimony? Read Act III to see what happens in the Salem courtroom.

◆ Reading Strategy

CATEGORIZE CHARACTERS BY ROLE

As you read a play, you'll often find it helpful to **categorize the characters** in some way. For example, one way you can classify characters in *The Crucible* is by their roles in the community:

Property owners and other community leaders
Reverend Parris, Thomas and Ann Putnam, John and Elizabeth Proctor, Francis and Rebecca Nurse, Giles Corey, Ezekiel Cheever, Marshal Herrick, Judge Hathorne
Servants, outcasts, and minors
Betty Parris, Tituba, Abigail Williams, Susanna Walcott, Mercy Lewis, Mary Warren, Sarah Good, Hopkins
Outsiders
Reverend John Hale, Deputy Governor Danforth

As you read Act III, think of other useful categories into which you might organize the characters.

◆ Grammar and Style

SUBJECT AND VERB AGREEMENT IN INVERTED SENTENCES

A **verb** must **agree** in number with its **subject,** regardless of the word order of subject and verb. In most sentences, the subject precedes the verb, but in an **inverted sentence** the verb comes first. Notice how the verb agrees in number with the subject of the following inverted sentences.

Singular: There is (V) a prodigious fear (S) in this country.

Plural: Now there are (V) no spirits (S) attacking her.

◆ Literary Focus

DRAMATIC AND VERBAL IRONY

Have you ever watched a horror film and wanted to yell, "Don't go in there, dummy!" as a character went to investigate noises? If so, you've experienced the riveting effects of dramatic irony. Irony arises when things are not what they seem. In **dramatic irony,** there is a contradiction between what a character thinks and what the audience knows to be true. In **verbal irony,** a character says one thing but means something quite different. For example, if John Proctor said, "Abigail is a sweet and innocent maiden," he would be using verbal irony. Look for both forms of irony in Act III.

◆ Build Vocabulary

LEGAL TERMS

The Crucible has several court scenes and contains a number of **legal terms.** *Deposition* is a term for the written testimony of a witness. A deposition, a legal document made under oath but not in open court, is used during a trial.

WORD BANK

Preview this list of words.

contentious
deposition
imperceptible
deferentially
anonymity
prodigious
effrontery
confounded
incredulously
blanched

Prepare and Engage

LESSON OBJECTIVES

1. **To develop vocabulary and word identification skills**
   - Legal Terms
   - Using the Word Bank: Synonym or Antonym?
2. **To use a variety of reading strategies to comprehend a drama**
   - Review and Anticipate
   - Reading Strategy: Categorize Characters by Role
3. **To increase knowledge of other cultures and to connect common elements across cultures**
   - Background for Understanding (ATE)
4. **To express and support responses to the text**
   - Critical Thinking
5. **To analyze literary elements**
   - Literary Focus: Dramatic and Verbal Irony
   - Idea Bank: Character Sketch
   - Cross-Curricular Connection: History (ATE)
6. **To research self-selected and assigned topics and produce reports in a variety of forms**
   - Idea Bank: Wanted Poster
   - Beyond the Classroom: Community Connection (ATE)
7. **To plan, prepare, organize, and present literary interpretations**
   - Idea Bank: Letter to the Editor
   - Idea Bank: Soliloquy
8. **To increase knowledge of the rules of grammar and usage**
   - Grammar and Style: Subject and Verb Agreement in Inverted Sentences

Interest Grabber Ask students if they have ever heard the phrase "miscarriage of justice." In what context? What does the phrase mean? After students have offered their responses—noting the phrase means "a failure in the administration of justice"—invite them to make predictions about how it may apply to the trials that take place in Act III.

Prentice Hall Literature Program Resources

REINFORCE / RETEACH / EXTEND

Selection Support Pages
Build Vocabulary: Legal Terms, p. 346
Grammar and Style: Subject and Verb Agreement in Inverted Sentences, p. 347
Reading Strategy: Categorize Characters by Role, p. 348
Literary Focus: Dramatic and Verbal Irony, p. 349

Strategies for Diverse Student Needs, Use a Story Map Organizer, p. 78

Beyond Literature Career Connection: Law, p. 78

Formal Assessment Selection Test, p. 332–334; Assessment Resources Software

Alternative Assessment, p. 78

Resource Pro CD-ROM *The Crucible,* Act III—includes all resource material and customizable lesson plan

Literature CD-ROM *The History of American Literature:* Part 2, Disk 2, Feature 4; *How to Read and Understand Drama,* Feature 12

Art Transparencies, "Trial By Jury," p. 15

Develop Understanding

One-Minute Insight Justice is traditionally shown wearing a blindfold, indicating that it is—or ought to be—an impersonal and objective force, ruled by principle alone, immune to the potentially corrupting influences of social pressure, private interests, and bias. The third act of *The Crucible* reveals, however, that the reality of justice can be very different from this ideal depiction of it. As characters with varying and often opposing motives take the stand, it becomes clear that the search for justice can be affected by human impulses, both well and ill meant.

◆ Grammar and Style

❶ Subject and Verb Agreement in Inverted Sentences Ask students to identify the verb and subject in this inverted sentence. Then ask: Do the subject and verb agree? Are they singular or plural? *The subject is* evidence, *and the verb is* is. *They agree in that both are singular.*

Customize for
English Language Learners
❷ Point out that much of the dialogue in the play does not reflect correct modern usage. The style of speaking is the author's concept of the English spoken in America three hundred years ago. Also, many characters, such as Martha Corey, are meant to sound relatively uneducated and use poor grammar. "I am innocent to a witch" in standard English might read, "I am innocent of the charge of being a witch."

◆ Critical Thinking

❸ Compare and Contrast Ask students if they can see any differences between the characters of Danforth and Hathorne, based on their reactions to Giles's interruption. *Students may point out that while Danforth only wants Giles taken from the room, Hathorne wants him arrested; this suggests that Hathorne is more harsh than Danforth.*

ACT III

The vestry room of the Salem meeting house, now serving as the anteroom of the General Court.

As the curtain rises, the room is empty, but for sunlight pouring through two high windows in the back wall. The room is solemn, even forbidding. Heavy beams jut out, boards of random widths make up the walls. At the right are two doors leading into the meeting house proper, where the court is being held. At the left another door leads outside.

There is a plain bench at the left, and another at the right. In the center a rather long meeting table, with stools and a considerable armchair snugged up to it.

Through the partitioning wall at the right we hear a prosecutor's voice, JUDGE HATHORNE'S, *asking a question; then a woman's voice,* MARTHA COREY'S, *replying.*

❶ **HATHORNE'S VOICE:** Now, Martha Corey, there is abundant evidence in our hands to show that you have given yourself to the reading of fortunes. Do you deny it?

❷ **MARTHA COREY'S VOICE:** I am innocent to a witch. I know not what a witch is.

HATHORNE'S VOICE: How do you know, then, that you are not a witch?

MARTHA COREY'S VOICE: If I were, I would know it.

HATHORNE'S VOICE: Why do you hurt these children?

MARTHA COREY'S VOICE: I do not hurt them. I scorn it!

GILES'S VOICE, *roaring:* I have evidence for the court!

Voices of townspeople rise in excitement.

DANFORTH'S VOICE: You will keep your seat!

GILES' VOICE: Thomas Putnam is reaching out for land!

DANFORTH'S VOICE: Remove that man, Marshal!

GILES' VOICE: You're hearing lies, lies! ❸

A roaring goes up from the people.

HATHORNE'S VOICE: Arrest him, excellency!

GILES' VOICE: I have evidence. Why will you not hear my evidence?

The door opens and GILES *is half carried into the vestry room by* HERRICK.

GILES: Hands off, damn you, let me go!

HERRICK: Giles, Giles!

GILES: Out of my way, Herrick! I bring evidence—

HERRICK: You cannot go in there, Giles; it's a court!

Enter HALE *from the court.*

HALE: Pray be calm a moment.

GILES: You, Mr. Hale, go in there and demand I speak.

HALE: A moment, sir, a moment.

GILES: They'll be hangin' my wife!

JUDGE HATHORNE *enters. He is in his sixties, a bitter, remorseless Salem judge.*

HATHORNE: How do you dare come roarin' into this court! Are you gone daft, Corey?

GILES: You're not a Boston judge, Hathorne. You'll not call me daft!

Enter DEPUTY GOVERNOR DANFORTH *and, behind him,* EZEKIEL CHEEVER *and* PARRIS. *On his appearance, silence falls.* DANFORTH *is a grave man in his sixties, of some humor and sophistication that does not, however, interfere with an exact loyalty to his position and his cause. He comes down to* GILES, *who awaits his wrath.*

DANFORTH, *looking directly at* GILES: Who is this man?

PARRIS: Giles Corey, sir, and a more contentious—

GILES, *to* PARRIS: I am asked the question, and I am old enough to answer it! *To* DANFORTH, *who*

Test Preparation Workshop

Grammar and Usage In the verbal sections of some standardized tests, students must identify sentence errors.

Use the following sample to demonstrate. Choose the letter that shows which portion of the sentence contains an error.

There was, in the distant past, many times when the progress of civilization seemed to stop.

A There was
B in the distant past
C when the progress
D to stop
E No error

Guide students to recognize that the correct answer is *A*. By omitting the interrupting phrase "in the distant past," students should be able to recognize that "There was many times" contains an error in subject-verb agreement.

impresses him and to whom he smiles through his strain: My name is Corey, sir, Giles Corey. I have six hundred acres, and timber in addition. It is my wife you be condemning now. *He indicates the courtroom.*

DANFORTH: And how do you imagine to help her cause with such contemptuous riot? Now be gone. Your old age alone keeps you out of jail for this.

GILES, *beginning to plead:* They be tellin' lies about my wife, sir, I—

DANFORTH: Do you take it upon yourself to determine what this court shall believe and what it shall set aside?

GILES: Your Excellency, we mean no disrespect for—

DANFORTH: Disrespect indeed! It is disruption, Mister. This is the highest court of the supreme government of this province, do you know it?

GILES, *beginning to weep:* Your Excellency, I only said she were readin' books, sir, and they come and take her out of my house for—

DANFORTH, *mystified:* Books! What books?

GILES, *through helpless sobs:* It is my third wife, sir; I never had no wife that be so taken with books, and I thought to find the cause of it, d'y'see, but it were no witch I blamed her for. *He is openly weeping.* I have broke charity with the woman, I have broke charity with her. *He covers his face, ashamed.* DANFORTH *is respectfully silent.*

4 **HALE:** Excellency, he claims hard evidence for his wife's defense. I think that in all justice you must—

DANFORTH: Then let him submit his evidence in proper affidavit.[1] You are certainly aware of our procedure here, Mr. Hale. *To* HERRICK: Clear this room.

1. **affidavit** (af´ ə dā´ vit) *n.*: Written statement made under oath.

◆ Build Vocabulary

contentious (kən ten´ shəs) *adj.*: Argumentative

HERRICK: Come now, Giles. *He gently pushes* COREY *out.*

FRANCIS: We are desperate, sir; we come here three days now and cannot be heard.

DANFORTH: Who is this man?

FRANCIS: Francis Nurse, Your Excellency.

HALE: His wife's Rebecca that were condemned this morning.

DANFORTH: Indeed! I am amazed to find you in such uproar. I have only good report of your character, Mr. Nurse.

HERRICK: I think they must both be arrested in contempt, sir. 5

DANFORTH, *to* FRANCIS: Let you write your plea, and in due time I will—

FRANCIS: Excellency, we have proof for your eyes; God forbid you shut them to it. The girls, sir, the girls are frauds.

DANFORTH: What's that?

FRANCIS: We have proof of it, sir. They are all deceiving you.

DANFORTH *is shocked, but studying* FRANCIS.

HATHORNE: This is contempt, sir, contempt! 6

DANFORTH: Peace, Judge Hathorne. Do you know who I am, Mr. Nurse?

FRANCIS: I surely do, sir, and I think you must be a wise judge to be what you are.

DANFORTH: And do you know that near to four hundred are in the jails from Marblehead to Lynn, and upon my signature?

FRANCIS: I—

DANFORTH: And seventy-two condemned to hang by that signature?

FRANCIS: Excellency, I never thought to say it to such a weighty judge, but you are deceived.

Enter GILES COREY *from left. All turn to see as he beckons in* MARY WARREN *with* PROCTOR. MARY *is keeping her eyes to the ground;* PROCTOR *has her elbow as though she were near collapse.*

PARRIS, *on seeing her, in shock:* Mary Warren!

Enrichment Discuss with students Abraham Lincoln's statement: "You may fool all the people some of the time; you can even fool some of the people all the time; but you can't fool all of the people all the time." How does this statement apply to periods of crisis, such as those of the Salem witch trials and the McCarthy hearings?

◆ Build Vocabulary

4 Legal Terms Point out that "hard evidence" means evidence that can be confirmed in some way, such as by supporting testimony.

◆ Build Vocabulary

5 Legal Terms *Contempt* in a court proceeding means disobedience to or open disrespect for the rules or authority of a court. A guilty party can be arrested and confined on a judge's order without trial. This still holds true today.

◆ Critical Thinking

6 Make Inferences Point out that Hathorne insists that Francis is guilty of contempt at this point, while Danforth wants to hear more. What can students infer about each judge from his action? *Students may say that Hathorne seems to be ready to treat any objection to court proceedings as criminal; Danforth seems slightly more willing to hold off on making a judgment until he has more information.*

Block Scheduling Strategies

Consider these suggestions to take advantage of extended class time:

- Before students begin reading the selection, introduce the Literary Focus, Dramatic and Verbal Irony. Extend learning by using the Literary Focus page in ***Selection Support,*** p. 349.
- To help students appreciate the intensity of Act III, ask volunteers to role-play some of the more dramatic excerpts of dialogue.
- Have students work on Build Vocabulary: Legal Terms, in ***Selection Support,*** p. 346, and then make a glossary of words in the selection associated with trials.
- Have students complete Grammar and Style: Subject and Verb Agreement in Inverted Sentences in ***Selection Support,*** p. 347.
- Students can work individually or in small groups to answer the Critical Thinking questions on p. 1151.

◆ Build Vocabulary

❶ **Legal Terms** "The state" refers to the prosecution in a criminal trial. Students may be familiar with the modern version of this term: "the people."

◆ Reading Strategy

❷ **Categorize Characters by Role** Ask students if they think that Parris would be so concerned about Mary Warren's testimony being heard in open court if he were not a community leader. Have them explain their reasoning. *Students should note that Parris's concern about Mary's testimony reflects his concern about his position and reputation in the community. He is afraid that Mary's testimony will open the door to a deeper inquiry into the girls' accusations—an inquiry that would involve his daughter Betty and his niece Abigail.*

◆ Reading Strategy

❸ **Categorize Characters by Role** Some students may say that Parris is the more villainous of the two. Motivated by self-interest, he seems willing to manipulate both people and the truth. Others may say that Danforth is the greater villain—he holds a position of greater responsibility and seems capable of abusing his power.

◆ Grammar and Style

❹ **Subject and Verb Agreement in Inverted Sentences** Ask students to identify the subject and verb in this inverted sentence and to indicate their number—that is whether they are singular or plural. *The subject is* desire, *and the verb is* lurks. *Both are singular.*

He goes directly to bend close to her face. What are you about here?

PROCTOR, *pressing* PARRIS *away from her with a gentle but firm motion of protectiveness:* She would speak with the Deputy Governor.

DANFORTH, *shocked by this, turns to* HERRICK: Did you not tell me Mary Warren were sick in bed?

HERRICK: She were, Your Honor. When I go to fetch her to the court last week, she said she were sick.

GILES: She has been strivin' with her soul all week, Your Honor; she comes now to tell the truth of this to you.

DANFORTH: Who is this?

PROCTOR: John Proctor, sir. Elizabeth Proctor is my wife.

PARRIS: Beware this man, Your Excellency, this man is mischief.

HALE, *excitedly:* I think you must hear the girl, sir, she—

DANFORTH, *who has become very interested in* MARY WARREN *and only raises a hand toward* HALE: Peace. What would you tell us, Mary Warren?

PROCTOR *looks at her, but she cannot speak.*

PROCTOR: She never saw no spirits, sir.

DANFORTH, *with great alarm and surprise, to* MARY: Never saw no spirits!

GILES, *eagerly:* Never.

PROCTOR, *reaching into his jacket:* She has signed a deposition, sir—

DANFORTH, *instantly:* No, no, I accept no depositions. *He is rapidly calculating this; he turns from her to* PROCTOR. Tell me, Mr. Proctor, have you given out this story in the village?

PROCTOR: We have not.

PARRIS: They've come to overthrow the court, sir! This man is—

❶ **DANFORTH:** I pray you, Mr. Parris. Do you know, Mr. Proctor that the entire contention of the state in these trials is that the voice of Heaven is speaking through the children?

PROCTOR: I know that, sir.

DANFORTH, *thinks, staring at* PROCTOR, *then turns to* MARY WARREN: And you, Mary Warren, how come you to cry out people for sending their spirits, against you?

MARY WARREN: It were pretense, sir.

DANFORTH: I cannot hear you.

PROCTOR: It were pretense, she says.

DANFORTH: Ah? And the other girls? Susanna Walcott, and—the others? They are also pretending?

MARY WARREN: Aye, sir.

DANFORTH, *wide-eyed:* Indeed. *Pause. He is baffled by this. He turns to study* PROCTOR'*s face.*

PARRIS, *in a sweat:* Excellency, you surely cannot think to let so vile a lie be spread in open court. ❷

DANFORTH: Indeed not, but it strike hard upon me that she will dare come here with such a tale. Now, Mr. Proctor, before I decide whether I shall hear you or not, it is my duty to tell you this. We burn a hot fire here; it melts down all concealment.

> **◆ Reading Strategy** ❸
> Would you classify either Parris or Danforth as a villain? Why or why not?

PROCTOR: I know that, sir.

DANFORTH: Let me continue. I understand well, a husband's tenderness may drive him to extravagance in defense of a wife. Are you certain in your conscience, Mister, that your evidence is the truth?

PROCTOR: It is. And you will surely know it.

DANFORTH: And you thought to declare this revelation in the open court before the public?

PROCTOR: I thought I would, aye—with your permission.

DANFORTH, *his eyes narrowing:* Now, sir, what is your purpose in so doing?

PROCTOR: Why, I—I would free my wife, sir.

DANFORTH: There lurks nowhere in your heart, nor hidden in your spirit, any desire to undermine this court? ❹

Speaking, Listening, and Viewing Mini-Lesson

Soliloquy

This mini-lesson supports the Speaking, Listening, and Viewing activity in the Idea Bank on page 1152.

Introduce the Concept A soliloquy is a speech describing a character's thoughts and feelings. It is usually addressed directly to the audience.

Develop Background Students can meet in small groups to discuss how Elizabeth might have reacted when she learned how her lie affected her husband's fate. As they discuss their ideas, they can jot down points to make in the soliloquies. They need not use the archaic speech style of the play, but they should write their notes in the first person.

Apply the Information Advise students to concentrate more on presenting soliloquies *clearly* than on showing emotion. Point out that, traditionally, soliloquies were meant to explain a state of mind, rather than to show feelings. Have students present their soliloquies.

Assess the Outcome Hold a discussion in which students compare and contrast the content and effectiveness of various soliloquies. Students can also complete Peer Assessment: Dramatic Performance in ***Alternative Assessment,*** p. 78.

PROCTOR, *with the faintest faltering:* Why, no, sir.

CHEEVER, *clears his throat, awakening:* I—Your Excellency.

DANFORTH: Mr. Cheever.

5 **CHEEVER:** I think it be my duty, sir—*Kindly, to* PROCTOR: You'll not deny it, John. *To* DANFORTH: When we come to take his wife, he damned the court and ripped your warrant.

PARRIS: Now you have it!

DANFORTH: He did that, Mr. Hale?

HALE, *takes a breath:* Aye, he did.

PROCTOR: It were a temper, sir. I knew not what I did.

DANFORTH, *studying him:* Mr. Proctor.

PROCTOR: Aye, sir.

DANFORTH, *straight into his eyes:* Have you ever seen the Devil?

PROCTOR: No, sir.

DANFORTH: You are in all respects a Gospel Christian?

PROCTOR: I am, sir.

PARRIS: Such a Christian that will not come to church but once in a month!

DANFORTH, *restrained—he is curious:* Not come to church?

PROCTOR: I—I have no love for Mr. Parris. It is no secret. But God I surely love.

6 **CHEEVER:** He plow on Sunday, sir.

DANFORTH: Plow on Sunday!

CHEEVER, *apologetically:* I think it be evidence, John. I am an official of the court, I cannot keep it.

PROCTOR: I—I have once or twice plowed on Sunday. I have three children, sir, and until last year my land give little.

GILES: You'll find other Christians that do plow on Sunday if the truth be known.

HALE: Your Honor, I cannot think you may judge the man on such evidence.

DANFORTH: I judge nothing. *Pause. He keeps watching* PROCTOR, *who tries to meet his gaze.* I tell you straight, Mister—I have seen marvels in this court. I have seen people choked before my eyes by spirits; I have seen them stuck by pins and slashed by daggers. I have until this moment not the slightest reason to suspect that the children may be deceiving me. Do you understand my meaning? 7

PROCTOR: Excellency, does it not strike upon you that so many of these women have lived so long with such upright reputation, and—

PARRIS: Do you read the Gospel, Mr. Proctor?

PROCTOR: I read the Gospel.

PARRIS: I think not, or you should surely know that Cain were an upright man, and yet he did kill Abel.[2]

PROCTOR: Aye, God tells us that. *To* DANFORTH: But who tells us Rebecca Nurse murdered seven babies by sending out her spirit on them? It is the children only, and this one will swear she lied to you. 8

DANFORTH *considers, then beckons* HATHORNE *to him.* HATHORNE *leans in, and he speaks in his ear.* HATHORNE *nods.*

HERRICK: Aye, she's the one.

DANFORTH: Mr. Proctor, this morning, your wife send me a claim in which she states that she is pregnant now.

PROCTOR: My wife pregnant!

DANFORTH: There be no sign of it—we have examined her body.

PROCTOR: But if she say she is pregnant, then she must be! That woman will never lie, Mr. Danforth.

DANFORTH: She will not?

2. **Cain . . . Abel:** In the Bible Cain, the oldest son of Adam and Eve, killed his brother, Abel.

◆ Build Vocabulary

deposition (dep′ ə zish′ ən) *n.*: The testimony of a witness made under oath but not in open court

◆ Build Vocabulary

5 Legal Terms A *warrant* is a written order giving authority for an action, such as an arrest warrant or a search warrant.

◆ Critical Thinking

6 Analyze Ask students if they agree with Cheever's assertion that he has a duty to reveal this information. Why or why not? *Most students will say that Cheever does not have a duty to reveal this information and that he is revealing it because of an inflated sense of self-importance he derives from being named an "official" of the court.*

◆ Literary Focus

7 Dramatic and Verbal Irony Ask students to explain what kind of irony this passage represents and why. *Students may point out that although Danforth believes that he has seen people choked, stabbed, and slashed by spirits, the reader knows that he has seen no such thing; therefore this passage is an example of dramatic irony.*

◆ Critical Thinking

8 Analyze Do students think that this is an effective response to Parris's observation about Cain and Abel? Why or why not? *Some students may say the response is effective because it undermines the trustworthiness of the statements made against the accused. Other students may say that Proctor's response is not effective because it is merely an opinion.*

Customize for
Less Proficient Readers
To help these students follow the twists in the plot of Act III, use ***Strategies for Diverse Student Needs,*** p. 78, "Use a Story Map Organizer."

Cross-Curricular Connection: History

The Legend of Salem One of the many characters in *The Crucible* taken from real life is John Hathorne, a judge who took part in the Salem witchcraft trials. Hathorne's most famous descendant is the writer Nathaniel Hawthorne (1804–1864). Hawthorne, a major figure in American literature, wrote both novels and short stories. He used the colonies of Hathorne's day as a setting for much of his work and explored the intolerance and cruelty of that time.

Two of Hawthorne's stories, "Young Goodman Brown" and "The May-Pole of Merrymount," focus on the grim aspects of New England's Puritan communities. His best-known novel, *The Scarlet Letter,* examines the repressive side of Puritanism and the hypocrisy and pain that such an atmosphere might produce.

Invite students to discuss what might have happened in Salem at the time of the trials if those in charge had known that future generations would look at their actions with disapproval.

◆ Build Vocabulary

❶ **Legal Terms** A *recess* is an unscheduled interruption in court proceedings.

◆ Literary Focus

❷ **Dramatic and Verbal Irony** Ask students which type of irony this statement exemplifies. *Students may need to be made aware that circumstances often arise when even the "pure in heart" need legal representation, as events in this play show. This assertion by Danforth is an example of dramatic irony.*

◆ Literary Focus

❸ **Dramatic and Verbal Irony** The statement literally means that the opinions are good, and not that the women are good.

◆ Grammar and Style

❹ **Subject and Verb Agreement in Inverted Sentences** Ask students to identify the subject and verb in this sentence and to indicate their number. *The subject is* farmers; *the verb is* are. *Both the subject and verb are plural.*

◆ Build Vocabulary

❺ **Legal Terms** To "summon" a person in legal terms means to formally call for the person's appearance in court. A summons, then, is not a request, but an order that the court can enforce.

◆ Critical Thinking

❻ **Make Inferences** Ask students what effect the thrust of Parris's statement would have on potential witnesses before the Salem court. *Students should note that Parris equates dissension from a position taken by the court with an attack. As a result, potential witnesses would feel intimidated.*

PROCTOR: Never, sir, never.

DANFORTH: We have thought it too convenient to be credited. However, if I should tell you now that I will let her be kept another month; and if she begin to show her natural signs, you shall have her living yet another year until she is delivered—what say you to that? JOHN PROCTOR *is struck silent.* Come now. You say your only purpose is to save your wife. Good, then, she is saved at least this year, and a year is long. What say you, sir? It is done now. *In conflict,* PROCTOR *glances at* FRANCIS *and* GILES. Will you drop this charge?

PROCTOR: I—I think I cannot.

DANFORTH, *now an almost imperceptible hardness in his voice:* Then your purpose is somewhat larger.

PARRIS: He's come to overthrow this court, Your Honor!

PROCTOR: These are my friends. Their wives are also accused—

DANFORTH, *with a sudden briskness of manner:* I judge you not, sir. I am ready to hear your evidence.

PROCTOR: I come not to hurt the court; I only—

❶ **DANFORTH,** *cutting him off:* Marshal, go into the court and bid Judge Stoughton and Judge Sewall declare recess for one hour. And let them go to the tavern, if they will. All witnesses and prisoners are to be kept in the building.

HERRICK: Aye, sir. *Very deferentially:* If I may say it, sir. I know this man all my life. It is a good man, sir.

DANFORTH—*it is the reflection on himself he resents:* I am sure of it, Marshal. HERRICK *nods, then goes out.* Now, what deposition do you have for us, Mr. Proctor? And I beg you be clear, open as the sky, and honest.

PROCTOR, *as he takes out several papers:* I am no lawyer, so I'll—

❷ **DANFORTH:** The pure in heart need no lawyers. Proceed as you will.

PROCTOR, *handing* DANFORTH *a paper:* Will you read this first, sir? It's a sort of testament. The people signing it declare their good opinion of Rebecca, and my wife, and Martha Corey. DANFORTH *looks down at the paper.*

> ◆ **Literary Focus**
> What makes this an example of verbal irony? ❸

PARRIS, *to enlist* DANFORTH'S *sarcasm:* Their good opinion! *But* DANFORTH *goes on reading, and* PROCTOR *is heartened.*

PROCTOR: These are all landholding farmers, members of the church. *Delicately, trying to point out a paragraph:* If you'll notice, sir— ❹ they've known the women many years and never saw no sign they had dealings with the Devil.

PARRIS *nervously moves over and reads over* DANFORTH'S *shoulder.*

DANFORTH, *glancing down a long list:* How many names are here?

FRANCIS: Ninety-one, Your Excellency.

PARRIS, *sweating:* These people should be summoned. DANFORTH *looks up at him questioningly.* ❺ For questioning.

FRANCIS, *trembling with anger:* Mr. Danforth, I gave them all my word no harm would come to them for signing this.

PARRIS: This is a clear attack upon the court!

HALE, *to* PARRIS, *trying to contain himself:* Is every defense an attack upon the court? Can no one—?

❻ **PARRIS:** All innocent and Christian people are happy for the courts in Salem! These people are gloomy for it. *To* DANFORTH *directly:* And I think you will want to know, from each and every one of them, what discontents them with you!

HERRICK: I think they ought to be examined, sir.

DANFORTH: It is not necessarily an attack, I think. Yet—

FRANCIS: These are all covenanted Christians, sir.

DANFORTH: Then I am sure they may have nothing to fear. *Hands* CHEEVER *the paper.* Mr. Cheever, have warrants drawn for all of these—arrest for examination. *To* PROCTOR: Now, Mister, what other information do you have for us?

Cross-Curricular Connection: History

The McCarthy Era Just as fears of witchcraft once besieged the citizens of colonial Massachusetts, the fear of Communists in the United States government obsessed millions of Americans after World War II. The man most responsible for this fear was Senator Joseph R. McCarthy.

McCarthy (1908–1957) was elected to the United States Senate from Wisconsin in 1946. He gained national attention when, in 1950, he claimed that many Communists occupied influential government positions. McCarthy had little evidence, but his charges raised a national outcry. The federal government launched security probes, and employees about whom doubts arose were fired. McCarthy even accused the Eisenhower administration of treason.

McCarthy's fall was as abrupt as his rise. During a televised investigation of the United States Army, his behavior alienated many. In 1954, the Senate censured him for "contemptuous" conduct. He died three years later. An atmosphere of reckless accusations of disloyalty, especially accusations not backed by evidence, is still called "McCarthyism."

Discuss with students how the reaction provoked by McCarthy resembles and differs from the panic over witchcraft in colonial Massachusetts.

FRANCIS *is still standing, horrified.* You may sit, Mr. Nurse.

FRANCIS: I have brought trouble on these people: I have—

7 **DANFORTH:** No, old man, you have not hurt these people if they are of good conscience. But you must understand, sir, that a person is either with this court or he must be counted against it, there be no road between. This is a sharp time, now, a precise time—we live no longer in the dusky afternoon when evil mixed itself with good and befuddled the world. Now, by God's grace, the shining sun is up, and them that fear not light will surely praise it. I hope you will be one of those. MARY WARREN *suddenly sobs.* She's not hearty, I see.

PROCTOR: No, she's not, sir. *To* MARY, *bending to her, holding her hand, quietly:* Now remember what the angel Raphael said to the boy Tobias.[3] Remember it.

MARY WARREN, *hardly audible:* Aye.

PROCTOR: "Do that which is good, and no harm shall come to thee."

MARY WARREN: Aye.

DANFORTH: Come, man, we wait you.

MARSHAL HERRICK *returns, and takes his post at the door.*

GILES: John, my deposition, give him mine.

PROCTOR: Aye. *He hands* DANFORTH *another paper.* This is Mr. Corey's deposition.

DANFORTH: Oh? *He looks down at it.* Now HATHORNE *comes behind him and reads with him.*

HATHORNE, *suspiciously:* What lawyer drew this, Corey?

GILES: You know I never hired a lawyer in my life, Hathorne.

DANFORTH, *finishing the reading:* It is very well phrased. My compliments. Mr. Parris, if Mr. Putnam is in the court, will you bring him in? HATHORNE *takes the deposition, and walks to the window with it.* PARRIS *goes into the court.* You have no legal training, Mr. Corey? 8

GILES, *very pleased:* I have the best, sir—I am thirty-three time in court in my life. And always plaintiff, too. 9

DANFORTH: Oh, then you're much put-upon.

GILES: I am never put-upon; I know my rights, sir, and I will have them. You know, your father tried a case of mine—might be thirty-five year ago, I think. 10

DANFORTH: Indeed.

GILES: He never spoke to you of it?

DANFORTH: No, I cannot recall it.

GILES: That's strange, he gave me nine pound damages. He were a fair judge, your father. 11 Y'see, I had a white mare that time, and this fellow come to borrow the mare—*Enter* PARRIS *with* THOMAS PUTNAM. *When he sees* PUTNAM, GILES' *ease goes; he is hard.* Aye, there he is.

DANFORTH: Mr. Putnam, I have here an accusation by Mr. Corey against you. He states that you coldly prompted your daughter to cry witchery upon George Jacobs that is now in jail.

PUTNAM: It is a lie.

DANFORTH, *turning to* GILES: Mr. Putnam states your charge is a lie. What say you to that?

GILES, *furious, his fists clenched:* A fart on Thomas Putnam, that is what I say to that!

DANFORTH: What proof do you submit for your charge, sir?

GILES: My proof is there! *Pointing to the paper.* If

3. **Raphael. . . Tobias:** In the Bible, Tobias is guided by the archangel Raphael to save two people who have prayed for their deaths. One of the two is Tobias's father, Tobit, who has prayed for his death because he has lost his sight; the other is Sara, a woman who is afflicted by a demon and has killed her seven husbands on their wedding day. With Raphael's assistance, Tobias exorcises the devil from Sara and cures his father of blindness.

◆ Build Vocabulary

imperceptible (im´ pər sep´ tə bəl) *adj.*: Barely noticeable

deferentially (def´ ər en´ shəl lē) *adv.*: In a manner that bows to another's wishes; very respectfully

◆ Critical Thinking

7 **Analyze** Ask students to explain how Danforth's statement might create problems for potential witnesses in this trial. *Elicit the following: In principle, witnesses should be more concerned with speaking the truth than with appearing to support the court. Danforth, however, suggests that the reverse is true in his courtroom.*

◆ Critical Thinking

8 **Speculate** Ask students what Danforth's decision to summon Putnam suggests about the contents of Giles Corey's deposition. *Students may surmise that Corey's deposition charges Putnam with a crime.*

◆ Build Vocabulary

9 **Legal Terms** A "plaintiff" is a person who starts a lawsuit. The party whom the plaintiff sues is known as the "defendant."

Customize for
English Language Learners

10 Point out that if Giles spoke correct modern English, he would say that Danforth's father had tried a case of his "thirty-five years ago." Here, as in many places in this selection, the author has chosen to have a character speak in an archaic or ungrammatical style.

◆ Build Vocabulary

11 **Legal Terms** *Damages,* in a legal context, means a sum of money awarded by a court for harm done to a plaintiff's person or property.

◆ Build Vocabulary

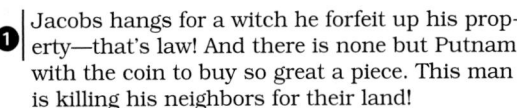

❶ **Legal Terms** To *forfeit* is to give up or lose some or all of one's property because of some fault, neglect, or illegal act. Make sure that students are aware that in modern usage, the term is simply "to forfeit" rather than "to forfeit up."

◆ Build Vocabulary

❷ **Legal Terms** *Hearing,* in this context, refers to a situation in which a judge listens to statements when the court is not officially in session; therefore, certain rules that apply while the court *is* in session are not in effect. Giles, who is familiar with such matters, knows that he cannot be held in contempt and put in jail for refusing to answer questions during a hearing; he is liable, however, once court reconvenes.

◆ Critical Thinking

❸ **Draw Conclusions** Point out that in his remarks to Giles, Danforth links the government and "the central church." Encourage students to draw conclusions about the colony's government, based on this reference. *Elicit the following: The government of the colony was a theocracy—a government in which the church and state are not considered separate entities.*

◆ Critical Thinking

❹ **Interpret** Ask students what role Hale seems to assume as the proceedings continue. *Sample responses: He acts as the court's conscience; he acts as the voice of reason.*

❶ Jacobs hangs for a witch he forfeit up his property—that's law! And there is none but Putnam with the coin to buy so great a piece. This man is killing his neighbors for their land!

DANFORTH: But proof, sir, proof.

GILES, *pointing at his deposition:* The proof is there! I have it from an honest man who heard Putnam say it! The day his daughter cried out on Jacobs, he said she'd given him a fair gift of land.

HATHORNE: And the name of this man?

GILES, *taken aback:* What name?

HATHORNE: The man that give you this information.

GILES, *hesitates, then:* Why, I—I cannot give you his name.

HATHORNE: And why not?

GILES, *hesitates, then bursts out:* You know well why not! He'll lay in jail if I give his name!

HATHORNE: This is contempt of the court, Mr. Danforth!

DANFORTH, *to avoid that:* You will surely tell us the name.

GILES: I will not give you no name. I mentioned my wife's name once and I'll burn in hell long enough for that. I stand mute.

DANFORTH: In that case, I have no choice but to arrest you for contempt of this court, do you know that?

GILES: This is a hearing; you cannot clap me for contempt of a hearing.

❷ **DANFORTH:** Oh, it is a proper lawyer! Do you wish me to declare the court in full session here? Or will you give me good reply?

GILES, *faltering:* I cannot give you no name, sir, I cannot.

DANFORTH: You are a foolish old man. Mr. Cheever, begin the record. The court is now in session. I ask you, Mr. Corey—

PROCTOR, *breaking in:* Your Honor—he has the story in confidence, sir, and he—

PARRIS: The Devil lives on such confidences! *To* DANFORTH: Without confidences there could be no conspiracy, Your Honor!

HATHORNE: I think it must be broken, sir.

DANFORTH, *to* GILES: Old man, if your informant tells the truth let him come here openly like a decent man. But if he hide in anonymity I must know why. Now sir, the government and central church demand of you the name of him who ❸ reported Mr. Thomas Putnam a common murderer.

HALE: Excellency—

DANFORTH: Mr. Hale.

HALE: We cannot blink it more. There is a prodigious fear of this court in the country—

DANFORTH: Then there is a prodigious guilt in the country. Are you afraid to be questioned here?

HALE: I may only fear the Lord, sir, but there is ❹ fear in the country nevertheless.

DANFORTH, *angered now:* Reproach me not with the fear in the country; there is fear in the country because there is a moving plot to topple Christ in the country!

HALE: But it does not follow that everyone accused is part of it.

DANFORTH: No uncorrupted man may fear this court, Mr. Hale! None! *To* GILES: You are under arrest in contempt of this court. Now sit you down and take counsel with yourself, or you will be set in the jail until you decide to answer all questions.

GILES COREY *makes a rush for* PUTNAM. PROCTOR *lunges and holds him.*

PROCTOR: No, Giles!

GILES, *over* PROCTOR'S *shoulder at* PUTNAM: I'll cut your throat, Putnam, I'll kill you yet!

PROCTOR, *forcing him into a chair:* Peace, Giles, peace. *Releasing him.* We'll prove ourselves. Now we will. *He starts to turn to* DANFORTH.

GILES: Say nothin' more, John. *Pointing at* DANFORTH: He's only playin' you! He means to hang us all!

MARY WARREN *bursts into sobs.*

DANFORTH: This is a court of law, Mister. I'll have no effrontery here!

PROCTOR: Forgive him, sir, for his old age. Peace, Giles, we'll prove it all now. *He lifts up* MARY's *chin.* You cannot weep, Mary. Remember the angel, what he say to the boy. Hold to it, now; there is your rock. MARY *quiets. He takes out a* 5 *paper, and turns to* DANFORTH. This is Mary Warren's deposition. I—I would ask you remember, 5 sir, while you read it, that until two week ago she were no different than the other children are 6 today. *He is speaking reasonably, restraining all his fears, his anger, his anxiety.* You saw her scream, she howled, she swore familiar spirits choked her; she even testified that Satan, in the form of women now in jail, tried to win her soul away, and then when she refused—

DANFORTH: We know all this.

PROCTOR: Aye, sir. She swears now that she never saw Satan; nor any spirit, vague or clear, that Satan may have sent to hurt her. And she declares her friends are lying now.

PROCTOR *starts to hand* DANFORTH *the deposition, and* HALE *comes up to* DANFORTH *in a trembling state.*

◆ Build Vocabulary

anonymity (an′ ə nim′ ə tē) *n.*: The condition of being unknown or unacknowledged

prodigious (prə dij′ əs) *adj.*: Of great size, power, or extent

effrontery (e frun′ tər ē) *n.*: Shameless boldness

◆ Build Vocabulary

5 Legal Terms Ask students to recall what a *deposition* is. If necessary, have them review Build Vocabulary on page 1131. *A deposition is the written testimony of a witness, made under oath, but not in open court, that is used during a trial.*

Customize for
English Language Learners

6 Proctor says, "... until two week ago she were no different than the other children are today." Have students restate this phrase in standard modern English. *Students should make the following changes: ... until two weeks ago she was no different from the other children as they are today.*

Humanities: Literature

Literature in the Massachusetts Bay colony was for the most part limited to sermons and chronicles of the colony's history. Colonists were fascinated by sermons and bought collections of them to read at their leisure. A typical sermon would cite a passage from the Bible, analyze its meaning, and apply it to daily life.

Some ministers became famous for their published sermons, none more so than Cotton Mather (1663–1728). His grandfather Richard and his father, Increase, had also been religious leaders in Massachusetts. Cotton Mather's four hundred published works include a defense of the Salem witchcraft trials. He also had a strong interest in the natural sciences.

Have students do library research to find examples of Cotton Mather's sermons. Suggest that they choose excerpts to share with the class.

◆ Critical Thinking

❶ Evaluate Ask students what they think this statement reveals about Hale's values and character. *Students may note that Hale has taken part in the sentencing of seventy-two people, but he is troubled by the possibility of making an error in this case. Although he is a prominent witch-hunter, he seems to have a sense of honesty and integrity.*

◆ Build Vocabulary

❷ Legal Terms When Danforth speaks of having "been thirty-two years at the bar," he means that he has practiced law for thirty-two years. "The bar" represents the courts. The term is believed to have originally referred to the rail at which defendants stand or the one behind the area where lawyers sit while trying a case. When a new lawyer is authorized to practice, he is said to have been "admitted to the bar."

◆ Reading Strategy

❸ Categorize Characters by Role Sample response: Danforth does not want to defend the accused; rather, he maintains there is no possible way to do so. Therefore, Danforth may be categorized as a witch hunter who wants to see all of the accused hang.

◆ Literary Focus

❹ Dramatic and Verbal Irony Ask students what kind of irony emerges in this passage, and encourage them to explain their reasoning. *Students should note that Danforth employs legal jargon and dry logic to discuss witchcraft, as though it were a demonstrable scientific phenomenon such as gravity. The opposition between his assumption that witchcraft is real and the reader's awareness that it is not results in dramatic irony.*

HALE: Excellency, a moment. I think this goes to the heart of the matter.

DANFORTH, *with deep misgivings:* It surely does.

HALE: I cannot say he is an honest man; I know him little. But in all justice, sir, a claim so weighty cannot be argued by a farmer. In God's name, sir, stop here; send him home and let him come again with a lawyer—

DANFORTH, *patiently:* Now look you, Mr. Hale—

HALE: Excellency, I have signed seventy-two death warrants; I am a minister of the Lord, and I dare not take a life without there be a proof so immaculate no slightest qualm of conscience may doubt it.

DANFORTH: Mr. Hale, you surely do not doubt my justice.

❶ **HALE:** I have this morning signed away the soul of Rebecca Nurse, Your Honor. I'll not conceal it, my hand shakes yet as with a wound! I pray you, sir, *this* argument let lawyers present to you.

DANFORTH: Mr. Hale, believe me; for a man of such terrible learning you are most bewildered—I hope you will forgive me. ❷ I have been thirty-two year at the bar, sir, and I should be <u>confounded</u> were I called upon to defend these people. Let you consider, now—*To* PROCTOR *and the others:* And I bid you all do likewise. ❸ In an ordinary crime, how does one defend the accused? One calls up witnesses to prove his innocence. But witchcraft is *ipso facto*,[4] on its face and by its nature, ❹ an invisible crime, is it not? Therefore, who may possibly be witness to it? The witch and the victim. None other. Now we cannot hope the witch will accuse herself; granted? Therefore, we must rely upon her victims—and they do testify, the children certainly do testify. As for the witches, none will deny that we are most eager for all their confessions. Therefore, what is left for a lawyer to bring out? I think I have made my point. Have I not?

> **◆ Reading Strategy**
> Based on this speech, how would you classify Danforth?

HALE: But this child claims the girls are not truthful, and if they are not—

DANFORTH: That is precisely what I am about to consider, sir. What more may you ask of me? Unless you doubt my probity?[5]

HALE, *defeated:* I surely do not, sir. Let you consider it, then.

DANFORTH: And let you put your heart to rest. Her deposition, Mr. Proctor.

PROCTOR *hands it to him.* HATHORNE *rises, goes beside* DANFORTH, *and starts reading.* PARRIS *comes to his other side.* DANFORTH *looks at* JOHN PROCTOR, *then proceeds to read.* HALE *gets up, finds position near the judge, reads too.* PROCTOR *glances at* GILES. FRANCIS *prays silently, hands pressed together.* CHEEVER *waits placidly, the sublime official, dutiful.* MARY WARREN *sobs once.* JOHN PROCTOR *touches her hand reassuringly. Presently* DANFORTH *lifts his eyes, stands up, takes out a kerchief and blows his nose. The others stand aside as he moves in thought toward the window.*

PARRIS, *hardly able to contain his anger and fear:* I should like to question—

DANFORTH—*his first real outburst, in which his contempt for* PARRIS *is clear:* Mr. Parris, I bid you be silent! *He stands in silence, looking out the window. Now, having established that he will set the gait:* Mr. Cheever, will you go into the court and bring the children here? CHEEVER *gets up and goes out upstage.* DANFORTH *now turns to* MARY. Mary Warren, how came you to this turnabout? Has Mr. Proctor threatened you for this deposition?

MARY WARREN: No, sir.

DANFORTH: Has he ever threatened you?

MARY WARREN, *weaker:* No, sir.

DANFORTH, *sensing a weakening:* Has he threatened you?

MARY WARREN: No, sir.

DANFORTH: Then you tell me that you sat in my court, callously lying, when you knew that people would hang by your evidence? *She does not answer.* Answer me!

---

4. ***ipso facto*** (ip´ sō fak´ tō): "By that very fact"; "therefore" (Latin).

5. **probity** (prō´ bə tē) *n.*: Complete honesty: integrity.

Cross-Curricular Connection: History

HUAC The Un-American Activities Committee of the United States House of Representatives, or *HUAC*, had a strong effect on American life for many years.

Starting in 1945, the committee held hearings to expose presumed Communists or Communist sympathizers. Anyone who had flirted with left-wing politics in the Depression was suspect, and anyone who was called upon to give the names of others to the committee but refused was stigmatized for being unpatriotic.

HUAC supporters created informal blacklists to get employers to fire, as well as not hire, people with a hint of radicalism in their background. Among those whose careers were ruined were many who had never been Communists. Some people even committed suicide.

Have a class discussion to compare the circumstances of witnesses before the HUAC with those of witnesses testifying at the witchcraft trials in Salem.

MARY WARREN, *almost inaudibly:* I did, sir.

5 **DANFORTH:** How were you instructed in your life? Do you not know that God damns all liars? *She cannot speak.* Or is it now that you lie?

MARY WARREN: No, sir—I am with God now.

DANFORTH: You are with God now.

MARY WARREN: Aye, sir.

6 **DANFORTH,** *containing himself:* I will tell you this—you are either lying now, or you were lying in the court, and in either case you have committed perjury and you will go to jail for it. You cannot lightly say you lied, Mary. Do you know that?

MARY WARREN: I cannot lie no more. I am with God, I am with God.

But she breaks into sobs at the thought of it, and the right door opens, and enter SUSANNA WALCOTT, MERCY LEWIS, BETTY PARRIS, *and finally* ABIGAIL. CHEEVER *comes to* DANFORTH.

CHEEVER: Ruth Putnam's not in the court, sir, nor the other children.

DANFORTH: These will be sufficient. Sit you down, children. *Silently they sit.* Your friend, Mary Warren, has given us a deposition. In which she swears that she never saw familiar spirits, apparitions, nor any manifest of the Devil. She claims as well that none of you have seen these things either. *Slight pause.* Now, children, this is a court of law. The law, based upon the Bible, and the Bible, writ by Almighty God, forbid the practice of witchcraft, and describe death as the penalty thereof. But likewise, children, the law and Bible damn all bearers of false witness. *Slight pause.* Now then. It does not escape me that this deposition may be devised to blind us; it may well be that Mary Warren has been conquered by Satan, who sends her here to distract our sacred purpose. If so, her neck will break for it. But if she speak true, I bid you now drop your guile and confess your pretense, for a quick confession will go easier with you. *Pause.* Abigail Williams, rise. ABIGAIL *slowly rises.* Is there any truth in this? 7

ABIGAIL: No, sir.

DANFORTH, *thinks, glances at* MARY *then back to* ABIGAIL: Children, a very augur bit[6] will now be turned into your souls until your honesty is proved. Will either of you change your positions now, or do you force me to hard questioning?

ABIGAIL: I have naught to change, sir. She lies.

DANFORTH, *to* MARY: You would still go on with this?

MARY WARREN, *faintly:* Aye, sir.

DANFORTH, *turning to* ABIGAIL: A poppet were discovered in Mr. Proctor's house, stabbed by a needle. Mary Warren claims that you sat beside her in the court when she made it, and that you saw her make it and witnessed how she herself stuck the needle into it for safe-keeping. What say you to that?

ABIGAIL, *with a slight note of indignation:* It is a lie, sir.

DANFORTH, *after a slight pause:* While you worked for Mr. Proctor, did you see poppets in that house?

ABIGAIL: Goody Proctor always kept poppets.

PROCTOR: Your Honor, my wife never kept no poppets. Mary Warren confesses it was her poppet. 8

CHEEVER: Your Excellency.

DANFORTH: Mr. Cheever.

CHEEVER: When I spoke with Goody Proctor in that house, she said she never kept no poppets. But she said she did keep poppets when she were a girl.

PROCTOR: She has not been a girl these fifteen years, Your Honor.

HATHORNE: But a poppet will keep fifteen years, will it not?

◆ Build Vocabulary

confounded (kən found′ id) *v.:* Confused; dismayed

6. **augur bit:** Sharp point of an augur, a tool used for boring holes.

◆ Critical Thinking

5 Evaluate Ask students what trait or traits of Danforth's this passage reveals. How do these traits affect his ability to function as a judge? *Students may observe that Danforth is severe and rigid in questioning Mary Warren and that he seems intent on frightening an answer out of her. His harshness and his predisposition to find her guilty prevent him from being an open-minded judge.*

◆ Build Vocabulary

6 Legal Terms *Perjury* means lying while testifying under oath in a court proceeding. Now, as then, a convicted perjurer could be punished with imprisonment.

◆ Grammar and Style

7 Subject and Verb Agreement in Inverted Sentences Ask students to identify the subject and verb in this sentence and to indicate their number. *The subject is truth, and the verb is is. Both subject and verb are singular.*

Customize for *English Language Learners*

8 Point out the presence of a double negative in this sentence (". . . never kept no poppets"). Students will find several other examples of double negatives throughout the selection. Although they are now considered incorrect, double negatives were often used in the past to add emphasis to a negative statement.

Customize for
Visual/Spatial Learners
Encourage these students to analyze the photograph on this page. Ask them to explain how the actors—and the director who blocked the scene—convey emotion. *Students should note the facial expressions. They should also see the varied heights at play in the photograph. Abigail is on her knees, looking up at the men; other girls look on from a distance.*

◆ Literary Focus

❶ Dramatic and Verbal Irony
Ask students to explain which form of irony John Proctor's remark represents. *Students should recognize the remark as an example of verbal irony. John Proctor says that "There might . . . be a dragon with five legs" in his house, but he in fact means the opposite—there is no dragon in his house, just as there are no poppets.*

PROCTOR: It will keep if it is kept, but Mary Warren swears she never saw no poppets in my house, nor anyone else.

PARRIS: Why could there not have been poppets hid where no one ever saw them?

PROCTOR, *furious:* There might also be a dragon with five legs in my house, but no one has ever seen it. ❶

PARRIS: We are here, Your Honor, precisely to discover what no one has ever seen.

Cross-Curricular Connection: History

John Calvin John Calvin (1509–1564), a major figure of the Protestant Reformation, was the progenitor of Puritanism in Great Britain and the American colonies.

Calvin was born in France but spent much of his life in Switzerland. Raised a Catholic, he declared himself a Protestant in 1533.

Calvin advocated constitutional government and separation between church and state. He opposed the monolithic structure of the Catholic Church, stating that all believers were priests. According to Calvin, only certain people, the *elect*, were to be saved by the grace of God from damnation, and God alone knew who they were.

Calvin believed that the Bible was the basis of all Christian teaching, and, at least implicitly, the foundation of civil government. He preached that faith mattered more than good works in evaluating a Christian life.

Calvin's followers founded the Presbyterian Church in Scotland. His French followers were known as Huguenots. In England, and later in America, they were known as Puritans.

PROCTOR: I do, sir. I believe she means to murder.

DANFORTH, *pointing at* ABIGAIL, *incredulously:* This child would murder your wife? ❷ ❸

PROCTOR: It is not a child. Now hear me, sir. In the sight of the congregation she were twice this year put out of this meetin' house for laughter during prayer.

DANFORTH, *shocked, turning to* ABIGAIL: What's this? Laughter during—!

PARRIS: Excellency, she were under Tituba's power at that time, but she is solemn now.

GILES: Aye, now she is solemn and goes to hang people!

DANFORTH: Quiet, man.

HATHORNE: Surely it have no bearing on the question, sir. He charges contemplation of murder.

DANFORTH: Aye. *He studies* ABIGAIL *for a moment, then:* Continue, Mr. Proctor.

PROCTOR: Mary. Now tell the Governor how you danced in the woods.

PARRIS, *instantly:* Excellency, since I come to Salem this man is blackening my name. He—

DANFORTH: In a moment, sir. *To* MARY WARREN, *sternly, and surprised.* What is this dancing? ❹

MARY WARREN: I—*She glances at* ABIGAIL, *who is staring down at her remorselessly. Then, appealing to* PROCTOR: Mr. Proctor—

PROCTOR, *taking it right up:* Abigail leads the girls to the woods, Your Honor, and they have danced there naked—

PARRIS: Your Honor, this—

PROCTOR: Mr. Danforth, what profit this girl to turn herself about? What may Mary Warren gain but hard questioning and worse?

DANFORTH: You are charging Abigail Williams with a marvelous cool plot to murder, do you understand that?

◆ Build Vocabulary

incredulously (in krej´ o͞o ləs lē) *adv.*: Skeptically

Comprehension Check ☑

❷ Have students restate Danforth's question to Proctor in contemporary English. *Possible paraphrase: Do you realize that you're accusing Abigail Williams of coldblooded murder?*

◆ Critical Thinking

❸ **Speculate** Have students speculate about whether Proctor will reveal Abigail's motives for wanting to murder his wife. How do students imagine that Danforth and Hathorne would respond to his revelation of this information? *Sample response: The fact that Proctor is claiming that Abigail wants to murder his wife shows that he is probably also willing to reveal Abigail's motives for wanting to do so. Danforth and Hathorne may respond to such a motive with disbelief, thinking that Proctor is merely making up the affair in order to save his wife from execution.*

◆ Background for Understanding

❹ **History** The Puritans held dancing—even when fully clothed—to be an unseemly and frivolous activity and, therefore, something to be condemned.

◆ **Reading Strategy**

❶ **Categorize Characters by Role** Ask students to suggest various categories into which characters connected with the trial may be placed. When categories are set, ask students to put Hathorne in one and to give their reasons. *Students may suggest various categories; two possibilities that work for discussion purposes are: (1) those who believe in witchcraft and those who do not; (2) those who have ulterior motives for their positions and those who do not. Students may say that Hathorne has no clear ulterior motive for his behavior and that he may genuinely believe in witches.*

◆ **Critical Thinking**

❷ **Analyze Causes and Effects** How do students explain the coldness of Mary Warren's skin during the earlier court proceedings? *Sample response: Mary Warren's cold skin could have been the result of nervousness or fear of being in court.*

◆ **Reading Strategy**

❸ **Categorize Characters by Role** Ask students into what category Parris fits and have them explain their choice. *Students should see that Parris has an ulterior motive—maintaining his position in Salem. Whether he genuinely believes in witches is less clear.*

◆ **Reading Strategy**

❹ **Categorize Characters by Role** Ask students to put John Proctor into a category and to explain their reasoning. *Students might say that John Proctor's motive is to save his wife—this is an overt rather than an ulterior motive. They may argue that he probably does not believe in witchcraft and definitely does not believe that the accused are witches.*

PROCTOR, *at once:* Mr. Parris discovered them himself in the dead of night! There's the "child" she is!

DANFORTH—*it is growing into a nightmare, and he turns, astonished, to* PARRIS: Mr. Parris—

PARRIS: I can only say, sir, that I never found any of them naked, and this man is—

DANFORTH: But you discovered them dancing in the woods? *Eyes on* PARRIS, *he points at* ABIGAIL. Abigail?

HALE: Excellency, when I first arrived from Beverly, Mr. Parris told me that.

DANFORTH: Do you deny it, Mr. Parris?

PARRIS: I do not, sir, but I never saw any of them naked.

DANFORTH: But she have *danced?*

PARRIS, *unwillingly:* Aye, sir.

DANFORTH, *as though with new eyes, looks at* ABIGAIL.

❶ **HATHORNE:** Excellency, will you permit me? *He points at* MARY WARREN.

DANFORTH, *with great worry:* Pray, proceed.

HATHORNE: You say you never saw no spirits, Mary, were never threatened or afflicted by any manifest of the Devil or the Devil's agents.

MARY WARREN, *very faintly:* No, sir.

HATHORNE, *with a gleam of victory:* And yet, when people accused of witchery confronted you in court, you would faint, saying their spirits came out of their bodies and choked you—

MARY WARREN: That were pretense, sir.

DANFORTH: I cannot hear you.

MARY WARREN: Pretense, sir.

❷ **PARRIS:** But you did turn cold, did you not? I myself picked you up many times, and your skin were icy. Mr. Danforth, you—

DANFORTH: I saw that many times.

PROCTOR: She only pretended to faint, Your Excellency. They're all marvelous pretenders.

HATHORNE: Then can she pretend to faint now?

PROCTOR: Now?

PARRIS: Why not? Now there are no spirits attacking her, for none in this room is accused of witchcraft. So let her turn herself cold now, let her pretend she is attacked now, let her faint. *He turns to* MARY WARREN. Faint! ❸

MARY WARREN: Faint?

PARRIS: Aye, faint. Prove to us how you pretended in the court so many times.

MARY WARREN, *looking to* PROCTOR: I—cannot faint now, sir.

PROCTOR, *alarmed, quietly:* Can you not pretend it? ❹

MARY WARREN: I—*She looks about as though searching for the passion to faint.* I—have no *sense* of it now, I—

DANFORTH: Why? What is lacking now?

MARY WARREN: I—cannot tell, sir, I—

DANFORTH: Might it be that here we have no afflicting spirit loose, but in the court there were some?

MARY WARREN: I never saw no spirits.

PARRIS: Then see no spirits now, and prove to us that you can faint by your own will, as you claim.

MARY WARREN, *stares, searching for the emotion of it, and then shakes her head:* I— cannot do it.

PARRIS: Then you will confess, will you not? It were attacking spirits made you faint!

MARY WARREN: No, sir, I—

PARRIS: Your Excellency, this is a trick to blind the court!

MARY WARREN: It's not a trick! *She stands.* I—I used to faint because I—I thought I saw spirits.

DANFORTH: *Thought* you saw them!

MARY WARREN: But I did not, Your Honor.

HATHORNE: How could you think you saw them unless you saw them?

MARY WARREN: I—I cannot tell how, but I did. I—I heard the other girls screaming, and you,

Your Honor, you seemed to believe them, and I—It were only sport in the beginning, sir, but then the whole world cried spirits, spirits, and I—I promise you, Mr. Danforth, I only thought I saw them but I did not.

DANFORTH *peers at her.*

PARRIS, *smiling, but nervous because* DANFORTH *seems to be struck by* MARY WARREN'S *story:* Surely Your Excellency is not taken by this simple lie.

DANFORTH, *turning worriedly to* ABIGAIL: Abigail. I bid you now search your heart and tell me this—and beware of it, child, to God every soul is precious and His vengeance is terrible on them that take life without cause. Is it possible, child, that the spirits you have seen are illusion only, some deception that may cross your mind when—

ABIGAIL: Why, this—this—is a base question, sir.

DANFORTH: Child, I would have you consider it—

5 **ABIGAIL:** I have been hurt, Mr. Danforth; I have seen my blood runnin' out! I have been near to murdered every day because I done my duty pointing out the Devil's people—and this is my reward? To be mistrusted, denied, questioned like a—

DANFORTH, *weakening:* Child, I do not mistrust you—

ABIGAIL, *in an open threat:* Let *you* beware, Mr. Danforth. Think you to be so mighty that the power of Hell may not turn *your* wits? Beware of it! There is—*Suddenly, from an accusatory attitude, her face turns, looking into the air above—it is truly frightened.*

DANFORTH, *apprehensively:* What is it, child?

6 **ABIGAIL,** *looking about in the air, clasping her arms about her as though cold:* I—I know not. A wind, a cold wind, has come. *Her eyes fall on* MARY WARREN.

MARY WARREN, *terrified, pleading:* Abby!

MERCY LEWIS, *shivering:* Your Honor, I freeze!

PROCTOR: They're pretending!

HATHORNE, *touching* ABIGAIL'S *hand:* She is cold, Your Honor, touch her!

MERCY LEWIS, *through chattering teeth:* Mary, do you send this shadow on me?

MARY WARREN: Lord, save me! 6

SUSANNA WALCOTT: I freeze, I freeze!

ABIGAIL, *shivering, visibly:* It is a wind, a wind!

MARY WARREN: Abby, don't do that!

DANFORTH, *himself engaged and entered by* ABIGAIL: Mary Warren, do you witch her? I say to you, do you send your spirit out?

With a hysterical cry MARY WARREN *starts to run.* PROCTOR *catches her.*

MARY WARREN, *almost collapsing:* Let me go, Mr. Proctor, I cannot, I cannot—

ABIGAIL, *crying to Heaven:* Oh, Heavenly Father, take away this shadow!

Without warning or hesitation, PROCTOR *leaps at* ABIGAIL *and, grabbing her by the hair, pulls her to her feet. She screams in pain.* DANFORTH, *astonished, cries, "What are you about?" and* HATHORNE *and* PARRIS *call, "Take your hands off her!" and out of it all comes* PROCTOR'S *roaring voice.*

PROCTOR: How do you call Heaven! Whore! Whore!

HERRICK *breaks* PROCTOR *from her.*

HERRICK: John!

DANFORTH: Man! Man, what do you—

PROCTOR, *breathless and in agony:* It is a whore!

DANFORTH, *dumfounded:* You charge—?

ABIGAIL: Mr. Danforth, he is lying!

PROCTOR: Mark her! Now she'll suck a scream to stab me with, but— 7

DANFORTH: You will prove this! This will not pass!

PROCTOR, *trembling, his life collapsing about him:* I have known her, sir. I have known her.

DANFORTH: You—you are a lecher?

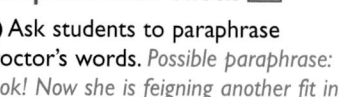

◆ Literary Focus

5 Dramatic and Verbal Irony
Ask students which kind of irony this passage demonstrates. Have them explain their answers. *Students should note that although Abigail claims that she was nearly murdered and that she has been doing her moral duty, readers know that this is false. Several other characters, however, do not know this, making the speech an example of dramatic irony.*

◆ Literary Focus

6 Dramatic and Verbal Irony
Invite seven volunteers to act out this scene. Then have students explain how dramatic irony adds to the scene's effect. *Like Proctor and Mary Warren, the audience knows that Abigail and the other girls are pretending; Danforth, however, seems to believe the girls. Since Danforth has power over people's lives, this dramatic irony makes the scene both intense and suspenseful.*

Comprehension Check ☑

7 Ask students to paraphrase Proctor's words. *Possible paraphrase: Look! Now she is feigning another fit in an attempt to discredit me. . . .*

Beyond the Classroom

Community Connection

Contemporary Courts In any community, large or small, there is a court, and perhaps more than one. Some courts are *federal* and work under federal law; others are *state* courts, authorized by state constitutions and laws.

The federal courts include *district courts,* where cases are first heard; *courts of appeals,* where cases are brought on appeal from district courts; and the *Supreme Court of the United States,* in Washington, D.C. There are ninety-five district courts, with at least one per state. Each of the twelve *circuits* into which the United States is divided has one court of appeals.

States control *county* and *local courts,* which handle local issues and ordinances, such as those having to do with traffic. Other state courts focus on special areas, such as juvenile and domestic affairs and probate (wills and estates). Many states have appeals courts and/or State Supreme Courts.

Interested students might visit a court when in session to see how it operates. They may also do research as to where the closest example of each type of court mentioned here is located.

Comprehension Check ☑

❶ Ask students what Proctor means by this sentence. *Sample answer: Francis is so virtuous that he cannot conceive of someone being guilty of such an immoral act as that committed by Proctor.*

◆ Critical Thinking

❷ **Make Inferences** Ask students why Proctor expects Danforth to believe what he says about Abigail and Elizabeth. *Students should note that Proctor, in saying that he has "made a bell" of his honor, acknowledges that he has destroyed his reputation in this extremely rigid and strict community, an extreme step that he would take only as a last measure to prevent injustice from being done.*

◆ Literary Focus

❸ **Dramatic and Verbal Irony** Have students describe the dramatic irony that is at work in this scene. *The audience knows that Elizabeth is being tested and that it is crucial that she tell the truth. Elizabeth, however, is not aware of the purpose of Danforth's questions.*

◆ Background for Understanding

Literature In discussing the "dilemma" he faced in trying to identify the similarities between the Salem witchcraft trials and the McCarthy hearings, Miller has noted: "The truth is that the more I worked at this dilemma the less it had to do with Communists and McCarthy and the more it concerned something very fundamental in the human animal: the fear of the unknown, and particularly the dread of social isolation." Have students discuss Miller's comment in relation to the events that have occurred in *The Crucible* up to this point.

FRANCIS, *horrified:* John, you cannot say such a—

❶ **PROCTOR:** Oh, Francis, I wish you had some evil in you that you might know me! *To* DANFORTH: A man will not cast away his good name. You surely know that.

DANFORTH, *dumfounded:* In—in what time? In what place?

PROCTOR, *his voice about to break, and his shame great:* In the proper place—where my beasts are bedded. On the last night of my joy, some eight months past. She used to serve me in my house, sir. *He has to clamp his jaw to keep from weeping.* A man may think God sleeps, but God sees everything. I know it now. I beg you, sir, I beg you—see her what she is. My wife, my dear good wife, took this girl soon after, sir, and put her out on the highroad. And being what she is, a lump of vanity, sir—*He is being overcome.* Excellency, forgive me, forgive me. *Angrily against himself, he turns away from the* GOVERNOR *for a moment. Then, as though to cry out is his only means of speech left:* She thinks to dance with me on my wife's grave! And well she might, for I thought of her softly. God help me, I lusted, and there *is* a promise in such sweat. But it is a whore's vengeance, and you must see it; I set myself entirely in your hands. I know you must see it now.

DANFORTH, *blanched, in horror, turning to* ABIGAIL: You deny every scrap and tittle of this?

ABIGAIL: If I must answer that, I will leave and I will not come back again!

DANFORTH *seems unsteady.*

❷ **PROCTOR:** I have made a bell of my honor! I have rung the doom of my good name—you will believe me, Mr. Danforth! My wife is innocent, except she knew a whore when she saw one!

ABIGAIL, *stepping up to* DANFORTH: What look do you give me? DANFORTH *cannot speak.* I'll not have such looks! *She turns and starts for the door.*

DANFORTH: You will remain where you are! HERRICK *steps into her path. She comes up short, fire in her eyes.* Mr. Parris, go into the court and bring Goodwife Proctor out.

PARRIS, *objecting:* Your Honor, this is all a—

DANFORTH, *sharply to* PARRIS: Bring her out! And tell her not one word of what's been spoken here. And let you knock before you enter. PARRIS *goes out.* Now we shall touch the bottom of this swamp. *To* PROCTOR: Your wife, you say, is an honest woman.

PROCTOR: In her life, sir, she have never lied. There are them that cannot sing, and them that cannot weep—my wife cannot lie. I have paid much to learn it, sir.

DANFORTH: And when she put this girl out of your house, she put her out for a harlot?

PROCTOR: Aye, sir.

DANFORTH: And knew her for a harlot?

PROCTOR: Aye, sir, she knew her for a harlot.

DANFORTH: Good then. *To* ABIGAIL: And if she tell me, child, it were for harlotry, may God spread His mercy on you! *There is a knock. He calls to the door.* Hold! *To* ABIGAIL: Turn your back. Turn your back. *To* PROCTOR: Do likewise. *Both turn their backs*—ABIGAIL *with indignant slowness.* Now let neither of you turn to face Goody Proctor. No one in this room is to speak one word, or raise a gesture aye or nay. *He turns toward the door, calls:* Enter! *The door opens.* ELIZABETH *enters with* PARRIS. PARRIS *leaves her. She stands alone, her eyes looking for* PROCTOR. Mr. Cheever, report this testimony in all exactness. Are you ready? ❸

CHEEVER: Ready, sir.

DANFORTH: Come here, woman. ELIZABETH *comes to him, glancing at* PROCTOR's *back.* Look at me only, not at your husband. In my eyes only.

ELIZABETH, *faintly:* Good, sir.

DANFORTH: We are given to understand that at one time you dismissed your servant, Abigail Williams.

ELIZABETH: That is true, sir.

DANFORTH: For what cause did you dismiss her? *Slight pause. Then* ELIZABETH *tries to glance at*

◆ Build Vocabulary

blanched (blancht) *adj.*: Paled; whitened

Art Transparencies

To emphasize the differences between the Salem witch trials and contemporary American trials, use Art Transparency 3: *Trial by Jury* in ***Art Transparencies,*** p. 15. Painted by Thomas Hart Benton in 1964, this painting is typical of his works, in which figures are painted in a stylized manner with smooth limbs and clearly defined facial features. Benton received much formal training, having studied art at the Corcoran School of Art in Washington, D.C., the School of the Art Institute of Chicago, and the Académie Julien in Paris. This training is evident in the composition of the painting, in which the sharp perspective of the room draws the viewer into the scene. The artist's use of light draws attention to the lawyers arguing the case, the attentive jury, and the presiding judge.

Discuss the painting with students. Ask students to determine from the painting whether Benton has a positive or a negative opinion of the criminal justice system in America. Contrast Benton's depiction of a trial with the scene from *The Crucible* on this page. Discuss with students the difference in the emotional levels of Benton's depiction and the scene from *The Crucible.* Discuss what effect emotions might have on the outcome of a trial. Where is a defendant more likely to receive a fair verdict: in a trial dominated by reason or in a trial in which emotions run high?

Cross-Curricular Connection: Science

Hysteria When Abigail and her friends have "spells," one reason why Danforth and others believe they are genuine is the presence of symptoms like icy skin and convulsions, which are hard to fake. There is, though, an explanation for such symptoms that puts them in the realm of biology rather than witchcraft. This is a condition called *hysteria.* Hysteria was first described by the ancient Greek physician Hippocrates, for whom the Hippocratic Oath is named.

Hippocrates wrongly thought that hysteria affected women exclusively. It is a mental condition that manifests itself—in men and women—in various physical symptoms, including those of heart disease, paralysis, pain, vomiting, weakness, tics, and chills. The symptoms can be convincing enough for doctors to authorize surgery.

One way in which hysterical symptoms can be brought about is by the influence of a strong leader—like Abigail—on suggestible followers. Thus, when Mary Warren attempts to duplicate the symptoms on her own, she cannot do so.

◆ Critical Thinking

❶ **Analyze** Have students summarize Elizabeth's response to Danforth's question. Then have them explain what motivated this response. *Students should note that in explaining why she dismissed Abigail, Elizabeth shifts much of the blame from Abigail to herself. She does not tell Danforth about the affair between John and Abigail because she does not want to implicate her husband in any wrongdoing.*

◆ Background for Understanding

❷ **History** Point out that the church-derived laws of the Massachusetts Bay Colony at that time regarded lechery (adultery) not only as a sin, but also a serious crime that could be punished by long imprisonment or even death.

◆ Critical Thinking

❸ **Make Inferences** Ask students why Elizabeth despairs as soon as she realizes that John had already confessed to his relationship with Abigail. *Sample response: She realizes that, in contradicting John's testimony, she has made Abigail look like an innocent party who has been wronged. By unintentionally clearing Abigail in this way, she has actually worsened not only her own situation but also that of all the other accused persons who stood to be acquitted if Abigail was proven a liar.*

◆ Critical Thinking

❹ **Analyze** Ask students what qualities in Hale's character are brought out by this speech. *Responses might include: his willingness to stand up to the other court officials; his sense of fairness and justice; his insight into people's motives.*

◆ Literary Focus

❺ **Dramatic and Verbal Irony** Responses might include the following: *Danforth does not know that Proctor told the truth and Elizabeth did not; he does not know that Abigail has been orchestrating all of the apparent "fits and spells."*

PROCTOR. You will look in my eyes only and not at your husband. The answer is in your memory and you need no help to give it to me. Why did you dismiss Abigail Williams?

ELIZABETH, *not knowing what to say, sensing a situation, wetting her lips to stall for time:* She—dissatisfied me. *Pause.* And my husband.

DANFORTH: In what way dissatisfied you?

ELIZABETH: She were— *She glances at* PROCTOR *for a cue.*

DANFORTH: Woman, look at me? ELIZABETH *does.* Were she slovenly? Lazy? What disturbance did she cause?

❶ **ELIZABETH:** Your Honor, I—in that time I were sick. And I—My husband is a good and righteous man. He is never drunk as some are, nor wastin' his time at the shovelboard, but always at his work. But in my sickness—you see, sir, I were a long time sick after my last baby, and I thought I saw my husband somewhat turning from me. And this girl— *She turns to* ABIGAIL.

DANFORTH: Look at me.

ELIZABETH: Aye, sir. Abigail Williams— *She breaks off.*

DANFORTH: What of Abigail Williams?

ELIZABETH: I came to think he fancied her. And so one night I lost my wits, I think, and put her out on the highroad.

DANFORTH: Your husband—did he indeed turn from you?

ELIZABETH, *in agony:* My husband—is a goodly man, sir.

DANFORTH: Then he did not turn from you.

ELIZABETH, *starting to glance at* PROCTOR: He—

❷ **DANFORTH,** *reaches out and holds her face, then:* Look at me! To your own knowledge, has John Proctor ever committed the crime of lechery? *In a crisis of indecision she cannot speak.* Answer my question! Is your husband a lecher!

ELIZABETH, *faintly:* No, sir.

DANFORTH: Remove her, Marshal.

PROCTOR: Elizabeth, tell the truth!

DANFORTH: She has spoken. Remove her!

PROCTOR, *crying out:* Elizabeth, I have confessed it! ❸

ELIZABETH: Oh, God! *The door closes behind her.*

PROCTOR: She only thought to save my name!

HALE: Excellency, it is a natural lie to tell; I beg you, stop now before another is condemned! I may shut my conscience to it no more—private vengeance is working through this testimony! ❹ From the beginning this man has struck me true. By my oath to Heaven, I believe him now, and I pray you call back his wife before we—

DANFORTH: She spoke nothing of lechery, and this man has lied!

HALE: I believe him! *Pointing at* ABIGAIL: This girl has always struck me false! She has—

ABIGAIL, *with a weird, wild, chilling cry, screams up to the ceiling.*

ABIGAIL: You will not! Begone! Begone, I say!

DANFORTH: What is it, child? *But* ABIGAIL, *pointing with fear, is now raising up her frightened eyes, her awed face, toward the ceiling—the girls are doing the same—and now* HATHORNE, HALE, PUTNAM, CHEEVER, HERRICK, *and* DANFORTH *do the same.* What's there? *He lowers his eyes from the ceiling, and now he is frightened; there is real tension in his voice.* Child! *She is transfixed—with all the girls, she is whimpering, open-mouthed, agape at the ceiling.* Girls! Why do you—?

MERCY LEWIS, *pointing:* It's on the beam! Behind the rafter!

DANFORTH, *looking up:* Where!

ABIGAIL: Why—? *She gulps.* Why do you come, yellow bird?

PROCTOR: Where's a bird? I see no bird!

ABIGAIL, *to the ceiling:* My face? My face?

PROCTOR: Mr. Hale—

DANFORTH: Be quiet!

PROCTOR, *to* HALE: Do you see a bird?

DANFORTH: Be quiet!!

> **◆ Literary Focus**
> What does the audience know that Danforth does not know? ❺

ABIGAIL, *to the ceiling, in a genuine conversation with the "bird," as though trying to talk it out of attacking her:* But God made my face; you cannot want to tear my face. Envy is a deadly sin, Mary.

MARY WARREN, *on her feet with a spring, and horrified, pleading:* Abby!

ABIGAIL, *unperturbed, continuing to the "bird":* Oh, Mary, this is a black art to change your shape. No, I cannot, I cannot stop my mouth; it's God's work I do. 6

MARY WARREN: Abby, I'm *here!*

PROCTOR, *frantically:* They're pretending, Mr. Danforth!

ABIGAIL—*now she takes a backward step, as though in fear the bird will swoop down momentarily:* Oh, please, Mary! Don't come down.

SUSANNA WALCOTT: Her claws, she's stretching her claws!

PROCTOR: Lies, lies.

ABIGAIL, *backing further, eyes still fixed above:* Mary, please don't hurt me!

MARY WARREN, *to* DANFORTH: I'm not hurting her!

DANFORTH, *to* MARY WARREN: Why does she see this vision?

MARY WARREN: She sees nothin'!

ABIGAIL, *now staring full front as though hypnotized, and mimicking the exact tone of* MARY WARREN'S *cry:* She sees nothin'!

MARY WARREN, *pleading:* Abby, you mustn't!

ABIGAIL AND ALL THE GIRLS, *all transfixed:* Abby, you mustn't!

MARY WARREN, *to all the girls:* I'm here, I'm here!

GIRLS: I'm here, I'm here!

DANFORTH, *horrified:* Mary Warren! Draw back your spirit out of them!

MARY WARREN: Mr. Danforth!

GIRLS, *cutting her off:* Mr. Danforth!

DANFORTH: Have you compacted with the Devil? Have you?

MARY WARREN: Never, never!

GIRLS: Never, never!

DANFORTH, *growing hysterical:* Why can they only repeat you?

PROCTOR: Give me a whip—I'll stop it!

MARY WARREN: They're sporting. They—!

GIRLS: They're sporting!

MARY WARREN, *turning on them all hysterically and stamping her feet:* Abby, stop it!

GIRLS, *stamping their feet:* Abby, stop it!

MARY WARREN: Stop it!

GIRLS: Stop it!

MARY WARREN, *screaming it out at the top of her lungs, and raising her fists:* Stop it!!

GIRLS, *raising their fists:* Stop it!!

MARY WARREN, *utterly confounded, and becoming overwhelmed by* ABIGAIL'S*—and the girls'—utter conviction, starts to whimper, hands half raised, powerless, and all the girls begin whimpering exactly as she does.*

DANFORTH: A little while ago you were afflicted. Now it seems you afflict others; where did you find this power? 7 8

MARY WARREN, *staring at* ABIGAIL: I—have no power.

GIRLS: I have no power.

PROCTOR: They're gulling[7] you, Mister!

DANFORTH: Why did you turn about this past two weeks? You have seen the Devil, have you not?

HALE, *indicating* ABIGAIL *and the* GIRLS: You cannot believe them!

MARY WARREN: I—

PROCTOR, *sensing her weakening:* Mary, God damns all liars!

DANFORTH, *pounding it into her:* You have seen the Devil, you have made compact with Lucifer, have you not?

PROCTOR: God damns liars, Mary!

---

7. **gulling:** Fooling.

◆ Literary Focus

6 Dramatic and Verbal Irony Ask students what type of irony Abigail's words represent. Have them explain their answers. *Students should indicate that by this point in the play readers are well aware that Abigail is not doing "God's work" but rather is driven by her own selfish and wicked motives. The contrast between what readers know and what several onlookers in the scene believe, including the judges, makes this passage an example of dramatic irony.*

◆ Critical Thinking

7 Analyze Encourage students to analyze the pressures under which Mary Warren finds herself at this point. *Sample response: The other girls are subjecting her to psychological torture by imitating her. At the same time, Danforth continues his harsh and leading interrogation, and Proctor continues to insist that she tell the truth. Mary is being tormented on all sides and must feel isolated and terrified.*

◆ Critical Thinking

8 Speculate Ask students if they think that Mary is about to turn away from John Proctor and rejoin Abby and the other girls. How does Miller make it clear that Mary is weakening? *Sample response: Mary may be about to turn away from Proctor and rejoin the girls because she is pressured by both the mimicking girls and the tough interrogation by Danforth. Miller makes it clear that Mary is weakening by having Mary scream "Stop it!!" and begin to whimper and by saying directly in the stage directions that Proctor can sense that Mary is weakening.*

Cross-Curricular Connection: History

Theocracy A government headed by religious authorities, with laws determined by the dictates of a particular religion or sect, is called a *theocracy.*

The Massachusetts Bay Colony was not begun as a theocracy, but a group of Puritans led by John Winthrop left Britain in 1630, determined to make it so. Winthrop and his allies wanted to create a model of the Puritan ideal for the world to emulate. They saw to it that only male members of their church, the Congregational Church, could vote and hold office. Congregational ministers defined the nature of lawful behavior. Dissent was not tolerated and led to severe punishment or expulsion. The best-known exiles were Anne Hutchinson and Roger Williams, who started a less restrictive colony, Rhode Island.

The end of the 1600's saw an easing of theocracy in the colony, due in part to growing public outcry over the Salem trials and their outcome.

◆ Critical Thinking

1 Synthesize Ask students to explain Mary's sudden shift in attitude. *Students may cite her sense of isolation from the rest of the girls and the pressure that has been applied to her from all sides, including the threat of hanging.*

◆ Literary Focus

2 Dramatic and Verbal Irony
Suggested response: *The words are "infinite charity." These words name a force that is quite opposite to the forces that drive Abigail.*

Customize for *AP Students*

Have students compare and contrast Mary Warren's sudden confession with Tituba's sudden confession in Act I. Suggest that students consider both the content of the confessions and the circumstances under which they were made.

◆ Background for Understanding

Literature When Miller's play was first performed, a number of critics claimed that the characters were simply "mouthpieces" for Miller's ideas. Among these critics was Walter Kerr, who wrote: "There are many times at the [performance] when one's intellectual sympathies go out to Mr. Miller and to his apt symbols of anguish on stage. But it is the intellect which goes out, not the heart."

"For Salem, and the people who live, love, fear, and die in it, are really only conveniences to Mr. Miller, props to his theme. He does not make them interesting in and for themselves, and you wind up analyzing them, checking their dilemmas against the latest headlines, rather than losing yourself in any rounded, deeply rewarding personalities."

Have students respond to Kerr's statement, explaining why they do or do not agree with it.

MARY *utters something unintelligible, staring at* ABIGAIL, *who keeps watching the "bird" above.*

DANFORTH: I cannot hear you. What do you say? MARY *utters again unintelligibly.* You will confess yourself or you will hang! *He turns her roughly to face him.* Do you know who I am? I say you will hang if you do not open with me!

PROCTOR: Mary, remember the angel Raphael—do that which is good and—

ABIGAIL, *pointing upward:* The wings! Her wings are spreading! Mary, please, don't, don't—!

HALE: I see nothing, Your Honor!

DANFORTH: Do you confess this power! *He is an inch from her face.* Speak!

ABIGAIL: She's going to come down! She's walking the beam!

DANFORTH: Will you speak!

MARY WARREN, *staring in horror:* I cannot!

GIRLS: I cannot!

PARRIS: Cast the Devil out! Look him in the face! Trample him! We'll save you, Mary, only stand fast against him and—

ABIGAIL, *looking up:* Look out! She's coming down!

She and all the girls run to one wall, shielding their eyes. And now, as though cornered, they let out a gigantic scream, and MARY, *as though infected, opens her mouth and screams with them. Gradually* ABIGAIL *and the girls leave off, until only* MARY *is left there, staring up at the "bird," screaming madly. All watch her, horrified by this evident fit.* PROCTOR *strides to her.*

PROCTOR: Mary, tell the Governor what they—*He has hardly got a word out, when, seeing him coming for her, she rushes out of his reach, screaming in horror.*

1 **MARY WARREN:** Don't touch me—don't touch me! *At which the girls halt at the door.*

PROCTOR, *astonished:* Mary!

MARY WARREN, *pointing at* PROCTOR: You're the Devil's man!

He is stopped in his tracks.

PARRIS: Praise God!

GIRLS: Praise God!

PROCTOR, *numbed:* Mary, how— ?

MARY WARREN: I'll not hang with you! I love God, I love God.

DANFORTH, *to* MARY: He bid you do the Devil's work?

MARY WARREN, *hysterically, indicating* PROCTOR: He come at me by night and every day to sign, to sign, to—

DANFORTH: Sign what?

PARRIS: The Devil's book? He come with a book?

MARY WARREN, *hysterically, pointing at* PROCTOR, *fearful of him:* My name, he want my name. "I'll murder you," he says, "if my wife hangs! We must go and overthrow the court," he says!

DANFORTH'S *head jerks toward* PROCTOR, *shock and horror in his face.*

PROCTOR, *turning, appealing to* HALE: Mr. Hale!

MARY WARREN, *her sobs beginning:* He wake me every night, his eyes were like coals and his fingers claw my neck, and I sign, I sign . . .

HALE: Excellency, this child's gone wild!

PROCTOR, *as* DANFORTH'S *wide eyes pour on him:* Mary, Mary!

MARY WARREN, *screaming at him:* No, I love God; I go your way no more. I love God, I bless God. *Sobbing, she rushes to* ABIGAIL. Abby, Abby, I'll never hurt you more!

They all watch, as ABIGAIL, *out of her infinite charity, reaches out and draws the sobbing* MARY *to her, and then looks up to* DANFORTH.

> **◆ Literary Focus**
> Which two words in these stage directions are an example of verbal irony? 2

DANFORTH, *to* PROCTOR: What are you? PROCTOR *is beyond speech in his anger.* You are combined with anti-Christ,[8] are you not? I have seen your power; you will not deny it! What say you, Mister?

HALE: Excellency—

8. **anti-Christ:** In the Bible, the great antagonist of Christ expected to spread universal evil.

DANFORTH: I will have nothing from you, Mr. Hale! *To* PROCTOR: Will you confess yourself befouled with Hell, or do you keep that black allegiance yet? What say you?

PROCTOR, *his mind wild, breathless:* I say—I say—God is dead!

PARRIS: Hear it, hear it!

PROCTOR, *laughs insanely, then:* A fire, a fire is burning! I hear the boot of Lucifer, I see his filthy face! And it is my face, and yours, Danforth! For them that quail to bring men out of ignorance, as I have quailed, and as you quail now when you know in all your black hearts that this be fraud—God damns our kind especially, and we will burn, we will burn together.

DANFORTH: Marshal! Take him and Corey with him to the jail!

HALE, *staring across to the door:* I denounce these proceedings!

PROCTOR: You are pulling Heaven down and raising up a whore!

HALE: I denounce these proceedings, I quit this court! *He slams the door to the outside behind him.*

DANFORTH, *calling to him in a fury:* Mr. Hale! Mr. Hale!

> ◆ **Reading Strategy**
> If you were classifying characters as static (unchanging) and dynamic (changing or growing), in which category would you place Reverend Hale? Why?

Guide for Responding

◆ Literature and Your Life

Reader's Response What incident in Act III provoked the strongest emotional response in you? Why?

Thematic Focus What dangers of the legal system does Act III point out?

Class Debate Hold an informal debate on this issue: Who bears more guilt for the fate of those hanged in the Salem witch trials—the young girls who accused innocent people or the judges and magistrates who sentenced them to death?

☑ Check Your Comprehension

1. Which three depositions are presented to the court?
2. Cory charges that Putnam is "killing his neighbors for their land." What does Danforth demand as proof?
3. Summarize the events leading to John Proctor's arrest.
4. After rejoining the other girls in their hysterical behavior, what accusation does Mary make about Proctor?
5. What does Reverend Hale denounce at the end of Act III?

◆ Critical Thinking

INTERPRET

1. How do the judges effectively discourage anyone from defending the good character or innocence of a person accused of witchcraft? Support your answer with an incident or quotation from the play. **[Analyze; Support]**
2. What does Proctor's decision to confess his involvement with Abigail reveal about his character? **[Infer]**
3. (a) Why does Elizabeth Proctor lie when questioned by Danforth? (b) What are the consequences of her lie? **[Analyze]**
4. Why does Mary Warren change her testimony and turn on John Proctor? **[Analyze]**

EVALUATE

5. Do you find Hale sympathetic? Why or why not? **[Evaluate]**

APPLY

6. Imagine that Elizabeth Proctor had told Danforth the truth. How might the outcome of the witchcraft hysteria have been different? **[Modify]**

EXTEND

7. Which qualities of a good judge do you think are lacking in Hathorne and Danforth? **[Career Link]**

◆ Reading Strategy

❸ Categorize Characters by Role Sample response: Hale is a dynamic character. His awareness of the unjust nature of the court has been growing throughout the act. At the end, he takes a bold and unexpected stand by denouncing the proceedings.

Reinforce and Extend

Answers

◆ Literature and Your Life

Reader's Response Accept all reasonable responses.

Thematic Focus Judges with preconceived notions can be very dangerous; public opinion is a poor court; hysteria or other excess emotion can be very dangerous in a court of law.

☑ Check Your Comprehension

1. Presented are citizens' good opinions of Martha Corey and Rebecca Nurse; Giles Corey's accusation that Thomas Putnam's accusations of witchcraft are motivated by greed; and Mary Warren's retraction of her testimony and claim that the other girls' charges of witchcraft are fraudulent.
2. Danforth demands as proof the name of the man who heard Putnam's intentions.
3. The key events leading to the arrest of John Proctor are Elizabeth's failure—in order to protect her husband from charges of adultery—to corroborate her husband's true admission that he had an affair with Abigail; Mary Warren's recantation—due to pressure from the girls—of her true statement that she lied; and Mary Warren's statement that John Proctor was the "Devil's man."
4. Mary accuses John Proctor of being a witch.
5. Reverend Hale denounces the court proceedings.

◆ Critical Thinking

1. The judges discourage people by making it likely that defenders might also be accused. The judge's admonition that anyone who is not *for* the court is *against* it illustrates this.
2. It shows that he is basically a good person who is willing to tell the truth, regardless of the consequences to himself.
3. (a) She lies because she does not want to humiliate her husband publicly. (b) Abigail's testimony is regarded as truth, and those she accused are considered witches.
4. Mary changes her testimony and turns on John because of the pressure of mimicry from the other girls that makes Mary appear to be a witch.
5. Sample response: Hale is sympathetic because he carefully listens to the testimony with an open mind, comes to believe the defendants, and denounces the court proceedings.
6. If Elizabeth had told the truth, Abigail's testimony would probably have been thrown out and all of the convicted "witches" would have been freed.
7. Suggested response: Danforth and Hathorne are not fair and objective.

Answers

◆ Reading Strategy

1. Have students explain the thinking behind their charts.
2. Sample response: Two possible categories are sympathetic and unsympathetic.

◆ Literary Focus

1. Examples include Parris's comment "Praise God!" when John Proctor is denounced and Proctor's bitter "God is dead" and "A fire, a fire is burning! I hear the boot of Lucifer; I see his filthy face! And it is my face, and yours, Danforth!" at the end of the act.
2. (a) John has already confessed to adultery, has told the court she never lies, and expects her to tell the truth. (b) She lies to protect her husband from the charge of adultery, thereby nullifying his testimony.

◆ Grammar and Style

Subject-Verb Agreement in Inverted Sentences

1. is, scene
2. sit, townspeople
3. are, Danforth and Hathorne
4. are, Abigail and her cohorts

◆ Build Vocabulary

Legal Terms

1. prosecutor: lawyer who argues the case against the accused
2. witness: someone who testifies in court under oath
3. contempt: open and punishable disrespect or disobedience in a court of law
4. perjury: lying under oath

Using the Word Bank

1. synonyms; 2. synonyms;
3. antonyms; 4. synonyms;
5. antonyms; 6. antonyms;
7. antonyms; 8. synonyms;
9. synonyms; 10. antonyms

Idea Bank

Customizing for
Performance Levels

Following are suggestions for matching Idea Bank topics with your students' performance levels:
Less Advanced Students: 1
Average Students: 2
More Advanced Students: 3

Guide for Responding, Act III (continued)

◆ Reading Strategy

CATEGORIZE CHARACTERS BY ROLE

As you've seen, the characters in the play can be classified into different categories according to their roles.

1. Organize a chart to categorize the characters in the play. You may categorize according to their attitudes toward the witchcraft trials or their roles in the trials: accuser and accused, or judge and other officials, for example.
2. What other categories, if any, do you think would be useful for classifying the characters? Explain.

◆ Literary Focus

DRAMATIC AND VERBAL IRONY

Irony arises when there is a discrepancy between the way things seem and the way they really are. In **dramatic irony,** there is a contrast between what a character thinks is true and what the audience knows. In **verbal irony,** words that seem to say one thing actually mean something quite different.

1. Find two examples of verbal irony in the dialogue in Act III. Explain what each speaker really means.
2. Consider the dramatic irony that occurs when Elizabeth testifies about her husband's behavior. (a) What does she not know that the audience knows? (b) Why is the effect of her testimony so ironic?

◆ Grammar and Style

SUBJECT AND VERB AGREEMENT IN INVERTED SENTENCES

In an **inverted sentence,** the common subject-verb order of a sentence is reversed. Even in an inverted sentence, a **verb** should **agree** in number with its **subject.**

Practice In your notebook, complete each sentence by choosing the correct form of the verb in parentheses and underlining the subject.

1. There (is, are) a courtroom scene in Act III of *The Crucible.*
2. In the courtroom (sits, sit) many townspeople.
3. Hearing the case (is, are) Danforth and Hathorne.
4. Here (is, are) Abigail and her cohorts.

◆ Build Vocabulary

LEGAL TERMS

The Crucible contains many terms from the specialized vocabulary of trials and the law. Determine the meaning of each of these words from the context in which it appears in Act III, and then use it in a sentence about a modern trial.

1. prosecutor
2. witness
3. contempt
4. perjury

USING THE WORD BANK: Synonym or Antonym?

For each item, indicate whether the paired words are synonyms or antonyms. Write your answers on a separate sheet of paper.

1. contentious, combative
2. deposition, testimony
3. imperceptible, obvious
4. deferentially, politely
5. anonymity, notoriety
6. prodigious, minuscule
7. effrontery, timidity
8. confounded, puzzled
9. incredulously, disbelievingly
10. blanched, darkened

Idea Bank

Writing

1. **Character Sketch** Write a character sketch of Mary Warren in which you describe her personality, including her strengths and weaknesses. Is she essentially good, bad, or just weak?
2. **Letter to the Editor** By the end of Act III, Reverend Hale has openly denounced the court he once supported. As Hale, write a letter to the editor of the *Salem Voice* in which you explain why you now oppose the court's actions.

Speaking, Listening, and Viewing

3. **Soliloquy** Show how Elizabeth Proctor might react when she learns the effects of her lie. Present her private thoughts in a soliloquy—a monologue she delivers while she is alone on stage.

✓ ASSESSMENT OPTIONS

Formal Assessment, Selection Test, pp. 332–334, and Assessment Resources Software. The selection test is designed so that it can be easily customized to the performance levels of your students.
Alternative Assessment, p. 78, includes options for less advanced students, more advanced students, intrapersonal learners, verbal/linguistic learners, and logical/mathematical learners.

PORTFOLIO ASSESSMENT
Use the following rubrics in the ***Alternative Assessment*** booklet to assess student writing:
Character Sketch: Description Rubric, p. 112
Letter to the Editor: Persuasion Rubric, p. 120

Guide for Interpreting, Act IV

◆ Review and Anticipate

"Is every defense an attack upon the court?" Hale asks in Act III; and Danforth observes, "A person is either with this court or he must be counted against it." Such remarks stress how little people like John Proctor and Giles Corey can do against the mounting injustices in Salem. Instead, their efforts backfire, and their own names join the list of those accused. What do you think the final outcome will be? Who will survive, and who will perish? Read the final act to see if your predictions are correct.

◆ Reading Strategy

Apply Themes to Contemporary Events

The Crucible was written during the McCarthy era of the 1950's, when fear of Communism swept America. The fears were understandable—eastern Europe and China had recently fallen to Communism—but they were also exploited for political ends. In Congress, a Republican senator named Joseph McCarthy leapt into the limelight when he charged that the State Department had been infiltrated by more than two hundred Communists. Leading a Senate investigation, McCarthy often charged that those who opposed his hearings were themselves Communists and began investigating them. The parallels between the Salem events, as Miller depicts them, and ongoing events in Congress at the time Miller wrote the play are clear. As you read Act IV, think about what **themes**, or messages, Miller was conveying that specifically **related to current events** of the time.

◆ Grammar and Style

Commonly Confused Words: *Raise* and *Rise*

Be careful not to confuse the verbs *raise* and *rise*. *Raise*, meaning "to lift up," always has a direct object, a noun or pronoun that receives the action of the verb. In contrast *rise*, meaning "to go up or get up," never has a direct object.

She *raises* the flask. [*flask* is direct object]
You'll never *rise* off the ground. [no direct object]

Forms of *raise*	*raise* or *raises, raising, raised,* (have) *raised*
Forms of *rise*	*rise* or *rises, rising, rose,* (have) *risen*

◆ Literary Focus

Theme

A **theme** is a central idea or insight into life that a writer tries to convey in a work of literature. Like most longer works, *The Crucible* has several themes. One theme is that fear and suspicion are infectious and can swell into a mass hysteria that destroys public order and rationality. As you read Act IV, consider how this theme is conveyed through the comments and actions of the characters. In addition, look for other themes, such as the idea that people can commit evil deeds in the name of good.

◆ Build Vocabulary

Words From Myths: *Tantalize*

In Greek mythology, the gods punished King Tantalus for his crimes. They placed him in a pool of water that shrank away whenever he tried to drink it. Fruit hanging above him receded whenever he tried to reach it. From this myth comes the word *tantalize*, which means "to entice with something that cannot be reached or achieved; to tease only to frustrate."

Word Bank

Preview this list of words from Act IV.

agape
conciliatory
beguile
floundering
retaliation
adamant
cleave
sibilance
tantalized
purged

LESSON OBJECTIVES

1. **To develop vocabulary and word identification skills**
   - Words From Myths: *Tantalize*
   - Using the Word Bank: *Synonyms*
2. **To use a variety of reading strategies to comprehend a drama**
   - Review and Anticipate
3. **To increase knowledge of other cultures and to connect common elements across cultures**
   - Cultural Connection (ATE)
   - Cross-Curricular Connection: Social Studies (ATE)
4. **To express and support responses to the text**
   - Critical Thinking
   - Idea Bank: Memorial
   - Idea Bank: Casting Profiles
   - Idea Bank: Critical Response
5. **To analyze literary elements**
   - Literary Focus: Theme
   - Reading Strategy: Apply Theme to Contemporary Events
   - Idea Bank: Literary Analysis
6. **To research self-selected and assigned topics and produce reports in a variety of forms**
   - Idea Bank: Compare-and-Contrast Chart
   - Beyond the Classroom: Career Connection (ATE)
7. **To plan, prepare, organize, and present literary interpretations**
   - Idea Bank: Group Discussion
   - Idea Bank: Mock Trial
   - Speaking, Listening, and Viewing Mini-Lesson (ATE)
8. **To increase knowledge of the rules of grammar and usage**
   - Grammar and Style: Commonly Confused Words: *Raise* and *Rise*

Interest Grabber Students may be familiar with television shows or movies in which a suspect lies in order to escape punishment. Point out to students that in this act of *The Crucible*, John Proctor faces death if he tells the truth. Read these lines from the play aloud:

Proctor: I want my life.

Hathorne *electrified, surprised:* You'll confess yourself?

Proctor: I will have my life.

Explain that Proctor's inner battle is between his honor and his desire to live. Have students discuss whether they believe, based on their knowledge of Proctor's character, that he will lie to save himself.

Prentice Hall Literature Program Resources

REINFORCE / RETEACH / EXTEND

Selection Support Pages
Build Vocabulary: Words From Myths, p. 350
Grammar and Style: *Raise* and *Rise*, p. 351
Reading Strategy: Apply Themes to Contemporary Events, p. 352
Literary Focus: Theme, p. 353

Strategies for Diverse Student Needs, p. 79

Beyond Literature
Workplace Skills: Research, p. 79

Formal Assessment Selection Test, pp. 335–337; Assessment Resources Software

Alternative Assessment, p. 79

Writing and Language Transparencies
Argument Organizer, p. 75

Resource Pro CD-ROM
The Crucible, Act IV

Literature CD-ROM
The History of American Literature: Part 2, Disk 2, Feature 4; *How to Read and Understand Drama,* Feature 12

Develop Understanding

One-Minute Insight In this final act of *The Crucible,* the action builds to a climax as the judges force John Proctor to decide whether he will live or die. Proctor must search his soul to discover if he is strong enough to face death rather than be dishonest. You might point out to students that in the McCarthy era, people brought before the Senate committee did not face death, but their decision—whether to remain silent or to name names—was enough to ruin their careers and devastate their families and friends.

Customize for
Less Proficient Readers
John Proctor is perhaps the most complex character in the play. To help students understand his character, have them create a chart showing how Proctor's character changes over time. For each act, they can list character traits, along with quotations that reveal the traits.

Customize for
Bodily/Kinesthetic Learners
Students who learn best through movement might benefit from acting out key scenes in Act IV. Encourage them to perform the scene with Hale and Danforth on pages 1158 and 1159, and the scene between Elizabeth and John Proctor on pages 1161–1163.

Comprehension Check ☑

❶ Who is Sarah Good talking about in this scene? *She is talking about the devil.*

ACT IV

A cell in Salem jail, that fall.

At the back is a high barred window; near it, a great, heavy door. Along the walls are two benches.

The place is in darkness but for the moonlight seeping through the bars. It appears empty. Presently footsteps are heard coming down a corridor beyond the wall, keys rattle, and the door swings open. MARSHAL HERRICK *enters with a lantern.*

He is nearly drunk, and heavy-footed. He goes to a bench and nudges a bundle of rags lying on it.

HERRICK: Sarah, wake up! Sarah Good! *He then crosses to the other benches.*

SARAH GOOD, *rising in her rags:* Oh, Majesty! Comin', comin'! Tituba, he's here, His Majesty's come! ❶

HERRICK: Go to the north cell; this place is wanted now. *He hangs his lantern on the wall.* TITUBA *sits up.*

TITUBA: That don't look to me like His Majesty; look to me like the marshal.

HERRICK, *taking out a flask:* Get along with you now, clear this place. *He drinks, and* SARAH GOOD *comes and peers up into his face.*

SARAH GOOD: Oh, is it you, Marshal! I thought sure you be the devil comin' for us. Could I have a sip of cider for me goin'-away?

HERRICK, *handing her the flask:* And where are you off to, Sarah?

TITUBA, *as* SARAH *drinks:* We goin' to Barbados, soon the Devil gits here with the feathers and the wings.

HERRICK: Oh? A happy voyage to you.

SARAH GOOD: A pair of bluebirds wingin' southerly, the two of us! Oh, it be a grand transformation, Marshal! *She raises the flask to drink again.*

HERRICK, *taking the flask from her lips:* You'd best give me that or you'll never rise off the ground. Come along now.

TITUBA: I'll speak to him for you, if you desires to come along, Marshal.

HERRICK: I'd not refuse it, Tituba; it's the proper morning to fly into Hell.

TITUBA: Oh, it be no Hell in Barbados. Devil, him be pleasure man in Barbados, him be singin' and dancin' in Barbados. It's you folks—you riles him up 'round here; it be too cold 'round here for that Old Boy. He freeze his soul in Massachusetts, but in Barbados he just as sweet and—*A bellowing cow is heard, and* TITUBA *leaps up and calls to the window:* Aye, sir! That's him, Sarah!

Test Preparation Workshop

Writing Skills: Grammar and Usage
Many standardized tests require students to identify errors in punctuation, capitalization, or spelling. Use the following sample test item to give students practice in this skill.

The playwright Arthur Miller wrote *The Crucible*, to communicate a message about mass hysteria.

A Spelling error
B Punctuation error
C Capitalization error
D No error

Guide students to see that a comma is incorrectly placed after the title of the play. Students should indicate the error by choosing B.

SARAH GOOD: I'm here, Majesty! *They hurriedly pick up their rags as* HOPKINS, *a guard, enters.*

HOPKINS: The Deputy Governor's arrived.

HERRICK, *grabbing* TITUBA: Come along, come along.

TITUBA, *resisting him:* No, he comin' for me. I
2 goin' home!

3 **HERRICK,** *pulling her to the door:* That's not Satan, just a poor old cow with a hatful of milk. Come along now, out with you!

TITUBA, *calling to the window:* Take me home, Devil! Take me home!

SARAH GOOD, *following the shouting* TITUBA *out:* Tell him I'm goin', Tituba! Now you tell him Sarah Good is goin' too!

In the corridor outside TITUBA *calls on—"Take me home, Devil: Devil take me home!" and* HOPKINS' *voice orders her to move on.* HERRICK *returns and begins to push old rags and straw into a corner. Hearing footsteps, he turns, and enter* DANFORTH *and* JUDGE HATHORNE. *They are in greatcoats and wear hats against the bitter cold. They are followed in by* CHEEVER, *who carries a dispatch case and a flat wooden box containing his writing materials.*

HERRICK: Good morning, Excellency.

DANFORTH: Where is Mr. Parris?

HERRICK: I'll fetch him. *He starts for the door.*

DANFORTH: Marshal. HERRICK *stops.* When did Reverend Hale arrive?

HERRICK: It were toward midnight, I think.

DANFORTH, *suspiciously:* What is he about here?

HERRICK: He goes among them that will hang, sir. And he prays with them. He sits with
4 Goody Nurse now. And Mr. Parris with him.

DANFORTH: Indeed. That man have no authority to enter here, Marshal. Why have you let him in?

HERRICK: Why, Mr. Parris command me, sir.

I cannot deny him.

DANFORTH: Are you drunk, Marshal?

HERRICK: No, sir; it is a bitter night, and I have no fire here.

DANFORTH, *containing his anger:* Fetch Mr. Parris.

HERRICK: Aye, sir.

DANFORTH: There is a prodigious stench in this place.

HERRICK: I have only now cleared the people out for you.

DANFORTH: Beware hard drink, Marshal.

HERRICK: Aye, sir. *He waits an instant for further orders. But* DANFORTH, *in dissatisfaction, turns his back on him, and* HERRICK *goes out. There is a pause.* DANFORTH *stands in thought.*

HATHORNE: Let you question Hale, Excellency; I should not be surprised he have been preaching in Andover lately.

DANFORTH: We'll come to that; speak nothing of Andover. Parris prays with him. That's strange. *He blows on his hands, moves toward the window, and looks out.*

HATHORNE: Excellency, I wonder if it be wise to let Mr. Parris so continuously with the prisoners. DANFORTH *turns to him, interested.* I think, sometimes, the man has a mad look these days. 5

DANFORTH: Mad?

HATHORNE: I met him yesterday coming out of his house, and I bid him good morning—and he wept and went his way. I think it is not well the village sees him so unsteady.

DANFORTH: Perhaps he have some sorrow.

CHEEVER, *stamping his feet against the cold:* I think it be the cows, sir.

DANFORTH: Cows?

CHEEVER: There be so many cows wanderin' the highroads, now their masters are in the jails, and much disagreement who they will belong to now. I know Mr. Parris be arguin' with farmers all yesterday—there is great contention, sir, about the cows. Contention make him weep, sir; it were always a man that weep for contention. *He turns, as do* HATHORNE *and* DANFORTH

Comprehension Check ☑

2 What seems to have happened to Tituba and Sarah Good? *They seem to have gone mad from being in prison a long time.*

◆ Background for Understanding

3 **History** Tell students that Tituba, whose character is last seen at this point in the play, spent the entire period of the trials languishing in jail. She was released in May of 1693 and sold by Samuel Parris. He used the proceeds of her sale to pay her prison fees.

◆ Critical Thinking

4 **Draw Conclusions** Have students discuss how Danforth's attitude toward Reverend Hale has changed. What has brought about this change? *Sample response: Danforth no longer perceives Reverend Hale as a friend. The change has come about because Hale's visits with the prisoners underscore the fact that he believes the trial was unfair and led to unjust verdicts.*

◆ Literary Focus

5 **Theme** Draw students' attention to Hathorne's description of Parris. Encourage them to speculate on what theme Miller might be raising here. *Students may say that Miller is raising the theme of guilt—Parris's participation in the trials has apparently taken a heavy toll on him.*

Block Scheduling Strategies

Consider these suggestions to take advantage of extended class time:

- Introduce the concept of theme by discussing the Literary Focus on page 1153. After students have read Act IV, have them complete the Literary Focus activities on page 1168. For more practice, use ***Selection Support,*** p. 353.
- After students have read the play, arrange for them to view all or part of the 1996 film version of *The Crucible*. Encourage them to discuss how the film compares with the text of the play.
- Arrange students in small groups to answer the Critical Thinking questions on page 1167.
- Encourage one or more groups of students to undertake the Group Discussion project outlined in the Speaking, Listening, and Viewing section of the Idea Bank, p. 1169. The information that the groups present will help students apply the themes that Miller raises to the McCarthy era.
- Suggest that students who are interested in the history of the Salem witchcraft trials work with partners to research and present compare-and-contrast charts, as outlined in the Projects section of the Idea Bank, p. 1169.

◆ Reading Strategy

❶ Apply Themes to Contemporary Events Students should note that the situation in Salem has deteriorated—the town seems to be in a constant state of chaos and contention. Miller may be warning that the anti-Communist hysteria will lead to similar results.

◆ Critical Thinking

❷ Analyze Ask students if they think Reverend Hale wants the prisoners to lie. Encourage them to give reasons to support their answers. *Students may recall that at the end of Act III, Hale denounced the court's proceedings. In his view, therefore, any confessions made at this point would be lies. He nevertheless urges the prisoners to confess to save their lives.*

◆ Critical Thinking

❸ Interpret What does Parris mean when he says that Abigail "had close knowledge of the town"? What does this knowledge have to do with her sudden departure? *Suggested response: He means that Abigail has a good sense of what was going on and what people were thinking. She must have sensed that the people of Salem, having heard about the events in Andover, would soon change their attitudes and turn against her.*

Comprehension Check ☑

❹ Ask students why they think Danforth is so insistent about there being no rebellion in Andover. *The failure of the witch trials in Andover is a threat to Danforth's authority in Salem. He fears that the same thing might happen there.*

◆ Reading Strategy ❶ What warning may the details about changes in Salem convey about the growing anti-Communist fear and suspicion in Miller's own time?

hearing someone coming up the corridor. DANFORTH *raises his head as* PARRIS *enters. He is gaunt, frightened, and sweating in his greatcoat.*

PARRIS, *to* DANFORTH, *instantly:* Oh, good morning, sir, thank you for coming. I beg your pardon wakin' you so early. Good morning, Judge Hathorne.

DANFORTH: Reverend Hale have no right to enter this—

PARRIS: Excellency, a moment. *He hurries back and shuts the door.*

HATHORNE: Do you leave him alone with the prisoners?

DANFORTH: What's his business here?

PARRIS, *prayerfully holding up his hands:* Excellency, hear me. It is a providence. Reverend Hale has returned to bring Rebecca Nurse to God.

DANFORTH, *surprised:* He bids her confess?

❷ **PARRIS,** *sitting:* Hear me. Rebecca have not given me a word this three month since she came. Now she sits with him, and her sister and Martha Corey and two or three others, and he pleads with them, confess their crimes and save their lives.

DANFORTH: Why—this is indeed a providence. And they soften, they soften?

PARRIS: Not yet, not yet. But I thought to summon you, sir, that we might think on whether it be not wise, to—*He dares not say it.* I had thought to put a question, sir, and I hope you will not—

DANFORTH: Mr. Parris, be plain, what troubles you?

PARRIS: There is news, sir, that the court—the court must reckon with. My niece, sir, my niece—I believe she has vanished.

DANFORTH: Vanished!

PARRIS: I had thought to advise you of it earlier in the week, but—

DANFORTH: Why? How long is she gone?

PARRIS: This be the third night. You see, sir, she told me she would stay a night with Mercy Lewis. And next day, when she does not return, I send to Mr. Lewis to inquire. Mercy told him she would sleep in *my* house for a night.

DANFORTH: They are both gone?!

PARRIS, *in fear of him:* They are, sir.

DANFORTH, *alarmed:* I will send a party for them. Where may they be?

PARRIS: Excellency, I think they be aboard a ship. DANFORTH *stands agape.* My daughter tells me how she heard them speaking of ships last week, and tonight I discover my—my strongbox is broke into. *He presses his fingers against his eyes to keep back tears.*

HATHORNE, *astonished:* She have robbed you?

PARRIS: Thirty-one pound is gone. I am penniless. *He covers his face and sobs.*

DANFORTH: Mr. Parris, you are a brainless man! *He walks in thought, deeply worried.*

PARRIS: Excellency, it profit nothing you should blame me. I cannot think they would run off except they fear to keep in Salem any more. *He is pleading.* Mark it, sir, Abigail had close knowledge of the town, and since the news of Andover[1] has broken here— ❸

DANFORTH: Andover is remedied. The court returns there on Friday, and will resume examinations.

PARRIS: I am sure of it, sir. But the rumor here speaks rebellion in Andover, and it—

DANFORTH: There is no rebellion in Andover! ❹

PARRIS: I tell you what is said here, sir. Andover

---

1. **news of Andover:** During the height of the terror in Salem Village, a similar hysteria broke out in the nearby town of Andover. There, many respected people were accused of practicing witchcraft and confessed to escape death. However, in Andover people soon began questioning the reality of the situation and the hysteria quickly subsided.

◆ Build Vocabulary

agape (a gāp′) *adj.*: Wide open

Cross-Curricular Connection: Social Studies

Barbados Explain to students that Tituba's homeland, Barbados, is one of the Lesser Antilles islands of the Caribbean, located about 250 miles northeast of Venezuela. It was settled in 1627 by the British, and it remained a British colony until it became an independent state in 1966. Today, much of the way of life in Barbados still reflects its British past, with all Barbadians—many of whom are descendants of slaves brought from Africa between 1636 and 1833—speaking English and with traffic driving on the left side of the road.

At the time represented in *The Crucible*, the main crop of Barbados was sugar, and huge plantations worked by slaves flourished. By 1684, there were around 20,000 white settlers and more than 45,000 slaves on the island. The plantation owners of Barbados had a reputation for being cruel masters.

Based on these facts, discuss with students whether life in Barbados during the time of the Salem witch trials was as carefree as Tituba implies.

have thrown out the court, they say, and will have no part of witchcraft. There be a faction here, feeding on that news, and I tell you true, sir, I fear there will be riot here.

5 **HATHORNE:** Riot! Why at every execution I have seen naught but high satisfaction in the town.

6 **PARRIS:** Judge Hathorne—it were another sort that hanged till now. Rebecca Nurse is no Bridget that lived three year with Bishop before she married him. John Proctor is not Isaac Ward that drank his family to ruin. *To* DANFORTH: I would to God it were not so, Excellency, but these people have great weight yet in the town. Let Rebecca stand upon the gibbet[2] and send up some righteous prayer, and I fear she'll wake a vengeance on you.

HATHORNE: Excellency, she is condemned a witch. The court have—

DANFORTH, *in deep concern, raising a hand to* HATHORNE: Pray you. *To* PARRIS: How do you propose, then?

PARRIS: Excellency, I would postpone these hangin's for a time. 7

DANFORTH: There will be no postponement.

PARRIS: Now Mr. Hale's returned, there is hope, I think—for if he bring even one of these to God, that confession surely damns the others in the public eye, and none may doubt more that they are all linked to Hell. This way, unconfessed and claiming innocence, doubts are multiplied, many honest people will weep for them, and our good purpose is lost in their tears.

2. **gibbet** (jib´ it) *n.*: Gallows.

5 Enrichment At the time, executions were public events that were intended to strike fear in the spectators and reinforce their awareness of the power of the authorities who governed their society.

◆ Critical Thinking

6 Draw Conclusions What does this passage reveal about Parris's chief concerns? *Parris is concerned chiefly about the public's possible adverse reactions to the hangings and not about whether the hangings are just or unjust.*

◆ Reading Strategy

7 Apply Themes to Contemporary Events Encourage students to speculate about what might have happened if the McCarthy hearings had been postponed. *Sample response: Some of the momentum that had built up would have been lost and people might have begun to doubt the legitimacy of the hearings.*

Customize for
Less Proficient Readers
To help these students gain greater insight into the play through dramatic performance, use ***Strategies for Diverse Student Needs,*** p. 79, "Prepare a Readers Theatre."

Cultural Connection

Tell students that many cultures have belief systems of good and evil. Many also have an antagonistic, "devil like" figure who interferes in people's lives. Ask students what they know about the devil and how he is portrayed in various cultures; discuss their responses.

To the Hebrews, for example, he was a satan, or opponent of God; hence, the name Satan. Mephistopheles is the devil's name in a German legend, later made famous in plays by Christopher Marlowe and Johann von Goethe, and in operas by Charles Gounod and Arrigo Boito.

Explain to students that despite the American common cultural impression that the devil is red and has horns and a tail, devils go by many names and faces in other cultures. To the Egyptians, both Apep, a giant serpent that lived in the Nile, and Set, a man with the head of a jackal and a forked tail, are "devil like" figures. The Native Americans in Chile have Ngurvilu, a water god who resembles both a wildcat and a scorpion. The Aztecs have Tezcatlipoca, who has the face of a bear. In India, the devil was a woman named Kali.

Ask students to research art books and other visual sources to find paintings and drawings of the devil in different times and cultures, to share with the class.

❶ **Clarification** Explain to students that in the Puritan church, excommunication occurred when a church member was deemed to have behaved in a way that went against church principles and regulations. When excommunicated, a person could no longer take part in the religious life of the community. Excommunication not only separated the excommunicant from the church, it also in effect removed him or her from society.

Comprehension Check ☑

❷ What does Parris make of the fact that a dagger was thrown onto his doorstep? *He interprets it as a death threat.*

◆ Literary Focus

❸ **Theme** Sample response: Danforth's speech reveals that he is determined to hold on to power and authority at any cost, whether it means hanging innocent people or striking out at anyone who dares to question his actions on behalf of "the law."

◆ Reading Strategy

❹ **Apply Themes to Contemporary Events** Ask students how this part of Danforth's statement might reflect what happened in the McCarthy hearings. *Sample response: McCarthy was willing to harm anyone he had to in order to keep the power the committee gave him.*

◆ Critical Thinking

❺ **Speculate** Have students predict whether Danforth will be able to convince John Proctor to confess. On what do they base their predictions? *Some students may say that John, because he thinks the trial was a sham, will confess in order to save his life. Other students may say that John, because he is headstrong and principled, will not resort to lying to save himself.*

DANFORTH, *after thinking a moment, then going to* CHEEVER: Give me the list.

CHEEVER *opens the dispatch case, searches.*

❶ **PARRIS:** It cannot be forgot, sir, that when I summoned the congregation for John Proctor's excommunication there were hardly thirty people come to hear it. That speak a discontent, I think, and—

DANFORTH, *studying the list:* There will be no postponement.

PARRIS: Excellency—

DANFORTH: Now, sir—which of these in your opinion may be brought to God? I will myself strive with him till dawn. *He hands the list to* PARRIS, *who merely glances at it.*

PARRIS: There is not sufficient time till dawn.

DANFORTH: I shall do my utmost. Which of them do you have hope for?

PARRIS, *not even glancing at the list now, and in a quavering voice, quietly:* Excellency—a dagger—*He chokes up.*

DANFORTH: What do you say?

❷ **PARRIS:** Tonight, when I open my door to leave my house—a dagger clattered to the ground. *Silence.* DANFORTH *absorbs this. Now* PARRIS *cries out:* You cannot hang this sort. There is danger for me. I dare not step outside at night!

REVEREND HALE *enters. They look at him for an instant in silence. He is steeped in sorrow, exhausted, and more direct than he ever was.*

DANFORTH: Accept my congratulations, Reverend Hale; we are gladdened to see you returned to your good work.

HALE, *coming to* DANFORTH *now:* You must pardon them. They will not budge.

HERRICK *enters, waits.*

DANFORTH, *conciliatory:* You misunderstand, sir; I cannot pardon these when twelve are already hanged for the same crime. It is not just.

PARRIS, *with failing heart:* Rebecca will not confess?

HALE: The sun will rise in a few minutes. Excellency, I must have more time.

DANFORTH: Now hear me, and beguile yourselves no more. I will not receive a single plea for pardon or postponement. Them that will not confess will hang. Twelve are already executed; the names of these seven are given out, and the village expects to see them die this morning. Postponement now speaks a floundering on my part; reprieve or pardon must cast doubt upon the guilt of them that died till now. While I speak God's law, I will not crack its voice with whimpering. If retaliation is your fear, know this—I should hang ten thousand that dared to rise against the law, and an ocean of salt tears could not melt the resolution of the statutes. Now draw yourselves up like men and help me, as you are bound by Heaven to do. Have you spoken with them all, Mr. Hale? ❸ ❹

> **◆ Literary Focus**
> What theme about authority or hypocrisy do you think Danforth's attitude here may convey?

HALE: All but Proctor. He is in the dungeon.

DANFORTH, *to* HERRICK: What's Proctor's way now?

HERRICK: He sits like some great bird; you'd not know he lived except he will take food from time to time.

DANFORTH, *after thinking a moment:* His wife—his wife must be well on with child now.

HERRICK: She is, sir.

DANFORTH: What think you, Mr. Parris? You have closer knowledge of this man; might her presence soften him? ❺

PARRIS: It is possible, sir. He have not laid eyes on her these three months. I should summon her.

DANFORTH, *to* HERRICK: Is he yet adamant? Has he struck at you again?

HERRICK: He cannot, sir, he is chained to the wall now.

DANFORTH, *after thinking on it:* Fetch Goody Proctor to me. Then let you bring him up.

HERRICK: Aye, sir. HERRICK *goes. There is silence.*

Cross-Curricular Connection: Social Studies

The Outcome of the Witchcraft Trials
When Danforth speaks of the executions in the town, he refers to twelve who had already been hanged. By the time the Salem witch hunt ended in 1693, twenty people had died—nineteen by hanging and one, Giles Corey, by being pressed to death by large stones. In addition, four more died in jail. Dorcas Good, the four-year-old daughter of Sarah Good, went mad in prison. The Salem trials marked the final time in America that people were executed for witchcraft. The other accused witches were released from prison in the spring of 1693.

HALE: Excellency, if you postpone a week and publish to the town that you are striving for their confessions, that speak mercy on your part, not faltering.

DANFORTH: Mr. Hale, as God have not empowered me like Joshua to stop this sun from rising,[3] so I cannot withhold from them the perfection of their punishment.

HALE, *harder now:* If you think God wills you to raise rebellion, Mr. Danforth, you are mistaken!

DANFORTH, *instantly:* You have heard rebellion spoken in the town?

6 **HALE:** Excellency, there are orphans wandering from house to house; abandoned cattle bellow on the highroads, the stink of rotting crops hangs everywhere, and no man knows when the harlots' cry will end his life—and you wonder yet if rebellion's spoke? Better you should marvel how they do not burn your province!

DANFORTH: Mr. Hale, have you preached in Andover this month?

HALE: Thank God they have no need of me in Andover.

DANFORTH: You baffle me, sir. Why have you returned here?

7 **HALE:** Why, it is all simple. I come to do the Devil's work. I come to counsel Christians they should belie themselves. *His sarcasm collapses.* There is blood on my head! Can you not see the blood on my head!!

3. **Joshua . . . rising:** In the Bible, Joshua, leader of the Jews after the death of Moses, asks God to make the sun and the moon stand still during a battle, and his request is granted.

◆ Build Vocabulary

conciliatory (kən sil′ ē ə tôr′ ə) *adj.*: Tending to soothe the anger of

beguile (bē gīl′) *v.*: Trick; delude

floundering (floun′ dər iŋ) *n.*: Awkward struggling

retaliation (ri tal′ ē ā′ shən) *n.*: Act of returning an injury or wrong

adamant (ad′ ə mənt) *adj.*: Firm; unyielding

cleave (clēv) *v.*: Adhere; cling

PARRIS: Hush! *For he has heard footsteps. They all face the door.* HERRICK *enters with* ELIZABETH. *Her wrists are linked by heavy chain, which* HERRICK *now removes. Her clothes are dirty; her face is pale and gaunt.* HERRICK *goes out.*

DANFORTH, *very politely:* Goody Proctor. *She is silent.* I hope you are hearty?

ELIZABETH, *as a warning reminder:* I am yet six months before my time.

DANFORTH: Pray be at your ease, we come not for your life. We—*uncertain how to plead, for he is not accustomed to it.* Mr. Hale, will you speak with the woman?

HALE: Goody Proctor, your husband is marked to hang this morning

Pause.

ELIZABETH, *quietly:* I have heard it.

HALE: You know, do you not, that I have no connection with the court? *She seems to doubt it.* I come of my own, Goody Proctor. I would save your husband's life, for if he is taken I count myself his murderer. Do you understand me? 8

ELIZABETH: What do you want of me?

HALE: Goody Proctor, I have gone this three month like our Lord into the wilderness. I have sought a Christian way, for damnation's doubled on a minister who counsels men to lie.

HATHORNE: It is no lie, you cannot speak of lies.

HALE: It is a lie! They are innocent!

DANFORTH: I'll hear no more of that!

HALE, *continuing to* ELIZABETH: Let you not mistake your duty as I mistook my own. I came into this village like a bridegroom to his beloved, bearing gifts of high religion; the very crowns of holy law I brought, and what I touched with my bright confidence, it died; and where I turned the eye of my great faith, blood flowed up. Beware, Goody Proctor—cleave to no faith when faith brings blood. 9 It is mistaken law that leads you to sacrifice. Life, woman, life is God's most precious gift; no principle, however glorious, may justify the taking of it. I beg you, woman, prevail upon your husband to

◆ Literary Focus

6 Theme Point out that this speech reinforces Cheever's earlier description of Salem (p. 1155). Ask students what theme or themes these descriptions raise. *Responses may include: fear and suspicion can destroy public order; revenge can backfire.*

Comprehension Check ☑

7 Have students explain in their own words Hale's response to the question "Why have you returned here?" *Sample response: At first he is bitter and sarcastic, stating that he has come to do "the Devil's work." He then expresses his profound sense of anguish and guilt, declaring that there is blood on his head.*

◆ Critical Thinking

8 Infer Have students discuss what Hale's remarks reveal about his character. *Sample response: Hale is honest, willing to admit when he has made a mistake and willing to take responsibility for his actions.*

◆ Critical Thinking

9 Connect Encourage students to recall Hale's arrival in Salem in Act I. Then have them explain what he means when he says that he came "bearing gifts of high religion." To what does he refer when he says that "blood flowed up"? *He is saying that when he first came to Salem, he genuinely believed in his mission; the result of his efforts, however, has been nothing but disaster and death.*

◆ Literary Focus

❶ **Theme** Responses may include: He states the theme that life is more important that any abstract principle; he expresses the idea that lying is justified under some circumstances.

◆ Critical Thinking

❷ **Analyze Character** Ask students what Elizabeth Proctor thinks of Hale's statements and what this reveals about her character. *She believes he is wrong to put life above faith; she reveals her integrity and deep faith.*

◆ Critical Thinking

❸ **Interpret** Have students explain what Reverend Hale means when he comments that "before the laws of God we are swine." *Suggested response: When compared with God's infinite wisdom, the knowledge that human beings possess is on the level of ignorance. Human beings cannot possibly understand the mind of God.*

◆ Literary Focus
What theme or themes does Reverend Hale state in this speech?

confess. Let him give his lie. Quail not before God's judgment in this, for it may well be God damns a liar less than he that throws his life away for pride. Will you plead with him? I cannot think he will listen to another.

ELIZABETH, *quietly:* I think that be the Devil's argument.

HALE, *with a climactic desperation:* Woman, before the laws of God we are as swine! We cannot read His will!

ELIZABETH: I cannot dispute with you, sir; I lack learning for it.

DANFORTH, *going to her:* Goody Proctor, you are not summoned here for disputation. Be there no wifely tenderness within you? He will die with the sunrise. Your husband. Do you understand it? *She only looks at him.* What say you? Will you contend with him? *She is silent.* Are you stone? I tell you true, woman, had I no other proof of your unnatural life, your dry eyes now would be sufficient evidence that you delivered up your soul to Hell! A very ape would weep at such calamity! Have the devil dried up any tear of pity in you? *She is silent.* Take her out. It profit nothing she should speak to him!

ELIZABETH, *quietly:* Let me speak with him, Excellency.

PARRIS, *with hope:* You'll strive with him? *She hesitates.*

DANFORTH: Will you plead for his confession or will you not?

ELIZABETH: I promise nothing. Let me speak with him.

A sound—the *sibilance* *of dragging feet on stone. They turn. A pause.* HERRICK *enters with* JOHN PROCTOR. *His wrists are chained. He is another man, bearded, filthy, his eyes misty as though webs had overgrown them. He halts inside the doorway, his eyes caught by the sight of* ELIZABETH. *The emotion flowing between them prevents anyone from speaking for an instant. Now* HALE, *visibly affected, goes to* DANFORTH *and speaks quietly.*

HALE: Pray, leave them Excellency.

DANFORTH, *pressing* HALE *impatiently aside:* Mr. Proctor, you have been notified, have you not? PROCTOR *is silent, staring at* ELIZABETH. I see light in the sky, Mister; let you counsel with your wife, and may God help you turn your back on Hell. PROCTOR *is silent, staring at* ELIZABETH.

HALE, *quietly:* Excellency, let—

DANFORTH *brushes past* HALE *and walks out.* HALE *follows.* CHEEVER *stands and follows,* HATHORNE *behind.* HERRICK *goes.* PARRIS, *from a safe distance, offers:*

PARRIS: If you desire a cup of cider, Mr. Proctor, I am sure I—PROCTOR *turns an icy stare at him, and he breaks off.* PARRIS *raises his palms toward* PROCTOR. God lead you now. PARRIS *goes out.*

4 *Alone,* PROCTOR *walks to her, halts. It is as though they stood in a spinning world. It is beyond sorrow, above it. He reaches out his hand as though toward an embodiment not quite real, and as he touches her, a strange soft sound, half laughter, half amazement, comes from his throat. He pats her hand. She covers his hand with hers. And then, weak, he sits. Then she sits, facing him.*

PROCTOR: The child?

ELIZABETH: It grows.

PROCTOR: There is no word of the boys?

ELIZABETH: They're well. Rebecca's Samuel keeps them.

◆ Build Vocabulary

sibilance (sib´ əl əns) *n.*: Hissing sound

PROCTOR: You have not seen them?

ELIZABETH: I have not. *She catches a weakening in herself and downs it.*

PROCTOR: You are a—marvel, Elizabeth.

ELIZABETH: You—have been tortured?

PROCTOR: Aye. *Pause. She will not let herself be drowned in the sea that threatens her.* They come for my life now. 5

ELIZABETH: I know it.

Pause.

PROCTOR: None—have yet confessed?

ELIZABETH: There be many confessed.

PROCTOR: Who are they?

ELIZABETH: There be a hundred or more, they say. Goody Ballard is one; Isaiah Goodkind is one. There be many.

PROCTOR: Rebecca?

ELIZABETH: Not Rebecca. She is one foot in Heaven now; naught may hurt her more.

PROCTOR: And Giles?

ELIZABETH: You have not heard of it?

PROCTOR: I hear nothin', where I am kept.

ELIZABETH: Giles is dead.

He looks at her incredulously.

PROCTOR: When were he hanged?

ELIZABETH, *quietly, factually:* He were not hanged. He would not answer aye or nay to his indictment; for if he denied the charge they'd hang him surely, and auction out his property. So he stand mute, and died Christian under the law. And so his sons will have his farm. It is the law, for he could not be condemned a wizard without he answer the indictment, aye or nay. 6

PROCTOR: Then how does he die?

ELIZABETH, *gently:* They press him, John.

PROCTOR: Press?

◆ Critical Thinking

4 Draw Conclusions What emotions do students imagine that the two characters are experiencing at this point? *Sample response: They are likely experiencing a flood of emotions, having to meet under the most difficult circumstances after such a long time in jail. They undoubtedly feel love for each other and quite possibly compassion, sorrow, sadness, and resignation over their fates.*

◆ Literary Focus

5 Theme Ask: What theme might Miller be expressing through his depiction of Elizabeth's attitude and behavior? *Responses might include the following: the strength of the human spirit; maintaining courage in the worst of times.*

Comprehension Check ☑

6 What did Giles do to help his sons? What tendency did he show through his life, including his final act? *By refusing to answer the charges, Giles died a Christian and made it possible for his sons to inherit his property. All his life he made a point of knowing the law and using it to his own advantage.*

Customize for *Bodily/Kinesthetic Learners*

The scene in which Elizabeth and John Proctor meet and speak with each other under the most trying of circumstances is a very powerful one, fraught with emotion. Perhaps some of your students would enjoy acting out this scene, trying to capture its emotion and mood.

Cross-Curricular Connection: Social Studies

In seventeenth-century America, witchcraft was one of the few crimes that carried a death sentence. The others were murder, rape, and insurrection. Though the usual method of execution was hanging, occasionally other methods were used. There is a record of two men found guilty of insurrection who were first hanged, then cut down while still alive and gutted. Then they were beheaded and their bodies cut in four parts.

When dealing with less serious crimes, officials tried to avoid imprisonment because of the cost. Offenders often paid fines instead. In addition, because public humiliation was deemed by the Puritans to be a greater punishment than incarceration, criminals sometimes had to suffer various public punishments. For example, criminals were often put in the stocks or pillory, devices that held the hands, feet, or neck in a wooden frame. At other times, they were publicly whipped.

Discuss with students why, in a Puritan community, such public punishment was felt to be more severe than imprisonment.

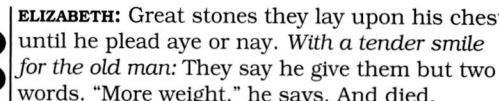

◆ Literary Focus

❶ Theme Ask students: What theme might these details about Giles Corey's death convey? *Responses may include the following: courage; defending the truth even in the face of death.*

❷ Enrichment Tell students that this is in fact the way in which the real Giles Corey died during the Salem witchcraft proceedings.

◆ Critical Thinking

❸ Analyze Have students explain Proctor's line of reasoning in this speech. Also have them explain his reasons for describing himself as he does. *Suggested response: According to Proctor, it doesn't matter if he lies by confessing, since he is already a sinner. He is referring to his guilt over his affair with Abigail when he says that he cannot pass himself off as a saint and that he is "no good man."*

◆ Critical Thinking

❹ Connect In what way does Elizabeth elaborate here on her earlier declaration: "I cannot judge you, John"? *Suggested response: She cannot pass judgment on his sins, because she feels that she, too, has sinned.*

Comprehension Check ☑

❺ What sins does Elizabeth think she has committed? *Because she felt insecure about herself, she doubted her husband's love and did not whole-heartedly offer him her love.*

ELIZABETH: Great stones they lay upon his chest
❶ until he plead aye or nay. *With a tender smile*
❷ *for the old man:* They say he give them but two
words. "More weight," he says. And died.

PROCTOR, *numbed—a thread to weave into his agony:* "More weight."

ELIZABETH: Aye. It were a fearsome man, Giles Corey.

Pause.

PROCTOR, *with great force of will, but not quite looking at her:* I have been thinking I would confess to them, Elizabeth. *She shows nothing.* What say you? If I give them that?

ELIZABETH: I cannot judge you, John.

Pause.

PROCTOR, *simply—a pure question:* What would you have me do?

ELIZABETH: As you will, I would have it. *Slight pause:* I want you living, John. That's sure.

PROCTOR, *pauses, then with a flailing of hope:* Giles' wife? Have she confessed?

ELIZABETH: She will not.

Pause.

PROCTOR: It is a pretense, Elizabeth.

ELIZABETH: What is?

PROCTOR: I cannot mount the gibbet like a saint.
It is a fraud. I am not that man. *She is silent.*
❸ My honesty is broke, Elizabeth; I am no good
man. Nothing's spoiled by giving them this lie
that were not rotten long before.

ELIZABETH: And yet you've not confessed till now. That speak goodness in you.

PROCTOR: Spite only keeps me silent. It is hard to give a lie to dogs. *Pause, for the first time he turns directly to her.* I would have your forgiveness, Elizabeth.

ELIZABETH: It is not for me to give, John, I am—

PROCTOR: I'd have you see some honesty in it. Let them that never lied die now to keep their souls. It is pretense for me, a vanity that will not blind God nor keep my children out of the wind. *Pause.* What say you?

ELIZABETH, *upon a heaving sob that always threatens:* John, it come to naught that I should forgive you, if you'll not forgive yourself. *Now he turns away a little, in great agony.* It is not my soul, John, it is yours. *He stands, as though in physical pain, slowly rising to his feet*
with a great immortal longing to find his answer. ❹
It is difficult to say, and she is on the verge of tears. Only be sure of this, for I know it now: Whatever you will do, it is a good man does it. *He turns his doubting, searching gaze upon her.* I have read my heart this three month, John. *Pause.* I have sins of my own to count. It needs a cold wife to prompt lechery.

PROCTOR, *in great pain:* Enough, enough—

ELIZABETH, *now pouring out her heart:* Better you should know me!

PROCTOR: I will not hear it! I know you!

ELIZABETH: You take my sins upon you, John—

PROCTOR, *in agony:* No, I take my own, my own!

ELIZABETH: John, I counted myself so plain, so poorly made, no honest love could come to me! Suspicion kissed you when I did; I never knew
how I should say my love. It were a cold house I ❺
kept! *In fright, she swerves, as* HATHORNE *enters.*

HATHORNE: What say you Proctor? The sun is soon up.

PROCTOR, *his chest heaving, stares, turns to* ELIZABETH. *She comes to him as though to plead, her voice quaking.*

ELIZABETH: Do what you will. But let none be your judge. There be no higher judge under Heaven than Proctor is! Forgive me, forgive me, John—I never knew such goodness in the world! *She covers her face, weeping.*

PROCTOR *turns from her to* HATHORNE; *he is off the earth, his voice hollow.*

PROCTOR: I want my life.

HATHORNE *electrified, surprised:* You'll confess yourself?

PROCTOR: I will have my life.

HATHORNE, *with a mystical tone:* God be praised! It is a providence! *He rushes out the door, and his voice is heard calling down the corridor:* He will confess! Proctor will confess!

PROCTOR, *with a cry, as he strides to the door:* Why do you cry it? *In great pain he turns back to her.* It is evil, is it not? It is evil.

ELIZABETH, *in terror, weeping:* I cannot judge you, John, I cannot!

PROCTOR: Then who will judge me? *Suddenly clasping his hands:* God in Heaven, what is John Proctor, what is John Proctor? *He moves as an animal, and a fury is riding in him, a* 6 *tantalized search.* I think it is honest, I think so; I am no saint. *As though she had denied this he calls angrily at her:* Let Rebecca go like a saint; for me it is fraud!

Voices are heard in the hall, speaking together in suppressed excitement.

ELIZABETH: I am not your judge, I cannot be. *As though giving him release:* Do as you will, do as you will!

PROCTOR: Would you give them such a lie? Say it. Would you ever give them this? *She cannot answer.* You would not; if tongs of fire were singeing you you would not! It is evil. Good, 7 then—it is evil, and I do it!

HATHORNE *enters with* DANFORTH, *and, with them,* CHEEVER, PARRIS, *and* HALE. *It is a businesslike, rapid entrance, as though the ice had been broken.*

DANFORTH, *with great relief and gratitude:* Praise to God, man, praise to God; you shall be blessed in Heaven for this. CHEEVER *has hurried to the bench with pen, ink, and paper.* PROCTOR *watches him.* Now then, let us have it. Are you ready, Mr. Cheever?

PROCTOR, *with a cold, cold horror at their efficiency:* Why must it be written?

DANFORTH: Why, for the good instruction of the village, Mister; this we shall post upon the church door! *To* PARRIS, *urgently:* Where is the marshal?

PARRIS, *runs to the door and calls down the corridor:* Marshal! Hurry!

DANFORTH: Now, then, Mister, will you speak slowly, and directly to the point, for Mr. Cheever's sake. *He is on record now, and is really dictating to* CHEEVER, *who writes.* Mr. Proctor, have you seen the Devil in your life? PROCTOR'S *jaws lock.* Come, man, there is light in the sky; the town waits at the scaffold; I would give out this news. Did you see the Devil?

PROCTOR: I did.

PARRIS: Praise God!

DANFORTH: And when he come to you, what were his demand?

PROCTOR *is silent.* DANFORTH *helps.* Did he bid you to do his work upon the earth?

PROCTOR: He did.

DANFORTH: And you bound yourself to his service? DANFORTH *turns, as* REBECCA NURSE *enters, with* HERRICK *helping to support her. She is barely able to walk.* Come in, come in, woman!

REBECCA, *brightening as she sees* PROCTOR: Ah, John! You are well, then, eh?

PROCTOR *turns his face to the wall.*

DANFORTH: Courage, man, courage—let her witness your good example that she may come to God herself. Now hear it, Goody Nurse! Say on, Mr. Proctor. Did you bind yourself to the Devil's service?

REBECCA, *astonished:* Why, John!

PROCTOR, *through his teeth, his face turned from* REBECCA: I did.

DANFORTH: Now, woman, you surely see it profit nothin' to keep this conspiracy any further. Will you confess yourself with him?

REBECCA: Oh, John—God send his mercy on you! 8

DANFORTH: I say, will you confess yourself, Goody Nurse?

REBECCA: Why, it is a lie, it is a lie; how may I damn myself? I cannot, I cannot.

◆ Build Vocabulary

tantalized (tan´ tə līzd) *adj.*: Tormented; frustrated

◆ Build Vocabulary

6 Word Origins: Words From Myths Have students research the Furies and determine how the meaning of the word "fury" reflects the myth. *The Furies were Greek divinities who punished criminals; their retribution was angry (furious) and swift.*

◆ Critical Thinking

7 Interpret Ask students what Proctor means by this paradoxical statement. *Responses may include the following: He is defiantly declaring his intention to save himself, no matter what the moral cost; he is declaring his hypocrisy to the world.*

◆ Literary Focus

8 Theme Have students determine how Rebecca Nurse embodies the theme of courage. *Sample response: Not only does she face death without flinching, but she also prays for mercy for those who are not as brave.*

◆ Background for Understanding

Literature On the occasion of a 1989 production of the play, Arthur Miller wrote: "What research showed me, and what I hoped the play would show the country and the world, was the continuity through time of human delusion, and the only safeguard, fragile though it may be, against it—namely, the law and the courageous few whose sacrifice illuminates delusion." Have students respond to Miller's comment. Then have them keep it in mind as they read the rest of the play. Is John Proctor one of the "courageous few" to whom Miller refers? Is Elizabeth?

Speaking, Listening, and Viewing Mini-Lesson

Mock Trial

This mini-lesson supports the Speaking, Listening, and Viewing activity in the Idea Bank on page 1169.

Introduce the Concept Explain to students that in a trial, the defense introduces witnesses who will help defend the accused and the prosecution introduces witnesses who will help prove the accused guilty. Both sides question all witnesses.

Develop Background Students can decide who will play the roles of defendants, attorneys, judge, and jury. Encourage them to consider these points as they develop their lines of questioning:

- What motives did Danforth and Hathorne have for their actions?
- Did Danforth and Hathorne act with the intent to harm the accused witches?
- Given the beliefs of the day, did Danforth and Hathorne present convincing cases against the accused?

Apply the Information Students can present their trial to the rest of the class. Remind students to speak clearly.

Assess the Outcome After the jury has rendered its verdict, encourage the class to discuss the trial. Was it fair? Were the arguments presented clearly and logically?

To evaluate the mock trial, have students use the *Peer Assessment* page for a Dramatic Performance, in ***Alternative Assessment,*** p. 79.

❶ **Enrichment** Explain to students that this type of questioning was frequently used during the McCarthy hearings. In fact, when Miller himself was called to testify before the committee in 1956, he was pressed to reveal the names of people who had attended meetings sponsored by the Communist party. To these requests, Miller responded, "My conscience will not permit me to use the name of another person and bring trouble on him."

Customize for
Bodily/Kinesthetic Learners
❷ These students may enjoy role-playing this scene featuring Danforth's intense questioning of Proctor to get the accused man to name others whom he had seen with the devil. Ask each student who takes the part of Danforth to be relentless in applying verbal pressure on Proctor.

❶ ❷ **DANFORTH:** Mr. Proctor. When the Devil came to you did you see Rebecca Nurse in his company? PROCTOR *is silent.* Come, man, take courage—did you ever see her with the Devil?

PROCTOR, *almost inaudibly:* No.

❶ ❷ **DANFORTH,** *now sensing trouble, glances at* JOHN *and goes to the table, and picks up a sheet—the list of condemned.*

DANFORTH: Did you ever see her sister, Mary Easty, with the Devil?

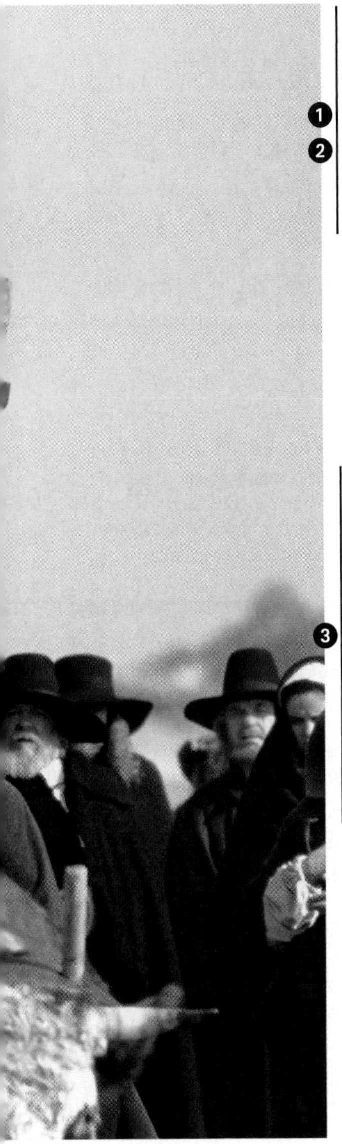

PROCTOR: No, I did not.

DANFORTH, *his eyes narrow on* PROCTOR: ❶ ❷ Did you ever see Martha Corey with the Devil?

PROCTOR: I did not.

DANFORTH, *realizing, slowly putting the sheet down:* Did you ever see anyone with the Devil?

PROCTOR: I did not.

DANFORTH: Proctor, you mistake me. I am not empowered to trade your life for a lie. You have most certainly seen ❸ some person with the Devil. PROCTOR *is silent.* Mr. Proctor, a score of people have already testified they saw this woman with the Devil.

PROCTOR: Then it is proved. Why must I say it?

DANFORTH: Why "must" you say it! Why, you should rejoice to say it if your soul is truly purged of any love for Hell!

PROCTOR: They think to go like saints. I like not to spoil their names.

DANFORTH, *inquiring, incredulous:* Mr. Proctor, do you think they go like saints?

PROCTOR, *evading:* This woman never thought she done the Devil's work.

DANFORTH: Look you, sir. I think you mistake your duty here. It matter nothing what she thought—she is convicted of the unnatural murder of children, and you for sending your spirit out upon Mary Warren. Your soul alone is the issue here, Mister, and you will prove its whiteness or you cannot live in a Christian country. Will you tell me now what persons conspired with you in the Devil's company? PROCTOR *is silent.* To your knowledge was Rebecca Nurse ever—

> ◆ **Reading Strategy**
> How might Proctor's insistence on not incriminating others relate to the McCarthy hearings of the 1950's? ❹

PROCTOR: I speak my own sins; I cannot judge another. *Crying out, with hatred:* I have no tongue for it.

HALE, *quickly to* DANFORTH: Excellency, it is enough he confess himself. Let him sign it, let him sign it.

PARRIS, *feverishly:* It is a great service, sir. It is a weighty name; it will strike the village that Proctor confess. I beg you, let him sign it. The sun is up, Excellency!

DANFORTH, *considers; then with dissatisfaction:* Come, then, sign your testimony. *To* CHEEVER: Give it to him. CHEEVER *goes to* PROCTOR, *the confession and a pen in hand.* PROCTOR *does not look at it.* Come, man, sign it.

PROCTOR, *after glancing at the confession:* You have all witnessed it—it is enough.

DANFORTH: You will not sign it?

PROCTOR: You have all witnessed it; what more is needed?

DANFORTH: Do you sport with me? You will sign your name or it is no confession, Mister! *His breast heaving with agonized breathing,* PROCTOR *now lays the paper down and signs his name.*

PARRIS: Praise be to the Lord!

◆ Build Vocabulary

purged (purjd) *v.*: Cleansed; purified

◆ Critical Thinking

❸ Draw Conclusions Ask students what effect they think Danforth's insistence on naming accomplices will have on Proctor. *Although Proctor is willing to damn himself by lying, he will probably not be willing to implicate others who are innocent.*

◆ Reading Strategy

❹ Apply Themes to Contemporary Events *Suggested response: Some of those questioned by McCarthy's committee refused to incriminate others as well; often this refusal led to the end of their careers because of blacklisting.*

◆ Background for Understanding

Literature Several years after the play was written, Arthur Miller discussed the character of Danforth. He commented, "Danforth was indeed dedicated to securing the status quo against such as Proctor. But I am equally interested in his *function* in the drama, which is that of the rule-bearer, the man who always guards the boundaries which, if you insist on breaking through them, have the power to destroy you. . . . When I say I did not make him evil enough, it is that I did not clearly demarcate the point at which he knows what he has done, and profoundly accept it as a good thing. This alone is evil." Have your students respond to Miller's comment and discuss whether they agree with his observation that he did not make Danforth "evil enough."

Beyond the Classroom

Career Connection

Judge Tell students that in the United States, there are two systems of courts: state courts and federal courts. In ten states, state court judges are appointed by the governor; in the others, they are elected by either voters or legislators. Federal judges are appointed by the President. Also explain that most trial judges, whether on the state or the federal level, start their careers as trial lawyers, while appeals judges often come from the ranks of office lawyers and law professors.

Have interested students do research to learn more about the education and experience needed to become a judge. They can report their findings to the class.

◆ Literary Focus

❶ **Theme** What notorious aspect of the McCarthy hearings might Miller be alluding to here? *Suggested response: He is alluding to the pressure that was put on witnesses to "name names"—that is, to incriminate others for having Communist ties.*

Comprehension Check ☑

❷ Why is Proctor's name so important to him, and why does it now cause him anguish? *It is something that he will hand down to his descendants. He cannot bear the thought that his name will be formally linked, by his signature, to the betrayal of the other accused.*

◆ Literary Focus

❸ **Theme** Ask students how Proctor's change of heart reflects the themes of integrity and courage. *Sample answer: He has found the courage within himself to tell the truth and face death; knowing that he has goodness in him gives him the strength he needs.*

◆ Background for Understanding

History Soon after the Salem witchcraft hysteria ended, Parris was voted out of office and forced to leave town. According to legend, Abigail Williams eventually ended up working in a Boston brothel. Elizabeth Proctor, on the other hand, managed to rebound from her husband's death, remarrying four years after his body was laid to rest.

Twenty years after the last execution, compensation was awarded to victims who were still living. In 1712, the government ordered the congregation to rescind the excommunications of the accused. Yet only one of the presiding judges, Samuel Sewall, ever publicly admitted that a dreadful mistake had been made.

PROCTOR *has just finished signing when* DANFORTH *reaches for the paper. But* PROCTOR *snatches it up, and now a wild terror is rising in him, and a boundless anger.*

DANFORTH, *perplexed, but politely extending his hand:* If you please, sir.

PROCTOR: No.

DANFORTH, *as though* PROCTOR *did not understand:* Mr. Proctor, I must have—

PROCTOR: No, no. I have signed it. You have seen me. It is done! You have no need for this.

PARRIS: Proctor, the village must have proof that—

PROCTOR: Damn the village! I confess to God, and God has seen my name on this! It is enough!

DANFORTH: No, sir, it is—

PROCTOR: You came to save my soul, did you not? Here! I have confessed myself; it is enough!

DANFORTH: You have not con—

PROCTOR: I have confessed myself! Is there no good penitence but it be public? God does not need my name nailed upon the church! God sees my name; God knows how black my sins are! It is enough!

DANFORTH: Mr. Proctor—

PROCTOR: You will not use me! I am no Sarah Good or Tituba, I am John Proctor! You will not use me! It is no part of salvation that you should use me!

DANFORTH: I do not wish to—

❶ **PROCTOR:** I have three children—how may I teach them to walk like men in the world, and I sold my friends?

DANFORTH: You have not sold your friends—

PROCTOR: Beguile me not! I blacken all of them when this is nailed to the church the very day they hang for silence!

DANFORTH: Mr. Proctor, I must have good and legal proof that you—

PROCTOR: You are the high court, your word is good enough! Tell them I confessed myself; say Proctor broke his knees and wept like a woman; say what you will, but my name cannot—

DANFORTH, *with suspicion:* It is the same, is it not? If I report it or you sign to it?

PROCTOR—*he knows it is insane:* No, it is not the same! What others say and what I sign to is not the same!

DANFORTH: Why? Do you mean to deny this confession when you are free?

PROCTOR: I mean to deny nothing!

DANFORTH: Then explain to me, Mr. Proctor, why you will not let—

PROCTOR, *with a cry of his whole soul:* Because it is my name! Because I cannot have another in my life! Because I lie and sign myself to lies! Because I am not worth the dust on the feet of them that hang! How may I live without my name? I have given you my soul; leave me my name! ❷

DANFORTH, *pointing at the confession in* PROCTOR's *hand:* Is that document a lie? If it is a lie I will not accept it! What say you? I will not deal in lies, Mister! PROCTOR *is motionless.* You will give me your honest confession in my hand, or I cannot keep you from the rope. PROCTOR *does not reply.* What way do you go, Mister?

His breast heaving, his eyes staring, PROCTOR *tears the paper and crumples it, and he is weeping in fury, but erect.*

DANFORTH: Marshal!

PARRIS, *hysterically, as though the tearing paper were his life:* Proctor, Proctor!

HALE: Man, you will hang! You cannot!

PROCTOR, *his eyes full of tears:* I can. And there's your first marvel, that I can. You have made your magic now, for now I do think I see some shred of goodness in John Proctor. Not enough to weave a banner with, but white enough to keep it from such dogs. ❸ ELIZABETH, *in a burst of terror, rushes to him and weeps against his hand.* Give them no tear! Tears pleasure them! Show honor now, show a stony

Beyond the Selection

FURTHER READING

Other Works by Arthur Miller

All My Sons
Death of a Salesman

Other Works About Social Pressures and Social Protest

A Raisin in the Sun, Lorraine Hansberry
A Doll's House, Henrik Ibsen

We suggest that you preview these works before recommending them to students.

INTERNET

You can find additional information about Miller and his work on the Internet. We suggest the following sites. Please be aware that sites may have changed from the time we published this information.

Visit the Arthur Miller Home Page at **http://www. penguin.com/usa/electronic/crucible/aboutarthur.html**

We *strongly recommend* that you preview the site before you send students to it.

heart and sink them with it! *He has lifted her, and kisses her now with great passion.*

REBECCA: Let you fear nothing! Another judgment waits us all!

DANFORTH: Hang them high over the town! Who weeps for these, weeps for corruption! *He sweeps out past them.* HERRICK *starts to lead* REBECCA, *who almost collapses, but* PROCTOR *catches her, and she glances up at him apologetically.*

REBECCA: I've had no breakfast.

HERRICK: Come, man.

HERRICK *escorts them out,* HATHORNE *and* CHEEVER *behind them.* ELIZABETH *stands staring at the empty doorway.*

PARRIS, *in deadly fear, to* ELIZABETH: Go to him, Goody Proctor! There is yet time!

From outside a drumroll strikes the air. PARRIS *is startled.* ELIZABETH *jerks about toward the window.*

PARRIS: Go to him! *He rushes out the door, as though to hold back his fate.* Proctor! Proctor!

Again, a short burst of drums.

HALE: Woman, plead with him! *He starts to rush out the door, and then goes back to her.* Woman! It is pride, it is vanity. *She avoids his eyes, and moves to the window. He drops to his knees.* Be his helper!—What profit him to bleed? Shall the dust praise him? Shall the worms declare his truth? Go to him, take his shame away! ❹

ELIZABETH, *supporting herself against collapse, grips the bars of the window, and with a cry:* He have his goodness now. God forbid I take it from him!

The final drumroll crashes, then heightens violently. HALE *weeps in frantic prayer, and the new sun is pouring in upon her face, and the drums rattle like bones in the morning air.*

Guide for Responding

◆ Literature and Your Life

Reader's Response How did you react to the ending of the play? Would you recommend this play to a friend? Why or why not?

Thematic Focus What does the ending of the play suggest about the value of integrity and holding fast to principles? How might that idea relate to the McCarthy era?

Journal Writing Write an epitaph for John Proctor or Rebecca Nurse.

☑ Check Your Comprehension

1. (a) What worries Parris when he meets with Danforth at the beginning of Act IV? (b) What does he propose to Danforth?
2. Summarize Hale's argument favoring Proctor's confession.
3. Why does Danforth arrange a meeting between John and Elizabeth Proctor?
4. What does Proctor have "no tongue for"?

◆ Critical Thinking

INTERPRET

1. (a) What might have motivated Abigail to leave Salem? (b) How does Parris exhibit his self-centeredness when he relates the news of Abigail's disappearence to Hathorne and Danforth? **[Infer]**
2. What motivates Reverend Hale to seek confessions from the condemned prisoners? **[Infer]**
3. Why is Elizabeth unable to offer her husband advice on whether to confess? **[Interpret]**
4. (a) Why does Proctor confess? (b) Why does he retract his confession? **[Analyze]**
5. Why does Elizabeth say her husband has "his goodness" as he is about to be hanged? **[Interpret]**

EVALUATE

6. Do you think John Proctor made the right decision? Why or why not? **[Evaluate]**

EXTEND

7. Could a tragedy like the Salem witchcraft trials occur today? Explain. **[Social Studies Link]**

◆ Critical Thinking

❹ **Make a Judgment** Ask students if they agree with Hale that Proctor's refusal to give in is due to "pride" and "vanity." *Suggested response: No, his refusal indicates that he has found goodness and honesty within himself; the refusal means his redemption.*

Reinforce and Extend

Answers

◆ Literature and Your Life

Reader's Response Responses should be supported by evidence from the play.

Thematic Focus It is vital to stick to one's principles; it is wrong to compromise one's principles and/or incriminate others simply because of fear for one's life, status, or livelihood.

☑ Check Your Comprehension

1. (a) Abby's disappearance and theft of his savings, the chaos in the community, the possibility of rebellion when respected people like Rebecca Nurse and John Proctor are executed, and the change of public opinion in neighboring towns worries him. (b) He asks Danforth to delay the executions.
2. Life is God's most precious gift; it is sinful to throw it away because of some misguided stubbornness or pride.
3. He hopes that Elizabeth will convince John to confess.
4. He has "no tongue for" accusing others.

◆ Critical Thinking

1. (a) Students might respond that she leaves because she realizes that many of the people of Salem are angry and may harm her. (b) Suggested response: He focuses on the fact that she has taken his money and left him penniless.
2. He feels guilty about his role in the proceedings and wants the accused to confess to avoid being executed.
3. She feels that it is wrong to instruct him to lie; yet she does not wish to see him die.
4. (a) Proctor confesses because he wants to save his life. (b) He retracts his confession because he does not want to ruin his good name by lying.
5. Elizabeth says John has "his goodness" because he refuses to let the fear of death keep him from being truthful about himself and others.
6. Many students will probably respond that he made the right decision because it enabled him to retain his dignity.
7. Accept all reasonable responses. Students who think a similar situation could arise may mention political or racial tensions, a frightening epidemic, or a natural or human-made disaster at its root.

Answers

◆ Reading Strategy

1. Miller might be criticizing the Senate committee's inquisitorial manner of questioning, its disregard of the legal rights of the accused, and its attitude that any failure to comply with the committee's wishes was an admission of guilt.
2. The motives are often a need to win petty personal quarrels, a desire for revenge, jealousy, greed, and a desire for more social or political power.

◆ Grammar and Style

Commonly Confused Words: *Raise* and *Rise*

Practice

1. rose
2. raising
3. raised
4. risen
5. raised

Grammar Reinforcement

For additional instruction and practice, use the lesson on Correct and Effective Use of Verbs in the **Language Lab CD-ROM,** and the practice page on the Correct Use of Tenses, page 57 in the *Writer's Solution Grammar Practice Book.*

◆ Literary Focus

1. (a) Possible evidence includes the description of Salem at the start of Act IV. (b) Possible evidence includes the noble behavior of John Proctor and Rebecca Nurse.
2. Accept all reasonable responses that students can support with examples from the play.

◆ Build Vocabulary

Using Words From Myths: *Tantalize*

Sample sentences follow.

1. I enjoy *cereal* for breakfast.
2. The *titanic* struggle between the two armies at last came to an end.
3. The *narcissistic* young man smiled at his reflection in the mirror.

Using the Word Bank

1. b 2. a 3. b 4. a 5. c
6. c 7. c 8. a 9. b 10. b

Guide for Responding, *Act IV* (continued)

◆ Reading Strategy

Apply Themes to Contemporary Events

As Arthur Miller himself mentions often in the background sections within *The Crucible*, there are several parallels between the witchcraft hysteria of 1692 and the events that occurred during the McCarthy era of the 1950's.

1. Based on the play's details, what criticisms might Miller be making about the way McCarthy's Senate committee dealt with those it questioned and those who criticized it?
2. What does the play suggest about the motives behind political "witch hunts" like Senator Joseph McCarthy's?

◆ Grammar and Style

Commonly Confused Words: *Raise* and *Rise*

To *raise* means "to lift up"; it takes a direct object. To *rise* means "to go up or get up"; it does not take a direct object. Study the forms of the two verbs on the chart below.

Verb	Present	Present Participle	Past	Past Participle
raise	raise, raises	raising	raised	(have) raised
rise	rise, rises	rising	rose	(have) risen

Practice Complete each sentence with the correct form of *rise* or *raise* in the tense indicated in parentheses.

1. All (past) when the judge entered.
2. They were (present participle) the flag outside the courthouse.
3. In 1692, cries of witchcraft (past) a ruckus in Salem.
4. Spirits were reported to have (past participle) to the courtroom ceiling.
5. Citizens in a nearby town had (past participle) a rebellion.

◆ Literary Focus

Theme

A **theme** is a central idea or insight about life conveyed in a work of literature. Longer works like *The Crucible* often express many themes.

1. Use evidence from the play to show how Miller conveys the following themes in *The Crucible*: (a) Fear and suspicion are infectious and can produce a mass hysteria that destroys public order and rationality. (b) It is more noble to die with integrity than to live with compromised principles that harm others.
2. State and support another theme that you feel the play expresses.

◆ Build Vocabulary

Using Words From Myths: *Tantalize*

Tantalize, from the myth about King Tantalus, is just one of several English words that come from Greek and Roman mythology. Review the three mythological figures below. Then, for each, write a sentence using the word in parentheses.

1. *Ceres*: The goddess of the harvest (cereal)
2. *Titan*: A race of giants with brute strength (titanic)
3. *Narcissus*: A boy punished by the gods for vanity (narcissistic)

Using the Word Bank: Synonyms

In your notebook, write the letter of the word that is most nearly the same in meaning as the first word.

1. agape: (a) dark, (b) open, (c) shocking
2. conciliatory: (a) soothing, (b) rude, (c) vengeful
3. beguile: (a) plead, (b) fool, (c) straighten
4. floundering: (a) groping, (b) jogging, (c) smelling
5. retaliation: (a) narration, (b) restatement, (c) revenge
6. adamant: (a) calm, (b) first, (c) stubborn
7. cleave: (a) depart, (b) grow, (c) stick
8. sibilance: (a) hissing, (b) humming, (c) screaming
9. tantalized: (a) freed, (b) tempted, (c) danced
10. purged: (a) soothed, (b) washed, (c) filled

Build Your Portfolio

Idea Bank

Writing

1. **Casting Profiles** As a casting director for this play, describe two or three of the main characters and the requirements for playing each.
2. **Literary Analysis** How is the play's title appropriate to its themes and content? Answer in a brief essay that begins with a definition of *crucible*.
3. **Critical Response** Some have claimed that *The Crucible*'s characters are only "mouthpieces" for Miller's ideas. In an essay, support or refute critic Walter Kerr, who said, "For Salem, and the people . . . in it, are really only conveniences to Mr. Miller, props to his theme. He does not make them interesting in and of themselves, and you wind up analyzing them . . . rather than losing yourself in any rounded, deeply rewarding personalities."

Speaking, Listening, and Viewing

4. **Mock Trial** Stage a mock trial to determine whether Danforth and Hathorne are guilty of murder for their roles in the Salem witch trials. Appoint a prosecutor, a defense attorney, defendants, witnesses, and a jury. **[Social Studies Link]**
5. **Group Discussion** Research the McCarthy era of the 1950's. Present your findings; then lead a group discussion about the accuracy of Miller's views of that era. **[Social Studies Link]**

Researching and Representing

6. **Compare-and-Contrast Chart** Working with a partner, research the facts of the Salem witchcraft trials. Then present a compare-and-contrast chart on differences between the trials and events in this play. Give possible reasons Miller had for making those changes. **[Social Studies Link]**
7. **Memorial** Design a memorial commemorating those killed in the Salem witch trials. **[Art Link]**

Online Activity www.phlit.phschool.com

Guided Writing Lesson

Defend a Character's Actions

Did John Proctor do the right thing in the end? What did you think of Reverend Hale's decisions, or Elizabeth Proctor's, or Judge Danforth's? Write an essay in which you defend a character's actions or final decision in the play. Like a good trial lawyer, you need not agree with your "client's" actions—just present the best defense possible.

Writing Skills Focus: Pro-and-Con Argument

To defend a character as effectively as possible, you need to anticipate and refute the attacks or criticisms that others may make. Your defense should include the following elements:

- **"Cons"**—reasons against your argument. In this case, list the reasons some people may find the character's actions or decisions to be wrong.
- **"Pros"**—reasons supporting your argument. In this case, list the reasons you find the character's actions or decisions to be right.
- **Refutation** Provide reasons that show the "pros" outweigh the "cons."

Prewriting Skim the play to decide which character's actions you will defend. Record possible "pros" and "cons" in a two-column chart. You might discuss the character with others to come up with as complete a list of "pros" and "cons" as possible.

Drafting Begin by presenting the "cons," then move on to the "pros." Use forceful, persuasive language to explain why the "pros" outweigh the "cons."

Revising Make sure you have effectively refuted the "cons" and included enough "pros" to support your argument. Is your word choice clear and precise? Do your sentences flow logically and smoothly?

✓ ASSESSMENT OPTIONS

Formal Assessment, Selection Test, pp. 335–337, and Assessment Resources Software. The selection test is designed so that it can be easily customized to the performance levels of your students.
Alternative Assessment, p. 79, includes options for less advanced students, more advanced students, musical/rhythmic learners, visual/spatial learners, and interpersonal learners.

PORTFOLIO ASSESSMENT
Use the following rubrics in the ***Alternative Assessment*** booklet to assess student writing:
Casting Profiles: Description Rubric, p. 112
Literary Analysis: Literary Analysis/Interpretation Rubric, p. 127
Critical Response: Critical Review Rubric, p. 126
Guided Writing Lesson: Persuasion Rubric, p. 120

Idea Bank

Customizing for *Performance Levels*
Following are suggestions for matching Idea Bank topics with your students' performance levels:
Less Advanced Students: 1
Average Students: 2
More Advanced Students: 3

Customizing for *Learning Modalities*
Following are suggestions for matching Idea Bank topics with your students' learning modalities:
Bodily/Kinesthetic: 4
Interpersonal: 5
Logical/Mathematical: 6
Visual/Spatial: 7

Guided Writing Lesson

Writing and Language Transparencies Have students use the Argument Organizer in ***Writing and Language Transparencies,*** p. 75, to organize their arguments in defense of a character.

Writers at Work Videodisc Have students view the videodisc segment (Ch. 4) featuring M. Gasby Greely, Vice-President of Communications for the Urban League, speaking about persuasive writing. Ask students what Greely says about the significance of words in the realm of persuasive writing.

Play frames 33643 to 43235

Writing Lab CD-ROM
Have students complete the tutorial on Persuasion. Follow these steps:
1. Use the Pros and Cons Chart to help evaluate arguments for and against justifying a character's actions.
2. Have students use the Persuasive Word Bin to select words and phrases that will make their argument more effective.
3. Use the Interactive Self-Evaluation Checklist to aid revision.

Sourcebook
Have students use Chapter 4, Persuasion (pp. 96–129), for additional support.

Prepare and Engage

LESSON OBJECTIVES

- To use recursive writing processes to write a position paper
- To recognize the connotations of words and use them to strengthen writing
- To use varied sentence structure

Distribute the scoring rubric for Persuasion (p. 120 in ***Alternative Assessment***) to make students aware of the criteria. See the note on page 1172 to customize the rubric to this workshop.

You may also want to present the Argument Organizer from the ***Writing and Language Transparencies***, p. 17.

Connect to Literature To familiarize students with the elements of a position paper, consider reviewing *The Declaration of Independence* (p. 140) and the excerpt from *The Crisis* by Thomas Paine (p. 144).

Writers at Work Videodisc To introduce students to the ways persuasive writing might shape public policy, play the videodisc segment featuring the National Urban League's Gasby Greely (Ch. 4).

Play frames 33643 to 43235

Writing Lab CD-ROM
If your students have access to computers, you may want to have them use the tutorial on Persuasion to write their position papers. Have students follow these steps:

1. Use the many interactive instructional activities that can be found in the Considering Audience and Purpose section.
2. Draft the position paper on the computer.
3. Use the Self-Evaluation Checklist to help in revising.

Position Paper — Writing Process Workshop

From the authors and signers of the Declaration of Independence to the creators of the social protest literature of recent decades, writers have tried, with reason or emotional appeal, to persuade readers to accept a wide range of ideas. A position paper presents one side of a controversial issue and tries to persuade its audience to take that side. The intended audience often has some power to shape policy on the issue.

These writing tips, introduced in this section's Guided Writing Lessons, will help you write your position paper:

Writing Skills Focus

- **Consider the knowledge level of readers.** Use language and details that they can understand. (See p. 1047.)
- **Elaborate** by providing both logical reasons and emotional appeals to support your argument. (See p. 1077.)
- **Use specific examples** to back up your position. (See p. 1057.)

This introduction to a position paper demonstrates many of these skills:

WRITING MODEL

A higher minimum wage destroys jobs by making it unprofitable to hire young, inexperienced job seekers. ① Its impact will be felt by the people with the fewest skills and the most to learn. I know because I'm proof. ②

I was a single mother when I started at Cousins Submarine shop in 1981. My first job was as a part-time cashier earning $2.90 per hour, less than I wanted, but more than I deserved. Within months, I had gotten a raise and moved up to making sandwiches. . . . Today, I supervise eight Cousins shops in Milwaukee and oversee nearly 300 employees. ③

① The author begins by stating her position.
② Clear, jargon-free language is appropriate for the average voter to understand.
③ The writer's personal experience supports her thesis.

Beyond the Classroom

Workplace Skills Connection

Proposals Formal proposals in the workplace combine elements of practical and persuasive writing. Like a position paper, a business proposal attempts to convince a person or a group in a position of power to adopt new practices or ideas. Employees generate proposals in order to initiate the funding, planning, and implementation of projects. Freelancers and business owners develop proposals to obtain work from other businesses or to attract investors to a new venture. Ask students how developing such proposals might differ from writing position papers. *Responses might include that proposal writers have more personal knowledge or experience of the intended audience, enabling them to tailor their language and examples more precisely. Position papers, in contrast, might attempt to appeal to universal values and beliefs and so contain appeals that are more emotional in nature.*

Prewriting

Choose a Topic Read the editorial page of a newspaper. Choose an issue from the paper that interests you or that evokes a strong personal response—either positive or negative. You may also take a position on one of the topics listed below.

Topic Ideas
- U.S. military intervention in foreign conflicts
- The use of dialect in literature
- Term limits for U.S. Congress members
- Required seat belts on school buses

Gather Facts and Examples Use current, credible resources to gather specific facts, examples, and evidence to support your position and persuade others to adopt it. You may run across information that disputes your position. Your ability to understand and refute the opposition can only strengthen your paper.

Drafting

Use Appropriate Vocabulary and Style Keep your readers in mind as you write. You will most likely be writing for a general audience, so remember to define any technical terms or jargon. At the same time, avoid "talking down" to your audience.

Avoid Faulty Logic In order to persuade your readers to adopt your position on an issue, you must present adequate supporting evidence. Avoid building your argument on faulty logic and unreasonable appeals, which a discerning audience will soon see through. Some tactics to avoid include the following:

- **Overgeneralization:** a statement that is too broad for the evidence that backs it up; for example: Modern poets have abandoned all traditional literary forms.
- **Circular reasoning:** an attempt to support a point by merely restating it in other words; for example: Sylvia Plath is a famous poet because many people know her work.
- **Either/or argument:** a statement that offers only two extremes, when there are other possibilities; for example: Either we lead the military peacekeeping effort or we risk a return to the foreign policy of isolationism.
- **Bandwagon appeal:** a statement that urges acceptance of an idea or action simply because "everyone" believes it or is doing it; for example: Anyone who is anybody has read the works of Arthur Miller.

Applying Language Skills: Connotation and Denotation

The **denotation** of a word is its literal definition. **Connotation** is a word's suggested meaning and the ideas associated with that word. Words with the same denotation may have different connotations:

Neutral Connotation: This bill overlooks environmental issues.

Negative Connotation: This bill neglects environmental issues.

Practice Rewrite the following passage, replacing each italicized word with a term that has the same denotation but a different connotation:

The Bidwell Ghost is a *skinny* young woman who waits by the side of a *desolate* road. Drivers who stop for her describe an *odor* like ripening orchard fruit as she *scrambles* into their cars.

Writing Application Use a thesaurus and a dictionary to find synonyms whose connotations can strengthen your writing.

Writer's Solution Connection
Language Lab

For other topic ideas, see the Inspirations in the tutorial on Persuasion.

Prewriting Strategy

To help students choose a topic for their position papers, consider reviewing the selections in the final part of this unit, which have a theme of social protest. Have students reflect on their reading to find a subject that particularly moved them. Then guide them to adapt and narrow these topics so that they are suitable for a position paper.

Customize for *Interpersonal Learners*

These students may find it helpful to rehearse aspects of their basic arguments orally with peers before drafting. Feedback from other students proves the effectiveness of certain lines of reasoning while causing students to question others. In order to achieve a balanced response, each student may want to engage two other students in this process—each representing either a pro or con position relative to the writer's.

Customize for *AP Students*

Encourage these students to contact a volunteer or nonprofit organization and offer to write a position paper that can be used for fund raising, as a form letter for members to sign and send to government officials, or as the basis for the organization's mission statement.

Writing Lab CD-ROM

The Gathering Evidence section of the tutorial on Persuasion includes tools that can help students shape their position papers: a Pros and Cons chart sorts opposing ideas to build a strong argument, while the interactive instruction on facts and opinions can help student evaluate claims they make.

Applying Language Skills

Connotation and Denotation Explain to students that though persuasive writing relies on the use of forceful language, writers need to temper emotional appeals by choosing words that reflect the writer's basic rational skills—a goal in which understanding the distinction between connotation and denotation is critical.

Suggested Answer

The Bidwell Ghost is a *gaunt* young woman who waits by the side of a *lonely* road. Drivers who stop for her describe a *stench* like ripening orchard fruit as she *shuffles* into their cars.

For additional instruction and practice, refer to the **Language Lab CD-ROM** lesson on Writing With Nouns and Verbs.

Elaboration Strategy

As students add details to their drafts, have them list connotations of potentially "loaded" words and evaluate whether they want to use these words.

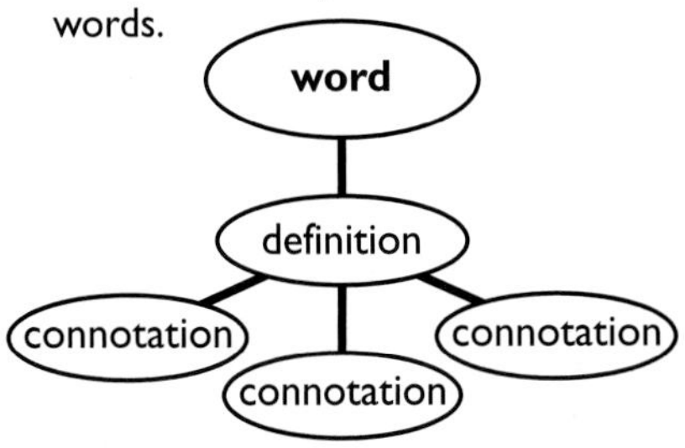

Revision Strategy

To enhance the effectiveness of the "read out loud" method of revising, encourage peers to rehearse their reading privately before reading to the writer. That way the reader can eliminate minor glitches in delivery that could be mistaken for awkward or unclear writing.

Publishing

If students choose to send their papers to editors or elected officials, remind them to follow up with phone calls to confirm receipt.

Applying Language Skills

Varying Sentence Length Explain to students that the rhythm created by varied sentence lengths can underscore the emotional appeal of their papers. For example, a short sentence can be used almost as a form of punctuation in its terseness of expression.

Suggested Answer

Puerto Rico is not a state but a protectorate. Recently, the citizens of this island that lies off the east coast of the United States voted on the issue of statehood.

Grammar Reinforcement

For additional instruction and practice, refer students to the Writing Style unit in the **Language Lab CD-ROM.**

Reinforce and Extend

Reflect on Writing To extend the assignment, ask students what actions they are committed to take as a result of writing their position papers.

Prentice Hall Writing and Grammar For more prewriting, elaboration, and revision strategies, see *Prentice Hall Writing and Grammar.*

APPLYING LANGUAGE SKILLS: Varying Sentence Length

Add interest to your writing and prevent it from becoming monotonous by **varying your sentence lengths.** Notice the varying lengths of these sentences from *The Rockpile*:

John took Delilah and sat down with her in the easy chair. His mother bent over Roy, and held him still, while his father, carefully—but still Roy screamed—lifted the bandage and stared at the wound. Roy's sobs began to lessen.

Practice Revise the following paragraph by varying the sentence lengths.

> Puerto Rico is not a state. It is a protectorate. It is also an island. Puerto Rico lies off the east coast of the United States. Recently, its citizens voted. They voted on the issue of statehood.

Writing Application Combine shorter sentences with conjunctions and appropriate punctuation to create longer, more complex, sentences.

Writer's Solution Connection Writing Lab

For help gathering forceful language, use the Persuasive Words Word Bin in the Revising and Editing section of the tutorial on Persuasion.

Use Persuasive Words Emphasize your main points with positive persuasive language—words such as *superior, intelligent, wise, brilliant*—to make your ideas seem more appealing. Use negative persuasive language—terms such as *implausible, misguided, unreasonable*—to convey criticism of opposing views.

Revising

Add Necessary Information Reread your position paper to be sure it explains the issue completely. Where necessary, add background or explanatory information

Read Out Loud Ask a classmate to read your paper out loud while you listen. Use the following revision checklist, based on this lesson's Writing Skills Focus, to guide your listening:

- How can I revise my choice of words or details to better suit my audience?
- Have I presented enough facts, quotations, reasons, or other evidence to support my opinion? How can I strengthen this evidence?
- What logical reasons have I used to make my point? Have I avoided faulty logic? What opposing arguments have I considered or should I consider to make my viewpoint seem more reasonable?

REVISION MODEL

~~You are about to consider cutting funds spent to support Public Television.~~ ① As you take up the issue of PBS, consider the far-reaching ramifications of canceling funding. ~~Everyone knows that the children's programming makes children smarter.~~ ② Current research indicates that high-school students who regularly watched Sesame Street as preschoolers routinely scored higher than peers who were not exposed to such programming.

① The author substitutes a more sophisticated sentence that is appropriate for the background and knowledge level of the intended audience.

② The author eliminates faulty logic; in this case, a bandwagon appeal. A verifiable fact adds credibility to the author's argument.

Publishing

- **Letter** Send your position paper to the editor of your local newspaper or to an elected official who may have power to impact the issue addressed in your paper.

✓ ASSESSMENT		4	3	2	1
PORTFOLIO ASSESSMENT Use the rubric on Persuasion in the ***Alternative Assessment*** booklet (p. 120) to assess students' writing. Add the following criteria to further customize the rubric to this assignment.	**Varying Sentence Length**	The writer effectively maintains an appealing rhythm by varying sentence length.	The writer varies the length of sentences, avoiding an overload of short or long sentences.	The writer provides little variety in terms of sentence length.	The writer uses sentences of nearly uniform length, lending a monotonous quality to the text.
	Connotation and Denotation	The writer consistently demonstrates an understanding of connotation, adding to the impact of the persuasive language.	The writer diplays an awareness of the connotative meanings of words.	The writer often uses words whose connotation hampers the effectiveness of the paper.	The writer consistently makes word choices without regard to connotation or denotation.

Student Success Workshop

Research Skills

Drawing Conclusions From Researched Information

Strategies for Success

Do you find it difficult to make sense of researched information? As you begin to prepare your report, have you ever wondered what to do with all the information you've collected? Gathering information about a research topic is the easy part. Drawing conclusions from the information gathered, however, is the most important aspect of research. Use the following strategies to help:

Organize the Information It is important to keep your research organized. Note cards help you do this. As you write down the information you find, label each card with a word or phrase that describes what is on the card. Then, assemble the related cards together.

Early Settlement
The Puritans arrived in America in 1620. Shortly thereafter, they founded the Massachusetts Bay Colony. Having made the journey for the freedom of religious expression, the Puritans based their society on moral codes and religious tenets.

Government
The Puritans created a government based upon religion. Ministers were among the most powerful figures in the Massachusetts Bay Colony. Magistrates used the Bible as their legal textbook. Citizens were required to obey religious laws and were punished if they didn't.

Anne Hutchinson
Among the first to challenge the Puritans' religious government was Anne Hutchinson. She interpreted religion differently from the leaders, and she openly criticized the colony's ministers. As a result of this conflict, Hutchinson was charged with sedition, or attempting to overthrow the government. She was tried, convicted, and banished from the colony. Others, after Hutchinson, were also persecuted for dissension.

Evaluate the Information Carefully read through the information you have gathered, including charts and illustrations. Try to recognize connections or links in the material. Do you notice a fact repeated more than once? What are the pervading themes? Many times, the important findings of your research are not directly stated but come from the connections you make in your gathered information.

Draw Conclusions From Information Once you've recognized common themes, the next step is to form conclusions. List the main ideas from your research, and write a summary in your own words. Draw a conclusion based upon this information. If you are presenting your research, use the conclusion and main ideas to prepare a rough outline. Then, fill in the supporting details.

Apply the Strategies

Read the sample note cards, and answer these questions:

1. What major themes of Puritan society are evident in these research notes?
2. Focusing the main ideas, create an outline using the researched information.
3. Using your own words, draw a conclusion about Puritan society from the information presented in the cards.

✔ *Here are situations in which to draw conclusions from researched information:*

- ▶ Presenting the results from a survey about community recycling efforts
- ▶ Comparing the facts when buying a new car
- ▶ Deciding your stance on a political issue

Prepare and Engage

LESSON OBJECTIVES

- To draw conclusions from information gathered
- To evaluate information

Customize for
Visual/Spatial Learners
Some students may benefit from visual methods of organizing research information. Encourage these students to organize information in graphic organizers, such as charts or webs, rather than on note cards. These visual presentations will help them evaluate the information more readily, leading to more valid conclusions.

Answers
Possible responses:

1. The importance of religion to the Puritans; the conflict between religion and government
2. Settling Massachusetts Bay Colony
   A. Early Settlement
   B. Forming a Government
   C. Dissension
3. The Puritans came to America seeking religious freedom. They had no tolerance for differing views or other religions.

Test Preparation Workshop

Drawing Conclusions From Researched Information
Standardized tests often require students to draw conclusions about information presented in passages on the test. Students should understand that conclusions may not be explicitly stated in what they have read.

Display the following item:

Which of the following conclusions about Puritan life may be drawn from the information presented in the workshop?

A Anne Hutchinson established her own religion when she was banished from the Massachusetts Bay Colony.
B Puritan intolerance for opposing viewpoints led to dissension in the Massachusetts Bay Colony.
C Puritan ministers were wise leaders for the Massachusetts Bay Colony.
D Citizens of the Massachusetts Bay Colony had a voice in running their government.

Students should explain why B is the correct answer.

Prepare and Engage

LESSON OBJECTIVES

- To prepare, organize, plan, and present literary interpretations; to present interpretations such as telling stories, performing original works, and interpreting poems and stories for a variety of audiences

Discuss with students how their language and style would differ in giving an opinion of a popular movie to a group of friends at lunch time and in reviewing the same film in a class presentation. Students should recognize that knowing the audience influences the way in which the information is delivered. Similarly, interpretations of literature will vary depending on the audience.

Customize for
Musical/Rhythmic Learners
Poetry is an excellent vehicle for students who have an interest in music and an awareness of the rhythm of language. Encourage students to use their knowledge of various rhythms to choose poems for interpretation. You may wish to have students who play musical instruments develop accompaniments that are appropriate for their interpretations.

Apply the Strategies

1. Students' interpretations should reflect an awareness of classmates' interests.
2. A story presented to a group of children might involve a more animated performance, perhaps including more obvious gestures and expressions. A story presented to a group of senior citizens could be presented with more subtle gestures.
3. Students may cite listeners' interests as one criterion that would make a work more appropriate for one audience than another. A work with complex language or a sophisticated theme may be wasted on a young or uninformed audience.

Speaking, Listening, and Viewing Workshop

Interpreting Literature for Varied Audiences

As in writing, when you interpret literature, you must think about your audience. The method, or style, you use to interpret literature can vary greatly, depending on your audience. You might be asked to tell a story, present an original work, or recite a poem for a community group, classmates, or a gathering of children. The way in which you present the material will differ for each of these groups.

Think About Your Audience An oral interpretation of literature is a type of performance. By thinking about your audience, you can develop a clear idea about the type of performance that would be most effective to express the meaning of the work. For example, a group of Shakespeare scholars might prefer a strict interpretation of the play *Romeo and Juliet,* but a casual gathering of young people might be more interested in a performance featuring animated expressions, music, and improvised humor.

Plan and Prepare An effective oral interpretation requires preparation. Take time to analyze the text you will interpret. Practice both verbal and nonverbal techniques, such as intonations, expressions, gestures, and pauses. Decide whether you want to introduce the work to your audience before you present your interpretation. Also, be sure to choose a work of literature suited to your audience.

Tips for Interpreting Literature Orally

Here are some points to keep in mind as you prepare and plan an oral interpretation:

- Keep your interpretation within the original meaning of the text.
- List the characteristics of your audience as you prepare your interpretation.
- Listen to a recording of yourself to identify your strong and weak points.

Apply the Strategies

1. Interpret a poem for your class. Think about three or four specific classmates as you prepare.
2. Choose a story to present to a group of children and to a group of senior citizens. How would your interpretations differ?
3. Why might certain works of literature be more appropriate for one particular audience than for another?

Beyond the Classroom

Community Connection
Many different community organizations provide opportunities to present interpretations of literature to varied audiences. Possibilities include day-care centers, public libraries, senior citizen centers, and historical societies.

Brainstorm with students for a list of places in the local community that might be interested in providing a forum for volunteers to present interpretations of literature. Have students identify works of literature that would be appropriate to interpret for each audience. Discuss as a group the characteristics of each audience and how the preparation of the interpretations will differ. Provide opportunities for volunteers to contact the various organizations to arrange the presentations.

Test Preparation Workshop

Writing Skills — Punctuation, Usage, and Sentence Structure

Strategies for Success

The writing sections of standardized tests examine your knowledge of the usage and mechanics of English. Use the following strategies to help you answer test questions regarding punctuation, grammar and usage, and sentence structure:

Punctuation These questions test your ability to use various punctuation marks correctly. For example, suppose you are asked to correct the underlined portion in the following sentence:

Some automobiles require diesel fuel in order to run properly, some do not.

1 Which of the following choices is correct?
A NO CHANGE
B properly . . . some do not.
C properly: some do not.
D properly; some do not.

The correct answer is **D.** A semicolon should be used to separate two independent clauses.

Grammar and Usage You will also need to recognize correct and incorrect grammar—specifically, subject-verb agreement and pronoun usage. For example:

2 Extreme sports like rock climbing grows in popularity among young people everywhere.
A NO CHANGE
B is growing
C grow
D grown

Answer **C** is correct because it is the only one that corrects the subject-verb agreement.

Sentence Structure These questions test your ability to correct structural errors like run-on sentences, fragments, misplaced modifiers, and mood or voice shifts. For example:

3 Good journalism provides all the vital information. *Who, what, when,* and *where.*
A NO CHANGE
B information, *who*
C information; *who*
D information: *who*

The right answer is **D** because it corrects a sentence fragment.

Apply the Strategies

Read the following passage, and answer the questions:

(1) It had been a long and hard-fought campaign, the voters were ready to make a choice. (2) With the qualifications of all the candidates in mind, the voters choose Dan O'Neill to be mayor. (3) Voters claimed they were impressed with the full range of his positive attributes. Experience and credibility.

1 How would you correct sentence 1?
A NO CHANGE
B campaign; the voters were ready to make a choice.
C campaign. the voters were ready to make a choice.
D campaign: the voters were ready to make a choice.

2 How would you correct sentence 2?
A NO CHANGE
B was choosing
C chose
D choosed

3 How would you correct sentence 3?
A NO CHANGE
B positive attributes: experience
C positively attributes: experience
D positive attributes; Experience

Correlations to Standardized Tests

The writing skills reviewed in this workshop correspond to the following standardized test section:
ACT Writing

Test Preparation

Each ATE workshop in Unit 6 supports the instruction here by providing teaching suggestions and a sample test item:

Punctuation
(ATE, pp. 877, 891, 956, 992, 1025)
Grammar and Usage
(ATE, pp. 913, 925, 947, 1067)
Sentence Structure
(ATE, pp. 903, 935, 977, 1047, 1078)
Identifying Errors
(ATE, pp. 1005, 1059)

LESSON OBJECTIVES

- To demonstrate control over grammatical elements
- To produce legible work that shows correct use of the conventions of punctuation and to produce error-free writing in the final draft
- To compose increasingly more involved sentences

Answers

1. (B) campaign; the voters were ready to make a choice.
2. (C) chose
3. (B) positive attributes: experience

Test-Taking Tip

Process of Elimination Point out to students that they can answer questions more efficiently on a standardized test by using a process of elimination. For example, question 1 in Apply the Strategies asks how you would correct sentence 1 in the passage. Answer *C* can be eliminated immediately, since starting a sentence with a lowercase letter would introduce a new error. A careful reading of sentence 1 shows that it contains two independent clauses, and so some change must be made. Therefore, answer *A* can also be eliminated. Students can then evaluate the two remaining choices to determine which uses the correct punctuation. Students should explain that they have chosen answer *B* because a semicolon is used to separate two independent clauses, while a colon may be used after a salutation, as a formal introduction, for emphasis, or to introduce a list.

Planning Instruction and Assessment

Unit Objectives

1. To read selections in different genre from world literature
2. To connect themes in literature across cultures
3. To analyze literary elements
4. To use elements of text to defend responses
5. To connect world literature to American literature

Meeting the Objectives

With each selection, you will find instructional material through which students can meet these objectives. Further, you will find additional practice pages in ***Selection Support*** in the ***Teaching Resources*** box.

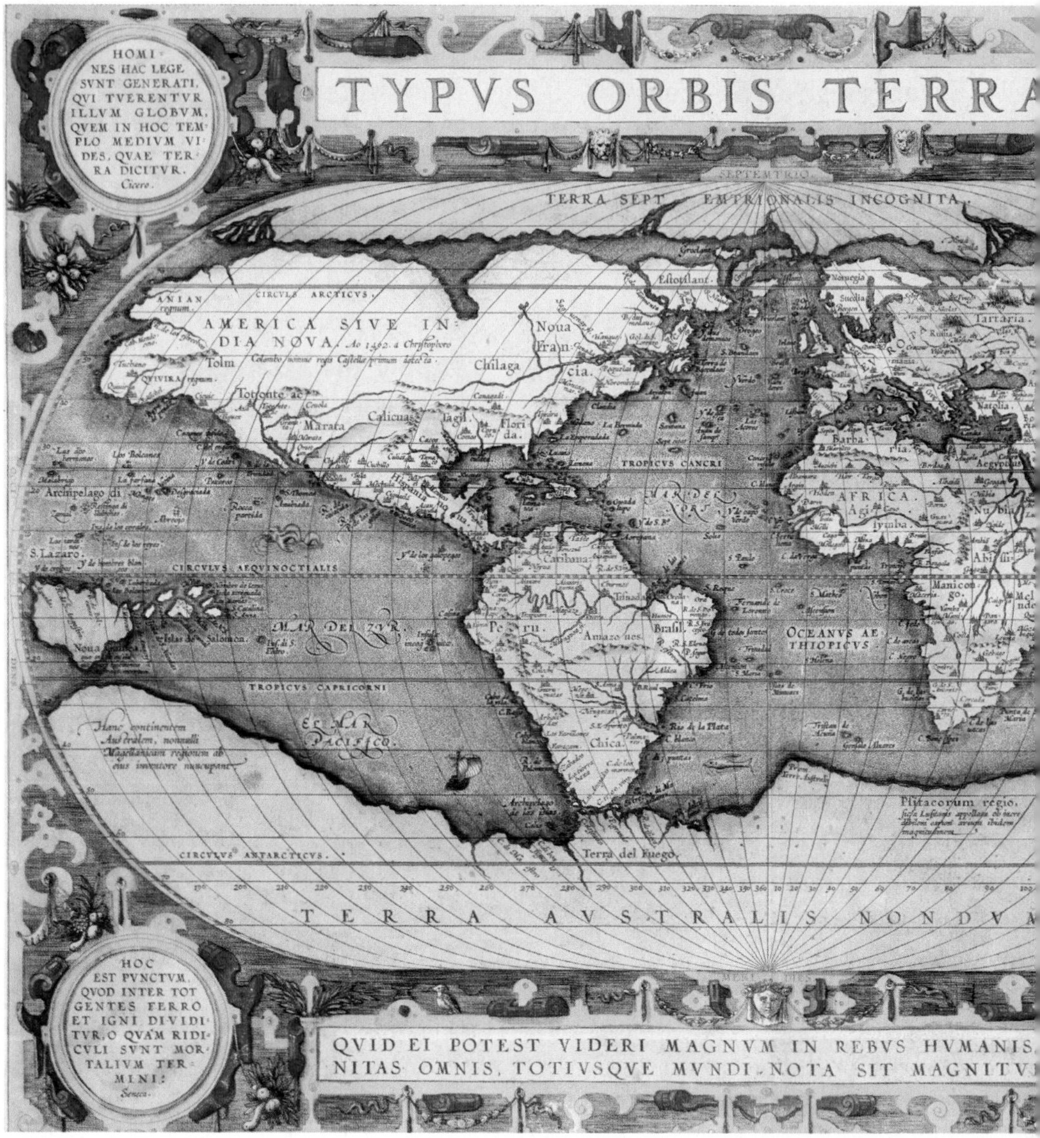

Oval World Map, Abraham Ortelius, Engraved 1587

Humanities: Art

Oval World Map, Abraham Ortelius, 1587.

Point out to students that this map was created in the sixteenth century. It reflects what Europeans knew about the world, based on the travels of European explorers. Help students connect this map to the unit of world literature by asking the following questions:

1. How is the map different from a contemporary map of the world? *Students will probably cite the changes to place names and to boundaries, as well as the style of the map.*
2. Compare and contrast the world view presented through a map like this one and through literature. *Students should note that the world view presented in a piece of literature often reflects the beliefs and knowledge of a particular culture. While a map such as this one reflects a European view in that the rendering is based on European exploration, the information is, by necessity, more objective.*
3. How can studying a map help you understand world literature? *Noting the physical relationships between places can help students identify possible reasons for similarities and differences in cultures.*

UNIT 7

Connections to World Literature

The stories, poems, and essays in Units 1 to 6 reflect the dominant voices and themes of American literature. Many of the themes that have been important to American writers have also been explored by writers around the world and throughout the ages. This unit presents classic and contemporary world literature that echoes the voices and themes of American writers. Each world literature selection is thematically connected to a specific work of American literature included in a previous unit.

Assessing Student Progress

The following tools are available to measure the degree to which students meet the unit objectives:

Informal Assessment

The questions following each selection are a first level of response to the concepts and skills presented with the selection. Students' responses are a brief informal measure of their grasp of the material. Their responses on this level can indicate where further instruction and practice are needed. You may then follow up with the practice pages in the ***Selection Support*** booklet.

You will find literature and reading guides in the ***Alternative Assessment*** booklet, which you may give students on an individual basis for informal assessment of their performance.

Formal Assessment

In the ***Formal Assessment*** booklet, you will find selection tests and a part test.

Selection Tests The selection tests measure comprehension and skills acquisition for each selection or group of selections.

Part Test The part test, which calls on students to read a passage of literature they have not previously seen, applies the unit skills on a broader level.

Alternative Assessment

Portfolios As you review individual pieces or the collected work in students' portfolios, you will find assessment sheets available in the portfolio section of the ***Alternative Assessment*** booklet.

Scoring Rubrics You will find scoring rubrics for writing modes in the ***Alternative Assessment*** booklet. You can apply these to Guided Writing Lessons and to Writing Process Workshop lessons.

Speaking, Listening, and Viewing The ***Alternative Assessment*** booklet contains assessment sheets for speaking, listening, and viewing activities.

Learning Modalities The ***Alternative Assessment*** booklet contains activities that appeal to different learning styles. You may use these too as an alternative measurement of students' growth.

LESSON OBJECTIVES

1. To develop vocabulary and word identification skills
- Extending Word Study: Word Origins (ATE)

2. To use a variety of reading strategies to comprehend a short story
- Tips to Guide Reading (ATE)
- Read to Be Entertained (ATE)

3. To increase knowledge of other cultures and to connect common elements across cultures
- About the King James Version (SE)
- Cultural Context (ATE)
- Connections to American Literature (ATE)

4. To express and support responses to the text
- Critical Thinking

Cultural Context Despite the wide range of books and topics in the Old Testament, it is unified by a few constant themes. Among these are the power, goodness, and mercy of the One God (most other peoples of that era worshipped many gods); the covenant, or solemn agreement, into which God enters with the Hebrew people; the tendency of humans to stray from the right path; and the forgiveness people win from God. Ask students to be aware of the presence of these themes as they read.

CONNECTIONS TO AMERICAN LITERATURE

Both "The Story of the Flood" and "Sinners in the Hands of an Angry God" use frightening images such as great floods and terrifying fires to describe God's wrath and His ability to punish people for their sins. Ask students to consider why the story of Noah's Ark is frequently told to young children, while Edwards's sermon would be considered much too horrifying to share with children. Encourage them to compare and contrast the language, tone, and imagery used in both stories.

About the Bible

Traditionally, the books of the Hebrew Bible (called the Old Testament by Christians) have been divided into three main sections. The Torah consists of the first five books of the Bible. Another section contains historical accounts, such as the Book of Samuel. Still another section consists of a variety of works: poetry, such as the Psalms; short stories, such as the Book of Ruth; and religious dialogues, such as the Book of Job.

About the King James Version

Translated into Greek, Latin, and every important Western language, the Bible has had a wide influence. One famous translation of the Bible was done by a committee of scholars for England's King James (1611). The phrases and cadences of the King James version of the Bible have influenced the prose and poetry of English for nearly four hundred years.

Connection to "Sinners in the Hands of an Angry God"

The Bible has long influenced the way people in many cultures and of many religions conduct themselves. Puritan preacher Jonathan Edwards's sermon "Sinners in the Hands of an Angry God" depicts a wrathful God and a merciful Christ, modeled on the teachings of the Bible.

King James Bible

The Story of the Flood

Genesis 6–8

Chapter 6

1 And it came to pass, when men began to multiply on the face of the earth, and daughters were born unto them,
2 That the sons of God saw the daughters of men that they were fair; and they took them wives of all which they chose.
3 And the Lord said, "My spirit shall not always strive with man, for that he also is flesh: yet his days shall be an hundred and twenty years."
4 There were giants in the earth in those days; and also after that, when the sons of God came in unto the daughters of men, and they bare children to them, the same became mighty men which were of old, men of renown.
5 And God saw that the wickedness of man was great in the earth, and that every imagination of the thoughts of his heart was only evil continually.
6 And it repented the Lord that he had made man on the earth, and it grieved him at his heart.
7 And the Lord said, "I will destroy man whom I have created from the face of the earth; both man, and beast, and the creeping thing, and the fowls of the air; for it repenteth me that I have made them."
8 But Noah found grace in the eyes of the Lord.
9 These are the generations of Noah: Noah was a just man and perfect in his generations, and Noah walked with God.
10 And Noah begat three sons, Shem, Ham, and Japheth.
11 The earth also was corrupt before God, and the earth was filled with violence.

Interest Grabber Allow students to access their prior knowledge of the story of Noah's ark for a brainstorming activity. Have students write on a clean sheet of paper everything they remember about the flood story. When they have exhausted their knowledge, allow them to read the story, keeping a list of the parts they either forgot or remembered incorrectly. Do they understand the story differently based on what they learned from this most recent reading?

Noah's Ark (After the Flood), Joseph Baker Fountain, Harrogate Museums and Art Gallery, North Yorkshire, UK

▲ **Critical Viewing** Does this painting depict a scene before or after the flood? Cite evidence to support your answer. **[Interpret]**

12 And God looked upon the earth, and, behold, it was corrupt; for all flesh had corrupted his way upon the earth.

13 And God said unto Noah, "The end of all flesh is come before me; for the earth is filled with violence through them; and, behold, I will destroy them with the earth.

14 "Make thee an ark of gopher wood; rooms shalt thou make in the ark, and shalt pitch it within and without with pitch.

15 "And this is the fashion which thou shalt make it of: The length of the ark shall be three hundred cubits,[1] the breadth of it fifty cubits, and the height of it thirty cubits.

16 "A window shalt thou make to the ark, and in a cubit shalt thou finish it above; and the door of the ark shall thou set in the side thereof; with lower, second, and third stories shalt thou make it.

17 "And behold, I, even I, do bring a flood of waters upon the earth, to destroy all flesh, wherein is the breath of life, from under heaven; and every thing that is in the earth shall die.

18 "But with thee will I establish my covenant;[2] and thou shalt come into the ark, thou, and thy sons, and thy wife, and thy sons' wives with thee.

19 "And of every living thing of all flesh, two of every sort shalt thou bring into the ark, to

1. **cubits** (kyōō´ bits) *n.*: Ancient units of linear measure, about 18–22 inches each.

2. **covenant** (kuv´ ə nənt) *n.*: A binding and solemn agreement.

Develop Understanding

One-Minute Insight

This Old Testament story tells of God's decision to destroy life on earth as a way of punishing men for their sins. He chooses Noah, who has stayed in God's grace by avoiding sin, to build an ark so his family and two of every kind of animal can survive the flood and later repopulate the earth. After the waters fall for 40 days and sit on the earth for 150 more, God remembers Noah and dries out the earth. Noah emerges after a dove returns to him with a sign that it is safe to do so. He offers sacrifices to God, who promises never again to destroy the earth because of man, as sinning is part of human nature. The story depicts a wrathful God who punishes the unfaithful and disobedient but rewards those who remain in His grace.

Tips to Guide Reading

Before they read silently, model to the students by reading the first few lines of the story aloud. Call their attention to why it is important to read according to punctuation. The first verse, for example, ends in a comma, indicating only a brief pause before the next line. The lines would have been difficult to comprehend had you paused longer simply because a new verse was about to begin. Discuss with students how reading according to punctuation can aid understanding.

▶Critical Viewing◀

Interpret The scene takes place after the flood. The animals seem to be exploring the earth, which looks desolate and lifeless as it recovers from the flood.

◆Critical Thinking

Analyze Explain to students that both God and Noah play a role in honoring the covenant. Ask them to explain the responsibilities of both. How is this covenant similar to covenants of today? *Noah's role is to remain in the grace of God by abstaining from sin and faithfully obeying His commands. God's role is to save Noah and his family from the flood if Noah fulfills his side of the promise. Students might discuss marriage vows or business contracts.*

Customize for
Less Proficient Readers

Encourage students to make a list of words and phrases from the story that are no longer commonly used in English, such as "shalt" and "said unto." Have students share their lists and write the terms on the board, on the left side of a two-column chart. Then, discuss the meaning of each word. Have students come up with a modern-day equivalent for each word or phrase and write these in the column on the right.

Customize for
Logical/Mathematical Learners

Students may be intrigued by the size and dimensions of the ark. Have them calculate its size and compare these measurements to those of modern ships. Have them share their findings with the class.

Clarification

The Hebrews divided beasts into those that were unclean, meaning unfit to eat, and those that were clean. These dietary laws are spelled out in Leviticus, the third book of the Old Testament.

Customize for
AP Students

Have students hypothesize about the reasons why God destroyed the earth by a flood as opposed to using other means, such as great fires or some type of pestilence or plague. Guide them to think about the connotations of water and its cleansing powers when they consider this question. Also, show how the flood reduces the earth to its appearance during the early stages of creation.

◆ Critical Thinking

Analyze Point out that although God tells Noah how long the rains will last, He does not reveal how long the earth will be flooded. Therefore, Noah does not know how long he will have to remain in the ark. Ask students why they think God kept this information from Noah. *Students might say that withholding this information was yet another test of Noah's faith in God.*

Extending Word Study

Prefixes Have students use their knowledge of Latin prefixes and roots to define the word *prevail*. If they do not know the meaning of the prefix *pre* or the root *-vail-*, encourage them to use the dictionary. Then, have them list other words with the root *-vail-* and decipher the definitions of the words.

keep them alive with thee; they shall be male and female.

20 "Of fowls after their kind, and of cattle after their kind, of every creeping thing of the earth after his kind, two of every sort shall come unto thee, to keep them alive.

21 "And take thou unto thee of all food that is eaten, and thou shalt gather it to thee; and it shall be for food for thee, and for them."

22 Thus did Noah; according to all that God commanded him, so did he.

Chapter 7

1 And the Lord said unto Noah, "Come thou and all thy house into the ark; for thee have I seen righteous before me in this generation.

2 "Of every clean beast thou shalt take to thee by sevens, the male and his female: and of beasts that are not clean by two, the male and his female.

3 "Of fowls also of the air by sevens, the male and the female; to keep seed alive upon the face of all the earth.

4 "For yet seven days, and I will cause it to rain upon the earth forty days and forty nights; and every living substance that I have made will I destroy from off the face of the earth."

5 And Noah did according unto all that the Lord commanded him.

6 And Noah was six hundred years old when the flood of waters was upon the earth.

7 And Noah went in, and his sons, and his wife, and his sons' wives with him, into the ark, because of the waters of the flood.

8 Of clean beasts, and of beasts that are not clean, and of fowls, and of every thing that creepeth upon the earth,

9 There went in two and two unto Noah into the ark, the male and the female, as God had commanded Noah.

10 And it came to pass after seven days, that the waters of the flood were upon the earth.

11 In the six hundredth year of Noah's life, in the second month, the seventeenth day of the month, the same day were all the fountains of the great deep broken up, and the windows of heaven were opened.

12 And the rain was upon the earth forty days and forty nights.

13 In the selfsame day entered Noah, and Shem, and Ham, and Japheth, the sons of Noah, and Noah's wife, and the three wives of his sons with them, into the ark;

14 They, and every beast after his kind, and all the cattle after their kind, and every creeping thing that creepeth upon the earth after his kind, and every fowl after his kind, every bird of every sort.

15 And they went in unto Noah into the ark, two and two of all flesh, wherein is the breath of life.

16 And they that went in, went in male and female of all flesh, as God had commanded him: and the Lord shut him in.

17 And the flood was forty days upon the earth; and the waters increased, and bare up the ark, and it was lift up above the earth.

18 And the waters prevailed, and were increased greatly upon the earth; and the ark went upon the face of the waters.

19 And the waters prevailed exceedingly upon the earth; and all the high hills, that were under the whole heaven, were covered.

20 Fifteen cubits upward did the waters prevail; and the mountains were covered.

21 And all flesh died that moved upon the earth, both of fowl, and of cattle, and of beast, and of every creeping thing that creepeth upon the earth, and every man:

22 All in whose nostrils was the breath of life, of all that was in the dry land, died.

23 And every living substance was destroyed which was upon the face of the ground, both man, and cattle, and the creeping things, and the fowl of the heaven; and they were destroyed from the earth: and Noah only remained alive, and they that were with him in the ark.

24 And the waters prevailed upon the earth an hundred and fifty days.

Chapter 8

1 And God remembered Noah, and every living thing, and all the cattle that was with him in the ark: and God made a wind to pass over

CONNECTIONS TO AMERICAN LITERATURE

Ask students to write a portion of "The Story of the Flood" as Jonathan Edwards would have written it. Have them tell the story with the language Edwards might have used, and make sure they keep in mind the audience and the purpose of his sermons. *Students' writing should reflect the urgency and the sense of warning that pervade Edwards's sermons. It should use repetition of words, figurative language, and other devices Edwards uses to convey his points. The audience should be involved and implicated in the story, rather than being innocent listeners.*

Read to
Be Entertained

Point out to students that biblical stories are some of the most well-known and beloved stories in the world. As they read, encourage them to think about what gives the stories such a widespread and long-lasting appeal. Why are certain images, like that of the great flood and the ark, so memorable?

the earth, and the waters asswaged.[3]

2 The fountains also of the deep and the windows of heaven were stopped, and the rain from heaven was restrained;

3 And the waters returned from off the earth continually: and after the end of the hundred and fifty days the waters were abated.

4 And the ark rested in the seventh month, on the seventeenth day of the month, upon the mountains of Ararat.

5 And the waters decreased continually until the tenth month: in the tenth month, on the first day of the month, were the tops of the mountains seen.

6 And it came to pass at the end of forty days, that Noah opened the window of the ark which he had made:

7 And he sent forth a raven, which went forth to and fro, until the waters were dried up from off the earth.

8 Also he sent forth a dove from him, to see if the waters were abated from off the face of the ground;

9 But the dove found no rest for the sole of her foot, and she returned unto him into the ark, for the waters were on the face of the whole earth: then he put forth his hand, and took her, and pulled her in unto him into the ark.

10 And he stayed yet other seven days; and again he sent forth the dove out of the ark;

11 And the dove came in to him in the evening; and, lo, in her mouth was an olive leaf pluckt off: So Noah knew that the waters were abated from off the earth.

12 And he stayed yet other seven days; and sent forth the dove; which returned not again unto him any more.

13 And it came to pass in the six hundredth and first year, in the first month, the first day of the month, the waters were dried up from off the earth: and Noah removed the covering of the ark, and looked, and, behold, the face of the ground was dry.

14 And in the second month, on the seven and twentieth day of the month, was the earth dried.

3. **asswaged** (ə swājd′) *v.*: Calmed; this is an archaic use of the word *assuaged* as an intransitive verb.

15 And God spake unto Noah, saying,

16 "Go forth of the ark, thou, and thy wife, and thy sons, and thy sons' wives with thee.

17 "Bring forth with thee every living thing that is with thee, of all flesh, both of fowl, and of cattle, and of every creeping thing that creepeth upon the earth; that they may breed abundantly in the earth, and be fruitful, and multiply upon the earth."

18 And Noah went forth, and his sons, and his wife, and his sons' wives with him:

19 Every beast, every creeping thing, and every fowl, and whatsoever creepeth upon the earth, after their kinds, went forth out of the ark.

20 And Noah builded an altar unto the Lord; and took of every clean beast, and of every clean fowl, and offered burnt offerings on the altar.

21 And the Lord smelled a sweet savor; and the Lord said in his heart, "I will not again curse the ground any more for man's sake; for the imagination of man's heart is evil from his youth; neither will I again smite any more every thing living, as I have done.

22 "While the earth remaineth, seedtime and harvest, and cold and heat, and summer and winter, and day and night shall not cease."

◆ Critical Thinking

1. Why did Noah have God's favor? **[Connect]**
2. How did Noah know when the flood waters had ebbed? **[Interpret]**
3. (a) What does God require of Noah and his sons before he makes the covenant? (b) What is the reason for these demands? **[Analyze]**

◆ Compare Literary Works

4. Would Jonathan Edwards most likely feel that God's actions—destroying every living thing on earth during the flood—were justified? Explain. **[Hypothesize]**

Cultural Connection

5. Is the lesson of "The Story of the Flood" also present in other cultures? Explain. **[Connect]**

◆ Critical Thinking

Speculate What are the connotations of doves and olive branches? What is the result of choosing the dove and the olive branch as opposed to a different type of bird or tree? *Olive branches and doves often symbolize peace. Perhaps they signify the end of a tumultuous and violent period and the beginning of a more tranquil time.*

Customize for *Bodily/Kinesthetic Learners*

Encourage students to act out the scene of various animals emerging from the ark for the first time since the flood. First, have them brainstorm for a list of emotions the animals might be feeling. Have them try to convey these emotions in their dramatic representations.

◆ Critical Thinking

Analyze Why was Noah's first action upon being released from the ark to build an altar to make sacrifices to God, rather than building some type of shelter for himself and his family? *Students might say that Noah wanted to demonstrate to God that his faith was still as strong as it was before the flood.*

Reinforce and Extend

Answers

◆ Critical Thinking

1. Noah was a just and righteous man who abstained from sin and showed faith in God.
2. Noah sent out a dove to survey the land. When the dove returned with an olive leaf, this signaled that the waters had abated enough so that life could once again exist on earth.
3. (a.) God requires that they not eat flesh with blood and that they not kill other humans.
   (b.) Students may say that God wants to avoid the evil that existed on earth before the flood.
4. Edwards would feel that those who do not attempt to convert their hearts by being born again deserve to suffer the wrath of God.
5. "The Story of the Flood" demonstrates the consequences of sinful behavior. This is a common topic in literature from around the world, including the *Panchatantra*.

Beyond the Selection

FURTHER READING

Books About Biblical Times

Ancient Israel: Its Life and Institutions, Roland De Vaux

Ancient Egypt and the Old Testament, John D. Corrid and Kenneth A. Kichen

We suggest that you preview these works before recommending them to students.

INTERNET

You and your students may find additional information about the Bible on the Internet. We suggest the following sites. Please be aware, however, that these sites may have changed since the time this information was published.

To read more from and about the Bible, visit these sites:

www.bythesea.org/Bible/

www.biola.edu/online_bible/

We *strongly recommend* that you preview the sites before you send the students to them.

LESSON OBJECTIVES

1. **To increase knowledge of other cultures and to connect common elements across cultures**
   - About Nelson Mandela (SE)
   - Connections to American Literature (ATE)
2. **To express and support responses to the text**
   - Critical Thinking

About Nelson Mandela

Nelson Mandela was born in 1918 in Umtata in the Transkei, South Africa. From an early age, he was passionate about the pursuit of justice. Declining to follow in his father's footsteps as a chieftain, Mandela instead became a lawyer and an activist for social justice. Openly critical of apartheid, Mandela was arrested several times throughout his life.

In 1961, Mandela left South Africa for military training, as a member of the militant wing of the African National Congress. Upon his return, he was sentenced to five years in prison for illegally leaving the country and for inciting workers to strike. While in prison, he was found guilty of sabotage and sentenced to life in prison.

In February 1990, Mandela was released from prison. His efforts with F.W. de Klerk to dismantle apartheid brought them both the Nobel Peace Prize in 1993. In 1994, Mandela was inaugurated as State President of South Africa.

Connection to
The Crisis, Number 1

The American patriot Thomas Paine issued a cry for freedom in *The Crisis, Number 1*, rallying the American colonists to support the fight for independence. Throughout history, many others led fights for freedom and equality. Nelson Mandela, in his fight for racial equality, is a notable example in the latter half of the twentieth century.

NELSON MANDELA
Political Leader

FOUR GOOD LINKS:

Nelson Rolihlahla Mandela
Thorough (and admiring) bio from the ANC

Alt. Culture: Nelson Mandela
Brief summing up of Mandela's place in the 1990's

The Noble Prize Internet Archive
Fine links and articles regarding Mandela's 1993 prize

Long Walk to Freedom
Notes and selected texts from Mandela's autobiography

From 1964 to 1990, Nelson Mandela was imprisoned for opposing South Africa's white minority government. Instead of disappearing from view, Mandela became a martyr and worldwide symbol of resistance to racism. In 1993, Mandela and the president who released him, F. W. de Klerk, shared the Nobel Peace Prize. In 1994, Mandela was elected the country's president.

Web Page

VITAL STATS:

- **Born:**
18 July 1918
- **Birthplace:**
Umtata, Transkei
- **Death:**
Still kicking
- **Best Known as:**
Leader of the South African anti-apartheid movement

Find a famous person! Enter a name: [ ] **Search**

◆ Critical Thinking

1. Which link would you click to learn about Nelson Mandela's early life? Why? **[Analyze]**

2. If Thomas Paine were alive today, what might his Web page contain? Explain. **[Speculate]**

Cultural Connection

3. Why might a leader such as Nelson Mandela inspire respect throughout the world and across cultures? **[Assess]**

Reinforce and Extend

Answers

◆ Critical Thinking

1. You would click the link entitled "Nelson Rolihlahla Mandela" because it contains biographical information on Mandela.
2. Paine's personal Web page might contain links to his inspirational writings about the Revolutionary War. The Web would be an excellent vehicle for increasing his readership and spreading his ideas.

Cultural Connection

3. Mandela might inspire respect around the world because of his fierce dedication to fighting for equality and justice. He has also shown great resiliency and bravery against seemingly insurmountable obstacles.

Prepare and Engage

LESSON OBJECTIVES

1. **To develop vocabulary and word identification skills**
   - Extending Word Study: Secondary Definitions (ATE)
2. **To use a variety of reading strategies to comprehend poetry**
   - Read to Discover Models for Writing (ATE)
3. **To increase knowledge of other cultures and to connect common elements across cultures**
   - About the Authors (SE)
   - Cultural Context (ATE)
   - Connections to American Literature (ATE)
4. **To express and support responses to the text**
   - Critical Thinking

Cultural Context Haiku, a form of Japanese poetry which consists of seventeen syllables arranged in three lines of five, seven, and five syllables evolved from another form of Japanese poetry called hokku. Hokku, which literally means "starting verse," is the first in a long chain of verses called haika. Because the hokku sets the tone for the rest of the chain, it holds a privileged position in haika, and it eventually became its own independent form. This new form was named haiku. Today, haiku poems often describe a single image or impression from nature and are characterized by their concise language, reflective tone, and imagistic feel.

CONNECTIONS TO AMERICAN LITERATURE

In James Russell Lowell's "The First Snowfall," a scene from nature is the instrument that reminds Lowell of a scene from his life. Ask students which of Issa's haiku call up memories or images from their lives.

About the Authors

Although his talent was not recognized until after his death, Japanese poet **Kobayashi Issa** (1763–1827) is now widely recognized as a great writer. Born into poverty, Issa struggled throughout his life to support himself and to overcome the emotional impact of the deaths of those close to him. His appreciation for the hardships faced by the common people is reflected in his haiku.

Shu Ting (1952–) is the pen name of Chinese writer Gong Peiyu. She began writing poetry when she was a teenager and gained famed by the time she was in her twenties. In both 1981 and 1983, she received official recognition in the form of China's National Poetry Award.

Connection to "The First Snowfall"

Poets through the ages have found inspiration in the natural world that surrounds them. James Russell Lowell's "The First Snowfall" explores how a snowfall evokes in the speaker intense memories of an extremely poignant event. In Issa's haiku, powerful images spring from his unique views of nature. In Shu Ting's "Fairy Tales," comparisons drawn from nature illustrate her statement that "The heart may be tiny / but the world's enormous."

▶ **Critical Viewing** Which haiku does this photograph best illustrate? Explain. **[Connect]**

Haiku

Kobayashi Issa
Translated by Geoffrey Bownas

Melting snow:
And on the village
Fall the children.

Beautiful, seen through holes
Made in a paper screen:
The Milky Way.

Far-off mountain peaks
Reflected in its eyes:
The dragonfly.

A world of dew:
Yet within the dewdrops—
Quarrels.

Viewing the cherry-blossom:
Even as they walk,
Grumbling.

With bland serenity
Gazing at the far hills:
A tiny frog.

Interest Grabber Choose some of the images in Issa's haiku, such as melting snow, a dragonfly, or a dewdrop, and ask students to write down the memories and feelings they associate with each. Have students share their answers and suggest that they keep these memories in mind as they read Issa's haiku.

Extending Word Study

Secondary Definitions In the fourth haiku, the word "quarrels" adds an interesting twist to the image of the dewdrop. Ask students to define a quarrel and then to consider how this very human term affects the way they picture the dewdrop. *Students will note that a quarrel is a dispute. The term adds a sense of complexity and life to the world within the seemingly simple dewdrop.* Then, tell students that a quarrel is also the name for a square or diamond-shaped pane of glass. Ask students how this definition affects the way they picture the dewdrop. Discuss with students why it is helpful to be aware of the possibilities of second and third definitions of words, especially when reading poetry.

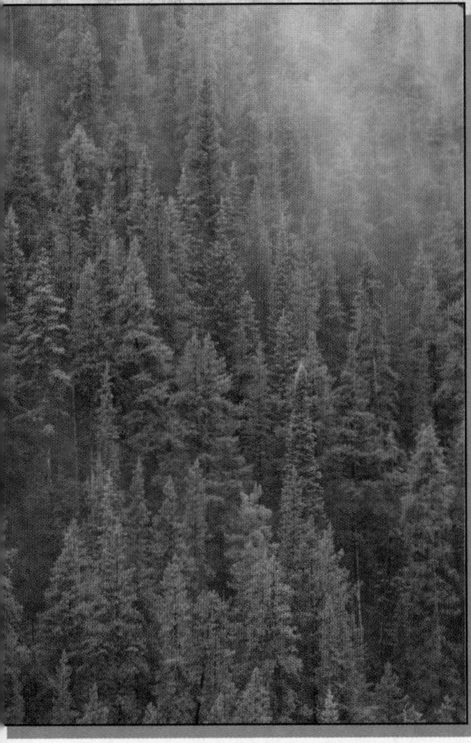

▲ Critical Viewing Why might "pine trees after rain" inspire faith within a viewer? **[Support]**

Fairy Tales

Shu Ting
Translated by Donald Finkel and Jinsheng Yi

You believed in your own story,
then climbed inside it—
a turquoise flower.
You gazed past ailing trees,
past crumbling walls and rusty railings.
Your least gesture beckoned a constellation
of wild vetch,[1] grasshoppers, and stars
to sweep you into immaculate distances.

The heart may be tiny
but the world's enormous.

And the people in turn believe—
in pine trees after rain,
ten thousand tiny suns, a mulberry branch
bent over water like a fishing-rod,
a cloud tangled in the tail of a kite.
Shaking off dust, in silver voices
ten thousand memories sing from your dream.

The world may be tiny
but the heart's enormous.

---

1. **wild vetch:** Any of a number of leafy climbing or trailing plants.

◆ Critical Thinking

1. Judging from these haiku, what was Issa's relationship with the natural world? Explain. **[Infer]**
2. In "Fairy Tales," what does Shu Ting mean by "The world may be tiny / but the heart's enormous"? **[Interpret]**
3. Why does Shu Ting interchange the words "heart" and "world" in the poem's refrain? **[Analyze]**

Cultural Connection

4. Arbor Day is an American celebration of an aspect of nature. Research to find one Japanese and one Chinese celebration of something in nature. **[Relate]**

Develop Understanding

One-Minute Insight Issa's haiku offer insights into the ways we look at the world by examining nature from inventive angles. Shu Ting's poem describes the importance of the feelings and acts of an individual as opposed to objective reality.

▶Critical Viewing◀

Support Pine trees remain sturdy and strong even after heavy rain or snow. They call up the idea of survival under adverse conditions.

Read to Discover Models for Writing

Simply by interchanging the words "heart" and "world," Shu Ting offers a refreshing new way to look at two commonly-used images. Have students think of common expressions or maxims. Encourage them to offer a new perspective on a common idea by changing just one or two words in the expression. For example, take the expression "love makes the world go round" and change it to "love makes the world stand still." This offers a different perspective on the way love affects people. The revised expression might become the seed for a poem.

Reinforce and Extend

Answers

◆ Critical Thinking

1. Issa finds wisdom about the world by examining scenes found in nature. For example, in the fourth haiku, he uses the image of a dewdrop to express situations that are not as simple as they appear on the surface.
2. Ting means that the human heart is powerful enough to change the world because it can change the way one views it.
3. By interchanging these words, she shows both the enormous possibilities in the world despite the apparent insignificance of individuals, and the importance of an individual's feelings compared to objective reality.

Cultural Connection

4. Answers will vary.

Beyond the Selection

FURTHER READING

Other Works by the Authors

The Spring of My Life: And Selected Haiku, Kobayashi Issa

Shu Ting: Selected Poems, Shu Ting

We suggest that you preview these works before recommending them to students.

INTERNET

You and your students may find additional information about Issa and Ting on the Internet. We suggest the following sites. Please be aware, however, that these sites may have changed since the time this information was published.

For more on haiku, see **home.sol.no/~keitoy/haiku.html#whatishaiku**

To read about contemporary Chinese literature, visit **www.yorku.ca/faculty/academic/iwai/three/martinj.htm**

We *strongly recommend* that you preview the sites before you send the students to them.

LESSON OBJECTIVES

1. **To develop vocabulary and word identification skills**
   - Extending Word Study: Precise Meanings (ATE)
2. **To use a variety of reading strategies to comprehend poetry**
   - Tips to Guide Reading (ATE)
3. **To increase knowledge of other cultures and to connect common elements across cultures**
   - About the Authors (SE)
   - Cultural Context (ATE)
   - Connections to American Literature (ATE)
4. **To express and support responses to the text**
   - Critical Thinking

Cultural Context Unlike the Romantic poets, Charles Baudelaire was not drawn to nature. In fact, he favored the artificial over the natural and the city over the countryside. He did not believe in the fundamental goodness of humanity, but rather in its inherent evil. Wordsworth, on the other hand, is often considered the greatest of the English Romantic poets. Though the Romantics took many different approaches to poetry, they generally shared a deep appreciation for nature, a sense of optimism, and an interest in the thoughts and emotions of the common man.

CONNECTIONS TO AMERICAN LITERATURE

Based on what they learned from reading "Nature," ask students how Emerson would react to the sailors' treatment of the albatross. Emerson believes in seeking harmony between man and nature. He would be saddened by the sailors' cruel treatment of the bird.

About the Authors

French poet **Charles Baudelaire** (1821–1867), one of the most colorful, startling, and innovative poets of the nineteenth century, strove for objectivity in his writing. His poetry nonetheless exhibits the imaginative and mystical qualities that are typical of much Romantic poetry.

Few poets have had more of an impact on the world than **William Wordsworth** (1770–1850). With Samuel Taylor Coleridge, he altered the course of English poetry. Their work was expressive of a movement known as Romanticism, and Wordsworth would come to be regarded as the greatest English Romantic poet.

Connections to the Excerpt From *Nature*

To Ralph Waldo Emerson, the natural world contains restorative powers and inspires joy. European writers of the nineteenth century seem to agree with him. The following poems contain powerful images that stem from the poets' observations of nature.

The Albatross

Charles Baudelaire
Translated by Kate Flores

◀ **Critical Viewing** In what way does this albatross seem like a king "of the blue"? **[Connect]**

Ofttimes, for diversion, seafaring men
Capture albatross, those vast birds of the seas
That accompany, at languorous[1] pace,
Boats plying their way through bitter straits.[2]

Having scarce been taken aboard
These kings of the blue, awkward and shy,
Piteously their great white wings
Let droop like oars at their sides.

This wingèd voyager, how clumsy he is and weak!
He just now so lovely, how comic and ugly!
One with a stubby pipe teases his beak,
Another mimics, limping, the cripple who could fly!

The Poet resembles this prince of the clouds,
Who laughs at hunters and haunts the storms;
Exiled to the ground amid the jeering pack,
His giant wings will not let him walk.

1. **languorous** (laŋ´ gər əs) *adj.*: Lacking vigor or vitality; slow or sluggish.
2. **straits** (strāts) *n.*: Narrow waterways.

Interest Grabber Have students think about the ideas they associate with the word "poet." What type of person is a poet? How do others respond to poets? Encourage them to create a metaphor or simile to express their conception of a poet. Have students share their answers and discuss where their impressions came from.

◆ Critical Thinking

Analyze Ask students how Baudelaire relates the treatment of the albatross to the life of a poet. *Baudelaire suggests that both have special gifts but suffer from misunderstanding and cruelty. Both may be awkward or shy but both have the ability to soar.*

To a Sky-lark

William Wordsworth

Ethereal[1] minstrel! pilgrim of the sky!
Dost thou despise the earth where cares abound?
Or, while the wings aspire, are heart and eye
Both with thy nest upon the dewy ground?
Thy nest which thou canst drop into at will,
Those quivering wings composed,[2] that music still!

Leave to the nightingale her shady wood;
A privacy of glorious light is thine;
Whence[3] thou dost pour upon the world a flood
Of harmony, with instinct more divine;
Type of the wise who soar, but never roam;
True to the kindred points of Heaven and Home!

---

1. **ethereal** (ē thir´ ē əl) *adj.*: Heavenly; delicate.
2. **composed** (kəm pōzd´) *adj.*: Calm; tranquil.
3. **whence** (hwens) *adv.*: From what place.

◆ Critical Thinking

1. How effective is Baudelaire's comparison of a poet to a seabird in "The Albatross"? Explain. **[Evaluate]**

2. With what human qualities does Wordsworth endow the sky-lark? With what divine qualities? **[Connect]**

◆ Compare Literary Works

3. Which poem—Baudelaire's or Wordsworth's—seems to express ideas more similar to those in Emerson's *Nature*? Explain. **[Compare and Contrast]**

Cultural Connection

4. Generally speaking, have people's views of nature changed much since the nineteenth century? Explain. **[Speculate]**

Develop Understanding

One-Minute Insight Baudelaire compares the poet to an albatross in his poem. He says that although both can be shy and awkward, they both have uncommon talents that are often overlooked. Wordsworth praises the beauty of the sky-lark in his poem, assigning it both earthly and heavenly qualities.

Tips to Guide Reading

Identify Main Ideas Ask students to keep in mind the major beliefs of the Romantic poets while reading "To a Sky-lark." Help them focus their reading by having them mark places in the poem that seem to express one of the ideas of Romanticism.

Extending Word Study

Dictionary Have students identify words in Wordsworth's poem with which they are only vaguely familiar. Have them write down these words and what they think they might mean. Then send them to the dictionary to learn the precise meanings. How does their understanding of the poem change with their new understanding of its language?

Reinforce and Extend

Answers

◆ Critical Thinking

1. Students may or may not agree with Baudelaire's opinion that poets often experience a sense of isolation or alienation from the rest of society.
2. Wordsworth gives the sky-lark the human qualities of wisdom and beauty. He gives it the divine qualities of a heavenly voice and a connection with God.
3. Like Emerson's work, Wordsworth's poem expresses deep appreciation for the natural world.
4. People seem to overlook the beauty of nature because today's world offers so many distractions. Also, nature no longer affects people's daily lives as it did before technology allowed us to live and travel in a wide variety of weather conditions.

Beyond the Selection

FURTHER READING

Other Works by the Authors

Baudelaire: Poems, Charles Baudelaire
Selected Poems, William Wordsworth

We suggest that you preview these works before recommending them to students.

INTERNET

You and your students may find additional information about Romanticism on the Internet. We suggest the following sites. Please be aware, however, that these sites may have changed since this information was published.

For more on Wordsworth, see **www.penguin.co.uk/Penguin/Authors/662.html**

To learn more about other Romantic poets, visit **tqd.advanced.org/3648/romaut.html**

We *strongly recommend* that you preview the sites before sending the students to them.

LESSON OBJECTIVES

1. To develop vocabulary and word identification skills
- Extending Word Study: Synonyms (ATE)

2. To use a variety of reading strategies to comprehend nonfiction
- Tips to Guide Reading (ATE)
- Read to Appreciate Author's Craft (ATE

3. To increase knowledge of other cultures and to connect common elements across cultures
- About the Selection (SE)
- Cultural Context (ATE)
- Connections to American Literature (ATE)

4. To express and support responses to the text
- Critical Thinking

Cultural Context In A.D. 79, the prosperous resort of Pompeii was buried almost instantaneously by the eruption of Mt. Vesuvius. Pliny the Elder, the uncle and role model of Pliny the Younger, was among those killed in this catastrophe. For the next 1,700 years Pompeii was hidden from view, until some workers digging a canal found some statues. Subsequent investigations revealed the complete city caught in action: villas of the rich, account ledgers of a devious banker, election posters, shops, and graffiti. Pliny the Younger was only seventeen at the time of the eruption; he was fifty-six when he described it in this letter to Tacitus. Have students think about what difference it might make to write about an event forty years later.

CONNECTIONS TO AMERICAN LITERATURE

Ask students to compare the language used in Pliny's epistle to that used in Mary Chesnut's diary. Does Chesnut's casual tone make her account more personal and gripping than Pliny's formal tone? What factors other than language can influence whether a piece feels personal?

About the Author

Son of a wealthy, distinguished family, Gaius Plinius Caecilius Secundus, or **Pliny the Younger** (A.D. 62–112), was born in the Po Valley, near what is now the Italian-Swiss border. With guidance from his uncle and guardian, Pliny the Elder, who was the author of the first Roman encyclopedia, the younger Pliny served his country in various civil-service posts.

Two great men were models for Pliny. Like his uncle, he used every spare moment for reading, note-taking, study, and reflection. From Cicero, an idol of the previous generation, Pliny learned the basics of oratory and writing for which he himself became famous.

About the Selection

Pliny's account is in the form of an epistle. An epistle differs from a private letter or personal note. Intended as a formal observation for the benefit of a group of readers, the epistle writer deliberately maintains an elevated tone.

Connection to "Mary Chesnut's Civil War"

Mary Chesnut's diary provides an eyewitness account of events of the Civil War. The language is informal and natural, allowing the reader to enter Chesnut's personal world. Pliny's letter is similar in that it gives a personal account of a historic event—the eruption of Mt. Vesuvius. Its language, however, is deliberately formal and the style less personal.

from Letters
The Eruption of Vesuvius

Pliny the Younger
Translated by Betty Radice

To Cornelius Tacitus[1]

Thank you for asking me to send you a description of my uncle's death[2] so that you can leave an accurate account of it for posterity; I know that immortal fame awaits him if his death is recorded by you. It is true that he perished in a catastrophe which destroyed the loveliest regions of the earth,[3] a fate shared by whole cities and their people, and one so memorable that it is likely to make his name live forever: and he himself wrote a number of books of lasting value: but you write for all time and can still do much to perpetuate his memory. The fortunate man, in my opinion, is he to whom the gods have granted the power either to do something which is worth recording or to write what is worth reading, and most fortunate of all is the man who can do both. Such a man was my uncle, as his own books and yours will prove. So you set me a task I would choose for myself, and I am more than willing to start on it.

My uncle was stationed at Misenum,[4] in active command of the fleet. On 24 August, in the early afternoon, my mother drew his attention to a cloud of unusual size and appearance. He had been out in the sun, had taken a cold bath, and lunched while lying down, and was then working at his books. He called for his shoes and climbed up to a place which would give him the best view of the phenomenon. It was not clear at that distance from which mountain

---

1. **Cornelius Tacitus** (kôr nēl´ yes tas´ i təs): Roman historian who wrote the *Annals*.
2. **my uncle's death:** Pliny the Elder.
3. **regions of the earth:** Pompeii.
4. **Misenum** (mī sē´ nəm): The northern arm of the bay of Naples.

Interest Grabber Accounts of natural disasters are ubiquitous in recent movies and television programs. Have students describe some of the natural disaster dramas they have seen. As a class, discuss the following questions: Why are these dramas so appealing? Why do they seem to be more appealing now than ever before? How might Pliny's purpose differ from that of a major motion picture studio, and how does this difference affect the way the story is told?

The Eruption of Vesuvius and the Death of Pliny, P.H. de Valencieme, Musée des Augustins, Toulouse, France

▲ **Critical Viewing** How does this depiction of the eruption match Pliny's written version? **[Support]**

the cloud was rising (it was afterwards known to be Vesuvius); its general appearance can best be expressed as a being like an umbrella pine, for it rose to a great height on a sort of trunk and then split off into branches, I imagine because it was thrust upwards by the first blast and then left unsupported as the pressure subsided, or else it was borne down by its own weight so that it spread out and gradually dispersed. Sometimes it looked white, sometimes blotched and dirty, according to the amount of soil and ashes it carried with it. My uncle's scholarly acumen[5] saw at once that it was important enough for a closer inspection, and he ordered a boat to be made ready, telling me I could come with him if I wished. I replied that I preferred to go on with my studies, and as it happened he had himself given me some writing to do.

As he was leaving the house he was handed a message from Rectina, wife of Tascius whose house was at the foot of the mountain, so that escape was impossible except by boat. She was terrified by the danger threatening her and implored him to rescue her from her fate. He changed his plans, and what he had begun in a spirit of inquiry he completed as a hero. He gave orders for the warships to be launched and went on board himself with the intention of bringing help to many more people besides Rectina, for this lovely stretch of coast was thickly populated. He hurried to the place which everyone else was hastily leaving, steering his course straight for the danger zone. He was entirely fearless, describing each new movement and phase of the portent[6] to be noted down exactly as he observed them. Ashes were already falling, hotter and thicker as the ships drew near, followed by bits of pumice and blackened stones, charred and cracked by the flames: then suddenly they were in shallow water, and the shore was blocked by the debris from the mountain. For a moment my uncle wondered whether to turn back, but when the helmsman[7] advised this he refused, telling him that Fortune stood by the courageous and they must make for Pomponianus at Stabiae.[8] He was cut off there by the breadth of the bay (for the shore gradually curves round a basin filled by the sea) so that he was not as yet in danger, though it was clear that this would come nearer as it spread. Pomponianus had therefore already put his belongings on board ship, intending to escape if the contrary wind fell. This wind was of course full in my uncle's favor, and he was able to bring his ship in. He embraced his terrified friend, cheered and encouraged him, and thinking he could calm his fears by showing his own composure, gave orders that he was to be carried to the bathroom. After his bath he lay down and dined; he was quite cheerful, or at any rate he pretended he was, which was no less courageous.

Meanwhile on Mount Vesuvius broad sheets of fire and leaping flames blazed at several

5. **acumen** (ə kyōō´ mən) *n.*: Keenness; shrewdness.

6. **portent** (pôr´ tent) *n.*: Here, an unfortunate, ominous event.

7. **helmsman** (helmz´ mən) *n.*: Person who steers a ship.

8. **Stabiae** (stə bī´ ə): Four miles south of Pompeii.

Humanities: Art

The Eruption of Vesuvius and the Death of Pliny, Artist Unknown.

In the latter part of the eighteenth century, the excavation of Pompeii greatly inspired the imaginations of European artists. The painting *The Eruption of Vesuvius and the Death of Pliny* reflects this interest. The mid-nineteenth-century painter was most likely familiar with the historic letter written by Pliny the Younger. Indeed the swirl of smoke is a prominent feature in this dramatic painting. Narrative scenes of antiquity continued to be a popular inspiration for artists through the end of the nineteenth century.

Use the following questions to discuss the art:

1. Does this artist's interpretation help you visualize the events in Pliny's letter?
2. What dimension of this illustration do you find most engaging?
3. How would a photographer today approach the dangerous assignment of capturing a catastrophe?

Develop Understanding

One-Minute Insight Pliny's letter to Tacitus is a response to the historian's request to learn the details of the death of Pliny the Elder. His account of the eruption of Mt. Vesuvius and the destruction of Pompeii is made particularly gripping by Pliny's involvement in it; his affection for his uncle is obvious throughout. Pliny is aware that his depiction of his uncle will influence the way Tacitus depicts him in his histories, and therefore the way future generations see him. He is careful to paint a portrait of his uncle as a courageous man who embodies the Stoic ideal of calmness under duress.

Tips to Guide Reading

Timeline As they read, have students fill in a timeline of the major events that occur between the first time Pliny the Elder sees the smoke cloud and the time of his death. Circulate around the room to make sure students write down the important events and that they understand the cause-and-effect relationships between them.

▶Critical Viewing◀

Support The ominous smoke cloud, the fiery mountain spewing charred debris, the roiling waves, and the general sense of terror and entrapment match Pliny's description.

Extending Word Study

Thesaurus Pliny uses the word *fearless* to describe his uncle. Have students brainstorm for a list of synonyms for this word and list them on the board. Then, send them to the thesaurus to learn more synonyms to add to the list. Discuss the ways in which some of the words differ in connotation, degree, or tone.

◆Critical Thinking

Evaluate Do students agree with Pliny that it was "no less courageous" of his uncle to pretend he was cheerful than to actually feel cheerful?
Students might say they agree with Pliny because in either case, his noble intent was to calm his terrified friend.

Read to
Appreciate Author's Craft

Although the literary epistle is not a popular genre today, it once enjoyed great attention. Ask students to consider why the epistle was so popular in antiquity and why it is not common today. Are there current genres or forms that contain the same combination of formal language and personal tone that the epistle conveyed?

◆ Critical Thinking

Interpret Why does Pliny take such pains to prove that his uncle certainly slept? Why is this detail important as part of the portrait of Pliny the Elder? *Anyone who could sleep during such a catastrophe definitely embodies the imperturbable calm admired by the Stoics.*

Connections to American Literature

Have students explain Pliny's final remark to Tacitus about the difference between a friendly letter and history. Then, have them determine which details of Mary Chesnut's diary would be included in or omitted from more formal histories of the Civil War. *Pliny means that the facts that make up a letter are vastly different from the events that fill historical accounts. The events described in Mary Chesnut's diary would be included in a formal history; the individual reactions to these events would not.*

points, their bright glare emphasized by the darkness of night. My uncle tried to allay the fears of his companions by repeatedly declaring that these were nothing but bonfires left by the peasants in their terror, or else empty houses on fire in the districts they had abandoned. Then he went to rest and certainly slept, for as he was a stout man his breathing was rather loud and heavy and could be heard by people coming and going outside his door. By this time the courtyard giving access to his room was full of ashes mixed with pumice stones, so that its level had risen, and if he had stayed in the room any longer he would never have got out. He was wakened, came out and joined Pomponianus and the rest of the household who had sat up all night. They debated whether to stay indoors or take their chance in the open, for the buildings were now shaking with violent shocks, and seemed to be swaying to and fro as if they were torn from their foundations. Outside on the other hand, there was the danger of falling pumice stones, even though these were light and porous;[9] however, after comparing the risks they chose the latter. In my uncle's case one reason outweighed the other, but for the others it was a choice of fears. As a protection against falling objects they put pillows on their heads tied down with cloths.

Elsewhere there was daylight by this time, but they were still in darkness, blacker and denser than any ordinary night, which they relieved by lighting torches and various kinds of lamp. My uncle decided to go down to the shore and investigate on the spot the possibility of any escape by sea, but he found the waves still wild and dangerous. A sheet was spread on the ground for him to lie down, and he repeatedly asked for cold water to drink. Then the flames and smell of sulfur which gave warning of the approaching fire drove the others to take flight and roused him to stand up. He stood leaning on two slaves and then suddenly collapsed, I imagine because the dense fumes choked his breathing by blocking his windpipe which was constitutionally[10] weak and narrow and often inflamed. When daylight returned on the 26th—two days after the last day he had seen—his body was found intact and uninjured, still fully clothed and looking more like sleep than death.

Meanwhile my mother and I were at Misenum, but this is not of any historic interest, and you only wanted to hear about my uncle's death. I will say no more, except to add that I have described in detail every incident which I either witnessed myself or heard about immediately after the event, when reports were most likely to be accurate. It is for you to select what best suits your purpose, for there is a great difference between a letter to a friend and history written for all to read.

9. **porous** (pôr′ əs) *adj.*: Full of openings.

10. **constitutionally** (kän′ sti to͞o′ shən əl ē) *adj.*: In physique; by nature.

◆ Critical Thinking

1. What picture of Pliny the Elder does his nephew want the reader to form? Support your answer with evidence from his letter. **[Interpret]**
2. (a) Why does Pliny the Younger admire people of action who can also express their actions in writing? (b) Would Pliny the Younger describe himself as such a person? Explain. **[Analyze; Speculate]**

◆ Compare Literary Works

3. Which account of history do you find more revealing: Chesnut's or Pliny the Younger's? Support your response with details. **[Compare and Contrast]**

Cultural Connection

4. Do you think Pliny's ideas about courage and bravery would hold true today? Why or why not? **[Relate]**

Reinforce and Extend

Answers
◆ Critical Thinking

1. Pliny wants the reader to picture his uncle as brave and calm.
2. (a) He admires those people because they seem to be doubly talented. (b) Pliny would not compare his tame life to that of his uncle; he might describe himself as respectable and his uncle as heroic.
3. Answers will vary. Students might find Chesnut's account revealing because of its very natural, casual tone. They might find Pliny's account revealing because of Pliny's great attachment to his uncle.
4. Answers will vary. Students might say that calmness in the face of danger is a trait that will always be valued.

Beyond the Selection

FURTHER READING

Works by Pliny the Younger and Pliny the Elder

Fifty Letters of Pliny, Pliny the Younger
Natural History: A Selection, Pliny the Elder

We suggest that you preview these works before recommending them to students.

INTERNET

You and your students may find additional information abut the eruption of Mt. Vesuvius on the Internet. We suggest the following site. Please be aware, however, that the site may have changed since the time this information was published.

For more on Mt. Vesuvius and Pompeii, visit **www.eliki.com/ancient/civilizations/pompeii/**

We strongly *recommend* that you preview this site before you send the students to it.

Why Is This Age Worse . . . ?

Anna Akhmatova
Translated by Stanley Kunitz with Max Hayward

About the Author

Anna Akhmatova was born Anna Gorenko (1889–1966) in Odessa, near the Black Sea. At the age of seventeen, when she began to publish her poetry, her father asked her to change her name to avoid disgracing the family. She adopted the name Akhmatova—her Tartar grandmother's name—because the southern Tartars always seemed mysterious and fascinating to her.

By the time of her death, Akhmatova was acclaimed as Russia's foremost woman poet. Her brilliant, intense poetry can be read as a chronicle of her country in the twentieth century.

About the Poems

The following poems stem from Akhmatova's experience of war—the Russian Revolution, during which the tsar and his family were executed and communism instated, and World War I. Akhmatova belonged to a school of poets referred to as the Acmeists, who emphasized the here and now in their poetry as a way of dealing with their experiences head on.

Connection to "Luke Havergal"

Edwin Arlington Robinson's "Luke Havergal" paints a scene of despair and hopelessness, as the speaker of the poem urges Havergal to choose death. Akhmatova's poems depict scenes of isolation and bleakness in the wake of war and destruction. Both poets use strong imagery to capture the grimness of their worlds.

Why is this age worse than earlier ages?
In a stupor of grief and dread
have we not fingered the foulest wounds
and left them unhealed by our hands?

In the west the falling light still glows,
and the clustered housetops glitter in the sun,
but here Death is already chalking the doors with crosses,
and calling the ravens, and the ravens are flying in.

◆ Critical Thinking

1. In line 8 of "Why Is This Age Worse . . .?" to whom does Akhmatova refer as ravens? **[Interpret]**
2. What three adjectives would you choose to describe the mood of Akhmatova's poem? Why? **[Evaluate]**

◆ Compare Literary Works

3. Which poem—"Luke Havergal" or "Why Is This Age Worse . . .?"—is more powerful? Support your response with details. **[Compare and Contrast]**

Cultural Connection

4. Do you think that Akhmatova's views about war are shared by those who experience war in the present? Why or why not? **[Relate]**

Prepare and Engage

LESSON OBJECTIVES

1. **To increase knowledge of other cultures and to connect common elements across cultures**
   - About the Poem (SE)
   - Connections to American Literature (ATE)
2. **To express and support responses to the text**
   - Critical Thinking

CONNECTIONS TO AMERICAN LITERATURE

Both Anna Akhmatova and Edward Arlington Robinson address people whose lives are filled with despair and frustration. Ask students which poem they can more easily identify with: the private grief of one man in Robinson's poem, or the communal grief of a nation in Akhmatova's poem.

Interest Grabber Hook students' interest by writing the first line of the poem on the board. Discuss with students whether the question in the line could refer to life in the United States today. Do they think this age is worse than previous ones, or better? What would their parents think? Their grandparents? What are the criteria by which they evaluate "an age"?

Reinforce and Extend

Answers

◆ Critical Thinking

1. The ravens create an ominous mood. They refer to the deadly forces that prey on and bring death to the people of Russia.
2. Answers will vary. Students might say grief-stricken, despondent, sorrowful, or other words that reflect Akhmatova's despair.
3. Answers will vary, depending on students' experiences and preferences.
4. Answers will vary. It is likely that the violence of war will always cause sorrow and frustration, regardless of time or place.

Beyond the Selection

FURTHER READING

Other Works by Akhmatova

Anno Domini MCMXXI

From Six Books

We suggest that you preview these works before recommending them to students.

INTERNET

You and your students may find additional information about Anna Akhmatova on the Internet. We suggest the following site. Please be aware, however, that the site may have changed since the time this information was published.

For more on Akhmatova, visit **dybka.home.mindspring.com/jill/akhmatova/links.html**

We *strongly recommend* that you preview the site before sending students to it.

LESSON OBJECTIVES

1. **To develop vocabulary and word identification skills**
   - Extending Word Study: Connotations (ATE)
2. **To use a variety of reading strategies to comprehend a short story**
   - Read to Appreciate Author's Craft (ATE)
3. **To increase knowledge of other cultures and to connect common elements across cultures**
   - About the Selection (SE)
   - Cultural Context (ATE)
   - Connections to American Literature (ATE)
4. **To express and support responses to the text**
   - Critical Thinking

Cultural Context Pirandello's native Italy stayed out of World War I during 1914, even though it was a member of the Triple Alliance with Austria-Hungary and Germany. Italy claimed it was not obliged to honor the agreement because Austria-Hungary went to war as an aggressor, rather than in self-defense. Italy entered the war in 1915 on the side of the Allies, and tried to help Russia by diverting the attention of Austria-Hungary away from the Eastern Front. This strategy proved unsuccessful and Italy suffered an enormous number of casualties in the process.

CONNECTIONS TO AMERICAN LITERATURE

Both Pirandello and Hemingway describe characters who try to devise methods to cope with the suffering caused by World War I. Ask students to compare the way the old man in "War" and the major in "In Another Country" deal with their hardships. Is one more successful than the other? *The old man tries to convince himself that his son died happily. The major tries to forget about the war and, instead, think about things like grammar, which follow rules and make sense. Both characters continue to suffer deeply.*

About the Author

Author **Luigi Pirandello** (1867–1936) gained worldwide renown as an innovative dramatist. His *Six Characters in Search of an Author* is a theatrical masterpiece that is often revived on stages the world over. The success of Pirandello's dramas, however, has overshadowed his other literary accomplishments. In his native Italy, for example, he is widely recognized as the master of the short story, and in 1934, his work received the ultimate recognition when he was awarded the Nobel Prize for Literature.

About the Story

This story takes place in Italy during World War I. Beginning in 1914, the war at first pitted France, Russia, and Great Britain against Germany, Austria-Hungary, and the Ottoman Empire. By the time the war ended in 1918, many other countries had taken part in the fighting.

Connection to "In Another Country"

World War I was brutal, and it took the lives of about nine million soldiers. In Hemingway's "In Another Country," an American soldier recovers from his war wounds in an Italian hospital. While there, he meets other soldiers who have suffered even greater losses. The horrors of combat are also revealed in Pirandello's "War," as passengers on a train traveling through Italy share tales of loss.

War

Luigi Pirandello
Translated by Samuel Putnam

The passengers who had left Rome by the night express had had to stop until dawn at the small station of Fabriano in order to continue their journey by the small old-fashioned "local" joining the main line with Sulmona.

At dawn, in a stuffy and smoky second-class carriage in which five people had already spent the night, a bulky woman in deep mourning was hoisted in—almost like a shapeless bundle. Behind her—puffing and moaning—followed her husband, a tiny man, thin and weakly, his face death-white, his eyes small and bright and looking shy and uneasy.

Having at last taken a seat, he politely thanked the passengers who had helped his wife and who had made room for her; then he turned round to the woman trying to pull down the collar of her coat and politely inquired:

"Are you all right, dear?"

The wife, instead of answering, pulled up her collar again to her eyes, so as to hide her face.

"Nasty world," muttered the husband with a sad smile.

And he felt it his duty to explain to his traveling companions that the poor woman was to be pitied, for the war was taking away from her her only son, a boy of twenty to whom both had devoted their entire life, even breaking up their home at Sulmona to follow him to Rome, where he had to go as a student, then allowing him to volunteer for war with an assurance, however, that at least for six months he would not be sent to the front and now, all of a sudden, receiving a wire saying that he was due to leave in three days' time and asking them to go and see him off.

The woman under the big coat was twisting and wriggling, at times growling like a wild animal, feeling certain that all those explanations would not have aroused even a shadow of sympathy from those people who—most likely—were in the same plight as herself. One of them, who had

Interest Grabber On the night before they read "War," ask students to ask their grandparents or other elders in the community to tell them stories about World War I. Perhaps these elders did not experience the war firsthand, but they may remember stories they were told by their own parents. Have willing students share the information they gathered, and tell them they are about to read another story about the grief caused by The Great War.

been listening with particular attention, said:

"You should thank God that your son is only leaving now for the front. Mine has been sent there the first day of the war. He has already come back twice wounded and been sent back again to the front."

"What about me? I have two sons and three nephews at the front," said another passenger.

"Maybe, but in our case it is our *only* son," ventured the husband.

"What difference can it make? You may spoil your only son with excessive attentions, but you cannot love him more than you would all your other children if you had any. Paternal love is not like bread that can be broken into pieces and split among the children in equal shares. A father gives *all* his love to each one of his children without discrimination, whether it be one or ten, and if I am suffering now for my two sons, I am not suffering half for each of them but double. . . ."

"True . . . true . . ." sighed the embarrassed husband, "but suppose (of course, we all hope it will never be your case) a father has two sons at the front and he loses one of them, there is still one left to console him . . . while . . ."

"Yes," answered the other, getting cross, "a son left to console him but also a son left for whom he must survive, while in the case of the father of an only son, if the son dies the father can die too and put an end to his distress. Which of the two positions is the worse? Don't you see how my case would be worse than yours?"

"Nonsense," interrupted another traveler, a fat, red-faced man with bloodshot eyes of the palest gray.

He was panting. From his bulging eyes seemed to spurt inner violence of an uncontrolled vitality which his weakened body could hardly contain.

"Nonsense," he repeated, trying to cover his mouth with his hand so as to hide the two missing front teeth. "Nonsense. Do we give life to our children for our own benefit?"

The other travelers stared at him in distress. The one who had had his son at the front since the first day of the war sighed: "You are right. Our children do not belong to us, they belong to the Country. . . ."

"Bosh," retorted the fat traveler. "Do we think of the Country when we give life to our children? Our sons are born because . . . well, because they must be born and when they come to life they take our own life with them. This is the truth. We belong to them but they never belong to us. And when they reach twenty they are exactly what we were at their age. We too had a father and mother, but there were so many other things as well . . . illusions, new ties . . . and the Country, of course, whose call we would have answered—when we

▲ **Critical Viewing** What details in this photograph link it to the setting of this story? **[Connect]**

Develop Understanding

One-Minute Insight

Pirandello's story takes place on a train traveling through Italy during World War I. The passengers share tales of loss and grief caused by the war, and they argue over which of them has been forced to endure the greatest hardships. One man surprises all the others when he claims he did not mourn at all over the death of his son, because the boy died happy and proud. By the end of the story though, he is overcome by grief and the passengers are united by their sorrows. There is no way for any of them to escape the horrors of war.

▶Critical Viewing◀

Connect The man dressed in a military uniform from World War I, the weapons he is transporting, and the countryside in the background link this photograph to the setting of the story.

◆ Critical Thinking

Analyze One of the passengers explains his theory about a father's love for his children when he says "A father gives all his love to each one without discrimination, whether it be one or ten. . . ." Ask students to explain what the man means by this. Do they believe this is possible? Why or why not? *The man means that parents have an infinite amount of love for their children, rather than a limited amount that they must divide among them.*

Read to Appreciate Author's Craft

The structure of Pirandello's story allows students to feel as though they too are passengers on the train, listening to the others discuss the horrors of the war. Have students imagine that one of the passengers turns and asks for their opinion about who is suffering the most. Have students come up with the answer they would give, and make sure that they, like the characters, have reasons to support their answers.

Extending Word Study

Connotations Pirandello uses the word bread in two different metaphors in the story. Have students identify the metaphors and what they mean. Then discuss why they think Pirandello chose bread as opposed to a different type of food. What qualities does bread have that make it suitable for these metaphors? What connotations does it bring to mind? *Students should note that bread is used in the description of paternal love and in the explanation of the importance of one's country. Bread connotes the idea of sustenance and life.*

Connections to American Literature

Would the main character in Hemingway's "In Another Country" agree with the old man's theory that young men who die at war die happy and proud deaths? Make sure students support their answers with evidence from the text. *Students might say that he would not agree with the old man's theory because he clearly does not believe that war is a glorious endeavor. However, he does fantasize about being a courageous fighter, so some students might say that he would agree with the old man.*

▶Critical Viewing◀

Interpret The soldiers in the photograph seem relieved to be taking a rest. They look as though they've traveled a great distance while carrying heavy equipment. Soldiers in World War I endured great physical strain.

▲ **Critical Viewing** What does this photograph reveal about conditions during World War I? **[Interpret]**

were twenty even if father and mother had said no. Now, at our age, the love of our Country is still great, of course, but stronger than it is the love for our children. Is there any one of us here who wouldn't gladly take his son's place at the front if he could?"

There was a silence all round, everybody nodding as to approve.

"Why, then," continued the fat man, "shouldn't we consider the feelings of our children when they are twenty? Isn't it natural that at their age they should consider the love for their Country (I am speaking of decent boys, of course) even greater than the love for us? Isn't it natural that it should be so, as after all they must look upon us as upon old boys who cannot move any more and must stay at home? If Country exists, if Country is a natural necessity like bread, of which each of us must eat in order not to die of hunger, somebody must go to defend it. And our sons go, when they are twenty, and they don't want tears, because if they die, they die inflamed and happy (I am speaking, of course, of decent boys). Now, if one dies young and happy, without having the ugly sides of life, the boredom of it, the pettiness, the bitterness of disillusion . . . what more can we ask for him? Everyone should stop crying: everyone should laugh, as I do . . . or at least thank God—as I do—because my son, before dying, sent me a message saying that he was dying satisfied at having ended his life in the best way he could have wished. That is why, as you see, I do not even wear mourning. . . ."

He shook his light fawn coat as to show it;

Beyond the Classroom

Career Connection

Photojournalist *Life* and *Look*, the first American picture magazines, were conceived in 1936 following the perfection of the process for reproducing photographs on a large scale. These magazines developed a formula which grouped a writer with a photographer, a researcher, and an editor to produce a story. The result was a form that depended on the photograph as much as on the written text to tell a story.

One of the most dangerous types of photojournalism is war correspondence. Since World War I, reporters and photographers have accompanied soldiers to the front lines to gather firsthand accounts of the battlefield. These photojournalists risk their lives to tell a dramatic story.

Today, most photojournalists work for newspapers or magazines. They must be skilled at seeking out and capturing dramatic moments in a wide array of situations, from politics to the environment to sports. They must also have in-depth knowledge of the techniques of taking and processing photos. Have interested students research famous American photojournalists such as Mathew Brady, Margaret Bourke-White, and Walker Evans.

his livid[1] lip over his missing teeth was trembling, his eyes were watery and motionless and soon after he ended with a shrill laugh which might well have been a sob.

"Quite so . . . quite so . . ." agreed the others.

The woman who, bundled in a corner under her coat, had been sitting and listening had—for the last three months—tried to find in the words of her husband and her friends something to console her in her deep sorrow, something that might show her how a mother should resign herself to send her son not even to death but to a probable danger of life. Yet not a word had she found among the many which had been said . . . and her grief had been greater in seeing that nobody—as she thought—could share her feelings.

But now the words of the traveler amazed and almost stunned her. She suddenly realized that it wasn't the others who were wrong and could not understand her but herself who could not rise up to the same height of those fathers and mothers willing to resign themselves, without crying, not only to the departure of their sons but even to their death.

She lifted her head, she bent over from her corner trying to listen with great attention to the details which the fat man was giving to his companions about the way his son had fallen as a hero, for his King and his Country, happy and without regrets. It seemed to her that she had stumbled into a world she had never dreamed of, a world so far unknown to her, and she was so pleased to hear everyone joining in congratulating that brave father who could so stoically[2] speak of his child's death.

Then suddenly, just as if she had heard nothing of what had been said and almost as if waking up from a dream, she turned to the old man, asking him:

"Then . . . is your son really dead?"

Everybody stared at her. The old man, too, turned to look at her, fixing his great, bulging, horribly watery light gray eyes, deep in her face. For some little time he tried to answer, but words failed him. He looked and looked at her, almost as if only then—at that silly, incongruous question—he had suddenly realized at last that his son was really dead . . . gone forever . . . forever. His face contracted, became horribly distorted, then he snatched in haste a handkerchief from his pocket and, to the amazement of everyone, broke into harrowing, heart-rending, uncontrollable sobs.

1. **livid** (liv´ id) *adj.*: Discolored, as if by a bruise.
2. **stoically** (stō´ i klē) *adv.*: In an indifferent or calm way.

◆ Critical Thinking

1. Compare and contrast the arguments of the two fathers who have sons at the front. **[Compare and Contrast]**
2. What reason does the man who lost his son in the war give for not wearing mourning? **[Connect]**
3. Why does the woman's question, "... is your son really dead?" break the man's composure? **[Infer]**

◆ Compare Literary Works

4. What can you infer from "In Another Country" and "War" about the scope and extent of World War I? **[Compare and Contrast]**

Cultural Connection

5. Could the conversation that took place on the train in "War" have occurred in the United States during World War II? Why or why not? **[Speculate]**

Beyond the Selection

FURTHER READING

Other Works by Luigi Pirandello

Six Characters in Search of an Author and Other Plays

The Oil Jar and Other Stories

We suggest that you preview these works before recommending them to students.

INTERNET

You and your students may find additional information about Luigi Pirandello on the Internet. We suggest the following site. Please be aware, however, that the site may have changed since the time this information was published.

For more on Pirandello and his influence on other playwrights, visit **www.kirjasto.sci.fi/pirandel.htm**

We *strongly recommend* that you preview this site before sending students to it.

◆ Critical Thinking

Interpret Have students consider why Pirandello describes the old man's shrill laugh as though it "might well have been a sob"? What does this description say about how the story might end? *Students might note that Pirandello is foreshadowing the fact that the man is actually deeply saddened by the loss of his son. He is indicating how the man feels beneath his stoic exterior.*

Connections to American Literature

Compare and contrast the last paragraph of "War" to the scene in "In Another Country" where the major lashes out at the speaker. In what way do these scenes reveal the true nature of the characters involved? *Students might say that both the major and the old man reveal their true emotions during these scenes.*

Reinforce and Extend

Answers

◆ Critical Thinking

1. The father with one son believes his is the more difficult situation because if he loses his son, he has no other son left to console him. The man with two sons at the front believes his case is worse because if he loses one son, he must somehow remain strong enough to be a good father to his other son.
2. The man claims he does not mourn for his son because he knows his son died feeling satisfied and proud.
3. The man's sadness was near the surface throughout the story. Her question broke his composure because it reminded him that despite his argument or his philosophy, his son was really gone.
4. Both works suggest that no one involved in a war is completely immune to its horrors.
5. Yes, because the fear and sadness experienced by the parents of the soldiers probably plague parents of soldiers in danger anywhere.

Prepare and Engage

LESSON OBJECTIVES

1. **To use a variety of reading strategies to comprehend poetry**
   - Tips to Guide Reading (ATE)
2. **To increase knowledge of other cultures and to connect common elements across cultures**
   - About the Author (SE)
   - Cultural Context (ATE)
   - Connections to American Literature (ATE)
3. **To express and support responses to the text**
   - Critical Thinking

Cultural Context In 1531, Diego de Almagro followed Spanish conquistador Francisco Pizarro to Peru in search of great riches. Though badly outnumbered, the Spanish forces defeated the Incas and captured Atahualpa, their chief. As ransom, they demanded a room filled with silver and another filled with gold. At the urgings of Almagro, however, the Spaniards took the riches and killed Atahualpa as well. Almagro then set out to add to his wealth by conquering Chile. This trip was unsuccessful, though, as both sides suffered many casualties and Almagro never found the riches he sought. Chile was later found to be exceedingly rich in mineral resources, an irony that Neruda celebrates in his poem.

CONNECTIONS TO AMERICAN LITERATURE

Ask students to sum up in a few words their general impressions of Chicago and Chile, based on the information provided by the poems. Which place do they find more appealing? Which would they be more interested in visiting, and why?

Interest Grabber Review the concept of personification with students. Then have them brainstorm for a list of the qualities they associate with their town. Encourage them to write a few lines describing their town, and to use personification in each.

About the Author

Pablo Neruda (1904–1973) was born in Parral, Chile. His original name was Neftali Ricardo Reyes. He took his pen name when he began to publish poetry because he was afraid if his poetry appeared under his given name, he would offend his father, a railway worker.

Neruda found early success as a poet and then spent several years of his life representing Chile abroad as a diplomat and an ambassador. Because of his interest in world affairs, Neruda's poetry became increasingly political, but it never suffered in quality. Neruda won the Nobel Prize for Literature in 1971.

About the Poem

This poem describes a period of Chile's history during which conquistadors from Spain waged war on the native Incas.

Connection to "Chicago"

Poems can be written for almost any reason: to paint an image, to persuade readers to take an action, or to extol someone's goodness or beauty. Just as Carl Sandburg's "Chicago" is a celebration of that great American city, Pablo Neruda's "Discoverers of Chile" celebrates a place: his native Chile.

Discoverers of Chile

Pablo Neruda
Translated by Robert Bly

Almagro[1] brought his wrinkled lightning down from
    the north,
and day and night he bent over this country
between gunshots and twilight, as if over a letter.
Shadow of thorn, shadow of thistle and of wax,
the Spaniard, alone with his dried-up body,
watching the shadowy tactics of the soil.
My slim nation has a body made up
of night, snow, and sand,
the silence of the world is in its long coast,
the foam of the world rises from its seaboard,
the coal of the world fills it with mysterious kisses.
Gold burns in its finger like a live coal
and silver lights up like a green moon
its petrified shadow that's like a gloomy planet.
The Spaniard, sitting one day near a rose,
near oil, near wine, near the primitive sky,
could not really grasp how this spot of furious stone
was born beneath the droppings of the ocean eagle.

---

1. **Almagro:** Diego de Almagro, a Spaniard who in 1531 came to Peru, following conquistador Francisco Pizarro. Greedy for gold and other precious minerals, he and Pizarro captured and held for ransom Atahualpa, the Incan chief. They eventually killed him. Pizarro then sent Almagro to conquer Chile, but the expedition was not successful, and hundreds of Spaniards and Incas were killed.

Develop Understanding

One-Minute Insight Neruda's poem celebrates the natural beauty and richness of his native Chile, which the greedy invader Diego de Almagro failed to appreciate. He ironically calls Almagro and his men "The Discoverers of Chile" to emphasize the fact that the Incas had been living on and appreciating this land for many years.

▲ Critical Viewing What would conquistadors hope to find in a landscape like this one? **[Deduce]**

◆ Critical Thinking

1. What poetic device does Neruda use when describing Chile's natural resources? **[Interpret]**
2. What is the speaker's attitude toward the Spaniards? **[Analyze]**

◆ Compare Literary Works

3. Which poet—Sandburg or Neruda—paints a more realistic view of his special place? Support your opinion with passages from the poems. **[Compare and Contrast]**

Cultural Connection

4. Is the speaker's attitude toward the Spaniards understandable, given Chile's history? Why or why not? **[Evaluate]**

Tips to Guide Reading

Shared Reading Read the first three lines of the poem aloud, and then discuss their meaning with students. This will help students to grasp the historical setting of the poem, which is important for understanding the rest of it.

▶Critical Viewing◀

Deduce Conquistadors would hope that the land, which looks untouched by humans, would be filled with undiscovered mineral riches.

◆ Critical Thinking

Interpret Have students point out lines where Neruda uses personification to describe Chile. What feelings or ideas might he be trying to evoke by giving the land human characteristics? *Neruda uses personification in lines 7, 11, and 12. He is trying to evoke love and empathy for his land, and to give it a strong sense of life.*

◆ Critical Thinking

Compare the description of Chile to that of Almagro. What is Neruda trying to say by contrasting the two? *Chile is described as rich and fertile, while Almagro is lifeless and dried-up. He stresses the fact that Almagro cannot appreciate the beauty and richness of Chile.*

Reinforce and Extend

Answers

◆ Critical Thinking

1. Neruda uses personification to describe Chile's natural resources.
2. The speaker resents the Spaniards' brutal attempts to conquer a land already inhabited by the Incas. He mocks them for failing to appreciate the true beauty of his land.

Compare Literary Works

3. Answers will vary. Students might say that Sandburg's view is more realistic because he exposes the ugliness of Chicago rather than just its beauty.

Cultural Connection

4. Answers will vary. Students might say his attitude is understandable because of all the strife brought to Chile by the Spaniards.

Beyond the Selection

FURTHER READING

Other Works by Pablo Neruda

Twenty Love Poems and a Desperate Song
Residence on Earth and Other Poems
Elementary Odes

We suggest that you preview these works before recommending them to students.

INTERNET

You and your students may find additional information about Pablo Neruda on the Internet. We suggest the following site. Please be aware, however that the site may have changed since the time this information was published.

For a wealth of information about Neruda, visit **members.aol.com/KatharenaE/private/Pweek/Neruda/neruda.html**

We *strongly recommend* that you preview this site before sending students to it.

LESSON OBJECTIVES

1. **To develop vocabulary and word identification skills**
   - Extending Word Study: Homophones (ATE)
2. **To use a variety of reading strategies to comprehend a short story**
   - Tips to Guide Reading (ATE)
   - Read to Be Entertained (ATE)
3. **To increase knowledge of other cultures and to connect common elements across cultures**
   - About the Story (SE)
   - Cultural Context (ATE)
   - Connections to American Literature (ATE)
4. **To express and support responses to the text**
   - Critical Thinking

Cultural Context Barbara Kimenye grew up in Uganda, which was a British protectorate until 1962. She now makes her home in Kenya, for political reasons: After Idi Amin Dada's coup in 1971, Uganda was plagued by a dictatorial government and a blatant disregard for human rights. Kimenye and many other writers moved to safer, neighboring countries, especially Kenya, to avoid persecution. Although this situation encouraged a spirit of cooperation and an open exchange of ideas among East African authors, Ugandan writing maintained its own identity. In "The Pig," Kimenye incorporates elements of her beloved Ugandan culture into a humorous story. Have students look for details which reveal information about everyday life in a Ugandan village.

CONNECTIONS TO AMERICAN LITERATURE

Have students explain the ways in which the setting plays a central role in "The First Seven Years" and "The Pig." They should consider how the setting determines the customs, beliefs, and actions of the main characters.

About the Author

Ugandan **Barbara Kimenye** (1940–) discovered when her sons were small that few children's books tell of African life. She decided to fill this void by writing stories that have meaning for African children.

In addition to her writing career, Kimenye worked for many years for His Highness the Kabaka of Uganda. She also worked in the Ministry of Education and later served as the Kabaka's librarian.

About the Story

This story takes place in Kalasanda, a Ugandan village. It is from a collection of stories entitled *Kalasanda Revisited* (1966). It is a follow-up to *Kalasanda* (1965), an earlier collection of Barbara Kimenye's stories.

Connection to "The First Seven Years"

The small, self-contained worlds of daily life can provide an effective backdrop for literature. These two short stories provide insights into the lives of two elderly men who live worlds apart. In Bernard Malamud's "The First Seven Years," an elderly shoemaker in New York City comes to an important realization about himself, his daughter, and his shop assistant. In "The Pig," Barbara Kimenye explores a short period in the life of an elderly Ugandan villager who receives from his grandson an unusual gift that proves to be a burden.

The Pig

Barbara Kimenye

Old Kibuka had long believed that retirement was no sort of life for a man like himself, who would, so he modestly believed, pass for not a day over forty-five. He had held a responsible post at the Ggombolola Headquarters, until the Government had sent somebody from the Public Service Commission to nose around the offices and root out all employees over retirement age. Then the next thing Kibuka knew, despite his youthfully dyed hair, he had a pension, a Certificate of Service, but no longer a job.

He still worried about the state his filing system must be in today, for having once called in at the Headquarters, merely to see if the youngster who had replaced him needed any advice or help, he had been appalled at the lack of order. Papers were scattered everywhere, confidential folders were open for all the world to read, and his successor was flirting madly with some pin-brained girl at the other end of the newly installed telephone.

The visit had not been anything near a success, for not even his former colleagues showed anything but superficial interest in what Kibuka had to say.

So there he was, destined to waste the remainder of his life in the little cottage beside the Kalasanda stream, with plenty indeed to look back on, but not very much to look forward to, and his greatest friend, Yosefu Mukasa, was away in Buddu County on business.

The self-pitying thought, "I might as well be dead," kept recurring in his mind as he pumped his pressure stove to boil a kettle of tea. Then the noise of a car, grinding its way along the narrow, uneven track, heading in his direction, sent him eagerly to the door. It was his eldest grandson who climbed out of the battered Landrover.[1] A tall, loose-limbed young man in a khaki shirt and blue jeans. Old Kibuka practically choked with happiness as his frail fingers were squeezed in a sinewy grip, and the bones of his shoulders almost snapped under an affectionate hug.

1. **Landrover:** Utility vehicle similar to a Jeep.

Interest Grabber Tell students they will read a story that takes place in a small village. Have them brainstorm for words and phrases they associate with the idea of a small village. What type of living conditions come to mind? What types of characters do they expect to read about? As they read, encourage students to be aware of how the story met or strayed from their expectations.

▲ **Critical Viewing** Why might Kibuka be delighted with a piglet like this one? **[Connect]**

"What a wonderful surprise! Come in, my boy. I was just making a cup of tea."

"Grandfather, this is a very short visit. I'm afraid I can't stay more than a few minutes." The boy's voice was musically deep, very much like his grandfather's once had been, before the tremor of age had changed it. "I just came to see how you are getting on, and I brought you a present."

"That's very kind of you, son!" The unexpected visit and now a present: in a matter of seconds Kibuka had completely reversed his opinion that life was no longer worth living. He was aglow with excitement.

"Yes. It's one of the piglets from the Farm School. The sow doesn't seem able to feed this new litter, so I thought you might like one for eating; it should make an excellent meal."

The boy strode back to the Landrover and returned with a black, squealing bundle under his arm.

Kibuka was more delighted than ever. He had never seen so small a pig before, and he spent a good ten minutes marveling at its tiny twinkling eyes, its minute[2] hoofs, and its wisp of a tail. When his grandson drove away, he waved happily from the doorstep, the piglet clutched tenderly to his chest.

He had told his grandson that he would take the creature up to the Mukasas and ask Miriamu to prepare it as a special "welcome home" supper for Yosefu, but he soon sensed a certain reluctance within himself to do this, because the piglet followed him about the house or squatted trustingly at his feet each time he sat down. Moreover, it obviously understood every word Kibuka said to it, for, whenever he spoke, it listened gravely with its dainty forefeet placed lightly upon his knee.

By nightfall Kibuka was enchanted with his

2. **minute** (mī no͞ot′) *adj.*: Tiny.

Cross-Curricular Connection: Social Studies

Idi Amin The ruler of Uganda from 1971 to 1979, Idi Amin was an army officer who came to power after leading his troops to overthrow his country's civilian government.

Amin is remembered as a violent dictator. In 1972, Amin forced about 50,000 Asians out of his country in what he said was an effort to put control of the country's economy back in the hands of Ugandans. Thousands of Ugandans who were opposed to Amin's policies were killed by Amin and his supporters. He also praised Adolf Hitler for trying to eliminate the Jews, and denounced many leaders around the world.

Amin's tyrannical rule ended in 1979 when Ugandans who opposed him joined forces with troops from neighboring Tanzania to overthrow his government. Amin then fled the country, and elections for a new civilian government were soon held.

Develop Understanding

One-Minute Insight Barbara Kimenye tells the story of an elderly man named Kibuka who receives a pig as a gift from his grandson. Kibuka's loneliness causes him to develop a strong affection for the pig. As he grows, though, the pig becomes a great burden to Kibuka. When the animal dies in a freak accident, it comes as a great relief to the old man, who eventually finds himself eating and enjoying his beloved pig. Kimenye's ironic and humorous tone make this a playful story about a man's relationship with his pet.

▶Critical Viewing◀

Connect The piglet's wide and affectionate eyes, his diminutive size, and his seeming helplessness might be attractive to Kibuka.

Tips to Guide Reading

Identify With Character At first glance, students might find it difficult to identify with Kibuka. Help them to connect with this character by having them make a list of any qualities they might have in common with Kibuka. If they have trouble, encourage them to think of a time when they felt lonely, a situation when they felt very attached to something, or their love for a pet. Encourage them to use this strategy to identify with characters they come across while reading.

Extending Word Study

Homophones Have students read the definition of *minute* provided in the footnote. Make sure they are aware of its pronunciation, and then ask them to think of other homophones—words that are spelled the same but have different pronunciations and meanings. For example, they might think of the forms of *read* or *live*. Discuss ways that students can be sure to choose the correct form of the word when they read or write.

▶Critical Viewing◀

Connect It might become a burden to feed and maintain such a large animal. It would require a lot of time and hard work to keep it clean and healthy.

◆Critical Thinking

Analyze Why does Kibuka take to the pig with such energy and passion? What does his relationship with the pig say about his character? *Students might note that Kibuka is lonely and feels as though he has no reason to live. Because the pig depends so much on him, Kibuka, he feels useful and loved once again. The pig also brings him some much-desired attention from his neighbors.*

Connections to American Literature

Kimenye and Malamud both write about elderly men who have unusual passions. Have students explore how the ages of Kibuka and Feld affect their thoughts and actions. *Feld's age makes him focus on his daughter's future rather than his own, which is why he tries to meddle in her affairs. Kibuka's age causes him to feel lonely, which allows him to feel so strongly for the pig.*

Customize for *Visual/ Spatial Learners*

Have students make an illustration of a passage in the story that they find particularly humorous. Have willing students share their drawings and explain why they were drawn to the passages they chose.

◀ **Critical Viewing** Why might such a pig present a burden to Kibuka? **[Connect]**

new companion, and would have as much considered eating it as he would consider eating the beloved grandson who had given it to him. He fed the piglet little scraps of food from his own plate, besides providing it with a rich porridge mixture. Nevertheless, within a few days it was clear that the pig's appetite was increasing out of all proportion to its size, and Kibuka had to resort to collecting matoke peelings[3] in an old bucket from his friends and nearest neighbors.

The news that Kibuka was keeping a pig, the first ever actually reared in Kalasanda, caused something of a sensation. In no time at all there was little need for him to cart the bucket from house to house, because the women and children, on their way to draw water from the stream, made a practice of bringing the peelings and food scraps with them as part of the excuse for calling on him, and being allowed to fondle the animal and discuss its progress as if it were a dear relative with a delicate hold on life.

No pig had ever had it so good. Fortunately, it proved to be a fastidiously clean creature, and for this reason Kibuka allowed it to spend its nights at the foot of his bed, although he was careful not to let his neighbors know of this. The pig, naturally enough, positively flourished in this cozy atmosphere of goodwill and personal attention. From a squealing bundle small enough to be held in one hand, it quickly developed into a handsome, hefty porker with eyes which held the faintest glint of malice even when it was at its most affectionate with Kibuka.

However, as the weeks went by, its rapid growth was accompanied by a variety of problems. For instance, it required more and more food, and, having been reared on the leavings of every kitchen in Kalasanda, was inclined to turn up its enormous snout at the idea of having to root in the shamba[4] whenever it felt

3. **matoke peelings:** Skins of plantains or bananas.

4. **shamba:** Vegetable garden.

like something to eat. Every time it started to kick its empty dish about noisily, pausing now and then to glare balefully at old Kibuka and utter snorts of derision, the old man was driven to taking up his bucket and trudging forth to see if any scraps in the village had been overlooked.

Also, while Kibuka had at first secretly enjoyed the warmth of a cuddly little piglet lying across his feet each night, he found himself at a distinct disadvantage when that same piglet acquired a bulk of some fifty or so pounds, and still insisted upon ponderously hoisting itself onto his bed as of right. Worse still, along with the weight, the piglet also produced a snore which regularly kept poor Kibuka awake until dawn. It was a grave decision he was finally called upon to make, yet one on which he simply dare not waver: in future, the pig would have to stay outside, tethered to a tree.

Who suffered most, Kibuka or his pig, would be hard to tell, for the animal's lamentations, continuing throughout the night, were equal in strength to the black remorse and wealth of recrimination churning in Kibuka's bosom. That pig never knew how often it was near to being brought indoors and pacified with a bowl of warm milk.

During the day it still was free to roam about until, that is, it adopted the irritating habit of falling into the stream. There it would be, placidly ambling after Kibuka as he pottered in his small shamba, or gently napping in the shade of a coffee tree, and then, for no apparent reason, off it would go to the water's edge, and either fall or plunge in before anybody could say "bacon."

The Kalasanda stream had no real depth; many Kalasandans often bathed there or waded in, but sometimes, after a drop or two of rain, the current had more strength, and was quite capable of sweeping a child off its feet. The pig seemed always to choose such times for its immersion, and there wasn't anything anybody could really do as it spluttered and floundered with its hoofs flaying madly, and terror written plainly across its broad, black face.

At first, Kibuka would rush back and forth along the bank, calling frantically in the hope that it would struggle towards him, but what usually happened in the end was that a particularly strong eddy[5] would sweep it round the bend into a thicket of weeds and rushes, and then the children playing there would have a good half-hour's fun driving it home.

This happened so often that Kibuka was forced to keep the pig tethered day and night. He visualized the time when no children would be playing in the reeds, and the pig would perhaps become entangled, dragged under and drowned.

By way of compensation he decided upon a regular evening walk for the animal, so by and by Kalasanda became accustomed to the sight of Kibuka, slight yet patriarchal in his kanzu and black waistcoat,[6] sedately traversing the countryside with a huge black pig at the end of a rope, and only strangers saw anything out of the ordinary in it. Without doubt, these walks were a source of great pleasure and exercise to the pig, who found them a wonderful change from the all too familiar view of Kibuka's shamba. Unfortunately, the same could not be said of their effect on old Kibuka. To be frank, Kibuka's corns were killing him, and the excruciating pain of every step sometimes brought tears to his eyes. Still, he tried to bear his discomfort with stoic fortitude, for, as he said to Daudi Kulubya, who showed concern over his limp, it was always the same before the heavy rains: in fact, his corns were as good as a barometer when it came to forecasting the weather. But he was always glad to return home, where he could sit for an

5. **eddy** (ed′ ē) *n.*: Small whirlpool current.
6. **kanzu and black waistcoat:** Ugandan male's traditional long cotton garment and black vest.

Read to Be Entertained

Kimenye creates humor by using elevated language. For example, she calls the pig's noises "lamentations" rather than "squeals," which suggests an expression of profound grief. In this way, she gently mocks the absurdity of the situation. Have students identify other places where Kimenye achieves humor by using elevated language.

◆ Critical Thinking

Predict Have students predict the fate of the pig. Make sure they support their predictions with evidence or hints from the text. For example, they might say that the description of the stream's dangers and the pig's tendency to fall into it bode poorly for his future.

Customize for *Less Proficient Readers*

Why does Kimenye use the word "bacon" in her description of the speed with which the pig falls into the stream? What does this suggest about his future? *Students should note the unmistakable suggestion that the pig might one day be turned into bacon.*

Customize for *Verbal/Linguistic Learners*

Have students choose a passage of the story to read aloud. As they prepare their readings, encourage students to note the ironic and humorous tone of the story. Discuss the best methods for using their voices to convey this tone as they read.

Cross-Curricular Connection: Social Studies

Raising Hogs

It is not surprising that Kibuka found it difficult to find enough food to feed the pig once it began to grow. Pigs require a great deal of food to stay healthy. In fact, hogs consume twenty per cent of the corn grown in the United States! For this reason, most of the hogs raised in this country live on corn-hog farms in the Midwest.

Though many people consider hogs to be dirty animals, they keep themselves cleaner than most farm animals. They are also thought to be among the most intelligent of domesticated animals.

Hogs are extremely useful to humans. About one fourth of the meat eaten in the United States comes from hogs, in the form of pork chops, ham, bacon, and sausage. Other parts of hogs, such as their fat, skin, and hair, are used to make a wide variety of everyday products like leather, brushes, and fertilizer. They are among the most useful animals raised in the country.

◆ Critical Thinking

Evaluate Ask students whether they think it is wrong for Kibuka to contemplate selling the pig to a farmer or butcher. Make sure students consider the facts of the story, rather than just their emotions, when making their decisions. For example, they should keep in mind Kibuka's old age and inability to keep the pig healthy, and the fact that the poor village might benefit from sharing the pig.

◆ Critical Thinking

Analyze Describe the scene of the motorcycle accident. What vivid images does Kimenye use? To which senses does she appeal? *Kimenye uses vivid descriptions of the sight and sound of the accident, including "the horrible grinding of brakes" and "a whirling kaleidoscope of disaster."*

Customize for *Interpersonal Learners*
Have students consider why so many of the villagers come to view the scene of the accident. Why would they be interested in such an event? *Students might say that news of the accident probably spread quickly in a small village, and that in such a place a motorcycle accident is a major event.*

◆ Critical Thinking

Predict What will Kibuka decide to do with the body of the pig? Which of his previous actions hint at the decision he will make? *Students might guess that he will consent to having the pig butchered. His wavering loyalty to the pig in the past hints at this outcome.*

hour with his poor feet in a bowl of hot water and try to keep his mind off the small fortune he was spending on corn plasters brought to Kalasanda by the peddlers in the market.

How long this state of affairs would have continued is anybody's guess. There were occasions when Kibuka actually entertained the notion of parting with his pet at the first good offer from a reputable farmer or butcher. And yet, one trusting glance or gesture of affection from that waddling hunk of pork was enough for him to feel ashamed of what he regarded as his own treachery.

The end came at last in the most unlikely manner. One minute there was Kibuka contemplating the sunset, and, incidentally, giving his feet a rest by one of the obscure paths leading to the Sacred Tree, while the pig scratched happily at the root of a clump of shrubs, its head hidden by foliage, while its carcass, broadside on, barricaded the path, and then, seconds later, there was the snarl of a motorcycle engine, the horrible grinding of brakes, followed by a whirling kaleidoscope of disaster. Kibuka, pig, bike and rider seemed to explode in all directions. Each had a momentary vision of the others sailing through the air.

When Kibuka eventually dared to open his eyes and cautiously move each limb, he was relieved to find he was still in one piece, although one shoulder felt painfully bruised and there was blood on both his hands. The rider, whom he now recognized as a certain Nathaniel Kiggundu, did not appear to have fared very badly either. He was staggering out of a tangled mass of weeds, wiping mud off his face, and fingering a long tear in the knee of his trousers.

Somewhere from behind the hedge came the raucous cries of a pig in distress, and it was in this direction that both men headed, once they had regained their bearings. They were only just in time to see the injured animal give up the ghost and join its ancestors in that heavenly piggery which surely must exist somewhere above. There was scarcely a mark on it, but its head lay at a strange and awkward angle, so it can be safely assumed that it died of a broken neck.

Old Kibuka was terribly upset, and the accident had left him in a generally shaky condition. He sat down beside the dead animal and wondered what would happen next. Nathaniel Kiggundu, however, seeing Kibuka was comparatively unhurt, showed more concern over his motorcycle, which lay grotesquely twisted in a ditch. The inevitable crowd collected almost as soon as the pig expired, so there was much coming and going, first to stare at the fatal casualty, and then to stare at the motorbike. Nantondo kept up a running commentary, her version of how the accident happened, although nobody believed she had seen it, and by the time Musisi the Ggombolola Chief arrived on the scene, she had fully adopted the role of Mistress of Ceremonies.

After taking a statement from Kiggundu, Musisi approached Kibuka and insisted upon taking him home in the Landrover. "You don't look at all well, Sir. Come. You can make your statement in the morning, when you have had a rest."

"But I can't leave my pig here." Kibuka refused to budge from the spot.

"Well, I can put it in the back of the Landrover, if you like. Only it would be better to have the butcher cut it up, because I don't think pork will keep for long in this weather."

The idea of eating the pig had never entered Kibuka's mind. While sitting beside the body, he had been seriously considering just whereabouts in the shamba he could bury it. Now he opened his mouth to tell Musisi in no uncertain terms that eating one's good friends was a practice reserved for barbarians: and then, he suddenly had a clear picture of himself struggling to dig a grave. He was sure no Kalasandans would want to help him do it. Then came the realization of the effect a perpetual reminder of his porking friend in his shamba would have on him. He did not think he could stand it. Far better, indeed, to let the past bury itself and, besides, why deprive his fellow villagers of a tasty treat? They were, after all, the people who had nourished the creature on their leftovers.

"Very well. Get somebody to carve it up and share it out among the people who eat pork, and do be sure to send a whole back leg up to the Mukasas," he said at last, suddenly feeling far too weary to care.

"Musa the butcher won't do it," Nantondo piped. "He's a Muslim."

"Well, I'll take it along to the Ggombolola Headquarters and ask one of the askaris[7] to carve it up. Anybody who wants pork must go there at about seven o'clock tonight," declared Musisi, and ordered two of the onlookers to help him lift the carcass into the back of his vehicle.

Back at his cottage, Kibuka rubbed his injured shoulder with a concoction he used to cure most of his ailments, be they loose bowels or a sore throat, and then sat brooding over a cup of tea. He went to bed very early and awoke next day to find the sun well risen. He decided he had had the best night's sleep he had enjoyed for many a month. Musisi arrived as Kibuka was leaving home to see if the leg of pork had been safely delivered to Yosefu and Miriamu.

"No, I'm taking the meat there now, Sir," Musisi said. "Would you care to come with me?"

Kibuka gladly accepted the lift, although he declined the lump of pork Musisi had brought for him, personally. "You have it, son. I'm not a great lover of pork."

7. **askaris:** Native African soldiers or police officers.

Miriamu went into raptures over the leg of pork, and Yosefu showed the keenest interest in the details of the accident. They pressed both Kibuka and Musisi to stay to lunch, but Musisi had to leave to attend a committee meeting in Mmengo, so only Kibuka remained. He and Yosefu, who lately had not seen as much of each other as usual, had plenty to discuss, and lunch was an exhilarating meal.

"I must say, you really are a wonderful cook!" Kibuka told Miriamu, helping himself to more food. Miriamu preened herself, shyly. "Well, that pork was as tender as a chicken, and very tasty, too!"

There was a moment of dismay when Kibuka realized he was eating and thoroughly enjoying the succulence of his late friend, but it quickly passed, and he continued piling his plate with meat, smiling to himself at the knowledge that there would be no need to take a walk in the late afternoon; he could have a good nap instead.

◆ Critical Thinking

1. What does Kibuka's reluctance to kill the pig reveal about his character? **[Infer]**
2. Following the death of the pig, why did Kibuka feel relief? **[Interpret]**

◆ Compare Literary Works

3. Judging from Malamud's or Kimenye's stories, what are some concerns the elderly have? **[Generalize]**

Cultural Connection

4. In what ways is life in Kibuka's small Ugandan village similar to life in a small American town? **[Relate]**

Clarify When Kimenye mentions "the people who eat pork," she is referring to the Islamic dietary laws which forbid the eating of pork. Muslims make up a minority of the population in Uganda. Ask students about other dietary restrictions they are familiar with.

◆ Critical Thinking

Infer Does Kibuka feel any qualms about his decision to have the pig slaughtered? How can you tell? *Students should note that Kibuka seems very relieved by his decision. He slept better than he had in a long while, and he experienced only a brief "moment of dismay" upon realizing he was eating and enjoying the pig.*

◆ Critical Thinking

Evaluate What general attitude does Kimenye have toward the people in the village of Kalasanda? Have students support their answers with evidence from the text. *Students should note that Kimenye conveys a humorous and gently mocking attitude toward the characters in the story.*

Reinforce and Extend

Answers

◆ Critical Thinking

1. Kibuka is a gentle and lonely man who finds himself easily attached to the adorable pig.
2. Kibuka feels relief because taking care of the pig had become a burden.

Compare Literary Works

3. The elderly characters in both stories are concerned for the well-being of their loved ones.

Cultural Connection

4. In a Ugandan village and a small American town, almost all the members of the community know one another and are aware of each other's problems and needs.

Beyond the Selection

FURTHER READING

Other Works by Barbara Kimenye

Kalasanda
Kalasanda Revisited
The Smugglers

We suggest that you preview these works before recommending them to students.

INTERNET

You and your students may find additional information about Uganda on the Internet. We suggest the following site. Please be aware, however, that the site may have changed since the time this information was published.

For more on the history and culture of Uganda, visit **www.nic.ug**

We *strongly recommend* that you preview this site before sending students to it.

LESSON OBJECTIVES

1. To increase knowledge of other cultures and to connect common elements across cultures
- About the Essay (SE)
- Cultural Context (ATE)
- Connections to American Literature (ATE)

2. To express and support responses to the text
- Critical Thinking

Cultural Context Though Solzhenitsyn received formal approval from Soviet prime minister Nikita Khrushchev to publish *One Day in the Life of Ivan Denisovich,* his period of acceptance in his native land was short-lived. Khrushchev soon fell from power and a reactionary leadership replaced him. This new government discouraged Solzhenitsyn's accounts of the atrocities of Stalin, and placed a ban on his books that was not lifted until 1989. He was quickly exiled by the Soviet Writers Union and settled in the United States. In 1970 he was awarded the Nobel Prize in Literature "for the ethical force with which he has pursued the indispensable traditions of Russian Literature." As they read, have students think about why it is so important for Solzhenitsyn to write about the horrors he witnessed.

CONNECTIONS TO AMERICAN LITERATURE

Solzhenitsyn laments the loss of religious freedom under the Communist regimes in the Soviet Union. Ask students why Solzhenitsyn finds this loss so devastating. Do they think Carson McCullers would consider religion a way to help eradicate loneliness? *Solzhenitsyn mourns the loss of religious freedom because of the connections and comforts it provides for people. McCullers might see religion as a source of connections between human beings.*

About the Author

Alexander Solzhenitsyn (1918–) was born in Kislovodsk, a town in southern Russia. When Germany invaded Russia in 1941, Solzhenitsyn was drafted and served in the army. While serving, he was charged with treason for writing letters that were critical of Stalin, the Soviet leader, to a friend. Solzhenitsyn spent the next eight years in prison.

In 1956, Solzhenitsyn wrote *One Day in the Life of Ivan Denisovich,* which describes life in prison camps. It catapulted Solzhenitsyn to fame. His later writings were read worldwide but banned in the Soviet Union. Solzhenitsyn was awarded the Nobel Prize for Literature in 1970.

About the Essay

For most of the twentieth century, Russia was part of the Soviet Union. Under the communist government, attending church, if not strictly illegal, was not encouraged. This essay explores Solzhenitsyn's feelings about the abandoned churches that dot the Russian countryside.

Connection to "The Mortgaged Heart"

In these essays, both writers explore emotional reactions to places. In "The Mortgaged Heart," McCullers explores the state of loneliness in New York City. Solzhenitsyn, in the following essay, shares his personal reactions as he walks along a path in the Russian countryside.

A Journey Along the Oka

Alexander Solzhenitsyn
Translated by Michael Glenny

Traveling along country roads in central Russia, you begin to understand why the Russian countryside has such a soothing effect.

It is because of its churches. They rise over ridge and hillside, descending towards wide rivers like red and white princesses, towering above the thatch and wooden huts of everyday life with their slender, carved and fretted belfries. From far away they greet each other; from distant, unseen villages they rise towards the same sky.

Wherever you may wander, over field or pasture, many miles from any homestead, you are never alone: above the wall of trees, above the hayricks, even above the very curve of the earth itself, the dome of a belfry is always beckoning to you, from Borki Lovetskie, Lyubichi, or Gavrilovskoe.[1]

But as soon as you enter a village you realize that the churches which welcomed you from afar are no longer living. Their crosses have long since been bent or broken off; the dome with its peeling paint reveals its rusty ribcage; weeds grow on the roofs and in the cracks of the walls; the cemetery is hardly ever cared for, its crosses knocked over and its graves ransacked; the ikons[2] behind the altar have faded from a decade of rain and are scrawled with obscene graffiti.

In the porch there are barrels of salt and a tractor is swinging round towards them, or a lorry[3] is backing up to the vestry door to collect some sacks. In one church, machine tools are humming away; another stands silent, simply locked up. Others have been turned into clubs where

1. **Borki Lovetskie, Lyubichi, or Gavrilovskoe:** Cities in the former Soviet Union.
2. **ikons** (ī´ känz) *n.*: Religious images or figures.
3. **lorry:** (lôr´ ē) *n.*: Truck.

Interest Grabber Ask students to consider an object or a structure in their town which somehow encapsulates something important about the town. For example, they might choose a very old home if the town prides itself on its rich history; or simply a pretty tree to express the natural beauty of the town. Have students explain their choices by writing a paragraph, and then have willing students share their ideas.

◆ Critical Thinking

Analyze Why do churches have such a soothing effect on Solzhenitsyn? What might churches symbolize to him? *The churches represent his faith and a link to the religious freedom of the past. They probably symbolize a less repressive time in his homeland.*

▲ **Critical Viewing** What distinctive features of the architecture of this church distinguish it from churches you've seen? **[Distinguish]**

propaganda meetings are held ("We Will Achieve High Yields of Milk!") or films shown: *Poem About the Sea, The Great Adventure.*

People have always been selfish and often evil. But the Angelus[4] used to toll and its echo would float over village, field, and wood. It reminded man that he must abandon his trivial earthly cares and give up one hour of his thoughts to life eternal. The tolling of the eventide bell, which now survives for us only in a popular song, raised man above the level of a beast.

Our ancestors put their best into these stones and these belfries—all their knowledge and all their faith.

Come on, Vitka, buck up and stop feeling sorry for yourself! The film starts at six, and the dance is at eight . . .

4. **Angelus** (an′ je ləs) *n.*: Bell rung to announce times for the Angelus, a prayer commemorating the Incarnation, said during morning, noon, and evening prayers.

◆ Critical Thinking

1. According to Solzhenitsyn, what "raised man above the level of a beast"? **[Connect]**
2. How does Solzhenitsyn feel about the condition of the churches in Russia? Support your answer with evidence from the text. **[Infer]**

◆ Compare Literary Works

3. Essays ultimately reveal something of the personality of their writers. Judging from these two essays, with which writer would you prefer to converse: McCullers or Solzhenitsyn? Why? **[Relate]**

Cultural Connection

4. "A Journey Along the Oka" was written when Russia was part of the Soviet Union. What banned aspect of Russian culture is Solzhenitsyn mourning? Why might that sort of ban cause distress for so many people? **[Infer]**

Develop Understanding

One-Minute Insight In this essay, Solzhenitsyn travels along the Russian countryside and describes how the churches he passes remind him of the loss of religious and other freedoms in his homeland. The churches look beautiful from a distance, but up close he can see that they are run-down and decrepit, and most of them are used for nonreligious purposes such as storage sheds or dance halls.

◆ Critical Thinking

Analyze Why does Solzhenitsyn include the farm production slogan "We Will Achieve High Yields of Milk!" in his essay? *This piece of Communist propaganda highlights the irony of the fact that the church, which was once used for spiritual inspiration, is now used for political indoctrination.*

Customize for
Interpersonal Learners
Considering what they know of the Solzhenitsyn's tumultuous history, do they think he is justified in saying that people have "always been selfish and sometimes evil"? Have students hold a discussion about why Solzhenitsyn feels this way.

Reinforce and Extend

Answers

◆ Critical Thinking

1. Solzhenitsyn believes that religion raised man above the level of a beast.
2. Solzhenitsyn feels dismayed that many of the churches are no longer holy places.

Compare Literary Works

3. Answers will vary based on the interests of the students.

Cultural Connection

4. Solzhenitsyn mourns the ban of religion in the Soviet Union. The ban might cause distress because it endangers people who believe and worship as they chose.

Beyond the Selection

FURTHER READING

Other Works by Alexander Solzhenitsyn

One Day in the Life of Ivan Denisovich
The Gulag Archipelago

We suggest that you preview these works before recommending them to students.

INTERNET

You and your students may find additional information about Solzhenitsyn on the Internet. We suggest this site. Please be aware, however, that the site may have changed since the time this information was published.

For more on this controversial writer, visit **nobelprizes.com/nobel/literature/1970a.html**

We *strongly recommend* that you preview this site before sending students to it.

How to Use Analyzing Real-World Texts

The Analyzing Real-World Texts section contains six nonfiction selections from real-world sources, such as Web sites, newspaper editorials, and journals. The instruction for each selection introduces a reading strategy, such as analyzing characteristics of texts. Questions requiring students to apply the strategy follow the selection. In addition, each real-world selection is thematically linked to a selection in the body of the book. Questions linking the two works appear at the end of the real-world selection.

LESSON OBJECTIVES

1. **To read for different purposes in varied sources**
   - Selection: Web site
2. **To read in order to research self-selected and assigned topics**
   - Reading Strategy: Locate Appropriate Information
3. **To use a variety of strategies to comprehend a text**
   - Compare Literary Forms

Answers

◆ Apply the Reading Strategy

1. "Difficulties faced"—site will contain information on this topic, since it is basic to the Pilgrims' story; "Religious doctrines"—site will contain some information, but will probably not go deeply into detail, since it is mainly directed at tourists, not scholars; "Structure of colony government"—(same as "Religious doctrines").
2. Answers include: the route followed by the Pilgrims; the origins of Thanksgiving; relations with Native Americans; the number of passengers on the Mayflower; directions to the "living history" museum Plimoth Plantation; and so on.

Analyzing Real-World Texts

Background

Plimoth Plantation, Inc., runs a museum in Plymouth, Massachusetts, the town founded in 1620 by the Pilgrims.

◆ Reading Strategy

Locate Appropriate Information To use reference works well, you must develop skills for **locating appropriate information.** For instance, if you search the Internet using the term *Pilgrim* for information on colonists, you must weed through sites about other kinds of Pilgrims. Your next step is to judge which site is worth visiting. (An elementary-school student's Web page may not be of use.) Finally, you need to choose which links on the page to explore. ("Membership" will not tell you about history.)

Use a graphic organizer like the one below to determine whether you can locate appropriate information on this site.

Topic	Will Site Have Information? Why?	Links to Use
Date of landing	Yes—it is a basic fact.	Pilgrim Story Plymouth Colony
Difficulties faced		
Religious doctrines		
Structure of colony government		

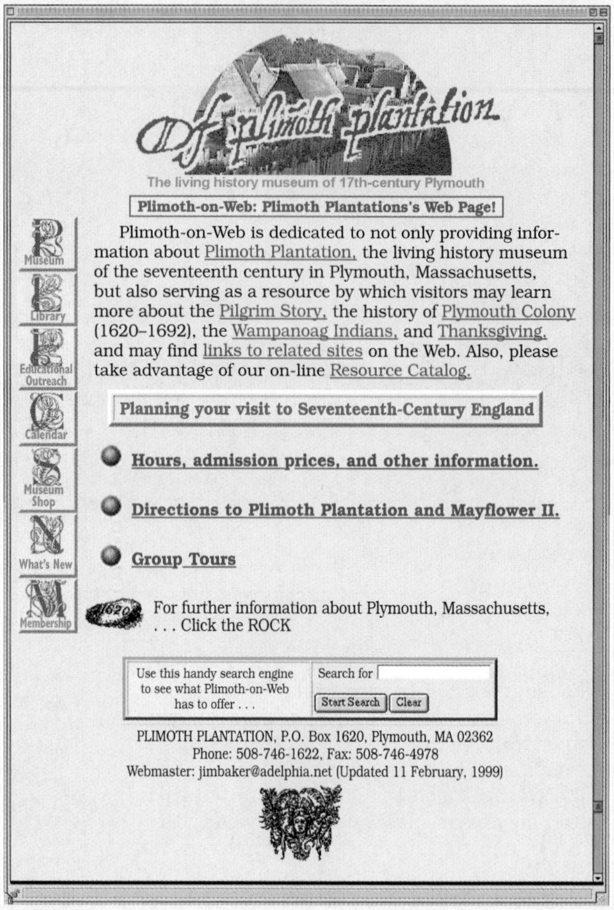

◆ Apply the Reading Strategy

1. Of the topics listed in the graphic organizer, which are likely to be covered on this site? Which are not? Explain your reasoning.
2. Name another topic for which this site might hold information.

◆ Compare Literary Forms

Read or review William Bradford's *Of Plymouth Plantation,* p. 71. Select a passage that you think belongs on this Web site. Explain your choice.

◆ Compare Literary Forms

Students may single out dramatic moments in the text, such as the description of the Pilgrims' prayers upon first arriving on dry land (beginning "Being thus arrived in a good harbor . . ." [p. 72]), or historically significant information, such as the agreement between the Pilgrims and Massasoit (beginning "1. That neither he nor any of his should injure . . ." [p. 75]).

Connecting to "Of Plymouth Plantation," William Bradford, p. 71

To connect this Web page to Bradford's firsthand account of the settling of Plymouth, ask students what springs to mind when they think of Pilgrims. *Possible answers: Thanksgiving, Squanto, round hats with silver buckles, religious dissent, and so on.* Explain that these images are all emblems of the Pilgrim experience. Then, have them read or review Bradford's "Plymouth Plantation," looking for passages that might also be "emblems" of the Pilgrim experience—passages representing something fundamental or singular in their history. Afterwards, have students study this Web site and answer the Compare Literary Forms question on this page.

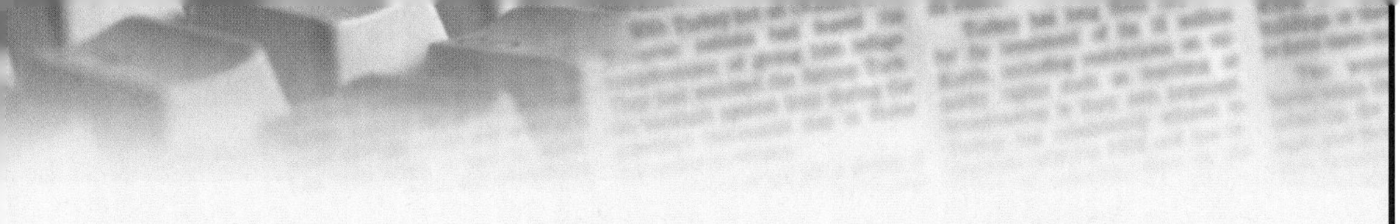

About the Authors

Martin Frost (1942–) has served more than ten terms as a congressperson from the Dallas–Fort Worth area in Texas. **Yeh Ling-Ling** (1953–), a naturalized citizen of Chinese ancestry, works on immigration policy issues.

◆ Reading Strategy

Logical and Faulty Modes of Persuasion Not every argument is clearly good or bad. When distinguishing **logical and faulty modes of persuasion,** you may need additional information before you can evaluate the argument.

Martin Frost cites a figure suggesting that immigrants are needed for jobs that "there are no American workers to fill." He gives a figure for employment, but he does not look at unemployment. You need to know whether unemployment among newcomers outweighs employment. Yeh Ling-Ling cites local experts who say that new immigrants hurt the chances of citizens to get jobs. She assumes that the opinions she cites apply to the big picture as well as to the local one. You need to know how immigration affects employment across the country.

Using a graphic organizer such as the one at right, note each instance in these articles in which more information would help you evaluate the arguments.

Where Freedom-Seekers Yearn to Be Free

Martin Frost

Newspaper editorial, Knight-Ridder/Tribune News Service, January 22, 1999

Throughout American history, this country has benefited tremendously from the extraordinary contributions made by the ingenuity, work ethic and profound sense of patriotism of legal immigrants.

We need a common-sense immigration policy that stops illegal immigration but allows America to continue to enjoy the many benefits of legal immigration without overburdening our social and economic systems.

Legal immigrants will continue to bring tangible benefits to our economy and American culture if we take sensible steps to adequately administer, fund, and enforce sensible immigration policy.

However, anti-immigrant interest groups and some in Congress are proposing that we take the extreme step of slamming America's door shut. These proponents of an immigration moratorium[1]—which would close our borders to all legal immigrants—are pushing a radical and possibly dangerous measure.

. . .

While sensible adjustments to this country's current limits on immigration are always worthy of

Persuasive Statement	Assumption	Additional Information Needed
It is a myth that immigrants take jobs from Americans: Each year 140,000 immigrants fill jobs Americans cannot.	1. If immigrants did not come, those jobs would remain unfilled. 2. ________	1. Would unemployed Americans take those jobs if they were retrained or moved? 2. ________

1. **moratorium** (môr′ ə tôr′ ē əm) *n.:* Official delay or stopping of an activity.

LESSON OBJECTIVES

1. **To read for different purposes in varied sources**
   - Selection: Newspaper editorials
2. **To read critically to evaluate texts**
   - Reading Strategy: Logical and Faulty Modes of Persuasion
3. **To analyze literary elements**
   - Compare Literary Forms

Connecting to *Letters From an American Farmer,* Michel-Guillaume Jean de Crèvecoeur, p. 197

To connect these newspaper editorials to Crèvecoeur's *Letters From an American Farmer,* ask students to discuss the meaning of the phrases "the land of liberty" and "the land of opportunity." *Possible responses: The United States is the "land of liberty" because it allows its people freedom of self-expression and belief. It is the "land of opportunity," because the nation's wealth is great and there are few restrictions on employment or on the wealth people can acquire.* Point out that this kind of opportunity and liberty were lacking in many European countries at the time that Crèvecoeur published his *Letters.* Explain that, in 1790, ten years after the *Letters* appeared, the United States had a population of only four million, excluding Native Americans. This non-Native American population was concentrated along the eastern seabord—only an intrepid few had reached the Mississippi River. Yet westward expansion seemed to offer limitless possibilities for new settlement. Forty years later, the population had tripled, and some whites had pushed beyond the Mississippi. From 1820 to 1870, nearly seven and a half million immigrants came to this new land, fueling the push westward.

Ask students to consider these facts as they read or review the excerpt from Crèvecoeur's Letters. Then, have them read these two newspaper editorials and answer the Compare Literary Forms question, p. 1209.

Answers

◆ Apply the Reading Strategy

1. Answers include: Readers need to know whether native citizens might retrain, relocate, or change their ideas of suitable employment if immigrant labor is not available to fill these jobs (in which case employment would go up); readers also need to know if unemployment among new immigrants is high (in which case new immigrants would add to overall unemployment).
2. Answers include: Readers need to know whether other causes of unemployment might keep Americans out of work, regardless of immigration rates; readers also need to know whether native citizens would be willing or able to fill the jobs currently taken by new immigrants (if not, lowering immigration rates would not necessarily increase employment).

public debate, a moratorium is an extreme measure that poses a threat to our economy and to our social fabric. A moratorium would block the entry of many people who play a pivotal role in our economy and are vital to our economic well-being as we enter the new millennium.

The calls for a moratorium on immigration are predicated on several myths. One such myth asserts that immigrants take jobs away from American workers. The truth is that legal immigrants do not supplant but supplement our native work force.

Each year, about 140,000 legal immigrants are hired in jobs that the U.S. Department of Labor has determined there are no American workers to fill. Clearly, American businesses would suffer without these immigrant workers.

Additionally, studies by the Rand Corporation, the Council of Economic Advisors, the National Research Council, and the Urban Institute[2] have all concluded that immigrants do not have a negative effect on the employment opportunities of native-born American workers.

Another myth perpetuated by moratorium advocates is that immigrants are overburdening our social services. In fact the opposite is true. An Urban Institute study recently concluded, "Immigrants actually generate significantly more in taxes paid than they cost in services." A freeze on immigration would actually wind up costing our social service agencies.

Yet another myth promoted by moratorium proponents is that immigrants are destroying our social fabric—that a halt in immigration is needed to allow us to assimilate the newcomers into the mainstream of American society.

In fact, a moratorium could have some very negative social side effects. Immigration allows many families already in our country to stay intact. Many are dependent upon immigrant relatives to care for their children while the two parents enter the work force. . . .

2. **Rand Corporation . . . and the Urban Institute:** Groups that study economic and social issues.

Legal Immigration Must Be Curbed, Too

Yeh Ling-Ling

Newspaper editorial, *USA Today*, January 1997, as prepared for the Carrying Capacity Network

Year after year, presidential candidates and members of Congress from both parties repeatedly have promised to reduce budget deficits, strengthen the economy, create jobs for Americans, and put welfare recipients back to work. [*In 1999, the author added:* The federal government continues to conceal the extent of its deficits by borrowing from the Social Security fund to balance the budget; the national debt is on the rise; real wages for lower- and middle-class workers have either declined or stagnated; and the gap between the rich and poor has been accentuated.] Yet, how can those goals possibly be achieved if the U.S. continues to allow an average of more than 800,000 legal immigrants to enter the

country every year? These newcomers need jobs, education, welfare, health care, and many other services that cannot even be provided to millions of native-born Americans.

As a naturalized citizen[1] of Chinese ancestry with extensive professional experience preparing family- and employment-based immigrant petitions, I am disappointed over the lack of will in Washington to reduce legal immigration. This hesitancy continues despite the fact that even strong immigration rights advocates have admitted the adverse[2] impact of mass immigration.

Antonia Hernandez, president of the Mexican American Legal Defense and Educational Fund, has stated that "migration, legal and undocumented, does have an impact on our economy. . . . Most of the competition is to the Latino community. We compete with each other for those low-paying jobs. There is an issue of wage depression, as in the garment industry, which is predominantly immigrant. . . . "

Chinese-American Prof. Paul Ong of UCLA,[3] a strong advocate of a liberal immigration policy, points out that, "in terms of adverse impact [of immigration] on wages and employment, the adverse impact will be most pronounced on minorities and established immigrants. . . ."

Po Wong, director of the Chinese Newcomers Service Center in San Francisco, indicated in 1993 that, of the 11,000 new Chinese immigrants looking for work through his agency, just two percent were placed successfully. "I don't think our community is equipped to welcome this large a number. . . . It's very depressing to see so many people come here looking for work."

Dolores Huerta, co-founder of the United Farm Workers Union, testified before the California Select Committee on immigration that, "With 1,500,000 legalized immigrants living in California, and only approximately 250,000 agricultural jobs in the state, there is no need for additional farm workers."

The pro-immigration Urban Institute has acknowledged that "less-skilled black workers and black workers in high immigration areas with stagnant economies are negatively affected [by immigration]."

. . .

The nation's leaders should be reminded that today's economy requires fewer and fewer workers due to automation, advances in technology, and corporate downsizing. Moreover, many jobs have been lost to foreign countries. If the Federal government continues to allow hundreds of thousands of low-skilled legal immigrants of working age to enter the U.S. every year, how can America's unemployed, low-skilled workers and welfare recipients be expected to find work? Rosy unemployment rates released by the Labor Department do not include millions of workers who are underemployed or never have found work. . . .

1. **naturalized** (nach´ ər əl īzd´) **citizen** *n.*: Person not born in a country, who legally becomes a citizen of that country.
2. **adverse** (ad vurs´) *adj.*: Unfavorable; harmful.
3. **UCLA:** University of California at Los Angeles.

◆ Apply the Reading Strategy

1. Frost suggests that immigration does not have a negative effect on native employment. What more do you need to know to evaluate this claim?
2. Yeh Ling-Ling suggests that unemployed Americans will be unable to find work if immigration rates do not change. What more do you need to know to evaluate this claim?

◆ Compare Literary Forms

Read or review Michel-Guillaume Jean de Crèvecoeur's *Letters From an American Farmer,* p. 197.
(a) What does Crèvecoeur take to be the essential meaning of immigration to the United States? (b) What issues do these editorials take to be essential? (c) Which approach to immigration do you think is more valid?

◆ Compare Literary Forms

(a) For Crèvecoeur, immigration is a kind of transformation of the past and a hope for the future: "Here [in America] individuals of all nations are melted into a new race of men, whose labors and posterity will one day cause great changes in the world" (p. 198). (b) The editorials take the economic well-being of the United States to be central to any discussion of immigration policy. (c) Some students may respond that Crèvecoeur's vision holds true to the essential meaning of the American dream, where debates about the economy seem petty; other students may respond that, unless backed up by economic facts, Crèvecoeur's idealism is unrealistic in today's world.

LESSON OBJECTIVES

1. **To read for different purposes in varied sources**
   - Selection: Historic memorandum
2. **To read critically to evaluate texts**
   - Reading Strategy: Analyze Text Structures: Patterns of Organization
3. **To use a variety of reading strategies to comprehend a memorandum**
   - Reading Strategy
4. **To analyze literary elements**
   - Compare Literary Forms

Connecting to "Crossing the Great Divide," Meriwether Lewis, p. 276

To connect Thomas Jefferson's "Commission of Meriwether Lewis" to Meriwether Lewis's journal entry "Crossing the Great Divide," ask students to consider the way in which documents make history as well as record it. When Jefferson asked Meriwether Lewis to explore the Missouri River, his "commission" of Lewis made the United States officially responsible for Lewis in the event that he ran into enemy agents in uncharted territory. Further, Lewis's records of his exploration would enable others to retrace his steps, laying open this western territory for further exploration and settlement.

Ask students to read or review Lewis's "Crossing the Great Divide," paying particular attention to the kind of history Lewis was trying to make—the future toward which he was preparing the way. Then, have them read Jefferson's "Commission" with the same focus. They should then answer the Compare Literary Forms questions, p. 1212.

About the Author

Thomas Jefferson (1743–1826), the main author of the Declaration of Independence, helped envision and establish an independent United States. He became president in 1801.

◆ Reading Strategy

Analyze Text Structures: Patterns of Organization

Writers can organize information in a variety of ways, including chronological order, spatial order, order of importance, point-by-point comparisons, and simple enumeration (listing items of equal importance).

In his commission of Meriwether Lewis, President Jefferson organizes some topics in the order of their importance. First, he describes the core of Lewis's mission: to "explore the Missouri River" in order to find a route to the Pacific. He then discusses points relating to the recording of information on the journey—a related point that is less important.

Using a graphic organizer such as this one, list another example in Jefferson's memorandum of items given in order of importance, one of items in chronological order, and one of enumeration.

Pattern of Organization	Examples
Order of Importance	1. Topic 1. Object of mission: explore the Missouri (main idea) Topic 2. Directions for taking observations (less important, related idea)
	2.
Chronological Order	
Enumeration	

Commission of Meriwether Lewis

Thomas Jefferson

Historic memorandum

June 20, 1803

To Meriwether Lewis,[1] esquire, captain of the first regiment of infantry of the United States of America:

Your situation as secretary[2] of the president of the United States, has made you acquainted with the objects of my confidential message of January 18, 1803, to the legislature; you have seen the act they passed, which, though expressed in general terms, was meant to sanction[3] those objects, and you are appointed to carry them into execution.

. . .

The object of your mission is to explore the Missouri river, and such principal streams of it, as, by its course and communication with the waters of the Pacific ocean, whether the Columbia, Oregan [*sic*], Colorado, or any other river, may offer the most direct and practicable water-communication across the continent, for the purposes of commerce.

Beginning at the mouth of the Missouri, you will take observations of latitude and longitude, at all remarkable points on the river, and especially at the mouths of rivers, at rapids, at islands, and other places and objects distinguished by such natural marks and characters, of a durable kind, as that they may with certainty be recognized hereafter. The courses of the river between these points of observation may be supplied by the compass, the log-line,[4] and by time, corrected by

1. **Meriwether Lewis** (1774–1809): Co-leader of the Lewis and Clark Expedition (1804–1806) to the Northwest.
2. **situation as secretary:** Lewis served as Jefferson's private secretary, handling his correspondence and so on.
3. **sanction** (saŋk′ shən) *v.*: Authorize or permit.
4. **log-line:** Device used to measure the speed of a vessel, consisting of rope tied to a log with known lengths marked off by knots.

the observations themselves. The variations of the needle, too, in different places, should be noticed.

The interesting points of the portage between the heads of the Missouri, and of the water offering the best communication with the Pacific Ocean, should also be fixed by observation; and the course of that water to the ocean, in the same manner as that of the Missouri.

Your observations are to be taken with great pains and accuracy; to be entered distinctly and intelligibly for others as well as yourself; to comprehend all the elements necessary, with the aid of the usual tables, to fix the latitude and longitude of the places at which they were taken; and are to be rendered to the war-office, for the purpose of having the calculations made concurrently by proper persons within the United States. Several copies of these, as well as of your other notes, should be made at leisure times, and put into the care of the most trustworthy of your attendants to guard, by multiplying them against the accidental losses to which they will be exposed. A further guard would be, that one of these copies be on the cuticular membranes of the paper-birch,[5] as less liable to injury from damp than common paper.

The commerce which may be carried on with the people inhabiting the line you will pursue, renders a knowledge of those people important. You will therefore endeavor to make yourself acquainted, as far as a diligent pursuit of your journey shall admit, with the names of the nations and their numbers;

The extent and limits of their possessions;

Their relations with other tribes or nations;

Their language, traditions, monuments;

Their ordinary occupations in agriculture, fishing, hunting, war, arts, and the implements for these;

Their food, clothing, and domestic accommodations;

The diseases prevalent among them, and the remedies they use;

Moral[6] and physical circumstances which distinguish them from the tribes we know;

Peculiarities in their laws, customs, and dispositions;

And articles of commerce they may need or furnish, and to what extent.

And, considering the interest which every nation has in extending and strengthening the authority of reason and justice among the people around them, it will be useful to acquire what knowledge you can of the state of morality, religion, and information[7] among them; as it may better enable those who may endeavor to civilize and instruct them, to adapt their measures to the existing notions and practices of those on whom they are to operate.

Other objects worthy of notice will be —

The soil and face of the country, its growth and vegetable productions, especially those not of the United States;

The animals of the country generally, and especially those not known in the United States;

The remains and accounts of any which may be deemed rare or extinct;

The mineral productions of every kind, but more particularly metals, limestone, pit-coal, and saltpeter;[8] salines and mineral waters, noting the temperature of the last, and such circumstances as may indicate their character;

Volcanic appearances;

Climate, as characterized by the thermometer, by the proportion of rainy, cloudy, and clear days; by lightning, hail, snow, ice; by the access and recess of frost; by the winds prevailing at different seasons; the dates at which particular plants put forth, or lose their flower or leaf; times of appearance of particular birds, reptiles or insects.

---

5. **cuticular** (kyo͞o tik´ yo͞o lər) **membranes of the paper birch:** Layer of bark, usable as paper.

6. **moral:** Having to do with conduct and character.

7. **information:** Here, "knowledge."

8. **saltpeter** (sôlt´ pēt´ ər): Potassium nitrate, mineral used to make gunpowder.

Answers

◆ Apply the Reading Strategy

1. Answers include: Jefferson uses *order of importance* in discussing first the general object of the mission (explore the Missouri to find a route to the Pacific), then turning to important details concerning the accomplishment of this object (methods of taking observation), and so on. Jefferson uses simple *enumeration* when he is listing the kinds of information the explorers should obtain regarding Native Americans (beginning with "the names of the nations and their numbers"). He uses *chronological order* in beginning the memorandum with the beginning of the journey and ending at the end—the safe return of the explorers.
2. Jefferson discusses the use of birch bark for paper as part of his general discussion of record-keeping. Though it is a more specific, less important topic than the one that follows (dealings with Native Americans), it "belongs with" the general discussion of record-keeping. Students may note that even when a writer puts information in the order of its importance, some minor details will still be grouped with more important ones, not saved until later.
3. Jefferson's main pattern of organization in the memorandum is order of importance. He starts with the most important aspect of the mission—to map the Missouri—and then gives more specific details regarding the accomplishment of that mission. He next turns to Native Americans—an important topic, but one less central to the mission than the object of mapping the Missouri. His concern for the safe return of the explorers, though also important, is even less central to his topic, so he deals with it last.

Analyzing Real-World Texts

. . .

In all your [dealings] with the natives, treat them in the most friendly and conciliatory manner which their own conduct will admit; allay all jealousies as to the object of your journey; satisfy them of its innocence; make them acquainted with the position, extent, character, peaceable and commercial dispositions of the United States; of our wish to be neighborly, friendly, and useful to them, and of our dispositions to a commercial [relationship] with them; confer with them on the points most convenient as mutual emporiums,[9] and the articles of most desirable interchange for them and us. If a few of their influential chiefs, within practicable distance, wish to visit us, arrange such a visit with them, and furnish them with authority to call on our officers on their entering the United States, to have them conveyed to this place at the public expense. If any of them should wish to have some of their young people brought up with us, and taught such arts as may be useful to them, we will receive, instruct, and take care of them. Such a mission, whether of influential chiefs, or of young people, would give some security to your own party. Carry with you some matter of the kine-pox; inform those of them with whom you may be of its efficacy as a preservative from the small-pox,[10] and instruct and encourage them in the use of it. This may be especially done wherever you winter.

As it is impossible for us to foresee in what manner you will be received by those people, whether with hospitality or hostility, so is it impossible to prescribe the exact degree of perseverance with which you are to pursue your journey. We value too much the lives of citizens to offer them to probable destruction. Your numbers will be sufficient to secure you against the unauthorized opposition of individuals, or of small parties; but if a superior force, authorized, or not authorized, by a nation, should be arrayed against your further passage, and inflexibly determined to arrest it, you must decline its further pursuit and return. In the loss of yourselves we should lose also the information you will have acquired. By returning safely with that, you may enable us to renew the essay with better calculated means. To your own discretion, therefore, must be left the degree of danger you may risk, and the point at which you should decline, only saying, we wish you to err on the side of your safety, and to bring back your party safe, even if it be with less information. . . .

9. **emporiums** (em pôr´ ē´ əmz) *n.*: Trading centers.

10. **kine-pox . . . small-pox:** Material taken from cattle suffering from the disease cowpox ("kine-pox") was used to vaccinate people against smallpox, a disease characterized by fever and eruptions of the skin.

◆ Apply the Reading Strategy

1. Review your pattern-of-organization diagram. Give examples of three patterns of organization Jefferson uses.
2. Why does Jefferson discuss the use of birch bark for paper, a minor detail, at the end of his discussion of record-keeping, an important topic?
3. Describe the main pattern of organization he uses in the memorandum.

◆ Compare Literary Forms

1. Read or review Meriwether Lewis's journal entry "Crossing the Great Divide," p. 276. In the events Lewis describes, what part of his instructions from Jefferson is he carrying out?
2. Give two reasons that the United States was concerned to secure good relations with Native Americans in the West.

◆ Compare Literary Forms

1. As Jefferson instructs, Lewis informs the Native Americans he has met of the purpose of his mission (Jefferson writes that he should "allay all jealousies as to the object of your journey"). He also informs them of the goodwill of the United States and its interest in doing business with them (Jefferson instructs him to tell Native Americans of the "peaceable and commercial dispositions" of the United States and its "wish to be neighborly, friendly, and useful to them").
2. Judging from Jefferson's memorandum and Lewis's journal, the United States wanted good relations with Native Americans in the West for business reasons. Jefferson and Lewis were also both concerned that Native Americans assist and not harm the explorers. In addition, Jefferson expresses a wish to "civilize and instruct" Native Americans.

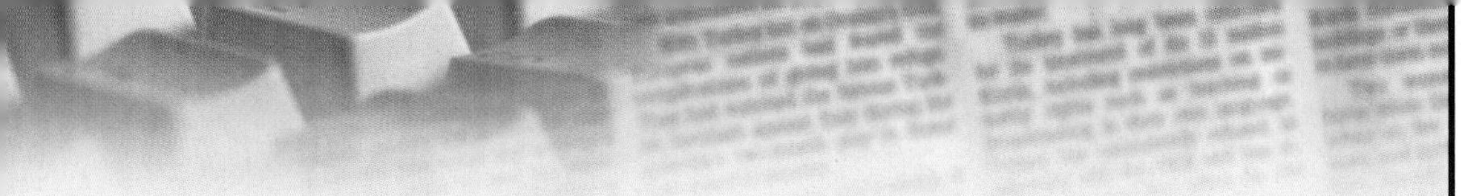

About the Author

John Graves (1920–), an award-winning essayist, often reflects on the land, wildlife, and history of Texas, his native state.

◆ Reading Strategy

Evaluate Credibility of Sources The **credibility** of an information source depends on the writer's methods and motives.

In "Old-Time Cowboys," John Graves's purpose is to draw a vibrant portrait of cowboys. He concludes that the way of the cowboy survived because of the "pride and pleasure" cowboys took in their work. This generalization is based only on anecdotal evidence (stories he has heard). It is not as credible as one based on statistical studies might be.

Using a graphic organizer like the one below, evaluate Graves's credibility on each kind of information listed.

	Example	Credibility: High–Low	My Reasoning
Biographical Details	Graves's friend "joined the Buffalo Bill Wild West Show."	Medium	There is no special reason to mistrust the story, but Graves probably has not fact-checked it.
Cowboys' Stories			
Cowboys' Way of Life			
Cowboy Character			
Historical Generalizations			

Old-Time Cowboys in the Modern World

John Graves

Anecdotal history

The bulk of those [real cowboys] whom I knew were Texans by birth and had done their cowboying chiefly in the state, some having worked on the Matadors or the Swensons or others of the old, large, established outfits in the Rolling Plains[1] and beyond, but most on more modest if still substantial spreads. A few had wandered farther. My favorite of the lot, a real friend who died in his eighties some years ago, had left his family's place south of Waco at eighteen and had cowboyed his way to Montana where he worked on several ranches . . . and joined the Buffalo Bill Wild West Show in its latter years. He could deliver verbatim the speech that Colonel Cody,[2] as he always called him, had made to introduce the Pony Express act in which he himself had ridden, and he had performed in the Roman Relays, one foot on each of two running horses, in Madison Square Garden in New York. Later he'd worked on a California ranch that furnished livestock for early Western movies, and had done stunt work there with Yakima Canutt[3] and played on Will Rogers'[4] cowboy polo team. He had, in short, heard the owl hoot in a good many different places and had led [quite] a life for a country boy from the Blacklands. And though by habit he spoke little of himself, he knew it had all been fine and if he liked you he'd tell you

1. **Rolling Plains:** Hilly region of northcentral Texas.
2. **Colonel Cody:** William F. "Buffalo Bill" Cody (1846–1917), frontiersman, buffalo hunter, and showman.
3. **Yakima Canutt** (1895–1986): Stuntman in westerns.
4. **Will Rogers** (1879–1935): Cowboy humorist.

LESSON OBJECTIVES

1. To read for different purposes in varied sources
- Selection: Anecdotal history

2. To read critically to evaluate texts
- Reading Strategy: Evaluate Credibility of Sources

3. To analyze literary elements
- Compare Literary Forms

Connecting to "A Wagner Matinée," Willa Cather, p. 614

To connect John Graves's anecdotal history "Old-Time Cowboys in the Modern World" to Cather's short story, ask students to consider the various ways people interpret suffering. Ask: How might a football fan view a football player's suffering? *Possible response: A fan might value the player's ability to endure suffering, to "take it" without complaint.* Ask: How might a political prisoner view his or her own suffering? *Possible response: A political prisoner might see suffering for a cause as a sign that he or she is faithful to his or her ideals.* Ask: How might a person view the suffering of a pet? *Possible response: A person might view a pet's suffering as unjustifiable, to be avoided if at all possible.* Then, ask students to read or review Cather's "A Wagner Matinée" and Graves's "Old-Time Cowboys . . . ," paying particular attention to the role suffering plays in each. They should then answer the Compare Literary Forms question, p. 1214.

Answers

◆ Apply the Reading Strategy

1. The essay is moderately credible as a source of information on the history of cattle ranching. On the one hand, Graves devotes much of his writing to the life and lore of Texas (see About the Author); presumably, he has got most of the facts straight. On the other hand, his motive in presenting this information is to get at the "essence" of the cowboy experience; his method is to reflect on cowboys he has known, not to examine all available evidence. Popular misconceptions or faulty generalizations may have crept into his account.
2. The essay is a very credible source for information on the stories cowboys tell of themselves. These stories are a main focus for Graves, so it is reasonable to assume that he was careful in collecting and reporting them. He received them firsthand, rather than transcribing them from another source and possibly compounding any errors that might appear in the transcript.

◆ Compare Literary Forms

(a) In "A Wagner Matinée," frontier hardships have reduced the scope of the aunt's life, leaving her lonely, deprived, and culturally out of touch; she bears physical marks of "isolation and monotony, and . . . frequent physical suffering" in the form of a nervous twitch. (b) For the cowboys Graves describes, facing frontier hardships was a source of joy, pride, and comradeship. Where hardship has beaten down Aunt Georgiana, it has elevated Graves's cowboys.

Analyzing Real-World Texts

about it, in the little shotgun rent house where he lived in his last years, raising large perfect tomatoes in five-gallon cans half full of horse manure.

The joy that was still in him—and in most cowboys, I think, even when you couldn't see it—was somehow epitomized in a browned, creased, Kodak snapshot he once showed me of himself when young on a big black horse by a spruce-bordered mountain lake, wearing a high-crowned Stetson and bearskin chaps, grinning like a possum, and clearly on top of his world. . . .

So I suppose that what my own personal perception of generalized cowboy character comes down to, as manifested in those few old-timers I've known, is mainly its strong flavor of dexterity[5] and joy and pride. Cowboys of this original breed were genuinely competent at horsemanship and roping and the other elements of their trade, because they had to be competent in order merely to get jobs and keep them, and to gain the acceptance of the men they worked with. . . .

Cowhands were thus an elite,[6] and like all elites were proud. And being proud and mainly young, most derived a lot of sheer fun from the life they led, as if it had been play. Work *is* play, in truth, if you like it and do it well, though I expect a majority of cowboys would have been ready for a fistfight if they'd heard described as play their customary labor. Nevertheless it's clear they took exultant pleasure and pride not only in its dexterous good parts but even in its worst ones. Pride in staying begrimed and sweaty . . . for however long a piece of work took, through days on days of twelve or fifteen hours or more devoted to the pursuit and management of the dim-witted recalcitrant creatures from which they took their name. Pride in the quantity of dust they breathed, in not only riding but making good use of horses that were sometimes only half broken to the work, in getting front teeth kicked out by calves, in the coarse heavy food they gulped down at intervals, in enduring such weather as presented itself with a minimum of raiment and shelter, in flopping down at night on the ground for a few hours of itchy, coughing sleep before being waked in the dark to start again. . . .

The work had to give such pride and pleasure, I think. If it hadn't, why else would quick and capable young men have stuck with it, for range-cook grub and wages of thirty or forty or fifty dollars a month or whatever the times were paying? In point of fact, I suspect these men's delight in doing what they did for a living, with their resultant willingness to do it for peanut pay, probably was a main reason the old way of working cattle survived past its logical time. It kept that way economic. Up through the 1930's, in much of the West, it furnished ranches with a steady supply of what were in a sense trained young slave workers, slaves not to the ranches themselves but to their own happy satisfaction in being good at what they did, and to their love for it. And if very often they hid all that behind a dry, laconic manner with which, like many elites, they sought to convey an impression that they didn't give a [darn], this was practically all front. They gave a [darn], all right. It was why they were there.

---

5. **dexterity** (deks ter´ ə tē) *n.*: Skill in using one's hands or body.
6. **elite** (ā lēt´) *n.*: An exceptional group, consisting of the most talented, finest, etc., in a given field.

◆ Apply the Reading Strategy

1. How credible is the essay as a source of information on the history of cattle ranching?
2. How credible is the essay as a source of information about stories cowboys tell of themselves?

◆ Compare Literary Forms

Read or review Willa Cather's short story "A Wagner Matinée," p. 614. (a) Describe the effect frontier hardships have had on the aunt. (b) Compare this effect with Graves's account of how cowboys responded to hardships.

LESSON OBJECTIVES

1. To read for different purposes in varied sources
- Selection: Historical essay

2. To read critically to evaluate texts
- Reading Strategy: Analyze Text Structures: Cause and Effect

3. To analyze literary elements
- Compare Literary Forms

Connecting to "From the Dark Tower," Countee Cullen, p. 848

To connect Veronica Chambers's historical essay "Harlem: A Paradise of My Own People" to Countee Cullen's poem "From the Dark Tower," ask students to consider the fact that, in 1910, African Americans were deprived of the vote in many states by discriminatory practices. They attended different schools from whites and were forced to use separate facilities in restaurants, trains, buses, and other public places.

Then, ask students to consider the blossoming of African American life in Harlem during the 1920's, when African American businesses, churches, poetry, and music thrived—the days of the composer Duke Ellington, painter Aaron Douglas, and the poet Langston Hughes. Ask: How might African Americans have viewed the Harlem Renaissance? *Possible response: African Americans may have viewed the Harlem Renaissance as an indication that, even in a white-dominated world, African Americans could achieve power over their own lives and culture, which suggested they might soon claim a place as the equals of whites.*

Then, ask students to read or review Countee Cullen's poem "From the Dark Tower" and Chambers's historical essay, focusing on the past out of which African American Harlem emerged and the new possibilities it suggested. They should then answer the Compare Literary Forms questions, p. 1217.

About the Author

Although **Veronica Chambers** (1970?–) grew up in a struggling family, at sixteen she had already enrolled in college. She went on to become a writer and journalist.

◆ Reading Strategy

Analyze Text Structures: Cause and Effect A **cause** is an event or condition that brings about another event or condition (the **effect**). A cause precedes its effect, so authors often discuss causes and effects in chronological sequence. A cause also explains an effect, so authors examining causes often look at alternative explanations.

In "Harlem," the author notes that a drop in real estate prices encouraged realtors to rent to blacks. The drop is one cause of the African American settlement of Harlem.

Use a graphic organizer like the one below to map each cause and effect in this essay.

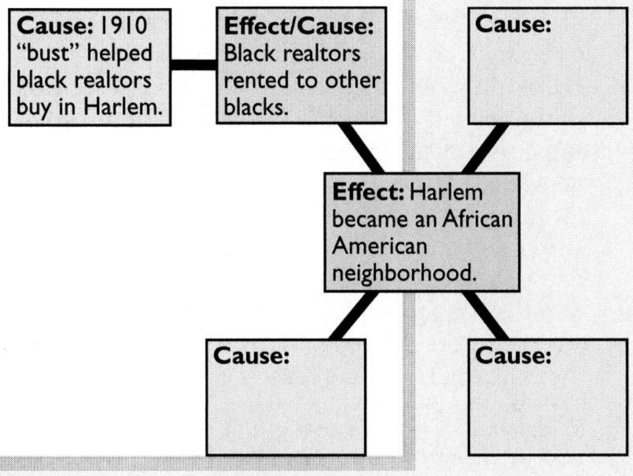

Harlem: A Paradise of My Own People

Veronica Chambers

Historical essay

In the 1920's Harlem[1] centered on 135th Street and Seventh Avenue and reached from 110th Street to 150th Street. The area stretched from the East River to St. Nicholas Avenue on the west, a space of less than two square miles. Still, this small neighborhood, known as Black Manhattan, was also hailed as "the city of refuge" and the "Negro Mecca."[2] To be in any part of Harlem during that period—to live there, to write or sing there, to dance there, even to visit there—was an immeasurable thrill. Better to "be a lamppost in Harlem than Governor of Georgia," as one popular saying described it.

Harlem was established in 1658 by Dutch settlers, who called it Nieuw Haarlem, after the city in Holland. It was a rural area until the 19th century, when improvements in transportation made it more accessible to lower Manhattan. Gradually, it became a fashionable residential community of New York City.

The Harlem Renaissance was in many ways the result of the Great Migration. Between 1900 and 1930, nearly three million African Americans left the South to seek their fortunes in the North, sending the black population of the North soaring by 400 percent. Although African Americans had been moving north since the time of the Civil War, the largest migration boom

---

1. **Harlem** (här′ ləm) *n.*: Section of New York City, in uptown Manhattan.
2. **Mecca** (mĕk′ ə) *n.*: Here, a place of significance to a particular group, to which members of that group travel.

Answers

◆ Apply the Reading Strategy

1. In the Great Migration, three million African Americans left the South for the cities of the North. This movement led to increased crowding in the old African American neighborhoods of New York, which made Harlem an appealing alternative.
2. Prejudice led to the Great Migration, which brought more African Americans north. It also limited the number of neighborhoods open to African Americans in the city, of which Harlem was the most attractive. Prejudice against recent European immigrants also led some Harlem landlords to favor renting to African Americans, against whom they were somewhat less biased.
3. Since the resistance of Harlem's whites was, in the end, ineffective, it is incidental to the main chain of events, and so may be discussed at the end. The contrast between white resistance and the dramatic, seemingly inevitable fact of Harlem's transformation also makes an effective conclusion.
4. (a) The rate of expansion of African American Harlem was greatest in the years between 1920 and 1930. In that time, African Americans expanded into new areas (marked in pink) of a size greater than the combined size of those areas settled before 1911 (red) and between 1911 and 1920 (orange). (b) Students may speculate that, by 1920, blacks were well-established in Harlem. This fact may have encouraged white landlords in the area to sell their properties or become resigned to renting to blacks. In the meantime, African American landlords accumulated funds from their Harlem properties, enabling them to acquire property in neighboring areas.

Analyzing Real-World Texts

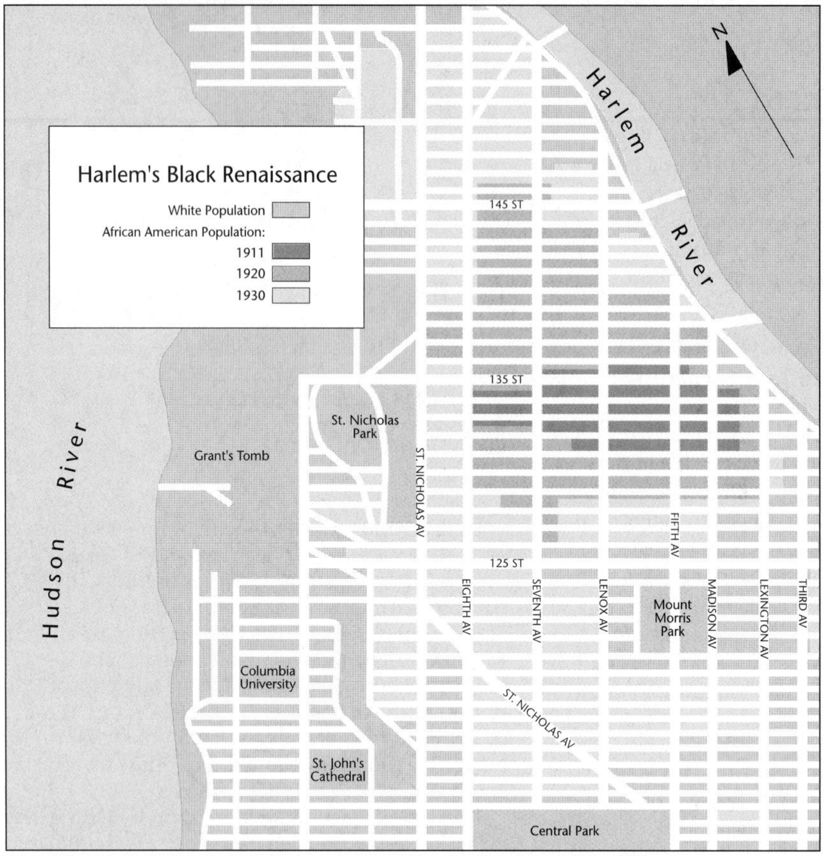

Acknowledgment: Adapted from *The Harlem Renaissance* by Steven Watson (New York: Pantheon Books, 1995).

occurred around World War I, when nearly half a million rural blacks left the South in search of racial equality and greater economic opportunity.

Thanks to these migrants, New York's black neighborhoods grew more and more crowded. At the same time, in the middle-class white district of Harlem, real estate speculators were driving up property prices far beyond their actual value. The bubble burst around 1910. As prices plummeted,[3] Harlem building owners panicked.

At this point, a number of black realtors also entered the volatile[4] Harlem scene. Among them was Philip A. Payton Jr., who, along with other fast-moving entrepreneurs,[5] knew that he could make large profits by opening this desirable neighborhood to blacks. He established the Afro-American Realty Company, leased or bought several Harlem buildings, and began renting to blacks. His move accelerated the local real estate panic; the remaining white property owners, certain that the presence of blacks would permanently depress prices, sold for whatever prices they could get and fled the neighborhood.

Of course, so many sellers brought still lower property prices, and black realtors

3. **plummeted** (plum´ it id) *v.*: Fell straight downwards.
4. **volatile** (väl´ ə təl) *adj.*: Likely to shift quickly.
5. **entrepreneurs** (än´ trə prə nʉrz´) *n.*: Persons who organize and manage their own businesses.

began snapping up even more bargains. Ironically, the white landlords who stayed in Harlem began renting to blacks and made out very well. Prejudice and custom sharply limited the neighborhoods available to blacks, and Harlem was by far the best one open to them. For this reason, landlords could bring in rents proportionately higher than those paid by whites, who had many more choices. However, not all white landlords were pleased by this situation. "We have endeavored for some time to avoid turning over this house to colored tenants," remarked one white nonresident owner in 1916, "but as a result of . . . rapid changes in conditions . . . this issue has been forced upon us."

Many observers, including photographer Jacob Riis,[6] also noted another irony: despite their protests, many white landlords favored African-American tenants over what they referred to as the "lower grades of foreign people"—recently arrived European immigrants who, like the millions of blacks who moved north, were searching for greater economic opportunities than they had in their native countries.

Harlem's whites did not surrender the neighborhood without a fight. The president of the Harlem Property Owners Protective Association led the attack, discouraging Harlem land holders from selling or renting to African Americans and even offering to build a 24-foot-high fence at 136th Street to keep blacks out of the neighborhood. A local newspaper, the *Harlem Home News*, shrilly announced in July 1911 that white homeowners "must wake up and get busy before it is too late to repel the black hordes[7] that stand ready to destroy the homes and scatter the fortunes of the whites living and doing business in the very heart of Harlem."

By that time, though, Harlem was already the neighborhood of choice for New York's African Americans. St. Philip's, New York's major black church, followed its parishioners[8] to Harlem and bought up choice pieces of property. Black newspapers moved their offices to Harlem, too, as did African-American social clubs and political organizations. Thus was born *the* Harlem, a city within a city.

6. **Jacob Riis** (rēs) (1849–1914): Journalist and social reformer, born in Denmark.

7. **hordes** (hôrdz) *n.*: Large, wandering group.
8. **parishioners** (pə rish′ ə nərz) *n.*: Members of a church.

◆ Apply the Reading Strategy

1. Explain the relationship between the Great Migration and the growth of black Harlem.
2. Explain how prejudice brought blacks to Harlem.
3. Given the cause-and-effect structure of "Harlem," why does the author discuss the resistance of Harlem's whites only at the end?
4. (a) Judging from the map, when was the rate of expansion of black Harlem greatest? (b) Give a possible cause for the change in rate.

◆ Compare Literary Forms

1. Read or review Countee Cullen's poem "From the Dark Tower," p. 848. (a) Cullen's poem (written during the Harlem Renaissance) reflects both past sorrow and hope for the future. Explain.
2. Explain why the birth of Harlem might have given Cullen new conviction about the prospects for justice.

◆ Compare Literary Forms

1. The poem lists a number of scenes of oppression—a people planting "while others reap" (l. 1), their downtrodden acceptance of the fact that some people should "hold their brothers cheap" (l. 4), and their perpetual weeping (l. 8). These scenes are announced with the phrase "We shall not always. . . ." This phrase indicates that, though oppression and sorrow fill the past and present, they will be overcome.
2. The birth of Harlem meant that African Americans had a cultural and business center of their own—African American newspapers, churches, and political organizations all moved into the new neighborhood. To writers like Cullen, the fact that African Americans were taking an active, governing role in their own lives presented a hopeful possibility, contrasting with their oppressed, marginal status in the white world.

LESSON OBJECTIVES

1. To read for different purposes in varied sources
- Selection: Critical commentary

2. To read critically to evaluate texts
- Reading Strategy: Syntax and Word Choice

3. To express and support responses to various types of texts
- Compare Literary Forms

4. To analyze literary elements
- Compare Literary Forms

Connecting to *The Crucible,* Arthur Miller, p. 1089

To connect Arthur Miller's commentary "On Social Plays" to his drama *The Crucible,* point out that both the essay and the play address a similar concern: the crushing power of society. Miller frequently writes about the powerlessness of common people who are pitted against strong social forces. Ask students to name some of the forces that may cause people to feel powerless. *Students may suggest the need to conform to a set of beliefs, actions, or behaviors to be accepted by others.* To encourage students to compare Miller's philosophy with his dramas, have students read or review *The Crucible,* looking for evidence of Miller's belief that modern society pits the individual against the group. Ask them to pay special attention to the different values held by the characters (e.g., respectability, survival, integrity) and to note whether the play offers an ideal for meaningful existence. Students can then read "On Social Plays" and answer the Compare Literary Forms questions, p. 1219.

Analyzing Real-World Texts

About the Author

An acclaimed playwright, **Arthur Miller** (1915–) writes plays that question modern society and its ability to grant individuals a meaningful life. *Death of a Salesman,* perhaps his best-known work, won a Pulitzer Prize in 1947.

◆ Reading Strategy

Analyze Characteristics of Texts: Syntax and Word Choice Through syntax and word choice, writers create a distinctive voice. **Syntax** is the ordering of words, phrases, and clauses in a sentence. **Word choice** concerns the kinds of words used—formal or informal, learned or common.

By combining learned words such as *mores* and informal phrases such as "or whatever," Miller creates an impression of sincerity. (Since he is comfortable using plain words, he must use fancy ones only when they best capture his ideas.) As in an excited conversation, his syntax is characterized by phrases restating ideas: for instance, "integers who have no weight, no *person.*"

Using a graphic organizer such as the one at right to examine Miller's word choices and syntax.

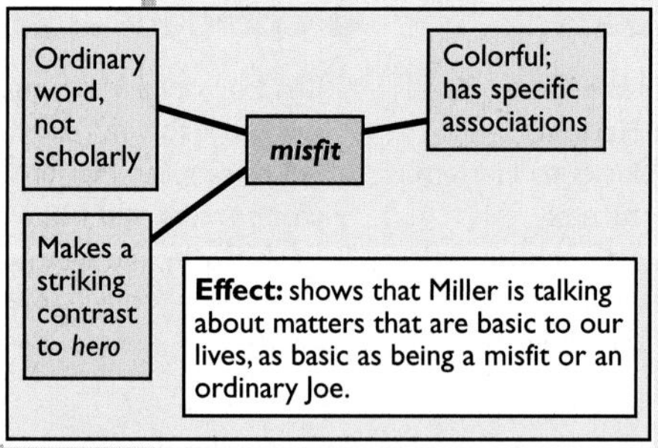

from On Social Plays

Arthur Miller

Critical commentary

Time is moving; there is a world to make, a civilization to create that will move toward the only goal the humanistic, democratic mind can ever accept with honor. It is a world in which the human being can live as a naturally political, naturally private, naturally engaged person, a world in which once again a true tragic victory may be scored.

But that victory is not really possible unless the individual is more than theoretically capable of being recognized by the powers that lead society. Specifically, when men live, as they do under any industrialized system, as integers[1] who have no weight, no *person,* excepting as customers, draftees, machine tenders, ideologists, or whatever, it is unlikely (and in my opinion impossible) that a dramatic picture of them can really overcome the public knowledge of their nature in real life. In such a society, be it communistic or capitalistic, man is not tragic, he is pathetic.[2] The tragic figure must have certain innate powers which he uses to pass over the boundaries of the known social law—the accepted mores[3] of his people—in order to test and discover necessity. Such a quest implies that the individual who has moved onto that course must be somehow recognized by the law, by the mores, by the powers that design—be they anthropomorphic[4] gods or economic and political laws—as having the worth, the innate value, of a whole people

---

1. **integers** (in´ tə jerz) *n.*: Numbers.
2. **pathetic** (pə the´ tik) *adj.*: Arousing pity.
3. **mores** (mōr´ āz´) *n.*: Customs; unwritten laws.
4. **anthropomorphic** (an´ thrə pō´ môr´ fik) *adj.*: Having human characteristics.

asking a basic question and demanding its answer. We are so atomized[5] socially that no character in a play can conceivably stand as our vanguard,[6] as our heroic questioner. Our society—and I am speaking of every industrialized society in the world—is so complex, each person being so specialized an integer, that the moment any individual is dramatically characterized and set forth as a hero, our common sense reduces him to the size of a complainer, a misfit. For deep down we no longer believe in the rules of the tragic contest; we no longer believe that some ultimate sense can in fact be made of social causation,[7] or in the possibility that any individual can, by a heroic effort, make sense of it. Thus the man that is driven to question the moral chaos in which we live ends up in our estimate as a possibly commendable but definitely odd fellow, and probably as a compulsively driven neurotic.[8] In place of a social aim which called an all-around excellence—physical, intellectual, and moral—the ultimate good, we have set up a goal which can best be characterized as "happiness"—namely, staying out of trouble. This concept is the end result of the truce which all of us have made with society. And a truce implies two enemies. When the truce is broken it means either that the individual has broken out of his ordained[9] place as an integer, or that the society has broken the law by harming him unjustly—that is, it has not left him alone to be a peaceful integer. In the heroic and tragic time the act of questioning the-way-things-are implied that a quest was being carried on to discover an ultimate law or way of life which would yield excellence; in the present time the quest is that of a man made unhappy by rootlessness and, in every important modern play, by a man who is essentially a victim. We have abstracted[10] from the Greek drama its air of doom, its physical destruction of the hero, but its victory escapes us. Thus it has even become difficult to separate in our minds the ideas of the pathetic and of the tragic. And behind this melting of the two lies the overwhelming power of the modern industrial state, the ignorance of each person in it of anything but his own technique as an economic integer, and the elevation of that state to a holy, quite religious sphere.

---

5. **atomized** (at´ ə mīzd´) *adj.*: Broken into small, disconnected pieces.
6. **vanguard** (van´ gärd´) *n.*: Leading part of an army or other group.
7. **social causation:** Social forces.
8. **neurotic** (no͞o rät´ ik) *n.*: Person suffering from mental or emotional imbalance.
9. **ordained** (ôr dānd´) *adj.*: Assigned; appointed.
10. **abstracted** (ab strak´ tid) *v.*: Taken; separated.

◆ Apply the Reading Strategy

1. Identify a casual phrase and a learned phrase in the following: "deep down we no longer believe in the rules of the tragic contest . . ."
2. Explain how Miller's syntax adds weight to the following sentence: "We have abstracted from the Greek drama its air of doom, its physical destruction of the hero, but its victory escapes us."

◆ Compare Literary Forms

1. Read or review Arthur Miller's own play *The Crucible*, p. 1089. Summarize Miller's analysis of modern society in the essay. Then, explain whether this analysis applies to the Salem of *The Crucible*.
2. (a) Explain whether society in *The Crucible* has "broken the law" by not leaving John Proctor "alone to be a peaceful integer." (b) Would Miller call Proctor a victim or a tragic hero? Explain.

Answers

◆ Apply the Reading Strategy

1. The phrase "deep down" is a casual phrase. The phrase "the tragic contest" is a learned one.
2. By "piling up" phrases—joining the phrase "its physical destruction of the hero" with "its air of doom" with just a comma—Miller shows that there are any number of nonessential features we have borrowed from Greek tragedy. After this pileup, the word *but* shifts the emphasis onto the next phrase, "its victory." The phrase rings out, since it is opposed to, but also linked with, the preceding phrases. Like them, it begins with *its* (referring back to "Greek drama"); unlike them, it names something that was possible for the Greeks but not for us. Through these syntactical devices, Miller gives the sentence strength and a rhythm that emphasizes its meaning.

◆ Compare Literary Forms

1. Students should recognize that in Miller's view, modern society is an impersonal power that "atomizes" individuals, treating them as no more than the fragmentary roles they fill. It has given up the idea of striving for an "overall excellence" or of struggling with questions about the meaning of life. Students may note that Salem society is different in important ways. First, it is small enough so that quarrels between individuals can threaten to tear the society apart. Each person's participation "counts" in a fundamental way—in this sense, Salem society is not as atomized as modern society. Second, the Puritanism of Salem society is intended to answer the question of the good life in a more meaningful way than modern ideas of "happiness." Like Miller's modern society, though, Salem society in the heat of the witch trials victimizes individuals, insisting on conformity as the price of peace. Rather than reducing its victims to modern "neurotics," though, Salem destroys them, as it does Giles, Proctor, and (in a subtler way) Hale.
2. (a) By persecuting Proctor and coercing him to make a false confession and false accusations, Salem society "breaks the law," invading Proctor's private life and disrupting his marriage rather than leaving him to live in peace. The "truce" it offers requires him to sign a lie, ruining his own good name. As in Miller's essay, society and the individual appear as enemies. Students may note, though, that more is at stake for Proctor than the modern goal of individual "happiness"; Proctor fights for his own integrity. (b) Students should note that Proctor's conflict with Salem is forced on him by events beyond his control. Unlike a tragic hero, he does not meet a fate that challenges and so underscores the power of his choices. Students may conclude that, in this way, Proctor is essentially a victim. Yet by the end of the play, Proctor does make a powerful choice. By sacrificing himself for his own good name, he asserts his integrity, proposing another kind of value than that recognized by Parris and Hathorne, society's representatives. He makes a statement about the good life—it must include integrity. Students may argue that, for this reason, Proctor fits Miller's definition of a tragic hero.

LESSON OBJECTIVES

1. To read in varied sources, including American and world literature, in order to understand different cultures and the common elements across cultures, to respond to the texts, and to analyze literary elements within the texts
- Critical Thinking
- Literature Selections

2. To acquire an extensive vocabulary through reading and systematic study
- Comparing Spanish and English Texts

About Literature in Translation

This section contains seven selections, each presented in its original Spanish and in an English translation. These bilingual selections are organized into three groups, according to literary or cultural affinities. Each of these smaller sections is accompanied by:
- an introduction containing background information on the authors and a relevant geographical or literary note
- a follow-up consisting of critical thinking questions and one or more questions requiring students to compare a Spanish original with its English translation.

The Art of Translation

This section contains literary works that were written in Spanish, and it shows the Spanish originals together with English translations. Such a format has several advantages. Even if you do not read Spanish, you can at least see what the original looks like and gain a greater awareness of literature written in Spanish. Also, a glance at the original will often reveal similarities between Spanish, a Romance language derived from Latin, and English, a Germanic language that has borrowed from Latin. Finally, seeing the original and the translation together will give you a greater appreciation for the work that translators do.

The Spanish Literary Tradition Spanish has a particularly rich literary tradition, both in Europe and the Americas. In Spain that tradition includes, among many other works, the classic novel *Don Quixote* [dän kē hōt′ ē] by Miguel de Cervantes [mē gel′ *the ther* vän′ tes] (1547–1616) and the poems of Federico García Lorca [fé de *rē*′ kô gär *thé* ä lôr′ kä] (1898–1936). As for the Americas, the poems and stories of the authors represented here hint at the wealth of literature that is available.

Translation If you can read only English, then you owe a debt to the translators who worked hard to render these Spanish originals in English. Translation *is* hard work because no language corresponds exactly to another. Translators must therefore make many choices, and qualified translators can disagree. The following versions of the title and first sentence of a poem by Peruvian César Vallejo [sā′ zär və yā′ hō] show this type of disagreement very clearly:

Sample Translations

	Original Poem	Translation by Robert Bly	Translation by Clayton Eshleman
Title	Voy a hablar de la esperanza	I Am Going to Talk About Hope	I Am Going to Speak of Hope
First Sentence	Yo no sufro este dolor como César Vallejo.	I do not feel this suffering as César Vallejo.	I don't suffer this pain as César Vallejo.

Traducción de literatura
Lecturas en Inglés y Español en pareja

About the Authors

Olivia Maciel [ô lí′ vē ə má′ sē əl] was born in Mexico and currently teaches at De Paul University, Chicago, Illinois.

María Herrera-Sobek [mə rē′ ə he rer′ ə sō′ bek] is featured in the anthology *Three Times a Woman.*

Octavio Paz [ôk tä′ vyô päs] (1914–1998) was a Nobel Prize-winner from Mexico.

Geographical Note

These three poets mention and describe various places in Mexico: the southeastern city of Villahermosa, meaning "beautiful city," located on the Grijalva River ("Mistress of Nothing"); the southern city of Oaxaca [wä hä′ kä], known for its sixteenth-century architecture ("Oaxaca III"); the crowded Boulevard Sebastó in the capital, Mexico City, located in central Mexico ("Pedestrian").

Mistress of Nothing

Translated by the author and Mary K. Hawley

The breeze presses essence from the sea
presses malanga, hibiscus flower, white
chrysanthemums.

The breeze sighs over the bridge of
Alvarado, over the river Grijalva,
beyond Chontalpa, Las Choapas, and
Teapa.
Smooths the feathers of Lorenzo the
parrot who eats oranges
beside the road, on the outskirts of
Oniaga—
as white butterflies shimmer in the air.

The breeze carries murmur of harp
rumor of guitar.

Beyond Agua Dulce,
beyond Juramento,
the breeze seeps into the House for
the Child,
inspires Salesia, enthralls dour Carmen,
quietly whispers "I am mistress of
nothing."

On the way to Villahermosa, Tabasco

Dueña de nada

Olivia Maciel

Esencia exprime la brisa del mar
Exprime malanga, flor de jamaica,
crisantemos blancos.

Suspira la brisa sobre el Puente de Al
varado, sobre el río Grijalva,
más allá de Chontalpa, Las Choapas, y
Teapa.
Le atuza la brisa las plumas al loro
Lorenzo que come naranja
a orilla del camino, a orilla de Oniaga—
mientras aletean en el aire varias
mariposas blancas.

Acarrea la brisa susurro de harpa
rumor de guitarra.

Más allá de Agua Dulce,
más allá del Juramento,
se cuela la brisa a la "Casa del Niño"
inspira a Salesia, arroba a la Carmen,
quedito musita "soy dueña de nada."

Rumbo a Villahermosa, Tabasco

How to Use Literature in Translation

Following are strategies for using Literature in Translation:

- Have students read and discuss The Art of Translation, p. 1220, paying special attention to the sample translations. Ask them to discuss their own previous ideas about translation.
- Have students who do not speak or read Spanish increase their knowledge of Spanish culture and literature by reading The Art of Translation, the introductory material for each section, and the English translations. Also have them answer the follow-up questions, including those that ask them to compare a translation with its original.
- Have students who speak and read Spanish read the Spanish originals aloud to the class and serve as experts in evaluating answers to questions comparing English and Spanish texts.
- Pair a Spanish-speaker with a student who does not speak Spanish, and have them alternate reading the Spanish original and the translation aloud to the class. Then have students work on the questions individually or in groups.
- Pair a Spanish-speaker with a student who does not speak Spanish, and have them read the selections together and answer the questions.
- Have a Spanish-speaker and a student who does not speak Spanish collaborate on a retranslation of one or more lines from a selection. Then have them discuss their translation with the class, comparing and contrasting it to the translation in the book.

Answers

◆ Critical Thinking

1. Students may realize that the breeze touches many things in passing, but it always moves on. In that sense, it does not own—and is not owned by—anything. It is therefore "Mistress of Nothing."
2. The poem seems to suggest that Oaxaca is a beautiful, mysterious, and romantic city where jasmine grows and fog hides everyday sights. Herrara-Sobek seems to love the city because its memory has a "sweet jasmin scent" for her.
3. Students may respond that the "fish" could be an airplane, a large advertisement showing a fish, or a sight that the pedestrian imagines. Students should support the interpretation they choose.

Compare English and Spanish Texts

4. The comparison reveals that the translator turned two lines into one and replaced the name of the city, Oaxaca, with the word *You*.
5. The Spanish words for *pedestrian* and *boulevard* are *peatón* and *bulevar,* respectively.

Oaxaca III

Translated by the author

You exist
Betwixt the fine gossamer fog
That lightly caresses your forehead
Like a bride's veil.

Tomorrow
I will cover my forehead
With the sweet jasmin scent
of your memories.

Oaxaca III

María Herrera-Sobek

Oaxaca
existes
entre la fina neblina
que cubre tu cara
como velo de novia.

Mañana
cubriré mi frente
con el jasmín
de tu recuerdo.

Pedestrian

Octavio Paz
Translated by Eliot Weinberger

He walked among the crowds
on the Boulevard Sebastó,
thinking about things.
A red light stopped him.
He looked up:
over
the gray roofs, silver
among the brown birds,
a fish flew.
The light turned green.
As he crossed the street he wondered
what he'd been thinking.

Peatón

Octavio Paz

Iba entre el gentío
por el bulevar Sebastó,
pensando en sus cosas.
El rojo lo detuvo.
Miró hacia arriba:
sobre
las grises azoteas, plateado
entre los pardos pájaros,
un pescado volaba.
Cambió el semáforo hacia el verde.
Se preguntó al cruzar la calle
en qué estaba pensando.

Critical Thinking

1. How is a breeze that touches so many things a "Mistress of Nothing"? **[Draw Conclusions]**
2. What does "Oaxaca III" suggest about the city of Oaxaca and about Herrera-Sobek's feelings concerning it? **[Infer]**
3. Discuss some possible explanations for what the "fish" in "Pedestrian" might be; then argue for the one you like best. **[Interpret]**

Compare English and Spanish Texts

4. Compare the first two lines of the Spanish original of "Oaxaca III" with the first line of the English translation. Explain how the author changed the original in translation. **[Compare and Contrast]**
5. Compare the two versions of "Pedestrian." What are the Spanish words for *pedestrian* and *boulevard?* **[Compare and Contrast]**

LESSON OBJECTIVES

1. **To read in varied sources, including American and world literature, in order to understand different cultures and the common elements across cultures, to respond to the texts, and to analyze literary elements within the texts**
   - Critical Thinking
   - Literature Selections
2. **To acquire an extensive vocabulary through reading and systematic study**
   - Comparing Spanish and English Texts

Clarification Be sure students realize that the English translation of "The Salamanders" continues in the left column of pp. 1224–1227 while the Spanish original continues in the right column of those same pages.

About the Authors

Tomás Rivera [tō mäs´ rē ve´ rä] (1935–1984) grew up as a migrant farm worker in Texas. He went on to write poems, essays, and fiction about the experience of Mexican American farm workers.

Tino Villanueva [tē´ nô vi yä nwä´ və] (1941–) is a Mexican American from Texas who has written four books of poetry.

Literary Note

These works, a story and a poem, show how a memory can haunt the mind. Also, they raise the question of why certain images of events and people last so much longer than others.

The *chiaroscuro* in Villanueva's poem refers to "an effect of combining light and shade." As you read the poem, think about how a scene preserved in memory can be made up of emotional light and shade, just as a painting is composed of visual light and shade.

The Salamanders

Translated by the author

What I remember most about that night is the darkness, the mud and the slime of the salamanders. But I should start from the beginning so you can understand all of this, and how, upon feeling this, I understood something that I still have with me. But I don't have this with me only as something I remember, but as something that I still feel.

It all began because it had been raining for three weeks and we had no work. We began to gather our things and made ready to leave. We had been with that farmer in Minnesota waiting for the rain to stop but it never did. Then he came and told us that the best thing for us to do was to leave his shacks because, after all, the beets had begun to rot away already. We understood, my father and I, that he was in fact afraid of us. He was afraid that we would begin to steal from him or perhaps that one of us would get sick, and then he would have to take the responsibility because we had no money. We told him we had no money, neither did we have anything to eat and no way of

Las salamandras

Tomás Rivera

Lo que más recuerdo de aquella noche es lo oscuro de la noche, el lodo y lo resbaloso de las salamandras. Pero tengo que empezar desde el principio para que puedan comprender todo esto que sentí y también de que, al sentirlo, comprendí algo que traigo todavía conmigo. Y no lo traigo como recuerdo solamente, sino también como algo que siento aún.

Todo empezó porque había estado lloviendo por tres semanas y no teníamos trabajo. Se levantó el campamento, digo campamento porque eso parecíamos. Con ese ranchero de Minesota habíamos estado esperando ya por tres semanas que se parara el agua, y nada. Luego vino y nos dijo que mejor nos fuéramos de sus gallineros porque ya se le había echado a perder el betabel. Luego comprendimos yo y mi 'apá que lo que tenía era miedo de nosotros, de que le fuéramos a robar algo o de que alguien se le enfermara y entonces tendría él que hacerse el responsable. Le dijimos que no teníamos dinero, ni qué comer, y ni cómo regresarnos a Texas; apenas tendríamos

English

making it all the way back to Texas. We had enough money, perhaps, to buy gasoline to get as far south as Oklahoma. He just told us that he was very sorry, but he wanted us to leave. So we began to pick up our things. We were leaving when he softened up somewhat and gave us two tents, full of spider webs, that he had in the loft in one of his barns. He also gave us a lamp and some kerosene. He told my dad that, if we went by way of Crystal Lake in northern Iowa, perhaps we would find work among the farmers and perhaps it had not been raining there so much and the beets had not rotted away. And we left.

In my father's eyes and in my mother's eyes, I saw something original and pure that I had never seen before. It was a sad type of love, it seemed. We barely talked as we went riding over the gravel roads. The rain seemed to talk for us. A few miles before reaching Crystal Lake, we began to get remorseful. The rain that continued to fall kept on telling us monotonously that we would surely not find work there. And so it was. At every farm that we came to, the farmers would only shake their heads from inside the house. They would not even open the door to tell us there was no work. It was when they shook their heads in this way that I began to feel that I was not part of my father and my mother. The only thing in my mind that existed was the following farm.

The first day we were in the little town of Crystal Lake everything went bad. Going through a puddle, the car's wiring got wet and my father drained the battery trying to get the car started. Finally, a garage did us the favor of recharging the battery. We asked for work in various parts of that little town, but then they got the police after us. My father explained that we were only

Español

con que comprar gasolina para llegarle a Oklahoma. Y él nomás nos dijo que lo sentía pero quería que nos fuéramos, y nos fuimos. Ya para salir se le ablandó el corazón y nos dio dos carpas llenas de telarañas que tenía en la bodega y una lámpara y kerosín. También le dijo a 'apá que, si nos íbamos rumbo a Crystal Lake en Iowa, a lo mejor encontrábamos trabajo en la ranchería que estaba por allí, y que a lo mejor no se les había echado a perder el betabel. Y nos fuimos.

En los ojos de 'apá y 'amá se veía algo original y puro que nunca les había notado. Era como cariño triste. Casi ni hablábamos al ir corriendo los caminos de grava. La lluvia hablaba por nosotros. Ya al faltar algunas cuantas millas de llegar a Crystal Lake, nos entró el remordimiento. La lluvia que seguía cayendo nos continuaba avisando que seguramente no podríamos hallar trabajo, y así fue. En cada rancho que llegamos, nomás nos movían la cabeza desde adentro de la casa, ni nos abrían la puerta para decirnos que no. Entonces me sentía que no era parte ni de 'apá ni de 'amá, y lo único que sentía que existía era el siguiente rancho.

El primer día que estuvimos en el pueblito de Crystal Lake nos fue mal. En un charco se le mojó el alambrado al carro y papá le gastó la batería al carro. Por fin un garage nos hizo el favor de cargarla. Pedimos trabajo en varias partes del pueblito pero luego nos echó la chota. Papá le explicó que sólo andábamos buscando trabajo pero él nos dijo que no quería húngaros en el pueblo y que nos saliéramos. El dinero ya casi se nos había acabado, y nos fuimos. Nos fuimos al oscurecer y paramos el carro a unas tres millas del pueblo, y allí vimos el anochecer.

La lluvia se venía de vez en cuando. Sentados todos en el carro a la orilla del camino, hablábamos un poco.

English

looking for work, but the policeman told us that he did not want any gypsies in town and told us to leave. The money was almost gone, but we had to leave. We left at twilight and we stopped the car some three miles from town and there we saw the night fall.

The rain would come and go. Seated in the car near the ditch, we spoke little. We were tired. We were hungry. We were alone. We sensed that we were totally alone. In my father's eyes and in my mother's eyes, I saw something original. That day we had hardly eaten anything in order to have money left for the following day. My father looked sadder, weakened. He believed we would find no work, and we stayed seated in the car waiting for the following day. Almost no cars passed by on that gravel road during the night. At dawn I awoke and everybody was asleep, and I could see their bodies and their faces. I could see the bodies of my mother and my father and my brothers and sisters, and they were silent. They were faces and bodies made of wax. They reminded me of my grandfather's face the day we buried him. But I didn't get as afraid as that day when I found him inside the truck, dead. I guess it was because I knew they were not dead and that they were alive. Finally, the day came completely.

That day we looked for work all day, and we didn't find any work. We slept at the edge of the ditch and again I awoke in the early morning hours. Again I saw my people asleep. And that morning I felt somewhat afraid, not because they looked as if they were dead, but because I began to feel again that I no longer belonged to them.

The following day we looked for work all day again, and nothing. We slept at the edge of the ditch. Again I awoke in the morning, and again I saw my people

Español

Estábamos cansados. Estábamos solos. En los ojos de 'apá y 'amá veía algo original. Ese día no habíamos comido casi nada para dejar dinero para el siguiente día. Ya 'apá se veía más triste, agüitado. Creía que no íbamos a encontrar trabajo. Y nos quedamos dormidos sentados en el carro esperando el siguiente día. Casi ni pasaron carros por ese camino de grava durante la noche.

En la madrugada desperté y todos estaban dormidos, y podía verles los cuerpos y las caras a mi 'apá, a mi 'amá y a mis hermanos, y no hacían ruido. Eran caras y cuerpos de cera. Me recordaron a la cara de 'buelito el día que lo sepultamos. Pero no me entró miedo como cuando lo encontré muerto a él en la troca. Yo creo porque sabía que estaban vivos. Y por fin amaneció completamente.

Ese día buscamos trabajo todo el día, y nada. Dormimos en la orilla del camino y volví a despertar en la madrugada y volví a ver a mi gente dormida. Pero esa madrugada me entró un poco de miedo. No porque se veían como que estaban muertos, sino porque ya me empezaba a sentir que no era de ellos.

El día siguiente buscamos trabajo todo el día, y nada. Dormimos en la orilla del camino y volví a despertar en la madrugada y volví a ver a mi gente dormida. Y esa madrugada, la tercera, me dieron ganas de dejarlos a todos porque ya no me sentía que era de ellos.

A mediodía paró de llover y nos entró ánimo. Dos horas más tarde encontramos a un ranchero que tenía betabel y a quien, según creía él, no se le había echado a perder la cosecha. Pero no tenía casas ni nada. Nos enseñó los acres de betabel que tenía y todo estaba por debajo del agua, todo enlagunado. Nos dijo que, si nos esperábamos

English

asleep. But that morning, the third one, I felt like leaving them because I truly felt that I was no longer a part of them.

On that day, by noon, the rain stopped and the sun came out and we were filled with hope. Two hours later we found a farmer that had some beets which, according to him, probably had not been spoiled by the rain. But he had no houses or anything to live in. He showed us the acres of beets which were still under water, and he told us that, if we cared to wait until the water went down to see if the beets had not rotted, and if they had not, he would pay us a large bonus per acre that we helped him cultivate. But he didn't have any houses, he told us. We told him we had some tents with us and, if he would let us, we would set them up in his yard. But he didn't want that. We noticed that he was afraid of us. The only thing that we wanted was to be near the drinking water, which was necessary, and also we were so tired of sleeping seated in the car, and, of course, we wanted to be under the light that he had in his yard. But he did not want us, and he told us, if we wanted to work there, we had to put our tents at the foot of the field and wait there for the water to go down. And so we placed our tents at the foot of the field and we began to wait. At nightfall we lit up the lamp in one of the tents, and then we decided for all of us to sleep in one tent only. I remember that we all felt so comfortable being able to stretch our legs, our arms, and falling asleep was easy. The thing that I remember so clearly that night was what awakened me. I felt what I thought was the hand of one of my little brothers, and then I heard my own screaming. I pulled his hand away, and, when I awoke, I found myself holding a salamander. Then I screamed and I saw that we were all

Español

hasta que se bajara el agua para ver si no estaba echado a perder, y si estaba bien el betabel, nos pagaría bonos por cada acre que le preparáramos. Pero no tenía casas ni nada. Nosotros le dijimos que teníamos unas carpas y que, si nos dejaba, podríamos sentarlas en su yarda. Pero no quiso. Nos tenía miedo. Nosotros lo que queríamos era estar cerca del agua de beber que era lo necesario, y también ya estábamos cansados de dormir sentados, todos entullidos, y claro que queríamos estar debajo de la luz que tenía en la yarda. Pero no quiso, y nos dijo que, si queríamos trabajar allí, que pusiéramos las carpas al pie de la labor de betabel y que esperáramos allí hasta que se bajara el agua. Y pusimos las carpas al pie de la labor de betabel, y nos pusimos a esperar.

Al oscurecer prendimos la lámpara de kerosín en una de las carpas y luego decidimos dormir todos en una sola carpa. Recuerdo que todos nos sentíamos a gusto al poder estirar las piernas, y el dormirnos fue fácil. Luego lo primero que recuerdo de esa noche y lo que me despertó fue el sentir lo que yo creía que era la mano de uno de mis hermanos, y mis propios gritos. Me quité la mano de encima y luego vi que lo que tenía en la mano yo era una salamandra. Estábamos cubiertos de salamandras que habían salido de lo húmedo de las labores, y seguimos gritando y quitándonos las salamandras del cuerpo. Con la ayuda de la luz de kerosín, empezamos a matar las salamandras. De primero nos daba asco porque al aplastarles les salía como leche del cuerpo, y el piso de la carpa se empezó a ver negro y blanco. Se habían metido en todo, dentro de los zapatos, en las colchas . . . Al ver fuera de la carpa con la ayuda de la lámpara, se veía todo negro el suelo. Yo realmente

English

covered with salamanders that had come out from the flooded fields. And all of us continued screaming and throwing salamanders off our bodies. With the light of the lamp, we began to kill them. At first we felt nauseated because, when we stepped on them, they would ooze milk. It seemed they were invading us, that they were invading the tent as if they wanted to reclaim the foot of the field. I don't know why we killed so many salamanders that night. The easiest thing to do would have been to climb quickly into our car. Now that I remember, I think that we also felt the desire to recover and to reclaim the foot of the field. I do remember that we began to look for more salamanders to kill. We wanted to find more to kill more. I remember that I liked to take the lamp, to seek them out, to kill them very slowly. It may be that I was angry at them for having frightened me. Then I began to feel that I was becoming part of my father and my mother and my brothers and sisters again.

What I remember most about that night was the darkness, the mud and the slime of the salamanders, and how hard they would get when I tried to squeeze the life out of them. What I have with me still is what I saw and felt when I killed the last one, and I guess that is why I remember the night of the salamanders. I caught one and examined it very carefully under the lamp. Then I looked at its eyes for a long time before I killed it. What I saw and what I felt is something I still have with me, something that is very pure—original death.

Español

sólo los veía como bultitos negros que al aplastarlos les salía leche. Luego parecía que nos estaban invadiendo la carpa, como que querían reclamar el pie de la labor. No sé por qué matamos tantas salamandras esa noche. Lo fácil hubiera sido subirnos al carro. Ahora que recuerdo, creo que sentíamos nosotros también el deseo de recobrar el pie de la labor, no sé. Sí recuerdo que hasta empezamos a buscar más salamandras, para matarlas. Queríamos encontrar más para matar más. Y luego recuerdo me gustaba aluzar con la lámpara y matar despacio a cada una. Sería que les tenía coraje por el susto. Sí, me empecé a sentir como que volvía a ser parte de mi 'apá y de mi 'amá y de mis hermanos.

Lo que más recuerdo de aquella noche fue lo oscuro de la noche, el zoquete, lo resbaloso de las salamandras y lo duro que a veces se ponían antes de que las aplastara. Lo que traigo conmigo todavía es lo que vi y sentí al matar la última. Y yo creo que por eso recuerdo esa noche de las salamandras. Pesqué a una y la examiné bien con la lámpara, luego le estuve viendo los ojos antes de matarla. Lo que vi y sentí es algo que traigo todavía conmigo, algo puro—la muerte original.

In the Chiaroscuro of the Years

Tino Villanueva
Translated by James Hoggard

Vigilant, keeping watch on myself,
I've gotten up, insomniac
in the night,
to drive back
the memory-loaded dreams
that almost by themselves
come vainly
through the alleys of childhood.
What a way to live,
blow to blow,
feeling myself driven
to ask what things mean.
If I stay awake between the sheets
it's because I'm overcome
by my inability to conquer
the night's thick spread
and to account for each event.

Living then
was an endless act of trusting
my soul to others.
And in the chiaroscuro of the years
I'm seeing
the scattered places I lived in
with my fully
bronzed body
and soul turned to rubble
by the scorn of those
driving my mind.

Now the time
of the scorched days emerges
and again
the memories of what I'm feeling
come clear.
It appears my only function
is to give this truth . . .
here, I, heir
of all my memories,
defending each moment
the awareness I lacked before.

En el claroscuro de los años

Tino Villanueva

Alertado vigía de mí mismo
me he parado
ante la noche insomne
a rechazar el sueño
cargado de memorias
que casi por sí solas
vanivienen
por los callejones de la infancia.
Qué manera de vivir
golpe a golpe
sintiéndome llamado a la exigencia
de pedir el sentido de las cosas.
Si me desvelo entre las sábanas
es que me relleva la torpeza
de no poder vencer
el despliegue denso de la noche,
de no poder contar cada suceso.

Vivir entonces
era acto perpetuo de confiar
el alma a los demás.
Y estoy viendo
en el claroscuro de los años
los sitios derramados que habité
con el tamaño bronceado
de mi cuerpo
y el alma hecha escombros
por el desdén
de los gobernantes en razón.

Ahora el tiempoatrás emerge
de las fechas requemadas
y de nuevo
se me notan los recuerdos
que estoy siendo.
Parece que no sirvo
más que para dar esta verdad . . .
aquí, yo, heredero
de todas mis memorias,
defendiendo a cada instante
la conciencia que antes me faltó.

Critical Thinking

1. In "The Salamanders," in what ways do the farmers and the policeman treat the narrator's family as if they were less than human? **[Support]**
2. Why do you think the narrator in "The Salamanders" felt more "part of" his family when he killed the salamanders? **[Interpret]**
3. In the poem "In the Chiaroscuro of the Years," are the memories that haunt the speaker pleasant ones? Explain. **[Infer]**
4. Explain what is positive about lines 36–39 of "In the Chiaroscuro of the Years." **[Analyze]**
5. In what ways is "In the Chiaroscuro of the Years" a chiaroscuro? **[Draw Conclusions]**
6. Referring to these literary works, explain what causes a memory to haunt a person's mind. **[Generalize]**

Compare English and Spanish Texts

7. Compare the English and Spanish texts of these works, looking for accent marks above letters. (a) Which language uses these marks? (b) How many different types of marks are there? **[Compare and Contrast]**

Compare English and Spanish Texts

7. (a) Accent marks appear in the Spanish originals. (b) There are two types of marks: the acute accent (´) and the tilde (~). You might want to explain to students that the acute accent indicates that a syllable is to be stressed and that the tilde over an *n* creates the sound *ny*, as in *señor*.

Answers

◆ Critical Thinking

1. Students may respond that all the farmers seem to be afraid of the family, almost as if these migrant farm workers were wild animals rather than people looking for work. The last farmer mentioned refuses to give them simple human necessities, like a place to sleep near drinking water and light. The policeman calls them "gypsies" and seems to use this word to mean worthless people.
2. Some students will say that in killing the salamanders the family was doing something together and also expressing their anger at the way they had been treated. Especially insightful students may realize that the salamanders, as alien creatures, embody the sense of alienation that had been imposed on the narrator. By killing the salamanders, the narrator therefore reclaimed his own sense of being human.
3. Students will probably realize that the memories are not pleasant. The title of the poem itself suggests the shadows of memory. Also, the speaker says that he lived "blow to blow," a phrase that suggests physical violence, emotional violence, or both. He also says that his soul had been "turned to rubble," an image that suggests a falling apart of identity.
4. Students may respond that these four lines are positive because the speaker says he inherits his memories and does not reject them: "heir/of all my memories." Also, he now seems to have an "awareness" of what the memories mean, an awareness he "lacked before."
5. Students may observe that the poem is a chiaroscuro in presenting both shade (dark and unpleasant memories) and light (a newfound feeling of "awareness").
6. Students should support their answers with passages and ideas from these literary works.

LESSON OBJECTIVES

1. **To read in varied sources, including American and world literature, in order to understand different cultures and the common elements across cultures, to respond to the texts, and to analyze literary elements within the texts**
   - Critical Thinking
   - Literature Selections
2. **To acquire an extensive vocabulary through reading and systematic study**
   - Comparing Spanish and English Texts

Literature in Translation
Paired Readings in English and Spanish

About the Authors

Berta G. Montalvo [män tälˊ vō] was born in Cuba and currently lives in Miami, Florida. Her books of poetry include *Miniaturas (Miniatures)* and *Gotas de rocío (Dewdrops)*.

Gabriela Mistral [gȧ brē eˊ lä mē strälˊ] (1889–1957) was a Chilean poet and the first Latin American woman to win a Nobel Prize for Literature. She was also a gifted teacher who helped and encouraged many young men and women. "Daybreak" sounds a note of love and hope that can often be heard in her poetry.

Literary Note

Montalvo and Mistral remind readers that a poem is where healing can begin and where joy can be shared.

Return

Berta G. Montalvo
Translated by Lori M. Carlson

Yesterdays: do not return
remain
in yesteryear.

Bad dreams: do not come back,
nor good dreams either.

Better that today
shine on tomorrow that
will lead us to the future.

Volver

Berta G. Montalvo

Que no vuelvan los ayeres
que se quedan así
en ayer.

Que no vuelvan los sueños malos,
ni los buenos tampoco.

Es mejor que el hoy
alumbre un mañana
que no tenga que volver.

Daybreak, *from* Time

Gabriela Mistral
Translated by Doris Dana

My heart swells that the Universe
like a fiery cascade may enter.
The new day comes. Its coming
leaves me breathless.
I sing. Like a cavern brimming
I sing my new day.

For grace lost and recovered
I stand humble. Not giving. Receiving.
Until the Gorgon night,
vanquished, flees.

Amanecer, *de* tiempo

Gabriela Mistral

Hincho mi corazón para que entre
como cascada ardiente el Universo.
El nuevo día llega y su llegada
me deja sin aliento.
Canto como la gruta que es colmada
canto mi día nuevo.

Por la gracia perdida y recobrada
humilde soy sin dar y recibiendo
hasta que la Gorgona de la noche
va, derrotada, huyendo.

Critical Thinking

1. In "Return," why does the speaker ask "Yesterdays" to "not return"? **[Interpret]**
2. Using your own words, restate the idea expressed in the last stanza of "Return." **[Interpret]**
3. In what way is "Daybreak" a victory song? **[Analyze]**
4. Suppose you are looking for a text to be read at the beginning of each day on a public radio station. Would you choose one of these two poems? Why? **[Evaluate]**

Compare English and Spanish Texts

5. In what ways is the English verb *revolve* similar to the Spanish verb that is the title of Montalvo's poem? **[Compare and Contrast]**

Answers

◆ Critical Thinking

1. Students may realize that the speaker wants to welcome "the future," not get bogged down in the bad or good of what has already happened.
2. No matter how students choose to restate the key idea, they should use their own words, not Montalvo's. Possible response: It is better to focus on the present moment and the opportunities that it brings than to think about the past.
3. Students may point out that night is described as a monster ("Gorgon") that is "vanquished" and "flees." In this sense, the poem is a victory of light over darkness, joy over despair.
4. Students should give specific reasons for their choice.

Compare English and Spanish Texts

5. (a) The English word *revolve* contains what appears to be the same root as the Spanish word *volver,* which means "return." Also, the words have a similar meaning because to *revolve* means "to circle, returning to the same point." Have students find the root in English and Spanish dictionaries and confirm that it is the same. You may then want to introduce the idea that the two languages share certain Latin roots. You can also point out that while English has many Latin-based words, it did not evolve from Latin as Spanish did. English evolved from the languages of Germanic tribes but has borrowed vocabulary from Latin, French, and a great many other sources. In contrast, Romance languages—such as Spanish, Portuguese, French, Italian, and Romanian—evolved directly from Latin. The term *Romance* derives from the term *Roman,* and Romans were speakers of Latin.

Planning Students' Sustained Reading

The works listed here are good choices for extending the themes explored in each unit. Included are descriptions of the books, tips for teaching them, and a guide to the related materials available for each. Use this information to help you decide which books to teach or to recommend to your students.

Literature Study Guides

Literature Study Guides are available for the titles listed below. These guides include section summaries, discussion questions, writing assignments, and activity ideas. They also provide helpful information about the author and the historical background of each book.

- *The Adventures of Huckleberry Finn*
- *The Great Gatsby*
- *Literature of the American Southwest*
- *Literature of the Expanding Frontier*
- *My Ántonia*
- *The Scarlet Letter*
- *Southern Writers*

Resources for Teaching Novels, Plays, and Literature Collections

This booklet includes graphic organizers, teaching strategies, and transparencies that will be useful when teaching any of these works. In addition, it includes formal tests for many of the selections.

Suggestions for Sustained Reading

Sustained Reading and Its Benefits Novels, plays, short-story collections, and full-length nonfiction works all provide a great opportunity for sustained reading—reading that takes place over an extended period of time. Through any of these types of writing, you can travel to new and distant worlds, follow a character's life from birth through adulthood, and experience events unlike anything that happens in your everyday life.

The Keys to Successful Sustained Reading Reading longer works can be more challenging than reading brief pieces because longer works usually involve more characters and plot events and because it is unlikely that you will read a longer work in a single sitting. Following are a few of the keys to successful sustained reading:

- **Set aside extended periods of time.** It is very hard to follow a longer work if you read it in short intervals of a few minutes at a time. Read in periods of a half hour or more. Do not allow yourself to be distracted by the television set or the telephone.
- **Make yourself comfortable.** You'll concentrate better if you make yourself comfortable each time you sit down to read. Choose a comfortable chair in a place you like.
- **Take notes as you read.** Jot down details of the settings, note information about the characters, and record important events.
- **Hold book-circle discussions.** Get together with classmates who are reading the same work. Share your reactions. Discuss what you learn about the characters, and try to analyze the message the writer is trying to convey.

The Prentice Hall Literature Library The Prentice Hall Literature Library includes many longer works that fit in well with the literature included in this book. Your teacher can provide you with access to many of these titles. In addition, you can find an unlimited array of other extended reading possibilities in bookstores and in your local libraries.

Suggested Works and Connections to Unit Themes Following are some suggestions for longer works that will give you the opportunity to experience the fun of sustained reading. Each of the suggestions further explores one of the themes in this book. Many of the titles are included in the Prentice Hall Literature Library.

Suggested Titles Related to Units

Unit One

The Scarlet Letter
Nathaniel Hawthorne

They were very few in number, but their courage, hard work, and intense perseverance enabled the Puritans who landed at Plymouth in 1620 to establish a colony. Though *The Scarlet Letter* was published in 1850, Nathaniel Hawthorne chose this setting—a world in which people lived simple lives and followed a strict moral code—for his masterpiece. The novel tells the story of Hester Prynne, who is branded as an outcast and struggles to create her own redemption.

Keepers of the Earth
Joseph Bruchac

In an effort to preserve the culture of his people—he is descended from the Abenaki—Joseph Bruchac has published many volumes of Native American tales and literature, both ancient and contemporary. In this collection, Bruchac presents a sampling of traditional tales. With each, Bruchac provides environmentally focused activities that highlight the relationship between Native American cultures and the natural world.

Unit Two

The Autobiography
Benjamin Franklin

Meet one of the greatest minds and sharpest wits in American history as Benjamin Franklin shares the story of his life in *The Autobiography*. This "rags to riches" tale recounts his rise from humble beginnings to a prosperous Renaissance man—a printer, scientist, inventor, diplomat, and witty commentator on human nature. Though Franklin died before he could complete *The Autobiography,* the book provides a fascinating look at the life and character of one of the greatest diplomats in our nation's history.

Unit Three

Walden
Henry David Thoreau

To read *Walden* is to understand why Henry David Thoreau still has the power to influence and inspire today's leaders, writers, and environmentalists. One of only two Thoreau books published in his lifetime, *Walden* received little attention when it appeared in 1845. Since then, it has been recognized as a literary masterpiece. It describes Thoreau's two-year experiment in self-sufficiency, in which he built and lived in a small wooden hut on the shores of Walden Pond, near Concord, Massachusetts.

Literature of the Expanding Frontier
Prentice Hall Collection

As our nation grew, the frontier was pushed farther and farther west as pioneers, lured by the promise of wide-open spaces, journeyed into untamed lands. This collection of stories, folk tales, songs, and poems captures the spirit of these courageous people who lived life on the edge of an expanding frontier. Their literature conveys the excitement of a time when both land and opportunities seemed limitless.

Unit Four

The Adventures of Huckleberry Finn
Mark Twain

Widely regarded as Twain's masterpiece, this action-packed novel captures the adventures of a young white orphan and a runaway slave. *Huckleberry Finn* is more than just a great story, however. Its uniquely American characters and speech convey the vitality of life in the United States as no other novel ever has. Read this book, and you'll understand why it's credited with changing the course of American literature.

My Ántonia
Willa Cather

The road to adulthood is never easy, especially when you live in the desolate wilderness described in Willa Cather's novel *My Ántonia*. For the young Bohemian immigrant Ántonia Shimerdas, the unforgiving, primitive Nebraska heartland is now home. Tough, self-sufficient, and spirited, she meets the daily challenges of frontier life with courage and

Customize for *Varying Student Needs*

When assigning the selections for each unit, keep in mind the following factors:

Unit 1

- Because of the difficulty of *The Scarlet Letter,* you may want to allow extra time to teach this novel.
- *Keepers of the Earth* is a collection of Native American tales paired with related activities and projects.
- *A Narrative of the Captivity and Restoration of Mrs. Mary Rowlandson* is a high-interest, first-person narrative.

Unit 2

- *The Autobiography of Benjamin Franklin* paints a colorful picture of eighteenth-century colonial life.
- The play *1776* had several successful runs on Broadway. It was also produced as a feature film that you may want to share with your students.
- *Citizen Tom Paine* is a lively and accessible historical novel.

Unit 3

- The pieces included in *The Great Short Works of Herman Melville* tend to be dense, demanding reading suitable for more proficient readers.
- The challenge of *Walden* is not the reading level but the content, which is highly introspective and philosophical.
- *Literature of the Expanding Frontier* is a high-interest collection that covers a wide range of reading levels.

Sensitive Issues

Some of these works contain potentially sensitive issues, such as the ones below. You might consider these issues when deciding what to teach.

- *The Scarlet Letter* tells of a woman who commits adultery and bears an illegitimate child. It addresses difficult issues of sin and redemption.
- Mary Rowlandson's book raises sensitive racial and ethnic issues involving the way early conflicts fed long-standing prejudice against Native Americans.
- The play *1776* contains some lighthearted sexual innuendoes and several references to drinking.

Customize for
Varying Student Needs
When assigning the selections for each unit, keep in mind the following factors:

Unit 4

- *The Adventures of Huckleberry Finn* is a classic adventure story with a high interest level and a great deal of satirical humor.
- The language and style of *My Ántonia,* a classic novel about life on the Nebraska frontier, are very accessible.
- The selections in *Literature of the Southwest* encompass a wide variety of reading levels and writing styles.

Unit 5

- *The Great Gatsby* is a classic novel of the Jazz Age and is accessible to the average reader.
- *Ethan Frome* is a relatively short novel of ill-fated love in a small New England town.
- Considered a modern classic, *The Grapes of Wrath* is long, dense, challenging reading.

Unit 6

- *The Kitchen God's Wife* is a highly readable, richly detailed, and emotionally powerful modern novel.
- *The Right Stuff* is a fast-paced, entertaining account of the early years of the NASA space program.
- *Southern Writers* is a high-interest collection that covers a broad range of reading levels and writing styles.

Sensitive Issues

Some of these works contain potentially sensitive issues such as the ones below. You might consider these issues when deciding what to teach.

- More than one hundred years after its publication, *The Adventures of Huckleberry Finn* continues to provoke controversy. The book has been noted for its treatment of slavery and racism, offensive language, and stereotypes. However, positive aspects of the novel, including its strong anti-racist stance, outweigh negative ones.
- Willa Cather's use of stereotypes in describing the immigrants who people the plains may be offensive to some students.
- F. Scott Fitzgerald writes about race and ethnicity in ways that some students might find offensive.
- *Ethan Frome* raises difficult questions about marital fidelity.
- Some parts of *The Kitchen God's Wife* contain disturbing scenes of domestic violence.

Prentice Hall Literature Library

The Prentice Hall Literature Library offers a wide variety of classic and contemporary works from around the world. You may choose to study these with your class or to recommend them to students for individual reading.

Suggested Titles Related to Units (continued)

determination. *My Ántonia* is a celebration of the pioneer spirit that realistically portrays both the beauty and hardship of life on the American frontier.

Literature of the American Southwest
Prentice Hall Collection

What comes to mind when you think of the American Southwest? For most, it's blue skies, sandy deserts and plains, cactuses, coyotes, and, of course, cowboys. Experience this exciting region through its literature—stories, tall tales, and songs that capture a time and place where people and events were larger than life.

Unit Five

The Great Gatsby
F. Scott Fitzgerald

The Great Gatsby is the quintessential Jazz Age novel; in it, you'll find all of the glamour, decadence, and emptiness that characterized the era. This tragic tale of broken dreams and ruined lives explores self-made millionaire Jay Gatsby's quest to win the love of the wealthy, beautiful—and married—Daisy Buchanan. Fitzgerald, who lived the life portrayed in his novels, gives us an inside look at the world of the idle rich.

Ethan Frome
Edith Wharton

A terrible twist of events lies at the heart of this bittersweet tale of a forbidden and ill-fated love. The setting—wintry, rural New England—is a departure for author Edith Wharton, whose novels and short stories are more often set against the backdrop of society life. The painful irony that brings the plot full circle results in a story that will haunt you long after you've read the last page.

The Grapes of Wrath
John Steinbeck

This powerfully moving book recounts one family's journey from the Oklahoma Dust Bowl in search of a better life in California's "promised land." Set in the depths of the Great Depression, it is a harsh yet uplifting tale of the strength of the human spirit in the face of adversity and injustice. The novel won a Pulitzer Prize and established John Steinbeck as one of the greatest authors of his day.

Unit Six

The Kitchen God's Wife
Amy Tan

As a young woman, Amy Tan rejected her Chinese heritage; as a mature writer, she celebrates it in her fiction. *The Kitchen God's Wife,* the follow-up to Tan's first blockbuster novel, *The Joy Luck Club,* recounts the fascinating yet tragic life story of a Chinese American widow. Told in the elderly woman's own distinctive voice, the eventful tale is rich in both history and heartache; it has earned the praise of critics and devoted readers alike.

The Right Stuff
Tom Wolfe

By the 1960's, the only frontier left to explore was outer space. The pioneers of old were replaced by high-tech astronauts, and America held its collective breath as the men of the Mercury space program broke from the confines of Earth to orbit the moon. If you're excited by the prospect of facing the unknown, of going where no one has gone before, you'll enjoy this gripping and satirical account of the first manned space mission.

Southern Writers
Prentice Hall Collection

From William Faulkner and Thomas Wolfe to Flannery O'Connor, Eudora Welty, and Alice Walker, many of America's greatest writers have come from the South. This collection features some of the best short works by many of the region's most famous traditional and contemporary authors. Their words paint a vivid picture of the language, landscapes, and personalities of southern life.

Test Practice Bank

Reading Comprehension

Summarizing Written Texts

Read the passage, and then answer the questions that follow. Mark the letter of your answer on a bubble sheet if your teacher provides one; otherwise, number from 1 to 4 on a separate sheet of paper, and write the letter of the correct answer next to each number.

Imagism was a literary movement originated by poets who rebelled against the sentimental poetry of the nineteenth century. Imagists used precise words to "paint" vivid images. The Imagists hoped that by freezing a single moment, they could capture the emotions of that moment.

The Imagists were influenced by Chinese and Japanese poetry. Like Imagist poems, haiku and tanka—two types of Japanese poetry—present an image or contrasting images to inspire a moment of enlightenment. The haiku and the tanka have rigid patterns of lines and syllables. Imagists, however, focused on the natural musical rhythms of language rather than on traditional metrical patterns.

1 Which of the following choices best expresses the main idea implied in the first paragraph?
A Imagists were rebels.
B Imagism was a literary movement.
C Imagism focused on the direct presentation of images.
D Imagists used the musical rhythms of everyday speech.

2 Which of the following statements best summarizes the first paragraph?
A Imagism originated in the nineteenth century.
B The Imagist movement was a reactionary movement.
C Imagist poems are simple.
D Imagist poems present striking images to evoke emotions.

3 Which of the following is the implied main idea in the second paragraph?
A Imagist poems resemble Chinese and Japanese poetry.
B Haiku and tanka are Japanese verse forms.
C Haiku and tanka record precise moments of enlightenment.
D Haiku and tanka follow strict patterns of lines and syllables.

4 Which of the following is the best summary of the second paragraph?
A The tanka and the haiku have rigid patterns.
B Imagists did not use strict patterns of lines and syllables.
C The Imagists used principles of Chinese and Japanese poetry.
D Chinese and Japanese poetry influenced the Imagists.

See the Test Preparation Workshop on page 115 for tips on answering questions about summarizing texts.

Using the Test Practice Bank

These tests provide practice test items in reading comprehension and writing skills, which correlate to standardized test objectives in content and format. For each standardized Test Preparation Workshop that appears in the book, you will find here a page of extra test items that focus on the same skill. In addition, several tests provide practice in a combination of skills, along with writing prompts.

You may choose to have your students use this Practice Bank from time to time in conjunction with the Test Preparation Workshops; alternatively, you may want students to spend a block of time working on the entire Practice Bank during a standardized test preparation period.

Correlations to Standardized Tests

The reading comprehension practice items on this page correspond to the following standardized test sections:

SAT Critical Reading
ACT Reading

Answers

1 (C) The focus of the paragraph is on how Imagists used words to "paint" vivid images and to try to capture the emotions of a single moment.
2 (D) That Imagist poems present striking images to evoke emotions best sums up the first paragraph.
3 (A) Saying that the Imagists were influenced by Chinese and Japanese poetry and that the images in Japanese poetry inspire a moment of enlightenment implies that Imagist poems resemble Chinese and Japanese poetry.
4 (C) Because the second paragraph describes the principles of Chinese and Japanese poetry and its influence on the Imagists, this choice is the best summary of the paragraph.

Correlations to Standardized Tests

The reading comprehension practice items on this page correspond to the following standardized test sections:

SAT Critical Reading
ACT Reading

Answers

1 (B) The first paragraph states that defeated France gave up its claims to North American territory.
2 (C) The second paragraph states that the British government wanted to raise revenue to pay its war debts.
3 (B) The second paragraph states that the colonists beat stamp distributors and destroyed their shops.
4 (A) The second paragraph states that the Stamp Act was eventually repealed.
5 (C) That the Boston massacre inflamed colonial passions suggests that the colonists became more determined.
6 (D) Because of their determination and inflamed passions, the colonists probably would have rebelled openly.

Test Practice Bank

Reading Comprehension

Recognize Cause and Effect; Predict Outcomes

Read the passage, and then answer the questions that follow. Mark the letter of your answer on a bubble sheet if your teacher provides one; otherwise, number from 1 to 6 on a separate sheet of paper, and write the letter of the correct answer next to each number.

The American Revolution was preceded by the French and Indian War, a struggle between England and France for control of North America. The conflict broke out in 1754 and continued for nearly a decade. When the war officially ended in 1763, defeated France gave up its claims to North American territory. There was general jubilation in the thirteen British colonies.

The good feelings were short-lived, however. The British government, wanting to raise revenue to pay its war debts, passed the Stamp Act in 1765, requiring colonists to buy stamps and affix them to each of 54 ordinary items. The colonists beat stamp distributors and destroyed their shops. The Stamp Act was eventually repealed. Other acts and reactions followed. The Townshend Acts, which taxed paper, paint, glass, lead, and tea, prompted a boycott. British troops sent to enforce the acts fired into a mob, killing five people. This so-called Boston massacre inflamed colonial passions.

1 What was the main reason France gave up its North American territories?
A They were too expensive.
B France lost a war with England.
C France could not get colonists to settle there.
D They were too far away to govern.

2 What was the main reason for the Stamp Act?
A a shortage of stamps
B inefficient postal service
C a need to pay war debts
D a need to regulate food quality

3 What immediate effect did the Stamp Act have?
A The colonists abided quietly.
B Stamp distributors were beaten.
C Stamps were thrown into Boston Harbor.
D The colonists cooperated.

4 What was the effect of the colonists' reactions to the Stamp Act?
A The act was repealed.
B Five colonists were shot.
C More stamps were printed.
D Parliament was dissolved.

5 When British troops shot five colonists, the colonists—
A realized they were outnumbered
B lost their initiative
C became more determined
D vowed to maintain peace

6 What would likely have been the colonists' reaction had the British not repealed the Stamp Act?
A compliance
B quiet resentment
C eventual acceptance
D open rebellion

See the Test Preparation Workshop on page 213 for tips on answering questions about recognizing cause and effect and predicting outcomes.

Reading Comprehension

Analyze Information to Make Inferences and Generalizations

Read the passage, and then answer the questions that follow. Mark the letter of your answer on a bubble sheet if your teacher provides one; otherwise, number from 1 to 6 on a separate sheet of paper, and write the letter of the correct answer next to each number.

> The canyon looked like a small dip in the horizon—a deceptive viewpoint, as the canyon walls towered over 1,500 feet. Felipe knew that his voyage would take days across rugged desert terrain. The idea of traveling so far with very little water unnerved him. He knew that if he did not make it to the canyon in four days, he could die. He must look for strawberry cactus in bloom to quench his thirst. There would not be any relief from the sun until he reached the cottonwoods on the riverbanks.
>
> Traveling at night seemed like a good idea until he nearly twisted his ankle in an unexpected gully. He vowed to make good time at dawn and dusk. He had managed to survive this long without getting caught. The canyon and Mexico were so close and yet a million miles away.

1 In this passage, Felipe's conflict is with—
A himself
B the desert
C the law
D lack of food

2 Which of the following best describes the mood in the passage?
A angry
B sunny and dry
C carefree
D determined

3 Based on the description in the passage, Felipe—
A knows this environment
B is out of place in the desert
C is lost
D is on a leisurely trip

4 Why does Mexico seem both close and distant to Felipe?
A Felipe cannot judge the distance very well.
B He can see Mexico, but he knows how long his trip will take.
C Felipe has not been to Mexico in many years.
D Felipe is only dreaming about Mexico.

5 Felipe does not travel at night because—
A he is afraid of the dark
B he would make too much noise
C he cannot see well enough to walk safely
D there are dangerous nocturnal animals

6 You can infer from this passage that Felipe—
A is running toward his freedom
B is running away from home
C committed a terrible crime
D was a slave

See the Test Preparation Workshop on page 427 for tips on answering questions about making inferences and generalizations.

Correlations to Standardized Tests

The reading comprehension practice items on this page correspond to the following standardized test sections:
SAT Critical Reading
ACT Reading

Answers

1 (B) If Felipe fails to make it across the rugged desert terrain in four days, he could die.
2 (D) That Felipe *vows* to make good time at dawn and dusk shows that his mood is determined.
3 (A) Felipe knows that the desert terrain is rugged, that he must look for strawberry cactus in bloom, and that he will find relief when he reaches the cottonwoods.
4 (B) To Felipe, the canyon and Mexico seem so close, but because of the desert he must cross, they feel a million miles away.
5 (C) Once he nearly twisted his ankle in an unexpected gully.
6 (A) That he managed to survive without getting caught suggests that he is running toward his freedom. There is no evidence that he was a slave or had committed a crime.

Correlations to Standardized Tests

The reading comprehension practice items on this page correspond to the following standardized test sections:

SAT Critical Reading
ACT Reading

Answers

1 (D) *Exaggerated* provides a context clue to help determine that *elaborated* means "added more detail."
2 (B) The mention of "heroes" provides a context clue to help determine that *feats* means "daring acts."
3 (B) The words "wrongful death" provide a context clue to help determine that *retribution* means "punishment."
4 (A) The words "walking more than 100 miles and riding another 400" provide a context clue to help determine that *fatigued* means "tired."
5 (D) That Cortez was out of ammunition suggests that he fought to the end and makes "resistant" the likely meaning of *defiant.*
6 (C) The words "but was sentenced to life" provide a context clue suggesting that *acquitted* means the opposite: cleared of the charges.

Test Practice Bank

Reading Comprehension

Using Context

Read the passage, and then answer the questions that follow. Mark the letter of your answer on a bubble sheet if your teacher provides one; otherwise, number from 1 to 6 on a separate sheet of paper, and write the letter of the correct answer next to each number.

The oral tradition of memorizing and telling stories has preserved many of the old myths, ballads, and legends of America's past. However, many stories have changed over time as tellers have elaborated and exaggerated details. Some stories create legends out of heroes, exalting the hero's life and immortalizing his or her attributes. Heroes may take on mythic qualities and perform extraordinary feats. One such legend is that of Gregorio Cortez, a famous fugitive in Texas.

As the legend has it, Cortez shot and killed a sheriff in retribution for the wrongful death of Cortez's brother. Cortez had to flee to Mexico, walking more than 100 miles and riding another 400. While on the run, he killed another sheriff. Three hundred men searched for Cortez to no avail. Fatigued and out of ammunition, a defiant Cortez was finally captured. He was acquitted for killing the first sheriff, but was sentenced to life for killing the second. Cortez served twelve years for his crime, receiving a pardon from the governor of Texas in 1913.

1 The word elaborated in this passage means—
A reinvented
B distorted
C left out detail
D added more detail

2 In this passage, the word feats means—
A peculiar language
B daring acts
C unusual dress
D snappy remarks

3 In this passage, the word retribution means—
A forgiveness
B punishment
C reward
D remembrance

4 The word fatigued in this passage means—
A tired
B hungry
C desperate
D dressed in military garb

5 In this passage, the word defiant means—
A confused
B meek
C agreeable
D resistant

6 The word acquitted in this passage means—
A sentenced
B given a second trial
C cleared of the charges
D found guilty

See the Preparation Workshop on page 631 for tips on answering questions about using context.

Test Practice Bank

Vocabulary

Sentence Completion

Read each sentence, and choose the word or group of words that correctly completes the sentence. Mark the letter of your answer on a bubble sheet if your teacher provides one; otherwise, number from 1 to 6 on a separate sheet of paper, and write the letter of the correct answer next to each number.

1 Saul began his intriguing story about his summer adventure, but then he ___ into a strange account about his backpack.
A progressed
B transferred
C digressed
D dipped

2 The woman was going to tell the investigators that she heard neighborhood dogs barking at 2:00 A.M. but decided this detail was too ___ for a case as big as theirs.
A urgent
B trivial
C important
D confusing

3 The increase in whales off the coast of Maui has made sighting these magnificent mammals a(n) ___ event.
A unusual
B boring
C everyday
D unique

4 New technology is advancing faster than ___ can produce new ___.
A manufacturers; products
B consumers; prices
C designers; ideas
D retailers; sales

5 Poetry can evoke several ___ depending on ___ clues.
A readings; mythical
B critiques; obscure
C imitations; reflective
D interpretations; contextual

6 When Rita ___ the force of the storm, she made a(n) ___ mistake by refusing to seek shelter on higher ground.
A evaluated; indiscrete
B apprised; languid
C underestimated; critical
D revered; apathetic

7 The gray day put everyone in a ___ mood.
A melancholic
B mellifluous
C frenzied
D gleeful

See the Test Preparation Workshop on page 863 for tips on answering questions about sentence completion.

Correlations to Standardized Tests

The vocabulary development practice items on this page correspond to the following standardized test section:
SAT Sentence Completions

Answers

1 (C) *Digress* means "strayed" or "wandered."
2 (B) *Trivial* means "irrelevant" or "trifling."
3 (C) *Everyday* means "common."
4 (A) *Manufacturers* are those who make things; *products* are what they make.
5 (D) One gives an *interpretation,* or explanation, based on *contextual* clues, or clues in the context of the poem.
6 (C) *Underestimated* means "minimized" or "made light of"; *critical* means "dangerous."
7 (A) *Melancholic* means "joyless" or "depressing" like the "gray day."

Correlations to Standardized Tests

The writing skills practice items on this page correspond to the following standardized test section:

ACT English: Usage/Mechanics

Answers

1 (B) A comma is needed to separate *masterpiece* from its appositive *Moby-Dick.*

2 (D) This choice completes the correlative conjunctions *not only . . . but also.*

3 (C) "*Moby-Dick* is" is correct because the discussion of the novel is written in entirely in the present tense.

4 (A) The semicolon correctly joins the two independent clauses in this compound sentence.

5 (B) The pronoun *its* agrees with its animal antecedent, Moby-Dick.

6 (D) By replacing the comma with *is,* a fragment is turned into a complete sentence.

Test Practice Bank

Writing Skills

Punctuation, Usage, and Sentence Structure

Read the passage, and then answer the questions that follow. Mark the letter of your answer on a bubble sheet if your teacher provides one; otherwise, number from 1 to 6 on a separate sheet of paper, and write the letter of the correct answer next to each number.

(1) In 1851, Herman Melville wrote his masterpiece. *Moby-Dick.* (2) This novel is not only the story of a whaling expedition, but is the story of a man's search for truth and revenge. (3) *Moby-Dick* was a symbolic examination of good and evil. (4) Melville's white whale is more than an animal; it is a symbol of everything inexplicable and uncontrollable in nature. (5) Like a storm that is both awe-inspiring and threatening, Moby-Dick attracts and harms her enemies. (6) Indifferent to the world, Moby-Dick, a true sea monster.

1 How would you correct sentence 1?
A No change needed
B masterpiece, *Moby-Dick.*
C masterpiece; *Moby-Dick.*
D masterpiece, it was *Moby-Dick.*

2 How would you correct sentence 2?
A No change needed
B expedition; but is
C expedition, but it is
D expedition, but is also

3 How would you correct sentence 3?
A No change needed
B *Moby-Dick* has
C *Moby-Dick* is
D *Moby-Dick* will be

4 How would you correct sentence 4?
A No change needed
B animal, it is
C animal it is
D animal . . . it is

5 How would you correct sentence 5?
A No change needed
B its enemies
C it's enemies
D their enemies

6 How would you correct sentence 6?
A No change needed
B *Moby-Dick,* is a true sea monster.
C *Moby-Dick*: a true sea monster
D *Moby-Dick* is a true sea monster.

See the Test Preparation Workshop on page 1175 for tips on answering questions about punctuation, usage, and sentence structure.

Combined Skills

Reading Comprehension; Vocabulary; Punctuation, Usage, and Sentence Structure

Read the passage, and answer questions 1–6. Then answer questions 7–12. Mark the letter of your answer on a bubble sheet if your teacher provides one; otherwise, number from 1 to 14 on a separate sheet of paper, and write the letter of the correct answer next to each number.

The persecution of witches began in the fourteenth century under the Spanish Inquisition. On a given day, up to a hundred alleged witches were burned. This strange hysteria renewed itself in 1692 when twenty persons were executed as witches in Salem, Massachusetts. The European witch hunts were largely political in nature. In New England, however, the motives were unique.

The colonists had to endure great hardships, many of which they could not control. They had to fight bitter winters, disease, failing crops, and death. They longed to blame this misfortune on someone, and so they blamed the Devil. Their Puritan faith taught that witches were real and dangerous and doing the Devil's work on Earth. In Salem, many people were quick to blame unusual behavior on witchcraft. It wasn't long until mass hysteria turned the quiet town into a paranoid mob.

1 According to the passage, why did the colonists accuse people of witchcraft?
- **A** They witnessed acts of witchcraft.
- **B** They wanted to dispose of political enemies.
- **C** They wanted to blame someone for their misfortunes.
- **D** They were compelled by the British government.

2 Based on this passage, what human characteristic did Puritan society display when faced with the unknown?
- **A** resentment
- **B** acceptance
- **C** understanding
- **D** paranoia

3 In this passage, the word nature means—
- **A** an inherent tendency
- **B** a sort or type
- **C** the uncivilized world
- **D** natural scenery

4 Which statement is the best summary of this passage?
- **A** Looking for a scapegoat, societies have executed people for being witches.
- **B** The Puritans in the 1600's took the lives of innocent people.
- **C** When hardships occur, there must be retribution to correct the situation.
- **D** The incident in Salem was the beginning of the separation of church and state.

5 What is the main idea of the first paragraph?
- **A** Political motives are the underlying force in witch hunts.
- **B** Witchcraft is a crime punishable by death.
- **C** People were accused and executed as witches for several hundred years.
- **D** The Spanish Inquisition was responsible for the Salem witch trials.

Correlations to Standardized Tests

The combined skills practice items on these two pages correspond to the following standardized test sections:

SAT Critical Reading
SAT Sentence Completions
ACT English: Usage/Mechanics

Answers

1 (C) The second paragraph states that the colonists longed to blame their misfortune on someone.
2 (D) The last line states that mass hysteria turned the quiet town into a paranoid mob.
3 (B) Here, the connotation of *nature* is "type": the European witch hunts were of a political *type*.
4 (A) The passage is an explanation of motives behind pursuit and execution of witches.
5 (C) The first paragraph shows that persecution of witches existed in the 1300's and as late as the 1600's.

Answers *(continued)*

6 (B) Continued misfortune will probably cause the colonists to continue to look for scapegoats.

7 (D) *Transposed,* meaning "reversed," is the logical answer.

8 (A) *Spurious,* meaning, "false," and *egregious,* meaning "glaring" or "gross," best complete the meaning of the sentence.

9 (B) *Prodigious,* meaning "great" or "tremendous" and *unsuccessful,* meaning "without success" most logically complete the sentence.

10 (C) A colon is needed to introduce a list.

11 (C) *His or her* properly agrees with the singular antecedent, *student.*

12 (C) It is best to repeat *Tomás* to avoid any confusion about the antecedent.

13 (D) This choice correctly eliminates the fragment, "When I took my bags to the counter."

14 (C) *Gone* is the correct past participle of *go.*

6 Based on this passage, what is the probable outcome if the people of Salem continue to experience misfortune after their witch trials?
A They will give up their faith.
B They will look for more witches.
C They will feel satisfied.
D They will blame themselves.

For questions 7–9, choose the word or group of words that best completes the sentence.

7 Laurel sent her résumé to several large firms but later discovered that she had __ the last two digits of her phone number.
A transmitted
B transversed
C transpired
D transposed

8 When the local news ran a ___ story about a gas leak, many people complained about the ___ mistake.
A spurious; egregious
B capricious; craven
C candid; modest
D sound; fraudulent

9 Despite John's ___ efforts to repair his bicycle, the continuous slipping of the gears showed he was ___.
A energetic; successful
B prodigious; unsuccessful
C cursory; productive
D exemplary; confused

For questions 10–14, choose the way you would correct each passage.

10 We were tested on the following concepts, allegory, apostrophe, and personification.
A No change needed
B concepts: allegory,
C concepts; allegory,
D concepts . . . allegory,

11 Each student is required to bring their registration card to the testing center.
A No change needed
B their own registration card
C his or her registration card
D her registration card

12 When the taxi driver asked Tomás where he wanted to go he looked confused.
A No change needed
B go, he
C go, Tomás
D go, they

13 When I took my bags to the counter. They were five pounds overweight.
A No change needed
B counter; they
C counter they
D counter, they

14 If she had finished her work on time, she might have went to the concert.
A go
B had gone
C have gone
D had went

Vocabulary

Antonyms, Analogies, and Sentence Completion

For questions 1–10, choose the pair of words whose relationship is most similar to that expressed by the pair of words in all capital letters. Mark the letter of your answer on a bubble sheet if your teacher provides one; otherwise, number from 1 to 10 on a separate sheet of paper, and write the letter of the correct answer next to each number.

1 FLAMBOYANT : OSTENTATIOUS ::
(A) obstinate : cooperative
(B) pristine : unspoiled
(C) defiant : adolescence
(D) insomnia : somnolent
(E) elixir : detrimental

2 WEDDING : JUBILATION ::
(A) valor : resilience
(B) ceremony : solemn
(C) demolition : construction
(D) fire : hysteria
(E) clergy : orator

3 DOCILE : TENACIOUS ::
(A) timid : conspicuous
(B) compliant : serene
(C) outgoing : dramatic
(D) venomous : serpentine
(E) affluent : wealthy

4 MITIGATE : ATTORNEY ::
(A) meticulous : perfectionist
(B) endurance : athlete
(C) navigate : aviator
(D) articulate : judge
(E) vindicate : suspicion

5 EVANESCENT : PERSISTENCE ::
(A) poignant : affection
(B) transparent : opacity
(C) garrulous : politician
(D) illuminate : luminosity
(E) titanic : immensity

6 CONTENT : ELATED ::
(A) confluence : fraternized
(B) aesthetic : culture
(C) baked : boiled
(D) preacher : divine
(E) adequate : superb

7 DISPASSIONATE : AGITATED ::
(A) obligated : required
(B) disinterested : impartial
(C) innocent : accused
(D) forthright : dishonest
(E) stranded : marooned

8 REPREHENSIBLE : SWINDLER ::
(A) brave : hero
(B) talented : actor
(C) stagnant : pond
(D) derivative : music
(E) luxurious : hotel

Correlations to Standardized Tests

The combined skills practice items on these two pages correspond to the following standardized test section:

SAT Antonyms, Analogies, Sentence Completions

Answers

1 (B) *Pristine* and *unspoiled* are synonymous adjectives, as are *flamboyant* and *ostentatious.*
2 (D) A fire is a cause for hysteria, just as a wedding is a cause for jubilation.
3 (A) *Docile* is the opposite of *tenacious,* as *timid* is the opposite of *conspicuous.*
4 (C) An aviator navigates, just as an attorney litigates.
5 (B) Something that is transparent has no opacity, just as something that is evanescent has no persistence.
6 (E) *Adequate* is less than *superb*, as *content* is less than *elated.*
7 (D) One who is dishonest is not forthright, just as one who is agitated is not dispassionate.
8 (A) A hero is generally characterized as brave, just as a swindler is generally characterized as reprehensible. However, an actor may or may not be talented; a pond may or may not be stagnant, and so on.

Answers *(continued)*

9 (B) Someone who is *greedy* is *avaricious,* just as something that is *alien* is *foreign.*

10 (C) Something *amorphous* is "without form," just as something that is *infallible* is "without error."

11 (C) *Refrain (from),* meaning "stop," most logically completes the sentence.

12 (E) *Camaraderie,* meaning "friendship," and *endured,* meaning "lasted," most logically complete the sentence.

13 (A) *Retained,* meaning "hired," and *incriminating,* meaning "implicating," most logically complete the sentence.

14 (B) *Emulate,* meaning "imitate," most logically completes the sentence.

15 (C) *Novice,* meaning "beginner," most logically completes the sentence.

16 (D) *Reconciliation,* meaning "agreement," and *contentious,* meaning "hostile" or "antagonistic" most logically complete the sentence.

9 ALIEN : FOREIGN ::

(A) key : unlock
(B) greedy : avaricious
(C) telephone : dial
(D) money : earnings
(E) poisonous : drinkable

10 INFALLIBLE : ERROR ::

(A) illusory : deception
(B) belligerent : temperament
(C) amorphous : form
(D) indecisive : responsibility
(E) tranquil : thought

For questions 11–16, choose the word of group of words that best completes each sentence.

11 After Tony's bypass surgery, the doctor ordered him to __ from eating fatty foods.

(A) circumvent
(B) discern
(C) refrain
(D) indulge
(E) satiate

12 The friendship between Savannah and Kristen while living overseas began a __ that __ many years after their tour of duty.

(A) resistance; concluded
(B) patronage; subsided
(C) dependency; resolved
(D) collaboration; toiled
(E) camaraderie; endured

13 Hoping to discredit the witness, the prosecutor __ the services of a private detective to find __ evidence.

(A) retained; incriminating
(B) deposed; veritable
(C) invoked; tenable
(D) conceived; auspicious
(E) affiliated; categorical

14 Many young authors try unsuccessfully to __ Hemingway's writing style.

(A) critique
(B) emulate
(C) canonize
(D) interrogate
(E) exacerbate

15 Sean had an excuse for misreading his lines; he was a __ in the theater.

(A) prodigy
(B) pundit
(C) novice
(D) disciple
(E) veteran

16 Even as the peace talks began, there was little hope of __ between the two __ countries.

(A) vacillation; neighboring
(B) negotiation; amicable
(C) antagonism; conservative
(D) reconciliation; contentious
(E) accomplishment; fortuitous

Writing Skills

Grammar and Usage

Follow the directions for each section. Mark the letter of your answer on a bubble sheet if your teacher provides one; otherwise, number from 1 to 6 on a separate sheet of paper, and write the letter of the correct answer next to each number.

Read the passage and choose the word or group of words that belongs in each space.

When McNeal woke up, he went down to the river. All the others (1) in their tents. Last night's dinner could not satisfy the growing boy's hunger, so he (2) to take care of breakfast himself. He never really thought of fish as a breakfast food, but his ideas (3) .

1 **A** is sleeping
B were sleeping
C will sleep
D will be sleeping

2 **A** would decide
B decides
C decided
D could decide

3 **A** have changed
B are changing
C will change
D were changing

Read the passage and decide which type of error, if any, appears in each underlined section.

(4) The Oak Bend Community Center had scheduled its meeting for memorial day. (5) Families were planning vacations, and requested that the date be changed. (6) Some members were not willing to be flexable, whereas others were happy to comply.

4 **A** Spelling error
B Capitalization error
C Punctuation error
D No error

5 **A** Spelling error
B Capitalization error
C Punctuation error
D No error

6 **A** Spelling error
B Capitalization error
C Punctuation error
D No error

Correlations to Standardized Tests

The writing skills practice items on this page correspond to the following standardized test section:

ACT English: Usage/Mechanics

Answers

1 (B) *Were sleeping* correctly indicates a continuing action in the past.
2 (C) *Decided* correctly indicates a past action completed in the past.
3 (D) *Were changing* correctly indicates a continuing action in the past.
4 (B) The proper noun *Memorial Day* must be capitalized.
5 (C) No comma is needed between two compound verbs *(were planning and requested).*
6 (A) *Flexible* is misspelled.

Correlations to Standardized Tests

The writing skills practice items on this page correspond to the following standardized test section:

ACT English Usage

Answers

1 (B) A comma is needed following an introductory subordinate clause.

2 (A) No comma is needed between two compound verbs *(weigh* and *measure).*

3 (D)

4 (C) Making a compound subject of *size, beauty, intelligence,* and *mystical songs* best combines the three sentences and eliminates the incorrect singular verb *(is)* following *size* and *beauty.*

5 (B) There is no need to break up this simple question with any internal punctuation.

Writing Skills

Sentence Construction

Read the passage. Choose the best way to write each underlined section. If the underlined section needs no change, choose "Correct as is." Mark the letter of your answer on a bubble sheet if your teacher provides one; otherwise, number from 1 to 5 on a separate sheet of paper, and write the letter of the correct answer next to each number.

When you think of a mammal you usually do not think of aquatic life. (1) However, whales are some of the largest mammals that have ever lived. The blue whale can weigh more than 150 tons, and measure up to 100 feet in length. (2)

We are attracted to whales. (3) Their size and beauty is captivating. So is their intelligence. Their mystical songs are captivating. (4) Why? Do they sing such haunting songs? (5)

1 **A** When you think of a mammal. You usually do not think of aquatic life.
B When you think of a mammal, you usually do not think of aquatic life.
C When you think of a mammal you usually do not think, of aquatic life.
D Correct as is

2 **A** The blue whale can weigh more than 150 tons and measure up to 100 feet in length.
B The blue whale can weigh more than 150 tons; and measures up to 100 feet in length.
C The blue whale can weigh more than 150 tons measuring up to 100 feet in length.
D Correct as is

3 **A** We are attracted. To whales.
B Attracted to whales are we.
C Whales can attract us to them.
D Correct as is

4 **A** Their size and beauty is captivating. So is their intelligence and mystical songs.
B Their size and beauty is captivating. Their intelligence and their mystical songs are captivating.
C Their size, beauty, intelligence, and mystical songs are captivating.
D Correct as is

5 **A** Why do they sing? Such haunting songs!
B Why do they sing such haunting songs?
C Haunting songs; why do they sing them?
D Correct as is

Writing Skills

Revising and Editing

Read the passage written in the style of a student essay. Then answer the questions that follow. Mark the letter of your answer on a bubble sheet if your teacher provides one; otherwise, number from 1 to 6 on a separate sheet of paper, and write the letter of the correct answer next to each number.

[1]Walt Whitman's poetic style had a strong influence on American poetry. [2]His book of poems, *Leaves of Grass,* was most influential, ___ many in his day did not applaud his innovative style. [3]Whitman's poems were political in nature, attacking slavery and celebrated individuality. [4]He also abandoned traditional poetic devices such as rhyme and meter. [5]Whitman was nicknamed the "Good Gray Poet." [6]*Leaves of Grass* was constantly being revised and enlarged by Whitman that grew to 383 poems in its final edition. [7]His collection has become the epitome of individual freedom, and American diversity.

1. Which of the following sentences could be added between Parts 1 and 2?
   A. *Leaves of Grass* contains the well-known poem, "Song of Myself."
   B. Today Whitman is revered as a poetic genius.
   C. Ralph Waldo Emerson, however, was an admirer, claiming Whitman's work to be "the most extraordinary piece of wit and wisdom that America has yet contributed."
   D. Whitman worked as a nurse, teacher, editor, and carpenter.

2. Which of the following changes is needed in the above passage?
   A. Part 1: change had to has
   B. Part 2: delete most
   C. Part 3: change celebrated to celebrating
   D. Part 4: change such as to as if

3. Which of the following draws attention away from the main idea of the paragraph?
   A. Part 3 C. Part 6
   B. Part 5 D. Part 7

4. Which word or phrase would, if inserted into the blank, help the reader understand the sequence of the writer's ideas?
   A. eventually
   B. nevertheless
   C. in addition
   D. although

5. Which of the following contains a misplaced modifier?
   A. Part 6 C. Part 4
   B. Part 5 D. Part 2

6. Which of the following should have a comma deleted?
   A. Part 1 C. Part 3
   B. Part 2 D. Part 7

Correlations to Standardized Tests

The writing skills practice items on these two pages correspond to the following standardized test section:

ACT English: Usage; Rhetorical Skills

Answers

1 (B) This sentence continues the idea of Whitman's influence on American poetry.
2 (C) *Celebrating* is needed to parallel *attacking*.
3 (C) Whitman's nickname has nothing to do with his poetry, which is the focus of the passage.
4 (B)The word *although* correctly signals a contrasting idea.
5 (D) *That* should be changed to *which* and moved to follow *Grass.* *(Leaves of Grass,* which was constantly being revised and enlarged by Whitman, grew . . .)
6 (D) No comma is needed when there are only two items in a series.

Answers (continued)

7 (A) This statement continues the idea of expressing individuality.

8 (B) A comma is needed following an introductory subordinate clause.

9 (D) The *constraints* refer to the *budget;* therefore, Part 10 should follow Part 11.

10 (D) The transition word *then* more logically follows "First." *Finally* would be used for the last three or more points being made.

11 (B) *Specified* should replace the incorrect "specificated."

12 (C) "This" has no clear antecedent and should be replaced by something more specific—"Budget considerations," for example.

Test Practice Bank

Read the following passage written in the style of a magazine article. Then answer the questions that follow. Mark the letter of your answer on a bubble sheet if your teacher provides one; otherwise, number from 7 to 12 on a separate sheet of paper, and write the letter of the correct answer next to each number.

8 Many people dream of building their own house, creating an expression of individuality. 9 However, until you begin the construction process you are blind to the limits and costs placed on artistic expression.

10 This of course can impose many constraints. 11 First, you must consider how your budget will accommodate the "ideal" house. 12 Finally, you must decide on details that you had no idea existed. 13 For example, you specificated solid oak doors for each inside door. 14 But what about the handles and hardware? 15 Why should you have to decide about minute details such as these?

7. Which of the following sentences could be added between Parts 8 and 9?
   A. A home is a reflection of who we are and how we live.
   B. Some houses have absolutely no personality.
   C. Individuality can be an expensive statement.
   D. Some people prefer leasing a house over buying or building.

8. Which of the following changes is needed in the above passage?
   A. Part 8: delete comma after house.
   B. Part 9: Add comma after process.
   C. Part 13: Replace comma after example with a semicolon.
   D. Part 14: Add a comma after handles.

9. Which of the following changes would make the sequence of ideas in the second paragraph clearer?
   A. Place Part 15 before 13.
   B. Reverse the order of Parts 13 and 14.
   C. Delete Part 11.
   D. Reverse the order of Parts 10 and 11.

10. Which of the following changes is needed in the second paragraph?
    A. Part 11: Delete ideal.
    B. Part 12: Change Finally to Then.
    C. Part 14: Delete But.
    D. Part 15: Move such before minute.

11. Which of the following parts uses an incorrect verb form?
    A. Part 9
    B. Part 10
    C. Part 13
    D. Part 15

12. In which part should the underlined word be replaced by a more precise word?
    A. Part 9
    B. Part 10
    C. Part 12
    D. Part 13

Writing Sample

In this section, you are required to write an essay of between 300 and 600 words on one of the writing topics that appear on this page. You should expect to spend approximately 60 minutes on your writing sample. During this time, you should organize your ideas, write a rough draft, and proofread and revise your draft essay.

Because of increasing numbers of underage smokers, state legislators are proposing that driving licenses of minors who are caught smoking be revoked. The goal is to reduce the number of teen smokers and promote a healthy lifestyle.

Your purpose is to write an essay, to be read by your state representative, in which you approve or disapprove of the proposed legislation. Be sure to defend your position with logical arguments and appropriate examples.

Many school districts have imposed strict dress codes for their students. Some parents and students believe that doing so violates their First Amendment rights. Others believe that a strict dress code improves students' behavior and self-esteem and enhances their learning ability.

Your purpose is to write a letter to your school board defending your position on this issue. Be sure to defend your position with logical arguments and appropriate examples.

You and four of your classmates have been chosen as candidates to take a trip to Europe with other students throughout the United States. Only one student from each school may go. How would you persuade the judges that you should be the one selected to represent your school on this trip.

Your purpose is to write an essay, to be read by your classroom instructor, in which you make a case in favor of your being chosen to represent your school. Be sure to defend your position with logical arguments and appropriate examples.

Because of increased violence and strong language on television, programs are now required to have ratings. Do you think this is an effective safeguard for young children watching television?

Your purpose is to write an essay, to be read by your classroom instructor, in which you take a position on whether or not you believe the new program ratings will safeguard young children. Be sure to defend your position with logical arguments and appropriate examples.

Rubric for Writing Tasks

0	1	2	3	4
Off topic Blank paper Foreign language Illegible, incoherent Not enough content to score	Incorrect purpose, mode, or audience Brief, vague Unelaborated Rambling Lack of language control Poor organization	Correct purpose, mode, audience Some elaboration Some details Gaps in organization Limited language control	Correct purpose, mode, audience Moderately well elaborated Clear, effective language Organized (perhaps with brief digressions)	Correct purpose, mode, audience Effective elaboration Consistent organization Sense of completeness, fluency

GLOSSARY

abeyance (ə bā´ əns) *n.*: Temporary suspension
ablutions (ab lo͞o´ shənz) *n.*: Washing or cleansing the body as part of a religious rite
abundance (ə bun´ dəns) *n.*: A great supply; more than enough
abyss (ə bis´) *n.*: Bottomless gulf; immeasurable depth
acquiesce (ak´ wē es´) *v.*: Agree without protest
admonitory (ad män´ i tôr´ ē) *adj.*: Warning
adversary (ad´ vər ser´ ē) *n.*: Opponent; enemy
affliction (ə flik´ shən) *n.*: Something causing pain or suffering
aggregation (ag´ grə gā´ shən) *n.*: Group or mass of distinct objects or individuals
aggrieved (ə grēvd´) *adj.*: Offended; wronged
agues (ā´ gyo͞oz) *n.*: Fits of shivering
alacrity (ə lak´ rə tē) *n.*: Speed
alliance (ə lī´əns) *n.*: Union of nations for a specific purpose
anarchy (an´ ər kē) *n.*: Absence of government
anathema (ə nath´ ə mə) *n.*: Curse
anomalous (ə näm´ ə ləs) *adj*: Abnormal
antagonism (an tag´ ə niz´ əm) *n.*: Hostility
apparition (ap´ ə rish´ ən) *n.*: The act of appearing or becoming visible
appellation (ap´ ə lā´ shən) *n.*: Name or title
apprised (ə prīzd´) *v.*: Informed; notified
arduous (är´ jo͞o wəs) *adj.*: Difficult
arrested (ə rest´ id) *adj.*: Stopped
artifice (ärt´ ə fis) *n.*: Artful trickery
aspiration (as´pə rā´shən) *n.*: Strong ambition
asylum (ə sī´ ləm) *n.*: Place of refuge
audaciously (ô dā´ shəs lē) *adv.*: Boldly or daringly
autonomous (ô tän´ ə məs) *adj.*: Independent
avarice (av´ ər is) *n.*: Greed for riches
aversion (ə vʉr´ zhən) *n.*: Object arousing an intense or definite dislike
avuncular (ə vuŋ´ kyo͞o lər) *adj.*: Having traits considered typical of uncles: jolly, indulgent, stodgy
bastions (bas´ chənz) *n.*: Fortifications
bayou (bī´ o͞o) *n.*: Sluggish, marshy inlet
beguile (bē gīl´) *v.*: Charm or delight
bellicose (bel´ ə kōs) *adj.*: Quarrelsome
benevolent (bə nev´ ə lənt) *adj.*: Kindly; charitable
bivouac (biv´ wak) *n.*: Temporary encampment
blaspheming (blas fēm´ iŋ) *v.*: Cursing
blithe (blīth) *adj.*: Carefree
brazenness (brā´ zən nis) *n.*: Shamelessness; boldness; impudence
brutal (bro͞ot´əl) *adj.*: Cruel and without feeling; savage; violent
buck (bək) *n.*: Male animal, especially a male deer
cacophony (kə käf´ ə nē) *n.*: Harsh, jarring sound
caper (kā´ pər) *n.*: Prank
capitulate (kə pich´ ə lāt´) *v.*: Surrender conditionally
celestial (sə les´ chəl) *adj.*: Of the heavens
chaos (kā´ äs) *n.*: Disorder of formless matter and infinite space, supposed to have existed before the ordered universe
circumspection (sʉr´ kəm spekt´ shən) *n.*: Cautiousness; prudence
claustrophobia (klôs´ trə fō´ bē ə) *n.*: Fear of being in a confined space
commiseration (kə miz´ ər ā´ shən) *n.*: Sympathy; condolence
compunctions (kəm puŋk´ shənz) *n.*: Anxieties; regrets
conceits (kən sētz´) *n.*: Strange or fanciful ideas
confederate (kən fed´ ər it) *adj.*: United with others for a common purpose
conflagration (kän´ flə grā´ shən) *n.*: Big, destructive fire
congealed (kən jēld´) *v.*: Thickened or solidified
congenial (kən jēn´ yəl) *adj.*: Agreeable
conjectural (kən jek´ chər əl) *adj.*: Based on guesswork
conjectured (kən jek´ chərd) *v.*: Guessed
connate (kän āt´) *adj.*: Existing naturally; innate
consanguinity (kän´ saŋ gwin´ ə tē) *n.*: Kinship
consecrate (kän´ sə krāt´) *v.*: Cause to be revered or honored
conspicuous (kən spik´ yo͞o əs) *adj.*: Obvious; easy to see or perceive
consternation (kän´ stər nā´ shən) *n.*: Great fear or shock that makes one feel helpless or bewildered
contingent (kən tin´ jənt) *adj.*: Unpredictable; accidental; dependent on
contrition (kən trish´ ən) *n.*: Remorse for having done wrong
copious (kō´ pē əs) *adj.*: Plentiful; abundant
cornice (kôr´ nis) *n.*: Projecting decorative molding along the top of a building
cosmopolitan (käz´ mə päl´ ə tən) *adj.*: Common to or representative of all or many parts of the world
countenance (koun´ tə nəns) *v.*: Approve; tolerate
covertly (kō vərt´ lē) *adv.*: Secretly; surreptitiously
craven (krā´ vən) *adj.*: Very cowardly
crux (kruks) *n.*: Essential point
cunning (kun´ iŋ) *adj.*: Skillful in deception; crafty; sly
deference (def´ ər əns) *n.*: Respect; courtesy; regard
defiance (dē fī´ əns) *n.*: Act of defying authority or opposition; open, bold resistance
degenerate (dē jen´ ər it) *adj.*: Morally corrupt
deliberation (di lib´ ə rā´ shən) *n.*: Careful consideration
demarcation (dē´ mär kā´ shən) *n.*: Separation
depravity (di prav´ ə tē) *n.*: Corruption; wickedness
deprecated (dep´ rə kāt´ id) *v.*: Expressed disapproval of; pleaded against
depredations (dep´ rə dā´ shənz) *n.*: Acts of robbing or plundering
derivative (də riv´ ə tiv) *adj.*: Not original; based on something else
despotic (de spät´ ik) *adj.*: Harsh; cruel; unjust
despotism (des´ pət iz´ əm) *n.*: Government by absolute rule; tyranny
dictum (dik´ təm) *n.*: Formal statement of fact or opinion
digress (dī gres´) *v.*: Depart temporarily from the main subject
dilapidated (di lap´ ə dā tid) *adj.*: In disrepair
discern (di sʉrn´) *v.*: Receive or recognize; make out clearly
disdainfully (dis dān´ fəl ē) *adv.*: Showing scorn or contempt
dispatched (dis pacht´) *v.*: Sent off on a specific assignment
disposition (dis´ pə zish´ ən) *n.*: An inclination or tendency
distillery (dis til´ ə rē) *n.*: Place where alcoholic liquors are distilled
divines (də vīnz´) *n.*: Clergy
dogma (dôg´ mə) *n.*: Formalized and authoritative doctrines or beliefs
dolorous (dō´ lər əs) *adj.*: Sad; mournful
dominion (də min´ yən) *n.*: Power to rule
dusky (dus´ kē) *adj.*: Dim; shadowy
dyspepsia (dis pep´ shə) *n.*: Indigestion
efface (ə fās´) *v.*: Erase; wipe out
effaced (ə fāsd´) *adj.*: Erased; wiped out
effuse (e fyo͞oz´) *v.*: Spread out; diffuse
elusive (ē lo͞o´ siv) *adj.*: Hard to grasp
embankment (em bangk´ mənt) *n.*: A mound of earth or stone built to hold back water or support a roadway
emigrants (em´ i grəntz) *n.*: People who leave one area to move to another
eminence (em´ ə nəns) *n.*: Greatness; celebrity
engrossed (in grōst´) *adj.*: Occupied wholly; absorbed
entreated (en trēt´ id) *v.*: Begged; pleaded
epitaph (ep´ ə taf) *n.*: Inscription on a tombstone or grave marker
equanimity (ek´ wə nim ə tē) *n.*: Composure
equivocal (i kwiv´ ə kəl) *adj*: Having more than one possible interpretation; uncertain
eradicate (e rad´ i kāt´) *v.*: Get rid of; wipe out; destroy
etiquette (et´ i kit) *n.*: Appropriate behavior and ceremonies
evitable (ev´ ə tə bəl) *adj.*: Avoidable
exalted (eg zôlt´ id) *adj.*: Filled with joy or pride; elated
excavated (eks´ kə vā tid) *v.*: Dug out; made a hole

expatriated (eks pā′ trē āt′ id) *adj.*: Deported; driven from one's native land
expedient (ik spē′ dē ənt) *n.*: Resource
expended (ek spend′ id) *v.*: To have spent or used by consuming
exquisite (eks′ kwi zit) *adj.*: Very beautiful; delicate; carefully wrought
extort (eks tôrt′) *v.*: To obtain by threat or violence
extricate (eks′ trə kāt′) *v.*: Set free
fallowness (fal′ ō nis) *n.*: Inactivity
fasting (fast′ iŋ) *v.*: Eating very little or nothing
feigned (fānd) *v.*: Pretended; faked
felicity (fə lis′ ə tē) *n.*: Happiness; bliss
filigree (fil′ i grē′) *adj.*: Resembling delicate, lacelike ornamental work of intertwined gold or silver wires
finite (fī′ nīt) *adj.*: Having measurable or definable limits
flagrant (flā′ grənt) *adj.*: Glaring; outrageous
foppery (fäp′ ər ē) *n.*: Foolishness
foreboding (fôr bōd′ iŋ) *n.*: Presentiment
foreknowledge (fôr′ näl′ ij) *n.*: Awareness of something before it happens or exists
forestall (fôr stôl′) *v.*: Prevent by acting ahead of time
fortuitous (fôr to͞o′ ə təs) *adj.*: Fortunate
frippery (frip′ ər ē) *n.*: Showy display of elegance
galvanic (gal van′ ik) *adj.*: Startling; stimulating as if by electric current
garrulous (gar′ ə ləs) *adj.*: Talking too much
genial (jēn′ yəl) *adj.*: Cheerful; friendly
geography (jē ôg′ rə fē) *n.*: The study of the surface of the Earth
glade (glād) *n.*: Open space in a wood or forest
glean (glēn) *v.*: Collect the remaining grain after reaping
gloaming (glō′ miŋ) *n.*: Evening dusk; twilight
grave (grāv) *adj.*: Serious; solemn
gregarious (grə ger′ ē əs) *adj.*: Sociable
guile (gīl) *n.*: Craftiness
hallow (hal′ ō) *v.*: Honor as sacred
heirs (erz) *n.*: People who carry on the tradition of predecessors
hovel (huv′ əl) *n.:* Low, open storage shed; hut
immersed (im murst′) *v.*: Plunged or completely submerged
impelled (im peld′) *v.*: Moved; forced
imperially (im pir′ ē əl ē) *adv.*: Majestically
imperious (im pir′ ē əs) *adj.:* Urgent; imperative
impertinent (im pur′ tən ənt) *adj.*: Not showing proper respect
impious (im′ pē əs) *adj.*: Lacking reverence for God
importunate (im pôr′ chə nit) *adj.*: Insistent
importunities (im′ pôr to͞on′ ə tēz) *n.*: Persistent requests or demands
imprecations (im′ prə kā′ shənz) *n.*: Curses
improvident (im präv′ ə dənt) *adj.*: Short-sighted; failing to provide for the future
inappeasable (in′ ə pē′ zə bəl) *adj.*: Unable to be quieted or calmed
increment (in′ krə mənt) *n.*: Increase, as in a series
indecorous (in dek′ ər əs) *adj.*: Improper
indications (in′ di kā′ shənz) *n.*: Signs; things that point out or signify
ineffable (in ef′ ə bəl) *adj.*: Inexpressible; unable to be spoken
inert (in urt′) *adj.*: Motionless
infallibility (in fal′ ə bil′ ə tē) *n.*: Inability to be wrong; reliability
infidel (in′ fə dəl) *n.*: A person who holds no religious belief
infinity (in fin′ i tē) *n.*: Endless or unlimited space, time, or distance
iniquity (in ik′ wə tē) *n.*: Sin
insatiable (in sā′ shə bəl) *adj.*: Constantly wanting more; unable to be satisfied
inscrutable (in skro͞ot′ ə bəl) *adj.*: Not able to be easily understood
insidious (in sid′ ē əs) *adj.*: Secretly treacherous
insurgents (in sur′ jənts) *n.*: Rebels; those who revolt against established authority
interminable (in tur′ mi nə bəl) *adj.*: Seeming to last forever
intuitively (in to͞o′ i tiv lē) *adv.*: Instinctively
invalided (in′ və lid′ id) *v.*: Released because of illness or disability
invective (in vek′ tiv) *n.*: Verbal attack; strong criticism
invoke (in vōk′) *v.*: Call on for help, inspiration, or support
jettisoned (jet′ ə sənd) *v.*: Thrown overboard to lighten the weight of a ship
jocularity (jäk′ yə lar′ ə tē) *n.*: Joking good humor
jubilant (jo͞o′ bəl ənt) *adj.*: Joyful and triumphant
labyrinth (lab′ə rinth′) *n.*: Intricate network of winding passages; maze
liberty (lib′ ər tē) *n.*: The condition of being free from control by others
limber (lim′ bər) *adj.*: Flexible
literalists (lit′ ər əl ists) *n.*: People who insist on taking words at their exact meaning
loath (lōth) *adj.*: Reluctant; unwilling
loathsome (lōth′ səm) *adj.*: Hateful; detestable
lulled (luld) *v.*: Calmed or soothed by a gentle sound or motion
luminary (lo͞o′ mə ner′ ē) *adj.*: Giving off light
magnanimity (mag′ nə nim′ ə tē) *n.*: Ability to rise above pettiness or meanness
malaise (ma lāz′) *n.*: Decline or slump
maledictions (mal′ ə dik′ shənz) *n.*: Curses
malevolence (mə lev′ ə ləns) *n.*: Malice; spitefulness
malevolent (mə lev′ ə lənt) *adj.*: Mean-spirited; showing ill will
malice (mal′ is) *n.*: Ill will; spite
malign (mə līn′) *adj.*: Malicious; very harmful
malingered (mə liŋ′ gərd) *v.*: Escaped work or duty by pretending to be ill
malingers (mə liŋ′ gərz) *v.*: Pretends to be ill
manifest (man′ ə fest′) *adj.*: Evident; obvious; clear
manifold (man′ ə fōld′) *adv.*: In many ways
manuscript (man′ yo͞o skript′) *n.*: Written or typed document, especially one submitted to a publisher or printer
meticulous (mə tik′ yo͞o ləs) *adj.*: Extremely careful about details
moiling (moi′ liŋ) *v.*: Churning; swirling
mollified (mäl′ ə fīd′) *v.*: Soothed; calmed
monotonous (mə nät′ ən əs) *adj.*: Tiresome because unvarying
monotony (mə nät′ ən ē) *n.*: Tiresome, unchanging sameness; lack of variety
mortality (môr tal′ ə tē) *n.*: Death on a large scale, as from disease or war
motives (mōt′ ivz) *n.*: Reasons for action; inner drives
multifarious (mul′ tə far′ ē əs) *adj.*: Having many parts or elements; diverse
multitudinous (mul′ tə to͞od′ ən əs) *adj.*: Numerous
mundane (mun dān′) *adj.*: Commonplace; ordinary
munificent (myo͞o nif′ ə sənt) *adj*: Generous
myriad (mir′ ē əd) *adj.*: Countless
negligence (neg′ li jəns) *n.*: An instance of failure, carelessness, or indifference
nonplused (nän′ plüsd′) *adj.*: Bewildered; perplexed
obeisance (ō bā′ səns) *n.*: Gesture of respect
obliterated (ə blit′ ər āt′ id) *v.*: Blotted out; destroyed
obstinacy (äb′ stə nə sē) *n.*: Stubbornness
obstinate (äb′ stə nit) *adj.*: Stubborn
obtuse (äb to͞os′) *adj.*: Slow to understand or perceive
ominous (äm′ ə nəs) *adj.*: Threatening
omnipotent (äm nip′ ə tənt) *adj.*: All-powerful
oppressed (ə prest′) *v.*: Kept down by cruel or unjust power or authority
oppresses (ə pres′ əz) *v.*: Weighs heavily on the mind
ornery (ôr′ nər ē) *adj.*: Having a mean disposition
oscillation (äs′ ə lā′ shən) *n.*: Act of swinging or moving regularly back and forth
ostentation (äs′ tən tā′ shən) *n.*: Boastful display
ostentatious (äs′ tən tā′ shəs) *adj*: Intended to attract notice
pacify (pas′ ə fī′) *v.*: Calm; soothe
palisades (pal′ə sādz′) *n.*: Large, pointed stakes set in the ground to form a fence used for defense
pall (pôl) *n.*: Cloth used to cover a coffin
palpable (pal′ pə bəl) *adj.*: Able to be touched, felt, or handled
paranoia (par′ ə noi′ ə) *n.*: Mental disorder characterized by delusions, especially of persecution
parsimony (pär′ sə mō′ nē) *n.*: Stinginess
patriarch (pā′ trē ärk′) *n.*: The father and ruler of a family or tribe
pensive (pen′ siv) *adj.*: Thinking deeply or seriously
penury (pen′ yə rē) *n.*: Lack of money, property, or necessities
perdition (pər dish′ ən) *n.*: Complete and irreparable loss; ruin
peremptorily (pər emp′ tər ə lē) *adj.*: Decisively; commandingly
perfidy (pur′ fə dē) *n.*: Betrayal of trust

peril (per´ əl) *n.*: Danger
persevere (pʉr sə vir´) *v.*: Persist; be steadfast in purpose
pertinaciously (pʉr´ tə nā´ shəs lē) *adv.*: Holding firmly to some purpose
pervading (pər vād´ iŋ) *adj.*: Spreading throughout
pestilential (pes´ tə len´ shəl) *adj.*: Likely to cause disease
piety (pī´ ə tē) *n.*: Devotion to religious duties
pilfer (pil´ fər) *v.*: Steal
pittance (pit´ əns) *n.*: Meager wage or remuneration
placid (plas´ id) *adj.*: Tranquil; calm; quiet
poignant (poin´ yənt) *adj.*: Sharply painful to the feelings
poise (poiz) *n.*: Balance; stability
polemics (pō lem´ iks) *n.*: Controversial arguments; branch of theology devoted to refuting errors
posterity (päs ter´ ə tē) *n.*: All succeeding generations
precipitate (prē sip´ ə tāt´) *v.*: Cause to happen before expected or desired
prelude (prel´ yōōd) *n.*: Introductory section or movement of a suite, fugue, or work of music
preposterous (pri päs´ tər əs) *adj.*: Ridiculous
prescient (presh´ ənt) *adj.*: Having foreknowledge
privations (prī vā´ shənz) *n.*: Loss of things previously possessed
prodigious (prə dij´ əs) *adj.*: Of great power or size
profundity (prō fun´ də tē) *n.*: Intellectual depth
profusion (prō fyōō´ zhən) *n.*: Abundance; rich supply
propitious (prō pish´ əs) *adj.*: Favorably inclined or disposed
protruded (prō trōōd´ id) *v.*: Jutted out
psychology (sī käl´ ə jē) *n.*: The science dealing with the mind and with mental and emotional processes
pugilistic (pyōō´ jə lis´ tik) *adj.*: Looking for a fight
purported (pʉr pôrt´ id) *adj.*: Supposed
querulous (kwer´ ə ləs) *adj.*: Inclined to find fault
radiant (rā´ dē ənt) *adj.*: Shining brightly
reaping (rēp´ iŋ) *v.*: Cutting or harvesting grain from a field
recompense (rek´ əm pens´) *n.*: Reward; repayment
recumbent (ri kum´ bənt) *adj.*: Resting
redolence (red´ əl əns) *n.*: Scent; smell
redolent (red´ əl ənt) *adj.*: Suggestive
redress (ri´ dres) *n.*: Atonement; rectification
refluent (ref´ lōō ənt) *adj.*: Flowing back
refulgent (ri ful´ jənt) *adj.*: Radiant; shining
reiterate (rē it´ ə rāt´) *v.*: Repeat or state over again
repose (ri pōz´) *n.*: State of being at rest
repression (ri presh´ ən) *n.*: Restraint
retrospective (re trə spek´ tiv) *adj.*: Looking back on or directed to the past
reverential (rev´ ə ren´ shəl) *adj.*: Showing or caused by a feeling of deep respect, love, and awe
rudiments (rōō´ də mənts) *n.*: Fundamental skills
rueful (rōō´ fəl) *adj.*: Feeling or showing sorrow or pity
sagacious (sə gā´ shəs) *adj.*: Shrewd
salient (sāl´ yənt) *adj.*: Standing out from the rest
sallow (sal´ ō) *adj.*: Sickly; pale yellow
salutary (sal´ yōō ter´ ē) *adj.*: Beneficial; promoting a good purpose
scepter (sep´ tər) *n.*: A rod or staff held by rulers as a symbol of sovereignty
scintillating (sint´ əl āt´ iŋ) *adj.*: Sparkling
scourge (skʉrj) *n.*: Cause of serious trouble or affliction
scrabbling (skrab´ liŋ) *v.*: Scrambling
semi-somnambulant (sem´ i säm nam´ byōō lənt) *adj.*: Half-sleepwalking
sentience (sen´ shəns) *n.*: Capacity of feeling
sepulcher (sep´əl kər) *n.*: Grave; tomb
serenity (sə ren´ ə tē) *n.*: Calmness
sinuous (sin´ yōō wəs) *adj.*: Moving in and out; wavy
slovenly (sluv´ ən lē) *adj.*: Untidy
smite (smīt) *v.*: To kill by a powerful blow
somnolent (säm´ nə lənt) *adj.*: Sleepy; drowsy
specious (spē´ shəs) *adj.*: Seeming to be good or sound without actually being so
squander (skwän´ dər) *v.*: Spend or use wastefully
stark (stärk) *adj.*: Stiff or rigid, as a corpse; severe
statistics (stə tis´ tiks) *n.*: The science of collecting and arranging facts about a particular subject in the form of numbers
stringency (strin´ jən sē) *n.*: Strictness; severity
subjugation (sub´ jə gā´ shən) *n.*: The act of conquering
sublime (sə blīm´) *adj.*: Inspiring awe or admiration through grandeur or beauty
subsistence (səb sis´ təns) *n.*: Means of support
subterranean (sub´ tə rā´nē ən) *adj.*: Underground
suffice (sə fīs´) *v.*: Be adequate; meet the needs of
suffrage (suf´ rij) *n.*: Vote or voting
sullen (sul´ ən) *adj.*: Sulky; glum
summarily (sə mer´ ə lē) *adv.*: Promptly and without formality
sundry (sun´ drē) *adj.*: Various; different
superfluous (soo pʉr´ flōō wəs) *adj.*: Excessive; not necessary
superseding (sōō´ pər sēd´ iŋ) *v.*: Overriding; making outmoded
surmised (sər mīzd´) *v.*: Guessed
swag (swag) *n.*: Suspended cluster of branches
switch (swich) *n.*: Slender, flexible twig or whip
tempest (tem´ pist) *n.*: Violent storm
tempo (tem´ pō) *n.*: Rate of activity of a sound or motion; pace
terra firma (ter´ ə fʉr´ mə) *n.*: Firm earth; solid ground (Latin)
timorous (tim´ ər əs) *adj.*: Full of fear
trajectory (trə jek´ tə rē) *n.*: The curved path of an object hurtling through space
transient (tran´ zē ənt) *adj.*: Not permanent
tremulous (trem´ yōō ləs) *adj.*: Characterized by trembling
tremulously (trem´ yōō ləs lē) *adv.*: Fearfully; timidly
tumultuous (tōō mult´ chōō wəs) *adj.*: Rough; stormy
tumultuously (tōō mul´ chōō wəs lē) *adv.*: In an agitated way
tyranny (tir´ ə nē) *n.*: Oppressive and unjust government
unalienable (un āl´ yən ə bəl) *adj.*: Not to be taken away
unanimity (yōō´ nə nim´ ə tē) *n.*: Complete agreement
untoward (un tō´ ərd) *adj.*: Inappropriate or improper
unwonted (un wän´ tid) *adj.*: Unusual; unfamiliar
usurers (yōō´ zhōō rərz) *n.*: Moneylenders who charge very high interest
usurpations (yōō´ sər pā´ shənz) *n.*: Unlawful seizures of rights or privileges
vagary (və ger´ ē) *n.*: Unpredictable occurrence
venerable (ven´ ər ə bəl) *adj.*: Worthy of respect
vigilance (vij´ ə ləns) *n.*: Watchfulness
vigilant (vij´ ə lənt) *adj.*: Alert to danger
visage (viz´ ij) *n.*: Appearance
vitality (vī tal´ ə tē) *n.*: Power to endure or survive; life force
vituperative (vī tōō´ pər ə tiv) *adj.*: Spoken abusively
vociferation (vō sif´ ər ā´ shən) *n.*: Loud or vehement shouting
voluminous (və lōōm´ ə nəs) *adj.*: Of enough material to fill volumes
waggery (wag´ ər ē) *n.*: Mischievous humor
wanton (wän´ tən) *adj.*: Senseless; unjustified

Literary Terms Handbook

ALLEGORY An *allegory* is a story or tale with two or more levels of meaning—a literal level and one or more symbolic levels. The events, setting, and characters in an allegory are symbols for ideas or qualities. Many of Nathaniel Hawthorne's short stories, such as "The Minister's Black Veil," on page 318, are allegories.

ALLITERATION *Alliteration* is the repetition of consonant sounds at the beginning of words or accented syllables. Sara Teasdale uses alliteration in the second stanza of her poem "Understanding":

> But you I never understood,
> Your spirit's secret hides like gold
> Sunk in a Spanish galleon
> Ages ago in water cold.

Poets and other writers use alliteration to link and to emphasize ideas as well as to create pleasing, musical sounds.

ALLUSION An *allusion* is a reference to a well-known person, place, event, literary work, or work of art. Writers often make allusions to stories from the Bible, to Greek and Roman myths, to plays by Shakespeare, to political and historical events, and to other materials with which they can expect their readers to be familiar. In "The Love Song of J. Alfred Prufrock," on page 647, T. S. Eliot alludes to, among other things, Dante's *Inferno*, Italian artist Michelangelo, Shakespeare's *Hamlet*, and to several incidents and people from the Bible. By using allusions, writers can bring to mind complex ideas simply and easily.

ALMANAC An *almanac* is a magazine or book, published monthly, seasonally, or yearly, that contains weather forecasts, tide tables, important dates, lists of upcoming events, statistics, and other information of use or interest to readers. The selection on page 188 is from *Poor Richard's Almanack* by Benjamin Franklin. Franklin's almanac is famous for its humorous and wise sayings.

ANECDOTE An *anecdote* is a brief story about an interesting, amusing, or strange event. An anecdote is told to entertain or to make a point. In the excerpt from *Life on the Mississippi*, on page 520, Mark Twain tells several anecdotes about his experiences on the Mississippi River.

ANTAGONIST An *antagonist* is a character or force in conflict with a main character, or protagonist. In Jack London's "To Build a Fire," on page 556, the antagonist is neither a person nor an animal but is rather the extreme cold of the Yukon. Not all stories contain antagonists. However, in many stories the conflict between the antagonist and the protagonist is the basis for the plot.

See also Conflict, Plot, *and* Protagonist.

APHORISM An *aphorism* is a general truth or observation about life, usually stated concisely and pointedly. Often witty and wise, aphorisms appear in many kinds of works. An essay writer may have an aphoristic style, making many such statements. Ralph Waldo Emerson was famous for his aphoristic style. His essay entitled "Fate" contains the following aphorisms:

> The book of Nature is the book of Fate.
> Men are what their mothers made them.
> Nature is what you may do.
> So far as a man thinks, he is free.
> A man's fortunes are the fruit of his character.

Used in an essay, an aphorism can be a memorable way to sum up or to reinforce a point or an argument.

APOSTROPHE An *apostrophe* is a figure of speech in which a speaker directly addresses an absent person or a personified quality, object, or idea. Phillis Wheatley uses apostrophe in this line from "To the University of Cambridge, in New England":

> Students, to you 'tis given to scan the heights

Apostrophe is often used in poetry and in speeches to add emotional intensity.

See also Figurative Language.

ASSONANCE *Assonance* is the repetition of vowel sounds in conjunction with dissimilar consonant sounds. Emily Dickinson uses assonance in the line "The mountain at a given distance." The *i* sound is repeated in the words *given* and *distance*, in the context of the dissimilar consonant sounds *g–v* and *d–s*.

ATMOSPHERE See Mood.

AUTOBIOGRAPHY An *autobiography* is a form of nonfiction in which a person tells his or her own life story. Notable examples of autobiographies include those by Benjamin Franklin and Frederick Douglass. *Memoirs*, a first-person account of personally or historically significant events in which the writer was a participant or an eyewitness, are a form of autobiographical writing.

See also Biography *and* Journal.

BALLAD A *ballad* is a songlike poem that tells a story, often one dealing with adventure and romance. Most ballads have the following characteristics:

1. Simple language
2. Four- or six-line stanzas
3. Rhyme
4. Regular meter

A *folk ballad* is one that originated in the oral tradition and was passed by word of mouth from generation to generation. Examples of folk ballads include "Yankee Doodle," "Casey Jones," and "John Henry." A *literary ballad* is one written by a specific person in imitation of the folk ballad. Henry Wadsworth Longfellow's "The Wreck of the Hesperus" is an example of a literary ballad.

BIOGRAPHY A *biography* is a form of nonfiction in which a writer tells the life story of another person. Carl Sandburg's *Abe Lincoln Grows Up* is a famous biography of President Lincoln.

See also Autobiography.

BLANK VERSE *Blank verse* is poetry written in unrhymed iambic pentameter. An iamb is a poetic foot consisting of one weak stress followed by one strong stress. A pentameter line is a line of five poetic feet. Robert Frost's "Birches," on page 804, is written in blank verse.

CHARACTER A character is a person or an animal that takes part in the action of a literary work. The following are some terms used to describe various types of characters:

The *main character* in a literary work is the one on whom the work focuses. *Major characters* in a literary work include the main character and any other characters who play significant roles. A *minor character* is one who does not play a significant role. A *round character* is one who is complex and multi-faceted, like a real person. A *flat character* is one who is one-dimensional. A *dynamic character* is one who changes in the course of a work. A *static character* is one who does not change in the course of a work.

See also Characterization *and* Motivation.

CHARACTERIZATION *Characterization* is the act of creating and developing a character. There are two primary methods of characterization: direct and indirect. In *direct characterization,* a writer simply states a character's traits, as when F. Scott Fitzgerald writes of the main character in his story "Winter Dreams," on page 670, "He wanted not association with glittering things and glittering people—he wanted the glittering things themselves." In *indirect characterization*, character is revealed by one of the following means:

1. By the words, thoughts, or actions of the character
2. By descriptions of the character's appearance or background
3. By what other characters say about the character
4. By the ways in which other characters react to the character

See also Character.

CINQUAIN *See* Stanza.

CLASSICISM *Classicism* is an approach to literature and the other arts that stresses reason, balance, clarity, ideal beauty, and orderly form in imitation of the arts of ancient Greece and Rome. Classicism is often contrasted with *Romanticism*, which stresses imagination, emotion, and individualism. Classicism also differs from *Realism*, which stresses the actual rather than the ideal.

See also Realism *and* Romanticism.

CLIMAX The *climax* is the high point of interest or suspense in a literary work. For example, Jack London's "To Build a Fire," on page 556, reaches its climax when the man realizes that he is going to freeze to death. The climax generally appears near the end of a story, play, or narrative poem.

See also Plot.

CONFLICT A *conflict* is a struggle between opposing forces. Sometimes this struggle is internal, or within a character, as in Bernard Malamud's "The First Seven Years," on page 892. At other times this struggle is external, or between a character and an outside force, as in Jack London's "To Build a Fire," on page 556. Conflict is one of the primary elements of narrative literature because most plots develop from conflicts.

See also Antagonist, Plot, *and* Protagonist.

CONNOTATION A *connotation* is an association that a word calls to mind in addition to the dictionary meaning of the word. Many words that are similar in their dictionary meanings, or denotations, are quite different in their connotations. Consider, for example, José García Villa's line, "Be beautiful, noble, like the antique ant." This line would have a very different effect if it were "Be pretty, classy, like the old ant." Poets and other writers choose their words carefully so that the connotations of those words will be appropriate.

See also Denotation.

CONSONANCE *Consonance* is the repetition of similar final consonant sounds at the ends of words or accented syllables. Emily Dickinson uses consonance in the following lines:

> But if he ask where you are hi*d*
> Until to-morrow,—happy lette*r*!
> Gesture, coquette, and shake your hea*d*!

COUPLET See Stanza.

CRISIS In the plot of a narrative, the *crisis* is the turning point for the protagonist—the point at which the protagonist's situation or understanding changes dramatically. In Bernard Malamud's "The First Seven Years," on page 892, the crisis comes when Feld recognizes that Sobel loves Miriam.

DENOTATION The *denotation* of a word is its objective meaning, independent of other associations that the word brings to mind.

See also Connotation.

DENOUEMENT See Plot.

DESCRIPTION A *description* is a portrayal, in words, of something that can be perceived by the senses. Writers create descriptions by using images, as John Wesley Powell does in the following passage from "The Most Sublime Spectacle on Earth," his description of the Grand Canyon, on page 278:

> When the clouds play in the canyon, as they often do in the rainy season, another set of effects is produced. Clouds creep out of canyons and wind into other canyons. The heavens seem to be alive, not moving as move the heavens over a plain, in one direction with the wind, but following the multiplied courses of these gorges.

Description is one of the major forms of discourse and appears quite often in literary works of all genres.

See also Image.

DEVELOPMENT See Plot.

DIALECT A *dialect* is the form of a language spoken by people in a particular region or group. Every dialect differs from every other dialect in the details of its vocabulary, grammar, and pronunciation. Writers often use dialect to make their characters seem realistic and to create local color. See, for example, Mark Twain's "The Notorious Jumping Frog of Calaveras County," on page 525.

See also Local Color.

DIALOGUE A *dialogue* is a conversation between characters. Writers use dialogue to reveal character, to present events, to add variety to narratives, and to arouse their readers' interest.

See also Drama.

DICTION *Diction* is a writer's or speaker's word choice. Diction is part of a writer's style and may be described as formal or informal, plain or ornate, common or technical, abstract or concrete. In the selection from *The Mortgaged Heart*, on page 994, Carson McCullers uses formal diction suitable to her essay's serious purpose.

See also Style.

DRAMA A *drama* is a story written to be performed by actors. The playwright supplies dialogue for the characters to speak, as well as stage directions that give information about costumes, lighting, scenery, properties, the setting, and the characters' movements and ways of speaking. The audience accepts as believable the many dramatic conventions that are used, such as soliloquies, asides, poetic language, or the passage of time between acts or scenes. An *act* is a major division in a drama. A *scene* is a minor division.

See also Genre.

DRAMATIC MONOLOGUE A *dramatic monologue* is a poem or speech in which an imaginary character speaks to a silent listener. T. S. Eliot's "The Love Song of J. Alfred Prufrock," on page 647, is a dramatic monologue.

See also Dramatic Poem *and* Monologue.

DRAMATIC POEM A *dramatic poem* is one that makes use of the conventions of drama. Such poems may be monologues or dialogues or may present the speech of many characters. Robert Frost's "The Death of the Hired Man" is a famous example of a dramatic poem.

See also Dramatic Monologue.

DYNAMIC CHARACTER See Character.

EPIGRAM An *epigram* is a brief, pointed statement, in prose or in verse, often characterized by use of some rhetorical device or figure of speech. Benjamin Franklin was famous for his epigrams, which include "Fools make feasts, and wise men eat them," and "A plowman on his legs is higher than a gentleman on his knees."

EPIPHANY An *epiphany* is a sudden revelation or flash of insight. The shoemaker in Bernard Malamud's "The First Seven Years," on page 892, experiences an epiphany when he suddenly and thoroughly comprehends that the actions of his apprentice, Sobel, are motivated by his secret love for Miriam.

ESSAY An *essay* is a short nonfiction work about a particular subject. Essays can be classified as *formal* or *informal*, *personal* or *impersonal*. They can also be classified according to purpose, such as *analytical* (see the excerpt from *The Mortgaged Heart* on page 994), *satirical* (see "Coyote v. Acme" on p. 998), or *reflective* (see Amy Tan's "Mother Tongue" on page 1012). Modes of discourse, such as *expository, descriptive, persuasive*, or *narrative*, are other means of classifying essays.

See also Satire, Exposition, Description, Persuasion, *and* Narration.

EXPOSITION *Exposition* is writing or speech that explains, informs, or presents information. The main techniques of expository writing include analysis, classification, comparison and contrast, definition, and exemplification, or illustration. An essay may be primarily expository, as is William Safire's "Onomatopoeia" on page 996, or it may use exposition to support another purpose, such as persuasion or argumentation, as in Ian Frazier's satirical essay "Coyote v. Acme" on page 998.

In a story or play, the exposition is that part of the plot that introduces the characters, the setting, and the basic situation.

See also Plot.

FALLING ACTION See Plot.

FICTION *Fiction* is prose writing that tells about imaginary characters and events. Short stories and novels are works of fiction.

See also Genre, Narrative, Nonfiction, *and* Prose.

FIGURATIVE LANGUAGE *Figurative language* is writing or speech not meant to be taken literally. Writers use figurative language to express ideas in vivid and imaginative ways. For example, Emily Dickinson begins one poem with the following description of snow:

> It sifts from leaden sieves,
> It powders all the wood

By describing the snow as if it were flour, Dickinson renders a precise and compelling picture of it.

See also Figure of Speech.

FIGURE OF SPEECH A *figure of speech* is an expression or a word used imaginatively rather than literally. Many types of figures of speech are used by writers in English, including apostrophe, hyperbole, irony, metaphor, oxymoron, paradox, personification, and simile.

See also Figurative Language. *See also the entries for individual figures of speech.*

FLASHBACK A *flashback* is a section of a literary work that interrupts the chronological presentation of events to relate an event from an earlier time. A writer may present a flashback as a character's memory or recollection, as part of an account or story told by a character, as a dream or a daydream, or simply by having the narrator switch to a time in the past. A flashback occurs in Part II of "An Occurrence at Owl Creek Bridge" on page 468, as the narrator recounts events that took place before those in the story's opening. Writers often use flashbacks as a dramatic way of providing background information.

FLAT CHARACTER See Character.

FOIL A *foil* is a character who provides a contrast to another character. In F. Scott Fitzgerald's "Winter Dreams," on page 670, Irene Scheerer is a foil for the tantalizing Judy Jones.

FOLK LITERATURE *Folk literature* is the body of stories, legends, myths, ballads, songs, riddles, sayings, and other works arising out of the oral traditions of peoples around the globe. The folk literature traditions of the United States, including those of Native Americans and of the American pioneers, are especially rich.

FOOT See Meter.

FORESHADOWING *Foreshadowing* in a literary work is the use of clues to suggest events that have yet to occur.

FREE VERSE *Free verse* is poetry that lacks a regular rhythmical pattern, or meter. A writer of free verse is at liberty to use any rhythms that are appropriate to what he or she is saying. Free verse has been widely used by twentieth-century poets such as Leslie Marmon Silko, who begins "Where Mountain Lion Lay Down With Deer" with these lines:

> I climb the black rock mountain
> stepping from day to day
> silently.

See also Meter.

GENRE A *genre* is a division, or type, of literature. Literature is commonly divided into three major genres: poetry, prose, and drama. Each major genre can in turn be divided into smaller genres. Poetry can be divided into lyric, concrete, dramatic, narrative, and epic poetry. Prose can be divided into fiction (novels and short stories) and nonfiction (biography, autobiography, letters, essays, and reports). Drama can be divided into serious drama, tragedy, comic drama, melodrama, and farce.

See also Drama, Poetry, *and* Prose.

GOTHIC *Gothic* refers to the use of primitive, medieval, wild, or mysterious elements in literature. Gothic elements offended eighteenth-century classical writers but appealed to the Romantic writers who followed them. Gothic novels feature places like mysterious and gloomy castles, where horrifying, supernatural events take place. Their influence on Edgar Allan Poe is evident in "The Fall of the House of Usher," on page 297.

GROTESQUE *Grotesque* refers to the use of bizarre, absurd, or fantastic elements in literature. The grotesque is generally characterized by distortions or striking incongruities. *Grotesque characters*, like those in Flannery O'Connor's "The Life You Save May Be Your Own," on page 879, are characters who have become ludicrous or bizarre through their obsession with an idea or a value or as a result of an emotional problem.

HARLEM RENAISSANCE The *Harlem Renaissance*, which occurred during the 1920's, was a time of African American artistic creativity centered in Harlem, in New York City. Writers of the Harlem Renaissance include Countee Cullen, Claude McKay, Jean Toomer, Langston Hughes, and Arna Bontemps.

HYPERBOLE A *hyperbole* is a deliberate exaggeration or overstatement. In Mark Twain's "The Notorious Jumping Frog of Calaveras County," on page 525, the claim that Jim Smiley would follow a bug as far as Mexico to win a bet is a hyperbole. As this example shows, hyperboles are often used for comic effect.

IAMBIC PENTAMETER *Iambic pentameter* is a line of poetry with five iambic feet, each containing one unstressed syllable followed by one stressed syllable (˘ ´). Iambic pentameter may be rhymed or unrhymed. Unrhymed iambic pentameter is called blank verse. These concluding lines from Anne Bradstreet's "The Author to Her Book" are in iambic pentameter:

> Ănd fór thy̆, Móthĕr, śhe ălás iš póor,
> Whĭch caúsed hĕr thús tŏ sénd theĕ óut
> ŏf dóor.

See also Blank Verse *and* Meter.

IDYLL An *idyll* is a poem or part of a poem that describes and idealizes country life. John Greenleaf Whittier's "Snowbound," on page 266, is an idyll.

IMAGE An *image* is a word or phrase that appeals to one or more of the five senses—sight, hearing, touch, taste, or smell.

See also Imagery.

IMAGERY *Imagery* is the descriptive or figurative language used in literature to create word pictures for the reader. These pictures, or images, are created by details of sight, sound, taste, touch, smell, or movement. The following stanza, from Kuangchi C. Chang's "Garden of My Childhood," shows how a poet can use imagery to appeal to several senses:

> I ran past the old maple by the terraced hall
> And the singing crickets under the latticed wall,
>
> And I kept on running down the walk
> Paved with pebbles of memory big and small
> Without turning to look until I was out of
> the gate
> Through which there be no return at all.

IMAGISM *Imagism* was a literary movement that flourished between 1912 and 1927. Led by Ezra Pound and Amy Lowell, the Imagist poets rejected nineteenth-century poetic forms and language. Instead, they wrote short poems that used ordinary language and free verse to create sharp, exact, concentrated pictures. "Oread," by H. D., illustrates how the Imagists concentrated on describing a scene or an object without making abstract comments:

> Whirl up, sea—
> whirl your pointed pines,
> splash your great pines
> on our rocks,
> hurl your green over us,
> cover us with your pools of fir.

IRONY *Irony* is a contrast between what is stated and what is meant, or between what is expected to happen and what actually happens. In *verbal irony*, a word or a phrase is used to suggest the opposite of its usual meaning. In *dramatic irony*, there is a contradiction between what a character thinks and what the reader or audience knows to be true. In *irony of situation*, an event occurs that directly contradicts the expectations of the characters, of the reader, or of the audience.

JOURNAL A *journal* is a daily autobiographical account of events and personal reactions. For example, Mary Chesnut's journal, on page 496, records events during the Civil War.

LEGEND A *legend* is a traditional story. Usually a legend deals with a particular person—a hero, a saint, or a national leader. Often legends reflect a people's cultural values. American legends include those of the early Native Americans and those about folk heroes such as Davy Crockett and Daniel Boone.

See also Myth.

LETTER A *letter* is a written message or communication addressed to a reader or readers and is generally sent by mail. Letters may be *private* or *public*, depending on their intended audience. Robert E. Lee's "Letter to His Son," on page 482, is an example of a *private* or *personal letter* because it was intended only for the writer's son, to whom it was addressed. A *public letter*, also called a *literary letter* or *epistle*, is a work of literature written in the form of a personal letter but created for publication. Michel-Guillaume Jean de Crèvecoeur's "Letters From an American Farmer," excerpted on page 197, are public letters.

LOCAL COLOR *Local color* is the use in a literary work of characters and details unique to a particular geographic area. Local color can be created by the use of dialect and by descriptions of customs, clothing, manners, attitudes, scenery, and landscape. Local-color stories were especially popular after the Civil War, bringing readers the West of Bret Harte, the Mississippi River of Mark Twain, and the New England of Sarah Orne Jewett.

See also Realism *and* Regionalism.

LYRIC POEM A *lyric poem* is a melodic poem that expresses the observations and feelings of a single speaker. Unlike a narrative poem, a lyric poem focuses on producing a single, unified effect. Types of lyric poems include the elegy, the ode, and the sonnet. Among contemporary American poets, the lyric is the most common poetic form.

MAIN CHARACTER *See* Character.

METAPHOR A *metaphor* is a figure of speech in which one thing is spoken of as though it were something else. The identification suggests a comparison between the two things that are identified, as in "death is a long sleep" or "the sleeping dead."

A *mixed metaphor* occurs when two metaphors are jumbled together. For example, thorns and rain are illogically mixed in "the thorns of life rained down on him." A *dead metaphor* is one that has been overused and has become a common expression, such as "the arm of the chair" or "nightfall." Metaphors are used to make writing, especially poetry, more vivid, imaginative, and meaningful.

METER The *meter* of a poem is its rhythmical pattern. This pattern is determined by the number and types of stresses, or beats, in each line. To describe the meter of a poem, you must scan its lines. *Scanning* involves marking the stressed and unstressed syllables, as follows:

> Sóon ăs thĕ sún fŏrsóok thĕ eástĕrn máin
>
> Thĕ péalĭng thúndĕr shóok thĕ héav'nly̆ pláin;
>
> —Phillis Wheatley, "An Hymn to the Evening"

As the example shows, each strong stress is marked with a slanted line (´) and each weak stress with a horseshoe symbol (˘). The weak and strong stresses are then divided by vertical lines (|) into groups called *feet*. The following types of feet are common in poetry written in English:

1. *Iamb*: a foot with one unstressed syllable followed by one stressed syllable, as in the word "ărоúnd"
2. *Trochee*: a foot with one stressed syllable followed by one unstressed syllable, as in the word "brókĕn"
3. *Anapest*: a foot with two unstressed syllables followed by one stressed syllable, as in the phrase "ĭn ă flásh"
4. *Dactyl*: a foot with one stressed syllable followed by two unstressed syllables, as in the word "árgŭmĕnt"
5. *Spondee*: a foot with two stressed syllables, as in the word "aírshíp"
6. *Pyrrhic*: a foot with two unstressed syllables, as in the last foot of the word "ĭmág|ĭnĭng"

Lines of poetry are often described as *iambic, trochaic, anapestic*, or *dactylic*. Lines are also described in terms of the number of feet that occur in them, as follows:

1. *Monometer*: verse written in one-foot lines

> Évĭl
> Bĕgéts
> Évĭl
>
> —Anonymous

2. *Dimeter:* verse written in two-foot lines

> This is | the time
> of the trag|ic man
>
> —Elizabeth Bishop, "Visits to St. Elizabeth's"

3. *Trimeter:* verse written in three-foot lines:

> Over | the win|ter glaciers
> I see | the sum|mer glow,
> And through | the wild-|piled snowdrift
> The warm | rosebuds | below.
>
> —Ralph Waldo Emerson, "Beyond Winter"

4. *Tetrameter:* verse written in four-foot lines:

> The sun | that brief | Decem|ber day
> Rose cheer|less ov|er hills | of gray
>
> —John Greenleaf Whittier, "Snowbound"

5. *Pentameter:* verse written in five-foot lines:

> I doubt | not God | is good, | well-mean|ing, kind,
> And did | He stoop | to quib|ble could | tell why
> The lit|tle bur|ied mole | contin|ues blind
>
> —Countee Cullen, "Yet Do I Marvel"

A complete description of the meter of a line tells both how many feet there are in the line and what kind of foot is most common. Thus, the lines from Countee Cullen's poem would be described as *iambic pentameter. Blank verse* is poetry written in unrhymed iambic pentameter. Poetry that does not have a regular meter is called *free verse.*

MONOLOGUE A *monologue* is a speech delivered entirely by one person or character.

See also Dramatic Monologue.

MOOD *Mood,* or atmosphere, is the feeling created in the reader by a literary work or passage. Elements that can influence the mood of a work include its setting, tone, and events.

See also Setting *and* Tone.

MOTIVATION A *motivation* is a reason that explains a character's thoughts, feelings, actions, or speech. Characters are motivated by their values and by their wants, desires, dreams, wishes, and needs. Sometimes the reasons for a character's actions are stated directly, as in Willa Cather's "A Wagner Matinée," on page 614, when Clark explains his reception of his aunt by saying, "I owed to this woman most of the good that ever came my way in my boyhood." At other times, the writer will just suggest a character's motivation.

MYTH A *myth* is a fictional tale that explains the actions of gods or heroes or the causes of natural phenomena. Myths that explain the origins of earthly life, as do the Onondaga, Najavo, and Modoc myths in this text, are known as origin myths. Other myths express the central values of the people who created them.

NARRATION *Narration* is writing that tells a story. The act of telling a story is also called *narration.* The *narrative,* or story, is told by a storyteller called the *narrator.* A story is usually told chronologically, in the order in which events take place in time, though it may include flashbacks and foreshadowing. Narratives may be true, as are the events recorded in Mary Chesnut's journal, on page 496, or fictional, as are the events in Flannery O'Connor's "The Life You Save May Be Your Own," on page 879. Narration is one of the forms of discourse and is used in novels, short stories, plays, narrative poems, anecdotes, autobiographies, biographies, and reports.

See also Narrative Poem *and* Narrator.

NARRATIVE A *narrative* is a story told in fiction, nonfiction, poetry, or drama. Narratives are often classified by their content or purpose. An *exploration narrative* is a firsthand account of an explorer's travels in a new land. Alvar Núñez Cabeza de Vaca's account of his exploration of the wilderness that is now Texas, "A Journey Through Texas," appears on page 34. "The Interesting Narrative of the Life of Olaudah Equiano," on page 44, is an example of a *slave narrative,* an autobiographical account of the experiences of an enslaved person. A *historical narrative* is a narrative account of significant historical events, such as John Smith's *The General History of Virginia,* on page 66, or William Bradford's *Of Plymouth Plantation,* on page 71.

See also Narration.

NARRATIVE POEM A *narrative poem* tells a story in verse. Three traditional types of narrative verse are *ballads,* songlike poems that tell stories; *epics,* long poems about the deeds of gods or heroes; and *metrical romances,* poems that tell tales of love and chivalry. Examples of American narrative poems include Stephen Vincent Benét's *John Brown's Body* and the ballad "John Henry."

See also Ballad.

1259

NARRATOR A *narrator* is a speaker or character who tells a story. A story or novel may be narrated by a main character, by a minor character, or by someone uninvolved in the story. The narrator may speak in the first person, as in John Updike's "The Brown Chest," on page 904, or in the third person, as in Anne Tyler's "Average Waves in Unprotected Waters," on page 926. In addition, the narrator may have an omniscient or a limited point of view. The *omniscient narrator* is all-knowing, while the *limited narrator* knows only what one character does. Because the writer's choice of narrator helps determine the point of view, this decision affects what version of a story is told and how readers will react to it.

See also Point of View.

NATURALISM *Naturalism* was a literary movement among novelists at the end of the nineteenth century and during the early decades of the twentieth century. The Naturalists tended to view people as hapless victims of immutable natural laws. Early exponents of Naturalism included Stephen Crane, Jack London, and Theodore Dreiser.

See also Realism.

NONFICTION *Nonfiction* is prose writing that presents and explains ideas or that tells about real people, places, objects, or events. Essays, biographies, autobiographies, journals, and reports are all examples of nonfiction.

See also Fiction *and* Genre.

NOVEL A *novel* is a long work of fiction. A novel often has a complicated plot, many major and minor characters, a significant theme, and several varied settings. Novels can be classified in many ways, based on the historical periods in which they are written, on the subjects and themes that they treat, on the techniques that are used in them, and on the literary movements that inspired them. Classic nineteenth-century novels include Herman Melville's *Moby-Dick*, an excerpt of which appears on page 332, and Nathaniel Hawthorne's *The Scarlet Letter*, an extended reading suggestion. Well-known twentieth-century novels include F. Scott Fitzgerald's *The Great Gatsby* and Edith Wharton's *Ethan Frome*, both of which are recommended selections for extended reading. A *novella* is not as long as a novel but is longer than a short story. Ernest Hemingway's *The Old Man and the Sea* is a novella.

ODE An *ode* is a long, formal lyric poem with a serious theme that may have a traditional stanza structure. An ode may be written for a private occasion or for a public ceremony. Odes often honor people, commemorate events, respond to natural scenes, or consider serious human problems.

See also Lyric Poem.

OMNISCIENT NARRATOR *See* Narrator *and* Point of View.

ONOMATOPOEIA *Onomatopoeia* is the use of words that imitate sounds. Examples of such words are *buzz, hiss, murmur*, and *rustle*. Isabella Stewart Gardner uses onomatopoeia in "Summer Remembered":

> Sounds sum and summon the remembering
> of summers.
> The humming of the sun
> The mumbling in the honey-suckle vine
> The whirring in the clovered grass
> The pizzicato plinkle of ice in an auburn uncle's
> amber glass.

ORAL TRADITION *Oral tradition* is the passing of songs, stories, and poems from generation to generation by word of mouth. The oral tradition in America has preserved Native American myths and legends, spirituals, folk ballads, and other stories or songs originally heard and memorized rather than written down.

See also Ballad, Folk Literature, Legend, Myth, *and* Spiritual.

ORATORY *Oratory* is public speaking that is formal, persuasive, and emotionally appealing. Patrick Henry's "Speech in the Virginia Convention," on page 168, is an example of oratory.

OXYMORON An *oxymoron* is a figure of speech that combines two opposing or contradictory ideas. An oxymoron, such as "freezing fire" or the often used "conspicuous by his absence," suggests a paradox in just a few words.

See also Figurative Language *and* Paradox.

PARADOX A *paradox* is a statement that seems to be contradictory but that actually presents a truth. Marianne Moore uses paradox in "Nevertheless" when she says, "Victory won't come / to me unless I go / to it." Because a paradox is surprising or even shocking, it draws the reader's attention to what is being said.

See also Figurative Language *and* Oxymoron.

PARALLELISM *Parallelism* is the repetition of a grammatical structure. Robert Hayden concludes his poem "Astronauts" with these questions in parallel form:

What do we want of these men?
What do we want of ourselves?

Parallelism is used in poetry and in other writing to emphasize and to link related ideas.

PARODY A *parody* is a humorous imitation of a literary work, one that exaggerates or distorts the characteristic features of the original. American author Donald Barthelme was noted for his parodic style, which he used to point out absurd aspects of modern life.

PERSONIFICATION *Personification* is a figure of speech in which a nonhuman subject is given human characteristics. In "April Rain Song," Langston Hughes personifies the rain:

Let the rain kiss you.
Let the rain sing you a lullaby.

Effective personification of things or ideas makes them seem vital and alive, as if they were human.

See also Figurative Language.

PERSUASION *Persuasion* is writing or speech that attempts to convince a reader to think or act in a particular way. During the Revolutionary War period, leaders such as Patrick Henry, Thomas Paine, and Thomas Jefferson used persuasion in their political arguments. Persuasion is also used in advertising, in editorials, in sermons, and in political speeches.

PLAIN STYLE *Plain style* is a type of writing in which uncomplicated sentences and ordinary words are used to make simple, direct statements. This style was favored by those Puritans who rejected ornate style because they wanted to express themselves clearly and directly, in accordance with the austerity of their religious beliefs. In the twentieth century, Ernest Hemingway was a master of plain style.

See also Style.

PLOT *Plot* is the sequence of events in a literary work. In most novels, dramas, short stories, and narrative poems, the plot involves both characters and a central conflict. The plot usually begins with an *exposition* that introduces the setting, the characters, and the basic situation. This is followed by the *inciting incident*, which introduces the central conflict. The conflict then increases during the *development* until it reaches a high point of interest or suspense, the *climax*. The climax is followed by the end, or *resolution*, of the central conflict. Any events that occur after the resolution make up the *denouement*. The events that lead up to the climax comprise the *rising action*. The events that follow the climax comprise the *falling action*.

See also Conflict.

POETRY *Poetry* is one of the three major types of literature. In poetry, form and content are closely connected, like the two faces of a single coin. Poems are often divided into lines and stanzas and often employ regular rhythmical patterns, or meters. Most poems make use of highly concise, musical, and emotionally charged language. Many also make use of imagery, figurative language, and special devices such as rhyme.

See also Genre.

POINT OF VIEW *Point of view* is the perspective, or vantage point, from which a story is told. Three commonly used points of view are first person, omniscient third person, and limited third person.

In the *first-person point of view*, the narrator is a character in the story and refers to himself or herself with the first-person pronoun "I." "The Fall of the House of Usher," on page 297, is told by a first-person narrator.

The two kinds of third-person point of view, limited and omniscient, are called "third person" because the narrator uses third-person pronouns such as "he" and "she" to refer to the characters. There is no "I" telling the story.

In stories told from the *omniscient third-person point of view*, the narrator knows and tells about what each character feels and thinks. "The Devil and Tom Walker," on page 236, is written from the omniscient third-person point of view.

In stories told from the *limited third-person point of view*, the narrator relates the inner thoughts and feelings of only one character, and everything is viewed from this character's perspective. "An Occurrence at Owl Creek Bridge," on page 468, is written from the limited third-person point of view.

See also Narrator.

PROSE *Prose* is the ordinary form of written language. Most writing that is not poetry, drama, or song is considered prose. Prose is one of the major genres of literature. It occurs in two forms: fiction and nonfiction.

See also Fiction, Genre, *and* Nonfiction.

PROTAGONIST The *protagonist* is the main character in a literary work. In "The Jilting of Granny Weatherall," on page 776, the protagonist is the dying grandmother.

See also Antagonist.

QUATRAIN See Stanza.

REALISM *Realism* is the presentation in art of the details of actual life. Realism was also a literary movement that began during the nineteenth century and stressed the actual as opposed to the imagined or the fanciful. The Realists tried to write truthfully and objectively about ordinary characters in ordinary situations. They reacted against Romanticism, rejecting heroic, adventurous, unusual, or unfamiliar subjects. The Realists, in turn, were followed by the Naturalists, who traced the effects of heredity and environment on people helpless to change their situations. American Realism grew from the work of local-color writers such as Bret Harte and Sarah Orne Jewett, and it is evident in the writings of major figures such as Mark Twain and Henry James.

See also Local Color, Naturalism, *and* Romanticism.

REFRAIN A *refrain* is a repeated line or group of lines in a poem or song. Most refrains end stanzas, as does "And the tide rises, the tide falls," the refrain in Henry Wadsworth Longfellow's poem on page 252; or "Coming for to carry me home," the refrain in "Swing Low, Sweet Chariot," on page 452. Although some refrains are nonsense lines, many increase suspense or emphasize character and theme.

REGIONALISM *Regionalism* in literature is the tendency among certain authors to write about specific geographical areas. Regional writers, like Willa Cather and William Faulkner, present the distinct culture of an area, including its speech, customs, beliefs, and history. Local-color writing may be considered a type of Regionalism, but Regionalists, like the southern writers of the 1920's, usually go beyond mere presentation of cultural idiosyncrasies and attempt, instead, a sophisticated sociological or anthropological treatment of the culture of a region.

See also Local Color *and* Setting.

RESOLUTION See Plot.

RHYME *Rhyme* is the repetition of sounds at the ends of words. Rhyming words have identical vowel sounds in their final accented syllables. The consonants before the vowels may be different, but any consonants occurring after these vowels are the same, as in *frog* and *bog* or *willow* and *pillow*. *End rhyme* occurs when rhyming words are repeated at the ends of lines. *Internal rhyme* occurs when rhyming words fall within a line. *Approximate*, or *slant*, *rhyme* occurs when the rhyming sounds are similar, but not exact, as in *prove* and *glove*.

See also Rhyme Scheme.

RHYME SCHEME A *rhyme scheme* is a regular pattern of rhyming words in a poem. To describe a rhyme scheme, one uses a letter of the alphabet to represent each rhyming sound in a poem or stanza. Consider how letters are used to represent the rhymes in the following example:

> With innocent wide penguin eyes, three *a*
>   large fledgling mocking-birds below *b*
> the pussywillow tree, *a*
>   stand in a row. *b*
>
> —Marianne Moore, "Bird-Witted"

The rhyme scheme of this section of Moore's poem is *abab*.

See also Rhyme.

RHYTHM *Rhythm* is the pattern of beats, or stresses, in spoken or written language. Prose and free verse are written in the irregular rhythmical patterns of everyday speech. Consider, for example, the rhythmical pattern in the following free verse lines by Gwendolyn Brooks:

> Life for my child is simple, and is good.
> He knows his wish. Yes, but that is not all.
> Because I know mine too.

Traditional poetry often follows a regular rhythmical pattern, as in the following lines by America's first great female poet, Anne Bradstreet:

> In critic's hands beware thou dost not come,
> And take thy way where yet thou art not
>   known
>
> —"The Author to Her Book"

See also Meter.

RISING ACTION See Plot.

ROMANTICISM *Romanticism* was a literary and artistic movement of the nineteenth century that arose in reaction against eighteenth-century Neoclassicism and placed a premium on fancy, imagination, emotion, nature, individuality, and exotica. Romantic elements can be found in the works of American writers as diverse as Cooper, Poe, Thoreau, Emerson, Dickinson, Hawthorne, and Melville. Romanticism is particularly evident in the works of the New England Transcendentalists.

See also Classicism *and* Transcendentalism.

ROUND CHARACTER See Character.

SATIRE *Satire* is writing that ridicules or criticizes individuals, ideas, institutions, social conventions, or other works of art or literature. The writer of a satire, the satirist, may use a tolerant, sympathetic tone or an angry, bitter tone. Some satire is written in prose and some, in poetry. Examples of satire in this text include W. H. Auden's "The Unknown Citizen," on page 696, and Ian Frazier's "Coyote v. Acme," on page 998.

SCANSION *Scansion* is the process of analyzing a poem's metrical pattern. When a poem is scanned, its stressed and unstressed syllables are marked to show what poetic feet are used and how many feet appear in each line. The last two lines of Edna St. Vincent Millay's "I Shall Go Back Again to the Bleak Shore" may be scanned as follows:

> But Í | shall fínd | the súl|len rócks |
> and skíes
> Unchánged | from whát | they wére |
> when Í | was yóung.

See also Meter.

SENSORY LANGUAGE *Sensory language* is writing or speech that appeals to one or more of the five senses.

See also Image.

SETTING The *setting* of a literary work is the time and place of the action. A setting may serve any of a number of functions. It may provide a background for the action. It may be a crucial element in the plot or central conflict. It may also create a certain emotional atmosphere, or mood. The setting of Ernest Hemingway's "In Another Country," on page 731, is Milan, Italy, during World War I. The story centers on the hospital in which the protagonist receives physical therapy for a war injury. The setting provides a backdrop for the action and is central to the plot.

SHORT STORY A *short story* is a brief work of fiction. The short story resembles the novel but generally has a simpler plot and setting. In addition, the short story tends to reveal character at a crucial moment rather than developing it through many incidents. For example, Thomas Wolfe's "The Far and the Near," on page 702, concentrates on what happens to the engineer when he visits the people who waved to him every day.

See also Fiction *and* Genre.

SIMILE A *simile* is a figure of speech that makes a direct comparison between two subjects using either like or as. Here are two examples of similes:

> The trees looked like pitch forks against the sullen sky.
>
> Her hair was as red as a robin's breast.

See also Figurative Language.

SLANT RHYME See Rhyme.

SONNET A *sonnet* is a fourteen-line lyric poem focused on a single theme. Sonnets have many variations but are usually written in iambic pentameter, following one of two traditional patterns: the *Petrarchan,* or *Italian, sonnet,* which is divided into two parts, the eight-line octave and the six-line sestet; and the *Shakespearean,* or *English, sonnet,* which consists of three quatrains and a concluding couplet.

See also Lyric Poem.

SPEAKER The *speaker* is the voice of a poem. Although the speaker is often the poet, the speaker may also be a fictional character or even an inanimate object or another type of nonhuman entity. Interpreting a poem often depends upon recognizing who the speaker is, whom the speaker is addressing, and what the speaker's attitude, or tone, is.

See also Point of View.

SPIRITUAL A *spiritual* is a type of African American folk song dating from the period of slavery and Reconstruction. A typical spiritual deals both with religious freedom and, on an allegorical level, with political and economic freedom. For example, in some spirituals the biblical river Jordan was used as a symbol for the Ohio River, which separated slave states from free states; and the biblical promised land, Canaan, was used as a symbol for the free northern United States. Most spirituals contained biblical allusions and made use of repetition, parallelism, and rhyme. Spirituals had a profound influence on the development of both poetry and song in the United States. See "Swing Low, Sweet Chariot," on page 452, and "Go Down, Moses," on page 453.

STAGE DIRECTIONS See Drama.

STANZA A *stanza* is a group of lines in a poem that are considered to be a unit. Many poems are divided into stanzas that are separated by spaces. Stanzas often function just like paragraphs in prose. Each stanza states and develops a single main idea.

Stanzas are commonly named according to the number of lines found in them, as follows:

1. *Couplet*: a two-line stanza
2. *Tercet*: a three-line stanza
3. *Quatrain*: a four-line stanza
4. *Cinquain*: a five-line stanza
5. *Sestet*: a six-line stanza
6. *Heptastich*: a seven-line stanza
7. *Octave*: an eight-line stanza

STATIC CHARACTER *See* Character.

STREAM OF CONSCIOUSNESS *Stream of consciousness* is a narrative technique that presents thoughts as if they were coming directly from a character's mind. Instead of being arranged in chronological order, the events of the story are presented from the character's point of view, mixed in with the character's feelings and memories just as they might spontaneously occur in the mind of a real person. Katherine Anne Porter uses this technique in "The Jilting of Granny Weatherall," on page 776, to capture Granny's dying thoughts and feelings. Ambrose Bierce also uses the stream-of-consciousness technique in his short story "An Occurrence at Owl Creek Bridge," which appears on page 468. Stream-of-consciousness writing reveals a character's complex psychology and presents it in realistic detail.

See also Point of View.

STYLE A writer's *style* is his or her typical way of writing. Style includes word choice, tone, degree of formality, figurative language, rhythm, grammatical structure, sentence length, organization—in short, every feature of a writer's use of language. Ernest Hemingway, for example, is noted for a simple prose style that contrasts with Thomas Paine's aphoristic style and with N. Scott Momaday's reflective style.

See also Diction *and* Plain Style.

SUSPENSE *Suspense* is a feeling of growing uncertainty about the outcome of events in a literary work. Writers create suspense by raising questions in the minds of their readers. Because readers are curious or concerned, they keep reading to find out what will happen next. Suspense builds until the climax of the plot, at which point the suspense reaches its peak. Thereafter, the suspense is generally resolved.

See also Climax *and* Plot.

SYMBOL A *symbol* is anything that stands for or represents something else. A *conventional symbol* is one that is widely known and accepted, such as a voyage symbolizing life or a skull symbolizing death. A *personal symbol* is one developed for a particular work by a particular author. Examples in this text include Hawthorne's black veil and Melville's white whale.

SYMBOLISM *Symbolism* was a literary movement during the nineteenth century that influenced many poets, including the Imagists and T. S. Eliot. Symbolists turned away from everyday, realistic details, trying instead to express emotions by using a pattern of symbols.

See also Imagism *and* Realism.

THEME A *theme* is a central message or insight into life revealed by a literary work. An essay's theme is often directly stated in its thesis statement. In most works of fiction, the theme is only indirectly stated: a story, poem, or play most often has an *implied theme*. For example, in "A Worn Path," on page 740, Eudora Welty does not directly say that Phoenix Jackson's difficult journey shows the power of love, but readers learn this indirectly by the end of the story.

TONE The *tone* of a literary work is the writer's attitude toward his or her subject, characters, or audience. A writer's tone may be formal or informal, friendly or distant, personal or pompous. For example, William Faulkner's tone in his "Nobel Prize Acceptance Speech," on page 798, is earnest and serious, whereas James Thurber's tone in "The Night the Ghost Got In," on page 818, is humorous and ironic.

See also Mood.

TRANSCENDENTALISM *Transcendentalism* was an American literary and philosophical movement of the nineteenth century. The Transcendentalists, who were based in New England, believed that intuition and the individual conscience "transcend" experience and thus are better guides to truth than are the senses and logical reason. Influenced by Romanticism, the Transcendentalists respected the individual spirit and the natural world, believing that divinity was present everywhere, in nature and in each person. The Transcendentalists included Ralph Waldo Emerson, Henry David Thoreau, Bronson Alcott, W. H. Channing, Margaret Fuller, and Elizabeth Peabody.

See also Romanticism.

Writing Handbook

The Writing Process

A polished piece of writing can seem to have been effortlessly created, but most good writing is the result of a process of writing, rethinking, and rewriting. The process can roughly be divided into stages: prewriting, drafting, revising, editing, proofreading, and publishing.

It's important to remember that the writing process is one that moves backward as well as forward. Even while you are moving forward in the creation of your composition, you may still return to a previous stage—to rethink or rewrite.

Following are stages of the writing process, with key points to address during each stage.

Prewriting

In this stage, you plan out the work to be done. You prepare to write by exploring ideas, gathering information, and working out an organization plan. Following are the key steps to take at this stage.

Step 1: Analyze the writing situation. Start by clarifying your assignment, so that you know exactly what you are supposed to do.

- *Focus your topic.* If necessary, narrow the topic—the subject you are writing about—so that you can write about it fully in the space you have.
- *Know your purpose.* What is your goal for this paper? What do you want to accomplish? Your purpose will determine what you include in the paper.
- *Know your audience.* Who will read your paper influences what you say and how you say it.

Step 2: Gather ideas and information. You can do this in a number of ways:

- *Brainstorm.* When you brainstorm, either alone or with others, you come up with possible ideas to use in your paper. Not all of your brainstormed ideas will be useful or suitable. You'll need to evaluate them later.
- *Consult other people about your subject.* Speaking informally with others may suggest an idea or approach you did not see at first.
- *Make a list of questions about your topic.* When your list is complete, find the answers to your questions.
- *Do research.* Your topic may require information that you don't have, so you will need to go to other sources to find information. There are numerous ways to find information on a topic. See the Research Handbook on p. 1282 for suggestions.

The ideas and information you gather will become the content of your paper. Not all of the information you gather will be needed. As you develop and revise your paper, you will make further decisions about what to include and what to leave out.

Step 3: Organize. First, make a rough plan for the way you want to present your information. Sort your ideas and notes; decide what goes with what and which points are the most important. You can make an outline to show the order of ideas, or you can use some other organizing plan that works for you.

There are many ways in which you can organize and develop your material. Use a method that works for your topic. Following are common methods of organizing information in the development of a paper:

- *Chronological Order* In this method, events are presented in the order in which they occurred. This organization works best for presenting narrative material or explaining in a "how to."
- *Spatial Order* In spatial order, details are presented as seen in space; for example, from left to right or from foreground to background. This order is good for descriptive writing.
- *Order of Importance* This order helps readers see the relative importance of ideas. You present ideas from most to least important or from least to most important.
- *Main Idea and Details* This logical organization works well to support an idea or opinion.

Drafting

When you draft, you put down your ideas on paper in rough form. Working from your prewriting notes and your outline or plan, you develop and present your ideas in sentences and paragraphs.

Don't worry about getting everything perfect at the drafting stage. Concentrate on getting your ideas down.

Draft in a way that works for you. Some writers

work best by writing a quick draft—putting down all their ideas without stopping to evaluate them. Other writers prefer to develop each paragraph carefully and thoughtfully, making sure that each main idea is supported by details.

As you are developing a draft, keep in mind your purpose and your audience. These determine what you say and how you say it.

Don't be afraid to change your original plans during drafting. Some of the best ideas are those that were not planned at the beginning. Write as many drafts as you like. You can draft over and over until you're happy with the results.

Most papers, regardless of the topic, are developed with an introduction, a body, and a conclusion. Here are tips for developing these parts:

Introduction In the introduction to a paper, you want to engage your readers' attention and let them know the purpose of your paper. You may use the following strategies in your introduction:

- State your main idea.
- Take a stand.
- Use an anecdote.
- Quote someone.
- Startle your readers.

Body of the paper In the body of your paper, you present your information and make your points. Your **organization** is an important factor in leading readers through your ideas. Your elaboration on your main ideas is also important. **Elaboration** is the development of ideas to make your written work precise and complete. You can use the following kinds of details to elaborate your main ideas:

- Facts and statistics
- Anecdotes
- Sensory details
- Examples
- Explanation and definition
- Quotations

Conclusion The ending of your paper is the final impression you leave with your readers. Your conclusion should give readers the sense that you have pulled everything together. Following are some effective ways to end your paper:

- Summarize and restate.
- Ask a question.
- State an opinion.
- Tell an anecdote.
- Call for action.

Revising

Once you have a draft, you can look at it critically or have others review it. This is the time to make changes—on many levels. Revising is the process of reworking what you have written to make it as good as it can be. You may change some details so that your ideas flow smoothly and are clearly supported. You may discover that some details don't work, and you'll need to discard them. Two strategies may help you start the revising process:

1. Read your work aloud. This is an excellent way to catch any ideas or details that have been left out and to notice errors in logic.
2. Ask someone else to read your work. Choose someone who can point out its strengths and suggest how to improve it.

How do you know what to look for and what to change? Here is a checklist of major writing issues. If the answer to any of these questions is no, then that is an area that needs revision.

1. Does the writing achieve your purpose?
2. Does the paper have unity? That is, does it have a single focus, with all details and information contributing to that focus?
3. Is the arrangement of information clear and logical?
4. Have you elaborated enough to give your audience adequate information?

Editing

When you edit, you look more closely at the language you have used to ensure that the way you express your ideas is the most effective.

- Replace dull language with vivid, precise words.
- Cut or change redundant expressions (unnecessary repetition).
- Cut empty words and phrases—those that do not add anything to the writing.
- Check passive voice. Usually active voice is more effective.
- Replace wordy expressions with shorter, more precise ones.

Proofreading

After you finish your final draft, you must proofread it, either on your own or with the help of a partner.

It's useful to have both a dictionary and a usage handbook to help you check for correctness. Here are the tasks in proofreading:

- Correct errors in grammar and usage.
- Correct errors in punctuation and capitalization.
- Correct errors in spelling.

Publishing

Now your paper is ready to be shared with others.

THE MODES OF WRITING

Description

Description is writing that creates a vivid picture, draws readers into a scene, and makes readers feel as if they are meeting a character or experiencing an event firsthand. A description may stand on its own or be part of a longer work, such as a short story.

When you write a description, bring it to life with sensory details, which tell how your subject looks, smells, sounds, tastes, or feels. You'll want to choose your details carefully so that you create a single main impression of your subject. Avoid language and details that don't contribute to this main impression. Keep these guidelines in mind whenever you are assigned one of the following types of description:

Observation In an observation, you describe an event that you have witnessed firsthand, often over an extended period of time. You may focus on an aspect of daily life or on a scientific phenomenon, such as a storm or an eclipse.

Remembrance When you write a remembrance, you use vivid, descriptive details to bring to life memorable people, places, or events from your past.

Reflective Essay A reflective essay is more than just a description of personal experiences or pivotal events from your life; it also describes your thoughts and feelings about the significance of those events.

Character Profile In a character profile, you capture a person's appearance and personality traits and reveal information about his or her life. Your subject may be a real person or a fictional character.

Travel Brochure Present details about culture, architecture, food, and scenery to describe a vacation destination in a way that appeals to potential visitors.

Narration

Whenever writers tell any type of story, they are using **narration.** While there are many kinds of narration, most narratives share certain elements—characters, a setting, a sequence of events (or plot, in fiction), and, often, a theme. You might be asked to write one of these types of narration:

Personal Narrative A personal narrative is a true story about a memorable experience or period in your life. In a personal narrative, your feelings about events shape the way you tell the story—even the way you describe people and places.

Myth, Legend, or Folk Tale When you write a myth, legend, or folk tale, you are setting down in writing a story—often fantastic—that has been handed down orally over the years.

Firsthand Biography A firsthand biography tells about the life (or a period in the life) of a person whom you know personally. Use your close relationship with the person to help you include personal insights not found in biographies based solely on research.

Short Story Short stories are short fictional, or made-up, narratives in which a main character faces a conflict that is resolved by the end of the story. In planning a short story, you focus on developing the plot, the setting, and the characters. You must also decide on a point of view: Will your story be told by a character who participates in the action or by someone who describes the action as an outside observer?

Exposition

Exposition is writing that informs or explains. The information you include in expository writing is factual or (when you're expressing an opinion) based on fact.

Your expository writing should reflect a well-thought-out organization—one that includes a clear introduction, body, and conclusion and is appropriate for the type of exposition you are writing. Here are some types of exposition you may be asked to write:

Cause-and-Effect Essay In a cause-and-effect essay, you consider the reasons something did happen or might happen. You may examine several causes of a single effect or several effects of a single cause.

Comparison-and-Contrast Essay When you write a comparison-and-contrast essay, you consider the similarities and differences between two or more subjects. You may organize your essay point by point—discussing each aspect of your subject in turn—or subject by subject—discussing all the qualities of one subject first, and then the qualities of the next subject.

Problem-and-Solution Essay In a problem-and-solution essay, you identify a conflict or problem and offer a resolution. Begin by clearly stating the problem and follow with a reasoned path to a solution.

Consumer Report A consumer report presents up-to-date information and relevant statistical data about one or more products in a given category.

Because readers use consumer reports to help them make purchasing decisions, you might also rate the product or products you profile and discuss the advantages or disadvantages of each.

Summary To write a summary or synopsis of an event or a literary work, you include only the details that your readers will need in order to understand the key features of the event or the literary work. Omit any personal opinions; include only factual details.

Persuasion

Persuasion is writing or speaking that attempts to convince people to agree with a position or to take a desired action. When used effectively, persuasive writing has the power to change people's lives. As a reader and a writer, you will find yourself engaged in many forms of persuasion. Here are a few of them:

Persuasive Essay In writing a persuasive essay, you build an argument, supporting your opinions with a variety of evidence: facts, statistics, examples, statements from experts. You also anticipate and develop counterarguments to opposing opinions.

Advertisement Advertisements are probably the most common type of persuasion. When you write an advertisement, you present information in an appealing way to make the product or service seem desirable.

Position Paper In a position paper, you try to persuade readers to accept your views on a controversial issue. Most often, your audience will consist of people who have some power to shape policy related to the issue. As they are in other types of persuasion, your views in a position paper should be supported with evidence.

Persuasive Speech A persuasive speech is a piece of persuasion that you present orally instead of in writing. As a persuasive speaker, you use a variety of techniques, such as repetition of key points, to capture your audience's interest and to add force to your argument.

Editorial An editorial expresses an opinion or a position on a current issue or concern. When you write an editorial, you state and then defend your opinion with logical reasons, facts, examples, and other details.

Research Writing

Writers often use outside research to gather information and explore subjects of interest. The product of that research is called **research writing.** In connection with your reading, you may occasionally be assigned one of the following types of research writing:

Research Paper A research paper uses information gathered from a variety of outside sources to explore a topic. In your research paper, you will usually include an introduction, in which your thesis, or main point, is stated; a body, in which you present support for the thesis; and a conclusion that summarizes, or restates, your main points. You should credit the sources of information, using footnotes or other types of citation, and include a bibliography, or general list of sources, at the end.

Multimedia Presentation In preparing a multimedia presentation, you will gather and organize information in a variety of media, or means of communication. You may use written materials, slides, videos, audiocassettes, sound effects, art, photographs, models, charts, and diagrams.

Annotated Bibliography An annotated bibliography is a list of materials about a certain topic. For each entry, you must provide source information (title, author, date of publication, and so on), as well as a summary of the material that includes your personal review or comments about it.

Statistical Report A statistical report uses numbers to support a thesis, or main idea. Before drafting your report, you must first interpret and draw conclusions from the numerical data you've gathered. Then present and support your findings in the report.

Creative Writing

Creative writing blends imagination, ideas, and emotions and allows you to present your own unique view of the world. Poems, plays, short stories, dramas, and even some cartoons are examples of creative writing. Many are found in this anthology; use them as an inspiration to produce your own creative works, such as the following:

Poem In a poem, you use sensory images, figurative language, and sound devices to communicate ideas, tell a story, describe feelings, or create a mood. Using exact and highly charged language will help you convey meaning and create vivid images for your readers.

Drama When you write a drama or a dramatic scene, you are writing a story that is intended to be performed. Since a drama consists largely of the words and actions of the characters, be sure to write dialogue that clearly shows the characters' personalities, thoughts, and emotions, as well as stage directions that convey your ideas about sets, props, sound effects, and the speaking style and movements of the characters.

Monologue A monologue is a speech delivered by a single character. You may create a monologue within the context of a longer drama or as a work to be read or performed in its own right.

Video Script A video script or screenplay is a drama written for television, film, or video production. In addition to dialogue and stage directions, you must also include detailed stage and camera directions in your video script. These instructions indicate the specific actions or effects necessary to telling the story clearly.

Imitation of an Author's Style In this type of creative writing, you take the recognizable elements of an author's style and use them to create your own piece of writing. You may write your imitation in a true attempt to replicate a writer's style or in the spirit of a humorous parody.

Response to Literature

In a **response to literature,** you express your thoughts and feelings about a work and often, in so doing, gain a better understanding of what the work is all about. Your response to literature can take many forms—oral or written, formal or informal. During the course of your reading, you may be asked to respond to a work of literature in one of these forms:

Retelling of a Literary Work When you retell a literary work, you restate the work in your own words. The subtle changes or emphases you bring to the retelling reveal your response to the work—what you particularly liked or what you wanted to change about the original piece of literature. You might also choose to adapt the work for another medium or literary genre.

Critical Review In a critical review of a literary work, you discuss various elements in the work and offer opinions about them. You may also give a summary of the work and a recommendation to readers.

Comparative Analysis of Two Literary Works A comparative analysis shows the similarities and differences between several elements—such as characters and plot—of two literary works. You might compare the works on a point-by-point basis or analyze one work before moving on to the next. Use quotations and specific details from the works to support your points.

Response to a Short Story In your response to a short story, you present your reactions to elements of the story—such as the setting, a particular character, or a plot twist—that made a strong impression on you. Include supporting quotations from the story, as well as a brief summary and personal evaluation of the work.

Literary Analysis In a literary analysis, you take a critical look at various important elements in the work. You then attempt to explain how the author has used those elements and how they work together to convey the author's message.

Practical and Technical Writing

Practical writing is fact-based writing that people do in the workplace or in their day-to-day lives. Business letters, memos, school forms, and job applications are examples of practical writing. **Technical writing,** which is also based on facts, explains procedures, provides instructions, or presents specialized information. You encounter technical writing every time you read a manual or a set of instructions.

In the following descriptions, you'll find tips for tackling several types of practical and technical writing:

Résumé A résumé is a written summary of your education background, work experience, and job qualifications presented in a concise format.

Cover and Follow-up Letters Accompany a résumé with a cover letter in which you introduce yourself and briefly explain your qualifications for the position. It's also a good idea to send a brief thank-you letter to follow up an interview. Use proper business letter format for both types of correspondence.

Proposal When you wish to present a new idea for consideration, describe your suggested plan of action in a proposal. While your proposal can take many different forms—from a simple business letter or memo to a formal plan—it should include specific information about the benefits of the proposed action. It should also provide relevant background information that a reader considering the proposal might need, such as costs or materials required to implement the plan.

Test Essay Good organization is key to writing an effective essay under test conditions. Adhering to an organizational plan will help you create a coherent essay, even under tight time restrictions. Your introduction should include a thesis statement—a one-sentence summary of your response to the test essay question. Make sure that each paragraph in the body of the essay supports this main idea, and conclude with a restatement of the thesis and a summary of the main points in the body.

Grammar and Mechanics Handbook

Summary of Grammar

Nouns A **noun** names a person, place, or thing. A **common noun** names any one of a class of people, places, or things. A **proper noun** names a specific person, place, or thing.

Common Nouns	Proper Nouns
essayist	William Safire, Carson McCullers
city	Boston, New Orleans

Pronouns A **pronoun** is a word that stands for a noun or for words that take the place of a noun. A **personal pronoun** refers to (1) the person speaking, (2) the person spoken to, or (3) the person, place, or thing spoken about.

	Singular	Plural
First Person	I, me, my, mine	we, us, our, ours
Second Person	you, your, yours	you, your, yours
Third Person	he, him, his, she, her, hers, it, its	they, them, their, theirs

A **reflexive pronoun** ends in *-self* or *-selves* and adds information to a sentence by pointing back to a noun or pronoun near the beginning of the sentence.

> . . . They click upon *themselves*
> as the breeze rises . . .
>
> —*Frost, p. 804*

An **intensive pronoun** ends in *-self* or *-selves* and simply adds emphasis to a noun or pronoun in the same sentence.

> The United States *themselves* are essentially the greatest poem.
>
> —*Whitman, p. 406*

A **demonstrative pronoun** directs attention to a specific person, place, or thing.

> *this* hat *these* coats *that* frame

A **relative pronoun** begins a subordinate clause and connects it to another idea in the sentence.

> The brave men, living and dead, *who* struggled here, have consecrated it . . .
>
> —*Lincoln, p. 480*

> I made a little book, in *which* I allotted a page for each of the virtues.
>
> —*Franklin, p. 132*

An **indefinite pronoun** refers to a noun or pronoun that is not specifically named.

> *Few* could refrain from twisting their heads toward the door; *many* stood upright and turned directly about; . . .
>
> —*Hawthorne, p. 319*

Verbs A **verb** is a word or group of words that expresses time while showing an action, a condition, or the fact that something exists.

An **action verb** is a verb that tells what action someone or something is performing.

> The sun that brief December day
> *Rose* cheerless over hills of gray, . . .
>
> —*Whittier, p. 267*

A **linking verb** is a verb that connects its subject with a word generally found near the end of the sentence. All linking verbs are intransitive.

> Her name *was* Phoenix Jackson.
>
> —*Welty, p. 740*

A **helping verb** is a verb that can be added to another verb to make a single verb phrase.

> Sir, we *have* done everything that could be done to avert the storm which is now coming on.
>
> —*Henry, p. 170*

Adjectives An **adjective** is a word used to describe a noun or pronoun or to give a noun or pronoun a more specific meaning. Adjectives answer these questions:

What kind?	*green* leaf, *tall* chimney
Which one?	*this* clock, *those* pictures
How many?	*six* days, *several* concerts
How much?	*more* effort, *enough* applause
Whose?	*Kennedy's* address, *my* name

The articles *the, a,* and *an* are adjectives. *An* is used before a word beginning with a vowel sound.

A noun or pronoun may sometimes be used as an adjective.

Adverbs An **adverb** is a word that modifies a verb, an adjective, or another adverb. Adverbs answer the questions *where, when, in what way,* or *to what extent.*

> She came *yesterday*. (modifies verb *came*)
> Please sit *here*. (modifies verb *sit*)
> We departed *immediately*. (modifies verb *departed*)
> They were *completely* unaware. (modifies adjective *unaware*)
> It rained *rather* often. (modifies adverb *often*)

Prepositions A **preposition** is a word that relates a noun or pronoun that appears with it to another word in the sentence. Prepositions are almost always followed by nouns or pronouns.

aboard the train　*among* us　*below* our plane
into view　*toward* them　*until* dark

Conjunctions A **conjunction** is a word used to connect other words or groups of words.

A **coordinating conjunction** connects similar kinds or groups of words.

dogs *and* cats　friendly *but* dignified

Correlative conjunctions are used in pairs to connect similar words or groups of words.

both Prem *and* Sanjay　*neither* she *nor* I

A **subordinating conjunction** connects two complete ideas by placing one idea below the other in rank or importance.

> *Even before they'd noticed anything wrong,* they'd wondered at his jittery, jerky catnaps . . .
>
> —*Tyler, p. 927*

A **conjunctive adverb** is an adverb used as a conjunction to connect complete ideas.

> Flannery O'Connor portrayed social outcasts in an unsentimental way; *nevertheless,* her underlying sympathy for their suffering is evident.

Interjections An **interjection** is a word that expresses feeling or emotion and functions independently of a sentence.

> *Oh,* woe is me!

Subject and Verb Agreement To make a subject and verb agree, make sure that both are *singular* or both are *plural.*

> All of it, all that the *land is* and *evokes,* its actual meaning as well as its metaphorical reverberation, *was* and *is* understood differently.
>
> —*"Arctic Dreams," Barry Lopez*

Phrases A **phrase** is a group of words, without a subject and verb, that functions in a sentence as one part of speech.

A **prepositional phrase** is a group of words that includes a preposition and a noun or pronoun.

beyond the horizon　inside the corral
in front of the store　throughout his life

An **adjective phrase** is a prepositional phrase that modifies a noun or pronoun by telling what kind or which one.

> And the concrete *of this city*
> the oily wind, the blazing windows,
> the shrieks *of automation* cannot,
> truly cannot answer for that hunger . . .
>
> —*Ortiz, p. 980*

An **adverb phrase** is a prepositional phrase that modifies a verb, an adjective, or an adverb by pointing out *where, when, in what way,* or *to what extent.*

> *During the intermission before the second half of the concert,* I questioned my aunt and found that the "Prize Song" was not new to her.
>
> —*Cather, p. 618*

An **appositive phrase** is a noun or pronoun with modifiers, placed next to a noun or pronoun to add information and details.

> I drop to Hawthorne, *the customs officer,* measuring coal and mostly trying to keep warm— . . .
>
> —*Lowell, p. 914*

A **participial phrase** is a participle that is modified by an adjective or adverb phrase or that has a complement. The entire phrase acts as an adjective.

> Two or three men, *conversing earnestly together,* ceased as he approached, . . .
>
> —*Harte, p. 534*

A **nominative absolute** is a noun or pronoun followed by a participle or participial phrase that functions independently of the rest of the sentence.

> *The preparations being complete,* the two private soldiers stepped aside and each drew away the plank upon which he had been standing.
>
> —*Bierce, p. 469*

An **infinitive phrase** is an infinitive with modifiers, complements, or a subject, all acting together as a single part of speech.

> . . . some set *to mow,* others *to bind thatch,* some *to build houses,* others *to thatch them* . . .
>
> —*Smith, p. 68*

Clauses A **clause** is a group of words with its own subject and verb.

An **independent clause** can stand by itself as a complete sentence. A **subordinate clause** cannot stand by itself as a complete sentence; it can only be part of a sentence.

An **adjective clause** is a subordinate clause that modifies a noun or pronoun by telling what kind or which one.

> In compliance with the request of a friend of mine, *who wrote me from the East,* I called on good-natured, garrulous old Simon Wheeler . . .
>
> —*Twain, p. 525*

A **subordinate adverb clause** modifies a verb, adjective, adverb, or verbal by telling *where, when, in what way, to what extent, under what condition,* or *why.*

> *Whenever Richard Cory went down town,*
> We people on the pavement looked at him.
>
> —*Robinson, p. 607*

A **noun clause** is a subordinate clause that acts as a noun.

> As I knew, or thought I knew, *what was right and wrong,* I did not see why I might not always do one and avoid the other.
>
> —*Franklin, p. 131*

Summary of Capitalization and Punctuation

CAPITALIZATION

Capitalize the first word in sentences, interjections, and incomplete questions. Also capitalize the first word in a quotation if the quotation is a complete sentence.

> And then I said in perfect English, "Yes, I'm getting rather concerned."
>
> —*Tan, p. 1013*

Capitalize all proper nouns and adjectives.

T. S. Eliot	Mississippi River	Harvard University
Turkish	November	Puerto Rican

Capitalize a person's title when it is followed by the person's name or when it is used in direct address.

Rev. Leonidas W. Smiley   General Robert E. Lee

Capitalize titles showing family relationships when they refer to a specific person, unless they are preceded by a possessive noun or pronoun.

Granny Weatherall   my grandfather Mammedaty

Capitalize the first word and all other key words in the titles of books, periodicals, poems, stories, plays, paintings, and other works of art.

The Crucible   "Anecdote of the Jar"

Capitalize the first word and all nouns in letter salutations and the first word in letter closings.

Dear Henry,   Yours truly,

PUNCTUATION

End Marks Use a **period** to end a declarative sentence, a mild imperative sentence, an indirect question, and most abbreviations.

> The early afternoon was clear and open and surrounded by pale blue sky.
>
> —*O'Connor, p. 886*

> Pile the bodies high at Austerlitz and Waterloo.
>
> —*Sandburg, p. 771*

Use a **period** after most abbreviations and after initials.

> Ask yourselves how this gracious reception of our petition comports with those warlike preparations which cover our waters and darken our land.
>
> —*Henry, p. 170*

Use a **question mark** to end an interrogative sentence, an incomplete question, or a statement that is intended as a question.

> Was it even Kentucky or Tennessee?
>
> —*Warren, p. 917*

Use an **exclamation mark** after an exclamatory sentence, a forceful imperative sentence, or an interjection expressing strong emotion.

> We wear the mask!
>
> —*Dunbar, p. 601*

> "Don't let him, sister!"
>
> —*Frost, p. 809*

Commas Use a comma before the conjunction to separate two independent clauses in a compound sentence.

> From my mother's sleep I fell into the State,
> And I hunched in its belly till my wet fur froze.
>
> —*Jarrell, p. 1045*

Use commas to separate three or more words, phrases, or clauses in a series.

> I spun, I wove, I kept the house, I nursed the sick, . . .
>
> —*Masters, p. 608*

Use commas to separate adjectives of equal rank. Do not use commas to separate adjectives that must stay in a specific order.

> She carried a thin, small cane made from an umbrella . . .
>
> —*Welty, p. 740*

> Feathery drifts of snow, shaken from the long pine boughs, flew like white-winged birds, and settled about them as they slept.
>
> —*Harte, p. 541*

Use a comma after an introductory word, phrase, or clause.

> Finding Tom so squeamish on this point, he did not insist upon it, . . .
>
> —*Irving, p. 242*

Use commas to set off parenthetical and nonessential expressions.

> My poor aunt's figure, however, would have presented astonishing difficulties to any dressmaker.
>
> —*Cather, p. 615*

Use commas with places, dates, and titles.

Boston, Massachusetts   November 17, 1915

Dr. Martin Luther King, Jr.

Use commas after items in addresses, after the salutation in a personal letter, after the closing in all letters, and in numbers of more than three digits.

Linden Lane, Princeton, N.J.   Dear Marian,

Affectionately yours,   6,778

Use a comma to indicate words left out of an elliptical sentence and to set off a direct quotation.

In T. S. Eliot's poetry, allusions are perhaps the most prominent device; in Ezra Pound's, images.

"Well, Granny," he said, "you must be a hundred years old and scared of nothing."

—*Welty, p. 743*

Semicolons Use a semicolon to join independent clauses that are not already joined by a conjunction.

The old woman didn't change her position until he was almost into her yard; then she rose with one hand fisted on her hip.

—*O'Connor, p. 879*

Use semicolons to avoid confusion when independent clauses or items in a series already contain commas.

Before these events, the day was glorious with expectancy; after them, the day was a dead and empty thing.

—*Twain, p. 521*

Colons Use a colon before a list of items following an independent clause.

Great literature provides us with many things: entertainment, enrichment, and inspiration.

Use a colon to introduce a formal or a lengthy quotation.

In *The Member of the Wedding,* the lonely twelve-year-old girl, Frankie Addams, articulates this universal need: "The trouble with me is that for a long time I have just been an *I* person."

—*McCullers, p. 994*

Quotation Marks A **direct quotation** represents a person's exact speech and is enclosed in quotation marks.

"Good," he said. "You will be able to play football again better than ever."

—*Hemingway, p. 731*

An **indirect quotation** reports only the general meaning of what a person said and does not require quotation marks.

One day I had said that Italian seemed such an easy language to me that I could not take a great interest in it, . . .

—*Hemingway, p. 733*

Always place a comma or a period inside the final quotation mark.

"Well, Missy, excuse me," Doctor Harry patted her cheek.

—*Porter, p. 776*

Place a question mark or an exclamation mark inside the final quotation mark if the end mark is part of the quotation; if it is not part of the quotation, place it outside the final quotation mark.

"Cornelia! Cornelia!" No footsteps, but a sudden hand on her cheek. "Bless you, where have you been?"

—*Porter, p. 777*

Use single quotation marks for a quotation within a quotation.

"'All right,' I say, 'I can't afford to pay
Any fixed wages, though I wish I could.'
'Someone else can.' 'Then someone else will
have to.'"

—*"The Death of the Hired Man," Robert Frost*

Underline or italicize the titles of long written works, movies, television and radio shows, lengthy works of music, paintings, and sculpture.

<u>The Great Gatsby</u>   *Mary Poppins*   <u>Aida</u>

Use quotation marks around the titles of short written works, episodes in a series, songs, and titles of works mentioned as parts of a collection.

"Winter Dreams"   "Go Down, Moses"

Dashes Use dashes to indicate an abrupt change of thought, a dramatic interrupting idea, or a summary statement.

She'd had moments herself of picturing some kind of evil gene in her husband's ordinary, stocky body—a dark little egg like a black jelly bean, she imagined it.

—*Tyler, p. 928*

Use dashes to set off a nonessential appositive or modifier when it is long, when it is already punctuated, or when you want to be dramatic.

. . . for some reason he was not completely sure of—it may have been the cold and his fatigue—he decided not to insist on seeing him.

—*Malamud, p. 896*

Hyphens Use a hyphen with certain numbers, after certain prefixes, with two or more words used as one word, with a compound modifier coming before a noun, and within a word when a combination of letters might otherwise be confusing.

fifty-four daughter-in-law
up-to-date report

Apostrophes Add an apostrophe and -s to show the possessive case of most singular nouns.

Taylor's poetry a poet's career

Add an apostrophe to show the possessive case of plural nouns ending in -s and -es.

the boys' ambition the Cruzes' house

Add an apostrophe and -s to show the possessive case of plural nouns that do not end in -s or -es.

the men's suits the deer's antlers

Use an apostrophe in a contraction to indicate the position of the missing letter or letters.

"You look like a saint, Doctor Harry, and I vow that's as near as you'll ever come to it."
—*Porter, p. 780*

GLOSSARY OF COMMON USAGE

adapt, adopt

Adapt is a verb meaning "to change." *Adopt* is a verb meaning "to take as one's own."

Washington Irving *adapted* many characters and situations from folk tales for his short stories.

Ezra Pound's followers *adopted* a spare, almost lean style in their verse.

advice, advise

Advice is a noun meaning "an opinion." *Advise* is a verb meaning "to give an opinion."

The man in Jack London's "To Build a Fire" ignores the *advice* of the old-timer from Sulphur Creek.

How might Lucinda Matlock *advise* the younger generation of today's world?

affect, effect

Affect is almost always a verb meaning "to influence." *Effect* is usually a noun meaning "result." *Effect* can also be a verb meaning "to bring about" or "to cause."

An understanding of T. S. Eliot's multiple allusions can *affect* one's appreciation of his poetry.

In Willa Cather's story, the Wagner concert has a profound *effect* on the emotions of Clark's Aunt Georgiana.

The aim of persuasive writing is often to *effect* a change in the attitudes of the audience.

among, between

Among is usually used with three or more items. *Between* is generally used with only two items.

Among the writers of the Harlem Renaissance, Langston Hughes stands out for his mastery of many literary genres.

At the end of Robert Frost's "Mending Wall," the speaker reports a conversation *between* himself and his neighbor.

as, because, like, as to

The word *as* has several meanings and can function as several parts of speech. To avoid confusion, use *because* rather than *as* when you want to indicate cause and effect.

Because Jonathan Edwards firmly believed that his listeners' souls were in danger, he desperately wanted them to repent.

Do not use the preposition *like* to introduce a clause that requires the conjunction *as*.

The Puritans reacted to music and dancing *as* one might expect: They considered that such entertainments were dangerous occasions for sin.

The use of *as to* for *about* is awkward and should be avoided.

Captain Ahab's bitter vehemence *about* the white whale must seem puzzling to the crew.

bad, badly

Use the predicate adjective *bad* after linking verbs such as *feel, look,* and *seem*. Use *badly* whenever an adverb is required.

Although Granny Weatherall looks *bad*, she is not at all happy to see Doctor Harry at the beginning of Katherine Anne Porter's story.

Elizabeth is *badly* shaken when Mr. Hooper refuses to remove the black veil.

because of, due to

Use *due to* if it can logically replace the phrase *caused by*. In introductory phrases, however, *because of* is better usage than *due to*.

Peyton Farquhar's failure to recognize the trap of the Federal scout may be *due to* his eagerness to aid the Confederate cause.

Because of Edgar Lee Masters's ability to sketch small-town characters accurately and accessibly, *Spoon River Anthology* became extremely popular.

being as, being that

Avoid using the expressions *being as* and *being that*. Use *because* or *since* instead.

Because Walt Whitman believed that new styles were needed in American poetry, he consciously broke with traditional forms and experimented with free verse.

Since Mr. Shiftlet is more interested in the car than in young Lucynell, it is hardly surprising that he abandons her at the roadside diner in Flannery O'Connor's "The Life You Save May Be Your Own."

beside, besides

Beside is a preposition meaning "at the side of" or "close to." Do not confuse *beside* with *besides*, which means "in addition to." *Besides* can be a preposition or an adverb.

When Clark sits *beside* his Aunt Georgiana at the concert, he tries to imagine her emotions as she hears the music.

Besides Mr. Oakhurst, which other characters are run out of town at the beginning of Bret Harte's "The Outcasts of Poker Flat"?

Thomas Jefferson was the third president of the United States; he was a gifted architect and inventor, *besides*.

can, may

The verb *can* generally refers to the ability to do something. The verb *may* generally refers to permission to do something.

One of Ralph Waldo Emerson's major themes is that human beings *can* acquire from nature a sense of their own potential and autonomy.

Robert Frost's poetry *may* appear to be simple, but it is rich with hidden meaning.

different from, different than

The preferred usage is *different from.*

In her powerful exploration of women's consciousness, Kate Chopin was *different from* the vast majority of her contemporaries.

due to the fact that

Replace this awkward expression with *because* or *since*.

Because Dexter Green cherishes his memories of the glamourous Judy Jones, it is not surprising that he is saddened by the knowledge that her youth and beauty have faded.

farther, further

Use *farther* when you refer to distance. Use *further* when you mean "to a greater degree."

The *farther* Phoenix Jackson travels in Eudora Welty's story "A Worn Path," the more her determination to reach her goal grows.

In his speech, Patrick Henry urges his countrymen to trust the British no *further*.

fewer, less

Use *fewer* for things that can be counted. Use *less* for amounts or quantities that cannot be counted.

William Carlos Williams's poem "The Red Wheelbarrow" uses *fewer* words than most other poems I've read.

The train engineer felt *less* anticipation with each step that drew him nearer to the house by the railroad tracks.

good, well

Use the predicate adjective *good* after linking verbs such as *feel, look, smell, taste,* and *seem*. Use *well* whenever you need an adverb.

At the end of F. Scott Fitzgerald's "Winter Dreams," Devon implies to Dexter that Judy Jones does not look as *good* as she used to.

Anne Tyler writes especially *well* about ordinary people and family relationships.

hopefully

You should not loosely attach this adverb to a sentence, as in "Hopefully, the rain will stop by noon." Rewrite the sentence so that *hopefully* modifies a specific verb. Other possible ways of revising such sentences include using the adjective *hopeful* or a phrase such as *everyone hopes that*.

In his Nobel Prize acceptance speech, William Faulkner wrote *hopefully* about mankind's ability to endure and prevail.

Mai was *hopeful* that she could locate some more biographical information about Jean Toomer at her local library.

Everyone hopes that Diane will win the oral interpretation contest with her rendition of Robert Frost's "Out, Out—."

its, it's

Do not confuse the possessive pronoun *its* with the contraction *it's*, standing for "it is" or "it has."

Perhaps the most memorable line in Emerson's poem "The Rhodora" is "Beauty is *its* own excuse for being."

Wallace Stevens's "Anecdote of the Jar" suggests that *it's* impossible to mediate completely between the wilderness and the world of civilization.

kind of, sort of

In formal writing, you should not use these colloquial expressions. Instead, use a word such as *rather* or *somewhat*.

Robert Lowell's train of thought in "Hawthorne" is *rather* difficult to follow.

In describing the events that launched the Civil War, Mary Chesnut is accurate but *somewhat* emotional.

lay, lie

Do not confuse these verbs. *Lay* is a transitive verb meaning "to set or put something down." Its principal parts are *lay, laying, laid, laid. Lie* is an intransitive verb meaning "to recline." Its principal parts are *lie, lying, lay, lain.*

Stream-of-consciousness narration *lays* a special responsibility on the reader to piece together the events in a story or narrative poem.

The speaker of Emily Dickinson's "I heard a Fly buzz—when I died—" lies in a silent room as her life slips away.

many, much

Use *many* to refer to a specific quantity. Use *much* for an indefinite amount or for an abstract concept.

Many of William Faulkner's novels deal with the themes of pride, guilt, and the search for identity.

Much of Mark Twain's fiction was influenced by his boyhood along the Mississippi.

may be, maybe

Be careful not to confuse the verb phrase *may be* with the adverb *maybe* (meaning "perhaps").

In some of Emily Dickinson's poems, the speaker *may be* the poet herself; in others, the speaker is clearly a different persona.

The most memorable, and *maybe* the most ineffectual, character in T. S. Eliot's poetry is J. Alfred Prufrock.

plurals that do not end in *-s*

The plurals of certain nouns from Greek and Latin are formed as they were in their original language. Words such as *criteria, media,* and *phenomena* are plural and should not be treated as if they are singular (*criterion, medium, phenomenon*).

In "Ars Poetica," Archibald MacLeish seems to deny that meaning is the most important *criterion* for the evaluation of poetry.

The *phenomena* discussed by the "learn'd astronomer" in Whitman's poem may have included planetary orbits and the influence of the moon on the tides.

raise, rise

Raise is a transitive verb that usually takes a direct object. *Rise* is intransitive and never takes a direct object.

Suspense *raises* readers' expectations and motivates them to continue reading a story to see how the plot will be resolved.

Some of Flannery O'Connor's best short stories can be found in her collection entitled *Everything That Rises Must Converge.*

set, sit

Do not confuse these verbs. *Set* is a transitive verb meaning "to put (something) in a certain place." Its principal parts are *set, setting, set, set. Sit* is an intransitive verb meaning "to be seated." Its principal parts are *sit, sitting, sat, sat.*

Phillis Wheatley's poem is so complimentary to Washington that it seems to *set* him on a pedestal.

As Mrs. Mallard *sits* upstairs alone, she suddenly realizes that the death of her husband has freed her to live for herself.

that, which, who

Use the relative pronoun *that* to refer to things or people. Use *which* only for things and *who* only for people.

The modern poet *that* Lee liked best was Sylvia Plath.

The Romantic movement, *which* emphasized inner feelings and emotions, took place during the early 1800's.

The poet *who* was the first to read his work at a presidential inauguration was Robert Frost.

unique

Because *unique* means "one of a kind," you should not use it carelessly instead of the words "interesting" or "unusual." Avoid such illogical expressions as "most unique," "very unique," and "extremely unique."

Some critics have argued that its themes and style make Herman Melville's *Moby-Dick* unique in the history of the American novel.

who, whom

In formal writing, remember to use *who* only as a subject in clauses and sentences and *whom* only as an object.

Walt Whitman, *who* grieved profoundly at Lincoln's assassination, rendered his tribute to the slain president in a long elegy entitled "When Lilacs Last in the Dooryard Bloom'd."

F. Scott Fitzgerald, *whom* many have heralded as the voice of the Jazz Age, wrote the American literary classic *The Great Gatsby.*

Speaking, Listening, and Viewing Handbook

Communication

Communication can be spoken, written, or nonverbal. The literature in this book is written, which is one form of communication, but much of your communication is probably oral or visual.

You use many different kinds of oral communication every day. When you communicate with your friends, when you communicate with your teachers or your parents, or when you interact with a cashier in a store, you are communicating orally. In addition to ordinary, everyday conversation, oral communication includes class discussions, speeches, interviews, presentations, and debates. When you communicate by telephone, you must rely solely on your verbal skills. When you communicate face to face, however, you usually use more than your voice to get your message across.

Interpreting visual messages is another important part of communication. Many messages are communicated with gestures, pictures, or other visual elements—with or without words.

Elements of Speaking, Listening, and Viewing

The following terms will give you a better understanding of the many elements that are involved in speaking, listening, and viewing:

ARTICULATION is the process of forming sounds into words; it is the way in which the tongue, teeth, lower jaw, and soft palate are used to produce speech sounds.

CONNOTATION is the set of associations a word calls to mind. The connotations of the words you choose influence the message you send. For example, most people respond more favorably to being described as "slim" rather than as "skinny." The connotation of *slim* is more appealing than that of *skinny*.

CRITICAL VIEWING is the act of evaluating visual presentations, such as art, reports, or media. Critical viewing involves understanding that visual presentations are not completely objective, evaluating the presentation's source and purpose, and developing opinions only after assessing the presentation.

ELEMENTS OF DESIGN are the components that make up a visual representation. Including shape, line, color, texture, and balance, elements of design are used to express meaning in visual representations.

FEEDBACK is the set of verbal and nonverbal reactions that indicate to a speaker that a message has been received and understood.

GESTURES are the movements made with arms, hands, face, and fingers to communicate.

INFLECTION refers to the rise and fall in the pitch of the voice in speaking; it is also called **intonation.**

LISTENING is understanding and interpreting sound in a meaningful way. You listen differently for different purposes.

Listening for key information: For example, when a teacher gives an assignment, or when someone gives you directions to a place, you listen for key information.

Listening for main points: In a classroom exchange of ideas or information, or while watching a television documentary, you listen for main points.

Listening critically: When you evaluate a performance, song, or a persuasive or political speech, you listen critically, questioning and judging the speaker's message.

NONVERBAL COMMUNICATION is communication without the use of words. People communicate nonverbally through gestures, facial expressions, postures, and body movements. Sign language is an entire language based on nonverbal communication.

VOCAL DELIVERY is the way in which you present a message. Your vocal delivery involves all of the following elements:

Volume: the loudness or quietness of your voice
Pitch: the high or low quality of your voice
Rate: the speed at which you speak; also called ***pace***
Stress: the amount of emphasis placed on different syllables in a word or on different words in a sentence

All of these elements individually, and the way in which they are combined, contribute to the meaning of a spoken message.

Speaking, Listening, and Viewing Outcomes

The following are some of the many types of situations in which you apply your speaking, listening, and viewing skills:

AUDIENCE Your audience in any situation refers to the person or people to whom you direct your message. An audience may be a group of people sitting in a classroom or an auditorium observing a performance, or it may be just one person to whom you address a question or a comment. When preparing for any speaking situation, it's useful to analyze your audience, learning what you can about their background, interests, and attitudes so that you can tailor your message to them.

DEBATE A debate is a formal public-speaking situation in which participants prepare and present arguments on opposing sides of a question, stated as a **proposition.** The proposition must be controversial: It must concern an issue that may be solved in two different, valid ways.

The two sides in a debate are the *affirmative* (pro) and the *negative* (con). The affirmative side argues in favor of the proposition, while the negative side argues against it. The affirmative side begins the debate, since it is seeking a change in belief or policy. The opposing sides take turns presenting their arguments, and each side has an opportunity for *rebuttal,* in which they may challenge or question the other side's argument.

FILM TECHNIQUE describes the methods used to present information through film. It includes special effects, camera angles, editing, and sequencing, all of which alter the way the information is presented. The use of film techniques can determine the effectiveness of a film or television program.

GROUP DISCUSSION results when three or more people meet to solve a common problem, arrive at a decision, or answer a question of mutual interest. Group discussion is one of the most widely used forms of interpersonal communication in modern society. **Meetings** are a kind of organized group discussion for a specific purpose.

INTERVIEW An interview is a form of interaction in which one person, the interviewer, asks questions of another person, the interviewee. Interviews may take place for many purposes: to obtain information, to discover a person's suitability for a job or a college, or to inform the public of a notable person's opinions.

MEDIA include all the forms of communication that deliver information to the public. Newspapers, magazines, radio, and television are types of media. Because media is the representation of information, it is seldom entirely objective.

MULTIMEDIA presentations use more than one media form to present information. Elements of video, music, and graphic displays can be combined for a multimedia presentation.

ORAL INTERPRETATION is the reading or speaking of a work of literature aloud for an audience. Oral interpretation involves giving expression to the ideas, meaning, or even the structure of a work of literature. The speaker interprets the work through his or her vocal delivery. **Storytelling,** in which a speaker reads or tells a story expressively, is a form of oral interpretation.

PANEL DISCUSSION is a group discussion on a topic of interest common to all members of a panel and to a listening audience. A panel is usually composed of four to six experts on a particular topic who are brought together to share information and opinions.

PANTOMIME is a form of nonverbal communication in which an idea or a story is communicated completely through the use of gesture, body language, and facial expressions, without any words at all.

READERS THEATRE is a dramatic reading of a work of literature. Participants take parts from a story or play and read aloud in expressive voices. Sets and costumes are not part of the performance; participants remain seated as they deliver their lines.

ROLE PLAY To role-play is to take the role of a person or character and act out a situation, speaking, acting, and responding in the manner of the character.

SPEECH A speech is an address given to an audience. A speech may be **impromptu**—delivered on the spur of the moment with no preparation—or formally prepared and delivered for a specific occasion.

- *Purposes*: The most common purposes of speeches are to persuade (e.g., political speeches), to entertain, to explain, and to inform.
- *Occasions*: Different occasions call for different types of speeches. Speeches given on these occasions could be persuasive, entertaining, or informative, as appropriate. The following are common occasions for speeches:

  Introduction: Introducing a speaker or presenter at a meeting or assembly

  Presentation: Giving an award or acknowledging the contributions of someone

  Acceptance: Accepting an award or a tribute

  Keynote: An inspirational address given at a large meeting or convention

  Commencement: A celebration honoring the graduates of a school or university

Research Handbook

Many of the assignments and activities in this literature book require you to find out more about your topic. Whenever you need ideas, details, or information, you must conduct research. You can find information by using library resources and computer resources, as well as by interviewing experts in a field.

Before you begin, create a research plan that lists the questions you want answered about your topic. Then decide which sources will best provide answers to those questions. When gathering information, it is important to use a variety of sources and not to rely on one main source of information. It is also important to document where you find different pieces of information you use so that you can cite those sources in your work.

The suggestions that follow can help you locate your sources.

Library Resources

Libraries contain many sources of information in both print and electronic form. You'll save time if you plan your research before actually going to the library. Make a list of the information you think you will need, and for each item list possible sources for the information. Here are some sources to consider:

NONFICTION BOOKS An excellent starting point for researching your topic, nonfiction books can provide either broad coverage or specific details, depending on the book. To find appropriate nonfiction books, use the library catalog, which may be in card files or in electronic form on computers. In either case, you can search by author, title, or subject; in a computer catalog, you can also search by key word. When you find the listing for a book you want, print it out or copy down the title, author, and call number. The call number, which also appears on the book's spine, will help you locate the book in the library.

NEWSPAPERS AND MAGAZINES Books are often not the best places for finding up-to-the-minute information. Instead, you might try newspapers and magazines. To find information about an event that occurred on a specific date, go directly to newspapers and magazines for that date. To find articles on a particular topic, use indexes like the *Readers' Guide to Periodical Literature*, which lists magazine articles under subject headings. For each article that you want, jot down the title, author (if given), page number or numbers, and the name and date of the magazine in which the article appears. If your library does not have the magazine you need, either as a separate issue or on microfilm, you may still be able to obtain photocopies of the article through an interlibrary loan.

REFERENCE WORKS The following important reference materials can also help you with your research.

- ***General encyclopedias*** have articles on thousands of topics and are a good starting point for your research, although they shouldn't be used as primary sources.
- ***Specialized encyclopedias*** contain articles in particular subject areas, such as science, music, or art.
- ***Biographical dictionaries and indexes*** contain brief articles on people and often suggest where to find more information.
- ***Almanacs*** provide statistics and data on current events and act as a calendar for the upcoming year.
- ***Atlases,*** or books of maps, usually include geographical facts and may also include information like population and weather statistics.
- ***Indexes and bibliographies,*** such as the *Readers' Guide to Periodical Literature*, tell you in what publications you can find specific information, articles, or shorter works (such as poems or essays).
- ***Vertical files*** (drawers in file cabinets) hold pamphlets, booklets, and government publications that often provide current information.

Computer Research

The Internet Use the Internet to get up-to-the-minute information on virtually any topic. The Internet provides access to a multitude of resource-rich sources such as news media, museums, colleges and universities, and government institutions. There are a number of indexes and directories organized by subject to help you locate information on the Internet, including Yahoo!, the World Wide Web Virtual Library, the Kids Web, and the Webcrawler. These indexes and directories will help you find direct links to information related to your topic.

Internet Sources and Addresses

- ***Yahoo! Directory*** allows you to do word searches or link directly to your topic by clicking on such subjects as the arts, computers, entertainment, or government.
  http://www.yahoo.com
- ***World Wide Web Virtual Library*** is a comprehensive and easy-to-use subject catalog that provides direct links to academic subjects in alphabetical order.
  http://celtic.stanford.edu/vlib/Overview.html
- ***Kids Web*** supplies links to reference materials, such as dictionaries, *Bartlett's Familiar Quotations*, a thesaurus, and a world fact book.
  http://www.npac.syr.edu/textbook/kidsweb/
- ***Webcrawler*** helps you to find links to information about your topic that are available on the Internet when you type in a concise term or key word.
  http://www.webcrawler.com

CD-ROM References

Other sources that you can access using a computer are available on CD-ROM. The Wilson Disk, Newsquest, the *Readers' Guide to Periodical Literature*, and many other useful indexes are available on CD-ROM, as are encyclopedias, almanacs, atlases, and other reference works. Check your library to see which are available.

Interviews as Research Sources

People who are experts in their field or who have experience or knowledge relevant to your topic are excellent sources for your research. If such people are available to you, the way to obtain information from them is through an interview. Follow these guidelines to make your interview successful and productive:

- Make an appointment at a time convenient to the person you want to interview, and arrange to meet in a place where he or she will feel comfortable talking freely.
- If necessary, do research in advance to help you prepare the questions you will ask.
- Before the interview, list the questions you will ask, wording them so that they encourage specific answers. Avoid questions that can be answered simply with *yes* or *no*.
- Make an audiotape or videotape of the interview, if possible. If not, write down the answers as accurately as you can.
- Include the date of the interview at the top of your notes or on the tape.
- Follow up with a thank-you note or phone call to the person you interviewed.

Sources for a Multimedia Presentation

When preparing a multimedia presentation, keep in mind that you'll need to use some of your research findings to illustrate or support your main ideas when you actually give the presentation. Do research to find media support, such as visuals, CDs, and so on—in addition to those media you might create yourself. Here are some media that may be useful as both sources and illustrations:

- Musical recordings on audiocassette or compact disk (CD), often available at libraries
- Videos that you prepare yourself
- Fine art reproductions, often available at libraries and museums
- Photographs that you or others have taken
- Computer presentations using slide shows, graphics, and so on
- Video- or audiocassette recordings of interviews that you conduct

Crediting Sources

Whatever form you use to present your research results, remember to credit your sources for any ideas you use that are not common knowledge and are not your own. In addition, be sure that you acknowledge passages or distinctive phrases that come from a source. In written work, credit others' ideas or words with footnotes, endnotes, or parenthetical notes.

Failure to credit sources properly is **plagiarism,** the presenting of someone else's words or ideas as your own. Plagiarism is a form of stealing. Words and ideas may not seem as tangible as physical property, but they are forms of intellectual property. As you know from your own experience, it takes hard work to formulate a new idea or to find just the right phrase to describe something. Acknowledge this work.

Index of Authors and Titles

Page numbers in *italics* refer to biographical information.

S

T

U

V

W

Y

Index of Skills

LITERARY TERMS

READING STRATEGIES

GRAMMAR AND STYLE

VOCABULARY

CRITICAL THINKING AND VIEWING

WRITING

WRITING SKILLS

SPEAKING, LISTENING, AND VIEWING

RESEARCHING AND REPRESENTING

LIFE AND WORK SKILLS

BACKGROUND

ACKNOWLEDGMENTS (continued)

Robert Bly "Discovers of Chile" by Pablo Neruda, translated by Robert Bly from *Neruda and Vallejo: Selected Poems,* edited by Robert Bly. Copyright © 1971 Robert Bly. Reprinted by permission of the translator.

Gwendolyn Brooks "The Explorer" from *Blacks* by Gwendolyn Brooks, published by The David Company, Chicago, IL. Copyright © 1987. Reissued by Third World Press, Chicago, IL, 1991. Reprinted by permission of the author.

Diana Chang "Most Satisfied by Snow" by Diana Chang. Reprinted by permission of the author.

Chelsea House Publishers, a division of Main Line Book Co. From "Harlem: A Paradise of My Own People" from *The Harlem Renaissance* by Veronica Chambers. Copyright © 1998 by Chelsea House Publishers, a division of Main Line Book Co. All rights reserved. Reprinted by permission.

Crown Publishing, a division of Random House, Inc. "Food for Thought" from *Dave Barry Is Not Making This Up,* by Dave Barry. Copyright © 1994 by Dave Barry. Published by Crown Publishers, Inc. Originally published in *The Miami Herald.*

Doris Dana c/o The Joan Daves Agency "Daybreak" from *Time*/"Amanecer" from *Tiempo* by Gabriela Mistral, translated by Doris Dana. From *Selected Poems of Gabriela Mistral,* translated and edited by Doris Dana. Copyright © 1971 by Doris Dana. Reprinted by arrangement with Doris Dana c/o The Joan Daves Agency.

Darhansoff & Verrill Literary Agency "Why Is This Age Worse. . .?" from *Poems of Akhmatova* by Anna Akhmatova, selected, translated and introduced by Stanley Kunitz with Max Hayward. Copyright © 1967, 1968, 1972, 1973 by Stanley Kunitz and Max Hayward. Used by permission of Darhansoff & Verrill Literary Agency.

J. M. Dent & Sons, Ltd. From "Letters from an American Farmer" by Michel-Guillaume Jean de Crèvecoeur in *An Everyman's Library.*

Sandra Dijkstra Literary Agency for Amy Tan "Mother Tongue" by Amy Tan. Copyright © 1989 by Amy Tan. First appeared in "Threepenny Review." Reprinted by permission of Sandra Dijkstra Literary Agency.

Doubleday, a division of Bantam Doubleday Dell Publishing Group, Inc. "An Occurrence at Owl Creek Bridge" from *The Complete Stories of Ambrose Bierce,* published by Doubleday & Company, Inc. From *Roots* by Alex Haley. Copyright © 1976 by Alex Haley. "The Adamant" and "The Light Comes Brighter," copyright 1938 by Theodore Roethke, from *The Collected Poems of Theodore Roethke* by Theodore Roethke. Used by permission of Doubleday, a division of Bantam Doubleday Dell Publishing Group, Inc.

Rita Dove Rita Dove, "For the Love of Books," first published as part of the introduction to *Selected Poems,* Pantheon Books/Vintage Books, © 1993 by Rita Dove. Reprinted by permission of the author.

Ecco Press "Where Is Here?" taken from *Where Is Here?* by Joyce Carol Oates. Copyright © 1992 by The Ontario Review, Inc. First published by The Ecco Press in 1992. Reprinted by permission of The Ecco Press.

Faber and Faber Ltd. "The Love Song of J. Alfred Prufrock" from *Collected Poems 1909–1962* by T. S. Eliot, copyright © 1936 by Harcourt Brace & Company, copyright © 1963, 1964 by T. S. Eliot. Reprinted by permission of Faber and Faber Ltd.

Farrar, Straus & Giroux, Inc. "Coyote v. Acme" from *Coyote v. Acme* by Ian Frazier. Copyright © 1996 by Ian Frazier. "The Death of the Ball Turret Gunner" and "Losses" from *The Complete Poems* by Randall Jarrell. Copyright © 1969 by Mrs. Randall Jarrell. "Hawthorne" from *The Union Dead* by Robert Lowell. Copyright © 1959 by Robert Lowell. Copyright renewed © 1987 by Harriot Lowell, Caroline Lowell, and Sheridan Lowell. "The First Seven Years" from *The Magic Barrel* by Bernard Malamud. Copyright © 1950, 1958 and copyright renewed © 1977, 1986 by Bernard Malamud. Excerpt from *The Right Stuff* by Tom Wolfe. Copyright © 1979 by Tom Wolfe. "A Journey Along the Oka" from *Stories and Prose Poems* by Alexander Solzhenitsyn, translated by Michael Glenny. Translation copyright © 1971 by Michael Glenny. Reprinted by permission of Farrar, Straus & Gilroux, Inc.

Fulcrum Publishing "The Earth on Turtle's Back" from *Keepers of the Earth: Native American Stories and Environmental Activities for Children* by Michael J. Caduto and Joseph Bruchac (© 1988) Fulcrum Publishing, 350 Indiana St., #350, Golden, CO 80401, 800-992-2908. Used by permission.

John Graves "Old Time Cowboys in the Modern World" from *A John Graves Reader.* Copyright © 1996 by John Graves. Used by permission of the author.

Harcourt Brace & Company "A Worn Path" from *A Curtain of Green and Other Stories,* copyright 1941 and renewed 1969 by Eudora Welty. "The Jilting of Granny Weatherall" from *Flowering Judas and Other Stories,* copyright 1930 and renewed 1958 by Katherine Anne Porter. "Chicago" and "Grass" from *Chicago Poems* by Carl Sandburg, copyright 1916 by Holt, Rinehart and Winston, Inc.; renewed 1944 by Carl Sandburg. "The Life You Save May Be Your Own" from *A Good Man Is Hard to Find and Other Stories,* copyright © 1953 by Flannery O'Connor and renewed 1981 by Regina O'Connor. "Everyday Use" from *In Love & Trouble: Stories of Black Women,* copyright © 1973 by Alice Walker. Reprinted by permission of Harcourt Brace & Company.

Joy Harjo "Suspended" by Joy Harjo from *In Short: A Collection of Brief Creative Nonfiction,* edited by Judith Kitchen and Mary Paumier Jones. Copyright © 1996. Reprinted by permission of the author.

HarperCollins Publishers, Inc. "The Boys' Ambition" from *Life on the Mississippi* by Mark Twain. "The Notorious Jumping Frog of Calaveras County" from *Sketches New and Old* by Mark Twain. Excerpt from *Pilgrim at Tinker Creek* by Annie Dillard. Copyright © 1974 by Annie Dillard. "Bidwell Ghost" from *Baptism of Desire* by Louise Erdrich. Copyright © 1990 by Louise Erdrich. From *Dust Tracks on a Road* by Zora Neale Hurston. Copyright 1942 by Zora Neale Hurston. Copyright renewed 1970 by John C. Hurston. "Here Is New York" from *Essays by E. B. White* by E. B. White. Copyright 1949 by E. B. White. Copyright renewed 1977 by E. B. White. All rights reserved. Reprinted by permission of HarperCollins Publishers, Inc.

HarperCollins Publishers, Inc., and Faber and Faber Ltd. "Mirror" from *Crossing the Water* by Sylvia Plath. Copyright © 1963 by Ted Hughes. Originally appeared in *The New Yorker.* Reprinted by permission of HarperCollins Publishers, Inc., and Faber and Faber Ltd.

Harvard University Press "I heard a Fly buzz—when I died" (#465), "There's a certain Slant of light" (#258), "My life closed twice before its close—" (#1732), "The soul selects her own Society—" (#303), "Because I could not stop for Death—" (#712), and "There is a solitude of space" (#1695) reprinted by permission of the publishers and the Trustees of Amherst College from *The Poems of Emily Dickinson,* Thomas H. Johnson, ed., Cambridge, Mass.: The Belknap Press of Harvard University Press, Copyright © 1951, 1955, 1979, 1983 by The President and Fellows of Harvard College.

Maria Herrera-Sobek The poem "Oaxaca III" by Maria Herrera-Sobek first appeared in *New Chicana/Chicano Writing 2,* edited by Charles M. Tatum (1992). Reprinted by permission of Maria Herrera-Sobek.

Hill and Wang, a division of Farrar, Straus & Giroux, Inc. Excerpts from "Sinners in the Hands of an Angry God" from *Jonathan Edwards: Representative Selections* edited by Clarence H. Faust and Thomas H. Johnson. Copyright © 1935, 1962 by Hill and Wang, Inc. Reprinted by permission of Hill and Wang, a division of Farrar, Straus & Giroux, Inc.

Henry Holt and Company, Inc. "The Gift Outright," "Acquainted With the Night," and "Stopping by Woods on a Snowy Evening" from *The Poetry of Robert Frost,* edited by Edward Connery Lathem. Copyright 1942, 1951, © 1956 by Robert Frost. Copyright © 1970 by Lesley Frost Ballantine, copyright 1923, 1928, © 1969 by Henry Holt and Company, Inc. Reprinted by permission of Henry Holt & Company, Inc. "Birches," "Out, Out—," and "Mending Wall" from *The Poetry of Robert Frost* edited by Edward Connery Lathem. Copyright 1944, © 1958 by Robert Frost, © 1967 by Lesley Frost Ballantine, copyright 1916, 1930, 1939, © 1969 by Henry Holt and Company, Inc. "Return" (English translation of "Volver" by Berta Montalvo), English translation by Lori M. Carlson from *Cool Salsa.* Copyright © 1994 by Lori M. Carlson.

Houghton Mifflin Company From "The Navajo Origin Legend" in *Navajo Legends*, collected and translated by Washington Matthews. "A Noiseless Patient Spider" and "When I Heard the Learn'd Astronomer" from *Complete Poetry and Selected Prose of Walt Whitman,* edited by J. E. Miller, Jr. From *The Mortgaged Heart* by Carson McCullers. Copyright 1940, 1941, 1942, 1945, 1948, 1949, 1953, © 1956, 1959, 1963, 1971 by Floria V. Lasky, Executrix of the Estate of Carson McCullers. "Ars Poetica" from *New and Collected Poems 1917–1982* by Archibald MacLeish. Copyright © 1985 by the Estate of Archibald MacLeish. Reprinted by permission of Houghton Mifflin Company. All rights reserved.

International Creative Management, Inc. "Ambush" from *The Things They Carried* by Tim O'Brien. Copyright © 1990 by Tim O'Brien. Reprinted by permission of International Creative Management, Inc.

Joelsongs "Allentown" by Billy Joel. Copyright © 1981 Joelsongs. All rights reserved. Used by permission of Joelsongs.

Johnson Publishing Company, Inc. From *My Bondage and My Freedom* by Frederick Douglass. Copyright 1970. Used by permission.

Barbara Kimenye "The Pig" by Barbara Kimenye from *Kalasanda Revisited*. Copyright © 1966 Oxford University Press.

Alfred A. Knopf, Inc. From *The Woman Warrior* by Maxine Hong Kingston. Copyright © 1975, 1976 by Maxine Hong Kingston. "The Brown Chest" from *The Afterlife and Other Stories* by John Updike. Copyright © 1994 by John Updike. "Dream Variations," "Ardella," and "Refugee in America" from *Collected Poems* by Langston Hughes. Copyright © 1994 by the Estate of Langston Hughes. "A Noiseless Flash" from *Hiroshima* by John Hersey. Copyright 1946 and renewed 1974 by John Hersey. Originally appeared in *The New Yorker*. "Anecdote of the Jar" from *Collected Poems* by Wallace Stevens. Copyright 1923 and renewed 1951 by Wallace Stevens. "Of Modern Poetry" from *Collected Poems* by Wallace Stevens. Copyright 1942 by Wallace Stevens and renewed 1970 by Holly Stevens. "The Negro Speaks of Rivers" and "I, Too" from *Selected Poems* by Langston Hughes. Copyright 1926 by Alfred A. Knopf, Inc., and renewed 1954 by Langston Hughes. From *Of Plymouth Plantation* by William Bradford, edited by Samuel Eliot Morison. Copyright 1952 by Samuel Eliot Morison and renewed 1980 by Emily M. Beck. Reprinted by permission of Alfred A. Knopf, Inc.

Latin American Literary Review Press "Freeway 280" by Lorna Dee Cervantes. Reprinted by permission of the publisher, *Latin American Literary Review*, Volume 15, No. 10, 1977, Pittsburgh, Pa.

Hal Leonard Corporation "Hammer and a Nail" words and music by Emily Saliers. Copyright © 1990 EMI Virgin Songs, Inc., and Godhap Music. All rights controlled and administered by EMI Virgin Songs, Inc. All rights reserved. International copyright secured. Used by permission.

Yeh Ling-Ling From "Legal immigration must be curbed, too." by Yeh Ling-Ling. The original article appeared in *USA Today Magazine*, January 1997, as prepared for Carrying Capacity Network. Reprinted by permission of the author.

Liveright Publishing Corporation "Runagate Runagate" copyright © 1966 by Robert Hayden, from *Collected Poems of Robert Hayden* by Frederick Glaysher, editor. "Frederick Douglass," copyright © 1966 by Robert Hayden, from *Angle of Ascent: New and Selected Poems* by Robert Hayden. "anyone lived in a pretty how town," copyright 1940, © 1968, 1991 by the Trustees for the E. E. Cummings Trust; "old age sticks," copyright © 1958, 1986, 1991 by the Trustees for the E. E. Cummings Trust, from *Complete Poems: 1904–1962* by E. E. Cummings. Edited by George J. Firmage. "Storm Ending" from *Cane* by Jean Toomer. Copyright 1923 by Boni & Liveright, renewed 1951 by Jean Toomer. Reprinted by permission of Liveright Publishing Corporation.

Olivia Maciel "Mistress of Nothing"/"Dueña de nada" by Olivia Maciel, translated into English by Olivia Maciel and Mary K. Hawley. Published in *shards of light/astillas de luz,* Tia Chucha Press, Chicago, 1998. Copyright © 1998. Reprinted by permission of the author.

Ellen C. Masters "Lucinda Matlock" from *Spoon River Anthology* by Edgar Lee Masters, published by Macmillan Publishing Company.

Archives of Claude McKay "The Tropics in New York" from *The Poems of Claude McKay* by Claude McKay, Harcourt Brace, publisher, copyright © 1981. Reprinted by permission of the Archives of Claude McKay, Carl Cowl, administrator.

N. Scott Momaday From *The Names: A Memoir by N. Scott Momaday,* published by Harper & Row Publishers, Inc., Copyright © 1976 by N. Scott Momaday. Reprinted by permission of the author.

Berta Montalvo "Volver" by Berta Montalvo from *Cool Salsa.* Copyright © Berta Montalvo. Reprinted by permission of the author.

New Directions Publishing Corporation "Heat" (Heat, Part II of Garden) and "Pear Tree" by H. D., *Collected Poems, 1912–1944.* Copyright © 1982 by the Estate of Hilda Doolittle. "In a Station of the Metro" and "The River-Merchant's Wife: A Letter" by Ezra Pound, from *Personae.* Copyright 1926 by Ezra Pound. "The Great Figure," "The Red Wheelbarrow" and "This Is Just to Say" by William Carlos Williams, from *Collected Poems Volume 1: 1909–1939.* Copyright 1938 by New Directions Publishing Corporation. Excerpts from "A Few Don'ts by an Imagist" (A Retrospect) from *Literary Essays of Ezra Pound.* Copyright © 1935 by Ezra Pound. "Peatón"/"Pedestrian" by Octavio Paz, from *Collected Poems 1957–1987.* Copyright © 1986 by Octavio Paz and Eliot Weinberger. Reprinted by permission.

The New York Times "Onomatopoeia" by William Safire from *You Could Look It Up.* Copyright © 1988 by The Cobbett Corporation. Originally appeared in *The New York Times.* Reprinted by permission.

North Point Press, a division of Farrar, Straus & Giroux, Inc. "Fairy Tales" by Shu Ting from *A Splintered Mirror: Chinese Poetry from the Democracy Movement,* translated by Donald Finkel. Translation copyright © 1991 by Donald Finkel. Reprinted by permission of North Point Press, a division of Farrar, Straus & Giroux, Inc.

W. W. Norton & Company, Inc. From "Civil Disobedience," reprinted from *Walden and Civil Disobedience* by Henry David Thoreau, edited by Owen Thomas. Copyright ©1966 by W. W. Norton & Company, Inc. "Who Burns for the Perfection of Paper" from *City of Coughing and Dead Radiators* by Martin Espada. Copyright © 1993 by Martin Espada. Reprinted by permission of W. W. Norton & Company, Inc.

W. W. Norton & Company, Inc., and Adrienne Rich "In a Classroom" from *Time's Power: Poems 1985–1988* by Adrienne Rich. Copyright ©1989 by Adrienne Rich. All rights reserved. Used by permission of W. W. Norton & Company, Inc., and the author.

Naomi Shihab Nye "Mint Snowball" by Naomi Shihab Nye. Reprinted by permission of the author.

Harold Ober Associates, Inc. "The Corn Planting" from *Sherwood Anderson Short Stories*, edited by Maxwell Geismar. © 1962 by Eleanor Anderson. "A Black Man Talks of Reaping" by Arna Bontemps. Copyright © 1963 by Arna Bontemps. Reprinted by permission of Harold Ober Associates Incorporated.

Simon J. Ortiz "Hunger in New York City" from *Going for the Rain: Poems* by Simon J. Ortiz. Published by Harper & Row. Reprinted by permission of Simon J. Ortiz.

Grace Paley c/o Elaine Markson Literary Agency, Inc. "Anxiety" from *Later the Same Day* by Grace Paley, Farrar, Straus and Giroux, 1985. Copyright © 1985 by Grace Paley. All rights reserved. Reprinted by permission of the author, c/o Elaine Markson Literary Agency, Inc.

Princeton University Press From *Walden: The Writings of Henry D. Thoreau*, edited by J. Lyndon Shanley. Copyright © 1971 Princeton University Press. Reprinted by permission of Princeton University Press.

Penguin Books UK "Melting Snow" from *The Penguin Book of Japanese Verse,* translated by Geoffrey Bownas and Anthony Thwaite (Penguin Books, 1964), translation copyright © Geoffrey Bownas and Anthony Thwaite 1964. From *The Letters of the Younger Pliny* translated by Betty Radice (Penguin Classics, 1963), copyright © Betty Radice, 1963.

The Permissions Company "The Albatross" by Charles Baudelaire, translated by Kate Flores. Reprinted with the permission of The Estate of Angel Flores, c/o The Permissions Company, P.O. Box 243, High Bridge, NJ 08829, USA.

Pirandello Estate and Toby Cole, Agent "War" by Luigi Pirandello from *The Medals and Other Stories,* © E. P. Dutton, N.Y., 1932, 1967. Reprinted by permission of the Pirandello Estate and Toby Cole, Agent.

Random House, Inc. "The Nobel Prize Acceptance Speech" by William

Faulkner, © 1950 The Nobel Foundation. "The Unknown Citizen" from *W. H. Auden: Collected Poems* by W. H. Auden, edited by Edward Mendelson. Copyright 1940 and renewed 1968 by W. H. Auden. "The Writer in the Family" from *Lives of the Poets* by E. L. Doctorow. Copyright © 1984 by E. L. Doctorow. "Cats" from *Living Out Loud* by Anna Quindlen. Copyright © 1987 by Anna Quindlen. "Race at Morning" from *Big Woods* by William Faulkner. Copyright © 1955 by The Curtis Publishing Company. "Gold Glade" from *Selected Poems 1923–1975* by Robert Penn Warren. Copyright © 1957 by Robert Penn Warren. Reprinted by permission of Random House, Inc.

Russell & Volkening as agents for the author "Average Waves in Unprotected Waters" by Anne Tyler. Copyright © 1977 by Anne Tyler. Originally published by *The New Yorker*. Reprinted by permission of Russell & Volkening as agents for the author.

Estate of Ricardo Sánchez "i yearn" by Ricardo Sánchez. Copyright © 1975 by Ricardo Sánchez. Reprinted by permission of the Estate of Ricardo Sánchez.

Scribner, A Division of Simon & Schuster, Inc. "In Another Country" from *Men Without Women* by Ernest Hemingway. Copyright 1927 by Charles Scribner's Sons. Copyright renewed 1955 by Ernest Hemingway. F. Scott Fitzgerald, "Winter Dreams" by F. Scott Fitzgerald from *All the Sad Young Men*. Copyright 1922 by Frances Scott Fitzgerald Lanahan; copyright renewed 1950. "Gulf War Journal" from *A Woman at War: Storming Kuwait With the U. S. Marines* by Molly Moore. Copyright © 1993 by Molly Moore. "Luke Havergal" from *Collected Poems* by Edwin Arlington Robinson, published by Charles Scribner's Sons. "Richard Cory" from *The Children of the Night* by Edwin Arlington Robinson, published by Charles Scribner's Sons. "The Far and the Near" from *Death to Morning* by Thomas Wolfe. Copyright 1935 by International Magazine Company; copyright renewed © 1963 by Paul Gitlin. Reprinted by permission of Scribner, a Division of Simon and Schuster.

Signet Classic, an imprint of Dutton Signet, a division of Penguin Books USA Inc. "Richard Bone" from *Spoon River Anthology* by Edgar Lee Masters, published by Penguin USA.

Simon & Schuster, Inc. From *Lonesome Dove* by Larry McMurtry, reprinted with the permission of Simon & Schuster. Copyright © 1985 by Larry McMurtry. "Poetry" by Marianne Moore is reprinted with the permission of Simon & Schuster from *Collected Poems of Marianne Moore*. Copyright 1935 by Marianne Moore; copyright renewed © 1963 by Marianne Moore and T. S. Eliot.

Estate of William Stafford "Traveling Through the Dark" from *Stories That Could Be True: New and Collected Poems* by William Stafford. Copyright © 1960 by William Stafford. Reprinted by permission of the Estate of William Stafford.

Estate of Donald E. Stanford "Huswifery" is reprinted from *The Poems of Edward Taylor* edited by Donald E. Stanford, copyright © 1960 Donald E. Stanford.

Sterling Lord Literistic, Inc. "The Crisis, Number 1," excerpts from "The Crisis, Number 1" by Thomas Paine, published in *Citizen Tom Paine*, edited by Howard Fast. Copyright © 1945 by Howard Fast. Reprinted by permission of Sterling Lord Literistic, Inc.

Syracuse University Press From "The Iroquois Constitution" from *Parker on the Iroquois;* edited with an introduction by William N. Fenton, Syracuse, N.Y., Syracuse University Press, 1968. By permission of the publisher.

Terry Teachout Excerpt from "The Case of the Missing Laugh Track" by Terry Teachout, published in *Civilization*, Aug/Sept 1997.

Rosemary A. Thurber "The Night the Ghost Got In" copyright 1933, © 1961 by James Thurber. From *My Life and Hard Times*, published by Harper & Row. Reprinted by permission.

Time Life Syndication "Iron Bird" by Steve Wulf from *Time Magazine*, September 11, 1995. Copyright ©1995 Time Inc. Reprinted by permission.

Tribune/Information Services, Inc. Excerpt from "Where freedom-seekers yearn to be free: Halting immigration deprives America of fresh talent that keeps it on top" by Rep. Martin Frost. Copyright 1999 Knight-Ridder/Tribune News Service. All rights reserved. Reprinted with permission of Knight-Ridder/Tribune Information Services.

The University of Nebraska Press Reprinted from *The Journals of the Lewis and Clark Expedition, July 28–November 1, 1805* (volume 5), edited by Gary Moulton, by permission of the University of Nebraska Press. Copyright 1988 by the University of Nebraska Press.

The University of North Carolina Press "To His Excellency, General Washington" and lines from "An Hymn to the Evening" from *The Poems of Phillis Wheatley*, edited by Julian D. Mason, Jr. Copyright © 1966, 1989 by The University of North Carolina Press. Used by permission of the publisher.

University of Texas Press and the author "El Corrido de Gregorio Cortez" from *With His Pistol in His Hand: A Border Ballad and Its Hero* by Americo Paredes, Copyright © 1958, renewed 1986. By permission of the author and the University of Texas Press.

University Press of New England Garrett Kaoru Hongo, "What For" from *Yellow Light*, © 1982 by Garrett Kaoru Hongo, Wesleyan University Press. Colleen McElroy, "For My Children" from *What Madness Brought Me Here*, © 1990 by Colleen McElroy, Wesleyan University Press. Yusef Komunyakaa, "Camouflaging the Chimera" from *Neon Vernacular*, © 1993 originally published in *Dien Cai Dau*, © 1988 by Yusef Komunyakaa, Wesleyan University Press. Reprinted by permission of University Press of New England.

Viking Penguin, a division of Penguin Books USA, Inc. *The Crucible* by Arthur Miller. Copyright 1952, 1953, 1954, renewed © 1980, 1981, 1982 by Arthur Miller. "The Turtle" from *The Grapes of Wrath* by John Steinbeck. Copyright 1939, renewed © 1967 by John Steinbeck. Used by permission of Viking Penguin, a division of Penguin Books USA Inc.

Tino Villanueva "In the Chiaroscuro of the Years" / "En el claroscuro de los años" by Tino Villanueva. Copyright 1987 by Tino Villanueva. All rights reserved. Used by permission of the author.

Albert Whitman & Co. "Pecos Bill Becomes a Coyote" from *Pecos Bill The Greatest Cowboy of All Time* by James Cloyd Bowman. Copyright © 1937, 1964 by Albert Whitman & Company. Reprinted by permission of the publisher. All rights reserved.

Darryl Babe Wilson "Diamond Island: Alcatraz" by Darryl Babe Wilson. Copyright © 1991 by Darryl Babe Wilson. Reprinted by permission of the author.

Writers House, Inc. "Why We Can't Wait," from "Letter From Birmingham Jail" by Martin Luther King, Jr., Copyright 1963 by Martin Luther King, Jr., copyright renewed 1991 by Coretta Scott King. Reprinted by arrangement with The Heirs to the Estate of Martin Luther King, Jr., c/o Writers House, Inc., as agent for the proprietor.

Note: Every effort has been made to locate the copyright owner of material reprinted in this book. Omissions brought to our attention will be corrected in subsequent editions.

Art Credits

Cover: © 1994, Terry Qing/FPG International Corp.; **ix:** *The Coming of the Mayflower*, N.C. Wyeth, from the Collection of Metropolitan Life Insurance Company, New York City; **x:** Reuters/Corbis-Bettmann; **xi:** *Retroactive I*, 1964, Robert Rauschenberg, Wadsworth Atheneum, Hartford, Connecticut, Gift of Susan Morse Hilles © Robert Rauschenberg/Licensed by VAGA, New York, NY; **xii:** *Quaker Meeting*, British, fourth quarter 18th century or first quarter 19th century, Bequest of Maxim Karolik, Courtesy, Museum of Fine Arts, Boston; **xiv:** (top) The Granger Collection, New York; (bottom) *The Lawrence Tree*, 1929, Georgia O'Keeffe, Wadsworth Atheneum, Hartford, The Ella Gallup Sumner and Mary Catlin Sumner Collection, © 1997 The Georgia O'Keeffe Foundation/Artists Rights Society (ARS), New York; **xv:** Sygma; **xvi:** *From Arkansas*, George Schreiber, Sheldon Swope Art Museum, Terre Haute, Indiana; **xvii:** Petrified Cole/The Image Bank; **xviii:** Corel Professional Photos CD-ROM™; **xix:** *Girls Skipping*, 1949, (detail) Hale Woodruff, oil on canvas, 24" x 32", Private Collection. Courtesy of Michael Rosenfeld Gallery, New York; **xx:** (left) © John LemkerAnimals Animals; (right) Corel Professional Photos CD-ROM™; **xxi:** Photofest; **xxii–1:** *World Map*, 1630, Jan Jansson, The Huntington Library, Art Collections and Botanical Gardens, San Marino, CA; **2:** (1492) Corbis-Bettmann; (1508) Corel Professional Photos CD-ROM™; (1520 Magellan) & (1640) North Wind Picture Archives; (1558) Victoria & Albert Museum/Art Resource, NY; (1608) National Portrait Gallery, Smithsonian Institution/Art Resource, NY; (1609) Scala/Art Resource, NY; (1620) & (1644) The Granger Collection, New York; **3:** (1675) North Wind Picture Archives; (1676) & (1721) & (1741) The Granger Collection, New York; (1727) Corel Professional Photos CD-ROM™; **5:** (top) North Wind Picture Archives; (bottom) *The Mason Children: David, Joanna, and Abigail*, 1670, attributed to the Freake-Gibbs painter. Fine Arts Museums of San Francisco, Gift of Mr. & Mrs. John D. Rockefeller 3rd; **6:** (top) © British Museum; (center) & (bottom) The Granger Collection, New York; **7:** (top) © Lee Boltin Picture Library; (center) & (bottom) Colonial Williamsburg Foundation; **8:** (top)The Bettmann Archive; (bottom) North Wind Picture Archives; **9:** (top) National Portrait Gallery, Smithsonian Institution/Art Resource, NY; **10:** *Sampler*, (detail) 1797 by Mary Wiggin. 18x 21 1/2." Philadelphia Museum of Art, Whitman Sampler Collection/Given by Pet, Incorporated.; **11:** *Oneida Chieftain Shikellamy*, Unknown American Artist, c.1820, 45½" x 32", oil on canvas, Philadelphia Museum of Art. The Collection of Edgar William and Bernice Chrysler Garbisch; **12:** Art Resource, NY; **15:** Astrolabe, Museum fur Kunst und Gewerbe, Hamburg; **16:** Corbis-Bettmann; **20:** ER Degginger/Bruce Coleman, Inc.; **23:** Nicole Galeazzi/ Omni-Photo Communications, Inc.; **24:** *Dreamwalker*, Nancy Wood Taber, colored pencil, courtesy of the artist; **26:** *The Place of Emergence and the Four Worlds* (Navajo), Courtesy of the Wheelwright Museum of the American Indian; **28:** *Red Jacket*, George Catlin, From the Collection of Thomas Gilcrease Institute of American History and Art, Tulsa, Oklahoma; **32:** The Granger Collection, New York; **34:** Corel Professional Photos CD-ROM™; **36:** (top)The Granger Collection, New York; (bottom) *Painting of Cabeza de Vaca, Esteban and their companions among various Texas Indian tribes*, Tom Mirrat, The Institute of Texan Cultures, San Antonio, Texas; **38–39:** Jeff Greenberg/ Photo Researchers, Inc.; **42:** *Olaudah Equiano* (detail), National Portrait Gallery, Smithsonian Institution, Washington, D.C./Art Resource, NY; **45:** *Slaves Below Deck* (detail), Lt. Francis Meynell, National Maritime Museum, Greenwich; **46:** Courtesy of the Library of Congress; **50:** (background) NASA; (top) Courtesy of the author; (bottom) UPI/Corbis-Bettmann; **51:** *San Francisco, 1849*, Attributed to Joshua Pierce, Oil on canvas, Photo by John Lei/Omni-Photo Communications, Inc.; **54:** *Native American male (Wailaki tribe)*, Edward S. Curtis, Southwest Museum, Los Angeles, Photo #N.40042.; **56–57:** Rafael Macia/Photo Researchers, Inc.; **58:** NASA; **59:** Architect of the Capitol; **63:** *Building the Fort*, ca. 1960, Julien Binford, oil on canvas, 86" x 101", The Jamestown Yorktown Educational Trust; **64:** (left) John Smith (detail), National Portrait Gallery, Smithsonian Institution, Washington, D.C./Art Resource, NY; (right) Corbis-Bettmann; **66:** *Founding the First Permanent English Settlement in America*, A.C. Warren, Print Collection, Miriam and Ira D. Wallach Division of Art, Prints and Photographs, The New York Public Library, Astor, Lenox and Tilden Foundations; **71:** *The Coming of the Mayflower*, N.C. Wyeth, from the Collection of Metropolitan Life Insurance Company, New York City; **73:** Cary Wolinsky/ Stock, Boston; **78:** (background): NASA; (right) AP/Wide World Photos; **79 & 82:** NASA; **83:** © 1992 Rob Goldman/FPG International Corp.; **87:** *Pilgrims Going to Church*, George Henry Boughton, oil on canvas, 1867, accession number S-117, Collection of The New-York Historical Society; **88:** *The Puritan*, Augustus Saint-Gaudens, The Metropolitan Museum of Art, Bequest of Jacob Ruppart, 1939 (39.65.53) All Rights Reserved.; **90:** 18th-century pastoral scene in needlework, attributed to Mary Whitehead of Connecticut, probably Norwich area, c. 1750, Lyman Allyn Art Museum, New London, Connecticut, USA; **92:** *Crewel Work Chair Seat Cover*, Gift of Samuel Bradstreet, Courtesy, Museum of Fine Arts, Boston; **96:** (top) Corbis-Bettmann; (bottom) Courtesy of the Library of Congress; **99:** *The Puritan*, c. 1898, Frank E. Schoonover, Oil on canvas, Collection of The Brandywine River Museum, Gift of Mr. and Mrs. Jacob J. Foster; **104:** (background) NASA; (br) Courtesy of the author; **105:** Reuters/Gary Hershorn/Archive Photos; **107:** Reuters/Corbis-Bettmann; **109:** NASA; **110:** Robert Daemmrich/Tony Stone Worldwide; **114:** ©Will McIntyre; Demi McIntyre/Allstock/PNI; **116–117:** *Washington Crossing the Delaware*, Emanuel Gottlieb Leutze, oil on canvas, H.149 in., W. 255 in. (378.5 x 647.7cm.) The Metropolitan Museum of Art, Gift of John S. Kennedy, 1897. (97.34), Copyright © 1992 By the Metropolitan Museum of Art; **118:** (1748) & (1752) & (1773 Phillis Wheatley) The Granger Collection, New York; (1755) North Wind Picture Archives; (1770) Stock Montage/Superstock; (1773 Boston) Courtesy of the Library of Congress; (1776) Courtesy, Independence National Historical Park Collection; **119:** (1781 Cornwallis) & (1791) & (1793) & (1796) The Granger Collection, New York; (1781 Uranus) NASA; (1789) *The Republican Court*, 1861 (detail), Daniel Huntington, The Brooklyn Museum; **120:** (top) National Museum of American History, Smithsonian Institution; (bottom) The Library Company of Philadelphia; **122:** (top) National Museum of American Art, Smithsonian Art Resource, NY; **123:** (top) New York Historical Society; (bottom) © Archive Photos; **124:** (top) Courtesy of the Library of Congress; (bottom) Courtesy, American Antiquarian Society; **125:** (top) & (center) The Granger Collection, New York; **126:** (top) *Sampler*, (detail) 1797 by Mary Wiggin. 18x 21 1/2". Philadelphia Museum of Art, Whitman Sampler Collection/ Given by Pet, Incorporated; (bottom) © Archive Photos; **127:** *Miss Liberty*, Abby Aldrich Rockefeller Folk Art Center, Williamsburg, VA; **128:** *Benjamin Franklin* (detail), c.1790, Pierre Michel Alix, National Portrait Gallery, Smithsonian Institution, Washington, D.C./Art Resource, New York; **131:** The Granger Collection, New York; **134:** *Quaker Meeting*, British, fourth quarter 18th century or first quarter 19th century, Bequest of Maxim Karolik, Courtesy, Museum of Fine Arts, Boston; **138:** (left) & (right) The Granger Collection, New York; **140–141:** (background) Corel Professional Photos CD-ROM™; **141:** (top) *The Declaration of Independence*, John Trumbull, © Yale University Art Gallery; **142:** (tl) *Washington's Headquarters Standard, the Standard of the Army in 1781*, Present-day copy, Courtesy of The Valley Forge Historical Society. Photo by Grace Davies/Omni-Photo Communications, Inc.; **142–143:** (background) Corel Professional Photos CD-ROM™; **144:** *Recruiting for the Continental Army*, c. 1857–59, William T. Ranney, Oil on canvas, 53¾" x 82¼", Munson-Williams-Proctor Institute, Museum of Art, Utica, New York; **148:** *Phillis Wheatley* (detail), Unidentified artist after Scipio Moorhead, National Portrait Gallery, Smithsonian Institution, Washington, D.C./Art Resource, New York; **149 & 150:** New York State Historical Association, Cooperstown; **152–153:** Corel Professional Photos CD-ROM™; **156:** (tl) NASA; (right) UPI/Corbis-Bettmann; **157:** (top) & (bottom) UPI/Corbis-Bettmann; **160:** NASA; **161:** *Recruiting for the Continental Army* (detail), c. 1857–59, William T. Ranney, Oil on canvas, 53¾" x 82¼", Munson-Williams-Proctor Institute, Museum of Art, Utica, New York; **164:** Corel Professional Photos CD-ROM™; **165:** *George Washington*, standing on the platform, Penn State Capitol, Harrisburg, Photo: Brian K. Foster. Courtesy Senate Communications; **166:** (left) *Patrick Henry* (detail), c.1835, James Barton Longacre after Lawrence Sully, The National Portrait Gallery, Smithsonian Institution, Washington, D.C./Art Resource, New York; (right) The Granger Collection, New York; **168:** *Patrick Henry Before the Virginia House of Burgesses 1851*, Peter F. Rothermel, Red Hill, The Patrick Henry National Memorial, Brookneal, Virginia; **172–173:** (background) The American Philosophical Society; **176:** (tl) NASA; (br) AP/Wide World Photos; **177:** *Retroactive I*, 1964, Robert Rauschenberg, Wadsworth Atheneum, Hartford, Connecticut, Gift of Susan Morse Hilles © Robert Rauschenberg/Licensed by VAGA, New York, NY; **180:** NASA; **181:** *Patrick Henry Before the Virginia House of Burgesses* (detail), 1851, Peter F. Rothermel, Red Hill, The Patrick Henry National Memorial, Brookneal, Virginia; **185:** 18th c. New England needlework, Colonial Williamsburg Foundation; **186:** *Benjamin Franklin in 1777* (detail), Augustus de Sainte Aubin after Cochin., Philadelphia Museum of Art, Given by Mrs. John D. Rockefeller; **187:** Culver Pictures, Inc.; **188 & 192:** (left) The Granger Collection, New York; **192:** (right) Corbis-Bettmann; **193:** Encyclopedia of US Postmarks & Postal History; **194:** *Building the First White House*, 1930, N.C. Wyeth, Copyrighted © by the White House Historical Association, photo by the National Geographical Society; **197:** *Independence (Squire Jack Porter)*, 1858, Frank Blackwell Mayer, National Museum of American Art, Smithsonian Institution, Bequest of Harriet Lane Johnson, Art Resource, New York; **202:** (tl) NASA; (bl) UPI/Corbis-Bettmann; (br) AP/Wide World Photos; **203:** Owen Franken/Stock, Boston; **205:** *Dance Africa*, 1996, Synthia Saint James, Third World Art Exchange; **207** NASA; **208:** © Sergio Renchansky/Black Star/PNI; **212:** Richard Hutchings/PhotoEdit; **214–215:** *Niagara Falls*, about 1832–1840, Thomas Chamber, © Wadsworth Atheneum, Harftord, Ella Gallup Sumner and Mary Catlin Sumner Collection; **216:** (1804 Lewis & Clark) Seltzer, *Lewis' First Glimpse of the Rockies*, 12/03/-008. The Thomas Gilcrease Institute of Art, Tulsa, Oklahoma; (1804 Napoleon) Giraudon/Art Resource, NY; (1813) & (1814) & (1824) The Granger Collection, New York; (1819) © Archive Photos; (1825) Samuel S. Spaulding Collection, Buffalo and Erie County Historical Society; (1829) Adam Woolfit/Corbis; **217:** (1830) & (1838) & (1852) The Granger Collection, New York; (1831 Notre Dame) Christie's Images/SuperStock; (1831 Reaper) Art Resource, NY; (1835) & (1837) Library of Congress/Corbis; **218:** (center) National Museum of American History, Smithsonian Institution; (bottom) Neg./Trans. no. 299397 (Photo by Logan, 1947), Courtesy Department of Library Services American Museum of Natural History; **219:** (top) & (bottom) National Museum of American History, Smithsonian Institution; **220:** (bottom) Museum of American Textile History/Rob Huntley/Lightstream; **221:** (top) Courtesy of the Library of Congress; (bottom) State Historical Society of Wisconsin; **222:** (top) National Museum of American History, Smithsonian Institution; (bottom) The National Portrait Gallery, Smithsonian Institution/Art Resource, NY; **223:** (bottom) American Steel Foundries; **224:** (top) *Sampler* (detail), 1797 by Mary Wiggin. 18 x 21 1/2." Philadelphia Museum of Art, Whitman Sampler Collection/Given by Pet, Incorporated.; (center) Copyrighted by the White House Historical Association; Photograph by the National Geographic Society; **225:** Gettysburg National Military Park Museum; **226:** (top) The Granger Collection, New York; (bottom) *Ralph Waldo Emerson* (detail), Frederick Gutenkust, National Portrait Gallery, Smithsonian Institution, Washington D.C./Art Resource, NY; **230:** Concord Free Public Library, Concord, Massachusetts; **234:** *Washington Irving* (detail): Daniel Huntington, National Portrait Gallery, Smithsonian Institution, Washington, D.C./Art Resource, New York; **237:** *The Devil and Tom Walker*, 1856, John Quidor, oil on canvas, 68.8 x 86.6. ©The Cleveland Museum of Art, Mr. and Mrs. William H. Marlatt Fund, 1967.18; **239:** Walking stick, King Georges County, Virginia, 1846, carved wood with ink decoration, 37 x 2 inches in diameter, Abby Aldrich Rockefeller Folk Art Center, Williamsburg VA; **240:** Yale University Art Gallery, New Haven. The Mabel Brady Garvan Collection; **241:** Leonard Lee Rue III/Stock, Boston; **242:** Index Stock Photography, Inc.; **248:** *Henry Wadsworth Longfellow* (detail), Thomas B. Read, The National Portrait Gallery, Smithsonian Institution, Washington, D.C./Art Resource, New York; **250–251:** Stephanie Maze/Woodfin Camp & Associates; **252:** *Breakers at Floodtide*, 1909, oil on canvas, 35" x 40", Signed lower right. Frederick J. Waugh, Butler Institute of American Art, Youngstown, Ohio; **256:** (top) *William Cullen Bryant* (detail), Unidentified photographer, National Portrait Gallery, Smithsonian Institution, Washington, D.C./Art Resource, New York; (center) The Granger Collection, New York; (bottom) Corbis-Bettmann; **257:** (tl) *John Greenleaf Whittier* (detail), 1881, William Notman, The National Portrait Gallery, Smithsonian Institution, Washington, D.C./Art Resource, New York; (br) The Granger Collection, New York; **259:** *Kindred Spirits*, Asher B. Durand, New York Public Library, Astor, Lenox and Tilden Foundations; **262:** Charles Krups/AP/Wide World Photos; **264:** © Ulrike Welsch; **266–267:** *Old Holley House, Cos Cob*, John Henry Twachtman, Cincinnati Art Museum, John J. Emery Endowment; **274:** (left) The Granger Collection, New York; (right) *John Wesley Powell* (detail), Edmund Clarence Messer, National Portrait Gallery, Smithsonian Institution, Washington, D.C./Art Resource, NY; **276:** (center) *White Salmon Trout*, ink on paper (Clark's drawing of salmon from his journal), Missouri Historical Society MHS Archives, entry before 17 March 1806. L/A #407b; (right) *Draught of the Falls and Portage of the Missouri River* (Clark's map of the Missouri River), Missouri Historical Society, Clark Papers, Voorhis #1, 2 July 1805, ink on paper, L/A 464b.; **277:** *Lewis and Clark with Sacajawea at the Great Falls of the Missouri*, Olaf C. Seltzer, #0137.871. The Thomas Gilcrease Institute of Art, Tulsa, Oklahoma; **278, 279, 280, 281:** (background) Corel Professional Photos CD-ROM™; **280:** (center) *Grand Canyon with Rainbow*, 1912, Thomas Moran, oil on canvas, 25" x 30" (63.5 x 76.3cm), Collection of the Fine Arts Museums of San Francisco, Gift of Mr. and Mrs. Robert Gill through the Patrons of Art and Music, (1981.89); **284:** (background) NASA; (br) Thomas Victor; **288:** NASA; **289:** PhotoEdit; **293:** *Mysterious Night*, ca. 1895, watercolor on board, 30½ x 21½ inches, Morris Museum of Art, Augusta GA; **294:** Corbis-Bettmann; **296:** *"I at length. . .,"* Edgar Allan Poe's *Tales of Mystery and Imagination* (London: George G. Harrap, 1935), Arthur Rackham, Print Collection, Miriam and Ira D. Wallach Division of Art, Prints and Photographs, The New York Public Library; Astor, Lenox and Tilden Foundations; **307:** *Separation, 1896*, Edvard Munch, Oil on canvas, Munch Museet, Oslo, Photo: Munch Museum (Svein Andersen/Sidsel de Jong); **311:** *The Raven*, 1845, Edmund Dulac, The Granger Collection, New York; **316:** *Nathaniel Hawthorne* (detail), 1862, Emanuel Gottlieb Leutze, The National Portrait Gallery, Smithsonian Institution, Washington, D.C./Art Resource, New York; **319:** *Winter Sunday in Norway, Maine*, c. 1860, Unidentified Artist, New York State Historical Association, Cooperstown; **325:** *Cemetery*, Peter McIntyre, Courtesy of the artist; **330:** The Granger Collection, New York; **332:** Corel Professional Photos CD-ROM™; **334:** *Captain Ahab on the deck of the Pequod*, 1930, pen and ink drawing, The Granger Collection, New York; **338 & 341:** *Moby Dick*, 1930, pen and ink drawing, The Granger Collection, New York; **343:** (tl), (tr), (rc) & (br) Culver Pictures, Inc.; **348:** (background) NASA; (br) Alex Oliveira/Globe Photos; **350–351:** *Summer Nights, #18*, 1985, Robert Adams, Gelatin-silver print, $15\frac{1}{8}$" x $14\frac{15}{16}$" (38.4 x 38.0 cm), The Museum of Modern Art, New York. Gift of Jeffrey Fraenkel. Transparency © 1997 The Museum of Modern Art, New York; **356:** NASA; **357:** Ken Karp Photography; **361:** *Early Morning at Cold Spring*, 1850, oil on canvas, 60" x 48", Asher B. Durand, Collection of the Montclair Art Museum, Montclair, New Jersey; **362:** *Ralph Waldo Emerson* (detail), Frederick Gutekunst/National Portrait Gallery, Smithsonian Institution, Washington, D.C./Art Resource, NY; **365:** *Sunset*, 1856, Frederick E. Church, Oil on canvas, 24" x 36", Collection of Munson-Williams-Proctor Institute Museum of Art, Utica, New York, Proctor Collection; **368:** (background) Frank Whitney/The Image Bank; **369:** Leonard Harris/Stock, Boston; **372:** The Granger Collection, New York; **374–375:** Owen Franken/PNI; **380:** The Granger Collection, New York; **384:** (background) NASA; (center) © Spencer Jarnagan; (bottom) Epic Records; **385** (top) & (bottom) **& 387:** Corel Professional Photos CD-ROM™; **388:** NASA; **389:** Corel Professional Photos CD-ROM™; **393:** *Walden Pond Revisited*, 1942, N.C. Wyeth, tempera, possibly mixed with other media on panel, 42" x 48" Collection of the Brandywine River Museum, Bequest of Miss Carolyn Wyeth; **394:** The Granger Collection, New York; **396:** *Room With a Balcony*, Adolph von Menzel, Staatliche Museen Preubischer Kulturbesitz, Nationgalerie, Berlin; **399:** Corel Professional Photos CD-ROM™; **400:** Frederic Edwin Church, American, 1826–1900. *Twilight in the Wilderness*, 1860s. Oil on canvas, 101.6 x 162.6 cm. © The

Cleveland Museum of Art, 1997, Mr. and Mrs. William H. Marlett Fund, 1965.233; **401:** Darrel Gulin/Tony Stone Images; **404:** The Granger Collection, New York; **408:** Culver Pictures, Inc.; **412–413:** *The Reaper*, c.1881, Louis C. Tiffany, oil on canvas, National Academy of Design, New York City; **414–415:** *The Lawrence Tree*, 1929, Georgia O'Keeffe, Wadsworth Atheneum, Hartford, The Ella Gallup Sumner and Mary Catlin Sumner Collection, © 1997 The Georgia O'Keeffe Foundation/ Artists Rights Society (ARS), New York; **418:** (background) NASA; (tr) *Langston Hughes* (detail), c. 1925, Winold Reiss, The National Portrait Gallery, Smithsonian Institution, Washington, D.C./Art Resource, New York; (br) Photo by M&A Productions; **419:** *Nobody Around Here Calls Me Citizen*, 1943, Robert Gwathmey, oil on canvas, H. 14¼" x W. 17", Collection Frederick R. Weisman Art Museum at the University of Minnesota, Minneapolis, Bequest of Hudson Walker from the Ione and Hudson Walker Collection. © Estate of Robert Gwathmey/Licensed by VAGA, New York, NY; **420:** *Mandolin*, Rosa Ibarra, Courtesy of the artist; **421:** NASA; **422:** Ken Karp Photography; **426:** Bob Daemmrich/Stock, Boston; **428–429:** *Detail of Battle of Cedar Creek* (partial study for larger painting), Julian Scott, Historical Society of Plainfield, New Jersey. Photograph by John Lei/Omni Photo-Communications; **429:** (left) *Portrait of Abraham Lincoln*, William Willard, National Portrait Gallery, Smithsonian Institution, Washington, D.C./Art Resource, New York; (right) The Granger Collection, New York; **430:** (tc) Chicago Historical Society; (1855) & (1859 Darwin) & (1859 John Brown) & (1865) & (1876) & (1877) The Granger Collection, New York; (1864) National Portrait Gallery, Smithsonian Institution/Art Resource, NY; **431:** (1881) Corbis-Bettmann; (1886) & (1888) & (1903) & (1908) The Granger Collection, New York; (1905) *Albert Einstein*, Tomassetti/ Superstock; **432:** (top) New York Public Library/ Rare Book Division; (bottom) Courtesy of the Library of Congress; **433:** (tl) & (tr) Courtesy of the Library of Congress; (bottom) Corbis-Bettmann; **434:** (top) Courtesy of the Library of Congress; (bottom) Nebraska State HIstorical Society; **436:** (bottom) North Wind Picture Archives; **437:** (tc) Chicago Historical Society; **438:** (top) *Sampler* (detail), 1797 by Mary Wiggin. 18x 21 1/2." Philadelphia Museum of Art, Whitman Sampler Collection/ Given by Pet, Incorporated; (center) *Samuel Longhorne Clemens (Mark Twain)* (detail), 1935, Frank Edwin Larson, National Portrait Gallery, Smithsonian Institution, Washington, D.C./Art Resource, New York; **439:** *Fight for the Standard*, oil on canvas, H 26¾ inches, W 21½ inches, Wadsworth Atheneum, Hartford. The Ella Gallup Sumner and Mary Catlin Sumner Collection Fund; **440:** (top) UPI/Corbis-Bettmann; (rc) Museum of the Confederacy, Richmond, Virginia, Photography by Katherine Wetzel; (bottom) The Granger Collection, New York; **443:** Courtesy of the Library of Congress; **444:** Courtesy National Archives; **446:** *Young Soldier: Separate Study of a Soldier Giving Water to a Wounded Companion*, 1861 (detail), Winslow Homer, Oil, gouache, black crayon on canvas, 36x17.5 cm., United States, 1836–1910, Cooper-Hewitt, National Museum of Design, Smithsonian Institution, Gift of Charles Savage Homer, Jr., 1912-12-110, Photo by Ken Pelka, Courtesy of Art Resource, New York; **450:** Sophia Smith Collection, Smith College; **452:** Courtesy of the Library of Congress; **456:** *Frederick Douglass* (detail), c.1844, Attributed to Elisha Hammond, The National Portrait Gallery, Smithsonian Institution, Washington, D.C./Art Resource, New York; **458:** *The Chimney Corner*, 1863, Eastman Johnson, oil on cardboard, 15½ x 13 in., Munson-Williams-Proctor Institute Museum of Art, Utica, New York; Gift of Edmund G. Munson, Jr.; **460:** *A Home on the Mississippi*, 1871, Currier & Ives, The Museum of the City of New York, Harry T. Peters Collection; **466:** Corbis-Bettmann; **468:** Superstock; **469:** The Kobal Collection; **473:** © David Muench 1994; **478:** (left) *Portrait of Abraham Lincoln* (detail), William Willard, National Portrait Gallery, Smithsonian Institution, Washington, D.C./Art Resource, New York; (right) *Robert E. Lee* (detail), 1864–1865, Edward Caledon Bruce, The National Portrait Gallery, Smithsonian Institution, Washington, D.C./Art Resource, New York; **480:** *Abraham Lincoln's Address at the Dedication of the Gettysburg National Cemetery, 19 November 1863*, lithograph, 1905, The Granger Collection, New York; **486:** (background) NASA; (bl) © 1969 Dennis Brack/Black Star; (right) AP/Wide World Photos; **488:** (background) NASA; **489:** *Robert E. Lee*, 1864–1865, Edward Caledon Bruce, The National Portrait Gallery, Smithsonian Institution, Washington, D.C./Art Resource, New York; **493:** *Newspapers in the Trenches '64*, William Ludwell Sheppard, Museum of the Confederacy, Richmond, Virginia, Photography by Katherine Wetzel; **494 & 498:** Courtesy of the Library of Congress; **501 & 502:** The Granger Collection, New York; **506:** (background) NASA; (bl) Sygma; (br) The Washington Post; **507:** D. Hudson/Sygma; **508:** Chip Hires/Liaison International; **510:** Sygma; **512:** (background) NASA; **513:** Courtesy of the Library of Congress; **517:** *The Old Stage Coach of the Plains*, 1901, Frederic Remington, oil on canvas, Amon Carter Museum, Forth Worth; **518:** *Samuel Langhorne Clemens (Mark Twain)* (detail), 1935, Frank Edwin Larson, National Portrait Gallery, Smithsonian Institution, Washington, D.C./Art Resource, New York; **520–521:** *Paddle Steamboat Mississippi*, Shelburne Museum, Shelburne, Vermont, Photo by Ken Burris; **522:** *Plantations on the Mississippi River - from Natchez to New Orleans 1858* (Norman Chart), Historic New Orleans Collection, accession no. 1947.11-v; **525:** *Mark Twain (Samuel L. Clemens) Riding the Celebrated Jumping Frog*, an English caricature, 1872, Frederic Waddy, The Granger Collection, New York; **527 & 532:** The Granger Collection, New York; **534–535:** *Edge of Town*, Charles Burchfield, The Nelson-Atkins Museum of Art, Kansas City, Missouri, (Gift of Friends of Art) 41–52; **540:** Esbin/Anderson/Omni-Photo Communications, Inc.; **544:** *Chief Joseph* (detail), 1878, Cyrenius Hall, National Portrait Gallery, Smithsonian Institution, Washington, D.C./Art Resource, New York; **546 & 549:** Kansas State Historical Society; **551:** National Museum of American History, Smithsonian Institution; **554:** Corbis-Bettmann; **558:** Wayne Lynch/DRK Photo; **562:** Annie Griffiths/DRK Photo; **568:** Courtesy of the Museum of Texas Tech University; **571:** The Granger Collection, New York; **572:** Index Stock Photography, Inc.; **574:** *Headin' Up the Range*, Edward Borein, oil on canvas, 30 by 20 inches, Signed Lower Right: Edward Borein, Photo courtesy of the Gerald Peters Gallery, Santa Fe, New Mexico; **578:** (background) NASA; (br) AP/Wide World Photos; **580–581:** *Open Range*, 1942, Maynard Dixon, oil on canvas, 34½" x 39", Museum of Western Art, Denver. #36.79. Bernard O. Milmoe, Photographer; **584:** (background) NASA; **585:** © Pete Winkle/Stock South/PNI; **589:** *Channel to the Mills*, 1913, Edwin M. Dawes, oil on canvas, 51 x 39½ in. Minneapolis Institute of Arts, anonymous gift; **590:** The Granger Collection, New York; **592–593:** *Afternoon in Piedmont*, c. 1911, Xavier Martínez, Collection of The Oakland Museum of California, Gift of Dr. William S. Porter; **598:** The Granger Collection, New York; **600:** Stock Montage, Inc.; **604:** (left) *Edwin Arlington Robinson* (detail), 1933, Thomas Richard Hood, National Portrait Gallery, Smithsonian Institution, Washington, D.C./Art Resource, New York; (right) *Edgar Lee Masters* (detail), 1946, Francis J. Quirk, National Portrait Gallery, Smithsonian Institution, Washington, D.C./Art Resource, New York; **606:** Horst Oesterwinter/International Stock Photography, Ltd.; **607:** *The Thinker (Portrait of Louis N. Kenton, 1900)*, Thomas Eakins, The Metropolitan Museum of Art, Kennedy Fund, 1917, Copyright © 1967, 1984 by The Metropolitan Museum of Art; **608:** *Barn Dance*, 1950, Grandma Moses, © 1989, Grandma Moses Properties Co., New York; **609:** Joel Greenstein/Omni-Photo Communications, Inc.; **612:** Corbis-Bettmann; **614:** *From Arkansas*, George Schreiber, Sheldon Swope Art Museum, Terre Haute, Indiana; **616:** The Granger Collection, New York; **622:** (background) NASA; (br) John Barrett/Globe Photos; **623:** Tim Davis/Photo Researchers, Inc.; **625:** (background) NASA; **626:** Corel Professional Photos CD-ROM™; **630:** Corbis; **632–633:** *Nighthawks*, 1942, Edward Hopper, oil on canvas, 76.2 x 144 cm, Friends of American Art Collection, 1942.51, The Art Institute of Chicago. All Rights Reserved; **634:** (1914) National Postal Museum, Smithsonian Institution Washington, DC; (1915 Lusitania) Courtesy of the Library of Congress; (1915 Olympics) Corbis-Bettmann; (1918) *Wilson* by Edmund Charles Tarbell, 1921, National Portrait Gallery, Smithsonian Institution, Washington, DC/Art Resource, N.Y.; (1919) National Archives; (1920) Museum of Connecticut History; (1928) David Ryan / Photo 20-20/PNI; (1922) & (1929) The Granger Collection, New York; **635:** (1930) & (1941) The Granger Collection, New York; (1931) *The Persistence of Memory*, Salvador Dali, The Museum of Modern Art, New York, © 1996 Demart Pro Arte, Geneva/ Artists Rights Society (ARS), New York; (1933) Franklin Delano Roosevelt Library, Hyde Park, NY; (1939) SuperStock; (1945–UN) Corel Professional Photos CD-ROM™; (1945–VJ Day) Alfred Eisenstaedt, Life Magazine © Time Warner; **636:** (top) Culver Pictures, Inc.; (bottom) Courtesy National Archives, photo no. (86-G-11F-7); **637:** (bottom) Historical Pictures/ Stock Montage, Inc.; **638:** (tr) Courtesy of the Atwater Kent Museum; (bottom) Culver Pictures, Inc.; **639:** (top) *Aspects of Negro*

Life: From Slavery Through Reconstruction, 1934, Aaron Douglas, Schomburg Center for Research in Black Culture, Art and Artifacts Division, The New York Public Library, Astor, Lenox and Tilden Foundations; (center) Corbis-Bettmann; (bottom) Courtesy of the Library of Congress; **640:** (bottom) Courtesy of the Library of Congress; **641:** (top) UPI/Corbis-Bettmann; (center) The Granger Collection, New York; (bottom) Library of Congress/ Corbis; **642:** (top) *Sampler* (detail), 1797 by Mary Wiggin. 18x 21 1/2", Philadelphia Museum of Art, Whitman Sampler Collection/Given by Pet, Incorporated,; **643:** *No Place to Go,* 1935, Maynard Dixon, Oil on canvas, 25 x 30 inches. The Herald Clark Memorial Collection, Courtesy of Brigham Young University Museum of Fine Arts. All Rights Reserved. Photo by David W. Hawkinson; **644:** *T.S. Eliot* (detail), 1888–1965, Sir Gerald Kelly, National Portrait Gallery, Smithsonian Institution, Washington, D.C./Art Resource, New York; **648:** *Moonlight, Dovehouse Street, Chelsea,* Algernon Newton, Fine Art Society, London/The Bridgeman Art Library International Ltd., London/New York; **650:** Corel Professional Photos CD-ROM™; **654:** (top) The Granger Collection, New York; (bottom) *William Carlos Williams* (detail), The National Portrait Gallery, Smithsonian Institution, Washington, D.C./Art Resource, NY; **655:** Corbis-Bettmann; **658:** The Granger Collection, New York; **660–661:** *Landscape Album in Various Styles,* ink and color on paper, 9$\frac{7}{16}$" x 12$\frac{3}{4}$", Ch'a Shih-piao, The Cleveland Museum of Art, Gift of Mr. and Mrs. Severance A. Millikin, 55.37; **662:** *The Figure 5 in Gold,* 1928, Charles Demuth, oil on composition board. H. 36 in. W. 29$\frac{3}{4}$ in. (91.4 x 75.6 cm) Signed (lower left): C.D. Inscribed (bottom center): W.C.W. (William Carlos Williams), The Metropolitan Museum of Art, Alfred Steiglitz Collection, 1949. (49.59.1). Photograph Copyright © 1996 By the Metropolitan Museum of Art; **664:** Adam Jones/Photo Researchers, Inc.; **665:** *Overhanging Cloud in July,* 1947/59, Charles Burchfield, Watercolor on paper, 39$\frac{1}{2}$" x 35$\frac{1}{2}$" Collection of Whitney Museum of American Art, Purchase, with funds from the Friends of the Whitney Museum of American Art; **668:** *F. Scott Fitzgerald* (detail), David Silvette, The National Portrait Gallery, Smithsonian Institution, Washington, D.C./Art Resource, New York; **670–671:** Corel Professional Photos CD-ROM™; **671:** (right) & **672:** Culver Pictures, Inc.; **674:** *Golf Course-California,* 1917, George Wesley Bellows, Oil on canvas, 30 x 38 inches, Collection Cincinnati Art Museum, The Edwin and Virginia Irwin Memorial, 1966.6; **675 & 676:** Culver Pictures, Inc.; **677:** *The Morning Sun,* c. 1920, 0/c, 50 x 40 ins., Pauline Palmer, Collection Rockford Art Museum, Gift of the Friends of American Art, 1922; **679, 680, & 683:** Culver Pictures, Inc.; **686:** UPI/Corbis-Bettmann; **688:** © The Stock Market/Milt/Patti Putnam; **692:** (left) *E. E. Cummings* (detail), 1958, Self Portrait, The National Portrait Gallery, Smithsonian Institution, Washington, D.C./Art Resource, New York; (right) BBC Hulton/Corbis-Bettmann; **695:** *Remember Now the Days of Thy Youth,* 1950, Paul Starrett Sample, Oil on canvas, 34 x 48 inches, Hood Museum of Art, Dartmouth College, Hanover, NH; Gift of Frank L. Harrington, class of 1954; **696:** *Turret Lathe Operator,* 1925, Grant Wood, oil on canvas 18" x 24", Cedar Rapids Museum of Art, Cedar Rapids, Iowa, Cherry Burrell Charitable Foundation Collection. Courtesy Associated American Artists, © Estate of Grant Wood/Licensed by VAGA, New York, NY; **700:** *Thomas Wolfe,* 1938, Soss Melik, National Portrait Gallery, Smithsonian Institution, Washington, D.C./Art Resource, New York; **703:** *Stone City, Iowa,* 1930, Grant Wood, Joslyn Art Museum, Omaha, Nebraska, Gift of the Art Institute of Omaha; © Estate of Grant Wood/Licensed by VAGA, New York, NY; **708:** (left) The Granger Collection, New York; (tr) Corbis-Bettmann; (br) AP/Wide World Photos; **710:** (background) John Wilkes/Photonica; **711:** Silver Burdett Ginn; **712–713:** Index Stock Photography, Inc.; **714:** *Untitled, 1964,* Alexander Calder (one of seven lithographs in series), 19$\frac{1}{2}$" x 25$\frac{1}{2}$", Solomon R. Guggenheim Museum, New York, Gift of the artist, 1965, Photo by Myles Aronowitz, © The Solomon R. Guggenheim Foundation, New York, © 1997 Artists Rights Society (ARS), New York/ADAGP, Paris; **718:** (background) NASA; (right) Water Weissman/Globe Photos; **719:** Petrified Cole/The Image Bank; **720–721:** © The Stock Market/Simon Nathan; **722:** NASA; **723:** Ken Karp Photography; **727:** *Do It Yourself Landscape,* 1962, Andy Warhol, Museum Ludwig, Cologne, photo courtesy of Rheinisches Bildarchiv Köln; **728:** (top) Larry Burrows/Life Magazine © Time Warner Inc.; (bottom) UPI/Corbis-Bettmann; **729:** (top) Thomas Victor; (bottom) Corel Professional Photos CD-ROM™; **731–734:** American Red Cross; **736–737:** © Animals Animals; **738:** *Farm Landscape,* 1932, Grant Wood, Oil on canvas, 23$\frac{1}{4}$ x 45$\frac{1}{2}$ in. (image), 43$\frac{3}{8}$ x 64$\frac{1}{2}$ in. (canvas), Coe College, Cedar Rapids, Iowa, Gift from the Eugene C. Eppley Foundation, © Estate of Grant Wood/Licensed by VAGA, New York, NY; **740–741:** *Georgia Red Clay,* 1946, Nell Choate Jones, oil on canvas, 25 x 30 inches, 1989.01.094, Morris Museum of Art, Augusta, Georgia; **743:** *Miz Emily,* Joseph Holston, 24" x16", Holston Reproductions; **748:** (background) NASA; (br) Thomas Victor; **749:** *Woman in a Window,* 1957, Richard Diebenkorn, oil on canvas, 59" x 56", Albright-Knox Art Gallery Buffalo, New York, Gift of Seymour H. Knox, 1958. Photo by Biff Henrich; **752:** NASA; **753:** Tony Freeman/PhotoEdit; **757:** *The Tower,* 1920, Charles Demuth, Tempera on pasteboard, 23$\frac{1}{4}$ x 19$\frac{1}{2}$ in. (58.4 x 49.4 cm) Initialed and inscribed in pencil on reverse: *After Christopher Wren* (?) Provincetown, Mass./1BO (?) - CD, Columbus Museum of Art, Ohio; Gift of Ferdinand Howald, 31.146; **758:** © Archive Photos; **761:** *Memories,* 1885–86, William Merritt Chase, oil on canvas, Munson-Williams-Proctor Institute Museum of Art, Utica, New York; **768:** *Carl Sandburg* (detail), Miriam Svet, The National Portrait Gallery, Smithsonian Institution, Washington, D.C./Art Resource, New York; **770:** (background) Stock Montage, Inc.; **771:** Corel Professional Photos CD-ROM™; **774:** Thomas Victor; **777:** *Garden of Memories,* Charles Burchfield, 1917, Watercolor, crayon, charcoal and pencil on paper, 25$\frac{3}{4}$" x 22$\frac{1}{2}$", The Museum of Modern Art, New York, Gift of Abby Aldrich Rockefeller (by exchange) Photograph ©1999 The Museum of Modern Art, New York; **784:** *William Faulkner* (detail), Soss Melik, The National Portrait Gallery, Smithsonian Institution, Washington, D.C./Art Resource, New York; **786:** Superstock; **790:** *Winter in Southern Louisiana,* 1911, Ellsworth Woodward, oil on canvas, Collection of Mississippi Museum of Art, Jackson, Purchase by Mississippi Art Association and Art Study Club, 1912.005.; **794:** *Old Man and The Boy,* John Head, Russell A. Fink Gallery; **795:** Corel Professional Photos CD-ROM™; **798:** UPI/Corbis-Bettmann; **802:** Dimitri Kessel/Life Magazine; **804–805:** Corel Professional Photos CD-ROM™; **806:** Dewitt Jones/Woodfin Camp & Associates; **808–809 & 810:** Corel Professional Photos CD-ROM™; **811:** Ellis Herwig/PNI; **812 & 816** (left) UPI/Corbis-Bettmann; **816:** (right) AP/Wide World Photos; **818, 820 & 821:** Copyright ©1933 by James Thurber. Copyright ©1961 renewed by Helen Thurber and Rosemary A. Thurber. Reprinted by arrangement with Rosemary A. Thurber and The Barbara Hogenson Agency; **822 & 823:** Culver Pictures, Inc.; **828:** Courtesy of the Estate of Carl Van Vechten, Joseph Solomon, Executor, The National Portrait Gallery, Smithsonian Institution, Washington, D.C./Art Resource, New York; **831:** *The Mather School,* 1988, Jonathan Green, oil on masonite, Courtesy of the artist; **833:** *School Bell Time,* 1978, From the Profile/Part I: The Twenties series (Mecklenburg County), Romare Bearden, 29$\frac{1}{4}$" x 41", Collection: Kingsborough Community College, The City University of New York; © Romare Bearden Foundation/Licensed by VAGA, New York, NY; **838:** (left) Langston Hughes (detail), c.1925, Winold Reiss, The National Portrait Gallery, Smithsonian Institution, Washington, D.C./Art Resource, New York; (right) The Granger Collection, New York; **840:** *Girl in Blue Dress,* 1936, Samuel Joseph Brown, Watercolor on paper, H. 30$\frac{1}{2}$ in., W. 21$\frac{1}{2}$ in., The Metropolitan Museum of Art, Gift of the Pennsylvania W.P.A., 1943, (43.46.13), Photograph ©1991 The Metropolitan Museum of Art; **841:** Corel Professional Photos CD-ROM™; **842:** *Girls Skipping,* 1949, Hale Woodruff, oil on canvas, 24" x 32", Private Collection. Courtesy of Michael Rosenfeld Gallery, New York; **843:** Michael Skott/The Image Bank; **846:** (top) *Countee Cullen* (detail), c.1925, Winold Reiss, The National Portrait Gallery, Smithsonian Institution, Washington, D.C./Art Resource, New York; (center) UPI/Corbis-Bettmann; (bottom) *Jean Toomer* (detail), c.1925, Winold Reiss, Gift of Laurence A. Fleischman and Howard Garfinkle with a matching grant from the National Endowment of the Arts, National Portrait Gallery, Smithsonian Institution, Washington, D.C./Art Resource, New York; **848:** *Aspiration,* Aaron Douglas, ©1936 The Estate of Thurlow E. Tibbs, Jr.; **850:** *Hoeing,* 1943, Robert Gwathmey, Oil on canvas, 40 by 60$\frac{1}{4}$ (101.6 by 153), Carnegie Institute Museum of Art, Pittsburgh, Pennsylvania, Patrons Art Fund, 44.3. Photograph by Richard Stoner, © Estate of Robert Gwathmey/Licensed by VAGA, New York, NY; **851:** Corel Professional Photos CD-ROM™; **854:** (background) NASA; (bottom) Rikard Sergei Sanchez/Arte Publico Press; **855 & 856:** Huipil (blouse) from the Tarascans of Michoacan. Embroidered cotton. Museo de Indumentaria Mexicana, Mexico City, D.F. Mexico. Schalkwijk/Art Resource, NY; **857:** NASA; **858:** © Laima Druskis/Stock, Boston/PNI; **862:** C. Blankenhorn/PNI; **864–865:** *Telephones,* (detail), 1954, Colleen Browning, oil on plywood, 14" x 32.5" (33.56 x 82.55 cm), Signed, lower right. Butler Institute of American Art. Museum purchase, 1955; **866:** (1952) Nancy Crampton; (1955) Leviton-Atlanta/Black Star; (1959) St. George Andrew/ Magnum Photos, Inc.; (1969) The Granger Collection, New York; (1972 China) UPI/Corbis-Bettmann; (1972 Vietnam) Peter Garfield/Folio, Inc.; (1974) Alex Webb/Magnum Photos; **867:** (1982) © 1985 Peter Marlow/ Magnum Photos, Inc.; (1987) © Larry Downing/Woodfin Camp & Associates; (1990 Carol Moseley Braun) National Organization of Women; (1990 Handicapped) ©The Stock Market/Wes Thompson; (1994) © Tomas Muscionico/Contact Press Images; (1997) © Dan Groshong/Sygma; **868:** (top) The Granger Collection, New York; (bottom) Wright/National Motor Museum; **869:** (bottom) UPI/Corbis-Bettmann; **870:** (top) AP/Wide World Photos; (bottom) Rick Smolan/Against All Odds; **871:** (bottom) Sven Simon; **872:** (bottom) © Les Stone/Sygma; **873:** (top) © Mark Bolster/International Stock Photography, Ltd.; (bottom) Courtesy of Apple Computer, Inc.; **874:** (top) *Sampler* (detail), 1797 by Mary Wiggin. 18x 21 1/2." Philadelphia Museum of Art, Whitman Sampler Collection/Given by Pet, Incorporated.; (center) Christopher Morris/Black Star/PNI; **875:** *Television Moon,* 1978–79, Alfred Leslie, oil on canvas, Wichita Art Museum, gift of Virginia and George Ablah; **876:** Flannery O'Connor Collection, Ina Dillard Russel Library, Georgia College; **880–881:** *Black Walnuts,* 1945, Joseph Pollet, Oil on canvas 30" x 40", Collection of Whitney Museum of American Art, Purchase, Gift of Gertrude Vanderbilt Whitney, by exchange; **884:** *Deep Fork Overlook,* Joan Marron-LaRue; **890:** Nancy Crampton; **892–893:** Culver Pictures, Inc.; **896:** © The Stock Market/Shiki; **902:** Thomas Victor; **904:** Corel Professional Photos CD-ROM™; **906:** *Winter Bouquet,* 1933, Charles Burchfield, Watercolor and gouache over graphite on paper, Sight: 35⅜ x 16¾ in. (91 x 69 cm) Ellen Gardner Fund, Courtesy, Museum of Fine Arts, Boston; **908:** © The Stock Market/Dick Frank Studios; **912:** (tl) Rollie McKenna; (tr) AP/Wide World Photos; (bl) *Robert Penn Warren* (detail), 1935, Conrad A. Albrizio, The National Portrait Gallery, Smithsonian Institution, Washington, D.C./Art Resource, New York; (br) Kit Stafford; **914:** *Crowninshield's Wharf, Around the Wharf are the Vessels America, Fame, Prudent, and Belisaurius,* George Ropes, Peabody Museum of Salem, Photo by Mark Sexton; **916–917 & 918:** Corel Professional Photos CD-ROM™; **920–921:** Tim Lynch/Stock, Boston; **924:** Diana Walker; **929:** *Girl Looking at Landscape,* 1957, Richard Diebenkorn, oil on canvas, 59 x 60⅜ inches, (149.9 x 153.4 cm), Gift of Mr. and Mrs. Alan H. Temple, 61.49, Collection of Whitney Museum of American Art, photograph by Geoffrey Clements, N.Y., Photograph copyright © 1997: Whitney Museum of American Art; **934:** (top) Thomas Victor; (center) Photo by Michael Nye; (bottom) Photo by Paul Abdoo; **937:** *Passion of Paints,* ©1997 Bob Peters, Exclusively represented by Applejack Licensing International; **938:** *Indian on Galloping Horse after Remington, No. 2, 1976,* Fritz Scholder, color lithograph, 30 x 22¼ in. Gift of Mr. and Mrs. Ben Q. Adams, 1979, Courtesy Museum of Fine Arts, Museum of New Mexico, Santa Fe NM; **940–941:** Culver Pictures, Inc.; **942:** *Getting Down,* Joseph Holston, 14" x 14", Holston Originals; **946:** Thomas Victor; **956:** © Anthony Barboza/Life Magazine; **964:** Prentice Hall; **966:** *Fruit Vendor,* 1951, Olga Costa, Museo de Arte Moderno, Mexico, ©Olga Costa - SOMAAP, Mexico, 1999; **976:** (lc) Shelley Rotner/Omni-Photo Communications, Inc.; (tl) Georgia McInnis/Courtesy of Arte Publico Press; (bl) Marlene Fostor; (tr) Rollie McKenna; **978:** *Untitled,* Peter Malone, Chen/Art Resource, NY; **979:** Colllins/ Monkmeyer; **980:** Mitchell Funk/The Image Bank; **981:** Corel Professional Photos CD-ROM™; **982, 983, 984:** © John Lemker/Animals Animals; **987:** Ken Karp Photography; **991:** *My Mother's Book of Life,* 1987, Lee Lawson, acrylic on panel, 34 x 30 in., Photo courtesy of Pomegranate Artbooks; **992:** (top) The Granger Collection, New York; (center) AP/Wide World Photos; (bottom) © 1996 Sigrid Estrada; **996:** *Blam,* 1962, © Roy Lichtenstein, oil on canvas, 68 x 80 in.; **999 & 1000:** Warner Bros./Photofest; **1004:** (top) AP/Wide World Photos; (center) Robert Severi/Liaison International; (bottom) Robert Foothorap; **1007:** *Biography,* 1988, Marina Gutierrez, Courtesy of the artist; **1012:** Jim McHugh; **1015:** Gary Gay/The Image Bank; **1019:** Bob Daemmrich / Stock, Boston; **1023:** *Choke,* 1964, Robert Rauschenberg, Oil and screenprint on canvas, 60" x 48", Washington University Gallery of Art, St. Louis, Gift of Mr. and Mrs. Richard K. Weil, 1972 © Robert Rauschenberg/Licensed by VAGA, New York, NY; **1024:** Thomas Victor; **1026:** *Push to Walk,* collage 48" x 48", Phoebe Beasley; **1034:** (left) AP/Wide World Photos; (right) Rollie McKenna; **1036–1038:** FPG International Corp.; **1041:** Courtesy National Archives; **1044–1045:** Stock Montage, Inc.; **1048:** (tl) AP/Wide World Photos; (tr) UPI/Corbis-Bettmann; (bl) Thomas Victor; (br) Pach/Corbis-Bettmann; **1050:** *Mirror II,* George Tooker, (1920–1938), Egg tempera on gesso panel, 20 x 20 in., 1968.4, Gift of R. H. Donnelley Erdman (PA 1956), Addison Gallery of American Art, Phillips Academy, Andover, Massachusetts. All Rights Reserved.; **1053:** *Part II, The Free Man, No. 30, The Frederick Douglass Series,* Jacob Lawrence, Hampton University Museum, Hampton, Virginia; **1058:** (left) Nihad Becirovic; (right) Thomas Victor; **1060:** *The Madonna And Child,* 1990, Momodou Ceesay, Dialogue Systems, Inc.; **1062:** *Winter,* Franca Ozz, Oil, 24" x 18", Edition of 999 s/n, Courtesy of The Hadley Companies; **1066:** Andrea Renault/Globe Photos; **1069:** *Laurence Typing,* 1952, Fairfield Porter, oil on canvas 40 x 30⅛ inches, The Parrish Art Museum, Southampton, New York, Gift of the Estate of Fairfield Porter; **1072:** *Letters and Postcards,* Reid Christman, 24" x 18" (61 cm x 45.7 cm), Fredrix linen canvas; **1078:** (left) Photo by Mandy Sayer; (right) AP/Wide World Photos; **1080–1081:** (background) Brian Parker/Tom Stack & Associates; **1080:** (bl) Corel Professional Photos CD-ROM™; **1082:** P.J. Griffiths/Magnum Photos, Inc.; **1086:** AP/Wide World Photos; **1087:** *The Trial of Two "Witches" at Salem, Massachusetts, in 1662,* Howard Pyle, The Granger Collection, New York; **1091:** *The Execution of the Reverend Stephen Burroughs for Witchcraft at Salem, Massachusetts, in 1692,* 19th century engraving, The Granger Collection, New York; **1097–1165:** Photofest; **1170:** John Neubauer/PhotoEdit; **1174:** © Mark C. Burnett/Stock, Boston/PNI; **1176–1177:** Bayerische Staatsbibliothek Munchen; **1179:** Noah's Ark *(After the Flood),* Joseph Baker Fountain, Harrogate Museums and Art Gallery, North Yorkshire, UK/The Bridgeman Art Library International Ltd., London/New York; **1182–1183:** www.Who2com; **1183:** Corel Professional Photos CD-ROM™; **1185:** Brian Parker/Tom Stack & Associates; **1186:** Corel Professional Photos CD-ROM™; **1189:** *The Eruption of Vesuvius and the Death of Pliny,* P.H. de Valencieme, Musee des Augustins, Toulouse, France; **1194:** Culver Pictures, Inc.; **1197:** Corel Professional Photos CD-ROM™; **1199:** Lisa J. Goodman /The Image Bank; **1200:** Paul McCormick/The Image Bank; **1205:** Super-Stock; **1206:** Plimouth Plantation, Plymouth, MA

Illustration Credits:

86, 113, 184, 211, 292, 360, 392, 425, 435, 437, 492, 516, 588, 627, 629, 642, 645, 726, 756, 861, 947, 990, 1022, 1173: Ernest Albanese.

12, 32, 42, 62, 274, 964: Ortelius Design.